THE
WRITERS
DIRECTORY
THIRTIETH EDITION

WOLVERHAMPTON LIBRARIES

CR			
02288688	C	√	

THE WRITERS DIRECTORY

THIRTIETH EDITION
VOLUME 6: V-Z

Editor
Lisa Kumar

ST. JAMES PRESS
A part of Gale, Cengage Learning

GALE
CENGAGE Learning·

Detroit · New York · San Francisco · New Haven, Conn · Waterville, Maine · London

GALE
CENGAGE Learning®

Writers Directory, 30th Edition

Project Editor: Lisa Kumar

Editorial Support Services: Natasha Mikheyeva

Manufacturing: Rita Wimberley

© 2012 Gale, Cengage Learning

ALL RIGHTS RESERVED. No part of this work covered by the copyright herein may be reproduced, transmitted, stored, or used in any form or by any means graphic, electronic, or mechanical, including but not limited to photocopying, recording, scanning, digitizing, taping, Web distribution, information networks, or information storage and retrieval systems, except as permitted under Section 107 or 108 of the 1976 United States Copyright Act, without the prior written permission of the publisher.

This publication is a creative work fully protected by all applicable copyright laws, as well as by misappropriation, trade secret, unfair competition, and other applicable laws. The authors and editors of this work have added value to the underlying factual material herein through one or more of the following: unique and original selection, coordination, expression, arrangement, and classification of the information.

For product information and technology assistance, contact us at
Gale Customer Support, 1-800-877-4253.
For permission to use material from this text or product,
submit all requests online at **www.cengage.com/permissions.**
Further permissions questions can be emailed to
permissionrequest@cengage.com

While every effort has been made to ensure the reliability of the information presented in this publication, Gale, a part of Cengage Learning, does not guarantee the accuracy of the data contained herein. Gale accepts no payment for listing; and inclusion in the publication of any organization, agency, institution, publication, service, or individual does not imply endorsement of the editors or publisher. Errors brought to the attention of the publisher and verified to the satisfaction of the publisher will be corrected in future editions.

EDITORIAL DATA PRIVACY POLICY: Does this product contain information about you as an individual? If so, for more information about our editorial data privacy policies, please see our Privacy Statement at www.gale.cengage.com.

Gale
27500 Drake Rd.
Farmington Hills, MI, 48331-3535

ISBN-13: 978-1-4144-8712-0 (set)   ISBN-10: 1-4144-8712-6 (set)
ISBN-13: 978-1-4144-8713-7 (vol. 1)   ISBN-10: 1-4144-8713-4 (vol. 1)
ISBN-13: 978-1-4144-8714-4 (vol. 2)   ISBN-10: 1-4144-8714-2 (vol. 2)
ISBN-13: 978-1-4144-9901-7 (vol. 3)   ISBN-10: 1-4144-9901-9 (vol. 3)
ISBN-13: 978-1-4144-9902-4 (vol. 4)   ISBN-10: 1-4144-9902-7 (vol. 4)
ISBN-13: 978-1-4144-9903-1 (vol. 5)   ISBN-10: 1-4144-9903-5 (vol. 5)
ISBN-13: 978-1-4144-9904-8 (vol. 6)   ISBN-10: 1-4144-9904-3 (vol. 6)

ISSN 0084-2699

Printed in the United States of America
1 2 3 4 5   16 15 14 13 12

FD156

Contents

Preface

The Writers Directory is the newly revised and expanded thirtieth edition of this acclaimed reference work. It lists 26,615 writers—writing under 29,776 names—from all countries of the world who have had at least one work published in English.

The Directory is published in 6 individual volumes, with content divided as follows:

Volume 1: Lists entries from A-C
Volume 2: Lists entries from D-G
Volume 3: Lists entries from H-L
Volume 4: Lists entries from M-Q
Volume 5: Lists entries from R-U
Volume 6: Lists entries from V-Z, Obituaries, Index to Writing Categories, and Country of Citizenship Index

The Directory lists approximately 26,526 living writers of fiction and non-fiction who have published at least one full-length work in English. Listees run the gamut from the best-known, best selling authors of fiction and the most prominent non-fiction writers to those writers just embarking on their literary careers. The thirtieth edition includes nearly 1,000 writers whose listings have not appeared in a previous edition of The Writers Directory.

The **Obituaries** Section contains the entries for approximately 89 writers whose listings have appeared in previous editions of The Writers Directory and whose passing was made known to us in preparing this edition.

Compilation Methods

Selection of writers to appear in The Writers Directory is based primarily on reference value. Biographical and career information is researched for each writer, then a copy of the entry is sent to the writer for his or her approval and updates. By this process, the editors can assure comprehensive, current information. At the same time, entries in the previous edition were rigorously reviewed with an eye toward their current research value. As a result, some writers' entries have been retired to make way for those of new writers.

How to Read a Citation

Entries in The Writers Directory contain some or all of the following elements (please note that this is a sample entry for demonstration purposes only):

▮ 1 ▮ WILLIAMS, Mae. ▮ 2 ▮ (Allison May Williams) ▮ 3 ▮ Also writes as William Allison. ▮ 4 ▮ American (born Malta), ▮ 5 ▮ b. 1945. ▮ 6 ▮ **Genres:** Novels, Biography. ▮ 7 ▮ **Career:** Freelance writer. ▮ 8 ▮ **Publications:** Paris, L'amour, 1972; (ed.) Running through the Weeds, 1982; (as William Allison) Louis, My Love (biography), 1987; The Waves at My Back, 1997. ▮ 9 ▮ **Address:** 27500 Drake Rd., Farmington Hills, MI 48331U.S.A. ▮ 10 ▮ **Online address:** maewil@aol.com ▮ 11 ▮ Died 1997.

▮ 1 ▮ Name of writer with fuller name information in parentheses

▮ 2 ▮ Full name of writer if different from writing name or pseudonyms but not used for writing

▮ 3 ▮ Pseudonym information

▮ 4 ▮ Nationality—if birthplace is different from nationality, it will follow the nationality in parentheses

▮ 5 ▮ Birth year

▮ 6 ▮ Genres—corresponds to **Index to Writing Categories**

▮ 7 ▮ Brief career information

▮ 8 ▮ Publications: title, year of publication, pseudonym if used, special awards

▮ 9 ▮ Address

▮ 10 ▮ Online address and/or web site

▮ 11 ▮ Death notation and year (in **Obituaries** Section only)

Cross references appear in the following form:

To main entry in main section: **ALLISON, William.** See **WILLIAMS, Mae.**

From main section to main entry in **Obituaries** section: **WILLIAMS, Mae.** See Obituaries.

From pseudonym in main section to main entry in **Obituaries** section: **ALLISON, William.** See **WILLIAMS, Mae** in the Obituaries.

Writers (and cross references) are listed alphabetically by surname which are sorted letter-by-letter. In cases where surnames are identical, writers are listed first by surname, then by given and middle names, and finally by suffixes such as Jr., Sr., II, or III. Surnames beginning with a prefix (such as Du, Mac, or Van), however spaced, are listed alphabetically under the first letter of the prefix and treated as if there were no space. Other compound surnames, hyphenated names, and names with apostrophes are alphabetized as if there were no space or punctuation. Surnames beginning with Saint or St. appear after names beginning with Sains and before names beginning with Sainu.

Entries in the **Obituaries** Section follow the same style as those in the main entries with the addition of the notation *Died* and the death year (if known) at the end of the entry.

Features

The Writers Directory contains many features to enhance its usefulness:

Boldface Rubrics allow quick and easy scanning for specifics on genre, career, publication, and mailing and online addresses.

The Obituaries Section lists the entries for those writers whose listing appeared in previous editions of The Writers Directory and whose passing was made known to us in preparing this edition. Cross references have been provided in the main body of the Directory to those deceased writers.

Indexing

The Writers Directory includes two indexes. In the **Index to Writing Categories**, one can locate writers by the type of works they write. New categories are added to The Writers Directory as needed to reflect new topics of interest and to define a writer's body of work more accurately. The **Country of Citizenship Index** lists writers by their country of citizenship as provided by the writer. Users are advised that one writer with multiple citizenship may appear under one country grouping (e.g., Canada-England) while another with the same citizenships may appear under a different grouping (e.g., England-Canada) depending on how the writer submitted the information.

The **Index to Writing Categories and Country of Citizenship Index** can be found in Volume 6 of the Directory following the **Obituaries** Section.

Also Available in Electronic Formats

Licensing. *The Writers Directory* is available for licensing. The complete database is provided in a fielded format and is deliverable on such media as disk or CD-ROM. For more information, contact Gale's Business Development Group at 1-800-877-GALE, or visit us on our web site at gale. cengage. com.

Online. *The Writers Directory* is accessible as part of Gale's Biography in Context database, as well as through the Gale Biographies database (File GALBIO) through Lexis-Nexis. For more information on Biography in Context, visit us on our web site at gale.cengage.com. For more information on Gale Biographies, contact LexisNexis, P.O. Box 933, Dayton, OH 45401-0933; phone (937) 865-6800; toll- free: 800-227-4908.

Suggestions Welcome

Comments and suggestions from users of *The Writers Directory* on any aspect of the product as well as suggestions for writers to be included in a future edition are cordially invited. Please write:

The Editor

The Writers Directory

St. James Press

Gale, a part of Cengage Learning

27500 Drake Rd.

Farmington Hills, Michigan 48331-3535.

Entry in *The Writers Directory* is at the discretion of the editor.

Abbreviations Used In The Writers Directory

A
AB	Alberta
ABC	American Broadcasting Company
ACT	Australian Capital Territory
AK	Alaska
AL	Alabama
Apt.	Apartment
AR	Arkansas
Assn.	Association
Assoc.	Associate
Asst.	Assistant
Ave.	Avenue
AZ	Arizona

B
b.	born
BBC	British Broadcasting Corporation
BC	British Columbia
Beds.	Bedfordshire
Berks.	Berkshire
Bldg.	Building
Blvd.	Boulevard
Brig.	Brigadier
Bros.	Brothers
Bucks.	Buckinghamshire

C
CA	California
Cambs.	Cambridgeshire
Can.	Canada
Capt.	Captain
CBC	Canadian Broadcasting Company
CBS	Columbia Broadcasting System (US)
CIA	Central Intelligence Agency (US)
CO; co.	Colorado; Company; County
Co-ed.	Co-editor
Co-trans.	Co-translator
Col.	Colonel
Contrib.	Contributor; Contributing
Corp.	Corporation
CPA	Certified Public Accountant
Cres.	Crescent
CT; Ct.	Connecticut; Court

D
DC	District of Columbia
DE	Delaware
Dept.	Department
Derbys.	Derbyshire
Dir.	Director
Div.	Division
Dr.	Doctor; Drive

E
E.	East
Ed.	Editor; Edition
Exec.	Executive

F
FBI	Federal Bureau of Investigation (US)
FL	Florida
Ft.	Fort

G
GA	Georgia
Gen.	General
Glam.	Glamorgan
Glos.	Glouchestershire
Gov.	Governor
Govt.	Government

H
Hants.	Hampshire
HE	His Eminence; His/Her Excellency
Herts.	Hertfordshire
HI	Hawaii
HM	His/Her Majesty
HMS	His/Her Majesty's Ship; His/Her Majesty's Service
Hon.	Honorable; Honorary

I
IA	Iowa
ID	Idaho
IL	Illinois
IN	Indiana
Inc.	Incorporated
Inst.	Institute
Intl.	International

J
Jr.	Junior

K
KS	Kansas
KY	Kentucky

L
LA	Louisiana
Lab.	Laboratory
Lancs.	Lancashire
Lelcs.	Leicestershire
LI	Long Island
Lincs.	Lincolnshire
Lt.	Lieutenant
Ltd.	Limited

M
MA	Massachusetts
Mag.	Magazine
Maj.	Major
MB	Manitoba
MD	Maryland
ME	Maine
Mgr.	Manager
MI	Michigan
Middx.	Middlesex
MN	Minnesota
MO	Missouri
MP	Member of Parliament
MT; Mt.	Montana; Mount, Mountain

N
N.	North
NASA	National Aeronautics and Space Administration
NATO	North Atlantic Treaty Organization
NB	New Brunswick
NBC	National Broadcasting System (US)
NC	North Carolina
NE	North East
NF	Newfoundland
NH	New Hampshire
NJ	New Jersey
NL	Newfoundland and Labrador
NM	New Mexico
No.	Number

Northants.	Northamptonshire
Notts.	Nottinghamshire
nr.	Near
NS	Nova Scotia
NSW	New South Wales
NT	Northern Territory (Australia); Northwest Territories (Canada)
NU	Nunavut
NV	Nevada
NW	North West
NWT	Northwest Territories
NY	New York
NYC	New York City

O

OH	Ohio
OK	Oklahoma
ON	Ontario
OR	Oregon
Orch.	Orchestra
Org.	Organization
Oxon.	Oxfordshire

P

PA	Pennsylvania
PE, PEI	Prince Edward Island
PEN	Poets, Playwrights, Essayists, Editors, Novelists
Pl.	Place
PO	Post Office
Pres.	President
Prof.	Professor
Prog.	Program
Publrs.	Publishers
Publs.	Publications

Q

QC	Quebec
QLD	Queensland

R

Rd.	Road
Rep.	Representative
Rev. ed.	Revised edition
RI	Rhode Island
RR	Rural Route
Rte.	Route

S

S.	South
SA	South Australia
Salop.	Shropshire
SC	South Carolina
Sch.	School
SD	South Dakota
SE	South East
Sec	Secretary
SK	Saskatchewan
Soc.	Society
Sq.	Square
Sr.	Senior
St.	Saint; Street
Staffs.	Staffordshire
Ste.	Suite
Supt.	Superintendent
SW	South West

T

Tas.	Tasmania
Terr.	Terrace
TN	Tennessee
Trans.	Translator; Translation
Treas.	Treasurer
TX	Texas

U

UK	United Kingdom
UN	United Nations
Unesco	United Nations Educational, Scientific and Cultural Organization
Unicef	United Nations Children's Emergency Fund
Univ.	University
US;	USA United States, United States of America
USS	United States Ship; United States Service
USSR	Union of Soviet Socialist Republics
UT	Utah

V

VA	Virginia
VIC	Victoria
Vol(s).	Volume(s)
VT	Vermont

W

W.	West
WA	Washington; Western Australia
Warks.	Warwicks; Warwickshire
WHO	World Health Organization
WI	Wisconsin
Wilts.	Wiltshire
Worcs.	Worcestershire
WV	West Virginia
WY	Wyoming

Y

YM-YWHA	Young Men's-Young Women's Hebrew Association
YMCA	Young Men's Christian Association
Yorks.	Yorkshire
YWCA	Young Women's Christian Association
YT	Yukon Territory

V

VACCHE, Angela Dalle. American/Italian (born Italy), b. 1954. **Genres:** Film, History, Theatre. **Career:** Yale University, Department of History of Art, faculty; Georgia Institute of Technology, associate professor, LCC-IFS Program, director; Vassar College, faculty; University of Udine, LCC-IFS Program, director; New York School of Literature, Communication and Culture, curatorial associate for performa-arts; University of Paris 7, visiting professor, 2008-09. **Publications:** The Body in the Mirror: Shapes of History in Italian Cinema, 1992; Cinema and Painting: How Art Is Used in Film, 1996; (ed. and intro.) The Visual Turn: Classical Film Theory and Art History, 2003; (ed. with B. Price) Color: The Film Reader, 2006; Diva: Defiance and Passion in Early Italian Cinema, 2008. Contributor to books. **Address:** Georgia Institute of Technology, Skiles 344, 686 Cherry St., Atlanta, GA 30332-0165, U.S.A. **Online address:** angela.dallevacche@lcc.gatech.edu

VACHSS, Andrew H(enry). American (born United States), b. 1942. **Genres:** Novels, Mystery/Crime/Suspense, Horror, Plays/Screenplays, Songs/Lyrics And Libretti, Criminology/True Crime, Law, Sociology, Sociology, Literary Criticism And History. **Career:** U.S. Public Health Service, program representative, 1965-66; Department of Social Services, unit supervisor, 1966-69; Community Development Foundation, urban coordinator, 1969-70; Calumet Community Congress, organizer and coordinator, 1970; Uptown Community Organization, director, 1970-71; Libra Inc., director, 1971-72; Medfield-Norfolk Prison Project, deputy director, 1971-72; Department of Youth Services, project director, 1972-73; Intensive Treatment Unit (ANDROS II), director, 1972-73; Advocacy Associates, director, 1973-75; Crime Control Coordinator's Office, planner and analyst, 1974-75; Juvenile Justice Planning Project, director, 1975-85; attorney and consultant, 1976-; College of New Resources, adjunct professor, 1980-81. Writer. **Publications:** BURKE SERIES: Flood, 1983; Strega, 1987; Blue Belle, 1988; Hard Candy, 1989; Blossom, 1990; Sacrifice, 1991; Down in the Zero, 1994; Footsteps of the Hawk, 1995; False Allegations, 1996; Safe House, 1998; Choice of Evil, 1999; Dead and Gone, 2000; Pain Management, 2001; Only Child, 2002; Down Here, 2004; Mask Market, 2006; Terminal, 2007; Another Life, 2008. NOVELS: Shella, 1993; The Getaway Man, 2003; Two Trains Running, 2005; Haiku, 2009; (with F. Caruso) Heart Transplant, 2010; The Weight, 2010; That's How I Roll, 2012; Blackjack, 2012. SHORT STORIES: Born Bad, 1994; Predator: Race War, 1995; Hard Looks: Adapted Stories, 1996; Everybody Pays, 1999. OTHERS: The Life-Style Violent Juvenile: The Secure Treatment Approach, 1979; The Child Abuse-Delinquency Connection: A Lawyer's View, 1989; Another Chance to Get It Right (prose-poem), 1993, 3rd ed., 2003; Batman: The Ultimate Evil, 1995; A Bomb Built in Hell, 2000; Crime Is On My Side, 2009; Pantheon, 2009. **Address:** 420 Lexington Ave., Ste. 2805, New York, NY 10170-2899, U.S.A.

VADINO, Diane. American (born United States) **Genres:** Novels. **Career:** McSweeney's (publishing house), original staff member. Writer. **Publications:** Smart Girls like Me, 2007. Contributor to periodicals. **Address:** New York, NY , U.S.A.

VAHANIAN, Gabriel. French (born France), b. 1927. **Genres:** Theology/Religion, Translations. **Career:** Princeton University, instructor, 1955-58; Syracuse University, assistant professor, 1958-62, associate professor, 1962-67, Eliphalet Remington professor, 1967-73, director of graduate studies in religion, 1967-75, Jeannette K. Watson professor of religion, 1975-84, adjunct professor of religion, 1984-; Universite des Sciences Humaines, visiting professor, 1972-75, 1975-76, 1979-80, professor de theologie ethique, 1984-95, professor emeritus, 1995-; University of Toronto, visiting professor, 1978; Rosary College, visiting professor, 1986-87; University of Metz, visiting professor, 1988-89, 1990-94; Centre College, visiting professor, 1993-95. Writer. **Publications:** (Trans.) J. Leuba and K. Barth, La Confession de foi de l'eglise (title means: 'The Faith of the Church'), 1960; The Death of God: The Culture of Our Post-Christian Era, 1961; Wait Without Idols, 1964; No Other God, 1966; La Condition de Dieu, 1970; Dieu et l'Utopie, 1977, rev. ed. as God and Utopia, 1977; (trans. and intro.) The Thought of Jacques Ellul, 1981; Sineui Jookeumkwa Hyundai Nunhak, 1984; L'Etre et Dieu, 1986; Hyundai Munhak, 1988; Dieu Anonyme ou la peur des mots, 1989, trans. as Anonymous God: An Essay on not Dreading Words, 2001; Hunanim gwa jutofia: gyo hoe wa teknik, 1991; L'Utopie Chrétienne (collection), 1992; Le Salut, 1994; (ed.) Le Siecle de Jacques Ellul, 1994; L'Europe a la croisee des religions, 1995; La foi une fois pour toutes, 1996; La transparence et le secret, 1998; Tillich and the New Religious Paradigm, 2004; Praise of the Secular, 2008. **Address:** 6 rue Schweighaeuser, Strasbourg, 67000, France.

VAID, Urvashi. American/Indian (born India), b. 1958. **Genres:** Gay And Lesbian Issues. **Career:** Pullman & Weitzen (law firm), legal secretary, administrative assistant, 1979-80; National Consumer Law Center, legal intern, 1981; American Civil Liberties Union, National Prison Project, legal intern, 1982, staff attorney, 1983-86; Geller & Weinberg (law firm), legal intern, 1982-83; Gay Community News, promotions manager, 1983, director, 1980-83; National Gay and Lesbian Task Force (NGLTF) and the National Gay and Lesbian Task Force Policy Institute, director of public information, 1986-89, executive director, 1989-92, think-tank director, 1997-2001; writer and lecturer, 1993-; National Network of Gay/Lesbian Statewide Political Groups, co-founder, 1996; Gill Foundation, director; Ford Foundation, Governance and Civil Society Unit, deputy director, 2001-05; Arcus Foundation, executive director, 2005-10; Arcus Operating Foundation, executive director, 2005-10; Vaid Group, president, 2010-, chief executive officer; City University of New York, Department of Sociology, visiting senior research fellow, 2010-; Columbia Law School, Center for Gender and Sexuality Law, Engaging Tradition Project, director, 2011-. Writer. **Publications:** Media Skills Workshop for Gay and Lesbian Activists and Organizations, 1988; (intro.) My American History, 1994; Virtual Equality: The Mainstreaming of Gay and Lesbian Liberation, 1995; (intro.) Hospital Time, 1997; (co-ed.) From Wrongs to Rights: Public Opinion on Gay and Lesbian Americans' Moves Toward Equality, 1997; (co-ed.) Income Inflation: The Myth of GLBT Affluence, 1998; (co-ed.) Out and Voting: The GLB Vote in Congressional House Elections, 1990-1998, 1998; (co-ed. and intro.) The Domestic Partnership Organizing Manual, 1999; (co-ed. and intro.) Outing Age: Public Policy Issues Affecting GLBT Seniors, 2000; (ed. with J. D'Emilio and W.B. Turner) Creating Change: Sexuality, Public Policy, and Civil Rights, 2000. Works appear in anthologies. Contributor of articles to books and periodicals. **Address:** Engaging Tradition Project, Center for Gender and Sexuality in the Law, Columbia Law School, 435 Jerome Greene Hall, New York, NY 10027, U.S.A. **Online address:** uvaid@law.columbia.edu

VAIDHYANATHAN, Siva. American (born United States), b. 1966.

Genres: Cultural/Ethnic Topics. Career: Dallas Morning News, reporter, 1988; Austin American-Statesman, reporter, 1989-91; Star-Telegram, reporter, 1992; Concordia University, history lecturer, 1996; Wesleyan University, visiting assistant professor of history, 1998-99; New York University, faculty fellow and assistant professor, 1999-2001, assistant professor of culture and communication and director of undergraduate program, 2002-, associate professor, through 2007; University of Wisconsin, assistant professor of information studies, 2001-02; University of Virginia, School Of Law, Department of Media Studies, associate professor, professor, Robertson professor in media studies, chair, 2011-; New York Institute for the Humanities, fellow; Institute for the Future of the Book, fellow; Columbia University, faculty. Writer. Publications: Copyrights and Copywrongs: The Rise of Intellectual Property and How It Threatens Creativity, 2001; The Anarchist in the Library: How the Clash between Freedom and Control Is Hacking the Real World and Crashing the System, 2004; (with C. Peña) Rewiring the Nation: The Place of Technology in American Studies, 2007; Googlization of Everything, 2011. Address: Department of Media Studies, University of Virginia, 224 Wilson Hall, PO Box 400866, Charlottesville, VA 22904-4866, U.S.A. Online address: sivav@virginia.edu

VAIL, Rachel. American (born United States), b. 1966. Genres: Children's Fiction, Adult Non-fiction, Young Adult Fiction, Novels, Novellas/Short Stories. Career: Writer. Publications: YOUNG-ADULT NOVELS: Wonder, 1991; Do-Over, 1992; Ever After, 1994; Daring to be Abigail, 1996; (with Avi) Never Mind!: A Twin Novel, 2004; If We Kiss, 2005. FRIENDSHIP RING SERIES: Please, Please, Please, 1998; Not That I Care, 1998; If You Only Knew, 1998; What Are Friends For?, 1999; Fill in the Blank, 2000; Popularity Contest, 2000; Justin Case, 2010. MAMA REX AND T SERIES: Mama Rex and T Shop for Shoes, 2000; Mama Rex and T Lose a Waffle, 2000; Mama Rex and T Run Out of Tape, 2001; The Horrible Play Date, 2001; The Sort-of-Super Snowman, 2002; Mama Rex and T Turn off the TV, 2002; Mama Rex and T Have Homework Trouble, 2002; The (Almost) Perfect Mother's Day, 2002; Halloween Knight, 2002; The Reading Champion, 2003; The Prize, 2003; Mama Rex and T Stay up Late, 2003. OTHER: Over the moon, 1998; Sometimes I'm Bombaloo, 2002; You, Maybe: The Profound Asymmetry of Love in High School, 2006; Righty and Lefty: A Tale of Two Feet, 2007; Jibberwillies at Night, 2008; Lucky, 2008; Gorgeous, 2009; Brilliant, 2010; School, Drool, and Other Daily Disasters, 2010; Flabbersmashed about You, 2012; Hello, My Name is Liam and I'll Be Your Easter Bunny, 2012; Shells, Smells, and the Horrible Flip-Flops of Doom, 2012; Piggy Bunny, 2012. Address: Writers House, 21 W 26th St., New York, NY 10010, U.S.A. Online address: rachelvailbooks@gmail.com

VAILL, Amanda. American (born United States) Genres: Biography, Novels, Young Adult Non-fiction. Career: Writer, 1992-; Viking Penguin, executive editor. Publications: (Ed.) O. Henry Selected Stories, 1994; Everybody was So Young: Gerald and Sara Murphy, A Lost Generation Love Story, 1998; (contrib.) Picasso et les Femmes, 2003; (co-author) Seaman Schepps: A Century of New York Jewelry Design, 2004; Somewhere: The Life of Jerome Robbins, 2006; (contrib.) Making It New: The Art and Style of Sara and Gerald Murphy, 2007; Hotel Florida: Love and Death in Spain, 1936-1939, forthcoming. Contributor to periodicals. Address: c/o Eric Simonoff, William Morris Endeavor, 1325 Ave. of the Americas, New York, NY 10019, U.S.A. Online address: author@amandavaill.com

VAILLANCOURT, Pauline Marie. See ROSENAU, Pauline Vaillancourt.

VAILLANT, Janet G. American (born United States), b. 1937. Genres: Education, History. Career: Queens College, instructor in English literature, 1965-66; Wheaton College, assistant professor of government, 1972-76; Harvard University, lecturer in government, 1976-80, National Resource Center For Russian, East European and Central Asian Studies, associate director, 1976-97, Davis Center for Russian Studies and Eurasian Studies, associate, 1997-, independent consultant, Russian and CIS education center associate; Soviet-American Institute on Teaching History, co-director, 1990-92. Writer. Publications: (With J. Richards) From Russia to USSR, 1985, 2nd ed., 1993; Black, French, and African: A Life of Leopold Sedar Senghor, 1990; (ed. with R.A. Cole) Activities for Teaching Russian and Soviet Studies in the High School, 1991, 2nd ed., 1993; Vie de Senghor, 2006. Contributor to periodicals. Address: Davis Center for Russian and Eurasian Studies, Harvard University, Rm. S301, 1730 Cambridge St., 3rd Fl., Cambridge, MA 02138, U.S.A. Online address: janet.vaillant@post.harvard.edu

VAITE, Célestine Hitiura. American/French (born France), b. 1966?. Genres: Novels, Young Adult Fiction. Career: Educator and writer. Publications: Breadfruit, 2000 in US as Breadfruit: A Novel, 2006; Frangipani, 2004; Tiare: The Husband Who Didn't Deserve his Wife and Everything that Happened Next, 2006 in US as Tiare in Bloom: A Novel, 2007; The Marriage Proposal, 2008. Address: c/o Author Mail, Little, Brown and Co., 1271 Ave. of the Americas, New York, NY 10020-1300, U.S.A. Online address: celestine_h_vaite@fast-email.com

VAIZEY, Marina. British/American (born United States), b. 1938. Genres: Art/Art History, History, Antiques/Furnishings. Career: Freelance writer, 1961-70; Financial Times Newspaper, art critic, 1970-74; Sunday Times, art critic, 1974-92; Now magazine, dance critic and feature writer, 1979-81; Art Quarterly and Review, National Art Collection Fund, consultant, editor, 1991-98. Writer. Publications: The St. Michael Guide to Famous Paintings, 1979; 100 Masterpieces of Art, 1979; Andrew Wyeth, 1980; (contrib.) The State of the Language, 1980; The Artist as Photographer, 1982; (co-author) Andre Kertesz, 1984; Peter Blake, 1985; Christo, 1990; Christiane Kubrick, 1990; Jørgen Hauges Sørensen: Et Udvalg af Billeder, 1994; Shining Through, 1995; Picasso's Ladies, 1998; (with C. Gere) Great Women Collectors, 1999; (ed.) Art, The Critics' Choice: 150 Masterpieces of Western Art Selected and Defined by the Experts, 1999; Sutton Taylor: A Lustrous Art, 1999; Felim Egan, 1999; (with C. Gere) Great Woman Collectors, 1999; Magdalene Odundo, 2001; The British Museum Smile, 2002; (with I. Thompson) Colin Rose: Edge to Edge, 2003; (with C. Phillips) Wendy Ramshaw: Jewellery, 2004. Address: 24 Heathfield Terr., Chiswick, London, GL W4 4JE, England.

VALDER, Peter. Australian (born Australia), b. 1928. Genres: Horticulture, Homes/Gardens, Botany. Career: Government of Australia, Department of Agriculture, plant pathologist, 1951-62; University of Sydney, mycologist and senior lecturer in botany, 1963-88; writer, television presenter and lecturer, 1988-. Publications: Wisterias: A Comprehensive Guide, 1995; The Garden Plants of China, 1999; Gardens in China, 2002. Contributor to magazines. Address: Timber Press Inc., 133 SW 2nd Ave., Ste. 450, Portland, OR 97204, U.S.A. Online address: valderpg@mac.com

VALDÉS, Mario J. Also writes as Mario Valdés San Martin. Canadian/American (born United States), b. 1934. Genres: Literary Criticism And History, Philosophy, Cultural/Ethnic Topics, Young Adult Fiction. Career: University of Michigan, instructor in Spanish, 1962-63; University of Toronto, assistant professor, 1963-66, associate professor, 1966-70, professor of Hispanic studies and comparative literature, 1970-99, Centre for Comparative Literature, director, 1978-83, Northern Telecom professor of Ibero-American studies 1996-2001, professor emeritus of comparative literature, 1999-; Revista Canadiense de Estudios Hispánicos, founding editor, 1976-92; University of Illinois, Department of Spanish, Italian and Portuguese, head, 1976-78; Canadian Review of Hispanic Studies, founding editor, 1976-92; ACLS, publications chair, 1988-96; Modern Language Association, vice president, president, 1988-91; Comparative Literary History Series, ICLA, general editor, 1992-2002. Publications: Death in the Literature of Unamuno, 1964; (with M.E. Valdés) An Unamuno Source Book, 1973; (co-author) Théorie Littéraire dans le Monde Hispanique, 1975; Shadows in the Cave: Phenomenological Theory of Literary Criticism, 1982; Phenomenological Hermeneutics and the Study of Literature, 1987; World-Making: The Literary Truth-Claim and the Interpretation of Texts, 1991; (with L. Hutcheon) Rethinking Literary History, 1994; La Interpretacion Abierta, 1996; Hermeneutics of Poetic Sense, 1997; Con Paul Ricoeur: Indagaciones Hermeneuticas, 2000; México: Fondo de Cultura Económica, 2006. EDITOR: Niebla, 1969; San Manuel Bueno, 1974; (with O.J. Miller) Interpretation of Narrative, 1978; (with O.J. Miller) Identity of the Literary Text, 1985; Inter-American Literary Relations, 1985; (with M.E. de Veldés) Approaches to Teaching Garcia Marquez's One Hundred Years of Solitude, 1990; Toward a Theory of Comparative Literature, 1990; A Ricoeur Reader: Reflection and Imagination, 1991; Comparative Literary History as Discourse, 1991; Leyendo a Paz, 1992; Latin America as Its Literature, 1995; O Condor Voa: Literatura e Cultura Latino Americanas, 2000; (with D. Kadir) Literary Cultures of Latin America, 3 vols., 2004. Contributor to periodicals. Address: Center for Comparative Literature, University of Toronto, 93 Charles St., 3rd Fl., Toronto, ON M5S 1K9, Canada. Online address: m.valdes@utoronto.ca

VALE-ALLEN, Charlotte. (Katharine Marlowe). Canadian (born Canada), b. 1941. Genres: Novels, Biography. Career: Writer and publisher. Publications: Hidden Meanings, 1976; Love Life, 1976; Sweeter Music, 1976; Another Kind of Magic, 1977; Becoming, 1977; Gentle Stranger, 1977; Mixed Emotions, 1977; Running Away, 1977; Gifts of Love, 1978; Julia's Sister, 1978; Meet Me in Time, 1978; Believing in Giants, 1978; Acts of Kindness, 1979; Moments of Meaning, 1979; Times of Triumph, 1979; Promises, 1980; Daddy's Girl (autobiography), 1980; The Marmalade Man (in paperback as Destinies), 1981; Perfect Fools, 1981; Intimate Friends, 1983; Pieces of Dreams, 1984; Matters of the Heart, 1985, Time/Steps, 1986; Illusions, 1987; Dream Train, 1988; Night Magic, 1989; Painted Lives, 1990; Leftover Dreams, 1992; Dreaming in Color, 1993; Somebody's Baby, 1995; Claudia's Shadow, 1996; Mood Indigo, 1997; Parting Gifts, 2001; Grace Notes, 2002; The Young Person's Dreambook, 2002; Fresh Air, 2003; Sudden Moves, 2004. AS KATHARINE MARLOWE: Hearts' Desires, 1991; Secrets, 1992; Nightfall, 1993. **Address:** 144 Rowayton Woods Dr., Norwalk, CT 06854, U.S.A. **Online address:** cvaleallen@earthlink.net

VALELLY, Richard M. American (born United States), b. 1953?. **Genres:** Social Sciences, Politics/Government. **Career:** College of the Holy Cross, Department of Political Science, lecturer and assistant professor, 1983-85; Massachusetts Institute of Technology, Department of Political Science, assistant professor and associate professor, 1985-93; Swarthmore College, Department of Political Science, associate professor, 1992-2000, professor, 2000-07, Claude C. Smith '14 professor, 2008-; Harvard University, visiting professor, 1993, University of Pennsylvania, visiting professor, 2003, 2004, 2007. Writer. **Publications:** Radicalism in the States: The Minnesota Farmer-Labor Party and the American Political Economy, 1989; The Two Reconstructions: The Struggle for Black Enfranchisement, 2004; (ed.) The Voting Rights Act: Securing the Ballot, 2006; (ed.) Princeton Readings in American Politics, 2009. Contributor to journals. **Address:** Department of Political Science, Swarthmore College, 500 College Ave., Swarthmore, PA 19081, U.S.A. **Online address:** rvalell1@swarthmore.edu

VALENSTEIN, Elliot S(piro). American (born United States), b. 1923. **Genres:** Psychology, Sciences. **Career:** Walter Reed Army Institute of Research, experimental psychologist, 1955-57, chief lab neuropsychologist, 1957-61; University of Maryland, lecturer in psychology, 1956-57; Catholic University of America, Graduate Experimental Psychology, lecturer, 1958; Fels Research Institute, Department of Psychophysiology-Neurophysiology, senior research associate, 1961-70; Antioch College (now Antioch University), associate professor, professor of psychology, 1961-70; Pahlavi University, visiting professor, 1968; Instituto Nacional de Neurologia, visiting professor, 1968; University of California, visiting professor, 1969-70; University of Michigan, Department of Psychology and Neuroscience Program, professor, 1970-94, chairman of biopsychology, 1980-91, professor emeritus, 1994-; Hebrew University, Department of Psychology, Fullbright fellow and visiting professor, 1980; Beijing University, visiting professor, 1983. Writer. **Publications:** Brain Control: A Critical Examination of Brain Stimulation and Psychosurgery, 1973; Persistent Problems in the Physical Control of the Brain, 1975; Great and Desperate Cures: The Rise and Decline of Psychosurgery and Other Radical Treatments for Mental Illness, 1986; Blaming the Brain: The Truth about Mental Health and Drugs, 1988; The War of the Soups and Sparks: The Discovery of Neurotransmitters and the History of the Dispute over How Nerves Communicate, 2005; Jai Hind: The Amazing Story of Subhas Chandra Bose, 2010. EDITOR AND CONTRIBUTOR: Brain Stimulation and Motivation: Research and Commentary, 1973; The Psychosurgery Debate: Scientific, Legal and Ethical Perspectives, 1980. **Address:** Department of Psychology, University of Michigan, 530 Church St., Ann Arbor, MI 48109-1043, U.S.A. **Online address:** esv@umich.edu

VALENTE, Claire. American (born United States), b. 1969. **Genres:** History, Humanities. **Career:** Harvard University, tutor and teaching assistant, 1994-97; University of Portland, assistant professor, 1997-2002; Whitman College, adjunct assistant professor of general studies. Writer. **Publications:** The Theory and Practice of Revolt in Medieval England, 2003; (contrib.) The Experience of Power in Medieval Europe: 950-1350, 2005; (contrib.) Essays on Medieval Childhood: Responses to Recent Debates, 2008. Contributor to books, journals and periodicals. **Address:** Whitman College, 345 Boyer Ave., Walla Walla, WA 99362, U.S.A.

VALENTI, Jessica. American (born United States), b. 1978. **Genres:** Women's Studies And Issues. **Career:** Feministing, founder and executive editor, 2004-; Real Hot 100 Campaign, co-founder, 2005; Rutgers University, part-time lecturer. **Publications:** Full Frontal Feminism: A Young Woman's Guide to Why Feminism Matters, 2007; (ed. with J. Friedman) Yes Means Yes! Visions of Female Sexual Power & a World without Rape, 2008; He's a Stud, She's a Slut and 49 Other Double Standards Every Woman Should Know, 2008; The Purity Myth: How America's Obsession with Virginity Is Hurting Young Women, 2009. Contributor to books and periodicals. **Address:** Seal Press, 1700 4th St., Berkeley, CA 94710, U.S.A. **Online address:** jessica@feministing.com

VALENTINE, Douglas. American (born United States), b. 1949. **Genres:** Military/Defense/Arms Control, Novels. **Career:** Worcester County Civil Liberties, board director, 1985-87; Telemarketing Media, copywriter, 1989-, consultant, 1990-; British Broadcasting Corp., consultant, 1990-92. Writer. **Publications:** The Hotel Tacloban, 1984; The Phoenix Program, 1990; TDY, 2000; The Strength of the Wolf: The Secret History of America's War on Drugs, 2004; The Strength Of The Pack: The Personalities, Politics, And Espionage Intrigues That Shaped The DEA, 2010. Contributor to periodicals. **Address:** c/o Joel Gotler, 8955 Norma Pl., Los Angeles, CA 90069, U.S.A. **Online address:** redspruce@douglasvalentine.com

VALENTINE, Fawn. American (born United States), b. 1949. **Genres:** Crafts, Trivia/Facts. **Career:** Cabin Creek Quilters, board director, 1990-94, vice president, 1992-94; West Virginia Heritage Inc., board director, 1991-; West Virginia Broadcasting Authority, producer, 1995; Greenbrier Housing Authority, section manager, 2000-; Mountain State University, School of Extended and Distance Learning, instructor, 2000-; West Virginia Quilters Inc., research staff. Writer. **Publications:** (Co-author) West Virginia Quilts and Quiltmakers: Echoes from the Hills, 2000. Contributor to periodicals. **Address:** School of Extended and Distance Learning, Mountain State University, 609 S Kanawha St., PO Box 9003, Beckley, WV 25801, U.S.A. **Online address:** fawn@citynet.net

VALENTINE, James. Australian (born Australia), b. 1961?. **Genres:** Novels, Children's Fiction, Westerns/Adventure. **Career:** Australian Broadcasting Corp., Radio, host; Showtime Movie News, reporter. **Publications:** JumpMan Rule No. 1: Dont Touch Anything, 2005, rev. ed. as The Past is Gone, 2007; Jump Man Rule No. 2: Don't Even Think about It!, 2005, rev. ed. as The Present Never Happens, 2007; JumpMan Rule No. 3: See Rule One, 2006, rev. ed. as The Future is Unknown, 2007; The Form Guide, 2007; Tom's Night Before Christmas, 2007; Spotfull, 2007; The True History of Stuff, 2008; Rolling Stone, forthcoming. Contributor to periodicals. **Address:** Curtis Brown Australia, PO Box 19, Paddington, NW 2021, Australia.

VALENTINE, Jean. American (born United States), b. 1934. **Genres:** Poetry, Literary Criticism And History. **Career:** Sarah Lawrence College, Department of Writing, professor, 1968-70, professor poetry writing workshops, 1974-2003; Barnard College, professor poetry writing workshops, 1968-70; Swarthmore College, teacher, 1968-70; City College of New York, professor poetry writing workshops, 1969-70; Yale University, Pierson College, professor poetry writing workshops, 1970-72; Hunter College, professor, 1970-75; 92nd Street Y, professor, 1975-83, 1987-; University of Cincinnati, poet-in-residence and professor, 1983; New York University, professor, 1989-2004; Bucknell University, poet-in-residence and professor, 1990; American University, poet-in-residence and professor, 1990; University of Columbia, professor, 2003; University of Pittsburgh, professor, 2003; Vermont College, professor, 2007, 2008; University of Alabama, professor, 2007; Drew University, poet-in-residence and professor, 2009-; state poet of New York, 2008-10. **Publications:** Dream Barker and Other Poems, 1965; Pilgrims, 1969; Ordinary Things, 1974; The Messenger, 1979; Home Deep Blue: New and Selected Poems, 1989; Night Lake, 1992; The River at Wolf, 1992; The Under Voice, 1995; Growing Darkness, Growing Light, 1997; The Cradle of the Real Life, 2000; (ed.) The Lighthouse Keeper: Essays on Eleanor Ross Taylor, 2001; Door in the Mountain: New and Collected Poems, 1965-2003, 2004; Little Boat, 2007; Lucy, 2009; (intro.) Tulips, Water, Ash, 2009; Break the Glass, 2010. **Address:** 527 W 110th St., Ste. 81, New York, NY 10025, U.S.A. **Online address:** jeanvalentine@mygait.com

VALENTINE, Mark. British (born England), b. 1959. **Genres:** Novels, Novellas/Short Stories, Science Fiction/Fantasy, Literary Criticism And History, Young Adult Fiction. **Career:** Department of Social Security, senior executive officer, 1977-. Writer. **Publications:** The Garden of Ruin (short story), 1980; (ed. with R. Dobson) Arthur Machen: Apostle of Wonder, 1985; (ed. with R. Dobson) Arthur Machen: Artist and Mystic, 1986; 14 Bellchamber Tower (short stories), 1988; Murmurings, 1991; (ed.) Haunted Pavilions (short stories), 1992; Arthur Machen, 1995; The Paravine Cries (short story), 1996; In Violet Veils (short stories), 1999; Time, a Falconer: A Study of Sarban, 2010. Works appear in anthologies. **Address:** Stable Cottage, Priest Bank Rd., Kildwick, Keighley, WY BD20 9BH, England. **Online address:** mark.valentine@btinternet.com

VALENTINO, Serena. American (born United States), b. 1970?. **Genres:** Novellas/Short Stories, Children's Fiction, Science Fiction/Fantasy. **Career:** Writer. **Publications:** GloomCookie, 1999; Nightmares & Fairy Tales, vol. I: Once upon a Time, 2003, vol. II: Beautiful Beasts, 2005, vol. III: 1140 Rue Royale, 2007, vol. IV: Dancing with the Ghosts of Whales, 2008; Fairest of All, 2008; How to be a Zombie: the Essential Guide for Anyone Who Craves Brains, 2010; How to be a Werewolf: The Claws-On Guide for the Modern Lycanthrope, 2011. **Address:** SLG Publishing, 577 S. Market St., San Jose, CA 95123, U.S.A. **Online address:** serena@serenavalentino.com

VALENTIS, Mary (Arensberg). American (born United States), b. 1945. **Genres:** Psychology, Self Help, Women's Studies And Issues, Education. **Career:** Hearst Newspapers, reporter, 1967-72; State University of New York, associate professor, professor of English, 1977-; University at Albany, Center for Humanities, Arts and Technoscience, co-founder and director; Technology Play Project, co-producer and director. Writer. **Publications:** The American Sublime, 1986; (with A. Devane) Female Rage, 1994; (with J. Valentis) Brave New You, 2001; (with J. Valentis) Romantic Intelligence: How to be as Smart in Love as You are in Life, 2003; (ed. with T.P. Monastaro and P. Yablonsky) TechKnowledgies: New Imaginaries in the Humanities, Arts and Technosciences, 2007. Contributor to periodicals. **Address:** Department of English, State University of New York, Humanities 337, 1400 Washington Ave., Albany, NY 12222, U.S.A. **Online address:** mbvbooks@aol.com

VALENZA, Joyce Kasman. American (born United States), b. 1954. **Genres:** Technology, Librarianship, Social Commentary, Adult Non-fiction, Education, Young Adult Non-fiction. **Career:** University of Pennsylvania, indexer, 1976-77; Franklin Institute, readers' services librarian, 1976-77; Free Library of Philadelphia, children's librarian, 1977-80, branch manager of children's and adult services, 1980-88; Wissahickon School District, teacher and librarian, 1988-98; Philadelphia Inquirer, columnist, 1996-2006; Springfield Township High School, library information specialist and teacher, 1998-; Schlessinger Library/Video Co., developer of instructional video series, 1998-2004; Chestnut Hill college, adjunct instructor, 2002-04; Mansfield University, adjunct instructor, 2002-04. Writer. **Publications:** Power Tools: 100+ Essential Forms and Presentations for Your School Library Information Program, 1998; Child Labor in America, 2002; Power Research Tools: Learning Activities and Posters, 2003; Power Tools Recharged: 125+ Essential Forms and Presentations for Your School Library Information Program, 2004; Super Searchers Go to School: Sharing Effective Online Strategies with K-12 Students Teachers and Librarians, 2005. **Address:** Springfield Township High School, 1801 E Paper Mill Rd., Erdenheim, PA 19038, U.S.A. **Online address:** joycevalenza@gmail.com

VALENZE, Deborah M. American (born United States), b. 1953. **Genres:** History, Women's Studies And Issues. **Career:** Brandeis University, Worcester Polytechnic Institute, Smith College, instructor; Columbia University, Barnard College, 1989-, associate professor, professor; Harvard Divinity School, acting director, 1997-98. Writer. **Publications:** Prophetic Sons and Daughters: Female Preaching and Popular Religion in Industrial England, 1985; The First Industrial Woman, 1995; The Social Life of Money in the English Past, 2006. Contributor to books and journals. **Address:** Department of History, Barnard College, Columbia University, 3009 Broadway, 415 Lehman Hall, New York, NY 10027, U.S.A. **Online address:** dvalenze@barnard.edu

VALENZUELA, Judith. *See* BEATTIE, Judith Hudson.

VALERI, Laura. American/Italian (born Italy) **Genres:** Novellas/Short Stories, Novels. **Career:** Nova Southeastern University, instructor, 1999-2002; University of Iowa, instructor, 1999-2002; Broward Community College, adjunct professor, 2002-03; Florida International University, adjunct professor, 2002-03; Georgia Southern University, Department of Writing and Linguistics, associate professor, 2003-. Writer. **Publications:** The Kind of Things Saints Do, 2002. Contributor to periodicals. **Address:** Department of Writing and Linguistics, Georgia Southern University, Newton Bldg. 1118, Ste. 2224B, PO Box 8026, Statesboro, GA 30460-1000, U.S.A. **Online address:** lvaleri@georgiasouthern.edu

VALERIO, Anthony. American (born United States), b. 1940. **Genres:** Adult Non-fiction, Biography, Novels. **Career:** Book editor, 1966-72; Writing instructor, 1986-88. **Publications:** The Mediterranean Runs Through Brooklyn, 1982; Valentino and the Great Italians (nonfiction), 1986; (comp.) Bart: A Life of A. Bartlett Giamatti, By Him and About Him, 1991; Conversation with Johnny: A Novel, 1997; Lefty and The Button Men, 2000; Anita Garibaldi: A Biography, 2001; Toni Cade Bambara's One Sicilian Night: A Memoir, 2007. Works appear in anthologies. Contributor to periodicals. **Address:** 6 Bellevue Pl., Middletown, CT 06457, U.S.A. **Online address:** avalerio@wesleyan.edu

VALESIO, Paolo. American/Italian (born Italy), b. 1939. **Genres:** Novels, Language/Linguistics. **Career:** Harvard University, lecturer and associate professor of romance languages; Yale University, professor of Italian, 1974-2004, Whitney Humanities Center, fellow, now professor emeritus; Wesleyan University, Center for the Humanities, fellow; Columbia University, Department of Italian, Giuseppe Ungaretti professor of Italian literature, 2005-, chair; American Association of Italian Studies, president. Writer. **Publications:** Strutture dell'allittterazione. Grammatica, retorica e folklore verbale, (title means: 'Structure of Alliteration, Grammar, Rhetoric and Verbal Folklore'), 1968; L'ospedale di Manhattan, 1978; Prose in poesia, 1979; Novantiqua: Rhetorics as a Contemporary Theory, 1980, rev. ed. as Ascoltare il silenzio: la retorica come teoria (Listening to Silence), 1986; Il regno doloroso, 1983; La rosa verde, 1987; Dialogo del falco e dell'avvoltoio, 1987; Le isole del lago (Islands of the Lake), 1990; La campagna dell'ottantasette: poesie e prose-in-poesia, 1990; Analogia del mondo (Analogy of the World), 1992; S'incontrano gli amanti: tre storie interoceaniche, 1993; Tradimenti (Betrayals) 1994; Sonetos profanos y Sacros (Profane and Sacred Sonnets), 1996; Dialogo coi volanti (Dialogue with the Flying Ones), 1997; Anniversari (Anniversaries), 1999; Piazza delle preghiere massacrate, 1999; Dardi, 2000; Cuore del girasole: poesie-dardi, 2001-2002, 2006, Volto quasi umano: poesie-dardi, 2003-2005, 2009. EDITOR: E. Sapir, Il linguaggio. Introduzione alla linguistica, 1969; (co-ed.) N. Zingarelli, Vocabolario della lingua italiana, 10th ed., 1970; Quaderni dannunziani: D'Annunzio a Yale, 1988; (with P. Carravetta) Poesaggio: poeti italiani d'America, 1993. **Address:** Department of Italian Literature, Columbia University, 513 Hamilton Hall, 1130 Amsterdam Ave., PO Box 2827, New York, NY 10027, U.S.A. **Online address:** pv2115@columbia.edu

VALIANTE, Gio. American (born United States), b. 1971. **Genres:** Sports/Fitness. **Career:** Golf Digest, editor, 1992-, travel editor, equipment editor; Park Springs Elementary School, teacher, 1995-96; Loggers Run Middle School, teacher, 1996-97; Rollins College, assistant professor, associate professor, professor. **Publications:** (With M. Stachura) Fearless Golf: Conquering the Mental Game, 2005. **Address:** Department of Education, Rollins College, 1000 Holt Ave., Ste. 2726, Winter Park, FL 32789-4499, U.S.A. **Online address:** gvaliante@rollins.edu

VALK, Anne M. American (born United States), b. 1964. **Genres:** Autobiography/Memoirs. **Career:** Southern Illinois University, history faculty, Women's Studies Program, director; Duke University, research coordinator, 1991-96; Brown University, John Nicholas Brown Center for Public Humanities and Cultural Heritage, associate director for programs and oral history teacher. Writer. **Publications:** Radical Sisters: Second- Wave Feminism and Black Liberation in Washington, DC, 2008; (ed. with L. Brown) Living with Jim Crow: African American Women and Memories of the Segregated South, 2010. **Address:** Brown University, PO Box 1880, Providence, RI 02912, U.S.A. **Online address:** anne_valk@brown.edu

VALKO, Peter. Hungarian (born Hungary), b. 1950. **Genres:** Information Science/Computers, Engineering, Sciences. **Career:** Eotvos L. University, Chemical Cybernetics Department, teaching assistant, 1975-76; Institute of Catalysis of the (then) Soviet Academy of Sciences, assistant professor, 1981-86, associate professor, 1987-88; Hungarian Hydrocarbon Institute, senior research scientist, 1989-91; Mining University Leoben, Institute of Drilling and Production, assistant professor, 1991-93; Texas AandM University, visiting associate professor and visiting research scientist, 1993-2000, associate professor, 2001-06, Harold Vance Department of Petroleum Engineering, professor, 2006-, Texas A&M Engineering Program, ConocoPhillips fellow, 2006. Writer. **Publications:** Sonnenbestrahlung von Gebäuden für verschiedene Bauformen und Fassadenrichtungen/Insolation bes bâtiments en fonction de leur formeet de leur orientation, 1975; (with V. Saandor) Miuszaki-tudomán-yosfeladatok megoldása személyi számítaógaéppel, 1987; Advanced Scientific Computing in BASIC: With Applications in Chemistry, Biology and

Pharmacology, 1989; (with M.J. Economides) Hydraulic Fracture Mechanics, 1995; (with M. Economides and R. Oligney) Unified Fracture Design: Bridging the Gap Between Theory and Practice, 2002. **Address:** Harold Vance Department of Petroleum Engineering, Texas A&M University, 3116 TAMU-501 E RichardsonBldg., 1403 LangfoRd., College Station, TX 77843-3116, U.S.A. **Online address:** p-valko@tamu.edu

VALLBONA, Rima de. American/Costa Rican (born Costa Rica), b. 1931. **Genres:** Novellas/Short Stories, Translations, Novels, Children's Fiction, Young Adult Fiction, Humanities, Education. **Career:** Liceo J.J. Vargas Calvo, San Pedro Montes de Oca, professor of Spanish and French, 1955-56; University of St. Thomas, professor, 1964-95, head of department, 1966-71, head of modern languages department, 1978-80, Cullen Foundation professor of Spanish, 1989-95, professor emeritus, 1995-; University of Houston, visiting professor, 1975-76; Casa Argentina de Houston, vice president, 1978-79; Rice University, visiting professor, 1980-83, emeritus professor, 1995-. Writer. **Publications:** IN SPANISH NOVELS: Noche en vela (title means: 'Night of the Wake'), 1968, 6th ed., 2000; Las sombras que perseguimos, 1983; Mundo, demonio y mujer, 1991. SHORT STORIES: Polvo del camino, 1971; Lasalamandra rosada, 1979; Mujeres y agonías, 1982, 4th ed., 2000; Baraja de soledades, 1983; Cosecha de pecadores, 1988; El arcangel delperdon, 1990; Los infiernos de la mujer y algo mas (stories), 1992; Tejedoras de suenosvs: realidad, 2003. OTHER: Yolanda Oreamuno, 1972; La obra en prosa de Eunice Odio (critical anthology), 1980; Vida i Sucesos de la Monja Alferez (critical ed.), 1992, 2nd ed., 1999; La narrativa de Yolanda Oreamuno, 1996; Tormy, La gata prodigiosa de Donaldito, 1997; (co-ed.) Palabra Innumerable: Eunice Odio ante la crítica, 2001; Tejedoras desueños versus realidad, 2003; A la deriva del tiempo y de la historia, 2007. **Address:** Latin Amer Literary Review Press, PO Box 17660, Pittsburgh, PA 15235, U.S.A. **Online address:** rvallbona@aol.com

VALLE, Teresa Del. Spanish (born Spain), b. 1937. **Genres:** History, Anthropology/Ethnology, Urban Studies, Women's Studies And Issues, Medicine/Health, Psychology. **Career:** University of Guam, lecturer in history, 1969-72; East-West Center, Communications Institute, research assistant, 1972-73, lecturer in anthropology, 1974-75; Universidad del Pais Vasco (University of the Basque Country), Donostia-San Sebastian, Department of Social Anthropology, assistant professor, 1980-84, head, 1981-85, professor of social anthropology, 1984-94, professor emeritus, 1994-, director of women's studies seminar, 1981-85, 1992-94; University of Nevada, Basque Studies Program, research associate, 1985-86, visiting professor, 1994. Script writer, field consultant for ethnographic documentary productions. **Publications:** Social and Cultural Change in the Community of Umatac, Southern Guam, 1979; Mujer vasca, 1985; Una introduccion a las culturas oceanicas: Micronesia, 1987; (co-author) La mujer y la palabra, 1987; Korrika: Rituales de la lengua en elespacio, 1988; The Importance of the Mariana Islands to Spain at the Beginning of the Nineteenth Century, 1991; (ed.) W.A. Douglass, Cultura vasca y su diaspora: Ensayosteoricos y descriptivos, 1991; (with C. Sanz) Genero y sexualidad, 1991; Mujeres en la ciudad: Un analisis, aplicado de Donostia, 1991; (ed.) Gendered Anthropology, 1993; Korrika Basque Ritual for Ethnic Identity, 1993; Andamiospara una nueva ciudad. Lecturas desde le antropolegia, 1997; (ed.) Perspectivas feministas desde la antropologia social, 2000; EmakumeakEuskal Herrian, 2001; (co-author) Modelos emergentes en los sistemas yen las relaciones de genero, 2002; Mujeres, Globalización Y DerechosHumanos, 2006. Contributor to books and journals. **Address:** Department of Philosophy, Values and Social, Anthropology, Universityersidad del Pais Vasco, 70 Tolosa Hiribidea, Donostia-San Sebastian, 20018, Spain. **Online address:** teresa.delvalle@ehu.es

VALLE, Victor Manuel. American (born United States), b. 1950. **Genres:** Poetry, Food And Wine, Social Sciences, Adult Non-fiction. **Career:** California Polytechnic State University, associate professor of ethnic studies; California Arts Council, artist-in-residence; Los Angeles Times, staff writer. **Publications:** Illegal, 1977; Autonomía universitaria, 1986; La educación universitaria en El Salvador: Un espejo roto en los 1980's, 1991; Siembra de vientos: El Salvador, 1960-69, 1993; (with M.L. Valle) Recipe of Memory: Five Generations of Mexican Cuisine, 1995; (with R.D. Torres) Latino Metropolis, 2000. Contributor of poems and periodicals. **Address:** c/o Author Mail, University of Minnesota Press, 111 3rd Ave. S, Ste. 290, Minneapolis, MN 55401, U.S.A.

VALLEE, Lillian (Bozenna). American/German (born Germany), b. 1949. **Genres:** Translations, Essays, Novellas/Short Stories, Poetry, Photography.

Career: University of California, teaching assistant, 1973-74, acting associate, 1977-78; University of Wisconsin, instructor in Polish and Russian language and lecturer in Polish literature, 1978-82; Modesto City Schools, substitute teacher and reader, 1986-87; Merced Community College, instructor in English literature and composition, 1987, 1989-94; Modesto Junior College, Yosemite Community College Distric, instructor in English literature and composition, 1987, 1989-94, instructor of English, 1991-. Writer. **Publications:** TRANSLATOR: (with C. Milosz) Milosz, Bells in Winter (poems), 1978; J. Mur, Prisoner of Martial Law, 1984; (with R. Findlay) Z. Osinski, Grotowski and His Laboratory, 1986; (with D. Miedzyrzecka) J. Kott, Bottom Translation: Marlowe and Shakespeare and the Carnival Tradition, 1987; W. Gombrowicz, Diary, vol. I, 1988, vol. II, 1989, vol. III, 1991; A. Wat, Lucifer Unemployed (stories), 1990; A. Zagajewski, Solitude and Solidarity (essays), 1990; A. Zagajewski, Two Cities: On Exile, History and the Imagination, 1994; Vision at Orestimba (poems); Erratics (poems), 1996; Handful of Snow (poems), 2000; (intro. and afterward) Two-hearted Oak, 2003. **Address:** Department of Literature & Language Arts, Yosemite Community College District, Founders Hall 226C, Modesto, CA 95352, U.S.A. **Online address:** valleel@yosemite.cc.ca.us

VALLE-FERRER, Norma. Puerto Rican (born Puerto Rico), b. 1947?. **Genres:** Biography, Social Sciences. **Career:** University of Puerto Rico, School of Communications, journalism teacher, professor; Pro Women, director. Writer. **Publications:** Fiestas de cruz: Tradición y devoción en la comunidad puertorriqueña, 1985; Luisa Capetillo: Historia de una mujer proscrita, 1990; (ed. and intro.) Works, 2008. **Address:** University of Puerto Rico, San Juan, PR 00936-5067, U.S.A.

VALLEJO, Armando. American/Mexican (born Mexico), b. 1949. **Genres:** Poetry, Novels, Autobiography/Memoirs. **Career:** Xalman (magazine), co-founder, 1977; Casa de la Raza, executive director. Writer and activist. **Publications:** Luna llena: ocho años de poesia chicana, 1971-1979, 1979; October: Memories of a Chicano, 1986; Copper Thunderbird/Pajarotrueno de cobre, 1989; Para morir en tus brazos y compromiso, 1989; Poemas de unemigrante/ Poems of an Immigrant, 1990; (co-author) Situacion de las Madresy los Ninos en Zones de Grandes Proyestos: Area de Shishufindi, 1992. Works appear in anthologies. Contributor to periodicals. **Address:** Casa de la Raza Inc., 601 E Montecito St., Santa Barbara, CA 93103, U.S.A.

VALLEJO, Boris. American (born United States), b. 1941. **Genres:** Art/Art History. **Career:** Freelance artist and writer. **Publications:** (Contrib.) When Hell Laughs, 1982; (contrib.) Endithor's Daughter, 1982; (contrib.) Against the Prince of Hell, 1983; Enchantment, 1984; Fantasy Art Techniques, 1985; The Fantastic Art of Boris Vallejo, 1987; Bodies: His Photographic Art, 1996; Hindsight: His Photographic Art, 1998; Dreams: The Art of Boris Vallejo, 1999; (with J. Bell) Titans, 2000; Hindsight, 2000; (with J. Bell) Twin Visions: The Fantasy Art Techniques of Boris Vallejo and Julie Bell, 2003; (with J. Bell) Fantasy Workshop, 2003; (with J. Bell) Fantasy of Flowers, 2006; (with J. Bell) Boris Vallejo and Julie Bell: Imaginistix, 2007; Boris Vallejo and Julie Bell: The Ultimate Illustrations, 2009. ART COLLECTIONS: The Fantastic Art of Boris, 1978; Mirage, 1982, new ed., 2001; The Boris Vallejo Portfolio, 1994; (foreword) Boris Vallejo's 3D Magic, 1995; (with J. Bell) Boris Vallejo and Julie Bell: The Ultimate Collection, 2005. Illustrator of books by others. **Address:** Alaska Momma Inc., 303 5th Ave., New York, NY 10016, U.S.A.

VALLERAND, April Hazard. American (born United States), b. 1957. **Genres:** Medicine/Health. **Career:** Little Company of Mary Hospital, registered nurse and acting charge nurse, 1979-81; Institute of Medical Studies, assistant director and lead instructor, 1981-83; Queen of Angels Medical Center, nurse educator, 1983-85; University of Florida, instructor, 1985-88, assistant professor of nursing, 1988-90; University of Medicine and Dentistry of New Jersey, assistant professor of clinical nursing, 1990-93, Grieder memorial lecturer, 1996; University of Pennsylvania, postdoctoral fellow in psychosocial oncology, 1995-98; Wayne State University, College of Nursing, associate professor. Writer. **Publications:** WITH J.H. DEGLIN: Nurse's Med Deck: The Only Med Cards Integrating Nursing Process, 1987, 11th ed., 2009; Davis's Drug Guide for Nurses, 1988, 11th ed., 2009; Drug Guide for Critical Care and Emergency Nursing, 1991; Nurse's Guide for IV Medications, 1991, 3rd ed., 1996; Davis's Guide to IV Medications, 2nd ed., 1994, 3rd ed., 1996; Pocket Companion to Accompany Davis's Drug Guide for Nurses: With Comprehensive Index, 2001; Guideline for the Management of Pain in Osteoarthritis, Rheumatoid Arthritis and Juvenile Chronic Arthritis,

2002; Med Notes: Nurses Pocket Pharmacology Guide, 2004. OTHER: (with G.E. Farr and D.D. Ignatavicius) Nursing Pharmacology, 1988, 3rd ed., 1997. Contributor to books and journals. **Address:** College of Nursing, Wayne State University, 364 Cohn, 5557 Cass Ave., Detroit, MI 48202, U.S.A. **Online address:** april.vallerand@wayne.edu

VALLONE, Lynne. American (born United States), b. 1962. **Genres:** Literary Criticism And History, Women's Studies And Issues. **Career:** SUNY Buffalo, Department of English, teaching assistant, 1984-88; Texas A&M University, Department of English, assistant professor, 1990-96, associate professor, 1996-2002, professor, 2002-07; Rutgers University, professor of childhood studies, 2007-08, Department of Childhood Studies, chair and professor, 2008-. Writer. **Publications:** (Ed. with C. Nelson) The Girl's Own: Cultural Histories of the Anglo-American Girl, 1830-1915, 1994; Disciplines of Virtue: Girls Culture in the Eighteenth and Nineteenth Centuries, 1995; (ed. with M.A. O'Farrell) Virtual Gender: Fantasies of Subjectivity and Embodiment, 1999; Becoming Victoria: A Royal Girlhood, 2001; (ed. with J. Mickenberg) Oxford Handbook of Children's Literature, 2011. **Address:** Department of Childhood Studies, Rutgers, The State University of NJ, 212B Blocker Bldg., Camden, NJ 08102, U.S.A. **Online address:** l-vallone@tamu.edu

VALLONE, Ralph. American (born United States), b. 1947. **Genres:** Law, Politics/Government. **Career:** Inter American University of Puerto Rico, professor of commercial law, 1971-72; Environmental Quality Board of Puerto Rico, chief hearing examiner, 1973-75; Ralph Vallone Law Firm, attorney, 1974-, attorney at Law. Writer. **Publications:** Tiene Usted Un Caso De Malapráctica Médica?, 1985; Second Vision, 1994. **Address:** Ralph Vallone Jr. Law Offices, Son Sid Condominium, Ste. 1, 1319 Ashford Ave., San Juan, PR 00907-1344, U.S.A. **Online address:** ralval@prtc.net

VALLVEY, Ángela. Spanish (born Spain), b. 1964?. **Genres:** Politics/Government. **Career:** Writer. **Publications:** El tamaño del Universo (title means: "The Size of the Universe"), 1998; A la Caza del Ultimo Hombre Salvaje, reprinted, 1999; Vias de Extincion, 2000; Los Estados Carenciales (title means: "The Deficient States"), 2002; No lo Llames Amor, 2003; Ciudad del Diablo, 2005; Todas las muñecas son Carnívoras, 2006; Nacida en Cautividad, 2006; El Viaje de Una Hoja de Lechuga, 2007; Muerte Entre Poetas, 2008; Artículos de Larra, 2008; El hombre del corazón negro, 2011. Contributor to periodicals. **Address:** c/o Author Mail, Seven Stories Press, 140 Watts St., New York, NY 10013, U.S.A.

VALMAN, Nadia. British (born England), b. 1968. **Genres:** Young Adult Non-fiction. **Career:** Queen Mary, University of London, lecturer. Writer. **Publications:** NONFICTION: (ed. with T. Kushner) Remembering Cable Street: Fascism and Anti-fascism in British Society, 2000; (ed. with B. Cheyette) The Image of the Jew in European Liberal Culture, 1789-1914, 2004; (ed. with T. Kushner) Philosemitism, Antisemitism and the Jews: Perspectives from the Middle Ages to the Twentieth Century, 2004; The Jewess in Nineteenth- Century British Literary Culture, 2007; (ed. with E. Bar-Yosef) The Jew in Late-Victorian and Edwardian Culture: Between the East End and East Africa, 2009. Contributor of articles to periodicals. **Address:** Department of English, Queen Mary, University of London, Mile End Rd., London, GL E1 4NS, England. **Online address:** n.d.valman@qmul.ac.uk

VANAK, Bonnie. American (born United States) **Genres:** Young Adult Fiction, Children's Fiction. **Career:** Journalist. **Publications:** The Falcon & the Dove, 2002; The Tiger & the Tomb, 2003; The Cobra & the Concubine, 2005; The Panther & the Pyramid, 2006; The Sword & the Sheath, 2007; Empath, 2007; Scorpion & the Seducer, 2008; Enemy Lover, 2008; Broken Souls, 2008; The Lady & the Libertine, 2009; Immortal Wolf, 2009; (co-author) Midnight Cravings, 2009; (with L.W. Jones and L. Childs) Holiday with a Vampire III, 2009; Courage of the Wolf, 2010; Shadow Wolf, 2011; The Covert Wolf (novel), 2012. ANCIENTS SERIES: Bitten by the Vampire, 2011; Hunted by the Jaguar, 2011; Mated to the Wolf, 2011; Seduced by the Wolf, 2012. **Address:** PO Box 4634, Deerfield Beach, FL 33442-4634, U.S.A. **Online address:** bonnievanak@aol.com

VAN ALLSBURG, Chris. American (born United States), b. 1949. **Genres:** Children's Fiction, Illustrations, Young Adult Fiction, Plays/Screenplays, Picture/Board Books, History, Mystery/Crime/Suspense. **Career:** Rhode Island School of Design, teacher, 1977-. Writer. **Publications:** SELF-ILLUSTRATED: The Garden of Abdul Gasazi, 1979; Jumanji, 1981; The Wreck of the Zephyr, 1983; The Polar Express, 1985; Zathura: A Space Adventure, 2002.

OTHERS: Ben's Dream, 1982; The Mysteries of Harris Burdick, 1984; The Stranger, 1986; The Z Was Zapped: A Play in Twenty-Six Acts, 1987; Two Bad Ants, 1988; Just a Dream, 1990; The Wretched Stone, 1991; The Widow's Broom, 1992; The Sweetest Fig, 1993; The Two Figs, 1993; Bad Day at Riverbend, 1995; All Aboard the Polar Express, 2004; Journey Begins, 2004; Gift of Christmas, 2004; (with R. Zemeckis, W. Broyles and E. Weiss) Trip to the North Pole, 2004; Polar Express: The Movie Shadow Book, 2004; (with R. Zemeckis and T. West) Magic Journey, 2004; Probuditi!, 2006; The Mysteries of Harris Burdick, 2011; Queen of the Falls, 2011; Chronicles of Harris Burdick: Fourteen Amazing Authors Tell the Tales, 2011. Illustrator of books by others. Contributor to periodicals. **Address:** Houghton Mifflin Harcourt Publishing Co., 222 Berkeley St., 9th Fl., Boston, MA 02116-3748, U.S.A. **Online address:** info@chrisvanallsburg.com

VAN ALPHEN, Ernst. Dutch (born Netherlands), b. 1958. **Genres:** Literary Criticism And History, Art/Art History, Photography. **Career:** University of Utrecht, instructor in modern Dutch literature, 1989-91; University of Nijmegen, assistant professor of comparative literature and financial manager of department of general arts, 1990-92; National University of Leiden, instructor, 1992, assistant professor of comparative literature, 1992-2000, professor of literary studies, 2000-; University of Hawaii, International Institute for Semiotic and Structural Studies, visiting professor, 1991; Leiden University, professor of literary studies, 2000-; University of California, Queen Beatrix professor of Dutch studies, professor of rhetoric, 2005. Writer. **Publications:** Francis Bacon and the Loss of Self, 1993; Caught by History: Holocaust Effects in Contemporary Art, Literature and Theory, 1997; Armando: Shaping Memory, 2000; Art in Mind: How Contemporary Images Shape Thought, 2005; (with M. Donnadieu) Marian Breedveld, 2010. IN DUTCH: Bang Voor Schennis? Inleiding in deIdeologiekritiek, 1987; Bij Wijze Van Lezen: Verleiding en Verzet van Willem Brakmans Lezer, 1988; Toekomst der Herinnering: Essays over Moderne Nederlandse Literatuur, 1993; (co-author) Literaire Magneet: Essays Over Willem Frederik Hermans en de Moderne Tijd, 1995; (co-author) Op Poetische Wijze, 1996; (contrib.) Moves: Schaken en kaarten Met Het Museum, 1997; Schaduw en Spel: Herbeleving, Historisering en Verbeelding Van de Holocaust, 2004. EDITOR: P.Hamon, Er staat meer Dan er Staat: Tekst, kennis en Leesbaarheid, 1985; (with I. de Jong) Door Het Oog Van de Tekst: Essays Voor Mieke Bal OverVisie, 1988; (Dutch trans.) Lector in Fabula, 1989; (with M.Meijer) DeCanon Onder Vuur: Nederlandse Literatuur Tegendraads Gelezen, 1991; (Dutch trans.) The Limits of Interpretation, 1992; (with I. Hoving and Frans-Willem Korsten) Africa and Its Significant Others: Forty Years of Intercultural Entanglement, 2003; (with M. Bal and C. Smith) The Rhetoric of Sincerity, 2008. Works appear in anthologies. Contributor of articles to journals. **Address:** Faculteit der Geesteswetenschappen, Inst for Cultural Disciplines/Literatuurwetenschap, Universiteit Leiden, Rm. 1.01A, Witte Singel-complex, van Wijkplaats 2, Leiden, 2311, Netherlands. **Online address:** e.j.van.alphen@hum.leidenuniv.nl

VAN ALSTYNE, William W. American (born United States), b. 1934. **Genres:** Law, History, Social Sciences. **Career:** California Department of Justice, deputy attorney general, 1958; U.S. Department of Justice, Civil Rights Division, attorney, 1959; Ohio State University, faculty, professor of law, 1960-64; Duke University, Perkins professor of law, 1965-, William R. and Thomas S. Perkins chair of law, 1974; American Civil Liberties Union, national board director, 1975-77; American Association of University Professors, national president, 1976-78; American Academy of Arts and Sciences, director, 1994-; University of Chicago, visiting faculty; Yale Law School, senior fellow; Hague International Court of Justice, fellow; College of William and Mary, Marshall-Wythe Law School, Lee professor, 2004-. Writer. **Publications:** (With J. O'Toole and R. Chait) Tenure, Three Views, 1979; Interpretations of the First Amendment, 1984; (co-author) Constitución y desarrollo social, 1988; The First Amendment: Cases and Materials, 1991, 2nd ed., 1995; (ed.) Freedom and Tenure in the Academy, Duke 1993; American First Amendment in the Twenty-First Century, Cases and Materials, 2002. Works appear in anthologies. Contributor to scholarly journals. **Address:** Marshall-Wythe Law School, College of William & Mary, Rm. 254B, 613 S Henry St., PO Box 8795, Williamsburg, VA 23185, U.S.A. **Online address:** wwvana@wm.edu

VANASSE, Deb. American (born United States), b. 1957. **Genres:** Young Adult Fiction, Picture/Board Books, Children's Fiction, Young Adult Non-fiction, Travel/Exploration, Young Adult Fiction, Novels. **Career:** University of Alaska, instructor, 1982-87; Fairbanks North Star Borough Schools, teacher, 1987-99; real estate sales and service, 1998-2004; freelance writer,

1999-; Advantage Alaska Realty, real estate broker and owner, 2004-06. **Publications:** YOUNG-ADULT NOVELS: A Distant Enemy, 1997; Out of the Wilderness, 1999; Under Alaska's Midnight Sun, 2005. PICTURE BOOKS: Alaska Animal Babies, 2005; A Totem Tale, 2006; The Insiders' Guide to Anchorage and Southcentral Alaska, 2007; (ed.) Picture this, Alaska: Historic Photographs from the Last Frontier, 2009; Amazing Alaska: A Raven's Eye View, 2010; Lucy's Dance, 2011. **Address:** PO Box 222451, Anchorage, AR 99522, U.S.A. **Online address:** debv@gci.net

VAN AUSDALE, Debra. American (born United States), b. 1954?. **Genres:** Race Relations, Cultural/Ethnic Topics, Young Adult Non-fiction, Novels. **Career:** Valdosta State University, assistant professor, 1995-96; Santa Fe Community College, instructor, 1996-97; University of Florida, lecturer, 1996-97; Syracuse University, assistant professor of sociology, 1997-, professor of sociology. Writer. **Publications:** (With J.R. Feagin) The First R: How Children Learn Race and Racism, 2001. Contributor to journals. **Address:** Syracuse University, 302 Maxwell Hall, Syracuse, NY 13244, U.S.A. **Online address:** dvanausd@syr.edu

VAN BELLE, Gerald. American/Dutch (born Netherlands), b. 1936. **Genres:** Medicine/Health. **Career:** Florida State University, assistant professor of statistics, 1967-72, associate professor; University of Washington, associate professor, 1975-76, professor of biostatistics, 1976-90, professor of environmental health and head of department, 1991-, Coordinating Center for the Study of Sudden Infant Death Syndrome, director, Department of Environmental and Occupational Health Sciences, director and chair, 1991-98, professor emeritus. Writer. **Publications:** (With F. Balcom and W.H. Le Riche) The Control of Infections in Hospitals, With Special Reference To A Survey In Ontario, 1966; (with L. Fisher) Biostatistics: A Methodology for the Health Sciences, 1993, 2nd ed., 2004; Statistical Rules of Thumb, 2002, 2nd ed., 2008. **Address:** Department of Environmental, & Occupational Health Science, School of Public Health, University of Washington, 1959 NE Pacific St., PO Box 357232, Seattle, WA 98195, U.S.A. **Online address:** vanbelle@u.washington.edu

VAN BEUSEKOM, Janneke. American/Dutch/Brazilian (born Brazil), b. 1956. **Genres:** Psychology, Social Work. **Career:** Life Management Associates, therapist, 1994-; Lancaster Cancer Center, visiting therapist. Writer. **Publications:** (With P. Lichtenberg and D. Gibbons) Encountering Bigotry: Befriending Projecting Persons in Everyday Life, 1997. **Address:** Life Management Associates, 1848 Charter Ln., Lancaster, PA 17601-5896, U.S.A.

VAN BOOY, Simon. American/British (born England), b. 1975?. **Genres:** Literary Criticism And History, Young Adult Fiction. **Career:** Long Island University, School of Visual Arts, teacher. Writer. **Publications:** The Secret Lives of People in Love, 2007; Love Begins in Winter: Five Stories, 2009; Pobble's Way, 2010. EDITOR: Why We Fight, 2010; Why We Need Love, 2010; Why Our Decisions Don't Matter, 2010. Contributor to periodicals. **Address:** New York, NY, U.S.A. **Online address:** info@simonvanbooy.com

VAN BRABANT, Jozef M(artin). American/Belgian (born Belgium), b. 1942. **Genres:** Economics, Business/Trade/Industry. **Career:** Catholic University of Louvain, economist, 1968-72; Free University of Berlin, wisschenschaftlicher mitarbeiter, 1972-75; United Nations, economic affairs officer, 1975-83, senior economic affairs officer, 1984-91, principal economic affairs officer, 1991-. Consultant and writer. **Publications:** The Program for Socialist Economic Integration, 1971; Planning and Economic Growth in a Socialist Economy, 1972; Een kwarteeuw socialistische economie in Oosteuropa (title means: 'A Quarter-Century of Socialist Economics in Eastern Europe'), 1973; Observations on Poland's Trade Performance and Foreign Economic Relations in Recent Years, 1973; Reflections on Poland's Economic Policies in the 1960s, 1973; Bilateralism and Structural Bilateralism in Intra-CMEA Trade, 1973; A Reconstruction of the Composition of Intra-CMEA Trade Relations, 1974; Essays on Planning, Trade and Integration in Eastern Europe, 1974; East European Cooperation, 1977; Socialist Economic Integration, 1980; Exchange Rates in Eastern Europe, 1985; Adjustment, Structural Change and Economic Efficiency, 1987; Regional Price Formation in Eastern Europe, 1987; Economic Integration in Eastern Europe, 1989; Remaking Eastern Europe, 1990; Il Difficile sentiero della perestroika: le economie dell'Est negli anni '80, 1990; The Planned Economies and International Economic Organizations, 1991; Integrating Eastern Europe into the Global Economy, 1991; A Central European Payments Union: Technical Aspects, 1991; Privatizing Eastern Europe, 1992; Unravelling the Ruble Regime, 1992; Ruble Convert-

ibility, External and Internal Equilibrium, and Perestroyka, 1992; Industrial Policy in Eastern Europe, 1993; The Transformation of Eastern Europe, 1995; Integrating Europe, 1996; The Political Economy of Transition, 1998. EDITOR: Economic Reforms in Centrally Planned Economies and Their Impact on the Global Economy, 1991; The New Eastern Europe and the World Economy, 1993; Remaking Europe: The European Union and the Transition Economies, 1999. **Address:** Department of Economics & Social Affairs, United Nations, Rm. DC2 2150, 2 United Nations Plz., New York, NY 10163-0020, U.S.A. **Online address:** brabant@un.org

VAN CAMP, Katie. Canadian (born Canada), b. 1981?. **Genres:** Children's Fiction. **Career:** Writer and educator. **Publications:** Harry and Horsie, 2009; Cookiebot, 2011. **Address:** c/o Susanna Einstein, LJK Literary Management, 708 3rd Ave., 16th Fl., New York, NY 10017, U.S.A. **Online address:** katie@harryandhorsie.com

VAN CAUWELAERT, Didier. French (born France), b. 1960. **Genres:** Novels. **Career:** Author. **Publications:** Vingt ans et des poussieres, 1982; Poisson d'amour, 1984; Lastronome, 1984; Madame et ses flics, 1985; Le nègre, 1986; Les vacances du fantôme, 1986; L'orange amère, 1988; Un objet en souffrance, 1991; Cheyenne, 1993; Un Aller Simple, 1994; Noces de sable, 1995; La vie interdite, 1997; Le passe-muraille, 1998; Corps étranger, 1998; La demi-pensionnaire, 1999; L'éducation dune fee, 2000; L'apparition, 2001; Amour, 2002; Rencontre sous X, 2002; Hors de moi, 2003; One-Way, 2003; L'evangile de Jimmy, 2004; Out of My Head, 2004; Le père adopté, 2007; La nuit dernière au XVe siècle, 2008; Thomas Drimm: Roman, 2009; Maison des Lumiéres: Roman, 2009; Témoins de la mariée: Roman, 2010; Le Rattachement, 2010. **Address:** Other Press L.L.C., 2 Park Ave., 24th Fl., New York, NY 10016, U.S.A.

VANCE, Jack. Also writes as Peter Held, Alan Wade. American (born United States), b. 1916. **Genres:** Novellas/Short Stories, Mystery/Crime/Suspense, Science Fiction/Fantasy, Novels, Young Adult Non-fiction, Science Fiction/Fantasy, Adult Non-fiction. **Career:** Writer. **Publications:** FICTION: The Space Pirate, 1950 as The Five Gold Bands, 1962; Big Planet, 1952; Vandals of the Void (juvenile), 1953; Slaves of the Klau, 1958; The Languages of Pao, 1958; The Dragon Masters, 1963; The Houses of Iszm, 1964; Son of the Tree, 1964; Future Tense (short stories), 1964; Space Opera, 1965; Monsters in Orbit, 1965; The World Between and Other Stories, 1965; The Brains of Earth, 1966; The Many Worlds of Magnus Ridolph (short stories), 1966; The Blue World, 1966; The Last Castle, 1967; Eight Fantasms and Magics: A Science Fiction Adventure (short stories), 1969 as Fantasms and Magics, 1978; Emphyrio, 1969; The Worlds of Jack Vance (short stories), 1973; The Anome, 1973 as The Faceless Man, 1987; The Brave Free Men, 1973; The Asutra, 1974; The Seventeen Virgins, 1974; The Gray Prince, 1974; Showboat World, 1975; The Moon Moth, and Other Stories, 1975; The Best of Jack Vance (short stories), 1976; Maske: Thaery, 1976; The Bagful of Dreams, 1979; Nopalgarth, 1980; Galactic Effectuator (short stories), 1980; Dust of Far Suns (short stories), 1981; The Narrow Land (short stories), 1982; Lost Moons (short stories), 1983; Suldrun's Garden, 1983 as Lyonesse, 1984; The Complete Magnus Ridolph (short stories), 1984; Light from a Lone Star, 1985; The Green Pearl, 1985; The Augmented Agent (short stories), 1986; The Dark Side of the Moon: Stories of the Future (short stories), 1986; Green Magic: The Fantasy Realms of Jack Vance (short stories), 1988; Araminta Station, 1988; Durdane, 1989; Madouc, 1990; Chateau d' If and Other Stories, 1990; Ecce and Old Earth, 1991; Throy, 1992; When the Five Moons Rise (short stories), 1992; Night Lamp, 1996; The Laughing Magician, 1997; Ports of Call, 1998; Coup de Grace and Other Stories, 2001; Gold and Iron; Clarges; The Languages of Pao (excerpts from novels), 2002; The Flesh Mask; Strange People, Queer Notions; Bird Island (excerpts from novels), 2002; The Domains of Koryphon, 2002; Mazirian the Magician, 2002; Golden Girl and Other Stories, 2002; Lurulu, 2004; Cugel the Clever, 2005; Cugel, the Skybreak Spatterlight, 2005; The Palace of Love, 2005; Wild Thyme and Violets: Other Unpublished Works and Addenda, 2005; The World Thinker and Other Stories, 2005; The Man in the Cage; The Deadly Isles, 2005; Son of the Tree and Other Stories, 2005; The Dogtown Tourist Agency and Freitzke's Turn, 2005; Gadget Stories, 2005; The Jack Vance Treasury, 2007; The Jack Vance Reader, 2008; The Kragen, 2008; Sjambak, 2009; This is Me, Jack Vance!, 2009; Wild Thyme, Green Magic, 2009; The Men Return, 2009; Hard Luck Diggings, 2010. FICTION IN DYING EARTH SERIES: The Dying Earth, 1950; The Eyes of the Overworld (short stories), 1966; Cugel's Saga, 1966; Rhialto the Marvellous, 1984. NOVELS IN KEITH GERSEN SERIES: To Live Forever, 1956; The View from Chickweed's Window, 1978; The House on Lily Street, 1979; The Dark Ocean, 1985; Strange Notions, 1985. NOVELS IN SHERIFF JOE BAIN SERIES: (as Alan Wade) Isle of Peril, 1957; (as Peter Held) Take My Face, 1957; The Man in the Cage, 1960; The Fox Valley Murders, 1966; The Pleasant Grove Murders, 1967; The Deadly Isles, 1969; Bad Ronald, 1973. FICTION IN DEMON PRINCE SERIES: The Star King, 1964; The Killing Machine, 1964; The Palace of Love, 1967; The Face, 1979; The Book of Dreams, 1981. FICTION IN PLANET OF ADVENTURE SERIES: City of the Chasch, 1968; Servants of the Wankh, 1969 as Wankh, 1986; The Dirdir, 1969; The Pnume, 1970. FICTION IN ALASTOR SERIES: Trullion: Alastor 2262, 1973; Marune: Alastor 933, 1975; Wyst: Alastor 1716, 1978. FICTION AS ELLERY QUEEN: The Four Johns (novel), 1964 as Four Men Called John, 1976; A Room to Die In (novel), 1965. OTHER: Bird Isle, 1988. Contributor to periodicals. **Address:** 6383 Valley View Rd., Oakland, CA 94611-1226, U.S.A.

VANCE, Laura L. (Laura Lee Vance). American (born United States), b. 1967. **Genres:** History, Theology/Religion, Women's Studies And Issues. **Career:** Georgia Southwestern State University, assistant professor, associate professor, professor of sociology, 1994-; Warren Wilson College, faculty of sociology, Department of Gender and Women's Studies, chair. Writer and sociologist. **Publications:** (Ed. with R.D.C. Bruno-Jofré as Laura Lee Vance) Women in Higher Education, 1991; Seventh-Day Adventism in Crisis: Gender and Sectarian Change in an Emerging Religion, 1999. **Address:** Department of Psychology and Sociology, Georgia Southwestern State University, 800 Wheatley St., Americus, GA 31709-4376, U.S.A. **Online address:** llv@canes.gsw.edu

VANCE, Laura Lee. See **VANCE, Laura L.**

VANCE, Steve. American (born United States), b. 1952. **Genres:** Novels, Mystery/Crime/Suspense, Illustrations, Young Adult Fiction, Horror, Novellas/Short Stories, Science Fiction/Fantasy, Graphic Novels, Graphic Novels. **Career:** Novelist and short story writer. **Publications:** Planet of the Gawfs, 1978; The Reality Weavers, 1979; All the Shattered Worlds, 1979; The Hybrid, 1981; The Hyde Effect, 1986; The Abyss, 1989; Not Available in Any Store: The Complete Catalog of the Most Amazing Products Never Made, 1990; Spook, 1990; The Asgard Run, 1990; Shapes, 1991; The Prince of Darkness: A Shane King Mystery Thriller, 1996; Pound for Pound, 1999; (coauthor) The Big Book of Vice, 1999; Superman Inc., 1999; Walpurgis Nights, 2001; Identity, 2001; Bad Girls, 2009; Mad Science, forthcoming. **Address:** c/o Author Mail, Five Star Books, 295 Kennedy Memorial Dr., Waterville, ME 04901, U.S.A.

VAN CITTERS, Darrell. American (born United States), b. 1956. **Genres:** Cartoons. **Career:** Walt Disney Studios, animation director, 1978-86; Warner Brothers Classic Animation, creative director, 1989-92; Renegade Animation, co-founder and supervising director, 1992-; Oxberry Press, manager, 2009-. Writer. **Publications:** Mister Magoo's Christmas Carol: The Making of the First Animated Christmas Special, 2009. **Address:** Renegade Animation, 111 E Broadway, Ste. 208, Glendale, CA 91205, U.S.A.

VANCLEAVE, Janice. (Janice Pratt VanCleave). American (born United States), b. 1942. **Genres:** Physics, Sciences, Biology, Chemistry, Earth Sciences, Mathematics/Statistics, Geography. **Career:** Teacher, 1966-91; writer, 1984-. **Publications:** JANICE VANCLEAVES'S SCIENCE FOR EVERY KID SERIES: Astronomy, 1989; Biology, 1990; Chemistry, 1991; Earth Science, 1991; Math, 1991; Physics, 1991; Geography, 1993; Dinosaurs, 1994; Geometry, 1994; Human Body, 1995; Oceans, 1996; Ecology, 1996; Constellations, 1997; Food and Nutrition for Every Kid, 1999; Energy for Every Kid, 2006. JANICE VANCLEAVE'S SPECTACULAR SCIENCE FAIR PROJECTS SERIES: Animals, 1992; Gravity, 1992; Molecules, 1992; Magnets, 1993; Earthquakes, 1993; Machines, 1993; Microscopes, 1993; Volcanoes, 1994; Electricity, 1994; Weather, 1995; Rocks and Minerals, 1996; Plants, 1997; Insects and Spiders, 1998; Solar System, 1999. THE BEST OF JANICE VANCLEAVE SERIES: 200 Gooey, Slippery, Slimy, Weird and Fun Experiments, 1993; 201 Awesome, Magical, Bizarre and Incredible Experiments, 1994; 202 Oozing, Bubbling, Dripping and Bouncing Experiments, 1996; 203 Icy, Freezing, Frosty, Cool and Wild Experiments, 1999. A+ PROJECT SERIES: A+ Biology, 1993; A+ Chemistry, 1993; A+ Earth Science, 1999; A+ Astronomy, 2001; A+ Physics, 2003. JANICE VANCLEAVE'S PLAY AND FIND OUT SERIES: Science, 1996; Nature, 1997; Math, 1998; Human Body, 1998; Bugs, 1999. OTHER: Janice VanCleave's Guide to the Best Science Fair Projects, 1997; Janice VanCleave's Science Experiment Sourcebook,

1997; Janice VanCleave's Science Around the Year, 2000; Janice VanCleave's Teaching the Fun of Science, 2001; Guide to More of the Best Science Fair Projects, 2001; Janice VanCleave's Help! My Science Project is Due Tomorrow: Easy Experiments You can Do Overnight, 2002; Janice Vancleave's 204 Sticky, Gloppy, Wacky, and Wonderful Experiments, 2002; Janice VanCleave's Science Project Workbook: Grades 3-6, 2003; Janice VanCleave's A-plus Science Fair Workbook and Project Journal. Grades 7-12, 2003; Janice VanCleave's A-plus Science Fair Projects, 2003; Janice VanCleave's Super Science Models, 2004; Janice VanCleave's Scientists through the Ages, 2004; Janice VanCleave's Science Around the World: Activities on Biomes from Pole to Pole, 2004; Janice VanCleave's Teaching the Fun of Math, 2005; Janice VanCleave's Engineering for Every Kid: Easy Activities that Make Learning Science Fun, 2006; Janice VanCleave's Big Book of Play and Find Out Science Projects, 2006; Janice VanCleave's Great Science Project Ideas from Real Kids, 2007; Hands on Bible Explorations: 52 Fun Activities for Christian Learning, 2007; Janice VanCleave's Teaching the Fun of Science to Young Learners, Grades Pre-K-2, 2008; Janice VanCleave's Super Science Challenges: Hands: On Inquiry Projects for Schools, Science Fairs, or Just Plain Fun!, 2008. **Address:** John Wiley & Sons Inc., 111 River St., Hoboken, NJ 07030-5774, U.S.A. **Online address:** jvccbs@aol.com

VANCLEAVE, Janice Pratt. See **VANCLEAVE, Janice.**

VAN CLEVE, Kathleen. See **DEMARCO, Kathy.**

VAN CLIEF-STEFANON, Lyrae N. American (born United States) **Genres:** Poetry. **Career:** Pennsylvania State University, instructor in English, 1996-99; Fairfax County Public Schools, teacher, 2001-04; Adult and Community Education-Fairfax County Public Schools, creative writing instructor, 2001-04; Cornell University, assistant professor of English, 2004-, associate professor of English; Auburn Correctional Facility, assistant professor. Writer. **Publications:** (Ed. with S.K. Harris) Adventures of Huckleberry Finn, 1999; (ed. with S.K. Harris) Adventures of Huckleberry Finn, 2000; Black Swan, 2002; (with E. Alexander) Poems in Conversation: And a Conversation, 2008; Open Interval, 2009. Works appear in anthologies. **Address:** Department of English, Cornell University, 41 Goldwin Smith Hall, 300 Day Hall, Ithaca, NY 14853-2801, U.S.A. **Online address:** lv48@cornell.edu

VAN COTT, Donna Lee. American (born United States) **Genres:** Politics/Government, Social Commentary, History. **Career:** Inter-American Dialogue, associate project director, 1992-95; Georgetown University, instructor, 1997; University of Tennessee, assistant professor, 1998-2004, associate professor, 2004; Tulane University, assistant professor, 2004-06, associate professor, 2006-07; University of Notre Dame, Helen Kellogg Institute for International Studies, visiting residential fellow, 2005; University of Connecticut, associate professor, 2007-, Center for Latin American and Caribbean Studies, affiliated faculty, 2007-. Writer. **Publications:** (Ed.) Indigenous Peoples and Democracy in Latin America, 1994; Defiant Again: Indigenous Peoples and Latin American Security, 1996; The Friendly Liquidation of the Past: The Politics of Diversity in Latin America, 2000; From Movements to Parties in Latin America: The Evolution of Ethnic Politics, 2005; Radical Democracy in the Andes, 2009. **Address:** Department of Political Science, University of Connecticut, 341 Mansfield Rd., Ste. 1024, Montieth 404, Storrs, CT 06269, U.S.A. **Online address:** donna.vancott@uconn.edu

VANDAL, Gilles. Canadian (born Canada) **Genres:** History. **Career:** University of Sherbrooke, department of political science and history, professor. Writer. **Publications:** The New Orleans Riot of 1866: Anatomy of a Tragedy, 1983; Rethinking Southern Violence: Homicides in Post-Civil War Louisiana, 1866-1884, 2000. Contributor to books and journals. **Address:** Department of History & Political Science, University of Sherbrooke, Sherbrooke, QC J1K 2R1, Canada. **Online address:** gilles.vandal@usherbrooke.ca

VAN DEBURG, William L. American (born United States), b. 1948. **Genres:** Cultural/Ethnic Topics, History, Race Relations. **Career:** University of Wisconsin, assistant professor, 1973-79, associate professor, 1979-85, chair of department, 1981-84, professor of Afro-American studies, 1985-2003, Evjue-Bascom professor, 2003-08. Writer. **Publications:** The Slave Drivers: Black Agricultural Labor Supervisors in the Antebellum South, 1979; Slavery and Race in American Popular Culture, 1984; New Dayin Babylon: The Black Power Movement and American Culture, 1965-1975, 1992; (ed.) Modern Black Nationalism: From Marcus Garvey to Louis Farrakhan, 1997; Black Camelot: African-American Culture Heroes in Their Times, 1960-1980,

1997; Hoodlums: Black Villains and Social Bandits in American Life, 2004; (ed.) African American Nationalism, 2005. **Address:** Department of Afro-American Studies, University of Wisconsin, 4131 H.C. White Hall, 600 N Park St., Madison, OR 53706, U.S.A. **Online address:** wlvandeb@wisc.edu

VAN DELDEN, Maarten. Dutch (born Netherlands), b. 1958. **Genres:** Literary Criticism And History. **Career:** New York University, Department of Spanish and Portuguese, assistant professor, 1990-97, Department of Comparative Literature, assistant professor, 1990-97; Rice University, Department of Hispanic Studies, associate professor, 1997-2007, Department of Hispanic Studies, chair, 2002-07; University of Southern California, Department of Spanish and Portuguese, associate professor, 2007-09; University of California, Department of Spanish and Portuguese, professor and chair, 2009-. Writer. **Publications:** Carlos Fuentes, Mexico and Modernity, 1998; (ed. with K.V. Berghe) Ellaberinto de la solidaridad: cultura y Política en México, 1910-2000, 2002; (with Y. Grenier) Gunshots at the Fiesta: Literature and Politics in Latin America, 2009; Polemical Continent: Culture Wars in Twentieth-Century Spanish America, forthcoming. **Address:** Department of Spanish and Portuguese, University of California, 5303 Rolfe Hall, Los Angeles, CA 90095, U.S.A. **Online address:** mvandelden@humnet.ucla.edu

VAN DE MIEROOP, Marc. American/Belgian (born Belgium), b. 1956. **Genres:** Archaeology/Antiquities, History, Urban Studies. **Career:** Yale University, lecturer, 1983-84; Columbia University, professor of history 1984-. Writer. **Publications:** Sumerian Administrative Documents from the Reigns of Isbi-Erra and Su-ilisu, 1987; Crafts in the Early Isin Period: A Study of the Isin Craft Archive from the Reigns of Isbi-Erra and Su-Ilisu, 1987; Society and Enterprise in Old Babylonian Ur, 1992; (trans. with Z. Bahrani) J. Bottero, Mesopotamia: Writing, Reasoning, and the Gods, 1992; The Ancient Mesopotamian City, 1997; Cuneiform Texts and the Writing of History, 1999; (with M. Hudson) Debt and Economic Renewal in the Ancient Near East, 2002; (ed. and trans. with Z. Bahrani) Invention of Cuneiform: Writing in Sumer, 2003; (ed. and intro. with Z. Bahrani) Myth and Politics in Ancient Near Eastern Historiography, 2004; History of the Ancient Near East, ca. 3000-323 B.C., 2004, 2nd ed., 2007; King Hammurabi of Babylon, 2005; (ed. and trans. with Z. Bahrani) Uruk, 2006; The Eastern Mediterranean in the Age of Ramesses II, 2007; A History of Ancient Egypt, 2010; (with S. Garfinkle and H. Sauren) Ur III Tablets from The Columbia University Libraries, 2010. **Address:** Department of History, Columbia University, 424 Fayerweather Hall, New York, NY 10027, U.S.A. **Online address:** mv1@columbia.edu

VAN DEN BRINK, H(ans) M(aarten). Dutch (born Netherlands), b. 1956?. **Genres:** Novels, Adult Non-fiction. **Career:** NRC Handelsblad, correspondent, 1982-95, art editor; VPRO (Dutch television network), editor-in-chief, 1995-2001; Witte de With, Center for Contemporary Art, director; Bonanza, freelance editor, 2001-02; Vrij Nederland, cultural and political columnist, 2002-06. **Publications:** Reis naar de West, 1986; Boven de grond in Washington en New York: berichte uit een nieuw Amerika, 1988; (co-author) Het Nieuwe Nederland (nonfiction), 1993; De vooruitgang (novel), 1993; De dertig dagen van Sint Isidoor, 1994; Over het water (novel), 1998; Hart van glas (novel), 1999; On the Water, 2001; Reizigers bij een herberg, 2003; (with M. Zeeman) Eeuwig leven: een briefwisseling over geloven, 2010. **Address:** Grove Press, 841 Broadway, New York, NY 10003, U.S.A.

VANDENBROUCKE, Lucien S. American/New Zealander (born New Zealand), b. 1951. **Genres:** International Relations/Current Affairs, Military/Defense/Arms Control, History. **Career:** U.S. Department of State, foreign service officer, 1985-86; U.S. Embassy, political officer, 1986-89; Office of Regional Affairs, Bureau of Near Eastern Affairs, political officer, 1989-90; U.S. Embassy, political/economic section, chief, 1993-95; U.S. Military Academy, visiting professor, 1995-. Writer. **Publications:** Perilous Options: Special Operations as an Instrument of U.S. Foreign Policy, 1993. **Address:** Department of Social Sciences, United States Military Academy, West Point, NY 10996-1798, U.S.A.

VANDENBURGH, Jane. American (born United States), b. 1948. **Genres:** Novels, Novellas/Short Stories, Autobiography/Memoirs. **Career:** University of California, teacher; George Washington University, faculty; Georgetown University, faculty; Saint Mary's College, writer-in-residence. **Publications:** NOVELS: Failure to Zigzag, 1989; The Physics of Sunset, 1999; Architecture

of the Novel: You Story's Shape, Force & Structure, 2007; A Pocket History of Sex in the Twentieth Century: A Memoir, 2009; Architecture of the Novel: A Writer's Handbook, 2010. Contributor to periodicals. **Address:** Counterpoint Press, 1919 5th St., Berkeley, CA 94710, U.S.A.

VANDERBES, Jennifer (Chase). American (born United States), b. 1974?. **Genres:** Novels, Mystery/Crime/Suspense, Romance/Historical, Young Adult Fiction. **Career:** Pittsburgh Post-Gazette, reporter; University of Wisconsin, James C. McCreight fiction fellow, 2000-01; Colgate University, Olive B. O'Connor fellow in creative writing, 2001-02; University of Iowa, Iowa Writers' Workshop, visiting assistant professor, 2003-04; New York Public Library, Guggenheim fellow and Cullman fellow, 2007-08. Writer. **Publications:** Easter Island (novel), 2003; Strangers At the Feast: A Novel, 2010. Contributor of articles to periodicals. **Address:** The Maxine Groffsky Literary Agency, 853 Bdwy., Ste. 708, 102 Dey House, 507 N Clinton St., New York, NY 10003, U.S.A. **Online address:** admin@jennifervanderbes.net

VANDERBILT, Tom. American (born United States), b. 1968. **Genres:** History, Psychology. **Career:** I.D., contributing editor; Print, contributing editor. **Publications:** The Sneaker Book: Anatomy of an Industry and an Icon, 1998; Survival City: Adventures among the Ruins of Atomic America, 2002; Traffic: Why We Drive the Way We Do (And What It Says about Us), 2008. Contributor to books and periodicals. **Address:** c/o Zoe Pagnamenta, Zoe Pagnamenta Agency L.L.C., 30 Bond St., New York, NY 10012-2452, U.S.A. **Online address:** info@howwedrive.com

VANDERHAM, Paul. Canadian (born Canada), b. 1959?. **Genres:** Literary Criticism And History, Young Adult Fiction. **Career:** King's University College, assistant professor of English. Writer. **Publications:** James Joyce and Censorship: The Trials of Ulysses, 1998. **Address:** King's University College, 9125-50 St. NW, Edmonton, AB T6B 2H3, Canada. **Online address:** pvanderh@kingsu.ab.ca

VANDERKAM, James C(laire). American (born United States), b. 1946. **Genres:** Theology/Religion, Translations. **Career:** North Carolina State University, assistant professor, 1976-81, associate professor, 1981-86, professor of religion, 1986-91; University of St. Andrews, lecturer, 1981; Society of Biblical Literature, chair, 1984-87; University of California, visiting professor of history, 1987; University of Notre Dame, professor of Hebrew scriptures, 1991-98, John A. O'Brien professor of theology, 1998-; Bible Review, book review editor, 1992-94; Seabury-Western Theological Seminary, William Copley Winslow lecturer, 1995; Johns Hopkins University, Samuel Iwry lecturer, 1998; Seminary of the Immaculate Conception, Denzer lecturer, 2000. Writer. **Publications:** Textual and Historical Studies in the Book of Jubilees, 1977; Enoch and the Growth of an Apocalyptic Tradition, 1984; (with M. Black) The Book of Enoch; or, 1 Enoch, 1985; The Book of Jubilees, 2 vols., 1989; The Dead Sea Scrolls Today, 1994, 2nd ed., 2010; Enoch: A Man for All Generations, 1995; Calendars in the Dead Sea Scrolls: Measuring Time, 1998; From Revelation to Canon: Studies in the Hebrew Bible and Second Temple Literature, 2000; An Introduction to Early Judaism, 2001; (with P. Flint) Meaning of the Dead Sea Scrolls: Their Significance for Understanding the Bible, Judaism, Jesus, and Christianity, 2002; From Joshua to Caiaphas: High Priests after the Exile, 2004; (with G.W.E. Nickelsburg) 1 Enoch: A New Translation; Based on the Hermeneia Commentary, 2004. EDITOR: (and trans.) Book of Jubilees: A Critical Text, 1989; No One Spoke Ill of Her: Essays on Judith, 1992; Qumran Cave 4 VIII: Parabiblical Texts, vol. I, 1994; Qumran Cave 4 XIV: Parabiblical Texts, vol. II, 1995; (with W. Adler) The Jewish Apocalyptic Heritage in Early Christianity, 1996; Qumran Cave 4 XVII: Parabiblical Texts, vol. III, 1996; Qumran Grotte 4 XVIII: Textes Hebreux (4Q521-4Q528, 4Q576-4Q579), 1998; (with M. Brady) Qumran Cave 4 VI: Poetical and Liturgical Texts, vol. I, 1998; (with P. Flint and contrib.) The Dead Sea Scrolls after Fifty Years, vol. I, 1998, vol. II, 1999; (with M. Brady) Qumran Cave 4 XX: Poetical and Liturgical Texts, vol. II, 1999; (with L. Schiffman) Encyclopedia of the Dead Sea Scrolls, 2 vols., 2000; (with M. Brady) Qumran Cave 4 XXVI: Cryptic Texts and Miscellanea, vol. I, 2000; (with M. Brady) Miscellaneous Texts from the Judaean Desert, 2000; (with L. Schiffman and E. Tov) The Dead Sea Scrolls 50 Years after Their Discovery, 2000; (with M. Brady) Qumran Grotte 4 XXII Textes Arameens Premiere Partie 4Q529-549, 2001; (with P.W. Flint and E. Tov) Studies in the Hebrew Bible, Qumran, and the Septuagint Presented to Eugene Ulrich, 2006; (with H.W. Attridge) Presidential Voices: The Society of

Biblical Literature in the Twentieth Century, 2006. Contributor of articles to books and journals. **Address:** Department of Theology, University of Notre Dame, 837 Flanner Hall, Notre Dame, IN 46556-5611, U.S.A. **Online address:** james.c.vanderkam.1@nd.edu

VAN DER KISTE, John (Patrick Guy). British (born England), b. 1954. **Genres:** History, Biography, Novels, Autobiography/Memoirs, Bibliography, Music, Young Adult Fiction, Romance/Historical, Romance/Historical. **Career:** Devon Library Services, library assistant, 1972-77; Land Registry, clerical assistant, 1977-78; College of Further Education, library assistant, 1978-; British Broadcasting Corp., TV, consultant, 2000. Writer. **Publications:** Roxeventies: Popular Music in Britain, 1970-79, 1982; Queen Victoria's Family: A Select Bibliography, 1982; Singles File: The Story of the 45 R.P.M. (music), 1987; Windsor and Habsburg: The British and Austrian Reigning Houses, 1848-1922 (history/biography), 1987; Crowns in a Changing World: The British and European Monarchies, 1901-36 (history), 1993; Kings of the Hellenes: The Greek Kings, 1863-1974, 1994; (comp.) Gilbert and Sullivan's Christmas, 2000; (with C. Hall) Once a Grand Duchess: Xenia, Sister of Nicholas II, 2002; The Man on the Moor (novel), 2004; William and Mary, 2003; Sons, Servants and Statesmen: The Men in Queen Victoria's Life, 2006; A Divided Kingdom: The Spanish Monarchy from Isabel to Juan Carlos, 2007; William John Wills, 2011. BIOGRAPHIES: Frederick III: German Emperor, 1888, 1981; (with B. Jordaan) Dearest Affie: Alfred, Duke of Edinburgh, Queen Victoria's Second Son, 1844-1900, 1984; The Roy Wood Story, 1986; Queen Victoria's Children, 1986; (with D. Wadeson) Beyond the Summertime: The Mungo Jerry Story, 1990; George V's Children, 1991; George III's Children, 1992; Childhood at Court, 1819-1914, 1995; Northern Crowns: Kings of Modern Scandinavia, 1996; King George II and Queen Caroline, 1997; The Romanovs 1818-1959: Alexander II of Russia and His Family, 1998, rev. ed., 2004; Kaiser Wilhelm II: Germany's Last Emperor, 1999; The Georgian Princesses, 2000; Dearest Vicky, Darling Fritz, 2001; (with C. Hall) One a Grand Duchess: Xenia, Sister of Tsar Nicholas II, 2002; Princess Victoria Melita: Grand Duchess Cyril of Russia, 1876-1936, 2003; Edward VII's Children, 2004; Emperor Francis Joseph: Life, Death and the Fall of the Hapsburg Empire, 2005; Jonathan Wild: Conman and Cutpurse, 2009; (with N. Sly) West Country Murders, 2009; Surrey Murders, 2009; Plymouth: History & Guide, 2009; A Grim Almanac of Cornwall, 2009; Durham Murders and Misdemeanours, 2009; Berkshire Murders, 2010; (with K.V.D. Kiste) Ivybridge and South Brent Through Time, 2010; More Cornish Murders, 2010; Dartmoor from Old Photographs, 2010. Contributor to periodicals and books. **Address:** Sutton Publishing Ltd., Phoenix Mill, Far Thrupp, Stroud, GC GL5 2BU, England.

VAN DER KOOI, Cornelis. Dutch (born Netherlands), b. 1952. **Genres:** Biography, Autobiography/Memoirs. **Career:** Reformed Church of Leimuiden, minister, 1984-92; VU-University Amsterdam, lecturer, 1992-2002, associated professor systematic theology, 2003-08, professor of systematic theology, Center of Evangelical and Reformation Theology, director, 2003-, Department for Dogmatics and Ecumenics, head, 2007-, chair of systematic theology, 2008-. Pastor and writer. **Publications:** Anfängliche Theologie: der Denkweg des jungen Karl Barth (1909 bis 1927), 1987; (with M.E. Brinkman) Het Calvinisme van Kuyper en Bavinck/Teksten bijeengezocht en ingeleid door, 1997; (ed. with J. de Bruijn) Kuyper Reconsidered: Aspects of His Life and Work, 1999; Hinkelen binnen de lijnen: enkele krijtstrepen voor een christologie, 1999; Als in een spiegel: God kennen volgens Calvijn en Barth: een tweeluik, 2002; As in a Mirror, 2005. **Address:** Vrije Universiteit Amsterdam, Faculteit der Godgeleerdheid, 14a-39, De Boelelaan 1105, Amsterdam, 1081 HV, Netherlands. **Online address:** vanderkooi@wanadoo.nl

VAN DER LEMME, Arie. See **VAN HENSBERGEN, Gijs.**

VAN DER LINDE, Laurel. American (born United States), b. 1952. **Genres:** Animals/Pets, Children's Non-fiction, Young Adult Non-fiction. **Career:** Broadway Plays, actress and dancer, 1976-82; Landmark Entertainment Group (multimedia entertainment), co-founder, 1982-86; writer, 1991-; Carousel Classics (audio books), founder, 1992-; Underground Audio Books, founder, 1997-; University of California, Writers' Program, instructor. **Publications:** The Devil in Salem Village, 1992; The Pony Express, 1993; The White Stallions: The Story of the Dancing Horses of Lipizza, 1994; Legends in Their Own Time, 1994; From Mustangs to Movie Stars: Five True Horse Legends of Our Time, 1995. Contributor to periodicals. **Address:** Writers' Program, University of California, 10995 Le Conte Ave., Ste. 440, Los Angeles, CA 90095-3001, U.S.A. **Online address:** vanderlinde@dslextreme.com

VAN DER MEER, Ron. Dutch (born Netherlands), b. 1945. **Genres:** Children's Fiction, Young Adult Fiction, Children's Non-fiction, Young Adult Non-fiction. **Career:** University of London, Goldsmiths College, research fellow, 1972-73, visiting lecturer, 1972-76; Chorley Wood School for Girls with Little or No Sight, visiting teacher in drawing techniques with a drawing aid, 1972-75; Eton College, visiting teacher, 1972-75; St. Martins School of Art, Graphic Design Department, visiting lecturer in graphic design, 1973-92; Eton College, Typography and Calligraphy, visiting teacher, 1974-77; Royal College of Art, Graphics Information Department, visiting lecturer, 1975-82; Middlesex Polytechnic, visiting lecturer, 1977-78; Van der Meer Books and Van der Meer Publishing, creative director, 1982-2001; Design Council, design consultant, 1985-87; Whizz Education Ltd., founder & director, 2004-; Maestro Education Ltd., director, 2007-11. Writer. **Publications:** SELF-ILLUSTRATED: Basil and Boris in London, 1978; Basil and Boris in North America, 1978; Sammy and Mara, 1978; My Brother Sammy, 1978; Naughty Sammy, 1979; Sammy and the Cat Party, 1979; Oh Lord!, 1980; Penny and the Piglets, 1980; I'm Fed Up, 1981; Funny Fingers, 1982; Fungus the Bogeyman Pop-Up Book, 1982; Who's Afraid?, 1983; The Ghost Book, 1983; Wheres the Mouse?, 1983; Where is the Baby?, 1983; What is Missing?, 1983; Who Eats What?, 1983; My Train, 1983; My Plane, 1983; My Motorbike, 1983; My Car, 1983; What Colour?, 1984; What Shape?, 1984; Who's Real?, 1984; Wheres the Apple?, 1984; Roaring Lion Tales Pop-Up Book, 1984; First Arabian Pop-Up Book, 1984; My Boat, 1985; My Lorry, 1985; My Rocket, 1985; My Circus, 1985; Your Amazing Senses: 36 Games, Puzzles, and Tricks that Show How Your Senses Work, 1987; Pigs at Home: A Picture Word Book, 1988; Fun with Shapes: A Spinning Wheel Book, 1990; Amazing Animal Senses, 1990; Fun with Animals: A Spinning Wheel Book, 1990; Fun with Numbers: A Spinning Wheel Book, 1990; Funny Hats, 1992. OTHER: (co-author) Frank Muirs Big Dipper, 1981; Monster Island Pop-Up Book, 1981; The Worlds First Ever Pop-Up Games Book, 1982; The Pop-Up Book of Magic Tricks, 1983; The Case of the Kidnapped Dog, 1983; (with A. McGowan) Sailing Ships Pop-Up Book, 1984; Majesty in Flight: Natures Birds of Prey in Three Dimensions, 1984; (with S. Gallagher) Inside the Personal Computer: An Illustrated Introduction in Three Dimensions, 1984; (with J. Hedgecoe) The Working Camera: The Worlds First Three-Dimensional Guide to Photography Made Easy, 1986; (R. Briggs) Snowman: A Pop-Up with Music, 1986; (with M. Jakubowski) The Great Movies-Live!: A Pop-Up Book, 1987; (with B. Cole) Babette Coles Beastly Birthday Book, 1990; The Birthday Cake: A Lift-the-Flap Pop-Up Book, 1992; (with C. and H. Frayling) The Art Pack: A Unique, Three-Dimensional Tour through the Creation of Art through the Centuries-What Artists Do, How They Do It, and the Masterpieces They Have Given Us, 1992; (with M. Berkeley) The Music Pack, 1994; (with T. Rohner) Family Bear Pop-up Book, 1994; (with R. Fisher) Earth Pack: Tornadoes, Earthquakes, Volcanoes: Natures Forces in Three Dimensions, 1995; (with A. Dudink) Brain Pack: An Interactive, Three-Dimensional Exploration of the Mysteries of the Mind, 1996; Kids Art Pack: A Hands-on Exploration of Art for the Whole Family, 1997; (with D. Sudjic) Architecture Pack: A Unique, Three-Dimensional Tour of Architecture Over the Centuries: What Architects Do, How They do It, and the Great Buildings They have Given Us Around the World, 1997; Learn About Numbers: With Flips, Flaps, Slides, Tabs, and Pop-up Surprises!, 1998; Learn About Shapes, 1998; How Many?: Spectacular Paper Sculptures: A Pop-up, 2007. Contributor to periodicals. **Address:** Rams Cottage, 39 Langley Rd., Langley, BR SL3 7AH, England. **Online address:** cdegroot@vandermeer.com

VANDERMERWE, Sandra. British/Irish (born Ireland) **Genres:** Business/Trade/Industry, Marketing, Administration/Management. **Career:** Witwatersrand University, professor of marketing; International Institute for Management Development, professor of marketing and international services; Imperial College, professor of international marketing and services, Tanaka Business School, chair of international marketing and services; Wellbeing University, International Health Insurance, director; London Business School, visiting professor; Manchester Business School, visiting professor; Templeton College of Oxford University, visiting professor; Vrije University, visiting professor. Writer. **Publications:** South African Marketing Strategy: Text and Cases, 1975; The Environment of South African Business, 1976; Business Policy and Strategy, 1977; From Tin Soldiers to Russian Dolls: Creating Added Value through Services, 1993; Competing through Services: Strategy and Implementation, 1994; Cases in European Marketing Management, 1994; The Eleventh Commandment: Transforming to Own Customers, 1996; Customer Capitalism: The New Business Model of Increasing Returns in New Market Spaces, 1999; Breaking Through: Implementing Customer Focus in Enterprises, 2004. Contributor to journals. **Address:** Tanaka Business School, Imperial College, South Kensington Campus, 53 Princes Gate, London, GL SW7 2PG, England. **Online address:** sandra.vandermerwe@btinternet.com

VAN DER PLAS, Rob(ert). American/Dutch (born Netherlands), b. 1938. **Genres:** Recreation, Technology, Sports/Fitness, Sciences, Illustrations, Reference. **Career:** Record Electrical, design engineer, 1960-63; Hebron & Medlock, design engineer, 1963-65; Ralph M. Parsons, design engineer, 1965-68; Standard Oil of California, engineering technologist, 1968-74; freelance technical translator, 1974-75; California Consulting, design engineer, 1975-78; independent consultant, writer, translator and researcher, 1979-85; ISA-Technik, project manager, 1986-90; Bicycle Books Inc., publisher and editor, 1990-96; Motorbooks Intl., publishing consultant, 1996-98; Cycle Publishing/Van der Plas Publications, publisher and editor, engineering consultant, freelance technical translator, 1998-. **Publications:** SELF-ILLUSTRATED: Roadside Bicycle Repairs: The Simple Guide to Fixing Your Bike, 1987, rev. ed., 1995; Bicycle Technology: Understanding, Selecting, and Maintaining the Modern Bicycle and Its Components, 1991, 3rd ed., 1996. OTHERS: The Penguin Bicycle Handbook: How to Maintain and Repair Your Bicycle, 1983; The Bicycle Repair Book: The Complete Manual of Bicycle Care, 1985, 2nd ed., 1993; Mountain Bike Book: Choosing, Riding and Maintaining the Off-Road Bicycle, 1985, rev. ed., 1993; Bicycle Racing Guide: Technique and Training for Bicycle Racers and Triathletes, 1986; The Bicycle Touring Manual: Using The Bicycle for Touring and Camping, 1987, 2nd ed., 1993; Bicycle Fitness Book, 1989; Mountain Bike Magic, 1991; Mountain Bike Maintenance, 1991, 3rd ed., 1993; Mountain Bike Technology, 1992; Bicycle Repair: Step by Step: The Full-Color Manual of Bicycle Maintenance and Repair, 1994; (ed.) Cycle History: Proceedings of the 6th International Cycle History Conference, Stellenbosch, South Africa, 4-8 March, 1995, 1996; (with C. Kelly) The Original Mountain Bike Book, 1997, 2nd ed., 1998; Road Bike Maintenance: Repairing and Maintaining the Modern Lightweight Bicycle, 1997; (co-author) The Original Mountain Bike Book, 1997; (ed.) Cycle History: Proceedings of the 7th International Cycle History Conference, Buffalo, NY, U.S.A., September 4-6, 1996, 1997; How To Fix Your Bike, 1998; Buying A Bike: How to Get the Best Bike for Your Money, 1999; Bicycle Repair Step by Step: How to Maintain and Repair Your Bicycle, 2002; (ed. with A. Ritchie) Cycle history 12: Proceedings of the 12th International Cycling History Conference, San Remo/Pigna, Italy, 25-28 September 2001, 2002; Simple Bicycle Repair: Fixing Your Bike Made Easy, 2004; (ed.) Cycle History 15: Proceedings, 15th International Cycling History Conference, 2005. **Address:** Cycle Publishing/ Van der Plas Publications, 1282 7th Ave., San Francisco, CA 94122, U.S.A. **Online address:** rvdp@vanderplas.net

VAN DER TOORN, Karel. Dutch (born Netherlands), b. 1956?. **Genres:** Theology/Religion, History, Young Adult Non-fiction. **Career:** University of Leiden, professor of ancient religions, 1987-98; Utrecht University, professor of ancient religions, 1987-93; University of Amsterdam, dean of faculty of humanities, 1998-2003, professor of religions of antiquity, 2003-06, university president, 2006-. Writer. **Publications:** NONFICTION: Sin and Sanction in Israel and Mesopotamia: A Comparative Study, 1985; (ed. with B. Becking and P.W. van der Horst) Dictionary of Deities and Demons in the Bible, 1995, 2nd ed., 1999; (ed. with J. Platvoet) Pluralism and Identity: Studies in Ritual Behaviour, 1995; Family Religion in Babylonia, Syria, and Israel: Continuity and Changes in the Forms of Religious Life, 1996; (ed.) The Image and the Book: Iconic Cults, Aniconism, and the Rise of Book Religion in Israel and the Ancient Near East, 1997; (ed. with A. van der Kooij) Canonization and Decanonization, 1998; (ed. with T. Abusch) Mesopotamian Magic: Textual, Historical, and Interpretative Perspectives, 1999; Scribal Culture and the Making of the Hebrew Bible, 2007. **Address:** University of Amsterdam, Spui 21, Amsterdam, 1012 WX, Netherlands.

VAN DERVEER, Tara. American (born United States), b. 1953. **Genres:** Sports/Fitness. **Career:** Stanford University, Department of Athletics, women's basketball coach, 1985-, Setsuko Ishiyama Director of Women's Basketball; U.S. National Women's Team, basketball coach, 1995-; U.S. Women's Olympic Team, basketball coach, 1996-. Writer. **Publications:** (With J. Ryan) Shooting from the Outside: How a Coach and Her Olympic Team Transformed Women's Basketball, 1997. Contributor to periodicals. **Address:** Department of Athletics, Stanford University, Stanford, CA 94305-6150, U.S.A. **Online address:** tarahoop@stanford.edu

VAN DER VEN, Johannes A. Dutch (born Netherlands), b. 1940. **Genres:** Theology/Religion. **Career:** Catholic University of Nijmegen, professor of pastoral theology, 1985-, dean of faculty, 1997-, Union of Faculty of Philosophy and Faculty of Theology, president, 1998-; International Academy of Practical Theology, board director, 1991-95, president, 1995-97; European Society for Catholic Theology, president, 1995-98; University of South Africa, extraordinary professor, 1998-; Radboud University, faculty. Writer. **Publications:** Katechetische leerplanontwikkeling, 1973; (with W.J. Berger) Graven Naar Geloof: Analyses Van Gesprekken Met Jongeren Vanuit Psychologie En Theologie, 1976; Kritische Godsdienstdidactiek, 1982; Vorming in Waarden en Normen, 1985; Bisschoppen en Theologen in Dialoog, 1987; Religie Tussen Oost en West, 1987; Entwurf Einer Empirischen Theologie, 1990; (with E. Vossen) Lijden en Pastoraat, 1990; (with L.G.M. Spruit) Kerk Op De Helling: Veranderingen in Katholiek Nederland En Gevolgen Voor De Pastoraal, 1993; Ecclesiologie in Context, 1993; (with H. Ziebertz) Religiöser Pluralismus und Interreligiöses Lernen, 1994; Religie in Fragmenten, Een Onderzoek Onder Studenten, Deutsche Studienverlag, 1994; Ecclesiology In Context, 1996; Botsende Culturen in Nederland, 1996; Formation of the Moral Self, 1998; Education for Reflective Ministry, 1998; Formation of the Moral Self, 1998; God Reinvented?, 1998; Kerk in Ontwikkeling: De Kerk Op Zoek Naar Haar Religieuze En Sociale Identiteit, 1998; (ed. with F. Schweitzer) Practical Theology: International Perspectives, 1999; Morele Zelf: Vorming en Ontwikkeling, 1999; Pastoraal Perspectief: Vorming tot Reflectief Pastoraat, 2000; (ed. with J.S. Dreyer) Divine Justice, Human Justice, 2002; (ed. with M. Scherer-Rath) Normativity and Empirical Research in Theology, 2004; (co-ed.) Forgiveness, Reconciliation and Moral Courage: Motives and Designs for Ministry in a Troubled World, 2004; (with J.S. Dreyer and H.J.C. Pieterse) Is There a God of Human Rights?: The Complex Relationship Between Human Rights and Religion, 2005; Human Rights or Religious Rules?, 2009. **Address:** Faculty of Theology, Radboud University, PO Box 9103, Nijmegen, 6500 HD, Netherlands. **Online address:** j.vanderven@rs.ru.nl

VAN DER VLIES, Andrew. British (born England), b. 1974?. **Genres:** History. **Career:** University of Sheffield, faculty, 2005-10; Queen Mary University of London, faculty, 2010-. Writer. **Publications:** South African Textual Cultures: White, Black, Read All Over, 2007; J.M. Coetzee's Disgrace, 2010. Contributor to periodicals and journals. **Address:** University of London, Senate House, Malet St., London, GL WC1E 7HU, England.

VANDERWAL, Andrew H. Canadian/Dutch (born Netherlands), b. 1956?. **Genres:** Bibliography, Children's Fiction. **Career:** PriceWaterhouseCoopers L.L.P., tax services partner. Writer and consultant. **Publications:** Canadian Development Assistance: A Selected Bibliography, 1978-1984, 1985; The Battle for Duncragglin, 2009. Contributor to periodicals. **Address:** Toronto, ON , Canada. **Online address:** avanderwalh@gmail.com

VAN DER ZEE, Barbara (Blanche). (Barbara Griggs). British (born England), b. 1932. **Genres:** History, Medicine/Health, Food And Wine. **Career:** Vogue, journalist, 1955-57; Daily Express, journalist, 1957-58; Evening Standard, journalist, 1958-68, fashion editor, 1961-69; Daily Mail, fashion editor, 1972-79; freelance author and journalist, 1979-. **Publications:** WITH H. ANTONY: William and Mary, 1973, A Sweet and Alien Land: The Story of Dutch New York, 1978, 1688: Revolution in the Family, 1988. Bibis Cook Book, 1976; Nouveau Poor, or, How to Live Better on Less, 1977; Green Pharmacy: A History of Herbal Medicine, 1981; The Food Factor, 1986; The Green Witch Herbal: Restoring Natures Magic in Home, Health & Beauty Care, 1994; Green Pharmacy: The History and Evolution of Western Herbal Medicine, 1997; Superfoods for Children, 2001. Contributor to periodicals. **Address:** c/o Richard Simon, 32 College Cross, London, GL N1 1PR, England.

VAN DER ZEE, Karen. (Mona van Wieren). Armenian/Dutch (born Netherlands), b. 1947. **Genres:** Romance/Historical, Novels, Young Adult Fiction, Literary Criticism And History. **Career:** Writer. **Publications:** Sweet Not Always, 1979; Love beyond Reason, 1980; A Secret Sorrow, 1981; Waiting, 1982; One More Time, 1983; Soul Ties, 1984; Going Underground, 1985; Staying Close, 1985; Pelangi Haven, 1985; Fancy Free, 1987; Time for Another Dream, 1987; Shadows on Bali, 1988; Hot Pursuit, 1988; (as Monavan Wieren) Rhapsody in Bloom, 1989; Brazilian Fire, 1989; Java Nights, 1990; Kept Woman, 1991; The Imperfect Bride, 1991; Something in Return, 1992; (as Mona van Wieren) A Prince among Men, 1992; Passionate Adventure, 1993; The Other Man, 1995; Making Magic, 1995; An Inconvenient Husband, 1996; Marriage Shy, 1996, rev. ed., 2001; A Love Untamed, 1997; Captive in Eden, 1997; Hired Wife, 1999, rev. ed., 2004; A Wife to Remember, 1999; Fire and Spice, 1999; Rand's Redemption, 2001; Midnight Rhythms, 2003; The Italian's Seduction, 2005. **Address:** Mills and Boon Ltd., Eton House, 18-24 Paradise Rd., Richmond, SR TW9 1SR, England. **Online address:** vanderzee.karen@gmail.com

VANDEVELDER, Paul. American (born United States), b. 1951?. **Genres:** History, Cultural/Ethnic Topics. **Career:** Journalist and film maker. **Publications:** Coyote Warrior: One Man, Three Tribes and the Trial That Forged a Nation, 2004, 2nd ed., 2009; Savages and Scoundrels: The Untold Story of America's Road to Empire Through Indian Territory, 2009. Contributor to periodicals and journals. **Address:** c/o Author Mail, Little, Brown and Company Inc., 1271 Ave. of the Americas, New York, NY 10020-1300, U.S.A.

VANDEWALLE, Dirk. American (born United States), b. 1953. **Genres:** Economics. **Career:** Dartmouth University, associate professor of government, chair of Asian and Middle Eastern studies program. Writer. **Publications:** (Ed.) Qadhafi's Libya, 1969-1994, 1995; (ed.) North Africa: Development and Reform in a Changing Global Economy, 1996; Libya since Independence: Oil and State-Building, 1998; A History of Modern Libya, 2006; Libya since 1969: Qadhafi's Revolution Revisited, 2008. Contributor to periodicals. **Address:** Dartmouth University, HB 6108, 211 Silsby Hall, Hanover, NH 03755, U.S.A. **Online address:** dirk.vandewalle@dartmouth.edu

VAN DIEPEN, Allison. Canadian (born Canada), b. 1977. **Genres:** Novels. **Career:** Alternative High School, head of English. Writer. **Publications:** YOUNG ADULT NOVELS: Street Pharm, 2006; Snitch, 2007; Raven, 2009; Oracle of Dating, 2010; Oracle Rebounds, 2010; Vampire Stalker, 2011. **Address:** c/o John Rudolph, Dystel and Goderich Literary Management, 1 Union Sq. W, Ste. 904, New York, NY 10003, U.S.A. **Online address:** allisonvandiepen@yahoo.com

VAN DOMELEN, John E(mory). American (born United States), b. 1935. **Genres:** Literary Criticism And History, Biography, Poetry, Autobiography/Memoirs. **Career:** University of Wisconsin, assistant professor, 1963-65, associate professor of English, 1965-67; University of Northern Iowa, assistant professor, 1967-69, associate professor of English, 1969-70; Texas A&M University, associate professor, 1970-74, professor of English, 1974-96, professor emeritus, 1996-. Writer. **Publications:** Tarzan of Athens, 1987; John Heath-Stubbs: A Checklist, 1987; The Haunted Heart, 1993. Contributor to periodicals. **Address:** Department of English, Texas A&M University, MS 4227 TAMU, College Station, TX 77843-1112, U.S.A. **Online address:** carat310@juno.com

VAN DOVER, J(ames) K(enneth). American (born United States), b. 1950. **Genres:** Literary Criticism And History, Mystery/Crime/Suspense. **Career:** Lincoln University, professor of English, 1978-; University of Tuebingen, Fulbright professor, 1980-81; University of Stuttgart, Fulbright professor, 1988-89; Nankai University, Fulbright professor, 2000; University of Vienna, American Studies, Fulbright professor, 2007. Writer. **Publications:** Murder in the Millions: Erle Stanley Gardner, Mickey Spillane, Ian Fleming, 1984; Defoe's World Mapped, 1988; At Wolfe's Door: The Nero Wolfe Novels of Rex Stout, 1991, rev. ed., 2003; Understanding William Kennedy, 1991; Polemical Pulps: The Martin Beck Novels of Maj Sjowall and Per Wahloo, 1993; You Know My Method: The Science of the Detective, 1994; (ed.) The Critical Response to Raymond Chandler, 1995; Centurions, Knights and Other Cops: The Police Novels of Joseph Wambaugh, 1995; (with J.F. Jebb) Isn't Justice Always Unfair?: The Detective in Southern Literature, 1996; We Must have Certainty: Four Essays on the Detective Story, 2005; Making the Detective Story American, 2010. Contributor to professional journals. **Address:** Department of English, Lincoln University, 1570 Baltimore Pk., PO Box 179, Lincoln University, PA 19352, U.S.A. **Online address:** vandover@lincoln.edu

VAN DUZER, Chet A. American (born United States), b. 1966. **Genres:** Environmental Sciences/Ecology, Geography, Literary Criticism And History, History, Young Adult Fiction. **Career:** Freelance writer. **Publications:** Duality and Structure in the Iliad and Odyssey, 1996; Floating Islands: A Global Bibliography, with an Edition and Translation of G.C. Munz's Exercitatio academica de insulis natantibus (1711), 2004; Johann Schoner's Globe of 1515: Transcription and Study, 2010. **Address:** 12177 Winton Way, Los Altos Hills, CA 94024-6431, U.S.A.

VAN DYKE, Henry. See Obituaries.

VAN EENWYK, John R. American (born United States), b. 1946. **Genres:** Psychology, Theology/Religion, Medicine/Health, Sciences. **Career:** Saint Anne's School, chairman, 1970-71; Church of Jamaica, priest-in-charge, 1971-72; State of Illinois, Department of Mental Health, mental health rehabilitation counselor II, 1973; Cathedral Shelter, alcohol rehabilitation counselor, 1977-78; private practice of clinical psychology and Jungian analysis, 1981-; C.G. Jung Institute, training analyst, 1984-92, director of access to clinical services, 1984-88, senior analyst, 1986-92; Pacific Northwest Society of Jungian Analysts, senior and training analyst, 1994-; St. Benedict's Episcopal Church, associate clergy, 2004-; University of Washington, School of Medicine, Department of Psychiatry and Behavioral Sciences, clinical faculty, 1995-; International Trauma Treatment Program, founder and clinical director. Writer. **Publications:** (Contrib.) Fractals of Brain, Fractals of Mind: In Search of a Symmetry Bond, 1996; (contrib.) Religion and the Clinical Practice of Psychology, 1996; Archetypes & Strange Attractors: The Chaotic World of Symbols, 1997; (contrib.) Changes in the Therapist, 2001. Contributor to journals. **Address:** 1026 State Ave. NE, Olympia, WA 98506, U.S.A. **Online address:** jrv@u.washington.edu

VAN ERVEN, Eugene. Dutch (born Netherlands), b. 1955. **Genres:** Plays/Screenplays, Theatre, Film. **Career:** University of Florida, Department of German, instructor, 1978; Victoria University of Wellington, researcher in drama and film, 1986-87, Theatre Studies Department, post doctoral fellow; Utrecht University, lecturer in American studies, 1988-99, senior lecturer and researcher, Theatre program, founder, 1999-2004, senior lecturer of community art, theory and practice, 2007-, Research Institute for History and Culture, associate professor; Instituto Pedagogica Arubano, staff, 2004-06; Foundation for International Film and Theater Projects, chair; RASA Intercultural Center, consultant; Vanderbilt University, Department of English, teaching fellow. Writer. **Publications:** Radical People's Theatre, 1988; Stages of People Power: The Philippine Educational Theater Association, 1989; (ed.) The Image and Imagination of America, vol. II, 1992; The Playful Revolution, 1992; Community Theatre: Global Perspectives, 2000; Living with Differences: Young Theatre Makers Searching for Themselves as Artists in Neighbourhoods, 2011. **Address:** Department of American Studies, University of Utrecht, Rm. 2.01, Muntstraat 2a, PO Box 80125, Utrecht, 3512EV, Netherlands. **Online address:** e.a.p.b.erven@uu.nl

VAN FRAASSEN, Bas C. American (born United States), b. 1941. **Genres:** Philosophy, Sciences, Physics. **Career:** Yale University, assistant professor, 1966-68, associate professor of philosophy, 1968-69; University of Toronto, professor of philosophy, 1969-81; Journal of Philosophical Logic, editor-in-chief, 1971-77; University of Southern California, professor of philosophy, 1976-81; Princeton University, McCosh professor of philosophy, 1982-2008, McCosh emeritus professor of philosophy, 2008-; San Francisco State University, College of Humanities, Department of Philosophy, professor, distinguished professor of philosophy. **Publications:** An Introduction to the Philosophy of Time and Space, 1970; Formal Semantics and Logic, 1971; (with K. Lambert) Derivation and Counterexample: An Introduction to Philosophical Logic, 1972; (co-author) Studies in Ontology: Essays, 1978; The Scientific Image, 1980; (ed. with E. Beltrametti) Current Issues in Quantum Logic, 1981; Images of Science: Essays on Realism and Empiricism, with a Reply from Bas C. van Fraassen, 1985; (with E. Bencivenga and K. Lambert) Logic Bivalence and Denotation, 1986; Laws and Symmetry, 1989; Quantum Mechanics: An Empiricist View, 1991; (ed. with W. Spohn and B. Skyrms) Existence and Explanation: Essays Presented in Honor of Karel Lambert, 1991; (ed.) Topics in the Foundation of Statistics, 1997; The Empirical Stance, 2002; (with J.C. Beall) Possibilities and Paradox: An Introduction to Modal and Many-Valued Logic, 2003; Bas C. van Fraassen: The Fortunes of Empiricism, 2006; Scientific Representation: Paradoxes of Perspective, 2008. **Address:** Department of Philosophy, College of Humanities, San Francisco State University, Humanities 443, 1600 Holloway Ave., San Francisco, CA 94132-1722, U.S.A. **Online address:** fraassen@sfsu.edu

VAN GEERT, Paul. Belgian (born Belgium), b. 1950. **Genres:** Psychology. **Career:** University of Groningen, lecturer, 1976, senior lecturer, 1978, professor of psychology, 1985-, chair of developmental psychology, Department of Psychology, dean, 1990-92; Center for Advanced Studies in the Behavioral Sciences, fellow, 1992-93; National Dutch Research Group on Developmental Psychology, chairman, 1993-98; British Journal of Developmental Psychology, associate editor, 1993-97; Nederlandse Tijdschrift voor de Psychologie, editor-in-chief, 1994-; Heijmans Institute for Psychological Research, director, 1997-2000; French Ministry of Scientific, Program on Invariants and Variability in the Cognitive Sciences, 1998-2000; Universit de Paris V, Department of Developmental and Cognitive Psychology, visiting professor, 2002; Harvard University, Summer Institute on Mind, Brain and Education, lecturer, 2002-03; University of Turin-Italy, Department of Psychology, visiting professor Lagrange project, 2002. Writer. **Publications:** The Development of Perception, Cognition, and Language: A Theoretical Approach, 1983; (ed.) Theory Building in Developmental Psychology, 1986; (trans. with L. Verhofstadt-Deneve and A. Vijdt) Handboek voor ontwikkelingspsychologie (title means: 'Handbook of Developmental Psychology'), 1990; (with L. Mos) Annals of Theoretical Psychology, vol. X, 1994; Dynamic Systems of Development: Change between Complexity and Chaos, 1994; (with J. Lautrey and B. Mazoyer) Invariants et Variabilits Dans les Sciences Cognitives, 2002. EDITOR: (with G. Breeuwsma) Psychologen over kindermishandeling: Een Ontwikkelingspsychologische Benadering (title means: 'Psychologists on Child Abuse: A Developmental Approach'), 1987; De Menselijke Levensloop (title means: 'The Human Lifespan'), vol. I: De Structuur van de Levensloop (The Structure of the Lifespan), vol. II: De chronologie van de levensloop (The Chronology of the Lifespan), vol. III: De Constructie van de Levensloop (The Construction of the Lifespan), 1990; (with L. Mos) Annals of Theoretical Psychology: Developmental Psychology, 1990. **Address:** Department of Developmental Psychology, State University of Groningen, Grote Kruisstraat 2-1, Groningen, 9712 TS, Netherlands. **Online address:** vangeert@inn.nl

VAN GINNEKEN, Jaap. Dutch (born Netherlands), b. 1943. **Genres:** Communications/Media, Psychology, Writing/Journalism, Intellectual History, History, Humanities, International Relations/Current Affairs, Film, Social Sciences, Third World. **Career:** University of Amsterdam, assistant professor of collective behavior and anthropology, 1970-75, International School, part-time assistant professor, associate professor of communication, 1990-2005; University of Leiden, assistant professor of theoretical psychology, 1982-85; University of Groningen, assistant professor of the history of psychology, 1987-90; Université de Nice Sophia-Antipolis, Ceram International Business School, associate professor of communication, 2006-08. Writer. **Publications:** The Rise and Fall of Lin Piao, 1976; The Third Indochina War, 1979; Crowds, Psychology & Politics, 1992; Understanding Global News, 1998; Collective Behavior and Public Opinion: Rapid Shifts, 2003; Screening Difference: How Hollywood Blockbuster Films Imagine Race, Ethnicity and Culture, 2007; Mass Movements, 2007; Mood Contagion: In a Hyperconnected World, 2012. **Address:** 9 All.d.l. Pierre à Tambour, Villeneuve Loubet, 06270, France. **Online address:** jaap.vanginneken@orange.fr

VAN HEERDEN, Etienne. South African (born South Africa), b. 1954. **Genres:** Novels, Children's Fiction, Poetry. **Career:** Supreme Court of South Africa, attorney, 1984; University of Zululand, lecturer in Afrikaans literature, 1985-87; Rhodes University, associate professor; University of Leiden, writer-in-residence; University of Cape Town, Department of Southern African Languages, Hofmeyr professor, Afrikaans and Netherlandic Studies Section, head. Writer. **Publications:** Matoli (children's novel), 1978; Obiter dictum (poems), 1981; My Kubaan, 1983; Om te awol, 1984; Toorberg, 1986; Die laaste kreef, 1987; Liegfabriek, 1988; Ancestral Voices, 1989; Casspirs en campari's: 'n historiese entertainment, 1991; Mad Dog and Other Stories, 1992; Die stoetmeester, 1993; Kikoejoe, 1996; Postmodernisme en prosa: vertelstrategieë in vyf verhale van Abraham H. de Vries, 1997; Stoetmeester, 1997; Leap Year, 1997; Lied van die Boeings: 'n kaberet, 1998; Die rooi roman: interaktiewe roman, 1999; Die mooiste liefde is verby, 1999; Die swye van Mario Salviati: 'n roman, 2000; Long Silence of Mario Salviati, 2002; Die stilte ná die boek: kitsessays, 2004; In stede van die liefde: 'n roman, 2005; Asbesmiddag, 2007; 30 Nagte in Amsterdam, 2009. Works appear in anthologies. **Address:** Department Southern African Languages, University of Cape Town, Lovers Walk St., PO Box X3, Rondebosch, 7701, South Africa. **Online address:** etiennev@mweb.co.za

VAN HENSBERGEN, Gijs. (Arie van der Lemme). British/Belgian (born Belgium), b. 1958. **Genres:** Art/Art History, Photography, Literary Criticism And History. **Career:** Knoedler Gallery, trainee art dealer, 1981-84; Martin Randall Travel Ltd., lecturer. Writer, historian, art critic and filmmaker. **Publications:** (As Arie van der Lemme) Art Deco, 1985; A Year in Castile, 1992; Gaudi: A Biography, 2001; In the Kitchens of Castile, 2003; Guernica: The Biography of a Twentieth-Century Icon, 2004; American Philanthropy, 2007. **Address:** c/o Euan Thorneycroft, Curtis Brown Group Ltd., Haymarket House, 28-29 Haymarket, 5th Fl., London, GL SW1Y 4SP, England. **Online address:** alexgijs@lineone.net

VAN HORN, Ray. American (born United States), b. 1970. **Genres:** Mystery/Crime/Suspense, Novels, Horror. **Career:** Bank of Baltimore, post-closer, 1993-95; Fairfax Mortgage, post-closer, 1995-98; Hockey Nut, hockey analyst; Valley Title, processor, 1997-99; Chase Title, senior processor, 1999-; Carroll County, Arts Council, faculty, 2002-; Maelstrom Zine, writer; Legends Magazine, staff writer. **Publications:** Mentor (thriller), 2002. Contributor to periodicals. **Address:** Publish America L.L.L.P., PO Box 151, Frederick, MD 21705, U.S.A. **Online address:** crtiger@adelphia.net

VANHUYSSE, Pieter. Israeli/Belgian (born Belgium), b. 1974. **Genres:** Politics/Government. **Career:** University of Haifa, lecturer, assistant professor of political science, 2005-. Writer. **Publications:** Divide and Pacify: Strategic Social Policies and Political Protests in Post-Communist Democracies, 2006. Contributor of essays, articles to periodicals. **Address:** University of Haifa, Education and Sciences Bldg., Haifa, 31905, Israel. **Online address:** pieterv@construct.haifa.ac.il

VAN HUYSSTEEN, Jacobus Wentzel Vrede. See **VAN HUYSSTEEN, J. Wentzel.**

VAN HUYSSTEEN, J. Wentzel. (Jacobus Wentzel Vrede van Huyssteen). American/South African (born South Africa), b. 1942. **Genres:** Theology/Religion, History, Sciences, Essays. **Career:** University of Port Elizabeth, professor of religious studies and chair, 1972-92; Princeton Theological Seminary, Department of Theology, James I. McCord professor of theology and science, 1992-. Writer and theologian. **Publications:** NONFICTION: Teologie van die Rede. Die Funksie van die Rasionele in die Denke van Wolfhart Pannenberg, 1970; Teologie as kritiese geloofsverantwoording: teorievorming in die sistematiese teologie, 1987; The Realism of the Text: A Perspective on Biblical Authority, 1987; Essays in Postfoundationalist Theology, 1997; Duet or Duel?: Theology and Science in a Postmodern World, 1998; (ed. with N.H. Gregersen) Rethinking Theology and Science: Six Models for the Current Dialogue, 1998; The Shaping of Rationality: Toward Interdisciplinarity in Theology and Science, 1999; (ed. as J. Wentzel Vrede van Huyssteen) Encyclopedia of Science and Religion, 2003; Alone in the World?: Human Uniqueness in Science and Theology, 2006; (ed. with E.P. Wiebe) In Search of Self, 2011. Contributor of articles to periodicals. **Address:** Department of Theology, Princeton Theological Seminary, 33 Carriage House, 64 Mercer St., PO Box 821, Princeton, NJ 08542-0803, U.S.A. **Online address:** wentzel.vanhuyssteen@ptsem.edu

VAN HYNING, Thomas E. American (born United States), b. 1954. **Genres:** Sports/Fitness. **Career:** Southern Illinois University, Office of Leisure Research, researcher, 1985-88; Keystone College, assistant professor of travel and tourism, sports information director and assistant women's softball coach, 1988-93; Endless Mountains Visitors Bureau, board director, 1992-93; Mississippi Development Authority, Division of Tourism, research program manager, 1994-; Hennig Associates, associate; San Juan Area Agency on Aging, planner; Municipality of Carolina, budget analyst and planner; Municipal Services Administration, economist; University of Scranton, consultant. Writer. **Publications:** Puerto Rico's Winter League: A History of Major League Baseball's Launching Pad, 1995; The Santurce Crabbers: Sixty Seasons of Puerto Rican Winter League Baseball, 1999. Contributor to magazines and newspapers. **Address:** 176 Zelma Ln., Florence, MS 39073, U.S.A. **Online address:** vanhyningt@cs.com

VAN ITALLIE, Jean Claude. American/Belgian (born Belgium), b. 1936. **Genres:** Plays/Screenplays, Writing/Journalism, Translations, Literary Criticism And History. **Career:** Transatlantic Review, associate editor, 1959-61; Columbia Broadcasting System, researcher, 1962; Open Theater, playwright-in-residence, 1963-68; New School for Social Research, instructor in playwriting, 1966-68, 1972; Yale University, School of Drama, instructor in playwriting, 1969, visiting critic in playwriting, 1984-85; Naropa Institute, teacher of playwriting, 1974-78, 1983, 1991; Princeton University, lecturer, 1976-86; Amherst College, visiting Mellon professor, 1976; New York University, lecturer in theater, 1984-85, 1988, 1992; Columbia University, instructor in playwriting, 1986; University of Colorado, instructor in playwriting, 1987-89, 1991; American Repertory Theater, instructor in playwriting, 1990; Middlebury College, visiting professor of theater, 1990. **Publications:** PLAYS: Children of the Shore, 1959; From an Odets Kitchen, 1963; The First Fool, 1964; The Murdered Woman, 1964; (with S. Thie) Thoughts on the Instant of Greeting a Friend on the Street, 1968; The King of the United States, 1972; (with M. Terry and S. Sheppard) Nightwalk, 1973; Seven Short and Very Short Plays, 1973; The Fable, 1975; Medea, 1979; Paradise Ghetto, 1982; The Tibetan Book of the Dead or How Not to Do It Again, 1983; Early Warnings, 1983; The Traveller, 1986; Calcutta, 1987; (with Chaikin) Struck Dumb, 1988; Ancient Boys, 1989; Master I Margarita, 1994; Guys Dreamin', 1998; Light, 2001; Fear Itself: Secrets of the White House, 2005. OTHERS: War and Four Other Plays, 1967; American Hurrah: Five Short Plays, 1967; The Serpent: A Ceremony, 1968; Mystery Play: A Farce, 1973; The Cherry Orchard: A Comedy in Four Acts, 1977, rev. ed., 1995; The Sea Gull: A Comedy in Four Acts, 1977; America Hurrah and Other Plays, 1978, rev. ed., 2001; Bag Lady, 1980; Chekhov: The Major Plays, 1995; (trans.) Anton Chekhov's Three Sisters: A Drama in Four Acts, 1995; Mikhail Bulgakov's Master & Margarita, or, The Devil Comes to Moscow, 1995; Playwright's Workbook, 1997; The Tibetan Book of the Dead for Reading Aloud, 1998; War Sex & Dreams, 1999. TRANSLATIONS: The Seagull, 1973; Anton Chekhov's The Three Sisters: A New English Version, 1979; Uncle Vanya: Scenes from Country Life in Four Acts, 1980; Jean Genet, The Balcony, 1986. **Address:** c/o Morgan Jenness, Abrams Artists Association, 275 7th Ave., New York, NY 10001, U.S.A.

VAN KESSEL, Ineke. Dutch (born Netherlands), b. 1948. **Genres:** History, Politics/Government, Area Studies, Homes/Gardens. **Career:** Dutch National News Agency, journalist at foreign desk, 1969-88; University of Leiden, African Studies Center, researcher, 1988-. **Publications:** Aspects of the Apartheid State: A Bibliographical Survey, 1989; Beyond Our Wildest Dreams: The United Democratic Front and the Transformation of South Africa, 2000; Zwarte Hollanders. Afrikaanse Soldaten in Nederlands-Indië, 2005. EDITOR: (with N.Tellegen) Afrikanen in Nederland, 2000; Merchants, Missionaries and Migrants: 300 Years of Dutch-Ghanaian Relations, 2002; (with J. Abbink) Vanguard or Vandals: Youth, Politics and Conflict in Africa, 2005; (with S. Ellis) Movers and Shaker: Social Movements in Africa, 2009; Nelson Mandela in een notendop, 2010. Contributor to books and periodicals. **Address:** African Studies Centre, University of Leiden, PO Box 9555, Leiden, 2300 RB, Netherlands. **Online address:** kessel@ascleiden.nl

VANKIN, Jonathan. American (born United States), b. 1962?. **Genres:** Novels, Criminology/True Crime, Politics/Government, History, Mystery/Crime/Suspense. **Career:** The Advocate, managing editor, 1985-86; Worcester magazine, staff writer, 1987-89; Metro, news editor, 1989-92; Daily Yomiuri, 1992-95; Vertigo, senior editor, 2004-11. **Publications:** Conspiracies Cover-ups and Crimes: Political Manipulation and Mind Control in America, 1992; Fifty Greatest Conspiracies of All Time: History's Biggest Mysteries Coverups and Cabals, 1995, rev. ed. as The Sixty Greatest Conspiracies of All Time: History's Biggest Mysteries, Coverups and Cabals, 1996, 2nd ed. as The Seventy Greatest Conspiracies of All Time: History's Biggest Mysteries, Coverups and Cabals, 1998, 3rd ed. as The Eighty Greatest Conspiracies of All Time: History's Biggest Mysteries, Coverups and Cabals, 2004; The Big Book of Scandal, 1997; The Big Book of Bad, 1998; The Big Book of Grimm, 1999; The Big Book of the 70s: True Tales from Ten Years of Tackiness and Tumult!, 2000; (with J. Whalen) Based on a True Story: Fact and Fantasy in 100 Favorite Movies, 2005; Tokyo Days, Bangkok Nights, 2009; (with J. Whalen) The World's Greatest Conspiracies, 2010. Contributor to periodicals. **Address:** Chicago Review Press, 814 N Franklin St., Chicago, IL 60610, U.S.A. **Online address:** jv@jonathanvankin.com

VAN LAAN, Nancy. American (born United States), b. 1939. **Genres:** Children's Fiction. **Career:** J. Walter Thompson Advertising Agency, assistant, 1961-62; ABC-TV, network censor, 1962-66; Solebury School, English teacher, 1984-89; Rutgers University, creative writing instructor, 1986-89. Writer, 1987-. **Publications:** The Big Fat Worm, 1987; Possum Come A-Knockin', 1990; A Mouse in My House, 1990; People, People Everywhere, 1992; This Is the Hat: A Story in Rhyme, 1992; The Tiny, Tiny Boy and the Big, Big Cow: A Scottish Folk Tale, 1993; Round and Round Again, 1994; Sleep, Sleep, Sleep: A Lullaby for Little Ones Around the World, 1995; This is the Hat: A Story in Rhyme, 1995; Mama Rocks, Papa Sings, 1995; In a Circle Long Ago: A Treasury of Native Lore from North America, 1995; La Boda: A Mexican Wedding Celebration, 1996; Little Baby Bobby, 1997; With a Whoop and a Holler: A Bushel of Lore from Way Down South, 1998; Little Fish, Lost, 1998; So Say the Little Monkeys, 1998; Moose Tales, 1999; Teeny Tiny Tingly Tales, 1999; Tree for Me, 2000; When Winter Comes, 2000; (with G. Booth) Laughing Man, 2001; Tickle Tum!, 2001; Busy, Busy Moose, 2003; Scrubba Dub, 2003; Nit-pickin'?, 2008. **Address:** c/o Gail Hochman, Brandt & Brandt Literary Agents Inc., 1501 Broadway, New York, NY 10036, U.S.A. **Online address:** nvanlaan@aol.com

VAN LAWICK-GOODALL, Jane. *See* **GOODALL, Jane.**

VAN LEMMEN, Hans. British/Dutch (born Netherlands), b. 1946. **Genres:** Antiques/Furnishings, Architecture, Design, Homes/Gardens, Art/Art History, Crafts. **Career:** Leeds College of Education, lecturer in art history, 1974-76; Leeds Polytechnic, lecturer in art history, 1976-92; Leeds Metropolitan University, associate lecturer in the history and theory, senior lecturer in art history, 1992-96. Writer. **Publications:** Tiles: A Collector's Guide, 1979, rev. ed., 1990; Victorian Tiles, 1981; Delftware Tiles, 1986, rev. ed., 1997; Tiled Furniture, 1989; (ed. with J. Malam) Fired Earth: 1000 Years of Tiles in Europe: A Scarborough Art Gallery Touring Exhibition, 1991; Tiles: 1000 Years of Architectural Decoration, 1993; Tiles in Architecture, 1993; Decorative Tiles Throughout the Ages, 1997; Art Nouveau Tiles, 1999; Blue and White Painting on China and Ceramics, 2001; (contrib.) Delft Ceramics at the Philadelphia Museum of Art, 2003; Ceramic Roofware, 2003. **Address:** 3 Castle View, Stonegate Rd., Leeds, WY LS17 5BY, England. **Online address:** juanlem@netcomuk.co.uk

VAN METER, Jonathan W. American (born United States), b. 1963. **Genres:** Business/Trade/Industry, Biography. **Career:** Vibe magazine, creator founding editor, editors-in-chief, 1992-94. **Publications:** The Last Good Time: Skinny D'Amato, the Notorious 500 Club, and the Rise and Fall of Atlantic City, 2003. Contributor to periodicals. **Address:** Crown Publicity, 1745 Broadway, New York, NY 10019-4368, U.S.A. **Online address:** jvanmeter@thelastgoodtime.com

VANMETER, Vandelia. (Vandelia L. Van Meter). American (born United States), b. 1934. **Genres:** History, Children's Non-fiction, Young Adult Non-fiction, Bibliography, Literary Criticism And History, Social Sciences. **Career:** Ottawa County Rural School, teacher, 1954-55; McClave High School, instructor in social sciences, 1957-58; Ellsworth Junior High School, instructor in social sciences, 1959-68, Ellsworth High School, media specialist, 1968-84; University of Southern Mississippi, assistant professor, 1986-90; Spalding University, associate professor of library and information sciences and chair of department, 1990-96, library director, 1991-. Writer. **Publications:** American History for Children and Young Adults, 1990; World History for Children and Young Adults, 1992; America in Historical Fiction, 1997. **Address:** Spalding University, 853 Library Ln., Louisville, KY 40203, U.S.A.

VAN METER, Vandelia L. *See* **VANMETER, Vandelia.**

VAN NATTA, Don. American (born United States), b. 1964. **Genres:** Biography, History. **Career:** Miami Herald, reporter, 1987-95; New York Times, metropolitan reporter, 1995-97, national correspondent; Washington bureau, reporter, 1997-; The Daily Free Press, editor-in-chief. Writer. **Publications:** First Off the Tee: Presidential Hackers, Duffers and Cheaters, from Taft to Bush, 2003; (with J. Gerth) Her Way: The Hopes and Ambitions of Hillary Rodham Clinton, 2007; Wonder Girl: The Magnificent Sporting Life of Babe Didrikson Zaharias, 2011. **Address:** c/o Author Mail, Editorial Office, Public Affairs, 250 W 57th St., Ste. 1321, New York, NY 10107, U.S.A. **Online address:** vannatta@nytimes.com

VAN NESS, Arthur Gordon. (Gordon Van Ness). American (born United States), b. 1950. **Genres:** Novels. **Career:** Longwood University, assistant professor, 1987-94, associate professor, 1994-2001, professor of English, 2001-, chair of department of English and modern languages. Writer. **Publications:** (As Gordon Van Ness) Outbelieving Existence: The Measured Motion of James Dickey, 1992; (ed. and intro.) Striking In: The Early Notebooks of James Dickey, 1996; (ed.) The One Voice of James Dickey: His Letters and Life, 1942-1969, 2003; (ed.) The One Voice of James Dickey: His Letters and Life, 1970-1997, 2005. **Address:** Department of English, Longwood University, 201 High St., Farmville, VA 23909, U.S.A. **Online address:** vannessag@longwood.edu

VAN NESS, Gordon. *See* **VAN NESS, Arthur Gordon.**

VAN NIEL, Kimberly. Australian (born Australia) **Genres:** Geography, Sciences, Information Science/Computers, Technology. **Career:** The University of Western Australia, School of Earth and Geographical Sciences, associate professor, senior lecturer. Writer and geographer. **Publications:** (With J. Delaney) Geographical Information Systems: An Introduction, 2nd ed., 2007.

Contributor to periodicals. **Address:** School of Earth and Environment, The University of Western Australia, 35 Stirling Hwy., M004, Crawley, WA 6009, Australia. **Online address:** kimberly.vanniel@uwa.edu.au

VAN ONSELEN, Charles. South African (born South Africa), b. 1944?. **Genres:** History, Local History/Rural Topics. **Career:** Institute of Commonwealth Studies, junior research fellow; International Labour Office, research officer; University of London, Centre for International and Area Studies, Ford Foundation research fellow, 1976-78; Yale University, visiting fellow, 1978; University of the Witwatersrand, Institute for Advanced Social Research and African Studies, director, 1979-99; University of Pretoria, Faculty of Humanities, research professor, 1999-; Stellenbosch Institute for Advanced Study, visiting fellow. Writer. **Publications:** Chibaro: African Mine Labour in Southern Rhodesia, 1900-1933, 1976; South Africa's Lumpenproletarian Army: Umkosi wa Ntaba, The Regiment of the Hills, 1890 to 1920, 1976; (with I.R. Phimister) Studies in the History of African Mine Labour in Colonial Zimbabwe, 1978; Studies in the Social and Economic History of the Witwatersrand, 1886-1914, 1982; Small Matter of a Horse: The Life of Nongoloza Mathebula, 1867-1948, 1984, 2nd ed., 2008; Seed Is Mine: The Life of Kas Maine, a South African Sharecropper, 1894-1985, 1996; New Babylon, new Nineveh: Everyday Life on the Witwatersrand, 1886-1914, 2001; The Fox and the Flies: The World of Joseph Silver, Racketeer and Psychopath in US as The Fox and the Flies: The Secret Life of a Grotesque Master Criminal, 2007; The Fox and the Flies: The Criminal Empire of the Whitechapel Murderer, 2008; Masked Raiders: Irish Banditry in Southern Africa: 1880-1899, 2010. **Address:** Faculty of Humanities, University of Pretoria, Humanities Bldg., Lynnwood Rd., PO Box X20, Hillcrest, 0028, South Africa. **Online address:** charles.vanonselen@up.ac.za

VANOOSTING, James. American (born United States), b. 1951?. **Genres:** Novels, Adult Non-fiction. **Career:** Southern Illinois University, professor of English, department chair; Seton Hall University, dean of arts and sciences, 1998-; Fordham University, visiting professor, St. Edmund Campion Fellow, 2005-, Communication and Media Studies, faculty, professor and department chair; University of California, visiting professor; Louisiana State University, visiting professor. Writer. **Publications:** NONFICTION: Business Correspondence: Writer, Reader, and Text, 1983; The Business Report: Writer, Reader, and Text, 1983; The Business Speech: Writer, Reader, and Text, 1985. YOUNG ADULT FICTION: Maxie's Ghost, 1987; Electing J.J., 1990; Practicing Business: Communication in the Workplace, 1992; (with P.H. Gray) Performance in Life and Literature, 1996; The Last Payback, 1997; And the Flesh Became Word: Reflections Theological and Aesthetic, 2005; Walking Mary, 2005. **Address:** Department of Communication & Media Studies, Fordham University, Faculty Memorial Hall 431, Rose Hill Campus, 441 E Fordham Rd., Bronx, NY 10458, U.S.A. **Online address:** vanoosting@fordham.edu

VAN OVERTVELDT, Johan. Belgian (born Belgium), b. 1955. **Genres:** Economics, Business/Trade/Industry. **Career:** Trends Magazine, editor, 1978-82, head editor, 1992-99, chief economist, 1999-2004; Brussels Lambert Bank, staff, 1982-87; Shoekonfex, general director, 1987-91; BTR, automotive group advisor, 1991-92; VKW Metena, general director, 2004-. **Publications:** (Co-author) Crash or Boom? De Wereldeconomie Op Het Einde Van Het Millennium, 1999; Fons Verplaetse, De Peetvader, 1999; Marktzege(n): Zes Aanklachten Tegen Het Antiglobalisme, 2002; De Euroscheppers: Macht En Manipulatie Achter De Euro, 2003; The Chicago School: How the University of Chicago Assembled the Thinkers Who Revolutionized Economics and Business, 2007; Bernanke's Test: Ben Bernanke, Alan Greenspan, and the Drama of the Central Banker, 2009, rev. ed., 2010; The End of the Euro, 2011. Contributor to periodicals. **Address:** VKW Metena, Sneeuwbeslaan 20, Wilrijk, 2610, Belgium.

VAN PARIJS, Philippe. Belgian (born Belgium), b. 1951. **Genres:** Economics, Social Sciences, Philosophy. **Career:** Belgian National Science Foundation, junior research fellow, 1974-80, senior research fellow, 1980-91; University of California, visiting fellow in sociology and economics, 1977-78; All Souls College, visiting fellow, 1977-78; Université catholique de Louvain, part-time lecturer, 1980-91, Hoover professor of economic and social ethics, 1991-, Hoover chair of economic and social ethics, director, 1991-; Victoria University of Manchester, visiting fellow, 1983; University of Amsterdam, Amsterdam, visiting lecturer, 1985; Centro Latino-Americano de Economia Humana, visiting lecturer, 1988; University of Wisconsin, visiting lecturer, 1990; European University Institute, Jean Monnet fellow, 1990-

91; University of Siena, Jean professor, 1993; Chinese Academy of Social Sciences, Institute of Marxism-Leninism, visiting professor, 1993; Universidad Autonoma de Barcelona, visiting professor, 1993; University of Bristol, Benjamin Meaker Visiting Professor, 1994; Federal University of Rio de Janeiro, visiting professor, 1994; Russian Academy of Sciences, Institute of Philosophy, visiting professor, 1994; University of Maine, visiting professor, 1996; All Souls College, visiting fellow, 1997-98; Yale University, Olmsted visiting professor, 2001; Harvard University, Department of Philosophy, visiting professor, 2004-; Katholieke Universiteit, visiting professor, 2006-; Nuffield College, senior research fellow, 2011-; University of Oxford, visiting professor, 2011-. Writer. **Publications:** Evolutionary Explanation in the Social Sciences: An Emerging Paradigm, 1981; Le Modele economique et ses rivaux: Introduction a la pratique de l'epistemologie des sciences sociales, 1990; Qu'est-ce qu'une societe juste? Introduction a la pratique de la philosophie politique, 1991; Marxism Recycled, 1993; Real Freedom for All: What (If Anything) Can Justify Capitalism?, 1995; Sauver la solidarite, 1995; Solidariteit voor de 21ste eeuw, 1996; Refonder la solidarité, 1999; (with C. Arnsperger) Ethique econmique et sociale, 2000; (co-author) What's Wrong with a Free Lunch?, 2001; (with B. Ackerman and A. Alstott) Redesigning Distribution: Basic Income and Stakeholder Grants as Alternative Cornerstones for a More Egalitarian Capitalism, 2006. EDITOR: (with J. Ladriere) Fondements d'une théorie de la justice: Essais critiques sur la philosophie politique de John Rawls, 1984; (with F. De Roose) La Pensee ecologiste: Essai d'inventaire a l'usage de ceux qui la pratiquent comme de ceux qui la craignent, 1991; (with J.M. Chaumont) Les Limites de l'ineluctable: Penser la liberte au seuil du troiseme millenaire, 1991; Arguing for Basic Income: Ethical Foundations for a Radical Reform, 1992; Ni ghetto ni tour d'ivoire: L'éthique économique et sociale aujourd'hui, 1993; Renta básica: más allá de la sociedad salarial, 2003; Cultural Diversity versus Economic Solidarity, 2003. **Address:** Chaire Hoover d'éthique, économique et Sociale, Université catholique de Louvain, Place Montesquieu 3, Louvain-la-Neuve, B-1348, Belgium. **Online address:** philippe.vanparijs@uclouvain.be

VAN PELT, Robert-Jan. Canadian/Dutch (born Netherlands), b. 1955. **Genres:** Cultural/Ethnic Topics, History, Architecture. **Career:** National University of Singapore, lecturer in architecture, 1984-85; University of Virginia, assistant professor of architecture, 1985-87; University of Waterloo, assistant professor, 1987-91, associate professor, 1991-96, professor of cultural history, 1996-. Writer. **Publications:** Tempel van de Wereld, 1984; Binnenhof, 1984; (with C.W. Westfall) Architectural Principles in the Age of Historicism, 1991; (with D. Dwork) Auschwitz: 1270 to the Present, 1996; The Science of Holocaust Research and the Art of Holocaust Denial, 1999; The Case for Auschwitz: Evidence from the Irving Trial, 2002; (with D. Dwork) Holocaust: A History, 2002; (contrib.) Letters to Sala: A Young Woman's Life in Nazi Labor Camps, 2006; (with D. Dwork) Flight from the Reich: Refugee Jews, 1933-1946, 2009. **Address:** Department of Architecture, University of Waterloo, 200 University Ave. W, Waterloo, ON N2L 3G1, Canada.

VAN PRAAGH, David. American (born United States), b. 1931. **Genres:** History, Politics/Government, Social Sciences, Third World, Writing/Journalism, Biography, Autobiography/Memoirs. **Career:** Trenton Times, political reporter, 1953-57; Providence Journal-Bulletin, United Nations special correspondent, 1958-61; Globe and Mail, reporter and Asia correspondent, 1962-72; Carleton University, associate professor of journalism, 1972-, adjunct professor; CJOH-TV, international analyst, 1981-; National Endowment for Democracy, consultant; International Development Research Centre, consultant. Writer. **Publications:** Alone on the Sharp Edge: The Story of M.R. Seni Pramoj and Thailand's Struggle for Democracy, 1989; Thailand's Struggle for Democracy: The Life and Times of M.R. Seni Pramoj, 1996; The Greater Game: India's Race with Destiny and China, 2003. Contributor to books. **Address:** School of Journalism and Communication, Carleton University, Saint Patrick's Bldg., Rm. 346, 1125 Colonel By Dr., Ottawa, ON K1S 5B6, Canada. **Online address:** dvanpraa@ccs.carleton.ca

VAN RADEN, Kristine. American (born United States), b. 1953. **Genres:** Human Relations/Parenting, Language/Linguistics, Theology/Religion. **Career:** City of Portland, community school director, 1975-80; Stedcraft, manager, 1980-82; writer, 1995-. **Publications:** (With M. Davis) Letters to Our Daughters: Mothers Words of Love, 1997. **Address:** 13652 NW Logie Trl., Hillsboro, OR 97124-8125, U.S.A.

VAN RIEL, C. B. M. Dutch (born Netherlands), b. 1951?. **Genres:** Communications/Media. **Career:** New York University, Stern School of Business, professor emeritus; Reputation Institute, executive director, managing director; Erasmus University, Rotterdam School of Management, professor; Corporate Reputation Review, co-founder & editor-in-chief; International Masters Program in Corporate Communications, founding director; Columbia University, faculty; Wharton School, faculty. **Publications:** (with J. Nedela) Profiles in Corporate Communication in Financial Institutions: A Cross-National Survey of Banks and Insurance Companies in Europe and the United States, 1989; Principles of Corporate Communication, 1995; (ed.) Strategic Corporate Communication: A Selection of Articles by Belgian and Dutch Authors in Leading International Journals, 2000; (with C.J. Fombrun) Fame & Fortune: How Successful Companies Build Winning Reputations, 2004; (with C.J. Fombrun) Essentials of Corporate Communication: Implementing Practices for Effective Reputation Management, 2007. **Address:** Rotterdam School of Management, Department of Business-Society Management, Rm. T11-56, PO Box 1738, Rotterdam, 3000 DR, Netherlands. **Online address:** criel@rsm.nl

VAN RULER, Han. *See* **VAN RULER**, J. A.

VAN RULER, J. A. (Han van Ruler). Dutch (born Netherlands), b. 1963. **Genres:** Philosophy, Intellectual History, Humanities. **Career:** Catholic University of Louvain, Belgian National Fund at Higher Institute for Philosophy, researcher, 1996-99; Erasmus University Rotterdam, professor of intellectual history, Dutch National Organisation for Scientific Research NWO, head and researcher, 2000-03, 2004-09. Writer. **Publications:** The Crisis of Causality: Voetius and Descartes on God, Nature, and Change, 1995; (ed. with H.A. Krop and A.J. Vanderjagt) Zeer Kundige Professoren: Beoefening van de Filosofie in Groningen van 1614 tot 1996, 1997; (ed. with A. Uhlmann and M. Wilson) Ethics/Arnold Geulincx, 2006. **Address:** Faculty of Philosophy, Erasmus University, Rm. H5-29, PO Box 1738, Rotterdam, 3000 DR, Netherlands. **Online address:** vanruler@fwb.eur.nl

VAN RYNBACH, Iris. American (born United States), b. 1952. **Genres:** Children's Fiction, Illustrations, Biography. **Career:** Writer and illustrator, 1979-; New Yorker magazine, illustrator, 1981-; Central Connecticut State University, adjunct art faculty, 1983-84, visiting professor, 1984-91; University of Hartford Art School, adjunct art faculty, 1984-89; Hartford College for Women, adjunct art faculty, 1992-; University of Connecticut, art department, art teacher, 1996, Greater Hartford Academy, faculty. **Publications:** (With P.D. Shea) The Taxing Case of the Cow, 2010. SELF-ILLUSTRATED: Cecily's Christmas, 1988; The Soup Stone, 1988; Everything from a Nail to a Coffin, 1991; Five Little Pumpkins, 1995; Captain Cook's Christmas Plum Pudding, 1997; Safely to Shore: America's Lighthouses, 2003. Contributor to periodicals. Illustrator of books by others. **Address:** Charlesbridge Publishing, 85 Main St., Watertown, MA 02472, U.S.A. **Online address:** irisvan@aol.com

VAN SCYOC, Sydney (Joyce). American (born United States), b. 1939. **Genres:** Science Fiction/Fantasy, Novels. **Career:** Science fiction writer, 1959-; freelance writer, 1962-; Starr King Unitarian Church, secretary, 1975-77, president, 1977-79. **Publications:** Saltflower, 1971; Assignment Nor'Dyren, 1973; Starmother, 1976; Cloudcry, 1977; Sunwaifs, 1981; Darkchild, 1982; Bluesong, 1983; Starsilk, 1984; Drowntide, 1987; Feather Stroke, 1989; Deepwater Dreams, 1991. **Address:** Avon Books, 10 E 53rd St., New York, NY 10022, U.S.A. **Online address:** sydnyvan@pacbell.net

VAN SLYCK, Abigail A(yres). American (born United States), b. 1959. **Genres:** Architecture, Cultural/Ethnic Topics, Geography. **Career:** University of California, visiting lecturer in urban planning, 1988; University of Arizona, assistant professor, 1989-95, associate professor of architecture, art history and women's studies, 1995-99; National Library of New Zealand, curator, 1996; Connecticut College, Dayton associate professor of art history and architectural studies, Dayton professor of art history, Architectural Studies Program, director, Art History Department, chair, 1999-; Vernacular Architecture Forum, president. Historian, educator and writer. **Publications:** Free to All: Carnegie Libraries and American Culture, 1890-1920, 1995; Manufactured Wilderness: Summer Camps and the Shaping of American Youth, 1890-1960, 2006. Contributor to books and journals. **Address:** Dept. of Art History & Architectural Studies, Connecticut College, 270 Mohegan Ave., PO Box 5565, New London, CT 06320-4196, U.S.A. **Online address:** aavan@conncoll.edu

VAN STEENHOUSE, Andrea. American (born United States), b. 1943.

Genres: Women's Studies And Issues. **Career:** Central Michigan University, teacher of guidance and counselor education, 1969-71; Michigan State University, teacher of psychiatry, 1974-79; Stress Management Inc., president, 1977-79; Stress Management Inc., president, 1979-; Simpler Life Press, founder and president. Writer, psychologist and commentator. **Publications:** Life Lines: A Personal Journal, 1987; A Woman's Guide to a Simpler Life, 1996; Empty Nest-Full Heart: The Journey From Home to College, 1998; (with I. Rawlings) Clothesline, 2002; (comp. with J. M. Martini) Deer Camp Dan's Cookbook, 2003. **Address:** Gibbs Smith, PO Box 667, Layton, UT 84041, U.S.A. **Online address:** vansteenhouse@gmail.com

VAN TILBURG, Christopher. American (born United States), b. 1966. **Genres:** Medicine/Health. **Career:** Physician and writer. **Publications:** Backcountry Snowboarding, 1998; Canyoneering: Beginning to Advanced Techniques, 2000; Backcountry Ski! Oregon: Classic Descents for Skiers & Snowboarders, Including Southwest Washington, 2001; Emergency Survival: A Pocket Guide: Quick Information for Outdoor Safety, 2001; (ed.) First Aid: A Pocket Guide: Quick Information for Mountaineering and Backcountry Use, 2001; Watersports Safety and Emergency First Aid: A Handbook for Boaters, Anglers, Kayakers, River Runners and Surfriders, 2002; Introducing Your Kids to the Outdoors, 2005; Mountain Rescue Doctor: Wilderness Medicine in the Extremes of Nature (memoir), 2007. Contributor to periodicals. **Address:** Joelle Delbourgo Associates Inc., 516 Bloomfield Ave., Ste. 5, Montclair, NJ 07042, U.S.A. **Online address:** vantilburg@gorge.net

VAN TILBURG, Hans (Konrad). American (born United States), b. 1961. **Genres:** History, Archaeology/Antiquities. **Career:** University of California, instructor in scientific diving techniques, 1985-87; East Carolina University, diving safety supervisor, crew chief and instructor, 1991-93; State Historical Society of Wisconsin, diving safety supervisor and crew chief, 1993; University of Hawaii, instructor maritime archaeology and history, 1996-2002; NOAA, maritime heritage coordinator, 2003-10. Writer. **Publications:** (Co-ed.) Maritime Archaeology: A Reader of Substantive and Theoretical Contributions, 1998; Chinese Junks on the Pacific: Views from a Different Deck, 2007; A Civil War Gunboat on Pacific Waters: Life on Board USS Saginaw, 2010. Contributor to books and periodicals. **Address:** NOAA Office of National Marine Sanctuaries, Pacific Islands Region, 6600 Kalanianaole Hwy., Ste. 302, Honolulu, HI 96825, U.S.A. **Online address:** hans.vantilburg@noaa.gov

VAN TILBURG, Jo Anne. American (born United States), b. 1942. **Genres:** Anthropology/Ethnology, Archaeology/Antiquities, Biography, Art/Art History. **Career:** School teacher, 1965-71; University of California, Psychology Clinic School, faculty, 1971-77, instructor in archaeology, 1983-; Cotsen Institute of Archaeology, research associate, 1993-, archaeologist, Rock Art Archive, director, 1997-; Smithsonian Institution, lecturer, 1993, 1999, 2003; Easter Island Statue Project, director, Rock Art Analysis, Archaeological Certificate Program, instructor, 1994, 1994, 1997, 1999, 2001-05; Universidad de Chile, Instituto de Estudios Isla de Pascua, research collaborator, 1982-86, 1989, 1990-98, 2002; Rapa Nui Outrigger Club, founder, 1989; British Museum, lecturer, 1990, 2002-08; Smithsonian Institution, lecturer, 1993, 1999, 2003; Archaeological Institute of America, national lecturer, 1994-; National Geographic Society, lecturer, 2002, 2003. Writer. **Publications:** (Ed. with C.W. Meighan) Prehistoric Indian Rock Art: Issues & Concerns, 1981; (ed. and comp.) Ancient Images on Stone: Rock Art of the Californias, 1983; (with F. Bock and A.J. Bock) The Church Rock Petroglyph Site: Field Documentation and Preliminary Analysis, 1987; H.M.S. Topaze on Easter Island, 1992; Easter Island Archaeology, Ecology, Culture, 1994; (contrib.) Splendid Isolation: Art of Easter Island, 2001; Among Stone Giants, 2003; Hoa Hakananai'a, 2004; Remote Possibilities: Hoa Hakananai'a and HMS Topaze On Rapa Nui, 2006; (contrib.) Stone: A Substantial Witness, 2006. Contributor to books and periodicals. **Address:** The Cotsen Institute of Archaeology, University of California, 308 Charles E. Young Dr. N, A210 Fowler Bldg., PO Box 951510, Los Angeles, CA 90095-1510, U.S.A. **Online address:** jvantil@ucla.edu

VAN TUYLL, Hubert P. American/Dutch (born Netherlands), b. 1957. **Genres:** International Relations/Current Affairs, Military/Defense/Arms Control, Economics, International Relations/Current Affairs, History. **Career:** Birmingham Area Legal Services, staff attorney, 1979-81; Texas A&M University, graduate assistant, 1984-85, Military Studies Institute, acting director, 1985-86; Union College, assistant professor, associate professor of history, 1986-91, director of planning and evaluation, 1987-91, History and Political

Science Program, coordinator, 1990-91; Augusta State University, Department of History, Anthropology, and Philosophy, assistant professor, professor of history, 1991-, chair. Writer. **Publications:** Feeding the Bear: American Aid to the Soviet Union, 1941-1945, 1989; America's Strategic Future: A Blueprint for National Survival in the New Millennium, 1998; The Netherlands and World War I: Espionage, Diplomacy, and Survival, 2001; (with J. Brauer) Castles, Battles, and Bombs: How Economics Explains Military History, 2008. Contributor to books and journals. **Address:** Department of History, Anthropology, and, Philosophy, Augusta State University, 2500 Walton Way, Augusta, GA 30904-2200, U.S.A. **Online address:** hvantuyl@aug.edu

VAN VUGT, William E. American (born United States), b. 1957. **Genres:** History, Biography, Autobiography/Memoirs. **Career:** Calvin College, Department of History, assistant professor, 1986-91, associate professor, 1991-94, professor, 1994-, chair. Writer. **Publications:** Britain to America: Mid-Nineteenth-Century Immigrants to the United States, 1999; (ed. with G.D. Cloete and contrib.) Race and Reconciliation in South Africa: A Multicultural Dialogue in Comparative Dialogue, 2000; British Buckeyes: The English, Scots, and Welsh in Ohio, 1700-1900, 2006; British Immigration to the United States: 1776-1914, 2009. Contributor to books and periodicals. **Address:** Department of History, Calvin College, 490 Hiemenga Hall, 3201 Burton SE, Grand Rapids, MI 49546-4402, U.S.A. **Online address:** wvanvugt@calvin.edu

VAN WILLIGEN, Anne. American (born United States), b. 1964. **Genres:** Food And Wine, History. **Career:** Kentucky Department for Libraries and Archives, regional consultant. Writer and consultant. **Publications:** (with J. van Willigen) Food and Everyday Life on Kentucky Family Farms, 1920-1950, 2006. **Address:** Bluegrass Regional Office, Kentucky Department for Libraries and Archives, 600 S Main St., Nicholasville, KY 40356-1839, U.S.A. **Online address:** anne.vanwilligen@ky.gov

VAN WILLIGEN, John. American (born United States), b. 1939. **Genres:** Anthropology/Ethnology, Bibliography, History. **Career:** University of Kentucky, professor, 1974-2009, professor emeritus, 2009-. Writer. **Publications:** Anthropology in Use: A Bibliographic Chronology of the Development of Applied Anthropology, 1980 as Anthropology in Use: A Source Book on Anthropological Practice, 1991; (with B.R. DeWalt) Training Manual in Policy Ethnography, 1985; Applied Anthropology: An Introduction, 1986, 3rd ed., 2002; Becoming a Practicing Anthropologist: A Guide to Careers and Training Programs in Applied Anthropology, 1987; (with S. Kedia) Applied Anthropology: Domains of Application, 2005. RURAL KENTUCKY SERIES: Gettin' Some Age on Me: Social Organization of Older People in a Rural American Community, 1989; (with S.C. Eastwood) Tobacco Culture: Farming Kentucky's Burley Belt, 1998; (with A.V. Willigen) Food and Everyday Life on Kentucky Family Farms, 1920-1950, 2006. INDIA SERIES: The Indian City: A Bibliographic Guide to the Literature on Urban India, 1979; (with N.K. Chadha) Social Aging in a Delhi Neighborhood, 1999. EDITOR: (with S. Abbott) Predicting Sociocultural Change, 1980; (with B. Rylko-Bauer and A. McElroy) Making Our Research Useful: Case Studies in the Utilization of Anthropological Knowledge, 1989; (with T.L. Finan) Soundings: Rapid and Reliable Research Methods for Practicing Anthropologists, 1991. Contributor of articles to books. **Address:** Lexington, KY , U.S.A. **Online address:** john.vanwilligen@uky.edu

VANZANT, Iyanla. American (born United States), b. 1953. **Genres:** Psychology, Self Help, Women's Studies And Issues. **Career:** Federation of Addiction Agencies, drug rehabilitation counselor, 1972-79; ordained Yoruba priestess, 1983; Medgar Evers College, director of alumni affairs, 1983-85; Philadelphia Public Defender's Association, attorney, 1988-90; writer, 1992- ; Inner Visions Institute for Spiritual Development, founder and executive director of training, 1998-; Inner Visions Intl., founder and executive director. **Publications:** Crowing Glory, 1989; Tapping the Power Within: A Path to Self-Empowerment for Black Women, 1992; Acts of Faith: Daily Meditations for People of Color, 1993; The Value in the Valley: A Black Woman's Guide through Life's Dilemmas, 1995; Faith in the Valley: Lessons for Women on the Journey to Peace, 1996; The Spirit of a Man: A Vision of Transformation for Black Men and the Women Who Love Them, 1996; The Big Book of Faith, 1997; In the Meantime: Finding Yourself and the Love That you Want, 1998; One Day My Soul Just Opened Up: 40 Days and 40 Nights toward Spiritual Strength and Personal Growth, 1998; Yesterday, I Cried: Celebrating the Lessons of Living and Loving, 1998; Don't Give It Away!, 1999; Until Today!: Daily Devotions for Spiritual Growth and Peace of Mind, 2000; Living

through the Meantime: Learning to Break the Patterns of the Past and Begin the Healing Process, 2001; Every Day I Pray: Awakening to the Grace of Inner Communion, 2001; (intro.) Best Black Women's Erotica, 2001; Up From Here: Reclaiming the Male Spirit: A Guide to Transforming Emotions Into Power and Freedom, 2002; Peace from Broken Pieces: How to Get through What You're Going Through, 2010. Contributor to periodicals. **Address:** Inner Visions Institute for Spiritual Development, PO Box 8517, Silver Spring, MD 20907-8517, U.S.A.

VAPNYAR, Lara. American/Russian (born Russia), b. 1971. **Genres:** Novels, Children's Fiction, Social Sciences, Literary Criticism And History, Young Adult Fiction. **Career:** City College of New York, faculty. Writer. **Publications:** There Are Jews in My House, 2003; Memoirs of a Muse, 2006; Broccoli and Other Tales of Food and Love, 2008. Contributor to periodicals. **Address:** 1745 Broadway, New York, NY 10019, U.S.A.

VARDAMIS, Frances (Diem). American (born United States), b. 1935. **Genres:** Mystery/Crime/Suspense, Translations, Young Adult Fiction, Novels. **Career:** Sugarbush Ski Resort, staff; Stavanger College, faculty; Robinson Jeffers Tor House Foundation, newsletter editor, 2000-; Carmel Harrison Memorial Library, treasurer. Translator. **Publications:** (Trans.) S. Hølmebakk, The Carriage Stone (fiction), 1996. MYSTERY NOVELS: Russian Doll, 2000; Ancestral Voices, 2001; Pity the Children, 2003; Vermont Sea Glass, 2006. Contributor to periodicals. **Address:** Robinson Jeffers Tor House Foundation, 26304 Ocean View Ave., Carmel, CA 93923, U.S.A. **Online address:** fdv@redshift.com

VARELDZIS, Georgia M. American (born United States), b. 1933. **Genres:** Food And Wine. **Career:** Duane Morris and Hecksher, legal secretary, 1953; McCallister, Burns and Gustafson, secretary and office manager, 1960-64; cooking instructor and writer, 1987-. **Publications:** Entertaining People, 1985; Very Entertaining, 1987; (with D. Morgan) The Basic Gourmet, 1993. **Address:** 13236 SW Buckfield Ln., Tigard, OR 97224-3078, U.S.A. **Online address:** gmvareldzis@aol.com

VARESI, Anthony G. Canadian (born Canada), b. 1972. **Genres:** Music, Popular Culture, Art/Art History. **Career:** Mair, Jensen, Blair Law Firm, associate attorney, 1999-2002; Gillespie Renkema Law Firm, associate attorney, 2002-. Writer. **Publications:** The Bob Dylan Albums: A Critical Study, 2002. **Address:** Gillespie Renkema Barnett Broadway L.L.P., 121 St. Paul St., 200 Ste., Kamloops, BC V2E 3K8, Canada. **Online address:** avaresi@kamloopslawyers.com

VARGAS, Fred. French (born France), b. 1957?. **Genres:** Novels. **Career:** Writer, archeologist and historian. **Publications:** NOVELS: Les jeux de l'amour et de la mort, 1986; L'homme aux cercles bleus, 1991; Ceux qui vont mourir te saluent, 1994; Debout les morts, 1995; Un Peu Plus Loin Sur la Droite, 1996; Sans feu ni lieu, 1997; This Night's Foul Work, 2008; Chalk Circle Man, 2009. CHIEF INSPECTOR ADAMSBERG SERIES: L'homme à l'envers, 1999; Les quatre fleuves, 2000; Pars vite et reviens tard, 2001; Petit traité de toutesvérités sur l'existence, 2001; Coule la Seine, 2002; Critique de l'anxiété pure, 2003; Sous les vents de Neptune, 2004; Dans les bois éternels, 2006; Seeking Whom He may Devour, 2006; Un lieu incertain, 2008; Armée Furieeuse, 2011; Jo Vargas, 2011. **Address:** c/o Author Mail, Publicity Department, Simon & Schuster Inc., 1230 Ave. of the Americas, New York, NY 10020, U.S.A.

VARGAS, Margarita. American (born United States), b. 1956. **Genres:** Translations, Women's Studies And Issues, Young Adult Fiction. **Career:** State University of New York, assistant professor of Spanish, 1985-94, associate professor of Spanish, 1994-, Institute on Research and Education on Women and Gender, co-director; Feministas Unidas, vice-president, 2003-04, president, 2004-05. Writer. **Publications:** (Trans. with J. Bruce-Novoa) The House on the Beach (novel), 1994; (ed. with T.C. Salas and intro.) Women Writing Women: An Anthology of Spanish-American Theater of the 1980s, 1997; (ed. with C. Larson) Latin American Women Dramatists: Theater, Texts and Theories, 1998. **Address:** Department of Romance Languages and Literatures, State University of New York at Buffalo, 910 Clemens Hall, Buffalo, NY 14260, U.S.A. **Online address:** mvargas@buffalo.edu

VARGAS LLOSA, (Jorge) Mario (Pedro). Spanish (born Spain), b. 1936. **Genres:** Novels, Novellas/Short Stories, Plays/Screenplays. **Career:** University of London, Queen Mary College and Kings College, faculty, 1966-68;

Washington State University, writer-in-residence, 1968; University of Puerto Rico, visiting professor, 1969; Libre, co-founder, 1971; Columbia University, Edward Laroque Tinker visiting professor, 1975; Harvard University, Robert Kennedy professor, 1992-; La Industria, journalist; Radio Panamericana, journalist; La Cronica, journalist; Woodrow Wilson Center, fellow; Agence France-Presse, journalist; L'Office de Radiodiffusion Télévision Française, broadcaster. **Publications:** FICTION: Los jefes, 1959, trans. as The Cubs and Other Stories; La ciudad y los perros (novel), 1963, trans. as The Time of the Hero, 1966; La casa verde (novel), 1966, trans. as The Green House, 1968; Los cachorros (title means: 'The Cubs'), 1967, trans. as The Cubs and Other Stories; Conversacion en la catedral (novel), 1969, trans. as Conversation in the Cathedral, 1975; Los cachorros, Los jefes, 1973; Pantaleon y las visitadoras (novel), 1973, trans. as Captain Pantoja and the Special Service, 1978; La tia Julia y el escribidor (novel), 1977, trans. as Aunt Julia and the Scriptwriter, 1982; The Cubs and Other Stories, 1979; La guerra del fin del mundo (novel), 1981, trans. as The War of the End of the World, 1984; Historia de Mayta (novel), 1985, trans. as The Real Life of Alejandro Mayta, 1986; Quien mato a Palomino Molero? (novel), 1986, trans. as Who Killed Palomino Molero?, 1987; El hablador (novel), 1987, trans. as The Storyteller, 1989; Elogio de la madrastra (novel), 1988, trans. as In Praise of the Stepmother, 1990; Lituma en los Andes (novel), 1993, trans. as Death in the Andes, 1996; The Notebooks of Don Rigoberto, 1998. OTHERS: La novela, 1968; (with G. Garcia Marquez) La novela en America Latina, 1968; (ed. with G. Brotherston) Seven Stories from Spanish America, 1968; Antologia minima de M. Vargas Llosa, 1969; Letra de batalla per Tirant lo Blanc, 1969, as Carta de batalla por Tirant lo Blanc, 1991; (with O. Collazos and J. Cortazar) Literatura en la revolucion y revolucion en la literatura, 1970; Los cachorros; El desafio; Dia domingo, 1970; Dia domingo, 1971; Garcia Marquez: Historia de un deicidio (title means: 'Garcia Marquez: The Story of a Deicide'), 1971; La historia secreta de una novela, 1971; (with M. de Riquer) El combate imaginario: Las cartas de batalla de Joanot Martorell, 1972; (with A. Rama) Garcia Marquez y la problematica de la novela, 1973; Obras escogidas: Novelas y cuentos, 1973; La orgia perpetua: Flaubert y Madame Bovary, 1975, trans. as The Perpetual Orgy: Flaubert and Madame Bovary, 1986; La orgia perpetua; Pantaleon y las visitadoras, 1978; Jose Maria Arguedas, entre sapos y halcones, 1978; La utopia arcaica, 1978; The Genesis and Evolution of Pantaleon y las visitadoras, 1979; Art, Authenticity and Latin American Culture, 1981; Entre Sartre y Camus, 1981; Contra viento y marea (title means: 'Against All Odds'), 3 vols., 1983-90; La cultura de la libertad, la libertad de la cultura, 1985; El debate, 1990; La verdad de las mentiras (title means: 'The Truth of Lies'), 1990; A Writer's Reality, 1991; El pez en el agua: Memorias, 1993, trans. as A Fish in the Water: A Memoir, 1994; Desafios a la libertad, 1994, trans. as Making Waves, 1997; La utopia arcaica, 1996; Ojos bonitos, cuadros feos, 1996; (with P. Bowles) Claudio Bravo: Paintings and Drawings, 1997; Cartas a un joven novelista, 1997; Los cuadernos de don Rigoberto, 1997; Historia no official, 1997; Making Waves, 1997; Notebooks of Don Rigoberto, 1998; na historia no official, 1998; Conversación en la catedral, 1999; La fiesta del chivo, 2000; El lenguaje de la passion, 2000; (co-author) El arte de la novela, 2000; (intro.) Manual del perfecto idiota latinoamericano-y español, 2000; Andes, 2001; Bases para una interpretación de Rubén Darío: tesis universitaria, 1958, 2001; Conferencia magistral, 2001; Feast of the Goat, 2001; Jefes; Lenguaje de la pasión, 2001; Literatura y política, 2001; Obra reunida: Teatro, 2001; Storyteller, 2001; In Praise of the Stepmother, 2002; Letters to a Young Novelist, 2002; Martín Chambi, 1920-1950, 2002; Verdad de las mentiras, 2002; Diario de Irak, 2003; Palma, valor nacional, 2003; (intro.) Escritos políticos y morales: Perú, 1954-1965, 2003; Paraiso en la otra esquina, 2003; Way to Paradise, 2003; (intro.) Flora Tristan, la paria et son rêve: correspondance, rev. ed., 2003; Fotos del paraíso, 2003; Obras completas, 2004; Tentación de lo imposible: Victor Hugo y Los miserables, 2004; Narraciones y novelas (1959-1967), 2004; Entrevistas escogidas, 2004; Donación Botero: Museo de Antioquia, 2005; Conversation in the Cathedral: A Novel, 2005; Ensayos literarios, 2005; Green House: A Novel, 2005; Mario Vargas Llosa: Doctor Honoris Causa 2005, 2005; Pez en el agua, 2005; Diccionario del amante de América Latina, 2006; Israel, Palestina: paz o guerra santa, 2006; Teatro: obra reunida, 2006; Travesuras de la niña mala, 2006; Bad Girl, 2007; (contrib.) Juan Diego Flórez: notas de una voz, 2007; Cachorros; Los jefes, 2007; Odiseo y Penélope, 2007; Temptation of the Impossible: Victor Hugo and Les misérables, 2007; Touchstones: Essays on Literature, Art and Politics, 2007; Wellsprings, 2008; Viaje a la ficción: el mundo de Juan Carlos Onetti, 2008; Al pie del Támesis, 2008; (with P. Yenne and A. Benavente) Arequipa en blanco y negro: el Estudio de Arte Vargas Hnos., 1912-1930, 2008; Sables y utopías: visiones de América Latina, 2009; Mil noches y una noche, 2009; Sueño del celta, 2010; Sueño y realidad de América Latina, 2010; Investidura como Doctor Honoris Causa del Excmo. Sr. D. Mario Vargas Llosa, 2010; In Praise of Reading and Fiction: The Nobel Lecture, December 7, 2010, 2011. **Address:** Agencia Carmen Balcells, Diagonal 580, Barcelona, 08021, Spain.

VARMUS, Harold E(lliot). American (born United States), b. 1939. **Genres:** Medicine/Health, Sciences. **Career:** Presbyterian Hospital, intern, resident, 1966-68; National Institutes of Health, clinical associate, 1968-70, director, 1993-99, National Cancer Institute, director, 2010-; University of California, postdoctoral fellow, lecturer in microbiology, 1970-72, Department of Microbiology and Immunology, assistant professor, 1972-74, Department of Biochemistry and Biophysics, assistant professor, 1972-74, associate professor, 1974-79, professor, 1979-83; American Cancer Society, research professor, 1984-93; Memorial Sloan-Kettering Cancer Center, president and chief executive officer, 2000-10. Writer. **Publications:** (Co-ed.) RNA Tumor Viruses: Molecular Biology of Tumor Viruses, 2nd ed., 1982; (ed. with A.J. Levine) Readings in Tumor Virology, 1983; (with R.A. Weinberg) Cells, Development and the Biology of Cancer, 1992; (with R.A. Weinberg) Genes and the Biology of Cancer, 1993; (ed. with J.M. Coffin and S.H. Hughes) Retroviruses, 1997; (ed. with N. Lane) Investing in Our Future: A National Research Initiative for America's Children for the 21st Century, 1999; Parity in Financing Mental Health Services: Managed Care Effects on Cost, Access and Quality, 1999; (with P.W. Majerus and R.M. Perimutter) The Molecular Basis of Blood Disease, 3rd ed., 2000; Art and Politics of Science, 2009. Contributor to journals and periodicals. **Address:** National Cancer Institute, National Institutes of Health, 6116 Executive Blvd., Ste. 300, Bethesda, MD 20892-8322, U.S.A.

VARNUM, Keith A. American (born United States), b. 1948. **Genres:** Self Help, Medicine/Health. **Career:** The Dream-A Gathering of Equals Seminars, founder and facilitator, 1994-. Writer. **Publications:** SELF-HELP BOOKS: (with M. Conrad) Living the Dream-It's Time!: A Chronicle of the Gathering of Equals, 1998; Inner Coach: Outer Power, 2002. **Address:** 11248 N 11th St., Phoenix, AZ 85020, U.S.A. **Online address:** keith@thedream.com

VARON, Sara. American (born United States) **Genres:** Novels. **Career:** Writer. **Publications:** SELF-ILLUSTRATED: Sweaterweather, 2003; Chicken and Cat, 2006; Robot Dreams, 2007; Chicken and Cat Clean Up, 2009; Bake Sale, 2011. **Address:** First Second Books, 175 5th Ave., New York, NY 10010, U.S.A. **Online address:** sara.varon@gmail.com

VAROUNIS, Athena. American (born United States), b. 1954?. **Genres:** Young Adult Non-fiction. **Career:** Edison Township, Police Department, crime analyst, identification and photography unit technician; Federal Bureau of Investigation (FBI), special agent, 1980-96, Office of Professional Responsibility, supervisory special agent, 1996-98, Special Photographic Unit, unit chief, 1998-2001, Defensive Programs Unit, unit chief, 2001-04; Vesuvius Investigative Consultants, co-founder; McDaniel College, adjunct professor. Writer. **Publications:** (With D. Heinecker) Franklin County Ghosts of Pennsylvania (nonfiction), 2009. **Address:** Vesuvius Investigative Consultants, PO Box 833, Reidsville, NC 27323, U.S.A. **Online address:** investigations@vesuvius-investigations.com

VARSAVSKY, Paula. Argentine (born Argentina), b. 1963?. **Genres:** Writing/Journalism. **Career:** Cultural writer and journalist. **Publications:** Nadie Alzaba la Voz, 1994; El Resto de su Vida, 2007. **Address:** Republica Arabe Siria 2885 1A, Buenos Aires, Argentina. **Online address:** pauvarsavsky@gmail.com

VARZI, Achille C. Italian (born Italy), b. 1958. **Genres:** Philosophy, Bibliography. **Career:** Istituto per la Ricerca Scientifica e Tecnologica, consultant and researcher, 1989-95; Columbia University, assistant professor of philosophy, 1995-2003, professor of philosophy, 2003-, chair of the department; The Journal of Philosophy, editor; Synthese, subject editor; Stanford Encyclopedia of Philosophy, subject editor. **Publications:** (With R. Casati) Holes and Other Superficialities, 1994; (ed. with Casati) Events: An Annotated Bibliography, 1994; (ed. with Casati) Events, 1996; (with R. Casati) 50 Years of Events: An Annotated Bibliography, 1947 to 1997, 1997; (with J. Nolt and D. Rohatyn) Schaum's Outline of Theory and Problems of Logic, 1998; (with Casati) Parts and Places: The Structures of Spatial Representation, 1999; Essay in Universal Semantics, 1999; (ed. with J. Higginbotham and F. Pianesi) Speaking of Events, 2000; Parole, Oggetti, Eventi e Altri Argomenti di Metafisica, 2001; (with R. Casati) Semplicità Insormontabili: 39 Storie Filosofiche, 2004; (ed. with L. Vieu) Formal Ontology in Information Systems, 2004; (with R. Casati) Insurmountable Simplicities: Thirty-Nine Philosophical Stories, 2006; (with J. Nolt and D. Rohatyn) Logic, 2006; (co-author) Stramaledettamente Logico: Esercizi Di Filosofia Su Pellicola, 2009; Mondo Messo A Fuoco: Storie Di Allucinazioni E Miopie Filosofiche, 2010. Contributor of articles to journals. **Address:** Department of Philosophy, Columbia University, 708 Philosophy Hall, 1150 Amsterdam Ave., PO Box 4971, New York, NY 10027, U.S.A. **Online address:** achille.varzi@columbia.edu

VARZI, Roxanne. American/Iranian (born Iran), b. 1971. **Genres:** History, Social Sciences, Sociology. **Career:** New York University, Department of Anthropology, instructor, 2002-04; University of London, School of Oriental and African Studies, visiting faculty, Department of Anthropology and Sociology, lecturer, Department of Anthropology and Near Eastern Studies, assistant professor, 2004-05; University of California, assistant professor of anthropology and film and media studies, 2005-09, associate professor of anthropology and film and media studies, 2009-; St. Antony's College, senior Iranian visiting fellow, 2005; University of Lund, UC/Lund Summer Exchange, assistant professor, 2007; Dr. Samuel M. Jordan Center for Persian Studies and Culture, Religious Studies, faculty; Center for Global Peace and Conflict Studies, faculty. Writer. **Publications:** Warring Souls: Youth, Media, and Martyrdom in Post-Revolution Iran, 2006. **Address:** Department of Anthropology, University of California, 4229 Social Science Plz. B, Irvine, CA 92697-5100, U.S.A. **Online address:** rvarzi@uci.edu

VAS DIAS, Robert. British/American (born United States), b. 1931. **Genres:** Poetry, Literary Criticism And History, Art/Art History. **Career:** Prentice-Hall Inc., assistant editor, 1955-56; Allyn & Bacon Inc., staff editor, 1956-57; freelance editor, 1957-65; Aspen Writers' Workshop, director, 1964-67; Long Island University, instructor in English, 1964-66; New York University, American Language Institute, instructor in English, 1966-71; Thomas Jefferson College, Grand Valley State University, tutor and poet-in-residence, 1971-74; Permanent Press, founder, 1972-, editor and publisher, 1973-; The Poetry Society, general secretary, 1975-78; Antioch Center for British Studies, lecturer in poetry, 1977-81; University of Maryland, European Division, lecturer, 1981-96; The Poetry School, London, tutor, 2002-. **Publications:** Ribbed Vision, A Poem, 1963; The Counted, 1967; (ed.) Inside Outer Space: New Poems of the Space Age, 1970; Written in Orbit, 1970; The Life of Parts: Or, Thanking You for the Book on Building Bird Feeders, 1972; Speech Acts & Happenings, 1972; Making Faces, 1975; Ode, 1977; Poems Beginning: The World, 1979; Time Exposures, 1999; Select Things, 2001; The Guts of Shadows, 2003; Leaping Down to Earth, 2008; Still Life and Other Poems of Art and Artifice, 2010. **Address:** 5 B, Compton Ave., Canonbury, London, GL N1 2XD, England. **Online address:** robertvasdias@blueyonder.co.uk

VASQUEZ, Ian. American (born United States), b. 1966. **Genres:** Novels. **Career:** St. Petersburg Times, copy editor. **Publications:** In the Heat (novel), 2008; Lonesome Point, 2009; Mr. Hooligan, 2010. **Address:** St. Petersburg Times, 490 1st Ave. S, St. Petersburg, FL 33701-4223, U.S.A. **Online address:** ian@ianvasquez.net

VASSANJI, M(oyez) G. Canadian/Kenyan (born Kenya), b. 1950. **Genres:** Novels, Novellas/Short Stories, Biography, Young Adult Non-fiction, Adult Non-fiction, Young Adult Fiction. **Career:** Atomic Energy of Canada Chalk River Power Station, postdoctoral fellow, 1978-80; University of Toronto, research associate and lecturer in physics, 1980-89; Toronto South Asian Review, co-founder and editor, 1980-; writer, 1989-; Indian Institute of Advanced Study, visiting professor, 2010; Emory University, faculty. **Publications:** Uhuru Street: Short Stories, 1990; Elvis, Raja: Stories, 2005. NOVELS: The Gunny Sack, 1989; No New Land, 1990; The Book of Secrets, 1993; Amriika, 1999; The In-Between World of Vikram Lall, 2003; When She Was Queen, 2005; The Assassin's Song, 2007. EDITOR: A Meeting of Streams: South Asian Canadian Literature, 1985; The Journey Prize Anthology: Short Fiction from the Best of Canada's New Writers, 1995; The Palm Leaf Fan & Other Stories, 2006. NON-FICTION: A Place Within: Rediscovering India, 2008; Mordecai Richler (biography), 2009. Contributor to periodicals. **Address:** c/o Cathy Paine, Westwood Creative Artists Ltd., 94 Harbord St., Toronto, ON M5S 1G6, Canada.

VASSBERG, David E(rland). American (born United States), b. 1936. **Genres:** Area Studies, History, Social Sciences, Sciences. **Career:** Pan American University, assistant professor, 1971-77, associate professor, 1977-83, professor of history, 1983-99, now professor emeritus. Writer. **Publications:** (With J. Arbena and H. Schmidt) Regionalism and the Musical Heritage of Latin America, 1980; La venta de tierras baldias: El comunitarismo agrario y la corona de Castilla durante el siglo XVI, 1983; Land and Society in Golden Age Castile, 1984; The Village and the Outside World in Golden Age Castile Mobility and Migration in Everyday Rural Life, 1996; Stockholm on the Rio Grande: A Swedish Farming Colony on the Mesquite Frontier of Southernmost Texas (1912-1985), 2003. Contributor to articles. **Address:** Department of History, University of Texas-Pan American, 1201 W University Dr., Edinburg, TX 78539, U.S.A.

VASTA, Edward. American (born United States), b. 1928. **Genres:** Novels, Novellas/Short Stories, Science Fiction/Fantasy, Children's Fiction, Plays/Screenplays, Literary Criticism And History, Autobiography/Memoirs, Translations, Translations. **Career:** Stanford University, instructor in English, 1956-58; University of Notre Dame, instructor, 1958-61, assistant professor, 1961-66, associate professor and director of graduate studies, 1966-69, professor, 1969-98, chair of department, 1972-78, professor emeritus, 1998-, Medieval Institute, fellow, 1993-97. Writer. **Publications:** The Spiritual Basis of Piers Plowman, 1965; Tales from the Hidden Apple, 2001; Novellas Back and Forth, 2002; Family Passions, 2003; Love and Redemption, 2003; Mud Pie Mysteries: Fables about Children in God's World, 2004; To Carthage We Came, 2011. EDITOR: Middle English Survey: Critical Essays, 1965; Interpretations of Piers Plowman, 1968; (with Z.P. Thundy) Chaucerian Problems and Perspectives: Essays Presented to Paul E. Beichner, C.S.C., 1979. TRANSLATOR: (with D.S. Cervigni) Vita Nuova, 1995; For She Distinguished Herself, First Among All, 2003. **Address:** Department of English, University of Notre Dame, 356 O'Shaughnessy Hall, Notre Dame, IN 46556-5639, U.S.A. **Online address:** evasta@nd.edu

VATIKIOTIS, Michael R. J. American (born United States), b. 1957. **Genres:** Politics/Government, Children's Fiction, Photography, History, Social Sciences. **Career:** BBC World Service, producer, 1984-87, correspondent, 1987-88; Far Eastern Economic Review, chief, 1987-99, managing editor, 1999-2001, editor-in-chief, 2001; Henry Dunant Centre for Humanitarian Dialogue, senior visiting fellow, regional director; Institute of Southeast Asian Studies, visiting fellow, visiting research fellow. **Publications:** (Contrib.) Over Indonesia, 1992; Indonesian Politics Under Suharto, 1993, 3rd ed. as Indonesian Politics Under Suharto: The Rise and Fall of the New Order, 1998; Political Change in Southeast Asia: Trimming the Banyan Tree, 1996; Debatable Land: Stories From Southeast Asia, 2001; The Spice Garden, 2004; (contrib.) Indonesia: Islands of the Imagination, 2005; Singapore Ground Zero, 2007. Contributor to books. **Address:** Centre for Humanitarian Dialogue, 114 rue de Lausanne, Geneva, CH 1202, Switzerland. **Online address:** vatikiotis@hdcentre.org

VAUCLAIR, Jacques. French/Swiss (born Switzerland), b. 1947. **Genres:** Psychology, Animals/Pets, Sciences. **Career:** International Center for Genetic Epistemology, general secretary, 1971-79; Emory University, visiting scientist, 1980-82; Institute of Neurophysiology and Psychophysiology, research associate, 1982-89; Centre National de la Recherche Scientifique, research director, 1989-98, head of comparative cognition group, 1990-; Université de Provence, professor, 1998-. Writer. **Publications:** L'intelligence de l'animal, 1992; La cognition animale, 1996; Animal Cognition: Recent Developments in Comparative Psychology, 1996; L'homme et le singe: Psychologie Comparee, 1998; Le developement du jeune enfant, 2004. **Address:** Department of Psychology, University of Provence, 29 av. Robert Schuman, Aix-en-Provence, 13621, France. **Online address:** jacques.vauclair@univ-provence.fr

VAUGHAN, Alden T(rue). American (born United States), b. 1929. **Genres:** History, Race Relations, Literary Criticism And History, Cultural/Ethnic Topics, Essays, Bibliography. **Career:** Columbia University, instructor, 1961-64, assistant professor, 1964-66, associate professor, 1966-69, professor of history, 1969-94, professor emeritus, 1994-; Harvard University, Charles Warren Center for Studies of American History, fellow; Clark University, affiliate professor of history. Writer. **Publications:** New England Frontier: Puritans and Indians 19620-75, 1965, 3rd ed., 1995; America before the Revolution, 1725-75, 1967; (contrib.) The Development of an American Culture, 1970; (comp.) The American Colonies in the 17th Century, 1971; (contrib.) The Columbia History of the World, 1972; American Genesis: Captain John Smith and the Founding of Virginia, 1975; (co-author) Crossing the Cultural Divide, 1980; (comp. with W. Washburn) A Comprehensive Bibliography of American Indian Captivity Narratives, 1982; (with V.M. Vaughan) Shakespeare's Caliban: A Cultural History, 1991; Roots of American Racism: Essays on the Colonial Experience, 1995; Transatlantic Encounters: American Indians in

Britain, 1500-1776, 2006. EDITOR: Chronicles of the American Revolution, 1965; (with R.B. Ross and J.B. Duff) The Structure of American History, 1970; The Puritan Tradition in America, 1620-1730, 1972, rev. ed., 1997; (with G.A. Billias) Perspectives on Early American History, 1973; (with F.J. Bremer) Puritan New England, 1977; New England's Prospect, 1977; Early American Indian Documents: Treaties and Laws, 1607-1789, 1979; (with E.W. Clark) Puritans among the Indians: Accounts of Captivity and Redemption, 1676-1724, 1981; (with V.M. Vaughan) Critical Essays on Shakespeare's The Tempest, 1998; New England Encounters: Indians and Euroamericans ca. 1600-1850: Essays Drawn from The New England Quarterly, 1999; (with V.M. Vaughan) Shakespeare, The Tempest, 2000; (with V.M. Vaughan and comp.) Shakespeare in American Life, 2007. **Address:** Department of History, Clark University, 950 Main St., Worcester, MA 01610, U.S.A. **Online address:** aldenvaughan@aol.com

VAUGHAN, Brian K. American (born United States), b. 1976. **Genres:** Air/Space Topics, Children's Fiction, Novels, Mystery/Crime/Suspense, Graphic Novels. **Career:** Writer, 1999-. **Publications:** Y: LAST MAN SERIES GRAPHIC NOVELS: Y: The Last Man: Unmanned, 2003; Y: The Last Man: One Small Step, 2004; Y: The Last Man, Whys and Wherefores, 2009. OTHERS: (co-author) Green Lantern: Circle of Fire, 2002; Pride of Baghdad: Inspired by a True Story=Kibriya Baghdad, 2006; Runaways, 2007; Batman: False Faces, 2008; Ex Machina, 8 vols., 2009. **Address:** c/o Author Mail, DC Comics, 1700 Broadway, New York, NY 10019, U.S.A. **Online address:** briankvaughan@aol.com

VAUGHAN, Marcia (K.). American (born United States), b. 1951. **Genres:** Children's Fiction, Animals/Pets, Children's Non-fiction, Young Adult Fiction. **Career:** Captain Charles Wilkes Elementary School, school librarian, 1975-80; Natangiia Primary School, school librarian, 1981; writer, 1981-; Blessed Sacrament School, school librarian, 1982-88. **Publications:** CHILDREN'S BOOKS: The Lucky Fun Book, 1984; Who?, 1984; Wombat Stew, 1986; Pewzer and Bonsai, 1985; Hands, Hands, Hands, 1987; Tails, 1987; Whose Toes and Nose Are Those?, 1987; A Cat's Eye Is One, 1987; Hiccups, 1987; Where Does the Wind Go?, 1987; Crosby Crocodile's Disguise, 1988; The Sticky Beak Mystery series (26 books), 1988; Still Room for More, 1989; The Wombat Stew Cookbook, 1989; (with R. Vaughan) Adam's Apple, 1989; (with R. Vaughan) Ships, Boats and Things That Float, 1989; As Fat as That, 1989; There's a Bunyip Under My Bed, 1989; The Sandwich That Max Made, 1989; Wake Up, Wallaby, 1989; At Night, 1989; Clouds, 1989; Numerals, 1989; Sleeping, 1989; T.J.'s Tree, 1989; Sleepy Bear, 1989; Monkey's Friends, 1989; Moonlight, 1989; Milly Fitzwilly's Most Magnificent Mousecatcher, 1990; (with P. Mullins) The Sea Breeze Hotel, 1990; An Abundance of Animals, 1990; Australian Spiders, 1990; Australian Snakes, 1990; Australian Crocodiles, 1990; Australian Insects, 1990; Australian Plants, 1990; Australian Sea Life, 1990; Deadly and Dangerous Australian Spiders, 1990; Deadly and Dangerous Australian Snakes, 1990; Deadly and Dangerous Australian Crocodiles, 1990; Deadly and Dangerous Australian Insects, 1990; Deadly and Dangerous Australian Plants, 1990; Deadly and Dangerous Australian Sea Life, 1990; The Giants' Child, 1991; A Skirt for Susan, 1991; The Mystery of the Missing Map, 1992; Sheep Shape, 1993; Hi-De-Hi, 1993; Jungle Parade, 1993; Otto the Otter, 1993; Something New, 1993; The Old Oak Tree, 1993; Animal Stretches, 1993; My Friends, 1993; Zither, 1993; (with R. Vaughan) Bon Voyage, 1994; How to Cook a Gooseberry Fool: Unusual Recipes From Around The World, 1994; Snap!, 1994, 2nd ed., 1996; Skateboard Bill, 1994; The Stick-around Cloud, 1994; Dorobo the Dangerous, 1994; Kapoc the Killer Croc, 1995; Riddle by the River, 1995; Tingo Tango Mango Tree, 1995; Whistling Dixie, 1995; Goldsworthy and Mort Blast Off, 1996; The Dancing Dragon, 1996; Happy Birthday, Mrs. Boedecker, 1996; Secret Friend, 1996; Catch the Cookie, 1996; Delilah Drink Water and the Clever Cloud, 1996; Boomer and Squeak's Lemonade Stand, 1999; Pirate Pie!, 1999; Abbie against the Storm: The True Story of a Young Heroine and a Lighthouse, 1999; Foiled Again, 2000; Foolish Ray, 2000; The Picky Prince, 2000; The Secret of Bunratty Castle, 2000; We're Going on a Ghost Hunt, 2001; The Secret to Freedom, 2001; Kissing Coyotes, 2002; Night Dancer: Mythical Piper of the Native American Southwest, 2002; Up the Learning Tree, 2003; The Treasure of Ghostwood Gully: A Southwest Mystery, 2004; (with R. Vaughan) Three Bears of the Pacific Northwest, 2011. GOLDSWORTHY AND MORT SERIES: Valentines and Easter Eggs, 1995; Spring Soup, 1995; Summer Fun, 1995; Holiday Hijinks, 1995; Blast Off, 1996. OTHERS:

I Howl, I Growl, 2003; Irena's Jars of Secrets, 2011. Contributor to books. **Address:** PO Box 13351, Burton Sta., Vashon, WA 98013, U.S.A.

VAUGHAN, Megan. British (born England), b. 1954. **Genres:** Local History/Rural Topics, Popular Culture, Humanities. **Career:** Cambridge University, King's College, Smuts professor of commonwealth history; University of Malawi, Chancellor College, professor of history; Oxford University, faculty. Writer. **Publications:** Kinship and Class: Stratification in the Zomba-Chilwa Area of Southern Malawi, 1800-1914, 1978; (with D. Hirschmann) Women Farmers of Malawi: Food Production in the Zomba District, 1984; (with G.H.R. Chipande) Women in the Estate Sector of Malawi: The Tea and Tobacco Industries, 1986; The Story of an African Famine: Gender and Famine in Twentieth-Century Malawi, 1987; Curing Their Ills: Colonial Power and African Illness, 1991; (with H.L. Moore) Cutting Down Trees: Gender, Nutrition, and Agricultural Change in the Northern Province of Zambia, 1890-1990, 1994; Creating the Creole Island: Slavery in Eighteenth-Century Mauritius, 2004. **Address:** Kings' College, Cambridge University, W Rd., Cambridge, CB CB3 9EF, England. **Online address:** mav26@cam.ac.uk

VAUGHAN, Richard Patrick. American (born United States), b. 1919. **Genres:** Psychology, Theology/Religion, Psychiatry. **Career:** Roman Catholic Priest (Jesuit); McAuley Neuropsychiatric Institute, clinical psychologist, 1956-61; Saint Mary's Hospital, clinical psychologist, 1956-57; University of San Francisco, associate professor, 1958-67, chair, 1957-67, psychological services, director, 1960-65, professor of psychology, 1967-69, College of Liberal Arts and Letters, dean, 1967-69; California Jesuit Province, vice-provincial for education, 1969-71, regional provincial, 1971-; Loyola Marymount University, instructor, 1977-87. Writer. **Publications:** Mental Illness and the Religious Life, 1962; Introduction to Religious Counseling: A Christian Humanistic Approach, 1969; Basic Skills for Christian Counselors, 1987; Pastoral Counseling and Personality Disorders: A Manual, 1994. Contributor to journals. **Address:** 15200 NBN Way, Blue Ridge Summit, PA 17214, U.S.A.

VAUGHAN, Ronald G(eorge). American/Canadian (born Canada), b. 1952. **Genres:** Music, How-to Books, Reference, Photography. **Career:** Professional drummer, 1964-; drumming instructor, 1967-; band leader, 1975-79; The Ronald Vaughan Trio, founder, 1975-; self-defense instructor, 1977-; personal security consultant, 1980-. Writer. **Publications:** The Drumset Owner's Manual: A Heavily Illustrated Guide to Selecting, Setting Up and Maintaining All Components of the Acoustic Drumset, 1993. Contributor to periodicals. **Address:** 29 Everingham Ct., North York, ON M2M 2J6, Canada. **Online address:** rvaughan@mycybernet.net

VAUGHAN, Susan C. American (born United States), b. 1941?. **Genres:** Medicine/Health, Psychology. **Career:** National Institute of Mental Health, research fellow; New York State Psychiatric Institute, staff; Columbia University, Center for Psychoanalytic Training and Research, senior candidate, Clinical Psychiatry, assistant professor. Writer. **Publications:** The Talking Cure: The Science Behind Psychotherapy, 1997; Viagra: A Guide to the Phenomenal Potency-Promoting Drug, 1998; Half Empty, Half Full: Understanding the Psychological Roots of Optimism, 2000. Contributor to periodicals. **Address:** Center for Psychoanalytic Training and Research, Columbia University, 25 W 81st St., Ste. 1C, New York, NY 10024, U.S.A. **Online address:** scv1@columbia.edu

VAUGHN, Carrie. American (born United States), b. 1973. **Genres:** Westerns/Adventure. **Career:** Novelist. **Publications:** Kitty and the Midnight Hour, 2005; Kitty Goes to Washington, 2006; Kitty Takes a Holiday, 2007; Kitty and the Silver Bullet, 2008; Kitty and the Dead Man's Hand, 2009; Kitty Raises Hell, 2009; Discord's Apple, 2010; Kitty's House of Horrors, 2010; Voices of Dragons, 2010; (contrib.) Songs of Love & Death, 2010; Kitty Goes to War, 2010; After the Golden Age, 2011; Kitty's Big Trouble, 2011; Steel, 2011; Kitty's Greatest Hits, 2011. Contributor to magazines. Works appear in anthologies. **Address:** Ashley Grayson Literary Agency, 1342 W 18th St., San Pedro, CA 90732, U.S.A. **Online address:** clvaughn@compuserve.com

VAUGHN, Elizabeth Dewberry. See DEWBERRY, Elizabeth.

VAUGHN, Ellen Santilli. American (born United States) **Genres:** inspirational/Motivational Literature, Novels, Theology/Religion. **Career:** Writer. **Publications:** (With C. Colson) Loving God, 1983; (with C. Colson) Who Speaks For God?, 1985; (with C. Colson) Kingdoms in Conflict, 1987; (with C. Colson) Against the Night: Living in the New Dark Ages, 1989; (with

C. Colson) The God of Stones and Spiders: Letters to a Church in Exile, 1990; (with C. Colson) The Body, 1992; (with C. Colson) Gideon's Torch, 1995; The Strand (novel), 1997; (with D. Peterson) Rags, Riches, & Real Success, 2000; (with D.I. Rosser) The God Who Hung on the Cross, 2003; (with C. Colson) Being the Body, 2003; Radical Gratitude: Discovering Joy Through Everyday Thankfulness, 2005; (with D. Jackson) It's All About Him: Finding the Love of My Life, 2007; Time Peace: Living Here and Now with a Timeless God, 2007; (with G. Laurie) Lost Boy: My Story, 2008; (with D. Jackson) Road Home, 2008; (with F. Pastore) Shattered: Struck Down, But Not Destroyed, 2010; (with M.B. Chapman) Choosing to See: A Journey of Struggle and Hope, 2010. **Address:** Word Publishing Group, Division of Thomas Nelson Inc., PO Box 141000, Nashville, TN 37214-1000, U.S.A. **Online address:** ellen@ellenvaughn.com

VAUGHN, Jacqueline. (Jacqueline Vaughn Switzer). American (born United States), b. 1950. **Genres:** Politics/Government, Environmental Sciences/ Ecology. **Career:** University of Redlands, Department of Political Science, assistant professor, 1979-81; Office of the District Attorney-San Bernardino, Victim-Witness Advocacy Program, program coordinator, 1980-81; Imagination Group, partner, 1982-88; Office of the District Attorney-Riverside, Child Abuse Recognition Program, program coordinator, 1983-87; Southern Oregon University, Department of Political Science, assistant professor, 1990-95, associate professor and department chair, 1995-97; Northern Arizona University, Department of Politics and International Affairs, assistant professor, 1997-2000, associate professor, 2000-04, professor, 2004-. Writer. **Publications:** AS JACQUELINE VAUGHN SWITZER: Environmental Politics: Domestic and Global Dimensions, 1994, 6th ed., 2011; The Play of Power, 1995; Green Backlash: The History and Politics of the Environmental Opposition in the U.S., 1997; Environmental Activism: A Reference Handbook, 2003; Disabled Rights: American Disability Policy and the Fight for Equality, 2003. OTHERS: (with H.J. Cortner) George W. Bush's Healthy Forests: Reframing the Environmental Debate, 2005; Conflicts over Natural Resources: A Reference Handbook, 2007; (with E. Otenyo) Managerial Discretion In Government Decision Making: Beyond the Street Level, 2007; Waste Management: A Reference Handbook, 2009. **Address:** Department of Political Science, Northern Arizona University, 214 SBS, PO Box 15036, Flagstaff, AZ 86011-5036, U.S.A. **Online address:** jacqueline.vaughn@nau.edu

VAUGHN, Patrika. American (born United States), b. 1933. **Genres:** Novels, Children's Fiction, Young Adult Fiction, Adult Non-fiction, Advertising/ Public Relations, Business/Trade/Industry, Education, Architecture, How-to Books, Money/Finance, Self Help, Writing/Journalism, Autobiography/ Memoirs, Biography, Ghost Writer, History. **Career:** A Cappela Publishing, president, chief executive officer, 1996-; e-Lit Agent, founder and chief executive officer; Editorial Associates, editorial director; Book Wrights, executive director; Advocate House, president, 1996-. Columnist and Writer. **Publications:** Siduri Revisioned: A Fictional History of the Future, 1987; Riding the Winds of Change, 1994; Everything You Need to Know to Write, Publish & Market Your Book, 1997. Contributor to periodicals. **Address:** Cappela Publishing, PO Box 3691, Sarasota, FL 34230-3691, U.S.A. **Online address:** acappub@aol.com

VAUSE, L(aurence) Mikel. American (born United States), b. 1952. **Genres:** Literary Criticism And History, Environmental Sciences/Ecology. **Career:** Weber State University, associate professor of English, 1983-, Honors Cortez professor, 1989, Lowe professor, 1995, director of honors program; Peregrine Smith Books, assistant fiction editor, 1983-91. Writer. **Publications:** (Ed.) Rock and Roses: Essays by Women on Mountaineering, 1991, 2nd ed. as Rock and Roses: Mountaineering Essay by Some of the World's Best Women Climbers of the 20th Century, 1999; (ed. with S.I. Zeveloff, W.H. McVaugh) A Wilderness Tapestry: An Eclectic Approach to Preservation, 1992; On Mountains & Mountaineers: A Critique of Mountaineering Literature, 1993; (ed. with C. Porter) The Peregrine Reader, 1997; I Knew It Would Come to This, 1999; (and ed.) Peering Over the Edge, 2005. **Address:** Department of English, Weber State University, 256 Elizabeth Hall, 1201 University Cir., Ogden, UT 84408-1201, U.S.A. **Online address:** mvause@weber.edu

VAVRA, Terry G. American (born United States), b. 1941. **Genres:** Marketing, Business/Trade/Industry, Economics, Social Sciences, Technology. **Career:** National Broadcasting Co., director of news audience research, 1972-78; Kenyon and Eckhardt, head of research group, 1979-80; Batten, Barton, Durstine and Osborn, director of research, 1980-82; Marketing Metrics Inc., president, 1983-, co-founder; Pace University, associate professor of market-

ing, 1983-99, Lubin School of Business, associate professor; Compaq Computer Corp., senior manager. Writer. **Publications:** (With A.J. Silk) Advertising's Affective Qualities and Consumer Response, 1974; Aftermarketing: How to Keep Customers for Life through Relationship Marketing, 1992, 2nd ed., 1995; Improving Your Measurement of Customer Satisfaction: A Guide to Creating, Conducting, Analyzing, and Reporting Customer Satisfaction Measurement Programs, 1997; The Customer Delight Principle: Exceeding Customers' Expectations for Bottom-Line Success, 2001; Customer Satisfaction Measurement Simplified: A Step-by-Step Guide for ISO 9001: 2000 Certification, 2002; (co-author) Loyalty Myths: Hyped Strategies That Will Put You Out of Business and Proven Tactics That Really Work, 2005. **Address:** Marketing Metrics Inc., 305 Rte. 17, PO Box 574, Paramus, NJ 07652, U.S.A. **Online address:** tvavra@marketingmetrics.com

VAYDA, Andrew P. American/Hungarian (born Hungary), b. 1931. **Genres:** Anthropology/Ethnology, Environmental Sciences/Ecology, Cultural/Ethnic Topics. **Career:** University of British Columbia, lecturer in anthropology, 1958-60; Columbia University, assistant professor, 1960-64, associate professor, 1964-68, professor, 1968-72; Rutgers University, professor of anthropology and ecology, 1972-2002, professor emeritus of anthropology and ecology, 2002-; Center for International Forestry Research , senior research associate. Writer. **Publications:** Maori Warfare, 1960; War in Ecological Perspective: Persistence, Change, and Adaptive Processes in Three Oceanian Societies, 1976; Methods and Explanations in the Study of Human Actions and Their Environmental Effects, 1996; Finding Causes of the 1997-98 Indonesian Forest Fires: Problems and Possibilities, 1999; Explaining Human Actions and Environmental Changes, 2009; (with B.B. Walters) Introduction: Pragmatic Methods and Causal-History Explanations, 2011. EDITOR: (with A. Leeds) Man, Culture and Animals: The Role of Animals in Human Ecological Adjustments, 1965; (and intro.) Peoples and Cultures of the Pacific: An Anthropological Reader, 1968; Environment and Cultural Behavior: Ecological Studies in Cultural Anthropology, 1969; Causal Explanation for Social Scientists: A Reader, 2011. Contributor to articles and periodicals. **Address:** Department of Human Ecology, Rutgers University, 55 Dudley Rd., Cook Office Bldg., New Brunswick, NJ 08901-8520, U.S.A. **Online address:** vayda@aesop.rutgers.edu

VAZ, Katherine. American (born United States), b. 1955. **Genres:** Sports/ Fitness, History. **Career:** University of California, associate professor; Harvard University, Briggs-Copeland lecturer in fiction. Writer. **Publications:** Cross-training: The Complete Book of the Triathlon, 1984; The High-performance Triathlete, 1985; Swim, Swim: A Complete Handbook for Fitness Swimmers, 1986; Saudade, 1994; Fado & Other Stories, 1997; Mariana, 1997; Our Lady of the Artichokes and Other Portuguese-American Stories, 2008. Contributor to periodicals. **Address:** Department of English, Harvard University, Barker Ctr., 12 Quincy St., Cambridge, MA 02138, U.S.A. **Online address:** kvaz@fas.harvard.edu

VAZQUEZ, Carmen Inoa. American (born United States), b. 1942. **Genres:** Medicine/Health, Psychology. **Career:** City University of New York, Queens College, 1973-76; City University of New York, City College, proctor supervisor, 1976-77, Hostos Community College, adjunct professor, 1977-79, 1999-2002; State University of New York, Empire State College, adjunct instructor, 1978-84; Morrisania Neighborhood Clinic, intern and consultant, 1979-80; New School for Social Research, faculty, 1980-; Nassau County Medical Center, psychology intern, 1980-81; South Bronx Mental Health Council Alcoholism Clinic, clinical supervisor, 1981-82; Bellevue Hospital Center, Bellevue Psychiatric Hospital, staff psychologist, 1981-84, Bellevue Hospital Center clinical psychology internship training program, director, 1984-2001, senior psychologist, 1984-90, Bilingual Treatment Program Clinic, founding director, 1988-96, supervisor and consultant, 1996-2005, 2006-, Institute for Multicultural Behavioral Health, founding director, 2001-05, forensic track training, coordinator, 2001-04, coordinated and supervised trainees clinical experience in health psychology, 2001-04; New York University, clinical instructor, 1982-84, clinical assistant professor, 1984-92, clinical professor of psychiatry, 1992-; Saint John's University, affiliate clinical professor, 1983-87; Association of Hispanic Mental Health Professionals, president, 1993-95; Psychology Licensure, panel reviewer, 1993-2003; Antioch University, adjunct faculty, 2000-01; Health Industries Enterprises Inc., director, 2001-. Consultant and writer. **Publications:** (With G.F. Simons and P.R. Harris) Transcultural Leadership: Empowering the Diverse Workforce, 1993; (with R. Gil) The Maria Paradox: How Latinas Can Merge Old World Traditions with New World Self-Esteem, 1996; Parenting With Pride, Latino

Style: How to Help Your Child Cherish Your Cultural Values and Succeed in Today's World, 2004; (ed. with E. Razin and M. Dijst) Employment Deconcentration in European Metropolitan Areas: Market Forces Versus Planning Regulations, 2007; (with D. Rosa) Grief Therapy with Latinos: An Integration of Culture for Clinicians, 2011. Contributor to books and magazines. **Address:** 110 E 40th St., Ste. 406, New York, NY 10016, U.S.A. **Online address:** drvazquez@drcarmenvazquez.com

VAZQUEZ-GOMEZ, Juana. American/Mexican (born Mexico), b. 1940. **Genres:** History, Biography, Autobiography/Memoirs, Social Sciences. **Career:** De Lorenz Travel, manager, 1959-69; Jani Pua Nani Boutique, owner, 1962-65; Russell Davis Boutique, sales representative, 1965; freelance writer and translator, 1979-; Platanos Restaurant, manager, 1986-88. **Publications:** Prontuario de Governantes de Mexico, 1325-1982, 1982, 3rd ed., 1998; Dictionary of Mexican Rulers, 1325-1997, 1997. Contributor to periodicals. **Address:** David Fugate Waterside Productions Inc., 2191 San Elijo Ave., Cardiff, CA 92007-1873, U.S.A.

VAZSONYI, Nicholas. American (born United States), b. 1963. **Genres:** Plays/Screenplays, Literary Criticism And History, Music. **Career:** Telemusic Inc., artistic director, 1984-86, 1988-90; Vanderbilt University, assistant professor of German, 1994-97; University of South Carolina, assistant professor, 1997-2001, associate professor, 2001-10, professor, 2010-, Jesse Chapman Alcorn memorial professor of foreign languages, 2011-, German Studies Program, director, 2002-06, graduate director, 2004-09. Writer. **Publications:** Lukacs Reads Goethe: From Aestheticism to Stalinism, 1997; (ed.) Searching for Common Ground: Diskurse zur deutschen Identität 1750-1871, 2000; (ed.) Wagner's Meistersinger: Performance, History, Representation, 2003; (ed.) Cambridge Wagner Encyclopedia, 2013. **Address:** Department of Languages, Literatures & Cultures, University of South Carolina, 1620 College St., Columbia, SC 29208-0001, U.S.A. **Online address:** vazsonyi@sc.edu

VEGA, Ana Lydia. (Talía Cuervo). American (born United States), b. 1946. **Genres:** Novels, Essays, Young Adult Fiction. **Career:** Writer, 1981-; University of Puerto Rico, lecturer, professor of French and Francophone literature, now retired; El Nuevo Dia Newspaper, columnist. **Publications:** (Co-author) Le françaisvécu, 1981; (as Talía Cuervo) (with L. Filippi) Vírgenes ymártires, 1982; Encancaranublado y otros Cuentos de Naufragio, 1982; (ed.) El Tramo Ancla: En Sayos Puertorriqueños de hoy, 1989, 2nd ed., 1991; Pasión de Historia y Otras Historias Depasión, 1991; Falsas crónicas del sur, 1991; Cuentos Calientes, 1992; Esperando a Loló y otros delirios degeneración, 1994; En la Bahía de Jobos: Celita y el Mangle Zapatero, 1998; Mirada de Doble Filo, 2008. Contributor to periodicals. Works appear in anthologies. **Address:** University of Puerto Rico, PO Box 21790, Rio Piedras, PR 00931-1790, U.S.A.

VEGA, Gina. American (born United States), b. 1946. **Genres:** Business/Trade/Industry, Economics, Information Science/Computers. **Career:** City University of New York, Queens College, Office of Community Studies, director, 1986-88; Health Insurance Plan of Greater New York, community programs coordinator, 1988-89; Institute for Rational-Emotive Therapy, administrative director, 1989-93; Organizational Ergonomics, owner and consultant, 1994-; University of Lethbridge, visiting faculty, 1995; St. John's University, adjunct assistant professor, 1995-96; Marymount Manhattan College, adjunct assistant professor, 1995-96; Hofstra University, adjunct assistant professor, 1996; Merrimack College, assistant professor, 1996-2001, associate professor of management and organization studies, 2001, department chair, 2002, co-chair, 2003-04; Trinity College, visiting professor 2000; Touro University Intl., mentor, 2004-. **Publications:** (With A. Ellis) Self-Management: Strategies for Personal Success, 1990; A Passion for Planning: Financials, Operations, Marketing, Management and Ethics 2001; Managing Teleworkers and Telecommunicating Strategies, 2003; (ed. with D.R. Comer) Moral Courage in Organizations: Doing the Right Thing at Work, 2011. Contributor of articles to books and periodicals. **Address:** Department of Management and Organization Studies, Francis E. Girard School of Business and, International Commerce, Merrimack College, 315 Turnpike St., North Andover, MA 01845, U.S.A. **Online address:** gina.veta@merrimack.edu

VEITCH, Kate. Australian/American (born United States), b. 1955?. **Genres:** Novels, Young Adult Non-fiction, Human Relations/Parenting. **Career:** Radio National, staff. Writer. **Publications:** (co-author) Feeling Our Way: Experiences of Pregnancy, Birth and Early Parenting (nonfiction), 1986; Listen

(novel), 2006 in US as Without a Backward Glance, 2008. Contributor to periodicals. **Address:** Faye Bender Literary Agency, 337 W 76th St., Ste. E1, New York, NY 10023-8010, U.S.A. **Online address:** kate@kateveitch.com

VEITCH, Rick. American (born United States), b. 1951. **Genres:** Novels. **Career:** King Hell Press (publishing imprint), founder, 1989; Comicon.com, co-founder. Comic artist and writer. **Publications:** COMIC BOOKS: Bratpack: A Novel, 1992; Greyshirt: Indigo Sunset, 2002; Aquaman: The Waterbearer, 2003; Can't Get No, 2006; Army@Love, 2007, vol. II: Generation Pwned, 2008. Contributor to periodicals. Works appear in anthologies. **Address:** VT , U.S.A. **Online address:** rarebit@sover.net

VEJJAJIVA, Jane. Thai (born Thailand), b. 1963?. **Genres:** Children's Fiction. **Career:** Media Focus Co., Business and Children Magazines, publisher and translator, 1988; Founded New Friends Children Magazine, executive editor, 1989-94; Translator Club, co-founder, 1994; Silkroad Publishers Agency, managing director, 1995-. **Publications:** The Happiness of Kati, 2003; Kwam Suk Kong Kati, 2006. **Address:** The Fielding Agency, 269 S Beverly Dr., Ste. 341, Beverly Hills, CA 90212, U.S.A.

VELARDE, Giles. (Peter Giles Velarde). British (born England), b. 1935. **Genres:** Design. **Career:** Designer of museum exhibitions, 1959-2001; Geological Museum, designer and head of design, 1977-88; Chartered Society of Designers, fellow; Museums Association, fellow; Royal Society of Arts, fellow. Writer and educator. **Publications:** Designing Exhibitions, 1989, 2nd ed. as Designing Exhibitions: Museums, Heritage, Trade and World Fairs 2001. Contributor to books. **Address:** Fir Trees Studio, Cliff End Ln., Pett Level, ES TN35 4EF, England. **Online address:** gilesvelarde@onetel.com

VELARDE, Peter Giles. See **VELARDE, Giles.**

VELÁSQUEZ, Gloria (Louise). American (born United States), b. 1949. **Genres:** Children's Fiction, Young Adult Fiction, Poetry. **Career:** Hewlett Packard, secretary, 1966-67; California Polytechnic State University, professor of Spanish, 1985-. Writer. **Publications:** NOVELS: Juanita Fights the School Board, 1994; Maya's Divided World, 1995; Tommy Stands Alone, 1995; Rina's Family Secret, 1998; Ankiza, 2000; J'aime qui je veux, 2002; Teen Angel, 2003; Tyrone's Betrayal 2005; Rudy's Memory Walk, 2009; Tommy Stands Tall, forthcoming; Toy Soldiers and Dolls/Soldaditos y muñecas, forthcoming. POETRY: I Used to Be a Superwoman, 1997; Xicana on the Run, 2004. **Address:** Modern Languages and Literatures, California Polytechnic State University, Rm. 28, Bldg. 47, San Luis Obispo, CA 93407, U.S.A. **Online address:** glvelasqu@gmail.com

VELEZ, Ivan. American (born United States) **Genres:** Novels, Humor/Satire, Children's Fiction. **Career:** Planet Bronx Productions, founder. Graphic novelist and Writer. **Publications:** Tales of the Closet, 2005; (co-ed.) Dead High Yearbook, 2007. FORTHCOMING: Laritza Versus the Space Aliens; Featuring A Story. **Address:** Planet Bronx Productions, PO Box 672146, Mosholu Sta., Bronx, NY 10467, U.S.A. **Online address:** ivanvelezjr@planetbronx.com

VELEZ-MITCHELL, Jane. American (born United States), b. 1955. **Genres:** Biography, Autobiography/Memoirs, Adult Non-fiction. **Career:** Warner Brothers/Telepictures television, reporter; KCAL-TV, anchor and reporter; WCBS-TV, anchor and reporter. Writer. **Publications:** Secrets Can Be Murder: What America's Most Sensational Crimes Tell Us about Ourselves, 2007; Secrets can be Murder: The Killer Next Door, 2008; IWant: My Journey from Addiction and Overconsumption to a Simpler, Honest Life, 2009; (with S. Mohr) Addict Nation: An Intervention for America, 2011. **Address:** Health Communications Inc., 3201 SW 15th St., Deerfield Beach, FL 33442, U.S.A. **Online address:** jane@secretscanbemurder.com

VELICKOVIC, Nenad. Croatian (born Croatia), b. 1962?. **Genres:** History. **Career:** Institute for Literature, secretary; University of Sarajevo, literature faculty. Writer. **Publications:** Konačari, 1997; Sexicon-Sexpressionism, 1998; Davo u Sarajevu, 1998; Sahib: Impresije iz depresije, 2002; Izdržite jos malo, nećete još dugo, 2003; Otac moje kćeri, 2003; (ed.) Inso(mno)lent P(r)ose, 2003; Lodgers, 2005; Viva sexico: Cosmoboy, Seksikon, Sekspresinizam, 2006; 100 Zmajeva, 2007. **Address:** Sandorf Literary Agency, Severinska 30, Zagreb, 10110, Croatia. **Online address:** omnibus@bih.net.ba

VELIKONJA, Mitja. Slovenian (born Yugoslavia), b. 1965. **Genres:** History. **Career:** University of Ljubljana, researcher, 1991-93, assistant, 1993-97, assistant professor, 1997-2002, associate professor of social sciences, 2002-. Writer. **Publications:** Bosanski religijski mozaiki: religije in nacionalne mitologije v zgodovini Bosne in Hercegovine, 1998; Urbana Plemena: Subkulture v Sloveniji v Devetdesetih, 1999; Religious Separation and Political Intolerance in Bosnia-Herzegovina, 2003; Mitografije Sedansosti, 2003; Eurosis: The Critique of the New Eurocentrism, 2005; Evroza: Kritika Novog Evrocentrizma, 2007. **Address:** Faculty of Social Sciences, University of Ljubljana, Kradeljeva P. 5, Ljubljana, 1000, Slovenia. **Online address:** mitja.velikonja@uni-lj.si

VELKLEY, Richard L. American (born United States), b. 1949. **Genres:** Literary Criticism And History, Philosophy, Politics/Government, Humanities, Social Sciences. **Career:** Alfred University, instructor, assistant professor, 1977-82; Rivier College, assistant professor, 1982-85; Stonehill College, Department of Philosophy, assistant professor, 1985-90, associate professor, 1990-96, chair, 1993-96; Wheaton College, visiting professor, 1988-89; Boston College, visiting professor, 1991; Catholic University of America, associate professor of philosophy, 1997-; Tulane University, Celia Scott Weatherhead professor of philosophy; The Review of Metaphysics, associate editor. **Publications:** Freedom and the End of Reason: On the Moral Foundation of Kant's Critical Philosophy, 1989; (ed. and intro.) The Unity of Reason: Essays on Kant's Philosophy, 1994; Being after Rousseau: Philosophy and Culture in Question, 2002; (ed.) Freedom and the Human Person, 2007; Heidegger, Strauss and the Premises of Philosophy on Original Forgetting, 2011. Contributor to books and journals. **Address:** Department of Philosophy, Tulane University, 111 Newcomb Hall, New Orleans, LA 70118-5698, U.S.A. **Online address:** rvelkley@tulane.edu

VELLA, Christina. American (born United States), b. 1952. **Genres:** History, Biography, Literary Criticism And History. **Career:** U.S. Department of State, Curatorial Division, writer and consultant; Tulane University, visiting professor of history. **Publications:** Intimate Enemies: The Two Worlds of the Baroness de Pontalba, 1997; (with R. Luza) The Hitler Kiss: A Memoir of the Czech Resistance, 2002; Indecent Secrets: The Infamous Murri Murder Affair, 2006. OTHERS: The Country for Men with Nerve in Degas in America, 1999; Dorothy Dix in Louisiana Portraits, 2007; Paris in the 18th Century in Concorde: Talleyrand/Marshall Center (U.S. State Dept.), 2007; El Corazon de Espana in Permanencia Cultural de Espana in Nueva Orleans, 2008. **Address:** 5500 Camp St., New Orleans, LA 70115, U.S.A. **Online address:** vellavella@aol.com

VELLEMAN, Daniel J. American (born United States), b. 1954. **Genres:** Mathematics/Statistics, Sciences. **Career:** University of Texas, instructor, 1980-83; University of Toronto, Erindale College, visiting assistant professor, 1982; Amherst College, assistant professor, 1983-87, associate professor, 1987-92, professor of mathematics, 1992-, Julian H. Gibbs '46 professor of mathematics. Writer. **Publications:** How to Prove It: A Structured Approach, 1994, 2nd ed., 2006; (with S. Wagon and J. Konhauser) Which Way Did the Bicycle Go?: And Other Intriguing Mathematical Mysteries, 1996; (with A. George) Philosophies of Mathematics, 2002. Contributor to mathematics journals. **Address:** Department of Mathematics, Amherst College, Amherst, MA 01002-5000, U.S.A. **Online address:** djvelleman@amherst.edu

VELTRI, George (M.). American (born United States), b. 1949. **Genres:** Novels, Literary Criticism And History, Young Adult Fiction. **Career:** Child Welfare Institute, curriculum designer and trainer, 1970-; Hello Studio, greeting card designer and manufacturer. Writer and therapist. **Publications:** Nice Boy: A Novel, 1995. **Address:** c/o Bill Corsa, Specialty Book Market, 443 Park Ave. S, Ste. 801, New York, NY 10016, U.S.A. **Online address:** geo@catskill.net

VENABLES, Stephen. British (born England), b. 1954. **Genres:** Travel/Exploration. **Career:** British Mountaineering Council, vice president, 1990-92; Alpine Club, president. Writer, teacher, broadcaster and public speaker. **Publications:** Painted Mountains: Two Expeditions to Kashmir, 1986; Everest: Kangshung Face, 1989; Island at the Edge of the World: A South Georgia Odyssey, 1991; M for Mountains (for children), 1993; Himalaya-Alpine-Style: The Most Challenging Routes On The Highest Peaks, 1996; A Slender Thread: Escaping Disaster In The Himalaya, 2000; Everest: Alone at the Summit, 2000; Lost Mountains: Two Expeditions to Kashmir, 2001; To The Top: The Story of Everest, 2003; Voices From The Mountains: 40 True-Life Stories of Unforgettable Adventure, Drama, and Human Endurance, 2006;

Meetings With Mountains, 2006; Ollie, 2006; Higher than the Eagle Soars: A Path to Everest, 2007; First Ascent, 2008. Contributor of articles to journals. **Address:** 6 Grosvenor Terr., St. Saviour's Rd., Bath, BA1 6SR, England. **Online address:** stephen@venables.ndo.co.uk

VENARDE, Bruce L. American (born United States), b. 1962?. **Genres:** Women's Studies And Issues, Translations. **Career:** Harvard University, teaching fellow, 1986-89, 1990-92, lecturer in history and literature, 1992-95; Tufts University, visiting assistant professor, 1995-96; University of Pittsburgh, assistant professor, 1996-99, associate professor of history, 1999-. Writer. **Publications:** Women's Monasticism and Medieval Society: Nunneries in France and England, 890-1215, 1997; (trans.) Robert of Arbrissel: A Medieval Religious Life, 2003; (trans. and intro.) J. Dalarun, Robert of Arbrissel: Sex, Sin, and Salvation in the Middle Ages, 2006. Contributor to books and periodicals. **Address:** Department of History, University of Pittsburgh, Pittsburgh, PA 15260, U.S.A. **Online address:** bvenarde@pitt.edu

VENARDOS, Thomas J(oseph). American (born United States), b. 1945. **Genres:** Administration/Management, Human Relations/Parenting, Public/Social Administration. **Career:** University of New Mexico, psychologist and professor, 1967-80; Eastern Washington University, adjunct professor, 1968-85; management consultant, 1975-; Venardos Management Group, president; National Institute for Consulting Ethics, executive director; IABC, president; Century University, adjunct professor; Olmstead and Associates Management Consultants, adjunct consultant; National Institute for Consulting Ethics, senior managing director; Professional Consulting Center, senior managing director. Writer. **Publications:** The Responsive Management Manual, 1994; Consulting Success Using Higher Performance Standards, 1997. **Address:** Venardos Management Group, 3925 S Jones Blvd., Apt. 2097, Las Vegas, NV 89103-7113, U.S.A. **Online address:** tvenardos@olmsteadassoc.com

VENCLOVA, Tomas. American/Lithuanian (born Lithuania), b. 1937. **Genres:** Poetry, Literary Criticism And History, Translations, History, Essays, Adult Non-fiction. **Career:** University of Vilnius, lecturer in literature, linguistics and semiotics, 1966-73, Faculty of Humanities, adjunct faculty; Academy of Sciences of the Lithuanian SSR, junior fellow of the institute of history, 1974-76; University of California, Department of Slavic Languages and Literatures, regents professor, 1977, lecturer, 1977-80; Ohio University, department of philosophy, Morton professor, 1978; Yale University, Department of Slavic Languages and Literatures, lecturer and acting instructor, 1980-85, assistant professor, 1985-90, associate professor, 1990-93, professor of Slavic languages and literatures, 1993-. Writer. **Publications:** POETRY: Kalbos zenklas (title means: 'A Sign of the Language'), 1972; 98 eileraščiai (title means: '98 Poems'), 1977; Pasnekesys ziema, 1981; Rozmowa w zimie, 1989; Tankejanti šviesa, 1990; Szesc wierszy (title means: 'Six Poems'), 1991; Cistost soli (title means: 'Purity of Salt'), 1991; Mondjatokmeg Fortinbrasnak (title means: 'Tell Fortinbras'), 1992; Rinktiue (title means: 'Selected Poems'), 1999; Vor Der Tur Das Ende Der Welt, 2000; Granenyï Vozdukh, 2002; Stati o Brodskom, 2004. NONFICTION: Neustoichivoe ravnovesie: vosem russkikh poeticheskikh tekstov (title means: 'Unstable Equilibrium: Eight Russian Poetic Texts'), 1986; Viltiesformos, 1991; Kształty nadziei, 1995; Aleksander Wat: Life and Art of an Iconoclast, 1996; Aleksander Wat: Obrazoburca, 1997; Forms of Hope, 1999; Vilnius, 2000; (co-author) Anna Akhmatova--posledniegody, 2001; Nieznniszczalny rytm: Eseje o literaturze, 2003; Nieznniszczalnyrytm: Eseje o literaturze, 2006; Tomas Venclova: doktor honoris causa Uniwersytetu Mikoaja Kopernika w Toruniu, 2006; (with I. Grudzińska-Gross) Miłosz i Brodski: Pole Magnetyczne, 2007; Junction: Selected Poems, 2008; Vilnius: A Personal History, 2009. TRANSLATIONS: Jaroslaw Iwaszkiewicz, Mergaite ir balandziai (title means: 'A Girl and Pigeons'), 1961; Tadeusz Breza, 1963; Curzio Malaparte, 1967; Iurii Olesha, 1971; Balsai, 1979; (with A. Shtromas) Politine Samone Lietuvoje ir joje atsispindinčios Krašto Ateities Vizijos, 1980; Lietuva pasaulyje: publicistika, 1981; Tekstai apie tekstus, 1985; T. S. Eliot, The Waste Land, 2007. OTHERS: Raketos, planetos ir mes, 1962; Golemas, arba dirbtinis zmogus, 1965; Atgimusi daina, 1986; Vilties Formos, 1991; (with L. Lempertienė) Josif Brodskij, 1999; Rinktine, 1999; Vilniaus Vardai, 2006. Contributor to journals. **Address:** Department of Slavic Languages & Literatures, Yale University, 432-1304, 2708 Hall of Graduate Studies, New Haven, CT 06520, U.S.A. **Online address:** tomas.venclova@yale.edu

VENDITTI, Robert. American (born United States), b. 1974?. **Genres:** Graphic Novels. **Career:** Top Shelf Productions, staff. Writer. **Publications:** SURROGATES SERIES: The Surrogates, 2005; Flesh & Bone, 2009. IRON

MAN SERIES: (co-author) Iron Man: Iron Protocols, 2009; (co-author) Iron Man: Tales of the Golden Avenger, 2010; The Homeland Directive, 2010. Contributor to books. **Address:** Top Shelf Productions, PO Box 1282, Marietta, GA 30061-1282, U.S.A. **Online address:** rob@topshelfcomix.com

VENDLER, Helen (Hennessy). American (born United States), b. 1933. **Genres:** Literary Criticism And History, Poetry, Humanities. **Career:** Cornell University, instructor in English, 1960-63; Haverford College, lecturer in English, 1963-64; Swarthmore College, lecturer in English, 1963-64; Smith College, assistant professor of English, 1964-66; Boston University, associate professor, 1966-68, professor of English, 1968-85, director of graduate studies, 1970-75, 1978-79; University of Bordeaux, Fulbright lecturer in American literature, 1968-69; Washington University, Fanny Hurst visiting professor, 1975; Harvard University, Department of English, visiting professor, 1981-85, professor of English, 1985-, William R. Kenan professor of English and American literature and language, 1986-, associate dean of arts and sciences, 1986-91, Arthur Kingsley Porter university professor, 1990-. Writer. **Publications:** Yeats's Vision and the Later Plays, 1963; On Extended Wings: Wallace Stevens Longer Poems, 1969; The Poetry of George Herbert, 1975; Part of Nature, Part of Us: Modern American Poets, 1980; The Odes of John Keats, 1983; Wallace Stevens: Words Chosen Out of Desire, 1984; The Music of What Happens: Poems, Poets, Critics, 1988; (contrib.) Poetry Manuscripts at Harvard, 1990; The Given and the Made: Strategies of Poetic Redefinition, 1995; The Breaking of Style: Hopkins, Heaney, Graham, 1995; Soul Says: Recent Poetry, 1995; The Art of Shakespeare's Sonnets, 1997; Seamus Heaney, 1998; (contrib.) Battle-Pieces and Aspects of the War: Civil War Poems, 2001; A Life of Learning: Charles Homer Haskins Lecture for 2001, 2001; Coming of Age as a Poet: Milton, Keats, Eliot, Plath, 2003; Poets Thinking: Pope, Whitman, Dickinson, Yeats, 2004; Invisible Listeners: Lyric Intimacy In Herbert, Whitman, And Ashbery, 2005; Our Secret Discipline: Yeats And Lyric Form, 2007; Primitivismus und das Groteske: Yeats' Supernatural Songs, 2007; Last Looks, Last Books: Stevens, Plath, Lowell, Bishop, Merrill, 2010; Dickinson: Selected Poems and Commentaries, 2010. EDITOR: (with R. Brower and J. Hollander) I. A. Richards: Essays in His Honor, 1973; Poems, 1985; The Harvard Book of Contemporary American Poetry, 1985 as The Faber Book of Contemporary American Poetry, 1987; Voices and Visions: The Poet in America, 1987; The Harper American Literature, 1987; Poems, Poets, Poetry: An Introduction and Anthology, 1997, 3rd ed., 2010. **Address:** Department of English, Harvard University, 205 Barker Ctr., 12 Quincy St., Cambridge, MA 02138-3929, U.S.A. **Online address:** vendler@fas.harvard.edu

VENET, Wendy Hamand. American (born United States), b. 1955. **Genres:** Women's Studies And Issues, Biography. **Career:** Eastern Illinois University, assistant professor, 1985-88, associate professor, 1988-95; Georgia State University, assistant professor, 1995-98, associate professor, 1998-2006, professor of history, 2006-, undergraduate studies director, 2001-06, associate chair, 2010-11. Writer. **Publications:** Neither Ballots nor Bullets: Women Abolitionists and the Civil War, 1991; (ed. with L.E. Murphy) Midwestern Women: Work, Community, and Leadership at the Crossroads, 1997; (ed. with R.W. Johannsen) The Union in Crisis, 1850-1877, 2003; A Strong-Minded Woman: The Life of Mary Livermore, 2005. Contributor to books and periodicals. **Address:** Women's Studies Institute, Georgia State University, PO Box 3969, Atlanta, GA 30302-3969, U.S.A. **Online address:** wvenet@gsu.edu

VENOLIA, Jan(et G.). American (born United States), b. 1928. **Genres:** How-to Books, Writing/Journalism, Reference, Language/Linguistics, Business/Trade/Industry, Education, Literary Criticism And History. **Career:** Freelance writer and editor, 1970-. **Publications:** Write Right! A Desktop Digest of Punctuation, Grammar and Style, 1979, 4th ed., 2001; Better Letters: A Handbook of Business and Personal Correspondence, 1981, 2nd ed., 1995; (ed. with M.G. Shirey and J.G. Hogness) Challiss Gore-The California I Saw, 1983; Rewrite Right!: How to Revise Your Way to Better Writing, 1987, 2nd ed. as Rewrite Right!: Your Guide to Perfectly Polished Prose, 2000; Kids Write Right!: What You Need to Be a Writing Powerhouse, 2000; The Right Word!: How to Say What You Really Mean, 2003; Right Letter!: How to Communicate Effectively in a Busy World, 2004. **Address:** Ten Speed Press, 1111 8th St., Ste. D, PO Box 7123, Berkeley, CA 94710-1203, U.S.A.

VENTER, J. Craig. American (born United States), b. 1946. **Genres:** Medicine/Health. **Career:** State University of New York, professor, 1976-82; Roswell Park Cancer Institute, professor; National Institutes of Health, researcher, 1983, section and lab chief of the national institute for neurological disorders and stroke, 1984-92; Institute for Genomic Research, founder, 1992-98; Celera Genomics, founder, president and chief executive, 1998-2002; J. Craig Venter Institute, chairman, president and founder, 2002-; Applera Corp., chair of the science advisory board; Institute for Genomic Research, board of trustees. Writer. **Publications:** (Ed. with L.C. Harrison) Receptor Purification Procedures, 1984; (ed. with L.C. Harrison) Membranes, Detergents, and Receptor Solubilization, 1984; (ed. with L.C. Harrison) Molecular and Chemical Characterization of Membrane Receptors, 1984; (ed. with C.M. Fraser and J. Lindstrom) Monoclonal and Anti-idiotypic Antibodies: Probes for Receptor Structure and Function, 1984; (ed. with R.W. Olsen) Benzodiazepine/GABA Receptors and Chloride Channels: Structural and Functional Properties, 1986; (ed. with D. Triggle) Structure and Physiology of the Slow Inward Calcium Channel, Liss, 1987; (ed. with C.Y. Jung) Target-size Analysis of Membrane Proteins, 1987; (co-author) The Sequence of the Human Genome, 2001; A Life Decoded: My Genome, My Life (memoir), 2007. **Address:** J. Craig Venter Institute, 9704 Medical Center Dr., Rockville, MD 20850, U.S.A.

VENTRESCA, Robert. (Robert A. Ventresca). Canadian (born Canada), b. 1970?. **Genres:** Politics/Government, History, Social Sciences. **Career:** University of Western Ontario, King's University College, assistant professor of history, chairman and associate professor of history. Writer and historian. **Publications:** (Ed. with F. Iacovetta and P. Draper) A Nation of Immigrants: Women, Workers and Communities in Canadian History, 1840s-1960s, 1998; From Fascism to Democracy: Culture and Politics in the Italian Election of 1948, 2004. **Address:** King's University College, University of Western Ontario, LH210, 9125 50 St. NW, Edmonton, AB T6B 2H3, Canada. **Online address:** rventres@uwo.ca

VENTRESCA, Robert A. See **VENTRESCA, Robert.**

VENTURA, Michael. American (born United States), b. 1945. **Genres:** Poetry, Documentaries/Reportage, Law, Photography. **Career:** Austin Sun, arts editor, 1974-77; Los Angeles Weekly, co-founder, 1978, senior editor, 1978-93; freelance writer, 1993-. Photographer. **Publications:** The Mollyhawk Poems, 1977; Shadow-Dancing in U.S., 1985; Night Time, Losing Time, 1989; South Bronx Hall of Fame: Sculpture by John Ahearn and Rigoberto Torre, 1991; (with J. Hillman) We've Had One Hundred Years of Psychotherapy and the World's Getting Worse, 1992; Sitting on Moving Steel, 1992; Letters at 3 A.M.: Reports on Endarkenment, 1993; The Zoo Where You're Fed to God: A Novel; 1994; The Death of Frank Sinatra: A Novel, 1996; Marilyn Monroe From Beginning to End, 1997; (with J. Hillman) Hundert Jahre Psychotherapie-und der Welt geht's immer schlechter, 1999; Cassavetes directs: On the Set of Love Streams, 2007; (with M. Tucker) Terry Allen, 2010; If I Was A Highway: Essays, 2011; The Tiger, the Rock, and the Rose, forthcoming; From Vegas to Nowhere, forthcoming. Contributor to magazines. **Address:** c/o Melanie Jackson, 250 W 57th St., PO Box 1119, New York, NY 10107, U.S.A. **Online address:** michael@michaelventura.com

VERBA, Joan Marie. American (born United States), b. 1953. **Genres:** Science Fiction/Fantasy, Air/Space Topics, Self Help. **Career:** Control Data Corporation and Unisys, computer programmer, 1978-87; Lerner Publications, word processor, 1989-95; Best Mark, quality editor, 1996-2008, Weight Watchers, 2000-09; Indiana University, associate instructor. **Publications:** Voyager: Exploring the Outer Planets, 1991; North Dakota, 1992; Boldly Writing: A Trekker Fan and Zine History 1967-1987, 1996; (co-author) Autumn World, 2000; Countdown to Action!, 2008; Action Alert, 2008; Deadly Danger, 2009; Situation: Critical, 2010, Weight Loss Success!, 2010; Extreme Hazard, 2011. **Address:** PO Box 1363, Minnetonka, MN 55345, U.S.A. **Online address:** verba001@tc.umn.edu

VERBOVEN, Agnes. Belgian (born Belgium), b. 1951. **Genres:** Children's Fiction, Humor/Satire. **Career:** Bell-ITT, market researcher, 1972-73; Universitaire Faculteiten SintIgnatius Te Antwerpen, economic researcher, 1973-75; Limburgs Universitair Centrum, economic researcher, 1975-79; Poespas (children's book store), owner, 1979-; Clavis (children's book publisher), editor and co-founder, 1984-. **Publications:** (Trans.) D. Barth, Alle Eendjes Zwemmen in Het Water (title means: 'Ducks Like to Swim'), 1997; A Day at the Playground, forthcoming. **Address:** Clavis, Vooruitzichtstraat 42, Hasselt, B-3500, Belgium.

VERDELLE, A. J. American (born United States), b. 1960?. **Genres:** Novels, Essays, Young Adult Fiction. **Career:** Freelance writer, 1995-; Radcliffe College, fellow in creative writing, 1996; Princeton University, lecturer in creative writing; statistics consultant, 1988-95; Vermont College, faculty; American Women's Economic Development Corp., staff; Lesley University, faculty. **Publications:** The Good Negress (novel), 1995; The Half Light of Manumission (essay), 1996; Beyond Shack Photography (essay), 1996; Meanwhile Back at the Ranch, forthcoming. **Address:** Wendy Weil Agency Inc., 232 Madison Ave., Ste. 1300, New York, NY 10016, U.S.A.

VERDON, Nicola. British (born England), b. 1970. **Genres:** Women's Studies And Issues, Sociology, History, Economics. **Career:** Harlaxton College, assistant lecturer, 1999-2001; University of Reading, research fellow, 2001-04; University of Sussex, senior lecturer in history, 2007-; University of Sheffield Hallam, instructor in history. Writer and historian. **Publications:** Rural Women Workers in Nineteenth-Century England: Gender, Work and Wages, 2002. Contributor to periodicals and journals. **Address:** University of Sussex, Sussex House, Brighton, ES BN1 9RH, England. **Online address:** n.j.verdon@sussex.ac.uk

VERDUIN, John Richard. American (born United States), b. 1931. **Genres:** Education, Business/Trade/Industry. **Career:** Teacher, 1954-59; State University of New York, assistant professor, 1962-64, associate professor of education, 1964-67; Southern Illinois University, associate professor, 1967-70, assistant dean, 1967-73, professor in department of educational administration and foundations, 1970-, now professor emeritus. Writer. **Publications:** Cooperative Curriculum Improvement, 1967; Conceptual Models in Teacher Education: An Approach to Teaching and Learning, 1967; (co-author) Pre-Student Teaching Laboratory Experiences, 1970; (co-author) Project Follow Through, 1971; (with H.G. Miller and C.E. Greer) Adults Teaching Adults: Principles and Strategies, 1977; (with H.G. Miller) The Adult Educator: A Handbook for Staff Development, 1979; Curriculum Building for Adult Learning, 1980; (with D.N. McEwen) Adults and Their Leisure: The Need for Lifelong Learning, 1984; (with H.G. Jellen) Handbook for Differential Education of the Gifted: A Taxonomy of 32 Key Concepts, 1986; (with H.G. Miller and C.E. Greer) The Lifelong Learning Experience: An Introduction, 1986; (co-author) Differentielle Erziehung Besonders Begabter: Ein Taxonomischer Ansatz, 1989; (with T.A. Clark) Distance Education: The Foundation for Effective Practice, 1991; (co-author) Strategic Planning for Health Professions, 1995; Helping Students Develop Investigative, Problem Solving, and Thinking Skills in a Cooperative Setting: A Handbook for Teachers, Administrators, and Curriculum Workers, 1996. **Address:** Department of Education Administration, Southern Illinois University, Woody Hall, Carbondale, IL 62901, U.S.A.

VERGHESE, Abraham. (Abraham Cheeran Verghese). American/Ethiopian (born Ethiopia), b. 1955. **Genres:** Medicine/Health, Adult Non-fiction, Social Sciences. **Career:** Madras Medical College, Government General Hospital, intern, 1979-80; East Tennessee State University, resident in medicine, 1980-82, chief resident and instructor in medicine, 1982-83, assistant professor, 1985-88, associate professor of medicine, 1988-90, special fellow in pulmonary diseases, 1985-88; Boston University, clinical and research fellow in infectious diseases and teaching assistant, 1983-85; American Board of Internal Medicine, certified in internal medicine, 1983, infectious diseases, 1987, pulmonary diseases, 1989, geriatrics, 1990, director, 2004-08; East Tennessee State University, assistant professor, 1985-88, associate professor of medicine, 1988-90, special fellow in pulmonary diseases, 1985-88; American Federation of Clinical Research, medical school representative, 1986-88; Veterans Administration Medical Center, chief of infectious diseases, 1986-90, chief of medicine, 1988-90, Research and Development Committee, chairman, 1987-88; University of Iowa, visiting associate in medicine, 1990-91; Thomason Hospital, Infection Control Committee, chairperson, 1992, 1996-97; Northeastern Ohio Universities, visiting professor, 1992; Texas Tech University, Division of Infectious Diseases, chief, 1991-95, professor of medicine, 1991-2002, Grover E. Murray distinguished professor, 2000-02, Faculty Development Committee, chair, 2000-02; University of Texas Health Science Center, Center for Medical Humanities and Ethics, director, 2002-05, Marvin Forland distinguished professor, 2002-05, Task Force on Professionalism, chair, 2002-03, Joaquin Cigarroa Jr. distinguished chair, 2005-07; Gemini Ink, director, 2003-06; Stanford University School of Medicine, Theory and Practice of Medicine, professor, Department of Internal Medicine, senior associate chair, 2007-, Department of Medicine, clerkship director, 2007-, Internal Medicine Residency, program director, 2009-. Writer. **Publications:** (Ed. with S.L. Berk) Infection in the Nursing Home, 1990; My Own Country: A Doctor's Story of a Town and Its People in the Age of AIDS, 1994 in UK as Soundings: A Doctor's Life in the Age of AIDS; My Own Country: A Doc-

tor's Story, 1995; The Tennis Partner: A Doctor's Story of Friendship and Loss, 1998; Cutting for Stone: A Novel, 2009. Works appear in anthologies. Contributor of articles to books and journals, magazines and newspapers. **Address:** Department of Medicine, Stanford University, S102, 300 Pasteur Dr., PO Box 5109, Stanford, CA 94305, U.S.A.

VERGHESE, Abraham Cheeran. See **VERGHESE, Abraham.**

VERLAG, Cora. See **CHURCHILL, E. Richard.**

VERLUISE, Pierre. French (born France), b. 1961. **Genres:** International Relations/Current Affairs, Local History/Rural Topics, History, Education. **Career:** Radio France Internationale, journalist, 1985-91; Le Quotidien de Paris, journalist, 1989-94; Sainte-Louise College, history teacher, 1992-, professor certified history and geography, 1997-, director of geopolitical, 2000-; Center for Transatlantic Studies, research associate, 2007; www.Diploweb. Com, founder and director. **Publications:** Arménie, la Fracture: Le Séime du 7 Décembre 1988: Suivi d'unTexte de Claude Mutafian, Le Karabagh de la fin du XIXe siècle à l'avènement de Gorbatchev, 1989; Le Nouvel Emprunt Russe, 1994; Géopolitique de l'Europe: L'Union Européenne élargie a-t-elle les Moyens de la Puissance?, 2005; Une Nouvelle Europe: Comprendre Une révolution géopolitique, 2006; La Russie, 2007; 20 ans après la Chute du Mur: l'Europe Recomposée, 2009. Contributor to periodicals. **Address:** 12 rue Cassette, Paris, 75006, France.

VERMAAS, Lori. American (born United States), b. 1966. **Genres:** Art/Art History, Natural History. **Career:** University of Iowa Press, copy editor and proofreader, 2001, Journal of Paleontology, production editor, 2003-06; State Historical Society of Iowa, editorial assistant, 2001; Texas Tech University Press, assistant editor and journals manager, 2006-08; Freedom Communications Inc., freelance journalist, 2008-10; e2M/HDR, staff consulting professional II, 2009-; freelance copy editor and proofreader, 2010-. **Publications:** Sequoia: The Heralded Tree in American Art and Culture, 2003. **Address:** Texas Tech University Press, 2903 4th St., Ste. 201, PO Box 41037, Lubbock, TX 79415, U.S.A. **Online address:** lori.vermaas@ttu.edu

VERMEIJ, Geerat J. American/Dutch (born Netherlands), b. 1946. **Genres:** Marine Sciences/Oceanography, Biology, Natural History. **Career:** University of Maryland, instructor, professor of zoology; University of California, Department of Geology, professor of geology, distinguished professor. Writer and biologist. **Publications:** Biogeography and Adaptation: Patterns of Marine Life, 1978; Evolution and Escalation: An Ecological History of Life, 1987; A Natural History of Shells, 1993; Privileged Hands: A Scientific Life, 1997; Nature: An Economic History, 2004; The Evolutionary World: How Adaptation Explains Everything from Seashells to Civilization, 2010. **Address:** Department of Geology, University of California, 1 Shields Ave., Davis, CA 95616-8605, U.S.A. **Online address:** gjvermeij@ucdavis.edu

VERMERRIS, Wilfred. American (born United States) **Genres:** Chemistry, Sciences. **Career:** University of Florida, Department of Agronomy, associate professor, Genetics Institute, member, Plant Molecular and Cellular Biology Graduate Program, member, 2006-; Purdue University, faculty member, 2001-06, Agricultural & Biological Engineering, adjunct associate professor. Agronomist, educator and writer. **Publications:** (with R. Nicholson) Phenolic Compound Biochemistry, 2006; (ed.) Genetic Improvement of Bioenergy Crops, 2008. **Address:** University of Florida, 1376 Mowry Rd., PO Box 103610, Gainesville, FL 32610-3610, U.S.A. **Online address:** wev@ufl.edu

VERMES, Géza. British/Hungarian (born Hungary), b. 1924. **Genres:** History, Theology/Religion. **Career:** Centre National de la Recherche Scientifique, researcher, 1954-57; University of Newcastle upon Tyne, lecturer, 1957-64, senior lecturer in religious studies, 1964-65; University of Oxford, Oriental Institute, reader, 1965-89, Wolfson College, professorial fellow, 1965-91, emeritus fellow, 1997-, chairman of curators, 1971-74, Faculty of Oriental Studies, board chairman, 1978-80, professor of Jewish studies, 1989-91, professor emeritus of Jewish studies, 1991-; Journal of Jewish Studies, editor, 1971-; Oxford Centre for Hebrew Studies, governor, 1972-92, director of publications, 1987-91, Forum for Qumran Research, director, 1991-, European Academy, fellow, 2001. **Publications:** Les Manuscrits du Desert de Juda, 1953, 2nd ed., 1954; Discovery in the Judean Desert, 1956; Scripture and Tradition in Judaism, 1961, rev. ed., 1973; (ed. and trans.) The Dead Sea Scrolls in English, 1967, (trans., ed. and intro.) rev. ed. as The Complete Dead Sea Scrolls in English, 1997, rev. ed., 2004; Jesus the Jew: A Historian's

Reading of the Gospels, 1973, 3rd ed., 1994; Post-Biblical Jewish Studies, 1975; The Dead Sea Scrolls: Qumran in Perspective, 1977, rev. ed., 1994; The Gospel of Jesus the Jew, 1981; Jesus and the World of Judaism, 1984; The Dead Sea Scrolls after Forty Years, 1987; Gesu Storico: Problema della Modernita, 1988; (with M.D. Goodman) The Essenes According to the Classical Sources, 1989; A Tribute to Geza Vermes: Essays on Jewish and Christian Literature and History, 1990; The Religion of Jesus the Jew, 1993; Zsido Jezus, 1995; Providential Accidents: An Autobiography, 1998; (with P.S. Alexander) Discoveries in the Judaean Desert, vol. XXVI, 1998; An Introduction to the Complete Dead Sea Scrolls, 1999; The Changing Faces of Jesus, 2000; Jesus in His Jewish Context, 2003; The Authentic Gospel of Jesus, 2003; Scrolls, Scriptures, and Early Christianity, 2005; Passion, 2006; The Nativity: History and Legend, 2007; Resurrection, 2008; Searching for the Real Jesus, 2010; The Story of the Scrolls, 2010; Jesus: Nativity-Passion-Resurrection, 2010; Real Jesus: Then and Now, 2010. CO-EDITOR: The History of the Jewish People in the Age of Jesus Christ, 3 vols., 1973-87; (with T.A. Burkill) On the Trial of Jesus, 2nd ed., 1974; (with J. Neusner) Essays in Honor of Yigael Yadin, 1983. **Address:** Westwood Cottage, Foxcombe Ln., Boars Hill, Oxford, OX OX1 5DH, England. **Online address:** geza.vermes@orinst.ox.ac.uk

VERMEULE, Adrian. American (born United States), b. 1968?. **Genres:** Law, Politics/Government. **Career:** U.S. Court of Appeals, Honorable David B. Sentelle, law clerk, 1993-94; U.S. Supreme Court, Honorable Antonin Scalia, law clerk, 1994-95; Kirkland & Ellis, associate, 1995-96; George Washington University, National Law Center, assistant professor, 1996-97; University of Chicago, School of Law, associate professor, 1998-2001, professor, 2001-05; Harvard Law School, visiting professor of law, 2005-06, professor of law, 2006-08, John H. Watson, Jr. professor of law, 2008-. Writer. **Publications:** (Co-author) The Constitution in Wartime: Beyond Alarmism and Complacency, 2005; Judging Under Uncertainty: An Institutional Theory of Legal Interpretation, 2006; (with E.A. Posner) Terror in the Balance: Security, Liberty and the Courts, 2007; Mechanisms of Democracy: Institutional Design Writ Small, 2007; Law and the Limits of Reason, 2008; (with E.A. Posner) Executive Unbound: After the Madisonian Republic, 2010; System of the Constitution, 2011. Contributor to journals. **Address:** Harvard Law School, Areeda 229, 1563 Massachusetts Ave., Cambridge, MA 02138-2903, U.S.A. **Online address:** avermeule@law.harvard.edu

VERMILYE, Jerry. American (born United States), b. 1931. **Genres:** Film, Novels, History, Literary Criticism And History, Art/Art History, Photography. **Career:** Berkshire Playhouse, actor and stage manager, 1954-56; Barrett Bookstore, chief stock clerk, 1954-60; Weston Playhouse, actor and stage manager, 1957-58; DeWolfe and Fiske Co., stock clerk, 1960-61; Boothbay Playhouse, actor and stage manager, 1960-66; Walter J. Johnson Inc., subscriptions clerk, 1962-64, 1965-67; Films in Review, editorial assistant, 1964-65; Independent Film Journal, writer and editor, 1967-68; TV Guide, senior writer and editor, 1968-99; freelance writer, 1999-. **Publications:** Burt Lancaster, 1971; Cary Grant, 1973; Bette Davis, 1973; Barbara Stanwyck, 1975; (with M. Ricci) The Films of Elizabeth Taylor, 1976, rev. ed., 1989; Ida Lupino, 1977; The Great British Films, 1978; The Films of Charles Bronson, 1980; The Films of the Thirties, 1982; The Films of the Twenties, 1985; The Last of My Gentleman Callers, 1988; (ed.) 500 Best British and Foreign Films to Buy Rent or Videotape, 1988; More Films of the Thirties, 1989; The Complete Films of Marlene Dietrich, rev. ed., 1992; The Complete Films of Laurence Olivier, 1992; Great Italian Films, 1994; The Complete Films of Audrey Hepburn, 1995; The Goulash Girls, 2002; Ingmar Bergman: His Life and Films, 2002; Buster Crabbe: Serial King, 2005; Boothbay Playhouse: A Professional History: 1937-1974, 2010. **Address:** 200 W 18th St., Ste. 6E, New York, NY 10011, U.S.A.

VERNEREY, Denise. French (born France), b. 1947. **Genres:** Art/Art History, Young Adult Non-fiction, Children's Non-fiction. **Career:** Teacher of German, English, and French, 1970-83; Le Louvre, researcher, 1986-89; Kairos Vision (multimedia editor), founder and manager, 1989-. Writer. **Publications:** Les antiques du musee de Laon, 1988; Le Parthenon, 1989; Au pays desdieux, les Grecs, 1989; Decovvertes Junior, 1990; Gothic Cathedrals of Europe, 1995; Palaces Old Gardens of Europe, 2000; Maltajne, 2002; Secrets d'Orsay, 2003. **Address:** 167 Bd Pereire, Paris, 75 017, France. **Online address:** kairosvision@hol.fr

VERNEY, Douglas (Vernon). American/Canadian/British (born England), b. 1924. **Genres:** Politics/Government, Chemistry. **Career:** University of Liverpool, assistant lecturer, lecturer, 1949-61; University of Florida, visiting professor, 1958-59; York University, associate professor, 1961-62, professor of political science, 1962-92, chair of department, 1962-67, professor emeritus, 1992-, Atkinson College, dean; Columbia University, visiting professor, 1967; Social Science Research Council of Canada, director, 1972-74; University of Pennsylvania, adjunct professor of South Asian studies, 1991, Center for the Advanced Study of India, fellow; Princeton University, visiting professor, 1993. Writer. **Publications:** Parliamentary Reform in Sweden 1866-1921, 1957; Public Enterprise in Sweden, 1959; The Analysis of Political Systems, 1959; (with D.W. Brogan) Political Patterns in Today's World, 1963, 2nd ed., 1968; (trans.) The Problems of Democracy, 1965; British Government and Politics: Life Without a Declaration of Independence, 1966, 3rd ed. 1976; (contrib.) Democracy in Crisis: New Challenges to Democracy in the Atlantic Area, 1971; Three Civilizations, Two Cultures, One State: Canada's Political Traditions, 1986; (with B. Arora) Indian Federalism from a Comparative Perspective, 1995. Contributor to journals. **Address:** Department of Political Science, York University, S672 Ross Bldg., 4700 Keele St., Toronto, ON M3J 1P3, Canada.

VERNEY, Michael Palmer. British (born England), b. 1923. **Genres:** Crafts, Recreation, Transportation, Young Adult Non-fiction. **Career:** River Severn Catchment Board, civil engineer, 1947-50; River Arun Catchment Board, deputy engineer, 1949-52; Marine Craft, consultant and chartered civil engineer, 1951-; West Sussex River Board, area engineer, 1952-65; Sussex River Authority, divisional engineer, 1965-74; Southern Water Authority, district engineer, 1974-81. Writer. **Publications:** (Foreword) Amateur Boat Building, 1948, 3rd ed. as Complete Amateur Boat Building, 1979; Practical Conversions and Yacht Repairs, 1951; Lifeboat into Yacht, 1953; Complete Amateur Boat Building, 1959; Building Chine Boats, 1960, new ed. 1991; Yacht Repairs and Conversions, 1961, 4th ed., 1966; Boat Maintenance by the Amateur, 1971; Boat Repairs and Conversions, 1972, 2nd ed., 1977; The Care and Repair of Hulls, 1979; The Complete Book of Yacht Care, 1993, 3rd ed., 1997. Contributor of articles to magazines. **Address:** 36 The Pkwy., Rustington, Sussex, WS BN16 2BU, England.

VERNEY, Peter (Vivian Lloyd). British (born England), b. 1930. **Genres:** Homes/Gardens, Biography, History, Biography. **Career:** Writer, 1970-. **Publications:** The Standard Bearer, 1963; The Micks-The Story of the Irish Guards, 1971; The Battle of Blenheim, 1976; The Gardens of Scotland, 1976; Here Comes the Circus, 1978; Anzio 1944: An Unexpected Fury, 1978; The Earthquake Handbook, 1979; Homo Tyrannicus, 1979; Animals in Peril: Man's War Against Wildlife, 1979; Weekend Athlete's Fitness Guide, 1980; (ed.) Book of Sporting Verse, 1980; (ed.) Fit for Golf, 1984; (ed.) Fit for Riding, 1984; (with M. Dunne) The Genius of the Garden, 1989. **Address:** A P Watt Literary Agency, 26/28 Bedford Row, London, GL WC1R 4HL, England.

VERNIERO, Joan C. American (born United States), b. 1949?. **Genres:** Children's Fiction, Children's Non-fiction, Race Relations, Science Fiction/Fantasy, History. **Career:** Naugatuck Valley Community Technical College, adjunct instructor; Masuk High School, language arts and reading teacher; University of Bridgeport, graduate-level instructor in education; Wonder Tots, consultant. Writer. **Publications:** You Can Call Me Willy: A Story for Children about AIDS, 1995; One-Hundred-and-one Read-Aloud Bible Stories: From the Old and New Testament, 1998; (with R. Fitzsimmons) One-Hundred-and-one Read-Aloud Myths and Legends, 1999; One-Hundred-and-one Read-Aloud Celtic Myths and Legends: Ten-Minute Readings from the Worlds Best-Loved Literature, 2000; One-Hundred-and-one Asian Read-Aloud Myths and Legends: Ten-Minute Readings from the Worlds Best-Loved Asian Literature, 2001; (with D. Rappaport) Victory or Death! Stories of the American Revolution, 2003; (with R. Fitzsimmons) An Illustrated Treasury of Read-Aloud Myths and Legends: The Worlds Best-Loved Myths and Legends for Parent and Child to Share, 2004; (with D. Rappaport) United No More! Stories of the Civil War, 2006. **Address:** HarperCollins Publishers, 10 E 53rd St., 18th Fl., New York, NY 10022, U.S.A. **Online address:** jvstory@aol.com

VERNON, Amelia Wallace. American (born United States), b. 1926. **Genres:** History, Social Sciences, Young Adult Non-fiction. **Career:** Medical College of South Carolina, instructor in nursing, 1949-51; Mercy Hospital, staff nurse, 1978-79; Cook County Hospital, staff nurse, 1980-82; freelance writer, 1983-. **Publications:** African Americans at Mars Bluff, South Carolina (history), 1993. Contributor to periodicals. **Address:** Presbyterian Home, 2350 Lucas St., PO Box 3, Florence, SC 29501, U.S.A.

VERNON, James. American/British (born England), b. 1965. **Genres:** Politics/Government, History. **Career:** Victoria University of Manchester, british academy fellow, 1991-94, lecturer and assistant professor, 1994-98, junior lecturer, senior lecturer and associate professor, 1998-2000; University of California, professor, 2000-. Writer. **Publications:** Politics and the People, 1993; (ed.) Re-Reading the Constitution: New Narratives in the Political History of England's Long Nineteenth Century, 1995; Hunger: A Modern History, 2007. **Address:** Department of History, University of California, 2214 Dwinelle Hall, Berkeley, CA 94720-2550, U.S.A. **Online address:** jvernon@berkeley.edu

VERONA, Stephen (Frederic). American (born United States), b. 1940. **Genres:** Plays/Screenplays, Biography. **Career:** Producer and Writer. **Publications:** The Making of the Lords of Flatbush, 2007. **Address:** 9595 Wilshire Blvd., Ste. 1020, Beverly Hills, CA 90212-2510, U.S.A. **Online address:** stephenverona@mac.com

VERRIER, Suzanne. American (born United States), b. 1942. **Genres:** Children's Fiction, Horticulture, Novels. **Career:** Illustrator of children's books, 1969-75; Forevergreen Farm, founder, owner and operator, 1983-93; White Flower Farm, consulting rosarian, 1994-2001; North Creek Farm, owner. Writer. **Publications:** SELF ILLUSTRATED: Titus Tidewater, 1970. OTHERS: Rosa Rugosa, 1991 Rosa Gallica, 1995; Rosa: Species, forthcoming. Contributor of articles to magazines. **Address:** North Creek Farm, 24 Sebasco Rd., Phippsburg, ME 04562, U.S.A. **Online address:** suzy@northcreekfarm.org

VERRILLO, Erica. (Erica F. Verrillo). American (born United States), b. 1953. **Genres:** Medicine/Health, Novels. **Career:** Guatemalan Refugee Crafts Project, co-founder, 1984. Writer, educator and public speaker. **Publications:** (As Erica F. Verillo with L.M. Gellman) Chronic Fatigue Syndrome: A Treatment Guide (adult nonfiction), 1998; World's End, 2009. PHOENIX RISING NOVEL TRILOGY: Elissa's Quest, 2007; Elissa's Odyssey, 2008. Contributor to periodicals. **Address:** MA , U.S.A. **Online address:** everrillo@yahoo.com

VERRILLO, Erica F. *See* **VERRILLO, Erica.**

VERSCHUUR, Gerrit L(aurens). American/South African (born South Africa), b. 1937. **Genres:** Astronomy. **Career:** Rhodes University, assistant professor of physics, 1960; Victoria University of Manchester, assistant professor of physics, 1964-67; National Radio Astronomy Observatory, research associate, 1967-69, assistant scientist, 1969-71, associate scientist, 1971-73, visiting associate scientist, 1984-85; University of California, visiting professor, 1970; University of Colorado, professor of astrogeophysics and director of Fiske Planetarium, 1973-79, lecturer, 1982-83; Aspen Research Institute, consultant, 1980-82; Advanced Energy Technology Inc., vice-president, 1982-84; University of Puerto Rico, Arecibo College, visiting professor, 1986; University of Maryland, lecturer in astronomy, 1987-92; Rhodes College, research professor of physics, 1992-96; University of Memphis, Department of Physics, adjunct faculty, 1996-. Chief scientist and writer. **Publications:** The Invisible Universe: The Story of Radio Astronomy, 1973, 2nd ed., 2007; (ed. with K.I. Kellermann) Galactic and Extragalactic Radio Astronomy (textbook), 1974, 2nd ed., 1988; Starscapes: Topics in Astronomy, 1977; Cosmic Catastrophes, 1978; (with G.B. Field and C. Ponnamperuma) Cosmic Evolution: An Introduction to Astronomy, 1978; The Invisible Universe Revealed: The Story of Radio Astronomy, 1987; Interstellar Matters: Essays on Curiosity and Astronomical Discovery, 1989; Hidden Attraction: The Mystery and History of Magnetism, 1993; Impact! The Threat of Comets and Asteroids, 1996. The Invisible Universe; Second edition, 2007. Works appear in anthologies. Contributor to journals and magazines. **Address:** Department of Physics, University of Memphis, 216 Manning Hall, Memphis, TN 38152, U.S.A. **Online address:** verschuur@aol.com

VERSÉNYI, Adam. American (born United States), b. 1957. **Genres:** Theatre, Theology/Religion, Politics/Government, Biography. **Career:** University of North Carolina, visiting assistant professor, 1988-90, assistant professor, 1990-95, associate professor, 1995-2003, professor of dramaturgy, 2003-, Institute for the Arts and Humanities, faculty fellow, 1993-, chair of international and area studies, Playmakers Repertory Co., resident dramaturg,

1988-, Milly S. Barranger distinguished term professor of dramatic art and dramaturg; Universidad de Caldas, Fulbright senior lecturer, 1990; Yale Repertory Theatre, staff; Florida Studio Theatre, staff; La Mama E.T.C., staff; The Mercurian (Online Journal), founder and editor. **Publications:** Theatre in Latin America: Religion, Politics and Culture from Cortes to the 1980s, 1993; El teatro en América Latino, 1996; (trans.) The Theater of Sabina Berman: The Agony of Ecstasy and Other Plays, 2003; (ed.) Dictionary of Literary Biography: Latin American Dramatists, 2005; Contributor to books and journals. **Address:** Department of Dramatic Art, University of North Carolina, CB 3230, Chapel Hill, NC 27599-3230, U.S.A. **Online address:** anversen@email.nc.edu

VERSLUIS, Arthur. American (born United States), b. 1959. **Genres:** Theology/Religion, Philosophy, History, Translations. **Career:** Washburn University, professor, 1990-94; Michigan State University, College of Arts and Letters, professor, 1995-, Department of Religious Studies, chair; Esoterica, founding editor; Journal for the Study of Radicalism, founding co-editor. **Publications:** The Philosophy of Magic, 1986; Telos, 1987; The Egyptian Mysteries, 1988; Song of the Cosmos: An Introduction to Traditional Cosmology, 1991; Sacred Earth: The Spiritual Landscape of Native America, 1992; The Elements of Native American Traditions, 1993; American Transcendentalism and Asian Religions, 1993; Theosophia: Hidden Dimensions of Christianity, 1994; Gnosis and Literature, 1996; The Mysteries of Love, 1996; (with R.W. Emerson) The Hermetic Book of Nature: An American Revolution in Consciousness, 1997; Wisdom's Children: A Christian Esoteric Tradition, 1999; Island Farm (memoir), 2000; Shakespeare the Magus, 2001; The Esoteric Origins of the American Renaissance, 2001; Restoring Paradise: Western Esotericism, Literature, Art, and Consciousness, 2004; Awakening the Contemplative Spirit: Writing, Gardening, and the Inner Life, 2004; (ed. and trans.) Awakening to Divine Wisdom: Christian Initiation into Three Worlds, 2004; The New Inquisitions: Heretic-Hunting and the Intellectual Origins of Modern Totalitarianism, 2006; Magic and Mysticism: An Introduction to Western Esotericism, 2007; (co-ed.) Esotericism, Art, and Imagination, 2008; The Secret History of Western Sexual Mysticism: Sacred Practices and Spiritual Marriage, 2008; (co-ed.) Esotericism, Religion, and Nature, 2010; The Mystical State, 2011. EDITOR AND AUTHOR OF INTRODUCTION: Wisdom's Book: The Sophia Anthology, 2000; The Wisdom of John Pordage, 2003; The Wisdom of Jacob Böhme, 2003; The Dawn of Wisdom Aurora Sapientiae and Letters of Spiritual Direction, 2005. Contributor of articles to periodicals. **Address:** Department of Religious Studies, College of Arts & Letters, Michigan State University, 116 Morrill Hall, East Lansing, MI 48824, U.S.A. **Online address:** versluis@msu.edu

VERTREACE-DOODY, Martha Modena. American (born United States), b. 1945. **Genres:** Children's Fiction, Poetry, Literary Criticism And History. **Career:** Kennedy-King College, poet-in-residence, 1977-, distinguished professor, 1995-. **Publications:** POETRY: Second House from the Corner, 1986; Oracle Bones, 1994; Maafa: When Night Becomes a Lion, 1996; Second Mourning, 1997; Smokeless Flame, 1998; Dragon Lady: Tsukimi, 1999. OTHERS: Under a Cat's-Eye Moon, 1991; Kelly in the Mirror (juvenile), 1993; Light Caught Bending, 1995; Cinnabar, 1995; Toni Cade Bambara, 1999; Glacier Fire, 2005. Contributor to magazines. **Address:** Kennedy-King College, 6300 S Halsted Ave., Chicago, IL 60621, U.S.A. **Online address:** poetmaeve@juno.com

VERYAN, Patricia. Also writes as Gwyneth Moore, Patricia Valeria Bannister. American/British (born England), b. 1923. **Genres:** Romance/Historical, Novels, History, Young Adult Fiction. **Career:** Columbia Pictures, staff, 1940-42; Pacific Telephone, staff, 1949; National Cash Register Co., staff, 1950; Southern Counties Gas Co., staff, 1951-52; Humble Oil and Refining Co., staff, 1952-55; University of California, secretary for graduate affairs, 1971-85; freelance novelist, 1978-. **Publications:** HISTORICAL ROMANCE NOVELS: The Lord and the Gypsy, 1978 in UK as Debt of Honour, 1980; Love's Duet, 1979 in UK as A Perfect Match, 1981; Mistress of Willowvale, 1980; Some Brief Folly, 1981; The Wagered Widow, 1984; Logic of the Heart, 1990; Poor Splendid Wings, 1992; (with L. Lynn, B. Metzger and J. Smith) Autumn Loves, 1993; Whimsy, forthcoming. SANGUINET SAGA: The Lord and the Gypsy, 1978; Love's Duet, 1979; Nanette, 1981; Some Brief Folly, 1981; Feather Castles, 1982; Married Past Redemption, 1983; The Noblest Frailty, 1983; Sanguinet's Crown, 1985; Give All to Love, 1987; Logic of the Heart, 1990; Lanterns, 1996. GOLDEN CHRONICLES: Practice to Deceive, 1985; Journey to Enchantment, 1986; Cherished Enemy, 1987; The Tyrant, 1987; Love Alters Not, 1987; The Dedicated Villain, 1989.

JEWELED MEN SERIES: Time's Fool, 1991; Had We Never Loved, 1992; Ask Me No Questions, 1993; A Shadow's Bliss, 1994; Never Doubt I Love, 1995; The Mandarin of Mayfair, 1995; The Riddle of Alabaster Royal, 1997; The Riddle of the Lost Lover, 1998; The Riddle of the Reluctant Rake, 1999; The Riddle of the Shipwrecked Spinster, 2001; The Riddle of the Deplorable Dandy, 2002. ROMANCE NOVELS AS GWYNETH MOORE: Men Were Deceivers Ever, 1989; The Dirty Frog, 1990; Love's Lady Lost, 1991. **Address:** 9805 NE 116th St., PO Box 7239, Kirkland, WA 98034, U.S.A.

VESETH, Michael. American (born United States), b. 1949. **Genres:** Economics, Politics/Government. **Career:** University of Puget Sound, professor of economics, 1975-, Political Economics Program, director, 1975-, International Political Economy Program, director, professor, Robert G. Albertson professor of international political economy; ILACA Program, director, 1990; Johns Hopkins Bologna Center, visiting professor, 1997. Writer. **Publications:** Introductory Macroeconomics, 1980, 2nd ed., 1984; Introductory Economics, 1981; Introductory Microeconomics, 1981; Public Finance, 1984; (with J.R. Clark) Economics: Cost and Choice, 1987; (with J.R. Clark) Microeconomics: Cost and Choice, 1987; (with J.R. Clark) Macroeconomics: Cost and Choice, 1987; Mountains of Debt: Crisis and Change in Renaissance Florence, Victorian Britain, and Postwar America, 1990; (with D.N. Balaam) Introduction to International Political Economy, 1996, 4th ed., 2008; (ed. with D.N. Balaam) Readings in International Political Economy, 1996; Selling Globalization: The Myth of the Global Economy, 1998; Unsettled Foundations: Chaos, Crisis, the Globalization Myth, 1998; (ed.) Rise of the Global Economy, 2002; Globaloney: Unraveling the Myths of Globalization, 2005, 2nd ed. as Globaloney 2.0: The Crash of 2008 and the Future of Globalization, 2010; Wine Wars: The Curse of the Blue Nun, the Miracle of Two Buck Chuck, and the Revenge of the Terroirists, 2011. **Address:** International Political Economy Program, University of Puget Sound, McIntyre 213M, 1500 N Warner St., PO Box 1057, Tacoma, WA 98416-1057, U.S.A. **Online address:** veseth@pugetsound.edu

VESEY, Godfrey. British (born England), b. 1923. **Genres:** Philosophy, Essays. **Career:** University of London, King's College, assistant lecturer, 1952-53, lecturer, 1953-65, reader in philosophy, 1965-69; Royal Institute of Philosophy, honorary director, 1966-79, fellow, 1979; Open University, Faculty of Arts, professor of philosophy, 1969-90, pro-vice-chancellor, 1975, professor emeritus of philosophy, 1990-. Writer. **Publications:** Embodied Mind, 1965; Perception, 1971; Other Minds?, 1973; Personal Identity: A Philosophical Analysis, 1973; (with A. Flew) Agency and Necessity, 1987; Inner and Outer: Essays on a Philosophical Myth, 1991. EDITOR: Body and Mind, 1964; The Human Agent, 1968; Talk of God, 1969; Knowledge and Necessity, 1970; The Proper Study, 1971; Reason and Reality, 1972; Philosophy and the Arts, 1973; (and foreword) Understanding Wittgenstein, 1974; Philosophy in the Open, 1974; Impressions of Empiricism, 1976; Communication and Understanding, 1977; Human Values, 1978; Idealism, Past and Present, 1982; Philosophers, Ancient and Modern, 1986; Philosophy in Christianity, 1989. **Address:** Department of Philosophy, Faculty of Arts, Open University, Walton Hall, Milton Keynes, BK MK7 6AA, England.

VESEY, Paul. See ALLEN, Samuel W.

VESPER, Karl H(amptom). American (born United States), b. 1932. **Genres:** Business/Trade/Industry, Engineering, Technology, Economics. **Career:** Marine Advisers Inc., business manager, 1961-62; Stanford University, research associate, lecturer in engineering, director of case development, 1963-69; Hosmer Machine Co., director, 1966-69; Rensselaer Polytechnic Institute, director of summer, 1966-67; University of Illinois, director, 1966-67; University of Washington, faculty, 1969, associate professor, professor of business administration in mechanical engineering and marine studies, 1974-2007, Academy of Management, Entrepreneurship Division, founder, Department of Management and Organization, chair, 1981-84, professor emeritus, 2007-; Baylor University, Joseph F. Schoen visiting professor of entrepreneurship, 1980; Babson College, Paul T. Babson visiting professor of entrepreneurship, 1981; University of Calgary, faculty, 1987; Trinity College, visiting professor, 1989; U.S. Department of State, consultant. Writer. **Publications:** Engineers at Work: A Casebook, 1974; (with L.T. Hosmer and A.C. Cooper) The Entrepreneurial Function: Text and Cases on Smaller Firms, 1977; (ed. and contrib.) Small Business and Entrepreneurship in the Pacific Northwest, 1979; New Venture Strategies, 1980, rev. ed., 1990; Entrepreneurship Education, 1980; Frontiers of Entrepreneurship Research, 1981; (ed. with C.A. Kent and D.L. Sexton) Encyclopedia of Entrepreneurship, 1982; Entrepreneurship

and National Policy, 1983; (with P. Larson) The Washington Entrepreneur's Guide, 1993; New Venture Mechanics, 1993; New Venture Experience, 1994, rev. ed., 1995. Contributor of articles to books and journals. **Address:** Management and Organization Department, Michael G. Foster School of Business, University of Washington, 314 Mackenzie Hall, PO Box 353200, Seattle, WA 98195-3200, U.S.A. **Online address:** kvesper@u.washington.edu

VEST, Herb D. American (born United States), b. 1944. **Genres:** Money/Finance, Business/Trade/Industry, Economics. **Career:** Certified public accountant, 1973-83; H.D. Vest Financial Services, founder, 1983, chair and chief executive officer, 1983-; University of Texas, lecturer; North Lake College, lecturer; U.S.-Mexico Chamber of Commerce, director; True.com, founder and chief executive officer; AdShuffle, founder and chief executive officer, 2005-. Writer. **Publications:** WITH L.R. NIEDERMEIER: Wealth: How to Get It, How to Keep It: The H.D. Vest System for Achieving Financial Security, 1994; Wealth Workout: H.D. Vest's Wealth Building Program for Life, 1996. Contributor to journals and newspapers. **Address:** H.D. Vest Financial Services, 6333 N State Hwy. 161 4th Fl., Irving, TX 75038, U.S.A. **Online address:** webmaster@hdvest.com

VICCHIO, Stephen (John). American (born United States), b. 1950. **Genres:** History, Philosophy, Social Commentary, Theology/Religion, Essays. **Career:** Johns Hopkins University, adjunct professor, 1973-, public safety program; University of Maryland, assistant professor of philosophy and religious studies, 1976-80, visiting associate professor, 1985-, visiting professor, 1986-87; St. Mary's Seminary and University, adjunct professor, 1979-, distinguished lecturer in systematic theology, 1988; College of Notre Dame, instructor, assistant professor, 1980-86, associate professor, 1986-92, professor of philosophy, 1992-; University of St. Andrews, tutor, 1983-84. Writer. **Publications:** A Careful Disorder: Chronicles of Life, Love, and Laughter (essays), 1987; The Voice from the Whirlwind: Reflections on the Problem of Evil, 1987; (ed.) On Vital Reserves, 1988; (ed. with V. Geiger and contrib.) Perspectives on the American Catholic Church, 1989; The Philosophy of Jacques Maritain, 1989; The Voice from the Whirlwind: The Problem of Evil and the Modern World, 1989; Ordinary Mysteries: More Chronicles of Life, Love, and Laughter (essays), 1991; I of the Beholder: Essays and Stories, 1995; Ivan and Adolph: the Last Man in Hell, 1997; Pieces of an Examined Life, 1999; Executioner's Hill (play), 2002; Ethics, Integrity, and American Policing, 2002; (with L.D. Edinberg) Sweet Uses Of Adversity: Images of the Biblical Job, 2002; The Image of the Biblical Job, a History: Volume One: Job in the Ancient World, 2006; The Image of the Biblical Job, a History: Volume Two: Job in the Medieval World, 2006; The Image of the Biblical Job, a History: Volume Three: Job in the Modern World, 2006; Jefferson's Religion, 2007; Biblical Figures in the Islamic Faith, 2008. Work appears in anthologies. Contributor of articles to periodicals. **Address:** Department of Philosophy, College of Notre Dame, 4701 N Charles St., Baltimore, MD 21210, U.S.A. **Online address:** svicchio@ndm.edu

VICK, Helen Hughes. American (born United States), b. 1950. **Genres:** Young Adult Fiction, Education, Literary Criticism And History. **Career:** Prescott Unified Schools, special education teacher; Northern Arizona University, part-time instructor. Writer. **Publications:** YOUNG ADULT FICTION: Walker of Time, 1993; Walker's Journey Home, 1995; Tag against Time, 1996. TEACHER'S GUIDES: Walker of Time Teacher's Guide: A Literature-Based Integrated Curriculum, 1995; Teacher's Guides: Walker's Journey Home, 1996; Teacher's Guide: Tag against Time, 1996. OTHER: Shadow, 1998; Charlotte, 1999. Contributor to periodicals. **Address:** PO Box 2851, Prescott, AZ 86301, U.S.A.

VICKERS, Adrian. Australian (born Australia), b. 1958?. **Genres:** Novels. **Career:** University of Sydney, professor of south east asian studies, 2007-. Writer. **Publications:** Bali: A Paradise Created, 1997; (ed. with David Walker and Julia Horne) Australian Perceptions of Asia, 1990; (comp. and author of intro.) Traveling to Bali: Four Hundred Years of Journeys, 1994; (ed.) Being Modern in Bali: Image and Change, 1996; (ed. with I Nyoman Darma Putra and Michele Ford) To Change Bali: Essays in Honour of I Gusti Ngurah Bagus, 2000; (with A. Wells) Explaining the Anti-globalisation Movement, 2001; A History of Modern Indonesia, 2005; Journeys of Desire: The Balinese Malat in Text and History, 2005. Contributor to books. **Address:** University of Sydney, Rm. 637, Brennan MacCallum Bldg. A18, Sydney, NW 2006, Australia. **Online address:** adrian.vickers@usyd.edu.au

VICKERS, Daniel. Canadian (born Canada), b. 1952?. **Genres:** History, Autobiography/Memoirs. **Career:** University of British Columbia, Department of History, professor, department head; Memorial University, faculty of history; University of California, faculty of history, department chair. Writer. **Publications:** Farmers and Fishermen: Two Centuries of Work in Essex County, Massachusetts, 1630-1850, 1994; (ed.) A Companion to Colonial America, 2003; (with V. Walsh) Young Men and the Sea: Yankee Seafarers in the Age of Sail, 2005; (ed.) The Autobiography of Ashley Bowen, (1728-1813), 2006. **Address:** Department of History, University of British Columbia, Rm. 1297, 1873 E Mall, Vancouver, BC V6T 1Z1, Canada. **Online address:** dvickers@interchange.ubc.ca

VICKERS, Joanne F. American (born United States), b. 1941. **Genres:** Women's Studies And Issues, Social Sciences, Adult Non-fiction. **Career:** Ohio Dominican College, professor of English language and literature and assistant dean of academic affairs, 1977-. Writer and consultant. **Publications:** (Contrib.) No More Frogs, No More Princes: Women Making Creative Choices in Midlife, 1993; (with B.L. Thomas) Men on Midlife: Eighteen Men Talk about Making New Choices in Careers, Relationships and What Really Matters in the Second Half of Life, 1996. **Address:** Department of Literature and English Language, Ohio Dominican University, 1216 Sunbury Rd., Columbus, OH 43219, U.S.A. **Online address:** vickersj@ohiodominican.edu

VICTOR, Barbara. American/Canadian (born Canada), b. 1946. **Genres:** Adult Non-fiction, Novels, Young Adult Non-fiction. **Career:** CBS Television, staff; U.S. News and World Report, staff, 1985-; Femme Magazine, staff, 1987-, contributing editor, 1990-97; ELLE USA, contributing editor, 1988-92; Madame Figaro, contributing editor, 1997-2001. Educator. **Publications:** Terrorism, 1986; Absence of Pain, 1988; Misplaced Lives, 1990; Friends, Lovers, Enemies, 1991; Coriander, 1993; The Derive Calculus Workbook, 1994; Voice of Reason: A Biography of Hanan Ashrawi, 1994; Hanan Ashrawi, 1995; (with R. Felder) Getting Away with Murder, 1996; The Lady: Aung San Suu Kyi, Nobel Laureate and Burma's Prisoner, 1998; Le Matignon de Jospin, 1999; Goddess, 2001; Army of Roses: Inside the World of Palestinian Women Suicide Bombers, 2003; The Last Crusade: Religion and the Politics of Misdirection, 2005; Charlotte Rampling: Biography, 2009; (with R. Felder) Breaking Up Is Hard To Do, 2009; (with R. Felder) The Good Divorce: How to Walk Away Financially Sound and Emotionally Happy, 2011; (with R. Nathan) Time Before Time, forthcoming. **Address:** InkWell Management, 521 5th Ave., 26th Fl, New York, NY 10175, U.S.A. **Online address:** barbaravictorsmecca@gmail.com

VICTOR, George. American (born United States) **Genres:** Psychology, Politics/Government. **Career:** Mental Health Clinic-Passaic, chief psychologist. Writer. **Publications:** Invisible Men: Faces of Alienation, 1974; The Riddle of Autism: A Psychological Analysis, 1983, rev. ed., 1995; Hitler: The Pathology of Evil, 1998; The Pearl Harbor Myth: Rethinking the Unthinkable, 2007; Death: The Religious Basis of the Holocaust, forthcoming; The Myth of Pearl Harbor and Fundamentalism, Defilement, forthcoming. Contributor to periodicals. **Address:** Brassey's Inc., 22883 Quicksilver Dr., Ste. 100, Dulles, VA 20166, U.S.A.

VICUNA, Cecilia. American/Chilean (born Chile), b. 1948. **Genres:** Poetry, Plays/Screenplays, History, Young Adult Fiction. **Career:** Freelance poet and performance artist. **Publications:** POETRY: Saborami, 1973; Siete Poemas, 1979; Luxumei o El Traspie de la Doctrina, 1983; Palabrarmas, 1984; Samara, 1986; La Wik'uña, 1990; Word and Thread, 1996; The Precarious: The Art and Poetry of Cecilia Vicuña, 1997; Instan, 2002; I tu, 2004; Otoño=Autumn, 2007; Soy Yos: Antologia, 1966-2006, 2010. EDITOR: (with M. Bogin and intro.) The Selected Poems of Rosario Castellanos, 1988; (ed. and intro.) ÜI: Four Mapuche Poets: An Anthology, 1998; (with E. Livon-Grosman) The Oxford Book of Latin American Poetry: A Bilingual Anthology, 2009. Contributor to books. Works appear in anthologies. **Address:** 135 Hudson St., New York, NY 10013-2102, U.S.A.

VIDAL, Gore. Also writes as Cameron Kay, Edgar Box, Katherine Everard. American (born United States), b. 1925. **Genres:** Novels, Novellas/Short Stories, Mystery/Crime/Suspense, Plays/Screenplays, Essays, Literary Criticism And History. **Career:** The New Party, co-chairman, 1968-72. Writer. **Publications:** NOVELS: Williwaw, 1946; In a Yellow Wood, 1947; The City and the Pillar, 1948, rev. ed., 1995; The Season of Comfort, 1949; A Search for the King: A Twelfth Century Legend, 1950; Dark Green, Bright Red, 1950; The Judgment of Paris, 1952; Messiah, 1954, rev. ed., 1980; Three, 1962; Ju-

lian, 1964; Washington D.C., 1967; Myra Breckinridge, 1968; Two Sisters: A Novel in the Form of a Memoir, 1970; Burr, 1973; Myron, 1974; 1876, 1976; Kalki, 1978; Creation, 1981; Duluth, 1983; Lincoln, 1984; Vidal In Venice, 1985; Myra Breckinridge, Myron, 1986; Empire, 1987; Armageddon?, 1987; Hollywood, 1990; Live from Golgotha, 1992; Smithsonian Institution, 1998; The Golden Age, 2000; Clouds and Eclipses: The Collected Short Stories, 2006. PLAYS: Visit to a Small Planet, 1957; The Best Man: A Play of Politics, 1960; Three Plays, 1962; Romulus: The Broadway Adaptation, 1966; Weekend, 1968; An Evening with Richard Nixon, 1972; (with W. Howard) Caligula, 1979. ESSAYS: Rocking the Boat, 1962; Sex, Death and Money, 1968; Reflections upon a Sinking Ship, 1969; Homage to Daniel Shays: Collected Essays, 1952-71 in UK as Collected Essays: 1952-71, 1972; Matters of Fact and of Fiction: Essays 1973-76, 1977; The Second American Revolution and Other Essays in UK as Pink Triangle and Yellow Star and Other Essays, 1982; At Home: Essays, 1982-1988, 1989; Virgin Islands: Essays, 1992; United States: Essays, 1952-1992, 1993; Palimpsest: A Memoir, 1995; Essential Vidal, 1998; The Last Empire: Essays 1992-2000, 2001; Perpetual War for Perpetual Peace, 2002; Dreaming War: Blood for Oil and the Cheney-Bush Junta, 2002; Selected Essays of Gore Vidal, 2008. OTHER: A Thirsty Evil: Seven Short Stories, 1956; (co-author) Great American Families, 1977; (intro.) Edith Wharton Omnibus, 1977; (with R.J. Stantion) Views from a Window: Conversations, 1980; (intro.) The Collected Stories Gore Vidal's Venice, 1985; The Decline and Fall of the American Empire, 1992; Screening History, 1992; Palimpest (memoir), 1995; The American Presidency, 1998; Sexually Speaking: Collected Sex Writings, 1999; Inventing a Nation, 2003; Imperial America: Reflections On the United States of Amnesia, 2004; Point to Point Navigation: A Memoir, 1964 to 2006, 2006; (with R. Scheer) Playing President: My Close Encounters with Nixon, Carter, Bush I, Reagan and Clinton: And How They Did Not Prepare Me for George W. Bush, 2006; Not Vital, 2007; (co-author) Zero: Perché La Versione Ufficiale Sull' 11/9 é Un Falso, 2007; (co-author) Zero: inchiesta sull'11 settembre, 2008; Gore Vidal: Snapshots in History's Glare, 2009. AS EDGAR BOX: Death in the Fifth Position, 1952; Death before Bedtime, 1953; Death Likes It Hot, 1954; Three by Box, 1978. AS KATHERINE EVERARD: A Star's Progress, 1950. AS CAMERON KAY: Thieves Fall Out, 1953. **Address:** Janklow & Nesbit Ltd., 445 Park Ave., New York, NY 10022-2606, U.S.A.

VIDMAR, John C. American (born United States) **Genres:** Theology/Religion, History. **Career:** Providence College, special lecturer, 2004-05, associate professor of theology, 2005-; Dominican House of Studies, associate professor and academic dean; Ohio Dominican University, instructor. Writer, theologian, Dominican friar and historian. **Publications:** The Catholic Church through the Ages: A History, 2005; English Catholic Historians and the English Reformation, 1585-1954, 2005; (with N. de Flon) 101 Questions and Answers on The Da Vinci Code and the Catholic Tradition, 2006; Praying with the Dominicans: To Praise, to Bless, to Preach, 2008. Contributor to periodicals. **Address:** Providence College, 549 River Ave., Providence, RI 02918-0001, U.S.A.

VIDRINE, Beverly Barras. American (born United States), b. 1938. **Genres:** Children's Non-fiction. **Career:** Elementary school teacher, 1960-62, 1964-65, 1970-76, 1988-91; Law office of Dennis J. Vidrine, office manager, legal secretary and bookkeeper, 1976-88. Writer. **Publications:** A Mardi Gras Dictionary, 1994; A Christmas Dictionary, 1997; St. Patrick's Day Alphabet, 2001; Easter Day Alphabet, 2003; Halloween Alphabet, 2004; Thanksgiving Day Alphabet, 2006. Contributor of articles to journals. **Address:** Pelican Publishing Company, 1000 Burmaster St., Gretna, LA 70053-2246, U.S.A. **Online address:** barras@iamerica.net

VIECELI, Emma. British (born England), b. 1979. **Genres:** Graphic Novels. **Career:** Artist and writer. **Publications:** (Illus.) William Shakespeare, Hamlet (graphic novel), 2007; (Illus.) William Shakespeare, Much Ado about Nothing (graphic novel), 2009. Work appears in anthology. **Address:** Cambridge, England. **Online address:** emma.vieceli@gmail.com

VIEIRA, Sergio. Mozambiquian (born Mozambique), b. 1941. **Genres:** Military/Defense/Arms Control, Area Studies, Third World, History. **Career:** FRELIMO (Mozambique's independence party), founding member, 1962-, representative-Algiers, 1964-67, representative-Cairo, 1969-70, secretary of the presidency, 1967-75; Cabinet of the President of Mozambique, director, 1975-77; Banco de Mozambique, governor, 1978-81; Economic Commission of the Non-Aligned Summit, chairperson, 1979; Niassa Province, governor, 1983-84; Mozambican/South African Joint Security Commission, minister of security and co-chairperson, 1984-87; University Eduardo Mondlane, professor, 1987-, Centre for African Studies, director, 1987-92; SAGE, general manager, 1992-93; Assembly of the Republic of Mozambique, Social Affairs Commission, chairperson; Estudos Mocambicanos, publisher, 1987-92; BPD, consultant, 1994; Zambezi Planning Office, director. Writer. **Publications:** Também Memória Do Povo, 1983; Conferência De Imprensa: Dada Por Sérgio Vieira Em 30 De Setembro De 1985 Em Maputo: Press Conference, 1985; Disarmament and Development: A Mozambican View, 1988; Southern Africa, Mozambique: From Rivalries to Global Convergence, 1988; War and Peace in Southern Africa: The Mozambican Reply to Pretoria's Undeclared War, 1989; Democracia e Desenvolvimento: Temas Para UmaReflexão Em Moçambique, 1990; (contrib.) How Fast the Wind?: Southern Africa, 1975-2000, 1992; The Possible Changes and Transformations, 1992; Governing During Transition, 1993; The History of the National Liberation Struggles: On the Relationship Between the Struggle and the Content and Direction of the Post-Colonial Society: The Case of Mozambique, 1993; Participei, por isso testemunho, 2010. Contributor to periodicals. **Address:** CEA UEM, C.P. 1993, Maputo, 99999, Mozambique.

VIGÉE, Claude (Andre Strauss). French/Israeli (born Israel), b. 1921. **Genres:** Poetry, Autobiography/Memoirs, Essays, Theology/Religion, Literary Criticism And History. **Career:** Ohio State University, professor of French and comparative literature, 1947-49; Wellesley College, professor, 1949-50; Brandeis University, professor, 1949-60; Hebrew University, professor, 1960-83; Claude Vigée Cultural Center, owner, 2000-. Writer. **Publications:** L'Aurore souterraine, 1952; La Come du Grand Pardon, 1954; Moisson de Canaan, 1967; La Lune d'hiver, 1970; Delivrance du souffle, 1977; Du bec al'oreille, 1977; Paque de la parole, 1983; Heimat des Hauches, 1985; Wenderowefir, 1988; La Manna e la rugiada, 1988; Leben in Jerusalem, 1990; La Terre el le Souffle, Claude Vigee, 1992; Les Cinq rouleaux (Bible studies), 1993; Treize inconnus de la Bible, 1996; La Maison des Vivants, 1996; La lucarne aux etoiles (notebooks), 1998; (with S. Parizet) Lesportes éiclairées de la nuit: entretiens, essais, cahier, récits inédits, 2000-2006, 2006; Être poéte, pour quevivent les hommes: choix d'essais, 1950-2005, 2006; (with Y.L. Men) Toutevie finit dans la nuit: entretiens, 2006; (with Y.L. Men) Toute vie finit dans la nuit: entretiens, 2007; Mélancolie solaire: nouveaux essais, cahiers, entretiens inédits, poèmes (2006-2008), 2008. POETRY: La Lutte avec l'ange, 1950; L'Ete indien, 1957; Le Soleil sous la mer, 1972; LesOrties noires, 1984; Le Feu d'une nuit d'hiver, 1989; Apprendre la nuit, 1991; Flow Tide, 1992; L'Heritage du feu, 1992; Aux portes du labyrinthe, 1996; Le passage du vivant, 2001; Dan le creuset du vent, 2003; Nostalgie du père: nouveaux essais, entretiens et poèmes (2000-2007), 2007; Double Voix, 2010. CRITICISM: Les Artistes de la faim, 1960; Revolte et louanges, 1962. ESSAYS: L'Art et le demonique, 1978; L'Extase et l'errance, 1982; La Manneet la Rosee, 1986; La Faille du regard (and interviews), 1987; Aux Sourcesde la litterature moderne I, 1989; Dans le silence de l'Aleph, 1992; Demain la seule demeure, 1999; Alle porte del silenzio, 2003. AUTOBIOGRAPHY/MEMOIRS: Le Parfum et la cendre, 1984; (with L. Balbont) Une Voix dans le defile, 1985; Un Panier de Houblon, vol. I, 1994, vol. II, 1995; Wintermond, 2004. Contributor to journals. Works appear in anthologies. **Address:** 12 bis rue des Marronniers, Paris, 75016, France.

VIGH, Henrik. (Henrik E. Vigh). Danish (born Denmark), b. 1969. **Genres:** Military/Defense/Arms Control, History. **Career:** Market Manager A/ S, consultant, 1994-96; Young & Rubicam, copywriter, 1998-99; GN-Resound, copywriter, 1998-99; University of Copenhagen, research fellow, 1999-2002, assistant professor, 2003-05; European Union, international observer for presidential election, 2005; Rehabilitation and Research Centre for Victims of Torture, researcher, 2005-07, senior researcher, 2007-. Writer and researcher. **Publications:** Navigating Terrains of War: Youth and Soldiering in Guinea-Bissau, 2006. Contributor of articles to periodicals. **Address:** Denmark. **Online address:** hv@rct.dk

VIGH, Henrik E. See **VIGH, Henrik.**

VIGIL, Diego. See **VIGIL, James Diego.**

VIGIL, James Diego. (Diego Vigil). American (born United States), b. 1938. **Genres:** Anthropology/Ethnology, Cultural/Ethnic Topics, History, Sociology, Women's Studies And Issues. **Career:** School teacher, 1962-68; Sacramento State College, lecturer in history, 1968-69; University of California, master instruction specialist in high potential program and lecturer in Chicano studies, 1969-71, Spanish-Speaking Mental Health Research Program,

research associate, 1974-76, Department of Criminology, law and Society, professor; Chaffey College, assistant professor, 1971-74, associate professor, 1974-80, professor of history and anthropology, 1980; California State University, instructor, 1977-80, lecturer, 1980-82; Whittier College, lecturer, 1977-79; University of Wisconsin-Milwaukee, research fellow in sociology, 1979-80, associate professor and director of Chicano studies, 1988-89; University of Southern California, associate professor of anthropology, 1984-, director of ethnic studies, 1981-87, professor of anthropology, 1992-, Center for Multi-ethnic and Transnational Studies, research fellow, 1992-; Harvard University, Graduate School of Education, visiting professor. Writer. **Publications:** (As Diego Vigil) Early Chicano Guerrilla Fighters, 1974; (contrib.) Chicano Perspectives on De-Colonizing Anthropology, 1978; From Indians to Chicanos: A Sociocultural History, 1980, 2nd ed. as From Indians to Chicanos: The Dynamics of Mexican American Culture, 1998; (contrib.) Twice a Minority: Mexican American Women, 1980; (with Arvizu and S. Rios) Cultura Chicana (monograph), 1985; (contrib.) The Broken Web: The Education of Hispanic Women, 1987; Barrio Gangs: Street Life and Identity in Southern California, 1988; (contrib.) Violence and Homicide in Hispanic Communities, 1988; Personas Mexicanas: Chicano High Schoolers in a Changing Los Angeles, 1997; From Indians to Chicanos: The Dynamics of Mexican-American Culture, 1998; A Rainbow of Gangs: Street Cultures in the Mega-City, 2002; The Projects: Gang and Non-Gang Families In East Los Angeles, 2007; Gang Redux: A Balanced Anti-gang Strategy, 2010; (with G.Q. Conchas) Streetsmart Schoolsmart, 2012. **Address:** Department of Criminology, Law and Society, University of California, 2355 SEII, 5300 Social and Behavioral Sciences Gateway, Irvine, CA 92697-7050, U.S.A. **Online address:** vigil@uci.edu

VIJAYARAGHAVAN, Vineeta. Indian (born India), b. 1972. **Genres:** Novels. **Career:** Katzenbach Partners L.L.C., consultant. Writer. **Publications:** Motherland: A Novel, 2001. **Address:** Katzenbach Partners L.L.C., 381 Park Ave. S, Ste. 501, New York, NY 10016, U.S.A.

VILANDER, Barbara. American (born United States), b. 1958. **Genres:** Photography, Sciences, Architecture. **Career:** Museum of Photographic Arts, education coordinator; Santa Barbara City College, adjunct faculty in art history. Historian and writer. **Publications:** Hoover Dam: The Photographs of Ben Glaha, 1999. **Address:** University of Arizona Press, 355 S Euclid Ave., Ste. 103, Tucson, AZ 85719-6654, U.S.A. **Online address:** bavilander@pipeline.sbcc.edu

VILAR, Irene. See **MENDES, Irene Vilar.**

VILEISIS, Ann. American (born United States), b. 1967. **Genres:** Environmental Sciences/Ecology, History, Food And Wine. **Career:** Colorado Outward Bound School, course director for educational river expeditions, 1990-95; writer, 1995-; National Museum of American History, fellow, 1999; Smithsonian Institution, fellow, 1999; Kalmiopsis Audubon Society, conservation director, 2003-06, president, 2007-10; Ford Family Foundation, community leadership fellow, 2008; Kalmiopsis Audubon Society Chapter, president. Writer, public speaker and lecturer. **Publications:** Discovering the Unknown Landscape: A History of America's Wetlands, 1997; Kitchen Literacy: How We Lost Knowledge of Where Food Comes From and Why We Need to Get it Back, 2008. Contributor to books and periodicals. **Address:** Kalmiopsis Audubon Society, PO Box 1265, Port Orford, OR 97465, U.S.A. **Online address:** avileisis@yahoo.com

VILLAFANE, Eldin. American (born United States), b. 1940. **Genres:** Ethics, Theology/Religion, Social Sciences. **Career:** Yabucoa Baseball Club, semi-professional baseball player, 1961-62; General Council of the Assemblies of God, editorial assistant, 1968-69; teacher, 1970-73; Spanish American Bible Institute, professor, 1971-72; minister-boston, 1973-; WHDH-Radio, moderator of the radio ministry, 1976-79; Gordon-Conwell Theological Seminary, assistant professor, 1976-82, associate professor, 1982-90, professor of Christian social ethics, 1990-, Center for Urban Ministerial Education, founding director, 1976-90, associate dean for urban and multicultural affairs, 1990-93, Contextualized Urban Theological Education Enablement Program, executive director, 1990-; Christian Center, interim pastor, 1984; North Central Bible College, visiting professor, 1991; Harvard Divinity School, visiting professor, 1998; Asociación para la Educación Teológica Hispana, co-founder and president; Society for Pentecostal Studies, president; La Comunidad of Hispanic American Scholars of Theology and Religion, founder and president. Writer. **Publications:** (With R. Sanchez and R. Dominguez) Ricardo

Tanon: El Poder y la Gloria de Dios, 1980; The Liberating Spirit: Toward an Hispanic American Pentecostal Social Ethic, 1992; An Evangelical Call to a Social Spirituality: Reflections on Urban Theology and Ministry, 1994; (trans. and author of preface) S. Mott, Biblical Ethics and Social Change, 1994; Seek the Peace of the City: Reflections on Urban Ministry, 1995; El Espíritu libera-dor: hacia una eética social pentecostal hispanoamericana, 1996; (co-author) Transforming the City: Reframing Education for Urban Ministry, 2002; (ed. with A. Padilla and R. Goizueta) Hispanic Christian Thought at the Dawn of the 21st Century: Apuntes in Honor of Justo L. Gonzalez, 2005; Beyond Cheap Grace: A Call to Radical Discipleship, Incarnation and Justice, 2006. Contributor to periodicals. Address: Gordon-Conwell Theological Seminary, 14542 Choate Cir., Charlotte, NC 28273-9103, U.S.A.

VILLA-GILBERT, Mariana. (Mariana Soledad Magdalena Villa-Gilbert). British (born England), b. 1937. Genres: Novels, Young Adult Fiction. Career: Writer. Publications: Mrs. Galbraith's Air, 1963; My Love All Dressed in White, 1964; Mrs. Cantello, 1966; A Jingle Jangle Song, 1968; The Others, 1970; Manuela: A Modern Myth (fantasy), 1973; The Sun in Horus, 1986. Address: c/o Herbert van Thal, London Management Ltd., 235241 Regent St., London, GL W1A 2JT, England.

VILLA-GILBERT, Mariana Soledad Magdalena. See **VILLA-GIL-BERT, Mariana.**

VILLAMIL, Victoria Etnier. American (born United States), b. 1940. Genres: Music, Biography, Art/Art History, Humanities. Career: Profes-sional opera and concert singer, 1967-89. Writer. Publications: A Singer's Guide to the American Art Song, 1870-1980, 1993; From Johnson's Kids to Lemonade Opera: The American Classical Singer Comes of Age, 2004. Ad-dress: 5 Caryl Ln., Philadelphia, PA 19118-2703, U.S.A.

VILLARI, Rosario. Italian (born Italy), b. 1925. Genres: History, Social Sciences. Career: University of Messina, teacher, 1959-70; St. Antony's College, visiting professor, 1974; University of Florence, teacher, 1971-78; University of Rome, teacher of early modern history, 1979-95, Department of Medieval and Modern History, director, 1992-94, emeritus professor, 1999-; Institute for Advanced Study, visiting professor, 1981-82. Writer. Publica-tions: La rivolta antispagnola a Napoli, 1967, trans. as The Revolt of Naples, 1993; (ed.) L'Uomo barocco, 1991; (ed.) Baroque Personae, 1995; Nation and Revolution in Seventeenth-Century Spanish Monarchy, forthcoming. UNTRANSLATED WORKS: Il Sud nella storia d'Italia: antologia della questione meridionale, 1961; Mezzogiorno e contadini nell'età moderna, 1961; Conservatori e democratici nell'Italia liberale, 1964; Storia dell'Europa contemporanea, 1971; Ribelli e riformatori dal XVI al XVIII secolo, 1979; Mezzogiorno e democrazia, 1979; Storia dell'Europa contemporanea, 1985; Elogio della dissimulazione: La lotta politica nel Seicento, 1987; Com'e nata l'Italia: Il Risorgimento, 1991; Per il re o per la patria: La fedelta nel Seicento, 1994; (with G. Parker) Política de Felipe II: dos estudios, 1996; (ed.) Scrittori politici dell'eta barocca, 1998; Mille anni di storia. Dalla citta medieva all' unita dell'Europa, 2000; Controllo Degli Stretti e Insediamenti Militari nel Mediterraneo, 2002; Filippo II e il Mediterraneo, 2003; Universalismo e Na-zionalit Nell'esperienza del Giacobinismo Italiano, 2003; Sommario di sto-ria, 2005; Storia Sociale e Politica, 2007. Address: Via Mecenate 77, Rome, 00184, Italy. Online address: r.villari@tiscali.it

VILLASMIL, Omar (Santiago). (Santiago Villasmil Stella). Venezuelan (born Venezuela), b. 1942. Genres: Adult Non-fiction, Theology/Religion. Career: Universidad de los Andes, professor of film-making and educational technology, 1971-, now professor emeritus. Writer and consultant. Publi-cations: (As Santiago Villasmil Stella) A Warrior on His Path (nonfiction), 2001. Address: Urb. San Cristóbal, Calle 5, Ste. 5-68, Mérida, 05101, Ven-ezuela. Online address: erick-villasmil@excite.com

VILLATORO, Marcos McPeek. American (born United States) Genres: Novels, Poetry, Documentaries/Reportage, Young Adult Fiction. Career: Mount St. Mary's College, teacher of creative writing and literature, assis-tant professor, Fletcher Jones endowed chair of writing, professor of English; Pacifica Radio, host; Public Broadcasting Service, commentator; National Public Radio, commentator. Writer. Publications: Walking to La Milpa: Liv-ing in Guatemala with Armies, Demons, Abrazos, and Death, 1996; A Fire in the Earth (novel), 1996; They Say That I Am Two: Poems, 1997; The Holy Spirit of My Uncle's Cojones (novel), 1999; On Tuesday, When the Home-less Disappeared: Poems, 2004. ROMILIA CHACÓN MYSTERY SERIES:

Home Killings, 2001; Minos, 2003; Venom Beneath the Skin, 2005; Blood Daughters, 2011. Address: Department of English, Mount St. Mary's Col-lege, Chalon Campus, 12001 Chalon Rd., Los Angeles, CA 90049, U.S.A. Online address: mvillatoro@msmc.la.edu

VILLEGAS, Halli. Canadian/American (born United States), b. 1967. Genres: Novels. Career: Guernica Editions Inc., editorial staff, 2001-; Tight-rope Books, founder and publisher. Publications: Red Promises, 2001; In the Silence Absence Makes, 2004; Human Cannonball: Poems, 2005; The Hair Wreath: And Other Stories, 2010; Artistic License, forthcoming; Love and Other Infidelities, forthcoming. Contributor of to periodicals. Address: Tight-rope Books, 602 Markham St., Postal Sta. P, Toronto, ON M6G 2L8, Canada. Online address: misshalli@netzero.com

VILLUM, Kjartan. See **FLOEGSTAD, Kjartan.**

VINCENT, Andrew. British/Welsh (born Wales), b. 1951. Genres: Philoso-phy, Politics/Government, Essays. Career: University of Salford, lecturer in politics, 1977-78; Nottingham Trent University, lecturer in politics, 1978-79; University of Wales, College of Cardiff, lecturer, 1979-90, senior lecturer in politics, 1990-94, reader in political theory, 1994-97, professor of political theory, 1997-2001; Cardiff University, professor of political theory, Collin-gwood and British Idealism Centre, co-director; University of Sheffield, professor of MA in political theory, 2001-, Centre for Political Ideologies, director; Australian National University, visiting fellow; Chinese University, visiting fellow. Writer. Publications: (With R. Plant) Philosophy, Politics, and Citizenship: The Life and Thought of the British Idealists, 1984; Theories of the State, 1987; Modern Political Ideologies, 1992, 3rd ed., 2009; (with D. Boucher) A Radical Hegelian: The Political and Social Philosophy of Henry Jones, 1993; (with D. Boucher) Pure Citizenship: The Contribution of Henry Jones to Philosophical and Political Argument in Britain, 1880-1922, 1993; (with D. Boucher) British Idealism and Political Theory, 2000; Nationalism and Particularity, 2002; The Nature of Political Theory, 2004; Politics of Human Rights, 2010; (with D. Boucher) British Idealism: A Guide for the Perplexed, 2012. EDITOR: (with M. George) The Philosophical Propaedeu-tic, 1986; (and contrib.) The Philosophy of T.H. Green (essays), 1986; Po-litical Theory: Tradition and Diversity, 1997. Works appear in anthologies. Address: Sheffield University, Arts Twr., Sheffield, SY S10 2TN, England. Online address: andrew.vincent@sheffield.ac.uk

VINCENT, Edgar. American (born United States) Genres: Biography, His-tory, Autobiography/Memoirs. Career: Imperial Chemical Industries, senior manager, now retired. Writer. Publications: Nelson: Love and Fame, 2003; (co-author) The Trafalgar Companion, 2005; (with T.G. Dickson) A Hand-book To Modern Greek, 2007. Address: c/o Author Mail, Yale University Press, 302 Temple St., PO Box 209040, New Haven, CT 06511-8909, U.S.A.

VINCENT, Erin. Australian (born Australia), b. 1969?. Genres: Novels, Psychology, Children's Fiction, Young Adult Fiction. Career: Author and actor. Publications: Grief Girl: My True Story, 2007. Contributor to periodi-cals. Address: Australia. Online address: erin@griefgirl.com

VINCENT, Isabel. Canadian (born Canada), b. 1965?. Genres: Young Adult Non-fiction, Biography, Autobiography/Memoirs. Career: Globe and Mail, reporter, Latin American Bureau Chief, 1991-95; National Post, investigative reporter. Publications: See No Evil: The Strange Case of Christine Lamont and David Spencer, 1995; Hitler's Silent Partners: Swiss Banks, Nazi Gold and the Pursuit of Justice, 1997; Bodies and Souls: The Tragic Plight of Three Jewish Women Forced into Prostitution in the Americas, 1860 to 1939, 2005; Gilded Lily: Lily Safra, The Making of One of the World's Wealthiest Wid-ows, 2010. Address: National Post, 300-1450 Don Mills Rd., Don Mills, ON M3B 3R5, Canada.

VINCENT, John James. British (born England), b. 1929. Genres: Interna-tional Relations/Current Affairs, Race Relations, Theology/Religion, Urban Studies. Career: Manchester and Salford Mission, minister, 1956-62; Ro-chdale Mission, superintend minister, 1962-69; British Council of Churches Commission on Defence and Disarmament, member, 1963-65, 1969-73; Ashram Community, leader, 1967-; University of Sheffield, Department of Biblical Studies, honorary lecturer, 1990-, British Liberation Theology Insti-tute, coordinator, 1990-, Doctoral Program in Contextual, Urban and Libera-tion Theologies, supervisor, 1993-, Urban Theology Unit, director, 1970-97, emeritus director and director of doctoral research degree programme, 1997-;

Sheffield Inner City Ecumenical Mission, superintendent minister, 1970-97; Alliance of Radical Methodists, founding member and chairman, 1971-74; New City Journal, editor, 1972-; Drew University, visiting professor, 1977; Guardian, contributor, 1985-; Methodist Church, president, 1989-90; University of Birmingham, Doctoral Program in Contextual, Urban and Liberation Theologies, supervisor, 2003-, Department of Theology, honorary lecturer, 2003-; St Deiniol's Library, fellow, 2003. **Publications:** Christ in a Nuclear World, 1962; (trans.) W.G. Kummel: Man in the New Testament, 1963; Christ and Our Stewardship, 1963; Christian Nuclear Perspective, 1964; Christ and Methodism, 1965; Here I Stand, 1967; Secular Christ, 1968; The Working Christ, 1968; The Race Race, 1970; The Jesus Thing, 1973; The Jesus Thing Workbook, 1973; Disciple and Lord, 1975; Alternative Church, 1976; Alternative Journeys, 1979; Inner City Issues, 1980; Starting All Over Again, 1981; Into the City, 1982; OK Let's Be Methodists, 1984; Radical Jesus, 1986, rev. ed., 2004; (with J.D. Davies) Mark at Work, 1986; Britain in the 90's, 1989; Gospel in the 90's, 1990; Discipleship in the 90's, 1991; Liberation Theology from the Inner City, 1992; Gospel from the City, 1997; Hope from the City, 2000; Journey: Explorations into Discipleship, 2004; (with W. Wooley) The Ethical Foundations of Socialism: The Influence of William Temple and R.H. Tawney on New Labour, 2007; (with N.J. Tro and E. Livingston) Chemistry: A Molecular Approach, 2008; (with J.W. Rogerson) City in Biblical Perspective, 2009; A Lifestyle of Sharing, 2009; (M.D. Hooker) The Drama of Mark, 2010. EDITOR: Stirrings: Essays Christian and Radical, 1977; Liberation Theology, U.K., 1995; Methodist Report on the Cities, 1997; Liberation Spirituality, 1999; Bible and Practice, 2001; Faithfulness in the City, 2003; (with J. Reiger) Methodist and Radical, 2004; Mark: Gospel of Action, 2006; Primitive Christianity, 2007; Stilling the Storm, 2011. **Address:** 178 Abbeyfield Rd., Sheffield, S4 7AY, England.

VINCENT, John (Russell). British (born England), b. 1937. **Genres:** History, Politics/Government, Biography, Humanities, Politics/Government, Social Sciences. **Career:** University of Cambridge, lecturer in modern British history, 1958-70, fellow of Peterhouse College, 1962-70; University of East Anglia, visiting professor, 1970; University of Bristol, professor of modern history, 1970-84, professor of history, 1984; The Times, columnist; The Sun, columnist. Writer. **Publications:** The Formation of the Liberal Party, 1857-68, 1966; Pollbooks: How Victorians Voted, 1967; (with A.B. Cooke) The Governing Passion: Cabinet Government and Party Politics in Britain, 1885-69, 1974; Gladstone and Ireland, 1979; The Later Derby Diaries: Home Rule, Liberal Unionism, and Aristocratic Life in Late Victorian England, 1981; Disraeli, 1990; Derby Diaries, 1869-1878, 1995; An Intelligent Person's Guide to History, 1996. EDITOR: (with A.B. Cooke) Lord Carlingford's Journal: Reflections of A Cabinet Minister, 1885, 1971; McCalmont's Parliamentary Poll Book: British Election Results, 1832-1918, 1971; Disraeli, Derby and The Conservative Party: Journals And Memoirs Of Edward Henry, Lord Stanley, 1849-1869, 1978; The Crawford Papers: The Journals of David Lindsay, Twenty-Seventh Earl Of Crawford And Tenth Earl of Balcarres (1871-1940), During The Years 1892 to 1940, 1984; Selection from the Diaries of Edward Henry Stanly, 15th Earl of Derby (1826-93): Between September 1969 and March 1878, 1994; Diaries of Edward Henry Stanley, 15th Earl of Derby (1826-93) between 1878 and 1893: A Selection, 2003. **Address:** 13 Woodland Rd., Bristol, GL BS8 1TB, England.

VINCENT, Norah. American (born United States), b. 1969?. **Genres:** Adult Non-fiction, Travel/Exploration, Medicine/Health. **Career:** Los Angeles Times, syndicated columnist; Baltimore Sun, contributor; Salon.com, bi-weekly columnist, 2001; Village Voice, writer of higher education column, 1999-2001; Foundation for the Defense of Democracies, senior fellow, 2001-03. Freelance writer and journalist. **Publications:** NONFICTION: Self-Made Man: One Woman's Journey into Manhood and Back Again, 2006; Self-Made Man: My Year Disguised as a Man, 2006; Voluntary Madness: My Year Lost and Found in the Loony Bin, 2008. OTHERS: (with C. Conway) The Instant Intellectual: The Quick and Easy Guide to Sounding Smart and Cultured, 1998; Thy Neighbor, 2012. Contributor of articles to periodicals. **Address:** c/o Author Mail, Viking Publicity, 375 Hudson St., New York, NY 10014-3658, U.S.A. **Online address:** norahvincent@gmail.com

VINCENT, Rachel. American (born United States), b. 1978?. **Genres:** Novels. **Career:** Fiction writer. **Publications:** SHIFTERS SERIES: YOUNG-ADULT NOVELS: Stray, 2007; Rogue, 2008; Prey, 2009; Pride, 2009; Shift, 2010; Alpha, 2010. SOUL SCREAMERS NOVEL SERIES: My

Soul to Take, 2009; My Soul to Save, 2010; My Soul to Keep, 2010; My Soul to Steal, 2011. **Address:** San Antonio, TX , U.S.A. **Online address:** rachel@rachelvincent.com

VINCENZI, Penny. British/American (born United States), b. 1939. **Genres:** Novels, Adult Non-fiction, Children's Fiction, Young Adult Fiction, Young Adult Non-fiction. **Career:** Vogue, junior secretary, secretary; Tatler, junior secretary, secretary; Mirror, secretary, personal assistant; Daily Mirror, fashion and beauty writer; Nova, fashion editor; Woman's Own, beauty editor; Looking Good, co-founder; Options, deputy editor. **Publications:** NON FICTION: The Compleat Liar, 1977; There's One Born Every Minute: A Survival Guide for Parents, 1984; Taking Stock: Over 75 Years of the OXO Cube, 1985. SPOILS OF TIME TRILOGY: No Angel, 2000; Something Dangerous, 2001; Into Temptation, 2002. NOVELS: Old Sins, 1989; Wicked Pleasures, 1992; An Outrageous Affair, 1993; Another Woman, 1994; Forbidden Places, 1995; The Glimpses, 1996; The Dilemma, 1996; Windfall, 1997; Almost a Crime, 1999; Sheer Abandon, 2005; An Absolute Scandal, 2007; The Best of Times, 2009; The Decision, 2011. Contributor to periodicals. **Address:** Overlook Press, 141 Wooster St., New York, NY 10012-3163, U.S.A. **Online address:** pennyvincenzi@headline.co.uk

VINE, Barbara. *See* RENDELL, Ruth.

VINES, Lois Davis. American (born United States), b. 1939. **Genres:** Literary Criticism And History, Language/Linguistics, History, Biography, Military/Defense/Arms Control. **Career:** Ohio University, instructor in French, 1963-66, instructor, 1969-73, assistant professor, 1973-81, associate professor, 1981-91, professor of French, 1991-, James S. Reid professor of humanities, The Charles J. Ping Institute, professor of humanities, professor of French, 1994-; International Center for Language Studies, instructor, 1968-69. Writer. **Publications:** MONOGRAPH: A Guide to Language Camps in the United States, 1980, vol. II, 1983; (co-ed.) Toward Excellence in Foreign Language Education, 1992; Foreign Language Requirements at Ohio Colleges and Universities, 1993. OTHERS: Valéry and Poe: A Literary Legacy, 1992; (ed.) Poe Abroad: Influence, Reputation, Affinities, 1999; (ed.) POW's Memoir of the First World War: The Other Ordeal, 2004. Works appear in anthologies. Contributor of articles to journals. **Address:** Department of Modern Languages, The Charles J. Ping Institute, Ohio University, Rm. 267, Gordy Hall, Trisolini House, Athens, OH 45701, U.S.A. **Online address:** vinesl@ohio.edu

VINEY, Donald Wayne. American (born United States), b. 1953. **Genres:** Philosophy, Race Relations, Education, Theology/Religion, Politics/Government. **Career:** East Central University, part-time instructor in English, 1982-84; University of Oklahoma, adjunct lecturer in philosophy, 1982-84; Pittsburg State University, Department of Social Sciences, assistant professor, 1984-89, associate professor, 1989-96, professor of philosophy, 1996-, university professor; The Practice of Social Science and History, co-editor, 1990-95; Midwest Quarterly, editor-in-chief, 1991; Universitas, editor, 1996; Logos-Sophia, editor-in-chief and founder, 1988. **Publications:** Charles Hartshorne and the Existence of God, 1985; Questions of Value: Readings for Basic Philosophy, 1989, rev. ed. as Questions of Value: Beginning Readings for Philosophy, 1998; A Philosopher Looks at the Bible, 1992; Logic for Nonvulcans: Introduction to Logic, 1997; A Brief Guide to Logic and Critical Thinking for Nonvulcans, 1998; (ed. and intro.) Translation of Works of Jules Lequyer, 1998; Jules Lequyer's Abel and Abel Followed by Incidents in the Life and Death of Jules Lequyer, 1999; (ed. with Jincheol O.) Creative Experiencing: A Philosophy of Freedom, 2011. Contributor of articles to journals. **Address:** Department of Social Sciences, Pittsburg State University, 412G Russ Hall, 1701 S Broadway, Pittsburg, KS 66762-3023, U.S.A. **Online address:** dviney@pittstate.edu

VINEY, Ethna. Irish (born Ireland), b. 1933. **Genres:** Essays, History, Sex, Social Sciences, Psychology, Biology. **Career:** Independent pharmacist, 1959-61; Westward Productions, managing director, producer, 1966-76, director. Writer. **Publications:** (With M. Viney) Another Life Again, 1981; Ancient Wars: Sexuality and Oppression, 1989; A Dozen Lips, 1994; Survival or Salvation, 1994; Dancing to Different Tunes: Sexuality and Its Misconceptions, 1996; (with M. Viney) A Wildlife Narrative: Eye on Nature, 1999; (with M. Viney) Ireland's Ocean: A Natural History, 2008. Contributor to periodicals. **Address:** Thallabawn, Carrowniskey PO, Westport, MA 4, Ireland. **Online address:** viney@anu.ie

VINEYARD, Jerry D. American (born United States), b. 1935. **Genres:**

Earth Sciences, Travel/Exploration, Sciences. **Career:** Metropolitan College, instructor, 1960-63; Missouri Department of Natural Resources, information services director, 1963-, deputy state geologist, through 1997, information services chief. Writer. **Publications:** Guidebook to the Geology between Springfield and Branson, Missouri, Emphasizing Stratigraphy and Cavern Development, 1967; (with J.W. Koenig and B.L. Happel) Bibliography of the Geology of Missouri, 1955-1965, 1967; (with W.C. Hayes) Environmental Geology in Town and Country, 1969; (with G.L. Feder) Springs of Missouri, 1974; (comp.) Geological Society of America 1989 Field Trip Guidebook, 1989; (with T.R. Beveridge) Geologic Wonders and Curiosities of Missouri, 1990; (with A.G. Unklesbay) Missouri Geology: Three Billion Years of Volcanoes, Seas, Sediments, and Erosion, 1992; Water Resource Sharing: The Realities of Interstate Rivers, 1997. **Address:** Missouri Department of Natural Resources, PO Box 176, Jefferson City, MO 65102, U.S.A. **Online address:** jelenvnyard@aol.com

VINGE, Vernor (Steffen). American (born United States), b. 1944. **Genres:** Science Fiction/Fantasy, Literary Criticism And History, Novels. **Career:** San Diego State University, assistant professor, 1972-78, associate professor of mathematics, 1978-2000, Department of Computer Science, professor, through 2002, professor emeritus, 2002-; Global Business Network, consultant and forecaster. Writer. **Publications:** Grimm's World, 1969, rev. ed. as Tatja Grimm's World, 1987; The Witling, 1976; Peace War, 1984; Marooned in Realtime, 1986; True Names and Other Dangers, 1987; Threats and Other Promises, 1988; A Fire Upon the Deep, 1991; Across Real Time, 1991; A Deepness in the Sky, 1999; Fast Times at Fairmont High, 2002; The Cookie Monster, 2004; Rainbows End, 2006; The Children of the Sky, 2011. **Address:** c/o Sharon Jarvis, Toad Hall Inc., PO Box 2090, Laceyville, PA 18623, U.S.A. **Online address:** vinge@cs.sdsu.edu

VINIKAS, Vincent. American (born United States), b. 1951. **Genres:** Communications/Media, History, Race Relations, Cultural/Ethnic Topics, Film. **Career:** University of Arkansas, assistant professor, 1983-89, professor, 1989-; Columbia University, president's fellow, 1974-75, university reader, 1975-76; Smithsonian Institution, Newberry Library, conferee, 1985; Educational Testing Service, Advanced Placement History Examinations, reader, 1994; NEH Institute on Public History, staff, 1984; NEH Institute on the Thirties, staff, 1992; NEH Institute on History of Death, staff, 1998; Sandage Symposium on History of Advertising, staff, 2000. Consultant, historian and writer. **Publications:** Soft Soap, Hard Sell: American Hygiene in an Age of Advertisement, 1992. Contributor of articles to periodicals. **Address:** Department of History, University of Arkansas, SH 604 B, Little Rock, AR 72204, U.S.A. **Online address:** vxvinikas@ualr.edu

VINJAMURI, David. American (born United States), b. 1964. **Genres:** Marketing, Business/Trade/Industry, Advertising/Public Relations. **Career:** Johnson & Johnson, marketing executive; Coca-Cola, marketing executive; DoubleClick, marketing executive; ThirdWay Brand Trainers, founder and president; New York University, adjunct professor of marketing. Writer. **Publications:** Accidental Branding: How Ordinary People Build Extraordinary Brands, 2008. Contributor to periodicals. **Address:** ThirdWay Brand Trainers, 804 W 180th St., Ste. 62, New York, NY 10033, U.S.A.

VIOLA, Lynne. American (born United States), b. 1955. **Genres:** History, Social Sciences, Politics/Government, Humanities. **Career:** Princeton University, lecturer in history, 1983-84; State University of New York, assistant professor of history, 1985-88; Boston College, visiting professor of history, 1985; University of Toronto, assistant professor, 1988-96, Department of History, professor, 1996-. Writer. **Publications:** The Best Sons of the Fatherland: Workers in the Vanguard of Soviet Collectivization, 1987; Peasant Rebels Under Stalin: Collectivization and the Culture of Peasant Resistance, 1996; Kollektivizatsiia i krest ianskoe Soprotivlenie na Ukraine: noiabr 1929-mart 1930 g.g., 1997; (co-author) Riazanskaia Derevnia v 1929-1930 gg.: khronika golovokruzheniia: dokumenty i materialy, 1998; (co-author) Tragediia Sovetskoĭ Derevni: Kollektivizatsiia Iraskulachivanie: Dokumenty i Materialy v 5 Tomakh, 1927-1939, 1999; Role of the OGPU in Dekulakization, Mass Deportations, and Special Resettlement in 1930, 2000; (co-ed.) War Against the Peasantry, 1927-1930: The Tragedy of the Soviet Countryside, 2005; The Unknown Gulag: The Lost World Of Stalin's Special Settlements, 2007. EDITOR: (with S. Fitzpatrick and contrib.) A Researcher's Guide to Sources on Soviet Social History in the 1930s, 1990; (with B. Farnsworth) Russian Peasant Women, 1992; Contending with Stalinism: Soviet Power and Popular Resistance in the 1930s, 2002. Contributor journals. **Address:** Department of

History, University of Toronto, Rm. 2074, Sidney Smith Hall, 100 St. George St., UC D-304, MU 112N, Toronto, ON M5S 3G3, Canada. **Online address:** lynne.viola@utoronto.ca

VIORST, Judith. American (born United States), b. 1931. **Genres:** Novels, Children's Fiction, Poetry, Psychology, Sciences, Children's Non-fiction, Human Relations/Parenting, Essays, Humor/Satire. **Career:** True Confessions, secretary, 1953-55; Women's Wear Daily, secretary, 1955-57; William Morrow (publisher), children's book editor, 1957-60; Science Service, science book editor, writer, 1960-63; Redbook Magazine, contributing editor, columnist, 1968-96; Washington Star Syndicate, columnist, 1970-72. **Publications:** (Ed. with S. Moore) Wonderful World of Science, 1961; Projects: Space, 1962; 150 Science Experiments, Step-by-Step, 1963; The Natural World: A Guide to North American Wildlife, 1965; The Village Square, 1965; The Changing Earth, 1967; Sunday Morning, 1968; It's Hard to Be Hip over Thirty and Other Tragedies of Married Life, 1968; I'll Fix Anthony, 1969; Try It Again, Sam: Safety When You Walk, 1970; (with M. Viorst) The Washington, D.C., Underground Gourmet, 1970; People and Other Aggravations, 1971; The Tenth Good Thing about Barney, 1971; Alexander and the Terrible, Horrible, No Good, Very Bad Day, 1972; Yes, Married: A Saga of Love and Complaint (prose pieces), 1972; My Mama Says There Aren't Any Zombies, Ghosts, Vampires, Creatures, Demons, Monsters, Fiends, Goblins, or Things, 1973; Rosie and Michael, 1974; How Did I Get to Be Forty and Other Atrocities, 1976; A Visit from St. Nicholas to a Liberated Household, 1976; Alexander Who Used to Be Rich Last Sunday, 1978; Love and Guilt and the Meaning of Life, Etc., 1979; If I Were in Charge of the World and Other Worries, 1981; Necessary Losses, 1986; When Did I Stop Being 20 Other Injustices, 1987; The Good-Bye Book, 1988; Forever Fifty and Other Negotiations (poetry), 1989; Earrings!, 1990; Murdering Mr. Monti: A Merry Little Tale of Sex and Violence (novel), 1994; The Alphabet from Z to A (with Much Confusion on the Way), 1994; Alexander, Who's Not (Do You Hear Me? I Mean It!) Going to Move, 1995; Sad Underwear and Other Complications: More Poems for Children and Their Parents, 1995; Absolutely Positively Alexander: The Complete Stories 1997; Imperfect Control: Our Lifelong Struggles with Power and Surrender, 1998; You're Officially a Grown-Up: The Graduate's Guide to Freedom, Responsibility, Happiness and Personal Hygiene, 1999; Super-Completely and Totally the Messiest, 2000; Suddenly Sixty and Other Shocks of Later Life, 2000; Grown-Up Marriage: What We Know, Wish We had Known, and Still Need to Know about being Married, 2003; I'm Too Young to be Seventy: And Other Delusions, 2005; Just in Case, 2006; Alexander and the Wonderful, Marvelous, Excellent, Terrific Ninety Days: An Almost Completely Honest Account of What Happened to Our Family When Our Youngest Son, His Wife, Their Baby, Their Toddler and Their Five-Year-Old Came to Live With Us for Three Months, 2007; Nobody Here but Me, 2008; Lulu and the Brontosaurus, 2010; Unexpectedly Eighty: And Other Adaptations, 2010; Lulu Walks the Dogs, 2012. Contributor of articles to periodicals. **Address:** c/o Robert Lescher, Lescher & Lescher Ltd., 47 E 19th St., 3rd Fl., New York, NY 10003-1323, U.S.A.

VIORST, Milton. American (born United States), b. 1930. **Genres:** International Relations/Current Affairs, Politics/Government. **Career:** Bergen Record, reporter, 1955-56; Newark Star Ledger, reporter, 1956-57; Washington Post, reporter, 1957-61; New York Post, correspondent, 1961-64; Fund for Investigative Journalism, chairman, 1969-79; Washington Star, syndicated political columnist, 1971-75; International Letter, correspondent, 1976-86; New Yorker Magazine, staff writer and correspondent, 1988-93; Princeton University, Ferris professor of journalism and public policy, 1995-96. **Publications:** Liberalism: A Guide to its Past, Present and Future in American Politics, 1963; Hostile Allies: FDR and de Gaulle, 1964; Fall from Grace: The Republican Party and the Puritan Ethic, 1968, rev. ed., 1971. (with Judith) The Washington, D.C., Underground Gourme, 1970; (with C.P. Anderson) Outsider in the Senate; Senator Clinton Anderson's Memoirs, 1970; Hustlers and Heroes: An American Political Panorama, 1971; Citizen Poor of the 1960's: An Examination into a Social Experiment, 1977; Fire in the Streets: America in the 1960's, 1980; UNRWA and Peace in the Middle East, 1984; Sands of Sorrow: Israel's Journey from Independence, 1987; Reaching for the Olive Branch: UNRWA and the Palestinians, 1989; Sand Castles: The Arabs in Search of the Modern World, 1994; In the Shadow of the Prophet: The Struggle for the Soul of Islam, 1998; What Shall I Do with This People? Jews and the Fractious Politics of Judaism, 2002; Fundamentalisms and the Conflicts in the Middle East, 2003; Storm from the East: The Struggle Between the Arab World and The Christian West, 2006. EDITOR: The Great Documents of Western Civilization, 1965; Making a Difference: The Peace

Corps at Twenty-five, 1986. Contributor to magazines and newspapers. **Address:** 3432 Ashley Terr. NW, Washington, DC 20008, U.S.A. **Online address:** mviorst@aol.com

VIPOND, Mary. Canadian (born Canada), b. 1943?. **Genres:** Communications/Media, History. **Career:** Canadian Historical Association, president, 2001-03; Concordia University, Department of History, professor, through 2008, now distinguished professor emeritus, Centre for Broadcasting Studies, fellow. Writer. **Publications:** The Mass Media in Canada, 1989, 4th ed. 2011; Listening In: The First Decade of Canadian Broadcasting, 1922-1932, 1992. **Address:** Department of History, Concordia University, Sir George Williams Campus, Rm. LB-1001.03, McConnell Bldg., 1400 de Maisonneuve Blvd. W, Montreal, QC H3G 1M8, Canada. **Online address:** vipond@alcor.concordia.ca

VIRDEN, Jenel. American/British (born England), b. 1954?. **Genres:** History. **Career:** University of Hull, senior lecturer in American history, 1992-, head of department; European Association of American Studies, secretary general. Writer. **Publications:** Good-bye Piccadilly: British War Brides in America, 1996; (ed. with J. Jařab and M. Arbeit) America in the Course of Human Events: Presentations and Interpretations, 2006; Americans and the Wars of the Twentieth Century, 2008. Contributor to books and periodicals. **Address:** Department of American Studies, University of Hull, Cottingham Rd., Hull, HB HU6 7RX, England. **Online address:** j.virden@hull.ac.uk

VIRGO, Seán. Canadian/Maltese (born Malta), b. 1940?. **Genres:** Novellas/Short Stories, Poetry, Novels, Essays, Literary Criticism And History. **Career:** University of Victoria, chancellor, writer-in-residence; Haig-Brown Institute, writer-in-residence. **Publications:** POETRY: Sea Change, 1971; Pieces for the Old Earth Man, 1973; (with S. Musgrave) Kiskatinaw Songs, 1977; Deathwatch on Skidegate Narrows and Other Poems, 1979; Selected Poems, 1991. SHORT STORIES: White Lies and Other Fictions, 1980; Through the Eyes of a Cat: Irish Stories, 1983; Wormwood: Fictions, 1989; Waking in Eden, 1990; (ed.) What Is Already Known, 1995; The Scream of the Butterfly, 1996; A Traveller Came By: Stories About Dying, 2000; Begging Questions, 2006. OTHERS: Island, 1975; Vagabonds, 1979; Selakhi, 1987; (ed.) Selected Verse of Thomas Darcy McGee, 1992; Telegony, 1998; (ed.) The Eye in the Thicket: Essays at a Natural History, 2002. **Address:** Thistledown Press, 633 Main St., Saskatoon, SK S7H 0J8, Canada.

VISCONTI, Tony. American (born United States), b. 1944. **Genres:** Autobiography/Memoirs, Biography, Music. **Career:** Essex Music Ltd., house record producer, 1967-69; freelance record producer, 1969-71; Good Earth Productions Ltd., managing director, 1972; Roar Music Ltd., director, 1988; Unique Records Ltd., director and label head, 1988; independent producer, 1988-. Writer. **Publications:** Tony Visconti: Bowie, Bolan and the Brooklyn Boy: The Autobiography, 2008. **Address:** Roar Music Ltd., 59 Dean St., London, GL WIV SHH, England. **Online address:** antonyv@earthlink.net

VISCUSI, Robert. American (born United States), b. 1941. **Genres:** Adult Non-fiction, Poetry. **Career:** New York University, teaching fellow, 1964-68, visiting assistant professor of Italian, 1980; City University of New York, Brooklyn College, adjunct lecturer, 1968-70, 1974-75; lecturer, 1973-74, 1979-80, instructor, 1980, assistant professor, 1981-83, associate professor, 1984-85, professor, 1986-, Claire and Leonard Tow professor of English, 1999-2000, Humanities Institute, faculty associate, 1981-82, director, 1982-88, executive officer, 1988-89; Kean College, instructor, 1970-73, adjunct instructor, 1975-78; Saint Peter's College, adjunct instructor, 1975-78; University of Paris, visiting professor, 1986; Ethyl R. Wolfe Institute for the Humanities, executive officer, 1989-; Italian American Writers Association, president. Writer. **Publications:** Max Beerbohm; or, The Dandy Dante: Re-reading with Mirrors, 1986; (ed.) Browning Institute Studies, 1988: Victorian Learning, 1989; An Oration upon the Most Recent Death of Christopher Columbus (poetry), 1993, 3rd ed., 1998; Astoria (novel), 1995, 2nd ed., 2002; A New Geography of Time (poetry), 2004; Buried Caesars, and Other Secrets of Italian American Writing, 2006. Contributor of books to journals. **Address:** Department of English, Wolfe Institute for the Humanities, Brooklyn College, 2308 Boylan Hall, Brooklyn, NY 11210, U.S.A. **Online address:** rviscusi@brooklyn.cuny.edu

VISCUSI, W. Kip. American (born United States), b. 1949. **Genres:** Business/Trade/Industry, Economics, History, Institutions/Organizations. **Career:** Harvard University, Harvard Law School, instructor in public policy, 1973-76, John F. Cogan, Jr. professor of law and economics, 1996-2006, Harvard Law School, Olin visiting professor of law and economics, 1995, Program on Empirical Legal Studies, director, John F. Kennedy School of Government, professor; Northwestern University, assistant professor, 1976-78, associate professor, 1979-81, professor of economics, 1985-88; Duke University, professor of business administration, 1981-85, George G. Allen professor of economics, 1988-96; President's Council on Wage and Price Stability, deputy director, 1979-81; National Bureau of Economic Research, research associate, 1978-88, 1995-; University of Chicago, John M. Olin visiting research professor, 1985-86; American Law Institute Project on Enterprise Liability for Personal Injury, chief economic consultant, 1986-87, associate reporter, 1988-91; Vanderbilt University Law School, university distinguished professor of law, economics and management, 2006-, Ph.D. Program in Law and Economics, co-director. Writer. **Publications:** Extending the Applicability of Stochastic Dominance Decision Rules, 1972; (with R. Berkman) Damming the West, 1973; Welfare of the Elderly, 1979; Employment Hazards, 1979; Risk by Choice, 1983; Regulating Consumer Product Safety, 1984; (co-author) Learning about Risk, 1987; (with M.J. Moore) Compensation Mechanisms for Job Risks, 1990; (co-author) Enterprise Responsibility for Personal Injury, vol. I: The Institutional Framework, vol. II: Approaches to Legal and Institutional Change, 1991; Reforming Products Liability, 1991; Smoking: Making the Risky Decision, 1991; (with J. Vernon and J.E. Harrington Jr.) The Economics of Regulation and Antitrust, 1992, 4th ed., 2005; (with W.A. Magat) Informational Approaches to Regulation, 1992; Fatal Tradeoffs, 1992; Product-Risk Labeling, 1993; (ed.) Mortality Costs of Regulatory Expenditures, 1994; Risk, Regulation and Responsibility, 1996; Rational Risk Policy, 1998; (with J.T. Hamilton) Calculating Risks?, 1999; (with R.W. Hahn and R.W.Lutter) Do Federal Regulations Reduce Mortality?, 2000; (with M.J. Moore) Product Liability Entering the Twenty-first Century: The U.S. Perspective, 2001; (ed.) Regulation through Litigation, 2002; Smoke-filled Rooms: A Postmortem on the Tobacco Deal, 2002; (ed.) Risks of Terrorism, 2003; (with T. Gayer) Classics in Risk Management, 2004; (with J.M. Vernon and J.E. Harrington, Jr.) Economics of Regulation and Antitrust, 2004; Societal Implications of Risk, forthcoming. Contributor to periodicals. **Address:** Law School, Vanderbilt University, Rm. 280, 131 21st Ave. S, Nashville, TN 37203-1181, U.S.A. **Online address:** kip.viscusi@vanderbilt.edu

VISOTZKY, Burton L. American (born United States), b. 1951. **Genres:** Theology/Religion, Bibliography, History, Literary Criticism And History, Young Adult Fiction. **Career:** Rabbi, 1977-; Jewish Theological Seminary of America (JTSA), faculty, 1977-, fellow, 1977-78, 1978-79, founding rabbi, 1984-85, associate professor of Talmud and Rabbinics, 1988-, professor, Nathan and Janet Appleman professor of midrash and interreligious studies, 1988-, associate dean of graduate school, 1991-96, Nathan and Janet Appleman chair of midrash and interreligious studies, Louis Finkelstein Institute for Religious and Social Studies, director; Union Theological Seminary, visiting lecturer, 1980; University of Cambridge, Clare Hall, fellow, 1985-86; Princeton Theological Seminary, visiting lecturer, 1987-89; Russian State University of the Humanities, visiting professor, 1994; Pontifical Gregorian University, master visiting professor. Writer. **Publications:** Louis Finkelstein: A Bibliography, 1977; Midrash Mishle (in Hebrew), 1990; Reading the Book: Making the Bible a Timeless Text, 1991; The Midrash on Proverbs, 1992; Fathers of the World: Essays on Rabbinic and Patristic Literature, 1995; (with C. Braun) Confronting Death: Four Stories of Consolation, 1995; The Genesis of Ethics, 1996; The Road to Redemption: Lessons From Exodus on Leadership and Community, 1998; (ed. and contrib.) From Mesopotamia to Modernity: Ten Introductions to Jewish History and Literature, 1999; (contrib.) Ot Avraama do sovremennosti, 2002; Golden Bells and Pomegranates: Studies in Midrash Leviticus Rabbah, 2003; Ginze Shekhter, 2003; Delightful Compendium of Consolation: A Fabulous Tale of Romance, Adventure and Faith in the Medieval Mediterranean, 2007; Sage Tales, 2011. Contributor of articles to journals. **Address:** Department of Talmud & Rabbinics, The Jewish Theological Seminary, Brush 511, 3080 Broadway, New York, NY 10027, U.S.A. **Online address:** buvisotzky@jtsa.edu

VISRAM, Rozina. British/Tanzanian (born Tanzania, United Republic of), b. 1939. **Genres:** Cultural/Ethnic Topics, Education, History, Women's Studies And Issues, Literary Criticism And History, Social Sciences. **Career:** History teacher, 1964-75; University of London, Institute of Education, Centre for Multicultural Education, fellow, 1983-85; Centre for Urban Education, Community Division, deputy director, 1988-90; Museum of London, researcher; University of North London, visiting lecturer. Writer. **Publications:** Ayahs, Lascars, and Princes: Indians in Britain, 1700-1947, 1986; Indians in Britain,

1987; Women in India and Pakistan: The Struggle for Independence from British Rule, 1992; Asians in Britain: 400 Years of History, 2002. Contributor to books and periodicals. **Address:** Cambridge University Press, Edinburgh Bldg., Shaftesbury Rd., Cambridge, CB CB2 8RU, England.

VISSON, Lynn. American (born United States), b. 1945. **Genres:** Food And Wine, Art/Art History, Language/Linguistics, Novellas/Short Stories, Translations. **Career:** Harvard University, teaching fellow, 1969; Barnard College, instructor in Russian, 1969-70; Columbia University, instructor, 1970-71, assistant professor of Russian, 1972-76; Bryn Mawr College, assistant professor of Russian, 1976-78; Middlebury College Russian Summer School, faculty, 1978; City University of New York, Hunter College, assistant professor of Russian, 1978-79; U.S. Department of State, contract interpreter, 1979-80; United Nations, simultaneous interpreter from Russian and French into English, 1981-2005; Hippocrene Books, consulting editor, editor-in-chief. **Publications:** (Co-author) The Moscow Gourmet: Dining Out in the Capital of the U.S.S.R., 1974; Sergei Esenin: Poet of the Crossroads, 1980; (trans.) Russian Women: Two Stories, 1983; (ed.) Vladimir Visson, Fair Warning: Memoirs of a New York Art Dealer, 1986; (trans.) Reason and Being, 1987; (trans.) Soviet Choreographers in the 1920's, 1990; (ed.) Small Fires: Letters From the Soviet People to Ogonyok Magazine, 1987-1990, 1990; From Russian into English: An Introduction to Simultaneous Interpretation, 1991, rev. ed., 1999; Wedded Strangers: The Challenges of Russian-American Marriages, 1998; The Art of Uzbek Cooking, 1999; The Russian Heritage Cookbook, 2003, rev. ed., 2009; Slova-khameleony i metamorfozy v sovremennom angliiskom iazzyke, 2010. **Address:** Hippocrene Books Inc., 171 Madison Ave., New York, NY 10016, U.S.A. **Online address:** lvisson@aol.com

VISWANATHAN, S(ubrahmanyam). Indian (born India), b. 1933. **Genres:** Literary Criticism And History, Art/Art History, History, Young Adult Fiction. **Career:** Madura College, tutor, 1953-56, lecturer in English, 1958-59; Sri Venkateswara University, lecturer in English, 1959-77; University of Kent, common-wealth staff fellow, 1974-75; University of Hyderabad, reader, 1977-83, professor of English, 1983-95, School of Humanities, dean, 1986-89, head of English department; Queen's University, visiting fellow, 1984-85, UGC national lecturer, 1986-87, emeritus fellow, 1995-97. Writer. **Publications:** The Shakespeare Play as Poem: A Critical Tradition in Perspective, 1980; (ed. with S. Nagarajan) Shakespeare in India, 1987; (ed. with C.T. Indra and T. Sriraman) Critical Essays, 1987; On Shakespeare's Dramaturgy: Word and Stage Image in the Plays, 1993; (ed.) Exploring Shakespeare: The Dynamics of Playmaking, 2005; (with V.V. Acharya) Leverage, Moral Hazard and Liquidity, 2010. Contributor to periodicals. **Address:** 8 Parthasarathypuram Ext., T. Nagar, Chennai, TN 600017, India.

VISWESWARAN, Kamala. American (born United States), b. 1962. **Genres:** Essays. **Career:** Fulbright fellow, 1987-88; University of Texas at Austin, assistant professor of anthropology, 1995-2001, associate professor, 2001-; Cultural Dynamics Journal, North American editor, 2000-05; Nepa School of Social Sciences and Humanities, visiting professor. Writer. **Publications:** Fictions of Feminist Ethnography (essays), 1994; Un/common Cultures: Racism and the Rearticulation of Cultural Difference, 2010; (ed. and intro.) Perspectives on Modern South Asia: A Reader in Culture, History, and Representation, 2011; Family Subjects: An Ethnography of the Female Question in Indian Nationalism, forthcoming. **Address:** Department of Anthropology, University of Texas, SAC 5.138, 1 University Sta., PO Box C3200, Austin, TX 78712, U.S.A. **Online address:** kvis@mail.utexas.edu

VITA-FINZI, Claudio. British/Australian (born Australia), b. 1936. **Genres:** Earth Sciences. **Career:** Cambridge University, St. John's College, research fellow, 1961-64; University College London, lecturer, 1964-88, professor, 1988-2001, professor emeritus, 2001-. Writer. **Publications:** (With J. Aarons) The Useless Land, 1960; (ed.) De bene instituta re publica, 1969; The Mediterranean Valleys, 1969; Recent Earth History, 1973; Archaeological Sites in Their Setting, 1978; (ed. with A. Ozer) Dating Mediterranean Shorelines, 1986; Recent Earth Movements: An Introduction to Neotectonics, 1986; Planet Earth: A Pop-up Guide, 1989; The Power Pop-up Book: Our Planet's Energy Resources: Production, Consumption, Conservation and Innovation, 1991; (ed. with L.A. Owen and I. Stewart) Neotectonics, Recent Advances, 1993; (ed. with L.A. Owen and I. Stewart) Neotectonics and Active Faulting: Papers Presented at the International Conference on Neotectonics, 1993; (ed. with I.S. Stewart) Coastal Tectonics, 1998; Monitoring the Earth, 2002; Planetary Geology, 2005; The Sun: A User's Manual, 2008; (ed. with A.B.

Mainwaring and R. Giegengack) Climate Crises in Human History, 2010. **Address:** University College London, Gower St., London, GL WC1E 6BT, England. **Online address:** cvitafinzi@hotmail.com

VITAL, David. Israeli/British (born England), b. 1927. **Genres:** History, International Relations/Current Affairs, Politics/Government, Theology/Religion. **Career:** Journalist, 1952-54; University of Sussex, lecturer, 1966-68; Bar-Ilan University, associate professor and professor of political science, 1968-72; University of California, visiting professor, 1969; Hebrew University of Jerusalem, visiting professor, 1969-70; Haifa University, professor, 1972-77; Australian National University, visiting fellow, 1974; University of Oxford, Wolfson College, visiting fellow, 1974-75; Tel Aviv University, professor of political science, 1977-95, Nahum Goldmann professor of diplomacy, 1977-95, professor emeritus, 1995-; Dartmouth College, visiting professor, 1981; Institute for Advanced Studies, Jerusalem, visiting fellow, 1981-82; University College London, visiting fellow, 1983-84; Northwestern University, professor of history and Klutznick professor of Jewish civilization, 1987-91. Writer. **Publications:** The Inequality of States: A Study of the Small Power in International Relations, 1967; The Making of British Foreign Policy, 1968; The Survival of Small States: Studies in Small Power/Great Power Conflict, 1971; Medinot Ketanot Be-Mivhan Ha-Kiyum, 1972; The Origins of Zionism, 1975; (co-author) Yiśra'el, dor ha-hithayut, 1979; Zionism: The Formative Years, 1982; Zionism: The Crucial Phase, 1987; The Future of the Jews, 1990; A People Apart: The Jews in Europe, 1789-1939, 1999. **Address:** Department of Political Science, Tel Aviv University, PO Box 39040, Tel Aviv, 69978, Israel. **Online address:** dvital@post.tau.ac.il

VITALI, Julius. American (born United States), b. 1952. **Genres:** How-to Books, Marketing, Art/Art History. **Career:** Photo journalist, 1980-2003; cultural journalist, 1980-2007; writing consultant, 1980-2007; Black Star Press Agency, photographer, 1980-82; Art For Social Change, assistant director, 1983; Hempstead Harbor Gallery, president, 1983, executive director, 1984-87; School Of Visual Arts, adjunct instructor, 1984-85; PA Governors School For The Arts, photography instructor, 1992; August House, director of development, 1992-96; Open Space Gallery, vice president, 1994-97, executive director, 1996-2002; Esma, director of development, 1994-97; Weaversville Intensive Treatment Unit, art instructor, 1997-2002; freelance curator, 2001-04; Saucon News, journalist, 2002-03; I.U. 20, creative therapies counselor, 2002-03; Kidspeace, creative therapies counselor, 2004-05; Lehigh Valley Writer's Academy, executive director, 2004-07; Hunger Through the Arts Foundation, director. Writer. **Publications:** (Contrib.) Terry Niedzialek: Hair Sculpture and its Roots: 36th Annual Contemporary American Art Exhibition, 1991; The Fine Artist's Guide to Marketing and Self-Promotion, 1996, rev. ed., 2003. Contributor to periodicals. **Address:** PO Box 701, Emmaus, PA 18049, U.S.A. **Online address:** vitali@ptd.net

VITALIS, Robert. American (born United States), b. 1955?. **Genres:** History. **Career:** University of Texas, instructor, 1987-88, assistant professor of government, 1988-91; Princeton University, visiting assistant professor of politics, 1990-91; Clark University, assistant professor, 1991-96, associate professor of government, 1996-99; University of Pennsylvania, associate professor of political science, 1999-2008, professor, 2008-, Penn Humanities Forum, fellow, 2000, Middle East Center, director, 2006. Writer. **Publications:** When Capitalists Collide: Business Conflict and the End of Empire in Egypt, 1995; (ed. with M. Al-Rasheed) Counter-narratives: History, Contemporary Society and Politics in Saudi Arabia and Yemen, 2003; America's Kingdom: Mythmaking on the Saudi Oil Frontier, 2007. **Address:** Department of Political Science, University of Pennsylvania, 208 S 37th St., Rm. 217, Philadelphia, PA 19104-6215, U.S.A. **Online address:** rvitalis@sas.upenn.edu

VITEBSKY, Piers. British (born England) **Genres:** Anthropology/Ethnology, Young Adult Non-fiction. **Career:** Agrarian Research and Training Institute, visiting researcher, 1982-93; University of Cambridge, Scott Polar Research Institute, assistant director of research, 1986-, Anthropology and Russian Northern Studies, head, 1986-; MacArthur Foundation project, consultant, 1991-94; European University, Department of Ethnology, secretary, 1998-2000; post-shamanic society, director, 2001-04. Writer. **Publications:** Policy Dilemmas for Unirrigated Agriculture in Southeastern Sri Lanka: A Social Anthropologist's Report on Shifting and Semi-Permanent Cultivation in an Area of Moneragala District, 1984; Dialogues with the Dead: The Discussion of Mortality among the Sora of Eastern India, 1993; The Saami of Lapland, 1994; The Shaman, 1995 as Shamanism, 2001; (with C. Humphrey) Sacred Architecture, 1997; (with M. Kerrigan and A. Lothian) Epics of Early

Civilization, 1998; (with T. Allan) Triumph of the Hero: Greek and Roman Myth, 1998; (with B. Leigh Molyneaux) Sacred Earth, Sacred Stones, 2001; Reindeer People: Living with Animals and Spirits in Siberia (memoir), 2005. **Address:** Scott Polar Research Institute, University of Cambridge, Lensfield Rd., Cambridge, CB2 1ER, England. **Online address:** pv100@cam.ac.uk

VITIELLO, Justin. American (born United States), b. 1941. **Genres:** Novellas/Short Stories, Poetry, Literary Criticism And History, Essays, Translations, Women's Studies And Issues, Adult Non-fiction. **Career:** University of Michigan, assistant professor of comparative literature, 1970-73; Temple University, assistant professor, 1974-80, associate professor, 1980-91, professor of Italian, 1991-2006, professor emeritus, 2006-. Writer. **Publications:** (Trans.) D. Dolci, Creature of Creatures: Selected Poems, 1980; Il carro del pesce di Vanzetti (poems), 1989 as Vanzetti's Fish Cart, 1991; Sicily Within (essay), 1992; (trans.) Italy's Ultramodern, Experimental Lyrics, 1992; Confessions of a Joe Rock (novella), 1992; Poetics and Literature of the Sicilian Diaspora: Studies in Oral History and Story Telling, 1993; Subway Home (poems), 1994; Labyrinths and Volcanoes: Windings through Sicily, 1998; (trans. with L. Bonaffini) G. Rimanelli, Viamerica=The Eyes, 1999; (ed. with A. Serrao and L. Bonaffini) Via Terra: An Anthology of Contemporary Italian Dialect Poetry, 1999; (ed. with M.A. Mannino) Breaking Open: Reflections on Italian American Women's Writing, 2003; Suicide of an Ethnic Poet, 2004; Amapolas y cardos, 2006. Contributor of articles to periodicals. **Address:** Department of French, German, Italian and Slavic Languages, Temple University, 525 Anderson Hall, 1114 W Berks St., Philadelphia, PA 19122-6090, U.S.A. **Online address:** jvitiell@nimbus.ocis.temple.edu

VITTITOW, Mary L(ou). American (born United States), b. 1937. **Genres:** Adult Non-fiction, Children's Non-fiction, Theology/Religion, Crafts, Education. **Career:** Commercial artist, 1954-61; Lowe Elementary School, teacher, 1971-. Writer. **Publications:** SELF-ILLUSTRATED: Games without Losers, 1975; Creative Bible Activities for Children, 1977; Everyday is a Special Day, 1978; Christians Celebrate, 1981; (with S. Liu) Learning Games without Losers, 1985; Fun Things for Kids at Christmas Time, 1991. **Address:** Lowe Elementary School, 210 Oxfordshire Ln., Louisville, KY 40222, U.S.A.

VITZ, Robert C. American (born United States), b. 1938. **Genres:** History, Intellectual History, Local History/Rural Topics. **Career:** Purdue University, assistant professor of history, 1971-72; Northern Kentucky University, assistant professor, 1972-75, associate professor, 1975-88, professor of history, 1988-, Department of History, chair, 1996-; Miami Purchase Association for Historic Preservation, board director, 1976-82; Cincinnati History Museum, consultant; Historic Southwest Ohio, board director, 1984-92, vice-president, 1986-88. Writer. **Publications:** The Queen and the Arts: Cultural Life in Nineteenth-Century Cincinnati, 1989. **Address:** Department of History & Geography, Northern Kentucky University, 415 Landrum Academic Ctr., Landrum 440, Highland Heights, KY 41099, U.S.A. **Online address:** vitz@nku.edu

VIVIANO, Frank. French/American (born United States), b. 1947?. **Genres:** Adult Non-fiction, Mystery/Crime/Suspense. **Career:** Journalist, 1977-; Pacific News Service, reporter; Chronicle, Asia correspondent, through 1990; San Francisco Chronicle, reporter/foreign correspondent-at-large, 1988-2002; Barga News, staff writer; KPIX, columnist; Afar Magazine, contributor. **Publications:** (With S. Silva) The Thrifty Gourmet: 250 Great Dinners in the Bay Area, 1987; (with S. Silva) Exploring the Best Ethnic Restaurants of the Bay Area, 1990; Dispatches from the Pacific Century, 1993; (intro.) In the Balkans, 1995; Blood Washes Blood: A True Story of Love, Murder and Redemption Under the Sicilian Sun, 2001. **Address:** c/o Author Mail, Pocket Books, 1230 Ave. of the Americas, New York, NY 10020, U.S.A. **Online address:** fviviano@sfchronicle.com

VIZENOR, Gerald (Robert). American (born United States), b. 1934. **Genres:** Novels, Novellas/Short Stories, Poetry, Anthropology/Ethnology, History, Literary Criticism And History, Mythology/Folklore, Autobiography/Memoirs, Bibliography, Essays. **Career:** Ramsey County Corrections Authority, group worker, 1957-58; Capital Community Center, roving group worker, 1958; Minnesota Department of Corrections, Minnesota State Reformatory, corrections agent, 1960-61; Minneapolis Tribune, staff writer, 1968-70; Park Rapids Public Schools, teacher trainer, 1971; Lake Forest College, instructor, 1971-73; Bemidji State University, instructor, 1971-73; University of Minnesota, professor of American Indian studies, 1980-87; University of California-Berkeley, lecturer, 1976-80, professor of Native American studies,

1991-, Richard and Rhoda Goldman distinguished professor, 2000-02, now professor emeritus, director of Native American studies; University of New Mexico, professor of American studies, distinguished professor of American studies; University of California-Santa Cruz, professor of literature, 1987-90, Kresge College, acting provost, 1990; University of Oklahoma, David Burke chair of letters, 1991; University of Nebraska Press, series editor; State University of New York Press, series editor; Tianjin University, visiting professor. **Publications:** POETRY: Born in the Wind, 1960; The Old Park Sleepers: A Poem, 1961; Two Wings the Butterfly: Haiku Poems in English, 1962; South of the Painted Stone, 1963; Raising the Moon Vines: Original Haiku in English, 1964; Seventeen Chirps: Haiku in English, 1964; (with J. Downes) Slight Abrasions: A Dialogue in Haiku, 1966; Empty Swings, 1967; Matsushima: Pine Islands, 1984; Crane Arise, Haiku, 1999. EDITOR: Summer in the Spring: Lyric Poems of the Ojibway, 1965, new ed. as Summer in the Spring: Anishinaabe Lyric Poems and Stories, 1993; Escorts to White Earth, 1868-1968: 100 Year Reservation, 1968; Anishinabe Adisokan: Stories of the Ojibwa, Tales of the People, 1970; The Everlasting Sky, 1972; Anishinabe Nagomon, 1974; Earthdivers, 1981; Touchwood: A Collection of Ojibway Prose, 1987; Narrative Chance: Postmodern Discourse on Native American Indian Literatures, 1989; Native American Literature: An Anthology, 1995; Survivance: Narratives of Native Presence, 2008; (and intro.) Native Storiers: Five Selections, trans. as Des Nouvelles des Indiens d'Amérique du Nord, 2008. NONFICTION: A Selected Bibliography of the Dakota and Ojibway Indians of Minnesota, 1967; Thomas James White Hawk, 1968; Tribal Scenes and Ceremonies, 1976; The People Named the Chippewa, 1984; Interior Landscapes: Autobiographical Myths and Metaphors, 1990, 2nd ed., 2009; Crossbloods: Bone Courts, Bingo and Other Reports, 1990; Manifest Manners: Postindian Warriors of Survivance, 1994, rev. ed., 1999; Fugitive Poses: Native American Indian Scenes of Absence and Presence, 1998; (with A.R. Lee) Postindian Conversations, 1999. NOVELS: Darkness in Saint Louis Bearheart, 1973 as Bearheart, 1990; Griever: An American Monkey King in China, 1987; The Heirs of Columbus, 1991; Dead Voices: Natural Agonies in the New World, 1992; Hotline Healers: An Almost Browne Novel, 1997; Chancers, 2000, trans. as Crâneurs, 2007. SHORT STORIES: Wordarrows: Indians and Whites in the New fur Trade, 1978; The Trickster of Liberty, 1988; Landfill Meditations: Crossblood Stories, 1991; Wordarrows: Native States of Literary Sovereignty, 2003. COLLECTED WORKS: Shadow Distance: A Gerald Vizenor Reader, 1994. OTHERS: Hiroshima Bugi: Atomu 57, 2003; Bear Island: The War at Sugar Point, 2006; Almost Ashore, 2006; Literary Chance: Essays on Native American Survivance, 2007; Father Meme, 2008; Native liberty: Natural Reason And Cultural Survivance, 2009; Shrouds of White Earth, 2010. Contributor to books. **Address:** American Studies, University of New Mexico, 309 Ortega Hall, Albuquerque, NM 87131, U.S.A. **Online address:** vizenor@unm.edu

VLASICH, James A(nthony). American (born United States), b. 1944. **Genres:** Sports/Fitness, History, Adult Non-fiction, Essays, Agriculture/Forestry, Social Sciences. **Career:** Southern Illinois University, instructor in physics, 1964-67; McDonnel Douglas Corp., associate engineer, 1967-68; State of Colorado, computer programmer, 1970-73; Fort Lewis College, KDUR-Radio, station manager, 1974-75; University of Utah, KUER-Radio, announcer, 1975-77; American West Center, research assistant, 1978-79, Archaeology Center, historian, 1980-81; Southern Utah University, associate professor of history, 1981-, professor of history. Writer. **Publications:** (Ed. with S.R. James, J.C. Janetski and S.R. James) Prehistory, Ethnohistory and History of Eastern Nevada: A Cultural Resources Summary of the Elko and Ely Districts, 1981; Legend for the Legendary: The Origin of the Baseball Hall of Fame, 1990; Pueblo Indian Agriculture, 2005; (ed.) Horsehide, Pigskin, Oval Tracks and Apple Pie: Essays on Sports and American Culture, 2005. Works appear in anthologies. Contributor of articles to journals. **Address:** Department of History & Sociology, Southern Utah University, 225I Centrum Arena, 351 W University Blvd., Cedar City, UT 84720, U.S.A. **Online address:** vlasich@suu.edu

VOEKS, Robert A(llen). American (born United States), b. 1950. **Genres:** Anthropology/Ethnology. **Career:** U.S. Fish & Wildlife Service, Unique Ecosystem Program, coordinator, 1978-80; California State University, associate professor, professor of geography, 1987-, Latin American Studies Program, coordinator, 1997-2000; Environmental Studies Graduate Program, chair, 2000-; U.S. Forestry Service, principal investigator, 1989; Federal University, visiting professor, 1990-91. Writer. **Publications:** Sacred Leaves of Candomblé: African Magic, Medicine and Religion in Brazil, 1997; The Roots of Rainforest Medicine: Medicinal Ethnobotany in the Humid Tropics, forthcoming; The Light Environment and Dipterocarp Seedling Survivorship in Northern Borneo, forthcoming. Contributor to periodicals. **Address:** Department of Geography, California State University, H-407, 800 N State College Blvd., Fullerton, CA 92834, U.S.A. **Online address:** rvoeks@fullerton.edu

VOERMANS, Paul. Australian (born Australia), b. 1960. **Genres:** Novels, Young Adult Fiction, Science Fiction/Fantasy. **Career:** Victoria College of the Arts, faculty. Novelist and actor. **Publications:** And Disregards the Rest, 1992; The Weird Colonial Boy, 1993. Works appear in anthologies. **Address:** Victor Gollanz Ltd., Wellington House, 125 Strand, London, GL WC2N 0BB, England. **Online address:** paul@vicnet.net.au

VOGEL, Carole Garbuny. American (born United States), b. 1954?. **Genres:** Children's Non-fiction, Environmental Sciences/Ecology, History, Marine Sciences/Oceanography, Young Adult Non-fiction, Biography, Essays, Genealogy/Heraldry, Genealogy/Heraldry. **Career:** Writer and genealogist. **Publications:** JUVENILE WITH K.A. GOLDNER: Why Mount St. Helens Blew Its Top, 1981; The Dangers of Strangers, 1983; HBJ Science Activity Workbooks for Levels 3-6, 1984; Humphrey, the Wrong Way Whale, 1987; The Great Yellowstone Fire, 1990. JUVENILE: The Great Midwest Flood, 1995; Will I Get Breast Cancer?: Questions and Answers for Teenage Girls, 1995; Shock Waves Through Los Angeles: The Northridge Earthquake, 1996; Legends of Landforms: Native American Lore and the Geology of the Land, 1999; Nature's Fury: Eyewitness Reports of Natural Disasters, 2000; Inside Earth, 2000; Breast Cancer: Questions & Answers for Young Women, 2001; Weather Legends: Native American Lore and the Science of Weather, 2001. RESTLESS SEA SERIES: Savage Waters, 2003; Shifting Shores, 2003; Human Impact, 2003; Ocean Wildlife, 2003; Dangerous Crossings, 2003; Undersea Exploration, 2003. JUVENILE WITH YOSSI LESHEM: The Man Who Flies with Birds, 2009. FOR ADULTS: (ed.) We Shall Not Forget: Memories of the Holocaust, 1994. Contributor to magazines and journals. Works appear in anthologies. **Address:** Little Brown & Co, 3 Center Plz., Boston, MA 02108-2084, U.S.A. **Online address:** cvogel@recognitionscience.com

VOGEL, Ezra F. American (born United States), b. 1930. **Genres:** Business/Trade/Industry, International Relations/Current Affairs. **Career:** Harvard University, research fellow, 1958-60, lecturer, 1958-67, postdoctoral fellow, 1961-64, research associate, 1961-67, professor, 1967-86, Henry Ford II research professor of the social sciences, 1986-2000, Henry Ford II research professor emeritus of the social sciences, 2000-, East Asian Research Center, associate director, 1967-72, director, 1972-77, Undergraduate Concentration in East Asian Studies, director, 1972-89, Council for East Asian Studies, chairman, 1977-80, Program on U.S.-Japan Relations, director, 1980-87, Center for International Affairs, director, 1980-87, honorary director, 1987-, Dillon Professor of International Affairs, 1986-, Fairbank Center, director, 1995-99, Asia Center, head, 1997-99; Reischauer Institute of Japanese Studies, faculty; Yale University, assistant professor, 1960-61; U.S. Government, national intelligence officer for East Asia, 1993-95; Keio University, Global Security Research Institute, director. Writer. **Publications:** Japan's New Middle Class, 1963, 2nd ed., 1971; (contrib.) Cadres, Bureaucracy, and Political Power in Communist China, 1967; Canton under Communism, 1969; Japan as Number One: Lessons for America, 1979; Ronsō Nichi-Bei masatsu, 1983; Comeback, 1985; Japan as Number One: Revisited, 1986; (with S. Sabōrō) Nichi-Bei tagaini nani o manabu ka, 1986; The Impact of Japan on a Changing World, 1987; One Step ahead in China: Guangdong under Reform, 1987; (with X.D. Yi) Guangdong gai ge, 1989; Marital Relationship of Parents and the Emotionally Disturbed Child, 1990; The Four Little Dragons: The Spread of Industrialization in East Asia, 1991; (with P. Giarra and M. Blaker) Case Studies in Japanese Negotiating Behavior, 2002; (with H. Keńichirōhen) Nitchū Sensōki Chūgoku no shakai to bunka, 2010; Deng Xiaoping and the Transformation of China, 20011. EDITOR: (with N.W. Bell) A Modern Introduction to the Family, 1960, rev. ed., 1968; Modern Japanese Organization and Decision Making, 1975; (with G. Lodge) Ideology and National Competitiveness, 1987; (with D. Davis) Chinese Society on the Eve of Tiananmen: The Impact of Reform, 1990; Living with China: U.S./China Relations in the Twenty-First Century, 1997; (with Y. Ming and T. Akihiko) Golden Age of the U.S.-China-Japan Triangle, 1972-1989, 2002; (with S.I. Levine) Deng Xiaoping Shakes the World: An Eyewitness Account of China's Party Work Conference and the Third Plenum, 2004; (with S.R. MacKinnon and D. Lary) China at War: Regions of China, 1937-1945, 2007; (with B. Kim) The Park Chung

Hee Era: The Transformation of South Korea, 2011. **Address:** Edwin O. Reischauer Institute of Japanese Studies, Harvard University, Center for Government and International Studies, South Bldg., 1730 Cambridge St., Cambridge, MA 02138-4317, U.S.A. **Online address:** efvogel@fas.harvard.edu

VOGEL, Lise. American (born United States) **Genres:** Women's Studies And Issues, Sociology. **Career:** Writer. **Publications:** The Column of Antoninus Pius, 1973; Marxism and the Oppression of Women: Toward a Unitary Theory, 1983; Mothers on the Job: Maternity Policy in the U.S. Workplace, 1993; Woman Questions: Essays for a Materialist Feminism, 1995. Contributor to periodicals. **Address:** 370 Riverside Dr., New York, NY 10025, U.S.A. **Online address:** lvogel@mindspring.com

VOGEL, Steve. (Steve Gregory Vogel). American (born United States), b. 1951. **Genres:** How-to Books, Novels, Biography. **Career:** Ford Motor Co., 1974-76; Corning Glass Works, plant controller, 1976-79; Ryder System Inc., controller, 1979-81, group controller, 1981-82, division planning staff, 1982-83; Dale Carnegie, teaching assistant, 1981-82; Guardian Industries Inc., group controller, 1983-86, director of finance, chief financial officer, acting chief financial officer, 1986-87; Bush Industries Inc., vice president of finance, 1987; Nastec Corp., vice president of finance and administration, chief financial officer, 1988; Sanguinity L.L.C., co-founder and chief executive officer. Writer and financial consultant. **Publications:** (As Steve G. Vogel) Take Control of Your Life: A Story of Wrestling with Personal Growth (novel), 2006. **Address:** Sanguinity L.L.C., 15425 Manchester Rd., Ste. 12, Ballwin, MO 63011-3077, U.S.A. **Online address:** stevegvogel@usa.net

VOGEL, Steve Gregory. *See* **VOGEL, Steve.**

VOGEL, Steven Kent. American (born United States), b. 1961. **Genres:** Business/Trade/Industry, Economics, Politics/Government, Sociology. **Career:** Japan Times, reporter; University of California, teacher; Harvard University, teacher; University of California, professor of political science. **Publications:** Freer Markets, More Rules: Regulatory Reform in Advanced Industrial Countries, 1996; (ed.) U.S.-Japan Relations in a Changing World, 2002; Japan Remodeled: How Government and Industry Are Reforming Japanese Capitalism, 2006; (ed. with N.H. Barma) The Political Economy Reader: Markets as Institutions, 2008. **Address:** Charles and Louise Travers Department of Political, Science, University of California, 210 Barrows Hall, Berkeley, CA 94720-1950, U.S.A. **Online address:** svogel@berkeley.edu

VOGT, Henri Hans Mikael. Finnish (born Finland), b. 1967. **Genres:** Politics/Government, Social Sciences, Humanities, Philosophy. **Career:** Finnish Institute of International Affairs, researcher, 2000-02, senior researcher, 2002-04; University of Helsinki, Department of Political Science, senior lecturer, 2004-05, 2006-07, adjunct professor, 2007-, Network for European Studies, director, 2007-08, Centre of Excellence (CoE) in Global Governance Research, research fellow, 2005-06. Writer. **Publications:** Between Utopia and Disillusionment: A Narrative of the Political Transformation in Eastern Europe, 2004; (ed. with H.Mayer) A Responsible Europe? Ethical Foundations of EU External Affairs, 2006. **Address:** CoE in Global Governance Research, University of Helsinki, Yliopistonkatu 3, PO Box 4, Helsinki, 00014, Finland. **Online address:** henri.vogt@helsinki.fi

VOGT, Peter. American (born United States), b. 1967?. **Genres:** Education, Fash Ion/Costume. **Career:** Career Planning Resources, president; University of Wisconsin, counselor; Edgewood College, counselor. Writer. **Publications:** Career Opportunities in the Fashion Industry, 2002, 2nd ed., 2007; (with T.C. Blanck and J. Anderson) The College to Career Roadmap: A Four Year Guide to Coaching Your Student, 2006; Career Wisdom for College Students: Insights You Won't Get in Class, on the Internet, or from Your Parents, 2007. **Address:** Career Planning Resources, 2400 Ivy Ln., Bloomington, MN 55431-2830, U.S.A. **Online address:** peter@careerplanningresources.com

VOIEN, Steven. American (born United States), b. 1954?. **Genres:** Novels, Novellas/Short Stories. **Career:** U.S. State Department, foreign service officer, 1989-94; writer, 1995-98; Business for Social Responsibility, manager/director, 1998-2003; Edelman Public Relations, Corporate Social Responsibility, vice president, 2003-06; Waggener Edstrom, Global Corporate Citizenship, vice president, 2007-08; Voien Consulting, principal, 2007, 2008-10; Ethics Resource Center, visiting senior fellow. **Publications:** NOVELS: In a High and Lonely Place, 1992; Black Leopard, 1997. **Address:** c/o Esther Newberg, International Creative Management, 825 8th Ave., New York, NY 10019, U.S.A.

VOIGT, Cynthia. American (born United States), b. 1942. **Genres:** Novels, Children's Fiction, Human Relations/Parenting, Young Adult Fiction. **Career:** J. Walter Thompson Advertising Agency, secretary, 1964; English teacher, 1965-67; The Key School, teacher in English, 1968-69, department chair, 1971-79, part-time teacher and department chair, 1981-88; writer, 1981-. **Publications:** TILLERMAN FAMILY SERIES: Homecoming, 1973; Dicey's Song, 1982; A Solitary Blue, 1983; The Runner, 1985; Sons from Afar, 1987; Seventeen Against the Dealer, 1989. KINGDOM SERIES: Jackaroo, 1985; On Fortune's Wheel, 1990; The Wings of a Falcon, 1993; Elske, 1999. BAD GIRLS SERIES: The Bad Girls, 1996; Bad, Badder, Baddest, 1997; It's Not Easy Being Bad, 2000; Bad Girls in Love, 2002; From Bad to Worse, 2003; Bad Girls, Bad Girls, Whatcha Gonna Do?, 2006. NOVELS: Tell Me If the Lovers Are Losers, 1982; The Callender Papers, 1983; Building Blocks, 1984; Come a Stranger, 1986; Izzy, Willy-Nilly, 1986, rev. ed., 2005; Stories About Rosie, 1986; Tree by Leaf, 1988; Tillerman Family Saga, 1990; The Vandemark Mummy, 1991; Glass Mountain, 1991; David and Jonathan, 1992; Orfe, 1992; When She Hollers, 1994; Born to Be Bad, 2001; The Rosie Stories, 2003; Angus and Sadie, 2005; When Bad Things Happen to Bad People, 2006; Young Fredle, 2011. **Address:** c/o Merrilee Heifetz, Writers House Inc., 21 W 26th St., New York, NY 10010-1003, U.S.A. **Online address:** cv@cynthiavoigt.com

VOIGT, Ellen Bryant. American (born United States), b. 1943. **Genres:** Poetry, Literary Criticism And History, Young Adult Fiction. **Career:** University of Iowa, College Pharmacy, technical writer, 1965-66; Iowa Wesleyan College, instructor in English, 1966-69; Goddard College, teacher of literature and writing, 1970-78, director of writing program, 1975-79; Arion's Dolphin, advisory editor, 1971-75; Guggenheim fellow, 1978-79; Massachusetts Institute of Technology, associate professor of creative writing, 1979-82, professor of poetry; Warren Wilson College, graduate professor for writers, visiting faculty member, 1981-; Vermont State poet, 1999-2003; Lila Wallace fellow, 1999-2001; American Academy of Poets, chancellor, 2002-05. **Publications:** Claiming Kin, 1976; The Forces of Plenty, 1983; The Lotus Flowers: Poems, 1987; Two Trees: Poems, 1992; Kyrie: Poems, 1995; (ed. with G. Orr) Poets Teaching Poets: Self and the World, 1996; The Flexible Lyric, 1999; Shadow of Heaven: Poems, 2002; (ed. with H. McGuth) Hammer and Blaze: A Gathering of Contemporary American Poets, 2002; (intro.) Beautiful Motion, 2004; Messenger: New and Selected Poems, 1976-2006, 2007; The Art of Syntax: Rhythm of Thought, Rhythm of Song, 2009. Contributor to periodicals. **Address:** Warren Wilson College, PO Box 9000, Asheville, NC 28815-9000, U.S.A.

VOLANTO, Keith J. (Keith Joseph Volanto). American (born United States), b. 1966?. **Genres:** History, Business/Trade/Industry. **Career:** Texas A&M University, lecturer and undergraduate advisor, 1998-2002; Blinn College, professor of history, 2002-04; Collin County Community College, professor of history, 2004-. Writer. **Publications:** Texas, Cotton, and the New Deal, 2005. (co-author) Beyond Myths and Legends: A Narrative History of Texas, 2008. Contributor to periodicals. **Address:** Social Sciences Division, Collin County Community College, 2800 E Spring Creek Pkwy., Plano, TX 75074-3300, U.S.A. **Online address:** kvolanto@ccccd.edu

VOLANTO, Keith Joseph. See **VOLANTO, Keith J.**

VOLCK, Brian. American (born United States), b. 1959?. **Genres:** Young Adult Fiction, Medicine/Health. **Career:** University Hospitals of Cleveland/Rainbow Babies and Children's Hospital, pediatrics resident, 1985-88, general academic pediatrics, 1988-89; U.S. Indian Health Service, general pediatrician, 1989-94; Federally Qualified Community Health Center, general pediatrician, 1994-96; University of Cincinnati, instructor; Cincinnati Children's Hospital Medical Center, adjunct assistant professor, assistant professor. Writer and pediatrician. **Publications:** (With J. Shuman) Reclaiming the Body: Christians and the Faithful Use of Modern Medicine, 2006. **Address:** Cincinnati Children's Hospital Medical Center, 3333 Burnet Ave., Cincinnati, OH 45229-3026, U.S.A. **Online address:** brian.volck@uc.edu

VOLK, Patricia (Gay). American (born United States), b. 1943. **Genres:** Novels, Novellas/Short Stories, Social Sciences, Literary Criticism And History. **Career:** Appelbaum and Curtis, art director, 1964-65; Seventeen maga-

zine, art director, 1967-69; Doyle, Dane, Bernbach Inc., copywriter, 1969-88, senior vice president and creative manager, 1969-87, senior vice president and associate creative director, 1987-88; writer, 1988-; Yeshiva College, adjunct instructor in fiction, 1991; New York Newsday, columnist, 1993-95; Playwright's Horizon Theater School, instructor, 1997-98; Marymount College, instructor, 1998-99. **Publications:** SHORT STORIES: The Yellow Banana, 1985; All It Takes, 1990. NOVELS: White Light, 1987; Stuffed: Adventures of a Restaurant Family, 2001; To My Dearest Friends, 2007. Contributor to periodicals. **Address:** c/o Gloria Loomis, Watkins/Loomis Agency Inc., 133 E 35th St., New York, NY 10016, U.S.A.

VOLK, Tyler. American (born United States), b. 1950. **Genres:** Earth Sciences, Environmental Sciences/Ecology. **Career:** New York University, professor of biology and science director of environmental studies; Utah State University, researcher; National Aeronautics and Space Administration, Ames Research Center, researcher, Kennedy Space Flight Center, researcher; School of Visual Arts, teacher. Writer. **Publications:** Metapatterns across Space, Time, and Mind, 1995; Gaia's Body: Toward a Physiology of Earth, 1998; What Is Death? A Scientist Looks at the Cycle of Life, 2002; Earth Science Success in 20 Minutes a Day, 2005; CO_2 Rising: The World's Greatest Environmental Challenge, 2008; Death & Sex, 2009. Contributor to books and periodicals. **Address:** Department of Biology, New York University, 1009 Silver Ctr., 100 Washington Sq. E, New York, NY 10003-6688, U.S.A. **Online address:** tyler.volk@nyu.edu

VOLKMAN, Ernest. American (born United States), b. 1940. **Genres:** Criminology/True Crime, History, Mystery/Crime/Suspense. **Career:** Newsday, national correspondent, 1974-77; Long Island Magazine, executive editor, 1978-82; Espionage, executive editor, 1984-88; Paumanok Institute, executive editor, 1988-. **Publications:** A Legacy of Hate: Anti-Semitism in America, 1982; Warriors of the Night: Spies, Soldiers and American Intelligence, 1985; (with J. Cummings) The Heist, 1986; (with B. Baggett) Secret Intelligence, 1988; (with J. Cummings) Goombata: The Improbable Rise and Fall of John Gotti and His Gang, 1990; Death Do Us Part, 1991; Spies: The Secret Agents Who Changed the Course of History, 1993; (with J. Cummings) Till Murder Do Us Part, 1994; Espionage: The Greatest Spy Operations of the Twentieth Century, 1995; Gangbusters: The Destruction of America's Last Mafia Dynasty, 1998; Science Goes to War: The Search for the Ultimate Weapon, from Greek Fire to Star Wars, 2002; Jian die de li shi=The History of Espionage, 2009. **Address:** Arcadia Ltd., 20A Old Neversink Rd., Danbury, CT 06811, U.S.A.

VOLKOV, Shulamit. Israeli (born Israel), b. 1942. **Genres:** History. **Career:** University of Tel Aviv, Department of History, instructor; Graduate School of History, head. Writer. **Publications:** The Rise of Popular Antimodernism in Germany: The Urban Master Artisans, 1873-1896, 1978; Yahadut prusyah: Mitos u- metsiut, 1993; Me-halukah le-ihud: Germanyah, 1945-1990, 1994; (with E. Muller-Lucker) Deutsche juden und die moderne, 1994; Die juden in Deutschland, 1780-1918, 1994; Ihud ve-herut be- Germanyah: Mi-Napoleon ead Bismark, 1997; Miutim, zarim ve-shonim: Kevutsot shulayim ba-historyah, 2000; Das judische projekt der moderne: Zehn essays, 2001; Ba-ma'agal ha- mekhushaf: Yehudim, antishemim ve-germanim aherim, 2002; Germans, Jews, and Antisemites: Trials in Emancipation (essays), 2006. **Address:** Tel Aviv University, PO Box 39040, Tel Aviv, 69978, Israel. **Online address:** volkov@post.tau.ac.il

VOLLENDORF, Lisa. American (born United States), b. 1969. **Genres:** History, Women's Studies And Issues, Literary Criticism And History. **Career:** Miami University, visiting assistant professor, 1995-97; Wayne State University, assistant professor, 1997-2003, associate professor, 2003-05; University of California, Summer Institute in Hispanic Languages and Culture, visiting associate professor and director, 2004-06; California State University, Department of Romance, German, Russian Languages and Literatures, associate professor, 2005-08, professor of Spanish and chair, 2008-. Writer. **Publications:** (Ed.) Recovering Spain's Feminist Tradition, 2001; Reclaiming the Body: Maria De Zayas's Early Modern Feminism, 2001; (ed.) Literatura y Feminismo en EspaNa, 2005; The Lives of Women: A New History of Inquisitional Spain, 2005; (ed. with D. Kostroun)Women, Religion, and the Atlantic World (1600-1800), 2009. **Address:** California State University, 1250 Bellflower Blvd., Long Beach, CA 90840, U.S.A. **Online address:** lvollend@csulb.edu

VOLLERS, Maryanne. American (born United States), b. 1955. **Genres:**

Documentaries/Reportage, Autobiography/Memoirs, Biography, Humor/Satire. **Career:** Rolling Stone, associate editor, 1977-82; freelance journalist, 1982-; NBC News, field producer, 1986-89. **Publications:** Ghosts of Mississippi: The Murder of Medgar Evers, the Trials of Byron DeLa Beckwith, and the Haunting of the New South, 1995; (with J. Nielsen) Ice Bound: A Doctor's Incredible Battle for Survival at the South Pole, 2001; Lone Wolf: Eric Rudolph: Murder, Myth, and the Pursuit of an American Outlaw, 2006; Lone Wolf: Eric Rudolph and the Legacy of American Terror, 2007; (with M. Vollers) All That is Bitter and Sweet: A Memoir, 2011. Contributor to periodicals. **Address:** c/o Kristine Dahl, International Creative Management Inc., 40 W 57th St., New York, NY 10019, U.S.A.

VOLLSTEDT, Maryana. American (born United States), b. 1925. **Genres:** Food And Wine. **Career:** Reed and Cross Inc., co-founder, 1952, owner, 1952-79; Vollstedt Associates, marketing and merchandising consultant, 1979-; The Register-Guard, food columnist. **Publications:** Oven Barbecue Cooking: For Kamoda and Other Barbecues, 1968; Pacific Fresh: Great Recipes from the West Coast, 1995; What's for Dinner?: Over 200 Delicious Recipes That Work Every Time, 1997; The Big Book of Casseroles, 2000; The Big Book of Soups and Stews, 2001; The Big Book of Breakfast, 2002; The Big Book of Potluck, 2003; (with P. Mitchell) The Simple Soups Deck, 2006; The Big Book of Easy Suppers, 2005; Meatloaf: Recipes for Everyone's Favorite, 2007; Big Book of Chicken: Over 275 Exciting Ways to Cook Chicken, 2008. **Address:** Chronicle Books L.L.C., 85 Second St., San Francisco, CA 94105, U.S.A. **Online address:** ovollstedt@aol.com

VOLPE, Vernon L(ewis). American (born United States), b. 1955. **Genres:** History, Civil Liberties/Human Rights, Politics/Government, Race Relations, Social Sciences. **Career:** University of Nebraska-Lincoln, teaching assistant, 1979-82, instructor, 1982-84, visiting assistant professor of history, 1984-86, Lewis and Clark project, assistant, 1985-86, Center for Great Plains Studies, resident fellow, 1990-; Texas A&M University, visiting assistant professor of history, 1986-87; University of Nebraska-Kearney, Department of History, associate professor, 1987, professor, department chair. Writer. **Publications:** Forlorn Hope of Freedom: The Liberty Party in the Old Northwest, 1838-1848, 1990. Contributor to history journals. **Address:** Department of History, University of Nebraska, Copeland Hall 103I, 905 W 25th St., Kearney, NE 68849, U.S.A. **Online address:** volpev@unk.edu

VOLSKY, Paula. American (born United States) **Genres:** Science Fiction/Fantasy, Novels, Young Adult Fiction. **Career:** U.S. Department of Housing and Urban Development, staff. Fantasy novelist. **Publications:** FANTASY NOVELS: The Curse of the Witch-Queen, 1982; The Sorcerer's Lady, 1986; The Luck of Relian Kru, 1987; The Sorcerer's Heir, 1988; The Sorcerer's Curse, 1989; Illusion, 1992; The Wolf of Winter, 1993; The Gates of Twilight, 1996; The White Tribunal, 1997; Grand Ellipse, 2000. Contributor of short stories to anthologies. **Address:** c/o Author Mail, Bantam Books, 1540 Broadway, New York, NY 10036, U.S.A.

VON AHNEN, Katherine. American (born United States), b. 1922. **Genres:** Poetry, Children's Fiction, Animals/Pets. **Career:** WCMC Radio, women's editor, 1945-55; Cape May Lighthouse, special events coordinator and admissions person; Fireglow, editor; Homespun, editor; Write-On, founder; Write-On-Two, founder. **Publications:** The Cape May Collection (poetry), 1991; (with J.A.Y. Bear) Charlie Young Bear, 1994; Lighthouse and Three Little Pigs, 1995; Heart of Naosaqua, 1996; Mary Elizabeth and the Cape May Point Lighthouse, 1997. **Address:** 304 St. James Pl., Cape May, NJ 08204-1754, U.S.A.

VON BENCKE, Matthew Justin. American (born United States), b. 1972. **Genres:** History, Politics/Government. **Career:** Boeing Co., manager of business development, 1995-97, Boeing Defense and Space Group, staff; University of California, researcher, 1997-; Robert Trent Jones II Firm, consultant, 1997-. Writer. **Publications:** The Politics of Space: A History of U.S.-Soviet/Russian Competition and Cooperation in Space, 1997; Reds on the Greens, 1998. **Address:** Westview Press, 2465 Central Ave., Boulder, CO 80301, U.S.A. **Online address:** matthew@bencke.com

VON DASSANOWSKY, Robert. *See* DASSANOWSKY, Robert.

VONDERPLANITZ, Aajonus. American (born United States), b. 1947. **Genres:** Plays/Screenplays, Medicine/Health, Sports/Fitness. **Career:** Optimal Ways of Living, nutritionist and managing director, 1983-; Carnelian

Bay Castle Press, nutrition writer, 1996-, scientist. **Publications:** The Garden of Date Eatin', 1976; We Want to Live, vol. I: Out of the Grips of Disease and Death, 1997, vol. II: Healthfully, 1997; The Recipe for Living without Disease, 2002. **Address:** Nutritional Foundation for Well Being, 3225 McLeod, Ste. 100, Las Vegas, NV 89121-2257, U.S.A. **Online address:** optimal@earthlink.net

VONDUNG, Klaus. German (born Germany), b. 1941. **Genres:** History, Literary Criticism And History, Politics/Government. **Career:** University of Munich, lecturer, 1968-71; University of Siegen, professor, 1976-2006, vice president, 1983-85; University of Florida, visiting professor, 1979; University of Houston, visiting professor, 1990; Kansai University, visiting professor, 1991, 2011; Kwansei Gakuin University, visiting professor, 1997, 2002; Zhejiang University, visiting professor, 2007, 2009, 2010. Writer. **Publications:** Magie und Manipulation: Ideologischer Kult und politische Religion des Nationalsozialismus, 1971; Volkisch-nationale und nationalsozialistische Literaturtheorie, 1973; Apokalypse in Deutschland, 1988; The Apocalypse in Germany, 2000; (with N. Binczek and N. Glaubitz) Anfang offen: Literarische ubergange ins 21 Jahrhundert, 2002; (with K.L. Pfeiffer) Jenseits Der Entzauberten Welt: Naturwissenschaft Und Mystik in Der Moderne, 2006. EDITOR: Das Wilhelminische Bildungsburgertum: zur Sozialgeschichte seiner Ideen (essays), 1976; Kriegserlebnis, 1980; The Collected Works of Eric Voegelin, 1997-98. **Address:** University of Siegen, Philosophische Fakultaet, Siegen, 57068, Germany. **Online address:** vondung@germanistik.uni-siegen.de

VON FINCKENSTEIN, Maria. (Maria Muehlen). Canadian/German (born Germany), b. 1942. **Genres:** Art/Art History, Social Sciences. **Career:** Indian and Northern Affairs Canada, curator, 1979-93, Inuit Art Section, head; Canadian Museum of Civilization, curator, 1997-. Contributor and writer. **Publications:** (Ed. as Maria Muehlen) Directory for Temporary Exhibition Facilities in Canadian Museums, 1979; Celebrating Inuit Art, 1948-1970, 1999; Nuvisavik: The Place Where We Weave, 2002. Contributor to periodicals. **Address:** Department of Inuit Art, Canadian Museum of Civilization, 100 Laurier St., PO Box 31000, Sta. B, Gatineau, QC J8X 4H2, Canada. **Online address:** maria.vonfinckenstein@civilization.ca

VON GUNDEN, Kenneth. American (born United States), b. 1946?. **Genres:** Film, Sciences, Young Adult Fiction, Literary Criticism And History, Novels. **Career:** Penn State University, part-time instructor in writing, popular culture, and film, instructor in writing, popular culture and film, professor of American studies, cinema art and integrative arts. **Publications:** (With S.H. Stock) Twenty All-Time Great Science-Fiction Films, 1982; Alec Guinness: The Films, 1987; Flights of Fancy: The Great Fantasy Films, 1989; StarSpawn, 1990; Five Postmodern Auteurs: Coppola, Lucas, DePalma, Spielberg, and Scorsese, 1991; K-9 Corps, 1991; K-9 Corps: Under Fire, 1991; K-9 Corps: Cry Wolf, 1992; K-9 Corps: Last Resort, 1992; The Sounding Stillness, 1993; The Pale Companion, 1994. Contributor to periodicals. **Address:** Department of English, Pennsylvania State University, 3000 Ivyside Pk., PO Box 6123, Altoona, PA 16601-3760, U.S.A. **Online address:** krv4@psu.edu

VON HABSBURG(-LOTHRINGEN), Géza. American/Hungarian (born Hungary), b. 1940. **Genres:** Art/Art History. **Career:** Christie, Manson & Woods Auctioneers, chairperson for Switzerland, 1966-84, chairperson of European operations, 1980-84; Kunsthalle der Hypokulturstiftung, chief curator and organizer of Faberge exhibition, 1984-87; Habsburg Fine Art International Auctioneers, chairperson, 1987-91; Faberge Arts Foundation, chief curator and organizer of Faberge exhibition, 1991-94; freelance writer and consultant, 1991-; New York School of Interior Design, adjunct faculty, 1993-95; Faberge Co., curator and consultant, 1994-; Bard University, Graduate Center for Studies of the Decorative Arts, adjunct professor, 1995-96; New York University, adjunct faculty, 1996, 1998; Metropolitan Museum of Art, lecturer. **Publications:** (Contrib.) Vom goldenen Überfluss der Welt: Bilder u. Skizzen, 1978; The Gilbert Collection of 18th-Century Gold Boxes, 1983; Fabergé, Hofjuwelier der Zaren, 1986; Fabergé, 1986; (with M. Lopato) Fabergé, Imperial Jeweler, 1994; Carl Fabergé: First Impressions, 1994; (co-author) Princely Taste: Treasures from Great Private Collections, 1995; Fabergé in America, 1996; Fabergé: Fantasies and Treasures, 1996; Princely Treasures, 1997; Fabergé, Imperial Craftsman and His World, 2000; Fabergé-Cartier: Rivalen am Zarenhof, 2003; Faberg Then and Now, 2005; Fabergé: Treasures of Imperial Russia, 2005; Fabergé Revealed: At the Virginia Museum of Fine Arts, 2011. Contributor of articles to journals. **Address:** 12 Governors Rd., Bronxville, NY 10708-1612, U.S.A.

VON HAGEN, Mark (L.). American (born United States), b. 1954. **Genres:** History, Area Studies. **Career:** Indiana University, instructor in Russian, 1981, Slavic Workshop, associate director, 1982; Stanford University, Western Culture Program, Humanities Track, teaching fellow, 1983-84, Department of History, Donald M. Kendall visiting associate professor in Soviet studies, 1992-95; Columbia University, Department of History, assistant professor, 1985-89, professor, 1989-2007, W. Averell Harriman Institute for the Advanced Study of the Soviet Union, associate director, 1989-92, The Harriman Institute, director, 1995-2001, Boris Bakhmeteff professor of Russian and East European studies, 2004-07, chair, 2006-07; Arizona State University, Department of History, professor and chair, 2007-09, School of Historical, Philosophical and Religious Studies, director, 2009-; Ukrainian Free University, professor of 20th century history of Ukraine, 2009; American Association for the Advancement of Slavic Studies, president. Writer. **Publications:** Soldiers in the Proletarian Dictatorship: The Red Army and the Soviet Socialist State, 1990; The Soviet Union and the Russian, Ottoman, and Habsburg Empires, 1997. EDITOR AND CONTRIBUTOR: (with P. Dotsenko) The Struggle for a Democracy in Siberia: Eyewitness Account of a Contemporary, 1983; (with K. Barkey) After Empire: Multiethnic Societies and Nation-Building, 1997; (co-ed.) Kazan, Moscow, St. Petersburg: Multiple Faces of the Russian Empire, 1997; (ed. with A. Kappeler, Z. Kohut and F. Sysyn) Culture, Nation and Identity: The Ukrainian-Russian Encounter, 1600-1945, 2003; (with J. Burbank and A. Remnev) Russian Empire: Space, People, Power, 1700-1930, 2007; War in a European Borderland: Occupations and Occupation Plans in Galicia and Ukraine, 1914-1918, 2007. Contributor of articles to journals and books. **Address:** Department of History, Arizona State University, PO Box 874302, Tempe, AZ 85287-4302, U.S.A. **Online address:** mark.vonhagen@asu.edu

VON HIPPEL, Eric. American (born United States), b. 1941. **Genres:** Social Work. **Career:** Graphic Sciences Inc., co-founder and manager of mechanism, 1966-69; McKinsey and Co., consultant, 1970-72; Massachusetts Institute of Technology, Sloan School of Management, assistant professor, 1973-79, associate professor, 1979-85, professor, 1985-2006, T. Wilson professor of management, 2006-, Entrepreneurship Program, co-founder, 1994-96, Innovation and Entrepreneurship Group, head, 2003-06, professor of engineering systems, 2006-; Canadian Institute for Advanced Research, fellow, 1995-97; University of New South Wales, Australian Graduate School of Management, Sir Walter Scott distinguished professor, 1997-98; Harvard Law School, Berkman Center for Internet and Society, fellow, 2007-09, faculty associate, 2009-10; George Washington University, Welling professor, 2009-10. Writer, economist, consultant and entrepreneur. **Publications:** The Sources of Innovation, 1988; Democratizing Innovation, 2005. Contributor to books and periodicals. **Address:** Sloan School of Management, Massachusetts Institute of Technology, Rm. E62-464, 50 Memorial Dr., Cambridge, MA 02142-1347, U.S.A. **Online address:** evhippel@mit.edu

VON KELLENBACH, Katharina. German (born Germany), b. 1960. **Genres:** Theology/Religion, History. **Career:** Temple University, teaching assistant and instructor, 1985-88; Lehigh University, visiting lecturer, 1989, Muhlenberg and Moravian College, visiting assistant professor, 1990-91; St. Mary's College of Maryland, Department of Philosophy and Religious Studies, assistant professor, 1991-2000, associate professor, 2000-06, chair, 2003-07, professor, 2006-, coordinator of interdisciplinary program in women's studies, 1991-200; U.S. Holocaust Memorial Museum, associate of center for advanced holocaust studies, 1999-2000. Writer. **Publications:** Anti-Judaism in Feminist Religious Writings, 1994; (ed. with S. Scholz) Zwischen-Räume: Deutsche Feministische Theologinnen im Ausland, 2000; (ed. with B. Krondorfer and N. Reck) Von Gott Reden im Land der Täter: Theologische Stimmen der dritten Generation nach der Shoah, 2001; (with B. Krondorfer and N. Reck) Mit Blick auf die Taäter: Fragen an die deutsche Theologie nach 1945, 2006. Contributor to books and periodicals. **Address:** Department of Philosophy and Religious Studies, St. Mary's College of Maryland, 18952 E Fisher Rd., St. Marys City, MD 20686-3001, U.S.A. **Online address:** kvonkellenbach@smcm.edu

VONNEGUT, Norb. American (born United States), b. 1958. **Genres:** Novels. **Career:** Morgan Stanley Financial Services, executive director, 1996-2006; Silvercrest Asset Management Group, managing director, 2006-09; Norb Vonnegut L.L.C., founder, 2009-. Writer and financial advisor. **Publications:** Top Producer (novel), 2009. **Address:** c/o Scott Hoffman, Folio Literary Management, 505 8th Ave., New York, NY 10018, U.S.A.

VON REDEN, Sitta. American/German (born Germany) **Genres:** History, Business/Trade/Industry. **Career:** Friedrich Meinecke Institute Free University, student assistant, 1983-85; The Queen's College, associate research fellow, 1990-91; University of Bristol, senior lecturer in ancient history and classics, 1992-2005; University of Augsburg, faculty of historisch-philologischen private lecturer, 2005-. Writer. **Publications:** Exchange in Ancient Greece, 1995; (ed. with P. Cartledge and P. Millett) Kosmos: Order, Individual and Community in Classical Athens, 1998; (ed. with W. Scheidel) The Ancient Economy, 2002; Money in Ptolemaic Egypt, 2007; Money in Classical Antiquity, 2010. **Address:** Department of Ancient History, Augsburg University, 10 University St., Augsburg, D-86135, Germany. **Online address:** sitta.vonreden@ukonline.co.uk

VON SCHLEGELL, Mark. American (born United States) **Genres:** Novels, Sciences, Science Fiction/Fantasy. **Career:** Rambler, newsletter editor. Teacher, art critic and writer. **Publications:** Venusia: A True Story, 2005; Mercury Station: A Transit, 2009. Contributor to anthologies and periodicals. **Address:** c/o Author Mail, MIT Press, 55 Hayward St., Cambridge, MA 02142-1493, U.S.A. **Online address:** schlegell@sff.net

VON TRIER, Lars. Danish (born Denmark), b. 1956. **Genres:** Plays/Screenplays, Biography. **Career:** Zentropa, co-founder, 1992. Director and screenwriter. **Publications:** The Element of Crime, 1984; Epidemic, 1987; Medea, 1988; The Kingdom, 1994; Breaking the Waves, 1996; The Kingdom II, 1997; The Idiots, 1998; Dogme 2, Idioterne: manuskript og dagbog, 1998; (contrib.) Il dogma della libertá, 1999; Dancer in the Dark, 2000; (contrib.) Trier om von Trier, 2003; Dogville, 2003; Lars fon Trier: Kontrol'nye Raboty, 2004. **Address:** Zentropa Productions, Filmbyen 24, Huidovre, DK-2650, Denmark.

VON TUNZELMANN, Alex. British (born England), b. 1977?. **Genres:** History, Biography. **Career:** Researcher and writer. **Publications:** Indian Summer: The Secret History of the End of an Empire, 2007. Contributor to books and periodicals. **Address:** A.P. Watt Ltd., 20 John St., London, GL WC1N 2DR, England.

VON TUNZELMANN, G(eorge) N(icholas). New Zealander (born New Zealand), b. 1943. **Genres:** Technology, Industrial Relations. **Career:** Cambridge University, St. John's College, lecturer and fellow, 1970-84; University of Sussex, Social Policy Research Unit, reader and professor of the economics of science and technology, 1984-2005, director of research, 2001-05; University of Sussex, R.M. Phillips professor of science and technology policy, 2005-. Writer. **Publications:** Steam Power and British Industrialization to 1860, 1978; (ed. with J. Fagerberg and B. Verspagen) The Dynamics of Technology, Trade and Growth, 1994; Technology and Industrial Progress: The Foundations of Economic Growth, 1995; Technical Change and the World Economy; (ed. with F. McGowan and S. Radoševic) Emerging Industrial Structure of the Wider Europe, 2004; (ed. with H. Hannula and S. Radoševic) Estonia, The New EU Economy: Building a Baltic Miracle?, 2006; (co-ed.) The Genesis of Innovation: Systemic Linkages Between Knowledge and the Market, 2008. **Address:** Science and Technology Policy Research, University of Sussex, Freeman Ctr. Ground Fl., International and Study Abroad Office, Brighton, ES BN1 9QE, England. **Online address:** g.n.von-tunzelmann@sussex.ac.uk

VON UNWERTH, Matthew. American (born United States), b. 1970?. **Genres:** Novels, Biography. **Career:** New York Psychoanalytic Institute, Abraham A. Brill Library, director; Philoctetes Center for the Multidisciplinary Study of the Imagination, coordinator. Writer. **Publications:** Freud's Requiem: Mourning, Memory, and the Invisible History of a Summer Walk, 2005. **Address:** c/o Author Mail, Publicity Department, Riverhead Books, 375 Hudson St., New York, NY 10014, U.S.A.

VON WARD, Paul. American (born United States), b. 1939. **Genres:** Psychology, Sciences, Social Sciences, Intellectual History, Natural History, Mythology/Folklore, Paranormal, Philosophy, Politics/Government, Social Commentary, Adult Non-fiction. **Career:** U.S. Department of State, foreign service officer, 1965-80; Delphi Intl., founder and chief executive officer, 1980-95; writer, 1995-. **Publications:** Dismantling the Pyramid: Government by the People, 1981; Solarian Legacy: Metascience and a New Renaissance, 1997; Our Solarian Legacy: Multidimensional Humans in a Self-Learning Universe, 2001; Gods, Genes, and Consciousness: Nonhuman Intervention in Human History, 2004; The Soul Genome: Science and Reincarnation, 2008;

We've Never Been Alone: History of Extraterrestrial Intervention, 2011. Contributor to periodicals. **Address:** PO Box 1776, Dahlonega, GA 30533, U.S.A. **Online address:** paul@vonward.com

VON WIESENBERGER, Arthur. American (born United States), b. 1953. **Genres:** Food And Wine. **Career:** Television Producer of Documentaries for European, African and Asian clients, 1975-78; Beverage industry, consultant, 1978-82; International Source Management, president and chairman, 1982-88; Berkeley Springs International Water Tasting, water master, 1991-; Ottledwater Web, founder; Santa Barbara Magazine, editor; Santa Barbara News-Press, co-publisher, 2006-, columnist; El Mexicano Newspaper, co-publisher. Writer. **Publications:** Oasis: The Complete Guide to Bottled Water Throughout the World, 1978; H2O: The Guide to Quality Bottled Water, 1988; The Santa Barbara Restaurant Guide, 1990, 3rd ed., 2001; The Pocket Guide to Bottled Water, 1991; Champagne and Caviar: A Connoisseur's Survival Guide, 1992; The Taste of Water, 1995. Contributor to periodicals. **Address:** Best Cellars L.L.C., PO Box 5658, Santa Barbara, CA 93150, U.S.A. **Online address:** nipperino@aol.com

VON ZELEWSKY, Alexander. Swiss (born Switzerland), b. 1936. **Genres:** Sciences, Chemistry. **Career:** University of California, A Miller Fellow, 1965-67; Eidgenössische Technische Hochschule Zürich, lecturer, 1967-69; University of Fribourg, Institute for Inorganic Chemistry, professor of inorganic chemistry and director, 1969-2006, now professor emeritus, Science Faculty, dean, 1974-75, 2000-02; Swiss National Science Foundation, vice president, 1980-92; Swiss Chemical Society, president, 1995-98. Writer. **Publications:** Science et Responsibilitaé: Wissenschaft und Verantwortung, 1982; Stereochemistry of Coordination Compounds, 1996. **Address:** Department of Chemistry, University of Fribourg, Ave. de l'Europe 2, Perolles, Fribourg, CH-1700, Switzerland. **Online address:** alexander.vonzelewsky@unifr.ch

VON ZIEGESAR, Cecily. American (born United States), b. 1970. **Genres:** Novels, Young Adult Fiction, Romance/Historical, Humor/Satire. **Career:** Writer. **Publications:** You Know You Love Me, 2002; Gossip Girl, 2002; All I Want Is Everything, 2003; Because I'm Worth It, 2003; You're the One That I Want, 2004; I Like It like That, 2004; Nobody Does It Better, 2005; Nothing Can Keep us Together: A Gossip Girl Novel, 2005; The It Girl, 2005; Reckless: An It Girl Novel, 2006; Would I Lie to You: A Gossip Girl Novel, 2006; Only in Your Dreams: A Gossip Girl Novel, 2006; Notorious: An It Girl Novel, 2006; Don't You Forget About Me: A Gossip Girl Novel, 2007; It Had To Be You: The Gossip Girl Prequel, 2007; Lucky: An It Girl Novel, 2007; Unforgettable: An It Girl Novel, 2007; You Just Can't Get Enough: A Gossip Girl the Carlyles Novel, 2008; The Carlyles, 2008; Tempted: An It Girl Novel, 2008; Infamous: An It Girl Novel, 2008; Take a Chance on Me, 2009; Adored, 2009; Love the One You're With, 2009; I Will Always Love You, 2009; Devious: An It Girl Novel, 2009; Classic: An It Girl Novel, 2010; Cum Laude, 2010; Gossip Girl, Psycho Killer, 2011. **Address:** Little Brown & Co., 1271 Ave. of the Americas, New York, NY 10020, U.S.A. **Online address:** blog@gossipgirl.net

VOOS, Paula B. American (born United States), b. 1949. **Genres:** Organized Labor, Business/Trade/Industry, Economics. **Career:** Institute on Aging, research assistant, 1974; Portland State University, instructor, 1974-76; Harvard University, teaching assistant, 1978-79; University of Massachusetts, instructor in economics, 1978-81; University of Wisconsin, assistant professor, 1981-86, associate professor, 1987-91, professor of economics and industrial relations, 1992-98, Industrial Relations Research Institute, director, 1993-98; Red Caboose Day Care Center, president, 1989; Institute for Wisconsin's Future, president, 1995-98; Rutgers University, School of Management and Labor Relations, Department of Labor Studies and Employment Relations, professor, 1998-, chair, 1999-2007, credit director, 2007-. Writer. **Publications:** (With A.E. Eaton) Unions and Contemporary Innovations in Work Organization, Compensation, and Employee Participation, 1989. EDITOR AND CONTRIBUTOR: (with L. Mishel) Unions and Economic Competitiveness, 1992; Contemporary Collective Bargaining in the Private Sector, 1994. Contributor to books and journals. **Address:** School of Management and Labor Relations, Rutgers University, Labor Education Ctr., 50 Labor Center Way, New Brunswick, NJ 08903, U.S.A. **Online address:** pbvoos@work.rutgers.edu

VORNBERGER, Cal Calvin. (Charles Calvin Vornberger). American (born United States), b. 1950. **Genres:** Photography, Natural History. **Career:** Freelance art director, 1978-80; Modern Telecommunications Inc., director of design, 1980-87; Tumble Interactive Media Inc., founder and president, 1988-

2000, chief creative officer, 2000-01; Epic Edge, chief creative officer, 2000; University of Texas, instructor; New York University, instructor; Hunter College, instructor; Pratt Institute, instructor; Katharine Gibbs School, instructor, adjunct professor; National Opera Institute, fellow. Writer. **Publications:** Birds of Central Park, 2005. **Address:** c/o Author Mail, Harry N. Abrams Inc., 115 W 18th St., 6th Fl., New York, NY 10011-4113, U.S.A. **Online address:** cal@calvorn.com

VORNBERGER, Charles Calvin. See **VORNBERGER, Cal Calvin.**

VORNHOLT, John. Also writes as Carolyn Goode, Carolyn Goode. American (born United States), b. 1951. **Genres:** Novels, Biography, Young Adult Fiction, Young Adult Non-fiction, Children's Fiction. **Career:** Writer. **Publications:** (With A. Grayson) Computers to Go: A Guide to the Briefcase Portables, 1985; Masks, 1989; Mummies, 1991; Contamination, 1991; Sanctuary, 1992; War Drums, 1992; The Fabulist, 1993; How to Sneak into the Girls Locker Room, 1993; Antimatter, 1994; Star Trek Generations, 1994; Capture the Flag, 1994; Break a Leg!: Famous Curses and Superstitions, 1994; Voices, 1995; Leather Wings, 1995; River Quest, 1995; The Witching Well, 1995; Blood Oath, 1995; First Contact, 1996; Rogue Saucer, 1996; Aftershock, 1996; (with S. Ciencin) Sabertooth Mountain, 1996; The Tale of the Ghost Riders, 1996; Crossfire, 1996; Mind Meld, 1997; Halloween Invaders!, 1997; Yun and the Sea Serpents, 1997; Yee and the Wolves, 1997; Tsun and the Rats, 1997; Lai and the Headhunters, 1997; Chi and the Giant, 1997; Primal Rage: The Avatars, 1997; Tunnel through the Stars, 1998; Valley of the Lizard, 1998; Haunted House Hijinks, 1998; Prisoner of Cabin 13, 1998; Coyote Moon, 1998; Dominion War Book One: Behind Enemy Lines, 1998; Insurrection, 1998; Haunts in the House, 1999; Witchopoly, 1999; Quarantine: Double Helix 4, 1999; Joyride, 2000; Gemworld, vol. I-II, 2000; Mascot Mayhem, 2000; Gone Fishin, 2000; Knock on Wood, 2000; The Genesis Wave, 3 vols., 2000-01; Final Fantasy: The Spirits Within: A Novel, 2001; The Troll King, 2002; Dolphin Watch, 2002; Star Trek Nemesis: A Novelization for Young Readers, 2002; The Genesis Force, 2003; The Troll Queen, 2003; The Troll Treasure, 2003; Seven Crows, 2003; A Time to Be Born, 2004; A Time to Die, 2004; (as Carolyn Goode) Cupidity, 2005; Seven: A Novelization, 2005; Return: A Novelization, 2005; The Curse of the Chain Veil, 2010. **Address:** c/o Author Mail, Pocket Books, 1230 Ave. of the Americas, New York, NY 10020, U.S.A. **Online address:** johnvorn@aol.com

VOSS, Ralph F. American (born United States), b. 1943. **Genres:** Literary Criticism And History, Writing/Journalism, Young Adult Fiction. **Career:** Teacher of English and history, 1965-66; Texas AandM University-Commerce, instructor in English, 1967-70; University of Texas at Austin, associate instructor in English, 1973-75; Atlanta Junior College, assistant professor of English, 1975-77; University of Utah, visiting assistant professor of English and director of writing center, 1977-78; University of Alabama, assistant professor, 1978-84, director of freshman English, 1978-83, associate professor, 1984-90, professor of English, 1990-, Writing Center, director, 1978-80, professor emeritus English; Fort Hays State University, visiting professor, 1992. Writer. **Publications:** Elements of Practical Writing: A Guide to Professional Writing, 1985; A Life of William Inge: The Strains of Triumph, 1989; (with M.L. Keene) The Heath Guide to College Writing, 1992, 2nd ed., 1995. EDITOR: Magical Muse: Millennial Essays on Tennessee Williams, 2002; (with D. Jolliffe and M. Trachsel) Against the Grain: A Volume in Honor of Maxine Hairston, 2002; Truman Capote and the Legacy of In Cold Blood, 2011; Works appear in anthologies. Contributor of articles to journals. **Address:** Department of English, University of Alabama, 229 Morgan Hall, PO Box 870244, Tuscaloosa, AL 35487, U.S.A. **Online address:** rvoss@english.as.ua.edu

VOSS, Sarah (Henderson). American (born United States), b. 1945?. **Genres:** inspirational/Motivational Literature, Mathematics/Statistics, Theology/Religion, Poetry, Education, Philosophy. **Career:** University of Nebraska, instructor of mathematics, 1981-86, department of philosophy and religion, community minister and research associate, 1995; College of St. Mary, assistant professor of mathematics and mathematics program director, 1986-90; First Unitarian Church of Chicago, ministerial intern, 1991-92; Peoples Church, interim minister, 1992-94; Nebraska's Eastern Regional Math and Science Coalition, community minister and director, 1994-95; First Unitarian Church of Sioux City, consulting minister, 1999-, Unitarian Universalist minister; Pi.zine Magazine, editor. Writer. **Publications:** Out of Our Prayers, Hope, 1991; What Number is God?: Metaphors, Metaphysics, Metamathematics, and the Nature of Things, 1995; Voice to Voice, Heart to Heart:

The Story of an Interim Ministry, 1996; Zero: Stories and Essays: Reflections about Nothing, 1998. Contributor of articles to periodicals. **Address:** Skinner House Books, 25 Beacon St., Boston, MA 02108, U.S.A. **Online address:** sarvoss@aol.com

VOS SAVANT, Marilyn. American (born United States), b. 1946. **Genres:** Self Help, Education, How-to Books, Humor/Satire, Psychology, Sciences. **Career:** Parade Magazine, contributing editor, 1986-; Jarvik Research Inc., vice president, 1988-; The Thinking American Inc., editor and publisher, 1996-; Jarvik Heart Inc., executive. **Publications:** Omni I.Q. Quiz Contest, 1985; (with L. Fleischer) Brain Building: Exercising Yourself Smarter, 1990; Ask Marilyn: Answers to America's Most Frequently Asked Questions, 1992; The World's Most Famous Math Problem: The Proof of Fermat's Last Theorem and Other Mathematical Mysteries, 1993; I've Forgotten Everything I Learned in School!: A Refresher Course to Help You Reclaim Your Education, 1994; More Marilyn: Some Like It Bright!, 1994; The Power of Logical Thinking: Easy Lessons in the Art of Reasoning-and Hard Facts about Its Absence in Our Lives, 1996; Of Course I'm for Monogamy; I'm also for Everlasting Peace and an End to Taxes, 1996; The Art of Spelling: The Madness and the Method, 2000; Growing Up: A Classic American Childhood: What Kids Should Know Before They Leave Home, 2002. Contributor to periodicals. **Address:** The Thinking American Inc., PO Box 967, Ansonia Sta., New York, NY 10023, U.S.A.

VOSTI, Stephen A. American (born United States), b. 1955. **Genres:** Agriculture/Forestry. **Career:** Federal University of Minas Gerais, Centro de Desenvolvimento e Planejamento Regional, visiting professor and postdoctoral research fellow in population sciences, 1985-87; International Food Policy Research Institute, Environment and Production Technology Division, research fellow, 1987-99; University of California, visiting professor, 1999-2001, Department of Agricultural and Resource Economics, assistant adjunct professor, 2001-, associate adjunct professor. Writer. **Publications:** Malaria Among Goldminers in Southern Pará: Preliminary Estimates of Determinants and Individual Costs, 1990; Links Between Rural Poverty and Environment in Developing Countries: Asset Categories and Investment Poverty, 1995; (with M. Nerlove and W. Basel) Role of Farm-level Diversification in the Adoption of Modern Technology in Brazil, 1996; (ed. with T. Reardon) Sustainability, Growth, and Poverty Alleviation: A Policy and Agroecological Perspective, 1997; (co-author) Cattle, Deforestation, and Development in the Amazon: An Economic, Agronomic, and Environmental Perspective, 1998; Intensified Small-scale Livestock Systems in the Western Brazilian Amazon, 2001; Intensifying Small-scale Agriculture in the Western Brazilian Amazon: Issues, Implications and Implementation, 2001; Intensified Production Systems on Western Brazilian Amazon Settlement Farms: Could They Save the Forest? 2001; (with J. Witcover and C.L. Carpentier) Agricultural Intensification by Smallholders in the Western Brazilian Amazon: From Deforestation to Sustainable Land Use, 2002; Rights to Forest Products, Deforestation and Smallholder Income: Evidence from the Western Brazilian Amazon, 2003; Are Agricultural Policies Making Us Fat? Likely Links between Agricultural Policies and Human Nutrition and Obesity, and Their Policy Implications, 2006. **Address:** Department of Agricultural & Resource Economics, University of California, 2135 Social Sciences & Humanities, 1 Shields Ave., Davis, CA 95616-5270, U.S.A. **Online address:** vosti@primal.ucdavis.edu

VOWELL, Sarah. American (born United States), b. 1969. **Genres:** Essays, History, Novels. **Career:** Public Radio Intl. (PRI), contributing editor and commentator, 1996-2008; Sarah Lawrence College, instructor in writing and art; School of the Art Institute, instructor in writing and art; New York University, New York Institute for the Humanities, fellow. Journalist. **Publications:** Radio On: A Listener's Diary, 1997; Take the Cannoli: Stories from the New World, 2000; Partly Cloudy Patriot, 2002; (contrib.) Family Ties: A Contemporary Perspective, 2003; Assassination Vacation, 2005; The Wordy Shipmates, 2008; A History of 19th Century Hawaii, 2011; Unfamiliar Fishes, 2011. Contributor to books and periodicals. **Address:** c/o Author Mail, Steven Barclay Agency, 12 Western Ave., Petaluma, CA 94952-2907, U.S.A.

VREELAND, Susan (Joyce). American (born United States), b. 1946. **Genres:** Novels, Novellas/Short Stories, Young Adult Fiction. **Career:** San Diego Unified School District, instructor in English, 1969-2000, instructor in ceramics, 1986-2000; writer, 1988-. **Publications:** NOVELS: What Love Sees, 1988; What English Teachers Want: a Survival Guide, 1995; Girl in Hyacinth Blue, 1999; The Passion of Artemisia, 2002; The Forest Lover, 2004; Life Studies, 2005; Luncheon of the Boating Party, 2007; Clara and Mr. Tiffany, 2011. Works appear in anthologies. Contributor of articles to magazines and journals. **Address:** 6246 Caminito Araya, PO Box 25523, San Diego, CA 92122-3402, U.S.A. **Online address:** susan@svreeland.com

VROOM, Victor H. American/Canadian (born Canada), b. 1932. **Genres:** Administration/Management, Psychology, Business/Trade/Industry. **Career:** University of Michigan, Institute for Social Research, assistant study director, 1955-58, Department of Psychology, instructor, 1958, lecturer, 1959; University of Pennsylvania, assistant professor of psychology, 1960-63; Carnegie Institute of Technology, associate professor, 1963-66; Carnegie-Mellon University, professor of psychology and industrial administration, 1966-72; Yale University, School of Organization and Management, professor of administrative sciences, 1972-73, professor of psychology, 1972-, John G. Searle professor, 1973-2007, Department of Administrative Sciences, chairman, 1972-75, Institute of Social and Policy Sciences, associate director, 1972-75, Bearing Point professor of management, 2007-; Society of Industrial-Organizational Psychology, president, 1980-81; AVT Business School, visiting professor, 2004-. Academy of Management, fellow. Writer. **Publications:** Some Personality Determinants of the Effects of Participation, 1960; (co-author) The Productivity of Work Groups, 1963; Work and Motivation, 1964, rev. ed., 1995; Motivation in Management, 1965; (ed.) Methods of Organizational Research, 1967; (with P.W. Yetton) Leadership and Decision-Making, 1973; Work and Motivation, 1982; (with A.G. Jago) The New Leadership: Managing Participation in Organizations, 1988; (foreword) The Acceptance of Human Resource Innovation: Lessons for Management, 1989; (intro.) Manage People, Not Personnel: Motivation and Performance Appraisal, 1990. EDITOR: Methods of Organization Research, 1967; (with E.L. Desi) Management and Motivation: Selected Readings, 1970. **Address:** Yale School of Management, 135 Prospect St., PO Box 208200, New Haven, CT 06520-8200, U.S.A. **Online address:** victor.vroom@yale.edu

VUIC, Jason. American (born United States), b. 1972. **Genres:** History. **Career:** Ohio State University, Center for Slavic and East European Studies, assistant director, 2002-06; Bridgewater College, assistant professor of history. Writer and historian. **Publications:** The Yugo: The Rise and Fall of the Worst Car in History, 2009. Contributor to journals and periodicals. **Address:** Staunton, VA , U.S.A. **Online address:** jvuic@bridgewater.edu

VUKCEVICH, Ray. American (born United States), b. 1946?. **Genres:** Novellas/Short Stories, Literary Criticism And History. **Career:** University of Oregon, computer programmer. Writer. **Publications:** The Man of Maybe Half-a-Dozen Faces, 2000; Meet Me in the Moon Room: Stories, 2001; The Best of Lady Churchill's Rosebud Wristlet, 2007; Alembical, 2008; Interfictions 2 Second Life Salon, 2009, Boarding Instructions, 2010. **Address:** c/o Author Mail, St. Martin's Minotaur, 175 5th Ave., New York, OR 10010, U.S.A. **Online address:** rayv@uoregon.edu

W

WABER, Bernard. American (born United States), b. 1924. **Genres:** Children's Fiction, Animals/Pets, Adult Non-fiction, Social Commentary. **Career:** Seventeen Magazine, commercial artist, 1952-54; Condé Nast Publications, staff, commercial artist, 1952-54; Life Magazine, graphic designer, 1955-72; author and illustrator of children's books, 1961-; People Magazine, graphic designer, 1974-88. **Publications:** SELF-ILLUSTRATED: Lyle at Christmas, 1998. OTHERS: Lorenzo, 1961; The House on East 88th Street, 1962 in UK as Welcome, Lyle, 1969; Rich Cat, Poor Cat, 1963; How to Go about Laying an Egg, 1963; Just Like Abraham Lincoln, 1964; Lyle, Lyle, Crocodile, 1965; Lyle and the Birthday Party, 1966; You Look Ridiculous, Said the Rhinoceros to the Hippopotamus, 1966; An Anteater Named Arthur, 1967; Cheese, 1967; A Rose for Mr. Bloom, 1968; Lovable Lyle, 1969; A Firefly Named Torchy, 1970; Nobody Is Perfick, 1971; Ira Sleeps Over, 1972; Lyle Finds His Mother, 1974; I Was All Thumbs, 1975; But Names Will Never Hurt Me, 1976; Goodbye, Funny Dumpy-Lumpy, 1977; Mice on My Mind, 1977; The Snake: A Very Long Story, 1978; You're a Little Kid with a Big Heart, 1980; Dear Hildegarde, 1980; Bernard, 1982; Funny, Funny Lyle, 1987; Ira Says Goodbye, 1988; Lyle at the Office, 1994; Do You See a Mouse?, 1995; Gina, 1995; A Lion Named Shirley Williamson, 1996; Bearsie Bear and the Surprise Sleepover Party, 1997; The Mouse That Snored, 2000; Fast Food! Gulp!, Gulp!, 2001; Courage, 2002; Evie & Margie, 2003; Betty's Day Off, 2005; Lyle Walks the Dogs: A Counting Book, 2009. **Address:** Houghton Mifflin Children's Books, 222 Berkeley St., 8th Fl., Boston, MA 02116-3764, U.S.A.

WABUDA, Susan. American (born United States), b. 1957. **Genres:** Theology/Religion, History. **Career:** Fordham University, Department of History, associate professor, 1991-, associate chair for undergraduate studies, 2001-03, St. Edmund Campion Institute for the Advancement of Intellectual Excellence, advisor, 2003-, St. Robert Southwell, S. J. Lecture Series, administrator, 2007-. Writer. **Publications:** (Contrib. and ed. with C. Litzenberger) Belief and Practice in Reformation England: A Tribute to Patrick Collinson from his Students, 1998; Preaching during the English Reformation, 2002. CONTRIBUTOR: Thomas Cranmer: Churchman and Scholar, 1993; Religion and the English People, 1500-1640: New Voices, New Perspectives, 1998; The Beginnings of English Protestantism, 2002; Studies in Church History, 38 vols., 2004. **Address:** Department of History, Fordham University, 623 Dealy Hall, 441 E Fordham Rd., Bronx, NY 10458-5159, U.S.A. **Online address:** wabuda@fordham.edu

WACH, Kenneth. Australian/German (born Germany), b. 1944. **Genres:** Art/Art History, Architecture. **Career:** University of Melbourne, School of Creative Arts, Department of Culture and Communication, principal fellow, associate professor and head of school, 1972-. Writer. **Publications:** (Contrib.) Surrealism: Revolution by Night, 1993; Salvador Dali: Masterpieces from the Collection of the Salvador Dali Museum, 1996. Contributor of articles to magazines. **Address:** School of Creative Arts, University of Melbourne, A203, Arts Ctr Bldg., Carlton, AC 3053, Australia. **Online address:** kenw@unimelb.edu.au

WACHSBERGER, Ken(neth). American (born United States), b. 1949. **Genres:** Writing/Journalism, Autobiography/Memoirs, How-to Books, inspirational/Motivational Literature. **Career:** Michigan State University, instructor in writing, 1982-87; Lansing Community College, instructor in writing,

1984-87; Eastern Michigan University, lecturer, 1987-; Azenphony Press, founder and editor, 1987-; Pierian Press, director of journals division and managing editor, 1988-99; MCB University Press, managing editor, 1999-2001; Gale Group, Cengage Learning, editor, 2001-; School for Compulsive Communicators, founder, instructor and dean; Jackson State Prison, teacher of writing classes. Educator and consultant. **Publications:** Beercans on the Side of the Road: The Story of Henry the Hitchhiker, 1988; (with S. Kalib) The Last Selection: A Child's Journey through the Holocaust, 1991; (with B. Mednicki) Never Be Afraid: A Jew in the Maquis, 1997; The Ballad of Ken and Emily: Or, Tales from the Counterculture, 1997; Your Partner Has Breast Cancer?: 21 Ways to Keep Sane as a Support Person, 2001; Transforming Lives: A Socially Responsible Guide to the Magic of Writing and Researching, 2004. EDITOR: Voices from the Underground: Insider Histories of the Vietnam Era Underground Press and Voices from the Underground: A Directory of Resources and Sources on the Vietnam Era Underground Press, 2 vols., 1993; Facts on File Banned Books Series, 4 vols. (Literature Suppressed on Religious/Political/Social/Sexual Grounds), 1998; 100 Banned Books, 1999; Voices from the Underground Series, 4 vols., 2011-12. Works appear in anthologies. Contributor to magazines and newspapers. **Address:** Azenphony Press, PO Box 130884, Ann Arbor, MI 48113-0884, U.S.A. **Online address:** ken@azenphonypress.com

WACHSMANN, Shelley. American (born United States), b. 1950?. **Genres:** Archaeology/Antiquities. **Career:** Hebrew University, assistant, 1975; Israel Department of Antiquities and Museums, inspector of underwater antiquities, 1976-89; Israel Antiquities Authority, archaeologist and researcher, 1990; Texas A&M University, Meadows visiting assistant professor of Biblical archeology, 1990-99, Meadows Associate professor of Biblical archeology, 1999-2010, Meadows professor of Biblical archeology, 2010-, Nautical Archaeology Program, coordinator, 2009-; The Persian War Shipwreck Survey, Canadian team archaeological principal investigator, 2003-06; The Danaos Project, archaeological principal investigator, 2007-09. Writer. **Publications:** Aegeans in the Theban Tombs, 1987; (co-author) The Excavations of an Ancient Boat from the Sea of Galilee (Lake Kinneret), 1990; The Sea of Galilee Boat: An Extraordinary 2000-Year-Old Discovery, 1995, 2nd ed. as Sea of Galilee boat, 2009; Seagoing Ships and Seamanship in the Bronze Age Levant, 1998; The Gurob Ship Cart Model and Its Mediterranean Context, forthcoming. Contributor of articles to books, journals and magazines. **Address:** Department of Anthropology, Texas A & M University, 122 Anthropology, College Station, TX 77843, U.S.A. **Online address:** swachsmann@tamu.edu

WACHTEL, Eleanor. Canadian (born Canada), b. 1947. **Genres:** Communications/Media, Writing/Journalism, Women's Studies And Issues, Biography, Autobiography/Memoirs, Literary Criticism And History, Young Adult Fiction. **Career:** Canadian Broadcasting Corporation (CBC-Radio), theater and film critic, 1979-87, writer and broadcaster, 1988-; Simon Fraser University, adjunct professor of women's studies, 1984-87; Kootenay School of Writing, teacher, 1985-87. **Publications:** (With A. Wachtel) Women's Cooperative Enterprise in Nakuru, 1977; How to Make it Work: A Report of the B.C. Human Rights Commission on Strengthening the Statutory Protection of Human Rights, February 1983, 1983; I'm Okay, We're not so Sure About You: A Report of the B.C. Human Rights Commission on Extensions to the Code, February 1983, 1983; What this Country did to Us, It Did to Itself:

A Report of the B.C. Human Rights Commission on the Farmworkers and Domestic Workers, February 1983, 1983; (co-author) Women and the Constitution, 1992; (co-author) A Feminist Guide to the Canadian Constitution, 1992; Writers & Company, 1993; More Writers & Company, 1996; Original Minds: Conversations with CBC Radio's Eleanor Wachtel, 2003; Random Illuminations: Conversations with Carol Shields, 2007. EDITOR: Battered and Blamed, 1980; A Perspective on Intervention in Cases of Wife Assault, 1980; Hitler's Holocaust: A Fact of History, 1986; (with R. Anderson) The Expo Story, 1986; (with L. Scheier and S. Sheard) Language in Her Eye: Views on Writing and Gender by Canadian Women Writing in English, 1990; Lost Classics, 2000. Contributor to periodicals. Works appear in anthologies. **Address:** Writers & Co., CBC Radio Arts and Entertainment, PO Box 500, Sta. A, Toronto, ON M5W 1E6, Canada. **Online address:** eleanor_wachtel@cbc.ca

WACHTEL, Shirley Russak. American (born United States), b. 1951. **Genres:** Children's Fiction, Essays, Novels, Young Adult Non-fiction. **Career:** Brooklyn Graphic Newspaper, editor-in-chief, 1976-77; Courier-Life Publications, freelancer; Ad Ventures Associates (advertising agency), creative partner, 1985-88; Middlesex County College, associate professor of English, 1988-, professor; James Madison High School, English teacher; The Brooklyn Times, columnist; The Staten Island Advance, feature writer. **Publications:** What Would I Be?, 1995; Addison Wesley Longman Interactive Guide to Newsweek, 1999; My Mother's Shoes-A Memoir, 2002; The Eight Days of Hanukkah, 2003; The Story of Blima: A Holocaust Survivor, 2005; In The Mellow Light: Collected Poems, 2009. Contributor of articles to newspapers and journals. **Address:** c/o Ben Camardi, Harold Matson Company Inc., 276 5th Ave., New York, NY 10001-4509, U.S.A. **Online address:** shirley_wachtel@middlesexcc.edu

WACHTER, Kenneth W. (Kenneth Willcox Wachter). American (born United States), b. 1947. **Genres:** History, Medicine/Health, Sciences. **Career:** Bell Telephone Laboratories, associate technical staff, 1968-69; St. Catherine's College, research fellow, 1971-74; Harvard University, assistant professor of statistics, 1974-77, head tutor of statistics, 1975-77, Eliot House, resident tutor, Harvard Center for Population Studies, research associate, associate professor of statistics, 1977-78; University of California, Miller fellow in statistics, 1977-79, Department of Demography, associate professor of demography and statistics, 1979-85, professor of demography and statistics, 1985-, chair, 1997-2008; National Bureau for Economic Research, associate, 1979-92; Social Science Research Council, director, 1993-2000; Social Science Research Council, board director, 1993-2000; Theoretical Population Biology, associate editor, 1993-2002; National Research Council Workshops on Biodemography, co-chair, 1995-97; American Academy of Arts and Sciences, fellow, 1996; Freshpond Institute, research associate, 1998-99; Population Association of America, board director, 1999-2002. Writer. **Publications:** (With E.A. Hammell and P. Laslett) Statistical Studies of Historical Social Structure, 1978; (with J. Bongaarts and T. Burch) Family Demography: Methods and their Applications, 1987; (with R. Floud and A. Gregory) Height, Health, and History: Nutritional Status in the United Kingdom, 1750-1980, 1990; (ed. with M.L. Straf) Future of Meta-Analysis, 1990; (ed. with C. Finch) Between Zeus and the Salmon, 1997; (ed. with R. Bulatao) Offspring, 2003; (ed. with M. Weinstein and J. Vaupel) Biosocial Surveys, 2008. **Address:** Department of Demography, University of California, 2232 Piedmont Ave., Berkeley, CA 94720-2120, U.S.A. **Online address:** wachter@demog.berkeley.edu

WACHTER, Kenneth Willcox. *See* **WACHTER, Kenneth W.**

WADDELL, Dan. British (born England), b. 1972?. **Genres:** Novels, Adult Non-fiction, Young Adult Non-fiction, Criminology/True Crime. **Career:** Journalist. **Publications:** NIGEL BARNES SERIES: The Blood Detective (novel), 2008; Blood Atonement, 2009. NONFICTION: Match of the Day Guide to Euro 2000, 2000; Survivor, 2001; Survivor-Panama: The Official Companion to the Second Series of TV's Biggest Challenge, 2002; (with F. Roddam) The Auf Wiedersehen Pet Story: That's Living Alright, 2003; (with T. Hart and P.D. Winder) The Cloud Garden, 2003; Who Do You Think You Are?, 2004; How To Be a Detective, 2012. Contributor to periodicals. **Address:** c/o Araminta Whitley, Lucas Alexander Whitley Ltd., 14 Vernon St., London, GL W14 0RJ, England. **Online address:** dan@danwaddell.net

WADDELL, Martin. (Catherine Sefton). Irish (born Ireland), b. 1941. **Genres:** Novels, Children's Fiction, Young Adult Fiction, Novellas/Short Stories, Picture/Board Books, Novellas/Short Stories, Children's Non-fiction. **Career:** Writer, 1966-. **Publications:** NOVELS: Otley, 1966; Otley Pursued,

1967; Otley Forever, 1968; Otley Victorious, 1969; Come Back When I'm Sober, 1969; A Little Bit British: Being the Diary of an Ulsterman, 1970. CHILDREN'S FICTION: Ernie's Chemistry Set, 1978; Ernie's Flying Trousers, 1978; You and Me, Little Bear, 1980; The Great Green Mouse Disaster, 1981; The House under the Stairs, 1983; (ed.) A Tale to Tell, 1983; Going West, 1983; Big Bad Bertie, 1984; The Budgie Said GRR, 1985; The School Reporter's Notebook, 1985; Owl and Billy, 1986; The Day It Rained Elephants, 1986; Our Wild Weekend, 1986; The Tough Princess, 1986; Owland Billy and the Space Days, 1987; The Tall Story of Wilbur Small, 1987; Can't You Sleep, Little Bear?, 1988; Great Gran Gorilla to the Rescue, 1988; Great Gran Gorilla and the Robbers, 1988; Alice the Artist, 1988; Class Three and the Beanstalk, 1988; Our Sleepysaurus, 1988; Tales from the Shop That Never Shuts, 1988; Fred the Angel, 1989; The Hidden House, 1989; Judy the Bad Fairy, 1989; Owl and Billy and the Space Days, 1989; Once There Were Giants, 1989; The Park in the Dark, 1989; We Love Them, 1989; Daisy's Christmas, 1990; Amy Said, 1990; Grandma's Bill, 1990; Little Obie and the Flood, 1990; My Great Grandpa, 1990; Rosie's Babies, 1990; Coming Home, 1991; Farmer Duck, 1991; The Happy Hedgehog Band, 1991; Herbie Whistle, 1991; Let's Go Home, Little Bear, 1991; Squeak-a-lot, 1991; Little Obie and the Kidnap, 1991; The Toymaker: A Story in Two Parts, 1991; Man Mountain, 1991; Sailor Bear, 1992; The Pig in the Pond, 1992; The Ghost Family Robinson at the Seaside, 1992; Sam Vole and His Brothers, 1992; Owl Babies, 1992; The School That Went to Sea, 1993; The Fishface Feud, 1993; Rubberneck's Revenge, 1993; Stories from the Bible: Old Testament Stories, 1993; Little Mo, 1993; Baby's Hammer, 1993; Big Bad Mole's Coming!, 1993; The Lucky Duck Song, 1993; The Big, Big Sea, 1994; When the Teddy Bears Came, 1994; Shipwreck at Old Jelly's Farm, 1994; Upside Down Harry Brown, 1994; The Kidnapping of Suzie Q, 1994; Tango's Baby, 1995; The Get-away Hen, 1995; Mimi and the Picnic, 1995; John Joe and the Big Hen, 1995; My Aunt Sal and the Mega Sized Moose, 1996; The Dump Gang, 1996; Small Bear Lost, 1996; Mimi and the Blackberry Pie, 1996; Bears Everywhere, 1996; What Use Is a Moose?, 1996; Cup Final Kid, 1996; Ben's Bring Your Bear Party, 1997; The Life and Loves of Zoe T. Curley, 1997; Mimi's Christmas, 1997; The Perils of Lord Reggie Parrott, 1997; The Adventures of Pete and Mary Kate, 1997; Little Frog and the Dog, 1997; Little Frog and the Frog Olympics, 1997; Little Frog and the Tadpoles, 1997; Little Frog in the Throat, 1997; Mimi and the Dream House, 1998; Yum Yum Yummy, 1998; The Hollyhock Wall, 1999; Who Do You Love?, 1999; Well Done, Little Bear, 1999; Good Job, Little Bear!, 1999; Night Night, Cuddly Bear, 2000; Little Bear's Baby Book, 2000; Mimi Mouse's Christmas, 2000; The Little Bear Stories, 2001; Webster J. Duck, 2001; The Ghost in the Blue Velvet Dress, 2001; Milly Bean, Jungle Queen, 2001; The Haunting of Ellen, 2001; Tom Rabbit, 2001; A Kitten Called Moonlight, 2001; Snow Bears, 2002; Cup Run, 2003; Going Up, 2003; Hi, Harry!, 2003; Room for a Little One: A Christmas Tale, 2004; Shooting Star, 2004; Star Striker Titch, 2004; Tiny's Big Adventure, 2004; It's Quacking Time!, 2005; Millie Bean, Jungle Queen Jigsaw Book, 2005; Sleep Tight, Little Bear!, 2005; Death and the Neighbours At Ness, 2005; Ernie and the Fishface Gang, 2006; Bee Frog, 2007; Charlie's Tasks, 2007; Tough Ronald, 2007; Arabian Nights, 2008; Super Hungry Dinosaur, 2009; The Dirty Great Dinosaur, 2009; Beowulf and Grendel: Hopscotch Adventures, 2009; Captain Small Pig, 2009; The Orchard Book of Ghostly Stories, 2009; Ben and Bobo, 2010; Baba Yaga, 2010; The Orchard Book of Hans Christian Andersen's Fairy Tales, 2010. LITTLE DRACULA SERIES: Little Dracula's Christmas, 1986; Little Dracula's First Bite, 1986; Little Dracula At the Seaside, 1987; Little Dracula Goes to School, 1987; Little Dracula At the Seashore, 1992; Little Dracula's Monstrous Poster Book, 1992; Little Dracula and Millicent, 2010. HARRIET SERIES: Harriet and the Crocodiles, 1984; Harriet and the Haunted School, 1984; Harriet and the Robot, 1987. SINBAD SERIES: Sinbad and the Diamond Valley, 2009; Sinbad and the Monkeys, 2009; Sinbad and the Ogres, 2010; Sinbad and the Giant Spider, 2010; Sinbad and the Pirates, 2010. NAPPER SERIES: Napper Goes for Goal, 1981; Napper Strikes Again, 1981; Napper's Golden Goals, 1984; Napper's Luck, 1993; Napper's Big Match, 1993; Napper, Super-Sub, 1993. THE MYSTERY SQUAD SERIES: The Mystery Squad and the Dead Man's Message, 1984; The Mystery Squad and the Whistling Thief, 1984; The Mystery Squad and Mr. Midnight, 1984; Mystery Squad and the Whistling Teeth, 1984; The Mystery Squad and the Artful Dodger, 1984; The Mystery Squad and the Creeping Castle, 1985; The Mystery Squad and Gemini Job, 1985; The Mystery Squad and the Candid Camera, 1985; The Mystery Squad and the Cannonball Kid, 1986; The Mystery Squad and the Robot's Revenge, 1986. CHILDREN'S FICTION: AS CATHERINE SEFTON: In a Blue Velvet Dress: Almost a Ghost Story, 1972 in US as In a Blue Velvet Dress, 1973; The Sleepers on the Hill, 1973; The Back House Ghosts, 1974 in US as The Haunting of Ellen: A Story of Suspense, 1975; The Ghost and Bertie Boggin, 1980; Emer's Ghost, 1981; The Finn Gang, 1981; A Puff of Smoke, 1982; The Emma Dilemma, 1982; Island of the Strangers, 1983; My Gang, 1984; The Blue Misty Monsters, 1985; The Ghost Girl, 1985; The Ghost Ship, 1985; Flying Sam, 1986; Starry Night, 1986; Shadows on the Lake, 1987; Bertie Boggin and the Ghost Again!, 1988; The Day the Smells Went Wrong, 1988; Frankie's Story, 1988; The Haunted Schoolbag, 1989; The Beat of the Drum, 1989; Horace the Ghost, 1991; Along a Lonely Road, 1991; The Boggart in the Barrel, 1991; The Ghosts of Cobweb, 1992; The Cast-off, 1993; The Ghosts of Cobweb and the Skully Bones Mystery, 1993; The Ghosts of Cobweb and the Circus Star, 1994; The Ghosts of Cobweb and the TV Battle, 1994; The Pocket Elephant, 1995; The Skeleton Club, 1995; Watch Out, Fred's About, 1996. **Address:** David Higham Associates Ltd., 5-8 Lower John St., Golden Sq., London, GL W1F 9HA, England.

WADDINGTON, Patrick (Haynes). New Zealander/British (born England), b. 1934. **Genres:** History, Language/Linguistics, Literary Criticism And History, Music, Biography, Humanities. **Career:** Teacher, 1956-63; Queen's University, lecturer, senior lecturer in modern languages and Slavonic studies, 1963-73; Northern Ireland Board, chief examiner in Russian, 1963-66; Belfast Russian Circle, founder and organizer, 1965-73; Victoria University of Wellington, visiting professor, 1973, professor of Russian literature and civilization, 1974-93, department head, 1974-91, professor emeritus, 1993-; University of Victoria, Canada, Lansdown visitor, 1983; University of Queensland, Russian departmental review, chairperson, 1986; Copyright Licensing Ltd., director, 1990-95; Cambridge University, Wolfson College, visiting fellow, 1991-92; Armstrong Browning Library (TX), visiting fellow, 1991-92; University of Maryland, lecturer; Yale University, lecturer; Cornell University, lecturer; Baylor University, lecturer; British Broadcasting Corp., broadcaster; Australian Broadcasting Co., broadcaster; Radio New Zealand, broadcaster. **Publications:** A Basic Russian-English Vocabulary, 1962; (with D. Buckley) O Level Tests in Russian, 1963, rev. ed., 1965; (ed.) Sud'ba cheloveka, 1964; (ed.) Dama s sobachkoy, 1964, rev. ed., 1984; Russian by Subjects, 1965, rev. ed., 1989; Advanced Translation from Russian Prose, 1965; (ed.) Dvoryanskoyegnezdo, 1969; (ed.) Rudin, 1970; (ed.) The Dodillon Copies of Letters by Turgenev to Pauline & Louis Viardot, 1970; Turgenev and England, 1980; Turgenev and George Sand: An Improbable Entente, 1981; Browning and Russia, 1985; Patrick: Or, That Awful Warning: The Autobiography of Patrick S. Waddington, 1986; Tennyson and Russia, 1987; A First Russian Vocabulary, 1988; From The Russian Fugitive to The Ballad of Bulgarie: Episodes in English Literary Attitudes to Russia from Wordsworth to Swinburne, 1994; From the Russian Fugitive to the Ballad of Bulgarie: Episodes in English Literary Attitudes to Russia from Wordsworth to Swinburne, 1994; (ed.) Ivan Turgenev and Britain, 1995; Theirs but to Do and Die: The Poetry of the Charge of the Light Brigade at Balaklava, 25 October 1854, 1995; (ed.) Fathers and Children, 1998; Russian Interests of the Rossetti Family: Gabriele Pasquale Giuseppe (1783-1854), Dante Gabriel (1828-82), Christina Georgina (1830-94), William Michael (1829-1919), 1998; Turgenev and Pavlovsky: A Friendship and a Correspondence, 1998; The Origins and Composition of Turgenev's Novel Dym (Smoke), 1998; A Catalogue of Portraits of Ivan Sergeyevich Turgenev (1818-83), 1999; Turgenev's Mortal Illness: From Its Origins to the Autopsy, 1999; Three Letters by Gustave Flaubert in the Library of Trinity College, Cambridge, 2000; Some Signed Books by French Authors from the Paris Library of Ivan Sergeyevich Turgenev, 2000; (comp.) The Musical Works of Pauline Viardot-Garcia (1821-1910): A Chronological Catalogue, With an Index of Titles, 2001; Modest Little Banquet at the Arts Club, or, How William Ralston Shedden-Ralston Gave a Grand Dinner Party for Sixteen Literary Men in London on 22 October 1881 to Honour Ivan Sergeyevich Turgenev, 2001; (co-ed.) Fighting Fans: Football Hooliganism as a World Phenomenon, 2002; Turgenev's Seventh, or, Whatever Became of that Novel about Russian and French Socialists?, 2003; Unsung Struggler for Humanity and Truth: The Mysterious Miss Emily Reeve (1817-65), 2003; Russian by Subjects: A Classified Vocabulary, 2008. Contributor of articles to journals and newspapers. **Address:** Victoria University of Wellington, PO Box 600, Wellington, 6140, New Zealand.

WADDINGTON, Raymond B(ruce). American (born United States), b. 1935. **Genres:** Literary Criticism And History, Poetry, Economics. **Career:** University of Houston, instructor in English, 1961-62; University of Kansas, assistant professor of English, 1962-65; University of Wisconsin, assistant professor, associate professor, professor of English, 1966-82; University of California, professor of English, now professor emeritus; National Endowment for the Humanities, senior fellow, 1983. Writer. **Publications:** (Con-

trib.) Calm of Mind, 1971; The Mind's Empire: Myth and Form in George Chapman's Narrative Poems, 1974; Aretino's Satyr: Sexuality, Satire and Self-Projection in Sixteenth-Century Literature and Art, 2004; Aretino, Titian and La Humanita di Cristo, 2009. EDITOR: (with T.O. Sloan) The Rhetoric of Renaissance Poetry: From Wyatt to Milton, 1974; (with C.A. Patrides) The Age of Milton: Backgrounds to Seventeenth-century Literature, 1980; (with A.H. Williamson) The Expulsion of the Jews: 1492 and After, 1994. Contributor to journals. **Address:** Department of English, University of California, Voorhies Hall, 1 Shields Ave., Davis, CA 95616, U.S.A. **Online address:** rbwaddington@ucdavis.edu

WADDINGTON-FEATHER, John Joseph. British (born England), b. 1933. **Genres:** Novels, Children's Fiction, Plays/Screenplays, Poetry, Romance/Historical, Literary Criticism And History, Mystery/Crime/Suspense, Essays, Essays. **Career:** Shrewsbury Prison, honorary assistant chaplain, 1975-; Poetry and Audience Magazine, co-editor, 1953-54; Summer Bulletin, editor, 1963-74; Feather Books, founder and director; The Poetry Church magazine, editor, 1996-2008. **Publications:** Century of Model-Village Schooling, 1958; A Collection of Poems, 1963; Of Mills, Moors and Men, 1966; Leeds, the Heart of Yorkshire, 1967, 3rd ed., 1985; Yorkshire Dialect, 1970, 4th ed., 2002; (ed. with B. Cowley and G. Wade) Dialect Verse from the Ridings, 1970; Garlic Lane, 1970, rev. ed., 2000; Easy Street, 1973, rev. ed., 2000; One Man's Road, 1977; Six More Characters in Search of an Author (play), 1978; Quill's Adventures in the Great Beyond, 1980; Tall Tales from Yukon, 1984; Khartoum Trilogy and Other Poems, 1985; Quill's Adventures in Wasteland, 1986; Quill's Adventures in Grozzieland, 1988; Six Christian Monologues, 1990; Six More Poems on New Testament Characters, 1994; Tales of Harry Hedgehog, 1994; Feather's Foibles, 1995; Wild Tales from the West, 1998; The Museum Mystery, 1999; The Bradshaw Mystery, 2000; The Poetry Church Collection: Lent and Easter 2000, 2000; The Marcham Mystery, 2002; Legends of Americada, 2002; Chance Child, vol. I, 2002, vol. II, 2003; Legend Land, 2003; Lollipop Man (play), 2003; The Graveyard Mystery, 2004; Quill's Adventures in Mereful, 2004; Quill's Adventures in Humanfolkland, 2005; Illingworth House, 2005; Behind Corridors of Power 2005; Bill Braithwaite's Miracle 2006; Jonah, 2006; The Allotment Mystery, 2006; Tyndale 2007. EDITOR/CO-EDITOR: Northern Aspect, 1964; Swing Back, 1971; Ipso Facto, 1975; The Poetry Church Anthology, 1999; Feather's Miscellany No: 1, 2007; Feather's Miscellany No: 2, 2009; New Hymns Seasons and Occasions (1) 2005; Seasons and Occasions (11) 2006; Hymns from the Classics 2007; The Crucifixion, 2009. **Address:** Feather Books, PO Box 438, Shrewsbury, SY3 0WN, England. **Online address:** john@waddysweb.freeuk.com

WADE, Alan. See VANCE, Jack.

WADE, Roger. See LANKFORD, Terrill Lee.

WADE, (Sarah) Virginia. American/British (born England), b. 1945. **Genres:** Autobiography/Memoirs, Reference, Sports/Fitness. **Career:** Tennis player, 1968-86. Writer and broadcaster. **Publications:** (With M.L. Mellace) Courting Triumph (autobiography), 1978; (with J. Rafferty) Ladies of the Court: A Century of Women at Wimbleton, 1984. **Address:** International Management Group, 1 Erieview Plz., Cleveland, OH 44114, U.S.A.

WADE, Sidney. American (born United States), b. 1951. **Genres:** Poetry. **Career:** University of Florida, lecturer in English, 1986-, assistant professor of English, 1993-, professor of English; University of Istanbul, senior Fulbright lecturer, 1989-90; Subtropics, poetry editor. **Publications:** POEMS: Empty Sleeves, 1991; Green, 1998; From Istanbul/Istanbul'dan, 1998; Celestial Bodies, 2002; Stroke: Poems, 2008. Contributor to periodicals. **Address:** Department of English, University of Florida, 4211D Turlington Hall, Gainesville, FL 32611-7310, U.S.A. **Online address:** swade@english.ufl.edu

WADE, Stephen. British (born England), b. 1948. **Genres:** Poetry, Military/Defense/Arms Control, Criminology/True Crime, Autobiography/Memoirs. **Career:** North Lindsey College (secondary school), lecturer in English, 1974-95; University of Huddersfield, senior lecturer in English, 1995-2003; University of Hull, part-time lecturer. Writer. **Publications:** Churwell Poems, 1987; Christopher Isherwood, 1991; The Imagination in Transit, 1996; More on the Word-Hoard, 1997; Jewish American Literature since 1945, 1999; Reading the Applause, 1999; Write Yourself a New Life, How to Pathways, 2000; Somewhere Else: Poems, 2001; (ed.) Gladsongs and Gatherings: Poetry and Its Social Context in Liverpool since the 1960s, 2001; In My Own Shire:

Region and Belonging in British Writing, 1840-1970, 2002; Foul Deeds and Suspicious Deaths in Halifax, 2004; Unsolved Yorkshire Murders, 2004; Spies in the Empire: Victorian Military Intelligence, 2007; Tracing Your Police Ancestors, 2009; Hauntings In Lincolnshire, 2009; DNA Crime Investigations/Cold Cases Revisited, 2009; Tracing Your Criminal Ancestors, 2009; Empire and Espionage: The Anglo-Zulu War 1879, 2010; Escapes from the Noose, 2010; Tracing your Legal Ancestors, 2010; Rowlandson's Human Comedy, 2011; Killers in the North East, forthcoming. **Address:** c/o Author Mail, Praeger Publishers, 88 Post Rd. W, Westport, CT 06881, U.S.A. **Online address:** stephen.wade@attworld.com

WADE, Susan. American (born United States), b. 1955. **Genres:** Novels, Young Adult Fiction. **Career:** Writer. **Publications:** Walking Rain, 1996; Burn Pattern, forthcoming. Contributor of articles to periodicals. Works appear in anthologies. **Address:** Bantam Books, 1540 Broadway, New York, NY 10036, U.S.A. **Online address:** susan.wade@genie.com

WADELL, Paul J(oseph). American (born United States), b. 1951. **Genres:** Theology/Religion, Humanities. **Career:** Catholic Theological Union of Chicago, assistant professor, 1984-90, associate professor, 1990-94, professor of ethics, 1994; St. Norbert College, professor of religious studies, 1998-. Writer. **Publications:** Friendship and the Moral Life, 1989; Friends of God: Virtues and Gifts in Aquinas, 1991; The Primacy of Love: An Introduction to the Ethics of Thomas Aquinas, 1992; Morality: A Course on Catholic Living, 1996; Becoming Friends: Worship, Justice, and the Practice of Christian Friendship, 2002; The Moral of the Story: Learning from Literature About Human and Divine Love, 2002; Happiness and the Christian Moral Life: An Introduction to Christian Ethics, 2008; (with P.J. Wadell) Christian Moral Life: Faithful Discipleship for a Global Society, 2010. **Address:** St. Norbert College, 100 Grant St., Rm. 431 Boyle Hall, De Pere, WI 54115-2099, U.S.A. **Online address:** paul.wadell@snc.edu

WADIA, Maneck S. American (born United States), b. 1931. **Genres:** Novels, Administration/Management, Adult Non-fiction, Anthropology/Ethnology. **Career:** Indiana University, assistant professor of management, 1958-60; University of Pittsburgh, Administrative Science Center, Ford Foundation fellow, 1960-61; Stanford University, Graduate School of Business and administration, faculty, 1961-65, International Center for the Advancement of Management Education, research associate, 1961-64, faculty resident, 1964-65; Wadia Associates, president and chief executive officer, 1971-. Writer. **Publications:** The Nature and Scope of Management, 1966; (with H.W. Boyd) Marketing Management: Cases from Emerging Countries, 1966; (comp.) Management and the Behavioral Sciences, 1968; Cases in International Business, 1970; Shukriya America; The Magic Yorii (novel); The Prophet Zoroaster: Wisdom for the Modern Age from an Ancient Sage. Contributor of articles to journals. **Address:** 1660 Luneta Dr., Del Mar, CA 92014, U.S.A. **Online address:** hfwadia@adelphia.net

WADSWORTH, Ginger. American (born United States), b. 1945. **Genres:** Children's Fiction, Children's Non-fiction. **Career:** Teacher and writer, 1986-. **Publications:** Julia Morgan, Architect of Dreams, 1990; Rachel Carson, Voice for the Earth, 1992; John Muir, Wilderness Protector, 1992; Along the Santa Fe Trail, 1993; Tomorrow Is Daddy's Birthday, 1994; Susan Butcher, Sled Dog Racer, 1994; Giant Sequoia Trees, 1995; Laura Ingalls Wilder, Story Teller of the Prairie, 1997; John Burroughs, the Sage of Slabsides, 1997; Desert Discoveries, 1997; One on a Web, 1997; One Tiger Growls, 1999; Laura Ingalls Wilder, On My Own Biography, 1999; Tundra Discoveries, 1999; River Discoveries, 2002; Benjamin Banneker, Pioneering Scientist, 2003; Words West: Voices of Young Pioneers, 2003; The Wright Brothers, 2003; Cesar Chavez, 2005; Annie Oakley, 2005; Woolly Mammoths, 2006; Camping with the President, 2009; Survival in the Snow, 2009; Up, Up, and Away, 2009; First Girl Scout: The Life of Juliette Gordon Low, 2011. **Address:** 2 Fleetwood Ct., Orinda, CA 94563-4004, U.S.A. **Online address:** plumepal@aol.com

WAEHLER, Charles A. American (born United States), b. 1956. **Genres:** Human Relations/Parenting, Psychology, Psychiatry. **Career:** Northwestern University, senior teaching fellow, 1986-87, Faculty Development Program, coordinator, 1988-89; Associated Clinical Psychologists, psychotherapist, 1986-89; Counseling Psychologists, private practice, 1990-95; Cornerstone Comprehensive Psychological Services, private practice, 1995-; University of Akron, assistant professor, 1989-95, associate professor, 1995-, Institute for Life-Span Development and Gerontology, fellow, Collaborative Program

in Counseling Psychology, training director, 2000-07. Writer. **Publications:** Bachelors: The Psychology of Men Who Haven't Married, 1996; (contrib.) Teaching and Learning Personality Assessment, 1998; (with L.N. Edelstein) What Do I Say?: The Therapists Guide to Answering Client Questions, 2011. Contributor to books and periodicals. **Address:** Department of Psychology, University of Akron, Rm. 354, Arts and Science Bldg., 302 Buchtel Common, Akron, OH 44325-6205, U.S.A. **Online address:** cwaehler@uakron.edu

WAELTI-WALTERS, Jennifer (Rose). Canadian/British (born England), b. 1942. **Genres:** Literary Criticism And History, Women's Studies And Issues, Translations, Young Adult Fiction, Social Sciences. **Career:** Goldsmith's College, lecturer, 1966-67; Sorbonne, lecturer in English, 1967-68; University of Victoria, Department of French, assistant professor of French, associate professor of French, professor of French, 1968-97, chair, 1979-84, professor of women's studies, 1979-97, director of women's studies, 1983-95, professor emeritus of French and women's studies, 1997-. Writer. **Publications:** Alchimie et litterature: Une étude de Portrait de l'artiste en Jeunesinge, 1975; J. M. G. LeClézio, 1977; Michel Butor: A Study of His View of the World and a Panorama of His Work, 1954-1974, 1977; Icare ou l'évasion Impossible: étude psycho-mythique de l'aeuvre de J.M.G. LeClézio, 1981; Fairy Tales and the Female Imagination, 1982; (with M. Verthuy-Williams) Jeanne Hyvrard, 1988; Feminist Novelists of the Belle Epoque: Love as a Lifestyle, 1990; (ed. with S.C. Hause and trans.) Feminisms of The Belle Epoque: A Historical and Literary Anthology, 1994; Jeanne Hyvrard: Theorist of the Modern World, 1996; (trans. with J.P. Mentha and intro.) The Dead Girl in a Lace Dress, 1996; Damned Women: Lesbians in French Novels 1796-1996, 2000. **Address:** Department of Women's Studies, University of Victoria, Rm. B111, Clearihue Bldg., 3800 Finnerty Rd., PO Box 3045, Sta. CSC, Victoria, BC V8W 3P4, Canada.

WAGENER, Leon. American (born United States) **Genres:** Biography, Travel/Exploration, Autobiography/Memoirs. **Career:** Boston Globe, correspondent. Journalist. **Publications:** (With B. Foster) Foster Child: A Biography of Jodie Foster, 1997; One Giant Leap: Neil Armstrong's Stellar American Journey, 2004. Contributor to periodicals. **Address:** c/o Author Mail, Forge Books, 175 5th Ave., New York, NY 10010-7703, U.S.A.

WAGMAN, Morton. American (born United States), b. 1925. **Genres:** Psychology, Sciences, Information Science/Computers. **Career:** University of Michigan, Department of Psychology, instructor, 1953-55; Veterans Administration Hospital, clinical psychologist, 1955-56; Veterans Administration, Michigan Regional Office, clinical psychologist, 1956-57; University of Illinois, instructor, 1957-59, clinical counselor at counseling center, 1957-86, assistant professor, 1959-65, associate professor, 1965-69, professor, 1969-86, professor emeritus of psychology, 1986-. Writer. **Publications:** The Dilemma and the Computer: Theory, Research, and Applications to Counseling Psychology, 1984; Computer Psychotherapy Systems: Theory and Research Foundations, 1988; Artificial Intelligence and Human Cognition: A Theoretical Intercomparison of Two Realms of Intellect, 1991; Cognitive Science and Concepts of Mind: Toward a General Theory of Human and Artificial Intelligence, 1991; Cognitive Psychology and Artificial Intelligence: Theory and Research in Cognitive Science, 1993; The Sciences of Cognition: Theory and Research in Psychology and Artificial Intelligence, 1995; Human Intellect and Cognitive Science: Toward a General Unified Theory of Intelligence, 1996; The General Unified Theory of Intelligence: Its Central Conceptions and Specific Application to Domains of Cognitive Science, 1997; Cognitive Science and The Symbolic Operations of Human and Artificial Intelligence: Theory and Research into the Intellective Processes, 1997; The Ultimate Objectives of Artificial Intelligence: Theoretical and Research Foundations, Philosophical and Psychological Implications, 1998; Language and Thought In Humans and Computers: Theory and Research in Psychology, Artificial Intelligence, and Neural Science, 1998; Cognitive Science and the Mind-Body Problem: From Philosophy to Psychology to Artificial Intelligence to Imaging of the Brain, 1998; The Human Mind According to Artificial Intelligence: Theory, Research, and Implications, 1999; Scientific Discovery Processes in Humans and Computers: Theory and Research in Psychology and Artificial Intelligence, 2000; Problem-solving Processes in Humans and Computers: Theory and Research in Psychology and Artificial Intelligence, 2002; Logical Processes in Humans And Computers: Theory and Research in Psychology and Artificial Intelligence, 2003; Reasoning Processes in Humans and Computers: Theory and Research in Psychology and Artificial Intelligence, 2003. Contributor to periodicals. **Address:** Department of Psychology, University of Illinois, 603 E Daniel St., Champaign, IL 61820, U.S.A.

WAGMAN-GELLER, Marlene. American/Canadian (born Canada), b. 1954?. **Genres:** Essays. **Career:** North Toronto Collegiate, faculty; Eastern High School of Commerce, teacher; Sweetwater High School, 1990-. Writer. **Publications:** Once Again to Zelda: The Stories behind Literature's Most Intriguing Dedications, 2008; Eureka! The Surprising Stories behind the Ideas That Shaped the World, 2010. **Address:** San Carlos, CA , U.S.A. **Online address:** onceagaintozelda@hotmail.com

WAGNER, Andreas. American/Austrian (born Austria), b. 1967. **Genres:** Sciences, Chemistry. **Career:** Institute for Advanced Study Berlin, fellow, 1995-96; Los Alamos National Laboratory, visiting scientist, 1996; Santa Fe Institute, postdoctoral fellow, 1996-98; University of New Mexico, Department of Biology, assistant professor, 1998, associate professor, 2002; Albuquerque High Performance Computing Center, associated faculty, 2000; University of Zurich, Department of Biochemistry, professor of bioinformatics, 2006-. Writer. **Publications:** Robustness and Evolvability in Living Systems, 2005. **Address:** Department of Biochemistry, University of Zurich, Winterthurestrasse 190, Zurich, 8057, Switzerland. **Online address:** aw@bioc.uzh.ch

WAGNER, Bruce. American (born United States), b. 1954. **Genres:** Novels, Plays/Screenplays. **Career:** Novelist, producer and director. **Publications:** NOVELS: Force Majeure, 1991; I'm Losing You, 1996; I'll Let You Go, 2001; Still Holding, 2003; The Chrysanthemum Palace, 2005; Memorial, 2006. OTHERS: (with W. Craven) Dream Warriors, 1992; Wild Palms, 1994. **Address:** c/o Miriam Altshuler, Russell & Volkening Inc., 50 W 29th St., Apt. 7E, New York, NY 10001-4227, U.S.A.

WAGNER, Daniel. Swiss/American (born United States), b. 1974?. **Genres:** Novels, Psychology, Young Adult Fiction. **Career:** Musician, construction worker and writer. **Publications:** A Movie... and a Book: A Novel, 2004. Contributor to periodicals. **Address:** Barbara J. Zitwer Agency, 525 W End Ave., Ste. 11H, New York, NY 10024, U.S.A.

WAGNER, David. American (born United States), b. 1950. **Genres:** Social Work, Sociology. **Career:** Service Employees International Union, labor organizer, 1978-, president; American Federation of State, County and Municipal Employees, labor organizer, through 1984; Columbia University, lecturer in social work and assistant director of field work, 1985-88; University of Southern Maine, Department of Sociology and Social Work, associate professor, 1988-99, professor of social work and sociology, chair and co-chair, 1998-2000, coordinator, 2000-06; M.S.W coordinator, 2006-. Writer. **Publications:** The Quest for a Radical Profession: Social Service Careers and Political Ideology, 1990; Checkerboard Square: Culture and Resistance in a Homeless Community, 1993; The New Temperance: The American Obsession with Sin and Vice, 1997; What's Love Got to Do with It?: A Critical Look at American Charity, 2000; The Poorhouse: America's Forgotten Institution, 2005; Ordinary People: In and Out of Poverty in the Gilded Age, 2008; The Miracle Worker and the Transcendentalist: Anne Sullivan, Franklin Sanborn, and the Education of Helen Keller, 2011. FORTHCOMING: The Irish Pauper; The Boston Brahmin; The Rise and Fall of Homelessness; From Poverty to Fame: What We Can Learn from Poor People Who Became Famous. Contributor to books and journals. **Address:** Department of Sociology, University of Southern Maine, 120 Bedford St., PO Box 9300, Portland, ME 04103, U.S.A. **Online address:** wagner@usm.maine.edu

WAGNER, Gillian (Mary Millicent). British (born England), b. 1927. **Genres:** Education, Social Commentary, Medicine/Health. **Career:** Incorporated Association of Preparatory Schools, governor, 1974, president, 1985-90; Skill: National Bureau for Students with Disabilities, president, 1978-91; Felixstowe College, chair of governors, 1980-87; National Centre for Volunteering, chair, 1984-89, vice-president, 1990-93, president, 1993-; Review of Residential Care, chair, 1986-88; National Institute for Social Work, governor, 1988-95, vice-chair, 1990-; Thomas Coram Foundation for Children, Court of Governors, chair, 1990-; London School of Economics and Political Science, governor, 1991-96; Residential Forum, founder, 1994. Writer. **Publications:** Camera and Dr. Barnardo, 1974; Barnardo, 1979; Children of the Empire, 1982; The Chocolate Conscience, 1987; (co-author) A Positive Choice, 1988; Residential Care, a Positive Choice: Report of the Independent Review of Residential Care, 1988; The Politics of Medical Encounters: How Patients and Doctors Deal with Social Problem, 1991; The Second Sickness: Contradictions of Capitalist Health Care, 2000; At the Front Lines of Medicine: How the Health Care System Alienates Doctors and Mistreats Patients and What We Can Do about It, 2001; Thomas Coram, Gent., 1668-1751, 2004. **Address:** 10 Physic Pl., Royal Hospital Rd., London, GL SW3 4HQ, England.

WAGNER, Linda Welshimer. See **WAGNER-MARTIN, Linda C.**

WAGNER, Matt. American (born United States), b. 1961. **Genres:** Cartoons, Novels, Humor/Satire. **Career:** Writer. **Publications:** GRAPHIC NOVELS/COMIC BOOK COLLECTIONS: Mage, 1984, 3 vols., 1987; (with R. Rankin) Grendel: Devil by the Deed, 1986; (co-author) Grendel: Devil's Legacy, 1988; (co-author) Batman: Faces, 1992; (co-author) Batman: Riddler, 1995; Matt Wagner's Grendel Cycle, 1995; (co-author) Sandman Mystery Theatre: The Tarantula, 1995; (co-author) Grendel Tales: Devils and Deaths, 1996; (co-author) Matt Wagner's Grendel Tales: The Devil in Our Midst, 1998; (co-author) Matt Wagner's Grendel Tales: Homecoming, 1998; (co-author) Neil Gaimon's Midnight Days, 1999; Mage: The Hero Defined, 4 vols., 1999; (with G. Rucka) Grendel: Past Prime, 2000; (co-author) Doctor Mid Nite, 2000; (with J.K. Snyder III) Doctor Mid Nite, 2000; Grendel: Black, White, & Red, 2000; (co-author) Grendel Tales: The Devil May Care, 2003; (with B. Mireault) Grendel: The Devil Inside, 2004; Trinity, 2004; (co-author) The Vamp: Sandman Mystery Theatre, vol. III, 2005; (co-author) Grendel: Red, White, & Black, 2005; Grendel: Behold the Devil, 2009; Madame Xanadu, vol. I: Disenchanted, 2009, vol. II: Exodus Noir, 2010, Broken House of Cards, 2010. **Address:** c/o Author Mail, Dark Horse Comics, 10956 SE Main St., Milwaukie, OR 97222, U.S.A. **Online address:** mattwagnercomics@gmail.com

WAGNER, Michele R. American (born United States), b. 1975. **Genres:** How-to Books, Geography, Travel/Exploration, Politics/Government. **Career:** Greehaven Press, editor and proofreader, 1998-2001. **Publications:** At Issue: How Should Prisons Treat Their Inmates?, 2000; Sweden, 2001; Haiti, 2002; (with V. Alexander) Welcome to Sweden, 2002; (with K. Brown) Welcome to Haiti, 2003. Contributor to periodicals. **Address:** c/o Author Mail, Gareth Stevens Inc., 330 W Olive St., Ste. 100, Milwaukee, WI 53212-1068, U.S.A.

WAGNER, Nike. Austrian/German (born Germany), b. 1945. **Genres:** Theatre, Biography, History. **Career:** Writer, musicologist and cultural critic. **Publications:** Geist und Geschlecht: Karl Kraus und die Erotik der Wiener Moderne, 1982; Terre étrangèr: Création au Théâtre des amandiers, 1984; Wagner Theater, 1998; The Wagners: The Dramas of a Musical Dynasty, 2001; Traumtheater: Szenarien der Moderne, 2001; (contrib.) Zeitversetzt: Ettersburger Klangräume=Shifted in Time: Ettersburg Sound Spaces, 2004. **Address:** Walfishgasse 12, Vienna, 1010, Austria. **Online address:** nikewagner@utanet.at

WAGNER, Ralph D. (Alonzo Boardman). American (born United States), b. 1951. **Genres:** Librarianship, History. **Career:** Peace Corps, staff, 1976-78; Northern Illinois University, business librarian, 1980-86; Western Illinois University, acting library director, 1986-89; Eureka College, library director, 1989-91; Westfield State College, reference librarian, 1994-2001. Writer. **Publications:** A History of the Farmington Plan, 2002. Contributor to periodicals. **Address:** 40 Taylor Ave., Westfield, MA 01085, U.S.A. **Online address:** rdwagner@dinsdoc.com

WAGNER, Rudolf G. German (born Germany), b. 1941. **Genres:** History, Politics/Government, Philosophy. **Career:** Harvard University, Harkness Fellow, 1969-71, visiting professor, 1990; University of California, Harkness fellow, 1970-71, Center for Chinese Studies, research linguist, 1984-86; Free University, assistant professor, 1972-77, lecturer of Chinese studies, 1978-81, privatdozent, 1982-83; Cornell University, Society for the Humanities, fellow, 1981-82; University of Heidelberg, Institute of Chinese Studies, Department of Chinese Studies, chair, 1987-, professor, 1987-2009, Centre for East Asian Studies, director, 2005-09, Cluster of Excellence Asia and Europe in a Global Context: Shifting Asymmetries in Cultural Flows, co-director, 2007-, senior professor, 2009-; European Center for Digital Resources in Chinese Studies, director, 2001-; Shanghai Academy of Social Sciences, professor, 1996-; Wissenschaftskolleg zu Berlin (Institute for Advanced Study), fellow, 2003-04. Writer. **Publications:** (Ed. and intro. with E. Neckermann) Wer erzieht wen: Dokumente zur Revolution im Erziehungswesen d. Volksrepublik China, 1976; Essays in Modern Chinese Literature and Literary Criticism,

1982; Reenacting the Heavenly Vision: The Role of Religion in the Taiping Rebellion, 1982; Literatur und Politik in der Volksrepublik China, 1983; The Contemporary Chinese Historical Drama: Four Studies, 1990; Inside a Service Trade: Studies in Contemporary Chinese Prose, 1992; The Craft of a Chinese Commentator: Wang Bi on the Laozi, 2000; A Chinese Reading of the Daodejing: Wang Bi's Commentary on the Laozi with Critical Text and Translation, 2003; Language, Ontology, and Political Philosophy in china: Wang Bis Scholarly Exploration of the Dark (Xuanxue), 2003; (ed.) Joining the Global Public: Word, Image, and City in Early Chinese Newspapers, 1870-1910, 2007. **Address:** Institute of Chinese Studies, Heidelberg University, Akademiestrasse 4, Heidelberg, 69117, Germany. **Online address:** wagner@gw.sino.uni-heidelberg.de

WAGNER, Sharon Blythe. Also writes as M. E. Cooper, Ann Sheldon, Casey Stephens, Blythe Bradley, Blythe Stephens. American (born United States), b. 1936. **Genres:** Mystery/Crime/Suspense, Romance/Historical, Children's Fiction, Novels, Young Adult Fiction. **Career:** Arizona State University, part-time clerk, 1966-68; writer, 1968-. **Publications:** Prairie Wind, 1967; Dude Ranch Mystery, 1968; Curse of Still Valley, 1969; Country of the Wolf, 1970; Maridu, 1970; Circle of Evil, 1971; Gypsy from Nowhere, 1971; Winter Evil, 1971; Moonwind, 1971; House of Shadows, 1972; Legacy of Loneliness, 1972; Cry of the Cat, 1973; Gypsy and Nimblefoot, 1973; Satan's Acres, 1974; Shades of Evil, 1974; Colors of Death, 1974; Havenhurst, 1974; Roses from Yesterday, 1974; Dark Waters of Death, 1975; Dark Side of Paradise, 1975; The Turquoise Talisman, 1975; Shadow of Her Eyes, 1979; Haunted Honeymoon, 1979; Gypsy and the Moonstone Stallion, 1980; House of Doom, House of Desire, 1980; Secrets, 1980; Embraces, 1980; The Chadwicks of Arizona, 1981; Charade of Love, 1981; Jaquelle's Shadow, 1982; New Dreams for Kendra, 1982; Jacquelle's Shadow, 1982; Journey to Paradise, 1982; Tour of Love, 1983; Strangers Who Love, 1983; Change Partners, 1983; House on the Hill, 1988; The Lost Lilacs of Latimer House, 1990; Moonglow, 1995. WITH B. CASEY: Shadow on the Sun, 1972; Cove in Darkness, 1972; Wind of Bitterness, 1973; Haitian Legacy, 1973; Dark Sun at Midnight, 1976; Echoes of an Ancient, 1976; Bride of the Dullahan, 1976; Love's Broken Promises, 1979. AS BLYTHE BRADLEY: To Love a Stranger, 1993; Moon Over Black Bayou, 1993; Dark Cloister, 1994. AS M.E. COOPER: Picture Perfect, 1986. AS ANN SHELDON: Linda Craig and the Palomino Mystery, 1962; Linda Craig and the Clue on the Desert Trail, 1962; Linda Craig and the Secret of Rancho del Sol, 1963; Linda Craig and the Mystery of Horseshoe Canyon, 1963; Linda Craig and the Mystery in Mexico, 1964; Linda Craig and the Ghost Town Treasure, 1964; Haunted Valley, 1982; Ghost Town Treasure, 1982; Emperor's Pony, 1983; Secret of the Old Sleigh, 1983; Phantom of Dark Oaks, 1984; Search for Scorpio, 1984; Silver Stallion, 1988; Glimmering Ghost, 1989; Star in the Saddle, 1989; Ride to Gold Canyon, 1989. AS BLYTHE STEPHENS: Rainbow Days, 1989; Gift of Mischief, 1991; Wake to Darkness, 1992. AS CASEY STEPHENS: Porterfield Legacy, 1980; The Shadows of Fieldcrest Manor, 1980. **Address:** 2137 E Bramble Ave., Mesa, AZ 85204-1445, U.S.A.

WAGNER, Wenceslas J. American/Polish (born Poland), b. 1917. **Genres:** Autobiography/Memoirs, Law, Politics/Government, History, Autobiography/Memoirs, Social Sciences, Essays. **Career:** French Institute of Air Transport, research associate, 1947-48; Fordham University, visiting professor of literature, 1948-49; Northwestern University, School of Law, teaching fellow in comparative law, 1950-53; University of Notre Dame, instructor, 1953-54, assistant professor, 1954-57, associate professor, 1957-61, professor of law, 1961-62; University of Paris, visiting professor, 1959-60; University of Rennes, visiting professor, 1959-60; Cornell University, visiting professor, 1961-62; Indiana University, Maurer School of Law, professor of law, 1962-; University of Detroit, professor of law, 1971-89. Writer. **Publications:** Les libertes de l'air, 1948; Gentleman from Tennessee is Wrong: The Truth About the Odra-Nysa Border, 1957; The Federal States and Their Judiciary: A Comparative Study in Constitutional Law and Organization of Courts in Federal States, 1959; (contrib.) Essays in Honor of Roscoe Pound, 1962; International Air Transportation as Affected by State Sovereignty, 1970; Obligations in Polish Law, 1974; Od Konspiracji Do Emigracji: Narodowa Organizacja Wojskowa: AK I Okreg Stoleczny Stronnictwa Narodowego Podczas II Wojny Swiatowej i Wspomnienia Powojenne, 1994. EDITOR: (with J.N. Hazard) Legal Thought in the United States under Contemporary Pressures: Reports From the United States of America on Topics of Major Concern as Established for the VIII Congress of the International Academy of Comparative Law, 1970; (and contrib.) Polish Law Throughout the Ages: One Thousand Years of Polish Law, 1970; (with D. Lasok) Polish Civil Law, 1973;

(with J.N. Hazard) The Law in the United States of America in Social and Technological Revolution, 1974; The Law in the U.S. in the Bicentennial Era, 1978; Law in the U.S. for the 1980's, 1982; Law in the U.S. Faces Social and Scientific Change, 1986; (with J.N. Hazard) U.S. Law in an Era of Democratization, 1990. Contributor of articles to books and journals. **Address:** Maurer School of Law, Indiana University, 211 S Indiana Ave., Bloomington, IN 47405-7001, U.S.A.

WAGNER-MARTIN, Linda C. (Linda Welshimer Wagner). American (born United States), b. 1936. **Genres:** Novels, Poetry, Literary Criticism And History, Women's Studies And Issues, Autobiography/Memoirs, Biography, Essays. **Career:** Teacher, 1957-60; Bowling Green State University, assistant professor, 1960-65; Wayne State University, assistant professor of English, 1966-68; Michigan State University, assistant professor of English, 1968-72, professor of English, 1972-88, graduate chair and associate chair, 1977-79, Internship Program, founder and director, 1977-79, associate dean, 1979-81, Michigan State University Press, faculty and president, 1981-88; The Centennial Review, poetry editor, 1968-88; University of North Carolina, Hanes professor of English and comparative literature, 1988-, Arts and Humanities Institute, fellow; American National Biography project, associate literary editor, 1989-95; American Literature Section, president, 1996; Mercer University, Lamar lecturer in Southern literature, 2000; Bethany College, Helen Louise McGuffie lecturer, 2001; University of Georgia, Eidson lecturer, 2002; Rockefeller Foundation Study Center, fellow, 2002; Ernest Hemingway Foundation and Society, president, 2003-05. **Publications:** The Poems of William Carlos Williams, 1964; Denise Levertov, 1967; Intaglios, 1967; The Prose of William Carlos Williams, 1970; Phyllis McGinley, 1971; (as Linda Welshimer Wagner) Hemingway and Faulkner: Inventors/Masters, 1975; (with C.D. Mead) Introducing Poems, 1976; (as Linda Welshimer Wagner) Speaking Straight Ahead: Interviews with William Carlos Williams, 1976; (as Linda Welshimer Wagner) Ernest Hemingway: A Reference Guide, 1977; Robert Frost: The Critical Heritage, 1977; William Carlos Williams: A Reference Guide, 1978; Dos Passos: Artist as American, 1979; American Modern (essays), 1980; Songs for Isadora, 1981; Ellen Glasgow: Beyond Convention, 1982; Sylvia Plath: A Biography, 1987, rev. ed., 2003; Sylvia Plath, the Critical Heritage, 1988; The Modern American Novel, 1914-1945, 1990; Wharton's The House of Mirth: A Novel of Admonition, 1990; Plath's The Bell Jar: A Novel of the Fifties, 1992; Telling Women's Lives, 1994; Favored Strangers, 1995; Wharton's The Age of Innocence, 1996; The Midcentury American Novel, 1997; Sylvia Plath: A Literary Life, 1999; Barbara Kingsolver, 2001; Hemingway's A Farewell to Arms, 2002; Zelda Sayre Fitzgerald, an American Woman's Story, 2004; Barbara Kingsolver, 2004. EDITOR: T.S. Eliot, 1974; (as Linda Welshimer Wagner) Ernest Hemingway, 5 Decades of Criticism, 1974; Joyce Carol Oates: Critical Essays, 1979; Sylvia Plath: Critical Essays, 1984; New Essays on The Sun Also Rises, 1987; Anne Sexton: Critical Essays, 1989; E. Glasgow, Virginia, 1989; Critical Essays on Denise Levertov, 1990; Denise Levertov: Critical Essays, 1991; J. Steinbeck, The Pearl, 1994; (ed. with C. Davidson) The Oxford Companion to Women's Writing in the U.S., 1995; Oxford Book of Women's Writing in the United States, 1995; The Age of Innocence, 1995; New Essays on Faulkner's Go Down, Moses, 1996; 7 Decades of Criticism, 1998; Over West: For Frederick Echman, 1999; The Bedford Cultural Edition of Stein's Three Lives, 2000; Historical Guide to Ernest Hemingway, 2000; Hemingway's The Sun Also Rises: A Casebook, 2001; William Faulkner: Six Decades of Criticism, 2002; (and intro.) The Portable Edith Wharton, 2003; (ed. and intro.) The Custom of the Country, 2006; Hemingway: Eight Decades of Criticism, 2008. Contributor to periodicals. **Address:** Department of English & Comparative Literature, University of North Carolina, Greenlaw Hall, PO Box 3520, Chapel Hill, NC 27599-3520, U.S.A. **Online address:** wagnerl@prodigy.net

WAGONER, David (Russell). American (born United States), b. 1926. **Genres:** Novels, Poetry, Young Adult Fiction. **Career:** De Paul University, instructor, 1949-50; Pennsylvania State University, instructor in English, 1950-54; University of Washington, associate professor, 1954-66, professor of English, 1966-, now professor emeritus; Poetry Northwest, editor, 1966-2002; University of Cincinnati, Ellison lecturer in modern poetry, 1968; Princeton University Press, Contemporary Poetry Series, editor, 1978-81; University of Missouri Press, editor, 1983-; Academy of American Poets, chancellor. **Publications:** POETRY: Dry Sun, Dry Wind, 1943; A Place to Stand, 1958; The Nesting Ground, 1963; Staying Alive, 1966; New and Selected Poems, 1969; Working Against Time, 1970; Riverbed, 1972; Sleeping in the Woods, 1974; Traveling Light, 1976; Collected Poems 1956-1976, 1976; Who Shall Be the Sun?, 1978; In Broken Country, 1979; Landfall, 1981; First Light,

1983; Through the Forest, 1987; Walt Whitman Bathing: Poems, 1996; The House of Song: Poems, 2002; Good Morning and Good Night: Poems, 2005; Map of the Night: Poems, 2008. NOVELS: The Man in the Middle, 1954; Money, Money, Money, 1955; Rock, 1958; The Escape Artist, 1965; Baby, Come On Inside, 1968; Where Is My Wandering Boy Tonight?, 1970; The Road to Many a Wonder, 1974; Tracker, 1975; Whole Hog, 1976; The Hanging Garden, 1980. OTHERS: (ed.) Straw for the Fire: From the Notebooks of Theodore Roethke, 1943-63, 1972, 2nd ed., 2006. **Address:** Department of English, University of Washington, B437, A101 Padelford, PO Box 354330, Seattle, WA 98195-4330, U.S.A. **Online address:** renogawd@aol.com

WAGSCHAL, Steven. American (born United States), b. 1967?. **Genres:** Literary Criticism And History. **Career:** Indiana University, associate professor and director of graduate studies. Writer. **Publications:** (ed.) Peribáñez y el comendador de ocaña, 2004; The Literature of Jealousy in the Age of Cervantes, 2006. Contributor to books and periodicals. **Address:** Bloomington, IN , U.S.A. **Online address:** swagscha@indiana.edu

WAHL, Jan. American (born United States), b. 1933. **Genres:** Children's Fiction, Plays/Screenplays, Poetry, Animals/Pets, Art/Art History. **Career:** Dance Magazine, correspondent, 1950. Writer. **Publications:** Pleasant Fieldmouse, 1964; The Howards Go Sledding, 1964; Hello Elephant, 1964; The Beast Book (poetry), 1964; Cabbage Moon, 1965; The Muffletumps: The Story of Four Dolls, 1966; Christmas in the Forest, 1967; Pocahontas in London, 1967; The Furious Flycycle, 1968; Push Kitty, 1968; Cobweb Castle, 1968; Rickety Rackety Rooster, 1968; Runaway Jonah and Other Tales, 1968; A Wolf of My Own, 1969; How the Children Stopped the Wars, 1969; The Fishermen, 1969; May Horses, 1969; The Norman Rockwell Storybook, 1969; The Prince Who Was a Fish, 1970; The Mulberry Tree, 1970; The Wonderful Kite, 1970; Doctor Rabbit, 1970; The Animals' Peace Day, 1970; Abe Lincoln's Beard, 1971; Anna Help Ginger, 1971; Crabapple Night, 1971; Margaret's Birthday, 1971; The Six Voyages of Pleasant Fieldmouse, 1971; Lorenzo Bear and Company, 1971; The Very Peculiar Tunnel, 1972; Magic Heart, 1972; Grandmother Told Me, 1972; Cristobal and the Witch, 1972; S.O.S. Bobomobile! or, The Future Adventures of Melvin Spitznagle and Professor Mickimecki, 1973; Crazy Brobobalou, 1973; The Five in the Forest, 1974; (with D.J. Garcia) Juan Diego and the Lady, 1974; Pleasant Fieldmouse's Halloween Party, 1974; Mooga Mega Mekki, 1974; Jeremiah Knucklebones, 1974; The Muffletump Storybook, 1975; The Clumpets Go Sailing, 1975; Bear, Wolf, and Mouse, 1975; The Screeching Door; or, What Happened at the Elephant Hotel, 1975; The Muffletumps' Christmas Party, 1975; The Woman with the Eggs, 1975; Follow Me, Cried Bee, 1976; Great-grandmother Cat Tales, 1976; Grandpa's Indian Summer, 1976; The Pleasant Fieldmouse Storybook, 1977; Doctor Rabbit's Foundling, 1977; Frankenstein's Dog, 1977; The Muffletumps' Halloween Scare, 1977; Pleasant Fieldmouse's Valentine Trick, 1977; Carrot Nose, 1978; Dracula's Cat and Frankenstein's Dog, 1978; Jamie's Tiger, 1978; Youth's Magic Horn, 1978; Drakestail, 1978; Who Will Believe Tim Kitten?, 1978; The Teeny Tiny Witches, 1979; Sylvester Bear Overslept, 1979; (reteller) Needle and Noodle, and Other Silly Stories, 1979; Doctor Rabbit's Lost Scout, 1979; Old Hippo's Easter Egg, 1980; Button Eye's Orange, 1980; The Cucumber Princess, 1981; The Little Blind Goat, 1981; Grandpa Gus's Birthday Cake, 1981; Tiger Watch, 1982; The Pipkins Go Camping, 1982; Small One, 1983; Peter and the Troll Baby, 1983; More Room for the Pipkins, 1983; Humphrey's Bear, 1983, rev. ed., 2005; So Many Raccoons, 1985; Cheltenham's Party, 1985; The Toy Circus, 1986; Rabbits on Roller Skates, 1986; Let's Go Fishing, 1987; The Golden Christmas Tree, 1988; Tales of Fuzzy Mouse: Six Cozy Stories for Bedtime, 1988; Tim Kitten and the Red Cupboard, 1988; Timothy Tiger's Terrible Toothache, 1988; Little Dragon's Grandmother, 1988; The Adventures of Underwater Dog, 1989; The Wizard of Oz Movie Storybook, 1989; The Rabbit Club, 1990; A Gift for Miss Milo, 1990; Mrs. Owl and Mr. Pig, 1991; (reteller) Tailypo, 1991; The Sleepytime Book, 1992; Little Eight John, 1992; My Cat Ginger, 1992; Suzy and the Mouse King, 1992; Little Gray One, 1993; Will Santa Come?, 1993; I Remember!: Cried Grandma Pinky, 1994; Cats and Robbers, 1995; Emily and the Snowflake, 1995; Once When the World Was Green, 1996; Jack Rabbit and the Giant, 1996; I Met a Dinosaur, 1997; (reteller) The Singing Geese, 1998; Rosa's Parrot, 1999; Little Johnny Buttermilk: After an Old English Folktale, 1999; Christmas Present, 1999; Three Pandas, 2000; The Field Mouse and the Dinosaur Named Sue, 2000; Mabel Ran Away with the Toys, 2000; Elf Night, 2002; Rabbits on Mars, 2003; Candy Shop, 2004; Knock! Knock!, 2004; The Enchanted Sled, 2005; Bear Dance, 2008;

Art Collector, 2011; Carl Theodor Dreyer and Ordet: My Summer with the Danish Filmmaker, 2012. Contributor of articles to magazines and periodicals. **Address:** Rogers, Coleridge & White Ltd., 20 Powis Mews, London, GL W11 1JN, England.

WAHRMAN, Dror. American (born United States), b. 1960. **Genres:** Politics/Government, Theology/Religion, History. **Career:** Indiana University, Department of History, Ruth N. Halls Professor, Center for Eighteenth-Century Studies, director. Writer. **Publications:** Adrikhalut bi- yerushalayim: tekufot ve-signonot, 1983; Yerushalayim: deyoknah shel rir bi-temurah, 1985 as Jerusalem, 1987; Ha-Bukharim u-shekhunatam bi-yerushalayim, 1991; (contrib.) Capturing the Holy Land: M.J. Diness and the Beginnings of Photography in Jerusalem, 1993; Imagining the Middle Class: The Political Representation of Class in Britain, c. 1780- 1840, 1995; Michael's Jerusalem: The New Guide, 1996; (ed. with C. Jones) The Age of Cultural Revolutions: Britain and France, 1750-1820, 2002; The Making of the Modern Self: Identity and Culture in Eighteenth-Century England, 2004. **Address:** Department of History, Indiana University, Ballantine 742, 1020 E Kirkwood, Bloomington, IN 47405-7103, U.S.A. **Online address:** dwahrman@indiana.edu

WAINSCOTT, Ronald H(arold). American (born United States), b. 1948. **Genres:** Theatre, Art/Art History, Literary Criticism And History. **Career:** University of Alabama, associate instructor in oral interpretation, voice and diction, 1975-76; Indiana University, associate instructor in acting and oral interpretation, 1977-79, professor of theatre and drama, 1999-, chair, 2002-04, director of graduate studies, 2004-; Illinois State University, assistant professor of theatre, 1981-84; Towson State University, assistant professor of theatre arts, 1984-89; University of Nebraska, associate professor of theatre history, dramatic literature, 1989-95, associate professor of theatre and drama, 1995-98, director of graduate studies, 1997-2002. Writer. **Publications:** Staging O'Neill: The Experimental Years, 1920-1934, 1988; The Emergence of the Modern American Theater, 1914-1929, 1997; (with K. Fletcher) Theatre: Collaborative Acts, 2004, 2nd ed., 2007, 3rd ed., 2009. Contributor of article to journals. **Address:** Department of Theater and Drama, Indiana University, 275 N Jordan, Bloomington, IN 47405-1101, U.S.A. **Online address:** wainscot@indiana.edu

WAINWRIGHT, Geoffrey. British (born England), b. 1939. **Genres:** Theology/Religion, History, Humanities. **Career:** Queen's College, lecturer in systematic theology, 1973-79; Studia Liturgica, editor, 1974-87; Union Theological Seminary, Roosevelt professor of systematic theology, 1979-83, Roosevelt chair, 1983; Duke University, professor of systematic theology, 1983-91, Robert Earl Cushman professor of Christian theology, 1991-; Societas Liturgica, president, 1983-85; Joint Commission for Dialogue between the World Methodist Council and the Roman Catholic Church, co-chair, chairman, 1986-; American Theological Society, president, 1996-97. **Publications:** Christian Initiation, 1969; Eucharist and Eschatology, 1971, 2nd ed., 1978; Doxology, 1980; The Ecumenical Moment, 1983; Geoffrey Wainwright on Wesley and Calvin, 1987; Henge Monuments, 1990; Methodists in Dialogue, 1995; Worship with One Accord, 1997; For Our Salvation: Two Approaches to the Work of Christ, 1997; (contrib.) Ecumenical Theology in Worship, Doctrine, and Life, 1999; Is the Reformation Over, 2000; Lesslie Newbigin: A Theological Life, 2000; Embracing Purpose: Essays on God, the World and the Church, 2007. EDITOR: The Study of Liturgy, 1978, rev. ed., 1992; Baptism and Eucharist: Ecumenical Convergence in Celebration, 1983; (with E. Yarnold and C. Jones) The Study of Spirituality, 1986; Keeping the Faith: Essays to Mark the Centenary of Lux Mundi, 1988; Dictionary of the Ecumenical Movement, 1991, rev. ed., 2002; (and intro.) Signs Amid the Rubble, 2003; The Oxford History of Christian Worship, 2006. **Address:** The Divinity School, Duke University, Rm. 301 Gray, PO Box 90968, Durham, NC 27708-0968, U.S.A. **Online address:** gwainwright@div.duke.edu

WAINWRIGHT, Gordon Ray. British (born England), b. 1937. **Genres:** How-to Books, Self Help, Medicine/Health, Communications/Media, Business/Trade/Industry. **Career:** Manvers Secondary High School, assistant English teacher, 1959-61; College of Technology, assistant lecturer in liberal studies, 1961-65; Hebburn Technical College, lecturer in general studies, 1965-68; Wearside College of Further Education, Department of Communication, head, 1968-83, head of communication and industrial development, 1983-85; North England Development Council, chairman, 1982. Writer. **Publications:** Efficiency in Reading, 1965; Towards Efficiency in Reading: Ten Passages for Practice in Faster and More Efficient Reading for Students and Adults, 1968; Rapid Reading Made Simple, 1972; How to Read for Speed and Comprehension, 1977; People and Communication, 1979; Report Writing, 1984; People and Communication: A Workbook, 1984; Teach Yourself Body Language, 1985; Teach Yourself Meetings and Committee Procedure, 1987; S.T.E.P.S. for Success, 1992, rev. ed., 1999; Essential Personal Skills for Life and Work, 1993; Body Language, 1993; Tricky Business Letters, 1993, rev. ed., 2000; Successful Business Writing in a Week, 1993; Read Faster, Recall More, 2001. Contributor to journals and newspapers. **Address:** 22 Hawes Ct., Seaburn Dene, Sunderland, SR6 8NU, England. **Online address:** gwainwright@btopenworld.com

WAINWRIGHT, Jeffrey. British (born England), b. 1944. **Genres:** Poetry, Translations, Mystery/Crime/Suspense. **Career:** Leeds University, Students Union Executive, cultural affairs secretary, 1965-66; University College of Wales, lecturer in English and American literature, 1967-73; Long Island University, visiting assistant professor, 1970-71; Manchester Polytechnic (now Manchester Metropolitan University), lecturer, 1973-, professor of English, 1999-2008. Writer. **Publications:** The Important Man, 1970; Heart's Desire, 1978; Selected Poems, 1985; The Red-Headed Pupil and Other Poems, 1994; Out of the Air, 1999; Poetry: The Basics, 2004, 2nd ed., 2011; Acceptable Words: Essays On The Poetry of Geoffrey Hill, 2005; Clarity or Death! Manchester, 2008. TRANSLATOR: The Mystery of the Charity of Joan of Arc, 1986; The Satin Slipper, 1988; Le Cid, 1994; In the Solitude of Cotton Fields, 1996. **Address:** Carcanet Press Ltd., Alliance House, 4th Fl., Cross St., Manchester, GM M2 7AP, England. **Online address:** jeffrey.wainwright@btinternet.com

WAISER, Bill. (W(illiam) A(ndrew) Waiser). Canadian (born Canada), b. 1953. **Genres:** History, Natural History, Social Sciences, Adult Non-fiction. **Career:** University of Saskatchewan, term lecturer, 1980-83, assistant professor, 1984-87, associate professor, 1987-90, graduate director, 1987-90, professor of history, 1990-, history department head, 1995-98; Parks Canada, Prairie and Northern Regional Office, Yukon historian, 1983-84. Writer. **Publications:** (As W.A. Waiser) The Field Naturalist: John Macoun, the Geological Survey and Natural Science, 1989; Saskatchewan's Playground: A History of Prince Albert National Park, 1989; (ed. with D. De Brou) Documenting Canada, 1992; The New Northwest: The Photographs of the Frank Crean Expeditions, 1908-1909, 1993; Park Prisoners: The Untold Story of Western Canada's National Parks, 1915-1946, 1995; (with B. Stonechild) Loyal Till Death: Indians and the North-West Rebellion, 1997; All Hell Can't Stop Us: The On-to-Ottawa Trek and Regina Riot, 2003; (with P. Dederick) Looking Back: True Tales from Saskatchewan History, 2003; (with P. Dederick) Saskatchewan: A New History, 2005; Portraits of an Era: The Aerial Photography of Howdy McPhail, 2010; (with S. Houston) Tommy's Team, 2010. **Address:** Department of History, University of Saskatchewan, Arts 714, 9 Campus Dr., Saskatoon, SK S7N 5A5, Canada. **Online address:** bill.waiser@usask.ca

WAISER, W(illiam) A(ndrew). *See* **WAISER, Bill.**

WAISMAN, Sergio Gabriel. American (born United States), b. 1967. **Genres:** Information Science/Computers, Translations, Children's Fiction, Novels, Autobiography/Memoirs. **Career:** San Diego State University, assistant professor of Spanish and Portuguese, 2001-04; George Washington University, Department of Romance, Germanic, and Slavic Languages and Literatures, associate professor of Spanish and international affairs, 2004-, chair, Elliott School of International Affairs, Judaic Studies Program, affiliate faculty. Writer. **Publications:** A Shortcut through Adventureland (computer book), 1984; (trans.) R. Piglia, Assumed Name, 1995; (trans.) N. Aguirre, Juan de la Rosa: Memoirs of the Last Soldier of the Independence Movement: A Novel, 1998; (trans.) J.M. Gorriti, Dreams and Realities: Selected Fiction of Juana Manuela Gorriti, 2003; Leaving, 2004; Borges and Translation: The Irreverence of the Periphery, 2005; (trans. with K. Washbourne) Anthology of Spanish American Modernismo, 2007; (trans. and intro.) M. Azuela, Underdogs: A Novel of the Mexican Revolution, 2008; (trans.) Leopoldo Lugones: Selected Writings, 2008. **Address:** Department of Romance, German, and Slavic, Languages and Literatures, George Washington University, Rm. 513 E, Phillips Hall, 801 22nd St. NW, Washington, DC 20052, U.S.A. **Online address:** waisman@gwu.edu

WAIT, Eugene M(eredith). American (born United States), b. 1936. **Genres:** History, Military/Defense/Arms Control, Social Sciences. **Career:** Writer. **Publications:** The March of the Teutons, 1972; America and the War of 1812, 1999; America and the Monroe Years, 1999; Opening of the Civil War, 1999; Jackson Years, 2000; Explorers and The New World, 2001; Ad-

ams vs. Jackson, 2001; Bull Run and Beyond, 2001; Civil War, 2001; Great Challenges of Reformation Europe, 2001; Zenith of Imperialism, 1896-1906, 2001; Explorers and the New World, 2002; Second Jackson Administration, 2002; Imperialism, 2003; Ancients to 500 B.C., 2003. Contributor of articles to periodicals. **Address:** 309 Lincoln Ave., Kerrville, TX 78028, U.S.A.

WAITE, Michael P(hillip). American (born United States), b. 1960. **Genres:** Children's Non-fiction, Children's Fiction, inspirational/Motivational Literature, Young Adult Fiction, Theology/Religion. **Career:** University of Oregon, instructor in English, 1991-92; Oregon State University, instructor in English, 1992-93; Sierra-CUC Software, game designer, 1993-. Writer. **Publications:** Handy-Dandy Helpful Hal: A Book about Helpfulness, 1987; Suzy Swoof: A Book about Kindness, 1987; Buzzle Billy: A Book about Sharing, 1987; Miggy and Tiggy: A Book about Overcoming Jealousy, 1987; Hoomania: A Journey into Proverbs, 1987; Emma Wimble, Accidental Astronaut, 1988; Eddy and His Amazing Pet, 1988; Eddy and the Rude Green Grood, 1988; Max and the Big Fat Lie: A Book about Telling the Truth, 1988; Casey the Greedy Young Cowboy: A Book about Being Thankful, 1988; Sir Maggie, the Mighty: A Book about Obedience, 1988; Boggin, Blizzy, and Sleeter the Cheater: A Book about Fairness, 1988; Leonard Greene and the Zapper Machine, 1990; Sammy's Gadget Galaxy: A Book about Patience, 1992; Gilly Greenweed's Gift for Granny: A Book about Showing Love, 1992; Sylvester the Jester: A Book about Accepting Others, 1992; The Hollyhonk Gardens of Gneedle and Gnibb: A Book about Forgiving, 1993; Daisy Doddlepaws and the Windy Woods Treasure, 1995; (with S. Lucas) Lady BugIsland: My First Helping Book, 1995; Bartholomew Beaver and the Stupendous Splash, 1995, 1996; Camp Windy Woods: Digger's Marvelous Moleberry Bush, 1995, 1996; Camp Windy Woods: Shelby the Magnificent, 1995, 1996; Butterflies for Two: My First Sharing Book, 1995; Jojofu, 1996; Windy Woods: Bartholomew and the Fabulous Bumbly-Flop, 1996; Windy Woods: Treasures of Willowbye Woods, 1996; The Parable of Bartholomew Beaver and the Stupendous Splash: In Which the Windy Woods Campers Learn the Biblical Value of Encouragement, 1996; The Parable of Daisy Doddlepaws and the Windy Woods Treasure: In Which the Windy Woods Campers Learn the Biblical Value of Friendship, 1996; The Parable of Shelby the Magnificent: In Which the Windy Woods Campers Learn the Biblical Value of Humility, 1996; The Parable of Digger's Marvelous Moleberry Patch: In Which the Windy Woods Campers Learn the Biblical Value of Generosity, 1996; Helpful Hal's Treasury of Christian Virtues, 1997; Rhyme-time Book of Christian Virtues, 1997. **Address:** c/o Publicity Director, Lothrop Lee & Shepard Books, 1350 Ave. of the Americas, New York, NY 10019, U.S.A. **Online address:** waites@earthlink.com

WAITE, P(eter) B(usby). Canadian (born Canada), b. 1922. **Genres:** History, Education, Institutions/Organizations, Social Sciences. **Career:** Dalhousie University, lecturer, 1951-55, assistant professor, 1955-60, associate professor, 1960, head of department, 1960-68, Thomas McCulloch professor of history, 1960-88, professor of history, 1961-88, professor emeritus, 1988-; University of Western Ontario, senior professor, 1963-64; Canadian Historical Association, president, 1968-69; Humanities Research Council of Canada, chairman, 1968-70. Writer. **Publications:** The Life and Times of Confederation 1864-1867, 1962, rev. ed., 2001; The Charlottetown Conference, 1864, 1963; Canada, 1874-1896, 1971; Arduous Destiny, 1971; Confederation 1854-1867, 1972; John A. Macdonald: His Life and World, 1975; (with R. Burt and R. Burnley) The Cumberland Mineral Statistics, 1982; The Durham and Northumberland Mineral Statistics, 1983; Reefs Unsuspected, 1983; The Man from Halifax: Sir John Thompson, Prime Minister, 1985; The French Canadians, 1985; (with Burt and Burnley) The Mines of Cardiganshire, 1985; Years of Struggle, 1867-1896, 1985; (with Burt and Burnley) Cornish Mines, 1987; Lord of Point Grey: N.A.M. MacKenzie 1894-1986, 1987; Candian History, 1988; The Loner: Three Sketches of The Personal Life and Ideas of R.B. Bennett, 1870-1947, 1992; The Lives of Dalhousie University: vol. I: 1818-1925, Lord Dalhousie's College, 1994, vol. II: 1925-1980, The Old College Transformed, 1998. EDITOR: The Confederation Debates in the Province of Canada, 1865, 1963, 2nd ed., 2006; Pre-Confederation: Documents of Canadian History, 1965; House of Commons Debates 1867-1868, 1968; (with W. Minchinton and C. King) Virginia Slave-Trade Statistics, 1698-1775, 1984; (with S. Oxner and T.G. Barnes) Law in a Colonial Society, 1984. **Address:** Dalhousie University, 1376 LeMarchant St., Halifax, NS B3H 3J5, Canada. **Online address:** pbwaite@istar.ca

WAITES, Martyn. British (born England), b. 1963?. **Genres:** Novels, Mystery/Crime/Suspense. **Career:** Huntercombe Young Offenders Institution, writer-in-residence; HMP Chelmsford, writer-in-residence; Essex University, RLF writing fellow. **Publications:** STEPHEN LARKIN SERIES: Mary's Prayer (crime novel), 1997; Little Triggers (crime novel), 1998; Candleland (crime novel), 2000; Born under Punches (novel), 2003. NOVEL: The White Room (novel), 2004. JOE DONOVAN CRIME NOVEL SERIES: The Mercy Seat, 2006; Bone Machine, 2007; White Riot, 2008; Speak No Evil, 2009. Works appear in anthologies. Contributor of articles to periodicals. **Address:** Gregory & Co., 3 Barb Mews, Hammersmith, London, GL W6 7PA, England.

WAITMAN, Katie. American (born United States), b. 1956. **Genres:** Science Fiction/Fantasy. **Career:** University of Southern California, School of Medicine, administrative assistant, 1980-82, Law School, administrative assistant, 1982-. Writer. **Publications:** SCIENCE FICTION: The Merro Tree, 1997; The Divided, 1999. **Address:** Law School, University of Southern California, Rm. 451, University Pk., Los Angeles, CA 90089-0071, U.S.A. **Online address:** kwaitman@law.usc.edu

WAITZKIN, Howard. (Howard Bruce Waitzkin). American (born United States), b. 1945. **Genres:** Medicine/Health, Sociology. **Career:** Summit County Children's Home, house parent, 1964; Summit County Community Action Council, coordinator of research, 1966; Stanford University, intern and postdoctoral fellow, 1972-73, Robert Wood Johnson Foundation, research associate in medicine and sociology, 1973-75, resident in medicine, 1974-75; University of California-Berkeley, lecturer, 1973-75, visiting associate professor, 1978-82; Massachusetts General Hospital, senior resident in medicine, 1977-78; La Clinica de la Raza, internist and primary care practitioner, 1978-82; University of California-San Francisco, assistant clinical professor of medicine, 1978-82; University of California-Irvine, professor of medicine and social sciences, 1982-96, Division of General Internal Medicine and Primary Care, chief, 1982-90; North Orange County Community Clinic, medical director, 1982-90; University of Vermont, associate professor and attending physician, 1975-77; University of Amsterdam, lecturer, 1977; Harvard Medical School, clinical fellow, 1977-78; Universidad Autonoma Metropolitana-Xochimilco, Fulbright senior lecturer, visiting professor, 1988-89; University of Arizona, visiting professor, 1992; University of Washington, visiting professor, 1992; University of New Mexico, Division of Community Medicine, professor and director, 1997-2000, Departments of Sociology, Family and Community Medicine, and Internal Medicine, faculty, 1997-, distinguished professor, 2005-. Writer. **Publications:** (With B. Waterman) The Exploitation of Illness in Capitalist Society, 1974; The Second Sickness, 1983, rev. ed., 2000; The Politics of Medical Encounters, 1991; At the Front Lines of Medicine, 2001; Medicine and Public Health at the End of Empire, 2011. Works appear in anthologies. Contributor to journals. **Address:** Department of Sociology, University of New Mexico, Rm. 1103, MSC 05 3080, 1070 Social Sciences Bldg., 1915 Roma NE, 1 University of New Mexico, Albuquerque, NM 87131-0001, U.S.A. **Online address:** waitzkin@unm.edu

WAITZKIN, Howard Bruce. See WAITZKIN, Howard.

WAITZKIN, Josh. American (born United States), b. 1976. **Genres:** How-to Books, Sports/Fitness. **Career:** The JW foundation, founder, 2008, president. Writer and educator. **Publications:** (With F. Waitzkin) Josh Waitzkin's Attacking Chess: Aggressive Strategies and Inside Moves from the U.S. Junior Chess Champion, 1995; The Art of Learning: A Journey in the Pursuit of Excellence, 2007; The Art of Learning: An Inner Journey to Optimal Performance, 2008. **Address:** Indian National Press Ltd., Free Press House 215, Nariman Pt., Mumbai, MH 400021, India. **Online address:** joshwaitzkin.web@gmail.com

WAJCMAN, Judy. Australian (born Australia), b. 1950. **Genres:** Women's Studies And Issues, Business/Trade/Industry, Economics, Social Sciences, Engineering. **Career:** Cambridge University, Sociology and Women in Society, instructor, 1975-80; University of Edinburgh, lecturer in sociology, Work and Technology, 1980-83; University of New South Wales, senior lecturer, associate professor, 1983-; University of Sydney, lecturer, 1983-85; University of Warwick, Industrial Relations Research Unit, principal research fellow, 1992-94; Australian National University, Research School of Social Sciences, professor of sociology, 1995; London School of Economics, Gender Institute and Sociology, Department of Sociology, head, 2009-; London Business School, visiting professor, 2000. University of Oxford, Oxford Internet Institute, visiting fellow, 2005-06, research associate, 2006-07, 2008-, senior research fellow, 2007-08; All Souls College, visiting fellow. Writer. **Publications:** (Co-author) Women in Society: Interdisciplin-

ary Essays, 1981; Women in Control: Dilemmas of a Workers' Cooperative, 1983; (ed. with D. Mackenzie) The Social Shaping of Technology: How the Refrigerator Got Its Hum, 1985, 2nd ed., 1999; (contrib.) Technology and the Labour Process, 1988; (contrib.) Women, Work and Computerization, 1988; Feminism Confronts Technology, 1991; Managing Like a Man: Women and Men in Corporate Management, 1998; Techno Feminism, 2004; (with P. Edwards) The Politics of Working Life, 2005; (co-ed.) The Handbook of Science and Technology Studies, 2008. **Address:** Department of Sociology, London School of Economics and Political Science, Rm. S203, Houghton St., London, GL WC2A 2AE, England. **Online address:** j.wajcman@lse.ac.uk

WAKEFIELD, Dan. American (born United States), b. 1932. **Genres:** Plays/Screenplays, Social Commentary, Novels, Autobiography/Memoirs, Psychology, Young Adult Fiction, Adult Non-fiction. **Career:** Princeton Packet, news editor, 1955; Columbia University, research assistant, 1955; Nation, staff writer, 1956-60; freelance writer, 1959-; University of Massachusetts, visiting lecturer, 1965-67, 1981-82, faculty; Atlantic Monthly, contributing editor, 1968-80; University of Iowa, visiting lecturer, 1972; Boston University, visiting lecturer, 1973-74, faculty; Emerson College, writer-in-residence, 1989-92, faculty; Shortridge Daily Echo, columnist; Indianapolis Star, sports correspondent; GQ Magazine, contributing writer, 1990-94; Florida International University, writer-in-residence, 1992, 1994-; Yoga Journal, contributing editor, senior writer, 1994-98; Converse College, Low Residency MFA in Writing Program, faculty. **Publications:** Island in the City: The World of Spanish Harlem, 1959; Revolt in the South, 1960; (ed.) The Addict: An Anthology, 1963; Between the Lines: A Reporter's Personal Journey Through Public Events, 1966; Supernation at Peace and War: Being Certain: Observations, Depositions, Testimonies, and Graffiti Gathered on a One-Man Fact-and-Fantasy-Finding Tour of the Most Powerful Nation in the World, 1968; (contrib.) Who We Are: An Atlantic Chronicle of the United States and Vietnam, 1969; All Her Children, 1976; Returning: A Spiritual Journey, 1988; The Story of Your Life: Writing a Spiritual Autobiography, 1990, 2nd ed., The Story of Your Life: How to Write a Spiritual Autobiography A Practical Guide to Explore Your Past and Understand Your Present, 2008; New York in the Fifties, 1992, rev. ed., 1999; Expect A Miracle: The Miraculous things that Happen to Ordinary People, 1995; Creating from the Spirit, 1996; How Do We Know When It's God?, 1999; (intro.) C. Wright Mills: Letters and Autobiographical Writings, 2000; Releasing the Creative Spirit: Unleash the Creativity in Your Life, 2001; New York in the Fifties, 2001; Spiritually Incorrect: Finding God in all the Wrong Places, 2004; The Hijacking of Jesus: How the Religious Right Distorts Christianity and Promotes Violence and Hate, 2006. NOVELS: Going All The Way, 1970; Starting Over, 1973; Home Free, 1977; Under The Apple Tree, 1982; Selling Out, 1985. **Address:** Department of English and Creative Writing, Florida International University, ACI-335, 11200 SW 8th St., Miami, FL 33199, U.S.A. **Online address:** wakespace@aol.com

WAKEFIELD, James L. American (born United States), b. 1954. **Genres:** Theology/Religion, Bibliography. **Career:** Salt Lake Theological Seminary, faculty, 1984-91, associate professor, 2002-; Good Shepherd Lutheran Church, associate pastor. Writer. **Publications:** Jürgen Moltmann: A Research Bibliography, 2002; Sacred Listening: Discovering the Spiritual Exercises of Ignatius Loyola, 2006. **Address:** Salt Lake Theological Seminary, PO Box 2096, Salt Lake City, UT 84110-2096, U.S.A. **Online address:** jwakefield@slts.edu

WAKLING, Christopher. (Christopher George Wakling). British (born England), b. 1970. **Genres:** Novels. **Career:** Educator; Lawyer and writer. **Publications:** The Immortal Part in UK as On Cape Three Points, 2003; Beneath the Diamond Sky, 2004; The Undertow, 2006; Towards the Sun, 2008; The Devils Mask, 2011; What I Did, 2011. **Address:** c/o Author Mail, Pan Macmillan-Picador, 20 New Wharf Rd., London, GL N1 9RR, England. **Online address:** responses@christopherwakling.com

WAKLING, Christopher George. See WAKLING, Christopher.

WAKOSKI, Diane. American (born United States), b. 1937. **Genres:** Poetry, Literary Criticism And History, Young Adult Fiction. **Career:** British Book Centre, clerk, 1960-63; Junior High School 22, teacher, 1963-66; New School for Social Research, lecturer, 1969; California Institute of Technology, writer-in-residence, 1972; University of Virginia, writer-in-residence, 1972-73; Willamette University, writer-in-residence, 1974; University of California, writer-in-residence, 1974; University of Wisconsin, writer-in-residence, 1975; Michigan State University, writer-in-residence, 1975, Department of English, professor, university distinguished professor in creative writing;

Whitman College, writer-in-residence, 1976; University of Washington, writer-in-residence, 1977; University of Hawaii, writer-in-residence, 1978; Emory University, writer-in-residence, 1980, 1981. **Publications:** Coins and Coffins, 1962; (co-author) Four Young Lady Poets, 1962; Dream Sheet, 1965; Discrepancies and Apparitions: Poems, 1966; The George Washington Poems, 1967; Greed, Parts One and Two, 1968; The Diamond Merchant, 1968; Inside the Blood Factory, 1968; (with R. Kelly and R. Loewinsohn) A Play and Two Poems, 1968; (with R. Kelly and R. Loewinsohn) The Well Wherein a Deer's Head Bleeds: A Play for Winter Solstice, 1968; Thanking My Mother for Piano Lessons, 1969; Some Black Poems for the Buddha's Birthday, 1969; Greed, Parts 3 and 4, 1969; Poems, 1969; The Moon Has a Complicated Geography, 1969; The Lament of the Lady Bank Dick, 1969; The Magellanic Clouds, 1970; The Wise Men Drawn to Kneel in Wonder at the Fact So of Itself, 1970; Love, You Big Fat Snail, 1970; Black Dream Ditty for Billy The Kid Seen in Dr. Generosity's Bar Recruiting for Hell's Angels and Black Mafia, 1970; Greed, Parts 5-7, 1971; Exorcism, 1971; On Barbara's Shore, 1971; The Motorcycle Betrayal Poems, 1971; This Water Baby: For Tony, 1971; The Pumpkin Pie, or Reassurances Are Always False, Though We Love Them, Only Physics Counts, 1972; The Purple Finch Song, 1972; Sometimes a Poet Will Hijack the Moon, 1972; Smudging, 1972; Form is an Extension of Content, 1972; The Owl and the Snake: A Fable, 1973; Dancing on the Grave of a Son of a Bitch, 1973; Greed, Parts 8, 9, 11, 1973; Winter Sequences, 1973; Stilllife: Michael, Silver Flute, and Violets, 1973; Trilogy: Coins and Coffins, Discrepancies and Apparitions, The George Washington Poems, 1974; Abalone, 1974; Wandering Tatler, 1974; Looking for the King of Spain, 1974; Fable of the Lion and the Scorpion, 1975; Creating a Personal Mythology (essays), 1975; Virtuoso Literature for Two and Four Hands, 1975; Waiting for the King of Spain, 1976; Variations on a Theme (essay), 1976; George Washington's Camp Cups, 1976; The Laguna Contract of Diane Wakoski, 1976; The Last Poem, 1976; The Ring, 1977; Overnight Projects with Wood, 1977; Spending Christmas with the Man from Receiving at Sears, 1977; The Man Who Shook Hands, 1978; Pachelbel's Canon, 1978; (intro.) Love at the Egyptian Theatre, 1978; Trophies, 1979; (intro.) Lust in Twenty-eight Flavors, 1979; The Managed World, 1980; Toward a New Poetry, 1980; Cap of Darkness: Including Looking For The King Of Spain and Pachelbel's Canon, 1980; Looking for Beethoven in Las Vegas, 1981; (with E. Lanyon) Making a Sacher Torte: Nine Poems, Twelve Illustrations, 1981; The Magician's Feastletters, 1982; Saturn's Rings, 1982; (with R. Creeley and C. Wright) National Poetry Competition, 1982, 1982; The Lady Who Drove Me to the Airport, 1982; Divers, 1982; The Collected Greed: Parts 1-13, 1984; Why My Mother Likes Liberace: A Musical Selection, 1985; The Rings of Saturn, 1986; Roses, 1987; Celebration of the Rose: For Norman on Christmas Day, 1987; Husks of Wheat, 1987; Emerald Ice: Selected Poems, 1962-1987, 1988, new ed., 2005; Unveilings, 1989; Medea the Sorceress, 1991; Jason the Sailor, 1993; The Ice Queen, 1994; The Emerald City of Las Vegas, 1995; Argonaut Rose, 1998; The Butcher's Apron: New and Selected Poems, Including Greed: Part 14, 2000; Diamond Dog, 2010. Contributor to books and periodicals. **Address:** Department of English, Michigan State University, 207 Morrill Hall, East Lansing, MI 48824-1036, U.S.A. **Online address:** wakoski@msu.edu

WALCOTT, Charles E(liot). American (born United States), b. 1943. **Genres:** Politics/Government, History, Biography, Social Sciences. **Career:** University of Minnesota, Department of Political Science, assistant professor, 1971-78, associate professor, 1978-89; Hamline University, adjunct professor, 1983-89; Virginia Polytechnic Institute and State University, Department of Political Science, associate professor, 1989-98, professor, 1998-. Writer. **Publications:** (With A. Walcott) Simple Simulations: A Guide to the Design and Use of Simulation/Games in Teaching Political Science, 1976; (ed.) Simple Simulations 2: A Collection of Simulation/Games for Political Scientists, 1980; (with K.M. Hult) Governing Public Organizations, 1990; (with K.M. Hult) Governing the White House, 1995; (with K.M. Hult) Empowering the White House: Governance under Nixon, Ford, and Carter, 2004. **Address:** Department of Political Science, Virginia Polytechnic Institute, 528 Major Williams Hall, Blacksburg, VA 24061, U.S.A. **Online address:** cwalcott@vt.edu

WALD, Diane. American (born United States), b. 1948?. **Genres:** Poetry. **Career:** Writer. **Publications:** My Hat That Was Dreaming, 1994; Double Mirror, 1996; Lucid Suitcase: Poems, 1999; The Yellow Hotel: Poems, 2002. Contributor to magazines. **Address:** Wave Books, 1938 Fairview Ave. E, Ste 201, Seattle, MA 98102, U.S.A. **Online address:** sleeperina@gmail.com

WALDBAUER, Gilbert (P.). (Gilbert Peter Waldbauer). American (born United States), b. 1928. **Genres:** Zoology, Biology. **Career:** University of Illinois-Urbana-Champaign, instructor, professor of entomology, 1953-95, professor emeritus, 1995-. Writer, 1995-. **Publications:** (With A.P. Marciano) Rice Leaf Folder: Mass Rearing and a Proposal for Screening for Varietal Resistance in the Greenhouse, 1979; Insects through the Seasons, 1996; Handy Bug Answer Book, 1998; Birder's Bug Book, 1998; Millions of Monarchs, Bunches of Beetles: How Bugs Find Strength in Numbers, 2000; What Good are Bugs?: Insects in the Web of Life, 2003; Insights from Insects: What Bad Bugs Can Teach Us, 2005; Walk Around the Pond: Insects in and Over the Water, 2006; Fireflies, Honey and Silk, 2009. **Address:** Department of Entomology, University of Illinois at Urbana-Champaign, 320 Morrill Hall, 505 S Goodwin Ave., Urbana, IL 61801, U.S.A.

WALDBAUER, Gilbert Peter. See **WALDBAUER, Gilbert (P.).**

WALDEN, Becky. See **USRY, Becky (S.).**

WALDEN, Mark. British (born England), b. 1973?. **Genres:** Novels, Young Adult Fiction, Children's Fiction. **Career:** Writer, video-game designer. **Publications:** Beyond the 13th Sun, 1981. H.I.V.E. NOVEL SERIES: Higher Institute of Villainous Education, 2006; The Overlord Protocol, 2007; Escape Velocity, 2008; Dreadnought, 2009, Rogue, 2010; Zero Hour, 2010; Aftershock, 2011. **Address:** Bloomsbury Publishing Plc, 36 Soho Sq., London, GL W1D 3QY, England. **Online address:** hivemind101@gmail.com

WALDFOGEL, Joel. American (born United States), b. 1962. **Genres:** Business/Trade/Industry. **Career:** F.W. Dodge/DRI, economist, 1985-87; University of Pennsylvania, Wharton School of Business, Department of Business and Public Policy, faculty, 1997-, Joel S. Ehrenkranz Family professor, 2003, chairperson, 2006-09, associate vice dean of doctoral programs, 2000-06; Federal Communications Commission Media Ownership Working Group, consultant, 2001-03; Yale University, faculty. Writer. **Publications:** (Ed. with J.B. Shoven) Debt, Taxes, and Corporate Restructuring, 1990; The Tyranny of the Market: Why You Can't Always Get What You Want, 2007; Scroogenomics: Why You Shouldn't Buy Presents for the Holidays, 2009. Contributor to periodicals. **Address:** Wharton School of Business, University of Pennsylvania, 3730 Walnut St., Philadelphia, PA 19104, U.S.A. **Online address:** waldfogj@wharton.upenn.edu

WALDINGER, Roger (David). American (born United States), b. 1953. **Genres:** Politics/Government, Sociology. **Career:** City University of New York, City College, assistant professor, professor of sociology, 1983-91, Graduate School and University Center, graduate faculty in Sociology, 1987; University of California, Department of Sociology, professor, 1990-, chair, 1999-2004, Lewis Center for Regional Policy Studies, director, 1995-98, distinguished professor of sociology, interim associate vice-provost for international studies. Writer. **Publications:** Through the Eye of the Needle: Immigrants and Enterprise in New York's Garment Trades, 1986; (co-author) Ethnic Entrepreneurs: Immigrant Business in Industrial Societies, 1990; (ed. with M. Bozorgmehr) Ethnic Los Angeles, 1996; Still the Promised City?: African-Americans and New Immigrants in Post Industrial New York, 1996; (ed.) Strangers at the Gates: New Immigrants in Urban America, 2001; (with M.I. Lichter) How the Other Half Works: Immigration and the Social Organization of Labor, 2002; Foreign Detachment: America's Immigrants and Their Homeland Connections, forthcoming. Contributor to books and periodicals. **Address:** Department of Sociology, University of California, 264 Haines Hall, PO Box 951551, Los Angeles, CA 90095-1551, U.S.A. **Online address:** waldinge@soc.ucla.edu

WALDMAN, Anne. American (born United States), b. 1945. **Genres:** Poetry. **Career:** St. Mark's Church-in-the-Bowery, assistant director, 1966-68, director of poetry project, 1968-78; Angel Hair and Angel Hair Books, editor, 1966-78; Full Court Press, founding editor, 1973; Naropa University, Jack Kerouac School of Disembodied Poetics, founding co-director and teacher, 1974-, director of summer writing program, 1984-, visiting lecturer, 1986-87, chair of summer writing program, distinguished professor of poetics, 1998-, artistic director; World Magazine, editor; Stevens Institute of Technology, visiting lecturer, 1981-82; New College of California, visiting lecturer, 1982; York University, Institute of American Indian Arts, visiting lecturer, 1985; University of Maine, visiting lecturer, 1986; New England College, faculty, 2003-; Giorno Poetry Systems Institute Inc., board director. Writer. **Publications:** On the Wing, 1968; O My Life!, 1969; Giant Night, 1970; Baby Breakdown, 1970; Icy Rose, 1971; No Hassles, 1971; (with T. Berrigan) Memorial Day, 1971; Holy City, 1971; Goodies from Anne Waldman, 1971; Light and Shadow, 1972; The West Indies Poems, 1972; Spin Off, 1972; (with J. Brainard) Self Portrait, 1973; Life Notes: Selected Poems, 1973; Fast Speaking Woman, 1975; Sun the Blond Out, 1975; Journals and Dreams: Poems, 1975; Shaman, 1977; (with R. Bye) 4 Travels, 1978; To a Young Poet, 1979; Countries, 1980; Cabin, 1982; First Baby Poems, 1982; Make-Up on Empty Space, 1984; Invention, 1985; Skin Meat Bones, 1985; The Romance Thing, 1987; Blue Mosque, 1988; Helping the Dreamer: New and Selected Poems, 1966-1988, 1989; Not a Male Pseudonym, 1990; Lokapala, 1991; (with G. Schneeman) Homage to Allen G., 1997; Iovis, 1993, Book II, 1997; Kill or Cure, 1994; (trans. with A. Schelling) Songs of the Sons & Daughters of Buddha, 1996; (contrib.) Kin, 1997; Marriage: A Sentence, 2000; Vow to Poetry, 2001; In the Room of Never Grieve: New and Selected Poems, 1985-2003, 2003; Structure of the World Compared to a Bubble, 2004; Outrider: Poems, Essays, Interviews, 2006; Manatee-Humanity, 2009; Lovis Trilogy: Colors in the Mechanism of Concealment, 2011. EDITOR: The World Anthology: Poems from the St. Mark's Poetry Project, and Another World, 1971; (with M. Webb) Talking Poetics from Naropa Institute, 2 vols., 1978-79; (and intro.) Nice to See You: Homage to Ted Berrigan, 1991; (and intro.) Out of This World, 1991; (with A. Schelling) Disembodied Poetics, Annals of the Jack Kerouac School, 1994; The Beat Book, 1996; (with L. Warsh) Angel Hair Sleeps with a Boy in My Head, 2001; (with L. Birman) Civil Disobediences: Poetics and Politics in Action, 2004; (with L. Wright) Beats at Naropa, 2009. **Address:** Naropa Institute, 2130 Arapahoe Ave., Boulder, CO 80302, U.S.A.

WALDMAN, Ayelet. American (born United States), b. 1964. **Genres:** Law, Mystery/Crime/Suspense, Novels. **Career:** Attorney, 1991-92; University of California, Boalt Hall School of Law, adjunct professor of law, 1997-2003; Drug Policy Alliance, consultant. Writer. **Publications:** Nursery Crimes, 2000; The Big Nap, 2001; A Playdate with Death, 2002; Death Gets a Time-Out, 2003; Daughter's Keeper (novel), 2003; Murder Plays House, 2004; Cradle Robbers, 2005; Love and Other Impossible Pursuits, 2006; Bye-bye, Black Sheep, 2006; Red Hook Road, 2010; Bad Mother: A Chronicle of Maternal Crimes, Minor Calamities, and Occasional Moments of Grace, 2010; Women in Prison Project, forthcoming. **Address:** c/o Author Mail, Berkley Books Publicity, 375 Hudson St., New York, NY 10014, U.S.A. **Online address:** ayeletwaldman@gmail.com

WALDMAN, Harry. American/Polish (born Poland), b. 1945. **Genres:** Film, Information Science/Computers, Language/Linguistics, Technology, Engineering, Biography, Literary Criticism And History, Humanities, Autobiography/Memoirs. **Career:** Bell Laboratories, technical analyst, 1968-74; Scholarly Press, editor and staff writer, 1975-81; Society of Manufacturing Engineers, editor, 1982-83; Mathematical Association of America, journal's editorial manager and senior writer, 1983-. **Publications:** (Co-ed.) Dictionary of Indians of North America, 1978; Dictionary of Robotics, 1985; Dictionary of SDI, 1988; Scenes Unseen: Unreleased and Uncompleted Films From the World's Master Filmmakers, 1912-1990, 1991; Beyond Hollywood's Grasp: American Filmmakers Abroad, 1914-1945, 1994; Hollywood and the Foreign Touch: A Dictionary of Foreign Filmmakers and Their Films from America, 1910-1995, 1996; Paramount in Paris: 300 Films Produced at the Joinville Studios, 1930-1933, with Credits and Biographies, 1998; Missing Reels: Lost Films of American and European Cinema, 2000 (paperback, 2008); Maurice Tourneur: The Life and Films, 2001 (paperback, 2008); Nazi Films in America, 1933-1942, 2008. **Address:** Mathematical Association of America, 1529 18th St. NW, PO Box 91112, Washington, DC 20036, U.S.A. **Online address:** hwaldman@maa.org

WALDMAN, Mark Robert. American (born United States) **Genres:** Psychology, Theology/Religion, Medicine/Health. **Career:** Heartline Psychological Information and Referral Service, director, 1986-94; Bruno Bettelheim, psychoanalytic supervisor, 1988-90; Transpersonal Perspectives in Psychology, founding editor, 1989-93; Stillpoint Foundation for Transpersonal Studies, faculty, 1992-93; Transpersonal Review, founding editor, 1994-96; Tarcher/Putnam, developmental editor, 1995-2005; Spiritual Emergence Network, regional coordinator, 1995-99; Jeff Herman Literary Agency, acquisitions editor, 2005-06; University of Pennsylvania, Center for Spirituality and the Mind, associate fellow, 2006-; Loyola Marymount University, Executive MBA Program, adjunct faculty, 2009-; Holmes Institute, faculty, 2011-. **Publications:** (Ed.) The Art of Staying Together: Embracing Love, Intimacy, and Spirit in Relationships, 1998; (ed. with S. Krippner) Dreamscaping: New and Creative Ways to Work with Your Dreams, 1999; (ed.) Love Games: How to Deepen Communication, Resolve Conflict, and Discover Who Your Partner

Really Is, 2000; (ed.) The Spirit of Writing: Classic and Contemporary Essays Celebrating the Writing Life, 2001; Archetypes of the Collective Unconscious: Reflecting American Culture through Literature and Art, 2003; (with T. Gilbert) Messages from the Archetypes: Using Tarot for Healing and Spiritual Growth: A Guidebook for Personal and Professional Use, 2004; (with A. Newberg) Why We Believe What We Believe: Uncovering Our Biological Need for Meaning, Spirituality, and Truth, 2006; (with A. Newberg) Born to Believe: God, Science, and the Origin of Ordinary and Extraordinary Beliefs, 2007; (with A. Newberg) How God Changes your Brain: Breakthrough Findings from a Leading Neuroscientist, 2009; (with A. Newberg) Words can Change Your Brain: 12 Conversation Strategies to Build Trust, Resolve Conflict, and Increase Intimacy, 2012. Contributor to periodicals. **Address:** 1601 Carmen Dr., Ste. 203, Camarillo, CA 93010, U.S.A. **Online address:** markwaldman@sbcglobal.net

WALDMAN, Sidney R. American (born United States), b. 1940. **Genres:** History, Military/Defense/Arms Control, Politics/Government. **Career:** Haverford College, professor. Writer. **Publications:** (with D.J. Vogler) Congress and Democracy, 1985; (ed. with S.J. Cimbala) Controlling and Ending Conflict: Issues before and after the Cold War, 1992; America and the Limits of the Politics of Selfishness, 2007. **Address:** U.S.A. **Online address:** swaldman@haverford.edu

WALDMAN, Steven. American (born United States), b. 1962. **Genres:** Law, Politics/Government. **Career:** Washington Monthly, editor; U.S. News & World Report, national editor; Newsweek, editor; Beliefnet.com, chief executive officer, cofounder and editor-in-chief, 1999-. **Publications:** The Bill: How the Adventures of Clinton's National Service Bill Reveal What Is Corrupt, Comic, Cynical, and Noble, about Washington, 1995, rev. ed. as The Bill: How Legislation Really Becomes Law: A Case Study of the National Service Bill, 1996; Founding Faith: Providence, Politics, and the Birth of Religious Freedom in America, 2008. Contributor to periodicals. **Address:** BeliefNet Inc., 303 Park Ave. S, PO Box 1062, New York, NY 10010-3601, U.S.A.

WALDMAN, Stuart. American (born United States), b. 1941. **Genres:** Travel/Exploration. **Career:** Mikaya Press, co-founder, 1995. Writer. **Publications:** Maritime Mile: The Story of the Greenwich Village Waterfront, 2002; We Asked for Nothing: The Remarkable Journey of Cabeza De Vaca, 2003; The Last River: John Wesley Powell & the Colorado River Exploration Expedition, 2005; Magellan's World, 2007. **Address:** Mikaya Press, 12 Bedford St., New York, NY 10014-4729, U.S.A. **Online address:** waldman@mikaya.com

WALDO, Anna Lee. American (born United States), b. 1925. **Genres:** Novels, History, Young Adult Fiction. **Career:** Miami Valley Hospital, research biochemist, 1950-56; Physicians and Surgeons Group, clinical chemist, 1956-65; Mercy Junior College, instructor in organic chemistry, 1965-69; Saint Johns Mercy Hospital, biochemist and instructor in biochemistry, 1969-74; Saint Louis Community College, instructor in chemistry and physical science, 1974-85; California Polytechnic State University, chemistry instructor, 1985-97; Midwest Medical Institute, instructor in biochemistry. Writer. **Publications:** Clinical Chemistry Methods: A Laboratory Manual, 1952; Sacajawea, 1979; Prairie: The Legend of Charles Burton Irwin and the Y Ranch, 1986; Circle of Stones, 1999; Circle of Stars, 2001; Watch the Face of the Sky, 2011. Contributor to journals. **Address:** Zova Books Inc., PO Box 21833, Long Beach, CA 90801, U.S.A. **Online address:** author@annaleewaldo.com

WALDOFF, Leon. American (born United States), b. 1935. **Genres:** Literary Criticism And History, Poetry, Art/Art History. **Career:** University of Illinois, professor of English, 1967-2000, professor emeritus, 2000-. Writer. **Publications:** Keats and the Silent Work of Imagination, 1985; Wordsworth in His Major Lyrics: The Art and Psychology of Self-Representation, 2001. **Address:** Department of English, University of Illinois, 608 S Wright St., Urbana, IL 61801, U.S.A. **Online address:** lwaldoff@illinois.edu

WALDREP, Christopher (Reef). American (born United States), b. 1951. **Genres:** History. **Career:** Teacher, 1974-90; Purdue University, teaching assistant, 1974; Eastern Illinois University, assistant professor, 1990-94, associate professor of history, 1994-99, professor, 1999-2000; San Francisco State University, Jamie and Phyllis Pasker professor of constitutional history, 2000-, Pasker chair of American history. Writer. **Publications:** Night Riders: Defending Community in the Black Patch, 1993; Roots of Disorder: Race and Criminal Justice in the American South, 1817-80, 1998; (ed. with D.

Nieman) Local Matters: Race, Crime and Justice in the Nineteenth-Century South, 2001; Racial Violence on Trial: A Handbook with Cases, Laws, and Documents, 2001; The Many Faces of Judge Lynch: Extralegal Violence and Punishment in America, 2002; (with L. Curry) The Constitution and the Nation, vol. I: Establishing the Constitution: 1215-1829, vol. II: The Civil War and American Constitutionalism: 1830-1890, vol. III: The Regulatory State: 1890-1945, vol. IV: A Revolution in Rights, 1937-2002, 2003; Vicksburg's Long Shadow: The Civil War Legacy of Race and Remembrance, 2005; (ed. with M. Bellesiles) Documenting American Violence: A Source Book, 2006; (ed.) Lynching in America: A History in Documents, 2006; African Americans Confront Lynching: Strategies of Resistance from the Civil War to the Civil Rights Era, 2009; Jury Discrimination: The Supreme Court, Public Opinion, and a Grassroots Fight for Racial Equality in Mississippi, 2010; (ed.) Race and National Power: A Sourcebook of Black Civil Ris from 1862 to 1954, 2010. Contributor to journals. **Address:** Department of History, San Francisco State University, 225 SCI, 1600 Holloway Ave., San Francisco, CA 94132, U.S.A. **Online address:** cwaldrep@sfsu.edu

WALDRON, Arthur (Nelson). American (born United States), b. 1948. **Genres:** History, Cultural/Ethnic Topics, Military/Defense/Arms Control. **Career:** Princeton University, assistant professor of history and East Asian studies, 1985-92; U.S. Naval War College, professor of strategy, 1991-97; University of Pennsylvania, Department of History, Lauder professor of international relations, 1997-, Institute for Strategic Threat Assessment and Response, associate; Intl. Assessment and Strategy Center, founder and vice president; Catholic University of Leuven, visiting professor; Institute for Southeast Asian Studies, visiting fellow; Brown University, faculty. Writer and consultant. **Publications:** The Great Wall of China: From History to Myth, 1990; (ed. and intro.) How the Peace Was Lost: The 1935 Memorandum Developments Affecting American Policy in the Far East, 1991; (ed.) Mao Tse-tung on Guerrilla Warfare, 1991; From War to Nationalism: China's Turning Point, 1924-1925, 1995; The Chinese Civil Wars, 1911-1949, 1995; (ed. with D. Moran); People in Arms: Military Myth and National Mobilization Since the French Revolution, 2003. **Address:** Department of History, University of Pennsylvania, 311C College Hall, Philadelphia, PA 19104-6228, U.S.A. **Online address:** awaldron2@mac.com

WALDROP, M(orris) Mitchell. American (born United States), b. 1947. **Genres:** Sciences, Technology, Information Science/Computers. **Career:** University Of Wisconsin, research assistant, 1969-77; Chemical and Engineering News, writer, 1977-78, West Coast bureau, head, 1978-80; American Association for the Advancement of Science, Science, senior writer, 1980-91, contributing correspondent, 1991-94; freelance writer, 1991-2003; National Science Foundation, staff, 2003-06; MMW Communications, principal, 2006-08; Nature, editor, 2008-. **Publications:** Man-Made Minds: The Promise of Artificial Intelligence, 1987; Complexity: The Emerging Science at the Edge of Order and Chaos, 1992; The Dream Machine: J.C.R. Licklinder and the Revolution That Made Computing Personal, 2001. Contributor of articles to periodicals. **Address:** 2430 39th St. NW, Washington, DC 20007, U.S.A.

WALKER, Anne Collins. American (born United States), b. 1939. **Genres:** History, Young Adult Fiction, Adult Non-fiction, Mystery/Crime/Suspense, Politics/Government. **Career:** Teacher, 1960-67; Dallas Market Center, staff, 1975-81; Ron Walker and Associates Inc., vice-president and corporate secretary, 1977-80; Abel Company Inc., payroll and bookkeeping clerk, 1978-81; Consumer Product Safety Commission, special assistant and deputy director of congressional relations, 1981-84; U.S. Department of Commerce, deputy director of public affairs, 1984-87. Writer. **Publications:** In the Sleep Room: The Story of the CIA Brainwashing Experiments in Canada, 1988; China Calls: Paving the Way for Nixon's Historic Journey to China, 1992. Contributor to newspapers. **Address:** 550 Golf Creek Ln., Jackson Hole, WY 83001-9076, U.S.A.

WALKER, Benjamin. Also writes as George Benjamin Walker. British/Indian (born India), b. 1913. **Genres:** Anthropology/Ethnology, History, Paranormal, Philosophy, Sciences, Theology/Religion, Reference. **Career:** British Consulate-General, confidential assistant, personal assistant; Asia, co-editor, 1951-52. Writer. **Publications:** Persian Pageant, 1950; Angkor Empire, 1955; Hindu World: An Encyclopedic Survey of Hinduism, vol. II, 1968; Sex and the Supernatural: Sexuality in Religion and Magic, 1970; (co-author) Encyclopedia of the Unexplained, 1974; Beyond the Body: The Human Double and the Astral Planes, 1974; The Human Double, 1974; Encyclopedia of Esoteric Man, 1977; Man and the Beasts Within: The Encyclopedia of the Occult,

the Esoteric and the Supernatural, 1977; Body Magic: Man and His Hidden Powers, 1977; Encyclopedia of Metaphysical Medicine, 1978; Masks of the Soul: The Facts behind Reincarnation, 1981; Tantrism: Its Secret Principles and Practices, 1982; Gnosticism: Its History and Influence 1983; Companion to the Kabala, 1990; Foundations of Islam, 1998; Caesar's Church: The Irrational in Science and Philosophy, 2001; Evolution under Scrutiny, 2005; Art and the Occult, forthcoming. **Address:** 84 Church Rd., Teddington, WM TW15 2TN, England.

WALKER, Charles F. American (born United States), b. 1959. **Genres:** History. **Career:** University of California, professor of history and director of the Hemispheric Institute on the Americas. Writer and historian. **Publications:** Smoldering Ashes: Cuzco and the Creation of Republican Peru, 1780-1840, 1999; Shaky Colonialism: The 1746 Earthquake-Tsunami in Lima, Peru, and Its Long Aftermath, 2008. Contributor to periodicals and journals. **Address:** Department of History, University of California, 2216 Social Sciences & Humanities, Davis, CA 95616, U.S.A. **Online address:** cfwalker@ucdavis.edu

WALKER, Clarence Earl. American (born United States), b. 1941. **Genres:** Human Relations/Parenting, Politics/Government, Military/Defense/Arms Control, History, Essays, Cultural/Ethnic Topics. **Career:** University of California, professor of history, 1985-. Writer. **Publications:** A Rock in a Weary Land: The African Methodist Episcopal Church during the Civil War and Reconstruction, 1982; Deromanticizing Black History: Critical Essays and Reappraisals, 1991; Biblical Counseling with African-Americans: Taking a Ride in the Ethiopian's Chariot, 1992; Breaking Strongholds in the African-American Family: Strategies for Spiritual Warfare, 1996; Booker T. Washington Family Relationships, 1843-1910: The Wrights and Burroughs, Ex-slaves of Bedford and Franklin Counties, Virginia, 1997; We Can't Go Home Again: An Argument about Afrocentrism, 2001; The Preacher and the Politician: Jeremiah Wright, Barack Obama, and Race in America, 2009; Mongrel Nation: The America Begotten by Thomas Jefferson and Sally Hemings, 2009. Contributor to journals. **Address:** University of California, 2216 Social Sciences and Humanities, Davis, CA 95616, U.S.A. **Online address:** cewalker@ucdavis.edu

WALKER, David (Maxwell). Scottish (born Scotland), b. 1920. **Genres:** History, Law. **Career:** University of London, researcher, 1953-54; University of Glasgow, School of Law, professor of jurisprudence, 1954-58, Faculty of Law and Financial Studies, dean, 1956-59, Regius professor of law, 1958-90, senior research fellow, 1990-, now emeritus Regius professor; Scottish University Law Institute, director, 1974-80; Royal Society of Edinburgh, vice-president, 1985-88. Writer. **Publications:** Law of Damages in Scotland, 1955; Scottish legal system; An Introduction to the Study of Scots law, 1959, 8th ed., 2001; The Law of Delict in Scotland, 1966, 2nd ed., 1981; Scottish Courts and Tribunals, 1969, 5th ed., 1985; Principles of Scottish Private Law, 1970, 4th ed., 4 vols., 1988-89; The Law of Civil Remedies in Scotland, 1974; The Law of Prescription in Scotland, 1976, 4th ed., 1992; The Law of Contracts in Scotland, 1979, 3rd ed., 1994; The Oxford Companion to Law, 1980; The Institutions of the Law of Scotland, 1981; The Scottish Jurists, 1985; Legal History of Scotland, 7 vols., 1988-2004; The Historical Evolution of Scots Law, 1998; Marx, Methodology and Science: Marx's Science of Politics, 2001. EDITOR: Faculty Digest of Decisions 1940-50, 1953; Topham and Ivamy's Company Law, 15th ed., 1974; Stair's Institutions, 6th ed., 1981; Stair Tercentenary Studies, 1981; (with P. Cane, J. Conaghan) New Oxford Companion to Law, 2001. **Address:** 1 Beaumont Gate, Glasgow, G12, Scotland.

WALKER, Donald E(dwin). American (born United States), b. 1941. **Genres:** Bibliography, Sports/Fitness, Cultural/Ethnic Topics. **Career:** Olivet College, assistant professor, 1965-, Department of Social Science, chairperson, Department of History and Political Science, professor and chairperson. Writer. **Publications:** (And comp. with B.L. Cooper) Baseball and American Culture: A Thematic Bibliography of Over 4, 500 Works, 1995. Contributor to periodicals. **Address:** Department of History and Political Science, Olivet College, 306-C Mott Bldg., Olivet, MI 49076, U.S.A. **Online address:** dwalker@olivetcollege.edu

WALKER, Geoffrey de Q(uincey). Australian (born Australia), b. 1940. **Genres:** Law, Politics/Government, Social Sciences. **Career:** Barrister-at-law, 1965-; University of Queensland, professor of law and head of department, 1985-96, dean of faculty of law, 1988-96, professor emeritus, 1996-; Administrative Appeals Tribunal of Australia, deputy president, 2004-. Writer. **Publications:** Australian Monopoly Law; Issues of Law, Fact and Policy,

1967; Initiative and Referendum: The People's Law, 1987; The Rule of Law: Foundation of Constitutional Democracy, 1988; Ten Advantages of a Federal Constitution: And How to Make the Most of Them, 2001; Australian Constitutional Law: Foundations and Theory, 2002; FEATURE: Out of the Tax Wilderness, 2004; People Power: The History and Future of the Referendum in Australia, 2011. **Address:** TC Beirne School of Law, The University of Queensland, Level 3, Forgan Smith Bldg., St Lucia, QL 4072, Australia. **Online address:** geoffrey.walker@aat.gov.au

WALKER, George Benjamin. *See* **WALKER, Benjamin.**

WALKER, Greg. British (born England), b. 1959?. **Genres:** Literary Criticism And History, History. **Career:** University of Leicester, professor of early-modern literature and culture, Medieval Research Centre, director, 1986-, Leverhulme Trust Major Research, fellow, 2001-04. Writer. **Publications:** John Skelton and the Politics of the 1520s, 1988; Plays of Persuasion: Drama and Politics at the Court of Henry VIII, 1991; Persuasive Fictions: Faction, Faith, and Political Culture in the Reign of Henry VIII, 1996; The Politics of Performance in Early Renaissance Drama, 1998; (ed.) Medieval Drama: An Anthology, 2000; The Private Life of Henry VIII, 2003; Writing under Tyranny: English Literature and the Henrician Reformation, 2005; (ed. with E. Treharne and W. Green) The Oxford Handbook of Medieval Literature in English, 2010. Contributor to periodicals. **Address:** Department of English, University of Leicester, University Rd., Leicester, LE1 7RH, England. **Online address:** gmw4@leicester.ac.uk

WALKER, Henry M(acKay). American (born United States), b. 1947. **Genres:** Information Science/Computers, Mathematics/Statistics. **Career:** Williams College, undergraduate teaching assistant for the computer laboratory, 1968-69; Mobil Oil Corp., computer systems analyst, 1969; Massachusetts Institute of Technology, Department of Mathematics, lecturer, 1973-74; Grinnell College, assistant professor of mathematics, 1974-80, associate professor, 1980-87, chair, 1981-83, professor, 1987-90, professor of mathematics, 1990-2006, chair, 1990-91, Samuel R. and Marie-Louise Rosenthal professor of natural science and mathematics, 2001-, distinguished educator, Department of Computer Science, chair, 1990-91, 2006-10, professor of computer science, 1990-; Bell Telephone Laboratories, technical staff, 1980-81; University of Texas, senior lecturer in computer sciences, 1988-89, 1990-93. Writer. **Publications:** Problems for Computer Solutions Using FORTRAN, 1980; Problems for Computer Solutions Using BASIC, 1980; Introduction to Computing and Computer Science with Pascal, 1986; Pascal: Problem Solving and Structured Program Design, 1987; Computer Science 2: Principles of Software Engineering, Data Types and Algorithms, 1989; The Limits of Computing, 1994; (with N. Dale) Abstract Data Types, 1996; The Proceedings of the Thirty-First SIGCSE Technical Symposium on Computer Science Education: SIGCSE 2000, 2000; Tao of Computing, 2005. Contributor to journals. **Address:** Department of Computer Science, Grinnell College, Noyce Science Ctr., 1116 8th Ave., Grinnell, IA 50112-1690, U.S.A. **Online address:** walker@cs.grinnell.edu

WALKER, James R(obert). American (born United States), b. 1950. **Genres:** Communications/Media, Reference. **Career:** Pennsylvania State University, producer and host of daily consumer education television and radio programs for agricultural extension service, 1976-78; University of Northern Iowa, assistant professor of speech and coordinator of radio and television division, 1981-83; University of Memphis, associate professor of communication and coordinator of graduate studies, 1983-93; Yale University, visiting fellow, 1990; Saint Xavier University, professor of mass communications and department chair, 1993-, Faculty Senate, president, 1996-97. Writer. **Publications:** (Ed. with R.V. Bellamy) The Remote Control in the New Age of Television, 1993; (with R.V. Bellamy) Television and the Remote Control: Grazing on a Vast Wasteland, 1996; (with D.F. Ferguson) The Commercial Television Industry, 1998; (with D.A. Ferguson) Broadcast Television Industry, 1998; (with R.V. Bellamy) Centerfield Shot: A History of Baseball on Television, 2008. Contributor of articles and to journals. **Address:** Department of Communication, St. Xavier University, Rm. N315, 3700 W 103rd St., Chicago, IL 60655, U.S.A. **Online address:** walker@sxu.edu

WALKER, Joel. *See* **WALKER, Joel Thomas.**

WALKER, Joel Thomas. (Joel Walker). American (born United States), b. 1968. **Genres:** Theology/Religion, History. **Career:** University of Washington, associate professor; Tahirler Project, field director, 1997-98, 2000-.

Writer, professor and archaeologist. **Publications:** (ed. as Joel Walker with S. Noegel and B. Wheeler) Prayer, Magic and the Stars in the Ancient and Late Antique World, 2003; The Legend of Mar Qardagh: Narrative and Christian Heroism in Late Antique Iraq, 2006. Contributor to periodicals and books. **Address:** Department of History, University of Washington, 315 Smith, PO Box 353560, Seattle, WA 98195-3560, U.S.A. **Online address:** jwalker@u.washington.edu

WALKER, Kate. Australian (born Australia), b. 1950. **Genres:** Children's Fiction, Young Adult Fiction, Young Adult Non-fiction, Picture/Board Books, Biography. **Career:** Writing teacher, 1987-. Writer. **Publications:** PICTURE BOOKS: Marty Moves to the Country, 1980; The Frog Who Would Be King, 1989; King Joe of Bogpeat Castle, 1989; The First Easter Rabbit, 1989; Our Excursion, 1994. FOR CHILDREN: The Alien Challenger, 1983; Suzie and the Pencil-Case Genie, 1988; The Letters of Rosie O'Brien: A Convict in the Colony of New South Wales, 1804, 1988; Tales from the Good Land, 1988; Burying Aunt Renie, 1989; The Dragon of Mith, 1989; I Hate Books!, 1995; Elephant's Lunch, 1998; Sticky Stuff, 2000; Mitch 2 Sue, 2003; Recycle, Reduce, Reuse, Rethink, 2004. FOR YOUNG ADULTS: Peter, 1993; Changes, 1995. NONFICTION: Writing Games, 1991; Step by Step Stories, 1991; Story Writing the Low Stress Way: A Manual for Primary and High School Teachers, 1992; Creativity and Story Writing, 1993; Story Writing: Teaching and Tapping Your Subconscious Mind (manual for adults), 1993; Writing Enrichment, 1994; Journal Writing, 1994; Bridging the Realms, 2004. OTHERS: Frog who would be King, 1995; (with E. Argaet) Famous Spy Cases, 2003; (with E. Argaet) Super Spies of World War II, 2003; (with E. Argaet) So You Want to be a Spy?, 2003; (with E. Argaet) Spies and Their Gadgets, 2003; (with E. Argaet) Spies in History, 2003; (with E. Argaet) Super Spies of World War I, 2003. Works appear in anthologies. Contributor to magazines and periodicals. **Address:** c/o Author Mail, Allen & Unwin, 83 Alexander St., PO Box 8500, Crows Nest, NW 2065, Australia. **Online address:** kw_writer@hunterlink.net.au

WALKER, Kathryn. American (born United States), b. 1943. **Genres:** Novels, Mystery/Crime/Suspense, Young Adult Fiction, History. **Career:** Athens Street Co., co-founder; Harvard University, Radcliffe College, Rothschild artist-in-residence, 1997. Writer and actress. **Publications:** A Stopover in Venice (novel), 2008; Mysteries of Alien Visitors and Abductions, 2009; Mysteries of Giant Humanlike Creatures, 2009; Mysteries of the Bermuda Triangle, 2009; Mysteries of UFOs, 2009; Mysteries of Water Monsters, 2009; The Mystery of Atlantis, 2009; The Mystery of the Ghosts of Flight 401, 2009. **Address:** Helen Brann Agency Inc., 94 Curtis Rd., Bridgewater, CT 06752-1204, U.S.A.

WALKER, Kenneth Roland. American (born United States), b. 1928. **Genres:** Education, History, Local History/Rural Topics, Autobiography/Memoirs, Administration/Management, Civil Liberties/Human Rights, Economics, International Relations/Current Affairs, Politics/Government, Race Relations, Theology/Religion, Essays. **Career:** Arkansas Tech University, associate professor and assistant dean of college, 1958-65, professor of history, 1965-98, School of Arts and Sciences, dean, 1970-72, head of social sciences and philosophy department, 1972-89, professor of history emeritus, 1998-; U.S. Air Force Academy, instructor and assistant professor of history. Writer. **Publications:** Days the Presidents Died, 1966; A History of the Midwest from the Beginning to 1970, 1972; History of First United Methodist Church of Russelville, 1973-1984, 1984, 2nd ed., 1993; History of Arkansas Tech University 1909-90, 1992. **Address:** Department of History & Political Science, Arkansas Tech University, WPN 255, 407 W Q St., Russellville, AR 72801, U.S.A.

WALKER, Lawrence R. American (born United States), b. 1951. **Genres:** Environmental Sciences/Ecology. **Career:** University of Nevada, professor of biology. Biologist and writer. **Publications:** (Ed.) Ecosystems of Disturbed Ground, 1999; (with R. del Moral) Primary Succession and Ecosystem Rehabilitation, 2003; (ed. with R.J. Hobbs and J. Walker) Linking Restoration and Ecological Succession, 2007; (with R. del Moral) Environmental Disasters, Natural Recovery and Human Responses, 2007; (ed. with K. Mehltreter and J.M. Sharpe) Fern Ecology, 2010; (with P. Bellingham) Island Environments in a Changing World, 2011. Contributor to academic journals. **Address:** School of Life Sciences, University of Nevada, 307 Juanita Greer White Hall, 4505 Maryland Pkwy., Las Vegas, NV 89154-4004, U.S.A. **Online address:** lawrence.walker@unlv.edu

WALKER, Marianne (Cascio). American (born United States), b. 1933. **Genres:** Literary Criticism And History. **Career:** University of Kentucky, Henderson Community College, professor of English and philosophy, 1976-2001, retired, 2001; St. Anthony's Hospice, co-founder, 1981-, board president, 1984-85, board director, 1987-88; Kentucky Humanities Council, board director, 1988-92. Writer. **Publications:** Margaret Mitchell and John Marsh: The Love Story behind Gone With the Wind, 1993, 2nd ed., 2000; When Cuba Conquered Kentucky, 1999. Contributor of articles to magazines and newspapers. **Address:** Rutledge Hill Press Inc., 501 Nelson Pl., PO Box 141000, Nashville, TN 37214-3600, U.S.A. **Online address:** walkerme33@bellsouth.net

WALKER, Martin. American/British (born England), b. 1947. **Genres:** Novels, History, Literary Criticism And History, Politics/Government, Travel/Exploration. **Career:** Harvard University, Harkness fellow and resident tutor of kirkland house, 1969-70; Guardian, reporter, columnist and foreign correspondent, 1972-99, Moscow bureau chief, 1983-88, U.S. bureau chief, 1989-97; United Press Intl., chief international correspondent, 1998-, editor-in-chief, 2003-, editor emeritus and international affairs columnist; Woodrow Wilson International Center for Scholars, fellow, 1999-2000; Global Business Policy Council, senior director, 2007-, head of A.T. Kearney's Global Business Policy Council; European Policy Institute, associate director; European Institute, vice-chairperson; British Broadcasting Corp., writer, BBC-TV, broadcaster, BBC-Radio, broadcaster; Radio Telefeis Eiran, commentator; ABC-TV, commentator; ABC-Radio, commentator; CNN, commentator; CBC, commentator; C-Span, commentator; CBS-TV, commentator; National Public Radio, commentator; New School for Social Research, World Policy Institute, senior fellow; Loyola College, H.L. Menken lecturer, 1994; Woodrow Wilson International Center for Scholars Public Policy fellow, 2000-01; National War College, lecturer; Hackney Community Defence Association, founder. **Publications:** Poor Man, Beggar Man, Thief: The Story of the New Horizon Youth Centre, 1972; The Happy Unicorns, 1972; The National Front, 1977, rev. ed. 1979; Identification Evidence: Practices and Malpractices, 1978; Daily Sketches: A History of Political Cartoons, 1978; The Money Soldiers, 1980; Powers of the Press, 1981; (with G. Coggan) Frightened for My Life: An Account of Deaths in British Prison, 1982; Turn of the Screw: The Aftermath of the 1984-85 Miners' Strike, 1985; State of Siege, 1985; The Waking Giant: Gorbachev and Perestroika, 1986; With Extreme Prejudice, 1987; Martin Walker's Russia, 1989; The Independent Traveller's Guide to the Soviet Union, 1990; (with J. Watson) The Insight Guide to Washington, DC, 1992; (as Martin J. Walker) Dirty Medicine: Science, Big Business and the Assault on Natural Health Care, 1993; Cold War and the Making of the Modern World, 1993; The Cold War: A History, 1994; President We Deserve: Bill Clinton, His Rise, Falls and Comebacks, 1996; America Reborn: A 20th Century Narrative in 26 Lives, 2000; (co-author) Europe in the 21st Century, 2001; (ed.) Iraq War: As Witnessed by the Correspondents and Photographers of United Press International, 2004; Bruno, Chief of Police, 2008; (ed.) Silenced Witnesses: vol. II: The Parents Story: The Denial of Vaccine Damage by Government, Corporations and the Media, 2009; The Dark Vineyard, 2010; Black Diamond, 2010; (as Martin J. Walker) Overthrowing The Temple, 2011. NOVELS: The Infiltrator, 1978; A Mercenary Calling, 1981; The Eastern Question, 1983; The Caves of Périgord, 2002. Contributor to periodicals. **Address:** United Press International, 1133 19th St. NW, Washington, DC 20036, U.S.A. **Online address:** mwalker@upi.com

WALKER, Melissa A. American (born United States), b. 1962. **Genres:** Business/Trade/Industry, Agriculture/Forestry, Women's Studies And Issues, History, Social Sciences. **Career:** Maryville College, office manager, 1985-86, director of alumni relations, 1986-87; Bryant College, associate director of alumni relations, 1987-92, assistant director of development research, 1992-96, professor, 1996; Community College of Rhode Island, adjunct professor, 1995; Converse College, assistant professor, 1996-2002, associate professor, 2002-07, George Dean Johnson, Jr., professor of history, 2007-; HubCulture Inc., president. Writer. **Publications:** All We Knew Was to Farm: Rural Women in the Upcountry South, 1919-1941, 2000; (ed. with J.R. Dunn and J.P. Dunn) Southern Women at the Millennium: A Historical Perspective, 2003; (ed.) Country Women Cope with Hard Times: A Collection of Oral Histories, 2004; (ed. and intro. with R. Sharpless) Work, Family, and Faith: Rural Southern Women in the Twentieth Century, 2006; Southern Farmers and Their Stories: Memory and Meaning in Oral History, 2006; (ed. with J.C. Cobb) The New Encyclopedia of Southern Culture, vol. XI: Agriculture and Industry, 2008; (intro. with T.M. Craig) Upcountry South Carolina Goes to War: Letters of the Anderson, Brockman, and Moore Families, 1853-1865,

2009. Contributor of articles to books and periodicals. **Address:** Converse College, 580 E Main St., Spartanburg, SC 29302-1931, U.S.A. **Online address:** melissa.walker@converse.edu

WALKER, Nigel (David). British/Chinese (born China), b. 1917. **Genres:** Criminology/True Crime, Philosophy, Psychology, Autobiography/Memoirs, Biography. **Career:** Scottish Office, staff, 1946-61; Nuffield College, Gwilym Gibbon fellow, 1958-59; Oxford University, reader in criminology, 1961-73; Howard League for Penal Reform, vice president, 1971-; Home Secretary's Advisory Council on Probation and After-Care, chairman, 1972-; Cambridge Institute of Criminology, director, 1973-80; Cambridge University, King's College, Wolfson professor of criminology and fellow, 1973-84, now emeritus Wolfson professor of criminology. Writer. **Publications:** Delphi, 1936; A Short History of Psychotherapy, 1957; Morale in the Civil Service, 1961; Crime and Punishment in Britain, 1965, 2nd ed., 2010; Aims of a Penal System, 1966; Crime and Insanity in England, 2 vols., 1968-72; Sentencing in a Rational Society, 1969; (co-author) Violent Offender: Reality or Illusion?, 1970; Crimes, Courts and Figures, 1971; Behaviour and Misbehaviour, 1977; Punishment, Danger, and Stigma, 1980; Sentencing Theory, Law and Practice, 1986, (co-author) 2nd ed., 1996; Crime and Criminology, 1987; (ed. with M. Hough) Public Attitudes to Sentencing, 1988; Why Punish, 1991; (co-author) Dangerous People, 1996; Aggravation, Mitigation and Mercy in English Criminal Justice, 1999; A Man without Loyalties: A Penologist's Afterthought, 2003. **Address:** Institute of Criminology, University of Cambridge, 7 West Rd., Sidgwick Ave., Cambridge, CB3 9DT, England.

WALKER, Paul E(rnest). American (born United States), b. 1941?. **Genres:** Intellectual History, Theology/Religion. **Career:** School teacher, 1967-68; Smithsonian Institution, National Museum of History and Technology, historian, 1973-76; American Research Center in Egypt Inc., director, 1976-80, executive director, 1980-86; Columbia University, part-time lecturer, 1981-86; McGill University, visiting assistant professor, 1984-86; Institute of Islamic Studies, associate professor, 1987-90; University of Michigan, visiting associate professor of Islamic studies, 1993-94, visiting professor of Islamic studies, 1997; University of Chicago, Center for Middle Eastern Studies, deputy director of academic programs, 2009-. Writer. **Publications:** Abū YaQūb al-Sijistānī and the Development of Ismaili Neoplatonism, 1974; Early Philosophical Shiism: The Ismaili Neoplatonism of Abū Ya'qūb al-Sijistānī, 1993; The Wellsprings of Wisdom: A Study of Abū Yaqūb al-Sijistānī's Kitābal-Yanābī, 1994; Abū Ya' qūb al-Sijistānī: Intellectual Missionary, 1996; An Ismaili Heresiography: The Bābal-shaytòan from Abū Tammām's Kitāb al-shajara, 1998; Hamid al-Din al-Kirmani: Ismaili Thought in the Age of al-Hakim, 1999; The Advent of the Fatimids: A Contemporary Shi'i Witness, 2000; (trans.) I. al-Juwayni, A Guide to Conclusive Proof for the Principles of Belief, 2000; Exploring an Islamic Empire: Fatimid History and Its Sources, 2001; Fatimids and Their Successors in Yaman: The History of an Islamic Community: Arabic Edition and English Summary of Idrīs Imād al-Dīn's Uyūn al-akhbār, vol. VII, 2002; Exploring an Islamic Empire: Fatimid History and its Sources, 2002; Fatimid History and Ismaili Doctrine, 2008; Orations of the Fatimid Caliphs: Festival Sermons of the Ismaili Imams: An Edition of the Arabic Texts and English Translation of Fatimid Khutbas, 2009; Caliph of Cairo, 2009. Works appear in anthologies. Contributor of articles to journals. **Address:** University of Chicago, 201 Pick Hall, 5828 S University Ave., Chicago, IL 60637, U.S.A. **Online address:** pwalker@uchicago.edu

WALKER, Randi Jones. American (born United States), b. 1952. **Genres:** History. **Career:** United Church of Christ, ordained pastor; California State University, adjunct faculty, 1990-91; Pacific School of Religion, assistant professor of church history, 1992-97, associate professor of church history, 1997-, professor of church history, now. Writer. **Publications:** (Ed.) Kept by Grace: A Centennial History of the First Congregational Church of Pasadena, 1986; Protestantism in the Sangre De Cristos, 1850-1920, 1991; Emma Newman, a Frontier Woman Minister, 2000; The Evolution of a UCC Style: History, Ecclesiology, and Culture of the United Church of Christ, 2005. Contributor to periodicals and journals. **Address:** Pacific School of Religion, Rm. 127 Holbrook, 1798 Scenic Ave., Berkeley, CA 94709-1323, U.S.A. **Online address:** rwalker@psr.edu

WALKER, R. B. J. Canadian/British (born England), b. 1947?. **Genres:** Politics/Government, Philosophy, International Relations/Current Affairs, Intellectual History. **Career:** Queen's University, Departments of Political Studies, Sociology and Geography, instructor, 1975-78; Princeton University, visiting fellow, 1977-79, Woodrow Wilson School of Public and International

Affairs, Center of International Studies, visiting associate professor of politics, 1988-89; Australian National University, visiting fellow, 1978, 1989, 1994; University of British Columbia, visiting lecturer, 1980-81; University of Victoria, Department of Political Science, visiting lecturer, 1980-81, assistant professor, 1981-86, associate professor, 1986-92, professor, 1992-, chair, 1994-96, Graduate Program in Cultural, Social and Political Thought, director, 1998-2000, 2004-; Royal Roads Canadian Military College, visiting instructor, 1986-88, 1990-94; Centre for the Study of Developing Societies, India, adjunct fellow, 1999-2002; Keele University, professor of international relations, 2000-09; Instituto de Relacionais Internacionais, Pontifica Universidade Catolica do Rio de Janeiro (PUC), visiting professor, 2004, 2009; CERI, Sciences-Po, Paris, visiting fellow, 2007. Writer. **Publications:** Political Theory and the Transformation of World Politics, 1980; World Politics and Western Reason, 1982; (ed.) Culture, Ideology and World Order, 1984; (co-ed.) The New Reality: The Politics of Restraint in British Columbia, 1986; (co-ed.) After Bennett: The New Politics of British Columbia, 1986; (ed. with S.H. Mendlovitz) Towards a Just World Peace: Perspectives from Social Movements, 1987; One World, Many Worlds, 1988; State Sovereignty, Global Civilization, and the Rearticulation of Political Space, 1988; (ed. with S.H. Mendlovitz) Contending Sovereignties: Redefining Political Community, 1990; Inside/Outside: International Relations as Political Theory, 1993; (ed. with R. Falk and L.E.J. Ruiz) Re-framing The International: Law, Culture(s), Politics, 2002; (co-author) Suspicion et exception, 2005; (ed. with B. Gokay) 11 September 2001: War, Terror, and Judgement, 2003; After the Globe/Before The World, 2009. **Address:** Department of Political Science, University of Victoria, SSM A343, PO Box 3050, Victoria, BC V8W 3R4, Canada. **Online address:** rwalker@uvic.ca

WALKER, Richard Averill. American (born United States), b. 1947. **Genres:** Business/Trade/Industry. **Career:** University of California, professor of geography. Writer and urban geographer. **Publications:** (With M. Storper) Systems and Marxist Theories of Industrial Location: A Review, 1979; (with M. Heiman) Land Use Control: Quiet Revolution for Whom?, 1980; (with M. Storper) Capital and Industrial Location, 1980; (with M. Storper) The Price of Water: Surplus and Subsidy in the California State Water Project, 1984; (with M. Storper) The Capitalist Imperative: Territory, Technology, and Industrial Growth, 1989; (with A. Sayer) The New Social Economy: Reworking the Division of Labor, 1992; Motivating and Rewarding Managers, 1999; The Conquest of Bread: 150 Years of Agribusiness in California, 2004; The Country in the City: The Greening of the San Francisco Bay Area, 2007. Contributor to books, journals and periodicals. **Address:** Department of Geography, University of California, 507 McCone Hall, Ste. 4740, Berkeley, CA 94720-4740, U.S.A. **Online address:** walker@berkeley.edu

WALKER, Rob. See ABBOTT, Lynn.

WALKER, Robert. Canadian (born Canada), b. 1945. **Genres:** Art/Art History, Photography, Business/Trade/Industry, Theology/Religion. **Career:** Galerie Optica, camerart exhibition curator, 1974; independent photographer, 1975-77, 1977-; International Center of Photography, exhibition curator, 1979. **Publications:** (Ed. with C. Capa) Halsman '79, 1979; (with A. Smith and K. Ashworth) Prospects of Part-Time Work: Preparing to Evaluaate the Back to Work Bonus: A Study Carried Out on Behalf of the Department of Social Security, 1998; Color Is Power, 2002; Live It: Optimism, 2009; Eid al-Adha, 2010. **Address:** 1477 Rue Viau, Montreal, QC HIV 3G8, Canada.

WALKER, Sally M(acArt). (Sally Fleming). American (born United States), b. 1954. **Genres:** Children's Non-fiction, Young Adult Non-fiction, Sciences, Novels, Animals/Pets, Mystery/Crime/Suspense. **Career:** Junction Book Store, children's book buyer, 1988-94; Children's literature consultant, 1988-; Anderson's Bookshops, children's book specialist, 1994-; Northern Illinois University, adjunct instructor, 1992-93. Author and literature consultant. **Publications:** FOR CHILDREN NONFICTION: Born near the Earth's Surface: Sedimentary Rocks, 1991; Fireflies, 2001; Mary Anning: Fossil Hunter, 2001; (as Sally Fleming) Ferocious Fangs, 2001; (as Sally Fleming) Rapid Runners, 2002; Fossil Fish Found Alive: Discovering the Coelacanth, 2002; Jackie Robinson (biography), 2002; Life in an Estuary, 2003. EARTH WATCH SERIES: Glaciers: Ice on the Move, 1990; Water up, Water Down: The Hydrologic Cycle, 1992; Volcanoes: Earth's Inner Fire, 1994; Earthquakes, 1996. NATURE WATCH SERIES: Rhinos, 1996; Hippos, 1998, rev. ed., 2008; Sea Horses, 1998; Dolphins, 1999, rev. ed., 2008; Manatees, 1999; Rays, 2003. EARLY BIRD PHYSICS SERIES: (with R. Feldmann) Work, 2002; (with R. Feldmann) Inclined Planes and Wedges, 2002; (with R. Feld-

mann) Levers, 2002; (with R. Feldmann) Pulleys, 2002; (with R. Feldmann) Screws, 2002; (with R. Feldmann) Wheels and Axles, 2002; (with R. Feldmann) Wedges, 2011; (with R. Feldmann) Inclined Planes, 2012. OTHERS: Opossum at Sycamore Road, 1997; The 18 Penny Goose (historical fiction), 1998; (comp. with S. Whiteley and K. Summers) The Teacher's Calendar, 1999-2000, 1999; Seahorse Reef: A Story of the South Pacific, 2000; Bessie Coleman: Daring to Fly, 2003; Crocodiles, 2004; 180 Creative Ideas for Getting Students Involved, Engaged and Excited, 2004; Secrets of a Civil War Submarine: Solving the Mysteries of the H.L. Hunley, 2005; Electricity, 2006; Heat, 2006; Matter, 2006; Light, 2006; Magnetism, 2006; Mystery Fish: Secrets of the Coelacanth, 2006; Shipwreck Search: Discovery of the H.L. Hunley, 2006; Sound, 2006; Supercroc Found, 2006; Palancas, 2006; Ruedas y ejes, 2006; Fossils, 2007; Minerals, 2007; Rocks, 2007; Soil, 2007; The Search for Antarctic Dinosaurs, 2008; El Sonido, 2008; Volcanoes, 2008; The Vowel Family: A Tale of Lost Letters, 2008; Caves, 2008; Glaciers, 2008; Opossums, 2008; Calor, 2008; Reefs, 2008; Written in Bone: Buried Lives of Jamestown and Colonial Maryland, 2009; Jaguars, 2009; Mosquitoes, 2009; Druscilla's Halloween, 2009; Frozen Secrets: Antarctica Revealed, 2010; Freedom Song: The Story of Henry Box Brown, 2011; Blizzard of Glass: The Halifax Explosion of 1917, 2011; (with R. Feldmann) Put to the Test: Pulleys, 2012; (with R. Feldmann) Put to the Test: Wheels and Axles, 2012; Put Wedges to the Test, 2012; Sound, 2012; (with D.W. Owsley) Their Skeletons Speak: Kennewick Man and the Paleoamerican World, 2012; Freedom Song: The Story of Henry Box Brown, 2012; (with R. Feldmann) Inclined Planes: Put to the Test, 2012; Investigating Electricity, 2012; Investigating Heat, 2012; Investigating Light, 2012; Investigating Magnetism, 2012; Investigating Matter, 2012; (with R. Feldmann) Put Levers to the Test, 2012; (with R. Feldmann) Put Screws to the Test: How do Simple Machines Work?, 2012. **Address:** c/o Author Mail, Lerner Publishing Group, 241 1st Ave. N, Minneapolis, MN 55401, U.S.A. **Online address:** sallymacwalker@hotmail.com

WALKER, Sam. American (born United States) **Genres:** Sports/Fitness. **Career:** Wall Street Journal, sports columnist, 1998-; Christian Science Monitor, staff writer, congressional correspondent and bureau chief. Journalist and writer. **Publications:** Fantasyland: A Season on Baseball's Lunatic Fringe, 2006. Contributor to periodicals. **Address:** The Christian Science Monitor, 210 Massachusetts Ave., Boston, MA 02115, U.S.A. **Online address:** sam@fantasylandthebook.com

WALKER, Stephen. (Steve Walker). British (born England), b. 1941. **Genres:** Psychology, Sciences, Sports/Fitness. **Career:** University of Tennessee, Department of Psychology, research associate, 1966-69, assistant professor, 1969-70; University of London, Birkbeck College, lecturer in psychology, 1970-88, School of Psychology, senior lecturer, 1988-2007, Resource Centre for Life Sciences, head, 1987-96, Resource Centre for Physical and Life Sciences, head, 1996-99, Faculty of Science, dean, 1999-2007, retired, 2007-. Writer. **Publications:** Learning and Reinforcement, 1975; Animal Thought, 1983; Learning Theory and Behaviour Modification, 1984; Animal Learning: An Introduction, 1987. **Address:** Department of Psychology, Birkbeck College, University of London, Malet St., London, WC1E 7HX, United Kingdom. **Online address:** s.walker@bbk.ac.uk

WALKER, Steve. See WALKER, Stephen.

WALKER, Susannah. American (born United States), b. 1970. **Genres:** History. **Career:** Virginia Wesleyan College, assistant professor of history. Writer. **Publications:** Style and Status: Selling Beauty to African American Women, 1920-1975, 2007. **Address:** Department of History, Virginia Wesleyan College, Virginia Beach, VA 23455, U.S.A.

WALKER, Thomas W(oodley). American (born United States), b. 1940. **Genres:** Area Studies, Politics/Government, Business/Trade/Industry. **Career:** Ohio University, professor of political science, 1972-, now professor emeritus of political science, director of Latin American studies, 1987-, now director emeritus; Latin American Studies Association, Task Force on Scholarly Relations-Nicaragua, founding co-chair, 1983-84. Writer. **Publications:** The Christian Democratic Movement in Nicaragua, 1970; Nicaragua: The Land of Sandino, 1981, 3rd ed., 1991; (with J.A. Booth) Understanding Central America, 1989, (with J.A. Booth and C.J. Wade) 5th ed., 2010; Doscoronéis à metrópole: Fios e tramas da sociedade e dapolítica em Ribeirão Preto no Século XX, 2000; Nicaragua: Living in the Shadow of the Eagle, 2003, (with C.J. Wade) 5th ed., 2011. EDITOR: Nicaragua in Revolution, 1982; Nicaragua: The First Five Years, 1985; Reagan Versus the Sandinistas: The

Undeclared War on Nicaragua, 1987; Revolution and Counterrevolution in Nicaragua, 1991; (with S.H .Kim) Perspectives on War and Peace in Central America, 1992; Nicaragua Without Illusions: Regime Transition and Structural Adjustment in the 1990s, 1997; (with A.C. Armony) Repression, Resistance and Democratic Transition in Central America, 2000. Contributor of articles to books and periodicals. **Address:** Department of Political Science, Ohio University, 228 Bentley Annex, Athens, OH 45701, U.S.A. **Online address:** walker@ohio.edu

WALKER, Wendy (Alison). American (born United States), b. 1951. **Genres:** Novels, Novellas/Short Stories, Romance/Historical, Science Fiction/Fantasy, Essays. **Career:** Harvard Advocate, poetry editor, 1971-72; art teacher, 1974-76; writer, 1981-82; St. Hilda's and St. Hugh's School, art teacher, 1982; MacDowell Colony, fellow, 1993; Hofstra University, adjunct associate professor of writing, 1995-99; Universidad de la Laguna, resident lecturer, 1998; Kentler International Drawing Space, visual consultant, advisor and curator; Grady Alexis Gallery, visual consultant, advisor and curator; Proteus Gowanus Gallery, core collaborator and proteotypes editor. **Publications:** The Sea-Rabbit, or, The Artist of Life (stories), 1988; The Secret Service (novel), 1992; Stories Out of Omarie (stories), 1995; Sexual Stealing, 2008; Blue Fire, 2009. Contributor to periodicals. **Address:** New York, NY 10025, U.S.A. **Online address:** wwalker102@rcn.com

WALKER-BLONDELL, Becky. American (born United States), b. 1951. **Genres:** Adult Non-fiction, Young Adult Fiction. **Career:** Teacher and consultant for the deaf and hard-of-hearing, 1982-. Writer. **Publications:** In My Mother's Arms, 1995. **Address:** c/o Winston-Derek Publishers Inc., 1722 W End Ave., Nashville, TN 37203-2602, U.S.A.

WALKERDINE, Valerie. British/Australian (born Australia) **Genres:** Psychology, Children's Fiction, Social Sciences, Humor/Satire. **Career:** University of London, Goldsmiths College, professor of the psychology of communication, 1991-97; University of Western Sydney, foundation professor of critical psychology, 1997-; Cardiff University, School of Social Sciences, professor of psychology, 2003-. Writer. **Publications:** Changing the Subject, 1984; (ed. with C. Urwin and C. Steedman) Language, Gender and Childhood, 1985; Surveillance, Subjectivity, and Struggle: Lessons from Pedagogic and Domestic Practices, 1987; The Mastery of Reason: Cognitive Development and the Production of Rationality, 1988; Democracy in the Kitchen, 1989; Schoolgirl Fictions, 1990; (ed. with J. Curran and D. Morley) Cultural Studies and Communication, 1996; Daddy's Girl, 1997; Counting Girls Out: Girls and Mathematics, 1998; Psychology, Postmodernity and the Media, 1998; (with H. Lucey and J. Melody) Growing Up Girl: Psychosocial Explorations of Gender and Class, 2001; (with L. Blackman) Mass Hysteria: Critical Psychology and Media Studies, 2001; (ed.) Challenging Subjects: Critical Psychology for a New Millennium, 2002; Children, Gender, Video Games: Towards a Relational Approach to Multi-Media, 2007. **Address:** School of Social Sciences, Cardiff University, 1.16 Glamorgan Bldg., King Edward VII Ave., Cardiff, SG CF10 3WT, Wales. **Online address:** walkerdinev@cf.ac.uk

WALKOWICZ, Chris. American (born United States), b. 1943. **Genres:** Animals/Pets. **Career:** Today Publications and Creative Marketing, typesetter and secretary, 1974-76, 1985-86; National War Dogs Memorial, vice-president, 1990-2000; Dog Writers Association of America, vice president, 1995-2000, president, 2000-04, president emeritus, 2004-; AKC Gazette, columnist. **Publications:** (With B. Wilcox) Successful Dog Breeding: The Complete Handbook of Canine Midwifery, 1985; The Bearded Collie, 1987; (with B. Wilcox) The Complete Question and Answer Book on Dogs, 1988; (with B. Wilcox) Atlas of Dog Breeds of the World, 1989; The German Shepherd Dog, 1991; (with B. Wilcox) Old Dogs, Old Friends: Enjoying your Older Dog, 1991; The Perfect Match: A Buyer's Guide to Dogs, 1996; Choosing a Dog for Dummies, 2001; For the Love of Dogs, 2006; Dog Show Judging: The Good, the Bad, and the Ugly, 2009. Contributor to magazines and newspapers. **Address:** Dogwise Inc., 403 S Mission St., Wenatchee, WA 98801, U.S.A. **Online address:** walkoway.dogbooks@mchsi.com

WALL, Cheryl A. American (born United States), b. 1948. **Genres:** Young Adult Non-fiction, Essays, Literary Criticism And History, Novellas/Short Stories, Literary Criticism And History. **Career:** Rutgers University, professor of English. Writer. **Publications:** NONFICTION: Women of the Harlem Renaissance, 1995; The Pasteboard Bandit, 1997; Worrying the Line: Black Women Writers, Lineage and Literary Tradition, 2005. EDITOR: Changing Our Own Words: Essays on Criticism, Theory and Writing by Black Wom-

en, 1989; Zora Neale Hurston, Novels and Short Stories, 1995; Zora Neale Hurston, Folklore, Memoirs and Other Writings, 1995; Zora Neale Hurston, Sweat, 1997; Zora Neale Hurston's Their Eyes Were Watching God: A Casebook, 2000; (with L.J. Holmes) Savoring the Salt: The Legacy of Toni Cade Bambara, 2007. **Address:** Department of English, Rutgers University, Murray Hall, College Ave. Campus, 510 George St., New Brunswick, NJ 08901-1167, U.S.A. **Online address:** cwall@rci.rutgers.edu

WALL, Ethan. See HOLMES, B(ryan) J(ohn).

WALL, James M(cKendree). American (born United States), b. 1928. **Genres:** Film, Politics/Government, Theology/Religion, Essays. **Career:** Atlanta Journal, sportswriter, 1947-50; Methodist church, assistant pastor, 1953; Claremont School of Theology, adjunct professor; ordained methodist minister, 1955; Together, associate editor, 1959-60; Christian Advocate, managing editor, 1960-63, editor, 1963-72; Christian Century, editor, 1972-99, senior contributing editor, 1999-. **Publications:** Church and Cinema: A Way of Viewing Film, 1971; Winning the War, Losing Our Soul, 1991; Hidden Treasures: Searching for God in Modern Culture, 1997. EDITOR: (and contrib.) Three European Directors, 1973; Theologians in Transition: The Christian Century How My Mind Has Changed Series, 1981; A Century of the Century, 1987; How My Mind has Changed, 1991. Contributor to periodicals. **Address:** The Christian Century, 104 S Michigan Ave., Ste. 700, Chicago, IL 60603, U.S.A.

WALL, James T. American (born United States), b. 1933. **Genres:** History, Essays. **Career:** Legislative aide, 1957-59; Central Intelligence Agency, operations officer, 1959-65; Northern Virginia Community College, faculty, 1969-, now professor emeritus; Command and General Staff College, instructor, 1972-77, 1986-88; First Army Intelligence School, instructor, 1973; State of Virginia, civilian aide and secretary of the army, 1979-81; Georgetown University, professorial lecturer in U.S. military history, 1979-82; University of Edinburgh, Fulbright visiting professor, 1983-84; U.S. Military Academy, adjunct professor, 1984-88; National University of Costa Rica, Fulbright visiting professor, 1986-87. Writer. **Publications:** From the Law of Moses to the Magna Carta: Essays in Ancient and Medieval History, 1979, rev. ed., 1985; (co-ed.) The Landscape of American History: Essays in Memoriam to Richard W. Griffin, 1979; Manifest Destiny Denied: America's First Intervention in Nicaragua, 1981; The Boundless Frontier: America from Christopher Columbus to Abraham Lincoln, 1999; Wall Street and the Fruited Plain: Money, Expansion, and Politics in the Gilded Age, 2008. Contributor to journals. **Address:** Department of History, Northern Virginia Community College, 8333 Little River Tpke., Annandale, VA 22003-3796, U.S.A. **Online address:** jimwall@aol.com

WALL, Kathryn R. American (born United States), b. 1945. **Genres:** Business/Trade/Industry, Mystery/Crime/Suspense, Young Adult Fiction, Children's Fiction, Novels. **Career:** St. Martin's Press, editor. **Publications:** BAY TANNER SERIES: In for a Penny, 2001, 2nd ed., 2002; And Not a Penny More, 2002; Perdition House, 2003; Judas Island, 2004; Resurrection Road, 2005; Bishop's Reach, 2006; Sanctuary Hill, 2007; The Mercy Oak, 2008; Covenant Hall, 2009; Canaan's Gate, 2010; Jericho Cay, 2011. **Address:** c/o Author Mail, St. Martin's Press, 175 5th Ave., New York, NY 10010, U.S.A. **Online address:** kwall645@aol.com

WALLACE, B. Alan. American (born United States), b. 1950. **Genres:** Theology/Religion, Translations. **Career:** Tibet Institute, lecturer, 1975-77; Center for Higher Tibetan Studies, lecturer, 1977-79; H.H. the Dalai Lama, interpreter, 1979; University of Washington, interpreter, 1982; American Institute of Buddhist Studies, lecturer, 1984-86; Amherst College, lecturer, 1987; Stanford University, teaching assistant, 1990-94, teaching intern, 1991, Innovative Academic Courses Program, lecturer, 1992, chief teaching assistant, 1994, instructor, 1997; Mind and Life Research Network, project director, 1991-93; University of California, Extension Program, instructor, 1997; University of California, Department of Religious Studies, lecturer, 1997-2001; Santa Barbara Institute, president and founder, 2003-; Mind and Life Institute, board director, 1991-; Phuket International Academy Mind Centre, director and chairman, 2010-. Writer. **Publications:** (Ed.) G.N. Dhargyey, Tibetan Tradition of Mental Development, 1974; (with K. McKenzie) Spoken Tibetan, 1985; Choosing Reality: A Contemplative View of Physics and the Mind, 1989 as Choosing Reality: A Buddhist View of Physics and the Mind, 1996; A Passage from Solitude: A Modern Commentary on Tibetan Buddhist Mind Training, 1992; Tibetan Buddhism From the Ground Up, 1993; The Bridge of Quiescence: Experiencing Tibetan Buddhist Meditation, 1998; Boundless Heart: The Four Immeasurables, 1999; The Taboo of Subjectivity: Toward a New Science of Consciousness, 2000; (ed.) Buddhism with An Attitude: The Tibetan Seven-Point Mind-Training, 2001; (ed.) Buddhism & Science: Breaking New Ground, 2003; Genuine Happiness: Meditation as the Path to Fulfillment, 2005; Attention Revolution: Unlocking the Power of the Focused Mind, 2006; Contemplative Science: Were Buddhism and Neuroscience Converge, 2007; Hidden Dimensions: The Unification of Physics and Consciousness, 2007; (with B. Hodel) Embracing Mind: The Common Ground of Science and Spirituality, 2008; Mind in the Balance: Meditation in Science, Buddhism and Christianity, 2009; Minding Closely: The Four Applications of Mindfulness, 2011; Stilling the Mind: Shamatha Teachings from Dudjom Lingpa's Vajra Essense, 2011; Meditations of a Buddhist Skeptic: A Manifesto for the Mind Sciences and Contemplative Practice, 2012. TRANSLATOR: (and ed.) The Ambrosia Heart Tantra, 1976; S.G. Amipa, Waterdrop from the Glorious Sea: a History of the Sakya Tradition of Tibetan Buddhism, 1976; (and ed.) The Life and Teachings of Geshe Rabten, 1980; H.H. the Dalai Lama, Four Essential Buddhist Commentaries, 1984; G.N. Dhargyey, The Kalchakra Tantra, 1986; (with J. Hopkins and L. Rabgyey) Y. Donden, Health Through Balance: An Introduction to Tibetan Medicine, 1986; (ed.) H.H. the Dalai Lama, A Commentary on the Ninth Chapter of Shantideva's Guide to the Bodhisattva Way of Life, 1988; (with G.T. Jinpa) H.H. the Dalai Lama, Worlds in Harmony: Dialogues on Compassionate Action, 1992; (with G.T. Jinpa) H.H. the Dalai Lama, Gentle Bridges: Conversations with the Dalai Lama on the Sciences of Mind, 1992; (with S. Khandro) G. Rinpoche, Ancient Wisdom: Nyingma Teachings of Dream Yoga, Meditation and Transformation, 1993; Gen Lamrimpa, Samantha Meditation: Tibetan Buddhist Teachings on Cultivating Meditative Quiescence, 1992, as Calming the Mind: Tibetan Buddhist Teachings on the Cultivation of Meditative Quiescence, 1995; (with V.A. Wallace) A Guide to the Bodhisattva Way of Life, 1997; (with G.T. Jinpa) Sleeping, Dreaming and Dying: An Exploration of Consciousness with the Dalai Lama, 1997; (with G.T. Jinpa) Healing Emotions: Conversations with the Dalai Lama on Mindfulness, Emotions and Health, 1997; Natural Liberation: Padmasambhava's Teachings on the Six Bardos, 1998; (and ed.) K. Chagme, A Spacious Path to Freedom: Practical Instructions on the Union of Mahamudra and Atiyoga, 1998; G. Lamrimpa, Realizing Emptiness: The Madhyamaka Cultivation of Insight, 1999; G. Lamrimpa, Transcending Time: The Kalacakra Six-Session Guruyoga, 1999; (and co-ed.) Consciousness at the Crossroads: Conversations with the Dalai Lama on Brainscience and Buddhism, 1999; Dhonden, Healing from the Sources: The Science and Lore of Tibetan Medicine, 2000; (and co-ed.) K. Chagme, Naked Awareness: Practical Teachings on the Union of Mahamudra and Dzogchen, 2000; D. Lingpa, The Vajra Heart Tantra: A Tantra Naturally Arisen from the Nature of Existence from the Matrix of Primordial Awareness of Pure Perception, 2001; (with S. Khandro) Meditation, Transformation and Dream Yoga, 2002; G. Lamrimpa, How to Realize Emptiness, 2010. Contributor to books and journals. Address: Santa Barbara Institute for Consciousness Studies, PO Box 3573, Santa Barbara, CA 93130, U.S.A. Online address: alanwallace@earthlink.net

WALLACE, Barbara Brooks. American/Chinese (born China), b. 1922. Genres: Children's Fiction, Novels, Picture/Board Books. Career: Foote, Cone & Belding, script secretary, 1946-49; Wright MacMahon Secretarial School, Beverly Hills, teacher, 1949-50; American Red Cross, Commerce and Industry Division, head of fund drive, 1950-52. Writer. Publications: Claudia, 1969; Andrew the Big Deal, 1970; The Trouble with Miss Switch, 1971; Victoria, 1972; Can Do, Missy Charlie, 1974; The Secret Summer of L.E.B., 1974; Julia and the Third Bad Thing, 1975; Palmer Patch, 1976; Hawkins, 1977; The Contest Kid Strikes Again, 1980; Peppermints in the Parlor, 1980; Hawkins and the Soccer Solution, 1981; Miss Switch to the Rescue!, 1981; Claudia and Duffy, 1982; Hello, Claudia!, 1982; The Barrel in the Basement, 1985; Argyle, 1987; The Interesting Thing That Happened at Perfect Acres Inc., 1988; The Twin in the Tavern, 1993; Cousins in the Castle, 1996; Sparrows in the Scullery, 1997; Ghosts in the Gallery, 2000; Secret in St. Something, 2001; Miss Switch Online, 2002; Perils of Peppermints, 2003; Peppermints in the Parlor, 2005; Have Dragon, Will Travel, 2009; Diary Of A Little Devil, 2011. Address: 5100 Fillmore Ave., Ste. 106, Alexandria, VA 22311-5038, U.S.A. Online address: jimbob4@comcast.net

WALLACE, Benjamin. American (born United States), b. 1968. Genres: Mystery/Crime/Suspense. Career: Prague Post, reporter; Budapest Post, reporter; Philadelphia Magazine, reporter and executive editor, 1996-2005; New York Magazine, contributing editor, 2011-; Czechoslovak Ministry of Foreign Affairs, proof reader. Journalist. Publications: (Ed. with R. Huber) The Philadelphia Reader, 2006; The Billionaire's Vinegar: The Mystery of the World's Most Expensive Bottle of Wine, 2008. Contributor to periodicals. Address: Brooklyn, NY, U.S.A. Online address: ben@benjaminwallace.net

WALLACE, Bruce. American (born United States), b. 1920. Genres: Biology, Environmental Sciences/Ecology, Sociology, Sciences. Career: Carnegie Institution of Washington, Department of Genetics, research associate, 1947-49; The Biological Lab, geneticist, assistant director, 1949-58; Cornell University, associate professor of genetics, 1958-61, professor of genetics, 1961-81; Virginia Polytechnic Institute and State University, professor of biology, 1981-83, university distinguished professor, 1983-94, university distinguished professor emeritus, 1994-. Writer. Publications: Studies on Sex Ratio in Drosophila Pseudoobscura. I. Selection and Sex-Ratio, 1948; (with T. Dobzhansky) Radiation, Genes and Man, 1959; (with A. Srb) Adaptation, 1961; Chromosomes, Giant Molecules and Evolution, 1966; Topics in Population Genetics, 1968; Genetic Load: Its Biological and Conceptual Aspects, 1970; Essays in Social Biology, 3 vols., 1972; Basic Population Genetics, 1981; (co-ed.) Dobzhansky's Genetics of Natural Populations, 1981; (ed. and comp.) Human Culture: A Moment in Evolution, 1983; (with G. Simmons, Jr.) Biology for Living, 1987; Fifty Years of Genetic Load: An Odyssey, 1991; (ed. with P.A. Distler and N.R. Krieg) AIDS, the Modern Plague, 1991; The Search for the Gene, 1992; (with J.O. Falkinham III) The Study of Gene Action, 1997; The Environment: As I See It, Science Is Not Enough, 1998; The Environment 2: As I See It, the Mold Must Be Broken, 2000. Address: Department of Biological Sciences, Virginia Polytechnic, Institute and State University, 2125 Derring Hall, Blacksburg, VA 24061-0002, U.S.A. Online address: kojima@swva.net

WALLACE, Carey Jean. American (born United States), b. 1974. Genres: Novels. Career: International Arts Movement, Working Artists Initiative, founder; Hillbilly Underground, founder, 2000. Writer. Publications: The Blind Contessa's New Machine, 2010. Contributor to periodicals. Address: Brooklyn, NY, U.S.A. Online address: theblindcontessa@gmail.com

WALLACE, Catherine M(iles). American (born United States), b. 1950. Genres: Ethics, Social Commentary, Women's Studies And Issues, Business/Trade/Industry, Theology/Religion. Career: Northwestern University, assistant professor of English, 1976-82; freelance writer, 1982-; Seabury Western Theological Seminary, Lilly Endowment writer-in-residence, 2000-04. Publications: The Design of Biographia Literaria, 1983; For Fidelity: How Intimacy and Commitment Enrich Our Lives, 1998; Dance Lessons: Moving to the Rhythm of a Crazy God, 1999 as Motherhood in the Balance: Children, Career, God, and Me, 2001; Selling Ourselves Short: Why We Struggle to Earn a Living and Have a Life, 2003. Address: 9828 N Keeler Ave., Skokie, IL 60076-1176, U.S.A. Online address: catherinewallace@compuserve.com

WALLACE, Deborah. American (born United States), b. 1945. Genres: Environmental Sciences/Ecology, Novels. Career: Consolidated Edison Co., ecologist, 1972-74; New York State Power Authority, environmental biologist, 1974-82; Public Interest Scientific, president and research scientist, 1976-; City University of New York, Queens College, staff scientist, 1986-91; Consumers Union, project leader, 1991-. Writer. Publications: Studies on the Collapse of Fire Service in New York City, 1972-1976: The Impact of Pseudoscience on Public Policy, 1977; In the Mouth of the Dragon: Toxic Fires in the Age of Plastics, 1990; (with R. Wallace) Plague on Your Houses: How New York was Burned Down and Public Health Crumbled, 1998; (with R. Wallace and R.G. Wallace) Farming Human Pathogens: Ecological Resilience and Evolutionary Process, 2009; (with R. Wallace) Gene Expression and Its Discontents: The Social Production of Chronic Disease, 2010. Contributor to journals. Address: c/o Douglas Storey, The Catalog, PO Box 2964, Vancouver, WA 98668, U.S.A.

WALLACE, Diana. Welsh/British (born England), b. 1964. Genres: Literary Criticism And History, Adult Non-fiction. Career: University of Glamorgan, lecturer in English literature, head of English division. Writer. Publications: Sisters and Rivals in British Women's Fiction, 1914-1939, 2000; The Woman's Historical Novel: British Women Writers, 1900-2000, 2004; (ed. with A. Smith) The Female Gothic: New Directions, 2009. Address: University of Glamorgan, Rm. FH105, Llantwit Rd., Treforest, Pontypridd, CF37 1DL, Wales. Online address: dwallace@glam.ac.uk

WALLACE, Don. American (born United States) Genres: Novels, Sports/Fitness, How-to Books, Young Adult Non-fiction. Career: Davis Daily Democrat, staff; Motor Boating & Sailing Magazine, staff; Kirkus Reviews, staff; Success Magazine, staff; Self Magazine, staff; The New School for Social Research, instructor of fiction and creative non fiction; Pace University, Graduate Division, adjunct professor of journalism; Golf Digest Woman Magazine, founding executive editor. **Publications:** Watersports Basics, 1985; Hot Water, 1991; A Tide in Time: The Log of Matthew Roving, 2000-03; One Great Game: Two Teams Two Dreams in the First-Ever National Championship High School Football Game, 2003. **Address:** c/o Author Mail, Atria Books, 1230 Ave. of the Americas, New York, NY 10020, U.S.A. **Online address:** donwallacebooks@prodigy.net

WALLACE, Ian. American/Canadian (born Canada), b. 1950. **Genres:** Children's Fiction, Young Adult Fiction, Illustrations, Literary Criticism And History, Art/Art History, Animals/Pets. **Career:** Kids Can Press, staff writer and illustrator, 1974-76; Art Gallery of Ontario, information officer, 1976-80. **Publications:** Julie News, 1974; The Sandwich, 1975, rev. ed., 1985; The Christmas Tree House, 1976; Chin Chiang and the Dragon's Dance, 1984; The Sparrow's Song, 1986; Mr. Kneebone's New Digs, 1991; A Winter's Tale, 1997; Boy of the Deeps, 1999; Duncan's Way, 2000; The Naked Lady, 2002; The True Story of Trapper Jack's Left Big Toe, 2002; The Man Who Walked the Earth, 2003; Mavis and Merna, 2005; The Sleeping Porch, 2008. SELF-ILLUSTRATED: Morgan the Magnificent, 1988. Illustrator of books by others. **Address:** Groundwood Books Ltd., 110 Spadina Ave., Ste. 801, Toronto, ON M5V 2K4, Canada. **Online address:** ianwallacebooks@gmail.com

WALLACE, James. American (born United States), b. 1947. **Genres:** Business/Trade/Industry, Biography, Autobiography/Memoirs. **Career:** Montgomery Advertiser, reporter, 1972-75; Yakima Herald-Republic, city editor, 1975-82; Seattle Post-Intelligencer, investigative reporter, 1982-96, aerospace reporter, 1996-. **Publications:** (With J. Erickson) Hard Drive: Bill Gates and the Making of the Microsoft Empire, 1992; Overdrive: Bill Gates and the Race to Control Cyberspace, 1997. **Address:** Seattle Post-Intelligencer, 101 Elliott Ave. W, Ste. 540, PO Box 1909, Seattle, WA 98119-4236, U.S.A. **Online address:** jameswallace@seattlepi.com

WALLACE, James D.(Donald). American (born United States), b. 1937. **Genres:** Ethics. **Career:** University of Illinois-Urbana-Champaign, instructor, 1962-63, assistant professor, 1963-68, associate professor, 1968-70, professor of philosophy, 1970-, professor emeritus of philosophy, department head, 1970-77, Program for the Study of Cultural Values and Ethics, fellow, 1991-92; American Council of Learned Societies, fellow, 1983-84; Cornell University, James H. Becker lecturer, 1990. Writer. **Publications:** Virtues and Vices, 1978; Moral Relevance and Moral Conflict, 1988; Ethical Norms, Particular Cases, 1996; Norms and practices, 2009. Contributor to books and periodicals. **Address:** Department of Philosophy, University of Illinois, 105 Gregory Hall, 810 S Wright St., Urbana, IL 61801, U.S.A.

WALLACE, John. British (born England), b. 1966. **Genres:** Children's Fiction, Young Adult Fiction, Human Relations/Parenting, Illustrations. **Career:** Writer. **Publications:** Little Bean, 1996; Little Bean's Friend, 1996; Little Bean's Holiday, 1997; Building a House with Mr. Bumble, 1997; Dressing up with Mr. Bumble, 1997; The Twins, 1998; Jungle Keds, 1998; Tiny Rabbit Goes to the Park, 1999; Tiny Rabbit, 2000; Pirate Boy, 2001; Monster Toddler, 2003; Anything for You, 2004; It's You, Daddy, 2005. Illustrator of books by others. **Address:** The Annexe, Belmont St., Brighton, BN1 4HN, England. **Online address:** john@johnwallace.co.uk

WALLACE, Karen. Canadian (born Canada), b. 1951. **Genres:** Children's Fiction, Children's Non-fiction, Novels, Young Adult Fiction. **Career:** Writer. **Publications:** The Battle for Gold Diggers' Forest, 1989; Fearless Fiona and the Mothproof Hall Mystery, 1992; Zizz Bear, 1992; Think of an Eel, 1992; Think of a Beaver, 1992; Zizz Bear, Busy Bear, 1993; Fearless Fiona and the Mystery of the Great Stone Haggis, 1993; Fearless Fiona and the Rolls-Royce Racket Mystery, 1993; Why Count Sheep?, 1993; My Hen Is Dancing, 1993; Red Fox, 1994; Bears in the Forest, 1994; King Henry VIII's Shoes, 1995; Queen Victoria's Swing, 1996; Imagine You Are a Tiger, 1996; Imagine You Are a Crocodile, 1996; Imagine You Are a Dolphin, 1996; Ace Ghosts, 1996; Ghouls Rule, 1996; Star Spooks, 1997; Funky Phantoms, 1997; It Takes Two, 1997; Rollerblading Royals, 1997; Postcards from Charlie, 1997; Tutankhamun's Arrow, 1998; Giant Gentle Octopus, 1998; A Hiccup on the High Seas, 1998; Hiding, 1998; Imagine You Are an Orang-utan, 1998; Seagull Beach, 1998; Tale of a Tadpole, 1998; Great Aunt Iris Goes Hunting, 1998; Albert's Raccoon; Crook Catchers, 1999; Quest for the Golden See-Saw, 1999; Scar-

lette Beane, 1999; Day at Seagull Beach, 1999; Whatever the Weather, 1999; Duckling Days, 1999; Madeleine the City Pig, 1999; Seagull Seashore, 1999; Weather Watching, 1999; Buzy Buzy Bee, 1999; Chomp! Munch! Chew!, 1999; Police Cat Fuzz, 2000; Bed for Winter, 2000; Big Machines, 2000; Born to be a Butterfly, 2000; City Pig, 2000; Cleopatra's Carpet, 2000; Crook Catchers, 2000; Rockets, 2000; Wild Baby Animals, 2000; Wolves, 2000; A Bed for the Winter, 2000; Esmeralda, 2000; Police Cat Fuzz Rides Again, 2001; Archie Hates Pink, 2001; Raspberries on the Yangtze, 2001; Diving Dolphin, 2001; My Cat's Secret, 2001; Rockets and Spaceships, 2001; Baby Animals, 2001; Climbing a Monkey Puzzle Tree, 2002; The Case of the Disappearing Necklace, 2002; Something Slimy on Primrose Drive, 2002; Raspberries on the Yangtze, 2002; Quirky Times at Quagmire Castle, 2003; I Am an Ankylosaurus, 2003; A Trip to the Zoo, 2003; The Case of the Howling Armor, 2004; Albert's Raccoon, 2004; I Am a Tyrannosaurus, 2004; Ooh La La, Lottie!, 2004; I Can Swim!, 2004; Marvin, The Blue Pig, 2005; Clever Cat, 2005; Wendy, 2005; Secret of the Crocodiles, 2005; Where are My Shoes?, 2006; Prince Marvin's Great Moment, 2006; Man With Tiger Eyes, 2006; Alice Goes to Hollywood, 2006; The Unrivalled Spangles, 2006; Aargh, it's an Alien, 2006; Something Slimy on Primrose Drive, 2007; Quirkytime at Quagmire Castle, 2007; The Minestrone Mob, 2007; The Peanut Prankster, 2007; The Emperor's New Clothes, 2007; Diamond Takers, 2007; Yikes, It's a Yeti!, 2008; King Cudgel's Challenge, 2008; Queen Carrion's Big Bear Hug, 2008; Princess Gusty Ox's Strange Change, 2008; I Wonder Why Flip the Flaps Farm Animals, 2008; I Wonder Why Flip the Flaps Creepy-Crawlies, 2008; (with B. Blake) Ghost Mouse, 2009; (with B. Blake) Detective Derek, 2009; Arthur the King, 2009; Round Table, 2009; Sir Lancelot and the Ice Castle, 2009; (with N. Chapman) Sword in the Stone, 2009; Alice Goes North, 2009; Bad Rat, 2012. **Address:** c/o Pat White, Rogers Coleridge and White, 11 Powis Mews, London, GL W11 1JN, England. **Online address:** patw@rcwlitagency.co.uk

WALLACE, Mark I. American (born United States), b. 1956. **Genres:** Theology/Religion, Adult Non-fiction. **Career:** University of Chicago, Divinity School, fellow, 1984-85, Institute for the Advanced Study of Religion, junior fellow, 1985-86; Merrimack College, lecturer in religious studies, 1986-87; Georgia State University, assistant professor of philosophy, 1987-89, Mortar Board distinguished professor, 1989; Swarthmore College, Department of Religion, assistant professor, 1989-95, associate professor of religion, chair/co-chair, 1995-; Princeton Theological Seminary Summer School, instructor, 1992; University of Pennsylvania, visiting lecturer, 2003. Theologian and writer. **Publications:** The Second Naiveté: Barth, Ricoeur and the New Yale Theology, 1990; (ed. with T.H. Smith) Curing Violence, 1994; (ed.) Figuring the Sacred: Religion, Narrative and Imagination, 1995; Fragments of the Spirit: Nature, Violence and the Renewal of Creation, 1996; Finding God in the Singing River: Christianity, Spirit, Nature, 2005; Green Christianity: Five Ways to a Sustainable Future, 2010. **Address:** Department of Religion, Swarthmore College, 216 Pearson, 500 College Ave., Swarthmore, PA 19081-1397, U.S.A. **Online address:** mwallac1@swarthmore.edu

WALLACE, Meredith. (Meredith Wallace Kazer). American (born United States), b. 1965. **Genres:** Medicine/Health. **Career:** Catholic Medical Center, nurse, 1988-89; Hesser College, adjunct instructor, 1989; Windsor Castle Health Care, Departments of Staff Development and Infection Control, director, 1989-90; Omni Home Health Service, nurse, 1990-92; Southern Connecticut State University, adjunct instructor, 1990, assistant professor, 1998-2002; Hospital of Saint Raphael, geriatric nurse specialist, 1992-96, manager of health promotion, 1996-98; Quinnipiac College, adjunct instructor, 1995-98; Geriatric Education Center, lecturer, 1996-; New York University, federal nurse trainee, 1997-98; Life Haven Shelter for Women and Children, director, 1997, vice president, 1999-2000, president, 2000-; Applied Nursing Research, managing editor, 2000-01; Brighton Gardens of Woodbridge, adult nurse practitioner, 2001-02; Fairfield University, assistant professor of gerontological nursing, community health, and nursing research, 2002-; Yale University School of Nursing, associate professor of adult, family, gerontological, and women's health primary care specialty; Fairfield University, School of Nursing, associate professor of nursing. Writer. **Publications:** (Ed. with L.L. Powel) Prostate Cancer: Nursing Assessment, Management, and Care, 2002; (ed.) Encyclopedia of Nursing Research, 2nd ed., 2006, (ed. with J.J. Fitzpatrick) 3rd ed., 2012; Essentials of Gerontological Nursing, 2007; (with S. Grossman) Gerontological Nurse Certification Review, 2008; (ed. with J.J. Fitzpatri) Doctor of Nursing Practice and Clinical Nurse Leader: Essentials of Program Development and Implementation for Clinical Practice, 2009; (ed. with L. Neal-Boylan) Case Studies in Gerontological Nursing for the Advanced Practice Nurse, 2012. Contributor of articles to periodicals. **Address:** School of Nursing, Fairfield University, Rm. 123, 1073 N Benson Rd., Fairfield, CT 06824-5171, U.S.A. **Online address:** mkazer@fairfield.edu

WALLACE, Naomi (French). American (born United States), b. 1960. **Genres:** Poetry, Plays/Screenplays. **Career:** Writer. **Publications:** To Dance a Stony Field (poems), 1995; Slaughter City (play), 1996; Birdy (play), 1997; One Flea Spare (play), 1997; The Trestle at Pope Lick Creek, 2001; In the Heart of America, and Other Plays, 2001; The Girl Who Fell Through a Hole in Her Sweater, 2003; The War Boys, 2004; Things of Dry Hours, 2007; Fever Chart: Three Visions of The Middle East, With One Short Sleepe, 2009. **Address:** Joyce Ketay Agency, 1501 Broadway, Ste. 1910, New York, NY 10036, U.S.A.

WALLACE, Rich. *See* **WALLACE, Richard (Alan).**

WALLACE, Richard (Alan). (Rich Wallace). American (born United States), b. 1957. **Genres:** Young Adult Fiction, Children's Fiction, Sports/Fitness, Novellas/Short Stories. **Career:** Herald News, editorial assistant, 1978-79, sports reporter, 1979-82; Daily Advance, sports editor, 1982-84, news editor, 1984-85; Trenton Times, copy editor, 1985-86, assistant city editor, 1986-87; Highlights for Children (magazine), copy editor, 1988-90, assistant editor, 1990-92, coordinating editor, 1992-98, senior editor, 1998-2004; freelance writer and editor, 2004-. **Publications:** AS RICH WALLACE: Wrestling Sturbridge, 1996; Shots on Goal, 1997; Playing Without the Ball: A Novel in Four Quarters, 2000; Losing is Not an Option, 2003; Restless: A Ghost's Story, 2003; The Roar of the Crowd, 2004; Technical Foul, 2004; Fast Company, 2005; Double Fake, 2005; Emergency Quarterback, 2005; Southpaw, 2006; Dunk Under Pressure, 2006; Takedown, 2006; Curveball, 2007; One Good Punch, 2007; Second-string Center, 2007; Dishes, 2008; Perpetual Check, 2009; Sports Camp, 2010; Kickers, vol. I: The Ball Hogs, 2010, vol. II: Fake Out, 2010, vol. III: Benched, 2010, vol. IV: Game-Day Jitters, 2011; War and Watermelon, 2011. Contributor to periodicals. **Address:** PO Box 178, Keene, NH 03431, U.S.A. **Online address:** richxw@aol.com

WALLACE, Vesna A. American/Croatian (born Croatia), b. 1952. **Genres:** Language/Linguistics, Theology/Religion. **Career:** University Extension, instructor, 1987-88; University of Washington, instructor, 1987-88; University of California-Berkeley, teaching assistant, 1990, research fellow, 1995-96; Stanford University, visiting lecturer, 1991, Department of Linguistics, visiting lecturer, 1993-95, Department of Religious Studies, teaching assistant, 1992-96; University of California-Santa Barbara, Department of Religious Studies, lecturer, 1997-2001, assistant professor, 2001-05, associate professor, 2005-08, professor, 2008-; Oxford Centre for Buddhist? Studies, academic director, 2008-10; University of Oxford, faculty of Oriental studies, professor, Numata chair in Buddhist studies; Open Society Institute, international supervisor, 2008-. Writer. **Publications:** Textbook for the First Year Intensive Serbo-Croatian, 1988; (trans. with B.A. Wallace) A Guide to the Bodhisattva Way of Life (Bodhicaryavatara), 1997; The Inner Kālacakratantra: A Buddhist Tantric View of the Individual, 2001; (trans.) The Kalacakratantra: The Chapter on the Individual Together with the Vimalaprabha, 2004; (intro.) The Kalacakra Tantra: The Chapter on Sadhana, Together with the Vimalaprabha Commentary, 2010. Contributor to journals. **Address:** Department of Religious Studies, University of California, 3065 Humanities and Social Sciences Bldg., 3rd Fl., Santa Barbara, CA 93105, U.S.A. **Online address:** vesna.wallace@orinst.ox.ac.uk

WALLACE-CRABBE, Christopher (Keith). Australian (born Australia), b. 1934. **Genres:** Poetry, Literary Criticism And History, Essays. **Career:** Royal Mint, junior technical officer, 1951-52; Gas & Fuel Corp., clerical officer, 1954-55; Haileybury College, teacher, 1957-58; University of Melbourne, Department of English, Lockie fellow, 1961-63, senior lecturer, 1963-76, head, 1974-76, 1984-85, reader, 1977-87, personal chair, 1987, professor, 1987-98, professor emeritus, 1998-, Australian Centre, founding director, 1989-94, fellow, 1998-; Yale University, Harkness fellow, 1965-67; University of Exeter, visiting fellow, 1973; Harvard University, visiting professor, 1987-88. Writer. **Publications:** The Music of Division, 1959; Order and Turbulence, 1961; Eight Metropolitan Poems, 1963; In Light and Darkness, 1964; The Rebel General, 1967; Where the Wind Came, 1971; Selected Poems, 1973; Chris Wallace-Crabbe Reads from His Own Work, 1973; Melbourne or the Bush: Essays on Australian Literature and Society, 1974; Act in the Noon, 1974; Shapes of Gallipoli, 1975; Foundations of Joy, 1976; The Emotions Are Not Skilled Workers: Poems, 1979; Toil and Spin: Two Di-

rections in Modern Poetry, 1979; Splinters (novel), 1981; Three Absences in Australian Writing, 1983; The Amorous Cannibal and Other Poems, 1985; I'm Deadly Serious, 1988; Sangue e L'Acqua, 1989; Falling into Language, 1990; For Crying Out Loud, 1990; Rungs of Time, 1992; Selected Poems 1956-1994, 1995; Whirling, 1998; By and Large, 2001; Next, 2004; The Universe Locks Down, 2005; Telling a Hawk from a Handsaw, 2008. EDITOR: Six Voices: Contemporary Australian Poets, 1963, rev. ed., 1974; Australian Poetry 1971, 1971; The Australian Nationalists, 1971; The Golden Apples of the Sun, 1980; (with P. Pierce) Clubbing of the Gunfire: 101 Australian War Poems, 1984; (with D. Goodman and D.J. O'Hearn) Multicultural Australia: The Challenges of Change, 1991; (with K. Flattley) From The Republic of Conscience: An International Anthology of Poetry, 1992; Approaching Australia: Papers from the Harvard Australian Studies Symposium, 1998; (with B. Bennett and J. Strauss) Oxford Literary History of Australia, 1998; Author, Author!: Tales of Australian Literary Life, 1998; Imagining Australia, 2004; Collected Poems, 2009. Contributor to periodicals. **Address:** The Australian Ctr., University of Melbourne, 137 Barry St., Carlton, VI 3053, Australia. **Online address:** ckwc@unimelb.edu.au

WALLACE-MURPHY, Tim. British/Irish (born Ireland) **Genres:** Social Commentary, Adult Non-fiction, History. **Career:** European Templar Heritage Research Network (ETHRN), co-founder. Lecturer, author and psychologist. **Publications:** An Illustrated Guidebook to Rosslyn Chapel, 1993; The Templar Legacy and Masonic Inheritance within Rosslyn Chapel, 1994; (with T. Ravenscroft) The Mark of the Beast: The Continuing Story of the Spear of Destiny, 1997; (with M. Hopkins) Rosslyn, Guardian of the Secrets of the Holy Grail, 1999; (with M. Hopkins and G. Simmans) Rex Deus: The True Mystery of Rennes-le-Chateau, 2000; (with M. Hopkins) Templars in America: From the Crusades to the New World, 2004; Cracking the Symbol Code, 2005; (with M. Hopkins) Custodians of Truth: The Continuance of Rex Deus, 2005; The Enigma of the Freemasons, 2006; What Islam Did for Us, 2006; Hidden Wisdom: The Secrets of the Western Esoteric Tradition, 2010; The Knights Templar: The Myth and the Reality, forthcoming. **Address:** c/o Author Mail, Red Wheel/Weiser/Conari, 65 Parker St., Ste. 7, Newburyport, MA 01950, U.S.A. **Online address:** twallace-murphy@supanet.com

WALLACH, Alan. American (born United States), b. 1942. **Genres:** Art/Art History, History, Business/Trade/Industry, Information Science/Computers. **Career:** Kean College, assistant professor, associate professor of art history, 1974-89; University of California-Los Angeles, visiting professor, 1982-83; New York University, faculty, 1984-85; Stanford University, faculty, 1987; University of California-New York, Graduate Center, faculty, 1988; University of Michigan, faculty, 1989; College of William and Mary, professor, Ralph H. Wark professor of art and art history and professor of American studies, 1989-; University of Delaware, faculty, 2006; Williams College, Graduate Program in the History of Art, Robert Sterling Clark distinguished visiting professor. Writer. **Publications:** (Ed. with W.H. Truettner) Thomas Cole: Landscape into History, 1994; The Year 2000 Hoax: Plain English Guide to the Year 2000 Problem, 1998; Exhibiting Contradiction: Essays on the Art Museum in the United States, 1998. **Address:** Department of Art and Art History, College of William and Mary, Andrews Hall 206B, PO Box 8795, Williamsburg, VA 23187-8795, U.S.A. **Online address:** axwall@wm.edu

WALLACH, Jeff. American (born United States), b. 1960?. **Genres:** Recreation, Sports/Fitness, Young Adult Fiction, Geography. **Career:** Milton Academy, faculty of writing; Lewis and Clark College, faculty; Oregon Graduate Institute, faculty; Oregon Writers Workshop, faculty of writing; The Critical Faculty, founder; Golf Media Network L.L.C., founding member and managing partner; Basalt Properties L.L.C., founder and managing partner; Porch Swing Properties L.L.C., founder and managing partner; Sol Brothers L.L.C., founder and managing partner. Freelance writer and environmentalist. **Publications:** Beyond the Fairway: Zen Lessons, Insights and Attitudes of Golf, 1995; What the River Says: Whitewater Journeys along the Frontier, 1996; Breaking 100: Eugene Country Club's First Century, 1999; Driven to Extremes: Uncommon Lessons from Golf's Unmanicured Terrain, 2002; Best Places to Golf Northwest: British Columbia to Northern Utah, the Western Rockies to the Pacific, 2004; Northwest Best Places to Golf, 2004; Pool and Drop: A Novel, 2009. Contributor to periodicals. **Address:** c/o Bob Mecoy, Bob Mecoy Literary Agency, 66 Grand St., Ste. 1, New York, NY 10013, U.S.A. **Online address:** jcw@teleport.com

WALLACH, Jennifer Jensen. American (born United States), b. 1974?. **Genres:** Autobiography/Memoirs, History. **Career:** Emory University, researcher, 1998; University of Massachusetts, research assistant, 1998-99, mentor and graduate student instructor, 1998-2002; Mount Ida College, adjunct instructor, 2002; Stonehill College, visiting professor, 2005-06; Georgia College and State University, assistant professor, 2006-09; University of North Texas, assistant professor, 2009-. Writer. **Publications:** Closer to the Truth Than Any Fact: Memoir, Memory, and Jim Crow, 2008; Richard Wright: From Black Boy to World Citizen, 2010. Contributor to journals and periodicals. **Address:** Department of History, University of North Texas, 1155 Union Cir., Ste. 310650, Denton, TX 76203, U.S.A. **Online address:** jennifer.wallach@unt.edu

WALLER, Douglas C. American (born United States), b. 1949. **Genres:** Military/Defense/Arms Control, Politics/Government, History. **Career:** Greensboro Record, staff; Charlotte News, staff; U.S. Congress, legislative assistant, 1980-88; Newsweek Magazine, defense and foreign policy correspondent, 1988-94; Time Magazine, correspondent, 1994-. **Publications:** (With E.J. Markey) Nuclear Peril: The Politics of Proliferation, 1982; Congress and the Nuclear Freeze: An Inside Look at the Politics of a Mass Movement, 1987; (with J.T. Bruce and D.M. Cook) The Strategic Defense Initiative, Progress and Challenges: A Guide to Issues and References, 1987; The Commandos: The Inside Story of America's Secret Soldiers, 1994; Air Warriors: The Inside Story of the Making of a Navy Pilot, 1998; Big Red: Three Months on Board a Trident Nuclear Submarine, 2001; Question of Loyalty: Gen. Billy Mitchell and the Court-Martial That Gripped the Nation, 2004; Wild Bill Donovan, 2010. Contributor to periodicals. **Address:** 5001 Dodson Dr., Annandale, VA 22003-6142, U.S.A.

WALLER, Jane (Ashton). British (born England), b. 1944. **Genres:** Children's Fiction, Young Adult Fiction, History, Recreation, How-to Books. **Career:** Artist and writer. **Publications:** A Stitch in Time: Knitting and Crochet Patterns from of the 1920s, 1930s & 1940s, 1972; Some Things for the Children, 1974; A Man's Book, 1977; The Thirties Family Knitting Book, 1981; Below the Green Pond (juvenile novel), 1982; The Man's Knitting Book, 1984; Classic Knitting Patterns from the British Isles: Men's Hand-Knits from the 20's to the 50's, 1985; (with M. Vaughan-Rees) Women in Wartime, 1987; (with M. Vaughan-Rees) Women in Uniform, 1989; Hand-Built Ceramics, 1990; (with M. Vaughan-Rees) Blitz: The Civilian War, 1940-1945, 1990; The Forties Knitting Book, 1991; Saving the Dinosaurs (juvenile novel), 1994; The Sludge Gulpers (juvenile novel), 1997; Colour in Clay, 1998; The Human Form in Clay, 2001. **Address:** Smith and Smith PR Ltd., Virginia House, 4th Fl., 5 Great Ancoats St., Manchester, GM M4 1AD, England. **Online address:** jane@smithandsmithpr.co.uk

WALLER, John. American/British (born England), b. 1972?. **Genres:** Sciences, History. **Career:** London University, lecturer; Harvard University, lecturer; University of Melbourne; Centre for Health and Society, lecturer, 2003-05; Michigan State University, assistant professor, 2006-09, associate professor, 2009-10. Writer and historian. **Publications:** The Discovery of the Germ: Twenty Years That Transformed the Way We Think about Disease, 2002; Einstein's Luck: The Truth behind Some of the Greatest Scientific Discoveries, 2002 in UK as Fabulous Science: Fact and Fiction in the History of Scientific Discovery, 2004; Leaps in the Dark, 2004; The Real Oliver Twist, 2005; A Time to Dance, a Time to Die: The Extraordinary Story of the Dancing Plague of 1518, 2008 in US as The Dancing Plague: The Strange, True Story of an Extraordinary Illness, 2009. **Address:** Lyman Briggs School of Medicine, 35 East Holmes Hall, East Lansing, MI 48825-1107, U.S.A. **Online address:** wallerj1@msu.edu

WALLER, P(hilip) J(ohn). British (born England), b. 1946. **Genres:** History, Reference. **Career:** University of Oxford, Magdalen College, fellow, 1968-71, Merton College, fellow and lecturer in modern history, 1971-2008, emeritus fellow, 2008- ; University of South Carolina, visiting professor, 1979; Colorado College, visiting professor, 1985; English Historical Review, editor, 2003-06. **Publications:** Democracy and Sectarianism: A Political and Social History of Liverpool 1868-1939, 1981; Town, City, and Nation: England, 1850-1914, 1983. EDITOR: Politics and Social Change in Modern Britain: Essays Presented to A.F. Thompson, 1987; (with N. Williams) Chronology of the Modern World, 1763-1992, 1994; (with N. Williams) Chronology of the 20th Century, 1995; (ed.) The English Urban Landscape, 2000; Writers, Readers and Reputations: Literary Life in Britain, 1870-1918, 2006. **Address:** Merton College, University of Oxford, Merton St., Oxford, OX OX1 4JD, England. **Online address:** philip.waller@merton.ox.ac.uk

WALLER, Robert James. American (born United States), b. 1939. **Genres:** Novellas/Short Stories, Essays, Novels, Photography. **Career:** University of Northern Iowa, professor of economics, applied mathematics, and management, 1968-91, Business School, dean, 1979-85. Writer. **Publications:** Just Beyond the Firelight: Stories and Essays, 1988; One Good Road Is Enough: Essays, 1990; Old Songs in a New Café: Selected Essays, 1994. NOVELS: The Bridges of Madison County in UK as Love in Black and White, 1992; Slow Waltz in Cedar Bend, 1993; Ballads of Madison County, 1993; Border Music, 1995; Puerto Vallarta Squeeze: The Run for el Norte, 1995; A Thousand Country Roads: An Epilogue to The Bridges of Madison Country, 2002; High Plains Tango: A Novel, 2005; The Long Night of Winchell Dear, 2006. OTHERS: Iowa: Perspectives on Today and Tomorrow, 1991; Images, 1994. Contributor to periodicals. **Address:** Aaron M. Priest Literary Agency Inc., 708 3rd Ave., 23rd Fl., New York, NY 10017-4201, U.S.A.

WALLEY, Christine J. American (born United States), b. 1965?. **Genres:** Social Sciences, Natural History, Economics, Business/Trade/Industry. **Career:** New York University, teaching assistant, 1989-97, instructor in anthropology, 1993-97; Massachusetts Institute of Technology, assistant professor, 1999-2003, associate professor of anthropology, 2003-. Writer. **Publications:** Rough Waters: Nature and Development in an East African Marine Park, 2004. Contributor to periodicals. **Address:** Anthropology Program, Massachusetts Institute of Technology, Rm. 16-255, 77 Massachusetts Ave., Cambridge, MA 02139-4307, U.S.A. **Online address:** cwalley@mit.edu

WALLIN, Pamela. American/Canadian (born Canada), b. 1953. **Genres:** Autobiography/Memoirs, Biography. **Career:** CBC Radio, host and producer, 1974-78; Toronto Star, reporter, 1978-80; Canada AM, co-host, 1980-85; CTV, parliamentary bureau chief, 1985-90; CBC TV, co-anchor, 1990-93; Pamela Wallin Productions, president, 1995-2002; Canadian Consulate, consulate general, 2002-06; Americas Society/Council of the Americas, senior advisor to president, 2006-. Writer. **Publications:** Since You Asked, 1998; Speaking of Success: Collected Wisdom, 2001; The Comfort of Cats, 2003. **Address:** Canadian Consulate General, 1251 Ave. of the Americas, New York, NY 10020-1175, U.S.A.

WALLINGFORD, Lee. American/Canadian (born Canada), b. 1947. **Genres:** Mystery/Crime/Suspense, Novels, Young Adult Fiction. **Career:** U.S. Forest Service, forestry technician, 1978-85; Freewater School, library media specialist, 1990-. Writer. **Publications:** Cold Tracks (novel), 1991; Clear-Cut Murder (novel), 1993. **Address:** Frances Collin Literary Agent, 110 W 40th St., PO Box 33, New York, NY 10018, U.S.A.

WALLIS, Velma. American (born United States), b. 1960?. **Genres:** Novels. **Career:** Writer. **Publications:** Two Old Women: An Alaska Legend of Betrayal, Courage and Survival, 1993, 2nd ed., 2004; Bird Girl and the Man Who Followed the Sun: An Athabaskan Indian Legend from Alaska, 1996; Raising Ourselves: A Gwich'in Coming of Age Story from the Yukon River, 2002. Contributor to periodicals. **Address:** Epicenter Press, 2112 Cowles St., Ste. 2, PO Box 82368, Kenmore, WA 98028, U.S.A.

WALLMEYER, Dick. (Richard Wallmeyer). American (born United States), b. 1931. **Genres:** Cartoons, Humor/Satire. **Career:** Newman-Rudolph Lithograph Co., proofreader, 1948-49; Montgomery-Ward, sales clerk in clothing department, 1949; WCHI-FM Radio, newscaster, 1950-51; Bundy Friday Studio, art studio apprentice, 1955; Filmack Studios, paste-up and line drawing artist, 1956; Children's Bootery, shoe salesman, 1956-61; Press-Telegram, editorial cartoonist, 1961-95, freelance cartoonist, 1995-. **Publications:** Today's Cartoon, 1962; Cartooning, 1975; Attack of the Political Cartoonists, 2004. **Address:** Press-Telegram, 300 Oceangate, Long Beach, CA 90844, U.S.A.

WALLMEYER, Richard. See **WALLMEYER, Dick.**

WALLS, Ian G. Scottish (born Scotland), b. 1922. **Genres:** Horticulture, Homes/Gardens, Agriculture/Forestry, Botany. **Career:** Dobbie & Company Ltd., staff, 1936-39; Asmer Seeds, staff, 1949-50; West of Scotland Agricultural College, horticultural adviser, 1950-78; D.T. Brown & Company Ltd., consultant; Clovis Lande Associates Ltd., consultant; Frederick Muller Ltd., consultant; R.D. Ltd., consultant. Writer. **Publications:** Tomato Cultivation for the Amateur, 1952; Gardening Month by Month, 1967; Creating Your Garden, 1967; The Lady Gardener, 1968; Greenhouse Gardening, 1970; Tomato Growing Today, 1972, 2nd ed., 1978; (with A. Berrie and D. Harris) Hydroponics, Growing Plants Without Soil: Easy-to-Follow Instructions for the Flatdweller, Modern Gardener and Commercial Grower, 1974; (with A.S. Horsburgh) Making Your Garden Pay: Profit From Garden and Nursery, 1974; Complete Book of the Greenhouse, 1974, 5th ed., 1993 in US as The Complete Book of Greenhouse Gardening, 1975; Making the Most of Your Greenhouse, 1975; Garden Problems A-Z, 1979; The Care and Maintenance of Bowling Greens, 1979; Collins A-Z of Garden Pests and Problems, 1979; Commercial Vegetable Growing Under Protection, 1981; Commercial Flower Growing Under Protection, 1981; Modern Greenhouse Methods: Flowers and Plants, Vegetables, 2 vols., 1982; Growing Vegetables, Fruit, and Flowers for Profit, 1986; Simple Tomato Growing, 1987; Growing Tomatoes, 1989; Low-Cost Gardening, 1992. Contributor to magazines and newspapers. **Address:** 17 Dougalston Ave., Milngaule, Glasgow, G62 6AP, Scotland.

WALSH, Ann. Canadian/American (born United States), b. 1942. **Genres:** Young Adult Fiction, History, Novels. **Career:** Teacher, 1964-78; Community College instructor, 1979-89; full-time writer, 1990-. **Publications:** YOUNG ADULT NOVELS: Your Time, My Time, 1984; Moses, Me and Murder!, 1988; The Ghost of Soda Creek, 1990; Across the Stillness, 1992; Shabash!, 1994; The Doctor's Apprentice, 1998; By the Skin of His Teeth, 2004; Flower Power, 2005; Horse Power, 2007; (with K.C. Waldron) Forestry, A-Z, 2008. EDITOR: Winds through Time: An Anthology of Canadian Historical Young Adult Fiction, 1998; Beginnings: Stories of Canada's Past, 2001; Dark Times, 2005. **Address:** 411 Winger Rd., Williams Lake, BC V2G 3S6, Canada. **Online address:** annwalshwrites@hotmail.com

WALSH, Edward N. American (born United States), b. 1925. **Genres:** Chemistry, Education. **Career:** Writer. **Publications:** (With A.D.F. Toy) Phosphorus Chemistry in Everyday Living, 2nd ed., 1987; (co-ed.) Phosphorus Chemistry: Developments in American Science, 1992. **Address:** 33 Concord Dr., New City, NY 10956, U.S.A.

WALSH, Gillian Paton. *See* **WALSH, Jill Paton.**

WALSH, Jill Paton. (Gillian Paton Walsh). British (born England), b. 1937. **Genres:** Young Adult Fiction, Novels, Children's Fiction, Picture/Board Books, Young Adult Non-fiction, History, Mystery/Crime/Suspense. **Career:** Enfield Girls Grammar School, English teacher, 1959-62; writer, 1962-; Library of Congress, Whittall Lecturer, 1978; Simmons College, Center for the Study of Children's Literature, visiting faculty, 1978-86; Green Bay Publications, co-founder, 1986-. **Publications:** (As Gillian Paton Walsh) Hengest's Tale, 1966; The Dolphin Crossing, 1967; Fireweed, 1969; (with K. Crossley-Holland) Wordhoard: Anglo-Saxon Stories, 1969; Goldengrove, 1972; Farewell, Great King, 1972; Toolmaker, 1973; The Dawnstone, 1973; The Emperor's Winding Sheet, 1974; The Butty Boy in US as The Huffler, 1975; (ed.) Beowulf, 1975; The Island Sunrise: Prehistoric Britain, 1975 in US as The Island Sunrise: Prehistoric Culture in the British Isles, 1976; Unleaving, 1976; Crossing to Salamis, 1977; The Walls of Athens, 1977; Persian Gold, 1978; Children of the Fox, 1978; A Chance Child, 1978; The Green Book, 1981, 3rd ed. as Shine, 1988; Babylon, 1982; A Parcel of Patterns, 1983; Lost and Found, 1984; Gaffer Samson's Luck, 1984; Five Tides, 1986; Lapsing, 1986; Torch, 1987; Birdy and the Ghosties, 1989; A School for Lovers, 1989; Can I Play Farmer, Farmer?, 1990; Can I Play Wolf?, 1990; Can I Play Jenny Jones?, 1990; Can I Play Queenie?, 1990; Grace, 1991; When Grandma Came, 1992; Matthew and the Sea Singer, 1992; The Wyndham Case, 1993; Knowledge of Angels, 1994; Pepi and the Secret Names, 1994; Thomas and the Tinners, 1995; Connie Came to Play, 1995; A Piece of Justice: An Imogen Quy Mystery, 1995; When I Was Little Like You, 1997; Goldengrove Unleaving, 1997; The Serpentine Cave, 1997; (with D.L. Sayers) Thrones, Dominations, 1998; A Desert in Bohemia, 2000; (with D.L. Sayers) A Presumption of Death, 2002; Debts of Dishonor: An Imogen Quy Mystery, 2006; The Bad Quarto: An Imogen Quy Mystery, 2007; The Attenbury Emeralds, 2010. **Address:** c/o Veronique Baxter, David Higham Associates Ltd., 5-8 Lower John St., Golden Sq., London, GL W1F 9HA, England.

WALSH, Kenneth T(homas). American (born United States), b. 1947. **Genres:** Biography. **Career:** New York Times, news clerk, 1969-70; Associated Press, newsman, 1972-76; Denver Post, reporter, statehouse correspondent and political editor, 1976-79, chief political writer and political columnist, 1979-81, Washington correspondent, 1981-84; U.S. News &

World Report, correspondent, 1984-86, White House correspondent, 1986-, chief White House correspondent; American University, adjunct professor, 1993-. **Publications:** Feeding the Beast: The White House Versus the Press, 1996; Ronald Reagan, 1997; Air Force One: A History of the Presidents and Their Planes, 2003; Mount Vernon to Crawford: A History of the Presidents and Their Retreats, 2005; From Mount Vernon to Crawford: A History Of The Presidents and Their Retreats, 2005; Family of Freedom: Presidents and African Americans in the White House, 2011. **Address:** U.S. News & World Report, 1050 Thomas Jefferson St. NW, Washington, DC 20007-3837, U.S.A. **Online address:** kennethtwalsh@kennethwalsh.com

WALSH, Lawrence. American (born United States), b. 1942?. **Genres:** Young Adult Fiction, Mystery/Crime/Suspense. **Career:** Bayer Corporation Quality Assurance Water Analysis Laboratory, chemist; Red Herring Mystery Magazine, founding editor; Whispering Prairie Press, president; Potpourri Publications, treasurer, 1993-95; Johnson County Community College, faculty; Maplewoods College, faculty. Writer. **Publications:** WITH S. WALSH: The Unicorn and Other Children's Stories, 1993; They Would Never Be Friends, 1996; Running Scared, 1999; Through a Dark Tunnel, 2001; Creating Fiction that Sells, 2002; The Last O'Neil, 2007; In the Middle of the Night, 2010. Contributor to books and periodicals. **Address:** Johnson County Community College, 12345 College Blvd., Overland Park, KS 66210-1299, U.S.A. **Online address:** landswalsh@prodigy.net

WALSH, Michael Stephen. *See* **WALSH, Stephen.**

WALSH, P(atrick) G(erard). Scottish/British (born England), b. 1923. **Genres:** Classics, Literary Criticism And History, Theology/Religion, Translations, Novels. **Career:** University College, lecturer in classics, 1952-59; University of Edinburgh, lecturer, 1959-66, reader in humanity, 1967-71, professor of medieval Latin, 1971-72; University of Toronto, visiting professor, 1966-67; Yale University, visiting professor, 1970-71; University of Glasgow, professor of humanity, 1972-93, honorary senior research fellow; University of North Carolina-Chapel Hill, visiting professor, 1978; Georgetown University, visiting professor, 1990; Pamona College, visiting professor, 1992. Writer. **Publications:** Livy: His Historical Aims and Methods, 1961; The Roman Novel The Satyricon of Petronius and the Metamorphoses of Apuleius, 1970; Courtly Love in the Carmina Burana, 1971; Livy, 1974. EDITOR: (with A. Ross) Aquinas, Courage, 1965; Livy Book XXI, 1973; Thirty Poems from the Carmina Burana, 1976; Andreas Capellanus on Love, 1982; Teubner Livy Books XXVI-VII, 1982; (with P. Sharratt) George Buchanan Tragedies, 1982; Divine Providence and Human Suffering, 1985; Livy, Book XXI, 1985; Teubner Livy Books XXVIII-XXX, 1986; (with M.J. Kennedy) William, History of English Affairs, 1988; William of Newburgh: History of English Affairs, 1988; Livy Book XXXVI, 1991; Livy Book XXXVII, 1992; Livy XXXVIII, 1993; (ed.) Love Lyrics from the Carmina Burana, 1993; Livy XXXIX, 1994; Livy XL, 1996; Livy XXXVI-XL, 1999; Augustine, The Good of Marriage, on Holy Virginity, 2001; Augustine, The City of God I-II, 2005. TRANSLATOR: Letters of Paulinus of Nola, vol., II, 1966-67; Poems of Paulinus of Nola, 1974; Cassiodorus, Explanation of the Psalms, 1990; (and intro.) Apuleius, The Golden Ass, 1994; Petronius, The Satyricon, 1996; (and intro.) Cicero, The Nature of the Gods, 1997; (and intro.) Boethius, The Consolation of Philosophy, 1999; (and intro.) Cicero, On Obligations, 2000; (ed. and intro.) Augustine, De civitate Dei, vol. I-II, 2005, vol. III, IV, 2007, vol. V, 2009, vol. VI-VII: City of God, 2009; (intro.) Pliny, Complete Letters, 2006; (and intro.) Selected Letters, 2008. Contributor to journals. **Address:** University of Glasgow, 11 Eldon St., Kelvingrove, Glasgow, G3 6NH, Scotland. **Online address:** patrick.walsh@glasgow.ac.uk

WALSH, Robb. American (born United States), b. 1952. **Genres:** Food And Wine, Children's Fiction. **Career:** Austin Chronicle, food editor, 1991-94; Natural History Magazine, food columnist, 1995-99; National Public Radio, commentator, 1998-; Chile Pepper, editor-in-chief, 1999-2000; Houston Press, lead restaurant reviewer and food feature writer, 2000-10. **Publications:** Kingdom of the Dwarfs, 1980; (with J. McCarthy) Traveling Jamaica with Knife, Fork & Spoon: A Righteous Guide to Jamaican Cookery, 1995; (with D. Garrido) Nuevo Tex-Mex: Festive New Recipes from Just North of the Border, 1998; (with G. Spears) A Cowboy in the Kitchen: Recipes from Reata and Texas West of the Pecos, 1998; Cowboy in the Kitchen, 1999; Legends of Texas Barbecue: Recipes and Recollections from the Pit Bosses, 2002; Are You Really Going to Eat That? Adventures of a Culinary Thrillseeker, 2003; The Tex-Mex Cookbook: A History in Recipes and Photos, 2004; The Texas Cowboy Cookbook, 2007; Sex, Death & Oysters: A Half-shell Lover's

World Tour, 2009; Tex-Mex Grill and Backyard Barbacoa Cookbook, 2010; Texas Eats, 2012. **Address:** Crown Publishing Group, 1745 Broadway, New York, NY 10019, U.S.A. **Online address:** robbwalsh@aol.com

WALSH, Stephen. (Michael Stephen Walsh). British (born England), b. 1942. **Genres:** Music, History. **Career:** The Times, writer; Daily Telegraph, writer; Financial Times, writer; British Broadcasting Corp., Department of Gramophone, producer, 1964-65; Listener, music critic, 1965; The Observer, deputy music critic, 1966-85; University of Cardiff, senior lecturer in music, 1976-, professor in music and chair; The Independent, music critic. **Publications:** The Lieder of Schumann, 1971; Bartók Chamber Music, 1982; The Music of Stravinsky, 1988; (trans.) P. Boulez, Stocktakings from an Apprenticeship, 1991; Stravinsky, Oedipus Rex, 1993; (ed. with A. Holden and N. Kenyon) The Viking Opera Guide, 1993; (ed. with A. Holden and N. Kenyon) The Penguin Opera Guide, 1996; Stravinsky, vol. I: A Creative Spring: Russia and France, 1882-1934, 1999, vol. II: The Second Exile: France and America, 1934-1971, 2006; The New Grove Stravinsky, 2002. Contributor to periodicals. **Address:** Cardiff School of Music, Cardiff University, Rm. 1.04, 33 Corbett Rd., Cardiff, SG CF10 3EB, Wales. **Online address:** walshs@cardiff.ac.uk

WALSH, Suella. American (born United States) **Genres:** Children's Fiction, Mystery/Crime/Suspense. **Career:** Whispering Prairie Press, board of directors; Potpourri Publications, secretary, 1991-95; Johnson County Community College, teacher; Maplewoods College, teacher. Writer. **Publications:** (With L. Walsh) The Unicorn and Other Children's Stories, 1993; (with L. Walsh) They Would Never Be Friends, 1996; (with L. Walsh) Running Scared, 1999; (with L. Walsh) Through a Dark Tunnel, 2001; (with L. Walsh) In the Middle of the Night, 2010. Contributor to books and periodicals. **Address:** 1803 Wornall Rd., Excelsior Springs, MO 64024, U.S.A. **Online address:** landswalsh@prodigy.net

WALSHE, Peter (Aubrey). American/South African (born South Africa), b. 1934. **Genres:** Politics/Government. **Career:** University of Notre Dame, Department of political science, assistant professor, 1967-77, Joan B. Kroc Institute for International Peace Studies, fellow, Department of Government and International Studies, professor, 1967-, now professor emeritus of political science. Writer. **Publications:** The Rise of African Nationalism in South Africa: African National Congress, 1912-52, 1970; Black Nationalism in South Africa, 1973; Church versus State in South Africa: The Case of the Christian Institute, 1983; Prophetic Christianity and the Liberation Movement in South Africa, 1995. Contributor to magazines. **Address:** Department of Government and International Studies, University of Notre Dame, Hesburgh Ctr., 217 O'Shaughnessy Hall, Notre Dame, IN 46556, U.S.A. **Online address:** a.p.walshe.1@nd.edu

WALSHE, R(obert) D(aniel). Australian (born Australia), b. 1923. **Genres:** Education, History, Language/Linguistics, Writing/Journalism. **Career:** High school teacher, 1952-63; Martindale Press Ltd., publisher and managing director, 1963-70; Sutherland Shire Evening College, teacher of creative writing, 1969-76; A.H. and A.W. Reed Publishers (Aust.) Private Ltd., editorial director, 1970-75; freelance writer, 1975-; Sutherland Shire Environment Centre, foundation chairman, 1991-99. **Publications:** Australia's Fight for Independence and Parliamentary Democracy: Centenary of Responsible Government, 1856-1956, 1956; (with P.M. Wheeler) Mastering Words, 1961; Guide to World History since 1789, 1962; (with P. O'Hara and D. Shirley) How to Study Better, 1963; (with P.M. Wheeler) Mastering English, 1969; (with J.J. Cosgrove and E.B. McKillop) Power and Persuasion: Twenty Modern Biographies of Great Men, 1974; Better Writing, Clearer Thinking, 1979; Every Child Can Write, 1981; (with B. Dwyer) Learning to Read the Media, 1984; Teaching Writing: K-12, 1988, 1986; Teaching Writing: K-12, 1988. EDITOR: Teaching the Process of Composition Writing, 1971; (with N.A. Little) Ways We Teach History, 1971; Exploring the New English, 1973; The New English in Action, 1974; Speaking of Writing: Seventeen Leading Writers of Australian and New Zealand Fiction Answer Questions on their Craft, 1975; Donald Graves in Australia: Children Want to Write, 1981; (with P. March) Writing and Learning in Australia, 1986. **Address:** 74 Linden St., Ste. 5, Sutherland, NW 2232, Australia.

WALSH SHEPHERD, Donna. American (born United States), b. 1948. **Genres:** Young Adult Fiction, Young Adult Non-fiction, Geography, Cultural/Ethnic Topics, Children's Non-fiction, Children's Fiction, Astronomy, Sciences, Sciences. **Career:** University of Alaska, instructor in literature and writing, 1988-. Technical writing consultant and children's book author. **Publications:** Trixie Belden and the Mystery at Mead's Mountain, 1978; The Aztecs, 1992; Uranus, 1994; Auroras: Light Shows in the Night Sky, 1995; Tundra, 1996; The Klondike Gold Rush, 1998; Alaska, 1999; South Dakota, 2001; Earth, 2002; New Zealand, 2002. Contributor to periodicals. **Address:** Department of English, University of Alaska, 3211 Providence Dr., Anchorage, AK 99504, U.S.A.

WALT, Stephen M. American (born United States), b. 1955. **Genres:** Politics/Government, International Relations/Current Affairs. **Career:** Center for Naval Analyses, staff, 1980-81; Harvard University, Center for Science and International Affairs, research fellow, 1981-84, Robert and Renee Belfer professor of international affairs, 1999-, John F. Kennedy School of Government, academic dean, 2002-06; Carnegie Endowment for International Peace, resident associate, 1986-87; Princeton University, assistant professor, 1984-89; University of Chicago, associate professor, 1989-95, professor, 1995-99, master of the social science collegiate division and deputy dean of social sciences, 1996-99. Writer. **Publications:** The Origins of Alliances, 1987; Analysts in War and Peace: MccGwire, McConnell, and Admiral Gorshkov, 1987; Revolution and War, 1996; Taming American Power: The Global Response to U.S. Primacy, 2005; (with J.J. Mearsheimer) Israeli Lobby and U.S. Foreign Policy, 2006. **Address:** John F. Kennedy School of Government, Harvard University, Littauer-367, 79 John F. Kennedy St., PO Box 53, Cambridge, MA 02138, U.S.A. **Online address:** stephen_walt@harvard.edu

WALTENBURG, Eric N. American (born United States), b. 1965. **Genres:** History, Law, Social Sciences. **Career:** Ohio State University, Department of Political Science, university fellow, 1989-90, graduate research assistant, 1990-94; Purdue University, Department of Political Science, assistant professor, 1994-2000, associate professor of political science, 2000-. Writer. **Publications:** (With B. Swinford) Litigating Federalism: The States before the U.S. Supreme Court, 1999; Choosing Where to Fight: Organized Labor and the Modern Regulatory State, 1948-1987, 2002; (with R.A. Clawson) Legacy and Legitimacy: Black Americans and the Supreme Court, 2009. Contributor to books and journals. **Address:** Department of Political Science, Purdue University, West Lafayette, IN 47907-2098, U.S.A. **Online address:** ewaltenb@purdue.edu

WALTER, Andrew. British (born England), b. 1961?. **Genres:** Money/Finance, Politics/Government, Economics. **Career:** London School of Economics, reader in international political economy, 1997-, TRIUM Global Executive MBA Program, academic director, 2001-, Internal Political Economy M.Sc. Program, director, Department of Management, research associate; Oxford University, St. Antony's College, fellow and university lecturer in international relations; University of Melbourne, Business School, visiting professor; University of British Columbia, visiting professor; International University of Japan, visiting professor; University of Southern California, Pacific Council for International Policy, visiting professor; Nanyang Technological University, Institute of Defense and Strategic Studies, visiting professor. Writer and political economist. **Publications:** World Power and World Money: The Role of Hegemony and International Monetary Order, 1991; Governing Finance: East Asia's Adoption of International Standards, 2008; (with G. Sen) Analyzing the Global Political Economy, 2009. Contributor to books, periodicals and journals. **Address:** Department of International Relations, London School of Economics and Political Science, Rm. D507, Houghton St., London, GL WC2A 2AE, England. **Online address:** a.walter@lse.ac.uk

WALTER, Denise Frances. *See* MCCONDUIT, Denise Walter.

WALTER, Jess. American (born United States), b. 1965?. **Genres:** Novels, Mystery/Crime/Suspense, Adult Non-fiction. **Career:** Writer. **Publications:** NON-FICTION: Every Knee Shall Bow: The Truth and Tragedy of Ruby Ridge and the Randy Weaver Family, 1995; (with C. Darden) In Contempt, 1996. FICTION: Over Tumbled Graves, 2001; Land of the Blind, 2003; Citizen Vince: A Novel, 2005; The Zero: A Novel, 2006; The Financial Lives of the Poets, 2009. **Address:** HarperCollins Publishers, 10 E 53rd St., New York, NY 10022, U.S.A. **Online address:** j.walter@comcast.net

WALTER, John. British (born England), b. 1948. **Genres:** History, Social Sciences. **Career:** University of Essex, lecturer, 1976-2000, Local History Center, director, 1978-, professor in history, 2000-. Writer. **Publications:** (Ed. with R. Schofield) Famine, Disease, and the Social Order in Early Modern History, 1989; Understanding Popular Violence in the English Revolution: the

Colchester Plunderers, 1999; Crowds and Popular Politics in Early Modern England, 2006. (ed. with M.J. Braddick) Negotiating Power in Early Modern Society: Order, Hierarchy, and Subordination in Britain and Ireland, 2001. **Address:** Department of History, University of Essex, Rm. 5NW.8.18, Wivenhoe Pk., Colchester, C04 3SQ, England. **Online address:** jwalter@essex.ac.uk

WALTERS, James W. American (born United States), b. 1945. **Genres:** Ethics, Theology/Religion, Bibliography. **Career:** Claremont Ecumenical Council, vice-president, 1978, president, 1979; Loma Linda University, School of Religion, assistant professor, 1980-86, associate professor, 1986-91, professor of Christian ethics, theological and philosophical ethics, biomedical ethics, 1991-, dean, Center for Christian Bioethics, co-founder, 1983, Ethics Center, associate director, 1985-91; Adventist Today, co-founding editor and publisher, 1993-, executive editor. **Publications:** Living is Loving: Relationships Matter Most, 1985; What Is a Person?: An Ethical Exploration, 1997; Martin Buber and Feminist Ethics: The Priority of the Personal, 2003. EDITOR: (with S. Kubo and C. Sandefur) Theological Bibliography of the SDA Theological Seminary, 1970; Bioethics Today: A New Ethical Vision, 1988; War No More?: Options in Nuclear Ethics, 1989; (with G.R. Winslow) Facing Limits: Ethics and Health Care for the Elderly, 1993; (with D.R. Larson) Beyond Limits: Advancing the Ethics and Aging Debate, 1993; Choosing Who's to Live: Ethics and Aging, 1996. Contributor to periodicals. **Address:** School of Religion, Loma Linda University, Rm. 216, Griggs Hall, Loma Linda, CA 92350, U.S.A. **Online address:** jwalters@llu.edu

WALTERS, Joel. Israeli/American (born United States), b. 1949. **Genres:** Education, Language/Linguistics. **Career:** University of Illinois, assistant professor of educational psychology, 1977-80; Bar-Ilan University, associate professor of English and department chair, 1981-, professor. Writer. **Publications:** (Ed. with R.L. Cooper and E. Shohamy) New Perspectives and Issues in Educational Language Policy: A Festschrift for Bernard Dov Spolsky, 2001; Bilingualism: The Sociopragmatic-Psycholinguistic Interface, 2005. **Address:** Department of English, Faculty of Humanities, Bar-Ilan University, SAL 209, Rm. 211, Bldg. 404, Ramat Gan, 52520, Israel. **Online address:** waltej@mail.biu.ac.il

WALTERS, Minette. British (born England), b. 1949. **Genres:** Romance/Historical. **Career:** IPC Magazine, sub-editor, editor, 1972-77; freelance writer, 1977-. **Publications:** The Ice House, 1992; The Sculptress, 1993; The Scold's Bridle, 1994; The Dark Room, 1996; The Echo, 1997; The Breaker, 1998; The Tinder Box, 1999; The Shape of Snakes, 2001; Acid Row, 2002; Fox Evil, 2003; Disordered Minds, 2003; Devil's Feather, 2005; Chickenfeed, 2006; Chameleon's Shadow, 2007. Contributor to periodicals. **Address:** Gregory and Company Authors, 3 Barb Mews, London, GL W6 7PA, England. **Online address:** minnettew@newcomuk.co.uk

WALTHAM, Tony (A. C.). British (born England), b. 1942?. **Genres:** Earth Sciences, Recreation, Natural History. **Career:** Nottingham Trent University, lecturer in geology, 1968-2004, now retired. Writer. **Publications:** (Ed.) Full Report, 1971; (comp. and ed. with M.M. Sweeting) Limestones and Caves of Northwest England, 1974; Caves, 1974; World of Caves, 1976; Catastrophe: The Violent Earth, 1978; Caves, Crags, and Gorges, 1984; (with J. Middleton) The Underground Atlas, 1986; Yorkshire Dales-Limestone Country, 1987; Yorkshire Dales National Park, 1987; Ground Subsidence, 1989; Xingwen, 1993; Foundations of Engineering Geology, 1994, 3rd ed., 2009; Sandstone Caves of Nottingham, 1996; (co-author) Karst and Caves of Great Britain, 1997; (with F. Bell and M. Culshaw) Sinkholes and Subsidence, 2005; The Yorkshire Dales: Landscape and Geology, 2007; Great Caves of the World, 2008. **Address:** 11 Selby Rd., Nottingham, NT NG2 7BP, England. **Online address:** tony@geophotos.co.uk

WALTNER-TOEWS, David. Canadian (born Canada), b. 1948?. **Genres:** Environmental Sciences/Ecology, Novels, Poetry. **Career:** University of Guelph, professor of population medicine. Writer. **Publications:** That Inescapable Animal, 1974; The Earth Is One Body, 1979; Good Housekeeping, 1983; (with J. Janzen and Y. Yaguchi) Three Mennonite Poets: Poetry, 1986; Endangered Species, 1988; Food, Sex, and Salmonella: The Risks of Environmental Intimacy, 1992; The Impossible Uprooting, 1995; The Fat Lady Struck Dumb, 2000; The Complete Tante Tina: Mennonite Blues and Recipes, 2004; Ecosystem Sustainability and Health: A Practical Approach, 2004; One Foot in Heaven, 2006; The Chickens Fight Back: Pandemic Panics and Deadly Diseases That Jump from Animals to Humans, 2007; Fear of Landing (novel), 2007; (ed. with J.J. Kay and N.E. Lister) The Ecosystem Approach:

Complexity, Uncertainty, and Managing for Sustainability, 2008; (with T. Gitau and M.W. Gitau) Integrated Assessment of Health and Sustainability of Agroecosystems, 2009. Works appear in anthologies. **Address:** Kitchener, ON , Canada. **Online address:** dwaltner@ovc.uoguelph.ca

WALTON, David. American (born United States), b. 1942?. **Genres:** Novels, Young Adult Fiction, Novellas/Short Stories. **Career:** Carnegie-Mellon University, teacher; University of Pittsburgh, faculty. Writer. **Publications:** Waiting in Line, 1975; Evening Out, 1983; Ride, 2002. Contributor to periodicals. **Address:** Department of English, University of Pittsburgh, 526 Cathedral of Learning, 4200 5th Ave., Pittsburgh, PA 15260, U.S.A. **Online address:** dwalt@pitt.edu

WALTON, Henry John. British/South African (born South Africa), b. 1924. **Genres:** Education, Medicine/Health, Psychiatry, Psychology, Reference. **Career:** Groote Schuur Hospital, resident physician, 1946-48, head of department of psychiatry, 1957-60; Maudsley Hospital, registrar, 1955-57, senior registrar, 1957; Columbia University, research fellow, 1960-61; University of Edinburgh, senior lecturer, professor of psychiatry, emeritus professor of international medical education and psychiatry, 1962-; Royal Edinburgh Hospital, consultant psychiatrist; Western General Hospital, Department of Psychiatry, consultant; World Federation for Medical Education, president. Writer. **Publications:** (With N. Kessel) Alcoholism, 1965; Know Your Own Mind, 1973, rev. ed., 1989; Small Group Methods in Medical Teaching, 1973; (co-author) Examinations in Medicine, 1976. EDITOR: (with G.F.M. Russell) Training of Psychiatrists, Proceedings of the Conference on Postgraduate Psychiatric Education, 6th-8th March, 1969, Held Under the Auspices of the Royal Medico-Psychological Association and the Association for the Study of Medical Education at the Institute of Psychiatry, 1970; (ed.) Small Group Psychotherapy, 1971; (co-ed.) Innovations in Medical Education, 1978; (co-ed.) Medical Education and Health Care, 1979; (ed.) Dictionary of Psychiatry, 1985; (ed.) Education and Training in Psychiatry: A Case Study in the Continuity of Medical Education, 1986; (co-ed.) Newer Developments in Assessing Clinical Competence, 1986; Proceedings of the World Summit on Medical Education, 1994; Medical Education, 1995. **Address:** University of Edinburgh, Old College, Edinburgh, EH8 9YL, United Kingdom. **Online address:** h.walton@ed.ac.uk

WALTON, James. South African (born South Africa), b. 1911?. **Genres:** Archaeology/Antiquities, Architecture, History, Young Adult Fiction. **Career:** Longman Group, publisher, 1960-, managing director, 1964-72. Writer. **Publications:** Homesteads of the Yorkshire Dales, 1947; Craftwork for African Schools, 1949; Vroeë Plase en Nedersettings in Die Orange Vrystaat, 1955; Early Timbered Buildings of the Huddersfield District, 1955; African Village, 1956; Father of Horses and Father of Kindness, 1958; Old Maseru, 1958; Early Ghoya Settlement in the Orange Free State, 1965; Homesteads and Villages of South Africa, 1952, 1965; Early Ghoya Settlement in the Orange Free State, 1965; Historic Buildings of Lesotho, 1972; Water-Mills, Windmills and Horse-Mills of South Africa, 1974; Cape Dovecots and Fowl-runs, 1985; Old Cape Farmsteads, 1989; South African Sledges, 1991; Portable Corn-Mills in South Africa, 1991; Double-Storeyed, Flat-Roofed Buildings of the Rural Cape, 1993; (contrib.) Cape Cottages, 1995; Beyond the Pale in Malwa, 1998; (with A. Pretorius) Windpumps in South Africa: Where Ever You Go, You See Them, 1998; Whenever You See Them, They Go, 1998; Homesteads and Villages of South Africa, 1999. EDITOR: The Mountain Bushmen of Basutoland, 1957; (with J.R. Wahl) Thomas Pringle in South Africa, 1970; The Josephine Mill and Its Owners: The Story of Milling and Brewing at the Cape of Good Hope, 1978. **Address:** 4 Mountain Rd., Claremont, Cape Town, 7708, South Africa.

WALTON, John (Nicholas). (Walton of Detchant). British (born England), b. 1922. **Genres:** Medicine/Health, Sciences, Autobiography/Memoirs. **Career:** Royal Victoria Infirmary, house physician, 1946-47, medical registrar, 1949-51; University of Durham, research assistant, 1951-56; University of Newcastle upon Tyne, assistant in neurology, 1956-58, professor of neurology, 1968-83, dean of medicine, 1971-81; Oxford University, Green College, warden, 1983-89. Writer. **Publications:** Subarachnoid Haemorrhage, 1956; (with R.D. Adams) Polymyositis, 1958; Essentials of Neurology, 1961, 6th ed., 1989; (ed.) Disorders of Voluntary Muscle, 1964, 6th ed. (with G. Karparti and D. Hilton-Jones), 1994; (ed. with N. Canal and G. Scarlato) Muscle Diseases: Proceedings of an International Congress, 1971; (ed. with W.G. Bradley and D.G. Medwin) Recent Advances in Myology: Proceedings of the Third International Congress on Muscle Diseases, Newcastle Upon Tyne,

15-21 September, 1974, 1975; (ed. with W.R. Brain) Brain's Diseases of the Nervous System, 8th ed., 1977, 10th ed., 1993; Introduction to Clinical Neuroscience, 1983, 2nd ed., 1987; (ed. with T.B. Binns) Medical Education and Manpower in the EEC, 1984; (ed. with P.B. Beeson and R.B. Scott) Oxford Companion to Medicine, 1986; (as Lord Walton of Detchant) (ed. with F.L. Mastaglia and contrib.) Skeletal Muscle Pathology, 1982, 2nd ed., 1992; The Spice of Life (autobiography), 1993; (as Lord Walton of Detchant) (ed. with S. Lock and J.A. Barondess) The Oxford Medical Companion, 1994. **Address:** The Old Piggery, Detchant, Belford, NM NE70 7PF, England. **Online address:** waldetch@aol.com

WALTON, Kendall L(ewis). American (born United States), b. 1939. **Genres:** Art/Art History, Literary Criticism And History, Music, Philosophy, Human Relations/Parenting, History. **Career:** University of Michigan, lecturer, 1965-67, assistant professor, 1967-72, associate professor, 1972-79, professor of philosophy, 1979-, James B. and Grace J. Nelson professor of philosophy, 1996-99, Charles L. Stevenson collegiate professor of philosophy, 1999-, School of Art and Design, professor, 2005-; University of Washington, visiting assistant professor, 1971; University of London, lecturer, 1974; Australian National University, visiting fellow, 1974; Trinity University, Stieren distinguished lecturer in the arts, 1991. Writer. **Publications:** Mimesis as Make-Believe: On the Foundations of the Representational Arts, 1990; Marvelous Images: On Values and the Arts, 2008; In Other Shoes: Music, Metaphor, Empathy, Existence, forthcoming; Aesthetics, forthcoming. Works appear in anthologies. **Address:** Department of Philosophy, University of Michigan, 2215 Angell Hall, 435 S State St., Ann Arbor, MI 48109-1003, U.S.A. **Online address:** klwalton@umich.edu

WALTON, Mary. American (born United States), b. 1941. **Genres:** Administration/Management, inspirational/Motivational Literature, Industrial Relations, Adult Non-fiction, Business/Trade/Industry. **Career:** Charleston Gazette, reporter, 1968-71; Philadelphia Inquirer, staff writer, 1970-80; Inquirer Magazine, reporter, 1972-92. **Publications:** The Deming Management Method, 1986; For Love of Money, 1987; Deming Management at Work: Six Successful Companies That Use the Quality Principles of the World-Famous W. Edwards Deming, 1990; Car: A Drama of the American Workplace, 1997; Woman's Crusade: Alice Paul and the Battle for the Ballot, 2010. Contributor to periodicals. **Address:** c/o Alice Martell, 545 Madison Ave., 7th Fl., New York, NY 10022-4219, U.S.A. **Online address:** marywalton2000@yahoo.com

WALTON, Priscilla L. Canadian/French (born France), b. 1957. **Genres:** Literary Criticism And History, Popular Culture, Women's Studies And Issues. **Career:** McMaster University, teaching assistant, 1985-86, 1989; University of Toronto, teaching assistant, 1986-89; University of Lethbridge, assistant professor, 1989-91; Carleton University, assistant professor, 1991-94, associate professor, 1994-98, professor of English, 1998-, associate faculty in film studies, Centre for Research in Cultural Studies, co-director; Canadian Review of American Studies, editor, Carleton American Studies Research Centre, director. Writer. **Publications:** The Disruption of the Feminine in Henry James, 1992; Patriarchal Desire and Victorian Discourse: A Lacanian Reading of Anthony Trollope's Palliser Novels, 1995; (ed.) Henry James, The Portrait of a Lady, 1995; (with M. Jones) Detective Agency: Women Re-Writing the Hard-Boiled Tradition, 1999; (ed. with L.V. Luven) Pop Can: Popular Culture in Canada, 1999; (with J. Andrews and A.E. Davidson) Border Crossings: Thomas King's Cultural Inversion, 2003; Our Cannibals, Ourselves, 2004. Contributor to books to journals. **Address:** Department of English, Carleton University, 1125 Colonel By Dr., Ottawa, ON K1S 5B6, Canada. **Online address:** percy_walton@carleton.ca

WALTON, Richard J(ohn). American (born United States), b. 1928. **Genres:** Children's Non-fiction, History, International Relations/Current Affairs, Politics/Government, Social Sciences. **Career:** WICE Radio Station, news editor and chief announcer, 1952-53; Providence Journal, reporter, 1954-55; New York World Telegram and The Sun, reporter, feature writer, columnist, assistant city editor, makeup editor, 1955-59; Western Connecticut State College, lecturer in international relations, political science and creative writing, 1968-73; New School for Social Research, lecturer in international relations, 1969-71; Rhode Island College, adjunct faculty, 1985-. **Publications:** The Remnants of Power: The Tragic Last Years of Adlai Stevenson, 1968; America and the Cold War, 1969; Beyond Diplomacy: A Background Book On American Military Intervention, 1970; Cold War and Counter Revolution: The Foreign Policy of John F. Kennedy, 1972; The United States and

Latin America, 1972; Canada and the U.S.A.: A Background Book About Internal Conflict and The New Nationalism, 1972; Congress and American Foreign Policy: A Background Book on the Presidential-Congressional Struggle, 1972; The United States and the Far East, 1974; Henry Wallace, Harry Truman and the Cold War, 1976; The Power of Oil: Economic, Social, Political, 1977; Swarthmore College: An Informal History, 1986; (with H.A.L. Brown) John Brown's Tract: Lost Adirondack Empire, 1988. Contributor to newspapers. **Address:** 5 Grenore St., Warwick, RI 02888, U.S.A. **Online address:** richard@richardjwalton.org

WALTON, Rick. American (born United States), b. 1957. **Genres:** Children's Fiction, Humor/Satire, Mystery/Crime/Suspense, Picture/Board Books. **Career:** Provo Cultural Affairs Board, resource assistant, 1981-86; freelance writer, 1982-; Provo Parks and Recreation Department, projects coordinator, 1983-84; WICAT Systems, Education Division, editor, 1984-85; Bacchus Elementary, Granite School District, teacher, 1987-88; Waterford School, teacher, 1988-89; International Business Machines Corp. (IBM), software designer and creative writer, 1989-90; freelance software designer, 1994-. **Publications:** MAKE ME LAUGH RIDDLE BOOK SERIES WITH A. WALTON: (ed. with F. Oviatt) Stories for Mormons, 1983; Dumb Clucks! Jokes about Chickens, 1987; Something's Fishy! Jokes about Sea Creatures, 1987; What's Your Name, Again? More Jokes about Names, 1988; Kiss a Frog! Jokes about Fairy Tales, Knights, and Dragons, 1989; Can You Match This? Jokes about Unlikely Pairs, 1989; What a Ham! Jokes about Pigs, 1989; Fossil Follies! Jokes about Dinosaurs, 1989; Clowning Around! Jokes about the Circus, 1989. YOU MUST BE JOKING RIDDLE BOOK SERIES WITH A. WALTON: Weather or Not: Riddles for Rain or Shine, 1990; On with the Show: Show Me Riddles, 1990; I Toad You So: Riddles about Frogs and Toads, 1991; Ho-Ho-Ho!: Riddles about Santa Claus, 1991; Alphabatty: Riddles about the Alphabet, 1991; Off Base: Riddles about Baseball, 1993; Hoop-La: Riddles about Basketball, 1993; Take a Hike: Riddles about Football, 1993; (comp.) Quacking Up!: Wacky Jokes for Feathered Folks, 2004; (co-author) The Sky's the Limit: Naturally Funny Jokes, 2005; Real Classy: Silly School Jokes, 2005. OTHER RIDDLE BOOKS: Riddle-Day Saints, 1994; Wholly Cowboy: Cowboy, Cow, and Horse Riddles, 1995; Dino-Might: Pre-hysterical Dinosaur Riddles, 1995; The Ghost Is Clear: Riddles about Ghosts, Goblins, Vampires, Witches and Other Creatures That Cause Shivers in the Night, 1995; Astro-Nuts! Riddles about Astronauts and the Planets They Love, 1995; Really Really Bad School Jokes!, 1998; Really Really Bad Summer Jokes, 1999. PICTURE BOOKS: Will You Still Love Me?, 1992; How Many How Many How Many, 1993; Noah's Square Dance, 1995; Once There Was a Bull...(frog), 1995, rev. ed. as Once There was a Bull...(frog): An Adventure in Compound Words, 2011; You Don't Always Get What You Hope For, 1996; (comp.) A Funny Thing Happened on the Way to Zion, 1996; One was Named Abel, He Slept on the Table, 1996; Pig, Pigger, Piggest, 1997, rev. ed. as Pig, Pigger, Piggest: An Adventure in Comparing, 2011; Dance, Pioneer, Dance!, 1997; So Many Bunnies: A Bed Time abc and Counting Book, 1998; Why the Banana Split, 1998, rev. ed. as Why the Banana Split: An Adventure in Idioms, 2011; Bullfrog Pops, 1999, rev. ed. as Bullfrog Pops!: An Adventure in Verbs and Direct Objects, 2011; Little Dogs Say Rough!, 2000; How Many?, 2000; My Two Hands/My Two Feet, 2000; One More Bunny: Adding from One to Ten, 2000; That's What You Get, 2000; That's My Dog!, 2001; The Bear Came Over to My House, 2001; How Can You Dance?, 2001; Bertie Was a Watchdog, 2002; Herd of Cows, Flock of Sheep! Quiet! I'm Tired! I Need My Sleep!, 2002, rev. ed. as Herd of Cows, Flock of Sheep: An Adventure in Collective Nouns, 2011; Bunny Day: Telling Time From Breakfast to Bedtime, 2002; (with A. Walton) Cars at Play, 2002; Bunnies On The Go: Getting from Place to Place, 2003; Bunny Christmas: A Family Celebration, 2004; Cinderella CTR, 2005; Bunny School: A Learning Fun-For-All, 2005; Around the House, the Fox Chased the Mouse, 2006, rev. ed., 2011; Just Me and 6, 000 Rats: A Tale of Conjunctions, 2007, rev. ed. as Just Me and 6, 000 Rats: An Adventure in Conjunctions, 2011; What Do We Do with the Baby?, 2008. OTHERS: What to Do When a Bug Climbs in Your Mouth and Other Poems to Drive You Buggy (poetry), 1995; Mrs. McMurphy's Pumpkin, 2004; Suddenly, Alligator!: An Adverbial Tale, 2004, rev. ed. as Suddenly Alligator: An Adventure in Adverbs, 2011; A Very Hairy Scary Story, 2004; Foul Play: Sports Jokes that Won't Strike Out, 2005; Magical Mischief: Jokes that Shock and Amaze, 2005; Around the House, the Fox Chased the Mouse: A Prepositional Tale, 2006; The Remarkable Friendship of Mr. Cat and Mr. Rat, 2006; Just Me and 6, 000 Rats: A Tale of Conjunctions, 2007; What Do We Do with the Bunny?, 2008; What Do We Do with the Baby?, 2008; Mr. President Goes to School, 2010; Baby's First Year, 2010; (with M. Gollaher) Where are Zebra's Stripes?: Little Tracker,

2011; (ed.) Much Ado about Mormons, 2011; Help! Giraffe!, 2011; (contrib.) Frankenstein, 2012. MYSTERIES: The African Mystery, 2002; The Candy Thieves Mystery, 2002; The Case of the Missing Heart, 2003; The Mystery of the Stolen Statue, 2003; The Case of a Very Secret Admirer, 2004; Is the Governor Calling?, 2004; Mini Mysteries: 20 Tricky Tales to Untangle, 2004; The Pine Street Girls Glub Mystery, 2004; Mini Mysteries 2: 20 More Tricky Tales to Untangle, 2006; Mini Mysteries 3: 20 More Tricky Tales to Untangle, 2007. ACTIVITY BOOKS AND GAMES: The Big Book of Scripture Activities, 1996; The Treasure Hunt Book, 2000; Friends Forever, 2001; Take a Hike 2002; Brain Waves, 2002; Coconut Puzzle Book, 2003; Puzzle Crazy, 2005; (with J. Adams) Packing Up a Picnic: Activities and Recipes for Kids, 2006. Contributor to magazines. **Address:** c/o Kendra Marcus, BookStop Literary Agency, 67 Meadow View Rd., Orinda, UT 94563-3246, U.S.A. **Online address:** rick@rickwalton.com

WALTON OF DETCHANT See **Walton, John (Nicholas).**

WALTZ, Kenneth N. American (born United States), b. 1924. **Genres:** International Relations/Current Affairs, Military/Defense/Arms Control, Politics/Government, Social Sciences, History. **Career:** Oberlin College, faculty, 1950-53; Columbia University, lecturer, 1953-56, assistant professor, 1956-57, Saltzman Institute of War and Peace Studies, adjunct professor, 1997-, research associate; Swarthmore College, associate professor, 1957-64, professor, 1964-66; Harvard University, Center for International Affairs, research associate, 1963-64, 1968-69, 1972, Guggenheim fellow, 1976; Brandeis University, professor, 1966-71, Adlai Stevenson professor of international politics, 1967-71; University of California, Ford professor of political science and comparative studies, 1971-94, retired, 1994, professor emeritus, 1994-; American Academy of Arts and Sciences, fellow, 1980; Kings College, senior research associate, 1986-87; Man, the Association, president, 1987-88. Writer and consultant. **Publications:** Man, The State and War: A Theoretical Analysis, 1959; Foreign Policy and Democratic Politics: The American and British Experience, 1967; (ed. with C.F. Hermann) Basic Courses in Foreign Policy; an Anthology of Syllabi, 1970; (ed. with S. Speigel) Conflict in World Politics, 1971; (ed. with R.J. Art) The Use of Force, International Politics and Foreign Policy, 1971, 7th ed., 2009; Theory of International Politics, 1979; The Spread of Nuclear Weapons: More May be Better, 1981; (with R.J. Art) Use of Force: Military Power and International Politics, 1988, 7th ed., 2009; (with S.D. Sagan) The Spread of Nuclear Weapons: A Debate, 1995, 2nd ed. as The Spread of Nuclear Weapons: A Debate Renewed, 2003; Realism and International Politics, 2008. **Address:** Department of Political Science, Columbia University, 1338 IAB, 420 W 118th St., PO Box 3347, New York, NY 10027, U.S.A. **Online address:** knw6@columbia.edu

WALTZER, Jim. American (born United States), b. 1950?. **Genres:** Novels, Adult Non-fiction. **Career:** Writer. **Publications:** (With T. Wilk) Tales of South Jersey: Profiles and Personalities, 2001; (with R. Kennedy, Jr.) Monopoly: The Story behind the World's Best-Selling Game, 2004; Sound of Mind, 2007; The Battle of the Century: Dempsey, Carpentier, and the Birth of Modern Promotion, 2011. Contributor to periodicals. **Address:** Five Star Publishing, 295 Kennedy Memorial Dr., Waterville, ME 04901, U.S.A. **Online address:** jmwaltzer@verizon.net

WALVIN, James. British (born England), b. 1942. **Genres:** History, Race Relations, Sports/Fitness, Social Sciences. **Career:** University of York, faculty to provost, now professor emeritus of history. Writer. **Publications:** (With M. Craton) A Jamaica Plantation: Worthy Park 1670-1870, 1970; (with M. Craton) Jamaican Plantation: The History of Worthy Park, 1670-1970, 1970; The Black Presence: A Documentary History of the Negro in England, 1555-1860, 1971; Black and White: The Negro and English Society, 1555-1945, 1973; The People's Game: A Social History of British Football, 1975; (with M. Craton and D. Wright) Slavery, Abolition, and Emancipation: Black Slaves and the British Empire: A Thematic Documentary, 1976; Beside the Seaside: A Social History of the Popular Seaside Holiday, 1978; Leisure and Society, 1830-1950, 1978; (ed. with D. Eltis) Abolition of the Atlantic Slave Trade: Origins and Effects in Europe, Africa, and the Americas, 1981; A Child's World: A Social History of English Childhood, 1800-1914, 1982; (ed.) Slavery and British Society, 1776-1846, 1982; (with E. Royle) English Radicals and Reformers, 1776-1848, 1982; Slavery and the Slave Trade: An Short Illustrated History, 1983; Black Personalities: Africans in Britain in the Era of Slavery, 1983; (ed. with J. Walton) Leisure in Britain, 1780-1939, 1983; Passage to Britain: Immigration in History and Politics, 1984; English Urban Life, 1776-1851, 1984; Urban England 1776-1851, 1984; (ed. with C.

Emsley) Artisans, Peasants, and Proletarians, 1760-1860: Essays presented to Gwyn A. Williams, 1985; Football and the Decline of Britain, 1986; England, Slaves, and Freedom, 1776-1838, 1986; (ed. with J.A. Mangan) Manliness and Morality: Middle-Class Masculinity in Britain and America, 1800-1940, 1987; Victorian Values, 1988; Black Ivory: A History of British Slavery, 1992, 2nd ed., 2001; Slaves and Slavery: The British Colonial Experience, 1992; The People's Game: The History of Football Revisited, 1994; The Life and Times of Henry Clarke of Jamaica, 1828-1907, 1994; Questioning Slavery, 1996; Fruits of Empire: Exotic Produce and British Taste, 1660-1800, 1997; The Quakers: Money and Morals, 1997; An African's Life: The Life and Times of Olaudah Equiano, 1745-1797, 1998; The Slave Trade, 1999; Britain's Slave Empire, 2000; Making the Black Atlantic: Britain and the African Diaspora, 2000; The Only Game, 2002; (ed. with J. Walvin) Slavery Reader, 2003; Atlas of Slavery, 2006; The Trader, the Owner, the Slave: Parallel in the Age of Slavery, 2007; A Short History of Slavery, 2007; Slavery to Freedom, 2007; Zong Slave Ship, 2008; The Slave Ship Zong, 2011; The Slave Trade, 2011; Zong: A Massacre, the Law and the End of Slavery, 2011. **Address:** Department of History, University of York, Heslington, York, NY YO10 5DD, England. **Online address:** jw26@york.ac.uk

WALWICZ, Ania. Australian/Polish (born Poland), b. 1951. **Genres:** Plays/Screenplays, Poetry, Songs/Lyrics And Libretti. **Career:** Experimental Arts Foundation, artist and writer-in-residence, 1986; Deakin University, writer-in-residence, 1987; University of Western Australia, writer-in-residence, 1988; Victorian College of the Arts, writer-in-residence; Melbourne University School of Creative Arts, writer-in-residence; Victorian Writers' Centre, writer-in-residence; Murdoch University, faculty; Royal Melbourne Institute of Technology University, lecturer. **Publications:** POETRY: Writing, 1982 as Travel/Writing, 1989; Boat, 1989; Red Roses (poetry), 1992; Palace of Culture, forthcoming. Works appear in anthologies. **Address:** Royal Melbourne Institute of Technology University, Rm. 6, Bldg. 94, Level 2, 124 La Trobe St., PO Box 2476, Melbourne, VI 3000, Australia. **Online address:** ania.walwicz@rmit.edu.au

WALZER, Michael. (Michael Laban Walzer). American (born United States), b. 1935. **Genres:** Philosophy, Politics/Government, Social Commentary. **Career:** Princeton University, assistant professor of politics, 1962-66; Harvard University, professor of government, 1966-80; Dissent, editor, 1976-; The New Republic, contributor editor, 1977-; Institute for Advanced Study, professor of social science, 1980-86, UPS Foundation, professor 1986-2007, professor emeritus, 2007-, fellow, 2010-. **Publications:** Cuba, The Invasion and the Consequences, 1961; The Revolution of the Saints: A Study in the Origins of Radical Politics, 1965; Obligations: Essays on Disobedience, War and Citizenship, 1970; Political Action, 1971; Regicide and Revolution, 1974; Just and Unjust Wars: A Moral Argument with Historical Illustrations, 1977, 4th ed., 2008; Radical Principles: Reflections of an Unreconstructed Democrat, 1980; (co-author) Politics of Ethnicity, 1982; Spheres of Justice, 1983; Exodus and Revolution, 1985; Interpretation and Social Criticism, 1987; The Company of Critics, 1988; What It Means to Be an American, 1992; Thick and Thin: Moral Argument at Home and Abroad, 1994; On Toleration, 1997; Politics and Passion: Toward a More Egalitarian Liberalism, 2004; Arguing About War, 2004; Thinking Politically: Essays in Political Theory, 2007. EDITOR: (with P. Green) The Political Imagination in Literature, 1969; Toward a Global Civil Society, 1995; (with D. Miller) Pluralism, Justice, and Equality, 1995; (co-ed.) The Jewish Political Tradition, vol. I: Authority, 2000, vol. II: Membership, 2003; Exilpolitik in der Hebräischen Bibel, 2001; (with N. Mills) 50 Years of Dissent, 2004; (intro.) Law, Politics and Morality in Judaism, 2006; (with N. Mills) Getting Out: Historical Perspectives on Leaving Iraq, 2009. **Address:** School of Social Science, Institute for Advanced Study, Einstein Dr., Princeton, NJ 08540, U.S.A. **Online address:** walzer@ias.edu

WALZER, Michael Laban. See **WALZER, Michael.**

WAMBAUGH, Joseph. American (born United States), b. 1937. **Genres:** Novels, Mystery/Crime/Suspense, Young Adult Non-fiction, Children's Nonfiction, Literary Criticism And History, Criminology/True Crime, Young Adult Fiction, Adult Non-fiction. **Career:** Los Angeles Police Department, patrolman, detective sergeant, 1960-74; writer, 1971-; National Broadcasting Co. (NBC-TV), creator and consultant, 1973-77; Columbia Broadcasting Co. (CBS-TV), creator and consultant, 1975-76. **Publications:** NOVELS: The New Centurions, 1971; The Blue Knight, 1972; The Choirboys, 1975; The Black Marble, 1978; The Glitter Dome, 1981; The Delta Star, 1983; The Secrets of Harry Bright, 1985; The Golden Orange, 1990; Fugitive Nights,

1992; Finnegan's Week, 1993; Floaters, 1996; Hollywood Station, 2006; Hollywood Crows, 2008; Hollywood Moon, 2009; Hollywood Hills, 2010. NONFICTION: The Onion Field, 1973; Lines and Shadows, 1984; Echoes in the Darkness, 1987; The Blooding, 1989; Fire Lover, 2002. Contributor to periodicals. **Address:** 3520 Kellogg Way, San Diego, CA 92106-3346, U.S.A.

WANDEL, Lee Palmer. American (born United States), b. 1954. **Genres:** History, Theology/Religion, Cultural/Ethnic Topics. **Career:** Stanford University, lecturer, 1985-87; Yale University, assistant professor, 1987-92, associate professor, 1992-97; Princeton University, Institute for Advanced Study, faculty, 1997-98; University of Wisconsin, assistant professor, 1998-99, associate professor, 1999-2001, professor of history, 2001-. Writer. **Publications:** Always Among Us: Images of the Poor in Zwingli's Zurich, 1990; Voracious Idols and Violent Hands: Iconoclasm in Reformation Zurich, Strasbourg, and Basel, 1995; (ed. with M.G.M. Curnen and H.M. Spiro) Facing Death: Where Culture, Religion, and Medicine Meet, 1996; (ed.) History has Many Voices, 2003; (with R.W. Winks) Europe in a Wider World, 1350-1650, 2003; The Eucharist in the Reformation: Incarnation and Liturgy, 2006. Contributor of articles to periodicals. **Address:** Department of History, University of Wisconsin, 3211 Mosse Humanities Bldg., 455 N Park St., Madison, WI 53706-1483, U.S.A. **Online address:** lpwandel@wisc.edu

WANDOR, Michelene. British (born England), b. 1940. **Genres:** Novels, Novellas/Short Stories, Plays/Screenplays, Poetry, Songs/Lyrics And Libretti, Literary Criticism And History, Music, Sex, Theatre, Women's Studies And Issues, Writing/Journalism. **Career:** Time Out, poetry editor and general arts reviewer, 1971-82; University of Kent, resident writer, 1982-83, senior lecturer in creative writing; Royal Literary Fund fellow, 2004-05; London Metropolitan University, Guildhall School of Music and Drama, faculty; Lancaster University, lecturer in creative writing. **Publications:** PLAYS: (with D. Brooke) Sink Songs, 1975; Wanted, 1988. FICTION: (co-author) Tales and More Tales I Tell My Mother, 2 vols., 1978-87; Guests in the Body, 1986; (with S. Maitland) Arky Types, 1987; False Relations, 2004. POETRY: Upbeat, 1982; (co-author) Touch Papers, 1982; Gardens of Eden, 1984; Collected Poems, 1990; Gardens of Eden Revisited, 1999. EDITOR: The Body Politic, 1972; (with M. Roberts) Cutlasses and Earrings, 1977; Strike While the Iron Is Hot, 1980; (and intro.) Plays by Women 1-4, 4 vols., 1982-85; On Gender and Writing, 1983; Wandor on Women Writers, 1989. OTHER: (co-author) The Great Divide, 1976; Understudies: Theatre and Sexual Politics, 1981, rev. ed. as Carry On, Understudies, 1986; Look Back in Gender, 1987; Wandor on Women Writers, 1989; Once a Feminist, 1990; Drama Today, 1993; Post-war British Drama: Looking Back in Gender, 2001; Music of the Prophets: The Resettlement of the Jews in England, 1655-56, 2006; Musica transalpina: Poetry Short, Narrative and Musical, 2006; Author is not Dead, Merely Somewhere Else: Creative Writing Reconceived, 2008; Fluviatile, 2010. **Address:** 71 Belsize Ln., London, GL NW3 5AU, England. **Online address:** mwandor@googlemail.com

WANG, Anyi. Chinese (born China), b. 1954. **Genres:** Novels, Novellas/Short Stories. **Career:** Shanghai Writers Association, chairwomen, 2001; Fudan University, professor of Chinese literature. Writer. **Publications:** Yu, sha sha sha, 1981; Wang Anyi zhong duan pian xiao shuo ji, 1983; Hei hie bai bai, 1983; Wei sheng, 1983; Yang qi li xiang di feng fan, 1983; Liu shi, 1983; 69 jie chuzhong sheng, 1984; Mu nütong you Meilijian, 1986; XiaoBao zhuang, 1986; Huanghe gudao ren, 1986; Mu nü man you Meilijian, 1986; Huang shan zhi lian (novel), 1986; Xiaocheng zhi lian (novel), 1986; Jinxiugu zhi lian (novel), 1987; Liushui sanshi zhang, 1988; Pu gong ying, 1988; Love In A Small Town, 1988; Pugong ying, 1989; Hai shang fanhua meng, 1989; Lü De di gushi, 1990; Shushu di gushi, 1990; Shen sheng ji tan, 1991; Mi Ni (short stories), 1991, as Mi Ni: zhang pain xiao shuo jiuan, 1996; Zhu lu zhong jie, 1992; Brocade Valley, 1992; (with Zhang Xinxin) Nan nan nü nü, 1992; Zhi qiung xioa shuo: cuo tuo sui yueyong tan diao, 1992; Ji shi he xu gou: Chuang zaoshi jie fang fa zhi yizhong, 1993; Wu tuo bang shi pian, 1993; Bian zou: Nu xing yi duan wenxue, 1993; (co-author) Fu xi he mu xi di shin hua, 1994; Xianggang deqing yu ai, 1994; Mei gui zhi men, 1995; Shangxin Taipingyang, 1995; Ziwu, 1995; Wang Anyi, 1995; Cheng huo che lü xing, 1995; Chang hen ge, 1996; Piao po de yu yan: san wen juan, 1996; Hai shang fan hua meng: zhongpian xiao shuo juan (short stories), 1996; Xiao cheng zhi lian: zhong pianxiao shuo juan (short stories), 1996; Xianggang de qing yu ai: zhong pianxiao shuo juan (short stories), 1996; Jishi yu xugou: Shanghaide gu shi (title means: Reality and Fiction: A Shanghai Story), 1996; Qingjie/Quin jie, 1996; Ren shi di chen fu, 1996; Zi mie men: Wang Anyi zhongduan pian xiao shuo zi xuan ji (short stories), 1996; Chenghen ge: changpian xiao

shuo juan, 1996; Wang Anyi zi xuan ji, 1996; Chong jian xiang ya ta, 1997; Wang Anyi xuan jin ren san wen, 1997; Xin ling shi jie: Wang Anyi xiaoshui jiang gao, 1997; Yi ge gu shi di san zhong jiang fa, 1997; Du yu, 1998; Chu nü dan, 1998; You shang de nian dai, 1998; Jie jin shi jichu: Wang Anyi san wen xin zuo, 1998; Fu Ping, 1998; Wo ai Bi'er, 1998; Yin ju di shi dai, 1999; Wang Anyi xiao shuo xuan, 1999; Nü ren er shi, 2000; Qing zhi shang, 2000; Mei tou, 2000; Gang shang de shi ji, 2000; Nan ren he nü ren nüren he cheng shi, 2000; Ti du, 2000; Mini, 2000; Ge xing Riben lai, 2000; San lian/Shan lian, 2001; Wen gong tuan: Wang Anyi xiao shuo (short stories), 2001; Fuping, 2001; Shang xin Taiping yang, 2001; Di xiong men, 2001; Xun zhao Shanghai, 2001; Wo du wo kan, 2001; Shang zhong hong lingxia zhong ou, 2002; Jiu tu, 2003; Ge Lou, 2003; Wang Anyi shuo/Wang Anyi talks, 2003; Xian shuo Zhongguo ren. Xu, 2003; Shanghai jie qing hua, 2003; Wang Anyi zhong pian xiao shuo xuan, 2004; (with J. Xiaoyan) Du zhi zui bi jiao yan jiu, 2004; Tao Zhi Yao Yao, 2004; Dao xiang lou: Wang an yi duan pian xiaoshuo dai biao zuo, 2005; Bei tong zhi di, 2006; Ru Zhijuan ri ji, 1947-1965, 2006; Qi meng shi dai, 2007; The Song of Everlasting Sorrow: A Novel of Shanghai, 2008; Yue se liao ren, 2008; (with Z. Xudong) Dui hua Qi meng shi dai, 2008; Wang Anyi duan pian xiao shuo bian nian, 2009; Shui shi weilat de zhongdui-zhang. Contributor to magazines. **Address:** c/o Author Mail, New Directions, 80 8th Ave., New York, NY 10011, U.S.A.

WANG, Dong. American (born United States), b. 1967. **Genres:** Novels. **Career:** Gordon College, professor of Chinese history and executive director of the east-west institute of international studies, 2002-09; Harvard University, research associate; University of Turku, professor of contemporary chinese history, Centre for East Asian Studies, director. Writer. **Publications:** China's Unequal Treaties: Narrating National History, 2005; Managing God's Higher Learning: US-China Cultural Encounter and Canton Christian College (Lingnan University), 1888-1952, 2007. **Address:** East-West Institute of International Studies, Gordon College, Wenham, MA 01984, U.S.A. **Online address:** dong.wang@gordon.edu

WANG, Jen. American (born United States), b. 1984. **Genres:** Mystery/Crime/Suspense. **Career:** Writer and artist. **Publications:** (With D. Roman) Agnes Quill: An Anthology of Mystery, 2007; Koko Be Good, 2010. **Address:** Los Angeles, CA , U.S.A. **Online address:** jwiggy@gmail.com

WANG, Jing. American/Taiwanese (born Taiwan), b. 1950. **Genres:** Literary Criticism And History. **Career:** Middlebury College, instructor, 1982-85; Duke University, assistant professor, 1985-92, Institutional Enchancement for Chinese Studies, principal investigator, 1999-2001, associate professor, 1992-2000, professor, 2000-01, Department of Asian and African Languages and Literature, director, 1993-96, chair, 1999-, Center for East Asian Cultural and Institutional Studies, director, 2000-01, Trinity College of Arts and Sciences, Bass chair, Susan B. King professor of Chinese literature, 2001; Princeton University, lecturer; Smith College, lecturer; McGill University, lecturer; Mount Holyoke College, Asian Studies Program, assistant professor, 1990-, associate professor of Asian studies; Massachusetts Institute of Technology, S.C. Fang professor of Chinese language and culture, professor of Chinese cultural studies, 2001-, Department of Comparative Media Studies, affiliated faculty, 2001-, Research Lab of Global Media and Culture, co-director, 2001, Department of Foreign Languages and Literatures, head, 2005-08, New Media Action Lab, director, 2009-; Chinese University of Science and Technology of China, Institute of Knowledge Management, visiting professor, 2009-12. Writer, consultant and researcher. **Publications:** The Story of Stone: Intertextuality, Ancient Chinese Stone Lore and the Stone Symbolism in Dream of the Red Chamber, Water Margin and The Journey to the West, 1992; High Culture Fever: Politics, Aesthetics and Ideology in Deng's China, 1996; Brand New China: Advertising, Media and Commercial Culture, 2008. EDITOR: (with Y. Wu) Perspectives on Contemporary Education in China, 1989; China's Avant-Garde Fiction: An Anthology, 1998; (with T. Barlow) Cinema and Desire: Feminist Marxism and Cultural Politics in the Work of Dai Jinhua, 1999; Locating China: Space, Place and Popular Culture, 2005. **Address:** Department of Asian Studies, Mount Holyoke College, Rm. 128, Ciruti Ctr., 50 College St., South Hadley, MA 01075, U.S.A. **Online address:** Yingwang@mtholyoke.edu

WANG, Lihua. American (born United States), b. 1947. **Genres:** Medicine/Health. **Career:** Oregon College of Oriental Medicine, teacher and supervisor of clinic, 1988-92; China Acupuncture Herb Center, acupuncturist, 1992. Writer. **Publications:** Chinese Home Remedies: Harnessing Ancient Wisdom for Self-Healing, 2005. **Address:** 14115 SE Division St., Portland, OR 97236, U.S.A. **Online address:** tom007star@yahoo.com

WANG, Sen. Canadian/Chinese (born China), b. 1959?. **Genres:** Agriculture/Forestry, Homes/Gardens, Natural History. **Career:** Chinese Ministry of Forestry, program officer, 1982-91, resource valuation, specialist; University of British Columbia, researcher, 1992-97; Canadian Forest Service, forest economist, 1997-, resource valuation specialist. Writer. **Publications:** (With G.C. Van Kooten) Forestry and the New Institutional Economics: An Application of Contract Theory to Forest Silvicultural Investment, 2001. Contributor to journals. **Address:** National Capital Region, Policy, Economics and Industry Branch, Canadian Forest Service, 580 Booth St., Ottawa, ON K1A 0E4, Canada. **Online address:** sen.wang@nrcan-rncan.gc.ca

WANG, Shuo. Chinese (born China), b. 1958. **Genres:** Plays/Screenplays, Novels, Novellas/Short Stories, Translations. **Career:** Novelist, playwright, short story writer and filmmaker. **Publications:** An Attitude (novella), 1989; Wang Shuo xie qu xiao shuo xuan, 1990; (co-author) Sao dong nian hua, 1991; Wo shi ni ba ba, 1992; (co-author) Bian ji bu di gu shi, 1992; Guo ba yin jiu si, 1992; Hai ma ge wu ting: si shi ji dian shi xi lie ju, 1993; Qing chun wu hui: Wang Shuo ying shi zuo pin ji, 1993; Dong wu xiong meng, 1994; Wan ti chiu shish hsin t'iao (novel), 1997; Kan shang qu hen mei, 1999; (with L. Zhu) Mei ren zeng wo meng han yao: Mei ren zeng wo meng han yao, 2000; Yin yue he zi: yin yue zai Zhongguo, 2001; Wen xue yang tai: wen xue zai Zhongguo, 2001; Mei shu hou chuang: Mei shu zai Zhongguo, 2001; Dian ying chu fang: Dian ying zai Zhongguo, 2001; Shi zuo jia pi pan shu, er, 2004; Wan zhu, 2005; Wo de qian sui han, 2007; Zhi nüer shu, 2007; He women de nüer tanhua, 2008. **Address:** William Morrow and Company Inc., 1350 Ave. of the Americas, New York, NY 10019-4702, U.S.A.

WANG, Wallace E. (Wally Wang). American (born United States), b. 1961. **Genres:** Information Science/Computers. **Career:** General Dynamics, technical writer, 1983-85; ComputorEdge (magazine), editor and writer, 1985-87; University of Zimbabwe, visiting professor of computer science, 1989; Top Bananas Entertainment, co-founder. Comedian. **Publications:** (With J. Mueller) Illustrated Ready, Set, Go! 4.5, 1989; (as Wally Wang with J. Mueller) Illustrated VP-Expert, 1989; The Best Free Time-Saving Utilities for the PC, 1989; (with S. Millard) Simple Computer Maintenance and Repair, 1990; 101 Computer Business Ideas, 1990; (as Wally Wang with J. Mueller) Illustrated Microsoft Word 5.0, 1990; (with J. Mueller) Illustrated PFS: First Publisher, 1990, 2nd. ed. as Illustrated PFS: First Publisher: For Versions 2.0 and 3.0, 1991; (with J. Mueller) Microsoft Macro Assembler 5.1: Programming in the 80386 Environment, 1990; (with J.Kraynak) The First Book of Personal Computing, 1990, 4th ed., 1993; (with J. Mueller) The Ultimate DOS Programmer's Manual, 1991; (as Wally Wang with K. Bibb) Illustrated Turbo C Plus Plus, 1991; (as Wally Wang) Software Buying Secrets, second edition, 1991; (as Wally Wang with D. Gookin and C. Van Buren) Illustrated Computer Dictionary for Dummies, 1993, 2nd ed., 1995; (as Wally Wang) Learn Quicken in a Day, 1993; Build Your Own Green PC, 1994; (as Wally Wang) CompuServe for Dummies, 1994, 3rd ed., 1996; More Word Perfect 6 for DOS for Dummies, 1994; ProComm Plus 2 for Windows for Dummies, 1994; Visual Basic 3 for Dummies, 1994; (with J.P. Mueller) OLE for Dummies, 1995; Visual Basic 4 for Windows for Dummies, 1995; (with J. Mueller) Dummies 101. Visual Basic Programming, 1996; More Visual Basic 4 for Windows for Dummies, 1996; (with R.C. Parker) Microsoft Office 97 for Windows for Dummies, 1996; More Microsoft Office for Windows 95 for Dummies, 1996; More Visual Basic 4 for Windows for Dummies, 1996; Surfing the Microsoft Network, 1996; (with J. Mueller) Dummies 101: Visual Basic 5 Programming, 1997; More Microsoft Office 97 for Windows for Dummies, 1997; Visual Basic 5 for Windows for Dummies, 1997; More Visual Basic 5 for Windows for Dummies, 1997; (as Wally Wang) Steal This Computer Book, 1998, 3rd ed. as Steal this Computer Book 3: What They Won't Tell You about the Internet, 2003; Visual Basic 6 for Dummies, 1998; Visual Basic 6 for Dummies Deluxe Compiler Kit, 1999; Beginning Programming for Dummies, 1999, 4th ed., 2007; (with R.C. Parker) Microsoft Office 2000 for Windows for Dummies, 1999; More Microsoft Office 2000 for Windows for Dummies, 1999; (with R. Hing) Print Shop Deluxe for Dummies, 2000; Office XP for Dummies, 2001; Web Cams for Dummies, 2001; (with L. Garrison) Breaking into Acting for Dummies, 2002; Visual Basic .NET for Dummies, 2002; (as Wally Wang) Totally Tasteless Photoshop Elements, 2003; Office 2003 for Dummies, 2003; Start! The No Nonsense Guide to Windows XP (Consumer), 2003; Totally Tasteless Photoshop Elements, 2003; (with W. Pollock) The Book of Nero 6, 2004; Steal this File Sharing Book, 2004; Vi-

sual Basic 2005 Express: Now Playing, 2006; Steal this Computer Book 4.0: What They Won't Tell You about the Internet, 2006; Book of Nero 7: CD and DVD Burning Made Easy, 2006; The Book of Nero 7, 2006; Office 2007 for Dummies, 2007; My New Mac: 52 Simple Projects to Get You Started, 2008; (with J.B. Fisher and G.A. Fisher) Strategic Entrepreneurism: Shattering the Start-Up Entrepreneurial Myths, 2008; Macs all-in-one Desk Reference for Dummies, 2008; My New iPhone, 2009; Office 2010 for Dummies, 2010; My New Ipad, 2010, 2nd ed., 2011; Mac Programming for Absolute Beginners, 2011; (with A. Rathbone) Windows 7 & Office 2010 for Dummies, 2011. **Address:** c/o Author Mail, No Starch Press, 38 Ringold St., San Francisco, CA 94103, U.S.A. **Online address:** bothecat@cox.net

WANG, Wally. *See* **WANG, Wallace E.**

WANG, XiaoHu. Chinese/American (born United States), b. 1962. **Genres:** Public/Social Administration, Economics, Business/Trade/Industry. **Career:** Renmin University of China, assistant professor of public finance, 1987-91; United States Agency for International Development, Local Governance Project, budget analyst, 1993-94; Town of Davie, budget analyst, 1993-94; Florida International University, School of Policy and Management, instructor, 1995-97, Florida Institute of Government, research associate, 1995-97; University of Central Florida, assistant professor, 1997-2003, associate professor of public administration, 2003-09, professor of public administration, 2009-11; City University of Hong Kong, Department of Public and Social Administration, professor, 2011-. Writer. **Publications:** Financial Management in the Public Sector: Tools, Applications, and Cases, 2006, 2nd ed., 2010; Performance Analysis for Public and Nonprofit Organizations, 2010; (with E.M. Berman) Essential Statistics for Public Managers and Policy Analysts, 2012. Contributor to periodicals. **Address:** Department of Public and Social Administration, City University of Hong Kong, Rm. AC1-Y7519, Academic Bldg., 83 Tat Chee Ave., Kowloon, Hong Kong, 1, Hong Kong. **Online address:** xwang65@cityu.edu.hk

WANG, Yun. American/Chinese (born China), b. 1964?. **Genres:** Air/Space Topics, Poetry. **Career:** University of Notre Dame, visiting professor; University of Oklahoma, Homer L. Dodge Department of Physics and Astronomy, assistant professor of theoretical cosmology, associate professor of theoretical cosmology. Writer. **Publications:** The Carp, 1994; The Book of Jade: Poems, 2002; Dark Energy, 2010; Journey to the Galactic River, forthcoming. Contributor of articles to journals. Works appear in anthologies. **Address:** Homer L. Dodge Department of Physics and Astronomy, University of Oklahoma, 327 Nielsen Hall, 440 W Brooks St., Norman, OK 73019, U.S.A. **Online address:** wang@nhn.ou.edu

WANGMO, Tsering. American/Indian (born India), b. 1967. **Genres:** Food And Wine, Poetry. **Career:** Chaksam-Pa Tibetan Opera Troupe, co-founder, 1991; Lhasa Moon (restaurant), owner and chef, 1995-; The Cultural Conservancy, Tibetan Cultural Preservation Project, founder, 1999. Writer and musician. **Publications:** (With Z. Houshmand) The Lhasa Moon Tibetan Cookbook, 1998. **Address:** Lhasa Moon, 2420 Lombard St., San Francisco, CA 94123-2604, U.S.A. **Online address:** akiwangmo@yahoo.com

WANKO, Cheryl L. American (born United States) **Genres:** Biography. **Career:** West Chester University of Pennsylvania, associate professor of English. Writer and historian. **Publications:** Roles of Authority: Thespian Biography and Celebrity in Eighteenth-Century Britain, 2003. **Address:** West Chester University of Pennsylvania, West Chester, PA 19383, U.S.A. **Online address:** cwanko@wcupa.edu

WAPNER, Leonard M. American (born United States), b. 1948. **Genres:** Mathematics/Statistics, Natural History, Humor/Satire. **Career:** El Camino College, professor of mathematics, 1974-. Writer. **Publications:** The Pea and the Sun: A Mathematical Paradox, 2005. Contributor to books. **Address:** Department of Mathematics, El Camino College, 16007 Crenshaw Blvd., Torrance, CA 90506-0001, U.S.A. **Online address:** lwapner@elcamino.edu

WAPSHOTT, Nicholas (Henry). British (born England), b. 1952. **Genres:** Biography, Autobiography/Memoirs, Politics/Government. **Career:** Scotsman, journalist, 1973-76; Times, journalist, 1976-84; Observer, features editor, 1984-88, political editor, 1988-92; Times Magazine, editor, 1992-96; Saturday Times, editor, 1996-; New York Sun, columnist and editor; Times of London, chief; The New School, adjunct professor; MSNBC, broadcaster; PBS, broadcaster; FOX News, broadcaster. **Publications:** Peter O'Toole,

1982; (with G. Brock) Thatcher, 1983; The Man Between: A Biography of Carol Reed, 1990; Rex Harrison, 1991; Carol Reed: A Biography, 1994; (with T. Wapshott) Older: A Biography of George Michael, 1998; Ronald Reagan and Margaret Thatcher: A Political Marriage, 2007. Contributor to periodicals. **Address:** The Times, 1 Pennington St., London, GL E1 9XN, England.

WARBER, Adam L. American (born United States), b. 1971. **Genres:** Politics/Government. **Career:** Western Michigan University, research assistant, 1994, teaching assistant, 1994-95; Texas A&M University, Department of Political Science, research assistant, 1996-2000, Center for Presidential Studies, research assistant, 1997-2000, assistant lecturer in political science, 2000-02; Clemson University, assistant professor of political science, 2002-. Writer, editor, political scientist and educator. **Publications:** Executive Orders and the Modern Presidency: Legislating from the Oval Office, 2006. Contributor to books. **Address:** Department of Political Science, Clemson University, 232 Brackett Hall, Clemson, SC 29634-1354, U.S.A. **Online address:** awarber@clemson.edu

WARBURTON, Nigel. British (born England), b. 1962?. **Genres:** Philosophy, History. **Career:** Nottingham University, lecturer in philosophy; Open University, senior lecturer, 1994-; Humanist Philosophers Group, founding member; University of London, School of Advanced Studies, Institute of Philosophy, honorary associate research fellow; Oxford University, Oxford Uehiro Centre, senior research associate. Writer. **Publications:** Philosophy: The Basics, 1992, 3rd ed., 1999; (ed.) Bill Brandt: Selected Texts and Bibliography, 1993; Thinking from A to Z, 1996, 2nd ed., 2000; Philosophy: The Classics, 1998, 3rd ed., 2006; (with B. Jay) Brandt: The Photography of Bill Brandt, 1999; Philosophy: The Basic Readings, 1999; Freedom: An Introduction with Readings, 2000; (with D. Maltravers and J. Pike) Reading Political Philosophy: Machiavelli to Mill, 2001; The Art Question, 2003; Ernö Goldfinger: The Life of an Architect, 2004; Philosophy: The Essential Study Guide, 2004, 3rd ed., 2006; Basics of Essay Writing, 2006; Free Speech: A Very Short Introduction, 2009; Philosophy Bites, 2010; A Little History of Philosophy, 2011. **Address:** Department of Philosophy, Open University, Walton Hall, Milton Keynes, BK MK7 6AA, England. **Online address:** n.warburton@open.ac.uk

WARD, Alan J. American/British (born England), b. 1937. **Genres:** History, Politics/Government. **Career:** University of Adelaide, lecturer in politics, 1963-67; College of William & Mary, assistant professor, 1967-71, associate professor, 1971-76, professor of government, 1976-2003, Department of Government, chair, 1987-93, director of graduate studies, 1971-77, professor emeritus, 2003-; University of Leicester, visiting professor, 1978; Flinders University, visiting professor; University of Vermont, visiting professor; American Conference for Irish Studies, president, 1981-83. Writer. **Publications:** Ireland and Anglo-American Relations 1899-1921, 1969; The Easter Rising: Revolution and Irish Nationalism, 1980, 2nd ed., 2003; (ed.) Northern Ireland: Living with the Crisis, 1987; The Irish Constitutional Tradition: Responsible Government and Modern Ireland, 1782-1992, 1994; (with D. DeBats) Degrees of Difference: Reshaping the University in Australia and the United States, 1998. **Address:** Department of Government, College of William & Mary, PO Box 8795, Williamsburg, VA 23187-8795, U.S.A. **Online address:** ajward@wm.edu

WARD, Amanda Eyre. American (born United States), b. 1972. **Genres:** Novels, Novellas/Short Stories, Mystery/Crime/Suspense. **Career:** Athens College, teacher; University of Texas, instructor in creative writing; University of Montana, Mansfield Library, staff. Writer. **Publications:** Butte as in Beautiful, 1999; Miss Montana's Wedding Day, 1999; Sleep Toward Heaven: A Novel, 2003; How to Be Lost: A Novel, 2004; Forgive Me: A Novel, 2007; Love Stories in this Town, 2009; Close Your Eyes: A Novel, 2011. Contributor to books. **Address:** c/o Michelle Tessler, Tessler Literary Agency, 27 W 20th St., Ste. 1003, New York, NY 10011, U.S.A. **Online address:** aeyreward@yahoo.com

WARD, Brian. American/British (born England), b. 1961?. **Genres:** History, Popular Culture, Race Relations. **Career:** University of Durham, lecturer, 1990-91; University of Newcastle upon Tyne, staff, 1991-2000, reader in American history, 1998; University of Virginia, Carter G. Woodson Institute for Afro-American and African Studies, post-doctoral fellow, 1995-96; University of Florida, Department of History, associate professor, 2000-, chairman, 2003-, professor. Writer. **Publications:** Just My Soul Responding: Rhythm and Blues, Black Consciousness, and Race Relations, 1998; Radio

and the Struggle for Civil Rights in the South, 2004. EDITOR: (with T. Badger) Making of Martin Luther King and the Civil Rights Movement, 1996; Media, Culture, and the Modern African American Freedom Struggle, 2001; The 1960s: A Documentary Reader, 2010. Works appear in anthologies. Contributor to journals and periodicals. **Address:** Department of History, University of Florida, 025C Keene-Flint Hall, PO Box 117320, Gainesville, FL 32611, U.S.A. **Online address:** wardb@ufl.edu

WARD, Chrissie. New Zealander (born New Zealand), b. 1949. **Genres:** History, Children's Non-fiction, Novellas/Short Stories. **Career:** Writer. **Publications:** Dear Lizzie: A Kiwi Soldier Writes from the Battlefields of World War One, 2000; Kia Ora Postie: A Love Affair With Kiwi Letter Boxes, 2006; Curious Kiwi Creatures, 2007. **Address:** New Holland Publishers (NZ) Ltd., Cnr Lake and Ocean View Rd., PO Box 34 321, Auckland, 1, New Zealand. **Online address:** cj.ward@xtra.co.nz

WARD, David. American/British (born England), b. 1938. **Genres:** Education, Geography, History, Social Sciences, Art/Art History. **Career:** Carleton University, lecturer in geography, 1963-64; University of British Columbia, assistant professor of geography, 1964-66; University of Wisconsin, Department of Geography, associate professor, 1966-71, professor of geography, 1971-, chair, 1974-77, Andrew Hill Clark professor of geography, through 2001, associate dean of the graduate school, 1980-87, vice chancellor for academic affairs and provost, 1989-2003, chancellor, 1993-2001, interim chancellor, 2011-, now chancellor emeritus; Journal of Historical Geography, editor, 1976-81; American Council on Education, president, 2001-08. **Publications:** Cities and Immigrants: A Geography of Change in Nineteenth-Century America, 1971; (ed.) Geographic Perspectives on America's Past, 1979; (with J.P. Radford) North American Cities in the Victorian Age, 1983; Poverty, Ethnicity, and the American City, 1840-1925, 1989; (ed. with O. Zunz) Landscape of Modernity, 1992; (ed. with N. Radomski) Proud Traditions and Future Challenges: The University of Wisconsin-Madison Celebrates 150 Years, 1999; The Bologna Process, 2008. Contributor of articles to periodicals and journals. **Address:** University of Wisconsin, 161 Bascom Hall, 500 Lincoln Dr., Madison, WI 53706-1314, U.S.A. **Online address:** david_ward@ace.nche.edu

WARD, David. Canadian (born Canada), b. 1967. **Genres:** Novels, Education. **Career:** Writer and educator. **Publications:** NOVELS: Escape the Mask 2001; Beneath the Mask 2003; Beyond the Mask 2006; The Hockey Tree, 2006; Archipelago, 2008; One Hockey Night, 2010; Between Two Ends, 2011. Contributor to periodicals. **Address:** 5580 SW Nevada Ct., 2034 Lower Mall, Portland, OR 97219, U.S.A. **Online address:** hello@davidward.ca

WARD, Elizabeth Honor. Also writes as Ward S. Leslie, Ward S. Leslie. British (born England), b. 1926. **Genres:** Children's Non-fiction, Literary Criticism And History, Physics, Theology/Religion, Sex. **Career:** Sutton Coldfield High School for Girls, teacher of physics, 1948-50; University of Ghana, demonstrator in physics, 1951-55; West African Examinations Council, part-time examiner in physics, 1951-63. Writer. **Publications:** (As Ward S. Leslie) Touchdown to Adventure, 1958; Senior Physics (Books 1 and 2), 1965-66; (with G. Osae-Addo) Newtown Families, 1966; The Story of Creation, 1973; (with A.H. Ward) Essential Senior Physics, 1974; (with K. Baker) AIDS, Sex, and Family Planning: A Christian View, 1989; Girl's Own Guide to the Girl's Own Paper, 1992. **Address:** Coaster, Hermitage, Gunville Ln., Dorchester, DT2 7BB, England. **Online address:** dorset2wards@hotmail.com

WARD, Frank A. American (born United States), b. 1948. **Genres:** Economics, Environmental Sciences/Ecology, Natural History, Sciences. **Career:** New Mexico State University, Department of Agricultural Economics and Agricultural Business, assistant professor, 1978-83, associate professor, 1983-88, professor, 1988-. Writer. **Publications:** (With E.V. Ness) Economic Impacts of New Mexico State Parks: An Input-Output Analysis, 1996; (with D.J. Beal) Valuing Nature with Travel Cost Models: A Manual, 2000; (co-author) Institutional Adjustments for Coping with Prolonged and Severe Drought in the Rio Grande Basin, 2001; Environmental and Natural Resource Economics, 2006. **Address:** Department of Agricultural Economics and, Agricultural Business, New Mexico State University, Rm. 371, Gerald Thomas Hall, PO Box 30003, Las Cruces, NM 88003-8003, U.S.A. **Online address:** fward@nmsu.edu

WARD, Geoffrey C(hampion). American (born United States), b. 1940. **Genres:** Plays/Screenplays, Biography, History, Military/Defense/Arms Control, Music, Essays, Art/Art History. **Career:** Encyclopedia Brittanica, senior picture editor, 1964-68; Reader's Digest, General Books Division, art director and writer, 1968-69; Audience Magazine, editor, 1970-73; freelance writer, 1973-75, 1982-; Lincoln Sites Project, research director and writer, 1975-76; American Heritage, managing editor, 1976-77, editor, 1977-82, columnist, 1983-94. Historian. **Publications:** Lincoln's Thought and the Present, 1978; The Maharajas, 1983; Treasures of the Maharajas, 1983; Before the Trumpet: Young Franklin Roosevelt, 1882-1905, 1985; A First-Class Temperament: The Emergence of Franklin Roosevelt, 1989; (with K. Burns and R. Burns) The Civil War: An Illustrated History, 1990; American Originals: The Private Worlds of Some Singular Men and Women, 1991; (with D.R. Ward) Tiger Wallahs: Encounters with the Men Who Tried to Save the Greatest of the Great Cats, 1993; (with K. Burns and J. O'Connor) Shadow Ball, 1994; (with K. Burns) Baseball: An Illustrated History, 1994; (with K. Burns and P.R. Walker) Who Invented the Game?, 1994; (with S.A. Kramer and K. Burns) 25 Great Moments, 1994; (ed.) Closest Companion: The Unknown Story of the Intimate Friendship Between Franklin D. Roosevelt and Margaret L. Suckley, 1995; The West: An Illustrated History, 1996; (ed.) The Best American Essays 1996, 1996; (with M. Nichols) The Year of the Tiger, 1998; (foreword) Black Bird Fly Away: Disabled in an Able-bodied World, 1998; Not for Ourselves Alone: The Story of Elizabeth Cady Stanton and Susan B. Anthony, 1999; Jazz: A History of American Music, 2000; (with D. Duncan) Mark Twain, 2001; Abraham and Mary Lincoln, 2001; Tigers and Tigerwallahs, 2002; Unforgivable Blackness: The Rise and Fall of Jack Johnson, 2004; (with K. Burns and L. Novick) The War: An Intimate History, 1941-1945, 2007; (with W. Marsalis) Moving to Higher Ground: How Jazz can Change Your Life, 2008; Disposition to Be Rich, 2012. Contributor to books and periodicals. **Address:** 290 W End Ave., Apt. 17C, New York, NY 10023, U.S.A.

WARD, Gregory. British (born England), b. 1951?. **Genres:** Novels, Mystery/Crime/Suspense, Young Adult Fiction, Biography, Autobiography/Memoirs. **Career:** Writer. **Publications:** The Carpet King, 1991; Water Damage, 1993; Kondor, 1997; The Internet Bride, 2000. **Address:** Little Brown & Company Inc., 1271 Ave. of the Americas, New York, NY 10020, U.S.A.

WARD, Harry Merrill. American (born United States), b. 1929. **Genres:** History, Biography, Military/Defense/Arms Control. **Career:** Georgetown College, assistant professor of history, 1959-61; Morehead State University, assistant professor, 1961-63, associate professor of history, 1963-65; University of Richmond, Department of history associate professor, 1965-78, professor, 1978-93, William Binford Vest professor, 1993-99, department chair, 1970-74, William Binford Vest professor emeritus, 1999-; Southern Illinois University, visiting associate professor, 1967-68; U.S.Bicentennial Media Group Inc., consultant, 1974-76. Writer. **Publications:** United Colonies of New England 1643-90, 1961; Department of War 1781-1795, 1962; Unite or Die: Intercolony Relations 1690-1763, 1971; Statism in Plymouth Colony, 1973; (with H.E. Greer, Jr.) Richmond during the Revolution, 1775-83, 1977; Duty, Honor, or Country: General George Weedon and the American Revolution, 1979; Richmond: An Illustrated History, 1985, rev. ed., 1988; Charles Scott and the Spirit of 76, 1988; Major General Adam Stephen and the Cause of American Liberty, 1989; Colonial America, 1607-1763, 1991; The American Revolution: Nationhood Achieved 1763-88, 1995; General William Maxwell and the New Jersey Continentals, 1997; The War for Independence and the Transformation of American Society, 1999; Between the Lines: Banditti of the American Revolution, 2002; George Washington's Enforcers: Policing the Continental Army, 2006; Going Down Hill: Legacies of the American Revolutionary War, 2009; For Virginia and for Independence, 2011. Contributor to books. **Address:** Department of History, University of Richmond, 319 Ryland Hall, 28 Westhampton Way, Richmond, VA 23173, U.S.A. **Online address:** rfugett@richmond.edu

WARD, James M. (James Michael Ward). American (born United States), b. 1951. **Genres:** Novels. **Career:** TSR Inc., games designer; Fast Forward Entertainment, president, 2000-05. Writer. **Publications:** The Prophets, 1982; (with M.L. Kirchoff) Light on Quests Mountain, 1983; (with R. Kuntz) Advanced Dungeons & Dragons, Legends & Lore, 1984; Operation, Weapons Disaster, 1986; (with J. Blashfield) Faerie Mound of Dragonkind, 1987; Greyhawk Adventures: A Compendium of Greyhawk Campaign Ideas for the AD&D Role Playing System, 1988; (with J. C. Hong) Pool of radiance, 1989; (with A.K. Brown) Pools of Darkness, 1992; (with A.K. Brown) Pool of Twilight, 1993; We Three Dragons: A Trio of Dragon Tales for the Holiday Season, 2005; Midshipwizard Halcyon Blithe, 2005; (contrib.) We Three Dragons: A Trio of Dragon Tales for the Holiday Season, 2005; Dragonfrigate Wizard Halcyon Blithe, 2006; Precious Presents, 2007; (contrib.) Timeshares, 2010. Contributor to periodicals. **Address:** Margaret Weis Productions, PO Box 1131, Williams Bay, WI 53191, U.S.A.

WARD, James Michael. See **WARD, James M.**

WARD, Jane (A.). American (born United States), b. 1960?. **Genres:** Novels, Poetry, Food And Wine. **Career:** 95th Restaurant, chef, director of private dining; Quebrada Bakery, pastry chef. Writer. **Publications:** Hunger, 2001; The Mosaic Artist, The Welcome Home, forthcoming. **Address:** c/o Author Mail, Forge Books, 175 5th Ave., New York, NY 10010-7703, U.S.A. **Online address:** janeaward@yahoo.com

WARD, Jesmyn. American (born United States), b. 1977?. **Genres:** Novels. **Career:** Random House, staff; University of New Orleans, faculty. Writer. **Publications:** Where the Line Bleeds, 2008. **Address:** De Lisle, MS , U.S.A. **Online address:** ojaccc@gmail.com

WARD, (John Stephen) Keith. British (born England), b. 1938. **Genres:** Philosophy, Theology/Religion. **Career:** University of Glasgow, lecturer in logic, 1964-66, lecturer in moral philosophy, 1966-69; University of St. Andrews, lecturer in moral philosophy, 1969-71; University of London, Kings College, lecturer in philosophy of religion, 1971-76, professor of moral theology, 1982-86, F.D. Maurice professor of moral and social theology, 1983-86, professor of philosophy of religion, 1986-91; Cambridge University, dean, 1974-82; University of Oxford, Regius professor of divinity, 1991-2003, professor emeritus, 2003-; Trinity Hall, honorary fellow, dean and director of studies in philosophy and in theology, 1976-83; Gresham College, Gresham professor of divinity, 2004-08; Heythrop College, professorial research fellow, 2009-; University of Wales, honorary fellow; World Congress of Faiths, president; Drake University, visiting professor; Claremont Graduate School, visiting professor, 1992; University of Tulsa, visiting professor; Cornell College, visiting professor; Hartford Seminary, visiting professor; Virginia Theological Seminary, visiting professor. Writer. **Publications:** Fifty Key Words in Philosophy, 1968; Ethics and Christianity, 1970; The Development of Kants View of Ethics, 1972; The Concept of God, 1974; The Christian Way, 1976; The Divine Image: The Foundations of Christian Morality, 1976; The Promise, 1980; Rational Theology and the Creativity of God, 1982; Holding Fast to God: A Reply to Don Cupitt, 1982; The Living God, 1984; The Battle for the Soul: An Affirmation of Human Dignity and Value, 1985, rep. as In Defence of the Soul, 1992; The Turn of the Tide, 1986; Evidence for the Virgin Birth, 1987; Images of Eternity: Concepts of God in Five Religious Traditions, 1987 as Concepts of God: Images of the Divine in Five Religious Traditions, 1998; The Rule of Love, 1989; Divine Action, 1990, rev. ed., 2007; A Vision to Pursue: Beyond the Crisis in Christianity, 1991; Is Christianity a Historical Religion?, 1992; Defending the Soul, 1992; Friends of Dr. Williamss Library Lecture 46, 1992; Religion and Revelation: A Theology of Revelation in the Worlds Religions, 1994; God, Chance and Necessity, 1996; Religion and Creation, 1996; Religion and Human Nature, 1998; God, Faith and the New Millennium: Christian Belief in an Age of Science, 1998; Religion and Community, 2000; Christianity: A Short Introduction, 2000; God: A Guide for the Perplexed, 2002; What the Bible Really Teaches: A Challenge for Fundamentalists, 2004; The Case for Religion, 2004; What the Bible Really Teaches: About Crucifixion, Resurrection, Salvation, the Second Coming, and Eternal Life, 2005; Is Religion Dangerous?, 2007; The Big Questions in Science and Religion, 2008; Why There Almost Certainly is a God: Doubting Dawkins, 2008; God and the Philosophers, 2009; Is Religion Irrational?, 2011; More than Matter?, 2011. Contributor to periodicals. **Address:** Christ Church, Oxford University, St. Aldates, Oxford, OX OX1 1DP, England. **Online address:** keith.ward@theology.ox.ac.uk

WARD, Jonas. See **GARFIELD, Brian (F. W.).**

WARD, Ken. Canadian (born Canada), b. 1949. **Genres:** Poetry, Children's Fiction, Animals/Pets, Illustrations. **Career:** Canadian Postal Service, mail carrier, 1983-. Writer and illustrator. **Publications:** SELF-ILLUSTRATED POETRY: Tiny Dreams and Secret Sighs, 1976; Another Slice of Goo, 1981; Twelve Kids, One Cow, 1989; Mrs. Kitchen's Cats, 1990. **Address:** Blue Moon Arts, 2013 Maynard St., Halifax, NS B3K 3T1, Canada.

WARD, Lee. Canadian (born Canada), b. 1970. **Genres:** Politics/Government. **Career:** University of Regina, Campion College, assistant professor of political science. Academic, political scientist and writer. **Publications:** The

Politics of Liberty in England and Revolutionary America, 2004; (ed. with A. Ward) The Ashgate Research Companion to Federalism, 2008. Contributor to periodicals and journals. **Address:** Campion College, University of Regina, 3737 Wascana Pkwy., Regina, SK S4S 0A2, Canada. **Online address:** lee.ward@uregina.ca

WARD, Logan. American (born United States), b. 1966. **Genres:** Biography, Autobiography/Memoirs. **Career:** Freelance writer. **Publications:** See You in a Hundred Years: Four Seasons in Forgotten America (memoir), 2007. Contributor to periodicals. **Address:** Staunton, VA , U.S.A. **Online address:** loganward@verizon.net

WARD, Margaret. Irish/British/German (born Germany), b. 1950. **Genres:** History, Area Studies, Gay And Lesbian Issues. **Career:** Queen's University, Institute of Irish Studies, junior research fellow, 1979-81; Belfast City Council, Department of Community Services, women's development officer, 1984-86; University of the West of England, lecturer, 1991-93; Bath Spa University College, research fellow in history, 1993-99; Democratic Dialogue, assistant director, 2000-05, Women's Resource and Development Agency, director, 2005-. Writer. **Publications:** Unmanageable Revolutionaries: Women and Irish Nationalism, 1983; Maud Gonne: A Life, 1990; The Missing Sex, 1991; (ed.) In Their Own Voice: Women and Irish Nationalism, 1995; Hanna Sheehy-Skeffington: A Life, 1997; The Female Line, 2003; (ed. with L. Ryan) Irish Women and Nationalism: Soldiers, New Women and Wicked Hags, 2004; (ed. with L. Ryan) Irish Women and Suffrage: Becoming Citizens, 2006; (ed. with L. Ryan) Irish Women and the Vote, 2007; Female Occupations, 2008. Contributor to books and journals. **Address:** Women's Resource & Development Agency, 6 Mount Charles, Belfast, BT7 1NZ, Northern Ireland. **Online address:** margaretg.ward@gmail.com

WARD, Matthew C. Scottish/British (born England), b. 1963. **Genres:** History, Social Commentary, Women's Studies And Issues, Social Sciences. **Career:** University of Dundee, School of Humanities, Department of Modern History, lecturer in American history, 1992-2006, senior lecturer in history, 2006-. Writer. **Publications:** Breaking the Backcountry: The Seven Years' War in Virginia and Pennsylvania, 1754-1765, 2003; The Battle for Quebec 1759: Britain's Conquest of Canada, 2005. **Address:** School of Humanities, University of Dundee, Nethergate, Dundee, DD1 4HN, Scotland. **Online address:** m.c.ward@dundee.ac.uk

WARD, Philip. (Darby Greenfield). British (born England), b. 1938. **Genres:** Novels, Novellas/Short Stories, Plays/Screenplays, Poetry, Travel/Exploration, Bibliography, Humor/Satire, Reference, Translations. **Career:** Wimbledon Public Libraries, chief cataloger, 1962-63; Oasis Oil Co. of Libya Inc., coordinator of library services, 1963-70; UNESCO, Shibinal-Kum, library consultant, 1973; UNESCO/Indonesia Development of National Library Service Project, project manager, 1973-74; Oxford University Press, editor, 1974-77; professional writer, 1975-; Oleander Press, managing director, 1976-. **Publications:** (With R. Cave) Simplified Cataloguing Rules for Private Libraries, 1959; Collected Poems, 1960; Periodicals in Libya, 1963; A Survey of Libyan Bibliographical Resources, 1964, 2nd ed., 1965; Loakrime: Idol of the Shattered Pyramid, 1967; Seldom Rains: Libyan Poems, 1967; Drama Workshop, 1967; Ambigamus: Or, the Logic Box, 1968; Apuleius on Trial at Sabratha, 1968; Poems for Participants: A Work-Book, 1968; At the Best of Times, 1968; A Musical Breakfast, 1968; The Poet and the Microscope, 1968; The Theory and Practice of Library Classification, 1968; The Okefani Song of Nij Zitru, 1969; A Lizard and Other Distractions, 1969; Fiction List of Murdoch Lenz, 1969; Maps on the Ceiling, 1970; Spanish Literary Appreciation, 1970; Garrity: Nine Plays, 1970; The Libyan Revolution, 1971; Pincers, 1973; A House on Fire, 1974; Indonesia: The Development of a National Library Service, 1975; A Maltese Boyhood, 1975; Television Plays, 1976; Impostors and Their Imitators, 1978; The Keymakers and Other Poems, 1978; A Dictionary of Common Fallacies, 1978, 2 vols., 1989; Cambridge Street Literature, 1978; Lose Nothing, 1979; (with A.J. Ward) The Small Publisher, 1979; Lost Songs and Other Political Poems, 1981; A Lifetime's Reading, 1982; Forgotten Games, 1984; Northern India, Rajasthan, Agra, Delhi, 1989; Wight Magic, 1990; Contemporary Designer Bookbinders, 1995; English Is a Foreign Language, 1996; (with A. Hawkyard) The Inventory of King Henry VIII, 1997; The Comfort of Women (novel), 2002; His Enamel Mug (poetry), 2003; Interplanetary Pastime, 2010. EDITOR: Evenyn Quell, The Quell-Finger Dialogues, 1965; The Libyan Civil Code, 1970; (and intro.) Indonesian Traditional Poetry (anthology), 1975; The Oxford Companion to Spanish Literature, 1978; The Gold-Mines of Midian,

1979. TRANSLATOR: Lope de Rueda, Las Aceitunas, 1962; Miguel Torga, Jesus, 1963; Angelo Pesce, Colours of the Arab Fatherland, 1972; The Scandalous Life of César Moro in His Own Words: Peruvian Surrealist Poetry, 1976; (ed. and intro.) Greguerías, 1982; The Pure-Bred Arabian Horse, 1984. TRAVEL GUIDES: Touring Libya: The Western Provinces, 1967; Touring Libya: The Southern Provinces, 1968; Touring Libya: The Eastern Provinces, 1969; Tripoli: Portrait of a City, 1969; Touring Iran, 1970; (with Pesce) Motoring to Nalut, 1970; Sabratha: Guide for Visitors, 1970; (with Ed van Weerd) The Way to Wadi al-Khail, 1970; Touring Lebanon, 1971; Come with Me to Ireland, 1972; Touring Cyprus, 1972; The Aeolian Islands, 1974; Bangkok: Portrait of a City, 1974; (as Darby Greenfield) Indonesia: A Traveler's Guide, vol. I: Java and Sumatra, 1975, vol. II: Bali and East Indonesia, 1976; Across Arabia, Saudi Arabian Airlines, 1976; Albania, 1982; Ha'il: Oasis City of Saudi Arabia, 1983; Japanese Capitals, 1985; Finnish Cities, 1987; Travels in Oman, 1987; Polish Cities, 1988; Rajasthan, Agra, Delhi, 1989; Bulgaria, 1989; South India: Tamil Nadu, Kerala, Goa, 1991; Bulgaria, a Travel Guide, 1991; Western India, 1992; Bulgarian Voices, 1992; Sofia: Portrait of a City, 1993; Bahrain: A Travel Guide, 1993; Gujarat, Daman, Diu, 1994. Contributor to books and periodicals. **Address:** Oleander Press, 17 Stansgate Ave., Cambridge, CB CB2 2QZ, England.

WARD, Ralph Gerard. Australian/New Zealander (born New Zealand), b. 1933. **Genres:** Geography, Social Sciences, Technology. **Career:** University of Auckland, junior lecturer, 1956-69, lecturer in geography, 1960-61; University College London, lecturer in geography, 1961-67; University of Papua New Guinea, foundation professor of geography, 1967-71; Australian National University, Research School of Pacific Studies, professor of human geography, 1971-98, director, 1980-93, professor emeritus, 1999-, visiting fellow; Pacific Science Association, president, 1999-2003. Writer. **Publications:** Islands of the South Pacific, 1961; Land Use and Population in Fiji, 1965; (with M. Levison and J.W. Webb) The Settlement of Polynesia: A Computer Simulation, 1973; (with A.V. Surmon) Port Moresby: 1973, rev. ed., 1973; (with T.G. McGee and D.W. Drakakis-Smith) Food Distribution in the New Hebrides, 1980; (with H.C. Brookfield and F. Ellis) Land, Cane, and Coconuts: Papers on the Rural Economy of Fiji, 1985; (with P. Ashcroft) Samoa: Mapping the Diversity, 1998. EDITOR: (with M.W. Ward) New Zealand's Industrial Potential, 1961; American Activities in the Central Pacific, 1790-1870, 1966; (with D.A.M. Lea) An Atlas of Papua and New Guinea, 1970; Man in the Pacific Islands, 1972; (with A. Proctor) South Pacific Agriculture: Choices and Constraints, 1980; (with M. Brookfield) New Directions in the South Pacific, 1988; (with E. Kingdon) Land, Custom, and Practice in the South Pacific, 1995; (with S.W. Serjeantson) And Then the Engines Stopped: Flying in Papua New Guinea, 2002; (with M.W. Ward) Tauponui a Tia: Tales of the Taupo Country, 2009. **Address:** Australian National University, Ellery Cres., Canberra, AC 0200, Australia. **Online address:** gerard.ward@anu.edu.au

WARD, (William) Peter. Canadian (born Canada), b. 1943. **Genres:** Cultural/Ethnic Topics, Politics/Government, Medicine/Health, Architecture, History, Homes/Gardens. **Career:** Queen's University, lecturer in history, 1972-73; University of British Columbia, Department of History, assistant professor, 1973-79, associate professor, 1979-90, professor, 1990-, university librarian, 2007-09. Writer. **Publications:** White Canada Forever: Popular Attitudes and Public Policy toward Orientals in British Columbia, 1978; (ed. with R.K. Carty) Entering the Eighties: Canada in Crisis, 1980; (ed. and intro., with R.A.J. McDonald) British Columbia: Historical Readings, 1981; (ed.) Mysteries of Montreal: Memoirs of a Midwife, 1984; (ed. with R.K. Carty) National Politics and Community in Canada, 1986; A Love Story from Nineteenth-Century Quebec: The Diary of George Stephen Jones, 1990; Courtship: Love and Marriage in Nineteenth-Century English Canada, 1990; Birth Weight and Economic Growth: Women's Living Standards in the Industrializing West, 1993; A History of Domestic Space: Privacy and the Canadian Home, 1999. **Address:** Department of History, University of British Columbia, 1107 Buchanan Twr., 1873 E Mall, Vancouver, BC V6T 1Z1, Canada. **Online address:** peter.ward@ubc.ca

WARDELL, Steven (William). American (born United States), b. 1971. **Genres:** Business/Trade/Industry, Sociology. **Career:** CPP Advisors L.L.C., principal. Author. **Publications:** Rising Sons and Daughters: Life Among Japan's New Young, 1995. Contributor to magazines and newspapers. **Address:** c/o Philip G. Spitzer, Spitzer Agency, 50 Talmage Farm Ln., East Hampton, NH 11937-4300, U.S.A.

WARDHAUGH, Ronald. Canadian (born Canada), b. 1932. **Genres:** Language/Linguistics. **Career:** University of Michigan, assistant professor, 1966-68, associate professor, 1968-72, professor of linguistics, 1972-75; Center for Research on Language and Language Behavior, director, 1969-71; University of Toronto, Department of Linguistics, professor, 1975-95, chairman, 1975-86, professor emeritus, 1995-. Writer. **Publications:** Teaching English to Speakers of Other Languages: The State of the Art, 1969; Reading: A Linguistic Perspective, 1969; Introduction to Linguistics, 1972; Topics in Applied Linguistics, 1974; Series R, 1975; The Contexts of Language, 1976; (ed. with H.D. Brown) A Survey of Applied Linguistics, 1976; Language and Nationhood: The Canadian Experience, 1983; How Conversation Works, 1985; An Introduction to Sociolinguistics, 1986, 6th ed., 2010; Languages in Competition, 1987; Investigating Language, 1993; Understanding English Grammar, 1995, 2nd ed., 2003; Proper English: Myths and Misunderstandings about Language, 1999; Understanding English Grammar: A Linguistic Approach, 2003. **Address:** Department of Linguistics, University of Toronto, 130 Saint George St., Rm. 6076, Toronto, ON M5S 3H1, Canada. **Online address:** rwardhaugh@shaw.ca

WARDLAW, Alvia J. American (born United States) **Genres:** Young Adult Fiction, Art/Art History. **Career:** Texas Southern University, assistant professor of art history, 1994, associate professor of art history, professor of art history, University Museum, director and curator; History of Fine Arts, Primitive Art and Education, associate curator; Museum of Fine Art, Modern and Contemporary art, curator, 1995-2009, research fellow; National Alliance of African and African American Art, co-founder, 1998; Barbara Jordan Archives, curator; Dallas Museum of Art, adjunct curator of African-American art. Art historian and writer. **Publications:** The Art of John Biggers: View from the Upper Room, 1995; (ed.) Something All Our Own: The Grant Hill Collection of African American Art, 2004; Notes from a Child's Odyssey: The Art of Kermit Oliver, 2005; Charles Alston, 2007; (with J.H. Franklin) Collecting African American Art: The Museum of Fine Arts, Houston, 2009. **Address:** Texas Southern University, 3100 Cleburne St., Houston, TX 77004, U.S.A. **Online address:** wardlaw_aj@tsu.edu

WARDLAW, Lee. American (born United States), b. 1955. **Genres:** Children's Fiction, Children's Non-fiction, Young Adult Non-fiction, Picture/Board Books, Young Adult Fiction, Novels. **Career:** Cold Spring Elementary School, summer program teacher's aide, 1974-76; KIST Radio, public ascertainment coordinator and copywriter, 1974-81; Los Ninos Head Start Pre-School, director's assistant, 1977-78; Montecito Library, storyteller, 1978-79; Goleta Head Start Pre-School, director and head teacher, 1978-79; Cornelia Moore Memorial Dental Foundation, teacher, 1979-82; Outlaw Communications, owner, 1982-85; Peabody Elementary School, library volunteer, 1985-93; Santa Barbara Community College, writing instructor, 1988-; Mountain View Elementary and Ellwood Elementary, author-in-residence, 1990-91; children's book author, 1986-; Santa Barbara Montessori School, community resource coordinator, 2010-. **Publications:** NONFICTION: Giggles & Grins: A Dental Health and Nutrition Curriculum Guide for Pre-School Teachers, 1985; Cowabunga! The Complete Book of Surfing, 1991; Bubblemania: The Chewy History of Bubble Gum, 1997; We All Scream for Ice Cream!, 2000. FICTION FOR CHILDREN: Me Plus Math Equals Headache, 1986, rev. ed., 1989; The Eye and I: Story, 1988; Corey's Fire, 1990; Operation Rhinoceros, 1992; Seventh-Grade Weirdo, 1992; The Ghoul Brothers, 1996; 101 Ways to Bug Your Parents, 1996; Dinosaur Pizza, 1998; Hector's Hiccups, 1999; My Life as a Weirdo, 2000; 101 Ways to Bug Your Teacher, 2004; Tripping Over the Lunch Lady, 2004; 101 Ways to Bug Your Friends and Enemies, 2011. PICTURE BOOKS: Tales of Grandpa Cat, 1994; (comp.) Punia and the King of Sharks: A Hawaiian Folktale, 1997; Bow-Wow Birthday, 1998; First Steps, 1999; Saturday Night Jamboree, 2000; The Chair Where Bear Sits, 2001; Peek-a-Book: A Lift-the-Flap Bedtime Rhyme, 2003; Won-Ton: A Cat Tale Told in Haiku, 2011; Red, White and Boom!, 2011. FOR YOUNG ADULTS: Alley Cat, 1987; Corey's Fire, 1990; Don't Look Back, 1993; See You in September, 1995. **Address:** Virginia Knowlton, Curtis Brown Ltd., 10 Astor Pl., Fl. 3, New York, NY 10003-6935, U.S.A. **Online address:** author@leewardlaw.com

WARDLE, (John) Irving. British (born England), b. 1929. **Genres:** Plays/Screenplays, Theatre, Biography. **Career:** The Times Literary Supplement, sub-editor, 1956-; Bolton Evening News, staff, 1958-; The Observer, deputy theatre critic, 1959-63; The Times (newspaper), drama critic, 1963-89; Gambit, editor, 1973-75; The Independent on Sunday, staff, 1989-95. **Publications:** The Theatres of George Devine, 1978; Theatre Criticism, 1992.

Address: Deborah Rogers Ltd., 5-11 Mortimer St., London, GL W1N 7RH, England. **Online address:** irving@ontheroad.demon.co.uk

WARDMAN, Gordon. British (born England), b. 1948. **Genres:** Novels, Poetry, Literary Criticism And History. **Career:** Kent & Yorkshire, probation officer, 1970-77; Yorkshire, communist party official, 1977-81. Writer. **Publications:** NOVELS: Crispin's Spur, 1985; Reparations, 1987. VERSE: High Country Hank, 1993; (ed.) Return to Sender: An Anthology of Poems for Elvis Presley, 1994; The Newfoundland Cantos, 1994; Trolleytown, 1996; Harlowski, 1998; Smaller Thoughts, 1998; The Trotskyist Cat Poems, 1999; Caedmon, 2001. Contributor to periodicals. **Address:** 26 Tithelands, Harlow, EX CM19 5, England.

WARDMAN, Sandy. *See* SMITH, Sandra Lee.

WARDROPER, John Edmund. British/Canadian (born Canada), b. 1923. **Genres:** History, Literary Criticism And History, Humor/Satire, Biography. **Career:** Cowichan Leader, reporter, 1941-43; Daily Colonist, reporter, 1943-45; News-Herald, desk man, 1948-49; Sunderland Echo, sub-editor, 1949; Liverpool Post, sub-editor, 1950; Daily Express, sub-editor, 1951-64; British national newspapers, staff, 1951-84; Sun, sub-editor, 1964-70; Sunday Times, sub-editor, 1970-. Freelance journalist. **Publications:** (Ed.) Love and Drollery: A Selection of Amatory, Merry and Satirical Verse of the 17th Century, 1969; Jest upon Jest: A Selection from the Jestbooks and Collections of Merry Tales Published from the Reign of Richard III to George III, 1970; (ed. and intro.) Demaundes Joyous: A Facsimile of the First English Riddle Book, 1971; Kings, Lords and Wicked Libellers: Satire and Protest, 1760-1837, 1973; The Caricatures of George Cruikshank, 1977; Juggernaut, 1981; (comp. and intro.) Lovers, Rakes, and Rogues: Amatory, Merry, and Bawdy Verse from 1580 to 1830, 1995; (comp. and intro.) The World of William Hone: A New Look at the Romantic Age in Words and Pictures of the Day, 1997; Wicked Ernest: The Truth about the Man Who was Almost Britain's King: An Extraordinary Royal Life Revealed, 2002. **Address:** 60 St. Paul's Rd., London, GL N1 2QW, England. **Online address:** jwardroper@blueyonder.co.uk

WARDROPPER, Ian. American (born United States), b. 1951. **Genres:** Art/Art History. **Career:** Sotheby's, Print Department, cataloger and general assistant, 1974-77; Metropolitan Museum of Art, graduate assistant, 1976, visiting assistant professor, Iris and B. Gerald Cantor curator, European sculpture and decorative Arts, chairman, 2001-; Art Institute, assistant curator of European painting and sculpture, 1982-85, associate curator of European decorative arts and sculpture, 1985-89, Eloise W. Martin curator of European decorative arts and sculpture and classical art, 1989-2001; Northwestern University, visiting professor; Drew University, visiting professor; College of New Rochelle, visiting professor; New York University, visiting professor. Writer. **Publications:** (Contrib.) A Decade of Decorative Arts: The Antiquarian Society of the Art Institute of Chicago, 1986; (with L.S. Roberts) European Decorative Arts in the Art Institute of Chicago, 1991; (with J. Zukowsky) Austrian Architecture and Design: Beyond Tradition in the Nineties, 1991; News from a Radiant Future: Soviet Propaganda Plates from the Tuber Collection, 1992; (with F. Licht) Chiseled with a Brush: Italian Sculpture, 1860-1925, from the Gilgore Collections, 1994; (co-author) From the Sculptor's Hand: Italian Baroque Terracottas from the State Hermitage Museum, 1998. EDITOR: (with T. Husband) Medieval Art from the Metropolitan Museum of Art and the Art Institute of Chicago (catalogue in Russian), 1990. Contributor to art and museum journals. **Address:** Dept. of European Sculpture & Decorative Arts, Metropolitan Museum of Art, 1000 5th Ave., New York, NY 10028, U.S.A. **Online address:** iwardrop@artic.edu

WARE, Alan. British (born England), b. 1949. **Genres:** Politics/Government, Social Sciences, History. **Career:** University of Warwick, faculty; University of Oxford, Worcesterr College, professor of politics, CUF University, lecturer, tutorial fellow in politics, 1990-. Writer. **Publications:** The Logic of Party Democracy, 1979; The Breakdown of Democratic Party Organization, 1940-1980, 1985; Citizens, Parties, and the State: A Reappraisal, 1987; (ed.) Charities and Government, 1989; Between Profit and State: Intermediate Organizations in Britain and the United States, 1989; (ed. with R.E. Goodin) Needs and Welfare, 1990; (with A. Reeve) Electoral Systems: A Comparative and Theoretical Introduction, 1992; Political Parties and Party Systems, 1996; (ed.) Democracy and North America, 1996; (ed.) The United States, 1997; (ed. with P. Burnell) Funding Democratization, 1998; The American Direct Primary: Party Institutionalization and Transformation in the North, 2002; The Democratic Party Heads North, 1877-1962, 2006; The Dynamics of Two-Party Politics: Party Structures and the Management of Competition, 2009; (ed. with M. Sánchez-Jankowski) The Management of Purpose, 2010; Political Conflict in America, 2011. Contributor to journals and periodicals. **Address:** Department of Politics and International Relations, University of Oxford, Manor Road Bldg., Manor Rd., Oxford, OX OX1 3UQ, England. **Online address:** alan.ware@worc.ox.ac.uk

WARE, Cheryl. American (born United States), b. 1963. **Genres:** Children's Fiction, Westerns/Adventure. **Career:** Belington Bank, general employee, 1981-85; One Valley Bank, bookkeeper, 1986-92; Fairmont State College, instructor, 1991-92; Alderson-Broaddus College, instructor, 1994-97. Writer. **Publications:** (Ed. with T. Fox) McNeese State University, 1939-1987: A Chronicle, 1990; Sea Monkey Summer, 1996 as Flea Circus Summer, 1997; Catty-Cornered, 1998; Venola in Love, 2000: Roberta Price Has Head Lice: A Story, 2003. **Address:** PO Box 561, Elkins, WV 26241-0561, U.S.A. **Online address:** venola@verizon.net

WARE, Jane (O.). (Jane Orth Ware). American (born United States), b. 1936. **Genres:** Architecture, Education, Local History/Rural Topics, Travel/Exploration, History, Education, Reference, Art/Art History, Art/Art History. **Career:** This Week, research editor, 1959-65; Ridgewood News, writer, 1978-80; freelance magazine journalist, 1983-. **Publications:** An Ohio State Profile: A Year in the Life of America's Biggest Campus, 1990; Other People's Business, 1993; Building Ohio, vol. I: A Traveler's Guide to Ohio's Urban Architecture, 2001, vol. II: A Traveler's Guide to Ohio's Rural Architecture, 2002; (ed.) Particular Places: A Traveler's Guide to Ohio's Best Road Trips, 2008. Contributor to magazines. **Address:** 2478 Bryden Rd., Columbus, OH 43209, U.S.A.

WARE, Jane Orth. *See* **WARE, Jane (O.).**

WARE, Kallistos. (Timothy Ware). British (born England), b. 1934. **Genres:** Theology/Religion, Philosophy, Translations. **Career:** Westminster Under School, classics master, 1958-59; Oxford University, researcher in church history, Magdalen College, 1960-63, Spalding lecturer in Eastern Orthodox studies, 1966-2001, now professor emeritus, Pembroke College, fellow, 1970-; Eastern Orthodox Church, priest, 1966-; Greek Orthodox Parish of Holy Trinity, priest-in-charge, 1966-; Anglican-Orthodox Joint Doctrinal Discussions, theological secretary, 1973-79, counselor, 1979-; Orthodox Archdiocese of Thyateira and Great Britain, titular bishop of Diokleia and assistant bishop, 1982-2001. Writer. **Publications:** (As Timothy Ware) The Orthodox Church, 1963, new ed., 1993; (as Timothy Ware) Eustratios Argenti: A Study of the Greek Church under Turkish Rule, 1964; The Power of the Name, 1974; The Orthodox Way, 1979, rev. ed., 1995; (co-author) Women and the Priesthood, 1983, rev. ed. (with T. Hopko), 1999; (intro.) The Ladder of Divine Ascent, 1982; Orthodoxos Dromos, 1984; (with R. Llewelyn and M. Clare) Praying Home: The Contemplative Journey, 1987; (foreword) The Jesus Prayer, 1987; Anthrōpos Kai Koinōnia: Dokimia Gia Te Thesetou Anthrōpou Sto Synchrono Kosmo, 1991; Act Out of Stillness: The Influence of Fourteenth-Century Hesychasm on Byzantine and Slav Civilization, 1995; How Are We Saved?: The Understanding of Salvation in the Orthodox Tradition, 1996; The Inner Kingdom, 2000; (with E. Behr-Sigel) The Ordination of Women in the Orthodox Church, 2000; (foreword) Spiritual World of Isaac the Syrian, 2000; Orthodox Church and the Orthodox Way Reviewed: A Traditionalist Critique of Two Popular Introductions to Eastern Orthodox Christianity, 2000; (as Timothy Ware) Pravoslavna Crkva, 2001; Ekklesia Kai Kosmos, 2002; Tout Ce Qui Vit Est Saint, 2003; In the Image of the Trinity: Collected Works, 2006. EDITOR: (intro.) The Art of Prayer: An Orthodox Anthology, 1966; (with C. Davey) Anglican-Orthodox Dialogue: The Moscow Statement Agreed by the Anglican-Orthodox Joint Doctrinal Commission 1976; (with G. Every and R. Harries) Seasons of the Spirit: Readings through the Christian Year, 1984; (with G. Every, R. Harries) Time of the Spirit: Readings through the Christian Year, 1984; (trans. with G.E.H. Palmer and P. Sherrard) Prayer of the Heart: Writings from the Philokalia: From the Complete Text, 1993; Abba: The Tradition of Orthodoxy in the West: Festschrift for Bishop Kallistos Ware of Diokleia, 2003; (trans. with G.E.H. Palmer and P. Sherrard) The Philokalia: Master Reference Guide: Master Indexes to the Four Primary Volumes, Authors w/Tables of Content, 2004; (G. Speake) Mount Athos: Microcosm of the Christian East, 2011. TRANSLATOR: (with M. Mary) The Festal Menaion, 1969; (with M. Mary) The Lenten Triodion, 1978; (with A.N. Papathanasiou and Z. Touraig) Ekklesia kai kosmos, 2002. **Address:** Greek Orthodox Archdiocese, Thyateira and Grt Britain, Thyateira House, 5 Craven Hill, London, GL W2 3EN, England.

WARE, Leland B. American (born United States), b. 1948?. **Genres:** Law, Biography, Autobiography/Memoirs. **Career:** Bar of the State of Georgia, staff, 1973; Wyatt and Associates, associate attorney, 1973-75; Hill, Jones, & Farrington, associate attorney, 1975-76; U.S. Department of Health, Education & Welfare, assistant regional attorney, 1976-79; U.S. Department of Justice, trial attorney, 1979-84; Howard University, university counsel, 1984-87; Bar of the District of Columbia, staff, 1985; St. Louis University, assistant professor, 1987-91, associate professor, 1991-94, professor of law, 1994-2000; Boston College Law School, visiting professor, 1992; Rühr University, visiting professor, 1997; University of Delaware, Louis L. Redding chair for the study of law and public policy, professor, 2000-; Christina Hospital Corp., trustee; National Board of the American Civil Liberties Union, vice president; Delaware Civil Liberties Union, board director. Writer. **Publications:** Thurgood Marshall: Freedom's Defender, 1999; (with R.J. Cottrol and R.T. Diamond) Brown v. Board of Education: Caste, Culture, and the Constitution, 2003; (ed. with R.L. Hayman, Jr.) Choosing Equality: Essays and Narratives on the Desegregation Experience, 2009. Contributor to periodicals and journals. **Address:** Institute for Public Administration, University of Delaware, 180 Graham Hall, Newark, DE 19716-7380, U.S.A. **Online address:** lware@udel.edu

WARE, Leslie. American (born United States) **Genres:** Business/Trade/Industry, Economics, Marketing. **Career:** National Audubon Society, Audubon Magazine, senior editor, 1979-89; Consumer Reports, editor-at-large, 1989-, features editor. **Publications:** (Co-author) Selling It: The Incredible Shrinking Package and Other Marvels of Modern Marketing, 2002. **Address:** Consumer Reports, 101 Truman Ave., Yonkers, NY 10703-1057, U.S.A.

WARE, Sandra J. American (born United States), b. 1972. **Genres:** Law, Young Adult Fiction, Education. **Career:** Rutgers Law School, Camden Academic Success Program, tutor; Law Student Success, principal. Writer. **Publications:** (With D. Edouard) Mortal Sins, 1991; (with D. Edouard) Sacred Lies, 1993; Guerrilla Tactics for Law School Academic Success, 2003. Contributor to journals. **Address:** Law Student Success, 140 Ford Ave., Woodbury, NJ 08096-5064, U.S.A. **Online address:** sanware@comcast.net

WARE, Susan. American (born United States), b. 1950. **Genres:** History, Women's Studies And Issues. **Career:** New York University, professor of history, 1986-95; Harvard University, faculty. Writer. **Publications:** (Comp.) Modern American Women: A Documentary History, 1969, 2nd ed., 2002; Beyond Suffrage, Women in the New Deal, 1981; Holding Their Own: American Women in the 1930s, 1982; Partner and I: Molly Dewson, Feminism, and New Deal Politics, 1987; (co-author) America's History, 2 vols., 1987, 5th ed., 2003; Still Missing: Amelia Earhart and the Search for Modern Feminism, 1993; (ed.) New Viewpoints in Women's History, 1994; (ed.) Forgotten Heroes: Inspiring American Portraits from Our Leading Historians, 1998; Letter to the World: Seven Women Who Shaped the American Century, 1998; (ed. with S. Braukman) Notable American Women: A Biographical Dictionary Completing the Twentieth Century, 2004; It's One O'clock and Here is Mary Margaret McBride: A Radio Biography, 2005; Title IX: A Brief History with Documents, 2007; Game, Set, Match: Billie Jean King and the Revolution in Women's Sports, 2011. Contributor to periodicals. **Address:** University of North Carolina Press, 116 S Boundary St., Chapel Hill, NC 27514-3808, U.S.A. **Online address:** sdware@aol.com

WARE, Timothy. *See* **WARE, Kallistos.**

WAREHAM, Dean Dean. (Michael Dean Wareham). American/New Zealander (born New Zealand), b. 1963. **Genres:** Music. **Career:** Galaxie 500, founder, 1987-91; Dean and Britta, co-founder, 2003-. Writer. **Publications:** Black Postcards: Unreleased B Sides and Notes from the Road, 2008. **Address:** NY , U.S.A. **Online address:** deanandbritta@gmail.com

WAREHAM, Michael Dean. *See* **WAREHAM, Dean Dean.**

WARFIELD, Gallatin. American (born United States), b. 1946. **Genres:** Novels, Mystery/Crime/Suspense, Young Adult Fiction, Literary Criticism And History. **Career:** Maryland Attorney General's Office, assistant attorney general, 1974-76; Howard County States Attorney's Office, Felony Division, chief, 1976-89. Writer. **Publications:** NOVELS: State versus Justice, 1992; Silent Son, 1994; Silent Witness, 1994; Raising Cain, 1996. **Address:** 2605 Alpine Blvd., PO Box 2378, Alpine, CA 91903-2378, U.S.A.

WARING, Belle. American (born United States), b. 1951?. **Genres:** Poetry. **Career:** The Nation's Children's Hospital, Children's National Medical Center, writer-in-residence; Vermont College, field faculty. Poet. **Publications:** Refuge, 1990; Dark Blonde: Poems, 1997; (trans.) J. Holbo, Reason & Persuasion: Three Dialogues by Plato, 3rd ed., 2010. **Address:** Sarabande Books Inc., 2234 Dundee Rd., Ste. 200, Louisville, KY 40205, U.S.A. **Online address:** bbwaring@yahoo.com

WARLICK, Ashley. American (born United States), b. 1972. **Genres:** Novels, Literary Criticism And History. **Career:** Queens University of Charlotte, MFA Creative Writing Program, instructor. Writer. **Publications:** The Distance from the Heart of Things, 1996; The Summer After June, 2000; Seek the Living: A Novel, 2005. Contributor to periodicals. **Address:** c/o Amanda Urban, International Creative Management Agency, 40 W 57th St., New York, NY 10019-4001, U.S.A.

WARMINGTON, William Allan. *See* Obituaries.

WARMUTH, Donna Akers. American (born United States), b. 1966. **Genres:** Geography. **Career:** Appalachian State University, adjunct instructor, 1999; Air Force Headquarters, cultural resource program manager; American Emergency Vehicles, vice president. Writer. **Publications:** Abingdon, Virginia: Images of America, 2002; Boone North Carolina: Images of America, 2003; Plumb Full of History: A Story of Abingdon, Virginia, 2003; Blowing Rock North Carolina: Images of America, 2004; Washington County: Images of America, 2006; Washington County Revisited: Images of America, 2008; (with B. Lambeth) Watauga County, 2008; Legends, Stories and Ghostly Tales of Abingdon and Washington County Virginia, 2005; Self-Rising Flowers; The Zinnia Tales, 2006. **Address:** PO Box 105, Deep Gap, NC 28618, U.S.A. **Online address:** info@donnaakers.com

WARNE, Randi R(uth). Canadian (born Canada), b. 1952. **Genres:** History, Women's Studies And Issues, Essays, Theology/Religion. **Career:** University of Toronto, fellow, 1976-77, 1982-83; St. Stephen's College, program director for continuing education and assistant professor of social ethics, 1988-93; University of Alberta, lecturer in religious studies and women's studies, 1993-94; Emmanuel College, Centre for the Study of Religion in Canada, research associate, 1993-95; University of Wisconsin-Oshkosh, director of women's studies and assistant professor of religious studies, 1994-97; Mount Saint Vincent University, co-ordinator of cultural studies, 2007-, Department of Religious Studies, chairman, 2007-, faculty. Writer. **Publications:** (Intro.) Purple Springs, 1992; Literature As Pulpit: The Christian Social Activism of Nellie L. McClung, 1993; (ed. with C.A. Cavanaugh) Standing on New Ground: Women in Alberta, 1993; (ed. with C.A. Cavanaugh) Telling Tales: Essays in Western Women's History, 2000; (ed. with P. Antes and A.W. Geertz) New Approaches to the Study of Religion, 2004. Contributor of articles to periodicals. **Address:** Philosophy/Religious Studies, Mount St. Vincent University, 326 Seton, 166 Bedford Hwy., Halifax, NS B3M 2J6, Canada. **Online address:** randi.warne@msvu.ca

WARNEKE, Georgia. *See* **WARNEKE, Sara.**

WARNEKE, Sara. Also writes as Georgia Warneke, Sara Douglass. Australian (born Australia), b. 1957. **Genres:** Novels, Romance/Historical, Science Fiction/Fantasy. **Career:** Latrobe University, senior lecturer in history, 1992-99; nurse. Novelist and historian. **Publications:** AXIS TRILOGY: Battle Axe, 1995; Enchanter, 1996; Star Man, 1997. WAYFARER REDEMPTION SERIES: Sinner, 1997; Pilgrim, 1998; Crusader, 1998. NOVELS: Beyond the Hanging Wall, 1996; Threshold, 1997. THE CRUCIBLE SERIES: The Nameless Day, 2000; The Wounded Hawk, 2001; Crippled Angel, 2006. TROY GAME: Hades' Daughter, 2003; Gods Concubine, 2004; Darkwitch Rising, 2005; Druid's Sword, 2006. DARKGLASS MOUNTAINS: The Serpent Bride, 2007; The Twisted Citadel, 2008; The Infinity Gate, 2009. AS SARA WARNEKE: Images of the Educational Traveller in Early Modern England, 1995; (trans.) Robert Mannyng of Brunne, Story of Arthur, 1995. AS SARA DOUGLASS: The Devil's Diadem, 2011. Works appear in anthologies. Contributor of articles to books. **Address:** c/o Author Mail, HarperCollins, 25 Ryde Rd., Pymble, NW 2073, Australia.

WARNER, Brad. American (born United States), b. 1964. **Genres:** Social Commentary, Adult Non-fiction, Theology/Religion, Humanities. **Career:** Dogen Sangha Intl., founder and leader; Hill Street Center, staff. Writer. **Publications:** Hardcore Zen: Punk Rock, Monster Movies & the Truth about Reality, 2003; Sit Down and Shut Up: Punk Rock Commentaries on Buddha, God, Truth, Sex, Death, and Dogen's Treasury of the Right Dharma Eye, 2007; Zen Wrapped in Karma Dipped In Chocolate: A Trip Through Death, Sex, Divorce, and Spiritual Celebrity in Search of the True Dharma, 2009; Sex, Sin, and Zen: A Buddhist Exploration of Sex from Celibacy to Polyamory and Everything in Between, 2010. **Address:** Hill Street Center, 237 Hill St., Santa Monica, CA 90405, U.S.A. **Online address:** doubtboy@mac.com

WARNER, Daniel. Swiss/American (born United States), b. 1946. **Genres:** International Relations/Current Affairs. **Career:** Associated Press, writer, 1986-; Graduate Institute of International Studies, International Security and Arms Control, International Training Course, assistant director, 1991-, deputy to the director for external relations and special programs, 1994-, secretary-general ad interim, 2000-01, deputy director, 2010-, executive director. **Publications:** An Ethic of Responsibility in International Relations, 1991; U.S. Foreign Policy after the End of the Cold War, 1996. EDITOR: Citizenship East and West, 1995; New Dimensions of Peacekeeping, 1995; (with M. Bertrand) A New Charter for a Worldwide Organisation?, 1996; Human Rights and Humanitarian Law: The Quest for Universality, 1997; (with V. Ghebali) OSCE and Preventive Diplomacy, 1999; Japan and Multilateral Diplomacy, 2001; (with V.Y. Ghebali) The Operational Role of the OSCE in South-Eastern Europe: Contributing to Regional Stability in the Balkans, 2001; (with J.M. Coicaud) Ethics and International Affairs: Extent and Limits, 2001; (with F. Sabahi) OSCE and the Multiple Challenges of Transition: The Caucasus and Central Asia, 2004; (with V.A. Leary) Social Issues, Globalisation and International Institutions: Labour Rights and the EU, ILO, OECD and WTO, 2006. **Address:** Graduate Institute of International Studies, 132 rue de Lausanne, PO Box 136, Geneva, CH-1211, Switzerland. **Online address:** warner@hei.unige.ch

WARNER, Elizabeth (Ann). British/American (born United States), b. 1940?. **Genres:** Essays, Music. **Career:** University of Durham, professor of Russian, Department of Slavonic Studies, head, Ustinov Institute for the Study of Central and Eastern Europe, director, now professor emeritus of Russian. Writer. **Publications:** The Russian Folk Theatre, 1977; Heroes, Monsters and Other Worlds from Russian Mythology, 1985; (with E.S. Kustovskii) Russian Traditional Folk Song, 1990; Russian Myths, 2002. **Address:** School of Modern Languages & Cultures, Durham University, Elvet Riverside, Durham, DU DH1 3JT, England.

WARNER, Francis. British (born England), b. 1937. **Genres:** Plays/Screenplays, Poetry, History, Literary Criticism And History. **Career:** Cambridge University, St. Catharine's College, teacher, 1958-65; Yeats International Summer School, assistant director, 1961-67; Oxford University, St. Peter's College, Lord White fellow and tutor in English literature, 1965-99, dean of degrees and emeritus fellow, 1999-; Samuel Beckett Theatre, founder, 1967. Writer. **Publications:** POETRY: Perennia, 1962; Early Poems, 1964; Experimental Sonnets, 1967; Madrigals, 1967; Poetry of Francis Warner, 1970; Lucca Quartet: For Lorraine, 1975; Poetry, 1978; Morning Vespers for Rosalind, 1980; Spring Harvest, 1981; Epithalamium, 1983; Collected Poems, 1960-1984, 1985; Nightingales: Poems 1985-96, 1997; Cambridge: A Poem, 2001; Oxford: A Poem, 2002. PLAYS: Maquettes: A Trilogy of one-set Plays, 1972; Lying Figures: A Play, 1972; Meeting Ends: A Play, 1974; Killing Time, 1976; A Conception of Love: A Play, 1978; Light Shadows, 1980; Moving Reflections, 1983; Living Creation, 1985; Healing Nature: The Athens of Pericles, 1988; Byzantium, 1990; Virgil and Caesar, 1993; Agora: An Epic, 1994; King Francis I: A Play, 1995; Goethe's Weimar, 1997; Rembrandt's Mirror, 2000. OTHERS: (comp.) Garland: A Little Anthology of Poetry and Engravings, 1968; Theatre and Nationalism in Twentieth Century Ireland, 1971; Francis Warner: Poet and Dramatist, 1977; Requiem Together with Its Maquettes, 1980; Transcendent Flame, 1987; By the Cam and the Isis, 1954-2000, 2005. **Address:** St. Peter's College, Oxford University, New Inn Hall St., Oxford, OX OX1 2DL, England.

WARNER, Jack. American (born United States), b. 1937. **Genres:** Novels. **Career:** United Press Intl., correspondent, bureau manager, 1956-86, national editor, 1986-87; Atlanta Journal and Constitution, journalist, 1987-2001. Writer, 2001-. **Publications:** Shikar, 2003. **Address:** Richard Curtis Associates., 171 E 74th St., 2nd Fl., New York, NY 10021-3221, U.S.A.

WARNER, Janine C. American (born United States), b. 1967. **Genres:** Information Science/Computers. **Career:** Visiontec Communications, principal, 1994-98; Miami Herald, online managing editor, director of new media, 1998-2000; Western Knight Center, multimedia program manager; CNET Networks, director of Latin-American operations; University of Southern California, lecturer; University of Miami, lecturer; Artesian Media Inc., co-founder; United States and Abroad, consultant. **Publications:** (With K. Reddy) Hybrid HTML Design: A Multi-Browser HTML Reference, 1996; (with K. Milburn and J. Burdman) Converting Content for Web Publishing: Time-saving Tools and Techniques, 1996; (with K. Milburn) Designing Web Pages with PageMill 2.0, 1997; The Flash 2 Web Animation Book: Advanced Animation Techniques from Successful Web Professionals, 1997; Dreamweaver for Dummies, 1998; Small Business Web Strategies for Dummies, 1998; (with K. Milburn) Flash 3 Web Animation F/X and Design, 1999; (with P. Vachier) Dreamweaver 3 for Dummies, 2000; Managing Web Projects for Dummies, 2001; Dreamweaver 4 for Dummies, 2001; Ebusiness Strategies for Dummies, 2001; (with I. Berkowitz) Dreamweaver MX for Dummies, 2002; (with I. Berkowitz) Teach Yourself Visually Dreamweaver MX, 2002; (with I. Berkowitz and Y. Gonzalez) Fifty Fast Dreamweaver MX Techniques, 2003; Teach Yourself Visually Dreamweaver, 2003; (with F. Vera) Macromedia Contribute for Dummies, 2003; (with S. Gardner) Dreamweaver MX 2004 for Dummies, 2004; (with S. Gardner) Teach Yourself Visually Dreamweaver MX 2004, 2004; Creating Family Web Sites for Dummies, 2005; Teach Yourself Visually Macromedia Dreamweaver 8, 2006; (with T. McCain and M. McCain) Digital Family Album Basics: Tools for Creating Digital Memories, 2006; Dreamweaver 8 for Dummies, 2006; Dreamweaver CS3, 2007; Dreamweaver CS3 for Dummies, 2007; Teach Yourself Visually Dreamweaver CS4, 2008; Web Sites for Dummies: Do-it-yourself, 2008; Adobe Dreamweaver CS5, 2010. **Address:** DigitalFamily Inc., 12335 Santa Monica Blvd., Ste. 101, 2187 Newcastle Ave., Ste. 204, Los Angeles, CA 90025, U.S.A. **Online address:** janine@jcwarner.com

WARNER, Judith. American (born United States), b. 1965. **Genres:** Biography, Human Relations/Parenting, History, Psychiatry, Women's Studies And Issues. **Career:** New York Times, news assistant, 1987-88, contributing columnist, 2001-06, freelance contributor, 2006-09, contributing writer, 2011- ; freelance writer, 1989-; Newsweek, special correspondent, 1996-98; The Washington Post, freelance contributor, 2001-06; XM Radio, host, 2005-07. **Publications:** Hillary Clinton: The Inside Story, 1993, rev. ed., 1999; (with M. Berley) Newt Gingrich, 1995; (with G. Mirabella) In and Out of Vogue, 1995; (with H. Dean) You Have the Power: How to Take Back Our Country and Restore Democracy in America, 2004; Perfect Madness: Motherhood in the Age of Anxiety, 2005; We've Got Issues: Children and Parents in the Age of Medication, 2010. **Address:** c/o Jennifer Rudolph Walsh, William Morris Endeavor, 1325 Ave. of the Americas, New York, NY 10019, U.S.A. **Online address:** judith@judithwarneronline.com

WARNER, Malcolm. American/British (born England), b. 1953. **Genres:** Art/Art History, Architecture, Biography. **Career:** University of Wisconsin's London Center, lecturer, 1979-87; Victoria University of Manchester, lecturer, 1982-83, 1984-85, visiting assistant professor, 1984-85; Cambridge University, lecturer, 1984-86; Lawrence University of Wisconsin, lecturer, 1985; independent curator, teacher and writer, 1985-88; School of the Art Institute of Chicago, lecturer, 1988; Art Institute of Chicago, Department of European Painting, research curator, 1988-90; University of Chicago, faculty, 1989; San Diego Museum of Art, curator of prints and drawings, 1990-96, curator of European art, 1992-96; University of California, lecturer, 1993; Yale University, Yale Center for British Art, curator of paintings and sculpture, 1996-2001; Kimbell Art Museum, senior curator, 2002-07, deputy director and acting director, 2007-. **Publications:** Portrait Painting, 1979; The Drawings of John Everett Millais, 1979; (with M. Jacobs) The Phaidon Companion to Art and Artists in the British Isles, 1980; James Tissot: Victorian Life, Modern Love, 1982; (ed. with M. Lutyens) Rainy Days at Brigo'Turk: The Highland Sketchbooks of John Everett Millais, 1853, 1983; (and intro.) The Image of London: Views by Travellers and Emigres, 1550-1920, 1987; The Art of the Print: Glossary, 1991; (co-author) The Pre-Raphaelites in Context, 1992; The Prints of Harry Sternberg, 1994; (with S. Wise) French and British Paintings from 1600 to 1800 in the Art Institute of Chicago: A Catalogue of the Collection, 1996; The Victorians: British Painting, 1837-1901, 1996; (ed.) New Dictionary of National Biography, 1997; (with J.M. Alexander) This Other Eden: Paintings from the Yale Center for British Art, 1998; (with R. Asleson) Great British Paintings From American Collections: Holbe in to Hockney/ Malcolm Warner and Robyn Asleson, 2001; (contrib. with J. Fleming and S. Cavell) Magic Markers: Objects of Transformation: Des Moines Art Center,

February 1 April 20, 2003: Georgia Blizzard, 2003; (with R. Blake) Stubbs & the Horse, 2004; (ed. with P. Alarco) El espejo y la máscara: el retrato en el siglo de Picasso, 2007; (and contrib. with P. Alarco) The Mirror & the Mask: Portraiture in the Age of Picasso, 2007; Friendship and Loss in the Victorian Portrait: May Sartoris by Frederic Leighton, 2009; (contrib.) Butchers, Dragons, Gods & Skeletons: Film Installations by Philip Haas, 2009. Contributor of articles to periodicals. **Address:** Kimbell Art Museum, Yale University, 3333 Camp Bowie Blvd., Fort Worth, TX 76107-2792, U.S.A. **Online address:** malcolm.warner@yale.edu

WARNER, Margaret. *See* **HUMPHREYS, Margaret.**

WARNER, Marina. British (born England), b. 1946. **Genres:** Novels, Novellas/Short Stories, Children's Fiction, Art/Art History, History, Literary Criticism And History, Mythology/Folklore. **Career:** Erasmus University, professor, 1991; University of London, visiting professor, 1994, Department of Humanities, visiting professor, 2009; University of Pittsburgh, visiting professor, 1997; Humanities Research Centre, visiting fellow, 1999; Stanford University, visiting professor, 2000; Columbia University, visiting fellow, 2003; University of Essex, Department of Literature, Film and Theatre Studies, professor of literature, 2004-; Royal College of Art, Department of Animation, visiting professor, 2008-; BBC TV, reviewer; Times Literary Supplement, staff; New York Times Book Review, reviewer; London Review of Books, reviewer. Writer. **Publications:** The Dragon Empress: Life and Times of Tzu-hsi, 1835-1908, Empress Dowager of China, 1972; Alone of All Her Sex: The Myth and the Cult of the Virgin Mary, 1976; Queen Victoria's Sketchbook, 1979; Joan of Arc: The Image of Female Heroism, 1981; Monuments and Maidens: The Allegory of the Female Form, 1985; Into the Dangerous World, 1989; The Mermaids in the Basement (short stories), 1993; (co-author) Cinema and the Realms of Enchantment: Lectures, Seminars, and Essays, 1993; Six Myths of Our Time: Little Angels, Little Monsters, Beautiful Beasts, and More (lectures), 1994; From the Beast to the Blonde: On the Fairy Tales and Their Tellers, 1994; (ed.) Wonder Tales, 1994; The Book of Signs & Symbols, 1996; (intro.) The Trial of Joan of Arc, 1996; (ed. and intro.) Wonder Tales, 1996; No Go the Bogeyman: Scaring, Lulling and Making Mock, 1999; David Nash: Forms Into Time, 2001; Fantastic Metamorphoses, Other Worlds: Ways of Telling the Self (lectures), 2002; Murderers I Have Known and Other Stories (short stories), 2002; (comp.) World of Myths, 2003; Signs & Wonders: Essays on Literature & Culture, 2003; Phantasmagoria: Spirit Visions, Metaphors, and Media into the Twenty-first Century, 2006; Monsters of Our Own Making: The Peculiar Pleasures of Fear, 2007; (contrib.) Sometimes I Think, Sometimes I Am, 2007. NOVELS: In a Dark Wood, 1977; The Skating Party, 1982; The Lost Father, 1988; Indigo, or Mapping the Waters, 1992; The Leto Bundle, 2001. FOR CHILDREN: The Crack in the Teacup: Britain in the 20th Century, 1979; The Impossible Day (Night, Bath, Rocket), 1981; The Wobbly Tooth, 1984. CATALOGS: Peter Randall-Page, 1992; Richard Wentworth, 1993; The Inner Eye, 1996; (with S. Bakewell) Metamorphing, 2002; (with W. Nekes and L. Mannoni) Eyes, Lies and Illusions, 2004. Contributor of articles to periodicals. **Address:** Department of Literature, Film & Theatre Studies, University of Essex, Rm. 5A.109, Colchester, Wivenhoe Park, CO4 3SQ, England. **Online address:** mswarner@essex.ac.uk

WARNER, Martin. British (born England), b. 1940. **Genres:** Philosophy. **Career:** University College of North Wales, lecturer, 1965-69; University of Warwick, lecturer, 1969-90, senior lecturer, 1990-2005, associate fellow, 2005-, Centre for Research in Philosophy and Literature, founding programme director, 1985-87. Writer. **Publications:** Philosophical Finesse: Studies in the Art of Rational Persuasion, 1989; A Philosophical Study of T.S. Eliot's Four Quartets, 1999; (comp.) Habit of Holiness: Daily Prayer, 2004; Known to the Senses, 2004; Between Heaven and Charing Cross, 2009. EDITOR: The Bible as Rhetoric: Studies in Biblical Persuasion and Credibility, 1990; (with R. Crisp) Terrorism, Protest and Power, 1990; (with M. Tudeau-Clayton) Addressing Frank Kermode: Essays in Criticism and Interpretation, 1991; Religion and Philosophy, 1992; (with A. Barker) The Language of the Cave, 1992; (with K. Vanhoozer) Transcending Boundaries in Philosophy and Theology: Reason, Meaning and Experience, 2007. Contributor to journals. **Address:** Department of Philosophy, University of Warwick, Coventry, WM CV4 7AL, England. **Online address:** martin.warner@warwick.ac.uk

WARNER, Penny. American/Japanese (born Japan), b. 1947. **Genres:** Children's Non-fiction, Mystery/Crime/Suspense, Writing/Journalism. **Career:** Writer. **Publications:** SELF-ILLUSTRATOR: Happy Birthday Parties!, 1985.

CONNOR WESTPHAL MYSTERY SERIES: Dead Body Language, 1997; Signs of Foul Play, 1998; Right To Remain Silent, 1998; Quiet Undertaking, 1999; Blind Side, 2001; Silence is Golden, 2003; Dead Mans Hand, 2007. PARTY BOOKS: Penny Warners Party Book, 1987; Best Party Book: 1001 Creative Ideas for Fun Parties, 1992; Kids Party Games And Activities: Hundreds of Exciting Things to Do at Parties for Kids 2-12, 1993; Kids Holiday Fun: Great Family Activities Every Month of the Year, 1994; Birthday Parties for Kids!: Creative Party Ideas Your Kids and Their Friends Will Love, 1996; Kids Party Cookbook!, 1996; Games People Play: The Biggest and Best Book of Party Games and Activities, 1997; The Kids Pick-A-Party Book: 50 Fun Themes for Happy Birthdays and Other Parties, 1997; The Big Book of Party and Holiday Fun, 1998; Kids Outdoor Parties: 25 Fun-Filled Party Themes, 1999; Baby Birthday Parties, 1999; Slumber Parties, 2000; Storybook Parties, 2001; Girls Night In, 2008. CHILD DEVELOPMENT AND ACTIVITY BOOKS: Super Toys, 1985; Splish Splash-Water Fun for Kids, 1995; Great Games for Kids on the Go: Over 240 Travel Games to Play on Trains, Planes, and Automobiles, 1998; Baby Play and Learn, 1999; Preschool Play and Learn, 2000; Smart Start for Your Baby: Your Babys Development Week by Week During the First Year and How You Can Help, 2001; Learn to Sign the Fun Way: Let Your Fingers Do the Talking With Games, Puzzles, and Activities in American Sign Language, 2001; Quality Time Any Time!: How to Make the Most of Every Moment with your Child, 2002; Summer Smarts for Cool Kids: Over 150 Fantastic and Fun Learning Activities to Help Kids Beat the Summer Blahs, 2002; Parents and Kids Complete Guide to Summer Camp Fun: Everything You Need to Prepare for an Incredible Camp Adventure!, 2002; 365 Baby Care Tips: Everything You Need to Know About Caring for Your Baby in the First Year of Life, 2002; (with P. Kelly) Toilet Training Without Tears or Trauma, 2003; (with P. Kelly) 365 Toddler Tips: A Helpful Handbook for the Early Years, 2004; Rock-A-Bye Baby: 200 Ways to Help Baby (and You!) Sleep Better, 2008. HEALTHY SNACK BOOKS: Healthy Snacks for Kids, 1983; Super Snacks for Kids, 1985; Healthy Treats and Super Snacks for Kids, 1994. MIDDLE GRADE MYSTERY FEATURING GIRL SCOUTS: Girls to the Rescue No. 7: Troop 13 Story, 2000; Mystery of the Haunted Caves, 2001. WITH T. WARNER: The Secret of the Bitter Sweets: A Murder Mystery Party for Eight People, 1986; Greetings From the Grave: A Murder Mystery Party for Eight People, 1986; A Deadly Game of Klew: A Murder Mystery Party for Six People, 1986. OTHERS: (with L.L. Oertel) Storybook Parties: 45 Parties Based on Childrens Favorite Stories, 2001; Signing Fun: American Sign Language Vocabulary, Phrases, Games and Activities, 2006; The Official Nancy Drew Handbook: Skills, Tips and Life Lessons from Everyones Favorite Girl Detective, 2007; Babys Favorite Rhymes to Sign, 2010; How to Host a Killer Party: A Party-planning Mystery, 2010; Baby's Favorite Rhymes to Sign, 2011; The Code Busters Club, Case #1: The Secret of the Skeleton Key, 2011; How to Party with a Killer Vampire: A Party-Planning Mystery, 2011; Secret of the Skeleton Key, 2012. Contributor to periodicals. **Address:** 710 Sinnet Ct., Danville, CA 94526, U.S.A. **Online address:** tpwarner@sbcglobal.net

WARNER, Sally. American (born United States), b. 1946?. **Genres:** Children's Fiction, Young Adult Fiction, Art/Art History, Novels. **Career:** Pasadena City College, teacher of art education. Artist and writer. **Publications:** SELF-ILLUSTRATED: Encouraging the Artist in Your Child (Even If You Can't Draw), 1989; Encouraging the Artist in Yourself: Even If It's Been a Long, Long Time, 1991; It's Only Temporary, 2008. JUVENILE: Making Room For Art, 1994; Dog Years, 1995; Some Friend, 1996; Elie and the Bunheads, 1997; Sort of Forever, 1998; Totally Confidential, 2000; Bad Girl Blues, 2001; Finding Hattie, 2001; How to Be a Real Person (in Just One Day), 2001; Sister Split, 2001; This Isn't about the Money, 2002; A Long Time Ago Today, 2003; Twilight Child, 2006. LILY SERIES: Sweet and Sour Lily, 1998; Private Lily, 1998; Accidental Lily, 1999; Leftover Lily, 1999. EMMA SERIES: Smart About the First Ladies, 2004; Not-So-Weird Emma, 2005; Only Emma, 2005; Super Emma, 2006; Best Friend Emma, 2007; Excellent Emma, 2009; Happily Ever Emma, 2010; EllRay Jakes Is not a Chicken, 2011; EllRay Jakes Is a Rock Star, 2011; Ellray Jakes Walks the Plank, 2012. OTHERS: Making Room for Making Art: A Thoughtful and Practical Guide to Bringing the Pleasure of Artistic Expression Back into Your Life, 1994. **Address:** c/o Author Mail, Viking Publicity, 345 Hudson St., New York, NY 10014, U.S.A.

WARNER, Sharon Oard. American (born United States), b. 1952. **Genres:** Novellas/Short Stories, Novels, Medicine/Health, Administration/Management, Women's Studies And Issues. **Career:** Oaks Treatment Center, educational activities coordinator, 1977-79; Spectrum/Focus on Deaf Artists, writer and grants coordinator, 1978-79; Lawrence Community Center, creative writing instructor, 1980; University of Kansas, instructor, 1980-84, lecturer in English, 1984-85; Lawrence Arts Center, creative writing instructor, 1983; Northeast Louisiana University, instructor in English, 1985-87; Iowa State University, instructor in English, 1987-88, instructor in creative writing, 1993; Drake University, visiting assistant professor of English, 1988-93; Des Moines Area Community College, instructor in composition and literature, 1993-94; University of Iowa, Summer Writing Festival, instructor in short fiction writing, novel writing and book reviewing, 1993-98, 2000; University of New Mexico, assistant professor in English, 1994-2000, associate professor, 2000-06, professor, 2006-, director of creative writing program, 1998-2008, Taos Summer Writer's Conference, founding director, 1998-. **Publications:** Learning to Dance and Other Stories, 1992; Deep in the Heart, 2000. EDITOR: (with M. Farley) Nineteen Stories: Contemporary Fiction by Kansas Writers, 1982; The Way We Write Now: Short Stories from the AIDS Crisis, 1995. Works appear in anthologies. Contributor of articles to periodicals. **Address:** Department of English Language & Literature, University of New Mexico, MSC 03 2170, Albuquerque, NM 87131-1106, U.S.A. **Online address:** swarner@unm.edu

WARNER, Val. British (born England), b. 1946. **Genres:** Poetry, Translations. **Career:** Inner London Education Authority, teacher, 1969-72; University College of Swansea, creative writing fellow, writer-in-residence, 1977-78; University of Dundee, writer-in-residence, 1979-81. Writer. **Publications:** These Yellow Photos, 1971; Under the Penthouse, 1973; (trans. and intro.) The Centenary Corbière: Poems and Prose of Tristan Corbière, 1974, new ed., 2003; (ed. and intro.) Charlotte Mew: Collected Poems and Prose, 1981, new ed., 2003; Before Lunch, 1986; Tooting Idyll, 1998; (trans. and afterword) T. Corbiere, The Centenary Corbière: Selected Poems and Prose, 2003. Contributor of periodicals and poems and short stories. **Address:** Carcanet Press Ltd., Alliance House, 30 Cross St., 4th Fl., Manchester, M2 7AQ, England. **Online address:** info@carcanet.co.uk

WARNICKE, Retha M. (Retha Marvine Warnicke). American (born United States), b. 1939. **Genres:** History, Women's Studies And Issues, Politics/Government. **Career:** Arizona State University, professor of history. Writer. **Publications:** William Lambarde, Elizabethan Antiquary, 1536-1601, 1973; Women of the English Renaissance and Reformation, 1983; The Rise and Fall of Anne Boleyn: Family Politics at the Court of Henry VIII, 1989; (intro.) Deaths Advantage Little Regarded, 1993; (intro.) The Monument or Tombe-stone: A Sermon Preached at the Funeral of Mrs. Elizabeth Juxon, 1996; (intro.) Deaths Sermon Unto the Living (1620), 1999; The Marrying of Anne of Cleves: Royal Protocol in Early Modern England, 2000; (intro.) The Praise of a Godly Woman (1627), 2001; (intro.) A True Guide to Glory (1619), 2004; (intro.) A Sermon Preached at Constantinople at the Funeral of Lady Anne Glover (1616), 2005; (intro.) A Sermon of Commemoration of the Lady Danvers, Late Wife of Sr. John Danvers (1627), 2006; Mary Queen of Scots, 2006. **Address:** Department of History, Arizona State University, Tempe, AZ 85287-4302, U.S.A. **Online address:** retha.warnicke@asu.edu

WARNICKE, Retha Marvine. See WARNICKE, Retha M.

WARNOCK, (Helen) Mary. See WARNOCK, Mary.

WARNOCK, Mary. ((Helen) Mary Warnock). British (born England), b. 1924. **Genres:** Ethics, Philosophy, Autobiography/Memoirs. **Career:** Oxford University, fellow and tutor, 1949-66, senior research fellow, 1976-84; Oxford Magazine, editor, 1959-61; Oxford High School, headmistress, 1966-72; Lady Margaret Hall, research fellow, 1972-76; Cambridge University, Girton College, life peer, 1985, mistress, 1986-89; Gresham College, visiting professor of rhetoric, 2000; Hertford College, principal. Writer. **Publications:** Ethics since 1900, 1960; The Philosophy of Jean-Paul Sartre, 1963; (ed.) Utilitarianism, 1964; Philosophy of Sartre, 1966; Existentialist Ethics, 1967; Existentialism, 1970; Sartre: A Collection of Critical Essays, 1971; Imagination, 1976; Schools of Thought, 1977; (with T. Devlin) What Must We Teach?, 1977; Concept of Educational Need, 1978; Meeting Special Educational Needs: A Brief Guide, 1978; Education: A Way Forward, 1979; Question of Life: The Warnock Report on Human Fertilisation and Embryology, 1985; (ed.) Vindication of the Rights of Woman, 1986; Memory, 1987; A Common Policy for Education, 1988; The Universities: Knowing Our Minds,

1989; The Uses of Philosophy, 1992; Imagination and Time, 1994; (ed.) Women Philosophers, 1996; The Intelligent Person's Guide to Ethics, 1998; Mary Warnock: A Memoir: People and Places, 2000; People and Places: A Memoir, 2000; Making Babies: Is there a Right to Have Children?, 2002; Nature and Mortality: Recollections of a Philosopher in Public Life, 2003; (intro.) Utilitarianism and on Liberty: Including Mill's Essay on Bentham' and Selections from the Writings of Jeremy Bentham and John Austin, 2003; Good Life: Thoughts on Life and Death, 2006; (with E. Macdonald) Easeful Death: Is there a Case for Assisted Dying?, 2008; (with B. Norwich) Special Educational Needs: A New Look, 2010; Dishonest to God, 2010. Contributor to periodicals. **Address:** 60 Church St., Great Bedwyn, Marlborough, WT SN8 3PF, England.

WARRACK, John (Hamilton). British (born England), b. 1928. **Genres:** Music. **Career:** Daily Telegraph, assistant music critic, 1954-61; Sunday Telegraph, chief music critic, 1961-72; Leeds Musical Festival, artistic director, 1977-83; Oxford University, lecturer in music, 1984-93. Writer. **Publications:** Six Great Composers, 1958; (with H. Rosenthal) Concise Oxford Dictionary of Opera, 1964, (with E. West) 3rd ed., 1996; Carl Maria von Weber, 1968; Tchaikovsky Symphonies and Concertos, 1969; Tchaikovsky, 1973; Tchaikovsky Ballet Music, 1979; (ed.) Writings on Music, 1981; (with E. West) Oxford Dictionary of Opera, 1992; Richard Wagner: Die Meistersinger von Nurnberg, 1994; German Opera, 2001; (ed. and trans. with R. Macnutt) Gunther Braam: The Portraits of Hector Berlioz, 2003. **Address:** Beck House, Rievaulx, Helmsley, York, NY Y062 5LB, England. **Online address:** warrack@aelred.demon.co.uk

WARREN, Cathy. American (born United States), b. 1951. **Genres:** Children's Fiction, Children's Non-fiction. **Career:** Methodist Hospital, assistant psychiatric counselor, 1973-75; Mother Earth Early Child Development Center, director, 1976-77; Beacon Hill Elementary School, teacher, 1977-78; Children's Schoolhouse, creative arts teacher and director, 1980-85; freelance writer, 1983-; Queen College, instructor in continuing education, 1988-; Warren Publishing, owner, 2002-. Writer. **Publications:** The Ten-Alarm Camp-Out, 1983; Victoria's ABC Adventure, 1984; Fred's First Day, 1984; Springtime Bears, 1986; Saturday Belongs to Sara, 1988; Roxanne Bookman: Live at Five, 1988. **Address:** 19809 N Cove Rd., Ste. 115, Cornelius, NC 28031, U.S.A.

WARREN, Charles. American (born United States), b. 1948. **Genres:** Film, Literary Criticism And History, Social Sciences. **Career:** New School for Social Research, teacher, 1979-81; Harvard University, teacher, 1981-90, 1995-2000; Tufts University, teacher, 1991-95; Boston University, teacher, 1999-2000, lecturer in film. Writer. **Publications:** T.S. Eliot on Shakespeare, 1987. EDITOR: (with M. Locke) Jean-Luc Godard's Hail Mary: Women and the Sacred in Film, 1993; Beyond Document: Essays on Nonfiction Film, 1996. Works appear in anthologies. Contributor to books and periodicals. **Address:** College of Communications, Boston University, 881 Commonwealth Ave., Boston, MA 02215, U.S.A.

WARREN, Dianne. American/Canadian (born Canada), b. 1950. **Genres:** Novellas/Short Stories, Young Adult Fiction, Art/Art History. **Career:** Regina Public Library, writer-in-residence, 1994-95. **Publications:** The Wednesday Flower Man (stories), 1987; Serpent in the Night Sky, 1992; Bad Luck Dog (stories), 1993; Club Chernobyl, 1994; (ed. with J.J. Lewis) Eureka!: Seven One-Act Plays for Secondary Schools, 1994; The Last Journey of Captain Harte, 1999; A Reckless Moon: And Other Stories, 2002; Cool Water, 2010. **Address:** c/o Author Mail, Publishers Group West, 1700 4th St., Berkeley, CA 94710, U.S.A.

WARREN, James Francis. Australian/American (born United States), b. 1942. **Genres:** Area Studies, History, Social Sciences, Anthropology/Ethnology. **Career:** Murdoch University, Southeast Asian Modern History, professor, 1976-, head of Asian studies program, 1977, 1981, 1987, 1993-96, Asia Research Centre, director, 1988-89, research associate; Yale University, visiting teaching fellow, 1983; Kyoto University, Centre for Southeast Asian Studies, visiting professorial research fellow, 1993, 1996-97; Asia Research Institute, professorial research fellow; National University of Singapore, professorial research fellow; McGill University, Indian Ocean World Centre, research associate; Australian National University, teacher. Writer. **Publications:** The North Borneo Chartered Company's Administration of the Bajauy, 1878-1909, 1971; The Sulu Zone, 1768-1898: The Dynamics of External Trade, Slavery, and Ethnicity in the Transformation of a Southeast Asian

Maritime State, 1981; Rickshaw Coolie: A People's History of Singapore, 1880-1940, 1986; Guide to the George L Peet Collection on Singapore and Malaysia, 1986; At the Edge of Southeast Asian History: Essays by James Francis Warren, 1987; Ah Ku and Karayuki-san: Prostitution in Singapore, 1870-1940, 1993; The Sulu Zone, the World Capitalist Economy and the Historical Imagination, 1998; Global Economy and the Sulu Zone: Connections, Commodities, and Culture, 2000; Iranun and Balangingi: Globalisation, Maritime Raiding and the Birth of Ethnicity, 2002; Pirates, Prostitutes and Pullers: Explorations in the Ethnoand Social History of Southeast Asia, 2008. **Address:** School of Social Sciences and Humanities, Murdoch University, Murdoch, Perth, WA 6150, Australia. **Online address:** j.warren@murdoch.edu.au

WARREN, Jeff. Canadian (born Canada), b. 1971?. **Genres:** Travel/Exploration. **Career:** Canadian Broadcasting Corporation Radio, freelance producer. Radio producer and freelance writer. **Publications:** Frommer's Algonquin Provincial Park, 2002; (and illus.) The Head Trip: Adventures on the Wheel of Consciousness, 2007. **Address:** Toronto, ON , Canada. **Online address:** jeff@headtrip.ca

WARREN, Karen J. American (born United States), b. 1947. **Genres:** Environmental Sciences/Ecology, Ethics, Humanities, Philosophy, Women's Studies And Issues, History, Social Sciences. **Career:** St. Olaf College, assistant professor, 1978-85; Macalester College, faculty, 1985-, professor, 1997-; Marquette University, women's chair in humanistic studies, 2004. Writer. **Publications:** (Co-ed.) Environmental Philosophy: From Animal Rights to Radical Ecology, 1993; (ed.) Ecological Feminism, 1994; (ed.) Ecological Feminist Philosophies, 1996; (with D.L. Cady) Bringing Peace Home: Feminism, Violence and Nature, 1996; (ed. with N. Erkal) Ecofeminism: Women, Culture, Nature, 1997; Ecofeminist Philosophy: A Western Perspective on What It Is and Why It Matters, 2000; Gendering Western Philosophy: Pairs of Men and Women Philosophers from 4th Century B.C.E. to the Present, 2004; Gendering the History of Western Philosophy: Pairs of Men and Women Philosophers from the 4th Century B.C.E. to the Present, 2007; (ed.) An Unconventional History of Western Philosophy: Conversations Between Men and Women Philosophers, 2009. Contributor of articles to periodicals. **Address:** Department of Philosophy, Macalester College, 1600 Grand Ave., St. Paul, MN 55105, U.S.A. **Online address:** warren@macalester.edu

WARREN, Kenneth. British (born England), b. 1931. **Genres:** Business/Trade/Industry, Geography, Regional/Urban Planning, Biography, Humor/Satire. **Career:** University of Leicester, lecturer in geography, 1956-66; University of Newcastle, lecturer in geography, 1966-70; Oxford University, lecturer in geography, 1970-90, Jesus College, fellow and tutor, 1970-91, emeritus fellow, 1991-. Writer. **Publications:** The British Iron & Steel Sheet Industry since 1840: An Economic Geography, 1970; (with G. Manners, D. Keeble and B. Rogers) Regional Development in Britain, 1972, 2nd ed., 1980; North East England, 1973; Mineral Resources, 1973; The American Steel Industry, 1850-1970: A Geographical Interpretation, 1973; World Steel: An Economic Geography, 1975; The Geography of British Heavy Industry Since 1800, 1976; Research on Selective Information Systems: A Bellagio Conference, October 23-27, 1979, 1980; Chemical Foundations: The Alkali Industry in Britain to 1926, 1980; Armstrong of Elswick: Growth in Engineering and Armaments, 1990; Consett Iron, 1840 to 1980: A Study in Industrial Location, 1990; John Meade Falkner, 1858-1932: A Paradoxical Life, 1995; Triumphant Capitalism: Henry Clay Frick and the Industrial Transformation of America, 1995; Steel, Ships and Men: Cammell Laird, 1824-1993, 1998; Wealth, Waste and Alienation: Growth and Decline in the Connellsville Coke Industry, 2001; Big Steel: The First Century of the United States Steel Corporation, 1901-2001, 2001; Industrial Genius: The Working Life of Charles Michael Schwab, 2007; Bethlehem Steel: Builder and Arsenal of America, 2008; Ken Warren Teaches Texas Hold'em 1, 2009. **Address:** School of Geography, Oxford University, Mansfield Rd., Oxford, OX1 3TB, England.

WARREN, Kenneth W. American (born United States), b. 1957. **Genres:** Literary Criticism And History. **Career:** University of Chicago, professor of English, 1991-, Fairfax M. Cone distinguished service professor of English. Writer. **Publications:** Let's Go! Budget Guide to the USA, 1980; Black and White Strangers: Race and American Literary Realism, 1993; So Black and Blue: Ralph Ellison and the Occasion of Criticism, 2003; Renewing Black Intellectual History: The Ideological and Material Foundations of African American Thought, 2010; What Was African American Literature?, 2011. Contributor to books. **Address:** Department of English, University of Chicago, Walker 507A, 1115 E 58th St., Chicago, IL 60637, U.S.A. **Online address:** kwarren@uchicago.edu

WARREN, Louis S. American (born United States) **Genres:** Humanities, Intellectual History, Local History/Rural Topics, Biography, Autobiography/ Memoirs. **Career:** Peterhouse School, teacher, 1985-87; University of San Diego, Department of History, assistant professor; University of California, Department of History, professor of history, W. Turrentine Jackson professor of western U.S. history. Writer. **Publications:** The Hunter's Game: Poachers and Conservationists in Twentieth-Century America, 1997; (ed.) American Environmental History, 2003; Buffalo Bill's America: William Cody and the Wild West Show, 2005. **Address:** Department of History, University of California, 3205 Social Sciences & Humanities, 1 Shields Ave., Davis, CA 95616, U.S.A. **Online address:** lswarren@ucdavis.edu

WARREN, Richard (Andrew). American (born United States), b. 1961. **Genres:** History, Translations, Politics/Government, Social Sciences. **Career:** University of the Americas, Department of International Studies, professor, 1993-94; Eastern Illinois University, assistant professor of history, 1994-. Writer. **Publications:** (Trans.) Enrique Tandeter, Coercion and Market: Silver Mining in Colonia Potosi, 1692-1826, 1993; Vagrants and Citizens: Politics and the Masses in Mexico City from Colony to Republic, 2001. **Address:** Department of History, Eastern Illinois University, 600 Lincoln Ave., Charleston, IL 61920, U.S.A.

WARREN, Rosanna. American (born United States), b. 1953. **Genres:** Novels, Poetry, Language/Linguistics, Literary Criticism And History. **Career:** Private art teacher, 1977-78; St. Martin's Press, clerical worker, 1977-78; Vanderbilt University, assistant professor of English, 1981-82; Boston University, visiting assistant professor, 1982-88, assistant professor, 1989-95, associate professor, 1995-99, Emma MacLachlan Metcalf professor of the humanities, professor of the humanities, university professor, professor of English and French, 2000-, University Professors Program, director of the translation seminar course; Robert Frost Farm, poet-in-residence, 1990; Academy of American Poets, chancellor, 1999-2005. Writer. **Publications:** The Joey Story (fiction), 1964; (trans. with S. Scully) Suppliant Women, 1995; Fables of the Self: Studies in Lyric Poetry, 2008. POETRY: Snow Day, 1981; Each Leaf Shines Separate, 1984; Stained Glass, 1993; Departure(poems), 2003; Ghost in a Red Hat, 2011. EDITOR: The Art of Translation: Voices from the Field, 1989; Cuttlefish Bones, 1993; (with M. Tyler) From this Distance: Poetry from Prison, 1997; Satura, 1998. Works appear in anthologies. Contributor to periodicals. **Address:** Department of English, Boston University, 236 Bay State Rd., Boston, MA 02215, U.S.A. **Online address:** rosanna@bu.edu

WARREN, Sandra K. American (born United States), b. 1944. **Genres:** Novels, Children's Fiction, Plays/Screenplays, Education, How-to Books, Autobiography/Memoirs, Biography. **Career:** Southland YWCA, teacher, 1976-78; Good Apple Inc., sales representative, 1984; Trillium Press, sales representative, 1987-90; Synergetics, sales representative, 1990-2002; Book Lures, sales representative, 1990-91; Pieces, editor, 1991-92; Creative Learning Consultants/Pieces of Learning, consultant, 1991-92; Arlie Enterprises, owner, 1992-. **Publications:** If I Were a Road (for children), 1987; If I Were a Table (for children), 1987; The Great Bridge Lowering, 1987; (ed.) Being Gifted: Because You're Special from the Rest (poetry for children), 1987; (with D. Rahimtoola) My School Calendar: Keeping Tracks, 1988, 3rd ed., 1990; Teacher's Guide to Parents of the Gifted/Parents of the Gifted Guide to Teachers, 1990, rev. ed., 1999; How to Publish Those Great Classroom Ideas, 1991, rev. ed., 2001; Arlie the Alligator (picture book), 1992; Arlie the Alligator Activity Guide, 1992; Celebrating Kwanzaa, 1994; Developing Creativity through Open-Ended Stories, 2003; When Duty Called: Even Grandma Had to Go, 2003; Hidden Casualties: Battles on the Home Front, 2003; Enhancing Creativity Through Open-ended Missing Parts Stories, 2006. **Address:** Arlie Enterprises, 216 Double Eagle Dr., Nebo, NC 28761, U.S.A. **Online address:** sandra@arliebooks.com

WARREN, Susan. American (born United States) **Genres:** Homes/Gardens, Sciences. **Career:** Wall Street Journal, deputy bureau chief; Houston Post, staff; Houston Chronicle, staff, 1991-. **Publications:** Backyard Giants: The Passionate, Heartbreaking, and Glorious Quest to Grow the Biggest Pumpkin Ever, 2007. **Address:** Arlington, TX , U.S.A. **Online address:** susan@backyardgiants.com

WARREN, Susan May. American (born United States), b. 1966. **Genres:** Novels, Military/Defense/Arms Control, Romance/Historical, Young Adult Fiction. **Career:** Writer. **Publications:** (With E. White and K. Fuller) Chance Encounters of the Heart, 2002; Tying the Knot, 2003; (co-author) The House

Love Built: Four Romances Are Built on the Foundation of Faith, 2003; (with S.K. Downs) Ekaterina, 2003; Happily Ever After, 2003; Letters from the Enemy, 2004; The Perfect Match, 2004; Nadia, 2004; Flee the Night, 2005; Escape to Morning, 2005; In Sheep's Clothing, 2005; Marina, 2005; Oksana, 2005; Reclaiming Nick: Noble Legacy, 2006; Expect the Sunrise, 2006; Everything's Coming Up Josey, 2006; Sands of Time, 2006; Chill Out, Josey!, 2007; Taming Rafe, 2007; Nothing but Trouble: A PJ Sugar Novel, 2008; Wiser than Serpents, 2008; Finding Stefanie, 2008; Get Cozy, Josey!, 2008; The Great Christmas Bowl, 2009; Double Trouble, 2010; Sons of Thunder, 2010; Licensed for Trouble, 2010; Nightingale, 2010; Undercover Pursuit, 2011; Point of No Return, 2011; Mission: Out of Control, 2011; My Foolish Heart, 2011; Heiress, 2011; Baby, It's Cold Outside, 2011; The Shadow of Your Smile, 2012. **Address:** PO Box 1290, Grand Marais, MN 55604, U.S.A. **Online address:** susan@susanmaywarren.com

WARREN, Victoria. American (born United States), b. 1971. **Genres:** Poetry, Young Adult Fiction. **Career:** Miami-Dade Community College, instructor in remedial courses for adults, 1989-; Dade County Public Schools, middle school language arts teacher, 1995-. Writer. **Publications:** Can You Feel Me? Intimate Poetry for the Woman, the Witch and the Whore in You, 2001; Loving in the Dark, 2001. **Address:** Favic Press, PO Box 4124, Hialeah, FL 33014-0124, U.S.A.

WARRINGTON, Freda. British (born England), b. 1956. **Genres:** Novels. **Career:** Leicester Royal Infirmary, medical artist, 1977-80. Freelance graphic designer and writer. **Publications:** NOVELS: The Rainbow Gate, 1989; A Taste of Blood Wine, 1992; Sorrow's Light, 1993; A Dance in Blood Velvet, 1994; The Dark Blood of Poppies: A Vampire Fantasy, 1995; Dark Cathedral, 1996; Pagan Moon, 1997; Dracula the Undead, 1997; The Court of the Midnight King, 2003. BLACKBIRD SERIES: A Blackbird in Silver, 1985; A Blackbird in Darkness, 1986; A Blackbird in Twilight, 1988; A Blackbird in Amber, 1988; Darker than the Storm, 1992. JEWELFIRE TRILOGY: The Amber Citadel, 1999; The Sapphire Throne, 2000; The Obsidian Tower, 2001; A Taste of Blood Wine, 2002; Elfland, 2009. **Address:** c/o John R. Parker, Literary Agents Ltd., 45 Fitzroy St., London, GL W1P 5HR, England. **Online address:** fredawarrington.author@gmail.com

WARSH, Lewis. American (born United States), b. 1944. **Genres:** Novels, Poetry, Translations. **Career:** Angel Hair Books, editor, 1966-77; Boston Eagle, editor, 1972-74; Saint Marks Church-in-the-Bowery Poetry Project, teacher, 1973-75, 1992-94, lecturer in creative writing and magazine editing, 1991-94, 1998, lecturer in creative writing, 1997-98; United Artists Books, editor, 1977-; Naropa Institute, lecturer in poetry and fiction, 1977, 1995, 2001, 2005, 2007, teacher, 1978, adjunct lecturer in literature and creative writing, 1980-81; New England College, teacher, 1979-80, adjunct lecturer in literature and creative writing, 1980-81; Long Island University, adjunct associate professor, 1984-, associate professor in English, 2000-, MFA Program in Creative Writing, director; Queens College, adjunct lecturer in literature, 1984-86; Yeshiva University, adjunct instructor in literature and creative writing, 1985-86; Fairleigh Dickinson University, adjunct instructor in creative writing, literature and composition, 1987-88; The World, editor, 1991-93; Pace University, adjunct instructor in literature, 1998-99; State University of New York, visiting assistant professor in fiction writing, 1999-2000; Angel Hairmagazine, editor; United Artists Magazine, editor and publisher; Angel Hair Magazine, editor. **Publications:** Angel Hair, 1966; The Suicide Rates, 1967; Highjacking, 1968; Moving through Air, 1968; (with T. Clark) Chicago, 1969; Two Poems, 1971; Dreaming as One, 1971; Long Distance, 1971; Part of My History, 1972; (trans.) R. Desnos, Night of Loveless Nights, 1973; Immediate Surrounding, 1974; The Maharajah's Son, 1977; Blue Heaven, 1978; Hives, 1979; Methods of Birth Control, 1983; Agnes and Sally (novel), 1984; Beowulf, 1984; Gustave Flaubert's Madame Bovary, 1985; Albert Camus's The Stranger, 1986; The Corset, 1987; Information from the Surface of Venus, 1987; A Free Man (novel), 1991; Avenue of Escape, 1995; Bustin's Island '68, 1996; Private Agenda, 1996; Money under the Table, 1997; The Origin of the World, 2001; Touch of the Whip, 2001; (with J. Harrison) Debtor's Prison, 2001; (with A. Waldman) The Angel Hair Anthology, 2001; Ted's Favorite Skirt, 2002; Reported Missing, 2003; The Flea Market in Kiel, 2006; Flight Test, 2006; Inseparable: Poems 1995-2005, 2008; Place in the Sun, 2010. **Address:** United Artists Books, 114 W 16th St. 5C, New York, NY 10011, U.S.A. **Online address:** lwarsh@mindspring.com

WARSH, Sylvia E. Maultash. Canadian/German (born Germany) **Genres:** Novels, Mystery/Crime/Suspense. **Career:** Toronto District School Board, writing instructor, 1989-. Writer. **Publications:** NOVELS: To Die in Spring, 2000; Find Me Again, 2003; Season of Iron, 2006; Queen of Unforgetting, 2010; Best Girl, 2012. Contributor to periodicals. **Address:** c/o Author Mail, Dundurn Press, 500-3 Church St., Toronto, ON M5E 1M2, Canada. **Online address:** sylviawarsh@yahoo.ca

WARSHAUER, Matthew. American (born United States), b. 1965?. **Genres:** Law, Politics/Government. **Career:** Central Connecticut State University, professor of history, 1997-; Connecticut History, editor, 2003-. Historian. **Publications:** Andrew Jackson and the Politics of Martial Law: Nationalism, Civil Liberties, and Partisanship, 2006; Andrew Jackson in Context, 2009. Contributor to books and periodicals. **Address:** Central Connecticut State University, 208 DiLoreto Hall, 1615 Stanley St., New Britain, CT 06050, U.S.A. **Online address:** warshauerm@ccsu.edu

WARUK, Kona. See HARRIS, (Theodore) Wilson.

WARWICK, Jacqueline. Canadian (born Canada), b. 1969?. **Genres:** Adult Non-fiction. **Career:** Dalhousie University, assistant professor of music, associate professor, Gender and Women's Studies Programme, coordinator, 2007-10; Echo, founding editor. **Publications:** Girl Groups, Girl Culture: Popular Music and Identity in the 1960s, 2007; (ed. with R. Knapp and S. Baur) Musicological Identities: Essays in Honor of Susan McClary, 2008. Contributor to Journals. **Address:** Department of Music, Dalhousie Arts Centre, Dalhousie University, Rm. 407, 6101 University Ave., Halifax, NS B3H 4R2, Canada. **Online address:** jacqueline.warwick@dal.ca

WASBY, Stephen L(ewis). American (born United States), b. 1937. **Genres:** Law, Politics/Government, Young Adult Non-fiction, Social Sciences. **Career:** Southeast Missouri State College, assistant professor, 1962-64; University of Minnesota, Extension Division, lecturer, 1965; Southern Illinois University, assistant professor to professor of political science, 1966-78; University at Albany-SUNY, professor of political science, 1978-99, director of program in public affairs, 1980-81. professor emeritus, 1999-; National Science Foundation, Law and Social Science Program, director, 1978-79; U.S. Naval Academy, Sec-Nav fellow, 1990-91; University of Victoria, visiting professor of law, 1995; University of Toronto, Canadian-American Relations, Bissell-Fulbright chair, 1997-98; University of Wisconsin-Milwaukee, visiting professor, 1972-73; Justice System Journal, editor-in-chief, 2005-07. Writer. **Publications:** (With D.R. Manwaring and D.R. Reich) Supreme Court as Policy-Maker: Three Studies on the Impact of Judicial Decisions, 1968; Political Science: The Discipline and Its Dimensions, 1970; The Impact of the United States Supreme Court: Some Perspectives, 1970; American Government and Politics, 1973; Continuity and Change: From the Warren Court to the Burger Court, 1976; Small Town Police and the Supreme Court: Hearing the Word, 1976; (with A. D'Amato & R. Metrailer) Desegregation from Brown to Alexander: An Exploration of Supreme Court Strategies, 1977; The Supreme Court in the Federal Judicial System, 1978, 4th ed., 1993; (co-author) Volume and Delay in State Appellate Courts: Problems and Responses, 1979; Vote Dilution, Minority Voting Rights and the Courts, 1982; Race Relations Litigation in an Age of Complexity, 1995. EDITOR: Civil Liberties: Policy and Policy-Making, 1976; (ed. with J.G. Grumm) The Analysis of Policy Impact, 1981; He Shall Not Pass This Way Again: The Legacy of Justice Douglas, 1990; (ed.) The Constitutional Logic of Affirmative Action, 1991; (ed.) Essentials of the American Constitution: The Supreme Court and the Fundamental Law, 2001. Contributor to journals. **Address:** Westview Press, 2465 Central Ave., Boulder, CO 80301, U.S.A. **Online address:** wasb@albany.edu

WASHBURN, Frances. American (born United States) **Genres:** Novels. **Career:** University of Arizona, American Indian Studies, assistant professor, professor. Writer. **Publications:** Elsie's Business, 2006; The Sacred White Turkey, 2010. **Address:** Department of American Indian Studies, University of Arizona, 237A Harvill Bldg., 1103 E 2nd St, PO Box 210076, Tucson, AZ 85721-0076, U.S.A. **Online address:** washburn@email.arizona.edu

WASHBURN, Livia J. Also writes as L. J. Washburn, Livia Reasoner, Livia Hallam, Elizabeth Hallam. American (born United States), b. 1957?. **Genres:** Mystery/Crime/Suspense. **Career:** Writer. **Publications:** A Peach of a Murder: A Fresh-baked Mystery, 2006; Murder by the Slice: A Fresh-baked Mystery, 2007; The Christmas Cookie Killer: A Fresh-baked Mystery, 2008; Frankly My Dear, I'm Dead, 2008; Killer Crab Cakes: A Fresh-baked Mystery, 2009; Huckleberry Finished, 2009. AS L.J. WASHBURN: Epitaph, 1987; Ghost River, 1988; (with L.D. Estleman and R.J. Randisi) The

Black Moon, 1989; Bandera Pass, 1989; Dead-Stick: A Lucas Hallam Mystery, 1989; Dog Heavies, 1990; Riders of the Monte, 1990; Red River Ruse, 1991; Wild Night: A Lucas Hallam Mystery, 1998. AS LIVIA REASONER: Mending Fences, 1998. AS ELIZABETH HALLAM: Spirit Catcher, 1998; Alura's Wish, 1999; Yesterday's Flame, 2000. AS LIVIA HALLAM: Call to Arms: A Novel, 2006; War Drums, 2006. WITH J. REASONER: Rivers of Gold, 1995; The Healer's Road, 1995; Healer's Calling, 1996; Cossack Three Ponies, 1997; Tie a Black Ribbon, 2000. **Address:** c/o Kim Lionetti, Book-Ends L.L.C., 136 Long Hill Rd., Gillette, NJ 07933, U.S.A. **Online address:** livia@flash.net

WASHBURN, L. J. See REASONER, Livia Jane Washburn.

WASHBURN, L. J. See WASHBURN, Livia J.

WASHBURN, Stan. American (born United States), b. 1943. **Genres:** Mystery/Crime/Suspense, Literary Criticism And History, Travel/Exploration, History, Young Adult Fiction. **Career:** College Preparatory School, trustee, 1986-; North Point Gallery, artist. Writer. **Publications:** The True Account of the Death by Violence of George's Dragon, 1974; Moral Alphabet of Vice and Folly: Embellished with Nudes and Other Exemplary Materials, 1986; Intent to Harm, 1994; Into Thin Air, 1996. Illustrator of books by A.Theroux. **Address:** Frederick Hill Associates, 1842 Union St., San Francisco, CA 94123, U.S.A.

WASHBURNE, Carolyn Kott. American (born United States), b. 1944. **Genres:** Women's Studies And Issues, Cultural/Ethnic Topics, Social Work. **Career:** Massachusetts Institute of Technology, administrative assistant, 1965-67; Philadelphia Tutorial Project Inc., administrative officer, 1967-69; Montgomery County (PA) Emergency Consultation and Referral Service, staff associate, 1970-71; Women in Transition Inc., co-founder and co-director, executive director, 1971-76; University of Wisconsin, Advanced Studies in Human Services, assistant director, 1976-77, School of Social Welfare, social worker, 1976-83, Region V Resource Center on Children and Youth Services, program associate, 1977-83, Department of English, adjunct assistant professor, 1983-, School of Architecture and Urban Planning, lecturer, 1991-, School of Business Administration-Business Writing, lecturer, 1998-; public relations consultant, 1983-; Wisconsin Business Journal, staff writer, 1984-85; Changing Homes Magazine, editor, 1986-88; Writer's Digest School, correspondence faculty, 1986-96; Cardinal Stritch College, lecturer, 1987-91; University Outreach, Business and Management of Effective Business Communication, lecturer, 1991-, Arts and Liberal Studies of Nonfiction Writing, Editing, Newsletters, lecturer, 1992-; Massachusetts Institute of Technology, administrative assistant, 1965-67; Philadelphia Tutorial Project Inc., administrative officer, 1967-69; Montgomery County (PA) Emergency Consultation and Referral Service, staff associate, 1970-71; Women in Transition Inc., co-founder and co-director, executive director, 1971-76; University of Wisconsin, Advanced Studies in Human Services, assistant director, 1976-77, School of Social Welfare, social worker, 1976-83, Region V Resource Center on Children and Youth Services, program associate, 1977-83, Department of English, adjunct assistant professor, 1983-, School of Architecture and Urban Planning, lecturer, 1991-, School of Business Administration-Business Writing, lecturer, 1998-; public relations consultant, 1983-; Wisconsin Business Journal, staff writer, 1984-85; Changing Homes Magazine, editor, 1986-88; Writer's Digest School, correspondence faculty, 1986-96; Cardinal Stritch College, lecturer, 1987-91; University Outreach, Business and Management of Effective Business Communication, lecturer, 1991-, Arts and Liberal Studies of Nonfiction Writing, Editing, Newsletters, lecturer, 1992-. Writer. **Publications:** Women in Transition, 1975; (with J.B. Fleming) For Better, for Worse: A Feminist Handbook on Marriage and Other Options, 1977; A Multicultural Portrait of Colonial Life, 1994; The 1930s, 1994; Italian Americans, 1995; America in the 20th Century, 1995; Drug Abuse, 1996. Contributor of articles to periodicals. **Address:** Washburne Literary Services, 1909 E. Menlo Blvd., Shorewood, WI 53211-2519, U.S.A. **Online address:** ckw@csd.uwm.edu

WASHINGTON, Donna L. American (born United States), b. 1967. **Genres:** Mythology/Folklore, Novellas/Short Stories, Picture/Board Books. **Career:** Teacher, 1995-. Writer. **Publications:** The Story of Kwanzaa (picture book), 1996; A Big, Spooky House (picture book), 2000; A Pride of African Tales, 2004; Li'l Rabbit's Kwanzaa, 2010. **Address:** DLW Storyteller Inc., 2 Haggis Ct., Durham, NC 27705-2166, U.S.A. **Online address:** qbot5@aol.com

WASIK, John F. (John Francis Wasik). American (born United States), b.

1957. **Genres:** Money/Finance, Business/Trade/Industry. **Career:** Consumers Digest, senior editor and special projects editor. Journalist, biographer, columnist, consultant, broadcaster, educator, poet, musician and public speaker. **Publications:** The Electronic Business Information Sourcebook, 1987; The Green Supermarket Shopping Guide, 1993; The Inve$tment Club Book, 1995; Green Marketing & Management: A Global Perspective, 1996; The Late-Start Investor: The Better-Late-than-Never Guide to Realizing Your Retirement Dreams, 1998; Retire Early-and Live the Life You Want Now: A 10-Step Plan for Reinventing Your Retirement, 2000; The Kitchen-Table Investor: Low-Risk, Low-Maintenance Wealth-Building Strategies for Working Families, 2001; The Bear-Proof Investor: Prospering Safely in Any Market, 2002; The Merchant of Power: Samuel Insull, Thomas Edison, and the Creation of the Modern Metropolis, 2006; (with T. Lydon) IMoney: Profitable ETF Strategies for Every Investor, 2008. Contributor to newspapers and periodicals. **Address:** Grayslake, IL , U.S.A. **Online address:** john@johnwasik.com

WASIK, John Francis. *See* **WASIK, John F.**

WASIL, Kenneth. American (born United States), b. 1951. **Genres:** Adult Non-fiction, Travel/Exploration, Novellas/Short Stories. **Career:** Writer and educator. **Publications:** The Car of the Future, 2008; Rivers of Words: An Adventure-Travel Tale of Teaching English in Cambodia, 2008. **Address:** Portable Press, PO Box 1117, Ashland, OR 97520-0038, U.S.A. **Online address:** thomaspaine101@gmail.com

WASIOLEK, Edward. American (born United States), b. 1924. **Genres:** Literary Criticism And History, Essays. **Career:** Ohio Wesleyan University, instructor in English, 1954-55; University of Chicago, assistant professor of English, 1955-60, associate professor of English and Russian, 1960-64, professor of Russian and comparative literature, 1964-69, distinguished service professor of Russian and comparative literature, 1969-, Department of Comparative Literature, chairman, 1965, Avalon Foundation distinguished service professor of Slavic and comparative literature, now Avalon Foundation distinguished service professor emeritus, Department of Slavic Languages and Literature, chairman, 1971-77, now distinguished service professor emeritus of Russian, English and comparative literature; Harvard University, visiting professor of Slavic and comparative literature, 1966-67. Writer. **Publications:** (With R. Bauer) Nine Soviet Portraits, 1955; Crime and Punishment and the Critics, 1961; Dostoevsky: The Major Fiction, 1964; The Brothers Karamazov and the Critics, 1967; Tolstoy's Major Fiction, 1978; Critical Essays on Tolstoy, 1986; Fathers and Sons: Russia at the Crossroads, 1993. EDITOR: (and trans.) The Notebooks for Crime and Punishment, 1967; (and intro.) The Notebooks for the Idiot, 1967; (and intro.) The Notebooks for the Possessed, 1968; The Notebooks for a Raw Youth, 1969; The Gambler with Polina Suslova's Diary, 1972. **Address:** Department of Slavic Languages and Literatures, University of Chicago, Rm. 406, Foster Hall, 1130 E 59th St., Chicago, IL 60637, U.S.A. **Online address:** ewasiole@uchicago.edu

WASS, Douglas (William Gretton). British (born England), b. 1923. **Genres:** Politics/Government, Law, History, Economics, Business/Trade/Industry. **Career:** His Majesty's Treasury, assistant principal, 1946-51, principal, 1951-62, assistant secretary, 1962-68, under secretary, 1968-70, deputy secretary, 1970-73, second permanent secretary, 1973-74, permanent secretary, 1974-83; International Monetary Fund, alternate executive director, 1965-67; British Embassy, financial counselor, 1965-67; Home Civil Service, joint head, 1981-83; Coopers and Lybrand, consultant, 1983-85; Barclay's Bank, director; Equity and Law Life Insurance Co., director and CEO; Policy Studies Institute, deputy chair; Centre for Economic Policy Research, governor. Writer. **Publications:** Government and the Governed, 1984; Policy Analysis and Constitutional Issues, Royal Institute of Public Administration, 1986; Decline to Fall: The Making of British Macro-Economic Policy and the 1976 IMF Crisis, 2008. Contributor to periodicals. **Address:** 6 Dora Rd., London, GL SW19 7HH, England.

WASSERMAN, Robin. American (born United States), b. 1978. **Genres:** Novels, Young Adult Fiction, Picture/Board Books. **Career:** Novelist. **Publications:** SCOOBY-DOO! PICTURE CLUE SERIES: Search for Scooby Snacks, 2000; Vanishing Valentines, 2001; Snow Ghost, 2001; Ghost School, 2002; Stormy Night, 2002. FACE TO FACE SERIES: Sharks, 2002; Wolves, 2002; Night Creatures, 2002; Penguins, 2002; Insects, 2002. JUVENILE NOVELS: Pizza Place Ghost, 2002; Oh, No! Why Me? II, 2002; Grind, 2003; Oops! I Did It (Again)!, 2003; A Cinderella Story, 2004; Raise Your Voice,

2004; Just My Luck! Embarrassing Moments and the Girls Who Survive Them, 2006; Callie for President, 2008; Life, Starring Me!, 2009; Wish You Were Here, Liza, 2010; Bedtime Stories: School's Out?, 2011; The Book of Blood and Shadow, 2012. UNFABULOUS SERIES: Keepin' It Real, 2005; Split Ends, 2005; Jinxed!, 2006; Just Deal, 2006; Meltdown, 2006; So You Want to Be... Unfabulous, 2006; Starstruck, 2006. YOUNG-ADULT NOVELS: Hacking Harvard, 2007. SEVEN DEADLY SINS SERIES: YOUNG-ADULT NOVELS: Lust, 2005; Envy, 2006; Pride, 2006; Wrath, 2006; Sloth, 2006; Gluttony, 2007; Greed, 2007. CHASING YESTERDAY SERIES: YOUNG-ADULT NOVELS: Awakening, 2007; Betrayal, 2007; Truth, 2007. SKINNED TRILOGY: YOUNG-ADULT NOVELS: Skinned, 2008; Crashed, 2009; Wired, 2010. OTHERS: Extraordinary Dangerous Animals, 2003; Extraordinary Sea Creatures, 2003; Extraordinary Solar System, 2003; Extraordinary Rain Forests, 2003; Extraordinary Wild Weather, 2003; Girl Talk: How to Deal with Friendship Conflicts, 2006. COLD AWAKENING: Frozen, 2011; Shattered, 2011; Torn, 2011. Works appear in anthologies. Contributor to periodicals. **Address:** Knopf Doubleday Group Foreign Rights, 1745 Broadway, New York, NY 10019, U.S.A. **Online address:** robin@robinwasserman.com

WASSERSTEIN, Bernard (Mano Julius). American/British (born England), b. 1948. **Genres:** History, International Relations/Current Affairs, Biography, Humanities, Politics/Government. **Career:** Nuffield College, research fellow, 1973-75; University of Sheffield, lecturer in modern history, 1976-80; Hebrew University of Jerusalem, visiting lecturer, 1979-80; Brandeis University, Department of History, associate professor, 1980-82, professor of history, 1982-96, chair, 1986-90, Tauber Institute, director, 1980-83, Graduate School of Arts and Sciences, dean, 1990-92; Oxford Centre for Hebrew and Jewish Studies, president, 1996-2000; University of Glasgow, professor of modern history, 2000-03; University of Chicago, Harriet and Ulrich E. Meyer professor of modern European Jewish history, 2003-. Writer. **Publications:** Wyndham Deedes in Palestine, 1973; The British in Palestine: The Mandatory Government and Arab-Jewish Conflict 1917-1929, 1978, 2nd ed., 1991; Britain and the Jews of Europe, 1939-1945, 1979, 2nd ed., 1999; (ed. with F. Malino) The Jews in Modern France, 1985; (with J.A.S. Grenville) The Major International Treaties since 1945: A History and Guide with Texts, 1987; The Secret Lives of Trebitsch Lincoln, 1988; Herbert Samuel: A Political Life, 1992; Vanishing Diaspora: The Jews in Europe since 1945, 1996; Secret War in Shanghai, 1999; (ed. with J. Grenville) The Major International Treaties of the Twentieth Century, 2000; Divided Jerusalem: The Struggle for the Holy City, 2001, 3rd ed., 2008; Israelis and Palestinians: Why Do They Fight? Can They Stop?, 2003, 3rd ed., 2008; Barbarism and Civilization: A History of Europe in Our Time, 2007; On the Eve: The Jews of Europe Before the Second World War, 2012. Contributor to periodicals. **Address:** Department of History, The University of Chicago, 1126 E 59th St., PO Box 67, Chicago, IL 60637-1580, U.S.A. **Online address:** bmjw@uchicago.edu

WASSERSTROM, Jeffrey N. American (born United States), b. 1961. **Genres:** History. **Career:** Indiana University, faculty, East Asian Studies Center, director; American Historical Review, editor; Journal of Asian Studies, editor; University of Kentucky, faculty; University of California-San Diego, faculty; University of California-Irvine, professor. Writer. **Publications:** Student Protests in Twentieth-Century China: The View from Shanghai, 1991; China's Brave New World: And Other Tales for Global Times, 2007; Global Shanghai, 1850-2010: A History in Fragments, 2009. EDITOR: (with E.J. Perry) Popular Protest and Political Culture in Modern China: Learning from 1989, 1992, 2nd ed. as Popular Protest and Political Culture in Modern China, 1994; (with L. Hunt and M.B. Young) Human Rights and Revolutions, 2000, 2nd ed., 2007; (with S. Brownell) Chinese Femininities, Chinese Masculinities: A Reader, 2002; Twentieth-Century China: New Approaches, 2003; (with K. Merkel-Hess and K.L. Pomeranz) China in 2008: A Year of Great Significance, 2009. **Address:** University of California, Irvine, CA 92697, U.S.A. **Online address:** jwassers@uci.edu

WÄSTBERG, Per. Swedish (born Sweden), b. 1933. **Genres:** Novels, Poetry, Urban Studies, Biography, Essays. **Career:** Stockholm newspaper Dagens, cultural editor and editor-in-chief; Swedish Amnesty, founder, 1963; Swedish PEN, president, 1967-78; International PEN, president, 1979-87; Dagens Nyheter, cultural editor and editor-in-chief. PEN, president, 1979-87; Dagens Nyheter, cultural editor and editor-in-chief. **Publications:** Enskilt arbete, 1952; (with L. af Petersens) Klara, 1957; (trans.) Afrika berattar, 1961; (with A. Ehnmark) Angola Mocambique, 1962 as Angola and Mozambique, 1963; Hjaltarnas uttag: Pojke med sapbubblor. Ur Enskilt arbete. Ett gammalt skuggspel (selected prose), 1964; Afrikas moderna litteratur, 1969; Afrika berattar; en antologi, 1970; (comp.) Afrikansk lyrik, 1970; (with A.-L. Wastberg) Roda huset: ett spel i Stockholm (drama), 1970; Afrika, ett uppdrag: reflexioner, beskrivninger, gissningar, 1976 as Assignments in Africa, 1986; Tal i Roda rummet, 1982; Kungstradgarden: en antologi, 1986; Stockholm i minnet och nuet, 1987; En forandrad varld=A World Transformed (in Swedish and English), 1988; Frusna tillgangar (title means: 'Frozen Assets'), 1990; Alice och Hjordis, tva systrar: dagbocker och brev, 1885-1964 (title means: 'Alice and Hjordis, Two Sisters: Diaries and Letters'), 1994; Kring Johannes (history), 1994; (with R. Millhagen) Sagerska huset, 1995 as The Sager House, 1995; (with A. Theorell) Minnets stiger (title means: 'Paths of Memory'), 2001; Tio anteckmingar om Stockholm (title means: 'Ten Notes on Stockholm'), 2003. AUTOBIOGRAPHY: Ung mans dagbok: fran tolv till sexton ar, 1946-1950 (title means: 'Young Man's Diary'), 1996; En ung forfattares dagbok: fran sjutton till tjugo ar, 1951-53 (title means: 'Young Writer's Diary'), 1997. BIOGRAPHY: Ernst och Mimmi (biography), 1964; Axel Hirsch: Folkbildare och filantrop, 2003; Hemliga rummen: en memoir, 2006. CRITICISM: Lovtal (title means: 'Words of Praise'), 1996; Werner Aspenstrom, 1997. DOCUMENTARIES: Forbjudet omrade (title means: 'Forbidden Territory'), 1960; Pa svarta listan (title means: 'On the Black List'), 1960; Ostermalm, 1962; Humlegardsmastaren. Ett skolkvarter pa ostermalm, 1971; Sommaroarna: en bok om stockhomarnas skargard, 1973; I Sydafrika: resan mot friheten, 1995; Sverige (title means: 'Sweden'), 2001. EDITOR: The Writer in Modern Africa, 1968; An Anthology of Modern Swedish Literature, 1979. ESSAYS: En dag pa varldsmarknaden, 1967; Berattarens oganblick, 1977; Ett horntorn vid Riddargatan, och andra Stockhomsskildringar, 1980; Obestamda artiklar (mini essays), 1981; Bestamda artiklar, 1982; Frukost med Gerard: och andra texter, 1993; Edith Wharton's hemliga tradgard (title means: 'Edith Wharton's Secret Garden'), 2000; Overgangsstallen (title means: 'Crossings'), 2003. NOVELS: Ett gammalt skuggspel, 1952; Halva kungariket, 1955; Arvtagaren, 1958; Vattenslottet (title means: 'The Water Castle'), 1968; Luftburen, 1969, as The Air Cage, 1972; Jordmanen, 1972, as Love's Gravity, 1977; Eldens skugga (title means: 'The Shadow of Fire'), 1986; Bergets kalla (title means: 'The Mountain Spring'), 1987; Ljusets hjarta, 1991 as Heart of Light, 1998; Vindens laga (title means: 'The Flame of the Wind'), 1993. POETRY: Tio atmosfarer (title means: 'Ten Atmospheres'), 1963; Enkel resa (title means: 'One-way Trip'), 1964; En avlagsen likhet, 1983; Fortojningar, 1995; Karleksdikter (anthology), 1995; Tre rader, 1998; Raderingar, 1999; Fortifikationer (title means: 'Fortifications'), 2001; Tillvaka i tid (title means: 'Back in Time'), 2004; Anders Sparrmans resa: en biografisk roman, 2008; Journey of Anders Sparrman, 2010. SHORT STORIES: Pojke med sapbubblor (title means: 'Boy Blowing Soap Bubbles'), 1949; Duvdrottningen: och andra berattelser, 1998. Contributor to periodicals. **Address:** Swedish Academy, PO Box 2118, Stockholm, 10313, Sweden.

WATADA, Terry. Canadian (born Canada), b. 1951. **Genres:** Novellas/Short Stories, Plays/Screenplays, Poetry, Children's Non-fiction, History, Mystery/Crime/Suspense, Young Adult Fiction, Literary Criticism And History, Literary Criticism And History. **Career:** Writer. **Publications:** POETRY: A Thousand Homes, 1995; Ten Thousand Views of Rain, 2001. SHORT STORY COLLECTION: Daruma Days, 1997. OTHERS: Bukkyo Tozen: A History of Jodo Shinshu Buddhism in Canada, 1996; Seeing the Invisible (children's non-fiction), 1998; Obon: The Festival of the Dead, 2006; Kuroshio: The Black Current, 2007. EDITOR: Asian Voices: Stories from Canada, Korea, China, Vietnam, and Japan, 1992; Face Kao: Portraits of Japanese Canadians Interned during WWII, 1996; Collected Voices: An Anthology of Asian North American Periodical Writing, 1997. Contributor to periodicals. **Address:** 6 Wildwood Cres., Toronto, ON M4L 2K7, Canada. **Online address:** tanea@sympatico.ca

WATENPAUGH, Keith David. American (born United States), b. 1966. **Genres:** History, Social Sciences. **Career:** Williams College, Middle East Studies, Andrew W. Mellon post-doctoral fellow, 1998-2000; University of Utah, Tanner Humanities Center, George S. and Dolores Dore Eccles distinguished visiting fellow, 2005-06; University of California, Religious Studies Program, associate professor of modern Islam, human rights and peace. Writer. **Publications:** Being Modern in the Middle East: Revolution, Nationalism, Colonialism, and the Arab Middle Class, 2006; Bread from Stones: The Middle East and the Making of Modern Humanitarianism, forthcoming. **Address:** United States Institute of Peace, 1200 17th St. NW, Washington, DC 20036-3006, U.S.A. **Online address:** kwatenpaugh@usip.org

WATERFIELD, Robin Anthony Herschel. British (born England), b. 1952?. **Genres:** Children's Fiction, Novels. **Career:** Saint Andrews University, lecturer, 1979-82; Penguin Books, copy editor and commissioning editor, 1982-84, 1988-91, consultant, 1991-99; freelance writer and editor, 1991; Newcastle College, faculty; Williams College, visiting lecturer, 2000; University of Sussex, writer-in-residence, 2001-02; Puffin Gamebooks, advisory editor. **Publications:** (Ed. and intro.) Jacob Boehme: Essential Readings, 1989; Before Eureka: The Presocratics and Their Science, 1989; (ed.) The Voice of Kahlil Gibran: An Anthology, 1995; (ed.) The Rime of the Ancient Mariner and Other Classic Stories in Verse, 1996; (author of intro.) Kahlil Gibran, Broken Wings: A Novel, 1998; Prophet: The Life and Times of Kahlil Gibran, 1998; Hidden Depths: The Story of Hypnosis, 2003; Athens: A History, from Ancient Ideal to Modern City, 2004; Xenophons Retreat: Greece, Persia, and the End of the Golden Age, 2006; Why Socrates Died: Dispelling the Myths, 2009; Dividing the Spoils: The War for Alexander the Great's Empire, 2011. FOR CHILDREN: (contrib.) Steve Jackson and Ian Livingstone Present Rebel Planet, illus. by Gary Mayes, 1985; Masks of Mayhem, 1986; Phantoms of Fear (game book), 1986; (with W. Davies) The Money Spider, 1988; (with W. Davies) The Water Spider, 1988; Deathmoor (game book), 1994. TRANSLATOR: (and intro.) Plato, Philebus, 1982; (contrib.) Theaetetus, 1985; The Theology of Arithmetic: On the Mystical, Mathematical and Cosmological Symbolism of the First Ten Numbers, 1988; (with H. Tredennick and intro.) Xenophon, Conversations of Socrates, 1990; Plato, Republic, 1993; (intro.) Plato, Gorgias, 1994; Epicurus, Letter on Happiness, 1994; Plato, Symposium, 1994; (and ed. with J. Annas) Plato, Statesman, 1996; Aristotle, Physics, 1996; Hiero the Tyrant and Other Treatises, 1997; Plutarch, Greek Lives: A Selection of Nine Greek Lives, 1998; Herodotus, The Histories, 1998; Plutarch, Roman Lives: A Selection of Eight Roman Lives, 1999; (contrib.) The First Philosophers: The Presocratics and Sophists, 2000; Euripides, Ion; Orestes; Phoenician Women; Suppliant Women, 2001; (intro.) Phaedrus, 2002; Euripides, Alcestis, Heracles, Children of Heracles, Cyclops, 2003; The Expedition of Cyrus, 2005; (and ed.) Streams of Grace: A New Selection from the Letters of the Abbé De Tourville with a Biographical Introduction, 2005; (intro.) Plato, Meno and Other Dialogues, 2005; Polybius, The Histories, 2010. Contributor to periodicals. **Address:** Elaia Molaon, Lakonia, 23052, Greece. **Online address:** rahwaterfield@hotmail.co.uk

WATERHOUSE, Carole A. American (born United States), b. 1957. **Genres:** Children's Fiction. **Career:** California University of Pennsylvania, professor of English, 1986-. Writer. **Publications:** Without Wings, 2002; The Paradise Ranch, 2003; The Tapestry Baby, 2011. Contributor to periodicals. **Address:** Department of English, California University of Pennsylvania, 230 Azorsky Hall, 250 University Ave., PO Box 36, California, PA 15419-1394, U.S.A. **Online address:** waterhouse@cup.edu

WATERMAN, Andrew (John). British (born England), b. 1940. **Genres:** Poetry. **Career:** University of Ulster, lecturer, 1968-78, senior lecturer in English, 1978-97. Writer. **Publications:** Living Room, 1974; From the Other Country, 1977; Over the Wall, 1980; Out for the Elements, 1981; (ed.) The Poetry of Chess, 1981; Selected Poems, 1986; In the Planetarium, 1990; The End of the Pier Show, 1995; Collected Poems, 1959-1999, 2000; The Captain's Swallow, 2007. **Address:** 5 Guernnsey Rd., Norwich, NF NR3 1JJ, England. **Online address:** andrew@andrewwaterman.co.uk

WATERMAN, Jonathan. American (born United States), b. 1956. **Genres:** Travel/Exploration. **Career:** Denali National Park, mountaineering ranger, 1982-85; Climbing, associate editor, 1987-89; American Alpine Club Press, director, 1993-96. Writer. **Publications:** Surviving Denali: A Study of Accidents on Mount McKinley, 1983, rev. ed., 1992; High Alaska: An Historical Guide to Denali, 1988; (ed.) Cloud Dancers: Profiles of North American Mountaineers, 1993; In the Shadow of Denali: Life and Death on Mount McKinley, 1994; Kayaking the Vermilion Sea: EightHundred Miles Down the Baja, 1995; A Most Hostile Mountain: Re-creating the Duke of Abruzzi's Historic Expedition on Alaska's Mount St. Elias, 1997; In the Shadow of Denali: Life and Death on Alaska's Mt. McKinley, 1998; (ed.) The Quotable Climber: Literary, Humorous, Inspirational and Fearful Moments of Climbing, 1998; Arctic Crossing: A Journey Through the Northwest Passage and Inuit Culture, 2001; Where Mountains Are Nameless: Passion and Politics in the Arctic National Wildlife Refuge: Including the Story of Olaus and Mardy Murie, 2005; The Mountain Why: Sailing After the Duke of Abruzzi to Saint Elias; Freeing Denali (novel); Running Dry: A Journey from Source to Sea Down the Colorado River, 2010; (contrib.) The Colorado River, 2011; How to Restore the Colorado River, forthcoming. **Address:** American Alpine Club, 710 10th St., Ste. 101, Golden, CO 80401, U.S.A.

WATERS, Barbara. American (born United States), b. 1929. **Genres:** Autobiography/Memoirs, Social Sciences. **Career:** Canyon del Oro High School, teacher of English, creative writing and southwestern literature, through 1985; Frank Waters Foundation, president and executive director, 1993-; Union Carbide's Computer Center, administrator; Southern Arizona Friends of C.G. Jung, consultant. Writer. **Publications:** (Foreword) The Woman at Otowi Crossing, 1987; Celebrating the Coyote: A Memoir, 1999; Pure Waters: Frank Waters and the Quest for the Cosmic, 2002; Rekindling the Inner Light, 2003. **Address:** Frank Waters Foundation, PO Box 1127, Taos, NM 87571, U.S.A. **Online address:** fwaters@laplaza.org

WATERS, Claire M. American (born United States) **Genres:** History, Biography, Literary Criticism And History. **Career:** University of California, associate professor of English, 2001-. Writer. **Publications:** Angels and Earthly Creatures: Preaching, Performance, and Gender in the Later Middle Ages, 2004; (ed.) Virgins and Scholars: A Fifteenth-Century Compilation of the Lives of John the Baptist, John the Evangelist, Jerome, and Katherine of Alexandria, 2008. **Address:** Department of English, University of California, 1 Shields Ave., Davis, CA 95616, U.S.A. **Online address:** cmwaters@ucdavis.edu

WATERS, David Watkin. British (born England), b. 1911. **Genres:** History, Marine Sciences/Oceanography, Travel/Exploration, Geography, Intellectual History, Art/Art History, Sports/Fitness. **Career:** Royal Navy, civilian historian, 1950-60; National Maritime Museum, curator of navigation and astronomy, 1960-76, assistant keeper, 1960-68, deputy keeper and secretary, 1968-71, keeper and deputy director, 1971-78; Smithsonian Institution, lecturer, 1966; British Society for the History of Science, president, 1976-78. Writer. **Publications:** The True and Perfecte Newes of Syr Frauncis Drake, 1955; (with F. Barley) Naval Staff History, Second World War: The Defeat of the Enemy Attack upon Shipping 1939-1945, 1957, 2nd ed., 1997; The Art of Navigation in England in Elizabethan and Early Stuart Times, 1958, 2nd ed., 1978; The Sea or Mariner's Astrolabe, 1966; The Rutters of the Sea: The Sailing Directions of Pierre Garcie: A Study of the First English and French Printed Sailing Directions, with Facsimile Reporductions, 1967; (contrib.) Art, Science and History in the Renaissance, 1967; (with H. Waters) The Saluki in History, Art and Sport, 1969, 2nd ed., 1984; (with G.P.B. Naish) The Elizabethan Navy and the Armada of Spain, 1975; Science and the Techniques of Navigation in the Renaissance, 1976; Navigational Books of Elizabethan and Stuart Times, 1977; (co-ed.) Ingrid and Other Studies: Papers, 1978; (comp. with T.R. Adams) English Maritime Books Printed before 1801: Relating to Ships, their Construction and their Operation at Sea: Including Articles in the Philosophical Transactions of the Royal Society and the Transactions of the American Philosophical Society, 1995. **Address:** c/o Cobwebs, Graffham, Petworth, Sussex, WS GU28 OPY, England.

WATERS, John F(rederick). American (born United States), b. 1930. **Genres:** Mystery/Crime/Suspense, Children's Fiction, Biology, Children's Non-fiction, Natural History, Essays, Picture/Board Books, Travel/Exploration, Travel/Exploration, Young Adult Fiction. **Career:** Cape Cod Standard Times, reporter, 1959-60; elementary teacher, 1960-66; full-time writer, 1966-. **Publications:** (With B. Waters) Salt-Water Aquariums, 1967; Marine Animal Collectors: How Creatures of the Sea Contribute to Science and our Knowledge of Man, 1969; The Sea Farmers, 1970; Saltmarshes and Shifting Dunes, 1970; The Crab From Yesterday: The Life-Cycle of a Horseshoe Crab, 1970; What Does an Oceanographer Do?, 1970; Turtles, 1971; Neighborhood Puddle, 1971; The Royal Potwasher, 1972; Green Turtle Mysteries, 1972; Some Mammals Live in the Sea, 1972; The Mysterious Eel, 1973; Hungry Sharks, 1973; Giant Sea Creatures, Real and Fantastic, 1973; Seal Harbor: The Life Story of the Harbor Seal, 1973; Camels, Ships of the Desert, 1974; Exploring New England Shores, 1974; Carnivorous Plants, 1974; Creatures of Darkness, 1975; Continental Shelves, 1975; Victory Chimes, 1976; Martime Careers, 1977; Maritime careers, 1977; Fishing, 1978; Summer of the Seals, 1978; A Jellyfish is Not a Fish, 1979; Crime Labs: The Science of Forensic Medicine, 1979; The Hatchlings: The Lives of Baby Turtles, 1979; Flood!, 1991; Watching Whales, 1991; Deep-Sea Vents: Living Worlds without Sun, 1994; Night Raiders on the Cape, 1997; Sharks: Dangerous or in Danger?, 1997. **Address:** 64 Meadowbrook Rd., North Chatham, MA 02650-1145, U.S.A. **Online address:** capefogbound@hotmail.com

WATERS, Sarah. British/Welsh (born Wales), b. 1966. **Genres:** Children's Non-fiction, Novels, Literary Criticism And History. **Career:** Open University, associate lecturer. Writer. **Publications:** How Newspapers Are Made, 1989; Growing Up, 1992; Hidden Animals, 1992; Keeping Safe, 1993; (ed. and intro.) Dancing with Mr. Darcy, 2009; (ed. with I. Cornils) Memories of 1968, 2010. NOVELS: Tipping the Velvet, 1999; Affinity, 2000; Fingersmith, 2002; Social Movements in France: Towards A New Citizenship, 2003; Night Watch, 2006; Little Stranger, 2009. **Address:** Little, Brown Book Group Ltd., 100 Victoria Embankment, 2nd Fl., London, GL EC4Y 0DY, England.

WATERS, Tony. American (born United States), b. 1958. **Genres:** Children's Fiction, Illustrations, Picture/Board Books, Young Adult Fiction, Animals/Pets. **Career:** Seabrook Island Resort Club, commercial reservations, 1982-88; Cricket Magazine Group, illustrator, 1994-; Frank Schaffer Publications, illustrator, 1995; Instructional Fair/T.S. Denison Publications, illustrator, 1996-97. Writer. **Publications:** SELF-ILLUSTRATED: The Sailor's Bride, 1991; Cinnamon's Busy Year, 2002; The Moon Smiles Down, 2002. Illustrator of books by P. Cuthbert and L.F. Wright. **Address:** 1830 2nd Dr., Charleston, SC 29407, U.S.A. **Online address:** redmouse58@hotmail.com

WATERSTON, Alisse. American (born United States), b. 1951?. **Genres:** Politics/Government, Economics, Social Sciences. **Career:** Pace University, adjunct instructor in anthropology and sociology, 1981-85; Tuckahoe After School Care Inc., president and founding vice president, 1985-89; Narcotic and Drug Research Inc., research fellow, 1986-91; State University of New York College, Division of Social Sciences, adjunct assistant professor of social sciences, 1991-92; Horowitz Associates Inc., senior analyst and project director, 1991-92; Surveys Unlimited, Ethnic Marketing Research Division, president, 1992-2003; Fordham University, adjunct assistant professor of anthropology and sociology, 1992-93; New School for Social Research, visiting associate professor of sociology, 1996-98; Columbia University, HIV Center for Clinical and Behavioral Studies, research associate, 1996-99; City University of New York, John Jay College of Criminal Justice, Department of Anthropology, associate professor, 2003-07, professor, 2008-. Writer. **Publications:** Street Addicts in the Political Economy, 1993; Love, Sorrow, and Rage: Destitute Women in a Manhattan Residence, 1999; (ed.) An Anthropology of War: Views From Frontline, 2009; (ed. with M.D. Vesperi) Anthropology Off the Shelf: Anthropologists on Writing, 2009. Contributor to journals. **Address:** Department of Anthropology, John Jay College of Criminal Justice, City University of New York, 899 10th Ave., New York, NY 10019-1069, U.S.A. **Online address:** awaterston@jjay.cuny.edu

WATFORD, Christopher M. American (born United States), b. 1978. **Genres:** History, Biography, Romance/Historical. **Career:** Davidson County Schools, teacher of at-risk students, 2000-05; Davidson County Community College, faculty; Mulkey Engineering and Consultants, staff, 2005; Campbell University, Norman Adrian Wiggins School of Law, faculty, 2005-, Federalist Society, president. Writer. **Publications:** The Civil War Roster of Davidson County, NC: Biographies of 1996 Men Before, During, and After the Conflict, 2001; (ed.) The Civil War in North Carolina: Soldiers' and Civilians' Letters and Diaries, 1861-1865, vol. I: The Piedmont, 2003; (ed.) The Civil War in North Carolina: Soldiers' and Civilians' Letters and Diaries, 1861-1965: The Mountains, 2003. **Address:** School of Law, Campbell University, PO Box 158, Buies Creek, NC 27506, U.S.A. **Online address:** cmwatford@hotmail.com

WA THIONG'O, Ngũgĩ. *See* NGUGI WA THIONG.

WATKINS, Graham. American (born United States), b. 1944. **Genres:** Horror, Plays/Screenplays, Novels, Young Adult Non-fiction, Ghost Writer. **Career:** Institute for Parapsychology, senior researcher, 1971-75; Duke University, electronics and computer systems worker, 1975-79; Pearson Music Co., electronic (computer) pipe organ worker, 1979-, senior engineer and technician. Writer. **Publications:** NOVELS: Dark Winds, 1989; The Fire Within, 1991; Kaleidoscope Eyes, 1993; Virus, 1995; Interception, 1997. NON FICTION: Ghosts and Poltergeists, 2001; (with B. Breman) Searching for Ghosts and Poltergeists, 2011. SHORT STORIES: A Moment of Ecstasy, 1994; A Night to Remember, 1994; The Red Sax, 1994; Here There Be Spyders, 1995; Comeback, 1997. Works appear in anthologies. **Address:** Rosen Publishing Group Inc., 29 E 21st St., New York, NY 10010, U.S.A. **Online address:** grahamwatkins@mindspring.com

WATKINS, John. American (born United States), b. 1960. **Genres:** Poetry, Literary Criticism And History. **Career:** University of Minnesota, Department of English, associate professor, professor, Department of History, professor, Center for Medieval Studies, faculty. Writer. **Publications:** The

Specter of Dido: Spenser and Virgilian Epic, 1995; Representing Elizabeth in Stuart England: Literature, History, Sovereignty, 2002; (with C. Levin) Shakespeare's Foreign Worlds, 2009; (ed. with C. Perry) Shakespeare and the Middle Ages, 2009. CONTRIBUTOR: The Cambridge History of Medieval Literature, 1999; Catholicism and Anti- Catholicism in Early Modern England, 1999; Early Modern English Poetry: A Critical Companion, 2nd ed., 2007. Contributor of articles to journals. **Address:** Department of English, University of Minnesota, 312 Lind Hall, 207 Church St. SE, Minneapolis, MN 55455, U.S.A. **Online address:** watki005@umn.edu

WATKINS, John Goodrich. American (born United States), b. 1913. **Genres:** Psychology, Medicine/Health. **Career:** High school teacher, 1933-39; Columbia University, assistant, 1940; Ithaca College, assistant professor, 1940-41; Alabama Polytechnic Institute (now Auburn University), professor, 1941-43; U.S. Army's Welch Hospital, chief clinical psychologist, 1945-46; Washington State College, associate professor of psychology, 1946-49; Veterans Administration Hospital, clinical psychologist, 1949-50; Veterans Administration Mental Hygiene Clinic, chief clinical psychologist, 1950-53; Veterans Administration Hospital, Psychology Service, chief, 1953-64; University of Montana, director of clinical training, 1964-80, professor, 1964-84, professor emeritus of psychology, 1984-; St. Patrick's Hospital, staff. Writer. **Publications:** Objective Measurement of Instrumental Performance, 1942; Hypnotherapy of War Neuroses: A Clinical Psychologist's Casebook, 1949; General Psychotherapy: An Outline and Study Guide, 1960; Watkins-Farnum Performance Scale - Form A Book, 1970; The Therapeutic Self: Developing Resonance: Key to Effective Relationships, 1978; (with R.J. Johnson) We, the Divided Self, 1982; Practice of Clinical Hypnosis, 1987; Hypnotherapeutic Techniques, 1987, (with A. Barabasz) 2nd ed., 2005; Hypnoanalytic Techniques, 1992; (with H.H. Watkins) Ego States: Theory and Therapy, 1997; Adventures in Human Understanding, 2001; Emotional Resonance: The Story of World-Acclaimed Psychotherapist Helen Watkins, 2005; (with A. Barabasz) Advanced Hypnotherapy: Hypnodynamic Techniques, 2008. Contributor to journals and books. **Address:** Department of Psychology, The University of Montana, Rm. 143, Skaggs Bldg., Missoula, MT 59812-1584, U.S.A.

WATKINS, Nicholas. British (born England), b. 1946. **Genres:** Biography, Art/Art History. **Career:** University of Leicester, research fellow art history, reader, lecturer, now reader emeritus. Writer. **Publications:** Matisse, 1977, rev. ed., 1992; Bonnard, 1994; Interpreting Bonnard: Color and Light, 1998; (contrib.) Beyond the Easel: Decorative Paintings by Bonnard, Vuillard, Denis and Roussel, 1890-1930, 2001; (contrib.) Behind the Mirror, 2008. **Address:** Department of History of Art & Film, University of Leicester, University Rd., Leicester, LE LE1 7RH, England.

WATKINS, Paul. American (born United States), b. 1964. **Genres:** Novels, Biography, Young Adult Non-fiction, Young Adult Fiction, Autobiography/Memoirs. **Career:** Lawrenceville School, teacher; The Peddie School, writer-in-residence. **Publications:** NOVELS: Night Over Day Over Night, 1988; Calm at Sunset, Calm at Dawn, 1989; In the Blue Light of African Dreams, 1990; The Promise of Light, 1992; Stand before your God, 1993; Archangel, 1995; The Story of My Disappearance, 1997; The Forger, 2000; Thunder God, 2004; Fellowship of Ghosts: A Journey Through the Mountains of Norway, 2004; Ice Soldier, 2006. OTHER: Stand before Your God (memoir), 1993. **Address:** The Peddie School, 201 South Main St, PO Box A, Hightstown, NJ 08520, U.S.A.

WATKINS, Ronald J(oseph). American (born United States), b. 1945. **Genres:** Criminology/True Crime, Ghost Writer, Mystery/Crime/Suspense. **Career:** Probation and hearing officer in Yreka, 1969-71; adult probation officer, 1972-85, administrative law judge, 1985-86, chief administrative law judge, 1986-92, assistant director, 1993-94. Watkins & Associates, founder and principal. Writer. **Publications:** High Crimes and Misdemeanors: The Term and Trials of Former Governor Evan Mecham, 1990; Evil Intentions: The Story of How an Act of Kindness Led to Senseless Murder, 1992; Birthright! Murder, Greed and Power in the U-Haul Family Dynasty, 1993; Against Her Will, 1995; A Suspicion of Guilt, 2001; Unknown Seas: How Vasco Da Gama Opened the East, 2003; Murder on Everest, 2010; Abandoned on Everest, 2010. **Address:** Mitchell Hamilburg Agency, 149 S Barrington Ave., Ste. 732, Los Angeles, CA 90049-2930, U.S.A. **Online address:** ronwatkins@ronwatkins.com

WATKINS, Steve. American (born United States), b. 1954. **Genres:** Race Relations, Cultural/Ethnic Topics, Young Adult Fiction. **Career:** Pelouze

Scale Co., assembly line worker, 1972; New Hanover Memorial Hospital, nurses' aide, 1974-75; Florida Flambeau, writer, 1975-76, associate editor, 1977-78, editor, 1978-80; Child Care Center, teacher, 1981; Tallahassee Democrat, assistant news editor, 1981-82, assistant features editor, 1982-83, arts and features writer, 1983; Therapeutic Concepts Inc., writer and editor, 1988; Red Letter Editorial Consultants, writer and editor, 1988; University of Mary Washington, assistant professor, 1990-96, associate professor of English, 1996-, professor of English, linguistics and communication. **Publications:** The Black O: Racism and Redemption in an American Corporate Empire, 1997; My Chaos Theory: Stories, 2006; Down Sand Mountain, 2008; What Comes After, 2011; The Grace Hotel, forthcoming. Contributor of articles to magazines and periodicals. **Address:** Department of English Linguistics and, Communication, Mary Washington College, 1301 College Ave., Fredericksburg, VA 22401, U.S.A. **Online address:** swatkins@umw.edu

WATKINS, William John. American (born United States), b. 1942. **Genres:** Science Fiction/Fantasy, Children's Fiction, Plays/Screenplays, Poetry, Urban Studies, Young Adult Fiction, Literary Criticism And History, Education, Education. **Career:** Delaware Valley College, instructor, 1965-68; Asbury Park High School, teacher, 1968-69; Brookdale Community College, instructor, 1969-70, assistant professor, 1970-71, associate professor, 1971-79, professor of humanities, 1979-, professor of English. Writer. **Publications:** Five Poems, 1968; A King of a Hole: A One-Act Play, 1969; The Judas Wheel (play), 1969; (with G. Snyder) Ecodeath, 1972; Clickwhistle, 1973; The God Machine, 1973; A Fair Advantage, 1975; (with G. Snyder) The Litany of Sh'reev, 1976; The Psychic Experiment Book, 1980; The Psychic Diet Book, 1980; What Rough Beast, 1980; Suburban Wilderness (non-fiction), 1981; Who's Who in New Jersey Wrestling, 1981; The Centrifugal Rickshaw Dancer, 1985; Going to See the End of the Sky, 1986; The Last Deathship off Antaries, 1989; Cosmic Thunder, 1996. Contributor to periodicals. **Address:** Brookdale Community College, 765 Newman Springs Rd., Lincroft, NJ 07738-1543, U.S.A. **Online address:** wwatkins@brookdalecc.edu

WATKINSON, John. British (born England), b. 1950. **Genres:** Technology, Information Science/Computers. **Career:** Digital Equipment Corp., lecturer, 1976-82; Sony Broadcast, lecturer, 1982-84; Ampex Great Britain, training manager, 1984-88; Run Length Ltd., founder and director, 1988-. Writer and consultant. **Publications:** The Art of Digital Audio, 1988, 3rd ed., 2001; The Art of Digital Video, 1990, 4th ed., 2008; The D-2 Digital Video Recorder, 1990; Coding for Digital Recording, 1990; RDAT, 1991; The D-3 Digital Video Recorder, 1992; (with F. Rumsey) The Digital Interface Handbook, 1993, 3rd ed., 2004; The Digital Video Tape Recorder, 1994; An Introduction to Digital Video, 1994, 2nd ed., 2001; The Art of Data Recording, 1994; An Introduction to Digital Audio, 1994; Compression in Video and Audio, 1995; Television Fundamentals, 1996; Audio for Television, 1997; The Art of Sound Reproduction, 1998; MPEG-2, 1999; Convergence in Broadcast and Communications Media: The Fundamentals of Audio, Video, Data Processing, and Communications Technologies, 2001; The MPEG Handbook: MPEG-1, MPEG-2, MPEG-4, 2001, 2nd ed., 2004. SNELL AND WILCOX HANDBOOK SERIES: The Engineer's Guide to Motion Compensation, 1994; The Engineer's Guide to Standards Conversion, 1994; The Engineer's Guide to Decoding and Encoding, 1994. Contributor to periodicals. **Address:** Run Length Ltd., 2 Hillside, Burghfield Common, Reading, BR RG7 3BQ, England.

WATMAN, Max. American (born United States), b. 1971?. **Genres:** Novels, History, Sports/Fitness. **Career:** New York Sun, turf correspondent, horse racing correspondent; The New Criterion, fiction chronicler; Nebraska Review, editor. **Publications:** Race Day: A Spot on the Rail with Max Watman, 2005. Chasing the White Dog: An Amateur Outlaw's Adventures in Moonshine, 2010. Contributor of articles. **Address:** New York Sun, 105 Chambers St., Ste. 2, New York, NY 10007, U.S.A. **Online address:** max@maxwatman.com

WATMOUGH, David. Canadian/British (born England), b. 1926. **Genres:** Novels, Novellas/Short Stories, Plays/Screenplays. **Career:** Cornish Guardian, junior reporter, 1943-44; Holy Cross Press, editor, 1953-54; British Broadcasting Corp., Third Programme, talks producer, 1956, broadcaster; Ace Books, editor, 1957; San Francisco Examiner, feature writer, reviewer and critic, 1958-60; Canadian Broadcasting Corp., music and theatre critic, 1960-64, 1967-80; The Vancouver Sun, drama and theatre critic, 1963-66; Vancouver STEP Magazine, arts columnist, 1992-94; XTRAWest!, book columnist, 1994-; KPFA-Radio, broadcaster. **Publications:** STORIES: Ashes for Easter & Other Monodramas, 1972; From a Cornish Landscape, 1975; Love and the Waiting Game, 1975; The Connecticut Countess, 1984; Fury, 1984; Vibrations in Time, 1986; Hunting with Diana, 1996. NOVELS: No More into the Garden, 1978; The Year of Fears, 1987; Thy Mother's Glass, 1992; The Time of the Kingfishers, 1994; The Moor is Dark beneath the Moon, 2002. OTHER: A Church Renascent: A Study in Modern French Catholicism, 1951; Names for the Numbered Years, 1967; The Unlikely Pioneer (history), 1986; (ed. and intro.) The Vancouver Fiction Book, 1985; Geraldine, 2007; Coming down the Pike, 2008; Eyes & Ears on Boundary Bay, 2009; To Each an Albatross, 2011. **Address:** Ekstasis Editions, 2808 Prior St., PO Box 8474, Victoria, BC V8T 3Y3, Canada. **Online address:** dwatmough@accnet.com

WATROUS, Livingston Vance. (L. Vance Watrous). American (born United States), b. 1943. **Genres:** Art/Art History, Archaeology/Antiquities, Sociology, Social Sciences. **Career:** State University of New York, professor of art history, 1976-. Writer. **Publications:** Lasithi, A History of Settlement on a Highland Plain in Crete, 1982; Kommos III: The Late Bronze Age Pottery, 1992. The Cave Sanctuary of Zeus at Psychro: A Study of Extra-Urban Sanctuaries in Minoan and Early Iron Age Crete, 1996; (as L. Vance Watrous with D. Hadzi-Vallianou and H. Blitzer) The Plain of Phaistos: Cycles of Social Complexity in the Mesara Region of Crete, 2004. Contributor to periodicals. **Address:** Department of Art History, State University of New York, 605 Clemens Hall, 202 Ctr. For the Arts, 262 W 38th St., Ste. 506, PO Box 604640, Buffalo, NY 14260, U.S.A. **Online address:** watrous@buffalo.edu

WATROUS, L. Vance. See **WATROUS, Livingston Vance.**

WATSON, Amy. See **WATSON, Amy Zakrzewski.**

WATSON, Amy Zakrzewski. (Amy Watson). American (born United States), b. 1965. **Genres:** Children's Non-fiction, Architecture. **Career:** Learning and Evaluation Center, writer and editor, 1987-90; Colonial Williamsburg Foundation, associate editor, 1989-92; Child Development Resources, editor, 1989-. **Publications:** The Folk Art Counting Book, 1992; Colonial Williamsburg from A to Z, 1993; Count with the Cooper, 1993; Colonial Animals, 1993; Animals at Colonial Williamsburg, 1993; Colonial Colors, 1993; Colonial Williamburg ABC, 1994; Ellicott Moon, 2005. **Address:** 117 Chestnut Dr., Williamsburg, VA 23185, U.S.A.

WATSON, Ben. See **WATSON, Benjamin A.**

WATSON, Ben. British (born England), b. 1956. **Genres:** Poetry, Music, Philosophy, Literary Criticism And History. **Career:** Trade Union and Community Resource and Information Centre, publications officer, 1981-85; MFT Computers, programmer, 1986-88; Kernel (now F1) Training, relational database trainer, 1988-91; music journalist, 1991-. Writer. **Publications:** Frank Zappa: The Negative Dialectics of Poodle Play, 1994; Art, Class and Cleavage: Quantulumcunque Concerning Materialist Esthetix, 1998; The Complete Guide to the Music of Frank Zappa, 1998; Mad Pride: A Celebration of Mad Culture, 2000; Shit-Kicks and Dough-Balls, 2003; Derek Bailey and the Story of Free Improvisation, 2004; (with E. Leslie) Academy Zappa, 2005; Honesty Is Explosive!: Selected Music Journalism, 2010; Adorno for Revolutionaries, 2011. POETRY COLLECTIONS AS OUT TO LUNCH: 1-2-3-4, 1980; 28 Sliverfish Macronix, 1992; Untrue Plonker Dunkin', 1994; Turnpike Ruler, 1994; Conductors of Chaos: A Poetry Anthology, 1996; Benison Fence-Off, 1999. Contributor to periodicals. **Address:** Quartet Books Ltd., 27 Goodge St., London, GL W1P 2LD, England. **Online address:** irritant@esemplasm.me.uk

WATSON, Benjamin A. Also writes as Ben Watson. American (born United States), b. 1961. **Genres:** Local History/Rural Topics, Food And Wine, Horticulture, Travel/Exploration, Natural History, Crafts. **Career:** Yankee Publishing Inc., managing editor, 1984-89; Storey Communications, editor, 1989-92; Chelsea Green Publishing, senior editor, 1994-, senior consulting editor. Author and journalist. **Publications:** Acts of God: The Old Farmer's Almanac Unpredictable Guide to Weather and Natural Disasters, 1993; AS BEN WATSON: (ed.) Taylor's Guide to Heirloom Vegetables, 1996; (with K. Laliberté) The Gardener's Supply Passport to Gardening, 1997; Cider, Hard and Sweet, 1999, 2nd ed., 2008; (ed. with C. Petrini) Slow Food: Collected Thoughts on Taste, Tradition, and the Honest Pleasures of Food, 2001; (with P. Martins) The Slow Food Guide to New York City, 2003. **Address:** Chelsea Green Publishing Inc., 85 N Main St., Ste. 120, PO Box 428, White River Junction, VT 05001, U.S.A. **Online address:** bwatson@chelseagreen.com

WATSON, Bruce. American (born United States), b. 1953?. **Genres:** Criminology/True Crime, Technology, Engineering, Adult Non-fiction, Social Sciences. **Career:** Writer and educator. **Publications:** The Man Who Changed How Boys and Toys Were Made, 2002; Bread and Roses: Mills, Migrants and the Struggle for the American Dream, 2005; Sacco and Vanzetti: The Men, the Murders and the Judgment of Mankind, 2007; Freedom Summer: The Savage Season that made Mississippi Burn and Made America a Democracy, 2010. **Address:** c/o Author Mail, Viking Press, 375 Hudson St., New York, NY 10014, U.S.A.

WATSON, C. G. American (born United States) **Genres:** Novels. **Career:** Songwriter, musician and educator. **Publications:** Quad (novel), 2007. **Address:** CA, U.S.A. **Online address:** carrie@cgwatson.com

WATSON, Clyde. American (born United States), b. 1947. **Genres:** Children's Fiction, Young Adult Fiction, Young Adult Non-fiction, Children's Non-fiction, Animals/Pets, Education, Theology/Religion, Poetry, Literary Criticism And History. **Career:** Elementary school teacher, 1968-72. Writer and composer. **Publications:** Father Fox's Pennyrhymes, 1971; Tom Fox and the Apple Pie, 1972; Quips and Quirks, 1975; Hickory Stick Rag, 1976; Binary Numbers, 1977; Catch Me and Kiss Me and Say It Again, 1978; Midnight Moon, 1979; How Brown Mouse Kept Christmas, 1980; Applebet: An ABC, 1982; Valentine Foxes, 1989; Mister Toad, 1992; Love's a Sweet, 1998; Father Fox's Christmas Rhymes, 2003; Midnight Moon, 2005. Illustrator of books by F. Morse. **Address:** 7 Low Rd., Hanover, NH 03755-2206, U.S.A. **Online address:** clydegone@yahoo.com

WATSON, Don. Australian (born Australia), b. 1949?. **Genres:** History. **Career:** Australian Broadcasting Corp.(ABC-TV), contributor, 1984-86. Professor and journalist. **Publications:** Brian Fitzpatrick: A Radical Life, 1979; Caledonia Australis: Scottish Highlanders on the Australian Frontier, 1984; Rabbit Syndrome: Australia and America, 2001; Recollections of a Bleeding Heart: A Portrait of Paul Keating PM, 2002; Death Sentence: The Decay of Public Language, 2003; Watson's Dictionary of Weasel Words, Contemporary Clichés, Cant & Management Jargon, 2004; Death Sentences: How Clichés, Weasel and Management-speak are Strangling Public Language, 2005; American Journeys, 2008; (with H. Smith) Bendable Learnings: The Wisdom of Modern Management, 2009; On-nibus, 2009. **Address:** The Whitlam Institute, University of Western Sydney, PO Box 1797, Penrith, NW 1797, Australia.

WATSON, Donald. British (born England), b. 1946?. **Genres:** Medicine/Health, Psychology, Theology/Religion, Language/Linguistics, Reference. **Career:** Writer, spiritual counsellor and educator. **Publications:** A Dictionary of Mind and Spirit, 1991; A Dictionary of Mind & Body, 1995. **Address:** 35 Collier Rd., Hastings, ES TN34 3JR, England. **Online address:** rev@donaldwatson.co.uk

WATSON, Ellen Dore. American (born United States), b. 1950. **Genres:** Poetry, Translations. **Career:** Massachusetts Review, managing editor, 1994-99. translation editor, 1994-; general editor and poetry editor, 2004-; Smith College, English Department, lecturer, Poetry Center, director, 1999-; Alice James Books, editorial board, 1997-. **Publications:** POETRY: Broken Railings, 1996; We Live in Bodies, 1997; Ladder Music, 2001; This Sharpening, 2006; Dogged Hearts, 2010. OTHERS: (trans.) The Companions, 1989; (trans. and intro.) The Alphabet in the Park: Selected Poems of Adelia Prado, 1990; (trans.) Zero, 2004; (trans.) The Tower of Glass, 2004; (trans.) Tale of a Certain Orient, 2004. Contributor to journals. **Address:** Department of English Language and Literature, Smith College, Wright Hall 211, Northampton, MA 01063, U.S.A. **Online address:** ewatson@smith.edu

WATSON, Esther Pearl. American (born United States), b. 1973. **Genres:** Children's Fiction, Illustrations. **Career:** Pratt Institute, teacher, 2000-03; Art Center College of Design, 2003-. Writer, painter and comic book creator. **Publications:** (Contrib. with M. Todd) The Pain Tree, and Other Teenage Angst-Ridden Poetry, 2000; (co-author) Whatcha Mean, What's a Zine? The Art of Making Zines and Minicomics, 2006. SELF-ILLUSTRATED: Romeo and Juliet (retelling of William Shakespeare's Romeo and Juliet), 2008; Unlovable, Fantagraphics, vol. I, 2009, vol. II, 2010. CHILDREN'S BOOKS SELF-ILLUSTRATED: Talking to Angels, 1996; The Adventures of Jules and Gertie, 1999; Trouble at Sugar Dip Well, 2002. **Online address:** funchicken@verizon.net

WATSON, George (Grimes). British/Australian (born Australia), b. 1927. **Genres:** Literary Criticism And History, Bibliography, Young Adult Nonfiction, Essays. **Career:** Cambridge University, St. John's College, fellow, Sandars reader in bibliography, lecturer in English, 1959-90. Writer. **Publications:** The Unservile State: Essays in Liberty and Welfare, 1957; Concise Cambridge Bibliography of English Literature, 600-1950, 1958, 2nd ed., 1965; The British Constitution and Europe, 1959; The Literary Critics: A Study of English Descriptive Criticism, 1962, 2nd ed., 1973; C.B.E.L.: The Making of the Cambridge Bibliography, 1965; Coleridge the Poet, 1966; Is Socialism Left?, 1967, rev. ed., 1986; The Study of Literature, 1968; The Literary Thesis: A Guide to Research, 1970; The English Ideology: Studies in the Language of Victorian Politics, 1973; Politics and Literature in Modern Britain, 1977; The Discipline of English: A Guide to Critical Theory and Practice, 1978; Modern Literary Thought, 1978; The Story of the Novel, 1979; The Idea of Liberalism: Studies for a New Map of Politics, 1985; Writing a Thesis: A Guide to Long Essays and Dissertations, 1987; The Certainty of Literature: Essays in Polemic, 1989; British Literature since 1945, 1991; Lord Acton's History of Liberty: A Study of his Library, with an Edited Text of his History of Liberty Notes, 1994; The Lost Literature of Socialism, 1998, 2nd ed., 2010; Never Ones for Theory?: England and the War of Ideas, 2002; Take Back the Past, 2007. EDITOR: Biographia Literaria, 1956, new ed., 1976; Radical Alternative: Studies in Liberalism, 1962; Of Dramatic Poesy, 1962; The English Mind: Studies in the English Moralists Presented to Basil Willey, 1964; The English Petrarchans: A Critical Bibliography of the Canzoniere, 1967; The New Cambridge Bibliography of English Literature, 1969; Literary English Since Shakespeare, 1970; (intro.) Castle Rackrent, 1980; The Shorter New Cambridge Bibliography of English Literature, 1981; (intro.) Biographia Literaria, or, Biographical Sketches of My Literary Life and Opinions, 1991; Critical Essays on C.S. Lewis, 1992. **Address:** Lutterworth Press, PO Box 60, Cambridge, CB CB1 2NT, England.

WATSON, Ian. British (born England), b. 1943. **Genres:** Novellas/Short Stories, Horror, Science Fiction/Fantasy, Plays/Screenplays, Poetry, Area Studies, Novels, Young Adult Non-fiction, Young Adult Non-fiction. **Career:** University of Dar es Salaam, lecturer, 1965-67; Tokyo University of Education, lecturer, 1967-70; Keio University, lecturer, 1967-70; Birmingham Polytechnic, School of the History of Art in Art and Design Center, lecturer, 1970-75, senior lecturer in complementary studies, 1975-76, Foundation Magazine, features editor, contributor; writer, 1976-; Nene College, writer-in-residence, 1984. **Publications:** Japan: A Cat's Eye View (non-fiction), 1969; The Embedding, 1973; The Jonah Kit, 1975; (with J. Watson) Orgasmachine, 1976; The Martian Inca, 1977; Japan Tomorrow (non-fiction), 1977; Alien Embassy, 1977; The Miracle Visitors, 1978; God's World, 1979; The Very Slow Time Machine (short stories), 1979; The Gardens of Delight, 1980; (with M. Bishop) Under Heaven's Bridge, 1980; Deathhunter, 1981; Conversations with Ayckbourn, 1981; Sunstroke and Other Stories, 1982; Chekhov's Journey, 1983; The Book of the River, 1984; Converts, 1984; The Book of the Stars, 1984; The Book of Being, 1985; Slow Birds and Other Stories, 1985; The Book of Ian Watson, 1985; Queenmagic, Kingmagic, 1986; (ed. with P. Sargent) Afterlives, 1986; Evil Water, 1987; The Power, 1987; Whores of Babylon, 1988, rev. ed., 2004; The Fire Worm, 1988; Meat, 1988; Salvage Rites and Other Stories, 1989; The Flies of Memory, 1990; Inquisitor, 1990; Nanoware Time, 1991; Stalin's Teardrops, 1991; Space Marine, 1993; Lucky's Harvest, 1993; The Coming of Vertumnus (short stories), 1994; The Fallen Moon, 1994; Harlequin, 1994; Chaos Child, 1995; Hard Questions, 1996; Oracle, 1997; A.I. Artificial Intelligence (screen story), 2001; The Lexicographer's Love Song, 2001; Draco, 2002; The Great Escape, 2002; Mockymen, 2003; Yaleen, 2004; The Butterflies of Memory, 2005; (co-author) Time Pieces, 2006; (with R. Quaglia) Beloved of My Beloved, 2009. Works appear in anthologies. **Address:** Daisy Cottage, Banbury Rd., Moreton Pinkney, Daventry, NH NN11 3SQ, England. **Online address:** ianwatson@cix.co.uk

WATSON, Irene. Canadian/American (born United States), b. 1946. **Genres:** Self Help, Women's Studies And Issues, Reference, Humanities, Human Relations/Parenting, Psychology, Writing/Journalism, Autobiography/Memoirs, Autobiography/Memoirs. **Career:** Nekoda Development Institute, chief executive officer; Higher Power Foundation Inc., president; Reader Views, managing editor. **Publications:** Gifts, 1996; The Sitting Swing (memoir), 2005, rev. ed., 2009; (ed. with V.R. Volkman) The Story that Must be Told, 2007; (with L. Desjardins and N. Oelklaus) Rewriting Life Scripts: Transformational Recovery for Families, 2009; (ed. with T. Tichelaar and V.R. Volkman) Authors Access: 30 Success Secrets for Authors and Publishers, 2009. **Address:** Loving Healing Press, 5145 Pontiac Trl., Ann Arbor, MI 48105-9627, U.S.A. **Online address:** irene@irenewatson.com

WATSON, James. British (born England), b. 1936. **Genres:** Novels, Novellas/Short Stories, Plays/Screenplays, Communications/Media, Education, Adult Non-fiction. **Career:** British Council, teacher of English, 1960-61; North East Evening Gazette, journalist and art critic, 1961-63; Dunlop Co., education officer and editor of educational literature, 1963-65; West Kent College, senior lecturer in English and liberal studies, 1965-. **Publications:** Sign of the Swallow, 1967; The Bull Leapers, 1970; Literal Studies in Further Education-An Informal Survey, 1973; Gilbert Makepeace Lives!, 1972; Legion of the White Tiger, 1973; The Freedom Tree, 1976; Venus Rising from the Sea, 1977; A Slight Insurrection, 1979; The Loneliness of a Long Distance Innovation: General Studies in a College of Further Education, 1980; What a Little Moonlight Can Do, 1982; Talking in Whispers, 1983; (with A. Hill) A Dictionary of Communication and Media Studies, 1984, 7th ed., 2006; What is Communication Studies?, 1985; When Nobody Sees, 1987; Make Your Move, 1988; No Surrender, 1990; Ticket to Prague, 1993; The Noisy Ducks of Buxlehude, 1993; Justice of the Dagger, 1997; Media Communication: An Introduction to Theory and Process, 1997, 3rd ed., 2008; The Ghosts of Izieu, 2000; Banned! Tom Paine, This Was Your Life, 2003; Fair Game-Steps of the Odessa, 2008; Gotcha!, 2006. **Address:** 9 Farmcombe Close, Tunbridge Wells, KT TN2 5DG, England. **Online address:** james.watson4@btinternet.com

WATSON, James D(ewey). American (born United States), b. 1928. **Genres:** Biology, Sciences. **Career:** University of Copenhagen, National Research Council, Merck fellow, 1950-51; Cambridge University, Cavendish Laboratory, research fellow, 1951-52, engaged in bio-chemical research with Crick, 1955-56; California Institute of Technology, senior research fellow in biology, 1953-55; Harvard University, assistant professor, 1956-58, associate professor, 1958-61, professor of molecular biology, 1961-76; Cold Spring Harbor Laboratory, director, 1968-94, president, 1994-2004; National Center for Human Genome Research, National Institutes of Science, director, 1989-92; Allen Institute for Brain Science, vice chairman, advisor, 2003-, now chancellor emeritus; Champalimaud Foundation, president, 2007-. Writer. **Publications:** Molecular Biology of the Gene, 1965, 6th ed., 2008; The Double Helix: A Personal Account of the Discovery of the Structure of DNA, 1968, rev. ed., 1998; (ed. with H.H. Hiatt and J.A. Winsten) Origins of Human Cancer, 1977; (with J. Tooze) The DNA Story: A Documentary History of Gene Cloning, 1981; (with J. Tooze and D.T. Kurtz) Recombinant DNA: A Short Course, 1983, (co-ed.) 3nd ed., 2007; (ed. with K. Mizobuchi and I. Watanabe) Nucleic Acid Research: Future Development, 1983; Recognition and Regulation in Cell-Mediated Immunity, 1985; Landmarks of Twentieth-Century Genetics: A Series of Essays (bound with Houses for Science: A Pictorial History of Cold Spring Harbor Laboratory, by Elizabeth L. Watson), 1991; Phage and the Origins of Molecular Biology, 1992; (co-author) The Molecular Biology of the Cell, 3rd ed., 1994; Passion for DNA: Genes, Genomes, and Society, 2000; Genes, Girls and Gamow: After the Double Helix (memoir), 2001; (with A. Berry) DNA: The Secret of Life, 2003; Francis Crick and James Watson: Pioneers in DNA Research, 2003; (ed. with J. Cairns and G.S. Stent) Phage and the Origins of Molecular Biology, rev. ed., 1992, centennial ed., 2007; (ed. and intro.) Darwin: The Indelible Stamp: The Evolution of an Idea, 2007; Avoid Boring People and Other Lessons from a Life in Science, 2007; The Annotated And Illustrated Double Helix, 2012. **Address:** Allen Institute for Brain Science, 551 N 34th St., PO Box 100, Seattle, WA 98103, U.S.A. **Online address:** pubaff@cshl.org

WATSON, Jan Elizabeth. American (born United States), b. 1972. **Genres:** Novels. **Career:** Columbia University, teaching fellow, editor, copywriter and adjunct professor; University of Maine, adjunct professor. **Publications:** Asta in the Wings (novel), 2009. **Address:** Denise Shannon Literary Agency Inc., 20 W 22nd St., Ste. 1603, New York, NY 10010, U.S.A. **Online address:** janelizabethwatson@gmail.com

WATSON, Jean. New Zealander (born New Zealand), b. 1933?. **Genres:** Novels, Novellas/Short Stories, Young Adult Fiction. **Career:** Karunai Illam Trust, Children's Home, founder and trustee, 1987. Novelist. **Publications:** The Balloon Watchers, 1975; The World Is an Orange and the Sun, 1978; Flowers from Happyever, 1980; Address to a King, 1986; Stand in the Rain: A Novel, 1986; Karunai Illam: The Story of an Orphanage, 1992; Three Sea Stories, 1994. **Address:** Karunai Illam Trust, 41 Maida Vale Rd., Roseneath, Wellington, 6011, New Zealand. **Online address:** jean@actrix.gen.nz

WATSON, J(ohn) R(ichard). British (born England), b. 1934. **Genres:** Literary Criticism And History, Poetry, History, Essays. **Career:** University of Glasgow, assistant lecturer in English, 1962-66; University of Leicester, lecturer, senior lecturer in English, 1966-78; University of Durham, professor of English, 1978-89, public orator, 1989-99, professor emeritus, 1999-, emeritus public orator; St Chad's College, Farmington fellow. Writer. **Publications:** Picturesque Landscape and English Romantic Poetry, 1970; A Leicester Calendar, 1976; Wordsworth's Vital Soul: The Sacred and Profane in Wordsworth's Poetry, 1982; Wordsworth, 1984; English Poetry of the Romantic Period 1789-1830, 1985, 2nd ed., 1992; The Poetry of Gerard Manley Hopkins, 1987; The English Hymn: A Critical and Historical Study, 1997; Romanticism and War: A Study of British Romantic Period Writers and the Napoleonic Wars, 2003. EDITOR: (and intro. with N.P. Messenger) Victorian Poetry: The City of Dreadful Night, and Other Poems, 1974; Browning: Men and Women and Other Poems, 1974; (with J.C. Hilson and M.M.B. Jones) Augustan Worlds, 1978; Everyman's Book of Victorian Verse, 1982; An Infinite Complexity: Essays in Romanticism, 1983; (co-ed.) Companion to Hymns and Psalms, 1988; Pre-Romanticism in English Poetry of the Eighteenth Century, 1989; (with J. Raimond) A Handbook to English Romanticism, 1992; (and contrib.) An Annotated Anthology of Hymns, 2002. Contributor to journals. **Address:** Durham University, Old Elvet, Durham, DU DH1 3HP, England. **Online address:** j.r.watson@durham.ac.uk

WATSON, Kathy. British (born England) **Genres:** Novels, Novellas/Short Stories, Ghost Writer, Horror, History. **Career:** British Broadcasting Corp., journalist. **Publications:** The Crossing: The Glorious Tragedy of the First Man to Swim the English Channel, 2001; The Devil Kissed Her: The Story of Mary Lamb, 2004. Contributor to periodicals. **Address:** c/o Author Mail, Jeremy P. Tarcher Publicity, Putnam, 80 Strand, London, GL WC2R 0RL, England.

WATSON, Ken D. Australian (born Australia) **Genres:** Novels, Children's Fiction. **Career:** University of Sydney, senior lecturer in education, professor, now professor emeritus; Indiana University, Institute for Advanced Study, fellow, 2002. Writer. **Publications:** Reading and Teaching the Novel, 1969; (co-author) Explore and Express, Book I & II, 1972, Book III, 1973, Book IV, 1974; (ed. with A. Ashworth) Towards a New English: A Handbook for Teachers of Secondary School English in the 1970s, 1972; (with R.V. Martin) Kenroy High School: A Simulation Designed for Use in Teacher Education Programmes Concerned with the Preparation of Secondary School Teachers, 1972; (ed.) New Directions, 1972; (ed. with R. King) Parental Involvement in Australian Schools: A Follow-Up Study, 1976; (with F. Christie) Language and the Mass Media, 1976; (ed. with S. Eagles) Around the Globe, 1977; (with R.D. Eagleson) English in Secondary Schools: Today and Tomorrow, 1977; (ed.) Aspects of Children's Literature, 1978; (with S. Eagles) The Climb and the Dream, 1978; (with D. Barnes and J. Thompson) Language in the Classroom, 1978; (co-ed.) Reading is Response: Suggestions for Teaching Novels, Short Stories, and Biography in Upper Primary and Secondary Schools, 1980; (ed. with L. Cairns) Six Interesting Schools, 1980; Reading is Response: First Supplement, 1981; English Teaching in Perspective, 1981; (ed.) Pamphlet Poems, 1982; (ed. with V. Bell) Language and Language Learning, Years 7-10: Some Questions and Answers, 1982; (ed. with W. Sawyer) English Teaching from A to Z, 1983; (ed. with W. Sawyer) Find That Poem!, 1984; (ed. with P. Richardson) Postcards from Planet Earth: An Anthology of International Poetry, 1990; (with B. Pinder) A Workshop Approach to Hamlet: Photocopiable Recourses, 1990; (with W. Michaels) The Dogs of War: A Workshop Approach to Julius Caesar, 1991; (with G. Shrubb) Star-Cross'd Lovers: A Workshop Approach to Romeo and Juliet, 1991; (with S. Wilson) The Green-Ey'd Monster: A Workshop Approach to Othello, 1991; (with G. Shrubb) The Food of Love: A Workshop Approach to Twelfth Night, 1991; (with W. Michaels) Gaze on Cleopatra: A Workshop Approach to Antony and Cleopatra, 1992; Such a Mad Marriage: A Workshop Approach to The Taming of the Shrew, 1993; (ed. with J. Stephens) From Picture Books to Literary Theory, 1994; (with W. Michaels and J. Hise) Shakespeare: A Teacher's Handbook, 1994; (co-author) English Teaching in Perspective in the Context of the 1990s, 1994; (co-author) Looking at Our Language: Language Investigations for Middle and Upper Secondary Classes, 1995; (co-ed.) Jigsaw: Poetry for Years 9, 10, 11, 12, 1995; (co-ed.) Word & Image: Using Picture Books in Years 6 to 10, 1997; (with C. Radcliffe and D. Nicholson) Bitter Bread: A Workshop Approach to Richard II and The Winter's Tale, 1997; (co-author) Does Class Size Matter?, 1997; (ed. with W. Sawyer and E. Gold) Re-viewing English, 1998; (with D. Robinson) Love's Keen Arrows: A Workshop Approach to As You Like It, 1998; (ed.) At the Round Earth's Imagined Corners:

A Multicultural Anthology of Contemporary Poetry, 1999; (co-ed.) Fiction, Literature and Media, 1999; (ed.) Film in English, 2000; My Best Poetry Unit: And Other Ideas for Teaching Poetry, 2001; (co-author) Binocular: Looking Closely at Country, 2004; (ed.) Shakespeare's Tragedies, 2004; (ed.) Shakespeare's Comedies, 2004; (ed.) Introducing Shakespeare, 2004; (ed. with P. Jones) Shakespeare's Histories: A Workshop Approach to Richard II, Henry IV Part 1, Henry V, Richard III, 2005; (ed. with M. Dunn) A Workshop Approach to Shakespeare's Sonnets: This Powerful Rhyme, 2005. **Address:** Australian Association for the Teaching of English, PO Box 3203, Norwood, SA 5067, Australia.

WATSON, Larry. American (born United States), b. 1947?. **Genres:** Novels, Poetry. **Career:** University of Wisconsin, professor of English and creative writing, 1979-2003; Marquette University, visiting professor, 2003-. Writer. **Publications:** NOVELS: In a Dark Time, 1980; Montana 1948: A Novel, 1993; Justice, 1995; White Crosses: A Novel, 1998; Laura, 2000; Orchard: A Novel, 2003; Sundown, Yellow Moon: A Novel, 2007; American Boy, 2011. POETRY COLLECTION: Leaving Dakota, 1983. Works appear in anthologies. Contributor of articles to journals. **Address:** Department of English, Marquette University, Rm. 328, Coughlin Hall, 607 N 13th St., PO Box 1881, Milwaukee, WI 53201-1881, U.S.A. **Online address:** readermail@larry-watson.com

WATSON, Mary Ann. American (born United States), b. 1944. **Genres:** Psychology. **Career:** Community College of Philadelphia, assistant professor of psychology, 1969-70; Public Health Service, clinical psychologist, 1970-72; Johns Hopkins University, School of Medicine, Psychohormonal Research Unit, research associate, 1972-73; University of Colorado, Health Sciences Center, Department of Biophysics and Genetics, research associate, 1973-77, Department of Psychiatry, research associate, 1973-77, Pediatric Psychology Masters Program, visiting professor, 1979-82; Metropolitan State College of Denver, assistant professor, 1974-78, associate professor, 1978-82, professor of psychology, 1982-; University of Denver, School of Social Work, visiting professor, 1986-88. Writer. **Publications:** Breaking the Bonds, 1982; Readings in Sexology, 1984, 2nd ed., 1991; Expanding Vista, 1991; Your Sexuality Workbook, 1996, rev. ed., 2002; Videocases in Human Sexuality, 1996; Videocases in Human Development, 1997; Defining Visions: Television and the American Experience since 1945, 1998, 2nd ed. as Defining Visions: Television and the American Experience in the 20th Century, 2008; (ed.) Modern Kenya: Social Issues and Perspectives, 2000; Rites of Passage: Videocases of Traditional African Peoples, 2001; The Changing American Indian in a Changing America: Videocase of American Indian Peoples, 2001; Africans in America; The Unfolding of Ethnic Identity, 2002; Colorado to Cairo: Voices of Youth, 2004; The Egyptian Family: Continuity and Change, 2004; Portraits in Human Sexuality with accompanying Instructor's Guide, 2005; Rocking the Cradle: Gay Parenting with Accompanying Instructor's Guide, 2008; (ed. with M.C. Keith) Norman Corwin's One World Flight, 2009. **Address:** Department of Psychology, Metropolitan State College of Denver, Rm. 054, 220 Plz., PO Box 173362, Denver, CO 80217-3362, U.S.A. **Online address:** watsonm@mscd.edu

WATSON, Ritchie Devon. American (born United States), b. 1943. **Genres:** History, Race Relations. **Career:** Randolph-Macon College, assistant professor, 1970-, A.G. Ingram professor of English, 1998-2008. Writer. **Publications:** The Cavalier in Virginia Fiction, 1985; Yeoman versus Cavalier: The Old Southwest's Fictional Road to Rebellion, 1993; Normans and Saxons: Southern Race Mythology and the Intellectual History of the American Civil War, 2008. **Address:** Randolph-Macon College, 204 Henry St., PO Box 5005, Ashland, VA 23005-5505, U.S.A. **Online address:** rwatson@rmc.edu

WATSON, Robert (Winthrop). American (born United States), b. 1925. **Genres:** Novels, Plays/Screenplays, Poetry, Art/Art History, Young Adult Fiction. **Career:** Williams College, instructor, 1946-48, 1952-53; Johns Hopkins University, instructor, 1950-52; University of North Carolina-Greensboro, faculty, 1953-87, professor of English, 1965-87, professor emeritus, 1987-; University of California-Northridge, visiting professor, 1968-69. Writer. **Publications:** Watson on the Beach, 1972; Betty Watson Paintings: Five Decades, 1999; Robert Watson the Complete Poems, 2011. POEMS: A Paper Horse, 1962; Advantages of Dark, 1966; Three Sides of the Mirror (novel), 1966; (ed. with G. Ruark) Greensboro Reader, 1967; Christmas in Las Vegas, 1971; Selected Poems, 1974; Island of Bones, 1976; Lily Lang(novel), 1977; Night Blooming Cactus, 1980; The Pendulum: New and Selected Poems, 1995. Contributor to periodicals. **Address:** Department of English and Comparative

Literature, University of North Carolina at Chapel Hill, Greenlaw Hall, Ste. 3520, Chapel Hill, NC 27599-3520, U.S.A.

WATSON, Roderick. (Rory Watson). Scottish (born Scotland), b. 1943. **Genres:** Poetry, Literary Criticism And History. **Career:** University of Victoria, lecturer in English, 1965-66; University of Stirling, lecturer in English, 1971-, professor in English, 1995, professor emeritus, 2009; Canongate Classics, series editor, 1987-2005; Fellow of Royal Society of Edinburgh, 1992; Scottish Book Trust, chairman, 1995-2000; Stirling Centre for Scottish Studies, director, 1999-2009. Writer. **Publications:** (With J. Rankin) 28 Poems, 1964; Poems, 1970; (with V. Simmons and P. Mills) Trio: New Poets from Edinburgh, 1971; Hugh MacDiarmid, 1976; True History on the Walls (poems), 1976; (with M. Gray) The Penguin Book of the Bicycle, 1978; The Literature of Scotland, 1985, 2nd ed., 2007; MacDiarmid, 1985; The Poetry of Norman MacCaig, 1989; Into the Blue Wavelengths (poems), 2004. EDITOR: (co-ed.) Scottish Poetry Seven, Eight and Nine, 3 vols., 1974-76; (with A. Ogilvy and G. Sutherland) Birds: An Anthology of New Poems, 1978; (with A. Ogilvie and G. Sutherland) Stones (poems), 1980; (and intro.) Three Scottish Poets, 1992; (and intro.) The Poetry of Scotland, 1995; (and intro.) Nan Shepherd, Grampian Quartet, 1996; (with A. Riach and intro.) Hugh MacDiarmid, Annals of the Five Senses and Other Stories, Sketches, and Plays, 1999; (and intro.) The Many Days, Selected Poems of Norman MacCaig, 2010. **Address:** Department of English Studies, University of Stirling, Stirling, CN FK9 4LA, Scotland. **Online address:** r.b.watson@virgin.net

WATSON, Rory. See WATSON, Roderick.

WATSON, Sophia. British (born England), b. 1962. **Genres:** Novels, Biography, Adult Non-fiction. **Career:** Quartet Books, assistant editor, 1983-84; Fisher Publishing, editor, 1984-85; Hamish Hamilton, editor, 1985-87; Mail on Sunday, feature writer, 1987; Daily Mail, feature writer, 1988-90, columnist; freelance writer, 1989-. **Publications:** Winning Women: The Price of Success in a Man's World (nonfiction), 1989; Marina, the Story of a Princess (biography), 1994; Meet Me at the Fair, 1996; Lazy Contentment: The History of the Carnarvon Arms Hotel, 1999. NOVELS: Her Husband's Children, 1995; Strange and Well-Bred, 1996; The Perfect Treasure, 1998; Only Pretending, 2000. Contributor to periodicals. **Address:** Great Highleigh, Exebridge, Dulverton, SM TA4 2LR, England. **Online address:** sophiawatson@royaloak18.fsnet.co.uk

WATSON, Stephanie. American (born United States), b. 1979. **Genres:** Children's Fiction, Literary Criticism And History, Novels. **Career:** Freelance writer. **Publications:** Elvis & Olive, 2008; Elvis & Olive: Super Detectives, 2010. **Address:** c/o Stephanie Watson, David Black Literary Agency, 156 5th Ave., New York, NY 10010-7002, U.S.A. **Online address:** sw@stephanie-watson.com

WATSON, Stephen. South African (born South Africa), b. 1954?. **Genres:** Poetry, Literary Criticism And History, Essays. **Career:** University of Cape Town, Department of English, acting director, professor of English, director of writing centre. Writer. **Publications:** Poems 1977-1982, 1982; In This City: Poems, 1986; Sydney Clouts and the Limits of Romanticism, 1986; Cape Town Days and Other Poems, 1989; Selected Essays, 1980-1990, 1990; Return of the Moon: Versions from the Xam, 1991, rev. ed as Song of the Broken String: After the Xam Bushmen: Poems from a Lost Oral Tradition, 1996; Sound from the Thinking Strings: A Visual, Literary, Archaeological and Historical Interpretation of the Final Years of /Xam life, 1991; Presence of the Earth: New Poems, 1995; A Writer's Diary, 1997; The Other City: Selected Poems, 1977-1999, 2000; The Light Echo & Other Poems, 2000-2006, 2007; The Music in the Ice: On Writers, Writing & Other Things, 2010. EDITOR: (and intro.) Essays and Lectures, 1949-1991, 1994; (and intro.) Selected Poems, 1961-1994, 1994; (with G. Huggan) Critical Perspectives on J.M. Coetzee, 1996; (with P. Cullinan) Dante in South Africa, 2005; (and intro.) A City Imagined, 2006. Contributor to books. **Address:** Department of English, UCT Creative Writing Ctr., University of Cape Town, Arts Bldg., Rondebosch, 7701, South Africa. **Online address:** swatson@humanities.uct.ac.za

WATSON, Steven. (Steven Peter Watson). American (born United States), b. 1947. **Genres:** Art/Art History, History, Politics/Government, Social Sciences, Photography. **Career:** Putnam County Mental Health, psychologist, 1976-95; Whitney Museum, consultant curator, 1995; Community mental health clinic, psychologist. Writer. **Publications:** Artifacts at the End of a Decade, 1981; (intro.) The Young and Evil, 1989; Strange Bedfellows: The First American Avant-Garde, 1991; The Harlem Renaissance: Hub of African-American Culture, 1995; The Birth of the Beat Generation: Visionaries, Rebels, and Hipsters, 1944-1960, 1995; Prepare for Saints: Gertrude Stein, Virgil Thomson, and the Mainstreaming of American Modernism, 1998; An Eye on the Modern Century: Selected Letters of Henry McBride, 2000; Factory Made: Warhol and the Sixties, 2003. Contributor to periodicals. **Address:** 603 W 111th St., New York, NY 10025, U.S.A.

WATSON, Steven Peter. See WATSON, Steven.

WATSON, William E. American (born United States), b. 1962. **Genres:** History, Adult Non-fiction, Ghost Writer. **Career:** Immaculata University, associate professor of history, 1998-, professor of history, chair, 2002-03, 2006-, The Duffy's Cut Project, director. Writer. **Publications:** (With A.V. Riasanovsky) Readings in Russian History, 1991; The Collapse of Communism in the Soviet Union, 1998; Tricolor and Crescent, 2003; (co-author) The Ghosts of Duffy's Cut: The Irish Who Died Building America's Most Dangerous Stretch of Railroad, 2006. Contributor of articles to periodicals. **Address:** Department of History, Immaculata University, 21 Faculty Ctr., 1145 King Rd., Immaculata, PA 19345, U.S.A. **Online address:** wwatson@immaculata.edu

WATT, Alan. Canadian/Scottish (born Scotland), b. 1965. **Genres:** Novels. **Career:** Writer. **Publications:** Diamond Dogs: A Novel, 2000; The 90-Day Novel: Unlock the Story Within, 2010. **Address:** LA Writers Lab, 5636 Melrose Ave., Los Angeles, CA 90038, U.S.A. **Online address:** alan@alanwatt.com

WATT, Ben. British (born England), b. 1962. **Genres:** Songs/Lyrics And Libretti, Autobiography/Memoirs, Biography, Music. **Career:** Musician and writer. **Publications:** Patient: The True Story of a Rare Illness, 1996. Contributor to periodicals. **Address:** c/o Jasmine Daines, J.F.D. Management, 106 Dalling Rd., London, GL W6 0JA, England.

WATT, David Harrington. American (born United States), b. 1957. **Genres:** History. **Career:** Temple University, instructor, 1986-87, assistant professor, 1987-92, associate professor of religion, 1992-99, associate professor of history, 1999-, director of general education, 2007-08, professor, 2009-; Lutheran Theological Seminary, lecturer, 1991; University of Dhaka, visiting lecturer, 2006. Writer. **Publications:** A Transforming Faith: An Exploration of Twentieth-Century American Evangelicalism, 1991; Bible-Carrying Christians: Conservative Protestants and Social Power, 2002. Work represented in anthologies. Contributor to periodicals. **Address:** Department of History, Temple University, 908 Gladfelter Hall, 1115 W Berks St., Philadelphia, PA 19122-6089, U.S.A. **Online address:** david.watt@temple.edu

WATT, Kelly. Canadian (born Canada), b. 1958. **Genres:** Novels, Novellas/Short Stories, Plays/Screenplays, Young Adult Fiction, Adult Non-fiction. **Career:** Stone Film, researcher and writer, 1985-86; Fitness Files, research writer, 1987-88; Canadian Broadcasting Corp., coordinator and scriptwriter for front page challenge, 1989-91; CTV, writer for the television program, 1992; Literary Press Group, publisher's representative for Ontario, 1995-98; freelance writer, 1998-. **Publications:** Letters (solo performance piece), 1982; Mad Dog (novel), 2001; She Waits: Love, Spaghetti and Other Stories by Youngish Women, 2002; The Fourteenth Year, 2007; The Ratfinks, 2010; Contributor to periodicals. Works appear in anthologies. **Address:** c/o Denise Bukowski, Bukowski Agency, 14 Prince Auttuer Ave., Ste. 202, Toronto, ON M5S 1M5, Canada. **Online address:** wattswords@cogeco.ca

WATTENBERG, Martin P(aul). American (born United States), b. 1956. **Genres:** Politics/Government. **Career:** University of Michigan, teaching assistant, 1978-82; University of California-Los Angeles, assistant professor of political science, 1982-83; University of California-Irvine, assistant professor, 1983-86, associate professor of political science and associate director of public policy research organization, 1986-91, professor, 1991-; Educational Testing Service, consultant, 1985. Writer. **Publications:** The Decline of American Political Parties, 1952-1980, 1984, 6th ed. as The Decline of American Political Parties, 1952-1996, 1998; The Rise of Candidate-Centered Politics: Presidential Elections of the 1980s, 1991; (with R.L. Lineberry and G.C. Edwards) Government in America: People, Politics and Policy, 11th ed., 2011; (ed. with R.J. Dalton) Parties without Partisans: Political Change in Advanced Industrial Democracies, 2000; (ed. with M.S. Shugart) Mixed-Member Electoral Systems: The Best of Both Worlds?, 2001; Where Have All the Voters Gone?, 2002; Is Voting for Young People?, 2007. Contributor to journals. **Address:** School of Political Sciences, University of California, 2285 Social Plz., PO Box 5100, Irvine, CA 92697-5100, U.S.A. **Online address:** mpwatten@uci.edu

WATTERS, Ethan. American (born United States), b. 1964. **Genres:** Psychology. **Career:** San Francisco Writers Grotto, co-founder, Writer. **Publications:** (With R. Ofshe) Making Monsters: False Memories, Psychotherapy, and Sexual Hysteria, 1994; (with R. Ofshe) Therapy's Delusions: The Myth of the Unconscious and the Exploitation of Today's Walking Worried, 1999; Urban Tribes: A Generation Redefines Friendship, Family, and Commitment, 2003; Crazy Like Us: The Globalization of the American Psyche, 2010. Contributor to magazines and periodicals. **Address:** U.S.A. **Online address:** ethan1@mindspring.com

WATTERSON, John Sayle. American (born United States), b. 1939?. **Genres:** Sports/Fitness, History. **Career:** James Madison University, assistant adjunct professor of history. Writer and sports historian. **Publications:** Thomas Burke, Restless Revolutionary, 1980; College Football: History, Spectacle, Controversy, 2000; The Games Presidents Play: Sports and the Presidency, 2006. **Address:** Department of History, James Madison University, Moody 1C, Jackson Hall, PO Box 2001, Harrisonburg, VA 22807, U.S.A. **Online address:** watterjs@jmu.edu

WATTS, Alan (James). British (born England), b. 1925. **Genres:** Meteorology/Atmospheric Sciences, Recreation, Sciences, Air/Space Topics, Natural History. **Career:** General Electric Company Research Laboratories, researcher on semiconductors, 1955-57; Colchester Institute, lecturer in physics, 1957-90; British Olympic Yachting Team, weather adviser, 1966-68; The Slide Centre, Science Slide Folios, editor and originator, 1970-89. **Publications:** Wind and Sailing Boats: The Structure and Behavior of the Wind as it Affects Sailing Craft, 1967, 3rd ed., 1987; Weather Forecasting Ashore and Afloat, 1968; Instant Weather Forecasting, 1968, 1988; The Wind Pilot, 1975; Instant Wind Forecasting, 1975; Basic Windcraft, 1976; The Course Builder's Handbook, 1979; Cruising Weather, 1982; Dinghy and Board Sailing Weather, 1984; Home Coursebuilding and Jumping, 1984; Reading the Weather: Modern Techniques for Yachtsmen, 1987; Sailing Off the Beach, 1990; Air Rider's Weather, 1992; UFO Quest: In Search of the Mystery Machines, 1994; The Weather Handbook, 1994, 2nd ed., 1999; UFO Visitation: Preparing for the Twenty-First Century, 1996; Unidentified Flying Objects, 1999; Weather Wise: Reading Weather Signs, 2008; Instant Storm Forecasting, 2009. **Address:** Ryelands, Elmstead Market, Colchester, EX CO7 7BB, England.

WATTS, Anthony John. British (born England), b. 1942. **Genres:** History, Military/Defense/Arms Control, Politics/Government, Air/Space Topics, Natural History, Business/Trade/Industry, Engineering. **Career:** British Broadcasting Corp., engineer, 1961-65; program operations assistant, 1965-78; Navy Intl., editor, 1978-. Consultant. **Publications:** Japanese Warships of World War II, 1966; Pictorial History of the Royal Navy 1816-1880, vol. I, 1970, 1880-1914, vol. II, 1971; The Loss of the Scharnhorst, 1970; (with B.G. Gordon) The Imperial Japanese Navy, 1872-1945, 1971; (comp.) A Source Book of Submarines and Submersibles, 1976; The U-Boat Hunters, 1976; A Source Book of Naval Aircraft and Aircraft Carriers, 1977, rev. ed., 1980; Fact File on Submarines, 2 vols., 1977; Axis Submarines, 1977; Allied Submarines, 1977; Source Book on Hovercraft and Hydrofoils, 1978; Battleships, 1978; Fact File on Battleships, 1978; Fact File on Cruisers, 2 vols., 1979; Axis Cruisers, 1979; Allied Cruisers, 1979; Source Book of Helicopters and Vertical Take-off Aircraft, 1982; (with A. English) Battle for the Falklands, 1982; The Imperial Russian Navy, 1990; Fast Attack Craft, 1992; The Royal Navy, An Illustrated History, 1994; Non-Nuclear Submarines-The World Market, 1996; Naval Mine Warfare Markets, 1996. EDITOR: Chronology of the War at Sea 1939-45, 2 vols., 1972-74; The Russian Fleet 1914-17, 1972; Scapa Flow 1919: The End of the German Fleet, 1973; Warships and Navies Review, 2nd ed., 1974; Chronology of the War at Sea, vol. II: 1943-1945, 1974; Warships and Navies 1974, 1974. **Address:** Hunters Moon, Hogspudding Ln., Newdigate, Dorking, SR RH5 5DS, England. **Online address:** anthony.watts@virgin.net

WATTS, Edward J. American (born United States), b. 1975. **Genres:** History, Education. **Career:** Indiana University, associate professor of history. Writer. **Publications:** City and School in Late Antique Athens and Alexan-

dria, 2006. Contributor to journals. **Address:** Department of History, Indiana University, Ballantine 742, 1020 E Kirkwood, Bloomington, IN 47405-7103, U.S.A. **Online address:** ejwatts@indiana.edu

WATTS, Sheldon J. American (born United States), b. 1934. **Genres:** History. **Career:** University of Ilorin, senior lecturer, 1977-84; American University, visiting associate professor, 1990-92; University of London, Friend of Institute of Historical Research, faculty. Writer. **Publications:** (With S. Watts) From Border to Middle Shire: Northumberland, 1586-1625, 1975; A Social History of Western Europe, 1450-1720: Tensions and Solidarities among Rural People, 1984; Epidemics and History: Disease, Power, and Imperialism, 1997; Disease and Medicine in World History, 2003. **Address:** American University in Cairo, PO Box 2511, Garden City, Cairo, 11511, Egypt.

WAUGH, Alexander. British (born England), b. 1963. **Genres:** Music, Autobiography/Memoirs, History. **Career:** Mail on Sunday, chief opera critic, 1990-91; Evening Standard, chief opera critic, 1991-96; entertainment manager; concert agent; documentary presenter; music critic; classical record producer. Writer. **Publications:** Classical Music: A New Way of Listening, 1995; Opera: A New Way of Listening, 1996; Time: From Micro-Seconds to Millennia, a Search for the Right Time, 1999; God, 2002; Fathers and Sons: The Autobiography of a Family, 2004; The House of Wittgenstein: A Family at War, 2008. Contributor to periodicals. **Address:** Aitken Alexander Associates, 18-21 Cavaye Pl., London, GL SW10 9PT, England. **Online address:** awaugh@luckhamfarm.com

WAUGH, Joan. American (born United States), b. 1950. **Genres:** Autobiography/Memoirs, Military/Defense/Arms Control. **Career:** University of California, Department of History, professor, 1993-. Historian and writer. **Publications:** Unsentimental Reformer: The Life of Josephine Shaw Lowell, 1997; Personal Memoirs of U.S. Grant: A History of the Union Cause, 2003; (ed. and contrib. with A. Fahs) The Memory of the Civil War in American Culture, 2004; (ed. and contrib. with G.W. Gallagher) Wars within a War: Controversy and Conflict over the American Civil War, 2009; U.S. Grant: American Hero, American Myth, 2009. Contributor to books. **Address:** Department of History, University of California, 6265 Bunche Hall, PO Box 951473, Los Angeles, CA 90095-1473, U.S.A. **Online address:** jwaugh@history.ucla.edu

WAUGH, John C(linton). American (born United States), b. 1929. **Genres:** History. **Career:** Arizona Wildcat and Arizona Daily Star, staff; Christian Science Monitor, Western News Bureau, bureau secretary, 1956-57, staff correspondent, 1957-65, focus editor, 1965-66, bureau chief, 1966-70, national series writer, 1970-73; freelance writer and editor, 1976-83, 1989-; U.S. Senator from New Mexico Jeff Bingaman, press secretary, 1983-89. **Publications:** NONFICTION: The Class of 1846: From West Point to Appomattox: Stonewall Jackson, George McClellan and Their Brothers, 1994; Sam Bell Maxey and the Confederate Indians, 1995; Reelecting Lincoln: The Battle for the 1864 Presidency, 1997; Last Stand at Mobile, 2001; Surviving the Confederacy, 2002; On the Brink of Civil War, 2003; Edwin Cole Bearss: History's Pied Piper, 2003; 20 Good Reasons to Study the Civil War, 2004; Kansai International Airport: Airport in the Sea, 2004; One Man Great Enough: Abraham Lincoln's Road to Civil War, 2007; Lincoln and McClellan: The Troubled Partnership Between a President and His General, 2010; (comp.) How Historians Work: Retelling the Past-From the Civil War to the Wider World, 2010. Contributor to periodicals. **Address:** 3408 Country Club Rd., Pantego, TX 76013, U.S.A. **Online address:** jcwaugh@flash.net

WAUGH, Louisa. Scottish/German (born Germany), b. 1970?. **Genres:** Travel/Exploration, Reference. **Career:** Writer. **Publications:** Hearing Birds Fly: A Nomadic Year in Mongolia, 2003. Contributor to journals. **Address:** c/o Author Mail, Little, Brown & Company Ltd., 100 Victoria Embankment, London, GL EC4Y 0DY, England.

WAUGH, Sylvia. British (born England), b. 1935?. **Genres:** Science Fiction/Fantasy, Children's Fiction, Young Adult Fiction, Autobiography/Memoirs. **Career:** Writer and teacher. **Publications:** FICTION: The Mennyms, 1994; Mennyms in the Wilderness, 1995; Mennyms Under Siege, 1996; Mennyms Alone, 1996; Mennyms Alive, 1997. SCIENCE FICTION: Space Race, 2000; Earthborn, 2002; Who Goes Home?, 2004. OTHERS: Bombs and Butterflies, forthcoming. Works appear in anthologies. **Address:** Random House Children's Books, 61-63 Uxbridge Rd., London, GL W5 5SA, England. **Online address:** sylvia@waugh001.freeserve.co.uk

WAUGH, Teresa (Lorraine). British (born England), b. 1940. **Genres:** Adult Non-fiction, Translations, History, Literary Criticism And History. **Career:** Writer and translator. **Publications:** Painting Water, 1984; Waterloo, Waterloo, 1986; (with A. Waugh) The Entertaining Book, 1986; An Intolerable Burden, 1988; A Song at Twilight, 1989; Sylvia's Lot, 1994; The Gossips, 1995; A Friend Like Harvey, 1999; The House, 2002. TRANSLATOR: M.R. Pahlavi, The Shah's Story, 1980; J. Gimpel, The Cathedral Builders, 1983; M. Bellonci, The Travels of Marco Polo: A Modern Translation, 1984; J. Tulard, Napoleon: The Myth of the Saviour, 1984; B. Craveri, Madame Du Deffand and Her World, 1994; A. Muhlstein, The Life of Astolphe de Custine, 1999; B. Craveri, Age of Conversation, 2005. Contributor to periodicals. **Address:** Combe Florey House, Taunton, SM TA4 3JD, England.

WAUZZINSKI, Robert A. American (born United States), b. 1950. **Genres:** Philosophy, Theology/Religion, History, Social Commentary. **Career:** Coalition for Christian Outreach, staff, 1972-76, education adviser for staff training and development, 1972-74; Chatham College, lecturer in philosophy and religion, 1978-80; Trinity Episcopal School for Ministry, lecturer, 1984; Geneva College, lecturer in religion and technology, 1985-86; Gordon-Conwell Theological Seminary, adjunct professor, 1985-86; Whitworth College, Edward B. Lindaman associate professor of communication, technology and change, 1986-92; Institute for Christian Studies, adjunct professor, 1988-92; Indiana University-Purdue University Indianapolis, research associate and coordinator, 1992-2004; Ball State University, Department of Philosophy and Religious Studies, associate professor, 2004-, religious studies professor; First Presbyterian Church, parish associate, pastor. Writer. **Publications:** Between God and Gold: Protestant Evangelicalism and the Industrial Revolution, 1820-1918, 1993; Discerning Prometheus: The Cry for Wisdom in Our Technological Society, 2001; The Transforming Story of Dwelling House Savings and Loan: A Pittsburgh Bank's Fight against Urban Poverty, 2003; Ruth: The Story of God's Unending Redemption, 2010. Works appear in anthologies. Contributor to periodicals. **Address:** First Presbyterian Church, 1400 W Riverside Ave., Muncie, IN 47303, U.S.A. **Online address:** wabber15@aol.com

WAWRO, Geoffrey. American (born United States), b. 1960. **Genres:** History. **Career:** World Banking Group, Chemical Bank, management trainee, 1983-87; Oakland University, assistant professor of history, 1992-97; Naval War College, visiting professor of strategy and policy, 1996-98, associate professor of history, 1997-2001, professor of strategic studies, 2000-05; University of North Texas, Major General Olinto Mark Barsanti professor of military history, 2005-, Military History Center, director, 2005-. Writer and historian. **Publications:** The Austro-Prussian War: Austria's War with Prussia and Italy in 1866, 1996; Warfare and Society in Europe, 1792-1914, 2000; The Franco-Prussian War: The German Conquest of France in 1870-1871, 2003; (contrib.) Historical Atlas: A Comprehensive History of the World, 2008; Quicksand: America's Pursuit of Power in the Middle East, 2010. Contributor to journals and periodicals. **Address:** Department of History, University of North Texas, PO Box 310650, Denton, TX 76203, U.S.A. **Online address:** wawro@unt.edu

WAX, Amy L. American (born United States), b. 1953. **Genres:** Business/ Trade/Industry, Economics. **Career:** Columbia Law Review, editor, 1985-87, senior revising editor, 1986-87; U.S. Court of Appeals for the District of Columbia Circuit, law clerk, 1987-88; United States Department of Justice, Office of the Solicitor General, assistant, 1988-94; University of Virginia, Law School, associate professor, 1994-99, professor, 1999-2000, Class of 1948 Professor of Scholarly Research in Law, 2000-01; University of Pennsylvania, Law School, professor, 2001-07, Robert Mundheim professor of law, 2007-. **Publications:** Race, Wrongs, and Remedies: Group Justice in the 21st Century, 2009. Contributor to books and periodicals. **Address:** Law School, University of Pennsylvania, 3400 Chestnut St., Philadelphia, PA 19104, U.S.A. **Online address:** awax@law.upenn.edu

WAX, Steven T. American (born United States), b. 1948. **Genres:** Law, Military/Defense/Arms Control. **Career:** U.S. District Court of Alaska, law clerk, 1974-75; County of King, assistant district attorney, 1975-79; Broome County Public Defender, public defender, 1979-83; State University of New York, lecturer, 1979-83; District of Oregon, federal public defender, 1983-; Northwestern University, School of Law, adjunct professor, 1983; Lewis & Clark Law School, faculty, 1985-93, 2001; U.S. Courts of Appeals, staff; U.S. Supreme Court, staff. Writer. **Publications:** Kafka Comes to America: Fighting for Justice in the War on Terror, 2008. **Address:** Office of the Federal Public Defender, 101 SW Main St., Ste. 1700, Portland, OR 97204-3225, U.S.A.

WAXMAN, Henry Arnold. American (born United States), b. 1939. **Genres:** Biography, Autobiography/Memoirs. **Career:** California State Assembly, assembly member, 1969-74; U.S. House of Representatives, representative, 1975-. Writer. **Publications:** (With J. Green) The Waxman Report: How Congress Really Works, 2009. Contributor to books and periodicals. **Address:** 2204 Rayburn House Office Bldg., Washington, DC 20515-0001, U.S.A.

WAYCOTT, Edon. American (born United States), b. 1943. **Genres:** Food And Wine. **Career:** La Brea Bakery, manager, 1989-90; cooking instructor, 1992-. Writer, artist, food stylist and creative consultant. **Publications:** Preserving the Taste, 1993; Summer Fruit, 1995; Breakfast All Day: 150 Recipes for Everybody's Favorite Meal, 1996. Contributor to periodicals. **Address:** LA Literary Agency, PO Box 46370, Los Angeles, CA 90046, U.S.A.

WAYMAN, Tom. Canadian (born Canada), b. 1945. **Genres:** Poetry, Essays, Novellas/Short Stories, Literary Criticism And History, Novels. **Career:** Colorado State University, assistant professor of English, 1968-69; University of Windsor, writer-in-residence, 1975-76; Wayne State University, assistant professor of English, 1976-77; University of Alberta, writer-in-residence, 1978-79; David Thompson University Centre, instructor, 1980-82; Simon Fraser University, writer-in-residence, 1983; Kootenay School of Writing, instructor, 1984-87; Kwantlen University College, instructor, 1988-89, faculty, 1998-2000; Okanagan University College, professor, 1990-91, 1992-95; Kootenay School of the Arts, writing program co-head, 1995-98, 2000-02; University of Toronto, writer-in-residence, 1996; University of Calgary, associate professor of English, 2002-10; Arizona State University, Fulbright visiting chair in creative writing, 2007. **Publications:** POEMS: (co-author) Mindscapes, 1971; Waiting for Wayman, 1973; For and Against the Moon, 1974; Money and Rain: Tom Wayman Live!, 1975; Free Time: Industrial Poems, 1977; A Planet Mostly Sea, 1979; Living on the Ground: Tom Wayman Country, 1980; Introducing Tom Wayman: Selected Poems 1973-1980, 1980; The Nobel Prize Acceptance Speech, 1981; Counting the Hours: City Poems, 1983; Inside Job: Essays on the New Work Writing, 1983; The Face of Jack Munro, 1986; In a Small House on the Outskirts of Heaven, 1989; A Country Not Considered: Canada, Culture, Work, 1993; Did I Miss Anything, Selected Poems 1973-1993, 1993; The Astonishing Weight of the Dead, 1994; I'll Be Right Back: New and Selected Poems 1980-1996, 1997; The Colours of the Forest, 1999; My Father's Cup, 2002; High Speed Through Shoaling Water, 2007. POETRY ANTHOLOGIES EDITOR: Beaton Abbott's Got the Contract, 1974; A Government Job at Last, 1975; Going for Coffee: Poetry on the Job, 1981; East of Main, 1989; Paperwork, 1991; The Dominion of Love, 2001. SHORT FICTION: Boundary Country, 2007; A Vain Thing, 2007. NOVEL: Woodstock Rising, 2009. **Address:** PO Box 163, Winlaw, BC V0G 2J0, Canada. **Online address:** appledor@netidea.com

WAYMAN, Vivienne. *See* Obituaries.

WAYNE, Donald. *See* DODD, Wayne.

WAYNE, Valerie. American (born United States), b. 1945. **Genres:** Literary Criticism And History. **Career:** Chicago State University, lecturer in composition, 1976-78; University of Illinois at Chicago, lecturer in composition, 1976-78; University of Hawaii, visiting assistant professor, associate professor of English, 1978-93, professor of English, 1993-, now professor emeritus, director of undergraduate honors program in English, 1988-91, graduate program in English, director, 1994-97; Society for the Study of Early Modern Women, president, 2000; Folger Shakespeare Library, Hinman Long-term Fellow, 2003; Shakespeare Association of America, trustee, 2007-10. Writer. **Publications:** EDITOR: The Matter of Difference: Materialist Feminist Criticism of Shakespeare, 1991; (and intro.) The Flower of Friendship: A Renaissance Dialogue Contesting Marriage, 1992; (with W. Burgwinkle and G. Man) Significant Others: Gender and Culture in Film and Literature, East and West: Selected Conference Papers, 1993; (ed. with C. Moore) Translations/ Transformations: Gender and Culture in Film and Literature, East and West: Selected Conference Papers, 1993; (intro.) Anne Cooke Bacon, 2000; (co-author) The Collected Works of Thomas Middleton, 2007; A Trick to Catch the Old One, 2007; (ed. with M.E. Lamb) Staging Early Modern Romance: Prose Fiction, Dramatic Romance, and Shakespeare, 2009. Works appear in anthologies. **Address:** Department of English, University of Hawaii, Kuykendall 325, 1733 Donaghho Rd., Honolulu, HI 96822, U.S.A. **Online address:** vwayne@hawaii.edu

WAYNER, Peter. American (born United States), b. 1964?. **Genres:** Documentaries/Reportage, Sciences, Information Science/Computers. **Career:** New York Times, technology reporter; Cornell University, teacher of computer science; Georgetown University, teacher of computer science. Writer. **Publications:** Agents Unleashed: A Public Domain Look at Agent Technology, 1995; Digital Cash: Commerce on the Net, 1996, 2nd ed., 1997; Disappearing Cryptography: Being and Nothingness on the Net, 1996, 3rd ed., 2009; Digital Copyright Protection, 1997; Java and Java Script Programming, 1997; (co-author) The Management of Risks Created by Internet-Initiated Value Transfers, 1997; Java Beans for Real Programmers, 1998; Compression Algorithms for Real Programmers, 1999; Free for All: How LINUX and the Free Software Movement Undercut the High-Tech Titans, 2000; Translucent Databases, 2002; Policing Online Games, 2003. Contributor to periodicals. **Address:** c/o Author Mail, HarperCollins Publishers, 10 E 53rd St., 7th Fl., New York, NY 10022, U.S.A. **Online address:** p3@wayner.org

WAZIYATAWIN. Also writes as Waziyatawin Angela Wilson, Angela Cavender Wilson. American (born United States), b. 1968. **Genres:** History, Language/Linguistics, Politics/Government, Race Relations, Social Commentary. **Career:** Arizona State University, assistant professor, 2000-06; University of Victoria, Indigenous Governance Program, indigenous peoples research chair and associate professor, 2008-; Oyate Nipi Kte, founder. Writer. **Publications:** (Ed. as Angela Cavender Wilson with D.A. Mihesuah) Indigenizing the Academy: Transforming Scholarship and Empowering Communities, 2004; (ed. as Waziyatawin Angela Wilson with M.Y. Bird) For Indigenous Eyes Only: A Decolonization Handbook, 2005; (as Waziyatawin Angela Wilson) Remember This! Dakota Decolonization and the Eli Taylor Narratives, 2005; (ed.) In the Footsteps of Our Ancestors: The Dakota Commemorative Marches of the 21st Century, 2006; What Does Justice Look Like? The Struggle for Liberation in Dakota Homeland, 2008. Contributor to journals and periodicals. **Address:** Indigenous Governance Program, University of Victoria, Rm. A260, 3800 Finnerty Rd., HSD Bldg., PO Box 1700 STN CSC, Victoria, BC V8P 5C2, Canada. **Online address:** waziyata@uvic.ca

WEAKS, Mary Louise. (Mary Weaks-Baxter). American (born United States), b. 1961. **Genres:** Literary Criticism And History. **Career:** Rockford College, assistant professor of American literature, 1988-95, associate professor, 1995-, Department of English, chair, 1994, Hazel E. Koch Professor of English; Westminster College, assistant professor of English, director of the writing. Writer. **Publications:** EDITOR: (with F.C. Watkins and J.T. Hiers) Talking With Robert Penn Warren, 1990; (with C. Perry) Southern Women's Writing: Colonial to Contemporary, 1995; (with C. Perry) The History of Southern Women's Literature, 2002. OTHERS: (as Mary Weaks Baxter) Reclaiming the American Farmer: The Reinvention of a Regional Mythology in Twentieth-century Southern Writing, 2006; (with C. Bruunand and C. Forslund) We Are a College at War: Women Working for Victory in World War II, 2010. **Address:** Department of English, Rockford College, 125 Scarborough Hall, 5050 E State St., Rockford, IL 61108-2311, U.S.A. **Online address:** mweaks-baxter@rockford.edu

WEAKS-BAXTER, Mary. *See* **WEAKS, Mary Louise.**

WEALES, Gerald. American (born United States), b. 1925. **Genres:** Novels, Children's Fiction, Literary Criticism And History, Theatre, Photography, Art/Art History. **Career:** Georgia Institute of Technology, instructor in English, 1951-53; Newark College of Engineering, instructor in English, 1953-55; Wayne State University, instructor in English, 1955-56; Brown University, assistant professor of English, 1957-58; University of Pennsylvania, assistant professor, 1958-63, associate professor, 1963-67, professor, 1967-87, professor emeritus, 1987-; Writer. **Publications:** Miss Grimsbee is a Witch, 1957; Tale for the Bluebird, 1960; Religion in Modern English Drama, 1961; American Drama since World War II, 1962; Edwardian Plays, 1962; A Play and Its Parts, 1964; Eleven Plays: An Introduction to Drama, 1964; Tennessee Williams, 1965; Miss Grimsbee Takes a Vacation, 1965; The Jumping-Off Place: American Drama in the 1960's, 1969; Clifford Odets, Playwright, 1971; Religion in Modern English Drama, 1976; Canned Goods as Caviar: American Film Comedy of the 1930's, 1985. EDITOR: (and intro.) The Complete Plays, 1966; Arthur Miller: Death of a Salesman: Text and Criticism, 1967; The Crucible: Text and Criticism, 1971; (with R.J. Nelson) Revolution: A Collection of Plays, 1975; (with R.J. Nelson) Enclosure: A Collection of Plays, 1975. **Address:** Department of English, University of Pennsylvania, Rm. 113, Fisher-Bennett Hall, Philadelphia, PA 19104-6273, U.S.A. **Online address:** gweales@english.upenn.edu

WEARNE, Alan. Australian (born Australia), b. 1948. **Genres:** Novels, Novellas/Short Stories, Poetry, Music. **Career:** Curtin University of Technology, teaching fellow, 2000-02; University of Wollongong, School of Journalism and Creative Writing, lecturer, senior lecturer and coordinator of creative writing. Writer. **Publications:** VERSE: Public Relations, 1972; New Devil, New Parish, 1976; The Australian Popular Songbook, 2008. NOVELS IN VERSE: The Nightmarkets, 1986; Out Here, 1987; The Lovemakers, vol. I: Saying All The Great Sexy Things, 2001, vol. II: Two, Money and Nothing, 2004. NOVELS: Kicking in Danger, 1997; Sarsaparilla A Calypso, 2007; The Australian Popular Songbook, 2008. **Address:** Faculty of Creative Arts, University of Wollongong, 25 G05c, Northfields Ave., Wollongong, NW 2522, Australia. **Online address:** alan_wearne@uow.edu.au

WEART, Spencer R(ichard). American (born United States), b. 1942. **Genres:** History, International Relations/Current Affairs, Physics, Earth Sciences, Popular Culture. **Career:** Mount Wilson and Palomar Observatories, research fellow, 1968-70; University of California, Department of History, research assistant, 1971-74; American Institute of Physics, Center for History of Physics, director, 1974-2009, retired, 2009. Writer, scientist and historian. **Publications:** SELF-ILLUSTRATED: How to Build a Sun, 1970. OTHERS: Light: A Key to the Universe, 1968; (with P. Forman and J. Heilbron) Physics Circa 1900: Personnel, Funding and Productivity of the Academic Establishments, 1975; Scientists in Power, 1979; Nuclear Fear: A History of Images, 1988; Never at War: Why Democracies Will Not Fight One Another, 1998; Discovery of Global Warming, 2003, rev. ed., 2008; Rise of Nuclear Fear, 2012. EDITOR: Selected Papers of Great American Physicists: The Bicentennial Commemorative Volume of the American Physical Society, 1976; (with G.W. Szilard) Leo Szilard, His Version of the Facts: Selected Recollections and Correspondence, 1978; (with M. Phillips) History of Physics: Readings from Physics Today, 1985; (co-ed. and contrib.) Out of the Crystal Maze: Chapters from the History of Solid State Physics, 1992. **Address:** Harvard University Press, 79 Garden St., Cambridge, MA 02138, U.S.A. **Online address:** sweart1@gmail.com

WEATHERFORD, Carole Boston. American (born United States), b. 1956. **Genres:** Children's Fiction, Poetry, Children's Non-fiction, Natural History. **Career:** Black Arts Review (radio talk show), creator, producer and host, 1979; Art Litho Co., account executive, 1981; National Bar Association, director of communications, 1981-85; B and C Associates Inc., creative director, 1985-88, 1993-95; freelance columnist, 2000-02; Fayetteville State University, visiting professor, 2002-. **Publications:** My Favorite Toy, 1994; The Tan Chanteuse (poetry for adults), 1995; Juneteenth Jamboree (novel), 1995; Me and My Family Tree, 1996; Grandma and Me, 1996; Mighty Menfolk, 1996; Mighty Men Talk, 1996; Sink or Swim: African-American Lifesavers of the Outer Banks, 1999; (with R.J. Weatherford) Somebody's Knocking at Your Door: AIDS and the African-American Church, 1999; The Tar Baby on the Soapbox, 1999; The Sound That Jazz Makes (poetry), 2000; The African-American Struggle for Legal Equality in American History, 2000; Princeville: The 500-Year Flood, 2001; Sidewalk Chalk: Poems of the City, 2001; Jazz Baby, 2002; Remember the Bridge: Poems of a People, 2002; Stormy Blues, 2002; Raising the Bar of Freedom: Great African American Lawyers, 2003; Freedom on the Move: The Greensboro Sit-Ins, 2005; A Negro League Scrapbook, 2005; The Carolinda Parakeet, 2005; Jesse Owens: The Fastest Man Alive, 2006; Moses: When Harriet Tubman Led her People to Freedom, 2006; Dear Mr. Rosenwald, 2006; Birmingham, 1963, 2007; Champions on the Bench, 2007; Becoming Billie Holiday, 2008; Racing Against the Odds, 2008; I, Matthew Henson: Polar Explorer, 2008; Before John was a Jazz Giant, 2008; Library Ghost, 2008; First Pooch: The Obamas Pick a Pet, 2009; Racing Against the Odds, 2009; Michelle Obama: First Mom, 2010; Sound that Jazz Makes, 2010; Obama: Only in America, 2010; Beatitudes: From Slavery to Civil Rights, 2010; Oprah: The Little Speaker, 2010. Contributor of articles to magazines and newspapers. **Address:** 3313 Sparrowhawk Dr., High Point, NC 27265, U.S.A. **Online address:** weathfd@earthlink.net

WEATHERHEAD, A(ndrew) Kingsley. American/British (born England), b. 1923. **Genres:** Literary Criticism And History, Biography. **Career:** University of Puget Sound, instructor, assistant professor, 1951-58; Louisiana State University, associate professor, 1958-60; University of Oregon, professor of English, 1960-89, professor emeritus of English, 1989-. Writer. **Publications:** A Reading of Henry Green, 1961; The Edge of the Image, 1967; (ed. with S.B. Greenfield) The Poem, 1968, 3rd ed., 1990; Stephen Spender and the Thirties, 1975; Leslie Weatherhead: A Personal Portrait, 1975; The British Dissonance, 1983; Upstairs: Writers and Residences, 2000. Contributor to periodicals. **Ad-**

dress: 2698 Fairmount Blvd., Eugene, OR 97403, U.S.A. **Online address:** akw@darkwing.uoregon.edu

WEATHERLY, Lee. (Titania Woods). British/American (born United States), b. 1967?. **Genres:** Novels, Young Adult Non-fiction. **Career:** Flying Frogs (writing consultancy), founder. Writer. **Publications:** NOVELS: Child X, 2002; Missing Abby, 2004; Breakfast at Sadie's, 2005; Them, Barrington Stoke, 2006; Kat Got Your Tongue, 2006; Watcher, 2007. GLITTERWINGS ACADEMY SERIES-AS TITANIA WOODS: Midnight Feast, 2007; Friends Forever, 2007; Fairy Dust, 2007; Fledge Star, 2007; Term-Time Trouble, 2007; New Girl, 2007; Seedling Exams, 2007; Flying High, 2008. NON-FICTION: (with H. Corner) How to Write a Blockbuster, 2008. **Address:** Caroline Sheldon Literary Agency, 70-75 Cowcross St., London, EC1MEJ, England. **Online address:** writetolee@ntlworld.com

WEAVER, Afaa Michael. (Michael S. Weaver). American (born United States), b. 1951. **Genres:** Plays/Screenplays, Poetry, Literary Criticism And History, Social Sciences. **Career:** Freelance journalist, 1980-; Seventh Son Press, editor and founder, 1985-95; Essex Community College, adjunct lecturer in English, 1987-88; City University of New York, Borough of Manhattan Community College, adjunct lecturer in English, 1988-90, Brooklyn College, adjunct lecturer in English, 1988-90; Seton Hall University, Law School, writing consultant, 1988-90; New York University, adjunct assistant professor, 1988-90; Rutgers University, associate professor of English, 1990-97; Simmons College, Department of English, endowed chair, professor, Alumnae professor of English, 1997-, The Zora Neale Hurston Literary Center, founder and director, 1997-. **Publications:** POETRY: Water Song, 1985; (as Michael S. Weaver) Poems, 1985; (as Michael S. Weaver) My Father's Geography, 1992; Stations in a Dream, 1993; (as Michael S. Weaver) Timber and Prayer: The Indian Pond Poems, 1995; Ten Lights of God, 2000; Sandy Point, 2000; Multitudes: Poems Selected & New, 2000; Plum Flower Dance: Poems 1985 to 2005, 2007. OTHERS: (as Michael S. Weaver ed. with D. Beaudouin and J. Taylor) Gathering Voices, 1986; (ed.) These Hands I Know: African-American Writers on Family, 2002. **Address:** Department of English, Simmons College, Rm. E211, 300 The Fenway, 3rd Fl., Boston, MA 02115-5898, U.S.A. **Online address:** michael.weaver@simmons.edu

WEAVER, Frederick S(tirton). American (born United States), b. 1939. **Genres:** Local History/Rural Topics, Economics. **Career:** University of California, assistant professor of economics, 1967-71; Hampshire College, professor of economics and history, 1971-, now professor emeritus. Writer. **Publications:** Regional Patterns of Economic Change in Chile, 1950-1964, 1968; Neo-classical Theory, Dependency Theory, and the Staple Theory: The Comparative Study of Foreign Trade and Investment in 19th Century Latin America, 1977; Class, State, and Industrial Structure: The Historical Process of South American Industrial Growth, 1980; Industrial Development and Cumulative Change: Historical Studies of England, Germany, and Brazil, 1989; (ed. and intro.) Promoting Inquiry in Undergraduate Learning, 1989; Liberal Education: Professions, Pedagogy, and Structure, 1991; (with I.E. Altuna) Presencia de la mujer en los programas de ingenieria, ciencia, y tecnologia, 1994; Inside the Volcano: History and Political Economy of Central America, 1994; Latin America in the World Economy: Mercantile Colonialism to Global Capitalism, 2000; Economic Literacy: Basic Economics with an Attitude, 2002, 3rd ed., 2010; (ed. with A. Mirsepassi and A. Basu) Localizing Knowledge in a Globalizing World: Recasting the Area Studies Debate, 2003; (with S.H. Strom) Confederates in the Tropics: Charles Swett's Travelogue of 1868, 2011. Contributor of articles to periodicals and books. **Address:** Department of Social Science, Hampshire College, 893 West St., Amherst, MA 01002-3372, U.S.A.

WEAVER, Karol K. American (born United States), b. 1970. **Genres:** History, Medicine/Health. **Career:** Susquehanna University, Department of History, assistant professor, 2004-08, associate professor, 2008-, Medical Humanities Initiative, coordinator, Women's Studies Program, coordinator. Writer. **Publications:** Medical Revolutionaries: The Enslaved Healers of Eighteenth-Century Saint Domingue, 2006; Medical Caregiving and Identity in Pennsylvania's Anthracite Region, 1880-2000, 2011. Contributor to books, periodicals and journals. **Address:** Department of History, Susquehanna University, Rm. 309, Steele Hall, 514 University Ave., Selinsgrove, PA 17870, U.S.A. **Online address:** weaverk@susqu.edu

WEAVER, Michael S. *See* **WEAVER, Afaa Michael.**

WEAVER, R(obert) Kent. American (born United States), b. 1953. **Genres:** Politics/Government. **Career:** Brookings Institution, Governmental Studies Program, research fellow, 1979-80, research associate, 1983-87, senior fellow, 1987-2002, co-director, 2002; Ohio State University, instructor in political science, 1981-83; Johns Hopkins School of Advanced International Studies, Centre of Canadian Studies, adjunct professor, 1984; Georgetown University, adjunct professor, 1990-, professor of public policy, 2002-, distinguished professor; Johns Hopkins University, visiting associate professor, 1991. Writer. **Publications:** The Politics of Industrial Change: Railway Policy in North America, 1985; Automatic Government: The Politics of Indexation, 1988; Ending Welfare as We Know It, 2000. EDITOR: (with B. Rockman) Do Institutions Matter? Government Capabilities in the United States and Abroad, 1992; The Collapse of Canada?, 1992; (with W.T. DIckens) Looking before We Leap, 1995; (with J. McGann) Think Tanks and Civil Societies: Catalysts for Ideas and Action, 2000; (with P. Stares) Guidance for Governance: Comparing Alternative Sources of Public Policy Advice, 2001; (with I.V. Sawhill, R. Haskins and A. Kane) Welfare Reform and Beyond, 2002; (with L.A. Pal) The Government Taketh Away: The Politics of Pain in the United States and Canada, 2003. Works appear in anthologies. Contributor to journals. **Address:** Department of Government, Georgetown University, 415 Old N., PO Box 571034, Washington, DC 20057, U.S.A. **Online address:** weaverrk@georgetown.edu

WEAVER, Will(iam Weller). American (born United States), b. 1950. **Genres:** Novels, Novellas/Short Stories, Young Adult Fiction, Philosophy, Biography. **Career:** Farmer, 1977-81; Bemidji State University, part-time writing instructor, 1979-81, associate professor, 1981-90, professor of English, 1990-2006, professor emeritus, 2006-; Will Weaver Racing (dirt track Midwest), owner. Lecturer, full time writer. **Publications:** Red Earth, White Earth (novel), 1986; A Gravestone Made of Wheat (stories), 1989; Snares, 1992; Barns of Minnesota, 2004; Sweet Land, 2006; The Last Hunter, An American Family Album (memoir), 2010; Libraries of Minnesota, 2011. YOUNG ADULT NOVELS: Striking Out, 1993; Farm Team, 1995; Hard Ball, 1998; Memory Boy, 2000; Claws, 2003; Full Service, 2005; Defect, 2007; Saturday Night Dirt, 2008; Super Stock Rookie, 2009; Checkered Flag Cheater, 2010; Survivors, 2012. Contributor to periodicals. **Address:** Bemidji, MN 56601, U.S.A. **Online address:** wweaver@paulbunyan.net

WEAVER-GELZER, Charlotte. American (born United States), b. 1950. **Genres:** Novels, Children's Fiction, Songs/Lyrics And Libretti, Theology/Religion, Autobiography/Memoirs. **Career:** Trans World Airlines, ticket agent, 1972; Redbook Magazine, secretary in editorial department, 1973-77. Writer, 1974-. Consultant. **Publications:** In the Time of Trouble, 1993; (co-author) Walk the Walk (youth musical), 1993; Glory Comes (youth musical), 1995. **Address:** 711 Ashbourne Ave., Lancaster, PA 17601, U.S.A. **Online address:** weavgelz@redrose.net

WEBB, Betty. American (born United States), b. 1942. **Genres:** Mystery/Crime/Suspense. **Career:** Phoenix College, teacher of creative writing. **Publications:** You Can Have It When I'm Through with It, 1976; Anteater of Death, 2008; Koala of Death, 2010; Desert Winds, 2012. MYSTERY NOVELS: Desert Noir, 2001; Desert Wives, 2003; Desert Shadows, 2004; Desert Run, 2006; Desert Cut: A Lena Jones Mystery, 2008; Desert Lost, 2009. Contributor to newspapers. **Address:** 7822 E Sheridan St., Scottsdale, AZ 85257, U.S.A. **Online address:** webbscottsdale@aol.com

WEBB, Clive. British (born England), b. 1970. **Genres:** History. **Career:** University of Sussex, reader in North American history, chair of history department, director of doctoral studies. Writer. **Publications:** Fight against Fear: Southern Jews and Black Civil Rights, 2001; (ed.) Massive Resistance: Southern Opposition to the Second Reconstruction, 2005; (with D. Brown) Race in the American South: From Slavery to Civil Rights, 2007; Rabble Rousers: The American Far Right in the Civil Rights Era, 2010. Contributor to books and periodicals. **Address:** United Kingdom. **Online address:** c.j.webb@sussex.ac.uk

WEBB, Harry Roger. *See* **RICHARD, Cliff.**

WEBB, Jacqueline. *See* **PEARCE, Margaret.**

WEBB, Janeen (S.). Australian (born Australia), b. 1951?. **Genres:** Novels,

Novellas/Short Stories, Science Fiction/Fantasy, Young Adult Fiction, Area Studies, Literary Criticism And History. **Career:** Australian Science Fiction Review, co-editor, 1987-91; Australian Catholic University, senior literature lecturer, associate professor of literature, reader in literature, Institute of Catholic Education, faculty; Eidolon, reviews editor. Consultant. **Publications:** (With A. Enstice) Aliens and Savages: Fiction, Politics, and Prejudice in Australia, 1998; (ed. with J. Dann) Dreaming Down-Under, 1998; (ed. with A. Enstice) The Fantastic Self, 1999; Sailing to Atlantis, 2001; Trends in the Modern Novel, 2001; (with G. McKay) Modern Australian Drama, 2001; The Silken Road to Samarkand, 2003; (ed. and intro. with A. Enstice) The Yellow Wave, 2003; Flying to Babylon, 2005. Contributor to books, journals and periodicals. **Address:** School of Arts and Sciences, Australian Catholic University, 1100 Nudgee Rd., Banyo, QL 4014, Australia. **Online address:** j.webb@patrick.acu.edu.au

WEBB, Lois Sinaiko. American (born United States), b. 1922. **Genres:** Cultural/Ethnic Topics, Food And Wine, Sports/Fitness. **Career:** Webb's Cove, owner, 1972-86; writer, 1988-. Consultant and interior designer. **Publications:** (With C.L. Albyn) Multicultural Cookbook for Students, 1993, rev. ed., 2009; Holidays of the World Cookbook for Students, 1995, (with L.G. Roten) rev. ed., 2011; Multicultural Cookbook of Life Cycle Celebrations, 2000. Contributor to magazines. **Address:** PO Box 784, Seabrook, TX 77586, U.S.A. **Online address:** loisswebb80@aol.com

WEBB, Michael (Jack). American (born United States), b. 1953. **Genres:** Novels, Young Adult Fiction. **Career:** The Obed Project, executive director, 2004-. Writer. **Publications:** NOVELS: The Master's Quilt, 1991; Balaam's Error, 1992; In The Cleft Of The Rock, 2007. **Address:** Golden Eagle School of Practical Ministry, 9821 W Vassar Way, Lakewood, CO 80227-2890, U.S.A. **Online address:** cleftofrock@earthlink.net

WEBB, Phyllis. Canadian (born Canada), b. 1927. **Genres:** Poetry, Essays, Literary Criticism And History. **Career:** University of British Columbia, staff, 1961-64; Canadian Broadcasting Corp.(CBC), program organizer, 1964-67, executive producer, 1967-69; Banff Centre, faculty; University of Victoria, sessional lecturer, 1977-78, 1982-84, visiting assistant professor, 1978-79; University of Alberta, writer-in-residence, 1980-81; Order of Canada, officer, 1992-. **Publications:** POEMS: (with G. Turnbull and E. Mandel) Trio, 1954; Even Your Right Eye, 1956; The Sea is also a Garden: Poems, 1962; Naked Poems, 1965; Selected Poems, 1954-1965, 1971; Wilson's Bowl, 1980; Sunday Water: Thirteen Anti Ghazals, 1982; The Vision Tree: Selected Poems, 1982; Water and Light: Ghazals and Anti Ghazals, 1984; Hanging Fire, 1990; (ed.) The Griffin Poetry Prize Anthology: A Selection of the 2004 Shortlist, 2004. OTHERS: Talking (essays), 1982; Nothing but Brush Strokes: Selected Prose, 1995. Contributor to periodicals. **Address:** RR 2, Mt. Baker Cr., C-9, Ganges, BC V8K 2L6, Canada.

WEBB, Stephen H. American (born United States), b. 1961. **Genres:** Theology/Religion, Education. **Career:** University of Chicago, research assistant, 1986-87, 1988-89; Wabash College, visiting instructor, 1987-88, Department of Religion and Theology, assistant professor, 1989-94, associate professor, 1994-2002, professor, 2002-. Writer. **Publications:** Refiguring Theology: The Rhetoric of Karl Barth, 1991; Blessed Excess: Religion and the Hyperbolic Imagination, 1993; The Gifting God: A Trinitarian Ethics of Excess, 1996; On God and Dogs: A Christian Theology of Compassion for Animals, 1998; Taking Religion to School: Christian Theology and Secular Education, 2000; Good Eating: The Bible, Diet, and the Proper Love of Animals, 2001; The Divine Voice: Christian Proclamation and the Theology of Sound, 2004; American Providence: A Nation with a Mission, 2004; Dylan Redeemed: From Highway 61 to Saved, 2006. Contributor to journals. **Address:** Wabash College, PO Box 352, Crawfordsville, IN 47933-0352, U.S.A. **Online address:** webbs@wabash.edu

WEBB, T(erry) D(ouglas). American (born United States), b. 1949. **Genres:** Librarianship, Education, Adult Non-fiction. **Career:** Phoenix Public Library, social sciences librarian, 1976-84; Brigham Young University-Hawaii Campus, assistant library director, 1984-87; University of Hawaii, Kapiolani College, library director, 1988-99; Monmouth University, Guggenheim Library, dean, 2000-02; California State University, director and dean of the library, 2002-. Writer. **Publications:** (Ed. with A.Gibb) Policy issues in small business research, 1980; (ed. with D. Watkins and T. Quince) Small Business Research: The Development of Entrepreneurs, 1982; Reorganization in the Public Library, 1985; The In-House Option: Professional Issues of Library Automation, 1987; Public Library Organization and Structure, 1989; (ed.) Building Libraries for the 21st Century: The Shape of Information, 2000; Re-Membering Libraries: Essays on the Profession, 2000. Contributor to periodicals. **Address:** California State University, 6000 J St., Sacramento, CA 95819, U.S.A.

WEBB, Veronica. American (born United States), b. 1965. **Genres:** Essays, Novels, Social Sciences, Adult Non-fiction. **Career:** Paper Magazine, contributing editor and columnist, 1989-; Interview Magazine, contributing editor, 1990-; Revlon, spokesmodel, 1992-96; Good Morning America, correspondent; HBO's Entertainment News, correspondent. Actor. **Publications:** Soul, 1997; Veronica Webb Sight: Adventures in the Big City, 1998. Contributor to books and periodicals. **Address:** Revlon Consumer Products Corp., 625 Madison Ave., New York, NY 10022, U.S.A.

WEBBER, Alan M. American (born United States), b. 1948?. **Genres:** Economics. **Career:** Willamette Week, editor; Oregon Times, co-founder; Harvard Business Review, managing editor and editorial director; Fast Company Magazine, founder and editor, 1995-. **Publications:** (With D. Dyer and M.S. Salter) Changing Alliances, 1987; (with W.C. Taylor) Going Global: Four Entrepreneurs Map the New World Marketplace, 1996; Rules of Thumb: 52 Truths for Winning at Business without Losing Your Self, 2009. Contributor to magazines. **Online address:** alan@ruleofthumb.com

WEBBER, Andrew Lloyd. British (born England), b. 1948. **Genres:** Songs/Lyrics And Libretti, Music. **Career:** Author and producer. **Publications:** (Contrib.) Medley from Jesus Christ Superstar for Orchestra, 1972; Variations, 1978; (with T. Rice) Evita: The Legend of Evita Perón, 1919-1952, 1978; Cats: The Book of the Musical, 1981; Performing World of the Musician, 1981; (with Rice) Joseph and the Amazing Technicolor Dreamcoat, 1982; Requiem for Soprano, Tenor, Treble, Chorus and Orchestra, 1985; Andrew Lloyd Webber, 1991; Sunset Boulevard: From Movie to Musical, 1993; Andrew Lloyd Webber for Piano: Piano Solos, 1993; Jesus Christ Superstar, 1997. **Address:** The Really Useful Group, 22 Tower St., London, GL WC2H 9TW, England.

WEBBER, Desiree Morrison. American (born United States), b. 1956. **Genres:** Children's Non-fiction, Librarianship. **Career:** Moore Public Library, head of children's services, 1990-97; writer 1997-; Oklahoma Department of Libraries, public library consultant, 1997-2002; Mustang Public Library, director, 2002-. **Publications:** CHILDREN'S NONFICTION: The Buffalo Train Ride, 1999; Bone Head: Story of the Longhorn, 2003. OTHERS: Travel the Globe: Multicultural Story Times, 1998; The Kid's Book Club: Lively Reading and Activities for Grades 1-3, 2001; (with S. Shropshire) Integrated Library Systems: Planning, Selecting and Implementing, 2010. **Address:** PO Box 667, Mustang, OK 73064, U.S.A. **Online address:** deswebber@yahoo.com

WEBBER, Mark (Alan). British (born England), b. 1964. **Genres:** International Relations/Current Affairs, Politics/Government, History, Social Sciences. **Career:** University of Warwick, lecturer, 1988-90; Loughborough University of Technology, lecturer in European studies, 1991-, professor of international politics. Writer. **Publications:** The International Politics of Russia and the Successor States, 1996; CIS Integration Trends: Russia and the Former Soviet South, 1997; (co-author) The Enlargement of Europe, 1999; (ed.) Russia and Europe: Conflict or Cooperation?, 2000; (co-author) Foreign Policy in a Transformed World, 2002; Inclusion, Exclusion and the Governance of European Security, 2007. Contributor to books, journals and periodicals. **Address:** Faculty of Social Sciences and Humanities, Loughborough University of Technology, Loughborough, LE LE11 3TU, England. **Online address:** m.a.webber@lboro.ac.uk

WEBBER, Ross A. American (born United States), b. 1934. **Genres:** Administration/Management, Institutions/Organizations, Cultural/Ethnic Topics, Business/Trade/Industry. **Career:** University of Pennsylvania, Wharton School, Department of Management, professor of management, 1964, vice president, 1981-86, chair, 1991-95, now professor emeritus. Writer. **Publications:** (With D.R. Hampton and C.E. Summer) Organizational Behavior and Practice of Management, 1968, 5th ed., 1987; Time and Management, 1972; Management: Basic Elements of Managing Organizations, 1975, 3rd ed., 1985; Time is Money!: The Key to Managerial Success: Essentials of Management, 1980; To be a Manager: Essential of Management, 1981; Guide to Getting Things Done, 1984; Becoming a Courageous Manager: Overcoming Career Problems of New Managers, 1991; Breaking Your Time Barriers: Becoming a Strategic Time Manager, 1992. EDITOR: Culture and Management: Text and Readings in Comparative Management, 1969; Management Pragmatics: Cases and Readings on Managing Organizations, 1979. **Address:** Department of Management, University of Pennsylvania, 2000 Steinberg-Deitrich Hall, 3620 Locust Walk, Philadelphia, PA 19104-6370, U.S.A. **Online address:** webber@wharton.upenn.edu

WEBER, David. American (born United States), b. 1952. **Genres:** Science Fiction/Fantasy, Novels. **Career:** Weber Associates, manager; Task Force Games, starfire game designer. Writer. **Publications:** HONOR HARRINGTON SERIES: On Basilisk Station, 1992; (with S. White) Stars at War, 1993; The Honor of the Queen, 1993; The Short Victorious War, 1994; Field of Dishonor, 1994; Flag in Exile, 1995; (contrib.) Triumphant, 1995; Honor among Enemies, 1996; In Enemy Hands, 1997; Echoes of Honor, 1998; (with D. Drake and S.M. Stirling) More Than Honor, 1998; (ed.) Worlds of Honor, 1999; Ashes of Victory, 2000; Changer of Worlds, 2001; War of Honor, 2002; (ed.) The Service of the Sword, 2003; The Shadow of Saganami, 2004; At All Costs, 2005. WITH S. WHITE: STARFIRE SERIES: Insurrection, 1990; Crusade: Starfire, 1992; In Death Ground, 1997; The Shiva Option, 2002; The Stars at War I (includes Crusade and In Death Ground), 2005; The Stars at War II (includes Insurrection and The Shiva Option), 2005. DAHAK SERIES: Mutineers Moon, 1991; The Armageddon Inheritance, 1993; Heirs of Empire, 1996; Empire From the Ashes (includes Mutineers Moon, The Armageddon Inheritance and Heirs of Empire), 2003. WAR GOD SERIES: Oath of Swords, 1995; The War Gods Own, 1998; Wind Riders Oath, 2004. WITH J. RINGO: MARCH UPCOUNTRY SERIES: March Upcountry, 2001; March to the Sea, 2001; (with J. Ringo) March to the Stars, 2003; (with J. Ringo) We Few, 2005. OTHERS: Path of the Fury, 1992; The Apocalypse Troll, 1999; The Excalibur Alternative, 2002; (with E. Flint) 1633, 2002; (with E. Flint and D. Drake) Warmasters, 2002; (with E. Flint) Crown of Slaves, 2003; Old Soldiers, 2005; Bolo!, 2005; (with L. Evans) Hells Gate, 2006; In Fury Born, 2006; Off Armageddon Reef (novel), 2007; (with L. Evans) Hell Hath No Fury, 2007; (with E. Flint) 1634: The Baltic War, 2007; By Schism Rent Asunder, 2008; By Heresies Distressed, 2009; Storm from the Shadows, 2009; Torch of Freedom, 2009; A Mighty Fortress, 2010; Mission of Honor, 2010; Out of the Dark, 2010; (ed.) In Fire Forged, 2011; A Beautiful Friendship, 2011; How Firm a Foundation, 2011; Rising Thunder, 2012; War Maid's Choice, forthcoming. Works appear in anthologies. Contributor to periodicals. **Address:** Baen Books, PO Box 1403, Riverdale, NY 10471, U.S.A.

WEBER, Doron. American/Israeli (born Israel), b. 1955. **Genres:** Novels, Plays/Screenplays, Adult Non-fiction, Gerontology/Senior Issues, How-to Books, Law, Medicine/Health. **Career:** United Jewish Appeal, speech writer, 1986-89; Reader's Catalog, senior editor, 1988-89; Society for the Right to Die, director of communications, 1989-91; Rockefeller University, director of communications, 1991-95; Alfred P. Sloan Foundation, program director and vice president, 1995-. **Publications:** NON FICTION: (with J. Feldschuh) Safe Blood: Purifying the Nation's Blood Supply in the Age of AIDS, 1990; (with E.R. Collins) Complete Guide to Living Wills: How to Safeguard Your Treatment Choices, 1991; (with J. Ahronlen) Final Passages: Positive Choices for the Dying and Their Loved Ones, 1992. NOVEL: The Deserters, 2002. OTHERS: Immortal Bird: A Family Memoir, 2012. **Address:** Alfred P. Sloan Foundation, 630 5th Ave., Ste. 2550, New York, NY 10111, U.S.A. **Online address:** weber@sloan.org

WEBER, Jennifer L. American (born United States), b. 1962?. **Genres:** History, Children's Non-fiction. **Career:** Hemet News, reporter and photographer, 1985-87; Daily Pilot, reporter, 1987-88; Times Advocate Escondido, reporter, 1988-92; Senator Lucy Killea, press secretary, 1992-93; Assemblywoman Dede Alpert, legislative aide, 1994-95; Sacramento Bee, celebrity gossip columnist and editor, 1995-98; Princeton University, lecturer, 2003-05; University of Kansas, Department of History, assistant professor, 2005-10, associate professor, 2010-. Writer. **Publications:** How Santa Came To Be, 1997; Copperheads: The Rise and Fall of Lincoln's Opponents in the North, 2006; Summer's Bloodiest Days: The Battle of Gettysburg as Told From All Sides, 2010. EDITOR: Colonialism, 2009; Progressivism, 2010; Terrorism, 2010; Federalism, 2010; Industrialism, 2010; Isolationism, 2010; Abolitionism, 2010; Nationalism, 2010; Expansionism, 2010; Internationalism, 2010; (with J. Podair and O.V. Burton) The Struggle for Equality, 2011. Contributor to periodicals. **Address:** Department of History, University of Kansas, 3633 Wescoe Hall, 1445 Jayhawk Blvd., Lawrence, KS 66045, U.S.A. **Online address:** jlweber@ku.edu

WEBER, Katharine. American (born United States), b. 1955. **Genres:** Novels, Autobiography/Memoirs, Biography, Intellectual History, Novellas/Short Stories, Songs/Lyrics And Libretti, Adult Non-fiction, Plays/Screenplays, Art/Art History, Literary Criticism And History, Humor/Satire, Popular Culture. **Career:** Kay Swift Memorial Trust, trustee, 1995-; Connecticut College, visiting writer-in-residence, 1996-97; Yale University, lecturer in fiction writing, 1996-2003; Star Foundation, staff facilitator, 2005-; Goucher College, Kratz Center for Creative Writing, writer-in-residence, 2006-; Columbia University, School of the Arts, thesis advisor, Graduate Writing Program, adjunct associate professor of creative writing, 2007-. **Publications:** Objects in Mirror Are Closer Than They Appear, 1995; The Music Lesson, 1999; The Little Women, 2003; Triangle, 2006; True Confections, 2010; The Memory of All That: George Gershwin, Kay Swift, and My Family's Legacy of Infidelities, 2011. **Address:** c/o Amy Williams, McCormick & Williams Literary Agency, 37 W 20th St., New York, NY 10011, U.S.A. **Online address:** katweber@snet.net

WEBER, Lori. Canadian (born Canada), b. 1959. **Genres:** Young Adult Fiction. **Career:** John Abbott College, teacher of English, 1996-. Writer. **Publications:** Klepto, 2004; Split, 2005; Tattoo Heaven, 2005; Strange Beauty, 2006; If You Live Like Me, 2009. Contributor to journals. **Address:** Pointe-Claire, QC , Canada. **Online address:** lorimaria_weber@yahoo.ca

WEBER, Ralph E. American (born United States), b. 1926. **Genres:** History, International Relations/Current Affairs, Politics/Government, Biography, Social Sciences. **Career:** University of Notre Dame, instructor, 1953-54; Marquette University, assistant, 1954-57, registrar and director of admissions, 1957-61; assistant professor, 1961-63, associate professor, 1963-69, professor of history, 1969-, chairman of the history department, 1993-96, now professor emeritus. Writer. **Publications:** Notre Dame's John Zahm: American Catholic Apologist and Educator, 1961; (with J. Arnold) Admission to College, 1964; Mathematics of the Shop, 1968; United States Diplomatic Codes and Ciphers 1775-1938, 1979; Masked Dispatches: Cryptograms and Cryptology in American History, 1775-1900, 1993. EDITOR: As Others See Us: American History in the Foreign Press, 1972, rev. ed. as From the Foreign Press: Two Centuries of American History, 1979; (with T.E. Hachey) Voices of Revolution: Rebels and Rhetoric, 1972; The Awakening of a Sleeping Giant: Third World Leaders and National Liberation, 1981; European Ideologies since 1789: Rebels, Radicals, and Political Ferment, 1981; (T.E. Hachey) American Dissent from Thomas Jefferson to Cesar Chavez: The Rhetoric of Reform and Revolution, 1981; The Final Memoranda: Major General Ralph H. Van Deman, U.S.A. ret., 1865-1952: The Father of U.S.Military Intelligence, 1988; Spymasters: Ten CIA Officers in Their Own Words, 1999; Talking with Harry: Candid Conversations with President HarryS. Truman, 2001; (intro.) Dear Americans: Letters from the Desk of Ronald Reagan, 2003. **Address:** Marquette University, 1103 W Wisconsin Ave., PO Box 1881, Milwaukee, WI 53201, U.S.A.

WEBER, Robert J(ohn). American (born United States), b. 1936. **Genres:** Psychology, Social Sciences, Sciences, Sports/Fitness. **Career:** Long Island University, C.W. Post Center, assistant professor of psychology, 1963-64; Kenyon College, assistant professor of psychology, 1964-67; Oklahoma State University, associate professor, professor of psychology, 1967-93, now professor emeritus; University of New Mexico, law and education, visiting professor, 1992-93, now professor emeritus. Writer. **Publications:** (Ed. with D.N. Perkins) Inventive Minds: Creativity in Technology, 1992; Forks, Phonographs, and Hot Air Balloons: A Field Guide to Inventive Thinking, 1993; The Created Self: Reinventing Body, Persona, and Spirit, 2000. Contributor to journals and periodicals. **Address:** W. W. Norton & Co., 500 5th Ave., New York, NY 10110, U.S.A. **Online address:** rweber63@comcast.net

WEBER, Samuel M. American (born United States), b. 1940?. **Genres:** Communications/Media, Translations. **Career:** Freie Universität, teacher; Johns Hopkins University, professor; University of California, professor of English and comparative literature, Paris Program in Critical Theory, director; Collège International de Philosophie, professor; Northwestern University, professor of German, adjunct professor of French, Avalon professor of humanities and co-director of Paris Program in Critical Theory, 2001-; European Graduate School, professor of philosophy and literature and Paul de Man chair. Writer. **Publications:** (Trans. with S. Weber and intro.) T.W. Adorno, Prisms, 1967; Rückkehr zu Freud: Jacques Lacans Ent-stellung D. Psychoanalyse, 1978; Freud-Legende: Drei Studien zum Psychoanalytischen Denken, 1979, trans. as The Legend of Freud, 1982; Unwrapping Balzac: A Reading of La Peau de Chagrin, 1979; Institution and Interpretation, 1987; Mass

Mediauras: Form, Technics, Media, 1996; Theatricality as Medium, 2004; Targets of Opportunity: On the Militarization of Thinking, 2005; Benjamin's-abilities, 2008. EDITOR: Demarcating the Disciplines: Philosophy, Literature, Art, 1986; (with F.A. Kittler and M. Schneider) Medien, 1987; (with H. de Vries) Violence, Identity, and Self-determination, 1997; (with H. de Vries) Religion and Media, 2001. **Address:** Department of German, Northwestern University, 2-540 Kresge Hall, 1880 Campus Dr., Evanston, IL 60208-2203, U.S.A. **Online address:** s-weber@northwestern.edu

WEBER, Sandra. American (born United States), b. 1961. **Genres:** Adult Non-fiction, Cultural/Ethnic Topics, History, Natural History, Women's Studies And Issues, Young Adult Non-fiction. **Career:** Author, storyteller, quality assurance analyst and educator. **Publications:** The Lure of Esther Mountain: Matriarch of the Adirondack High Peaks, 1995; The Finest Square Mile: Mount Jo and Heart Lake, 1998; Mount Marcy: The High Peak of New York, 2001; Yemen, 2003; The Internet, 2004; The Personal Computer, 2004; Breaking Trail: Remarkable Women of the Adirondacks, 2004; Two in the Wilderness: Adventures of a Mother and Daughter in the Adirondack Mountains, 2005. Contributor to periodicals. **Address:** 431 Perkiomen Ave., Lansdale, PA 19446, U.S.A. **Online address:** weber@sandraweber.com

WEBER, Thomas. Scottish/German (born Germany), b. 1974. **Genres:** History, Photography. **Career:** University of Aberdeen, lecturer in modern European, international, and global political history, Department of History, postgraduate research coordinator. Writer. **Publications:** Lodz Ghetto Album: Photographs by Henryk Ross, 2004; Our Friend The Enemy: Elite Education in Britain and Germany before World War I, 2008; Hitler's First War: Adolf Hitler, the Men of the List Regiment and the First World War, 2010. **Address:** University of Aberdeen, Crombie Annexe, Meston Walk, Aberdeen, AB24 3FX, Scotland. **Online address:** t.weber@abdn.ac.uk

WEBER, Thomas. Australian (born Australia), b. 1950. **Genres:** History, Philosophy, Biography, International Relations/Current Affairs. **Career:** La Trobe University, Institute for Peace Research, teacher of politics and peace studies, peace studies area coordinator, 1996-, School of Social Sciences, reader and associate professor. Writer. **Publications:** (With K.L. Milte) Police in Australia: Development, Functions, and Procedures, 1977; (with K.L. Milte and S.I. Miller) Principles of Police Planning: Armed Robbery, 1978; (with R. Douglas) Guilty, Your Worship: A Study of Victoria's Magistrates' Courts, 1980; Hugging the Trees: The Story of the Chipko Movement, 1988; Conflict Resolution and Gandhian Ethics, 1991; Gandhi's Peace Army: The Shanti Sena and Unarmed Peacekeeping, 1996; On the Salt March: The Historiography of Gandhi's March to Dandi, 1997; (ed. with Y. Moser-Puangsuwan) Nonviolent Intervention across Borders: A Recurrent Vision, 2000; Gandhi as Disciple and Mentor, 2004; (contrib.) Gandhi, Gandhism and the Gandhians, 2006; The Shanti Sena: Philosophy, History and Action, 2009; Going Native: Gandhi's Relationship with Western Women, 2011. Contributor to periodicals. **Address:** School of Social Sciences, La Trobe University, 312 Social Sciences Bldg., Bundoora, Melbourne, VI 3086, Australia. **Online address:** t.weber@latrobe.edu.au

WEBER, Timothy P. American (born United States), b. 1947. **Genres:** Politics/Government. **Career:** Denver Seminary, assistant professor of church history, 1976-81, associate professor of church history, 1981-87, professor of church history, 1987-92; Southern Baptist Theological Seminary, David T. Porter professor of church history, 1992-96; Northern Baptist Theological Seminary, professor, dean and vice president of academic affairs, 1997-2003; Memphis Theological Seminary, president, 2003-05; Fuller Theological Seminary, visiting professor of church history, 2006-; consultant, 2005-07; EFL Associates, senior consultant for higher education practice, 2007-09; Religion Matters, executive director, 2011-; Colorado Christian University, College of Adult and Graduate Studies, affiliate professor, 2011-. Writer. **Publications:** The Future Explored, 1978; Living in the Shadow of the Second Coming: American Premillennialism, 1875-1925, 1979, new ed. as Living in the Shadow of the Second Coming: American Premillennialism, 1875-1982, 1987; On the Road to Armageddon: How Evangelicals Became Israel's Best Friend, 2004. Works appear in anthologies. **Address:** Religion Matters, PO Box 1902, Castle Rock, CO 80104-1902, U.S.A. **Online address:** tweber@religionmatters.org

WEBER, William. American (born United States), b. 1950?. **Genres:** Adult Non-fiction, Sciences. **Career:** Wildlife observer, 1978-; Mountain Gorilla Project, co-founder; Wildlife Conservation Society, senior conservationist,

North American Programs, director. Writer. **Publications:** African Rain Forest Ecology and Conservatism: An Interdisciplinary Perspective, 2001; (with A. Vedder) In the Kingdom of Gorillas: Fragile Species in a Dangerous Land, 2001 in UK as In the Kingdom of Gorillas: The Quest to Save Rwanda's Mountain Gorillas, Aurum, 2002; Gorillas to Grizzlies: Natural Reflections on Saving the Wild, forthcoming. **Address:** Wildlife Conservation Society, 2300 Southern Blvd., Bronx, NY 10460, U.S.A. **Online address:** bweber@wcs.org

WEBSTER, Brenda. American (born United States), b. 1936?. **Genres:** Novels, Psychology, Novellas/Short Stories, Autobiography/Memoirs, Young Adult Fiction, Translations. **Career:** PEN American Center, president, chair. Psychoanalytic critic and freelance writer. **Publications:** Yeats: A Psychoanalytic Study, 1973; Blake's Prophetic Psychology, 1983; Sins of the Mothers (novel), 1993; (ed. with J.E. Johnson) Hungry for Light: The Journal of Ethel Schwabacher, 1993; Tattoo Bird (short stories), 1996; Paradise Farm (novel), 1999; The Last Good Freudian (memoir), 2000; The Beheading Game, 2006; (trans. with G. Romani) E. Bruck, Letter to My Mother, 2006; Vienna Triangle: A Novel, 2009. Contributor to periodicals. **Address:** PEN American Center, 588 Broadway, Ste. 303, New York, NY 10012, U.S.A. **Online address:** websterbrenda1@aol.com

WEBSTER, Catherine. American (born United States), b. 1944?. **Genres:** Poetry. **Career:** University of the Pacific, teacher. Poet. **Publications:** (Ed. and comp.) Handspan of Red Earth: An Anthology of American Farm Poem, 1991; The Thicket Daybreak: Poems, 1997; The Concept of Bodily Objects, 1997; (ed. and comp.) Over This Soil: An Anthology of World Farm Poems, 1998. **Address:** University of Iowa Press, 119 W Park Rd., 100 Kuhl House, Iowa City, IA 52242-1000, U.S.A. **Online address:** cweb552@aol.com

WEBSTER, Ernest. British (born England), b. 1923. **Genres:** Novels, Mystery/Crime/Suspense. **Career:** Writer. **Publications:** NOVELS: The Friulan Plot, 1980; Madonna of the Black Market, 1981; Cossack Hide-Out, 1981; Red Alert, 1982; The Venetian Spy-Glass, 1983; The Verratoli Inheritance, 1983; Million-Dollar Stand-In, 1983; The Watchers, 1984. **Address:** 17 Chippendale Rise, Otley, WY LS21 2BL, England.

WEBSTER, Jason. American/British (born England), b. 1970?. **Genres:** Travel/Exploration, History, Cultural/Ethnic Topics, Area Studies, Mystery/Crime/Suspense, Novels. **Career:** Author. **Publications:** Duende: A Journey into the Heart of Flamenco, 2003; Andalus: Unlocking the Secrets of Moorish Spain, 2004; Guerra Living in the Shadows of the Spanish Civil War, 2006; Sacred Sierra: A Year on a Spanish Mountain, 2009; Or The Bull Kills You, 2011. Contributor to periodicals. **Address:** Minotaur Books, Macmillan Publishers, 175 5th Ave., New York, NY 10010, U.S.A. **Online address:** jason.webster@mac.com

WEBSTER, John. British (born England), b. 1925. **Genres:** Botany. **Career:** University of Nottingham, researcher in mycology, 1945-46; University of Hull, assistant lecturer, 1946-48, lecturer in botany, 1948-50; University of Sheffield, lecturer, 1950-59, senior lecturer, 1959-65, reader in botany, 1965-69; University of Exeter, Department of Biological Sciences, department head, 1969-85, professor of biological sciences, 1985-90, professor emeritus, 1990-; British Mycological Society, president, 1969, 1996; International Mycological Association, vice president, 1977-83; Indian Medical Association, president, 1983-90. Writer. **Publications:** Introduction to Fungi, 1970, (with R. Weber) 3rd ed., 2007; (trans. with M.J. Hackston) K. Esser, Cryptogams, 1983; (with N.J. Dix) Fungal Ecology, 1994; (ed.) Brief Biographies of British Mycologists, 1996. Contributor to journals. **Address:** College of Life and Environmental Sciences, University of Exeter, Geoffrey Pope Bldg., Stocker Rd., Exeter, DN EX4 4QD, England. **Online address:** j.webster@exeter.ac.uk

WEBSTER, Len. British (born England), b. 1948?. **Genres:** Novels, Novellas/Short Stories, Poetry, Local History/Rural Topics, Autobiography/Memoirs, History, Language/Linguistics. **Career:** Writer. **Publications:** POETRY: Behind the Painted Veil, 1972; Flight From the Sibyl, 1993. NOVELS: The Turban-Wallah: A Tale of Little India, 1984; Beneath The Blue Moon, 1992. STORIES: Hell-Riders and Other Stories, 1994. MEMOIRS: Lone Wolf: Memoirs in the Form of Short Stories, forthcoming. **Address:** 48 Marshall Rd., Warley, B68 9ED, England. **Online address:** lenspoems@yahoo.ie

WECKER, David. American (born United States), b. 1950. **Genres:** Adult Non-fiction, Human Relations/Parenting, Antiques/Furnishings, Business/Trade/Industry, Economics, Travel/Exploration. **Career:** Cincinnati Post, newspaper columnist, 1980-2005; Kentucky Post, newspaper columnist, 1980-2005; Eureka! Ranch, writer, workshop presenter, 1990-; 700WLW Clear Channel, talk show host, 1993-2002; Fingerprint Brand Storytelling, founding partner, 2005-07; BrandFlick, founding partner and creative director, 2009-. Journalist and writer. **Publications:** (With D.B. Hall) Jump Start Your Brain, 1995; (with D.B. Hall) Maverick Mindset: Finding the Courage to Journey from Fear to Freedom, 1997; (with R. Sweet) Mastering the Universe: He-Man and the Rise and Fall of A Billion-Dollar Idea, 2005, Now We Are One: Faces Of International Adoption, 2007; (with A. Humphries) Spinning Beneath My Feet: An Irishman Treks to the North Pole, 2010. **Address:** BrandFlick, 474 Joann Ln., Alexandria, KY 41001-8920, U.S.A. **Online address:** sambets@choice.net

WECKMANN, Luis. See Obituaries.

WEDDE, Ian. New Zealander (born New Zealand), b. 1946. **Genres:** Novels, Novellas/Short Stories, Poetry, Translations, Young Adult Fiction, Essays. **Career:** British Council, teacher, 1969-70; London Magazine, poetry reviewer, 1970-71; New Zealand Broadcasting Corp., broadcasting editor, 1972; Victoria University, writer-in-residence, 1984; The Evening Post, art critic, 1983-90; Te Papa Tongarewa, project manager, 1994-2004. **Publications:** Homage to Matisse (poems), 1971; (intro. and trans. with F. Tuqan) Selected Poems, 1973; Made Over (poems), 1974; Pathway to the Sea (poems), 1975; Earthly: Sonnets for Carlos, 1975; Dick Seddon's Great Dive, 1976; Spells for Coming Out (poems), 1977; Castaly (poems), 1980; The Shirt Factory and Other Stories, 1981; Georgicon, 1984; (ed. with H. McQueen and intro. with M. Orbell) The Penguin Book of New Zealand Verse, 1985; Symmes Hole, 1986; Tendering: New Poems, 1988; Survival Arts, 1988; (ed. with G. Burke) Now See Hear!: Art, Language, and Translation, 1990; The Drummer, 1993; (ed.) Fomison: What Shall We Tell Them?, 1994; How to Be Nowhere: Essays and Texts, 1971-1994, 1995; (with J. Walsh and A. Johnston) Dream Collectors: One Hundred Years of Art In New Zealand, 1998; (ed.) Ralph Hotere: Black Light, 1999; Making Ends Meet: Essays and Talks, 1992-2004, 2005; Three Regrets And A Hymn To Beauty: New Poems, 2005; The Viewing Platform, 2006; (with R. McWhannell) Allen Maddox, 2006; Chinese Opera, 2008; Bill Culbert: Making Light Work, 2009; Good Business: New Poems, 2005-2008, 2009. **Address:** 11 Albany Ave., Mt. Victoria, Wellington, 6011, New Zealand. **Online address:** ian.wedde@paradise.net.nz

WEDDINGTON, Elizabeth Gardner. See **GARDNER, Jerome.**

WEDDINGTON, Sarah (Ragle). American (born United States), b. 1945. **Genres:** Law, Social Sciences, Biography, Autobiography/Memoirs, Women's Studies And Issues. **Career:** Individual law practice in Austin, 1967-77; attorney, 1969-70; Department of Agriculture-Washington, general counsel, 1977-78; special assistant, 1978-79, assistant, 1979-81; Interdepartmental Task Force on Women, chair, 1978-81; Wheaton College, visiting professor of government, 1981-83; Glamour magazine, contributing editor, 1981-83; Texas Women's University, distinguished lecturer, 1981-90, Department of History and Government, adjunct professor, 1993; University of New Mexico, Carl Hatch professor of law and public administration, 1982-83; Texas Office of State-Federal Relations, director, 1983-85; private law practice, 1985-; University of Texas, Department of Government, adjunct associate professor, 1986-, adjunct professor; The Weddington Center, founder and director. Writer. **Publications:** The Legal Status of Homemakers in Texas, 1977; (contrib.) Texas Women in Politics: A Project of Sarah Weddington, Jane Hickie, and Deanna Fitzgerald, 1977; A Question of Choice, 1992. **Address:** Department of Government, College of Liberal Arts, University of Texas, 3 232 Batts Hall, PO Box A1800, 1 University Sta., Austin, TX 78712-0119, U.S.A. **Online address:** sweddington@mail.utexas.edu

WEDDLE, David. American (born United States), b. 1956. **Genres:** Young Adult Non-fiction, Biography, Autobiography/Memoirs. **Career:** Author and producer. **Publications:** If They Move-Kill Em!: The Life and Times of Sam Peckinpah, 1994; (with J. Lang) Abyss, 2001; Among the Mansions of Eden: Tales of Love Lust and Landin Beverly Hills, 2003; (with S.D. Perry, J. Land and K.R.A. DeCandido) Twist of Faith, 2007. Contributor to periodicals. **Address:** c/o Kristine Dahl, International Creative Management Inc., 730 5th Ave., New York, NY 10019, U.S.A.

WEDDLE, Kevin J. American (born United States), b. 1957. **Genres:** Biography, Autobiography/Memoirs, History. **Career:** United States Army War College, professor of military theory and strategy and deputy dean of

academics, Advanced Strategic Art Program, director. Writer. **Publications:** Lincoln's Tragic Admiral: The Life of Samuel Francis Du Pont, 2005. **Address:** Department of Academic Affairs, United States Army War College, 122 Forbes Ave., Carlisle, PA 17013-5234, U.S.A.

WEDEEN, Richard Peter. American (born United States), b. 1934. **Genres:** Environmental Sciences/Ecology, Medicine/Health. **Career:** Beth Israel Hospital, intern, 1959-60, medical resident, 1960-61; National Institutes of Health trainee in renal diseases, research fellow, 1961-63, research assistant and research associate, 1961-66, medical resident, 1963-64; Mount Sinai Hospital, medical resident, 1963-64; Mount Sinai School of Medicine, instructor, 1966-68, assistant professor of medicine, 1968-72; Harvard Medical School, visiting lecturer, 1968-69; Jersey City Medical Center, chief of renal section, 1971-75, Department of Medicine, director, 1976-78; University of Medicine and Dentistry of New Jersey, associate professor, 1972-76, professor of medicine, 1976-, clinical professor of interdisciplinary studies, 1990, professor of preventive medicine and community health, 1990-; Veterans Administration Medical Center, associate chief of staff for research and development, 1978-, acting chief of staff, 1988-89; University of Antwerp, visiting professor, 1985; Veterans Biomedical Research Institute, president, 1989-2001. Writer. **Publications:** Poison in the Pot: The Legacy of Lead, 1984; (co-ed. and contrib.) Toxic Circles: Environmental Hazards from the Workplace into the Community, 1993. Works appear in anthologies. Contributor to journals. **Address:** 574 S Forest Dr., Teaneck, NJ 07666, U.S.A. **Online address:** dwedeen@attglobal.net

WEDELL, Eberhard George. Also writes as George Wedell. British/Belgian/German (born Germany), b. 1927. **Genres:** Communications/Media, Education, Autobiography/Memoirs. **Career:** Ministry of Education, staff, 1950-60; Independent Television Authority, secretary, 1960-64; University of Manchester, professor of adult education, 1964-75, honorary professor of employment policy, 1975-83, professor of communications policy, 1983-92, professor emeritus, 1992-; Employment and Vocational Training of European Economic Community Commission, senior official and adviser, 1973-82, head, 1973-; European Institute for the Media, director, 1983-90, director general, 1991-93, vice president, 1993-97. Writer. **Publications:** The Use of Television in Education, 1963; Broadcasting and Public Policy, 1968; (with H.D. Perraton) Teaching at a Distance: An Appraisal of the Co-Ordinated Teaching of O Level Physics using Television, Correspondence and Special Aids, 1968; The Place of Education by Correspondence in Permanent Education, 1970; (co-author) Study by Correspondence: An Enquiry into Correspondence Study for Examinations for Degrees and Other Advanced Qualifications, 1971; Correspondence Education in Europe, 1971; Teachers and Educational Development in Cyprus, 1971; (as George Wedell with E. Katz, M. Pilsworth and D. Shinar) Broadcasting in the Third World: Promise and Performance, 1977; (as George Wedell with G. Luyken) Media in Competition: The Future of Print and Electronic Media in 22 Countries, 1986; (as George Wedell with P. Crookes, A. Daws and K. Ryan) Radio 2000: The Opportunities for Public and Private Radio Services in Europe, 1991; (with R. Rocholl) Vom Segen des Glaubens: Aufzeichnungen über das Leben und Wirken von Gertrud und Hans Wedell, 1995; (with B. Luckham) Television at the Crossroads, 2001. EDITOR: Structures of Broadcasting: A Symposium, 1970; Education and the Development of Malawi, 1973; (as George Wedell with R. Leonard and G.M. Luyken) Mass Communications in Western Europe: An Annotated Bibliography, 1986; (as George Wedell) Making Broadcasting Useful: The African Experience: The Development of Radio and Television in Africa in the 1980s, 1986; No Discouragement, 1997; (as Gertrude Wedell with R. Rocholl) Memoir of Troubled Times, 2008. Contributor to books. **Address:** University of Manchester, Oxford Rd., Manchester, GM M13 9PL, England.

WEDELL, George. See **WEDELL, Eberhard George.**

WEEDMAN, Lauren. American (born United States), b. 1969?. **Genres:** Women's Studies And Issues, Humor/Satire. **Career:** The Daily Show with Jon Stewart, correspondent, 2001; Seattle Children's Theatre, intern; Empty Space Theatre, intern. Writer and comedian. **Publications:** A Woman Trapped in a Woman's Body: Tales from a Life of Cringe, 2007. **Address:** c/o Marissa Devins, United Talent Agency, 9560 Wilshire Blvd., Ste. 500, Beverly Hills, CA 90212-2401, U.S.A. **Online address:** contact@laurenweedman.net

WEEKS, Jeffrey. British/Welsh (born Wales), b. 1945. **Genres:** History, Politics/Government, Sex, Sociology. **Career:** University of London, London School of Economics and Political Science, research officer, 1970-77;

University of Essex, fellow, 1978-79; Kent University, lecturer in sociology, 1980-83; University of Southampton, Social Work Studies, research fellow, 1983-85; CNAA, academic administrator, 1985-90; University of the West of England, professor of social relations, 1990-94; London South Bank University, research professor of sociology, 1994-, now professor emeritus, School of Education, Politics and Social Science, head, 1995-98, dean of humanities and social science, 1998-2003, Arts and Human Sciences, executive dean, 2003-07, university director of research; Social Policy and Urban Regeneration Research Institute, director, 2005-. Writer. **Publications:** (With S. Rowbotham) Socialism and the New Life: The Personal and Sexual Politics of Edward Carpenter and Havelock Ellis, 1977; Coming Out: Homosexual Politics in Britain from the Nineteenth Century to the Present, 1977; Sex, Politics, and Society, 1981, 2nd ed., 1989; Sexuality and Its Discontents, 1985; Sexuality, 1986, 3rd ed., 2009; Family Studies-Information Needs and Resources: The Report of the Review Panel on Family Studies, 1986; Against Nature: Essays on History, Sexuality, and Identity, 1991; Invented Moralities: Sexual Values in an Age of Uncertainty, 1995; Making Sexual History, 2000; (with B. Heaphy and C. Donovan) Same Sex Intimacies: Families of Choice and Other Life Experiments, 2001; The World We Have Won: The Remaking of Erotic and Intimate Life, 2007; Languages of Sexuality, 2011. EDITOR: (co-ed.) Sources in British Political History, 5 vols., 1974-78; Family Directory, 1986; (with K. Porter) Between the Acts: Lives of Homosexual Men, 1885-1967, 1991, 2nd ed., 1998; The Lesser Evil and The Greater Good, 1994; (with J. Holland) Sexual Cultures: Communities, Values, and Intimacy, 1996; (with J. Holland and M. Waites) Sexualities and Society, 2003. **Address:** Faculty of Arts and Human Sciences, London South Bank University, 103 Borough Rd., London, GL SE1 0AA, England. **Online address:** weeksj@lsbu.ac.uk

WEEKS, John F. British/American (born United States), b. 1941. **Genres:** Economics, Third World. **Career:** American University, professor, 1976-87; Middlebury College, professor, 1987-91; University of London, London School of Oriental and African Studies, director of Center for Development Studies, professor of development economics, now professor emeritus of development economics, Centre for Development Policy and Research, senior researcher, Research on Money and Finance Group, senior researcher; Kadir Has University, visiting professor, 2009-; Addis Ababa University, Institute for the Study of African Economies, senior researcher. Writer. **Publications:** Employment Growth in Kenya Manufacturing: Another Look at Labour Absorption, 1974; Acumulación e imperialismo, 1978; (with E. Dore) Basic Needs in Development Strategies: The Journey of a Concept, 1979; Capital and Exploitation, 1981; Development Strategy and the Economy of Sierra Leone, 1982; The Economies of Central America, 1985; The Limits to Capitalist Development: The Industrialization of Peru, 1950-1980, 1985; A Critique of Neoclassical Macroeconomics, 1989; (ed.) Debt Disaster?: Banks, Governments and Multilaterals Confront the Crisis, 1989; Centroamérica: el futuro de la integración económica, 1990; (with A. Zimbalist) Panama at the Crossroads: Economic Development and Political Change in the Twentieth Century, 1991; (ed.) Beyond Superpower Rivalry: Latin America and the Third World, 1991; (with P. Gunson) Panama: Made in the USA, 1991; (with V. Jamal) Africa Misunderstood or Whatever Happened to the Rural-Urban Gap?, 1993; (with W. Pelupessy) Economic Maladjustment in Central America, 1993; (ed.) Structual Adjustment and the Agricultural Sector in Latin America and the Caribbean, 1995; (with G. Standing and J. Sender) Restructing the Labour Market: The South African Challenge, 1996; (ed. with C. Brundenius) Globalization and Third World Socialism: Cuba and Vietnam, 2001; Capital, Exploitation and Economic Crisis, 2010; Irreconcilable Inconsistencies of Neoclassical Macroeconomics, 2011. **Address:** Centre for Development Policy & Research, London School of Oriental and African Studies, University of London, Thornhaugh St. Russell Sq., London, GL WC1H 0XG, England. **Online address:** jw10@soas.ac.uk

WEEKS, Sarah. American (born United States), b. 1955. **Genres:** Children's Fiction, Children's Non-fiction, Picture/Board Books, Novels. **Career:** The New School, Writing Program, adjunct faculty; Authors Readers Theatre, founding member. Children's book author. **Publications:** Hurricane City, 1993; Follow the Moon, 1995; Red Ribbon, 1995; The Opposite of Pig, 1996; Noodles, 1996; Shoes, 1997; Soup, 1997; Little Factory, 1998; Mrs. McNosh Hangs Up Her Wash, 1998; Regular Guy, 1999; Splish, Splash!, 1999; Piece of Jungle, 1999; Happy Birthday, Frankie, 1999; Guy Time, 2000; Drip, Drop, 2000; The Perfect Garden, 2000; Mrs. McNosh and the Great Big Squash, 2000; My Busy Day, 2001; Noisy Friends, 2001; My Big, Bright World, 2001; My Guy, 2001; Bite Me, I'm a Shape, 2002; Bite Me, I'm a Book, 2002; My Somebody Special, 2002; Guy Wire, 2002; A Box for Bobo, 2002; Angel

Face, 2002; Oh My Gosh, Mrs. McNosh!, 2002; Two Eggs, Please, 2003; Without You, 2003; Crocodile Smile: Ten Songs of the Earth as the Animals See It, 2003; If I Were a Lion, 2004; Paper Parade, 2004; So B. It: A Novel, 2004; Baa-Choo!, 2004; Get Well Soon, or Else!, 2004; Danger! Boys Dancing!, 2004; Beware of Mad Dog!, 2004; I'm a Pig, 2005; Baah Choo, 2005; Who's Under That Hat?: A Lift-The-Flap Adventure, 2005; Be Mine, Be Mine, Sweet Valentine, 2005; Brass Bone, 2006; Ruff! Ruff! Where's Scruff?: A Lift-The-Flap Adventure, 2006; Jumping the Scratch: A Novel, 2006; (co-author) Tripping Over the Lunch Lady, 2006; Fink's Funk, 2006; Counting Ovejas, 2006; Overboard!, 2006; PIP Squeak, 2007; Ella, Of Course!, 2007; Peek In My Pocket, 2007; The Brass Bone, 2008; Bunny Fun, 2008; Oggie Cooder, 2008; (co-author) Up All Night, 2008; Oggie Cooder, Party Animal, 2008; Catfish Kate, 2009; Woof, 2009; Catfish Kate and the Sweet Swamp Band, 2009; Mac and Cheese, 2009; Sophie Peterman tells the Truth!, 2009; Mac and Cheese and the Perfect Plan, 2010; As Simple as it Seems, 2010; Pie, 2011. **Address:** c/o Author Mail, Scholastic Inc., 557 Broadway, New York, NY 10012-3999, U.S.A. **Online address:** authorweeks@aol.com

WEEMS, David B(urnola). American (born United States), b. 1922. **Genres:** Engineering, How-to Books, Novels, Engineering, Homes/Gardens. **Career:** Neosho High School, science instructor, 1957-68; mayor of Newtonia, 1983-85. Writer. **Publications:** NONFICTION: How to Design, Build, and Test Complete Speaker Systems, 1978; 21 Custom Speaker Enclosure Projects You Can Build, 1980; 30 Projects to Improve Your Stereo System, 1981; Designing, Building and Testing Your Own Speaker System with Projects, 1981, 4th ed., 1997; Designing and Building Your Own Stereo Furniture, 1981; (with M. Murphy) How to Collect & Restore Cars, 1981; Raising Goats: The Backyard Dairy Alternative, 1983; Great Sound Stereo Speaker Manual with Projects, 1990, 2nd ed., 2000. FICTION: Son of an Earl: Sold for a Slave, 1993. Contributor to periodicals. **Address:** 416 E Hickory St., Neosho, MO 64850, U.S.A.

WEENOLSEN, Patricia. (Patricia Otway-Ward). American/French (born France), b. 1930. **Genres:** Novellas/Short Stories, Mystery/Crime/Suspense, Psychology. **Career:** Educator and Writer. **Publications:** Transcendence of Loss over the Life Span, 1988; The Art of Dying: How to Leave This World with Dignity and Grace, at Peace with Yourself and Your Loved Ones, 1996; Cave of Storms: A Novel, 2009; Daughter of the Morning Star, 2010; Mindstalker: A Psychological Thriller, 2011. Contributor of articles to periodicals. **Address:** Rubythroat Press L.L.C., 4026 Stone Way N, Ste. 501, Seattle, WA 98103-8028, U.S.A. **Online address:** pweenolsen@earthlink.net

WEGELA, Karen Kissel. American (born United States), b. 1945?. **Genres:** Psychology, Self Help. **Career:** Psychologist and teacher, 1968-; Naropa University, professor. Writer. **Publications:** How to Be a Help Instead of a Nuisance: Practical Approaches to Giving Support, Service and Encouragement to Others, 1996; The Courage to Be Present: Buddhism, Psychotherapy, and the Awakening of Natural Wisdom, 2009; What Really Helps: Using Mindfulness and Compassionate Presence to Help, Support and Encourage Others, 2011. **Address:** M.A. Contemplative Psychotherapy Program (MACP), Naropa University, 2130 Arapahoe Ave., Boulder, CO 80304, U.S.A. **Online address:** kkwegela@naropa.edu

WEGMAN, William (George). American (born United States), b. 1943. **Genres:** History, Photography, Illustrations, Adult Non-fiction, Animals/Pets. **Career:** University of Wisconsin-Madison, associate professor, 1968-70; California State University, associate professor, 1970; University of Wisconsin-Wausau, instructor. Writer. **Publications:** Man's Best Friend: Photographs and Drawings, 1982; William Wegman: 1 October-14 November 1982, 1982; (co-author) Wegman's World: 5 December 1982 to 16 January 1983, Walker Art Center, 1982; Everyday Problems (drawings), 1984; Nineteen Dollars & Eighty-Four Cents, 1984; The History of Travel: The Catalogue of an Exhibition of Paintings by William Wegman, 1990; William Wegman: Paintings, Drawings, Photographs, Videotapes, 1990; William Wegman Photographic Works, 1969-1976, 1991; Sofort-Bild-Geschichten: Instant-Imaging-Stories, 1992; (with C. Kismaric and M. Heiferman) Cinderella, 1993; (with C. Kismaric and M. Heiferman) Little Red Riding Hood, 1993; Photographic Works 1969-1976, 1993; L'oeuvre Photographique, 1993; ABC, 1994; Wildlife: October 1 Through December 31, 1994, California Center for the Arts Museum, 1994; 123, 1995; Triangle, Square, Circle, 1995; William Wegman's Mother Goose, 1996; William Wegman's Farm Days: Or how Chip Learnt an Important Lesson on the Farm or a Day in the Country, or Hip Chip's Trip, or Farmer Boy, 1997; Puppies, 1997; My Town, 1998; Strange But True:

William Wegman, October 31-December 24, 1998, 1998; What Do You Do?, 1999; William Wegman's Pups, 1999; Fay, 1999; (with I. Sischy) Fashion Photographs, 1999; Surprise Party, 2000; Wegmanology, 2001; How Do You Get To MOMAQNS?, 2002; William Wegman Polaroids, 2002; I Want a Dog, 2003; Chip Wants a Dog, 2003; Dress up Batty, 2004; William Wegman: Funney, Strange, 2006; (contrib.) Dogs, 2007. Contributor to magazines. **Address:** Yale University Press, 302 Temple St., PO Box 209040, New Haven, CT 06520-9040, U.S.A. **Online address:** wegman@wegmanworld.com

WEGMANN, Peter. Swiss (born Switzerland), b. 1957. **Genres:** Art/Art History, Romance/Historical, History. **Career:** Museum of the Oskar Reinhart Foundation, curator, 1983-. Writer. **Publications:** Gottfried Semper und das Winterthurer Stadthaus: Sempers Architektur im Spiegel Seiner Kunsttheorie, 1985; (co-ed.) Grenzbereiche der Architektur, 1985; Caspar David Friedrich to Ferdinand Hodler, 1993. **Address:** Stiftung Oskar Reinhart, Stadthausstrasse 6, Winterthur, CH-8400, Switzerland.

WEIDEMAN, Ryan. American (born United States), b. 1941. **Genres:** Photography, Travel/Exploration. **Career:** Photographer and artist, 1981-. Writer. **Publications:** In My Taxi: New York after Hours, 1991. **Address:** 309 W 43rd St., New York, NY 10036-6423, U.S.A.

WEIDENBAUM, Murray. American (born United States), b. 1927. **Genres:** Business/Trade/Industry, Economics, Politics/Government, Military/Defense/Arms Control. **Career:** State of New York, Department of Labor, junior economist, 1948-49; U.S. Bureau of the Budget, Executive Office of the President, fiscal economist, 1949-57; General Dynamics Corp., Convair Division, economist, 1957-58; Boeing Co., corporate economist, 1958-63; Stanford Research Institute, senior economist, 1963-64; National Aeronautics and Space Administration, director of economic research program, 1964-69; Washington University, associate professor, 1964-66, Department of Economics, professor of economics, 1966-, chairman, 1966-69, 1971-74, Edward Mallinckrodt distinguished university professor, 1971-, Center for the Study of American Business, founder, director, 1975-2001, Weidenbaum Center on the Economy, honorary chairman, 2001-; University of California, visiting professor, 1972; U.S. Council of Economic Advisers, assistant secretary of the treasury for economic policy, 1969-71, chairman, 1981-82; President's Council of Economic Advisors, chairman, 1981-82; Midwest Economics Association, president, 1985-86. Writer and consultant. **Publications:** The Military Market, 1963; Federal Budgeting, 1964; Congress and the Federal Budget: Federal Budgeting, The Choice of Government Programs, 1965; The Federal Budget and the Outlook for Defense Spending, 1966; Strategies for Diversification of Defense/Space Companies, 1967; Economic Impact of the Vietnam War, 1967; Prospects for the American Economy During the Post-Vietnam Period, 1967; Arms and the American Economy: A Domestic Convergence Hypothesis, 1967; Competition in High Technology Government Markets, 1967; Prospects for Reallocating Public Resources, 1967; The Modern Public Sector, 1969; The Defense Budget, 1972; Fiscal Responsibility, 1973; Matching Needs and Resources, 1973; (with M.H. Halperin and J.A. Stockfish) Political Economy of the Military-Industrial Complex, 1973; Economics of Peacetime Defense, 1974; Government Mandated Price Increases: A Neglected Aspect of Inflation, 1975; Government Credit Subsidies for Energy Development, 1977; Business, Government and the Public, 1977, 3rd ed., 1986; (with R. DeFina) Cost of Federal Regulation of Economic Activity, 1978; The Future of Business Regulation, 1979; Report Card on Reaganomics, 1984; (ed. with J. Tobin) Two Revolutions in Economic Policy, 1988; (ed. with K.W. Chilton) Public Policy toward Corporate Takeovers, 1988; Rendezvous with Reality: The American Economy after Reagan, 1988; Military Spending and the Myth of Global Overstretch, 1989; The Changing Economic Role of Defense, 1989; (with E.S. Christian) The Allure of Value-added Taxes: Examining the Pros and Cons, 1989; (ed. with D.G. Raboy and E.S. Christian, Jr.) Value-added Tax: Orthodoxy and New Thinking, 1989; (with M. Jensen) Threats and Opportunities in the International Economy, 1990; (ed. with K.W. Chilton and M.E. Warren) American Manufacturing in a Global Market, 1990; Small Wars, Big Defense: Paying for the Military after the Cold War, 1992; (with H.S. James) When Businesses Cross International Borders, 1993; (co-author) Reagan and the Economy: Nine Intimate Perspectives, 1994; Business and Government in the Global Marketplace, 5th ed., 1995, 7th ed., 2004; (with S. Hughes) Bamboo Network: How expatriate Chinese Entrepreneurs are Creating a New Economic Superpower in Asia, 1996; (ed. with K. Chilton and R. Batterson) The Dynamic American Firm, 1996; An Agnostic Examination of the Case for Action on Global Warming, 1998; Looking for Common Ground on U.S. Trade Policy, 2001; One-armed Economist: The Intersection of Busi-

ness and Government, 2004; The Competition of Ideas: The World of Washington Think Tanks, 2009. **Address:** Department of Economics, Washington University, 1 Brookings Dr., PO Box 1208, St. Louis, MO 63130-4899, U.S.A. **Online address:** moseley@wustl.edu

WEIDENSAUL, Scott. American (born United States), b. 1959?. **Genres:** History, Social Sciences. **Career:** Pottsville Republican, weekly columnist, full-time reporter, 1978-88; freelance writer, 1988; Philadelphia Inquirer, columnist; Harrisburg Patriot-News, columnist. Lecturer and field researcher. **Publications:** (ed.) The Practical Ornithologist, 1990; The Birder's Miscellany: A Fascinating Collection of Facts, Figures and Folklore from the World of Birds, 1991; (contrib.) Discover Birds, 1991; Seasonal Guide to the Natural Year: A Month by Month Guide to Natural Events; Mid- Atlantic, 1992; Seasonal Guide to the Natural Year: A Month by Month Guide to Natural Events; New England & New York, 1993; Mountains of the Heart: A Natural History of the Appalachians, 1994; (with B.V. Patter) Max Bonker and the Howling Thieves, 1996; Raptors: The Birds of Prey, 1996; National Audubon Society First Field Guide to Birds, 1998; Living on the Wind: Across the Hemisphere with Migratory Birds, 1999; The Ghost with Trembling Wings: Science, Wishful Thinking and the Search for Lost Species, 2002; The Wildlife Art of Ned Smith, 2003; The Raptor Almanac: A Comprehensive Guide to Eagles, Hawks, Falcons and Vultures, 2004; Return to Wild America: A Yearlong Search for the Continent's Natural Soul, 2005; (intro.) Ned Smith's Game News Covers: The Complete Collection, 2006; Of a Feather: A Brief History of American Birding, 2007. Contributor to periodicals. **Address:** c/o Peter Matson, Sterling Lord Literistic, 65 Bleecker St., New York, NY 10012, U.S.A. **Online address:** scottweidensaul@scottweidensaul.com

WEIDT, Maryann N. American (born United States), b. 1944. **Genres:** Biography, Children's Non-fiction. **Career:** Hennepin County Library, children's librarian, 1969-78; Duluth Public Library, head of children's services, 1978-88; Duluth Transit Authority, director, 1979-82; Duluth Community Schools, director, 1981-83; AFSCME delegate, director, 1982-83; University of Minnesota, adjunct professor of children's literature, 1984-85; Loft Literary Center, faculty. Writer. **Publications:** BIOGRAPHIES FOR CHILDREN: Presenting Judy Blume, 1989; Mr. Blue Jeans: A Story about Levi Strauss, 1990; Stateswoman to the World: A Story about Eleanor Roosevelt, 1991; Wild Bill Hickok, 1992; Oh, the Places He Went: A Story about Dr. Seuss-Theodor Seuss Geisel, 1994; Revolutionary Poet, 1997; Voice of Freedom, 2001; Matthew Henson, 2002; Rosa Parks, 2003; Harriet Tubman, 2003; Fighting for Equal Rights: A Story About Susan B. Anthony, 2004. OTHER: (with H. Sorensen) Daddy Played Music for the Cows (picture book), 1995. Contributor to periodicals. **Address:** 1975 Lakeview Dr., Carlton, MN 55718, U.S.A. **Online address:** mweidt@hotmail.com

WEIHS, Jean (Riddle). (Jean Riddle). Canadian (born Canada), b. 1930. **Genres:** Children's Non-fiction, Librarianship, Bibliography, Education. **Career:** University of Toronto, bibliographer, 1953-59; North York Public Library, general reference librarian, 1960-64; Public Schools, librarian, 1965-66; head of technical services, 1967-69; Ontario Institute for Studies in Education, cataloger, 1966; Ontario Ministry of Education, instructor, 1968-69; Seneca College of Applied Arts and Technology, director of library techniques course, 1969-86; Technical Services Group, principal consultant, 1986-; University of California, visiting professor, 1988; Simmons College, visiting professor, 1989. Writer. **Publications:** (As Jean Riddle with S. Lewis and J. Macdonald) Nonbook Materials: The Organization of Integrated Collections, 1970, 3rd ed. (as Jean Weihs, with S. Lewis), 1989; Accessible Storage of Nonbook Materials, 1984; (with L. Howarth) A Brief Guide to AACR2: 1988 Revision and Implications for Automated Systems, 1988; (with S.S. Intner) Standard Cataloging for School and Public Libraries, 1990, 4th ed., 2007; The Integrated Library: Encouraging Access to Multimedia Materials, 2nd ed., 1991; Facts About Canada, Its Provinces and Territories, 1995; (co-author) Special Libraries: A Cataloging Guide, 1998; (ed.) The Principles and Future of AACR: Proceedings of the International Conference on the Principles and Future Development of AACR, Toronto, Ontario, Canada, October 23-25, 1997, 1998; (with E. Evans and S. Intner) Introduction to Technical Services for Library Technicians, 2002; (with S.S. Intner and S.S. Lazinger) Metadata and Its Impact on Libraries, 2006; (with S.S. Intner) Beginning Cataloging, 2009. (ed. with S.S. Intner and J.F. Fountain) Cataloging Correctly for Kids, 2011; CHILDREN'S NONFICTION: Nunavut: Our Land, 1999; Ontario, 2000; British Columbia, 2001; (with J. Caven) Aspects of Government in Canada, 2001. Contributor to books and journals. **Address:** Technical

Services Group, 4 Fairview Blvd., Toronto, ON M4K 1L9, Canada. **Online address:** jean.weihs@rogers.com

WEIL, Debbie. American (born United States) **Genres:** Sociology. **Career:** Jonesboro News-Daily, reporter, 1978-79; Atlanta Constitution, staff feature writer, 1980-82, reporter, editor; Cox Newspapers Washington Bureau, national reporter, 1982-84; American University, School of Communication, adjunct professor, 1986-90; Roll Call, policy editor, 1990-92, reporter, editor; DC Web Women, co-founder, 1995-; Network Solutions Inc., web content marketing manager, 1998-2000; marketing consultant, 1998-2000; WordBiz.com Inc., founder and president, 2000-; Voxie Media, founder. **Publications:** The Corporate Blogging Book: Everything You Need to Know to Get It Right in US as Corporate Blogging Book: Absolutely Everything You Need to Know to Get It Right, 2006. **Address:** WordBiz.com Inc., 3601 Newark St. NW, PO Box 3766, Washington, DC 20016, U.S.A. **Online address:** wordbiz@gmail.com

WEIL, Elizabeth. American (born United States) **Genres:** Biography, Self Help. **Career:** Freelance journalist. **Publications:** They All Laughed at Christopher Columbus: An Incurable Dreamer Builds the First Civilian Spaceship, 2002; (with A. Maniatis) Crib Notes: A Random Reference for the Modern Parent, 2004; (with N. Bondy and A. Maniatis) Love Notes: A Random Reference for the Modern Romantic, 2006; (with D. Torres) Age is Just a Number: Achieve Your Dreams at Any Stage in Your Life, 2009. **Address:** c/o Author Mail, Chronicle Books, 85 2nd St., 6th Fl., San Francisco, CA 94105, U.S.A. **Online address:** liz.weil@me.com

WEIMANN, Gabriel. Israeli (born Israel), b. 1950. **Genres:** Communications/Media, Politics/Government, Law, Information Science/Computers. **Career:** University of Haifa, Department of Communication, lecturer, 1981-84, senior lecturer, 1984-88, associate professor, 1989-96, professor, 1996-, chairman of department of sociology and anthropology, 1988-91, chairman of department of communication, 1994-97, 2000-03, Emek Izrael College, academic director, 1989-90; Hebrew University of Jerusalem, lecturer, 1981-84; Carleton University, visiting professor, 1984; Stanford University, visiting professor, 1985; Israeli Academy for National Security, faculty, 1987-; University of Mainz, visiting professor, 1988-89; University of Pennsylvania, The Annenberg School of Communication, visiting professor, 1991-92; Lehigh University, visiting professor, 1991-92; Hofstra University, visiting professor, 1996; National University of Singapore, visiting professor, 1997-98; United States Institute of Peace, senior fellow, 2003-04; American University, visiting professor, 2005. Writer. **Publications:** (With C. Winn) Hate on Trial: The Zundel Affair, the Media, Public Opinion in Canada, 1986; (with C. Winn) The Theater of Terror: Mass Media and International Terrorism, 1993; The Influentials: People Who Influence People, 1994; Communicating Unreality: Mass Media and Reconstruction of Realities, 2000; Ha-Hidah Ha-Singaporit, 2000; (with B. Nevo) The Singaporean Enigma, 2001; Terror on the Internet: The New Arena, the New Challenges, 2006; (with A. Kaplan) Freedom and Terror: Reason and Unreason in Politics, 2011. Contributor of articles to books, journals and magazines. **Address:** Department of Communication, University of Haifa, Rm. 8032, Rabin Complex, Mount Carmel, Haifa, 31905, Israel. **Online address:** weimann@soc.haifa.ac.il

WEIMER, Joan. (Joan Myers Weimer). American (born United States), b. 1936. **Genres:** Autobiography/Memoirs, Literary Criticism And History, Biography. **Career:** Drew University, instructor, 1968-70, assistant professor, 1970-75, associate professor, 1975-82, professor of English, 1982-, department head, 1982-86, 1991, now emeritus; University of North Carolina, Frey Foundation distinguished visiting professor. Writer. **Publications:** Back Talk: Teaching Lost Selves to Speak (memoir), 1994; Awestruck: A Skeptic's Pilgrimage, 2005. EDITOR: (with D.R. Weimer) Literature of America, 1973; Women Artists, Women Exiles: Miss Grief and Other Stories by C.F. Woolson, 1988. Work appears in anthologies. Contributor to journals. **Address:** Department of English, Drew University, 36 Madison Ave., Madison, NJ 07940, U.S.A.

WEIMER, Joan Myers. See **WEIMER, Joan.**

WEIN, Elizabeth E(ve). American (born United States), b. 1964. **Genres:** Young Adult Fiction, Science Fiction/Fantasy, Romance/Historical, Ghost Writer, Horror, Military/Defense/Arms Control, Cultural/Ethnic Topics, Area Studies, Mythology/Folklore. **Career:** U.S. Postal Service, conference man-

ager, 1993-94; Harrisburg Area Community College, English Department, adjunct faculty, 1994. Writer. **Publications:** The Winter Prince, 1993; A Coalition of Lions, 2003; The Sunbird, 2004; Rush Hour: Reckless, 2006; The Coyote Road: Trickster Tales, 2007; Lion Hunter: The Mark of Solomon Book 1, 2007; Empty Kingdom: The Mark of Solomon Book 2, 2008; Firebirds Soaring, 2009; Code Name Verity, 2012. Contributor to books. **Address:** c/o Ginger Clark, Curtis Brown Ltd., 10 Astor Pl., New York, NY 10003, U.S.A. **Online address:** ewein2412@yahoo.co.uk

WEINBAUM, Marvin G. American (born United States), b. 1935. **Genres:** Politics/Government, History, Technology, Military/Defense/Arms Control, Engineering, Young Adult Non-fiction, Politics/Government. **Career:** Colby College, instructor in political science, 1961-65; University of Illinois, assistant professor, 1965-69, associate professor, 1969-82, professor of political science, 1982-98, professor emeritus, 1998-, South Asian and Middle Eastern Studies Program, director; United States Institute of Peace, senior fellow, 1996-97, U.S. Department of State, foreign affairs analyst, 1999-2003. Writer. **Publications:** (With M. Davis) Metropolitan Decision Processes, 1969; (L.H. Gold) Presidential Elections: A Simulation with Readings, 1969; Food, Development and Politics in the Middle East, 1982; Egypt and the Politics of U.S. Economic Aid, 1986; Pakistan and Afghanistan: Resistance and Reconstruction, 1994; (ed. with C. Kumar) South Asia Approaches the Millennium, 1995; International Interventions in Local Conflict: Crisis Management and Conflict Resolution Since the Cold War, 2010. **Address:** Middle East Institute, 1761 North St. NW, Washington, DC 20036-2882, U.S.A. **Online address:** m.weinbaum@mideasti.org

WEINBERG, Florence Byham. See **WEINBERG, Florence M(ay).**

WEINBERG, Florence M(ay). (Florence Byham Weinberg). American (born United States), b. 1933. **Genres:** Novels, Literary Criticism And History. **Career:** St. John Fisher College, instructor, 1967, assistant professor, 1967-71, associate professor, 1971-75, professor, 1975-89, Division of Modern Languages and Classical Studies, chairman, 1972-79, International Studies Program, director, 1983-86; Trinity University, professor, 1989-99, Department of Modern Languages and Literatures, chair, 1989-95, professor emeritus, 1999-. Writer. **Publications:** The Wine and the Will: Rabelais's Bacchic Christianity, 1972; Gargantua in a Convex Mirror, 1986; The Cave, 1987; Rabelais et les lecons du rire, 2000; Sonora Wind, Ill Wind, 2002; I'll Come to Thee by Moonlight, 2002; Long Desirs: Louise Labe, Lyonnaise, 2002; The Storks of La Caridad, 2004; Apache Lance, Franciscan Cross, 2005; Seven Cities of Mud, 2008; Sonora Moonlight, 2008; Sonora Wind, 2009; Home, Fond Illusion, forthcoming. **Address:** F.M. Weinberg Co., 331 Royal Oaks Dr., San Antonio, TX 78209, U.S.A. **Online address:** florenceweinberg@juno.com

WEINBERG, Helene Barbara. American (born United States), b. 1942. **Genres:** Art/Art History, History. **Career:** City University of New York, Queens College, instructor, 1972-73, assistant professor, 1973-78, associate professor, 1978-86, professor of art history, 1987-94, Graduate School and University Center, assistant professor, 1977-78, associate professor, 1978-86, professor of art history, 1987-94, professor emeritus, 1994-; The Metropolitan Museum of Art, Department of American Paintings and Sculpture, curator of American paintings and sculpture, 1990-, Alice Pratt Brown curator of American paintings and sculpture. Writer. **Publications:** The Decorative Work of John La Farge, 1977; The American Pupils of Jean-Léon Gérôme, 1984; The Lure of Paris: Nineteenth-Century American Painters and Their French Teachers, 1991; (with D. Bolger, N.M. Brennecke and D.P. Curry) American Impressionism and Realism: The Painting of Modern Life, 1885-1915, 1994; American Impressionism, 1994; John Singer Sargent, 1994; (with M. Simpson and R. Ormond) Uncanny Spectacle: The Public Career of the Young John Singer Sargent, 1997; (with S.L. Herdrich) American Drawings and Watercolors in the Metropolitan Museum of Art: John Singer Sargent, 2000; (with S.G. Larkin) American Impressionists Abroad and at Home: Paintings from the Collection of the Metropolitan Museum of Art, 2000; Childe Hassam, American Impressionist, 2004; (ed. with C.R. Barratt) American Stories: Paintings of Everyday Life, 1765-1915, 2009. **Address:** The Metropolitan Museum of Art, 1000 5th Ave., 82nd St., New York, NY 10028, U.S.A.

WEINBERG, Louise. American (born United States) **Genres:** Law, Military/Defense/Arms Control. **Career:** Bingham, Dana & Gould, associate, 1969-71; law clerk, 1971-72; Suffolk University, associate professor of law, 1974-76, professor of law, 1977-80; Brandeis University, lecturer in law,

1975; Hebrew University, visiting professor; Stanford University, visiting associate professor of law, 1976-77; University of Texas, School of Law, visiting professor, 1979, professor of law, 1980-, William B. Bates chair for the administration of justice, 1997-; World Economic Forum, faculty fellow, 1995-; United States District Court, District of Massachusetts, clerk. Writer. **Publications:** (With D.H. Vernon) Conflict of Laws: Cases, Materials and Problems, 1990, (co-author) rev. ed., 2002; Federal Courts: Cases and Comments on Judicial Federalism and Judicial Power, 1994; Our Marbury, 2003; Overcoming Dred, 2008; American Tragedy: The Supreme Court And The Coming Of The Civil War, 2009. Contributor to journals and periodicals. **Address:** School of Law, University of Texas, 727 E Dean Keeton St., Austin, TX 78705-3299, U.S.A. **Online address:** lweinberg@mail.law.utexas.edu

WEINBERG, Steve. American (born United States), b. 1948. **Genres:** Documentaries/Reportage, Biography. **Career:** Journalist, 1968-78; Drake University, adjunct professor of journalism, 1976-78; University of Missouri School of Journalism, director of reporting program and associate professor, 1978-, professor, now professor emeritus; Alicia Patterson fellow, 1997-98; Investigative Reporters and Editors, executive director, 1983-90, writer and copy editor. **Publications:** SELF-ILLUSTRATOR: Trade Secrets of Washington Journalists: How to Get the Facts about What's Going on in Washington, 1981. OTHERS: (with S. Goettsch) Terrace Hill: The Story of a House and the People Who Touched It, 1978; (ed. with J. Colbert) The Investigative Journalist's Morgue, 1986; Armand Hammer: The Untold Story, 1989; Telling the Untold Story: How Investigative Reporters are Changing the Craft of Biography, 1992; For Their Eyes Only: How Presidential Appointees Treat Public Documents as Personal Property, 1992; The Reporter's Handbook: An Investigator's Guide to Documents and Techniques, 1995, 4th ed. as The Investigative Reporter's Handbook: A Guide to Documents, Databases, and Techniques, 2002; A Journalism of Humanity: A Candid History of the World's First Journalism School, 2008; Taking on the Trust: The Epic Battle of Ida Tarbell and John D. Rockefeller, 2008. Contributor to books and periodicals. **Address:** Missouri School of Journalism, University of Missouri, 213 Lee Hills Hall, 120 Neff Hall, Columbia, MO 65211-1200, U.S.A. **Online address:** weinbergs@missouri.edu

WEINBERG, Steven. American (born United States), b. 1933. **Genres:** Astronomy, Physics, Education, Sciences. **Career:** Columbia University, instructor, 1957-59; Institute for Defense Analyses, consultant, 1960-73; University of California, Lawrence Radiation Laboratory, research associate, 1959-60, assistant professor, 1960-62, associate professor, 1962-64, professor of physics, 1964-69; Massachusetts Institute of Technology, visiting professor, 1967; professor, 1969-73; College de France, chair in physics, 1971; Arms Control and Disarmament Agency, consultant, 1973; Harvard University, Higgins Professor of Physics, 1973-83, visiting professor, 1983-; Smithsonian Astrophysical Observatory, senior scientist, 1973-83, senior consultant, 1983-; University of Texas, Jack S. Josey-Welch Foundation chair in science and regental professor of physics, 1982-, Theory Research Group, director; Jerusalem Winter School for Theoretical Physics, director, 1983-. Writer. **Publications:** Gravitation and Cosmology: Principles and Applications of the General Theory of Relativity, 1972; The First Three Minutes: A Modern View of the Origin of the Universe, 1977; The Discovery of Subatomic Particles, 1982, rev. ed., 2003; (with W.H. McCrea and M.J. Rees) The Constants of Physics: proceedings of a Royal Society Discussion Meeting held on 25 and 26 May 1983, 1983; (ed. with T. Piran) Intersection Between Elementary Particle Physics and Cosmology: Jerusalem Winter School for Theoretical Physics, 1986; (ed. with T. Piran) Physics in Higher Dimensions, 1986; (with R.P. Feynman) Elementary Particles and the Laws of Physics, 1987; (with J. Bahcall and T. Piran) Dark Matter in the Universe, 1987, 2nd ed., 2004; (ed. with T. Piran) Strings and superstrings, 1988; (ed. with J.C. Wheeler and T. Piran) Supernovae, 1990; Dreams of a Final Theory, 1993; The Quantum Theory of Fields, 1995; Facing Up-Science and Its Cultural Adversaries, 2001; (ed. with D. Nelson and T. Piran) Statistical Mechanics of Membranes and Surfaces, 2004; Glory and Terror: The Growing Nuclear Danger, 2004; Cosmology, 2008; Lake Views: This World and the Universe, 2009. **Address:** Department of Physics, University of Texas, 1 University Sta. C1600, Austin, TX 78712-0264, U.S.A. **Online address:** weinberg@physics.utexas.edu

WEINBERGER, Peter. See **WEINBERGER, Peter Ezra.**

WEINBERGER, Peter Ezra. (Peter Weinberger). American (born United States), b. 1974?. **Genres:** Politics/Government, History. **Career:** George Mason University, Institute for Conflict Analysis and Resolution, research

professor, 2003-04; American University, School of International Service, assistant professor, 2004-08; United States Institute of Peace, Education and Training Center/Domestic, adviser, 2008-. Writer. **Publications:** Co-opting the PLO: A Critical Reconstruction of the Oslo Accords, 1993-1995, 2006; (with P. Cullen) Reframing the Defense Outsourcing Debate: Merging Government Oversight with Industry Partnership, 2007. **Address:** Lexington Books, 4501 Forbes Blvd., Ste. 200, Lanham, MD 20706, U.S.A. **Online address:** pweinberger@usip.org

WEINER, Anita. American/Israeli (born Israel), b. 1935. **Genres:** Social Sciences. **Career:** Haifa University, senior lecturer, 1969-96, coordinator, 1975-91, Department of Continuing Education, director, 1988-91, now senior lecturer emeritus. Writer. **Publications:** Outside the Family: The History of Child Placement in the Land of Israel during the British Mandate, 1985; (with E. Weiner) Israel-A Precarious Sanctuary: War, Death, and the Jewish People, 1989; (with E. Weiner) Expanding the Options in Child Placement: Israel's Dependent Children in Care from Infancy to Adulthood, 1990; (with E. Weiner) The Martyr's Conviction: A Sociological Analysis, 1990; (ed. with A. Bar-On and E. Weiner) The Abraham Fund Directory of Institutions and Organizations Fostering Coexistence between Jews and Arabs in Israel, 1992; Expanding Historical Consciousness: The Development of the Holocaust Educational Foundation, 2002; Renewal: Reconnecting Soviet Jewry to the Jewish People; A Decade of American Jewish Joint Distribution Committee (AJJDC) Activities in the Former Soviet Union, 1988- 1998, 2003. **Address:** University of Haifa, Mount Carmel, Haifa, 31905, Israel. **Online address:** a.weiner@worldnet.att.net

WEINER, Edmund. (E. S. C. Weiner). British (born England), b. 1950. **Genres:** Language/Linguistics, Biography, Autobiography/Memoirs. **Career:** Oxford University, Christ Church, lecturer, 1974-76, Kellogg College, Rewley House, supernumerary fellow; Oxford University Press, assistant editor, 1977-84, Oxford English Dictionary, co-editor, 1984-93, deputy chief editor, 1993-, principal philologist, 1998-2001. **Publications:** AS E. S. C. WEINER: (comp.) Oxford Guide to English Usage, 1983, (with A. Delahunty) 2nd ed., 1994; (comp.) The Oxford Miniguide to English Usage, 1983, (with A. Delahunty) 2nd ed., 1994; Oxford Guide to the English Language, 1984; (ed. with J.A. Simpson) The Oxford English Dictionary, 2nd ed., 1989; (comp.) The Compact Oxford English Dictionary: Complete Text Reproduced Micrographically, 2nd ed., 1991; (ed. with M. Waite and A. Delahunty) The Oxford Dictionary and English Usage Guide, 1996; (with S. Greenbaum) The Oxford Reference Grammar, 2000. OTHERS: (with S. Chalker) The Oxford Dictionary of English Grammar, 1994, rev. ed., 1998; (with P. Gilliver and J. Marshall) The Ring of Words: Tolkien and the Oxford English Dictionary, 2006. **Address:** Oxford University Press, Great Clarendon St., Oxford, OX OX2 6DP, England. **Online address:** edmund.weiner@oup.com

WEINER, E. S. C. See **WEINER, Edmund.**

WEINER, Hollace Ava. American (born United States), b. 1946. **Genres:** History. **Career:** Baltimore New American, 1968-71; Fort Worth Star-Telegram, news and feature reporter, 1986-97. Historian. **Publications:** Jewish Stars in Texas: Rabbis and Their Works, 1999; Beth-El Congregation, Fort Worth, Texas Centennial, 1902-2002, 2002; (comp. and ed. with K.D. Roseman) Lone Stars of David: The Jews of Texas, 2007; Jewish Junior League: The Rise and Demise of the Fort Worth Council of Jewish Women, 2008; River Crest...The First Hundred Years, 2011. Contributor of articles to books and periodicals. Works appear in anthologies. **Address:** Ft. Worth, TX , U.S.A. **Online address:** hollacelist@charter.net

WEINER, Jennifer Agnes. American (born United States), b. 1970. **Genres:** Novels. **Career:** Centre Daily Times, education reporter, 1991-94; Lexington Herald-Ledger, features reporter, 1994-95; Philadelphia Inquirer, features reporter, 1995-2001; Mademoiselle Magazine, contributing editor, 1998; freelance writer, 2001-. **Publications:** Good in Bed, 2001; In Her Shoes, 2002; Little Earthquakes, 2004; (co-author) American Girls about Town, 2004; Goodnight Nobody, 2005; The Guy not Taken: Stories, 2006; Certain Girls: A Novel, 2008; Best Friends Forever: A Novel, 2009; Half Life, 2010; Fly Away Home, 2010; Then Came You, 2011. **Address:** Atria Books, 1230 Ave. of the Americas, New York, NY 10020, U.S.A. **Online address:** jen@jenniferweiner.com

WEINER, Kay Bain. American (born United States), b. 1932. **Genres:** Art/Art History, Crafts, Design, How-to Books. **Career:** Canfield Solder Co., consultant; Eastman Corp., president; Kay Bain Weiner Glass Art Educational Foundation, founder, 2006-. Writer. **Publications:** Stained Glass Magic: Mix and Match Patterns and Projects, 1980; The Solder Magic Book: Instructions and Patterns, 1989; Line and Color Magic for Glass Design, 1990; Baubles, Dangles, and Beads: The Stained Glass Jewelry Book, 1991; More Solder Magic/In Your Wildest Imagination, 1992; Brush on Color Magic, 1994; Stained Glass: A Guide to Today's Tiffany Copper Foil Technique, 1994, rev. ed., 2000; Glass Enameling, 1996; Tooling Around, 2000; Solder Sculpting and Beyond, 2002; Creative Designing, Innovative Glass Art, 2003; Contemporary Glass Enameling: Fusing with Powders, Paints and Frit, 2005; Designs for Glass Enameling: Techniques and Patterns, 2005. **Address:** Kay Bain Weiner Foundation, 7447 Via De Fortuna, Carlsbad, CA 92009-6938, U.S.A.

WEINER, Marc A. American (born United States), b. 1955. **Genres:** Music, Communications/Media, Film, Humanities, Intellectual History, Novellas/Short Stories, Novels. **Career:** Indiana University-Bloomington, assistant professor of Germanic studies, 1985-92, associate professor of Germanic studies, 1992-96, professor of Germanic studies, associate professor of film studies, 1996-, adjunct professor of comparative literature, 1996-, adjunct professor of communication and culture, 1996-, adjunct professor of cultural studies, 1996-, Institute of German studies, director, 1997-2004; Harvard University, Center for Cultural and Literary Studies, Andrew W. Mellon faculty fellow, 1987-88; The German Quarterly, editor, 1995-97. **Publications:** Arthur Schnitzler and the Crisis of Musical Culture, 1986; Undertones of Insurrection: Music, Politics and the Social Sphere in the Modern German Narrative, 1993 as (intro.) Undertones of Insurrection: Music & Cultural Politics in the Modern German Narrative, 2009; Richard Wagner and the Anti-Semitic Imagination, 1995; Antisemitische Fantasien: Die Musikdramen Richard Wagners, 2000. Contributor to journals. Works appear in anthologies. **Address:** Department of Germanic Studies, Indiana University-Bloomington, Ballantine Hall 644, 1020 E Kirkwood Ave., Bloomington, IN 47405-7103, U.S.A. **Online address:** weiner@indiana.edu

WEINER, Mark S(tuart). American (born United States) **Genres:** Law, Adult Non-fiction, History, Politics/Government. **Career:** Rutgers School of Law, professor of law. Writer. **Publications:** Black Trials: Citizenship from the Beginnings of Slavery to the End of Caste, 2004; Americans Without Law: The Racial Boundaries Of Citizenship, 2006. **Address:** Rutgers School of Law, Center for Law and Justice, 123 Washington St., Newark, NJ 07102, U.S.A. **Online address:** mweiner@kinoy.rutgers.edu

WEINER, Stephanie Kuduk. American (born United States), b. 1972. **Genres:** Politics/Government, Poetry, History. **Career:** Wesleyan University, associate professor of English. Writer. **Publications:** Republican Politics and English Poetry, 1789-1874, 2005. Contributor of articles to periodicals. **Address:** Department of English, Wesleyan University, 294 High St., Middletown, CT 06459-3207, U.S.A. **Online address:** sweiner@wesleyan.edu

WEINER, Stephen. American (born United States), b. 1955. **Genres:** Librarianship, Literary Criticism And History, Adult Non-fiction, Writing/Journalism, History. **Career:** Somerville Public Library, branch librarian, reference librarian and young adult/children's librarian, 1988-95; Maynard Public Library, director, 1995-. Writer. **Publications:** Bring an Author to Your Library, 1993; 100 Graphic Novels for Public Libraries, 1996; The 101 Best Graphic Novels, 2001, rev. ed., 2006; Faster than a Speeding Bullet: The Rise of the Graphic Novel, 2003; (with N.C.C. Couch) The Will Eisner Companion: The Pioneering Spirit of the Father of the Graphic Novel, 2004; (with P. Crawford) Using Graphic Novels in the Classroom including Bone: A Guide for Teachers and Librarians, 2005; Hellboy: The Companion, 2008. Contributor to periodicals. **Address:** Maynard Public Library, 77 Nason St., Maynard, MA 01754, U.S.A. **Online address:** sweiner101@yahoo.com

WEINER, Susan. American (born United States), b. 1946. **Genres:** Education, Humanities, Law, Literary Criticism And History, Sociology, Anthropology/Ethnology. **Career:** State Technical Institute, teacher of composition, 1973-75; University of Miami, part-time teacher, 1984-86; Miami-Dade Community College, part-time teacher, 1984-86; Yale University, professor of French. Writer. **Publications:** Law in Art: Melville's Major Fiction and Nineteenth-Century American Law, 1992; Enfants Terribles: Youth and Femininity in the Mass Media in France, 1945-1968, 2001. Contributor to magazines and newspapers. **Address:** 140 W 79th St., Apt. 10B, New York, NY 10024-6422, U.S.A. **Online address:** mssrweiner@aol.com

WEINER, William J(errold). American (born United States), b. 1945. **Genres:** Medicine/Health, Sports/Fitness. **Career:** Rush Presbyterian-St. Luke's Medical Center, intern, 1969-70, neurology resident, 1971-73; University of Chicago, assistant professor of neurology, 1975-77; Rush University, associate professor of neurology and pharmacology, 1977-83; University of Miami, professor of neurology, Movement Disorders Center, director, 1983-; University of Maryland, School of Medicine, department of neurology, professor and chairman, 2000-, Medical Center, chief of neurology, Maryland Parkinson's Disease and Movement Disorders Center, director. Writer. **Publications:** (With H.L. Klawans, P.A. Nausieda and C.G. Goetz) A Textbook of Clinical Neuropharmacology, 1981; (with A.E. Lang) Movement Disorders: A Comprehensive Survey, 1989; (with L.M. Shulman and A.E. Lang) Parkinson's Disease: A Complete Guide for Patients and Families, 2001, rev. ed., 2007. EDITOR: Respiratory Dysfunction in Neurologic Disease, 1980; (with C.G. Goetz) Neurology for the Non-Neurologist, 1981, 6th ed., 2010; (with F. Hefti) Progress in Parkinson Research, 1988; (with F. Hefti) Progress in Parkinson's Disease Research-2, 1992; Emergent and Urgent Neurology, 1992, (with L.M. Shulman) 2nd ed., 1999; (with A.E. Lang) Drug-Induced Movement Disorders, 1992, rev. ed., 2005; (with F. Hefti) Progress in Parkinson's Disease Research-2, 1992; (with A.M. Cohen) The Comprehensive Management of Parkinson's Disease, 1994; (with C. Singer) Sexual Dysfunction: A Neuro-Medical Approach, 1994; (with A.E. Lang) Behavioral Neurology of Movement Disorders, 1995, (with K.E. Anderson and A.E. Lang) rev. ed., 2005; (with L.M. Shulman) Emergent and Urgent Neurology, 1999; (with S.A. Factor) Parkinson's Disease: Diagnosis and Clinical Management, 2002, rev. ed., 2008; (with E. Tolosa) Hyperkinetic Movement Disorders, 2011. Contributor to periodicals. **Address:** University of Maryland School of Medicine, University of Maryland, 110 S Paca St., 03-072, 655 W Baltimore St., Baltimore, MD 21201-1595, U.S.A. **Online address:** wweiner@som.umaryland.edu

WEINER-DAVIS, Michele. American (born United States), b. 1952. **Genres:** Psychiatry, Self Help, Sex, Social Commentary, Romance/Historical. **Career:** Private practice of marriage and family therapy; workshop presenter; The Divorce Busting Center, director. Writer. **Publications:** (With W. O'Hanlon) In Search of Solutions: A New Direction in Psychotherapy, 1989; Divorce Busting: A Revolutionary and Rapid Program for Staying Together, 1992; Divorce Busting: A Step-by-Step Approach to Making Your Marriage Loving Again, 1992; Fire Your Shrink!: Do-It-Yourself Strategies for Changing Your Life and Everyone in It, 1995; Change Your Life and Everyone in It, 1996; Getting through to the Man You Love, 1998; A Woman's Guide to Changing Her Man: Without His Even Knowing It, 1998; The Divorce Remedy: The Proven 7-Step Program for Saving Your Marriage, 2001; The Sex-Starved Marriage: A Couple's Guide to Boosting Their Marriage Libido, 2003; Sex-Starved Wife: What to do When He's Lost Desire, 2008. **Address:** The Divorce Busting Ctr., PO Box 271, Boulder, CO 80306, U.S.A. **Online address:** michele@divorcebusting.com

WEINGARTNER, Herbert J. American/German (born Germany), b. 1935. **Genres:** Medicine/Health, Psychology. **Career:** Johns Hopkins University, instructor, 1966-, associate professor of psychology, through 1975; University of Maryland, professor of psychology, 1970-76; George Washington University, professor and chairperson of psychology and pharmacology department, 1986-90; National Institute on Alcohol Abuse and Alcoholism, Cognitive Neurosciences Section, chief, Cognitive Neuroscience Systems, president, 1987-; Johns Hopkins University, professor of psychology; University of Maine, Shibles distinguished visiting university professor; National Institutes of Health, director, consultant, now retired. Writer. **Publications:** (Ed. with E.S. Parker) Memory Consolidation: Psychobiology of Cognition, 1984; (ed. with R.G. Lister) Perspectives on Cognitive Neuroscience, 1991; (co-ed.) Memory Improvement: Implication for Memory Theory, 1992. **Address:** National Institute on Health Clinical Ctr., Rm. 3B-19, Bldg. 10, 9000 Rockville Pke., Bethesda, MD 20892, U.S.A.

WEINHEIMER, Beckie. American (born United States), b. 1958?. **Genres:** Young Adult Fiction. **Career:** Writer. **Publications:** Converting Kate, 2007. **Address:** Viking Children's Books, 375 Hudson St., New York, NY 10014-3658, U.S.A. **Online address:** beckieweinheimer58@yahoo.com

WEINKAUF, Mary Louise Stanley. *See* **WEINKAUF, Mary S(tanley).**

WEINKAUF, Mary S(tanley). (Mary Louise Stanley Weinkauf). American (born United States), b. 1938. **Genres:** Poetry, Literary Criticism And History, Mystery/Crime/Suspense. **Career:** University of Tennessee, instructor in English, through 1966; Adrian College, assistant professor of English, 1966-69; Dakota Wesleyan University, professor and department head, 1969-89, chairman of humanities division; Siloa Lutheran Church, pastor, 1993-; Calvary Lutheran Church, pastor, 1997-2005. Writer. **Publications:** Early Poems by a Late Beginner, 1976; Hard-Boiled Heretic: The Lew Archer Novels of Ross Macdonald, 1994; S. Fowler Wright: Sermons in Stone, 1994; Sermons in Science Fiction: The Novels of S. Fowler Wright, 1994; Ngaio Marsh, 1996; Murder Most Poetic: The Mystery Novels of Ngaio Marsh, 1996. Contributor to periodicals. **Address:** 8991 Highland Dr., Woodruff, WI 54568, U.S.A. **Online address:** woodwork@nnex.net

WEINMAN, Lynda (Susan). American (born United States), b. 1955. **Genres:** Information Science/Computers, Technology, Adult Non-fiction, Communications/Media. **Career:** Art Center College of Design, instructor in interactive media design, digital imaging, motion graphics, and web design, 1989-96; Center for Creative Imaging, instructor, 1991-95; American Film Institute, instructor, 1993-96; University of California, School of Visual Arts, instructor, 1994-95; San Francisco State University, instructor in the multimedia studies program, 1994-96; lynda.com, co-founder, 1995-, executive chair; writer, 1996-; Ojai Digital Arts Center, co-founder, 1999; The Net., contributing editor. Consultant. **Publications:** NONFICTION: (with B. Heavin) Coloring Web Graphics, 1996, rev. ed. as Coloring Web Graphics. 2, 1997; Deconstructing Web Graphics, 1996, (with J.W. Lentz) rev. ed. as Deconstructing Web Graphics. 4, 2003; (with R. Pirouz) Click Here: Web Communication Design, 1997; Inspiring Web Graphics, 1997; Lynda Weinman's Web Graphics Resource Library, 1997; Preparing Web Graphics, 1997; (with W. Weinman) Creative HTML Design, 1998, rev. ed. as Creative HTML Design.2, 2001; Dreamweaver 2/H.O.T., 1999, rev. ed. as Dreamweaver 3: H-O-T, 2000; Photoshop 5.5/ Image Ready 2 Hands-on Training, 2000, rev. ed. as Photoshop7/ Image Ready for the Web: Hands-on Training, 2003; (with G. Green and K. Weil) Flash 5 H.O.T.: Hands-on Training, 2002; (with C. Newman) After Effects 5.0/5.5, H-O-T Hands-on Training, 2003, rev. ed. as Adobe After Effects 6 H.O.T.: Hands-on Training, 2004; (with A. Rudner and G. Green) Dreamweaver MX H.O.T.: Hands-on Training, 2003; (with G. Green) Macromedia Dreamweaver MX 2004: Hands-onTraining, 2003; (contrib.) Mac OS X Jaguar H.O.T.: Hands-on Training, 2003; (with G. Chow) Acrobat 5 H.O.T.: Hands-on Training, 2003, rev. ed. as Adobe Acrobat 6 H.O.T.: Hands-on Training, 2004; (with G. Chow) Mac OSX Panter Hands-on Training, 2004; (with S. Rebenschied) Macromedia Flash MX 2004 beyond the Basics: Hands-on Training, 2004; (with S. Rebenscheid) Photoshop Elements 2 H.O.T.: Hands-on Training, 2004; (with T. Staples) Adobe Photoshop CS/Image Read CS for the Web, 2004; (with J.V. West) Adobe Illustrator CS Hands-on Training, 2004; (with R. Yeung) Macromedia Flash MX 2004: Hands-on Training, 2004; (with C. Fahs) Adobe After Effects 7, 2007. SOFTWARE: COSA After Effects, 1993; VideoFusion 1.5, 1993. OTHERS: Designing Web Graphics, 1996, 3rd ed. as Designing Web Graphics.3, 1999; (with J. Kabili) Photoshop 7, 2003; (with G. Chow) Mac OS X Panther Hands-on Training, 2004. Contributor to periodicals. **Address:** New Riders Publishing, 201 W 103rd St., Indianapolis, IN 46290, U.S.A. **Online address:** lynda@lynda.com

WEINREB, Michael. American (born United States) **Genres:** Adult Non-fiction, Sports/Fitness. **Career:** Grantland, staff writer. **Publications:** (With P. Williams) How to be Like Mike: Life Lessons about Basketballs Best, 2001; Girl Boy etc., 2004; Kings of New York: A Year among the Geeks, Oddballs, and Geniuses Who Make Up America's Top High School Chess Team, 2007; Bigger than the Game: Bo, Boz, the Punky QB, and the Making of the Modern Athlete in the Eighties, 2010. **Address:** 375 Hudson St., New York, NY 10014, U.S.A. **Online address:** michael@michaelweinreb.com

WEINRICH, A. K. H. British/German (born Germany), b. 1933. **Genres:** Anthropology/Ethnology, Psychology, Race Relations, Sociology, Urban Studies, Women's Studies And Issues, Politics/Government, Bibliography, Bibliography. **Career:** School of Social Work, lecturer in social anthropology, 1965-66; University of Zimbabwe, lecturer, 1966-71, senior lecturer in social anthropology, 1972-75; United Nations Social, Educational and Cultural Organization (UNESCO), researcher, 1975-77; University of Dar-es-Salaam, associate professor of sociology, 1977-80; Government of Zimbabwe, senior research officer in the parliament, 1981-82; psychologist and therapist, 1986-. Writer. **Publications:** Chiefs and Councils in Rhodesia: Transition from Patriarchal to Bureaucratic Power, 1971; Rhodesia: The Ousting of the

Tangwena, 1972; Black and White Elites in Rural Rhodesia, 1973; African Farmers in Rhodesia: Old and New Peasant Communities in Karangaland, 1975; Cold Comfort Farm Society: A Christian Commune in Rhodesia, 1975; Mucheke: Race, Status and Politics in a Rhodesian Community, 1976; The Tonga People on the Southern Shore of Lake Kariba, 1977; (trans. with I. Fischer) H. Vocke, The Lebanese War: Its Origins and Political Dimensions, 1978; Women and Racial Discrimination in Rhodesia, 1979; Situation de la femme au Zimbabwe avant l'indépendence, 1981; African Marriage in Zimbabwe and the Impact of Christianity, 1983; Der Kelch und die Schlange, 1989, trans. as The Chalice and the Snake, 1991; Journeys of Self-Discovery, 1991. **Address:** 38 Cranhurst Rd., London, GL NW2 4LP, England. **Online address:** akh.weinrich@virgin.net

WEINROTH, Michelle. American (born United States), b. 1959. **Genres:** Politics/Government, History, Literary Criticism And History. **Career:** University of Birmingham, Centre for Contemporary Cultural Studies, staff of popular memory workshop, 1982-85, lecturer, 1985; McGill University, lecturer, 1987, 1991; University of Regina, lecturer, 1989; Laval University, lecturer, 1989; University of Ottawa, part-time lecturer in sociology, 1989-90; York University, lecturer, 1992; Carleton University, teacher. Writer. **Publications:** (Trans. with P.L. Browne) G. Laforest, Trudeau and the End of a Canadian Dream, 1995; Reclaiming William Morris: Englishness, Sublimity and the Rhetoric of Dissent, 1996; (trans. with P.L. Browne) Gérard Bouchard, The Making of the Nations and Cultures of the New World: An Essay in Comparative History, 2008. Contributor of articles to periodicals and books. **Address:** 146 1st Ave., Ottawa, ON K1S 2G4, Canada. **Online address:** brownep@comnet.ca

WEINSTEIN, Allen. American (born United States), b. 1937. **Genres:** History, International Relations/Current Affairs, Politics/Government. **Career:** University of Maryland, lecturer in history, 1964-66, visiting professor of history, professor; Smith College, assistant professor, professor, 1966-81, American studies program, chairman, director, 1972-77; Georgetown University, professor, 1981-84; The Washington Post, editorial staff, 1981; The Washington Quarterly, executive editor, 1981-83; Robert Maynard Hutchins CSDI, president, 1984; Democracy Program, executive director, 1982-84; National Endowment for Democracy, acting president, 1983-84; Boston University, professor and university professor of history, 1985-89; U.S. Institute for Peace, founding member, director, 1985-2001; Center for Democracy, president and chief executive officer, 1985-2003; International Institute of Democracy, officer, 1989-2001; Global Panel, chair, 1993-98; International Foundation for Election Systems, senior advisor, 2003, senior strategist; archivist of the United States, 2005-08. **Publications:** Prelude to Populism, 1970; Origins of Modern America, 1865-1900, 1970; (with R.J. Wilson) Freedom and Crisis, 1974, (with F.O. Gatell) 3rd ed., 1981; Between the Wars: American Foreign Policy from Versailles to Pearl Harbor, 1978; Perjury: The Hiss-Chambers Case, 1978; (contrib.) Evolution and Revolutions, 1990; (with A. Vassiliev) The Haunted Wood: Soviet Espionage in America, 1997; (with A. Vassiliev) The Haunted Wood: Soviet Espionage in America-The Stalin Era, 1999; (with D. Rubel) The Story of America: Freedom and Crisis from Settlement to Superpower, 2002. EDITOR/CO-EDITOR: (with F.O. Gatell) American Themes: Essays in Historiography, 1968; (with F.O. Gatell and D. Sarasohn) American Negro Slavery: A Modern Reader, 1968, 3rd ed., 1979; (with F.O. Gatell) The Segregation Era 1863-1954, 1970; Random House Readings in American History, 6 vols., 1970; (with F.O. Gatell and P. Goodman) The Growth of American Politics, 1972; (with F.O. Gatell and P. Goodman) Readings in American political history, 1972; (with M. Maoz) Harry S. Truman and the Founding of Israel, 1981; (with M. Maoz) Truman and the American Commitment to Israel, 1981; (with P. Reeves and S. Sobol) The Status of Human Rights under the Helsinki Accords, 1990. **Address:** College of Information Studies, University of Maryland, Rm. 4121D, Hornbake Bldg. S, College Park, MD 20742-4325, U.S.A.

WEINSTEIN, Cindy. American (born United States), b. 1960. **Genres:** Literary Criticism And History, Social Sciences, Young Adult Fiction. **Career:** University of California, teaching assistant, 1985-86, graduate instructor, 1986-87, research assistant, 1987-88; California Institute of Technology, assistant professor, 1989-95, associate professor of English, 1995-2004, professor of English, 2005-, Division of the Humanities and Social Sciences, executive officer for the humanities, 2008-. Writer. **Publications:** The Literature of Labor and the Labors of Literature: Allegory in Nineteenth-Century American Fiction, 1995; (ed.) The Cambridge Companion to Harriet Beecher Stowe, 2004; Family, Kinship, and Sympathy in Nineteenth-Century American Literature, 2004; (ed. with P. Stoneley) A Concise Companion to American Fiction, 1900-1950, 2008; Introduction to the Oxford Classical Edition of Nathaniel Hawthorne's The Scarlet Letter, forthcoming. Contributor to books and journals. **Address:** Division of the Humanities and Social Sciences, California Institute of Technology, MC 101-40, 311 Dabney Hall, 1200 E California Blvd., Pasadena, CA 91125-0002, U.S.A. **Online address:** caw@hss.caltech.edu

WEINSTEIN, Jay. American (born United States), b. 1965. **Genres:** Food And Wine. **Career:** Freelance writer, 1996-; freelance editor, 1999-2003; Natural Gourmet Institute, instructor. **Publications:** A Cup of Comfort Cookbook: Favorite Comfort Foods to Warm Your Heart and Lift Your Spirit, 2002; The Everything Vegetarian Cookbook: 300 Healthy Recipes Everyone Will Enjoy, 2002; The Ethical Gourmet: How to Enjoy Great Food That is Humanely Raised, Sustainable, Nonendangered and That Replenishes the Earth, 2006; (ed.) Southeast Asian Flavors, 2008. Contributor to periodicals. **Address:** Natural Gourmet Institute, 48 W 21st St., 2nd Fl., New York, NY 10010, U.S.A. **Online address:** jweinstein@attg.net

WEINSTEIN, Mark Allen. American (born United States), b. 1937. **Genres:** Literary Criticism And History, Biography. **Career:** Bronx Community College, instructor, 1964-65; Brooklyn College, instructor, 1965-68, assistant professor of English, 1968-70; University of Nevada, associate professor of English, 1970-74, professor of English, 1974-, distinguished professor, 2001-, now emeritus; University of Edinburgh, Institute for Advanced Studies in the Humanities, honorary fellow, 1979; University of Aberdeen, Institute of Cultural Studies, research fellow. Writer. **Publications:** William Edmondstoune Aytoun and the Spasmodic Controversy, 1968; (ed.) Prefaces to the Waverley novels, 1978; Saint Ronan's Well, 1995; (ed. with A. Lumsden) The Pirate/Walter Scott, 2000. **Address:** Department of English, University of Nevada, 6th Fl., Flora Dungan Humanities Bldg., 4505 Maryland Pkwy., PO Box 455011, Las Vegas, NV 89154-5011, U.S.A. **Online address:** weinstei@unlv.nevada.edu

WEINSTEIN, Miriam. American (born United States), b. 1946. **Genres:** Food And Wine, History, Human Relations/Parenting. **Career:** Journalist and filmmaker. **Publications:** Yiddish: A Nation of Words, 2001; (ed.) Prophets and Dreamers: A Selection of Great Yiddish Literature, 2002; The Surprising Power of Family Meals: How Eating Together Makes Us Smarter, Stronger, Healthier and Happier, 2005. Contributor to journals. **Address:** c/o Author Mail, Steerforth Press, 45 Lyme Rd., Ste. 208, Hanover, NH 03755, U.S.A.

WEINSTEIN, Philip M. American (born United States), b. 1940. **Genres:** Literary Criticism And History, Biography, Autobiography/Memoirs, Humanities, Young Adult Fiction, Novels. **Career:** Harvard University, assistant professor of English, 1968-71; Swarthmore College, Department of English, associate professor, professor and head, 1971-, Alexander Griswold Cummins professor of English, 1992-. Writer. **Publications:** Henry James and the Requirements of the Imagination, 1971; The Semantics of Desire: Changing Models of Identity from Dickens to Joyce, 1984; Faulkner's Subject: A Cosmos No One Owns, 1992; (ed.) The Cambridge Companion to William Faulkner, 1995; What Else but Love?: The Ordeal of Race in Faulkner and Morrison, 1996; Unknowing: The Work of Modernist Fiction, 2005; Becoming Faulkner: The Art and Life of William Faulkner, 2009. **Address:** Department of English, Swarthmore College, 304 LPAC, 500 College Ave., Swarthmore, PA 19081-1397, U.S.A. **Online address:** pweinst1@swarthmore.edu

WEINSTOCK, Nicholas. American (born United States) **Genres:** Gay And Lesbian Issues, Novels, Autobiography/Memoirs, Literary Criticism And History, Young Adult Fiction. **Career:** Turtle Bay Books, editorial assistant; Villard Books, editorial assistant; Riverhead Books, editorial assistant; Random House Publishers, editor; 20th Century Fox Television, vice president. **Publications:** The Secret Love of Sons: How We Men Feel about Our Mothers, and Why We Never Tell, 1997; (with J. Quinn) The Mentor: A Memoir of Friendship and Gay Identity, 2000; As Long as She Needs Me, 2001; Golden Hour, 2006. Contributor to periodicals. **Address:** HarperCollins Publishers, 10 E 53rd St., 20th Fl., New York, NY 10022-5244, U.S.A.

WEINTRAUB, Andrew N. American (born United States), b. 1962. **Genres:** Theatre, Music. **Career:** University of California, lecturer in music, 1996-97; University of Pittsburgh, Department Of Music, visiting assistant professor of music, 1997-98, assistant professor of music, 1998-2004, associate professor of music, 2004-, professor, director of graduate studies, 2007-; Mid-Atlantic Society for Ethnomusicology, vice president, 1999-2001; National Univer-

sity of Malaysia, Institute for Ethnic Studies, visiting fellow, 2009. Writer and ethnomusicologist. **Publications:** Power Plays: Wayang Golek Puppet Theater of West Java, 2004; (ed. with B. Yung) Music and Cultural Rights, 2009; Dangdut Stories: A Social and Musical History of Indonesia's Most Popular Music, 2010; (ed.) Islam and Popular Culture in Indonesia and Malaysia, 2011. Contributor to journals. **Address:** University of Pittsburgh, 305 Music Bldg., 4337 5th Ave., Pittsburgh, PA 15260, U.S.A. **Online address:** anwein@pitt.edu

WEINTRAUB, David. (David A. Weintraub). American (born United States), b. 1949. **Genres:** Travel/Exploration, Sciences, Astronomy. **Career:** Oregon Journal, staff photographer, 1975-76; Salem Statesman-Journal, staff photographer, 1976-79; Oregon Journal/Oregonian, staff photographer, 1980-83; freelance writer and photographer, 1980-; University of California Extension, Academy of Art College, instructor; City College of San Francisco, instructor; Photo District News, staff writer; Vanderbilt University, professor of astronomy. **Publications:** East Bay Trails, 1998; North Bay Trails, 1999; Adventure Kayaking: Cape Cod and Martha's Vineyard, 2000, 2nd. ed., 2001; Monterey Bay Trails, 2001; Peninsula Tales & Trails: Commemorating the Thirtieth Anniversary of the Midpeninsula Regional Open Space District, 2004; Walking the Cape and Islands: A Comprehensive Guide to the Walking and Hiking Trails of Cape Cod, Martha's Vineyard and Nantucket, 2006; Is Pluto a Planet?, 2006. Contributor of articles to books and magazines. **Address:** Wilderness Press, 2440 Bancroft Way, Berkeley, CA 94710, U.S.A.

WEINTRAUB, David A. See **WEINTRAUB, David.**

WEINTRAUB, Linda. American (born United States), b. 1942. **Genres:** Art/Art History, Social Commentary, Environmental Sciences/Ecology. **Career:** Bard College, Edith C. Blum Art Institute, director, 1981-92; Oberlin College, Henry Luce professor for emerging art, 2000-03; Artnow Publications, founder. Writer. **Publications:** Thomas Hart Benton: Chronicler of America's Folk Heritage, 1986; Maximal Implications of the Minimal Line, 1987; Process and Product, 1988; Isabel Bishop, 1989; Art What Thou Eat, 1990; Raquel Rabinovich: The Dark is the Source of Light, 1996; Art on the Edge and Over: Searching for Art's Meaning in Contemporary Society, 1997; Animal, Anima, Animus, 1998; Arcana Mundi: Selected Works, 1979-2000, 2001; In the Making: Creative Options for Contemporary Art, 2003; Making Contemporary Art: How Today's Artists Think and Work, 2003; Ecocentric Topics: Pioneering Themes for Eco-Art, 2006; Cycle-Logical Art: Recycling Matters for Eco-Art, 2007. **Address:** ArtNow Publications, 28 Olsen Rd., Rhinebeck, NY 12572-2260, U.S.A. **Online address:** linda@artnowpublications.com

WEINTRAUB, Sidney. American (born United States), b. 1922. **Genres:** Novels, Business/Trade/Industry, International Relations/Current Affairs, Economics. **Career:** U.S. Department of State, foreign service officer, 1949, chief of commercial policy, U.S. AID Program, economic counselor and director, deputy assistant secretary of state for international finance and development, 1969-74, U.S. Agency for International Development, assistant administrator; Brookings Institution, senior fellow, 1978-79; University of Texas, Lyndon B. Johnson School of Public Affairs, Dean Rusk chair, Dean Rusk professor, 1976-94, now Dean Rusk professor emeritus; Center for Strategic and International Studies (CSIS), expert, 1994-, William E. Simon chair in political economy. Writer. **Publications:** Mexican Slay Ride (novel), 1962; The Siamese Coup Affair (novel), 1963; The Foreign-exchange Gap of the Developing Countries, 1965; Trade Preferences for Less-developed Countries: An Analysis of United States Policy, 1966; United States: Latin American Trade and Financial Relations: Some Policy Recommendations, 1977; (ed. with N.V. Walbek) Conflict, Order, and Peace in the Americas, 1978; Government-Private Joint Venture as a Confidence Builder in Non-fuel Minerals Investment, 1979; (with S.R. Ross) Illegal Alien from Mexico: Policy Choices for an Intractable Issue, 1980; (ed. with W.R. Cline) Economic Stabilization Policies in Developing Countries, 1981; (with S.R. Ross) Temporary Alien Workers in the United States: Designing Policy from Fact and Opinion, 1982; (ed.) Economic Coercion and U.S. Foreign Policy: Implications of Case Studies from the Johnson Administration, 1982; Free Trade between Mexico and the United States, 1984; (ed.) Industrial Strategy and Planning in Mexico and the United States, 1986; Mexican Trade Policy and the North American Community, 1988; (ed. with F.D. Bean and J. Schmandt) Mexican and Central American Population and U.S. Immigration Policy, 1989; A Marriage of Convenience: Relations Between the United States, 1990; Transforming the Mexican Economy: The Salinas Sexenio, 1990; (ed. with S. Díaz-Briquets) Determinants of Emigration from Mexico, Central America, and the Caribbean, 1991; (ed. with S. Díaz-Briquets) Migration Impacts of Trade and Foreign Investment: Mexico and Caribbean Basin Countries, 1991; (ed. with S. Díaz-Briquets) Effects of Receiving Country Policies on Migration Flows, 1991; (ed. with A.D. Jones and L.F. Rubio) U.S.-Mexican Industrial Integration: The Road to Free Trade, 1991; (ed. with S. Díaz-Briquets) Regional and Sectoral Development in Mexico as Alternatives to Migration, 1991; (ed. with R.F. de Castro and M.V. Campos) Sectoral Labor Effects of North American Free Trade, 1993; (ed.) Integrating the Americas: Shaping Future Trade Policy, 1994; (ed. with M.D. Baer) NAFTA Debate: Grappling with Unconventional Trade Issues, 1994; NAFTA: What Comes Next, 1994; (ed. with J. Hoebing and M.D. Baer) NAFTA and Sovereignty: Trade-offs for Canada, Mexico, and the United States, 1996; NAFTA at Three: A Progress Report, 1997; (ed. with C. Sands) North American Auto Industry Under NAFTA, 1998; Technical Cooperation Needs for Hemispheric Trade Negotiations, 1999; Financial Decision-Making in Mexico: To Bet a Nation, 2000; Development and Democracy in the Southern Cone: Imperatives for U.S. Policy in South America, 2000; Commentaries on International Political Economy: Constructive Irreverence, 2003; (ed.) NAFTA's Impact on North America: The First Decade, 2004; (ed. with A.M. Rugman and G. Boyd) Free Trade in the Americas: Economic and Political Issues for Governments and Firms, 2004; Issues in International Political Economy: Constructive Irreverence, 2004; (ed. with A. Hester and V.R. Prado) Energy Cooperation in the Western Hemisphere: Benefits and Impediments, 2007; Unequal Partners: The United States and Mexico, 2010; (with D. Wood) Cooperative Mexican-U.S. Antinarcotics Efforts, 2010. **Address:** Center for Strategic and International Studies, 1800 K St. NW, Washington, DC 20006-2202, U.S.A. **Online address:** sweintraub@csis.org

WEINTRAUB, Stanley. American (born United States), b. 1929. **Genres:** Art/Art History, History, Intellectual History, Literary Criticism And History, Military/Defense/Arms Control, Biography. **Career:** Pennsylvania State University, instructor, 1953-59, assistant professor, 1959-62, associate professor, 1962-65, professor of English, 1965-70, research professor, 1970-86, Evan Pugh professor of arts and humanities, 1986-2000, Evan Pugh professor emeritus of arts and humanities, 2000-, Institute for the Arts and Humanistic Studies, director, 1970-90; University of California, visiting professor, 1963; University of Hawaii, visiting professor, 1973; University of Singapore, visiting professor; University of Malaya, visiting professor; University of Delaware, adjunct professor of English, 2003-. Writer. **Publications:** Private Shaw and Public Shaw, A Dual Portrait of Lawrence of Arabia and G.B.S., 1963; The War in the Wards, Korea's Unknown Battle In A Prisoner-Of-War Hospital Camp, 1964; (with B.S. Oldsey) The Art of William Golding, 1965; Reggie: A Portrait of Reginald Turner, 1965; Beardsley, 1967; Biography and Truth, 1967; Last Great Cause: The Intellectuals and the Spanish Civil War, 1968; (with R. Weintraub) Evolution of a Revolt, 1968; Journey to Heartbreak; The Crucible Years of Bernard Shaw, 1914-1918, 1971; Whistler: A Biography, 1974; (with R. Weintraub) Lawrence of Arabia: The Literary Impulse, 1975; Aubrey Beardsley, Imp of the Perverse, 1976; War in the Wards: Korea's Unknown Battle In A Prisoner-Of-War Hospital Camp, 1976; Four Rossettis: A Victorian Biography, 1977; London Yankees: Portraits of American Writers and Artists in England, 1894-1914, 1979; Unexpected Shaw: Biographical Approaches to G.B.S. and His Work, 1982; A Stillness Heard Round the World: The End of the Great War, November 1918, 1985; Bernard Shaw, the Diaries, 1885-1897: With Early Autobiographical Notebooks and Diaries, and An Abortive 1917 Diary, 1986; (with R. Ploog) Benjamin West Drawings from the Historical Society of Pennsylvania, May 31 through September 17, 1987; Victoria: An Intimate Biography, 1987; Long Day's Journey into War: December 7, 1941, 1991; Bernard Shaw: A Guide to Research, 1992; Disraeli: A Biography, 1993; The Last Great Victory-The End of World War II, July/August 1945, 1995; Shaw's people: Victoria to Churchill, 1996; Uncrowned King: The Life of Prince Albert, 1997; MacArthur's War: Korea and the Undoing of An American Hero, 2000; (with R. Weintraub) Dear Young Friend, 2000; Edward the Caresser: The Playboy Prince Who Became Edward VII, 2001; Silent Night: The Story of World War I Christmas Truce, 2001; Charlotte and Lionel: A Rothschild Love Story, 2003; General Washington's Christmas Farewell: A Mount Vernon Homecoming, 1783, 2003; Silent Night: The Remarkable Christmas Truce of 1914, 2003; Iron Tears: America's Battle for Freedom, Britain's Quagmire, 1775-1783, 2005; 11 Days in December: Christmas at the Bulge, 1944, 2006; 15 Stars: Eisenhower, MacArthur, Marshall: Three Generals Who Saved the American Century, 2007; General Sherman's Christmas: Savannah, 2009; Pearl Harbor Christmas: A World at War, December 1941, 2011; Victorian Yankees at Queen Victoria's Court: American Encounters with Victoria and Albert, 2011; Who's Afraid of Ber-

nard Shaw?: Some Personalities in Shaw's Plays, 2011; Final Victory: FDR's Extraordinary Campaign for President During World War II, 2012. EDITOR: G.B. Shaw, An Unfinished Novel, 1958; C.P. Snow, a Spectrum: Science, Criticism, Fiction, 1963; (and intro.) The Yellow Book: Quintessence of the Nineties, 1964; The Savoy: Nineties Experiment, 1966; The Court Theatre 1904-1907: A Commentary and Criticism, 1966; Shaw, Cashel Byron's Profession, 1968; The Literary Criticism of Oscar Wilde, 1968; Shaw: An Autobiography, 2 vols., 1969-70; (and intro.) The Green Carnation, 1970; Shaw, Saint Joan, 1971; Bernard Shaw's Nondramatic Literary Criticism, 1972; (with P. Young) Directions in Literary Criticism, Contemporary Approaches to Literature, 1973; Saint Joan: 50 Years After, 1923/24-1973/74, 1973; The Portable Bernard Shaw, 1977; (with A. Wright) Heartbreak House: A Facsimile of the Revised Typescript, 1981; (with R. Aldington) The Portable Oscar Wilde, 1981; Modern British Dramatists 1900-1945, 2 vols., 1982; The Playwright and the Pirate: Bernard Shaw and Frank Harris, a Correspondence, 1982; British Dramatists since World War II, 2 vols., 1982; (intro.) Bernard Shaw on the London Art Scene, 1885-1950, 1989. Contributor to periodicals. **Address:** Department of English, University of Delaware, 212 Memorial Hall, Newark, DE 19716, U.S.A. **Online address:** sqw4@comcast.net

WEIR, Ben(jamin M.). American (born United States), b. 1923. **Genres:** Autobiography/Memoirs, Biography, Theology/Religion. **Career:** Presbyterian Church (U.S.A.), missionary-fraternal worker in Lebanon and Syria, 1953-61; San Francisco Theological Seminary, Hewlett professor of evangelism and mission chair, 1987-95, Flora Lamson Hewlett professor of evangelism and mission emeritus. Writer. **Publications:** (With C. Weir and D.C. Benson) Hostage Bound, Hostage Free, 1987. **Address:** San Fransico Theological Seminary, 105 Seminary Rd., San Anselmo, CA 94960, U.S.A.

WEIR, Charlene. American (born United States), b. 1937. **Genres:** Mystery/Crime/Suspense, Young Adult Fiction. **Career:** Writer. **Publications:** MYSTERY NOVELS: The Winter Widow, 1992; Consider the Crows, 1993; Family Practice, 1995; Murder Take Two, 1998; A Cold Christmas, 2001; Up in Smoke, 2003; Edge of Midnight, 2006. **Address:** c/o Meg Ruley, Jane Rotrosen Agency, 318 E 51st St., New York, NY 10022, U.S.A. **Online address:** charweir@sbcglobal.net

WEIR, David A. American (born United States) **Genres:** History, Theology/Religion. **Career:** Nyack College, professor of history. Writer and educator. **Publications:** The Origins of the Federal Theology in Sixteenth-Century Reformation Thought, 1990; Early New England: A Covenanted Society, 2005. **Address:** Department of History, Nyack College, Rm. 214, North Campus, 1 South Blvd., Nyack, NY 10960, U.S.A. **Online address:** david.weir@nyack.edu

WEIR, Gary E. American (born United States), b. 1951?. **Genres:** Military/Defense/Arms Control, History, Politics/Government. **Career:** University of Tennessee, instructor, 1977-78; Sacred Heart School, teacher, 1978-82; St. Ann's Academy, teacher, 1982-86; U.S. Naval Academy, professor of history, 1986-87; University of Maryland University College, adjunct professor of history, 1987-; U.S. Naval Historical Center, historian of science and technology, 1987-; Naval Historian's Support Group, founder. Writer. **Publications:** (With C. Tuggle) The Department of Energy, 1989; Building American Submarines: 1914-1940, 1991; Building the Kaiser's Navy: The Imperial Naval Office and German Industry in the Tirpitz Era, 1890-1919, 1992; Forged in War: The Naval Industrial Complex and American Submarine Construction, 1940-1961, 1993; Ocean in Common: American Naval Officers, Scientists, and the Ocean Environment, 2001; (with W.J. Boyne) Rising Tide: The Untold Story of the Russian Submarines that Fought the Cold War, 2003. Contributor to books and journals. **Address:** University College, University of Maryland, 3501 University Blvd. E, Adelphi, MD 20783, U.S.A.

WEIR, Ronald Blackwood. British (born England), b. 1944?. **Genres:** Economics, History, Business/Trade/Industry, Humanities. **Career:** University of York, Derwent College, senior lecturer in economic and social history, provost, 1980-2009. Writer. **Publications:** The History of the North of Scotland Malt Distillers Association 1874-1926, 1970; A History of the Scottish American Investment Company Limited, 1873-1893, 1973; (with A. Peacock) The Composer in the Market Place, 1975; The History of the Malt Distillers Association of Scotland, 1975; The History of the Distillers Company, 1877-1939, 1995. **Address:** Department of Economics, University of York, Heslington, NY YO10 5DD, England. **Online address:** rbw1@york.ac.uk

WEIR, Theresa. Also writes as Anne Frasier, Anne Frasier. American (born United States), b. 1954?. **Genres:** Romance/Historical, Novels, Young Adult Fiction, Autobiography/Memoirs. **Career:** Novelist. **Publications:** Forever Man, 1988; Amazon Lily, 1988; Loving Jenny, 1989; Iguana Bay, 1990; Pictures of Emily, 1990; Forever, 1991; Last Summer, 1992; Long Night Moon, 1994; One Fine Day, 1994; American Dreamer, 1997; Some Kind of Magic, 1998; Cool Shade, 1998; Bad Karma, 1999. AS ANNE FRASIER: Hush, 2002; Sleep Tight, 2003; Play Dead, 2004; Before I Wake, 2005; Pale Immortal, 2006; Garden of Darkness, 2007; Max Under the Stars, 2010; The Lineup, 2010; The Orchard, 2011. **Address:** Penguin/Putnam Inc., 375 Hudson St., New York, NY 10014, U.S.A. **Online address:** annefrasier@comcast.net

WEIS, Lois. American (born United States), b. 1948. **Genres:** Education, Sociology. **Career:** University of Missouri-Columbia, Midwest Center for Equal Educational Opportunity, program coordinator, 1977-78; State University of New York, assistant professor, 1978-84, associate professor, 1984-89, professor of educational organization, administration and policy, 1989-, Graduate School of Education, associate dean, 1986-92, distinguished professor, 2005; Alvan Ikoku College of Education, lecturer, 1980; University of Wisconsin-Madison, visiting assistant professor, 1982; Ontario Institute for Studies in Education, visiting associate professor of sociology, 1986-87; American Educational Studies Association, president. Writer. **Publications:** Between Two Worlds: Black Students in an Urban Community College, 1985; Working Class without Work: High School Students in a De-Industrializing Economy, 1990; High School as a Site for the Encouragement of White Male Dominance, 1990; (with M. Fine) The Unknown City: The Lives of Poor and Working Class Young Adults, 1998; (with M. Fine) Speed Bumps: A Student-Friendly Guide to Qualitative Research, 2000; Class Reunion: The Remaking of the American White Working Class, 2004; (with M. Fine) Silenced Voices and Extraordinary Conversations: Re-Imagining Schools, 2003; (with M. Fine) Working Method: Research and Social Justice, 2004. EDITOR: (intro.) Issues in Education: Schooling and the Reproduction of Class and Gender Inequalities, 1982; Race, Class, and Schooling, 1986; (co-ed. and intro.) Crisis in Teaching, 1988; (with Petrie and E. Farrar) Dropouts from Schools: Issues, Dilemmas, and Solutions, 1989; (co-ed.) Curriculum for Tomorrow's Schools, 1990; (co-ed. and intro.) Perspectives on Early Childhood Education, 1991; (co-ed.) Textbooks in American Society, 1991; (with M. Fine) Construction Sites: Excavating Race, Class, and Gender among Urban Youth, 2000; (with C. McCarthy and G. Dimitriadis) Ideology, Curriculum, and the New Sociology of Education: Revisiting the Work of Michael Apple, 2006; Way Class Works: Readings on School, Family, and the Economy, 2008. EDITOR and CONTRIBUTOR: (with M. Apple) Ideology and Practice in Schooling, 1983; (with P. Altbach and G. Kelly) Excellence in Education: Perspectives on Policy and Practice, 1985; Class, Race, and Gender in American Schools, 1987; (with M. Fine) Beyond Silenced Voices: Class, Race, and Gender in United States Schools, 1992, rev. ed., 2005; (co-ed.) Off White, 1997; (with M. Seller) Beyond Black and White: New Faces and Voices in United States Schools, 1997. Contributor to books and journals. **Address:** Graduate School of Education, State University of New York, 430 Baldy Hall, Amherst, NY 14260-1000, U.S.A. **Online address:** weis@buffalo.edu

WEISBERG, Herbert F. American (born United States), b. 1941. **Genres:** Politics/Government, Social Sciences. **Career:** University of Michigan, assistant professor, 1969-73, associate professor, 1973-74; Ohio State University, Department of Political Science, professor of political science, 1974-, chair, 2005-11, Polimetrics Laboratory, director, 1993-99, 2002-05, Center for Survey Research, director, 2004-05. Writer. **Publications:** (With B.D. Bowen) Introduction to Survey Research and Data Analysis, 1977, 2nd ed., 1989; (with B.D. Bowen) Introduction to Data Analysis, 1980; (with H.B. Asher and B.M. Richardson) Political Participation: An ISSC Workbook in Comparative Analysis, 1984; Central Tendency and Variation (monograph), 1992; (with J. Krosnick and B. Bowen) Introduction to Survey Research, Polling and Data Analysis, 1996; Total Survey Error Approach: A Guide to the New Science of Survey Research, 2005; (co-author) The American Voter Revisited, 2008. EDITOR: (with R.G. Niemi) Probability Models of Collective Decision Making, 1972; (with R.G. Niemi) Controversies in Voting Behavior, 1976, 5th ed., 2010; Political Science: The Science of Politics, 1986; (with R.G. Niemi and D.C. Kimball) Classics in Voting Behavior, 1993; Democracy's Feast: Elections in America, 1995; (with S.C. Patterson) Great Theatre: The American Congress in the 1990s, 1998; (with E.S. Heberlig and L.M. Campoli) Classics in Congressional Politics, 1999; (with J.M. Box-Stefensmeier) Reelection 1996: How Americans Voted, 1999; (with C. Wilcox) Models of Voting in Presidential Elections: The 2000 U.S. Election, 2004.

Address: Department of Political Science, Ohio State University, 2140 Derby Hall, 154 N Oval Mall, Columbus, OH 43210-1373, U.S.A. **Online address:** weisberg.1@osu.edu

WEISBERG, Joseph. American (born United States), b. 1937. **Genres:** Earth Sciences, Education, Marine Sciences/Oceanography, Meteorology/Atmospheric Sciences, Novels, Medicine/Health. **Career:** Wayne Township Public Schools, teacher, 1960-64; New Jersey City University, Department of Geoscience and Geography, assistant professor, 1964-67, associate professor, 1967-72, chair, 1970-83, professor, 1972-83, School of Arts and Sciences, dean, 1983-93; councilman, 1988-94, mayor, 1994-2002; New Jersey State Alliance for Environmental Education, vice president, 1976-78; Alliance for Creative Education, director, 1996-; Parsippany Board of Education, vice president, 1980-; North Jersey Computer Academy, founder, director; U.S. Central Intelligence Agency, officer; Joseph S. Weisberg Associates, director; Lake Hiawatha Jewish Center, president. Writer. **Publications:** (With M.H. Friedman) Temporomandibular Joint Disorders: Diagnosis and Treatment, 1985; (ed. with B. Hecox and T.A. Mehreteab) Physical Agents: A Comprehensive Text for Physical Therapists, 1994; 10th Grade: A Novel, 2002; (with H. Shink) 3 Minutes to a Pain-Free Life: The Groundbreaking Program for Total Body Pain Prevention and Rapid Relief, 2005; Ordinary Spy: A Novel, 2008. Contributor to periodicals. **Address:** 4 Camelot Way, Parsippany, NJ 07054, U.S.A. **Online address:** contact@josephweisberg.com

WEISBERGER, Lauren. American (born United States), b. 1977. **Genres:** Novels, Women's Studies And Issues, Young Adult Fiction. **Career:** Vogue magazine, personal assistant, 2001; Departures magazine, staff writer, 2003. Writer. **Publications:** The Devil Wears Prada, 2003; Everyone Worth Knowing, 2005; People Or Not People, 2006; Chasing Harry Winston, 2008; Last Night at Chateau Marmont: A Novel, 2010. Contributions to periodicals. **Address:** c/o Author Mail, Simon & Schuster, 1230 Ave. of the Americas, New York, NY 10020, U.S.A. **Online address:** lauren@laurenweisberger.com

WEISBLAT, Tinky. (Tinky Dakota Weisblat). American (born United States) **Genres:** Food And Wine, Adult Non-fiction. **Career:** Paris en Films, assistant; singer and freelance journalist, 1991-; Museum of Television and Radio, senior editor of catalog, 2000-02. **Publications:** The Pudding Hollow Cookbook, 2004; Pulling Taffy, forthcoming; TV Diners, forthcoming; In Our Grandmothers' Kitchens, forthcoming. Contributor of articles to periodicals. **Address:** c/o Author Mail, Merry Lion Press, 84 Middle Rd., Hawley, MA 01339-9623, U.S.A. **Online address:** tinky@merrylion.com

WEISBLAT, Tinky Dakota. See **WEISBLAT, Tinky.**

WEISBROT, Robert (S.). American (born United States), b. 1951. **Genres:** History, Civil Liberties/Human Rights, Race Relations, Politics/Government. **Career:** Colby College, assistant professor of history, 1980-85, associate professor of history, 1985-90, professor of history, 1990-, Christian A. Johnson distinguished teaching professor of history, 1993-; Harvard University, Du-Bois Institute for Afro-American Studies, research associate, 1983-84. Writer. **Publications:** The Jews of Argentina: From the Inquisition to Peron, 1979; Father Divine and the Struggle for Racial Equality, 1983; Freedom Bound: A History of America's Civil Rights Movement, 1990; Marching toward Freedom, 1957-1965: From the Founding of the Southern Christian Leadership Conference to the Assassination of Malcolm X, 1994; Xena: Warrior Princess: The Official Guide to the Xenaverse, 1998; Hercules: The Legendary Journeys: The Official Companion, 1998; Maximum Danger: Kennedy, the Missiles, and the Crisis of American Confidence, 2001; (with G.C. Mackenzie) Liberal Hour: Washington and the Politics of Change in the1960s, 2008. **Address:** Department of History, Colby College, 5329 Mayflower Hill, Miller 252, Waterville, ME 04901, U.S.A. **Online address:** rsweisbr@colby.edu

WEISER, Philip J. American (born United States), b. 1968?. **Genres:** Technology, Communications/Media. **Career:** Tenth Circuit Court of Appeals, Judge David M. Ebel, law clerk, 1994-95; United States Supreme Court, Justices Byron R. White and Ruth Bader Ginsburg, law clerk, 1995-96; United States Department of Justice, Antitrust Division, senior counsel to the assistant attorney general, 1996-98, deputy assistant attorney general, 2009-10; Hillel Council of Colorado, board director, 1999-2001; University of Colorado School of Law, associate professor, 1999-2006, professor of law and interdisciplinary telecommunications program, 2006-, associate dean for research, 2007-, dean, 2011-; Silicon Flatirons Center for Law, Technology and Entrepreneurship, founder and executive director, 2000-; Princeton Law and

Public Affairs Program, visiting professor, fellow, 2001-02; Princeton University, Law and Public Affairs Program fellow, 2001-02; Colorado Public Utilities Commission, special master, 2001-02; Journal on Telecommunications and High Tech Law, founder, advisor, 2001-06; White House, senior advisor, 2010-11. Writer. **Publications:** (With J.E. Nuechterlein) Digital Crossroads: American Telecommunications Policy in the Internet Age, 2005; (with S.M. Benjamin, D.G. Lichtman and H.A. Shelanski) Telecommunications Law and Policy, 2nd ed., 2006; Clearing the Air: Convergence and the Safety Enterprise, 2006; The Future of Video: New Approaches to Communications Regulations, 2007; A Framework for National Broadband Policy, 2008; (co-author) Jury and Democracy, 2010. Contributor to journals. **Address:** University of Colorado Law School, 401 UCB, 404 Wolf Law Bldg., 2450 Kittredge Loop Rd., Boulder, CO 80309-0401, U.S.A. **Online address:** phil.weiser@colorado.edu

WEISGALL, Jonathan M. American (born United States), b. 1949. **Genres:** Military/Defense/Arms Control, History, Sciences, Young Adult Non-fiction. **Career:** Paul, Weiss, Rifkind, Wharton & Garrison, associate, 1972; United States Court of Appeals for the Ninth Circuit, law clerk, 1973-74; Covington and Burling, associate, 1975-79; Ginsburg, Feldman, Weil and Bress, associate, 1980-81, partner, 1982-83; Jonathan M. Weisgall Esq Inc., president and attorney, 1983-; Georgetown University, Law Center, adjunct professor of law; MidAmerican Energy Holdings Co., vice president of legislative and regulatory affairs. Writer. **Publications:** Operation Crossroads: The Atomic Tests at Bikini Atoll (nonfiction), 1994. Contributor to periodicals. **Address:** MidAmerican Energy Holdings Co., 1200 New Hampshire Ave. NW, Ste. 300, Washington, DC 20036, U.S.A. **Online address:** jweisgall@aol.com

WEISMAN, Brent Richards. American (born United States), b. 1952. **Genres:** Archaeology/Antiquities, Cultural/Ethnic Topics. **Career:** Florida Department of State, Division of Historical Resources, Bureau of Archaeological Research, archaeologist, director of Conservation and Recreation Lands Archaeological Survey, 1989-95; University of South Florida, Graduate School, Department of Anthropology, associate dean and professor, 2005-08, professor and department chair. **Publications:** Like Beads on a String: A Culture History of the Seminole Indians in North Peninsular Florida, 1989; Excavations on the Franciscan Frontier: Archaeology at the Fig Springs Mission, 1992; Crystal River: A Ceremonial Mound on the Florida Gulf Coast, 1995; Unconquered People: Florida's Seminole and Miccosukee Indians, 1999; Pioneer in Space and Time: John Mann Goggin and the Development of Florida Archaeology, 2002; (ed. with P.E. Kolianos) Lost Florida Manuscript of Frank Hamilton Cushing, 2005; (ed. with P.E. Kolianos) Florida Journals of Frank Hamilton Cushing, 2005. **Address:** Department of Anthropology, University of South Florida, SOC 104, 4202 E Fowler Ave., Tampa, FL 33620-7200, U.S.A. **Online address:** bweisman@cas.usf.edu

WEISMAN, Leslie Kanes. American (born United States), b. 1945. **Genres:** Architecture, Women's Studies And Issues. **Career:** University of Detroit, assistant professor, 1968-75; New Jersey Institute for Technology, associate professor of architecture, 1975-97, associate dean, 1984-85, professor of architecture, 1998-2004, professor emerita of architecture 2004-; Detroit City Planning Commission, consultant, 1969-75; Detroit Historical Society, consultant, 1969-75; Women's School of Planning and Architecture, co-founder, 1974-81; Networks, Women in Architecture (professional organization), co-founder, 1977-82; Brooklyn College, visiting professor of women's studies, 1980; Massachusetts Institute of Technology, visiting associate professor of architecture, planning and women's studies, 1986; Sheltering Ourselves (international educational forum on housing and economic development for low income women and their families), co-founder, 1987-; University of Illinois Urbana-Champaign, George A. Miller endowment professor, 1995-96. Writer. **Publications:** Discrimination by Design: A Feminist Critique of the Man-Made Environment, 1992; (ed. with D. Agrest and P. Conway) The Sex of Architecture, 1996. Contributor to books. **Address:** College of Architecture, Art and Design, New Jersey Institute of Technology, University Heights, Newark, NJ 07102-1982, U.S.A. **Online address:** weisman@njit.edu

WEISS, Andrea. American/British (born England), b. 1956?. **Genres:** Plays/Screenplays, Gay And Lesbian Issues, History, Women's Studies And Issues, Biography. **Career:** City College of New York, chair of media and communications arts, professor, 2003-; Jezebel Productions, owner, director; New York University, faculty; National Film and Television School of Great Britain, faculty. Writer and artist-in-residence. **Publications:** NONFICTION: Before Stonewall: The Making of a Gay and Lesbian Community, 1988; Vampires

and Violets: Lesbians in Film, 1993; Paris Was a Woman: Portraits from the Left Bank, 1995; Escape to Life, 2005; In the Shadow of the Magic Mountain: The Erika and Klaus Mann Story, 2008. OTHER: (with H. Winterer) Stalking und häusliche Gewalt, 2005. **Address:** Department of Media Arts Production, City College of New York, S-471 Shepard Hall, 138th St., Convent Ave., New York, NY 10013, U.S.A. **Online address:** andrea@jezebel.org

WEISS, Avraham. American (born United States), b. 1944?. **Genres:** Theology/Religion, Women's Studies And Issues. **Career:** Hebrew Institute of Riverdale, senior rabbi and director; Yeshivat Chovevei Torah, founder and dean. Writer and activist. **Publications:** Women at Prayer: A Halakhic Analysis of Women's Prayer Groups, 1990; Principles of Spiritual Activism, 2002; (contrib.) The Yeshivat Chovevei Torah Rabbinical School Tanakh Companion to the Book of Samuel: Bible Study in the Spirit of Open Orthodox Judaism, 2006; Spiritual Activism: A Jewish Guide to Leadership and Repairing the World, 2008. **Address:** Hebrew Institute of Riverdale, 3700 Henry Hudson Pkwy., Bronx, NY 10463, U.S.A. **Online address:** hirshuli@yahoo.com

WEISS, Brian L(eslie). (Michael L. Weiss). American (born United States), b. 1944. **Genres:** Medicine/Health, Psychology, Self Help. **Career:** Mount Sinai Hospital, chair of psychiatry, through 1990, now chairman emeritus of psychiatry; University of Miami Medical School, professor, through 1992, now chairman emeritus of psychiatry; Yale University Medical School, Department of Psychiatry, speaker on past-life regression therapy. Writer, psychiatrist and researcher. **Publications:** Many Lives, Many Masters, 1988; Through Time into Healing, 1992; Only Love is Real: A Story of Soulmates Reunited, 1996; Messages from the Masters: Tapping into the Power of Love, 2000; Mirrors of Time: Using Regression for Physical, Emotional and Spiritual Healing, 2002; Meditation: Achieving Inner Peace and Tranquility in Your Life, 2002; Eliminating Stress, Finding Inner Peace, 2003; Same Soul, Many Bodies: Discover the Healing Power of Future Lives Through Progression Therapy, 2004. Contributor of articles to journals. **Address:** Warner Books Inc., 1271 Ave. of the Americas, New York, NY 10020, U.S.A.

WEISS, Daniel Evan. American (born United States), b. 1953. **Genres:** Novels, Young Adult Fiction, Young Adult Non-fiction. **Career:** Writer. **Publications:** 100% American, 1988; Unnatural Selection, 1990 in US as The Roaches Have No King, 1994; The Great Divide: How Females and Males Really Differ, 1991; Hell on Wheels, 1991; The Swine's Wedding, 1996; Honk If You Love Aphrodite, 1999. Contributor to books. **Address:** Serpent's Tail, 3A Exmouth House, Pine St., London, GL EC1R 0JH, England. **Online address:** contact@pointedprose.com

WEISS, Michael L. See **WEISS, Brian L(eslie).**

WEISS, Raymond L. American (born United States), b. 1930. **Genres:** Ethics, Philosophy, Theology/Religion, Adult Non-fiction, Humanities. **Career:** University of Chicago, lecturer in liberal arts, 1963-65, Institute for the Advanced Study of Religion, research fellow, 1982; University of Wisconsin-Milwaukee, instructor, 1965-, professor of philosophy, now professor emeritus of philosophy. Writer. **Publications:** (Ed. with C.E. Butterworth) Ethical Writings of Maimonides, 1975; Maimonides' Ethics: The Encounter of Philosophic and Religious Morality, 1991. Works appear in anthologies. Contributor to periodicals. **Address:** Department of Philosophy, University of Wisconsin-Milwaukee, Curtin Hall, Ste. 612, 2200 E Kenwood Blvd., PO Box 413, Milwaukee, WI 53201-0413, U.S.A. **Online address:** weiss@uwm.edu

WEISS, Tamara. American (born United States) **Genres:** Food And Wine, Self Help, Regional/Urban Planning. **Career:** Midnight Farm, Marthas Vineyard, co-owner. Writer. **Publications:** Potluck at Midnight Farm: Celebrating Food Family Friends on Marthas Vineyard, 2002. Contributor to periodicals. **Address:** c/o Author Mail, Clarkson Potter, 1745 Broadway, New York, NY 10019, U.S.A.

WEISS, Thomas Fischer. American/Czech (born Czech Republic), b. 1934. **Genres:** Physics, Biology, Sciences. **Career:** Massachusetts Institute of Technology, research assistant in dynamic analysis and control laboratory, 1956-57, research assistant at research laboratory of electronics, 1957-63, consultant to Lincoln laboratory, 1961-65, assistant professor, 1963-68, associate professor, 1968-78, professor of electrical engineering and computer science, 1978-92, Thomas and Gerd Perkins professor of electrical and bioelectrical engineering, 1992-97, professor emeritus, 2000-; Douglas Aircraft

Co., engineer, 1957; Harvard University, research associate in preventive medicine, 1964-69, instructor, 1969-74, Harvard-MIT Division of Health Sciences and Technology, faculty, 1980-; Massachusetts Eye and Ear Infirmary, research associate in otolaryngology, 1964-. Writer. **Publications:** Cellular Biophysics, vol. I: Transport, vol. II: Electrical Properties, 1996; Solutions to Problems in Cellular Biophysics, vol. I: Transport, vol. II: Electrical Properties, 1997. Contributor to books and journals. **Address:** Massachusetts Institute of Technology, Rm. 36-881, 77 Massachusetts Ave., Cambridge, MA 02139-4307, U.S.A. **Online address:** tfweiss@mit.edu

WEISS, Thomas G. American (born United States), b. 1946. **Genres:** International Relations/Current Affairs, Politics/Government. **Career:** International Labor Organization, research associate, 1971; Institute for World Order, assistant director of university program, 1972-73; UN Institute for Training and Research, research associate, 1974-75; New School for Social Research, part-time instructor, 1974-84; UN Conference on Trade and Development, senior economic affairs officer, 1975-85; Office of the UN Commissioner for Namibia, senior aid coordinator, 1978; International Peace Academy, executive director, 1985-89; Brown University, Thomas J. Watson Jr. Institute for International Studies, associate director, 1990-98, associate dean of faculty for international faculty affairs, 1992-95; Academic Council on the UN System, executive director, 1992-98; City University of New York, Graduate Center, Ralph Bunche Institute for International Studies, presidential professor of political science, director, 1998-, UN Intellectual History Project, co-director, International Studies Association, chair, 2007-9, president, 2009-10; Global Governance, editor, 2000-05; International Commission on Intervention and State Sovereignty, director, 2000-02; Colgate University, visiting professor; Princeton University, visiting professor. Writer. **Publications:** International Bureaucracy, 1975; (with R.S. Jordan) The World Food Conference and Global Problem Solving, 1976; (with A. Jennings) More for the Least?, 1983; Multilateral Development Diplomacy in UNCTAD, 1986; (with A.R. Norton) UN Peacekeepers, 1990; Humanitarianism under Siege, 1991; (with L. Minear) Humanitarian Action in Times of War, 1993; (with L. Minear) Mercy under Fire, 1995; Humanitarian Conflict, 1995; (with L. Minear and C. Scott) The News Media, Civil War, and Humanitarian Action, 1996; (with C. Collins) Humanitarian Challenges and Intervention, 1996, (with C. Collins) 2nd ed., 2000; Military-Civilian Interactions, 1999, 2nd ed., 2004; (with L. Emmerij and R. Jolly) Ahead of the Curve?, 2001; The Responsibility to Protect, 2001; (with P. Aall and D.T. Miltenberger) Guide to IGOs, NGOs, and the Military in Peace and Relief Operations, 2001; (co-author) UN Voices, 2005; (with D.A. Korn) Internal Displacement, 2006; Sword & Salve, 2006; Humanitarian Intervention, 2007; What's Wrong with the United Nations and How to Fix It, 2009; (with R. Jolly and L. Emmerij) UN Ideas That Changed the World, 2009; (co-author) The United Nations and Changing World Politics, 6th edition, 2010; (with R. Thakur) Global Governance and the UN, 2010; (with M. Barnett) Humanitarianism Contested: Where Angels Fear to Tread, 2011; Thinking About Global Governance: Why People and Ideas Matter, 2011. EDITOR: (with A. Jennings) The Challenge of Development in the 80s, 1982; (with D. Pitt) The Nature of United Nations Bureaucracies, 1986; American, Soviet, and Third World Perceptions of Regional Conflicts, 1989; The United Nations in Conflict Management, 1990; Humanitarian Emergencies and Military Help in Africa, 1990; Peacekeepers, Soldiers, and Disasters, 1991; (with M.A. Kessler) Third World Security in the Post-Cold War Era, 1991; (with J.G. Blight) The Suffering Grass, 1992; Collective Security in a Changing World, 1993; (with L. Minear) Humanitarianism across Borders, 1993; The United Nations and Civil Wars, 1995; From Massacres to Genocide, 1996; (with L. Gordenker) NGOs, the UN, and Global Governance, 1996; (with J. Lepgold) Collective Conflict Management, 1998; (co-ed.) Political Gain and Civilian Policy, 1997; Beyond UN Subcontracting, 1998; (with J. Boulden) Terrorism and the UN, 2004; (with M.E. Crahana and J. Goering) Wars on Terrorism and Iraq, 2004; (with S. Daws) Oxford Handbook on the UN, 2007; (with M. Barnett) Humanitarianism in Question, 2008; The UN and Nuclear Orders, 2009. Contributor to professional journals and periodicals. **Address:** The Graduate Center, The City University of New York, 365 5th Ave., Ste. 5203, New York, NY 10016, U.S.A. **Online address:** tweiss@gc.cuny.edu

WEISS, Timothy F. Hong Kong/American (born United States), b. 1949. **Genres:** Literary Criticism And History. **Career:** University of Illinois, assistant professor of English, 1985-91; University of Maine, director of professional writing, 1991-, associate professor; The Chinese University of Hong Kong, Department of English, professor. Writer. **Publications:** Fairy Tale and Romance in the Works of Ford Madox Ford, 1984; On the Margins: The Art of Exile in V.S. Naipaul, 1992; Translating Orients: Between Ideology and Uto-

pia, 2004; (ed. with K. Tam) English and Globalization: Perspectives From Hong Kong and Mainland China, 2004. **Address:** Department of English, The Chinese University of Hong Kong, Fung King Hey 323, 3/F Fung King Hey Bldg., Shatin, 1, Hong Kong. **Online address:** tweiss@cuhk.edu.hk

WEISSBACH, Lee Shai. American/Israeli (born Israel), b. 1947. **Genres:** Novels, Social Work, History, Theology/Religion. **Career:** Boston College, lecturer, 1975-76; Harvard University, research associate, 1976-78; Regis College, lecturer, 1977-78; University of Louisville, Department of History, assistant professor, 1978-84, associate professor, 1984-90, professor of history, 1990-, chair, 1992-95, associate dean, 2000-03. Writer. **Publications:** Child Labor Reform in Nineteenth-Century France: Assuring the Future Harvest, 1989; The Synagogues of Kentucky: Architecture and History, 1995; Jewish Life in Small-Town America: A History, 2005. Contributor to books. **Address:** Department of History, University of Louisville, 103C Gottschalk Hall, Louisville, KY 40292, U.S.A. **Online address:** weissbach@louisville.edu

WEISSBORT, Daniel. American/British (born England), b. 1935. **Genres:** Poetry, Translations. **Career:** Albion Knitwea, director, 1957-61; Modern Poetry in Translation Magazine, editor, 1965-83; Poetry Intl., advisory director, 1970-73; Carcanet Press, director, 1972-80; University of Iowa, visiting professor of comparative literature, 1974-75, Translation Workshop, director, 1974, professor of English and comparative literature, 1980-, International Writing Program, acting director, 1986, chair of comparative literature, 1987, emeritus professor; University of Warwick, Centre for Translation and Comparative Cultural Studies, honorary professor; London University, King's College, Department of English, research fellow. **Publications:** (Trans.) P. Sorlin, The Soviet People and Their Society, 1969; (trans.) L.M. Vega, Guerillas in Latin America, 1969; (trans. and ed.) N. Zabolotsky, Scrolls: Selected Poems of Nikolai Zabolotsky, 1970; (trans.) A History of the Peoples' Democracies, 1971; (trans.) The Trial of the Four, 1971; The Leaseholder, 1971; (trans. and ed.) Natalya Gorbanevskaya, 1972; (trans.) The History of Holy Russia, 1972; (trans. and ed.) Nose! Nose? No-se! and Other Plays by Andrei Amalrik, 1972; In an Emergency, 1972; (ed.) Post-War Russian Poetry, 1974; (trans. with A. Rudolf) E. Vinokurov, The War is Over, 1976; Soundings, 1977; (ed.) From the Night and other Poems, 1978; (trans. and ed.) Russian Poetry: The Modern Period, 1978; (trans.) E. Evtushenko, Ivan the Terrible and Ivan the Fool, 1979; (trans.) P. Modiano, Missing Person, 1980; (trans.) The World About Us, by Claude Simon, 1983; Leaseholder: New and Collected Poems 1965-1985, 1986; (ed.) Translating Poetry: The Double Labyrinth, 1989; Fathers, 1991; (ed.) The Poetry of Survival: Post-War Poets of Central and Eastern Europe, 1992; (ed. with J. Glad) Twentieth-Century Russian Poetry, 1992; Inscription, 1993; Lake, New and Selected Poems, 1993; (ed. with A.K. Mehrotra) Periplus: Poetry in Translation, 1993; (ed. with G. Rathi) Survival, an Experience and an Experiment in Translating Modern Hindi Poetry, 1994; Theme & Version: Plath & Ronsard, 1995; What Was All the Fuss About?, 1998; Nikolay Zabolotsky Selected Poems, 1999; Letters to Ted, 2002; From Russian with Love: Joseph Brodsky in English, 2004; (ed. with V. Polukhina) Anthology of Contemporary Russian Women Poets, 2005; (ed.) Translation: Theory and Practice, 2006; (ed.) Selected Translations, 2007; Ted Hughes and Translation, 2011. **Address:** Department of Comparative Literature, University of Iowa, Iowa City, IA 52242, U.S.A.

WEISSBOURD, Richard. American (born United States), b. 1957?. **Genres:** Sociology, Human Relations/Parenting, Self Help, Psychology. **Career:** Harvard University, John F. Kennedy School of Government, lecturer on education, professor, Harvard Graduate School of Education, lecturer on education, professor; Lee Academy, founder. Writer. **Publications:** The Vulnerable Child: What Really Hurts America's Children and What We Can Do about it, 1996; The Parents We Mean To Be, How Well-intentioned Adults Undermine Children's Moral And Emotional Development, 2009. Contributor to periodicals. **Address:** c/o Taryn Roeder, Houghton Mifflin Harcourt Publicity, 222 Berkeley St., Boston, MA 02116, U.S.A. **Online address:** weissbri@gse.harvard.edu

WEISSKOPF, Thomas E. American (born United States), b. 1940. **Genres:** Economics, Politics/Government, Essays, History. **Career:** Indian Statistical Institute, research and teaching associate, 1961-62, visiting professor of economics, 1966-67; Massachusetts Institute of Technology, assistant research economist, 1963; American Institute of Indian Studies, junior fellow, 1964-65; United Nations Industrial Development Organization, consultant and workshop leader, 1966-68; Harvard University, assistant professor of economics, 1968-72, associate professor of economics, 1972-79; University of Michigan, professor of economics, 1979-2010, professor emeritus, 2010-, Residential College, director, 1996-2001, 2002-05. Writer. **Publications:** (Ed. with A. MacEwan) Perspectives on the Economic Problem: A Book of Readings in Political Economy, 1970, 2nd ed., 1973; (ed. with H. Chenery) Studies in Development Planning, 1971; (ed. with R. Edwards and M. Reich) The Capitalist System: A Radical Analysis of American Society, 1972, 3rd ed., 1986; (with D.M. Gordon and S. Bowles) Beyond the Waste Land: A Democratic Alternative to Economic Decline, 1983; (with D.M. Gordon and S. Bowles) After the Waste Land: A Democratic Economics for the Year 2000, 1991; (co-ed.) Economics and Social Justice: Essay on Power, Labor and Institutional Change, 1998; (with N. Goodwin, F. Ackerman and J.A. Nelson) Microeconomics in Context, 2003, 3rd ed., 2008; Affirmative Action in the United States and India: A Comparative Perspective, 2004. Contributor to journals. **Address:** Residential College, University of Michigan, East Quadrangle, 200 Greene, Ann Arbor, MI 48109-1245, U.S.A. **Online address:** tomw@umich.edu

WEISSMAN, Karen. American (born United States) **Genres:** Medicine/Health. **Career:** Writer, educator, consultant and research scientist. **Publications:** (With T. Coyne) The Spiritual Chicks Question Everything: Learn to Risk, Release, and Soar, 2002. **Address:** c/o Author Mail, Red Wheel/Weiser L.L.C., 65 Parker St., Ste. 7, Newburyport, MA 01950, U.S.A. **Online address:** info@spiritualchicks.com

WEISSTUB, David N(orman). Canadian (born Canada), b. 1944. **Genres:** Poetry, Law, Medicine/Health. **Career:** Yale University, lecturer, 1969-70, visiting Hoyt fellow, 1971; York University, Osgoode Hall Law School, assistant professor, professor of law, 1970-; University of Toronto, Department of Interdisciplinary Studies, lecturer, 1971-72, 1972-73, special lecturer; Gerstein Lecture Series, chairman, 1972; Oxford University, lecturer, 1973; Ontario Psychiatric Association, lecturer, 1974; Canadian Bar Association, lecturer, 1975; Harvard Law School, lecturer, 1975; Ontario College of Physicians and Surgeons, legal consultant, 1975; McMaster University Medical School, lecturer, 1976; Clarke Institute of Psychiatry, visiting associate professor of psychiatry, 1976-77, forensic consultant, 1976; Universite de Montreal, Philippe Pinel professor of legal psychiatry and biomedical ethics, 1993, Centre de Recherche, director, Department de Psychiatry, professor; Federal Government of Canada, special consultant; International Academy of Law and Mental Health, honorary life president; International Journal of Law and Psychiatry, editor-in-chief; International Library on Ethics Law and the New Medicine, editor-in-chief. **Publications:** Heaven, Take My Hand (poetry), 1968; (with C.C. Gotlieb) The Nature of Privacy, 1971; (ed. with L.V. Kaplan) Symposium, Dialectics in the Discourse of Law and Psychiatry, 1981; (with J.C. Smith) The Western Idea of Law, 1983; (with W. Winslade) Ethical Issues in Forensic Theory and Practice, 1990; Socio-Legal Studies of Obscenity, 1991; Le consentement et la recherche épidémiologique, 2001; Les populations vulnérables, 2001; Réflexions philosophiques et historiques, 2001; (with D.C. Thomasma and C. Hervé) Personhood and Health Care, 2001; La régulation de la recherche, 2001. EDITOR and CONTRIBUTOR: Law, Growth and Technology, 1972; Creativity and the University, 1973; Law and Policy, 1976; Law and Psychiatry, 3 vols., 1978-80; Law and Psychiatry in the Canadian Context, 1980; Law and Mental Health: International Perspectives, 1984; Law and Mental Health, 6 vols., 1985-91; (with C. Mitchell) Intoxication and Criminal Responsibility, 1990; Research on Human Subjects: Ethics, Law, and Social Policy, 1998; (co-ed.) Aging: Caring for Our Elders, 2001; (co-ed.) Aging: Culture, Health and Social Change, 2001; (co-ed.) Aging: Decisions at the End of Life, 2001; (with G.F. Tomossy) Human Experimentation and Research, 2003. Contributor to books and periodicals. **Address:** Universite de Montreal, Chaire de Psychiatrie Legal, Faculte de Medecine, CP 6128, Succ Centre-Ville, Montreal, QC H3C 3J7, Canada. **Online address:** david.norman.weisstub@umontreal.ca

WEITEKAMP, Margaret A. American (born United States), b. 1971?. **Genres:** Women's Studies And Issues. **Career:** Mellon fellow in the humanities, 1993-94; American Historical Association/NASA, aerospace history, fellow, 1997-98; Hobart and William Smith Colleges, assistant professor of women's studies, 2001-04; Smithsonian Institution National Air & Science Museum, curator, 2004. Writer. **Publications:** Right Stuff, Wrong Sex: America's First Women in Space Program, 2004. **Address:** Smithsonian Institution, National Air & Space Museum, Division of Space History, PO Box 37012, Washington, DC 20013-7012, U.S.A. **Online address:** weitekampm@si.edu

WEITZ, Eric D. American (born United States), b. 1953. **Genres:** Business/Trade/Industry, Economics, History. **Career:** University of Minnesota, faculty, College of Liberal Arts, Arsham and Charlotte Ohanessian chair, 2001-, Department of History, chair, 2006-09. Writer. **Publications:** Creating German Communism, 1890-1990: From Popular Protests to Socialist State, 1997; A Century of Genocide: Utopias of Race and Nation, 2003; Weimar Germany: Promise and Tragedy, 2007. EDITOR: (with N.N. Kozlov) Nikolai Ivanovich Bukharin: A Centenary Appraisal, 1990; (with D.E. Barclay) Between Reform and Revolution: German Socialism and Communism from 1840 to 1990, 1998; (with A. Fenner) Fascism and Neofascism: Critical Writings on the Radical Right in Europe, 2004. Contributor to books and periodicals. **Address:** Department of History, University of Minnesota, 1110 Heller Hall, 271 19th Ave. S, Minneapolis, MN 55455, U.S.A. **Online address:** weitz004@umn.edu

WEITZMAN, Susan. American (born United States), b. 1958?. **Genres:** Psychology, Criminology/True Crime. **Career:** University of Chicago, Department of Adult Outpatient Psychiatry, staff member, Graham School for Continuing Studies, teacher, School of Social Service Administration, Professional Development Program, lecturer; Loyola University, School of Social Work, lecturer; Weitzman Center, founder and president. Psychotherapist and writer. **Publications:** Not to People Like Us: Hidden Abuse in Upscale Marriages, 2000. Contributor to periodicals. **Address:** Weitzman Center, 203 N Wabash Ave., Ste. 2000, Chicago, IL 60601, U.S.A.

WEK, Alek. American (born United States), b. 1977. **Genres:** Autobiography/Memoirs, Photography. **Career:** Ford Models, model, 1996; IMG Models, model, 1997-; Alek Wek 1933 Ltd., founder, 2001-; Working to Educate Kids, founder, 2006-; Refugees Advisory Council, activist. Writer. **Publications:** Alek: From Sudanese Refugee to International Supermodel, 2007. Contributor to periodicals. **Address:** IMG Models, 304 Park Ave. S, New York, NY 10010, U.S.A.

WEKESSER, Carol A. American (born United States), b. 1963. **Genres:** Adult Non-fiction, Social Commentary, Ethics, Young Adult Non-fiction. **Career:** Curriculum Concepts, book editor, 1988-90; Greenhaven Press, senior editor, 1990-93; freelance writer and editor, 1993-; school psychologist, 2000-. **Publications:** Reproductive Technologies, 1996. EDITOR: Social Justice: Opposing Viewpoints, 1990; Central America: Opposing Viewpoints, 1990; America's Children, 1991; The Death Penalty: Opposing Viewpoints, 1991; (with M. Polesetsky) Women in the Military, 1991; America's Defense, 1991; Africa: Opposite View Point, 1992; (with M. Biskup) Suicide, 1992; (with K.L. Swisher and C. Pierce) Sexual Harassment, 1992; (with S.L. Tipp) Politics in America, 1992; American Foreign Policy, 1993; Alcoholism, 1994; Health Care in America, 1994; Water, 1994; (with W. Barbour) Breakup of the Soviet Union, 1994; (with K.L. Swisher and W. Barbour) Violence Against Women, 1994; Feminism, 1995; Ethics, 1995; Euthanasia, 1995; Violence in the Media, 1995; Reproductive Technologies, 1996; Genetic Engineering, 1996; Smoking, 1997; Pornography, 1997; Chemical Dependency: Opposing Viewpoints, 1997; Child Welfare: Opposing Viewpoints, 1998. **Address:** 4606 53rd Terr., Roeland Park, KS 66205, U.S.A.

WELCH, Amy. American (born United States) **Genres:** Criminology/True Crime, Social Sciences. **Career:** Ohio University, Institute for Local Government Administration and Rural Development, staff; Health Recovery Services, performance and quality improvement associate, 2000-02; Institute for Local Government Administration and Rural Development, public service associate, 2000-02; University of Tennessee, Law Enforcement Innovation Center, program specialist, 2002-07; Lone Star College System, manager of grant compliance, 2008-10, Government Affairs and Institutional Advancement, director of completion by design, 2010-. Writer. **Publications:** (With J. Hallcox) Bodies We've Buried: Inside the National Forensic Academy, The World's Top CSI Training School, 2006; (with J. Hallcox) Behind the Yellow Tape: On the Road with Some of America's Hardest Working Crime Scene Investigators, 2009. **Address:** Lone Star College System, 5000 Research Forest Dr., The Woodlands, TX 77381-4356, U.S.A. **Online address:** amy.m.welch@lonestar.edu

WELCH, David A. Canadian (born Canada), b. 1960. **Genres:** History. **Career:** University of Toronto, assistant professor, 1990-94, associate professor of political science, 1994-2002; University of Toronto, associate professor, 2002-05, George Ignatieff chair of peace and conflict studies, 2002-07, professor of political science, 2005-09; Rockefeller Research and Study Center, resident fellow, 2005; National Defense Academy, visiting professor, 2007; University of Otago, William Evans fellow, 2007; Balsillie School of International Affairs, CIGI chair of global security, 2009-, interim director; University of Waterloo, professor of political science, 2009-. Writer. **Publications:** (With J.G. Blight) On the Brink: Americans and Soviets Reexamine the Cuban Missile Crisis, 1989, 2nd ed., 1990; (ed. with J.G. Blight and D. Lewis) Cuba Between the Superpowers: The Antigua Conference on the Cuban Missile Crisis, Center for Foreign Policy Development, 1992; Justice and the Genesis of War, 1993; (with J.G. Blight and B.J. Allyn) Cuba on the Brink: Castro, the Missile Crisis, and the Soviet Collapse, 1993, rev. ed., 2002; (ed. with J.G. Blight) Intelligence and the Cuban Missile Crisis, 1998; Decisions, Decisions: The Art of Effective Decision Making, 2002; Painful Choices: A Theory of Foreign Policy Change, 2005; (with D. Munton) The Cuban Missile Crisis: A Concise History, 2007, 2nd ed., 2011; (with J.G. Blight and J.M. Lang) Vietnam if Kennedy Had Lived: Virtual JFK, 2009; (ed. with Y. Soeya and M. Tadokoro) Japan as a 'Normal Country'?: A Nation in Search of Its Place in the World, 2011; (with J.S. Nye, Jr.) Understanding Global Conflict and Cooperation: An Introduction to Theory and History, 9th ed., 2013. CONTRIBUTOR: Canada, the United States, and New Challenges to Security, 1992; Canada Among Nations, 1992-1993: A New World Order?, 1992; The Essence of Japan's National Security, 1996; Decision-Making on War and Peace: The Cognitive-Rational Debate, 1997; The Oxford Companion to American Military History, 1999; The Oxford Companion to Politics of the World, 2nd ed., 2001; Ethics in International Affairs: Theory and Cases, 2006. Contributor to periodicals. **Address:** Balsillie School of International Affairs, 67 Erb St., W, Waterloo, ON N2L 6C2, Canada. **Online address:** david@davidwelch.ca

WELCH, D. Don. (Don Welch). American (born United States), b. 1947?. **Genres:** Social Work, Law, Social Sciences. **Career:** Nashville Tennessean, reporter, 1971-74; Meharry Medical College Community Mental Health Center, director of west nashville youth service, 1975-76; Nashville University Center, assistant director, 1976-77; Vanderbilt University, assistant dean for academic services, 1977-80, associate dean, 1980-84, Law School, lecturer, 1984-90, assistant dean of law school, 1984-85, associate dean of administration, 1985-, senior lecturer, 1990-93, associate professor of law and ethics and public policy, 1993-98, professor of law, 1998-, professor of religion, Center for the Study of Religion and Culture, fellow, 2007-09. Writer. **Publications:** (As Don Welch) Macho Isn't Enough!: Family Man in a Liberated World, 1985; (ed. and intro.) Law and Morality, 1987; Conflicting Agendas: Personal Morality in Institutional Settings, 1994; Vanderbilt Law School: Aspirations and Realities, 2008. Contributor of articles to journals, periodicals and magazines. **Address:** Vanderbilt Law School, Vanderbilt University, Rm. 152E, 131 21st Ave. S, Nashville, TN 37240, U.S.A. **Online address:** don.welch@vanderbilt.edu

WELCH, Don. *See* **WELCH, D. Don.**

WELCH, Evelyn S. British (born England), b. 1959?. **Genres:** Art/Art History. **Career:** University of Sussex, pro-vice chancellor, through 2004; University of London, Department of English, professor of renaissance studies and academic dean for arts, 2004-, Research and International Affairs, vice principal. Art historian and writer. **Publications:** Art and Authority in Renaissance Milan, 1995; Art and Society in Italy, 1350-1500, 1997; Shopping in the Renaissance: Consumer Cultures in Italy, 1400-1600, 2005; (with M. O'Malley) The Material Renaissance, 2007; (with J. Shaw) Making and Marketing Medicine in Renaissance Florence, 2011. **Address:** School of English and Drama, University of London, Mile End Rd., London, GL E1 4NS, England. **Online address:** e.welch@qmul.ac.uk

WELCH, Kathleen E(thel). American (born United States), b. 1951. **Genres:** Classics, Communications/Media, Cultural/Ethnic Topics, Humanities. **Career:** University of Iowa, International Writing Program, research assistant, 1975-77, Department of English, instructor, 1977-82; University of Oklahoma, assistant professor, 1982-88, associates distinguished lecturer, 1985, associate professor of English, 1988-94, senior faculty research fellow, 1990, professor of English, 1994-, Samuel Roberts Noble Family Foundation presidential professor of English, 2001-; Coalition of Women Scholars in the History of Rhetoric and Composition, founding president, 1990-95; Association of Teachers of Advanced Composition, president, 1989-91; University of Colorado, associate professor, 1991, visiting professor; Rhetoric Society of America, president, 1995-97; Ohio State University, lecturer, distinguished visiting professor; Old Dominion University, lecturer; School of the Art

Institute of Chicago, lecturer; Texas Christian University, lecturer, visiting professor; University of Wisconsin, lecturer; University of Texas, lecturer; University of Utah, visiting professor. Writer. **Publications:** The Contemporary Reception of Classical Rhetoric: Appropriations of Ancient Discourse, 1990; Electric Rhetoric: Classical Rhetoric, Oralism, and A New Literacy, 1999. Contributor to periodicals and journals. Works appear in anthologies. **Address:** Department of English, University of Oklahoma, 760 Van Vleet Oval, Gittinger Hall, Norman, OK 73019-2055, U.S.A. **Online address:** kwelch@ou.edu

WELCH, Richard F. American (born United States), b. 1945. **Genres:** Social Sciences, History, Business/Trade/Industry. **Career:** Glen Cove High School, history teacher, 1972-2001; Long Island University, C.W. Post Campus, adjunct professor of history, 1982-; State University of New York, adjunct professor, 2008-. Writer. **Publications:** Memento Mori: The Gravestones of Early Long Island, 1680-1810, 1983; An Island's Trade: Nineteenth-Century Shipbuilding on Long Island, 1993; (ed. with R.B. MacKay) Long Island: An Illustrated History, 2000; The Boy General: The Life and Careers of Francis Channing Barlow, 2003; (contrib.) The Encyclopedia of New York State, 2004; King of the Bowery: Big Tim Sullivan, Tammany Hall, and New York City from the Gilded Age to the Progressive Era, 2008. Contributor to journals. **Address:** Fairleigh Dickinson University Press, 285 Madison Ave., Madison, NJ 07940, U.S.A. **Online address:** rfw67@yahoo.com

WELCH, Robert. Irish (born Ireland), b. 1947. **Genres:** Novels, Poetry, Literary Criticism And History, Young Adult Fiction, Novellas/Short Stories. **Career:** University of Leeds, lecturer, 1971-73, 1974-84; University of Ife, lecturer, 1973-74; National University of Ireland, visiting lecturer, 1982; University of Ulster, Department of English, professor, 1984-, Media and Theatre Studies, head, 1984-94, Centre for Irish Literature and Bibliography, director, 1994-2000, Faculty of Arts, dean, 2000-, now professor emeritus; Saint John's College, Oxford, visiting fellow, 1989; O'Casey Theatre School, director, 1994-96; University of Missouri, Jefferson-Smurfitt visiting lecturer. Writer. **Publications:** Irish Poetry from Moore to Yeats, 1980; A History of Verse Translation from the Irish, 1789-1897, 1988; Changing States: Transformations in Modern Irish Writing, 1993; Irish Myths, 1996; A History of the Abbey Theatre, 1999; Structure of Process: John Montague's Poetry, 1999; (trans.) Forty Four, 2005; Protestants: A Play in Seven Scenes, 2006; Evergreen Road, 2006; Constanza, 2009. POETRY: Muskerry, 1991; Secret Societies, 1997; The Blue Formica Table, 1998. NOVELS: The Kilcolman Notebook, 1994; Groundwork, 1997; Tearmann (in Irish), 1997; The Kings Are Out, 2004. EDITOR: (and contrib.) The Way Back: George Moore's The Untilled Field and The Lake, 1982; (with S.B. Bushrui) Literature and the Art of Creation: Essays in Honour of A.N. Jeffares, 1988; (intro.) Irish Writers and Religion, 1992; (intro.) Writings on Irish Folklore, Legend and Myth, 1993; The Oxford Companion to Irish Literature, 1996; (with G. Delanty) Patrick Galvin: New and Selected Poems, 1996; Concise Oxford Companion to Irish Literature, 2000. Contributor to periodicals. **Address:** School of Languages and Literature, University of Ulster, Cromore Rd., Coleraine, BT52 1SA, Northern Ireland. **Online address:** ra.welch@ulster.ac.uk

WELCH, Sheila Kelly. American (born United States), b. 1945. **Genres:** Children's Fiction, Children's Non-fiction. **Career:** Special education teacher, 1967-73; writer and illustrator, 1983-; Highland Community College, children's literature telecourse instructor, 1993-. **Publications:** A Horse for All Seasons, 1995; Horses of the Air, 1996; A Horse for All Seasons, 1997. SELF-ILLUSTRATED: Don't Call Me Marda, 1990; Land of Another Sun, 1995; Little Prince Know-It-All, 1998; Lazy Bones Jones, 1999; The Shadowed Unicorn, 2000; Leaping Lena, 2000. Contributor of short stories to magazines. **Address:** c/o Author Mail, Scott Foresman, 1900 E Lake Ave., Glenview, IL 60025, U.S.A. **Online address:** sheilawelch@juno.com

WELCHER, Rosalind. American (born United States), b. 1922. **Genres:** Children's Fiction, Poetry, Cartoons, Humor/Satire, Young Adult Fiction, Literary Criticism And History. **Career:** Joan and Ginger's Magazine, art director, 1944-45; Panda Prints Inc., co-founder, 1946, art director, editor and principal, 1946-77; Fisher Hill Studios, partner and art director, 1977-. **Publications:** (With S.R. Diamond) Where Is Christmas?, 1944; The Runaway Angel: Or, A Dream All Your Own, 1963; The Split-Level Child, 1963. SELF-ILLUSTRATED: The Magic Top, 1965; It's Wonderful to Be in Love, 1966; Somebody's Thinking of You, 1966; I Wish You a Merry Christmas, 1967; It Must Be Hard to Be a Mother, 1967; Do You Ever Feel Lonely, 1967;

Please Don't Feel Blue, 1967; Thank You for So Many Things, 1967; There Is Nothing Like a Cat, 1967; Squeeking by, 1968; Moonlight, Cobwebs and Shadows, 1969; Do You Believe in Magic, 1970; Wouldn't You Like to Run Away, 1970; When You're Away, 1970; The Wonderful Season, 1970; Maybe the Sky Is Falling, 1970; This Could Be Such a Beautiful World, 1970; I Want to Be Somebody's Cat, 1986; My Brother Says There's a Monster Living in Our Toilet, 1987; Dear Tabby: (or Letters from the Purr-plexed), 1989; Social Insecurities, 1989; When Nino Flew, 1996. Illustrator of books by T. Kitt. **Address:** W. Hill Press Inc., 572 Rhododendron Rd., Fitzwilliam, NH 03447, U.S.A. **Online address:** rws@monad.net

WELCH-TYSON, Delorys. American (born United States) **Genres:** Novels, Social Sciences. **Career:** Writer. **Publications:** Gingersnaps, 1998; Ladyfingers, 2005; Almond Cookie, forthcoming. **Address:** c/o Author Mail, Random House, 1745 Broadway, New York, NY 10019, U.S.A. **Online address:** welchtysondelorys@yahoo.com

WELDON, Fay. British (born England), b. 1931. **Genres:** Novels, Novellas/Short Stories, Children's Fiction, Plays/Screenplays, Young Adult Non-fiction, Children's Non-fiction, Autobiography/Memoirs, inspirational/Motivational Literature, inspirational/Motivational Literature. **Career:** The Savoy Hotel, writer-in-residence, 2002; Brunel University, Department of English, chair of creative writing and professor of creative writing, 2006-; British Foreign Office, propaganda writer; The Daily Mirror, market researcher. **Publications:** The Fat Woman's Joke, 1967 in US as ... and the Wife Ran Away, 1968; (co-author) Mixed Doubles, 1970; Down among the Women, 1972; Female Friends: A Novel, 1974; Words of Advice, 1974 as Little Sisters, 1978; Remember Me, 1976; Praxis: A Novel, 1978; (ed. with E. Feinstein) New Stories 4: An Arts Council Anthology, 1979; Puffball, 1979; Action Replay, 1980; Watching Me Watching You (stories), 1981; The President's Child, 1982; I Love My Love, 1984; Life and Loves of a She Devil, 1984; Letters to Alice: On First Reading Jane Austen, 1984; Polaris and Other Stories, 1985; Rebecca West, 1985; The Shrapnel Academy, 1986; The Hearts and Lives of Men, 1987; The Rules of Life, 1987; The Heart of the Country, 1988; Leader of the Band, 1988; Wolf the Mechanical Dog (for children), 1988; Party Puddle (for children), 1989; The Cloning of Joanna May, 1990; Darcy's Utopia, 1991; Moon over Minneapolis, or, Why She Couldn't Stay (stories), 1991; Growing Rich, 1992; So Very English, 1992; Life Force, 1992; Affliction in US as Trouble, 1993; Splitting, 1994; (with D. Bailey) The Lady is a Tramp, 1995; Worst Fears, 1996; Wicked Women (stories), 1997; Big Women in US as Big Girls Don't Cry, 1997; Nobody Likes Me (for children), 1997; Hard Time to Be a Father, 1998; Growing Rich, 1998; The Reading Group: A Play, 1999; Godless in Eden (essays), 1999; Rhode Island Blues, 2000; The Bulgari Connection (novel), 2001; Nothing to Wear and Nowhere to Hide, 2002; Auto da Fay (memoir), 2002; (adapter) Madame Bovary: Breakfast with Emma, 2003; Flood Warning, 2003; Mantrapped, 2004; She May Not Leave, 2005; What Makes Women Happy, 2006; The Spa Decameron, 2007; (co-author) Poolside, 2007; The Stepmother's Diary, 2008; (co-author) Great Escapes, 2008; The Spa, 2009; Chalcot Crescent, 2009; Kehua!, 2010; Habits of the House, 2012. **Address:** Capel & Land Ltd., 29 Wardour St., London, GL W1D 6PS, England. **Online address:** fay.weldon@brunel.ac.uk

WELDON, Phaedra M. American (born United States) **Genres:** Novels, Mystery/Crime/Suspense, Art/Art History. **Career:** Graphic artist and Writer. **Publications:** (Contrib.) Out of the Cocoon, 2005; Wraith: A Zoë Martinique Novel, 2007; Spectre: A Zoë Martinique Investigation, 2008; Phantasm: A Zoë Martinique Investigation, 2009; Revenant: A Zoë Martinique Investigation, 2010. Works appear in anthologies. Contributor to periodicals. **Address:** Writers House, 21 W 26th St., New York, NY 10010, U.S.A. **Online address:** zam007@comcast.net

WELDT-BASSON, Helene Carol. American (born United States), b. 1958. **Genres:** Literary Criticism And History, Young Adult Fiction, History. **Career:** Columbia University, visiting assistant professor, 1988-90; Fordham University, assistant professor, 1990-, associate professor of Spanish. Writer. **Publications:** Augusto Roa Bastos's I the Supreme: A Dialogic Perspective, 1993; Subversive Silences: Nonverbal Expression and Implicit Narrative Strategies in the Works of Latin American Women Writers, 2009; (ed.) Postmodernism's Role in Latin American Literature: The Life and Work of Augusto Roa Bastos, 2010. Contributor to Hispanic studies journals. **Address:** Fordham University, Rose Hill Campus, Bronx, NY 10458, U.S.A.

WELFORD, Sue. New Zealander/British (born England), b. 1942. **Genres:** Mystery/Crime/Suspense, Children's Fiction, Young Adult Fiction, Literary Criticism And History. **Career:** Writer. **Publications:** NOVELS: Catch the Moon, 1989; Secrets, 1990; Ghost in the Mirror, 1993; (as Fiona Kelly) Mischief at Midnight, 1993; Snowbird Winter, 1994; Monkey Business, 1994; The Other Guest, 1994; The Night After Tomorrow, 1995; The Shadow of August, 1996; Siren Song, 1996; Secret Love, 1996; Dreamstalker, 1997; Starlight City, 1998; You've Got to Have the Heart, 1998; Nowhere to Run, 1999; Out of the Blue, 2001; Turning Point, 2002; Whispers on the Wind, 2002; Waiting for Mermaids, 2002. CHARLIE SCROGGINS SERIES: Charlie in the Pink, 1992; Charlie on the Spot, 1995. ST. JO'S HOSPITAL: Dangerous Obsession, 1997; Desperate Measures, 1997; Harmful Internet, 1997; High Hopes, 1997; Lucky Escape, 1997; Harmful Intent, 1997; Shattered Dreams, 1997. NON FICTION: Devoted Dogs, 1999; Heroic Horses, 1999. OTHER: The Young Oxford Book of Aliens, 1998. JUST GEORGE: George, Timmy and the Haunted Cave, 2000; George, Timmy and the Curious Treasure, 2000; George, Timmy and the Footprint in the Sand, 2000; George, Timmy and the Secret in the Cellar, 2000; George, Timmy and the Stranger in the Storm, 2000; George, Timmy and the Lighthouse Mystery, 2000. Contributor to periodicals. **Address:** c/o Lesley Hadcroft, Laurence Pollinger Ltd., 18 Maddox St., Mayfair, GL W1R 0EU, England.

WELISH, Marjorie. American (born United States), b. 1944. **Genres:** Poetry, Art/Art History, Literary Criticism And History. **Career:** Cambridge University, Judith E. Wilson visiting poetry fellow, 2005; Pratt Institute, faculty; Pratt Institute, faculty, adjunct professor. Poet. **Publications:** POETRY: Handwritten, 1979; The Windows Flew Open, 1991; Casting Sequence, 1993; The Annotated Here and Selected Poems, 2000; Word Group: Poems, 2004. ART CRITICISM: George Wardlaw: Exodus II, 1992; Donald Lipski, 1992; Thomas Nozkowski: David Reed, 1992. OTHERS: Signifying Art: Essays On Art After 1960, 1999; (with B. Spector) The Napkin and its Double, 2007; Isle of the Signatories, 2008. OTHER: (contrib.) Of the Diagram, 2003. Contributor of articles to periodicals. **Address:** Pratt Institute, 200 Willoughby Ave., Brooklyn, NY 11205, U.S.A.

WELIVER, Phyllis. (Phyllis Rebecca Weliver). American (born United States), b. 1968. **Genres:** Music, Women's Studies And Issues. **Career:** Wilkes University, assistant professor of English; St. Louis University, assistant professor of English. Writer. **Publications:** Women Musicians in Victorian Fiction, 1860-1900: Representations of Music, Science, and Gender in the Leisured Home, 2000; (ed.) The Figure of Music in Nineteenth-Century British Poetry, 2005; The Musical Crowd in English Fiction: Class, Culture, and Nation, 2006. Contributor to periodicals. **Address:** Department of English, St. Louis University, 127 Humanities Bldg., 3800 Lindell Blvd., St. Louis, MO 63108-3414, U.S.A. **Online address:** pweliver@slu.edu

WELIVER, Phyllis Rebecca. See **WELIVER, Phyllis.**

WELLAND, Michael. British (born England), b. 1946. **Genres:** Sciences, Natural History. **Career:** Writer and geologist. **Publications:** Sand: The Never-Ending Story, 2009. **Address:** England. **Online address:** mw@throughthesandglass.com

WELLAND, Sasha Su-Ling. American (born United States), b. 1969?. **Genres:** Biography, History, Women's Studies And Issues. **Career:** University of Washington, Department of Anthropology, assistant professor, 2006-, Department of Gender, Women and Sexuality Studies, assistant professor, 2006-. Writer. **Publications:** A Thousand Miles of Dreams: The Journeys of Two Chinese Sisters, 2006. Contributor of articles to journals. **Address:** Department of Gender, Women and Sexuality Studies, University of Washington, B-110 Padelford Hall, PO Box 354345, Seattle, WA 98195-4345, U.S.A. **Online address:** swelland@u.washington.edu

WELLER, Vann K. American (born United States) **Genres:** Novels. **Career:** Modular Sound (audio services firm), manager and operator, 1977-87; First Word Productions, founder and owner. Writer. **Publications:** NOVELS: Urge2merge, 1995; The Thirteenth Book, 2000. **Address:** First Word Productions, 574 Rte. 206, Trenton, NJ 08610-4332, U.S.A. **Online address:** vkw@ix.netcom.com

WELLFORD, Lin(da). American (born United States), b. 1951. **Genres:** Children's Non-fiction, Crafts, How-to Books, Art/Art History, Humor/Satire. **Career:** Green Forest Band Boosters, vice president. Writer. **Publications:**

The Art of Painting Animals on Rocks, 1994; Painting Houses, Cottages, and Towns on Rocks, 1996; Painting More Animals on Rocks, 1998; Painting Flowers on Rocks, 1999; Painting Pets on Rocks, 2000; Painting on Rocks, 2001; Painting on Rocks for Kids, 2002; Painting Zoo Animals on Rocks, 2004; Rock Painting Fun for Everyone!, 2006; Lin Wellford's Painted Garden Art Anyone Can Do, 2007; The New Grandparents Name Book, 2009. **Address:** Stone Managerie, 9328 Hwy. 62 E, Green Forest, AR 72638, U.S.A. **Online address:** linwell@cswnet.com

WELLINGTON, Jean Susorney. American (born United States), b. 1945. **Genres:** Classics, Art/Art History, History, Humanities, Theology/Religion, Archaeology/Antiquities. **Career:** University of Cincinnati, Classics Library, head, 1970-2003. Writer. **Publications:** Dictionary of Bibliographic Abbreviations Found in the Scholarship of Classical Studies and Related Disciplines, 1983, rev. ed., 2003. **Address:** 24 Rolling Hills Dr., Cincinnati, OH 45215, U.S.A. **Online address:** jean.wellington@uc.edu

WELLINGTON, Monica. American/British (born England), b. 1957. **Genres:** Children's Fiction, Children's Non-fiction, Illustrations, Picture/ Board Books, Education, Reference. **Career:** School of Visual Arts, teacher, 1994-. Writer. **Publications:** SELF-ILLUSTRATED: Molly Chelsea and Her Calico Cat, 1988; All My Little Ducklings, 1989; In Between, 1989; Seasons of Swans, 1990; The Sheep Follow, 1992; Mr. Cookie Baker, 1992, rev. ed., 2006; Night Rabbits, 1995; Baby in a Buggy, 1995; Baby in a Car, 1995; Baby Goes Shopping, 1997; Baby at Home, 1997; Night House, Bright House, 1997; Night City, 1998; Bunny's Rainbow Day, 1999; Squeaking of Art: The Mice go to the Museum, 1999; Bunny's First Snowflake, 2000; Apple Farmer Annie, 2001; Firefighter Frank, 2002; Crepes by Suzette, 2004; Ana Cultiva Manzanas: Apple Farmer Annie, 2004; Zinnia's Flower Garden, 2005; Pizza at Sally's, 2006; Truck Driver Tom, 2007; Riki's Birdhouse, 2009; Gabby and Grandma Go Green, 2010. **Address:** Dutton Children's Books, 345 Hudson St., New York, NY 10014, U.S.A. **Online address:** monicaaw@earthlink.net

WELLINGTON, Sheila W(acks). American (born United States), b. 1932. **Genres:** Women's Studies And Issues, Administration/Management, Business/Trade/Industry, Adult Non-fiction. **Career:** Yale University, School of Medicine, lecturer in psychiatry, 1974-93, vice president and secretary, 1987-93; Hill-West Haven, Connecticut Mental Health Center, director, 1977-80; Greater Bridgeport Community Mental Health Center, director, 1980-86; Catalyst, president, 1993-2003; New York University, Leonard N. Stern School of Business, Department of Management and Organizations, clinical professor, 2003-, executive-in-residence. Writer. **Publications:** Women on Boards: Challenge of Change, 1993; (foreword) Advancing Women in Business-The Catalyst Guide: Best Practices from the Corporate Leaders, 1998; (foreword) Creating Women's Networks: A How-to Guide for Women and Companies, 1998; (with B. Spence) Be Your Own Mentor: Strategies from Top Women on the Secrets of Success, 2001. **Address:** Leonard N. Stern School of Business, New York University, Rm. 709, Tisch Hall, 40 W 4th St., New York, NY 10012, U.S.A. **Online address:** swelling@stern.nyu.edu

WELLMAN, Carl Pierce. American (born United States), b. 1926. **Genres:** Civil Liberties/Human Rights, Philosophy. **Career:** Lawrence University, instructor, 1953-57, assistant professor, 1957-62, associate professor, 1962-66, professor and chairman of philosophy, 1966-68; Washington University, professor of philosophy, 1968-, Hortense and Tobias Lewin distinguished professor in humanities, 1988-, professor emeritus of philosophy. Writer. **Publications:** The Language of Ethics, 1961; Challenge and Response: Justification in Ethics, 1971; Morals and Ethics, 1975; (ed.) Equality and Freedom, Past, Present and Future: IVR-IX, 1977; Welfare Rights, 1982; Theory of Rights: Persons Under Laws, Institutions and Morals, 1985; (with P. Sack and M. Yasaki) Monismus oder Pluralismus der Rechtskulturen?: Anthropologische and Ethnologische Grundlagen Traditioneller und Moderner Rechtssysteme, 1991; Real Rights, 1995; Approach to Rights: Studies in the Philosophy of Law and Morals, 1997; Proliferation of Rights: Moral Progress or Empty Rhetoric?, 1999; (with M. Friedman) Rights and Reason: Essays in Honor of Carl Wellman, 2000; (ed. and intro.) Rights and duties, 2002; Medical Law and Moral Rights, 2005; Moral Dimensions of Human Rights, 2011. Contributor to journals. **Address:** Department of Philosophy, Washington University, 1 Brookings Dr., PO Box 1073, St. Louis, MO 63130-4899, U.S.A. **Online address:** cpwellma@artsci.wustl.edu

WELLMAN, John McDowell. American (born United States), b. 1945. **Genres:** Plays/Screenplays, Poetry, Novels. **Career:** Montgomery College,

associate professor of English, 1969-72; Black Box Magazine, editor, 1977; New York University, playwright-in-residence, 1981-82; Mentor Playwrights' Project, teacher of playwriting, 1984-92; Rockefeller Foundation, Bellagio Study and Conference Center, resident, 1991; University of New Mexico, PNM distinguished chair in playwriting, 1991; Atlantic Center for the Arts, master artist, 1991; Yale University School of Drama, playwright-in-residence, 1992; Princeton University, playwright-in-residence, 1992-93; Brooklyn College, associate professor of play writing, 1998-99, Donald I. Fine professor of play writing, 2000-10, distinguished professor, 2010-; Brown University, associate professor of play writing, 1999-2000. **Publications:** POETRY: In Praise of Secrecy, 1977; Satires, 1985; A Shelf in Woop's Clothing, 1990. NOVELS: Whirligig, 1989; The Fortuneteller, 1991; Two Plays: A Murder of Crows and The Hyacinth Macaw, 1994; The Bad Infinity, 1994; The Land beyond the Forest: Dracula and Swoop, 1995; Annie Salem: An American Tale, 1996. EDITOR: Theatre of Wonders: Six Contemporary American Plays, 1985; Seven Different Plays, 1988; Slant Six, 1990. **Address:** c/o Buddy Thomas, International Creative Management, 40 W 57th St., New York, NY 10019, U.S.A. **Online address:** mwellman@brooklyn.cuny.edu

WELLS, Cheryl A. American (born United States), b. 1972?. **Genres:** Military/Defense/Arms Control, History, Medicine/Health. **Career:** University of Wyoming, associate professor of history. Writer. **Publications:** Civil War Time: Temporality & Identity in America, 1861-1865, 2005; A Surgeon in the Army of the Potomac, 2008. **Address:** Department of History, College of Arts and Sciences, University of Wyoming, Rm. 158, History Bldg., 1000 E University Ave., Laramie, WY 82071-2000, U.S.A. **Online address:** cwells@uwyo.edu

WELLS, Ken. American (born United States), b. 1948. **Genres:** Essays, Novels, Travel/Exploration, Young Adult Fiction. **Career:** Houma Courier, reporter, 1967-75; Columbia Missourian, staff, 1975-77; Miami Herald, reporter, 1978-82; Wall Street Journal, New York, San Francisco Bureau, reporter, 1982-90, London Bureau, reporter, 1990-93, Page One, writer and senior editor, 1993-2006; Condé Nast Portfolio Magazine, senior editor, 2006-08. **Publications:** Meely LaBauve, 2000; Junior's Leg, 2001; (ed.) Floating off the Page: The Best Stories from the Wall Street Journal's Middle Column, 2002; Logan's Storm: A Novel, 2002; (ed.) Herd on the Street: Animal Stories from the Wall Street Journal, 2003; Travels with Barley: A Journey Through Beer Culture in America, 2004; Crawfish Mountain: A Novel, 2007; Travels with Barley: The Quest for the Perfect Beer Joint, 2008; The Good Pirates of the Forgotten Bayous: Fighting to Save a Way of Life in the Wake of Hurricane Katrina, 2008; Rascal: A Dog and His Boy, 2010. Contributor to periodicals. **Address:** Timoth J. Seldes Russell & Volkening, 50 W 29th St., Ste. 7E, New York, NY 10001-4227, U.S.A.

WELLS, Mary Ann. (Mary Janet Wells). American (born United States), b. 1944. **Genres:** History, Local History/Rural Topics, Travel/Exploration, Biography, Social Sciences. **Career:** Freelance photographer, 1972-76; American, photojournalist, 1977-81; freelance photographer and public relations consultant, 1981-87; freelance writer, 1981-. **Publications:** A History Lover's Guide to Mississippi, 1988; Guide to Mississippi's Festivals, Fairs and Flea Markets, 1988; A History Lover's Guide to Louisiana, 1990; (co-author) Discovering Mississippi, 1994; Native Land: Mississippi, 1540-1798, 1994; Searching for Red Eagle: A Personal Journey into the Spirit World of Native America, 1998; (with J.D. Elliot, Jr.) Cotton Gin Port: A Frontier Settlement on the Upper Tombigbee, 2003. Contributor to periodicals. **Address:** 9900 Spain Rd. NE, Albuquerque, NM 87111-1988, U.S.A. **Online address:** wellsmaryann@yahoo.com

WELLS, Mary Janet. See WELLS, Mary Ann.

WELLS, Melanie. American (born United States), b. 1965?. **Genres:** Novels, Mystery/Crime/Suspense, Theology/Religion. **Career:** LifeWorks Group (psychotherapy community), founder and director, LPC and LMFT, supervisor. Writer, musician and psychotherapist. **Publications:** When the Day of Evil Comes: A Novel of Suspense, 2005; The Soul Hunter: A Novel of Suspense, 2006; My Soul to Keep: A Novel of Suspense, 2008. **Address:** LifeWorks Group, 2515 Cedar Springs Rd., Dallas, TX 75201, U.S.A. **Online address:** mwells@wefixbrains.com

WELLS, Patricia. American (born United States), b. 1946. **Genres:** Food And Wine, Travel/Exploration, Reference. **Career:** Milwaukee Journal, copy editor, reporter, 1966-68; Washington Post, copy editor, 1972-76; New York Times, copy editor and food writer, 1976-80; International Herald Tribune, restaurant critic, 1980-; New York Times Paris Bureau, contributor, 1980-. **Publications:** New Wise Cookbook, 1981; Food Lover's Guide to Paris, 1984, 4th ed., 1999; Food Lover's Guide to France, 1987; Bistro Cooking, 1989; Simply French, 1991; Patricia Wells Trattoria: Healthy, Simple, Robust Fare Inspired bythe Small Family Restaurants of Italy, 1993; Patricia Wells at Home in Provence: Recipes Inspired by Her Farmhouse in France, 1996, 2nd. ed., 1999; Atelier of Joel Robuchon: The Artistry of a Master Chef and His Proteges, 1998; Paris Cookbook, 2001; Provence Cookbook: 175 Recipes and a Select Guide to the Markets, Shops, & Restaurants of France's Sunny South, 2004; Guy Savoy: Simple French Recipes for the Home Cook, 2004; Guy Savoy: Simple French Recipes for the Home Cook, 2004; Vegetable Harvest, 2007; (with W. Wells) We've Always had Paris and Provence: A Scrapbook of Our Life in France, 2008; Salad as a Meal: Healthy Main-dish Salads for Every Season, 2011; Simply Truffles: Recipes and Stories that Capture the Essence of the Black Diamond, 2011. Contributor to periodicals. **Address:** Lescher & Lescher, 155 E 71st St., New York, NY 10021, U.S.A. **Online address:** mail@patriciawells.com

WELLS, Peter S. American (born United States), b. 1938. **Genres:** Anthropology/Ethnology, History, Economics. **Career:** University of Minnesota, Department of Anthropology, professor of anthropology, Graduate Studies, director, 2000-03, Center for German & European Studies, affiliated faculty. Writer. **Publications:** Culture Contact and Culture Change: Early Iron Age Central Europe and the Mediterranean World, 1980; The Emergence of an Iron-Age Economy: The Mecklenburg Grave Groups from Hallstatt and Sticna, 1981; Rural Economy in the Early Iron Age: Excavations at Hascherkeller, 1978-1981, 1983; Farms, Villages, and Cities: Commerce and Urban Origins in Late Prehistoric Europe, 1984; (ed. with C.B. Kendall) Voyage to the Other World: The Legacy of Sutton Hoo, 1992; Settlement, Economy, and Cultural Change at the End of the European Iron Age: Excavations at Kelheim in Bavaria, 1987-1991, 1993; The Barbarians Speak: How the Conquered Peoples Shaped Roman Europe, 1999; Beyond Germans, Celts and Scythians: Archaeology and Identity in Iron-Age Europe, 2001; The Iron Age, 2002; The Battle That Stopped Rome: Emperor Augustus, Arminius, and the Slaughter of the Legions in the Teutoburg Forest, 2003; Barbarians to Angels: The Dark Ages Reconsidered, 2008; Creating an Imperial Frontier: Archaeology of the Formation of Rome's Danube Borderland, forthcoming. **Address:** Department of Anthropology, University of Minnesota, 395 Humphrey Ctr., 301 19th Ave. S, Minneapolis, MN 55455, U.S.A. **Online address:** wells001@umn.edu

WELLS, Rebecca. American (born United States), b. 1952?. **Genres:** Novels, Plays/Screenplays, Young Adult Fiction, Literary Criticism And History. **Career:** Writer. **Publications:** Little Altars Everywhere (novel), 1992; Divine Secrets of the Ya-Ya Sisterhood: A Novel, 1996; Ya-Yas in Bloom: A Novel, 2004; Crowning Glory of Calla Lily Ponder: A Novel, 2009. **Address:** Witherspoon Associates, 521 5th Ave., 26th Fl., New York, NY 10175, U.S.A. **Online address:** rebecca@rebeccawellsbooks.com

WELLS, Roger. British (born England), b. 1947. **Genres:** History, Social Sciences. **Career:** University of Wales, lecturer, 1972-73; University of Exeter, lecturer, 1973-75; University of York, lecturer, 1975-76; University of Brighton, Brighton Polytechnic, senior lecturer, 1976-95; Christ Church University College, professor, 1995-. Writer. **Publications:** Dearth and distress in Yorkshire, 1793-1802, 1977; Insurrection: The British Experience 1795-1803, 1983; Wretched Faces: Famine in Wartime England 1793-1801, 1988; (ed. with M. Reed) Class, Conflict and Protest in the English Countryside, 1700-1880, 1990; (ed.) Victorian Village: The Diaries of the Reverend John Coker Egerton, Curate and Rector of Burwash, East Sussex, 1857-1888, 1992; Crime, Protest and Popular Protest in Southern England, 1740-1850, 1997. **Address:** Department of History, Christ Church University College, North Holmes Rd., Canterbury, KT CT1 1QU, England. **Online address:** r.wells@cant.ac.uk

WELLS, Rosemary. American (born United States), b. 1943. **Genres:** Children's Fiction, Illustrations, Novels, Essays. **Career:** Allyn & Bacon, staff; Macmillan Publishing Co., staff; freelance writer and illustrator, 1968-. **Publications:** SELF-ILLUSTRATED: The First Child, 1970; Martha's Birthday, 1970; Miranda's Pilgrims, 1970; The Fog Comes on Little Pig Feet, 1972; Noisy Nora (verse), 1973; Timothy Goes to School, 1981; Through the Hidden Door, 1987; Max's Valentine, 2003; Max's Christmas Stocking, 2003; Hands off, Harry!, 2011. OTHERS: John and the Rarey, 1969; Michael and the Mitten Test, 1969; Unfortunately Harriet, 1972; Benjamin and Tulip, 1973; None of the Above, 1974; Abdul, 1975; Morris's Disappearing Bag: A Christmas Story, 1975; Leave Well Enough Alone, 1977; Don't Spill It Again, James (verse), 1977; Stanley and Rhoda, 1978; Max's Ride, 1979; Max's First Word, 1979; Max's New Suit, 1979; Max's Toys: A Counting Book, 1979; When No One Was Looking, 1980; Good Night, Fred, 1981; A Lion for Lewis, 1982; Peabody, 1983; The Man in the Woods, 1984; Hazel's Amazing Mother, 1985; Max's Bath, 1985; Max's Bedtime, 1985; Max's Birthday, 1985; Max's Breakfast, 1985; Max's Christmas, 1986; (with S. Jeffers) Forest of Dreams, 1988; Shy Charles, 1988; Max's Chocolate Chicken, 1989; (with J. Hurley) Cooking for Nitwits, 1989; Little Lame Prince, 1990; Fritz and the Mess Fairy, 1991; Max's Dragon Shirt, 1991; The Island Light, 1992; Moss Pillows, 1992; First Tomato, 1992; Max and Ruby's First Greek Myth: Pandora's Box, 1993; Waiting for the Evening Star, 1993; Lucy Comes to Stay, 1994; Night Sounds, Morning Colors, 1994; Max and Ruby's Midas: Another Greek Myth, 1995; Lassie Come-home, 1995; Edward in Deep Water, 1995; Edward Unready for School, 1995; Edward's Overwhelming Overnight, 1995; The Language of Doves, 1996; Bunny Cakes, 1997; McDuff Comes Home, 1997; McDuff Moves In, 1997; McDuff Shows the Way, 1997; Bunny Money, 1997; McDuff and the Baby, 1997; Jack and the Beanstalk, 1997; Nora la revoltosa, 1997; Mary on Horseback: Three Mountain Stories, 1998; Yoko, 1998; McDuff's New Friend, 1998; The Fisherman and His Wife, 1998; Itsy-bitsy Spider, 1998; Bear Went Over the Mountain, 1998; Read to Your Bunny, 1998; (with M. Tallchief) Tallchief, 1999; Streets of Gold, 1999; Rachel Field's Hitty, 1999; Bingo, 1999; Emily's First 100 Days of School, 2000; Goodnight Max, 2000; McDuff Stories, 2000; Timothy's Lost and Found Day, 2000; World Around Us, 2001; Yoko's Paper Cranes, 2001; Halloween Parade, 2001; Mama, Don't Go!, 2001; How Many? How Much, 2001; McDuff Goes to School, 2001; Ready to Read, 2001; Doris's Dinosaur, 2001; Felix Feels Better, 2001; Adding It Up, 2001; Be My Valentine, 2001; Bunny Party, 2001; Discover and Explore, 2001; (with T. Wells) House in the Mail, 2002; McDuff Saves the Day, 2002; Read Me a Story, 2002; Wingwalker, 2002; Ruby's Beauty Shop, 2002; The Germ Busters, 2002; Yoko & Friends: When I Grow Up, 2003; When I Grow Up, 2003; Small World of Binky Braverman, 2003; Only You, 2003; Max Drives Away, 2003; Max and Ruby Play School, 2003; Felix and the Worrier, 2003; Emily's World of Wonders, 2003; Ruby's Tea for Two, 2003; Ruby's Rainy Day, 2004; My Kindergarten, 2004; McDuff Steps Out, 2004; Max and Ruby's Snowy Day, 2004; Max's Halloween, 2004; Bunny Mail, 2004; McDuff's Favorite Things, 2004; McDuff's Hide-and-Seek, 2004; Yoko's World of Kindness: Golden Rules for a Happy Classroom, 2005; (with S. Jeffers) McDuff's Wild Romp, 2005; Miraculous Tale of the Two Maries, 2006; Max's ABC, 2006; Carry Me!, 2006; My Shining Star: Raising a Child Who is Ready to Learn, 2006; Red Moon at Sharpsburg: A Novel, 2007; Max Counts His Chickens, 2007; Gulps, 2007; Ruby's Falling Leaves, 2007; (contrib.) Max & Ruby's Christmas Tree, 2007; Happy Halloween!, 2008; Max's Easter Surprise, 2008; Max's Bunny Business, 2008; Otto Runs for President, 2008; Voyage to the Bunny Planet, 2008; Yoko Writes Her Name, 2008; Hide-and-seek, 2008; Lincoln and His Boys, 2009; Baby Max and Ruby: Red Boots, 2009; Baby Max and Ruby: Clean-Up Time, 2009; Baby Max and Ruby: Shopping, 2009; Baby Max and Ruby: Peek-a-Boo, 2009; Max's Worm Cake, 2009; Max's Apples, 2009; (with S. Fernandez) My Havana: Memories of a Cuban Boyhood, 2010; On the Blue Comet, 2010; Max & Ruby's Bedtime Book, 2010; Love Waves, 2011; Yoko's Show-and-Tell, 2011; Max & Ruby's Treasure Hunt, 2012; Yoko Learns to Read, 2012. Illustrator of books by others. **Address:** Hyperion Editorial Department, 77 W 66th St., 11th Fl., New York, NY 10023-6201, U.S.A.

WELLS, Shirley. Also writes as Holly Graham, Ruth Bennett, Shirley Worrall. British (born England), b. 1955?. **Genres:** Mystery/Crime/Suspense, Novels. **Career:** British Broadcasting Corp., staff. Writer. **Publications:** AS SHIRLEY WORRALL: All Our Tomorrows, 1990; A New Future Beckoning, 1990; The Call of the Isles, 2000; Hold Fast These Family Ties, 2000; Where the Island Waits, 2002; Flight of the Mandarins, 2006; These Promises to Keep, 2006; The Mystery at Kingsley Hall, 2007; Where the Rainbow Ends, 2011. AS HOLLY GRAHAM: A Scandalous Affair, 2000. AS RUTH BENNETT: Where Angels Wait, 2004. CRIME FICTION: Into the Shadows, 2007; A Darker Side, 2008; Where Petals Fall, 2009; Presumed Dead, 2010; The Broken Circle, 2010; Shades of Evil, 2011; Dead Silent, 2011; Silent Witness, 2012. Contributor to magazines. **Address:** Soho Press Inc., 853 Broadway, New York, NY 10003, U.S.A. **Online address:** shirley@shirleywells.com

WELLS, Simon. American (born United States), b. 1961?. **Genres:** Film, Business/Trade/Industry, Social Sciences. **Career:** WCRS, board member; Enteraction TV, Branded Programming Division, head, 2002-. Director and writer. **Publications:** (With A. Catterall) Your Face Here: British Cult Movies since the Sixties, 2001; The Beatles: 365 Days, 2005; The Rolling Stones: 365 Days, 2006. Contributor to periodicals. **Address:** Enteraction TV, 8 Park Pl., 12 Lawn Ln., London, GL SW8 1UD, England.

WELLS, Spencer. American (born United States), b. 1969. **Genres:** Photography. **Career:** National Geographic Society, explorer-in-residence and director of the genographic project; Cornell University, Frank H.T. Rhodes Class of '56 professor; Oxford University, Wellcome Trust Centre for Human Genetics, Population Genetics Research Group, director. Writer, geneticist, paleoanthropologist and documentary filmmaker. **Publications:** The Journey of Man: A Genetic Odyssey, Photographs by Mark Read, 2002; Deep Ancestry: Inside the Genographic Project, 2006; Pandora's Seed: The Unforeseen Costs of Civilization, 2010. Contributor to periodicals. **Address:** Washington, DC , U.S.A. **Online address:** rsw96@cornell.edu

WELLS, Stanley (William). British (born England), b. 1930. **Genres:** Literary Criticism And History, Theatre, Bibliography. **Career:** University of Birmingham, Shakespeare Institute, reader in English, 1962-77, professor of Shakespeare Studies, 1988-97, director, 1988-97, professor emeritus, 1997-; Royal Shakespeare Theatre, governor, 1974-, vice-chairman, 1991-; Oxford Shakespeare, general editor, 1978-; Balliol College, senior research fellow, 1980-88; Shakespeare Survey, editor, 1981-; Shakespeare Birthplace Trust, chairman. **Publications:** Shakespeare: A Reading Guide, 1969, 1970; Literature and Drama, 1970; Royal Shakespeare, 1977; Shakespeare: An Illustrated Dictionary, 1978; Shakespeare: The Writer and His Work, 1978; Re-Editing Shakespeare for the Modern Reader, 1984; (co-author) William Shakespeare: A Textual Companion, 1987; An Oxford Anthology of Shakespeare, 1987; Shakespeare: A Dramatic Life, 1994; Four Histories, 1994; Shakespeare on the Stage: An Anthology of Criticism, 1997; Shakespeare: The Poet and his Plays, 1997; The Oxford Dictionary of Shakespeare, 1998; William Shakespeare: The Quiz Book, 1998; Shakespeare: For All Time, 2003; (with P. Edmondson) Shakespeare's Sonnets, 2004; Looking for Sex in Shakespeare, 2004; Shakespeare and Co., 2006; Is it True What they Say About Shakespeare?, 2007; Shakespeare, Sex, & Love, 2010. EDITOR: Thomas Nashe: Selected Writings, 1964; A Midsummer Night's Dream, 1967; Richard II, 1969; The Comedy of Errors, 1972; Select Bibliographical Guides: Shakespeare, 1973, rev. ed., 1990; English Drama Excluding Shakespeare, 1975; (ed. with K. Muir) Aspects of Hamlet, 1979; (with R.L. Smallwood) The Shoemaker's Holiday, 1979; (ed. with K. Muir) Aspects of King Lear, 1982; (and intro.) Shakespeare's Sonnets: And, a Lover's Complaint, 1985; (with G. Taylor) The Complete Oxford Shakespeare, 1986; The Cambridge Companion to Shakespeare Studies, 1986; (with A. Davies) Shakespeare and the Moving Image, 1994; (with R. Warren) Twelfth Night, or, What You Will, 1994; Shakespeare and the Globe, 1999; (with C.M.S. Alexander) Shakespeare and Race, 2000; History of King Lear, 2000; (with C.M.S. Alexander) Shakespeare and Sexuality, 2001; (with L.C. Orlin) Shakespeare: An Oxford Guide, 2003; (with M. De Grazia) New Cambridge Companion to Shakespeare, 2010; (with C. Jansohn and L.C. Orlin) Shakespeare without Boundaries, 2010. **Address:** Sheil Land Associates Ltd., 52 Doughty St., London, GL WC1N 2LS, England. **Online address:** s.w.wells@bham.ac.uk

WELLS, Sue. See **WELLS, Susan (Mary).**

WELLS, Susan (Mary). (Sue Wells). Kenyan/British (born England), b. 1951. **Genres:** Natural History, Geography, Medicine/Health, Animals/Pets. **Career:** Natural History Museum, scientific officer, 1974; Station Biologique de la Tour du Valat, researcher, 1974-77; International Union for Conservation of Nature and Natural Resources (IUCN) SSC Traffic Group, researcher, 1978-80; IUCN Conservation Monitoring Center, research officer, 1980-83; IUCN/United Nations Environment Programme (UNEP), senior research officer and senior editor, Coral Reefs of International Importance, directory, 1983-87; International Council for Bird Preservation (ICBP), assistant director of information, 1988; World Birdwatch, editor, 1988; independent environmental consultant, 1989-91; University of Newcastle-upon-Tyne, research associate, 1991-92; International Center for Living Aquatic Resources Management (ICLARM), consultant, 1992. **Publications:** (With R.M. Pyle, S.A. Hughes and N.M. Collins) The IUCN Invertebrate Red Data Book, 1983;

(with M. Haywood) Manual of Marine Invertebrates, 1989; (ed. and contrib.) Coral Reefs of the World, vol. I: Atlantic and Eastern Pacific, vol. II: Indian Ocean, Red Sea and Gulf, vol. III: Central and Western Pacific, 1989; The Illustrated World of Oceans, 1991; Explore the World of Mighty Oceans, 1992; (with N. Hanna) The Greenpeace Book of Coral Reefs, 1992; (with P. Holthus and J. Maragos) Environmental Guidelines for Reef Coral Harvesting Operations, 1994; (ed. with G. Kelleher and C. Bleakley) Global Representative System of Marine Protected Areas, 1995; Sweet Reason: Rhetoric and the Discourses of Modernity, 1996; Giant Clams: Status, Trade and Mariculture, and the Role of CITES in Management, 1997; Out of the Dead House: Nineteenth Century Women Physicians and the Writing of Medicine, 2000; Conservation of Coastal and Marine Biodiversity in the Eastern African Region: Progress in Implementation of the Jakarta Mandate, 2001; (ed. with M. Samoilys and S. Makoloweka) Putting Adaptive Management into Practice: Collaborative Coastal Management in Tanga, Northern Tanzania, 2007; Coral Reef (pop-up book), 2009. Contributor to journals and periodicals. **Address:** PO Box 68200, Nairobi, 1, Kenya.

WELLS (DIMENSTEIN), Catherine. American (born United States), b. 1952. **Genres:** Science Fiction/Fantasy, Novels, inspirational/Motivational Literature, Literary Criticism And History. **Career:** University of Arizona, adjunct librarian, 1991-. Writer. **Publications:** NOVELS: The Earth Is All That Lasts, 1991; Children of the Earth, 1992; The Earth Saver, 1993; Mother Grimm, 1997; Beyond the Gates, 1999; Stones of Destiny, 2007. SHORT FICTION: The Nechtanite and the Inforat, 2000; Artie's Angels, 2001; The Sea-Maid, 2002; Sysop, 2004; Point of Origin, 2005. OTHERS: Political Profiles: Hillary Clinton, 2007; Political Profiles: John McCain, 2007; Crystal Desert, 2010. Works appear in anthologies. **Address:** College of Social and Behavioral Sciences, University of Arizona, 9000 S Rita Rd., PO Box 210028, Tucson, AZ 85742, U.S.A. **Online address:** cdimenst@u.arizona.edu

WELPTON, Ann Carolyn. See **FISHER-WIRTH, Ann W.**

WELS, Susan. American (born United States) **Genres:** History, Biography, Travel/Exploration, Cultural/Ethnic Topics. **Career:** Author. **Publications:** Fifteen Seconds: The Great California Earthquake of 1989, 1989; America: Then And Now, 1992; (co-author) The African Americans, 1993; (with D.E. Cohen and L. Liberman) A Day in the Life of Israel, 1994; (with D.E. Cohen) Requiem for the Heartland, 1995; (with D.E. Cohen and S. van Beek) A Day in the Life of Thailand, 1995; The Olympic Spirit: 100 Years of the Games, 1995; (with D.E. Cohen and L. Liberman) Jerusalem: In the Shadow of Heaven, 1996; The Story of Mothers and Daughters, 1997; Titanic: Legacy of the World's Greatest Ocean Liner, 1997; Stanford: Portrait of a University, 1999; Pearl Harbor: America's Darkest Day, 2001; Domain Names for Dummies, 2001; (with D.E. Cohen and L. Liberman) A Day in the Life of Africa, 2003; California Academy of Sciences: Architecture in Harmony with Nature, 2008; Amelia Earhart: The Thrill of it, 2009. EDITOR: Investing with the Best, 1986; The Stanford Health & Exercise Handbook, 1987; Jasper Ridge: A Stanford Sanctuary, 1990; Canyons of Color, 1995; Yellowstone: Land of Fire and Ice, 1995; Grand Canyon: The Great Abyss, 1995; Glacier and Waterton, 1996; Grand Teton: Citadels of Stone, 1996; Yosemite: Valley of Thunder, 1996; The Other Parent, 2002; Off Mike, 2008; The Co-Presidency of Bush and Cheney, 2009; The Life and Letters of Kate Gleason, 2010. **Address:** 740 Castro St., San Francisco, CA 94114, U.S.A. **Online address:** susanwels@ameliaearhartbook.net

WELSBACHER, Anne. American (born United States), b. 1955. **Genres:** Zoology, Physics, Earth Sciences, Children's Fiction, Natural History. **Career:** Freelance writer and editor, 1980-; Science Museum of Minnesota, publications director, 1990-. **Publications:** Hammerhead Sharks, 1995; Mako Sharks, 1995; Tiger Sharks, 1995; Whale Sharks, 1995; Wading Birds, 1999; Flying Brown Pelicans, 1999; Leopards Abdo, 2000; Jaguars, 2000; Lions, 2000; Pumas, 2000; Tigers, 2000; Pulleys, 2001; Levers, 2001; Screws, 2001; Wheels and Axles, 2001; Wedges, 2001; Anacondas, 2001; Vampire Bats, 2001; Wolves, 2001; Inclined Planes, 2001; Cheetahs, 2002; Killer Whales, 2002; Komodo Dragons, 2002; Cougars, 2003; Crocodiles, 2003; Life in a Rain Forest, 2003; Green Design, 2008; Rain Forests, 2009; Earth-friendly Design, 2009; Protecting Earth's Rain Forests, 2009. UNIVERSE SERIES: The Earth, 1997; Galaxies, 1997; Moons, 1997; The Planets, 1997; The Solar System, 1997; Sun and Stars, 1997. STATES SERIES: Alabama, 1998; Arkansas, 1998; California, 1998; Colorado, 1998; Connecticut, 1998; Delaware, 1998; Indiana, 1998; Iowa, 1998; Kansas, 1998; Kentucky, 1998; Louisiana, 1998; Nebraska, 1998; New Hampshire, 1998; New Jersey, 1998; New York, 1998; North Dakota, 1998; Pennsylvania, 1998; Puerto Rico, 1998; South Dakota, 1998; Texas, 1998; Washington, 1998; Missouri, 2002. PRESI-DENTS SERIES: George Washington, 1998, rev. ed., 2002; Andrew Jackson, 1998; James Monroe, 1998; John Adams, 1998; Theodore Roosevelt, 1998, rev. ed., 2002; James Madison, 1998, rev. ed., 2002; Thomas Jefferson, 1998, rev. ed., 2002; Andrew Johnson, 2000, rev. ed., 2002; John Tyler, 2000, rev. ed., 2002; Abraham Lincoln, 2001; Franklin Pierce, 2001; James K. Polk, 2001; Rutherford B. Hayes, 2001; Ulysses S. Grant, 2001; Martin Van Buren, 2001. **Address:** Science Museum of Minnesota, 120 W Kellogg Blvd., St. Paul, MN 55102, U.S.A.

WELSCH, Roger L(ee). American (born United States), b. 1936. **Genres:** Mythology/Folklore, Young Adult Fiction. **Career:** Dana College, instructor in German, 1960-64; Nebraska Wesleyan University, assistant professor of folklore and German, 1964-73; University of Nebraska, teacher of folklore in Extension Division, 1966-88, faculty, 1973-88, adjunct professor, 1988-; Smithsonian Institution, field operative, 1974-; CBS News, Sunday Morning essayist, 1988-, senior correspondent. **Publications:** An Outline-Guide to Nebraska Folklore (syllabus), 1966; A Treasury of Nebraska Pioneer Folklore, 1966; Sod Walls: The Story of the Nebraska Sod House, 1968; (trans.) K. Krohn, Folklore Methodology, 1971; Shingling the Fog and Other Plains Lies, 1972; Tall Tale Postcards: A Pictorial History, 1976; Omaha Tribal Myths and Trickster Tales, 1981; Mister, You Got Yourself a Horse: Tales of Old-Time Horse Trading, 1981; Of Trees and Dreams: The Fiction, Fact and Folklore of Tree-Planting on the Northern Plains, 1982; (with L.K. Welsch) Catfish at the Pump: Humor and the Frontier, 1982; Inside Lincoln, 1984; You Know You're a Nebraskan, 1985; You Know You're a Husker, 1986; (with L.K. Welsch) Cather's Kitchens: Foodways in Literature and Life, 1987; It's Not the End of the Earth but You Can See It from Here (fiction), 1990; Touching the Fire: Buffalo Dancers, the Sky Bundle and Other Tales (fiction), 1992; Liars Too: The Legend Continues, 1993; Uncle Smoke Stories: Four Nehawka Coyote Stories from the Big Belly Lodge (young adult), 1994; (ed. with D. Mowitz and D. Ohrtman) Ageless Iron, 1994; Old Tractors and the Men Who Love Them: How to Keep Your Tractors Happy and Your Family Running, 1995; Roger Welsch, Busted Tractors and Rusty Knuckles: Norwegian Torque Wrench Techniques and Other Fine Points of Tractor Restoration, 1997; Diggin' I and Piggin' Out: The Truth about Food and Men, 1997; Touching the Fire: Buffalo Dancers, the Sky Bundle and Other Tales, 1997; Love, Sex and Tractors, 2000; Postcards from Nebraska, 2000; Old Tractors Never Die: Roger's Guide to the Care and Feeding of Ageless Iron, 2001; Everything I Know about Women I Learned from My Tractor, 2002; Outhouses, 2003; My Life with Dogs, 2004; From Tinkering to Torquing: A Beginner's Guide to Tractors and Tools, 2005; Forty Acres and a Fool: How to Live in the Country and Still Keep Your Sanity, 2006; Weed 'em and Reap: A Weed Eater Reader, 2006; My Nebraska: The Good, the Bad and the Husker: With Original Sketches of Nebraska Scenic Sites by the Author, 2006; (ed. with J.R. Dow) Wyoming Folklore: Reminiscences, Folktales, Beliefs, Customs and Folk Speech, 2010. EDITOR: Germans and German-Russians in Nebraska, 1980; P.M. Hannibal, Beautiful Dannebrog, 1986. Contributor to books. **Address:** Primrose Farm, RR 1, Dannebrog, NE 68831-0160, U.S.A. **Online address:** captneb@micrord.com

WELSH, Alexander. American (born United States), b. 1933. **Genres:** Literary Criticism And History, Philosophy. **Career:** Yale University, Department of English, instructor, 1960-63, assistant professor, 1963-66, associate professor of English, 1966-67, Emily Sanford professor of English, 1991-, now Emily Sanford professor emeritus of English; University of Pittsburgh, professor of English, 1967-72; University of California, professor of English, 1972-91; Nineteenth Century Fiction, editor, 1975-81. **Publications:** The Hero of the Waverley Novels, 1963; (ed. and intro.) Old Mortality, 1966; Thackeray: A Collection of Critical Essays, 1968; The City of Dickens, 1971, 3rd ed., 1999; Reflections on the Hero as Quixote, 1981; George Eliot and Blackmail, 1985; From Copyright to Copperfield: The Identity of Dickens, 1987; Strong Representations: Narrative and Circumstantial Evidence in England, 1992; Freud's Wishful Dream Book, 1994; Dickens Redressed: The Art of Bleak House and Hard Times, 2000; Hamlet in His Modern Guises, 2001; What is Honor?: A Question of Moral Imperatives, 2008. Contributor to periodicals. **Address:** Department of English, Yale University, SSS 802, 63 High St., PO Box 208302, New Haven, CT 06520-8302, U.S.A. **Online address:** alexander.welsh@yale.edu

WELSH, Frank (Reeson). British (born England), b. 1931. **Genres:** History,

Documentaries/Reportage, Industrial Relations, Literary Criticism And History, Young Adult Fiction. **Career:** John Lewis Partnership, affiliate, 1954-58; CAS Group, affiliate, 1958-64; William Brandt's Sons & Company Ltd., managing director, 1965-72; Hadfields Ltd., chair, 1967-79; Jensen Motors Ltd., chair, 1968-72; Grindlays Bank, director, 1971-85; Cox & Kings, chair, 1972-76; Henry Ansbacher & Co., director, 1976-82; University of Tennessee, visiting lecturer, 1979-; Trireme Trust, director, 1983-. Writer. **Publications:** The Profit of the State: Nationalised Industries and Public Enterprises, 1982; The Afflicted State: A Survey of Public Enterprise, 1983; First Blood: Tales of Horror from the Border Country, 1985; (with G. Ridley) Bend'Or, Duke of Westminster: A Personal Memoir, 1985; Uneasy City: An Insider's View of the City of London, 1986; Building the Trireme, 1988; Hong Kong: A History in US as A Borrowed Place: The History of Hong Kong, 1993; Companion Guide to the Lake District, 1997; South Africa: A Narrative History, 1999; Dangerous Deceits, 1999; The Four Nations: A History of the United Kingdom, 2003; Great Southern Land: A New History of Australia, 2004; Australia: A New History of the Great Southern Land, 2006; (co-author) Victoria's Empire, 2007; The Battle for Christendom: The Council of Constance, 1415 and the Struggle to Unite Against Islam, 2008. **Address:** Curtis Brown Ltd., Haymarket House, 28-29 Haymarket 4th Fl., London, GL SWIY 4SP, England. **Online address:** fw@frankwelsh.com

WELSH, Irvine. Irish/Scottish (born Scotland), b. 1958. **Genres:** Novels, Novellas/Short Stories, Young Adult Fiction. **Career:** Hackney Council, staff; Writer, 1993-; 4 Ways (film production company), partner. **Publications:** Trainspotting, 1994; The Acid House (short stories), 1995; Marabou Stork Nightmares: A Novel, 1995; Ecstasy: Three Tales of Chemical Romances, 1996; Children of Albion Rovers, 1996; (with N. Waplington) The Wedding, 1996; Filth: A Novel, 1998; You'll Have Had Your Hole, 1998; Glue, 2001; (intro.) 4-Play, 2001; Porno, 2002; Bedroom Secrets of the Master Chefs, 2006; (with A.M. Smith and I. Rankin) One City, 2006; (with D. Cavanagh) Babylon Heights, 2006; (with R. Todd) Leonard Pepper and Other Stories, 2007; If You Liked School, You'll Love Work, 2007; Crime, 2008; Reheated Cabbage: Tales of Chemical Degeneration, 2009; (co-author) Because I am a Girl, 2009; Days Like This: A Portrait of Scotland Through the Stories of its People, 2009; Skagboys, 2012. **Address:** c/o Jonathan Cape, Random House UK Ltd., 20 Vauxhall Bridge Rd., London, GL SW1V 2SA, England.

WELSING, Frances Cress. American (born United States), b. 1935. **Genres:** Psychiatry, Race Relations, Social Sciences. **Career:** Cook County Hospital, intern, 1962-63; St. Elizabeth Hospital, resident in general psychiatry, 1963-66; Howard University College of Medicine, assistant professor of pediatrics, 1968-75; Hillcrest Children's Center, clinical director, 1975-76; Paul Robeson School for Growth and Development, clinical director, 1976-90; Cress Welsing Institute for Psychiatry and Social Research, founder. Writer. **Publications:** The Cress Theory of Color Confrontation and Racism, 1970; The Isis Papers: The Keys to the Colors, 1991. **Address:** 7603 Georgia Ave. NW, Ste. 402, Washington, DC 20012, U.S.A.

WELTGE, Sigrid W(ortmann). (Sigrid Weltge-Wortmann). American/German (born Germany), b. 1935. **Genres:** Art/Art History, Design, Women's Studies And Issues, Writing/Journalism, History. **Career:** Goddard College, artist, 1977; Philadelphia University (formerly Philadelphia College of Textiles and Science), professor of art history, design, textiles and costumes, 1978-2005, now professor emeritus; Penland School of Crafts, artist, 1994; Danmarks Design Skçle, artist, 1996; Kansas City Art Institute, artist, 1996; Anderson Ranch, seminar leader, 2004, 2005. Writer. **Publications:** Die Ersten Maler in Worpswede, 1976, rev. ed., 1998; (as Sigrid Weltge-Wortmann) Ersten Maler in Worpswede, 1979; (contrib.) History of Clothing, 1989; Bauhaus Textiles: Women Artists and the Weaving Workshop, 1993; Women's Work: Textile Art from the Bauhaus, 1993, rev. ed., 1998; ITessuti del Bauhaus: L'arte e l'artigianator di un laboratorio femminile, 1993; Bauhaus-Textilien.Kunst und Kuenstlerinnen der Webwerkstatt, 1933; Lore Kadden Lindenfeld: A Life in Textiles 1945-1997, 1997; Dictionary of Women Artists, 1997; (contrib.) Lenore Tawney: Celebrating Five Decades of Work, 2000. Contributor to periodicals. **Address:** School of Textiles and Materials Technology, Philadelphia University, 4201 Henry Ave., Philadelphia, PA 19144-5497, U.S.A. **Online address:** weltges@philau.edu

WELTGE-WORTMANN, Sigrid. See **WELTGE, Sigrid W(ortmann).**

WELTNER, Peter (Nissen). American (born United States), b. 1942. **Genres:** Novellas/Short Stories, Novels, Literary Criticism And History,

Young Adult Fiction. **Career:** San Francisco State University, faculty, 1969-, professor of English, through 2006, professor emeritus of English, 2006-. Writer. **Publications:** Beachside Entries/Specific Ghosts (short stories), 1989; Identity and Difference (novel), 1990; In a Time of Combat for the Angel (three short novels), 1991; The Risk of His Music (short stories), 1997; How the Body Prays (novel), 1999. **Address:** Department of English, San Francisco State University, 1600 Holloway Ave., San Francisco, CA 94132, U.S.A.

WELTON, Jude. British (born England), b. 1955. **Genres:** Art/Art History, Children's Non-fiction, Young Adult Non-fiction, Homes/Gardens, Sports/Fitness, Children's Fiction, Sciences. **Career:** Marshall Cavendish, editor, 1981-88; George Philip Ltd., editor, 1989; freelance author, 1990-. **Publications:** EYEWITNESS ART SERIES: Monet, 1993; Impressionism, 1993; Looking at Paintings, 1994; Gauguin, 1994. ARTISTS IN THEIR TIME SERIES: Henri Matisse, 2002; Marc Chagall, 2003. OTHERS: Impressionist Gardens, 1993; Impressionist Landscapes, 1993; Mothers in Art, 1994; Drawing: A Young Artist's Guide, 1994; Can I Tell You About Asperger Syndrome?: A Guide for Friends and Family, 2004; What Did You Say? What Do You Mean?: An Illustrated Guide to Understanding Metaphors, 2004; Adam's Alternative Sports Day: An Asperger Story, 2005; Water Supplies, 2006. Contributor to periodicals. **Address:** c/o Author Mail, Franklin Watts, 338 Euston Rd., London, GL NW1 3BH, England.

WEN, Chihua. American (born United States), b. 1958. **Genres:** Documentaries/Reportage, History. **Career:** Xinhua News Agency (New China News Agency), reporter and editor, 1982-87. **Publications:** (With B. Jones) The Red Mirror: Children of China's Cultural Revolution (anthology), 1995. Contributor to magazines and newspapers. **Address:** PO Box 23, Imperial Beach, CA 91933-0023, U.S.A.

WENDEROTH, Joe. American (born United States), b. 1966. **Genres:** Poetry, Adult Non-fiction, Essays, Literary Criticism And History. **Career:** New York University, instructor in creative writing, 1990-91; Harford Community College, instructor in English, 1993; Catonsville Community College, instructor in English, 1993-94; Johns Hopkins University, Center for Talented Youth, instructor, 1994-95; Baltimore International Culinary College, instructor in English, 1995; University of California, Department of English, associate professor, 1995-, professor. Poet. **Publications:** Disfortune: Poems, 1995; It is If I Speak, 2000; Letters to Wendy's, 2000; Holy Spirit of Life: Essays Written for John Ashcroft's Secret Self, 2005; Agony: A Proposal (non-fiction), 2007; No Real Light, 2007. Contributor to magazines. **Address:** Department of English, University of California at Davis, Rm. 208 Voorhies, 1 Shields Ave., Davis, CA 95616, U.S.A. **Online address:** jlwenderoth@ucdavis.edu

WENDLING, Ronald C(harles). American (born United States), b. 1939. **Genres:** Intellectual History, Literary Criticism And History, Theology/Religion, Adult Non-fiction. **Career:** Canisius College, instructor in English, 1963-65; Saint Joseph's University, instructor in English, 1965-66, assistant professor, 1972-81, associate professor, 1981-95, professor of English, 1995-, director of honors program, 1986-90, now professor emeritus; Hamilton College, instructor, 1969-70, assistant professor of English, 1970-72. Writer. **Publications:** Coleridge's Progress to Christianity: Experience and Authority in Religious Faith, 1995. Contributor of articles to periodicals. **Address:** Department of English, Saint Joseph's University, Bellarmine 111, 5600 City Ave., Philadelphia, PA 19131-1395, U.S.A. **Online address:** rwendlin@sju.edu

WENDOVER, Robert W(arren). American (born United States), b. 1955. **Genres:** Administration/Management, How-to Books. **Career:** Neshaminy School District, teacher, 1977-81; Colorado State University, assistant residence hall director, 1981-82, acting assistant director of career services, 1982-83; Villanova University, career counselor, 1983-84; University of Denver, education director, 1984-88; Career Track, trainer, 1986-87; The Center for Generational Studies, managing director, 1988-, GenTrends Newsletter, editorial director; Leadership Resources Inc., president, 1988-; University of Phoenix, faculty, 1990-2002; National Speakers Association, president, 2005-09; The American Productivity and Quality Center, special advisor, 2007-08; Colorado Speakers Association, president; Rocky Mountain Chapter of the American Society, president; National Meetings Industry Council, chair. Writer. **Publications:** Smart Hiring For Small Companies, 1988; Smart Hiring: The Complete Guide for Recruiting Employees, 1989, 3rd ed., 2002; High Performance Hiring, 1991, rev. ed., 2003; The 2 Minute Motivator: How to Inspire Superior Performance, 1992; Smart Hiring for Your Business, 1994;

Hand-Picked: The Complete Guide to Finding and Hiring the Best Employees, 1996; Recruiting for High Performance: Attracting the Best, 2003; (with T.L. Gargiulo) On Cloud Nine: Weathering the Challenge of Many Generations in the Workplace, 2006; Smart Hiring at the Next Level, 2006. Contributor to magazines and newspapers. **Address:** The Center for Generational Studies, 15200 E Girard Ave., Ste. 3000, Aurora, CO 80014, U.S.A. **Online address:** wendover@gentrends.com

WENDT, Albert. New Zealander/Western Samoan (born Western Samoa), b. 1939. **Genres:** Novels, Poetry, Novellas/Short Stories, Plays/Screenplays, Young Adult Non-fiction. **Career:** Samoa College, teacher, 1964-69, principal, 1969-73; Bulletin (now Samoa Times), editor, 1966; University of the South Pacific, senior lecturer, 1974-75, Extension Services, assistant director, 1976-77, professor of pacific literature, 1982-87, University of the South Pacific Center, director, 1988; Mana Publications, editor, 1978; Unesco Program on Oceanic Cultures, coordinator, 1975-79; University of Auckland, Department of English, professor of English, 1988-, now professor emeritus. **Publications:** NOVELS: Sons for the Return Home, 1973; Pouliuli, 1977; Leaves of the Banyan Tree, 1979; The Banyan: A Novel About Samoa, 1989; Ola, 1991, Black Rainbow 1992; Mango's Kiss: A Novel, 2003; Songmaker's Chair, 2004; The Adventures of Vela, 2009. STORIES: Flying Fox in a Freedom Tree, 1974; The Birth and Death of the Miracle Man, 1986; The Best of Albert Wendt's Short Stories, 1999. POETRY: Inside Us the Dead, 1976; Shaman of Visions, 1984; Photographs, 1995; Book of the Black Star, 2002. EDITOR: Some Modern Poetry from Fiji, 1974; Some Modern Poetry from Western Samoa, 1974; Some Modern Poetry from the New Hebrides, 1975; Some Modern Poetry from the Solomons, 1975; (and intro.) Lali: A Pacific Anthology, 1980; Nuanua: An Anthology of Pacific Writing, 1995; (with R. Whaitiri and R. Sullivan) Whetu Moana: Contemporary Polynesian Poems in English, 2003; (with R. Whaitiri and R. Sullivan) Mauri Ola: Contemporary Polynesian Poems in English, 2010. **Address:** Department of English, University of Auckland, Arts 1 Bldg., 14a Symonds St., Auckland, 1, New Zealand. **Online address:** a.wendt@auckland.ac.nz

WENGER, Beth S. American (born United States), b. 1963. **Genres:** Theology/Religion, Cultural/Ethnic Topics. **Career:** University of Pennsylvania, Katz Family associate professor of American Jewish history, professor of history, Katz Family term chair in American Jewish history and director of Jewish studies program; National Museum of American Jewish History, Organization of American Historians distinguished lecturer and historical consultant; University of Pennsylvania's Center for Advanced Judaic Studies, the Jewish Women's Archive, director. Writer. **Publications:** New York Jews and the Great Depression: Uncertain Promise, 1996; (ed. with J. Shandler) Encounters with the Holy Land: Place, Past and Future in American Jewish Culture (museum catalog), 1997; (ed. with H.R. Diner and J. Shandler) Remembering the Lower East Side: American Jewish Reflections, 2000; The Jewish Americans: Three Centuries of Jewish Voices in America, 2007; History Lessons: The Creation of American Jewish Heritage, 2010. Contributor to journals. Works appear in anthologies. **Address:** Department of History, University of Pennsylvania, 320 College Hall, 3451 Walnut St., Philadelphia, PA 19104, U.S.A. **Online address:** bwenger@sas.upenn.edu

WENGER, Etienne. American/Swiss (born Switzerland), b. 1952. **Genres:** Information Science/Computers. **Career:** Alliance Française, French teacher, 1974-77; Unity School, assistant principal, 1977-79; Battelle Institute, systems analyst, 1981-82; Institute for Research on Learning, teacher, research scientist, 1987-97, affiliated; writer, speaker, researcher and consultant, 1997-; University of Aalborg, honorary professor, 2005-; CPsquare, founder, director. **Publications:** Artificial Intelligence and Tutoring Systems: Computational and Cognitive Approaches to the Communication of Knowledge, 1987; (with J. Lave) Situated Learning: Legitimate Peripheral Participation, 1991; Communities of Practice: Learning, Meaning and Identity, 1998; (with R. McDermott and W. Snyder) Cultivating Communities of Practice: A Guide to Managing Knowledge, 2002; (ed. with M. Huysman and V. Wulf) Communities and Technologies: Proceedings of the First International Conference on Communities and Technologies, 2003; Digital Habitats, 2009; (with N. White and J. Smith) Digital Hanitats, 2010. **Address:** PO Box 810, North San Juan, CA 95960, U.S.A. **Online address:** etienne@ewenger.com

WENGERT, Timothy J. American (born United States), b. 1950. **Genres:** Theology/Religion, Law. **Career:** Lutheran church, assistant pastor, 1977-78, pastor, 1983-89; Lutheran Theological Seminary, professor, 1989-, Ministerium of Pennsylvania professor. Writer. **Publications:** Philip Melanchthon's Annotationes in Johannem, 1987; Law and Gospel, 1997; Human Freedom, Christian Righteousness, 1998; The 1529 Holy Week and Easter Sermons of Dr. Martin Luther, 1999; (with G.W. Lathrop) Christian Assembly: Marks of the Church in a Pluralistic Age, 2004; Formula for Parish Practice: Using the Formula of Concord in Congregations, 2006; Priesthood, Pastors, Bishops: Public Ministry for the Reformation and Today, 2008; Martin Luther's Catechisms: Forming the Faith, 2009; Philip Melanchthon, Speaker of the Reformation: Wittenberg's Other Reformer, 2010. EDITOR: (with C. Brockwell) Telling the Churches Stories, 1995; (with M.P. Graham) Philip Melanchthon and the Commentary, 1997; (with R. Kolb) Book of Concord: the Confessions of the Evangelical Lutheran Church, 2000; Harvesting Martin Luther's Reflections on Theology, Ethics and the Church, 2004; Pastoral Luther, 2009. **Address:** Lutheran Theological Seminary, 7301 Germantown Ave., Philadelphia, PA 19119-1794, U.S.A. **Online address:** twengert@ltsp.edu

WENHAM, David. British (born England), b. 1945. **Genres:** Theology/Religion, History, Social Sciences. **Career:** Inter-Varsity Fellowship, secretary, 1971-74; Union Biblical Seminary, lecturer in new testament studies, 1974-79; Tyndale House, head of gospels research project, 1979-83; University of Oxford, Wycliffe Hall, tutor in New tTestament studies, 1983-2007, vice-principal and dean; Shelswell Group of Parishes, associate priest, 1995-2002; Histon Parish Church, lay reader; University of Bristol, research fellow; Trinity College, senior tutor, 2008-, vice-principal. Writer. **Publications:** (Ed. with R.T. France) Studies in Midrash and historiography, 1983; The Rediscovery of Jesus's Eschatological Discourse, 1984; (ed. with C. Blomberg) The Miracles of Jesus, 1986; The Parables of Jesus, 1989; Paul: Follower of Jesus or Founder of Christianity?, 1995; (with S. Walton) Exploring the New Testament, vol. I, 2001; Paul and Jesus: The True Story, 2002; (intro.) The Elements of New Testament Greek, 3rd ed., 2005; Did St Paul Get Jesus Right? The Gospel According to Paul, 2010. Contributor to periodicals. **Address:** Trinity College, Stoke Hill, Stoke Bishop, Bristol, BS9 1JP, England. **Online address:** david.wenham@trinity-bris.ac.uk

WERBACH, Adam. American (born United), b. 1973?. **Genres:** Autobiography/Memoirs, Business/Trade/Industry, Engineering. **Career:** Sierra Student Coalition, founder and director, 1991-; Sierra Club, president and head, 1996-; Act Now Productions (now Saatchi & Saatchi), founder and global chief executive officer, 1998-, chief sustainability officer. Writer, producer and director. **Publications:** Act Now, Apologize Later: If You Don't Stand Up for Something, You'll Fall for Anything, 1997; Strategy for Sustainability: A Business Manifesto, 2009. **Address:** Saatchi & Saatchi S, 501 York St., San Francisco, CA 94110-1438, U.S.A. **Online address:** adam.werbach@sierraclub.org

WERBER, Bernard. French (born France), b. 1961. **Genres:** Novels, Sciences, Young Adult Fiction. **Career:** Freelance journalist, 1983; New Observer, scientific journalist, 1984-90. **Publications:** L

es fourmis, 1991; Le Jour des fourmis, 1992; Les Thanatonautes, 1994; La Révolution des fourmis, 1996; Le Père de nos Pères, 1998; L'empire des Anges: Roman, 2000; L'Ultime Secret, 2001; Arbre des Possibles et Autres Histoires, 2002; Nous les Dieux, 2004; Le papillon des étoiles: roman, 2006; Le mystère des dieux, 2007; Paradis sur mesure, 2008; Nouvelle encyclopédie du savoir relatif et Absolu, 2009; Le miroir de Cassandre, 2009; Rire du Cyclope: Roman, 2010. **Address:** c/o Albin Michel, 22 rue Huyghens, Paris, 75680, France.

WERBNER, Pnina. British/South African (born South Africa), b. 1944. **Genres:** Anthropology/Ethnology, Politics/Government. **Career:** Keele University, School of Sociology and Criminology, reader in social anthropology, 1997-2001, professor of social anthropology, 2001-, now professor emeritus, Research Institute in Law, Politics and Justice, Centre for Social, Cultural and Postcolonial Research, chair, 2004-. Writer and social anthropologist. **Publications:** The Migration Process: Capital, Gifts, and Offerings among British Pakistanis, 1990; (ed. with H. Donnan) Economy and Culture in Pakistan: Migrants and Cities in a Muslim Society, 1991; (ed. with M. Anwar) Black and Ethnic Leaderships in Britain: The Cultural Dimensions of Political Action, 1991; (ed. with T. Modood) Debating Cultural Hybridity: Multi-cultural Identities and the Politics of Anti-racism, 1997; (ed. with T. Modood) The Politics of Multiculturalism in the New Europe: Racism, Identity, and Com-

munity, 1997; (ed. with H. Basu) Embodying Charisma: Modernity, Locality, and Performance of Emotion in Sufi Cults, 1998; (ed. with N. Yuval-Davis) Women, Citizenship and Difference, 1999; Imagined Diasporas among Manchester Muslims: The Public Performance of Pakistani Transnational Identity Politics, 2002; Pilgrims of Love: The Anthropology of a Global Sufi Cult, 2003; (ed.) Anthropology and the New Cosmopolitanism: Rooted, Feminist and Vernacular Perspectives, 2008. **Address:** School of Sociology and Criminology, Keele University, Rm. CBB1.008, Keele, ST ST5 5BG, England. **Online address:** p.werbner@keele.ac.uk

WERCKMEISTER, O(tto) K(arl). American/German (born Germany), b. 1934. **Genres:** Art/Art History, Essays, Politics/Government, Cultural/Ethnic Topics. **Career:** University of California, professor of art history, 1971-84; Northwestern University, Mary Jane Crowe distinguished professor of art history, 1984-, now Mary Jane Crowe distinguished professor emeritus of art history. Writer. **Publications:** Der Deckel des Codex aureus von St. Emmeram: Ein Goldschmiedewerk des S. Jahrhunderts, 1963; Die Bilder der drei Propheton in der BibliaHispalense, 1963; Three Problems of Tradition in Pre-Carolingian Figure Style: From Visigothic to Insular Illumination, 1963; Irisch-northumbrische Buchmalerei des S. Jahrhunderts und monastische Spiritualitæt, 1967; Ende der æsthetik, 1971; Ideologie und Kunst bei Marx und andere Essays, 1974; The Political Ideology of the BayeuxTapestry, 1976; Versuche über Paul Klee, 1981; The Making of Paul Klee's Career, 1914-1920, 1989; Zitadellenkultur: die Schöne Kunst des Untergangs in der Kultur der Achtziger Jahre, 1989; (ed. with R. Rumold) The Ideological Crisis of Expressionism: The Literary and Artistic German War Colony in Belgium, 1914-1918, 1990; Citadel Culture, 1991; Linkelkonen, 1997; Icons of the Left: Benjamin and Eisenstein, Picasso and Kafka after the Fall of Communism, 1999; (Contrib.) Paul Klee 1933/Pamela Kort, 2003; Der Medusa-Effekt: Politische Bildstrategien seit dem 11. September 2001, 2005; Surrealistische Kriegsbild bei Max von Moos, 2005; The Political Confrontation of the Arts: From the Great Depression to the Second World War, 1929-1939, forthcoming. **Address:** Department of Art History, Northwestern University, Rm. 3-400, Kresge Hall, 1880 Campus Dr., 1881 Sheridan Rd., Evanston, IL 60208-0818, U.S.A. **Online address:** okw2002@aol.com

WERLOCK, Abby Holmes P(otter). American (born United States), b. 1942. **Genres:** Literary Criticism And History, Young Adult Fiction. **Career:** Madeira School, instructor in English, 1968-69; American University Association, instructor in English, 1970-72; International School of Bangkok, instructor in English, 1970-72; University of Maryland, instructor, 1971-72; University of Sussex, lecturer in English, 1972-74; Columbus International College, instructor in English, chairperson of department, 1974-77; National Cathedral School, instructor in English, 1979-84; Hamilton College, visiting assistant professor of English, 1984-87; St. Olaf College, associate professor of English, 1987-98, associate professor emerita, 1999-; writer, 1998-. **Publications:** (With M. Pearlman) Tillie Olsen, 1991; (ed.) British Women Writing Fiction, 2000; (ed.) The Facts on File Companion to the American Short Story, 2000, (ed. with J.P. Werlock) 2nd ed., 2009; Carol Shields' The Stone Diaries: A Reader's Guide, 2001; The Facts on File Companion to the American Novel, 2004. Contributor of articles to periodicals. **Address:** St Olaf College, 1520 St. Olaf Ave., Northfield, MN 55057, U.S.A. **Online address:** abby@werlock.com

WERMAN, Golda. Israeli/German/American (born United States), b. 1930. **Genres:** Literary Criticism And History, Translations, Biography. **Career:** Indiana University, director of program in Jerusalem, 1972-91; University of Wisconsin, Madison, director of overseas program in Jerusalem, 1985-. Writer. **Publications:** Milton and Midrash, 1995. TRANSLATION: The Dybbuk and Other Writings, 1992; (and intro.) The Stories of David Bergelson, 1996; (with R. Werman) Strange Ways, 2007. Contributor to periodicals. **Address:** 1 Nachalat Zadok St., Jerusalem, 95458, Israel. **Online address:** rwerman@vms.huji.ac.il

WERNER, Marta L. American (born United States), b. 1964?. **Genres:** Literary Criticism And History, Poetry. **Career:** Georgia State University, assistant professor of literature; D'Youville College, assistant professor of English, associate professor of English, Literary journal Sketch, faculty advisor. Writer. **Publications:** (Ed.) Emily Dickinson's Open Folios: Scenes of Reading, Surfaces of Writing, 1995; Radical Scatters: Emily Dickinson's Fragments and Related Texts, 1870-1886, 2000; (ed.) Ordinary Mysteries: The Common Journal of Nathaniel and Sophia Hawthorne, 1842-1843, 2005. Contributor to books and journals. **Address:** Department of English, D'Youville College,

320 Porter Ave., ALT 426, Buffalo, NY 14201-9985, U.S.A. **Online address:** wernerm@dyc.edu

WERNICK, Andrew (Lee). Canadian/British (born England), b. 1945. **Genres:** Cultural/Ethnic Topics, Sociology, Advertising/Public Relations, Communications/Media, Gerontology/Senior Issues, Intellectual History, Theology/Religion, Social Sciences, Young Adult Non-fiction, Humanities. **Career:** Trent University, assistant professor, 1972-78, associate professor, 1978-83, professor of cultural studies and sociology, 1983-, Graduate Program in Methodologies for the Study of Western History and Culture, director, Trent's Cultural Studies Program, chairperson, 1983-88, 2003-07, now professor emeritus of cultural studies and sociology; Institute for Contemporary Arts, lecturer; Ivan Franko National University, visiting professor. Writer. **Publications:** Promotional Culture: Advertising, Ideology and Symbolic Expression, 1991; (ed. with P. Berry and contrib.) Shadow of Spirit: Religion and Postmodernism, 1992; (ed. with M. Featherstone) Images of Aging: Cultural Representations of Later Life, 1995; Auguste Comte and the Religion of Humanity: The Post-Theistic Program of French Social Theory, 2001. Contributor to periodicals and books. **Address:** Department of Cultural Studies, Trent University, Rm. 202, Scott House, 300 London St., Peterborough, ON K9H 7P4, Canada. **Online address:** awernick@trentu.ca

WERRIS, Wendy. American (born United States), b. 1950?. **Genres:** Literary Criticism And History, Young Adult Non-fiction, Autobiography/Memoirs. **Career:** Pickwick Bookshop, sales associate, 1970; Rolling Stone/Straight Arrow Books, sales representative, 1975-. Writer and photographer. **Publications:** An Alphabetical Life: Living It Up in the World of Books, 2006. Contributor to magazines and journals. **Address:** B.J. Robbins Literary Agency, 5130 Bellaire Ave., North Hollywood, CA 91607, U.S.A. **Online address:** whenwhere2@sbcglobal.net

WERSBA, Barbara. American (born United States), b. 1932. **Genres:** Children's Fiction, Poetry, Novels, Young Adult Fiction, Animals/Pets, Romance/Historical, Young Adult Non-fiction. **Career:** Actress, 1944-59; writer, 1959-; The Bookman Press, founder, 1994-; Rockland Center for the Arts, instructor of writing. **Publications:** The Boy Who Loved the Sea, 1961; The Brave Balloon of Benjamin Buckley, 1963; The Land of Forgotten Beasts, 1964; A Song for Clowns, 1965; Do Tigers Ever Bite Kings? (verse), 1966; The Dream Watcher, 1968; Run Softly, Go Fast, 1970; Let Me Fall Before I Fly, 1971; Amanda Dreaming, 1973; The Country of the Heart, 1975; Tunes for a Small Harmonica: A Novel, 1976; Twenty-Six Starlings Will Fly Through Your Mind (verse), 1980; The Crystal Child, 1982; The Carnival in My Mind, 1982; Crazy Vanilla, 1986; Fat: A Love Story, 1987; Love Is the Crooked Thing, 1987; Beautiful Losers, 1988; Just Be Gorgeous: A Novel, 1988; Wonderful Me: A Novel, 1989; The Farewell Kid: A Novel, 1990; The Best Place to Live is the Ceiling: A Novel, 1990; Brother Mouky and the Falling Sun, 1990; You'll Never Guess the End, 1992; Life Is What Happens While You're Making Other Plans, 1994; Whistle Me Home, 1997; Walter: The Story of a Rat, 2005. Contributor to books and magazines. **Address:** McIntosh & Otis Inc., 310 Madison Ave., New York, NY 10017, U.S.A. **Online address:** wersba@frontstreetbooks.com

WERSHLER-HENRY, Darren Sean. Canadian (born Canada), b. 1966?. **Genres:** Poetry, Literary Criticism And History, Cartoons. **Career:** Technical writer, 1996-97; Coach House Books, senior editor, 1998-2002; York University, Communication Studies program, instructor, 2002-05; Canadian Film Centre, CFC Media Lab, instructor, 2002-07, faculty, 2008-; Wilfrid Laurier University, Department of Communication Studies, assistant professor of communications, 2005-10, graduate studies, 2006; Concordia University, Technoculture, Art and Games Group, faculty, 2010-, Department of English, assistant professor, 2010-, chair in media and contemporary literature, 2011-. **Publications:** Nicholodeon: A Book of Lowerglyphs (poetry), 1997; (with S. Mitchell) Internet Directory 2000, 1999; (with M. Surman) Commonspace: Beyond Virtual Community, 2000; The Tapeworm Foundry andor the Dangerous Prevalence of Imagination (poetry), 2000; (with H. Niedzviecki) The Original Canadian City Dweller's Almanac: Facts, Rants, Anecdotes and Unsupported Assertions for Urban Residents, 2002; Free as in Speech and Beer: Open Source, Peer-to-Peer and the Economics of the Online Revolution, 2002; (ed. with M. Higgins and S. Pender) The Common Sky: Canadian Writers against the War, 2003; (with B. Kennedy) Apostrophe, 2006; The Iron Whim: A Fragmented History of Typewriting, 2007; Guy Maddin's My Winnipeg, 2010. **Address:** Department of Communication Studies, Wilfrid Laurier University, DAWB 3-142, Alvin Woods Bldg., 75 University Ave. W,

Waterloo, ON N2L 3C5, Canada. **Online address:** dwershlerhenry@wlu.ca

WERT, Jonathan (Maxwell). American (born United States), b. 1939. **Genres:** Administration/Management, Education, Environmental Sciences/Ecology, Bibliography, Genealogy/Heraldry, Biography, Sciences, Poetry, History. **Career:** Bays Mountain Park, Department of Environmental Education, program director and chief of interpretive services, 1969-71; Tennessee Valley Authority, supervisor, Environmental Education Section, staff, 1971-74, Energy Conservation Education Section and Energy Resource Materials Center, staff, 1974-75, consultant; Journal of Environmental Education, editor, 1975-; Management Diagnostics Inc., president, 1985-; Fermi, Perry, Brunswick, Palo Verde, and FitzPatrick Nuclear Generating Plants, management and organization consultant; Oglethorpe Power Corp., consultant; Pennsylvania Power & Light Co., work process consultant; Calvert Cliffs Nuclear Generating Station, consultant; Maine Yankee Nuclear Generating Station, management and work process consultant; Wisconsin Electric Power Co., consultant; U. S. Department of Energy, consultant; Butler, Porter, Gay and Day, Attorneys, consultant; United States Energy Association, executive consultant; Jay Fulkroad & Sons Inc., consultant; Empire Kosher Foods Inc., consultant; Blair County Commissioners and Director of Personnel, consultant; Connecticut Department of Public Utility Control, management consultant; Clinton Power Station, management and organization contractor. Writer. **Publications:** Tombstone Inscriptions for Wirth's Evangelical Lutheran Church Cemetery, 1968; Environmental Education Study Projects for College Students and for High School Students, 1974; Developing Environmental Education Curriculum Material, 1974; Developing Environmental Study Areas, 1974; Process Model Showing How a Federal Government Agency, Such as the Tennessee Valley Authority, Can Utilize Its Resources to Cooperate with Other Agencies in the Development of Environmental Education Programs for the Tennessee Valley Region: A Dissertati, 1974; Finding Solutions to Environmental Problems... A Process Guide, 1975; Energy: Selected Resource Materials for Developing Energy Education/Conservation Programs, 1975; (co-author) Energy Conservation Education in the Public Schools of Tennessee, 1975; Assessing an Issue in Relation to Environmental, Economic and Social Impact, 1976; Energy Education/Conservation, 1976; Selected Energy Conservation Options for the Home, 1978; Energy Conservation Measures for Mobile Home Dwellers, 1978; Selected Energy Management Options for Small Business and Local Government, 1978; Life Lines: A Book of Poetry, Prose and Axioms, 1983; Survivorship and Growth in Employment, 1983; Chronology of Events: History of Wirth's Evangelical Lutheran Church, 1770-1815, 1995; (comp.) Wert Ancestors of Jonathan M. Wert, 1995; Organizational Culture Characteristics, 1996; Violations of Good Business Practices, 1996; The Wert Family of Dauphin County, Pennsylvania, 1996; Safety Culture at Nuclear Plants, 1996. **Address:** Management Diagnostics Inc., PO Box 240, Port Royal, PA 17082-0240, U.S.A. **Online address:** jwert@mdi-wert.com

WERTENBAKER, Timberlake. British/American (born United States), b. 1951?. **Genres:** Plays/Screenplays, Translations, Novels. **Career:** Time-Life Books, staff writer; Shared Experience, resident writer, 1983; Royal Court Theatre, writer-in-residence, 1984-85. Journalist, teacher and translator. **Publications:** New Anatomies, 1980; Inside Out, 1982; Abel's Sister, 1983; The Grace of Mary Traverse, 1985, rev. ed., 1999; Our Country's Good: Based on The Playmaker, a novel by Thomas Keneally, 1989; The Love of the Nightingale, 1989; Three Birds Alighting on a Field, 1993; The Break of Day, 1995; (and intro.) Plays One, 1996; After Darwin, 1998; After Darwin: A Play in Two Acts, 1999; The Ash Girl, 2000; Credible Witness, 2001; Timberlake Wertenbaker: Plays Two, 2002; Credible Witness: A Full-Length Play, 2003; (with D. Short and G. Preissova) Jenufa, 2007; (with Euripides) Hecuba, 2009; Line, 2009. TRANSLATOR: A. Mnouchkine, Mephisto, 1986; J. Anouilh, Leocadia, 1987; (adapted) The Thebans, 1992; P. Marivaux, False Admissions, 1990; P. Marivaux, La Dispute, 1990; P.Marivaux, Successful Strategies, 1990; Eduardo de Filippo, Filumena, 1999; M. Maeterlink, Pelléas and Mélisande, 1999; F.G. Lorca, The House of Bernarda Alba, 1999; (with M. Williamson) Euripides' Hippolytus: A New Version, 2009. **Address:** Casarotto Ramsay & Associates Ltd., Waverley House, 7-12 Noel St., London, GL W1F 8GQ, England.

WERTH, Barry. American (born United States), b. 1952. **Genres:** Documentaries/Reportage. **Career:** Writer. **Publications:** The Billion-Dollar Molecule: One Companys Quest for the Perfect Drug, 1994; Damages: One Family's Legal Struggles in the World of Medicine, 1998; The Scarlet Professor: Newton Arvin: A Literary Life Shattered by Scandal, 2001; (with A. Tsiaras)

From Conception to Birth: A Life Unfolds, 2002; The Architecture and Design of Man and Woman: The Marvel of the Human Body, Revealed, 2004; 31 Days: The Crisis That Gave Us the Government We Have Today, 2006; Banquet At Delmonicos: Great Minds, the Gilded Age, and the Triumph of Evolution in America, 2009. **Address:** c/o Amanda Urban, International Creative Management, 40 W 57th St., New York, NY 10019, U.S.A. **Online address:** info@barrywerth.com

WERTHEIMER, Jack. American (born United States), b. 1948. **Genres:** Cultural/Ethnic Topics, History. **Career:** City University of New York, adjunct instructor, 1972-78, Queens College, adjunct instructor, 1972-78; City College, adjunct instructor, 1972-78; Herbert H. Lehman College, adjunct instructor, 1972-78; York College, adjunct instructor, 1972-78; College of Mount St. Vincent, adjunct instructor, 1972-78; Vassar College, visiting assistant professor, 1978-79; Jewish Theological Seminary of America, provost and professor of Jewish history, 1979-, Joseph and Martha Mendelson professor of American Jewish history, 1993-; Joseph and Miriam Ratner Center for the Study of Conservative Judaism, founding director, 1987-2008; Reconstructionist Rabbinical College, adjunct associate professor, 1988-89; U.S. Military Academy, adjunct associate professor, 1992; Columbia University, presidents fellow, National Foundation for Jewish Culture, presidents fellow. Writer. **Publications:** Understanding the Holocaust: How It Happened-Why It Happened, 1981; Unwelcome Strangers: East European Jews in Imperial Germany, 1987; A People Divided: Judaism in Contemporary America, 1993; Jewish Identity and Religious Commitment: The North American Study of Conservative Synagogues and Their Members, 1995-1996, 1997; Talking Dollars and Sense about Jewish Education, 2001; All Quiet on the Religious Front: Jewish Unity, Denominationalism, and Postdenominationalism, 2005; Linking the Silos: How to Accelerate the Momentum in Jewish Education Today, 2005; Recent Trends in Supplementary Jewish Education, 2007; A Census of Jewish Supplementary Schools in the United States, 2006-2007, 2008; Schools that Work: What We Can Learn From Good Jewish Supplementary Schools, 2009; Generation of Change: How Leaders in Their Twenties and Thirties are Reshaping American Jewish Life, 2010. EDITOR AND CONTRIBUTOR: The American Synagogue: A Sanctuary Transformed, 1987; Uses of Tradition: Jewish Continuity in the Modern Era, 1992; The Modern Jewish Experience: A Reader's Guide, 1993; (and comp.) Conservative Synagogues and Their Members: Highlights of the North American Survey of 1995-1996, 1996; Tradition Renewed: A History of the Jewish Theological Seminary, 2 vols., 1997; Jews in the Center: Conservative Synagogues and Their Members (essay), 2000; Jewish Religious Leadership: Image and Reality (essay), 2004; (ed. with E. Lederhendler) Text and Context: Essays in Modern Jewish History and Historiography in Honor of Ismar Schorsch Family Matters: Jewish Education in an Age of Choice, 2007; Imagining the American Jewish Community, 2007; Learning and Community: Jewish Supplementary Schools in the Twenty-first Century, 2009; The New Jewish Leaders: Reshaping the American Jewish Landscape, 2011. **Address:** Department of Jewish History, Jewish Theological Seminary of America, 3080 Broadway, New York, NY 10027, U.S.A. **Online address:** jawertheimer@jtsa.edu

WESCHLER, Lawrence. American (born United States), b. 1952. **Genres:** Biography, Art/Art History, Humanities, International Relations/Current Affairs, Writing/Journalism, Politics/Government. **Career:** University of California-Los Angeles, Oral History Project, editor and interviewer, 1974-78, faculty, Ernst Toch Archive, director; freelance writer, 1978-80; New Yorker, staff writer, 1981-2002; University of California-Santa Cruz, Regents lecturer, 1989, Bard Center, fellow, 1992; New York Institute for Humanities, director, 1990-; Sarah Lawrence College, faculty; McSweeney's, contributing editor; Threepenny Review, contributing editor; Wholphin DVD, curator; Virginia Quarterly Review, art wrangler; New York University, faculty; Columbia University, faculty; Princeton University, faculty; Chicago Humanities Festival, artistic director, 2006. **Publications:** Ernst Toch, 1887-1964: A Biographical Essay Ten Years After His Passing, 1974; Seeing Is Forgetting the Name of the Thing One Sees: A Life of Contemporary Artist Robert Irwin, 1982; Solidarity, Poland in the Season of its Passion, 1982; The Passion of Poland, from Solidarity Through the State of War, 1984; (trans.) True to Life, 1984; (ed.) Being and Circumstance: Notes Toward a Conditional Art, 1985; (trans.) Hanna Krall, Shielding the Flame: An Intimate Conversation with Marek Edelmen, the Last Surviving Leader of the Warsaw Ghetto Uprising, 1986; Shapinsky's Karma, Boggs's Bills, and Other True Life Tales, 1988; A Miracle, a Universe: Settling Accounts with Torturers, 1990; Mr. Wilson's Cabinet of Wonder, 1995; Calamaties of Exile: Three Nonfiction Novellas, 1998; A Wanderer in the Perfect City: Selected Passion Pieces, 1998; Calami-

ties of Exile, 1998; Boggs: A Comedy of Values, 1999; Robert Irwin Getty Garden, 2002; Vermeer in Bosnia: A Reader, 2004; Everything That Rises: A Book of Convergences, 2006; (with N. Baume, J. Mergel) Tara Donovan, 2008; Seeing is Forgetting the Name of the Thing One Sees: Over Thirty Years of Conversations with Robert Irwin, 2008; Uncanny Valley: Adventures in the Narrative, 2011. **Address:** New York Institute for Humanities, New York University, New York, NY 10036, U.S.A.

WESKER, Arnold. British (born England), b. 1932. **Genres:** Novellas/Short Stories, Young Adult Fiction, Plays/Screenplays, Autobiography/Memoirs, Essays, Novels, Young Adult Non-fiction, Music, Music. **Career:** Playwright, 1958-; Centre Forty Two, co-founder, 1961, artistic director, 1961-70; director, 1968-; British Centre on International Theatre Institute, chairman, 1978-82. **Publications:** PLAYS: Chicken Soup with Barley, 1958; Roots, 1959; I'm Talking about Jerusalem, 1960; The Wesker Trilogy, 1960; The Kitchen: A Play in Two Parts with an Interlude, 1961; Chips with Everything: A Play in Two Acts, 1962; The Nottingham Captain: A Moral for Narrator, Voices and Orchestra, 1962; Master, 1966; Their Very Own and Golden City: A Play in Two Acts and Twenty-Nine Scenes 1966; The Four Seasons: A Play in Two Parts, 1966; The Friends: A Play in Two Acts, 1970; The Old Ones, 1973, rev. ed., 1974; The Journalists, 1975, as The Journalists: A Triptych, 1979; Three Plays, 1976; The Plays of Arnold Wesker, vol. I, 1976, vol. II, 1977; The Merchant, 1977, rev. ed., 1983; Love Letters on Blue Paper, 1978; Caritas, 1981; Cinders, 1982; Annie Wobbler, 1986; Longitude: A Play, 2006; Arnold Wesker's Love Plays, 2008; Arnold Wesker's Social Plays, 2009; Groupie, 2010; Political Plays, 2010; Joy and Tyranny, 2011; Wesker's Comedies, 2012; Wesker's Domestic Plays, 2012; Wesker's Historical Plays, 2012. OTHERS: Labour and the Arts: II, or What, Then, is to Be Done?, 1960; The Modern Playwright; or, O Mother, is it Worth it?, 1961; (intro.) The Serving Boy, 1968; Fears of Fragmentation (essays), 1970; Six Sundays in January, 1971; Love Letters on Blue Paper: Three Stories, 1974; (contrib.) Say Goodbye, You May Never See Them Again: Scenes from Two East-End Backgrounds, 1974; Words as Definitions of Experience, 1976; Journey into Journalism: A Very Personal Account in Four Parts, 1977; Fatlips: A Story for Children, 1978; Said the Old Man to the Young Man: Three Stories (short stories), 1978; Love Letters on Blue Paper, 1980; Distinctions, 1985; Three Women Talking, 1990; Letter to a Daughter, 1990; Blood Libel, 1991; Wild Spring, 1992; As Much As I Dare, 1932-1959 (autobiography), 1994; The Birth of Shylock and the Death of Zero Mostel: Diary of a Play 1973 to 1980, 1997; Honey: A Novel, 2005; The Rocking Horse, 2007; All Things Tire of Themselves, 2008; Wesker's Monologues, 2009; On Theatre, 2010; Ambivalences, 2011. **Address:** Hay on Wye, Hereford, HW HR3 5RJ, England. **Online address:** wesker@compuserve.com

WESLEY, Carolyn. See **CRANE, Caroline.**

WESLEY, Patricia Jabbeh. American (born United States) **Genres:** Poetry. **Career:** University of Liberia, instructor in English and writing, 1980-90; Grand Valley State University, instructor in writing, 1992-94; Davenport College of Business, instructor, 1992-96; Aquinas College, instructor in literature and writing, 1993-96; Kalamazoo Institute of Arts, storyteller and Africa outreach researcher, 1995-; Kalamazoo College, Lee Stryker Center, instructor, 1997-98; Western Michigan University, research associate, 1998-, Department of English, doctoral associate, 1998-2002, assistant professor, 2002-03; Indiana University of Pennsylvania, Department of English, assistant professor, 2003-05; Pennsylvania State University, assistant professor of English, 2005-, associate professor of English. Writer. **Publications:** (Contrib.) New to North America, 1997; Before the Palm Could Bloom: Poems of Africa, 1998; Becoming Ebony, 2003; The River is Rising: Poems, 2007; Where the Road Turns: Poems, 2010; Remnants: A Family's Story, forthcoming; The A.B.C. of Children's African Name Book: Children Meeting Children, forthcoming. Contributor to books and periodicals. **Address:** Division of Arts and Humanities, Pennsylvania State University, 125 Misciagna Family Center for Performing Arts, 3000 Ivyside Pk., Altoona, PA 16601, U.S.A. **Online address:** jlajeh@gmail.com

WESLEY, Richard (Errol). American (born United States), b. 1945. **Genres:** Plays/Screenplays. **Career:** United Airlines, passenger service agent, 1967-69; Black Theatre, editor, 1969-73; Frank Silvera Writers Workshop, founding member, 1974-82; Manhattanville College, faculty, 1975; Wesleyan University, faculty, 1973-74; Manhattan Community College, lecturer in black art and creative writing, 1980-81, 1982-83; Rutgers University, faculty, 1984; New York University, Tisch School of the Arts, Department of

Dramatic Writing, assistant professor, associate professor in playwriting and screenwriting, Goldberg Department of Dramatic Writing, acting chair, chair, 2005-. **Publications:** The Black Terror (in The New Lafayette Theatre Presents), 1974; The Sirens, 1975; The Mighty Gents, 1979; The Past Is the Past, and Gettin' It Together, 1979; On the Road to Babylon, 1982; The Dream Team, 1987; Heaven and the Homeboy, 1997. **Address:** Goldberg Department of Dramatic Writing, Tisch School of the Arts, New York University, Rm. 742, 721 Broadway, 7th Fl., New York, NY 10003, U.S.A. **Online address:** rew3@nyu.edu

WESLEY, Valerie Wilson. American (born United States), b. 1947. **Genres:** Mystery/Crime/Suspense, Young Adult Fiction, Young Adult Non-fiction, Children's Fiction, Novels. **Career:** Scholastic News, associate editor; Essence Magazine, senior editor, executive editor, contributing editor; Sisters of Crime, director; Newark Arts Council, director; Ramapo College, adjunct faculty. **Publications:** NON FICTION: (with W. Hudson) Afro-Bets Book of Black Heroes from A to Z: An Introduction to Important Black Achievers for Young Readers, 1988. JUVENILE FICTION: Where Do I Go From Here? (young adult novel), 1993; Freedom's Gifts: A Juneteenth Mystery, 1997; Ain't Nobody's Business If I Do, 1999; Always True to You in My Fashion, 2002; No Way of Dying, 2004; Playing My Mother's Blues, 2005. TAMARA HAYLE MYSTERY NOVELS: When Death Comes Stealing, 1994; Devil's Gonna Get Him, 1995; Where Evil Sleeps, 1996; No Hiding Place, 1997; Easier to Kill, 1998; The Devil Riding, 2000; Dying in the Dark, 2004; Of Blood and Sorrow, 2008. OTHERS: Willimena and the Cookie Money, 2001. WILLIMENA RULES! SERIES: How to Lose Your Class Pet, 2003; How to Fish Your Trouble, 2004; How to Lose Your Cookie Money, 2004; How to Almost Ruin Your Class Play, 2005; 23 Ways to Mess Up Valentine's Day, 2006; How to Face Up to the Class Bully, 2007; How to Have the Best Kwanzaa Ever, 2007. Contributor to periodicals. **Address:** Essence Magazine, 1500 Broadway, 6th Fl., New York, NY 10036, U.S.A. **Online address:** valwilwes@aol.com

WESS, Jane A. British (born England), b. 1953. **Genres:** Sciences, Bibliography. **Career:** Science Museum, curator of mathematics and astronomy, George III collection, science teaching, astronomy and weights and measures, 1979-. Writer. **Publications:** (With A.Q. Morton) Public and Private Science: The King George III Collection, 1993. **Address:** Science Museum, Exhibition Rd., London, GL SW7 2DD, England. **Online address:** j.wess@nmsi.ac.uk

WESSELL, Eva. (Eva-Maria Gawlyta). American/German (born Germany), b. 1939. **Genres:** Literary Criticism And History, Biography. **Career:** University of California, lecturer, 1987; Saddleback Community College, adjunct faculty, 1987-94; University of Southern California, lecturer, 1988-. Writer. **Publications:** (With H. Lehnert) Nihilismus Der Menschenfreundlichkeit: Thomas Manns Wandlung und sein Essay Goethe und Tolstoi, 1991; (ed. and contrib. with H. Lehnert) A Companion to the Works of Thomas Mann, 2004. **Address:** School of Humanities, University of California, 177 Humanities Instructional Bldg., Irvine, CA 92697-3390, U.S.A. **Online address:** ewessell@uci.edu

WESSELMANN, Debbie Lee. American (born United States), b. 1959. **Genres:** Novels, Novellas/Short Stories. **Career:** Fairleigh Dickinson University, creative writing instructor; Albright College, adjunct lecturer; Lehigh University, adjunct lecturer of English. Writer. **Publications:** Trutor & the Balloonist (novel), 1997; The Earth and the Sky (short story collection), 1998; Vibrissa, 2003; Captivity (novel), 2008. Contributor to journals. **Address:** 1518 Noah's Cir., Hellertown, PA 18055, U.S.A. **Online address:** dlw@trutor.net

WESSON, Joan. See **PITTOCK, Joan (Hornby).**

WEST, Bing. See **WEST, Francis J.**

WEST, Carter. See **WHITEHEAD, David (Henry).**

WEST, Colin. British (born England), b. 1951. **Genres:** Children's Fiction, Animals/Pets, Illustrations, Poetry. **Career:** Writer and illustrator. **Publications:** Out of the Blue From Nowhere, 1976; Step in the Wrong Direction: Poems and Pictures, 1984; The King's Toothache, 1988; I Bought My Love a Tabby Cat, 1988; Granny's Jungle Garden, 1999. SELF-ILLUSTRATED FOR CHILDREN: Not to Be Taken Seriously, 1982; (and ed.) The Land of Utter Nonsense, 1983; A Step in the Wrong Direction, 1984; Fat Puss and

Friends, 1984; It's Funny When You Look at It, 1984; Have You Seen the Crocodile?, 1986; Pardon? Said the Giraffe, 1986; The King of Kennelwick Castle, 1986; Hello! Great Big Bullfrog, 1987; Not Me! Said the Monkey, 1987; (and ed.) The Beginner's Book of Bad Behaviour, 1987; (with J. Banyard) A Moment in Rhyme, 1987; Once There Was an Elephant, 1987; Fat Puss on Wheels, 1988; One Little Elephant, 1988; Two Hooks, 1988; The Owl and the Pussy-Cat, 1988; Ten Little Crocodiles, 1988; What Would You Do With a Wobble-Dee-Woo?, 1988; Trotting Off to Market, 1988; Monty, the Dog Who Wears Glasses, 1990; The Royal Huddle, 1990; The Best of West, 1990; Go Tell It to the Toucan, 1990, rev. ed., 1996; Between the Sun, the Moon, and Me, 1990; Monty Bites Back, 1990; Monty: Up to His Neck in Trouble, 1991; Shape Up, Monty!, 1991; Monty Must Be Magic, 1992; Howard Helps Out, 1993; Hooray for Howard, 1993; Everything Happens to Howard, 1993; Hurry Up, Howard, 1993; Monty Ahoy!, 1994; Vanessa, the Pig with the Wiggly Waggly Ears, 1995; Messy Murray Brown, 1995; Long Tales, Short Tales and Tall Tales, 1995; Mum in a Million, 1995; Only Joking! Laughed the Lobster, 1995; One Day in the Jungle, 1995; I Don't Care said the Bear, 1996; Buzz, Buzz, Buzz, Went Bumblebee, 1996; Monty's Ups and Downs, 1996; Marmaduke the Magic Cat, 1996; The Wandering Bear, 1996; The Big Book of Nonsense, 2001; Moose and Mouse, 2004; Toby and his Old Tin Tub, 2006; Jenny the Joker, 2007; Grandpa's Boneshaker Bicycle, 2007; A Crocodile's Teeth, 2007; Uncle Pat and Auntie Pat, 2007; Crocodile Tears, 2008. **Address:** 14 High Rd., Epping, EX CM16 4AB, England.

WEST, Cornel (Ronald). American (born United States), b. 1953. **Genres:** Philosophy, Theology/Religion. **Career:** Union Theological Seminary, assistant professor of philosophy of religion, 1977-83, 1988; Yale University Divinity School, faculty, 1984-87; Princeton University, professor of religion, 1988-94, director of African American studies, 1988-94; Center for African American Studies, class of 1943 university professor, 2002-; Harvard University, professor of religion and Afro-American studies, 1994-99, Alphonse Fletcher Jr. university professor, 1999-2002; Haverford College, faculty. Writer. **Publications:** Prophesy Deliverance!: An Afro-American Revolutionary Christianity, 1982; Prophetic Fragments, 1988; The American Evasion of Philosophy: A Genealogy of Pragmatism, 1989; (with B. Hooks) Breaking Bread: Insurgent Black Intellectual Life, 1991; The Ethical Dimensions of Marxist Thought, 1991; Race Matters, 1993; Keeping Faith: Philosophy and Race in America, 1993; Beyond Eurocentrism and Multiculturalism, 1993; (with J.A. Snead) White Screens, Black Images, 1994; (with M. Lerner) Jews and Blacks: Let the Healing Begin, 1995; (with H.L. Gates) Future of the Race, 1996; Restoring Hope, 1997; (with R.M. Unger) Future of American Progressivism, 1998; (with S.A. Hewlett) The War against Parents, 1998; Cornel West: A Critical Reader, 1999; (with H.L. Gates) African-American Century, 2000; The Cornel West Reader, 2000; (foreword) Making it on Broken Promises: Leading African American Male Scholars Confront the Culture of Higher Education, 2002; Democracy Matters: Winning the Fight Against Imperialism, 2004; Covenant in Action, 2007; Hope on a Tightrope: Words & Wisdom, 2008; (with D. Ritz) Brother West: Living and Loving out Loud: A Memoir, 2009. CO-EDITOR: (with C. Guidote and M. Coakley) Theology in the Americas: Detroit II Conference Papers, 1982; (with J. Rajchman) Post-Analytic Philosophy, 1985; Out There: Marginalization and Contemporary Cultures, 1991; Encyclopedia of African-American Culture and History, 1996; Struggles in the Promised Land, 1997; (with Q.H. Dixie) Courage to Hope: From Black Suffering to Human Redemption, 1999; Other Malcolm, 2001; (with S.A. Hewlett and N. Rankin) Taking Parenting public: The Case for a New Social Movement, 2002; (with E.S. Glaude) African American Religious Thought: An Anthology, 2003; (K. Keeling, C. MacCabe) Racist Traces and Other Writings: European Pedigrees/African Contagions, 2003. Contributor to periodicals. **Address:** Center for African American Studies, Princeton University, Stanhope Hall, Princeton, NJ 08544, U.S.A. **Online address:** maryannr@princeton.edu

WEST, Darrell M. American (born United States), b. 1954. **Genres:** Politics/Government, Communications/Media. **Career:** Brookings Institution, research fellow, 1980-81; University of Pennsylvania, lecturer in political science, 1981-82; Brown University, John Hazen White distinguished professor of public policy and political science, 1982-, Taubman Center and the Center's Public Opinion Laboratory, director; Brookings Instituition, Center for Technology Innovation, director and vice-president; WJAR-TV, political commentator; WLNE-TV, political commentator. Writer. **Publications:** Making Campaigns Count: Leadership and Coalition-building in 1980, 1984; Congress and Economic Policymaking, 1987; Air Wars: Television Advertising in Election Campaigns, 1952-1992, 1993, 4th ed. as Air Wars: Television

Advertising in Election Campaigns, 1952-2008, 2010; (with T.J. Anton and J.D. Combs) Public Opinion in Rhode Island, 1984-1993: From the Greenhouse Compact to the Banking Crisis, 1984-1993, 1994; (with B.A. Loomis) Sound of Money: How Political Interests Get What They Want, 1998; Checkbook Democracy: How Money Corrupts Political Campaigns, 2000; Patrick Kennedy: The Rise to Power, 2001; (with T.J. Anton and J.D. Combs) Rhode Island Opinion, 1994-2000, 2001; Rise and Fall of the Media Establishment, 2001; (with J. Orman) Celebrity Politics, 2002; (ed. with L.S. Maisel) Running on Empty?: Political Discourse in Congressional Elections, 2004; Digital Government: Technology and Public Sector Performance, 2005; The Science-Industrial Complex: Biotechnology Policy Across National Boundaries, 2007; (with L.S. Maisel and B.M. Clifton) Evaluating Campaign Quality: Can the Electoral Process be Improved?, 2007; (with E.A. Miler) Digital Medicine: Health Care in the Internet Era, 2009; Brain Gain: Rethinking U.S. Immigration Policy, 2010. **Address:** Taubman Center for Public Policy, Brown University, Rm. 202, 67 George St., PO Box 1977, Providence, RI 02912-1977, U.S.A. **Online address:** darrell_west@brown.edu

WEST, Diana. American (born United States), b. 1961. **Genres:** Adult Non-fiction, Social Commentary. **Career:** Washington Times, journalist, 1999-2002, columnist; Scripps Howard News Service, columnist. **Publications:** The Death of the Grown-Up: How America's Arrested Development Is Bringing Down Western Civilization, 2007; The Hollow Center, forthcoming. Contributor to periodicals. **Address:** c/o Torie Hajdu, St. Martin's Press, 175 5th Ave., New York, NY 10010, U.S.A. **Online address:** deathofthegrownup@verizon.net

WEST, Donald James. British (born England), b. 1924. **Genres:** Criminology/True Crime, Gay And Lesbian Issues, Paranormal, Sex. **Career:** University of Cambridge, Institute of Criminology, professor, 1960-, now emeritus, Darwin College, emeritus fellow; Cambridge Psychiatric Service, honorary consultant psychiatrist; Society for Psychical Research, president, 1984-88. Writer. **Publications:** Eleven Lourdes Miracles, 1957; Psychical Research Today, 1962; The Habitual Prisoner, 1963; Murder Followed by Suicide, 1966; The Young Offender, 1967; Homosexuality, 1968; Present Conduct and Future Delinquency, 1969; (ed.) The Future of Parole, 1972; (with D.P. Farrington) Who Becomes Delinquent?, 1973; The Delinquent Way of Life, 1977; Homosexuality Re-Examined, 1977; (ed. with A. Walk) Daniel McNaughton: His Trial and the Aftermath, 1977; (with C. Roy and F.L. Nichols) Understanding Sexual Attacks, 1978; Delinquency, 1982; Sexual Victimisation, 1985; Sexual Crimes and Confrontations, 1987; (with C.K. Li and T.P. Woodhouse) Children's Sexual Encounters with Adults, 1990; (with B. De Villiers) Male Prostitution, 1993; (ed.) Sex Crimes, 1994; (ed. with R. Green) Socio-Legal Control of Homosexual Behavior: A Multi-Nation Comparison, 1997; Homosexuality: Its Nature and Causes, 2008. **Address:** Institute of Criminology, Cambridge University, 7 West Rd., Cambridge, CB3 9DT, England. **Online address:** donjwest@dial.pipex.com

WEST, Edward. American (born United States), b. 1949?. **Genres:** Photography, Travel/Exploration. **Career:** School of the Art Institute, assistant professor, 1973-80; University of Hawaii, staff, 1981-89; School of the Art Institute of Chicago, chair of photography; University of Michigan, School of Art and Design, professor and director of international program, 1990-, Center for Afroamerican and African Studies, professor of art. Writer and photographer. **Publications:** Casting Shadows: Images from a New South Africa: Photographs, 2001. **Address:** Center for Afroamerican and African Studies, University of Michigan, 505 S State St., 4700 Haven Hall, Ann Arbor, MI 48109-1045, U.S.A. **Online address:** ewest@umich.edu

WEST, Elliott. American (born United States), b. 1945. **Genres:** Essays, History. **Career:** University of Texas, assistant professor, 1971-75, associate professor, 1975-79; University of Arkansas, faculty, 1979-, alumni distinguished professor of American history, 2003-. Writer. **Publications:** (Ed. with M.F. Morris) Essays on Urban America, 1975; (ed. with K.R. Philp) Essays on Walter Prescott Webb, 1976; The Saloon on the Rocky Mountain Mining Frontier, 1979; Growing up with the Country: Childhood on the Farwestern Frontier, 1989; (ed. with P. Petrik) Small Worlds: Children and Adolescents in America, 1850-1950, 1992; The Way to the West: Essays on the Central Plains, 1995; Growing up in Twentieth-century America: A History and Reference Guide, 1996; The Contested Plains: Indians, Goldseekers, and the Rush to Colorado, 1998; Trail of Tears: National Historic Trail, 2000; Mining Frontiers of the Far West, 1848-1880, rev. ed., 2001; The Last Indian War: The Nez Perce Story, 2009. Contributor of articles to journals. **Address:**

Department of History, University of Arkansas, 416 Old Main, Fayetteville, AR 72701, U.S.A. **Online address:** ewest@uark.edu

WEST, Ewan (D.). British (born England), b. 1960. **Genres:** Music, Reference. **Career:** Oxford University, Worcester College, lecturer, 1986-94; Mansfield College, junior research fellow, 1988-92; Somerville College, director of studies in music and lecturer, 1989-94. Writer. **Publications:** (With J. Warrack) The Oxford Dictionary of Opera, 1992, (with J. Warrack) 3rd ed. as The Concise Oxford Dictionary of Opera, 1996. Contributor to journals. **Address:** 8 Drakes Pl., Cheltenham, GC GL50 2JF, England. **Online address:** ewan_west@mail.com

WEST, Francis J. (Bing West). American (born United States), b. 1940. **Genres:** Novels, Military/Defense/Arms Control, Adult Non-fiction. **Career:** Defense for International Security Affairs, director of program development, 1971-72, assistant secretary, deputy secretary, 1974-75; Naval War College, professor, 1973-74, dean of research, 1977-81; Tufts University, The Fletcher School, visiting professor, 1975-77; Hudson Institute, vice president; GAMA Corp., president; Rand Corp., analyst; Atlantic Monthly, correspondent. Writer. **Publications:** Small Unit Action in Vietnam, Summer 1966, 1967; The Village, 1972; (co-author) Naval Forces and Western Security, 1987. AS BING WEST: The Pepperdogs: A Novel, 2003; (with R.L. Smith) The March Up: Taking Baghdad with the 1st Marine Division, 2003; No True Glory: A Frontline Account Of The Battle For Fallujah, 2005; Strongest Tribe: War, Politics, And The Endgame In Iraq, 2008; Wrong War: Grit, Strategy, and the Way Out of Afghanistan, 2011; (with D. Meyer) Into the Fire: A Firsthand Account of the Most Extraordinary Battle in the Afghan War, 2012. **Address:** GAMA Corp., 6417 Loisdale Rd., Ste. 300, Springfield, VA 22150, U.S.A. **Online address:** westbing@yahoo.com

WEST, Harry G. British (born England), b. 1966. **Genres:** Politics/Government, Social Sciences. **Career:** University of London, lecturer in social anthropology & chair of the School of Oriental and African Studies Food Studies Center; Conducted anthropological research in Mueda, 1991-2005. Writer and educator. **Publications:** (ed. with G.W. Myers) Proceedings do Workshop Internacional Sobre a Politica da Terra em Africa: Maputo, 18-20 de Fevereiro de 1992, 1992; (ed. with G.W. Myers) Land Tenure Security and State Farm Divestiture in Mozambique: Case Studies in Nhamatanda, Manica and Montepuez Districts, 1993; (ed. with K.W. Thompson) Conflict and Its Resolution in Contemporary Africa, 1997; (ed. with T. Sanders) Transparency and Conspiracy: Ethnographies of Suspicion in the New World Order, 2003; Kupilikula: Governance and the Invisible Realm in Mozambique, 2005; (ed. with T.J. Luedke) Borders and Healers: Brokering Therapeutic Resources in Southeast Africa, 2006; Ethnographic Sorcery, 2007. Contributor of articles to periodicals. **Address:** School of Oriental & African Studies, University of London, Thornhaugh St., Russell Sq., London, WC1H0 XG, England. **Online address:** hw16@soas.ac.uk

WEST, James L(emuel) W(ills). American (born United States), b. 1946. **Genres:** Literary Criticism And History, Biography, Bibliography. **Career:** Virginia Polytechnic Institute and State University, instructor, 1971-72, assistant professor, 1972-77, associate professor, 1977-83, professor of English, 1983-86; University of South Carolina, professor, 1983; Pennsylvania State University, professor of English, 1986-92, distinguished professor of English, 1992-2000, Center for the History of the Book, director, 1992, Edwin Erle Sparks professor of English, 2000-. Writer. **Publications:** William Styron: A Descriptive Bibliography, 1977; (ed.) Gyascutus: Studies in Antebellum Southern Humorous and Sporting Writing, 1978; Making of F. Scott Fitzgerald's This Side of Paradise, 1980; (ed.) Sister Carrie, 1981; (comp.) Additional Apparatus for the Pennsylvania Edition of Dreiser's Sister Carrie: Emendations in the Copy-text, Rejected Proof Alterations, Sample Historical Collation, 1981; (ed. with A.D. Casciato) Critical Essays on William Styron, 1982; (ed. with T.P. Riggio and N.M. Westlake) American Diaries, 1902-1926, 1982; Making of This Side of Paradise, 1983; (ed.) Conversations With William Styron, 1985; Sister Carrie Portfolio, 1985; (with S. Wright) Reynolds Price: A Bibliography, 1949-1984, 1986; (ed. with A.D. Casciato) Waiting for Nothing and Other Writings, 1986; American Authors and the Literary Marketplace Since 1900, 1988; (ed.) Cambridge Edition of the Works of F. Scott Fitzgerald, 1990; (ed.) Jennie Gerhardt, 1992; (ed.) Dreiser's Jennie Gerhardt: New Essays on the Restored Text, 1995; (ed.) This Side of Paradise, 1995; (ed. with T.P. Riggio) Dreiser's Russian Diary, 1996; William Styron: A Life, 1998; (ed.) Flappers and Philosophers, 2000; (ed.) Trimalchio: An Early Version of The Great Gatsby, 2000; (ed.) Tales of the Jazz Age, 2002;

(ed.) My Lost City: Personal Essays, 1920-1940, 2005; The Perfect Hour: The Romance of F. Scott Fitzgerald and Ginevra King, 2006; (ed.) All the Sad Young, 2007; (ed. with R. Sirlin) Sophie's Choice: A Contemporary Casebook, 2007; (ed.) All the Sad Young Men, 2007; (ed.) Lost Decade: Short Stories from Esquire, 1936-1941, 2008; (ed.) Beautiful and Damned, 2008; (ed.) Basil, Josephine and Gwen Stories, 2009; (ed.) Suicide Run: Five Tales of the Marine Corps, 2009; (ed.) Letters to My Father, 2009; (ed.) Spires and Gargoyles: Early Writings, 1909-1919, 2010; (ed.) Backwoods Tales: Paddy McGann, Sharp Snaffles and Bill Bauldy: Selected Fiction of William Gilmore Simmons, 2010; Making the Archives Talk, 2011; (ed.) Short Autobiography, 2011; Tender is the Night, A Romance, 2012. **Address:** Department of English, Pennsylvania State University, 13 Burrowes Bldg., University Park, PA 16802, U.S.A. **Online address:** jlw14@psu.edu

WEST, Karen. *See* **BARTELL, Karen Hulene.**

WEST, Mark D. American (born United States) **Genres:** Law. **Career:** United States District Court, clerk; Paul, Weiss, Rifkind, Wharton & Garrison, attorney; University of Michigan, professor of law, Center for Japanese Studies, director, 2003-. Writer, attorney and educator. **Publications:** (with C.J. Milhaupt) Economic Organizations and Corporate Governance in Japan: The Impact of Formal and Informal Rules, 2004; Law in Everyday Japan: Sex, Sumo, Suicide and Statutes, 2005; The Japanese Legal System: Cases, Codes and Commentary, 2006; Secrets, Sex and Spectacle: The Rules of Scandal in Japan and the United States, 2006. **Address:** Ctr. for Japanese Studies, University of Michigan, 1080 S University Ave., Ste. 3640, Ann Arbor, MI 48109-1106, U.S.A. **Online address:** markwest@umich.edu

WEST, M(artin) L(itchfield). British (born England), b. 1937. **Genres:** Classics, Translations, Philosophy. **Career:** St. John's College, Woodhouse Junior Research Fellow, 1960-63; University College, fellow and praelector, 1963-74; University of London, Bedford/Royal Holloway College, professor of Greek, 1974-91; All Souls College, senior research fellow, 1991-2004, emeritus fellow, 2004-. Writer. **Publications:** Early Greek Philosophy and the Orient, 1971; Textual Criticism and Editorial Technique Applicable to Greek and Latin Texts, 1973; Studies in Greek Elegy and Iambus, 1974; Immortal Helen, 1975; Greek Metre, 1982; The Orphic Poems, 1983; The Hesiodic Catalogue of Women: Its Nature, Structure and Origins, 1985; Introduction to Greek Metre, 1987; Studies in Aeschylus, 1990; Ancient Greek Music, 1992; The East Face of Helicon: West Asiatic Elements in Greek Poetry and Myth, 1997; Studies in the Text and Transmission of the Iliad, 2001; (with E. Poehlmann) Documents of Ancient Greek Music: The Extant Melodies and Fragments Edited and Transcribed with Commentary, 2001; Indo-European Poetry and Myth, 2007; The Making of the Iliad, 2010; Hellenica, 2011; The Making of the Lliad, 2011; Old Avestan Syntax and Stylistics, 2011. TRANSLATOR: Sing Me, Goddess, 1971; (and intro.) Hesiod: Theogony and Works and Days, 1988; (and intro.) Greek Lyric Poetry: The Poems and Fragments of the Greek Iambic, Elegiac, and Melic Poets, 1993; (and intro.) Homeric Hymns, Homeric Apocrypha, Lives of Homer, 2003; (and intro.) Greek Epic Fragments From the Seventh to the Fifth Centuries BC, 2003; (and intro.) The Hymns of Zoroaster, 2010. EDITOR: Hesiod, Theogony, 1966; (with R. Merkelbach) Fragmenta Hesiodea, 1967; Iambi et elegi Graeci ante Alexandrum cantati, 1971, 2nd ed., 1989; Theognidis et Phocylidis fragmenta et adespota quaedam gnomica, 1978; Hesiod, Works and Days, 1978; Delectus ex iambis et elegis Graecis, 1980; (with F. Solmsen and R. Merkelbach) Hesiodi Theogonia; Opera et dies; Scutum, 1983; Carmina Anacreontea, 1984; (and trans.) Euripides, Orestes, 1987; Aeschyli Tragoediae cum incerti poetae Prometheo, 1990; Aeschyli Persae, 1991; Aeschyli Choephoroe, 1991; Aeschyli Agamemnon, 1991; Aeschyli Eumenides, 1991; Aeschyli Septem contra Thebas, 1992; Aeschyli Supplices, 1992; Aeschyli Prometheus, 1992; Homeri Ilias, 1998; W.S. Barrett, Greek Lyric, Tragedy, and Textual Criticism: Collected Papers, 2007. Contributor to periodicals. **Address:** All Souls College, 14 High St., Oxford, OX OX1 4AL, England. **Online address:** martin.west@all-souls.ox.ac.uk

WEST, Michael Rudolph. American (born United States), b. 1962. **Genres:** Politics/Government, Race Relations, Education, Biography. **Career:** College of the Holy Cross, associate professor of history. Writer. **Publications:** The Education of Booker T. Washington: American Democracy and the Idea of Race Relations, 2006. **Address:** Department of Africana Studies, College of the Holy Cross, 1 College St., Worcester, MA 01610-2322, U.S.A. **Online address:** mwest@holycross.edu

WEST, Nigel. *See* **ALLASON, Rupert (William Simon).**

WEST, Owen. *See* **KOONTZ, Dean R(ay).**

WEST, Sandra L. American (born United States), b. 1947. **Genres:** History, Literary Criticism And History. **Career:** City of Newark, journalist, 1975-79; Seton Hall University, adjunct faculty, 1990; Telfair Museum of Art, docent, 1991-92; Savannah State University, staff public relations writer, 1996; Zora Neale Hurston/Richard Wright Foundation, official documentary photographer, 1997-2001; Virginia Commonwealth University, adjunct faculty, 2000-02; Virginia Union University, adjunct humanities faculty, 2000-03; Polished Papers (proofreading and editing service), owner and proofreader, 2002-; Rutgers University, lecturer in African-American literature, composition and communication skills, 2003-; Black History Museum of Virginia, docent, 2003; Harlem Renaissance 101, owner and touring lecturer, 2004-; The Camden Street Neighborhood Association, founder. **Publications:** (With Aberjhani) Encyclopedia of the Harlem Renaissance, 2003; Newark's Literary Lights, 2008. **Address:** Celeste Bateman & Associates, 68 Shephard Ave., Newark, NJ 07112-2559, U.S.A. **Online address:** lavonne_07112@yahoo.com

WESTAD, Odd Arne. British/Norwegian (born Norway), b. 1960. **Genres:** History, International Relations/Current Affairs. **Career:** University of Oslo, adjunct professor of history, 1991-; University of North Carolina, faculty; Johns Hopkins University, faculty; University of London, London School of Economics and Political Science, Department of International History, professor of international history, 1998-, head, 2004-07, Cold War Studies Centre (now LSE IDEAS), co-director, 1998-, Asia Research Centre, director, Cold War History Journal, editor; Norwegian Nobel Institute, director of research. Political scientist. **Publications:** Cold War and Revolution: Soviet-American Rivalry and the Origins of the Chinese Civil War, 1944-1946, 1993; Decisive Encounters: The Chinese Civil War, 1946-1950, 2003; The Global Cold War: Third World Interventions and the Making of Our Times, 2005. EDITOR: (with G. Lundestad) Beyond the Cold War: New Dimensions in International Relations, 1993; (with S. Holtsmark and I.B. Neumann) The Soviet Union in Eastern Europe, 1945-89, 1994; The Fall of Détente: Soviet-American Relations during the Carter Years, 1997; Brothers in Arms: The Rise and Fall of the Sino-Soviet Alliance, 1945-1963, 1998; Reviewing the Cold War: Approaches, Interpretations, and Theory, 2000; (with C. Moon and G. Kahng) Ending the Cold War in Korea: Theoretical and Historical Perspectives, 2001; (with J. Hanhimäki) The Cold War: A History in Documents and Eyewitness Accounts, 2003; (with S. Quinn-Judge) The Third Indochina War: Conflict between China, Vietnam and Cambodia, 1972-79, 2006; (with M.P. Leffler) Cambridge History of the Cold War, 2009; (with P. Villaume) Perforating the Iron Curtain: European Détente, Transatlantic Relations, and the Cold War, 1965-1985, 2010. **Address:** London School of Economics and Political Science, University of London, Rm. COL.B206, Houghton St., London, GL WC2A 2AE, England. **Online address:** a.westad@lse.ac.uk

WESTBROOK, Peter (J.). American (born United States), b. 1952. **Genres:** Sports/Fitness, Autobiography/Memoirs, Biography. **Career:** Peter Westbrook Foundation, founder and executive director, 1991-; writer, 1996-. **Publications:** (With T. Hazarika) Harnessing Anger: The Way of an American Fencer, 1997. Contributor to periodicals. **Address:** Peter Westbrook Foundation, PO Box 7554, New York, NY 10116, U.S.A. **Online address:** pwestb@peterwestbrook.org

WESTBURG, Barry (Richard). American (born United States), b. 1938. **Genres:** Literary Criticism And History, Poetry, Novellas/Short Stories, Novels, History, Young Adult Fiction. **Career:** Bennington College, instructor, 1967-68; University of Rochester, assistant professor of English, 1968-75; Adelaide University, senior lecturer, 1975-, honorary visiting research fellow; Southern Review, fiction editor, 1998-. **Publications:** The Confessional Fictions of Charles Dickens (criticism), 1977; The Fernhouse Cure (poems), 1988; (co-ed.) No. 13 Friendly St., 1989; Wingwalking and Other Tales (short stories), 1990; The Progress of Moonlight (novel), 1990; (ed. with J. Kroll) Tuesday Night Live: Fifteen Years of Friendly Street, 1993; Rage of Angels: Expatriate Tales, 1998. Contributor to journals. **Address:** Department of English, School of Humanities, University of Adelaide, English DX 650 335, Adelaide, SA 5005, Australia. **Online address:** bwestbur@arts.adelaide.edu.au

WESTCOTT, Jan (Vlachos). *See* Obituaries.

WESTCOTT, Wayne L. American (born United States), b. 1949. **Genres:** Medicine/Health, Sports/Fitness, Education. **Career:** Pennsylvania State University, instructor and assistant track coach; Eastern Connecticut State University, professor and assistant track coach; Florida State University, professor of physical education and undergraduate co-director; Old Colony Young Men's Christian Association, fitness director; South Shore Young Men's Christian Association, fitness research director, senior fitness research director. Writer. **Publications:** Strength Fitness: Physiological Principles and Training Techniques, 1982, 4th ed., 1995; Building Strength at the YMCA, 1987, 2nd ed., 2003; Keeping Fit, 1987; Be Strong: Strength Training for Muscular Fitness for Men and Women, 1992; Nautilus Strength Training Certification Textbook, 1995; Building Strength and Stamina, 1996, 2nd ed., 2003; Strength Training Past Fifty, 1998; (with T.R. Baechle) Strength Training for Seniors, 1999; (with P. Draovitch) Complete Conditioning for Golf, 1999; (with A.D. Faigenbaum) Strength and Power for Young Athletes, 2000; (with A.D. Faigenbaum) Youth Fitness, 2001; (with S.F. Ramsden) Specialized Strength Training, 2001; (with T. D'Arpino) High Intensity Strength Training, 2003; (with R.L.R. Loud) No More Cellulite: A Proven 8-week Program for a Firmer, Fitter Body, 2003; (with A.D. Faigenbaum) Youth Strength Training, 2005; (with G. Reinl) Get Stronger, Feel Younger: The Cardio and Diet-Free Plan to Firm Up and Lose Fat, 2007; (with T.R. Baechle) Strength Training Past 50, 2007; (with A.D. Faigenbaum) Youth Strength Training: Programs for Health, Fitness, and Sport, 2009; (with T.R. Baechle) Fitness Professional's Guide to Strength Training Older Adults, 2010. Contributor to books and journals. **Address:** South Shore YMCA, 79 Coddington St., Quincy, MA 02169, U.S.A.

WESTCOTT-JONES, K. See **WESTCOTT-JONES, Kenneth.**

WESTCOTT-JONES, Kenneth. Also writes as Eric Taunton, K. Westcott-Jones. British (born England), b. 1921. **Genres:** Business/Trade/Industry, Transportation, Travel/Exploration. **Career:** Rail Passengers Assurance Co., staff, 1939; Marconi Marine Co., radio officer, 1946-51; freelance author and travel writer, 1951-; East Anglian Daily Times Series, travel correspondent, 1952-93; Uganda Government, travel consultant, 1959-66; Business Travel World, focus columnist, 1960-85; Welcome South Tours Inc., honorary director, 1979. **Publications:** To the Polar Sunrise, 1957; America Beyond the Bronx, 1961; Great Railway Journeys of the World, 1964; Exciting Railway Journeys of the World, 1967; By Rail to the Ends of the Earth, 1967; (with D. Green) Business Air Traveller's Guide, 1970; Romantic Railways, 1971; Steam in the Landscape, 1971; (co-author) The Great Trains, 1974; Wotton Tramway, 1974; (co-author) Fodor's Railways of the World, 1976; Railways for Pleasure, 1980; Scenic America, 1985; Where to Go in America, 1990; Rail Tales of the Unexpected, 1991; Passenger Liners of the Western Ocean, 1997. Contributor to periodicals. **Address:** Hillswick, Michael Rd., London, GL SE25 6RN, England.

WESTEN, Drew. American (born United States), b. 1959. **Genres:** Psychology, Medicine/Health. **Career:** Emory University, professor of psychology and director of Laboratory of Personality and Psychopathology; University of Michigan, lecturer; Harvard Medical School, lecturer; Boston University, lecturer; Cambridge Hospital, chief psychologist; National Public Radio, commentator; Western Strategies L.L.C., owner. Writer. **Publications:** Self and Society: Narcissism, Collectivism and the Development of Morals, 1985; Psychology: Mind, Brain and Culture, 1996, 5th ed. (with R.M. Kowalski), 2009; The Political Brain: The Role of Emotion in Deciding the Fate of the Nation, 2007. CONTRIBUTOR: The Self In Emotional Distress: Cognitive And Psychodynamic Perspectives, 1992; Emotions in Psychopathology: Theory and Research, 1998; Personality and Psychopathology, 2006. Contributor to periodicals and journals. **Address:** Department of Psychology, Emory University, 489 Psychology Bldg., 36 Eagle Row, Atlanta, GA 30322, U.S.A. **Online address:** dwesten@emory.edu

WESTERN, Jon W. American (born United States), b. 1963?. **Genres:** Advertising/Public Relations, Business/Trade/Industry, Economics, Politics/Government, International Relations/Current Affairs, Social Sciences. **Career:** U.S. Department of State, Bureau of Intelligence and Research, country analyst for Bosnia, Croatia and Poland, 1990-93; Columbia University, School of International and Public Affairs, Andrew Wellington Cordier teaching fellow, 1996-98; United States Institute of Peace, Jennings Randolph Peace Scholar Dissertation Fellow, 1998-99; Dayton Upgrade Project, project coordinator, 2000; George Washington University, adjunct assistant professor, 2000; Mount Holyoke Colleges and the Five Colleges Inc., assistant pro-

fessor, 2000-06, associate professor of international relations, 2006. Writer. **Publications:** Selling Intervention and War: The Presidency, the Media and the American Public, 2005; (ed. with E. Paus and P.B. Prime) Global Giant: Is China Changing the Rules of the Game?; (ed. with P.C. McMahon) International community and Statebuilding: Getting Its Act Together?. Contributor to books. **Address:** Mount Holyoke College, 50 College St., South Hadley, MA 01075, U.S.A. **Online address:** jwestern@mtholyoke.edu

WESTERVELT, Saundra D(avis). American (born United States), b. 1968. **Genres:** Law, Philosophy. **Career:** University of Virginia, lecturer in sociology, 1996-97; University of North Carolina, assistant professor, 1997-2003, associate professor of sociology, 2003-. Writer. **Publications:** Shifting the Blame: How Victimization Became a Criminal Defense, 1998; (ed. with J.A. Humphrey) Wrongly Convicted: Perspectives on Failed Justice, 2001. Contributor to journals. **Address:** Department of Sociology, University of North Carolina, 337 Graham Bldg., PO Box 26170, Greensboro, NC 27402-6170, U.S.A. **Online address:** sdwester@uncg.edu

WESTHEIMER, (Karola) Ruth. American/German (born Germany), b. 1928. **Genres:** Psychology, Sex, Autobiography/Memoirs, Human Relations/Parenting, Romance/Historical. **Career:** Planned Parenthood Clinic, project director, 1967-70; Lehman College, Department of Sex Counseling, associate professor, 1970-77; Cornell University Medical Center, New York Hospital, adjunct associate professor; Brookdale Hospital, lecturer; Brooklyn College, faculty; Adelphi University, faculty; Columbia University, faculty; Yale University, Calhoun College, associate fellow; New York University, adjunct professor. Writer. **Publications:** Dr. Ruth's Guide to Good Sex, 1983; (with N. Kravetz) First Love: A Young People's Guide to Sexual Information, 1985; Dr. Ruth's Guide for Married Lovers, 1986; (with B. Yagoda) All in a Lifetime: An Autobiography, 1987: (with N. Kravetz) First Love: A Young People's Guide to Sexual Information, 1988; (with L. Leiberman) Sex and Morality: Who is Teaching Our Sex Standards?, 1988; (with L. Lieberman) Dr. Ruth's Guide to Erotic and Sensuous Pleasures, 1991; (with S. Kaplan) Surviving Salvation: The Ethiopian Jewish Family in Transition, 1992; Dr. Ruth's Guide to Safer Sex, 1992; Dr. Ruth Talks to Kids: Where You Came from, How Your Body Changes, and What Sex is All About, 1993; The Art of Arousal, 1993; (ed.) Dr. Ruth's Encyclopedia of Sex, 1994, rev. ed. as Encyclopedia of Sex, 2000; Heavenly Sex, 1995; Sex for Dummies, 1995, (with P.A. Lehu) 3rd ed., 2006; (with B. Yagoda) The Value of Family: A Blueprint for the Twenty-first Century, 1996; (with P.A. Lehu) Dr. Ruth Talks about Grandparents: Advice for Kids on Making the Most of a Special Relationship, 1997; (with S. Kaplan) Grandparenthood, 1998; (with A. Grünebaum) Dr. Ruth's Pregnancy Guide for Couples: Love, Sex, and Medical Facts, 1999; (with P. Lehu) Dr. Ruth's Guide to College Life: The Savvy Student's Handbook, 2000; (with P. Lehu) Rekindling Romance for Dummies, 2001; Power: The Ultimate Aphrodisiac, 2001; Who Am I? Where Did I Come From?, 2001; (with P. Lehu) Rekindling Romance for Dummies, 2001; (contrib.) Lover's Companion: Art and Poetry of Desire, 2002; (with S. Lopater) Human Sexuality: A Psychosocial Perspective, 2002, 2nd ed., 2005; Musically Speaking: A Life through Song, 2003; (with P.A. Lehu) Conquering the Rapids of Life: Making the Most of Midlife Opportunities, 2003; (with P.A. Lehu) Fifty-two Lessons on Communicating Love: Tips, Anecdotes, and Advice for Connecting with the One You Love from America's Leading Relationship Therapist, 2004; (with P.A. Lehu) Dr. Ruth's Guide to Talking about Herpes, 2004; (with P.A. Lehu) Dr. Ruth's Sex After 50: Revving up the Romance, Passion & Excitement!, 2005; (with P.A. Lehu) Dr. Ruth's Guide to Teens & Sex Today: From Social Networking to Friends with Benefits, 2008; (with P.A. Lehu) Dr. Ruth's Top 10 Secrets for Great Sex: How to Enjoy It, Share It, and Love It Each and Every Time, 2009. Contributor to periodicals. **Address:** c/o Pierre A. Lehu, Communications Connection, 145 W 45th St., Ste. 1009, New York, NY 10036-4008, U.S.A.

WESTLING, Louise H. See **WESTLING, Louise (Hutchings).**

WESTLING, Louise (Hutchings). (Louise H. Westling). American (born United States), b. 1942. **Genres:** Autobiography/Memoirs, Literary Criticism And History, Young Adult Fiction. **Career:** Centre College of Kentucky, instructor in English, 1965-67; Pacific Northwest Educational Laboratory, research associate, 1968-71; University of Oregon, graduate teaching fellow, 1971-74, Honors College, assistant professor, 1978-81, instructor in English, 1981-84, assistant professor of English, 1985-88, associate professor of English, 1988-94, professor of English, 1994-, now professor emeritus, Environmental Studies Program, core professor, 2003-; Oregon State University, instructor in English, 1974-77; Ecole Nationale de la Statistique et de l'Administration Economique, professor, 1978; Universities of Tübingen and Stuttgart, visiting professor, 1981; Philological Association of the Pacific Coast, executive director 1984-87; University of Heidelberg, senior Fulbright lecturer, 1996. Writer. **Publications:** Evolution of Michael Drayton's Idea, 1974; Sacred Groves and Ravaged Gardens, 1985; Eudora Welty, 1989; The Green Breast of the New World: Landscape, Gender and American Fiction, 1996; (co-author) World of Literature, 1999; The Voice of the Things, the Waves and the Forest, forthcoming. EDITOR: He Included Me: The Autobiography of Sarah Rice, 1989; Witness to Injustice, 1995. **Address:** Department of English, University of Oregon, PLC 827, Eugene, OR 97403, U.S.A. **Online address:** lhwest@uoregon.edu

WESTMACOTT, Richard N. (Richard Noble Westmacott). American/Singaporean (born Singapore), b. 1941. **Genres:** Local History/Rural Topics, Geography, Environmental Sciences/Ecology, Horticulture. **Career:** Land Use Consultants, London, staff, 1966-68; Consulting landscape architect in private practice, 1970-77; University of Georgia, assistant professor, 1977-83, associate professor, 1983-91, professor of environmental design, 1991-, senior teaching fellow, 1998-. Writer. **Publications:** (With T. Worthington) New Agricultural Landscapes, 1974; Lakes and Ponds, 1976, 2nd ed., 1992; (with J.T. Tourbier) Water Resources Protection Technology, 1981; Agricultural Landscapes: A Second Look, 1984; African-American Gardens and Yards in the Rural South, 1992, 2nd ed., 1998; (with T. Worthington) Agricultural Landscapes: 33 Years Of Change: Report Of A Study Undertaken During 2005 On Behalf of The Countryside Agency's Landscape, Access And Recreation Division, 2006. **Address:** School of Environmental Design, University of Georgia, 609 Caldwell Hall, Athens, GA 30602-1845, U.S.A. **Online address:** westmac@uga.edu

WESTMACOTT, Richard Noble. See **WESTMACOTT, Richard N.**

WESTMEIER, Karl-Wilhelm. American/German (born Germany), b. 1939. **Genres:** History, Theology/Religion, Social Commentary. **Career:** Christian and Missionary Alliance, staff, 1965-86, itinerant minister, 1971, 1976, 1981; University of Cauca, lecturer in humanities, 1967; Instituto Biblico Alianza de Colombia, Department of Systematic Theology, instructor in Bible and theology, chairperson, 1975-86; Nyack College, Alliance Theological Seminary, assistant professor, 1982-88, associate professor, 1988-92, professor of theology, 1992-, resident professor of missiology and theology, 1992-, adjunct professor in missiology and theology. Writer. **Publications:** Reconciling Heaven and Earth: The Transcendental Enthusiasm and Growth of an Urban Protestant Community, Bogotá, Colombia, 1986; The Evacuation of Shekomeko and the Early Moravian Missions to Native North Americans, 1994; Protestant Pentecostalism in Latin America: A Study in the Dynamics of Missions, 1999; El dolor y la gloria: historia de la Alianza Cristiana y Misionera en Puerto Rico, 2000. Contributor of articles to periodicals. **Address:** Alliance Theological Seminary, Nyack College, PO Box 195343, San Juan, PR 00919-5343, U.S.A. **Online address:** kwestmeier@cs.com

WESTMINSTER, Ayn. See **MUNDIS, Hester (Jane).**

WESTOFF, Charles F. (Charles Francis Westoff). American (born United States), b. 1927. **Genres:** Demography, Sociology. **Career:** University of Pennsylvania, instructor in sociology, 1950-52; Milbank Memorial Fund, research associate, 1952-55; Princeton University, research associate, 1955-62, professor of demographic studies and sociology, 1962-, Maurice P. During 22 professor emeritus of demographic studies, head of department, 1965-70, Office of Population Research, research associate, 1955-59, senior research demographer, associate director, 1962-75, director, 1975-92, Department of Sociology, chairman, 1965-70; New York University, associate professor of sociology, 1958-62, Washington Square College, Department of Sociology, head, 1959-62; Commission on Population Growth and America's Future, executive director, 1970-72; Alan Guttmacher Institute, vice-chair; United Nations Educational, Scientific and Cultural Organization, consultant. Writer. **Publications:** Family Growth in Metropolitan America, 1961; The Third Child: A Study in the Prediction of Fertility, 1963; College Women and Fertility Values, 1967; The Later Years of Childbearing, 1970; Reproduction in the United States: 1965, 1971; From Now to Zero: Fertility, Contraception and Abortion in America, 1971; (with C.F. Westoff) The Contraceptive Revolution, 1977; (with W.J. Cohen) Demographic Dynamics in America, 1977; (with E.F. Jones) Patterns of Aggregate and Individual Changes in Contraceptive Practice: United States, 1965-1975, 1979; (with W.D. Mosher) Trends in

Contraceptive Practice, United States, 1981; (co-author) Peru Experimental Study: An Evaluation of Fertility and Child Health Information, 1989; (co-author) Dominican Republic Experimental Study: An Evaluation of Fertility and Child Health Information, 1990; Reproductive Preferences: A Comparative View, 1991; Age at Marriage, Age at First Birth, and Fertility in Africa, 1992; (with L. Nyblade and A.K. Blanc) Marriage and Entry Into Parenthood, 1994; (with A. Bankole) Childbearing Attitudes and Intentions, 1995; Unmet Need: 1990-1994, 1995; (with A. Bankole) Mass Media and Reproductive Behavior in Africa, 1997; Replacement of Abortion by Contraception, 1998; (with H. Rafalimanana) Gap Between Preferred and Actual Birth Intervals in Sub-Saharan Africa: Implications for Fertility and Child Health, 2001; (with A. Bankole) Contraception-Fertility Link in Sub-Saharan Africa and in Other Developing Countries, 2001; Contraception-Abortion Connections in Armenia, 2002; Trends in Marriage and Early Childbearing in Developing Countries, 2003; Recent Trends in Abortion and Contraception in 12 Countries, 2005; New Estimates of Unmet Need and the Demand for Family Planning, 2006; (with A.R. Cross) Stall in the Fertility Transition in Kenya, 2006; Desired Number of Children: 2000-2008, 2008; New approach to estimating abortion rates, 2008; (with F.I. Serbanescu) The Relationship Between Contraception and Abortion in the Republic of Georgia, 2008. EDITOR: Aspects of Population Growth Policy, 1972; Demographic and Social Aspects of Population Growth, 1972; Toward the End of Growth, 1973. **Address:** Office of Population Research, Princeton University, 251 Wallace Hall, Princeton, NJ 08544, U.S.A. **Online address:** westoff@princeton.edu

WESTOFF, Charles Francis. See **WESTOFF, Charles F.**

WESTON, Mark. American (born United States), b. 1953?. **Genres:** Young Adult Non-fiction, History, Travel/Exploration. **Career:** ABC News, staff; River Path Associates, associate. Lawyer, consultant and writer. **Publications:** The Land and People of Pakistan, 1992; Meet George Orwell, 1994; Giants of Japan: The Lives of Japans Greatest Men and Women, 1999; Prophets and Princes: Saudi Arabia from Muhammad to the Present, 2008; Honda: The Boy who Dreamed of Cars, 2008. **Address:** Peter Rubie Literary Agency, 240 W 35th St., New York, NY 10001, U.S.A. **Online address:** mark@riverpath.com

WESTON, Susan. Also writes as Susan B. Weston. American (born United States), b. 1943. **Genres:** Novels, Literary Criticism And History, Novellas/Short Stories, Education. **Career:** University of Hawaii, instructor, 1972-74, assistant professor of English, 1974-; Hawaii Literary Arts Council, vice president, 1978-. Writer. **Publications:** (As Susan B. Weston) Wallace Stevens: An Introduction to the Poetry, 1977; Children of the Light (novel), 1985. Contributor of articles to periodicals. **Address:** 80 Park St., Ste. 55, Brookline, MA 02446, U.S.A. **Online address:** susanweston@erols.com

WESTON, Susan B. See **WESTON, Susan.**

WESTRUM, Dexter. American (born United States), b. 1944. **Genres:** Novels, Novellas/Short Stories, Literary Criticism And History, Autobiography/Memoirs, Essays, Young Adult Fiction. **Career:** Windsor High School, English teacher, 1967-68; Woodstock Union High School, English teacher, 1968-72; Academy of the Holy Angels, English teacher, 1973-78, 1979-80; University of Minnesota, teaching associate of English and composition, 1978-79, 1980-85, professor; Ottawa University, assistant professor, 1985-91, associate professor of English, 1991-; Concordia University Wisconsin, adjunct faculty. Writer. **Publications:** Thomas McGuane, 1991; Elegy for a Golf Pro, 1994. **Address:** Concordia University Wisconsin, 12800 N Lake Shore Dr., Mequon, WI 53097-2402, U.S.A. **Online address:** dwestrum@msn.com

WESTRUP, Hugh. Canadian (born Canada) **Genres:** Sciences, Animals/Pets, Medicine/Health, Children's Non-fiction. **Career:** Weekly Reader Publishing, Current Science Magazine, managing editor. **Publications:** Maurice Strong: Working for Planet Earth, 1994; The Mammals, 1996; Bite Size Science: 150 Facts You Won't Believe!, 1997; Bite Size Geography, 1997; Bite-Size Biography, 2000, Know-It-All Animals, 2000. **Address:** Weekly Reader Publishing, 44 S Broadway, 18th Fl., White Plains, NY 10601, U.S.A.

WESTWICK, Peter J. American (born United States), b. 1967?. **Genres:** Sciences. **Career:** California Institute of Technology, senior research fellow in humanities, 2000-04; Yale University, International Security Studies, John M. Olin fellow, 2005-06; University of California, lecturer & visiting researcher in history, 2006-. Writer. **Publications:** The National Labs: Science in an American System, 1947-1974, 2003; Into the Black: JPL and the American Space Program, 1976-2004, 2007. Contributor to periodicals and journals. **Address:** Department of History, University of California, Santa Barbara, CA 93106-9410, U.S.A. **Online address:** westwick@history.ucsb.edu

WESTWOOD, John Norton. British (born England), b. 1931. **Genres:** History, Transportation, Military/Defense/Arms Control, Economics, Business/ Trade/Industry. **Career:** Canadian National Railways, economist, 1957-59; McGill University, lecturer in Russian language and literature, 1959-64; Florida State University, associate professor of modern history, 1967-69; University of Sydney, senior lecturer in modern history, 1970-72; University of Birmingham, honorary research fellow, 1976-. Writer. **Publications:** Soviet Railways Today, 1964; A History of Russian Railways, 1964; Russia, 1917-1964, 1966; Witnesses of Tsushima, 1970; Soviets Historia 1917-1970, 1971; Endurance and Endeavour: Russian History, 1973, 5th ed., 2002; An Illustrated History of the Russo-Japanese War, 1973; Railways of India, 1974; Fighting Ships of World War II, 1975; (comp.) Trafalgar, 1976; Locomotive Designers in the Age of Steam, 1977; British-built Steam Locos Overseas, 1977; All Colour World of Trains, 1978; Trains, 1979; Railways at War, 1980; Russia since 1917, 1980; St. Michael Book of Steam, 1980; Railways at War, 1980; Soviet Locomotive Technology during Industrialization, 1981; (contrib.) Atlas of the 20th century, 1982; (ed.) Illustrated History of Britain, 1983; Railway Data Book, 1983; History of the Middle East Wars, 1984; The Eastern Front: The Soviet-German War, 1941-1945, 1984; Russia against Japan 1904-1905: A New Look at the Russo-Japanese War, 1986; Atlas of American Wars, 1986; Pictorial History of Railroads, 1988; Golden Age of British Steam, 1991; Russian Naval Construction, 1905-45, 1994; Russian Transport 1913-1945: A Supplement to Economic Transformation in the USSR, 1994; (ed.) The New Illustrated Encyclopedia of Railways, 1998, rev. ed., 2000; The Age of Steam: The Locomotives, the Railroads and Their Legacy, 2000; Soviet Railways to Russian Railways, 2002; The Historical Atlas of World Railroads, 2009. **Address:** Centre for Russian and East European Studies, University of Birmingham, Edgbaston, Birmingham, WM B15 2TT, England. **Online address:** jnwestwood@tiscali.co.uk

WETENHALL, John. American (born United States), b. 1957. **Genres:** Art/ Art History, History, Autobiography/Memoirs. **Career:** Sterling and Francine Clark Art Institute, curatorial assistant, 1981; Williamstown Regional Art Conservation Laboratory, apprentice, 1981-82; University of Santa Clara, visiting lecturer, 1985; National Museum of American Art, Smithsonian fellow, 1986-87; University of Minnesota, visiting lecturer, 1988; Birmingham Museum of Art, curator of painting, sculpture and graphic arts, 1989-95; Cheekwood Museum of Art, director, 1995-; Vietnam Women's Memorial Project, consultant; Miami Art Museum, interim director; The John and Mable Ringling Museum of Art, executive director. Writer. **Publications:** (With D.B. Cass) Italian Paintings, 1850-1960: From Collections in the Northeastern United States: Catalogue and Exhibition, 1982; (ed.) Splendors of the American West: Thomas Moran's Art of the Yellowstone and Grand Canyon, 1990; (with K.A. Marling) Iwo Jima: Monuments, Memories, and the American Hero, 1991; The Ascendency of Modern Public Sculpture in America: A History of American Public Sculpture from the New Deal to the Early 1970s, 1992. Contributor to periodicals. **Address:** The John & Mable Ringling Museum of Art, 5401 Bay Shore Rd., Sarasota, FL 34243, U.S.A.

WETHERELL, W(alter) D(avid). American (born United States), b. 1948. **Genres:** Novels, Novellas/Short Stories, Essays. **Career:** Writer. **Publications:** NOVELS: Souvenirs, 1981; Chekhov's Sister, 1990; The Wisest Man in America, 1995; Morning, 2001; Century of November: A Novel, 2004; Soccer Dad: A Father, a Son and a Magic Season, 2008. ESSAYS: Vermont River, 1984; Upland Stream: Notes on the Fishing Passion, 1991; North of Now, 1998; One River More, 1999. STORIES: The Man Who Loved Levittown, 1985; Hyannis Boat and Other Stories, 1989; Wherever that Great Heart May Be, 1996; Hills like White Hills: Stories, 2009. OTHER: The Smithsonian Guides to Natural America. Northern New England-Vermont, New Hampshire and Maine, 1995; Place of the Long River: A Connecticut River Anthology of Poetry and Prose, with Views from the Source to the Sound, 1995; North of Now: A Celebration of Country and the Soon to be Gone, 1998; One River More, 1998; Morning, 2001; This American River: Five Centuries of Writing About the Connecticut, 2002; Yellowstone Autumn: A Season of Discovery in a Wondrous Land, 2009. On Admiration: Heroes, Heroines, Role Models and Mentors, 2010. **Address:** Skyhorse Publishing Inc., 307 W 36th St., 11th Fl., New York, NY 10018, U.S.A. **Online address:** wdwetherell@valley.net

WETHERINGTON, Mark V. American (born United States), b. 1949. **Genres:** Young Adult Fiction, Economics. **Career:** Writer. **Publications:** (With C.F. Bryan, jr.) Finding Our Past: A Guidebook for Group Projects in Community History, 1983, 2nd ed., 1984; The New South Comes to Wiregrass Georgia, 1860-1910, 1994; Plain Folk's Fight: The Civil War and Reconstruction in Piney Woods Georgia, 2005. Contributor to periodicals. **Address:** The Filson Historical Society, 1310 S 3rd St., Louisville, KY 40208-2306, U.S.A. **Online address:** markweth@filsonhistorical.org

WETMORE, Kevin J. (Jr.). American (born United States), b. 1969. **Genres:** Theatre, Film, Novels, Literary Criticism And History. **Career:** Denison University, professor of theater, 1999-2002; California State University, assistant professor, professor of theater, 2002-; Loyola Marymount University, associate professor of theater, professor; Association for Theatre in Higher Education, secretary and treasurer. Writer. **Publications:** The Athenian Sun in an African Sky, 2002; Black Dionysus, 2003; The Empire Triumphant: Race, Religion and Rebellion in the Star Wars Films, 2005; Modern Japanese Drama and Performance, 2005; Dude Where's My Bard, 2005; (co-author) Shakespeare and Youth Culture, 2006; (co-ed.) Modern Japanese Theatre and Performance, 2006; (ed. with A.S. Howard) Suzan-Lori Parks: A Casebook, 2007; (ed.) Revenge Drama in European Renaissance and Japanese Theater: From Hamlet to Madame Butterfly, 2008. **Address:** Department of Theatre, California State University, 18111 Nordhoff St., Northridge, CA 91330-8320, U.S.A. **Online address:** kwetmore@lmu.edu

WETTENHALL, Roger L. Australian (born Australia), b. 1931. **Genres:** Administration/Management, Institutions/Organizations, Politics/Government, Public/Social Administration. **Career:** Australian Commonwealth Public Service, personnel officer, 1948-59; University of Tasmania, Department of Political Science, lecturer, 1961-65, senior lecturer, 1966-69, reader 1969-71; University of Canberra, School of Administrative Studies, head, 1971-85, college fellow in administrative studies, 1985-89, professor of public administration, 1990-94, professor of public administration emeritus, 1994-; University of Manchester, Hallsworth Research Fellow, 1964-65; Australian Journal of Public Administration, editor, 1989-95; Asian Journal of public administration, associate editor, 2010-. Writer. **Publications:** Railway Management and Politics in Victoria, 1856-1906, 1961; A Guide to Tasmania Government Administration, 1968; The Iron Road and the State: W.M. Acworth as Scholar, Critic, and Reformer, 1970; Bushfire Disaster: An Australian Community in Crisis, 1975; Organising Government: The Uses of Ministries and Departments, 1986; Public Enterprise and National Development: Selected Essays, 1987; (co-author) Governance of Public Enterprise: An African Spotlight on the Role of the Board, 1994; (co-author) Reluctant Democrats: The Transition to Self-Government in the Australian Capital Territory, 1996; (co-author) Contracting Out in Australia, 1997; (co-author) Public Enterprise Divestment: Australian Case Studies, 2001. EDITOR: (with M. Painter) The First Thousand Days of Labor, 1975; (with J.M. Power and J.A. Halligan) Local Government Systems of Australia, 1981; (with G.R. Curnow) Understanding Public Administration, 1981; (with A. Kouzmin and J.R. Nethercote) Australian Commonwealth Administration: Essays in Review, 1984; (with C.O. Nuallain) Getting Together in Public Enterprise, 1987; (with C.O. Nuallain) Public Enterprise: The Management Challenge, 1987; (with C.O. Nuallain) Public Enterprise Performance Evaluation: Seven Country Studies, 1990; (with J. Halkligan) Hawke's Third Government: Australian Commonwealth Administration 1987-1990, 1992; (with I. Thynne and B.S. Ghuman) Symposiums on Public Enterprise, Privatizations and the Public-Private Mix, 1995; (with J. Halligan) A Decade of Self-Government in the Australian Capital Territory 2002; (with G. Pirotta and L. Briguglio) Governance of Small States, 2001; (with I. Thynne) Organizations in Public Management, 2003; (with C. Aulich) Howard's Second and Third Governments 1998-2004, 2005; Howard's Fourth Government 2004-2007, 2008. Contributor to professional periodicals. **Address:** ANZSOG Institute for Governance, University of Canberra, Canberra, AC 2601, Australia. **Online address:** roger.wettenhall@canberra.edu.au

WETTIG, Gerhard. German (born Germany), b. 1934. **Genres:** History, International Relations/Current Affairs, Politics/Government. **Career:** Historical-Political Commission of the Evangelical Research Corp., research associate, 1961-62; German Society for Foreign Affairs, research staff, 1962-66; Federal Institute for East European and International Studies, senior research staff, 1966-88, director of international relations and international security research, 1989-99; Institute of Contemporary History, external research staff, 2000-. Writer. **Publications:** Der Dialog zwischen SPD und SED vom Februar bis Juni 1966 als Teil der Deutschland-Politik des Ostblocks, 1966; The Dialogue of SED and SPD: Patterns of Communist Political Strategy in Germany, 1967; Entmilitarisierung und Wiederbewaffnung in Deutschland 1943-55: Internationale Auseinandersetzungen um die Rolle der Deutschen in Europa, 1967; Sowjetunion vor der deutschen Frage, 1967; Die Rolle der russischen Armee im revolutionaeren Machtkampf 1917: Forschungen zur osteuropaeischen Geschichte, 1967; Politik im Rampenlicht: Aktionweisen moderner Aussenpolitik, 1967; The Soviet Decision to Rearm East Germany: A Case Study of the Early Cold War Period, 1968; Soviet Non-Proliferation Policy: An Analysis of Soviet Public Statements from November 1966 to January 1968, 1968; The Soviet Policy of European Security: Behavior and Motivation Analysis, 1968; Die Deutschland-Politik der DDR und dieosteuropäischen Staaten, 1969; Zur russischen Aussenpolitikgegenüber Deutschland vom Wiener Kongress bis zur Gegenwart, 1969; Bedrohungsvorstellungen als Faktor der internationalen Politik: der Bedrohungsnexus u, seine Rolle in zwischenstaatl, Konflikten, 1970; Betrachtungen zum gegenwärtigen Stand der Berlin-Frage, 1970; Dassowjetische Programm der europäischen Sicherheit alte Parole und neue Politik, 1970; Zur sowjetischen Strategie der europäischen Sicherheit, 1970; Die Ost-Berliner Konferenz der Warschauer-Pakt-Staaten und die Aussichten für eine befriedigende Berlin-Regelung, 1971; Europäische Sicherheit: Das europäische Staatensystem in dersowjetischen Aussenpolitik 1966-72, 1972; Deutschlandpolitischen Interessen der Sowjetunion und der Deutsche Demokratische Republik, 1972-73, 1975; Gesamteuropäische kollektive Sicherheit undosteuropäische kollektive Souveränität als Elemente dessowjetischen Europa-Programms, 1972; Die Wertung der Bundesrepublik durch USSR und DDR 1966-1972, 1972; Etappen der sowjetischen Europa-Politik im Blick auf KSZE und MBFR, 1973; Kontakt und Kommunikation: einwünschenswertes Element europäischer Friedensforschung?, 1973; Die Auseinandersetzungen um das Verhalten genüber der Bundesrepublik Deutschland im Jahre 1969, 1974; Die Berlin-Frage als Angelpunkt dersowjetischen Westpolitik 1970/71, 1974; Entwicklungen der sowjetischenRüstungs politik, 1974; Koexistenz-Konzept und Europa-Politik aussowjetischer Sicht: überlegungen zu Thesen von Michail Voslenskij, 1974; Kontakt und Kommunikation als Problem der Ost-West-Beziehungen in Europa, 1974; Sowjetische Vorstellungen über eine Neuordnung derzwischenstaatlichen Beziehungen in Europa, 1974; Die Verhandlungen mit der Bundesrepublik von Januar bis August 1970, 1974; Die sowjetische MBFR-Politik als Problem der Ost-West-Entspannung in Europa, 1974; Dilemmas der SED-Abgrenzungspolitik: eine zusammenfassende Analyse, 1975; Der Kampf um die freie Nachricht, 1975; Frieden und Sicherheit in Europa: Problem der KSZE und der MBFR, 1975; Die sowjetische Portugal-Politik 1974-1975, 1975; Zu den Beziehungen zwischen der Sowjetunion und der DDR in den Jahren 1969-75: eine zusammenfassende Analyse, 1975; Zum Ergebnis der KSZE, 1975; Die praktische Anwendung des Berlin-Abkommens durch UdSSR und DDR (1972-1976), 1976; Die Sowjetunion, die Deutsche Demokratische Republik und die Deutschland-Frage 1965-1976: Einvernehmen u, Konflikt im sozialist, Lager, 1976; Zur Lage Berlins vordem Viermächte-Abkommen, 1976; Argumentationslinien der USSR und der DDR im Blick auf die Verwirklichung ihrer KSZE-Verpflichtungen, 1977; Broadcasting and Détente: Eastern Policies and Their Implication for East-West Relations, 1977; Die Folgen der KSZE aus östlicher Sicht, 1977; Die östliche Entspannungspolitik im Lichte von Theorie und Praxis, 1977; Die Schlussakte der KSZE und die seitherige Politik in der Frage der Informationsverbreitung, 1977; Menschenrechte als Element einesgerechten und dauerhaften Friedens, 1978; Die Berliner Zugangsproblematikvor dem Vier-Mächte-Abkommen von 1971, 1978; Die Bindungen West-Berlins seit dem Vier-Mächte-Abkommen, 1978; Das Problem des Transits nach West-Berlin, 1978; Die sicherheitspolitischen Auseinandersetzungen auf der KSZE-Folgekonferenz, 1978; Sowjetische Entspannungspolitik: Eine zusammenfassende Bewertung, 1978; Die Warschauer-Pakt-Staaten auf der Belgrader Folgekonferenz, 1978; (with F. Oldenburg) Der Sonderstatus der DDR in den europäischen Ost-West-Beziehungen, 1979; Das Abschreckungskonzept als Theorie der Friedenssicherung: Darstellung, Analyse, Kritik, 1979; Ansätze zueiner Theorie der Entspannung, 1979; Entspannungskonzepte in Ost und West, 1979; Das Funktionieren der Besuchregelung auf Grund desVier-Mächte-Abkommens, 1979; Das Konzept der stabilen Abschreckung inden Ost-West-Beziehungen, 1979; Die Auseinandersetzungen um dieeurostrategische Nachrüstung der NATO, 1980; East-West Security Relations on the Eurostrategic Level, 1980; Die Mittelstreckenproblematikaus sowjetischer Sicht, 1980; Die Statusprobleme Ost-Berlins 1949-1980, 1980; Die Durchführung des Berlin-Transits nach demVier-Mächte-Abkommen 1972-1981, 1981; Entspannungsinteressen in Ostund West, 1981; Der euro-strategische

Datenvergleich als Instrument dersowjetischen Politik, 1981; Instrumentarien der Entspannungspolitik, 1981; Konflikt und Kooperation zwischen Ost und West: Entspannung in Theorie und Praxis: Ausses-und sicherheitspolitische Analyse, 1981; Diesicherheitspolitische Debatte in Europa, 1981; Die sowjetische Note vom 10. März 1952: Wiedervereinigungsangebot oder Propagandawerkzeug?, 1981; Das Vier-Maechte-Abkommen in der Bewaehrungsprobe: Berlin im Spannungsfeld zwischen Ost und West, 1981; Chancen für einen Wandel in Osteuropa?: Generationswechsel im Kreml als Herausforderung für die Politik des Westens, 1982; Die Beziehungen der Sowjetunion zur Bundesrepublik Deutschland, 1982; Die Einmischung als politisches Problemder Ost-West-Beziehungen, 1982; Die Friedensbewegung der beginnenden 80erJahre, 1982; Grundlinien der sowjetischen Sicherheitspolitik, 1982; Die Instrumentalisierung der Bedrohungsvorstellungen und der Streitkräftedaten im INF-Bereich, 1982; The Relations of the USSR with the Federal Republic of Germany, 1982; The Role of West Germany in Soviet Policies Toward Western Europe, 1982; Zum Abbruch der INF-Verhandlungen, 1983; Die Rolle von Bedrohungsvorstellungen in der sowjetischen Westpolitik, 1983; Psychoanalyse, Friedensbewegung und Sicherheitspolitik, 1983; Wege zur Kriegsverhütung und Friedenssicherung, 1983; Modelle der zwischenstaatlichen Sicherheit, 1984; Information und Sicherheit in sowjetkommunistischer Sicht, 1984; Kleineren Warschauer-Pakt-Staaten in den Ost-West-Beziehungen, 1985; Alternativen der Sicherheit, 1986; Soviet Attitudes Toward Arms Control, 1986; USA-UdSSR, 1986; Gorbatschows Ausreichende Verteidigung in der sowjetischen Sicherheitspolitik, 1987; A New Soviet Approach to Negotiating on Arms Control, 1987; Zur gegenwärtigen Entwicklung der sowjetischen Militärdoktrin, 1988; New Thinking in Soviet Foreign Policy, 1989; The Role of Military Power in Soviet Policy, 1989; High Road, Low Road, 1989; Zur Quellenlage bei der Analyse der sowjetischen Aussen- und Sicherheitspolitik, 1989; Die NATO im amtlichen sowjetischen Denken und Handeln, 1989; (ed.) Sowjetische Militärmacht und die Stabilität in Europa, 1990; West European Integration and Pan-Europeanism in Soviet Foreign Policy, 1990; Soviet Concept of Security in a Common European House, 1990; Soviet Union and German Unification, 1990; Gesellschaftliche Ebene der Aussenpolitik Gorbatschows, 1990; UdSSR und der politische Wandel in Osteuropa, 1990; Zu den innen-und wirtschaftspolitischen Voraussetzungen der sowjetischen Aussenpolitik, 1990; Sowjetunion und die Entwicklungsperspektiven des Kommunismus in Europa, 1990; Probleme der Friedenssicherung in Europa, 1991; Basic Concepts of Gorbachev's New Security Thinking, 1991; Sicherheit in einem neuen Europa, 1991; Changes in Soviet policy towards the West, 1991; Nation und Konflikt in Osteuropa nach dem Zusammenbruch des Kommunismus, 1992; Russland und Deutschland in einem neuen System der europäischen Sicherheit, 1992; Russische Truppenrückzug aus den baltischen Staaten, 1993; (ed.) Sicherheits-und Bedrohungsperzeptionen in Ost-und Mitteleuropa, 1993; Ende der DDR 1989-90: Ergebnis geschichtlichen Zufalls?, 1994; Central European Security After the End of the Soviet Empire, 1994; (ed.) Sicherheits-und Bedrohungsvorstellungen in Ostmitteleuropa, 1995; Herkömmliche und neuartige Herausforderungen für die Sicherheit in Europa, 1995; (ed.) Sowjetische Deutschland-Politik in der ära Adenauer, 1997; (ed. with H. Timmermann) Rumänien und die NATO, 1997; (ed. with A. Eckner) Slovenia's National Security in a New European Environment, 1997; Europäische System nach dem Ende des Kalten Krieges, 1997; (ed. with B. Bentlin) Russland und der Jugoslawienkonflikt, 1997; Bereitschaft zu Einheit in Freiheit?: die sowjetische Deutschland-Politik 1945-1955, 1999; Die Stalin-Note vom 10. März 1952, 2002; Chruschtschows Berlin-Krise 1958 bis 1963: Drohpolitik und Mauerbau, 2006; Stalin and the Cold War in Europe: The Emergence and Development of East-West Conflict, 1939-1953, 2008. **Address:** Institute of Contemporary History, Leonrodstr. 46 B, Muenchen, 80636, Germany.

WETTSTEIN, Robert M. American (born United States), b. 1950. **Genres:** Law, Psychiatry, Criminology/True Crime, Psychology, Law, Medicine/Health. **Career:** University of Pittsburgh, faculty psychiatrist and assistant professor of psychiatry, 1984-96, clinical associate professor of psychiatry; Behavioral Sciences and the Law, editor, 1990-96. Writer. **Publications:** (With B.A. Weiner) Legal Issues in Mental Health Care, 1993; (ed.) Treatment of Offenders with Mental Disorders, 1998. **Address:** 401 Shady Ave., Ste. B103, Pittsburgh, PA 15206, U.S.A. **Online address:** wettsteins@aol.com

WETZEL, James. American (born United States), b. 1959. **Genres:** Theology/Religion, Philosophy. **Career:** Colgate University, Department of Philosophy and Religion, faculty, 1988, associate professor, 1994-2004, professor, 2004-05; University of Notre Dame, visiting assistant professor, 1991-92; Princeton University, Eli Lilly lecturer in Christian thought, 2001-02; Villanova University, Augustinian chair in the thought of Saint Augustine and professor of philosophy, 2005-. Writer. **Publications:** Augustine and the Limits of Virtue, 1992; Augustine: A Guide for the Perplexed, 2010. Works appear in anthologies. Contributor to periodicals. **Address:** Department of Philosophy, Villanova University, 800 Lancaster Ave., 177 St. Augustine Ctr., Villanova, PA 19085, U.S.A. **Online address:** james.wetzel@villanova.edu

WEXLER, Alan. American (born United States), b. 1947. **Genres:** History, Travel/Exploration, Biography, Humor/Satire, Sciences, Geography. **Career:** The Maverick Group, senior copywriter, 1993-. Author. **Publications:** The Scandal Annual, 1986; (with C. Waldman) Who Was Who in World Exploration, 1992; The Atlas of Westward Expansion, 1994; Encarta '97, 1996; (with C. Waldman and J. Cunningham) Encyclopedia of Exploration, 2004. Writer. **Address:** 26 Van Dam St., New York, NY 10013-1230, U.S.A. **Online address:** alanwexler@hotmail.com

WEXLER, Alice (Ruth). American (born United States), b. 1942. **Genres:** History, Medicine/Health, Women's Studies And Issues, Autobiography/Memoirs, Biography, Education. **Career:** Sonoma State University, assistant professor, 1972-76, associate professor of history, 1976-82; University of California, visiting professor of history, Center for the Study of Women, research fellow, 1994-; Claremont Graduate School, visiting professor of history; Occidental College, visiting professor of history. Writer. **Publications:** Emma Goldman: An Intimate Life, 1984; Emma Goldman in Exile: From the Russian Revolution to the Spanish Civil War, 1989; (contrib.) The Challenge of Feminist Biography, 1992; Mapping Fate: A Memoir of Family, Risk, and Genetic Research, 1995; The Woman Who Walked Into the Sea: Three Stories in the Making of a Genetic Disease, 2008; Art and Disability: The Social and Political Struggles Facing Education, 2009. Contributor to periodicals. **Address:** Center for the Study of Women, University of California, PO Box 957222, Los Angeles, CA 90095-7222, U.S.A. **Online address:** arwexler@ucla.edu

WEXLER, Bruce E. American (born United States) **Genres:** Biology, Sciences, Medicine/Health. **Career:** Yale Medical School, professor of psychiatry; Connecticut Mental Health Center, Neurocognitive Research Laboratory, director; A Different Future, founder; Council of Religious Institutions of the Holy Land, co-facilitator, 2002; West Bank, staff. Writer. **Publications:** Brain and Culture: Neurobiology, Ideology and Social Change, 2006. Contributor of articles to journals. **Address:** Connecticut Mental Health Center, 34 Park St., New Haven, CT 06519, U.S.A. **Online address:** bruce.wexler@yale.edu

WEXLER, Jay D. American (born United States), b. 1969. **Genres:** Theology/Religion, Travel/Exploration. **Career:** Teacher, 1991-92; Berlitz Inc., English teacher, 1992; Lewis, D'Amato, Brisbois, Bisgaard, Buxbaum & Choy, Xiamen P.R.C., legal assistant, 1993-94; United States Supreme Court, law clerk, 1997-99; Unites States Department of Justice, Office of Legal Counsel, attorney, 1999-2001; Boston University, law professor, 2001-; Institut de Droit comparé Edouard Lambart, visiting professor, 2008. Writer. **Publications:** Holy Hullabaloos: A Road Trip to the Battlegrounds of the Church/State Wars, 2009. **Address:** School of Law, Boston University, 765 Commonwealth Ave., Boston, MA 02215, U.S.A. **Online address:** jaywex@bu.edu

WEXLER, Merin. American (born United States) **Genres:** Young Adult Fiction, Novellas/Short Stories. **Career:** Writer. **Publications:** The Porno Girl, and Other Stories 2003 as Save Yourself, and Other Stories, 2004. **Address:** c/o Author Mail, St. Martin's Press, 175 5th Ave., New York, NY 10010, U.S.A.

WEXLER, Richard. American (born United States), b. 1953. **Genres:** Civil Liberties/Human Rights, Documentaries/Reportage, Human Relations/Parenting, Young Adult Non-fiction, Politics/Government. **Career:** Freelance journalist, 1974-76; WMHT-TV, associate producer, 1976; Wisconsin Public Radio, assistant news director and reporter, 1977-79; WGBY-TV, news director and reporter, 1979-81; WXXI-TV, reporter and producer, 1981-84; City Newspaper, reporter and columnist, 1985-86; Times Union, reporter, 1986-; Pennsylvania State University, assistant professor of communications; National Coalition for Child Protection Reform, executive director. **Publications:** Wounded Innocents: The Real Victims of the War against Child Abuse, 1990. Contributor to periodicals. **Address:** National Coalition for Child Protection Reform, 53 Skyhill Rd., Ste. 202, Alexandria, VA 22314, U.S.A. **Online address:** rwexler@nccpr.org

WEXLER, Robert Freeman. American (born United States), b. 1961. **Genres:** Novels, Novellas/Short Stories. **Career:** Writer. **Publications:** In Springdale Town (novella), 2003; Circus of the Grand Design (novel), 2004; Psychological Methods to Sell Should Be Destroyed: Stories (chapbook), 2008; The Painting and the City (novel), 2009. **Address:** Yellow Springs, OH , U.S.A. **Online address:** robertfwexler@gmail.com

WEYERMANN, Debra. American (born United States), b. 1954. **Genres:** Criminology/True Crime, Young Adult Fiction. **Career:** Norfolk Ledger-Star, reporter, 1976-78; Arizona Daily Star, reporter, 1978-86; Denver Post, reporter, 1986-88; Santa Barbara News-Press, reporter, 1988-90. Writer. **Publications:** The Gang They Couldn't Catch: The Story of America's Greatest Modern-Day Bank Robbers-and How They Got Away with It (nonfiction), 1993; Answer Them Nothing: Bringing Down the Polygamous Empire of Warren Jeffs, 2011; American Hero, forthcoming; Shurtleff's War, forthcoming. **Address:** c/o Suzanne Gluck, Inernational Creative Management, 825 8th Ave., New York, NY 10019, U.S.A. **Online address:** weyerman@bellsouth.net

WEYLAND, Jack. American (born United States), b. 1940. **Genres:** Young Adult Fiction, Novels, Picture/Board Books. **Career:** South Dakota School of Mines and Technology, professor of physics, 1968-93; The American Indian Science and Engineering Society, adviser, 1989-93; Brigham Young University (formerly Ricks College), professor of physics, 1993-. Writer. **Publications:** Charly, 1980; First Day of Forever, and Other Stories for LDS Youth, 1980; Sam, 1981; Punch and Cookies Forever: And Other Stories for LDS Youth, 1981; The Reunion, 1982; Pepper Tide, 1983; A New Dawn, 1984; The Understudy: A Novel, 1985; Last of the Big-Time Spenders, 1986; If Talent Were a Pizza, You'd Be a Supreme, 1986; Sara, Whenever I Hear Your Name, 1987; A Small Light in the Darkness: And Other Stories, 1987; Brenda at the Prom, 1988; Stephanie, 1989; Michelle & Debra, 1990; Kimberly, 1992; Megapowers: Can Science Fact Defeat Science Fiction?, 1992; Nicole, 1993; Weyland: Five Complete Novels, 1994; On the Run, 1995; Night on Lone Wolf Mountain and Other Short Stories, 1996; Lean on Me, 1996; Brittany, 1997; Jake, 1998; Emily, 1999; Ashley & Jen, 2000; Megan, 2001; King Daryl of Dread, 2002; Cheyenne in New York: A Novel, 2003; Adam's Story: A Novel, 2004; Everyone Gets Married in the End, 2004; Saving Kristen, 2005; Alone, Together, 2006; As Always, Dave, 2007; Forever, 2008; Brianna, My Brother, and the Blog, 2009; The Samaritan Bueno, 2009; Cameron Meets Madison, 2010; Mother's Day Boot Camp, 2010; It All Started with Autumn Jones, 2010. **Address:** 369 Yale Ave., Rexburg, ID 83440-2524, U.S.A. **Online address:** weylandj@byui.edu

WEYR, Thomas. (Thomas Hector Weyr). American/Austrian (born Austria), b. 1927. **Genres:** Translations, Cultural/Ethnic Topics, Military/Defense/Arms Control, Adult Non-fiction, History. **Career:** United Press Intl., reporter, 1953-59; freelance journalist, 1959-63; ABC Radio Network, news writer, 1963-66; Curtis Hoxter Public Relations, account executive, 1966-67; Research Institute of America, managing editor, 1968-86; NIBM Business Publications, directing editor, 1986-93; DM News Intl., editor, 1994-99. **Publications:** (Trans.) The Twilight Men, 1968; World War II (military history), 1969; (trans.) Erwin Fischer, The Berlin Indictment, 1971; (trans.) The Curse of the Pharohs, 1975; Reaching for Paradise: The Playboy Vision of America, 1978; (trans.) Saul Friedlaender, Reflections of Nazism, 1984; Hispanic U.S.A.: Breaking the Melting Pot, 1988; Setting of the Pearl: Vienna Under Hitler, 2005. Contributor to periodicals. **Address:** Brandt & Brandt Literary Agency, 1501 Broadway, New York, NY 10036, U.S.A.

WEYR, Thomas Hector. *See* **WEYR, Thomas.**

WHALEN, Richard James. American (born United States), b. 1935. **Genres:** Politics/Government, Social Commentary, History. **Career:** Richmond News Leader, reporter, 1957-58, associate editor, 1958-59; Time Magazine, contributing editor, 1959-60; Wall Street Journal, editorial writer, 1960-62; Fortune, associate editor, 1962-65; Time Inc., senior writer, 1963; Georgetown University, Center for Strategic and International Studies, writer-in-residence, 1967-69; U.S. State Department, consultant, 1969-72; Worldwide Information Resources Ltd. (WIRES), chairman, 1971-; Bear, Stearns & Co., advisor, 1971, limited partner, 1981-; Whalen Consulting Group, chairman, 1996-. **Publications:** The Founding Father: The Story of Joseph P. Kennedy, 1964; New York: A City Destroying Itself: An Angry View of New York, 1965; Catch the Falling Flag: A Republican's Challenge to His Party, 1972; Taking Sides: A Personal View of America from Kennedy to Nixon to

Kennedy, 1974; (with B.J. Wattenberg) The Wealth Weapon: U.S. Foreign Policy and Multinational Corporations, 1980; Trade Warriors: An Inside Look at Trade Activists in Congress andHow to Reach Them, 1986. **Address:** c/o Owen Laster, William Morris Agency, 1740 Broadway, New York, NY 10019, U.S.A.

WHALEN, Thomas J. American (born United States), b. 1964. **Genres:** History, Politics/Government. **Career:** Boston University, College of General Studies, Department of Social Science, assistant professor, associate professor. Writer and journalist. **Publications:** Kennedy versus Lodge: The 1952 Massachusetts Senate Race, 2000; Dynasty's End: Bill Russell and the 1968-69 World Champion Boston Celtics, 2004; A Higher Purpose: Profiles in Presidential Courage, 2007; When the Red Sox Ruled: Baseball's First Dynasty, 1912-1918, 2011. **Address:** Department of Social Science, College of General Studies, Boston University, 871 Commonwealth Ave., 1 Silber Way, Boston, MA 02215, U.S.A. **Online address:** tjw64@bu.edu

WHALIN, W. Terry. American (born United States), b. 1953. **Genres:** Business/Trade/Industry, Children's Non-fiction, inspirational/Motivational Literature, Medicine/Health, Self Help, Theology/Religion, How-to Books. **Career:** Wycliffe Bible Translators, Editorial Department, manager; In Other Words, linguist and Bible translator, managing editor, 1975-93; Billy Graham Evangelistic Association, associate editor, 1993-94; Decision Magazine, associate editor, 1993-94; Whalin and Associates, president and chief executive officer, 1994; Christianity.com, feature writer, 2000-01; Cook Communications Ministries, acquisitions editor, 2001-03; Intermedia Publishing Group, publisher. **Publications:** Jumpstart Your Publishing Dreams, Insider Secrets To Skyrocket Your Success, 2009. CHILDREN'S BOOKS: When I Grow Up, I Can Go Anywhere for Jesus, 1992; Never Too Busy: Mark 10: 13-16, 1993; Chuck Colson, 1994; A Strange Place to Sing, 1994; The Brave But Gentle Shepherd: I Samuel 17: 34-37, 1996; John Perkins, 1996; Luis Palau, 1996; Billy Sunday, 1996; Sojourner Truth: American Abolitionist, 1997; Samuel Morris: The Apostle of Simple Faith, 1999; Billy Graham, 2002. STORYBOARD THE PRAYER SERIES: Prayers for My Son, 1999; Prayers for My Daughter, 1999; Prayers for My Wife, 1999; Prayers for My Husband, 1999. OTHERS: (with C. Woehr) One Bright Shining Path, 1993; (with L. Kreider) Bottom-Line Faith, 1995; (with P.H. Porter, Jr.) Let the Walls Fall Down: A Call for Men to Bridge Barriers That Prevent Them From Finding Success in Life, 1996; (with T. Phillips and B. Norsworthy) The World at Your Door, 1997; (with P.H. Porter) Better Men: On the Path to Purity, 1998; (with C. Lewis) First Place: The Original Spiritually Based Weight Loss Plan for Whole Person Fitness, 1998, rev. ed., 2001; (with P.H. Porter) Seven Paths to Purity: Spiritual Solutions to Everyday Problems, 1998; (with S.L. Shaiklin) The Book of Prayers: A Mans Guide to Reaching God, 1998; (with B.J. Leninger) Lessons from the Pit: A Successful Veteran of the Chicago Mercantile Exchange Shows Executives How to Thrive in a Competitive Environment, 1999; (with S. Bolt) Money for Life, 1999; Lighthouse Psalms, 1999; Love Psalms, 1999; Alpha Teach Yourself the Bible in 24 Hours, 2003; (with V. Flowers) Complete Idiots Guide to Teaching the Bible, 2003; (with V. Flowers) Running On Ice: The Overcoming Faith of Vonetta Flowers, 2005; Book Proposals That Sell, 21 Secrets to Speed Your Success, 2005; Inspiring Women of the Faith: Sojourner Truth, Florence Nightengale, Amy Carmichael, Corrie ten Boom, 2008. FOR YOUNG READERS: Moses and the Great Escape, 1998; Joshua and the Jericho Project, 1998; Daniel and the Babylon Adventure, 1998; Jesus and His Miracles, 1998. BOOKS BIBLE FRIENDS BOOKSTORE SERIES: The Lord Is My Shepherd: Psalm 23; Make a Joyful Noise to the Lord: Psalm 100; Dont Worry: The Sermon on the Mount; Ruth Follows God; Queen Esther Rescues Her People; Miriam Saves Moses; When Fire Fell from Heaven: Elijah; Two Special Friends: David and Jonathan; A Promise Kept: Samson; Jesus and the Children; Jesus Calms the Storm; Zaccheus Climbs a Tree to See Jesus; Two Different Sisters: Mary and Martha; A Lame Man Walks: Peter in the Temple; The Seller of Purple: Lydia. Contributor to periodicals. **Address:** 23623 N Scottsdale Rd., Ste. D-3 481, Scottsdale, AZ 85255, U.S.A. **Online address:** terry@terrywhalin.com

WHALLEY, Joyce Irene. British (born England) **Genres:** Art/Art History, Crafts, History, Photography. **Career:** Victoria and Albert Museum, staff, 1950-81; Beatrix Potter Studies, editor, 1991-2001; Beatrix Potter Society Newsletter, editor, 1995-. **Publications:** English Handwriting, 1540-1843, 1969; (contrib.) Illuminated Manuscripts, 1972; Cobwebs to Catch Flies: Illustrated Books for the Nursery and Schoolroom, 1700-1900, 1974; Writing Implementsand Accessories, 1975; The Pen's Excellencie: Calligraphy in Western Europe and America, 1980; Book of Verse, 1980; Pliny's Histo-

ria Naturalis, 1982; Beatrix Potter's Derwentwater Sketchbook (facsimile), 1984; A Student's Guide to Western Calligraphy, 1984; Beatrix Potter: The V and A Collections (catalog), 1985; Two Victorian Railway Alphabets, 1986; (co-author) Beatrix Potter 1866-1945: The Artist and Her World, 1987, rev. ed., 1996; (with W. Bartlett) Beatrix Potter's Derwentwater, 1988; (with T.R. Chester) Bright Stream: A History of Children's Book Illustration, 1994. Contributor to books. **Address:** High Banks, 26 Stoneborough Ln., Budleigh Salterton, DN EX9 6HL, England.

WHALLEY, Peter. British (born England), b. 1946. **Genres:** Mystery/Crime/Suspense, Plays/Screenplays, Young Adult Fiction, Novels. **Career:** Writer and educator. **Publications:** NOVELS: Postmortem, 1982; The Mortician's Birthday Party, 1988; Old Murders, 1989; Love and Murder, 1989; Blackmailer's Summer, 1990; The Baby War, 1993; The Allegation, 1994. HARRY SOMMERS SERIES: Rogues, 1986; Robbers, 1987; Villains, 1987; Crooks, 1988. OTHERS: Local Murder, 1987; Dead of Night, 1990. **Address:** Crosswinds, 28, Hest Bank Ln., Hest Bank, Lancaster, ES W11 4LZ, England.

WHARTON, Thomas. Canadian (born Canada), b. 1963?. **Genres:** Science Fiction/Fantasy. **Career:** University of Alberta, assistant professor of English and film studies; Grant MacEwan College, faculty; Athabasca College, faculty. Writer. **Publications:** Icefields, 1995; Salamander, 2001; The Logogryph, 2004; The Shadow of Malabron, 2008. **Address:** Department of English and Film Studies, University of Alberta, Edmonton, AB T6G 2R3, Canada. **Online address:** twharton@ualberta.ca

WHAT, Leslie. American/German (born Germany), b. 1955?. **Genres:** Science Fiction/Fantasy, Popular Culture, Literary Criticism And History, Theology/Religion, Writing/Journalism, Essays, Novels, Humor/Satire, Humor/Satire. **Career:** UCLA Extension Writers Program, instructor. Writer. **Publications:** The Sweet and Sour Tongue, 2000; Olympic Games, 2004; Crazy Love: Stories, 2008; Editor Phantom Drift: New Fabulism, 2011. **Address:** Tachyon Publications, 1459 18th St., Ste. 139, San Francisco, CA 94107, U.S.A. **Online address:** lesliewhat@comcast.net

WHEATCROFT, John Stewart. American (born United States), b. 1925. **Genres:** Novels, Novellas/Short Stories, Plays/Screenplays, Poetry. **Career:** University of Kansas, instructor in English, 1950-52; Bucknell University, instructor, 1952-57, assistant professor, 1957-62, associate professor, 1962-66, professor of English, 1966-95, Homer Price Rainey professor of English emeritus, 1996-, Stadler Center for Poetry, director, 1979-96; University of Montana, distinguished visiting professor, 1969. Writer. **Publications:** POETRY: Death of a Clown, 1964; Prodigal Son, 1967; A Voice from the Hump and A Fourteenth Century Poet's Vision of Christ, 1977; Ordering Demons, 1981; The Stare on the Donkey's Face, 1990; Random Necessities, 1999; The Fugitive Self: New and Selected Poems, 2009; Telling Tales, 2010. NOVELS: Edie Tells: A Portrait of the Artist as a Middle-Aged Cleaning Woman, 1975; Catherine, Her Book, 1984; The Beholder's Eye, 1987; Killer Swan, 1992; Mother of All Loves, 1994; Trio with Four Players, 1995; The Education of Malcolm Palmer, 1997. OTHER: Ofoti, 1970; (with P. Balakian) Declaring Generations, 1982; (with K. Patten) Gowpen: A Double Handful of Poems, 1982; Slow Exposures (stories), 1986; (ed.) Our Other Voices (interviews with poets), 1991; Answering Fire, 2006. **Address:** Department of English, Bucknell University, 121 Vaughan Literature Bldg., Lewisburg, PA 17837, U.S.A. **Online address:** jsw015@bucknell.edu

WHEATLE, Alex. British (born England), b. 1963. **Genres:** Novels. **Career:** Writer. **Publications:** NOVELS: Brixton Rock, 1999; East of Acre Lane, 2001; The Seven Sisters, 2002; Island Songs, 2002; The Dirty South, 2002; (with M. Parham) Checkers, 2003. **Address:** Susijn Agency, 64 Great Titchfield St., 3rd Fl., London, GL W1W 7QH, England.

WHEATLEY, Nadia. Australian (born Australia), b. 1949. **Genres:** Children's Fiction, Plays/Screenplays, Bibliography, Biography, Children's Non-fiction, Adult Non-fiction. **Career:** University of Canberra's, May Gibbs Fellow. Writer. **Publications:** CHILDREN'S FICTION: Five Times Dizzy, 1982; Dancing in the Anzac Deli, 1984; The House That was Eureka, 1984; The Blooding, 1987; (with D. Rawlins) My Place, 1992; Lucy in the Leap Year, 1993; The Night Tolkien Died (short stories), 1995; The Greatest Treasure of Charlemagne the King, 1997; Highway, 1998; Luke's Way of Looking, 1999; Vigil, 2000; A Banner Bold, 2000. TELEPLAYS: (with T. Larsen) Five Times Dizzy (series), 1986. OTHER: (comp.) Adolescents and Family

Problems: Books for Young Children, 1988; (comp.) Children and Family Problems: Books for Young Children, 1988; 1 is for One, 1996; The Life and Myth of Charmian Clift (biography), 2001; Going Bush, 2007. EDITOR: (and intro.) Trouble in Lotus Land, 1990; Being Alone with Oneself, 1991; Landmarks, 1993; The Selected Essays of Charmian Clift, 2001; Listening to Mondrian, 2006. **Address:** Barbara Mobbs, PO Box 126, Edgecliff, NW 2027, Australia.

WHEELER, Deborah (Jean Ross). (Deborah J. Ross). American (born United States), b. 1947. **Genres:** Science Fiction/Fantasy, inspirational/Motivational Literature, Literary Criticism And History. **Career:** California Institute of Arts, library assistant, 1971-75; Pasadena College of Chiropractic, instructor of physiology, microbiology and neurology, 1976-80, dean, 1980; private practice, chiropractor, 1979-91; Beethoven St. Elementary School, PTA volunteer coordinator and librarian, 1993-. Writer. **Publications:** SCIENCE FICTION NOVELS: Jaydium, 1993; Northlight, 1995. AS DEBORAH J. ROSS: CLINGFIRE: (with M.Z. Bradley) The Fall of Neskaya, 2001; (with M.Z. Bradley) Zandru's Forge, 2003; (with M.Z. Bradley) A Flame in Hali, 2004. CHILDREN OF KINGS: (with M.Z. Bradley) The Alton Gift, 2007; Lace and Blade, 2008; (ed.) Lace and Blade 2, 2009; Hastur Lord, 2010; The Seven-Petaled Shield, forthcoming. Works appear in anthologies. **Address:** c/o Russell Galen, Scovil Chichak Galen Agency, 276 5th Ave., Ste. 708, New York, NY 10001, U.S.A. **Online address:** deborahjross@sff.net

WHEELER, Elizabeth. (Elizabeth A. Wheeler). American (born United States), b. 1959. **Genres:** Young Adult Fiction. **Career:** University of Oregon, Department of English, assistant professor of English, associate professor of English, director of undergraduate studies, Literacy Initiative, co-director. Writer. **Publications:** Uncontained: Urban Fiction in Postwar America, 2001. **Address:** Department of English, University of Oregon, PLC 238, 1098 E 13th Ave., Eugene, OR 97403-5275, U.S.A. **Online address:** ewheeler@uoregon.edu

WHEELER, Elizabeth A. See **WHEELER, Elizabeth.**

WHEELER, Helen Rippier. American (born United States) **Genres:** Communications/Media, Education, Gerontology/Senior Issues, Social Sciences, Women's Studies And Issues, Bibliography, Librarianship. **Career:** Hicksville Public Library, library director, 1951-53; University of Chicago, Laboratory School, staff and part-time foreign student adviser of International House, 1953-55; Chicago High School, teacher and librarian, 1955-56; Columbia University, Teachers College, Agnes Russell Center, staff, 1956-58, Latin American coordinator, 1962-64; City Colleges of Chicago, library director and audio-visual coordinator, 1958-62; Drexel University, adjunct assistant professor, 1964-65; University of Hawaii, associate professor and community colleges system consultant, 1965-66; Indiana State University, associate professor, 1966-68; St. John's University, associate professor, 1968-69; consultant and writer, 1969-71, 1973-; Louisiana State University, associate professor, 1971-73; Womanhood Media Consulting, sole proprietor, 1973-93. **Publications:** The Community College Library: A Plan for Action, 1965; A Basic Book Collection for the Community College Library, 1968; Womanhood Media: Current Resources About Women, 1972; Supplement, 1975; The Bibliographic Instruction-Course Handbook: A Skills and Concepts Approach to the Undergraduate, Research Methodology, Credit Course: For College and University Personnel, 1988; Getting Published in Women's Studies: An International, Interdisciplinary Professional Development Guide Mainly for Women, 1989; Women & Aging: A Guide to the Literature, 1997; Making It Out, forthcoming. Contributor to periodicals. **Address:** 2701 Durant Ave., Ste. 14, Berkeley, CA 94704-1733, U.S.A. **Online address:** pen136@inreach.com

WHEELER, Jill. American (born United States), b. 1964. **Genres:** Children's Non-fiction, Animals/Pets. **Career:** Adculture Group Inc., supervisor, 2003-. Writer. **Publications:** NONFICTION: Lost in London, 1988; (ed.) Bound for Boston, 1988; Adventure in Athens, 1988; There's No Place Like Rome, 1988; Light-Haired One: The Story of Crazy Horse, 1989; Wolf of the Desert: The Story of Geronimo, 1989; Forest Diplomat: The Story of Hiawatha, 1989; Forest Warrior: The Story of Pontiac, 1989; Lame One: The Story of Sequoyah, 1989; Dakota Brave: The Story of Sitting Bull, 1989; The Air We Breathe, 1990; The Animals We Live with, 1990; The City We Live In, 1990; The Land We Live on, 1990; The Water We Drink, 1990; Corazon Aquino, 1991; Earth Day Every Day, 1991; Earth Moves: Get there with Energy to Spare, 1991; The Food We Eat, 1991; Healthy Earth, Healthy Bodies, 1991; Throw Away Generation, 1991; Nancy R. Reagan, 1991; The People

We Live With, 1991; The Throw-Away Generation, 1991; Princess Caroline of Monaco, 1992; A.A. Milne, 1992; Coretta Scott King, 1992; Dr. Seuss, 1992; Laura Ingalls Wilder: A Tribute to the Young at Heart, 1992; Michael Landon, 1992; Mother Teresa, 1992; Princess Caroline, 1992; Raisa Gorbachev, 1992; Beastly Neighbors: A Book About Animals, 1993; Branch Out: A Book About Land, 1993; Earth Kids, 1993; Every Drop Counts: A Book About Water, 1993; For the Birds!: A Book About Air, 1993; Let's Explore the Heartland, 1994; The Midwest and the Heartland, 1994; Let's Explore the Northeast, 1994; Let's Explore the Southeast, 1994; Let's Explore the Pacific West: This Land is Your Land, 1994; The Southeast and Gulf States, 1994; Let's Explore the West, 1994; Tiger Woods: Lion on the Links, 1995; Bill Peet, 1996; Everyday Heroes of the Heart, 1996; Everyday Heroes at Home, 1996; Everyday Heroes on the Move, 1996; Everyday Heroes Overcome Challenges, 1996; Everyday Heroes Take a Stand, 1996; Everyday Heroes to the Rescue, 1996; The Forces with Us: A Book about Energy, 1996; Gaps in Space: A Book about Black Holes, 1996; Heather Whitestone: Miss America with a Mission, 1996; It's a Very Small World: A Book about Atoms, 1996; Judy Blume, 1996; Louisa May Alcott, 1996; Mark Twain, 1996; Move It!: A Book about Motion, 1996; R.L. Stine, 1996; See Hear: A Book about Sound and Light, 1996; Selena: The Queen of Tejano, 1996; Mark Twain, 1996; The Stuff Life's Made Of: A Book about Matter, 1996; Gwendolyn Brooks, 1997; Judith Viorst, 1997; L. Frank Baum, 1997; Lloyd Alexander, 1997; Peggy Parish, 1997; Virginia Hamilton, 1997; Brett Favre, 1998; Tara Lipinski, 1998; Princess Diana, 2000; Jim Carrey, 2001; Julia Roberts, 2001; Shania Twain, 2001; Tom Cruise, 2001; Michael J. Fox, 2001; Tom Hanks, 2001; Amelia Earhart, 2002; Clara Barton, 2002; Madeleine Albright, 2002; Oprah Winfrey, 2002; Nelson Mandela, 2002; Colin Powell, 2002; September 11, 2001: The Day That Changed America, 2002; Enrique Iglesias, 2002; America's Leaders, 2002; George W. Bush, 2002; Mel Gibson, 2003; Pope John Paul II, 2003; Red Cross Workers, 2003; Rosa Parks, 2003; Susan B. Anthony, 2003; Thurgood Marshall, 2003; Brad Pitt, 2003; Cesar Chavez, 2003; Denzel Washington, 2003; ER Doctors, 2003; Faith Hill, 2003; Firefighters, 2003; Gandhi, 2003; George Washington Carver, 2003; Harriet Tubman, 2003; Hillary Rodham Clinton, 2003; Jackie Robinson, 2003; Jennifer Lopez, 2003; Kelly Clarkson, 2003; Laura Bush, 2003; Madonna, 2003; Martin Luther King Jr., 2003; Beetle, 2004; Benazir Bhutto, 2004; Camaro, 2004; Coalition Leaders, 2004; Condoleezza Rice, 2004; Golda Meir, 2004; Hilary Duff, 2004; Indira Gandhi, 2004; Margaret Thatcher, 2004; Mary Robinson, 2004; Maserati, 2004; Mercedes-Benz, 2004; Norman Bridwell, 2004; Rolls-Royce, 2004; Saddam Hussein, 2004; Violetta Chamorro, 2004; Chris Van Allsburg, 2005; David Wiesner, 2005; Ezra Jack Keats, 2005; Garth Williams, 2005; Gertrude Chandler-Warner, 2005; Jessica Simpson, 2005; Judy Blume, 2005; Lindsay Lohan, 2005; Marjorie Weinman-Sharmat, 2005; Mercer Mayer, 2005; Robert McCloskey, 2005; William Steig, 2005; Bumblebee Bats, 2006; Crab Spiders, 2006; Daddy Longlegs Spiders, 2006; Fringe-Lipped Bats, 2006; Funnel-Web Spiders, 2006; Ghost-Faced Bats, 2006; Hobo Spiders, 2006; Honduran White Bats, 2006; Little Brown Bats, 2006; Recluse Spiders, 2006; Slit-Faced Bats, 2006; White-tailed Spiders, 2006; Andy Roddick, 2007; Barbara Park, 2007; Christopher Paolini, 2007; David Beckham, 2007; Lebron James, 2007; Lemony Snicket, 2007; Margaret Wise Brown, 2007; Mary Pope Osborne, 2007; Michael Vick, 2007; Michelle Wie, 2007; Nuclear Power, 2007; Roald Dahl, 2007; Tom Brady, 2007; Alternative Cars, 2008; Cockapoos, 2008; Fossil Fuels, 2008; Everyday Conservation, 2008; Nature Power, 2008; Goldendoodles, 2008; Renewable Fuels, 2008; Labradoodles, 2008; Puggles, 2008; Schnoodles, 2008; Yorkiepoos, 2008; Barack Obama, 2009; Kate DiCamillo, 2009; Avi, 2009; Patricia Nixon, 2009; C.S. Lewis, 2009; Cynthia Rylant, 2009; J.R.R. Tolkien, 2009; Pam Muñoz Ryan, 2009; Bengal Cats, 2010; Edith Wilson, 2010; Abigail Adams, 2010; Mamie Eisenhower, 2010; Harriet Lane, 2010; New Jersey, 2010; Kansas, 2010; Iowa, 2010; New Mexico, 2010; Pennsylvania, 2010; Portuguese Water Dogs, 2010; Bernese Mountain Dogs, 2010; Savannah Cats, 2010; Chausie Cats, 2010; Toyger Cats, 2010; Pixiebob Cats, 2010; Safari Cats, 2010; Michelle Obama, 2010; Welsh Corgis, 2010; Newfoundlands, 2010; Weimaraners, 2010; Boston Terriers, 2010; Nikki Grimes, 2011; Christopher Paul Curtis, 2011; Ragdoll Cats, 2012; Julia Alvarez, 2012; Japanese Bobtail Cats, 2012; Havana Brown Cats, 2012; Grace Lin, 2012; Egyptian Mau Cats, 2012; British Shorthair Cats, 2012; American Wirehair Cats, 2012. **Address:** 13025 Court Pl., Burnsville, MN 55337, U.S.A. **Online address:** jillewheeler@hotmail.com

WHEELER, Kate. American (born United States), b. 1955. **Genres:** Novels, Novellas/Short Stories, Travel/Exploration. **Career:** Writer, 1984-; CFTO, reporter; Miami Herald, news reporter, 1977-79; Middlesex Community

College, teacher of English composition, 1991; Insight Meditation Society, teacher of meditation, 1991-; Texas State University, faculty. **Publications:** (Trans. with E. Marquez) E. Marquez, Lo Esperado y Lo Vivido (title means: 'Borrowed Time'), 1984; (ed.) In This Very Life: The Liberation Teachings of the Buddha, 1992; Not Where I Started From (short stories), 1993; When Mountains Walked (novel), 2000; (ed.) Nixon under the Bodhi Tree and Other Works of Buddhist Fiction, 2004; (ed.) State of Mind Called Beautiful, 2006. Contributor to journals. **Address:** 72 Rev Nazareno Properzi Way, Somerville, MA 02143, U.S.A.

WHEELER, Lesley. American (born United States), b. 1967. **Genres:** Poetry, History. **Career:** Washington and Lee University, assistant professor, 1994-2000, associate professor, 2000-06, professor of English, 2006-, Henry S. Fox professor of English, chair of women's studies, 2003-05; American Association of University Women, fellow, 1996. Writer. **Publications:** The Poetics of Enclosure: American Women Poets from Dickinson to Dove, 2002; Voicing American Poetry: Sound and Performance From the 1920s to the Present, 2008; (ed. with M. Richards and R. Starace) Letters to the World: Poems from Members of the Women's Poetry Listserv, 2008; Heathen, 2009; Heterotopia, 2010. **Address:** Department of English, Washington & Lee University, Baker Hall 312, Lexington, VA 24450, U.S.A. **Online address:** wheelerlm@wlu.edu

WHEELER, Lonnie. American (born United States), b. 1952. **Genres:** Sports/Fitness, Autobiography/Memoirs. **Career:** Anderson Independent, staff, 1977-84; Clarion Ledger, staff, 1977-84; Cincinnati Enquirer, staff, 1977-84; Cincinnati Post, sports columnist, 1999-2007; USA Today, feature writer. **Publications:** (With J. Baskin) The Cincinnati Game, 1988; Bleachers: A Summer in Wrigley Field, 1988; The Official Baseball Hall of Fame Story of Mickey Mantle, 1990; (with H. Aaron) I Had a Hammer: The Hank Aaron Story, 1991; (with C. Young) Hard Stuff: The Autobiography of Coleman Young, 1994; (with B. Gibson) Stranger to the Game: The Autobiography of Bob Gibson, 1994; (with J. Marshall) Street Soldier: One Man's Struggle to Save a Generation, One Life at a Time, 1996; Blue Yonder: Kentucky, the United State of Basketball, 1998; The Road Back: The Cincinnati Bengals, 2006; (with B. Gibson and R. Jackson) Sixty Feet, Six Inches: A Hall of Fame Pitcher & a Hall of Fame Hitter Talk about How the Game Is Played, 2009. Contributor of articles to periodicals. **Address:** New Richmond, OH , U.S.A. **Online address:** lonniewheeler@gmail.com

WHEELER, Penny Estes. American (born United States), b. 1943. **Genres:** Novels, Adult Non-fiction, Children's Fiction, Women's Studies And Issues, Theology/Religion, Education, Human Relations/Parenting. **Career:** Teacher of second grade, 1967-68; Guide Magazine, editor, 1983-86; book acquisitions editor, 1986-94; Women of Spirit, editor, 1994-. **Publications:** Your Career in Elementary Education, 1970; A Time of Tears and Laughter: And a Story, The Darkness Had No Answer, 1971; (ed.) Journal of a Happy Woman, 1973; Don't Be Lonely, 1973; Three for the Show, 1973; VD, 1974; Alcohol, 1974; With Long Life, 1978; The Appearing, 1979; More Than Harps of Gold, 1981; The Beginning, 1982; (ed.) Give Me a Break, 1988; Longing for Home: A Personal View of Heaven, 1991; (with R. Jacobsen) Because You Prayed: Heartwarming Stories About Our Listening God, 1999; Tugging on God's Hand: Stories You Love from Women of Spirit, 2003; (ed.) Elasti-Brain: 365 Devotions to Stretch Your Mind and Shape Your Faith: A Daily Devotional for Juniors and Earliteens, 2008. Contributor to magazines. **Address:** Review and Herald Publishing Association, 55 W Oak Ridge Dr., Hagerstown, MD 21740-7301, U.S.A.

WHEELER, Richard S. (Richard Shaw Wheeler). American (born United States), b. 1935. **Genres:** Novels, Westerns/Adventure, History. **Career:** Phoenix Gazette, editorial writer, 1961-62; Oakland Tribune, page editor, 1963-65; Reader's Digest, staff writer, 1966; Billings Gazette, reporter, 1968-69; copy editor and city editor, 1970-72; Carson City Nevada Appeal, reporter, 1969-70; Open Court Publishing Co., book editor, 1973-74; Icarus Press, book editor, 1980-81; Green Hill Publishers, book editor, 1982-85; Walker and Co., editor, 1985-87; Big Timber, editor, 1987-97; Livingston, editor, 1998-. **Publications:** WESTERNS: Bushwack, 1978; Beneath the Blue Mountain, 1979; Winter Grass, 1983; Sam Hook, 1986; Richard Lamb, 1987; Dodging Red Cloud, 1987; Stop, 1988; Fool's Coach, 1989; Where the River Runs, 1990; Montana Hitch, 1990; Badlands, 1992; The Two Medicine, 1993; The Witness, 2000; Restitution, 2001; Drum's Ring, 2001; Cutthroat Gulch, 2003; The Bounty Trail, 2004; Vengeance Valley, 2004. SKYE'S WEST SERIES: Sun River, 1989; Bannack, 1989; The Far Tribes, 1990; Yellowstone,

1990; Bitterroot, 1991; Sundance, 1992; Wind River, 1993; Santa Fe, 1994; Rendezvous, 1997; Dark Passage, 1998; Going Home, 2000; Downriver, 2001; The Deliverance, 2003; The First Dance, 2010. SANTIAGO TOOLE SERIES: Incident at Fort Keogh, 1990; The Final Tally, 1991; Deuces and Ladies Wild, 1991; The Fate, 1992. SAM FLINT SERIES: Flint's Gift, 1997; Flint's Truth, 1998; Flint's Honor, 1999. NOVELS: The Rocky Mountain Company, 1991; Fort Dance, 1991; Cheyenne Winter, 1992; Cashbox, 1994; Goldfield, 1995; Sierra, 1996; Second Lives, 1997; The Buffalo Commons, 1998; Aftershocks, 1999; Sun Mountain, 1999; Masterson, 1999; The Fields of Eden, 2001; Eclipse, 2002; The Exile, 2003; Trouble in Tombstone, 2004; An Obituary for Major Remo, 2004; Seven Miles to Sundown, 2005; Fire in the Hole, 2005; From Hell to Midnight, 2006; The Honorable Cody, 2006; Fire Arrow: A Barnaby Skye Novel, 2006; Accidental Novelist: A Literary Memoir, 2007; Canyon of Bones, 2007; Virgin River, 2008; North Star, 2009; Bad Apple: A Cletus Parr Mystery, 2009; Owl Hunt: A Barnaby Skye Novel, 2010; Yancey's Jackpot, 2010; Snowbound, 2010. OTHER: The Children of Darkness, 1973; Pagans in the Pulpit, 1974; (ed.) Tales of the American West, 2000; The Richest Hill on Earth, 2011. Works appear in anthologies. Contributor to periodicals. **Address:** c/o Robin Rue, Writers House L.L.C., 21 W 26th St., New York, NY 10010, U.S.A. **Online address:** rwheeler@imt.net

WHEELER, Richard Shaw. *See* **WHEELER, Richard S.**

WHEELER, Ron. American (born United States), b. 1954. **Genres:** Cartoons. **Career:** Ralston Purina Co., staff, 1977; Maritz Motivation Co., creative director, 1978-79; cartoonist/humor illustrator, 1980-. Writer. **Publications:** (Contrib.) Terrible Plight of Oliver B, 1990; Cartoon Clip-Art for Youth Leaders 2, 1991; Help I'm Late for School and I Can't Get Up!, 1994; Love & Dating and Other Natural Disasters!, 1993; Jeremiah: I Wouldn't Be Tempted If Temptation wasn't so Tempting!, 1995; Jeremiah: Let My Words Be Sweet & Tender 'Cause I May Have to Eat 'Em!, 1996; Dr. Frenchy's Bible ABCs, 2005; Stinky Stevens and the Plight of the One-Armed Doll, 2009; Stinky Stevens and the Time Machine Adventure, 2009; Power of Shaolin Kung Fu: Harness the Speed and Devastating Force of Jow Ga Kung Ku, 2011. Illustrator of books by others. **Address:** CartoonWorks, 9818 Summit St., Kansas City, MO 64114-3806, U.S.A. **Online address:** ron@cartoonworks.com

WHEELER, Sara. British (born England), b. 1961. **Genres:** Travel/Exploration, Biography, Sciences, Environmental Sciences/Ecology. **Career:** U.S. Polar Program, writer-in-residence, 1995; BBC Radio, contributor; travel journalist. **Publications:** An Island Apart: Travels in Evia, 1993; Travels in a Thin Country: A Journey through Chile, 1994; Terra Incognita: Travels in Antarctica, 1996; (co-ed.) Amazonian: The Penguin Book of Womens New Travel Writing, 1998; (contrib.) Greetings from Antarctica, 1999; Cherry: A Life of Apsley Cherry-Garrard, 2002; Too Close to the Sun: The Audacious Life and Times of Denys Finch Hatton, 2006; The Magnetic North: Notes From the Arctic Circle, 2009. **Address:** c/o Gillon Aitken, Aitken Alexander Associates Ltd., 18-21 Cavaye Pl., London, GL SW10 9PT, England.

WHEELER, Shannon L. American (born United States), b. 1966. **Genres:** Cartoons. **Career:** Austin American-Statesman, cartoonist, 1990-99; Will Vinton Studio, animator, 1991-2002; Dark Horse Comics, cartoonist, 1991-; Beanworld Press Inc., reader, 1993-; Marvel Comics, brief contributor, 1994; MTV Animation, creator, 1996; Will Vinton Studios for WB, animator, 1998-2000; Dark Horse, comic book artist, 1998-; CDForge, co-partier, 1999-; Penguin Books, cartoonist, 2002-09; Adhesive Comics and Press, publisher and editor-in-chief; The New Yorker, cartoonist. **Publications:** Too Much Coffee Man: Guide for the Perplexed, 1998; Too Much Coffee Man's Parade of Tirade, 1999; Too Much Coffee Man's Amusing Musings, 2001. Contributor to periodicals. **Address:** Adhesive Press, PO Box 14549, Portland, OR 97293-0549, U.S.A. **Online address:** wheeler@tmcm.com

WHEELER, Susan. American (born United States), b. 1955. **Genres:** Poetry, Novels. **Career:** Art Institute of Chicago, director of public programs and information, 1981-85; freelance editor and writer, 1983-91; New York University, School of the Art Institute, instructor, 1984-85, director of public affairs arts and sciences, 1989-95, instructor, 1997-98, visiting instructor, 2006-08; Poets in Public Service, instructor, 1989-91; New School for Social Research, instructor, 1994-; Rutgers University, instructor, 1995-96; Princeton University, visiting lecturer, 1999-2010, associate professor, 2010-, Lewis Center for the Arts, director of creative writing, 2011-; University of Iowa Writers' Workshop, visiting professor, 2000; Columbia University, visiting professor, 2004. Writer. **Publications:** Bag O' Diamonds, 1993; Smokes, 1998; Source Codes, 2001; Record Palace: A Novel, 2005; Ledger, 2005; Assorted Poems, 2009. Contributor to journals. Works appear in anthologies. **Address:** Lewis Center for Arts, Princeton University, 185 Nassau St., Princeton, NJ 08544, U.S.A. **Online address:** swheeler@princeton.edu

WHEELER, Thomas. American (born United States) **Genres:** Novels, Literary Criticism And History. **Career:** American Broadcasting Corp., executive producer, 2005-; National Broadcasting Co., executive producer and show runner. Screenwriter and novelist. **Publications:** The Arcanum, 2004. Contributor to periodicals. **Address:** c/o Author Mail, Random House, 1745 Broadway, New York, NY 10019, U.S.A.

WHELAN, Gloria (Ann). American (born United States), b. 1923. **Genres:** Young Adult Fiction. **Career:** Minneapolis Family and Children's Service, social worker, 1948-49; Children's Center of Wayne County, supervisor of group services and day care program, 1963-68; Spring Arbor College, instructor in American literature, 1979-; Interlochen Academy for the Arts, writer-in-residence. **Publications:** YOUNG ADULT NOVELS: Clearing in the Forest, 1978; A Time to Keep Silent, 1979; The Pathless Woods, 1981; Next Spring an Oriole, 1987; A Week of Raccoons, 1988; Silver, 1988; Playing with Shadows, 1988; The Secret Keeper, 1990; Hannah, 1991; Bringing the Farmhouse Home, 1992; Goodbye, Vietnam, 1992; A Time to Keep Silent, 1993; Night of the Full Moon, 1993; That Wild Berries Should Grow: The Story of a Summer, 1994; Once on this Island, 1995; The President's Mother, 1996; The Indian School, 1996; The Ambassador's Wife, 1997; The Shadow of the Wolf, 1997; The Miracle of St. Nicholas, 1997; Friends, 1997; Forgive the River, Forgive the Sky, 1998; Farewell to the Island, 1998; Miranda's Last Stand, 1999; Pathless Woods: Ernest Hemingway's Sixteenth Summer in Northern Michigan, 1999; Welcome to Starvation Lake, 2000; Return to the Island, 2000; Homeless Bird, 2000; Rich and Famous in Starvation Lake, 2001; Angel on the Square, 2001; Fruitlands: Louisa May Alcott made Perfect, 2002; Jams and Jellies by Holly and Nellie, 2002; Are There Bears in Starvation Lake?, 2002; Wanigan, 2002; Impossible Journey, 2003; Haunted House in Starvation Lake, 2003; Chu Ju's House, 2004; Burying the Sun, 2004; Friend on Freedom River, 2004; Listening for Lions, 2005; Mackinac Bridge: The Five Mile Poem, 2006; Summer of the War, 2006; Turning, 2006; Parade of Shadows, 2007; Disappeared, 2008; Yuki and the One Thousand Carriers, 2008; Locked Garden, 2009; Waiting for the Owl's Cal, 2009; (with J. Nolan) K is for Kabuki: A Japan Alphabet, 2009; After the Train, 2009; Listeners, 2009; R the Train, 2009; Small Acts of Amazing Courage, 2011; See What I See, 2011; The Boy Who Wanted to Cook, 2011; Megan's Year: An Irish Traveler's Story, 2011. Contributor of articless to journals and newspapers. **Address:** c/o Liza Vogues, 866 United Nations Plz., New York, NY 10017, U.S.A. **Online address:** gloriawhelan@comcast.net

WHELAN, Irene. American (born United States) **Genres:** Social Sciences, History, Theology/Religion. **Career:** Manhattanville College, professor of history and director of Irish Studies. Writer and historian. **Publications:** The Bible War in Ireland: The Second Reformation and the Polarization of Protestant-Catholic Relations, 1800-1840, 2005. Contributor to books. **Address:** Department of History, Manhattanville College, Founders Hall G16, 2900 Purchase St., Purchase, NY 10577, U.S.A. **Online address:** whelani@mville.edu

WHELAN, Ruth. Irish (born Ireland), b. 1956. **Genres:** History, Local History/Rural Topics, Language/Linguistics, Social Commentary, Adult Non-fiction, Humanities. **Career:** French teacher, 1977-78; école Normale Supérieure, instructor in English as a foreign language, 1981-82; école Nationale Supérieurede la Statistique et des Affairs économiques, instructor in English as a foreign language, 1983-84; Trinity College, lecturer, 1984-96, senior lecturer in French, 1996-97, fellow, 1990; Herzog August Bibliothek, visiting fellow, 1988; Linacre College, senior visiting fellow, 1992; National University of Ireland, professor of French and head of department, 1997-, research professor, 2004-05; University of Nantes, research associate, 2005. Writer. **Publications:** The Anatomy of Superstition: A Study of the Historical Theory and Practice of Pierre Bayle, 1989; (co-ed. and contrib.) De l'humanisme aux Lumières, Bayle et leprotestantisme, 1996; (co-ed.) Correspondance de Pierre Bayle, vol. I: 1662-1674, vol. II: Novembre 1674- novembre 1677, 1999; (co-ed., trans. and contrib.) Encyclopedia of the Enlightenment, four vols., 2003; (ed. with C. Baxter, trans. and contrib.) Toleration and Religious Identity: The Edict of Nantes and Its Implications in France, Britain and Ireland, 2003; (ed.

with B. Tribout) Narrating the Self in Early Modern Europe, 2007; Refugees for Religion's Sake: The Huguenots in Early Modern Ireland, forthcoming. **Address:** Department of French, National University of Ireland, Rm. 29 Arts Bldg., Maynooth, KL 1, Ireland. **Online address:** ruth.whelan@nuim.ie

WHELAN, Yvonne. British (born England) **Genres:** Politics/Government, Social Sciences. **Career:** University of Ulster, lecturer in human geography; University College Dublin, Department of Geography, faculty; Concordia University, Irish Studies at the Centre for Canadian-Irish Studies, O'Brien visiting professor, 2004; University of Bristol, School of Geographical Sciences, Department of Human Geography, senior lecturer, 2005-. University of Toronto, Armstrong visiting professor, 2008. Writer. **Publications:** Reinventing Modern Dublin: Streetscape, Iconography and the Politics of Identity, 2003; Ireland: Space, Text, Time, 2005; (ed. with N. Moore) Heritage, Memory and the Politics of Identity: New Perspectives on the Cultural Landscape, 2007; (ed. with L. Harte) Ireland beyond Boundaries: Mapping Irish Studies in the Twenty-first Century, 2007. Contributor of articles to periodicals. **Address:** School of Geographical Sciences, University of Bristol, 2.7N University Rd., Senate House, Tyndall Ave., Clifton, Bristol, BS8 1SS, England. **Online address:** yvonne.whelan@bristol.ac.uk

WHELDON, David. British (born England), b. 1950. **Genres:** Novels, Poetry, inspirational/Motivational Literature. **Career:** Yeovil General Hospital, house surgeon, 1973-74; Frenchay Hospital, house physician, 1974; Radcliffe Infirmary, resident pathologist, 1974-75, registrar in pathology, 1975-77, senior registrar in microbiology, 1977-79; Bedford General Hospital, consultant microbiologist, 1980-92. Writer. **Publications:** The Chaos Contract, 1970; The Viaduct, 1982; The Course of Instruction, 1984; A Vocation, 1986; At the Quay, 1990; Onesimus, 1997; The Uncompliant Stranger, 1997; Days and Orders, 1998; Language in a Narrow Place, 1998; The Present Perennial, 1998; Night Altitude, 1999; Changes, Days, Lives, 2000; A Lens to the Sun, 2000; A Road Assumed, 2000. Contributor to periodicals. **Address:** The Bodley Head, 9 Bow St., London, GL WC2E 7AH, England. **Online address:** dwauthor@berkeleybooks.co.uk

WHELEHAN, Imelda. British (born England), b. 1960. **Genres:** Women's Studies And Issues, Young Adult Non-fiction, Literary Criticism And History, Social Sciences. **Career:** De Montfort University, principal lecturer, 1989, professor of English and women's studies, Research for the Faculty of Humanities, head, Centre for Adaptations, visiting professor; University of Tasmania, Faculty of Arts, research professor; Oxford Journals, Adaptation Journal, co-editor; Contemporary Women's Writing Journal, associate editor. **Publications:** Modern Feminist Thought: From the Second Wave to Post-Feminism, 1995; (ed. with D. Cartmell) Adaptations: From Text to Screen, Screen to Text, 1999; Overloaded: Popular Culture and The Future of Feminism, 2000; (ed. with D. Cartmell and I.Q. Hunter) Retrovision: Reinventing the Past in Film and Fiction, 2001; Helen Fielding's Bridget Jones's Diary: A Reader's Guide, 2002; (with J. Pilcher) Fifty Key Concepts in Gender Studies, 2004; The Feminist Bestseller: From Sex and the Single Girl to Sex and the City, 2005; (ed. with D. Cartmell) The Cambridge Companion to Literature on Screen, 2007; (with D. Cartmell) Screen Adaptation: Impure Cinema, 2010. Contributor to books. **Address:** Faculty of Arts, University of Tasmania, 408 Arts Bldg., Ground Fl., 2nd Level, Sandy Bay Campus, PO Box 44, Hobart, 7001, Tasmania. **Online address:** imelda.whelehan@utas.edu.au

WHELPTON, John Francis. Chinese/British (born England), b. 1950. **Genres:** Politics/Government, Ethics, Sociology. **Career:** Tribhuvan University, lecturer, 1972-74; Ministry of Defense, trainee, 1975-78, officer, 1978-81; Kiangsu-Chekiang College, teacher, 1987-91; Cheung Sha Wan Catholic Secondary School, teacher, 1991-96; Hong Kong Technical College, lecturer, 1996-97; Baptist Lui Ming Choi Secondary School, 1997-. Writer. **Publications:** Jang Bahadur in Europe: The First Nepalese Mission to the West, 1983; Nepal, 1990; Kings, Soldiers, and Priests: Nepalese Politics and the Rise of Jang Bahadur Rana, 1830-1857, 1991; (ed.) Nationalism and Ethnicity in a Hindu Kingdom: The Politics of Culture in Contemporary Nepal, 1997; People, Politics & Ideology: Democracy and Social Change in Nepal, 1999; (ed.) A History of Nepal, 2005. **Address:** Baptist Lui Ming Choi Secondary School, 11 Yuen Wo Rd., Lek Yuen Estate, Shatin, 511330, China. **Online address:** jfwhelpt@hkstar.com

WHICKER, Alan (Donald). British/Egyptian (born Egypt), b. 1925. **Genres:** Travel/Exploration, Autobiography/Memoirs, History, Biography. **Career:** Exchange Telegraph News Agency, foreign correspondent, 1947-, war correspondent, 1951; British Broadcasting Corp. (BBC), reporter, 1957-, presenter, 1958-68; Yorkshire Television, presenter, 1968-83; BBC, associate, 1983-. Writer. **Publications:** Away-with Alan Whicker, 1963; Within Whicker's World (autobiography), 1982; Whicker's New World, 1985; Whicker's World Down Under, 1988; Whicker's World: Take 2!, 2000; Whicker's War, 2005. Contributor to periodicals. **Address:** Le Gallais Chambers, St. Helier, Jersey, CI JE3 5BA, England.

WHIGHAM, Thomas. American (born United States), b. 1955. **Genres:** Politics/Government. **Career:** San Francisco State University, visiting lecturer, 1985; California State University, visiting lecturer, 1985-86; California State Polytechnic University, visiting lecturer, 1985-86; University of California, visiting lecturer, 1985-86; University of Georgia, assistant professor, 1986-91, associate professor, 1991-99, professor, 1999-. Writer. **Publications:** The Politics of River Trade: Tradition and Development in the Upper Plata, 1780-1870, 1991; Yerba Mate del Paraguay, 1780-1870, 1991; (with J.W. Cooney) El Paraguay Bajo los Lopez: Algunos Ensayos de Historia Social y Política, 1994; (with J.W. Cooney) A Guide to Collections on Paraguay in the United States, 1995; (comp. with J.W. Cooney) El Paraguay Bajo el Doctor Francia: Ensayos Sobre la Sociedad Patrimonial, 1814-1840, 1996; Paraguay, Corrientes y la Politica Fluvial: Tradiciòn y Desarrolloen el Alto Plata, 1780-1870, 1999; Paraguayan War, 2002; (ed. with H. Kraay) I Die with My Country: Perspectives on the Paraguayan War, 1864-1870, 2004; (ed. with R.S. Yegros) Escritos Históricos, 2006; (ed. with J.W. Cooney) Campo y Frontera: El Paraguay Al Fin De La Era Colonial, 2006; (ed. and comp. with J.M. Casal) La diplomacia estadounidense durante la Guerra de la Triple Alianza, 2008; (with J.M. Casal) Charles Ames Washburn sobre Paraguay, 1861-1868, 2008; Lo que el río se llevó: Estado y comercio en Paraguay y Corrientes, 1776-1870, 2009; (ed. with J.M. Casal) Paraguay: el nacionalismo y la guerra: actas de las primeras Jornadas Internacionales de Historia del Paraguay en la Universidad de Montevideo, 2009. **Address:** Department of History, University of Georgia, 314 LeConte Hall, 382 E Broad St., Athens, GA 30602, U.S.A. **Online address:** twhigham@uga.edu

WHISMAN, Dale. American (born United States) **Genres:** Novels. **Career:** Writer and private investigator. **Publications:** Friends and Other Perishables, 2004. Contributor to periodicals. **Address:** Tulsa Night Writers, 3436 S 96th East Ave., Tulsa, OK 74145, U.S.A. **Online address:** dale@dalewhisman.com

WHITAKER, Katie. British (born England), b. 1967. **Genres:** Novels, Biography, Autobiography/Memoirs, Literary Criticism And History, Philosophy. **Career:** University of Chicago, Century Fellow. Writer. **Publications:** Mad Madge: The Extraordinary Life of Margaret Cavendish, Duchess of Newcastle, the First Woman to Live by Her Pen, 2002; A Royal Passion: The Turbulent Marriage of King Charles I of England and Henrietta Maria of France, 2010. **Address:** c/o Author Mail, Basic Books, 387 Park Ave. S, New York, NY 10016, U.S.A.

WHITAKER, Matthew C. American (born United States) **Genres:** History, Civil Liberties/Human Rights. **Career:** Arizona State University, School of Historical, Philosophical, and Religious Studies, Department of History, teaching assistant, 1995-97, assistant professor, 2001-06, associate professor of history, 2006-11, Foundation professor of history, 2011-, School of Justice and Social Inquiry, affiliate faculty, 2001-, affiliate faculty of African and African American studies, 2001-, Center for the Study of Race and Democracy, founding director, 2010-; Michigan State University, Department of History, teaching assistant, 1997-2001; Whitaker Group L.L.C., co-owner and chief executive officer. Writer. **Publications:** (Contrib.) Organizing Black America: An Encyclopedia of African American Associations, 2000; Race Work: The Rise of Civil Rights in the Urban West, 2005; (ed.) African American Icons of Sport: Triumph, Courage, and Excellence, 2008; (ed. and intro. with J.I. Levitt) Hurricane Katrina: America's Unnatural Disaster, 2009; (ed.) Icons of Black America: Breaking Barriers and Crossing Boundaries, 2011; (contrib.) African American Urban History since World War II; Oxford Encyclopedia of African American History; Dictionary of American History; Over Jordan: African Americans in the Twentieth Century, forthcoming; Facing the Rising Sun: A History of African Americans in Arizona, forthcoming; Black Power Principals, forthcoming; Over Jordan: A History of Modern Black America, forthcoming; I Shook Up the World: The Life and Times of Muhammad Ali, forthcoming. **Address:** Department of History, Arizona State University, 4490 Coor Hall, 975 S Myrtle Ave., PO Box 874302, Tempe, AZ 85287-4302, U.S.A. **Online address:** matthew.whitaker@asu.edu

WHITAKER, Phil. British (born England), b. 1966?. **Genres:** Novels. **Career:** Alternative Medical Center, general practitioner and director; Guardian, book reviewer; Literary Intelligence (manuscript critiquing service), co-founder, 2001-; Arvon Foundation, tutor. Writer. **Publications:** NOVELS: Eclipse of the Sun, 1997; Triangulation, 1999; The Face, 2003; Freak of Nature, 2007. **Address:** c/o Jonny Geller, Curtis Brown Group Ltd., Haymarket House, 28-29 Haymarket, London, GL SW1 4SP, England. **Online address:** info@literaryintelligence.co.uk

WHITCHER, Susan (Godsil). American/Japanese (born Japan), b. 1952. **Genres:** Children's Fiction, Novels, Picture/Board Books, Mystery/Crime/Suspense, Horror. **Career:** Writer and teacher. **Publications:** Moonfall, 1993; Real Mummies Don't Bleed: Friendly Tales for October Nights, 1993; Something for Everyone, 1995; Enchanter's Glass, 1996; The Key to the Cupboard, 1996; The Fool Reversed, 2000. Contributor to periodicals. **Address:** c/o Emilie Jacobson, Curtis Brown Ltd., 10 Astor Pl., New York, NY 10003, U.S.A.

WHITCOMB, John C(lement). American (born United States), b. 1924. **Genres:** Astronomy, Earth Sciences, History, Theology/Religion. **Career:** Grace Theological Seminary, professor, 1951-90, director of post-graduate studies, 1961-86; Spanish-World Gospel Mission Inc., president, 1962-90; Grace Theological Journal, editor, 1980-89; Whitcomb Ministries Inc., president; Christian Workman Schools of Theology, founder and professor. **Publications:** Darius the Mede: A Study in Historical Identification, 1959; (with H.M. Morris) The Genesis Flood: The Biblical Record and its Scientific Implications, 1961; The Origin of the Solar System, 1964; Chart of the Old Testament Kings and Prophets, 1968; Solomon to the Exile: Studies in Kings and Chronicles, 1971; The Early Earth: An Introduction to Biblical Creationism, 1972, 3rd ed., 2010; The World That Perished: An Introduction to Biblical Catastrophism, 1973, 3rd ed., 2009; (with D.B. DeYoung) The Moon: Its Creation, Form and Significance, 1978; Esther: The Triumph of God's Sovereignty, 1979; (with J.J. Davis) Israel: From Conquest to Exile, 1980; The Bible and Astronomy, 1984; Daniel, 1985; (foreword) Astronomy and the Bible, 2000; (with D.B. DeYoung) Our Created Moon: Earth's Fascinating Neighbor, 2003; (intro.) The Grand Canyon: A Different View, 2003; The Rapture, the Great Tribulation, and the Millennium, 2010; (foreword) The Judgment Seat of Christ, 2011. Contributor to journals. **Address:** Whitcomb Ministries Inc., 6147 Hythe Rd., Indianapolis, IN 46220-4149, U.S.A. **Online address:** jcwhitcomb@juno.com

WHITCOMB, Laura. American (born United States) **Genres:** Novels, Young Adult Non-fiction, Young Adult Fiction. **Career:** Educator and writer. **Publications:** A Certain Slant of Light, 2005; (with A. Rittenberg) Your First Novel: A Published Author and a Top Agent Share the Keys to Achieving Your Dream, 2006; The Fetch, 2009; Novel Shortcuts: Ten Techniques that Ensure a Great First Draft, 2009. **Address:** c/o Author Mail, Houghton Mifflin, 222 Berkeley St., Boston, MA 02116-3764, U.S.A. **Online address:** lwhitcomb23@aol.com

WHITE, Andrea. American (born United States), b. 1942. **Genres:** Literary Criticism And History, Young Adult Fiction. **Career:** California State University, lecturer in English, 1976-, lecturer in interdisciplinary studies, 1990-; University of Southern California, lecturer in English, 1991-. Writer. **Publications:** (Co-author) Choices: A Text of Reading and Writing, 1983; Joseph Conrad and the Adventure Tradition: Constructing and Deconstructing the Imperial Subject, 1993; (co-ed.) Conrad in the Twenty-First Century: Contemporary Approaches and Perspectives, 2005. Work represented in anthologies. Contributor of articles to journals. **Address:** 4625 White Oak Ave., Encino, CA 91316, U.S.A.

WHITE, Bailey. American (born United States), b. 1950. **Genres:** Humor/Satire, Novels, Social Sciences, Young Adult Fiction, Novellas/Short Stories. **Career:** Thomasville City School System, teacher of first grade, now retired; National Public Radio, periodic commentator. Writer. **Publications:** Mama Makes Up Her Mind: And Other Dangers of Southern Living, 1993; Sleeping at the Starlite Motel, 1995; Quite a Year for Plums, 1998; Nothing with Strings, 2008. **Address:** c/o Jonathon Lazear, The Lazear Agency Inc., 430 1st Ave. N, Ste. 416, Minneapolis, MN 55401, U.S.A.

WHITE, Barbara Ehrlich. (Elliott White). American (born United States), b. 1936. **Genres:** Art/Art History, Biography, Architecture, Psychology. **Career:** Queens College, lecturer, 1959-61; Boston University, lecturer, 1965;

Tufts University, lecturer, 1965-66, assistant professor, 1966-87, adjunct professor of art history, 1987-. Writer. **Publications:** (Ed.) Impressionism in Perspective, 1978; Renoir: His Life, Art and Letters, 1984; Impressionists Side by Side: Their Friendships, Rivalries, and Artistic Exchanges, 1996. Contributor to journals. **Address:** 47 Circle Rd., Lexington, MA 02420, U.S.A.

WHITE, Bill. American (born United States), b. 1967. **Genres:** History, Military/Defense/Arms Control. **Career:** Operation Support (charitable organization), founder, 1991; Intrepid Sea, Air & Space Museum, Intrepid Fallen Heroes Fund, president, 1992-2010; Constellations Group, chairman and chief executive officer, 2010-. **Publications:** (With R. Gandt) Intrepid: The Epic Story of America's Most Legendary Warship, 2008. **Address:** Constellations Group, 1 Penn Plz., Ste. 3600, New York, NY 10119, U.S.A. **Online address:** bw@constellationsgroup.com

WHITE, Caramine. American (born United States), b. 1966. **Genres:** Novels. **Career:** Pet Publishing Inc., contributing editor; University of North Carolina-Greensboro, lecturer, 1993-97; Guilford Technical Community College, assistant professor, 1998-; Regent University, associate professor of language and literature. **Publications:** Reading Roddy Doyle, 2001; Running Naked Through the Streets, 2009. Contributor to magazines. **Address:** School of Undergraduate Studies, Regent University, 1000 Regent University Dr., Virginia Beach, VA 23464, U.S.A. **Online address:** cwhite@regent.edu

WHITE, Carolinne. British (born England), b. 1955. **Genres:** Classics, History, Theology/Religion, Biography, Translations, Literary Criticism And History. **Career:** University of South Africa, tutor in Latin, 1986-87; Oxford University, tutor and lecturer, 1987-, faculty research fellow; Liddell and Scott Greek Lexicon, editorial assistant, 1988-92; Dictionary of Medieval Latin From British Sources, editorial assistant, 1992-. **Publications:** Christian Friendship in the Fourth Century, 1992; Early Christian Latin Poets, 2000. TRANSLATOR: (and intro.) The Correspondence (394-419) Between Jerome and Augustine of Hippo, 1990; (and ed.) Gregory of Nazianzus: Autobiographical Poems, 1996; (intro. and ed.) Early Christian Lives: Life of Antony by Athanasius, Life of Paul of Thebes by Jerome, Life of Hilarion by Jerome, Life of Malchus by Jerome, Life of Martin of Tours by Sulpicius Severus, Life of Benedict by Gregory the Great, 1998; (and comp.) The Confessions of St. Augustine, 2001; (and ed.) Autobiographical Poems, 2005; (ed. and intro.) The Rule Of St. Benedict, 2008; (ed.and intro.) Lives of Roman Christian Women, 2010. **Address:** Ioannou Centre for Classical and Byzantine Studies, Faculty of Classics, University of Oxford, 66 St. Giles, Oxford, OX OX1 3LU, England. **Online address:** carolinne.white@classics.ox.ac.uk

WHITE, Carolyn. American (born United States), b. 1948. **Genres:** Poetry, Mythology/Folklore, Children's Fiction, Novels, History. **Career:** Writer. **Publications:** A History of Irish Fairies, 1976, rev. ed., 2001; Ghostroad: A Silver Spur Western, 1989; The Voyage of Penelope (poetry), 1993; The Tree House Children: An African Tale, 1994; Whuppity Stoorie: A Scottish Folktale, 1997; Gribbly-Boo!, 2000; The Adventure of Louey and Frank, 2001. Contributor to periodicals. **Address:** 1661 Mt. Vernon Ave., East Lansing, MI 48823, U.S.A. **Online address:** carolynw@pilot.msu.edu

WHITE, Christopher. American (born United States), b. 1956. **Genres:** Natural History, Biography. **Career:** Mare Nostrum Foundation, executive director; Chesapeake Bay Foundation, staff biologist. Writer and naturalist. **Publications:** Endangered and Threatened Wildlife of the Chesapeake Bay Region: Delaware, Maryland, and Virginia, 1982; Chesapeake Bay: Nature of the Estuary: a Field Guide, 1989; Skipjack: The Story of America's Last Sailing Oystermen, 2009. **Address:** Santa Fe, NM , U.S.A. **Online address:** chris@christopherwhitebooks.com

WHITE, Christopher (John). British (born England), b. 1930?. **Genres:** Art/Art History, Architecture, Photography. **Career:** British Museum, Department of Prints and Drawings, assistant keeper, 1954-65, Art of the Netherlands, professor, 1992-97, Art of the Netherlands, professor emeritus, 1997-; P.D. Colnaghi, director, 1965-71; Master Drawings, reviews editor, 1967-80; National Gallery of Art, curator of graphic arts, 1971-73; Paul Mellon Centre for Studies in British Art, director of studies, 1973-85; Yale University, Yale Center for British Art, adjunct professor of history of art, 1976-85, associate director, 1976-85; Ashmolean Museum, acting director, director, 1985-97, now director emeritus; Worcester College, fellow, 1985-97, now professor

emeritus. Writer. **Publications:** Drawings of Rembrandt, 1962; Rembrandt and His World, 1964; The Flower Drawings of Jan van Huysum, 1964; Rubens and His World, 1968; (intro.) Late Etchings of Rembrandt: A Study in the Development of a Print: An Arts Council Exhibition at the British Museum Gallery of Prints & Drawings, 20 March-11 May 1969, 1969; Rembrandt as an Etcher: A Study of the Artist at Work, 1969; (co-author) Rembrandt's Etchings: An Illustrated Critical Catalogue, 1970; Dürer: The Artist and His Drawings, 1971; (comp.) Loan Exhibition of Drawings by old Masters from the Collection of Mr. Geoffrey Gathorne-Hardy, 1972; (co-ed.) Liber Amicorum Karel G. Boon, 1974; English Landscape 1630-1850: Drawings, Prints & Books from the Paul Mellon Collection: An Exhibition, April19-July 17, 1977, 1977; Dutch Pictures in the Collection of Her Majesty the Queen, 1982; (ed.) Rembrandt in Eighteenth Century England, 1983; Peter Paul Rubens: Man and Artist, 1987; (co-author) Drawing in England from Hilliard to Hogarth, 1987; Segno Del Genio: Cento Disegni di Grandi Maestri del Passato dall Ashmolean Museum di Oxford, 1991; Old Master Drawings From the Ashmolean Museum, 1992; Hidden Treasures: Works of Art from Oxfordshire Private Collections, 1993; (with C. Crawley) Dutch and Flemish Drawings of the Fifteenth to the Early Nineteenth Centuries in the Collection of Her Majesty the Queen at Windsor Castle, 1994; Anthony van Dyck: Thomas Howard, the Earl of Arundel, 1995; (ed. with Q. Buvelot) Rembrandt by Himself, 1999; Ashmolean Museum, Oxford, Catalogue of the Dutch, Flemish and German Paintings, 1999; Later Flemish Pictures in the Collection of Her Majesty The Queen, 2007. **Address:** Ashmolean Museum, Beaumont St., Oxford, OX OX1 2PH, England.

WHITE, Courtney. (J. C. White). American (born United States), b. 1960. **Genres:** Social Sciences, Mathematics/Statistics. **Career:** Quivera Coalition, co-founder and executive director. Writer. **Publications:** (As J.C. White) In the Land of the Delight Makers: An Archaeological Survey in the American West, 1992; (as J.C. White) Adobe Typology and Site Chronology: A Case Study from Pecos National Historical Park, 1995; Revolution on the Range: The Rise of a New Ranch in the American West, 2008; (ed. with R.L. Knight) Conservation for a New Generation: Redefining Natural Resources Management, 2009. **Address:** Quivira Coalition, 1413 2nd St., Ste. 1, Santa Fe, NM 87505, U.S.A. **Online address:** admin@quiviracoalition.org

WHITE, C. Todd. American (born United States), b. 1965. **Genres:** History. **Career:** Hobart and William Smith Colleges, assistant professor of anthropology and sociology; James Madison University, visiting assistant professor of anthropology. Writer and anthropologist. **Publications:** Pre-Gay L.A.: A Social History of the Movement for Homosexual Rights, 2009. **Address:** Department of Anthropology & Sociology, Hobart and William Smith Colleges, Stern Hall, Geneva, NY 14456, U.S.A. **Online address:** ctwhite2@buffalo.edu

WHITE, Dan. American (born United States), b. 1967. **Genres:** Travel/Exploration, Medicine/Health, Environmental Sciences/Ecology, Essays. **Career:** Journalist and humorist. **Publications:** The Cactus Eaters: How I Lost My Mind and Almost Found Myself on the Pacific Crest Trail, 2008. Contributor of articles to periodicals. **Address:** HarperCollins Publishers, 10 E 53rd St., New York, NY 10022, U.S.A. **Online address:** cactus.eaters@yahoo.com

WHITE, Dave. American (born United States), b. 1979. **Genres:** Novels. **Career:** Middle-school, English teacher. Educator and writer. **Publications:** JACKSON DONNE SERIES-NOVELS: When One Man Dies, 2007; The Evil That Men Do, 2008. Works appear in anthologies. **Address:** NJ , U.S.A. **Online address:** davewhitenovels@yahoo.com

WHITE, David Gordon. American (born United States), b. 1953. **Genres:** Theology/Religion. **Career:** University of Virginia, Department of Religious Studies, lecturer, 1984-94, assistant professor, 1994-96; University of California, associate professor, 1996-2000, professor, 2000-06, J. F. Rowny professor of comparative religion, 2011-; Princeton University, Stewart fellow in anthropology and visiting professor, 2007. Writer. **Publications:** Other Gives Rise to Self: Dog-Men on the Borders of Medieval Europe, India and China, 1988; Myths of the Dog-Man, 1991; The Alchemical Body: Siddha Traditions in Medieval India, 1996; (ed.) Tantra in Practice, 2000; Kiss of the Yogini: Tantric Sex in Its South Asian Contexts, 2003; Sinister Yogis, 2009; (intro.) Yoga: Immortality and Freedom, 2009; (ed.) Yoga in Practice, 2011; The Yoga Sutras of Patanjali: A Biography, 2012. Contributor to books and periodicals. **Address:** Department of Religious Studies, University of California, 3077 Humanities and Social Sciences Bldg., Santa Barbara, CA 93106-3130,

U.S.A. **Online address:** white@religion.ucsb.edu

WHITE, Edmund. American (born United States), b. 1940. **Genres:** Novels, Gay And Lesbian Issues, Essays, Adult Non-fiction, Biography, Young Adult Non-fiction, Art/Art History. **Career:** Time Inc., Life Book Division, staff writer, 1962-70; The Saturday Review, senior editor, 1972-73; Horizon, associate editor, 1974-75; Johns Hopkins University, assistant professor of writing seminars, 1977-79; Columbia University, School of the Arts, adjunct professor of creative writing, 1980-82; New York Institute for the Humanities, executive director, 1980-82; Brown University, professor of English, 1990-92; Princeton University, Lewis Center for the Arts, professor of creative writing, 1998-. **Publications:** (With P. Wood) When Zeppelins Flew, 1969; Forgetting Elena, 1973; (with D. Brown) The First Men, 1973; (with C. Silverstein) The Joy of Gay Sex: An Intimate Guide for Gay Men to the Pleasures of a Gay Lifestyle, 1977; Nocturnes for the King of Naples, 1978; States of Desire: Travels in Gay America (non-fiction), 1980; A Boy's Own Story, 1982; (co-author) Aphrodisiac (short stories), 1984; Caracole, 1985; (with A. Mars-Jones) The Darker Proof: Stories from a Crisis, 1987; The Beautiful Room is Empty, 1988; Genet: A Biography, 1993; The Burning Library: Essays, 1994; Sketches from Memory: People and Places in the Heart of Our Paris in US as Our Paris: Sketches from Memory, 1995; Skinned Alive: Stories, 1995; Farewell Symphony: A Novel, 1997; Marcel Proust, 1999; The Married Man, 2000; The Flaneur: A Stroll Through The Paradoxes Of Paris, 2001; Fanny: A Fiction, 2003; Arts and Letters, 2004; My Lives, 2006; Hotel de Dream: A New York Novel, 2007; Chaos: A Novella and Stories, 2007; (intro.) Elles, 2007; Terre Haute, 2007; Rimbaud: The Double Life of a Rebel, 2008; Corps à Corps: Entretiens avec Augustin Trapenard diffusés sur France Culture du 7 au 11 juin 2004, 2009; City Boy: My Life in New York during the 1960s and '70s, 2009; Jack Holmes and His Friends, 2012. EDITOR: The Faber Book of Gay Short Fiction, 1991; (and intro.) The Selected Writings of Jean Genet, 1993; Loss Within Loss: Artists in the Age of AIDS, 2001. Works appear in anthologies. **Address:** c/o Amanda Urban, International Creative Management Inc., 730 5th Ave., New York, NJ 10019, U.S.A. **Online address:** ewhite@princeton.edu

WHITE, Edward M. American (born United States), b. 1933. **Genres:** Adult Non-fiction, Literary Criticism And History, Writing/Journalism, Autobiography/Memoirs, Essays. **Career:** Harvard University, teaching assistant, 1958-60; Wellesley College, instructor, 1960-63, assistant professor of English, 1963-65; California State University, Department of English, associate professor, 1965-69, chair, 1966-75, professor of English, 1969-96, professor emeritus, 1996-; University of Arizona, visiting professor, 2000-09. Writer. **Publications:** (Ed.) The Writer's Control of Tone, 1970; (ed.) The Pop Culture Tradition: Readings, with Analysis for Writing, 1972; Comparison and Contrast: The California State University English Equivalency Examination, 8 vols., 1974-81; (contrib.) Equivalency Testing, 1974; (contrib.) The Continuing Challenge: The Program for Innovation and Improvement in the Instructional Process, 1977; Teaching and Assessing Writing, 1985, 2nd ed. as Teaching and Assessing Writing: Recent Advances in Understanding, Evaluating, and Improving Student Performance, 1998; Developing Successful College Writing Programs, 1989; Assigning, Responding, Evaluating: A Writing Teacher's Guide, 1992, 4th ed., 2006; (ed. with L.Z. Bloom) Inquiry: A Cross-curricular Reader, 1993, (with L.Z. Bloom and S. Borrowman) 2nd ed. as Inquiry: Questioning, Reading, Writing, 2004; (ed. with L.Z. Bloom and D.A. Daiker) Composition in the Twenty-first Century: Crisis and Change, 1996; (ed. with W.D. Lutz and S. Kamusikiri) Assessment of Writing: Politics, Policies, Practices, 1996; (ed. with L.Z. Bloom and D.A. Daiker) Composition Studies in the New Millennium: Rereading the Past, Rewriting the Future, 2003; (ed. with S. Borrowman) The Promise of America, 2007. **Address:** Department of English, California State University, 334 University Hall, 5500 University Pkwy., San Bernardino, CA 92407-2318, U.S.A. **Online address:** ewhite@csusb.edu

WHITE, Elliott. *See* **WHITE, Barbara Ehrlich.**

WHITE, Emily. Canadian/American (born United States), b. 1971?. **Genres:** Autobiography/Memoirs. **Career:** Writer, lawyer, educator and consultant. **Publications:** Lonely: A Memoir, 2010. Contributor to books and periodicals. **Address:** St. John's, NL , Canada. **Online address:** emily@lonelythebook.com

WHITE, Evelyn C. American (born United States), b. 1954. **Genres:** Medicine/Health, Biography, Women's Studies And Issues, Autobiography/Memoirs. **Career:** San Francisco Chronicle, reporter, 1986-95. **Publications:** Chain, Chain, Change: For Black Women Dealing with Physical and Emotional Abuse, 1985, 2nd ed., 1995; (ed.) The Black Women's Health Book: Speaking for Ourselves, 1990, 2nd ed., 1994; (foreword) Black Like Us: A Century of Lesbian, Gay and Bisexual African American Fiction, 2002; Alice Walker: A Life, 2004; Every Goodbye ain't gone: A Photo Narrative of Black Heritage on Salt Spring Island, 2009. Contributor to periodicals. **Address:** Faith Childs Literary Agency, 915 Broadway, Ste. 1009, New York, NY 10010, U.S.A.

WHITE, Franklin. American (born United States) **Genres:** Novels, Young Adult Fiction, inspirational/Motivational Literature, Young Adult Non-fiction. **Career:** Blue/Black Press, founder. Writer. **Publications:** Fed Up With the Fanny (novel), 1996; Cup of Love: A Novel, 1999; Til Death Do Us Part, 2000; (with B. Stewart) No Matter What, 2002; (with L. Anderson) Change of Heart, 2002; Money for Good, 2003; Potentially Yours, 2004; First Round Lottery Pick, 2005; Joy and Pain, 2008. **Address:** Simon & Schuster Inc., 1230 Ave. of the Americas, New York, NY 10020, U.S.A. **Online address:** franklinwhite111@aol.com

WHITE, Howard. Canadian (born Canada), b. 1945. **Genres:** History, Area Studies, Poetry, Biography, Travel/Exploration. **Career:** Peninsula Voice, founder, editor, publisher, 1969-74; Raincoast Chronicles, editor, 1972-; Harbour Publishing, founder, president and publisher, 1974-. **Publications:** (With B. White) A Hard Man to Beat: The Story of Bill White, Labour Leader, Historian, Shipyard Worker, Raconteur: An Oral History, 1983; The Men There Were Then, 1983; (with J. Spilsbury) Spilsbury's Coast: Pioneer Years in the Wet West, 1987; The Accidental Airline, 1988; Writing in the Rain (essays and poetry), 1990; Patrick and the Backhoe (children's story), 1991; Ghost in the Gears (poetry), 1993; The Sunshine Coast: From Gibsons to Powell River; 1996; (ed.) Stories and History of the British Columbia Coast, 2003; (ed.) Raincoast Chronicles. Fourth Five: Stories and History of the BC Coast from Raincoast Chronicles Issues 16-20, 2005; The Airplane Ride, 2006. works appears in anthologies. Contributor to periodicals. **Address:** Harbour Publishing, PO Box 219, Madeira Park, BC V0N 2H0, Canada.

WHITE, J. C. *See* **WHITE, Courtney.**

WHITE, Jenny. (Jenny B. White). American/German (born Germany), b. 1953. **Genres:** Novels. **Career:** Marmara University, Department of Economics and Business Administration, lecturer, 1987-88; University of Nebraska, Department of Sociology and Anthropology, assistant professor, 1992-96; Boston University, associate professor of anthropology, 1996-, director of undergraduate studies, Women's Studies Program, director, 2000-01; American Anthropological Association, Middle East Section, president, 2004-06; Turkish Studies Association, president, 2004-06. Novelist. **Publications:** Money Makes Us Relatives: Women's Labor in Urban Turkey, 1994, 2nd ed., 2004; Islamist Mobilization in Turkey: A Study in Vernacular Politics, 2002; The Sultan's Seal, 2006; The Abyssinian Proof, 2008; The Winter Thief, 2010. Contributor to periodicals. **Address:** Department of Anthropology, Boston University, 232 Bay State Rd., Ste. 410, Boston, MA 02215, U.S.A. **Online address:** jbwhite@bu.edu

WHITE, Jenny B. *See* **WHITE, Jenny.**

WHITE, John Kenneth. American (born United States), b. 1952. **Genres:** Politics/Government. **Career:** University of Connecticut, Department of Political Science, graduate teaching assistant, 1977-78, Institute for Social Inquiry, graduate research assistant, 1979-80; Governor's Office of Policy and Management, Energy Division, staff, 1980; State University, College of Arts and Science, visiting assistant professor of political science, 1980-81, assistant professor of political science, 1981-86, associate professor of political science, 1986-88; Catholic University of America, associate professor of politics, 1989-94, professor of politics, 1994-, Life Cycle Institute, director, 2004-05. Writer. **Publications:** The Fractured Electorate: Political Parties and Social Change in Southern New England, 1983; The New Politics of Old Values, 1988, 3rd ed., 1998; Still Seeing Red: How the Old Cold War Shapes the New American Politics, 1997, rev. ed., 1998; (with D.M. Shea) New Party Politics: From Jefferson and Hamilton to the Information Age, 2000, 2nd ed., 2004; The Values Divide: American Politics and Culture in Transition, 2002; The Making of the Candidates, 2003; Barack Obama's America: How New Conceptions of Race, Family, and Religion Ended the Reagan Era, 2009; (with

M. Kerbel) Party On!: From Hamilton and Jefferson to Today's Networked Age, 2012. CO-EDITOR: New York State Today: Politics, Government, Public Policy, 2nd ed., 1989; Challenges to Party Government, 1992; Governing New York State, 1994; The Politics of Ideas: Intellectual Challenges to the Party After 1992, 1995; Political Parties and The Collapse of the Old Orders, 1998; Politics of Ideas: Intellectual Challenges Facing the American Political Parties, 2001; Contemporary Readings in American Government, 2002; Winning the White House, 2005. Contributor to books and periodicals. **Address:** Department of Politics, Catholic University of America, Washington, DC 20064, U.S.A. **Online address:** white@cua.edu

WHITE, Jonathan (Bruce). American (born United States), b. 1956. **Genres:** Novels, Environmental Sciences/Ecology, Sciences. **Career:** High school teacher, 1994-; Resource Institute, founder and president. General contractor and writer. **Publications:** Talking on the Water: Conversations About Nature and Creativity, 1994; (with S. Searcy and T. Stimmel) Cliffsnotes Basic Math and Pre-Algebra Practice Pack, 2010. Contributor to periodicals. **Address:** PO Box 299, Orcas, WA 98280, U.S.A.

WHITE, Jon Manchip. American/Welsh (born Wales), b. 1924. **Genres:** Novels, Poetry, History, Biography, Plays/Screenplays, Young Adult Nonfiction, Young Adult Fiction. **Career:** British Broadcasting Corp. (BBC-TV), story editor and screenwriter, 1950-51; H.M. Foreign Service, senior executive officer, 1952-56; Hammer Film Productions Ltd., scenario editor, 1956-57; freelance writer, 1956-67; Samuel Bronston Productions, screenwriter, 1960-64; University of Texas, professor of English, 1967-77; University of Tennessee, Lindsay Young professor of humanities and professor of English, 1977-97; Minsterworth Productions, Ltd., director. **Publications:** Dragon, 1943; Salamander, 1943; The Rout of San Romano, 1952; Ancient Egypt, 1952, 1970; Mask of Dust, 1953; The Last Race, 1953; Anthropology, 1954; Build Us a Dam, 1955; The Girl from Indiana, 1956; No Home but Heaven, 1957; The Mercenaries, 1958; Hour of the Rat, 1962; Marshal of France, 1962, Everyday Life in Ancient Egypt, 1963; The Rose in the Brandy Glass, 1965; Nightclimber, 1968; Diego Velazquez: Painter and Courtier, 1969; The Land God Made in Anger, 1969; Cortes and the Downfall of the Aztec Empire, 1971; The Game of Troy, 1971; The Mountain Lion, 1971; (with V. Guest) The Camp on Blood Island, 1972; The Garden Game, 1973; Send for Mr. Robinson!, 1975; A World Elsewhere, 1975 in UK as The Great American Desert, 1977; Robinson Factor, 1976; Everyday Life of the North American Indian, 1979; The Moscow Papers, 1979; Death by Dreaming, 1981; Fevers and Chills: Three Extravagant Tales, 1983; What to Do When the Russians Come, 1984; The Last Grand Master: A Novel of Revolution, 1985; The Journeying Boy: Scenes from a Welsh Childhood, 1991; Whistling Past the Churchyard: Strange Tales from a Superstitious Welshman, 1992; Solo Goya: Goya and the Duchess of Alba At Sanlcar, 2000; Echoes and Shadows, 2003; Rawlins White: Patriot to Heaven, 2011. EDITOR: The Glory of Egypt, 1955; Life in Ancient Egypt, 1971; Tomb of Tutankhamen, 1971; Manners and Customs of the Modern Egyptians, 1972. **Address:** 5620 Pinellas Dr., Knoxville, TN 37919-4118, U.S.A.

WHITE, Joseph B. American (born United States), b. 1958. **Genres:** Documentaries/Reportage, Business/Trade/Industry. **Career:** Vineyard Gazette, reporter, 1979-82; St. Petersburg Times, reporter, 1982-86; Connecticut Law Tribune, reporter, 1986-87; Wall Street Journal, reporter, 1987-90, deputy bureau chief, 1990-94, news editor, 1994-, Detroit bureau chief, 1998-2007, senior editor. **Publications:** (With P. Ingrassia) Comeback: The Fall and Rise of the American Automobile Industry, 1994. **Address:** The Wylie Agency Inc., 250 W 57th St., Ste. 2114, New York, NY 10107-2114, U.S.A. **Online address:** joseph.white@wsj.com

WHITE, Julie. See **ASNER, Jules.**

WHITE, Karen. American (born United States), b. 1964. **Genres:** Romance/ Historical, Novels, Young Adult Fiction, Mystery/Crime/Suspense. **Career:** Writer. **Publications:** ROMANCE NOVELS: In the Shadow of the Moon, 2000; Whispers of Goodbye, 2001; Falling Home, 2002; After the Rain, 2003; (co-author) Blessings of Mossy Creek, 2004; Color of Light, 2005; Pieces of the Heart, 2006; Learning to Breathe, 2007; A Year of Rain, 2008; Memory of Water, 2008; House on Tradd Street, 2008; Girl on Legare Street, 2009; Lost Hours, 2009; On Folly Beach, 2010; Beach Trees, 2011. Works appear in anthologies. **Address:** PO Box 623, Roswell, GA 30077-0623, U.S.A. **Online address:** authorkarenwhite@aol.com

WHITE, Kenneth. French/Scottish (born Scotland), b. 1936. **Genres:** Poetry, Travel/Exploration, Autobiography/Memoirs, Essays, Translations, Literary Criticism And History. **Career:** University of Glasgow, lecturer in French literature, lecturer in English and American literature, 1963-83; University of Paris VII, lecturer, 1969-83; Sorbonne University of Paris, professor of poetics, 1983-96; International Institute of Geopoetics, founder, 1989; University of Bordeaux, lecturer; UHI Millennium Institute, visiting professor. Writer. **Publications:** Wild Coal, 1963; En toute Candeur, 1964; The Cold Wind of Dawn, 1966; Letters from Gourgounel, 1966; The Most Difficult Area, 1968; (trans.) Selected Poems by Andre Breton, 1969; (trans.) A. Breton, Ode to Charles Fourier, 1969; Travels in the Drifting Dawn, 1972; The Tribal Dharma, 1974; On the Haiku Path, 1975; Scènes d'un monde flottant, 1976; Terre de diamant, 1977; A Walk along the Shore, 1977; Dérives (fiction), 1978; The Life-Technique of John Cowper Powys, 1978; Segalen: Theorie et pratique du voyage, 1979; Mahamudra, 1979; Le Grand Rivage, 1980; L'Ecosseavec Kenneth White, 1980; Le Visage du vent d'est, 1980; La Figure dudehors, 1982; Scenes d'un monde flottant, 1983; La Route bleue, 1983, trans. as The Blue Road, 1990; Atlantica, 1986; L'anorak du goéland, 1986; L'esprit nomade, 1987; The Bird Path: Collected Longer Poems, 1989; LeMonde d'Antonin Artaud, 1989; Handbook for the Diamond Country: Collected Shorter Poems 1960-1990, 1990; In the Sand Parishes, 1990; Hokusai, ou l'horizon sensible, 1990; Les Cygnes sauvages, 1990; Pilgrim of the Void, 1992; éloge du livre, 1994; Le Plateau del'Albatros, 1994; Van Gogh, 1994; (with Basserode) Déambulations dans l'espace nomade, 1995; (with J. Roux) Le livre des abîmes et des hauteurs, 1996; (with J. Camacho) La danse du chamane sur le glacier, 1996; Les Rives du silence, 1997; Le lieu et la parole: entretiens 1987-1997, 1997; Les bijoux, 2nd ed., 1998; Pisma iz Srbije i Crne Gore, 1998; On Scottish Ground, 1998; Le chemin des crêtes, 1999; Limites et Marges, 2000; House of Tides, 2000; Richard Texier: latitude atlantique, 2000; House of Tides: Letters from Brittany and other Lands of the West, 2000; (with O. Mériel) Regard photographique sur Trouville, 2002; Open Worlds: Collected Poems 1960-2000, 2003; Across the Territories: Travels from Orkney to Rangiroa, 2004; Le passage extérieur, 2005; La Maison des mares, 2005; Ermitage des brumes: occident, orient et au-delà, 2005; Le Rodeur des confins, 2006; Dialogue avec Deleuze: politique, philosophie, géopóique, 2007; (ed. with R. Bouvet) Le nouveau territoire, 2008; Affinités extrêmes, 2009; La Carte de Guido, 2011. **Address:** Gwenved, Chemin du Goaquer, Trebeurden, 22560, France.

WHITE, Kevin. British (born England), b. 1959. **Genres:** Sex, History, Psychology. **Career:** Ohio State University, Center for Comparative Studies, lecturer, 1986-90; Thames Valley University, part-time lecturer in American studies, 1992-93; University of Sussex, tutorial fellow in American studies, 1993-; Portsmouth University, School of Education, access programme in contemporary studies, lead tutor, 2000-, School of Education, senior lecturer, 2003-. Writer. **Publications:** The First Sexual Revolution: The Emergence of Male Heterosexuality in Modern America, 1993; Sexual Liberation or Sexual License?: The American Revolt against Victorianism, 2000. Contributor to periodicals. **Address:** School of Education and Continuing Studies, University of Portsmouth, Saint George's Bldg., 141 High St., Portsmouth, HM PO1 2HY, England. **Online address:** kevin.white@port.ac.uk

WHITE, Kimberley. American (born United States), b. 1966?. **Genres:** Novels, Romance/Historical. **Career:** Write2Win educational seminars, founder; Kimberly's Critiquing and Consulting Services, founder. Teacher, nurse and writer. **Publications:** NOVELS: Sweet Tomorrows, 2000; Tango, 2003; Acquisitions, 2003; Only in My Dreams, 2003; Forever After, 2004; Hard to Love, 2004; Conquering Dr. Wexler's Heart, 2005; Sweet Repercussions, 2005; To Love a Ballantyne, 2005; Ballantyne's Destiny, 2006; (with N. Bryant and M. Schuster) You Never Know, 2006; All the Way, 2008; I Need More, 2009. Contributor to books and journals. **Address:** PO Box 672, Novi, MI 48376-0672, U.S.A. **Online address:** kwhite_writer@hotmail.com

WHITE, Lawrence J. American (born United States), b. 1943. **Genres:** Business/Trade/Industry, Economics, Education. **Career:** Harvard Development Advisory Service, economic adviser and consultant, 1969-70; Harvard University, teaching assistant, 1965-69; Princeton University, assistant professor of economics, 1970-76; New York University, Stern School of Business Administration, Department of Economics, associate professor, 1976-79, professor, 1979-, Arthur E. Imperatore professor, chair, 1990-95, Robert Kavesh Professor, deputy chair, 2005-; U.S. Council of economic advisers, senior staff economist, 1978-79; U.S. Department of Justice, Antitrust Division, chief economist, 1982-83; Journal of Financial Intermediation, associate editor, 1989-95; consultant to U.S. government bodies; Review of Industrial Organization, co-editor, 2003-04, general editor, 2004-. Writer. **Publications:** The Automobile Industry since 1945, 1971; Industrial Concentration and Economic Power in Pakistan, 1974; (ed.) Technology, Employment, and Development, 1974; (ed. with L.G. Goldberg) Deregulation of the Banking and Securities Industries, 1979; Reforming Regulation: Processes and Problems, 1981; Corporate Governance in the 1980s, 1981; The Regulation of Air Pollutant Emissions from Motor Vehicles, 1982; (ed. with M. Keenan) Mergers and Acquisitions, 1982; Measuring the Importance of Small Business in the American Economy, 1982; The Public Library in the 1980's: The Problems of Choice, 1983; (ed. with A. Saunders) Technology and the Regulation of Financial Markets, 1986; International Trade in Ocean Shipping Services: The United States and the World, 1988; (ed.) Private Antitrust Litigation, 1988; (ed. with J.E. Kwoka) The Antitrust Revolution: Economics, Competition and Policy, 1989, 5th ed., 2009; Community Reinvestment Act, 1990; The S and L Debacle: Public Policy Lessons for Bank and Thrift Regulation, 1991; (comp. with A. Saunders and G.F. Udell) Bank Management and Regulation, 1992; Why Now? Change and Turmoil in U.S. Banking, 1992; (with M. Klausner) Structural Change in Banking, 1993; U.S. Public Policy Toward Network Industries, 1999; Reducing the Barriers to International Trade in Accounting Services, 2001. **Address:** Department of Economics, Leonard N Stern School of Business, New York University, Rm. 7-65, 44 W 4th St., New York, NY 10012-1126, U.S.A. **Online address:** lwhite@stern.nyu.edu

WHITE, Linda (Louise). American (born United States), b. 1949?. **Genres:** Humanities, Translations, Language/Linguistics. **Career:** Getchell Library, library assistant, 1976-79; University of Nevada, Basque Studies Program, library assistant, 1981-84, lexicographer, 1985-87, 1987-89, assistant coordinator, 1989-99, assistant professor, 2000-03, associate professor, 2003-06, emeritus faculty of Basque studies, 2006-. Freelance writer. **Publications:** WITH G. AULESTIA: English-Basque Dictionary, 1990; Basque-English, English-Basque Dictionary, 1992; The Basque Poetic Tradition, 2000. TRANSLATOR: J.M. de Barandiaran, A View From the Witch's Cave: Folktales of the Pyrenees, 1991; T. del Valle, Korrika: Basque Ritual for Ethnic Identity, 1993; (with L. Corcostegui) Aulestia, Improvisational Poetry From the Basque Country, 1995; Dancing Flea, 1996; Karmentxu and The Little Ghost, 1996; The Old Law of Bizkaia (1452): Introductory Study and Critical Edition, 2005; Nerea and I, 2005. EDITOR: Basque Cultural Studies, 2000; Basque Politics and Nationalism on the Eve of the Millennium, 2000; The Basque Diaspora/La Diaspora Vasca, 2000; (with C. Watson) Amatxi, Amuma, Amona: Writings in Honor of Basque Women, 2003; Anthology of Basque Short Stories, 2004; Aurrera!: A Textbook for Studying Basque, 2008. Contributor of articles to journals. **Address:** Basque Studies Program, University of Nevada, Morrill Hall, 1664 N Virginia St., PO Box 0166, Reno, NV 89557-0208, U.S.A. **Online address:** linda@unr.edu

WHITE, Mark J. British (born England), b. 1965?. **Genres:** History. **Career:** Queen Mary University of London, professor of history; University of St Andrews, faculty; Eastern Illinois University, faculty; University of Wisconsin, faculty; University of Illinois, faculty. **Publications:** The Cuban Missile Crisis, 1996; Missiles in Cuba: Kennedy, Khrushchev, Castro, and the 1962 Crisis, 1997; (ed.) Kennedy: The New Frontier Revisited, 1998; (ed. and intro.) The Kennedys and Cuba: The Declassified Documentary History, 1999, (with S. Plunkett) rev. ed., 2001; Miss Layard Excavates: A Palaeolithic Site at Foxhall Road, Ipswich, 1903-1905, 2004; Kenneth Branagh, 2005; Against the President: Dissent and Decision-making in the White House: A Historical Perspective, 2007. **Address:** Queen Mary University of London, 327 Mile End Rd., London, GL E1 4NS, England. **Online address:** m.j.white@qmul.ac.uk

WHITE, Mary Wheeling. American (born United States), b. 1965. **Genres:** Literary Criticism And History, Biography. **Career:** University of North Carolina, graduate teaching assistant, 1989-94; Longwood University, visiting assistant professor of English, 1994-96; Methodist University, assistant professor of English, 1996-2000, associate professor of English, 2000-01, adjunct online professor of English, 2002-04, Southern Writers Symposium, director, Women's Studies Program, coordinator; New Leaf Editing, editor, 2006-10; Goldey-Beacom College, associate professor of English, 2002-04, adjunct professor of English, 2009, 2011-; Strayer University, adjunct online professor of English, 2010. Writer. **Publications:** Fighting the Current: The Life and Work of Evelyn Scott, 1998. **Address:** Department of English,

Goldey-Beacom College, Arts & Sciences Business Training Skills Pavilion, 4701 Limestone Rd., Ste. 6, Wilmington, DE 19808, U.S.A. **Online address:** mwhite@methodist.edu

WHITE, Merry (I.). American (born United States), b. 1941. **Genres:** Food And Wine, Education, Anthropology/Ethnology, Women's Studies And Issues, Area Studies, Social Sciences. **Career:** Harvard University, Departmet of East Asian Studies, administrator and head tutor, 1977-81, 1984-87, Edwin O. Reischauer Institute of Japanese Studies, research associate, 1981-, Harvard Graduate School of Education, Project on Human Potential, director, 1981-84, director of international education, 1985-87, U.S.-Japan Program, faculty affiliate, 1990-; Boston University, Department of Anthropology, professor, 1987-. Writer. **Publications:** Cooking for Crowds (cook book), 1974; Noodles Galore (cook book), 1976; Pasta and Noodles, 1981; (with R.A. LeVine) Human Conditions, 1986; (ed. with S. Pollak) The Cultural Transition: Human Experience and Social Transformation in the Third World and Japan, 1986; The Japanese Educational Challenge: A Commitment to Children, 1987; The Japanese Overseas: Can They Go Home Again?, 1988; The Material Child: Coming of Age in Japan and America, 1993; (ed. with S. Barnet) Comparing Cultures: Readings on Contemporary Japan for American Writers, 1995; Perfectly Japanese: Making Families in an Era of Upheaval, 2002; Coffee Life in Japan, 2012. Contributor to periodicals. **Address:** Department of Anthropology, Boston University, 232 Bay State Rd., Ste. 410, Boston, MA 02215, U.S.A. **Online address:** corky@bu.edu

WHITE, Michael C(harles). American (born United States), b. 1952. **Genres:** Novels, Novellas/Short Stories. **Career:** New York Institute of Technology, faculty; University of Southern Maine, Stonecoast MFA Program in Creative Writing, faculty; Springfield College, associate professor of writing; Fairfield University, Department of English, professor of English, Low Residency MFA in Creative Writing Program, founder and director. Writer. **Publications:** (Ed. with A. Davis) Birch Lane Presents American Fiction: The Best Short Stories by Emerging Writers, 1990, vol. III, 1992, vol. IV, 1993; A Brother's Blood (novel), 1996; The Blind Side of the Heart, 1999; Marked Men (stories), 2000; A Dream of Wolves (novel), 2000; The Garden of Martyrs, 2004; Soul Catcher, 2007; Beautiful Assassin, 2010. Contributor to magazines and journals. **Address:** Department of English, Fairfield University, Rm. 121, Donnarumma Hall, 1073 N Benson Rd., Fairfield, CT 06824, U.S.A. **Online address:** mcwhite@fairfield.edu

WHITE, Michael J. American (born United States), b. 1977. **Genres:** Young Adult Fiction. **Career:** Garage Theatre Troupe, writer. Educator. **Publications:** Weeping Underwater Looks a Lot Like Laughter, 2010. **Address:** Denver, CO , U.S.A. **Online address:** mjwhite32@gmail.com

WHITE, Mimi. American (born United States), b. 1953. **Genres:** Communications/Media, Social Sciences. **Career:** Northwestern University, assistant professor, 1982-88, associate professor of radio, television and film, 1988-, Department of Radio/Television/Film, professor, chair, Gender Studies Program, director, Communication Program, associate dean, senior associate dean; University of Helsinki, Bicentennial Fulbright professor of North American studies, 2004-05. Writer. **Publications:** Tele-Advising: Therapeutic Discourse in American Television, 1992; (with J. Schuoch and S. Reilly) Media Knowledge: Readings in Popular Culture, Pedagogy and Critical Citizenship, 1992; (ed. with J. Schwoch) Questions of Method in Cultural Studies, 2006. **Address:** Department of Radio Television and Film, Northwestern University, Annie May Swift Hall, 1920 Campus Dr., Ste. 210, Evanston, IL 60208-2952, U.S.A. **Online address:** m-white@northwestern.edu

WHITE, Morton (Gabriel). American (born United States), b. 1917. **Genres:** Intellectual History, Philosophy, Sciences, Cultural/Ethnic Topics, Sciences. **Career:** Columbia University, instructor of philosophy, 1942-46; City College (now City College of the City University of New York), instructor of physics, 1942-43, visiting professor, 1968-69; University of Pennsylvania, assistant professor of philosophy, 1946-48; Harvard University, assistant professor, 1948-50, associate professor, 1950-53, professor of philosophy, 1950-70, Department of Philosophy, chair, 1954-57; Tokyo University, visiting professor, 1952, 1960, 1966; Institute for Advanced Study, professor, 1970-87, emeritus professor, 1987-; University of Oslo, visiting professor, 1977-78. Writer. **Publications:** The Origin of Dewey's Instrumentalism, 1943; Social Thought in America, the Revolt against Formalism, 1949; Toward Reunion in Philosophy, 1956; Religion, Politics and the Higher Learning, 1959; (with L. White) The Intellectual Versus the City, from Thomas

Jefferson to Frank Lloyd Wright, 1962; Foundations of Historical Knowledge, 1965; Science and Sentiment in America; Philosophical Thought from Jonathan Edwards to John Dewey, 1972; Pragmatism and the American Mind; Essays and Reviews in Philosophy and Intellectual History, 1973; The Philosophy of the American Revolution, 1978; What is and What Ought to Be Done: An Essay on Ethics and Epistemology, 1981; (with L. White) Journeys to the Japanese 1952-1979, 1986; Pragmatism and the Politics of Epistemology, 1986; Philosophy, the Federalist, and the Constitution, 1987; The Question of Free Will: A Holistic View, 1993; A Philosopher's Story, 1999; Philosophy of Culture: The Case for Holistic Pragmatism, 2002; From a Philosophical Point of View: Selected Studies, 2005. EDITOR: (and intro.) Age of Analysis; 20th Century Philosophers, Selected, with Introd. and Interpretive Commentary, 1955; (with A. Schlesinger, Jr.) Paths of American Thought, 1963; (with S. Morgenbesser and P. Suppes) Philosophy, Science, and Method; Essays in Honor of Ernest Nagel, 1969; Documents in the History of American Philosophy, from Jonathan Edwards to John Dewey, 1972. **Address:** Institute for Advanced Study, Einstein Dr., Princeton, NJ 08540-4907, U.S.A.

WHITE, Neil. American (born United States), b. 1960. **Genres:** Autobiography/Memoirs. **Career:** Progressive Forensic (magazine), editor, 1982-84; PC Opportunities (magazine), 1984-85; Oxford Times, founder and publisher, 1985-88; Coast Business Journal, publisher, 1988-; New Orleans (magazine), publisher, 1992-93; Nautilus Publishing, president, 1994-2000; Oxford Health & Fitness, publisher and editor, 1998-99; Health 101 (magazine), creative director and publisher, 1998-2000; Life 101 (magazine), creative director and publisher, 1998-2001. **Publications:** In the Sanctuary of Outcasts: A Memoir, 2009. Contributor to periodicals. **Address:** Oxford, MS , U.S.A. **Online address:** stella@theconnellagency.com

WHITE, Pamela C. (Pamela Cooper White). American (born United States), b. 1955. **Genres:** Civil Liberties/Human Rights. **Career:** Lutheran Theological Seminary of Philadelphia, professor; Columbia Theological Seminary, professor of pastoral theology, care and counseling; San Francisco Partnership Ministry, executive director; Church of Christ, ordained minister & priest; Episcopal Church, ordained minister & priest, 1979-; Graduate Theological Union, Center of Women and Religion, director. Writer, educator, Episcopal priest, pastoral psychotherapist and administrator. **Publications:** (As Pamela C. White) Schoenberg and the God-Idea: The Opera Moses And Aron, 1985; The Cry of Tamar: Violence against Women and the Church's Response, 1995; Shared Wisdom: Use of the Self in Pastoral Care and Counseling, 2004; Many Voices: Pastoral Psychotherapy in Relational and Theological Perspective, 2007. Contributor to periodicals and journals. **Address:** Columbia Theological Seminary, PO Box 520, Decatur, GA 30031, U.S.A. **Online address:** cooperwhitep@ctsnet.edu

WHITE, Pamela Cooper. See **WHITE, Pamela C.**

WHITE, Peter (O. G.). British (born England), b. 1932. **Genres:** Theology/Religion, History, Race Relations, Military/Defense/Arms Control. **Career:** Wellington College, schoolmaster, 1957-82, second master, 1982-92. Writer. **Publications:** Predestination, Policy and Polemic: Conflict and Consensus in the English Church from the Reformation to the Civil War, 1992. Contributor of articles to periodicals. Works appear in anthologies. **Address:** Rudhall Barns, Phocle Green, Ross-on-Wye, Herefordshire, HW HR9 7TL, England. **Online address:** peterwhite@onetel.net

WHITE, Phillip M. American (born United States), b. 1950. **Genres:** Bibliography, Anthropology/Ethnology, Theology/Religion, History. **Career:** Southwest Texas State University, reference librarian, 1979-81; University of Texas, Perry-Castaneda Library, reference librarian, 1982-85; San Diego State University, Love Library, reference librarian, 1985-, bibliographer of American Indian studies, 1989-; California State University, reference librarian. Writer. **Publications:** American Indian Studies: A Bibliographic Guide, 1995; (with S.D. Fitt) Bibliography of the Indians of San Diego County: The Kumeyaay, Diegueño, Luiseño and Cupeño, 1998; (comp.) The Native American Sun Dance Religion and Ceremony: An Annotated Bibliography, 1998; (comp.) The Kickapoo Indians Their History And Culture An Annotated Bibliography, 1999; The Peyotism and the Native American Church: An Annotated Bibliography, 2000; (comp.) Bibliography Of Native American Bibliographies, 2004; American Indian Chronology: Chronologies of the American Mosaic, 2006. **Address:** University Library, San Diego State University, Love Library Addition 108F, 5500 Campanile Dr., San Diego, CA 92182-6742, U.S.A. **Online address:** pwhite@rohan.sdsu.edu

WHITE, Randy Wayne. American (born United States), b. 1950. **Genres:** Mystery/Crime/Suspense, Regional/Urban Planning, Ethics, Young Adult Fiction. **Career:** Boat captain and fishing guide, 1977-90; writer, 1989-. **Publications:** ECO-ADVENTURE MYSTERIES: Sanibel Flats, 1990; Batfishing in the Rainforest, 1991; The Heat Islands, 1992; The Man Who Invented Florida, 1993; Captiva, 1996; North of Havana, 1998; The Sympathy for the Devil, 1998; The Mangrove Coast, 1998; The Sharks of Lake Nicaragua, 1999; Ten Thousand Islands, 2000; Shark River, 2001; Twelve Mile Limit, 2002; Last Flight Out, 2002; Everglades, 2003; An American Traveler: True Tales of Adventure, Travel, and Sport, 2003; Tampa Burn, 2004; Dead of Night, 2005; Dark Light, 2006; Hunter's Moon, 2007; Black Widow, 2008; Dead Silence, 2009; Deep Shadow, 2010; (ed. with C.F. Brennen) Randy Wayne White's Ultimate Tarpon Book, 2010; Night Vision, 2011; Chasing Midnight, 2012. Contributor to periodicals. **Address:** PO Box 486, Pineland, FL 33945, U.S.A. **Online address:** rwwhite1@aol.com

WHITE, Stephen E. American (born United States), b. 1947. **Genres:** Earth Sciences, Geography, Psychology, Human Relations/Parenting, Theology/Religion. **Career:** Kansas State University, Department of Geography, assistant professor, 1975-80, associate professor, 1980-85, professor of geography, 1985-, department head, 1979-87, 1994-97, presidential lecturer, 1992-96, College of Arts and Sciences, associate dean, 1997-2002, interim dean, 2002-. Writer. **Publications:** (Ed. with D.E. Kromm) Groundwater Exploitation in the High Plains, 1992; So Long for Now: Dealing with the Death of a Loved One, 2010. Contributor to journals. **Address:** Department of Geography, Kansas State University, 118 Seaton Hall, Manhattan, KS 66506-2904, U.S.A. **Online address:** sewhite@k-state.edu

WHITE, Stephen K. American (born United States), b. 1949. **Genres:** Politics/Government, Philosophy. **Career:** Fulbright fellow, 1978-79; University of Hartford, assistant professor of political science, 1980-81; Virginia Polytechnic Institute and State University, assistant professor, 1981-87, associate professor, 1987-91, professor of political science, 1991-2001; Alexander Von Humboldt, fellow, 1987-88, 1997-98; University of Frankfurt, research fellow, 1987-88, 1997-98; Erasmus University, visiting professor, 1997; Political Theory, editor, 1999-; University of Virginia, professor of government and foreign affairs, 2001-, James Hart professor of political theory. Writer. **Publications:** Recent Work of Jurgen Habermas: Reason, Justice and Modernity, 1988; (ed. and contrib.) Life-World and Politics: Between Modernity and Post-Modernity, 1989; Political Theory and Postmodernism, 1991; Edmund Burke: Modernity, Politics and Aesthetics, 1994; (ed. and contrib.) Cambridge Companion to Habermas, 1995; Sustaining Affirmation: The Strengths of Weak Ontology in Political Theory, 2000; (ed. with J.D. Moon) What is Political Theory?, 2003; Ethos of a Late-modern Citizen, 2009. Works appear in anthologies. Contributor of articles to journals and books. **Address:** Department of Political Science, Virginia Polytech Inst and State University, 531 Major Williams Hall, PO Box 0130, Blacksburg, VA 24063-0130, U.S.A. **Online address:** skw2n@virginia.edu

WHITE, Stephen (Leonard). Irish (born Ireland), b. 1945. **Genres:** Politics/Government, Area Studies. **Career:** University of Glasgow, lecturer, 1971-85, reader in politics, 1985-, professor of politics, 1991-, James Bryce professor of politics. Writer. **Publications:** Political Culture and Soviet Politics, 1979; Britain and the Bolshevik Revolution: A Study in the Politics of Diplomacy, 1920-1924, 1980; (ed. with D. Nelson) Communist Legislatures in Comparative Perspective, 1982; Communist Political Systems: An Introduction, 1982; (ed. with W.B. Simons) Party Statutes of the Communist World, 1984; The Origins of Detente: The Genoa Conference and Soviet-Western Relations, 1921-1922, 1986; (ed. with D. Nelson) Communist Politics, 1986; The Bolshevik Poster, 1988; (ed. with A. Pravda) Ideology and Soviet Politics, 1988; Bolshevik Poster, 1988; (co-ed.) Gorbachev and Gorbachevism, 1989; (co-ed.) Developments in Soviet Politics, 1990; Gorbachev in Power, 1990; Gorbachev and After, 1991; (co-ed.) Developments in Soviet and Post-Soviet Politics, 1992, 6th ed., 2005; (ed.) New Directions in Soviet History, 1992; (co-ed.) Soviet Transition: From Gorbachev to Yeltsin, 1993; After Gorbachev, 1991, 4th ed., 1993; (co-author) Politics of Transition: Shaping a Post-Soviet Future, 1993; Russia Goes Dry, 1996; (with R. Rose and I. McAllister) How Russia Votes, 1997; (with W. Miller and P. Heywood) Values and Political Change in Postcommunist Europe, 1998; Russia's New Politics, 2000; (with E. Mawdsley) The Soviet Elite from Lenin to Gorbachev, 2000; Russia's New Politics: The Management of a Postcommunist Society, 2000; (ed.) Politics of the Postcommunist World, 2001; Communism and Its Collapse, 2001; (ed. with R. Fawn) Russia After Communism, 2002; (co-ed.) Developments in Central and East European Politics 3, 2003; (co-ed.) Postcommunist Belarus, 2005; (co-author) Putin's Russia and the Enlarged Europe, 2006; (ed. with P. Webb) Party Politics in New Democracies, 2007; (with J. Lowenhardt) Russian Regions: A Bibliography, 2007; (ed.) Media, Culture and Society in Putin's Russia, 2008; (ed.) Politics and the Ruling Groupin Putin's Russia, 2008; (co-ed.) Developments in Russian Politics 7, 2010; Understanding Russian Politics, 2011. **Address:** Department of Politics, University of Glasgow, Glasgow, G12 8RT, Scotland. **Online address:** s.white@socsci.gla.ac.uk

WHITE, Warren H. American (born United States), b. 1935. **Genres:** Novels, Reference, History. **Career:** Fourdee Inc., staff, 1972-81; Emerson Electric, staff, 1972-81; Certified Slings Inc., vice president, 1981-98; consultant, 1998-2004. Writer. **Publications:** Covered Bridges in the Southeastern United States: A Comprehensive Illustrated Catalog, 2003; Covered Bridges in the New England States: A Comprehensive Illustrated Catalog, 2006. **Address:** 1311 Harbour Dr., Longwood, FL 32750, U.S.A.

WHITEHEAD, Barbara Dafoe. American (born United States), b. 1944. **Genres:** Documentaries/Reportage, Human Relations/Parenting. **Career:** Institute for American Values, vice president; Rutgers, The State University of New Jersey, National Marriage Project, co-director. Writer. **Publications:** The Divorce Culture, 1997; (with D. Popenoe) Should We Live Together?: What Young Adults Need to Know About Cohabitation Before Marriage: A Comprehensive Review of Recent Research, 1999, 2nd ed., 2002; Why There Are No Good Men Left: The Romantic Plight of the New Single Woman, 2003; (ed. with D. Blankenhorn and S. Brophy-Warren) Franklin's Thrift: The Lost History of an American Virtue, 2009. Contributor to periodicals. **Address:** Random House Inc., 1745 Broadway, 3rd Fl., New York, NY 10019, U.S.A. **Online address:** bdw@newsinglewoman.com

WHITEHEAD, Catherine Sarah. (Kate Whitehead). British (born England), b. 1960. **Genres:** Literary Criticism And History, Criminology/True Crime, History, Social Sciences, Reference. **Career:** Natural Environment Research Council, press officer, 1986-87; British Broadcasting Corp., radio producer, 1987-. Writer. **Publications:** The Third Programme: A Literary History, 1989; Hong Kong Murders, 2001. Contributor to periodicals. **Address:** British Broadcasting Corp., Whiteladies Rd., Bristol, AV BS82LR, England.

WHITEHEAD, Colson. American (born United States), b. 1969?. **Genres:** Novels, History. **Career:** Village Voice, pop culture critic and columnist. **Publications:** The Intuitionist, 1999; John Henry Days: A Novel, 2001; The Colossus of New York: A City in Thirteen Parts, 2003; Apex Hides the Hurt, 2006; Sag Harbor: A Novel, 2009; Zone One: A Novel, 2011. Contributor to periodicals. **Address:** c/o Author Mail, Doubleday Publishers, 1540 Broadway, New York, NY 10036-4039, U.S.A.

WHITEHEAD, David (Henry). Also writes as Leonard F. Meares, Carter West, Glenn Lockwood, Matt Logan, Ben Bridges. British (born England), b. 1958. **Genres:** Romance/Historical, Westerns/Adventure, Horror, Science Fiction/Fantasy, Mystery/Crime/Suspense, Criminology/True Crime. **Career:** BBC Books Registry, assistant-in-charge, 1981-92. Librarian and writer. **Publications:** WESTERNS AS DAVID WHITEHEAD: Hang 'Em All, 1989; Heller, 1990; Starpacker, 1990; Riding for Justice, 1990; Law of the Gun, 1991; Heller in the Rockies, 1992; Trial by Fire, 1993; Barbed Wire Noose, 1994; Judgement Day, 1994; Cougar Valley, 1996; It Had its Moments, 2007. WESTERNS AS BEN BRIDGES: The Silver Trail, 1986; Hard as Nails, 1987; Mexico Breakout, 1988; Hangman's Noose, 1988; The Wilde Boys, 1988; The Deadly Dollars, 1988; Wilde Fire, 1988; Squaw Man, 1988; Wilde's Law, 1990; North of the Border, 1990; Shoot to Kill, 1990; Aces Wilde, 1991; Hell for Leather, 1992; Marked for Death, 1993; Gunsmoke Is Grey, 1994; Rattler Creek, 1995; Cold Steel, 1995; Blood Canyon, 1996; Thunder Gorge, 1997; Mean as Hell, 1999; Draw Down the Lightning, 2007; Three for the Trail, 2011. ROMANCE NOVELS AS JANET WHITEHEAD: Yours for Eternity, 1991; Patterns in the Snow, 1991; Far Eastern Promise, 1993; A Time to Run, 1996; Winterhaven, 2007; Yesterday's Child, 2008; Hold Me Forever, 2008; Autumn Leaves, 2008. WESTERNS AS GLENN LOCKWOOD: Ride for the Rio!, 2000; Back With a Vengeance, 2001; Blaze of Glory, 2001. WESTERNS AS MATT LOGAN: Tanner's Guns, 1991; Coffin Creek, 1992; Gunsmoke Legend, 1993; Ride the High Lines, 1995; Storm in the Saddle, 1996; The Spurlock Gun, 1998. WESTERNS AS LEONARD F. MEARES: Tin Star Trio, 1994; A Quest of Heroes, 1996. WESTERNS AS CARTER WEST: Montana Gunsmoke, 1999; Apacheria, 2000; Lockwood's

Law, 2000. WESTERNS AS DOUG THORNE: All Guns Blazing, 2008; Cannon for Hire, 2011. HORROR AS DAVID WHITEHEAD: The Fluttering, 2008; Scare Tactics, 2009; The Dead are Awake, forthcoming. THRILLERS WITH STEVE HAYES: Feral, 2010; Dead End, 2010; Tomorrow, Utopia, 2010; Killer Smile, 2010; Fanatics, 2010; Sherlock Holmes and the Queen of Diamonds, 2011; Cast a Deadly Shadow, 2011; Under the Knife, 2011. SCIENCE FICTION AS DOUGLAS THORNE: Earth-Shattering, 2010. **Address:** c/o Robert Hale Ltd., Clerkenwell House, 23-27 Hatton Wall, London, GL EC1N 8JJ, England. **Online address:** davewhitehead2003@yahoo.co.uk

WHITEHEAD, Kate. See **WHITEHEAD, Catherine Sarah.**

WHITEHORN, Alan (James). Canadian (born Canada), b. 1946. **Genres:** Politics/Government, Poetry. **Career:** Carleton University, Institute of Canadian Studies, research associate and lecturer in politics, 1975-78; Royal Military College of Canada, assistant professor, 1978-81, associate professor, 1981-88, professor of political science, 1988-94, 1996-; Simon Fraser University, J.S. Woodsworth professor of humanities, J.S. Woodsworth chair in humanities, 1994-96. Writer and parliament member. **Publications:** Canadian Socialism: Essays on the CCF-NDP, 1992; (with K. Archer) Canadian Trade Unions and the New Democratic Party, 1993; (with K. Archer) Political Activists: The NDP in Convention, 1997; (ed. with H. Thorburn) Party Politics in Canada, 8th ed., 2001; (with L. Shirinian) The Armenian Genocide: Resisting the Inertia of Indifference, 2001; Poems: Political and Philosophical, 2002; Ancestral Voices: Ethnic Roots, Identity and a Genocide Remembered, 2007; Just Poems: Reflections on the Armenian Genocide, 2009. Contributor of articles and journals to books. **Address:** Department of Political and Economic Science, Royal Military College of Canada, PO Box 17000, Sta. Forces, Kingston, ON K7K 7B4, Canada. **Online address:** whitehorn_a@rmc.ca

WHITEHOUSE, David (Bryn). American/British (born England), b. 1941. **Genres:** Archaeology/Antiquities, Art/Art History, History. **Career:** Siraf Expedition, director, 1966-73; Oxford University, Wainwright fellow in Near Eastern archeology, 1966-73; British Institute of Afghan Studies, director, 1973-74; British School, director, 1974-84; Corning Museum of Glass, chief curator, 1984-87, deputy director of collections, 1987-88, deputy director of museum, 1988-92, director, 1992-98, executive director and curator of ancient and Islamic glass, 1998-. Writer. **Publications:** (With D. Collins, M. Henig and R. Whitehouse) Background to Archeology, 1972; (with R. Whitehouse) Archaeological Atlas of the World, 1975; Lübbes Archäologischer Welt-Atlas, 1976; (with D. Andrews and J. Osborne) Papers in Italian Archeology 1: The Lancaster Seminar: Recent Research in Prehistoric, Classical, and Medieval Archeology, 1978; AtlasArchéologique Universel, 1978; Siraf III: The Congregational Mosque, 1980; (with R. Hodges) Mohammed, Charlemagne, and the Origins of Europe: The Pirenne Thesis in the Light of Archeology, 1983; (co-author) Glass of the Caesars, 1987; Glass of the Roman Empire, 1988; Masterpieces of Glass: A World History From the Corning Museum of Glass, 1990; (co-author) Treasures from the Corning Museum of Glass, 1992; (comp.) Glass: A Pocket Dictionary of Terms Commonly Used to Describe Glass and Glass Making, 1993, rev. ed., 2006; English Cameo Glass in the Corning Museum of Glass, 1994; Roman Glass in the Corning Museum of Glass, vol. I, 1997, vol. II, 2001, vol. III, 2003; Excavations at ed-Dur, (Ummal-Qaiwain, UAE), vol. I: The Glass Vessel, 1998; The Corning Museum of Glass: A Decade of Glass Collecting, 1990-1999, 2000; (with S. Carboni) Glass of the Sultans, 2001; The Moon: A Biography, 2001; The Sun, 2004; Sasanian and Post-Sasanian Glass in the Corning Museum of Glass, 2005; (ed. and intro. with S.M. Rossi-Wilcox) Drawing Upon Nature: Studies for the Blaschkas' Glass Models, 2007; Reflecting Antiquity: Modern Glass Inspired by Ancient Rome, 2007; Siraf I: History, Topography and Environment, 2009; One Small Step, 2009; Galileo, 2009; Islamic Glass in the Corning Museum of Glass, 2010; Medieval Glass for Popes, Princes and Peasants, 2010; Glass: A Short History, 2012. **Address:** Corning Museum of Glass, 1 Museum Way, Corning, NY 14830-2253, U.S.A. **Online address:** whitehou@cmog.org

WHITELAW, Ian. Canadian (born Canada), b. 1953?. **Genres:** Humor/Satire, Reference, Education. **Career:** Writer. **Publications:** Habitus Disgustica: The Encyclopedia of Annoying, Rude and Unpleasant Behavior, 2006; A Measure of All Things: The Story of Man and Measurement, 2007; (with J. Whitaker) The Horse: A Miscellany of Equine Knowledge, 2007; Snow Dogs!, 2008; (with K. Heidorn) The Field Guide to Natural Phenomena, 2010. **Address:** Plume, 375 Hudson St., New York, NY 10014-3657, U.S.A.

WHITELAW, Nancy. American (born United States), b. 1933. **Genres:**

Biography, Intellectual History, Science Fiction/Fantasy, Autobiography/ Memoirs. **Career:** Malden Schools, teacher, 1954-55; Amerikan Kiz Koleji, teacher, 1955-58; Amherst Public School System, teacher, 1968-88; Institute of Children's Literature, instructor, 1988-. Writer. **Publications:** Biography of General Charles de Gaulle: I am France, 1991; A Beautiful Pearl, 1991; Charles de Gaulle, 1991; Theodore Roosevelt Takes Charge, 1992; Joseph Stalin: From Peasant to Premier, 1992; Margaret Sanger: Every Child a Wanted Child, 1994; They Wrote Their Own Headlines: American Women Journalists, 1994; Mr. Civil Rights: The Story of Thurgood Marshall, 1995, 2nd ed., 2003; Grace Hopper: Programming Pioneer, 1995; Nathaniel Hawthorne: American Storyteller, 1996, 2nd ed., 2003; William Tecumseh Sherman: Defender and Destroyer, 1996; More Perfect Union: The Story of Alexander Hamilton, 1997, 2nd ed., 2003; Clara Barton: Civil War Nurse, 1997; Bram Stoker: Author of Dracula, 1998, rev. ed. 2004; Lady Diana Spencer: Princess of Wales, 1998; Let's Go! Let's Publish!: Katharine Graham and the Washington Post, 1999; Joseph Pulitzer and the New York World, 2000; William Randolph Hearst and the American Century, 2000, rev. ed., 2004; Andrew Jackson: Frontier President, 2001; Shot Heard Round the World: The Battles of Lexington and Concord, 2001; The Battles of Lexington and Concord, 2001; Thomas Jefferson: Philosopher and President, 2002; Jimmy Carter: President and Peacemaker, 2004; Queen Victoria and the British Empire, 2005; Catherine de' Medici and the Protestant Reformation, 2005; Queen Isabella and the Unification of Spain, 2005; Catherine the Great and the Enlightenment in Russia, 2005; Victory in Destruction: The Story of William Tecumseh Sherman, 2005; Homestead Steel Strike of 1892, 2006; Dark Dreams: The Story of Stephen King, 2006; Rebels and Revolutionaries: Voices of American Labor, 2007; Supreme Court Justices: Thurgood Marshall, 2011. Contributor to newspapers and periodicals. **Address:** 3212 Salisbury Rd., Jamestown, NY 14701, U.S.A.

WHITELAW, Stella. British (born England), b. 1941?. **Genres:** How-to Books, Novels, Young Adult Non-fiction. **Career:** Swanwick Wirters's Summer School, lecturer; P & Co. Cruise Ships, lecturer; House of Commons, Parliamentary Press Gallery, secretary, through 2002; full-time writer, 2002-. **Publications:** (With J. Gardiner and M. Ronson) Grimalkin's Tales: Strange and Wonderful Cat Stories, 1983. NOVELS: Weave a Loving Web, 1971; Love Is a Star Garden, 1974; Another Word for Love, 1977; Sweet Chastity, 1979; Desert Storm, 1983; Baptism of Fire, 1989; Pennyroyal, 1989; Eagle's Eye, 1990; This Savage Sky, 1990; Dragon Lady, 1991; A Certain Hunger, 1993; The Owl and the Pussycats, 1993; No Darker Heaven, 1996; Sweet Seduction, 1997; Veil of Death, 2004; Mirror Mirror, 2005; Midsummer Madness, 2009; Portrait of a Murder, 2011. RAINBOW ROMANCE SERIES: Secret Taj, 1984; Flood Tide, 1986. LOVE ON CALL SERIES: Deluge, 1994; Cruise Doctor, 1996. NONFICTION: How to Write and Sell a Synopsis, 1993; How to Write a Short Short Story, 1996; How to Write Short Short Stories, 1996; How to Write and Sell a Book Proposal, 2000; Book Proposals: The Essential Guide, 2011. JORDAN LACEY SERIES: Pray and Die, 2000; Wave and Die, 2001; Spin and Die, 2002; Hide and Die, 2003; Jest and Die, 2004; Ring and Die, 2005; Turn and Die, 2007; Fold and Die, 2009. CASEY JONES CRUISE SHIP MYSTERY SERIES: Second Sitting, 2008; Dead Slow Ahead, 2008; A Wide Berth, 2010. **Address:** Pollinger Ltd., 9 Staple Inn, Holborn, London, GL WC1V 7QH, England.

WHITELEY, Nigel. British (born England) **Genres:** Adult Non-fiction, History. **Career:** Lancaster University, professor of visual art and head of art department. Writer. **Publications:** Pop Design: Modernism to Mod, 1987; (ed. with M. Wheeler) The Lamp of Memory: Ruskin, Tradition and Architecture, 1992; Design for Society, 1993; (ed. with R. Keat and N. Abercrombie) The Authority of the Consumer, 1994; (contrib.) Modernism, Gender and Culture, 1997; (contrib.) Interpreting Visual Culture, 1998; (contrib.) Utility Reassessed, 1999; (ed.) Detraditionalisation and Art: Aesthetic, Authority, Authenticity, 2000; Reyner Banham: Historian of the Immediate Future, 2002; Rogina: Digitalizzazione Della Realta, 2007. Contributor to journals and periodicals. **Address:** Lancaster Institute for the Contemporary Arts, Lancaster University, Bailrigg, Lancaster, LC LA1 4YD, England. **Online address:** n.whiteley@lancaster.ac.uk

WHITEMAN, (David) Bruce. Canadian (born Canada), b. 1952. **Genres:** Literary Criticism And History, Writing/Journalism, Poetry, Bibliography, Art/Art History. **Career:** McMaster University, research collections librarian, 1979-88; McGill University, head of department of rare books and special collections, 1988-96; University of California, William Andrews Clark Memorial Library, head librarian, 1996-2010. Writer. **Publications:** Sun at Your Thighs, The Moon at Your Lips, 1978; Leonard Cohen: An Annotated Bibliography, 1980; Raymond Souster: A Descriptive Bibliography, 1984; (ed.) A Literary Friendship: The Correspondence of Ralph Gustafson and W.W.E. Ross, 1984; Raymond Souster and His Works, 1985; (with C. Stewart and C. Funnell) A Bibliography of Macmillan of Canada Imprints, 1906-1980, 1985; The Letters of John Sutherland, 1942-1956, 1992; Lasting Impressions: A Short History of English Publishing in Quebec, 1994; J.E.H. MacDonald, 1995; The Forger Contemplates Rossetti, 2000; (ed. with C. Burlingham) World from Here: Treasures of the Great Libraries of Los Angeles, 2001. POETRY: 12 Poems, 12 Drawings, 1978; Inventions, 1979; Ten Lessons in Autobiography, 1981; The Cold Engineering of the World, 1983; Recesses in the Heart: The Thera Poems, 1984; Collected Poems of Raymond Souster, 1984; The Invisible World Is in Decline, 1984, vol. II-IV, 1989, vol. V, 2000; A Nature Murder, 1985; En avoir fini avec le corps seul, 1987; Polyphonic Windows, 1993; (trans. with F. Farley-Chevrier) F. Charron, After Ten Thousand Years, Desire: Selected Recent Poems, 1995; Visible Stars: New and Selected Poems, 1995; XXIV Short Love Poems, 2002; Tristia, 2002; The Invisible World Is in Decline Bks. I-VI, 2006; (trans.) Catullus LXXXV & CV, 2006; (trans.) Tiberianus, Pervigilium Veneris, 2009. **Address:** 1326 Elm St., Grinnell, IA 50112, U.S.A. **Online address:** dbrucewhiteman@gmail.com

WHITEMAN, Robin. British (born England), b. 1944. **Genres:** Homes/ Gardens, Horticulture, Travel/Exploration, History, Art/Art History. **Career:** United Motion Pictures, writer and director, 1968-70; freelance filmmaker, 1970-80; Video Tracks Ltd., director and producer, 1980-85; Talbot-Whiteman, writer and partner, 1985-. **Publications:** The Cotswolds, 1988; Shakespeare's Avon: A Journey from Source to Severn, 1989; The English Lakes, 1989; Cadfael Country, 1990; In the North of England: The Yorkshire Moors and Dales, 1991; The Cadfael Companion, 1991; The Benediction of Brother Cadfael, 1992; The West Country, 1993; The Garden of England: The Counties of Kent, Surrey and Sussex, 1995; The Heart of England, 1995; English Landscapes, 1995; The Cadfael Companion: The World of Brother Cadfael, 1995; (with R. Talbot) East Anglia and the Fens, 1996; Brother Cadfael's Herb Garden, 1996; Wessex, 1997; The Peak District, 1997; Lakeland Landscapes, 1997; Northumbria: English Border Country, 1998; Yorkshire Landscapes, 1998; Cotswold Landscapes, 1999; Brother Cadfael's Book of Days, 2000; England, 2000; East Anglia, 2002. **Address:** Weidenfeld and Nicolson, Orion House, 5 Upper St. Martin Ln., London, GL WC2H 9EA, England. **Online address:** t-w@cw.com

WHITE-PARKS, Annette. American (born United States), b. 1935. **Genres:** Novels, Novellas/Short Stories, History, Autobiography/Memoirs, Biography. **Career:** Sacramento State University, teaching assistant, 1967-69, instructor, 1969-72; University of California, teaching assistant, 1970-71; Old Sacramento Historical Project, executive coordinator, 1971-73; City of Ukiah, bicentennial coordinator, 1975-77; Sonoma State University, faculty, 1977-80; Mendocino College, instructor in composition, poetry, folklore, creative writing and literature, 1978-85; California State Chancellor's Office, Women Writers Project, director, 1979-81; Washington State University, teaching assistant, 1985-91, instructor in women's studies, 1988-89, teaching assistant in writing and literature, 1990-91; University of Wisconsin, assistant professor, 1991-93, associate professor of English, 1993-97, professor, 1997-, now professor emeritus; Wisconsin-in-Scotland, professor of English, 1994, 1997, 2000. Writer. **Publications:** When Grownups Were Children, 1976; Qh awála li: Water Coming Down Place: A History of Gualala, California, 1980; (intro.) Valleys of Mendocino County, 1981; Sui Sin Far/Edith Maude Eaton: A Literary Biography, 1995; Bridge Work (novel), 2004; Grandma's Lost House: Restoring a Memory, 2006; Cuttings from the Violas: Traveling with My Scots Grannies, 2008. EDITOR: A Gathering of Voices on the Asian American Experience, 1994; (with E. Ammons) Tricksterism in Turn-of-the-Century American Literature: A Multicultural Perspective, 1994; (with A. Ling) Mrs. Spring Fragrance and Other Writings by Sui Sin Far, 1995. Contributor to books and periodicals. **Address:** Department of English, University of Wisconsin, 1725 State St., La Crosse, WI 54601, U.S.A. **Online address:** white-pa.anne@uwlax.edu

WHITEWAY, Doug. See WHITEWAY, Doug(las) Alfred.

WHITEWAY, Doug(las) Alfred. Also writes as Doug Whiteway, C. C. Benison. Canadian (born Canada), b. 1951. **Genres:** Mystery/Crime/Suspense, Young Adult Non-fiction. **Career:** Winnipeg Tribune, journalist; Winnipeg Free Press, feature writer and reporter, 1981-86; freelance writer, 1981-; The Beaver Magazine, associate editor, 1998-2006, editor, 2006-; Winnipeg Public Library, writer-in-residence, 2007-08. **Publications:** MYSTERY NOVELS AS C.C. BENISON: What's Cooking in Ethnic Winnipeg, 1987; Death at Buckingham Palace, 1996; Death at Sandringham House, 1997; Death at Windsor Castle, 1998; (co-author) In Search of Ancient Alberta, 1998; (co-author) One Hundred Years at St. Charles Country Club, 2004; Death in Cold Type, 2005; (ed.) Front Porch Mannequins, 2009; Twelve Drummers Drumming, 2011. Contributor to magazines and newspapers. **Address:** The Beaver Magazine, Lombard Ave., Ste. 478-167, Winnipeg, MB R3B 0T6, Canada. **Online address:** ccbenison@shaw.ca

WHITFIELD, Roderick. British (born England), b. 1937?. **Genres:** Archaeology/Antiquities, Area Studies, Art/Art History, Theology/Religion, Translations, Photography. **Career:** Princeton University, research associate and lecturer, 1965-66; St. John's College, Cambridge, research fellow, 1966-68; British Museum, Department of Oriental Antiquities, assistant keeper first class, 1968-84; University of London, Percival David Foundation of Chinese Art, head, 1984-93, Percival David professor of Chinese and East Asian art, 1984-2002, professor emeritus, 2002-, School of Oriental and African Studies, CIAA president, professor, Department of the History of Art and Archaeology, professorial research associate; University of Toronto, Teetzel lecturer, 1995; Dunhuang Academy, fellow, 2000-. Writer. **Publications:** In Pursuit of Antiquity, 1969; Art of Central Asia: The Stein Collection in the British Museum, 1982; Tonkō Kaiga, 1982; Seiiki Bijutsu: Daiei Hakubutsukan Stain Korekushon, 1982; (with R. Goepper) Treasure from Korea: Art Through 5000 Years, 1984; Senshoku Chōso Hekiga, 1984; (with Y.S. Pak) Korean Art Treasures, 1986; (with A. Farrer) Caves of the Thousand Buddhas: Chinese Art from the Silk Route, 1990; Fascination of Nature: Plants and Insects in Chinese Painting and Ceramics of the Yuan Dynasty, 1993; Dunhuang, Caves of the Singing Sands, Buddhist Art from the Silk Road, 1995; Cave Temples of Mogao: Art and History on the Silk Road, 2000; (with Y. Pak) Handbook of Korean Art: Buddhist Sculpture, 2002; (with Y.S. Pak) Handbook of Korean Art: Pottery and Celadon, 2002; (contrib.) Treasury of Writings on Qingming shanghe tu, 2007; (with C.L. Yang) Catalogue of the Wou Lien Pai Museum of Chinese Art, 2010; (contrib.) Chinese Prints, 7th-21st centuries, 2010. EDITOR: Treasures from Korea: Art Through 5000 Years, 1984; The Problem of Meaning in Early Chinese Bronzes, 1993; (with W. Tao) Exploring China's Past: New Discoveries and Studies in Archaeology and Art, 1999; Dictionary of Korean Art and Archaeology, 2004; (with Y. Pak) Korean True-View Landscape: Paintings by Chong Son (1676-1759), 2005; (with T. Chan) National Museum of Korea, 2009. **Address:** School of Oriental and African Studies, University of London, Thornhaugh St., Russell Sq., London, GL WC1H 0XG, England. **Online address:** rw5@soas.ac.uk

WHITFIELD, Sarah. British (born England), b. 1942. **Genres:** Art/Art History, Photography. **Career:** Joanna Drew Travel Bursary, founding member; The Elephant Trust, chair; curator and writer. **Publications:** Impressionismo e postimpressionismo: Collezione Thyssen-Bornemisza, 1990; Fauvism, 1991; Magritte: The Hayward Gallery, 1992; (co-author) René Magritte: Catalogue Raisonné, vol. I: Oil Paintings, 1916-1930; (with F. Hergott) Georges Rouault: The Early Years 1903-20, 1993; Fauvism, 1996; (with J. Elderfield) Bonnard, 1998; Malcolm Morley: In Full Colour, 2001. Work represented in books. **Address:** 21 Denbigh Rd., London, GL W11 2SJ, England.

WHITING, Cécile. American (born United States), b. 1958. **Genres:** Art/Art History, Humanities. **Career:** University of California-Los Angeles, Department of Art History, faculty, 1998-2003; University of California-Irvine, School of Humanities, associate dean of graduate studies, Department of Art History, professor and chair, professor of visual studies, Graduate Program in Visual Studies, director. Writer and art historian. **Publications:** Antifascism in American Art, 1989; A Taste for Pop: Pop Art, Gender, and Consumer Culture, 1997; Pop L.A.: Art and the City in the 1960s, 2006; (contrib.) Chicago Imagists, 2011; (contrib.) Anglo-American: Artistic Exchange Between Britain and the USA, 2012. **Address:** Department of Art History, University of California, 2216 Humanities Gateway, PO Box 2785, Irvine, CA 92697, U.S.A. **Online address:** cwhiting@uci.edu

WHITING, Robert. Japanese/American (born United States), b. 1942. **Genres:** Social Commentary, Popular Culture, Adult Non-fiction. **Career:** Encyclopedia Britannica, editor, 1969-72; Grolier Intl., project editor, 1972-73; Time-Life Books, project director, 1975-76; Creative Resources Group, president and co-owner, 1977-; Encyclopaedia Britannica, consultant, 1977; Daily Sports, columnist, 1979-85; British Broadcasting Corp., consultant, 1979; Shukan Asahi, columnist, 1988-92; News Station, reporter and com-

mentator, 1990-93. **Publications:** The Chrysanthemum and the Bat: Baseball Samurai Style, 1977; You Gotta Have Wa, 1989; (with W. Cromartie) Slugging It Out in Japan: An American Major Leaguer in the Tokyo Outfield, 1991; Tokyo Underworld: The Fast Times and Hard Life of an American Gangster in Japan, 1999; Meaning of Ichiro: The New Wave from Japan and the Transformation of Our National Pastime, 2004. Works appear in anthologies. **Address:** 313 Nikaido, Kamakura 248, Kanagawa, 221-0045, Japan.

WHITLAM, (Edward) Gough. Australian (born Australia), b. 1916. **Genres:** Politics/Government, History. **Career:** University of Melbourne, Chifley memorial lecturer, 1957, 1975; Australian Labor Party, deputy leader, 1960-67, leader of the opposition, 1967-77, leader, 1967-77; Prime Minister of Australia, 1972-75; Australian foreign minister, 1972-73; Harvard University, visiting professor of Australian studies, 1979-80; University of Sydney, fellow of Senate, 1981-83, 1986-89; UNESCO, Australian ambassador, 1983-86; Australia-China Council, chairman, 1986-91; Australian National Gallery Council, chairman, 1987-90; Hanoi Architectural Heritage Foundation, founder, 1993-. Writer. **Publications:** The Constitution versus Labor, 1957; Australian Foreign Policy, 1963; Socialism within the Constitution, 1965; Australia: Base or Bridge, 1966; Responsibilities For Urban and Regional Development, 1968; Beyond Vietnam: Australia's Regional Responsibility, 1968; Labor's Role Today, 1968; An Urban Nation, 1969; Australia: An Urban Nation, 1970; A New Federalism, 1971; Australian Public Administration, 1973; Australia's Foreign Policy: New Directions, New Definitions, 1973; Road to Reform, 1975; The New Federalism, 1976; On Australia's Constitution, 1977; Reform During Recession, 1978; The Truth of the Matter, 1979, 3rd ed., 2005; The Italian Inspiration in English Literature, 1980; A Pacific Community (Harvard lectures), 1981; Australian Federalism in Crisis, 1983; The Whitlam Government, 1972-1975, 1985; International Law-Making, 1989; Australia's Administrative Amnesia, 1990; National Collecting Institutions, 1990; Living with the United States: British Dominions and New Pacific States, 1990; A Century of Social Change, 1992; National and International Maturity, 1991; Coordination of Transportation, 1992; Human Rights in One Nation, 1992; Abiding Interests, 1997; My Italian Notebook, 2002; Road to China, 2010. **Address:** 100 William St., Sydney, NW 2011, Australia.

WHITLEY, David S(cott). American (born United States), b. 1953. **Genres:** Archaeology/Antiquities, Art/Art History, Anthropology/Ethnology, Adult Non-fiction. **Career:** W&S Consultants (cultural resource management consultants), president, owner, 1982-; University of California, Institute of Archaeology, chief archaeologist, lecturer, 1983-87, extension instructor, 1989-; State of California Historical Resources Commission, prehistoric archaeologist, 1986-87; University of the Witwatersrand, Rock Art Research Unit, lecturer, research fellow, 1987-89; International Council on Monuments and Sites, United States representative, 1992-2004, council of directors, 1997-2004; Alta Mira Press, Archaeology of Religion, series editor, 2002-; Arizona State University, adjunct professor of geography, 2003-. Writer. **Publications:** Rock Art Treasures of Ancient America (documentary film), 1982; Guide to Rock Art Sites: Southern California and Southern Nevada, 1996; Following the Shamans Path: A Walking Tour of Little Petroglyph Canyon, 1998; The Art of the Shaman: Rock Art of California, 2000. EDITOR: (with E.L. McCann and C.W. Clewlow, Jr.) Inland Chumash Archaeological Investigations, 1980; (with M.P. Beaudry) Investigaciones arqueológicas en la costasur de Guatemala, 1989; (with L.L. Loendorf) New Light on Old Art: Recent Advances in Hunter-Gatherer Rock Art Research, 1994; (with K. Hays-Gilpin and contrib.) Reader in Gender Archaeology, 1998; Reader in Archaeological Theory: Postprocessual and Cognitive Approaches, 1998; Handbook of Rock Art Research, 2001; (with G. Gumerman IV and contrib.) Reader in the Archaeology of Civilizations, 2001; (and contrib.) Ethnography and North American Rock Art, 2004; (with L.L. Loendorf and C. Chippindale) Discovering North American Rock Art, 2005; Introduction to Rock Art Research, 2005; The Idea of Nature In Disney Animation, 2007; (with K. Hays-Gilpin) Belief in the Past: Theoretical Approaches to the Archaeology of Religion, 2008; Cave Paintings and the Human Spirit: The Origin of Creativity and Belief, 2009. Contributor to periodicals and magazines. **Address:** 447 3rd St., Fillmore, CA 93015, U.S.A. **Online address:** huitli@impulse.net

WHITLEY, Gershonah C. (Gershonah Cynthia Whitley). American (born United States), b. 1955. **Genres:** Self Help. **Career:** US Department of Education, teacher; Motivational Enterprises, literary director and managing staff. Writer. **Publications:** (As Gershonah Cynthia Whitley) Looking for Self in All the Wrong Places, 2007. **Address:** Motivational Enterprises, 1015 Winthrop St., 3rd Fl., Brooklyn, NY 11212, U.S.A. **Online address:**

keziayisrael@yahoo.com

WHITLEY, Gershonah Cynthia. *See* **WHITLEY**, Gershonah C.

WHITLEY, Peggy. (Peggy J. Whitley). American (born United States), b. 1938. **Genres:** Education. **Career:** Lone Star College, Kingwood Library, dean of educational services, director of teaching, learning and distance education librarian. Writer. **Publications:** (With C.C. Olson and S.W. Goodwin) 99 Jumpstarts to Research: Topic Guides for Finding Information on Current Issues, 2001, 2nd ed., 2010; (with S.W. Goodwin as Peggy J. Whitley) 99 Jumpstarts for Kids: Getting Started in Research, 2003; (with S.W. Goodwin as Peggy J. Whitley) 99 Jumpstarts for Kids' Science Research, 2006; (with S.W. Goodwin as Peggy J. Whitley) 99 Jumpstarts for Kids' Social Studies Reports: Research Help for Grades 3-8, 2007. **Address:** Kingwood Library, Lone Star College, 20000 Kingwood Dr., Kingwood, TX 77339, U.S.A. **Online address:** pwhitley@lonestar.edu

WHITLEY, Peggy J. *See* **WHITLEY**, Peggy.

WHITLOCK, Dean. American (born United States) **Genres:** Young Adult Fiction, Novels, History. **Career:** Writer. **Publications:** Sky Carver (young adult novel), 2005; Raven, 2007; Fireboy, forthcoming. Contributor to periodicals. **Address:** c/o Author Mail, Clarion Books, 215 Park Ave. S, New York, NY 10003, U.S.A. **Online address:** boatman@deanwhitlock.com

WHITLOCK, Flint. American/Indian (born India), b. 1916. **Genres:** Civil Liberties/Human Rights, Military/Defense/Arms Control. **Career:** Military historian, 1986; Colorado Military History Museum Inc., president. Writer. **Publications:** Soldiers on Skis: A Pictorial Memoir of the 10th Mountain Division, 1992; Denver Mile-High Magic: Hundreds of Things to See and Do in and around the Mile-High City, 1996; The Rock of Anzio: From Sicily to Dachau a History of the 45th Infantry Division, 1998; The Fighting First: The Untold Story of the Big Red One on D-Day, 2004; Given up for Dead: American GI's in the Nazi Concentration Camp at Berga, 2005; Distant Bugles, Distant Drums: The Union Response to the Confederate Invasion of New Mexico, 2006; (with R. Smith) The Depths of Courage: American Submariners at War with Japan, 1941-1945, 2007; (with T.L. Barnhart) Capt. Jepp and the Little Black Book: How Barnstormer and Aviation Pioneer Elrey B. Jeppesen made the Skies Safer for Everyone, 2007; Turbulence before Takeoff: The Life and Times of Aviation Pioneer Marlon Dewitt Green, 2009; Internal Conflicts, 2009. **Address:** Basic Books, 387 Park Ave. S, 12th Fl., New York, NY 10016, U.S.A. **Online address:** flint@flintwhitlock.com

WHITLOCK, Luder (G.). American (born United States), b. 1940. **Genres:** Theology/Religion. **Career:** Reformed Theological Seminary, faculty, 1975-, acting president, 1978, president, 1979-2001, associate professor of mission and evangelism emeritus; Teleios, president; Trinity Forum, executive director, 2003-08, senior fellow; Key Life Network Inc., director; Barna Institute, director; World Reformed Fellowship, co-founder, director; National Commission on Higher Education, director; Graduate Institute for Applied Linguistics, director; Spirit of the Reformation Study Bible, executive director; CareNet, director; International Reformed Fellowship, co-president. Writer. **Publications:** The Spiritual Quest: Pursuing Christian Maturity, 2000. Contributor to books. **Address:** Teleios, 455 S Orange Ave., 2nd Fl., PO Box 4920, Orlando, FL 32801, U.S.A. **Online address:** luder.whitlock@excelsis.cc

WHITMAN, Alice. *See* **MARKER**, Sherry.

WHITMAN, Nancy C(hong). American (born United States), b. 1932. **Genres:** Mathematics/Statistics, Education. **Career:** Wisconsin State College, instructor in mathematics, 1958-60; University of Hawaii, mathematics supervisor at university high school, 1961-63, Educational Research and Development Center, researcher, 1962-64, professor of mathematics education, 1962-, associate professor of mathematics, 1967-72, teacher at university laboratory school, 1972-81, Department of Curriculum and Instruction, chair, 1989-92, co-chair of secondary education, 1995-96, chair of secondary and middle level education, 1996-97, now professor emeritus mathematics education. Writer. **Publications:** Project D: Program for Talented Students in Mathematics in Secondary Schools in Hawaii, 1965; (with F. Baum) The Metric System, 1978; (ed. and trans.) S. Maehara, Atarashii Sansuu (title means: 'New Mathematics'), 1994; A Case Study of Japanese Middle Schools, 1983-1998: A Reflection on Practices, Trends, and Issues, 2000; Learning from Jap-

anese Middle School Math Teachers, 2003; Standard-Based Math Activities for K-8 Students: Meeting the Needs of Today's Diverse Student Population, 2006; Counting Petals: Using Flowers of Hawai'i, 2009. Contributor of books to journals. **Address:** Dept. of Teacher Education and Curriculum Studies, University of Hawaii, 1776 University Ave., Honolulu, HI 96822, U.S.A. **Online address:** nanwhitman@aol.com

WHITMAN, Sylvia (Choate). American (born United States), b. 1961. **Genres:** Novellas/Short Stories, History, Literary Criticism And History. **Career:** Phillips Junior College, English instructor, 1985; Berlitz Language School, English as a second language instructor, 1985; University of Texas, teaching assistant, 1988-89; Orlando Sentinel, copy editor on the international/national desk, 1989-93; Vassar College, public relations coordinator, 1993-95; Daily Progress, copy, photograph and layout editor, 1995-96; Rollins College, Thomas P. Johnson Student Resource Center, learning specialist, 1997-98, Writing Center, coordinator, 1998-. **Publications:** Hernando de Soto and the Explorers of the American South, 1991; V is for Victory: The American Home Front during World War II, 1993; Uncle Sam Wants You: Military Men and Women of World War II, 1993; This Land Is Your Land: The American Conservation Movement, 1994; Get up and Go: The History of American Road Travel, 1996; Children of the Frontier, 1998; Immigrant Children, 2000; Children of the World War II Home Front, 2000; What's Cooking?: The History of American Food, 2001; World Poverty, 2008; Under the Ramadan Moon, 2008. Contributor of articles to books and periodicals. **Address:** 1534 16th Rd. N, Ste. 12, Arlington, VA 22209-2773, U.S.A. **Online address:** sylviawhitman@hotmail.com

WHITMAN, T(orrey) Stephen. American (born United States), b. 1950. **Genres:** History, Social Sciences, Politics/Government. **Career:** Citibank, systems analyst, 1974-75; U.S. Department of State, human resources manager, 1975-90; District of Columbia, Office of the Prosecuting Attorney, mediator, 1979-84; University of Houston, adjunct professor, 1983; Gettysburg College, instructor, 1993-94; Mount St. Mary's College, assistant professor of history, 1994-, associate professor, professor. Writer. **Publications:** The Price of Freedom: Slavery and Manumission in Baltimore and Early National Maryland, 1997; Challenging Slavery in the Chesapeake: Black and White Resistance to Human Bondage, 1775-1865, 2007. Contributor of articles to periodicals. **Address:** Department of History, Mount St. Mary's College, 16300 Old Emmitsburg Rd., Emmitsburg, MS 21727, U.S.A. **Online address:** whitman@msmary.edu

WHITMORE, Benette. American (born United States), b. 1955. **Genres:** Novels. **Career:** Cazenovia College, Office of Communications, public relations director and instructor of communications, 1980-82; Sargent-Webster-Crenshaw & Folley, publications director, 1982-90; Community General Hospital, media specialist, 1990-95; Onondaga Community College, EXCEL Learning Center, instructor, 1992-95; State University of New York, College of Environmental Science and Forestry, Department of Environmental Studies, instructor, 1993-, ESF Writing Program, director, 2009-; Cornell University, Engineering Communications Program, instructor, 1995-97; Syracuse University, senior writing instructor, 1995-2009, Creative Writing Graduate Program, visiting instructor, 2007. Writer. **Publications:** A Quilt for Elizabeth, 1992; Pappyland Activity Book, vol. I-II, 1995; The Little Shoe Book, 1995; Real Stuck, Way Up, 1996; Ghost Bat in a Gum Tree, 1998; Shelter, 2006. Contributor to journals and periodicals. **Address:** Department of Environmental Studies, State University of New York, 105 Moon Library, 106 Marshall Hall, 1 Forestry Dr., Syracuse, NY 13210-2787, U.S.A. **Online address:** bwhitmor@esf.edu

WHITMORE, Cilla. *See* **GLADSTONE**, Arthur M.

WHITSON, Kathy J. American (born United States) **Genres:** Language/Linguistics, Literary Criticism And History. **Career:** Eureka College, associate professor of English, professor of English. Writer. **Publications:** Native American Literatures: An Encyclopedia of Works Characters Authors and Themes, 1999; Encyclopedia of Feminist Literature, 2004. Contributor to books and journals. **Address:** Humanities Division, Eureka College, 300 E College Ave., Eureka, IL 61530, U.S.A. **Online address:** kwhitson@eureka.edu

WHITSON, Stephanie Grace (Irvin). American (born United States), b. 1952?. **Genres:** Novels, Young Adult Non-fiction. **Career:** Prairie Pieceworks Inc., owner. Writer. **Publications:** PRAIRIE WINDS SERIES: Walks the Fire: A Novel, 1995; Soaring Eagle, 1996; Red Bird, 1997. KEEPSAKE LEGACIES SERIES: Sarah's Patchwork, 1998; Karyn's Memory Box, 1999; Nora's Ribbon of Memories, 1999. DAKOTA MOONS SERIES: Valley of the Shadow, 2000, rev. ed., 2004; Edge of the Wilderness, 2001; Heart of the Sandhills, 2002. PINE RIDGE PORTRAITS SERIES: Watchers on the Hill, 2004; Footprints on the Horizon, 2005. QUILT CHRONICLES SERIES: The Key on the Quilt, 2012; The Shadow of a Name, 2012. NON-FICTION: The Friendship Bear, 2003; How to Help a Grieving Friend: A Candid Guide For Those Who Care, 2005; (with K.L. Moore) Home on the Plains: Quilts and the Sod House Experience, 2011. NOVELS: A Garden in Paris, 2005; A Hilltop in Tuscany, 2006; Jacob's List, 2007; Unbridled Dreams, 2008; A Claim of Her Own, 2009; Sixteen Brides, 2010; A Most Unsuitable Match, 2011. Contributor to periodicals. **Address:** c/o Author Mail, Thomas Nelson Inc., PO Box 141000, Nashville, TN 37214, U.S.A.

WHITTEMORE, (Edward) Reed. American (born United States), b. 1919. **Genres:** Poetry, Literary Criticism And History, Biography, Essays, Novellas/ Short Stories, Autobiography/Memoirs. **Career:** Furioso Magazine, founder, editor, 1939-53; Carleton College, faculty, 1947-62, English Department, chairman, 1962-64, professor of English, 1962-67; Carleton Miscellany, editor, 1960-64; Library of Congress, consultant in poetry, 1964-65, honorary consultant, 1968-71, interim consultant, 1984-85; National Institute of Public Affairs, 1966-68; Princeton University, Bain-Swiggett Lecturer, 1967-68; University of Maryland, professor, 1967-84, professor emeritus of English, 1984-; New Republic Magazine, literary editor, 1969-73; Delos Magazine, editor, 1988-92. **Publications:** Furioso, 1939; Heroes & Heroines: Poems, 1946; An American Takes a Walk and Other Poems, 1956; The Self-Made Man and Other Poems, 1959; (ed.) Browning, 1960; The Boy from Iowa: Poems and Essays, 1962; Little Magazines, 1963; The Fascination of the Abomination: Poems, Stories and Essays, 1963; Return, Alpheus: A Poem for the Literary Elders of Phi Beta Kappa, 1965; Ways of Misunderstanding Poetry, 1965; Poems, New and Selected, 1967; From Zero to the Absolute: Essays, 1967; Fifty Poems Fifty, 1970; The Mother's Breast and the Father's House, 1974; William Carlos Williams: Poet from Jersey, 1975; The Poet as Journalist: Life at the New Republic, 1976; The Feel of Rock: Poems of Three Decades, 1982; Pure Lives: The Early Biographers, 1988; Whole Lives: The Shapers of Modern Biography, 1989; Poets and Anthologists, 1986; The Past, the Future, the Present: Poems Selected and New, 1990; Six Literary Lives, 1992; Six Literary Lives: The Shared Impiety of Adams, London, Sinclair, Williams, Dos Passos and Tate, 1993; Ten from Ten & One More, 2007; Against the Grain: The Literary Life of a Poet: A Memoir, 2007. **Address:** Department of English, University of Maryland, 2119 Tawes Hall, College Park, MD 20742, U.S.A.

WHITTEN, Leslie Hunter. American (born United States), b. 1928. **Genres:** Novels, Children's Fiction, Poetry, Biography, Translations, Autobiography/ Memoirs. **Career:** Radio Free Europe, news editor, 1952-55, news chief, 1955-57; International News Service, desk editor, 1957-58; Washington Post, reporter, 1958-62; United Press Intl., newsman, 1958; Hearst Newspapers, reporter, 1963-66, assistant bureau chief, 1966-69; Washington Merry-Go-Round, chief assistant, 1969-78, senior investigator, 1969-92. Writer. **Publications:** MYSTERY NOVELS: Progeny of the Adder, 1965; Moon of the Wolf in UK as Death of the Nurse, 1967; A Day without Sunshine, 1985; The Fangs of Morning, 1994. NOVELS: The Alchemist, 1973; Conflict of Interest, 1976; Sometimes a Hero, 1979; A Killing Pace, 1983, 2nd ed., 1985; The Lost Disciple: The Book of Demas, 1989; Moses: The Lost Book of the Bible: A Novel, 1999. OTHER: Pinion, the Golden Eagle, 1968; (trans.) The Abyss, by Baudelaire, 1970; F. Lee Bailey, 1971; Washington Cycle, 1979; Sad Madrigals, 1997. **Address:** 3142 Gracefield Rd., Apt. 303, Silver Spring, MD 20904, U.S.A.

WHITTEN, Norman E. American (born United States), b. 1937. **Genres:** Anthropology/Ethnology, Cultural/Ethnic Topics, Race Relations, Mythology/Folklore. **Career:** Washington University, assistant professor, associate professor, 1965-70; University of California, visiting associate professor, 1970-79; University of Illinois, professor of anthropology and Latin American studies, 1970-, head of the department, 1983-86; Spurlock Museum of World Cultures, curator, 2001-; Center for Latin American and Caribbean Studies, director, 2000-03; American Ethnologist, editor, 1979-84. **Publications:** Class, Kinship and Power in an Ecuadorian Town, 1965; Black Frontiersmen: A South American Case, 1974; Sacha Runa: Ethnicity and Adaptation of Ecuadorian Jungle Quichua, 1976; Temas sobre la Continuidad y Adaptacion Cultural Ecuatoriana, 1984; Amazonia Ecuatoriana: La Otra Cara del Pro-

greso, 1985; (with D.S. Whitten) Art, Knowledge and Health, 1985; Sicuanga Runa: The Other Side of Development in Amazonian Ecuador, 1985; (with D.S. Whitten) From Myth to Creation: Art from Amazonian Ecuador, 1988; Pioneros Negros: La Cultura Afro-Latinoamericana del Ecuador y de Colombia, 1993; Transformaciones Culturales en la Sierra Ecuatoriana, 1993; Clase, Parentesco y Poder en un Pueblo Ecuatoriano: Los Negros de San Lorenzo, 1997; (with D.S. Whitten) Puy.o Runa: Imagery and Power in Modern Amazonia, 2008; (with D.S. Whitten) Histories of the Present: People and Power in Ecuador, 2011. EDITOR: (with J.F. Szwed) Afro-American Anthropology, 1970; Cultural Transformations and Ethnicity in Modern Ecuador, 1981; (with D.S. Whitten) Imagery and Creativity: Ethnoaesthetics and Art Worlds in the Americas, 1993; (with A. Torres) Blackness in Latin America and the Caribbean, 2 vols., 1998; Millennial Ecuador: Critical Essays on Cultural Transformations and Social Dynamics, 2003. **Address:** Department of Anthropology, University of Illinois at Urbana-Champaign, 607 S Mathews, Urbana, IL 61801, U.S.A. **Online address:** nwhitten@uiuc.edu

WHITTINGTON, Brad. American (born United States), b. 1956. **Genres:** Humor/Satire, Young Adult Fiction. **Career:** Educator and editor. **Publications:** Welcome to Fred, 2003; Living With Fred: A Novel, 2005; Escape from Fred, 2006; (with P. Little) Hell in a Briefcase: A Matt Cooper Novel, 2006. Contributor of articles to magazines. **Address:** Broadman & Holman Publishers, 127 9th Ave., Nashville, TN 37234-0002, U.S.A. **Online address:** author@fred.texas.com

WHITTINGTON, Geoffrey. British (born England), b. 1938. **Genres:** Money/Finance. **Career:** University of Cambridge, Department of Applied Economics, senior research officer, 1962-72, Price Waterhouse Coopers professor of financial accounting, 1988-2001, Price Waterhouse Coopers professor emeritus of financial accounting, 2001-, Fitzwilliam College, fellow, 1966-72, director of studies, 1967-72, professorial fellow, 1988-2001, life fellow, 2001-, Judge Business School, Centre for Financial Analysis and Policy, senior research associate; University of Edinburgh, Department of Accounting and Business Method, professor of accountancy and finance and head, 1972-75; University of Bristol, Department of Economics, professor of accounting and finance, 1975-88, head, 1981-84, Faculty of Social Sciences, dean, 1985-87; Institute of Chartered Accountants of Scotland, professorial research fellow, 1996-2001. Writer. **Publications:** (With A. Singh and H.T. Burley) Growth, Profitability and Valuation, 1968; Prediction of Profitability and Other Studies of Company Behaviour, 1971; Company Taxation and Dividends, 1974; (with G. Meeks) Financing of Quoted Companies in the United Kingdom, 1976; Inflation Accounting, 1983; (with D. Tweedie) The Debate on Inflation Accounting, 1984; (ed. and intro. with R.H. Parker and G.C. Harcourt) Readings in the Concept and Measurement of Income, 1986; The Elements of Accounting: An Introduction, 1992; (with V. Saporta and A. Singh) Effects Of Hyper-Inflation On Accounting Ratios: Financing Corporate Growth In Industrial Economies, 1997; Profitability, Accounting Theory and Methodology, 2007. Contributor to books and journals. **Address:** Centre for Financial Analysis & Policy, Judge Business School, University of Cambridge, Trumpington St., Cambridge, CB CB2 1AG, England. **Online address:** gw12@cam.ac.uk

WHITTINGTON, Keith E. American (born United States), b. 1968. **Genres:** Law, Politics/Government. **Career:** Yale University, teaching fellow, 1991-93; Houston Community College, instructor, 1993-95; Catholic University of America, assistant professor, 1995-97; Princeton University, public law field coordinator, 1997-2003, Department of Politics, assistant professor, 1997-2002, associate professor, 2002-05, professor, 2005-06, William Nelson Cromwell professor of politics, 2006-, Law and Public Affairs Program, faculty associate, 1999-, 2006-09, John Maclean Jr. Presidential preceptor, 2000-03, James Madison Program in American Ideals and Institutions, faculty associate, 2000-, departmental affirmative action officer, 2002-03, Public Law Colloquium, founder and organizer, 2002-04, 2006-, director of undergraduate program and senior advisor, 2002-05, senior and junior independent work advisor, 2003-05, James Madison Program in American Ideals and Institutions, acting director, 2004-05, director of graduate studies, 2007-; University of Texas School of Law, visiting professor of law, 2005-06. Writer. **Publications:** Constitutional Construction: Divided Powers and Constitutional Meaning, 1999; Constitutional Interpretation: Textual Meaning, Original Intent and Judicial Review, 1999; (ed. with N. Devins) Congress and the Constitution, 2005; Political Foundations of Judicial Supremacy: The

Presidency, the Supreme Court and Constitutional Leadership in U.S. History, 2007; (ed. with R.D. Kelemen and G.A. Calderia) The Oxford Handbook of Law and Politics, 2008. Contributor to books and periodicals. **Address:** Department of Politics, Princeton University, 240 Corwin Hall, Princeton, NJ 08544, U.S.A. **Online address:** kewhitt@princeton.edu

WHITTLE, Chris. American (born United States), b. 1947. **Genres:** Education, Administration/Management. **Career:** Media entrepreneur, chairman and publisher, 1979-86; Channel One, founder and chairman, 1989-94; Edison Schools, founder, 1992-; Whittle Communications, founder and chairman; Avenues: The World School, CEO. Writer. **Publications:** Crash Course: Imagining a Better Future for Public Education, 2005. Contributor to periodicals. **Address:** Edison Schools, 521 5th Ave., 11th Fl., New York, NY 10175, U.S.A.

WHITTLE, Peter. British/New Zealander (born New Zealand), b. 1927. **Genres:** Genealogy/Heraldry, Mathematics/Statistics. **Career:** University of Cambridge, lecturer, 1959-61, Churchill professor of mathematics, 1967-94, Churchill professor emeritus of mathematics, 1994-, Statistical Laboratory, director, 1973-86; University of Manchester, professor of mathematical statistics, 1961-67. Writer. **Publications:** Hypothesis Testing in Time Series Analysis, 1951; Prediction and Regulation by Linear Least-square Methods, 1963, 2nd ed., 1983; Probability, 1970, 2nd ed., 1976; Optimisation under Constraints: Theory and Applications of Nonlinear Programming, 1971; Optimisation over Time: Dynamic Programming and Stochastic Control, 2 vols., 1982; Systems in Stochastic Equilibrium, 1986; Risk-Sensitive Optimal Control, 1990; Probability via Expectation, 1992, 4th ed., 2000; (contrib.) Probability, Statistics, and Optimisation: A Tribute to Peter Whittle, 1994; Optimal Control: Basics and Beyond, 1996; Neural Nets and Chaotic Carriers, 1998; A Family History of the Oku Street Whittles, 2001; Networks: Optimisation and Evolution, 2007. **Address:** 268 Queen Edith's Way, Cambridge, CB CB1 8NL, England. **Online address:** whittle@statslab.cam.ac.uk

WHITTON, David. (David William Whitton). British (born England), b. 1947. **Genres:** Theatre. **Career:** Lancaster University, Faculty of Arts and Social Sciences, lecturer, senior lecturer, 1972-95, professor of French theater, 1995-, Department of European Languages and Cultures, now professor emeritus, dean of arts and humanities; University of California-Davis, visiting professor, 1996; International Federation for Theatre Research, joint secretary. Writer. **Publications:** Stage Directors in Modern France, 1987; Molière: Le Misanthrope, 1991; Molière: Le Bourgeois Gentilhomme, 1992; Molière: Don Juan, 1995. **Address:** Department of European Languages & Cultures, Faculty of Arts & Social Sciences, University of Lancaster, Bowland North 356, Lancaster, LC LA1 4YD, England. **Online address:** d.whitton@lancaster.ac.uk

WHITTON, David William. *See* **WHITTON, David.**

WHITTON, Kenneth S(tuart). British/Scottish (born Scotland), b. 1925. **Genres:** Plays/Screenplays, Language/Linguistics, Literary Criticism And History, Music, Theatre, Biography, Translations, Social Sciences, Social Sciences. **Career:** School teacher of German, 1952-66; University of Bradford, lecturer of German studies, 1966-84, Department of European Studies, chair, 1972-92, professor of European cultural studies, 1984-92, professor emeritus, 1992-. Writer. **Publications:** (Trans.) B. Lohse, Australia and the South Seas, 1959; Hundert Nacherzahlungen, 1965; Wirwaren Vier, vol. I, 1966, vol. II, 1967; (comp.) Advanced Nacherzählungen for University and Sixth Form Classes, 1969; (ed. and trans.) D. Fischer-Dieskau, Schubert's Songs: A Biographical Study of His Songs, 1976; (with J.M. Whitton) Zusammen, 1980; The Theatre of Friedrich Dürrenmatt: A Study in the Possibility of Freedom, 1980; Dietrich Fischer-Dieskau, Mastersinger: A Documented Study, 1981; Lieder: An Introduction to German Song, 1984; (ed. with A.J. Jones) German in the Classroom, 1984; Dürrenmatt: Reinterpretation in Retrospect, 1990; Durrenmatt: Der Besuch Der Alten Dame and Die Physiker, 1994; (ed. and trans.) H.A. Neunzig, Dietrich Fischer-Dieskau: A Biography, 1998; Goethe and Schubert: The Unseen Bond, 1999; Ossian, Goethe, and Schubert: The Poetry of the Heart, forthcoming. Contributor to periodicals. **Address:** University Of Bradford, Richmond Rd., Bradford, WY BD7 1DP, England.

WHITTY, Julia. American (born United States), b. 1958?. **Genres:** Novellas/Short Stories, Natural History, Documentaries/Reportage, Environmental Sciences/Ecology. **Career:** Producer and writer. **Publications:** A Tortoise for the Queen of Tonga (short stories), 2002; The Fragile Edge: Diving and Other Adventures in the South Pacific, 2007. NATURE DOCUMENTARIES: Return of the Great Whales; In the Kingdom of the Dolphins; Deep Blue Home: An Intimate Ecology of Our Wild Ocean, 2010. Contributor of short stories and essays to periodicals. **Address:** c/o Author Mail, Houghton Mifflin, 222 Berkeley St., Boston, MA 02116-3764, U.S.A.

WHITWORTH, John. British/Indian (born India), b. 1945. **Genres:** Poetry. **Career:** Teacher, 1969-84, 1990-; literary journalist and reviewer, 1984-. **Publications:** POETRY: Unhistorical Fragments, 1980; Poor Butterflies, 1982; Lovely Day for a Wedding, 1985; Tennis and Sex and Death, 1989; (ed.) The Faber Book of Blue Verse, 1990; Landscape with Small Humans, 1993; (intro.) The Complete Poetical Works of Phoebe Flood (for children), 1996; From the Sonnet History of Modern Poetry, 1999; Writing Poetry, 2001, rev. ed., 2006; The Whitworth Gun, 2002. OTHER: Being the Bad Guy, 2007. **Address:** 20 Lovell Rd., Rough Common, Canterbury, KT CT2 9D9, England. **Online address:** jwhitworthpoet@btopenworld.com

WHITZMAN, Carolyn. Canadian (born Canada), b. 1963. **Genres:** Regional/Urban Planning. **Career:** Safe Cities Collaborative Consultants, partner, 1999-; University of Melbourne, senior lecturer in urban planning, faculty of architecture, building and planning, associate professor. Writer. **Publications:** (With L. Wekerle) Safe Cities: Guidelines for Planning, Design and Management, 1995; The Handbook of Community Safety, Gender and Violence Prevention: Practical Planning Tools, 2008; Suburb, Slum, Urban Village: Transformations in Toronto's Parkdale Neighbourhood, 1875-2002, 2009. Contributor to books and journals. **Address:** University of Melbourne, 500 Yarra Blvd., Richmond, VI 3121, Australia. **Online address:** whitzman@unimelb.edu.au

WHYMAN, Matt. British (born England), b. 1969?. **Genres:** Novels, Novellas/Short Stories, Young Adult Non-fiction. **Career:** 19 Magazine, advice columnist, 1995-; TheSite.org, relationship advisor; Eve Magazine, columnist. **Publications:** WISE GUIDES SERIES: Wise Guides: Divorce and Separation: How to Survive Your Parents' Break-Up, 1999; Wise Guides: Smoking, 2000; Wise Guides: Drinking, 2002; Wise Guides: Family Breakup, 2005. NOVELS: Man or Mouse, 2000; Columbia Road, 2002; Superhuman (young adult), 2003; Boy Kills Man, 2004; The Wild (young adult), 2005; Street Runners (young adult), 2008. CARL HOBBES THRILLER SERIES: Icecore: A Carl Hobbes Thriller, 2007; Inside the Cage, 2007; Goldstrike, 2009. YOUNG ADULT SELF-HELP BOOKS XL: A Tool Kit for Life, 2002; XY 100: One Hundred Strategies for Life, 2004; Unzipped: Toolkit for Life, 2007. SO BELOW SERIES: CHILDREN'S STORIES: So Below: Key to the City, 2005; So Below: Siege under the City, 2005. Contributor to books. **Address:** Lucas Alexander Whitley Ltd., 14 Vernon St., London, GL W14 0RJ, England. **Online address:** matt.whyman@gmail.com

WHYNOTT, Douglas (Vernon). American (born United States), b. 1950. **Genres:** History, Local History/Rural Topics, Reference, Adult Non-fiction. **Career:** Freelance writer, 1978-; University of Massachusetts, lecturer in writing and faculty resident, 1985-, tuner; Mount Holyoke College, lecturer in English and journalism, 1989-97; Emerson College, associate professor of creative writing, 1997-, director of MFA program, 2002-09; Columbia University, adjunct professor of creative writing program, 2000. **Publications:** Following the Bloom: Across America with the Migratory Beekeepers, 1991; Lessons in the Blues: Studying Piano with Sammy Price, the King of Boogie Woogie; Giant Bluefin, 1995; A Unit of Water, A Unit of Time: Joel White's Last Boat, 1999; Country Practice: Scenes From the Veterinary Life, 2004. Contributor to periodicals. **Address:** Deparment of Writing, Literature & Publishing, Emerson College, 120 Boylston St., Boston, MA 02216-4624, U.S.A. **Online address:** douglas_whynott@emerson.edu

WHYTE, Jack. (John D. Whyte). Canadian/Scottish (born Scotland), b. 1940. **Genres:** Science Fiction/Fantasy. **Career:** Teacher, 1963-68; professional musician, entertainer, performer, 1968-78; CBC national television, writer, copy chief and creative director, 1978-80, corporate communications, 1980-96; Simon Fraser University, part-time teacher. **Publications:** Eagles' Brood, 1994; The Saxon Shore, 1995; The Singing Sword, 1996; The Skystone, 1996; The Sorcerer, 1997; The Sorcerer: Metamorphosis, 1999; The Fort at River's Bend, 1999; Uther, 2000; Clothar the Frank, 2003; The Lance Thrower, 2004; Eagle, 2005; The Knights of the Black and White: Book I of the Templar Trilogy, 2006; Jack Whyte: Forty Years In Canada, 2007; The Eagle: The Concluding Volume Of The Camulod Chronicles, 2007; Standard Of Honor, 2007; Order in Chaos, 2009; The Forest Laird, 2010; Rebel, 2012.

Address: c/o Author Mail, Penguin Books of Canada Ltd., 10 Alcorn Ave., Ste. 300, Toronto, ON M4V 3B2, Canada.

WHYTE, John D. *See* **WHYTE, Jack.**

WHYTE, Mary. American (born United States), b. 1953. **Genres:** Art/Art History, Illustrations. **Career:** Professional artist, 1976-. Writer. **Publications:** SELF-ILLUSTRATED: Watercolor for the Serious Beginner, 1997; Alfreda's World, 2003. OTHERS: An Artist's Way of Seeing, 2005; Working South: Paintings And Sketches, 2011; Painting Portraits and Figures in Watercolor, 2011. Contributor to magazines. Illustrator of books by others. **Address:** c/o Katie Lindler, Coleman Fine Art, 79 Church St., Charleston, SC 29401-2503, U.S.A. **Online address:** info@colemanfineart.com

WIATER, Stan. *See* **WIATER, Stanley.**

WIATER, Stanley. (Stan Wiater). American (born United States), b. 1953. **Genres:** Horror, Science Fiction/Fantasy, Film, Writing/Journalism, Documentaries/Reportage, Reference. **Career:** Freelance writer, 1970-; Dark Dreamers, creator and host, 2000-01; ShadoWind Inc., owner. **Publications:** Dark Dreamers: Conversations with the Masters of Horror, 1990; (as Stan Wiater) The Official Teenage Mutant Ninja Turtles Treasury, 1991; Dark Visions: Conversations with the Masters of the Horror Film, 1992; (with S.R. Bissette) Comic Book Rebels: Conversations with the Creators of the New Comics, 1993; Mysteries of the Word, 1994; Dark Thoughts: On Writing, Advice and Commentary from Fifty Masters of Fear and Suspense, 1997; (with B. Gwinn) Dark Dreamers: Facing the Masters of Fear, 2001; (with C. Golden and H. Wagner) The Stephen King Universe, 2001; (with C. Golden and H. Wagner) The Complete Stephen King Universe: A Guide to the Worlds of Stephen King, 2006; Dark Dreamers: On Writing, 2010. EDITOR: Night Visions 7, 1989; After the Darkness, 1993; Richard Matheson's The Twilight Zone Scripts, 1998; (with B. Lumley) The Brian Lumley Companion, 2002; (with M.R. Bradley and P. Stuve) The Twilight and Other Zones: The Dark Worlds of Richard Matheson, 2009. Works appear in anthologies. Contributor to periodicals. **Address:** ShadoWind Inc., 48 Bevier St., Springfield, MA 01107, U.S.A. **Online address:** stanleywiater@hotmail.com

WIBER, Melanie G(ay). Canadian (born Canada), b. 1954. **Genres:** Anthropology/Ethnology, Law, Earth Sciences. **Career:** University of Alberta, lecturer in anthropology, 1986-87; University of New Brunswick, Department of Anthropology, assistant professor, 1987-90, associate professor, 1991-95, full professor, 1995-, acting chair; International Commission on Legal Pluralism, commission secretariat, 2001-06; Oceans Management Research Network, socio-economics of integrated management, head. Writer. **Publications:** (Ed. with R. Kuppe and A. Griffithe) Law and Anthropology: Group Rights Strategies for Assisting the Fourth World, 1990; Politics, Property and Law in the Philippine Uplands, 1993; Erect Men/Undulating Women: The Visual Imagery of Gender, Race, and Progress in Reconstructive Illustrations of Human Evolution, 1996; (ed. with J. Spiertz) The Role of Law in Natural Resource Management, 1996; (ed. with F. V. Benda-Beckmann and K. V. Benda-Beckman) Changing Properties of Property, 2006. Contributor to books and journals. **Address:** Department of Anthropology, University of New Brunswick, Annex C Bldg., Ste. 28, 13 MacAulay Ln., PO Box 4400, Fredericton, NB E3B 5A3, Canada. **Online address:** wiber@unb.ca

WICCLAIR, Mark R. American (born United States), b. 1944. **Genres:** Philosophy, Ethics. **Career:** Columbia University, instructor, 1972-74; City University of New York, adjunct lecturer, 1974-75; Lafayette College, instructor, 1975-76, assistant professor of philosophy, 1976-78; West Virginia University, assistant professor, 1978-83, associate professor, 1983-88, professor of philosophy, 1988-, adjunct professor of community medicine, 1990-, associate director of Center for Health Ethics and Law, 1990-94; University of Pittsburgh Center for Bioethics and Health Law, adjunct professor of medicine, 1989-. Writer. **Publications:** Ethics and the Elderly, 1993; Conscientious Objection in Health Care: An Ethical Analysis, 2011. Contributor to books and journals. **Address:** Department of Philosophy, West Virginia University, PO Box 6312, Morgantown, WV 26506-6312, U.S.A. **Online address:** wicclair@pitt.edu

WICK, Steve. American (born United States), b. 1951. **Genres:** Adult Nonfiction, Sciences, History. **Career:** Newsday, reporter, 1978-84, East End bureau chief, 1984-2005, deputy editor, 2005-. Writer. **Publications:** Bad Company: Drugs, Hollywood, and the Cotton Club Murder, 1990; Heaven and Earth: The Last Farmers of the North Fork, 1996; The Long Night: William L. Shirer and the Rise and Fall of the Third Reich, 2011. Contributor to periodicals. **Address:** Newsday, 235 Pinelawn Rd., Melville, NY 11747-4226, U.S.A. **Online address:** wick@newsday.com

WICK, Walter. American (born United States), b. 1953. **Genres:** Children's Non-fiction, Picture/Board Books, Illustrations, Literary Criticism And History. **Career:** Writer and photographer, 1992-. **Publications:** Veo: Un Libro de Adivinanzas Ilustradas, 1994; Veo Navidad: Un Libro de Adivinanzas Ilustradas, 1995; A Drop of Water: A Book of Science and Wonder, 1997; Walter Wick's Optical Tricks, 1998; Can You See What I See?: Picture Puzzles to Search and Solve, 2002; Can You See What I See? Dream Machine, 2003; Can You See What I See? Cool Collections, 2004; Can You See What I See? Seymour and the Juice Box Boat, 2004; Can You See What I see? The Night Before Christmas: Picture Puzzles To Search and Solve, 2005; Can You See What I See?: Dinosaurs, 2006; Can You See What I See?: Once Upon a Time, 2006; Can You See What I See? Seymour Makes New Friends, 2006; Can You See What I See?: Animals Read-and-Seek, 2007; Can You See What I See?: Trucks & Cars, 2007; Can You See What I See?: Nature Read-and-Seek, 2008; Can You See What I See?: On a Scary, Scary Night, 2008; Can You See What I See?: Toys Read-snd-Seek, 2008; Can You See What I See?: 100 Fun Finds Read-and-Seek, 2009; Can You See What I See?: Treasure Ship, 2010. I SPY SERIES: (with J. Marzollo): Christmas: A Book of Picture Riddles, 1992; A Book of Picture Riddles, 1992; Fun House: A Book of Picture Riddles, 1993; Mystery: A Book of Picture Riddles, 1993; Fantasy: A Book of Picture Riddles, 1994; School Days: A Book of Picture Riddles, 1995; More than Meets the Eye, 1996; Spooky Night: A Book of Picture Riddles, 1996; Super Challenger: A Book of Picture Riddles, 1997; Spooky Mansion, 1999; A Dinosaur's Eye, 2003; A Christmas Tree, 2010. **Address:** c/o Author Mail, Scholastic Books, 557 Broadway, New York, NY 10012, U.S.A.

WICKER, Brian John. British (born England), b. 1929. **Genres:** International Relations/Current Affairs, Literary Criticism And History, Philosophy, Theology/Religion, Military/Defense/Arms Control. **Career:** L.C.C., careers advisory officer, 1953-56; University of Birmingham, assistant secretary, 1956-60, senior lecturer in English, 1960-68, Department of Extramural Studies, staff tutor; The Guardian, columnist, 1963-68; Eastern Michigan University, visiting professor, 1968-69; Manhattanville College, visiting professor, 1968-69; Fircroft College, principal, 1980-88; Pax Christi (UK), vice president. **Publications:** Culture and Liturgy, 1963; God and Modern Philosophy, 1964; Work and the Christian Community, 1964; Culture and Theology, 1966 in US as Toward a Contemporary Christianity, 1967; First the Political Kingdom, 1967; (co-ed. and contrib.) From Culture to Revolution, 1968; The Story-Shaped World, 1975; Nuclear Deterrence: What Does the Church Teach?, 1986; (ed.) Studying War-No More?, 1993; (ed. with F. van Iersel) Humanitarian Intervention and the Pursuit of Justice: A Pax Christi Contribution to a Contemporary Debate, 1995; (with H. Haleem, S. Risahuddin and O. Ramsbotham) The Crescent and the Cross: Muslim and Christian Approaches to War and Peace, 1998; (ed.) Witnesses to Faith: Martyrdom in Christianity and Islam, 2006; (ed. with D. Fisher) Just War on Terror?: A Christian and Muslim Response, 2010. **Address:** Chimney Pots, 33 Westcroft Rd., Carshalton, SR SM5 2TG, England. **Online address:** brian.wicker@ukgateway.net

WICKER, Christine. American (born United States), b. 1953. **Genres:** Adult Non-fiction, Novels. **Career:** Dallas Morning News, feature writer, columnist and religion reporter. **Publications:** NONFICTION: (with J. Matthews) The Eyeball Killer, 1996; God Knows My Heart (autobiography), 1999; Lily Dale: The True Story of the Town That Talks to the Dead, 2003; Not in Kansas Anymore: A Curious Tale of How Magic Is Transforming America, 2005; Fall of the Evangelical Nation: The Surprising Crisis Inside the Church, 2008. **Address:** c/o Jandy Nelson, Manus & Associates Literary Agency Inc., 425 Sherman Ave., Ste. 200, Palo Alto, CA 94306-1850, U.S.A. **Online address:** christine@christinewicker.com

WICKER, Tom. *See* Obituaries.

WICKHAM, Chris. *See* **WICKHAM, Christopher J.**

WICKHAM, Christopher J. (Chris Wickham). American/British (born England), b. 1950. **Genres:** Film, Language/Linguistics, Literary Criticism And History. **Career:** University of Regensburg, lecturer in English, 1974-76; Allegheny College, assistant professor of German, 1982-85; University of Illinois, assistant professor of German, 1985-91; Middlebury College, German School, instructor, 1986, 1991, 1993, 1997, 1999, 2001, 2003; University of Texas, assistant professor, 1991-97, associate professor of German, 1997-, College of Liberal and Fine Arts, associate dean. **Publications:** AS CHRIS WICKHAM: Early Medieval Italy: Central Power and Local Society, 400-1000, 1981; Diendorf Kr. Nabburg (phonological study of a Bavarian dialect), 1987; (ed. with K.H. Schoeps) Was in den alten Buechern steht: Neue Interpretationen von der Aufklaerung zur Moderne (title means: What the Old Books Say: New Interpretations from the Enlightenment to the Present), 1991; (with J. Fentress) Social Memory, 1992; Community and Clientele in Twelfth-Century Tuscany: The Origins of the Rural Commune in the Plain of Lucca, 1998; (ed. with I.L. Hansen) Long Eighth Century, 2000; Courts and Conflict in Twelfth-Century Tuscany, 2003; Framing the Early Middle Ages: Europe and the Mediterranean 400-800, 2005; (ed.) Marxist History-Writing for the Twenty-First Century, 2007; (co-ed.) Rodney Hilton's Middle Ages: An Exploration of Historical Themes, 2007; Inheritance of Rome: A History of Europe from 400 to 1000, 2009. AS CHRISTOPHER J. WICKHAM: Mountains and the City: The Tuscan Appennines in the Early Middle Ages, 1988; (ed. with B.A. Murray) Framing the Past: The Historiography of German Cinema and Television, 1992; Constructing Heimat in Postwar Germany: Longing and Belonging, 1999. **Address:** College of Liberal and Fine Arts, University of Texas at San Antonio, 1 UTSA Cir., San Antonio, TX 78249-1644, U.S.A.

WICKHAM, David. British/Egyptian (born Egypt), b. 1944. **Genres:** Poetry, Politics/Government, Sports/Fitness. **Career:** British Broadcasting Corp., producer and director. Writer. **Publications:** (With S. Coe and D. Teasdale) More Than a Game: Sport in Our Time, 1992. Contributor to periodicals. **Address:** 110 Euston Rd., London, GL NW1 2DQ, England.

WICKHAM, DeWayne. American (born United States), b. 1946. **Genres:** Documentaries/Reportage, Autobiography/Memoirs. **Career:** U.S. News and World Report, correspondent, 1974-75; Baltimore Sun, reporter, 1975-78; WBAL-TV, host, 1976-89; Gannett News Service, columnist, 1985-; USA Today, columnist, 1988-; Howard University School of Journalism, chair, 1992-94; Delaware State University, distinguished professor of journalism, 2001-; North Carolina Agricultural and Technical State University, Institute for Advanced Journalism Studies, director, 2001-; Poynter Institute, journalism ethics fellow, 2002; Black Enterprise Magazine, washington correspondent; Baltimore Evening Sun Newspapers, reporter; CBS News, analyst; BlackAmericaWeb.com, executive editor; University of Maryland's college of journalism, adjunct faculty; The Trotter Group, co-founder; National Association of Black Journalists, founding member and president. **Publications:** Fire at Will, 1989; Woodholme: A Black Man's Story of Growing up Alone (memoir), 1995; (ed.) Thinking Black: Some of the Nation's Best Black Columnists Speak Their Minds, 1996; Bill Clinton and Black America, 2002; (co-ed.) Black Voices in Commentary, 2006. **Address:** USA Today/USA Today.com, 7950 Jones Branch Dr., Mc Lean, VA 22108-0605, U.S.A. **Online address:** dewaynewickham@aol.com

WICKHAM, Madeleine. See KINSELLA, Sophie.

WICKHAM-CROWLEY, Timothy P. American (born United States), b. 1951. **Genres:** Sociology, History. **Career:** Cornell University, teaching assistant, 1974-75, instructor, 1980; Hamilton College, visiting assistant professor, 1983-84; University of Rochester, assistant professor, 1984-85, visiting assistant professor, 1985-86; Georgetown University, Department of Sociology, assistant professor, 1986-92, associate professor, 1992-, Center for Latin American Studies, M.A. program director, 2001-07, 2009-10, Department of Sociology, chair, 2010-. Writer. **Publications:** Exploring Revolution: Essays on Latin American Insurgency and Revolutionary Theory, 1991; Guerrillas and Revolution in Latin America: A Comparative Study of Insurgents and Regimes since 1956, 1992; (ed. with S.E. Eckstein) Struggles for Social Rights in Latin America, 2003; (ed. with S.E. Eckstein) What Justice? Whose Justice?: Fighting for Fairness in Latin America, 2003. **Address:** Department of Sociology, Georgetown University, 595 Intercultural Ctr., PO Box 571037, Washington, DC 20057-1037, U.S.A. **Online address:** wickhamt@georgetown.edu

WICKRAMASINGHE, Nalin Chandra. Welsh/Sri Lankan (born Sri Lanka), b. 1939. **Genres:** Poetry, Astronomy, Mathematics/Statistics, Physics. **Career:** Jesus College, tutor, 1965-73, fellow; Vidyodaya University of Ceylon, professor of mathematics, 1966-; University of Wales, College of Cardiff,

professor, 1973-, Department of Applied Mathematics and Astronomy, head, 1973-89, professor of applied mathematics and astronomy, 1989-, Cardiff Centre for Astrobiology, director, 2000-, honorary professor; Institute of Fundamental Studies, director, 1983-84; Institute of Mathematics and its Applications, fellow; University of Cambridge, Institute of Astronomy, staff; Glamorgan University, honorary professor, 2007. Writer. **Publications:** Interstellar Grains, 1967; Light Scattering Functions with Applications in Astronomy, 1973; The Cosmic Laboratory, 1975; (with D.J. Morgan) Solid State Astrophysics, 1976; Is Life a Cosmic Phenomenon?, 1982; Fundamental Studies and the Future of Science, 1984; (with F. Hoyle) Lifecloud, The Origin of Life in 1978; (with F. Hoyle) Diseases from Space, 1979; (with F. Hoyle) Evolution from Space, 1981; (with F. Hoyle) Space Travellers, The Bringers of Life, 1981; Why Neo-Darwinism Does Not Work, 1982; (with F. Hoyle) Proofs That Life Is Cosmic, 1983; (with F. Hoyle) From Grains to Bacteria, 1984; (ed.) Living Comets, 1985; (with J. Watkins) Viruses from Space, 1985; Archaeopteryx-The Primordial Bird: A Case of Fossil Forgery, 1986; (with F. Hoyle) Cosmic Life Force, 1988; (with F. Hoyle) The Theory of Cosmic Grains, 1991; (with F. Hoyle) Our Place in the Cosmos, 1993; (with D. Ikeda) The Wonders of Life and The Universe, 1993; Glimpses of Life, Time and Space (anthology of poems), 1994; Life on Mars? The Case for a Cosmic Heritage, 1997; Space and Eternal Life, 1998; (ed. with F. Hoyle) Astronomical Origins of Life, 2000; Cosmic Dragons: Life and Death on Our Planet, 2001; (ed. with G. Burbidge and J. Narlikar) Fred Hoyle's Universe, 2003; A Journey with Fred Hoyle: The Search for Cosmic Life, 2005; (with J. Wickramasinghe and W. Napier) Comets and the Origin of Life, 2010. **Address:** Cardiff Centre for Astrobiology, Cardiff University, 2 North Rd., Cardiff, CT10 3DY, Wales. **Online address:** wickramasinghe@cf.ac.uk

WICKS, Susan. British (born England), b. 1947. **Genres:** Novels, Poetry, Autobiography/Memoirs. **Career:** University of Kent, senior lecturer in English and American literature, director of creative writing. Writer. **Publications:** POETRY: Singing Underwater, 1992; Open Diagnosis, 1994; The Clever Daughter, 1997; Night Toad: New & Selected Poems, 2003; De-iced, 2007. NOVELS: The Key, 1997; Little Thing, 1998. OTHERS: Driving My Father (memoir), 1995; Roll Up for the Arabian Derby, 2008; House of Tongues, 2011. **Address:** School of English, University of Kent, Canterbury, KT CT2 7NX, England. **Online address:** s.j.wicks@kent.ac.uk

WIDDECOMBE, Ann (Noreen). British (born England), b. 1947. **Genres:** Communications/Media, Young Adult Fiction. **Career:** Oxford Union, secretary, 1971, treasurer, 1972; Unilever, marketing department staff, 1973-75; London University, senior administrator, 1975-87; Runnymeade District Councillor, 1976-78, member of Parliament for Maidstone, 1987-97, member of Parliament for The Weald, 1997-2010; Foreign Office, PPS, staff, 1990; State Department of Employment, under secretary, 1993; State Department of Employment, minister, 1994; State Home Office, prisons and immigration minister, 1995; Shadow Cabinet, health secretary, 1998, home secretary, 1999-2001; novelist, 2000-; Canterbury Christ Church University, honorary fellow, 2009. **Publications:** Layman's Guide to Defence, 1984; Inspired and Outspoken, 1999; The Clematis Tree, 2000; Right From the Beginning, 2001; An Act of Treachery, 2002; Father Figure, 2005; An Act Of Peace, 2005; The Idealists, forthcoming. **Address:** United Agents, 12-26 Lexington St., London, GL W1F 0LE, England.

WIDDICOMBE, Richard Toby. See WIDDICOMBE, Toby.

WIDDICOMBE, Toby. (Richard Toby Widdicombe). American/British (born England), b. 1955. **Genres:** Literary Criticism And History, Bibliography, Photography. **Career:** University of California-Irvine, teaching assistant, teaching associate, 1977-84; Orange Coast College, instructor in literature and language, 1981-82; University of California-Santa Barbara, visiting lecturer, 1984-86, lecturer in English, 1987-89; New York Institute of Technology, assistant professor of English, 1989-92; University of Alaska-Anchorage, assistant professor, 1992-95, associate professor, 1996-2000, professor of English, 2001-. Writer. **Publications:** (As Richard Toby Widdicombe) Edward Bellamy: An Annotated Bibliography of Secondary Criticism, 1988; (ed. and intro. as Richard Toby Widdicombe) America and the Americans in 1833-1834, by an Emigrant, 1994; A Reader's Guide to Raymond Chandler, 2001; Simply Shakespeare, 2002; (ed. with H.S. Preiser) Revisiting the Legacy of Edward Bellamy (1850-1898), American Author and Social Reformer: Uncollected and Unpublished Writings, Scholarly Perspectives for a New Millennium, 2002; Vango Notes on Shakespeare, 2006; (with M. Greer) Screening Shakespeare, 2nd ed., 2009. Contributor to magazines. **Address:**

Department of English, University of Alaska-Anchorage, Admin 103-E, 3211 Providence Dr., Anchorage, AK 99508-4614, U.S.A. **Online address:** afrtw@uaa.alaska.edu

WIDDIFIELD, Stacie G(raham). American (born United States), b. 1953. **Genres:** Art/Art History. **Career:** University of Arizona, assistant professor, 1987-96, associate professor of art, 1996-, professor, Latin American Studies, associate faculty. Writer. **Publications:** The Embodiment of the National in Late Nineteenth-Century Mexican Painting, 1996; (ed.) La Amplitud del Modernismo y la Modernidad, 2003. Contributor to journal. **Address:** College of Fine Arts, University of Arizona, Rm. 288, Art Bldg., 1017 N Olive Rd., PO Box 210004, Tucson, AZ 85721-0004, U.S.A. **Online address:** staciew@email.arizona.edu

WIDMAIER, Eric P(aul). American (born United States), b. 1957. **Genres:** Biology, Sciences. **Career:** Boston University, assistant professor, 1988-94, associate professor, 1994-99, professor of biology, 1999-, Boston Nutrition Obesity Research Center, staff, 1994-; WABU-TV, lecturer, 1994-97. Writer. **Publications:** Why Geese Don't Get Obese (and We Do): How Evolution's Strategies for Survival Affect Our Everyday Lives, 1998; The Stuff of Life: Profiles of the Molecules That Make Us Tick, 2002; Vander, Sherman, & Luciano's Human Physiology: The Mechanisms of Body Function, 2004; (with H. Raff and K.T. Strang) Vander's Human Physiology: The Mechanisms of Body Function, 10th ed., 2006, 12th ed., 2011. Contributor to books and periodicals. **Address:** Department of Biology, Boston University, 5 Cummington St., Boston, MA 02215-2406, U.S.A. **Online address:** widmaier@bu.edu

WIDNER, Jennifer A(nne). American (born United States), b. 1958. **Genres:** Area Studies, Politics/Government, Law, Autobiography/Memoirs, Biography, Economics, Social Sciences. **Career:** Yale University, acting instructor in political science, 1986; Duke University, assistant professor of public policy, 1986-87; Harvard University, assistant professor, 1987-91, associate professor of government, 1991-94; University of Michigan, associate professor of political science, 1995-2002, professor of political science, 2002-04; Princeton University, professor of politics and international affairs, 2004-, Mamdouha S. Bobst Center for International Peace and Justice, director, 2005-, Woodrow Wilson School of Public and International Affairs, Institutions for Fragile States Program, director. Writer. **Publications:** The Rise of a Party-State in Kenya: From Harambee! to Nyayo!, 1992; (ed.) Economic Change and Political Liberalization in Sub-Saharan Africa, 1994; Building the Rule of Law: Francis Nyalali and the Road to Judicial Independence in Africa, 2001. Contributor to journals. **Address:** Department of Politics and International Affairs, Princeton University, 441 Robertson Hall, Princeton, NJ 08544, U.S.A. **Online address:** jwidner@princeton.edu

WIEBE, Katie Funk. Canadian (born Canada), b. 1924. **Genres:** Gerontology/Senior Issues, Theology/Religion, Autobiography/Memoirs, Biography. **Career:** Tabor College, instructor, associate professor of English, 1966-90, professor emeritus, 1991. Writer. **Publications:** Day of Disaster, 1976; Alone: A Widow's Search for Joy, 1976, as Alone: A Search for Joy, 1987; Our Lamps were Lit: An Informal History of the Bethel Deaconess Hospital School of Nursing, 1978; Women among the Brethren, 1979; Good Times with Old Times: How to Write Your Memoirs, 1979; Second Thoughts, 1981; Who Are the Mennonite Brethren?, 1981; Bless Me Too, My Father, 1988; (co-ed.) Your Daughters shall Prophesy: Women in Ministry in the Church, 1992; Life after 50: A Positive Look at the Aging in the Faith Community, 1993; Prayers of an Omega: Facing the Transitions of Aging, 1994; Border Crossing, 1995, rev. ed., 2002; The Storekeeper's Daughter, 1997; Bridging the Generations, 2001; You Never Gave Me a Name, 2009; How to Write Your Personal or Family History, 2009. **Address:** Tabor College, 400 S Jefferson Dr., Hillsboro, KS 67063, U.S.A. **Online address:** kfwiebe@aol.com

WIECK, Carl F. Finnish/American (born United States), b. 1937. **Genres:** Novels. **Career:** University of Louisville, assistant professor, 1966-68; Morehouse College, associate professor, 1968-73; University of Abidjan, Fulbright professor, 1973-76; University of Joensuu, acting senior lecturer, 1988-89; University of Tampere, senior lecturer in American literature and American studies, 1989-2003, senior lecturer emeritus and docent, 2003-. Writer. **Publications:** Refiguring Huckleberry Finn, 2000; Lincoln's Quest for Equality: The Road to Gettysburg, 2002. **Address:** Department of Translation Studies, School of Language, Translation & Literary Studies, University of Tampere, Pinni B, 4th Fl., Tampere, 33014, Finland. **Online address:** carl.wieck@uta.fi

WIEDEMANN, Barbara. American (born United States), b. 1945. **Genres:** Poetry, Literary Criticism And History. **Career:** University of Alabama, assistant professor of English, 1986-87; University of Florida, lecturer in English, 1987-88; Auburn University, assistant professor, 1988-93, associate professor, 1993-2000, professor of English, 2000-. Writer. **Publications:** (Ed. with R.C. Evans) My Name was Martha: A Renaissance Woman's Autobiographical Poem, 1993; (with R.C. Evans and A.C. Little) Short Fiction: A Critical Companion, 1997; Josephine Herbst's Short Fiction: A Window to Her Life and Times, 1998; Half-Life of Love (a chapbook), 2008; Sometime in October (a chapbook), 2010. Contributor to books, journals and newspapers. **Address:** Department of English & Philosophy, Auburn University, 351 Liberal Arts, PO Box 244023, Montgomery, AL 36124-4023, U.S.A. **Online address:** bwiedema@aum.edu

WIEDER, Alan. American (born United States), b. 1974?. **Genres:** Autobiography/Memoirs. **Career:** Writer and producer. **Publications:** Year of the Cock: The Remarkable True Account of a Married Man Who Left His Wife and Paid the Price (memoir), 2009. **Address:** c/o Kim Witherspoon, InkWell Management, 521 5th Ave., 26th Fl., New York, NY 10175, U.S.A. **Online address:** anneeducoq@hotmail.com

WIEDMAN, John Charles. American (born United States), b. 1949. **Genres:** Humor/Satire, Medicine/Health, Sports/Fitness. **Career:** Leader Federal Savings and Loan, vice president, 1976-82; Verex, sales representative, 1982-84; Union Planters Investment Banking Group, sales representative, 1984-90; Wiedman Mortgage Inc., owner, 1990-. Writer. **Publications:** Desperately Seeking Snoozin': The Insomnia Cure from Awake to Zzzzz, 1999. **Address:** Towering Pines Press Inc., 860 River Park Dr., Memphis, TN 38103-0804, U.S.A. **Online address:** weed6442@aol.com

WIEGAND, Shirley A. American (born United States), b. 1947. **Genres:** Librarianship. **Career:** University of Oklahoma, College of Law, faculty, 1988-95; American University, faculty; Marquette University, Law School, faculty, 1997-, associate dean, Cooperative Program, director, now professor emeritus. Writer and lawyer. **Publications:** Library Records: A Retention and Confidentiality Guide, 1994; (with W.A. Wiegand) Books on Trial: Red Scare in the Heartland, 2007; Books on Trial: Witch Hunt in the Heartland and a Nation's Response, forthcoming. **Address:** Law School, Marquette University, Sensenbrenner Hall, 1103 W Wisconsin Ave., PO Box 1881, Milwaukee, WI 53201, U.S.A. **Online address:** shirley.wiegand@marquette.edu

WIEGAND, Wayne A. American (born United States), b. 1946. **Genres:** Area Studies, History, Librarianship. **Career:** University of Wisconsin-Milwaukee, history teacher, 1969; John A. Logan College, instructor in history, 1973; Kalamazoo College, Upjohn Library, supervisor, 1973-74; Urbana College, college librarian, 1974-76; University of Kentucky, assistant professor, 1976-82, associate professor of library and information science, 1982-86; University of Wisconsin-Madison, associate professor, 1987-89, professor of library and information studies, 1989-2002, Center for Print Culture History in Modern America, co-founder and co-director, 1992-2002, fellow of teaching academy, 1996-2002, Institute for Research in the Humanities, fellow; University of Arizona, visiting distinguished professor, 1993, 1995, 1997; University of North Carolina, visiting professor, 1994; University of North Carolina, William Rand Kenan Jr. visiting professor, 1994; Florida State University, F. William Summers professor of library and information studies and professor of American studies, 2003-; Library Quarterly, co-editor, 2003-. **Publications:** The History of a Hoax: Edmund Lester Pearson, John Cotton Dana and the Old Librarian's Almanack, 1979; Politics of an Emerging Profession: The American Library Association, 1876-1917, 1986; Patrician in the Progressive Era: A Biography of George von Lengerke Meyer, 1988; (with D. Steffens) Members of the Club: A Look at One Hundred ALA Presidents, 1988; An Active Instrument for Propaganda: The American Public Libraries during World War I, 1989; Irrepressible Reformer: A Biography of Melvil Dewey, 1996; (with S.A. Weigand) Books on Trial: Red Scare in the Heartland, 2007; Main Street Public Library, 2011. EDITOR: Leaders in American Academic Librarianship, 1925-1975, 1983; Supplement to the Dictionary of American Library Biography, 1990; (with D.G. Davis, Jr.) Encyclopedia of Library History, 1994; (with J. Danky) Print Culture in a Diverse America, 1998; (with T. Augst) Libraries as Agencies of Culture; (with A. Lundin) Defining Print Culture for Youth, 2003; (with J.P. Danky) Women in Print: Essays on the Print Culture of American Women from the Nineteenth and Twentieth Centuries, 2006; Genreflecting: A Guide to Popular Reading Interests, 2006. Contributor to books and journals. **Address:** College of Information, Florida State University, 101 Louis Shores Bldg., Tallahassee, FL 32306-2100, U.S.A. **Online address:** wwiegand@mailer.fsu.edu

WIELAND, Liza. American (born United States), b. 1960. **Genres:** Novels, Novellas/Short Stories, Literary Criticism And History. **Career:** Dickinson College, assistant professor of English, 1987-90; Colorado College, assistant professor of English, 1990-91; California State University, associate professor, 1991-, professor; East California University, assistant professor. Writer. **Publications:** STORIES: The Names of the Lost, 1992; Discovering America, 1993; You Can Sleep While I Drive, 1999. NOVELS: Bombshell, 2001; Near Alcatraz, 2005; A Watch of Nightingales, 2009; Quickening, 2010. **Address:** Department of English, East California University, Erwin 317, Bate 2201, Greenville, NC 27858-4353, U.S.A. **Online address:** wielandl@ecu.edu

WIELER, Diana. (Diana J. Wieler). Canadian (born Canada), b. 1961. **Genres:** Children's Fiction, Young Adult Fiction, Picture/Board Books, Poetry, Novels. **Career:** CKXL Radio, advertising copywriter, 1980-82; Western Producer Prairie Books, editor, 1980-90; CJWW Radio, advertising copywriter, 1982-84; Star Phoenix, creative features writer, 1984-89. **Publications:** FICTION: FOR YOUNG ADULTS: (as Diana J. Wieler) Last Chance Summer, 1986; Bad Boy, 1989; Drive, 1999. FOR CHILDREN: A Dog on His Own, 1983; To the Mountains by Morning, 1995. RANVAN SERIES: The Defender, 1993; A Worthy Opponent, 1995; Magic Nation, 1997. OTHERS: Prairie Jungle: Songs, Poems and Stories for Children, 1985; Canadian Children's Annual: Number Twelve, 1987. **Address:** 133 Spruce Thicket Walk, Winnipeg, MB R2V 3Z1, Canada. **Online address:** djwieler@home.com

WIELER, Diana J. *See* **WIELER, Diana.**

WIENER, Antje. German (born Germany), b. 1960. **Genres:** Politics/Government, Social Commentary, Adult Non-fiction, Law, Social Sciences. **Career:** Free University of Berlin, tutuor, 1988, Institute for Latin American Studies, research assistant, 1987-89, Otto-Suhr Institute, lecturer in political science, 1990; Stanford University, lecturer in political science, 1990-91; Carleton University, Department Comparative Government & International Relations, teaching assistant, 1991-93, sessional lecturer, 1993-95; University of Sussex, Sussex European Institute, human capital and mobility postdoctoral fellow, 1995-97; University of Hanover, assistant professor of political science, 1997-99; Queen's University, reader, 1999-2002, Jean Monnet professor of European politics, 2001, Jean Monnet chair, 2000-07, professor of international relations, 2002-07, Jean Monnet Centre of Excellence, director, 2003; University of Bath, professor of politics and international relations, 2007-09; University of Hamburg, professor of politics and global governance, 2009-; European Political Science Review (EPSR), associate editor; ConWEB, founding co-editor. Writer. **Publications:** Geschlecht, Klasse, Ethnie: Alte Konflikte und Neue Soziale Bewegungen in Lateinamerika, 1991; European Citizenship Practice: Building Institutions of a Non-State, 1998; (with T. Diez) European Integration Theory, 2004, 2nd ed., 2009; Invisible Constitution of Politics: Contested Norms and International Encounters, 2008. EDITOR: (with W. Reusch) Gender, Class, Ethnicity: Old Conflicts and New Social Movements in Latin America, 1991; (with K. Neunreither) European Integration after Amsterdam: Institutional Dynamics and Prospects for Democracy, 2000; (with T. Christiansen and K.E. Jørgensen) The Social Construction of Europe, 2001. Contributor to books and periodicals. **Address:** Department of European Studies and Modern, Languages, University of Bath, 21 University Sq., Bath, BA2 7AY, United Kingdom. **Online address:** a.wiener@bath.ac.uk

WIENER, Joel Howard. American (born United States), b. 1937. **Genres:** History, Social Sciences. **Career:** Skidmore College, assistant professor of history, 1964-67; City University of New York, City College, associate professor, 1967-76, professor of history, 1977-2000, chair, 1981-85, professor emeritus of history, 2000-; University of York, visiting lecturer, 1971-73; New Dictionary of National Biography, associate editor. **Publications:** The War of the Unstamped: The Movement to Repeal the British Newspaper Tax, 1830-1836, 1969; A Descriptive Finding List of Unstamped British Periodicals, 1830-1836, 1970; Radicalism and Freethought in Nineteenth-Century Britain: The Life of Richard Carlile, 1983; William Lovett, 1989; Americanization of the British Press, 1830s-1914, 2011. EDITOR: Great Britain: Foreign Policy and the Span of Empire, 4 vols., 1972; Great Britain: The Lion at Home: A Documentary History of Domestic Policy, 1689-1973, 4 vols., 1974; Innovators and Preachers: The Role of the Editor in Victorian England, 1985; Papers for the Millions: The New Journalism in Britain, 1850s to

1914, 1988; (with M. Hampton) Anglo-American Media Interactions, 1850-2000, 2007. **Address:** Department of History, City College, City University of New York, 160 Convent Ave., New York, NY 10031-9101, U.S.A. **Online address:** jwiener267@aol.com

WIENER, Jonathan B(aert). American (born United States), b. 1962. **Genres:** Law. **Career:** National Bureau of Economic Research, researcher and editor, 1982-84; American Law Institute, research assistant, 1985-88; Hazardous Air Pollutant Strategy Group, chair, 1988-89; U.S. Department of Justice, Environment Division, special assistant, 1989-91; White House Office of Science and Technology Policy, policy counsel, 1992; White House Council of Economic Advisers, senior staff economist, 1992-93; Duke University, associate professor of law, 1994-98, Nicholas School of the Environment, professor of environmental policy, 1994-, professor of law, 1999-2004, Resources for the Future, university fellow, 2002-, Sanford Institute of Public Policy, professor of public policy studies, 2003-, William R. and Thomas L. Perkins professor of law, 2004-, Duke Center for Environmental Solutions, faculty director, 2000-05, Duke Law School, director, 2007-, SRA's World Congress on Risk, co-chair, 2012-; Society for Risk Analysis, president, 2008; Harvard University, Law School, visiting professor, 1999, 2010, NBER, research assistant, Harvard Law, review editor; University of Chicago, Law School, visiting professor; Ecole des Hautes Etudes en Sciences Sociales, visiting professor; le Centre International de Recherche sur Environnement et le Dévelopement, visiting professor, 2005-06. **Publications:** (Ed. with J. Graham) Risk versus Risk: Tradeoffs in Protecting Health and the Environment, 1995; (with D. Dudek) Joint Implementation, Transaction Costs and Climate Change, 1996; (with R.B. Stewart) Reconstructing Climate Policy: Beyond Kyoto, 2003; (co-ed.) The Reality of Precaution: Comparing Risk Regulation in the United States and Europe, 2010. Contributor to law periodicals. **Address:** School of Law, Duke University, 1111 E 60th St., PO Box 90360, Durham, NC 27708-0360, U.S.A. **Online address:** wiener@law.duke.edu

WIENER, Joshua M(ark). American (born United States), b. 1949. **Genres:** Gerontology/Senior Issues, Medicine/Health, Social Sciences, Law, Women's Studies And Issues. **Career:** University of Tokyo, European Political, research fellow, 1951-54, associate professor, 1954-64, professor of international politics, 1964-88, professor emeritus, 1988-; Meiji Gakuin University, professor of peace studies, 1988-93; International Christian University, Peace Research Institute, senior research fellow, 1993-96. Writer. **Publications:** (Ed.) Swing Beds: Assessing Flexible Health Care in Rural Communities, 1987; (with A. Rivlin, R. Hanley and D. Spence) Caring for the Disabled Elderly: Who Will Pay?, 1988; (with J. Engel) Improving Access to Health Services for Children and Pregnant Women, 1991; (with M.A. Strosbert, R. Baker and I.A. Fein) Rationing America's Medical Care: The Oregon Plan and Beyond, 1992; (with L.H. Illston and R. Hanley) Sharing the Burden: Strategies for Public and Private Long-Term Care Insurance, 1994; Persons with Disabilities, 1995; (co-ed.) Persons with Disabilities: Issues in Health Care Financing and Service Delivery, 1995; (with J. Holahan and S. Wallin) Health Policy for the Low-Income Population: Major Findings from the Assessing the New Federalism Case Studies, 1998; Health Policy for Low-Income People in Alabama, 1998; (ed. with J. Holahan and A. Weil) Federalism and Health Policy, 2003. Contributor to books. **Address:** 8-29-19 Shakujii-machi, Nerima-ku, Tokyo, 177-0041, Japan.

WIENER, Nancy H. American (born United States), b. 1958. **Genres:** Theology/Religion, Homes/Gardens, Adult Non-fiction. **Career:** Columbia University, president's fellow, 1986; Hebrew Union College, fieldwork coordinator, 1991, Jacob and Hilda Blaustein Center for Pastoral Counseling, clinical director, 2000-, adjunct professor of pastoral care and counseling, 2004-, Dr. Paul M. and Trudy Steinberg professor in human relations and counseling, 2010-. Writer. **Publications:** Beyond Breaking the Glass: A Spiritual Guide to Your Jewish Wedding, 2001; (with D. Judson) Meeting at the Well: A Jewish Spiritual Guide to Being Engaged, 2002; (with N. Fuchs-Kreimer) Judaism for Two: A Spiritual Guide for Strengthening and Celebrating Your Loving Relationship, 2005. **Address:** Jacob and Hilda Blaustein Center for Pastoral, Counseling, Hebrew Union College, 1 W 4th St., New York, NY 10012-1186, U.S.A. **Online address:** nwiener@huc.edu

WIEREN, Mona van. *See* **VAN DER ZEE, Karen.**

WIESEL, Elie. American/Romanian (born Romania), b. 1928. **Genres:** Novels, Plays/Screenplays, Theology/Religion, Writing/Journalism, Autobiography/Memoirs, Documentaries/Reportage, Essays, Translations, Translations.

Career: City University of New York, City College, distinguished professor of Judaic studies, 1972-76; Boston University, College of Arts and Sciences, Andrew W. Mellon professor in the humanities, university professor, professor of religious studies, 1976-, professor of philosophy, 1988-; United States President's Commission on the Holocaust, chair, 1979-80; United States Holocaust Memorial Council, chair, 1980-86; Florida International University, distinguished visiting professor, 1982; Eckerd College, distinguished visiting professor, 1994, 1995. Writer. **Publications:** Un Di Velt Hot Geshvign, 1956, trans. as La Nuit, 1958; L'Aube, 1961; Le Jour, 1961; La Ville de la chance, 1962; Les Portes de la foret, 1964; Le Chant des morts, 1966, trans. as Legends of Our Time, 1968; The Jews of Silence: A Personal Report on Soviet Jewry, 1966; Zalmen ou la Folie de Dieu (play), 1966; Le Mendiant de Jerusalem, 1968, trans. as (with L. Edelman) A Beggar in Jerusalem, 1970; La Nuit, L'Aube, and Le Jour, 1969, trans. as Night, Dawn, and The Accident: Three Tales, 1972 as The Night Trilogy: Night, Dawn, The Accident, 1987 as Night, Dawn, Day, 1985; Entre deux soleils, 1970, trans. as (with L. Edelman) One Generation After, 1970; Celebration Hassidique: Portraits et legendes, 1972; Le Serment de Kolvillag, 1973; Ani maamin: A Song Lost and Found Again, 1974; Celebration Biblique: Portraits et legendes, 1975; Un Juif aujourd 'hui: Recits, essais, dialogues, 1977; (co-author) Dimensions of the Holocaust, 1977; Four Hasidic Masters and Their Struggle against Melancholy, 1978; Le Proces de Shamgorod tel qu'il se deroula le 25 fevrier 1649: Piece en trois actes, 1979; Images from the Bible, 1980; Le Testament d'un poete Juif assassine, 1980; Five Biblical Portraits, 1981; Somewhere a Master, 1982 as Somewhere a Master: Further Tales of the Hasidic Masters, 1984; Paroles d'etranger, 1982; The Golem: The Story of a Legend As Told by Elie Wiesel (fiction), 1983; Le Cinquieme Fils, 1983; Against Silence: The Voice and Vision of Elie Wiesel, 3 vols., 1985; Signes d'exode, 1985; Job ou Dieu dans latempete, 1986; Le Crepuscule au loin, 1987; (with A.H. Friedlander) The Six Days of Destruction, 1989; L'Oublie: Roman, 1989; (with P. Saint-Cheron) Evil and Exile, 1990; From the Kingdom of Memory: Reminiscences, 1990; The Forgotten (novel), 1992; (with S. Malka) Monsieur Chouchani: L'Enigme d'un maitre du XX siecle: Entretiensavec Elie Wiesel, suivis d'une enquete, 1994; Tous les fleuves vont a lamer: Memoires, 1994 as All Rivers Run to the Sea: Memoirs, 1995; (with F. Mitterrand) Memoire a deux voix, 1995 as Memoir in Two Voices, 1996; Das Gegenteil von Gleichgueltigkeit ist Erinnerung: Versuche zu Elie Wiesel, 1995; Jorge Semprun, Semprun, Wiesel: Se taire est impossible, 1995; (intro.) Medical and Psychological Effects of Concentration Camps on Holocaust Survivors, 1997; Ethics and Memory, 1997; Celebration Prophetique: Portraits et Legendes, 1998; Celebrating Elie Wiesel: Stories, Essays, Reflections, 1998; King Solomon and His Magic Ring, 1999; Les Juges: Roman, 1999; Hope against Hope: Johann Baptist Metz and Elie Wiesel Speak Out on the Holocaust, 1999; And the Sea Is Never Full: Memoirs 1969-, 1999; (with R.D. Heffner) Conversations with Elie Wiesel, 2001; The Judges: A Novel, 2002; After the Darkness: Reflections on the Holocaust, 2002; (co-author) Po Obu Stronach Muru: Wspomnienia Z Warszawskiego Getta, 2003; Le Temps Des Déracinés: Roman, 2003; Wise Men and Their Tales: Portraits of Biblical, Talmudic, and Hasidic Masters, 2003; (with J. Russell and N.F. Weber) Marc Klionsky, 2004; Somewhere a Master: Hasidic Portraits and Legends, 2005; The Time of the Uprooted: A Novel, 2005; Un Désir Fou de Danser: Roman, 2006; The Night Trilogy: Night; Dawn; Day, 2008; Cas Sonderberg: Roman, 2008; Mad Desire to Dance: A Novel, 2009; Rashi, 2009; Sonderberg Case: A Novel, 2010; Otage: Roman, 2010; (trans.) Hostage, 2012. Contributor to periodicals. **Address:** Department of Religion, College of Arts & Sciences, Boston University, 147 Bay State Rd., Boston, MA 02215-1719, U.S.A.

WIESEN, S. Jonathan. American (born United States), b. 1968. **Genres:** History. **Career:** Colgate University, visiting assistant professor, 1997-98; Southern Illinois University, assistant professor, 1998-2003, associate professor of modern European history, 2003-. Writer. **Publications:** West German Industry and the Challenge of the Nazi Past, 1945-1955, 2001; (ed. with P.E. Swett and J.R. Zatlin) Selling Modernity: Advertising in Twentieth Century Germany, 2007; Creating the Nazi Marketplace: Commerce and Consumption in the Third Reich, 2010. Contributor to books. **Address:** Department of History, Southern Illinois University, Rm. 3374 Faner Hall, 1000 Faner Dr., PO Box4519, Carbondale, IL 62901-2594, U.S.A. **Online address:** jwiesen@siu.edu

WIESENFARTH, Joseph (John). American (born United States), b. 1933. **Genres:** Literary Criticism And History, Novels, Social Sciences. **Career:** St. Joseph's High School, teacher, 1956-58; De La Salle College, lecturer in English, 1958-62; La Salle College, assistant professor, 1962-64; Manhattan College, assistant professor, 1964-67, associate professor, 1967-70; University of Wisconsin, associate professor, 1970-76, professor of English, 1976, chairman, 1983-86, 1989-92, Hands-Bascom professor, 1992, Nathan S. Blount professor, 1994, professor emeritus, 2000-, Graduate School, associate dean, 1995-96, College of Letters and Science, associate dean, 1996-97, director of university reaccreditation project, 1997-2000. Writer. **Publications:** Henry James and the Dramatic Analogy, 1963; The Errand of Form, 1967; Plane Words: 3 Poems Written in the Jet Stream, 1975; George Eliot's Mythmaking, 1977; George Eliot: A Writer's Notebook and Uncollected Writings, 1854-1879, 1981; Gothic Manners and the Classic English Novel, 1988; Ford Madox Ford and the Arts, 1989; Jane Austen's Jack and Alice, 2001; Jane Austen's The Three Sisters, 2004; History and Representation in Ford Madox Ford's Writings, 2004; Ford Madox Ford and the Regiment of Women: Violet Hunt, Jean Rhys, Stella Bowen, Janice Biala, 2005; Ford Madox Ford's No More Parades, 2011. Contributor to periodicals. **Address:** Department of English, University of Wisconsin, 7187 Helen C. White Hall, 600 N Park St., Madison, WI 53706-1475, U.S.A. **Online address:** jjwiesen@wisc.edu

WIESENTHAL, Christine S. Canadian (born Canada), b. 1963. **Genres:** Young Adult Fiction. **Career:** University of Alberta, associate professor of English, 2000-. Writer. **Publications:** Figuring Madness in Nineteenth-Century Fiction, 1997; Instruments of Surrender, 2001; The Half-lives of Pat Lowther, 2005. Works appear in anthologies. Contributor to periodicals and journals. **Address:** University of Alberta, 4-9 Humanities Ctr., Edmonton, AB T6G 2E5, Canada. **Online address:** christine.wiesenthal@ualberta.ca

WIESEPAPE, Betty Holland. American (born United States), b. 1941. **Genres:** Young Adult Fiction, Literary Criticism And History, Romance/Historical. **Career:** Teacher of developmental reading, 1964-76; BEL Publishing, curriculum writer and teaching consultant, 1976-92; University of Texas, School of Arts and Humanities, lecturer, 1998-2001, senior lecturer in English and assistant director of creative writing, 2001-; North Lake Community College, lecturer, 2000-01. Writer. **Publications:** Lone Star Chapters: The Story of Texas Literary Clubs, 2004. Contributor of articles to periodicals. Works appear in anthologies. **Address:** School of Arts and Humanities, University of Texas, JO 5.205, 800 W Campbell Rd., PO Box JO 31, Richardson, TX 75080-3021, U.S.A. **Online address:** bet@utdallas.edu

WIESNER, Karen Sue. American (born United States), b. 1969. **Genres:** Novels, Mystery/Crime/Suspense. **Career:** Writer. **Publications:** AS KAREN WIESNER: Leather and Lace, 1999; Mistletoe Marriages, 1999; Fire and Ice vol. I, 1999, vol. III, 2002; Falling Star, 1999; Vows and the Vagabond, 2000; Sweet Dream, 2001; Leather and Lace/Flesh and Blood, 2001; Reluctant Hearts, 2002; Restless as Rain, 2002; First Love, vol. II, 2002; Sweet Dreams, 2003; Waiting for an Eclipse, 2003; (with C. Spindler) Degrees of Separation, 2004; (with C. Spindler) Tears on Stone, 2005; First Draft in 30 days, 2005; Mirror Mirror, 2005; No Ordinary Love, 2006; Until Death Do Us Part, 2006; Bounty on the Rebel's Heart, 2007; Under the Spell, 2007; Restless as Rain, 2007; The Bloodmoon Curse, 2007; Dead Drop, 2007; The Bloodman Curse, 2007; Renegade's Rose, 2008; Undercover Angel, 2008; Shadow Boxing, 2009; Baby, Baby, 2009; Foolish Games, 2010; Hard To Handle, 2011; Dance in Shadows, 2011; Shards of Ashley, 2011; Hypnotized, 2011; Souls On (B)oring Street, 2011; Mind Games, 2011; Dark Approach, 2011; Worlds Collide, 2012; Clumsy Girl's Guide to Falling in Love, 2012; Bewitched, 2012; Michael's Angel, 2013; The Deep, 2013; Drifter's Heart, 2013; (with L.N. Childers, R.R. Mallory and J. Toombs) Silver Bells, Wedding Bells, forthcoming. AS KAREN S. WIESNER: Electronic Publishing: The Definitive Guide, Petals of Life Publishing, 1999; Weave Your Web: The Promotional Companion to Electronic Publishing, the Definitive Guide, 2003; (with C. Splinder) Romantic Notions, 2008; From First Draft to Finished Novel, 2008; (with C. Splinder) Fifteenth Letter, 2008; (with C. Splinder) Falcon's Bend Case Files, vol. I, 2009; Glass Angels, 2011. AS KAREN SUE WIESNER: Taking Responsibility Builds Trust, 2003; (with L. Derkez) Cody Knows, 2003; (with L. Derkez) Cody Knows II, forthcoming; Taking Care of Your Things, forthcoming. OTHER: (as K.S. Wiesner) Soul Bleeds: The Dark Poetry and Other Wanderings of K.S. Wiesner, 2001. **Address:** c/o Author Mail, Hard Shell Word Factory, 8946 Loberg Rd., PO Box 161, Amherst Junction, WI 54407, U.S.A. **Online address:** kwiesner@cuttingedge.net

WIESNER-HANKS, Merry E. American (born United States), b. 1952. **Genres:** History, Women's Studies And Issues. **Career:** Augustana College, assistant professor of history, 1979-85; University of Wisconsin, assistant professor, 1985-87, director of undergraduate studies, 1986-90, associate professor, 1987-94, professor of history, 1994-, Center for Women's Studies, director, 1992-96, 2001-05, department chair, 1998-2001, Comparative Study of Religion Program, coordinator, 2001-04, Center for 21st Century Studies, interim director, 2006-07, distinguished professor, 2007-; Stanford University, visiting associate professor, 1988; Marquette University, women's chair in humanistic studies, 1996-97. Writer. **Publications:** Women in the Sixteenth Century: A Bibliography, 1983; Working Women in Renaissance Germany, 1986; (with J. Ruff and B. Wheeler) Discovering the Western Past: A Look at the Evidence, 1988, 6th ed., 2007; Women and Gender in Early Modern Europe, 1993, 3rd ed., 2007; Discovering the World's Past, 1996, 3rd ed., 2007; (ed. and trans. with J. Skocir) Convents Confront the Reformation: Catholic and Protestant Nuns in Germany, 1996; (co-author) Discovering the Global Past: A Look at the Evidence, vol. I: To 1600, 1997, vol. II: From 1500, 1997, rev. ed. as vol. I: To 1650, vol. II: since 1400, 2001; (ed.) Encyclopedia of the Reformation, 1996; Gender, Church and State in Early Modern Germany: Essays by Merry E. Wiesner, 1998; (ed. with R. Bridenthal and S.M. Stuard) Becoming Visible: Women in European History, 1998; Christianity and Sexuality in the Early Modern World: Regulating Desire, Reforming Practice, 2000; (co-author) Experiencing World History, 2000; (with L. Di Caprio) Lives and Voices: Sources on Women in European History, 2001; (as Merry E. Wiesner-Hanks) Gender in History, 2001; (ed. with M. Chojnacka) Ages of Woman, Ages of Man: Sources on European Social History, 1250-1750, 2002; (ed. And trans. With Susan C. Karant-Nunn) Luther on Women: A Sourcebook, 2003; (ed. with W.B. Wheeler and K.R. Curtis) Discovering the Medieval Past: A Look at the Evidence, 2003; (ed. And intro. With T.A. Meade) A Companion to Gender History, 2004; (co-author) Discovering the Ancient Past: A Look at the Evidence, 2004; Age of Voyages, 1350-1600, 2005; Early Modern Europe, 1450-1789, 2006; (ed. And intro.) Witchcraft in Early Modern Europe, 2007; Historical Comparisons, 2007; Marvelous Hairy Girls: The Gonzales Sisters and Their Worlds, 2009; The Renaissance and Reformation, forthcoming; Religious Transformations in the Early Modern World: A Brief Study with Documents, forthcoming. Contributor to books. **Address:** Department of History, University of Wisconsin, Rm. 347, Holton Hall, 2200 E Kenwood Blvd., PO Box 413, Milwaukee, WI 53201-0413, U.S.A. **Online address:** merrywh@uwm.edu

WIEST, Andrew A. (Andrew Allen Wiest). American (born United States), b. 1960. **Genres:** Novels. **Career:** University of Illinois, teaching assistant, 1984-86; University of Southern Mississippi, adjunct faculty member, 1988-89, visiting assistant professor, 1990-92, professor of record in the british studies program, 1992, 1993, 1996-, assistant professor, 1993-97, deputy director of british studies program, 1993-96, associate professor, 1997-2001; founder and director of the center for the study of war and society, 1998-2005,codirector, 2006-, director of vietnam studies program, 2000-, professor of record in vietnam studies program, 2000-01, professor of history 2002-, assistant director of british studies program, 2002-04, director of university honors forum, 2003-, director of graduate studies in the History department, 2004-05, Royal Military Academy, War Studies Department, visiting senior lecturer, 1996; United States Air Force Air War College, Department of Warfighting Strategy, visiting professor, 2005-06. Writer. **Publications:** (as Andrew A. Wiest) Passchendaele and the Royal Navy, 1995; (as Andy Wiest with C. McNab) The Illustrated History of the Vietnam War, 2000; (ed. and contrib. with G. Jensen) War in the Age of Technology: Myriad Faces of Modern Armed Conflict, 2001; (with G.L. Mattson) The Pacific War, 2001; (with G.L. Mattson) The Pacific War: From Pearl Harbor to Hiroshima, 2001; The Illustrated History of World War I, 2001; (with M.K. Barbier) Infantry Warfare: Strategy and Tactics, 2002; (as Andy Wiest) The Vietnam War, 1956-1975, 2003; (with D. Jordan) Atlas of World War II, 2004; (as Andrew A. Wiest) Haig: The Evolution of a Commander, 2005; (ed. and contrib.) Rolling Thunder in a Gentle Land: The Vietnam War Revisited, 2006; Vietnam's Forgotten Army: Heroism and Betrayal in the ARVN, 2008; The Vietnam War, 1956- 1975, 2009. Contributor to books. **Address:** Department of History, University of Southern Mississippi, 118 College Dr., Rm. 5407, Hattiesburg, MS 39406-0001, U.S.A. **Online address:** andrew.wiest@usm.edu

WIEST, Andrew Allen. See **WIEST, Andrew A.**

WIGGERS, Raymond. American (born United States), b. 1952. **Genres:** Earth Sciences, Horticulture, Geography, Sciences, Natural History, Botany. **Career:** Illinois Environmental Protection Agency, environmental protection geologist, 1979-80; horticulturist, 1980-92; host for public radio, 1988-90;

national park service ranger and environmental education specialist, 1992-93; Illinois State Museum, museum editor and curator of publications, 1993-, The Natural History Exploration Guild, founder. **Publications:** Picture Guide to Tree Leaves, 1991; The Amateur Geologist: Explorations and Investigations, 1993; The Plant Explorer's Guide to New England, 1994; Geology Underfoot in Illinois, 1997. **Address:** Natural History Exploration Guild, 9808 Michigan Blvd., Ste. 204, Beach Park, IL 60099, U.S.A. **Online address:** raywiggers@nheg.org

WIGGIN, Eric E(llsworth). American (born United States), b. 1939. **Genres:** Novels, Mystery/Crime/Suspense, Natural History, Human Relations/Parenting. **Career:** Palermo Baptist Churches, pastor, 1965-68; teacher, 1966-73; Faith Christian School, English teacher and librarian, 1973-74; Piedmont Bible College, instructor in English, 1974-78; Glen Cove Bible College, instructor in English, 1978-79; freelance reporter, 1979-84; full-time writer, 1979-. **Publications:** MAGGIE'S WORLD SERIES: Maggie: Life at the Elms, 1994; Maggie's Homecoming, 1994; Maggie's Secret Longing, 1994. HANNAH'S ISLAND SERIES: The Hills of God, 1993; A Hound for Hannah, 1995; The Mystery of the Sunken Steamboat, 1995; The Mysterious Stranger, 1995; The Lesson of the Ancient Bones, 1996; The Secret of the Old Well, 1997; The Texas Rodeo Showdown, 1999. OTHER: The Heart of a Grandparent: Investing Yourself in Your Grandchildren's Future, 1993; Blood Moon Rising (novel), 2000; The Gift of Grandparenting: Building Meaningful Relationships with Your Grandchildren, 2001; An Heir to Murder, 2003. **Address:** 3420 Cline Rd., Muskegon, MI 49444-8706, U.S.A.

WIGGINS, David. American/British (born England), b. 1933. **Genres:** Philosophy. **Career:** Colonial Office, assistant principal, 1957-58; Princeton University, Janie Eliza Proctor visiting fellow, 1958-59; New College, lecturer to fellow, 1959-67, emeritus fellow, 2000-; Bedford College, professor of philosophy, 1967-80; University College, professor in philosophy, 1981-90; Center for Advanced Study in Behavioral Sciences, fellow, 1985-86; Birkbeck College, professor of philosophy, 1990-94; Brasenose College, reader of philosophy; University of Oxford, Wykeham professor of logic, 1993-2000; Aristotelian Society, president, 1999-2000; Boston University, Findlay visiting professor, 2001. Writer. **Publications:** Identity and Spatio-Temporal Continuity, 1967; Truth, Invention and the Meaning of Life, 1977; Sameness and Substance, 1980; Needs, Values, Truth, 1987, 3rd ed., 1998; Essays for David Wiggins: Identity, Truth and Value, 1996; (ed.) Conditionals, 1997; Sameness and Substance Renewed, 2001; Ethics: Twelve Lectures on the Philosophy of Morality, 2006; Solidarity and the root of the ethical, 2008. Contributor to journals and periodicals. **Address:** New College, Holywell St., Oxford City Ctr., Oxford, OX OX1 3BN, England.

WIGGS, Susan. American (born United States) **Genres:** Novels. **Career:** Teacher, 1980-91; writer, 1983-. **Publications:** Texas Wildflower, 1987; Briar Rose 1988; Winds of Glory, 1988; Moonshadow, 1989; The Canary Who Sailed with Columbus (juvenile), 1989; The Lily and the Leopard, 1991; The Raven and the Rose, 1991; October Wind: A Novel of Christopher Columbus, 1991; The Mist and Magic, 1992; Jewel of the Sea, 1993; Kingdom of Gold, 1994; Circle in the Water, 1994 as At the King's Command, 2009; Vows Made in Wine, 1995, as The Maiden's Hand, 2009; Dancing on Air, 1996, as At the Queens Summons, 2009; The Lightkeeper, 1997; The Drifter, 1998; Briar Rose, 1998; The Charm School, 1999, rev. ed., 2008; Husband for Hire, 1999; The Horsemaster's Daughter, 1999, rev. ed., 2008; The Mistress, 2000, rev. ed., 2010; The You I Never Knew, 2000; The Hostage, 2000, rev. ed., 2010; The Firebrand, 2001, rev. ed., 2010; Halfway to Heaven, 2001; Passing through Paradise, 2002; The Lightkeeper, 2002; Enchanted Afternoon, 2002; Summer Affair, 2003; Home before Dark, 2003; The Ocean between Us, 2004; Summer by the Sea, 2004; Table for Five, 2005; Lakeside Cottage, 2005; Summer at Willow Lake, 2006; The Winter Lodge, 2007; Dockside, 2007; Snowfall at Willow Lake, 2008; Just Breathe, 2008; Lakeshore Christmas, 2009; Fireside, 2009; The Summer Hideaway, 2010; The Story of Us, 2010; How I Planned Your Wedding, 2010; The Borrowed Bride, 2010; The Goodbye Quilt, 2011; Marrying Daisy Bellamy, 2011. **Address:** Jane Rotrosen Agency, 318 E 51st St., New York, NY 10022, U.S.A. **Online address:** susanwiggs@pobox.com

WIGNALL, Kevin. (K. J. Wignall). British/Belgian (born Belgium) **Genres:** Novels, Criminology/True Crime, Horror, Mystery/Crime/Suspense. **Career:** Educator and writer. **Publications:** People Die, 2001; Among the Dead, 2002; For the Dogs, 2004; Who is Conrad Hirst?, 2007; (as K.J. Wignall) Blood, 2011. Contributors to periodicals. **Address:** c/o Curtis Brown, Curtis

Brown Group Ltd, Haymarket House, 28/29 Haymarket, London, GL SW1Y 4SP, England. **Online address:** kevin@kevinwignall.com

WIGNALL, K. J. *See* **WIGNALL, Kevin.**

WIJNBERG, Ellen. British/American (born United States), b. 1952?. **Genres:** Young Adult Non-fiction, Sociology, Medicine/Health. **Career:** Writer and television producer. **Publications:** Alcohol, 1994; Parental Unemployment, 1994. Contributor to periodicals. **Address:** 2 Melody Rd., Wandsworth, London, GL SW18 2QF, England.

WIKAN, Unni. Norwegian (born Norway), b. 1944. **Genres:** Anthropology/Ethnology. **Career:** University of Bergen, assistant professor, 1971-74; University of Oslo, assistant professor, 1974-80, professor of sociology, 1981-, Norwegian professor of social anthropology; Johns Hopkins University, visiting assistant professor, 1977; Ethnographic Museum, director, 1983-85; UNICEF, consultant, 1985, 1989-91; Ben-Gurion University, visiting professor, 1989; Beersheba University, visiting professor, 1989; World Food Program, consultant, 1993-94; École des Hautes Études en Sciences Sociales, visiting professor, 1996; London School of Economics, visiting professor, 1996; Johann Wolfgang Goethe University, visiting professor, 2000; Harvard University, visiting professor; Norwegian Agency for Development Cooperation, consultant. Writer. **Publications:** Fattigfolk i Cairo, Gyldendal, 1976; Life among the poor in Cairo, 1980; Behind the Veil in Arabia: Women in Oman, 1982; Imorgen, hvis God vid, 1983; Managing Turbulent Hearts: A Balinese Formula for Living, 1990; Mot en ny norsk underklasse: innvandrere, kultur og integrasjon, 1995; Tomorrow God Willing: Self-Made Destinies in Cairo, 1996; Generous Betrayal: Culture and Identity Politics in the New Europe, 2002; For Arens skyld: Fadime til ettertanke, 2003; Medmennesker: 35 aisr i Kairos bakgater, 2004; Omaere, 2008; In Honor of Fadime: Murder and Shame, 2008. **Address:** Department of Social Anthropology, University of Oslo, Eilert Sundt's House, 6th Fl., PO Box 1091, Oslo, 0317, Norway. **Online address:** unni.wikan@sai.uio.no

WIKTOROWICZ, Quintan. American (born United States), b. 1970. **Genres:** Theology/Religion, Social Sciences. **Career:** American Enterprise Institute for Public Policy Research, research assistant, 1991; Shippensburg University, assistant professor of political science, 1998-2000; Rhodes College, Department of International Studies, assistant professor, 2001-, professor, J.S. Seidman Research Fellow; Dartmouth College, visiting assistant professor of government, 2000-01; U.S. National Security Council, senior director. Writer. **Publications:** The Management of Islamic Activism: Salafis, the Muslim Brotherhood and State Power in Jordan, 2001; (ed. and contrib.) Islamic Activism: A Social Movement Theory, 2004; Radical Islam Rising: Muslim Extremism in the West, 2005. Contributor of articles to books and periodicals. **Address:** Department of International Studies, Rhodes College, 2000 N Pkwy., Memphis, TN 38112-1690, U.S.A. **Online address:** wiktorowiczq@rhodes.edu

WILBUR, Richard (Purdy). American (born United States), b. 1921. **Genres:** Poetry, Songs/Lyrics And Libretti, Literary Criticism And History, Translations, Humor/Satire, Education, Illustrations. **Career:** Harvard University, Society of Fellows, junior fellow, 1947-50, assistant professor of English, 1950-54; Wellesley College, associate professor of English, 1955-57; Wesleyan University, professor of English, 1957-77; Smith College, writer-in-residence, 1977-86; Library of Congress, consultant, 1987; Dell Publishing Co., general editor; Amherst College, faculty; Academy of American Poets, now chancellor emeritus. **Publications:** SELF-ILLUSTRATED: Opposites: Poems and Drawings, 1973; More Opposites, 1991; Opposites, More Opposites, and a Few Differences, 2000. OTHERS: The Beautiful Changes and Other Poems, 1947; Ceremony and Other Poems, 1950; (comp.) A Bestiary (anthology), 1955; Things of This World: Poems, 1956; (with L. Hellman) Candide (comic operetta), 1957; Poems 1943-1956, 1957; Anniversary Lectures, 1959; Poems, 1959; (with L. Bogan and A. MacLeish) Emily Dickinson: Three Views, 1960; Advice to a Prophet and Other Poems, 1961; The Poems of Richard Wilbur, 1963; The Pelican from a Bestiary of 1120, 1963; Prince Souvanna Phouma: An Exchange between Richard Wilbur and William Jay Smith, 1963; Loudmouse, 1963; Complaint, 1968; Walking to Sleep: New Poems and Translations, 1969; Digging to China, 1970; Seed Leaves: Homage to R. F., 1974; The Mind Reader (poems), 1976; Responses: Prose Pieces, 1953-1976, 1976; (with W.J. Smith) Verses on the Times, 1978; Seven Poems, 1981; Pedestrian Flight: Twenty-one Clerihews for the Telephone, 1981; A Finished Man, 1985; New and Collected Poems, 1988; Conversa-

tions with Richard Wilbur, 1990; (foreword) A Life in Photography, 1991; A Game of Catch, 1994; Runaway Opposites, 1995; L'invitation au voyage, or Invitation to the Voyage: A Poem from the Flowers of Evil, 1854, 1997; The Catbirds Song, 1997; The Disappearing Alphabet, 1998; (contrib.) A Stable-Lamp is Slighted: TTBB Chorus with Piano or Organ, 1999; (contrib.) A Stable-Lamp is Lighted: For Solo Voice with Piano or Organ, 1999; (contrib.) A Stable-Lamp is Lighted: SSAA Chorus with Piano or Organ, 1999; Mayflies: New Poems and Translations, 2000; The Pig in the Spigot, 2000; Writer, 2004; Collected Poems: 1943-2004, 2004; (contrib.) And Every Stone Shall Cry, 2005; Seven American Poets in Conversation: John Ashbery, Donald Hall, Anthony Hecht, Donald Justice, Charles Simic, W.D. Snodgrass, Richard Wilbur, 2008; Anterooms: New Poems and Translations, 2010. TRANSLATOR: J.B.P. de Molière, The Misanthrope: Comedy in Five Acts, 1666, 1955; J.B.P. de Molière, Tartuffe: Comedy in Five Acts, 1669, 1963; J.B.P. de Molière, The School for Wives, 1971; J.B.P. de Molière, The Learned Ladies, 1978; J. Racine, Andromache, 1982; J.B.P. de Molière, Four Comedies, 1982; The Whale, 1982; J. Racine, Phaedra, 1986; (and intro.) J.B.P. de Molière, The School for Husbands, 1992; J.B.P. de Molière, The Imaginary Cuckold, 1993; (and intro.) J.B.P. de Molière, School for Husbands and, Sganarelle, or, The Imaginary Cuckold, 1993; J.B.P. de Molière, Amphitryon, 1995; J.B.P. de Molière, Don Juan, 1998 as Don Juan: Comedy in Five Acts, 1665, 2001; J.B.P. de Molière, The Bungler, 2000; J. Racine, The Suitors, 2001; (and intro.) P. Corneille, Illusion Comique (title means: 'The Theatre of Illusion'), 2007; J.B.P. de Molière, Lovers' Quarrels, 2009; (and intro.) P. Corneille, Le Cid, 2009. EDITOR: (with L. Untermeyer and K. Shapiro) Modern American and Modern British Poetry, 1955; (and intro.) Complete Poems of Poe, 1959; (with A. Harbage) Poems, 1966, rev. ed. as The Narrative Poems, and Poems of Doubtful Authenticity, 1974; (intro.) The Narrative of Arthur Gordon Pym, 1974; (and intro.) Selected Poems, 1978; Poems and Poetics, 2003. Contributor to periodicals. **Address:** Academy of American Poets, 75 Maiden Ln., Ste. 901, New York, NY 10038, U.S.A.

WILBY, Basil Leslie. (Gareth Knight). British (born England), b. 1930?. **Genres:** Paranormal. **Career:** Free-lance writer, 1960-; Longman Group Ltd., educational representative, 1965-70, university sales manager, 1970-76, education publisher, 1976-91; consultant, 1991-; Helios Book Service Ltd., director, 1963-82; C.G. Jung Foundation, consultant; New Dimensions, editor. **Publications:** (Ed.) The New Dimensions Red Book, 1968; Meeting the Occult, 1973. AS GARETH KNIGHT: A Practical Guide to Qabalistic Symbolism, 1965; The Practice of Ritual Magic, 1969, 4th ed., 2003; Occult Exercises and Practices, 1969, 4th ed., 2003; Experience of the Inner Worlds, 1975; The Occult: An Introduction, 1975; A History of White Magic, 1978, rev. ed. as Magic and the Western Mind, 1991; The Secret Tradition in Arthurian Legend, 1983; The Rose Cross and the Goddess, 1985, rev. ed. as Evoking the Goddess, 1993; The Gareth Knight Tarot Deck, 1985; The Treasure House of Images, 1986, rev. ed. as Tarot and Magic, 1991; The Magical World of the Inklings: J.R.R. Tolkien, C.S. Lewis, Charles Williams, Owen Barfield, 1990, new ed., 2010; The Magical World of the Tarot, 1991; Dion Fortune's Magical Battle of Britain, 1993; Magical Images and the Magical Imagination, 1997, 2nd ed., 2003; (with D. Fortune) Introduction to Ritual Magic, 1997; (with D. Fortune) The Circuit of Force, 1998; (with D. Fortune) Principles of Hermetic Philosophy, 1999; (ed.) Spiritualism and Occultism, 2000; (ed. and author of intro.) Principles of Esoteric Healing, 2000; Dion Fortune and the Inner Light, 2000; (ed. and intro.) Pythoness: The Life and Work of Margaret Lumley Brown, 2000; Merlin and the Grail Tradition, 2000; Esoteric Training in Everyday Life, 2001; The Magical World of C.S. Lewis, 2001; The Magical World of J.R.R. Tolkien, 2001; The Magical World of Charles Williams, 2001; The Magical World of Owen Barfield, 2001; The Wells of Vision, 2002; Dion Fortune and the ThreeFold Way, 2002; The Abbey Papers, 2002; (with D. Fortune) Practical Occultism, 2002; Granny's Magic Cards, 2004; The Magical Fiction of Dion Fortune, 2003; (with D. Fortune and M.L. Brown) The Arthurian Formula, 2005; Dion Fortune and the Lost Secrets of the West, 2006; Magic and the Power of the Goddess: Initiation, Worship and Ritualin the Western Mystery Tradition, 3rd ed., 2008: The Faery Gates of Avalon, 2008; Melusine of Lusignan and the Cult of the Faery Woman, 2010; To the Heart of the Rainbow, 2010; Yours Very Truly Gareth Knight, 2010; (trans.) A. Lebey, The Romance of the Faery Melusine, 2011. **Address:** Society of Inner Light, 38 Steeles Rd., London, GL NW3 4RG, England. **Online address:** garethknight.basil@googlemail.com

WILCE, Ysabeau S. American (born United States) **Genres:** Young Adult Fiction. **Career:** Califa Society for Historiography and Graphic Maps, archivist. Historian and writer. **Publications:** Flora vs. the Butler of Crackpot

Hall, 2006; Flora Segunda: Being the Magickal Mishaps of a Girl of Spirit, Her Glass-Gazing Sidekick, Two Ominous Butlers (One Blue), a House with Eleven Thousand Rooms, and a Red Dog, 2006; Flora's Dare: How a Girl of Spirit Gambles All to Expand Her Vocabulary, Confront a Bouncing Boy Terror, and Try to Save Califa from a Shaky Doom (Despite Being Confined to Her Room), 2008. Contributor to periodicals. **Address:** Harcourt Children's Books, 222 Berkeley St., Boston, MA 02116, U.S.A. **Online address:** denizen@yswilce.com

WILCKEN, Lois. American (born United States), b. 1949. **Genres:** Music. **Career:** La Troupe Makandal Inc. (music and dance company), business manager, executive director, 1981-, musicologist; Hunter College, adjunct associate professor, 1989-98; City Lore, accounts manager, 1994-. Writer. **Publications:** The Drums of Vodou, 1992; (ed. with R. Allen) Island Sounds in the Global City: Caribbean Popular Music and Identity in New York, 1998. **Address:** City Lore, 72 E 1st St., New York, NY 10003-9322, U.S.A. **Online address:** makandal-ny@juno.com

WILCOX, James. American (born United States), b. 1949. **Genres:** Novels, Humor/Satire. **Career:** Random House, editorial assistant, 1971-72, assistant editor, 1973-76, associate editor, 1976-77; Doubleday, associate editor, 1977-78; Louisiana State University, Department of English, professor, MacCurdy professor; writer, 1978-. **Publications:** NOVELS: Modern Baptists, 1983; North Gladiola, 1985; Miss Undine's Living Room. 1987; Sort of Rich, 1989; Polite Sex, 1991; Guest of a Sinner, 1993; Plain and Normal, 1998; North Gladiola, 2000; Heavenly Days, 2003; Hunk City, 2007. **Address:** Department of English, University of Louisiana, 211-A Allen Hall, Baton Rouge, LA 70803, U.S.A. **Online address:** jwilcox1@lsu.edu

WILCOX, Laird (M.). American (born United States), b. 1942. **Genres:** Politics/Government, Bibliography, Novels, Social Sciences. **Career:** University of Kansas, Wilcox Collection on Contemporary Political Movements, founder, 1965; Editorial Research Service, writer, editor and owner. Investigator. **Publications:** (Ed.) Guide to the American Right: Directory and Bibliography, 1978; (ed.) Guide to the American Left: Directory and Bibliography, 1984; Directory of the American Left, 1984; Spectrum, 1985; (contrib.) Guide to the American Occult, 1986; Terrorism, Assassination, Espionage, and Propaganda: A Master Bibliography, 1989; (with J. George) Nazis, Communists, Klansmen, and Others on the Fringe: Political Extremism in America, 1992; (ed. with J. George) Be Reasonable: Selected Quotations for Inquiring Minds, 1994; Crying Wolf: Hate Crime Hoaxes in America, 1995; American Extremists: Militias, Supremacists, Klansmen, Communists and Others, 1996; The Watchdogs: Anti-Racist Watchdog Groups, 1998. **Address:** Editorial Research Service, PO Box 2047, Olathe, KS 66061, U.S.A. **Online address:** lwilcox3@aol.com

WILCOX, Paula. British (born England), b. 1951. **Genres:** Social Sciences, Sociology. **Career:** University of Sheffield, Centre for Criminological and Legal Research, research associate, 1990; University of Bradford, Violence, Abuse and Gender Relations Research Unit, researcher; University of Brighton, senior lecturer, School of Applied Social Science, principal lecturer. Sociologist and writer. **Publications:** Surviving Domestic Violence: Gender, Poverty and Agency, 2006. Contributor to books and periodicals. **Address:** School of Applied Social Science, University of Brighton, Falmer, Lewes Rd., Brighton, ES BN2 4AT, England. **Online address:** p.s.wilcox@brighton.ac.uk

WILCOX, Sherman. American (born United States) **Genres:** Psychology. **Career:** U.S. Air Force, staff, 1969-73; Saint Margaret's Center for Children, assistant director & teacher, 1977-78; New Mexico Division of Vocational Rehabilitation, state co-ordinator of services for the deaf, 1978-82; Sperry Flight Systems, technical editor, 1982- 83; University of New Mexico, part-time instructor of American Deaf Culture, 1982-87, linguistics teaching assistant, 1985-86, part-time instructor, 1986, linguistics teaching associate, 1987, assistant professor, 1988-95, associate professor of linguistics, 1995-, chair of the department of linguistics, 2002-; Albuquerque Public Schools, teacher of the hearing impaired, 1983-85. Writer and consultant. **Publications:** (ed.) American Deaf Culture: An Anthology, 1989; (ed.) Academic Acceptance of American Sign Language, 1992; The Phonetics of Fingerspelling, 1992; (with D.F. Armstrong and W.F. Stokoe) Gesture and the Nature of Language, 1995; (with P.P. Wilcox) Learning to See: Teaching American Sign Language as a Second Language, 2nd ed., 1997; (ed., with M. Hiraga and C. Sinha) Cultural, Psychological and Typological Issues in Cognitive Linguistics: Selected Papers of the Bi-annual ICLA Meeting in Albuquerque, July 1995, 1999; (with

D.F. Armstrong) The Gestural Origin of Language, 2007. Contributor to periodicals and academic journals. **Address:** Department of Linguistics, University of New Mexico, Albuquerque, NM 87131, U.S.A. **Online address:** wilcox@unm.edu

WILCOX, Stephen F. American (born United States), b. 1951. **Genres:** Mystery/Crime/Suspense, Novels, Novellas/Short Stories, Young Adult Fiction. **Career:** Rochester Democrat and Chronicle, reporter, 1977-81; freelance writer, 1981-. **Publications:** The Dry White Tear, 1989; The St. Lawrence Run, 1990; The Twenty Acre Plot, 1991; All the Dead Heroes: A T.S.W. Sheridan Mystery, 1992; The Nimby Factor, 1992; The Painted Lady, 1994; The Green Mosaic, 1994; The Hard Time Cafe, 1998; Purgatory Prayers, 1998; The Hidden Men, 1999; The Jericho Flower: A Hackshaw Mystery, 2001; Niagara Fall: A Novel of Crime and Comedy, 2001. **Address:** 25 Hulburt Ave., Fairport, NY 14450, U.S.A.

WILCOX, (William) Clyde. American (born United States), b. 1953. **Genres:** Politics/Government, Business/Trade/Industry. **Career:** Federal Election Commission, statistician, 1984-86; Union College, visiting assistant professor, 1986-87; Georgetown University, assistant professor, 1987-91, associate professor, 1991-95, professor, 1996-. Writer and consultant. **Publications:** God's Warriors: The Christian Right in Twentieth Century America, 1992; (with T.G. Jelen and E.A. Cook) Between Two Absolutes: Public Opinion and the Politics of Abortion, 1992; (with S.J. Wayne) The Quest for National Office, 1992; The Latest American Revolution?: The 1994 Elections and Their Implications for Governance (monograph), 1995; (with T.G. Jelen) Public Attitudes toward Church and State, 1995; (with C.W. Brown Jr. and L.W. Powell) Serious Money: Fundraising and Contributing in Presidential Nomination Campaigns, 1995; (with T.G. Jelen) Public Attitudes on Church and State, 1995; (with M.J. Rozell) Second Coming: The New Christian Right in Virginia Politics, 1996; Onward Christian Soldiers?: The Religious Right in American Politics, 1996, (with C. Robinson) 4th ed., 2011; (with M.J. Rozell) Interest Groups in American Campaigns: The New Face of Electioneering, 1999, (with M.M. Franz and M.J. Rozell) 3rd ed., 2012; Public Opinion, 1999; (with S.J. Wayne) The Election of the Century and What It Tells Us about the Future of American Politics, 2002; (with J.C. Green and M.J. Rozell) The Christian Right in American Politics: Marching to the Millennium, 2003; (with J.M. Berry) The Interest Group Society, 5th ed., 2009. EDITOR AND CONTRIBUTOR: (with S.J. Wayne) The Quest for Office: National Electoral Politics, 1992; (with E.A. Cook and S. Thomas) The Year of the Woman: Myths and Realities, 1994; (with P. Herrnson and R. Biersack) Risky Business?: PAC Decisionmaking in Congressional Elections, 1994; (with M.J. Rozell) God at the Grass Roots: The Christian Right in the 1994 Elections, 1995; (with B. Norrander) Understanding Public Opinion, 1995, 3rd ed., 2010; (with S. Thomas) Women in Elected Office: Past, Present and Future, 1996; (with D.M. Hassler) Political Science Fiction, 1997; (with P.S. Herrnson and R.G. Shaiko) The Interest Group Connection: Electioneering, Lobbying and Policymaking in Washington, 1998; (with J.M. Bruce) The Changing Politics of Gun Control, 1998. EDITOR: (with M.J. Rozell) God at the Grass Roots, 1996: The Christian Right in the American Elections, 1997; (with S. Thomas) Women and Elective Office: Past, Present and Future, 1998, 2nd ed., 2005; (with R. Biersack and P.S. Herrnson) After the Revolution: PACs, Lobbies and the Republican Congress, 1999; (with C.A. Rimmerman and K.D. Wald) The Politics of Gay Rights, 2000; (with J.C. Green and M.J. Rozell) Prayers in the Precincts: The Christian Right in the 1998 Elections, 2000; (with M.J. Rozell) The Clinton Scandal and the Future of American Government, 2000; (with T.G. Jelen) Religion and Politics in Comparative Perspective: The One, the Few and the Many, 2002; (with H.F. Weisberg) Models of Voting in Presidential Elections: The 2000 U.S. Election, 2004; (with P.C. Manuel and L.C. Reardon) The Catholic Church and the Nation-State: Comparative Perspectives, 2006; (with J.C. Green and M.J. Rozell) The Values Campaign?: The Christian Right and the 2004 Elections, 2006; (with C.A. Rimmerman) The Politics of Same-Sex Marriage, 2007; New Boundaries in Political Science Fiction, 2008; (with C. Wilcox) Faith, Politics, and Sexual Diversity in Canada and the United States, 2011. Contributor to books and newspapers. **Address:** Department of Government, Georgetown University, ICC 679, PO Box 571034, Washington, DC 20057-1034, U.S.A. **Online address:** wilcoxc@georgetown.edu

WILCZEK, Frank. American (born United States), b. 1951. **Genres:** Young Adult Non-fiction. **Career:** University of California, professor of physics, 1981-88; Princeton University, instructor, professor of physics, 1974-81, 1989-2000; Massachusetts Institute of Technology, professor of physics,

2000-, Herman Feshbach professor of physics. Writer. **Publications:** NON-FICTION: (with B. Devine) Longing for the Harmonies: Themes and Variations from Modern Physics, 1988; (ed. with A. Shapere) Geometric Phases in Physics, 1989; Fractional Statistics and Anyon Superconductivity, 1990; (with B. Devine) Fantastic Realities: 49 Mind Journeys and a Trip to Stockholm, 2006; The Lightness of Being: Mass, Ether and the Unification of Forces, 2008. **Address:** MIT Center for Theoretical Physics, Department of Physics, Massachusetts Institute of Technology, 6-301 Bldg., 77 Massachusetts Ave., Cambridge, MA 02139, U.S.A. **Online address:** wilczek@mit.edu

WILD, Henry Mark. *See* **WILD, Mark.**

WILD, Kate. British (born England), b. 1954?. **Genres:** Novels. **Career:** Author and filmmaker. **Publications:** Fight Game (novel), 2007. **Address:** c/o Darley Anderson, Darley Anderson Literary, TV & Film Agency, Estelle House, 11 Eustace Rd., London, SW6 1JB, England. **Online address:** kate@katewild.co.uk

WILD, Mark. (Henry Mark Wild). American (born United States), b. 1970. **Genres:** History. **Career:** California State University, College of Natural and Social Sciences, associate professor of history. Writer and historian. **Publications:** Street Meeting: Multiethnic Neighborhoods in Early Twentieth-Century Los Angeles, 2005. **Address:** College of Natural and Social Sciences, California State University, King Hall A4025, 5151 State University Dr., Los Angeles, CA 90032-4226, U.S.A. **Online address:** mwild@calstatela.edu

WILDE, Kelley (Cotter). American (born United States), b. 1947?. **Genres:** Novels, Poetry, Young Adult Fiction, Horror. **Career:** Toronto Star, freelance writer. Novelist. **Publications:** The Suiting, 1988; Makoto, 1990; Mastery, 1991; Angel Kiss, 1993. Contributor to periodicals. **Address:** Dell Publishing, 1540 Broadway, New York, NY 10036, U.S.A.

WILDE, Lyn Webster. British (born England) **Genres:** Women's Studies And Issues, Young Adult Non-fiction, Young Adult Fiction, Literary Criticism And History. **Career:** University of Worcester, fellow, 2005-08. Writer. **Publications:** Working with Your Dreams: Linking the Conscious and Unconscious in Self-Discovery, 1995; Celtic Women: In Legend, Myth and History, 1997; On the Trail of the Women Warriors: The Amazons in Myth and History, 2000; Becoming the Enchanter: A Journey into the Heart of the Celtic Mysteries, 2002; Celtic Inspirations: Essential Meditations and Texts, 2010. **Address:** Isle of Avalon Foundation, 2-4 High St., Glastonbury, SM BA6 9DU, England. **Online address:** lynww@talktalk.net

WILDENTHAL, Bryan H. American (born United States), b. 1964?. **Genres:** Law. **Career:** U.S. Court of Appeals, 11th Circuit, law clerk, 1989-90; Michigan Supreme Court, law clerk, 1990-92; Wilmer, Cutler & Pickering, attorney, 1992-94; Chicago-Kent College of Law, visiting professor, 1994-96; Thomas Jefferson School of Law, professor, 1996-. Writer. **Publications:** Native American Sovereignty on Trial: A Handbook with Cases, Laws, and Documents, 2003. **Address:** Thomas Jefferson School of Law, 1155 Island Ave., San Diego, CA 92101, U.S.A. **Online address:** bryanw@tjsl.edu

WILDER, Gene. (Jerome Silberman). American (born United States), b. 1935. **Genres:** Plays/Screenplays, Humor/Satire, Autobiography/Memoirs, Young Adult Fiction. **Career:** Writer, actor, director and producer. **Publications:** Millionairess, 1963; Silver Streak, 1976; (with M.S. Piver) Gilda's Disease: Sharing Personal Experiences and a Medical Perspective on Ovarian Cancer, 1996; Kiss Me Like a Stranger: My Search For Love and Art, 2005; My French Whore, 2007; The Woman Who Wouldn't, 2008; What is the Thing Called Love?, 2010. **Address:** c/o Ames Cushing, William Morris Agency, 1 William Morris Pl., Beverly Hills, CA 90212, U.S.A. **Online address:** info@genewilder.net

WILDERSON, Frank B. American (born United States), b. 1956?. **Genres:** Autobiography/Memoirs, Film, Race Relations. **Career:** University of California, professor of African American studies. Writer. **Publications:** Incognegro: A Memoir of Exile and Apartheid, 2008; Red, White & Black: Cinema and the Structure of U.S. Antagonisms, 2010. **Address:** University of California, Irvine, Irvine, CA 92697, U.S.A. **Online address:** fwilders@uci.edu

WILDGEN, Michelle. American (born United States), b. 1974?. **Genres:** Novels, Food And Wine, Writing/Journalism. **Career:** Tin House Magazine, executive editor. **Publications:** You're Not You (novel), 2006; Food

& Booze: A Tin House Literary Feast (anthology), 2007; But Not For Long, (novel), 2009. Contributor to journals and periodicals. **Address:** c/o Emilie Stewart, Emilie Stewart Literary Agency, 241 E Broadway, Ste. B, New York, NY 10002, U.S.A. **Online address:** michelle@michellewildgen.com

WILDING, Michael. British/Australian (born Australia), b. 1942. **Genres:** Novels, Novellas/Short Stories, Literary Criticism And History, Adult Non-fiction, Young Adult Fiction, Young Adult Non-fiction. **Career:** Primary school teacher, 1960; University of Sydney, lecturer in English, 1962-66, senior lecturer, 1969-72, reader, 1973-92, professor of English and Australian literature, 1993-2000, professor emeritus, 2001-; University of Birmingham, assistant lecturer, 1967, lecturer in English, 1968; Wild & Woolley Ltd. (publisher), director, 1974-79; Paper Bark Press, co-editor, 1987-97; University of California, visiting professor, 1987; University of Queensland, George Watson visiting fellow, 1990; James Cook University, Colin Roderick lecturer, 1992; New South Wales State Literary Awards Judging Panel, chair, 1994; National University of Singapore, Center for the Arts, visiting professor, 1996; New South Wales Writers Center, chairman, 1997-2002. Writer. **Publications:** Milton's Paradise Lost, 1969; (with M. Green and R. Hoggart) Cultural Policy in Great Britain, 1970; Aspects of the Dying Process: Short Stories, 1972; Living Together, 1974; The Short Story Embassy: A Novel, 1975; The West Midland Underground: Stories, 1975; Scenic Drive, 1976; Marcus Clarke, 1977; The Phallic Forest, 1978; Political Fictions, 1980; Pacific Highway, 1981; Reading the Signs, 1984; The Paraguayan Experiment, 1985; The Man of Slow Feeling: Selected Short Stories, 1986; Dragons Teeth: Literature in the English Revolution, 1987; Under Saturn: Four Stories, 1988; Great Climate, 1990; Her Most Bizarre Sexual Experience, 1991; Social Visions, 1993; The Radical Tradition: Lawson, Furphy, Stead, 1993; This Is for You, 1994; Book of the Reading, 1994; Somewhere New: New and Selected Stories, 1996; Studies in Classic Australian Fiction, 1997; Wildest Dreams, 1998; Raising Spirits, Making Gold and Swapping Wives, the True Adventures of Dr John Dee and Sir Edward Kelly, 1999; Among Leavisites, 1999; Academia Nuts, 2002; Wild Amazement, 2006; National Treasure, 2007; Superfluous Men, 2009; The Prisoner of Mount Warning, 2010; The Magic of It, 2011. EDITOR: (with C. Higham) Australians Abroad, 1967; Three Tales by Henry James, 1967; Marvell: Modern Judgments, 1969; The Tragedy of Julius Caesar and Marcus Brutus, 1970; (with S. Cass, R. Cheney and D. Malouf) We Took Their Orders and Are Dead: An Anti-War Anthology, 1971; The Portable Marcus Clarke, 1976, 2nd ed., 1988; (with S. Knight) The Radical Reader, 1977; The Tabloid Story Pocket Book, 1978; The Workingman's Paradise by William Lane, 1980; Stories by Marcus Clarke, 1983; (with R. Krausmann) Airmail from Down Under, 1990; The Oxford Book of Australian Short Stories, 1994; (with M. Lee) History, Literature and Society: Essays in Honour of S.N. Mukherjee, 1997; (with D. Myers) Best Stories Under the Sun 1-3, 2004, rev. ed., 2006; (with D. Brooks) Running Wild: Essays, Fictions and Memoirs Presented to Michael Wilding, 2004; (with D. Myers) Confessions & Memoirs, 2006; (with L. Hergenhan and K. Stewart) Cyril Hopkins' Marcus Clarke, 2009; (with P. Corris) Heart Matters, 2010. **Address:** School of Letters, Art & Media, University of Sydney, Sydney, NW 2006, Australia. **Online address:** mwilding@austarnet.com.au

WILDMAN, Steven S. American (born United States), b. 1948. **Genres:** Film, International Relations/Current Affairs, Economics, Technology, Business/Trade/Industry, Adult Non-fiction. **Career:** University of California, Department of Economics, assistant professor of economics, 1979-83; Rand Corp., consultant, 1981-83; Economists Inc., senior economist, 1983-88; Northwestern University, Department of Communication Studies, associate professor of communication studies, 1988-99, Ameritech research professor, 1989-90, Program in Telecommunications Science, Management and Policy, director, 1990-99, Van Zelst research professor of communication, 1996-97; Michigan State University, Quello Center for Telecommunication Management and Law, co-director, Department of Telecommunication, Information Studies and Media, James H. Quello professor of telecommunication studies; Lecg L.L.C., director. Writer. **Publications:** (With S.E. Siwek) International Trade in Films and Television Programs, 1988; (ed. with M.E. Guerin-Calvert) Electronic Services Networks: A Business and Public Policy Challenge, 1991; (with B.M. Owen) Video Economics, 1992; (ed. with B.A. Cherry and A.S. Hammond, IV) Making Universal Service Policy: Enhancing the Process Through Multidisciplinary Evaluation, 1999; (ed. with L.F. Cranor) Rethinking Rights and Regulations: Institutional Responses to New Communication Technologies, 2003. Contributor of articles to journals. Works appear in anthologies. **Address:** Department of Telecommunication, Information, Studies and Media, Michigan State University, 406 Communication Arts & Sciences Bldg., East Lansing, MI 48824-1212, U.S.A. **Online address:** swildman@msu.edu

WILDWIND, Sharon Grant. Canadian/American (born United States) **Genres:** Novels, Mystery/Crime/Suspense, Adult Non-fiction, Young Adult Fiction, Autobiography/Memoirs. **Career:** Writer. **Publications:** ELIZABETH PEPPERHAWK/AVIVAH ROSEN MYSTERY SERIES: Some Welcome Home, 2005; First Murder in Advent, 2006; Missing, Presumed Wed, 2009; OTHERS: Dreams That Blister Sleep: A Nurse in Vietnam (memoir), 1999; Soldier on the Porch, 2007. **Address:** Five Star Publishing, 1517 3rd Ave. NW, Fort Dodge, IA 50501, U.S.A. **Online address:** cml@wildwindauthor.com

WILE, Mary Lee. American (born United States), b. 1947. **Genres:** Novels, inspirational/Motivational Literature, Biography, Theology/Religion, Young Adult Fiction, Mystery/Crime/Suspense. **Career:** Colorado State University, instructor in English, 1976, 1981-82; Fort Collins High School, history teacher, 1984-86; Mount Ararat High School, English teacher, 1986-2009; Episcopal Diocese of Maine, Deacon Formation, program coordinator, 2001-. Writer. **Publications:** Ancient Rage (novel), 1995; I Will, with God's Help: Episcopal Confirmation for Youth and Adults, 2000; Christ's Own Forever: Episcopal Baptism of Infants and Young Children: Leader's Guide, 2002. Contributor to periodicals. **Address:** c/o Regula Noetzli, Charlotte Sheedy Literary Agency, 65 Bleeck er St., New York, NY 10012-2420, U.S.A. **Online address:** wilem@remove_melink75.org

WILENSKY, Amy S. American (born United States), b. 1969. **Genres:** Autobiography/Memoirs, Young Adult Non-fiction. **Career:** Freelance writer. **Publications:** Passing for Normal: A Memoir of Compulsion, 1999; Dandelion: Celebrating the Magical Blossom, 2000; The Weight of It: A Story of Two Sisters (memoir), 2004; Knack Healthy Snacks for Kids: Recipes for Nutritious Bites at Home or On the Go, 2010. **Address:** c/o Amanda Urban, International Creative Management, 730 5th Ave., New York, NY 10019, U.S.A.

WILENTZ, Amy. American (born United States), b. 1954. **Genres:** Area Studies, History, Sociology, Social Sciences. **Career:** Time, staff writer, 1980-89; New Yorker, Jerusalem correspondent, 1995-97; The Nation, contributing editor and columnist, 1998-; Columbia Journalism School, faculty 2000-03; University of California, Irvine, Literary Journalism Program, professor, 2005-. **Publications:** The Rainy Season: Haiti since Duvalier, 1989; (with M.J. Camejo) Harvesting Oppression: Forced Haitian Labor in the Dominican Sugar Industry, 1990; (trans. and ed.) In the Parish of the Poor: Writings from Haiti, 1990; (with A. Fuller) Return to the Darkest Days: Human Rights in Haiti since the Coup, 1991; Martyrs' Crossing: A Novel, 2001; I Feel Earthquakes More Often than They Happen: Coming to California in the Age of Schwarzenegger, 2006. Contributor to newspapers. **Address:** Simon & Schuster Publishing, 1230 Ave. of the Americas, New York, NY 10020, U.S.A. **Online address:** amy@amywilentz.com

WILENTZ, Sean. American (born United States), b. 1951. **Genres:** History, Essays, Biography, Music. **Career:** Princeton University, Department of History, assistant professor, 1979-85, associate professor, 1985-87, professor, 1987-98, Dayton-Stockton professor of history, 1998-2005, Sidney and Ruth Lapidus professor of the American Revolutionary era, 2007-10, Program in American Studies, director, 1995-2006, George Henry Davis 1886 professor of American history, 2005-06, 2011-. Writer. **Publications:** Chants Democratic: New York and the Rise of the American Working Class, 1788-1850, 1984; (ed.) Rites of Power: Symbolism, Ritual, and Politics since the Middle Ages, 1985; (ed.) Major Problems in the Early Republic, 1787-1848: Documents and Essays, 1992, (with J. Earle) 2nd ed., 2008; (with M. Merrill) The Key of Liberty: The Life and Democratic Writings of William Manning, A Laborer, 1747-1814, 1993; (with P.E. Johnson) The Kingdom of Matthias: A Story of Sex and Salvation in 19th Century America, 1994; (ed.) David Walker's Appeal to the Coloured Citizens of the Word, 1996; (ed. with G. Marcus) The Rose & the Briar: Death, Love, and Liberty in the American Ballad, 2004; The Rise of American Democrac y: Jefferson to Lincoln, 2005; Andrew Jackson, 2005; Best American History Essays on Lincoln, 2009; Bob Dylan in America, 2010. **Address:** Department of History, Princeton University, 129 Dickinson Hall, Princeton, NJ 08544-1017, U.S.A. **Online address:** swilentz@princeton.edu

WILES, Deborah. American (born United States), b. 1953. **Genres:** Children's Non-fiction, Picture/Board Books, Novels. **Career:** Towson University, instructor in writing and oral-history gatherer; Lesley University, instructor in writing and oral-history gatherer; Vermont College, instructor in writing and oral-history gatherer. Journalist. **Publications:** Love, Ruby Lavender, 2001; Freedom Summer, 2001; One Wide Sky: A Bedtime Lullaby, 2003; Each Little Bird That Sings, 2005; Hang the Moon, 2006; Moves the Symphony True, 2007; The Aurora County All-Stars, 2007; Countdown, 2010; End of the Rope, forthcoming. **Address:** c/o Steven Malk, Writers House Inc., 21 W 26th St., New York, NY 10010-1083, U.S.A. **Online address:** deborah@deborahwiles.com

WILEY, Kim Wright. American (born United States), b. 1955?. **Genres:** Novels, Young Adult Non-fiction. **Career:** Charlotte Taste, food and wine editor. **Publications:** Love in Mid Air (novel), 2010. NONFICTION: Walt Disney World with Kids, 1990; Disneyland and Southern California with Kids, 1992; (with N.L. Teaff) Perimenopause: Preparing for the Change: A Guide to the Early Stages of Menopause and Beyond, 1995, rev. ed., 1999; (with L.C. Wiley) Walt Disney World 4 Teens by Teens, 2000; Walt Disney World & Universal Orlando with Kids, 2005. Contributor of articles to periodicals. **Address:** Charlotte, NC , U.S.A. **Online address:** kwwiley@aol.com

WILEY, Michael. American (born United States), b. 1961. **Genres:** Geography, Romance/Historical, Mystery/Crime/Suspense. **Career:** University of North Florida, College of Arts and Sciences, Department of English, associate professor, professor. Writer. **Publications:** Romantic Geography: Wordsworth and Anglo-European Spaces, 1998; The Last Striptease (novel), 2007; Romantic Migrations: Local, National and Transnational Dispositions, 2008; Bad Kitty Lounge, 2010; Bad Night's Sleep, 2011. **Address:** Department of English, University of North Florida, Rm. 2641, Arts & Sciences Bldg., 1 University of North Florida Dr., Jacksonville, FL 32224, U.S.A. **Online address:** mwiley@unf.edu

WILEY, Peter (Booth). American (born United States), b. 1942. **Genres:** Adult Non-fiction, Writing/Journalism, History, Travel/Exploration. **Career:** Leviathan, founder and editor, 1968-71; Bulkhead, reporter, 1970-72; Pacific News Service, staff reporter and associate editor, 1975-79; Points West, syndicated columnist, 1981-87; John Wiley & Sons, board director, 1984, chair, 2002. **Publications:** (With R. Gottlieb) Empires in the Sun: The Rise of the New American West, 1982; (with R. Gottlieb) America's Saints: The Rise of Mormon Power, 1984; (with K. Ichiro) Yankees in the Land of the Gods: Commodore Perry and the Opening of Japan, 1990; A Free Library in this City: The Illustrated History of the San Francisco Public Library, 1996; National Trust Guide, San Francisco: America's Guide for Architecture and History Travelers, 2000. **Address:** John Wiley & Sons Inc., 111 River St., Hoboken, NJ 07030-5774, U.S.A. **Online address:** pwiley@wiley.com

WILEY, Tatha. American (born United States) **Genres:** Theology/Religion. **Career:** United Theological Seminary of the Twin Cities, staff; University of St. Thomas, College of Arts and Sciences, Department of Theology, professor; St. Catherine University, professor; Metropolitan State University, professor. Writer. **Publications:** Original Sin: Origins, Developments, Contemporary Meanings, 2002; (ed.) Thinking of Christ: Proclamation, Explanation, Meaning, 2003; Paul and the Gentile Women: Reframing Galatians, 2005; Creationism and the Conflict over Evolution, 2009; Encountering Paul: Understanding the Man and His Message, 2010. **Address:** Department of Theology, University of St. Thomas, JRC 153, 2115 Summit Ave., St. Paul, MN 55105, U.S.A. **Online address:** twiley@stthomas.edu

WILFORD, Hugh. British (born England), b. 1965. **Genres:** Documentaries/Reportage. **Career:** University of Keele, lecturer in American studies, 1991; Victoria University of Manchester, lecturer in American studies, 1991-92; Middlesex University, lecturer in American studies, 1992-; University of Sheffield, lecturer in history, 1998-2006; California State University, associate professor of history. Writer. **Publications:** The New York Intellectuals: From Vanguard to Institution, 1995; CIA, the British Left, and the Cold War: Calling the Tune?, 2003; (ed. with H. Laville) U.S. Government, Citizen Groups, and the Cold War: The State-private Network, 2005; Mighty Wurlitzer: How the CIA Played America, 2008. Contributor to books and periodicals. **Address:** Department of History, The University of Sheffield, Rm. 3 Clarkehouse Rd., 1 Upper Hanover St., Sheffield, S3 7RA, England. **Online address:** h.wilford@sheffield.ac.uk

WILFORD, John Noble. American (born United States), b. 1933. **Genres:** Air/Space Topics, Archaeology/Antiquities, Astronomy, Sciences, History. **Career:** Wall Street Journal, reporter, 1956-57, 1959-61; Time, contributing editor, 1962-65; New York Times, science reporter, 1965-73, assistant national news editor, 1973-75, director of science news, 1975-79, science correspondent, 1979-, senior science correspondent, now retired; Corpcom Services Inc., director, 1962-88; Duke University, visiting journalist, 1984; Princeton University, McGraw distinguished professor in writing, 1985; University of Tennessee, chair of excellence in science journalism, 1989-90. **Publications:** We Reach the Moon, 1969, rev. ed., 1971; (with W. Stockton) Spaceliner: The New York Times Report on the Columbia's Voyage into Tomorrow, 1981; The Mapmakers: The Story of the Great Pioneers of Cartography from Antiquity to the Space Age, 1982, rev. ed., 2000; The Riddle of the Dinosaur, 1985; (co-author) The New York Times Guide to the Return of Halley's Comet, 1985; Mars Beckons: The Mysteries the Challenges, the Expectations of Our Next Great Adventure in Space, 1990; The Mysterious History of Columbus: An Exploration of the Man, the Myth, the Legacy, 1991. EDITOR: Scientists at Work, 1979; Cosmic Dispatches: The New York Times Reports on Astronomy and Cosmology, 2001, new ed., 2002. **Address:** 232 W 10th St., New York, NY 10014, U.S.A.

WILHELM, Doug. American (born United States), b. 1952?. **Genres:** Novels, Young Adult Non-fiction. **Career:** Bernardsville News, journalist, 1976-78; Randolph Reporter, founding editor, 1978-80; English teacher and freelance writer, 1981-82; freelance writer, 1985-; Boston Globe, correspondent, 1985-90. **Publications:** YOUNG-ADULT NONFICTION: Alexander the Great: Master of the Ancient World, 2010. YOUNG-ADULT NOVELS: Raising the Shades, 2001; The Revealers, 2003; Falling, 2007; True Shoes, 2011. CHOOSE YOUR OWN ADVENTURE SERIES: The Forgotten Planet, 1993; Scene of the Crime, 1993; The Secret of Mystery Hill, 1993; Search the Amazon!, 1994; Gunfire at Gettysburg, 1994; Shadow of the Swastika, 1995; The Gold Medal Secret, 1996; The Underground Railroad, 1996; Curse of the Pirate Mist, 2011. **Address:** Farrar, Straus and Giroux, 18 W 18th St., New York, NY 10011, U.S.A. **Online address:** doug@dougwilhelm.com

WILHELM, Kate. American (born United States), b. 1928. **Genres:** Novels, Novellas/Short Stories, Mystery/Crime/Suspense, Science Fiction/Fantasy, Young Adult Non-fiction, Writing/Journalism. **Career:** Full-time writer, 1956-; Milford Science Fiction Writers Conference, co-director, 1963-76; Michigan State University, Clarion Fantasy Workshop, lecturer, 1968-96. **Publications:** More Bitter than Death (mystery), 1963; The Mile-Long Spaceship (collection), 1963 in UK as Andover and the Android, 1966; (with T.L. Thomas) The Clone: A Science Fiction Novel, 1965; The Nevermore Affair, 1966; The Killer Thing, 1967; The Downstairs Room and Other Speculative Fiction (collection), 1968; Let the Fire Fall, 1969; (with T. Thomas) The Year of the Cloud, 1970; Margaret and I, 1971; Abyss: Two Novellas, 1971; City of Cain, 1973; The Infinity Box (collection), 1975; The Clewiston Test, 1976; Where Late the Sweet Birds Sang, 1976; Fault Lines: A Novel, 1976; Somerset Dreams and Other Fictions, 1978; Juniper Time: A Novel, 1979; Axoltl, 1979; (with D. Knight) Better Than One (anthology), 1980; A Sense of Shadow, 1981; Listen, Listen (collection), 1981; Oh, Susannah!, 1982; Welcome, Chaos, 1983; Huysmans' Pets, 1986; (with R. Wilhelm) The Hills are Dancing, 1986; The Hamlet Trap, 1987; Crazy Time, 1988; Dark Door, 1988; Smart House, 1989; Children of the Wind (collection), 1989; Cambio Bay, 1990; Sweet, Sweet Poison (mystery), 1990; Death Qualified: A Mystery of Chaos, 1991; State of Grace, 1991; Seven Kinds of Death, 1992; And the Angels Sing: Stories, 1992; Justice for Some, 1993; The Best Defense, 1994; A Flush of Shadows: Five Short Novels Featuring Constance Leidl and Charlie Meiklejohn, 1995; Malice Prepense, 1996; The Good Children, 1998; Defense for the Devil, 1999; No Defense, 2000; The Casebook of Constance and Charlie, 2000; The Deepest Water, 2000; Moongate, 2000; Desperate Measures, 2001; Skeletons: A Novel of Suspense, 2002; The Clear and Convincing Proof, 2004; The Unbidden Truth, 2004; Storyteller: Writing Lessons and More From 27 Years of the Clarion Writer's Workshop, 2005; The Price of Silence, 2005; Sleight of Hand, 2006; A Wrongful Death, 2007; Cold Case, 2008; Fear is a Cold Black, 2010; Heaven is High, 2011; Death of an Artist: A Mystery, 2012. EDITOR: Nebula Award Stories Nine, 1974; Clarion SF (anthology), 1977. Works appear in anthologies. **Address:** c/o Jonathan Knight, 1645 Horn Ln., Eugene, OR 97404-2957, U.S.A. **Online address:** kate@katewilhelm.com

WILHOIT, James C. American (born United States), b. 1951?. **Genres:** Theology/Religion, Education. **Career:** Wheaton College, faculty, 1981-, Scripture Press Chair of Christian Formation & Ministry. Writer. **Publications:** Christian Education and the Search for Meaning, 1986, 2nd ed., 1991; (with L. Ryken) Effective Bible Teaching, 1988; (ed. with K.O. Gangel) The Christian Educator's Handbook on Adult Education, 1993; (ed. with K.O. Gangel) The Christian Educator's Handbook on Spiritual Formation, 1994; (ed. with J.M. Dettoni) Nurture That Is Christian, 1995; (ed. with K.O. Gangel) The Christian Educator's Handbook on Family Life Education, 1996; (ed. with L. Ryken and T. Longman III) Dictionary of Biblical Imagery, 1998; (ed.) Nelson's Personal Handbook on Prayer, 2002; (with L. Ryken and P. Ryken) Ryken's Bible Handbook, 2005; Spiritual Formation as If the Church Mattered: Growing in Christ through Community, 2008. Contributor to periodicals and journals. **Address:** IL, U.S.A. **Online address:** james.wilhoit@wheaton.edu

WILKER, Josh. American (born United States), b. 1968. **Genres:** Autobiography/Memoirs. **Career:** Writer. **Publications:** The Lenape Indians, 1994; Julius Erving, 1995; Classic Cons and Swindles, 1997; The Head Coaches, 1998; Confucius: Philosopher and Teacher, 1999; Organized Crime, 1999; Wayne Gretzky, 2000; A.J. Foyt, 2007; Cardboard Gods: An All-American Tale Told through Baseball Cards (memoir), 2010. **Address:** Chicago, IL, U.S.A. **Online address:** jawilker68@yahoo.com

WILKIE, Curtis. American (born United States), b. 1941?. **Genres:** Documentaries/Reportage. **Career:** Clarksdale Press Register, reporter and editor on the staff, 1963-69; Wilmington New Journal, reporter and editor on the staff, 1971-74; Boston Globe, journalist, national and foreign correspondent, 1975-2000, White House correspondent, 1977-82, Washington Bureau, chief, Middle East Bureau, founder, 1984-87, retired, 2000; University of Mississippi, Meek School of Journalism and New Media, Department of Journalism, visiting professor of journalism, 2002-, associate professor of journalism, Kelly G. Cook chair, 2004-, Overby Center for Southern Journalism and Politics, Overby fellow, 2007-; Louisiana State University, journalism professor-in-residence, 2003. **Publications:** (With J. McDougal) Arkansas Mischief: The Birth of a National Scandal, 1998; Dixie: A Personal Odyssey through Events that Shaped the Modern South, 2001; The Fall of the House of Zeus: The Rise and Ruin of America's Most Powerful Trial Lawyer, 2010. **Address:** Overby Center for Southern Journalism and Politics, Meek School of Journalism and New Media, University of Mississippi, 555 Grove Loop, Ste. 247, University, MS 38677, U.S.A. **Online address:** cwilkie@olemiss.edu

WILKIE, Pamela. Scottish/British (born England), b. 1935. **Genres:** Poetry, Literary Criticism And History. **Career:** Writer and teacher. **Publications:** Voyager, 1997; In the Lexicographer's Bedroom, 2001. Contributor to periodicals. **Address:** Peterloo Poets, 2 Kelly Gardens, Calstock, CW PL18 9SA, England.

WILKINS, Arnold. British (born England), b. 1946. **Genres:** Medicine/Health, Psychology, Adult Non-fiction, Business/Trade/Industry, Reference. **Career:** Montreal Neurological Institute, research fellow, 1972-74; Medical Research Council, scientist, 1974-78, grade 1 scientist, 1978-84, senior scientist, 1984-91, special appointment, 1991-97; University of Essex, professor of psychology, 1997-, Visual Perception Unit, director. Writer. **Publications:** NONFICTION: Visual Stress, 1995; Reading Through Colour: How Coloured Filters Can Reduce Reading Difficulty, Eye Strain, and Headaches, 2003. Contributor to journals and periodicals. **Address:** Department of Psychology, University of Essex, Rm. 3.716, Wivenhoe Park, Colchester, EX CO4 3SQ, England. **Online address:** arnold@essex.ac.uk

WILKINS, Mira. American (born United States), b. 1931. **Genres:** Business/Trade/Industry, Economics, History, Money/Finance. **Career:** Columbia University, affiliate, 1957-66; Wayne State University, affiliate, 1958-60; Union College, faculty, 1966-68; Smith College, faculty, 1968-71; Florida International University, professor of economics, 1974-; Chase Federal Bank, director, 1976-93. Writer. **Publications:** (With F. Hill) American Business Abroad: Ford on Six Continents, 1964; The Emergence of Multinational Enterprise: American Business Abroad from the Colonial Era to 1914, 1970; The Maturing of Multinational Enterprise: American Business Abroad from 1914 to 1970, 1974; Foreign Enterprise in Florida: The Impact of Non-U.S. Direct Investment, 1979; New Foreign Enterprise in Florida, 1980; The History of Foreign Investment in the United States to 1914, 1989; The History of Foreign Investment in the United States, 1914-1945, 2004; (with W.J. Hausman and P. Hertner) Global Electrification: Multinational Enterprise and International Finance in the History of Light and Power, 2008. EDITOR: European Foreign

Investments as Seen by the U.S. Department of Commerce, 1977; Foreign Investments in the United States: Department of Commerce and Department of Treasury Estimates, 1977; Issues and Insights on International Investment, 1977; British Overseas Investments, 1907-1948, 1977; The Growth of Multinational Enterprise, 1991; (with H. Schröter) The Free-Standing Company in the World Economy, 1830-1996, 1998; International Finance Series, 53 vols.; European Business: Four Centuries of Foreign Expansion, 59 vols.; The World Economy Series, 37 vols. Contributor to periodicals. **Address:** Department of Economics, Florida International University, DM 319C, 11200 SW 8th St., Miami, FL 33199, U.S.A. **Online address:** wilkinsm@fiu.edu

WILKINS, Sally (E. D.). American (born United States) **Genres:** Young Adult Non-fiction, Children's Non-fiction, Adult Non-fiction, History, Women's Studies And Issues. **Career:** Wilkins Lumber Co., vice president. Writer. **Publications:** When Jesus was Little, 1999; When Mary was Little, 1999; Insiders Guide to New Hampshire, 1999; Deserts, 2001; Grasslands, 2001; Temperate Forests, 2001; Sports and Games of Medieval Cultures, 2002; (co-author) Women of Granite, 2008; (co-author) Women of the Bay State, 2009; (co-author) Women of the Golden State, 2009; (co-author) Women of the Lone Star State, 2010; Women of the Constitution State, forthcoming. Contributor to books. **Address:** Apprentice Shop Books L.L.C., PO Box 375, Amherst, NH 03031-0393, U.S.A. **Online address:** sally@sallywilkins.com

WILKINSON, Alec. American (born United States), b. 1952. **Genres:** Essays. **Career:** Provincetown Art Association, researcher, 1978; New Yorker, staff writer, 1980, reporter, 1981-. **Publications:** Midnights: A Year With the Welfleet Police, 1982, 2nd ed., 2000; Moonshine: A Life in Pursuit of White Liquor, 1985, 2nd ed., 1998; Big Sugar: Seasons in the Cane Fields of Florida, 1989; The Riverkeeper, 1991; A Violent Act, 1992, 2nd ed., 1994; My Mentor: A Young Man's Friendship with William Maxwell, 2002; Mr. Apology and Other Essays, 2003; The Happiest Man in the World: An Account of the Life of Poppa Neutrino, 2007; The Protest Singer: An Intimate Portrait of Pete Seeger, 2009; The Ice Balloon: S.A. Andrée and the Heroic Age of Arctic Exploration, 2011. Contributor to magazines and periodicals. **Address:** New Yorker, 20 W 43rd St., New York, NY 10036, U.S.A. **Online address:** info@alecwilkinson.com

WILKINSON, Beth. American (born United States), b. 1925. **Genres:** Human Relations/Parenting, Medicine/Health, Art/Art History, Crafts, Psychology, Sciences, Reference. **Career:** Educator and writer. **Publications:** Coping When a Grandparent Has Alzheimer's Disease, 1992; Coping with Jealousy, 1992; Drugs and Depression, 1994; Careers Inside the World of Health Care, 1995, rev. ed., 1999; Papermaking for Kids: Simple Steps to Handcrafted Paper, 1997; Coping with the Dangers of Tattooing, Body Piercing, and Branding, 1998. **Address:** 1715 E Kearney St., Laramie, WY 82070, U.S.A.

WILKINSON, Bruce H. American (born United States), b. 1947. **Genres:** inspirational/Motivational Literature, Theology/Religion. **Career:** Walk Thru the Bible Ministries, founder and president, 1977-2002. Writer. **Publications:** (With K. Boa) Talk Thru the Old Testament, 1983; (with K. Boa) Talk Thru the New Testament, 1983; (with K. Boa) Talk Thru the Bible, 1983; Talk Thru Bible Personalities, 1983; (co-author) The Daily Walk Bible with 365 Devotional Helps to Guide You Through the Bible in One Year, 1987; How to Teach Almost Anything to Practically Anyone, 1992; (co-author) A Closer Walk, 1992; (with G.A. Getz) Nehemiah: Becoming a Disciplined Leader, 1995; (co-author) Family Walk Devotional Bible, 1996; Personal Holiness in Times of Temptation, 1998; Experiencing Spiritual Breakthroughs: The Powerful Principle of the Three Chairs, 1999; The Prayer of Jabez: Breaking Through to the Blessed Life, 2000; (with D. Kopp) The Prayer of Jabez Devotional, 2001; (with D. Kopp) Secrets of the Vine: Breaking Through to Abundance, 2001; (with D. Kopp) The Prayer of Jabez for Teens, 2001; The Prayer of Jabez for Kids, 2001; (with M. Carlson) The Prayer of Jabez for Little Ones, 2001; The Prayer of Jabez Devotions for Kids Living Big for God, 2001; (with D. Kopp) Experiencing Spiritual Breakthroughs, 2002; (with D. Kopp) Secrets of the Vine Devotional, 2002; Secrets of the Vine for Kids, 2002; (with M. Carlson) Secrets of the Vine for Little Ones, 2002; Secrets of the Vine for Young Hearts, 2002; (with M. Thomas) A Life God Rewards for Guys Only, 2002; (with M. Thomas) A Life God Rewards for Kids, 2002; (with D. Kopp) A Life God Rewards for Teens, 2002; (with M. Thomas) A Life God Rewards: Girls Only, 2002; (with D. Kopp) Reflections from A Life God Rewards, 2002; (with M. Thomas) A Life God Rewards for Little Ones, 2002; (with K. Boa) The Wilkinson and Boa Bible Handbook: The Ultimate Guide to Help You Get More Out of the Bible, 2002; (with D. Kopp) Secrets

of the Vine for Teens, 2003; Set Apart: Discovering Personal Victory Through Holiness, 2003; (with D. Kopp and H. Kopp) Dream Giver, 2003; (with J. Wilkinson) Dream Giver for Teens, 2004; (with D.M. Wilkinson) Dream Giver for Parents, 2004; Dream Giver for Couples, 2004; (with A. Murray) Daily in His Presence, 2004; My 100 Best-loved Bible Stories, 2005; (with B. Smith) Beyond Jabez, 2005; (co-author) The Greatest Gift, 2006; (with D. Kopp) You Were Born for This: 7 Keys to a Life of Predictable Miracles, 2009; (with D. Kopp) The God Pocket: He Owns It, You Carry It: Suddenly, Everything Changes, 2011. EDITOR: (with P.M. Wallace and J.W. Hoover) Daily Walk Bible, 1987; (C.W. Edwards and P. Kirk) Closer Walk New Testament, 1990; (with L. Woods and P.A. Kirk) Youthwalk, 1991, rev. ed., 2003; (with P.A. Kirk and C.W. Edwards) Family Walk, 1991; (with J.W. Hoover and P.A. Kirk) Your Daily Walk: 365 Daily Devotionals to Read through the Bible in a Year, 1991; (with M.R. Hodges and P.A. Kirk) Closer Walk: 365 Daily Devotionals that Nurture a Heart for God, 1992; Almost Every Answer for Practically Any Teacher!: A Resource Guide for All Who Desire to Teach for Lifechange, 1992; (with P.A. Kirk and C.W. Edwards) More Family Walk, 1992; (with L. Woods and P.A. Kirk) More Youthwalk, 1992; (co-ed.) Youthwalk Devotional Bible, 1992; (with L. Wooks and P.A. Kirk) Youthwalk Again, 1993; (with P.A. Kirk and J.W. Hoover) New Daily Walk Bible, 1995; (co-ed.) NIV Youthwalk Devotional Bible, 1997; Victory Over Temptation, 1998; Thirty Days to Experiencing Spiritual Breakthroughs, 1999; Youthwalk 2: Commitment, Stress, Forgiveness, & Other Topics for Teen Survival, 2003. Contributor to periodicals. **Address:** c/o Author Mail, Multnomah Publishers Inc., 204 W Adams Ave., PO Box 1720, Sisters, OR 97759, U.S.A.

WILKINSON, Carole. Australian/British (born England), b. 1950?. **Genres:** Novels, Young Adult Non-fiction. **Career:** Writer. **Publications:** DRAGON KEEPER SERIES: Dragon Keeper, 2003; Garden of the Purple Dragon, 2005; Dragon Moon, 2007; Dragon Dawn, 2008. RAMOSE SERIES: Prince in Exile, 2001; Ramose and the Tomb Robbers, 2001; Sting of the Scorpion, 2001; The Wrath of Ra, 2002; Ascent to the Sun, 2007; Fury of the Gods, 2007. NOVELS: Watery Grave, 1999; Out of Orbit, 1999; Bertrand's Quest, 2000; A Knight's Journey, 2001. OTHERS: Stagefright, 1996; Deepwater, 1999; Who Shot the Movies? (nonfiction), 2000; (contrib.) Real Sci-fi, 2000; Knights' Progress, 2000; Wheels Around, 2001; Black Snake: The Daring of Ned Kelly, 2002; Fire in the Belly: The Inside Story of the Modern Olympics (nonfiction), 2004; Alexander the Great: Reckless Conqueror, 2004; Ned Kelly's Jerilderie Letter, 2007; The Dragon Companion: An Encyclopedia, 2007; Hatshepsut: The Lost Pharaoh of Egypt, 2008. **Address:** Black Dog Books, 15 Gertrude St., Fitzroy, VI 3065, Australia. **Online address:** mail@carolewilkinson.com.au

WILKINSON, Charles F. American (born United States), b. 1941. **Genres:** Novels. **Career:** Lewis & Roca, associate, 1966-68; Bronson, Bronson & McKinnon, associate, 1968-71; Native American Rights Fund, staff attorney, 1971-75; University of Oregon, School of Law, assistant professor, 1975-78, associate professor, 1978-81, professor of law, 1981-87; University of Minnesota, visiting professor, 1981; University of Colorado, School of Law, visiting professor, 1984-85, professor of law, 1987-, Moses Lasky professor of law, 1989-, distinguished professor, 1997-, faculty, Center of the American West, co-founder, 1987, co-chair, 1987-97, vice chair, 1997-; University of Michigan, visiting professor, 1986; Northern Lights Institute, board director, 1986-97; Center for Environmental Law and Policy, board director; Western Environmental Law Center, board director. Writer. **Publications:** Cases and Materials on Federal Indian Law, 1979, 5th ed., 2005; Federal Public Land and Resources Law, 1981, 6th ed., 2007; American Indians Time and the Law: Native Societies in a Modern Constitutional Democracy, 1987; Land and Resource Planning in the National Forests, 1987; The American West: A Narrative Bibliography and a Study in Regionalism, 1989; Federal Public Land and Resources Law: Statutory Supplement, 1990; Values and Western Water: A History of the Dominant Issues, 1990; Crossing the Next Meridian: Land Water and the Future of the West, 1992; The Eagle Bird: Mapping a New West, 1992, rev. ed., 1999; Searching out the Headwaters: Change and Rediscovering in Western Water Policy, 1993; Atlas of the New West: Portrait of a Changing Region, 1997; Fire on the Plateau: Conflict and Endurance in the American Southwest, 1999; Messages from Franks Landing: A Story of Salmon Treaties and the Indian Way, 2000; Away Out Over Everything: The Olympic Peninsula and the Elwha River, 2004; Blood Struggle: The Rise of Modern Indian Nations, 2005; People are Dancing Again: The History of the Siletz Tribe of Western Oregon, 2010. Contributor to periodicals. **Address:** Office of Admissions, University of Colorado School of Law, 405 Wolf Law Bldg., 401 UCB, Boulder, CO 80309-0403, U.S.A. **Online address:**

fore.wilkinson@colorado.edu

WILKINSON, David Marion. American (born United States), b. 1957?. **Genres:** Education. **Career:** Loffland Brothers, Contractor, 1981-85; Townlake Mortgage Inc., loan officer, 1985-86; Nu-Design Construction Inc., supervisor, 1986-88; The Bratton Firm, P.C., case manager, 1988-94; writer, 1994-; Sul Ross State University, writer-in-residence, 2004-08. **Publications:** Not between Brothers: An Epic Novel of Texas, 1996; The Empty Quarter, 1998; Oblivion's Altar: A Novel of Courage, 2002; One Ranger: A Memoir, 2004. Contributor of short fiction to publications. **Address:** 2007 Vista Ln., Austin, TX 78703-2955, U.S.A. **Online address:** mylogan@austin.rr.com

WILKINSON, Denys (Haigh). British (born England), b. 1922. **Genres:** Physics, Education. **Career:** Cambridge University, demonstrator, 1947-51, lecturer, 1951-56, reader in nuclear physics, 1956-57; Oxford University, professor of nuclear physics, 1957-59, head of nuclear physics laboratory, 1957-76, professor of experimental physics, 1959-76; Oxford Studies in Physics (formerly Oxford Library of the Physical Sciences), editor, 1957-; International Monographs on Physics, staff, 1960-; Jesus College, honorary fellow, 1961-; Erice International School of Nuclear Physics, director, 1975-83; University of Sussex, vice-chancellor, 1976-87, professor emeritus of physics, 1987-; Progress in Particle and Nuclear Physics, editor, 1976-84. **Publications:** Ionization Chambers and Counters, 1950; (ed. as D.H. Wilkinson) Isospin in Nuclear Physics, 1970; (ed.) Mesonic Interface Between Nuclear Structure and Particle Physics: Proceedings of the International School of Nuclear Physics, Erice, 2-14 September 1976, 1978; (ed. with M. Rho) Mesons in Nuclei, 1979; Progress in Particle and Nuclear Physics, vol. IV, 1980; (contrib.) Solly Gabriel Cohen: 1920-1984: In Memoriam, 1985; (contrib.) Interactions and Structures in Nuclei: Proceedings of a Conference to Celebrate the 65th Birthday of Sir Denys Wilkinson, FRS, University of Sussex, 7-9th September 1988, 1988; Our Universes, 1991. **Address:** University of Sussex, 1 Pevensey Bldg., Sussex House, Brighton, ES BN1 9QH, England.

WILKINSON, Marian. Australian (born Australia), b. 1954?. **Genres:** History, Politics/Government. **Career:** Sydney Morning Herald, correspondent, deputy editor, environment editor; The Age, correspondent; Australian Broadcasting Corp. (ABC-TV), Four Corners Program, executive producer; The Australian, senior reporter. **Publications:** (With B. Toohey) Book of Leaks: Exposes in Defence of the Public's Right to Know, 1987; Fixer: The Untold Story of Graham Richardson, 1996; (with D. Marr) Dark Victory, 2003. Contributor to periodicals. **Address:** Four Corners Program, ABC-TV, PO Box 9994, Sydney, NW 2001, Australia.

WILKINSON, Richard H(erbert). American (born United States), b. 1951. **Genres:** Archaeology/Antiquities, History, Adult Non-fiction. **Career:** University of Arizona, lecturer, 1988-93, Egyptian Expedition, director, 1990-, senior lecturer, 1994-97, associate professor, 1997-2000, professor, 2000-, Department of Classics, Regents professor; American Research Center in Egypt, president of Arizona chapter, 1990-2000; Journal of Ancient Egyptian Interconnections, editor; Directory of North American Egyptologists, editor. **Publications:** Reading Egyptian Art: A Hieroglyphic Guide to Ancient Egyptian Painting and Sculpture, 1992; Symbol & Magic in Egyptian Art, 1994; (ed.) Valley of the Sun Kings, 1995; (with N. Reevers) The Complete Valley of the Kings: Tombs and Treasures of Egypt's Greatest Pharaohs, 1996; The Complete Temples of Ancient Egypt, 2000; The Complete Gods and Goddesses of Ancient Egypt, 2003. (ed.) Egyptology Today, 2008; Egyptian Scarabs, 2008; (ed.) Tausert: Female Pharaoh of Egypt, 2011. Contributor of articles to journals. **Address:** Department of Classics, University of Arizona, PO Box 210076, Tucson, AZ 85721-0076, U.S.A.

WILKINSON, Sylvia J. American (born United States), b. 1940. **Genres:** Novels, Education, Sports/Fitness, History. **Career:** University of North Carolina, instructor in English, art and drama, 1963-65; College of William and Mary, instructor in English and creative writing, 1966-67; University of North Carolina, lecturer in creative writing and visiting writer, 1967-70; Creative Writing Learning Institute of North Carolina, visiting writer, 1968-69; Hollins College, writer-in-residence, 1969, 1975; Richmond Humanities Center, writer-in-residence, 1972-80; Sweet Briar College, writer-in-residence, 1973-75, 1977; Washington College, visiting writer, 1974-75, 1984; University of Wisconsin, visiting writer, 1985. **Publications:** Moss on the North Side, 1966; A Killing Frost, 1967; Cale, 1970; Change, 1971; The Stainless Steel Carrot, 1973; Shadow of the Mountain, 1977; Bone of My Bones, 1980; Dirt Tracks to Glory, 1983; World of Racing, 10 vols., 1981-85; Sprint Cars, 1981;

Can-Am, 1981; Stock Cars, 1981; Super Vee, 1981; Endurance Racing, 1981; Formula One, 1981; Formula Atlantic, 1981; Automobiles, 1982; Trans-Am, 1983; Dirt Tracks to Glory, 1983; Kart Racing, 1985; I Can Be a Race Car Driver, 1986; On the 7th Day, God Created the Chevrolet, (novel) 1993; Lying Dog, forthcoming; Sewer Lily, forthcoming. Contributor of articles to periodicals. **Address:** 2101 Scenic Hwy. L104, Pensacola, FL 32503-6658, U.S.A.

WILKINSON, Tracy. American (born United States) **Genres:** History, inspirational/Motivational Literature. **Career:** United Press Intl., reporter; Los Angeles Times, reporter, 1987-, journalist. Writer. **Publications:** The Vatican's Exorcists: Driving Out the Devil in the 21st Century, 2007. **Address:** Warner Books Pty Ltd., 2 Westall Rd., F1 Hallmarc Business Pk., Clayton, VI 3168, Australia. **Online address:** wilkinson@latimes.com

WILKINSON, Winifred. *See* HAUSMANN, Winifred Wilkinson.

WILKS, Burrel Lee. American (born United States), b. 1967. **Genres:** Novellas/Short Stories. **Career:** Strategies for Millionaire Magnetism program, creator; Diamond Developments Inc. (property development), partner; Burrel Streetwise Inc., founder, owner & president; Ready-Set-Work (nonprofit), staff. Writer, businessman, speaker and life coach. **Publications:** Tattoos on My Soul: From the Ghetto to the Top of the World: A Sizzling Story of Grit, Glitz and Personal Growth, 2006. **Address:** Burrel Streetwise Inc., 6240 W 3rd St., Ste. 2404, Los Angeles, CA 90036, U.S.A.

WILKS, Mike. British (born England), b. 1947?. **Genres:** Illustrations. **Career:** TWD (design firm), founder and designer, 1970-75. Artist, freelance writer and illustrator. **Publications:** SELF-ILLUSTRATED, The Weather Works, 1983; The Ultimate Alphabet, 1986; The Annotated Ultimate Alphabet, 1988; BBC Drawing Course, 1990; The Ultimate Noah's Ark, 1993; Metamorphosis: The Ultimate Spot-the-Difference Book, 1997. NOVELS, Mirrorscape, 2007; Mirrorstorm, 2010. Illustrator of books by others. **Address:** c/o Kate Shaw, Viney Agency, 8 Goodrich Rd., East Dulwich, London, GL SE22 9EH, England. **Online address:** feedback@mike-wilks.com

WILL, Clifford M(artin). American (born United States), b. 1946. **Genres:** Physics. **Career:** California Institute of Technology, instructor in physics, 1971-72; University of Chicago, fellow of Enrico Fermi Institute, 1972-74; Stanford University, assistant professor of physics, 1974-81; Washington University, associate professor, 1981-85, professor of physics, 1985-2005, Department of Physics, chairman, 1991-96, 1997-2002, College of Arts and Sciences, James S. McDonnell professor of physics, 2005-. Writer. **Publications:** Theory and Experiment in Gravitational Physics, 1981, rev. ed., 1993; Was Einstein Right?: Putting General Relativity to the Test, 1986, 3rd ed., 1993. Contributor to periodicals. **Address:** Department of Physics, Washington University, 375 Compton, 1 Brookings Dr., St. Louis, MO 63130, U.S.A. **Online address:** cmw@wuphys.wustl.edu

WILL, George F. American (born United States), b. 1941. **Genres:** Politics/Government, Social Commentary, Essays, Psychology, Social Sciences, History. **Career:** Michigan State University, professor of politics, 1967-68; University of Toronto, professor of politics, 1968-69; U.S. Senate, congressional aide to Senator Allott, 1970-72; National Review, Washington editor, 1972-78; Washington Post, syndicated columnist, 1974-; Newsweek, contributing editor, 1976-; American Broadcasting Co. (ABC-TV), World News Tonight, news analyst and political commentator, 1984-, contributing analyst; Harvard University, faculty, 1995, 1998. **Publications:** (Ed.) Press, Politics and Popular Government, 1972; The Pursuit of Happiness and Other Sobering Thoughts, 1978; (with M. Novak) Solzhenitsyn and American Democracy, 1980; The Pursuit of Virtue and Other Tory Notions, 1982; Statecraft as Soulcraft: What Government Does, 1983; The Morning After: American Successes and Excesses, 1981-1986, 1986; The New Season: A Spectators Guide to the 1988 Election, 1987; Men at Work: The Craft of Baseball, 1990; Political Essays, 1990; Suddenly: The American Idea Abroad and at Home, 1986-1990, 1990; Restoration: Congress, Term Limits and the Recovery of Deliberative Democracy, 1992; The Leveling Wind: Politics, the Culture and Other News, 1990-1994, 1994; The Woven Figure: Conservatism and America's Fabric, 1994-1997, 1997; Bunts: Curt Flood, Camden Yards, Pete Rose and Other Reflections on Baseball (essays), 1998; With a Happy Eye But...: America and the World, 1997-2002, 2002; One Man's America: The Pleasures and Provocations of Our Singular Nation, 2008. Contributor to periodicals. **Address:** Washington Post Writers Group, 1150 15th St. NW, Washington, DC 20071-0001, U.S.A.

WILLARD, Dale C. American (born United States) **Genres:** Novels, Science Fiction/Fantasy. **Career:** Writer and Educator. **Publications:** My Son, My Brother, My Friend: A Novel in Letters, 1978; The Linnet's Tale, 2002. **Address:** c/o Stacey Glick, Dystel & Goderich Literary Management, 1 Union Sq. W, New York, NY 10003, U.S.A.

WILLARD, Pat. American (born United States) **Genres:** Food And Wine. **Career:** Writer and educator. **Publications:** Pie Every Day: Recipes and Slices of Life, 1997; A Soothing Broth: Tonics, Custards, Soups, and Other Cure-alls for Colds, Coughs, Upset Tummies, and Out-of-Sorts-Days, 1998; Secrets of Saffron: The Vagabond Life of the World's Most Seductive Spice, 2001; America Eats!: On the Road with the WPA: The Fish Fries, Box Supper Socials, and Chitlin Feasts That Define Real American Food, 2008. FORTHCOMING: The Reluctant Bride; He and I: A Life Through Marriage. **Address:** c/o Author Mail, Beacon Press, 25 Beacon St., Boston, MA 02108, U.S.A. **Online address:** kattwillard@gmail.com

WILLBANKS, James H. American (born United States), b. 1947?. **Genres:** Military/Defense/Arms Control, International Relations/Current Affairs, History, Biography. **Career:** U.S. Army Command and General Staff College, instructor, 1992-96, professor of national security affairs, 1998-, chair of the history department, Department of Military History, director; Kansas City Kansas Community College, adjunct faculty, 1992-96, 1998; University of Kansas, adjunct faculty, 2001. Writer. **Publications:** Thiet Giap! The Battle of An Loc, April 1972, 1993; Abandoning Vietnam: How America Left and South Vietnam Lost Its War, 2004, 2nd ed., 2008; Machine Guns: An Illustrated History of Their Impact, 2004; Battle of An Loc, 2005; (ed.) The Vietnam War, 2006; The Tet Offensive: A Concise History, 2007; Vietnam War Almanac, 2010; (ed.) America's Heroes, 2011. Contributor of articles to books and magazines. **Address:** University Press of Kansas, 2502 Westbrooke Cir., Lawrence, KS 66045-4444, U.S.A. **Online address:** jwillbanks@kc.rr.com

WILLE, Lois. American (born United States), b. 1931. **Genres:** Urban Studies, History. **Career:** Chicago Daily News, reporter, 1956-77, editorial page editor, 1977-, national correspondent and associate editor; Chicago Sun-Times, editorial page editor, 1978-84; Chicago Tribune, deputy editor, editorial page editor, 1984-91; freelance writer, 1991-. **Publications:** Forever Open, Clear, and Free: The Historic Struggle for Chicago's Lakefront, 1972, 2nd ed. as Forever Open, Clear, and Free: The Struggle for Chicago's Lakefront, 1991; At Home in the Loop: How Clout and Community Built Chicago's Dearborn Park, 1997. **Address:** 1530 S State St., Chicago, IL 60605-2987, U.S.A. **Online address:** lowille@aol.com

WILLEMEN, Paul. Scottish/Belgian (born Belgium), b. 1944. **Genres:** Film, Cultural/Ethnic Topics, Art/Art History. **Career:** Napier University, professor of Critical Studies, 1996-. Writer. **Publications:** Le Cinema Neerlandais Sonore, 1971; Pasolini, 1977; Ophuls, 1978; (with T. Milne) The Encyclopedia of Horror Movies, 1986; The Films of Amos Gitai, 1993; Looks and Frictions: Essays in Cultural Studies and Film Theory, 1994; (with A. Rajadhyaksha) Encyclopaedia of Indian Cinema, 1995, rev. ed., 1999; (contrib.) Horror, 1996. EDITOR: (with D. Will) Roger Corman: The Millennic Vision, 1970; (with C. Johnston) Frank Tashlin, 1973; (with C. Johnston) Jacques Tourneur, 1975; Pier Paolo Pasolini, 1977; (with B. Gandhy) Indian Cinema, 1980; (with J. Pines) Questions of Third Cinema, 1989; The Films of Amos Gitai: A Montage, 1993; (with J. Pines) The Essential Framework: Classic Film and TV Essays, vol. I, 1998. **Address:** 14 Drummond Pl., Edinburgh, EH3 6PJ, Scotland.

WILLETT, Ralph. British (born England), b. 1935?. **Genres:** Area Studies, History, Literary Criticism And History, Social Commentary, Adult Nonfiction, Film, Essays. **Career:** University of Hull, senior lecturer in American studies, 1966-95, senior fellow, 1995, now retired. Writer. **Publications:** (With J. White) Slavery in the American South, 1970; The Merrill Studies in Pierre, 1971; (ed. with A. Pollard) Webster's New World Companion to English and American Literature, 1973; The Open Cage: American Film (1935-1960), 1980; (ed. and intro. with S.W. Baskerville) Nothing Else to Fear: New Perspectives on America in the Thirties (essays), 1985; The Americanization of Germany, 1945-1949, 1989; Hard-Boiled Detective Fiction, 1992; The Naked City: Urban Crime Fiction in the USA (criticism), 1996. **Address:** Manchester University Press, Oxford Rd., Manchester, GM M13 9NR, England. **Online address:** r.w.willett@hull.ac.uk

WILLEY, Margaret. American (born United States), b. 1950. **Genres:** Young Adult Fiction, Novels, Animals/Pets, Picture/Board Books. **Career:** Writer. **Publications:** YOUNG ADULT NOVELS: The Bigger Book of Lydia, 1983; Finding David Dolores, 1986; If Not for You, 1988; Saving Lenny, 1990; The Melinda Zone, 1993; Facing the Music, 1996; Thanksgiving with Me, 1998; Clever Beatrice: An Upper Peninsula Conte, 2001; Clever Beatrice and the Best Little Pony, 2004; A Clever Beatrice Christmas, 2006; The 3 Bears and Goldilocks, 2008; A Summer of Silk Moths, 2009; The Pact, 2012. Contributor to journals. **Address:** 2019 Jane Ct., Grand Haven, MI 49417-2506, U.S.A. **Online address:** margwilley@hotmail.com

WILLIAMS, Adam. American/Hong Kong (born Hong Kong), b. 1953?. **Genres:** Novels, Young Adult Fiction, History. **Career:** Sino-British Trade Council, staff; Jardine Matheson, chief representative, 1986-; British Chamber of Commerce, chair, 1996-98. Speaker and novelist. **Publications:** The Palace of Heavenly Pleasure, 2004; The Emperor's Bones, 2006; The Dragon's Tail, 2007; The Book of the Alchemist, 2009. **Address:** c/o Araminta Whitley, LAW Agency, 14 Vernon St., London, GL WR14 0RJ, England.

WILLIAMS, Alan. British (born England), b. 1935. **Genres:** Sciences. **Career:** Leeds University, lecturer, senior lecturer, Livesey professor of fuel and combustion science, now professor emeritus. Writer. **Publications:** (With W.L. Lom) Liquefied Petroleum Gases: Guide to Properties, Applications, and Usage of Propane and Butane, 1974, rev. ed., 1982; (with W.L. Lom) Substitute Natural Gas, Manufacture and Properties, 1976; Combustion of Sprays of Liquid Fuels, 1976; (with A. Gilpin) Dictionary of Energy Technology, 1982; Combustion of Liquid Fuel Sprays, 1989; (ed.) Methane Emissions: Report of a Working Group Appointed by the Watt Committee on Energy, 1994; (co-author) Combustion and Gasification of Coal, 2000. **Address:** Energy and Resources Research Institute, School of Process, Environmental & Materials Eng., University of Leeds, Rm. 533, Clarendon Rd., Leeds, LS2 9JT, England. **Online address:** a.williams@leeds.ac.uk

WILLIAMS, Alan L(arson). American (born United States), b. 1947. **Genres:** Film, Communications/Media. **Career:** Media Study-Buffalo, film and video programmer, 1975-76; University of Iowa, visiting assistant professor of film studies, 1977-81; Rutgers University, Department of French, assistant professor, 1981-87, associate professor of French and cinema studies, 1987-93, professor, 1993-, Interdisciplinary Program in Cinema Studies, acting director, 1985-86, 1987-88, 1989-90. Writer. **Publications:** Max Ophuls and the Cinema of Desire: Style and A Spectacle in Four Films, 1948-1955, 1980; Republic of Images: A History of French Filmmaking, 1992; (ed. and intro.) Film and Nationalism, 2002. Contributor to journals. Works appear in anthologies. **Address:** Department of French, Rutgers University, 107C RAB, 131 George St., New Brunswick, NJ 08901-1414, U.S.A.

WILLIAMS, Alan Lee. British (born England), b. 1930. **Genres:** Military/Defense/Arms Control, Politics/Government, History. **Career:** H.M. Government Delegation to 24th General Assembly of the UN, leader, 1969; European Movement, deputy director, 1970-72; Secretary of State Defense, parliamentary private secretary, 1974-79; Transport on Water, chairman, 1974-; CSIS European Working Group, chairman, 1974-; State for Defense, secretary, 1974-76, PPS to secretary of state for Northern Ireland, 1976-79; English-Speaking Union, director, 1979-86; Toynbee Hall, warden and chief executive, 1987-92; Atlantic Council, director, 1992-, honorary vice-president, 2000-; University of London, politics department visiting professor, 2003-; Parliament for Hornchurch, member. Writer. **Publications:** WITH G.L. WILLIAMS: A Book of Radical Essays, 1966; (with F. Barnaby) The Nuclear Future, 1969; Europe or the Open Sea, 1970; Crisis in European Defence, 1974; The European Defence Initiative: Europe's Bid for Equality, 1985; Labour's Decline and the Social Democrats' Fall, 1989; Islamic Resurgence, 1991; International Terrorism, 1996; European Foreign and Security Policy, 1996; WEU Challenge for NATO, 1996; Strategy for Security in the Future, 1999; Does NATO Have a Future?, 2002. **Address:** 6 N Several Blackheath, London, GL SE3 0QR, England.

WILLIAMS, Alex. British (born England), b. 1969?. **Genres:** Children's Fiction. **Career:** Writer. **Publications:** The Talent Thief: An Extraordinary Tale of an Ordinary Boy, 2006; The Deep Freeze of Bartholomew Tullock in UK as The Storm Maker: A Hair-Raising Adventure for All Weathers, 2008. **Address:** David Higham Associates, 508 Lower John St., Golden Sq., London, GL W1F 9HA, England.

WILLIAMS, Amanda Kyle. American (born United States), b. 1957.

Genres: Novellas/Short Stories, Mystery/Crime/Suspense, Novels, Young Adult Fiction, Children's Fiction. **Career:** Sovereign Carpet Mills Inc., Dalton, vice president of manufacturing. Writer. **Publications:** SUSPENSE NOVELS: Club Twelve, 1990; The Providence File, 1991; A Singular Spy, 1992; The Spy in Question: A Madison McGuire Espionage Thriller, 1993; Stranger you Seek, 2011; Stranger in the Room, 2012; Don't Talk to Strangers, 2013. Works appear in anthologies. Contributor to periodicals. **Address:** 820 Derrydown Way, PO Box 666011, Decatur, GA 30030-4161, U.S.A. **Online address:** amanda@amandakylewilliams.com

WILLIAMS, Andrew. British (born England), b. 1962?. **Genres:** History, Biography, Food And Wine. **Career:** British Broacasting Corp., Newsnight, producer, 1986, Panorama, assistant editor, history unit, producer; BBC, senior current affairs producer. **Publications:** The Battle of the Atlantic: The Allies Submarine Fight Against Hitler's Gray Wolves of the Sea, 2002; The Battle of the Atlantic: Hitlers Gray Wolves of the Sea and the Allies Desperate Struggle to Defeat Them, 2003; Cannibal Trout: Tying & Fishing Flesh, Fry and Egg Flies, 2005; Spon's Practical Guide to Alterations and Extensions, 2008; Toxic Morsel: T.E. Lawrence and the Mint, 2008. **Address:** c/o Author Mail, Basic Books, 387 Park Ave. S, 12th Fl., New York, NY 10016, U.S.A.

WILLIAMS, Arlene. American (born United States) **Genres:** Young Adult Fiction, Animals/Pets, Children's Fiction. **Career:** Writer and illustrator. **Publications:** SELF-ILLUSTRATED: Tales from the Dragon's Cave: Peacemaking Stories for Everyone, 1995. OTHERS: Fairy Tales for the New Age, 1992, 2nd ed., 1995; Winker, Buttercup, and Blue, 1994; Dragon Soup, 1996; Tales of Spirit, Tales of Light, 1997; How to Be a Dragon without Burning Your Tongue, 2003; Tiny Tortilla, 2004. **Address:** c/o Author Mail, Dutton Publishers, Penguin Group, 375 Hudson St., New York, NY 10014-3658, U.S.A. **Online address:** arlene@arlenewilliamsbooks.com

WILLIAMS, Austin. British (born England), b. 1959. **Genres:** History, Illustrations. **Career:** ManTownHuman: Manifesto Towards a New Humanism in Architecture, founder; Future Cities Project, director; NBS Learning Channels, architectural producer; Royal College of Art, visiting tutor; British Broadcasting Corp., architecture critic; NBS TV, editor; Architects' Journal, technical editor. **Publications:** (With K. Trant) The Macro World of Microcars, 2004; The Enemies of Progress: The Dangers of Sustainability, 2008; (ed. with D. Clements, A. Donald and M. Earnshaw) The Future of Community: Reports of a Death Greatly Exaggerated, 2008. SELF-ILLUSTRATED: Structure and Fabric, 2008; Sustainability and Practice, 2009. Contributor to periodicals and journals. **Address:** Future Cities Project, 66 Portland Pl., London, GL W1B 1AD, England.

WILLIAMS, Barry. British (born England), b. 1932. **Genres:** Education, History, Biography. **Career:** History master, 1957-63; Rank Film Organization, Education Division, history adviser, 1962-70; Clee Humberstone Foundation School, senior history master, 1964-69; Gillingham School, head of history department and sixth form master, 1969-72; Sherborne School for Girls, university adviser and head of history side, 1971-. Writer. **Publications:** Struggle for Canada, 1967; Modern Japan, 1969, 2nd ed., 1987; Struggle for North America, 1969; Emerging Japan, 1969; Modern Africa 1870-1970, 1970; Making of Modern World: Asia, 1970; Asia: Food and People, 1970; Congo Tragedy, 1970; Making of Modern World: Africa, 1972; Modern France, 1974; (co-author) The Teaching of History, 1975; Modern France 1870-1976, 1979; Elusive Settlement: England's Revolutionary Years 1637-1701, 1984; So Many Opportunities: A Historical Portrait of Sherborne School for Girls, 1998. EDITOR: The First Industrial Revolution, 1973; Transport, 1974. **Address:** Herons Reach, 30A Lincoln Rd., Glinton, Peterborough, PE6 7JS, England.

WILLIAMS, Bert (Nolan). Canadian (born Canada), b. 1930. **Genres:** Novels, Romance/Historical, Plays/Screenplays, History, Young Adult Nonfiction. **Career:** Scarborough Board of Education, teacher, 1953-67, librarian, 1968-75. Writer. **Publications:** Food for the Eagle, 1970; Master of Ravenspur, 1970; The Rocky Mountain Monster, 1973; Son of Egypt, 1977. **Address:** 10 Muirhead Rd., Apt. 504, Toronto, ON M2J 4P9, Canada.

WILLIAMS, Bronwyn. See BROWNING, Dixie Burrus.

WILLIAMS, Brooke. American (born United States) **Genres:** Local History/Rural Topics, Travel/Exploration. **Career:** Murie Center, executive director, through 2008. Speaker, writer and consultant. **Publications:** (Ed. with J. Deel and F.E. Kruse) Frontiers in Semiotics, 1986; Utah Ski Country, 1986; (with T. Till) Utah: A Centennial Celebration, 1995; Halflives: Reconciling Work and Wildness, 1999, rev. ed., 2003; (with C. Noble) Escalante: The Best Kind of Nothing, 2006. **Address:** University of Arizona Press, Main Library Bldg., 5th Fl., 1510 E University Blvd., PO Box 210055, Tucson, AZ 85721-0055, U.S.A.

WILLIAMS, Carla. American (born United States), b. 1965?. **Genres:** Architecture, Art/Art History, Photography. **Career:** J. Paul Getty Museum, Department of Photographs, intern, 1991-92, Collections Information Planning Department, writer, 1997-99; New York Public Library, Schomburg Center for Research in Black Culture, Prints and Photographs Division, curator, 1992-93; Pomona College, instructor in photography, 1994; freelance writer and editor, 1995-; Thaw Art History Center, College of Santa Fe, visual resource curator, 1999-2002; Carlagirl Photo, founder, 1999; Stanford University, Department of Drama, lecturer, 2003. **Publications:** Thurgood Marshall: 1908-1993, 2002; The Underground Railroad, 2002; (with D. Willis) The Black Female Body: A Photographic History, 2002; Pleasure and Beauty: Self-Portraits 1985-1990, 2009. Works appears in anthology. Contributor to journals. **Address:** c/o Author Mail, Temple University Press, 1852 N 10th St., Philadelphia, PA 19122, U.S.A. **Online address:** carla@carlagirl.net

WILLIAMS, Charles. British (born England), b. 1933. **Genres:** Biography. **Career:** House of Lords, front bench spokesman, 1985-; opposition spokesperson for trade and industry, 1987-92; deputy leader of the opposition, 1989-92; opposition spokesperson for defence, 1990-97; opposition spokesperson for the environment 1992-97. Writer. **Publications:** (With T. Dennis) An Investment Bank for the U.K., 1987; The Last Great Frenchman: A Life of General de Gaulle, 1993; Bradman, An Australian Hero, 1996; Adenauer: The Father of the New Germany, 2000; Pétain: How the Hero of France Became a Convicted Traitor and Changed the Course of History, 2005; Harold Macmillan, 2010. Contributor to periodicals. **Address:** House of Lords, London, GL SW1A 0PW, England. **Online address:** williamscc@parliament.uk

WILLIAMS, C(harles) K(enneth). American (born United States), b. 1936. **Genres:** Poetry, Autobiography/Memoirs, Essays, Translations, Children's Fiction. **Career:** Franklin and Marshall College, visiting professor, 1977; University of California-Irvine, visiting professor, 1978; Boston University, visiting professor, 1979-80; Brooklyn College, visiting professor, 1982-83; Columbia University, lecturer, 1982-85; George Mason University, professor of English, 1982-95; University of California-Berkeley, Holloway lecturer, 1986; Princeton University, professor, 1995-. Writer. **Publications:** A Day for Anne Frank, 1968; Lies, 1969; I Am the Bitter Name, 1972; With Ignorance, 1977; (co-trans.) The Women of Rachis, 1978; The Lark, The Thrush, The Starling, 1983; Tar, 1983; Flesh and Blood, 1987; (trans.) The Bacchae of Euripedes, 1990; A Dream of Mind, 1992; Selected Poems, 1994; (co-trans.) The Selected Poems of Francis Ponge, 1994; The Vigil, 1997; Poetry and Consciousness (essays), 1998; Repair, 1999; Misgivings, 2000; The Singing, 2003; Collected Poems, 2006; Wait, 2010; On Whitman, 2010. **Address:** Department of Creative Writing, Princeton University, 6 New South, Princeton, NJ 08544, U.S.A. **Online address:** ckwms@princeton.edu

WILLIAMS, Charlie. British (born England), b. 1971?. **Genres:** Novels. **Career:** Writer. **Publications:** Deadfolk, 2004; King of the Road, 2006; Fags and Lager, 2006; Stairway to Hell, 2010. **Address:** Worcester, England. **Online address:** cs_will@btopenworld.com

WILLIAMS, Christine L. American (born United States), b. 1959?. **Genres:** Women's Studies And Issues, Gay And Lesbian Issues, Social Commentary. **Career:** University of Oklahoma, assistant professor of sociology, 1986-88; University of Texas, Department of Sociology, assistant professor, 1988-94, associate professor, 1994-99, professor, 1999-, chair; Current Perspectives in Social Theory, associate editor, 1988-94; University of Sydney, visiting professor, 1992; Gender and Society, advisory editor, 1992-95, editor, 2004-06. **Publications:** Gender Differences at Work: Women and Men in Nontraditional Occupations, 1989; (ed.) Doing Women's Work: Men in Nontraditional Occupations, 1993; Still a Man's World: Men Who Do Women's Work, 1995; (ed. with A. Stein) Sexuality and Gender, 2002; (ed. with J.C. Alexander and G.T. Marx) Self, Social Structure, and Beliefs: Explorations in Sociology, 2004; Inside Toyland: Working, Shopping, and Social Inequality, 2006. CONTRIBUTOR: A Case for the Case Study, 1991; Required Reading: Sociology's Most Influential Books, 1998; Daring to Find Our Names: The

Search for Lesbigay Library Librarianship, 1998; Qualitative Sociology as Everyday Life, 1999; Social Inequalities in Comparative Perspective, 2004; Encyclopedia of Sociology, 2007. Contributor to periodicals and journals. **Address:** Department of Sociology, University of Texas, 536 BUR, 1 University Sta., PO Box A1700, Austin, TX 78712, U.S.A. **Online address:** cwilliams@austin.utexas.edu

WILLIAMS, Cindy. American (born United States), b. 1947. **Genres:** Mathematics/Statistics, Military/Defense/Arms Control, Economics. **Career:** Rand Corp., mathematician, 1979-82; Pentagon Senior Executive Service, Strategic Offensive Forces Division in the Directorate of Program Analysis and Evaluation of the Office of the Secretary of Defense, division director, 1982-87; MITRE Corp., associate department head, department head, associate technical director, 1988-94, director of command and control integration environment, 1997-98; Congressional Budget Office, assistant director for national security, 1994-97; Massachusetts Institute of Technology, Security Studies Program, principal research scientist, 1998-; Dartmouth College, Dickey Center for International Understanding, visiting fellow, 2010-. Writer. **Publications:** (With G. Crawford) Analysis of Subjective Judgement Matrices, 1980; (ed.) Holding the Line: U.S. Defense Alternatives for the Early 21st Century, 2001; (ed.) Filling the Ranks: Transforming the U.S. Military Personnel System, 2004; Buying National Security: How America Plans and Pays for its Global Role and Safety at Home, 2010. Contributor to books, journals and periodicals. **Address:** Department of Political Science, Massachusetts Institute of Technology, E40 Bldg., 77 Massachusetts Ave., 4th Fl., Cambridge, MA 02139-4307, U.S.A. **Online address:** cindywil@mit.edu

WILLIAMS, David. American (born United States), b. 1959. **Genres:** History, Young Adult Non-fiction. **Career:** Valdosta State University, professor of history, 1988-. Writer. **Publications:** NONFICTION: The Georgia Gold Rush: Twenty-niners, Cherokees and Gold Fever, 1993; Rich Man's War: Class, Caste and Confederate Defeat in the Lower Chattahoochee Valley, 1998; Johnny Reb's War: Battlefield and Homefront, 2000; (with T.C. Williams and D. Carlson) Plain Folk in a Rich Man's War: Class and Dissent in Confederate Georgia, 2002; A People's History of the Civil War: Struggles for the Meaning of Freedom, 2005; Bitterly Divided: The South's Inner Civil War, 2008. **Address:** Department of History, Valdosta State University, Valdosta, GA 31698, U.S.A. **Online address:** william@valdosta.edu

WILLIAMS, David B. American (born United States), b. 1965?. **Genres:** Travel/Exploration. **Career:** Canyonlands Field Institute, special programs coordinator, 1987-92; Arches National Park, interpretive ranger, 1993, 1995, 1996; Frederick Law Olmsted National Historical Site, interpretive ranger, 1997; Burke Museum of Natural History and Culture, education assistant, 1999-. Writer. **Publications:** Grand Views of Canyon Country: A Driving Guide, 2000; A Naturalist's Guide to Canyon Country, 2000; The Street-Smart Naturalist, 2005 as The Seattle Street-Smart Naturalist: Field Notes from the City, 2009; Stories in Stone: Travels through Urban Geology, 2009. Contributor to books. **Online address:** wingate@seanet.com

WILLIAMS, Diane. American (born United States), b. 1946. **Genres:** Novellas/Short Stories, Novels. **Career:** J.G. Ferguson, textbook editor, 1969-71; Scott Foresman, textbook editor, 1971-74; freelance writer, 1976-; StoryQuarterly, fiction editor, 1985-97; Syracuse University, visiting assistant professor, 1999; Bard College, visiting assistant professor, 2001, 2004; NOON, publisher and founding editor, 2000-. **Publications:** This Is about the Body, the Mind, the Soul, the World, Time, and Fate: Stories, 1990; (ed. with A. Brashler and M. Pritchard) The American Story: The Best of Story-Quarterly, 1990; Some Sexual Success Stories: Plus Other Stories in Which God Might Choose to Appear, 1992; The Stupefaction, 1996; Excitability: Selected Stories, 1986-1996, 1998; Romancer Erector: Novella and Stories, 2001; It Was Like My Trying To Have A Tender-Hearted Nature: A Novella and Stories, 2007. Contributor to journals. **Address:** NOON Magazine, 1369 Madison Ave., Ste. 298, New York, NY 10128, U.S.A.

WILLIAMS, Donna. Australian (born Australia), b. 1963. **Genres:** Poetry, Education, Psychology, Social Work, Sociology, Autobiography/Memoirs. **Career:** Writer. **Publications:** Autism: An Inside-Out Approach: An Innovative Look at the Mechanics of Autism and Its Developmental Cousins, 1996; Autism and Sensing: The Unlost Instinct, 1998; Exposure Anxiety: The Invisible Cage-An Exploration of Self Protection Responses in the Autism Spectrum and Beyond, 2003; Not Just Anything: A Collection of Thoughts on Paper, 2004; The Jumbled Jigsaw: An Insider's Approach to the Treatment of Autistic Spectrum Fruit Salads, 2006. AUTOBIOGRAPHY: Nobody Nowhere: The Extraordinary Autobiography of an Autistic, 1992; Somebody Somewhere: Breaking Free from the World of Autism, 1994; Like Color to the Blind, 1996; Everyday Heaven: Journeys beyond the Stereotypes of Autism, 2004. **Address:** Jessica Kingsley Publishers, 116 Pentonville Rd., London, GL N1 9JB, England. **Online address:** bookings@donnawilliams.net

WILLIAMS, Duncan Ryûken. American/Japanese (born Japan), b. 1969. **Genres:** Theology/Religion, History. **Career:** Harvard University, teaching fellow, 1992-95; Trinity College, visiting lecturer of religion, 1996, assistant professor of Japanese religions and culture, 2000-02; Brown University, visiting lecturer in religious studies, 1997-98; Sophia University, lecturer in religious studies, 1997-2001; Komazawa University, postdoctoral fellow in Zen Buddhist history, 2002-03; University of California-Irvine, assistant professor of East Asian Buddhism and culture, 2002-05, associate professor of East Asian Buddhism and culture, 2005-06; University of California-Berkeley, associate professor of Japanese Buddhism, 2006-, Center for Japanese Studies, director, 2007-, Shinjo Ito distinguished chair in Japanese Buddhism, 2009-; University of Southern California, School of Religion, associate professor and chair, 2011-, Center for Japanese Religions and Culture, director, 2011-. Writer. **Publications:** (Ed. with M.E. Tucker) Buddhism and Ecology: The Interconnection of Dharma and Deeds, 1997; (ed. with C.S. Queen) American Buddhism: Methods and Findings in Recent Scholarship, 1999; The Other Side of Zen: A Social History of Sōtō Zen: Buddhism in Tokugawa Japan, 2005; (ed. with T. Moriya) Issei Buddhism in the Americas, 2010. **Address:** School of Religion, University of Southern California, ACB 130, 825 Bloom Walk, Los Angeles, CA 90089-1481, U.S.A. **Online address:** duncanwi@usc.edu

WILLIAMS, Dwight. American (born United States), b. 1966. **Genres:** Documentaries/Reportage, Novels, Autobiography/Memoirs, Biography, Romance/Historical. **Career:** Writer. **Publications:** (With R.J. Pensack) Raising Lazarus, 1994; (with E. Mitchell) The Way of the Explorer: An Apollo Astronaut's Journey through the Material and Mystical Worlds, 1996, rev. ed., 2008; Rumors in the Blood, 1997; From the Garden of Memory (novel), 1998; (with O.B. Revell) A G-Man's Journal: A Legendary Career Inside the FBI from the Kennedy Assassination to the Oklahoma City Bombing, 1998. **Address:** PO Box 771134, Steamboat Springs, CO 80477, U.S.A. **Online address:** dwight@cmn.net

WILLIAMS, Forman A. American (born United States), b. 1934. **Genres:** Engineering, Technology, Young Adult Fiction, Physics, Sciences. **Career:** Harvard University, assistant professor of engineering and applied physics, 1958-64; University of California, professor of aerospace engineering, 1964-81, professor of engineering physics and combustion, Center for Energy Research, director, 1988-, presidential chair in energy and combustion research, 1993; Princeton University, Robert H. Goddard professor of mechanical and aerospace engineering, 1981-88, Robert H. Goddard chair; Yale University, adjunct professor of mechanical engineering and materials science. Writer. **Publications:** Combustion Theory, 1965, 2nd ed., 1985; Fundamental Aspects of Solid Propellant Rockets, 1969; (with T.J. Hendricks and M.K. Liu) Boundary Layer Flow Problems in Desalination by Reverse Osmosis, 1971; (co-ed.) Turbulent Reacting Flows, 1980, rev. ed., 1994; (ed. with P.C. Fife and A. Linan) Dynamical Issues in Combustion Theory, 1991; (co-ed.) Modern Developments in Energy, Combustion and Spectroscopy: In Honor of SS Penner, 1993; (with A. Linan) Fundamental Aspects of Combustion, 1993. **Address:** Department of Mechanical & Aerospace Engineering, University of California, 9500 Gilman Dr., La Jolla, CA 92093, U.S.A. **Online address:** faw@ucsd.edu

WILLIAMS, Geoff. (Geoffrey Williams). American (born United States), b. 1970?. **Genres:** Adult Non-fiction, Novels, Business/Trade/Industry, History, Autobiography/Memoirs. **Career:** Popular Ceramics Magazine, associate editor, 1992; BOP Magazine, associate editor, 1993-96; Cincinnati Post, features reporter, 1999-2001; Babytalk magazine, contributing editor and writer, 2002-07; Geoff Williams (writing and editing), freelance journalist and author, 1996-. **Publications:** (As Geoffrey Williams) Ingenuity in a Can: The Ralph Stolle Story, 2004; C.C. Pyle's Amazing Foot Race: The True Story of the 1928 Coast-to-Coast Run across America, 2007; (with C. Balish) Living Well with Bad Credit: Buy a House, Start a Business and Even Take a Vacation-No Matter How Low Your Credit Score is, 2010. Contributor to magazines and periodicals. **Address:** Health Communications Inc., 3201 SW 15th St., Deerfield Beach, FL 33442, U.S.A. **Online address:** gwilliams1@cinci.rr.com

WILLIAMS, Geoffrey. *See* **WILLIAMS, Geoff.**

WILLIAMS, Gerhild Scholz. (Gerhild Scholz-Williams). American/German (born Germany), b. 1942. **Genres:** Sciences, Literary Criticism And History, Bibliography. **Career:** Washington University, assistant professor, 1975-80, associate professor, 1980-86, professor, 1986-, German Languages department chair, 1986-92, associate provost, 1988, 1989-98, associate vice chancellor, 1995-, special assistant to the chancellor for academic affairs/associate vice chancellor, 1997-, Barbara Schaps Thomas and David M. Thomas Professor in the Humanities in Arts and Sciences, 1999-; Lausanne University, visiting professor, 1990, 1996. Writer. **Publications:** The Vision of Death: A Study of the Memento Mori Expressions in Some Latin, German and French Didactic Texts of the 11. and 12. Centuries, 1976; The Literary World of Maximilian I: An Annotated Bibliography, 1982; (with J.F. Poag) Das weiterleben des mittelalters in der Deutschen literatur, 1983; (with P.M. Luzeler and H. Lehnert) Zeitgenossenschaft: Zur Deutschsprachigen literatur im 20. jahrhundert: festschrift fur Egon Schwarz zum 65. geburtstag, 1987; Defining Dominion: The Discourses of Magic and Witchcraft in Early Modern France and Germany, 1995; (with A. Schwarz) Existentielle vergeblichkeit: vertrage in der melusine, im eulenspiegel und im Dr. Faustus, 2003; Ways of Knowing in Early Modern Germany: Johannes Praetorius as a Witness to His Time, 2006. EDITOR: (with S.K. Schindler) Knowledge, Science and Literature in Early Modern Germany, 1996; (with C.D. Gunnoe, Jr.) Paracelsian Moments: Science, Medicine & Astrology in Early Modern Europe, 2002; (with M. Giesenkirchen and J. Morris and trans. with H. Stone) P. De Lancre, On the Inconstancy of Witches: Pierre De Lancre's Tableau De L'inconstance Des Mauvais Anges Et Demons (1612), 2006. Contributor to books and periodicals. **Address:** Department of Germanic Languages & Literatures, Washington University, CB 1104, 1 Brookings Dr., St. Louis, MO 63130, U.S.A. **Online address:** gerhild_williams@aismail.wustl.edu

WILLIAMS, Gregory Howard. American (born United States), b. 1943. **Genres:** Law, Race Relations, Politics/Government. **Career:** Delaware County, deputy sheriff, 1963-66; Virginia Public Schools, teacher, 1966-70; U.S. Senate, legislative assistant, 1971-73; George Washington University, director of experimental programs, 1973-77, administrator; Foreign Lawyer Training Program, consultant, 1975-77; University of Iowa, College of Law, professor, 1977-93, associate vice president of academic affairs, 1991-93; Ohio State University, Michael E. Moritz College of Law, dean and professor of law, 1993-2001, Carter C. Kissell professor of law, chair in civil rights and civil liberties; City College of New York, president, 2001-09; University of Cincinnati, College of Law, president, 2009-. Writer. **Publications:** The Law and Politics of Police Discretion, 1984; Iowa Guide to Search and Seizure, 1986; Life on the Color Line: The True Story of a White Boy Who Discovered He Was Black, 1995. Contributor to periodicals. **Address:** College of Law, University of Cincinnati, Clifton Ave. and Calhoun St., PO Box 210040, Cincinnati, OH 45221-0040, U.S.A. **Online address:** gwilliams@ccny.cuny.edu

WILLIAMS, Helen. Canadian/British (born England), b. 1948. **Genres:** Novellas/Short Stories, Art/Art History, Mythology/Folklore, Illustrations. **Career:** Redbourne Upper School, teacher of general art, graphics and textiles, 1971-73; Stamford High School for Girls, instructor in art and calligraphy, 1973-74; artist, designer and illustrator, 1974-; teacher, 1977-79; Churchdown School, artist-in-residence, 1989; Stroud High School, instructor in art, textiles fashion and design, 1989-; Jackson County Star, copy editor. **Publications:** T.S. Eliot: The Waste Land, 1968; (comp.) In Abigail's Garden, 1987; (with C. Ritson) Impact of the E.E.C.'s Reference Price System on the Marketing of Fruit and Vegetables in the U.K., 1987; (comp.) Garland for Isabella: A language of Flowers, 1988; (comp.) Language of Flowers, 1988; (with Perry and R. Illing) Illustrated Catalogue of the Early Editions of Handel in Australia, A Second Supplement, 1988; Stories in Art, 1992; People in Art, 1992; Mental Maths Homework for 7 Year Olds, 1999; Mental Maths Homework for 9 Year Olds, 2000; Behind the Veil, 2002; Moving On, 2002; Village Brother, 2002; (with C. Smith) The Islamic Year: Surahs, Stories and Celebrations, 2003; (ed. and comp.) Roy Romer is Alive and Well and Living in California, 2004; Feng Shui Solutions: Feng Shui Solutions For Home, Business And Garden, 2005; Feng Shui Solutions for Home, Business and Garden: Conscious Living for the Modern Age, 2009. **Address:** Walden Press Inc., PO Box 1177, Walden, CO 80480, U.S.A. **Online address:** hmwden@hotmail.com

WILLIAMS, (Henry) Nigel. British (born England), b. 1948. **Genres:** Plays/Screenplays, Novels, Adult Non-fiction, Young Adult Non-fiction, Young Adult Fiction. **Career:** Writer and television executive; British Broadcasting Corp., production assistant, assistant director and producer of arts programs, executive producer. **Publications:** PLAYS: Class Enemy, 1978; Sugar and Spice, 1980; Line Em, 1980; Trial Run, 1980; W.C.P.C., 1982; My Brother's Keeper: A Play, 1985; Country Dancing, 1987; Harry and Me, 1996. NOVELS: My Life Closed Twice, 1977; Jack Be Nimble, 1980; Johnny Jarvis, 1983; Charlie, 1984; Star Turn, 1985; Witchcraft, 1987; The Wimbledon Poisoner, 1990; They Came from SW19, 1993; East of Wimbledon, 1993; 2 1/2 (Three) Men in a Boat, 1993; Scenes From a Prisoner's Life, 1994; From Wimbledon to Waco, 1995; William Golding's Lord of the Flies, 1996; Stalking Fiona, 1998; Forty Something, 1999; Hatchett and Lycett, 2002; School-Marm Murders, 2002; Love Letters Straight from the Heart: True Stories of Passion and Heartbreak, 2003; Acoustic Troubadours, 2003; (foreword) The Mountain Skills Training Handbook, 2004. **Address:** Judy Daish Associates, 2 St. Charles Pl., London, GL W10 6EG, England. **Online address:** wimbledon@compuserve.com

WILLIAMS, Herbert (Lloyd). Welsh (born Wales), b. 1932. **Genres:** Novels, Novellas/Short Stories, Children's Fiction, Plays/Screenplays, Poetry, History, Biography, Documentaries/Reportage, Documentaries/Reportage. **Career:** Welsh Gazette, reporter, 1951-53; Reading Standard, reporter, 1953; Cambrian News, reporter and sub-editor, 1953-56; South Wales Echo, reporter, industrial correspondent and sub-editor, 1956-60, chief feature writer, 1961-72; Scottish Daily Mail, sub-editor, 1960-61; Birmingham Evening Mail, features sub-editor, 1972-73; British Broadcasting Corp., general producer, 1973-79. Writer. **Publications:** Too Wet for the Devil, 1962; The Dinosaurs, 1966, The Trophy, 1967; A Lethal Kind of Love, 1968; Battles in Wales, 1975; Come Out Wherever You are The Great Escape in Wales, 1976; Stage Coaches in Wales, 1977; The Welsh Quiz Book, 1978; Railways in Wales, 1981; Pembrokeshire Coast National Park Guide, 1987; Davies the Ocean: Railway King and Coal Tycoon, 1991; Ghost Country: A Collection of Poems, 1991; The Stars in Their Courses, 1992; John Cowper Powys, 1997; Stories of King Arthur, 1997; Looking Through Time, 1998; Voices of Wales, 1999; A Severe Case of Dandruff, 1999; (ed. and intro.)Renewals: Selected Poems, 1958-1998, 1999; The Woman in Back Row, 2000; Punters, 2002; Wrestling in Mud: New and Selected Poems, 2007; The Marionettes, 2008; Tiger in the Park, 2010; Nice Work If You Can Get It, 2011; Love Child, 2011. **Address:** 63 Bwlch Rd., Fairwater, Cardiff, SG CF5 3BX, Wales. **Online address:** h.williams13@ntlworld.com

WILLIAMS, Hugh Steadman. British (born England), b. 1935. **Genres:** Plays/Screenplays, Literary Criticism And History. **Career:** Westminster Productions Ltd., artistic director, 1975-87, chairperson, 1987; Christian Arts Trust, executive secretary, 1996-. Writer. **Publications:** PLAYS: Grass is Greener, 1960; Past Imperfect, 1966; The Flip Side, 1969; Let's All Go Down the Strand, 1969; (with A. Thornhill) Return Trip, 1974; Poor Man, Rich Man: A One-Man Show Based on the Life of St. Francis of Assisi, 1979; Everywoman: A Verse Drama, 1981; Gavin and the Monster (children's book), 1981; Skeletons, 1987. **Address:** 6 Acton Pl., Vicarage Rd., Yalding, KT ME18 6DN, England. **Online address:** hugh@actonplace.demon.co.uk

WILLIAMS, Ian. American/British (born England), b. 1949. **Genres:** Young Adult Non-fiction. **Career:** Writer. **Publications:** NONFICTION: The Alms Trade: Charities, Past, Present and Future, 1989; The U.N. for Beginners, 1995; Deserter: Bush's War on Military Families, Veterans, and His Past, 2004; Rum: A Social and Sociable History of the Real Spirit of 1776, 2005. Contributor to books. **Address:** Catskills, NY, U.S.A. **Online address:** deadlinepundit@igc.org

WILLIAMS, Jacqueline (B.). American (born United States), b. 1934. **Genres:** Food And Wine, History, Local History/Rural Topics, Sciences, Medicine/Health. **Career:** Writer, 1981-. Public speaker. **Publications:** (With G. Silverman) No Salt, No Sugar, No Fat Cookbook, 1981, rev. ed., 1993; (with G. Silverman) Hold the Fat, Sugar, and Salt, 1984; (with G. Silverman) The Quick and Delicious Low-Fat, Low-Salt Cookbook, 1986; (with G. Silverman) Lowfat American Favorites, 1990; Wagon Wheel Kitchens: Food on the Oregon Trail, 1993; The Way We Ate: Pacific Northwest Cooking, 1843-1900, 1996; The Hill with a Future: Seattle's Capitol Hill, 1900-1946, 2001; The Handbag Book of Diet Emergencies, 2004; The Handbag Book of Girly Love Emergencies, 2004; (ed. with P. Okunieff and Y. Chen) Oxygen Transport to Tissue XXVI, 2005. Contributor of articles to periodicals. **Address:** 1235 22nd Ave. E, Seattle, WA 98112, U.S.A. **Online address:** jbwill2@mindspring.com

WILLIAMS, James C. American (born United States), b. 1942. **Genres:** History, Environmental Sciences/Ecology, Local History/Rural Topics, Humanities. **Career:** Gavilan College, professor of history, 1971-85; California History Center Foundation, executive director, 1985-93, project director and exhibition curator, 1986-91; De Anza College, professor of history, 1993-2004, department chairman, 2000-04, emeritus professor, 2004-. Writer. **Publications:** The Rise of Silicon Valley, 1993; Energy and the Making of Modern California, 1997. EDITOR: Old Town Santa Barbara: A Narrative History of State Street from Gutierrez to Ortega, 1850-1975 (monograph), 1977; Sketches of Gilroy, 1980. Contributor to books and periodicals. **Address:** Department of History, De Anza College, 21250 Stevens Creek Blvd., Cupertino, CA 95014, U.S.A. **Online address:** techjunc@pacbell.net

WILLIAMS, Jeanne. Also writes as Jeanne Crecy, Kristin Michaels, Megan Castell, Jeanne Foster, Diedre Rowan. American (born United States), b. 1930. **Genres:** Novels, Children's Fiction, Mystery/Crime/Suspense. **Career:** Unitarian Universalist Church, board director, 1972-75, president, 1975-76; Western Writers of America, president. Writer. **Publications:** To Buy a Dream, 1958; Promise of Tomorrow, 1959; Coyote Winter, 1965; Beasts with Music, 1967; Oil Patch Partners, 1968; New Medicine, 1971; Trails of Tears, 1972; Freedom Trail, 1973; Winter Wheat, 1975; A Lady Bought with Rifles, 1976; A Woman Clothed in Sun, 1977; Voyage to Love, 1978; Bride of Thunder, 1978; Daughter of the Sword, 1979; The Valiant Women, 1981; Harvest of Fury, 1982; The Heaven Sword, 1983; A Mating of Hawks, 1983; The Cave Dreamers, 1985; The Heaven Sword, 1985; So Many Kingdoms, 1986; Texas Pride, 1987; Lady of No Man's Land, 1988; No Roof but Heaven, 1990; Home Mountain, 1990; The Island Harp, 1991; Animal Rights and Welfare, 1991; (ed. with L. Hayes-Sierra) The Key to Understanding the Federal Budget Process, 1992; The Longest Road, 1993; Daughter of the Storm, 1994; The Unplowed Sky, 1994; Home Station, 1995; Wind Water, 1997; Beneath the Burning Ground, vol. I: The Underground River, 2004, vol. II: The Hidden Valley, 2004; Trampled Fields: A Frontier Story, 2005. AS MEGAN CASTELL: The Queen of a Lonely Country, 1980. AS JEANNE CRECY: Hands of Terror, 1972; The Lightning Tree, 1972; My Face Beneath the Stone, 1975; The Winter Keeper, 1975; The Night Hunters, 1975. AS JEANNE FOSTER: Deborah Leigh, 1981; Wyoming Glory, Eden Richards, 1982; Woman of Three Worlds, 1984. AS KRISTIN MICHAELS: To Begin with Love, 1975; Enchanted Twilight, 1975; A Special Kind of Love, 1976; Enchanted Journey, 1977; Song of the Heart, 1977; Make Believe Love, 1978. AS DEIRDRE ROWAN: Dragon's Mount, 1973; Silver Wood, 1974; Shadow of the Volcano, 1975; Time of the Burning Mask, 1976; Ravensgate, 1976. AS J.R. WILLIAMS: Tame the Wild Stallion, 1957; Mission in Mexico, 1959; The Horse Talker, 1960; The Confederate Fiddle, 1962, (as Jeanne Williams) 2nd ed., 1997; River Guns, 1962; Oh Susanna!, 1963. **Address:** PO Box 16335, Portal, AZ 85632, U.S.A. **Online address:** author@jeannewilliams.net

WILLIAMS, John A(lfred). American (born United States), b. 1925. **Genres:** Novels, Poetry, Biography, History, Military/Defense/Arms Control, Social Sciences, Autobiography/Memoirs, Literary Criticism And History, Literary Criticism And History. **Career:** Doug Johnson Associates, public relations officer, 1952-54; Comet Press Books, publicity director, 1955-56; Negro Market Newsletter, editor and publisher, 1956-57; Abelard-Schuman Inc., assistant to publisher, 1957-58; Ebony Magazine and Jet Magazine, European correspondent, 1958-59; Newsweek Magazine, Africa correspondent, 1964-65; City University of New York, La Guardia Community College, distinguished professor, 1973-79; Cooper Union, distinguished visiting professor, 1974-75; Boston University, visiting professor, 1978-79; Rutgers University, professor, 1979-90, Paul Robeson professor of English, 1990-94; New York University, visiting professor, 1986-87; Bard College, visiting professor, 1994-95. **Publications:** NOVELS: The Angry Ones (One for New York), 1960; Night Song, 1961; Sissie, 1963 in UK as Journey Out of Anger, 1965; The Man Who Cried I Am, 1967; Sons of Darkness, Sons of Light, 1969; Captain Blackman, 1972; Mothersill and the Foxes, 1975; The Junior Bachelor Society, 1976; Click Song, 1982; The Berhama Account, 1985; Jacob's Ladder, 1987; Clifford's Blues, 1998. NONFICTION: Africa: Her History, Lands and People, 1962; The Protectors, 1964; This Is My Country Too, 1965; The Most Native of Sons: Richard Wright, 1970; The King God Didn't Save Martin Luther King, Jr., 1970; Flashbacks, 1972; Minorities in the City, 1975; (with D.A. Williams) If I Stop I'll Die: The Comedy and Tragedy of Richard Pryor, 1991. EDITOR: The Angry Black, 1962; Beyond the Angry

Black, 1966; Amistad I and II, 1970, 1971; Y'Bird No.2, 1978; Introduction to Literature, 1985, 2nd ed., 1994; Street Guide to African Americans in Paris, 1992, 2nd ed., 1996; Bridges: Literature across Cultures, 1993; Dear Chester, Dear John: Letters between Chester Himes and John A. Williams, 2008. OTHER: Last flight from Ambo Ber, 1981; Ways In: Approaches to Literature, 1994, 2nd ed., 2003; Safari West (poetry), 1998; Vanqui (libretto), 1999. **Address:** 693 Forest Ave., Teaneck, NJ 07666, U.S.A.

WILLIAMS, John Hartley. British (born England), b. 1942. **Genres:** Poetry, Literary Criticism And History, Mystery/Crime/Suspense. **Career:** Catholic University of Lille, lecturer in English language and literature, 1965-66; National Institute for Applied Sciences, lecturer in English literature and language, 1966-67; Bishop Road School, teacher of English as a foreign language, 1967-68; University of Novi Sad, lecturer in English language, 1968-70; University of Yaounde, lecturer in English language and literature, 1970-72; Herndon College and Technology, lecturer in liberal studies, 1975-76; Free University of Berlin, lecturer in English language, 1976-. Writer. **Publications:** POETRY: Hidden Identities, 1982; Bright River Yonder, 1988; Cornerless People, 1990; Double, 1994; Ignoble Sentiments, 1995; Canada, 1997; (trans. with H. Ottschofksi) Censored Poems, 2001; Spending Time with Walter, 2001; Blues, 2004. OTHERS: (with M. Sweeney) Teach Yourself Writing Poetry and Getting Published, 1996, rev. ed., 2003; Writing Poetry and Getting Published, 1997; Mystery in Spiderville: A Romance, 2002, rev. ed., 2003; North Sea Improvisation, 2003; The Ship, 2007; Café des Artistes, 2009; (with M. Sweeney) Write Poetry and Get It Published, 2010. CONTRIBUTOR: Poetry with An Edge 2, 1993; Poems for Bosnia, 1993; The Long, Pale Corridor, 1996; (trans.) The Scarin the Stone: Contemporary Poems from Bosnia, 1998. Contributor to periodicals. **Address:** 18 Jenbacher Weg, Berlin, 12209, Germany.

WILLIAMS, Jon. See **WILLIAMS, Walter Jon.**

WILLIAMS, Joy. American (born United States), b. 1944. **Genres:** Novels, Novellas/Short Stories, Travel/Exploration, Essays, Young Adult Fiction. **Career:** University of Houston, visiting instructor of creative writing, 1982; University of Florida, visiting instructor of creative writing, 1983; University of California, visiting instructor of creative writing, 1984; University of Iowa, visiting instructor of creative writing, 1984; University of Arizona, visiting instructor of creative writing, 1987-92; University of Montana, visiting instructor, 2000; University of Texas, visiting instructor, 2000; Washington University, visiting instructor, 2004; University of Wyoming, eminent writer-in-residence, 2008-09. Writer. **Publications:** State of Grace, 1973, rev. ed., 1990; The Changeling, 1978; Taking Care, 1982, rev. ed., 1985; The Florida Keys: A History and Guide, 1987, 10th ed., 2003; Breaking and Entering, 1988; Escapes: Stories, 1990, 2nd ed., 1991; Florida, 1999; The Quick and the Dead, 2000; Ill Nature: Rants and Reflections on Humanity and Other Animals, 2001; Honored Guest: Stories, 2004. Works appear in anthologies. **Address:** c/o Amanda Urban, International Creative Management, 40 W 57th St., New York, NY 10019-4001, U.S.A.

WILLIAMS, Karen Lynn. American (born United States), b. 1952. **Genres:** Children's Fiction, Young Adult Fiction, Adult Non-fiction. **Career:** Teacher of the deaf, 1975-76; Green Acres School, teacher of the deaf, 1977-80; writer, 1984-; Pittsburgh Center for the Arts, teacher, 1994-96; Seton Hill College, adjunct instructor, 1998-; Institute of Children's Literature, instructor, 1998-2001; Hospital Albert Schweitzer, director of public relations, 2001-02, part-time public relations staff, 2002-04; Chatham University, MFA Creative Writing Program, adjunct instructor. **Publications:** When Africa Was Home, 1991. FOR CHILDREN: Galimoto, 1990; Baseball and Butterflies, 1990; First Grade King, 1992; Applebaum's Garage, 1994; Tap-Tap, 1994; Painted Dreams, 1998; Circles of Hope, 2005; (with K. Mohammed) Four Feet, Two Sandals, 2007; (with K. Mohammed) My Name is Sangoel, 2009; Beach Tail, 2010; Lubuto Means Light, 2010. FOR YOUNG ADULTS: A Real Christmas This Year, 1995; One Thing I'm Good At, 1999; Not Alone, forthcoming. Contributor of articles to magazines. **Address:** c/o Lynn Bennett, Transatlantic Literary Agency Inc., 2 Bloor St. E, Ste. 3500, Toronto, ON M4W 1A8, Canada. **Online address:** karen@karenlynnwilliams.com

WILLIAMS, Kate. British (born England), b. 1974. **Genres:** Biography, History, Novels. **Career:** Lectures to society and groups; Sunday Telegraph, writer; The Daily Telegraph, writer; The Independent, writer; The Spectator, writer; Time Out, writer; BBC History Magazine, writer; History Today, reviewer; Financial Times, reviewer; University of London, Royal Holloway, faculty in creative writing. **Publications:** England's Mistress: The Infamous Life of Emma Hamilton, 2006; Becoming Queen Victoria: The Tragic Death of Princess Charlotte and the Unexpected Rise of Britain's Greatest Monarch, 2010; The Pleasures of Men, 2011; (contrib.) The Enchantress, Emma, Lady Hamilton: The Jean Kislak Collection, 2011; (with A. Weir, T. Borman and S. Gristwood) The Ring and the Crown: A History of Royal Wedding 1066-2011, 2011. Contributor to journals and periodicals. **Address:** c/o Simon Trewin, United Agents, 12-26 Lexington St., London, GL W1F OLE, England.

WILLIAMS, Kathryn. (Lucy Ruggles). American (born United States), b. 1981. **Genres:** Novels. **Career:** Sideshow Media (book packager), freelance project editor. Journalist. **Publications:** YOUNG-ADULT NOVELS: The Debutante, 2008; The Lost Summer, 2009. OTHERS: (adaptor as Lucy Ruggles) Minutemen (motion-picture novelization), 2007; (as Lucy Ruggles) Tales from Halloweentown: The Witch's Amulet, 2007; (adaptor as Lucy Ruggles) Camp Rock: The Junior Novel, 2008; (as Lucy Ruggles) Camp Rock, Second Session: For the Record, 2008; Roomies: Sharing Your Home with Friends, Strangers, and Total Freaks, 2008; (as Lucy Ruggles) Camp Rock, Second Session: Rock Royalty, 2009. Contributor to periodicals. **Address:** Nashville, TN , U.S.A. **Online address:** kathryn@kathrynswilliams.com

WILLIAMS, Kimmika L(yvette Hawes). American (born United States), b. 1959. **Genres:** Adult Non-fiction, Biography, Poetry, Autobiography/Memoirs, Plays/Screenplays. **Career:** Philadelphia Tribune, reporter and columnist, 1984-86; Pennsylvania Prison Society, instructor, 1985-89; Bob Lott Productions, scriptwriter, 1986-89; WXPN-FM, arts host and producer, 1989-90; Village Arts Center, instructor, 1990-; Walnut Street Theatre, outreach instructor, 1990-; Bushfire Theatre, writer-in-residence; Temple University, faculty. **Publications:** It Ain't Easy to Be Different, 1986; Negro Kinship to the Park, 1990; Envisioning a Sea of Dry Bones, 1994; Epic Memory: Places and Spaces I've Been, 1995; Signs of the Time: Culture Pop, 1999; Di-Verse City 2000; Mine Eyes Have Seen Into the Millennium, 2000; Brother Love, 2005. **Address:** Writer in Residence, Bushfire Theatre, 224 S 52nd and Locust Sts., Philadelphia, PA 19139, U.S.A. **Online address:** kwilli01@temple.edu

WILLIAMS, Kristen P. American (born United States), b. 1964. **Genres:** Politics/Government, Social Commentary. **Career:** University of California, visiting assistant professor of political science; Clark University, associate professor of government and international relations, associate professor of political science. Writer. **Publications:** Despite Nationalist Conflicts: Theory and Practice of Maintaining World Peace, 2001; (contrib.) The New Great Power Coalition, 2001; (with S.L. Spiegel, J.M. Taw and F.L. Wehling) World Politics in a New Era, 3rd ed., 2004; (contrib.) Ethnic Conflict and International Politics: Explaining Diffusion and Escalation, 2004; (with N.G. Jesse) Identity and Institutions: Conflict Reduction in Divided Societies, 2005; (with J.P. Kaufman) Women, the State, and War: A Comparative Perspective on Citizenship and Nationalism, 2007; (with J. Kaufman) Women and War: Gender Identity and Activism in Times of Conflict, 2010; (with N.G. Jesse) Ethnic Conflict: A Systematic Approach to Cases of Conflict, 2011; (ed. with S.E. Lobell and N.G. Jesse) Beyond Great Powers and Hegemons: Why Secondary States Support, Follow or Challenge, 2012. Contributor to periodicals. **Address:** Department of Government, Clark University, Worcester, MA 01610-1477, U.S.A. **Online address:** kwilliams@clarku.edu

WILLIAMS, Len. American/Canadian (born Canada), b. 1937?. **Genres:** Novels, Young Adult Fiction, Mystery/Crime/Suspense. **Career:** Gold Circle, chief executive officer; Lion-Nathan's retail operations, chief executive officer; Coca-Cola New Zealand, president; J.C. Penney, president; Pic 'n' Save Corp., president and chief executive officer, 1990-. Writer. **Publications:** Justice Deferred: A Novel, 2002. Contributor to periodicals. **Address:** Welcome Rain Publishers, 225 W 35th St., New York, NY 10001, U.S.A.

WILLIAMS, Lena (Marguerite). American (born United States), b. 1950. **Genres:** Race Relations, Social Sciences, Psychology. **Career:** WHUR-FM, reporter; Washington Post, reporter-intern, 1972; Black Sports, associate editor; New York Times, clerk in sports department, reporter and senior writer, 1974-2005, now retired; Duke University, visiting journalist fellow, 1993. **Publications:** It's the Little Things: Everyday Interactions That Get under the Skin of Blacks and Whites, 2000, It's the Little Things: The Everyday Interactions That Anger, Annoy, and Divide the Races, 2001. **Address:** New York Times, 229 W 43rd St., New York, NY 10036, U.S.A.

WILLIAMS, Lillian Serece. American (born United States), b. 1944. **Genres:** Race Relations, History. **Career:** Buffalo Board Education, teacher, 1966-69; State University of New York, assistant professor, 1972-76, lecturer, 1976-79, associate professor of history, 1987-, Institute for Research on Women, director, 1987-, chair; Afro-American New York Life and History, associate editor, 1977-; Howard University, assistant professor of American history, 1979-; American Security Bank of Washington, consultant, 1979-80; New York State Museum's permanent, consultant; National Association of Colored Women's Clubs, editor. **Publications:** A Bridge to the Future: The History of Diversity in Girl Scouting, 1996; Strangers in the Land of Paradise: The Creation of an African-American Community, Buffalo, New York, 1900-1940, 1999. Contributor to books and periodicals. **Address:** Department of African-American Studies, State University of New York, 732 Clemens Hall, Buffalo, NY 14260-4600, U.S.A. **Online address:** lsw4@buffalo.edu

WILLIAMS, Liz. British (born England), b. 1965?. **Genres:** Novels, Horror, Science Fiction/Fantasy, Novellas/Short Stories. **Career:** Brighton Women's Center, information technology manager. Writer and consultant. **Publications:** NOVELS: The Ghost Sister, 2001; Empire of Bones, 2002; The Poison Master, 2003; Nine Layers of Sky, 2003; Banner of Souls, 2004; Winterstrike, 2008. DETECTIVE INSPECTOR CHEN SERIES: (with J. Foster) Snake Agent, 2005; The Demon and the City, 2006; Precious Dragon, 2007; The Shadow Pavilion, 2008; The Iron Khan, 2009; Morningstar, 2011. DARK-LAND SERIES: Darkland, 2006; Bloodmind, 2007. COLLECTIONS: The Banquet of the Lords of Night and Other Stories, 2004; (co-author) Time Pieces, 2006; (co-author) Anniversaries: The Write Fantastic, 2010; A Glass of Shadow, 2011. **Address:** c/o Author Mail, Random House Inc., 1745 Broadway, New York, NY 10019-4368, U.S.A. **Online address:** liz@arkady.org

WILLIAMS, Marcia (Dorothy). British (born England), b. 1945. **Genres:** Children's Fiction, History, Animals/Pets. **Career:** Writer, 1986-. **Publications:** SELF-ILLUSTRATED: The First Christmas, 1987; The Amazing Story of Noah's Ark, 1988; When I Was Little, 1989; Jonah and the Whale, 1989; Not a Worry in the World, 1990; Joseph and His Magnificent Coat of Many Colors, 1992; Greek Myths for Young Children, 1992; Mr. William Shakespeare's Plays in US as Tales from Shakespeare: Seven Plays, 1998; Psyche and Eros, 1998; Bravo, Mr. William Shakespeare!, 2000; No Worries!, 2000; Hooray for Inventors!, 2005; Three Cheers for Inventors!, 2005; Archie's War: My Scrapbook of the First World War, 1914-1918, 2007; My Secret War Diary, by Flossie Albright: My History of the Second World War, 1939-1945, 2008; My Great Lost Dog Adventure!, 2010; Ancient Egypt, 2011. OTHERS: (reteller) King Arthur and the Knights of the Round Table, 1996; (reteller) Fabulous Monsters, 1999; (reteller) God and His Creations, 2004. Illustrator of books by others. **Address:** Walker Books Ltd., 87 Vauxhall Walk, London, GL SE11 5HJ, England.

WILLIAMS, Marie S(heppard). American (born United States), b. 1931. **Genres:** Novellas/Short Stories, History. **Career:** Minneapolis Society for the Blind, social worker and manager, 1971-81; Walker Methodist Home Care, home health aide and companion for Alzheimer's patients, 1986-95. Writer. **Publications:** STORIES: The Worldwide Church of the Handicapped: And Other Stories, 1996; The Weekend Girl and Other Stories, 2003. Contributor to magazines. **Address:** Folio Bookworks, 3241 Columbus Ave. S, Minneapolis, MN 55407-2030, U.S.A.

WILLIAMS, Mark. New Zealander (born New Zealand), b. 1951. **Genres:** Literary Criticism And History, Poetry, Essays. **Career:** University of Auckland, junior lecturer, 1976-78, tutor in English, 1984; University of Canterbury, lecturer in American studies, 1985, lecturer, 1992-93, senior lecturer in English, 1994-, associate professor, 2001-; University of Waikato, lecturer in English, 1986-91; Victoria University, Department of English, associate professor, 2008-. Writer. **Publications:** Leaving the Highway: Six Contemporary New Zealand Novelists, 1990; Patrick White, 1993; Exercise Testing and Training in the Elderly Cardiac Patient, 1994; (comp.) Post-Colonial Literatures in English: Southeast Asia, New Zealand and the Pacific, 1996; (with J. Stafford) Maoriland: New Zealand Literature, 1872-1914, 2006. EDITOR: The Caxton Press Anthology: New Zealand Poetry, 1972-1986, 1987; (with G. McGregor) Dirty Silence: Aspects of Language and Literature in New Zealand: Essays Arising From the University of Waikato Winter Lecture Series of 1990, 1991; (with A. Riach) The Radical Imagination: Lectures and Talks by Wilson Harris, 1992; (with E. Alley) In the Same Room: Conversations with New Zealand Writers, 1992; (with M. Leggott) Opening the Book: New

Essays on New Zealand, 1995; The Source of the Song: New Zealand Writers on Catholicism, 1995; (with J. Bornholdt and G. O'Brien) Anthology of New Zealand Poetry in English, 1997; (with G. Berendse) Terror and Text: Representing Political Violence in Literature and the Visual Arts, 2002. Contributor to periodicals. **Address:** School of English Film Theatre and Media Studies, Victoria University, Rm. 911, von Zedlitz Bldg., Kelburn Pde, Kelburn Campus, PO Box 600, Wellington, 6140, New Zealand. **Online address:** mark.williams@vuw.ac.nz

WILLIAMS, Mark London. American (born United States), b. 1959. **Genres:** Children's Fiction. **Career:** California State University-Northridge Extension and Learning Tree University, instructor; Digital Coast Reporter, executive editor; Below the Line, columnist. Journalist, editor and free-lance writer. **Publications:** Ancient Fire, 2001; Dino Sword, 2001; Dragon Sword, 2004; Trail of Bones, 2005; City of Ruins, 2007; (adapter) Curious George, Tadpole Trouble, 2007; Curious George Storybook Collection, 2010; Fortune's Fool, forthcoming. Contributor of articles to periodicals. **Address:** PO Box 4381, North Hollywood, CA 91617, U.S.A. **Online address:** scribe@dangerboy.com

WILLIAMS, Martin Anthony Joseph. Australian/British (born England), b. 1941. **Genres:** Archaeology/Antiquities, Earth Sciences, Environmental Sciences/Ecology, Geography, Meteorology/Atmospheric Sciences, History. **Career:** Hunting Technical Services Ltd., soil surveyor, 1963-64; Commonwealth Scientific and Industrial Research Organisation, Division of Land Research and Regional Survey, geomorphologist, 1964-66; Macquarie University, lecturer, 1969-72, senior lecturer, 1973-77, associate professor of earth sciences, 1978-84; Monash University, Department of Geography, professor and chair, 1985-88, Graduate School of Environmental Science, director, 1988-90, professor of geography and environmental science, 1988-92; University of Adelaide, foundation professor of environmental studies, 1993-2007, affiliate professor in geology and geophysics, 1993-2008, Mawson Graduate Center, director, 1993-98, Department of Geographical and Environmental Studies, faculty, 1998-2007, emeritus professor, 2007-. Writer. **Publications:** (With D. Adamson) Origins of the Soils Between the Blue and White Nile Rivers, Central Sudan, With Some Agricultural and Climatological Implications, 1976; (co-author) Quaternary Environments, 1993, 2nd ed., 1998; (with R.J. Balling, Jr.) Interactions of Desertification and Climate, 1994. EDITOR: (with J.L. Davies) Land form Evolution in Australasia, 1978; (with H. Faure) The Sahara and the Nile: Quaternary Environments and Prehistoric Occupation in Northern Africa, 1980; (with D.A. Adamson) A Land between Two Niles: Quaternary Geology and Biology of the Central Sudan, 1982; (with C.D. Haynes and M.G. Ridpath) Monsoonal Australia: Landscape, Ecology, and Man in the Northern Lowlands, 1991; (with P. De Deckker and A.P. Kershaw) The Cainozoic in Australia: A Re-appraisal of the Evidence, 1991. OTHER: (co-author) Di si ji huan jing, 1997. Contributor to books and periodicals. **Address:** Geographical and Environmental Studies, University of Adelaide, Rm. G 37, Napier Bldg., North Terr., Adelaide, SA 5000, Australia. **Online address:** martin.williams@adelaide.edu.au

WILLIAMS, Mary E. American (born United States), b. 1960. **Genres:** Adult Non-fiction, Novels, Young Adult Fiction. **Career:** Salon, staff writer; Public Radio Internationals Morning Show, culture correspondent. **Publications:** Issues in Racism, 2000. EDITOR: The Jury System, 1997; (with T.L. Roleff) Marriage and Divorce, 1997; Readings on Maya Angelou, 1997; Discrimination: Opposing Viewpoints, 1997; (with T.L. Roleff) Sexual Violence: Opposing Viewpoints, 1997; Family: Opposing Viewpoints, 1998; Child Labor and Sweatshops, 1998; (with B. Stalcup and K.L. Swisher) Working Women: Opposing Viewpoints, 1998; Date Rape, 1998; Minorities, 1998; (with C.P. Cozic and T.L. Roleff) Tobacco and Smoking: Opposing Viewpoints, 1998; Human Rights: Opposing Viewpoints, 1998; Culture Wars: Opposing Viewpoints, 1999; The Middle East: Opposing Viewpoints, 2000; Homosexuality: Opposing Viewpoints, 1999; Hate Groups: Opposing Viewpoints, 1999; Legalized Gambling, 1999; Education: Opposing Viewpoints, 2000; Capital Punishment, 2000; Smoking, 2000; Teen Smoking, 2000; Sex: Opposing Viewpoints, 2000; Race Relations: Opposing Viewpoints, 2001; Interracial America: Opposing Viewpoints, 2001; Terminal Illness: Opposing Viewpoints, 2001; Rape, 2001; Readings on West Side Story, 2001; Abortion: Opposing Viewpoints, 2002; The White Separatist Movement, 2002; The Sexual Revolution, 2002; Civil Rights, 2002; Death Penalty, 2002; Terrorist Attack on America, 2003; Vaccinations, 2003; Is Global Warming a Threat?, 2003; Is the Death Penalty Fair?, 2003; Abortion, 2003; Marijuana, 2003; Paranormal Phenomena: Opposing Viewpoints, 2003; 1968, 2004; Hate

Groups: Opposing Viewpoints, 2004; Immigration: Opposing Viewpoints, 2004; Poverty and the Homeless, 2004; Racism, 2004; American Values: Opposing Viewpoints, 2005; Constructing a Life Philosophy, 2005; Epidemics, 2005; Hallucinogens, 2005; Is it Unpatriotic to Criticize One's Country?, 2005; Adoption, 2006; Catholic Church, 2006; Global Warming, 2006; Religion in America, 2006; Smoking: An Opposing Viewpoints Guide, 2006; Mental Illness, 2007; Self-Mutilation, 2008; Epilepsy, 2010; Media Bias, 2011; Aids, 2011; Lyme Disease, 2011; Growth Disorders, 2011; Perspectives on Diseases and Disorders, 2011; Gangs, 2012. NOVEL: All the Lurking Mothers of God, forthcoming. **Address:** c/o Author Mail, Greenhaven Press, 15822 Bernardo Center Dr., San Diego, CA 92127-2320, U.S.A. **Online address:** embeedub@yahoo.com

WILLIAMS, Maurice. Canadian/Australian (born Australia), b. 1944?. **Genres:** Social Work, Sociology. **Career:** University of Maryland's European Division, member of faculty; Notre Dame University, member of faculty; University of British Columbia Okanagan (formerly Okanagan University College), professor of history. Writer. **Publications:** Gau, Volk, and Reich: Friedrich Rainer and the Paradox of Austrian National Socialism, 2005; My Internment and Testimony at the Nuremberg War Crimes Trial: The Account of Friedrich Rainer, Austrian Nazi, 2006; Myra's Men: Building the Kettle Valley Railway, Myra Canyon to Penticton, 2008. **Address:** Irving K. Barber School of Arts & Sciences, University of British Columbia, 3333 University Way, Okanagan, Kelowna, BC V1V 1V7, Canada. **Online address:** maurice.williams@ubc.ca

WILLIAMS, Michael. *See* Obituaries.

WILLIAMS, Nancy S. American (born United States), b. 1943. **Genres:** Education, Reference. **Career:** Art teacher, 1965-66; University of Texas at Austin, instructor, 1967-68; Episcopal school, reading specialist, 1968-70; learning strategist and learning disabilities resource room teacher, 1971-79; St. Joseph Hospital, learning specialist and cognitive rehabilitation therapist, 1983-84; Xavier College, assistant professor, 1984-85; St. DePaul University, lecturer, 1984-85, assistant professor, 1985-91, associate professor, 1991-2001, professor of education, 2001, program coordinator for language literacy and specialized instruction, 1996-97, 2002, associate dean of education, 1999-2001. Writer. **Publications:** (With M. Brogan) Developing Literacy in At-Risk Readers: Using Literature in Clinic and Classroom, 1991; Children's Literature and Reading for Students with Reading Difficulties, 2000; Children's Literature Selections and Strategies for Students with Reading Difficulties: A Resource for Teachers, 2000; Selecting and Using Good Books for Struggling Readers: A Resource for Parents and Caregivers, 2002; Using Literature to Support Skills and Critical Discussion for Struggling Readers, Grades 3-9, 2004. **Address:** Christopher-Gordon Publishers Inc., 1420 Providence Hwy, Ste. 120, Norwood, MA 02062, U.S.A. **Online address:** nancy.s.williams@comcast.net

WILLIAMS, Niall. Irish (born Ireland), b. 1958. **Genres:** Autobiography/Memoirs, Novels, Plays/Screenplays, Adult Non-fiction, Young Adult Fiction, Travel/Exploration, Reference. **Career:** Writer, 1985-; Avon Books, copywriter; County Sligo, writer-in-residence. Publisher. **Publications:** Nonfiction (with C. Breen): O Come Ye Back to Ireland: Our First Year in County Clare, 1987; When Summer's in the Meadow, 1989; The Pipes are Calling: Our Jaunts Through Ireland, 1990; The Luck of the Irish: Our Life in County Clare, 1995. FICTION: Four Letters of Love, 1997; As It is in Heaven, 1999; The Way You Look Tonight, 2000; The Fall of Light, 2002; Only Say the Word, 2005; The Unrequited, 2006; Boy in the World, 2007 as Boy and Man, 2008; John: A Novel, 2008. **Address:** Soho Press, 853 Broadway, New York, NY 10003, U.S.A. **Online address:** nwilliams@literati.net

WILLIAMS, Patricia J(oyce). American (born United States), b. 1951. **Genres:** Race Relations, Law. **Career:** Los Angeles Office of the City Attorney, deputy city attorney, 1975-78; Los Angeles City Attorney's Office, deputy city attorney, 1976-78; Western Center on Law and Poverty, staff attorney, 1978-80; Golden Gate University, associate professor of law, 1980-84; City University of New York, associate professor, 1984-88; University of Wisconsin, professor of law, 1988-93; Stanford University, visiting associate professor of law, 1988-89; Columbia University, professor of law, 1992-, Columbia Law School, James L. Dohr professor of law; Harvard University, visiting professor of women's studies, 1992; Wellesley College, fellow; Dartmouth College, School of Criticism and Theory, fellow, Center for Advanced Study in the Behavioral Sciences, fellow, MacArthur Fellow, 2000-. Writer.

Publications: The Alchemy of Race and Rights, 1991; The Rooster's Egg: On the Persistence of Prejudice, 1995; Seeing a Color-blind Future: The Paradox of Race, 1998; Open House of Family, Friends, Food, Piano Lessons and the Search for a Room of My Own, 2004. Contributor to books and periodicals. **Address:** Columbia Law School, Columbia University, Rm. 505, Jerome Greene Hall, 435 W 116th St., New York, NY 10027-7201, U.S.A. **Online address:** williams@law.columbia.edu

WILLIAMS, Paul K. American (born United States), b. 1966. **Genres:** Novels, History, Adult Non-fiction. **Career:** U.S. Air Force Pentagon Headquarters, legacy resource management program director, 1992-97; Kelsey and Associates Inc. (consulting firm), owner, operator, 1995-. Writer. **Publications:** The Historic Homes of J.F.K.: A Self-guided Walking Tour Through Central Georgetown, 1992; Dupont Circle, 2000; The Neighborhoods of Logan, Scott and Thomas Circles, 2001; Greater U Street, 2002; Washington, D.C., Then and Now, 2002; Skaneateles Lake, 2002; Owasco Lake, 2002; Woodley Park, 2003; Cleveland Park, 2003; Georgetown University, 2003; Capitol Hill, 2004; Washington, D.C.: The World War II Years, 2004; Nostalgic Views of Washington, D.C., 2005; Southwest Washington, D.C., 2005; (with M.L. Elfin) Forest Hills, 2006; How to Research Your House History, forthcoming. Contributor to periodicals. **Address:** Kelsey and Associates Inc., 1730 Corcoran St. NW, Washington, DC 20009, U.S.A. **Online address:** paul@washingtonhistory.com

WILLIAMS, Peter. British/Welsh (born Wales), b. 1937. **Genres:** Music. **Career:** University of Edinburgh, lecturer, 1962-72, reader, 1972-82, professor and dean, 1982-85, Russell Collection of Harpsichords, director; Friends of St. Cecilia's Hall, president, 1968-; Duke University, distinguished professor, 1985-90, Center for Performance Practice Studies, director, 1990-, university organist, 1985-90, Department of Music, chairman, 1985-88; Cardiff University, John Bird professor of music. Writer. **Publications:** The European Organ, 1450-1850, 1966; (comp. with S. Newman) Russell Collection and Other Early Keyboard Instruments in Saint Cecilia's Hall, Edinburgh, 1968; Figured Bass Accompaniment: Harpsichord, 1970; Bach Organ Music, 1972; A New History of the Organ from the Greeks to the Present Day, 1980; The Organ Music of J.S. Bach, vols. I-II, 1980, vol. III, 1984, 2nd ed., 2003; Playing the Organ Works of Bach: Some Case Studies, 1987; (with B. Owen) Organ, 1988; The Organ in Western Culture, 750-1250, 1993; How Do Churches Come to Have Organs?, 1993; The Chromatic Fourth during Four Centuries of Music, 1997; Bach, the Goldberg Variations, 2001; The Life of Bach, 2004; J.S. Bach: A Life in Music, 2007. EDITOR: The Organ Yearbook, 1969; Bach, Handel, Scarlatti, Tercentenary Essays, 1985; Musicalisches Opfer: BWV 1079, 1986; Kunst Der Fuge: BWV 1080, 1986; Organ concertos, 1988; (with R.L. Todd) Perspectives on Mozart Performance, 1991. **Address:** Department of Music, Cardiff University, Corbett Rd., Cardiff, CF10 3EB, Wales. **Online address:** williamsp2@cf.ac.uk

WILLIAMS, R. D. American (born United States), b. 1975. **Genres:** Mythology/Folklore, Novels, Novellas/Short Stories, Science Fiction/Fantasy, Literary Criticism And History. **Career:** Writer. **Publications:** The Lost Gate, 2007. **Address:** 603 Hawthorne Ave., Cincinnati, OH 45205, U.S.A. **Online address:** rdwilliams@writing.com

WILLIAMS, Redford. American (born United States), b. 1940. **Genres:** Psychology, Medicine/Health, Sciences. **Career:** Yale-New Haven Medical Center, intern, resident, 1967-70; U.S. Public Health Service, senior surgeon, 1970-72; Duke University Medical Center, assistant professor, 1972-77, professor of psychiatry, 1977-, Behavioral Medicine Research Center, director, 1985-, professor of psychology, 1990-; North Carolina Heart Association, director, 1980-83; Williams LifeSkills Inc., co-founder and chairman, 1997-; Duke University Graduate School, professor of psychology; University of North Carolina, School of Public Health, adjunct professor of epidemiology; International Society of Behavioral Medicine, president, 2006-08. Writer. **Publications:** NONFICTION: (ed. with W.D. Gentry) Psychological Aspects of Myocardial Infarction and Coronary Care, 1975, 2nd ed., 1979; (ed. with W.D. Gentry) Behavioral Approaches to Medical Treatment, 1977; (with R.S. Surwit and D. Shapiro) Behavioral Approaches to Cardiovascular Disease, 1982; (ed.) Neuroendocrine Control and Behavior, 1985; The Trusting Heart: Great News about Type A Behavior, 1989; (with V. Williams) Anger Kills: Seventeen Strategies for Controlling the Hostility That Can Harm Your Health, 1993; (with V. Williams) Lifeskills: 8 Simple Ways to Build Stronger

Relationships, Communicate More Clearly and Improve Your Health, 1997; (with V. Williams) The Type E Personality: 10 Steps to Emotional Excellence in Love, Work and Life, 2004; (with V. Williams) In Control: No More Snapping at Your Family, Sulking at Work, Steaming in the Grocery Line, Seething at Meetings, Stuffing Your Frustration, 2006. Contributor to periodicals. **Address:** Williams LifeSkills Inc., 2020 W Main St., Ste. 100, Durham, NC 27705, U.S.A. **Online address:** redfordw@duke.edu

WILLIAMS, R(obert) J(oseph) P(aton). British (born England), b. 1926. **Genres:** Biology, Chemistry, Sciences. **Career:** Oxford University, Napier Royal Society Research Professor, Merton College, junior research fellow, 1951-55, now professor emeritus; Wadham College, fellow, 1955-72, university lecturer, 1955-72, reader in chemistry, 1972-74, senior research fellow, through 1991, fellow emeritus, 1991-; Harvard University, faculty, 1965-66, biochemistry faculty, through 1974; California Institute of Technology, Buchman Memorial Lecturer, 1972; Royal Society Napier, research professor, 1974-91; Princeton University, visiting lecturer, 1976; Indiana University, Frank C. Mathers Lecturer, 1978; University of Toronto, visiting lecturer, 1980; University of Zurich, Biochemistry Institute, commemoration lecturer, 1981; Royal Society, Bakerian Lecturer, 1981; University of Newfoundland, visiting lecturer, 1983; Dalhousie University, Walter J. Chute Lecturer, 1984; University of Norwich, Katritsky Lecturer, 1986; Pennsylvania State University, Chermeda Lecturer, 1986; University of Lund, Sunner Memorial Lecturer, 1986; Swedish Academy, A. Scheele Memorial Lecturer, 1986; University of Sussex, Alan Johnson Memorial Lecturer, 1987; University of London, Drummond Lecturer in Biology, 1988; University of Southern California, Stauffer Lecturer, 1990; Royal Free Hospital, visiting professor, 1991-; Massachusetts Institute of Technology, Arthur D. Little Lecturer, 1991; Institute of Neurology, Pewterers Lecturer, 1992; University of Nottingham, Jesse Boot Lecturer, 1993. Writer. **Publications:** (With C.S.G. Phillips) Inorganic Chemistry, 1965; Bioinorganic Chemistry, 1978; (ed. with J.R.R.F. da Silva) New Trends in Bio-inorganic Chemistry, 1978; (ed. with P.B. Garland) Mobility and Migration of Biological Molecules, 1981; (ed. with A. Miller and D. Phillips) Mineral Phases in Biology: Proceedings of a Royal Society Discussion Meeting Held on 1 and 2 June 1983, 1983; (ed. with S. Mann and J. Williams) Biomineralization: Chemical and Biochemical Perspectives, 1989; (with J.J.R.F. da Silva) The Biological Chemistry of the Elements: The Inorganic Chemistry of Life, 1991, 2nd ed., 2001; (with J.J.R.F. da Silva) The Natural Selection of the Chemical Elements: The Environment and Life's Chemistry, 1996; (with J.J.R.F. Da Silva) Bringing Chemistry to Life: From Matter to Man, 1999; Chemistry of Evolution: The Development of our Ecosystem, 2006; (ed. with J.S. Rowlinson and A. Chapman) Chemistry at Oxford: A History from 1600 to 2005, 2009. Contributor to journals. **Address:** Wadham College, Oxford University, Parks Rd., Oxford, OX OX1 3PN, England. **Online address:** bob.williams@chem.ox.ac.uk

WILLIAMS, Robyn. Australian/British (born England), b. 1944. **Genres:** Adult Non-fiction, Autobiography/Memoirs, History. **Career:** Australian Science Communicators, president. Writer. **Publications:** NON-FICTION: The Uncertainty Principle, 1991; And Now for Something Completely Different (autobiography), 1995; This is the Science Show, 1995; Normal Service Won't Be Resumed: The Future of Public Broadcasting, 1996; Scary Monsters & Bright Ideas, 2001; (with T. Frame and N. Drayson) Charles Darwin: An Australian Selection, 2008. NOVELS: 2007: A True Story Waiting to Happen, 2002; Unintelligent Design: Why God isn't as Smart as She Thinks She Is, 2006. Contributor to periodicals. **Address:** Australian Broadcasting Corp., ABC Ultimo Ctr., 700 Harris St., PO Box 9994, Sydney, WA 2001, Australia. **Online address:** williams.robyn@abc.net.au

WILLIAMS, Sheila J. American (born United States), b. 1948?. **Genres:** Novels, Young Adult Fiction. **Career:** Writer. **Publications:** NOVELS: Dancing on the Edge of the Roof, 2002; The Shade of my Own Tree, 2003; On the Right Side of a Dream, 2005; Girls Most Likely, 2006. **Address:** c/o Author Mail, Random House Publishing Group, 1745 Broadway, 18th Fl., New York, NY 10019, U.S.A. **Online address:** sheila@sheilajwilliams.com

WILLIAMS, Sheron. American (born United States), b. 1955. **Genres:** Children's Fiction, Adult Non-fiction, Music, Westerns/Adventure. **Career:** Columbia College, part-time faculty, 1990-, instructor. Writer. **Publications:** And in the Beginning, 1992; Hip Hop City Saturday, 1992; Imani's Music, 2002. **Address:** Department of Arts Management, Columbia College, 600 S Michigan Ave., Chicago, IL 60605, U.S.A. **Online address:** sheron.williams@loop.colum.edu

WILLIAMS, Stanley Tookie. American (born United States), b. 1953. **Genres:** Humanities. **Career:** Crips gang, cofounder, 1971-. Writer. **Publications:** (with B.C. Becnel) Gangs and Self-esteem, 1996; (with B.C. Becnel) Gangs and Weapons, 1996; (with B.C. Becnel) Gangs and Your Friends, 1996; (with B.C. Becnel) Gangs and Your Neighborhood, 1996; (with B.C. Becnel) Gangs and Drugs, 1996; (with B.C. Becnel) Gangs and Violence, 1996; (with B.C. Becnel) Gangs and the Abuse of Power, 1996; (with B.C. Becnel) Gangs and Wanting to Belong, 1996; (with B.C. Becnel) Life in Prison, 1998; Blue Rage, Black Redemption, 2007.

WILLIAMS, Stephanie. British/Canadian (born Canada), b. 1948?. **Genres:** Novels. **Career:** Childrens Express (now Headliners), founder; The Sunday Times, journalist; The Wall Street Journal, journalist; Access Project, chair; New Statesman, journalist. **Publications:** NONFICTION: HongKong Bank: The Building of Norman Foster's Masterpiece, 1989; London Docklands, 1990; Olga's Story: Three Continents, Two World Wars and Revolution-One Woman's Epic Journey through the Twentieth Century (biography), 2005. **Address:** c/o Bill Hamilton, A M Heath & Company Ltd, 6 Warwick Ct., London, GL WC1R 5 DJ, England. **Online address:** stephanie@stephanie-williams.com

WILLIAMS, Susan. American (born United States), b. 1960. **Genres:** Sciences, Business/Trade/Industry, Biography. **Career:** Investor Responsibility Research Center Inc., manager special projects, 1984-; Plainfield Recycling Shed, coordinator, 1990-. Writer. **Publications:** (With D.S. Cogan) Generating Energy Alternatives: Conservation, Load Management, Renewable Energy at America's Electric Utilities, 1983; (with S. Fenn and D. Cogan) Power Plays: Profiles of America's Independent Renewable Electricity Developers, 1986; (with D.S. Cogan) Generating Energy Alternatives: Demand-side Management, Renewable Energy at America's Electric Utilities, 1987; Trash to Cash: New Business Opportunities in the Post-consumer Waste Stream, 1991; (ed.) The McClellanville Coast Cookbook, 1992; Hydro-Québec and the Great Whale Project: Hydroelectric Development in Northern Québec, 1993; Equal Employment and Disclosure: A Report on U.S. Corporate Practices, 1996; Food in the United States, 1820s-1890, 2006. Contributor to periodicals. **Address:** City County Office, 200 E Washington St., Ste. 241, Indianapolis, IN 46204, U.S.A.

WILLIAMS, Terrie (Michelle). American (born United States), b. 1954. **Genres:** Adult Non-fiction. **Career:** New York Hospital, medical social worker, 1977-80; Black Filmmaker Foundation, program administrator, 1980-81; Black-owned Community Alliance, executive director, 1981-82; World Institute of Black Communications, executive director, 1982; Essence Communications Inc., vice president and director of corporate communications, 1982-87; Terrie Williams Agency, owner, 1988-; The Stay Strong Foundation, co-founder, 2001-, board director. Writer. **Publications:** (With J. Cooney) The Personal Touch: What You Really Need to Succeed in Today's Fast-paced Business World, 1994; Stay Strong: Simple Life Lessons for Teens, 2001; A Plentiful Harvest: Creating Balance and Harmony through the Seven Living Virtues, 2002; Black Pain: It Just Looks Like We're Not Hurting, 2008. **Address:** Terrie Williams Agency, 382 Central Pk. W, Ste. 7R, New York, NY 10025, U.S.A. **Online address:** tmwms@terriewilliams.com

WILLIAMS, Terry Tempest. American (born United States), b. 1955. **Genres:** Natural History, Adult Non-fiction, Children's Non-fiction, Sciences, Essays. **Career:** Navajo Reservation in Montezuma Creek, teacher; Utah Museum of Natural History, curator, naturalist-in-residence; University of Utah, Shirley Sutton Thomas visiting professor of English, 1999; Dartmouth College, Montgomery fellow, faculty. Writer. **Publications:** (With T. Major) The Secret Language of Snow (for children), 1984; Pieces of White Shell: A Journey to Navajo Land, 1984; Between Cattails (verse; for children), 1985; Coyote's Canyon, 1989; Refuge: An Unnatural History of Family and Place, 1991; The Graywolf Annual Ten: Changing Community, 1993; (with B. McKibben and W.L. Heat-Moon) Three Essays, 1993; Stone Time, Southern Utah: A Portrait and a Meditation, 1994; An Unspoken Hunger: Stories from the Field (essays), 1994; Atomic Ghost: Poets Respond to the Nuclear Age, 1995; Desert Quartet: An Erotic Landscape, 1995; (ed. with T. Lyon) Great and Peculiar Beauty: A Utah Reader, 1995; (comp. with S. Trimble) Testimony: Writers of the West Speak on Behalf of Utah Wilderness, 1996; (ed. with W.B. Smart and G.M. Smith) New Genesis: A Mormon Reader on Land and Community, 1998; (intro.) All My Rivers are Gone: A Journey of Discovery through Glen Canyon, 1998; Leap: A Traveler in the Garden of Twilights,

2000; Red: Passion and Patience in the Desert, 2001; Emmet Gowin, 2002; Open Space of Democracy, 2004; Illuminated Desert, 2008; Mosaic: Finding Beauty in a Broken World, 2008. Works appear in anthologies. Contributor to periodicals. **Address:** Brandt & Brandt Literary Agency, 1501 Broadway, New York, NY 10036, U.S.A.

WILLIAMS, Theresa. American (born United States), b. 1956. **Genres:** Meteorology/Atmospheric Sciences, Novels, Mystery/Crime/Suspense, Romance/Historical. **Career:** Bowling Green State University, lecturer of literature and writing, senior lecturer, Creative Writing Program, core faculty. Novelist. **Publications:** The Secret of Hurricanes: A Novel, 2002. Contributor to periodicals. **Address:** Creative Writing Program, Department of English, Bowling Green State University, 419 East Hall, Bowling Green, OH 43403-0001, U.S.A. **Online address:** terria@bgsu.edu

WILLIAMS, Tony. American/British (born England), b. 1946. **Genres:** Cultural/Ethnic Topics, Film, History. **Career:** Southern Illinois University at Carbondale, associate professor of English, 1984-, professor. Writer. **Publications:** (With L. Staig) Italian Western: Opera of Violence, 1975; Jack London: The Movies, 1992; Hearths of Darkness: The Family in the American Horror Film, 1996; Radical Allegories: The Films of Larry Cohen, 1997; Structures of Desire: British Cinema 1939-1955, 2000; Video Versions: Film Adaptations of Plays on Video, 2000; The Cinema of George A. Romero, 2003; Body and Soul: The Cinematic Vision of Robert Aldrich, 2004. EDITOR: (with J.-J. Malo) Vietnam War Films, 1994; (with R. Fumento) Jack London's the Sea Wolf, 1998; (with S.J. Schneider) Horror International, 2005. Contributor to periodicals. **Address:** Department of English, Southern Illinois University, Faner 2266, 1000 Faner Dr., PO Box 4503, Carbondale, IL 62901, U.S.A. **Online address:** tonyw@siu.edu

WILLIAMS, Vera B. American (born United States), b. 1927. **Genres:** Children's Fiction, Illustrations, Music, Literary Criticism And History, Young Adult Fiction. **Career:** Gate Hill Cooperative Community, co-founder and teacher, 1953-70; Collaberg School (alternative school for children), co-founder and teacher, 1960-69; Everdale School, teacher, 1970-73; author and illustrator of books for children, 1975-; Goddard College, instructor, 1980-82. Writer. **Publications:** It's a Gingerbread House: Bake It, Build It, Eat It!, 1978; (contrib.) Our Class Presents Ostrich Feathers: A Play in Two Acts, 1978; The Great Watermelon Birthday, 1980; Three Days on a River in a Red Canoe, 1981; A Chair for My Mother, 1982; Something Special for Me, 1983; Music, Music for Everyone, 1984; Cherries and Cherry Pits, 1986; My Mother, Leah and George Sand, 1986; (with J. Williams) Stringbean's Trip to the Shining Sea, 1988; More More More, Said the Baby: Three Love Stories, 1990; Scooter, 1993; Lucky Song, 1997; Amber Was Brave, Essie Was Smart, 2001; Best Sandwich, 2001; A Chair for Always, 2009. Illustrator of books by B. Brenner, R. Charlip and L. Moore. Contributor to periodicals. **Address:** c/o Author Mail, Greenwillow Books, 1350 Ave. of the Americas, New York, NY 10019-4702, U.S.A.

WILLIAMS, Vernon J(ohnson). American (born United States), b. 1948. **Genres:** Anthropology/Ethnology, History, Race Relations, Sociology, Philosophy. **Career:** University of Rhode Island, instructor in history, 1978; Clark University, lecturer in history, 1978-79; Northwestern University, research associate in history, 1979-84; Elmhurst College, lecturer, 1981; University of Iowa, visiting adjunct assistant professor of history, 1985; Rhode Island College, assistant professor of history, 1985-90; University of Massachusetts-Boston, William Monroe Trotter Institute, research associate, 1987-88; Boston University, Afro-American Studies Center, lecturer and research associate, 1989-90; Purdue University, Department of History, associate professor, 1990-97, professor of history, 1997-2004; Indiana University, Department of African American and African Diaspora Studies, professor, 2004-. Writer. **Publications:** Race and Class in American Race Relations Theory, 1894-1939, 1989; From a Caste to a Minority: Changing Attitudes of American Sociologists toward Afro-Americans, 1896-1945, 1989; Rethinking Race: Franz Boas and His Contemporaries, 1996; The Social Sciences and Theories of Race, 2006. Contributor to books and journals. **Address:** Department of African American/Diaspora Studies, Indiana University, M-23 Memorial Hall E, 1021 E 3rd St., Bloomington, IN 47405, U.S.A. **Online address:** vewillia@indiana.edu

WILLIAMS, Walter E(dward). American (born United States), b. 1936. **Genres:** Economics, Politics/Government, Race Relations, History. **Career:**

Los Angeles County Probation Department, staff, 1963-67; Los Angeles City College, economics instructor, 1967-68; California State University, assistant professor, 1967-71; Urban Institute, research staff, 1971-73; Temple University, associate professor of economics, 1973-80; Hoover Institute, fellow, 1976, director; Reason Foundation, director; Grove City College, faculty, director; George Mason University, Department of Economics, John M. Olin istinguished professor of economics, 1980-, department chairman, 1995-2001; Media General, board director, 2001-11, retired, 2011. Writer. **Publications:** Youth and Minority Unemployment, 1977; (with L.A. Smith and W.W. Gunn) Black America and Organized Labor: A Fair Deal?, 1979; (with J.T. Bennett) Strategic Minerals: The Economic Impact of Supply Disruptions, 1981; America, A Minority Viewpoint, 1982; The State against Blacks, 1982; Explaining the Economic Gender Gap, 1983; Legislating Black Unemployment, 1984; All It Takes Is Guts: A Minority View, 1987; South Africa's War against Capitalism, 1989; Do the Right Thing: The People's Economist Speaks, 1995; More Liberty Means Less Government: Our Founders Knew this Well, 1999; (foreword) A Cure Worse Than The Disease: Fighting Discrimination Through Government Control, 1999; Liberty Versus the Tyranny of Socialism, 2008; Up from the Projects: An Autobiography, 2010; Race & Economics: How Much Can be Blamed on Discrimination?, 2011. Contributor to periodicals. **Address:** Department of Economics, George Mason University, 333 Enterprise Hall, MSN 3G4, 3rd Fl., 4400 University Dr., Fairfax, VA 22030-4444, U.S.A. **Online address:** wwilliam@gmu.edu

WILLIAMS, Walter Jon. (Jon Williams). American (born United States), b. 1953. **Genres:** Science Fiction/Fantasy. **Career:** Teacher and writer. **Publications:** Ambassador of Progress, 1984; Knight Moves, 1985; Hardwired, 1986; The Crown Jewels, 1987; Voice of the Whirlwind, 1987; House of Shards, 1988; Solip: System, 1989; Hardwired: The Sourcebook, 1989; Angel Station, 1989; Facets (short stories), 1990; Elegy For Angels and Dogs (novella), 1990; Days of Atonement, 1991; Dinosaurs (novella), 1991; Aristoi, 1992; Wall, Stone, Craft, 1993; Metropolitan, 1995; Rock of Ages, 1995; City on Fire, 1997; Rift, 1999; Destiny's Way, 2002; The Praxis, 2002; Sundering, 2004; Conventions of War, 2005; (with S.M. Stirling, H. Turtledove and M. Gentle) Worlds that weren't, 2005; Implied Spaces, 2008; This is not a Game, 2009; Deep State, 2011; Fourth Wall, 2012. AS JON WILLIAMS: The Privateer, 1981; The Yankee, 1981; The Raider; Privateers and Gentlemen, 1981; The Macedonian, 1984; Cat Island, 1984. Works appear in anthologies. **Address:** c/o Tor Books, 175 5th Ave., 14th Fl., 14th Fl., New York, NY 10010, U.S.A. **Online address:** dubjay@walterjonwilliams.net

WILLIAMS, Wendy. American (born United States), b. 1950?. **Genres:** Sciences, Sports/Fitness, Recreation, Environmental Sciences/Ecology. **Career:** Author and journalist, 1996. Duke University, Hastings Center for Medical Ethics, journalist-in-residence; University of Colorado Center for Environmental Journalism, fellow; Marine Biological Laboratory, fellow. **Publications:** The Best Bike Paths of New England: Safe, Scenic, and Traffic-Free Bicycling, 1996; The Best Bike Paths of the Southwest: Safe, Scenic, and Traffic-Free Bicycling, 1996; Cape Wind: Money, Celebrity, Class, Politics, and the Battle for Americas Energy Future on Nantucket Sound, 2007; Kraken: The Curious, Exciting and Slightly Disturbing Science of Squid, 2010. **Address:** Abrams Image, 115 W 18th St., 6th Fl., New York, NY 10011, U.S.A. **Online address:** wesuwi@comcast.net

WILLIAMS, W. S. C. British (born England), b. 1929. **Genres:** Physics. **Career:** University of Glasgow, lecturer, 1955-61; Oxford University, lecturer in physics, 1961-96, Department of Nuclear Physics, senior research officer, St. Edmund Hall, fellow and tutor, 1963-96. Writer. **Publications:** Introduction to Elementary Particle Physics, 1961, 2nd ed., 1971; Nuclear and Particle Physics, 1991; Solutions Manual for Nuclear and Particle Physics, 1994; Introducing Special Relativity, 2002. **Address:** CRC Press, 6000 Broken Sound Pkwy. NW, Ste. 300, Boca Raton, FL 33487, U.S.A. **Online address:** b.williams1@physics.ox.ac.uk

WILLIAMSON, Chet. American (born United States), b. 1948. **Genres:** Novels, Mystery/Crime/Suspense, Horror, Science Fiction/Fantasy, Children's Fiction, Graphic Novels. **Career:** Teacher, 1971-72; actor, 1973-77; Armstrong World Industries, writer and producer of business theater pieces, 1977-86; freelance writer, 1986-. **Publications:** HORROR NOVELS: Soulstorm, 1986; Ash Wednesday, 1987; Lowland Rider, 1988; Dreamthorp: A New Novel, 1989; Reign, 1990; Mordenheim, 1994; Atmosfear: A Novel, 1995; Clash by Night, 1998. AS CHET WILLIAMSON: OTHER: McKain's Dilemma, 1988; (with G. Brandner, R. Laymon and S. Wiater) Night Visions

7, 1989; The House of Fear: A Study in Comparative Religions, 1989; Aliens: Music of the Spears, 1994; Second Chance, 1995; Cross, 1995; The Crow: City of Angels, 1996; Murder in Cormyr, 1996; The Searchers vol. I: City of Iron, 1998, vol. II: Empire of Dust, 1998, vol. III: Siege of Stone, 1999; Pennsylvania Dutch Night before Christmas, 2000; Uniting Work and Spirit: A Centennial History of Elizabethtown College, 2001; Figures in Rain, 2002; Pennsylvania Dutch Alphabet, 2007; The Story of Noichi the Blind, 2007; (co-author) Tales From the Crossroad vol. I, 2011; Defenders of the Faith, 2011; Hunters, 2011. AS CHET WILLIAMSON: SCIENCE FICTION: Hell: A Cyberpunk Thriller, 1995; The Searchers: City of Iron, 1998; The Searchers: Empire of Dust, 1998; The Searchers: Siege of Stone, 1999. Contributor to magazines. **Address:** 605 Mount Gretna Rd., Elizabethtown, PA 17022, U.S.A. **Online address:** chet.williamson@gmail.com

WILLIAMSON, Denise. American (born United States), b. 1954. **Genres:** Novels, Children's Fiction, History, Race Relations, Theology/Religion, Young Adult Fiction, Biography. **Career:** Pennsylvania Bureau of State Parks, environmental education specialist, through 1982. Writer. **Publications:** JUVENILE: Bible Readings on God's Creation, 1987; Quiet Times with Active Preschoolers: Activity Devotions for Families with Young Children, 1989; River of Danger: A Story of Samuel Kirkland, 1990; Forbidden Gates: A Story of Stephen, the First Martyr, 1990; Chariots to China: A Story of Eric Liddell, 1991; The King's Reward: A Story of Vincent de Paul, 1991; Silent Road to Rescue, 2008. ROOTS OF FAITH SERIES: The Dark Sun Rises, 1998; When Stars Begin to Fall, 2001. **Address:** PO Box 574, Shippensburg, PA 17257-9421, U.S.A.

WILLIAMSON, Donald I. British (born England), b. 1922. **Genres:** Sciences, Zoology, Marine Sciences/Oceanography. **Career:** University of Liverpool, Port Erin Marine Laboratory, assistant lecturer, reader in marine biology, 1948-87, emeritus reader, 1987-, honorary fellow, 1987; International Indian Ocean Expedition, senior specialist on decapod crustacean larvae, 1967-. Writer and carcinologist. **Publications:** On a Collection of Planktonic Decapoda and Stomatopoda (Crustacea) from the East Coast of the Sinai Peninsula, Northern Red Sea, 1970; Larvae and Evolution: Toward a New Zoology, 1992; The Origins of Larvae, 2003. CO-EDITOR: The Evolutionary Biology Papers of Elie Metchnikoff, 2000. Works appear in anthologies. Contributor to books and journals. **Address:** 14 Pairk Beg, Port Erin, IM IM9 6NH, England. **Online address:** diwilliamson@manx.net

WILLIAMSON, Edwin. British (born England), b. 1949. **Genres:** Language/Linguistics. **Career:** Edinburgh University, Forbes professor of Hispanic studies; Oxford University, King Alfonso XIII chair of Spanish, King Alfonso XIII professor of Spanish Studies, professor; Exeter College, professorial fellow, 2003-; Stanford University, visiting professor; Trinity College, faculty; University of London, Birkbeck College, faculty; Universidade de Sao Paulo, visiting professor. Writer. **Publications:** The Half-Way House of Fiction: Don Quixote and Arthurian Romance, 1984; The Penguin History of Latin America, 1992; (ed. and intro.) Cervantes and the Modernists: The Question of Influence, 1994; Borges: A Life, 2004; (co-ed.) Autoridad y Poder en el Siglo de Oro, 2009. **Address:** Department of Medieval and Modern Languages, Oxford University, 41 & 47 Wellington Sq., Oxford, OX OX1 2JF, England. **Online address:** edwin.williamson@mod-langs.ox.ac.uk

WILLIAMSON, Greg. American (born United States), b. 1964. **Genres:** Poetry. **Career:** Johns Hopkins University, The Writing Seminars, lecturer in writing, 1989-, senior lecturer; Waywiser Press, associate editor. **Publications:** The Silent Partner (poems), 1995; What's the Recipe for Friends?, 1999; Errors in the Script: Poems, 2001; Most Marvelous Piece of Luck, 2008. Contributor to journals. **Address:** The Writing Seminars, Johns Hopkins University, 081 Gilman Hall, 3400 N Charles St., Baltimore, MD 21218, U.S.A. **Online address:** wmson@jhu.edu

WILLIAMSON, J(erry) W(ayne). American (born United States), b. 1944. **Genres:** Local History/Rural Topics, Film, History. **Career:** Appalachian State University, Department of English, assistant professor, associate professor, professor, 1970-, professor emeritus, Appalachian Journal, editor emeritus. **Publications:** Myth of the Conqueror: Prince Henry Stuart, A Study of 17th Century Personation, 1978; Southern Mountaineers in Silent Films: Plot Synopses of Movies about Moonshining, Feuding, and Other Mountain Topics, 1904-1929, 1994; Hillbillyland: What the Movies Did to the Mountains and What the Mountains Did to the Movies, 1995. EDITOR: A Guide to Appalachian Studies, 1977; An Appalachian Symposium: Essays Written in

Honor of Cratis D. Williams, 1977; (with E.T. Arnold) Interviewing Appalachia: The Appalachian Journal Interviews, 1978-1992, 1994. **Address:** Carol Grotnes Belk Library & Information Commons, Appalachian State University, 218 College St., PO Box 32026, Boone, NC 28608-2026, U.S.A. **Online address:** willimsonjw@appstate.edu

WILLIAMSON, Joel. American (born United States), b. 1929. **Genres:** History, Literary Criticism And History, Race Relations, Social Sciences. **Career:** University of North Carolina, instructor in history, 1960-64, assistant professor, 1964-66, associate professor, 1966-69, professor, 1969-85, Lineberger professor in the humanities, 1985-, now professor emeritus, CSAS, associate director; Center for Advanced Study in the Behavioral Sciences, fellow, 1977-78; Harvard University, visiting professor of history, 1981-82, Charles Warren Center, fellow, 1981-82; Rockefeller Center, fellow. Writer. **Publications:** After Slavery: The Negro in South Carolina during Reconstruction 1861-1877, 1965; (ed. and intro.) The Origins of Segregation, 1968; New People: Miscegenation and Mulattoes in the United States, 1980; The Crucible of Race: Black-White Relations in the American South since Emancipation, 1984; A Rage for Order: Black/White Relations in the American South since Emancipation, 1986; William Faulkner and Southern History, 1993. **Address:** Department of History, University of North Carolina, Hamilton Hall, CB 3195, Chapel Hill, NC 27599-3195, U.S.A. **Online address:** annaleoww@aol.com

WILLIAMSON, John (Gordon). British/Scottish (born Scotland), b. 1949. **Genres:** Music, History. **Career:** University of Liverpool, lecturer in music, 1974-93, senior lecturer in music 1993-97, reader in music 1998-2002, professor of music, 2003-, now professor emeritus. Writer. **Publications:** The Music of Hans Pfitzner, 1992; Richard Strauss: Also Sprach Zarathustra, 1993; (ed.) The Cambridge Companion to Bruckner, 2004; Words and Music, 2005. Contributor to journals and books. **Address:** School of Music, University of Liverpool, 80 Bedford St. S, PO Box 147, Liverpool, MS L69 3BX, England. **Online address:** j.g.williamson@liv.ac.uk

WILLIAMSON, Kate T. American (born United States), b. 1979?. **Genres:** Photography, Education. **Career:** Writer and artist. **Publications:** SELF-ILLUSTRATED: A Year in Japan, 2006; At a Crossroads: Between a Rock and My Parents' Place, 2008. OTHER: Hello Kitty Through the Seasons, 2006. Contributor to periodicals. **Address:** New York, NY , U.S.A. **Online address:** hello@katetwilliamson.com

WILLIAMSON, Margaret. American/British (born England), b. 1947. **Genres:** Classics, Poetry. **Career:** University of Toronto, Department of English, teaching assistant, 1970-71; London University, Department of Workers Educational Association and Extra-Mural, tutor in English literature, 1973-75; City Literary Institute, part-time tutor of Greek and Latin language and literature, 1975-79; University of Reading, lecturer in classics, 1979-82; Paddington Institute, tutor of Greek and Latin, 1982-83; Cambridge University, supervisor in classics, 1982-83; Open University, tutor and counsellor, 1982-92, assistant senior counsellor, 1985-89; St. Paul's Girls School, teacher of English and classics, 1983-85; Joint Association of Classical Teachers, 1985-89; University of London, Goldsmiths, Department of Drama, part-time tutor of classical drama, 1987, Centre for Extra-Mural Studies, tutor, 1988-89; University of Surrey, St. Mary's University College, senior lecturer in classical studies, 1989-99, Director of Classical Studies Programme, 1997-99; Oxford University, Magdalen College, lecturer, 1990-91; Dartmouth College, associate professor of classics and comparative literature, 1999-. Writer. **Publications:** Sappho's Immortal Daughters (monograph), 1995; (ed. with S. Blundell) The Sacred and the Feminine in Ancient Greece, 1998; (trans. with T. Wertenbaker) Euripides Hippolytus: A New Version, 2009. **Address:** Department of Classics, Dartmouth College, 311A Reed Hall, Dartmouth College, Hanover, NH 03755, U.S.A. **Online address:** margaret.williamson@dartmouth.edu

WILLIAMSON, Miryam Ehrlich. American (born United States) **Genres:** Information Science/Computers, Medicine/Health. **Career:** Freelance writer, 1983-. **Publications:** Artificial Intelligence for Microcomputers: The Guide for Business Decision Makers, 1986; Fibromyalgia: A Comprehensive Approach: What You Can Do about Chronic Pain and Fatigue, 1996; The Fibromyalgia Relief Book: 213 Ideas for Improving Your Quality of Life, 1998; Blood Sugar Blues: Overcoming the Hidden Dangers of Insulin Resistance, 2001; Type 2: A Book of Support for Type 2 Diabetics, 2003; (with V.C. Giampapa) Breaking the Aging Code: Maximizing Your DNA Function for Optimal Health and Longevity, 2004; (with R. Mann) Forensic Detective: How I Cracked the World's Toughest Cases, 2006. Contributor to periodicals and journals. **Address:** The Ballantine Publishing Group, 1540 Broadway, New York, NY 10036, U.S.A. **Online address:** miryam@mwilliamson.com

WILLIAMSON, Philip G. Also writes as Joe Fish, Philip First. British (born England), b. 1955. **Genres:** Science Fiction/Fantasy, Novels, Children's Fiction. **Career:** Writer. **Publications:** NOVELS: Moonblood (fantasy), 1994; Heart of Shadows, 1994; Citadel, 1995; Enchantment's Edge, 1996; Orbus's World, 1997; The Soul of the Orb, 1998. FIRSTWORLD CHRONICLES: Dinbig of Khimmur, 1991; The Legend of Shadd's Torment, 1993; From Enchantery, 1993. NOVELS AS PHILIP FIRST: The Great Pervader, 1983; Paper Thin and Other Stories, 1986; Dark Night, 1986. **Address:** c/o Charles Walker, Peters Fraser Dunlop, 503/4, The Chambers, Chelseaharbour, GL SW10 0XF, England. **Online address:** philwil@chug.screaming.net

WILLIAMSON, Robert C(lifford). American (born United States), b. 1916. **Genres:** Sociology, Cultural/Ethnic Topics, History, Young Adult Non-fiction, Social Sciences, Anthropology/Ethnology. **Career:** Los Angeles City College, faculty, 1946-60, professor of sociology and psychology; National University of El Salvador, Smith-Mundt professor, 1958; National University of Colombia, Fulbright professor, 1961; Haverford College, visiting professor of sociology, 1962-63; Peace Corps, lecturer and consultant, 1962-63; Lehigh University, adjunct professor of sociology, associate professor, professor of sociology, Department of Social Relations, chairman, 1963-; American Friends Service Committee, Latin American section, chairman, 1965-67; Catholic University, Fulbright professor, 1967-68. Writer. **Publications:** (With S. Sargent) Social Psychology, 4th ed. (with S. Sargent and P.G. Swingle), 1982; Marriage and Family Relations, 1966, 2nd ed., 1972; (ed. with G.H. Seward) Sex Roles in Changing Society, 1970; (ed. with J.A. van Eerde) Language Maintenance and Language Shift, 1980; Minority Languages and Bilingualism: Case Studies in Maintenance and Shift, 1991; (with A. Rinehart and T. Blank) Early Retirement: Promises and Pitfalls, 1992; Latin American Societies in Transition, 1997; Latin America: Cultures in Conflict, 2006. Contributor to journals. **Address:** Department of Sociology and Anthropology, Lehigh University, 681 Taylor St., Bethlehem, PA 18015, U.S.A. **Online address:** rw01@lehigh.edu

WILLIFORD, (G.) Craig. American (born United States), b. 1953?. **Genres:** Theology/Religion. **Career:** Grace Baptist Church, assistant pastor, 1975-79; Judson Baptist Church, associate pastor, 1979-81; William Jennings Bryan College, assistant professor, 1981-87, associate pastor of education, 1987-92; The Chapel, chief operating officer and senior associate pastor, 1992-99; Woodmen Valley Chapel, chief operating officer and senior associate pastor, 1999-2000; Denver Seminary, president, 2000-08; Trinity International University, president, 2010-. Writer. **Publications:** WITH C. WILLIFORD: Faith Tango: A Liberating Approach to Spiritual Growth in Marriage, 2002; Questions from the God Who Needs No Answers: What Is He Really Asking of You?, 2003; How to Treat a Staff Infection: Resolving Problems in Your Church or Ministry Team, 2006. Contributor to books and periodicals. **Address:** Trinity International University, 2065 Half Day Rd., Deerfield, IL 60015, U.S.A. **Online address:** president@denverseminary.edu

WILLIFORD, Lex. American (born United States), b. 1954. **Genres:** Novellas/Short Stories, Novels, Film. **Career:** Trinity university, graduate teaching assistant, 1979-80; Stephen F. Austin State University, graduate teaching assistant, 1980-82, assistant instructor, 1982-83, instructor in English and supervisor of writing center, 1983; University of Arkansas, graduate teaching assistant, 1984-87, Arkansas Writers in the Schools, visiting writer and co-director, 1986-87, Arkansas Poetry in the Schools, co-director, 1986-87; Auburn University, instructor in English, 1987-90, editor, 1988-91, director of writing center, 1989-90; Southern Illinois University, lecturer in creative writing, 1990-94, faculty advisor, 1993, founding editor, 1994; University of Alabama, assistant professor of creative writing, 1994-99; University of Texas, associate professor of creative writing, 2000-, faculty senate, 2002-, MFA Student Organisation, faculty advisor, 2002-04, Rio Grande Review, faculty advisor, 2004-, director, 2008. **Publications:** Macauley's Thumb (stories), 1994; (ed. with M. Martone) Scribner Anthology of Contemporary Short Fiction: Fifty North American Stories Since 1970, 1999, 2nd ed., 2007; Touchstone Anthology of Contemporary Nonfiction: Work From 1970 to the Present, 2007. Works appear in anthologies. Contributor of articles to magazines. **Address:** Department of Creative Writing, University of Texas, Liberal Arts 415, 500 W University Ave., El Paso, TX 79968, U.S.A. **Online address:** lex@utep.edu

WILLIMON, William H(enry). American (born United States), b. 1946. **Genres:** History, Theology/Religion, Biography, Essays. **Career:** Ordained United Methodist, minister, 1971; associate pastor, 1972-74; pastor, 1974-76; Duke University, Divinity School, assistant professor of liturgy and worship and presiding minister at the chapel, 1976-80, visiting associate professor, 1980-83, parish minister, 1980-83, minister and professor of the practice of Christian ministry, 1984-89, professor of Christian ministry and dean of chapel, 1989-2004; Northside United Methodist Church, pastor, 1980-84; University of Bonn, theology faculty, 1988; The United Methodist Church, bishop, North Alabama Conference, bishop, 2004-. Writer. **Publications:** Lord of the Congaree: Wade Hampton of South Carolina, 1971, rev. ed. as Lord of the Congaree: Wade Hampton of South Carolina, 1991; (with P.P. Willimon) Turning the World Upside Down: The Grimke Sisters of South Carolina, 1972; The Gospel for the Person Who Has Everything, 1978; Between Two Advents, 1978; Saying Yes to Marriage, 1978; Worship as Pastoral Care, 1979; Remember Who You Are: Baptism, a Model for Christian Life, 1979; (with R. Wilson) Preaching and Worship in the Small Church, 1980; (with J. Westerhoff) Liturgy and Learning through the Life Cycle, 1980, rev. ed., 1994; Word, Water, Wine and Bread: How Worship Has Changed over the Years, 1980; (with H.W. Cabell) Family Friends and Other Funny People: Memories of Growing Up Southern, 1980; Integrative Preaching: The Pulpit at the Center, 1981; The Way: Confirmation for Discipleship in the United Methodist Church, 1981; Sunday Dinner: The Lord's Supper and Christian Life, 1981; The Bible: A Sustaining Presence in Worship, 1981; The Service of God: How Worship and Ethics Are Related, 1983; On a Wild and Windy Mountain: Meditations for the Christian Year, 1984; Preaching and Leading Worship, 1984; Handbook on Preaching and Worship, 1984; What's Right with the Church, 1984; Sighing for Eden: Sin, Evil and the Christian Faith, 1985; (ed.) And The Laugh Shall Be First: A Treasury of Religious Humor and Satire, 1986; With Glad and Generous Hearts: A Personal Look at Sunday Worship, 1986; The Chapel, Duke University, 1986; (with R. Wilson) Rekindling the Flame: Strategies for a Vital United Methodism, 1987; Preaching about Conflict in the Local Church, 1987; The Promises of Marriage, 1988; Acts of the Apostles: Interpretation, a Commentary for Teaching and Preaching, 1988; Clergy and Laity Burnout, 1988; (with S. Hauerwas) Resident Aliens: The Church as Colony, 1989; Why I Am a United Methodist, 1990; (with M. Flynn) Confirmation: A New Approach to Making Disciples, 1990; The Bible Shapes Us, 1990; William H. Willimon's Last Laugh (religious humor), 1991; Goodbye High School, Hello College (meditations), 1992; Peculiar Speech: Preaching to the Baptized, 1992; (with S.M. Hauerwas) Preaching to Strangers: Evangelism and Preaching, 1992; Proclamation: Advent/Christmas (Year C), 1993; The Intrusive Word: Preaching to the Unbaptized, 1994; (with T.H. Naylor and M. Naylor) The Search for Meaning, 1994; (with T.H. Naylor) The Abandoned Generation: The Crisis in Higher Education, 1995; (with R. Lischer) The Concise Encyclopedia of Preaching, 1995; On Your Own, But Not Alone: Life after College (meditations for college graduates), 1995; (with A. Langford) A New Connection: Reforming the United Methodist Church, 1995; Reinventing the Connection: The Reform of the United Methodist Church, 1996; (with S.M. Hauerwas and S.C. Saye) Lord, Teach Us: The Lord's Prayer and the Christian Life, 1996; (with T.H. Naylor and R. Osterberg) The Search for Meaning in the Workplace, 1996; (with S.M. Hauerwas) Where Resident Aliens Live: Exercises for Christian Practice, 1996; (with T.H. Naylor) Downsizing the U.S.A., 1997; Reading with Deeper Eyes: The Love of Literature and the Life of Faith, 1998; (with M.B. Copenhaver and A.B. Robinson) Good News in Exile: Three Pastors Offer a Hopeful Vision for the Church, 1999; (with S.M. Hauerwas) The Truth about God: The Ten Commandments in Christian Life, 1999; Calling and Character: Virtues of the Ordained Life, 2000; The Last Word: Insights about the Church and Ministry, 2000; Pastor: The Theology and Practice of Ordained Ministry, 2002; (co-author) Pastor's Guide to Effective Ministry, 2002; (ed.) Pastor: A Reader for Ordained Ministry, 2002; (with T. Campolo) Survival Guide for Christians on Campus, 2002; (comp. and ed.) Sunday after Tuesday, 2002; A Peculiar Prophet: William H. Willimon and the Art of Preaching, 2004; (co-author) The Pastor's Guide to Personal Spiritual Formation, 2005; (ed.) Sermons from Duke Chapel: Voices from A Great Towering Church, 2005; (ed. with D.L. Weaver-Zercher) Vital Christianity: Spirituality, Justice, and Christian Practice, 2005; Proclamation and Theology, 2005; Sinning like a Christian: A New Look at the Seven Deadly Sins, 2005; Conversations with Barth on Preaching, 2006; Thank God it's Friday: Encountering the Seven Last Words from the Cross, 2006; United Methodist Beliefs: A Brief Introduction, 2007; The Stewardship Companion: Lectionary Resources for Preaching, 2007; A Guide to Preaching and Leading Worship, 2008; Who Will Be Saved?, 2008; (with K. Barth) Early Preaching of Karl Barth: Fourteen Sermons, 2009; Undone by Easter: Keeping Preaching Fresh, 2009; This We Believe: The Core of Wesleyan Faith and Practice, 2010; Preaching Master Class, 2010; Collected Sermons of William H. Willimon, 2010; Why Jesus?, 2010; A Will to Lead and the Grace to Follow: Letters on Leadership from a Peculiar Prophet, 2011. Contributor to periodicals. **Address:** The United Methodist Center, 898 Arkadelphia Rd., Birmingham, AL 35204-3436, U.S.A. **Online address:** will@duke.edu

WILLINGHAM, Bill. American (born United States), b. 1956. **Genres:** Animals/Pets. **Career:** TSR Inc., staff artist. Novelist. **Publications:** COMIC BOOKS: Fables: Legends in Exile, 2002; Sandman Presents: Taller Tales, 2003; Fables: The Last Castle, 2003; Fables: Animal Farm, 2004; Fables: Storybook Love, 2004; Robin: Unmasked!, 2004; Sandman Presents Thessaly, 2005; Jack of Fables, 2006; Fables: 1001 Nights of Snowfall, 2006; Shadowpact: Darkness and Light, 2008; Peter & Max: A Fables Novel, 2009; Fables: The Dark Ages, 2009; Literals, 2009; Batman: Under the Cowl, 2010; (with M. Sturges) The Bad Seed, 2010; (contrib.) House of Mystery: Under New Management, 2011. Contributor to periodicals. **Address:** c/o Author Mail, DC Comics, 1700 Broadway, New York, NY 10019, U.S.A.

WILLIS, Alan Scot. American (born United States), b. 1968. **Genres:** Theology/Religion. **Career:** Northern Michigan University, Department of History, assistant professor of history, associate professor. Writer and historian. **Publications:** All According to God's Plan: Southern Baptist Missions and Race, 1945-1970, 2005. **Address:** Department of History, Northern Michigan University, 208DD Cohodas Hall, 1401 Presque Isle Ave., Marquette, MI 49855-5305, U.S.A. **Online address:** awillis@nmu.edu

WILLIS, Barry. (Barry Donald Willis). American (born United States), b. 1952. **Genres:** Education, Young Adult Fiction, Reference. **Career:** Utah State University, Department of Instructional Technology, director, 1977-79; Alaska Pacific University, Department of Training and Education, staff, 1986-89; University of Alaska, associate vice chancellor, 1987-89, state wide director of distance learning, 1989-93, director of instructional development; Boston University, Department of Administration, Training and Policy, staff, 1989; University of Idaho, College of Education, professor and director, 1993-, associate dean for engineering outreach, associate vice-president for educational outreach. Writer. **Publications:** Effective Distance Education: A Primer for Faculty and Administrator, 1992; Distance Education: A Practical Guide, 1993; (ed.) Distance Education: Strategies and Tools, 1994; The Strange Case of the Lost Elvis Diaries, 1995. **Address:** College of Engineering, University of Idaho, PO Box 441011, Moscow, ID 83844-1011, U.S.A. **Online address:** bwillis@uidaho.edu

WILLIS, Barry Donald. See WILLIS, Barry.

WILLIS, Connie. American (born United States), b. 1945. **Genres:** Science Fiction/Fantasy, Novellas/Short Stories, Young Adult Fiction. **Career:** Teacher, 1967-69; full-time writer, 1969-; substitute teacher, 1974-81. **Publications:** (With C. Felice) Water Witch (novel), 1982; Fire Watch (short stories), 1985; (co-author) Berserker Base, 1985; Lincoln's Dreams, 1987; (with C. Felice) Light Raid, 1989; Doomsday Book, 1992; Impossible Things (short story collection); 1994, (co-ed.) The New Hugo Winners, vol. III, 1994; Uncharted Territory, 1994; Remake, 1994; Bellwether, 1996; (with C. Felice) Promised Land, 1997; To Say Nothing Of The Dog, Or, How We Found The Bishop's Bird Stump At Last, 1997; Miracle and Other Christmas Stories, 1999; Passage, 2000; (with S. Williams) Woman's Liberation: A Choice of Futures By and About Women, 2001; Inside Job, 2005; The Winds of Marble Arch and Other Stories: A Connie Willis Compendium, 2007; All Seated on the Ground, 2008; D.A, 2007; Blackout, 2010; All Clear, 2010. **Address:** c/o Ralph Vicinanza, 111 8th Ave., Ste. 1501, New York, NY 10011, U.S.A.

WILLIS, Deborah. American (born United States), b. 1948. **Genres:** Adult Non-fiction, Photography, Biography, Bibliography. **Career:** New York Public Library, curator, 1980-92; City University of New York, adjunct professor, 1989-90; Smithsonian Institution, Center for African-American History and Culture, exhibition curator, 1992; Columbia University, visiting artist, 1996; Art Institute of Boston, visiting artist, 1996; Duke University Center for Documentary Studies, Lehman Brady chair, 2000-; Duke University, joint professor in documentary studies and American studies, 2000-; University of North Carolina, joint professor in documentary studies and American studies, 2000-; Harvard College, Department of African and African Americans Studies, visiting professor, 2006; Tisch School of the Arts, New York University, professor of photography and imaging, university professor, chair. **Publications:** Black Photographers, 1840-1940: An Illustrated Bio-Bibliography, 1985; An Illustrated Bio-Bibliography of Black Photographers, 1940-1988, 1989; Early Black Photographers, 1840-1940: Twenty-three Postcards, 1992; Lorna Simpson, 1992; (ed.) J.P. Ball, Daguerrean and Studio Photographer, 1993; Van Der Zee: Photographer, 1886-1983, 1993; (ed.) Picturing Us: African-American Identity in Photography, 1994; (ed. with J. Lusaka) Visual Journal: Harlem and DC in the Thirties and Forties, 1996; Reflections in Black: A History of Black Photographers, 1840 to the Present, 2000; (with C. Williams) The Black Female Body: A Photographic History, 2002; (with D.L. Lewis) A Small Nation of People: Portraits of Progress in Black America, 2003; (contrib.) Seconds of My Life, 2007; Let Your Motto Be Resistance: African American Portraits, 2007; (with K. Merida) Obama: The Historic Campaign in Photographs, 2008; Posing Beauty: African American Images from the 1890s to the Present, 2009; (ed.) Black Venus 2010: They Called Her Hottentot, 2010; (with E. Bernard) Michelle Obama: The First Lady in Photographs, 2010. **Address:** Tisch School of the Arts, New York University, 721 Broadway Rm. 821, New York, NY 10003, U.S.A. **Online address:** deb.willis@nyu.edu

WILLIS, Edgar E(rnest). American/Canadian (born Canada), b. 1913. **Genres:** Communications/Media, History, Biography, Autobiography/Memoirs. **Career:** Detroit Public Schools Radio Department, writer, 1935-38, 1940-43; Wayne University, assistant professor of speech, 1946; San Jose State College, associate professor, professor of speech, 1946-52; Stanford University, Radio-Television Institute, lecturer, 1949-52; University of Michigan, Department of Communication, associate professor, 1952-57, professor, 1957-, department chairman, now professor emeritus; Station WWJ-TV, news analyst, 1953-54; National Educational Television, program associate, 1958-59. Writer. **Publications:** Foundations in Broadcasting, 1951; A Radio Directors Manual, 1961; Writing Television and Radio Programs, 1967, 5th ed. 1978; (with G. Chester and G. Garrison) Television and Radio, 4th ed., 1971, 5th ed., 1978; (with C. D'Arienzo) Writing Scripts for Television, Radio and Film, 1981, 3rd ed., 1993; (with H. Aldridge) Television, Cable and Radio: A Communications Approach, 1992; (with R.L. Weaver) How To Be Funny on Purpose, 2005; Civilian in an Ill-fitting Uniform: A Memoir of World War II, 2010. **Address:** Department of Communication Studies, University of Michigan, 1225 S University Ave., Ann Arbor, MI 48104-2523, U.S.A.

WILLIS, Gerri. American (born United States) **Genres:** Business/Trade/Industry, Economics. **Career:** Smart Money Magazine, columnist and senior financial correspondent; CNN Business News, personal finance editor, 2003-; Fox Business Network, host, 2010-. **Publications:** The SmartMoney Guide to Real Estate Investing, 2003; Home Rich: Increasing the Value of the Biggest Investment of Your Life, 2008. **Address:** Fox News Network L.L.C, 1211 Ave. of the Americas, 15th Fl., New York, NY 10036, U.S.A. **Online address:** gerri@cnn.com

WILLIS, Jack D. American (born United States), b. 1940. **Genres:** Biography, Medicine/Health. **Career:** Daily Phoenix, reporter and editor, 1971-89; Northeastern State University, part-time instructor; University of Oklahoma, adjunct professor of journalism, 1990-2007; Oklahoma Daily, editorial advisor. Journalist. **Publications:** Saving Jack: A Man's Struggle with Breast Cancer, 2008. **Address:** Edmond, OK , U.S.A. **Online address:** savingjack@gmail.com

WILLIS, Julia. American (born United States), b. 1949. **Genres:** Humor/Satire, Gay And Lesbian Issues. **Career:** Red Clay Books, associate editor, 1974-76; freelance writer, 1975-; North Carolina Arts Council, poet-in-residence, 1977-78; producer, 1979-85; playwright, 1979-94; comedy writer and performer, 1979-. **Publications:** Who Wears the Tux? The Original Great American Dyke Quiz: Accept No Substitute! (humor), 1990; We Oughta Be In Pictures (humor), 1993; Meow-Mories: A Place for Kitten Notes and Cat Fancies Recorded by Non-biological Parents of Fabulous Felines (humor), 1996; Reel Time (novel), 1998. Works appear in anthologies. Contributor of articles to periodicals. **Address:** 31 Francis Ave., Quincy, MA 02169, U.S.A. **Online address:** eggrocketx@comcast.net

WILLIS, Paul J. American (born United States), b. 1955. **Genres:** Novels, Adult Non-fiction, Poetry. **Career:** Sierra Treks, instructor, 1974; Whitworth College, adjunct instructor, 1982-85; Houghton College, assistant professor of English, 1985-88; Westmont College, assistant professor, 1988-92, associate professor, 1992-98, professor of English, 1998-. Writer. **Publications:**

NOVELS: No Clock in the Forest, 1991; The Stolen River, 1992; The Alpine Tales, 2010. ADULT NON-FICTION: Best Spiritual Writing 1999: Anthology, 1999; Best American Spiritual Writing 2004: Anthology, 2004; Bright Shoots of Everlastingness: Essays on Faith and the American Wild, 2005; Best Christian Writing 2006: Anthology, 2006. POETRY: Frog at Midnight, 1992; Genesis Poems, 1994; Best American Poetry 1996: Anthology, 1996; Poison Oak, 1999; The Deep and Secret Color of Ice, 2003; How to Get There, 2004; (ed. with D. Starkey) In a Fine Frenzy: Poets Respond to Shakespeare, 2005; Visiting Home, 2006; Rosing from the Dead, 2009. Contributor to journals. **Address:** Department of English, Westmont College, 955 La Paz Rd., 104 Reynolds Hall, Santa Barbara, CA 93108, U.S.A. **Online address:** willis@westmont.edu

WILLIS, Resa. American (born United States), b. 1949. **Genres:** Novels, Novellas/Short Stories, History, Literary Criticism And History, Biography. **Career:** Drury College, Department of English, professor of English, 1980-, Department of Languages and Literature, chair, 1989-. Writer. **Publications:** Mark and Livy: The Love Story of Mark Twain and the Woman Who Almost Tamed Him, 1992; FDR and Lucy: Lovers and Friends, 2004. Contributor of articles to magazines and journals. **Address:** Department of English, Drury University, 900 N Benton Ave., Springfield, MO 65802-3712, U.S.A. **Online address:** rwillis@drury.edu

WILLIS, Val. British (born England), b. 1946. **Genres:** Children's Fiction, Mystery/Crime/Suspense. **Career:** Primary School Houghton Regis, teacher, 1967-73; Nursery School Cublington, headmistress, 1974-85; Swanbourne House School, Pre-Preparatory Department, deputy head teacher, 1985-. Writer. **Publications:** Secret in the Matchbox, 1988; Silly Little Chick, 1989; Secret in the Wardrobe, 1990; Sally's Circus Hat, 1990; The Surprise in the Wardrobe, 1990; The Mystery in the Bottle, 1991. Contributor to periodicals. **Address:** Beach Helm, Beachwood off Redhills Rd., Arnside, CM LA5 0AX, England.

WILLMOTT, Phyllis. British (born England), b. 1922?. **Genres:** Local History/Rural Topics, Social Commentary, Social Work, Autobiography/Memoirs, Biography, Social Sciences, History. **Career:** Hackney Hospital, hospital social worker, 1947-49; London School of Economics and Political Science, research assistant, 1955-56; Institute of Community Studies, social research officer, 1956-67, senior research officer, 1972-82; Croydon College, part-time lecturer in social administration, 1967-72; writer, 1982-. **Publications:** (Ed. with A. Hancock) Social Workers, 1965; Consumer's Guide to the British Social Services, 1967, 4th ed., 1978; (ed.) Public Social Services, 1973; Growing Up in a London Village: Family Life Between the Wars (autobiography), 1979; (with S. Mayne) Families at the Centre: A Study of Seven Action Projects, 1981; (with R. Mitton and P. Willmott) Unemployment, Poverty and Social Policy: A Comparative Study in The United Kingdom, France and Germany: Extended Report to the Commission of the European Communities, 1981; A Green Girl, 1983; Under One Roof: Manor Gardens Centre, 1913-1988, 1988; Coming of Age in Wartime, 1988; A Singular Woman: The Life of Geraldine Aves, 1898-1986, 1992; Joys and Sorrows: Fragments from the Post-War Years, 1995; (co-author) 100 Years of Health Related Social Work, 1996; From Rural East Anglia to Suburban London: A Century of Family History, 1998. **Address:** 27 Kingsley Pl., Highgate, London, GL N6 5EA, England. **Online address:** phylliswillmott@yahoo.co.uk

WILLOUGHBY, Pamela R. Canadian (born Canada), b. 1952. **Genres:** Bibliography. **Career:** University of Alberta, assistant professor, 1987-95, associate professor, 1995-2007, professor of anthropology, 2007-. Writer and educator. **Publications:** Spheroids and Battered Stones in the African Early and Middle Stone Age, 1987; (trans.) Bibliographie des travaux des archeologues canadiens sur L'Afrique (title means: 'Bibliography of Works by Canadian Archaeologists on Africa'), 1992; The Evolution of Modern Humans in Africa: A Comprehensive Guide, 2007. Contributor of articles to periodicals. **Address:** Department of Anthropology, University of Alberta, Edmonton, AB T6G 2H4, Canada. **Online address:** pam.willoughby@ualberta.ca

WILLOW, Shannon. *See* **HALL, Gimone.**

WILLRICH, Mason. American (born United States), b. 1933. **Genres:** International Relations/Current Affairs, Politics/Government, Public/Social Administration, Technology, History. **Career:** Pillsbury, Madison & Sutro, associate attorney, 1960-62; U.S. Arms Control & Disarmament Agency, attorney adviser, 1962-64, assistant general counsel, 1964-65; writer, 1965-;

University of Virginia, associate professor, 1965-68, professor of law, 1968-76, John C. Stennis professor of law, 1976-79, Center for the Study of Science, Technology and Public Policy, director, 1968-73; Stanford University, lecturer, 1974; Royal Institute of International Affairs, visiting research fellow, 1975; Rockefeller Foundation, International Relations Division, director, 1976-79; Massachusetts Institute of Technology, visiting professor, 1976; Princeton University, Woodrow Wilson School of Public and International Affairs, visiting professor, 1977; PG&E Enterprises, executive vice president, 1979-88, chief executive officer, 1989-94; Energy Works L.L.P., founding chairman, 1995-98; Nth Power L.L.C., partner, 1996-2002; California Independent System Operator, chair, 2005-10. Independent consultant. **Publications:** Non-Proliferation Treaty: Framework for Nuclear Arms Control, 1969; (ed. with B. Boskey) Nuclear Prolifereration, 1970; (ed.) Civil Nuclear Power and International Security, 1971; Global Politics of Nuclear Energy, 1971; (ed.) International Safeguards and Nuclear Industry, 1973; (ed. with J.B. Rhinelander) SALT: The Moscow Agreements and Beyond, 1974; (with T.B. Taylor) Nuclear Theft: Risks and Safeguards, 1974; (co-author) Energy and World Politics, 1975; (with P.M. Marston, D.G. Norrell and J.K. Wilcox) Administration of Energy Shortages: Natural Gas and Petroleum, 1976; (co-author) Radioactive Waste Management and Regulation, 1977; Adventures Between History's Pages: A Memoir, 2007. Contributor of articles to periodicals and journals. **Address:** 38 Dudley Ct., Piedmont, CA 94611-3442, U.S.A. **Online address:** willrichm@aol.com

WILLS, Alfred J(ohn). British (born England), b. 1927. **Genres:** History, Politics/Government, Children's Fiction. **Career:** Northern Rhodesia Government, education officer, 1951-58; Northwestern Polytechnic, Modern History and British Constitution, assistant lecturer, 1960-63; Norwich School, History and Politics, assistant master, 1964-89, now retired. Writer. **Publications:** An Introduction to the History of Central Africa, 1964, 4th ed. as An Introduction to the History of Central Africa: Zambia, Malawi, and Zimbabwe, 1985; The Story of Africa from the Earliest Times, vol. I, 1968, vol. II, 1972. **Address:** King Edward VI School, Norwich, NF NR6 7AU, England. **Online address:** ajwills@freeuk.com

WILLS, Garry. American (born United States), b. 1934. **Genres:** History, Literary Criticism And History, Social Commentary, Theology/Religion, Military/Defense/Arms Control, Biography, Translations. **Career:** Richmond News Leader, associate editor, 1961; Center for Hellenic Studies, fellow, 1961-62; Johns Hopkins University, associate professor, 1962-67, assistant professor of humanities, 1968-80; University of California, regents lecturer, 1971; Northwestern University, Henry R. Luce professor of American culture and public policy, 1980-88, adjunct professor of history, 1988-2005, professor emeritus, 2005-. Writer. **Publications:** Chesterton, Man and Mask, 1961; Solomon the Wise, 1961; Animals of the Bible, 1962; Politics and Catholic Freedom, 1964; (ed.) Roman Culture: Weapons and the Man, 1966; (with O. Demaris) Jack Ruby, 1968; The Second Civil War: Arming for Armageddon, 1968; Nixon Agonistes: The Crisis of the Self-Made Man, 1970, rev. ed., 2002; Bare Ruined Choirs: Doubt, Prophecy, and Radical Religion, 1972; (ed.) Values Americans Live By, 1974; Inventing America: Jeffersons Declaration of Independence, 1978; At Button's (novel), 1979; Confessions of a Conservative, 1979; Explaining America: The Federalist, 1980; The Kennedy Imprisonment: A Meditation on Power, 1982; Cincinnatus: George Washington and the Enlightenment, 1982; Lead Time: A Journalist's Education, 1983; Reagan's America: The Innocents at Home, 1987; Under God: Religion and American Politics, 1990; Lincoln at Gettysburg: The Words that Remade America, 1992; Certain Trumpets, 1993; Witches and Jesuits: Shakespeares Macbeth, 1994; John Waynes America: The Politics of Celebrity, 1997; Saint Augustine, 1999; A Necessary Evil: A History of American Distrust of Government, 1999; Papal Sin: Structures of Deceit, 2000; Chesterton, 2001; Venice: Lion City, The Religion of Empire, 2001; (intro.) Saint Augustines Childhood, 2001; Why I Am a Catholic, 2002; James Madison, 2002; Mr. Jefferson's University, 2002; James Madison, 2002; (intro.) Saint Augustine's Memory, 2002; (intro.) Saint Augustines Sin, 2003; Negro President: Jefferson and the Slave Power, 2003; (intro.) Saint Augustine's Conversion, 2004; Henry Adams and the Making of America, 2005; Rosary: Prayer Comes Round, 2005; (trans. and intro.) Confessions, 2006; What Jesus Meant, 2006; What Paul Meant, 2006; Bushs Fringe Government, 2006; Head and Heart: American Christianities, 2007; What the Gospels Meant, 2008; (trans. and intro.) Martials Epigrams: A Selection, 2008; Bomb Power: The Modern Presidency and the National Security State, 2010; Outside Looking In: People Observed, 2010; Augustines Confessions: A Biography, 2011; Verdi's Shakespeare, 2011; Rome and Rhetoric, 2011; Font of Life, 2012. Contributor to

periodicals. **Address:** Department of History, Northwestern University, 1881 Sheridan Rd., Ste. 202, Evanston, IL 60208-2220, U.S.A. **Online address:** g-wills@northwestern.edu

WILLUMSON, Glenn. American (born United States), b. 1949. **Genres:** Art/Art History, Photography, Area Studies. **Career:** Public High Schools, mentor teacher, 1977-81; University of California, Nelson Art Gallery, associate curator, 1982-83, University Art Museum, faculty, 1985-86, visiting professor, 1990; J. Paul Getty Research Institute, curator, 1988-92; Pennsylvania State University, Palmer Museum of Art, senior curator, 1992-2001, adjunct professor of art history, 1994-2001; University of Florida, professor of art history and director of graduate program in museum studies, 2001-. Writer. **Publications:** (Contrib.) Anthony Van Dyck's Antwerp, 1599-1641, 1991; W. Eugene Smith and the Photographic Essay, 1992; Collecting with a Passion: Selections from the Pincus Collection of Contemporary Art, Palmer Museum of Art, 1993; L'Album Photographique: Historire and Conservation d'un objet, 2000; Photographs, Objects, Histories, 2004; Contribution of Historic Preservation to the Quality of Life in Florida, 2006; From Periphery to Center, 2007; Framing the West, 2010; The Crocker Art Museum Collection Unveiled, 2010. Contributor to periodicals. **Address:** School of Art and Art History, University of Florida, 116 FAC, PO Box 115801, Gainesville, FL 32611-5801, U.S.A. **Online address:** gwillumson@arts.ufl.edu

WILMER, Clive. British (born England), b. 1945. **Genres:** Poetry, Art/Art History, Economics, Literary Criticism And History, Recreation, Social Commentary, Translations. **Career:** British Institute, teacher of English, 1968; Oxford School of English, teacher of English, 1971-72; University of Padua, assistant lecturer in English literature, 1971-72; Bell School of Languages, teacher of English, 1973-86; Corpus Christi College, research associate, 1979-99; Numbers Magazine, co-founder and editor, 1986-90; University of California, creative writing instructor, 1986; Anglia Polytechnic University, writer-in-residence and research fellow, 1998; Fitzwilliam College, associate teaching officer, 1999; University of Cambridge, faculty of English, affiliated lecturer, 2008; Fitzwilliam College, Bye-fellow; Anglia Ruskin University, honorary fellow; Sidney Sussex College, fellow-commoner; Times Literary Supplement, contributor; PN Review, contributor. Journalist. **Publications:** (With D. Davis and R. Wells) Shade Mariners, 1970; Devotions, 1982; Poets Talking: The Poet of the Month Interviews from BBC Radio 3, 1994; (contrib.) Three Poets in Conversation, 2006. POETRY: The Dwelling-Place, 1977; A Catalogue of Flowers, 1986; Amores, 1986; The Infinite Variety, 1989; Of Earthly Paradise, 1992; Selected Poems, 1995; The Falls, 2000; Stigmata, 2005; The Mystery of Things, 2006. TRANSLATOR (with G. Gomori) M. Radnoti, Forced March: Selected Poems, 1979, rev. ed., 2003; G. Petri, Night Song of the Personal Shadow: Selected Poems, 1991; G. Gomori, My Manifold City, 1996; G. Petri, Eternal Monday: New and Selected Poems, 1999; G. Gomori, Poems for Mari, 2006. EDITOR: T. Gunn, The Occasions of Poetry: Essays in Criticism and Autobiography, 1982; J. Ruskin, Unto This Last and Other Writings, 1985; D.G. Rossetti, Selected Poems and Translations, 1991; W. Morris, News from Nowhere and Other Writings, 1993; (with C. Moseley) Cambridge Observed: An Anthology, 1998; D. Davie, With the Grain: Essays on Thomas Hardy and Modern British Poetry, 1998; (with G. Gomori) The Life and Poetry of Miklos Radnoti, 1999; D. Davie, Modernist Essays: Yeats, Pound, Eliot, 2004. Contributor to periodicals. **Address:** A. M. Heath & Company Ltd., 79 St. Martin's Ln., London, GL WC2N 4AA, England. **Online address:** clive.wilmer@ntlworld.com

WILMOT, Jeanne. (Jean Wilmot Carter). American (born United States), b. 1950. **Genres:** Food And Wine, Mythology/Folklore, Music, History, Social Sciences. **Career:** Attorney and writer. **Publications:** (With M. Dorson) Tales from the Rain Forest: Myths and Legends from the Amazonian Indians of Brazil, 1997; Dirt Angel: Stories, 1997. AS JEANNE WILMOT CARTER: (with D. Halpern) Halpern's Guide to the Essential Restaurants of Italy: From Milan to Rome with Notes on the Food and Wine, 1990; (ed. with D. Halpern) On Music, 1994. Contributor to periodicals. **Address:** c/o George Braziller Inc., 171 Madison Ave., New York, NY 10016, U.S.A.

WILNER, Isaiah. American (born United States), b. 1978?. **Genres:** Biography. **Career:** Time Magazine, consultant; New York Magazine, writer. **Publications:** The Man Time Forgot: A Tale of Genius, Betrayal, and the Creation of Time Magazine, 2006. Contributor to magazines. **Address:** c/o Author Mail, HarperCollins Publishers, 10 E 53rd St., 11th Fl., New York, NY 10022-5244, U.S.A. **Online address:** isaiahwilner@gmail.com

WILSFORD, David. American (born United States), b. 1956. **Genres:** Politics/Government, International Relations/Current Affairs, Education. **Career:** University of California, instructor in social sciences, 1978-80; Universite de Paris VII, Institut d'Anglais, lecturer in politics and history, 1981-82, U.F.R. de Lettres et de Sciences Humaines, lecturer in politics and economics, 1984-85; Universite de Paris III, U.E.R. des Etudes Anglophones, lecturer in politics and history, 1981-82; University of Oklahoma, assistant professor of political science, 1987-90; Georgia Institute of Technology, assistant professor, 1990-92, associate professor of international affairs, 1992-95; Institute for American Universities, president and professor, 1995-2005; Yale University, distinguished faculty fellow, 2004; London School of Economics, visiting senior fellow, 2006; George Mason University, Ras al Khaimah, vice president, 2006-, Public and International Affairs, faculty. Writer. **Publications:** Doctors and the State: The Politics of Health Care in France and the United States, 1991; (ed.) Political Leaders of Contemporary Western Europe: A Biographical Dictionary, 1995; (ed. with M.M.L. Crepaz and T.A. Koelble) Democracy and Institutions: The Life Work of Arend Lijphart, 2000. Contributor of articles to journals. **Address:** Public & International Affairs, George Mason University, Robinson Hall A, Rm. 229, 4400 University Dr., 3F4, Fairfax, VA 22030, U.S.A. **Online address:** dwilsfor@gmu.edu

WILSON, Andrew. British (born England), b. 1967. **Genres:** Biography, Young Adult Non-fiction, Sex, Literary Criticism And History. **Career:** Magazine journalist, 1989-92; freelance journalist, 1992-. **Publications:** Beautiful Shadow: A Life of Patricia Highsmith, 2004; Harold Robbins: The Man Who Invented Sex, 2007; The Lying Tongue, 2007. Contributor to periodicals. **Address:** c/o Clare Alexander, Gillon Aitken Associates, 18-21 Cavaye Pl., London, GL SW10 9PT, England.

WILSON, Andrew. British (born England), b. 1961. **Genres:** History, Politics/Government, Social Sciences. **Career:** University of Cambridge, Sidney Sussex College, senior research fellow; University College, School of Slavonic and East European Studies, reader in Ukrainian studies, senior lecturer in Russian and Ukrainian studies; Royal Institute of International Affairs, honorary fellow; European Council for Foreign Relations, senior policy fellow, through 2010. Writer. **Publications:** (With N. Bachkatov) Nouveaux Soviétiques de A à Z, 1991; (with T. Kuzio) Ukraine: Perestroika to Independence, 1994; Ukrainian Nationalism in the 1990s: A Minority Faith, 1996; (contrib.) Nation-Building in the Post-Soviet Borderlands: The Politics of National Identities, 1998; The Ukrainians: Unexpected Nation, 2000, 3rd ed., 2009; (ed. with W. Slater) The Legacy of the Soviet Union, 2004; Virtual Politics: Faking Democracy in the Post-Soviet World, 2005; Ukraine's Orange Revolution, 2005; Belarus: The Last European Dictatorship, 2011. **Address:** School of Slavonic & East European Studies, University College London, 16 Taviton St., London, GL WC1H 0BW, England. **Online address:** a.wilson@ssees.ucl.ac.uk

WILSON, Andrew. British/Belgian (born Belgium), b. 1923. **Genres:** International Relations/Current Affairs, Military/Defense/Arms Control. **Career:** Daily Express, assistant, 1950-52; The Observer newspaper, chief African correspondent, 1960-62, Defence and Aviation correspondent, 1963-79, associate editor, 1971-89, foreign editor, 1979-82, Moscow correspondent, 1986-89; The European Press Agency, director, 1992-. **Publications:** Flame Thrower, 1956; (trans. with E. Wilson) The Schlieffen Plan, 1957; North from Kabul, 1961; The Bomb and the Computer, 1968, as War Gaming, 1970; The Bomb and the Computer, Wargaming from Ancient Chinese Mapboard to Atomic Computer, 1969; (ed.) The Observer Atlas of World Affairs, 1971; The Concorde Fiasco, 1973; Flame Thrower, 1973; Aegean Dispute, 1979; The Aegean Question, 1980; Eagle has Wings: The Story of American Space Exploration, 1945-1975, 1982; The Disarmer's Handbook, 1983; (with N. Bachkatov) Living with Glasnost, 1988; (with N. Bachkatov) Russia Revised, 1992 in US as Russia and the Commonwealth A to Z, 1992. **Address:** Bolt & Watson Ltd., 8 Storey's Gate, London, GL B-1000, England. **Online address:** editors@russia-eurasia.net

WILSON, A(ndrew) N. British (born England), b. 1950. **Genres:** Novels, Children's Fiction, Literary Criticism And History, Theology/Religion, Biography, Poetry, Adult Non-fiction, Young Adult Fiction, Essays. **Career:** St. Hugh's College, lecturer, 1976-82; Oxford University, faculty, 1975; New College, lecturer, 1977-81; Merchant Taylor's School, schoolmaster, 1975-80; Stanford University, teacher, 1978-80; Spectator, literary editor, 1981-83; Evening Standard, columnist. **Publications:** NOVELS: Sweets of Pimlico, 1977; Unguarded Hours, 1978; Kindly Light, 1979; Healing Art, 1980; Who Was Oswald Fish, 1981; Wise Virgin, 1982; Scandal, Or Priscilla's Kindness, 1983; Gentlemen in England: A Vision, 1985; Love Unknown, 1986; Incline Our Hearts, 1988; A Bottle in the Smoke, 1990; Daughters of Albion, 1991; The Vicar of Sorrows, 1993; Hearing Voices, 1995; A Watch in the Night, 1996; Dream Children, 1998; My Name Is Legion, 2004; A Jealous Ghost, 2005; Winnie and Wolf, 2006. BIOGRAPHY: The Laird of Abbotsford: A View of Sir Walter Scott, 1980; Life of John Milton, 1983, 2nd ed., 1984; Hilaire Belloc, 1984; Tolstoy: A Biography, 1988; Eminent Victorians, 1989 in US as The Victorians, 2003; C.S. Lewis: A Biography, 1990; Against Religion, 1990; Jesus, 1992; London: A Short History, 2004; Betjeman: A Life, 2006. EDITOR: Ivanhoe, 1982; Essays by Divers Hands 44, 1986; (intro.) The Lion and the Honeycomb: The Religious Writings of Tolstoy, 1987; (intro.) Prayers, Poems and Meditations, 1989; The Faber Book of Church and Clergy, 1992; The Rise and Fall of the House of Windsor, 1993; The Faber Book of London, 1994; The Norton Book of London, 1994; God's Funeral, 1999; Iris Murdoch as I Knew Her, 2003; England: A Collection of the Poetry of Place, 2008; Our Times, 2008; Our Times: The Age of Elizabeth II, 2010. POETRY: Lilibet: An Account in Verse of the Early Years of the Queen Until the Time of Her Accession, 1984. OTHERS: (intro.) Dracula, 1983; How Can We Know? An Essay on the Christian Religion, 1985; (with C. Moore and G. Stamp) The Church in Crisis, 1986; (contrib.) Landscape in France, 1987; Stray, 1987; Penfriends from Porlock: Essays and Reviews 1977-1986, 1988; The Tabitha Stories, 1989; Hazel the Guinea-Pig, 1989; The Rise and Fall of the House of Windsor, 1993; (intro.) How Much Land Does a Man Need?: And Other Stories, 1993; Paul: The Mind of the Apostle, 1997; (foreword) Tolstoy the Man, 2005; After the Victorians: The Decline of Britain in the World, 2005; Betjeman: A Life, 2006; Elizabethans, 2011; Dante in Love, 2011. **Address:** Author Mail, Farrar, Straus & Giroux, 18 W 18th St., New York, NY 10011, U.S.A.

WILSON, Angela Cavender. *See* **WAZIYATAWIN.**

WILSON, Antoine Leonide Thomas. American/Canadian (born Canada), b. 1971?. **Genres:** Novels, Young Adult Non-fiction. **Career:** University of California, Extension Writing Program, teacher of writing; A Public Space, contributing editor. **Publications:** The Young Zillionaire's Guide to Distributing Goods and Services, 2000; You and a Death in Your Family (young adult), 2001; The Assassination of William McKinley, 2002; S.E. Hinton, 2003; The Interloper: A Novel, 2007; (with L. Murley) Distribution of Goods and Services, 2012; Panorama City, 2012. **Address:** c/o Anna Stein, Aitken Alexander Associates Ltd., 80 5th Ave., Ste. 1101, New York, NY 10011-8011, U.S.A. **Online address:** info@antoinewilson.com

WILSON, Barbara (Ellen). American (born United States), b. 1950. **Genres:** Novellas/Short Stories, Mystery/Crime/Suspense, Translations, Young Adult Fiction, Travel/Exploration. **Career:** Seal Press, co-founder, 1976, publisher, 1982-94; Women in Translation Press, co-founder, director, 1989-2004. Writer, editor, teacher and translator. **Publications:** CRIME FICTION: Murder in the Collective, 1984; Sisters of the Road, 1986; Dog Collar Murders, 1989; Gaudí Afternoon, 1990; Trouble in Transylvania, 1993; The Death of a Much-Travelled Woman and Other Adventures with Cassandra Reilly, 1998; The Case of the Orphaned Bassoonists, 2000. SHORT STORY COLLECTIONS: Talk & Contact, 1978; Thin Ice, 1981; Walking on the Moon: Six Stories and a Novella, 1983; Miss Venezuela, 1988; Salt Water and Other Stories, 1999. TRANSLATIONS: Cora Sandel: Collected Short Stores, 1985; Backstreets, 1992; Nothing Happened, 1999. OTHERS: Geography Lesson, 1977; Murder in the Collective, 1984; Ambitious Women, 1985; (ed. with F. Conlon and R. da Silva) The Things that Divide Us, 1985; Cows and Horses, 1988; If You Had a Family, 1996; Blue Windows: A Christian Science Childhood, 1997; Sugarfootn'!, 2001; Clear Spring, 2002; (ed.) Steady as She Goes: Women's Adventures at Sea, 2003; Pirate Queen: In Search of Grace O'Malley and Other Legendary Women of the Sea, 2004; Incognito Street: How Travel Made Me a Writer, 2006; Palace of the Snow Queen: Winter Travels in Lapland, 2007. Contributor to books and periodicals. **Address:** Seal Press, 1700 4th St., Berkeley, CA 94710, U.S.A. **Online address:** seaisland@seanet.com

WILSON, Barbara Ker. Australian/British (born England), b. 1929. **Genres:** Novels, Novellas/Short Stories, Children's Fiction, Children's Non-fiction, Mythology/Folklore, History, Literary Criticism And History. **Career:** Oxford University Press, junior children's editor, 1949-54; Bodley Head, managing editor in children's books section, 1954-57; William Collins, managing editor, 1958-61; Angus & Robertson, children's books editor, 1965-73; Hodder & Stoughton, children's books editor, 1973-76; Readers Digest Condensed Books, editor, 1978-84; University of Queensland Press, editor. **Publications:** Scottish Folk-Tales and Legends, 1954, rev. ed. as Fairy Tales from Scotland, 1999; Path-through-the-Woods, 1958; The Wonderful Cornet, 1958; Fairy Tales of Germany, 1959; Fairy Tales of Ireland, 1959; Fairy Tales of Russia, 1959; Fairy Tales of England, 1960; Fairy Tales of France, 1960; Fairy Tales of India, 1960; Fairy Tales of Mexico, 1960; The Lovely Summer, 1960; Look at Books, 1960; Writing for Children, 1960; Noel Streatfeild: A Monograph, 1961; Fairy Tales of Persia, 1961; Last Year's Broken Toys, 1962 in US as In Love and War, 1963; Ann and Peter in Paris (and in London), 2 vols., 1963-65; A Story to Tell: Thirty Tales for Little Children, 1964; Beloved of the Gods in US as In the Shadow of Vesuvius, 1965; Legends of the Round Table, 1966; Greek Fairy Tales, 1966; A Family Likeness, 1967 in US as The Biscuit-Tin Family, 1968; Animal Folk Tales, 1968; Australia: Wonderland Down Under, 1969; Hiccups and Other Stories: Thirty Tales for Little Children, 1971; Tales Told to Kabbarli: Aboriginal Legends Collected by Daisy Bates, 1972; The Magic Fishbones and Other Fabulous Tales of Asia, 1974; The Magic Bird and Other Fabulous Tales from Europe, 1976; Just for a Joyride (reader), 1977; The Turtle and the Island: Folk Tales from Papua New Guinea, 1978, rev. ed., 1990; The Willow Pattern Story, 1978; (with J. Cadry) The Persian Carpet Story, 1981; Kelly the Sleepy Koala, 1983; Kevin the Kookaburra, 1983; Molly, 1983; Jane Austen in Australia (adult novel), 1984 in US as Antipodes Jane: A Novel of Jane Austen in Australia, 1985; Daisy Bates, 1986; Acacia Terrace, 1988; The Quade Inheritance (adult novel), 1988; The Turtle and the Island, 1990; Wishbones: A Folk Tale from China, 1993; Fairy Tales from Scotland, 1999; The Lost Years of Jane Austen: A Novel, 2008; Stories from Scotland, 2009. EDITOR: The Second Young Eve, 1962; Wha ta Girl (and Boy) Should Know about Sex, 2 vols., 1962; Australian Kaleidoscope, 1968; Alitjinya ngura tjukurtjarangka: Alitji in the Dream Time, 1975; A Handful of Ghosts: Thirteen Eerie Tales by Australian Authors, 1976; The Illustrated Treasury of Australian Stories and Verse for Children, 1987; Brief Encounters: Short Stories, 1992; Alitji in Dreamland: Alitjinya Ngura Tjukurmankuntjala: An Aboriginal Version of Lewis Carroll's Alice's Adventures in Wonderland, 1992; (comp.) Hands Up!: Who Enjoyed Their School Days, 1994. **Address:** University of Queensland Press, Staff House Rd., PO Box 6042, Saint Lucia, QL 4067, Australia.

WILSON, Barrie A. Canadian (born Canada), b. 1940?. **Genres:** Theology/Religion, Business/Trade/Industry, Humanities. **Career:** St. Louis University, faculty; York University, professor, now professor emeritus, Atkinson College, chair of religious studies. Writer. **Publications:** (Co-author) Interpretation, Meta-interpretation, and Oedipus Tyrannus: Protocol of the Thirty-ninth Colloquy, 26 May 1980, 1980; The Anatomy of Argument, 1980, rev. ed., 1986; To the Point: Effective Business Communication, 1988; (comp.) About Interpretation: From Plato to Dilthey, a Hermeneutic Anthology, 1989; Hermeneutical Studies: Dilthey, Sophocles, and Plato, 1990; How Jesus Became Christian, 2008. Contributor to journals. **Address:** Department of Humanities, Vanier College, York University, 4700 Keele St., Toronto, ON M3J 1P3, Canada. **Online address:** barrie@yorku.ca

WILSON, Barry K. Canadian (born Canada), b. 1948. **Genres:** History, Biography, Local History/Rural Topics, Politics/Government, Agriculture/Forestry. **Career:** Saint John Telegraph Journal, reporter, 1970-71; Oshawa Times, reporter, 1971-73; Saskatoon Star-Phoenix, reporter, 1973-76; Western Producer, national correspondent, 1977-79, 1980-. **Publications:** Politics of Defeat: The Decline of the Liberal Party in Saskatchewan, 1980; Beyond the Harvest: Canadian Grain at the Crossroads, 1981; Farming the System: How Politics and Farmers Shape Agricultural Policy, 1990; Benedict Arnold: A Traitor in Our Midst, 2001. Contributor to periodicals. **Address:** Western Producer, 702-150 Wellington St., Ottawa, ON K1P 5A4, Canada. **Online address:** barry.wilson@producer.com

WILSON, B. G. See **WILSON, (Brian) Geoffrey.**

WILSON, Brandon. American (born United States), b. 1953. **Genres:** Adult Non-fiction, Travel/Exploration, Inspirational/Motivational Literature, Autobiography/Memoirs. **Career:** Author, photographer and peace activist. **Publications:** Yak Butter Blues: A Tibetan Trek of Faith, 2004, 2nd ed., 2006; Dead Men Don't Leave Tips: Adventures X Africa, 2005; Along the Templar Trail: Seven Million Steps for Peace, 2008; (intro.) On a Donkey's Back (collection of Nepalese poetry and paintings), 2008; Over the Top & Back Again: Hiking X the Alps, 2010. Contributor of articles to newspapers and maga-zines. **Address:** Pilgrim's Tales Inc., PO Box 854, Volcano, HI 96785, U.S.A. **Online address:** pilgrimstales@yahoo.com

WILSON, (Brian) Geoffrey. (B. G. Wilson). British (born England), b. 1920?. **Genres:** Songs/Lyrics And Libretti, Communications/Media, History, Transportation, Biography, Art/Art History. **Career:** The Railway Gazette, assistant editor, 1938-39, 1946-56; Railway World, editor, 1956-61; World Book Encyclopedia, editor, 1961-63; International Railway Journal, editor, 1963-68; British Government Information Service, press officer; Ministry of Public Building and Works, press officer. **Publications:** (As B.G. Wilson with V.S. Haram) The Central London Railway, 1950; (with J.R. Day) Famous Railways of the World, 1956; (with J.R. Day) Unusual Railways, 1957; The Old Telegraphs, 1976; Libretti from French: The Bells of Corneville, 1978; (with C. Spencer) Elbow Room: The Story of John Sydney Brocklesby, 1984. **Address:** 20 Old School Close, Melrose Rd., Merton Pk., London, GL SW19 3HY, England.

WILSON, Bronwen. Canadian/American (born United States) **Genres:** Art/Art History, History, Politics/Government. **Career:** David Vance Design, principal designer, 1984-94; University of British Columbia, Renaissance Art and Culture, lecturer, 1998-99, associate professor, 2006-, Department of Art History, Visual Art and Theory, associate professor, 2007-; McGill University, Department of Art History and Communication Studies, assistant professor, 2000-05, associate professor, 2005-07, adjunct professor, 2007-. Writer. **Publications:** The World in Venice: Print, the City, and Early Modern Identity, 2005; (ed. with P. Yachnin) Making Publics in Early Modern Europe: People, Things, Forms of Knowledge, 2010. Contributor to books and periodicals. **Address:** Department. of Art History, Visual Art and Theory, University of British Columbia, 403-6333 Memorial Rd., Vancouver, BC V6T 1Z2, Canada. **Online address:** bronwen@interchange.ubc.ca

WILSON, Budge. Canadian (born Canada), b. 1927. **Genres:** Novels, Novellas/Short Stories, Children's Fiction, Young Adult Fiction, History. **Career:** Halifax Ladies' College (now Armbrae Academy), teacher of English and art, 1951-52; University of Toronto, Institute of Child Study, filing clerk, staff artist, 1953-57; Toronto Public Library, librarian, 1954; teacher at nursery school, 1956-57; Peterborough Country Board of Education, fitness instructor, 1970-. Writer. **Publications:** FOR CHILDREN: The Best/Worst Christmas Present Ever, 1984; Mr. John Bertr and Nijinsky and Charlie, 1986; A House Far from Home, 1986; Mystery Lights at Blue Harbour, 1987; Going Bananas, 1989; Madame Belzile and Ramsay Hitherton Hobbs, 1990; Leaving and Other Stories, 1992; Cassandra's Driftwood, 1994; Harold and Harold, 1995; Duff the Giant Killer, 1997; The Long Wait, 1997; The Cat That Barked, 1998; The Fear of Angelina Domino, 2000; Duff's Monkey Business, 2000; Manfred, the Unmanageable Monster, 2001; A Fiddle for Angus, 2001; The Christmas That Almost Wasn't, 2002. FOR YOUNG ADULTS: Breakdown, 1988; Thirteen Never Changes, 1989; Lorinda's Diary, 1991; Oliver's Wars, 1992; Sharla, 1997. SHORT STORIES FOR YOUNG ADULTS AND ADULTS: The Sale, 1977; Three Voices, 1983; The Metaphor, 1983; The Leaving, 1985; Big Little Jerome, 1985; Mr. Manuel Jenkins, 1986; The Diary, 1987; Cordelia Clark, 1994; The Dandelion Garden, 1995; Mothers and Other Strangers, 1996; Friendships, 2006. FOR ADULTS: The Courtship, 1994; Fractures: Family Stories, 2002. OTHERS: Jill Quinn, 2001; Izzie: The Christmas That Almost Wasn't, 2002; Imperfect Perfect Christmas, 2004; Izzie: Trongate Fury, 2005; Patricia's Secret, 2005; Homecoming, 2006; Before Green Gables, 2008. Contributor of articles to periodicals. **Address:** 37 SW Cove Rd., North West Cove, RR 1, Hubbards, NS B0J 1T0, Canada. **Online address:** budgewilson@ns.sympatico.ca

WILSON, Carter. American (born United States), b. 1941. **Genres:** Novels, Plays/Screenplays, Anthropology/Ethnology, Children's Fiction. **Career:** Stanford University, lecturer in English, 1965-66; Harvard University, Briggs-Copeland lecturer in English and general education, 1966-69; Tufts University, lecturer, 1969-71, assistant professor of English and director of writing program, 1971-72; University of California, assistant professor, 1972-74, associate professor, 1974-79, professor of community studies, 1979-2002, professor emeritus of community studies, 2002-. Writer. **Publications:** Crazy February, 1966; I Have Fought the Good Fight, 1967; Appeals to Santiago, 1968; On Firm Ice, 1969; A Green Tree & a Dry Tree: A Novel of Chiapas, 1972; (contrib.) Drinking in the Mayan Highlands of Chiapas, 1973; (contrib.) The Best from Fantasy and Science Fiction, 1973; (trans. with M.L.

Davila) E. Abreu Gomez, Canek: Legend and History of a Mayan Hero, 1979; Treasures on Earth: A Novel, 1981; (with J. Coburn) The Times of Harvey Milk, 1983; Common Threads, 1989; Queen of Hearts, 1992; (contrib.) Best American Erotica, 1993; Hidden in the Blood: A Personal Investigation of AIDS in the Yucatán, 1995. **Address:** Department of Community Studies, University of California, 1156 High St., Santa Cruz, CA 95064, U.S.A. **Online address:** georgec@ucsc.edu

WILSON, Catharine Anne. Canadian (born Canada), b. 1958?. **Genres:** History. **Career:** University of Guelph, lecturer. Writer and historian. **Publications:** A New Lease on Life: Landlords, Tenants, and Immigrants in Ireland and Canada, 1994; Tenants in Time: Family Strategies, Land, and Liberalism in Upper Canada, 1799-1871, 2009. **Address:** Department of Rural History, University of Guelph, 50 Stone Rd. E, Guelph, ON N1G 2W1, Canada. **Online address:** cawilson@uoguelph.ca

WILSON, Catherine. American (born United States), b. 1951. **Genres:** Philosophy, Animals/Pets, History, Natural History, Sciences. **Career:** University of Oregon, assistant professor, associate professor, professor, 1978-92, head of philosophy, 1989-92; University of Konstanz, Alexander von Humboldt fellow, 1984-86; University of Alberta, professor, 1992-99, chair, 1992-97; Canadian Journal of Philosophy, executive editor, 1993-98; History of Philosophy Quarterly, editor, 1998-2003; University of British Columbia, professor of philosophy, 1999-2003, distinguished professor of philosophy, 2003-05; Trinity College, visiting fellow commoner, 2004-05; Enzyklopaedie der Neuzeit, sub-editor, 2004-10; Princeton University, Department of Philosophy, visiting professor, 2008-09; City University of New York, The Graduate Center, distinguished professor of philosophy. **Publications:** Leibniz's Metaphysics: A Historical and Comparative Study, 1989; The Invisible World: Early Modern Philosophy and the Invention of the Microscope, 1995; (ed.) Civilization and Oppression, 1999; (ed.) Leibniz, 2001; Descartes's Meditations: An Introduction, 2003; Responsibility, 2003; Moral Animals: Ideals and Constraints in Moral Theory, 2004; Epicureanism at the Origins of Modernity, 2008; (ed. with D.M. Clarke) Oxford Handbook of Philosophy in Early Modern Europe, 2011; Life According to Nature, forthcoming. Contributor of articles to periodicals. **Address:** The Graduate Center, City University of New York, 365 5th Ave., New York, NY 10016, U.S.A. **Online address:** cwilson@gc.cuny.edu

WILSON, Christine. See GEACH, Christine.

WILSON, Christopher R. British (born England), b. 1952?. **Genres:** Music, Poetry, Photography. **Career:** University of Reading, lecturer, senior lecturer; University of Hull, professor of music history; Globe Theatre music exhibition, music consultant. Writer. **Publications:** Words and Notes Coupled Lovingly Together: Thomas Campion, A Critical Study, 1989; (ed. and intro.) A New Way of Making Fowre Parts in Counterpoint and Giovanni Coprario, Rules How to Compose, 2003; (with M. Calore) Music in Shakespeare: A Dictionary, 2005. Contributor to books. **Address:** University of Hull, L220, Hull, HU6 7RX, United Kingdom. **Online address:** christopher.wilson@hull.ac.uk

WILSON, Colin (Henry). British (born England), b. 1931. **Genres:** Novels, Criminology/True Crime, Paranormal, Psychology, Young Adult Non-fiction, Novellas/Short Stories, History. **Career:** Cranbourne Products Ltd., staff, 1947; Gateway Secondary Technical School, laboratory assistant, 1947-48; tax collector, 1947-49; Hollins College, writer-in-residence, 1966-67; University of Washington, visiting professor, 1967-68; Rutgers University, visiting professor, 1974. Writer. **Publications:** The Outsider, 1956; Religion and the Rebel, 1957; The Age of Defeat in US as The Stature of Man, 1959; Ritual in the Dark, 1960; (with P. Pitman) Encyclopedia of Murder, 1961; Adrift in Soho, 1961; The Strength to Dream, 1962; The World of Violence, 1963 in US as The Violent World of Hugh Greene, 1963; Origins of the Sexual Impulse, 1963; Man Without a Shadow in US as The Sex Diary of Gerard Sorme, 1963; Necessary Doubt, 1964; Rasputin and the Fall of the Romanovs, 1964; The Brandy of the Damned, 1964 in US as Chords and Dischords, 1966; Beyond the Outsider, 1965; Eagle and Earwig, 1965; Sex and the Intelligent Teenager, 1966; The Glass Cage, 1966; Introduction to the New Existentialism, 1966; The Mind Parasites, 1967; Voyage to a Beginning, 1969; Bernard Shaw and Reassessment, 1969; Poetry and Mysticism, 1969; Case Book of Murder, 1969; The Philosopher's Stone, 1969; Poetry and Mysticism, 1969; The Killer, 1970 in US as Lingard, 1970; The God of the Labyrinth in US as The Hedonists, 1970; (with J.B. Pick and E.H. Visiak) The Strange Genius of David Lindsay, 1970; L'Amour: The Ways of Love,

1970; The Occult, 1971; The Black Room, 1971; Strindberg (play), 1972; New Pathways in Psychology, 1972; Order of Assassins: The Psychology of Murder, 1972; Strange Powers, 1973; Tree by Tolkien, 1973; Reich, Borges, Hesse, 1973; The Hermann Hesse, 1974; The Return of the Lloigor, 1974; A Book of Booze, 1974; The Craft of the Novel, 1975; Mysterious Powers, 1975 as They Had Strange Powers, 1975; The Space Vampires, 1976; Men of Strange Powers, 1976; Enigmas and Mysteries, 1976; The Geller Phenomenon, 1976; Mysteries of the Mind, 1978; Science Fiction as Existentialism, 1978; Starseekers, 1980; Frankenstein's Castle, 1980; The War against Sleep, 1980; The Quest for Wilhelm Reich, 1981; Poltergeist!, 1981; Anti-Sartre, 1981; Access to Inner Worlds, 1982; The Criminal History of Mankind, 1983; (with D. Seaman) Modern Encyclopaedia of Murder, 1983; Psychic Detectives, 1983; (with G. Finley-Day and D. Gibbons) Rogue Trooper, Book One, Titan (London), 1984; The Janus Murder Case, 1984; C.G. Jung: The Lord of the Underworld, 1984; Afterlife, 1985; Rudolf Steiner: The Man and His Vision, 1985; The Personality Surgeon, 1985; Existential Essays, 1985; The Essential Colin Wilson, 1985; (with D. Seaman) An Encyclopaedia of Scandal, 1986; Aleister Crowley: The Man and the Myth, 1987; Spider World-The Tower, 1987; (with R. Odell) Jack the Ripper, 1987; Spider World-The Delta, 1988; The Sex Diary of a Metaphysician, 1988; The Misfits, 1988; Beyond the Occult, 1988; The Magician from Siberia, 1988; The Decline and Fall of Leftism, 1989; Written in Blood, 1989; (with D. Seaman) Serial Killers, 1990; Mozart's Journey to Prague (play), 1991; (with D. Wilson) Unsolved Mysteries Past and Present, 1992; Spider World-The Magician, 1992; The Strange Life of P.D. Ouspensky, 1993; (intro.) Silent Circles of Truth, 1995; From Atlantis to the Sphinx, 1996; Atlas of Holy Places and Sacred Sites, 1996; Below the Iceberg, 1996; World Famous UFOs, 1996; World Famous Unsolved, 1996; (with D. Wilson) World Famous Spies, 1996; (contrib.) Tree of Life: The Inaugural Exhibition of the American Visionary Art Museum, 1996; (with S. Wilson) World Famous Love Stories, 1996; Mysteries of the Universe, 1997; UFOs and Aliens, 1997; Strange Vanishings, 1997; Ghost Sightings, 1997; Psychic Powers, 1998; Alien Dawn, 1998; Ghosts and the Supernatural, 1998; Books in My Life, 1998; Introduction to James Drought, 1999; Nikos Kazantzakis, 1999; (with R. Fle'math) The Atlantis Blue Print, 2000; The Devil's Party, 2000 in US as Rogue Messiahs, 2000; After Life: Survival of the Soul, 2nd ed., 2000; (with D. Wilson) The Mammoth Encyclopedia of the Unsolved, 2000; The Tower, 2001; The Delta, 2001; (with J. Grant) Qinmeartha and the Girl-Child LoChi and The Tomb of the Old Ones, 2002; Spider World-Shadowland, 2003; Autobiography: Dreaming to Some Purpose, 2004; (with O. Cyriax and D. Wilson) The Encyclopedia of Crime, 2006; Serial Killer Investigations, 2006; Atlantis and the Kingdom of the Neanderthals: 100, 000 Years of Lost History, 2006; The Angry Years: The Rise and Fall of The Angry Young Men, 2007; Manhunters: Criminal Profilers & Their Search for the World's Most Wanted Serial Killers, 2007; Super Consciousness: The Quest for the Peak Experience, 2009; (with D. Wilson) Strange: True Stories of the Mysterious and Bizarre, 2009; Existential Criticism: Selected Book Reviews, 2009; (with D. Wilson) Evil, 2009. EDITOR: (with J. Grant) The Directory of Possibilities, 1981; (with C. Evans) Great Mysteries, 1986; (with R. Duncan) Marx Refuted, 1987. Contributor to books and periodicals. **Address:** Tetherdown, Trewallock Ln., Gorran Haven, CW PL26 6NT, England.

WILSON, Cynthia. American (born United States), b. 1953?. **Genres:** Medicine/Health, Environmental Sciences/Ecology, Chemistry, Social Sciences. **Career:** Chemical Inquiry Information Network, executive director and founder, 1990-. Writer. **Publications:** Chemical Exposure and Human Health: A Reference to 314 Chemicals With A Guide to Symptoms and A Directory of Organizations, 1993; (with C. Duehring) The Human Consequences of the Chemical Problem, 1994. **Address:** Chemical Injury Information Network, PO Box 301, White Sulphur Springs, MT 59645, U.S.A.

WILSON, Darryl B(abe). American (born United States), b. 1939. **Genres:** History, Autobiography/Memoirs, Biography, Translations, Romance/Historical. **Career:** University of Arizona, American Indian Language Development Institute, affiliate, 1994-; Yaqui Reservation, Lawrence Intermediate School, teacher, 1995; San Francisco State University, instructor; Foothill College, faculty. Writer. **Publications:** (Trans.) Wellen Auf Dem Meer Der Zeit (title means: 'Waves upon the Ocean of Time'), 1974; (co-ed.) Dear Christopher (a collection of letters addressed to Columbus), 1993; The Sound of Rattles and Clappers, 1993; Wilma Mankiller, Principal Chief of the Cherokee Nation, 1995; Beginning Biographies, 1995; (with L. Crozier-Hogle) Voices from the Earth (anthology of Native American interviews), 1997; (comp. with L. Crozier-Hogle) Surviving in Two Worlds: Contemporary Native American Voices, 1997; The Morning the Sun Went Down (autobiography), 1998. Works appear in anthologies. **Address:** 4733 S Carson St., Apt. 61, Carson City, NV 89701-6628, U.S.A.

WILSON, David Dana. *See* **WILSON, David Niall.**

WILSON, David Henry. British (born England), b. 1937. **Genres:** Novels, Children's Fiction, Plays/Screenplays, Translations, Young Adult Fiction, Animals/Pets. **Career:** Teacher, 1960-64; University of Cologne, lecturer in English, 1964-67; University of Konstanz, lecturer, 1967-2000; Bristol University, lecturer, 1972-2000. Writer. **Publications:** TRANSLATOR: W. Iser, The Cathedral of Monreale, 1965; Nepal: Art Treasures from the Himalayas, 1969; The Implied Reader, 1974; Act of Reading, 1978; New Perspectives in German Literary Criticism, 1979; Walter Pater: The Aesthetic Moment, 1988; Sterne's Tristram Shandy, 1988; O. Wilde: Works of a Conformist Rebel, 1989; The18th Century Mock-Heroic Poem, 1990; Wales, 1991; The Fictive and the Imaginary, 1993; Staging Politics: The Lasting Impact of Shakespeare's Histories, 1993; East Anglia, 1994; The West Country, 2000; Kolomon Moser, 2002; Tibet: Turning the Wheel of Life, 2003; The Art Director's Handbook of Professional Magazine Design, 2003; Goya: To Every Story There Belongs Another, 2003; K. Boie, Princess Plot, 2009; (trans.) K. Boie, Verrat in Skogland (title means: 'The Princess of Trap'), 2010. CHILDREN FICTION: Der Elefant Auf Papas Auto, 1972; Elephants Don't Sit on Cars, 1977; The Fastest Gun Alive and Other Night Adventures, 1978; Never Say Moo to a Bull, 1978; Getting Rich with Jeremy James, 1979; Beside the Sea with Jeremy James, 1980; How the Lion Lost His Lunch, 1980; How to Stop a Train with One Finger, 1984; Superdog, 1984; Can a Spider Learn to Fly?, 1984; Do Goldfish Play the Violin?, 1985; Superdog the Hero, 1986; There's a Wolf in My Pudding, 1986; Yucky Ducky, 1988; Superdog in Trouble, 1988; Gander of the Yard, 1989; Little Billy and the Wump, 1990; Please Keep off the Dinosaur, 1993; Gideon Gander Solves the World's Greatest Mysteries, 1993; The Castle of Inside Out, 1997; Do Gerbils Go to Heaven?, 1999; Never Steal Wheels from a Dog, 2000; Triple Trouble with Jeremy James, 2006; Causing Chaos with Jeremy James, 2006; Making Mischief with Jeremy James, 2008; Elephants: A Book for Children with 80 Color Photographs, 2008. NOVELS: Asmadi, 1985; The Coachman Rat, 1989; Der Fluch der Achten Fee, 1989. OTHERS: All the World's a Stage, 1968; The Make-up Artist, 1973; On Stage, Mr. Smith, 1975; Monster Man, 1983; Shylock's Revenge, 1986; Are You Normal, Mr. Norman?: And Other Short Plays, 1984; We're Looking for Mary Pickford and Other Plays, 1987; How to Make Your Theatre Pay: A Comedy, 2002; My Favorite Animal Families, 2010. **Address:** c/o Herta Ryder, Toby Eady Associates Ltd., 7 Gledhow Gardens, London, GL SW5 0BL, England.

WILSON, David M(ackenzie). British (born England), b. 1931. **Genres:** Archaeology/Antiquities, Art/Art History, Crafts, History, Social Sciences. **Career:** British Museum, assistant keeper, 1954-64, director, 1977-92; British Archaeological Association, president, 1962-68; University of London, reader, 1964-71, professor of medieval archaeology, 1971-76; University College, Department of Scandinavian Studies, joint head, 1973-76; Viking Society, president, 1968-70; Cambridge University, Slade professor, 1985-86. Writer. **Publications:** The Anglo-Saxons, 1960, rev. ed., 1971; Anglo-Saxon Medalwork 700-1100 in the British Musuem, 1964; (with O. Klindt-Jensen) Viking Art, 1966; (with G. Bersu) Three Viking Graves in the Isle of Man, 1966; The Vikings and Their Origins: Scandinavia in the First Millennium, 1970, new ed., 1980; Reflections on the St. Ninian's Isle Treasure, 1970; (with P.G. Foote) The Viking Achievement, 1970; (with P.G. Foote) Viking Achievement: A Survey of the Society and Culture of Early Medieval Scandinavia, 1970; (co-author) St. Ninian's Isle and Its Treasure, 1973; The Viking Age in the Isle of Man, 1974; Civil and Military Engineering in Viking Age Scandinavia, 1978; Economic Aspects of the Vikings in the West-the Archaeological Basis, 1980; The Forgotten Collector: Augustus Wollaston Franks of the British Museum, 1984; Anglo-Saxon Art: From the Seventh Century to the Norman Conquest, 1984; The Bayeux Tapestry: The Complete Tapestry in Color, 1985; The British Museum: Purpose and Politics, 1990; Awful Ends, The British Museum Book of Epitaphs, 1992; Showing the Flag, 1992; Vikingetidens Konst, 1995; Gods and Heroes: The Vikings in European Art, 1997; The British Museum: A History, 2002; Vikings in the Isle of Man, 2008. EDITOR: Archaeology of Anglo-Saxon England, 1976; The Northern World, 1980; The Collections of the British Museum, 1989; (with E. Roesdahl) From Viking to Crusader: The Scandinavians and Europe, 800-1200, 1992. **Address:** The Lifeboat House, Castletown, IM 1M9 1LD, England.

WILSON, David Niall. (David Dana Wilson). American (born United States), b. 1959?. **Genres:** Science Fiction/Fantasy, Mystery/Crime/Suspense, Novels, Novellas/Short Stories, Poetry, Literary Criticism And History. **Career:** Freelance writer, 1997-. **Publications:** Chrysalis, 1997; (with B. Savory, J. Pelan and E. Lee) Of Pigs and Spiders, 1999; This Is My Blood, 1999; The Temptation of Blood, 2000; (with R. Graves and M. McLaughlin) The Gossamer Eye, 2002; Dark Ages: Lasombra, 2003; Relic of the Dawn, 2004; Deep Blue, 2004; The Mote in Andrea's Eye, 2006; Defining Moments, 2007; Ancient Eyes, 2007; Ennui And Other States of Madness, 2008; Vintage Soul, 2009; Maelstrom, 2010. GRAILS COVENANT SERIES: To Sift Through Bitter Ashes, 1997; To Speak in Lifeless Tongues, 1998; To Dream of Dreamers Lost, 1998. Works appear in anthologies. Contributor to books and magazines. **Address:** Terminal Fright Publications, PO Box 100, Black River, NY 13612, U.S.A. **Online address:** david@macabreink.com

WILSON, David S(cofield). American (born United States), b. 1931. **Genres:** Art/Art History, Mythology/Folklore, Natural History, Adult Nonfiction, Homes/Gardens, Essays, Illustrations. **Career:** Morris and Forest Lake, English teacher, 1957-62; University of Minnesota, instructor, 1962-64, 1967-68; State University of New York, assistant professor of English, 1964-67; University of California-Davis, associate professor of American studies, through 1968, now senior lecturer emeritus. Writer. **Publications:** SELF-ILLUSTRATED: Beyond Mediation, 1979. OTHERS: In the Presence of Nature, 1978; (co-author) American Wildlife in Symbol and Story, 1978; (with J. Mechling and R. Merideth) Morning Work: A Trialogue on Issues of Knowledge and Freedom in Doing American Culture Studies, 1979; (with D. Robertson) Signs of Life in the Valley, 1981; (ed. with A.K. Gillespie) Rooted in America: Foodlore of Popular Fruits and Vegetables, 1999. Contributor to books. **Address:** Department of American Studies, University of California, 2134A Hart Hall, 1 Shields Ave., Davis, CA 95616, U.S.A. **Online address:** dswilson@ucdavis.edu

WILSON, Des. British/New Zealander (born New Zealand), b. 1941. **Genres:** Business/Trade/Industry, History, Novels, Natural History, Ghost Writer, Autobiography/Memoirs, Biography. **Career:** Journalist, 1956-59; Melbourne Sun, journalist, 1959-60; Observer, columnist and reporter, 1971-74; Royal Shakespeare Co., head of public affairs, 1974-76; Social Work Today, managing editor, 1976-79; Illustrated London News, deputy editor, 1979-81; political campaigner and activist, 1982-91; Friends of the Earth (a political activist group), co-founder and director, 1983; Burson-Marsteller, director of public affairs, 1992-94; British Airports Authority, director of corporate and public affairs, 1994-2000; New Statesman, columnist; Guardian, columnist; Shelter (a social services organization), co-founder and director. Journalist, columnist, political campaign organizer, public relations specialist, environmental activist, public speaker, documentary filmmaker and biographer. **Publications:** (Ed.) Notice to Quit, 1969; I Know It Was the Place's Fault, 1970; Des Wilson's Minority Report, 1973; So You Want to Be Prime Minister: An Introduction to British Politics Today, 1979; The Lead Scandal: The Fight to Save Children from Damage by Lead in Petrol, 1983; The Environmental Crisis: A Handbook for All Friends of the Earth, 1984; The Secrets File: The Case for Freedom of Information in Britain Today, 1984; Pressure: The A to Z of Campaigning in Britain, 1984; An End to Silence, 1985; Costa Del Sol (novel), 1990, rev. ed., 2005; Campaign (novel), 1992; (ed.) Cultism: Evil Unlimited, 2000; (with J. Egan and Susan C. King) Private Business-Public Battleground: The Case for Twenty-first Century Stakeholder Companies, 2002; Swimming with the Devilfish: Under the Surface of Professional Poker, 2006; Ghosts at the Table, 2007 in US as Ghosts at the Table: Riverboat Gamblers, Texas Rounders, Internet Games, and the Living Legends Who Made Poker What It Is Today, 2008; Memoirs of A Minor Public Figure, 2011. **Address:** Pryors Cottage, Nancegollan, CW TR13 0A2, England. **Online address:** des.wilson@talk21.com

WILSON, D. Harlan. American (born United States), b. 1971. **Genres:** Young Adult Fiction, Plays/Screenplays. **Career:** Wright State University, associate professor of English. Writer. **Publications:** FICTION: The Kafka Effekt, 2001; Stranger on the Loose, 2003; Pseudo-City, 2005; The Bizarro Starter Kit, 2006; Dr. Identity: Or, Farewell to Plaquedemia, 2007; Counting Earps & Other Rejekts, 2008; Blankety Blank: A Memoir of Vulgaria, 2008; Peckinpah: An Ultraviolent Romance, 2009; They Had Goat Heads, 2010. CRITICISM: Technologized Desire: Selfhood and the Body in Postcapitalist Science Fiction, 2009; Codename Prague, 2011; The Kyoto Man, 2013. Contributor to books. **Address:** Eraserhead Press, 205 NE Bryant St., Portland, OR 97211, U.S.A. **Online address:** david.wilson@wright.edu

WILSON, Diane. American (born United States), b. 1954?. **Genres:** Young Adult Non-fiction. **Career:** Minnesota Literature, editor, 2002-04; SASE, board chair; The Artists Voice, founder and editor. **Publications:** Spirit Car: Journey to a Dakota Past, 2006; Beloved Child: A Dakota Way of Life, 2011. Contributor to periodicals. **Address:** Shafer, MN , U.S.A. **Online address:** diane@wilsonwords.com

WILSON, D. J. See **WILSON, Dolores J.**

WILSON, Dolores J. (D. J. Wilson). American (born United States) **Genres:** Novels, Young Adult Fiction. **Career:** Writer. **Publications:** Big Hair and Flying Cows, 2004; Little Big Heart, 2005; Barking Goats and the Redneck Mafia, 2006; Jail Bertie and the Peanut Ladies, 2007; (as D.J. Wilson) Flight to Freedom, 2008; Dark Secrets of the Old Oak Tree, 2010. **Address:** c/o Author Mail, Medallion Press, 1020 Cedar Ave., Ste. 216, St. Charles, IL 60174, U.S.A. **Online address:** dj@doloresjwilson.com

WILSON, Duff. American (born United States), b. 1954?. **Genres:** Documentaries/Reportage, Young Adult Non-fiction, Law. **Career:** Seattle Post-Intelligencer, staff; Associated Press, staff; Omak Chronicle, staff; Seattle Times, investigative reporter, 1989-2004; The New York Times, sports investigative reporter, 2004-, reporter; Investigative Reporters and Editors, board director. **Publications:** Fateful Harvest: The True Story of a Small Town, a Global Industry, and a Toxic Secret, 2001. Contributor to books. **Address:** The New York Times, 620 8th Ave., New York, NY 10018-1618, U.S.A. **Online address:** dwilson@nytimes.com

WILSON, Elizabeth. British (born England), b. 1936?. **Genres:** Novels. **Career:** University of North London, faculty, 1987-2001; University of the Arts, London College of Fashion, visiting professor of cultural studies. Writer and activist. **Publications:** Women and the Welfare State, 1977; Only Halfway to Paradise: Women in Postwar Britain, 1945-1968, 1980; Mirror Writing: An Autobiography, 1982; Adorned in Dreams, 1985, 2nd ed., 2003; (with A. Weir) Hidden Agendas: Theory, Politics, and Experience in the Women's Movement, 1986; (with L. Taylor) Through the Looking Glass: A History of Dress from 1860 to the Present Day, 1991; The Sphinx in the City: Urban Life, the Control of Disorder and Women, 1991; (ed. with J. Ash) Chic Thrills: A Fashion Reader, 1992; (ed. with A. de la Haye) Defining Dress: Dress as Object, Meaning and Identity, 1999; Bohemians: The Glamorous Outcasts, 2000; (ed. with J. Entwistle) Body Dressing, 2001; The Contradictions of Culture: Cities, Culture, Women, 2001. NOVELS The Lost Time Cafe, 1993; Poisoned Hearts, 1995; The Twilight Hour, 2006; The Love that Kills, 2008. **Address:** Serpent's Tail, 3A Exmouth House, Pine St., London, GL EC1R 0JH, England. **Online address:** mail@elizabethwilson.net

WILSON, Emma. American (born United States), b. 1967?. **Genres:** Adult Non-fiction, Sex. **Career:** Cambridge University, Corpus Christi College, Department of French, lecturer in modern and medieval languages, senior lecturer, reader in contemporary French literature and film, head of department, fellow, professor of French literature and the visual arts. Writer. **Publications:** Sexuality and the Reading Encounter: Identity and Desire in Proust, Duras, Tournier and Cixous, 1996; French Cinema since 1950: Personal Histories, 1999; Memory and Survival: The French Cinema of Krzysztof, 2000; Investigación bibliográfica sobre estudios de sexualidad de la mujer rural, 2002; Cinema's Missing Children, 2003; Alain Resnais, 2006; Atom Egoyan, 2009; (ed.) The Cambridge History of French Literature, 2011. **Address:** Department of French, Corpus Christi College, University of Cambridge, Trumpington St., Sidgwick Ave., Cambridge, CB3 9DA, England. **Online address:** efw1000@cam.ac.uk

WILSON, Eric (P.). American (born United States) **Genres:** Novels, Young Adult Fiction, Mystery/Crime/Suspense. **Career:** Writer. **Publications:** Dark to Mortal Eyes: A Novel, 2004; Expiration Date: A Novel, 2005; The Best of Evil: A Novel, 2006; A Shred of Truth: A Novel, 2007; Facing the Giants, 2008; Field of Blood, 2008; Fireproof, 2008; Flywheel, 2008; Haunt of Jackals, 2009; Valley of Bones, 2010. **Address:** c/o Author Mail, WaterBrook Press, 12265 Oracle Blvd., Ste. 200, Colorado Springs, CO 80921, U.S.A.

WILSON, Eva. British/Swedish (born Sweden), b. 1925. **Genres:** Art/Art History, Design, Illustrations, History. **Career:** Lund University, Department of Archaeology, illustrator and photographer, 1950-55; freelance archaeological illustrator and writer, 1955-. **Publications:** Early Medieval Designs from Britain, 1983; North American Indian Designs, 1984; North American Indian Designs for Artists and Craftspeople, 1987; Ancient Egyptian Designs for Artists and Craftspeople, 1987; Celtic and Early Medieval Designs from Britain for Artists and Craftspeople, 1987; Islamic Designs, 1988; Islamic Designs for Artists and Craftpeople, 1988; 8000 Years of Ornament: An Illustrated Handbook of Motifs in US as Ornament-8000 Years: An Illustrated Handbook of Motifs, 1994; Roman Designs, 1999. **Address:** The Lifeboat House, The Quay, Castletown, IM 1M9 1LD, England.

WILSON, Fran. See **WILSON, Frances Engle.**

WILSON, Frances Engle. (Fran Wilson). American (born United States), b. 1922. **Genres:** Romance/Historical, Novels, Young Adult Fiction, Literary Criticism And History. **Career:** KTUL-Radio, announcer, 1943-44; writer, 1975-. **Publications:** ROMANCE NOVELS: Until Summer, 1981; Love's Sweet Design, 1987; Candles in the Snow, 1988; Dangerous Masquerade, 1988; Yesterday's Secrets, 1990; Golden Spring, 1993: Love's Legacy, 1994; Summer Stranger, 1994; A Heart Divided, 1995; All the Tomorrows, 1995; Bridestown, 1996; A Forever Kind of Guy, 1997; A Scotsman's Kiss, 1998; Summer Rain, 1999; To Saddle a Dream, 2000. AS FRAN WILSON: Where Mountains Wait, 1980; Amber Wine, 1982; Winter Promise, 1983; After Autumn, 1983; Souvenirs, 1983; Together in Lisbon, 1984; Clouds Against the Sun, 1985. **Address:** 4165 E 44th St., Tulsa, OK 74135, U.S.A.

WILSON, Francille Rusan. American (born United States), b. 1947. **Genres:** History, Biography. **Career:** Smithsonian Institution, Center for African American History and Culture, research fellow, 1996-98; City of Los Angeles, Commission on the Status of Women, commissioner, 2007-12; University of Southern California, associate professor, director of African American Studies, American Studies and Ethnicity, 2008-09; Mills College, Ethnic Studies Program, director; University of Maryland, associate professor of African American studies; Eastern Michigan University, faculty; University of Michigan-Flint, faculty; University of Michigan-Ann Arbor, Rockefeller Foundation, postdoctoral fellow. Writer. **Publications:** The Segregated Scholars: Black Social Scientists and the Creation of Black Labor Studies, 1890-1950, 2006. Contributor to books and journals. **Address:** Department of African American Studies, University of Maryland, 2169 LeFrak Hall, College Park, MD 20742, U.S.A. **Online address:** fwilson@aasp.umd.edu

WILSON, F(rancis) Paul. Also writes as Mary Elizabeth Murphy, Colin Andrews. American (born United States), b. 1946. **Genres:** Science Fiction/Fantasy, Horror, Mystery/Crime/Suspense, Children's Fiction. **Career:** Cedar Bridge Medical Group, physician, 1974-. Writer. **Publications:** Healer, 1976; Wheels Within Wheels, 1978; An Enemy of the State, 1980; The Keep, 1981; The Tomb: A Repairman Jack Novel, 1984; The Touch, 1986, rev. ed., 2009; Black Wind, 1988; (contrib.) The 100 Best Horror Books, 1988; Soft and Others: 16 Stories of Wonder and Dread, 1989; Dydeetown World, 1989; The Tery, 1989; Midnight Mass, 1990; Pelts, 1990; Reborn, 1990; Buckets, 1991; Sibs, 1991; Reprisal, 1991; Nightworld, 1992, rev. ed., 2012; The Barrens, 1992; The La Nague Chronicles, 1992; (ed. and contrib.) Freak Show, 1992; Foundation, 1993 in US as The Select, 1994; (as C. Andrews) Implant, 1995; (as M. Murphy) Virgin, 1995; (with M.J. Costello) Mirage, 1996; (ed. and contrib.) Diagnosis: Terminal: An Anthology of Medical Terror, 1996; Deep as the Marrow, 1997; (with S. Lyon) Nightkill, 1997; Legacies: A Repairman Jack Novel, 1998; (with M.J. Costello) Masque, 1998; The Barrens and Others, 1998; Conspiracies: A Repairman Jack Novel, 1999; All the Rage: A Repairman Jack Novel, 2000; The Christmas Thingy, 2000; Hosts: A Repairman Jack Novel, 2001; The Beast and Me, 2001; The Haunted Air: A Repairman Jack Novel, 2002; Sims, 2003; The Fifth Harmonic, 2003; Gateways: A Repairman Jack Novel, 2003; (co-author) Artifact, 2003; Crisscross: A Repairman Jack Novel, 2004; Infernal: A Repairman Jack Novel, 2005; Harbingers: A Repairman Jack Novel, 2006; Bloodline: A Repairman Jack Novel, 2007; Do-Gooder, 2007; (co-author) Completely Doomed, 2007; Jack: Secret Histories, 2008; By the Sword: A Repairman Jack Novel, 2008; Aftershock and Others, 2009; Ground Zero: A Repairman Jack Novel, 2009; Jack: Secret Circles, 2010; Fatal Error: A Repairman Jack Novel, 2010; Jack: Secret Vengeance, 2011; The Dark at the End: A Repairman Jack Novel, 2011. Contributor to periodicals. **Address:** c/o Albert Zuckerman, Writers House, 21 W 26th St., New York, NY 10010, U.S.A. **Online address:** fpaul46@aol.com

WILSON, Frank R. American (born United States) **Genres:** Medicine/Health, Sciences, How-to Books, Music. **Career:** University of California, School of Medicine, Peter F. Ostwald Health Program for Performing Artists, medical director; Stanford University, School of Medicine, writer, lecturer and consultant; physician and author. **Publications:** Mind, Muscle and Music: Physiological Clues to Better Teaching, 1981; Tone Deaf and All Thumbs? An Invitation to Music-Making for Late Bloomers and Non-Prodigies, 1986; The Hand: How Its Use Shapes the Brain, Language, and Human Culture, 1998 as Die Hand, Geniestreich der Evolution, 2000 in Spanish as LA Mano, 2002. EDITOR: Biology of Music Making: Proceedings of the 1984 Denver Conference, 1987; (with F.L. Roehmann) Music and Child Development: The Biology of Music Making: Proceedings of the 1987 Denver Conference, 1990. **Address:** School of Medicine, Stanford University, 300 Pasteur Dr., Stanford, CA 94305, U.S.A. **Online address:** fwilson@handoc.com

WILSON, Gina. British/Welsh (born Wales), b. 1943. **Genres:** Children's Fiction, Young Adult Fiction, Poetry. **Career:** Scottish National Dictionary, assistant editor, 1967-73; Dictionary of the Older Scottish Tongue, assistant editor, 1972-73; Arvon Foundation, faculty. **Publications:** Ricky's Birthday, 1973; Cora Ravenwing, 1980; A Friendship of Equals, 1981; The Whisper, 1982; All Ends Up, 1984; Family Feeling, 1986; Just Us, 1988; Polly Pipes Up, 1989; I Hope You Know..., 1989; Jim-Jam Pyjamas, 1990; Wompus Galumpus, 1990; Riding the Great White, 1992; Prowlpuss, 1995; Ignis, 2001; Grandma's Bears, 2004. Works appear in anthologies. Contributor to periodicals. **Address:** David Higham Associates Ltd., 5-8 Lower John St., Golden Sq., London, GL W1F 9HA, England.

WILSON, Gretchen. (Gretchen Frances Wilson). American (born United States), b. 1973. **Genres:** Novels, Music, Biography, Autobiography/Memoirs. **Career:** Printers Alley, bar singer, 1996-2003; Epic Records, contracted singer, 2003-. Writer. **Publications:** (With J. Rich and K. Alphin) Here for the Party: Piano, Vocal, Guitar, 2004; (with J. Rich) Redneck Woman, 2004; (with V. McGehee and J. Rich) All Jacked Up, 2005; (with A. Rucker) Redneck Woman: Stories from My Life, 2006. **Address:** Club 27, PO Box 708, Lebanon, TN 37088, U.S.A. **Online address:** gw@bubbleup.net

WILSON, Gretchen. *See* **KELBAUGH, Gretchen.**

WILSON, Gretchen Frances. *See* **WILSON, Gretchen.**

WILSON, G. Willow. American (born United States), b. 1982. **Genres:** Autobiography/Memoirs, Graphic Novels. **Career:** Teacher, 2003. Writer. **Publications:** (Intro.) Cairo: A Graphic Novel, 2007; (intro.) Air, vol. I: Letters from Lost Countries, 2009; (intro.) Vixen: Return of the Lion, 2009; (intro.) Air, vol. II: Flying Machines, 2009; The Butterfly Mosque: A Young American Woman's Journey to Love and Islam (memoir), 2010. Contributor to books and periodicals. **Address:** c/o Warren Frazier, John Hawkins and Associates Inc., 71 W 23 St., Ste. 1600, New York, NY 10010, U.S.A. **Online address:** info@gwillowwilson.com

WILSON, Jacqueline (Aitken). British (born England), b. 1945. **Genres:** Mystery/Crime/Suspense, Children's Fiction, Young Adult Fiction. **Career:** D.C. Thomson Newspapers, journalist, 1963-65; freelance writer, 1965-; Jackie magazine, journalist; Roehampton University, professorial fellow, 2008, pro vice chancellor, Children's Literature MA, teacher, Creative Writing MA, teacher. **Publications:** Hide and Seek, 1972; Ricky's Birthday, 1973; Truth or Dare, 1973; Snap, 1974; Let's Pretend, 1976; Making Hate, 1977; Nobody's Perfect, 1982; Waiting for the Sky to Fall, 1983; The Other Side, 1984; The School Trip, 1984; The Killer Tadpole, 1984; How to Survive Summer Camp, 1985; Amber, 1986; The Monster in the Cupboard, 1986; Glubbslyme, 1987; The Power of the Shade, 1987; Supersleuth, 1987; Lonely Hearts, 1987; This Girl, 1988; Rat Race, 1988; Vampire, 1988; The Party in the Lift, 1989; The Left-Outs, 1989; Falling Apart, 1989; Is There Anybody There?, 1990; Take a Good Look, 1990; The Dream Palace, 1991; The Story of Tracy Beaker, 1991; Video Rose, 1992; The Suitcase Kid, 1992; Mark Spark, 1992; Mark Spark in the Dark, 1993; The Werepuppy, 1993; Deep Blue, 1993; The Mum-Minder, 1993; The Bed and Breakfast Star, 1994 in US as Elsa, Star of the Shelter!, 1996; Twin Trouble, 1994; Teddy Goes Swimming, 1994; Teddy at the Fair, 1994; Teddy in the Garden, 1994; Teddy Likes the Little One, 1994; Teddy Plays Hide and Seek, 1994; Come Back, Teddy!, 1994; Freddy's Teddy, 1994; The Werepuppy on Holiday, 1995; The Dinosaur's Packed Lunch, 1995; Cliffhanger, 1995; Jimmy Jelly, 1995; Love from Katy, 1995; Sophie's Secret Diary, 1995; Double Act, 1995; Beauty and the Beast, 1996; Mr.Cool, 1996; Bad Girls, 1996; Connie and the Water Babies, 1996; The Monster Story-Teller, 1997; The Lottie Project, 1997; Girls in Love, 1997; The Wooden Horse, 1998; Rapunzel, 1998; Buried Alive!, 1998; Girls under Pressure, 1998; Monster Eyeballs, 1999; The Illustrated Mum,

1999; Girls out Late, 1999; Lizzy Zip Mouth, 2000; Vicky Angel, 2000; The Dar Game, 2000; My Brother Bernadette, 2001; The Cat Mummy, 2001; Dustbin Baby, 2001; Sleepovers, 2001; Jacqueline Wilson Journal, 2001; The Jacqueline Wilson Diary 2002, 2001; Jacqueline Wilson Address Book, 2002; Jacqueline Wilson Diary 2003, 2002; Jacqueline Wilson Diary 2004, 2003; Secrets, 2002; The Worry Web Site, 2002; Girls in Tears, 2002; Lola Rose, 2003; Midnight, 2003; Best Friends, 2004; The Diamond Girls, 2004; Clean Break, 2005; Candyfloss, 2007; Totally Jacqueline Wilson, 2007; Secrets and Dreams Slipcase, 2007; Starring Tracy Beaker, 2007; Jacqueline Wilson Diary 2008, 2007; Kiss, 2008; Jacky Daydream, 2008; My Sister Jodie, 2008; Cookie, 2008; Tracy Beaker's Thumping Heart, Comic Relief, 2009; Hetty Feather, 2009; Jacqueline Wilson Diary 2010, 2009; Lily Alone, 2011. **Address:** David Higham Associates, 5-8 Lower John St., Golden Sq., London, GL W1R 4HA, England.

WILSON, Jan Doolittle. American (born United States), b. 1972. **Genres:** Politics/Government, Women's Studies And Issues. **Career:** Central Michigan University, assistant professor of history; Grinnell College, visiting assistant professor of history, 2000-01; Ft. Hays State University, assistant professor of history, creator and director of the women's and gender studies program, 2001-05; University of Tulsa, assistant professor of history and women's studies and director of women's and gender studies. Writer. **Publications:** The Women's Joint Congressional Committee and the Politics of Maternalism, 1920-30, 2007. **Address:** University of Tulsa, 800 S Tucker Ave., Tulsa, OK 74104-9700, U.S.A. **Online address:** jan-wilson@utulsa.edu

WILSON, Joan Hoff. *See* **HOFF, Joan.**

WILSON, John K. American (born United States), b. 1969. **Genres:** Politics/Government, History. **Career:** Institute for College Freedom, founder; Independent Press Association, Campus Journalism Project, coordinator. Writer, liberal activist and political consultant. **Publications:** The Myth of Political Correctness: The Conservative Attack on Higher Education, 1995; Newt Gingrich: Capitol Crimes and Misdemeanors, 1996; How the Left Can Win Arguments and Influence People: A Tactical Manual for Pragmatic Progressives, 2001; Barack Obama: This Improbable Quest, 2008; Patriotic Correctness: Academic Freedom and Its Enemies, 2008. **Address:** Chicago, IL , U.S.A. **Online address:** collegefreedom@yahoo.com

WILSON, John Morgan. American (born United States), b. 1945?. **Genres:** Novels, Young Adult Non-fiction, Literary Criticism And History, Mystery/Crime/Suspense. **Career:** University of California, Extension Writers' Program, instructor, 1980-2009; Los Angeles Times, assistant editor, 1985-92; Easy Reader (newspaper), founder. Freelance journalist. **Publications:** The Complete Guide to Magazine Article Writing, 1993; Inside Hollywood: A Writer's Guide to Researching the World of Movies and TV, 1998. BENJAMIN JUSTICE MYSTERY NOVELS: Simple Justice, 1996; Revision of Justice, 1997; Justice at Risk, 1999; The Limits of Justice, 2000; Blind Eye, 2003; Moth and Flame, 2004; Rhapsody in Blood, 2006; Spider Season, 2008. PHILIP DAMON MYSTERY WITH P. DUCHIN: Blue Moon, 2002; Good Morning, Heartache, 2003. Contributor to periodicals. **Address:** St. Martin's Press, 175 5th Ave., New York, NY 10010-7703, U.S.A. **Online address:** john@johnmorganwilson.com

WILSON, Jonathan. American/British (born England), b. 1950. **Genres:** Novels, Novellas/Short Stories, Literary Criticism And History, Sports/Fitness, Recreation, Young Adult Fiction. **Career:** Hebrew University, English Department, teaching assistant, 1977-81; Tufts University, English Department, part-time lecturer, 1982-84, assistant professor, 1984-91, associate professor, 1991-2000, chair, 1998-2005, Fletcher professor of rhetoric and Debate and professor of English, 2000-, director of creative writing, 2005-07, Center for the Humanities, director, 2007-; Boston University, visiting professor, 2002. Writer. **Publications:** CRITICISM: On Bellow's Planet: Readings from the Dark Side, 1985; Herzog: The Limits of Ideas, 1990. SHORT STORIES: Schoom, 1995; Ambulance is on the Way: Stories of Men in Trouble, 2005. NOVELS: The Hiding Room, 1995; A Palestine Affair, 2003; Marc Chagall, 2007. OTHER: Inverting the Pyramid: The History of Football Tactics, 2009. Contributor to periodicals. **Address:** Department of English, Tufts University, 215 East Hall, Medford, MA 02155, U.S.A. **Online address:** jonathan.wilson@tufts.edu

WILSON, Joseph (Charles). American (born United States), b. 1949. **Genres:** Politics/Government, Autobiography/Memoirs. **Career:** US State

Department, general services officer, 1976-78, administrative officer, 1978-82; United States National Security Council, senior director for African affairs, 1997-98; J.C. Wilson International Ventures, chief executive officer, 1998-; consultant, 1998-; Jarch Capital L.L.C., vice chairman, 2007-. Writer. **Publications:** The Politics of Truth: Inside the Lies That Led to War and Betrayed My Wife's CIA Identity, 2004; The Politics of Truth: Inside the Lies That Put the White House on Trial and Betrayed My Wife's CIA Identity, 2005. Contributor to periodicals. **Address:** 1717 Pennsylvania Ave. NW, Ste. 300, Washington, DC 20006-4619, U.S.A. **Online address:** joewilson@politicsoftruth.com

WILSON, June. *See* **BADENI, June.**

WILSON, Justine. *See* **MUSK, Justine.**

WILSON, Kathleen. American (born United States), b. 1954. **Genres:** History, Social Sciences, Cultural/Ethnic Topics. **Career:** Yale University, instructor, 1981-85; Harvard University, lecturer, 1985-89; State University of New York, associate professor of history, professor of history, 1990-; Australian National University, visiting fellow, 2001; University of Canterbury, visiting fellow, 2005; Huntington Library, John Brockton fellow, 2010. Writer. **Publications:** The Sense of the People: Politics, Culture and Imperialism in England, 1715-1785, 1995; The Island Race: Englishness, Empire and Gender in the Eighteenth Century, 2003; (ed.) A New Imperial History: Culture, Identity and Modernity in Britain and the Empire, 1660-1840, 2004; Child of Mine, 2011. CONTRIBUTOR: Gender and Empire: The Oxford History of the British Empire, 2004; Re-Discovering Nelson, 2005; Women's History: Britain, 1660-1850, 2006. **Address:** Department of History, State University of New York, N-331 Social & Behavioral Sciences Bldg., 100 Nicolls Rd., Stony Brook, NY 11794-4348, U.S.A. **Online address:** kawilson@notes.cc.sunysb.edu

WILSON, Ken. American (born United States), b. 1943. **Genres:** Recreation, Sports/Fitness, Travel/Exploration, Autobiography/Memoirs, Natural History, Environmental Sciences/Ecology. **Career:** Ken Wilson Realty and Development, owner and broker, 1971-; Sportsmen on Film, president, 1984-; Wilson Asset management, president, 1999-. Public accountant and writer. **Publications:** Sport Hunting on Six Continents: Hunting around the World-from Alaska to Australia-from the Americas to Africa, Asia and Europe, 1998. Contributor to hunting magazines. **Address:** Sportsmen on Film Inc., 231 Earl Garrett, Ste. 300, PO Box 291818, Kerrville, TX 78028, U.S.A. **Online address:** kwilson@sportsmenonfilm.com

WILSON, Kevin. American (born United States), b. 1978?. **Genres:** Novellas/Short Stories. **Career:** University of the South, visiting instructor; Sewanee Writers' Conference, staff; MacDowell Colony, fellow; Yaddo, fellow; Kimmel Harding Nelson Center for the Arts, fellow. Writer. **Publications:** Tunneling to the Center of the Earth: Stories, 2009. Works appear in anthologies. Contributor to periodicals and journals. **Address:** Department of English, University of the South, 735 University Ave., Sewanee, TN 37383, U.S.A. **Online address:** kevin@wilsonkevin.com

WILSON, Laura. British (born England), b. 1964?. **Genres:** Novels, Criminology/True Crime. **Career:** Guardian, crime fiction reviewer. Writer. **Publications:** CRIME NOVELS: A Little Death, 2000; Dying Voices, 2000; My Best Friend, 2002; Hello Bunny Alice, 2003 as Telling Lies to Alice, 2004; The Lover, 2004; A Thousand Lies, 2006. TED STRATTON SERIES: CRIME NOVELS: Stratton's War, 2008 as The Innocent Spy, 2009; An Empty Death, 2009; Austerity, 2010; A Capital Crime, 2010. FOR CHILDREN: Daily Life in a Victorian House, 1993; Daily Life in a Tudor House, 1995; Daily Life in a Wartime House, 1995; How I Survived the Oregon Trail: The Journal of Jesse Adams (fiction), 1999; How I Survived the Irish Famine: The Journal of Mary O'Flynn (fiction), 2001; Investigating Childhood in Tudor and Victorian Times, 2001. Contributor to periodicals. **Address:** c/o Jane Gregory, Gregory and Co., 3 Barb Mews, London, GL W6 7PA, England.

WILSON, Lyle (Giles). Canadian (born Canada), b. 1955?. **Genres:** Art/Art History, Anthropology/Ethnology, History. **Career:** University of British Columbia, Museum of Anthropology, curatorial assistant and artist-in-residence, 1987-. Writer. **Publications:** (With A. Drake) Eulachon: A Fish to Cure Humanity (exhibition catalog), 1992. **Address:** Museum of Anthropology, University of British Columbia, 9393 NW Marine Dr., Vancouver, BC V6T 1Z2, Canada.

WILSON, Marc. American (born United States), b. 1951. **Genres:** Military/Defense/Arms Control, History. **Career:** International Newspaper Network, chief executive officer and founder, 1989-; Associated Press, assistant chief of bureau; Bigfork Eagle, editor and publisher; TownNews.com, chief executive officer and general manager. Journalist. **Publications:** Hero Street, U.S.A.: The Story of Little Mexico's Fallen Soldiers, 2009. Contributor to periodicals. **Address:** TownNews.com, 1510 47th Ave., Moline, IL 61265, U.S.A. **Online address:** marcus@townnews.com

WILSON, Martin. American (born United States), b. 1973?. **Genres:** Novels, Travel/Exploration, Young Adult Fiction. **Career:** Writer. **Publications:** (With A. McClellan) Uniquely North Carolina, 2004; Uniquely Alabama, 2004; Uniquely Mississippi, 2004; What They Always Tell Us (novel), 2008. Contributor to books. **Address:** c/o George M. Nicholson, Sterling Lord Literistic Inc., 65 Bleecker St., New York, NY 10012, U.S.A. **Online address:** martin@martinwilsonwrites.com

WILSON, Melba (Jean). American (born United States), b. 1947. **Genres:** Medicine/Health, Psychology. **Career:** Writer. **Publications:** Crossing the Boundary: Black Women Survive Incest, 1994; Healthy and Wise: The Essential Health Handbook for Black Women, 1994; (with S. Fernando and D. Ndegwa) Forensic Psychiatry, Race and Culture, 1998. **Address:** c/o Seal Press, 3131 Western Ave., Ste. 410, Seattle, WA 98121-1028, U.S.A. **Online address:** wilson@compuserve.com

WILSON, Myoung Chung. American/Korean (born Korea (South)), b. 1943. **Genres:** Bibliography. **Career:** Slippery Rock State College, instructor, 1969-71; The Free Public Library, adult services librarian, 1972-74; Rutgers, the State University of New Jersey, School of Communication and Information, Archibald S. Alexander Library, information services librarian, 1974-, social sciences librarian and liaison; National Center for Science Information Systems, consultant. Writer. **Publications:** (Co-author) Building a Scholarly Communications Center: Modeling the Rutgers Experience, 1999; Korean Government Publications: An Introductory Guide, 2000. Contributor to periodicals. **Address:** Archibald S. Alexander Library, School of Communication and Information, Rutgers, the State University of New Jersey, 169 College Ave., New Brunswick, NJ 08901-1163, U.S.A. **Online address:** mywilson@rulmail.rutgers.edu

WILSON, Nancy Hope. American (born United States), b. 1947. **Genres:** Children's Fiction, Young Adult Fiction, Plays/Screenplays, Animals/Pets. **Career:** Lycee Clemenceau, English teacher, 1969-70; preschool teacher, 1971-72; The Pilot School, English teacher, 1972-73; The Cambridge School, English teacher, 1973-76; consultant, 1975-83; Specialized Home Care, education supervisor, 1982-87; Mohawk Trail Regional Schools, enrichment coordinator, 1987-89. Writer. **Publications:** Bringing Nettie Back, 1992; The Reason for Janey, 1994; A Nose for Trouble, 1994; Helen and the Hudson Hornet (picture book), 1994; Becoming Felix, 1996; A Whiff of Danger, 1996; Old People, Frogs and Albert, 1997; Flapjack Waltzes, 1998; Mountain Pose, 2001. **Address:** c/o Susan Cohen, Writers' House, 21 W 26th St., New York, NY 10010, U.S.A.

WILSON, Nathan David. *See* **WILSON, N. D.**

WILSON, N. D. (Nathan David Wilson). American (born United States), b. 1978. **Genres:** Young Adult Non-fiction, Young Adult Fiction, Children's Fiction. **Career:** Credenda/Agenda Magazine, managing editor; New Saint Andrews College, part-time lecturer in English, 2001-04, fellow of literature, 2004-. **Publications:** 100 CUPBOARDS SERIES: 100 Cupboards, 2007; Dandelion Fire, 2009; The Chestnut King, 2010. OTHERS: (as Nathan D. Wilson) Right Behind: A Parody of Last Days Goofiness, 2001; (as Nathan D. Wilson) Supergeddon: A Really Big Geddon, 2003; The Dragon and the Garden, 2007; In the Time of Noah, 2007; Leepike Ridge, 2007; Notes from the Tilt-a-Whirl: Wide-Eyed Wonder in God's Spoken World, 2009; (intro.) Twilight Land, 2010; Three Smiths, 2010; The Dragon's Tooth, 2011; (with D. Wilson) The Rhetoric Companion: A Student's Guide to Power in Persuasion, 2011; (with D. Wilson) The Rhetoric Companion Answer Key, 2011; The Drowned Vault, 2012. Contributor to periodicals. **Address:** New Saint Andrews College, 405 S Main St., PO Box 9025, Moscow, ID 83843, U.S.A. **Online address:** contact@ndwilson.com

WILSON, Patricia Potter. American (born United States), b. 1946. **Genres:** Librarianship, Biography, Autobiography/Memoirs. **Career:** England Air

Force Base, teacher, 1967-68, 1972-77; library media specialist, 1979-81; University of Houston-Central Campus, lecturer in children's literature, 1983-86; University of Houston-Clear Lake, lecturer, 1984-87, assistant professor, 1988-94, associate professor of library and information science and reading education, 1994-2001, associate professor emeritus, 2001-; consultant, 2001-; librarian. Writer. **Publications:** (With A. Kimzey) Happenings: Developing Successful Programs for School Libraries, 1987; The Professional Collection for Elementary Educators, 1996; (with R. Leslie) Premiere Events: Library Programs That Inspire Elementary School Patrons, 2001; (with R. Leslie) Igniting the Spark: Library Programs That Inspire High School Patrons, 2001; (with J.A. Lyders) Leadership for Today's School Library: A Handbook for the Library Media Specialist and the School Principal, 2001; (with R. Leslie) Center Stage: Library Programs That Inspire Middle School Patrons, 2002; (with R. Leslie) Eagle on Ice: Eagle Scout Paul Siple's Antarctic Adventures with Commander Byrd, 2008. **Address:** PO Box 890653, Houston, TX 77289-0653, U.S.A.

WILSON, Peter H. British (born England), b. 1963. **Genres:** History, Military/Defense/Arms Control, Theology/Religion. **Career:** University of Sunderland, faculty; Newcastle University, faculty; German Historical Institute, modern German history workshop coordinator, 2002-; University of Hull, G.F. Grant professor of history, 2007-, director of research, deputy head of department, Marvel Centre for Medieval and Early Modern Studies, associate director, 2010-. Writer and historian. **Publications:** War, State, and Society in Württemberg, 1677-1793, 1995; German Armies: War and German Politics, 1648-1806, 1998; The Holy Roman Empire, 1495-1806, 1999; Absolutism in Central Europe, 2000; From Reich to Revolution: German History, 1558-1806, 2004; Europe's Tragedy: A History of the Thirty Years War in US as The Thirty Years War: Europe's Tragedy, 2009. EDITOR AND CONTRIBUTOR: Warfare in Europe, 1815- 1914, 2006; 1848: The Year of Revolutions, 2006; A Companion to Eighteenth-Century Europe, 2008; (with A. Forrest) The Bee and the Eagle: Napoleonic France and the End of the Holy Roman Empire, 1806, 2009. **Address:** Department of History, University of Hull, Hull, HU6 7RX, England. **Online address:** p.h.wilson@hull.ac.uk

WILSON, Rob. See **GORE, Patrick Wilson.**

WILSON, Robin J. British (born England), b. 1943. **Genres:** Mathematics/Statistics, Education. **Career:** Jesus College, lecturer in mathematics, 1969-72; Lady Margaret Hall in Oxford, lecturer in mathematics, 1988-94; Keble College, lecturer in mathematics, 1980-99; Gresham College, professor of geometry, 2001-02, 2004-; Open University, Milton Keynes, lecturer, 1972-79, dean, 1995-96, department head, 2003-05, professor of pure mathematics, 2005-. Writer. **Publications:** NONFICTION: (with N.L. Biggs and E.K. Lloyd) Graph Theory, 1736-1936, 1976; (with S. Fiorini) Edge-colourings of Graphs, 1977; Selected Topics in Graph Theory, 1978, 2nd ed., 1983; Combinatorics and Graph Theory, P1979; (ed. with L.W. Beineke) Applications of Graph Theory, 1979; (ed.) Applications of Combinatorics, 1982; (ed. with F.C. Holroyd) Geometrical Combinatorics, 1984; (with F. Lloyd) Gilbert & Sullivan: The Official D'Oyly Carte Picture History, 1984; Introduction to Graph Theory, 1985; (ed. with A. Borthwick) Sir Arthur Sullivan, 1986; (ed. with A. Borthwick) Songs: Book Two, 1987; (ed. with A. Borthwick) Songs: Book Three, 1988; (ed. with R. Nelson) Graph Colourings, 1990; (with J.J. Watkins) Graphs: An Introductory Approach: A First Course in Discrete Mathematics, 1990; (ed. with J. Fauvel and R. Flood) Mobius and His Band: Mathematics and Astronomy in Nineteenth-Century Germany, 1993; (with O. Oacho and O. Yasuhiko) Yasashiku Kuwashii Gurafu Riron Nyumon, 1993; (ed. with L.W. Beineke) Graph Connections: Relationships between Graph Theory and Other Areas of Mathematics, 1997; (with R.C. Read) An Atlas of Graphs, 1998; (ed. with J. Fauvel and R. Flood) Oxford Figures: 800 Years of the Mathematical Sciences, 2000; (with J.M. Aldous) Graphs and Applications: An Introductory Approach, 2000; (with J. Gray) Mathematical Conversations: Selections from the Mathematical Intelligencer, 2001; Stamping through Mathematics, 2001; Four Colors Suffice: How the Map Problem Was Solved, 2002; (ed. with J. Fauvel and R. Flood) Music and Mathematics: From Pythagoras to Fractals, 2003; (ed. with M. Anderson and V. Katz) Sherlock Holmes in Babylon: And Other Tales of Mathematical History, 2004; (ed. with L.W. Beineke) Topics in Algebraic Graph Theory, 2004; (ed. with R. Balakrishnan and G. Sethuraman) Graph Theory and Its Applications, 2004; How to Solve Sudoku: A Step-by-Step Guide, 2005; Hidden Word Sudoku: The Last Word in Sudoku Puzzles, 2006; Lewis Carroll in Numberland: His Fantastical Mathematical Logical Life: An Agony in Eight Fits, 2008; Topics in Topological Graph Theory, 2009; Anderson, Marlow, Who Gave You the

Epsilon?, and Other Tales of Mathematical History, 2009. **Address:** England. **Online address:** r.j.wilson@open.ac.uk

WILSON, Robley. American (born United States), b. 1930. **Genres:** Novels, Novellas/Short Stories, Poetry, Literary Criticism And History, Plays/Screenplays. **Career:** Raymondville Chronicle, reporter, 1950-51; New York State Fair, assistant publicity director, 1956; Valparaiso University, instructor, 1958-63; University of Northern Iowa, assistant professor, 1963-69, associate professor, 1969-75, professor of English, 1975-99, professor emeritus, 2000-; North American Review, editor, 1969-2000; Guggenheim fellow in fiction, 1983-84; Nicholl fellow in screen writing, 1995-96. Writer. **Publications:** POETRY: All That Lovemaking, 1961; Returning to the Body, 1977; Kingdoms of the Ordinary, 1987; A Pleasure Tree, 1990; A Walk through the Human Heart, 1996; Everything Paid For, 1999. SHORT STORY COLLECTIONS: The Pleasures of Manhood, 1977; Living Alone, 1978; Dancing for Men, 1983; Terrible Kisses, 1989; The Book of Lost Fathers, 2001; Who Will Hear Your Secrets, 2012. NOVELS: The Victim's Daughter, 1991; Splendid Omens, 2004; The World Still Melting, 2005. EDITOR: (with S. Minot) Three Stances of Modern Fiction: A Critical Anthology of the Short Story, 1972; (intro.) Four Minute Fictions: 50 Short Stories from the North American Review, 1987; The Place That Holds Our History: The Missouri Writer's Biennial Anthology, 1990; Adventures of Gertrude Stein, Detective, 1999; (with S. Hubbard) 100% Pure Florida Fiction: An Anthology, 2000. **Address:** Blue Garage Co., PO Box 4009, Winter Park, FL 32793-4009, U.S.A. **Online address:** robley3@earthlink.net

WILSON, Sandra. (Sandra Heath). British/Welsh (born Wales), b. 1944. **Genres:** Romance/Historical, Novels, Novellas/Short Stories. **Career:** Writer. **Publications:** Less Fortunate than Fair: The story of Cicely Plantagenet, 1974; The Queen's Sister, 1974; The Lady Cicely, 1974; Wife to the Kingmaker, 1974; Alice, 1976; The Penrich Dragon, 1977; Jessica, 1979; A Woman of Property, 1981; The Chalbourne Sapphires, 2007. ROMANCE NOVELS AS SANDRA HEATH: The Whispering Rocks, 1978; Green Girl, 1979; The Smuggler's Daughter, 1979; Lily of the Sun, 1980; The Courting of Jenny Bright, 1980; Mally, 1980; The Opera Dancer, 1981; A Commercial Enterprise, 1981; Unwilling Heiress, 1981; The Makeshift Marriage, 1981; The Sherborne Sapphires, 1982; Fashion's Lady, 1982; My Lady Domino, 1983; Rakehell's Widow, 1984; A Perfect Likeness, 1985; A Change of Fortune, 1985; Mannerby's Lady, 1986; A Scandalous Publication, 1986; The Absent Wife, 1987; Lady Jane's Ribbons, 1987; A Matter of Duty, 1988; An Impossible Confession, 1988; The Wrong Miss Richmond, 1989; The Pilfered Plume, 1989; The Second Lady Southvale, 1990; A Christmas Courtship, 1990; Lord Buckingham's Bride, 1991; Lord Kane's Keepsake, 1992; A Country Cotillion, 1992; (co-author) A Regency Christmas: Five New Stories, 1992; Lady Sabrina's Secret, 1993; Cruel Lord Cranham, 1993; A Highland Conquest, 1994; The Halloween Husband, 1994; Shades of the Past, 1994; Camilla's Conscience, 1995; The Haunting of Henrietta, 1995; Magic at Midnight, 1995; Lucy's Christmas Angel, 1995; Command Performance, 1996; Halloween Magic, 1996; Summer's Secret, 1997; The Faun's Folly, 1998; Marigold's Marriages, 1999; (co-author) A Regency Sampler, 1999; The Magic Jack O'Lantern, 1999; Counterfeit Kisses, 2000; Mistletoe Mischief, 2000; Breaking the Rules, 2001; Hide and Seek, 2001; An Easy Conquest, 2001; Playing with Fire, 2002; Second Thoughts, 2002; Lavender Blue, 2003; Fine Feathers, 2003; False Steps, 2003; Winter Dreams, 2004; Regency Christmas Magic: Five Stories, 2004; Diamond Dreams, 2005; (with E. Jensen, C. Kelly and A. McCabe) A Homespun Regency Christmas, 2008. Works appear in anthologies. **Address:** David Bolt Associates, 12 Heath Dr., Send, SR GU23 7EP, England.

WILSON, Sandy. American/British (born England), b. 1924. **Genres:** Songs/Lyrics And Libretti, Autobiography/Memoirs, Humor/Satire, Novellas/Short Stories, Social Sciences. **Career:** Writer. **Publications:** This Is Sylvia: Her Lives and Loves, 1954, rev. ed., 1955; The Boy Friend (libretto), 1954, rev. ed., 1972; The Buccaneer, 1955; Who's Who for Beginners, 1957; Valmouth: A Musical, 1958, rev. ed., 1985; The Poodle from Rome (short stories), 1962; Divorce Me, Darling!, 1965, 2nd ed., 1981; His Monkey Wife, 1971; I Could Be Happy: An Autobiography, 1975; Ivor, 1975; Caught in the Act, 1976; The Roaring Twenties, 1976; The Clapham Wonder, 1978; Aladdin, 1979. **Address:** 2 Southwell Gardens, London, GL SW7 4SB, England.

WILSON, S. G. See **WILSON, Stephen G.**

WILSON, Sharon Rose. American (born United States), b. 1941. **Genres:**

Literary Criticism And History, Art/Art History. **Career:** Purdue University, teaching assistant, 1963-65; University of Wisconsin, teaching assistant, 1965-70; University of Northern Colorado, instructor, 1970-73, assistant professor, 1974-78, associate professor of English and women's studies, 1978-84, professor of English and women's studies, 1985-, director of writing minor, 1985-88; Middlesex Polytechnic, Fulbright exchange teacher, 1978-79; Boulder County Women's Resources Center, visiting humanist, 1980. Writer. **Publications:** Margaret Atwood's Fairy-Tale Sexual Politics, 1993; (ed. with T.B. Friedman and S. Hengen) Approaches to Teaching Atwood's The Handmaid's Tale and Other Works, 1996; (ed.) Margaret Atwood's Textual Assassinations: Recent Poetry and Fiction, 2003; Myths and Fairy Tales in Contemporary Women's Fiction: From Atwood to Morrison, 2008. Contributor to books and periodicals. **Address:** Department of English, University of Northern Colorado, Ross 1170B, PO Box 109, Greeley, CO 80639, U.S.A. **Online address:** sharon.wilson@unco.edu

WILSON, Stephen G. (S. G. Wilson). Canadian (born Canada), b. 1942?. **Genres:** Law, Theology/Religion, History, Essays. **Career:** Carleton University, professor of religion. Writer. **Publications:** The Gentiles and the Gentile Mission in Luke-Acts, 1973; Luke and the Pastoral Epistles, 1979; (ed. with M.D. Hooker as S.G. Wilson) Paul and Paulinism: Essays in Honour of C.K. Barrett, 1982; Luke and the Law, 1983; Related Strangers: Jews and Christians, 70-170 C.E., 1995; (ed. with J.S. Kloppenborg) Voluntary Associations in the Graeco-Roman World, 1996; (ed. with M. Desjardins) Text and Artifact in the Religions of the Mediterranean Antiquity: Essays in Honour of Peter Richardson, 2000; Leaving the Fold: Apostates and Defectors in Antiquity, 2004. **Address:** Carleton University, 1125 Colonel By Dr., Ottawa, ON K1S 5B6, Canada.

WILSON, Susan. American (born United States), b. 1951. **Genres:** Novels. **Career:** Connecticut Bank and Trust Co., portfolio accounting cashier, 1974-79; Waterbury School System, substitute teacher, 1979; Uniroyal Chemical Co., Crop Protection Division, secretary, 1980-86; Rochambeau Middle School, secretary, 1986-88; Last Word Word Processing Service, proprietor, 1988-; Martha's Vineyard Hospital, medical records clerk, 1988-89; Martha's Vineyard Hospital Foundation, project coordinator, 1989-91, assistant director of development, 1991-94, director of development, 1994-95; Polly Hill Arboretum, development coordinator, 1998-2004; Martha's Vineyard Museum, development coordinator, 2004-. Writer. **Publications:** Beauty: A Novel, 1996; Hawke's Cove, 2000; Cameo Lake, 2001; The Fortune Teller's Daughter, 2002; Summer Harbor: A Novel, 2003; One Good Dog, 2010; The Dog Who Danced, 2012. Contributor to periodicals. **Address:** c/o Andrea Cirillo, Jane Rotrosen Agency, 318 E 51st St., New York, NY 10022, U.S.A. **Online address:** susanwilsonwrites@yahoo.com

WILSON, Tim. See **WILSON, T. R.**

WILSON, Timothy R. See **WILSON, T. R.**

WILSON, T. R. Also writes as Jude Morgan, Tim Wilson, Timothy R. Wilson. British (born England), b. 1962?. **Genres:** Novels, Young Adult Fiction. **Career:** Peterborough College of Adult Education, tutor. Writer and educator. **Publications:** (As Timothy Wilson) Master of Morholm: A Novel of the Fenland, 1986; The Ravished Earth, 1988; Treading on Shadows, 1989; The Straw Tower, 1990; Beauty for Ashes, 1992; Roses in December, 1992; Heartsease, 1993; Hester Verney, 1993; Purgatory, 1993; Close to You, 1994; A Green Hill Far Away, 1994; Freezing Point, 1995; John Twopenny, 1995; The Strawberry Sky, 1996; I Spy, 1996; Cruel to Be Kind, 1997; The Poppy Path, 1997; (as Tim Wilson) In a Child's Eye, 1998; A Singing Grave, 1998; A Ruling Passion, forthcoming. AS JUDE MORGAN: The King's Touch, 2002; Passion: A Novel of the Romantic Poets, 2004; Symphony, 2006; Indiscretion, 2006; An Accomplished Woman, 2007; The Taste of Sorrow, 2009; A Little Folly, 2010; Charlotte and Emily, 2010; The Secret Life of William Shakespeare, 2012. **Address:** St. Martin's Griffin, 175 5th Ave., New York, NY 10010, U.S.A.

WILSON, Trevor Gordon. New Zealander/American (born United States), b. 1928. **Genres:** History, Politics/Government. **Career:** Canterbury University, faculty, 1952; Auckland University, assistant lecturer in history, 1953-55; Manchester University, research assistant, 1957-59; University of Adelaide, lecturer, senior lecturer in history, 1960-67, professor of history, 1968-, honorary visiting research fellow, now professor emeritus; St. John's College, commonwealth fellow, 1972; Marshall University, Drinko distinguished

professor of history, 1989; Australian National University, visiting fellow; Magdalen College, visiting fellow; London School of Economics, academic visitor. Writer. **Publications:** The Downfall of the Liberal Party 1914-1935, 1966; (ed. and intro.) The Political Diaries of C.P. Scott 1911-1928, 1970; The Myriad Faces of War: Britain and the Great War 1914-1918, 1986; (with R. Prior) Command on the Western Front: The Military Career of Sir Henry Rawlinson 1914-1918, 1992; (with R. Prior) Passchendaele: The Untold Story, 1996; (with R. Prior) The First World War, 1999; (with R. Prior) Somme, 2005; (ed. with N. Cheesman and M. Skidmore) Ruling Myanmar: From Cyclone Nargis to National Elections, 2010. **Address:** John Deaver Drinko Academy, Marshall University, 211 Old Main, 1 John Marshall Dr., Huntington, WV 25755-2014, U.S.A. **Online address:** tjwilson@senet.com.au

WILSON, Waziyatawin Angela. See **WAZIYATAWIN.**

WILSON, Wesley M. American (born United States), b. 1927. **Genres:** Anthropology/Ethnology, History, International Relations/Current Affairs, Language/Linguistics, Law, Mythology/Folklore, Travel/Exploration, Social Sciences, Social Sciences. **Career:** Western Electric Co., equipment engineer, 1952-54; West Coast Telephone Co., personnel assistant, 1954-56, personnel director, 1956-57; National Labor Relations Board, attorney, 1960-69; labor relations attorney, 1970-85. Writer. **Publications:** Labor Law Handbook, 1963; Labor Relations Primer, 1973; Know Your Job Rights, 1976; Countries of the World, Then and Now, 3 vols., 1996; Five Languages Made Simpler: French, Italian, English, Spanish and German, Grammar, Vocabulary, Phrases and Conversation, 1997; Curious Customs & Bizarre Beliefs Around the World, 1999. **Address:** 3300 Carpenter Rd. SE, Ste. 113E, Olympia, WA 98503, U.S.A. **Online address:** weswilson@highstream.net

WILSON, William Scott. Japanese/American (born United States), b. 1944?. **Genres:** Novels, Translations, History. **Career:** Author. **Publications:** (Trans. and intro.) Ideals of the Samurai: Writings of Japanese Warriors, 1982; Hagakure: The Book of the Samurai, 1983; Budoshoshinshu: The Warrior's Primer, 1984; (trans.) The Roots of Wisdom: Saikontan, 1985; (trans.) The Unfettered Mind: Writings of the Zen Master to the Sword Master, 1986; The Lone Samurai: The Life of Miyamoto Musashi, 2004; (trans.) I. Chozanshi, Tengu geijutsuron (title means: 'The Demon's Sermon on the Martial Arts and Other Tales'), 2006; The Flowering Spirit: Classic Teachings on the Art of Nō, 2006; Yojokun: Life Lessons from a Samurai, 2008; The 36 Secret Strategies of the Martial Arts: The Classic Chinese Guide for Success in War, Business and Life, 2008; (trans.) H. Ying-ming, Cai gen tan (title means: 'The Unencumbered Spirit: Reflections of a Chinese Sage'), 2009. **Address:** Kodansha International, 1-17-14, Otowa YK Bldg., Bunkyo-ku, Tokyo, 112-8652, Japan.

WILT, David (Edward). American (born United States), b. 1955. **Genres:** Communications/Media, Film. **Career:** WMUC-Radio, announcer, sports director, program producer and record librarian, 1973-80; University of Maryland, McKeldin Library, circulation desk supervisor, 1980-85, University of Maryland Libraries, Circulation and Serials, Engineering and Physical Sciences Library, head, 1986-2009, EPSL, acting head, 1986-87, systems librarian, 2009-; George Washington University, professorial lecturer in film studies, 2008-. Writer. **Publications:** (With M. Shull) Doing Their Bit: Wartime American Animated Films, 1939-1945, 1987, rev. ed., 2004; Hardboiled in Hollywood: Five Black Mask Writers and the Movies, 1991; (with M. Shull) Hollywood War Films, 1937-1945: An Exhaustive Filmography of American Feature-length Motion Pictures Relating to World War II, 1996; (ed. with M.A. Smith and J.B. Erickson) Encyclopedia of Physical Sciences and Engineering Information Sources, 2nd ed., 1997; The Mexican Filmography 1916-2001, 2004; (contrib.) Film and Comics, 2007; (contrib.) Latsploitation, Latin America, and Exploitation Cinema, 2009. Contributor to books, magazines and newspapers. **Address:** Information Technology Division, University of Maryland Libraries, University of Maryland, College Park, MD 20742, U.S.A. **Online address:** dwilt@umd.edu

WILTSE, Jeff. American (born United States), b. 1970. **Genres:** History, Social Sciences. **Career:** University of Montana, assistant professor of history, 2002-, associate professor of history. Writer. **Publications:** Contested Waters: A Social History of Swimming Pools in America, 2007. Contributor to periodicals. **Address:** Department of History, University of Montana, Rm. 263 Liberal Arts, 32 Campus Dr., Missoula, MT 59812-0864, U.S.A. **Online address:** jeff.wiltse@mso.umt.edu

WILTSHIRE, Susan Ford. American (born United States), b. 1941. **Genres:** Classics, Autobiography/Memoirs, Essays, Poetry, Novellas/Short Stories. **Career:** University of Illinois, assistant professor of classics, 1967-69; Fisk University, director of the honors program, 1969-71; Vanderbilt University, assistant professor, 1971-75, associate professor, 1975-89, professor of classics, 1989-2007, department chair, 1989-95, 1999-2006, professor emeritus, 2007-, Phi Beta Kappa associate lecturer, 1991-93. Writer. **Publications:** Public and Private in Vergil's Aeneid, 1989; Greece, Rome, and the Bill of Rights, 1992; Seasons of Grief and Grace: A Sister's Story of AIDS, 1994; (co-author) Classical Nashville: Athens of the South, 1996; (ed.) Prairie Laureate: The Collected Poems of Robert Lee Brothers, 1998; Athena's Disguises: Mentors in Everyday Life, 1998; Windmills and Bridges: Poems Near and Far, 2002. Works appear in anthologies. Contributor to periodicals. **Address:** Department of Classical Studies, Vanderbilt University, 2301 Vanderbilt Pl., Sta. B350018, Nashville, TN 37235-0018, U.S.A. **Online address:** susan.f.wiltshire@vanderbilt.edu

WIMBERLEY, (Amos) Darryl. American (born United States) **Genres:** Mystery/Crime/Suspense. **Career:** Communications Properties Inc., assistant regional manager, 1979-80; University of Texas, instructor, 1981-93. Writer. **Publications:** BARRETT RAINES SERIES: (with J. Samsel) Writing For Interactive Media, 1998; A Rock And A Hard Place, 1999; Dead Man's Bay, 2000; Strawman's Hammock, 2001; Devil's Slew: A Detective Barrett Raines Mystery, 2010. OTHERS: A Tinker's Damn, 2000; The King Of Colored Town, 2007; Pepperfish Keys: A Detective Barrett Raines Mystery, 2007; Kaleidoscope (novel), 2008; Devil's Slew: A Barrett Raines Mystery, 2011. **Address:** 3902 Sycamore Dr., Austin, TX 78722, U.S.A. **Online address:** adarrylw@gmail.com

WIMSATT, William C. American (born United States), b. 1941. **Genres:** Philosophy, Young Adult Non-fiction, Sciences. **Career:** NCR Corp., designer in engineering department, 1962-63; University of Chicago, Department of Philosophy, assistant professor, 1971-74, associate professor, 1974-81, professor, 1981-2007, Fishbein Center, faculty of studies in history of science and medicine, 1997-, Big Problems Program, founder and director, 1998-, Peter B. Ritzma professor of philosophy, 2007-, now professor emeritus of philosophy; Ohio State University, university visiting distinguished professor, 1983-84; University of Minnesota, Winton professor of the liberal arts, Minnesota Center for Philosophy of Science, residential fellow. Writer. **Publications:** Re-engineering Philosophy for Limited Beings: Piecewise Approximations to Reality, 2007. Contributor to books. **Address:** Department of Philosophy, University of Chicago, 1115 E 58th St., Chicago, IL 60637, U.S.A. **Online address:** wwim@midway.uchicago.edu

WINANS, Christopher. American (born United States), b. 1950. **Genres:** Biography, Autobiography/Memoirs, Business/Trade/Industry. **Career:** Trentonian, reporter, 1978; Philadelphia Journal, reporter, 1979; United Press Intl., reporter in Philadelphia, 1980-81; Delaware County Daily Times, community news editor, 1981-83; Wall Street Journal, news editor, occasional book reviewer and financial reporter, 1983-93; Best Week, Best's Review, executive editor, 1993-. **Publications:** Malcolm Forbes: The Man Who Had Everything, 1990; The King of Cash: The Inside Story of Laurence Tisch, 1995. **Address:** Acton & Dystel, 928 Broadway, New York, NY 10010, U.S.A.

WINAWER, Sidney Jerome. American (born United States), b. 1931. **Genres:** Medicine/Health, Human Relations/Parenting. **Career:** Harvard Medical School, assistant in medicine, 1962-66; Harvard Medical Service Boston City Hospital, assistant physician, 1964-66; Memorial Sloan-Kettering Cancer Center, staff, 1968-, Laboratory for Gastrointestinal Cancer Research, head, 1978-98, chief of gastrointestinal and nutrition service, 1988-98, Paul Sherlock chair, 1991-; Cornell University, College of Medicine, professor of medicine, 1980-; Center for Prevention Colon Cancer WHO, head, 1985; American College of Gastroenterology, president; International Digestive Cancer Alliance, co-chair. Writer. **Publications:** (With M. Shike) Cancer Free: The Comprehensive Cancer Prevention Program, 1995; (with N. Taylor) Healing Lessons: A Doctor's Story of Love, Loss and Transformation, 1998. EDITOR: (with P. Rozen and C.B. Reich) Large Bowel Cancer: Policy, Prevention, Research and Treatment, 1991; (with R.C. Kurtz) Gastrointestinal Cancer, 1992; Management of Gastrointestinal Diseases, 1992; (with A.M. Cohen) Cancer of the Colon, Rectum and Anus, 1995. Contributor to books and professional journals. **Address:** Laboratory for Gastrointestinal Cancer Research, Memorial Sloan-Kettering Cancer Center, 1275 York Ave., Ste. 90, New York, NY 10021, U.S.A. **Online address:** winawers@mskcc.org

WINCHELL, Donna Haisty. American (born United States), b. 1952. **Genres:** Communications/Media, Literary Criticism And History. **Career:** Clemson University, coordinator of writing laboratory, 1983-88, Department of English, assistant professor, 1983-89, associate professor, 1989-94, professor, 1994-2008, professor emeritus, 2008-, director of composition and rhetoric, 1988-91. Writer. **Publications:** (With M.S. Ply) Writer, Audience, Subject: Bridging the Communication Gap, 1989; Alice Walker, 1992; (contrib.) Trifles, 2004; (with M.R. Winchell) Ideas In Conflict: Writing About The Great Issues Of Civilization, 2008; (with A. Rottenberg) Elements of Argument, 2009; (with A.T. Rottenberg) Structure of Argument, 2009, 7th ed., 2011. Works appear in anthologies. Contributor to periodicals. **Address:** Department of English, Emeritus College, Clemson University, E-301A Martin Hall, Clemson, SC 29634, U.S.A. **Online address:** winched@clemson.edu

WINCHESTER, Simon. American/British (born England), b. 1944. **Genres:** Documentaries/Reportage, Travel/Exploration, Geography. **Career:** Canadian Mining Co., staff, 1966; Journal, Newcastle, reporter, 1967-70; Guardian, correspondent, 1969-79; Daily Mail, chief U.S. correspondent, 1979-80, American bureau chief, 1980; Sunday Times, chief foreign feature writer, senior feature writer, 1981-; University of Chicago, writer-in-residence, 2001; San Jose State University, Lurie professor, 2004; St. Catherine's College, honorary fellow, 2009; Order of the British Empire, officer. **Publications:** In Holy Terror: Reporting the Ulster Troubles, 1974 in US as Northern Ireland in Crisis: Reporting the Ulster Troubles, 1975; American Heartbeat: Notes from a Midwestern Journey, 1976; Their Noble Lordships: The Hereditary Peerage Today, 1981 in US as Their Noble Lordships: Class and Power in Modern Britain, 1982; (with J. Morris) Stones of Empire: The Buildings of the Raj, 1983; Prison Diary, Argentina, 1983; The Sun Never Sets: Travels to the Remaining Outposts of the British Empire in UK as Outposts, 1985; Korea: A Walk through the Land of Miracles, 1988; Pacific Rising: The Emergence of a New World Culture, 1991; Hong Kong: Here Be Dragons, 1992; Pacific Nightmare: How Japan Starts World War III: A Future History, 1992; (with M. Parr) Small World, 1995; The River at the Center of the World: A Journey up the Yangze and Back in Chinese Time, 1996; The Professor and the Madman: A Tale of Murder, Insanity and the Making of the Oxford English Dictionary in UK as The Surgeon of Crowthorne, 1998; The Fracture Zone: A Return to the Balkans, 1999; The Map That Changed the World: William Smith and the Birth of Modern Geology, 2001; Dictionary of Modern English Usage, 2002; Krakatoa: The Day the World Exploded, 2003; The Meaning of Everything: The Story of the Oxford English Dictionary, 2003; Outposts: Journeys to the Surviving Relics of the British Empire, 2004; Crack in the Edge of the World: America and the Great California Earthquake of 1906, 2005; Korea: A Walk through the Land of Miracles, 2005; Korea zu Fuss durch das Land der Wunder Simon Winchester, 2006; Man Who Loved China: Joseph Needham and the Making of a Masterpiece, 2008; Bomb, Book and Compass: Joseph Needham and the Great Secrets of China, 2008; The Best American Travel Writing, 2009; Atlantic: A Vast Ocean of a Million Stories, 2010; Atlantic: The Biography of an Ocean, 2010; Alice Behind Wonderland, 2011. **Address:** William Morris Agency, 1325 Ave. of the Americas, New York, NY 10019, U.S.A.

WINCKLER, Edwin A. American (born United States), b. 1941. **Genres:** Politics/Government, History, Sciences, Social Sciences, Philosophy, Economics, Business/Trade/Industry. **Career:** Soros Reproductive Health and Rights, fellow, 2003-04; Harvard University, lecturer; University of California, lecturer. Writer. **Publications:** (Ed. with S. Greenhalgh) Contending Approaches to the Political Economy of Taiwan, 1988; (co-ed.) Elections in Japan, Korea, and Taiwan under the Single Non-Transferable Vote: The Comparative Study of an Embedded Institution, 1999; (ed.) Transition from Communism in China: Institutional and Comparative Analyses, 1999; (with S. Greenhalgh) Governing China's Population: From Leninist to Neoliberal Biopolitics, 2005. **Address:** Weatherhead East Asian Institute, Columbia University, 420 W 118th St., 9th Fl., New York, NY 10027, U.S.A. **Online address:** eaw9@columbia.edu

WINCKLER, Martin. (Marc Zaffran). Armenian/South African/Canadian (born Canada), b. 1955. **Genres:** Novels, Mystery/Crime/Suspense. **Career:** Prescrire, editor and deputy editor, 1983, 1989. Translator. **Publications:** La Vacation: Roman, 1989; La Maladie de Sachs, 1998; Contraceptions mode d'emploi, 2001; Case of Doctor Sachs, 2001; Le Mystére Marcoeur, 2001; Légendes, 2002; Mort in Vitro, 2003; Plumes d Ange, 2003; Trois médecins, 2004; Noirs Scalpels, 2005; Rire de Zorro, 2005; Camisoles, 2006; À ma bouche, 2007; (with S. Viviana) Droits du patient, 2007; Le Numéro 7, 2007; Trilogie Twain, 2008; Histoires en lair: Fictions, récits, projets, 2008; Choeur des Femmes: Roman, 2009; Invisibles, 2011. Contributor of essays on social and medical issues to periodicals. **Address:** c/o Publicity Director, Seven Stories Press, 140 Watts St., New York, NY 10013, U.S.A.

WINDER, Michael. American (born United States), b. 1977?. **Genres:** Biography, Autobiography/Memoirs, Military/Defense/Arms Control. **Career:** United States Army, commissioned officer. Author and motivational speaker. **Publications:** An Officer and a Junkie: From West Point to the Point of No Return, 2008. **Address:** U.S.A. **Online address:** mhwinder@aol.com

WINDER, Simon. British (born England), b. 1963?. **Genres:** History, Psychology, Young Adult Non-fiction, Literary Criticism And History, Social Sciences. **Career:** Penguin Books, publishing director. Writer. **Publications:** (Comp.) Sea Longing, 1998; The Man Who Saved Britain: A Personal Journey into the Disturbing World of James Bond, 2006; Germania: In Wayward Pursuit of the Germans and Their History, 2010. **Address:** c/o Andrew Wylie, The Wylie Agency, 17 Bedford Sq., London, GL WC1B 3JA, England.

WINDLE, Janice Woods. American (born United States) **Genres:** Women's Studies And Issues, Novels, Young Adult Non-fiction, Food And Wine. **Career:** Texas State House of Representatives, executive secretary, 1958-61; El Paso Bicentennial Commission, director, 1975-77; El Paso Community Foundation, president, now president emeritus. Writer. **Publications:** NOVELS: True Women, 1993; Hill Country, 1998; Will's War, 2001. NON-FICTION: The True Women Cookbook, 1997. **Address:** c/o Marika Flatt, Phenix & Phenix Literary Publicists, 8716 N Mopac Expy., Ste. 330, Austin, TX 78759-8357, U.S.A. **Online address:** windle@phenixpub.com

WINDLEY, Carol. Canadian (born Canada), b. 1947. **Genres:** Novellas/Short Stories, Novels, Young Adult Fiction. **Career:** Malaspina University-College, instructor of fiction writing workshops, 1995-97. Writer and librarian. **Publications:** COLLECTIONS: Visible Light, 1993; Home Schooling: Stories, 2006. NOVEL: Breathing under Water, 1998. **Address:** Oolichan Books, PO Box 2278, Fernie, BC V0B 1M0, Canada. **Online address:** cwindley@shaw.ca

WINDSOR, Linda. (Linda Covington). American (born United States), b. 1950. **Genres:** Novels, Romance/Historical, Novellas/Short Stories, Young Adult Fiction. **Career:** Demco Inc., comptroller, 1966-98; Windsor Enterprises Inc., financial consultant, 1999-. Writer. **Publications:** Pirate's Wild Embrace, 1990; Hawaiian Caress, 1990; Hawaiian Temptress, 1991; Wings of Love, 1991; Texas Lovestorm, 1991; Midnight Lovestorm, 1992; Delta Moonfire, 1992; Mexican Caress, 1993; The Knight and the Raven, 1994; Island Flame, 1995; Autumn Rose, 1996; Winter Rose, 1997; Border Rose, 1998; Hi Honey, I'm Home, 1999; Not Exactly Eden, 2000; It Had to Be You, 2001; Along Came Jones, 2003. FIRES OF GLEANNMARA SERIES HISTORICAL NOVELS: Maire, 2000; Riona, 2001; Deirdre, 2002. BRIDES OF ALBA SERIES: Healer, 2010; Thief, 2011; Rebel, 2012. MOONSTRUCK SERIES: Paper Moon, 2005; Fiesta Moon, 2005; Blue Moon, 2006. PIPER COVE CHRONICLES: Wedding Bell Blues, 2007; For Pete's Sake, 2008. AS LINDA COVINGTON: Wild Tory Rose, 1992; Liberty's Flame, 1994. Work appears in anthologies. **Address:** Alive Communications, 7680 Goddard St., Ste. 200, Colorado Springs, CO 80920, U.S.A. **Online address:** linda@lindawindsor.com

WINEAPPLE, Brenda. American (born United States), b. 1949. **Genres:** Writing/Journalism, Biography, Essays, Autobiography/Memoirs. **Career:** Union College, assistant professor, 1976-82, associate professor, 1983-90, professor of English, 1990-94, Doris Zemurray Stone and Washington Irving professor of modern literary and historical studies, 1994-; New York University, associate, 1989-90; New York State Council for the Humanities, lecturer, 1990-92; Yale University, Donald C. Gallup senior fellow in American literature, 1991-92; Indiana University, Institute for Advanced Study, honorary fellow, 1994; Columbia University, MFA Program, adjunct, 2004-10; The New School, MFA Program, professor, 2004-; Sarah Lawrence College, writer, 2004; City University of New York, Leon Levy Center for Biography, director and distinguished writer-in-residence, 2009-11. **Publications:** Genêt: A Biography of Janet Flanner, 1989; Sister Brother: Gertrude and Leo Stein, 1996, 2nd ed., 1997; (intro.) The Wings of the Dove, Henry James, 1999; Hawthorne: A Life, 2003; Three Lives, 2003; (intro.) Representative Men: Seven Lectures, Ralph Waldo Emerson, 2004; (ed.) Selected Poems, 2004;

White Heat: The Friendship of Emily Dickinson and Thomas Wentworth Higginson, 2008; (ed.) Nineteenth-Century American Writers on Writing, 2010; (ed. and intro.) Selected Stories, 2011. Contributor to periodicals and newspapers. **Address:** Janklow & Nesbit Associates, 445 Park Ave., 13th Fl., New York, NY 10022, U.S.A. **Online address:** bw@brendawineapple.com

WINEARLS, Joan. Canadian (born Canada), b. 1937. **Genres:** Art/Art History, Geography, Local History/Rural Topics, Natural History, Bibliography, Illustrations. **Career:** Toronto Public Library System, Metropolitan Bibliographic Centre, librarian; University of Toronto, map librarian, 1964-98, associate instructor of library science, 1970, Librarian IV, 1980, head the map library, through 1998, adjunct professor, faculty of library science, 1974-98, retired, 1998; Royal Ontario Museum, co-curator of exhibition, 1983. Writer. **Publications:** (With Y. Tessier) Directory of Canadian Map Collections, 1969; (contrib.) Ontario's History in Maps, 1984; Mapping Upper Canada, 1780-1867: An Annotated Bibliography of Manuscript and Printed Maps, 1991; The Atlas as a Book, 1490 to 1900, 1993; Editing Early and Historical Atlases, 1995; Art on the Wing: British, American and Canadian Illustrated Bird Books from the Eighteenth to the Twentieth Century, 1999. Contributor to periodicals. **Address:** University of Toronto Library, 130 St. George St., Toronto, ON M5S 1A5, Canada.

WINEGARTEN, Renee. British (born England), b. 1922. **Genres:** Literary Criticism And History, Biography, Essays, Politics/Government, Adult Non-fiction. **Career:** British Foreign Office, Research Department, Latin American Section, research assistant 1943-45; Cambridge University, Girton College, supervisor, 1946-47; Westminster Tutors, tutor in French and Spanish, 1947-54; freelance literary critic, 1954-. Writer. **Publications:** French Lyric Poetry in the Age of Malherbe, 1954; Writers and Revolution: The Fatal Lure of Action, 1974; The Double Life of George Sand: Woman and Writer, 1978; Mme. de Staël, 1985; Simone de Beauvoir: A Critical View, 1988; Accursed Politics: Some French Women Writers and Political Life 1715-1850, 2003; Germaine de Staël & Benjamin Constant: a dual biography, 2008. Contributor to journals. **Address:** Georges Borchardt Inc., 145 E 52nd St., New York, NY 10022, U.S.A.

WINER, Andrew. American (born United States), b. 1966?. **Genres:** Novels. **Career:** University of California, Department of Creative Writing, assistant professor, associate professor and chair. Writer. **Publications:** NOVELS: The Color Midnight Made, 2002; The Marriage Artist, 2010. **Address:** c/o Author Mail, Simon & Schuster Inc., 1230 Ave. of the Americas, New York, NY 10020-1513, U.S.A. **Online address:** andrew@andrewwiner.com

WINER, Deborah Grace. (Deborah Grace). American (born United States), b. 1961. **Genres:** Plays/Screenplays, Writing/Journalism, Biography. **Career:** Journalist and playwright; lyrics and lyricists; artistic director. **Publications:** (With D. McGovern) I Remember Too Much: 89 Opera Stars Speak Candidly of Their Work, Their Lives and Their Colleagues, 1990; (with D. McGovern) Sing Out, Louise!: 150 Broadway Musical Stars Remember 50 Years (interviews), 1993; The Night and the Music: Rosemary Clooney, Barbara Cook and Julie Wilson inside the World of Cabaret, 1995; The Last Girl Singer (play), 1995; On the Sunny Side of the Street: The Life and Lyrics of Dorothy Fields, 1997. **Address:** Sterling Lord Literistic, 65 Bleecker St., New York, NY 10012, U.S.A.

WINERIP, Michael. American (born United States), b. 1951. **Genres:** Documentaries/Reportage, Children's Fiction, Young Adult Non-fiction. **Career:** The Miami Herald, staff; Rochester Times-Union, staff; Louisville Courier-Journal, staff; New York Times, reporter, suburban columnist, investigative reporter, national political writer, education writer, deputy metro editor, national education columnist, national political correspondent and parenting columnist, Sunday Magazine, staff writer. **Publications:** 9 Highland Road (nonfiction), 1994. ADAM CANFIELD OF THE SLASH SERIES: Adam Canfield of the Slash, 2005; Watch your Back!, 2007; The Last Reporter, 2009. Contributor of articles to periodicals. **Address:** New York Times, 229 W 43rd St., New York, NY 10036-3959, U.S.A. **Online address:** mike@michaelwinerip.com

WINFIELD, Jess M. (Jess Borgeson). American (born United States), b. 1961. **Genres:** Novels. **Career:** Playwright, screenwriter, producer and novelist, 1981-; Reduced Shakespeare Co., founder and actor, 1981-92; Walt Disney Productions, writer, story editor and executive producer, 1998-2006. **Publications:** (As Jess Borgeson with A. Long and D. Singer and ed. as J.M.

Winfield) The Reduced Shakespeare Company's the Complete Works of William Shakespeare, 1994; What Would Shakespeare Do? Personal Advice from the Bard, 2000; My Name Is Will: A Novel of Sex, Drugs, and Shakespeare, 2008. **Address:** c/o Jason Dravis, Monteiro Rose Dravis Agency Inc., 17514 Ventura Blvd., Ste. 205, Encino, CA 91316, U.S.A. **Online address:** jess@jesswinfield.com

WINFIELD, Julia. *See* **ARMSTRONG, Jennifer.**

WINFORD, Donald C. American/Trinidadian (born Trinidad and Tobago), b. 1945. **Genres:** Language/Linguistics. **Career:** University of York, graduate assistant in linguistics, 1968-72; University of the West Indies, lecturer in English language and linguistics, 1972-78, lecturer on indefinite tenure, 1978-84, senior lecturer in indefinite tenure, 1984-88; University of Texas, Department of Linguistics, visiting lecturer, 1982-83; Ohio State University, Department of Linguistics, assistant professor, 1988-93, associate professor, 1993-99, professor, 1999-. Writer. **Publications:** Predication in Caribbean English Creole, 1993; Introduction to Contact Linguistics, 2003. EDITOR: (with W.F. Edwards) Verb Phrase Patterns in Black English and Creole, 1991; (with F. Byrne) Focus and Grammatical Relations in Creole Languages, 1993; (with A.K. Speers) The Structure and Status of Pidgin and Creoles: Including Selected Papers from the Meetings of the Society for Pidgin and Creole Linguistics, 1997; (with L. Isurin and K. de Bot) Multidisciplinary Approaches to Code Switching, 2009. Contributor to journals. **Address:** Department of Linguistics, Ohio State University, 222 Oxley Hall, 1712 Neil Ave., Columbus, OH 43210, U.S.A. **Online address:** dwinford@ling.ohio-state.edu

WING, Betsy. American (born United States), b. 1936. **Genres:** Novels, Novellas/Short Stories, Translations, Poetry, Sociology, Literary Criticism And History. **Career:** Oberlin College, visiting instructor, 1989. Freelance translator and writer. **Publications:** Look Out for Hydrophobia (novella and stories), 1990. TRANSLATOR: The Newly Born Woman, 1986; The Private Picasso, 1987; The College of Sociology, 1988; Opera or the Undoing of Women, 1988; Against Architecture, 1989; Look Out for Hydrophobia: Stories, 1990; (intro.) The Book of Promethea, 1991; Michel Foucault (biography), 1991; (with K. Bieber) Outwitting the Gestapo, 1993; E. Gloussant, Poetics of Relation, 1997; E. Gloussant, Black Salt (poems), 1997; P. Constant, The Governor's Daughter, 1998; In Praise of the Variant, 1999; The Riddle of Nostradamus, 1999; A. Djebar, So Vast the Prison, 1999; The Fourth Century/Le quatriémesiécle, 2001; P. Constant, Trading Secrets, 2001; P. Constant, White Spirit, 2005; C. Montalbetti, Western, 2009; E. Gloussant, Overseer's Cabin, 2011. Contributor to periodicals. **Address:** Faith Childs Literary Agency, 275 W 96th St., New York, LA 10025, U.S.A. **Online address:** wingtran@ix.netcom.com

WING, Natasha. American/Ukranian (born Ukraine), b. 1960. **Genres:** Children's Fiction, Children's Non-fiction, Picture/Board Books, Biography, Poetry. **Career:** Arizona Republic, staff, 1982-88; MTC Associates (advertising agency), account representative, 1988-90; Write Ideas, owner and writer, 1990-2008; reading tutor, 1997-98. **Publications:** Hippity Hop, Frog on Top, 1994; Jalapeno Bagels, 1996; The Night Before Easter, 1999; The Night Before Halloween, 1999; The Night Before Valentine's Day, 2000; The Night Before Kindergarten, 2001; The Night Before Thanksgiving, 2001; The Night Before Summer Vacation, 2002; The Night Before the New Baby, 2002; The Night Before the Night Before Christmas, 2002; The Night Before the Tooth Fairy, 2003; A Slice of Humboldt Pie, 2004; Merry Thanksgiving, 2005; The Night Before the 100th Day of School, 2005; The Night Before Summer Camp, 2007; Go to Bed, Monster!, 2007; An Eye for Color: The Story of Josef Albers, 2009; Pearl vs. the Tooth Fairy, 2009; The Night Before St. Patrick's Day, 2009; The Night Before New Year's, 2009; The Night Before Mother's Day, 2010; How to Raise a Dinosaur, 2010; The Night Before Preschool, 2011; The Night Before Kindergarten Sticker Stories, 2011; The Night Before Father's Day, 2012. **Address:** 1527 Hearthfire Dr., Fort Collins, CO 80524, U.S.A. **Online address:** natashawing@gmail.com

WINGATE, Steven. American (born United States), b. 1964. **Genres:** Novellas/Short Stories, Novels. **Career:** South Dakota State University, assistant professor, 2011-; College of the Holy Cross, visiting assistant professor of creative writing, 2010-11; University of Colorado, Writing Workshop, instructor, 2001-10; Fiction Writers Review, contributing editor. **Publications:** Wifeshopping: Stories, 2008. Works appear in anthologies. Contributor to books and periodicals. **Address:** Department of English, South Dakota State University, PO Box 0504, Brookings, SD 57007, U.S.A. **Online address:** stevenwingate@mac.com

WINGER, Anna. German/American (born United States), b. 1970?. **Genres:** Novels. **Career:** Author, photographer and artist. **Publications:** This Must Be the Place, 2008. Contributor to magazines. **Address:** Berlin, Germany. **Online address:** annawinger@gmail.com

WINGERTER, J. Richard. Canadian (born Canada), b. 1942. **Genres:** Education, Philosophy, Theology/Religion. **Career:** Writer. **Publications:** Beyond Metaphysics Revisited, 2002; Science, Religion, and the Meditative Mind, 2003; Teaching, Learning, and the Meditative Mind, 2003; Observerless Observations, 2005; Living Beyond the One and the Many: Silent-Mind Transcendence of All Traditional and Contemporary Monism and Dualism, 2011. **Address:** Edmonton Trail RPO, 311-16th Ave. NE, PO Box 52078, Calgary, AB T2E 8K9, Canada. **Online address:** jrwingerter@shaw.ca

WINGFIELD, Paul. British (born England), b. 1961?. **Genres:** Music. **Career:** University of Sydney, research fellow in music, 1987-88; Cambridge University, Caius College, research fellow in music, 1988-90, Trinity College, fellow and director of studies in music, 1990-, tutor for admissions. Writer. **Publications:** Leoš Janáček: Glagolitic Mass, 1992; (ed.) Janáček Studies, 1999. **Address:** Trinity College, Cambridge University, Saint John's St., Cambridge, CB CB2 1TQ, England. **Online address:** admissions@trin.cam.ac.uk

WINIK, Marion (Lisa). American (born United States), b. 1958. **Genres:** Poetry, Novellas/Short Stories, Autobiography/Memoirs, Biography. **Career:** Creative Rapid Learning Center, curriculum coordinator, 1978-80; Research and Planning Consultants, managing editor, 1980-81, direct mail manager, 1983-84; Stanley H. Kaplan Educational Center Inc., researcher, teacher, 1981-84; City University of New York, Brooklyn College, lecturer, 1982-83; Unison-Tymlabs, marketing, technical writer, 1984-94; All Things Considered, National Public Radio, commentator, 1991-. Writer and commentator. **Publications:** Nonstop (poetry), 1981; Boy Crazy (poetry and short stories), 1986; Telling: Confessions, Concessions, and Other Flashes of Light (essays), 1994; First Comes Love (memoir), 1996; The Lunch-Box Chronicles: Notes from the Parenting Underground (memoir), 1998; Rules for the Unruly: Living an Unconventional Life, 2001; Above Us Only Sky, 2005; Glen Rock Book of the Dead, 2008; Dona Schwartz: In the Kitchen (poems), 2009. Contributor to periodicals. **Address:** University of Baltimore, 1420 N Charles St., Baltimore, MD 21201, U.S.A. **Online address:** maliwali@aol.com

WININGER, Kathleen J. American (born United States), b. 1955. **Genres:** Philosophy, Humanities, Art/Art History, Film, Ethics. **Career:** Union College, assistant professor, 1984-85; Earlham College, assistant professor, 1985-89; University of Southern Maine, Department of Philosophy, associate professor, 1989-, chair, professor of philosophy; Villanova University, instructor. Writer. **Publications:** Nietzsche's Reclamation of Philosophy, 1997; (ed. with R.B. Baker and F.A. Elliston) Philosophy and Sex, 3rd ed., 1998, (ed. with R.B. Baker) 4th ed., 2009. Contributor to books and periodicals. **Address:** Department of Philosophy, University of Southern Maine, 47 Exeter St., Portland, ME 04102, U.S.A. **Online address:** wininger@usm.maine.edu

WINKLER, Anthony C. American/Jamaican (born Jamaica), b. 1942. **Genres:** Novels, Novellas/Short Stories, Plays/Screenplays, Writing/Journalism, Plays/Screenplays, Speech/Rhetoric, Reference. **Career:** Appleton-Century-Crofts, field representative, 1968-70; Scott Foresman & Co., field representative, 1971-75; Moneague Teachers College, tutor in English, 1975-76; freelance writer, 1976-; Dekalb Community College, adjunct professor. **Publications:** Poetry as System, 1971; (with J.R. McCuen-Metherell) Rhetoric Made Plain, 1974, 6th ed., 1995; (comp. with J.R. McCuen-Metherell) Readings for Writers, 1974, (comp. with J.R. McCuen-Metherell) 13th ed., 2010; (with J.R. McCuen-Metherell) From Idea to Essay, 1977, 13th ed., 2012; (with D. Ochs) A Brief Introduction to Speech, 1979, 2nd ed., 1983; (with J.R. McCuen-Metherell) Writing the Research Paper: A Handbook, 1979, 8th ed., 2012; (with J.R. McCuen-Metherell) Writing Sentences, Paragraphs and Essays, 1981; (comp. with J.R. McCuen-Metherell) Exposition: Model Paragraphs and Essays, 1982; The Painted Canoe, 1983; (with J.R. McCuen-Metherell) Rewriting Writing, 1987, 2nd ed., 1990; The Lunatic, 1987; (with J.R. McCuen-Metherell) From Reading, Writing, 1988, 2nd ed., 1993; (with J.R. McCuen-Metherell) Reading, Writing and the Humanities, 1991; The Great Yacht Race, 1992; (with J.R. McCuen-Metherell) The Journal Reader, 1993; (with J.R. McCuen-Metherell) Prentice Hall Pocket Guide for Writers, 1995; Going Home to Teach, 1995; (with C. Marley Booker)

Bob Marley: An Intimate Portrait by His Mother, 1996; (with J.R. McCuen-Metherell) Grammar Talk, 1997; The Duppy, 1997; (with J. McEuen) Writing Talk: Sentences and Paragraphs with Readings, 1997, 5th ed., 2009; (with J.R. McCuen-Metherell) Writing Talk: Paragraphs and Short Essays with Readings, 1997, 5th ed., 2009; (with J.R. McCuen-Metherel) Writing the Research Paper: Pocket Guide, 2000; (with C.M. Booker) Bob Marley, My Son, 2003; The Annihilation of Fish and Other Stories, 2004; Dog War, 2007; The Lunatic, 2007; Writing the Research Paper: A Handbook, (with J.R. McCuen-Metherell) 7th ed., 2008; Trust the Darkness: My Life As a Writer, 2008; Writing Talk: Sentences and Paragraphs with Readings, 2009; (with J.R. McCuen-Metherell) From Idea to Essay: A Rhetoric, Reader and Handbook, 2009; (with J.R. McCuen-Metherell) Grammar Matters: Sentence Basics and Essential Grammar, 2011. Contributor to periodicals. **Address:** 1670 Berkford Ct. NE, Atlanta, GA 30319, U.S.A.

WINKLER, Henry Ralph. American (born United States), b. 1916. **Genres:** History, Social Sciences. **Career:** University of Cincinnati, instructor in history, 1939-40, university professor of history, 1977-, executive vice-president, 1977, president, 1977-84, university professor emeritus of history and president emeritus, 1984-; U.S. Office of War Information, information analyst, 1942-43; Roosevelt College of Chicago (now Roosevelt University), assistant professor of history, 1946-47; Rutgers University, assistant professor, 1947-52, associate professor, 1952-58, professor of history, 1958-70, chair of department, 1960-64, university professor of history, 1970-77, Faculty of Liberal Arts, dean, 1967-68, vice-provost, 1968-70, vice-president for academic affairs, 1970-72, senior vice-president for academic affairs, 1972-76, acting president, 1976, executive vice-president, 1976-77. Writer. **Publications:** Development of the League of Nations Idea in Great Britain, 1914-1919, 1947; The League of Nations Movement in Great Britain 1914-1919, 1952; (ed. with K.M. Setton) Great Problems in European Civilization, 1954, 2nd ed., 1966; Great Britain in the Twentieth Century, 1960; (ed. and intro.) Twentieth-Century Britain: National Power and Social Welfare, 1976; Paths Not Taken: British Labor and International Policy in the 1920s, 1994; British Labour Seeks a Foreign Policy, 1900-1940, 2005. **Address:** Office of the President, University of Cincinnati, 2600 Clifton Ave., Cincinnati, OH 45221, U.S.A. **Online address:** henry.winkler@uc.edu

WINKLER, John. British (born England), b. 1935?. **Genres:** Marketing, Economics, Money/Finance. **Career:** J. Lyons Group of Companies, marketing director; Winkler International Ltd., owner, managing director, 1969-; The Times, marketing correspondent. **Publications:** Marketing for the Developing Company, 1969; Winkler on Marketing Planning, 1972; Company Survival During Inflation: A Systematic Approach to Profit Improvement, 1975; Bargaining for Results, 1984; Pricing for Results, 1984; Winning Sales and Marketing Tactics, 1991. **Address:** Winkler International Ltd., PO Box 104, East Sussex, SU BN10 7WD, England. **Online address:** website@thewinklers.co.uk

WINKLER, Jonathan Reed. American (born United States), b. 1975?. **Genres:** History, Military/Defense/Arms Control. **Career:** Wright State University, associate professor. Writer. **Publications:** Nexus: Strategic Communications and American Security in World War I, 2008. **Address:** U.S.A. **Online address:** jonathan.winkler@wright.edu

WINLAND, Daphne N. Canadian (born Canada), b. 1957?. **Genres:** History. **Career:** York University, associate professor and director of the graduate program. Writer. **Publications:** We Are Now a Nation: Croats between Home and Homeland, 2007. Contributor to periodicals. **Address:** York University, 2054C Vari Hall, 4700 Keele St., Toronto, ON M3J 1P3, Canada. **Online address:** winland@yorku.ca

WINN, Tracy. American (born United States), b. 1953?. **Genres:** Young Adult Fiction, Novellas/Short Stories. **Career:** Writer. **Publications:** Mrs. Somebody Somebody: Stories, 2009. Contributor to periodicals. **Address:** Boston, MA , U.S.A. **Online address:** tracy@winnwriter.com

WINNER, Lauren F. American (born United States), b. 1975?. **Genres:** Autobiography/Memoirs, Theology/Religion. **Career:** Christianity Today, senior writer; Beliefnet.com, book review editor; Duke Divinity School, faculty; Princeton University, Center for the Study of Religion, visiting fellow, 2007-08; Yale University, Institute of Sacred Music, visiting fellow, 2010-11. **Publications:** (With R. Balmer) Protestantism in America, 2002; Girl Meets God: On the Path to a Spiritual Life, 2002; Mudhouse Sabbath, 2003; Real Sex: The Naked Truth About Chastity, 2005; (co-author) 5 Paths to the Love of Your Life: Defining Your Dating Style, 2005; Cheerful and Comfortable Faith, 2010; Still: Notes on a Mid-faith Crisis, 2012. Contributor to periodicals. **Address:** Christianity Today, 465 Gundersen Dr., PO Box OL1009, Carol Stream, IL 60188-2415, U.S.A. **Online address:** lauren@laurenwinner.net

WINNER, Michael Robert. American/British (born England), b. 1935. **Genres:** Plays/Screenplays, Biography. **Career:** Film critic and columnist for English newspapers and magazines, 1951-; Scimitar Films Ltd., chairman, 1957-; film producer and director, 1960-; theater producer, 1974-; Sunday Times and News of the World, weekly columnist. **Publications:** Winner's Dinners, 1999, rev. ed., 2001; Shocking Cinema of the Seventies: Necronomicon Presents, 2000; Winner Guide, 2002; Winner Takes All Biography, 2004; Fat Pig Diet, 2007. Contributor to periodicals and newspapers. **Address:** Scimitar Films Ltd., 219 Kensington High St., London, GL W8 6BD, England.

WINNICK, R. H. American (born United States), b. 1947. **Genres:** Administration/Management, Literary Criticism And History, Young Adult Fiction. **Career:** Prentice-Hall Inc., editor, 1976-79; Norback and Company Inc., managing editor, 1980-81; Ford Foundation, reports editor, 1982-84; The Research Board Inc., editor and writer; Kekst and Co. (public relations firm), partner, 1986-. **Publications:** (With L. Thompson) Robert Frost: The Later Years, 1938-1963, 1977; (with L. Thompson) Robert Frost, A Biography, 1982; (ed.) Letters of Archibald MacLeish, 1907 to 1982, 1983; (with S. Donaldson) Archibald MacLeish: An American Life, 1992. Contributor to periodicals. **Address:** Kekst & Company Inc., 437 Madison Ave., New York, NY 10022-7001, U.S.A.

WINNIFRITH, T(homas) J(ohn). British (born England), b. 1938. **Genres:** Literary Criticism And History, Translations, Adult Non-fiction, History, Novels, Poetry. **Career:** Eton College, assistant master, 1961-66; University of Liverpool, William Noble fellow, 1968-70; University of Warwick, lecturer, 1970-77, senior lecturer in English and comparative literary studies, 1977-98, Graduate School of Comparative Literature, chairman, 1975-79, Joint School of Classics, chairman, 1982-88, European Humanities Research Center, director, 1985-90, Department of English and Comparative Literary Studies, chairman, 1989-92, Leverholme Emeritus Fellow, 1999-2000; All Souls College, visiting research fellow, 1984. Writer. **Publications:** The Brontës and Their Background: Romance and Reality, 1973, 2nd ed., 1988; The Brontës, 1977; (trans. with J. O'Malley) J. Nyiri, Streets, 1979; (intro.) Life and Works of the Sisters Brontë, 1982; (with E. Chitham) Brontë Facts and Problems, 1983; (with W.V. Whitehead) 1984 and All's Well?, 1984; The Vlachs: The History of the Balkan People, 1987; A New Life of Charlotte Brontë 1988; (with E. Chitham) Charlotte and Emily Brontë: A Literary Life, 1989; The Fallen Women in the Nineteenth-Century Novel, 1994; Shattered Eagles: Balkan Fragments, 1995; The Sayings of Charlotte Brontë, 1996; Tom Winnifrith's Ultimate Stock Market Success, 2000; Badlands, Borderlands: A History of Northern Epirus/Southern Albania, 2002. EDITOR: (and intro. with P. Murray) Greece Old and New, 1983; Poems of Patrick Branwell Brontë: A New Annotated and Enlarged Edition of the Shakespeare Head Brontë, 1983; The Poems of Branwell Brontë, 1983; The Poems of Charlotte Brontë, 1984; (with P. Murray and K. Gransden) Aspects of the Epic, 1983; (with E. Chitham) Selected Brontë Poems, 1985; (with C. Barrett) The Philosophy of Leisure, 1989; (with C. Barrett) Leisure in Art and Literature, 1992; Perspectives on Albania, 1992; Charlotte Brontë: Unfinished Novels, 1993; Critical Essays on Emily Brontë, 1997; The Sayings of Charlotte Brontë, 1997. **Address:** 50 Sheep St., Shipston on Stour, WW CV36 4AE, England. **Online address:** twinnifr@fish.co.uk

WINOCK, Michel. French (born France), b. 1937. **Genres:** History, Politics/Government. **Career:** Lycee Joffre, teacher, 1961-63; Lycee Hoche, teacher, 1963-66; Lycee Lakanal, teacher, 1966-68; University of Paris VIII, lecturer, 1968-78; Editions du Seuil, publisher, 1969-; Institut d'Etudes Politiques (Sciences-Po), professor, 1978-, now professor emeritus; radio producer, 1983-85. Writer and historian. **Publications:** (With J. Azéma) Les communards, 1964; (with J. Azéma and M. Lidove) La Classe D'histoire en euxieme T, 1969; (with J. Azéma) IIIe République, 1870-1940, 1970; Histoire Politique de la Revue Esprit, 1930-1950, 1975; (with J. Azéma) La Troisieme Republique, 1870-1940, 1976; La République se Meurt: Chronique 1956-1958, 1978; (with P. Aries) Un Historien de Dimanche, 1980; (intro.) Le Congrès de Londres devant la presse, 1980; (intro.) Congrès international socialiste des travailleurs et des chambres syndicales ouvrières, Londres 26 juillet-2 août 1896, 1980; Edouard Drumont et Cie: Antisemitisme et Fascisme en France, 1982; La Fièvre Hexagonale: Les Grandes Crises Politiques de 1871-1968, 1986; Chronique des Annees Soixante, 1987; 1978: l'Annee sans Pareille: Chronique, 1988; Nationalisme, Antisemitisme, et Fascisme en France, 1990; L'echec au Roi: 1791-1792, 1991; 1991, les Frontieres Vives, 1992; (with J. Azéma) Histoire de l'Extreme Droite en France, 1993; Parlez-Moi de la France, 1995; (co-ed.) Dictionnaire des Intellectuels Francais: Les Personnes, les Lieux, les Moments, 1996; Le Siècle des Intellectuels, 1997; 1914-1918, 1998; La France Politique XIXe-XXe Siecle, 1999; Les voix de la liberté: les è crivains engagè s au XIXe siè cle, 2001; Le Belle Epoque, 2002; Jeanne et les siens, 2003; La rance et les Juifs, de 1789 a nos jours, 2004; La France et les juifs: de 1789 à nos jours, 2004; Victor Hugo dans larène politique, 2005; Pierre Mendès France, 2005; La gauche au pouvoir: l'héritage du Front populaire, 2006; L'agonie de la IVe République: 13 mai 1958, 2006; Clémenceau, 2007; La mêlée présidentielle, 2007; La droite, 2008; Trahison de Munich: Emmanuel Mounier et la Grande Débâcle des Intellectuels, 2008; (co-ed.) Dictionnaire des Intellectuels Français: Les Personnes, Les Lieux, Les Moments, 2009; XXe Siècle Idéologique et Politique, 2009; Madame de Staël, 2010; L'effet de génération: une brève histoire des intellectuels français, 2011. Contributor to books, journals and periodicals. **Address:** Editions du Seuil, 25 bd Romain Rolland, Paris, 75014, France.

WINOKUR, Jon. American (born United States), b. 1947. **Genres:** Essays, Humor/Satire, Reference, Autobiography/Memoirs. **Career:** Advertising copywriter, 1971-75; partner of a marketing agency, 1975-77; real estate investor, 1977-83; writer, 1983-. **Publications:** Master Tips, 1985; The Pride Method, 1986; Je Ne Sais What?: A Guide to de Rigueur Frenglish for Readers, Writers and Speakers, 1995; (with N. Epstein) Happy Motoring!: Canine Life in The Fast Lane, 1997; How to Win at Golf Without Actually Playing Well, 2000; Ennui to Go, 2005; In Passing: Condolences and Complaints on Death, Dying and Related Disappointments, 2005; Encyclopedia Neurotica, 2005; The Big Book of Irony, 2007; (with J. Garner) Garner Files, 2011. EDITOR AND COMPILER: Writers on Writing, 1986; The Portable Curmudgeon, 1987; Zen to Go, 1988; A Curmudgeon's Garden of Love, 1989; Friendly Advice, 1990; Mondo Canine, 1991; True Confessions, 1992; Portable Curmudgeon Redux, 1992; Fathers, 1993; The Rich Are Different, 1996; Advice to Writers: A Compendium of Quotes and Anecdotes and Writerly Wisdom from a Dazzling Array of Literary Lights, 1999; The Traveling Curmudgeon: Irreverent Notes, Quotes and Anecdotes on Dismal Destinations, Excess Baggage, the Full Upright Position and Other Reasons Not to Go There, 2003; The War Between the State: Northern California vs Southern California, 2004; Zen to Go: Bite-Sized Bits of Wisdom, 2005; The Big Curmudgeon: 2500 Outrageously Irreverent Quotations and Interviews with World-Class Grumps and Cantankerous Commentators, 2007. **Address:** c/o Reid Boates, PO Box 328, Pittstown, NJ 08867-0328, U.S.A.

WINSEY, Valentine Rossilli. American (born United States) **Genres:** Genealogy/Heraldry, Psychology, History. **Career:** Columbia University, adjunct lecturer and assistant professor, 1961-66; New School for Social Research, adjunct lecturer and assistant professor, 1961-66; City University of New York, Bernard M. Baruch College, adjunct lecturer and assistant professor, 1961-66, John Jay College of Criminal Justice, teacher, 1970-76, Manhattan Community College, teacher, 1970-76; Pace University, associate professor of anthropology, sociology and psychology, 1966-70, professor of anthropology, sociology and psychology, 1976-; Cornell University, Assimilation and Absorption of Immigrants Project, director of research, 1971-73. Writer. **Publications:** Your Self as History: Family History and its Effects on your Personality, 1992; (ed.) Feminism among First Generation Immigrant Women, 1992; Your Self as History: Tracing Your Past to Enrich Your Future, 1996. Works appear in anthologies. Contributor of articles to journals, magazines and newspapers. **Address:** Pace University, 1 Pace Plz., New York, NY 10038, U.S.A. **Online address:** valwinsey@aol.com

WINSHIP, Michael P. American (born United States), b. 1952. **Genres:** History, Law, Biography, Autobiography/Memoirs, Theology/Religion. **Career:** State University of New York, Department of History, instructor, 1991-92; Cornell University, visiting assistant professor, 1992-93; University of Georgia, assistant professor, 1993-97, associate professor, 1997-2002, professor of history, 2002-, E. Merton Coulter professor, 2005-, E. Merton Coulter chair of history, 2006-. Writer. **Publications:** Seers of God: Puritan Providentialism in the Restoration and Early Enlightenment, 1996; Making Heretics: Militant Protestantism and Free Grace in Massachusetts, 1636-1641, 2002; The Times

and Trials of Anne Hutchinson: Puritans Divided, 2005; (with M.C. Carnes) The Trial of Anne Hutchinson: Liberty, Law and Intolerance in Puritan New England, 2nd ed., 2005; (with E.J. Larson) Constitutional Convention: A Narrative History: From the Notes of James Madison, 2005; Godly Republicanism: Puritans, Pilgrims and ACity on Hill, 2012; Hot Protestants: A History of Puritanism in England and North America, forthcoming. **Address:** Department of History, University of Georgia, 329 LeConte, 212 Leconte Hall, Athens, GA 30602, U.S.A. **Online address:** mwinship@uga.edu

WINSLADE, John (Maxwell). American/New Zealander (born New Zealand), b. 1953. **Genres:** Education, Psychology, Social Sciences. **Career:** Counselor for family courts, director, 1990-99; University of Waikato, senior lecturer in education, 1993-2003, director of counselor education programs, 1999-2003; Waikato Mediation Services, founding member, mediator, 1994-99; California State University, associate professor, 2003-06, professor, 2006-, Educational Counseling Program, coordinator. Writer. **Publications:** (With G. Monk) Narrative Counseling in Schools, 1999, 2nd ed., 2007; (with G. Monk) Narrative Mediation, 2000; New Horizons in Multicultural Counseling, 2007; Practicing Narrative Mediation, 2008. EDITOR: (with P. Low and T. Locke) White Feathers (poetry), 1991; (co-author and contrib.) Narrative Therapy in Practice, 1997; A Place to Stand, 1999; (with L. Hedtke) Remembering Lives: Conversations with the Dying and the Bereaved, 2004; (with G. Monk and S. Sinclair) New Horizons in Multicultural Counseling, 2008. Contributor to books and periodicals. **Address:** Deptartment of Educational, Psychology and Counseling, California State University, 5500 University Pkwy., San Bernardino, CA 92407-2397, U.S.A. **Online address:** jwinslad@csusb.edu

WINSLOW, Barbara. American (born United States), b. 1947. **Genres:** Adult Non-fiction, Children's Fiction. **Career:** Bureau of Indian Affairs, teacher, 1970-80; Maine School Administrative District 54, elementary school teacher, 1985-; Sunday School Classes, teacher. Writer. **Publications:** Dance on a Sealskin, 1995. Contributor to periodicals. **Address:** Maine School Administrative District 54, 196 W Front St., Skowhegan, ME 04976, U.S.A. **Online address:** bwinslow@tdstelme.net

WINSLOW, Don. American (born United States), b. 1953. **Genres:** Mystery/Crime/Suspense, Novels. **Career:** Writer. **Publications:** NEAL CAREY MYSTERY SERIES: A Cool Breeze on the Underground, 1991; The Trail to Buddha's Mirror, 1992; Way Down on the High Lonely, 1993; A Long Walk Up the Water Slide, 1994; While Drowning in the Desert: A Neal Carey Mystery, 1996. OTHERS: Ironwood Revisited, 1989; Isle of Joy, 1996; The Death and Life of Bobby Z, 1997; Blue Butterfly, 1998; California Fire and Life, 1999; Images of Ironwood, 1999; Master of Ironwood, 2000; Captive Women, 2000; Many Pleasures of Ironwood, 2002; Fall of the Ice Queen, 2002; Slave Girls of Rome, 2002; Claire's Uptown Girls, 2003; Best of Ironwood, 2003; Don Winslow's Victorian Erotica, 2003; (with P. Maslowski) Looking for a Hero: Staff Sergeant Joe Ronnie Hooper and the Vietnam War, 2004; Katerina in Charge, 2004; Pleasure Machine, 2004; Gloria's Indiscretion, 2004; The Power of the Dog, 2005; French Postcards, 2005; Little Red Dress, 2006; The Winter of Frankie Machine, 2006; The Dawn Patrol, 2008; The Gentlemen's Hour, 2009; Satori, 2010; Savages, 2010; About Tommy Flynn, 2011. **Address:** 1537 Orchard Ln., Julian, CA 92036, U.S.A. **Online address:** winslowfans@yahoo.com

WINSTEAD, Linda. *See* **JONES, Linda Winstead.**

WINSTON, Daoma. American (born United States), b. 1922. **Genres:** Mystery/Crime/Suspense, Romance/Historical, Novels, Mystery/Crime/Suspense, Young Adult Fiction, Literary Criticism And History. **Career:** Novelist. **Publications:** Doubtful Mercy, 1949; Tormented Lovers, 1962; Love Her, She's Yours, 1963; The Secrets of Cromwell Crossing, 1965; Sinister Stone, 1966; The Wakefield Witches, 1966; The Mansion of Smiling Masks, 1967; (with G. John) The Castle of Closing Doors, 1967; Shadow of an Unknown Woman, 1967; The Carnaby Curse, 1967; Shadow on Mercer Mountain, 1967; Pity My Love, 1967; The Traficante Treasure, 1968; The Long and Living Shadow, 1968; Braken's World No. 1, 1969; Mrs. Berrigan's Dirty Book, 1970; Beach Generation, 1970; Wild Country, 1970; Dennison Hill, 1970; Sound Stage, 1970; The Love of Lucifer, 1971; The Vampire Curse, 1971; The Mayeroni Myth, 1971; Flight of a Fallen Angel, 1971; The Devil's Daughter, 1971; The Devil's Princess, 1971; Seminar in Evil, 1972; The Victim, 1972; The Return, 1972; The Inheritance, 1972; Kingdom's Castle, 1972; Skeleton Key, 1972; Moorhaven, 1973; The Trap, 1973; The Unforgotten,

1973; The Sorcerers, 1973; The Haversham Legacy, 1974; A Visit after Dark, 1975; Walk Around the Square, 1975; The Golden Valley, 1975; Emerald Station, 1976; Gallows Way, 1976; The Dream Killers, 1976; The Adventuress: A Novel, 1978; House of Mirror Images, 1979; Mills of the Gods, 1979; Secret of an Unknown Woman, 1979; The Lotteries, 1980; A Sweet Familiarity: A Novel, 1981; Mira, 1981; Hands of Death, 1982; Family of Strangers, 1983; A Story of the Fall River Line 1847 to 1937, 1983; The Fall River Line, 1985; Death Wish, 1986; Maybe This Time, 1988; The Moderns, 1988; Hannah's Gate, 1992; Curse of Hannah's Gate, 1993; A Double Life, 1993; Silent Witness, 1995. Address: Jay Garon Brooke Associates Inc., 101 W 55th St., Ste. 5K, New York, NY 10019-5347, U.S.A.

WINSTON, Lois. American (born United States) Genres: Mystery/Crime/ Suspense, Romance/Historical, Novels, Crafts. Career: Writer. Publications: Talk Gertie to Me, 2006; Love, Lies and a Double Shot of Deception, 2007; Assault with a Deadly Glue Gun, 2010; Death By Killer Mop Doll, 2011. Address: Midnight Ink, 2143 Wooddale Dr., Woodbury, MN 55125-2989, U.S.A. Online address: lois@loiswinston.com

WINSTON, Lolly. American (born United States), b. 1962?. Genres: Novels, Young Adult Fiction. Career: Automotive News, stringer. Freelance journalist. Publications: Good Grief, 2004; Happiness Sold Separately, 2006; Bad Girls, forthcoming. Contributor of articles to periodicals. Works appear in anthologies. Address: Warner Books, 1271 Ave. of the Americas, New York, NY 10020, U.S.A. Online address: lolly@lollywinston.com

WINSTON, Mark L. American (born United States), b. 1950. Genres: Biology, Essays, Sciences. Career: Woods Hole Oceanographic Institution, research assistant, 1972-73; U.S. Department of Agriculture, Gypsy Moth Section, research assistant, 1973; Africanized bee Management, consultant, 1977-80; Idaho State University, visiting assistant professor, 1979-80; Simon Fraser University, assistant professor, 1980-84, associate professor, 1984-88, professor of biological sciences, 1988-, university research professor, 1990-91, M.J. Wosk Centre for Dialogue, fellow, 2002-09, Undergraduate Semester in Dialogue, director, 2002-09; British Columbia Pollination Working Group, organizer, 1984; Hebrew University, visiting Fulbright professor, 1986-87; Cornell University, lecturer, 1991; Burquest Jewish Community Association, board director, 1992-; Phero Tech Inc., senior industrial fellow, 1995-96; Canadian Broadcasting Corp., consultant; Vancouver's Science World, consultant. Writer. Publications: (With C.D. Michener and R. Jander) Pollen Manipulation and Related Activities and Structures in Bees of the Family Apidae, 1978; Proboscis of the Long-Tongued Bees: A Comparative Study, 1979; The Biology of the Honey Bee, 1987; Killer Bees: The Africanized Honey Bee in the Americas, 1992; Nature Wars: People vs. Pests, 1997; From Where I Sit: Essays on Bees, Beekeeping, and Science, 1998; Travels in the Genetically Modified Zone, 2002. Works appear in anthologies. Contributor to journals and magazines. Address: Department of Biological Sciences, Simon Fraser University, Rm. B8276, 8888 University Dr., Burnaby, BC V5A 1S6, Canada. Online address: winston@sfu.ca

WINSTON, Wayne L. American (born United States), b. 1950. Genres: Information Science/Computers, Technology. Career: Indiana University, Kelley School of Business, professor. Writer. Publications: Operations Research: Applications and Algorithms, 1987, 4th ed., 2004; Introduction to Mathematical Programming: Applications and Algorithms, 1991; Simulation Modeling Using @Risk, 1996 as Simulation Modeling Using @Risk: Updated for Version 4, 2001; Practical Management Science: Spreadsheet Modeling and Applications, 1997, 3rd ed., 2009; (with S.C. Albright) Data Analysis and Decision Making with Microsoft Excel, 1999, 3rd ed., 2006; (with S.C. Albright and C. Zappe) Managerial Statistics, 2000; (with S.C. Albright and C. Zappe) Data Analysis and Decision Making with Microsoft Excel, 2002, 3rd ed., 2009; Operations Research, vol. I: Introduction to Mathematical Programming, 2003, vol. II: Introduction to Probability Models, 2004; Data Analysis for Managers with Microsoft Excel, 2004; Microsoft Excel Data Analysis and Business Modeling, 2004 as Microsoft Office Excel 2007: Data Analysis and Business Modeling, 2007; Spreadsheet Modeling and Applications: Essentials of Practical Management Science, 2005; Mathletics: How Gamblers, Managers, and Sports Enthusiasts Use Mathematics in Baseball, Basketball, and Football, 2009. Address: Kelley School of Business, Indiana University, Godfrey Graduate and Executive Education Ctr., 1275 E 10th St., Bloomington, IN 47405, U.S.A. Online address: winston@indiana.edu

WINSTON-ALLEN, Anne. American (born United States), b. 1942.

Genres: Women's Studies And Issues. Career: University of Munich, DAAD graduate research fellow, 1973-74; Phillips University, assistant professor, 1980-85, associate professor, 1986-91; Southern Illinois University, lecturer, 1991-93, assistant professor, 1994-98, associate professor of German, 1998-, German section head of the department, 2006-. Academic and writer. Publications: Stories of the Rose: The Making of the Rosary in the Middle Ages, 1997; Convent Chronicles: Women Writing about Women and Reform in the Late Middle Ages, 2004. Contributor to periodicals and journals. Address: Department of Foreign Language & Literatures, Southern Illinois University, Faner Hall 2162, PO Box 4521, Carbondale, IL 62901-4521, U.S.A. Online address: winston@siu.edu

WINTER, David Brian. British (born England), b. 1929. Genres: Theology/ Religion, Biography, inspirational/Motivational Literature, Novels. Career: Ware Church of England Secondary School, teacher of English and religious education, 1954-58; Tottenham County Mixed Grammar School, teacher of English and religious education, 1958-59; Crusade, editor, 1959-71; British Broadcasting Corp. (BBC-Radio), producer, 1971-82, head of religious programmes, 1982-89; Church of England, priest, 1989-. Publications: The Christian's Guide to Church Membership, 1963; Ground of Truth, 1964; Old Faith, Young World, 1966; For All the People, 1966; New Singer, New Song, 1968; (with S. Linden) Two a Penny (novel), 1969; How to Walk with God, 1969; What Now?, 1969 as How to Walk with God, 1978; Laurie, The Happy Man in US as Closer than a Brother, 1971; (with J. Bryant) Well God, Here We Are Again, 1971; Hereafter: A New Look at an Old Question: What Happens Beyond Death?, 1972 in US as Hereafter: What Happens After Death?, 1973; (ed.) Matthew Henry's Commentary, 2 vols., 1975; After the Gospels in US as One Hundred Days in the Arena, 1978; But This I Can Believe, 1980; The Search for the Real Jesus, 1982; Believing the Bible, 1983; Truth in the Son, 1985; (with S. Augustine) Walking in the Light: Confessions of St. Augustine for the Modern Reader, 1985; Living through Loss, 1986; Walking into Light (The Confessions of St. Augustine), 1986; Battered Bride?, 1988; What Happens after Death?, 1991; (ed.) Christian Classics in Modern English, 1991; What's in a Word?, 1994; Forty Days with the Messiah: Day-by-Day Reflections on the Words of Handel's Oratorio, 1996; Where Do We Go from Here?, 1996; (intro.) The Way in New Testament: New Revised Standard Version, 1997; (comp. and intro.) The Wisdom of St. Augustine, 1997; (comp.) The Master Haunter: An Anthology of Poetry Exploring the Meaning and the Mystery of Jesus Christ, 1998; Why Marry?: Choosing the Way You Live Together, 1999; Message for the Millennium, 1999; (with C. Winter) The Best for Your Child: Help for New Parents, 1999; The Poets' Christ, 2000; Winter's Tale: An Autobiography Living Through an Age of Change in Church and Media, 2001; After the Gospels: Readings from Great Christians of the Early Church, 2001; With Jesus in the Upper Room: Forty Gospel Reflections for Lent and Easter, 2002; Hope in the Wilderness, 2003; Making Sense of the Bible, 2004; Old Words, New Life: Reflections on 40 Key Old Testament Words, 2005; The Nation's Favourite Prayers, 2006; Journey to Jerusalem: Bible Readings from Ash Wednesday to Easter Sunday, 2007; (comp.) Espresso Prayers: Perfect Shots for Any Time of Day, 2008; Pilgrim's Way: Journeying Through the Year with the Bible, 2008; Seasons of the Son: A Journey Through the Christian Year, 2008; The Bible Made Clear, 2008; The Espresso Bible: The Bible In Sips, 2009; The One-stop Guide To Christianity, 2009; The Road Well Travelled: Exploring Traditional Christian Spirituality, 2009; Prayers to Go: Kurze Gebete fur jede Gelegenheit, 2009; Bible to Go: Kleine Portionen fur den Alltag, 2009; Facing the Darkness and Finding the Light: Reflections for Troubled Times from the Book of Revelation, 2011. Address: 51 Nideggen Close, Thatcham, BR RG19 4HS, England. Online address: david_winter1@btinternet.com

WINTER, John (Anthony). British (born England), b. 1930. Genres: Architecture, Young Adult Fiction, Art/Art History. Career: Stillman and Eastwick-Field, assistant architect, 1953-54; Yale University, instructor, 1956-57; Skidmore Owings and Merrill, assistant architect, 1957-59; Erno Goldfinger, assistant architect, 1959-60; John Winter and Associates, principal, 1960-; Architectural Association, instructor, 1960-64; Toronto University, visiting professor, 1962; University College, instructor, 1976-79; Cambridge University, instructor, 1977-78; Syracuse University, visiting professor, 1978. Writer. Publications: Modern Building, 1969; Industrial Architecture, 1969; Industrial Buildings, 1971; (ed.) EPA Method Study 8, Total Mercury in Water, 1977; (contrib.) The Open Hand: Essays on Le Corbusier, 1977; (co-author) Architecture: Style, Structure and Design, 1982; Le statue del Marchese Ginori: Sculture in porcellana bianca di Doccia, 2003; (contrib.) Studies Using Scientific Methods: Pigments in Later Japanese Paintings, 2003. Address:

John Winter & Associates, 80 Lamble St., London, GL NW5 4AB, England.

WINTER, Kari J. American (born United States), b. 1960. **Genres:** Literary Criticism And History, Race Relations, Autobiography/Memoirs, History, Novels, Civil Liberties/Human Rights, Gay And Lesbian Issues, Politics/Government, Women's Studies And Issues, Cultural/Ethnic Topics. **Career:** Indiana University, research assistant, associate program coordinator, 1980-81; Nes Ammim Education Office, interfaith relations program, co-editor, 1982-83; University of Minnesota, instructor in English and composition, 1984-90; Fisk University, assistant professor of English, 1990-92; University of Vermont, assistant professor of English, 1992-97, associate professor of English, 1997-2003; University at Buffalo, State University of New York, associate professor of American studies, 2003-07, professor of American studies, 2007-. **Publications:** Subjects of Slavery, Agents of Change: Women and Power in Gothic Novels and Slave Narratives, 1790-1865, 1992; (ed. and intro.) The Blind African Slave: Or, Memoirs of Boyrereau Brinch, Nick-named Jeffrey Brace, 1810, 2004; The American Dreams of John B. Prentis, Slave Trader, 2011. Works appear in anthologies. Contributor to periodical and journals. **Address:** Department of American Studies, State University of New York, 1010B Clemens Hall, Buffalo, NY 14260-4630, U.S.A. **Online address:** kwinter2@buffalo.edu

WINTER, Michael. Canadian/British (born England), b. 1965?. **Genres:** Novels, Autobiography/Memoirs, Literary Criticism And History, Young Adult Fiction. **Career:** The Burning Rock Collective, founder. Writer. **Publications:** Creaking in Their Skins, 1994; (ed.) Extremities: Fiction from the Burning Rock, 1994; One Last Good Look, 1999; This All Happened: A Fictional Memoir, 2000; The Big Why: A Novel, 2004; The Architects are Here, 2007. Contributor to periodicals. **Address:** c/o Author Mail, Bloomsbury USA, 175 5th Ave., New York, NY 10010-7703, U.S.A.

WINTERBOTTOM, Michael. British (born England), b. 1934?. **Genres:** Classics, History. **Career:** University College London, lecturer in Latin and Greek, 1962-67; Worcester College, fellow and tutor in classics, 1967-92, reader in classical languages, 1990-92; Corpus Christi College, Corpus Christi professor of Latin, fellow, 1993-2001. Writer. **Publications:** Problems in Quintilian, 1970; Institutionis Oratoriae Libri Duodecim; Recognovit Brevique Adnotatione Critica Instruxit M. Winterbottom, 1970; (with D.A. Russell) Ancient Literary Criticism: The Principal Texts in New Translations, 1972; Three Lives of English Saints, 1972; Cornelii Taciti Opera Minora, 1975; Roman Declamation, 1980; (with D.C. Innes) Sopatros the Rhetor: Studies in the Text of the Diairesis zetematōn, 1988. EDITOR: Quintilian, 1970; (with R.M. Ogilvie) Tacitus: Opera Minora, 1975; The Minor Declamations Ascribed to Quintilian, 1984; History of the Church of York, 1066-1127, 1990; (with M. Lapidge) Life of St. Aethelwold, 1991; M. Tulli Ciceronis De officiis, 1994. EDITOR AND TRANSLATOR: The Elder Seneca Declamations, 1974; Gildas, 1978; (with R.A.B. Mynors and R.M. Thomson) William of Malmesbury, Gesta Regum Anglorum, vol. I, 1998; (with R.M. Thomson) William of Malmesbury, Saints' Lives, 2002; Aspects of The Language of Latin Prose, 2005; (ed. with T. Reinhart) Institutio Oratoria. Book 2 / Quintilian, 2006; Gesta pontificum Anglorum=The History of the English Bishops, 2007; (with D.A. Russell) Classical Literary Criticism, 2008. **Address:** Corpus Christi College, Merton St., Oxford, OX OX1 4JF, England.

WINTERHALDER, Edward. American (born United States), b. 1955?. **Genres:** Young Adult Non-fiction, Young Adult Fiction. **Career:** Writer. **Publications:** NONFICTION: Out in Bad Standings: Inside the Bandidos Motorcycle Club: The Making of a Worldwide Dynasty, 2005; (with W.D. Clercq) The Assimilation: Rock Machine to Bandidos, 2008; (with A. Veno and W.D. Clercq) Biker Chicks: The Magnetic Attraction of Women to Bad Boys and Motorbikes, 2009; (with J.R. Lawson) All Roads Lead to Sturgis: A Biker's Story (fiction), 2009; The Mirror: A Biker's Story (fiction), 2010; (with W.D. Clercq) Biker Chicz of North America, 2010. **Address:** Block-head City Entertainment, PO Box 1654, Owasso, OK 74055-1654, U.S.A. **Online address:** bhcpressoffice@aol.com

WINTERS, Kay. American (born United States), b. 1936. **Genres:** Children's Fiction, Children's Non-fiction, History, Novels, Poetry, Adult Non-fiction. **Career:** Massachusetts Public Schools, elementary education teacher, 1960-63; Palisades School District, elementary education teacher and supervisor, 1968-92; American International Schools, education consultant, 1970-80. Writer. **Publications:** Did You See What I Saw?: Poems about School, 1996; The Teeny Tiny Ghost, 1997; Wolf Watch, 1997; Where Are the Bears?, 1998; How Will the Easter Bunny Know?, 1999; Whooo's Haunting the Teeny Tiny Ghost?, 1999; Tiger Trail, 2000; But Mom, Everybody Else Does, 2002; Abe Lincoln, the Boy Who Loved Books, 2003; Echoes of Ancient Egypt, 2003; Voices of ancient Egypt, 2003; My Teacher for President, 2004; The Teeny Tiny Ghost and the Monster, 2004; And Fly She Did!: The Amazing Childhood Adventures of Amelia Earhart, 2005; John Appleseed: A Trail of Trees, 2007; Colonial Voices Hear them Speak, 2008; Whooo's That?: A Lift-the-Flap Pumpkin Fun Book, 2009; Who's Coming for Christmas?, 2010; This School Year Will Be the Best!, 2010; Voices of the Oregon Trail, 2012; Bears go to Town, 2012. FOR ADULTS: (with M. Felber) The Teachers Copebook: How to End the Year Better Than You Started, 1980. **Address:** PO Box 339, Richlandtown, PA 18955, U.S.A. **Online address:** kaywinters@kaywinters.com

WINTERS, Rebecca. See **BURTON, Rebecca B(rown).**

WINTLE, Francis Edward. See **RUTHERFURD, Edward.**

WINTZ, Cary D. American (born United States), b. 1943. **Genres:** History, Social Sciences, Politics/Government. **Career:** Texas Southern University, instructor, 1971-74, assistant professor, 1974-77, associate professor of history, professor, 1977-2011, department chairman, 1995-2001, distinguished professor, 2011-, coordinator of assessment; U.S. Information Service, lecturer on race and ethnicity, 1985, 1990, 2006-08. Writer. **Publications:** Black Culture and the Harlem Renaissance, 1988, rev. ed., 1997; (with A. Anderson) Texas: The Lone Star State, 2001. EDITOR: (with H. Beeth) Black Dixie: Afro-Texan History and Culture in Houston, 1992; African American Political Thought, 1890-1930: Washington, DuBois, Garvey, and Randolph, 1995; The Harlem Renaissance, 1920-1940, 7 vols., 1996; (intro.) Politics and Aesthetics of New Negro Literature, 1996; (intro.) Emergence of the Harlem Renaissance, 1996; (intro.) Critics and the Harlem Renaissance, 1996; (intro.) Black Writers Interpret the Harlem Renaissance, 1996; (intro.) Remembering the Harlem Renaissance, 1996; The Clansman: A Historical Romance of the Ku Klux Klan, 2001; (with S. Haynes) Major Problems in Texas History: Documents and Essays, 2002; The Harlem Renaissance: A History and an Anthology, 2003; (with P. Finkelman) Encyclopedia of the Harlem Renaissance, 2004; (ed.) Harlem Speaks: A Living History of the Harlem Renaissance, 2007; (with B.A. Glasrud) African Americans and the Presidency: The Road to the White House, 2009; (with B.A. Glasrud) The Harlem Renaissance in the American West: The New Negro's Western Experience, 2011. Contributor of articles to journals. **Address:** Department of History, Geography and Economics, Texas Southern University, BJML 305D, 3100 Cleburne St., Houston, TX 77004, U.S.A. **Online address:** wintz_cd@tsu.edu

WIPRUD, Brian M. American (born United States), b. 1961?. **Genres:** Novels, Food And Wine, Children's Fiction. **Career:** Weidlinger Associates Inc., utility specialist. Photographer and writer. **Publications:** Sleep with the Fishes, 2001; Pipsqueak, 2002; Stuffed, 2005; Crooked, 2006; Tailed, 2007; Feelers, 2009; Buy Back, 2010; Ringer, forthcoming. **Address:** Trident Media, 41 Madison Ave., 36th Fl., New York, NY 10010-2257, U.S.A. **Online address:** wiprud@wai.com

WIRSING, Robert G. American (born United States), b. 1936. **Genres:** Politics/Government, History. **Career:** University of South Carolina, assistant professor, 1971-76, associate professor, 1976-83, professor, 1983-2000, professor emeritus, 2000-; School of International Studies, United States Army JFK Special Warfare Center, visiting professor, 1982-84; Fulbright lecturer in Pakistan, 1985; Quaid-i-Azam University, visiting faculty, 1985-86; Asian Affairs Journal, executive editor, 1992-; Asia-Pacific Center for Security Studies, College of Security Studies, professor, 2000-08; Georgetown University's, School of Foreign Service, visiting professor, professor. **Publications:** (With N. Wirsing) Ancient India and its Influence in Modern Times, 1973; (ed.) International Relations and the Future of Ocean Space, 1973; Socialist Society and Free Enterprise Politics, 1977; (contrib.) Protection of Ethnic Minorities: Comparative Perspectives, 1981; Baluchis and Pathans, 1981, rev. ed., 1987; Pakistan's Security under Zia, 1977-1988, 1991; India, Pakistan and the Kashmir Dispute, 1994; War or Peace on the Line of Control?: The India-Pakistan Dispute Over Kashmir Turns Fifty, 1998; Kashmir in the Shadow of War: Regional Rivalries in a Nuclear Age, 2003; (ed. with S.P. Limaye and M. Malik) Religious Radicalism and Security in South Asia, 2004; (with C. Jasparro) Spotlight on Indus River Diplomacy: India, Pakistan and the Baglihar Dam dispute, 2006; Baloch Nationalism and the Geopolitics of Energy Resources: The Changing Context of Separatism in Pakistan,

2008; (ed. with E. Ahrari) Fixing Fractured Nations: Ethnic Separatism in the Asia-Pacific, 2010. **Address:** School of Foreign Service at Qatar, Georgetown University, A128 LAS Bldg., GU-Q Bldg., PO Box 23689, Doha, 1, Qatar. **Online address:** rgw22@georgetown.edu

WIRZBA, Norman. American (born United States), b. 1964?. **Genres:** Philosophy, Humanities. **Career:** Northern Illinois University, lecturer; Loyola University, lecturer in philosophy, 1992-93; University of Saskatchewan, St. Thomas More College, assistant professor of philosophy, 1993-95; Georgetown College, associate professor, 1995-2006, professor of philosophy, 2006-, department chair, 1995-. Writer. **Publications:** (Ed. and intro.) The Art of the Commonplace: Agrarian Essays of Wendell Berry, 2002; (ed.) (ed.) The Essential Agrarian Reader: The Future of Culture, Community and the Land, 2003; The Paradise of God: Renewing Religion in an Ecological Age, 2003; (ed. with B.E. Benson) The Phenomenology of Prayer, 2005; Living the Sabbath: Discovering the Rhythms of Rest and Delight, 2006; (ed. with B.E. Benson) Transforming Philosophy and Religion: Love's Wisdom, 2008; (ed.) Gift of Creation, 2009; (ed. with B.E. Benson) Words of Life: New Theological Turns in French Phenomenology, 2010; Food and Faith: A Theology of Eating, 2011; (with F. Bahnson) Making Peace with the Land: God's Call to Reconcile with Creation, 2012. **Address:** Department of Philosophy, Georgetown College, 400 E College St., Georgetown, KY 40324, U.S.A. **Online address:** norman_wirzba@georgetowncollege.edu

WISDOM, Linda Randall. American (born United States), b. 1950. **Genres:** Romance/Historical, Novels. **Career:** Writer. **Publications:** ROMANCE NOVELS: Dancer in the Shadows, 1980; Fourteen Karat Beauty, 1981; A Man with Doubts, 1982; Bright Tomorrow, 1982; Dreams from the Past, 1982; Guardian Angel, 1983; Snow Queen, 1983; Unspoken Past, 1983; Business as Usual, 1984; Island Rogue, 1984; A World of Their Own, 1985; Double Jeopardy, 1994; Midnight Lady, 1994; O'Hara vs. Wilder, 1994; Tess and the Tenderfoot, 2001. HEX PARANORMAL ROMANCE NOVELS: Fifty Ways to Hex Your Lover, 2008; Hex Appeal, 2008; Wicked by Any Other Name, 2009; Hex in High Heels, 2009. ROMANCE NOVELS: Caution: Man at Work, 1984; For Better or Worse, 1984; Birds of a Feather, 1985; Gentle Protector, 1985; Love Has Many Voices, 1985; All a Man Could Want, 1986; A Love to Last Forever, 1986; Murphy's Charm, 1986; Splendor at Dawn, 1986; Written in the Stars, 1986; A Perilous Affair, 1987; Only Love, 1988; We Give Thanks, 1988; Appearances Are Deceiving, 1989; Code of Silence, 1989; Lady's Choice, 1989; A Man for Maggie, 1990; O'Malley's Quest, 1990; Sins of the Past, 1990; Free Spirits, 1991; Voices in the Night, 1991; Sometimes a Lady, 1992; This Old House, 1992; Under His Spell, 1992; A Man for Mom, 1993; No Room at the Inn, 1993; Sudden Impulse, 1993; The Countess and the Cowboy, 1993; He's a Rebel, 1994; Vegas Vows, 1994; Counterfeit Husband, 1995; Mommy Heiress, 1995; Do You Take This Man ..., 1996; No More Mister Nice Guy, 1996; Twist of Fate, 1996; Bells, Rings, and Angels' Wings, 1997; In Memory's Shadow, 1997; Mr. and Mrs. ... and Mrs.?, 1997; Naughty 'n Nice, 1997; A Stranger Is Watching, 1998; She's Having His Baby, 1998; The Last Two Bachelors, 1999; Mirror, Mirror, 2000; My Little One, 2000; Bride of Dreams, 2001; Small-Town Secrets, 2002; Two Little Secrets, 2002; Pregnancy Countdown, 2003; Roses after Midnight, 2003; After the Midnight Hour, 2005; Single Kid Seeks Dad, 2005; Memories after Midnight, 2006. OTHER: Ballet Surprise, 1996. Contributor to periodicals. **Address:** Murrieta, CA , U.S.A. **Online address:** linda@lindawisdom.com

WISE, David. American (born United States), b. 1930. **Genres:** Politics/Government, Institutions/Organizations, Adult Non-fiction, Novels. **Career:** New York Herald Tribune, reporter, 1951-53, New York City Hall bureau chief, 1953-57, Albany bureau chief, 1956-57, Washington bureau staff, 1958-60, White House correspondent, 1960-62, chief of Washington bureau, 1963-66; Woodrow Wilson International Center for Scholars, fellow, 1970-71; University of California, Santa Barbara, lecturer in political science, 1977-79. Writer. **Publications:** (With T.B. Ross) The U-2 Affair, 1962; (with Ross) The Invisible Government, 1964; (with Ross) The Espionage Establishment, 1967; O Govêrno invisível, 1968; (with M. Cummings) Democracy under Pressure: An Introduction to the American Political System, 1971, 10th ed., 2005; The Politics of Lying: Government Deception, Secrecy and Power, 1973; The American Police State, 1976, 2nd ed. as The American Police State: The Government Against the People, 1978; The Spy Who Got Away: The Inside Story of Edward Lee Howard, the CIA Agent Who Betrayed His Country's Secrets and Escaped to Moscow, 1988; Molehunt: The Secret Search for Traitors that Shattered the CIA, 1992; Nightmover, 1995; Cassidy's Run: The Secret Spy War over Nerve Gas, 2000; Spy: The Inside Story of How the FBI's Robert

Hanssen Betrayed America, 2002; Tiger Trap: America's Secret Spy War with China, 2011. NOVELS: Spectrum, 1981; The Children's Game, 1983; The Samarkand Dimension, 1987. Contributor to magazines and periodicals. **Address:** Sterling Lord Literistic Inc., 65 Bleecker St., New York, NY 10012-2420, U.S.A. **Online address:** dwise@neh.gov

WISE, Joe. American (born United States), b. 1939. **Genres:** Novels, History, Medicine/Health, Travel/Exploration, Biography, Autobiography/Memoirs, Sports/Fitness. **Career:** Physician, cardiologist and writer. **Publications:** Cannibal Plateau: A Novel, 1997; In the Moro, 1999; A Primer on Heart Disease for Patients and Their Families, 2000; The Fish: A Novel, 2002; A Sense of Place: A Conversation with Perk Vickers, 2003; If You Go: One Man's Travels to Special Places in the American Southwest and Beyond, 2003. Contributor to magazines and newspapers. **Address:** 29 Calle Pagosa, Santa Fe, NM 87506, U.S.A. **Online address:** pagoda@rt66.com

WISE, Mike. American (born United States), b. 1964. **Genres:** Sports/Fitness. **Career:** New York Times, reporter, 1994-2004; Washington Post, sports columnist, 2004-, sportswriter, feature writer. **Publications:** (With F. Isola) Just Ballin': The Chaotic Rise of the New York Knicks, 1999; (with S. O'Neal) Shaq Talks Back, 2002. Contributor to periodicals. **Address:** Washington Post, 1150 15th St. NW, Washington, DC 20071-0001, U.S.A.

WISE, Robert L. American (born United States), b. 1939. **Genres:** Novels, Theology/Religion, inspirational/Motivational Literature, Young Adult Non-fiction. **Career:** United Methodist Church, pastor, 1966-74; First United Methodist Church, pastor, 1974; Lake Hills Community Church, pastor, 1974-77; Our Lord's Community Church, pastor, 1977-89; Church of the Redeemer, pastor, 1989-2000; Communion of Evangelical Episcopal Churches, elected bishop, 1997-; Roman Catholic Church, spiritual director. Writer. **Publications:** NON-FICTION: Your Churning Place, 1977; When There Is No Miracle, 1977; How Not to Go Crazy, 1980; The Pastor's Barracks, 1986; The Church Divided, 1986; When the Night Is Too Long, 1990; The Comfort Book (miniature book), 1994; (with P. Meier) Windows of the Soul: A Look at Dreams and Their Meanings, 1995; Quest for the Soul, 1996; Spiritual Abundance, 2000. FICTION: The Scrolls of Edessa, 1987; All That Remains, 1995; (with P. Meier) The Secret Code, 1999; (with M. Evans) The Jerusalem Scrolls, 1999; (with W.L. Wilson Jr.) The Tail of the Dragon, 2000; Be Not Afraid, 2000; The Empty Coffin: A Sam and Vera Sloan Mystery, 2001; The Dead Detective: A Sam and Vera Sloan Mystery, 2002; Deleted!: A Sam and Vera Sloan Mystery, 2003. PEOPLE OF THE COVENANT SERIES: The Dawning, 1991; The Exiles, 1993; The Fall of Jerusalem, 1994. MILLENNIUM SERIES: (with P. Meier) The Third Millennium, 1993; (with P. Meier) The Fourth Millennium: The Sequel, 1996; (with P. Meier) Beyond the Millennium, 1998; Mega-Millennium, 1998; Wired, 2004; The Nanar Road to Colditz, 2004. OTHERS: (with S. Arterburn and P. Meier) Fear Less for Life, 2002; Crazy Makers: Getting Along with the Difficult People in Your Life, 2003; Tagged, 2004; Narrow Door at Colditz, 2004; Bitter Road to Dachau, 2005; The Secret Road Home, 2006; Crossing the Threshold of Eternity: What the Dying can Teach the Living, 2007; The Son Rises: Resurrecting the Resurrection, 2008; Shrouded in Silence, 2011. **Address:** 4100 Rankin Rd., Oklahoma City, OK 73120, U.S.A. **Online address:** revwise@aol.com

WISE, Steven W. American (born United States), b. 1948. **Genres:** Novels. **Career:** North Carolina Highway Commission, Department of Transportation, staff, 1971-83; Cannon Blaylock & Wise, co-owner. Writer. **Publications:** NOVELS: Midnight, 1992; Chambers, 1994; Long Train Passing, 1996; Chimborazo, 2001; The Jordan Tracks, 2005. **Address:** Cannon, Blaylock & Wise, 2100 E Broadway, Ste. 208, Columbia, MO 65201-6082, U.S.A. **Online address:** stevewise48@gmail.com

WISE, Tim J. American (born United States), b. 1968. **Genres:** Politics/Government, Race Relations. **Career:** Louisiana Coalition Against Racism and Nazism, youth coordinator and associate director; Fisk University, Race Relations Institute, advisor; Poynter Institute, visiting faculty; Smith College School for Social Work adjunct faculty. Writer. **Publications:** Little White Lies: The Truth about Affirmative Action and Reverse Discrimination, 1995; Affirmative Action: Racial Preference in Black and White, 2005; White Like Me, 2005, rev. ed. as White Like Me: Reflections on Race from a Privileged Son, 2008; Speaking Treason Fluently: Anti-Racist Reflections from an Angry White Male, 2008; Between Barack and a Hard Place: Racism and White Denial in the Age of Obama, 2009; Colorblind: The Rise of Post-Racial Politics and the Retreat from Racial Equity, 2010. **Address:** U.S.A. **Online ad-**

dress: timwise@timwise.org

WISE, Victoria (Jenanyan). American (born United States), b. 1944. **Genres:** Food And Wine. **Career:** Chez Panisse Restaurant, chef, 1971-73; Pig-by-the-Tail (delicatessen), founder, owner, operator and chef, 1973-85; writer, 1985-; California College of Arts and Crafts, Good and Plenty Café, co-founder, chef, co-designer and operator, 1989-91; Norman's Restaurant, executive chef and general manager, 1990-91. **Publications:** (With J. Potenziani and A. Jenanyan) American Charcuterie: Recipes from Pig-by-the-Tail, 1986; (with S. Hoffman) Good and Plenty: America's New Home Cooking, 1988; (with S. Hoffman) The Well-Filled Tortilla Cookbook, 1990; Mexican Cooking: Foods of the World, 1993; The Vegetarian Table: Mexico, 1995; (with S. Hoffman) The Well-Filled Microwave Cookbook, 1996; The Vegetarian Table: Japan, 1998; Garden House: Bringing the Outdoors In, 1999; (and comp.) The Smith and Hawken Gardeners' Community Cookbook, 1999; The Pressure Cooker Gourmet, 2003; (with A. Roberts and M.B. Mondavi) Annie and Margrit: Recipes and Stories from the Robert Mondavi Kitchen, 2003; (with S. Hoffman) The Olive and the Caper: Adventures in Greek Cooking, 2004; The Armenian Table, 2004; Sausage: Recipes for Making and Cooking with Homemade Sausage, 2010. Contributor to books. **Address:** 743 Calmar Ave., Oakland, CA 94610, U.S.A. **Online address:** wisekitchen@comcast.net

WISEMAN, Alan. British (born England), b. 1936. **Genres:** Biology, Engineering. **Career:** University of Surrey, School of Biological Science, senior lecturer in biochemistry, 1978-. Writer. **Publications:** Organization for Protein Biosynthesis, 1965; (with B.J. Gould) Enzymes: Their Nature and Role, 1971; (with J.M. Lynch) Environmental Biomonitoring: The Biotechnology Ecotoxicology Interface, 1998. EDITOR AND CONTRIBUTOR: Handbook of Enzyme Biotechnology, 1975, 3rd ed., 1995; (with J.M. Lynch) Enzymic and Non-Enzymic Catalysis, 1980; Principles of Biotechnology, 1983; Enzyme Induction, Mutagen Activation, and Carcinogen Testing in Yeast, 1987. **Address:** Cambridge University Press, 32 Ave. of the Americas, New York, NY 10013-2473, U.S.A.

WISEMAN, Eva. Canadian/Hungarian (born Hungary), b. 1947?. **Genres:** Children's Fiction. **Career:** Winnipeg Free Press, journalist; Winnipeg Tribune, journalist. Educator. **Publications:** A Place Not Home, 1996; My Canary Yellow Star, 2002; No One Must Know, 2004; Kanada, 2006; Puppet, 2009. **Address:** Winnipeg, MB , Canada. **Online address:** evakwiseman@gmail.com

WISEMAN, James A. American (born United States), b. 1942. **Genres:** Theology/Religion. **Career:** Ordained Benedictine monk, 1970; St. Anselm's Abbey, abbot, 1975-83, novice master, 1983-94, prior of the monastic community, 1990-2006; Catholic University of America, Department of Theology, visiting professor, 1985-86, assistant professor, 1986-92, associate professor, 1992-2007, chair, 1995-98, 2001-03, professor, 2007-, School of Theology and Religious Studies, associate dean for undergraduate studies, 2006-07. Writer and theologian. **Publications:** (Ed. and trans.) John Ruusbroec: The Spiritual Espousals and Other Works, 1985; (ed. with L. Dupré) Light from Light: An Anthology of Christian Mysticism, 1988, 2nd ed., 2001; (ed. with D.W. Mitchell) The Gethsemani Encounter: A Dialogue on the Spiritual Life by Buddhist and Christian Monastics, 1997; Theology and Modern Science: Quest for Coherence, 2002; (ed. with D.W. Mitchell) Transforming Suffering: Reflections on Finding Peace in Troubled Times, 2003; Spirituality and Mysticism: A Global View, 2006. **Address:** School of Theology and Religious Studies, Catholic University of America, 106 Caldwell Hall, 620 Michigan Ave. NE, Washington, DC 20064, U.S.A. **Online address:** wiseman@cua.edu

WISEMAN, Richard. British (born England), b. 1966?. **Genres:** Psychology, Adult Non-fiction. **Career:** University of Hertfordshire, Perrot-Warrick Research Unit, director, 1994-, professor of psychology, 2003-, Public Understanding of Psychology, chair; Channel 4, staff; Twitter, psychologist. Writer. **Publications:** (With R.L. Morris) Guidelines for Testing Psychic Claimants, 1995; Deception & Self-Deception: Investigating Psychics, 1997; (with J.Milton) Guidelines for Extrasensory Perception Research, 1997; (with P. Lamont) Magic in Theory, 1999; The Luck Factor: Changing Your Luck, Changing Your Life, the Four Essential Principles, 2003; Did You Spot the Gorilla?: How to Recognize Hidden Opportunities, 2004; (ed. with C. Watt) Parapsychology, 2005; Quirkology: How We Discover the Big Truths In Small Things, 2007; 59 Seconds: Think a Little, Change a Lot, 2009; Paranormality, 2011. **Address:** Department of Psychology, University of Hert-

fordshire, College Ln., Hatfield, HF AL10 9AB, England. **Online address:** r.wiseman@herts.ac.uk

WISEMAN, Rosalind. American (born United States), b. 1969. **Genres:** Adult Non-fiction, Human Relations/Parenting, Novels, Medicine/Health, Young Adult Non-fiction. **Career:** Empower Program (national violence-prevention program), co-founder and president, 1992-2000, contractor, 2000-06; Family Circle Magazine, contributing editor and monthly columnist. Public speaker. **Publications:** NONFICTION: Defending Ourselves: A Guide to Prevention, Self-Defense, and Recovery from Rape, 1994; Queen Bees & Wannabes: Helping Your Daughter Survive Cliques, Gossip, Boyfriends, and Other Realities of Adolescence, 2002, 2nd ed. as Queen Bees & Wannabes: Helping Your Daughter Survive Cliques, Gossip, Boyfriends, and the New Realities Of Girl World, 2009; (with E. Rapoport) Queen Bee Moms & Kingpin Dads: Dealing with the Parents, Teachers, Coaches, and Counselors Who Can Make-or Break-Your Child's Future, 2006; Owning Up Curriculum: Empowering Adolescents To Confront Social Cruelty, Bullying, and Injustice, 2009; Boys, Girls, and Other Hazardous Materials, 2010. **Address:** Levine Greenberg Literary Agency Inc., 307 7th Ave., Ste. 2407, New York, NY 10001, U.S.A. **Online address:** rosalind@rosalindwiseman.com

WISHINSKY, Frieda. Canadian/German (born Germany), b. 1948. **Genres:** Children's Fiction, Children's Non-fiction, Picture/Board Books, Education. **Career:** Montcrest School, special education teacher, 1980-; York University, research assistant. Full-time writer. **Publications:** Oonga Boonga, 1990, rev. ed., 1999; Why Can't You Fold Your Pants Like David Levine?, 1992; Jennifer Jones Won't Leave Me Alone, 1995; Crazy for Chocolate, 1998; Each One Special, 1998; The Man Who Made Parks: The Story of Parkbuilder Frederick Law Olmsted, 1999; No Frogs for Dinner, 1999; Give Maggie a Chance, 1999; So Long Stinky Queen, 2000; A Quest in Time, 2000; Nothing Scares Us, 2000; Whats the Matter with Albert?: A Story of Albert Einstein, 2002; Jennifer Jones Wont Leave Me Alone, 2003; Maryas Dream: A Story of Marie Curie, 2003; Just Call Me Joe, 2003; Just Mabel, 2004; A Noodle up Your Nose, 2004; (with L.A. Laliberte) A Bee in Your Ear, 2004; Queen of the Toilet Bowl, 2005; Albert Einstein, 2005; Just Imagine ABC, 2005; Dimple Delight, 2005; Could we Live on the Moon?, 2005; (with J. Weaver) Its Your Room: A Decorating Guide for Real Kids, 2006; Pioneer Kids, 2007; Crazy For Gold, 2007; Yikes! Vikings!, 2007; Please, Louise!, 2007; Beware, Pirates!, 2007; Danger, Dinosaurs, 2007; Hurry, Freedom, 2008; Whale Tale, 2008; A Frog in My Throat, 2008; Lost in the Snow, 2008; Flying High, 2008; (with E. MacLeod) Everything But The Kitchen Sink: Weird Stuff You Didnt Know about Food, 2008; Far from Home, 2008; All Aboard!, 2008; The Man Who Made Parks: The Story of Parkbuilder Frederick Law Olmsted, 2009; Stop that Stagecoach, 2009; On the Case!, 2009; Sos! Titanic!, 2010; Make it Fair!, 2010; Where Are You, Bear?: A Canadian Alphabet Adventure, 2010; Blob, 2010; Arctic storm!, 2011; Youre Mean, Lily Jean!, 2011. EDUCATIONAL: Airplanes, 1997; Construction, 1997; Farm, 1997; Cars & Trucks, 1997; Boats & Ships, 1997; Nelson Language Arts 5, 1998; Nelson Language Arts 6, 1998; Nelson Language Arts 3, Supplemental Readings, 1999; My Dog Kam, 2003; Moving Away, 2003; Picnic Plans, 2003; Grandpa Moves In, 2003; First Day, 2003; A Trip by Train, 2003; Ten Blue Things, 2003; A Hat for Me, 2003; All about Miss Miller, 2003; My Little House, 2004; (with S. Siamon) Canada Day, 2004; Family Night, 2004; Around the World in a Day, 2004; The Worrywart, 2004; Breakfast in the Bathtub, 2004; David Thompson: Map-Maker, 2005; Alexander Graham Bell: Man of Ideas, 2005; Halifax Explodes!, 2011; You're mean, Lily Jean!, 2011; Arctic Storm!, 2011; (with S.L. Moore) What's up, Bear?, 2012. Contributor to periodicals. **Address:** 292 Horsham Ave., Willowdale, ON M2R 1G4, Canada. **Online address:** frieda.wishinsky@gmail.com

WISKER, Gina. British (born England), b. 1951. **Genres:** Education, Literary Criticism And History, Women's Studies And Issues, Writing/Journalism, Horror. **Career:** Anglia Ruskin University, principal lecturer in English and educational development, 1978-2006, coordinator of women's studies; University of Brighton, Centre for Learning and Teaching, head, professor of higher education and contemporary literature. Writer. **Publications:** EDITOR: Black Women's Writing, 1993; It's My Party: Reading Twentieth-Century Women's Writing, 1994; (with S. Brown) Enabling Student Learning: Systems and Strategies, 1996; (with L. Pearce) Fatal Attractions: Re-scripting Romance in Literature on Film, 1998; Postcolonial and African American Women's Writing, 2000; Postgraduate Student's Research Handbook, 2001; Working One-to-One With Students: Supervising, Coaching, Mentoring and Personal Tutoring, 2008; (with P. Dodgson-Katiyo) Rites of Passage in Postcolonial Women's Writing, 2010; Teaching African American Women's Writing, 2010; A BEGINNER'S GUIDE SERIES: Virginia Woolf, 2000; Sylvia Plath, 2001; Toni Morrison, 2002; Margaret Atwood's Alias Grace: A Reader's Guide, 2002; Angela Carter, 2003; The Postgraduate Research Handbook: Succeed With Your MA, MPhil, EdD and PhD, 2008. OTHER: Empowering Women in Higher Education, 1996; Post Colonial and African and American Women's Writing: A Critical Introduction, 2000; Good Supervisor: Supervising Postgraduate and Undergraduate Research for Doctoral Theses and Dissertations, 2005, 2nd ed., 2010; Horror Fiction: An Introduction, 2005; Key Concepts in Post Colonial Literature, 2007; One-to-one Teaching: Supervising, Mentoring and Coaching, 2008; The Undergraduate Research Handbook, 2009; Atwood's The Handmaid's Tale: A Reader's Guide, 2010. Contributor to journals. **Address:** Centre for Learning and Teaching, University of Brighton, M104 Mayfield House, Falmer, Brighton, ES BN1 9PH, England. **Online address:** g.wisker@brighton.ac.uk

WISMAN, Ken. American (born United States), b. 1947. **Genres:** Novels, Science Fiction/Fantasy. **Career:** Writer. **Publications:** Frost on the Window: 14 Stories of Christmas, 1984; Weird Family Tales: A Journal of Familial Maledictions, 1993; Weird Family Tales II: The Curse Continues, 1995; Fourteen Fantasies from a Shop Called Imagination, 2001; Eden, 2002. Works appear in anthologies. Contributor of articles to journals. **Address:** Applewood Village, 91 Cortland Ln., Boxborough, MA 01719, U.S.A.

WITEK, Terri. American (born United States), b. 1952. **Genres:** Poetry. **Career:** Stetson University, professor of English, Melissa Sullivan Creative Writing Program, chair and director, now professor emeritus. Writer. **Publications:** Robert Lowell and Life Studies: Revising the Self, 1993; Fools and Crows (poetry), 2003; Carnal World (poetry), 2006; The Shipwreck Dress (poetry), 2008; Exit Island, 2012. Contributor of articles to journals. **Address:** Department of English, Stetson University, 421 N Woodland Blvd., Ste. 8300, DeLand, FL 32723, U.S.A. **Online address:** twitek@stetson.edu

WITEMEYER, Hugh Hazen. American (born United States), b. 1939. **Genres:** Literary Criticism And History, Poetry. **Career:** University of California, assistant professor of English, 1966-73; University of New Mexico, professor of English, 1973-2004, professor emeritus, 2004-; Friends of D.H. Lawrence, founder and vice president. Writer. **Publications:** The Poetry of Ezra Pound: Forms and Renewal 1908-1920, 1969; George Eliot and the Visual Arts, 1979; (intro.) The Letters of William Carlos Williams & Charles Tomlinson, 1992. EDITOR: (with G. Bornstein) Letters to the New Island, 1989; William Carlos Williams and James Laughlin: Selected Letters, 1989; George Eliot's Originals and Contemporaries: Essays in Victorian Literary History and Biography, 1991; (with E.P. Walkiewicz) Ezra Pound and Senator Bronson Cutting: A Political Correspondence, 1930-1935, 1995; Pound/Williams: Selected Letters of Ezra Pound and William Carlos Williams, 1996; The Future of Modernism, 1997; (with B. Magid) William Carlos Williams and Charles Tomlinson: A Transatlantic Connection, 1999. **Address:** Department of English Language and Literature, University of New Mexico, PO Box 032170, Albuquerque, NM 87131-0001, U.S.A. **Online address:** hughwit@unm.edu

WITHAM, Larry. (Larry Alan Witham). American (born United States), b. 1952?. **Genres:** Natural History, Theology/Religion, Economics, History, Novels, Young Adult Fiction. **Career:** Washington Times, reporter; Science & Spirit, editor, 2007. **Publications:** Rodzianko: An Orthodox Journey from Revolution to Millennium, 1917-1988, 1991; The Negev Project: A Novel, 1994; Dark Blossom: A Novel of East and West, 1997; (as Larry A. Witham) Where Darwin Meets the Bible: Creationists and Evolutionists in America, 2002; By Design: Science and the Search for God, 2003; (as Larry A. Witham) Who Shall Lead Them?: The Future of Ministry in America, 2005; The Measure of God: Our Century-Long Struggle to Reconcile Science and Religion, 2005; City upon a Hill: How Sermons Changed the Course of American History, 2007; The Proof of God: The Debate that Shaped Modern Belief, 2008; Marketplace of the Gods: How Economics Explains Religion, 2010; The God Biographers, 2010; Art Schooled: A Year Among Prodigies, Rebels, and Visionaries at a World-Class Art College, 2012. Contributor to periodicals. **Address:** c/o Author Mail, Oxford University Press, 198 Madison Ave., New York, NY 10016-4308, U.S.A.

WITHAM, Larry Alan. See **WITHAM, Larry.**

WITHERINGTON, Ben. American (born United States), b. 1951. **Genres:**

Theology/Religion, History, Money/Finance. **Career:** 4-Point Charge, senior minister, 1980-83; Duke University, The Divinity School, adjunct professor of Wesleyan studies, 1982-83; High Point College, adjunct professor of New Testament, 1982-83; 2-Point Charge, senior minister, 1983-84; Ashland Theological Seminary, professor of biblical and Wesleyan studies, 1984-95; Gordon-Conwell Divinity School, visiting professor of New Testament, 1988, 1990, 1993; Cambridge University, Robinson College, bye fellow, 1992; Asbury Theological Seminary, professor of New Testament interpretation, 1995-, Jean R. Amos professor of New Testament for doctoral studies; Vanderbilt Divinity School, visiting professor of New Testament, 2004; Duke Divinity School, faculty; Gordon-Conwell Theological Seminary, faculty. Writer. **Publications:** Women in the Ministry of Jesus: A Study Of Jesus' Attitudes To Women and Their Roles as Reflected in His Earthly Life, 1984; Women and the Genesis of Christianity, 1990; The Christology of Jesus, 1990; Jesus, Paul and the End of the World: A Comparative Study in New Testament Eschatology, 1992; Jesus the Sage: The Pilgrimage of Wisdom, 1994; Friendship and Finances in Philippi, 1994; Paul's Narrative Thought World: The Tapestry of Tragedy and Triumph, 1994; The Jesus Quest: The Third Search for the Jew of Nazareth, 1995; Conflict and Community in Corinth: A Socio-Rhetorical Commentary on 1 and 2 Corinthians, 1995; John's Wisdom: A Commentary on the Fourth Gospel, 1995; (ed.) History, Literature and Society in the Book of Acts, 1996; The Many Faces of Christ: The Christologies of the New Testament and Beyond, 1998; Grace in Galatia: A Commentary on St. Paul's Letter to the Galatians, 1998; The Acts of the Apostles: A Socio-Rhetorical Commentary, 1998; Paul Quest: The Search for the Jew from Tarsus, 1998; The Many Faces of the Christ: The Christologies of the New Testament and Beyond, 1998; (with C.G. González and C.E. Tilson) How United Methodists Study Scripture, 1999; Jesus the Seer: The Progress of Prophecy, 1999; The Realm of The Reign: Reflections On The Dominion of God, 1999; New Testament History: A Narrative Account, 2001; The Gospel of Mark: A Socio-Rhetorical Commentary, 2001; The Shadow of The Almighty: Father, Son and Spirit In Biblical Perspective, 2002; The Poetry of Piety: An Annotated Anthology of Christian Poetry, 2002; (with B.W. Longenecker) The Lost Letters of Pergamum: A Story From the New Testament World, 2003; The Brother of Jesus: The Dramatic Story and Meaning of The First Archaeological Link to Jesus and His Family, 2003; Revelation, 2003; New Testament Story, 2004; (with D. Hyatt) Paul's Letter To The Romans: A Socio-Rhetorical Commentary, 2004; The Gospel Code: Novel Claims About Jesus, Mary Magdalene, and Da Vinci, 2004; Grace in Galatia: A Commentary on St. Paul's Letter To The Galatians, 2004; The New Testamentstory, 2004; The Problem with Evangelical Theology: Testing the Exegetical Foundations of Calvinism, Dispensationalism, and Wesleyanism, 2005; Letters and Homilies for Hellenized Christians, 2006; Matthew, 2006; Incandescence: Light Shed Through the Word, 2006; What Have They Done with Jesus?: Beyond Strange Theories and Bad History Why We Can Trust the Bible, 2006; 1 and 2 Thessalonians: A Socio-Rhetorical Commentary, 2006; The Letters to Philemon, The Colossians, and the Ephesians: A Socio-Rhetorical Commentary On The Captivity Epistles, 2007; Letters And Homilies For Jewish Christians: A Socio-Rhetorical Commentary On Hebrews, James and Jude, 2007; Troubled Waters: The Real New Testament Theology of Baptism, 2007; The Living Word of God: Rethinking The Theology of The Bible, 2007; (contrib.) Prayers of Jesus: Participant's Guide, 2007; Making a Meal of It: Rethinking The Theology of The Lord's Supper, 2007; Letters to Philemon, the Colossians and the Ephesians, 2007; Imminent Domain: The Story of the Kingdom of God and Its Celebration, 2009; What's in the Word: Rethinking the Socio-rhetorical Character of the New Testament, 2009; New Testament Rhetoric: An Introductory Guide to the Art of Persuasion in and of the New Testament, 2009; Indelible Image: The Theological and Ethical Thought World of the New Testament, 2009; We Have Seen His Glory: A Vision of Kingdom Worship, 2010; Work: A Kingdom Perspective on Labor, 2010; Revelation and the End Times: Unraveling God's Message of Hope, 2010; Jesus and Money: A Guide for Times of Financial Crisis, 2010; (with A. Witherington) Papias and the Mysterious Menorah, 2010; Is There a Doctor in the House?: An Insider's Story and Advice on Becoming a Bible Scholar, 2011; Corinthian Leather, 2011; Paul's Letter to the Philippians, 2011; A Week in the Life of Corinth, 2012; On the Road with Jesus, 2012. FORTHCOMING: The Gospel of Matthew; (with A.J. Levine) The Gospel of Luke; Paul's Letters to the Thessalonians, A Socio-Rhetorical Commentary; The Inner Circle of Jesus; New Testament Theology; Letters and Homilies of the New Testament, 2 vols.; (with D. Hyatt) Paul's Letters to Philemon, the Colossians and the Ephesians. **Address:** Asbury Theological Seminary, 204 N Lexington Ave., Wilmore, KY 40390-1129, U.S.A. **Online address:** benw333@hotmail.com

WITHROW, Sarah. Canadian (born Canada), b. 1966. **Genres:** Young Adult Fiction, Picture/Board Books. **Career:** Freelance corporate writer, 1989-98; Fireworks, glass blowers' assistant, 1998-2000; St. Lawrence College, School of Continuing Studies, instructor in writing, 2000-; Queen's University, communications officer, 2005-07; City of Kingston, communications officer, 2007-. **Publications:** Bat Summer, 1998; Box Girl, 2001; The Black Sunshine of Goody Pryne, 2003; What Gloria Wants, 2005; Be a Baby (picture book), 2007. **Address:** Kingston, ON , Canada. **Online address:** swithrow@kingston.net

WITT, Christopher. American (born United States), b. 1951. **Genres:** Economics, Human Relations/Parenting. **Career:** Witt Communications, founder and president, 1993-. Speech consultant, coach and writer. **Publications:** (With D.A. Morrison) From Loneliness to Love, 1989; (with G.M. Nelson) Sacred Threshold: Rituals and Readings for a Wedding with Spirit, 1998; (with G.M. Nelson) A Wedding with Spirit: A Guide to Making Your Wedding (and Marriage) More Meaningful, 2006; (with D. Fetherling) Real Leaders Don't Do PowerPoint: How to Sell Yourself and Your Ideas, 2009. **Address:** Witt Communications, 1010 University Ave., Ste. 1677, San Diego, CA 92103, U.S.A. **Online address:** chris@wittcom.com

WITT, John Fabian. American (born United States), b. 1972. **Genres:** Law, Young Adult Fiction. **Career:** United States Court of Appeals for the Second Circuit, clerk to Judge Pierre N. Leval, 2000-01; Columbia Law School, associate professor, 2001-05, professor of law, 2005-06, professor of law and history, 2006-08, George Welwood Murray Professor of Legal History, 2008-09; University of Tokyo, visiting lecturer, 2004; University of Texas, Harrington faculty fellow, 2004; Harvard Law School, visiting associate professor, 2005; Yale Law School, professor, 2009-; Columbia Law School Program in Legal History, co-director. Writer. **Publications:** NONFICTION: The Accidental Republic: Crippled Workingmen, Destitute Widows and the Remaking of American Law, 2004; Patriots and Cosmopolitans: Hidden Histories of American Law, 2007. Contributor to books, law journals and magazines. **Address:** Yale Law School, PO Box 208215, New Haven, CT 06520, U.S.A.

WITT, Martha. American (born United States) **Genres:** Novels, Young Adult Fiction. **Career:** Writer. **Publications:** Broken As Things Are: A Novel, 2004. Contributor to journals and anthologies. **Address:** c/o Annsley Rosner, Henry Holt & Co., 115 W 18th St., New York, NY 10011, U.S.A. **Online address:** inquiries@marthawitt.com

WITTE, Glenna Finley. See **FINLEY, Glenna.**

WITTE, John. Canadian (born Canada), b. 1959. **Genres:** Novels. **Career:** Emory Law School, assistant professor, 1989-91, associate professor, 1991-93, director; Pew Charitable Trusts Project on Christianity and Democracy, Law and Religion Program, director, 1989-95; Alexander von Humboldt-Stiftung, fellow, 1995; Pew Charitable Trusts Project on the Problem of Proselytizing, director, 1995-99; Pew/Notre Dame Project on Law and Human Nature: codirector, 2001- 04; McDonald Foundation Project on the Foundations of Religious Liberty and Rule of Law, director, 2007-. Writer. **Publications:** (ed. and author of intro.) Herman Dooyeweerd, A Christian Theory of Social Institutions, 1986; (ed. with Frank S. Alexander) The Weightier Matters of the Law: Essays on Law and Religion: A Tribute to Harold J. Berman, 1988; (ed. with Johan D. van der Vyver) Religious Human Rights in Global Perspective: Legal Perspectives, 1996; From Sacrament to Contract: Marriage, Religion, and Law in the Western Tradition, 1997; (ed. with Michael J. Broyde) Human Rights in Judaism: Cultural, Religious, and Political Perspectives, 1998; (ed. with Michael Bourdeaux) Proselytism and Orthodoxy in Russia: The New War for Souls, 1999; John E. Coons and Patrick M. Brennan, By Nature Equal: The Anatomy of a Western Insight, 1999; (ed. with Richard C. Martin) Sharing the Book: Religious Perspectives on the Rights and Wrongs of Proselytism, 1999; Religion and the American Constitutional Experiment: Essential Rights and Liberties, 2nd ed., 2004; Law and Protestantism: The Legal Teachings of the Lutheran Reformation, 2002; (with E. Ellison) Covenant Marriage in Comparative Perspective, 2005; (ed. with Frank S. Alexander) The Teachings of Modern Christianity: Human Nature, Politics, and Law, 2005; (ed. with Steven M. Tipton) Family Transformed: Religion, Values, and Society in American Life, 2005; (with R.M. Kingdon) Sex, Marriage, and Family in John Calvin's Geneva, 2005; (ed. with Frank S. Alexander) The Teachings of Modern Christianity on Law, Politics, and Human Nature, 2006; God's Joust, God's Justice: Law and Religion in the Western Tradition, 2006; (ed. with Don S. Browning and M. Christian Green) Sex, Marriage, and Family in World Religions, 2006; (ed. with M. Christian Green and Amy Wheeler) The Equal-regard Family and Its Friendly Critics: Don Browning and the Practical Theological Ethics of the Family, 2007; (ed. with Frank S. Alexander) The Teachings of Modern Roman Catholicism on Law, Politics, and Human Nature, 2007; The Reformation of Rights: Law, Religion and Human Rights in Early Modern Calvinism, 2007; (ed. with Philip L. Reynolds) To Have and to Hold: Marrying and Its Documentation in Western Christendom, 400-1600, 2007; (ed. with Frank S. Alexander) The Teachings of Modern Protestantism on Law, Politics, and Human Nature, 2007; (ed. with Frank S. Alexander) The Teachings of Modern Orthodox Christianity on Law, Politics, and Human Nature, 2007. **Address:** Emory Law School, 1301 Clifton Rd., Atlanta, GA 30322, U.S.A. **Online address:** jwitte@law.emory.edu

WITTENBORN, Dirk. American (born United States), b. 1951. **Genres:** Novels, Literary Criticism And History. **Career:** Novelist. **Publications:** Johnson versus Johnson: A Real Life Dynasty Torn Apart by Lust and Greed, 1990. NOVELS: Eclipse, 1977; Zoë, 1983; Fierce People, 2002; Pharmakon, 2008. Contributor to periodicals. **Address:** c/o Caroline Dawnay, Peters Fraser & Dunlop Group Ltd., Drury House, 34-43 Russell St., London, GL WC2B 5HA, England.

WITTES, Benjamin. American (born United States), b. 1969. **Genres:** Law, Politics/Government. **Career:** Brookings Institution, senior fellow; Atlantic Monthly, contributing editor. **Publications:** Starr: A Reassessment, 2002; Confirmation Wars: Preserving Independent Courts in Angry Times, 2006; Law and the Long War: The Future of Justice in the Age of Terror, 2008. Contributor of articles to journals. **Address:** Brookings Institution, 1775 Massachusetts Ave. NW, Washington, DC 20036, U.S.A.

WITTLINGER, Ellen. American (born United States), b. 1948. **Genres:** Novels, Novellas/Short Stories, Plays/Screenplays, Poetry, Young Adult Fiction. **Career:** Writer, 1970-; Swampscott Public Library, children's librarian, 1989-92; Emerson College, writing instructor. **Publications:** Breakers (poetry), 1979; Lombardo's Law, 1993; Noticing Paradise, 1995; Hard Love, 1999; What's in a Name, 2000; Gracie's Girl, 2000; Razzle, 2001; The Long Night of Leo and Bree, 2002; Zigzag, 2003; Raziel, 2003; Heart on My Sleeve, 2004; Sandpiper, 2005; Blind Faith, 2006; Parrotfish, 2007; Love & Lies, 2008; This Means War!, 2010. Works appear in anthologies. Contributor to periodicals. **Address:** Simon & Schuster Inc., 1230 Ave. of the Americas, New York, NY 10020, U.S.A. **Online address:** ellwitt@hotmail.com

WITTMANN, Rebecca. Canadian (born Canada), b. 1970. **Genres:** Young Adult Fiction. **Career:** Marquette University, assistant professor of History, 2002-03; University of Toronto at Mississauga, assistant professor of history, 2003-08, associate professor of history, 2008-. Writer. **Publications:** Beyond Justice: The Auschwitz Trial, 2005. Contributor to journals. **Address:** Department of Historical Studies, University of Toronto at Mississauga, UTM 272, 3359 Mississauga Rd. N, Mississauga, ON L5L 1C6, Canada. **Online address:** wittmann@chass.utoronto.ca

WITTMER, Pierre (Jean). French (born France), b. 1942. **Genres:** Art/Art History, Children's Non-fiction, Children's Fiction, Homes/Gardens. **Career:** D. Feau Conseil Immobilier, executive assistant, 1965-67; Societe des Centres Commerciaux, legal and administrative director, 1969-81; Societe Europeenne d'Assurance et de Reassurance, secretary general, 1981-83; private business consultant, 1984-. Writer. **Publications:** Caillebotte au jardin: La periode d'Yerres, 1869-1879, 1990, trans. as Caillebotte and His Garden at Yerres, 1991; Cent jardins à Paris et en Ile-de-France, 1992; (with S. Dannaud) Mon ete avec Caillebotte (children's), 1994, trans. as My Summer in Caillebotte's Garden, 1995; (with S. Dannaud) Mon voyage avec Monet (children's), 1995; Sur les pas de Delacroix a Champrosay 1844-1863, 1998; (with F. d'Ormesson) Aux jardins de Mereville pittoesque 1895-1905, 1999; (with M. Genthon) Paul Landowski à Paris: une promenade de sculpture de 1897 à 1960, 2001; (with Y. Farinaux-Le Sidaner and J. Galiegue) Henri Le Sidaner en son jardin de Gerberoy 1901-1939, 2001. Contributor to art journals. **Address:** Altitude 95, 15 rue des Rossignols, Yerres Essonne, 91330, France.

WITTNER, Lawrence Stephen. American (born United States), b. 1941. **Genres:** History, Politics/Government. **Career:** Hampton Institute, assistant professor, 1967-68; Vassar College, assistant professor, 1968-73, senior Fulbright lecturer, 1973-74; State University of New York at Albany, lecturer 1974-76, assistant professor, 1976-77, associate professor, 1977-83, professor of history, 1983-2010, professor emeritus of history, 2010-. Writer. **Publica-

tions: Rebels against War: The American Peace Movement 1941-60, 1969; (ed.) MacArthur, 1971; Cold War America: From Hiroshima to Watergate, 1974, 1978; American Intervention in Greece 1943-1949, 1982; Rebels against War: The American Peace Movement 1933-1983, 1984; (ed.) Biographical Dictionary of Modern Peace Leaders, 1985; One World or None: A History of the World Nuclear Disarmament Movement through 1953, 1993; Resisting the Bomb: A History of the World Nuclear Disarmament Movement, 1954-1970, 1997; Toward Nuclear Abolition: A History of the World Nuclear Disarmament Movement, 1971 to the Present, 2003; (co-ed.) Peace Action: Past, Present, and Future, 2007; Confronting the Bomb: A Short History of the World Nuclear Disarmament Movement, 2009; The Outsider: Memoirs of an Activist Intellectual, 2012. **Address:** Department of History, State University of New York, 1400 Washington Ave., Albany, NY 12222, U.S.A. **Online address:** wittner@albany.edu

WITZEL, Michael Karl. American (born United States), b. 1960. **Genres:** Adult Non-fiction, Novels, Autobiography/Memoirs, Food And Wine, Cultural/Ethnic Topics, History, Social Sciences. **Career:** Freelance writer. **Publications:** The American Gas Station: History and Folklore of the Gas Station in American Car Culture, 1992; The American Drive-In: History and Folklore of the Drive-In Restaurant, 1994; Gas Station Memories, 1994; Route 66 Remembered, 1996; Drive-In Deluxe, 1997; (with K. Bash) Cruisin: Car Culture in America, 1997; (with G.Y. Witzel) Soda Pop!: From Miracle Medicine to Pop Culture, 1998; The American Diner, 1999; The American Motel, 2000; Gas Stations Coast to Coast, 2000; (with G.Y. Witzel) The Sparkling Story of Coca-Cola: An Entertaining History Including Collectibles, Coke Lore and Calendar Girls, 2002; Barns: Style & Structure, 2003; (with G.Y. Witzel) Legendary Route 66: A Journey Through Time along America's Mother Road, 2007; Barbecue Road Trip: Recipes, Restaurants & Pitmasters from America's Great Barbecue, 2008. Contributor of articles to magazines. **Address:** Motorbooks International Publishing Co., 729 Prospect Ave., PO Box 1, Saint Paul, MN 55101-3885, U.S.A. **Online address:** witzelwords@yahoo.com

WIXSON, Douglas. American (born United States), b. 1933. **Genres:** Literary Criticism And History, Economics, History. **Career:** Shell Oil Co., roustabout, 1955; Institut Zugerberg, teacher, 1961; University of Colorado, mathematics instructor, 1962-64; University of North Carolina, Chapel Hill, English instructor, 1969-71; Universitéde St. Etienne, professor, 1971-72; Université de Chambéry, professor, 1972-74; University of North Carolina, Greensboro, assistant professor, 1974-76; University of Missouri, professor, 1976-92; Jack Conroy Estate, literary executor, 1990-. Writer. **Publications:** (Ed. and intro.) The Weed King and Other Stories, 1985; (ed. and intro.) The Disinherited, 1991; Worker-Writer in America: Jack Conroy and the Tradition of Midwestern Literary Radicalism, 1898-1990, 1994; (ed. and intro.) The Lost Traveler, 1995; (ed. and intro.) A World to Win, 2000; (ed. and intro.) On the Dirty Plate Trail: Remembering the Dust Bowl Refugee Camps, 2007. **Address:** 2108 Griswold Ln., Austin, TX 78703-3010, U.S.A. **Online address:** solvitur@texas.net

WIZOWATY, Suzi. American (born United States), b. 1954. **Genres:** Novels. **Career:** Interstate Consortium, assistant to the director, 1980; Princeton Theological Seminary, bookstore manager, 1980-85; Princeton Nursery School, board director, 1983-84; Champlain College, editor and assistant director of marketing, 1986; Burlington Peace and Justice Center, board director, 1986-87; Goddard College, adjunct faculty, 1986-2001; Fletcher Free Library, director of outreach services, 1987-91; Vermont New Jewish Agenda, board director, 1986-88; Trinity College, adjunct faculty, 1990-91; St. Michael's College, adjunct faculty, 1991-93, adjunct faculty in creative writing, 2001-; South Burlington Community Library, program director, 1991-95; Vermont Council on the Humanities, coordinator of literacy program, 1995-96, program director, 1996-99; Northern New England Tradeswomen, associate director, 2001-02; Vermont Works for Women, associate director. **Publications:** The Round Barn, 2002; A Tour of Evil, 2005. **Address:** Curtis Brown Ltd., 10 Astor Pl., Fl. 3, New York, NY 10003, U.S.A. **Online address:** wizowaty@sover.net

WODHAMS, Herbert Jack. See **WODHAMS, Jack.**

WODHAMS, Jack. (Herbert Jack Wodhams). Australian/British (born England), b. 1931. **Genres:** Novellas/Short Stories, Science Fiction/Fantasy, Theology/Religion, Biography, Young Adult Fiction, Theology/Religion. **Career:** Australian Post Office, driver, 1975-. Writer. **Publications:** Anchor Man, 1969; Split Personality, 1969; The Authentic Touch, 1971; Budnip,

1972; One Clay Foot, 1979; Looking for Blücher, 1980; Ryn, 1982; Future War (stories), 1982; (with P. Collins) Generation X, 1999; Magus Malefic, 2000; Small Book of Controversies, 2004; Pumfenpuffenwagen, forthcoming. Contributor of short stories and periodicals. **Address:** PO Box 48, Caboolture, QL 4510, Australia.

WODZIŃSKI, Marcin. Polish (born Poland), b. 1966?. **Genres:** Young Adult Non-fiction, Theology/Religion. **Career:** University of Wroclaw, Department of Jewish Studies, professor, Centre for the Culture and Languages of the Jews, director. Writer. **Publications:** NONFICTION: Hebrajskie Inskrypcje na śląsku XIII-XVIII wieku, 1996; Groby cadyków w Polsce: o chasydzkiej literaturze nagrobnej i jej kontekstach, 1998; (with A. Trzciński) Cmentarz żydowski w Lesku, vol. I: Wiek XVI i XVII, 2001; (ed. with J. Spyra) Jews in Silesia, 2001; Oświecenie żydowskie w Królestwie Polskim Wobec Chasydyzmu: Dzieje Pewnej Idei, 2003; (ed. with A. Michałowska-Mycielska) Małżeństwo z rozsadku? Zdydzi w społeczeństwie dawnej Rzeczypospolitej, 2007; Władze Królestwa Polskiego Wobec Chasydyzmu: Z dziejów Stosunków Politycznych, 2008; Judaica w Aktach Centralnych Władz Wyznaniowych Królestwa Polskiego Archiwum Głównego Akt Dawnych: Informator Archiwalny, 2010. Contributor to journals. **Address:** Studium Kultury i Jezykow Zydowskich, Uniwersytet Wrocawski, pl. Nankiera 15, Wroclaw, 50-140, Poland. **Online address:** wodzinsk@uni.wroc.pl

WOELL, Edward J. American (born United States), b. 1965. **Genres:** History, Theology/Religion, Military/Defense/Arms Control. **Career:** University of Wisconsin, visiting professor of history, 1997; Cardinal Stritch University, instructor of history, 1997-98; Marist College, assistant professor of history, 1998-2003; Marquette University, Institute for the Transformation of Learning, researcher, 1998; Western Illinois University, associate professor of history, 2003-09. Writer. **Publications:** Small-Town Martyrs and Murderers: Religious Revolution and Counterrevolution in Western France, 1774-1914, 2006. Contributor to journals. **Address:** Department of History, Western Illinois University, 432 Morgan Hall, 1 University Cir., Macomb, IL 61455-1390, U.S.A. **Online address:** eJ-woell@wiu.edu

WOGAMAN, J(ohn) Philip. American (born United States), b. 1932. **Genres:** Ethics, Social Commentary, Theology/Religion. **Career:** United Methodist Church, ordained minister, pastor, 1956-58, Division of World Missions, staff, 1960-61; University of the Pacific, associate professor of Bible and social ethics and director of Pacific center for the study of social issues, 1961-66; Wesley Theological Seminary, associate professor, 1966-69, professor of Christian social ethics, 1969-92, affiliated professor of Christian ethics, 1992, dean, 1972-83, dean emeritus, professor emeritus of Christian social ethics, 1992-; Foundry United Methodist Church, senior minister, 1992-2002; Iliff School of Theology, interim president, 2004-06; St. Luke United Methodist Church, senior pastor, 2008-09. Writer. **Publications:** Methodism's Challenge in Race Relations: A Study of Strategy, 1960; Protestant Faith and Religious Liberty, 1967; Guaranteed Annual Income: The Moral Issues, 1968; A Christian Method of Moral Judgment, 1977; The Great Economic Debate: An Ethical Analysis in UK as Christians and the Great Economic Debate, 1977; (with P. McCleary) Quality of Life in a Global Society, 1978; Faith and Fragmentation: Christianity for a New Age, 1985; Economics and Ethics, 1986; Christian Perspectives on Politics, 1988, rev. ed., 2000; Christian Moral Judgment, 1989; Making Moral Decisions, 1990; Christian Ethics: A Historical Introduction, 1993, 2nd ed., 2010; To Serve the Present Age: The Gift and Promise of United Methodism, 1995; Speaking the Truth in Love: Prophetic Preaching to a Broken World, 1998; From the Eye of the Storm: A Pastor to the President Speaks Out, 1998; An Unexpected Journey: Reflections on Pastoral Ministry, 2004; Faith and Fragmentation: Reflections on the Future of Christianty, 2004; An Unexpected Journey: Reflections on Pastoral Ministry, 2004; Moral Dilemmas: An Introduction to Christian Ethics, 2009. EDITOR: The Population Crisis and Moral Responsibility, 1973; (with D.M. Strong) Readings in Christian Ethics, 1996; Communitarian Ethics: Later Writings of Walter G. Muelder, 2007. Contributor to periodicals. **Address:** Wesley Theological Seminary, 4500 Massachusetts Ave. NW, Washington, DC 20016, U.S.A. **Online address:** jpwogaman@aol.com

WOGINRICH, Jenna. American (born United States), b. 1982?. **Genres:** Young Adult Non-fiction. **Career:** Oakpaw Art, illustrator, 2001-; HGTV.com, interactive designer, 2005-; ITSAFARWALK, art director, designer and illustrator, 2005-; Eldon Design Associates, interactive designer, 2005-06; Orvis Co., website designer. Writer. **Publications:** Made from Scratch: Discovering the Pleasures of a Handmade Life (nonfiction), 2008; Barnheart:

The Incurable Longing for a Farm of One's Own, 2011. **Address:** Storey Publishing, 210 MASS MoCA Way, North Adams, MA 01247, U.S.A. **Online address:** jenna@itsafarwalk.com

WOHLGELERNTER, Maurice. American/Polish (born Poland), b. 1921. **Genres:** Literary Criticism And History, Humanities, Autobiography/Memoirs, Essays. **Career:** Yeshiva University, faculty, visiting professor, 1955-70; Bar-Ilan University, New School for Social Research, faculty, 1966-68, 1992-93; City University of New York, Baruch College, professor of English, 1972-, now professor emeritus; New York University, faculty, 1993. Writer. **Publications:** Israel Zangwill: A Study, 1964; Frank O'Connor: An Introduction, 1977; Jewish Writers/Irish Writers: Selected Essays on the Love of Words, 2000. EDITOR: The King of Schnorrers, 1964; (co-ed.) History, Religion and Spiritual Democracy: Essays in Honor of Joseph Leon Blau, 1980; The Great Hatred, 1988; (and intro.) History, Religion and American Democracy, 1993; Level Sunlight, 1998. **Address:** Department of English, Baruch College, City University of New York, 17 Lexington Ave., Ste. 411, New York, NY 10010, U.S.A.

WOIK, Julie. American (born United States), b. 1963. **Genres:** Children's Fiction, Picture/Board Books. **Career:** Sarasota Memorial Hospital, psychiatric technician, 1984-90. Writer. **Publications:** The Garden Gathering, 2007; (with M. Tobin) The Life and Times of Lilly Lash: The Garden Gathering, 2009. **Address:** Snow In Sarasota Publishing, 5170 Central Sarasota Pkwy., Apt. 309, PO Box 1360, Sarasota, FL 34238-7624, U.S.A. **Online address:** finnwoik@verizon.net

WOIROL, Gregory R. American (born United States), b. 1948. **Genres:** Economics, History, Sociology. **Career:** Whittier College, Department of Economics, instructor, 1976-80, assistant professor, 1980-83, associate professor, 1983-86, head, 1984-87, 1990-93, professor of economics, 1986-, chair, associate academic dean of liberal education, 1986-90, Douglas W. Ferguson chair in economics and business administration, Richard and Billie Deihl distinguished chair. Writer. **Publications:** In the Floating Army: F.C. Mills on Itinerant Life in California, 1914, 1992; Technological Unemployment and Structural Unemployment Debates, 1996. Contributor to periodicals. **Address:** Department of Economics, Whittier College, Hoover 121, 13406 E Philadelphia St., Whittier, CA 90601-4446, U.S.A. **Online address:** gwoirol@whittier.edu

WOIWODE, L. *See* **WOIWODE, Larry (Alfred).**

WOIWODE, Larry (Alfred). (L. Woiwode). American (born United States), b. 1941. **Genres:** Novels, Poetry, Novellas/Short Stories, Theology/Religion, Essays, Biography, Autobiography/Memoirs. **Career:** Freelance writer, 1964-; University of Wisconsin, writer-in-residence, 1973-74; State University of New York, visiting professor, 1983-85, professor, director of creative writing, 1985-88; Jamestown College, writer-in-residence, 2006-. **Publications:** (As L. Woiwode) What I'm Going to Do, I Think, 1969; (co-author) Poetry North, 1970; Beyond the Bedroom Wall: A Family Album, 1975, Even Tide (poems), 1977; Poppa John, 1981; Born Brothers, 1988; The Neumiller Stories, 1989; Indian Affairs: A Novel, 1992; Reflection on the Church, Writing and His Own Life, 1993; Silent Passengers: Stories, 1993; Acts, 1993; The Aristocrat of the West: The Story of Harold Schafer, 2000; What I Think I Did: A Season of Survival in Two Acts, 2000; Behind the Bathroom Door, 2003; My Dinner with Auden, 2004; A Step from Death: A Memoir, 2008; A Step from Death: A Father's Album, 2008; Invention of Lefse: A Christmas Story, 2011; Words Made Fresh: Essays on Literature and Culture, 2011. **Address:** c/o Don Fehr, Basic Books, 10 E 53rd St., New York, NY 10022-5244, U.S.A. **Online address:** woiwode@ndsupernet.com

WOJAHN, David (Charles). Also writes as Mudrooroo Johnson. American (born United States), b. 1953. **Genres:** Poetry. **Career:** University of Alabama, faculty; University of Chicago, faculty; University of New Orleans, assistant professor of English, 1981-82; University of Arkansas, assistant professor of English, 1982-85; Vermont College of Fine Arts, adjunct professor, 1983-; Indiana University, Lilly professor of poetry, 1985-; University of Houston, visiting professor, 1985; Virginia Commonwealth University, Department of English, professor, 2003-, Creative Writing Program, director. Writer. **Publications:** POETRY: Icehouse Lights, 1982; Glassworks, 1987; Mystery Train, 1990; Late Empire, 1994; The Falling Hour, 1997; Strange Good Fortune, 2001 Spirit Cabinet, 2002; Collected Poems, 2006; Interrogation Palace: New and Selected Poems, 1982-2004, 2006; World Tree, 2011.

EDITOR: (with B. Henderson and P. Levine) The Pushcart Prize XI: Best of the Small Presses, 1986; (with J. Myers) A Profile of Twentieth-Century American Poetry, 1991; (and foreword) Only World, 1995. **Address:** Department of English, Virginia Commonwealth University, 108 Anderson House, 900 Park Ave., PO Box 842005, Richmond, VA 23284-2005, U.S.A. **Online address:** dcwojahn@vcu.edu

WOJNAROWSKI, Adrian. American (born United States), b. 1970?. **Genres:** Biography, Trivia/Facts, Autobiography/Memoirs, Sports/Fitness. **Career:** Record, sports columnist; Yahoo Sports online, sports columnist; ESPN, sports columnist. Author. **Publications:** The Miracle of St. Anthony: A Season with Coach Bob Hurley and Basketball's Most Improbable Dynasty, 2005; Jimmy V: The Life and Death of Jim Valvano, 2008. Contributor to periodicals. **Address:** Glen Rock, NJ , U.S.A. **Online address:** espnwoj10@aol.com

WOKECK, Marianne Sophia. American (born United States) **Genres:** Novels, Adult Non-fiction, History, Business/Trade/Industry. **Career:** The Papers of William Penn, associate editor, 1982-86; Indiana University-Purdue University Indianapolis, assistant professor, professor of history, 1991-, adjunct professor of American studies and womens studies, 1992-, director of American studies department, 2003-06, fellow, 2003-, associate dean of academic affairs, 2006-; Santayana Edition, general editor, 1999-, director, 2003-. Educator, writer and historian. **Publications:** The Papers of William Penn 1701-1718, 1986, (ed. with J. Wiltenburg, C. Horle and A. Hirsch) vol. IV, 1987; Lawmaking and Legislators in Pennsylvania. A Biographical Dictionary: 1682-1709, 1991; Trade in Strangers: The Beginnings of Mass Migration to North America, 1999; (ed. with M.A. Coleman) The Life of Reason or The Phases of Human Progress, 2011. Contributor to periodicals. **Address:** Department of History, Indiana University-Purdue University, CA 441D, 425 University Blvd., Indianapolis, IN 46202-5143, U.S.A. **Online address:** mwokeck@iupui.edu

WOLCOTT, Patty. American (born United States), b. 1929. **Genres:** Children's Fiction, Education, Sports/Fitness. **Career:** Teacher, 1952-56; Houghton Mifflin Co., Elementary School Textbooks, editor, 1956-59; Artists and Writers Press, Juvenile Trade Books, editor, 1960-61; Columbia University Teachers College, Agnes Russell Center, faculty, 1963-66; full-time writer, 1969-. **Publications:** The Reef of Coral, 1969; The Marvelous Mud Washing Machine, 1974; The Cake Story, 1974; Where Did That Naughty Little Hamster Go?, 1974; The Forest Fire, 1974; I'm Going to New York to Visit the Queen, 1974; Tunafish Sandwiches, 1975; Beware of a Very Hungry Fox, 1975; Super Sam and the Salad Garden, 1975; My Shadow and I, 1975; Pickle Pickle Pickle Juice, 1975; The Dragon and the Wild Fandango, 1980; Double-Decker Double-Decker Bus, 1980; Pirates, Pirates over the Salt, Salt Sea, 1981; Eeeeeek!, 1981; The Dragon and the Gold, 1983; This Is Weird, 1985. Contributor to periodicals. **Address:** 245 Aspen Cir., Lincoln, MA 01773-9422, U.S.A.

WOLD, Donald J. American (born United States), b. 1945?. **Genres:** Sex, Gay And Lesbian Issues, Theology/Religion. **Career:** Writer and educator. **Publications:** Out of Order: Homosexuality in the Bible and the Ancient Near East, 1998. Contributor to periodicals. **Address:** c/o Author Mail, Baker Books, PO Box 6287, Grand Rapids, MI 49516-6287, U.S.A.

WOLENSKY, Kenneth C. American (born United States), b. 1962. **Genres:** History, Technology. **Career:** Pennsylvania Historical & Museum Commission, historian, 1996-; Pennsylvania State University, Capital College, American studies faculty, 1998; Pennsylvania Humanities Council, commonwealth speaker, 1999-2003; Organization of American Historians, distinguished lecturer, 2004-; Smithsonian Institution, national affiliate. Writer. **Publications:** (With R.P. Wolensky and N.H. Wolensky) The Knox Mine Disaster, January 22, 1959: The Final Years of the Northern Anthracite Industry and the Effort to Rebuild a Regional Economy, 1999; Living for Reform, 2001; (with R.P. Wolensky and N.H. Wolensky) Fighting for the Union Label: The Women's Garment Industry and the ILGWU in Pennsylvania, 2002; (ed.) The Great Strike: Perspectives on the 1902 Anthracite Coal Strike, 2002; Remembering a Twentieth Century Public Servant, 2005; (with R.P. Wolensky and N.P. Wolensky) Voices of the Knox Mine Disaster: Stories, Remembrances, and Reflections of the Anthracite Coal Industry's Last Major Catastrophe, January 22, 1959, 2005; (with G.M. Leader) The Life of Pennsylvania Governor George M. Leader: Challenging Complacency, 2011. Contributor of articles to books and periodicals. **Address:** Pennsylvania Historical & Museum Commission, Commonwealth Keystone Bldg., 400 North St., Harrisburg, PA 17120-0211, U.S.A. **Online address:** kwolensky@state.pa.us

WOLF, Allan. American (born United States), b. 1963. **Genres:** Poetry, Novels. **Career:** Virginia Tech, instructor in writing and composition, 2005-; Poetry Alive!, educational director & co-ordinator of national residency program, 1990-2003. Author, performer and educator. **Publications:** POETRY: Something Is Going to Happen: Poem Performance for the Classroom, 1990; It's Show Time: Poetry from the Page to the Stage, 1993; The Blood-Hungry Spleen and Other Poems about Our Parts, 2003; Immersed in Verse: An Informative, Slightly Irreverent and Totally Tremendous Guide to Living the Poet's Life, 2006; Haiku Stickies: 100 Haiku to Write and Leave Behind, 2007; (with S. Holbrook) More Than Friends: Poems from Him and Her, 2008. NOVELS: New Found Land: Lewis and Clark's Voyage of Discovery, 2004; Zane's Trace, 2007. **Address:** Asheville, NC , U.S.A. **Online address:** allanwolf@earthlink.net

WOLF, Anthony E. American (born United States), b. 1940. **Genres:** How-to Books, Human Relations/Parenting, Humor/Satire. **Career:** Writer. **Publications:** I'll be Home before Midnight and I Won't get Pregnant: Stories of Adolescence, 1988; Get Out of My Life, but First Could You Drive Me and Cheryl to the Mall? A Parent's Guide to the New Teenager, 1991; It's Not Fair, Jeremy Spencer's Parents Let Him Stay Up All Night! A Guide to the Tougher Parts of Parenting, 1995; Why Did You Have to Get a Divorce? And When Can I Get a Hamster? A Guide to Parenting through Divorce, 1998; The Secret of Parenting: How to Be in Charge of Today's Kids-from Toddlers to Preteens-without Threats or Punishment, 2000; Mom, Jason's Breathing on Me! The Solution to Sibling Bickering, 2003; Why Can't You Shut Up? How We Ruin Relationships-How Not To, 2006; I'd Listen to My Parents if They'd just Shut Up: What to Say and not Say When Parenting Teens Today, 2011. Contributor to periodicals. **Address:** C033, 813 Williams St., Ste. 205, Longmeadow, MA 01106-2052, U.S.A. **Online address:** info@anthonywolf.com

WOLF, Eva Sheppard. American (born United States), b. 1969. **Genres:** History, Race Relations. **Career:** San Francisco State University, associate professor of history, 2003-. Writer. **Publications:** Race and Liberty in the New Nation: Emancipation in Virginia from the Revolution to Nat Turner's Rebellion, 2006; Almost Free: A Story About Family and Race in Antebellum Virginia, 2012. **Address:** Department of History, San Francisco State University, Rm. SCI 267, 1600 Holloway Ave., San Francisco, CA 94132, U.S.A. **Online address:** shepwolf@sfsu.edu

WOLF, Gita. Indian (born India), b. 1956. **Genres:** Mythology/Folklore, Education, Animals/Pets. **Career:** Tara Publishing, publisher, 1993-. Writer. **Publications:** Mala: A Women's Folk Tale, 1994; (ed.) Landscapes, Children's Voices, 1995; The Very Hungry Lion: A Folktale, 1995; (with K. Arna) Child Art with Everyday Materials, 1996; Picturing Words and Reading Pictures, 1997; (contrib.) Hensparrow Turns Purple, 1998; (co-author) Trash!: On Ragpicker Children and Recycling, 1999; (with S. Khanna and A. Ravishankar) Toys and Tales with Everyday Materials, 1999; (with S. Rao) Tree Girl, 2001; (comp.with S. Rao and V. Geetha) Ideal boy, 2001; (with S. Rao and E. Scanziani) Legend of the Fish, 2003; (with V. Geetha and A. Ravishankar) Masks and Performance with Everyday Materials, 2003; (ed. with K. Arni) Beasts of India, 2003; (with S. Rao and B. Shyam) London Jungle Book, 2004; (co-author) Puppets Unlimited: With Everyday Materials, 2005; (with L. Andradis) SSSS: Snake Art & Allegory, 2010; (ed. with B. Shyam and J. Yamakami) Signature, 2010; (contrib.) Flight of The Mermaid, 2010; (contrib.) Monkey Photo, 2010. **Address:** Tara Publishing House, 38/GA Shoreham, Besant Nagar 5th Ave., Besant Nagar, Chennai, TN 600090, India. **Online address:** helmut@giasmd01.vsnl.net.in

WOLF, J.M. See **WOLF, Joan M.**

WOLF, Joan M. (J.M. Wolf). American (born United States), b. 1966?. **Genres:** Novels, Young Adult Fiction, Reference, Children's Fiction. **Career:** Writer. **Publications:** The Beanstalk and Beyond: Developing Critical Thinking through Fairy Tales, 1997; Someone Named Eva, 2007. AS J.M. WOLF: Cinderella Outgrows the Glass Slipper, and Other Zany Fractured Fairy-Tale Plays, 2002; Journal Activities That Sharpen Students' Writing, 2005; Leveled Read-Aloud Plays: U.S. Civil Holidays, 2007. **Address:** Scholastic Inc., 557 Broadway, New York, NY 10012, U.S.A. **Online address:** joan@joanmwolf.com

WOLF, Kenneth Baxter. American (born United States), b. 1957. **Genres:** Theology/Religion, History. **Career:** Whiting fellow in the humanities, 1983-84; Stanford University, lecturer in history, 1984-85; Pomona College, visiting assistant professor, 1985-86, Department of History, assistant professor, 1986-93, associate professor, 1993-2001, chair, 1995-98, professor, 2001-, John Sutton Miner professor of history, 2006-, associate dean of the college, 2006-09, faculty of history and classics, 2011-; Princeton Institute for Advanced Study, fellow, 1989-91; National Endowment for the Humanities, fellow, 2004-05. Academic, historian and writer. **Publications:** Christian Martyrs in Muslim Spain, 1988; (trans. and intro.) Conquerors and Chroniclers of Early Medieval Spain, 1990; Making History: The Normans and Their Historians in Eleventh-Century Italy, 1995; The Poverty of Riches: St. Francis of Assisi Reconsidered, 2003; (trans.) Geoffrey Malaterra, The Deeds of Count Roger of Calabria and Sicily and of His Brother Duke Robert Guiscard, 2005; (trans. and intro.) Life and Afterlife of St. Elizabeth of Hungary: Testimony From Her Canonization Hearings, 2011. Contributor to periodicals and journals. **Address:** Department of History, Pomona College, 008 Pearsons Hall, 551 N College Way, Claremont, CA 91711, U.S.A. **Online address:** kwolf@pomona.edu

WOLF, Kirsten. American/Danish (born Denmark), b. 1959. **Genres:** Novellas/Short Stories, Translations, Area Studies. **Career:** University of Wisconsin, Department of Scandinavian Studies, lecturer, 1986-87, professor of Scandinavian studies, 2001-, Torger Thompson Chair; University of Copenhagen, Arnamagnaean Dictionary, editor, 1987-88; University of Manitoba, Department of Icelandic Language and Literature, associate professor, professor, chair, 1988-2001. **Publications:** An Annotated Bibliography of North American Doctoral Dissertations on Old Norse Icelandic, 1998; Daily Life of the Vikings, 2004. TRANSLATOR: (with Á. Hjaltadóttir) Western Icelandic Short Stories, 1992; (with J. Jensen) A. Olrik, Some Principles for Oral Narrative Research, 1992. EDITOR: (co-ed.) Medieval Scandinavia: An Encyclopedia, 1993; Gydinga Saga, 1995; (and trans.) Writings by Western Icelandic Women, 1996; The Icelandic Legend of Saint Dorothy, 1997; The Old Norse-Icelandic Legend of Saint Barbara, 2000; Saga Heilagrar Onnu, 2001; (with A.N. Doane) Beatus Vir: Studies in Early English and Norse Manuscripts: In Memory of Phillip Pulsiano, 2006. **Address:** Department of Scandinavian Studies, University of Wisconsin, 1370 Van Hise Hall, 1220 Linden Dr., Madison, WI 53706, U.S.A. **Online address:** kirstenwolf@wisc.edu

WOLF, Margery. American (born United States), b. 1933. **Genres:** Anthropology/Ethnology, Area Studies, Young Adult Non-fiction, Sociology. **Career:** Lewis Henry Morgan lecturer, 1983; Duke University, visiting associate professor, 1984-85; University of Iowa, professor of anthropology, 1985, now professor emeritus; Rockefeller Residency Program in the Humanities, principal investigator, 1987-93. Anthropologist and writer. **Publications:** The House of Lim: A Study of a Chinese Farm Family, 1968; Women and the Family in Rural Taiwan, 1972; (ed. with R. Witke) Women in Chinese Society, 1975; Revolution Postponed: Women in Contemporary China, 1985; A Thrice Told Tale: Feminism, Postmodernism and Ethnographic Responsibility, 1992. **Address:** Department of Anthropology, University of Iowa, 114 MacBride Hall, Iowa City, IA 52242-1322, U.S.A. **Online address:** margeryw@sonic.net

WOLF, Maryanne. American (born United States), b. 1947. **Genres:** Language/Linguistics, Art/Art History. **Career:** The Childrens Hospital Medical Center, clinic intern, 1978; Veterans Administration Medical Center, Aphasia Research Center, naming group research associate, 1978-84; Harvard University, instructor, 1978-79, Harvard Institute of Reading, Language and Learning Disorders, director, 1980-81, Harvard Medical School, Livingston fellow, 1979, research scientist, 1992-; Brandeis University, assistant professor of psychology, 1979-80; Tufts University, Eliot-Pearson Department of Child Development, assistant professor of child study, 1980-86, associate professor, 1987-98, professor of child development, 1999-, John DiBiaggio professor of citizenship and public service, 2006-, Center for Reading and Language Research, director, 1996-, adjunct faculty, 2006-, Tisch Fellow, 2006-08. Writer. **Publications:** (Ed. with M.K. McQuillan and E. Radwin) Thought and Language/Language and Reading, 1980, 2nd ed., 1983; (ed. and contrib.) Dyslexia, Fluency, and the Brain, 2001; (with M. Denckla) Rapid Automatized Naming and Rapid Alternating Stimulus Tests, 2005; Proust and the Squid: The Story and Science of the Reading Brain, 2007. Contributor to books and periodicals. **Address:** Department of Child Development, Tufts University, 105 College Ave., Medford, MA 02155, U.S.A. **Online address:** maryanne.wolf@tufts.edu

WOLF, Reva. American (born United States), b. 1956. **Genres:** Art/Art History, Humanities, Intellectual History, Literary Criticism And History, Film. **Career:** Art historian; Boston College, assistant professor of fine art, 1988-95; State University of New York, assistant professor of art history, 1996-99, associate professor of art history, 1999-2008, professor of art history, 2008-; Harvard University, Andrew W. Mellon junior faculty fellow in the humanities, 1990-91; Institute for Advanced Study, fellow, 1995-96. Writer. **Publications:** Essay in Fatal Consequences: Callot, Goya and the Horrors of War, 1990; Goya and the Satirical Print in England and on the Continent, 1730 to 1850, 1991; Essay in Goya: Neue Forschungen, 1994; Andy Warhol, Poetry and Gossip in the 1960s, 1997; Essay in Andy Warhol Photography, 1999; (contrib.) Essay in Goya's Realism, 2000; Essay in Experimental Cinema: The Film Reader, 2002; Essay in Andy Warhol, Work and Play, 2003; (intro.) I'll Be Your Mirror: The Collected Andy Warhol Interviews, 2004; The Scholar and the Fan in What Is Research in the Visual Arts, 2008; (ed.) Andy Warhol: Private and Public in 151 Photographs, 2010; Goya's Red Boy, in Art in Spain and the Hispanic World: Essays in Honor of Jonathan Brown, 2010; (co-author) The Spanish Manner Drawings from Ribera to Goya, 2010. Contributor to journals. **Address:** Department of Art History, State University of New York, 1 Hawk Dr., SAB 108G, New Paltz, NY 12561, U.S.A. **Online address:** wolfr@newpaltz.edu

WOLF, Sarah (Elizabeth). Also writes as S. K. Wolf, Sarah Shoemaker. American (born United States), b. 1936. **Genres:** Novels, Mystery/Crime/Suspense, Administration/Management, Adult Non-fiction. **Career:** High school teacher, 1961-62, 1964-65; University of Michigan, librarian, 1983-87; writer, 1987-. **Publications:** NOVELS: Long Chain of Death, 1987; (as S.K. Wolf) The Harbinger Effect, 1989; (as S.K. Wolf) MacKinnon's Machine, 1991; Ingrained Memories, 2000. EDITOR: (as Sarah Shoemaker) Collection Management: Current Issues, 1989. OTHER: Unterseeische rohrleitungen und meeresumweltschutz, 2011. **Address:** Jean V. Naggar Literary Agency Inc., 216 E 75th St., Ste 1E, New York, NY 10021, U.S.A.

WOLF, S. K. *See* **WOLF, Sarah (Elizabeth).**

WOLFE, Alan (Stephen). American (born United States), b. 1942. **Genres:** Sociology, Politics/Government, Philosophy, History. **Career:** Rutgers University, assistant professor of political science, 1966-68; State University of New York, College at Old Westbury, assistant professor of political science, 1968-70; City University of New York, Richmond College, assistant professor, associate professor of sociology, 1970-78; University of California, visiting associate professor, 1978-80; Queens College, associate professor, professor of sociology, 1979-89; University of Aarhus, visiting professor, 1987-88; Columbia University, Department of Sociology, adjunct professor, 1989; New School for Social Research, dean of graduate faculty of political and social science, 1991-93, Michael E. Gellert professor of sociology and political science, 1991-93; Boston University, university professor and professor of sociology and political science, 1993-99; Boston College, Boisi Center for Religion and American Public Life, director, 1999-, professor of political science, 1999-. Writer. **Publications:** (Ed. with M. Surkin) An End to Political Science, 1970; (with C.A. McCoy) Political Analysis: An Unorthodox Approach, 1972; The Seamy Side of Democracy: Repression in America, 1973, 2nd ed., 1978; The Limits of Legitimacy, 1977; The Rise and Fall of the Soviet Threat: Domestic Sources of the Cold War Consensus, 1979; (co-author) A Questão da Democracia, 1980; America's Impasse: The Rise and Fall of the Politics of Growth, 1981; Whose Keeper?: Social Science and Moral Obligation, 1989; (ed.) America at Century's End, 1991; The Human Difference: Animals, Computers, and the Necessity of Social Science, 1993; Marginalized in the Middle, 1996; One Nation, After All: What Middle-Class Americans Really Think about: God, Country, Family, Racism, Welfare, Immigration, Homosexuality, Work, the Right, the Left, and Each Other, 1998; Moral Freedom: The Impossible Idea that Defines the Way We Live Now, 2001; (ed.) School Choice: The Moral Debate, 2003, An Intellectual in Public, 2003; The Transformation of American Religion, 2003; The Free Press, 2003; Return to Greatness: How America Lost Its Sense of Purpose and What it Needs to Do to Recover It, 2005; Does American Democracy Still Work?, 2006; (with J.D. Hunter) Is there a Culture War?: A Dialogue on Values and American Public Life, 2006; (contrib.) Christianity and American Democracy, 2007; (ed. with E.C. Owens) Gambling: Mapping the American Moral Landscape, 2009; Future of Liberalism, 2009; Political Evil: What It Is and How To Combat It, 2010; (ed. with I. Katznelson) Religion and Democracy in the United States, 2010. **Address:** Boisi Center for Religion and American Public Life, Boston College, 24 Quincy Rd., Chestnut Hill, MA 02467,

U.S.A. **Online address:** wolfe@bc.edu

WOLFE, Art. American (born United States), b. 1952. **Genres:** Natural History, Photography, Travel/Exploration. **Career:** Photographer, painter and writer. **Publications:** The Imagery of Art Wolfe (monograph), 1985; The Sierra Club Alaska Postcard Collection: A Portfolio, 1989; Light on the Land, 1991; The Art of Nature Photography, 1993; (with M. Gardner) Photography Outdoors: A Field Guide for Travel & Adventure Photographers, 1995, 2nd ed., 2002; (with D. Skillman) Tribes, 1997; Rhythms from the Wild, 1997; The Living Wild, 2000; (with G. Jecan) Colorado, 2000; Alaska, 2000; The High Himalaya, 2001; California, 2001; Africa, 2001; Northwest Wild: Celebrating our Natural Heritage, 2004; Alaska Wild: Celebrating Our Natural Heritage, 2004; The Elements: Earth, Air, Fire, Water, 2004; Vanishing Act, 2005; Seven Summits: the High Peaks of the Pacific Northwest, 2005; (with P. Kramer) On Puget Sound, 2007; Inside Passage to Alaska, 2008; Travels to the Edge, 2009. Contributor to periodicals. **Address:** Art Wolfe Inc., 1944 1st Ave. S, Seattle, WA 98134, U.S.A. **Online address:** info@artwolfe.com

WOLFE, Barbara (Lea). American (born United States), b. 1943. **Genres:** Economics, Education, Medicine/Health, Mathematics/Statistics, Social Sciences. **Career:** University of Pennsylvania, instructor in economics, 1970-72; Federal Reserve Bank of Philadelphia, economic consultant, 1972-76; Bryn Mawr College, Department of Economics, assistant professor of economics, 1973-76; University of Wisconsin, Institute for Research on Poverty, research associate, 1976-77, research affiliate, 1977-, director, 1994-2000, Department of Economics, assistant professor, 1977-81, associate professor, 1981-87, professor of economics and population health sciences, 1987-, vice-chair, 2001-04, Department of Population Health Sciences, assistant professor, 1977-81, associate professor, 1981-87, Office of the Vice Chancellor for the Health Sciences, senior staff associate, 1982-91, Robert M. La Follette School of Public Affairs, professor, 1990-, director, 2006-08, Center for Health Policy and Program Evaluation, executive chairperson, 1985-92; National Bureau of Economic Research, research associate, 1987-; Wisconsin Consortium for Health Services Research, facilitator, 1988-93; Netherlands Institute for Advanced Study, fellow-in-residence, 1984-85, 1996-97; Australia National University, adjunct professor, 2002-12. Writer. **Publications:** (With M.R. Olneck) Intelligence and Family Size: Another Look, 1977; (with J.R. Behrman and J. Flesher) A Monte Carlo Study of Alternative Approaches for Dealing with Randomly Missing Data, 1979; Earnings Lost and Income Gained: The Equity and Adequacy of Transfers to the Disabled: Or, How Well Do the Disabled Fare?, 1980; (with R.H. Haveman and J. Warlick) Behavioral Responses to Social Security Retrenchment, 1985; Health Care Expenditures for the Elderly: Are Prospective Payment Systems and Community Care the Paths to Cost Reduction?, 1985; Health Status and Medical Expenditures: Is There a Link?, 1985; (ed. with H.M. van de Kar) Relevance of Public Finance for Policy-Making: De la Pertinence Des Finances Publiques Dans L'élaboration Des Politiques économiques: Proceedings of the 41st Congress of the International Institute of Public Finance, Madrid, Spain, 1985, 1987; (with R. Haveman) Succeeding Generations, 1994; (co-author) Making Schools Work, 1994; (ed. with L. Wu) Out of Wedlock: Causes and Consequences of Nonmarital Fertility, 2001. Contributor of articles to books and periodicals. **Address:** Department of Economics, University of Wisconsin, 7424 William H. Sewell Social Science Bldg., 1180 Observatory Dr., Madison, WI 53706-1393, U.S.A. **Online address:** wolfe@lafollette.wisc.edu

WOLFE, Gene (Rodman). American (born United States), b. 1931. **Genres:** Novels, Mystery/Crime/Suspense, Science Fiction/Fantasy, Children's Fiction, Poetry, Young Adult Fiction, Novellas/Short Stories. **Career:** Periodical Plant Engineering, editor; Procter and Gamble, project engineer, 1956-72; Plant Engineering Magazine, senior editor, 1972-84; writer, 1984-. **Publications:** Operation ARES, 1970; The Fifth Head of Cerberus (SF short stories), 1972; Peace (novel), 1975; (with U.K. Le Guin and J. Tiptree, Jr.) The New Atlantis and Other Novellas of Science Fiction, 1975; (with R.A. Lafferty and W. Moudy) In the Wake of Man: A Science Fiction Triad, 1975; The Devil in a Forest (juvenile novel), 1976; The Island of Doctor Death and Other Stories and Other Stories, 1980; The Shadow of the Torturer, 1980; The Claw of the Conciliator, 1981; Gene Wolfe's Book of Days (short stories), 1981; The Sword of the Lictor, 1981; The Citadel of the Autarch, 1984; Free Live Free, 1984; Soldier of the Mist, 1986; Empires of Foliage and Flower, 1987; The Urth of the New Sun, 1987; There Are Doors, 1988; Storeys from the Old Hotel, 1988; For Rosemary (poetry), 1988; Endangered Species, 1989; Soldier of Arete, 1989; Pandora by Holly Hollander (mystery), 1990; Letters Home, 1991; Castle of Days, 1992; Young Wolfe (early stories), 1992; Nightside the

Long Sun, 1993; Lake of the Long Sun, 1994; Shadow & Claw, 1994; Sword & Citadel, 1994; Caldé of the Long Sun, 1994; Peace, 1995; Storeys from the Old Hotel, 1995; Exodus from the Long Sun, 1996; Devil in a Forest, 1996; Urth of the New Sun, 1997; Free Live Free, 1999; On Blue's Waters, 1999; Strange Travelers, 2000; In Green's Jungles, 2000; Return to the Whorl, 2001; (with N. Gaiman) A Walking Tour of the Shambles, 2002; Latro in the Mist, 2003; Innocents Aboard: New Fantasy Stories, 2004; Knight, 2004; Wizard, 2004; The Wizard Knight, 2005; Starwater Strains, 2005; Soldier of Sidon, 2006; Pirate Freedom, 2007; Evil Guest, 2008; The Very Best of Gene Wolfe: A Definitive Retrospective of his Finest Short Fiction, 2009; The Very Best of Gene Wolfe: A Definitive Retrospective of His Finest Short Fiction Sorcerer's House, 2010; Home Fires, 2011. **Address:** PO Box 69, Barrington, IL 60011, U.S.A.

WOLFE, George C. American (born United States), b. 1954. **Genres:** Plays/Screenplays, Songs/Lyrics And Libretti, Art/Art History. **Career:** Playwright, actor, director, 1978-; Joseph Papp Public Theater, producer, 1993-, trustee and director, 2004-; New York Shakespeare Festival/Public Theater, artistic director and producer, 1993-2004; Center for Civil & Human Rights, chief executive officer; Inner City Cultural Center, executive director. **Publications:** The Colored Museum, 1988; Jelly's Last Jam, 1991; Blackout, 1991; (adapted) Spunk: Three Tales, 1992, rev. ed., 2000. **Address:** New York Shakespeare Festival, 425 Lafayette St., New York, NY 10003, U.S.A.

WOLFE, Linda. American (born United States), b. 1935. **Genres:** Novels, Criminology/True Crime, History, Sex, Horror. **Career:** Oxford University Press, editorial assistant, 1958-59; Partisan Review, editorial assistant, 1959-60; Time-Life, researcher and writer, 1960-71; New York, contributing editor, 1971-. **Publications:** Literary Gourmet: The Pleasure of Reading about Wonderful Food in Scenes from Great Literature, the Delight of Savoring it in the Recipes of Master Chefs and All Seasoned with Anecdotes and Little Known Facts about the Art of Cooking, 1962; The Cooking of the Caribbean Islands, 1970; Playing Around: Women and Extramarital Sex, 1975; Private Practices (novel), 1979; The Cosmo Report: An In-Depth Landmark Work Revealing the Sexual Behavior of 106,000 Cosmopolitan Readers, 1981; Literary Gourmet: Menus From Masterpieces, 1985; The Professor and the Prostitute and Other True Tales of Murder and Madness, 1986; Wasted: The Preppie Murder, 1989; Double Life: The Shattering Affair between Chief Judge Sol Wachtler and Socialite Joy Silverman, 1994; Love Me to Death, 1998; The Murder of Dr. Chapman: The Legendary Trials of Lucretia Chapman and Her Lover, 2004; Kinsey: Public and Private, 2004; Sano y salvo/ Healthy and Alive: Primeros Auxilios Y Tratamientos De Urgencia Para Ninos Y Adolescentes, 2007. EDITOR: McCall's Introduction to Scandinavian Cooking, 1971; McCall's Introduction to Mexican Cooking, 1971; McCall's Introduction to German Cooking, 1972; McCall's Introduction to British Cooking, 1972. Contributors to periodicals. **Address:** c/o Irene Skolnick, Irene Skolnick Literary Agency, 2095 Broadway, Ste. 307, New York, NY 10023, U.S.A. **Online address:** wolfelinda@aol.com

WOLFE, Peter. American (born United States), b. 1933. **Genres:** Literary Criticism And History, Essays, Adult Non-fiction. **Career:** University of Nebraska, assistant professor of English, 1964-67; University of Missouri, Department of English, assistant professor, 1967-68, associate professor, 1968-76, professor, 1976-2000, curator's professor of English, 2000-; University of Windsor, visiting professor, 1971; University of California, visiting professor, 1975; University of Waikato, visiting professor, 1980; University of Queensland, visiting professor, 1980; National Taiwan Normal University, visiting professor, 1982; Moscow State University, visiting professor, 1984; Catholic University of Lublin, visiting professor, 1991; University of Sczcecin, visiting professor, 1992; Flinders University, visiting professor, 1995. Writer. **Publications:** The Disciplined Heart: Iris Murdoch and Her Novels, 1966; Mary Renault, 1969; Rebecca West: Artist and Thinker, 1971; Graham Greene: The Entertainer, 1972; John Fowles: Magus and Moralist, 1976, 2nd ed., 1979; Dreamers Who Live Their Dreams: The Novels of Ross Macdonald, 1976; Beams Falling: The Art of Dashiell Hammett, 1980; Jean Rhys, 1980; Laden Choirs: The Fiction of Patrick White, 1983; Something More Than Night: The Case of Raymond Chandler, 1985; (ed.) Essays in Graham Greene, 1987; Corridors of Deceit: The World of John le Carré, 1987; Yukio Mishima, 1989; (comp.) Critical Essays on Patrick White, 1990; Alarms and Epitaphs: The Art of Eric Ambler, 1993; In the Zone: The Twilight World of Rod Serling, 1997; A Vision of His Own: The Mind and Art of William Gaddis, 1997; Understanding Alan Bennett, 1999; August Wilson, 1999; Understanding Penelope Fitzgerald, 2004; Like Hot Knives to the Brain: James

Ellroy's Search for Himself, 2005; Havoc in the Hub: A Reading of George V. Higgins, 2007; Simon Gray Unbound: The Journey of a Dramatist, 2011. **Address:** Department of English, University of Missouri, 465 Lucas Hall, 1 University Blvd., St. Louis, MO 63121-4400, U.S.A. **Online address:** spwolfe@umsl.edu

WOLFE, Tom. American (born United States), b. 1931. **Genres:** Novels, Social Commentary, Documentaries/Reportage, Illustrations, Theology/Religion, Young Adult Non-fiction, Novellas/Short Stories, Young Adult Fiction, Young Adult Fiction, Adult Non-fiction. **Career:** Springfield Union, reporter, 1956-59; Washington Post, reporter, Latin American correspondent, 1960-62; New York Herald Tribune, reporter, New York Sunday Magazine (now New York magazine), writer, 1962-66, contributing editor, 1968-76; New York World Journal Tribune, writer, 1966-67; Esquire Magazine, contributing editor, 1977-; Harper's Magazine, contributing artist, 1978-81. **Publications:** SELF-ILLUSTRATED: Mauve Gloves and Madmen, Clutter and Vine, and Other Stories, Sketches, and Essays, 1976. OTHERS: (co-author) New York Herald Tribune Presents New York, New York, 1964; The Kandy-Kolored Tangerine-Flake Streamline Baby, 1965; The New York Spy, 1967; The Pump House Gang, 1968 as The Mid-Atlantic Man and Other New Breeds in England and America, 1969; The Electric Kool-Aid Acid Test, 1968; Radical Chic and Mau-Mauing the Flak Catchers, 1970; (ed. with E.W. Johnson) The New Journalism, 1973; The Painted Word, 1975; (contrib.) Marie Cosindas, Color Photographs, 1978; The Right Stuff, 1979, new ed., 1983; In Our Time, 1980; From Bauhaus to Our House, 1981; The Purple Decades: A Reader, 1982; The Bonfire of the Vanities, 1987; Two Complete Books, 1994; Caricatures in Clay, 1994; A Man in Full: A Novel, 1998; Hooking Up, 2000; I am Charlotte Simmons, 2004; Carving Down-Home Angels with Tom Wolfe, 2005; Carving Santas for Today with Tom Wolfe, 2008; Carving Bottle Stoppers with Tom Wolfe, 2009; Back to Blood, 2012. Contributor of articles to periodicals. **Address:** Farrar, Straus & Giroux, 19 Union Sq. W, New York, NY 10003-3304, U.S.A.

WOLFER, Dianne. Australian (born Australia), b. 1961. **Genres:** Novels, Novellas/Short Stories, Children's Fiction, Young Adult Fiction, Plays/Screenplays, Picture/Board Books, Animals/Pets. **Career:** Western Australian Education Department, teacher, 1984-87, 1991-92; Japan International School and American School, teacher, 1987-90; TAFE Intl., lecturer to adults; Western Australia for Society of Children's Book Writers and Illustrators, advisor. Writer. **Publications:** FOR YOUNG ADULTS: Dolphin Song, 1995; Border Line, 1998; Choices, 2001. CHAPTER BOOKS: Butterfly Notes, 2002; Iron Kid, 2003; Being Billy, 2003; Scuba Kid, 2004; Jungle Trek, 2004; Village Rules!, 2004. OTHERS: Photographs in the Mud (picturebook), 2004; Horse-Mad, 2005; The Kid Whose Mum Kept Possums In Her Bra, 2006; Lighthouse Girl, 2009. Contributor to magazines. **Address:** 1/7 Finlay St., Albany, WA 6330, Australia. **Online address:** dianne@westnet.com.au

WOLFERMAN, Kristie C(arlson). American (born United States), b. 1948. **Genres:** Young Adult Non-fiction, Women's Studies And Issues, Adult Non-fiction, History. **Career:** Petit Appetit Cooking School for Young Cooks, founder and co-director, 1980-86; Pembroke Hill School, elementary teacher, 1986-96, teacher, 1994-96, middle school teacher, 1996-. Writer. **Publications:** (With M.D. Beachy) When Peanut Butter Is Not Enough, 1986; The Nelson-Atkins Museum of Art: Culture Comes to Kansas City, 1993; The Osage in Missouri, 1997; The Indomitable Mary Easton Sibley: Pioneer of Women's Education in Missouri, 2008. **Address:** 1005 Brentwood Cir., Kansas City, MO 64112, U.S.A.

WOLFERS, Michael. British (born England), b. 1938. **Genres:** Race Relations, Biography, International Relations/Current Affairs, Translations. **Career:** Times Newspapers Ltd., Africa correspondent, 1965-72; free-lance writer, 1972-; University of Juba, visiting senior lecturer in African politics and government, 1979-82; South West Africa People's Organization, consultant. **Publications:** The Black Man's Burden Revisited, 1974; Politics in the Organization of African Unity, 1976; (with J. Bergerol) Angola in the Frontline, 1983; Hamlet and Cybernetics, 1991; (ed. with E. Hodgkin) Thomas Hodgkin: Letters from Africa, 1947-56, 2000; Thomas Hodgkin: Wandering Scholar, 2007. TRANSLATOR: J.L. Vieira, The Real Life of Domingos Xavier, 1978; A. Cabral, Unity and Struggle, 1979; (ed. and intro.) Poems from Angola, 1979; Pepetela, Mayombe, 1982; S. Machel, An African Revolutionary, 1985; C. Lopes, Guinea Bissau: From Liberation Struggle to Independent Statehood, 1987; S. Machel, An African Revolutionary: Selected Speeches and Writings, 1987; L. Magaia, Dumba Nengue: Run for Your Life, 1988; S. Amin, Delinking: Towards a Polycentric World, 1990; S. Amin, Maldevelopment: Anatomy of a Global Failure, 1990; S. Amin, Re-Reading the Postwar Period, 1994. **Address:** 66 Roupell St., London, GL SE1 8SS, England. **Online address:** mwolfers@dircon.co.uk

WOLFF, Craig (Thomas). American (born United States) **Genres:** Biography, Sports/Fitness, Autobiography/Memoirs. **Career:** New York Times, reporter, 1983-94; Columbia University School of Journalism, assistant professor, 2003-05, professor; New York University, Department of Journalism, clinical associate professor, 2005-. Writer. **Publications:** Tennis Superstars: The Men, 1980; Wayne Gretzky: Portrait of a Hockey Player, 1983; Outrage: The Story behind the Tawana Brawley Hoax, 1990; My Heart Will Cross This Ocean: My Story, My Son, Amadou, 2003; Mays, forthcoming. Contributor to periodicals. **Address:** Department of Journalism, New York University, Arthur Carter Hall, 10 Washington Pl., New York, NY 10003, U.S.A. **Online address:** cw54@nyu.edu

WOLFF, Cynthia Griffin. American (born United States), b. 1936. **Genres:** Novellas/Short Stories, Literary Criticism And History, Biography, Women's Studies And Issues, Humanities. **Career:** Boston University, part-time instructor, 1961-62, instructor, 1963-64; Illinois Institute of Technology, part-time instructor, 1962-63; City University of New York, Queens College, instructor, 1965-68; Manhattanville College, assistant professor of English, 1968-71; University of Massachusetts, assistant professor, 1971-74, associate professor, 1974-76, professor of English, 1976-80; Massachusetts Institute of Technology, professor of humanities, 1980-85, professor of humanities, 1985-2003, emeritus professor of literature, 2003-. Writer. **Publications:** Samuel Richardson and the Eighteenth-Century Puritan Character, 1972; A Feast of Words: The Triumph of Edith Wharton, 1977, 2nd ed., 1995; Emily Dickinson, 1986. EDITOR: Other Lives, 1973; (and intro.) Classic American Women Writers: Sarah Orne Jewett, Kate Chopin, Edith Wharton, Willa Cather, 1980; The House of Mirth, 1985; (and intro.) Four Stories by American Women, 1990; (with K.O. Lauer) Ehan Frome: Authoritative Text, Backgrounds and Contexts, Criticism, 1995; (and intro.) The Age of Innocence, 1996. Contributor to journals. **Address:** Massachusetts Institute of Technology, 77 Massachusetts Ave., Cambridge, MA 02139-4307, U.S.A.

WOLFF, Edward N(athan). American (born United States), b. 1946. **Genres:** Economics. **Career:** New York University, assistant professor, 1974-79, associate professor, 1979-84, professor of economics, 1984-, Institute for Economic Analysis, director, 1998-2001; National Bureau of Economic Research, research associate, 1974-77, 2001-; Review of Income and Wealth, managing editor, 1987-2004. **Publications:** Social Security, Pensions, and the Wealth Holdings of the Poor, 1985; Growth, Accumulation, and Unproductive Activity, 1987; (with W. Baumol and S.A.B. Blackman) Productivity and American Leadership, 1989; (with W. Baumol and L. Osberg) The Information Economy, 1989; (with D. Dollar) Competitiveness, Convergence, and International Specialization, 1993; Top Heavy: A Study of the Increasing Inequality of Wealth in America, 1994; Economics of Poverty, Inequality, and Discrimination, 1997; Retirement Insecurity, 2002; (with W.J. Baumol and A.S. Blinder) Downsizing in America, 2003; (with A. Zacharias and A. Caner) Levy Institute Measure of Economic Well-Being: Concept, Measurement, and Findings: United States, 1989 and 2000, 2004; (with A. Zacharias and A. Caner) Levy Institute Measure of Economic Well-Being: United States, 1989, 1995, 2000, and 2001, 2004; (with A. Zacharias and A. Caner) Levy Institute Measure of Economic Well-Being: How Much does Public Consumption Matter for Well-Being?, 2004; Does Education Really Help?: Skill, Work, and Inequality, 2006; Poverty and Income Distribution, 2009. EDITOR: International Comparisons of the Distribution of Household Wealth, 1987; (with F. Moseley) International Perspectives on Profitability and Accumulation, 1992; (with D.B. Papadimitriou) Poverty and Prosperity in the USA in the Late Twentieth Century, 1993; Research in Economic Inequality, 1993; (with W.J. Baumol and R.R. Nelson) Convergence of Productivity, 1994; The Economics of Productivity, 1997; (with T.M. Shapiro) Assets of the Poor, 2001; What Has Happened to the Quality of Life in the Advanced Industrialized Nations?, 2004; International Perspectives on Household Wealth, 2006. **Address:** Department of Economics, New York University, 19 W 4th St., 6th Fl., New York, NY 10012, U.S.A. **Online address:** edward.wolff@nyu.edu

WOLFF, Geoffrey. American (born United States), b. 1937. **Genres:** Novels, Biography, Young Adult Fiction, Literary Criticism And History. **Career:** Robert College, lecturer in literature, 1961-63; Istanbul University, lecturer

in American literature and chairman, 1962-63; The Washington Post, book critic, 1964-69; Maryland Institute, College of Art, lecturer in aesthetics, 1965-69; Corcoran School of Art, lecturer, 1968-69; Newsweek, literary critic, 1969-71; Princeton University, resident writer, 1970-74; New Times, literary editor, 1974-79; Middlebury College, lecturer, 1976, adjunct associate professor, 1977-78; Washington University, Fannie Hurst visiting lecturer, 1978; Columbia University, graduate writing program, William Jovonovich lecturer in fiction, 1979; Esquire Magazine, contributor editor, 1979-82; Princeton University, Ferris professor, 1980, 1992; Brown University, lecturer, 1981, 1988; Warren Wilson College, program for writers, trustee, 1981-84; Brandeis University, writer-in-residence, 1982-94; Boston University, Graduate Writing Program, visiting professor, 1982; University of California, program in writing, director, 1995-2006, professor of English, now professor emeritus. **Publications:** Bad Debts, 1969; The Sightseer, 1974; Black Sun: The Brief Transit and Violent Eclipse of Harry Crosby (biography), 1976; Inklings, 1977; The Duke of Deception, 1979; (ed. and intro.) Edward Hoagland Reader, 1979; Providence, 1985; (ed. with R. Atwan) Best American Essays 1989, 1989; The Final Club, 1990; A Day at the Beach: Recollections, 1992; The Age of Consent, 1995, The Art of Burning Bridges: A Life of John O'Hara, 2003, The Edge of Maine, 2005; Hard Way Around: The Passages of Joshua Slocum, 2010; Two Faces, forthcoming. **Address:** Department of English, University of California, 435 Humanities Instructional Bldg., MC 2650, Irvine, CA 92697-2650, U.S.A. **Online address:** gwolff@uci.edu

WOLFF, Jonathan. British (born England), b. 1959. **Genres:** Young Adult Non-fiction. **Career:** Prudential Assurance, Legal Department, faculty; University College London, lecturer, 1986-94, senior lecturer, 1994-96, reader, 1996-2000, professor of philosophy, 2000-, head of department, 1997-, School of Advanced Study, founding director of philosophy program, 1995-98, Centre for Philosophy, Justice and Health, director, 2008-; Guardian, columnist, 2005-09. Writer. **Publications:** NONFICTION: Robert Nozick: Property, Justice and the Minimal State, 1991; An Introduction to Political Philosophy, 1996, rev. ed., 2006; (ed. with M. Rosen) Political Thought, 1999; (ed. with M.W.F. Stone and intro.) The Proper Ambition of Science, 2000; Why Read Marx Today?, 2003; (with A. de Shalit) Disadvantage, 2007; (ed. with M. Hannam) Southern Africa, 2020 Vision: Public Policy Priorities for the Next Decade, 2010; Ethics and Public Policy: A Philosophical Inquiry, 2011; Human Right to Health, 2012. Contributor to books. **Address:** Department of Philosophy, University College London, Gower St., London, GL WC1E 6B, England. **Online address:** j.wolff@ucl.ac.uk

WOLFF, Justin. American (born United States), b. 1969. **Genres:** Biography. **Career:** San Diego Reader, staff writer and columnist, 1999-2002; Providence Phoenix, staff writer, 1999; Harvard University, preceptor in expository writing, 2002-06; National Endowment for the Humanities, fellow, 2005; Roanoke College, Joanne Leonhardt Cassullo assistant professor of art history, 2006-. **Publications:** Richard Caton Woodville: American Painter, Artful Dodger, 2002. **Address:** Roanoke College, 221 College Ln., Salem, VA 24153, U.S.A. **Online address:** jwolff@fas.harvard.edu

WOLFF, Robert P(aul). American (born United States), b. 1933. **Genres:** Education, Philosophy, Politics/Government, Social Commentary, Young Adult Non-fiction. **Career:** Harvard University, instructor in philosophy and social science, 1958-61; University of Chicago, assistant professor of philosophy, 1961-63; Wellesley College, visiting lecturer in philosophy, 1963-64; Columbia University, associate professor, 1964-71, professor of philosophy, 1971-81; Rutgers University, visiting professor, 1967-68; University of Wisconsin, Matchette Lecturer, 1969; University of Massachusetts, professor, 1971-92, professor of Afro-American studies, 1992-2008, professor emeritus, 2008-; Vanderbilt University, Raphael P. Demos memorial lecturer, 1974; Goethe Institute of Boston, Kant memorial lecturer, 1974; Trent University, Gilbert Ryle memorial lecturer, 1980; Brandeis University, professor of philosophy, 1981-. Writer. **Publications:** Kant's Theory of Mental Activity, 1962; (with H. Marcuse and B. Moore) Critique of Pure Tolerance, 1965; The Poverty of Liberalism, 1968; The Ideal of the University, 1969; In Defence of Anarchism, 1970; The Autonomy of Reason, 1973; About Philosophy, 1976, 10th ed., 2009; Understanding Rawls, 1977; Understanding Marx, 1985; Moneybags Must Be So Lucky, 1988. EDITOR: Political Man and Social Man, 1965; Kant: A Collection of Critical Essays, 1967; Kant's Foundations: Text and Commentary, 1968; The Essential Hume, 1969; Ten Great Works of Philosophy, 1969; Philosophy: A Modern Encounter, 1971; The Rule of Law, 1971; Styles of Political Action in America, 1972; 1984 Revisited: Prospects for American Politics, 1973; Introductory Philosophy, 1979. **Address:** Department of Afro-American Studies, University of Massachusetts, Rm. 316, New Africa House, Amherst, MA 01003, U.S.A.

WOLFF, Ruth. American (born United States), b. 1932. **Genres:** Plays/Screenplays. **Career:** Playwright and screenwriter. **Publications:** PLAY: The Abdication, 2002. **Address:** Dramatic Publishing, 311 Washington St., Woodstock, IL 60098-3308, U.S.A.

WOLFF, Sally. American (born United States), b. 1954. **Genres:** Literary Criticism And History, Biography. **Career:** Emory University, assistant dean, 1989-97, associate dean, 1997-, Department of English, assistant vice president and adjunct professor. Writer. **Publications:** (With F.C. Watkins) Talking about William Faulkner, 1996; (ed. with N. Warren) Southern Mothers: Fact and Fictions in Motherhood in Southern Women's Writing, 1999; Ledgers of History: William Faulkner, an Almost Forgotten Friendship, and an Antebellum Plantation Diary, 2010. **Address:** Department of English, Emory University, 410-A Administration Bldg., N-302 Callaway Ctr., Atlanta, GA 30322, U.S.A. **Online address:** swolff@emory.edu

WOLFF, Theodore F. American (born United States), b. 1926. **Genres:** Art/Art History, Education, Young Adult Non-fiction. **Career:** Artist, 1950-; Christian Science Monitor, art critic, 1977-90. Writer. **Publications:** Enrico Donati: The Most Recent Work, 1984; The Many Masks of Modern Art, 1989; Morris Graves: Flower Paintings, 1994; Enrico Donati: Surrealism and Beyond, 1996; (with G. Geahigan) Art Criticism and Education, 1997; Joyce Treiman, 1997; John Steuart Curry, 1998; (contrib.) Morris Graves, the Early Works, 1998; (contrib.) Wildeworld: The Art of John Wilde, 1999; Jessie Benton Evans and Don Gray, 2004; (contrib.) Contrasts that Complement: Eileen Monaghan Whitaker & Frederic Whitaker, 2004. **Address:** PO Box 396, Planetarium Sta., New York, NY 10024, U.S.A.

WOLFF, Tobias (Jonathan Ansell). American (born United States), b. 1945. **Genres:** Novels, Novellas/Short Stories, Education. **Career:** Stanford University, Jones lecturer in creative writing, 1975-78, professor of English and creative writing, 1997-, Creative Writing Program, director, 2000-02, Ward W. and Priscilla B. Woods professor; Syracuse University, Peck professor of English, 1980-97. Writer. **Publications:** Ugly Rumors, 1975; In the Garden of the North American Martyrs: A Collection of Short Stories, 1981 in UK as Hunters in the Snow, 1982; (ed.) Matters of Life and Death: New American Stories, 1982; The Barracks Thief, 1984; Back in the World, 1985; (ed.) A Doctor's Visit: The Short Stories of Anton Chekhov, 1987; The Stories of Tobias Wolff, 1988; This Boy's Life: A Memoir, 1989; (ed.) The Picador Book of Contemporary American Stories, 1993; (ed. and intro.) The Vintage Book of Contemporary American Short Stories, 1994; In Pharaoh's Army: Memories of the Lost War, 1994; (ed.) Best American Short Stories, 1994; The Night in Question: Stories, 1996; (ed. and intro.) Writers Harvest 3, 2000; Old School, 2003; Our Story Begins: New and Selected Stories, 2008; (foreward) On Writing Short Stories, 2011. Contributors to periodicals. **Address:** Department of English, Stanford University, Rm. 218, Bldg. 460, Margaret Jacks Hall, Stanford, CA 94305-2087, U.S.A. **Online address:** twolff@stanford.edu

WOLFGANG, Kurt. American (born United States) **Genres:** Graphic Novels, Children's Fiction. **Career:** Noe Fie Monomedia, founder and editor. **Publications:** (Ed. and contrib.) LowJinx 2: Understanding Minicomics, 2000; (ed. and contrib.) LowJinx 3: The Big Rip-Off!, 2001; Where Hats Go, 2001. **Address:** 14 Allen Pl., Collinsville, CT 06022, U.S.A. **Online address:** noefiepub@aol.com

WOLFINGER, Raymond E(dwin). American (born United States), b. 1931. **Genres:** Politics/Government, Essays, History, Social Sciences. **Career:** Yale University, Department of Political Science, instructor, 1958-59; Stanford University, visiting assistant professor of political science, 1961-62, assistant professor, 1962-66, associate professor, 1966-70, professor of political science, 1970-71; University of California, Charles and Louise Travers Department of Political Science, professor of political science, 1971-95, Heller professor of political science, 1995-, now professor emeritus, Data Archive and Technical Assistance, director, 1980-92. Writer. **Publications:** (Ed.) Readings in American Political Behavior, 1966, 2nd ed., 1970; (ed.) Readings on Congress, 1971; The Politics of Progress, 1973; (with M. Shapiro and F.I. Greenstein) Dynamics of American Politics, 1976, 2nd ed., 1980; (with S.J. Rosenstone) Voter Turnout in Midterm Elections, 1978; (with S.J. Rosenstone) Who Votes?, 1980; (co-author) A Common Destiny: Blacks and American Society, 1989; (co-author) The Myth of the Independent Voter, 1992; (ed. with N.W.

Polsby) On Parties: Essays Honoring Austin Ranney, 1999. Contributor to periodicals. **Address:** Charles and Louise Travers Department of Political, Science, University of California, 646 Barrows Hall, PO Box 1950, Berkeley, CA 94720-1950, U.S.A. **Online address:** vturnout@socrates.berkeley.edu

WOLFMAN, Judy. American (born United States), b. 1933. **Genres:** Children's Fiction, Plays/Screenplays, Young Adult Non-fiction, Young Adult Fiction, inspirational/Motivational Literature. **Career:** York City School District, teacher, 1968-93; York College of Pennsylvania, adjunct professor, 1993-, York College Storytelling Troupe, founder and coach; Western Maryland College, adjunct professor, 1999-; Back Mt. Nursery School, owner and operator; Little People Day Care School, owner and administrator; Pennsylvania State University, adjunct professor. Writer. **Publications:** Life on a Pig Farm, 1998, 2nd ed., 2002; The Golden Goose, 2001; Life on a Horse Farm, 2001; Life on a Crop Farm, 2001; Life on a Goat Farm, 2002; Life on a Cattle Farm, 2002; Life on a Sheep Farm, 2004; Life on a Dairy Farm, 2004; Life on an Apple Orchard, 2004; Life on a Chicken Farm, 2004; How and Why Stories for Readers Theatre, 2004; Not My Time, forthcoming. Works appear in anthologies. Contributor of articles to periodicals. **Address:** 2770 Hartford Rd., York, PA 17402, U.S.A. **Online address:** jbwolfman@verizon.net

WOLFSON, Jill. American (born United States) **Genres:** Young Adult Fiction, Novels, Young Adult Non-fiction. **Career:** San Jose Mercury News, staff reporter, journalist and editor; University of California, faculty; San Jose State University, faculty; The Beat Within, staff; Sun-Sentinel Newspaper, journalist. **Publications:** (With J. Hubner) Somebody Else's Children: The Courts, the Kids, and the Struggle to Save America's Troubled Families, 1996; What I Call Life (novel), 2005; Home, and Other Big, Fat Lies (novel), 2006; Cold Hands, Warm Heart, 2009. **Address:** Henry Holt and Co., 175 5th Ave., New York, NY 10010, U.S.A. **Online address:** jill@jillwolfson.com

WOLFSON, Richard. American (born United States) **Genres:** Physics, Environmental Sciences/Ecology. **Career:** Massachusetts General Hospital, cyclotron engineer, 1969-70; Kearsarge Regional High School, science teacher, 1971-73; Middlebury College, professor of physics, 1971-, Benjamin F. Wissler professor of physics, 2000; National Center for Atmospheric Research, affiliated, 1980-81, visiting scientist, 1986-87; St. Andrew's University, visiting scientist, 1993; Stanford University, visiting scientist, 1998-99. Writer. **Publications:** (With J.M. Pasachoff) Physics, 1987; (with J.M. Pasachoff) Physics: Extended With Modern Physics, 1990; Nuclear Choices: A Citizen's Guide to Nuclear Technology, 1991, rev. ed., 1993; (with S.Z. Aker) PowerBook companion, 1992, 2nd ed., 1993; (with J.M. Pasachoff) Physics for Scientists and Engineers, 2nd ed., 1995, 3rd ed., 1999; (with J.M. Pasachoff) Physics, with Modern Physics for Scientists and Engineers, 2nd ed., 1995, 3rd ed., 1999; Simply Einstein: Relativity Demystified, 2003; Physics in Your Life, 2004; Earth's Changing Climate, 2007; Essential University Physics, 2007, 2nd ed., 2012; Energy, Environment and Climate, 2008, 2nd ed., 2012; (with A.F. Rex) Essential College Physics, 2010. **Address:** Department of Physics, Middlebury College, Middlebury, VT 05753, U.S.A. **Online address:** wolfson@middlebury.edu

WOLFSON, Susan J. American (born United States), b. 1948. **Genres:** Literary Criticism And History, Romance/Historical, Novels. **Career:** Rutgers University, assistant professor, 1978-84, chairperson of sophomore English, 1984-85, associate professor, 1984-90, chairperson of English honors program, 1984-86, 1987-88, professor, 1990-91, chairperson of graduate admissions, 1990-91; University of California, visiting fellow, 1986-87; Princeton University, visiting fellow, 1988-89, 1989-90, professor of English, 1991-; Association of Literary Scholars and Critics, vice president, 2008, president, 2009-. Writer. **Publications:** The Questioning Presence: Wordsworth, Keats and the Interrogative Mode in Romantic Poetry, 1986; Formal Charges: The Shaping of Poetry in British Romanticism, 1997; Borderlines: The Shiftings of Gender in British Romanticism, 2006; John Keats, 2011; The Annotated Frankenstein, 2011; The Annotated Northanger Abbey, 2013. EDITOR: (with B.V. Qualls and intro.) The Strange Case of Dr. Jekyll and Mr. Hyde, 1995; (with P.J. Manning) Lord Byron: Selected Poems, 1996; (with P.J. Manning) The Romantics and Their Contemporaries, 1999; Felicia Hemans: Selected Poems, Letters and Reception Materials, 2000; (with P.J. Manning) Selected Poems of Thomas Hood, Winthrop Mackworth Praed, Thomas Lovell Beddoes, 2000; The Cambridge Companion to Keats, 2001; (with E. Fay) The Siege of Valencia, by Felicia Hemans: The 1823 Publication and the Manuscript, 2002; Mary Shelley's Frankenstein, 2002; (with C.L. Johnson) Jane Austen's Pride and Prejudice, 2003; Mary Wollstonecraft Shelley's Frankenstein or The Modern Prometheus, 2003, 2nd ed., 2007; (with M. Brown) Reading for Form, 2006; John Keats, 2007; Soundings of Things Done: The Poetry and Poetics of Sound in the Romantic Ear and Era, 2008; (with B.V. Qualls) Dr. Jekyll and Mr. Hyde, The Secret Sharer, Transformation: Three Tales of Doubles, 2009; Romantic Interactions: Social Being & the Turns of Literary Action, 2010. FORTHCOMING: Figures on the Margin: The Language of Gender in British Romanticism; Romantic Conversations of Gender. Contributor to books and journals. **Address:** Department of English, Princeton University, 18 McCosh Hall, Princeton, NJ 08544, U.S.A. **Online address:** wolfson@princeton.edu

WOLFTHAL, Diane (Bette). American (born United States), b. 1949. **Genres:** Art/Art History. **Career:** City University of New York, Hunter College, adjunct lecturer, 1976-77; Kean College of New Jersey, Adjunct lecturer, 1978; Manhattan College, adjunct lecturer, 1983; New York University, adjunct assistant professor, 1983; Metropolitan Museum of Art, lecturer, 1983; Brooklyn Museum, research assistant in European paintings, 1983-94; Columbia University, assistant professor of art history, 1984-88; Pratt Institute, visiting assistant professor, 1990-91; Manhattanville College, assistant professor, 1991-93, associate professor of art history, 1993-95; Arizona State University, Women's Studies Affiliated, faculty, 1995-2008; assistant professor, 1995-99, affiliated professor of humanities, 1997-2004, Jewish Studies Affiliated Faculty, 1998-, associate professor, 1999-2005; professor, 2005-08; Historians of Netherlandish Art, director; Rice University, David and Caroline Minter endowed chair in the humanities and professor of art history, 2008-, core faculty in Jewish studies, 2009-, Center for the Study of Women, Gender and Sexuality, faculty, 2009-, chair of art history department, 2009-. Writer. **Publications:** The Beginnings of Netherlandish Canvas Painting, 1400-1530, 1989; Images of Rape: The Heroic Tradition and Its Alternatives, 1999; (ed.) Peace and Negotiation: Strategies for Co-Existence in the Middle Ages and Renaissance, 2000; Picturing Yiddish: Gender, Identity, and Memory in Illustrated Yiddish Books of Renaissance Italy, 2004; (ed. with R. Voaden) Framing the Family: Narrative and Representation in the Medieval and Early Modern Periods, 2005; In and Out of the Marital Bed: Seeing Sex in Renaissance Europe, 2010; (ed. with J. Vitullo) Money, Morality and Culture in Late Medieval and Early Modern Europe, 2010; Corpus of Fifteenth-Century Painting in the Southern Netherlands, forthcoming; (with C.Metzger) Principality of Liège: Early Netherlandish Paintings in Los Angeles, forthcoming; (ed. with J. Garton) New Studies on Old Masters: Essays in Renaissance Art in Honor of Colin Eisler, 2011. Contributor to journals. **Address:** Department of Art History, Rice University, MS 21, Herring Hall 117, 6100 Main St., Houston, TX 77005-1827, U.S.A. **Online address:** wolfthal@rice.edu

WOLIN, Steven J. American (born United States), b. 1940. **Genres:** Medicine/Health, Psychology, Social Work, Social Commentary, Self Help. **Career:** Jewish Hospital of Brooklyn, intern in medicine and pediatrics, 1966-67; Bronx Municipal Hospital, resident in psychiatry, 1967-70; George Washington University, Medical Center, Department of psychiatry, assistant clinical professor, 1972-78, associate clinical professor, 1978-83, clinical professor, 1983-, family therapy instructor, 1980-; University of Judaism, visiting professor, 1991-92; Training and Treatment in the Challenge Model, co-director and project resilience. Writer. **Publications:** (With P. Steinglass, L.A. Bennett and D. Reiss) The Alcoholic Family, 1987; (with S. Wolin) The Resilient Self: How Survivors of Troubled Families Rise above Adversity, 1993; (co-author) Three Spiritual Perspectives on Resilience: Buddhism, Christianity, and Judaism, 1999; Contributor to books and journals. **Address:** Department of Psychiatry and Behavioral Sciences, George Washington University Medical Ctr., 2150 Pennsylvania Ave., 8th Fl. NW, Washington, DC 20037, U.S.A. **Online address:** swolin@projectresilience.com

WOLIN, Sybil. American (born United States) **Genres:** Adult Non-fiction, Psychology, Self Help. **Career:** Jerusalem Avenue Junior High School, English teacher, 1962-63; New York State Youth Board, East Harlem Youth Employment Center, remedial reading teacher, 1963-64; New Rochelle High School, English teacher, 1964-69, teacher, 1969-70; Tri-Services Center, education specialist, 1964-79; Parent Education Advocacy Training Center, education consultant, 1979-91; University of Judaism, adjunct professor, 1992-93; United States Memorial Holocaust Museum, Oral History Project, consultant; Project Resilience, writer and co-director. Writer. **Publications:** (With S.J. Wolin) The Resilient Self: How Survivors of Troubled Families Rise above Adversity, 1993; (ed. with A Desetta) The Struggle to Be Strong: True Stories by Teens About Overcoming Tough Times, 2000; (with V. Taylor) New Normal: How FDNY Firefighters are Rising to the Challenge of

Life After September 11, 2002. Contributor to journals. **Address:** Project Resilience, 5410 Connecticut Ave. NW, Washington, DC 20015, U.S.A. **Online address:** sybilwolin@projectresilience.com

WOLITZER, Hilma. American (born United States), b. 1930. **Genres:** Novels, Children's Fiction, Young Adult Fiction. **Career:** Middlebury College, Bread Loaf Writers Conference, staff assistant, 1975-76, staff, 1977-78, 1980-92; University of Iowa, visiting lecturer in writing, 1978-79, 1983; Wichita State University, distinguished writer-in-residence, 1979; Columbia University, visiting lecturer in writing, 1979-80; New York University, visiting lecturer in writing, 1984; Swarthmore College, visiting lecturer in writing, 1985. Teacher and writer. **Publications:** NOVELS: Ending, 1974; In the Flesh, 1977; Hearts, 1980; In the Palomar Arms, 1983; Silver, 1988; Tunnel of Love (novel), 1994; The Company of Writers: Fiction Workshops and Other Thoughts on the Writing Life, 2001; Doctor's Daughter: A Novel, 2006; Summer Reading: A Novel, 2007; An Available Man, 2012. JUVENILE: Introducing Shirley Braverman, 1975; Out of Love, 1976; Toby Lived Here, 1978; Wish You Were Here, 1984. Contributor to magazines. Works appear in anthologies. **Address:** 500 E 85th St., Ste. 18H, New York, NY 10028-7456, U.S.A. **Online address:** hwolitzer@nyc.rr.com

WOLK, Josh. American (born United States), b. 1969. **Genres:** Adult Nonfiction, Biography. **Career:** Vanity Fair, fact checker; Entertainment Weekly, senior editor; Tufts University, Zamboni (campus humor magazine), founder, 1988-. **Publications:** Cabin Pressure: One Man's Desperate Attempt to Recapture His Youth as a Camp Counselor, 2007. Contributor to magazines and periodicals. **Address:** Hyperion Books, 114 5th Ave., New York, NY 10011-5604, U.S.A. **Online address:** josh@joshwolk.com

WOLKE, Robert L. American (born United States), b. 1928. **Genres:** Food And Wine, Sciences, Reference. **Career:** University of Pittsburgh, associate, professor of chemistry, professor emeritus of chemistry, 1990-; The Washington Post, food columnist. **Publications:** (Ed.) Impact, Science on Society, 1975; Chemistry Explained, 1980; Why Do Batteries Die?, 1996. EINSTEIN SERIES: What Einstein Didn't Know: Scientific Answers to Everyday Questions, 1999; What Einstein Told His Barber: More Scientific Answers to Everyday Questions, 2000; What Einstein Told His Cook: Kitchen Science Explained, 2002; What Einstein Told His Cook 2, the Sequel: Further Adventures in Kitchen Science, 2005. **Address:** Department of Chemistry, Chevron Science Center, University of Pittsburgh, 234 CHVRN, 219 Parkman Ave., Pittsburgh, PA 15260, U.S.A. **Online address:** wolke@pitt.edu

WOLL, Peter. American (born United States), b. 1933. **Genres:** Administration/Management, Law, Politics/Government. **Career:** University of California, instructor, 1958-60, assistant professor, 1960-64; Brandeis University, associate professor, 1964-76, professor, 1976-; U.S. Civil Service Commission, lecturer. Writer. **Publications:** American Bureaucracy, 1963, 2nd ed., 1977; Administrative Law: The Informal Process, 1963, 1974; Public Policy, 1974; (co-author) America's Political System, 5th ed., 1991; (co-author) America's Political System: State and Local, 3rd ed., 1979; (with R. Jones) The Private World of Congress, 1979; Constitutional Law, 1981; Congress, 1985; Constitutional Democracy, 2nd ed., 1986; American Government: The Core, 1989, 2nd ed., 1992; (with S.J. Rockwell) American Government: Competition and Compromise, 2001; (with J.E. Davis and P. Fernlund) Civics: Government and Economics in Action, 2009. EDITOR: American Government: Readings and Cases, 1962, 18th ed., 2010; Public Administration and Policy, 1966; American Government: Readings and Cases, 1962, 13th ed., 1999; Behind the Scenes in American Government, 1977, 9th ed., 1993; Debating American Government, 2nd ed., 1988; (with S.J. Rockwell) American Political Ideals and Realities, 1999; American Government: Readings and Cases, 19th ed., 2011. **Address:** Department of Politics, Brandeis University, 415 South St., Golding 117, Waltham, MA 02454-9110, U.S.A. **Online address:** woll@brandeis.edu

WOLLEN, Peter. American/British (born England), b. 1938. **Genres:** Plays/Screenplays, Film, Literary Criticism And History, Art/Art History, Social Sciences, Politics/Government. **Career:** University of California, School of Theatre, Film and Television, chairman of film department, 1993, professor, now professor emeritus; Vassar College, distinguished Luce professor; Brown University, faculty; New York University, faculty; Columbia University, faculty; Northwestern University, faculty. Writer. **Publications:** FILM THEORY AND CRITICISM: Signs and Meaning in the Cinema, 1969, 4th ed., 1998; Readings and Writings: Semiotic Counter-strategies, 1982; Komar

& Melamid: The Fruitmarket Gallery, Edinburgh, 10 August-21 September 1985: Museum of Modern Art, Oxford, 6 October-1 December 1985, 1985; On the Passage of a Few People through a Rather Brief Moment in Time: The Situationist International 1957-1972, 1989; Singin' in the Rain, 1992; Raiding the Icebox: Reflections on Twentieth-century Culture, 1993; (contrib.) Scene of the Crime, 1997; Addressing the Century: 100 Years of Art and Fashion, 1998; (with F. Pacteau and N. Bryson) Victor Burgin: Una exposición Retrospectiva, Fundació Antoni Tapies, 6 abril-17 junio 2001, 2001; Paris Hollywood: Writings on Film, 2002; (with R. Dyer and J. Fisher) Electronic Shadows: The Art of Tina Keane, 2003; Paris/Manhattan: Writings on Art, 2004; Raiding the Icebox: Reflections on Twentieth-Century Culture, 2008. EDITOR: Working Papers on the Cinema: Sociology and Semiology, 1969; (with J. Hillier and contrib.) Howard Hawks, American Master, 1996; (with C. MacCabe and M. Francis) Who is Andy Warhol?, 1997; (with L. Cooke) Visual Display: Culture Beyond Appearances, 1998; (with A. Cappellazoo and A. Pedrosa) Making Time: Considering Time As a Material, 2000; (with J. Kerr) Autopia: Cars and Culture, 2002. **Address:** School of Theatre, Film and Television, University of California, 3335 Macgowan, PO Box 951622, Los Angeles, CA 90095-1622, U.S.A. **Online address:** pwollen@tft.ucla.edu

WOLOCH, Cecilia G. American (born United States), b. 1956. **Genres:** Poetry. **Career:** Patton State Mental Hospital, writer-in-residence, 1988; Idyllwild Arts, director of summer poetry program, 1989-; University of Southern California, adjunct creative writing faculty, 1997-99, lecturer in creative writing, 2006-; University of Redlands, adjunct creative writing faculty, 1999-2000; California State University, adjunct creative writing faculty, 2000-01; New England College, MFA Program in Poetry, faculty, 2002-04; Paris Poetry Workshop, director, 2003-; Western Connecticut State University, MFA Program in Writing, faculty, 2005-. Writer. **Publications:** Sacrifice (poetry), 1997; (co-author) Tsigan: The Gypsy Poem, 2002; Late (poetry), 2003; Narcissus, 2008; Carpathia: Poems, 2009. Works appear in anthologies. Contributor of articles to periodicals. **Address:** University of Southern California, THH 442, 3551 Trousdale Pkwy., ADM 304, Los Angeles, CA 90089, U.S.A. **Online address:** ceciwo@aol.com

WOLOCH, Isser. American (born United States), b. 1937. **Genres:** History. **Career:** Indiana University, lecturer, 1963-64, assistant professor, 1964-66; University of California, assistant professor, 1966-69; Columbia University, associate professor, 1969-75, professor of history, 1975-98, Moore Collegiate professor of history, 1998-2007, Moore Collegiate professor emeritus of history, 2007-. Writer. **Publications:** Jacobin Legacy, 1970; (ed.) The Peasantry in the Old Regime, 1970; (co-author) The Western Experience, 1974; The French Veteran from the Revolution to the Restoration, 1979; Eighteenth-Century Europe: Tradition and Progress, 1715-1789, 1982, (with G.S. Brown) 2nd ed., 2012; The New Regime: Transformations of the French Civic Order, 1789-1820s, 1994; (ed.) Revolution and The Meanings of Freedom in the Nineteenth Century, 1996; Napoleon and His Collaborators: The Making of a Dictatorship, 2001. **Address:** Department of History, Columbia University, Fayerweather Hall, 1180 Amsterdam Ave., New York, NY 10027, U.S.A. **Online address:** iw6@columbia.edu

WOLPER, Carol. American (born United States) **Genres:** Novels, Plays/Screenplays, Romance/Historical, Young Adult Fiction. **Career:** Writer. **Publications:** (With L. Obst) Dirty Dreams, 1990; The Cigarette Girl, 1999; Secret Celebrity, 2002; Mr. Famous, 2004; Anne of Hollywood, 2012. **Address:** Riverhead Books Publicity, Penguin Group, 375 Hudson St., New York, NY 10014, U.S.A.

WOLPERT, Stanley Albert. American (born United States), b. 1927. **Genres:** History, Novels, Biography, Politics/Government, Law. **Career:** University of California, Department of History, instructor, 1959-60, assistant professor, 1960-63, associate professor, 1963-66, professor of history, 1966-95, chairman, 1968-, distinguished professor of South Asian history, professor emeritus, 1996-; University of Hawaii, visiting professor, 1960; University of Pennsylvania, visiting professor, 1961. Writer. **Publications:** Aboard the Flying Swan, 1954; Nine Hours to Rama, 1962; Tilak and Gokhale: Revolution and Reform in the Making of Modern India, 1962, 4th ed., 2009; Morley and India, 1906-1910, 1967; The Expedition, 1967; An Error of Judgment, 1970; A New History of India, 1977, 8th ed., 2009; Roots of Confrontation in South Asia: Afghanistan, Pakistan, India, and the Superpowers, 1982; Jinnah of Pakistan: A Life, 1984; (ed. with R. Sisson) Congress and Indian Nationalism: The Pre-Independence Phase, 1988; Massacre at Jallianwala Bagh, 1988; Zulfi Bhutto of Pakistan: His Life and Times, 1993; Nehru: A Tryst with Destiny, 1996; Gandhi's Passion: The Life and Legacy of Mahatma Gandhi, 2001; (ed.) Encyclopedia of India, 2006; Shameful Flight: The Last Years of the British Empire in India, 2006; India and Pakistan: Continued Conflict or Cooperation?, 2010. **Address:** Department of History, University of California, 5385 Bunche Hall, PO Box 951473, Los Angeles, CA 90095-1473, U.S.A. **Online address:** wolpert@history.ucla.edu

WOLTERS, Raymond. American (born United States), b. 1938. **Genres:** History. **Career:** University of Delaware, instructor, 1965-67, assistant professor, 1967-70, associate professor, 1970-75, professor of history, 1975-96, Thomas Muncy Keith professor, 1996-. Writer. **Publications:** Negroes and the Great Depression: The Problem of Economic Recovery, 1970; The New Negro on Campus: Black College Rebellions of the 1920s, 1975; The Burden of Brown: Thirty Years of School Desegregation, 1984; Right Turn: William Bradford Reynolds, the Reagan Administration, and Black Civil Rights, 1996; Du Bois and His Rivals, 2002; Race and Education, 1954-2007, 2008. **Address:** Department of History, University of Delaware, 220 John Munroe Hall, Newark, DE 19716, U.S.A. **Online address:** wolters@udel.edu

WOLTON, Thierry. French (born France), b. 1951. **Genres:** History, Writing/Journalism, Business/Trade/Industry. **Career:** Liberation, journalist, 1974-79; Le Point, journalist, 1982-87; Gourmet Magazine, staff, 1991-2005; ELLE Magazine, staff, 1991-2005. **Publications:** (With C. Jelen) L'Occident des dissidents, 1979; (with C. Jelen) Le Petit Guide De La Farce Tranquille, 1982; (with A. Glucksmann) Silence, on Tue, 1986; Le KGB en France, 1986; Le Grand Recrutement, 1991; La France Sous Influence: Paris-Moscou, 30 ans Derelations Secrétes, 1997; L'histoire Interdite, 1998; Rouge-brun: Lemal Du Siéle, 1999; La Fin Des Nations, 2002; Comment Guérir Ducomplexe De Gauche, 2003; Bréve Psychanalyse De La France, 2004; Quatriéme Guerre Mondiale, 2005; Le Grand Bluff Chinois: Comment Pékin Nous Vend Sa Révolution Capitaliste, 2007; KGB Au Pouvoir: Le Systéme Poutine, 2008. **Address:** 59 rue Notre Dame des Champs, Paris, 75006, France.

WOLVEN, Scott. American (born United States), b. 1965?. **Genres:** Novellas/Short Stories, Novels, Literary Criticism And History, Young Adult Fiction. **Career:** State University of New York, creative-writing instructor; University of Southern Maine, Stonecoast MFA in creative writing, faculty. Writer. **Publications:** Controlled Burn: Stories of Prison Crime and Men, 2005; False Hopes, 2011; King Zero, 2011. Contributor to periodicals. **Address:** Simon & Schuster Inc., 1230 Ave. of the Americas, New York, NY 10020-1513, U.S.A.

WOLVERTON, Cheryl. American (born United States), b. 1963. **Genres:** Romance/Historical, Novels, Children's Fiction, Young Adult Fiction, Literary Criticism And History, Theology/Religion. **Career:** Writer. **Publications:** A Matter of Trust, 1997; A Fathers Love, 1998; This Side of Paradise, 1998; The Best Christmas Ever, 1998; For Love of Zach, 1999; A Mothers Love, 1999; For Love of Hawk, 2000; For Love of Mitch, 2000; Healing Hearts, 2000; What the Doctor Ordered, 2000; A Husband to Hold, 2001; In Search of a Hero, 2003; Shelter From The Storm, 2003; Once Upon a Chocolate Kiss, 2003; Among the Tulips, 2004; A Wife for Ben, 2005; Storm Clouds, 2005; Home to You, 2006; Ayiana, 2008. **Address:** PO Box 207, Slaughter, LA 70777, U.S.A. **Online address:** cheryl@cherylwolverton.com

WOLVERTON, Dave. Also writes as Dave Farland, David Farland. American (born United States), b. 1957?. **Genres:** Science Fiction/Fantasy. **Career:** Brigham Young University, Department of English, professor. Writer. **Publications:** NOVELS: On My Way to Paradise, 1989; Serpent Catch, 1991; Path of the Hero, 1993; Wheatfields Beyond, 1993; The Courtship of Princess Leia, 1994; Very Strange Trip: A Novel, 1999; Heart of the Pharaoh, 2001; Flight of the Phoenix, 2001; Curse of the Nile, 2001; Revenge of the Scorpion King, 2001; Monmouth Council Boy Scouts, 2003; Of Mice And Magic, 2005. AS DAVID FARLAND: The Sum of All Men, 1998; Runelords, 1998; Brotherhood of the Wolf, 1999; Wizardborn, 2001; The Lair of Bones, 2003; Worlds of the Golden Queen, 2005; Sons of the Oak, 2006; Worldbinder, 2007; The Wyrmling Horde, 2008; Chaosbound, 2009; Freaky Flyday, 2009. THE GOLDEN QUEEN SPACE OPERA SERIES: The Golden Queen, 1994; Beyond the Gate, 1995; Lords of the Seventh Swarm, 1997; Rising Force, 1999. STAR WARS MISSIONS SERIES: The Search for Grubba the Hut, 1998; The Hunt For Han Solo, 1998; Ithorian Invasion, 1997. STAR WARS EPISODE I ADVENTURES SERIES: The Ghostling Children, 2000; The Hunt for Anakin Skywalker, 2000; Capture Arawynne, 2000; Trouble on Tattooine, 2000. EDITOR: L. Ron Hubbard Presents the Writers of the Future, vols. IX-X, 1993-94. OTHERS: Voyage to the Underworld, 1998; Imperial Jailbreak, 1998. OTHERS: (contrib.) Tales of the Bounty Hunters, 1996; The Wizard of Ooze, 2007; (contrib.) L. Ron Hubbard Presents Writers of the Future, 2008; (as Dave Farland) In the Company of Angels, 2011. **Address:** St. Martin's Press, 175 5th Ave., Rm. 1715, New York, NY 10020-1513, U.S.A. **Online address:** davidfarland@xmission.com

WOLVERTON, Lisa. American (born United States), b. 1966. **Genres:** Language/Linguistics, Art/Art History. **Career:** Harvard University, Society of Fellows, junior fellow, 1996-99; University of Oregon, assistant professor, 2000-07, associate professor of history, 2007-. Writer. **Publications:** Hastening toward Prague: Power and Society in the Medieval Czech Lands, 2001; (with I.F. McNeely) Reinventing Knowledge: From Alexandria to the Internet, 2008; (trans.) Cosmas of Prague, The Chronicle of the Czechs, 2009. Contributor to boks and periodicals. **Address:** Department of History, University of Oregon, 325 McKenzie Hall, 1288 University of Oregon, Eugene, OR 97403-1288, U.S.A. **Online address:** lwolvert@uoregon.edu

WOLVERTON, Mark. American (born United States), b. 1960?. **Genres:** Air/Space Topics, Biography. **Career:** Writer and dramatist. **Publications:** The Depths of Space: The Story of the Pioneer Planetary Probes, 2004; A Life in Twilight: The Final Years of J. Robert Oppenheimer, 2008. Contributor of articles to periodicals. **Address:** PO Box 40322, Philadelphia, PA 19106, U.S.A. **Online address:** mark@markwolverton.com

WOLVERTON, Robert E. American (born United States), b. 1925. **Genres:** Classics, Education, Humanities, Language/Linguistics, Literary Criticism And History, Mythology/Folklore, Theology/Religion, Sports/Fitness, Sports/Fitness. **Career:** Florida State University, instructor, 1951-52, assistant professor, 1962-65, associate professor of classics, 1965-67, director of honors program, 1966-67; University of Georgia, assistant professor of classics, 1954-59; Tufts University, assistant professor of classics and history, 1959-62, assistant, 1960-62, Department of Classics, acting head, 1961-62; Mills College, Academic Administration Internship Program, fellow, 1965-66; University of Illinois, associate professor of classics, associate dean of graduate college, 1967-69; Miami University, professor of classics, dean of graduate school and research, 1969-72; College of Mount St. Joseph, president, 1972-77; Mississippi State University, vice-president, 1977-, professor of classics, 1977-86, professor of classics, Robert Holland Faculty Senate, chair, 2006-07, president, 2007-. U.S. Office of Education, consultant; University Associates Inc., consultant. Writer. **Publications:** (With M.G. Brown) A Primer of Foreign Language Study, 1958; (contrib.) Studies in Honor of B. L. Ullman, 1963; (contrib.) Studies in Honor of W.E. Caldwell, 1964; Classical Elements in English Words, 1965; An Outline of Classical Mythology, 1966; In Other Words: A Lexicon of Sports for Winners and Losers - and More, 2005. **Address:** Department of Foreign Languages, Mississippi State University, Rm. 301C, Lee Hall, PO Box 9517, Mississippi State, MS 39762, U.S.A. **Online address:** rew1@ra.msstate.edu

WOLVERTON, Terry. American (born United States), b. 1954. **Genres:** Novels, Plays/Screenplays, Gay And Lesbian Issues, Poetry. **Career:** Lesbian Art Project, co-founder, 1977, co-director, 1977-80; White Women's Anti-Racism Consciousness Raising, founder, 1980; Woman's Building, calendar editor, 1977-81, administrative assistant, 1981-84, director, 1982-86, development director, 1984-88, executive director, 1988-89; Incest Awareness Project, co-organizer, 1979-81; Consult'Her Consulting Firm, principal, 1982-; California Arts Council, artist-in-residence, 1984-96; L.A. Gay and Lesbian Center, creative writing instructor, 1988-97; Writers at Work, founder, 1997. **Publications:** Blue Moon (poems), 1977; Black Slip (poems), 1992; Bailey's Beads (novel), 1996. PERFORMANCE TEXTS: In Silence Secrets Turn to Lies/Secrets Shared Become Sacred Truth, 1979; (with V. Stolsen) Ya Got Class, Real Class, 1980; Medium: Memory/Muse, 1983; Familiar, 1984; Me and My Shadow, 1984; (with C. Stifter) Dis-a-Buse: To Free from a Misconception or Delusion, 1986; A Merry Little Christmas (three-act play), 1987; Mystery Bruise: Poems, 1999. EDITOR: (with B. Weissman) Harbinger: Poetry and Fiction by Los Angeles Writers, 1990; (with R. Drake) Indivisible: New Short Fiction by Gay and Lesbian West Coast Writers, 1991; Blood Whispers: L.A. Writerson AIDS, vol. I, 1991, vol. II, 1994; Creating Visibility: Providing Lesbian-Sensitive and Lesbian-Specific Alcoholism Recovery Services, 1993; (with R. Drake) Hers: Brilliant New Fiction by Lesbian Writers, 1995; (with R. Drake) His: Brilliant New Fiction by Gay Writers, 1995; (with R. Drake) His 2: Brilliant New Fiction by Gay Writers, 1997; (with R. Drake) Hers 2: Brilliant New Fiction by Lesbian Writers, 1997; (with R.

Drake) His 3: Brilliant New Fiction by Gay Writers, 1999; (with R. Drake) Hers 3: Brilliant New Fiction by Lesbian Writers, 1999; (with R. Drake) Circa 2000: Gay Fiction at the Millennium, 2000; Insurgent Muse: Life and Art at the Woman's Building, 2002; Embers, 2003; Shadow and Praise: Poems, 2007; The Labrys Reunion, 2009. Contributor to magazines. **Address:** c/o Robert Drake, Drake Literary Agency, 314 S Iseminger St., Philadelphia, PA 19107-5904, U.S.A.

WOLZIEN, Valerie. American (born United States), b. 1948?. **Genres:** Mystery/Crime/Suspense, Novels, Literary Criticism And History, Mystery/Crime/Suspense. **Career:** Mystery novelist. **Publications:** SUSAN HENSHAW SUBURBAN MYSTERIES NOVEL: Murder at the PTA Luncheon, 1988; The Fortieth Birthday Body, 1989; We Wish You a Merry Murder, 1991; All Hallows' Evil, 1992; An Old Faithful Murder, 1992; A Star-Spangled Murder, 1993; A Good Year For a Corpse, 1994; Tis the Season to Be Murdered, 1994; Remodeled to Death, 1995; Elected For Death, 1996; Weddings Are Murder, 1998; The Student Body, 1999; Death at a Discount, 2000; An Anniversary to Die for, 2002; Death in a Beach Chair, 2004; Death in Duplicate, 2005. JOSIE PIGEON SEASHORE MYSTERIES NOVEL: Shore to Die, 1995; Permit for Murder, 1997; Deck the Halls With Murder, 1998; This Old Murder, 2000; Murder in the Forecast, 2001; A Fashionable Murder, 2003; Death at a Premium: A Josie Pigeon Mystery, 2005. Contributor to periodicals. **Address:** Fawcett Book Group, 201 E 50th St., New York, NY 10022, U.S.A. **Online address:** valerie@wolzien.com

WOMACK, Jack. American (born United States), b. 1956. **Genres:** Novels, Science Fiction/Fantasy, Young Adult Fiction. **Career:** Amalgamated Clothing and Textile Workers Union, managing editor, 1989-; HarperCollins Publishers, staff; Hachette Book Group USA, publicity manager for the Orbit and Yen imprints. **Publications:** Ambient, 1987; Terraplane, 1988; Heathern, 1990; Elvissey, 1993; Random Acts of Senseless Violence, 1994; Let's Put the Future Behind Us, 1996; Going, Going, Gone, 2000. Contributor of short stories and articles to periodicals. **Address:** 515 W 111th St., Ste. 5E, New York, NY 10025, U.S.A.

WOMACK, Philip. British (born England), b. 1981?. **Genres:** Novels. **Career:** Literary Review, contributing editor; Periscope Post, contributing editor; PORT, contributing editor. **Publications:** The Other Book (novel for young adults), 2008; The Liberators (novel for young adults), 2010. Contributor to newspapers and magazines. **Address:** GL , England. **Online address:** philipwomack@yahoo.co.uk

WOMACK, Steven (James). American (born United States), b. 1952. **Genres:** Novels, Plays/Screenplays, Mystery/Crime/Suspense. **Career:** Daily Record, city editor, reporter and photographer, 1975-77; Vanderbilt University, development researcher, 1977-78; United Press International (UPI), reporter, 1978; freelance photographer and writer, 1978; American Bible Society, writer and photographer for news bureau, 1979-80, typographer, graphic artist and photographer, 1980-82; Thomas Nelson Publishers, operations manager of typesetting department, 1983-86; Tennessee State University, instructor in screenwriting, 1988-91; Nashville State Technical Institute, adjunct professor of English, 1991-95; Watkins College of Art & Design, Watkins Film School, faculty, 1995-. **Publications:** MYSTERIES: Murphy's Fault 1990; Smash Cut, 1991; The Software Bomb, 1993; Dead Folk's Blues, 1993; Torch Town Boogie, 1993; Way Past Dead, 1995; Chain of Fools, 1996; Murder Manual, 1998; Dirty Money, 2000; By Blood Writers, 2005. Contributor to periodicals. **Address:** 214 Timberline Ct., Franklin, TN 37069-7177, U.S.A.

WONG, Janet S. American (born United States), b. 1962. **Genres:** Poetry, Children's Fiction, Young Adult Fiction, Young Adult Non-fiction, inspirational/Motivational Literature. **Career:** Attorney, 1987-91; Arts Arbitration and Mediation Services, arbitrator/mediator, 1989-95; public speaker and performer, 1994-; University of Southern California Writing Project, writer-in-residence, 1995; Singapore Society for Reading and Literacy, visiting author, 1997; Yale University, Yale Law School, Yale Law and Technology Association, director; University of California, Immigrant Children's Art Project, founder; Writer, 1991-. **Publications:** Good Luck Gold and Other Poems, 1994; A Suitcase of Seaweed, and other Poems, 1996; Behind the Wheel: Poems about Driving, 1999; The Rainbow Hand: Poems about Mothers and Children, 1999; Night Garden: Poems from the World of Dreams, 2000; Buzz, 2000; This Next New Year, 2000; The Trip Back Home, 2000; Grump, 2001;

Apple Pie 4th of July, 2002; You Have to Write, 2002; Minn and Jake, 2003; Knock on Wood: Poems about Superstitions, 2003; Alex and the Wednesday Chess Club, 2004; Hide & Seek, 2005; Before it Wriggles Away, 2006; The Dumpster Diver, 2007; Twist: Yoga Poems, 2007; Minn and Jake's Almost Terrible Summer, 2008; Homegrown House, 2009; Me and Rolly Maloo, 2010. Works appear in anthologies. **Address:** Simon & Schuster Children's Publicity, 1230 Ave. of the Americas, New York, NY 10020, U.S.A. **Online address:** janet@janetwong.com

WONG, Shawn (Hsu). American (born United States), b. 1949. **Genres:** Novels. **Career:** University of Washington, American Ethnic Studies Department, assistant professor, 1984-90, associate professor, 1990-95, Creative Writing Program, director, 1995-97, professor of English, 1996-, Department of English, chair, 1997-2002, University Honors Program, director, 2003-06; University of Tubingen, faculty; Jean Moulin University, faculty; University of Washington Rome Center, faculty. Writer. **Publications:** NOVELS: Homebase, 1979; American Knees, 1995. OTHERS: (ed. with I. Reed and K. Trueblood) Before Columbus Foundation Fiction Anthology: Selections from the American Book Awards 1980-1990, 1992; (ed.) Asian American Literature: A Brief Introduction and Anthology, 1996; (ed. with R.B.H. Goh) Asian Diasporas: Cultures, Identities, Representations, 2004. **Address:** Department of English, University of Washington, B423 Padelford Hall, PO Box 354330, Seattle, WA 98195, U.S.A. **Online address:** homebase@u.washington.edu

WONNACOTT, Paul. American/Canadian (born Canada), b. 1933. **Genres:** Economics, History. **Career:** Columbia University, instructor and assistant professor of economics, 1958-62; University of Maryland, associate professor, 1962-67, professor of economics, 1967-92, professor emeritus, 1992-; Council of Economic Advisers, senior staff economist, 1968-70; University of California at Irvine, regents lecturer, 1993; Middlebury College, Alan R. Holmes professor of economics, 1994-2000. Writer. **Publications:** The Canadian Dollar, 1960; (with R.J. Wonnacott) Free Trade between the United States and Canada: The Potential Economic Effects, 1967; (with H. Johnson and H. Shibata) Harmonization of National Economic Politics under Free Trade, 1968; (with R.J. Wonnacott) U.S.-Canadian Free Trade: The Potential Impact on the Canadian Economy, 1968; Floating Canadian Dollar; Exchange Flexibility and Monetary Independence, 1972; Macroeconomics, 1974, 4th ed., 1990; (with R. Wonnacott) Economics, 1979, 4th ed., 1990; Introduction to Macroeconomics, 1979; Introduction to Microeconomics, 1979, 4th ed., 1990; U.S. Intervention in the Exchange Market for DM, 1977-80, 1982; The United States and Canada: The Quest for Free Trade, 1987; U.S. and Canadian Auto Policies in a Changing World Environment, 1987; The Last Good War: A Novel, 2007; The 38th President, 2008. **Address:** Department of Economics, University of Maryland, 3105 Tydings Hall, College Park, MD 20742, U.S.A. **Online address:** paulwon@refraction.org

WONNACOTT, Ronald Johnston. Canadian (born Canada), b. 1930. **Genres:** Economics. **Career:** Harvard Law School, lecturer, 1956-57; Harvard University, Department of Economics, lecturer, 1958; University of Western Ontario, Department of Economics, assistant professor, 1958-61, associate professor, 1962-65, professor, 1965-, chairman, 1969-72, William G. Davis professor emeritus, 1996-, Centre for the Study of International Economic Relations, senior research fellow, 1996-; University of Minnesota, visiting associate professor, 1961-62; Canadian Economics Assignment, president, 1981; Canadian Economics Association, president, 1981-82; Stanford University, Mellon Fellow, 1993-94. Writer. **Publications:** Canadian-American Dependence: An Inter-industry Analysis, 1961; (with G.L. Reuber) Cost of Capital in Canada, 1961; Manufacturing Costs and the Comparative Advantage of United States Regions, 1963; (with P. Wonnacott) Free Trade between the United States and Canada: The Potential Economic Effects, 1967; (with D.E. Bond) Trade Liberalization and the Canadian Furniture Industry, 1968; (with P. Wonnacott) U.S.-Canadian Free Trade, 1968; (with T.H. Wonnacott) Introductory Statistics, 1969, 5th ed., 1990; (with T.H. Wonnacott) Econometrics, 1970, rev. ed., 1979; (with T.H. Wonnacott) Introductory Statistics for Business and Economics, 1972, 4th. ed., 1990; Options Commerciales du Canada, 1975; Canada's Trade Options, 1975; (with P. Wonnacott) Economics, 1979, 4th ed., 1990; Introduction to Microeconomics, 1979; Introduction to Macroeconomics, 1979, rev. ed., 1986; (with T.H. Wonnacott) Regression: A Second Course in Statistics, 1981, rev. ed., 1986; (with T.H. Wonnacott) Statistics: Discovering Its Power, 1982; Aggressive U.S. Reciprocity Evaluated with a New Analytical Approach to Trade Conflicts, 1984; Selected New

Developments in International Trade Theory, 1984; Canada-U.S. Free Trade: Problems and Opportunities, 1985; (with R. Hill) Canadian and U.S. Adjustment Policies in a Bilateral Trade Agreement, 1987; U.S. Hub-and-Spoke Bilaterals and the Multilateral Trading System, 1990; Macroeconomics, 1990; Microeconomics, 1990; The Economics of Overlapping Free Trade Areas and the Mexican Challenge, 1991. Contributor to periodicals and journals. **Address:** Department of Economics, University of Western Ontario, Rm. 4090, Social Science Centre, London, ON N6A 5C2, Canada. **Online address:** wonnacot@uwo.ca

WOO, Sung J. American/Korean (born Korea (South)), b. 1971. **Genres:** Novels, Novellas/Short Stories, Adult Non-fiction. **Career:** Writer. **Publications:** Everything Asian (novel), 2009. Contributor to periodicals. **Address:** Washington, NJ , U.S.A. **Online address:** sungjwoo@gmail.com

WOO, Wing Thye. American/Malaysian (born Malaysia), b. 1954. **Genres:** Economics. **Career:** University of Maryland, lecturer in economics, 1982-84; Brookings Institution, research associate in economic studies, 1982-85, International Trade and Economics in the Global Economy and Development Program, new century chair in international trade and economics, 2006-09, nonresident senior fellow, 2009-, John L. Thornton China Center, Foreign Policy Studies Program, senior fellow, 2006-09; University of California, professor of economics, Pacific Rim Studies Program at Institute of Governmental Affairs, head, 1987-95; People's University of China, visiting professor, 1989; National Taiwan University, visiting professor, 1990; Institute of Southeast Asian Studies, visiting research fellow, 1990; U.S. Treasury, special adviser, 1997-98; Harvard University, Harvard Institute for International Development, faculty associate, 1997-2000, Center for International Development, associate, 2000-02; Chinese Economists Society, vice-president, 2000-01, 2002-03; Chinese Economic Association of North America, president; Columbia University, Center for Globalisation and Sustainable Development, East Asia Program, director; University of Nottingham, fellow; Institute for Strategic and International Studies, fellow, 2004-06. Writer. **Publications:** (With G. Fan) Decentralized Socialism and Macroeconomic Stability: Lessons from China, 1993; (with B. Glassburner and A. Nasution) Macroeconomic Policies, Crises, and Long-Term Growth in Indonesia, 1965-1990, 1994; (with C. Heady and P.W. Wong) Fiscal Management and Economic Reform in the People's Republic of China, 1995; (ed. with J.D. Sachs and S. Parker) Economies in Transition: Asia and Europe, 1997; Economics and Politics of Transition to an Open Market Economy: China, 1999; (ed. with J.D. Sachs and K. Schwab) Asian Financial Crisis: Lessons for a Resilient Asia, 2000; (ed. with L. Song) China's Dilemma: Economic Growth, the Environment, and Climate Change, 2008; (ed. with K. Lee and J. Kim) Power and Sustainability of the Chinese State, 2008. Contributor of articles to journals, magazines, books and newspapers. **Address:** Department of Economics, University of California, 1 Shields Ave., Davis, CA 95616-5270, U.S.A. **Online address:** wtwoo@ucdavis.edu

WOOD, Ann. American (born United States), b. 1970?. **Genres:** Novels. **Career:** Provincetown Banner, staff reporter. Dancer. **Publications:** Bolt Risk, 2005. **Address:** c/o Author Mail, Leapfrog Press, PO Box 2110, Teaticket, MA 02536, U.S.A.

WOOD, Anthony C. American (born United States), b. 1954. **Genres:** History, Humanities. **Career:** Landmarks Preservation Commission, confidential assistant, 1979-81; Municipal Arts Society, deputy director, 1981-83, director of special projects, 1983-84, director of public affairs, 1984-86; J.M. Kaplan Fund, program officer, 1986-92, chief program officer, 1992-93; Columbia University, adjunct associate professor of historic preservation, 1991-; New York Preservation Archive Project, founder and chair, 1993-; Ittleson Foundation, executive director, 1993-; Drayton Hall, site council chair, 2008-; Preservation League of New York State, chair; Historic Districts Council of New York City, chair; Partners for Sacred Places, chair. Writer. **Publications:** Preserving New York: Winning the Right to Protect a City's Landmarks, 2007. Contributor to periodicals. **Address:** New York, NY , U.S.A. **Online address:** acw5@columbia.edu

WOOD, Brian. American (born United States), b. 1972. **Genres:** Graphic Novels, Mystery/Crime/Suspense, Romance/Historical, Science Fiction/Fantasy, Young Adult Fiction, Social Commentary, Westerns/Adventure. **Career:** Writer and graphic artist. **Publications:** (Intro.) Channel Zero, 1998; Generation X, Counter-X, 2000; (intro.) Couscous Express, 2002; (intro.) Fight for Tomorrow, 2002; (intro.) Pounded, 2002; (intro.) Channel Zero: Jennie

One, 2003; The Couriers, 2003, vol. II: Dirtbike Manifesto, 2004, vol. III: The Ballad of Johnny Funwrecker, 2005; (intro.) Supermarket, 2006; (intro.) The Tourist, 2006; (intro.) Demo, 2008, vol. II, 2011; Local, 2008; The New York Four, 2008; The New York Five, 2010; DV8: Gods And Monsters, 2011. DMZ: On the Ground, 2006; Body of a Journalist, 2007; Public Works, 2007; Friendly Fire, 2008; The Hidden War, 2008; Blood in the Game, 2009; War Powers, 2009; Hearts and Minds, 2010; M.I.A., 2011; Collective Punishment, 2011; Free States Rising, 2012; The Five Nations of New York, 2012. NORTHLANDERS: vol.I: Sven the Returned, 2008; The Cross and The Hammer, 2009; Blood In The Snow, 2010; The Plague Widow, 2010; Metal, 2011; Thor's Daughter, 2011; The Icelandic Trilogy, 2012. **Address:** Brooklyn, NY , U.S.A. **Online address:** brian@brianwood.com

WOOD, Bridget. Also writes as Frances Gordon, Sarah Rayne. British (born England), b. 1947. **Genres:** Novels, Mystery/Crime/Suspense, Horror, Science Fiction/Fantasy, Literary Criticism And History, Psychology. **Career:** Writer, 1992-. **Publications:** FANTASY NOVELS: Wolfking, 1991; The Lost Prince, 1992; Rebel Angel, 1993; Sorceress, 1994. OTHER NOVELS: Mask of the Fox, 1982; The Chessmen, 1983; The Devil in Amber, 1984; The Rose Window, 1985; The Minstrel's Lute, 1987; Satanic Lute, 1987. HORROR NOVELS: AS FRANCES GORDON: Blood Ritual, 1994; The Devil's Piper, 1995; The Burning Altar, 1996; Thorn, 1997; Changeling, 1998; Wildwood, 1999. PSYCHOLOGICAL THRILLERS: AS SARAH RAYNE: Tower of Silence, 2003; A Dark Dividing, 2004; Roots of Evil, 2005; Spider Light, 2007; The Death Chamber, 2008; Ghost Song, 2009; House of the Lost, 2010. **Address:** c/o Jane Conway Gordon, 1 Old Compton St., London, GL W1V 5PH, England. **Online address:** sarah@sarahrayne.co.uk

WOOD, C. E. (Clyde Edward Wood). American (born United States) **Genres:** Novels, Adult Non-fiction. **Career:** Glenville State College, Department of Social Sciences, assistant professor of history, adjunct faculty, associate professor of history, 2004-; Peru State College, adjunct professor; University of Nebraska, instructor; Concordia College, instructor; West Virginia University, study board advisor. Historian and writer. **Publications:** (Contrib.) Magill's Guide to Military History, 2001; (contrib.) Land Warfare: An Encyclopedia, 2002; Mud: A Military History, 2006. **Address:** Department of Social Sciences, Glenville State College, Rm. 231, Louis Bennett Hall, 200 High St., Glenville, WV 26351, U.S.A. **Online address:** ed.wood@glenville.edu

WOOD, Clyde Edward. *See* **WOOD, C. E.**

WOOD, Curtis W(illiam). American (born United States), b. 1941. **Genres:** History. **Career:** Western Carolina University, professor of history, 1969-, now professor emeritus; Mountain Heritage Center, senior research associate. Writer. **Publications:** (With H.T. Blethen) A Mountain Heritage: The Illustrated History of Western Carolina University, 1989; (ed. with H.T. Blethen) Ulster and North America, 1997; (with H.T. Blethen) From Ulster to Carolina, 1998. **Address:** Department of History, Western Carolina University, 225 McKee Bldg., Cullowhee, NC 28723, U.S.A. **Online address:** woodcw@email.wcu.edu

WOOD, David. British (born England), b. 1944. **Genres:** Children's Fiction, Plays/Screenplays. **Career:** Freelance actor, writer, director, producer and magician. **Publications:** PLAYS AND MUSICAL PLAYS FOR CHILDREN: The Owl and the Pussycat Went to See..., 1970; The Plotters of Cabbage Patch Corner, 1972; Flibberty and the Penguin, 1974; Hijack over Hygenia, 1974; Old Mother Hubbard, 1976; The Papertown Paperchase, 1976; Larry the Lamb in Toytown, 1977; Rock Nativity (for adults), 1977; The Gingerbread Man, 1977; Old Father Time, 1977; Tickle, 1978; Mother Goose's Golden Christmas, 1978; Babes in the Magic Wood, 1979; Cinderella, 1980; There Was an Old Woman, 1980; Nutcracker Sweet, 1981; Aladdin, 1981; The Ideal Gnome Expedition, 1982; Dick Whittington and Wondercat, 1983; Meg and Mog Show, 1984; Robin Hood, 1985; The Old Man of Lochnagar, 1986; The Selfish Shellfish, 1986; Jack and the Giant, 1987; The See-Saw Tree, 1987; Save the Human, 1990; Dinosaurs and All That Rubbish, 1990; Jack the Lad, 1991; The Pied Piper, 1991; The BFG, 1991; The Witches, 1993; Noddy, 1995; Rupert and the Green Dragon, 1997; More Adventures of Noddy, 1998; Babe the Sheep-Pig, 1998; The Twits, 2000; Tom's Midnight Garden, 2001; Spot's Birthday Party, 2001; Fantastic Mr Fox, 2003; James and the Giant Peach, 2004; Lady Lollipop, 2005; Danny the Champion of the World, 2006; The Lighthouse Keeper's Lunch, 2006; George's Marvellous Medicine, 2006; The Tiger Who Came to Tea, 2008; Guess How Much I Love You, 2010; Goodnight Mister Tom, 2011. CHILDREN'S FICTION: The Operats

of Rodent Garden, 1984; The Discorats, 1985; The Gingerbread Man, 1985; Playtheatres, 1987; Chish 'n' Fips, 1987; Sidney the Monster, 1988; Happy Birthday Mouse!, 1991; Baby Bear's Buggy Ride, 1993; The BFG: Plays for Children, 1993; Pop-Up Theatre: Cinderella, 1994; Meg and Mog: Four Plays for Children, 1994; Bedtime Story, 1996; The Magic Show, 1996; The Christmas Story, 1996; Mole's Summer Story, 1997; Mole's Winter Story, 1998; Silly Spider, 1998; Funny Bunny's Magic Show, 1999; The Phantom Cat of the Opera, 2000; The Toy Cupboard, 2000; The Witches: Plays for Children, 2002; The Twits: Plays for Children, 2003; Under the Bed!, 2006; (with R. Fowler) Mole's Bedtime Story, 2007; A Present for Father Christmas, 2008; Danny the Champion of the World: Plays for Children, 2009; Cinderella, 2010. **Address:** Casarotto Ramsay Ltd., Waverley House, 7-12 Noel St., London, GL W1F 8GQ, England. **Online address:** david.woodplays@virgin.net

WOOD, (David) Ira. American (born United States), b. 1950. **Genres:** Novels, Plays/Screenplays. **Career:** Meta Information Applications, technical writer, 1978-79; Coleco and Grolier Education Corp., software designer, 1983-84; Leapfrog Press, editor and publisher, 1997-. Director, actor and writer. **Publications:** (With M. Piercy) The Last White Class: A Play About Neighborhood Terror, 1980; The Kitchen Man (novel), 1985; Going Public (novel), 1991; (with M. Piercy) Storm Tide (novel), 1998; (with M. Piercy) So You Want to Write: How to Master the Craft of Fiction and the Personal Narrative, 2001; Sharks: Learning the SH Sound, 2002; Fort Sumter: Where the Civil War Began, 2006. INTERACTIVE COMPUTER-BASED FICTION FOR CHILDREN AND YOUNG ADULTS: Treasure Hunter, 1984; Max Dublin's Treasure, 1984; Wacky Word Games, 1984; The Lost Dinosaur, 1985; Hospital, 1985; Farewell, Alaska!, 1985. Contributor of articles to periodicals. Works appear in anthologies. **Address:** c/o Erika Spellman, William Morris Agency, 1350 Ave. of the Americas, New York, NY 10019, U.S.A. **Online address:** ira@leapfrogpress.com

WOOD, Dennis (Michael). British (born England), b. 1947. **Genres:** Literary Criticism And History, Biography, Autobiography/Memoirs, Novels. **Career:** University of Birmingham, Department of French Studies, lecturer, 1972-86, senior lecturer, 1986-89, reader in French literature, 1989-94, personal chair of French Literature, 1994-97, head, 1997-2002, professor emeritus of French Literature and Chevalier dans l'Ordre des Palmes Académiques, 2002-; Université Paul-Valéry, exchange lecturer, 1977. Writer. **Publications:** Benjamin Constant, Adolphe, 1987; Constant: Adolphe, 1987; Benjamin Constant: A Biography, 1993; The Novels of Isabelle de Charrière (1740-1805), 1994. EDITOR: Oeuvres completes, vol. VIII: Romans, contes etnouvelles I, 1763-1797, 1980, vol. IX: Romans, contes et nouvelles II, 1798-1806, 1981; Oeuvres complètes, Romans, vol. I: 1973-1797, 1980, vol. I: 1798-1806, 1981; Ecrits littéraires (1800-1813), 1995; (with C. Crossley) Annales Benjamin Constant 7: Constant in Britain/Constant etla Grande-Bretagne, 1987; (with C.P. Courtney) Correspondancegénérale, vol. II: 1793-1794, 1994, vol. III: 1795-1805, forthcoming; (with P. Baron and W. Perkins) Femmes et littérature: Colloque des Universités de Birmingham et de Besançon, 2003. Works appear in anthologies. Contributor to periodicals. **Address:** Department of French Studies, School of Humanities, University of Birmingham, Ashley Bldg., Edgbaston, Birmingham, WM B15 2TT, England. **Online address:** d.m.wood@bham.ac.uk

WOOD, Don. American (born United States), b. 1945. **Genres:** Children's Fiction, Illustrations, Young Adult Non-fiction. **Career:** Blue Moon (book and import shop), co-owner and operator, 1970-75; editorial and magazine illustrator, graphic designer, author and illustrator of children's books, 1976-. **Publications:** SELF-ILLUSTRATED WITH A. WOOD: The Big Hungry Bear, 1984; The Little Mouse, the Red Ripe Strawberry and the Big Hungry Bear (play), 1990; Piggies, 1991; Merry Christmas, Big Hungry Bear!, 2002. SELF-ILLUSTRATED: Into the Volcano, 2008. OTHER: A World-Class Boxer, 2005. Illustrator of books by A. Wood. **Address:** Harcourt Trade Publishers, 15 E 26th St., 15th Fl., New York, NY 10010-1520, U.S.A.

WOOD, Douglas (Eric). American (born United States), b. 1951. **Genres:** Adult Non-fiction, Children's Non-fiction, Earth Sciences, Environmental Sciences/Ecology, Children's Fiction. **Career:** Music teacher, 1973-77; naturalist and wilderness guide, 1977-. Writer, musician and recording artist. **Publications:** SELF-ILLUSTRATED: Paddle Whispers, 1992; Fawn Island, 2001. FOR CHILDREN. NONFICTION: Old Turtle, 1992; Making the World, 1998; Grandad's Prayers of the Earth, 1999; What Moms/Dads Can't Do, 2001. FICTION: The Windigo's Return: A North Woods Story, 1996; Northwoods Cradle Song: From a Menominee Lullaby, 1996; Rabbit and the

Moon, 1998; What Dads Can't Do, 2000; What Moms Can't Do, 2001; A Quiet Place, 2002; What Teachers Can't Do, 2002; What Santa Can't Do, 2003; Old Turtle and the Broken Truth, 2003; Secret of Saying Thanks, 2005; What Grandmas Can't Do, 2005; Nothing to Do, 2006; Lessons of Old Turtle: The Broken Truth, forthcoming. ADULT NONFICTION: Minnesota: The Spirit of the Land, 1995; Breathe the Wind, Drink the Rain: Notes on Being Alive, 2002. OTHERS: Prescriptions from the Dock, 2005; The Things Trees Know, 2005; Find True North, 2005; How Does Your Garden Grow?, 2005; The Thing With Feathers, 2006; When Mama Mirabelle comes home, 2007; Old Turtle: a Story, 2007; Chickadee's Message, 2009; Miss Little's Gift, 2009; Aunt Mary's Rose, 2010; No One But You, 2010; Franklin and Winston: A Christmas that Changed the World, 2010; Where the Sunrise Begins, 2010. Contributor to magazines. **Address:** 3835 Pine Point Rd., Sartell, MN 56377, U.S.A. **Online address:** doug@douglaswood.com

WOOD, Edward John. Also writes as Ted Wood, Jack Barnao. Canadian/British (born England), b. 1931. **Genres:** Mystery/Crime/Suspense, Plays/Screenplays, Ghost Writer, Children's Fiction. **Career:** London & Manchester Assurance, sales representative, 1953-54; Toronto City Police, constable, 1954-57; MacLaren Advertising, copywriter, 1957-66; Foster Advertising, creative director, 1966-69; Cockfield Brown Advertising, staff, 1969-74; Crime Writers of Canada, president, 1987-88. **Publications:** REID BENNETT SERIES AS TED WOOD: Somebody Else's Summer, 1973; Dead in the Water, 1983; Murder on Ice, 1984 in UK as The Killing Cold, 1984; Live Bait, 1985 in UK as Dead Centre, 1985; Fool's Gold, 1986; Corkscrew, 1987; When the Killing Starts, 1989; On the Inside, 1990; Flashback, 1992; Snowjob, 1992; (with J. Schmidt) Two Lands, One Heart: An American Boy's Journey to his Mother's Vietnam, 1995; Iditarod Dream: Dusty and his Sled Dogs Compete in Alaska's Jr. Iditarod, 1996; Ghosts of the Southwest: The Phantom Gunslinger and Other Real-Life Hauntings, 1997; Ghosts of the West Coast: The Lost Souls of the Queen Mary and Other Real-Life Hauntings, 1999; A Clean Kill, 1995; Importance of Being Ambiguous, 2003. JOHN LOCKE SERIES AS JACK BARNAO: Hammerlocke, 1986; Lockestep, 1987; Timelocke, 1991. Works appear in anthologies. **Address:** 24 Tremaine Terr., Cobourg, ON K9A 5A8, Canada.

WOOD, Frances. British (born England), b. 1948. **Genres:** History, Librarianship, Translations, Literary Criticism And History. **Career:** British Library, research assistant, 1971-72, curator of Chinese collections; University of London, School of Oriental and African Studies, library assistant, 1972-79. Writer and librarian. **Publications:** EDITOR AND CONTRIBUTOR: Chinese Studies: Papers Presented at a Colloquium at the School of Oriental and African Studies, University of London, 24-26 August 1987, 1988; The House of Confucius, 1988; Blue Guide: China, 1993; (with S. Whitfield) Dunhuang and Turfan: Contents and Conservation of Ancient Documents from Central Asia, 1996. NONFICTION: (with J. Lust) Catalogue of Publications of Translation and Monitoring Services and of Periodicals Dealing with the People's Republic of China in the Library of the School of Oriental and African Studies, 1974; Through the Year in China, 1981; Chinese Illustration, 1985; (trans.) Stones of the Wall, 1986; People at Work in China, 1987; A Companion to China, 1988; (with A. Scott-James and R. Desmond) The British Museum Book of Flowers, 1989; (with N. Sivin, P. Brooke and C.R. Sivin) The Contemporary Atlas of China, 1989; (with N. Titley) Oriental Gardens: An Illustrated History, 1992; 19th Century Paintings of Life in China, 1995; Did Marco Polo Go to China?, 1995; No Dogs and Not Many Chinese: Treaty Port Life in China, 1843-1943, 2000; Hand Grenade Practice in Peking: My Part in the Cultural Revolution, 2000; The Silk Road: Two Thousand Years in the Heart of Asia, 2002; The First Emperor of China, 2007; Di Guo Lue Ying: Yingguo Shi Tuan Hua Jia Bi Xia De Zhongguo, 2007; China's First Emperor and His Terracotta Warriors, 2008; The Lure of China: History and Literature from Marco Polo to J.G. Ballard, 2008. **Address:** Asia, Pacific & Africa Collections, British Library, 96 Euston Rd., London, GL NW1 2DB, England. **Online address:** frances.wood@bl.uk

WOOD, Frances M. American (born United States), b. 1951. **Genres:** Novels. **Career:** Writer and reference librarian. **Publications:** Becoming Rosemary, 1997; Daughter of Madrugada, 2002; When Molly was a Harvey Girl, 2010. Contributor to periodicals. **Address:** c/o Frances Kuffel, Jean V. Naggar Literary Agency Inc., 216 E 75th St., Ste. 1E, New York, NY 10021-2921, U.S.A. **Online address:** fmw@francesmwood.com

WOOD, Gaby. British (born England), b. 1971?. **Genres:** Adult Non-fiction, History. **Career:** The Observer, staff writer, senior writer, deputy literary editor, arts editor, Review Section, editor, correspondent; Telegraph Media Group Ltd., Daily Telegraph, head of books. **Publications:** The Smallest of All Persons Mentioned in the Record of Littleness, 1998; Edison's Eve: A Magical History of the Quest for Mechanical Life in UK as Living Dolls: A Magical History of the Quest for Mechanical Life, 2002. Contributor to books, magazines and periodicals. **Address:** Faber and Faber Ltd., Bloomsbury House, 74-77 Great Russell St., London, GL WC1B 3DA, England.

WOOD, Gerald C. American (born United States), b. 1944. **Genres:** Literary Criticism And History, Film, Plays/Screenplays, Popular Culture, Theatre, Essays. **Career:** Carson-Newman College, assistant professor, professor of English, 1971-, department head, 1985-2008, Horton Foote Center for Theater and Film, director, 2008-; University of Tennessee, visiting associate professor, 1982, 1985. Writer. **Publications:** (Ed.) Selected One-Act Plays of Horton Foote, 1989; Galbraith Springs, 1992; (ed.) Horton Foote: A Casebook, 1998; Horton Foote and the Theater of Intimacy, 1999; Conor McPherson: Imagining Mischief, 2003; Neil La Bute: A Casebook, 2006; (ed. with A. Hazucha) Northsiders: Essays on the History and Culture of the Chicago Cubs, 2008. Contributor to books and periodicals. **Address:** McFarland, 960 NC Hwy., 88 W, PO Box 611, Jefferson, NC 28640, U.S.A. **Online address:** gwood@cn.edu

WOOD, Gillen D'Arcy. American/Australian (born Australia) **Genres:** Novels, Cultural/Ethnic Topics. **Career:** University of Illinois, Department of English, faculty, 2000-, associate professor, Nicholson professor of English, Center for Advanced Study, associate, 2010-11, Sustainability Studies Initiative in the Humanities, director, 2011-. Writer. **Publications:** The Shock of the Real: Romanticism and Visual Culture, 1760-1860, 2001; (intro.) A Tale of Two Cities, 2003; Hosack's Folly: A Novel of Old New York, 2005; (intro.) Ivanhoe, 2005; Romanticism and Music Culture in Britain, 1770-1840: Virtue and Virtuosity, 2010; Tambora: The Global Climate Emergency of 1815-17, forthcoming; Frankenstein's Weather: Mt. Tambora and the Global Climate Dystopia, 1815-18, forthcoming. Contributor to periodicals. **Address:** Other Press, 2 Park Ave., 24th Fl., New York, NY 10016, U.S.A. **Online address:** gdwood@illinois.edu

WOOD, Gordon S(tewart). American (born United States), b. 1933. **Genres:** History, Politics/Government. **Career:** Harvard University, teaching fellow, 1960-64, assistant professor, 1966-67; College of William and Mary, assistant professor, 1964-66; University of Michigan, associate professor, 1967-69; Brown University, Department of History, associate professor, 1969-71, professor of history, 1971-, chairman, 1983-86, university professor, 1990-, Alva O. Way university professor, 1997-, now Alva O. Way university professor emeritus; University of Cambridge, Pitt P professor, 1982-83; Northwestern University, School of Law, Pritzker visiting professor, 2001, professor of law and history, 2003. Writer. **Publications:** Representation in the American Revolution, 1969; The Creation of the American Republic, 1776-1787, 1969; (intro. and ed.) The Rising Glory of America, 1760-1820, 1971, rev. ed., 1990; The Confederation and the Constitution: The Critical Issues, 1973; Revolution and the Political Integration of the Enslaved and Disenfranchised, 1974; (contrib.) Leadership in the American Revolution, 1974; (with J.R. Pole) Social Radicalism and the Idea of Equality in the American Revolution, 1976; (co-author) The Great Republic, 1977; The Making of the Constitution, 1987; The Radicalism of the American Revolution, 1992; (ed. with L.G. Wood) Russian-American Dialogue on the American Revolution, 1995; (ed. with A. Molho) Imagined Histories: American Historians Interpret the Past, 1998; The American Revolution: A History, 2002; (ed.) Common Sense and Other Writings, 2003; The Americanization of Benjamin Franklin, 2004; Revolutionary Characters: What Made the Founders Different, 2006; The Purpose of the Past: Reflections on the Uses of History, 2008; Empire of Liberty: A History of the Early Republic, 1789-1815, 2009; Idea of America: Reflections on the Birth of the United States, 2011. Contributor to periodicals. **Address:** Department of History, Brown University, 79 Brown St., PO Box N, Providence, RI 02912, U.S.A. **Online address:** gordon_wood@brown.edu

WOOD, Ian N(icholas). British (born England), b. 1950. **Genres:** History. **Career:** University of Leeds, lecturer, 1976-89, senior lecturer in history, 1989-95, professor of early medieval history, 1995-. Writer. **Publications:** (Ed. with P.H. Sawyer) Early Medieval Kingship, 1977; (ed. with B. Sawyer and P. Sawyer) The Christianization of Scandinavia: Report of a Symposium Held at Kungälv, Sweden 4-9 August 1985, 1987; (ed. with N. Lund) People and Places in Northern Europe, 500-1600: Essays in Honour of Peter Hayes

Sawyer, 1991; (ed. with G.A. Loud) Church and Chronicle in the Middle Ages: Essays Presented to John Taylor, 1991; (ed. with J. Harries) The Theodosian Code, 1993; The Merovingian Kingdoms, 450-751, 1994; The Most Holy Abbot Ceolfrid, 1995; (ed.) Franks and Alamanni in the Merovingian Period: An Ethnographic Perspective, 1998; (ed. with E. Chrysos) East and West: Modes of Communication: Proceedings of the First Plenary Conference at Merida, 1999; The Missionary Life: Saints and the Evangelisation of Europe, 400-1050, 2001; (ed. with W. Pohl and H. Reimitz) The Transformation of Frontiers from Late Antiquity to the Carolingians, 2001; (ed. with K. Mitchell) The World of Gregory of Tours, 2002; (with D. Shanzer) Avitus of Vienne, Letters and Selected Prose, 2002; (with F. Orton and C. Lees) Fragments of History: Rethinking the Ruthwell and Bewcastle Monuments, 2007. **Address:** School of History, University of Leeds, Leeds, WY LS2 9JT, England. **Online address:** i.n.wood@leeds.ac.uk

WOOD, James. British (born England), b. 1965?. **Genres:** Novels, Literary Criticism And History, Essays. **Career:** The Guardian, chief literary critic, 1992-96; The New Republic, senior editor, 1996-2007; Boston University, visiting professor; Kenyon College, visiting professor; Harvard University, visiting professor, 2003-, professor of the practice of literary criticism, 2010-; The New Yorker, staff writer, 2007-. Literary critic and novelist. **Publications:** Selected Stories of D.H. Lawrence, 1999; The Broken Estate: Essays on Literature and Belief, 1999; The Book Against God, 2003; The Irresponsible Self: On Laughter and the Novel, 2004; How Fiction Works, 2008; Novels, 1970-1982, 2010; Fun Stuff and Other Essays, 2012. **Address:** The New Yorker, 6300 Wilshire Blvd., 12th Fl., Los Angeles, CA 90048, U.S.A. **Online address:** wood2@fas.harvard.edu

WOOD, John A. American (born United States), b. 1947. **Genres:** Photography, Poetry, Art/Art History. **Career:** McNeese State University, Department of English and Foreign Languages, director of graduate studies in English, 1976, professor, professor emeritus, 2006-, Master of Fine Arts Program in Creative Writing, founder and director; 21st: The Journal of Contemporary Photography, editor, 1998-. **Publications:** Orbs, 1968; (ed.) The Daguerreotype: A Sesquicentennial Celebration, 1989; (ed.) America and the Daguerreotype, 1991; The Art of the Autochrome: The Birth of Color Photography, 1993; In Primary Light (poetry), 1994; (with M.A. Foresta) Secrets of the Dark Chamber: The Art of the American Daguerreotype, 1995; The Scenic Daguerreotype: Romanticism and Early Photography, 1995; The Photographic Arts, 1997; The Gates of the Elect Kingdom (poetry), 1997; Selected Poems, 1968-1998, 1999; (ed.) Gardens of DeCosse, 2000; (contrib.) Cowboy Code, 2000; (ed.) Clandestine Mind, 2000; (ed. and intro.) Songs of Experience, 2002; (ed.) Cante Jondo, 2002; (contrib.) Animalerie, 2004; (ed.) Sally Mann, 2005; (ed. and intro.) Toward Omega, 2006; (trans. and intro.) Flowers of Evil, 2006; (intro.) Duino Elegies, 2006; (ed. and contrib.) Book of Life, 2006; (ed.) Shadows of the Dream, 2007; (ed. and afterword with J. Baldridge) Everywhere Chronicles, 2008; (ed. and intro.) Mont-Saint-Michel, 2008; (intro.) William Ropp, 2009. **Address:** Department of English and Foreign Languages, McNeese State University, PO Box 92655, Lake Charles, LA 70609, U.S.A.

WOOD, Kieron. Irish/British (born England), b. 1949. **Genres:** Law, Civil Liberties/Human Rights. **Career:** Journalist, attorney and writer. Radio Telefis Eireann, senior television reporter and radio sub-editor, 1978, religious affairs correspondent, 1987, legal affairs correspondent, 1990; Sunday Business Post, senior assistant editor, 2000-. **Publications:** The Most Beautiful Thing This Side of Heaven: The Tridentine Mass-and How to Say/Pray It, 1989; The Latter Day Saints, 1990; The Kilkenny Incest Case, 1993; (with P. O'Shea) Divorce in Ireland: The Options, The Issues, The Law, 1997, rev. ed. as Divorce in Ireland: Marital Breakdown, Answers and Alternatives, 2003; The High Court: A User's Guide, 1998, 2nd ed., 2002. **Address:** Sunday Business Post, 80 Harcourt St., Dublin, 2, Ireland. **Online address:** kwood@sbpost.ie

WOOD, Marcia (Mae). American (born United States), b. 1956. **Genres:** Young Adult Fiction, Money/Finance, Biography, Novels. **Career:** Richmond Heights Public Library, Board of Trustees, secretary, 1988-90; St. Louis Community College, instructor, 1992-. Writer. **Publications:** YOUNG ADULT NOVELS: The Secret Life of Hilary Thorne, 1988; The Search for Jim McGwynn, 1989; Always, Julia, 1993; Consolidating Financial Statements, 1995. OTHER: (contrib.) Before You Go, 1970. Contributor to journals. **Address:** John Hawkins & Associates Inc., 71 W 23rd St., Ste. 1600, New York, NY 10010-4185, U.S.A.

WOOD, Margaret. American (born United States), b. 1950. **Genres:** Fashion/Costume. **Career:** Window Rock School District, schoolteacher, 1971-72; Navajo Community College, director of library services, 1973-74; librarian, 1975-78; Heard Museum, intern lecturer, 1986, Fashion Fusion Exhibit, consultant/researcher/co-curator, 1999-2000; Native American Fashions Inc., owner/designer; Waverly Fabric Corp., lecturer, 1986; Wheelwright Museum of the American Indian, textile artist. Education consultant and writer. **Publications:** Native American Fashions: Adaptations of Traditional Designs, 1981, 2nd ed., 1997. Contributor to periodicals. **Address:** Native American Fashions Inc., PO Box 44802, Phoenix, AZ 85064, U.S.A. **Online address:** margaretwood44@aol.com

WOOD, Marguerite N. British (born England), b. 1923?. **Genres:** Poetry, Literary Criticism And History, Social Sciences. **Career:** Chartered physiotherapist, now retired; Poetry Society, General Council, staff, 1963-69; Suffolk Poetry Society, chairman, 1976-88. **Publications:** (Ed. with J.H. McMaster) Supplementary Report on the Manuscripts of His Grace the Duke of Hamilton, 1932; The Lord Provosts of Edinburgh, 1296-1932, 1932; Warrender Letters, 1935; (contrib.) The Abbey of Dryburgh, Berwickshire, 2nd ed., 1948; (ed.) Edinburgh Poll Tax Returns for 1694, 1951; (ed.) Register of Edinburgh Apprentices, 1756-1800, 1963; Stone of Vision, 1964; Windows Are Not Enough, 1971; Crack Me the Shell, 1975; A Line Drawn in Water, 1980; A Wall Cracks, 1993; Seascape, Selected Poems, 1994; The Day's Canvas, 1998. Works appear in anthologies. **Address:** Sandy Hill, Sandy Ln., Woodbridge, SU IP12 4DJ, England. **Online address:** m-d-wood@lineone.net

WOOD, Michael. American/British (born England), b. 1936. **Genres:** Plays/Screenplays, Film, Literary Criticism And History. **Career:** St. John's College, research fellow, 1961-64; Columbia University, instructor, 1964-66, assistant professor, 1968-71, associate professor, 1971-74, professor of comparative literature, 1974-82; freelance writer, 1966-68; Guggenheim fellow, 1973-74; National Endowment for the Humanities fellow, 1978-79; National University of Mexico, visiting professor, 1981-82; University of Exeter, professor of English literature, 1982-95; Princeton University, visiting fellow, 1993, Department of English and Comparative Literature, professor, 1995-, Charles Barnwell Straut Class of 1923 professor, acting associate chair, chair, 1998-2004. Writer. **Publications:** Stendhal, 1971; America in the Movies: Or Santa Maria, It Had Slipped My Mind, 1975; Literature: Fiction, Poetry, Drama (textbook), 1977; Gabriel García Márquez: One Hundred Years of Solitude, 1990; The Magician's Doubts: Nabokov and the Risks of Fiction, 1995; Children of Silence: On Contemporary Fiction, 1998; Belle de Jour, 2000; Franz Kafka, 2002; Road to Delphi: The Life and Afterlife of Oracles, 2003; Literature and the Taste of Knowledge, 2005; (ed. with S. Bermann) Nation, Language, and the Ethics of Translation, 2005; Yeats and Violence, 2010. **Address:** Department of English, Princeton University, 52 McCosh Hall, Princeton, NJ 08544, U.S.A. **Online address:** mwood@princeton.edu

WOOD, Monica. American (born United States), b. 1953. **Genres:** Novels, Novellas/Short Stories, Writing/Journalism, Young Adult Non-fiction. **Career:** High school guidance counselor, 1980-86; freelance writer, 1986-; University of Southern Maine, teacher of fiction writing, 1988-; Virginia Center for Creative Arts, fellow. **Publications:** (Ed.) Short Takes: 15 Contemporary Stories, 1992; Secret Language: A Novel, 1993; Description, 1995; (with J.M. Bickham and K. Reed) More about How to Write a Million: The Essential Guide to Becoming a Successful Author, 1996; 12 Multicultural Novels: A Reading and Teaching Guide, 1997; My Only Story: A Novel, 2001; Ernie's Ark: Stories, 2001; The Pocket Muse: Ideas & Inspirations for Writing, 2002; Any Bitter Thing: A Novel, 2005; The Pocket Muse: Endless Inspiration: New Ideas for Writing, 2006; When We Were the Kennedys: A Memoir from Mexico, Maine, 2012. Works appear in anthologies. Contributor to periodicals. **Address:** Houghton Mifflin Harcourt, 222 Berkeley St., Boston, MA 02116, U.S.A. **Online address:** monica@monicawood.com

WOOD, N. Lee. American (born United States), b. 1955?. **Genres:** Science Fiction/Fantasy, Novels. **Career:** Author. **Publications:** Looking for the Mahdi, 1996; Faraday's Orphans, 1997; Bloodrights, 1999, rev. ed., 2000; Master of None, 2004; Kingdom of Lies, 2005; Kingdom of Silence, 2009. Contributor to periodicals. **Address:** Ace Books/Berkeley Publishing Group, 200 Madison Ave., New York, NY 10016, U.S.A.

WOOD, Nuria. *See* **NOBISSO, Josephine.**

WOOD, Patricia. American (born United States), b. 1953. **Genres:** Novels,

Literary Criticism And History. **Career:** Writer. **Publications:** Lottery, 2007. Contributor to periodicals. **Address:** c/o Dorian Karchmar, William Morris Endeavor Entertainment, 1325 Ave. of the Americas, New York, NY 10019, U.S.A. **Online address:** patricia@patriciawoodauthor.com

WOOD, Ralph C. American (born United States), b. 1942. **Genres:** Theology/Religion. **Career:** North Park College, lecturer in English, 1966-67; Wake Forest University, instructor, 1971-75, assistant professor, 1975-79, associate professor, 1979-87, professor of religion, 1987-90, John Allen Easley professor of religion, 1990-97; Samford University, distinguished professor of religion, 1997-98; Baylor University, Department of Religion, university professor of theology and literature, 1998-. Writer. **Publications:** (Co-ed.) The Glad Irony of the Gospel: Sermons Preached at Wake Forest Baptist Church, 1985; (ed. with J.E. Collins) Civil Religion and Transcendent Experience: Studies in Theology and History, Psychology and Mysticism, 1988; The Comedy of Redemption: Christian Faith and Comic Vision in Four American Novelists, 1988; Gospel According to Tolkien: Visions of the Kingdom in Middle-Earth, 2003; Contending for the Faith: The Church's Engagement with Culture, 2003; Flannery O'Connor and the Christ-haunted South, 2004; Literature and Theology, 2008; Preaching and Professing: Sermons by a Teacher Seeking to Proclaim the Gospel, 2009; Chesterton: The Nightmare Goodness of God, 2011. Works appear in anthologies. Contributor of articles to journals and magazines. **Address:** Department of Religion, Baylor University, 601 Tidwell Bible Bldg., 1 Bear Pl., PO Box 97284, Waco, TX 76798-7284, U.S.A. **Online address:** ralph_wood@baylor.edu

WOOD, Stephanie. American (born United States), b. 1954. **Genres:** History. **Career:** University of California, Department of History, teaching associate 1980-83; University of Maine, assistant professor of Latin American and U.S. history, 1984-89; University of Oregon, Department of History, adjunct assistant professor of Latin American history, 1988-, faculty affiliate, 1999-2002, Center for the Study of Women in Society, Wired Humanities Project, coordinator, 2002-04, associate director, 2004-09, Yamada Language Center, Wired Humanities Projects, director, 2009-; Meridian Productions, director of research for the videotape documentary. Writer. **Publications:** (Ed. with S. Schroeder and R. Haskett) Indian Women of Early Mexico, 1997; (ed. with X.N. Ramirez) De Tlacuilos y Escribanos: Estudios sobre Documentos Indigenas Coloniales del Centro de Mexico, 1998; Transcending Conquest: Nahua Views of Spanish Colonial Mexico, 2003. Contributor of articles to academic journals. **Address:** Center for the Study of Women in Society, University of Oregon, 340 Hendricks Hall, Eugene, OR 97403-1201, U.S.A. **Online address:** swood@uoregon.edu

WOOD, Ted. See **WOOD, Edward John.**

WOODARD, J. David. American (born United States), b. 1947. **Genres:** Politics/Government, History. **Career:** Auburn University, assistant professor, 1978-80; Clemson University, professor of political science, 1983-. Writer. **Publications:** The Burden of Busing: The Politics of Desegregation in Nashville, Tennessee, 1985; American Conservatism from Burke to Bush: An Introduction, 1991; The Conservative Tradition in America, 1996; The Conservative Tradition in America, 2003; The America That Reagan Built, 2006; The New Southern Politics, 2006; Why We Whisper: Restoring Our Right to Say It's Wrong, 2008. Contributor of articles to periodicals. **Address:** Central, SC , U.S.A. **Online address:** judithw@clemson.edu

WOODARD, Michael D. American (born United States), b. 1946. **Genres:** Sex, Race Relations, Business/Trade/Industry, Economics, Social Sciences. **Career:** Neighborhood Youth Corps, job placement counselor and training coordinator, 1966-70; Indiana National Bank, assistant manager, 1970-72; Project Equality of Indiana, state director, 1973-75; employment management consultant, 1975-81; U.S. Department of Agriculture, Forest Service, North Central Forest Experiment Station, research associate, 1979-80; Governors State University, research associate, 1980-81; University of Missouri-Columbia, assistant professor, 1986-89, acting assistant dean for minority affairs, 1987-88; Center for Advanced Study in the Behavioral Sciences, Stanford, fellow, 1986; Woodard & Associates (consulting firm), president and chief executive officer, 1990-; University of Chicago, William Burgess fellow; University of Maryland, faculty; University of Missouri, faculty; University of California, Los Angeles, faculty. Writer. **Publications:** (Co-author) The Sexual Harassment Test, 1992; (co-author) The Problem of Sexual Harassment: A Supervisor's Guide, 1992; Black Entrepreneurs in America: Stories of Struggle and Success, 1996, 2nd ed., 1998. Contributor to books. **Address:**

Woodard & Associates Inc., 325 P St. SW, Ste. 706, PO Box 70594, Washington, DC 20024-0594, U.S.A. **Online address:** mdwnmdr@aol.com

WOODBURY, Heather. American (born United States), b. 1964?. **Genres:** Plays/Screenplays, Art/Art History, Photography. **Career:** CafÉ Bustelo, founder and director, 1987-89; Joseph Papp Public Theater, playwright-in-residence, 2001-02; Atlantic Arts Center, master-artist-in-residence, 2009; Fomenting ARTS Unlimited Inc., artistic director. Performance artist, playwright and screenwriter. **Publications:** What Ever: A Living Novel, 2003; Tale of 2Cities: An American Joyride on Multiple Tracks, 2006. Contributor to books. **Address:** Fomenting ARTS Unlimited Inc., 1166 Glendale Blvd., Los Angeles, CA 90026-3203, U.S.A. **Online address:** heather@heatherwoodbury.com

WOODFORD, Peggy. British (born England), b. 1937. **Genres:** Novels, History, Music, Biography, Novellas/Short Stories, Young Adult Fiction. **Career:** British Broadcasting Corp., research and script assistant, 1961-63; College of Padworth, senior tutor in English, 1963-66; freelance writer, 1966-. **Publications:** Abraham's Legacy, 1963; Schubert: His Life and Times, 1969, 2nd ed., 1978; Please Don't Go, 1972, 2nd ed., 2007; Backwater War, 1974; Mozart: His Life and Times, 1977; (ed. and contrib.) The Real Thing: Seven Stories of Love, 1977 in US as Looking for Love: Seven Uncommon Love Stories, 1979; Rise of the Raj, 1978; See You Tomorrow, 1979; New Stories, 1980; (ed. and contrib.) You Can't Keep Out the Darkness, 1980; Love Me, Love Rome, 1981; The Girl With a Voice, 1984; (ed.) Misfits: An Anthology of Short Stories, 1984; Monster in Our Midst, 1989; Out of the Sun, 1990; Blood and Mortar, 1994; Cupid's Tears, 1995; On the Night, 1997; One Son is Enough, 2006; Powder Boy, forthcoming. **Address:** Laura Morris Literary Agency, 21 Highshore Rd., London, GL SE15 5AA, England. **Online address:** peggywoodford@talktalk.net

WOODGER, Elin. British/American (born United States), b. 1954. **Genres:** Art/Art History, Literary Criticism And History, Travel/Exploration, History. **Career:** Linguistics Intl., operations manager and customer service manager, 1979-88; Massachusetts General Hospital, executive secretary, 1989-98; freelance writer, 1997-. **Publications:** (With B. Toropov) Encyclopedia of the Lewis and Clark Expedition, 2004; (with D.F. Burg) The 1980s, 2006. **Address:** James Peter Associates Inc., PO Box 358, New Canaan, CT 06840, U.S.A. **Online address:** ewoodgerm@aol.com

WOODHOUSE, Emma. See **HARROD-EAGLES, Cynthia.**

WOODHOUSE, Sarah. British (born England) **Genres:** Romance/Historical, Education. **Career:** Writer. **Publications:** ROMANCE NOVELS: A Season of Mists, 1984; The Indian Widow, 1986; Daughter of the Sea, 1986; The Peacock's Feather, 1988; The Native Air, 1991; Enchanted Ground, 1993; Meeting Lily, 1995; Other Lives, 1997; My Summer with Julia, 2000; (co-author) Helping Children With Yoga: A Guide for Parents and Teachers, 2006; (with M. Patmore) Minimum Core for Numeracy: Audit and Test, 2009. Contributor to periodicals. **Address:** c/o Century, 20 Vauxhall Bridge Rd., London, GL SW1V 2SA, England.

WOODHOUSE, S(usan) T. (Liz Carlyle). American (born United States), b. 1958. **Genres:** Romance/Historical, inspirational/Motivational Literature, Literary Criticism And History. **Career:** Writer. **Publications:** ROMANCE FICTION: UNDER PSEUDONYM LIZ CARLYLE: My False Heart, 1999; A Woman Scorned, 2000; Beauty Like the Night, 2000; A Woman of Virtue, 2001; No True Gentleman, 2002; The Devil You Know, 2003; A Deal with the Devil, 2004; The Devil to Pay, 2005; One Little Sin, 2005; Two Little Lies, 2006; Three Little Secrets, 2006; Never Lie to a Lady, 2007; Never Deceive a Duke, 2007; Never Romance a Rake, 2008; Tempted All Night, 2009; Wicked All Day, 2009; One Touch of Scandal, 2010. CO-AUTHOR: (with C. Maxwell) Tea for Two: Two Novellas, 2002; Big Guns Out of Uniform, 2003; The One That Got Away, 2004; The School for Heiresses, 2006. Contributor of articles to periodicals. **Address:** c/o Nancy Yost Lowenstein, Lowenstein-Yost Associates, 121 W 27th St., Ste. 601, New York, NY 10001, U.S.A. **Online address:** lizcarlyle@aol.com

WOODHULL, Winifred. (Winnie Woodhull). American (born United States), b. 1950. **Genres:** Administration/Management, Social Sciences. **Career:** University of Virginia, instructor, 1980-81; Dickinson College, instructor, 1981-86; University of Minnesota, instructor, 1986-87, 1988-89; Carleton College, instructor, 1987-88; University of California, associate professor of

French and cultural studies, 1989-. Writer. **Publications:** Transfigurations of the Maghreb: Feminism, Decolonization, and Literatures, 1993; In Postcolonial Francophone Studies: A Critical Introduction, 2003; (ed. with R. Cancel) African Diasporas: Ancestors, Migrations and Borders, 2008. **Address:** Department of Literature, University of California, LIT 332, Literature Dept. 0410, 9500 Gilman Dr., La Jolla, CA 92093-0410, U.S.A. **Online address:** wwoodhull@ucsd.edu

WOODHULL, Winnie. *See* **WOODHULL, Winifred.**

WOODING, Sharon L(ouise). American (born United States), b. 1943. **Genres:** Children's Fiction, Human Relations/Parenting, Illustrations. **Career:** New York Public Schools, teacher, 1965-66; Walter C. Black Elementary School, teacher, 1966-69; Climbing Tower School, teacher, 1973-78; Colorado Rocky Mountain School, director of publications, 1978-79; Indian Hill Arts, Groton Center for the Arts, art teacher, 1979-84; Groton Public Schools, elementary art teacher, 1987-2004, middle school art teacher, 2004-; Lawrence Academy, art teacher. Painter and writer. **Publications:** SELF-ILLUSTRATOR: Hilary's Story, 1980; Arthur's Christmas Wish, 1986; A Dance for Phoebe, 1986; The Painter's Cat, 1994. POEMS: The Box, the Party, Feet, 2003. **Address:** Lawrence Academy, 26 Powderhouse Rd., PO Box 992, Groton, MA 01450, U.S.A.

WOODLAND, Alan D(onald). Australian (born Australia), b. 1943. **Genres:** Economics. **Career:** University of New England, lecturer, 1967-69; University of Sydney, professor of Econometrics; University of British Columbia, assistant professor, 1969-74, associate professor, 1975-77, professor, 1978-81; The Economic Record, editor, 1986-92; Review of International Economics and Public Finance, associate editor; University of New South Wales, Australian School of Business, School of Economics, professor and ARC Australian professorial fellow, Academy of the Social Sciences in Australia, fellow, scientia professor; Econometric Society, fellow; Academy of the Social Sciences of Australia, fellow; ARC Centre of Excellence in Population Ageing Research, chief investigator. **Publications:** On Testing Weak Separability, 1946; International Trade and Resource Allocation, 1982; (ed. with J. Piggott) International Trade Policy and the Pacific Rim: Proceedings of the IEA Conference Held in Sydney Australia, 1999; (ed.) Economic Theory and International Trade: Essays in Honour of Murray C. Kemp, 2002; (with C. Yoshida) Economics of Illegal Immigration, 2005. **Address:** School of Economics, University of New South Wales, Rm. 416, Australian School of Business Bldg., Sydney, NW 2052, Australia. **Online address:** a.woodland@unsw.edu.au

WOODLAND, Malcolm. Canadian (born Canada), b. 1958. **Genres:** Literary Criticism And History, Poetry, History. **Career:** University of Toronto, Department of English, associate professor. Writer. **Publications:** Wallace Stevens and the Apocalyptic Mode, 2005. Contributor of articles to periodicals. **Address:** Department of English, University of Toronto, 170 Saint George St., Toronto, ON M5R 2M8, Canada. **Online address:** mal.woodland@utoronto.ca

WOODMAN, Allen. American (born United States), b. 1954. **Genres:** Novels, Novellas/Short Stories, Children's Fiction. **Career:** Northern Arizona University, associate professor of English, 1986-, professor of creative writing, department chair. Writer. **Publications:** (Ed.) Stories About How Things Fall Apart and What's Left When They Do, 1985; The Shoebox of Desire and Other Tales, 1987; (with D. Kirby) The Cows Are Going to Paris, 1991; (with D. Kirby) The Bear Who Came to Stay, 1994; All-You-Can-Eat, Alabama (novel), 1994; Saved by Mr. F. Scott Fitzgerald and Other Stories, 1997. **Address:** Department of English, Northern Arizona University, Rm. 325, BAA Bldg. 23, PO Box 6032, Flagstaff, AZ 86011, U.S.A. **Online address:** allen.woodman@nau.edu

WOODMAN, David C(harles). Canadian (born Canada), b. 1956. **Genres:** Travel/Exploration, Mystery/Crime/Suspense, History. **Career:** Writer. **Publications:** Unravelling the Franklin Mystery: Inuit Testimony, 1991; Strangers Among Us, 1995. Contributor to journals. **Address:** 27 Eaton Ave., Victoria, BC V8Z 5C9, Canada.

WOODMAN, Harold David. American (born United States), b. 1928. **Genres:** History. **Career:** Roosevelt University, lecturer in American history, 1962-63; University of Missouri, assistant professor, 1963-66, associate professor of American history, 1966-69, professor of history, 1969-71;

Purdue University, Department of History, professor, 1971-, American Studies, chair, 1981-, Louis Martin Sears distinguished professor of history, now professor emeritus; Purdue University Press, chairman, 1979-80; Business History Conference, president, 1980; Southern Historical Association, president. writer. **Publications:** (Ed. with A.F. Davis) Conflict and Consensus in American History, 1966, 9th ed., 1997; King Cotton and His Retainers, 1968; New South-New Law, 1995. EDITOR: Slavery and the Southern Economy, 1966; The Legacy of the American Civil War, 1973. Contributor of articles to journals. **Address:** Department of History, Purdue University, University Hall, 672 Oval Dr., West Lafayette, IN 47907-2087, U.S.A. **Online address:** hwoodman@purdue.edu

WOODMAN, Marion (Boa). Canadian (born Canada), b. 1928. **Genres:** Psychology, Women's Studies And Issues, Medicine/Health. **Career:** Private practice, Jungian analyst, 1949-93; high school teacher of English and creative drama, 1950-74; Marion Woodman Foundation, senior faculty. Writer. **Publications:** The Owl Was A Baker's Daughter: Obesity, Anorexia Nervosa and the Repressed Feminine: A Psychological Study, 1980; Addiction to Perfection: The Still Unravished Bride: A Psychological Study, 1982; The Pregnant Virgin: A Process of Psychological Transformation, 1985; (contrib.) Betwixt and Between: Rites of Initiation, 1987; (contrib.) Family Secrets: Life Stories of Adult Children of Alcoholics, 1987; The Ravaged Bridegroom: Masculinity in Women, 1990; (contrib.) To Be a Woman, 1990; (contrib.) Mothers and Fathers, 1990; (with K. Dotson, M. Hamilton and R. Greer-Allen) Leaving My Father's House: A Journey to Conscious Femininity, 1992; (contrib.) We Two, 1992; Conscious Femininity: Interviews with Marion Woodman, 1993; (with E. Dickson) Dancing in the Flames: The Dark Goddess in the Transformation of Consciousness, 1996; (with J. Mellick) Coming Home to Myself: Reflections for Nurturing a Woman's Body and Soul, 1998; (with R. Bly) The Maiden King: The Reunion of Masculine and Feminine, 1998; (with L. van Der Post, T. Berry and R. Woodman) The Forsaken Garden, 1998; Bone, Dying into Life, 2000. Contributor to books and periodicals. **Address:** Shambhala Publications Inc., 300 Massachusetts Ave., Horticultural Hall, Boston, MA 02115, U.S.A.

WOODRING, Jim. American (born United States), b. 1952. **Genres:** Cartoons, Illustrations, Novels. **Career:** Cartoonist, storyboard artist, commercial illustrator and writer. **Publications:** Tantalizing Stories Presents Frank in the River, 1992; The Book of Jim, 1993; Star Wars: Jabba the Hutt, 1995; (with K. Plunkett) Aliens: Labrinth, 1997; Frank, 2 vols., 1997; (co-author) Aliens: Kidnapped, 1999; Trosper, 2002; The Frank Book, 2003; Oneiric Diary, 2003; Jim Woodring Dream Journal, 2003; Pupshaw and Pushpaw, 2004; Seeing Things, 2005; The Museum of Love and Mystery, 2008; The Portable Frank, 2009; Weathercraft, 2010; Congress of the Animals, 2011. Works appear in anthologies. Contributor to periodicals. **Address:** c/o Author Mail, Fantagraphics Books Inc., 7563 Lake City Way NE, Seattle, WA 98115, U.S.A. **Online address:** jimwoodring@mindspring.com

WOODRUFF, Joan Leslie. American (born United States), b. 1953. **Genres:** Novels, Mystery/Crime/Suspense, Mythology/Folklore, Young Adult Nonfiction. **Career:** San Bernardino Community Hospital, Hand Rehabilitation Clinic, director of occupational therapy services, 1975-77, director and administrator of clinic, 1976-87; Redlands Hospital, administrator and clinical representative, 1980; Martin Luther Memorial Hospital, administrator, 1982; Hemet Valley Hospital, staff, 1984; Riverside American Indian Center, board director, 1987-91. Writer. **Publications:** Traditional Stories and Foods: An American Indian Remembers, 1990; Neighbors (novel), 1993; The Shiloh Renewal (novel), 1998; Ghost in the Rainbow (suspense novel), 2002; Wishes and Windmills, 2003; Polar Bears in the Kitchen, 2009. Contributor to journals, magazines and newspapers. **Address:** PO Box 687, Mountainair, NM 87036-0687, U.S.A. **Online address:** pekoes7152@mypacks.net

WOODRUFF, Lee McConaughy. American (born United States), b. 1960?. **Genres:** Autobiography/Memoirs, Essays. **Career:** Hill and Knowlton (communications company), account supervisor, 1988; Porter Novelli (public relations firm), senior vice president; Bob Woodruff Foundation, co-founder. Writer and public relations and marketing consultant. **Publications:** (With B. Woodruff) In an Instant: A Family's Journey of Love and Healing (memoir), 2007; Perfectly Imperfect: A Life in Progress (essays), 2009. Contributor to periodicals. **Address:** Bob Woodruff Foundation, PO Box 955, Bristow, VA 20136, U.S.A. **Online address:** info@remind.org

WOODRUFF, Nancy. American (born United States), b. 1963?. **Genres:**

Novels. **Career:** Columbia University, adjunct assistant professor; State University of New York, faculty; The American International University, Richmond College, adjunct assistant professor; New York University, College of Arts and Science, faculty. Writer. **Publications:** Someone Else's Child, 2000; My Wife's Affair, 2010. **Address:** c/o Elizabeth Tobin, NAL, Penguin Group USA, 375 Hudson St., 5th Fl., New York, NY 10014, U.S.A. **Online address:** nancy@nancywoodruff.com

WOODRUFF, Nan Elizabeth. American (born United States), b. 1949. **Genres:** History. **Career:** University of Illinois, assistant editor, 1977-78; College of Charleston, assistant professor of history, 1979-88; Pennsylvania State University, assistant professor of history, 1988-92, associate professor of history, 1992-2004, professor of history, 2004-; University of Arkansas, Donovan distinguished lecturer, 1992; Tulane University, Andrew Mellon lecturer, 1998; Delta State University, Crandall lecturer, 2003. **Publications:** As Rare As Rain: Federal Relief in the Great Southern Drought of 1930-31, 1985; American Congo: The African American Freedom Struggle in the Delta, 2003. Contributor of articles to books and periodicals. **Address:** Department of History & Religious Studies Program, Pennsylvania State University, 302 Weaver Bldg., University Park, PA 16802-5503, U.S.A. **Online address:** new7@psu.edu

WOODRUM, Robert H. American (born United States), b. 1965. **Genres:** Race Relations. **Career:** Clark Atlanta University, visiting assistant professor of history. Writer. **Publications:** Everybody Was Black Down There: Race and Industrial Change in the Alabama Coalfields, 2007. **Address:** Clark Atlanta University, 25 McPheeters-Dennis SW, Atlanta, GA 30314, U.S.A. **Online address:** rwoodrum@cau.edu

WOODS, Brenda. American (born United States) **Genres:** Novels, History, Literary Criticism And History. **Career:** Physical therapist and writer. **Publications:** The Red Rose Box, 2002; Emako Blue, 2004; My Name is Sally Little Song, 2006; A Star on the Hollywood Walk of Fame, 2010. **Address:** c/o Author Mail, G. P. Putnam, 375 Hudson St., New York, NY 10014-3658, U.S.A.

WOODS, Eldrick. *See* **WOODS, Tiger.**

WOODS, Janet. (Bryanna Fox). Australian/British (born England), b. 1939?. **Genres:** Novels. **Career:** Author. **Publications:** (As Bryanna Fox) Thread of Destiny, 1992; Daughter of Darkness, 2001; Angelina, 2002; Pandora's Girl, 2002; From This Day Forth, 2002; Against the Tide, 2003; A Dorset Girl, 2003; A Grace of Day, 2003; A Fair Pretender, 2004; Beyond the Plough, 2004; A Handful of Ashes, 2004; The Stonecutter's Daughter, 2005; Amaranth Moon, 2005; Where Seagulls Soar, 2006; Cinnamon Sky, 2006; More Than a Promise, 2006; The Convict's Woman, 2007; Broken Journey, 2007; The Coal Gatherer, 2007; Edge of Regret, 2008; Without Reproach, 2008; Hearts of Gold, 2009; Salting the Wound, 2009; Straw in the Wind, 2010; Paper Doll 2010; Lady Lightfingers, 2011. **Address:** Woodcott Writing Services, PO Box 2099, Kardinya, WA 6163, Australia. **Online address:** woods@iinet.net.au

WOODS, Jeannie Marlin. American (born United States), b. 1947. **Genres:** Theatre, Bibliography, Biography, Translations. **Career:** Jeannie Marlin, actor, 1972-80; Third Eye Theater, principal actor, 1972-74; Germinal Stage Denver, principal actor, 1977-80; City University of New York, City College, lecturer, 1987; Bernard M. Baruch College, lecturer, 1988; Winthrop University, assistant professor, 1989-95, associate professor, 1995-2000, Winthrop's outstanding junior professor, 1995, professor and interim department chair, 2000-, College of Visual and Performing Arts, associate dean, 2001-, director; National Institute of the Arts, Fulbright professor, 1998-99, senior Fulbright lecturer, 1998-99; New Stage Ensemble Theatre, co-founder and artistic director, 1993, 2001-; Starry Night Repertory Theatre, founder, 2004, artistic director and president of the board; Western Illinois University, Department of Theatre and Dance, chairperson, 2006-08; Association for Theatre in Higher Education, mentor. Writer. **Publications:** Maureen Stapleton: A Bio-Bibliography, 1992; Theatre to Change Men's Souls: The Artistry of Adrian Hall, 1993; (trans.) Chi-Mei Wang, The Bride and Her Double, 1999. Contributor to periodicals. **Address:** College of Visual and Performing Arts, Winthrop University, 133 McLaurin Hall, Rock Hill, SC 29733, U.S.A. **Online address:** woodsj@winthrop.edu

WOODS, Lawrence T(imothy). Canadian (born Canada), b. 1960. **Genres:** International Relations/Current Affairs, Politics/Government. **Career:** University of British Columbia, Institute of International Relations, research assistant, 1982-83; honorary research associate, 1993, Institute of Asian Research, visiting professor, 1998-99; Queen's University, Department of Political Studies, teaching assistant, 1983-84; Oakangan College, Continuing Education Division, instructor, 1985; substitute teacher, 1984-85; Bishop's University, assistant professor of political studies, 1988-93, head men's soccer coach, 1989; University of Northern British Columbia, associate professor of international studies, 1993-2001, Office of International Programmes, acting director, 1993-94; Canadian Consortium on Asia Pacific Security, director, 1997, co-chair, 1998-2001, vice president, 1998-2000, president, 2000-01; American University of Sharjah, associate professor of political science and international studies, 2001-, professor of political science and international studies; University of Victoria, Centre for Asia Pacific Initiatives, visiting professor, 1998-99; East Timor Action Group, conveyor, 1999; Prince George Immigration and Multicultural Services Society, director, 2000. Writer. **Publications:** Asia-Pacific Diplomacy: Nongovernmental Organizations and International Relations, 1993; (ed. with P. Bowles) Japan after the Economic Miracle: In Search of New Directions, 2000; (ed.) Japan's Emergence as a Modern State: Political and Economic Problems of the Meiji Period, 2000; (ed.) Understanding Japan: Essays Inspired by Frank Langdon, 2004. Contributor of articles to journals. **Address:** Department of Arab & International Studies, College of Arts & Sciences, American University of Sharjah, PO Box 26666, Sharjah, 26666, United Arab Emirates. **Online address:** lwoods@aus.edu

WOODS, Macdara. Irish (born Ireland), b. 1942?. **Genres:** Poetry, Translations. **Career:** Cyphers (literary review), founding co-editor, 1975-. Poet, translator, broadcaster and educator. **Publications:** POETRY: Decimal D. Sex Drinks in a Bar in Marrakesh, 1970; Early Morning Matins, 1973; Stopping the Lights in Ranelagh, 1987; Miz Moon, 1988; The Hanged Man Was Not Surrendering, 1990; (ed.) The Kilkenny Anthology, 1991; Notes from the Countries of Blood-Red Flowers, 1994; Selected Poems, 1996; Knowledge in the Blood: New and Selected Poems, 2000; The Nightingale Water, 2000; (ed. with J. Vaughan) Present Tense: Words and Pictures, 2006; Artichoke Wine, 2006; This Time This Place, 2007. OTHER: (trans.) R. Abuswesha, The King of the Dead and Other Libyan Tales, 1978. **Address:** Dublin, DU , Ireland. **Online address:** macdarawoods@gmail.com

WOODS, Michael. British (born England), b. 1952. **Genres:** Art/Art History, Photography, Biography. **Career:** Freelance photographer. **Publications:** Two Deaths (art photography), 1999; (with N. Roeg) Sound, 2000; (with V. Stern, L. Summers and V. V. Horne) Roadmaps and Rampways: Profiles of Students with Disabilities in Science, Mathematics, Engineering, and Technology, 2001. Contributor to periodicals. **Address:** c/o William Hamilton, A. M. Heath & Company Ltd., 6 Warwick Ct., London, GL WC1R 5DJ, England.

WOODS, Paula L. American (born United States), b. 1953?. **Genres:** Race Relations, Mystery/Crime/Suspense, Novels, Young Adult Fiction, Essays. **Career:** Writer, 1992-. **Publications:** (With F.H. Liddell) I, Too Sing America: The African American Book of Days, 1992; (ed. with F.H. Liddell) I Hear a Symphony: African Americans Celebrate Love, 1994; (ed.) Spooks, Spies and Private Eyes: Black Mystery, Crime and Suspense Fiction, 1995; (ed. with F.H. Liddell) Merry Christmas, Baby: A Christmas and Kwanzaa Treasury, 1996. CHARLOTTE JUSTICE MYSTERY NOVELS: Inner City Blues, 1999, rev. ed., 2000; Stormy Weather, 2001, rev. ed., 2002; Dirty Laundry, 2003; Strange Bedfellows, 2006. **Address:** Faith Childs Literary Agency Inc., 915 Broadway, Ste. 1009, New York, NY 10010, U.S.A. **Online address:** carolt@woodsontheweb.com

WOODS, Peter. *See* **SHAW, Thurstan.**

WOODS, Stuart. American (born United States), b. 1938. **Genres:** Novels, Travel/Exploration, Autobiography/Memoirs, Adult Non-fiction, Young Adult Fiction, Romance/Historical. **Career:** Consultant, 1960-73; freelance writer, 1973-. **Publications:** FICTION: Chiefs, 1981; Run before the Wind, 1983; Deep Lie, 1986; Under the Lake, 1987; White Cargo, 1988; Grass Roots, 1989; Palindrome, 1991; New York Dead, 1991; Santa Fe Rules, 1992; L.A. Times, 1993; Dead Eyes, 1994; Heat, 1994; Imperfect Strangers, 1995; Choke, 1995; Dirt, 1996; Dead in the Water, 1997; Swimming to Catalina, 1998; Orchid Beach, 1998; Worst Fears Realized, 1999; Run, 2000; L.A. Dead, 2000; Cold Paradise, 2001; Orchid Blues, 2001; The Short Forever, 2002; Blood Orchid, 2002; Capital Crimes, 2003; Dirty Work, 2003; The Prince of Beverly Hills, 2004; Reckless Abandon, 2004; Iron Orchid,

2005; Two-Dollar Bill, 2005; Dark Harbor, 2006; Dead Paradise, 2006; Short Straw, 2006; Beverly Hills Dead, 2007; Fresh Disasters, 2007; Shoot Him If He Runs, 2007; Santa Fe dead, 2008; Hot Mahogany, 2008; Hothouse Orchid, 2009; Mounting Fears, 2009; Loitering with Intent, 2009, Kisser, 2009; Lucid Intervals, 2010; Santa Fe Edge, 2010; Strategic Moves, 2011; Bel-Air Dead, 2011. NON-FICTION: Blue Water, Green Skipper (memoir), 1977; A Romantic's Guide to the Country Inns of Britain and Ireland, 1979. OTHER: Son of Stone, 2011; D.C. Dead, 2011; Unnatural Acts, 2012. Contributor to magazines. **Address:** Janklow and Nesbit Associates, 445 Park Ave., New York, NY 10022-2606, U.S.A. **Online address:** stuart@stuartwoods.com

WOODS, Tiger. (Eldrick Woods). American (born United States), b. 1975. **Genres:** Sports/Fitness. **Career:** Tiger Woods Foundation, co-founder, 1996-; Tiger Woods Design, founder & chair, 2006-. Writer. **Publications:** (co-author) How I Play Golf, 2001; Quotable Tiger: A Grand Slam Compendium of Compelling Quotes by and about Tiger Woods, Golf Champion Extraordinaire, 2001. **Address:** PGA, 100 Avenue of Champions, PO Box 10960, Palm Beach Gardens, FL 33418-3665, U.S.A.

WOODS, Titania. *See* **WEATHERLY**, Lee.

WOODS, Vanessa. American/Australian (born Australia), b. 1977?. **Genres:** Autobiography/Memoirs, Children's Fiction. **Career:** Duke University, research scientist; Discovery Channel, writer; Friends of Bonobos, board director. **Publications:** It's Every Monkey for Themselves: A True Story of Sex, Love, and Lies in the Jungle (memoir), 2007; Bonobo Handshake: A Memoir of Love and Adventure in the Congo, 2010. CHILDREN'S NONFICTION: It's True! There Are Bugs in Your Bed, 2004; It's True! Space Turns You into Spaghetti, 2006; It's True! Pirates Ate Rats, 2007. Contributor to periodicals. **Address:** Duke University, PO Box 90383, Durham, NC 27708, U.S.A. **Online address:** v.woods@duke.edu

WOODSON, Jacqueline. American (born United States), b. 1963. **Genres:** Children's Non-fiction, Young Adult Non-fiction, Novels, Children's Fiction, Young Adult Fiction. **Career:** Goddard College, M.F.A. Writing Program, associate faculty, 1993-95; Eugene Lang College, associate faculty, 1994; National Book Foundation, writer-in-residence, 1995-96; Vermont College, M.F.A. Program, associate faculty, 1996. **Publications:** FOR CHILDREN: Martin Luther King, Jr., and His Birthday, 1990; We Had a Picnic This Sunday Past, 1997; Sweet, Sweet Memory, 2000; The Other Side, 2001; Visiting Day, 2002; Our Gracie Aunt, 2002; Coming on Home Soon, 2004; Show Way, 2005. FICTION FOR YOUNG ADULTS: Last Summer with Maizon, 1990; The Dear One, 1991; Maizon at Blue Hill, 1992; Between Madison & Palmetto, 1993; Book Chase, 1994; I Hadn't Meant to Tell You This, 1994; From the Notebooks of Melanin Sun, 1995; The House You Pass on the Way, 1997; If You Come Softly, 1998; Lena, 1999; Miracle's Boys, 2000; Hush, 2002; Locomotion, 2003; Behind You, 2004. OTHERS: Autobiography of a Family Photo: A Novel, 1995; (ed. with N.F. Mazer) Just a Writer's Thing: A Collection of Prose and Poetry From the National Book Foundation's 1995; (ed.) A Way Out of No Way: Writing about Growing Up Black in America (short stories), 1996; Summer Writing Camp, 1996; Feathers, 2007; After Tupac & D Foster, 2008; Peace, Locomotion, 2009; Pecan Pie Baby, 2010; Beneath a Meth Moon, 2012; Each Kindness, 2012. **Address:** Charlotte Sheedy Literary Agency, 65 Bleeker St., Ste. 12, New York, NY 10012, U.S.A. **Online address:** letters@jacquelinewoodson.com

WOODWARD, Bob. American (born United States), b. 1943. **Genres:** Politics/Government, Military/Defense/Arms Control, Social Sciences, History, Adult Non-fiction. **Career:** Montgomery County Sentinel, reporter, 1970-71; Washington Post, reporter, 1971-79, Metro Section, assistant managing editor, 1979-81, Investigative News Section, assistant managing editor, 1981-, associate editor. **Publications:** (With C. Bernstein) All the Presidents Men, 1974; (with C. Bernstein) The Final Days, 1976; (with S. Armstrong) The Brethren: Inside the Supreme Court, 1979; Wired: The Short Life and Fast Times of John Belushi, 1984; Veil: The Secret Wars of the CIA, 1981-1987, 1987; The Secret Wars of the CIA, 1987; The Commanders, 1991; (with D.S. Broder) The Man Who Would Be President: Dan Quayle, 1992; The Agenda: Inside the Clinton White House, 1994; The First Act: Inside the Clinton White House, 1994; The Choice, 1996; Shadow: Five Presidents and the Legacy of Watergate, 1999; Maestro: Greenspans Fed and the American Boom, 2000; Bush at War, 2002; Plan of Attack, 2004; The Secret Man, 2005; State of Denial, 2006; The War Within: A Secret White House History, 2006-2008, 2008; Obamas Wars, 2010. Contributor to books and periodicals. **Address:**

Washington Post, 1150 15th St. NW, Washington, DC 20071-0001, U.S.A. **Online address:** woodwardb@washpost.com

WOODWARD, Caroline (Hendrika). Canadian (born Canada), b. 1952. **Genres:** Novels, Novellas/Short Stories, Adult Non-fiction, Education. **Career:** Writer, 1968-; Polestar Press, manuscript reader, managing editor; teacher in creative writing, 1985-; B.C. Arts Council, vice-chair, 1996-98; Kate Walker & Co., publishers representative, through 2008. **Publications:** A Blue Fable, 1981; Disturbing the Peace, 1990; Alaska Highway Two-Step (novel), 1993; Work is a 4-Letter Word (short stories and illustrations), 1999; Penny Loves Wade, Wade Loves Penny, 2010; Singing Away the Dark, 2011. Works appear in anthologies. Contributor to magazines. **Address:** PO Box 249, New Denver, BC V0G 1S0, Canada. **Online address:** carojeff@netidea.com

WOODWARD, Kenneth L. American (born United States), b. 1935. **Genres:** Adult Non-fiction. **Career:** Omaha Sun, journalist, 1962-64; Newsweek Magazine, religion editor, 1964-2002, section editor, 1974-78, senior writer, 1988-2002, contributing editor, 2002-; University of California, regents lecturer in religion, National Humanities Center, fellow. **Publications:** (With A. Kornhaber) Grandparents, Grandchildren: The Vital Connection, 1981; Making Saints: How the Catholic Church Determines Who Becomes a Saint, Who Doesn't, and Why, 1990; The Book of Miracles: The Meaning of the Miracle Stories in Christianity, Judaism, Buddhism, Hinduism, 2000. Contributor to periodicals. **Address:** Newsweek, 555 W 18th St., PO Box 433172, New York, NY 10011, U.S.A. **Online address:** kennethlwoodward@msn.com

WOODWARD, Margaret E. American (born United States), b. 1950. **Genres:** Novels, Young Adult Fiction. **Career:** Writer and lawyer. **Publications:** NOVELS: Still Waters, 1995 as The Indictment, 1996; Now We Are Seven, 1997. OTHER: No Place Called Home, 1997. **Address:** c/o Pamela Ahearn, Ahearn Agency Inc., 2021 Pine St., New Orleans, LA 70118, U.S.A.

WOODWARD, Ralph Lee. American (born United States), b. 1934. **Genres:** History. **Career:** Tulane University, Department of History, part-time instructor, 1958-60; Instituto Guatemalteco Americano, part-time instructor of English, 1960-61; Wichita University, assistant professor of history, 1961-62; University of Southwestern Louisiana, assistant professor of history, 1962-63; University of North Carolina, assistant professor, associate professor of history, 1963-70; Tulane University, professor of history, 1970-99, professor emeritus, 1999-; College of Arts and Sciences, Department of History, head, 1973-75; Tulane Summer Sessions in Central America, director, 1975-78; Tulane-Newcomb Junior Year Abroad, professor-in-charge, 1975-76, Department of History, chairperson, 1986-88; U.S. Military Academy, Department of Social Sciences, visiting professor, 1989-, Department of History, graduate coordinator, 1991-92; Texas Christian University, Neville G. Penrose professor of Latin American studies, 1999-2003, Latin American Studies Program, coordinator, 2001-02; Tarleton State University, Joe and Teresa Long professor of social science, 2007. Writer and historian. **Publications:** Political Economy in Guatemala, 1962; Latin American History. Chapel Hill, 1965; Class Privilege and Economic Development: The Consulado de Comercio of Guatemala, 1793-1871, 1966, rev. ed. 1981; Robinson Crusoe's Island: A History of the Juan Fernandez Islands, 1969, rev. ed., 1981; (co-author) Applied Enlightenment: 19th Century Liberalism, 1972; Central America: A Nation Divided, 1976, 3rd ed., 1999; (comp.) Belize, 1980; (comp.) Nicaragua, 1983, rev. ed., 1992; (comp.) El Salvador, 1988; (comp.) Guatemala, 1992; Belize, 1993; Rafael Carrera and the Emergence of the Republic of Guatemala, 1993; Rafael Carrera y la emergencia de la República de Guatemala, 1821-1871, 2002; A Short History of Guatemala, 2005, rev. ed., 2008. EDITOR: Positivism in Latin America, 1850-1900: Are Order and Progress Reconcilable?, 1971; (trans.) Tribute to Don Bernardo de Gálvez: Royal Patents and An Epic Ballad Honoring the Spanish Governor of Louisiana, 1979; Central America, Research Guide to Central America and the Caribbean, 1985; Central America: Historical Perspectives on the Contemporary Crises, 1987; Central America: The Contemporary Crises in Historical Perspective, 1988; Encyclopedia of Latin American History and Culture, 1996; Here and There in Mexico: The Travel Writings of Mary Ashley Townsend, 2001; The Fayette Round Table Club, 1910-2010, 2010. Works appear in anthologies. **Address:** 303 N Linn, Fayette, MO 65248, U.S.A. **Online address:** clioclio@sbcglobal.net

WOODWELL, George M. American (born United States), b. 1928. **Genres:** Environmental Sciences/Ecology, Natural History, Biology. **Career:** University of Maine, assistant professor, associate professor of botany, 1957-61; Brookhaven National Laboratory, assistant scientist, senior scientist, 1961-

75; Yale University, School of Forestry and Environmental Science, lecturer, 1969-75; Marine Biological Laboratory, deputy director, assistant director for education and distinguished scientist, 1975-77, Ecosystems Center, founder and director, 1975-85; Woods Hole Research Center, founder and director, 1985-2005, director emeritus and senior scientist, 2005-. Writer. **Publications:** (Ed.) Diversity and Stability in Ecological Systems, 1967; Watch on the Earth, 1972; (ed. with E.V. Pecan) Carbon and the Biosphere: Proceedings of the 24th Brookhaven Symposium in Biology, Upton, N.Y., May 16-18, 1972, 1973; (co-author) Ecological and Biological Effects of Air Pollution, 1973; (ed.) The Role of Terrestrial Vegetation in the Global Carbon Cycle: Measurement by Remote Sensing, 1984; (ed.) The Earth in Transition: Patterns and Processes of Biotic Impoverishment, 1990; (ed. with K. Ramakrishna) World Forests for the Future: Their Use and Conservation, 1993; (ed. with F.T. MacKenzie) Biotic Feedbacks in the Global Climatic System: Will the Warming Feed the Warming?, 1995; Forests in a Full World, 2001; The Nature of a House: Building a World that Works, 2009. Contributor to journals. **Address:** Woods Hole Research Center, 149 Woods Hole Rd., Falmouth, MA 02540-1644, U.S.A. **Online address:** gmwoodwell@whrc.org

WOODWELL, William H. American (born United States) **Genres:** Advertising/Public Relations, Biography, Autobiography/Memoirs. **Career:** U.S. Senator John Heinz, assistant press secretary, 1985-87; League of Women Voters of the United States, press secretary, 1987-89; Hager Sharp Inc., account supervisor, 1989-91; editorial consultant, 1991-; International Herald Tribune, editor. **Publications:** (Ed. with J.M. Woodwell) A Watershed Primer for Pennsylvania: A Collection of Essays on Watershed Issues, 1999; Choosing the President: The Citizen's Guide to the 2000 Election, 2000; Coming to Term: A Father's Story of Birth, Loss, and Survival, 2001. Contributor to periodicals. **Address:** 1292 Jadwyn Rd., Maurertown, VA 22644, U.S.A. **Online address:** bill@whwoodwell.com

WOODWORTH, Stephen. American (born United States), b. 1967?. **Genres:** Novels, Horror, Mystery/Crime/Suspense, Young Adult Fiction. **Career:** Writer. **Publications:** Through Violet Eyes, 2004; With Red Hands, 2005; In Golden Blood, 2005; From Black Rooms, 2006. **Address:** c/o Author Mail, Bantam Dell Publishing Group, 1745 Broadway, New York, NY 10019, U.S.A.

WOODWORTH, Steven E(dward). American (born United States), b. 1961. **Genres:** History. **Career:** Baptist school, teacher, 1984-86; Houston Community College, adjunct instructor, 1984-87; Rice University, Jefferson Davis Papers, research assistant, 1985-87; Bartlesville Wesleyan College, instructor in history, 1987-89; Toccoa Falls College, assistant professor of history, 1989-94, associate professor, 1994-97; Texas Christian University, assistant professor, 1997-2000, associate professor, 2000-05, professor, 2005-. Writer. **Publications:** Jefferson Davis and His Generals: The Failure of Confederate Command in the West, 1990; The Essentials of United States History, 1841 to 1877: Westward Expansion and the Civil War, 1990; The Essentials of United States History, 1500 to 1789: From Colony to Republic, 1990; (with J. McDuffie and G. Piggrem) The Advanced Placement Examination in United States History, 1990; (with J. McDuffie and G. Piggrem) Best Test Preparation for the Advanced Placement Examination in United States History, 1990; (co-author) The Graduate Record Examination in History, 1993; Davis and Lee at War, 1995; (ed.) Leadership and Command in the American Civil War, 1995; A Deep Steady Thunder: The Battle of Chickamauga, 1996; Essentials of United States History: 1500-1789 from Colony to Republic, 1996; The American Civil War: A Handbook of Literature and Research, 1996; (ed.) Art of Command in the Civil War, 1998; Six Armies in Tennessee, 1998; (ed.) Musick of the Mocking Birds, the Roar of the Cannon: The Civil War Diary and Letters of William Winters, 1998; Chickamauga: A Battlefield Guide with a Section on Chattanooga, 1999; No Band of Brothers: Problems in the Rebel High Command, 1999; (ed.) Civil War Generals in Defeat, 1999; (ed.) Human Tradition in the Civil War and Reconstruction, 2000; Cultures in Conflict -The American Civil War, 2000; (ed.) Grant's Lieutenants. From Cairo to Vicksburg, 2001; While God Is Marching On, 2001; (ed.) Loyal, True and Brave: America's Civil War Soldiers, 2002; A Scythe of Fire, 2002; Beneath a Northern Sky: A Short History of the Gettysburg Campaign, 2003, 2nd ed., 2008; (with K.J. Winkle) Atlas of the Civil War, 2004; (intro.) Southern Sons, Northern Soldiers: The Civil War Letters of the Remley Brothers, 22nd Iowa Infantry, 2004; Nothing but Victory, 2005; (with G. Piggrem) United States History, 2005; (with S.E. Woodworth) Shiloh: A Battlefield Guide, 2006; Decision in the Heartland: The Civil War in the West, 2008; (ed.) Grant's Lieutenants From Chattanooga to Appomattox, 2008; (ed.) American Civil War, 2008; (ed.) Shiloh Campaign, 2009; Sherman, 2009; (ed.) Chickamauga Campaign, 2010; Manifest Destinies: America's Westward Expansion and the Road to the Civil War, 2010; This Great Struggle: America's Civil War, 2011. Contributor to periodicals. **Address:** Department of History, Texas Christian University, Reed Hall 310, PO Box 297260, Fort Worth, TX 76129, U.S.A. **Online address:** s.woodworth@tcu.edu

WOODY, Elizabeth. American (born United States), b. 1959. **Genres:** Novellas/Short Stories, Poetry, Cultural/Ethnic Topics, Environmental Sciences/Ecology, Literary Criticism And History, Autobiography/Memoirs, Essays. **Career:** Institute of of American Indian Arts, professor of creative writing, 1994-96, program assistant; Ecotrust, Indigenous Leadership Program, director, Shorebank Enterprise Cascadia, program associate for economic development; National Science Foundation, Center for Coastal Margin Observation and Prediction, program coordinator; Northwest Native American Writers Association, founding member. Writer. **Publications:** POETRY: Hand into Stone, 1988; Luminaries of the Humble, 1994; Seven Hands, Seven Hearts: Prose and Poetry, 1994; (contrib.) Salmon Nation: People and Fish at the Edge (essays), 1999, rev. ed. as Salmon Nation: People, Fish, and Our Common Home, 2003; Elenco Racconti Raccolta Scrittrici Indianoamericane. Contributor to magazines and periodicals. **Address:** Ecotrust, 721 NW 9th Ave., Ste. 200, Portland, OR 97209-3448, U.S.A. **Online address:** liz@ecotrust.org

WOOG, Adam. American (born United States), b. 1953. **Genres:** Area Studies, Local History/Rural Topics, Young Adult Non-fiction, Biography, Children's Non-fiction. **Career:** Freelance writer, 1982-; Kansai Time Out, music editor, 1982-84; International Christian University, writing instructor, 1984-86; Kodansha Intl., copy editor, 1984-86; Seattle Times, book reviewer, author and interviewer, 1986-, jazz critic, 1986-90, staff reporter, 1987; Seattle Home and Garden, contributing editor, 1989-91; Appleton Public Library, staff. **Publications:** FOR ADULTS: Sexless Oysters and Self-Tipping Hats: 100 Years of Invention in the Pacific Northwest, 1991; (with H. Baskas) Atomic Marbles and Branding Irons: Guide to Museums, Collections, and Roadside Curiosities in Washington and Oregon, 1993; (with R. Marino) Be Elvis! A Guide to Impersonating the King, 2000; The Gift, 2000; Crossroads: The Experience Music Project Collection, 2000. FOR YOUNG ADULTS: The United Nations, 1993; Poltergeists: Opposing Viewpoints, 1995; Harry Houdini, 1995; Louis Armstrong, 1995; Duke Ellington, 1995; Elvis Presley, 1997; Suicide, 1997; Marilyn Monroe, 1997; Amelia Earhart, 1997; Roosevelt and the New Deal, 1998; The Shark, 1998; Whale, 1998; The Beatles, 1998; The History of Rock and Roll, 1999; The 1900s, 1999; Bill Gates, 1999; Steven Spielberg, 1999; Magicians and Illusionists, 2000; George Lucas, 2000; Gangsters, 2000; Frank Sinatra, 2001; Rock and Roll Legends, 2001; New York (13 Colonies), 2002; Lucille Ball, 2002; Sweatshop During the Industrial Revolution, 2003; History of the Elizabethan Theater, 2003; Fidel Castro, 2003. FOR CHILDREN: Slammers, Stacks, and Hitters, 1995; Killer Whales, 2002; A Cowboy in the Wild West, 2002; Medieval Knights, 2003; Prohibition, 2003. OTHER: Microscope, 2004; 1970s, 2004; 1990s, 2004; Anne Frank, 2004; What Makes Me a Jew?, 2004; What Makes Me a Catholic?, 2004; Godzilla, 2004; Roald Dahl, 2005; Mummy, 2005; What Makes me a Protestant?, 2005; What Makes Me a Quaker?, 2005; E.B. White, 2005; Samurai Warrior, 2005; Ray Charles And the Birth of Soul, 2006; History of American Folk Music, 2006; Fight Renewed: The Civil Rights Movement, 2006; Frankenstein, 2006; Bigfoot, 2006; History of Gospel Music, 2006; Jyotirmayee Mohapatra, 2006; Carlos Santana: Legendary Guitarist, 2007; From Ragtime to Hip-Hop: A Century of Black American Music, 2007; King Kong, 2007; Jennifer Lopez, 2008; Pierre M. Omidyar: Creator of eBay, 2008; Walter Payton, 2008; Ballard Locks, 2008; Joe Montana, 2008; Oprah Winfrey, 2009; YouTube, 2009; Palestinian National Authority, 2009; Syria, 2009; Emancipation Proclamation: Ending Slavery in America, 2009; Jacques Cartier, 2009; John Lasseter: Pixar Animator, 2009; Mark Zuckerberg, Facebook Creator, 2009; Mirror Image: How Guys See Themselves, 2009; Mummies, 2009; Bionic Hand, 2010; Jesse James, 2010; Wyatt Earp, 2010. OTHER: The History of Gospel Music, 2006; Reality TV, 2007; Ripped from the Headlines: Food Safety, 2007; SCRATCHbot, 2010; Calamity Jane, 2010; Billy the Kid, 2010; Derrick Rose, 2010; Vampires in the Movies, 2011; Reggie Bush, 2011; LaDainian Tomlinson, 2011; Nubia, 2011; The Early Middle Ages, 2011; Food Myths and Facts, 2011; Zombies, 2011; Giants, 2012; The Late Middle Ages, 2012; Military Might and Global Intervention, 2012; Matt Damon, 2012; Careers in the FBI, 2013; Careers in the Secret Service, 2013; Careers in Homeland Security, 2013; Careers in Forensic Science, 2013; Careers in the ATF, 2013; Careers in State, County, and City Police Forces, 2013. Contributor to periodicals. **Address:** Seattle Times, PO Box 70, Seattle, WA

98111, U.S.A. **Online address:** awoog@earthlink.net

WOOG, Dan. American (born United States), b. 1953. **Genres:** Gay And Lesbian Issues, Sports/Fitness, Essays. **Career:** Westport News, sports editor, 1976-78, columnist; Soccer America, executive editor of youth soccer letter, 1987-2003; Westport Soccer Association, coaching director, 1995-98; Monster.com, contributing writer, 2003-; freelance writer. **Publications:** Woog's World: The Book (essays), 1991; School's Out: The Impact of Gay and Lesbian Issues in America's Schools, 1995; Jocks: True Stories of America's Gay Male Athletes, 1998; Ultimate Soccer Almanac, 1998, rev. ed., 2000; Friends and Family: True Stories of Gay America's Straight Allies, 1999; Parents' Guide to Soccer, 1999; (with B. Steffens) Jesse Jackson, 2000; Jobs: Gay Men, Straight Work, 2001; Dear Dan-: Apologies from an Imperfect World, 2001; Jocks 2: Coming Out to Play, 2002; Staples High School: 120 Years of A-plus Education, 2005. **Address:** Monster.com, 622 3rd Ave., 39th Fl., New York, NY 10017, U.S.A. **Online address:** dwoog@optonline.net

WOOLDRIDGE, Adrian. British (born England), b. 1959. **Genres:** Administration/Management, Education, History, Politics/Government, Psychology, Economics, Business/Trade/Industry. **Career:** Oxford University, All Souls College, fellow, 1980-94; The Economists, journalist, Schumpeter Columnist, 1988-, management editor, Los Angeles correspondent, social policy editor, bureau chief and Lexington columnist, through 2009; University of California, Harkness fellow, 1984-85. **Publications:** Measuring the Mind: Education and Psychology in England, 1880-1990, 1994; Masters of Management, 2011. WITH J. MICKLETHWAIT: The Witch Doctors: Making Sense of the Management Gurus, 1996; A Future Perfect: The Challenge and Promise of Globalization, 2000; The Company: A Short History of a Revolutionary Idea, 2003; The Right Nation: Conservative Power in America, 2004; God is Back: How the Global Rise of Faith will Change the World, 2009. **Address:** The Economist, 25 St. James's St., London, SW1 1LT, England. **Online address:** adrianwooldridge@economict.com

WOOLDRIDGE, Connie Nordhielm. American (born United States), b. 1950. **Genres:** Children's Non-fiction, Biography. **Career:** American Airlines, flight attendant, 1972-73; Seoul Foreign School, first grade teacher, 1973-75; Sieden Prairie Elementary School, school librarian, 1977-78; freelance writer, 1978-. **Publications:** Wicked Jack, 1995; When Esther Morris Headed West, 2001; The Legend of Strap Buckner, 2001; Thank You Very Much, Captain Ericsson, 2005; The Brave Escape of Edith Wharton, 2010: Just Fine the Way They Are 2011. Contributor to periodicals. **Address:** Connie Nordhielm Wooldridge, 1831 S B St., Richmond, IN 47374, U.S.A. **Online address:** connwool@aol.com

WOOLEY, Marilyn J. American (born United States), b. 1951. **Genres:** Novels. **Career:** University of Arizona, teaching assistant, 1973-75; NIMH, research trainee, 1975-77; Long Beach Medical Center, postdoctoral intern, 1977-78; County of Orange Human Services Agency, postdoctoral intern, 1978-79; Switzer Center, postdoctoral trainee, 1978; Breakthru Consultations, coordinator of psychological services, 1978-79; Shasta County Mental Health Services, clinical psychologist, 1979-81; Group Foster Home Inc., board director, 1980-; University of California, Family Practice Residency Program, assistant clinical professor, 1981-; Association of Traumatic Stress Specialists, staff, 2009-; West Coast Post-trauma Retreat, staff. Writer. **Publications:** Jackpot Justice (novel), 2000; Covenant's Child, forthcoming. Contributor of articles to books and journals. **Address:** c/o Laurie Liss, Sterling Lord Literistic Inc., 65 Bleecker St., New York, NY 10012-2420, U.S.A. **Online address:** wooleymj@aol.com

WOOLEY, Susan Frelick. American (born United States), b. 1945. **Genres:** Education, Medicine/Health. **Career:** Duke University, Medical Center, research technician, 1969-71, Electron Microscopy Laboratory, supervisor, 1969-71; Central High School, substitute teacher, 1971-72; American Red Cross, director of safety services and nursing, 1975-77, Nursing and Health Programs, director, 1975-77; Delaware State College, Department of Health, Physical Education, and Recreation, assistant professor of health education, 1978-87; BSCS, curriculum writer and staff associate, 1987-91; Centers for Disease Control and Prevention, National Center for Chronic Disease Prevention and Health Promotion, Division of Adolescent and School Health, health education specialist, 1991-96, Program Development and Services Branch, acting section chief, 1995, editor, writer and consultant, 1997; Emory University, Rollins School of Public Health, Department of Behavioral Sciences and Health Education, adjunct faculty, 1996; American Association for Health Ed-

ucation, development consultant, 1997; Society of State Directors of Health, Physical Education, and Recreation, project coordinator, 1997; American School Health Association, executive director, 1997-2010, consultant; Kent State University, adjunct faculty, 2000-. **Publications:** (Co-author) Science for Life and Living: Integrating Science, Technology, and Health, 14 vols., 1992; (ed. with E. Marx and D. Northrop) Health is Academic: A Guide to Coordinated School Health Programs, 1998; (co-ed.) Health, Mental Health, and Safety Guidelines for Schools, 2005; (with L.B. Chu) Give it a Shot!: A Toolkit for Nurses and Other Immunization Champions Working with Secondary Schools, 2006, 2nd ed., 2008; (with M. Rubin) Partners in Prevention: Whole School Approaches to Prevent Adolescent Pregnancy and Sexually Transmitted Infections, 2006; (with M. Rubin) Tell Me about AIDS: A Curriculum for K-6 Students and Their Families, 2007; (with C. Glimpse and S. Johnson) Sharing the Dream: Engaging Families as Partners in Supporting Student Success in Leadership for Family and Community Involvement, 2010; (co-author) Guidelines for 2008 AAHE/NCATE Health Education Preparation Standards, 2010. Contributor to books and periodicals. **Address:** American School Health Association, 4340 East West Hwy., Ste. 403, Bethesda, MD 20814, U.S.A. **Online address:** swooley@ashaweb.org

WOOLF, Daniel. *See* **WOOLF, D. R.**

WOOLF, D. R. (Daniel Woolf). Canadian/British (born England), b. 1958. **Genres:** History, Essays. **Career:** University of Birmingham, sessional lecturer, 1983; Queen's University, Social Science and Humanities Research Council of Canada (SSHRCC), postdoctoral fellow in history, 1984-86, principal and vice-chancellor, 2009-, Department of History, professor, 2009-; Bishop's University, assistant professor of history, 1986-87; Dalhousie University, assistant professor, 1987-90, associate professor, 1990-94, professor of history, 1994-99, associate dean of graduate studies, 1998-99; McMaster University, professor of history and dean of humanities, 1999-2002; University of Alberta, professor of history and dean of faculty of arts, 2002-09. Writer. **Publications:** (Ed.) Intellectual History: New Perspectives, 1989; The Idea of History in Early Stuart England: Erudition, Ideology, and The Light of Truth from the Accession of James I to the Civil War, 1990; (ed. with J. Morrill and P. Slack as Daniel Woolf) Public Duty and Private Conscience in Seventeenth-Century England: Essays Presented to G.E. Aylmer, 1993; (ed. with T.F. Mayer) The Rhetorics of Life-Writing in Early Modern Europe: Forms of Biography from Cassandra Fedele to Louis XIV, 1995; (ed.) A Global Encyclopedia of Historical Writing, 2 vols., 1998; Reading History in Early Modern England, 2000; (ed. with A. Fox as Daniel Woolf) The Spoken Word: Oral Culture in Britain, 1500-1850, 2002; (as Daniel Woolf) The Social Circulation of the Past: English Historical Culture, 1500-1730, 2003; (ed. with N.L. Jones) Local Identities in Late Medieval and Early Modern England, 2007; (as Daniel Woolf) Global History of History, 2011; (ed. as Daniel Woolf) Oxford History of Historical Writing, 2011. Contributor to journals. **Address:** Office of the Principal, Queen's University, 351 Richardson Hall, 74 University Ave., Kingston, ON K7L 3N6, Canada. **Online address:** principal@queensu.ca

WOOLF, F. X. *See* **ENGEL, Howard.**

WOOLF, Greg. American (born United States) **Genres:** History. **Career:** Magdalen College, teaching fellow, 1990-; Brasenose College, teaching fellow, 1990-; Christ's College, research fellow, 1990; University of St. Andrews, chair of ancient history, 1998-, professor of ancient history and head of school of classics; Laboratoired'Archéologie, école Normale Supérieure, researcher; University of Leicester, part-time teacher; Journal of Roman Studies, editor. **Publications:** (Ed. with A.K. Bowman) Literacy and Power in the Ancient World, 1994; Becoming Roman: The Origins of Provincial Civilization in Gaul, 1998; Cambridge Illustrated History of the Roman World, 2003; (ed. with C. Edwards) Rome the Cosmopolis, 2003; (ed.) Cambridge Illustrated History of the Roman World, 2003; (ed.) Ancient Civilizations: The Illustrated Guide to Belief, Mythology and Art, 2005; Et tu, Brute?: The Murder of Caesar and Political Assassination, 2006; Tales of the Barbarians: Ethnography and Empire in the Roman West, 2011; Rome: An Empire's Story, 2012. **Address:** School of Classics, University of St. Andrews, Rm. C 28, Swallowgate, St. Andrews, FF KY16 9AL, Scotland. **Online address:** gdw2@st-andrews.ac.uk

WOOLF, Paula. American (born United States), b. 1950. **Genres:** Children's Fiction, Novellas/Short Stories. **Career:** Teacher, 1973-75, 1976-78, 1981-88, 1991-93; Fulton County Schools, teacher of the gifted, 1997-2002.

Writer. **Publications:** Old Ladies with Brooms Aren't Always Witches, 1998. **Address:** 15245 Highgrove Rd., Alpharetta, GA 30004-3192, U.S.A. **Online address:** paulajwoolf@yahoo.com

WOOLF, Stuart Joseph. British (born England), b. 1936. **Genres:** History, Politics/Government, Social Sciences. **Career:** Pembroke College, fellow and assistant director of studies in history, 1961-65; University of Reading, reader in Italian history, Centre for the Advanced Study of Italian History, director, 1965-74; University of Essex, professor of history, 1975-92; European University Institute, professor of history, 1983-93; University of Venice, professor of contemporary history, 1996-2006, professor emeritus, 2006-, European Doctorate in the Social History of Europe and the Mediterranean, coordinator, 1996-2006. Writer. **Publications:** Studi sulla nobilta piemontese nell'epoca dell' assolutismo, 1963; (with M.V. Posner) Italian Public Enterprise, 1967; (comp.) The Italian Risorgimento, 1969; (co-author) Storia d'Italia: Dal primo Settecento all'Unita, 1973; L'Epoca della Reazione, 1978; A History of Italy 1700-1860, 1979; (with J.C. Perrot) State and Statistics in France 1789-1815, 1984; The Poor in Western Europe in the Eighteenth and Nineteenth Centuries, 1986; Napoleon's Integration of Europe, 1991; TRANSLATOR: P. Levi, If This is a Man, 1961; P. Levi, The Truce: A Survivor's Journey Home from Auschwitz, 1965; A. Marongiu, Medieval Parliaments: A Comparative Study, 1968; F. Venturi, Italy and the Enlightenment: Studies in a Cosmopolitan Century, 1973. EDITOR: European Fascism, 1968, rev. ed. as Fascism in Europe, 1981; The Nature of Fascism, 1968; (with E.L. Jones) Agrarian Change and Economic Development, 1969; The Rebirth of Italy, 1943-50, 1972; Domestic Strategies: Work and Family in France and Italy, 1600-1800, 1988; Espaces et familles dans l'Europe du Sud a l'age moderne, 1993; Storia d'Italia, Le regioni dall'Unita a oggi. La Valle d'Aosta, 1995; Nationalism in Europe, 1815 to the Present: A Reader, 1996; Regional and National Identities in Europe in the XIXth and XXth Centuries: Les Identites Regionales et Nationales en Europe aux XIXe et XXe Siecles, 1998; Identita Regionali nelle Alpi, 1999; (with P.P. Viazzo) L'alpeggio e il mercato, 2001; Formaggi e mercati: Economia d'Alpeggio e Mercato in Valle d'Aosta e Haute-Savoie, 2002; Storia di Venezia: L'Ottocento, 1797-1918, 2002; L'Italia Repubblicana Vista da Fuori, 1945-2000, 2007. **Address:** 237 Via G. D'Annunzio, Firenze, 50135, Italy. **Online address:** woolfstuart@gmail.com

WOOLFE, Jennifer A(nne). British (born England), b. 1944. **Genres:** Food And Wine, Medicine/Health, Sciences, Environmental Sciences/Ecology, Agriculture/Forestry. **Career:** Cambridge University, junior research fellow in nutrition, 1970-72; University of Ghana, researcher and teacher, 1972-76; University of Pernambuco, food microbiologist and teacher, 1977-81; International Potato Center, affiliate, 1982-; Ministry of Agriculture, Fisheries, and Food, senior scientific officer (nutrition), 1990-. Writer. **Publications:** The Potato in the Human Diet, 1987; Sweet Potato: An Untapped Food Resource, 1992. **Address:** Cambridge University Press, Shaftesbury Rd., Cambridge, CB CB2 8BS, England. **Online address:** mark.woolfe@btinternet.com

WOOLFE, Sue. Australian (born Australia), b. 1950. **Genres:** Novels, Literary Criticism And History. **Career:** Sydney TAFE, secondary school teacher and tutor; SBS television, director and producer; Rollins College, writer-in-residence, 1996; Iowa University, writer-in-residence; University of New South Wales, writer-in-residence; University of Sydney, lecturer in creative writing. **Publications:** Language in Literature (nonfiction), 1975; Briga, 1976; A Place for Everything, 1977; About Literature (nonfiction), 1984; (with K. Grenville) Making Stories: How Ten Australian Novels Were Written (nonfiction), 1993; (ed.) Wild Minds: Stories of Outsiders and Dreamers, 1999; Mystery of the Cleaning Lady: A Writer Looks at Creativity and Neuroscience, 2007. NOVELS: Painted Woman, 1990; Leaning towards Infinity: How My Mother's Apron Unfolds into My Life, 1996; The Secret Cure, 2003. Contributor to periodicals. **Address:** Department of English, University of Sydney, Rm. A20, John Woolley Bldg., Sydney, NW 2006, Australia. **Online address:** sue.woolfe@arts.usyd.edu.au

WOOLHOUSE, Roger. British (born England), b. 1940. **Genres:** Humanities, Sciences, Adult Non-fiction, Biography, Philosophy. **Career:** University College, assistant lecturer, 1964-66, lecturer, 1966-68; University of York, lecturer, 1968-73, senior lecturer, 1973-84, reader, 1984, professor, 1994-2001, professor emeritus, 2001-, chair of philosophy department, 1984-94; University of Pennsylvania, visiting professor, 1982; University of California, visiting professor, 1987; Princeton University, visiting professor, 1992; Rutgers University, visiting professor, 1996, 1997. Writer. **Publications:** Locke's Philosophy of Science and Knowledge: A Consideration of Some Aspects of an Essay Concerning Human Understanding, 1971; (ed.) Leibniz, Metaphysics and Philosophy of Science, 1981; (with R. Hall) 80 Years of Locke Scholarship: A Bibliographical Guide, 1983; Locke, 1983; (ed.) Metaphysics and Philosophy of Science in the Seventeenth and Eighteenth Centuries: Essays in Honour of Gerd Buchdahl, 1988; (ed.) George Berkeley, Principles of Human Knowledge: And Three Dialogues between Hylas and Philonous, 1988; The Empiricists, 1988; Descartes, Spinoza, Leibniz: The Concept of Substance in Seventeenth-Century Metaphysics, 1993; (ed.) Gottfried Wilhelm Leibniz: Critical Assessments, 1994; (ed.) Leibniz's New System (1695), 1996; (trans. and ed. with R. Francks) Leibniz's "New System" and Associated Contemporary Texts, 1997; (ed.) John Locke, An Essay Concerning Human Understanding, 1997; (trans. with R. Francks) Philosophical Texts, 1998; Locke: A Biography, 2007; Starting with Leibniz, 2010. **Address:** Department of Philosophy, University of York, Heslington, York, NY YO10 5DD, England. **Online address:** rsw3@york.ac.uk

WOOLLEN, Geoff. British (born England), b. 1945. **Genres:** Literary Criticism And History, Young Adult Fiction. **Career:** University of Glasgow, senior lecturer in nineteenth-century French literature, 1972-, School of Modern Languages and Cultures, reader in French, 1972-, French and German Publications, general editor. **Publications:** (Trans.) Balzac: Le Cure De Tours, 1988; (trans. and intro.) The Last Day of a Condemned Man and Other Prison Writings, 1992; Rostand: Cyrano De Bergerac, 1994. **Address:** School of Modern Languages & Cultures, University of Glasgow, Modern Languages Bldg., Rm. 110, 16 University Gardens, Glasgow, G12 8QL, Scotland. **Online address:** g.woollen@french.arts.gla.ac.uk

WOOLLEY, Benjamin. British (born England) **Genres:** Novels, Young Adult Fiction, History. **Career:** British Broadcasting Corp. (BBC), broadcaster and journalist. Writer. **Publications:** Virtual Worlds: A Journey in Hype and Hyperreality, 1992; The Bride of Science: Romance, Reason and Byron's Daughter, 1999; The Queen's Conjurer: The Science and Magic of Dr. John Dee, Adviser to Queen Elizabeth I, 2001; Heal Thyself: Nicholas Culpeper and the Seventeenth-Century Struggle to Bring Medicine to the People, 2004; The Herbalist: Nicholas Culpeper and the Fight for Medical Freedom, 2004; Savage Kingdom: The True Story of Jamestown, 1607 and the Settlement of America, 2007. Contributor to periodicals. **Address:** c/o Anthony Sheil, Gillon Aitken Associates, 18-21 Cavaye Pl., London, GL SW10 9PT, England.

WOOLLEY, Bryan. American (born United States), b. 1937. **Genres:** Novels, History, Novellas/Short Stories, Documentaries/Reportage, Essays, Autobiography/Memoirs. **Career:** High school English teacher, 1958-59; Christian Church, minister, 1963-67; Christian Board of Publication, magazine editor, 1966-67; Associated Press, night editor, 1967-68; Anniston Star, city editor, 1968-69; Louisville Courier-Journal and Times, writer, 1969-76; Dallas Times Herald, editorial writer and columnist, 1976-78, writer, 1976-89. **Publications:** Some Sweet Day, 1974; (contrib.) We Be Here When The Morning Comes, 1975; Time & Place, 1977; November 22, 1981; Sam Bass: A Novel, 1983; The Time of My Life, 1984; (contrib.) Where Texas Meets the Sea: A Coastal Portrait, 1985; Edge of the West and Other Texas Stories, 1990; (contrib.) The Way Home: Photographs From the Heart of Texas, 1992; The Bride Wore Crimson and Other Stories, 1993; Generations and Other True Stories, 1995; Mythic Texas: Essays on the State and its People, 2000; (co-author) Final Destinations: A Travel Guide for Remarkable Cemeteries in Texas, New Mexico, Oklahoma, Arkansas and Louisiana, 2000; (contrib.) Charreada: Mexican Rodeo in Texas (essays), 2002; Mr. Green's Magnificent Machine, 2003; Where I Come From, 2003; Home is Where The Cat Is, 2004; Texas Road Trip: Stories From Across The Great State and a Few Personal Reflections, 2004; Wonderful Room: The Making of a Texas Newspaperman, 2010. Contributor to periodicals. **Address:** 18040 Midway Rd., Ste. 215, Dallas, TX 75287-6503, U.S.A.

WOOLLEY, Peter J. American (born United States), b. 1964. **Genres:** Politics/Government, Area Studies, International Relations/Current Affairs, Adult Non-fiction. **Career:** Fairleigh Dickinson University, professor of comparative politics, 1987-, PublicMind, executive director, 2001-; U.S. Naval War College, advanced research fellow, 1994-95; The Journal of Conflict Studies, book review editor, 1997-2007; Lafayette College, American Council on Education, fellow, 2001-02. **Publications:** (Ed. with A.R. Papa) American Politics: Core Argument/Current Controversy, 1998, 2nd ed., 2002; Japan's Navy: Politics and Paradox, 1971-2000, 2000; Geography and Japan's Strategic Choices: From Seclusion to Internationalization, 2005. Contributor of articles to journals. **Address:** PublicMind, Fairleigh Dickinson University,

M-MS3-02, 285 Madison Ave., Madison, NJ 07940, U.S.A. **Online address:** woolley@fdu.edu

WOOLVERTON, John F(rederick). American (born United States), b. 1926. **Genres:** History, Biography. **Career:** The Episcopal Church, Virginia Theological Seminary, professor, 1958-83, The Historical Society, Anglican and Episcopal History, editor-in-chief, 1977-, director; Trinity Church, rector, 1983-89. **Publications:** Colonial Anglicanism in North America (history), 1984; The Education of Phillips Brooks (biography), 1995; The Skeptical Vestryman and Plato's Heavenly Way of Justice: George Whitney Martin, 1887-1959, Vestryman, St. George's Church, New York City, 1948-1959 (biography), 1997; Robert H. Gardiner and the Reunification of Worldwide Christianity in the Progressive Era, 2005. **Address:** Anglican and Episcopal History, The Historical Society, The Episcopal Church, PO Box 1749, Harlingen, TX 78551, U.S.A. **Online address:** john_woolverton@ecunet.org

WOOTSON, Alice (G.). American (born United States), b. 1937. **Genres:** Romance/Historical, Novels, Young Adult Fiction. **Career:** Teacher, 1964-92. Writer. **Publications:** ROMANCE NOVELS: Snowbound with Love, 2000; Dream Wedding, 2001; Home for Christmas, 2001; Trust in Me, 2002; To Love Again, 2002; Escape to Love, 2003; Kindred Spirits, 2004; Aloha Love, 2005; Perfect Wedding, 2005; Ready to Take a Chance, 2006. **Address:** PO Box 18832, Philadelphia, PA 19119, U.S.A. **Online address:** agwwriter@email.com

WOOTTON, David. British (born England), b. 1952. **Genres:** Medicine/Health, Translations, Politics/Government. **Career:** Cambridge University, Peterhouse, research fellow, 1975-76; University of London, Westfield College, lecturer in history, 1976-82, Queen Mary College, professor of intellectual history, 1998-2004; McGill University, visiting professor of political science, 1980-82; Dalhousie University, Department of history, assistant professor, 1982-85, associate professor, 1985-87; University of Western Ontario, associate professor of political science, 1987-89; University of Victoria, Lansdowne chair in the humanities, 1989-95, associate professor, 1989-91, professor of history, 1991-95, Humanities Center, founding director, 1991-95; Washington University, Center for the History of Freedom, visiting fellow, 1990; Princeton University, Shelby Cullom Davis Center, Department of History, visiting fellow, 1992-93; Brunel University, professor of politics and head of the department of government, 1994-96, professor of history and dean of faculty of arts, 1996-98, acting head of performing arts, 1996-98; University of York, anniversary professor of history, 2004-. Writer. **Publications:** Paolo Sarpi: Between Renaissance and Enlightenment, 1983; (trans. and intro.) Candide and Related Texts, 2000; Bad Medicine: Doctors Doing Harm since Hippocrates, 2006; Galileo: Watcher of the Skies, 2010. EDITOR: Divine Right and Democracy: An Anthology of Political Writing in Stuart England, 1986; (with M. Hunter) Atheism from the Reformation to the Enlightenment, 1992; Republicanism, Liberty, and Commercial Society, 1649-1776, 1994; (and trans.) N. Machiavelli, Selected Political Writings, 1994; (and trans.) N. Machiavelli, The Prince, 1995; (and intro.) Modern Political Thought: Readings from Machiavelli to Nietzsche, 1996, 2nd ed., 2007; (trans. and intro.) T. More, Utopia, 1999; (and intro.) The Essential Federalist and Anti-Federalist Papers, 2003; (and intro.) Political Writings, 2003; (and intro.) Doctor Faustus, 2005; (with G. Holderness) Gender and Power in Shrew-taming Narratives, 1500-1700, 2010; (with G. Nowell-Smith) The Coming of the Book, 2010. **Address:** Department of History, University of York, Heslington, York, NY YO10 5DD, England. **Online address:** dw504@york.ac.uk

WORBOYS, Anne. Also writes as Anne Eyre Worboys, Vicky Maxwell, Annette Eyre, Annette Isobel Worboys. British (born England), b. 1920?. **Genres:** Mystery/Crime/Suspense, Romance/Historical, Young Adult Fiction. **Career:** Novelist. **Publications:** Tread Softly in the Sun, 1969; Magnolia Room, 1972; The Lion of Delos, 1974; Every Man a King, 1975 in US as Rendezvous with Fear, 1977; The Barrancourt Destiny, 1977; The Bhunda Jewels, 1980; Run, Sara, Run, 1981; A Kingdom for the Bold, 1986 in US as Aurora Rose, 1988; China Silk, 1992; Alice, 1993; Village Sins, 1994; You Can't Sing without Me, 1996; Season of the Senses, 1996; Hotel Girl, 1997; House of Destiny, 1998; Shifting Sands, 1998; Relative Strangers, 1998. AS ANNE EYRE WORBOYS: Dream of Petals Whim, 1961; Palm Rock and Paradise, 1961; Call from a Stranger, 1962. AS ANNETTE EYRE: Three Strings to a Fortune, 1962; Visit to Rata Creek, 1964; The Valley of Yesterday, 1965; A Net to Catch the Wind, 1966; Return to Bellbird Country, 1966; The House of Five Pines, 1967; The River and Wilderness, 1967 in US as Give Me Your Love, 1975; A Wind from the Hill, 1968; Thorn-Apple,

1968; Tread Softly in the Sun, 1969; The Little Millstones, 1970; Dolphin Bay, 1970; Rainbow Child, 1971; The Magnolia Room, 1972; Venetian Inheritance, 1973. AS VICKY MAXWELL: Chosen Child, 1973; Flight to the Villa Mistra, 1973; The Way of the Tamarisk, 1974 (in US as Anne Worboys, 1975); High Hostage, 1976; The Other Side of Summer, 1977. **Address:** c/o David Higham Associates, 5-8 Lower John St., Golden Sq., London, GL W1R 4HA, England. **Online address:** anneworboys@aol.com

WORBOYS, Anne Eyre. *See* **WORBOYS, Anne.**

WORBOYS, Annette Isobel. *See* **WORBOYS, Anne.**

WORCESTER, Kent. (Kenton W. Worcester). American (born United States), b. 1959. **Genres:** Organized Labor, Politics/Government, Adult Nonfiction, Essays. **Career:** Columbia University, instructor, 1986-91, chair of division of social sciences and associate professor of political science and international studies; Social Science Research Council, program director, 1991-; Marymount Manhattan College, Department of Political Science, associate professor, professor. Writer. **Publications:** (Ed. with G. Perusek) Trade Union Politics: American Unions and Economic Change, 1960s-1990s (nonfiction), 1995; C.L.R. James: A Political Biography, 1995; (as Kenton W. Worcester) Social Science Research Council, 1923-1998, 2001; (ed. as Kenton Worcester with S.A. Bermanzohn and M. Ungar) Violence and Politics: Globalization's Paradox, 2002; (ed. with J. Heer) Arguing Comics: Literary Masters on a Popular Medium, 2004; (ed. with J. Heer) A Comics Studies Reader, 2008. **Address:** Department of Political Science, Marymount Manhattan College, 221 E 71st St., New York, NY 10021, U.S.A. **Online address:** kworcester@mmm.edu

WORCESTER, Kenton W. *See* **WORCESTER, Kent.**

WORCESTER, Robert. (Robert Milton Worcester). British/American (born United States), b. 1933. **Genres:** Marketing, Environmental Sciences/Ecology, Politics/Government, Business/Trade/Industry. **Career:** McKinsey & Co., consultant, 1962-65; Opinion Research Corp., controller, chief financial officer and assistant, 1965-69; Market & Opinion Research Intl. (MORI now Ipsos MORI), founder, 1969-, managing director, 1969-94, chairman, 1973-; University of Kent, honorary professor of politics, 2002-, chancellor, 2006-; Institute of Business Ethics, president, 2010-. Writer. **Publications:** AS ROBERT M. WORCESTER: (ed. with J. Downham) Consumer Market Research Handbook, 1972, (ed. with J. Downham) 3rd ed., 1986; (ed. with M. Harrop) Political Communications: The General Election Campaign of 1979, 1982; (ed.) Political Opinion Polling: An International Review, 1983; (with L. Watkins) Private Opinions Public Polls, 1986; British Public Opinion: A Guide to the History and Methodology of Political Opinion Polling, 1991; (with S. Barnes) Dynamics of Societal Learning about Global Environmental Change, 1991; (with R. Mortimore) Explaining Labour's Landslide, 1999. OTHERS: (with E. Jacobs) We British: Britain under the MORIscope, 1990; (with E. Jacobs) Typically British?: The Prudential MORI Guide, 1991; (with R. Mortimore) Explaining Labour's Second Landslide, 2001. **Address:** Ipsos MORI, 79-81 Borough Rd., London, GL SE1 1FY, England. **Online address:** bob.worcester@ipsos-mori.com

WORCESTER, Robert Milton. *See* **WORCESTER, Robert.**

WORDEN, J. William. American (born United States), b. 1932?. **Genres:** Medicine/Health. **Career:** Gordon College, lecturer in psychology, 1959-60, lecturer in pastoral psychology, 1962-64, associate professor, 1962-66, dean of students and counseling psychologist, 1962-66, Department of Psychology, head, 1963-66; Boston University, School of Fine Arts, director of counseling services and lecturer in psychology, 1966-68; Harvard University, Medical School, research associate, 1968-72, assistant professor, 1972-86, lecturer in psychology, 1986-; Massachusetts General Hospital, lecturer, 1969-86, psychologist, 1969-; private practice of clinical psychology, 1970-; Radcliffe College, lecturer, 1977-80; Biola University, Rosemead Graduate School of Professional Psychology, professor, 1986-; American Psychological Association, fellow. Consultant and writer. **Publications:** (With W. Proctor) PDA-Personal Death Awareness, 1976; (with A.D. Weisman) Coping and Vulnerability in Cancer Patients: Research Report, 1977; (with A.D. Weisman and H.J. Sobel) Psychosocial Screening and Intervention with Cancer Patients: Research Report, 1980; (with H.J. Sobel) Helping Cancer Patients Cope: A Problem Solving Intervention for Health Care Professionals, 1982; Grief Counseling and Grief Therapy: A Handbook for the Mental Health Practitioner, 1982, 4th ed., 2008; Children and Grief: When a Parent Dies, 1996. Contributor to journals. **Address:** Department of Psychology, Biola University, 13800 Biola Ave., La Mirada, CA 90639-0001, U.S.A. **Online address:** william.worden@biola.edu

WORK, James C. American (born United States), b. 1939. **Genres:** Novels, Young Adult Fiction, Essays. **Career:** College of Southern Utah, teacher; Colorado State University, professor of literature, retired, 2003. Writer. **Publications:** KEYSTONE RANCH SERIES: Ride South to Purgatory, 1999; Ride West to Dawn, 2001; Ride to Banshee Cañon, 2002; The Dead Ride Alone, 2004; Riders of Deathwater Valley, 2005; The Outcast of Spirit Ridge, 2006. OTHERS: (ed.) Shane: The Critical Edition, 1984; (ed.) Prose & Poetry of the American West, 1991; Following Where the River Begins: A Personal Essay on an Encounter with the Colorado River (memoir), 1991; Following Where the River Begins, 1992; (ed.) Gunfight!: Thirteen Western Stories, 1996; The Tobermory Manuscript, 2000; A Title to Murder: The Carhenge Mystery (second in the series begun with The Tobermory Manuscript), 2004; Windmills, the River and Dust: One Man's West, 2005; Don't Shoot the Gentile, 2011. **Address:** 1540 Westview Ave., Fort Collins, CO 80521, U.S.A.

WORKMAN, Jeremiah W. American (born United States), b. 1983. **Genres:** Autobiography/Memoirs. **Career:** Writer. **Publications:** (With J.R. Bruning) Shadow of the Sword: A Marine's Journey of War, Heroism, and Redemption (memoir), 2009. Contributor to newspapers. **Address:** c/o Jim Hornfischer, Hornfischer Literary Management L.P., PO Box 50544, Austin, TX 78763, U.S.A.

WORMELL, Mary. Scottish/British (born England), b. 1959. **Genres:** Children's Fiction, Children's Non-fiction, Animals/Pets. **Career:** Children's book author and illustrator. **Publications:** Hilda Hen's Search, 1994; Hilda Hen's Happy Birthday, 1995; Hilda Hen's Scary Night, 1996; Why Not?, 2000; Bernard the Angry Rooster, 2001. Illustrator of books by D. King-Smith. **Address:** Hartwoodmyres Farm, Ettrick Valley, Selkirk, TD7 5HA, Scotland. **Online address:** mary.wormell@btinternet.com

WORMSER, Richard. American (born United States), b. 1933. **Genres:** Young Adult Non-fiction, Novels, Young Adult Fiction. **Career:** Shamokin Citizen, journalist; University of Bridgeport, faculty; The New School, instructor; University of New Haven, faculty. **Publications:** The Invader (novel), 1972; History of Childhood, 1995; Rise and Fall of Jim Crow: The African-American Struggle Against Discrimination, 1865-1954, 1999; Islam in America, 1999; Defense Lawyers, 2000; To A Young Filmmaker, 2001; Defending the Accused: Stories from the Courtroom, 2001; To the Young Filmmaker: Conversations with Working Filmmakers, 2002. NONFICTION FOR YOUNG ADULTS: Allan Pinkerton: America's First Private Eye, 1990; Lifers: Learn the Truth at the Expense of Our Sorrow, 1991; Countdown to Crisis: A Look at the Middle East, 1992; Three Faces of Vietnam, 1993; The Iron Horse: How Railroads Changed America, 1993; Growing up in the Great Depression, 1994; Hoboes: Wandering in America, 1870-1940, 1994; Juveniles in Trouble, 1994; American Islam: Growing up Muslim in America, 1994; The Titanic, 1994; American Childhoods: Three Centuries of Youth at Risk, 1996. Contributor to periodicals. **Address:** Videoline Productions, 103 Whitney Ave., Ste. 1, New Haven, CT 06510, U.S.A. **Online address:** rwormser@aol.com

WOROBEC, Christine D. Canadian (born Canada), b. 1955?. **Genres:** History. **Career:** University of Toronto, history tutor, 1979-81, 1983-84; Kent State University, assistant professor, 1984-92, associate professor of history, 1992-99, Soviet and East European Studies Program, director, 1991-99, Department of History, graduate coordinator, 1992-96; Harvard University, visiting associate professor of history, 1998; Northern Illinois University, associate professor, 1999-2001, professor of history, 2001-, Presidential research professor, 2003-07, distinguished research professor, 2007-10, board of trustees professor, 2008-10, professor emeritus, 2010-. Writer. **Publications:** (With H. Myroniuk) Ukrainians in North America: A Select Bibliography, 1981; Peasant Russia: Family and Community in the Post-Emancipation Period, 1991; (ed. with B.E. Clements and B.A. Engel) Russia's Women: Accommodation, Resistance, Transformation, 1991; Possessed: Women, Witches and Demons in Imperial Russia, 2001; (ed.) Human Tradition in Imperial Russia, 2009. **Address:** Department of History, Northern Illinois University, Zulauf 702, DeKalb, IL 60115, U.S.A. **Online address:** worobec@niu.edu

WORONOV, Mary. American (born United States), b. 1946. **Genres:** Art/Art History, Natural History, Animals/Pets. **Career:** Actress, painter and writer. **Publications:** Wake for the Angels: Paintings and Stories, 1994; Swimming Underground: My Years in the Warhol Factory, 1995; Snake, 2000, 2nd ed., 2002; Niagara, 2002; Blind Love, 2004. **Address:** c/o Phil Brock, Studio Talent Group, 1328 12th St., Santa Monica, CA 90401-2051, U.S.A. **Online address:** mail@maryworonov.com

WORRALL, Shirley. See WELLS, Shirley.

WORRELL, R. DeLisle. See WORRELL, (Rupert) DeLisle.

WORRELL, (Rupert) DeLisle. (R. DeLisle Worrell). Barbadian (born Barbados), b. 1945. **Genres:** Economics, Politics/Government, Social Sciences. **Career:** Central Bank of Barbados, Department of Research, manager, division director of research, 1973-84, director of research and information, 1985-89, deputy governor, 1990-2000, governor, 2009-; Princeton University, Woodrow Wilson School, faculty, 1980-81; Yale University, Economic Growth Center, faculty, 1985; Inter-American Development Bank, consultant; International Monetary Fund, senior economist, Monetary and Exchange Affairs Department, technical assistance adviser; University of West Indies, Caribbean Center for Money and Finance, executive director, director, Sir Arthur Lewis Institute of Social and Economic Studies, professor of economics. Writer. **Publications:** The Caribbean Economy in the Nineties: Challenge and Response, 1986; Small Island Economies: Structure and Performance in the English-Speaking Caribbean Since 1970, 1987; Common Currency for the Caribbean: A Study, 1992; Economic Policies in Small Open Economies: Prospects for the Caribbean, 1992. EDITOR: (and contrib.) The Economy of Barbados, 1946-80, 1982; (with C. Bourne) Economic Adjustment Policies for Small Nations: Theory and Experience in the English-Speaking Caribbean, 1989; (with Bourne and D. Dodhia) Financing Development in the Commonwealth Caribbean, 1991; (ed. with J.I. Dominguez and R.A. Pastor) Democracy in the Caribbean: Political, Economic and Social Perspectives, 1993; (with T. Farrell) Caribbean Monetary Integration, 1994. Contributor of articles to books. **Address:** Central Bank of Barbados, Tom Adams Financial Cre., Spry St., Bridgetown, BB11126, Barbados. **Online address:** delisle.worrell@sta.uwi.edu

WORSHAM, Lynn. American (born United States), b. 1953. **Genres:** Literary Criticism And History, Art/Art History, Politics/Government, Social Sciences, Women's Studies And Issues. **Career:** University of Wisconsin-Milwaukee, assistant professor, 1988-94, Graduate Program in Rhetoric and Composition Studies, coordinator, 1992-94, Graduate Program in Modern Studies, coordinator, 1994-96, associate professor of English, 1994-98; University of South Florida, professor of English, 1998-2005, Graduate Program in Rhetoric and Composition, coordinator, 2003; Illinois State University, professor of English, 2005-, JAC, editor, 2005-, Department of English and Philosophy, faculty. **Publications:** (Ed. with S.C. Jarratt) Feminism and Composition Studies: In Other Words, 1998; (ed. with G.A. Olson and intro.) Race, Rhetoric and the Postcolonial, 1999; (ed. with G.A. Olson and S.I. Dobrin) The Kinneavy Papers: Theory and the Study of Discourse, 2000; (ed. with G.A. Olson) Critical Intellectuals on Writing, 2003; (ed. with G.A. Olson) Postmodern Sophistry: Stanley Fish and the Critical Enterprise, 2004; (ed. with G.A. Olson) Politics of Possibility: Encountering the Radical Imagination, 2007; (ed. with G.A. Olson) Plugged In: Technology, Rhetoric and Culture in a Posthuman Age, 2008. **Address:** Department of English, Illinois State University, WIH 206, PO Box 4100, Normal, IL 61790-4240, U.S.A. **Online address:** lworsha@ilstu.edu

WORTHEN, John. British (born England), b. 1943. **Genres:** Biography, Novels. **Career:** University of Nottingham, professor of D.H. Lawrence Studies, Faculty of Arts, professor emeritus. Writer and biographer. **Publications:** D.H. Lawrence and the Idea of the Novel, 1979; D.H. Lawrence: A Literary Life, 1989; D.H. Lawrence, 1991; D.H. Lawrence, the Early Years, 1885-1912, 1991; The Gang: Coleridge, the Hutchinsons and Wordsworths in 1802, 2001; D.H. Lawrence: The Life of An Outsider, 2005; Robert Schumann: Life and Death of a Musician, 2007; T.S. Eliot: A Short Biography, 2009; An Introduction to Samuel Taylor Coleridge, 2010. EDITOR: The Lost Girl, 1981; (and intro.) The Rainbow, 1981; The Prussian Officer and Other Stories, 1983; Love Among the Haystacks and Other Stories, 1987; (with D. Farmer and L. Vasey) Women in Love, 1987; (with P. Eggert) Lawrence and Comedy, 1996; (with L. Vasey) The First Women in Love, 1998; (with H. Schwarze) The Plays, 1999; (with E. Greenspan and L. Vasey) Studies in Classic American Literature, 2003; (with A. Harrison) D.H. Lawrence's Sons and Lovers: A Casebook, 2005; (with N.H. Reeve) Introductions and Reviews, 2005. **Address:** School of English Studies, University of Nottingham, Trent Bldg., University Park Campus, Nottingham, NT NG7 2RD, England. **Online address:** english-enquiries@nottingham.ac.uk

WORTHEN, Molly. American (born United States), b. 1981?. **Genres:** Biography, Education, History. **Career:** Writer. **Publications:** The Man on Whom Nothing Was Lost: The Grand Strategy of Charles Hill, 2005. Contributor to periodicals. **Address:** c/o Author Mail, Trade Division, Adult Editorial, Houghton Mifflin Co., 222 Berkeley St., Fl. 8, Boston, MA 02116-3764, U.S.A. **Online address:** molly.worthen@yale.edu

WORTHING, Peter. American (born United States), b. 1964. **Genres:** History, Military/Defense/Arms Control. **Career:** Muskingum College, faculty; University of North Florida, faculty; Texas Christian University, associate professor of history, 2002-. Writer. **Publications:** Occupation and Revolution: China and the Vietnamese August Revolution of 1945, 2001; A Military History of Modern China: From the Manchu Conquest to Tian'anmen Square, 2007. **Address:** Texas Christian University, 2800 S University Dr., Fort Worth, TX 76129, U.S.A. **Online address:** p.worthing@tcu.edu

WORTHINGTON, Everett L. American (born United States), b. 1946. **Genres:** Novels. **Career:** Virginia Commonwealth University, professor of psychology. Writer. **Publications:** When Someone Asks for Help: A Practical Guide for Counseling, 1982; How to Help the Hurting: When Friends Face Problems with Self-Esteem, Self-Control, Fear, Depression, Loneliness, 1985; Counseling for Unplanned Pregnancy and Infertility, 1987; Marriage Counseling: A Christian Approach to Counseling Couples, 1989; Counseling before Marriage, 1990; (ed.) Psychotherapy and Religious Values, 1993; (with D. McMurry) Value Your Mate: How to Strengthen Your Marriage, 1993; Hope for Troubled Marriages: Overcoming Common Problems & Major Difficulties, 1993; (with D. McMurry) Marriage Conflicts: Resources for Strategic Pastoral Counseling, 1994; I Care about Your Marriage, 1994; (with K. Worthington) Helping Parents Make Disciples: Strategic Pastoral Counseling Resources, 1995; (with K. Worthington) Value Your Children: Becoming Better Parental Disciple-Makers, 1995; (ed.) Christian Marital Counseling: Eight Approaches to Helping Couples, 1996; (with M.E. McCullough and S.J. Sandage) To Forgive Is Human: How to Put Your Past in the Past, 1997; (ed.) Dimensions of Forgiveness: Psychological Research & Theological Perspectives, 1998; Five Steps to Forgiveness: The Art and Science of Forgiving, 2003; Hope-Focused Marriage Counseling: A Guide to Brief Therapy, 2005; (ed.) Handbook of Forgiveness, 2005; The Power of Forgiving, 2005; Forgiveness and Reconciliation: Theory and Application, 2006; Humility: The Quiet Virtue, 2007. Contributor to periodicals. **Address:** Department of Psychology, College of Humanities & Sciences, Virginia Commonwealth University, 808 W Franklin St., Richmond, VA 23284-2018, U.S.A. **Online address:** eworth@vcu.edu

WORTSMAN, Peter. American (born United States), b. 1952. **Genres:** Novellas/Short Stories, Essays, Translations, Theatre, Travel/Exploration, Writing/Journalism. **Career:** Sing Out magazine, managing editor, 1976-78; Adelphi University, instructor in writing, 1978-81; Adtech Translations, German consultant, 1982-85; Columbia University, speech writer for dean of law, 1985-87, College of Physicians and Surgeons, staff writer and managing editor of alumni publications, 1987-; Courants d'ombre, New York correspondent, 1996-2001. **Publications:** (Trans.) G. Schiff, German Essays in Art History, 1988; (trans.) R. Musil, Posthumous Papers of a Living Author, 1988; (trans.) H. Belting, Max Beckmann: Tradition as a Problem in Modern Art, 1989; (trans.) J. Laederach, Sixty-Nine Ways to Play the Blues, 1990; A Modern Way to Die: Small Stories and Microtales, 1991; (trans.) A. von Chamisso, Peter Schlemihl, 1993; The Tattooed Man Tells All (play), 2000; (trans.) Telegrams of the Soul: Selected Prose of Peter Altenberg, 2005; (trans.) Posthumous Papers of a Living Author, 2006; (trans.) Travel Pictures, 2008; (trans.) Selected Prose of Heinrich von Kleist, 2010. Work appears in anthologies. **Address:** Faculty of Medicine, Columbia University, 2960 Broadway, New York, NY 10027-6902, U.S.A. **Online address:** pw8@columbia.edu

WOŚ, Joanna H(elena). American (born United States), b. 1951. **Genres:** Novellas/Short Stories, Young Adult Fiction. **Career:** Octagon Museum, curator, 1982-84; Institute of Musical Services, museum program specialist, 1984; New York State Museum, development consultant, 1985; Albany Institute of History and Art, director of development, 1987-89; New York State

Writers Institute, program assistant, 1989-92; Junior Museum, development coordinator, 1990-92; Santa Fe Literary Center, coordinator, 1992-93; Hudson Valley Writers Center, program assistant, 1994-95; Sycamore School, teaching assistant, 1995-97; Hussey-Mayfield Memorial Public Library, youth services reference librarian, 1999-. Writer. **Publications:** A House of Butter (short stories), 1999; The Three Properties of Life, forthcoming. Contributor to periodicals. Works appear in anthologies. **Address:** 8148 Lieber Rd., Indianapolis, IN 46260, U.S.A. **Online address:** jhwriter@indy.net

WOUK, Herman. American (born United States), b. 1915. **Genres:** Novels, Plays/Screenplays, Young Adult Non-fiction, Theology/Religion. **Career:** Fred Allen, staff writer, 1936-41; writer, 1946-; Yeshiva University, visiting professor, 1953-58; College of the Virgin Islands, trustee, 1961-69; Washington National Symphony, board director, 1969-71. **Publications:** The Man in the Trenchcoat, 1941; Aurora Dawn, 1947; City Boy: The Adventures Of Herbie Bookbinder and His Cousin, Cliff, 1948; The Caine Mutiny, 1951; The Caine Mutiny Court-Martial, 1954; Marjorie Morningstar, 1955; Slattery's Hurricane, 1956; Nature's Way, 1958; This is My God, 1959, rev. ed., 1970; Youngblood Hawke, 1962; Don't Stop the Carnival, 1965; (intro.) Now, Hear This!, 1965; The Lomokome Papers, 1968; The Winds of War, 1971; War and Remembrance, 1978; Inside, Outside, 1985; Hajsza, 1990; The Hope, 1994; The Glory, 1994; Agnon in Jerusalem: A Reminiscence and a Teaching, 1998; The Will to Live On: This is Our Heritage, 2000; A Hole in Texas, 2004; (intro.) Hearst to Hughes: Memoir of a Forensic Psychiatrist, 2007; The Language God Talks, 2010. Contributor to periodicals. **Address:** c/o Author Mail, BSW Literary Agency, 3255 N St. NW, Washington, DC 20007-2845, U.S.A.

WRANGHAM, Richard W. American (born United States), b. 1948. **Genres:** Biology. **Career:** Bristol University, postdoctoral fellow, 1976; Stanford University, postdoctoral associate, 1976-77; Harvard University, visiting lecturer in anthropology, 1977-80, professor of anthropology, chair biological anthropology, 1991-98; King's College, research fellow, 1980-84; University of Michigan, assistant professor, 1984-89, associate professor of anthropology, 1985-89, associate professor of biology, 1986-87, Program in Evolution and Human Behavior, coordinator, 1989-; Kibale Chimpanzee Project, director, 1987-; Jane Goodall Institute, trustee, 1993-. writer. **Publications:** (Ed. with B.C.R. Bertram, T.H. Clutton-Brock, R.I.M. Dunbar and D.I. Rubenstein) Current Problems in Sociobiology, 1982. (ed. with D.I. Rubenstein) Ecological Aspects of Social Evolution: Birds and Mammals, 1986; (ed. with B.B. Smuts, D.L. Cheney, R.M. Seyfarth and T.T. Struhsaker) Primate Societies, 1987; (co-author) Chimpanzee Cultures, 1994; (with D. Peterson) Demonic Males: Apes and the Origins of Human Violence, 1996; (ed. with E. Ross) Science and Conservation in African Forests: The Benefits of Long-term Research, 2008; Catching Fire: How Cooking Made Us Human, 2009. (ed. with M.N. Muller) Sexual Coercion in Primates and Humans: An Evolutionary Perspective on Male Aggression against Females, 2009. Contributor to books, journals and periodicals. **Address:** Museum of Comparative Zoology, Harvard University, 26 Oxford St., Cambridge, MA 02138, U.S.A. **Online address:** wrangham@fas.harvard.edu

WRAY, John. American (born United States), b. 1971?. **Genres:** Novels, Literary Criticism And History, Young Adult Fiction. **Career:** Writer. **Publications:** The Right Hand of Sleep, 2001; Canaan's Tongue, 2005; Lowboy, 2009. Contributor to periodicals. **Address:** c/o Author Mail, Knopf Publishing, 1745 Broadway, New York, NY 10019, U.S.A.

WRAY, Matt. American (born United States), b. 1964. **Genres:** Young Adult Non-fiction. **Career:** University of California, research assistant in health sciences, 1997-98; Humboldt State University, visiting assistant professor in department of ethnic studies, 2000-01; University of Nevada, assistant professor of sociology, 2001-08; Temple University, assistant professor of sociology, 2008-, affiliated faculty in American studies program, 2009-. Writer. **Publications:** (ed. with A. Newitz) White Trash: Race and Class in America, 1997; Not Quite White: White Trash and the Boundaries of Whiteness, 2006. Contributor to books, periodicals and journals. **Address:** Department of Sociology, Temple University, 751 Gladfelter Hall, 1115 W Berks St., Philadelphia, PA 19122, U.S.A. **Online address:** wray.matt@gmail.com

WREDE, Patricia C(ollins). American (born United States), b. 1953. **Genres:** Science Fiction/Fantasy, Children's Fiction, Novels, Novellas/Short Stories. **Career:** Minnesota Hospital Association, rate review analyst, 1977-78; B. Dalton Bookseller, financial analyst, 1978-80; Dayton-Hudson Corp., financial analyst, 1980-81, senior financial analyst, 1981-83, senior accountant, 1983-85; full-time writer, 1985-. **Publications:** LYRA SERIES: Shadow Magic, 1982; Daughter of Witches, 1983; The Harp of Imach Thyssel, 1985; Caught in Crystal, 1987; The Raven Ring, 1994. ENCHANTED FOREST SERIES: Talking to Dragons, 1984; Dragonsbane, 1990; Searching for Dragons, 1991; Calling on Dragons, 1993. CECELIA AND KATE SERIES WITH C. STEVERMER: Sorcery and Cecelia: Or The Enchanted Chocolate Pot, 1988; The Grand Tour, 2004; The Mislaid Magician: Or Ten Years After, 2006. MAIRELON SERIES: Mairelon the Magician, 1991; Magician's Ward, 1997. FRONTIER MAGIC SERIES: Thirteenth Child, 2009; Across the Great Barrier, 2011. NOVELS: The Seven Towers, 1984; Snow White and Rose Red, 1989. COLLECTION: Book of Enchantments, 1996. **Address:** c/o Ginger Clark, Curtis Brown Ltd., 10 Astor Pl., 3rd Fl., New York, NY 10003, U.S.A. **Online address:** pcwrede@pcwrede.com

WREN, Jill Robinson. American (born United States), b. 1954?. **Genres:** Law, Librarianship, How-to Books, Education, Information Science/Computers. **Career:** Wisconsin Attorney General, law clerk, 1979; Food Service Marketing Magazine, assistant editor, 1980-81; Dane County Circuit, Judge P. Charles Jones, judicial law clerk, 1981, Judge Angela B. Bartell, judicial law clerk, 1981-83; State Bar of Wisconsin Continuing Legal Education Division, editor, 1984-86; Adams & Ambrose Publishing (formerly American Academic Press), senior editor, 1986-. **Publications:** (With C.G. Wren) The Legal Research Manual: A Game Plan for Legal Research and Analysis, 1983, 2nd ed., 1986; (with C.G. Wren) Using Computers in Legal Research: A Guide to LEXIS and WESTLAW, 1994. **Address:** Adams & Ambrose Publishing, PO Box 259684, Madison, WI 53725-9684, U.S.A. **Online address:** jrwren@adamsambrose.com

WRENN, Lynette Boney. American (born United States), b. 1928. **Genres:** Business/Trade/Industry, Economics, History, Politics/Government, Social Sciences. **Career:** Teacher, 1949-51, 1953-54; Southwestern at Memphis (now Rhodes College), teacher, 1958; Memphis State University, instructor in history, 1983-84. Writer. **Publications:** (Contrib.) Governors of Tennessee, 1790-1835, 1979; The Taxing District of Shelby County: A Political and Administrative History of Memphis, Tennessee, 1879-1893, 1985; (contrib.) Southern Cities, Southern Schools, 1990; Cinderella of the New South: A History of the Cottonseed Industry, 1855-1955, 1995; Crisis and Commission Government in Memphis: Elite Rule in a Gilded Age City, 1998; A History of Memphis during the Late Nineteenth Century, 1998; (ed.) A Bachelor's Life in Antebellum Mississippi: The Diary of Dr. Elijah Millington Walker, 1849-1852, 2004. Contributor of articles to journals. **Address:** 4209-B Trillium Ln., Greensboro, NC 27410-8877, U.S.A.

WRESZIN, Michael. American (born United States), b. 1926. **Genres:** Politics/Government, History. **Career:** Wayne State University, instructor in American history, 1959-62; Brown University, assistant professor of American history and civilization, 1962-64; City University of New York, Queens College, assistant professor, 1965-67, associate professor, 1968-70, professor of American history, 1971-98, now professor emeritus. Writer. **Publications:** Oswald Garrison Villard: Pacifist at War, 1965; (ed. with F.A. Warren) The New Deal: An Anthology, 1968; The Superfluous Anarchist: Albert Jay Nock, 1972; A Rebel in Defense of Tradition: The Life and Politics of Dwight Macdonald, 1994; (ed. with intro.) Moral Temper: The Letters of Dwight Macdonald, 2001; (ed.) Interviews with Dwight Macdonald, 2003. Works appear in anthologies. Contributor to periodicals. **Address:** Department of History, Queens College, City University of New York, 65-30 Kissena Blvd., Flushing, NY 11367, U.S.A.

WRIGHT, Alex. American (born United States), b. 1966. **Genres:** Adult Non-fiction, History. **Career:** New York Times, User Experience and Product Research, director. Writer and information architect. **Publications:** Glut: Mastering Information through the Ages, 2007. Contributor to periodicals. **Address:** Joseph Henry Press, 500 5th St. NW, Washington, DC 20001-2736, U.S.A. **Online address:** alex@alexwright.com

WRIGHT, Alexandra. American (born United States), b. 1979. **Genres:** Children's Fiction, Children's Non-fiction. **Career:** Writer. **Publications:** FOR CHILDREN. NONFICTION: Will We Miss Them?: Endangered Species, 1992; At Home in the Tide Pool, 1992; Can We Be Friends?: Nature's Partners, 1994. FICTION: Alice in Pastaland: A Math Adventure, 1997. **Address:** Charlesbridge Publishing, 85 Main St., Watertown, MA 02472, U.S.A. **Online address:** awright@drew.edu

WRIGHT, Alexis. Australian (born Australia), b. 1950. **Genres:** Novels, Adult Non-fiction, History, Literary Criticism And History, Humanities. **Career:** Northern Territory Aboriginal Constitutional Convention, researcher and planner, 1993; Kalkaringi Convention, researcher and planner, 1998; Flinders University, Center for Remote Area Health, Central Australia Indigenous Community Initiative Injury Prevention Project, senior research manager, 2001-02; Leaders in Medical Education Network, coordinator; University of Melbourne, Onemda VicHealth Koori Health Unit, project officer. **Publications:** Grog War (nonfiction), 1997; Plains of Promise (novel), 1997; (ed.) Take Power Like This Old Man Here: An Anthology of Writings Celebrating Twenty Years of Land Rights in Central Australia, 1977-1997, 1998; Carpentaria (novel), 2006; (with C. Tsiolkas and G. Haigh) Tolerance, Prejudice and Fear: Sydney PEN Voices, the 3 Writers Project, 2008. **Address:** Onemda VicHealth Koori Health Unit, University of Melbourne, Rm. 415, Level 4, 207 Bouverie St., Melbourne, VI 3010, Australia. **Online address:** alexisw@unimelb.edu.au

WRIGHT, A(mos) J(asper). American (born United States), b. 1952. **Genres:** Poetry, Criminology/True Crime, History. **Career:** Auburn University, Draughon Library, Microforms and Documents Department, library assistant, 1973-81; University of Alabama, Health Sciences Library, graduate assistant and library assistant, 1981-82; Tuscaloosa (Alabama) Public Library, cataloger, 1982-83; School of Medicine, Department of Anesthesiology Library, director, 1983-, associate professor, 2002-. Writer. **Publications:** Frozen Fruit, 1978; Right Now I Feel Like Robert Johnson, 1980; Criminal Activity in the Deep South, 1700-1930: An Annotated Bibliography, 1989; Included In: Alabama Poets: A Contemporary Anthology, 1990. Contributor of articles to periodicals. **Address:** School of Medicine, University of Alabama, 619 S 19th St., JT 965, Birmingham, AL 35249-6810, U.S.A. **Online address:** ajwright@uab.edu

WRIGHT, Barbara. American (born United States), b. 1951. **Genres:** Novels, Plays/Screenplays, Literary Criticism And History. **Career:** University of New Hampshire, instructor in English, 1980-81; Creative Communications, public relations writer, 1981-83; San Salvador, freelance writer, 1983; APM Inc., health care management writer, 1984-86; freelance writer, 1986-. **Publications:** (With R.T. Craig) Mental Health Financing and Programming: A Legislator's Guide, 1988; (co-author) American with Developmental Disabilities: Policy Directions for the States, 1991; What Legislators Need to know About Traumatic Brain Injury, 1993. NOVELS: Easy Money, 1995; Plain Language, 2003; White Hands, 2010; Crow, 2012. Contributor to journals. **Address:** c/o Gail Hochman, Brandt & Hochman Literary Agents Inc., 1501 Broadway, Ste. 2310, New York, NY 10036, U.S.A. **Online address:** wribar@kcnet.com

WRIGHT, Betty Ren. (Revena Wright). American (born United States), b. 1927. **Genres:** Children's Fiction, Novels, Mystery/Crime/Suspense, Young Adult Fiction, Ghost Writer. **Career:** Western Publishing Co., editorial assistant and editor, 1949-67, Editorial Department, managing editor, 1967-78; Racine Editorial, managing editor, 1967-78; writer, 1978-. **Publications:** Willy Woo-oo-oo, 1951; Snowball, 1952; The Yellow Cat, 1952; Bunny Button, Whitman, 1953; Jim Jump, 1954; Poppyseed, 1954; (as Revena) Mr. Moggs Dogs, 1954; My Big Book, 1954; Train Coming!, 1954; (adapter) Bear Country, 1954; (adapter) Beaver Valley, 1954; (adapter with A. Hanson) Water Birds, 1955; American Folkore, 1956; Roundabout Train, 1958; Good Morning, Farm, 1964; I Want to Read, 1965; (as Revena) Histoire dun lap ingris, 1965; This Room is Mine, 1966; Teddy Bears Book of 1-2-3, 1969; (with J. Wylie) Elephants Birthday Party: A Story about Shapes, 1971; The Cat Who Stamped His Feet, 1975; The Rabbits Adventure, 1977; Rogers Upside-Down Day, 1979; The Day Our TV Broke Down, 1980; Why Do I Daydream?, 1981; (adapter) H.G. Wells, The Time Machine, 1981; (adapter) Stephen Crane, The Red Badge of Courage, 1981; I Like Being Alone, 1981; My New Mom and Me, 1981; My Sister is Different, 1981; Getting Rid of Marjorie, 1981; The Secret Window, 1982; (adapter) Emily Brontë, Wuthering Heights, 1982; The Dollhouse Murders in UK as The Ghosts in the Attic, 1983; Ghosts beneath Our Feet, 1984; Christinas Ghost, 1985; The Summer of Mrs. MacGregor, 1986; A Ghost in the Window, 1987; The Pike River Phantom, 1988; Rosie and the Dance of the Dinosaurs, 1989; The Ghost of Ernie P., 1990; A Ghost in the House, 1991; The Cat Next Door, 1991; The Scariest Night, 1991; The Ghost of Popcorn Hill, 1993; The Ghosts of Mercy Manor, 1993; The Ghost Witch, 1993; The Ghost Comes Calling, 1994; Out of the Dark, 1995; Nothing but Trouble, 1995; Haunted Summer, 1996; Getting Rid of Katherine, 1996; Too Many Secrets, 1997; The Ghost in Room 11, 1997; A Ghost in the

Family, 1998; The Phantom of Five Chimneys, 1998; Pet Detectives, 1999; The Moonlight Man, 2000; The Wish Master, 2000; Blizzard, 2003; Crandalls Castle, 2003; Princess for a Week, 2006. Contributor to periodicals. **Address:** Sternig & Burne Literary Agency, 2370 S 107th St., Apt. 4, Milwaukee, WI 53227-2036, U.S.A.

WRIGHT, Carolyn D. *See* **WRIGHT, C. D.**

WRIGHT, C. D. (Carolyn D. Wright). American (born United States), b. 1949. **Genres:** Poetry, Essays, Humanities. **Career:** San Francisco State University, lecturer in poetry writing and publishing, 1979-81, Poetry Center, office manager, 1979-81; Brown University, assistant professor, 1983-88, associate professor, Graduate Creative Writing Program, director, 1988-95, professor of English, 1995-, Israel J. Kapstein professor of literary arts. Writer. **Publications:** POETRY: Alla Breve Loving, 1976; Room Rented by a Single Woman, 1977; Terrorism, 1979; Translations of the Gospel Back into Tongues, 1982; Further Adventures with You, 1986; String Light, 1991; Just Whistle: A Valentine, 1993; The Lost Roads Project: A Walk-In Book of Arkansas, 1994; The Reader's Map of Arkansas, 1994; Tremble, 1996; Deepstep Come Shining, 1998; A Reader's Map of Rhode Island, 1999; (ed.) Run Through Rock: Selected Short Poems of Besmilr Brigham, 2000; Steal Away: Selected and New Poems, 2002; One Big Self: Prisoners of Louisiana, 2003; Cooling Time: An American Poetry Vigil, 2005; One Big Self: An Investigation, 2007; Like Something Flying Backwards: New & Selected Poems, 2007; Rising, Falling, Hovering, 2008; One with Others: A Little Book of Her Days, 2010. **Address:** Literary Arts Program, Brown University, 68 1/2 Brown St., PO Box 1923, Providence, RI 02912, U.S.A. **Online address:** carolyn_wright@brown.edu

WRIGHT, Charles (Penzel). American (born United States), b. 1935. **Genres:** Poetry, Translations, History. **Career:** University of California, Department of English, assistant professor, professor of English, 1966-83; Universita Degli Studi, Fulbright lecturer, 1968-69, distinguished visiting professor, 1992; University of Iowa, visiting lecturer, 1974-75; Princeton University, visiting lecturer, 1978; Columbia University, visiting lecturer, 1978; University of Virginia, Souder Family professor of English, 1983-; The Academy of American Poets, chancellor, 1999-2002. Writer. **Publications:** The Voyage, 1963; Six Poems, 1965; The Dream Animal, 1968; Private Madrigals, 1969; The Grave of the Right Hand, 1970; The Venice Notebook, 1971; Backwater, 1973; Hard Freight, 1973; Bloodlines, 1975; Colophons: Poems, 1977; China Trace, 1977; (trans.) E. Montale, The Storm and Other Poems, 1978; Wright: A Profile, 1979; Dead Color: Poems, 1980; The Southern Cross, 1981; (trans.) Motets, 1981; Country Music: Selected Early Poems, 1982, 2nd ed., 1991; Four Poems of Departure, 1983; The Other Side of the River: Poems, 1984; (trans.) D. Campana, Orphic Songs, 1984; Five Journals, 1986; Zone Journals, 1988; Halflife: Improvisations and Interviews, 1977-87, 1988; Xionia, 1990; The World of the Ten Thousand Things: Poems 1980-1990, 1990; Chickamauga, 1995; Quarter Notes: Improvisations and Interviews, 1995; Black Zodiac, 1997; Appalachia, 1998; Negative Blue: Selected Later Poems, 2000; A Short History of the Shadow, 2002; Snake Eyes, 2004; (trans. with J. Galassi and D. Young) E. Montale, Selected Poems, 2004; Buffalo Yoga, 2004; The Wrong End of The Rainbow: Poems, 2005; Scar Tissue, 2006; Littlefoot, 2007; Sestets: Poems, 2009; Outtakes: Sestets, 2010; Bye-and-bye: Selected Late Poems, 2011. **Address:** Department of English, University of Virginia, 219 Bryan Hall, PO Box 400121, Charlottesville, VA 22904-4121, U.S.A. **Online address:** cpw9b@virginia.edu

WRIGHT, Christopher. *See* **WRIGHT, Kit.**

WRIGHT, Christopher J.H. (Christopher Joseph Herbert Wright). British/Irish (born Ireland), b. 1947. **Genres:** Ethics. **Career:** Ordained Anglican pastor, 1977; Parish Church of St. Peter & St. Paul, assistant pastor, 1977-; Union Biblical Seminary, teacher, 1983-88; All Nations Christian College, academic dean, 1988-93, principal, 1993-2001; Langham Partnership International, international ministries director, 2001-. Writer. **Publications:** An Eye for an Eye: The Place of Old Testament Ethics Today, 1983; User's Guide to the Bible, 1984; God's People in God's Land: Family, Land and Property in the Old Testament, 1990; Walking in the Ways of the Lord: The Ethical Authority of the Old Testament, 1995; Knowing Jesus through the Old Testament, 1995; Deuteronomy, 1996; The Message of Ezekiel: A New Heart and a New Spirit, 2001; (ed. with P. Gardner and C. Green) Fanning the Flame: Bible, Cross & Mission-Meeting the Challenge in a Changing World, 2003; Old Testament Ethics for the People of God, 2004; The Mission of God: Un-

locking the Bible's Grand Narrative, 2006; Knowing the Holy Spirit through the Old Testament, 2006; Knowing God the Father through the Old Testament, 2007; Salvation Belongs to Our God: Celebrating the Bible's Central Story, 2008. **Address:** Langham Partnership Intl., PO Box 997, Guildford, GU1 9DS, England. **Online address:** chris@langhampartnership.org

WRIGHT, Christopher Joseph Herbert. *See* **WRIGHT, Christopher J.H.**

WRIGHT, Cliff. British (born England), b. 1963. **Genres:** Children's Fiction, Illustrations, Novels. **Career:** Elemental Eye Gallery, founder, 2011. Writer and illustrator. **Publications:** SELF-ILLUSTRATED PICTURE BOOKS: When the World Sleeps, 1989; Crumbs!, 1990; The Tangleweed Troll, 1993; Santa's Ark, 1997; Bear and Box, 2007; Bear and Boat, 2007. OTHERS: The Explorers, 1992; (with M. Moss) Henry's Kite, 1996; (with M. Moss) Windswept, 1997; Bear and Kite, 2004; Bear and Ball, 2005; Three Bears, 2006; The Magic Of Drawing, 2008. Illustrator of books by A. Geras, A. Jungman and K. White. **Address:** Greenways, Pevensey Rd., New Haven, ES BN9 9TU, England. **Online address:** info@cliffwright.co.uk

WRIGHT, Clifford A. American (born United States), b. 1951. **Genres:** Food And Wine, International Relations/Current Affairs. **Career:** Brookings Institution, researcher; Institute of Arab Studies, staff fellow; American Middle East Peace Research Institute, executive director; University of California, Gustav E. von Grunebaum Center for Near-Eastern Studies, center affiliate; ZesterDaily.Com, contributing editor; Rhode Island School of Design, teacher; Institute for Culinary Education, teacher; Sur la Table, teacher; Venice Cooking School, co-founder. Writer. **Publications:** (With K. Nakhleh) After the Palestine-Israel War, 1983; Facts and Fables: The Arab-Israeli Conflict, 1989; Cucina Paradiso, 1992; Cucina Rapida, 1994; Lasagne, 1995; Grill Italian, 1996; Italian Pure and Simple, 1998; A Mediterranean Feast, 1999; Mediterranean Vegetables, 2001; Real Stew, 2002; Little Foods of the Mediterranean, 2003; Some Like It Hot, 2005; Bake Until Bubbly: The Ultimate Casserole Book, 2008; The Best Soups in the World, 2010; Hot & Cheesy, 2012. Contributor to magazines. **Address:** c/o Angela Miller, Miller Agency-Film Ctr., 630 9th Ave., Ste. 1102, New York, NY 10036, U.S.A. **Online address:** cwright@cliffordawright.com

WRIGHT, Cora M. American (born United States), b. 1944. **Genres:** Children's Non-fiction, Education, Young Adult Non-fiction, Literary Criticism And History, Social Commentary. **Career:** California State University, instructor; Chapman University, instructor. Writer. **Publications:** Hot Links: Literature Links for the Middle-School Curriculum, 1998; More Hot Links: Linking Literature with the Middle-School Curriculum, 2002. **Address:** ABC-CLIO, 130 Cremona Dr., Santa Barbara, CA 93117, U.S.A. **Online address:** tandcwrigh@yahoo.com

WRIGHT, Courtni C(rump). American (born United States), b. 1950. **Genres:** Theatre, Romance/Historical, Children's Fiction. **Career:** C&P Telephone Co., account executive, 1972-75, manager, 1972-86; Waterloo Middle School, English teacher, 1975-77; Howard County Schools, English teacher, 1975-77; Bell Atlantic Corp., marketing manager, 1977-87; Grace Episcopal Day School, English teacher, 1987-90; National Cathedral School, English teacher, 1990-97; freelance writer, 1997-98; The Hebrew Academy of Greater Washington, high school English teacher, 1998-99; Montgomery County Public Schools, high school English teacher, 1999-; National Endowment for the Humanities, fellow. **Publications:** ADULT NONFICTION: Women of Shakespeare's Plays, 1993; (with R.Gayle and M. Walker) Season's Greetings, 1998. FOR CHILDREN: Journey to Freedom: A Story of the Underground Railroad, 1994; Jumping the Broom, 1994; Wagon Train: A Black Family's Westward Journey in 1865, 1995. ADULT FICTION: Blush, 1997; It had to be you, 1998; Paradise, 1999; A Sure Thing, 1999; All That Matters, 2000; A New Beginning, 2000; A Forgotten Love, 2000; Very Special love, 2000; Recipe For Love, 2001; Uncovered Passion, 2002; A Charmed Love, 2002; The Music of Love, 2003; The Last Christmas Gift, 2003; Summer Breeze, 2004; Espresso for Two, 2004; Windswept Love, 2005; Love Under Construction, 2006. Contributor to periodicals. **Address:** 12612 Springloch Ct., Silver Spring, MD 20904, U.S.A. **Online address:** courtni@erols.com

WRIGHT, Daphne. Also writes as Clare Layton, Natasha Cooper, N. J. Cooper, Kate Hatfield. British (born England), b. 1951. **Genres:** Novels. **Career:** Chatto & Windus (publisher), secretary and editorial assistant, 1976-77; Hutchinson (publisher), editor, 1977-83; Quartet (publisher), editorial director, 1983-84; Bellew Publishing, staff, 1984-86. **Publications:** NOV-

ELS: The Distant Kingdom, 1987; The Longest Winter, 1989; The Parrot Cage, 1990; Never Such Innocence, 1991; Dreams of Another Day, 1992; The Tightrope Walkers, 1993. AS KATE HATFIELD: Drowning in Honey, 1995; Angels Alone, 1996; Marsh Light, 1997. AS NATASHA COOPER: WILLOW KING MYSTERY SERIES: A Common Death, 1990 as Festering Lilies, 1990; Poison Flowers, 1991; Bloody Roses, 1992; Bitter Herbs, 1993; Rotten Apples, 1995; The Drowning Pool, 1996; Sour Grapes, 1997. AS NATASHA COOPER: TRISH MAGUIRE MYSTERY SERIES: Creeping Ivy, 1998; Fault Lines, 1999; Prey to All, 2000; Out of the Dark, 2002; A Place of Safety, 2003; Keep Me Alive, 2004; Gagged and Bound, 2005; Evil Is Done, 2007 as A Greater Evil, 2007; A Poisoned Mind, 2008. NOVEL AS NATASHA COOPER: No More Victims, 2008. AS N.J. COOPER: KAREN TAYLOR SERIES: No Escape, 2009; Life Blood, 2010; Face of the Devil, 2011. NOVEL AS N.J. COOPER: Suspicion, 2011. AS CLARE LAYTON: Clutch of Phantoms, 2000; Those Whom the Gods Love, 2001. Contributor to periodicals. **Address:** c/o Jane Gregory, Gregory & Co., 3 Barb Mews, Hammersmith, London, GL W6 7PA, England.

WRIGHT, Donald Andrew. Canadian (born Canada), b. 1965. **Genres:** History. **Career:** University of Ottawa, lecturer, 1995, 1996; St. Thomas University, lecturer, 1997, 1999-2000; University of New Brunswick, lecturer, 1999, residence don, 1999-2000, associate professor of political science, 2005-; Brock University, assistant professor of history and Canadian studies, 2000-05. Academic and writer. **Publications:** (Ed.) Canadian Studies: An Introductory Reader, 2004; The Professionalization of History in English Canada, 2005. Contributor of articles to periodicals. **Address:** University of New Brunswick, 100 Tucker Park Rd., PO Box 5050, St. John, NB E2L 4L5, Canada. **Online address:** wrightd@unb.ca

WRIGHT, Donald R(ichard). American (born United States), b. 1944. **Genres:** History, Area Studies, Humanities. **Career:** American Historical Review, editorial assistant, 1975-76; State University of New York College at Cortland, assistant professor, 1976-79, associate professor, 1979-84, department head, 1983-85, professor, 1984-90, distinguished teaching professor of history, 1990-2007, distinguished teaching professor of history emeritus, 2007-; New York State Council for the Social Studies, presenter of workshops, 1980-2008; National Museum of the Gambia, collector and curator, 1982; University of Witwatersrand, lecturer, 2000; The Citadel, Mark Clark visiting distinguished professor of history, 2005-06; Geographical Expeditions and Travel Dynamics International Excursions in Africa, lecturer, 2008-. **Publications:** The Early History of Niumi: Settlement and Foundation of a Mandinka Stateon the Gambia River, 1977; Oral Traditions from the Gambia, vol. I: Mandinka Griots, 1979, vol. II: Family Elders, 1980; What to Teach about Africa: A Guide for Secondary Teachers, 1990; African Americans in the Colonial Era: From African Origins through the American Revolution, 1990, 3rd ed., 2010; African Americans in the Early Republic, 1789-1831, 1993; The World and a Very Small Place in Africa, 1997, 3rd ed. 2010; (coauthor) The Atlantic World, A History, 1400-1888, 2007. Contributor of articles to journals and books. **Address:** 4355 Locust Ave., Homer, NY 13077, U.S.A. **Online address:** wrightd21@gmail.com

WRIGHT, Eric. Canadian/British (born England), b. 1929. **Genres:** Novels, Novellas/Short Stories, Mystery/Crime/Suspense, Autobiography/Memoirs. **Career:** Ryerson Polytechnic, teacher of English, 1958-89. Writer. **Publications:** CHARLIE SALTER DETECTIVE NOVELS: The Night the Gods Smiled: Introducing Inspector Charlie Salter, 1983; Smoke Detector: An Inspector Charlie Salter Mystery, 1984; Death in the Old Country: An Inspector Charlie Salter Mystery, 1985; The Man Who Changed His Name in UK as A Single Death, 1986; A Body Surrounded by Water: An Inspector Charlie Salter Novel, 1987; A Question of Murder, 1988; A Sensitive Case, 1990; Final Cut, 1991; A Fine Italian Hand: An Inspector Charlie Salter Novel, 1992; Death by Degrees, 1993; Buried in Stone: A Mel Pickett Mystery, 1995; Death of a Sunday Writer, 1996; Death on the Rocks, 1999; The Kidnapping of Rosie Dawn: A Joe Barley Mystery, 2000; Death of a Hired Man, 2001; The Last Hand, 2002; A Charlie Salter Omnibus, 2003; Finding Home, 2007. WITH H. ENGEL: My Brother's Keeper (novel), 2003; The Hemingway Caper (novel), 2003; A Killing Climate: The Collected Mystery Stories (short stories), 2003. OTHER: (contrib.) Fingerprints, 1984; Moodie's Tale (comic novel), 1994; Always Give a Penny to a Blind Man (memoir), 1999; Twins, 2001; A Likely Story: A Joe Barley Mystery, 2010. **Address:** Bella Pomer Agency Inc., 355 St. Clair Ave. W, Ste. 801, Toronto, ON M5P 1N5, Canada.

WRIGHT, Franz. American (born United States), b. 1953. **Genres:** Poetry, Literary Criticism And History, Translations, Young Adult Fiction. **Career:** Brandeis University, Jacob Ziskind visiting poet-in-residence, 2009. **Publications:** (Trans. and intro.) R.M. Rilke, The Unknown Rilke, 1983; (trans.) R. Char, No Siege Is Absolute, 1984; (co-trans.) V. Mort Factory of Tears, 2008. POETRY: Tapping the White Cane of Solitude, 1976; The Earth Without You, 1980; Eight Poems, 1981; The One Whose Eyes Open When You Close Your Eyes, 1982; No Siege is Absolute, 1984; Going North in Winter, 1986; Entry in an Unknown Hand, 1989; Midnight Postscript, 1990; And Still the Hand Will Sleep in Its Glass Ship, 1990; Rorschach Test, 1991; The Night World and the Word Night, 1993; Ill Lit: Selected and New Poems, 1998; The Beforelife: Poems, 2001; Walking to Martha's Vineyard, 2003; God's Silence, 2006; Earlier Poems, 2007; Wheeling Motel: Poems, 2009. Works appear in anthologies. Contributor to periodicals. **Address:** c/o Alison Granucci, Blue Flower Arts, 373 Mabbettsville Rd., Millbrook, NY 12545, U.S.A. **Online address:** marthamc@tiac.net

WRIGHT, George Thaddeus. American (born United States), b. 1925. **Genres:** Poetry, Literary Criticism And History. **Career:** Harry S. Goodman Productions (television, radio), assistant producer, 1949-51; University of California, lecturer, 1956-57; University of Kentucky, instructor and assistant professor of English, 1957-60; San Francisco State College, assistant professor of English, 1960-61; University of Tennessee, associate professor of English, 1961-68; Universite d'Aix-Marseille, Fulbright lecturer in American literature, 1964-66; University of Minnesota, professor of English, 1968-89, chairman, 1974-77, regents' professor, 1989-93, regents' professor emeritus, 1993-; University of Thessaloniki, staff, 1977-78. Writer. **Publications:** The Poet in the Poem: The Personae of Eliot, Yeats and Pound, 1960; W.H. Auden, 1969, rev. ed., 1981; (ed.) Seven American Literary Stylists from Poe to Mailer: An Introduction, 1973; Shakespeare's Metrical Art, 1988; Aimless Life: Poems, 1961-1995, 1999; Hearing the Measures: Shakespearean and Other Inflections, 2001; Poetic Craft and Authorial Design in Shakespeare, Keats, T.S. Eliot, and Henry James, with Two Essays on the Pygmalion Legend, 2011. Contributor to journals. **Address:** University of Minnesota, 207 Lind Hall, 207 Church St SE, Minneapolis, MN 55455, U.S.A. **Online address:** wrightg@smccd.net

WRIGHT, Helen L(ouise). American (born United States), b. 1932. **Genres:** Cultural/Ethnic Topics, Music, Literary Criticism And History. **Career:** Meharry Medical College and Hospital, secretary, 1953-54; New York Hospital, Payne Whitney Psychiatric Clinic, dictaphone operator, 1954-58; Columbia University, New York School of Social Work, secretary, 1958-62; Chase Manhattan Bank, secretary, 1973-78; Stanley P. Wagman, P.C., administrative manager, 1978-81; Cadwalader, Wickersham & Taft, word processing operator, 1981-; Helen L. Wright Inc., president. Writer. **Publications:** Metropolitan Opera House, 1979. Contributor to periodicals. **Address:** PO Box 78264, Nashville, TN 37207-8264, U.S.A. **Online address:** hwr1561160@aol.com

WRIGHT, James D(avid). (Jim Wright). American (born United States), b. 1947. **Genres:** Sociology. **Career:** University of Massachusetts, assistant professor, 1973-76, associate professor, 1976-79, professor of sociology, 1979-88; Social and Demographic Research Institute, associate director, 1975-82, director, 1982-85, director of research, 1985-88; Tulane University, Charles A. and Leo M. Favrot professor of human relations, 1988-2001, Department of Biostatistics and Epidemiology, adjunct professor, 1990-2001; University of Central Florida, provost distinguished research professor of sociology, 2001-, Survey Research Laboratory, director, Institute for Social and Behavioral Science, director; UCF Institute for Social and Behavioral Sciences, director. Writer. **Publications:** (With R.F. Hamilton) New Directions in Political Sociology, 1975; The Dissent of the Governed: Alienation and Democracy in America, 1976; (with P.H. Rossi, S.R. Wright and E. Weber-Burdin) After the Clean-up: Long Range Effects of Natural Disasters, 1979; (ed. with P.H. Rossi) Social Science and Natural Hazards, 1981; (with P.H. Rossi) Weapons, Crime and Violence in America: Executive Summary, 1981; (coauthor) Weapons, Crime and Violence in America: A Literature Review and Research Agenda, 1981; (with P.H. Rossi, E. Weber-Burdin and J. Pereira) Natural Hazards and Public Choice: The State and Local Politics of Hazard Mitigation, 1982; (with P.H. Rossi, E. Weber-Burdin and J. Pereira) Victims of the Environment: Loss from Natural Hazards in the United States, 1970-1980, 1983; (with P.H. Rossi and K. Daly) Under the Gun: Weapons, Crime and Violence in America, 1983; (ed. with P.H. Rossi and A. Anderson) The Handbook of Survey Research, 1983; (with P.H. Rossi) The Armed Criminal in America: A Survey of Incarcerated Felons, 1985; (with P.H. Rossi) Armed and Considered Dangerous: A Survey of Felons and Their Firearms, 1986,

2nd ed., 2008; (with R.F. Hamilton) The State of the Masses, 1986; (with E. Weber) Homelessness and Health, 1987; Address Unknown: The Homeless in America, 1989; (with J.A. Devine) The Greatest of Evils: Urban Poverty and the American Underclass, 1993; (with J.F. Sheley) Gun Acquisition and Possession in Selected Juvenile Samples, 1993; (with J.A. Devine) Drugs as a Social Problem, 1994; (with J.F. Sheley) In the Line of Fire: Youths, Guns and Violence in Urban America, 1995; (with J.F. Sheley and Z.T. McGee) Weapon-Related Victimization in Selected Inner-City High School Samples, 1995; (with B.A. Rubin and J.A. Devine) Beside the Golden Door: Policy, Politics and the Homeless, 1998; (as Jim Wright) Fixin' to Git: One Fan's Love Affair with NASCAR's Winston Cup, 2002; (with S.L. Nock and L.A. Sanchez) Covenant Marriage: The Movement to Reclaim Tradition in America, 2008; (with A.M. Donley) Poor and Homeless in the Sunshine State: Down and Out in Theme Park Nation, 2011. **Address:** Department of Sociology, University of Central Florida, 403-Q, Phillips Hall, PO Box 25000, Orlando, FL 32816-1360, U.S.A. **Online address:** jwright@mail.ucf.edu

WRIGHT, J. B. *See* **BARKAN, Joanne.**

WRIGHT, Jim. *See* **WRIGHT, James D(avid).**

WRIGHT, John S. (John Samuel Wright). American (born United States), b. 1946?. **Genres:** Biography. **Career:** Carleton College, chair and associate professor of African and African-American studies and associate professor of English, 1973-84, Afro-American and African Studies Program, chair, 1974-82; University of Minnesota, associate professor, 1984-2007, professor of African American and African studies, 2007-, professor of English, 2007-. Writer. **Publications:** (Intro.) My bondage and My Freedom, 2003; Shadowing Ralph Ellison, 2006. Works appear in anthologies. Contributor to periodicals. **Address:** Department of African American & African Studies, University of Minnesota, 812 Social Science Bldg., 267 19th Ave. S, Minneapolis, MN 55455-0499, U.S.A. **Online address:** wrigh003@umn.edu

WRIGHT, John Samuel. *See* **WRIGHT, John S.**

WRIGHT, Julie. American (born United States), b. 1972. **Genres:** Novels, Romance/Historical, Adult Non-fiction, Literary Criticism And History. **Career:** Writer. **Publications:** To Catch a Falling Star, 2001; Loved like That, 2002; Writing Secrets, 2004; Publishing Secrets, 2004; My Not-so-fairy-tale Life: A Novel, 2005; Seeking Zion, 2008; Eyes Like Mine, 2009; Cross My Heart, 2010; The Hazzardous Universe, 2011; The Day My Subconscious Betrayed Me, forthcoming; The Sand Prophets, forthcoming; The Thirteenth Month, forthcoming; Spell Check, forthcoming. **Address:** c/o Author Mail, Bonneville Books, 925 N Main St., Springville, UT 84663, U.S.A. **Online address:** stars@juliewright.com

WRIGHT, Kai. American (born United States), b. 1974?. **Genres:** History. **Career:** Washington Blade, staff reporter, 1997-; Freelance journalist, 2000-; Foreign Policy, editorial assistant; Public Broadcasting Service television show NewsHour, desk assistant; City Limits magazine, senior editor, 2002-; Black AIDS Institute, project editor, 2000, 2002, 2004; National Newspaper Publishers Association, project editor, 2000, 2002, 2004. **Publications:** (ed.) The African-American Archive: The History of the Black Experience in Documents, 2001; Soldiers of Freedom: An Illustrated History of African Americans in the Armed Forces, 2002; Drifting toward Love: Black, Brown, Gay and Coming of Age on the Streets of New York (nonfiction), 2008. Contributor to periodicals. **Address:** Brooklyn, NY , U.S.A. **Online address:** press@kaiwright.com

WRIGHT, Keith. (Keith Charles). British (born England), b. 1963. **Genres:** Mystery/Crime/Suspense, Novellas/Short Stories, Novels, Horror. **Career:** Nottinghamshire Constabulary, detective, 1982-, now retired. Writer and consultant. **Publications:** One Oblique One (crime novel), 1991; Trace and Eliminate (crime novel), 1992; Addressed to Kill (crime novel), 1993; Fair Means or Foul? (crime novel), 1995; (ed.) Perfectly Criminal (short story), 1996; Psychic Detective, 2000. **Address:** c/o Jeffrey Simmons, 10 Lowndes Sq., London, GL SW1X 9HA, England.

WRIGHT, Kit. (Christopher Wright). British (born England), b. 1944. **Genres:** Young Adult Fiction, Poetry, Children's Fiction, Animals/Pets, Reference, Young Adult Non-fiction. **Career:** Poetry Society, education officer, through 1975; Brock University, lecturer in English; Cambridge University, Trinity College, fellow-commoner in creative arts, 1977-79. Writer. **Publica-**

tions: (With S. Miller and E. Maslen) Treble Poets 1, 1974; (ed.) Soundings: A Selection of Poems for Speaking Aloud, 1975; The Bear Looked over the Mountain, 1977; Arthur's Sister, 1978; Arthur's Uncle, 1978; Arthur's Granny, 1978; Arthur's Father, 1978; Rabbiting On and Other Poems (juvenile), 1978; Hot Dog and Other Poems (juvenile), 1981; The Day Room, 1983; Bump-Starting the Hearse, 1983; (ed.) Poems for 9-Year Olds and Under Over 10-Year Olds, 2 vols., 1984; Cat Among the Pigeons (juvenile), 1987; One of Your Legs is Both the Same: A Poem, 1987; Poems 1974-1983, 1988; Real Rags and Red, 1988; Short Afternoons, 1989; Funnybunch: New Puffin Book of Funny Verse, 1993; Tigerella, 1993; Great Snakes!, 1994; Dolphinella, 1995; Rumpelstiltskin, 1998; Hoping it Might Be So, 2000; Write Away, 2000. **Address:** c/o Viking Kestrel, 80 Strand, London, GL WC2R 0RL, England.

WRIGHT, Leslie B(ailey). American (born United States), b. 1959. **Genres:** Human Relations/Parenting, Psychology, Self Help, Children's Non-fiction. **Career:** Writer. **Publications:** (With M.B. Loiselle) Shining Through: Pulling It Together after Sexual Abuse, 1997; (with M.B. Loiselle) Back on Track: The Boys Book for Dealing with Sexual Abuse, 1997; (with M.B. Loiselle) Rewind, Rebound: A Teenage Guy's Book for Dealing with Sexual Abuse, 2010. **Address:** 11300 Edgewood Farm Ct., Richmond, VA 23233, U.S.A.

WRIGHT, (Mary) Patricia. (Mary Napier). British (born England), b. 1932. **Genres:** Romance/Historical, History, Race Relations, Young Adult Fiction. **Career:** Writer, 1959-; Hughes & Wilbraham, agricultural surveyor and agent, 1955-57; Turnbridge Wells Grammar School for Girls, part-time teacher, 1966-80. Educator. **Publications:** Conflict on the Nile: Study of Fashoda Incident 1897-1900, 1972; A Space of the Heart, 1976; Journey into Fire, 1977; Shadow of the Rock, 1979; Storm Harvest, 1979; Heart of the Storm, 1980; Blind Chance, 1980; Storms of Fate, 1981; This, My City, 1981; While Paris Danced, 1982; History of Frant, 1982; I Am England, 1987; That Near and Distant Place, 1988; The Strange History of Buckingham Palace: Patterns of People, 1996. AS MARY NAPIER: Woman's Estate (sketches), 1959; Waiting, 1980; Forbidden Places, 1981; A State of Fear, 1984; Heartsearch, 1988; Budapest Risk, 1989; Powers of Darkness, 1990. **Address:** 10 Shernfold Pk., Frant, ES TN3 9DX, England.

WRIGHT, M(aureen) R(osemary). British (born England), b. 1933?. **Genres:** Philosophy, Classics, History. **Career:** University of Wales-Aberystwyth, lecturer in classics, 1964-84, senior lecturer, 1984-89; Center for Hellenic Studies, fellow, 1967-68; University of Reading, senior lecturer in classics, 1989-95; University of Wales-Lampeter, professor and head of classics 1995-2000, professor emeritus, 2000-. Writer. **Publications:** Empedocles: The Extant Fragments, 1981; The Presocratics, 1984; Cicero: On Stoic Good and Evil, 1990; Cosmology in Antiquity, 1995; Reason and Necessity, 2000; Introducing Greek Philosophy, 2010. **Address:** Department of Classics, University of Wales, Lampeter, SA48 7ED, Wales. **Online address:** mow@aber.ac.uk

WRIGHT, Melinda. *See* **JORDAN, Penny.**

WRIGHT, Michael. *See* **WRIGHT, Michael J(ohn).**

WRIGHT, Michael J(ohn). (Michael Wright). New Zealander/British (born England), b. 1944. **Genres:** Literary Criticism And History, Sciences, Poetry, Photography. **Career:** Australian National University, tutor, senior tutor, lecturer, 1972-81; University of Auckland, lecturer in English, 1981-, honorary research fellow. Writer. **Publications:** Phīangkhwāmkhlúanwai, 1980; (ed.) Angkarn Kalyanapong: A Contemporary Siamese Poet, 1986; Angkhān Kanlayānaphong, kawī Sayāmrūamsamai, 1987; (with S.J. Hollis) Old English Prose of Secular Learning, 1992; Guitar Stories, 1995; Farang khlang Sayām, 1998; (contrib.) Electric Guitars: The Illustrated Encyclopedia, 2000; Ōngkān Chaeng Nam, 2000; Digital Family Photography, 2003; Transitions in End of Life Care: Hospice and Related Developments in Eastern Europe and Central Asia, 2003; Farang Lang Tawantok, 2004; New Normal, 2004; Phra Phikkhanet, mahā thep HindūChomphūthawīp Lae Usākhane, 2005; (ed.) Discovering Ayutthaya, 2007; (contrib.) Securing Citrix XenApp Server in the Enterprise, 2008. **Address:** Department of English, University of Auckland, Rm. 418, Arts 1 Bldg., 14 A Symonds St., Auckland, 1011, New Zealand. **Online address:** mj.wright@auckland.ac.nz

WRIGHT, Nicholas Thomas. *See* **WRIGHT, N. T(om).**

WRIGHT, Nina. American (born United States), b. 1964. **Genres:** Novels, Young Adult Fiction, Mystery/Crime/Suspense. **Career:** Writer and educator. **Publications:** Homefree, 2006; Sensitive, 2007. WHISKEY MATTIMOE MYSTERY SERIES: Whiskey on the Rocks, 2005; Whiskey Straight Up, 2006; Whiskey and Tonic, 2007; Whiskey and Water, 2008; Whiskey with a Twist, 2009. **Address:** Midnight Ink, 2143 Wooddale Dr., Woodbury, MN 55125-2989, U.S.A. **Online address:** nina@ninawright.net

WRIGHT, N. T(om). Also writes as Tom Wright, Nicholas Thomas Wright. Scottish/British (born England), b. 1948. **Genres:** Theology/Religion, inspirational/Motivational Literature. **Career:** Merton College, junior research fellow, 1975-78; Downing College, fellow and chaplain, 1978-81; McGill University, assistant professor of New Testament language and literature, 1981-86, Montreal Diocesan Theological College, honorary professor, 1981-86; Yale Divinity School, visiting lecturer, 1982; Oxford University, lecturer in New Testament studies, 1986-93, Worcester College, fellow, 1986-93; Vacation Term for Biblical Studies, visiting lecturer, 1988; Institute for Christian Studies, visiting lecturer, 1988, 1989, 1991, fellow; Sheffield University, visiting lecturer, 1989; St. George's College, visiting professor, 1989; Mansfield College, North American Summer School, lecturer, 1989, 1990; Lincoln College, lecturer, 1989; University College, lecturer, 1989; Wadham College, lecturer, 1989; Hebrew University, visiting professor, 1989; New College School, parent governor, 1990-93; Birmingham University, School for Continuing Studies, visiting lecturer, 1990; Journal for the Study of the New Testament, assistant editor, 1991-96; Lichfield Cathedral, dean, 1994-99; Canon of Westminster, 2000-03; Bishop of Durham, 2003-10; University of Durham, visitor, 2003-; Auckland Castle Enterprises, chairman, 2003-06; University of St. Andrews, New Testament and Early Christianity, chair and research professor, 2010-. Writer. **Publications:** Small Faith, Great God, 1978, rev. ed., 2010; The Epistles of Paul to the Colossians and to Philemon, 1987; (with S. Neill) The Interpretation of the New Testament, 1861-1986, 1988; The Climax of the Covenant: Christ and the Law in Pauline Theology, 1991; Bringing the Church to the World, 1992 in UK as New Tasks for a Renewed Church, 1992; The Crown and the Fire, 1992; Christian Origins and the Question of God, vol. I: The New Testament and the People of God, 1992, vol. II: Jesus and the Victory of God, 1996; Who Was Jesus?, 1992; Following Jesus: Biblical Reflections on Christian Discipleship, 1994; The Lord and His Prayer, 1996; The Original Jesus, 1996; For All God's Worth, 1997; What St. Paul Really Said, 1997; A Moment of Prayer, 1997; A Moment of Quiet, 1997; A Moment of Peace, 1997; A Moment of Celebration, 1997; Reflecting the Glory, 1997; The Way of the Lord: Christian Pilgrimage in the Holy Land and Beyond, 1999; The Millennium Myth, 1999; The Challenge of Jesus: Rediscovering Who Jesus Was and Is, 1999; (with M.J. Borg) The Meaning of Jesus: Two Visions, 1999; Holy Communion for Amateurs, 1999; Twelve Months of Sundays: Reflections on Bible Readings, 2002; Mark for Everyone, 2001, 2nd ed., 2004; Luke for Everyone, 2001, 2nd ed., 2004; Paul for Everyone: Galatians and Thessalonians, 2002; Matthew for Everyone, 2002, 2nd ed., 2004; The Contemporary Quest for Jesus, 2002; Paul for Everyone: The Prison Letters, 2002, 2nd ed., 2004; John for Everyone, 2002, 2nd ed., 2004; Paul for Everyone: 1 Corinthians, 2003, 2nd ed. as Paul for Everyone: 2 Corinthians, 2004; Hebrews for Everyone, 2004; Scripture and the Authority of God, 2005; The Last Word: Beyond the Bible Wars to a New Understanding of the Authority of Scripture, 2005; Judas and the Gospel of Jesus: Have We Missed the Truth about Christianity?, 2006; The Scriptures, the Cross and the Power of God: Reflections for Holy Week, 2006; Simply Christian: Why Christianity Makes Sense, 2006; Evil and the Justice of God, 2006; The Resurrection of Jesus, 2006; Colossians & Philemon: An Introduction and Commentary, 2007; The Gospel and Our Culture, 2007; Christians at the Cross: Finding Hope in the Passion, Death, and Resurrection of Jesus, 2007; (as Tom Wright) Acts for Everyone, 2008; Surprised by Hope: Rethinking Heaven, the Resurrection and the Mission of the Church, 2008; (with C.A. Evans) Jesus, the Final Days: What Really Happened, 2009; (with P. Pell) Romans: 18 Studies for Individuals and Groups, 2009; (with D. Larsen and S. Larsen) Philippians, 2009; (with D. Larsen and S. Larsen) Matthew, 2009; (with L. Johnson) Mark, 2009; (with L. Johnson) Ephesians, 2009; Justification, 2009; Challenge of Easter, 2009; (with D. Larsen and S. Larsen) 1 Corinthians, 2009; (with P. Pell) 1 & 2 Thessalonians, 2009; (with P.J. le Peau) 1 & 2 Timothy and Titus, 2009; (with K. Berglund) John, 2009; (contrib.) Jesus, Paul and the People of God, 2010; After You Believe, 2010; (with P. Pell) 2 Corinthians, 2010; (with S. Larsen and Dale) Galatians: 10 Studies for Individuals or Groups, 2010; The Kingdom New Testament, 2011. EDITOR:

The Work of John Frith, 1983; (with L.D. Hurst) The Glory of Christ in the New Testament: Studies in Christology in Memory of George Bradford Caird, 1987; (with S.K. Soderlund) Romans and the People of God, 1999; (with K.J. Vanhoozer, C.G. Bartholomew and D.J. Treier) Dictionary for Theological Interpretation of the Bible, 2005; (with D.J. Treier and K.J. Vanhoozer) Theological Interpretation of the New Testament, 2008. **Address:** School of Divinity, University of St Andrews, South St., St Andrews, FF KY16 9JU, Scotland.

WRIGHT, Revena. *See* **WRIGHT, Betty Ren.**

WRIGHT, Robert Lee. American (born United States), b. 1920. **Genres:** Cultural/Ethnic Topics, History, Mythology/Folklore, Education. **Career:** University of Minnesota, instructor in English, 1946-48; Michigan State University, assistant professor of written and spoken English, 1948-57, communication skills, associate professor, 1957-61, professor of American thought and language, and comparative literature, 1961-, now professor emeritus; Columbia University Teachers College, instructor in English, 1953-54. Writer. **Publications:** Writing Without Rules, 1951, rev. ed., 1955; (ed.) Swedish Emigrant Ballads, 1965; (contrib.) University College and the Decade Ahead: General Education in a Changing University, 1969; (with D. Anderson) The Dark and Tangled Path: Race in America, 1971; (ed.) Irish Emigrant Ballads and Songs, 1975; (ed. with R. Wright) Danish Emigrant Ballads and Songs, 1983. Contributor to books. **Address:** Department of American Thought and Language, Michigan State University, East Lansing, MI 48824, U.S.A.

WRIGHT, Sharon D. *See* **AUSTIN, Sharon D. Wright**

WRIGHT, Theodore Paul. American (born United States), b. 1926. **Genres:** Theology/Religion, International Relations/Current Affairs, Politics/Government, Social Sciences, Third World, Young Adult Non-fiction. **Career:** Bates College, instructor, 1955-57, assistant professor, 1957-64, associate professor, 1964-65; State University of New York, Graduate School of Public Affairs, associate professor, 1965-72, professor of political science, 1971-95, professor emeritus, 1995-; Dutch Settlers Society, officer; New Netherlands Institute, officer. Writer. **Publications:** American Support of Free Elections Abroad, 1964; The Muslim Minority in India, 1975. Contributor of articles to periodicals. **Address:** Department of Political Science, University at Albany, State University of New York, 1400 Washington Ave., Albany, NY 12222, U.S.A. **Online address:** wright15@juno.com

WRIGHT, Tom. *See* **WRIGHT, N. T(om).**

WRIGHT, Vinita Hampton. American (born United States), b. 1958?. **Genres:** inspirational/Motivational Literature, Novels, Young Adult Fiction, Theology/Religion, Classics. **Career:** Missouri public school system, music teacher, 1982-88; Harold Shaw Publishers, editor; Tyndale House, editor; Loyola Press, editorial director of trade books division, senior book editor. **Publications:** (Ed.) Prayers across the Centuries: Abraham, Jesus, St. Augustine, Martin Luther, Susanna Wesley, 1993; Grace at Bender Springs: A Novel, 1999; Velma Still Cooks in Leeway (novel), 2000; (ed. with L.A. Jackson) Parents Guide to Teen Health: Raising Physically & Emotionally Healthy Teens, 2001; Simple Acts of Moving Forward: A Little Book about Getting Unstuck, 2004, rev. ed., 2009; Winter Seeking: A Novella, 2003; 2005: A Book of Grace-Filled Days, 2005; 2006: A Book of Grace-Filled Days, 2005; The Soul Tells a Story: Engaging Creativity With Spirituality in the Writing Life, 2005; Dwelling Places: A Novel, 2006; A Catalogue of Angels: The Heavenly, the Fallen and the Holy Ones Among Us, 2006; St. Thérèse of Lisieux Prayer Book, 2008; Days of Deepening Friendship: For the Woman Who Wants Authentic Life with God, 2009. COMPILER: (with C. Plueddemann) World Shapers: A Treasury of Quotes from Great Missionaries, 1991; (with C. Plueddemann) Prayers around the Family Table: Dinner-time Discussion and Prayer, 1992; (with M. Horner) Women's Widsom through the Ages: Timeless Quotations on Life and Faith, 1994; (with C. Plueddemann) Family Prayers for All Occasions, 1995; (with K. Call) A Dickens Christmas Collection, 1995. Contributor to periodicals. **Address:** Loyola Press, 3441 N Ashland Ave., Chicago, IL 60657, U.S.A. **Online address:** vinitawright@sbcglobal.net

WRIGHT, William Edward. American (born United States), b. 1926. **Genres:** History, Literary Criticism And History. **Career:** University of Minnesota, instructor, 1957-59, assistant professor, 1959-61, associate professor, 1961-73, professor of history, 1973-, now professor emeritus, Center for

Immigration Studies, director, 1966-67, Graduate History Studies, director, 1967-69, International Programs, associate dean, 1969-70, associate to the vice-president for international programs, 1970-76, Center for Austrian Studies, director, 1977-88. Writer. **Publications:** Serf, Seigneur and Sovereign: Agrarian Reform in Eighteenth-Century Bohemia, 1966. EDITOR: Austria since 1945, 1982; Austria in the Age of the French Revolution, 1789-1815, 1990; (intro.) Austria, 1938-1988: Anschluss and Fifty Years, 1995. **Address:** Department of History, University of Minnesota, 1110 Heller Hall, 271 19th Ave S, Minneapolis, MN 55455, U.S.A. **Online address:** wrigh001@umn.edu

WRIGHT AUSTIN, Sharon D. (Sharon D. Wright). American (born United States), b. 1965. **Genres:** Politics/Government, Race Relations, Social Sciences, History. **Career:** University of Louisville, assistant professor of Pan-African studies, 1992-95; University of Missouri, assistant professor, 1995-2000, associate professor of political science and black studies, 2000-02; University of Florida, visiting associate professor, 2001-04, associate professor of political science, 2004-. Writer. **Publications:** NONFICTION: (as Sharon D. Wright) Race, Power, and Political Emergence in Memphis, 2000; The Transformation of Plantation Politics: Black Politics, Concentrated Poverty, and Social Capital in the Mississippi Delta, 2006. Contributor to books and journals. **Address:** Department of Political Science, University of Florida, 234 Anderson Hall, P O Box 117325, Gainesville, FL 32611-7325, U.S.A. **Online address:** polssdw@polisci.ufl.edu

WRIGLEY, Robert. American (born United States), b. 1951. **Genres:** Poetry. **Career:** Southern Illinois University, Department of English, adjunct professor, 1976-77; Lewis-Clark State College, poet-in-residence, assistant professor, 1977-84, associate professor of English, 1984-89, professor, 1989-99; Warren Wilson College, MFA Program for Writers, core faculty, 1990, 1991, 1998; University of Montana, Richard Hugo distinguished professor of poetry, 1990; University of Oregon, visiting assistant professor, 1990-91, Creative Writing Program, director, 1990-91; University of Idaho, professor of English, 1999-, MFA Creative Writing Program, director, 2000-07. Writer. **Publications:** POETRY: The Sinking of Clay City, 1979; Moon in a Mason Jar, 1986; What My Father Believed, 1991; In the Bank of Beautiful Sins, 1995; Reign of Snakes, 1999; Lives of the Animals, 2003; Earthly Meditations: New and Selected Poems, 2006; Beautiful Country, 2010. CHAPBOOKS: The Glow, 1982; In the Dark Pool, 1988; Clemency, 2002. Works appear in anthologies. Contributor to magazines and journals. **Address:** Department of English, University of Idaho, 217 Brink Hall, 709 Deakin Ave., PO Box 441102, Moscow, ID 83844-9802, U.S.A. **Online address:** rwrigley@uidaho.edu

WROBEL, David M. American/British (born England), b. 1964. **Genres:** History, Business/Trade/Industry, Economics. **Career:** Ohio University, John Cady fellow, 1988-89; College of Wooster, visiting instructor, 1990-91, visiting assistant professor of history, 1991-92; Hartwick College, visiting assistant professor of history, 1992-94; Widener University, assistant professor of history, 1994-98, chair, 1997-98, associate professor of history, 1998-2000; University of Nevada, associate professor of history, 2000-04, professor of history, 2004-, department chair, 2008-; American History Content Enhancement Institute, co-coordinator and instructor, 2002-04; Yale University, senior fellow in western history, 2005-06. Writer. **Publications:** The End of American Exceptionalism: Frontier Anxiety from the Old West to the New Deal, 1993; (ed. with M.C. Steiner) Many Wests: Place, Culture, and Regional Identity, 1997; (ed. with P.T. Long) Seeing and Being Seen: Tourism in the American West, 2001; Promised Lands: Promotion, Memory, and the Creation of the American West, 2002; (intro.) Golden West: Fifty Years of Bison Books, 2011; (with D. Tanenhaus) The Progressive Era, forthcoming. **Address:** Department of History, University of Nevada, 4050 Maryland Pkwy., PO Box 455020, Las Vegas, NV 89154-5020, U.S.A. **Online address:** david.wrobel@unlv.edu

WRONSKY, Gail (F.). American (born United States), b. 1956. **Genres:** Poetry, Women's Studies And Issues, Theology/Religion, Young Adult Fiction. **Career:** Foxcroft School, teacher in english; Loyola Marymount University, professor of English, 1986-. Writer. **Publications:** Again the Gemini Are in the Orchard, 1991; Dying for Beauty, 2000; The Love-Talkers, 2003; Poems for Infidels, 2005; Blue Shadow Behind Everything Dazzling, 2009; (with M. Bendall) Bling & Fringe, 2009; So Quick Bright Things, 2010. AS CALAMITY WRONSKY: (with B. Bendall) Calamity & Belle, 1993; (with B. Bendall) Dear Calamity...Love, Belle, 1994. **Address:** Department of English, Loyola

Marymount University, University Hall 3873, University Hall, Ste. 4600, Los Angeles, CA 90045, U.S.A. **Online address:** gwronsky@lmu.edu

WROUGHTON, John Presbury. British (born England), b. 1934?. **Genres:** History, Social Sciences. **Career:** King Edward's School, History Department, head, 1965-74, second master, 1974-82, headmaster, 1982-93. Writer. **Publications:** Cromwell and the Roundheads, 1969; Plots, Traitors and Spies 1953-1985, 1970; (with J. Paxton) Smuggling, 1971; Documents on British Political History, vol. III, 1971; (ed.) Bath in the Age of Reform 1830-1841, 1972; The Civil War in Bath and North Somerset, 1973; (with D. Cook) Documents on World History, vol. II, 1976; Documents and Debates, 17th Century Britain, 1980; (with C. Cook) English Historical Facts, 1603-1689, 1980; King Edward's School at Bath 1552-1982, 1982; A Community at War: The Civil War in Bath and North Somerset, 1642-1650, 1992; The Stuart Age, 1603-1714, 1997; Longman Companion to the Staurt Age, 1603-1714, 1997; An Unhappy Civil War, 1999; Mr Colston's Hospital, 2002; 450 Years: King Edward's School, Bath 1552-2002, 2002; Stuart Bath: Life in the Forgotten City, 1603-1714, 2004; Routledge Companion to the Stuart Age, 1603-1714, 2005; Tudor Bath: Life and Strife in the Little City, 1485-1603, 2006; The Battle of Lansdown 1643: An Explorer's Guide, 2008. **Address:** 41 The Empire, Grand Parade, Bath, SM BA2 4DF, England.

WU, C(hien-) F(u) Jeff. American/Taiwanese (born Taiwan), b. 1949. **Genres:** Mathematics/Statistics, Technology. **Career:** University of California, Tse-Wei Liu fellow, 1973-74, Earl C. Anthony fellow, 1974-76, lecturer in statistics, 1976-77; University of Wisconsin, assistant professor, 1977-80, associate professor, 1980-83, professor of statistics and mathematics, 1983-88; Alfred P. Sloan Foundation, Sloan fellow, 1983; Mathematical Sciences Research Institute, faculty, 1983; University of Waterloo, professor of statistics, GM/NSERC chair, 1988-93, adjunct professor, 1995-; University of Michigan, professor, 1995-98, H.C. Carver professor of statistics, 1997-2003, Department of Statistics and of Industrial and Operations Engineering, chair and professor, 1993-2003; National Statistics Bureau of China, advisor, 1994-; Indian Statistical Institute, P.C. Mahalanobis memorial lecturer, 1998; Nankai University, Applied Statistics and Information Center, chair, 2001-; Georgia Institute of Technology, College of Engineering, Coca-Cola chair in engineering statistics and professor, 2003-; Institute of Mathematical Statistics, American Society for Quality, fellow; American Statistical Association, fellow. Writer. **Publications:** (With M.S. Hamada) Experiments: Planning, Analysis and Parameter Design Optimization, 2000, 2nd ed. as Experiments: Planning, Analysis and Optimization, 2009; (with R. Mukerjee) Modern Theory of Factorial Design, 2006. Contributor to books and journals. **Address:** H. Milton Stewart School, Georgia Institute of Technology, Rm. 233, ISyE Main Entrance Bldg., 765 Ferst Dr., Atlanta, GA 30332-0205, U.S.A. **Online address:** jeff.wu@isye.gatech.edu

WU, Chin-Tao. Taiwanese (born Taiwan) **Genres:** Art/Art History, History, Humanities. **Career:** Bethnal Green Museum of Childhood, part-time art worker, 1991-2000; University of East Anglia, School of World Art Studies and Museology, J. Paul Getty Post-doctoral Research Fellow, 1998-99; University College London, Department of History of Art, honorary research fellow, 1999-; Graduate School of Arts Administration, assistant professor, 2000-01; Nanhua University, Department of Aesthetic and Art Management, assistant professor, 2001-04; Institute of European and American Studies, Academic Sinica, assistant research fellow, 2004-09, associate research fellow, 2009-. Writer and art historian. **Publications:** Privatising Culture: Corporate Art Intervention since the 1980s, 2002. Contributor to periodicals. **Address:** Institute of European and American Studies, Academia Sinica, 128 Academia Rd., Taipei, 115, Taiwan. **Online address:** chintao@sinica.edu.tw

WU, David Y(en) H(o). American/Chinese (born China), b. 1940. **Genres:** Anthropology/Ethnology, Area Studies, Cultural/Ethnic Topics, Food And Wine. **Career:** Academia Sinica Institute of Ethnology, technician, 1958-59, research assistant, 1963-66, adjunct fellow, 1976-; University of Hawaii, anthropology instructor, 1969, graduate school faculty, 1980-; East-West Center, research associate, 1974-; Chiang Ching-Ko Foundation for International Scholarly Exchange, consultant, 1989-93. Writer. **Publications:** Traditional Chinese Concepts of Food and Medicine in Singapore, 1979; The Chinese in Papua New Guinea, 1880-1980, 1982; (with J.J. Tobin and D.H. Davidson) Preschool in Three Cultures: Japan, China and the United States, 1989. EDITOR: Ethnicity and Interpersonal Interaction: A Cross Cultural Study,

1982; (with W.S. Tseng) Chinese Culture and Mental Health, 1985; (with V.R. Domínguez) From Beijing to Port Moresby: The Politics of National Identity in Cultural Policies, 1998; (with T. Chee-beng) Changing Chinese Foodways in Asia, 2001; (with S.C.H. Cheung) Globalization of Chinese Food, 2002. **Address:** Institute for Culture and Communication, East-West Center, 1777 East-West Rd., Honolulu, HI 96848, U.S.A. **Online address:** wuyenhe@aol.com

WU, Edna. *See* WU, Qingyun.

WU, Fan. American/Chinese (born China), b. 1973. **Genres:** Literary Criticism And History, Young Adult Fiction. **Career:** Yahoo!, Web editor and marketer. **Publications:** NOVELS: February Flowers, 2006; Beautiful as Yesterday, 2009. Contributor to periodicals. **Address:** Toby Eady Associates Literary Agency, 9 Orme Ct., 3rd Fl., London, GL W2 4RL, England. **Online address:** sailingwu@gmail.com

WU, Harry. American/Chinese (born China), b. 1937. **Genres:** Area Studies, Civil Liberties/Human Rights, Humanities, International Relations/Current Affairs. **Career:** China Geoscience University, teacher, 1980-85; Stanford University, Hoover Institution on War, Revolution and Peace, research fellow, 1987-; Laogai Research Foundation (LRF), founder and executive director, 1992-; China Information Center, executive director. Writer. **Publications:** (As Hongda Harry Wu) Laogai: The Chinese Gulag, 1992; (with C. Wakeman) Bitter Winds: A Memoir of My Years in China's Gulag, 1994; (with G. Vecsey) Troublemaker: One Man's Crusade against China's Cruelty, 1996; Yi ge ren de liang ge gu shi, 2003; Lao dong jiao yang he liu chang jiu ye, 2004; Lao gai: Zhongguo te se de zui yu fa, 2009; Zui zai dang dai yi huo qian qiu: Zhongguo ji hua sheng yü zheng ce shi shi san shi zhou nian yan jiu bao gao, 2010. Contributor to periodicals. **Address:** Laogai Research Foundation, 1109 M St. NW, Washington, DC 20005-4306, U.S.A.

WU, Ningkun. American/Chinese (born China), b. 1920. **Genres:** Poetry, Biography, Essays, Translations. **Career:** Institute of International Relations, professor of English, 1956-92, professor emeritus of English, 1992-; University of Montana, Mansfield visiting professor of Chinese studies, 1992. Writer. **Publications:** (With Y. Li) A Single Tear: A Family's Persecution, Love, and Endurance in Communist China, 1993; Yi di lei, 2002. **Address:** 2231 Colts Neck Rd., Reston, VA 20191, U.S.A. **Online address:** ningkunwu@aol.com

WU, Norbert. American (born United States), b. 1961. **Genres:** Marine Sciences/Oceanography, Photography. **Career:** The Cousteau Society, photographer; Smithsonian Tropical Research Institute, Republic of Panama, research diver; Cucoloris Films, director, 1992; Survival Anglia, director, 1995; First Breath, Hardy Jones Productions for Audubon Films, staff, 1996; National Geographic Television, Deep Flight, staff, 1997. Writer and cinematographer. **Publications:** Life in the Oceans, 1991; Beneath the Waves: Exploring the Hidden World of the Kelp Forest, 1992; Fish Faces, 1993; Splendors of the Seas, 1994; How to Photograph Underwater, 1994; A City Under the Sea: Life in a Coral Reef, 1996; Selling Nature Photographs, 1997; Scholastic Encyclopedia of Animals, 2001; Under Antarctic Ice, 2004; Diving the World, 2004. Contributor to magazines. **Address:** Norbert Wu Productions, 1065 Sinex Ave., Pacific Grove, CA 93950, U.S.A. **Online address:** office@norbertwu.com

WU, Qingyun. (Edna Wu). American/Chinese (born China), b. 1950. **Genres:** Novels, Literary Criticism And History, Translations. **Career:** Zhengzhou University, lecturer in English, 1978-85; Pennsylvania State University, lecturer in Chinese, 1987-90; University of Texas, lecturer in Chinese, 1990-91; California State University, professor of Chinese, 1991-, Chinese Studies Center, director, Chinese Program, coordinator. Writer. **Publications:** (As Edna Wu) Clouds and Rain: A China-to-America Memoir (novel), 1994; Female Rule in Chinese and English Literary Utopias, 1995. TRANSLATOR: (with S. Tianting) K. Graham, Liushu Fengsheng (title means: 'The Wind in the Willows'), 1985; Nuowei Tonghua Xuan (title means: 'Norwegian Fairy Tales'), 1986; E.R. Burroughs, Renyuan Taishan (title means: 'Tarzan of the Apes'), 1987; (with T. Beebee) B. Hua, The Remote Country of Women (novel), 1994; W. Yun, Fan hua meng (title means: 'A dream of glory'), 2008; Z. Sujin, Di san zhi yan, (title means: 'A Novel About the Chinese People's Liberation Army: The Third Eye'), 2010; (as Edna Wu) A Single-winged Bird (Bilingual Edition Fiction and Poetry), 2010. Contributor of articles to periodicals. **Address:** Chinese Studies Center, California State University, 11381 Bunche Hall, 5151 State University Dr., Los Angeles, CA 90032, U.S.A. **Online address:** qwu@calstatela.edu

WU, Yenna. American/Taiwanese (born Taiwan), b. 1957?. **Genres:** Area Studies, Language/Linguistics, Literary Criticism And History, Women's Studies And Issues, Humor/Satire, Translations. **Career:** University of Vermont, assistant professor, 1986-92, Chinese Language Program, director, 1986-92; University of California, assistant professor, 1992-96, associate professor, 1996-99, professor of Chinese, 1999-, Asian Languages and Civilization Program, director, 2002-, distinguished teaching professor, director of asian literatures and cultures. Writer. **Publications:** (Trans.) K. Hamsun, E (title means: 'Hunger'), 1982; The Lioness Roars: Shrew Stories from Late Imperial China, 1995; The Chinese Virago: A Literary Theme, 1995; (ed. with P.F. Williams) Zhongguo fu nü yu wen xue lun ji (essays), vol. I, 1999, vol. II, 2001; (with P.F.C. Williams) Chinese, the Easy Way, 1999, 2nd ed. as Mandarin Chinese the Easy Way, 2008; Ameliorative Satire and the Seventeenth-Century Chinese Novel, Xingshi Yinyuan Zhuan-Marriage As Retribution, Awakening the World, 1999; (with P.F. Williams) Great Wall of Confinement: The Chinese Prison Camp Through Contemporary Fiction and Reportage, 2004; (ed. with P.F. Williams) Remolding and Resistance Among Writers of the Chinese Prison Camp: Disciplined and Published, 2006; Wan li da qiang, 2007; (with S. Livescu) Human Rights, Suffering, and Aesthetics in Political Prison Literature, 2011. Contributor of articles to journals. **Address:** Department of Comparative Literature & Foreign, Languages, University of California, 2413 HMNSS Bldg., Riverside, CA 92521-0321, U.S.A. **Online address:** yenna.wu@ucr.edu

WUBBELS, Lance. (Robert Hall). American (born United States), b. 1952. **Genres:** Novels, Theology/Religion, inspirational/Motivational Literature, Sports/Fitness, Psychology. **Career:** Bethany College of Mission, professor of biblical studies, 1980-91; Bethany House Publishers, managing editor, 1983-99; Solo Source Inc., vice president of editorial, 2000; Koethel Peterson & Associates Inc., vice president of literary development. **Publications:** EDITOR AS ROBERT HALL: The Power of Prayer in a Believer's Life, 1993; Spiritual Warfare in a Believer's Life, 1993; What the Holy Spirit Does in a Believer's Life, 1993; Grace Abounding in a Believer's Life, 1994; The Triumph of Faith in a Believer's Life, 1994; A Passion for Holiness in a Believer's Life, 1994. NOVELS: Far from the Dream, 1994; One Small Miracle, 1995; Whispers in the Valley, 1995; Keeper of the Harvest, 1995; Some Things Last Forever, 1996; The Bridge Over Flatwillow Creek, 1998; In the Shadow of a Secret, 1999; The Omega Code, 1999. EDITOR: (and comp.) The Power of Christ's Miracles, 1995; (and comp.) The Power of Christ's Prayer Life, 1995; (and comp.) The Power of the Cross of Christ, 1995; The Life of Paul: A Servant of Jesus Christ, 1995; The Life of David: The Man After God's Own Heart, 1995; The Life of Joseph: Beloved, Hated and Exalted, 1995; (and comp.) The Power of Christ's Tears, 1996; (and comp.) The Power of Christ's Second Coming, 1996; The Life of Abraham: The Obedience of Faith, 1996; (and comp.) The Life of Moses: The Servant of God, 1996; The Life of Peter: Fisherman, Disciple, Apostle, 1996; (and comp.) The Power of Christ the Warrior, 1997; (and comp.) In His Presence: Daily Devotionals, 1998; R.A. Torrey on the Holy Spirit, 2002. OTHERS: A Woman in the Making: Guidance from a Father's Heart, 2003; (comp. and adaptor with T. McDowell) Bible Nobodies who Became Somebodies, 2004; (with M. Anderson) To a Child Love Spelled T-I-M-E: What a Child Really Needs From You, 2004; Champions Speak Out On Golf, 2005; Champions Speak Out On Racing, 2005; Champions Speak Out On Baseball, 2006; (and comp.) Champions Speak Out On Football, 2007. **Address:** Koechel Peterson & Associates, 2600 E 26th St., Minneapolis, MN 55406-1201, U.S.A.

WUERCH, William L. American (born United States), b. 1952. **Genres:** History, Social Sciences. **Career:** Assistant territorial librarian of Guam, 1982-85; University of Guam, instructor, 1985-88, assistant professor, 1988-91, associate professor, 1991-99, professor, 1999-, department head, 1986-89, 1998-. Writer. **Publications:** The governor's Palace During the American Navy Administration of Guam, 1984; A Fine Place for Water and Wood: A Guide to the Logbooks of American Whalers and Traders in the Nieves M. Flores Memorial Library, 1985; (comp. with N. Goetzfridt) Micronesia, 1975-1987: A Social Science Bibliography, 1989; (with D.E. Haynes) Historical Survey of the Spanish Mission Sites on Guam, 1669-1800, 1990, 2nd ed., 1993; (with D.A. Ballendorf) Historical Dictionary of Guam and Micronesia, 1994; (with D. Haynes) Micronesian Religion and Lore, 1995; (ed. with L.D. Carter and R.R. Carter) Guam History: Perspectives, 1997, vol. II, 2003; (with M. Storie) Micronesia, 1999. Contributor of articles. **Address:** University of Guam, UOG Sta., Mangilao, GU 96923, U.S.A. **Online address:**

wwuerch@uguam.uog.edu

WU HUNG. American/Chinese (born China), b. 1945. **Genres:** Art/Art History, Architecture. **Career:** Palace Museum, research staff, 1973-78; Harvard University, assistant professor, associate professor of fine arts, 1987-93; University of Chicago, Harrie A. Vanderstappen distinguished service professor, 1994-, Center for the Art of East Asia, director, Smart Museum of Art, consulting curator. Art historian and author. **Publications:** The Wu Liang Shrine: The Ideology of Early Chinese Pictorial Art, 1989; Monumentality in Early Chinese Art and Architecture, 1995; The Double Screen: Medium and Representation in Chinese Painting, 1996; (co-author) Three Thousand Years of Chinese Painting, 1997; Remaking Beijing, 1998; Transience: Chinese Experimental Art at the End of the Twentieth Century, 1999, rev. ed., 2005; Exhibiting Experimental Art in China, 2000; (contrib.) The Art of Mu Xin: The Landscape Paintings and Prison Notes, 2001; The First Guangzhou Triennial Reinterpretation: A Decade of Experimental Chinese Art (1990-2000), 2002; Rong Rong's East Village, 2003; Han Tang zhi jian de Shi jue Wen Hua yu wu zhi wen Hua, 2003; (co-author) Between Past and Future: New Photography and Video from China, 2004; Phantasmagoria: Recent Photographs by Miao Xiaochun, 2004; (ed. with K.R. Tsiang) Body and Face in Chinese Visual Culture, 2005; Remaking Beijing: Tiananmen Square and the Creation of a Political Space, 2005; Celestial Realm: The Yellow Mountains of China, 2005; Li yi Zhong De Mei Shu: Wu Hong Zhongguo Gu Dai Mei Shu Shi Wen Bian/Art in its Ritual Context: Essays on Ancient Chinese Art by Wu Hung, 2005; Zuo pin yu zhan chang: Wu Hong lun Zhongguo dang dai yi shu, 2005; (co-author) 3000 Years of Chinese Sculpture, 2006; (with J. McGrath and S. Smith) Displacement: The Three Gorges Dam and Contemporary Chinese Art, 2008; Zou zi ji de lu: Wu Hong lun Zhongguo dang dai yi shu jia, 2008; Cities here and now, 2009; Art of the Yellow Springs: Understanding Chinese Tombs, 2010; (ed.) Reinventing the Past: Archaism and Antiquarianism in Chinese Art and Visual Culture, 2010; (contrib.) Miao Xiaochun, 2010; (contrib.) Xu Bing, 2010; (ed.) Contemporary Chinese Art, 2010; Heaven, Earth and Men: The Universe in Chinese Art, 9 vols., forthcoming; Art of the Yellow Spring: Rethinking East Asian Tombs, forthcoming. Contributor to journals. **Address:** Department of Art History, University of Chicago, 274 Cochrane-Woods Art Ctr., 5540 S Greenwood Ave., Chicago, IL 60637, U.S.A. **Online address:** hungwu@uchicago.edu

WULLSCHLÄGER, Jackie. British (born England), b. 1962?. **Genres:** Literary Criticism And History, Biography, Autobiography/Memoirs, Science Fiction/Fantasy. **Career:** Financial Times, literary critic and European arts correspondent, 1986-. **Publications:** Inventing Wonderland: The Lives and Fantasies of Lewis Carroll, Edward Lear, J.M. Barrie, Kenneth Grahame, and A.A. Milne, 1995; Hans Christian Andersen: The Life of a Storyteller, 2000; (ed. and intro.) Fairy Tales/Hans Christian Andersen, 2004; (with P. Vann) Joash Woodrow: Landscapes, 2007; Chagall: A Biography, 2008. **Address:** Financial Times Ltd., 1 Southwark Bridge, London, GL SE1 9HL, England. **Online address:** jackie.wullschlager@ft.com

WULSIN, Lawson R. American (born United States), b. 1951. **Genres:** Medicine/Health. **Career:** Mood Disorders Center, founder, 1989; University of Cincinnati, College of Medicine, professor of psychiatry and family medicine; Massachusetts Mental Health Center, Clinical Research Training Program, NIMH fellow; University of Pennsylvania, Center for Cognitive Therapy extramural, fellow; Cincinnati Edition, radio programs host. Writer and psychiatrist. **Publications:** Treating the Aching Heart: A Guide to Depression, Stress, and Heart Disease, 2007; (ed. with M. Riba and M. Rubenfire) Psychiatry and Heart Disease: The Mind, Brain, and Heart, 2011. Contributor to periodicals and journals. **Address:** Department of Psychiatry, University of Cincinnati, Stetson Bldg., 260 Stetson St., Ste. 3200, Cincinnati, OH 45219, U.S.A. **Online address:** lawson.wulsin@uc.edu

WUNDERLI, Richard (M.). American (born United States), b. 1940. **Genres:** History. **Career:** University of Utah, instructor, 1965-66; University of Maryland, European Division, instructor, 1968-69; University of California, instructor, 1975-76; University of Colorado, Department of History, assistant professor, 1976-82, associate professor, 1982-91, chair, 1984-89, professor of history, 1991-, now professor emeritus; Learning Unlimited, education director, 1991-2009. Writer. **Publications:** London Church Courts and Society on the Eve of the Reformation, 1981; Peasant Fires: The Drummer of Niklashausen, 1992. **Address:** 1848 S Marshall Cir., Lakewood, CO 80232-7086, U.S.A. **Online address:** rwunderl@uccs.edu

WUNDERLICH, Ray Charles. American (born United States), b. 1929. **Genres:** Education, Medicine/Health, Psychology, Essays, Human Relations/Parenting, Sciences, Sports/Fitness, Reference, Reference. **Career:** All Children's Hospital, staff and director of diagnostic and evaluation clinic, 1966-68; The Real Doctor Articles, staff, 1996-; Wunderlich Center for Nutritional Medicine, director. Writer. **Publications:** Kids, Brains and Learning: What Goes Wrong-Prevention and Treatment, 1970; Allergy, Brains and Children Coping: Allergy and Child Behavior, the Neuro-Allergic Syndrome, 1973; Improving Your Diet and Fatigue, 1976; Fatigue: What Causes It, What It Does to You, What You Can Do About It, 1976; (contrib.) Developmental Vision in Lifelong Learning, 1977; Sugar and Your Health: Nutritional Problems, Diabetes and Low Blood Sugar, 1982; (with D.K. Kalita) Nourishing Your Child: A Bioecologic Approach, 1984; Help for New Parents and Parents-to-Be, 1989; Carpal Tunnel Syndrome, 1993. **Address:** Wunderlich Center for Nutritional Medicine, 8821 Dr. Martin Luther King Jr. St. N, St. Petersburg, FL 33702, U.S.A. **Online address:** manager@wunderlichcenter.com

WUNSCH, James S(tevenson). American (born United States), b. 1946. **Genres:** Politics/Government, Public/Social Administration, Third World, Economics. **Career:** Indiana University, Department of Political Science, associate instructor, 1969-70, 1972-73; University of Ghana, research fellow, 1971-72, affiliate; Creighton University, instructor, 1973, assistant professor, 1973-78, associate professor, 1978-86, professor of political science, 1986-, Washington, D.C. Internship Program, director, 1980-2002, Public Affairs Internship Program, director, 1973-, Interdisciplinary Program in African Studies, director, Department of Political Science, chairman, 1982-92, 1996-2007, African Studies Program, founder and director, 1998-, Graduate Program in International Relations, acting director, 1996-97; U.S. Agency for International Development, social science analyst for office of rural development and development administration, 1978-80; United States Department of Agriculture, project design and evaluation specialist, 1978-79; Indiana University-Bloomington, visiting associate professor and senior fellow of workshop on political theory and policy analysis, 1985-86; Associates in Rural Development Inc., senior associate and project manager, 1987-88; University of Maryland, World Academy of Development and Cooperation, external fellow. Writer. **Publications:** (With M. Landau, L. Carina and S. Bhakti) The Provincial Development Assistance Project, 1980; Rural Development, Decentralization, and Administrative Reform: Toward a New Analytical Framework (monograph), 1988; (ed. with D. Olowu) The Failure of the Centralized State: Institutions for Self Governance in Africa, 1990; (and contrib.) La Faillite de l'Etat centralisé en Afrique, 1995; (with D. Olowu) Local Governance in Africa: The Challenges of Democratic Decentralization, 2004. **Address:** Department of Political Science, Creighton University, Rm. 428, Creighton Hall, 2500 California Plz., Omaha, NE 68178, U.S.A. **Online address:** jwunsch@creighton.edu

WUORI, G. K. American (born United States) **Genres:** Novellas/Short Stories, Essays, Travel/Exploration, Young Adult Fiction. **Career:** Writer. **Publications:** Reflections In A Keyhole Eye, 1998; Nude in Tub: Stories of Quillifarkeag, Maine, 1999; An American Outrage: A Novel of Quillifarkeag, Maine, 2000. Contributor to magazines. **Address:** c/o Author Mail, Algonquin Books of Chapel Hill, PO Box 2225, Chapel Hill, NC 27515-2225, U.S.A. **Online address:** gkwuori@hotmail.com

WURMAN, Richard Saul. American (born United States), b. 1935. **Genres:** Adult Non-fiction, Architecture, Regional/Urban Planning, Travel/Exploration. **Career:** Architect, graphic designer, author, publisher, educator, entrepreneur; Louis I. Kahn (architect), 1960-62; North Carolina State University, faculty, 1962-64, 1977; Washington University, faculty, 1965; Princeton University, faculty, 1965-67; Cambridge University, faculty, 1967-68; Cornell University, faculty, 1968-70; California State Polytechnic Institute Group for Environmental Education, founding director, 1968; City College of New York, faculty, 1968-70; University of California, faculty, 1976; University of Southern California, faculty, 1976; California State Polytechnic Institute, professor of architecture and dean of school of environmental design; Housing and Community Development, deputy director, 1977; Otis/Parsons, chair of department of environmental design; Access Press Ltd., founder and president. Writer. **Publications:** NONFICTION: The Notebooks and Drawings of Louis I. Kahn; Aspen Visible: And Our Man-Made Environment; The City, Form and Intent, Raleigh, NC, 1963; (with J.R. Passioneau) Urban Atlas: 20 American Cities, 1966; Making the City Observable, 1971; (with J.A. Gallery) Man-Made Philadelphia, 1972; (co-author) The Nature of Recreation:

A Handbook in Honor of Frederick Law Olmstead, Using Examples from His Work, 1972; (co-author) Cities-Comparisons of Form and Scale, 1974; Information Anxiety, 1989; Hawaii: Focusing in on Paradise, 1989; (with A. Siegel and K.M. Morris) Wall Street Journal Guide to Understanding Money and Markets, 1989; (with D. Goodman) Danny Goodmans Macintosh Handbook Featuring System 7, 1992; Information Architects, 1996; Understanding, 1999; Wills, Trusts and Estate Planning, 2000; Drugs: Prescription, Non-prescription and Herbal, 2000; Can I Afford to Retire?, 2000; Heart Disease & Cardiovascular Health, 2000; Information Anxiety, 2001; Diagnostic Tests for Men, 2001; Diagnostic Tests for Women, 2001; Understanding Children, 2002; 1000: Richard Saul Wurmans Whos Really Who, 2002; Understanding Healthcare, 2004. TRAVEL GUIDES: LA Access, 1982; Hawaii Access, 1982; NYC Access, 1982; San Francisco, Access, 1982, 8th ed., 1999; 1984 Olympic Access, 1983; Football Access 1983; Los Angeles: Things to See & Do in 1984, 1984; Baseball Access, 1984; Dog Access, 1984; Tokyo Access, 1984; New Orleans Access, 1984; Washington, DC Access, 1984, rev. ed., 1994; Medical Access, 1986; London Access, 1987; SF Access, 1987, 6th ed., 1994; Rome Access, 1987, 5th ed., 1997; Summer Games, 1988; USATLAS, 1989, rev. ed., 1991; Boston Access, 1991; Summer Games Access, 1992: Barcelona, 1992; Northern California Wine Country Access, 1992; Chicago Access, 1993; Paris Access, 4th ed., 1994; Florence-Venice-Milan Access, rev. ed., 1994; Seattle Access, 1995. EDITOR: Yellow Pages of Learning Resources: Resources Directory Area Code 800, 1972; What Will Be Has Always Been: The Words of Louis I. Kahn, 1986; (with L. Leifer) Follow the Yellow Brick Road: Learning to Give, Take, and Use Instructions, Drawings by Ed Koren and Larry Gonick, Introduction by John Sculley, 1992; (ed.) Understanding, 2000. OTHERS: Information Anxiety 2, 2001. Contributor to journals. **Address:** The Orchard, 180 Narragansett Ave., Newport, RI 02840, U.S.A. **Online address:** rsw@wurman.com

WURST, Karin A. American (born United States), b. 1955. **Genres:** Cultural/Ethnic Topics, Literary Criticism And History, Language/Linguistics. **Career:** German Quarterly, book review editor, 1997-2001; Michigan State University, Department of Linguistics and Germanic, professor of German, 1988, Slavic, Asian and African Languages, chair, 2005, University Graduate Council, chair, 2005, College of Arts and Letters dean, 2006-. Writer. **Publications:** Familiale Liebe ist die wahre Gewalt: Die Repräsentation der Familie in G.E. Lessings dramatischem Werk, 1988; (intro.) Elenore Thon, Adelheit von Rastenberg: An English Translation, 1996; (with A.C. Leidner) Unpopular Virtues: The Critical Reception of J.M.R. Lenz, 1999; Fabricating Pleasure: Fashion, Entertainment and Cultural Consumption in Germany, 1780-1830, 2005. EDITOR: (intro.) Frauen und Drama im achtzehnten Jahrhundert, 1991; (intro.) J.R.M. sic Lenz als Alternative? Positionsanalysen zum 200. Todestag, 1992; Adelheit von Rastenberg: The Original German Text, 1996. **Address:** College of Arts and Letters, Michigan State University, East Lansing, MI 48824, U.S.A. **Online address:** wurst@msu.edu

WURTS, Janny. American (born United States), b. 1953. **Genres:** Science Fiction/Fantasy, Young Adult Fiction, Novellas/Short Stories, Novels. **Career:** Hampshire College, Astronomy College, laboratory assistant. Fantasy and science-fiction writer and illustrator. **Publications:** NOVELS: Sorcerer's Legacy, 1982; The Master of White Storm, 1992; That Way Lies Camelot, 1994; To Ride Hell's Chasm, 2002. CYCLE OF FIRE SERIES: Stormwarden, 1984; Keeper of the Keys, 1988; Shadowfane, 1988. EMPIRE SERIES WITH R.E. FEIST: Daughter of the Empire, 1987; Servant of the Empire, 1990; Mistress of the Empire, 1992. WARS OF LIGHT AND SHADOW SERIES (SHIPS OF MERIOR): The Curse of the Mistwraith, 1993; Ships of Merior, 1994; Warhost of Vastmark, 1995. SHORT STORIES: Triad, 1998. WARS OF LIGHT AND SHADOW (ALLIANCE OF LIGHT) SERIES: Fugitive Prince, 1997; Grand Conspiracy, 1999; Peril's Gate, 2001; Traitor's Knot, 2004; Stormed Fortress, 2007. WARS OF LIGHT AND SHADOW SERIES (SWORD OF THE CANON): Initiate's Trial, 2009. **Address:** HarperCollins Publishers, 77-85 Fulham Palace Rd., Hammersmith, London, GL W6 8JB, England. **Online address:** jannywurts@paravia.com

WURTZEL, Elizabeth (Leigh). American (born United States), b. 1967. **Genres:** Documentaries/Reportage, Novels, Self Help. **Career:** Dallas Morning News, reporter, 1987-88; New York Magazine, pop music critic, 1989-91; New Yorker, pop music critic, 1991-93; Nerve.com, film critic. **Publications:** Prozac Nation: Young and Depressed in America, 1994, 2nd ed., 1995; (contrib.) Next: Young Writers on the New Generation, 1994; Bitch: In Praise of Difficult Women, 1998; Radical Sanity: Commonsense Advice for Uncommon Women, 1999; Bitch Rules: Common Sense Advice for an Uncommon

Life, 2001; More, Now, Again: A Memoir of Addiction, 2002; Secret of Life: Commonsense Advice for Uncommon Women, 2004. Contributor to periodicals. **Address:** c/o Mort Janklow, Janklow & Nesbit Associates, 445 Park Ave., New York, NY 10022-2606, U.S.A.

WÜRZBACH, Natascha. German (born Germany), b. 1933. **Genres:** Literary Criticism And History, History. **Career:** University of Munich, Federal Republic of Germany, Department of English, research assistant and lecturer, 1965-75; University of Cologne, Department of English, professor of English and head, 1975-99, professor emeritus, 1999-; Gender Inn, founder, 1987-. Writer. **Publications:** Die Struktur des Briefromans und seine Entstehung in England, 1964; (with E. Weber) Geschichten um die Baukunst, 1965; Anfänge und gattungstypische Ausformung der englischen Strassenballade 1550-1650, 1981. EDITOR: (and intro.) The Novel in Letters: Epistolary Fiction in the Early English Novel, 1678-1740, 1969; British Theatre: Eighteenth-century English Drama, 1969; (with M. Kannen) Herzdame: Freundschaft und Liebe zwischen Frauen, 1993; Raumerfahrung in der klassischen Moderne-Grostadt, Reisen, Wahrnehmungssinnlichkeit und Geschlecht in englischen Erzahltexten, 2006. Contributor of articles to journals. **Address:** Department of English, University of Cologne, Albertus-Magnus-Platz, Cologne, 50923, Germany. **Online address:** natascha.wuerzbach@t-online.de

WYATT, Clarence R. American (born United States), b. 1956. **Genres:** Writing/Journalism, Documentaries/Reportage. **Career:** Centre College, research associate, 1979-82, development consultant, 1982-88, executive assistant to the president, 1988-90, assistant professor of history and consultant on planning and resources, 1990-, Claude D. Pottinger professor of history, special assistant to the president, chief planning officer; Garner-Wyatt Consulting, partner; Teagle Foundation, consultant; United Negro College Fund, consultant; Heart of Danville, founder. Writer. **Publications:** Paper Soldiers: The American Press and the Vietnam War, 1993; (ed. with M.J. Manning) Encyclopedia of Media and Propaganda in Wartime America, 2011. Contributor of articles to periodicals. **Address:** Centre College, 600 W Walnut St., Danville, KY 40422-1309, U.S.A. **Online address:** wyattc@centre.edu

WYATT, David M. American (born United States), b. 1948. **Genres:** Literary Criticism And History, Young Adult Fiction, History. **Career:** University of Virginia, assistant professor of English, 1975-82; Virginia Foundation for the Humanities, program associate, 1982-87; Princeton University, visiting lecturer in English, 1984-85; University of Maryland, associate professor, 1987-89, professor of English, 1989-. Writer. **Publications:** Prodigal Sons: A Study in Authorship and Authority, 1980; The Fall Into Eden: Landscape and Imagination, 1986; (ed.) New Essays on The Grapes of Wrath, 1990; Out of the Sixties: Storytelling and the Vietnam Generation, 1993; (ed. with intro.) Selected Stories and Sketches, 1995; Five Fires: Race, Catastrophe and the Shaping of California, 1997; And the War Came: An Accidental Memoir, 2004; Secret Histories: Reading Twentieth American literature, 2010. **Address:** Department of English, University of Maryland, 3107 Tawes Hall, 2119 Tawes Hal, College Park, MD 20742, U.S.A. **Online address:** dwyatt@umd.edu

WYATT, Don J. American (born United States), b. 1953. **Genres:** Cultural/Ethnic Topics, History, Philosophy, Biography. **Career:** Clark University, visiting lecturer in history, 1984; Harvard University, lecturer in East Asian languages and civilizations, 1985-86; Middlebury College, visiting assistant professor, 1986-87, assistant professor, 1987-91, associate professor, 1991-96, professor of history, 1996-, John M. McCardell Jr. distinguished professor, 2010-, vice-president for undergraduate affairs and dean of the college, 1994-97; Vermont Academy of Arts and Sciences, board trustee, 1994-97; Beloit College, alumni trustee, 1995-98, term trustee, 2002-; Phi Beta Kappa Society, senator, 2000-12; Wheaton College, visiting assistant professor of history. Writer. **Publications:** (Co-author) Sung Dynasty Uses of the I Ching, 1990; The Recluse of Loyang: Shao Yung and the Moral Evolution of Early Sung Thought, 1996; (with N. DiCosmo) Political Frontiers, Ethnic Boundaries and Human Geographies in Chinese History, 2003; Battlefronts Real and Imagined: War, Border and Identity in the Chinese Middle Period, 2008; The Blacks of Premodern China, 2010. Contributor to books and periodicals. **Address:** Department of History, Middlebury College, 343 Axinn Ctr., Starr Library, 15 Old Chapel Rd., Middlebury, VT 05753, U.S.A. **Online address:** wyatt@middlebury.edu

WYATT, Robert Lee. American (born United States), b. 1940. **Genres:** Education, History. **Career:** English teacher, 1963-69; General Dynamics

Corp., writer and director of airplane construction films, 1969-70; teacher of English, journalism and drama, 1970-87; Big Pasture News, owner and publisher, 1976-86; University of Oklahoma, instructor, 1987-90; East Central University, professor of education, 1990-2006, emeritus professor, 2006-; Ada Community Theater, president, director. Writer. **Publications:** Devol: Gateway to the Big Pasture, 1974; Grandfield: Hub of the Big Pasture, vol. I, 1975, vol. II, 1976; The History of the Haverstock Tent Show, 1997; (with S. Looper) So You Have to Have a Portfolio: Planning, Producing, and Presenting a Professional Portfolio, 1998, 2nd ed., 2004; (with J.E. White) Making Your First Year a Success: The Secondary Teacher's Survival Guide, 2002, 2nd ed., 2007. **Address:** College of Education, East Central University, PO Box J-1, Ada, OK 74820, U.S.A. **Online address:** bwyatt@wilnet1.com

WYATT-BROWN, Anne M(arbury). American (born United States), b. 1939. **Genres:** Literary Criticism And History, Gerontology/Senior Issues, Humanities, Language/Linguistics. **Career:** Cleveland Institute of Art, instructor, associate professor of English, 1974-83; University of Florida, lecturer, 1983-89, coordinator of scholarly writing, 1983-2003, assistant instructor and research assistant, 1989-92, assistant professor of linguistics, 1992-96, associate professor, 1996-2004, Women Studies Program, graduate coordinator, 1996-98, Undergraduate Director, 2000-03, associate professor emeritus, 2004-; Case Western Reserve University, lecturer, 1976, adjunct assistant professor, 1982-83; Cleveland State University, adjunct lecturer, 1980. Psyart, editor; Journal of Aging, Humanities, and the Arts, editor, co-editor; International Journal of Aging and Human Development, editor. **Publications:** Barbara Pym: A Critical Biography, 1992; (ed. with J. Rossen and contrib.) Aging and Gender in Literature: Studies in Creativity, 1993. (with B.F. Waxman) Aging in literature, 1999; Works appears in anthologies. Contributor to periodicals. **Address:** Department of Linguistics, University of Florida, 4131 Turlington Hall, PO Box 115454, Gainesville, FL 32611-5454, U.S.A. **Online address:** awyatt@nervm.nerdc.ufl.edu

WYER, Robert S. American (born United States), b. 1935. **Genres:** Psychology. **Career:** Bell Telephone Laboratories, staff, 1957-59; Hughes Aircraft Co., staff, 1961-63; University of Iowa, assistant professor, 1963-65; University of Illinois, assistant professor, 1965-67, associate professor, 1967-71, professor, 1971-95, professor emeritus, 1995-, chair professor of marketing, 2009-10; Hong Kong University of Science and Technology, visiting professor, 1997-2009; Chinese University of Hong Kong, visiting professor, 2010-. Writer. **Publications:** (With G. Terrell) Non-intellective Factors Associated with Scholastic Achievement, 1966; Cognitive Organization and Change, 1974; (with D.E. Carlston) Social Cognition, Inference, and Attribution, 1979; (with T.K. Srull) Memory and Cognition in Its Social Context, 1989; Social Comprehension, Inference and Attribution, 2004. EDITOR: (with T.K. Srull) Handbook of Social Cognition, 3 vols., 1984, 2nd ed., 1994; (and contrib.) Advances in Social Cognition, vol. I: A Dual Process Model of Impression Formation, 1988, vol. II: Social Intelligence and Cognitive Assessments of Personality, 1989, vol. III: Content and Process Specificity in the Effects of Prior Experiences, 1990, vol. IV: The Content, Structure, and Operation of Thought Systems, 1991, vol. V: The Representation of Trait and Behavioral Knowledge about Self, 1992, vol. VI: Towards a General Theory of Anger and Emotion, 1993, vol. VII: Associated Systems Theory, 1994, vol. VIII: Knowledge and Memory, 1995, vol. IX: Ruminative Thoughts, 1996, vol. X: The Automutuality of Everyday Life, 1997, vol. XI: Stereotype Activation and Inhibition, 1998, vol. XII: Perspectives on Behavioral Self-Regulation, 1999; (with C. Chiu and Y. Hong) Understanding Culture: Theory, Research, and Application, 2009. Contributor to books and journals. **Address:** Department of Marketing, Chinese University of Hong Kong, Shatin, 852, Hong Kong. **Online address:** r-wyer@uiuc.edu

WYETH, Sharon Dennis. American (born United States) **Genres:** Novels, Young Adult Fiction. **Career:** Daycare Center, family counselor. Writer. **Publications:** Rocky Romance, 1988; Too Cute for Words, 1989; P.S. Forget It!, 1989; Boys Wanted!, 1989; Amy's Song, 1989; Win or Lose, 1989; Sam The Sham, 1989; No Creeps Need Apply, 1989; Dream Holiday, 1990; Roommate Trouble, 1990; The Dinosaur Tooth, 1990; The Ghost Show, 1990; Lisa's Secret, 1990; Stolen Pen Pals, 1990; Sealed With A Kiss, 1990; The Mighty Dolphin, 1990; Palmer At Your Service, 1990; Lisa We Miss You, 1990; Mystery About Maxie, 1990; Heartbreak Guy, 1990; Chicken Pox Party, 1990; Boy Crazy, 1991; Handle With Care, 1991; Summer Sizzle, 1991; The Boy Project, 1991; Double Date, 1991; The World of Daughter McGuire, 1994; Always My Dad, 1995; Vampire Bugs: Stories Conjured from the Past, 1995; Ginger Brown: Too Many Houses, 1995; Splash Party,

1996; Winning Stroke, 1996; Human Shark, 1996; In Deep Water, 1996; Ginger Brown: The Nobody Boy, 1997; Tomboy Trouble, 1998; Once on This River, 1998; Something Beautiful, 1998; A Piece of Heaven, 2001; Freedoms Wings, 2001; Flying Free, 2002; Message in the Sky, 2003; Orphea Proud, 2004; (with J. Bauer) This Family Is Driving Me Crazy, 2009. **Address:** Delacorte Press, 1540 Broadway, New York, NY 10036, U.S.A. **Online address:** sdw@sharondenniswyeth.com

WYKE, Maria. British (born England), b. 1957. **Genres:** History. **Career:** University of North London, part-time lecturer in classics, 1985-87; Cambridge University, Newnham College, fellow and joint college lecturer in classics, 1987-92, Corpus Christi College, joint college lecturer in classics, 1987-92, director of studies in classics, 1987-92; University College, honorary research fellow, 1992-93, postdoctoral fellow, 2005-08, Department of Greek and Latin, professor of Latin and head, 2005-; University of Reading, lecturer, professor of classics, 1993-2005; Manchester University, Joseph and Hannah Maria Lees fellow in Latin, 1984-85; Oxford University, Queen's College, junior research fellow in Classical languages and literature, 1985-87; British School at Rome, Balsdon fellow, 1997-98; Oxford University, Somerville College, Alice Horsman traveling fellow. Writer. **Publications:** (Ed. with L.J. Archer and S. Fischler) Women in Ancient Societies: An Illusion of the Night, 1994; Projecting the Past: Ancient Rome, Cinema, and History, 1997; (ed.) Gender and the Body in the Ancient Mediterranean, 1998; (ed.) Parchments of Gender: Deciphering the Bodies of Antiquity, 1998; (ed. with M. Biddiss) The Uses and Abuses of Antiquity, 1999; The Roman Mistress: Ancient and Modern Representations, 2002; (ed. with A. Hopkins) Roman Bodies: Antiquity to the Eighteenth Century, 2005; (ed.) Julius Caesar in Western Culture, 2006; Caesar: A Life in Western Culture, 2007; (ed. with L.B.T. Houghton) Perceptions of Horace: A Roman Poet and His Readers, 2009. Contributor of articles to academic books and journals. **Address:** Department of Greek and Latin, University College London, Gower St., London, GL WC1E 6BT, England. **Online address:** m.wyke@ucl.ac.uk

WYLD, Evie. British/Australian (born Australia), b. 1980?. **Genres:** Novels. **Career:** Review (an independent bookshop), staff. Writer. **Publications:** After the Fire, a Still Small Voice (novel), 2009. Contributor to books. Works appear in anthologies. **Address:** Mulcahy Conway Associates Ltd., 15 Canning Passage, Kensington, GL W8 5AA, England. **Online address:** evie@eviewyld.com

WYLE, Dirk. See **HAYNES, Duncan H(arold).**

WYLIE, Diana. American (born United States), b. 1948. **Genres:** Race Relations, History. **Career:** Chinga Girls Secondary School, teacher, 1970-71; Holmes and Meier publisher Inc., editor, 1974-82; University of Oran, instructor in history, 1975-76; University of Legon, research fellow, 1977-; Yale University, teaching fellow, 1977, 1982-83, assistant professor, 1985-91, associate professor of history, 1991-94, associate director of Southern African research program, 1985-94; Vassar College, instructor in history, 1978-79; Mount Holyoke College, visiting assistant professor of history, 1982, 1985; Swarthmore College, external honors examiner, 1986-88, 1991; Boston University, associate professor, 1994-2003, professor of history, 2003-; Harvard University, visiting associate professor of history, 1999-2000. Writer. **Publications:** A Little God: The Twilight of Patriarchy in a Southern African Chiefdom, 1990; Starving on a Full Stomach: Hunger and the Triumph of Cultural Racism in Modern South Africa, 2001; Art and Revolution: The Life and Death of Thami Mnyele, South African Artist, 2008; Enchantment: Pictures from the Tangier American Legation Museum, 2010. Contributor to books and periodicals. **Address:** Department of History, Boston University, Rm. 517, African Studies Ctr., 226 Bay State Rd., Boston, MA 02215, U.S.A. **Online address:** dwylie@bu.edu

WYLLIE, Peter J(ohn). American/British (born England), b. 1930. **Genres:** Earth Sciences, Sciences, Geography, Mathematics/Statistics. **Career:** British North Greenland Expedition, geologist, 1952-54; University of Saint Andrews, assistant lecturer in geology, 1955-56; Pennsylvania State University, research assistant, 1956-58, assistant professor of geochemistry, 1958-59, associate professor of petrology, 1961-65, acting head of department of geochemistry and mineralogy, 1962-63; University of Leeds, research fellow in chemistry, 1959-60, lecturer in experimental petrology, 1960-61; University of Chicago, professor, 1965-83, associate dean of college and of physical sciences division, 1972-73, master of physical sciences in collegiate division, 1972-73, Homer J. Livingston professor of geology, 1978-83, Department of

Geophysical Sciences, chairman, 1979-82; Journal of Geology, editor, 1967-83; Springer-Verlag Minerals and Rocks monograph series, editor-in-chief, 1968-99; California Institute of Technology, division of geological and planetary sciences, professor of geology, 1983-99, chairman, 1983-87, professor emeritus, 1999-; China School of Geosciences, honorary professor, 1996-, divisional academic officer, 1994-99. **Publications:** Geological Reconnaissance through South Germania Land, 1957; (with H. Lister) Geomorphology of Dronning Louise Land, 1957; (ed.) Ultramafic and Related Rocks, 1967; The Dynamic Earth: Textbook in Geosciences, 1971; The Way the Earth Works: An Introduction to the New Global Geology and Its Revolutionary Development, 1975; (ed.) Solid Earth Sciences and Society, 1993. CONTRIBUTOR: Northice: The Story of the British North Greenland Expedition, 1957; Venture to the Arctic, 1958; High Pressure Physics and Chemistry, 1963; Methods and Techniques in Geophysics, 1966; The Carbonatites, 1966; The Earth's Crust and Upper Mantle (monograph), 1969; The Structure and Physical Properties of the Earth's Crust (monograph), 1971; The Great Ideas Today, 1971; Alkaline Rocks, 1974; High Pressure Research: Applications to Geophysics, 1977; Evolution of the Igneous Rocks, 1979; Kimberlites, Diatremes and Diamonds: Their Geology, Petrology and Geochemistry, 1979. **Address:** Division of Geological and Planetary Sciences, California Institute of Technology, 066 Arms Laboratory, MC 170-25, Pasadena, CA 91125, U.S.A. **Online address:** wyllie@caltech.edu

WYMAN, Andrea. American (born United States) **Genres:** Novels, Illustrations, Education. **Career:** Waynesburg College, professor of early childhood education; Edinboro University, Baron-Forness Library, assistant professor, associate professor and curriculum materials librarian. Writer. **Publications:** SELF-ILLUSTRATED: Rural Women Teachers in the United States: A Sourcebook, 1996. OTHERS: Red Sky at Morning, 1991; Faith, Hope, and Chicken Feathers, 1994. **Address:** Baron-Forness Library, Edinboro University, Rm. 237, 200 Tartan Dr., Edinboro, PA 16444, U.S.A. **Online address:** awyman@edinboro.edu

WYMAN, Bruce C. American (born United States), b. 1947. **Genres:** Environmental Sciences/Ecology, Sciences, Technology. **Career:** Texas Air Control Board, project officer and data analyst, 1978-81; McNeese State University, associate professor of biological and environmental sciences, 1983-; U.S. Environmental Protection Agency, Air Pollution Resource Training Center, director, 1983-; Greater Lake Charles Water Co., board director, 1990-91. Writer. **Publications:** (With L.H. Stevenson) The Facts on File Dictionary of Environmental Science, 1991, 3rd ed., 2007. **Address:** McNeese State University, 4205 Ryan St., PO Box 92000, Lake Charles, LA 70609, U.S.A. **Online address:** wyman@mcneese.edu

WYMAN, Carolyn. American (born United States), b. 1956. **Genres:** Food And Wine, Young Adult Non-fiction. **Career:** Narragansett Times, feature writer, 1978-80; New Haven Register, feature writer, 1980-. **Publications:** (With B.T. Leblang) Supermarket Sampler Picks the Best New Products of 1991, 1991; Ella Fitzgerald: Jazz Singer Supreme (young adult biography), 1993; I'm a Spam Fan: America's Best-Loved Foods (non-fiction), 1993; Kitchen Sink Cookbook: Offbeat Recipes from Unusual Ingredients, 1997; Spam: A Biography, 1999; Jell-O: A Biography, 2001; Better Than Homemade: Amazing Foods That Changed the Way We Eat, 2004; The Great Philly Cheesesteak Book, 2009. Contributor to periodicals. **Address:** New Haven Register, 40 Sargent Dr., New Haven, CT 06511, U.S.A. **Online address:** carolyn@greatphillycheesesteakbook.com

WYMAN, Max. Canadian/British (born England), b. 1939. **Genres:** Cultural/Ethnic Topics, Dance/Ballet, Biography, Young Adult Fiction. **Career:** Vancouver Sun, music, dance and theater critic, 1967-79, editor, 1991-96; Simon Fraser University, Centre for Communications and the Arts, governor, 1972-74; Canada Broadcasting Corp., commentator and interviewer, 1975-; Vancouver Province, arts columnist, dance and theater critic and books editor, 1980-91; Review of Books, founding editor, 1996-99, senior writer, 1999-2003; Canadian Commission for UNESCO, president; Lions Bay, mayor, 2005-08. **Publications:** The Royal Winnipeg Ballet: The First Forty Years, 1978; Dance Canada: An Illustrated History, 1989; Evelyn Hart: An Intimate Portrait, 1991; (ed.) Vancouver Forum: Old Powers, New Forces, 1992; Toni Cavelti: A Jeweller's Life, 1996; Max Wyman Revealing Dance: Selected Writings, 1970's-2001, 2001; The Defiant Imagination: Why Culture Matters, 2004. Works appear in anthologies. Contributor to magazines. **Address:** c/o Denise Bukowsk, Bukowski Agency, 14 Prince Arthur Ave., Ste. 202, Toronto, ON M5R 1A9, Canada. **Online address:** maxwyman@telus.net

WYMARK, Olwen (Margaret). American (born United States), b. 1932. **Genres:** Plays/Screenplays, Theatre, Young Adult Fiction, Literary Criticism And History. **Career:** Dramatist, 1966-. Writer. **Publications:** Three Plays, 1967; The Gymnasium and Other Plays, 1971; Find Me: A Play, 1980; Loved: A Play, 1980; (adaptor) Female Parts: One Woman Plays (adaptation of Plays by Dario Fo and Franca Rame), 1981; Nana, 1981; Best Friends and Other Plays, 1984; Lessons and Lovers: D.H. Lawrence in New Mexico, 1986; Strike Up the Banns, 1990; Brezhnev's Children, 1992; Mothering Sunday, 2002. Contributor to periodicals. **Address:** The Agency, 24 Pottery Ln., London, GL W11 4LZ, England. **Online address:** olwen@olwenwymark.demon.co.uk

WYMELENBERG, Suzanne. American (born United States), b. 1929. **Genres:** Medicine/Health, Philosophy, Sports/Fitness, Sciences. **Career:** Time, stringer, 1965-89. Writer. **Publications:** (With D. Matthews and S.C. Cowley) Secondhand Is Better (2H=B), 1975; Science and Babies: Private Decisions, Public Dilemmas, 1990; (with B. Winikoff) The Contraceptive Handbook: A Guide to Safe and Effective Choices, 1992; (with B. Winikoff) Whole Truth about Contraception: A Guide to Safe and Effective Choices, 1997. **Address:** Joseph Henry Press, 500 5th St. NW, Washington, DC 20001, U.S.A. **Online address:** swymelenberg@earthlink.net

WYNDHAM, Francis (Guy Percy). British (born England), b. 1924. **Genres:** Novels, Biography, Novellas/Short Stories, Young Adult Fiction. **Career:** Andre Deutsch, publisher's reader and editor, 1955-58; Queen (magazine), theater and film critic and literary editor, 1959-63; Sunday Times (newspaper), Sunday Times Magazine, staff writer and assistant editor, 1964-80. **Publications:** (Intro.) Box of Pin-Ups, 1965; Graham Greene, rev. ed., 1968; (with D. King) Trotsky: A Documentary, 1972; Out of the War (short stories), 1974; Mrs. Henderson (short stories), 1985 in UK as Mrs. Henderson and Other Stories; The Other Garden (novel), 1987; The Theatre of Embarrassment (essays), 1991; Collected Fiction of Francis Wyndham, 1992; Other Garden and Collected Stories, 2008; Complete Fiction, 2009. EDITOR: (with D. Melly) The Letters of Jean Rhys, 1984 in UK as Jean Rhys Letters, 1931-1966; (and intro. With D. King) Far Journeys: Photographs and Notebooks, 1993. **Address:** Rogers, Coleridge & White Ltd., 20 Powis Mews, London, GL W11 1JN, England.

WYNES, Charles E. (Charles Eldridge Wynes). American (born United States), b. 1929. **Genres:** History, Race Relations, Essays, Social Sciences. **Career:** Texas A&M University, instructor, assistant professor of history, 1958-62; University of Georgia, assistant professor, 1962-66, associate professor, 1966-70, professor of history, 1970-, now professor emeritus. Writer. **Publications:** Race Relations in Virginia 1870-1902, 1961; (co-author) A History of Georgia, 1977; Charles Richard Drew: The Man and the Myth, 1988; (intro.) Ten Years on a Georgia Plantation Since the War, 1866-76, 1992; (intro.) Journal of a Residence on a Georgia Plantation in 1838-39, 1992. EDITOR: Southern Sketches from Virginia 1881-1901, 1964; The Negro in The South Since 1865, 1965; Forgotten Voices, 1967. **Address:** Department of History, University of Georgia, 220 LeConte Hall, Athens, GA 30602-1602, U.S.A.

WYNES, Charles Eldridge. See **WYNES, Charles E.**

WYNIA, Gary W. See Obituaries.

WYNN, Charles M. American (born United States), b. 1939. **Genres:** Paranormal, Sciences. **Career:** University of Michigan, instructor in chemistry, 1965-66; Oakland Community College, professor of physical science, 1969-79; Eastern Connecticut State University, Department of Chemistry, professor of chemistry, 1979-, assistant chair. Writer. **Publications:** (With L. Graeser) Teachers Manual for Higher School Certificate in Chemistry, 1967; Laboratory Experiments for Chemistry: A Basic Introduction, 1978, 4th ed., 1993. WITH A.W. WIGGINS: Natural Science: Bridging the Gaps, 1991, 4th ed., 1998; The Five Biggest Ideas in Science, 1997; Quantum Leaps in the Wrong Direction: Where Real Science Ends and Pseudoscience Begins, 2001; The Five Biggest Unsolved Problems in Science, 2003; (ed.) And God said, Let there be Evolution!: Reconciling the Book of Genesis, the Qur'an, and the Theory of Evolution, 2009, 2nd ed., 2011. Contributor to journals. **Address:** Department of Chemistry, Eastern Connecticut State University, Science 456, 83 Windham St., Willimantic, CT 06226-2211, U.S.A. **Online address:** wynnc@easternct.edu

WYNNE, Ben. American (born United States), b. 1961. **Genres:** History,

Adult Non-fiction. **Career:** University of Mississippi, history instructor, 2000-02; Florida State University, visiting assistant professor, 2003-05; Gainesville State College, assistant professor of history, 2005-, associate professor of history. Writer. **Publications:** A Hard Trip: A History of the 15th Mississippi Infantry, CSA, 2003; (intro.) Recollections and letters, 2004; Mississippi's Civil War: A Narrative History, 2006; (intro.) Mosby's Memoirs: The Memoirs of Colonel John Singleton Mosby, 2006; Mississippi, 2008; (ed. and intro.) The Personal Observations of a Man of Intelligence: Notes of a Tour in North America in 1861, 2009. Contributor to books. **Address:** Division of Social Sciences, Gainesville State College, GC - Academic II, Rm. 117, 3820 Mundy Mill Rd., Oakwood, GA 30566, U.S.A. **Online address:** brw22@earthlink.net

WYNNE, Frank. Irish (born Ireland), b. 1962?. **Genres:** Biography, Autobiography/Memoirs, Translations, Art/Art History, Photography, Criminology/True Crime. **Career:** Revolver Magazine, staff; Crisis Magazine, staff; Deadline Magazine, managing editor; America Online, editorial director. Freelance writer and translator. **Publications:** I was Vermeer: The Rise and Fall of the Twentieth Century's Greatest Forger, 2006. TRANSLATOR: D. Sigaud, Somewhere in a Desert, 1998; M. Houellebecq, Atomised, 2000; M. Houellebecq, The Elementary Particles, 2000; D. Guedj, The Parrot's Theorem: A Novel, 2001; M. Houellebecq, Lanzarote, 2003; M. Houellebecq, Platform: A Novel, 2003; P. Besson, In the Absence of Men, 2003; A. Comte-Sponville, The Little Book of Philosophy, 2004; F. Beigbeder, Windows on the World: A Novel, 2004; P. Mérot, Mammals, 2006; A. Kourouma, Allah is Not Obliged (novel), 2007; F. Beigbeder, Holiday in a Coma: AND Love Lasts Three Years, 2007; A. Zaoui, Banquet of Lies, 2008; (with M. Frendo) B.H. Lévy and M. Houellebecq, Public Enemies: Dueling Writers Take on Each Other and the World, 2010; Y. Khadra, What the Day Owes the Night, 2010; M. Figueras, Kamchatka, 2010; B. Sansal, An Unfinished Business, 2010; A. Cueto, The Blue Hour, 2010; C. Lanzmann, The Patagonian Hare, 2011; E. de Hériz, Manual of Darkness, 2011; T.E. Martinez, Purgatory, 2011. **Address:** c/o David Miller, Rogers, Coleridge & White Literary Agency, 20 Powis Mews, London, GL W11 1JN, England.

WYNNE, John (Stewart). (David Howell). American (born United States) **Genres:** Novels, Novellas/Short Stories, Mystery/Crime/Suspense. **Career:** Writer. **Publications:** The Sighting (chapbook containing title story), 1978; (As David Howell) Aftershock (novel), 1981; Crime Wave: A Novel, 1982; The Other World: Stories, 1994; The Listener's Guide to Audio Books: Reviews, Recommendations, and Listings for More than 2, 000 Titles (reference), 1995. Contributor to periodicals. **Address:** Harold Schmidt Literary Agency, 415 W 23rd St., Ste. 6F, New York, NY 10011, U.S.A.

WYNNE, Marcus. American (born United States) **Genres:** Mystery/Crime/ Suspense, Young Adult Fiction, Literary Criticism And History. **Career:** Writer, consultant and photographer. **Publications:** THRILLERS: No Other Option, 2001; Warrior in the Shadows, 2002; Brothers in Arms, 2004. Contributor to periodicals and magazines. **Address:** Trident Media Group L.L.C., 41 Madison Ave., 36th Fl., New York, NY 10010, U.S.A. **Online address:** marcus@marcuswynne.com

WYNNE-JONES, Tim(othy). Canadian/British (born England), b. 1948. **Genres:** Novels, Children's Fiction, Plays/Screenplays, Poetry, Novellas/ Short Stories, Picture/Board Books. **Career:** PMA Books, book designer, 1974-76; University of Waterloo, instructor in visual arts, 1976-78; York University, instructor in visual arts, 1978-80; Solomon and Wynne-Jones, graphic designer, 1976-79; Vermont College of Fine Arts, faculty. Writer. **Publications:** FOR CHILDREN FICTION: Madelaine and Ermadello, 1977; Zoom at Sea, 1983; Zoom Away, 1985; I'll Make You Small, 1986; Architect of the Moon, 1988 in US as Builder of the Moon, 1989; The Hour of the Frog, 1989; Zoom Upstream, 1992; Mouse in the Manger, 1993; The Last Piece of Sky, 1993; Some of the Kinder Planets (short stories), 1993; (with A. Lewis) Rosie Backstage, 1994; The Book of Changes (short stories), 1994; The Maestro, 1995; On Tumbledown Hill, 1998; Lord of the Fries and Other Stories, 1999; Ned Mouse Breaks Away, 2003; Zoom, 2009. POETRY: Mischief City, 1986. FOR ADULTS NOVELS: Odd's End, 1980; The Knot, 1982; Le Matou Marin, 1984; Fastyngange, 1988; Voices, 1990; Stephen Fair: A Novel, 1998; Boy in the Burning House, 2000; A Thief in the House of Memory, 2005; (ed.) My Dad's a Punk: 12 Stories About Boys and Their Fathers, 2006; Rex Zero and the End of the World, 2007; (co-author) Click, 2007; Boat in the Tree, 2007; Rex Zero, King of Nothing, 2008; Uninvited, 2009; Pounce de Leon, 2009; Rex Zero, the Great Pretender, 2010; Blink & Caution, 2011. **Address:** Barry Goldblatt Literary L.L.C., 320 7th Ave., Ste. 266, Brooklyn, NY 11215, U.S.A. **Online address:** author.author@timwynne-jones.com

WYNVEEN, Tim. Canadian (born Canada), b. 1951. **Genres:** Novels, Young Adult Fiction. **Career:** Freelance copyeditor and journalist. **Publications:** Angel Falls, 1997; Balloon, 1999; Sweeter Life: A Novel, 2002. Contributor of book reviews. **Address:** c/o Bruce Westwood, Westwood Creative Artists Ltd., 94 Harbord St., Toronto, ON M5S 1G6, Canada.

WYNYARD, Robin (Norman). British (born England), b. 1945. **Genres:** Essays, Humanities. **Career:** University of London, faculty; Gonzaga University, visiting professor; Hamdard University, professor emeritus; Canterbury Christ Church University College, visiting lecturer. Writer. **Publications:** (With M. Alfino and J. Caputo) McDonaldization Revisited: Critical Essays on Consumer Culture, 1998; (ed.) McDonaldization of higher education, 2002. Contributor to books and periodicals. **Address:** 51 Cromwell Rd., Whitstable, Kent, CT5 1NW, England.

X

XI, **Xi.** American/Chinese (born China), b. 1938. **Genres:** Novellas/Short Stories, Novels, Poetry, Literary Criticism And History. **Career:** Teacher, 1958-79; TV screenplay writer, 1960-; Chinese Students Weekly, editor, 1960-; Damuzhi zhoubao (literary magazine), editor, 1975-77; Suye wenxue (literary magazine), editor, 1981-84. **Publications:** Wo cheng, 1974; Jiao he, 1981; Chun wang, 1982; Shao lu, 1982; Shi qing, 1982; Xiang wo zhe yang di yi ge nü zi, 1984; Xiang wo zhe yang di yige du zhe, 1986; Hu zi you lian, 1986; A Girl Like Me And Other Stories, 1986; My City: A Hong Kong Story, 1993; Marvels of a Floating City and Other Stories, 1997; Fei zhan, 2000; Flying Carpet: A Tale Of Fertillia: A Novel, 2000. **Address:** Hong Kong University Press, 14/F Hing Wai Ctr., Tin Wan Praya Rd., Aberdeen, 45101, Hong Kong.

XIANG, **Lanxin.** Swiss/Chinese (born China), b. 1956. **Genres:** History, Area Studies. **Career:** Clemson University, assistant professor, 1991-94, associate professor of political science, 1995-96; Graduate Institute of International Studies, International History and Politics, associate professor, 1996-, professor; Fudan University-Shanghai, International Affairs, chair. Writer. **Publications:** Recasting the Imperial Far East: Britain and America in China, 1945-1950, 1995; Mao's Generals: Chen Yi and the New Fourth Army, 1998; Chinese Military: Problems of Modernization, 1999; Origins of the Boxer War: A Multinational Study, 2003; Yi he tuan zhan zheng de qi yuan: kua guo yan jiu, 2003; (with F. Shaolei) Zhuan xing zhong de Eluosi dui wai zhan lue, 2005; (with F. Shaolei) Eluosi yu da guo ji zhou bian guan xi, 2005; (with F. Shaolei) Zhuan xing li lun yu Eluosi zheng zhi gai ge, 2005; (with F. Shaolei) Zhuan xing zhong de Eluosi she hui yu wen hua, 2005; (with F. Shaolei) Eluosi jing ji zhuan xing, 2005; (with F. Shaolei) Chuan tong yu dui wai guan xi, 2007. **Address:** Graduate Institute of International Studies, Rue de Lausanne 132, PO Box 136, Geneva, CH - 1211, Switzerland. **Online address:** lanxin.xiang@graduateinstitute.ch

XIAOKANG, **Su.** American/Chinese (born China), b. 1949?. **Genres:** Plays/Screenplays, Autobiography/Memoirs, Translations, Biography. **Career:** Magazine Democratic China, editor, journalist. **Publications:** (With W. Luxiang and X. Jun) He Shang, 1988; Dang dai hun bian chen si lu, 1988; (with L. Shixu and Z.Z. Zhu) Wu tuo bang ji: Lushan hui yi ji shi, 1989; Yin yang da lie bian: Guan yu xian dai hun yin di tong ku si kao, 1989; Zi you bei wang lu, 1989; Long de bei chang, 1989; Gendai Chugoku no kiga to hinkon, 1990; He shang ji wai ji, 1990; Yuan si zhong sheng sui, 1996; Li hu li jie zi xu, 1997. **Address:** c/o Author Mail, Random House Inc., 1745 Broadway 18th Fl., New York, NY 10019, U.S.A.

XINGJIAN, **Gao.** French/Chinese (born China), b. 1940. **Genres:** Plays/Screenplays, Novels, Young Adult Fiction. **Career:** Beijing People's Art Theatre, resident playwright, 1981-87; China Reconstructs and Chinese Writers Association, translator. Writer. **Publications:** IN ENGLISH TRANSLATION: One Man's Bible, 1991; Ink Paintings, 1995; The Other Shore: Plays, 1999; Soul Mountain (novel), 1999; Return to Painting, 2002; Snow in August, 2003; Buying a Fishing Rod for My Grandfather, 2004; The Case for Literature, 2007. OTHERS: Xian Dai Xiao Shuo Ji Qiao Chu Tan, 1981; Juedui Zinghao (title means: 'The Alarm Signal'), 1982; Chezhan (title means: 'Bus Stop'), 1983; You Zhi Ge Zi Jiao Hong Chun Er, 1984; Ye Ren (title means: 'Wild Man'), 1985; Gao Xingjian Xi Ju Ji, 1985; Ling Shan, 1990; Dialoguer-interloquer (two-act play, title means: 'Dialogue and Rebuttal'), 1992; Flucht: Eine Moderne Tragödie, 1992; Shan Hai Jing zhuan, 1993; Le Somnambule (title means: 'The Sleepwalker'), 1994; La Montagne De l'âme, 1995; Gao Xingjian Xi Ju Liu Zhong, 1995; Tao Wang, 1995; Ming Cheng, 1995; Dui Hua Yu Fan Jie, 1995; Mei You Zhu Yi, 1996; Auplus Près du Reel: Dialogues Sur L'écriture (1994-1997), 1997; Unecanne à pèche Pour Mon Grand-père, 1997; Yi Ge Ren de Shengjing, 1999; Le Livre d'un Homme Seul (novel), 2000; Gao Xingjian: Tuschmalerei 1983-1993, 2000; Gei Wo Lao ye Mai yu Gan, 2001; Gao Xingjian duan Pian Xiao Shuo Ji, 2001; Pour Une Autre Esthétique, 2001; Gao Xingjian: Le Goût de L'encre, 2002; Dui yi Zhong xian dai xi ju Dezhui Qiu, 2003; (contrib.) Autour de Gao Xingjian, 2003; Témoignage de la Littérature, 2004; Quêteur Dela Mort; Suivi de, L'autre Rive et La Neige en Août, 2004; La Neige Enaoût de Xu Shuya: Epopée Lyrique en Deux Actes D'après Lapièce Homonyme Publièe aux èditions du Seuil, 2005; Lun Chuang Zuo, 2008; (with G.C.F. Fong) Of Mountains and Seas: A Tragicomedy of the Gods in Three Acts, 2008; Gao Xingjian, 2010; (with F.Z. Zhu) Lun xi ju, 2010. **Address:** c/o Author Mail, Editions de l' Aube, 13 pl Andre Masson, La Tour-d' Aigues, 84240, France.

Y

YABLONSKY, Linda. American (born United States), b. 1948?. **Genres:** Novels, Young Adult Fiction, Art/Art History. **Career:** Viking Press, editor, 1970-74; Night Light Readings, creator and host, 1991-; WPS1.org Art Radio, program director; ARTnews, contributing editor; The New York Times Style Magazine, columnist. Writer. **Publications:** The Story of Junk: A Novel, 1997; The Concert I Can't Forget; The Creative Time Book; Okay You Mugs: Writers on Movie Actors; Curve: The Nude in Contemporary Art; Time Out Book of New York Walks: 23 Walks Around the Big Apple; Bomb! Speak Fiction and Poetry; Low Rent: A Decade of Prose and Photographs from the Portable Lower East Side; (co-author) Face Addict. Contributor to periodicals. **Address:** Donadio and Olson Inc., 121 W 27th St., Ste. 704, New York, NY 10001, U.S.A.

YABUKI, Susumu. Japanese (born Japan), b. 1938. **Genres:** Area Studies. **Career:** Oriental Economist, staff writer, 1962-67; Institute of Developing Economies, researcher, 1967-76; Yokohama City University, associate professor, 1976-85, professor, 1985-, now professor emeritus; Consulate General of Japan, special assistant, 1979-80. **Publications:** MōTaku-To Shakaishugi Kensetsu o Kataru, 1975; A Crumbling Red China-signs and omens, 1981; 2000-nen no Chūgoku, 1984; Gendai Chūgoku no rekishi, 1949-1985: Mō Takutō jidai kara Tō Shō hei jidai e, 1986; Chaina shindorō mu: kagirinaku shihon shugi ni chikai shakai sugi, 1986; Chaina uotchingu: keizai kaikaku kara seiji kaikaku e, 1986; Zusetsu Chū goku no keizai suijun, 1987; Chū goku kaihū no bure n torasuto, 1987; Posuto Tō Shō hei: kaikaku to kaihō no yukue, 1988; Bunka daikakumei, 1989; The Great Cultural Revolution, 1989; Ten'anmon Jiken no shinsō, 1990; Mō Takutō to Shū Onrai, 1991; Mao Zedong and Zhou Enlai, 1991; Deng Xiaoping di jiu shi nian, 1994; China's New Political Economy: The Giant Awakes, 1995, (with S.M. Harner) rev. ed., 1999; The People's Liberation Army, 1996; Pō tsumasu kara kesareta otoko: Asakawa Kan'ichi no Nichi-Ro Sensō ron, 2002; Asakawa Kan'ichi hikaku hōkensei ronshū, 2007; Asakawa Kan'ichi to sono jidai, 2007; Nihon No Hakken: Asakawa Kan'ichi To Rekishigaku, 2008. **Address:** Yokohama City University, 22-2 Seto Kanazawa-ward, Yokohama City, 236-0027, Japan. **Online address:** yabuki@ca2.so-net.ne.jp

YAEGER, Don. American (born United States), b. 1962. **Genres:** Sports/Fitness, Documentaries/Reportage. **Career:** San Antonio Light, reporter, 1984-85; Dallas Morning News, reporter, 1986; Florida Times-Union, reporter and capitol bureau chief, 1986-90; University of Florida, adjunct professor; Florida State University, College of Communications, adjunct professor; Sports Illustrated, writer and associate editor, 1996; One Eighty Consulting, staff; One Eighty Communications, staff. Consultant. **Publications:** Undue Process: The NCAA's Injustice for All, 1990; Shark Attack: Jerry Tarkanian and His Battle with the NCAA and UNLV, 1992; (with D.S. Looney) Under the Tarnished Dome: How Notre Dame Betrayed Its Ideals for Football Glory, 1993; (with D. Brown) Tiger in a Lion's Den: Adventures in LSU Basketball, 1994; (with G. Karl) This Game's the Best! (So Why Don't They Quit Screwing with It?), 1997; (with D. Richardson) Living the Dream, 1997; (with D. Rosenhaus and J. Rosenhaus) A Shark Never Sleeps: Wheeling and Dealing With the NFL's Most Ruthless Agent, 1997; (with J. Benedict) Pros and Cons: The Criminals Who Play in the NFL, 1998; (with W. Payton) Never Die Easy: The Autobiography of Walter Payton, 2000; (with D. Wetzel) Sole Influence: Basketball, Corporate Greed and the Corruption of America's Youth, 2000;

(with T. McGraw) Ya Gotta Believe!: My Roller-Coaster Life as a Screwball Pitcher and Part-Time Father and My Hope-Filled Fight Against Brain Cancer, 2004; (S. Cunningham and J. Papadakis) Turning of the Tide: How One Game Changed the South, 2006; (with M. Pressler) It's Not About The Truth: The Untold Story of the Duke Lacrosse Case and the Lives it Shattered, 2007; (with W. Dunn) Running for My Life: My Journey in the Game of Football and Beyond, 2008; (with J. Henry) Tarnished Heisman: Did Reggie Bush Turn His Final College Season into a Six-figure Job?, 2008; (with M. Flynt) Senior, 2008; (with W. Moon) Never Give up on Your Dream: My Journey, 2009; (with J. Wood) Game Plan for Life: John Wooden's Lessons on Mentoring, 2009; (with D. Hoyt) Devoted: The Story of a Father's Love for His Son, 2009; (with M. Oher) I Beat the Odds: From Homelessness, to the Blindside and Beyond, 2011; (with J. Craig) Gold Medal Strategies: Business Lessons from America's Miracle Team, 2011; (with R. Ryan) Play like you mean it, 2011; Greatness, 2011; (with R. Blair) Nothing to Lose, Everything to Gain, 2011. **Address:** One Eighty Consulting, 413 N Meridian Dr., Tallahassee, FL 32301, U.S.A. **Online address:** don@donyaeger.com

YAEGER, Don. See **LOONEY, Douglas S.**

YAFFE, James. American (born United States), b. 1927. **Genres:** Novels, Plays/Screenplays, Mystery/Crime/Suspense. **Career:** United States Navy, staff, 1945-46; Colorado College, writer-in-residence, professor of English, 1968-2002, director of general studies, 1982-99, professor emeritus of English, 2002-. Writer. **Publications:** Poor Cousin Evelyn, 1950; The Good-for-Nothing, 1953; What's the Big Hurry?, 1954; Nothing but the Night, 1957; The Deadly Game (play), 1960; Mister Margolies, 1962; (with G. Berg) Dear me, the Sky is Falling, 1963; This Year's Genie (play), 1965; Nobody Does You Any Favors, 1966; The American Jews, 1968; (with J. Weidman) Ivory Tower (play), 1969; The Voyage of the Franz Joseph, 1970; So Sue Me! The Story of a Community Court, 1972; Saul and Morris, Worlds Apart, 1982; Cliffhanger: A Thriller in Two Acts (play), 1985; A Nice Murder for Mom, 1988; Mom Meets Her Maker, 1990; Mom Doth Murder Sleep, 1991; Mom among the Liars, 1992; My Mother, the Detective (short stories), 1997; Mom Lights a Candle, 2002. Contributor to magazines. **Address:** Department of English, Colorado College, 14 E Cache La Poudre St., Colorado Springs, CO 80903, U.S.A.

YAGAMI, Kazuo. American/Japanese (born Japan) **Genres:** Biography, Autobiography/Memoirs, History. **Career:** University of North Florida, visiting assistant professor, 2002-03; University of Northern Colorado, lecturer, 2004-06; Savannah State University, assistant professor, 2006-; Florida State University, faculty. Writer. **Publications:** Konoe Fumimaro and the Failure of Peace in Japan, 1937-1941: A Critical Appraisal of the Three-Time Prime Minister, 2006. contributor to journals. **Address:** Department of Social & Behavioral Sciences, Savannah State University, Rm. SSB 209, 3219 College St., Savannah, GA 31404, U.S.A. **Online address:** yagamik@savannahstate.edu

YAGHER, Kevin. American (born United States), b. 1962. **Genres:** Plays/Screenplays, History, Children's Non-fiction. **Career:** Kevin Yagher Productions Inc. (producers of special effects makeup for film and television), president, 1985-; Writer, director and producer. **Publications:** SELF-ILLUS-

TRATED: Heverly (picture book), 2001. **Address:** Kevin Yagher Productions Inc., 6615 Valjean Ave., Van Nuys, CA 91406, U.S.A.

YAGHMAIAN, Behzad. American/Iranian (born Iran), b. 1953?. **Genres:** Social Commentary, Adult Non-fiction, Politics/Government, History. **Career:** Ramapo College, professor of political economy; Neshat, columnist, 1998-99; PBS/Channel 4, consultant, 2003. Writer. **Publications:** Social Change in Iran: An Eyewitness Account of Dissent, Defiance, and New Movements for Rights, 2002; Embracing the Infidel: Stories of Muslim Migrants on the Journey West, 2005. Contributor to periodicals. **Address:** c/o Author Mail, Delacorte Press, 1745 Broadway, New York, NY 10019, U.S.A. **Online address:** behzad.yaghmaian@gmail.com

YAGODA, Ben. American (born United States), b. 1954. **Genres:** Biography, Young Adult Non-fiction, Autobiography/Memoirs. **Career:** New Leader Magazine, assistant editor, 1976-78; New Jersey Monthly, staff editor, 1980-82; Philadelphia Magazine, articles editor, 1982-85, book critic, 1989-2001; Daily News, staff, 1986-88; University of Delaware, assistant professor, 1992-96, associate professor, 1996-2001, professor of English, 2001-, professor of journalism, director of journalism program. **Publications:** (With R. Westheimer) All in a Lifetime: An Autobiography, 1987; Will Rogers (biography), 1993; (with R. Westheimer) Value of Family: A Blueprint for the 21st Century, 1996; (ed. with K. Kerrane) The Art of Fact: A Historical Anthology of Literary Journalism, 1997; About Town: The New Yorker and the World It Made, 2000; Scott Arboretum of Swarthmore College: The First 75 Years, 2003; The Sound on the Page: Style and Voice in Writing, 2004; When You Catch an Adjective, Kill It: The Parts of Speech for Better and/or Worse, 2006; Memoir: A History, 2009. Contributor to periodicals. **Address:** English Department, University of Delaware, 223 Memorial Hall, Newark, DE 19716, U.S.A. **Online address:** byagoda@udel.edu

YAKHLIF, Yahya. Palestinian (born Palestine), b. 1944?. **Genres:** Novels, Young Adult Fiction, History. **Career:** Writer. **Publications:** Maharah, 1974; Najrān taḥta al-ṣ ifr: riwāyah, 1975; Tuffāḥ al-majānīn: riwāyah, 1982; Nashīd al-ḥayāh: riwāyah, 1985; Tilka al-laylah al-tawīlah: riwāyah tasjīlīyah li-waqāi ḥadīth ṭāirat al-Raīs Arafāt fī al-ṣ aḥrā al-Lībīyah, 1992; Buhayrah warā' al-rīḥ: riwāyah, 1997; Nahr yastahimmu f'i bu hayrah: riwāyah, 2000; Yawm'īy'āt al-ijtiy'āḥ wa-al-ṣ um'ūd: shah'adāh mayd'ān'īyah, 2003; Ma al-sama: riwayah, 2008. **Address:** c/o Author Mail, Interlink Books, 46 Crosby St., Northampton, MA 01060-1804, U.S.A.

YALOM, Irvin D(avid). American (born United States), b. 1931. **Genres:** Novels, Psychology. **Career:** Mount Sinai Hospital, intern, 1956-57; Johns Hopkins University, Henry Phipps Psychiatric Clinic, resident, 1957-60; Patuxent Institution, consultant, 1959-60; Stanford University, School of Medicine, instructor, 1962-63, assistant professor, 1963-68, associate professor, 1968-73, professor of psychiatry, 1973-94, emeritus professor, 1994-, Adult Psychiatric Clinic, assistant director, 1973-88, Stanford University Hospital, Psychiatry Inpatient Unit, medical director, 1981-94, Inpatient and Outpatient Units, consultant, 1984-94; Center for Advanced Study in Behavioral Sciences, fellow, 1977-78. Writer. **Publications:** The Theory and Practice of Group Psychotherapy, 1970, 5th ed., 2005; (with M.A. Lieberman and M.B. Miles) Encounter Groups, 1973; (with G. Elkin) Every Day Gets a Little Closer, 1974; Existential Psychotherapy, 1980; Inpatient Group Psychotherapy, 1983; (with S. Vinogradov) Concise Guide to Group Psychotherapy, 1989; Love's Executioner and Other Tales of Psychotherapy, 1989; When Nietzsche Wept (novel), 1992; (ed. with J. Werne) Treating Eating Disorders, 1995; (ed. with C. Classen) Treating Women Molested in Childhood, 1995; (ed. with S. Brown) Treating Alcoholism, 1995; Lying on the Couch (novel), 1996; A Yalom Reader, 1998; Momma and the Meaning of Life, 1999; Gift of Therapy: An Open Letter to a New Generation of Therapists and Their Patients, 2002; Schopenhauer Cure: A Novel, 2005; Staring at the Sun: Overcoming the Terror of Death, 2008; The Spinoza Problem: A Novel 2012. Contributor to books and periodicals. **Address:** 951 Matadero Ave., Palo Alto, CA 94306, U.S.A. **Online address:** idy@stanford.edu

YAMADA, Nanako. American/Chinese (born China), b. 1939. **Genres:** Art/Art History, Photography. **Career:** College of DuPage, instructor in Japanese language, 1990-; Northern Illinois University, instructor in Japanese language, 1991-; University of Chicago, Center for East Asian Studies, associate; freelance art historian. Writer. **Publications:** (With H. Meritt) Guide to Modern Japanese Woodblock Prints, 1900-1975, 1992: (with H. Meritt) Woodblock Kuchi-e Prints: Reflections of Meiji Culture, 2000; Mokuhan kuchie sōran,

2005; Kuchie meisaku monogatarishū, 2006; Bijinga kuchie saijiki, 2008. Contributor to journals. **Address:** Center for East Asian Studies, University of Chicago, 302 Judd Hall, 5835 S Kimbark Ave., Chicago, IL 60637, U.S.A.

YAMAGUCHI, Yōji. American/Japanese (born Japan), b. 1963?. **Genres:** Novels, Genealogy/Heraldry, Children's Fiction, Biography. **Career:** Writer. **Publications:** Face of a Stranger: A Novel, 1995; A Student's Guide to Japanese American Genealogy, 1996; Nihongo No Kiseki: "Aiueo" to "Iroha" No Hatsumei, 2007. **Address:** HarperCollins Publishers Inc., 10 E 53rd St., New York, NY 10022, U.S.A.

YAMASHITA, Karen Tei. American (born United States), b. 1951. **Genres:** Novels, Plays/Screenplays, Literary Criticism And History. **Career:** University of California, assistant professor, 1997-, associate professor of literature, professor of literature and creative writing, undergraduate program director. Writer. **Publications:** NOVELS: Through the Arc of the Rain Forest, 1990; Brazil-Maru, 1992; Tropic of Orange, 1997. OTHER: Circle K Cycles, 2001; I Hotel, 2010. Contributor to periodicals. **Address:** Department of Language Program, Kresge College, University of California, Humanities 1 231, 1156 High St., Santa Cruz, CA 95064, U.S.A. **Online address:** ktyamash@ucsc.edu

YAMBA, C(hristian) Bawa. Swedish/Ghanaian (born Ghana), b. 1944. **Genres:** Anthropology/Ethnology, History. **Career:** University of Stockholm, lecturer, 1980-98; Ethnographical Museum of Sweden, curator, 1988-90; Karolinska Institute, Division of International Health Care Research, senior research fellow, 1991-; Swedish International Development Agency, senior research officer, 1996-98; Karlinska Institute, Division of International Health Care Research, senior research fellow, 1998-; Nordic Africa Institute, Nordic research fellow, 1999-; University of Hull, honorary research fellow; Diakonhjemmet University College, associate professor, 2003-08, professor, 2009-. Writer. **Publications:** Permanent Pilgrims: The Role of Pilgrimage in the Lives of West African Muslims in Sudan, 1995; (ed. with L. Haram) Dealing with Uncertainty in Contemporary African Lives, 2009. Contributor to journals. **Address:** Edinburgh University Press, 22 George Sq., Edinburgh, EH8 9LF, Scotland. **Online address:** bawa.yamba@nai.uu.se

YAN, Yunxiang. American (born United States), b. 1954?. **Genres:** Social Sciences, Sociology. **Career:** Peking University, lecturer, 1984-86; Chinese University of Hong Kong, lecturer, 1993-94; Johns Hopkins University, assistant professor of anthropology, 1994-96; University of California, assistant professor, 1996-98, associate professor, 1998-2003, professor of anthropology, 2003-, Center for Chinese Studies, co-director, 2005-. Writer and anthropologist. **Publications:** The Flow of Gifts: Reciprocity and Social Networks in a Chinese Village, 1996; Private Life under Socialism: Love, Intimacy, and Family Change in a Chinese Village, 1949-1999, 2003; The ren sheng huo de bian ge, 2006; Individualization of Chinese Society, 2009. Contributor to periodicals and journals. **Address:** Department of Anthropology, University of California, 381 Haines Hall, 375 Portola Plz., PO Box 951553, Los Angeles, CA 90095-1553, U.S.A. **Online address:** yan@anthro.ucla.edu

YANCEY, Diane. American (born United States), b. 1951. **Genres:** Children's Non-fiction, Young Adult Non-fiction, Adult Non-fiction. **Career:** Writer, 1985-. **Publications:** Desperadoes and Dynamite: Train Robbery in the United States, 1991; The Reunification of Germany, 1994; The Hunt for Hidden Killers, 1994; Zoos, 1995; Schools, 1995; Camels for Uncle Sam, 1995; Life in War-Torn Bosnia, 1996; Life in the Elizabethan Theater, 1997; Life in a Japanese-American Internment Camp, 1998; Life in Charles Dickens's England, 1999; Civil War Generals of the Union, 1999; Eating Disorders, 1999; Strategic Battles, 2000; Leaders of the North and South, 2000; (ed.) The Vietnam War: Life of an American Soldier, 2001; The Internment of the Japanese, 2001; Life on the Pony Express, 2001; Tuberculosis, 2001; Spies, 2002; STD's: What You Don't Know Can Hurt You, 2002; Life during the Roaring Twenties, 2002; Travel Guide to Al Capone's Chicago, 2003; Frederick Douglass, 2003; Al Capone, 2003; Leaders and Generals, 2003; Life during the Dust Bowl, 2004; Life of an American Soldier in Afghanistan, 2004; Middle East: An Overview, 2005; German Americans, 2005; Homefront, 2005; Terrorism, 2006; Forensic Anthropologist, 2006; Murder, 2006; Tracking Serial Killers, 2007; Case of the Green River Killer, 2007; Unabomber, 2007; The Case of the Zodiac Killer, 2008; Forensic Entomologist, 2009; Body Farms, 2009; Art Deco, 2010; Basketball, 2011. **Address:** c/o Kendra Marcus, Bookstop Literary Agency, 67 Meadow View Rd., Orinda, CA 94563, U.S.A. **Online address:** d.yancey@worldnet.att.net

YANCEY, George. (George Allan Yancey). American (born United States), b. 1962. **Genres:** Sociology, Social Sciences, Humanities. **Career:** University of Texas-Austin, Department of Economics, teaching assistant, 1987-89, Department of Sociology, teaching assistant, 1989-91, assistant instructor, 1991-93; University of Texas-San Antonio, Division of Social and Policy Science, visiting assistant professor, 1993-96; Round Top Consulting Associates, special projects consultant, 1994-96; University of Wisconsin, assistant professor, 1996-99; University of North Texas, Department of Sociology, assistant professor, 1999-2001, associate professor, 2002-, professor. Writer. **Publications:** Beyond Black and White: Reflections on Racial Reconciliation, 1996; (ed. with S.W. Yancey) Just Don't Marry One: Interracial Dating Marriage and Parenting, 2002; United by Faith: The Multiracial Congregation as an Answer to the Problem of Race, 2003; Who Is White?: Latinos Asians and the New Black/Nonblack Divide, 2003; One Body One Spirit: Principles of Successful Multiracial Churches, 2003; Beyond Racial Gridlock: Embracing Mutual Responsibility, 2006; Interracial Contact and Social Change, 2007; (with R. Lewis, Jr.) Interracial Families: Current Concepts and Controversies, 2009; Compromising Scholarship: Religious and Political Bias in American Higher Education, 2010; (with M.O. Emerson) Transcending Racial Barriers: Toward a Mutual Obligations Approach, 2010; (as George Allan Yancey) Neither Jew Nor Gentile: Exploring Issues of Racial Diversity on Protestant College Campuses, 2010. **Address:** Department of Sociology, University of North Texas, Rm. 397F, Chilton Hall, 1155 Union Cir., Ste. 311157, Denton, TX 76203, U.S.A. **Online address:** gyancey@unt.edu

YANCEY, George Allan. See **YANCEY, George.**

YANG, Belle. American (born United States), b. 1960. **Genres:** Children's Fiction, Autobiography/Memoirs, Picture/Board Books. **Career:** Artist and writer. **Publications:** SELF-ILLUSTRATED: Baba: A Return to China upon My Father's Shoulders, 1994; The Odyssey of a Manchurian, 1996; Chili-Chili-Chin-Chin, 1999; Hannah is My Name, 2004; Always Come Home to Me, 2007; Foo the Flying Frog of Washtub Pond, 2009; Forget Sorrow: An Ancestral Tale, 2010; Happy Birth Day!, 2012. **Address:** c/o Deborah Warren, East West Literary Agency, 1158 26th St., Ste. 462, Santa Monica, CA 90403, U.S.A. **Online address:** belleyang@comcast.net

YANG, Dali. See **YANG, Dali L.**

YANG, Dali L. (Dali Yang). American (born United States), b. 1964?. **Genres:** International Relations/Current Affairs, Social Sciences. **Career:** University of Chicago, assistant professor of political science, 1992-99, associate professor, 1999-2004, professor, 2004-, Chicago Center in Beijing, faculty director, 2010-; Department of Political Science, chairman, Committee on International Relations, director, Center for East Asian Studies, director. National University of Singapore, East Asian Institute, director, 2007-08. Writer and consultant. **Publications:** (Ed. and intro.) Yan Jiaqi, Zouxiang Minzhu Zhengzhi: Yan Jiaqi Zhongguo Zhengzhi Lunwenji, 1991; Calamity and Reform in China: State, Rural Society and Institutional Change Since the Great Leap Famine, 1996; Beyond Beijing: Liberalization and the Regions in China, 1997; Remaking the Chinese Leviathan: Market Transition and the Politics of Governance in China, 2004; (ed. with B.J. Naughton) Holding China Together: Diversity and National Integration in the Post-Deng Era, 2004; (ed.) Discontented Miracle: Growth, Conflict and Institutional Adaptations in China, 2007; (ed. with L. Zhao) China's Reforms At 30: Challenges and Prospects, 2009. Contributor to periodicals. **Address:** Department of Political Science, University of Chicago, Pick 422A, 5828 S University Ave., Chicago, IL 60637, U.S.A. **Online address:** daliyang@uchicago.edu

YANG, Kao Kalia. American/Thai (born Thailand), b. 1980. **Genres:** Autobiography/Memoirs. **Career:** Words Wanted LLP (an editorial services company), co-founder and co-owner. Writer, entrepreneur, memoirist, educator, documentary filmmaker and advocate. **Publications:** The Latehomecomer: A Hmong Family Memoir, 2008. Contributor to periodicals. **Address:** Words Wanted L.L.P., 501 Dale St., Ste. 300, St. Paul, MN 55103-1914, U.S.A. **Online address:** kaokaliayang@gmail.com

YANNI, Carla. American (born United States), b. 1965. **Genres:** Art/Art History, Adult Non-fiction, Social Sciences. **Career:** University of New Mexico, assistant professor, 1994-97; Rutgers University, assistant professor, 1997-, professor of art history, Undergraduate Academic Affairs, assistant vice president, 2007-11; National Gallery of Art, Center for Advanced Study in the Visual Arts, senior fellow, 2002-03; Society of Architectural Historians,

board director, 2003-07. Writer. **Publications:** Nature's Museums: Victorian Science and the Architecture of Display, 1999; The Architecture of Madness: Insane Asylums in the United States, 2007. **Address:** Department of Art History, Rutgers University, Voorhees Hall, 71 Hamilton St., New Brunswick, NJ 08901, U.S.A. **Online address:** cyanni@rci.rutgers.edu

YANOW, Scott. American (born United States), b. 1954. **Genres:** Music, Novels. **Career:** Record Review, jazz editor, 1976-84; freelance writer, 1983-. Historian. **Publications:** (Co-ed.) All Music Guide to Jazz, 1998; Duke Ellington, 1999; Swing, 2000; Bebop, 2000; Afro-Cuban Jazz, 2000; Classic Jazz: 1895-1933, 2001; The Trumpet Kings, 2001; Jazz on Record: The First Sixty Years 1917-76, 2003; Jazz on Film, 2004; Jazz: A Regional Exploration, 2005; The Jazz Singers, 2008. **Address:** PO Box 1220, Lake Hughes, CA 93532, U.S.A. **Online address:** scottyanowjazz@yahoo.com

YANSKY, Brian. American (born United States), b. 1957?. **Genres:** Novels, Humor/Satire, Novellas/Short Stories, Young Adult Fiction, Writing/Journalism. **Career:** Austin Community College, adjunct instructor, 1995-2002, assistant professor, 2002-. Writer. **Publications:** My Road Trip to the Pretty Girl Capital of the World, 2003; Wonders of the World, 2007; Alien Invasion & Other Inconveniences, 2010. Contributor to periodicals. **Address:** Austin, TX , U.S.A. **Online address:** brian@brianyansky.com

YAPP, Malcolm E(dward). British (born England), b. 1931?. **Genres:** History, Politics/Government, Social Sciences. **Career:** University of London, School of Oriental and African Studies (SOAS), professor of the modern history of Western Asia, 1985-98, professor emeritus of the modern history of Western Asia, 1998-. Writer. **Publications:** The Enlightenment, 1974; Chingis Khan and the Mongol Empire, 1974; Ibn Sina and the Muslim World, 1975; (ed. with V.J. Parry) War, Technology and Society in the Middle East, 1975; The Growth of the State, 1976; Nationalism, 1976; The British Raj and Indian Nationalism, 1977; Gandhi, 1977; (ed. with D. Taylor) Political Identity in South Asia, 1979; (with J.S. Read) Law, 1979; (with Read) Man and Law, 1979; Strategies of British India: Britain, Iran, and Afghanistan, 1798-1850, 1980; The Making of the Modern Near East, 1792-1923, 1987; The Near East since the First World War, 1991, 2nd ed., 1996; (ed.) Politics and Diplomacy in Egypt: The Diaries of Sir Miles Lampson 1935-1937, 1997; (ed.) British Documents on Foreign Affairs, Reports and Papers from the Foreign Office Confidential Print Part III, From 1940 through 1945 Series B, Near and Middle East, 1997; Mizrahh ha-Ķarov le-min Milḥemet ha-'Olam ha-Rishonah, 1999; (ed.) British Documents on Foreign Affairs: Reports and Papers from the Foreign Office Confidential Print. Part IV, From 1946 through 1950. Series B, Near and Middle East, 1946, 1999. **Address:** School of Oriental and African Studies, University of London, Thornhaugh St., Russell Sq., London, GL WC1H 0XG, England.

YARBOROUGH, Sharon C(lare). American (born United States), b. 1937. **Genres:** Novels, Natural History, Biology. **Career:** New Mexico State Heritage Program, management analyst, 1977-79; freelance botanist, teacher, photographer and consultant, 1980-91; Sul Ross State University, assistant curator of herbarium, 1995-. Writer. **Publications:** (With A.M. Powell) Ferns and Fern Allies of the Trans-Pecos and Adjacent Areas, 2002; Good Vibrations, forthcoming. Contributor to journals. **Address:** 701 N 2nd St., Alpine, TX 79830-3707, U.S.A. **Online address:** sharony@overland.net

YARBRO, Chelsea Quinn. Also writes as Vanessa Pryor, Quinn Fawcett, Trystam Kith, Terry Nelson Bonner. American (born United States), b. 1942. **Genres:** Novellas/Short Stories, Mystery/Crime/Suspense, Horror, Romance/Historical, Science Fiction/Fantasy, Westerns/Adventure, Young Adult Fiction, Paranormal, Essays, Novels. **Career:** Mirthmakers Children's Theatre, theatre manager and playwright, 1961-64; children's counselor, 1963-64; C.E. Erickson and Associates, cartographer, 1963-70; writer, 1968-; Sampo Productions, program director, 1970-71, 1973; Science Fiction Writers of America, secretary, 1970-72; Magic Cellar, tarot reader, 1974-79. **Publications:** (Ed. with T.N. Scortia) Two Views of Wonder, 1973; Time of the Fourth Horseman (science fiction), 1976; Ogilvie, Tallant & Moon, 1976; Bad Medicine, 1976; Hotel Transylvania, 1978; False Dawn (science fiction), 1978; The Palace, 1978; Cautionary Tales (short stories), 1978; Music When Sweet Voices Die, 1979; Blood Games, 1979; Sins of Omission, 1980; Ariosto: Ariosto Furioso, A Romance for an Alternate Renaissance, 1980; Dead and Buried, 1980; Path of the Eclipse, 1981; Tempting Fate, 1982; The Saint-Germain Chronicles (short stories), 1983; The Godforsaken (novel), 1983; Hyacinths (science fiction), 1983; Locadio's Apprentice (juvenile fiction),

1984; Nomads (novelization), 1984; Signs and Portents (short stories), 1984; Four Horses for Tishtry (juvenile fiction), 1985; A Mortal Glamour (novel), 1985; To the High Redoubt (novel), 1985; A Baroque Fable (novel with music), 1986; Floating Illusions (juvenile fiction), 1986; Firecode (novel), 1987; A Flame in Byzantium (novel), 1987; Crusader's Torch (novel), 1988; Taji's Syndrome (novel), 1988; The Law in Charity (western), 1989; A Candle for D'Artagnan (novel), 1989; Beastnights (novel), 1989; Out of the House of Life (novel), 1990; Poison Fruit, 1991; Spider Glass, 1991; (with G.R. Dickson, S. Lewitt and S. Perry) The Harriers, 1991; Cat's Claw, 1992; Darker Jewels, 1993; Crown of Empire, 1993; (with G.R. Dickson, D. Drake and C. Stasheff) Blood and War, 1993; Charity, Colorado, 1993; Better in The Dark, 1993; The Vampire Stories of Chelsea Quinn Yarbro, 1994; Monet's Ghost, 1995; Mansions of Darkness, 1996; Writ in Blood, 1997; Blood Roses, 1998; Kelene: The Angry Angel, 1998; Communion Blood, 1999; Fenice: Soul of an Angel, 1999; Dark Light: Shattered Light, 1999; Magnificat, 2000; Come Twilight, 2000; A Feast in Exhile, 2001; Zhameni: The Angel of Death, 2001; Night Blooming, 2002; (with A. Shimerman) Outrageous Fortune, 2002; Midnight Harvest, 2003; Apprehensions and Other Delusions, 2003; Dark of the Sun, 2004; States of Grace, 2005; Roman Dusk, 2006; Borne in Blood, 2007; The Lost Prince, 2007; A Dangerous Climate, 2008; Burning Shadows, 2009; An Embarrassment of Riches, 2011. AS TERRY NELSON BONNER: The Making of Australia No.5: The Outback, 1983. AS QUINN FAWCETT (with B. Fawcett): Napoleon Must Die, 1993; Death Wears a Crown, 1993; The Adventures of Mycroft Holmes, 1994; The Further Adventures of Mycroft Holmes, 1995; Against the Brotherhood, 1997; Embassy Row, 1998; The Flying Scotsman, 1999; The Scottish Ploy, 2000; Death to Spies, 2002; Siren Song, 2003; Honor Among Spies, 2004. AS VANESSA PRYOR: A Taste of Wine, 1982. AS TRYSTAM KITH: Trouble in the Forest, 2004; A Bright Winter Sun, 2005. OTHER: In the Face of Death, 2001. NON-FICTION: Messages from Michael: On the Nature of the Evolution of the Human Soul, 1979; More Messages from Michael, 1986; Michael's People: Continuing the Michael Teaching, 1988; Michael for the Millennium, 1995. Works appear in anthologies. **Address:** c/o Irene Kraas, Kraas Literary Agency, 13514 Winter Creek Ct., Houston, TX 77077, U.S.A.

YARBROUGH, Stephen R. American (born United States), b. 1950. **Genres:** Cultural/Ethnic Topics, Humanities, Intellectual History, Language/ Linguistics, Literary Criticism And History, Philosophy, Speech/Rhetoric, Theology/Religion, Biography. **Career:** Lake Forest College, lecturer in English, 1981; University of Wisconsin, instructor in English, 1982; Texas A&M University, College Station, assistant professor, 1982-88, associate professor of English, 1988-89; Skidmore College, associate professor of English, 1989-92; Aristotle University, Fulbright professor, 1990; University of North Carolina, associate professor of English, 1992-97, professor and director of undergraduate studies, 1997-; Bogazici University, lecturer; Carnegie-Mellon University, lecturer; University of Tulsa, lecturer. Writer. **Publications:** (With S.C. Brennen) Irving Babbitt, 1987; Deliberate Criticism: Toward a Postmodern Humanism, 1992; (with J.C. Adams) Delightful Conviction: Jonathan Edwards' Rhetoric of Conversion, 1993; After Rhetoric: Studies in Discourse beyond Language and Culture, 1999; Inventive Intercourse: From Rhetorical Conflict to the Ethical Creation of Novel Truth, 2006; Richard Rorty, Feminism and the Annoyances of Pragmatism, forthcoming. Works appear in anthologies. Contributor of articles to journals. **Address:** Department of English, University of North Carolina, 3105 MHRA, 121 McIver Bldg., Greensboro, NC 27412-5001, U.S.A. **Online address:** sryarbro@uncg.edu

YARBROUGH, Steve. American (born United States), b. 1956. **Genres:** Novellas/Short Stories, Novels, Young Adult Fiction. **Career:** Author, 1984-; Virginia Polytechnic Institute, faculty, 1984-89; California State University, professor of English, 1988-; University of Mississippi, Grisham writer-in-residence, 1999-2000; Emerson College, faculty, Department of Writing, Literature and Publishing, professor, 2009-. **Publications:** STORIES: Family Men, 1990; Mississippi History, 1994; Veneer, 1998. NOVELS: The Oxygen Man, 1999; Visible Spirits, 2001; Prisoners of War, 2004; The End of California, 2006; Safe from the Neighbors, 2010. **Address:** Department of Writing, Literature and Publishing, Emerson College, 180 Tremont St., 10th Fl., 120 Boylston St., Boston, MA 02116-4624, U.S.A. **Online address:** stevey@csufresno.edu

YĀRID, Nāzik Sābā. Lebanese/Palestinian (born Palestine), b. 1928. **Genres:** Novels, Literary Criticism And History, Young Adult Fiction, Young Adult Non-fiction. **Career:** French Protestant College, teacher of Arabic literature, 1950-78; Lebanese American University, assistant professor of Arabic literature, 1978-98, retired, 1998. Writer. **Publications:** Anthology and Study of Ibn ar-Rumi's Satirical Poetry, 1988; Arab Travellers and the Western Civilization, 1991; (with N. Bayyumi) Al-Kātib'āt al-Lubnāniyāt: bibliyughrāfiya, 1850-1950, 2000; A Complete Bibliography of Lebanese Women Writers from 1850 to 1950, 2001; Secularism and the Arab World: 1850-1939, 2002. NOVELS: Nuqtat ad-Dāira, 1980; Assada al-Makhnuq, 1986; Kana al-Amsu Ghadan, 1988; Taqāsim ala Watarin Da'ia (novel), 1992, trans. as Improvisations on a Missing String, 1997; Fi Dhill al-Qal'a, 1996; Al-Dhikrayāt al-Mulghāt, 1998; Ba'idan 'an Dhillal-Qal'a, 1998; Ayam fi Beirut, 2002. IN ARABIC: LITERARY CRITICISM: Elias Abu-Shabuki, 1969; Ibn ar-Rumi, 1980; Ahmad Shauqi, 1981; Hammad Ajrad, 1983; In the Wake of Abu Nuwas, 1992. OTHERS: Ahomad, Shawqi lahonal-mujtama wa-al-watoan, 1968; Ibn al-Rumi, 1969; Rahhā ilun al-'Arab wa-'Arab wa-ḥ aḍ ārat al-Gharb fi al-nahḍ ah al-'Arabiyah al-ḥ adithah, 1979; (with J.K. Jibran) Nabī, 1983; (co-author) Al-Siyasah wa-al-hoilah Inda al-Arab: Raqaiq al-hoilalfi Daqaiq al-hoiyal, 1992; Fi falak Abi Nuwas: Walibah ibn al-Houbab, Kulthum ibn Amr al-Attabi, Aban ibn Abd al-Hoamid al-Lahoiqi, 1992; Al-Nisa al-Arabiyat fi al-ishrinat: houdouran wa-huwiyah, 2001; (contrib.) Art of Rawas: Conversations with Nazik Yared, 2004; Al-Aqniah: riwāyah, 2004; Dhikrayāt lam taktamil, 2008; Canceled Memories: A Novel, 2009. Contributor to books. **Address:** Syracuse University Press, 621 Skytop Rd., Ste. 110, Syracuse, NY 13244, U.S.A. **Online address:** nsyared@inco.net.lb

YARNOLD, Barbara M(aria). American (born United States), b. 1961. **Genres:** Public/Social Administration, Theology/Religion, Politics/Government, Law, History. **Career:** Saginaw Valley State University, assistant professor of political science, 1988-90; Florida International University, assistant professor, 1990-95, associate professor of public administration, 1995-. Writer. **Publications:** Refugees without Refuge: Formation and Failed Implementation of U.S. Political Asylum Policy in the 1980's, 1990; International Fugitives: A New Role for the International Court of Justice, 1991; (ed.) The Role of Religious Organizations in Social Movements, 1991; Politics and the Courts: Toward a General Theory of Public Law, 1992; Abortion Politics in the Federal Courts: Right Versus Right, 1995; (contrib.) Controlling State Crime, 1995; Adolescents at Risk: Substance Abuse Among Miami's Adolescents in the 1990's, 1997; Paris and Other Poems: 1980-1997, 1998; Religious Wars in the Courts, 1999. Contributor of articles to journals and newspapers. **Address:** Department of Public Administration, Florida International University, N Miami Campus, North Miami, FL 33181, U.S.A.

YAROSHINSKAYA, Alla. Russian/Ukranian (born Ukraine), b. 1953. **Genres:** Novellas/Short Stories, Environmental Sciences/Ecology, Documentaries/Reportage, Social Sciences. **Career:** Radyanska Zhitomirshina (newspaper), journalist, 1976-89; U.S.S.R. Parliament, member, 1989-91; European Parliament, member, 1990-91; Ministry of Press and Information of the Russian Federation, Mass Media Department, chief, 1991-92; Federal Information Center of the President of the Russian Federation, International Liaison of Mass Media Department, chief, 1992-93; adviser to Russian President Boris N. Yeltsin, 1993-2000; Ecological Center, president, 1999-; adviser to former Russian president Mikhail Gorbachev, 2000-; Alla Yaroshinskaya Charity Fund to assist victims of nuclear disasters, president and founder, 1993-2000; Ecological Charity Fund, president; Russian Ecological Congress, co-chair; Federal Council of the Russian Social Democratic movement, director. Writer. **Publications:** Chernobyl is with Us (non-fiction), 1991, trans. as Chernobyl: Prohibited Truth, 1994; Chernobyl: Top Secret (non-fiction), 1992; Testimony of Zenon Matkiwsky, M.D. President of the Children of Chornobyl Relief Fund before the Subcommittee on Nuclear Safety, Senate Committee on the Environment and Public Works: July 22, 1992, 1992; Chernobyl, the Forbidden Truth, 1994, 2nd ed., 1995; Philosophy of Nuclear Security, 1997; Kremlin Kiss (novel), 2 vols., 2001; The Opposite Door (stories), 2002; Chernobyl' 20 let spustia: prestuplenie bez nakazaniia, 2006; Zhytomyrs kyi proryv: spetsvypusk chasopysu svitlo spilkuvannia, 2009. CO-AUTHOR: Earth is Alarmed (nonfiction), 1990; (and ed.) Nuclear Encyclopedia, 1996; Dimensions of Sustainability, 1997; Human Dimension of Nuclear Security, 1998; Vanunu and the Bomb, 1998; New Security Concerns and Approaches, 1998; Ambiente e cultura, 1999; Time for Changing, Time for Hopes, 1999; Chernobyl 20 Years Later: Crime without Punishment, 2006. Die grosse Lüge-Tschernobyl 20 Jahre danach, 2006; Chernobyl: Crime Without Punishment, 2011. Contributor to periodicals. **Address:** Alla Yaroshinskaya Fund, Bersenevskaya Naberezkaya, 20/2, Moscow, 103790, Russia. **Online address:** ayaro@mail.domonet.ru

YARROW, Andrew. American (born United States), b. 1957. **Genres:** Economics. **Career:** Public Agenda (think tank), vice president and director; American University, adjunct professor of history; New York Times, reporter; U.S. Department of Labor, speech writer; Brookings Institution, Economic Studies Program, Outreach for Special Projects, director; Export-Import Bank of the United States, staff; U.S. Department of Education, straff; United Nations Children's Fund (UNICEF), staff; National Endowment for the Arts, staff; World Bank. **Publications:** Latecomers: Children of Parents over 35, 1991; Forgive Us Our Debts: The Intergenerational Dangers of Fiscal Irresponsibility, 2008; Measuring America: How Economic Growth Came to Define American Greatness in the Late Twentieth Century, 2010. Contributor to journals, newspapers and magazines. **Online address:** yarrow@american.edu

YARSHATER, Ehsan (Ollah). American/Iranian (born Iran), b. 1920. **Genres:** Area Studies, International Relations/Current Affairs, Language/Linguistics. **Career:** University of Teheran, associate professor, professor of old Persian and Avestan, 1953-60; Royal Institute for Translation and Publication, director, 1953-61; UNESCO, Council of Philosophy and Humanistic Sciences, secretary, 1954-58; Columbia University, visiting associate professor of Indo-Iranian, 1958-60, Hagop Kevorkian professor of Iranian studies, 1961, Hagop Kevorkian professor emeritus of Iranian studies, Hagop Kevorkian chair, 1961-, Department of Middle East Languages and Cultures, chair, 1967-73, Center for Iranian Studies, founding director, 1968-; Persian Heritage Series, editor, 1962-; Rahnema-ye Ketab, Literary and Book Review Journal, founding editor, 1975-79; Institute of Central and West Asian Studies, honorary fellow, 1990-; Encyclopedia Iranica, editor. **Publications:** Shir-i Fārsīdar ahd-i Shāhrukh (nīmah-i avval-i qarn-inuhum), yā, āghāz-i inhòitòàtò dar Panj ris Fārsī, trans. as Persian Poetry Under Shah-Rukh: The Second Half of the Fifteenth Century, 1955; Dāstānhā-yi īrān-ibāstān, trans. as Old Iranian Myths and Legends, 1957; Dāstānhā-yi Shāhnām, trans. as Legends of the Epic of Kings, 1957, 4th ed., 1982; al-Asātòīr al-Irānīyahal-qadīmah, 1965; A Grammar of Southern Tati Dialects, 1969; Dānishnāmah-i īraMCNn va Islām, 1976; Iranica Varia: Papers In Honor of Professor Ehsan Yarshater, 1990; (co-author) Azarī, yā, Zabān-i bāstān-i Azarbāygān, 1993; Lion and the Throne, 1998; Dāstānhā-yi īrān-i bāstān, 2000. EDITOR: Tarjumah-iFārsī-i Ishārāt va tanbīhāt, 1954; Panj risālah, 1954; Iran Faces the Seventies, 1971; Sadeq Hedayat: An Anthology, 1971; (with D. Bivar) The Inscriptions of Eastern Mazandaran, 1979; (with R. Ettinghausen) Highlights of Persian Art, 1981; Encyclopedia Iranica, 1981; Cambridge History of Iran, vol. III, 1982; Encyclopædia Iranica, 1983; Persian Literature, 1988; History of Medicine in Iran, 2004; Mystical Poems of Rumi, 2009. Contributor of articles to journals. **Address:** Center for Iranian Studies, 450 Riverside Dr., Ste. 24, New York, NY 10027, U.S.A. **Online address:** ey4@columbia.edu

YARWOOD, Doreen. British (born England), b. 1918. **Genres:** Homes/Gardens, Architecture, Fash Ion/Costume, Antiques/Furnishings, Biography, Art/Art History. **Career:** Educator, 1945-48; freelance writer and artist, 1949-; University of Sussex, Extra-mural Courses, lecturer; NADFAS, lecturer and chairman. **Publications:** English Costume from the Second Century B. C. to 1952, with Introductory Chapters on the Ancient Civilizations, 1953, 5th ed., 1979; The English Home, a Thousand Years of Furnishing and Decoration, 1956; The Architecture of England, 1963; Outline of English Architecture, 1965, new ed., 1977; English Houses, 1966; Architecture of England: From Prehistoric Times to the Present Day, 1967; Outline of English Costume, 1967, 4th ed., 1977; The Architecture of Italy, 1970; Robert Adam, 1970; The Architecture of Europe, 1974, 3rd ed., 1987; European Costume: 4000 Years of Fashion, 1975; The Architecture of Britain, 1976, 3rd ed., 1980; The Encyclopedia of World Costume, 1978, 3rd ed., 1988; The Encyclopaedia of World Costume, 1978; The English Home, rev. ed., 1979; Costume of the Western World: Pictorial Guide and Glossary, 1980; The British Kitchen: Housewifery since Roman Times, 1981; Five Hundred Years of Technology in the Home, 1983; English Interiors, 1984; Encyclopaedia of Architecture, 1985; Encyclopedia of Architecture, 1986; A Chronology of Western Architecture, 1987; Science and the Home, 1987; The Architecture of Europe: 19th and 20th Centuries, 1991; Fashion in the Western World: 1500-1990, 1992; The Architecture of Europe: Classical Architecture, 1420-1800, 1992; (contrib.) International Dictionary of Architects and Architecture, 1993; Illustrated Encyclopedia of World Costume, 2011. Contributor to books and journals. **Address:** Flat 2 Forest Lodge, Portland Rd., East Grinstead, WS RH19 4EZ, England.

YATES, Dwight. American (born United States), b. 1942?. **Genres:** Young Adult Fiction, Novels. **Career:** Tabora Boys School, instructor, 1965-67; University of Montana, graduate assistant, 1967-70, instructor, 1970-72; University of Arizona, graduate assistant and associate in teaching, 1972-79,

McKale Writing Clinic, director, 1979-80; University of California, lecturer, 1981-; University of Redlands, adjunct faculty, 1987. Writer. **Publications:** (Ed. with N. Carrick) A Student's Guide to Freshman Composition, 1980; Haywire Hearts and Slide Trombones, 2005; Bring Everybody: Stories, 2006. Contributor to periodicals. **Address:** Department of Creative Writing, University of California, ARTS 121, 900 University Ave., Riverside, CA 92521, U.S.A. **Online address:** dyates@ucr.edu

YATES, Jean. American (born United States), b. 1951. **Genres:** Fash Ion/Costume. **Career:** Author. **Publications:** Links: Inspired Bead and Wire Jewelry Creations, 2008. **Address:** Westchester County, NY , U.S.A. **Online address:** jean@prettykittydogmoonjewelry.com

YATES, Nigel. *See* Obituaries.

YAZDANFAR, Farzin. American/Iranian (born Iran), b. 1953. **Genres:** Novellas/Short Stories, Literary Criticism And History, Women's Studies And Issues, Translations. **Career:** Richard J. Daley College, instructor in English as a second language, 1986-; University of Chicago, Persian bibliographer, 1994-96. Writer. **Publications:** Stories from Iran: A Chicago Anthology 1921-1991, 1991; The Downhearted: A Collection of Eighteen Short Stories, 1999; EDITOR: (with J. Green) Walnut Sapling on Masih's Grave, and Other Stories by Iranian Women, 1993; (trans. and intro.) In a Voice of Their Own: A Collection of Stories by Iranian Women Written since the Revolution of 1979, 1996; (trans.) Marxism and Literary Criticism, 1997; (comp. and trans.) Loneliness, the Thin Skin of Porcelain: A Collection of Fourteen Short Stories, 2003; Chīnī-i nāzuk-i tanhāī, 2003; Contributor to periodicals. **Address:** Adult Education Program, Richard J. Daley College, 7500 S Pulaski Rd., Chicago, IL 60652, U.S.A. **Online address:** farzin1953@netzero.net

YE, Sang. *See* SHEN, Dajun.

YE, Ting-Xing. Canadian/Chinese (born China), b. 1952. **Genres:** Children's Fiction, Young Adult Fiction, Young Adult Non-fiction, Picture/Board Books, History, Children's Non-fiction. **Career:** Da Feng Labor Camp, staff, 1968-74; Municipality of Shanghai, Foreign Affairs Office, English translator, 1978-87; Canadian Manufacturers' Association, Canadian Trade Index, assistant editor, 1990-92; Harriett Todd Public School, library secretary, 1993-95; freelance writer and translator, 1995-. **Publications:** Three Monks, No Water, 1997; A Leaf in the Bitter Wind: A Memoir, 1997, 2nd ed., 1999; Weighing the Elephant, 1998; Share the Sky, 1999; White Lily, 2000; (with W. Bell) Throwaway Daughter: A Novel, 2003; My Name is Number Four, 2007; Mountain Girl, River Girl, 2008; The Chinese Thought of It, 2009. **Address:** Annick Press, 15 Patricia Ave., Toronto, ON M2M 1H9, Canada. **Online address:** greenleaf@orillia.org

YEAGER, Peter C(leary). American (born United States), b. 1949. **Genres:** Sociology, Law, Criminology/True Crime, Institutions/Organizations, Ethics, Business/Trade/Industry, Social Sciences. **Career:** Sun Newspapers, reporter, 1971-72; Yale University, lecturer to assistant professor of sociology, 1979-82; Boston University, assistant professor, associate professor of sociology, 1982-; Harvard University, ethics fellow, 1989-90. Writer. **Publications:** (Co-author) Illegal Corporate Behavior, 1979; (with M.B. Clinard) Corporate Crime, 1980; The Limits of Law: The Public Regulation of Private Pollution, 1991. **Address:** Department of Sociology, Boston University, 96-100 Cummington St., Boston, MA 02215, U.S.A. **Online address:** pcyeager@bu.edu

YEARGERS, Edward K. American (born United States), b. 1938. **Genres:** Biology, Sciences, How-to Books. **Career:** Georgia Institute of Technology, associate professor, professor of biology, 1968-, now emeritus. Writer. **Publications:** Basic Biophysics for Biology, 1992; (with R.W. Shonkwiler and J.V. Herod) An Introduction to the Mathematics of Biology: With Computer Algebra Models, 1996. **Address:** School of Biology, Georgia Institute of Technology, 310 Ferst Dr., Atlanta, GA 30332-0001, U.S.A.

YEATS, Robert S(heppard). American (born United States), b. 1931. **Genres:** Earth Sciences, Natural History. **Career:** Shell Oil Co., engineer, senior staff geologist, 1958-67; Ohio University, associate professor, 1967-70, professor of geology, 1970-77; Oregon State University, professor of geosciences, 1977-97, professor of oceanography, 1991-97, Richard H. Jahns distinguished lecturer In engineering geology, 1995, professor emeritus, 1997-, department chair, 1977-85; International Lithosphere Program, chair of working group 1, 1987-90; U.S. Geological Survey, geologist, 1968, 1969, 1975;

Glomar Challenger, scientist, 1971, chief scientist, 1973-74, 1978; Geological Survey of Japan, visiting scientist, 1992; Institut de Physique du Globe de Paris, physicien associé, 1993; Earth Consultants Intl., senior consultant, 1997-, partner, 2001-; Institute of Geological and Nuclear Sciences, visiting scientist, 1999; International Commission of Scientific Unions, Task Group on Present Earth Deformation and Paleoseismology, chairman. Writer. **Publications:** (With K. Sieh and C.R. Allen) The Geology of Earthquakes, 1997; Living with Earthquakes in the Pacific Northwest, 1998, 2nd ed., 2004; Living with Earthquakes in California: A Survivor's Guide, 2001. Contributor to journals. **Address:** Department of Geosciences, Oregon State University, 244 Wilkinson Hall, Corvallis, OR 97331-5506, U.S.A. **Online address:** yeatsr@geo.oregonstate.edu

YEE, Shirley J. American (born United States), b. 1959. **Genres:** Women's Studies And Issues, Cultural/Ethnic Topics, Social Sciences. **Career:** Indiana-Purdue University, visiting assistant professor, 1987-88; University of Washington, Department of Women Studies, assistant professor, 1988-94, associate professor, 1994-, chair, 1995-2001, Department of American Ethnic Studies, adjunct associate professor, Department of History, adjunct associate professor. Writer. **Publications:** Black Women Abolitionists: A Study in Activism, 1828-1860, 1992; An Immigrant Neighborhood, 2011. Works appear in anthologies. **Address:** Department of Women Studies, University of Washington, Rm. B110, Padelford Hall, PO Box 354345, Seattle, WA 98195-4345, U.S.A. **Online address:** sjyee@u.washington.edu

YEGÜL, Fikret K. American/Turkish (born Turkey), b. 1942. **Genres:** Archaeology/Antiquities, Architecture. **Career:** Wellesley College, assistant professor of art history, 1975-76; University of California, Department of Art History, assistant professor, 1976-82, associate professor, 1983-88, chairperson, 1987-93, professor, 1988-; Bilkent University, visiting professor, 1993-94. Writer. **Publications:** The Roman Bath Gymnasium Complex at Sardis, 1986; Gentlemen of Instinct and Breeding: Architecture at the American Academy in Rome, 1894-1940, 1991; (ed.) Vitruvius ve Mimarlik Uzerine On Kitap, 1991; Baths and Bathing in Classical Antiquity, 1992; (co-author) The City of Sardis: Approaches in Graphic Recording, 2003; Antik Cag'da Hamamlar ve Yikanma, 2006; Bathing in the Roman World, 2010. Contributor to journals. **Address:** Department of the History of Art and Architecture, University of California, 2814 Ellison Hall, Santa Barbara, CA 93106-7080, U.S.A. **Online address:** yegul@arthistory.ucsb.edu

YEH, Catherine Vance. American (born United States) **Genres:** Cultural/Ethnic Topics, Social Sciences, Women's Studies And Issues. **Career:** Harvard University, Department of East Asian Languages and Civilizations, lecturer in Chinese literature, 1990-91; University of Heidelberg, Institute of Chinese Studies, research associate, 1994-; Meiji University, visiting professor, 1998-99; Boston University, Department of Modern Languages and Comparative Literature, visiting professor, 2005-06, associate professor of Chinese, 2006-, Department of Foreign Language and Literature, Chinese language and Literature Section, head. Writer. **Publications:** Shanghai Love: Courtesans, Intellectuals and Entertainment Culture, 1850-1910, 2006; (ed. with D. Croissant and J.S. Mostow) Performing Nation: Gender Politics in Literature, Theater and the Visual Arts of China and Japan, 1880-1940, 2008. **Address:** Boston University, Rm. 201D, 712 Commonwealth Ave., Boston, MA 02138, U.S.A. **Online address:** yeh@bu.edu

YEIDE, Harry. American (born United States), b. 1960. **Genres:** History, Military/Defense/Arms Control, Biography. **Career:** U.S. Federal Government, foreign affairs analyst. Writer. **Publications:** Steel Victory: The Heroic Story of America's Independent Tank Battalions at War in Europe, 2003; The Tank Killers: A History of America's World War II Tank Destroyer Force, 2004; The Longest Battle: September 1944 to February 1945, from Aachen to the Roer and Across, 2005; Weapons of the Tankers: American Armor in World War II, 2006; (with M. Stout) First to the Rhine: The 6th Army Group in World War II, 2007; Steeds of Steel: A History of American Mechanized Cavalry in World War II, 2008; Infantry's Armor: The U.S. Army's Separate Tank Battalions in World War II, 2010; Fighting Patton: George S. Patton Jr. Through the Eyes of His Enemies, 2011. **Address:** Stackpole Books, 5067 Ritter Rd., Mechanicsburg, PA 17055-6921, U.S.A. **Online address:** yeide@gwu.edu

YEKELCHYK, Serhy. Canadian (born Canada), b. 1966. **Genres:** History. **Career:** University of Michigan, postdoctoral fellow and visiting assistant professor, 2000-01; University of Victoria, Department of Germanic and Slavic Studies, associate professor of Slavic studies and chair, 2001-. Writer. **Publications:** Stalin's Empire of Memory: Russian-Ukrainian Relations in the Soviet Historical Imagination, 2004; Ukraine: Birth of a Modern Nation, 2007; (ed. with O. Schmidtke) Europe's Last Frontier? Belarus, Moldova and Ukraine between Russia and the European Union, 2008. **Address:** University of Victoria, Rm. D243, Clearihue Bldg., PO Box 3045, Victoria, BC V8W 3P4, Canada. **Online address:** serhy@uvic.ca

YELLIN, Emily. American (born United States), b. 1961?. **Genres:** Adult Non-fiction, Business/Trade/Industry, Politics/Government, Sciences. **Career:** Journalist. **Publications:** Our Mothers' War: American Women at Home and at the Front during World War II, 2004; Your Call Is (Not That) Important to Us: Customer Service and What It Reveals About Our World and Our Lives, 2009. Contributor to periodicals. **Address:** c/o Nicole Kalian Abbott, Free Press, Simon & Schuster, 1230 Ave. of the Americas, New York, NY 10020, U.S.A. **Online address:** emily@emilyyellin.com

YEN, Ching-hwang. Chinese (born China), b. 1937. **Genres:** History, Politics/Government. **Career:** Nanyang University, tutor in history, 1963-65, Centre for Chinese Language and Culture, Tan Lark Sye professor, 2000; University of Adelaide, lecturer in history, 1968-76, senior lecturer, 1976-86, reader, 1987-88, reader and associate professor, in history, 1991-2002, School of History and Politics, adjunct associate professor and reader; University of Hong Kong, chair professor of history and department head, 1988-90; Chinese Association of South Australia, president and vice-president. Writer. **Publications:** The Overseas Chinese and the 1911 Revolution: With Special Reference to Singapore and Malaya, 1976; Coolies and Mandarins: China's Protection of Overseas Chinese during the Late Ch'ing Period, 1985; A Social History of the Chinese in Singapore and Malaya, 1800-1911, 1986; (ed. and contrib.) Ethnic Chinese Abroad: A Special Issue of Asian Culture, 1990; Studies in Overseas Chinese History, 1992; Studies in Modern Overseas Chinese History, 1995; Community and Politics: Chinese in Colonial Singapore and Malaysia, 1995; The Ethnic Chinese in Eastern Southeast Asia, 2002. **Address:** Department of History, University of Adelaide, 5 08, Napier Bldg., Adelaide, SA 5005, Australia. **Online address:** chinghwang.yen@adelaide.edu.au

YENAWINE, Philip. American (born United States), b. 1942. **Genres:** Art/Art History, Photography. **Career:** Metropolitan Development Association, assistant, 1963-65; New York State Council on the Arts, program associate (visual arts), 1965-68; Metropolitan Museum of Art, High School Exhibition Service, coordinator, 1969-70, Department of High School Programs, associate museum educator-in-charge, 1970-74; South Street Seaport Museum, Museum Programs, director, 1974-76; University of Illinois, visiting faculty in art education, 1976-77; Chicago Consortium of Colleges and Universities, MA Program in Interrelated Arts, instructor, 1976-77; Museum of Contemporary Art, director of education, 1977-78; Aspen Art Museum, director, 1978-82; Aspen Co., curatorial consultant, 1982-83; Museum of Modern Art, director of education, 1983-93; Institute of Contemporary Art, visiting curator, 1992-94; lecturer, writer and consultant, 1992-; Massachusetts College of Art, visiting professor, 1993-94; Development through Art, partner, 1994-97; Visual Understanding in Education, co-founding director, 1997-. Writer. **Publications:** FOR CHILDREN: How to Show Grown-ups the Museum, 1986; Colors, 1991, 3rd ed., 2006; Lines, 1991, 3rd ed., 2006; Shapes, 1991, 2nd ed., 2006; Stories, 1991, 2nd ed., 2006; People, 1993; Places, 1993. OTHERS: Inheriting the Theory: New Voices and Multiple Perspectives on DBAE, 1990; How to Look at Modern Art, 1991; (with A. Housen and N.L. Miller) Reports on Audience Research, 1981-1993, 1994; Key Art Terms for Beginners, 1995; (with A. Housen) Visual Thinking Strategies Starter Lessons, 1998; (ed. with B. Wallis and M. Weems) Art Matters: How the Culture Wars Changed America, 1999; (with A. Housen) VTS Basic Manual, 2000; (intro.) John Kelly, 2001. Contributor to periodicals. **Address:** 959 W Kensington Rd., Los Angeles, CA 90026-4313, U.S.A. **Online address:** pyenawine@vue.org

YENNE, Bill. American (born United States), b. 1949. **Genres:** History, Air/Space Topics, Transportation, Picture/Board Books, Military/Defense/Arms Control, Travel/Exploration, Ghost Writer. **Career:** American Graphic Systems Inc. (AGS BookWorks), founder and president, 1983-. Writer and photographer. **Publications:** The History of the US Air Force, 1984; S.A.C.: A Primer of Modern Strategic Airpower, 1985; McDonnell Douglas: A Tale of Two Giants, 1985; Southern Pacific, 1985; The Encyclopedia of North American Indian Tribes: A Comprehensive Study of Tribes from the Abitibi to the Zuni, 1986; Atlas of the Solar System, 1987; Lockheed, 1987; U.S. Air Power, 1989; Black '41: The West Point Class of 1941 and the American Triumph in

World War II, 1991; Into the Sunset: The Convair Story, 1995; Legends of Flight: With the National Aviation Hall of Fame, 1997; San Francisco Then and Now, 1998; The Field Guide to Elvis Shrines, 1999; Lost Treasure: A Guide to Buried Riches, 1999; Inside Boeing: Building the 777, 2002; (with J.G. Real) The Asylum of Howard Hughes, 2003; The American Brewery, 2003; Secret Weapons of World War II, 2003; San Francisco's Noe Valley, 2004; Attack of the Drones: A History of Unmanned Aerial Combat, 2004; A Damned Fine War (novel), 2004; Great American Beers: Twelve Brands That Became Icons, 2004; The Missions of California, 2004; Operation Cobra and the Great Offensive: Sixty Days That Changed the Course of World War II, 2004; Indian Wars: The Campaign for the American West, 2005; Atlas of North American Railroads, 2005; Great Northern Empire Builder, 2005; The Story of the Boeing Company, 2005, rev. ed., 2010; On the Trail of Lewis and Clark: Yesterday and Today, 2005; Santa Fe Chiefs, 2005; Secret Weapons of the Cold War, 2005; The American Aircraft Factory in World War II, 2006; B 17 at War, 2006; Glacier National Park, 2006; (with C.E. LeMay) Superfortress: The Story of the B 29 and American Air Power in World War II, 2006; Raptor Force: 2006; Holy Fire, 2007; Raptor Force: Corkscrew, 2007; Guinness: The 250 Year Quest for the Perfect Pint, 2007; Rising Sons: The Japanese American GIs Who Fought for the United States in World War II, 2007; (with C. Rosica) The Authentic Brand, 2007; The Evergreen Story, 2008; Sitting Bull, 2008; Tommy Gun: How General Thompson's Submachine Gun Wrote History, 2009; Convair Deltas, 2009; Aces High: The Historic Saga of the Two Top-Scoring American Aces of WWII, 2009; Hitler's Master of the Dark Arts, 2010; Birds of Prey: Predators, Reapers and America's Newest UAVs, 2010; Alexander the Great, 2010. Address: American Graphic Systems Inc., PO Box 460313, San Francisco, CA 94146-0313, U.S.A. Online address: bill_yenne@sbcglobal.net

YEP, Laurence (Michael). American (born United States), b. 1948. Genres: Science Fiction/Fantasy, Children's Fiction, Young Adult Fiction, Novellas/Short Stories, Young Adult Non-fiction, Picture/Board Books, Novels, Adult Non-fiction, Adult Non-fiction. Career: Foothill College, part-time instructor of English, 1975; San Jose City College, part-time instructor in English, 1975-76; Spinnaker, writer, 1985; Alice in Wonderland, writer, 1985; Jungle Book, writer, 1986; University of California-Berkeley, visiting lecturer in Asian-American studies, 1987-89; University of California-Santa Barbara, writer-in-residence, 1990. Publications: FOR CHILDREN AND YOUNG ADULTS: Sweetwater (juvenile science fiction), 1973; Dragon of the Lost Sea, 1982; Kind Hearts and Gentle Monsters, 1982; The Mark Twain Murders, 1982; Liar, Liar, 1983; The Tom Sawyer Fires, 1984; Dragon Steel, 1985; The Curse of the Squirrel, 1987; Pay the Chinaman, 1987; The Rainbow People, 1989; Dragon Cauldron, 1991; The Star Fisher, 1991; The Lost Garden, 1991; Tongues of Jade, 1991; Dragon War, 1992; The Shell Woman and the King, 1993; (ed.) American Dragons: Twenty-five Asian American Voices, 1993; The Butterfly Boy, 1993; The Man Who Tricked a Ghost, 1993; The Boy Who Swallowed Snakes, 1994; The Tiger Woman, 1994; Foxfire, 1994; The Ghost Fox, 1994; The Junior Thunder Lord, 1994; The Thief of Hearts, 1995; Hiroshima: A Novella, 1995; Later, Gator, 1995; The City of Dragons, 1995; Tree of Dreams: Ten Tales from the Garden of Night, 1995; Ribbons, 1996; The Khan's Daughter: A Mongolian Folktale, 1997; The Dragon Prince: A Chinese Beauty and the Beast Tale, 1997; The Cook's Family, 1998; The Imp That Ate My Homework, 1998; The Amah, 1999; Cockroach Cooties, 2000; Dream Soul, 2000; The Journal of Wong Ming-Chung: A Chinese Miner: California, 1852, 2000; The Magic Paintbrush, 2000; Angelfish, 2001; Lady Ch'iao Kuo: Warrior of the South, 2001; Lady of Ch'iao Kuo: Warrior of the South, 2001; When the Circus Came to Town, 2002; Spring Pearl: The Last Flower, 2002; Skunk Scout, 2003; The Earth Dragon Awakes: The San Francisco Earthquake of 1906, 2006; (with K.S. Yep) Angel Island: Conversations with My Father, 2008; Bravo, Mia!: Girl of the Year, 2008; Mia, 2008; (with K.S. Yep) The Dragon's Child: A Story of Angel Island, 2008; Auntie Tiger, 2009; City of Fire, 2009; The Star Maker, 2011; City of Ice, 2011. GOLDEN MOUNTAIN CHRONICLES FOR CHILDREN: Dragonwings, 1975; Child of the Owl, 1977; Sea Glass, 1979; The Serpent's Children, 1984; Mountain Light, 1985; Dragon's Gate, 1993; The Traitor, 2003; Dragon Road, 2008. CHINATOWN MYSTERY SERIES FOR CHILDREN: The Case of the Goblin Pearls, 1997; The Case of the Lion Dance, 1998; The Case of the Firecrackers, 1999. TIGER'S APPRENTICE SERIES FOR CHILDREN: The Tiger's Apprentice, 2003; Tiger's Blood, 2005; Tiger Magic, 2006. FOR ADULTS: Seademons, 1977; Shadow Lord, 1985; Monster Makers, Inc., 1986. OTHER: Dragons of Silk, 2011. Works appear in anthologies. Address: Maureen Walters, Curtis Brown Ltd., 10 Astor Pl., New York, NY 10003-6935, U.S.A.

YERMAKOV, Nicholas Valentin. See HAWKE, Simon.

YERXA, Donald A(llan). American (born United States), b. 1950. Genres: History. Career: Eastern Nazarene College, instructor of history, 1977-80, assistant professor of history, 1980-83, associate professor of history and director of admissions, 1983-88, professor of history, 1990-2009, professor emeritus, 2009-; Boston University, The Historical Society, assistant director, 2001-08, director, 2009-11, Religion and Innovation Grants Program, director, 2011-, Historically Speaking, editor, 2001-08, senior editor, 2009-; Fides et Historia, editor, 2011-. Publications: The Burning of Falmouth, 1775: A Case Study in British Imperial Pacification, 1975; Admirals and Empire: The United States Navy and the Caribbean, 1991; (with K.W. Giberson) Species of Origins: America's Search for a Creation Story, 2002; (ed.) Recent Themes in Military History, 2008; (ed.) Recent Themes in Historical Thinking, 2008; (ed.) Recent Themes in the History of Africa and the Atlantic World, 2008; (ed.) Recent Themes in Early American History, 2008; (ed.) Recent Themes in World History and the History of the West, 2009; (ed.) Recent Themes on Historians and the Public, 2009; (ed.) Recent Themes at the Interface of Science, Religion and History, 2009; (ed.) British Abolitionism and the Question of Moral Progress, 2012. Contributor to journals. Address: Boston University, The Historical Society, 656 Beacon St., Mezzanine, Boston, MA 02215, U.S.A. Online address: yerxad@bu.edu

YESALIS, Charles E(dward). American (born United States), b. 1946. Genres: Medicine/Health, Sports/Fitness. Career: University of Michigan School of Public Health, tutor in epidemiology and statistics, 1970-71; John Hopkins University, instructor in health care organization, 1975-76, Health Services Research and Development Center, research associate, 1975-76, senior research associate, 1976; University of Iowa, assistant professor of epidemiology, 1976-81, associate professor, 1981-86; Pennsylvania State University, professor of exercise and sport science and of health policy and administration, 1986-2006, professor emeritus of health policy and administration and kinesiology, 2006-, Department of Communications Disorders, acting head, 1993-94, Writer. Publications: (With G.J. Norwood and D. Lipson) Capitation for Pharmacy Services, 1982; (with V.S. Cowart) The Steroids Game, 1998; (with R.M. politzer and H.D. Holt) U.S. Health Care Simplified: Principles and Perspectives, 2012. EDITOR AND CONTRIBUTOR: Anabolic Steroids in Sport and Exercise, 1993, 2nd ed., 2000; (with M.S. Bahrke) Performance Enhancing Substances in Sport & Exercise, 2002. Contributor to magazines. Address: Department of Health Policy and Administration, Pennsylvania State University, 604 Ford Bldg., University Park, PA 16802-4705, U.S.A. Online address: cey2@psu.edu

YEUNG, Henry Wai-Chung. Singaporean/Chinese (born China), b. 1968. Genres: Business/Trade/Industry. Career: National University of Singapore, assistant professor, 1996-99, associate professor, 2000-05, professor of economic geography, 2005-, East Asia Institute research associate, 2000; Royal Geographic Society, fellow; Henan University, adjunct professor; Institute of Geographical Sciences and Natural Resources Research, Chinese Academy of Sciences, adjunct professor; University of Manchester, Commonwealth fellow, 2002; University of Washington, Fulbright foreign researcher, 2003; Kitakyushu International Center for the Study of East Asian Economies, visiting researcher, 2006; University of Auckland, distinguished visitor, 2006; University of Hong Kong, visiting professor, 2006; University of Manchester, School of Environment and Development, honorary professorial fellow, 2007-10. Academic, geographer and writer. Publications: Transnational Corporations and Business Networks: Hong Kong Firms in the ASEAN Region, 1998; (ed.) The Globalization of Business Firms from Emerging Economies, 2 vols., 1999; Singapore's Global Reach: An Executive Report, 1999; Globalisation and the Asia-Pacific: Contested Territories, 1999; (with K. Olds) Globalization of Chinese Business Firms, 2000; Entrepreneurship and the Internationalisation of Asian Firms: An Institutional Perspective, 2002; (ed. with J. Peck) Remaking the Global Economy: Economic-Geographical Perspectives, 2003; Chinese Capitalism in a Global Era: Towards Hybrid Capitalism, 2004; (ed.) Handbook of Research on Asian Business, 2006; (with N.M. Coe and P.F. Kelly) Economic Geography: A Contemporary Introduction, 2007. Contributor to journals. Address: National University of Singapore, Department of Geography, 1 Arts Link, Kent Ridge, 117570, Singapore. Online address: henryyeung@nus.edu.sg

YEZZI, David Dalton. American (born United States), b. 1966?. Genres: Poetry. Career: New Criterion, executive editor; Unterberg Poetry Center, director. Poet. Publications: The Hidden Model, 2003; Azores: Poems, 2008;

(ed.) The Swallow Anthology of New American Poets, 2009. Contributor to periodicals. **Address:** New Criterion, 900 Broadway, Ste. 602, New York, NY 10003, U.S.A.

YGLESIAS, Rafael. American (born United States), b. 1954. **Genres:** Novels, Plays/Screenplays, Young Adult Fiction, Literary Criticism And History. **Career:** Writer. **Publications:** Hide Fox and All After, 1972; The Work is Innocent, 1976; The Game Player, 1978; Hot Properties, 1986; Only Children, 1988; The Murderer Next Door, 1990; Fearless, 1993; Dr. Neruda's Cure for Evil, 1996; A Happy Marriage, 2009. **Address:** 18 E 12th St., New York, NY 10003, U.S.A. **Online address:** rjy2@mac.com

YIANNOPOULOS, A(thanassios) N. American/Greek (born Greece), b. 1928. **Genres:** Law, Civil Liberties/Human Rights. **Career:** Louisiana State University, Law School, research associate professor, 1958-62, professor of law and coordinator of law institute program and research, 1962-79; Ohio State University, Law School, visiting associate professor, 1959; Law Institute, reporter, 1962-; Tulane University, Law School, W. R. Irby professor of law, 1979-2007, Eason-Weinmann Center for Comparative Law, Eason-Weinmann professor of law and chair, 2007-08, professor emeritus, 2008-. Writer. **Publications:** (Co-author) American, Greek Private International Law, 1957; Negligence Clauses in Ocean Bills of Lading: Conflict of Laws and the Brussels Convention of 1924: A Comparative Study, 1962; Civil Law Property, 1962, 4th ed., 2001; (trans.) Aubry and Rau, Obligations, 1965; Civil Law in the Modern World, 1965; Civil Law of Property: The Law of Things, Real Rights and Real Actions, 1966, 4th ed., 2001; Personal Servitudes: Usufruct, Habitation and Rights of Use, 1968, 5th ed., 2011; Civil Law Property Coursebook: Louisiana Legislation, Jurisprudence and Doctrine, 1975, 9th ed., 2010; Louisiana Civil Law System, 1977, 2d ed. 1999; Predial Servitudes, 1983, 3d ed., 2004; (with T. Schoenbaum) Admiralty and Maritime Law: Cases and Materials, 1984; (ed.) Ocean Bills of Lading: Traditional Forms, Substitutes and EDI Systems, 1995; Louisiana Civil Treatise, vol. II, 1999, vol. III, 2000, vol. IV, 2001. **Address:** Admiralty Law Institute, Tulane University, Rm. 355-G, Weinmann Hall, 6329 Freret St., New Orleans, LA 70118-6231, U.S.A. **Online address:** ayianno@tulane.edu

YIFTACHEL, Oren. Israeli (born Israel), b. 1956. **Genres:** Politics/Government, Geography, History. **Career:** Planning Collaborative, planning assistant, 1983-84; Perth City Council, Planning Department, planning officer, 1984-86; Curtin University of Technology, lecturer, senior lecturer, 1987-93; Israel 2020 National Plan, planning consultant, 1991-93; Ben Gurion University of the Negev, faculty member, 1994-98, assistant professor, 1998-2004, professor, 2004-; University of Pennsylvania, Fulbright fellow, 1996-97; Royal Melbourne Institute of Technology, visiting fellow, 1997-; Hagar: Studies in Culture, Politics and Place, founding editor, 1999-2004; Management College, adjunct professor, 2000-06; Metropolitan Plan for Beer-Sheva, planning consultant, 2003; U.S. Institute of Peace, senior research fellow, 2003-04; University of California, visiting professor, 2004; Geography Research Forum, editor. **Publications:** The Role of Theory in Urban Planning: A Study of Metropolitan Planning in Perth, Western Australia, 1987; Planning a Mixed Region in Israel: The Political Geography of Arab-Jewish Relations in the Galilee, 1992; Ukhlusiyat Yisrael u- meafyeneha: netune yesod ve-tahaziyot le-tsorkhe tikhnun merhavi, 1993; (ed. with A. Meir) Ethnic Frontiers and Peripheries: Landscapes of Development and Inequality in Israel, 1996; Shomrim al ha-kerem mag'd el-kurum ke-mashal, 1997; (co-ed.) The Power of Planning: Spaces of Control and Transformation, 2001; Ethnocracy: Land and Identity Politics in Israel/Palestine, 2006. Contributor to books and periodicals. **Address:** Israel. **Online address:** yiftach@bgu.ac.il

YLVISAKER, Anne. (Anne E. Hanson). American (born United States), b. 1965. **Genres:** Children's Non-fiction, Novels. **Career:** Teacher and writer. **Publications:** Your Stomach, 2002; Your Muscles, 2002; Your Lungs, 2002; Dear Papa, 2002; Ice Storms, 2003; The Arctic Ocean, 2003; The Atlantic Ocean, 2003; Avalanches, 2003; Droughts, 2003; The Indian Ocean, 2003; The Pacific Ocean, 2003; Landslides, 2003; The Antarctic Ocean, 2003; Lake Erie, 2004; Lake Huron, 2004; Lake Superior, 2004; Lake Ontario, 2004; Lake Michigan, 2004; Lake Erie, 2004; Lake Huron, 2004; Little Klein, 2007; Luck of the Buttons, 2011. AS ANNE E. HANSON: Ambulances, 2001; Fire Engines, 2001; Fire Trucks in Action, 2012; Ambulances in Action, 2012. **Address:** c/o Anne Irza-Leggat, Candlewick Press Inc., 99 Dover St., Somerville, MA 02144, U.S.A. **Online address:** anne.irza-leggat@candlewick.com

YOCKEY, Hubert P(almer). American (born United States), b. 1916. **Genres:** Biology, Information Science/Computers, Travel/Exploration, Sciences. **Career:** University of California Radiation Laboratory, staff, 1942-44; Tennessee Eastman Corp., staff, 1944-46; North American Aviation Inc., staff, 1946-52; Convair, staff, 1952-53; Oak Ridge National Laboratory, assistant director of Health Physics Division, 1953-59; Aerojet-General Nucleonics, staff, 1959-62; Boy Scouts of America, cubmaster, 1962-64, scoutmaster, 1965-68, explorer post advisor, 1968-75; Hughes Research Laboratories, principal scientist, 1962-64; U.S. Army, supervisory nuclear engineer, GM-15, 1964-87. Writer, 1987-. **Publications:** (Ed. with R.P. Platzman and H. Quastler) Symposium on Information Theory in Biology, 1958; Information Theory and Molecular Biology, 1992; Information Theory, Evolution and the Origin of Life, 2005. Contributor books and journals. **Address:** 1507 Balmoral Dr., Bel Air, MD 21014-5638, U.S.A.

YODER, Edwin Milton. American (born United States), b. 1934. **Genres:** History, Essays, Biography. **Career:** Charlotte News, columnist and editorial writer, 1958-61; Greensboro Daily News, columnist and editorial writer, 1961-64, associate editor and editorial pages editor, 1965-75; University of North Carolina at Greensboro, assistant professor of history, 1964-65; Washington Star, editorial writer, editorial page editor, 1975-81; Washington Post Writers Group Syndicate, columnist, 1982-97; Washington and Lee University, professor of journalism and humanities, 1992-, now professor emeritus. **Publications:** The Unmaking of a Whig and Other Essays in Self-Definition, 1990; Night of the Old South Ball: And Other Essays and Fables, 1994; Joe Alsop's Cold War: A Study of Journalistic Influence and Intrigue, 1995; The Historical Present: Uses and Abuses of the Past, 1997; Telling Others What to Think: Recollections of a Pundit, 2004; Lions at Lamb House, 2007. **Address:** Department of Journalism and Mass Communications, Washington and Lee University, Reid Hall, 204 W Washington St., Lexington, LA 24450, U.S.A.

YODER, John C. American (born United States), b. 1942. **Genres:** History, Third World, Animals/Pets, Politics/Government. **Career:** Social Science Research Council, fellow, 1974-76; North Park College, assistant professor of politics, 1977-80; Whitworth College, Department of History and Politics, assistant professor, associate professor, 1980-89, professor, 1989-, Fulbright program adviser; Cuttington University College, Fulbright professor, 1987-88; University of Liberia, Fulbright professor, 1988; Daystar University, Fulbright lecturer, 1998, 2001. Writer. **Publications:** (Ed.) The Encyclopedia Africana Dictionary of African Biography, vol. II: Sierra Leone-Zaire, 1979; The Kanyok of Zaire: An Institutional and Ideological History to 1895, 1992; Popular Political Culture, Civil Society and State Crisis in Liberia, 2003. Works appear in anthologies. Contributor to periodicals and journals. **Address:** Department of History and Politics, Whitworth College, Weyerhaeuser Hall, 300 W Hawthorne Rd., Ste. 210J, Spokane, WA 99251, U.S.A. **Online address:** johnyoder@whitworth.edu

YOERG, Sonja I. American (born United States), b. 1959?. **Genres:** Zoology, Animals/Pets, Biology. **Career:** University of California, researcher, lecturer and project director of the captive breeding program; Museum of Vertebrate Zoology, researcher and lecturer; biological psychologist. Writer. **Publications:** Clever As a Fox: Animal Intelligence and What It Can Teach Us about Ourselves, 2001. Contributor to periodicals. **Address:** c/o Bloomsbury USA, 175 5th Ave., New York, NY 10010, U.S.A.

YOGGY, Gary A. American (born United States), b. 1938. **Genres:** Communications/Media, Essays, Humor/Satire. **Career:** Corning Community College, instructor, 1963-65, assistant professor, 1965-67, associate professor, 1967-83, director of continuing education, 1969-77, professor of history, 1983-2001, professor emeritus, 2001-; Steuben County Economic Opportunity Program, director, 1972-79, president, 1973-79; Boces Board of Education, president, 1977-79; Elmira Psychiatric Center, president, 1987; Elmira Little Theatre, president, 1995-, director. Writer. **Publications:** Riding the Video Range: The Rise and Fall of the Western on Television, 1995; (ed.) Back in the Saddle: Essays on Western Film and Television Actors, 1998. Contributor to books. **Address:** Corning Community College, 1 Academic Dr., Corning, NY 14830-3297, U.S.A.

YOLEN, Jane. American (born United States), b. 1939. **Genres:** Novels, Novellas/Short Stories, Science Fiction/Fantasy, Children's Fiction, Young Adult Fiction, Poetry, Songs/Lyrics And Libretti, Children's Non-fiction, Children's Non-fiction, Food And Wine, History, Music, Mythology/Folklore, Photography, Sciences, Young Adult Non-fiction, Biography, Graphic Novels. **Career:**

Bridgeport Sunday Herald, cub reporter, 1957; Newsweek Magazine, intern, 1959; writer, 1960-; Saturday Review, production assistant, 1960-61; Gold Medal Books, assistant editor, 1961-62; Rutledge Books, associate editor, 1962-63; Alfred A. Knopf Inc., assistant juvenile editor, 1963-65; Jane Yolen Books, Harcourt Brace Jovanovich Imprint, editor, 1988-98. **Publications:** See This Little Line? (poetry), 1963; Pirates in Petticoats, 1963; The Witch Who Wasn't, 1964; Gwinellen, the Princess Who Could Not Sleep, 1965; The Emperor and the Kite, 1967; The Minstrel and the Mountain: A Tale of Peace, 1967; (with A. Huston) Trust a City Kid, 1966; Isabel's Noel, 1967; Greyling: A Picture Story from the Islands of Shetland, 1968; The Longest Name on the Block, 1968; World on a String: The Story of Kites, 1968; The Wizard of Washington Square, 1969; The In Way Investigators; Or, The Mystery at McCracken's Place, 1969; It All Depends, 1970; The Seventh Mandarin, 1970; Hobo Toad and the Motorcycle Gang, 1970; The Bird of Time, 1971; The Girl Who Loved the Wind, 1972; Friend: The Story of George Fox and the Quakers, 1972; (co-ed.) The Fireside Song Book of Birds and Beasts, 1972; The Wizard Islands, 1973; (comp. and intro.) Zoo, 2000: Twelve Stories of Science Fiction and Fantasy Beasts, 1973; Writing Books for Children, 1973, rev. ed., 1983; The Girl Who Cried Flowers and Other Tales, 1974; The Boy Who Had Wings, 1974; The Adventures of Eeka Mouse, 1974; The Rainbow Rider, 1974; The Magic Three of Solatia, 1974; Ring Out! A Book of Bells, 1974; The Little Spotted Fish, 1975; The Transfigured Hart, 1975; The Moon Ribbon and Other Tales, 1976; Milkweed Days, 1976; Simple Gifts: The Story of the Shakers, 1976; An Invitation to the Butterfly Ball: A Counting Rhyme (poetry), 1976; The Seeing Stick, 1977; The Sultan's Perfect Tree, 1977; The Hundredth Dove and Other Tales, 1977; Hannah Dreaming, 1977; The Lady and the Merman, 1977; The Giants' Farm, 1977; (comp.) Rounds about Rounds, 1977; The Simple Prince, 1978; No Bath Tonight, 1978; The Mermaid's Three Wisdoms, 1978; Spider Jane, 1978; (comp. and intro.) Shape Shifters: Fantasy and Science Fiction Tales about Humans Who Can Change Their Shape, 1978; The Giants Go Camping, 1979; Dream Weaver and Other Tales, 1979 as Dream Weaver, 1989; All in the Woodland Early: An ABC Book (poetry), 1979; Spider Jane on the Move, 1980; Mice on Ice, 1980; How Beastly! A Menagerie of Nonsense Poems (poetry), 1980; Dragon Night and Other Lullabies (poetry), 1980; Commander Toad in Space, 1980; The Robot and Rebecca: The Mystery of the Code-Carrying Kids, 1980; Sleeping Ugly, 1981; Uncle Lemon's Spring, 1981; Brothers of the Wind, 1981; The Boy Who Spoke Chimp, 1981; Shirlick Holmes and the Case of the Wandering Wardrobe, 1981; The Acorn Quest, 1981; The Robot and Rebecca and the Missing Owser, 1981; The Gift of Sarah Barker, 1981; Touch Magic: Fantasy, Faerie and Folklore in the Literature of Childhood, 1981; Dragons Blood, 1982, 2nd ed., 2004; Commander Toad and the Planet of the Grapes, 1982; Neptune Rising: Songs and Tales of the Undersea Folk, 1982; Merlin's Booke, 1982; Commander Toad and the Big Black Hole, 1983; Tales of Wonder, 1983; Cards of Grief, 1984; Children of the Wolf, 1984; Heart's Blood, 1984, 2nd ed., 2004; The Stone's Silenus, 1984; Dragonfield and Other Stories, 1985; Commander Toad and the Dis-Asteroid, 1985; (ed. with M.H. Greenberg and C.G. Waugh) Dragons and Dreams: A Collection of New Fantasy and Science Fiction Stories, 1986; (ed.) The Lullaby Songbook, 1986; Commander Toad and the Intergalactic Spy, 1986; Ring of Earth: A Child's Book of Seasons, 1986; (ed.) Favorite Folktales from Around the World, 1986; The Sleeping Beauty, 1986; Piggins, 1987; The Three Bears Rhyme Book, 1987; A Sending of Dragons, 1987, 2nd ed., 2004; Owl Moon, 1987; Commander Toad and the Space Pirates, 1987; (ed. with M.H. Greenberg and C.G. Waugh) Spaceships and Spells: A Collection of New Fantasy and Science-fiction Stories, 1987; Sister Light, Sister Dark, 1988; The Devil's Arithmetic, 1988; Picnic with Piggins, 1988; (ed. with M.H. Greenberg) Werewolves: A Collection of Original Stories, 1988; Piggins and the Royal Wedding, 1988; Dove Isabeau, 1989; (ed. with M.H. Greenberg) Things that Go Bump in the Night: A Collection of Original Stories, 1989; Best Witches: Poems for Halloween, 1989; (ed.) Lap-Time Song and Play Book, 1989; White Jenna, 1989; The Faery Flag: Stories and Poems of Fantasy and the Supernatural, 1989; Guide to Writing for Children, 1989; Sky Dogs, 1990; Bird Watch: A Book of Poetry, 1990; Baby Bear's Bedtime Book, 1990; Elfabet: An ABC of Elves, 1990; The Dragon's Boy, 1990; Dinosaur Dances, 1990; Tam Lin: An Old Ballad, 1990; All Those Secrets of the World, 1991; All in the Woodland Early: An ABC Book, 1991; (ed. with M.H. Greenberg) Vampires: A Collection of Original Stories, 1991; Pulphouse Science-fiction Short Stories, 1991; (ed.) 2041 AD: Twelve Stories about the Future by Top Science Fiction Writers, 1991; Hark! A Christmas Sampler, 1991; Wings, 1991; Wizard's Hall, 1991; Sword and the Stone, 1991; (ed. and intro.) Jane Yolen's Mother Goose Songbook, 1992; (ed.) Street Rhymes Around the World, 1992; Briar Rose, 1992; Eeny, Meeny, Miney Mole, 1992; Encounter, 1992; Letting Swift River Go, 1992; A Letter from Phoenix Farm, 1992; Storyteller, 1992; (ed. and intro.) Jane Yolen's Songs of Summer, 1993; Weather Report: Poems, 1993; Xanadu, 1993; (intro.) Cut From the Same Cloth: American Women of Myth, Legend and Tall Tale, 1993; Here There Be Dragons, 1993; Honkers, 1993; Mouse's Birthday, 1993; Raining Cats and Dogs, 1993; Welcome to the Green House, 1993; What Rhymes with Moon?, 1993; Hands, 1993; Travelers Rose, 1993; (ed.) Jane Yolen's Old MacDonald Songbook, 1994; (ed.) Sleep Rhymes Around the World, 1994; Xanadu 2, 1994; And Twelve Chinese Acrobats, 1994; Animal Fare: Poems, 1994; Beneath the Ghost Moon, 1994; Here There Be Unicorns, 1994; Grandad Bill's Song, 1994; Good Griselle, 1994; The Girl in the Golden Bower, 1994; Old Dame Counterpane, 1994; (ed. with M.H. Greenberg) The Haunted House: A Collection of Original Stories, 1995; (ed.) Camelot, 1995; Alphabestiary: Animal Poems From A to Z, 1995; (ed.) Xanadu 3, 1995; Among Angels: Poems, 1995; Ballad of the Pirate Queens, 1995; Before the Storm, 1995; Here There Be Witches, 1995; Merlin and the Dragons, 1995; A Sip of Aesop, 1995; The Three Bears Holiday Rhyme Book, 1995; Water Music: Poems for Children, 1995; The Wild Hunt, 1995; Sky Scrape, City Scape: Poems of City Life, 1996; Sing Noel: Christmas Carols, 1996; Mother Earth, Father Sky: Poems of Our Planet, 1996; Milk and Honey: A Year of Jewish Holidays, 1996; Musicians of Bremen: A Tale From Germany, 1996; O Jerusalem, 1996; Meet the Monsters, 1996; Little Mouse & Elephant: A Tale from Turkey, 1996; Hobby: The Young Merlin Trilogy, 1996; Here There Be Angels, 1996; Encuentro, 1996; Sea Watch: A Book of Poetry, 1996; Sacred Places, 1996; Passager: The Young Merlin Trilogy, Book One, 1996; Welcome to the Sea of Sand, 1996; Child of Faerie, Child of Earth, 1997; Books of Great Alta, 1997; Once Upon Ice and Other Frozen Poems, 1997; Nocturne, 1997; Miz Berlin Walks, 1997; Merlin: The Young Merlin Trilogy, Book Three, 1997; Twelve Impossible Things Before Breakfast: Stories, 1997; Sea Man, 1997; Once Upon a Bedtime Story: Classic Tales, 1997; Commander Toad and the Voyage Home, 1998; Book of Fairy Holidays, 1998; Armageddon Summer, 1998; Liars' Book, 1998; King Long Shanks, 1998; House, House, 1998; Here There Be Ghosts, 1998; Welcome to the Ice House, 1998; Tea With an Old Dragon: A Story of Sophia Smith, Founder of Smith College, 1998; Snow, Snow: Winter Poems for Children, 1998; Raising Yoder's Barn, 1998; Prince of Egypt, 1998; Pegasus, the Flying Horse, 1998; Originals, 1998; The One-armed Queen, 1998; Poetry Play Any Day with Jane Yolen, 1999; (ed.) Gray Heroes: Elder Tales from Around the World, 1999; (with H.E.Y. Stemple) Mary Celeste: An Unsolved Mystery from History, 1999; Moon Ball, 1999; Fairies' Ring: A Book of Fairy Stories & Poems, 1999; Wizard's Map, 1999; Pictish Child, 1999; Boots and the Seven Leaguers: A Rock-and-troll Novel, 2000; Color Me a Rhyme: Nature Poems for Young People, 2000; (ed.) Sherwood: Original Stories from the World of Robin Hood, 2000; (ed. and intro. with H.E.Y. Stemple) Mirror, Mirror: Forty Folktales for Mothers and Daughters to Share, 2000; Not One Damsel in Distress: World Folktales for Strong Girls, 2000; How Do Dinosaurs Say Goodnight?, 2000; Harvest Home, 2000; Off We Go!, 2000; (with R.J. Harris) Queen's Own Fool: A Novel of Mary Queen of Scots, 2000; Sister Emily's Lightship and Other Stories, 2000; Where Have the Unicorns Gone?, 2000; Touch Magic: Fantasy, Faerie & Folklore in the Literature of Childhood, 2000; Dear Mother, Dear Daughter: Poems for Young People, 2001; (with R.J. Harris) Odysseus in the Serpent Maze, 2001; Hurrying Child, 2001; (with S. Oppenheim) Fish Prince and Other Stories: Mermen Folk Tales, 2001; Welcome to the River of Grass, 2001; (with H.E.Y. Stemple) The Wolf Girls: An Unsolved Mystery from History, 2001; Bedtime For Bunny: A Book to Touch and Feel, 2002; Bagpiper's Ghost, 2002; Animal Train: A Lift-the-flap Concept Book, 2002; Horizons: Poems as Far as the Eye Can See, 2002; (with R.J. Harris) Hippolyta and the Curse of the Amazons, 2002; (with R.J. Harris) Girl in a Cage, 2002; Firebird, 2002; Time for Naps, 2002; Wild Wings: Poems for Young People, 2002; (with R.J. Harris) Atalanta and the Arcadian Beast, 2003; How Do Dinosaurs Get Well Soon?, 2003; Least Things: Poems About Small Natures, 2003; Mightier Than the Sword: World Folktales for Strong Boys, 2003; My Brothers' Flying Machine: Wilbur, Orville, and Me, 2003; Hoptoad, 2003; Flying Witch, 2003; (with H.E.Y. Stemple) Roanoke: The Lost Colony: An Unsolved Mystery from History, 2003; (with S. Oppenheim) The Sea King, 2003; Sword of the Rightful King: A Novel of King Arthur, 2003; Take Joy: A Book for Writers, 2003; (with H.E.Y. Stemple) Barefoot Book of Ballet Stories, 2004; Fine Feathered Friends: Poems for Young People, 2004; How Do Dinosaurs Clean Their Rooms?, 2004; How Do Dinosaurs Count to Ten?, 2004; Jason and the Gorgon's Blood, 2004; The Perfect Wizard: Hans Christian Andersen, 2004; (with R.J. Harris) Prince Across the Water, 2004; Count Me a Rhyme: Animal Poems by the Numbers, 2005; Baby Bear's Chairs, 2005; Apple for the Teacher: Thirty Songs for Singing While You Work, 2005; (ed. with P.N. Hayden) Years Best Science Fiction and Fantasy for Teens, 2005; (ed.) Trot, Trot to Boston: Lap Songs, Finger Plays, Clapping Games and Pantomime Rhymes, 2005; Meow: Cat Stories from Around the World, 2005; Grandma's Hurrying Child, 2005; Holding On to the Past, 2005; How Do Dinosaurs Eat Their Food?, 2005; Soft House, 2005; Pay the Piper, 2005; Dimity Duck, 2006; Baby Bear's Books, 2006; How Do Dinosaurs Play With Their Friends?, 2006; How Do Dinosaurs Learn Their Colors?, 2006; Fairy Tale Feasts: A Literary Cookbook for Young Readers and Eaters, 2006; Take Joy: A Writer's Guide to Loving the Craft, 2006; (with A. Stemple) Troll Bridge: A Rock 'n' Roll Fairy Tale, 2006; Baby Bear's Big Dreams, 2007; How do Dinosaurs Go To School?, 2007; (with R.J. Harris) Rogue's Apprentice, 2007; Shape Me a Rhyme: Nature's Forms in Poetry, 2007; (with H.E.Y. Stemple) Sleep, Black Bear, Sleep, 2007; Johnny Appleseed, 2008; Mama's Kiss, 2008; Sea Queens: Women Pirates Around the World, 2008; My Uncle Emily, 2009; Dragon's Heart, 2009; Mirror to Nature: Poems about Reflection, 2009; Scarecrow's Dance, 2009; (with H.E.Y. Stemple) The Barefoot Book of Dance Stories, 2009; Under the Star 2009; An Egret's Day, 2009; How Do Dinosaurs Say I Love You 2009; How Do Dinosaurs Learn Colours and Numbers?, 2009; Come to the Faeries' Ball, 2009; Hush, Little Horsie, 2010; Switching on the Moon: A Very First Book of Bedtime Poems, 2010; Good Night, Little Bunny, 2010; Foiled, 2010; My Father Knows the Names of Things, 2010; My Father Knows the Names of Things, 2010; (with M. Snyder) Except the Queen, 2010; How Do Dinosaurs Laugh Out Loud?, 2010; How Do Dinosaurs Love Their Cats?, 2010; How Do Dinosaurs Love Their Dogs?, 2010; Lost Boy: The Story of the Man Who Created Peter Pan, 2010; Elsie's Bird, Pig 2010; (with H.E.Y. Stemple) Not All Princesses Dress in Pink, 2010; All Star!: Honus Wagner and the Most Famous Baseball Card Ever, 2010; How Do Dinosaurs Play All Day?, 2011; (with J.P. Lewis) Self-portrait with Seven Fingers: The Life of Marc Chagall in Verse, 2011; Birds of a Feather, 2011; Day Tiger Rose Said Good-bye, 2011; Pretty Princess Pig, 2011; How Do Dinosaurs Say Happy Birthday?, 2011; Creepy Monsters, Sleepy Monsters, 2011; Bug Off!, 2012; Snow in Summer, 2011; How Do Dinosaurs Go Up and Down, 2011; Creepy Monsters, Sleepy Monsters, 2011; Sister Bear, 2011; Things to Say to a Dead Man, 2011; Waking Dragons, 2012; (with J.P. Lewis) Take Two, 2012; How Do Dinosaurs Eat Cookies?, 2012; How Dinosaurs Celebrate Christmas, 2012; How Do Dinosaurs Celebrate Chanukah, 2012; Curse of the Thirteenth Fey, 2012; (with H.E.Y. Stemple) Bad Girls, 2012; (with J.P. Lewis) Last Laughs: Animal Epitaphs, 2012. **Address:** c/o Elizabeth Harding, Curtis Brown Ltd., 10 Astor Pl., New York, NY 10003-6935, U.S.A. **Online address:** janeyolen@aol.com

YONG, Amos. American/Malaysian (born Malaysia), b. 1965. **Genres:** Theology/Religion. **Career:** Regent University, J. Rodman Williams professor of theology. Writer and theologian. **Publications:** (Ed.) Discerning the Spirit(s): A Pentecostal-Charismatic Contribution to Christian Theology of Religions, 2000; (ed.) Toward a Pneumatological Theology: Pentecostal and Ecumenical Perspectives on Ecclesiology, Soteriology, and Theology of Mission, 2002; Spirit-Word-Community: Theological Hermeneutics in Trinitarian Perspective, 2002; Beyond the Impasse: Toward a Pneumatological Theology of Religions, 2003; (ed. with P.G. Heltzel) Theology in Global Context: Essays in Honor of Robert Cummings Neville, 2004; The Spirit Poured Out on All Flesh: Pentecostalism and the Possibility of Global Theology, 2005; Theology and Down Syndrome: Reimagining Disability in Late Modernity, 2007; Hospitality and the Other: Pentecost, Christian Practices, and the Neighbor, 2008; (ed. with E. Alexander) Philip's Daughters: Women in Pentecostal-Charismatic Leadership, 2009; (ed. with J.K.A. Smith) Science and the Spirit: A Pentecostal Engagement with the Sciences, 2010; In the Days of Caesar: Pentecostalism and Political Theology: The Cadbury Lectures 2009, 2010; (ed. with B.B. Zikmund) Remembering Jamestown: Hard Questions about Christian Mission, 2010; (ed. with C. Clarke) Global Renewal, Religious Pluralism, and the Great Commission: Towards a Renewal Theology of Mission and Interreligious Encounter, 2011; (ed. with E.Y. Alexander) Afro-Pentecostalism: Black Pentecostal and Charismatic Christianity in History and Culture, 2011. Contributor to journals. **Address:** School of Divinity, Regent University, 247 Robertson Hall, 1000 Regent University Dr., Virginia Beach, VA 23464, U.S.A. **Online address:** ayong@regent.edu

YOO, John C. American/Korean (born Korea (South)), b. 1967. **Genres:** History, Politics/Government, Military/Defense/Arms Control, Law. **Career:** University of California, acting professor of law, 1993-99, professor of law, 1999-, Advanced Law Program, director, 2004-; Free University, visiting professor, 1998; U.S. Department of Justice, Office of Legal Counsel, deputy assistant attorney general, 2001-03; University of Chicago, Law School, visiting professor, 2003; University of Trento, distinguished Fulbright chair in

law, 2006. Writer and journalist. **Publications:** The Powers of War and Peace: The Constitution and Foreign Affairs after 9/11, 2005; War by Other Means: An Insider's Account of the War on Terror, 2006; Crisis and Command: The History of Executive Power from George Washington to George W. Bush, 2009; Confronting Terror: 9/11 and the Future of American National Security, 2011; Taming Globalization: International Law, the U.S. Constitution, and the New World Order, 2012. Contributor to periodicals. **Address:** School of Law, University of California, 890 Simon Hall, 215 Boalt Hall, Berkeley, CA 94720-7200, U.S.A. **Online address:** yoo@law.berkeley.edu

YOO, Paula. American (born United States), b. 1969?. **Genres:** Novels, Children's Non-fiction. **Career:** Detroit News, journalist; People Magazine, entertainment correspondent; Glendale Community College, instructor in English. Educator, screenwriter and musician. **Publications:** Sixteen Years in Sixteen Seconds: The Sammy Lee Story (nonfiction children's book), 2005; Good Enough (young-adult novel), 2008; Shining Star: The Anna May Wong Story (nonfiction children's book), 2009. **Address:** Writers House, 21 W 26th St., New York, NY 10010-1003, U.S.A.

YORBURG, Betty. American (born United States), b. 1926. **Genres:** Social Commentary, Sociology, Human Relations/Parenting. **Career:** City University of New York, City College, lecturer, 1967-68, assistant professor, 1969-71, associate professor, 1972-74, professor, 1974-, now professor emeritus. Writer. **Publications:** Utopia and Reality: A Collective Portrait of American Socialists, 1969; The Changing Family, 1973; Sexual Identity: Sex Roles and Social Change, 1974; (with I. Arafat) The New Women: Attitudes Behavior, and Self-image, 1976; Introduction to Sociology, 1982; Families and Societies, 1983; Family Relationships, 1993; Sociological Reality, 1995; Family Realities: A Global View, 2002. **Address:** Department of Sociology, City College, City University of New York, 6/124 N Academic Bldg., 160 Convent Ave., New York, NY 10031, U.S.A. **Online address:** bettyyorburg@att.net

YORINKS, Adrienne. American (born United States), b. 1956. **Genres:** Geography, History, How-to Books, Natural History, Children's Fiction, Animals/Pets. **Career:** Brookdale Community College, instructor in psychodrama and creative-arts therapy. Writer. **Publications:** SELF-ILLUSTRATED: (co-author) Quilt of States, 2005; (with J. Larson) Hummingbirds: Facts and Folklore from the Americans, 2011. OTHER: The Home Grooming Guide for Dogs, 1988. **Address:** 10 Edwards Pl., Short Hills, NJ 07078, U.S.A. **Online address:** adrienne@adrienneyorinks.com

YORK, Alissa. Canadian (born Canada), b. 1970?. **Genres:** Novels, Young Adult Fiction. **Career:** Writer. **Publications:** Any Given Power, 1999; Mercy: A Novel, 2003; Effigy: Mormons, Polygamy, Taxidermy, Love, 2007; Fauna: A Novel, 2010. Contributor to periodicals. Works appear in anthologies. **Address:** c/o Nicola Makoway, Random House of Canada Ltd., 1 Toronto St., Ste. 300, Toronto, ON M5C 2V6, Canada. **Online address:** mail@alissayork.com

YORK, Lynn. American (born United States), b. 1957?. **Genres:** Novels, Children's Fiction, Music. **Career:** Writer, consultant and educator. **Publications:** The Piano Teacher (novel), 2004; The Sweet Life (novel), 2007. **Address:** Plume, 375 Hudson St., New York, NY 10014-3657, U.S.A. **Online address:** lyork@alumni.duke.edu

YORK, Phyllis. American (born United States), b. 1937. **Genres:** Human Relations/Parenting, Self Help, Psychology, Medicine/Health, Politics/Government. **Career:** Eagleville Hospital, psychotherapist, 1971-73, director of training, 1973-75; independent family therapist, consultant and trainer, 1975-78; Toughlove, founding member, 1978-. Writer. **Publications:** (With D. York) Toughlove: A Self-Help Manual for Parents Troubled by Teenage Behavior, 1980; (with D. York and T. Wachtel) Toughlove, 1982; (co-author) Toughlove: A Self-Help Manual for Kids in Trouble, 1983; (with D. York and T. Wachtel) Toughlove Solutions, 1984; (with D. York) Toughlove Cocaine, 1985; (with D. York) Toughlove for Teachers, 1987; (with D. York) Getting Strong in All the Hurting Places, 1989. **Address:** Toughlove, 100 Mechanics St., PO Box 1069, Doylestown, PA 18901-3700, U.S.A.

YORK, R. A. Irish/British (born England), b. 1941. **Genres:** Literary Criticism And History, Novels, Poetry. **Career:** University of Ulster, lecturer, 1969-2006, professor in European literature, now professor emeritus. Writer. **Publications:** The Poem as Utterance, 1986; Strangers and Secrets: Communication in the Nineteenth-Century Novel, 1994; The Rules of Time: Time and Rhythm in the Twentieth-Century Novel, 1999; The Extension of Life: Fiction and History in the American Novel, 2003; Agatha Christie: Power and Illusion, 2007. **Address:** School of Languages, Literatures & Cultures, University of Ulster, Cromore Rd., Coleraine, BT52 1SA, Northern Ireland. **Online address:** ra.york@ulst.ac.uk

YORKE, Katherine. See **ELLERBECK, Rosemary.**

YORKE, Malcolm. British (born England), b. 1938. **Genres:** Children's Fiction, Art/Art History, Children's Non-fiction, Novels, Adult Non-fiction, Biography, Autobiography/Memoirs. **Career:** University of Jyvaskyla, lecturer, 1965-67; University of Northumbria, senior lecturer, 1968-96. Writer. **Publications:** Wood and Paper, 1978; Eric Gill: Man of Flesh and Spirit, 1982; The Spirit of Place: Nine Neo-Romantic Artists and Their Times, 1988; Keith Vaughan: His Life and Work, 1990; Miss Butterpat Goes Wild!, 1993; Matthew Smith: His Life and Reputation, 1997; Mervyn Peake, a Life: My Eyes Mint Gold, 2000. FOR CHILDREN: Reginald F. Dweebly Thunders On, 1993; Molly the Mad Basher, 1994; Cushy Butterpat Goes Wild, 1994; The Wishing Horse, 1995; Class Four's Wild Week, 1995; Scarem's House, 1995; Beastly Tales: Yeti, Bigfoot and the Loch Ness Monster, 1998; The Wishing Horse Rides Again, 1999; A Lifetime of Drawing: The Sketchbooks of Rigby Graham, 2004; The Inward Laugh: Edward Bawden and His Circle, 2005. **Address:** David Higham Associates Ltd., 5-8 Lower John St., Golden Sq., London, GL W1F 9HA, England.

YORKE, Margaret. British (born England), b. 1924. **Genres:** Novels, Mystery/Crime/Suspense, Young Adult Fiction, Criminology/True Crime, Literary Criticism And History. **Career:** WRNS, 1942-45; Oxford University, Saint Hilda's College, Oxford, assistant librarian, 1959-61; Christ Church, library cataloger, 1963-65; Crime Writer's Association, chairman, 1979-80. Writer. **Publications:** Summer Flight, 1957; Pray Love, Remember, 1958; Christopher, 1959; Deceiving Mirror, 1960; The China Doll, 1961; Once a Stranger, 1962; The Birthday, 1963; Full Circle, 1965; No Fury, 1967; The Apricot Bed, 1968; The Limbo Ladies, 1969; No Medals for the Major, 1974; The Small Hours of the Morning: A Thriller, 1975; The Cost of Silence, 1977; The Point of Murder, 1978; The Come-On, 1978; Death on Account, 1979; The Scent of Fear, 1980; The Hand of Death, 1981; Devil's Work, 1982; Find Me a Villain, 1983; The Smooth Face of Evil, 1984; Intimate Kill, 1985; Safely to the Grave, 1986; Evidence to Destroy, 1987; Speak for the Dead, 1988; Crime in Question, 1989; Admit to Murder, 1990; A Small Deceit, 1991; Criminal Damage, 1992; Dangerous to Know, 1993; Almost the Truth, 1994; Serious Intent, 1995; A Question of Belief, 1997; Act of Violence, 1998; False Pretences, 1998; The Price of Guilt, 1999; A Case to Answer, 2000; Cause for Concern, 2001. PATRICK GRANT SERIES: Dead in the Morning, 1970; Silent Witness, 1972; Grave Matters, 1973; Mortal Remains, 1974; Cast for Death, 1976. STORY COLLECTIONS: Pieces of Justice, 1994; A Dead Giveaway, 1995. Works appear in anthologies. **Address:** Curtis Brown Group Ltd., Haymarket House, 4th Fl., 28/29 Haymarket, London, GL SW1Y 4SP, England.

YOSHIMASA, Aoyama. See **AOYAMA, Gosho.**

YOSHIMOTO, Banana. (Mahoko). Japanese (born Japan), b. 1964. **Genres:** Novels, Novellas/Short Stories, Young Adult Fiction. **Career:** Writer. **Publications:** Kitchen, 1988; Asleep, 1989; Shirakawa yofune, 1989; Goodbye Tsugumi, 1989, new ed. 2002; NP, 1990; Fruits Basket, 1990; Lizard, 1993; Tokage, 1993; Amrita, 1994; Banana No Banana, 1994; Hardboiled & Hard Luck, 2005; The Lake, 2011. **Address:** Japan Foreign-Rights Center, 27-18-804 Naka Ochiai 2-chome, Shinjuku-ku, Tokyo, 161, Japan.

YOSHINO, Kenji. American (born United States), b. 1969?. **Genres:** Social Work. **Career:** Yale University, Yale Law School, associate professor of law, 1997-2003, professor of law, 2003-06, deputy dean of intellectual life, 2005-06, Guido Calabresi professor of law, 2006-08; New York University, School of Law, visiting professor of law, 2006-07, Chief Justice Earl Warren professor of constitutional law, 2008-; Yale Law Journal, articles editor. **Publications:** Covering: The Hidden Assault on Our Civil Rights, 2006; Thousand Times More Fair, 2011; Constitutional Displacement, 2012. Contributor to journals. **Address:** School of Law, New York University, 40 Washington Sq. S, Ste. 501, New York, NY 10012-1005, U.S.A. **Online address:** kenji.yoshino@nyu.edu

YOST, J. T. American (born United States), b. 1973?. **Genres:** Novellas/

Short Stories, Illustrations. **Career:** J.T. Yost Illustration, founder and owner; Primarily Pet Portraits, founder and owner; Birdcage Bottom Books, founder and owner. Writer and artist. **Publications:** SELF-ILLUSTRATED: Old Man Winter and Other Sordid Tales (collection of short comics), 2009. Contributor to periodicals. **Address:** New York, NY , U.S.A. **Online address:** jtyost@gmail.com

YOTHERS, Brian. American (born United States), b. 1975?. **Genres:** Literary Criticism And History. **Career:** University of Texas, visiting assistant professor, 2004-05, assistant professor, 2005-10, IMPACT fellow, 2007-08, associate professor of English, 2010-; Purdue University, Early American Reading Group, founding member. Writer. **Publications:** The Romance of the Holy Land in American Travel Writing, 1790-1876, 2007. Contributor to books, periodicals and journals. **Address:** Department of English, University of Texas, Rm. 113, Hudspeth Hall, 500 W University Ave., El Paso, TX 79968-0526, U.S.A. **Online address:** byothers@utep.edu

YOUD, Samuel. See Obituaries.

YOUMANS, Marly. American (born United States), b. 1953. **Genres:** Novels, Poetry, Children's Fiction, Science Fiction/Fantasy, Young Adult Fiction. **Career:** Writer. **Publications:** NOVELS: Little Jordan: A Novel, 1995; Catherwood, 1996; The Wolf Pit, 2001; Val/Orson, 2009; FANTASY: The Curse of the Raven Mocker (juvenile), 2003; Ingledove, 2005; POETRY: Claire: Poems, 2004; The Throne of Psyche, 2011. OTHERS: Thaliad, 2011; Glimmerglass, 2011; A Death at the White Camellia Orphanage, 2012; Maze of Blood, 2012. Contributor to periodicals. **Address:** c/o Author Mail, Farrar Straus and Giroux Inc., 18 W 18th St., New York, NY 10011, U.S.A.

YOUNG, Antony. New Zealander/Chinese (born China), b. 1964. **Genres:** Marketing, Business/Trade/Industry. **Career:** Publicis Groupe, Saatchi & Saatchi, advertising executive, 1987-95; regional head of media, 1995-96; Zenith Media, chief executive, 1996-2003; ZenithOptimedia UK Group, chief executive officer, 2003-06; Optimedia US, president, 2006-, chief executive officer. Writer. **Publications:** (with L. Aitken) Profitable Marketing Communications: A Guide to Marketing Return on Investment, 2007. **Address:** U.S.A. **Online address:** antony.young@optimedia-us.com

YOUNG, Bette Roth. American (born United States), b. 1937. **Genres:** History, Theology/Religion, Biography, Social Sciences, Romance/Historical, Literary Criticism And History. **Career:** Jewish Community Center of Metropolitan Detroit, library director, 1979-82; Wayne State University, instructor, 1980; Jewish Parents Institute, educational director, 1980-82; The Jewish News, book critic, 1980-82; Adult College of Jewish Studies, lecturer, 1985-87; Columbus Jewish Historical Society, consultant, membership director, writer, 1987-90, oral historian, 1990-; Ohio Jewish Chronicle, book critic, 1991-; Columbus Dispatch, book critic, 1992-. **Publications:** (With E. Grad) Congregation Shaarey Zedek, 1861-1981, 1981; The History of the Association of Jewish Community Organization Personnel, 1969-1987, 1987; (ed. with B.M. Mandelkorn) The Columbus Jewish Foundation, 1955-1990: Where the Road of Tomorrow Is Paved, 1994; Emma Lazarus in Her World, Life and Letters, 1995; To Dwell Together in Unity: The Jewish Community Council of Detroit, 1937-1945, forthcoming. **Address:** 4776 Smoketalk Ln., Westerville, OH 43081-7838, U.S.A. **Online address:** ubette@asacomp.com

YOUNG, Carol. American (born United States), b. 1945?. **Genres:** Children's Fiction, Animals/Pets. **Career:** Imagination Unlimited (art studio for children's art and creative problem-solving), art teacher, owner, 1978-; desktop publishing, editing, graphic design, photography, 1989-97; Westport Continuing Education Outreach, coordinator. Writer. **Publications:** Halloween Scene, 1981; Legacy, 1996; Little Walrus Warning, 1996. Contributor to periodicals. **Address:** Imagination Unlimited, 100 Compo Rd. S, Westport, CT 06880, U.S.A.

YOUNG, C. Dale. American (born United States), b. 1969. **Genres:** Poetry, Novels. **Career:** New England Review, poetry editor, 1995-; University of California, senior resident physician, 1998-2002; Warren Wilson College, MFA Program, faculty. **Publications:** The Day Underneath the Day, 2001; The Second Person, 2007; Torn, 2011. **Address:** c/o Author Mail, TriQuarterly Books, Northwestern University Press, 629 Noyes St., Evanston, IL 60208-4210, U.S.A. **Online address:** cdaleyoung@cdaleyoung.com

YOUNG, David (Pollock). American (born United States), b. 1936. **Genres:**

Poetry, Literary Criticism And History, Autobiography/Memoirs, Translations, Essays, Food And Wine, Young Adult Fiction. **Career:** Oberlin College, instructor, 1961-65, assistant professor, 1965-68, associate professor, 1969-73, professor of English, 1973-, Donald R. Longman professor, 1986-, Donald R. Longman emeritus professor; Field: Contemporary Poetry and Poetics, editor, 1969-. **Publications:** Something of Great Constancy: The Art of A Midsummer Night's Dream, 1966; Sweating Out the Winter: Poems, 1969; The Heart's Forest: A Study of Shakespeare's Pastoral Plays, 1972; Boxcars, 1973; Work Lights; 32 Prose Poems, 1977; The Names of a Hare in English: Poems, 1979; Foraging: Poems, 1986; Troubled Mirror: A Study of Yeats': The Tower, 1987; Earthshine, 1988; The Action to the Word: Style and Structure in Shakespeare's Tragedies, 1990; The Planet on the Desk: Selected and New Poems, 1991; Shakespeare's Middle Tragedies: A Collection of Critical Essays, 1993; Night Thoughts and Henry Vaughan, 1994; Seasoning: A Poets's Year: With Seasonal Recipes. 1997; At the White Window, 2000; Six Modernist Moments in Poetry, 2006; Black Lab, 2006; Field of Light and Shadow, 2010. TRANSLATOR: Rilke's Duino Elegies, 1978; (intro.) Wang Wei, Li Po, Tu Fu, Li Ho: Four T'Ang Poets, 1980; Valuable Nail: Selected Poems of Gunter Eich, 1981; Interferon, or On Theatre: Poems by Miroslav Holub, 1982; The Heights of Macchu Picchu, 1987; Sonnets to Orpheus, 1987; Five T'Ang Poets, 1990; Vanishing Lung Syndrome, by Holub, 1990; The Dimension of the Present Moment, by Holub, 1990; Selected Poems of Rainer Maria Rilke: Book of Fresh Beginnings, 1994; (with J.I. Lin) Clouds Float North: The Complete Poems of Yu Xuanji, 1998; The Poetry of Petrarch, 2004; Du Fu: A Life in Poetry, 2008. EDITOR: Twentieth Century Interpretations of Henry IV, vol. II: A Collection of Critical Essays, 1968; (with S. Friebert) A Field Guide to Contemporary Poetry and Poetics, 1980; (with S. Friebert) Longman Anthology of Contemporary American Poetry, 1950-1980, 1983; (with K. Hollaman) Magical Realist Fiction, 1984; Dimension of the Present Moment: Essays, 1990; (with S. Friebert and D. Walker) Field Guide to Contemporary Poetry & Poetics, 1997; (intro.) Selected Poems, 2004. Contributor to periodicals. **Address:** Department of English, Oberlin College, Rm. Peters G04, 101 N Professor St., Oberlin, OH 44074, U.S.A. **Online address:** david.young@oberlin.edu

YOUNG, Dean. American (born United States), b. 1955?. **Genres:** Poetry. **Career:** University of Wisconsin, visiting assistant professor, 1989; Loyola University, assistant professor, 1989-95, associate professor of English, 1995-2000; Vermont College, Low-Residency M.F.A. Program, faculty, 1994; University of Iowa, Writers' Workshop, visiting professor, 1998, 2001-03, associate professor, 2003-06, professor, 2006-08; Vermont Studio Center, visiting poet, 2000, 2002, 2004; University of Texas, Department of English, William Livingston chair of poetry, 2008-. Writer. **Publications:** POETRY: Design with X, 1988; Beloved Infidel, 1992; Strike Anywhere, 1995; First Course in Turbulence, 1999; Skid, 2002; True False, 2002; Original Monkey, 2004; Elegy on Toy Piano, 2005; Ready-made Bouquet, 2005; Embryoyo, 2007; Primitive Mentor, 2008; The Art of Recklessness, 2010; Fall Higher, 2011. Contributor to periodicals. Works appear in anthologies. **Address:** Department of English, University of Texas, CAL 312, PO Box B5000, 1 University Sta., Austin, TX 78712, U.S.A. **Online address:** deanyoung@mail.utexas.edu

YOUNG, Dean (Wayne). American (born United States), b. 1938. **Genres:** Cartoons, Humor/Satire, Young Adult Fiction, Graphic Novels. **Career:** Sisson and Barrett Advertising, account executive, 1960-63; "Blondie" Comic Strip, cartoonist, 1963-. Writer. **Publications:** (With R. Marschall) Blondie & Dagwood's America, Harper, 1981; (with S. Drake) Another Masterpiece!: Blondie, 1991; (with M. Ryzik) Blondie: The Complete Bumstead Family History, 2007. **Address:** PO Box 3531, Clearwater Beach, FL 33767, U.S.A. **Online address:** dana@blondie.com

YOUNG, Dianne. Canadian (born Canada), b. 1959. **Genres:** Children's Fiction, Children's Non-fiction, Food And Wine. **Career:** University of Saskatchewan, Neuropsychiatry Research Unit, research technician, 1982-98; Saskatoon Public School Division, teacher assistant, 2000-. Writer. **Publications:** Adventures in Microwave Cooking, 1976; The Abaleda Voluntary Firehouse Band, 1990; (with J. Juliano) Diabetic's Innovative Cookbook: A Positive Approach to Living with Diabetes, 1994; Purple Hair? I Don't Care!, 1995; A World of Difference, 1999; Honey Trouble, 2001, new ed., 2009. **Address:** PO Box 343, Martensville, SK S0K 2T0, Canada. **Online address:** dianne.young@sasktel.net

YOUNG, Donald R. (Toby Young). American (born United States), b. 1933. **Genres:** Natural History, Politics/Government, Travel/Exploration, History,

Children's Non-fiction. **Career:** Indianapolis Star, copy editor, 1955-63; Encyclopedia Americana, American History and Political Science, senior editor, 1967-77; freelance writer and photographer, 1978-; Collier's and Funk and Wagnalls, seasonal staff editor, 1984-86, 1992-; Aperture Foundation, managing editor, 1986-87. **Publications:** American Roulette: The History and Dilemma of the Vice Presidency, 1965; The Great American Desert, 1980; (with C.O. Bix) The Sierra Club Book of Our National Parks, 1990; Natural Monuments of America, 1990; Historic Monuments of America, 1990; National Parks of America, 1994. EDITOR: Adventure in Politics: The Memoirs of Philip LaFollette, 1970; The Sierra Club to the National Parks, vol. III, 1984, vol. V, 1986, rev. ed., 5 vols., 1995; The Smithsonian Guides to Historic America, 12 vols., rev. ed., 1998; Rocky Mountain States, 1998; The Audubon Guides to National Wildlife Refuges, 3 of 9 vols., 2000. CONTRIBUTOR: The American Heritage Pictorial History of the Presidents of the United States, 1968; Desert States, 1998; Mid-Atlantic States, 1998; Plains States, 1998; Great Lakes States, 1998; Virginia and the Capital Region, 1998; Southern New England, 1998; Texas and the Arkansas River Valley, 1998. **Address:** 166 E 61st St., Apt. 3-C, New York, NY 10065-8513, U.S.A. **Online address:** numiscribe@aol.com

YOUNG, E. L. Australian (born Australia), b. 1973?. **Genres:** Novels, Technology. **Career:** New Scientist, editor. **Publications:** STORM SERIES: YOUNG ADULT NOVELS: The Infinity Code, 2007; The Ghostmaster, 2007 in US as The Ghost Machine, 2008; The Black Sphere, 2008; The Viper Club, 2008; The Death Web, 2008. **Address:** New Scientist, Twr. 2, 475 Victoria Ave., Chatswood, NW 2067, Australia.

YOUNG, Elizabeth. British (born England), b. 1923. **Genres:** Poetry, Architecture, History, International Relations/Current Affairs, Travel/Exploration. **Career:** Writer. **Publications:** (With W. Young) Old London Churches, 1956; Time Is as Time Does (poetry), 1958; Nations and Nuclear Weapons, 1963; Control of Proliferation, 1969; (co-ed. and contrib.) Quiet Enjoyment: Arms Control and Police Forces for the Ocean, 1971; A Farewell to Arms Control?, 1972; (with B. Johnson) Law of the Sea, 1973; (with P. Fricke) Sea-Use Planning, 1975; (with W. Kennet) Neither Red nor Dead: The Case for Disarmament, 1981; Men and Women: Equal But Not Interchangeable, 1982; (with W. Young) London's Churches, 1986; The Gorbachev Phenomenon, 1987; (with W. Kennet) Northern Lazio: An Unknown Italy, 1990. Contributor of articles to journals and newspapers. **Address:** 100 Bayswater Rd., London, GL W2 3HJ, England. **Online address:** lizyoung@gn.apc.org

YOUNG, Glennys. American (born United States), b. 1959. **Genres:** History, Theology/Religion. **Career:** Stanford University, Hoover Institution on War, Revolution and Peace, postdoctoral fellow, 1989-90, lecturer, 1990-92; University of Washington, Department of History, assistant professor, 1992-, associate professor of history, director of graduate studies, Jackson School of International Studies, faculty. Writer. **Publications:** Power and the Sacred in Revolutionary Russia: Religious Activists in the Village, 1997; The Communist Experience in the Twentieth Century, 2011. **Address:** Henry M. Jackson School of International Studies, University of Washington, THO 423, 315 Smith, PO Box 353560, Seattle, WA 98195-3650, U.S.A. **Online address:** glennys@uw.edu

YOUNG, Ian. Canadian/British (born England), b. 1945. **Genres:** Poetry, Gay And Lesbian Issues, History, Bibliography, Translations, Essays, Novellas/Short Stories, Young Adult Fiction, Young Adult Fiction. **Career:** Catalyst Press, director, 1969-81; Ian Young Books, proprietor, 1988-; TMW Communications, director, 1990-; Sykes Press, director, 2008-. Writer and publisher. **Publications:** POEMS: White Garland: 9 Poems for Richard, 1969; Year of the Quiet Sun, 1970; Double Exposure, 1970, rev. ed., 1974; (with R. Phelan) Cool Fire: 10 Poems by Ian Young and Richard Phelan, 1970; Some Green Moths, 1972; Autumn Angels, 1973; Yuletide Story, 1973; Don, 1973; Invisible Words, 1974; Common or Garden Gods, 1976; Alamo, 1976; Whatever Turns You On in the New Year, 1976; Schwule Poesie, 1978; (with R. Phelan) Lions in the Stream, 1979; Sex Magick, 1986; Between the Cracks, 1996; The Mammoth Book of Gay Short Stories, 1997; A Day for a Lay, 1999; Autobibliography, 2001; The AIDS Dissidents 1993-2000, 2001. EDITOR: (contrib.) The Male Muse: A Gay Anthology, 1973; On the Line: New Gay Fiction, 1981; Overlooked & Underrated: Essays on Some Twentieth-Century Writers, 1982; The Son of the Male Muse: New Gay Poetry, 1983; (with J. Lauritsen) The AIDS Cult: Essays on the Gay Health Crisis, 1997. OTHERS: (trans.) Count J. Fersen, Curieux d'Amour, 1970; The Male Homosexual in Literature: A Bibliography, 1975, 2nd ed., 1982; Gay Resistance: Homosexuals in the Anti-Nazi Underground, 1985; The AIDS Dissidents: An Annotated Bibliography, 1993; The Stonewall Experiment: A Gay Psychohistory, 1995; Out in Paperback: A Visual History of Gay Pulps, 2007. **Address:** Ian Young Books, 2483 Gerrard St. E, Toronto, ON M1N 1W7, Canada. **Online address:** info@ianyoungbooks.com

YOUNG, James E. (James Edward Young). American (born United States), b. 1951. **Genres:** History, Humanities, Literary Criticism And History. **Career:** Bryn Mawr College, visiting assistant professor, 1983-84; University of Washington, visiting professor; Harvard University, visiting professor; Princeton University, visiting professor; New York University, assistant professor, Dorot professor of English and Hebrew/Judaic studies, 1984-88; University of Massachusetts, professor of English and Judaic studies, 1988-, Department of Judiac and Near Eastern Studies, chair; The Art of Memory, editor, 1994; State Museum at Terezin, board director. **Publications:** Writing and Rewriting the Holocaust: Narrative and the Consequences of Interpretation, 1988; The Texture of Memory: Holocaust Memorials and Meaning, 1993; (ed.) The Art of Memory: Holocaust Memorials in History, 1994; At Memory's Edge: After-Images of the Holocaust in Contemporary Art and Architecture, 2000; The Stages of Memory at Ground Zero: A Juror's Report on the World Trade Center Memorial Process, forthcoming. Contributor to books and periodicals. **Address:** Department of English, University of Massachusetts, 170 Bartlett Hall, Herter 739, Amherst, MA 01003, U.S.A. **Online address:** jeyoung@english.umass.edu

YOUNG, James Edward. See **YOUNG, James E.**

YOUNG, Jeff C. American (born United States), b. 1948. **Genres:** Children's Non-fiction, History, Politics/Government, Sports/Fitness, Young Adult Non-fiction, Biography, Transportation, Military/Defense/Arms Control, Military/Defense/Arms Control. **Career:** The Ledger, news clerk and sports correspondent, 1985-86; Avon Park Sun, sports editor, 1986-87; Department of Corrections, prison librarian, 1989-91, 1993; Enid Baa Library, librarian, 1991-92; Montverde Academy, media specialist, 1993-95; Polk County School Board, media specialist, 1995-2001; Keiser College, librarian, 2001-02; Florida Technical College, librarian, 2003-04; Meridian College, librarian, 2009-. **Publications:** The Fathers of American Presidents: From Augustine Washington to William Blythe and Roger Clinton, 1997; Top 10 Basketball Shot-Blockers, 2000; Top10 World Series MVPs, 2001; Dwight D. Eisenhower: Soldier and President, 2001; Benjamin Harrison, 2002; Chester A. Arthur, 2002; Franklin Pierce, 2002; James Buchanan, 2003; James Garfield, 2003; Great Communicator: The Story of Ronald Reagan, 2003; The Korean War, 2003; Operation Iraqi Freedom, 2003; Grover Cleveland, 2003; Yao Ming: Basketball's Big Man, 2005; Bleeding Kansas and the Violent Clash Over Slavery in the Heartland, 2006; The Pony Express and Its Death-Defying Mail Carriers, 2006; Cesar Chavez, 2007; Hugo Chavez Leader of Venezuela, 2007; Henry Ford Genius Behind the Affordable Car, 2007; Burning Up the Court The Miami Heat, 2008; Political Profiles Arnold Schwarzenegger, 2008; Xtreme Athletes Kelly Slater, 2009; Xtreme Athletes Shaun White, 2009; Devin Hester, 2009; Dwyane Wade, 2009; Henry Hudson: Discoverer of the Hudson River, 2009; Hernando de Soto: Spanish Conquistador in the Americas, 2009; Michelle Obama, 2009; Motorcycles: the Ins and Outs of Superbikes; Choppers and Other Motorcycles, 2010; Political Profiles: Joe Biden, 2010; Trucks: the Ins and Outs of Trucks, Semis, Pickups and Other Trucks, 2010; True Underground Rescue Stories, 2011; Belaying the Line: Mountain, Rock and Ice Climbing, 2011; Dropping the Flag: Auto Racing, 2011; Leading the Pack: Dogsled Racing, 2011; Pulling the Ripcord: Skydiving, 2011; Running the Rapids: White-water Rafting, Canoeing and Kayaking, 2011; Shooting the Curl: Surfing, 2011. Contributor of articles to newspapers and magazines. **Address:** 242 Granada Blvd., North Port, FL 34287, U.S.A. **Online address:** jcyauth@copper.net

YOUNG, Jock. American/Scottish (born Scotland), b. 1942. **Genres:** Communications/Media, Criminology/True Crime, Sociology. **Career:** Enfield College of Technology, faculty; Middlesex Polytechnic, lecturer, 1967, senior lecturer, 1967-72, principal lecturer, 1972-78, reader in sociology, 1978-, professor and head of centre for criminology, 1986-2002; Polytechnic of Central London, honorary professor of sociology, 1982-84; University of Leicester, Scarman Centre for the Study of Public Order, honorary fellow, 1996-; City University of New York, distinguished professor of sociology, 2000-01, John Jay College of Criminal Justice, distinguished professor of sociology, 2002-03, distinguished professor of criminal justice, 2002-; University of Kent, professor of sociology, 2004-08, visiting professor of sociology, 2005-07, hon-

orary professor of criminology, 2009-. Writer and consultant. **Publications:** The Zookeepers of Deviancy, 1970; The Drugtakers: The Social Meaning of Drug Use, 1971; (with I. Taylor and P. Walton) The New Criminology: For a Social Theory of Deviance, 1973; (with V. Greenwood) Abortion in Demand, 1976; (with M. Fitzgerald) Know Your Own Society, 1981; Polytechnics in Transition, 1982; Media as Myth, 1982; Contemporary Criminology Theory, 1982; (with R. Kinsey and J. Lea) Losing the Fight against Crime, 1986; (with T. Jones and B. MacLean) The Islington Crime Survey: Crime, Victimization, and Policing in Inner-City London, 1986; (with J. Lea) What Is to Be Done about Law and Order?: Crisis in the Nineties, 1993; (co-author) Sistema Penal e Intervenciones Sociales: Algunas Experiencias Nacionales, Regionales y Locales en Europa, 1993; The Exclusive Society: Social Exclusion, Crime, and Difference in Late Modernity, 1999; Vertigo of Late Modernity, 2007; (with J. Ferrelll and K. Hayward) Cultural Criminology: An Invitation, 2008; The Criminological Imagination, 2011. EDITOR: (with S. Cohen) The Manufacture of News, 1973, 2nd ed., 1981; (with R. Bailey) Contemporary Social Problems in Britain, 1973; (with I. Taylor and P. Walton) Critical Criminology, 1975; Capitalism and the Rule of Law, 1980; Permissiveness and Control, 1980; Policing the Riots, 1982; (with R. Matthews) Confronting Crime, 1986; (with R. Matthews) Issues in Realist Criminology, 1992; (with R. Matthews) Rethinking Criminology: The Realist Debate, 1992; (with P. Walton) The New Criminology Revisited, 1998; (with R. Matthews) New Politics of Crime and Punishment, 2003. **Address:** John Jay College, City University of New York, 899 10th Ave., New York, NY 10019-1069, U.S.A. **Online address:** jyoung@jjay.cuny.edu

YOUNG, John. Australian/British (born England), b. 1934. **Genres:** Environmental Sciences/Ecology, Ethics, History, Intellectual History, Politics/Government, Language/Linguistics. **Career:** University of Auckland, tutor in New Zealand history, 1958-59; University of Adelaide, Department of History, senior lecturer in history, 1963-87, chair, 1982-84, Mawson Graduate Centre for Environmental Studies, director, 1988-90; Shipwrights Point School of Wooden Boat Building, manager, 1992-, association chair. Writer. **Publications:** Australia's Pacific Frontier, 1968; Adventurous Spirits: Australian Migrant Society in Pre-cession Fiji, 1984; A Touch of Magic: The Building of the One and All, 1985; Post-Environmentalism, 1990 in US as Sustaining the Earth: A Post-Environmentalist View, 1990; (ed. with K. Dyer) Changing Directions: The Proceedings of the Conference, 1990. **Address:** Pentarba, Huon Hwy., Hobart Campus, Geography-Geology Bldg. 403, South Franklin, TA 7113, Australia. **Online address:** leofleda@primus.com.au

YOUNG, John. See **MACINTOSH, Brownie.**

YOUNG, John K(arl). American (born United States), b. 1951. **Genres:** Biology, Chemistry, Sciences. **Career:** Howard University, Department of anatomy, assistant professor, 1979-84, associate professor, 1984-97, professor, 1997-. Writer. **Publications:** Cells: Amazing Forms and Functions, 1990; (trans.) Boris Kotlyar, Plasticity in the Nervous System, 1991; Hormones: Molecular Messengers, 1994; (trans. and ed.) V.M. Dilman, Development, Aging, and Disease, 1994; Sacred Sites of the Knights Templar, 2003; (with B. Karg) Everything Freemasons Book: Unlock the Secrets of this Ancient and Mysterious Society, 2006. Integrated Histology by Alvin Telser and John Young, with Kate Baldwin, 2007; The Building Blocks of Human Life: Understanding Mature Cells and Stem Cells, 2007; Human Anatomy: The Beauty of Form and Function, 2008; Wheater's Review of Histology and Basic Pathology by Kate Baldwin, Ray Hakim, Leki Tadesse-Heath, and John Young, 2009; Introduction to Cell Biology, 2010. **Address:** Department of Anatomy, College of Medicine, Howard University, 520 West St. NW, Washington, DC 20059, U.S.A. **Online address:** jyoung@howard.edu

YOUNG, John Sacret. American (born United States), b. 1947. **Genres:** Novels, Plays/Screenplays, Autobiography/Memoirs, Art/Art History. **Career:** Sacret Inc., president and treasurer, 1977-; Samoset Inc., president, 1990-. Writer and director. **Publications:** NOVELS: Gallitzin and Sons, 1978; The Weather Tomorrow, 1981. OTHER: Remains: Non-viewable (memoir), 2005. Contributor to periodicals. **Address:** Samoset Inc./Sacret Inc., 127 Broadway, Ste. 220, Santa Monica, CA 90401-2392, U.S.A.

YOUNG, Ken. American (born United States), b. 1956. **Genres:** Sports/Fitness, Biography, Politics/Government, Young Adult Fiction. **Career:** Sports Illustrated, staff; CBS Sports, staff. Writer. **Publications:** Civil Liberties and Service Recruitment: The Plight of Reluctant Servicemen, 1970; Local Politics and the Rise of Party: The London Municipal Society and the Conservative Intervention in Local Elections, 1894-1963, 1975; (ed.) Essays on the Study of Urban Politics, 1975; (with J. Kramer) Strategy and Conflict in Metropolitan Housing: Suburbia Versus the Greater London Council, 1965-75, 1978; (with L. Mills) Public Policy Research: A Review of Qualitative, 1980; (with L. Mills and C. Mason) Urban Governments and Economic, 1980; (with N. Connelly) Policy and Practice in the Multi-Racial, 1981; (with P.L. Garside) Metropolitan London, Politics and Urban Change, 1837-1981, 1982; (with L. Mills) Managing the Post-Industrial City, 1983; (ed. with N. Glazer and C.S. Schelling) Ethnic Pluralism and Public Policy: Achieving Equality in the United States and Britain, 1983; (ed.) National Interests and Local Government, 1983; (ed. with M. Loughlin and M.D. Gelfand) Half a Century of Municipal Decline, 1935-1985, 1985; (co-author) London Employment, 1986; (ed.) New Directions for County Government, 1989; (with L. Grayson) Quality of Life in Cities: An Overview and Guide to the Literature, 1994; Cy Young Award Winners, 1994; (with N. Rao) Local Government Since 1945, 1997; Index to Death Registrations, Waterloo County, 1869 to 1880, 1998. Contributor of articles to periodicals. **Address:** 51 Simpson Dr., Old Bethpage, NY 11804-1222, U.S.A.

YOUNG, Kenneth Ray. American (born United States), b. 1939. **Genres:** History, Biography, Social Sciences. **Career:** Western Connecticut State University, instructor, associate professor, 1966-80, professor of history and non-western cultures, 1980-, now professor emeritus of history. Writer. **Publications:** (Ed. with R. Tanter) Politics of Middle Class Indonesia, 1990; The General's General: The Life and Times of Arthur MacArthur, 1994; Islamic Peasants and The State: The 1908 Anti-Tax Rebellion in West Sumatra, 1994. Contributor of articles to journals. **Address:** Department of History & Non-Western Cultures, Western Connecticut State University, 224 Warner Hall, 181 White St., Danbury, CT 06810, U.S.A.

YOUNG, Kevin. American (born United States), b. 1970. **Genres:** Poetry, Young Adult Fiction. **Career:** University of Georgia, Department of English, assistant professor; Indiana University, Ruth Lilly professor of poetry, 2001; Emory University, Atticus Haygood professor of English and creative writing, Raymond Danowski Poetry Library, curator; Stanford University, fellow in poetry. Poet. **Publications:** Most Way Home (poetry), 1995; To Repel Ghosts: Five Sides in B Minor, 2001; (ed.) Blues Poems, 2003; Jelly Roll: A Blues, 2003; (ed.) Selected Poems, 2004; Black Maria: Being the Adventures of Delilah Redbone and A.K.A. Jones, 2005; To Repel Ghosts: Remixed from the Original Masters, 2005; (ed.) Jazz Poems, 2006; For the Confederate Dead, 2007; Dear Darkness: Poems, 2008; (ed.) The Art of Losing, 2010; (as Kevin Lowell Young) Ardency: A Chronicle of the Amistad Rebels, 2011. Contributor of poetry to periodicals. **Address:** Department of English, Emory University, N 302 Callaway Ctr., 537 Kilgo Cir., Atlanta, GA 30322, U.S.A. **Online address:** kevin.young@emory.edu

YOUNG, Margaret Labash. American (born United States), b. 1926. **Genres:** Humanities, Business/Trade/Industry, International Relations/Current Affairs, Social Sciences. **Career:** Mechanics and Farmers Savings Bank, clerk, 1948-49; Emma Willard Day School, science teacher, 1952-53; Arthur D. Little Inc., Central Sales Office, secretary, 1953-55, assistant in operations research group, 1955-57; Cambridge Public Library, paraprofessional librarian, 1957-58; University of Michigan, reference and circulation librarian, 1959-62; Gale Research Co., bibliographer, 1965-68, associate editor, 1969-71, editor, 1972-88; Henry Ford Community College, reference and documents librarian, 1965-67; Salzburg Seminar in American Studies, librarian, 1981-83; publishing information consultant, 1989-. **Publications:** EDITOR/CO-EDITOR: Directory of Special Libraries and Information Centers, 1974, 6th ed., vol. II, 1981; Health Sciences Libraries: Including All Aspects of Basic and Applied Medical Sciences, 1975, rev. ed., 1979; Science and Technology Libraries: Including Agriculture, Environment/Conservation, and Food Science Libraries, 1975, 6th ed. as Science and Technology Libraries: Including Agriculture, Energy, Environment/Conservation and Food Sciences Libraries, 1981; Education and Information Science Libraries: Including Audiovisual, Picture, Publishing, Rare Book, and Recreational Libraries, 1975, rev. ed., 1979; Business and Law Libraries: Including Military and Transportation Libraries, 1975, rev. ed., 1979; Subject Directory of Special Libraries and Information Centers: A Subject Classified Edition of Material Taken from Directory of Special Libraries and Information Centers, vol. V, 1975, 6th ed., 1981; (with H.C. Young and A.T. Kruzas) New Special Libraries: A Periodic Supplement for the Fourth Edition of Directory of Special Libraries and Information Centers, 1977; Scientific and Technical Organizations and Agencies Directory, vol. II, 2nd ed., 1987; (with B.T. Darnay) Life Sciences Organiza-

tions and Agencies Directory, 1988; (with C. Halverson) Systems for Success: A How-to Manual for Today's Interior Designer, 2000. OTHER: Social Sciences and Humanities Libraries: Including Area/Ethnic, Art, Geography/Map, History, Music, Religion/Theology, Theater and Urban/Regional Planning Libraries, 1975, rev. ed., 1979. **Address:** 313 Farmdale Rd., Hopkins, MN 55343, U.S.A.

YOUNG, Patrick. American (born United States), b. 1937. **Genres:** Medicine/Health, Sciences, Sports/Fitness, Education. **Career:** United Press Intl., reporter, 1961-62; USN, journalist, 1963-64; National Observer, staff writer, 1965-77; freelance writer, 1977-79, 1995-; Newhouse News Service, chief science and medical writer, 1980-88; Science News, editor, 1988-95. **Publications:** Drifting Continents, Shifting Seas: An Introduction to Plate Tectonics, 1976; Asthma and Allergies: An Optimistic Future, 1980; Drugs and Pregnancy, 1987; Mental Disturbances, 1988; Schizophrenia, 1988; (with A.R. Figelman) Keeping Young Athletes Healthy, 1991. Contributor to periodicals. **Address:** Chelsea House Publishers, 1974 Sproul Rd., Ste. 400, PO Box 914, Broomall, PA 19008-3402, U.S.A.

YOUNG, Robert A. Canadian (born Canada), b. 1950. **Genres:** International Relations/Current Affairs, Politics/Government, Social Sciences, Young Adult Non-fiction. **Career:** McGill University, assistant professor of political science, 1980-81; University of Western Ontario, assistant professor, 1981-85, associate professor, 1985-92, professor of political science, 1992-, Canada Research Chair in Multilevel Governance, chair; University of Toronto, visiting associate professor, 1987-88; Queen's University, Institute of Intergovernmental Relations, visiting research fellow, 1991-92; C.D. Howe Institute, research fellow; Political Economy Research Group, co-director; Economic Policy Research Institute, co-director. Writer. **Publications:** (Ed.) Confederation in Crisis, 1991; (ed. with D. Brown and D. Herperger) Constitutional Commentaries: An Assessment of the 1991 Federal Proposals: Conference Report, 1992; (ed. with G. Lachappelle and J.E. Trent) Quebec Canada: New Challenges and Opportunities, 1996; The Secession of Quebec and the Future of Canada, 1998; (ed.) Stretching the Federation: The Art of the State in Canada, 1999; The Struggle for Quebec: From Referendum to Referendum?, 1999; (with C. Leuprecht) Canada: The State of the Federation 2004 Municipal Federal Provincial Relations in Canada, 2006; (ed. with A. Sancton) Foundations of Governance: Municipal Government in Canada's Provinces, 2009. **Address:** Department of Political Science, University of Western Ontario, Rm. 4223, Social Science Ctr., Rm. 4154, London, ON N6A 5C2, Canada. **Online address:** young@uwo.ca

YOUNG, Robert J.C. American (born United States), b. 1950. **Genres:** Politics/Government, History. **Career:** New York University, Silver professor of English and comparative literature, 2005-; Wadham College, professor of English and critical theory and fellow; Southampton University, faculty Rutgers Universit, faculty. Writer. **Publications:** (Ed. with D. Attridge and G. Bennington) Post-structuralism and the Question of History, 1987; White Mythologies: Writing History and the West, 1990, rev. ed., 2004; Colonial Desire: Hybridity in Theory, Culture, and Race, 1995; Torn Halves: Political Conflict in Literary and Cultural Theory, 1996; (Ed. with B. Kah Choon and R.B.H. Goh) The Silent Word: Textual Meaning and the Unwritten, 1998; Postcolonialism: An Historical Introduction, 2001; Postcolonialism: A Very Short Introduction, 2003; The Idea of English Ethnicity, 2007. Contributor to periodicals. **Address:** 5th Fl., 19 University Pl., New York, NY 10003, U.S.A. **Online address:** mail@nyupoco.com

YOUNG, Robin. American (born United States) **Genres:** Literary Criticism And History, History, Biography. **Career:** California State University, lecturer; Chapman College, lecturer; Los Angeles Police Department Academy, instructor; Children' Museum, founder. Writer and historian. **Publications:** Time's Disinherited Children: Childhood, Regression, and, Sacrifice in the Plays of Henrik Ibsen, 1989; For Love & Liberty: The Untold Civil War Story of Major Sullivan Ballou & His Famous Love Letter, 2006. Contributor to periodicals. **Address:** c/o Author Mail, Thunder's Mouth Press, 245 W 17th St., 11th Fl., New York, NY 10011-5300, U.S.A.

YOUNG, Roger (E.). American (born United States), b. 1942. **Genres:** Plays/Screenplays. **Career:** National Broadcasting Co., Channel 6, director. Writer and producer. **Publications:** Modern Cooking Equipment and its Applications, 1979. **Address:** c/o Steve Glick, William Morris Agency Inc., 151 S El Camino Dr., Beverly Hills, CA 90212, U.S.A. **Online address:** roger@rogyoung.net

YOUNG, Rose. See HARRIS, Marion (Rose).

YOUNG, Ruth. American (born United States), b. 1946. **Genres:** Children's Fiction, Food And Wine, Humor/Satire, Young Adult Fiction, Songs/Lyrics And Libretti, Plays/Screenplays, Young Adult Fiction, Literary Criticism And History, Literary Criticism And History. **Career:** Composer and playwright, 1975-. Consultant and writer. **Publications:** JUVENILE: The Great-Catsby, 1985; My Blanket: Me and Silkie, 1987; My Babysitter, 1987; My New Baby, 1987; My Potty Chair, 1987; Starring Francine & Dave, 1988; A Trip to Mars, 1990; (with M. Rose) Spider Magic, 1990; (with M. Rose) Turtle Magic, 1990; Daisy's Taxi, 1991; Golden Bear, 1992; Who Says Moo, 1993. OTHER: (with M. Rose) To Grill a Mockingbird and Other Tasty Titles, 1985; Trumpet of the Swan (libretto). **Address:** 1443 Willard St., San Francisco, CA 94117, U.S.A.

YOUNG, Sheila. British (born England), b. 1943?. **Genres:** Art/Art History, Antiques/Furnishings, Crafts. **Career:** Writer. **Publications:** The Queen's Jewellery, 1968; The Queen's Jewellery: The Jewels of H.M. Queen Elizabeth II, 1969; (contrib.) Great Collections: The Unique Jewels of Queen Elizabeth, 1971. **Address:** 50 Moor Ct., Westfield, Gosforth, Newcastle upon Tyne, NM NE3 4YD, England.

YOUNG, T. Kue. Canadian (born Canada), b. 1948. **Genres:** Medicine/Health, Social Sciences. **Career:** Community Health Centre, general practitioner, 1974-75; University of Toronto Sioux Lookout Project, general practitioner, 1975-77; Canadian Government, Department of National Health and Welfare, medical director, 1980-83; University of Manitoba, Department of Community Health Sciences, assistant professor, 1983-87, associate professor, 1987-92, professor, 1992-, Northern Health Research Unit, director, 1988-94, department head, 1998-2001; Royal College of Physicians and Surgeons, fellow, 1984; Medical Research Council, senior scientist, 1998-2008; University of Toronto, Dalla Lana School of Public Health, professor, 2002-, TransCanada Pipelines chair in aboriginal health, 2004. Writer. **Publications:** Health Care and Cultural Change, 1988; (co-author) The Health Effects of Housing and Community Infrastructure on Canadian Indian Reserves, 1991; The Health of Native Americans, 1994; (with J.B. Waldram and D.A. Herring) Aboriginal Health in Canada, 1995, 2nd ed., 2006; (ed. with P. Bjerregaard) Population Health, 1998, 2nd ed., 2005; The Circumpolar Inuit, 1998; (ed. with P. Bjerregaard) Health Transitions in Arctic Populations, 2008. **Address:** Dalla Lana School of Public Health, Universit of Toronto, Rm. 547, 155 College St., Toronto, ON M5T 3M7, Canada. **Online address:** kue.young@utoronto.ca

YOUNG, Toby. See YOUNG, Donald R.

YOUNGBLOOD, Denise J. (Denise Jeanne Youngblood). American (born United States), b. 1952?. **Genres:** Film, History, Humor/Satire. **Career:** San Jose City College, visiting instructor in history, 1980; Russian Review, editorial assistant, copy editor, 1980-82; Stanford University Libraries, Slavic bibliographic assistant, 1980-82; American Association for the Advancement of Slavic Studies, assistant, 1982-88; University of Vermont, Burlington, assistant professor, 1988-94, associate professor, 1994-99, professor, 1999-, department chair, 1999-2003, Provost's Office, vice provost for faculty and academic affairs, 2003-05; Middlebury College, visiting associate professor, 1995. Writer and consultant. **Publications:** Soviet Cinema in the Silent Era, 1918-1935, 1985; Movies for the Masses: Popular Cinema and Soviet Society in the 1920s, 1992; The Magic Mirror: Moviemaking in Russia, 1908-1918, 1999; (with J. Woll) Repentance, 2001; Russian War Films: On the Cinema Front, 1914-2005, 2007; (with T. Shaw) Cinematic Cold War: The American and Soviet Struggle for Hearts and Minds, 2010. Contributor of articles to journals. **Address:** Department of History, University of Vermont, Wheeler House, 133 S Prospect St., Burlington, VT 05405, U.S.A. **Online address:** denise.youngblood@uvm.edu

YOUNGBLOOD, Denise Jeanne. See YOUNGBLOOD, Denise J.

YOUNGBLOOD, Ronald Fred. American (born United States), b. 1931. **Genres:** Theology/Religion, History, Philosophy, Reference. **Career:** Bethel Seminary, assistant professor, 1961-65, associate professor, 1965-70, professor of Old Testament, 1970-2001, professor emeritus, 2001-; Wheaton College, professor of Old Testament, 1978-81, associate dean, 1978-80, dean of graduate school, 1980-81; Trinity Evangelical Divinity School, professor of Old Testament and Semitic languages, 1981-82. Writer. **Publications:** Great Themes of the Old Testament, 1968, rev. ed. as The Heart of the Old Testament, 1971, 2nd ed., 1998; Special Day Sermons, 1973, 2nd ed., 1989; Faith of Our Fathers, 1976; How it all Began, 1980; Exodus, 1983; Themes from Isaiah, 1983; The Book of Genesis: An Introductory Commentary, 1991; New Compact Key Reference Concordance, 1992; The Book of Isaiah: An Introductory Commentary, 1993; Bible Concordance, 1993; Nelson's Comfort Print Bible Concordance, 1995; (with F.F. Bruce and R.K. Harrison) Compact Bible dictionary, 2004; (with F.F. Bruce and R.K. Harrison) Nelson's Student Bible Dictionary, 2005; (with F.F. Bruce and R.K. Harrison) International Children's Bible Dictionary: A Fun and Easy-to-Use Guide to the Words, People, and Places in the Bible, 2006. EDITOR: (and trans.) New International Version, 1978; (with M. Inch) The Living and Active Word of God, 1983; (with M.C. Tenney) What the Bible Is All About, rev. ed., 1983; (ed.) Evangelicals and Inerrancy, 1984; (with W.C. Kaiser, Jr.) A Tribute to Gleason Archer, 1986; The Genesis Debate: Persistent Questions about Creation and the Flood, 1986; Nelson's New Illustrated Bible Dictionary, 1995; (exec.) New International Reader's Version, 1998; The Challenge of Bible Translation: Communicating God's Word to the World, 2003; (with J.H. Stek) Zondervan TNIV Study Bible: Personal Size, 2006; Unlock the Bible, 2011. (trans.) Today's New International Version New Testament, forthcoming; New International Version Study Bible, forthcoming. **Address:** Bethel Seminary, 6116 Arosa St., San Diego, CA 92115, U.S.A. **Online address:** r-youngblood@bethel.edu

YOUNGBLOOD, Shay. American (born United States), b. 1959?. **Genres:** Plays/Screenplays, Novellas/Short Stories, Novels. **Career:** Washington Entertainment Television, public information assistant; Peace Corps, agriculture information officer; Syracuse Community Writer's Project, instructor in creative writing; Rhode Island Adult Correctional Institution for Women, instructor in playwrighting; Brown University, instructor in playwrighting, 1992-93; New School for Social Research, instructor in creative writing; Rhode Island Women's Prison, creative writing instructor, 1992; Wheaton College, Cole visiting professor, 1995-97; New School University, Eugene Lang College, lecturer, 1998; New York University, Graduate Program in Creative Writing, visiting professor, 2001-02; New York University, faculty of creative writing, 2002-03; University of Mississippi, John & Renee Grisham writer-in-residence, 2002-03; Texas A&M University, visiting professor, 2008-10, writer-in-residence. **Publications:** Shakin' the Mess Outta Misery (play), 1988; The Big Mama Stories (stories), 1989; Talking Bones (play), 1992; Square Blues (play), 1992; Amazing Grace (play), 1995; Soul Kiss (novel), 1997; Black Girl in Paris, (novel), 2000. **Address:** Texas A&M University, Bizzell Hall West, 1st Fl., Blocker Bldg., College Station, TX 77843, U.S.A. **Online address:** youngbloodarts@gmail.com

YOUNG-BRUEHL, Elisabeth. See Obituaries.

YOUNG-EISENDRATH, Polly. American (born United States), b. 1947. **Genres:** Psychology. **Career:** New York Bell Telephone, Personnel Assessment Center, research assistant, 1966, special assistant, 1967; Richardson Foundation, NC Fellows Program, coordinator of internship program, 1969-70; Guilford Technical Community College, instructor in English and social sciences, 1970-73; Goddard College, Graduate Program, assistant regional director, 1974-75; Lindenwood Colleges, instructor, 1975-76, associate director, 1975-76, College for Individualized Education, national program coordinator, 1976-77, administrator of master's program in art therapy and counseling psychology, 1977-78; Washington University, instructor in counseling and social work, George Warren Brown School of Social Work, supervisor of counseling program, 1978-79; Bryn Mawr College, assistant professor of social work and social research, 1980-86, visiting lecturer in human development, 1986-89; Clinical Associates West, chief psychologist, Jungian analyst and president, 1986-94; Institute of Pennsylvania Hospital, research psychologist, 1989-95; University of Vermont, clinical associate professor of psychiatry and clinical associate professor of psychology; Norwich University, clinical supervisor and consultant in leadership development. Writer. **Publications:** Hags and Heroes: A Feminist Approach to Jungian Psychotherapy with Couples, 1984; (ed. with J. Hall) The Book of the Self: Person, Pretext, and Process, 1987; (with F.L. Wiedemann) Female Authority: Empowering Women through Psychotherapy, 1987; (with J. Hall) Jung's Self Psychology: A Constructivist Perspective, 1991; You're Not What I Expected: Learning to Love the Opposite Sex, 1993; The Gifts of Suffering: Finding Insight, Compassion, and Renewal, 1996; (ed. with T. Dawson) The Cambridge Companion to Jung, 1997, rev. ed., 2008; (ed. with R. Martin) Awakening to Zen: The Teachings of Roshi Philip Kapleau, 1997; You're Not What I Expected: Love

After the Romance Has Ended, 1997; Gender and Desire: Uncursing Pandora, 1997; Resilient Spirit: Transforming Suffering into Insight and Renewal, 1997; Women and Desire: Beyond Wanting to Be Wanted, 1999; (ed. with M. Miller) The Psychology of Mature Spirituality: Integrity, Wisdom, Transcendence, 2000; (ed. with S. Muramoto) Awakening & Insight: Zen Buddhism and Psychotherapy, 2002; Subject to Change: Jung, Gender, and Subjectivity in Psychoanalysis, 2004; The Self-Esteem Trap: Raising Confident and Compassionate Kids in an Age of Self-Importance, 2008. Works appear in anthologies. Contributor of articles to journals. **Address:** 195 Calais Rd., Worcester, VT 05682-9799, U.S.A. **Online address:** pollye@comcast.net

YOUNGER, James. American/British (born England), b. 1967?. **Genres:** Economics, Sciences. **Career:** Economist, freelance science journalist, 1989-94; New York Times, freelance science journalist, 1989-94; British Broadcasting Corp. (BBC), BBC Science, documentary producer, 1994-2004; Termite Art Productions, supervising producer, 2004-; Creative Differences Productions, series producer; Fox Television Studios, executive producer. **Publications:** (Contrib.) Economic Impact of Oil Resource Development on the Alaskan Economy, 1975-1985, 1976; (with D. McNab) The Planets, 1999. **Address:** c/o Author Mail, Yale University Press, 302 Temple St., PO Box 209040, New Haven, CT 06511-8909, U.S.A. **Online address:** james@grondle.com

YOUNGHOLM, Thomas. American (born United States), b. 1949. **Genres:** Novels, Theology/Religion. **Career:** Cook County Sheriff's Youth Services Department, family counselor and public educator. Novelist and business consultant. **Publications:** The Celestial Bar: A Spiritual Journey, 1994; In the Shadow of the Sphere: An Adventure of Spirit and Heart, 2000. **Address:** Creative Information Concepts, PO Box 1504, Lemon Grove, CA 91946-1504, U.S.A. **Online address:** creativeic@aol.com

YOUNGKIN, Stephen D. American (born United States) **Genres:** Biography, Autobiography/Memoirs. **Career:** Writer. **Publications:** (With J. Bigwood and R.G. Cabana, Jr.) The Films of Peter Lorre, 1982; (with F. Hofmann) Peter Lorre: Portrait des Schauspielers auf der Flucht, 1998; The Lost One: A Life of Peter Lorre, 2005. **Address:** The University Press of Kentucky, 663 S Limestone St., Lexington, KY 40508-4008, U.S.A. **Online address:** derverloren@hotmail.com

YOUNGMAN, Paul A. American (born United States), b. 1965. **Genres:** Cultural/Ethnic Topics, Technology, History. **Career:** East Chapel Hill High School, teacher, 1996-2003; University of North Carolina, assistant professor of German, 2003-08, associate professor of German, 2008-, Center for Humanities, Technology, and Science, director, 2007-10, Complex Systems Institute, faculty associate, 2010-, Center for Advanced Research in the Humanities, director, 2010-. Writer. **Publications:** Black Devil and Iron Angel: The Railway in Nineteenth-Century German Realism, 2005; We are the Machine: The Computer, the Internet, and Information in Contemporary German Literature, 2009; Digital Realities or Digital Myths?: The Computer and Its Network in Contemporary German Literature, forthcoming. **Address:** Department of Languages and Culture Studies, University of North Carolina, 458 College of Education, 9201 University City Blvd., Charlotte, NC 28223-0001, U.S.A. **Online address:** pyoungman@uncc.edu

YOUNGS, Betty F. (Betty Ferrell Youngs). American (born United States), b. 1928. **Genres:** Education, Writing/Journalism, Psychology. **Career:** Baptist Board, editorial assistant, 1950-54, style editor, vocational guidance consultant and editor of vocational guidance materials, 1958-66; First Baptist Church, pastor's assistant, 1954-57; State Baptist Board, assistant to state missions director, 1957-58. **Publications:** Let's Explore Jobs, 1971; What's Bugging You?, 1973. **Address:** 2720 Oberlin Dr., Durham, NC 27705, U.S.A.

YOUNGS, Betty Ferrell. See **YOUNGS, Betty F.**

YOUNGS, Tim. British (born England) **Genres:** Anthropology/Ethnology, Travel/Exploration, Writing/Journalism. **Career:** Loughborough University, research fellow in black British drama, 1986-87; Trent Polytechnic, research assistant in travel narratives of Africa, 1987-90; Nottingham Trent University, School of Arts and Humanities, lecturer in English, 1990-, professor of English and travel studies, Centre for Travel Writing Studies, director, Studies in Travel Writing, founding editor, 1997-. **Publications:** Travellers in Africa: British Travelogues, 1850-1900, 1994; (ed.) Writing and Race, 1997; (ed. with P. Hulme) The Cambridge Companion to Travel Writing, 2002; (ed. with

C. Taylor) Ballistic Missile Defence, 2003; (ed. with G. Hooper) Perspectives on Travel Writing, 2004; (ed. with G. Hooper) Nineteenth-Century Travels, Explorations and Empires, vol. VII, 2004; Sudan: Conflict in Darfur, 2004; (with C. Taylor) Iraq: Political and Security Issues at the Handover, 2004; (ed.) Rose nere e guerrieri sentimentali, 2004; (ed.) Travel Writing in the Nineteenth-Century: Filling the Blank Spaces, 2006; (with P. Hulme) Talking About Travel Writing: A Conversation Between Peter Hulme and Tim Youngs, 2007. Contributor to periodicals. **Address:** School of Arts and Humanities, Nottingham Trent University, Clifton Ln., Nottingham, NT NG11 8NS, England. **Online address:** tim.youngs@ntu.ac.uk

YOUNIE, William J(ohn). American (born United States), b. 1932. **Genres:** Education, Reference. **Career:** Fordham University, adjunct associate professor, 1958-67; Southbury Training School, director of education, 1959-64; Columbia University, Teachers College, associate professor of education, 1964-70; Elwyn Institute, consultant, 1965-; New York Federation, Council for Exceptional Children, president, 1966-67; William Paterson College of New Jersey, professor of special education and counseling, 1970-97, professor emeritus, 1998-. Writer. **Publications:** Guidelines for Establishing School-Work Study Programs for Educable Mentally Retarded Youth, 1966; (ed.) Preparation of Work Study Teachers of the M. R., 1966; Instructional Approaches to Slow Learning, 1967; (with H. Rusalem) The World of Rehabilitation: An Atlas for Special Educators, 1971; Basic Speech Improvement, 1976; Marking Time, 1978. CONTRIBUTOR: Educational Therapy, 1966; A Selected Bibliography in Special Education, 1967. Contributor to journals. **Address:** William Paterson University, 300 Pompton Rd., Wayne, NJ 07470, U.S.A.

YOUNT, Lisa. American (born United States), b. 1944. **Genres:** Sociology, Biology, Children's Non-fiction, Medicine/Health, Women's Studies And Issues, Young Adult Non-fiction, Biography, Reference, Reference. **Career:** Freelance writer, 1967-. **Publications:** Too Hot, Too Cold, Just Right: How Animals Control Their Temperatures, 1981; The Telescope, 1983; Lore of Our Land, 1984; Stones and Bones, 1986; Black Scientists, 1991; Cancer, 1991, rev. ed., 2000; True Adventure Readers, 1992; Contemporary Women Scientists, 1994; Louis Pasteur, 1994; William Harvey: Discoverer of How Blood Circulates, 1994, rev. ed., 2008; (with M.M. Rodgers) Our Endangered Planet: Air, 1995; Women Aviators, 1995; Pesticides, 1995; Twentieth-Century Woman Scientists, 1996; Antonivan Leeuwenhoek: First to See Microscopic Life, 1996, rev. ed., 2008; Memory, 1996; (with H. Henderson) The Scientific Revolution, 1996; Genetics and Genetic Engineering, 1997; (with Henderson) Twentieth-Century Science, 1997; Antoine Lavoisier: Founder of Modern Chemistry, 1997, rev. ed., 2008; Frontier of Freedom: African Americans in the West, 1997; Issues in Biomedical Ethics, 1998; Asian-American Scientists, 1998; Medical Technology, 1998; A-Z of Women in Science and Math, 1999, rev. ed., 2008; Epidemics, 2000; (ed.) Cloning, 2000; Physician-Assisted Suicide and Euthanasia, 2000; Library in a Book: Biotechnology and Genetic Engineering, 2000, 3rd ed., 2008; History of Medicine, 2001; Euthanasia, 2001; Disease Detectives, 2001; Library in a Book: Patients' Rights in the Age of Managed Health Care, 2001; Patients' Rights in the Age of Managed Health Care, 2001; Pirates, 2002; (ed.) The Ethics of Genetic Engineering, 2002; (ed.) Genetic Engineering, 2002; Gene Therapy, 2002; A-Z of Biologists, 2003; (ed.) The Discovery of the AIDS Virus, 2003; Fighting Bioterrorism, 2004; Animal Rights, 2004, rev. ed., 2008; Antibiotics, 2005; Energy Supply, 2005; Virtual Reality, 2005; (ed.) Does the Internet Increase the Risk of Crime?, 2006; How can Domestic Violence be Prevented?, 2006; Modern Astronomy: Expanding the Universe, 2006; Modern Genetics: Engineering Life, 2006; Modern Marine Science: Exploring the Deep, 2006; Forensic Science: From Fibers To Fingerprints, 2007; Right to Die and Euthanasia, 2007; Robert Ballard: Explorer and Undersea Archaeologist, 2009; Rita Levi-Montalcini: Discoverer of Nerve Growth Factor, 2009; Alfred Wegener: Creator of the Continental Drift Theory, 2009; The Father of Anatomy: Galen and his Dissections, 2010; Rosalind Franklin: Photographing Biomolecules, 2011; Nikola Tesla: Harnessing Electricity, 2011; Luc Montagnier: Identifying the AIDS Virus, 2011; Craig Venter: Dissecting the Genome, 2011; Edward Pickering and his Women Computers, 2011; Alfred Blalock, Helen Taussig and Vivien Thomas: Mending Children's Hearts, 2011. Contributor of articles to periodicals. **Address:** 2631 Mira Vista Dr., El Cerrito, CA 94530-1429, U.S.A. **Online address:** lisaleo@well.com

YOUNT, Steven. American (born United States), b. 1948. **Genres:** Novels, Plays/Screenplays, Literary Criticism And History. **Career:** Writer, 1982-87, 1991-; University of Texas, Humanities Research Center, film historian, 1987-88; Lyndon B. Johnson Presidential Library, archivist, 1989-90. **Publications:** Wandering Star (novel), 1994; Blue Suede Shoes (novel), 2003. **Address:** 6329 Rushingbrook Dr., Raleigh, NC 27612, U.S.A. **Online address:** stevenyount@earthlink.com

YOURDON, Ed. See **YOURDON, Edward Nash.**

YOURDON, Edward Nash. (Ed Yourdon). American (born United States), b. 1944. **Genres:** Information Science/Computers. **Career:** Digital Equipment Corp., senior programmer, 1964-66; General Electric, Medinet Division, project manager, 1966-67; Mandate Systems Corp., senior consultant, 1968; E.L.I. Computer Time-Sharing Inc., director of R&D, 1968-70; independent consultant, 1970-74; Yourdon Inc., founder and chief executive officer, 1974-86; University of North Texas, Information Systems Research Center, faculty fellow; DeVRY Inc., vice president, 1986-87; Nodruoy Inc., chief executive officer, 1987-; Technology Transfer, research project advisor on software industry opportunities; Mastech, board director; Cutter Consortium, chairman, senior consultant; Cutter IT Journal, founding editor, now emeritus. **Publications:** COMPUTER DESIGN AND SOFTWARE: Design of On-Line Computer Systems, 1972; Techniques of Program Structure and Design, 1975; How to Manage Structured Programming, 1976; (with T.R. Lister) Learning to Program in Structured COBOL, vol. I, 1978, vol. II, 1979; (with L.L. Constantine) Structured Design: Fundamentals of a Discipline of Computer Program and Systems Design, 1979; Structured Walkthroughs, 1979; Managing the System Life Cycle: A Software Development Methodology Overview, 1982; Coming of Age in the Land of Computers: A Parent's Guide to Computers for Children, 1985; The Perils of Personal Computing, 1985; Nations at Risk: The Impact of the Computer Revolution, 1986; Modern Structured Analysis, 1989, rev. ed. as Just Enough Structured Analysis, 2007; (with P. Coad) Object-Oriented Analysis, 1990; (with P. Coad) Object-Oriented Design, 1991; Decline and Fall of the American Programmer, 1992; Object-Oriented Systems Design: An Integrated Approach, 1994; Mainstream Objects: An Analysis and Design Approach for Business, 1995; (with C. Argila) Case Studies in Object-Oriented Analysis and Design, 1995; Rise and Resurrection of the American Programmer, 1997; Death March: Managing Mission Impossible Projects, 1997, 2nd ed., 2004; (with J. Yourdon) Time Bomb 2000! What the Year 2000 Computer Crisis Means to You!, 1997; (with R.A. Roskind) The Complete Y2K Home Preparation Guide, 1999; (with J. Yourdon and P.G. Crane) The Y2K Financial Survival Guide: Sound Investment Through the Year 2000, 2000; Byte Wars: The Impact of September Eleventh on Information Technology, 2002; Managing High-Intensity Internet Projects, 2002; Outsource: Competing in the Global Productivity Race, 2005. OTHER: Silent Witness: A Novel of Computer Crime, 1982. EDITOR: Classics in Software Engineering, 1979; Managing the Structured Techniques, 1979; Writings of the Revolution: Selected Readings on Software Engineering, 1982. Contributor to periodicals. **Address:** Nodruoy Inc., 275 W 96th St., Apt. 21G, New York, NY 10025-6269, U.S.A. **Online address:** ed@yourdon.com

YOURDON, Jennifer. American (born United States) **Genres:** Communications/Media, Sciences, Information Science/Computers, Business/Trade/Industry. **Career:** Financial analyst and author. **Publications:** (With E. Yourdon) Time Bomb 2000: What the Year 2000 Computer Crisis Means to You!, 1998; (with E. Yourdon and P.G. Crane) The Y2K Financial Survival Guide: Sound Investment Strategies through the Year 2000, 2000. **Address:** c/o Author Mail, Prentice Hall, 200 Old Tappan Rd., Old Tappan, NJ 07675-7095, U.S.A.

YOURGRAU, Palle. American/South African (born South Africa), b. 1950. **Genres:** Novels, History, Philosophy, Science Fiction/Fantasy. **Career:** Brandeis University, Department of Philosophy, assistant professor, associate professor, professor, Harry A. Wolfson professor of philosophy, Harry A. Wolfson chair of philosophy, 2005-. Writer. **Publications:** (Ed.) Demonstratives, 1990; The Disappearance of Time: Kurt Godel and the Idealistic Tradition in Philosophy, 1991; Godel Meets Einstein: Time Travel in the Godel Universe, 1999; A World without Time: The Forgotten Legacy of Godel and Einstein, 2005. **Address:** Department of Philosophy, Brandeis University, Rabb 332, 415 S St., PO Box 549110, Waltham, MA 02454, U.S.A. **Online address:** yourgrau@brandeis.edu

YOUST, Lionel. American (born United States), b. 1934. **Genres:** Local His-tory/Rural Topics, Biography, Documentaries/Reportage. **Career:** Air Force, jet engine technician, Writer. **Publications:** Above the Falls: An Oral and Folk History of Upper Glenn Creek, Coos County, Oregon, 1991, 2nd ed., 2003; She's Tricky Like Coyote: Annie Miner Peterson, an Oregon Coast Indian Woman, 1997; (with W.R. Seabury) Coquelle Thompson, Athabaskan Witness: A Cultural Biography, 2002; Sawdust in the Western Woods: A Personal, Pictorial and Primarily Oral History of the Small Sawmill in the Douglas Fir Region, 1926-1956, 2009. **Address:** Golden Falls Publishing, 12445 Hwy 241, Coos Bay, OR 97420, U.S.A. **Online address:** lionel@youst.net

YOW, Valerie Raleigh. American (born United States), b. 1934. **Genres:** Plays/Screenplays, History, Biography. **Career:** Brooklyn College, instructor in history, 1966-70; University of Rhode Island, assistant professor of history, 1974-80, professor; Northern Illinois University, assistant professor of women's studies, 1984-90; C.G. Jung Society of the Triangle, board director, 2000-; Oral History Review, book review editor. Historian. **Publications:** The History of Hera: A Woman's Art Cooperative, 1974-1989, 1989; Bryant College: The First Hundred Years, 1991; Patient Care: A History of Butler Hospital, 1994; Recording Oral History: A Practical Guide for Social Scientists, 1994, 2nd ed., Recording Oral History: A Guide for the Humanities and Social Sciences, 2005; Bernice Kelly Harris: A Good Life Was Writing (biography), 1999; Betty Smith: Life of the Author of A Tree Grows in Brooklyn, 2008. **Address:** 12 Davie Cir., Chapel Hill, NC 27514, U.S.A. **Online address:** reeyownc@mindspring.com

YSRAEL, Elie-Pierre. See **RENAUD, Jacques.**

YU, Anthony C. American/Hong Kong (born Hong Kong), b. 1938. **Genres:** Literary Criticism And History, Theology/Religion, Translations, Humanities. **Career:** University of Illinois, instructor, 1967-68; University of Chicago, Divinity School, assistant professor, 1968-74, associate professor, 1974-78, professor of religion and literature, 1978-88, Carl Darling Buck distinguished service professor emeritus, 1988-2005, professor emeritus of religion and literature, 2005-; Indiana University, associate visiting professor, 1975; Journal of Asian Studies, assistant editor, 1975-77; Journal of Religion, co-editor, 1980-90; Stanford University, Evans-Wentz lecturer in Oriental religions, 1982; University of Alberta, distinguished visiting professor, 1992; University of Hong Kong, visiting professor, 1997; Asia Research Institute, distinguished lecturer; National Singapore University, Wu Teh Yao lecturer, 2005; Academia Senicia, distinguished lecturer, 2005; Chinese University of Hong Kong, Chung Chi College, Siu Lien Ling Wong visiting fellow, 2005-06; Australian National University, Institute and School of Asian and Pacific Studies, senior visiting fellow, 2008. **Publications:** Dissertation: The Fall: The Poetic and Theological Realism of Aeschylus, Milton, and Camus, 1969; Rereading the Stone: Desire and the Making of Fiction in Dream of the Red Chamber, 1997; State and Religion in China: Historical and Textual Perspectives, 2005; Comparative Journeys: Essays on Literature and Religion East and West, 2008. EDITOR: (intro.) Parnassus Revisited: Modern Critical Essays on the Epic Tradition, 1973; (and trans.) The Journey to the West, 1977, vol. IV, 1983; (with M. Gerhart) Morphologies of Faith: Essays in Religion and Culture in Honor of Nathan A. Scott, Jr., 1990; The Monkey & the Monk: A Revised Abridgment of the Journey to the West, 2006. Contributor to magazines, books, journals and newspapers. **Address:** Divinity School, University of Chicago, 024 Swift Hall, 1025 E 58th St., Chicago, IL 60637-1509, U.S.A. **Online address:** acyu@uchicago.edu

YU, Michelle. American (born United States) **Genres:** Women's Studies And Issues, Novels. **Career:** College Sports Television, sports writer; Sports Illustrated for Kids, reporter; TVG, intern, 2004-06, production assistant and fill-in on-air talent, 2006-10, freelance/on-site reporter, 2010, reporter, analyst, anchor and host, 2010-. **Publications:** (With B. Kan) China Dolls (novel), 2007; (with B. Kan) Young, Restless, and Broke, 2010. **Address:** Thomas Dunne Books, 175 5th Ave., New York, NY 10010, U.S.A. **Online address:** michelleandblossom@chinadollsnovel.com

YU, Miri. Korean/Japanese (born Japan), b. 1968. **Genres:** Young Adult Fiction. **Career:** Tokyo Kid Brothers, actress and assistant director. Writer. **Publications:** Seibutsuga, 1991; Uo no matsuri, 1992; Himawari no hitsugi, 1993; Hinemi. Uo no matsuri, 1993; Hinemi. Sakan no matsuri, 1993; Green Bench, Kawade Shobo, 1994; Yu Miri no jisatsu, 1995; Kazoku no hyohon, 1995; Kotoba no ressun, 1996; Mado no aru shoten kara, 1996; Shigo jiten, 1996; Furu hausu, 1996; Mizube no yurikago, 1997; Kazoku shiniema, 1997; Nau andozen Yu Miri: Yu Miri jishin ni yoru zensakuhin kaisetsu purasu gojuichino shitsumon, 1997; Now and then Yu Miri: Yu Miri jishin ni yoru-zensakuhin kaisetsu purasu gojuichi no shitsumon, 1997; Tairu, 1997; Kazoku shinema, 1997; Ijime ǔi sigan, 1998; Kamen no kuni, 1998; Gorudu rasshu, 1998; Jisatsu, 1999; Jogakusei no tomo, 1999; Saengmyŏng, 2000; Inochi, 2000; Otoko, 2000; Yŏhaksaeng ui Ch'ing'u, 2000; Kajok sǔk'ech'i, 2000; sakana ga mitayume, 2000; Koe, 2001; Sekai no hibiware to tamashii no kuhaku o, 2001; Mulkogi kwa kkun kkum, 2001; Ruju, 2001; Ikiru, 2001; Kotoba wa shizuka ni odoru, 2001; Turu, 2001; Tamashii, 2001; Gold Rush, 2003. **Address:** c/o Author Mail, Welcome Rain Publishers L.L.C., 532 Laguardia Pl., Ste. 473, New York, NY 10012-1428, U.S.A.

YUAN, Gao. (Hai Lan). American/Chinese (born China), b. 1952. **Genres:** Cultural/Ethnic Topics, Ethics, History. **Career:** Shijiazhuang Diesel Engine Factory, foundry workshop engineer, 1975-76; Hebei Provincial Foreign Trade Bureau, agent for fruit exports, 1976-78; China Daily, feature writer, 1981-82; Asia Cable, political and legal correspondent, 1984-86. **Publications:** Born Red: A Chronicle of the Cultural Revolution, 1988; Lure the Tiger Out of the Mountains: the Thirty-six Stratagems of Ancient China, 1991. Contributor to periodicals. **Address:** 6-B Escondido Village, Stanford, CA 94305, U.S.A.

YUDELMAN, David. Canadian/South African (born South Africa), b. 1944. **Genres:** Politics/Government, Money/Finance, Communications/Media, Industrial Relations, Organized Labor, Writing/Journalism, Documentaries/Reportage, Business/Trade/Industry, Business/Trade/Industry. **Career:** African Night School, teacher, 1962-67; Rand Daily Mail, political and financial journalist, 1964-67; Times, political and financial journalist, 1967-70; Financial Mail, political and financial journalist, 1970-72, 1975-76; University of the Witwatersrand, senior lecturer, political science, 1979-82; Queen's University, Centre for Resource Studies, senior research associate, 1982-86, adjunct professor of political studies, 1985-86; Frost and Sullivan (political risk analysts), associate, 1983-87; Bank of Montreal, adviser on legislation and government, manager of policy analysis and manager of information and analysis, 1986-89; Ontario Hydro, planning officer, senior strategic projects officer and section head of executive writing projects, 1989-93; Executive Writing Projects, founder and principal, 1993-. Writer. **Publications:** The Emergence of Modern South Africa, 1982; (ed.) Financing Canadian Mining in the 1980s, 1984; Political Risk in Extractive Industries, vol. II, 1985; Canadian Mineral Policy, Past and Present, 1985; Mining and the MacDonald Commission: The State of the Industry in the Mid-1980s, 1985; (with J. Crush and A. Jeeves) South Africa's Labor Empire, 1991. **Address:** 153 Wolfrey Ave., Toronto, ON M4K 1L4, Canada. **Online address:** yudelman@tellitbetter.com

YUDKIN, Leon Israel. British (born England), b. 1939. **Genres:** Literary Criticism And History, Language/Linguistics, Young Adult Fiction. **Career:** University of London, lecturer in modern Hebrew, 1964-65; University of South Africa, lecturer in Judaica, 1965-66; University of Manchester, lecturer in modern Hebrew, 1966-96; University College London, lecturer, 1996-2002; University of Paris VIII, visiting professor. Writer. **Publications:** Isaac Lamdan: A Study in Twentieth-Century Hebrew Poetry, 1971; Escape into Siege, 1974; U.Z. Greenberg: On the Anvil of Hebrew Poetry, 1980; Jewish Writing and Identity in the Twentieth Century, 1982; 1948 and After: Aspects of Israeli Fiction, 1984; Else Lasker-Schueler: A Study in German-Jewish Literature, 1990; Beyond Sequence: Current Israeli Fiction and Its Context, 1992; A Home Within: Varieties of Jewish Expression in Modern Fiction, 1996; Public Crisis and Literary Response: The Adjustment of Modern Jewish Literature, 2001; Literature in the Wake of the Holocaust, 2003. EDITOR: (with B. Tammuz) Meetings with the Angel (short story anthology), 1973; Modern Hebrew Literature in English Translation, 1986; Agnon: Texts and Contexts in English Translation, 1988; The Israeli Writer and the Holocaust, 1993; The Other in Israeli Literature, 1993; Hebrew Literature in the Wake of the Holocaust, 1993; Israeli Writers Consider the Outsider, 1993; Israel: The Vision of a State and its Literature, 2005. In and Out: Bohemian Jewry and the Prague Circle, 2010. Contributor of articles to periodicals. **Address:** 51 Hillside Ct., 409 Finchley Rd., London, GL NW3 6HQ, England. **Online address:** yudk4@aol.com

YUILL, Nicola M. British (born England), b. 1965. **Genres:** Psychology, Human Relations/Parenting, Children's Fiction, Education. **Career:** University of Sussex, research fellow in experimental psychology, 1983-86, lecturer in psychology, 1988-, senior lecturer in psychology; Cambridge University, research fellow in unit on the development and integration of behaviour, 1986-88. Writer. **Publications:** (With J. Oakhill) Children's Problems in Text

Comprehension: An Experimental Investigation, 1991. CONTRIBUTOR: Handbook of Educational Ideas and Practices, 1990; Dyslexia: Integrating Theory and Practice, 1991; The Child as Psychologist, 1993. Contributor to periodicals. **Address:** School of Cognitive and Computing Sciences, University of Sussex, Pevensey 2 4b02, Falmer, Brighton, ES BN1 9QH, England. **Online address:** nicolay@sussex.ac.uk

YUMOTO, Kazumi. Japanese (born Japan), b. 1959?. **Genres:** Novels, Children's Fiction. **Career:** Writer. **Publications:** Natsu No Niwa, 1996; Popura no aki, 1997; Haru No Orgugan, 1999; Letters from the Living, 2003. Contributor to periodicals. **Address:** Farrar, Straus and Giroux, 19 Union Sq. W, New York, NY 10003-3304, U.S.A.

YUN, Ch'oe. Korean (born Korea (South)), b. 1953?. **Genres:** Novellas/Short Stories. **Career:** University of California, lecturer, 1997; Sogang University, assistant professor, 1984-87, associate professor, 1987-92, professor of French literature, 1992-. Writer and translator. **Publications:** Nŏ nŭn tŏ isang nŏ ka anida, 1991; (co-author) Hoesaek nun saram, 1992; Chŏgi sori ŏpsi hanjŏm kkonnip i chigo, 1992; Soksagim, soksagim, 1994; Yŏlse kaji irŭm ǔi kkot hyanggi, 1999; (with P. Maurus) Littérature coréenne devant le modernisme et le colonialisme, ou, Lère des revues, 2000; (contrib.) Uri saengae ǔi kkot oe, 2009. **Address:** Sogang University, 35 Baekbeom-ro, Mapo-gu, 1, Korea (South). **Online address:** choey@sogang.ac.kr

YURCHAK, Alexei. American/Russian (born Russia), b. 1960. **Genres:** History, Politics/Government, Sociology. **Career:** University of California, associate professor of anthropology; St. Petersburg University, researcher; Popov Institute of Communications and Acoustics, scientist. Writer and educator. **Publications:** Everything Was Forever, until It Was No More: The Last Soviet Generation, 2006. Contributor to books and periodicals. **Address:** Department of Anthropology, University of California, 232 Kroeber Hall, Berkeley, CA 94720, U.S.A. **Online address:** yurchak@berkeley.edu

YURICK, Sol. American (born United States), b. 1925. **Genres:** Novels, Literary Criticism And History, Mystery/Crime/Suspense, Romance/Historical, Young Adult Fiction. **Career:** New York University, librarian, 1945-53; New York City Department of Welfare, social investigator, 1954-59; writer, 1961-. **Publications:** The Warriors, 1965; Fertig, 1966; The Bag, 1968; Someone Just Like You (short stories) 1973; (ed.) Voices of Brooklyn: An Anthology, 1973; An Island Death, 1975; Richard A, 1981; Behold Metatron, 1985; Confession, 1999. **Address:** Georges Borchardt Inc., 136 E 57th St., New York, NY 10022, U.S.A. **Online address:** syu9085551@aol.com

YURYENÉN, Sergey. German (born Germany), b. 1948. **Genres:** Novellas/Short Stories, Novels, Literary Criticism And History. **Career:** Druzhba Narodov (literary monthly), correspondent and editor, 1974-75; Radio Free Europe/Radio Liberty, freelance journalist, 1978-84, researcher, 1984-86, program specialist, 1986-. **Publications:** Po puti k domu: Povest i rasskazy, 1977; Volnyǐ strelok, roman, 1985; Narushitel granitsy, 1986; Syn imperii: infantilnyǐ roman, 1986; U mikrofona Aleksandr Galich-: izhrannye teksty i zapisi, s dopolnitel, 1990; Skoryǐ v Peterburg (short stories), 1991; Doch general nogo sekretaria: roman (novel), 1999; Beglyǐ, 2002; Vkhodit Kaliban, 2006. Contributor of articles to periodicals and journals. **Address:** Bulowstrasse 20, Munich, 81679, Germany.

YUSA, Michiko. American/Japanese (born Japan), b. 1951. **Genres:** Philosophy, Biography. **Career:** Western Washington University, assistant professor, 1983-88, associate professor, 1988-94, professor, 1994-. Writer. **Publications:** (With M. Soga) Basic Kanji, 1989; Denki: Nishida Kitaro, 1998; Zen and Philosophy: An Intellectual Biography of Nishida Kitarō, 2002; Japanese Religious Traditions, 2002; (ed. with S. Clark-Langager) Isamu Noguchi and Skyviewing Sculpture, 2004; (with M.K. Yaku) Nihon no Shūkyō, 2007. **Address:** Department of Modern and Classical Languages, Western Washington University, Humanities 205, 516 High St., Bellingham, WA 98225-5946, U.S.A. **Online address:** michiko.yusa@wwu.edu

Z

ZABEL, Diane. American (born United States), b. 1957. Genres: Business/Trade/Industry. Career: Fluvanna County Library, librarian and director, 1983-84; Bosler Free Library, cataloger, 1984-85; Pennsylvania State University, Schreyer Business Library, assistant librarian, 1985-86, social science reference librarian, 1986-97, business librarian, 1998-2000, Louis and Virginia Benzak business librarian, 2000-, acting head, 2009-11; Reference and User Services Quarterly, editor, 1999-. Publications: Flexible Work Arrangements in ARL Libraries, 1992; (ed. with N.L. Herron) Bridging the Gap: A Focus on Polarity in America, 1995; (with C. Avery) The Quality Management Sourcebook: An International Guide to Materials and Resources, 1996; (with C. Avery) The Flexible Workplace: A Sourcebook of Information and Research, 2000; (ed.) Reference Reborn: Breathing New Life into Public Services Librarianship, 2011. Contributor to books. Address: Schreyer Business Library, Pennsylvania State University, 309 Paterno Library, University Park, PA 16802, U.S.A. Online address: dxz2@psu.edu

ZABOR, Rafi. American (born United States), b. 1946. Genres: Novels, Music, Biography. Career: Jazz drummer, 1967-; journalist, 1977-89; Musician Magazine, jazz critic, 1977, editor. Publications: The Bear Comes Home (novel), 1997; I, Wabenzi, 2005. Works appear in anthologies. Contributor of articles to periodicals. Address: 140 E 2nd St., New York, NY 10009, U.S.A. Online address: zabor@concentric.net

ZABOROWSKA, Magdalena J. American/Polish (born Poland), b. 1963. Genres: Gay And Lesbian Issues, Cultural/Ethnic Topics, Literary Criticism And History, Women's Studies And Issues, Architecture. Career: Furman University, assistant professor of English, 1992-96; Aarhus University, assistant professor, 1996-97, associate professor, 1998-2000, research fellow, 1999-2000; University of Michigan, visiting associate professor, 2000-01, Program in American Culture and Center for Afro-American and African Studies, associate professor, 2001-10; professor of American and Afro-American studies, 2010-. Writer. Publications: How We Found America: Reading Gender Through East European Immigrant Narratives, 1995; James Baldwin's Turkish Decade: Erotics of Exile, 2009. EDITOR: Modern Polish Poems, 1986; Other Americans, Other Americas, 1998; The Puritan Origins of American Sex, 2001; Over the Wall/After the Fall, 2004. Contributor to books and journals. Address: Program in American Culture, Center for Afro-American & African Studies, University of Michigan, 3700 Haven Hall, Ann Arbor, MI 48109-1045, U.S.A. Online address: mzaborow@umich.edu

ZABUS, Chantal J. Belgian (born Belgium), b. 1955. Genres: Novels, Cultural/Ethnic Topics, Gay And Lesbian Issues, Language/Linguistics, Sex, Third World, Women's Studies And Issues, Autobiography/Memoirs, Autobiography/Memoirs. Career: Université Paris 13, professor of comparative postcolonial and gender studies; Universite de Paris 3, researcher. Author. Publications: The African Palimpsest: Indigenization of Language in the West African Europhone Novel, 1991; Changements au féminin en Afrique noire: anthropologie et littérature, 1999; Le secret: motif et moteur de la littérature, 1999; Tempests after Shakespeare, 2002; Between Rites and Rights: Excision in Women's Experiential Texts and Human Contexts, 2007; (ed. with S. Nagy-Zekmi) Colonization or Globalization? Postcolonial Explorations of Imperial Expansion, 2010; (ed. with S. Nagy-Zekmi) Perennial Empires: Postcolonial, Transnational, and Literary Perspectives, 2011. Address:

Université Paris 13, 99 avenue Jean-Baptiste Clément, Paris, 93430, France. Online address: czabus@hotmail.com

ZACCARIA, Jerry A. American (born United States), b. 1945. Genres: Travel/Exploration, Transportation, Photography, Reference. Career: Elementary school teacher, 1965-67; Augusta County School Board, assistant principal, 1973-87, principal, 1988-97; TR XIV Publishing, founder and president, 1998-. Writer. Publications: Lighthouses of Virginia: The Quick and Easy Guide to All Virginia Lighthouses: Includes Rare Interior Photographs of All Remaining Virginia Lighthouses, 1997. Address: Family Resource & Referral Center, 934 N Augusta St., Staunton, VA 24401-3282, U.S.A. Online address: jerryzac@cfw.com

ZACCARO, Stephen J. American (born United States) Genres: Psychology, Economics, Business/Trade/Industry. Career: George Mason University, associate professor of psychology, professor of psychology; Journal of Business and Psychology and Military Psychology, associate editor. Publications: (Ed. with A.W. Riley) Occupational Stress and Organizational Effectiveness, 1987; Models and Theories of Executive Leadership: A Conceptual-Empirical Review and Integration, 1996; The Nature of Executive Leadership: A Conceptual and Empirical Analysis of Success, 2001; (ed. with R.J. Klimoski) The Nature of Organizational Leadership: Understanding the Performance Imperatives Confronting Today's Leaders, 2001; (ed. with S.M. Halpin and D.V. Day) Leader Development for Transforming Organizations: Growing Leaders for Tomorrow, 2004; (ed. with M.A. Marks and L.A. DeChurch) Multiteam Systems: An Organization Form for Dynamic and Complex Environments, 2011. Address: Department of Psychology, George Mason University, Rm. 3066B, David King Hall, 3F5, 4400 University Dr., Fairfax, VA 22030-4422, U.S.A. Online address: szaccaro@gmu.edu

ZACHARASIEWICZ, Waldemar. Austrian (born Austria) Genres: Literary Criticism And History. Career: University of Graz, lecturer, 1973-74; University of Vienna, professor of English and American studies, 1974, Canadian Studies Center, director; University of Mainz, Erasmus visiting professor, 1994, Department of English and American Studies, head, 1997-99; Princeton University, fellow, 2006; University of Texas, fellow, 2006. Writer. Publications: Die Cosmic Voyage und die Excursion in der Englischen Dichtung des 17. und 18. Jahrhunderts, 1969; Die Klimatheorie in der Englischen Literatur und Literaturkritik von der Mitte des 16. bis zum Frühen 18. Jahrhundert, 1977; (ed. with F.K. Stanzel) Encounters and Explorations: Canadian Writers and European Critics, 1986; Die Erzählkunst des Amerikanischen Südens, 1990; (ed. with H. Foltinek and W. Riehle) Tales and Their Telling Difference: Zur Theorie und Geschichte der Narrativik, Festschrift zum 70. Geburtstag von Franz K. Stanzel, 1993; Images of Central Europe in Travelogues and Fiction by North American Writers, 1995; Das Deutschlandbild in der Amerikanischen Literatur, 1998; (ed. with M. Draxlbauer) Remembering the Individual/Regional/National Past, 1999; (contrib.) Europäischer Völkerspiegel: Imagologisch-ethnographische Studien zu den Völkertafeln des Frühen 18. Jahrhunderts, 1999; (ed.) The Many Souths: Class in Southern Culture, 2003; (ed.) Transatlantische Differenzen, 2004; Images of Germany in American Literature, 2007; (ed. with R. Gray) Transatlantic Exchanges: The American South in Europe-Europe in the American South, 2007; Imagology revisited, 2010. CO-EDITOR: Encounters and Explorations, 1986; Possibilities and Limits of Multiculturalism, 2001; Sites of Memory and Collective Identities, 2001; Interculturality Canadian and the Transatlantic Heritage, 2005. **Address:** Institut fur Anglistik und Amerikanistik, Universitat Wien, Universitatcampus, Hof 8, Spitalgasse 2-4, Vienna, A-1090, Austria. **Online address:** waldemar.zacharasiewicz@univie.ac.at

ZACHARIAS, Karen Spears. German/American (born United States), b. 1956. **Genres:** Military/Defense/Arms Control, Young Adult Fiction, Autobiography/Memoirs. **Career:** Tri-City Herald, Tri-Cities, reporter, 2000; Vietnam Veterans Events, lecturer; Central Washington University, adjunct professor of journalism; Fairhope Center for the Writing Arts, writer-in-residence; Carson McCullers Center, writer-in-residence. **Publications:** (With R. McCombs) Benched: The Memoirs of Judge Rufe McCombs, 1997; Hero Mama: A Daughter Remembers the Father She Lost in Vietnam-and the Mother Who Held Her Family Together, 2005; After the Flag Has Been Folded, 2006; Where's Your Jesus Now?: Examining How Fear Erodes Our Faith, 2008; Will Jesus Buy Me a Double-wide?, 2010; A Silence of Mockingbirds, 2012. Contributor to periodicals. **Address:** HarperCollins, 10 E 53rd St., New York, NY 10022-5299, U.S.A. **Online address:** kzacharias@tri-cityherald.com

ZACHARIAS, Ravi K. American/Indian (born India), b. 1946. **Genres:** Theology/Religion. **Career:** Alliance Theological Seminary, professor and chair of evangelism and contemporary thought, 1981-84; Ravi Zacharias International Ministries, founder and president, 1984-, chairman; Staley Foundation, distinguished lecturer; University of Oxford, Wycliffe Hall, visiting professor, senior research fellow. Writer. **Publications:** A Shattered Visage: The Real Face of Atheism, 1990; Can Man Live without God, 1994; Deliver Us from Evil: Restoring the Soul in a Disintegrating Culture, 1996; Cries of the Heart: Bringing God Near When He Feels So Far, 1998; The Merchant and the Thief (juvenile): A Folktale of Godly Wisdom, 1999; (with K. Johnson) Jesus among Other Gods: The Absolute Claims of the Christian Message, 2000; The Broken Promise (juvenile), 2000; The Lotus and the Cross: Jesus Talks with Buddha, 2001; Light in the Shadow of Jihad, 2002; Sense and Sensuality: Jesus Talks with Oscar Wilde on the Pursuit of Pleasure, 2002; Is Your Church Ready?: Motivating Leaders to live an Apologetic Life, 2003; (ed. with N. Geisler) Who Made God?: And Answers to Over 100 Other Tough Questions of Faith, 2003; (ed.) Kingdom of the Cults, 2003; Recapture the Wonder, 2003; I, Isaac, Take Thee, Rebekah: Moving From Romance to Lasting Love, 2004; Real Face of Atheism, 2004; Lamb and the Führer: Jesus Talks with Hitler, 2005; Walking from East to West: God in the Shadows, 2006; (ed. with S. Mcknight and D. DuRant) Who was Jesus?, 2007; (and ed.) Beyond Opinion: Living the Faith that We Defend, 2007; Grand Weaver: How God Shapes Us Through the Events of Our Lives, 2007; New Birth or Rebirth?: Jesus Talks with Krishna, 2008; End of Reason: A Response to the New Atheists, 2008; Is There Not a Cause, 2008; There is a Plan, 2009; Has Christianity Failed You?, 2010; From Oprah to Chopra: Almost Right, 2011; Merchant and the Thief: A Folktale of Godly Wisdom, 2012; The Merchant and the Thief: A Folktale from India, 2012; Why Jesus?, 2012. Works appear in anthologies. **Address:** Ravi Zacharias International Ministries, 4725 Peachtree Corners Cir., Ste. 250, Norcross, GA 30092, U.S.A.

ZACHARY, G(regg) Pascal. American (born United States), b. 1955. **Genres:** Information Science/Computers, Adult Non-fiction. **Career:** The Wall Street Journal, senior writer, 1989-2001; Stanford University, visiting lecturer; Johns Hopkins University, Institute for Applied Economics, fellow; Arizona State University, professor; Nautilus Institute, senior associate; San Jose Mercury News, staff; Willamette Week, staff; Santa Barbara News and Review, staff; Time Inc., writer and editor; Berkeley Barb, staff; Innovation Beat, managing editor; Journalists for Human Rights, co-founder, 2003; Gates Foundation, consultant. **Publications:** Show-Stopper!: The Breakneck Race to Create Windows NT and the Next Generation at Microsoft, 1994; Endless Frontier: Vannevar Bush, Engineer of the American Century, 1997; Global Me: New Cosmopolitans and the Competitive Adge-Picking Globalism's Winners and Losers, 2000; The Diversity Advantage: Multicultural Identity in the New World Economy, 2000, rev. ed., 2003; Married to Africa: A Love Story, 2009. **Address:** Journalists for Human Rights, 147 Spadina Ave., Ste. 206, Toronto, ON M5V 2L7, Canada. **Online address:** g.zachary@gmail.com

ZACHTER, Mort. American (born United States), b. 1958?. **Genres:** Autobiography/Memoirs, Biography. **Career:** New York University, Stern School of Business, adjunct tax professor. Writer and attorney. **Publications:** Dough (memoir), 2007. Contributor to periodicals and magazines. **Address:** Princeton, NJ, U.S.A. **Online address:** mortzachter@msn.com

ZACK, Naomi. American (born United States), b. 1944. **Genres:** Ethics, Cultural/Ethnic Topics, Intellectual History, Philosophy, Cultural/Ethnic Topics. **Career:** Columbia University, preceptor of philosophy, 1968-69; State University of New York, adjunct instructor, 1990-91, assistant professor, 1991-98, associate professor, 1998-2000, professor, 2000-01, Empire State College, tutor, 1990-99, Doctor of Arts in Humanistic Studies Program, director, 2000-01; Rensselaer Polytechnic Institute, adjunct assistant professor of philosophy, 1990-91; University of Oregon, professor of philosophy, 2001-. Writer. **Publications:** Race and Mixed Race, 1993; Bachelors of Science: Seventeenth-Century Identity, Then and Now, 1996; Thinking about Race (textbook), 1998, 2nd ed., 2006; Philosophy of Science and Race, 2002; Inclusive Feminism: A Third Wave Theory of Women's Commonality, 2005; Ethics For Disaster, 2009; Handy Philosophy Answer Book, 2010; Ethics and Mores of Race, 2011. EDITOR: American Mixed Race; Race/Sex: Their Sameness, Difference, and Interplay, 1997; Women of Color and Philosophy, 2000. **Address:** Department Philosophy, University of Oregon, 338 PLC, 1415 Kincaid St., 1295 University of Oregon, Eugene, OR 97403-1295, U.S.A. **Online address:** nzack@uoregon.edu

ZACKS, Shelemyahu. American (born United States), b. 1932. **Genres:** Mathematics/Statistics. **Career:** Kansas State University, professor of statistics, 1965-68; George Washington University, Program in Logistics, consultant, 1967-87; University of New Mexico, professor of mathematics, 1968-70; Case Western Reserve University, Department of Mathematics, professor and chair, 1974-79; Virginia Polytechnic Institute, Department of Statistics, faculty, 1979-80; State University of New York-Binghamton, Department of Mathematical Sciences, professor and chair, 1980-, Center for Statistics, Quality Control and Design, director, 1983-; Technion University, faculty; New York University, faculty; Stanford University, faculty; Tel Aviv University, faculty; University of New Mexico, faculty. Writer. **Publications:** The Theory of Statistical Inference, 1971; Parametric Statistical Inference: Basic Theory and Modern Approaches, 1981; Introduction to Reliability Analysis: Probability Models and Statistical Methods, 1992; (with H. Bolfarine) Prediction Theory for Finite Populations, 1992; Stochastic Visibility in Random Fields, 1994; (with R. Kenett) Modern Industrial Statistics: The Design and Control of Quality and Reliability, 1998; Stage-Wise Adaptive Designs, 2009. Contributor of articles to journals. **Address:** Department of Mathematical Sciences, Binghamton University, LN 2202, PO Box 6000, Binghamton, NY 13902-6000, U.S.A. **Online address:** shelly@math.binghamton.edu

ZADOFF, Allen. American (born United States), b. 1967?. **Genres:** Autobiography/Memoirs, Social Sciences. **Career:** Author and motivational speaker. **Publications:** Hungry: Lessons Learned on the Journey from Fat to Thin (memoir), 2007; Food, Girls, and Other Things I Can't Have, 2009; My Life, the Theater, and Other Tragedies, 2011. **Address:** Los Angeles, CA , U.S.A. **Online address:** allenzadoff@gmail.com

ZAFFRAN, Marc. *See* **WINCKLER, Martin.**

ZAFÓN, Carlos Ruiz. *See* **ZAFÓN, Carlos Ruiz.**

ZAFÓN, Carlos Ruiz. Also writes as Carlos Ruiz Zafón. American/Spanish (born Spain), b. 1964. **Genres:** Young Adult Fiction, Novels, Mystery/Crime/Suspense. **Career:** Writer, 1993-. **Publications:** La sombra del viento, 2001; The Shadow of the Wind, 2004; El Príncipe de la Niebla, 2006; El Palacio de la Medianoche, 2006; El Juego del ángel, 2008; The Angel's Game, 2009; The Prince of Mist, 2010; Midnight Palace, 2011. **Address:** Penguin Group (USA) Inc., 375 Hudson St., New York, NY 10014-3658, U.S.A. **Online address:** publicity.enquiries@orionbooks.co.uk

ZAGORSKI, Paul W. American (born United States), b. 1946. **Genres:** Politics/Government, Military/Defense/Arms Control. **Career:** College of Idaho, assistant professor, 1974-75; Pittsburg State University, professor, 1975-, International Studies Program, director. Writer. **Publications:** Democracy vs. National Security: Civil-Military Relations in Latin America, 1992; Comparative Politics: Continuity and Breakdown in the Contemporary World, 2009. Contributor to periodicals. **Address:** Department of Social Sciences, Pittsburg State University, 412 Russ Hall, 1701 S Broadway, Pittsburg, KS 66762-5856, U.S.A. **Online address:** zagorski@pittstate.edu

ZAHARIADIS, Nikolaos. American (born United States), b. 1961. **Genres:** Politics/Government, Social Sciences. **Career:** University of Alabama, associate professor of political science and director of the political science program, Department of Government, professor and director of international studies. Writer and political scientist. **Publications:** Markets, States, and Public Policy: Privatization in Britain and France, 1995; Theory, Case, and Method in Comparative Politics, 1996; (ed.) Contending Perspectives in International Political Economy, 1999; Ambiguity and Choice in Public Policy: Political Decision Making in Modern Democracies, 2003; Essence of Political Manipulation: Emotion, Institutions, and Greek Foreign Policy, 2005; State Subsidies in the Global Economy, 2008. Contributor to periodicals. **Address:** Department of Government, University of Alabama, 410 Heritage Hall Bldg., 1401 University Blvd., Birmingham, AL 35294-1152, U.S.A. **Online address:** nzaharia@uab.edu

ZAHN, Timothy. American (born United States), b. 1951. **Genres:** Science Fiction/Fantasy, Novellas/Short Stories. **Career:** Writer. **Publications:** The Blackcollar, 1983; A Coming of Age, 1984; Cobra, 1985; Spinneret, 1985; The Backlash Mission, 1986; Cascade Point and Other Stories, 1986; Cobra Strike, 1986; Triplet, 1987; Cobra Bargain, 1988; Time Bomb and Zahndry Others, 1988; Deadman Switch, 1988; Warhorse, 1990; Heir to the Empire, 1991; Distant Friends, 1992; Dark Force Rising, 1992; Last Command, 1993; Conquerors' Pride, 1994; Conquerors' Heritage, 1995; Conquerors' Legacy, 1996; Specter of the Past, 1997; Vision of the Future, 1998; (with M.A. Stackpole) Star Wars. Mara Jade: by the Emperor's Hand, 1998; The Icarus Hunt, 1999; Angelmass, 2001; Star Song and Other Stories, 2002; Manta's Gift, 2002; Dragon and Thief: A Dragonback Adventure, 2003; Dragon and Soldier: The Second Dragonback Adventure, 2004; Green and the Gray, 2004; Star Wars. Survivor's Quest, 2004; Cobra Trilogy, 2004; Night Train to Rigel, 2005; Dragon and Slave: The Third Dragonback Adventure, 2005; Star Wars. Outbound Flight, 2006; Dragon and Herdsman: The Fourth Dragonback Adventure, 2006; Blackcollar: The Judas Solution, 2006; Dragon and Judge, 2007; Third Lynx, 2007; Star Wars. Allegiance, 2007; Dragon and Liberator: The Sixth Dragonback Adventure, 2008; Odd Girl Out, 2008; Terminator Salvation: From the Ashes, 2009; Cobra Alliance, 2009; Domino Pattern, 2010; Terminator Salvation: Trial by Fire, 2010; (contrib.) Star Wars Omnibus, 2010; (adapted) Star Wars: The Thrawn Trilogy, 2010; Cobra Guardian, 2011. **Address:** Bantam Books Inc., 1540 Broadway, New York, NY 10036-4039, U.S.A.

ZAID, Gabriel. Mexican (born Mexico), b. 1934. **Genres:** Poetry, Essays. **Career:** Monterrey Institute of Technology, industrial engineer, 1955; Ibcon, president, 1958-; El Colegio Nacional, fellow; Academia Mexicana de la Lengua, fellow. Writer. **Publications:** Fábula de Narciso y Ariadna (poem), 1958; La poesía, fundamento de la ciudad (essays), 1963; Seguimiento (poems), 1964; La Máquina de cantar (essays), 1967; Campo nudista (poems), 1969; Leer poesía (criticism), 1972, 9th ed., 2009; Los demasiados libros (essays), 1972, 12th ed., 2010; Práctica mortal (poems), 1973; Cómo leer en bicicleta (essays), 1975, 6th ed., 2010; Cuestionario (poems), 1976; El progreso improductivo (essays), 1979, 9th ed., 2009; La feria del progreso (essays), 1982; La poesía en la Práctica (essays), 1985, 4th ed., 2009; La economía presidencial (essays), 1987, 7th ed., 2010; De los libros al poder (essays), 1988, 8th ed., 2010; Sonetos y canciones (poems), 1992; Ensayos sobre poesía (essays), 1993, 2nd ed., 2004; La nueva economía presidencial, 1994, 7th ed., 2010; Adís al PRI (essays), 1995; Hacen falta empresarios creadores de empresarios (essays), 1995, 10th ed., 2004; Reloj de sol (poems), 1995, 8th ed., 2009; Tres poetas católicos (criticism), 1997; Crítica del mundo cultural (essays), 1999, 2nd ed., 2009; So Many Books: Reading and Publishing in an Age of Abundance, 2003; El costo de leer (essays), 2004; Encuesta nacional de lectura: informes y evaluaciones, 2006; The Secret of Fame, 2008; El secreto de la fama, 2009; Empresarios oprimidos, 2009. EDITOR: ómnibus de poesía mexicana, 1971, 27th ed., 2008; Asamblea de poetas jóvenes de México, 1980, 4th ed., 1991. COMPILER AND AUTHOR OF PROLOGUE: (with J.E. Pacheco) J.C. Becerra: El otoño recorre las islas, 1973, 8th ed., 2002; Manuel Ponce: Antología poética, 1980; Daniel Cosío Villegas: Imprenta y vida pública, 1985; Carlos Pellicer: Antología mínima, 2001; Tout est si clair que ça fait peur=Todo tan claro que da miedo, 2001. Contributor to periodicals. **Address:** Ibcon S.A., Gutenberg 224, Mexico City, DF 11590, Mexico. **Online address:** ibcon1@ibcon.com.mx

ZAILCKAS, Koren. American/Saudi (born Saudi Arabia), b. 1980?. **Genres:** Novels, Autobiography/Memoirs, Women's Studies And Issues. **Career:** Men's Journal, advertising assistant. Writer. **Publications:** Smashed: Story of a Drunken Girlhood, 2005; Fury, 2010. Contributor to books and periodicals. **Address:** c/o Amanda Urban, International Creative Management Inc., 825 8th Ave., New York, NY 10019, U.S.A. **Online address:** smashedbook@hotmail.com

ZAK, William F. American (born United States), b. 1945. **Genres:** Literary Criticism And History, History. **Career:** Salisbury State University, graduate faculty, professor of English, 1972-2002, professor emeritus, 2002-. Writer. **Publications:** Sovereign Shame: A Study of King Lear, 1984; The Polis and the Divine Order: The Oresteia, Sophocles, and the Defense of Democracy, 1995. Contributor to journals. **Address:** Department of English, Salisbury State University, 1101 Camden Ave., Salisbury, MD 21801-6837, U.S.A. **Online address:** wfzak@ssu.edu

ZAKARIA, Fareed. American/Indian (born India), b. 1964. **Genres:** Politics/Government, Geography, Social Sciences. **Career:** The New Republic, reporter, 1987; Harvard University, Olin Institute, executive coordinator, 1991-92; Foreign Affairs, managing editor, 1993-2000; Newsweek Intl., contributing editor, 1996-2000, editor, 2000-10; Columbia University, Department of Political Science, adjunct professor, 1997; Foreign Exchange, host, 2005-07; Yale University, trustee, 2006-; Newsweek, columnist, editor, 2000-10; Washington Post, columnist; CNN, Fareed Zakaria GPS, host, 2008-; Time (magazine), contributing editor, editor-at-large and columnist, 2010-. **Publications:** (Ed. with J.F. Hoge, Jr.) The American Encounter: The United States and the Making of the Modern World, 1997; From Wealth to Power: The Unusual Origins of America's World Role, 1998; The Future of Freedom: Illiberal Democracy at Home and Abroad, 2003, rev. ed., 2007; The Post-American World, 2008; Post-American World: Release 2.0, 2011. Contributor to periodicals. **Address:** c/o Royce Carlton, 866 United Nations Plz., Ste. 587, New York, NY 10017, U.S.A. **Online address:** fzassist@newsweek.com

ZAKARIA, Haji Ahmad. Singaporean (born Singapore), b. 1947. **Genres:** Politics/Government, Institutions/Organizations. **Career:** University of Malaya, faculty; Universiti Sains Malaysia, faculty; University Kebangsaan Malaysia, political science and strategic studies and head, 1978-82, Faculty of Social Sciences and Humanities, head of the strategic and security studies unit, 1987-99, dean of social sciences and humanities, 1999-; Australian National University, Strategic and Defence Studies Centre, visiting fellow, 1982-83; ISIS Malaysia, deputy director-general, 1983-85; Hoover Institution on War, professor, 1983-; Resource Systems Institute, East-West Center, senior fellow, 1985; National University of Singapore, Department of Political Science, senior fellow, 1992-93; Help University College, deputy vice chancellor. Writer. **Publications:** Police and Political Development in Malaysia: Change, Continuity, and Institution-Building of a Coercive Apparatus in a Developing, Ethnically Divided Society, 1977; (with M. Shibusawa and B. Bridges) Pacific Asia in the 1990s, 1992. EDITOR: (with H. Crouch) Military-Civilian Relations in Southeast Asia, 1985; Government and Politics of Malaysia, 1987; (with N. Mahmood) Political Contestation: Case Studies from Asia, 1990. **Address:** Fakulti Sains Sosial Dan Kemanusiaan, Universiti Kebangsaan Malaysia, Bangi, Selangor, 43600, Malaysia. **Online address:** profzak@pkrisc.cc.ukm.my

ZAKI, Hoda M. American (born United States), b. 1950. **Genres:** Politics/Government, Civil Liberties/Human Rights. **Career:** Hood College, professor of political science, African American Studies Program, director. Writer. **Publications:** Phoenix Renewed: The Survival and Mutatation [i.e. Mutation] of Utopian Thought in North American Science Fiction, 1965-1982, 1988, rev. ed. as Phoenix Renewed: The Survival and Mutation of Utopian Thought in North American Science Fiction, 1965-1982, 1993; Civil Rights and Politics at Hampton Institute: The Legacy of Alonzo G. Moron, 2007. **Address:** MD, U.S.A. **Online address:** hzaki@hood.edu

ZAKNIC, Ivan. American/Croatian (born Croatia), b. 1938. **Genres:** Art/Art History, Translations, Architecture, Humanities. **Career:** Jean Royer (architect and urbanist), draftsperson, 1960-62; Henry George Green (architect), draftsperson, 1969-70; Hoberman and Wasserman (architects and planners), architect, 1972-73; Todd Williams (architect), architect, 1973; University of Texas, assistant professor in architecture and planning, 1975-79; Cornell University, visiting assistant professor in architecture, 1980-82; Gwathmey Siegel and Associates (architects), architect, designer, consultant, editor and archivist, 1983-85; Pratt Institute, adjunct assistant professor in architectural design, 1984-85; John Burgee Architects with Philip Johnson, consultant, editor and archivist, 1985-86; Lehigh University, professor of architecture,

1986-94, chair of department of art and architecture, 1990-96; Princeton University, visiting fellow. **Publications:** Pompidou Center, 1983; (trans.) Max Fourny and Gerard Xuriguera, Milinkov: An Itinerary of Nostalgia, 1990; Le Corbusier, Pavillon Suisse, 2004. EDITOR: Charles Gwathmey and Robert Siegel: Buildings and Projects, 1984; (and comp.) Philip Johnson/John Burgee Architecture, 1979-1985, 1986; (and comp. and trans. with N. Pertuiset) C. Jeanneret (Le Corbusier), Journey to the East, 1987; (and trans.) The Final Testament of Pere Corbu, 1997. Contributor to periodicals. **Address:** Department of Art & Architecture, Lehigh University, Chandler Ullmann 17, Bethlehem, PA 18015, U.S.A.

ZALBEN, Jane Breskin. American (born United States), b. 1950. **Genres:** Novels, Novellas/Short Stories, Children's Fiction, Young Adult Fiction, Poetry, Westerns/Adventure, Illustrations, Picture/Board Books, Picture/Board Books. **Career:** Dial Press, Children's Book Department, assistant, 1971-72; Holt, Rinehart and Winston Inc., freelance book designer, 1973-74; writer and illustrator of children's books and novels, 1973-; Thomas Y. Crowell Co., senior designer of children's books, 1974-75; Scribner's, art director of children's books, 1975-76; School of Visual Arts, instructor of illustration, design and writing of children's books, 1976-93; Vassar Publishing Institute, writer-in-residence, 1988. **Publications:** SELF-IILLUSTRATED: Cecilia's Older Brother, 1973; Lyle and Humus, 1974; Basil and Hillary, 1975; Penny and the Captain, 1978; Norton's Nightime, 1979; Will You Count the Stars Without Me?, 1979; Norton's Nighttime, 1979; Oh, Simple!, 1981; Porcupine's Christmas Blues, 1982; Beni's First Chanukah, 1988; Leo and Blossom's Sukkah, 1990; Goldie's Purim, 1991; Beni's Little Library, 1991; Buster Gets Braces, 1992; Happy New Year, Beni, 1993; Papa's Latkes, 1994; Miss Violet's Shining Day, 1995; Pearl Plants a Tree, 1995; Beni's Family Cookbook for Jewish Holidays, 1996; Pearl's Marigolds for Grandpa, 1997; Beni's Family Treasury: Stories for the Jewish Holidays, 1998; Beni's First Wedding, 1998; To Every Season: A Family Holiday Cookbook, 1999; Don't Go!, 2001; (and comp.) Let There Be Light: Poems and Prayers for Repairing the World, 2002; Pearl's Passover: A Family Celebration Through Stories, Recipes, Crafts, and Songs, 2002. NOVELS: Maybe It Will Rain Tomorrow, 1982; Here's Looking at You, Kid, 1984; Water from the Moon, 1987; Earth to Andrew O. Blechman, 1989; The Fortuneteller in 5B, 1991; Unfinished Dreams, 1996. OTHERS: Jabberwocky, 1977; Oliver and Alison's Week, 1980; A Perfect Nose for Ralph, 1980; Happy Passover, Rosie, 1990; Pearl's Eight Days of Chanukah, 1998; To Every Season: A Family Holiday Cookbook, 1999; The Magic Menorah: A Modern Chanukah Tale, 2001; Baby Babka, the Gorgeous Genius, 2004; (with S. Zalben) Saturday Night at the Beastro, 2004; Hey, Mama Goose, 2005; Paths to Peace: People Who Changed the World, 2006; Leap, 2007; Light, 2007; Brenda Berman: Wedding Expert, 2009; Four Seasons, 2011; Mousterpiece, 2012. Illustrator of books by others. Contributor to periodicals. **Address:** c/o Elizabeth Harding, Curtis Brown Ltd., 10 Astor Pl., New York, NY 10003, U.S.A. **Online address:** janezalben@hotmail.com

ZALD, Mayer Nathan. American (born United States), b. 1931. **Genres:** Institutions/Organizations, Sociology. **Career:** University of Chicago, Department of Psychology, instructor, assistant professor, 1960-64, Department of Sociology, instructor, assistant professor, 1960-64; American Journal of Sociology, associate editor, 1962-63; Vanderbilt University, Department of Sociology, associate professor, 1964-68, professor, 1968-77, chairman, 1971-75; Social Forces, advisory editor, 1974-78; Administration and Society, advisory editor, 1976-90; University of Michigan, professor of sociology, social work and business administration, 1977-2001, chairman, 1981-86, 1990-92, professor emeritus, 2001-, Intersections: Initiative on Social Sciences and the Humanities, co-director, 2002-04, Organizational Studies Program, faculty affiliate, 2007-; American Sociological Review, associate editor, 1979-82; Elsevier Scientific Publications, consulting editor, 1980-81; Academy of Management, Organization and Management Theory Division, distinguished lecturer, 1989; University of North Carolina, Department of Sociology, Elaine Selo memorial lecturer, 1989; University of California, visiting professor, 2002; Renmin University, Workshop on Social Movement Theory and Research, lecturer, 2007. **Publications:** Organizational Change: The Political Economy of the YMCA, 1970; Occupations and Organizations in American Society, 1971; (with G.L. Wamsley) The Political Economy of Public Organizations: A Critique and Approach to the Study of Public Administration, 1973. EDITOR: Social Welfare Institutions, 1965; (and intro.) Organizing for Community Welfare, 1967; Power in Organizations, 1970; (with W.A. Rushing) Organizations and Beyond: Selected Essays of James D. Thompson, 1976; (with J.D. McCarthy) The Dynamics of Social Movements: Resource Mobilization, Social Control, and Tactics, 1979; (with G.T. Martin, Jr.) Social Welfare in Society, 1981; (with G.D. Suttles) The Challenge of Social Control: Citizenship and Institution Building in Modern Society, 1985; (with J.D. McCarthy) Social Movements in an Organizational Society, 1987; (with R.L. Kahn) Organizations and Nation-States, 1990; (with D. McAdam and J.D. McCarthy) Comparative Perspectives on Social Movements: Political Opportunities, Mobilizing Structures, and Cultural Framings, 1996; (with J.A. Guidry and M.D. Kennedy) Globalizations and Social Movements: Culture, Power, and the Transnational Public Sphere, 2000; (with J.C. Banaszak-Holl and S.R. Levitsky) Social Movements and the Transformation of American Health Care, 2010. Works appear in anthologies. Contributor to books. **Address:** Department of Sociology, University of Michigan, Rm. 3155, LSA Bldg., 500 S State St., Ann Arbor, MI 48109-1382, U.S.A. **Online address:** mayerz@umich.edu

ZALOGA, Steven J(oseph). American (born United States), b. 1952. **Genres:** Military/Defense/Arms Control, History, Theatre. **Career:** DMS Inc., managing editor of special studies and defense analyst, 1978-86; Video Ordnance Inc., writer and producer, 1987-92; Technology Training Inc., lecturer, 1987-91; Teal Group Corp., senior analyst, 1993-; Institute for Defense Analyses, adjunct staff, 1995-. **Publications:** (With J. Milsom) Russian Tanks of World War Two, 1977; Handbook for American Graduate Students in Poland, 1978; Modern Soviet Armor: Combat Vehicles of the USSR and Warsaw Pact Today, 1979; Stuart: U.S. Light Tanks in Action, 1979; Blitzkrieg: Armour Camouflage and Markings, 1939-40, 1980; Squadron Signal, 1981; Soviet Heavy Tanks, 1981; Armour of the Middle East Wars, 1948-78, 1981; (with J. Loop) Modern U.S. Armour, 1982; (with J. Grandsen) The Eastern Front: Armour Camouflage and Markings, 1941-45, 1983; Battle of the Bulge (photographic survey), 1983; Israeli Armour, 1948-82 (photographic survey), 1983; (with J. Grandsen) Soviet Tanks and Combat Vehicles of World War II, 1984; Soviet Tanks Today (photographic survey), 1984; (with M. Green) Tanks Illustrated: U.S. Battle Tanks Today (photographic survey), 1984; Patton's Tanks (photographic survey), 1984; (with V. Madej) The Polish Campaign of 1939, 1985; U.S. Infantry Combat Vehicles Today (photographic survey), 1985; U.S. Halftracks of WW2 (photographic survey), 1985; The Soviet Army Today (photographic survey), 1985; The Soviet Army of World War Two (photographic survey), 1985; Operation Barbarossa 1941 (photographic survey), 1985; Soviet Army Uniforms in World War Two, 1985; Air Defense for the U.S. Army, 1985; U.S. Tank Destroyers of World War Two (photographic survey), 1985; Future Fighters, 1986; (with J.W. Loop) Soviet Tanks and Combat Vehicles, 1946 to the Present, 1987; U.S. Mechanized Firepower Today (photographic survey), 1987; Inside the Soviet Army Today, 1987; U.S. Marine Tanks in World War Two, 1988; Soviet Air Defense Missiles: Design, Development, and Tactics, 1989; Red Thrust: Attack on the Central Front, Soviet Tactics and Capabilitiesin the 1990s, 1989; Soviet Mechanized Firepower Today (photographic survey), 1989; (with Grandsen) Soviet Mechanized Firepower 1941-45 (photographic survey), 1989; The Road to Berlin 1944-45 (photographic survey), 1989; The Soviet T-72 Tank, 1989; The Soviet BMP Infantry Combat Vehicle, 1990; (with M. Green) Tank Attack: A Primer on Modern Tank Warfare, 1991; Soviet Wheeled Armored Vehicles, 1991; Modern Soviet Warplanes: Fighters, 1991; Modern Soviet Warplanes: Helicopters and Strike Aircraft, 1991; (with W. Luczak) Armor of the Afghanistan War, 1991; The Soviet T-64 and T-80 Tanks, 1992; Soviet Warships Today, 1992; The Red Army of the Great Patriotic War, 1941-5, 1992; Russian Falcons: The New Wave of Soviet Combat Aircraft, 1992; Target America: The Soviet Union and the Strategic Arms Race, 1945-64, 1993; The Soviet T-54, T-55, and T-62 Tanks, 1993; The ZSU-23-4 Shilka and Other Soviet Air Defense Gun Vehicles, 1993; The Sherman Tank at War: The European Theatre, 1942-45, 1994; (with G. Balin) D-Day Tank Warfare, 1994; (with Balin) Tank Warfare in Korea 1950-53, 1994; Inside the Blue Berets: The Combat History of the Soviet and Russian Airborne Assault Force, 1995; Tank Battles of the Pacific War 1941-45, 1995; U.S. Tank Destroyers at War 1941-45, 1995; Red Army Handbook, 1939-45, 1998; The Kremlin's Nuclear Sword: The Rise and Fall of Russia's Strategic Nuclear Forces, 1945-2000, 2002; Operation Cobra 1944: Breakout from Normandy, 2004; Poland 1939: The Birth of Blitzkrieg, 2004; D-Day 1944: Omaha Beach, 2004; D-Day 1944: Utah Beach & U.S. Airborne Landings, 2004; Bagration 1944: The Destruction of Army Group Center, 2004; Lorraine 1944: Patton Versus Manteuffel, 2004; (with J. Loop) Soviet Bloc Elite Forces, 2005; U.S. Armored Units in the North African and Italian Campaigns 1942-45, 2006; Modelling the U.S. Army M4 (75mm) Sherman Medium Tank, 2006; Remagen 1945: Endgame Against the Third Reich, 2006; German Panzers, 1914-18, 2006; The Atlantic Wall, 2007; U.S. Field Artillery of World War II, 2007; Red SAM: The SA-2

Guideline Anti-aircraft Missile, 2007; U.S. Airborne Divisions in the ETO, 1944-45, 2007; Japanese Tanks: 1939-45, 2007; Modelling the US Army M4 (76mm) Sherman Medium Tank, 2007; The Siegfried Line, 1944-45: Battles on the German Frontier, 2007; New Vanguard 140: Armored Trains, 2008; Armored Thunderbolt: The U.S. Army Sherman in World War II, 2008; German V-Weapon Sites 1943-45, 2008; Unmanned Aerial Vehicles: Robotic Air Warfare, 1917-2007, 2008; Liberation of Paris 1944: Patton's Race for the Seine, 2008; Panther vs. Sherman: Battle of the Bulge, 1944, 2008; M1 Abrams vs T-72 Ural: Operation Desert Storm 1991, 2009; Staghound Armored Car, 1942-62, 2009; Modeling Us Armor of World War II, 2009; T-80 Standard Tank: The Soviet Army's Last Armored Champion, 2009; (with K. Ford) Overlord: The D-Day Landings, 2009; M551 Sheridan: US Airmobile Tanks, 1941-2001, 2009; T-62 main Battle Tank, 1965-2005, 2009; Operation Dragoon 1944: France's Other D-Day, 2009; Rangers Lead the Way: Pointe-du-hoc D-day, 1944, 2009; (with L.S. Ness) Companion to the Red Army 1939-45, 2009; Defense of Japan, 1945, 2010; Operation Nordwind 1945, 2010; French Tanks of World War I, 2010; Spanish Civil War Tanks: The Proving Ground for Blitzkrieg, 2010; T-34-85 vs M26 Pershing: Korea 1950, 2010; George S. Patton: Leadership, Strategy, Conflict, 2010; Armored Attack 1944, 2011; Most Daring Raid of World War II, 2011; Defense of the Rhine 1944-45, 2011; (ed.) Battle Ground: The Greatest Tank Duels in History, 2011; Kamikaze: Japanese Special Attack Weapons, 1944-45, 2011; Operation Pointblank 1944: Defeating the Luftwaffe, 2011; Panzer IV vs Char B1 bis: France 1940, 2011; Armored Victory 1945: U.S. Army Tank Combat in the European Theater From the Battle of the Bulge to Germany's Surrender, 2012. **Address:** Teal Group Corp., 3900 University Dr., Ste. 220, Fairfax, VA 22030-2513, U.S.A. **Online address:** szaloga@tealgroup.com

ZAMBRANO, Myrna M. American (born United States), b. 1958. **Genres:** Women's Studies And Issues, Education. **Career:** City of San Diego, Office of Senator, district director. Writer. **Publications:** NONFICTION: Mejor Sola Que Mal Acompañada: Para La Mujer Golpeada/For the Latina in an Abusive Relationship (bilingual; title means Better Alone Than in Bad Company), 1985; No Más: Guia para la Mujer Golpeada, 1994. Contributor to periodicals. **Address:** Planning Division, City of San Diego, 202 C St., MS 5A, San Diego, CA 92101, U.S.A.

ZAMBRENO, Mary Frances. (Robyn Tallis). American (born United States), b. 1954. **Genres:** Science Fiction/Fantasy, Mythology/Folklore, Young Adult Fiction, Literary Criticism And History. **Career:** Rich South High School, English teacher, 1977-80; Chicago State University, instructor, 1981; Loyola University, lecturer, 1981-88; DePaul University, instructor, 1986; University of Illinois, lecturer, 1987-91; Rosary College, visiting assistant professor, 1991-92; Elmhurst College, assistant professor of English. Writer. **Publications:** (As Robyn Tallis) Children of the Storm, 1989; A Plague of Sorcerers, 1991; Journeyman Wizard, 1994; Fire Bird, 2001. Contributor to periodicals. **Address:** Department of English, Elmhurst College, 190 Prospect Ave., Elmhurst, IL 60126-3296, U.S.A. **Online address:** maryz@elmhurst.edu

ZAMIR, Israel. (Israel Singer Zamir). Israeli/Polish (born Poland), b. 1929. **Genres:** Biography, Novellas/Short Stories, Novels, Autobiography/Memoirs. **Career:** Hotam (weekly magazine), editor; Al-Hamishmar (daily newspaper), journalist, 1973-, editor, through 1995; Daf-Yarok (kibbutz weekly magazine), editor; Kar-Lamoshav (agricultural magazine), editor, 1989-; University of Tel-Aviv, instructor of journalism, 1985-95. **Publications:** Sandal Shel Sus: Sipurim, 1979; Horshoe (short story collection), 1980; Avi, Yitshak Bashevis-Zinger, 1994; MóUj Ojciec Bashevis Singer, 1995; Agil ba-ozen: Sipurim, 1998; Shoket Sedukah, 2001; Aravah Bukhiyah: Sipurim, 2009. Contributor to books. **Address:** Kibbutz Beit-Alfa, M.P. Gilboa, 19140, Israel.

ZAMIR, Israel Singer. See ZAMIR, Israel.

ZAMORA, Bernice (B. Ortiz). American (born United States), b. 1938. **Genres:** Poetry, Literary Criticism And History, Third World, Women's Studies And Issues, Adult Non-fiction, Anthropology/Ethnology, History. **Career:** University of California, instructor in Chicano studies, 1976-78; University of San Francisco, instructor in English and ethnic studies, 1978-79; Santa Clara University, assistant professor of English, 1990-; Stanford University, assistant visiting professor, 1994; California Council for the Humanities, educational consultant; California State Department of Education, educational consultant; De Colores, editor. **Publications:** (With J.A. Burciaga) Restless

Serpents (poems), 1976; Releasing Serpents (poems), 1994; Bellow, 1997; Recalling Richard, 1997. EDITOR: (with J. Armas) Chicano Literary Criticism, Chicano Short Stories, Barrio Oral History, Chicano Poetry Anthology, 1980; (with J. Armas and M. Reed) Flor y Canto IV and V: An Anthology of Chicano Literature, 1980. Works appear in anthologies. Contributor to periodicals. **Address:** Department of English, Santa Clara University, 500 El Camino Real, Santa Clara, CA 95053, U.S.A.

ZAMORA, Lois Parkinson. American (born United States), b. 1944?. **Genres:** Literary Criticism And History, Art/Art History. **Career:** University of California, teaching fellow, 1971-73; George Mason University, visiting assistant professor, 1977-78; University of Houston, Department of English, assistant professor, 1978-84, associate professor, 1984-89, professor, 1989-, John and Rebecca Moores distinguished professor, College of Humanities, interim dean of fine arts and communication, 1996-99, Department of History, professor, 1999-, School of Art, professor, 1999-, Center for the America, co-director, 2009-, Department of Comparative Cultural Studies, chair, 2011-. Writer. **Publications:** (Ed. and intro.) The Apocalyptic Vision in America: Interdisciplinary Essays on Myth and Culture, 1982; (trans.) A. Muñiz-Huberman, Enclosed Garden, 1988; Writing the Apocalypse: Historical Vision in Contemporary U.S. and Latin American Fiction, 1989; (ed. and intro. with W.B. Faris) Magical Realism: Theory, History, Community, 1995; The Usable Past: The Imagination of History in Recent Fiction of the Americas, 1997; (ed. with W. Watriss) Image and Memory: Photography from Latin America, 1866-1994, 1998; (ed. and intro.) Contemporary American Women Writers: Gender, Class, Ethnicity, 1998; (comp.) Guillermo Floris Margadant y su mundo, 2002; How Far Is America from Here?, 2005; The Inordinate Eye: New World Baroque and Latin American Fiction, 2006; (ed. with M. Kaup) Baroque New Worlds: Representation, Transculturation, Counterconquest, 2007. **Address:** Department of English, University of Houston, 227C Roy Cullen Bldg., 4800 Calhoun Rd., Houston, TX 77004, U.S.A. **Online address:** lzamora@uh.edu

ZAMORA, Narciso. American (born United States), b. 1959. **Genres:** History. **Career:** Writer. **Publications:** Walking Man: A Modern Missions Experience in Latin America, 2008. **Address:** Quill Driver Books/Word Dancer Press, 2006 S Mary St., Fresno, CA 93721-3311, U.S.A. **Online address:** narcisozf@hotmail.com

ZANCANELLA, Don. American (born United States), b. 1954. **Genres:** Novellas/Short Stories, Young Adult Fiction. **Career:** University of New Mexico, College of Education, Department of Language, Literacy and Sociocultural Studies, assistant professor, associate professor, 1988-, professor, chair. Writer. **Publications:** Western Electric (short stories), 1996. Contributor to periodicals. **Address:** College of Education, University of New Mexico, Rm. 143, Hokona Hall, 1 University of New Mexico, Albuquerque, NM 87131-0001, U.S.A. **Online address:** zanc@unm.edu

ZANE See ROBERTS, Kristina LaFerne.

ZANG, David W(illiam). American (born United States), b. 1950. **Genres:** Biography, Sports/Fitness. **Career:** Internal Revenue Service, revenue officer, 1975-78; University of Maryland, assistant instructor in physical education, 1985-86, visiting lecturer in kinesiology, 1988-91; American Alliance for Health, Physical Education, Recreation, and Dance, assistant archivist, 1986-87; Towson State University, senior lecturer in physical education, 1987-88, 1992-95, assistant professor of physical education, 1995-99, associate professor of kinesiology, 1999-, professor of kinesiology, department chair; Museum of American Sport, project director, 1991-92; Pennsylvania State University, lecturer, 1993; George Mason University, lecturer; Washington Bible College, lecturer. Writer. **Publications:** (With M. Everman) AAHPERD Archives Oral History Guidelines, 1988; (with B. Kessler) Play Life of A City: Baltimore's Recreation and Parks, 1900-1955, 1989; (contrib. and ed.) The Columbia Encyclopedia, 1993; Fleet Walker's Divided Heart: The Life of Baseball's First Black Major Leaguer, 1995; Sportswars: Athletes in the Age of Aquarius, 2001. Contributor of articles to journals and magazines. **Address:** Department of Kinesiology, Towson University, TC 204, 8000 York Rd., Towson, MD 21252, U.S.A. **Online address:** dzang@towson.edu

ZANGANA, Haifa. British/Iraqi (born Iraq), b. 1950?. **Genres:** Novels, Women's Studies And Issues, Military/Defense/Arms Control. **Career:** Novelist and educator. **Publications:** Through the Vast Halls of Memory, 1991; Nisa 'alá Safar: Riwayah (novel), 2001; City of Widows: An Iraqi Woman's

Account of War and Resistance, 2007; Dreaming of Baghdad, 2009. Contributor to newspapers. **Address:** London, GL , England. **Online address:** haifa-zangana@yahoo.co.uk

ZANGGER, Eberhard. Swiss/German (born Germany), b. 1958. **Genres:** Communications/Media, Archaeology/Antiquities, Earth Sciences, Geography, Technology, Young Adult Fiction. **Career:** Senckenberg Museum, Frankfurt am Main, technician in museum design, 1974-76; Ruhr University, preparator and restorer, 1976-78; German Mining Museum, technician, 1978-80; Stanford University, researcher, geoarchaeologist, 1984-88; Cambridge University, Department of Earth Sciences, senior research associate, 1988-91; Klaus J. Stohlker AG (strategic public relations), senior consultant, 1999-2000; Eberhard Zangger Public Relations, founder and director, 2000- ; KPNQwest N.V., director of corporate communications, 2000-02; Science Communications GmbH, founder and chief executive officer, 2002-. Writer. **Publications:** The Flood from Heaven: Deciphering the Atlantis Legend, 1992; Geoarchaeology of the Argolid, 1993; Ein Neuer Kampf Um Troia: Archäologie in Der Krise, 1994; Zukunft Der Vergangenheit: Archäologieim 21, Jahrhundert, 1998; Future of the Past: Archaeology in the Twenty-First Century, 2001; Splügen, Wo Sich Wege Treffen: Das Bodenhaus Erzählt Seine Geschichte, 2003. Contributor to books and journals. Works appear in anthologies. **Address:** Science Communications GmbH, Sonnhaldenstrasse 14, Zurich, 8032, Switzerland. **Online address:** e.zangger@science-communications.ch

ZANUSSI, Krzysztof. Swiss/Polish (born Poland), b. 1939. **Genres:** Plays/Screenplays. **Career:** Director of motion pictures; Association of Polish Filmmakers, vice president, 1971-83; Federation of European Film Directors (FERA), president, 1990-94; Katowice University, professor, 1992; Silesian University, professor; European Graduate School, professor of European film; TOR Film Studio, director; theater director; Association Eurovisioni, president. Writer. **Publications:** On editing an amateur film, 1968; Nowele filmowe, 1976; Rozmowy o filmie amatorskim, 1978; Scenariusze filmowe, 1978; Discourse on an Amateur Film, 1978; Zanussi: sei film, 1979; Wherever You Are, 1992; Scenariusze filmowe III, 1992; Przed nieznanym trybunałem, 1997; Opowieści weekendowe: cykl nowel telewizyjnych, 1997; Giovanni Paolo II: il profeta del terzo millennio, 1997; Time to Die, 1999; In Full Gallop: And Six Other Screenplays, 2001; Bigos nie zginie!-: w rodzinnej Europie. Rozmawia Dorota Maciejewska, 2003; Persona non grata, 2005. **Address:** Media and Communications Division, European Graduate School, Alter Kehr 20, Leuk-Stadt, CH-3953, Switzerland. **Online address:** tov@tov.com.pl

ZARAGOZA, Federico Mayor. *See* **MAYOR, Federico.**

ZARB, Janet M. Canadian/American (born United States), b. 1941. **Genres:** Psychology, Medicine/Health. **Career:** Toronto Board of Education, psychologist, 1978-86; Providence Centre Hospital, psychologist, 1986-92, director of psychological services, 1992-; St. Michael's Hospital, psychologist, 1986-92. Writer. **Publications:** Cognitive-Behavioral Assessment and Therapy with Adolescents, 1992; Developmental Cognitive Behavioral Therapy With Adults, 2007. Contributor to journals. Works appear in anthologies. **Address:** Providence Centre Hospital, 3276 St. Clair Ave. E, Scarborough, Ontario, ON M1L 1W1, Canada.

ZAREMBA, Alan Jay. American (born United States), b. 1949. **Genres:** Administration/Management. **Career:** State University of New York at Fredonia, assistant professor, 1976-81; Northeastern University, associate professor of communication studies, 1981-. Writer. **Publications:** Mass Communication and International Politics: A Case Study of Press Reactions to the 1973 Arab-Israeli War, 1988; Management in a New Key: Communication in the Modern Organization, 1989, rev. ed., 1993; Organizational Communication: Foundations for Business & Management, 2003, 3rd ed. as Organizational Communication: Foundations for Business and Collaboration, 2010; Speaking Professionally: A Concise Guide, 2006; The Madness of March: Bonding and Betting with the Boys in Las Vegas, 2009; Crisis Communication: Theory and Practice, 2009. **Address:** Northeastern University, 360 Huntington Ave., Boston, MA 02115, U.S.A. **Online address:** a.zaremba@neu.edu

ZARETSKY, Natasha. American (born United States), b. 1970?. **Genres:** History. **Career:** Graduate Council, research fellow, 1995-97; Duke University, J. Walter Thompson research fellow, 1999; Southern Illinois University, assistant professor, 2002-08, associate professor of history, 2008-. Writer

and historian. **Publications:** No Direction Home: The American Family and the Fear of National Decline, 1968-1980, 2007. Contributor books and periodicals. **Address:** Department of History, Southern Illinois University, Rm. 3374, 1000 Faner Dr., PO Box 4519, Carbondale, IL 62901, U.S.A. **Online address:** zaretsky@siu.edu

ZARETSKY, Robert David. American (born United States), b. 1955. **Genres:** Politics/Government. **Career:** University of Houston, associate professor, 1991-, professor of French History. Writer. **Publications:** Nîmes at War: Religion, Politics, and Public Opinion in the Gard, 1938-1944, 1995; (trans.) Voices from the Gulag: Life and Death in Communist Bulgaria, 1999; (trans. with J.T. Scott) Tzvetan Todorov, Frail Happiness: An Essay on Rousseau, 2001; Cock & Bull Stories: Folco de Baroncelli and the Invention of the Camargue, 2004; (with A.L. Conklin and S. Fishman) Modern France and Its Empire, 1870 to the Present, 2009 as France and Its Empire since 1870, 2010; (with J.T. Scott) The Philosophers' Quarrel: Rousseau, Hume, and the Limits of Human Understanding, 2009; Albert Camus, Elements of a Life, 2010. Contributor to periodicals. **Address:** University of Houston, 17C Roy G. Cullen Bldg., Houston, TX 77204-3303, U.S.A. **Online address:** rzaretsky@uh.edu

ZARINS, Joyce Audy. *See* **DOS SANTOS, Joyce Audy.**

ZARNOW, Teryl. American (born United States), b. 1951. **Genres:** Human Relations/Parenting, Essays, Humor/Satire, Social Sciences. **Career:** Indianapolis News, editorial writer, 1975-82; The Orange County Register, staff writer, 1982-89, family columnist, 1987-2009; local columnist, 2009-. **Publications:** Husband Is the Past Tense of Daddy and Other Dispatches from the Front Lines of Motherhood, 1990; The Mother Side of Midnight: Nocturnal Confessions of a Lunch Box Queen, 1992. Contributor of articles to magazines. **Address:** The Orange County Register, 625 N Grand Ave., Santa Ana, CA 92701, U.S.A. **Online address:** familywriter@aol.com

ZARR, Sara. American (born United States), b. 1970. **Genres:** Novels, Adult Non-fiction. **Career:** Writer. **Publications:** NOVEL: Story of a Girl, 2007; Sweethearts, 2008; Once was Lost, 2009; How to Save a Life, 2011. Works appear in anthologies. Contributor to books and periodicals. **Address:** Little, Brown and Co., 1271 Ave. of the Americas, New York, NY 10020-1300, U.S.A. **Online address:** contact@sarazarr.com

ZARUCCHI, Jeanne Morgan. (Jeanne Morgan). American (born United States), b. 1955. **Genres:** Art/Art History, Literary Criticism And History. **Career:** University of Missouri, Department of Foreign Language, assistant professor, 1985-91, associate professor of French, 1991-99, associate professor of art history, 1995-99, chair of the university senate, 1998-2000; professor of French and art history, 1999-, art history coordinator, 2003-06, chair of the department, 2006-, Campus Mediation Service, coordinator, Interdisciplinary Studies Committee, chairman, The Honor Society of Phi Kappa Phi, president. Writer. **Publications:** (As Jeanne Morgan) Perrault's Morals for Moderns, 1985; Charles Perrault's Memoirs of My Life, 1989; (with W.S. Brooks and B. Norman) La Querelle d'Alceste, 1994; Johnson Brothers in America: A Century of Design, 2000. Contributor of articles to journals. **Address:** Department of Foreign Languages & Literatures, College of Fine Arts, University of Missouri, 503 Lucas Hall, 8001 Natural Bridge, St. Louis, MO 63121, U.S.A. **Online address:** zarucchi@umsl.edu

ZASLAVSKAIA, Tatiana (Ivanovna). Russian/Ukranian (born Ukraine), b. 1927. **Genres:** Social Sciences, Sociology. **Career:** Institute of Economics, researcher, senior researcher, 1950-63; Institute of Economics and Industrial Engineering, Department of Sociology, head, 1963-88; Novosibirsk State University, professor of political economy, 1975-88; Soviet Center for Public Opinion Studies (UCIOM), director, 1988-92, president, 1992-; Congress of People's Deputies, people's deputy, 1989-92; Interdisciplinary Academic Center of Social Sciences, co-president, 1992-; Moscow School of Social and Economic Sciences, professor, 1995-. Writer. **Publications:** The Labor Payment in the Collective Farms, 1966; Migration of Rural Population, 1970; A Voice of Reform: Essays, 1989; Die Gorbatschow-Strategie Wirtschafts und Sozialpolitik in der U.S.S.R., 1990; Sociology of Economic Life, 1991; The Second Socialist Revolution: An Alternative Soviet Strategy, 1991; (ed.) Kuda idet Rossiĭa?, 2000; (ed. with M. Shabanova) Sotsiologiĭa svobody, 2000; (ed.) Kto i kuda stremitsia vesti Rossiiu?, 2001; Kuda idet Rosiia?, 2002; Sotsietal'naia transformatsiia rossiĭskogo obshchestva, 2002; Rossiia, kotoruiu my obretaem, 2003; Kuda prishla Rossiia?, 2003; Izbrannye proizvedenia, 2007; Russian Society at the Social Breakdown: View from Inside, forthcoming. **Address:** Moscow School of Social and Economic Sciences, 82-2-256 Vernadskogo prospect, Moscow, 119571, Russia. **Online address:** tiz@msses.ru

ZASLOW, Jeffrey L. American (born United States), b. 1958. **Genres:** Autobiography/Memoirs. **Career:** Norfolk Ledger-Star, reporter intern; Orlando Sentinel, feature writer, 1980-83; Wall Street Journal, columnist, 1983-87, senior writer and columnist, 2003-; Chicago Sun-Times, advice columnist, 1987-2001; USA Weekend, columnist, 1994-2002. Writer. **Publications:** NONFICTION: Tell Me All about It: A Personal Look at the Advice Business, 1990; Take It from Us: Advice from 262 Celebrities on Everything That Matters-to Them and to You, 1994; (comp.) Talk of Fame, illustrated by David Small, 1997; (with R. Pausch) The Last Lecture, 2008; (with C. Sullenberger) Highest Duty: My Search for What Really Matters, 2009; The Girls from Ames: A Story of Women and Friendship, 2009. Contributor to periodicals. **Address:** West Bloomfield, MI , U.S.A. **Online address:** jeffrey.zaslow@wsj.com

ZATLIN, Jonathan R. American (born United States), b. 1963. **Genres:** Politics/Government, Social Sciences. **Career:** University of Bonn, lecturer in English, 1986-88; Agence France-Presse/Extel, correspondent, 1991-92; University of California, lecturer in history, 2001; Massachusetts Institute of Technology, assistant professor of history, 2001-02; Boston University, assistant professor of history, 2002-08, associate professor of history, 2008-, humanities foundation fellow, 2004-05, German History Workshop, founder and chair, 2005-; Harvard University, Minda de Gunzburg Center for European Studies, affiliate, 2002-. Writer and historian. **Publications:** (Ed. with P.E. Swett and S.J. Wiesen) Selling Modernity: Advertising in Twentieth-Century Germany, 2007; The Currency of Socialism: Money and Political Culture in East Germany, 2007. Contributor to books and journals. **Address:** Department of History, Boston University, 226 Bay State Rd., Boston, MA 02215, U.S.A. **Online address:** jzatlin@bu.edu

ZATSIORSKY, Vladimir M. American/Russian (born Russia), b. 1932. **Genres:** Biology, Sports/Fitness, Medicine/Health, Sciences, Education, Engineering. **Career:** Lvov Institute of Physical Culture, assistant professor, 1954-57; Central Institute of Physical Culture, associate professor, professor, 1960-74, head and professor of the biomechanics, chair, 1974-87, head of the chair of biomechanics, 1989; U.S.S.R.'s National Olympic Teams, fitness and biomechanics consultant, 1960-90; All-Union Research Institute of Physical Culture, director, 1987-89; University of Calgary, visiting professor, 1990-91; University of California, Los Angeles, visiting professor, 1991; Pennsylvania State University, Department of Exercise and Sport Sciences, visiting professor, 1991-93, professor of exercise and sports science, 1993-, professor of kinesiology, 1993-, Biomechanics Laboratory, director, 1995-2004, professor of kinesiology, 1996-. Writer and consultant. **Publications:** Motor Abilities of Athletes, 1966; Cybernetics, Mathematics, Sport, 1969; (with D.D. Donskoj) Biomechanics, 1979; Basis of Sports Metrology, 1979; (with A.S. Aruin and V.N. Selayanov) Biomechanics of the Human Musculoskeletal System, 1981; (with S.Y. Aleshinsky and N.A. Yakunin) Biomechanical Basis of Endurance, 1982; (with A.S. Aruin) Occupational Biomechanics, 1989; (with A.S. Aruin) Ergonomicheskaia Biomekhanika, 1989; Science and Practice of Strength Training, 1995, 2nd ed., (with W.J. Kraemer), 2006; Kinematics of Human Motion, 1998 new ed. 2002. EDITOR: (and contrib.) Biodynamics of Sport Technique, 1978; Sports Metrology, 1982; Biomechanics in Sports: Performance Enhancement and Injury Prevention, 2000; (with M.L. Latash) Classics in Movement Science, 2001; Kinetics of Human Motion, 2002; (with B.I. Prilutsky) Biomechanics of Skeletal Muscles, 2012. **Address:** Department of Kinesiology, Pennsylvania State University, 039 Recreation Bldg., 417 Old Main St, University Park, PA 16802, U.S.A. **Online address:** vxz1@psu.edu

ZATTI, Sergio. Italian (born Italy), b. 1950?. **Genres:** Theology/Religion, History. **Career:** University of Genoa, professor of history of literary criticism; University of Pisa, associate professor of the history of literary criticism and faculty of humanities, professor of Italian literature. Writer. **Publications:** L'uniforme cristiano e il multiforme pagano: Saggio sulla Gerusalemme liberata, 1983; L'ombra del Tasso: Epica e romanzo bel Cinquecento, 1996; La rappresentazione dell'altro nei testi del Rinascimento, 1998; (with G.B. Squarotti and T. Tasso) Ludovico Ariosto, 2000; (ed.) Eroe e l'ostacolo, 2010. **Address:** Dipartimento di Studi Italianistici, Universitá di Pisa, Via Del Collegio Ricci, Pisa, 10-56126, Italy. **Online address:** s.zatti@ital.unipi.it

ZAVODNYIK, Peter. American (born United States), b. 1969. **Genres:** History. **Career:** Kralovec & Marquard Chartered, attorney. Writer. **Publications:** The Age of Strict Construction: A History of the Growth of Federal Power, 1789-1861, 2007; The Rise and Fall of the Federal Colossus: The Growth of Federal Power from Lincoln to FDR, 2011. **Address:** Kralovec & Marquard Chartered, 55 W Monroe St., Ste. 1000, Chicago, IL 60603, U.S.A. **Online address:** pzavodnyik@yahoo.com

ZAWODNY, J(anusz) K. American/Polish (born Poland), b. 1921. **Genres:** International Relations/Current Affairs, Politics/Government, History. **Career:** Princeton University, instructor, 1955-57, assistant professor, 1957-58; Center for Advanced Study in the Behavioral Sciences, fellow, 1961-62; University of Pennsylvania, associate professor, 1962-63, professor of international relations, 1965-75; Washington University, professor, 1963-65; Harvard University, Center for International Affairs, research associate, 1968; Oxford University, Saint Antony's College, senior associate, 1968-69; Institute for Advanced Study, faculty, 1971-72; Claremont Graduate University and Pomona College, professor of international relations, 1975-82; National Security Council, advisor, 1979-82. Writer. **Publications:** Death in the Forest: The Story of the Katyn Forest Massacre, 1962, 5th ed., 1989; Guide to the Study of International Relations, 1965; Morte nella foresta. La vera storia del massacro di Katyn, 1973; Nothing but Honour: The Story of the Warsaw Uprising 1944, 1978; Katyn, 1989; Pamiętniki znalezione w Katyniu, 1990; Uczestnicy i Swiadkowie Powstania Warszawskiego: Wywiady, 1994, rev. ed., 2004; Powstanie Warszawskie w Walce i Dyplomacji, 1994. EDITOR and CONTRIBUTOR: Unconventional Warfare, 1962; (and comp. with A.Z.B. Kruger) Man and International Relations: Contributions of the Social Sciences to the Study of Human Conflict and Integration, 2 vols., 1967; Motyl Na Swiegu, 2004. **Address:** 23703 NE Margaret Rd., Brush Prairie, WA 98606, U.S.A.

ZAYD, Laylá Abū. *See* **ABOUZEID, Leila.**

ZAZOVE, Philip. American (born United States), b. 1951. **Genres:** Autobiography/Memoirs, Medicine/Health. **Career:** West Jordan Medical Center, president, 1981-89; University of Michigan Medical Center, assistant professor of family practice, 1989-95, assistant chair of clinical programs, 1995-, associate medical director, Department of Family Medicine, clinical professor, professor, interim chair; Trails Camp, medical director and volunteer physician, 1990-94. Writer. **Publications:** When the Phone Rings, My Bed Shakes: Memoirs of a Deaf Doctor, 1993; Four Days in Michigan, 2010. Contributor to journals. **Address:** University of Michigan Health System, Dexter Family Medicine, 7300 Dexter-Ann Arbor Rd., Ste. 110, Dexter, MI 48130, U.S.A. **Online address:** pzaz@umich.edu

ZEBROWSKI, George. American (born United States), b. 1945. **Genres:** Novellas/Short Stories, Science Fiction/Fantasy, Young Adult Fiction, Writing/Journalism, Novels, Children's Fiction. **Career:** Binghamton Evening Press, copy editor, 1967; State University of New York, lecturer in science fiction, 1971; SFWA Bulletin, freelance writer and lecturer, 1970-75, 1983-91; Crown Publisher, consultant, general editor, 1983-85; Omni Magazine, science essayist; Amazing Stories magazine, film essayist. **Publications:** SCIENCE FICTION EXCEPT AS NOTED: The Omega Point, 1972; The Star Web, 1975; Tomorrow Today, 1975; The Monadic Universe and Other Stories, 1977; (with P. Anderson and J. Dann) A World Named Cleopatra, 1977; Ashes and Stars, 1977; Macrolife, 1979; The Omega Point Trilogy, 1983; Sunspacer, 1984; Monadic Universe, 1985; The Stars Will Speak (young adult), 1985; Stranger Suns, 1991; (with C. Pellegrino) The Killing Star, 1995; Beneath the Red Star: Studies on International Science Fiction (essays), 1996; The Sunspacers Trilogy, 1996; (with P. Sargent) A Fury Scorned, 1996; (with P. Sargent) Heart of the Sun, 1997; Brute Orbits, 1998; Cave of Stars, 1999; (with C. Pellegrino) Dyson Sphere, 1999; (with P. Sargent) Across the Universe, 1999; Swift Thoughts (stories), 2002; In the Distance, and Ahead in Time, 2002; (with P. Sargent) Garth of Izar, 2003; Black Pockets And Other Dark Thoughts, 2005; Empties, 2009. EDITOR: (and intro. with T.N. Scortia) Human Machines: An Anthology of Stories about Cyborgs, 1975; (with J. Dann) Faster Than Light: An Original Anthology About Interstellar Travel, 1976; The Best of Thomas N. Scortia, 1981; (with I. Asimov and M.H. Greenberg) Creations: The Quest for Origins in Story and Science, 1983; Crown Classics of Science Fiction, 10 vols., 1984-85; Nebula Awards 20 (21, 22), 3 vols., 1985-88; Synergy, 4 vols., 1987-89; (ed. and intro. with G. Benford) Skylife: Space Habitats in Story and Science, 2000; Synergy SF: New Science Fiction, 2004. Contributor to periodicals. **Address:** Richard

Curtis Associates Inc., 171 E 74th St., 2nd Fl., New York, NY 10021, U.S.A. **Online address:** sarzeb1@cs.com

ZECHENTER, Katarzyna Anna. American (born United States) **Genres:** Young Adult Fiction, History, Military/Defense/Arms Control. **Career:** University of Kansas, Polish lecturer; University College London, lecturer in Polish literature. Writer. **Publications:** The Fiction of Tadeusz Konwicki: Coming to Terms with Post-War Polish History and Politics, 2007; Kraków in the Immediate Post-War Period (1945-1968), forthcoming. Contributor of articles to journals. **Address:** School of Slavonic and East European Studies, University College London, 16 Taviton St., London, GL WC1H 0BW, England. **Online address:** k.zechenter@ssees.ucl.ac.uk

ZEDRIC, Lance Q. American (born United States), b. 1961. **Genres:** Novels, Military/Defense/Arms Control, How-to Books, Self Help, History. **Career:** Monmouth College, director of public information, 1983-85; U.S. Army Intelligence, staff, 1988-92; photographer, 1995-; Children's Home, teacher therapist, 1997-. Writer, researcher and consultant. **Publications:** Silent Warriors of World War II: The Alamo Scouts Behind the Japanese Lines, 1995; (with M.F. Dilley) Elite Warriors: 300 Years of America's Best Fighting Troops, 1996; Losers, Users, and Parasites: A Host's Guide to Ridding Your Life of Unwanted People, 1996; (with E.J. Moriconi) Sir John Jervis, Earl of St. Vincent: A Man for the Occasion, 2007; The Last Rubicon (novel), 2009; (with D. Graybill) Pink Heals: The Mending of America, 2011. **Address:** 1816 W Broughton Ct., Peoria, IL 61614-4624, U.S.A. **Online address:** zee61@aol.com

ZEE, A. American/Chinese (born China) **Genres:** Food And Wine, History, Mythology/Folklore, Physics, Third World. **Career:** The Rockefeller University, assistant professor, 1972-73; Princeton University, assistant professor, 1973-78; University of Pennsylvania, associate professor, 1978-80; University of Washington, professor, 1980-85; Ecole Normale Supérieure, visiting professor, 1981, 1992-93; University of California, professor of physics, 1985-, Institute for Theoretical Physics, professor; The Institute for Advanced Study, Dyson distinguished visiting professor, 1996-97; Harvard University, Radcliffe Institute for Advanced Study, visiting professor and fellow, 2006-07. Writer. **Publications:** Unity of Forces in the Universe, 1982; Fearful Symmetry: The Search for Beauty in Modern Physics, 1986, rev. ed., 1999; (co-ed.) Cosmology and Particle Physics, 1988; An Old Man's Toy: Gravity at Work and Play in Einstein's Universe, 1989, rev. ed. as Einstein's Universe, 2000; Swallowing Clouds, 1990; Mysteries of Life and the Universe, 1992; Quantum Field Theory in a Nutshell, 2003, 2nd ed., 2010. **Address:** Institute for Theoretical Physics, University of California, Kohn 2321, Broida Hall, Santa Barbara, CA 93106-9530, U.S.A. **Online address:** zee@kitp.ucsb.edu

ZEGURA, Elizabeth Chesney. (Elizabeth Anne Chesney). American (born United States), b. 1949?. **Genres:** Literary Criticism And History, Humanities, Intellectual History. **Career:** Duke University, instructor in French, 1973-75, visiting assistant professor of Italian, 1977; Davidson College, instructor in French, 1975-76; University of Arizona, visiting assistant professor, 1978-80, adjunct lecturer, 1985, 1987-88, adjunct assistant professor, 1989-93, lecturer, 1993-96, senior lecturer in French and Italian, 1993-94, 1996-2001, associate professor, 2001-, director of graduate studies; DePauw University, assistant professor of French, 1981-82. Writer. **Publications:** AS ELIZABETH ANNE CHESNEY: The Countervoyage of Rabelais and Ariosto: A Comparative Study of Two Renaissance Mock Epics, 1982; (with M. Tetel) Rabelais Revisited, 1993; (ed.) The Rabelais Encyclopedia, 2004. Contributor to Journal. **Address:** Department of French & Italian, University of Arizona, Modern Languages 556, Tucson, AZ 85721-0067, U.S.A. **Online address:** zegurae@u.arizona.edu

ZEIDNER, Lisa. American (born United States), b. 1955. **Genres:** Novels, Poetry, History, Young Adult Fiction. **Career:** Rutgers University, professor of English, 1979-, MFA Program, director. Writer. **Publications:** NOVELS: Customs, 1981; Alexandra Freed, 1983; Limited Partnerships, 1989; Layover, 1999. POETRY: Talking Cure, 1982; Pocket Sundial, 1988. OTHERS: Brandywine: A Legacy of Tradition in du Pont-Wyeth Country, 1995; Love Bomb, 2012. **Address:** Department of English, Rutgers University, 419 Armitage Hall, 311 N 5th St., Camden, NJ 08102, U.S.A. **Online address:** lz@lisazeidner.com

ZEIDNER, Moshe. Israeli/German (born Germany), b. 1948. **Genres:** Psychology. **Career:** Hebrew University, research and teaching assistant, 1974-

76; University of Haifa, Faculty of Education, Department of Counseling and Human Development, teaching assistant, 1977-82, instructor, 1983-84, lecturer, 1984-89, senior lecturer, 1989-94, professor, 1994-, Laboratory for Cross Cultural Research in Personality and Individual Differences, founder and director, 1995-, Center for the Interdisciplinary Research on Emotions, co-founder and director, 1997-2006, dean of research, 2000-03, 2004-05; Consulting Psychologists Press, psychological test editor, 1988-90; Indiana University-Purdue University, lecturer. **Publications:** Hashpaot Matsaviyot Aadot Be-vitsua Evutsot Be-mivane Kosher Metuhnanim, 1983; Test Anxiety: The State of the Art, 1998; (with G. Matthews and R.D. Roberts) Emotional Intelligence: Science and Myth, 2002; (with G. Matthews and R.D. Roberts) What We Know About Emotional Intelligence: How It Affects Learning, Work, Relationships, and Our Mental Health, 2009; (G. Matthews) Anxiety 101, 2010; (with G. Matthews and R.D. Roberts) Emotional Intelligence 101, 2011. EDITOR: (with C. Schwarze) Stress, Anxiety and Coping in Academic Settings: First Colloquium of Educational Researchers of the University of Haifa, Israel and the Heinrich-Heine-University Düsseldorf, Germany in Düsseldorf, 1996; (with M. Boekaerts and P.R. Pintrich) Handbook of Self-Regulation, 2000; (with G. Matthews and R.D. Roberts) The Science of Emotional Intelligence: Knowns and Unknowns, 2007. EDITOR AND CONTRIBUTOR: (with R. Most) Psychological Testing: An Inside View, 1992; (with D.H. Saklofske) International Handbook of Personality and Intelligence, 1995; (with N.S. Endler) Handbook of Coping: Theory, Research, Applications, 1996. Contributor to books and journals. **Address:** Faculty of Education, University of Haifa, Rm. 534, Education and Sciences Bldg., 5th Fl., Mt. Carmel, Haifa, 31905, Israel. **Online address:** zeidner@research.haifa.ac.il

ZEIER, Joan T(heresa). American (born United States), b. 1931. **Genres:** Children's Fiction, Poetry, Children's Non-fiction, Local History/Rural Topics, Young Adult Fiction. **Career:** Lee & Becker Law Firm, secretary, 1948-51; Freelance writer, 1978-; Madison Metropolitan School District, secretary, 1980-; Madison Area Technical College, creative writing instructor, 1998-. **Publications:** The Elderberry Thicket, 1990; Stick Boy, 1993; (co-author) Celebrating a Community of Faith, 1996; It's Franny's Move, forthcoming; The End of Autumn, forthcoming; Ticket to Touchstone, forthcoming; Only in Your Dreams, forthcoming. EDITOR: South of the North Woods (anthology), 1985; Fine Lines: A Collection, 1989. **Address:** 4213 Major Ave., Madison, WI 53716, U.S.A. **Online address:** jazz1948@aol.com

ZEILER, Thomas W. American (born United States), b. 1961?. **Genres:** History, Military/Defense/Arms Control. **Career:** University of Colorado, Department of History, lecturer, 1990-93, assistant professor, 1993-98, associate professor, 1998-2001, chair, 2000-04, professor of history, 2001-, Internship Program, director and organizer, 1995-96, director of graduate studies, 1999-2000, Secretaries of Defense Program, director, 2006-08, Program on International Affairs, professor, 2006-, Global Studies Residential Academic Program, director, 2008-; Diplomatic History: Journal of the Society for Historians of American Foreign Relations, executive editor, 2001-; Japan Women's University, visiting professor, 2004-05; University of Tokyo, visiting professor, 2004-05. **Publications:** American Trade and Power in the 1960's, 1992; Free Trade, Free World: The Advent of GATT, 1999; Dean Rusk: Defending the American Mission Abroad, 2000; (with A.E. Eckes, Jr.) Globalization and the American Century, 2003; Unconditional Defeat: Japan, America, and the End of World War II, 2004; Ambassadors in Pinstripes: The Spalding World Baseball Tour and the Birth of the American Empire, 2006; American Foreign Relations Since 1600: A Guide to the Literature, 3rd ed., 2010; Annihilation: A Global Military History of World War II, 2011; (ed. with R.J. McMahon) Guide to U.S. Foreign Policy: A Diplomatic History, 2012; Global Games: The Spalding World Tour of 1888-1889, forthcoming; World War II: A Global History, forthcoming. **Address:** Department of History, University of Colorado, 204 Hellems Hall, PO Box 234, Boulder, CO 80309-0234, U.S.A. **Online address:** thomas.zeiler@colorado.edu

ZEILIK, Michael. American (born United States), b. 1946. **Genres:** Astronomy, Education. **Career:** Southern Connecticut State University, instructor in astronomy, 1969-72; Cambridge Center for Adult Education, instructor, 1973; Harvard University, instructor in astronomy, 1974-75; University of New Mexico, assistant professor, 1975-79, associate professor, 1979-85, Institute for Astrophysics, associate director, 1985-88, Center for Graduate Studies, director, 1987-91, professor of physics and astronomy, 1985-2004, professor emeritus of physics, 2004-; University of Wisconsin-Madison, National Institute for Science Education, research fellow, 1989-99. Smithsonian Institution, Smithsonian Astrophysical Observatory predoctoral fellow. Writer. **Publica-**

tions: Film Notes for Explorations in Space and Time, 1974; Astronomy, the Evolving Universe, 1976, 9th ed., 2002; (with J. Gaustaud) Astronomy: The Cosmic Perspective, 1983; (ed. with D.M. Gibson) Cool Stars, Stellar Systems and the Sun, 1986; (with E.V.P. Smith) Introductory Astronomy and Astrophysics, 1987, 4th ed., 1998; Conceptual Astronomy, 1993; Interactive Lesson Guide in Astronomy, 1998, 2nd ed., 2001; (with J. Jacobs) Spectra Quest!. Contributor to journals. **Address:** Department of Physics and Astronomy, University of New Mexico, Rm. 25, P&A Campus, 1919 Lomas Blvd. NE, Albuquerque, NM 87131, U.S.A. **Online address:** mzeilik@cnsp.com

ZELDIN, Theodore. British/Israeli (born Israel), b. 1933. **Genres:** History, Politics/Government, Biography. **Career:** Oxford University, research fellow, 1957-63, St. Antony's College, senior tutor and dean, 1963-77, fellow in history, 1977-; Harvard University, visiting professor of history, 1970; University of Southern California, visiting professor; Oxford Muse Foundation, founder, 2001, president; Paris Business School, professor; World Economic Forum, fellow; HEC, professor; Oxford Food Symposium, co-founder; Wytham Hall Medical Charity, trustee. English philosopher, sociologist, historian, writer and public speaker. **Publications:** The Political System of Napoleon III, 1958; Émile Ollivier and the Liberal Empire of Napoleon III, 1963; (ed. and contrib.) Conflicts in French Society: Anticlericalism, Education and Morals in the Nineteenth Century, 1970; France, 1848-1945, vol. I: Ambition, Love and Politics, 1973, vol. II: Intellect, Taste and Anxiety, 1977, vol. III: Intellect and Pride, 1980, vol. IV: Taste and Corruption, 1980; vol. V: Anxiety and Hypocrisy, 1981; The French, 1982; Happiness, 1988; An Intimate History of Humanity, 1994; Conversation: How Talk Can Change Your Life, 2000. Contributor to books. **Address:** St. Antony's College, Oxford University, 62 Woodstock Rd., Oxford, OX OX2 6JF, England.

ZELIKOW, Philip. (Philip David Zelikow). American (born United States), b. 1954. **Genres:** History, International Relations/Current Affairs. **Career:** Texas Court of Criminal Appeals, briefing attorney, 1979-80; David Berg and Associates (now Berg and Androphy), trial attorney, 1980-83, of counsel, 1983-85, 1991-98; Naval Postgraduate School, adjunct professor of national security affairs, 1984-85; United States Department of State, political officer and political adviser, 1985-89, Operations Center, watch officer, 1985-89, Secretariat Staff, line officer, 1985-89, counselor, 2005-07; National Security Council, director for European security affairs, 1989-91; Harvard University, associate professor of public policy, 1991-98; University of Virginia, Corcoran Department of History, White Burkett Miller professor of history, 1998-, director of graduate studies, 2010-, Miller Center of Public Affairs, director, 1998-2005; National Commission on Terrorist Attacks Upon the United States, executive director, 2003-04; Office of the Secretary of Defense, consultant, 2010-. Writer. **Publications:** (Ed. with G. Allison, A. Carter and S. Miller) Cooperative Denuclearization: From Pledges to Deeds, 1993; (with C. Rice) Germany Unified and Europe Transformed: A Study in Statecraft, 1995; American Intelligence and the World Economy, 1996; (ed. with J.S. Nye, Jr. and D.C. King) Why People Don't Trust Government, 1997; (ed. with E.R. May) The Kennedy Tapes: Inside the White House during the Cuban Missile Crisis, 1997; (ed. with R.B. Zoellick) America and the Muslim Middle East: Memos to a President, 1998; (with G. Allison) Essence of Decision: Explaining the Cuban Missile Crisis, 1999; (ed. with R.B. Zoellick) America and Russia: Memos to a President, 2000; (ed. with R.B. Zoellick) America and the East Asian Crisis: Memos to a President, 2000; (ed.) American Military Strategy: Memos to a President, 2001; (ed. with R.B. Zoellick) America and the Balkans: Memos to a President, 2001; (contrib.) John F. Kennedy: The Great Crises, 2001; (ed. with E.R. May) Dealing with Dictators: Dilemmas of U.S. Diplomacy and Intelligence Analysis, 1945-1990, 2006; (afterword) The 9/11 Commission Report: The Attack from Planning to Aftermath, 2011. Contributor to books and periodicals. **Address:** Corcoran Department of History, University of Virginia, Rm. 421, Nau Hall, South Lawn, Charlottesville, VA 22904, U.S.A. **Online address:** zelikow@virginia.edu

ZELIKOW, Philip David. See ZELIKOW, Philip.

ZELINSKY, Wilbur. American (born United States), b. 1921. **Genres:** Geography, Bibliography. **Career:** University of Georgia, assistant professor, 1948-52; University of Wisconsin, research associate, 1952-54; Chesapeake and Ohio Railway Co., industrial analyst, 1954-59; Wayne State University, special instructor in geography, 1955-59; Southern Illinois University, professor, 1959-63; Pennsylvania State University, professor of geography, 1963-87, emeritus professor of geography and demography, 1987-. Writer. **Publications:** CONTRIBUTOR: Field Study in American Geography, 1959;

Tropical Africa, vol. I, 1960; Readings in Cultural Geography, 1962; A Prologue to Population Geography, 1966; (comp. and ed. with M. Church and R.E. Huke) A Basic Geographical Library, 1966; (ed. with L.A. Kosiński) An Abridged Version of the Discussions at the Symposium on Population Pressures upon Physical and Social Resources in the Developing Lands, Pennsylvania State University, 1967, 1969; (with L.A. Kosiński and R.M. Prothero) Geography and a Crowding World, 1970; This Remarkable Continent: An Atlas of United States and Canadian Society and Culture, 1982; Nation into State, 1988; (with L.A. Kosiński) The Emergency Evacuation of Cities: A Cross-National Historical and Geographical Study, 1991. OTHERS: A Bibliographic Guide to Population Geography, 1962; The Cultural Geography of the United States, 1973, rev. ed., 1992; Exploring the Beloved Country: Geographic Forays into American Society and Culture, 1994; The Enigma of Ethnicity: Another American Dilemma, 2001; Not Yet a Placeless Land, 2011; (with S.A. Matthews) Place of Religion in Chicago, 2011. Contributor to journals and periodicals. **Address:** Department of Geography, Pennsylvania State University, 302 Walker Bldg., University Park, PA 16802, U.S.A. **Online address:** wxz1@psu.edu

ZELITCH, Simone E. American (born United States), b. 1962. **Genres:** Novels, Literary Criticism And History. **Career:** University of Veszprem, peace corps teacher, 1991-92; Southern Illinois University, creative writing instructor; Community College of Philadelphia, instructor and director of poets and writers series, assistant professor and co-director of the certificate program in creative writing, associate professor, coordinator of the creative writing program. Writer. **Publications:** The Confession of Jack Straw: A Novel, 1991; Louisa, 2000; Moses in Sinai, 2001. Contributor to periodicals. **Address:** Community College of Philadelphia, 1700 Spring Garden St., Philadelphia, PA 19130-3936, U.S.A. **Online address:** szelitch@ccp.edu

ZELIZER, Barbie. American (born United States), b. 1954. **Genres:** Communications/Media, History. **Career:** Jerusalem Post, section editor, 1973-76; Van Leer Institute, project assistant and materials coordinator, 1976-78; Ben-Gurion University of the Negev, project assistant and materials co-ordinator, 1976-78; Jewish Telegraphic Agency, reporter and feature writer, 1978-80; Israel Television, News Department, onsite analyst, 1979-80; Reuters News Agency, reporter and feature writer, 1980-83; Communications Institute, Hebrew University of Jerusalem, course coordinator, 1981-83; University of Pennsylvania, instructor in communication and urban studies, 1988-90, Annenberg School of Communication, instructor, 1988-89, associate professor of communications, 1997, Raymond Williams Term chair of communication, 1999, professor of communications, 2002, Raymond Williams professor of communication; University of Delaware, instructor, 1988-89; Temple University, assistant professor of rhetoric and communication, 1990-94, Department of Broadcasting, Telecommunications and Mass Media, associate professor, 1995-97; Columbia University, Freedom Forum Center for Media Studies, research fellow, 1994-95, visiting lecturer; Central European University, visiting professor, 2005; Stockholm University, visiting professor, 2005; Universidad Catholica Portuguesa, visiting professor, 2007; Joint Summer School Universidad Catholica Portuguesa, visiting professor, 2008; Georgetown University, visiting professor, 2008; Israel Department of Immigrant Absorption and Jewish Agency, Ruder & Finn Public Relations, editor and translator for Israel Foreign Ministry. **Publications:** (Co-author) Almost Midnight: Reforming the Late-Night News, 1980; Covering the Body: The Kennedy Assassination, the Media and the Shaping of Collective Memory, 1992; Remembering to Forget: Holocaust Memory through the Camera's Eye, 1998; (ed. and intro.) Visual Culture and the Holocaust, 2001; (ed. with S. Allan) Journalism After September 11, 2002, 2nd ed., 2011; (ed. with S. Allan) Reporting War: Journalism in Wartime, 2004; Taking Journalism Seriously: News and the Academy, 2004; (ed.) Explorations in Communication and History, 2008; (ed.) The Changing Faces of Journalism: Tabloidization, Technology and Truthiness, 2009; (with S. Allan) Keywords in News and Journalism Studies, 2009; (co-ed.) Handbook of Journalism Studies, 2010; About to Die: How News Images Move the Public, 2010; (ed.) Making the University Matter, 2011; About to Die: Journalism, Memory and the Voice of the Visual, forthcoming. Contributor of articles to journals. **Address:** The Annenberg School for Communication, University of Pennsylvania, 3620 Walnut St., Philadelphia, PA 19104, U.S.A. **Online address:** bzelizer@asc.upenn.edu

ZELIZER, Julian E. American (born United States), b. 1969. **Genres:** Politics/Government. **Career:** Johns Hopkins University, Department of History, fellow, 1991-95; Brookings Institution, research fellow, 1995-96; State University of New York, assistant professor, 1996-99, associate professor of history, 1999-2002, associate professor of public administration and policy, 2002-04, affiliated faculty, 2002-04; Gilder Lehrman Institute of American History, research fellow, 2000; Princeton University Press, co-editor, 2002-; American Politics and History Initiative, director, 2003-05; Boston University, professor of history, 2004-07; Harvard University, Center for American Political Studies, faculty associate, 2004-07, 2007-; Princeton University, professor of history and public affairs, 2007-; Center for the Study for the Study of Democratic Politics, faculty associate, 2007-; Dirksen Congressional Center, director; Organization of American Historians, distinguished lecturer, 2007-08. Writer. **Publications:** Taxing America: Wilbur D. Mills, Congress, and the State, 1945-1975, 1998; (ed. with M. Jacobs and W.J. Novak) The Democratic Experiment: New Directions in American Political History, 2003; (ed.) The American Congress: The Building of Democracy, 2004; On Capitol Hill: The Struggle to Reform Congress and Its Consequences, 1948-2000, 2004; (ed.) New Directions in Policy History, 2005; (ed. with B.J. Schulman) Rightward Bound: Making America Conservative in the 1970s, 2008; (ed. with B.J. Schulman) Constitution and Public Policy in U.S. History, 2008; (ed.) Presidency of George W. Bush: A First Historical Assessment, 2010; Jimmy Carter: The 39th President, 1977-81, 2010; Arsenal of Democracy: The Politics of National Security- from World War II to the War on Terrorism, 2010; Governing America: Essays on Political History, 2011; (with M. Jacobs) Conservatives in Power: The Reagan Years, 1981-1989: A Brief History with Documents, 2011; (ed. with K. Phillips-Fein) What's Good for Business: Business and American Politics since World War II, 2012; A History of the Reagan Revolution, forthcoming. Contributor to books and periodicals. **Address:** Department of History, Woodrow Wilson School, Princeton University, 136 Dickinson Hall, Princeton, NJ 08544-1174, U.S.A. **Online address:** jzelizer@princeton.edu

ZELL, Steve. See **PITZEL, Steve.**

ZELLAR, Gary. Canadian (born Canada), b. 1953. **Genres:** History. **Career:** Sam Houston State University, lecturer, 1999-2000, adjunct lecturer, 2002; Blinn College, adjunct history instructor, 2000-02; City of Huntsville Cultural Services, historical consultant, 2001-07; Montgomery College, adjunct history instructor, 2003-07; Angelina College, adjunct history instructor, 2004-07; Lee College, adjunct history instructor, 2006-07; University of Saskatchewan, assistant professor of history. Writer and historian. **Publications:** (With N. Wyatt) History of the Bumpers College: Evolution of Education in the Agricultural, Food and Life Sciences in Arkansas, 1999; (comp. with L. Salisbury) Bibliographical Resources to the Literature of Agriculture and Rural Life in Arkansas, 1820-1945, 2000; African Creeks: Estelvste and the Creek Nation, 2007. Contributor to books and journals. **Address:** Department of History, University of Saskatchewan, 518 Arts, 9 Campus Dr., Saskatoon, SK S7N 5A5, Canada. **Online address:** gary.zellar@usask.ca

ZELLMAN, Shelley. American (born United States), b. 1948. **Genres:** Autobiography/Memoirs, Plays/Screenplays, Young Adult Non-fiction. **Career:** Television writer and producer, 1978-. **Publications:** (With B. Bennett) Autobiography of an Angel (nonfiction), 1998. **Address:** c/o Roger Strull, Preferred Artists, 16633 Ventura, Ste. 1421, Encino, CA 91436, U.S.A.

ZELONY, Susan. See **BREEN, Susan.**

ZELTSERMAN, Dave. American (born United States), b. 1959. **Genres:** Novels, Young Adult Fiction. **Career:** Novelist and software engineer. **Publications:** FICTION: In His Shadow, 2002 as Fast Lane, 2004; Small Crimes, 2008; Pariah, 2009; Killer, 2010; The Caretaker of Lorne Field, 2010; Outsourced, 2011. BILL SHANNON SERIES: NOVELS: Bad Thoughts, 2007; Bad Karma, 2009. **Address:** Boston, MA , U.S.A. **Online address:** dave.zeltserman@gmail.com

ZELVIN, Elizabeth. American (born United States), b. 1944?. **Genres:** Mystery/Crime/Suspense, Novels, Novellas/Short Stories, Poetry, Adult Nonfiction. **Career:** Writer. **Publications:** I Am the Daughter, 1981; (ed. with S.L.A. Straussner) Gender & Addictions: Men and Women in Treatment, 1997; Gifts & Secrets: Poems of the Therapeutic Relationship, 1999; Death Will Get You Sober, 2008; Death Will Help You Leave Him, 2009; Death Will Extend Your Vacation, 2012. **Address:** 115 W 86th St., New York, NY 10024, U.S.A. **Online address:** lizzelvin@aol.com

ZENCEY, Eric. American (born United States), b. 1953?. **Genres:** Novels,

Environmental Sciences/Ecology, Autobiography/Memoirs, History. **Career:** Goddard College, professor of history, faculty, 1982-95; Vermont College, professor; University of New York in Prague, professor; University of New York in Tirana, professor; Empire State College, visiting associate professor of historical and political studies, 2004-, associate professor, 2002-, chair, 2002-04; North American Review, contributing editor. **Publications:** NOVEL: Panama, 1995; Virgin Forest: Meditations on History, Ecology, and Culture, 1998. **Address:** Empire State College, 2 Union Ave., Saratoga Springs, NY 12866, U.S.A. **Online address:** eric.zencey@esc.edu

ZENITH, Richard. Portuguese/American (born United States), b. 1956. **Genres:** Novellas/Short Stories, Poetry, Essays, Translations. **Career:** Universidade Federal de Santa Catarina, instructor in English, 1979, 1982-83; Tilton School, Spanish teacher, 1984-85; Poetry Intl., national editor, 2004-; Portuguese Book and Library Institute, consultant. Translator. **Publications:** Terceiras Pessoas (in Portuguese; short stories), 2003; Fernando Pessoa, 2008. TRANSLATOR: L. Vieira, The Loves of Joao Vencio, 1991; A.L. Antunes, An Explanation of the Birds, 1991; A.L. Antunes, Act of the Damned, 1993; 113 Galician-Portuguese Troubadour Poems, 1995; (and intro.) F. Pessoa, Book of disquietude, 1996; S. de M. Breyner, Log Book: Selected Poems, 1997; (and ed.) Fernando Pessoa and Co.: Selected Poems, 1998; A.L. Antunes, The Natural Order of Things, 2000; (and ed.) The Selected Prose of Fernando Pessoa, 2001; (and ed.) F. Pessoa, Book of Disquiet, 2003; A.L. Antunes, The Inquisitors' Manual, 2003; J.C. de M. Neto, Education by Stone: Selected Poems, 2005; (and ed.) F. Pessoa, A Little Larger than the Entire Universe: Selected Poems, 2006; J.L. Peixoto, The Implacable Order of Things: A Novel, 2007; L.D. Camões, 2008; L. de Camões, Sonnets and Other Poems, 2009. Contributor to periodicals. **Address:** Rua Francisco Sanches, 132-4, Lisbon, 1170-144, Portugal. **Online address:** rzenith@mail.telepac.pt

ZENTGRAF, Kristine M. American (born United States) **Genres:** History, Sociology. **Career:** California State University, part-time instructor, 1995-98, assistant professor, 1998-, associate professor, Haynes faculty fellow, 2007. Writer and sociologist. **Publications:** (With G. Hytrek) America Transformed: Globalization, Inequality and Power, 2008; (ed. with A. Leon-Guerrero) Contemporary Readings in Social Problems, 2009. **Address:** Department of Sociology, California State University, 1250 Bellflower Blvd., Long Beach, CA 90840, U.S.A. **Online address:** kzentgra@csulb.edu

ZENTNER, Peter. British/Czech (born Czech Republic), b. 1932. **Genres:** Business/Trade/Industry, Politics/Government, Social Sciences. **Career:** Procter & Gamble, brand manager, 1954-58; Greenlys Advertising, account executive, 1958-59; Envoy Journals Ltd., director, 1960-70; consultant, 1970-. Writer. **Publications:** East-West Trade: A Practical Guide to Selling in Eastern Europe, 1967; Social Democracy in Britain: Must Labour Lose?, 1982. Contributor to journals and periodicals. **Address:** 38 Woodland Gardens, London, GL N10 3UA, England.

ZEPEDA, Gwendolyn. American (born United States), b. 1971. **Genres:** Novels, Novellas/Short Stories. **Career:** Novelist and educator. **Publications:** To the Last Man I Slept with and All the Jerks Just Like Him (short stories), 2004; Growing Up with Tamales=Los tamales de Ana (juvenile), 2008; Houston, We Have a Problema (novel), 2009; Sunflowers (juvenile), 2009; Lone Star Legend (novel), 2010. **Address:** c/o Jenny Bent, The Bent Agency, 204 Park Pl., Brooklyn, NY 11238, U.S.A. **Online address:** gwendolyn.zepeda@gmail.com

ZEPHANIAH, Benjamin (Obadiah Iqbal). British (born England), b. 1958. **Genres:** Novels, Plays/Screenplays, Poetry. **Career:** Africa Arts Collective, writer-in-residence, 1989; Memphis State University, writer-in-residence, 1991, 1995; Self-Help Organization for Ex-Prisoners, president; Farendg, and Dread Poets Society, president; Hackney Empire Theatre, chairperson; Umoja Housing Co-op, chairperson; recording artist. Playwright. **Publications:** POETRY: Pen Rhythm, 1980; The Dread Affair, 1985; In a Liverpool, 1988; Rasta Time in Palestine, 1990; City Psalms, 1992; Talking Turkeys (children's poetry), 1994; Out of the Night, 1994; Funky Chickens (children's poetry), 1996; Propa Propaganda, 1996, Schools Out, 1997; Face, 1999; Wicked World, 2000; Too Black, Too Strong, 2001; We are Britain, 2002. NOVELS: Refugee Boy, 2001; Face, 2002; Gangsta Rap, 2004; Teacher's Dead, 2007. OTHERS: Rasta Time in Palestine, 1990. Contributor to periodicals. **Address:** PFD, Drury House, 34-43 Russell St., London, GL WC2B 5HA, England.

ZÉPHIR, Flore. American/Haitian (born Haiti), b. 1958. **Genres:** Sociology. **Career:** Indiana University, Department of French and Italian, associate instructor in French, 1982-86; Virginia Commonwealth University, Department of Foreign Languages, instructor in French, 1986-88; University of Missouri, Department of Romance Languages and Literatures, assistant professor of French language and linguistics, 1988-90, assistant professor, 1991-97, associate professor of French, linguistics and curriculum and instruction, 1997-2000, associate professor of French, linguistics, and African diaspora studies, 1997-2003, director of undergraduate studies, 2000-08, professor of French, linguistics, and African diaspora studies, 2003-, associate chair, 2007-08, chair, 2008-, College of Education, Department of Curriculum and Instruction, Foreign Language Education Program, coordinator, 1991-2000, Master of Arts in Language Teaching, coordinator, 1993-, Linguistics Area Program, chair, 2004-07, Afro-Romance Institute for Languages and Literatures, acting director, 2008-; University of Delaware, assistant professor of French and coordinator for foreign language education, 1990-91. Writer. **Publications:** (Ed. with E. Smith) Proceedings of the 1992 Mid-America Linguistics Conference and Conference on Siouan and Caddoan Languages, 1993; Haitian Immigrants in Black America: A Sociological and Sociolinguistic Portrait, 1996; Trends in Ethnic Identification among Second-Generation Haitian Immigrants in New York City, 2001; The Haitian Americans, 2004. Contributor of articles to books and journals. **Address:** Department of Romance Languages, University of Missouri, 126 Arts & Science Bldg., Columbia, MO 65211, U.S.A. **Online address:** zephirf@missouri.edu

ZESCH, Scott. American (born United States) **Genres:** Novels, Young Adult Fiction, Agriculture/Forestry. **Career:** Writer, 1993-. **Publications:** (With T.W. Dichter) Thinking Economically: Applying Two Classical Concepts to Grassroots Enterprise Development, 1987; Food Crops Versus Cash Crops: A Spurious Controversy?, 1987; Alamo Heights, 1999; The Captured: A True Story of Indian Abduction on the Texas Frontier, 2004. **Address:** c/o Author Mail, St. Martins Press, 175 5th Ave., New York, NY 10010, U.S.A.

ZETTEL, Sarah. American (born United States), b. 1966. **Genres:** Science Fiction/Fantasy, Novels, Literary Criticism And History. **Career:** Science fiction novelist and short-story writer. **Publications:** NOVELS: Reclamation, 1996; Fool's War, 1997; Saving All Cradle, 1998; Playing God, 1998; The Quiet Invasion, 2000; Kingdom of Cages, 2001; A Sorcerer's Treason, 2002; The Usurper's Crown, 2003; The Firebird's Vengeance: A Novel of Isavalta, 2004; Sword of the Deceiver: A Novel of Isavalta, 2007; Bitter Angels, 2009; A Taste of the Nightlife, 2011; Let Them Eat Stake, 2012. OTHERS: In Camelot's Shadow, 2004; For Camelot's Honor, 2005; Under Camelot's Banner, 2006; Camelot's Blood, 2008. Contributor of short stories to periodicals. **Address:** c/o Author Mail, Warner Books Inc., Time and Life Bldg., 9th Fl., 1271 Ave. of the Americas, New York, NY 10020, U.S.A. **Online address:** szettel@umich.edu

ZETTLER, Steve. (Nero Blanc). American (born United States), b. 1947. **Genres:** Mystery/Crime/Suspense, Novels, Young Adult Fiction, Literary Criticism And History. **Career:** Writer. **Publications:** CROSSWORD MYSTERY AS NERO BLANC: The Crossword Murder, 1999; Two Down: A Crossword Murder Mystery, 2000; The Crossword Connection, 2001; A Crossword to Die For, 2002; A Cross Worder's Holiday, 2002; Corpus de Crossword, 2003; A Crossworder's Gift, 2003; Wrapped up in Crosswords, 2004; Anatomy of a Crossword, 2004; Another Word for Murder, 2005; A Crossworder's Delight, 2005; Death on the Diagonal, 2066. OTHERS: The Second Man, 1996; Double Identity, 1997; Ronin, 1998. **Address:** c/o Alice Martell, 545 Madison Ave., 7th Fl., New York, NY 10022, U.S.A. **Online address:** neroblanc@crosswordmysteries.com

ZEVELOFF, Samuel I. American (born United States), b. 1950. **Genres:** Environmental Sciences/Ecology, Zoology, Earth Sciences, Biology. **Career:** Teacher, 1972-74; North Carolina State University, instructor in zoology, 1976-78, Department of Zoology and Physiology, instructor, 1976-78, 1982, Executive Board, president, 1982-84; visiting assistant professor of zoology, 1982-84; University of Wyoming, instructor in zoology, 1982; Weber State University, assistant professor, 1984-86, associate professor, 1986-91, professor of zoology and chairperson of department, 1987-, Academic Affairs, administrative intern, 1986-87; Council on Undergraduate Research, institutional liaison, 1994-2004; The World Conservation Union, staff, 2004-08; Ogden Nature Center, director, 2003-05. Writer. **Publications:** Mammals of the Intermountain West, 1988; (ed. with C.M. McKell) Wilderness Issues in the Arid Lands of the Western United States, 1992; (ed. with L.M. Vause and

W.H. McVaugh) Wilderness Tapestry: An Eclectic Approach to Preservation, 1992; Raccoons: A Natural History, 2002. Works appears in anthology. **Address:** Department of Zoology, Weber State University, SL 402, Ogden, UT 84408-2505, U.S.A. **Online address:** szeveloff@weber.edu

ZEVON, Crystal. American (born United States), b. 1949. **Genres:** Biography, Autobiography/Memoirs, Art/Art History. **Career:** Writer. **Publications:** I'll Sleep When I'm Dead: The Dirty Life and Times of Warren Zevon, 2007. **Address:** The Young Agency, 41 W 86th St., Ste. 6L, New York, NY 10024, U.S.A. **Online address:** czevon@gmail.com

ZHANG, Song Nan. Canadian/Chinese (born China), b. 1942. **Genres:** Mythology/Folklore, Cultural/Ethnic Topics, Children's Non-fiction, Illustrations. **Career:** Central Institute of Fine Arts, art professor, 1985-88, deputy director, 1985-87, Mural Department, associate professor, 1985-88; Dominion Gallerie/Westmont Gallerie, Shayne Gallery, artist, 1988-. Writer. **Publications:** SELF-ILLUSTRATED: A Little Tiger in the Chinese Night: An Autobiography in Art, 1993; Five Heavenly Emperors: Chinese Myths of Creation, 1994; The Children of China: An Artist's Journey, 1995; Cowboy on the Steppes, 1997; The Ballad of Mulan, 1998; (with H.Y. Zhang) A Time of Golden Dragons, 2000; (with H.Y. Zhang) The Great Voyages of Zheng He=Hai hành phi thường cua Trinh Hòa, 2005. Illustrator of books by others. **Address:** Tundra Books, 345 Victoria Ave., Ste. 604, Montreal, QC H3Z 2N2, Canada.

ZHAO, Yuezhi. Canadian (born Canada), b. 1965. **Genres:** Communications/Media, Writing/Journalism, History, Social Sciences, Politics/Government. **Career:** University of California, assistant professor of communication, 1997-; Simon Fraser University, associate professor of communication; Political Economy of Global Communication, Canada research chair. **Publications:** (With R.A. Hackett) Sustaining Democracy?: Journalism and the Politics of Objectivity, 1998; Media, Market, and Democracy in China: Between the Party Line and the Bottom Line, 1998; (ed. with R.A. Hackett) Democratizing Global Media: One World, Many Struggles, 2005; (ed. with P. Chakravarthy) Global Communications: Toward a Transcultural Political Economy, 2008; Communication in China: Political Economy, Power and Conflict, 2008. **Address:** Department of Communication, Simon Fraser University, K 9678, 8888 University Dr., Burnaby, BC V5A 1S6, Canada. **Online address:** yzhao@sfu.ca

ZHEUTLIN, Peter. American (born United States) **Genres:** Geography. **Career:** Lawyer, freelance journalist and public speaker. **Publications:** Around the World on Two Wheels: Annie Londonderry's Extraordinary Ride, 2007; (with T. Graboys) Life in the Balance: A Physician's Memoir of Life, Love, and Loss with Parkinson's Disease and Dementia, 2008. Contributor to periodicals. **Address:** Needham, MA , U.S.A. **Online address:** info@annielondonderry.com

ZHU, Ha Jin. *See* **JIN, Ha.**

ZHU, Lin. Chinese (born China), b. 1949?. **Genres:** Novels, Young Adult Fiction, Children's Fiction, Novellas/Short Stories. **Career:** Shanghai Childrens Press, editor, 1974-90. **Publications:** Sheng huo di lu, 1979; Xin hua (juvenile), 1981; Ye ming zhu (juvenile), 1982; Di yu yu tian tang (fiction), 1984; Chen lu, 1984; She zhen tou hua, 1984; Ku lian shu (fiction), 1985; Fang she hua xue, 1985; Hunan shu, 1985; Tui (fiction), 1989; (with A. li and G. Chen) Hai ti, 1989; Hong men zi, 1989; Wu ye di Lancang jiang, 1990; Tian shi dao, 1990; Da shi fu ren hui yi lu: Xiongyali, Yinni, Faguo, Meiguo, 1991; (with X. Ji and Z. Zhao) Qu lu po cheng, 1991; Nü wu, 1993; Jie tou sketch, 1993; Nü xing-ren, 1993; Zhi ai zai ren jian (fiction), 1994; Nian nian sui sui hua xiang si, 1996; (with Q. Zhang) Tian tang li zai xiang hui, 1998; (with Q. Zhang) Zhu Lin wen ji (fiction), 1998; (with Q. Zhang) Ku lian shu: Zhi ai zai ren jian (fiction), 1998; Ge lou shang de tian kong (juvenile), 1999; Zou xiang Nuobei'er, 2002. **Address:** c/o Author Mail, University of Hawaii Press, 2840 Kolowalu St., Honolulu, HI 96822-1888, U.S.A.

ZHU, Liping. American (born United States), b. 1957. **Genres:** History. **Career:** National Park Service, contract historian, 1991-92; University of New Mexico, instructor in history, 1994-95; Eastern Washington University, assistant professor, 1996-2001, associate professor of history, 2001-06, professor, 2006-. Writer. **Publications:** Fort Union National Monument: An Administrative History, 1992; A Chinaman's Chance: The Chinese on the Rocky Mountain Mining Frontier, 1997; (with R.E. Fosha) Ethnic Oasis: The Chinese in the Black Hills, 2004. Contributor of articles to periodicals. **Address:** Department of History, Eastern Washington University, RRL 129A, PO Box 27, Cheney, WA 99004, U.S.A. **Online address:** lzhu@ewu.edu

ZHU, Tianwen. *See* CHU, Tien-wen.

ZHUOYUN YU. Chinese (born China), b. 1918. **Genres:** Architecture. **Career:** Beijing Cultural Relics Committee, engineer, 1941-54; Palace Museum, senior engineer, 1954-84, Design Section, chief, 1954-79, Department of Ancient Architecture, vice-director, 1980-84, chief engineer, 1984-89; Buddhist Association of China, technical adviser, 1957-58; Beijing University of Industry, lecturer, 1984, 1986; Graduate School of Southeast China University, visiting professor, 1994-. Writer. **Publications:** (Comp.) Palaces of the Forbidden City, 1984; (contrib.) Gong dian jian zhu, 1987; Zi jin cheng gong dian, 1988; (with S. Shiyuan) Zhongguo Zi jin cheng xue hui lun wen ji, 1997; Zhongguo gong dian jian zhu lun wen ji, 2002; (ed.) Gu gong jian zhu tu dian, 2007. Contributor to anthologies and journals. **Address:** Administrative Department for Ancient Architecture, Palace Museum, Beijing, 100020, China.

ZICREE, Mark Scott. American (born United States), b. 1955. **Genres:** Communications/Media, Plays/Screenplays, Adult Non-fiction, Art/Art History, Young Adult Fiction, Science Fiction/Fantasy, Humor/Satire. **Career:** National Public Radio, Morning Edition, commentator, 1991-93. Freelance writer and editor. **Publications:** The Twilight Zone Companion, 1982, 2nd ed., 1989; (with B. Hamably) Magic Time, 2001; (with M.K. Bohnhoff) Magic Time: Angelfire, 2002; (with R.C. Wilson) Magic Time: Ghostlands, 2005. **Address:** 7521 W Norton Ave., Ste. 8, West Hollywood, CA 90046, U.S.A. **Online address:** marc@zicree.com

ZIEFLE, Helmut W(ilhelm). American/German (born Germany), b. 1939. **Genres:** Language/Linguistics, Theology/Religion, Biography, Reference, Education. **Career:** Teacher, 1965-67; Wheaton College, instructor, 1967-72, assistant professor, 1972-77, associate professor, 1977-82, professor of German, 1982-2001, Wheaton in Germany Program, director, 1977-2001, professor emeritus of German, 2001-; German Evening School, president, 1978-80. Writer. **Publications:** Sibylle Schwarz: Leben und Werk, 1975; One Woman Against the Reich, 1981, rev. ed. as One Woman against the Reich: The True Story of a Mother's Struggle to Keep Her Family Faithful to God in a World Gone Mad, 2003; Dictionary of Modern Theological German, 1982, 2nd ed., 1992; Gegen Hitler und das Reich, 2000. EDITOR: Sibylle Schwarz: Deutsche Poetische Gedichte, 1980; Theological German: A Reader, 1986; Hermann Hesse und das Christentum, 1994; Modern Theological German: A Reader and Dictionary, 1997. **Address:** Wheaton College, 501 College Ave., Wheaton, IL 60187-5593, U.S.A. **Online address:** helmut.w.ziefle@wheaton.edu

ZIEGLER, Jennifer. (Jennifer Lynn Ziegler). American (born United States), b. 1967. **Genres:** Novels. **Career:** Journalist and educator. **Publications:** Alpha Dog (novel), 2006; How Not to Be Popular (novel), 2008. **Address:** Austin, TX , U.S.A. **Online address:** jennifer@jenniferziegler.net

ZIEGLER, Jennifer Lynn. *See* ZIEGLER, Jennifer.

ZIEGLER, Philip (Sandeman). British (born England), b. 1929. **Genres:** History, Biography, Essays. **Career:** William Collins Sons and Company Ltd., staff, 1966-84; Collins, editor-in-chief, 1979-80. **Publications:** The Black Death, 1969; Omdurman, 1973; Crown and People, 1978; Elizabeth's Britain, 1926-1986, 1986; (intro.) An Illustrated Short History of the World, 1987; The Sixth Great Power: A History of One of the Greatest of All Banking Families, the House of Barings, 1762-1929, 1988; London at War, 1939-1945, 1995; Osbert Sitwell, 1998; Britain Then and Now, 1999; Soldiers: Fighting Men's Lives, 1901-2001, 2002; Duchess of Dino: Chatelaine of Europe, 2003; Omdurman, 2003; Man Of Letters: The Extraordinary Life and Times of Literary Impresario, 2005; Legacy: Cecil Rhodes, the Rhodes Trust and Rhodes Scholarships, 2008. BIOGRAPHIES: The Duchess of Dino, 1962; Addington: A Life of Henry Addington, First Viscount Sidmouth, 1965; King William IV, 1971; Melbourne: A Biography of William Lamb, 2nd ed. as Viscount Melbourne 1976; Diana Cooper: A Biography, 1981; Mountbatten: The Official Biography, 1985, rev. ed., 2001; King Edward VIII: The Official Biography, 1990; Harold Wilson: The Authorized Life of Lord Wilson of Rievaulx, 1993; Edward Heath: The Authorised Biography, 2010. EDITOR: The Diaries of Lord Louis Mountbatten, 1920-1922, 1987; The Personal Diary of Admiral the Lord Louis Mountbatten, Supreme Allied Commander, South-East Asia, 1943-1946, 1988; From Shore to Shore: The Diaries of Earl

Mountbatten of Burma, 1953-1979, 1989; (with D. Seward) Brooks's: A Social History, 1991; Essays Catholic and Critical: By George P.Schner, S.J., 2002. Contributor to newspapers. **Address:** 22 Cottesmore Gardens, London, GL W8 5PR, England.

ZIELENZIGER, Michael. American (born United States), b. 1955. **Genres:** History, Economics, Business/Trade/Industry. **Career:** Daily Princetonian, chairman, 1976-77; Kansas City Star, national correspondent; Chicago Sun-Times, reporter; San Jose Mercury News, Pacific Rim correspondent; Stanford University, John S. Knight fellow, 1991; Knight-Ridder Newspapers, bureau chief, 1996-2003. **Publications:** Shutting Out the Sun: How Japan Created Its Own Lost Generation, 2006. Contributor to periodicals. **Address:** Nan A. Talese Books, 1745 Broadway, New York, NY 10019-4368, U.S.A. **Online address:** z@shuttingoutthesun.com

ZIETLOW, E(dward) R(obert). Canadian/American (born United States), b. 1932. **Genres:** Literary Criticism And History, Novels, Natural History, Young Adult Fiction. **Career:** University of Victoria, assistant professor, 1965-77, associate professor of English, professor of English, 1977-98. Writer. **Publications:** These Same Hills, 1960; A Country for Old Men and Other Stories, 1977; Transhominal Criticism, 1978; The Indian Maiden's Captivity and The Heart of the Country, 1978; Matada Rose, 1997. **Address:** 2124 Ferndale Rd., Victoria, BC V8N 2Y7, Canada.

ZIETZ, Karyl Lynn. Also writes as Karyl Charna Lynn. American (born United States), b. 1943. **Genres:** Architecture, Music, Reference, Photography. **Career:** Kope Productions, producer and director, 1984-; Smithsonian Institution, lecturer, moderator and coordinator. Writer. **Publications:** Abriss der Kinder- und Jugendpsychologie, 1967; Kind und physische Welt, 1969; Opera! The Guide to Western Europe's Great Houses, 1991; Opera Companies and Houses of the United States, 1994; The National Trust Guide to Great Opera Houses in America, 1996; Opera Companies and Houses of Western Europe, Canada, Australia and New Zealand, 1999; Breve Storia dei Teatrid' Opera Italini, 2001; Italian Opera Houses and Festivals, 2005. Contributor to periodicals. **Address:** Kope Productions, PO Box 40103, Palisades Sta., Washington, DC 20016, U.S.A.

ZIFF, Larzer. American (born United States), b. 1927. **Genres:** Cultural/Ethnic Topics, History, Literary Criticism And History. **Career:** Education Testing Service, test constructor in English, 1951-52; University of Chicago, lecturer in humanities, 1952-53, director of academic programs, 1953-56; University of California, assistant professor, professor of English, 1956-73, chairman of graduate studies and vice chairman of the department of English, 1965-69, Education Abroad Program, director, 1969-71; University of Copenhagen, Fulbright professor and lecturer, 1959-60; University of Warsaw, visiting professor, 1963; Modern Language Association, Literature & Society Group, chairman, 1965; English Institute, Criticism & History Section, chairman, 1966; Oxford University, university lecturer, 1973-78, Exeter College, fellow, 1973-78; University of Pennsylvania, professor of English, 1978-81; Johns Hopkins University, Department of English, Caroline Donovan professor of English, 1981-99, chair, 1991-95, Caroline Donovan professor emeritus of English, 1999-, research professor. Writer. **Publications:** The Career of John Cotton, 1962; The American 1890s, 1966; Literature of America: Colonial Period, 1970; (comp. with R. Macauley) America and Its Discontents, 1971; Puritanism in America, 1973; Literary Democracy, 1981; Writing in the New Nation, 1991; Return Passages, 2000; Mark Twain, 2004. EDITOR: (and intro.) Autobiography, 1959; Walden, 1961; The Scarlet Letter, 1963; The Genius, 1967; The Financier, 1967; John Cotton on the Churches of New England, 1968; Selected Writings of Benjamin Franklin, 1979; (and intro.) Selected Essays, 1982; (and intro.) Maggie, a Girl of the Streets, and Other Tales of New York, 2000; (and intro.) Nature and Selected Essays, 2003; (and intro.) Portable Benjamin Franklin, 2005. Contributor to journals. **Address:** Department of English, Johns Hopkins University, 30D Gilman Hall, 3400 N Charles St., Baltimore, MD 21218, U.S.A. **Online address:** lziff@jhu.edu

ZIFFRIN, Marilyn J. American (born United States), b. 1926. **Genres:** Music, Biography, Autobiography/Memoirs, Photography, Art/Art History. **Career:** Northwest Mississippi Agriculture High School and Junior College (now Northwest Mississippi Junior College), head of music department, 1949-50; WGN-Radio and TV, assistant head of transcription department, 1950-52; W.M. Simeral and Co., office manager, 1952-56; Chicago Public Schools, elementary school teacher, 1956-61; Northeastern Illinois University, assistant professor of music, 1961-67; New England College, associate professor of music, 1967-82; Saint Paul's School, teacher of musical composition, 1972-82. Writer. **Publications:** Colors: An Orchestra Piece, 1979; Sono: For Cello and Piano, 1980; Four Pieces for Tuba, 1982; Fantasia for Bassoon Solo, 1986; Carl Ruggles: Composer, Painter and Storyteller, 1994. Contributor to periodicals. **Address:** PO Box 179, Bradford, NH 03221-0179, U.S.A. **Online address:** ziffrin@iamnow.net

ZIGAL, Thomas. American (born United States), b. 1948. **Genres:** Novellas/Short Stories, Mystery/Crime/Suspense, Novels, Essays. **Career:** Writer. **Publications:** Western Edge (stories), 1982; (ed. with D. Oliphant) Joyce at Texas, 1983. MYSTERY NOVELS: Playland, 1981; Into Thin Air, 1995; Hardrock Stiff: A Kurt Muller Mystery, 1996; Pariah: A Kurt Muller Mystery, 1999; The White League, 2005. EDITED WITH D. OLIPHANT: Perspectives on Photography, 1982; Perspectives on Music: Essays on Collections at the Humanities Research Center, 1985; WCW & Others: Essays on William Carlos Williams and his Association with Ezra Pound, Hilda Doolittle, Marcel Duchamp, Marianne Moore, Emanuel Romano, Wallace Stevens, and Louis Zukofsky, 1985. **Address:** c/o Bill Contardi, Brandt & Hochman Literary Agents Inc., 1501 Broadway, Ste. 2310, New York, NY 10036, U.S.A. **Online address:** thomaszigal@gmail.com

ZIGMAN, Laura. American (born United States), b. 1962. **Genres:** Novels. **Career:** Vintage Books, senior publicist, 1986-89; Atlantic Monthly Press, marketing manager, 1989-91; Random House Inc., Turtle Bay Books, publicity director, 1991-93; Alfred A. Knopf Inc., promotion manager, 1993-95; writer, 1995-; Smithsonian Institution, project manager, 1996. **Publications:** NOVELS: Animal Husbandry, 1998; Dating Big Bird, 2000; Her, 2002; Piece of Work, 2006; (with P. Novak) Get Over Yourself!: How To Get Real, Get Serious, And Get Ready To Find True Love, 2008. Contributor to periodicals. **Address:** c/o Author Mail, Warner Books, Hachette Book Group USA, 1271 Ave. of the Americas, New York, NY 10020-1300, U.S.A. **Online address:** laura@laurazigman.com

ZIHLMAN, Adrienne L. American (born United States) **Genres:** Sciences, Social Sciences, Anthropology/Ethnology, History. **Career:** University of California, Department of Anthropology, assistant professor, 1967-79, associate professor, 1967-79, chairman, 1975-78, professor, 1979-. Writer. **Publications:** (Contrib. and ed. with M.E. Morbeck and A. Galloway) The Evolving Female: A Life-History Perspective (anthropology), 1997; The Human Evolution Coloring Book, 2nd ed., 2000. **Address:** Department of Anthropology, University of California, 355, Social Sciences I, 1156 High St., Santa Cruz, CA 95064, U.S.A. **Online address:** azihlman@ucsc.edu

ZILBOORG, Caroline (Crawford). American/British (born England), b. 1948. **Genres:** Literary Criticism And History, Essays, Biography. **Career:** Lake Erie College, assistant professor, 1977-84, associate professor, 1984-92, professor of English, 1992-95, coordinator of women's studies program, 1984-88, division of humanities, chair, 1986-88; University of Cambridge, Clare Hall, visiting fellow, 1992-93, faculty of English, 1995-. Writer. **Publications:** American Prose and Poetry in the 20th Century, 2000; The Masks of Mary Renault: A Literary Biography, 2001; Richard Aldington and H.D: Their Lives in Letters, 1918-1961, 2003; Women Writers, Past and Present, 2004; Critical edition of H.D.'s Bid Me to Live, 2011; Transgressions, 2011. EDITOR: (intro.) Richard Aldington and H.D: The Early Years in Letters, 1992; Richard Aldington: Essays in Honour of the Centenary of His Birth, 1994; (intro.) Richard Aldington and H.D.: The Later Years in Letters, 1995; Women's Firsts, 1997; Sergeant Lamb of the Ninth, 1999. Contributor to periodicals. **Address:** University of Cambridge, Clare Hall, Cambridge, CB CB3 9AL, England. **Online address:** caroline.zilboorg@gmail.com

ZIMBALIST, Andrew S. American (born United States), b. 1947. **Genres:** Economics, Sports/Fitness, History, Politics/Government. **Career:** Smith College, professor of economics, 1974-, Robert A. Woods professor of economics, 1991-; Doshisha University, visiting professor, 1974; Harvard University, visiting research fellow, 1980. Writer and consultant. **Publications:** (With J.G. Espinosa) Economic Democracy: Worker's Participation in Chilean Industry, 1970-1973, 1978, rev. ed., 1981; (with H.J. Sherman) Comparing Economic Systems: A Political-Economic Approach, 1984, (with H.J. Sherman and S. Brown) 2nd ed., 1989; (with C. Brundenius) The Cuban Economy: Measurement and Analysis of Socialist Performance, 1989; (with J. Weeks) Panama at the Crossroads: Economic Development and Political Change in the Twentieth Century, 1991; Baseball and Billions: A Probing Look Inside the Big Business of Our National Pastime, 1992; Unpaid Profes-

sionals: Commercialism and Conflict in Big-Time College Sports, 1999; May the Best Team Win: Baseball Economics and Public Policy, 2003; (with S. Szymanski) National Pastime: How Americans Play Baseball and the Rest of the World Plays Soccer, 2005; Bottom Line: Observations and Arguments on the Sports Business, 2006; In the Best Interests of Baseball?: The Revolutionary Reign of Bud Selig, 2006; Circling the Bases: Essays on the Challenges and Prospects of the Sports Industry, 2011. EDITOR: Case Studies on the Labor Process, 1979; Comparative Economic Systems: An Assessment of Knowledge, Theory and Method, 1984; Cuba's Socialist Economy Toward the 1990s, 1987; Cuban Political Economy: Controversies in Cubanology, 1988; (co-ed.) Cuba in Transition, 1992; (with R.G. Noll) Sports, Jobs & Taxes: The Economic Impact of Sports Teams and Stadiums, 1997; The Economics of Sport, 2001; (with N. Hogshead-Makar) Equal Play: Title IX and Social Change, 2007. Contributor of articles to periodicals. **Address:** Department of Economics, Smith College, 103 Wright Hall, Northampton, MA 01063, U.S.A. **Online address:** azimbali@email.smith.edu

ZIMBARDO, Philip G. American (born United States), b. 1933. **Genres:** Psychology, Self Help, Social Sciences. **Career:** Yale University, assistant professor of psychology, 1959-60, visiting professor, 1962; New York University, assistant professor of psychology, 1960-67; Columbia University, associate professor of psychology, 1968; Stanford University, professor of psychology, 1968-, now professor emeritus; PBS-TV Series, host, 1990. Writer. **Publications:** (Ed.) The Cognitive Control of Motivation: The Consequences of Choice and Dissonance, 1969; (with E.B. Ebbesen) Influencing Attitudes and Changing Behavior: a Basic Introduction to Relevant Methodology, Theory, and Applications, 1969, 2nd ed., 1977; (with F. Ruch) Psychology and Life, 8th ed., 1971, (with R. Gerrig) 19th ed., 2010; (comp. with C. Maslach) Psychology for our Times: Readings, 1973, (with C. Maslach) 2nd ed., 1977; (with F.L. Ruch) Lehrbuch der Psychologie: eine Einführung für Studenten der Psychologie, Medizin und Pädagogik, 1975; Shyness: What It Is, What to Do about It, 1977; (with D. Dempsey) Psychology & You, 1978; (with S. Radl) The Shyness Workbook, 1980; (ed.) Social Psychology, 1980; Essentials of Psychology and Life, 1980; Readings on Human Behavior, 1988; (with M. Leippe) The Psychology of Attitude Change and Social Influence, 1991; (with A.L. Weber) Psychology, 1994, 4th ed., 2005; (with S. Radl) Shy Child: A Parent's Guide to Preventing and Overcoming Shyness from Infancy to Adulthood, 1999; (with M.K. Huggins and M. Haritos-Fatouros) Violence Workers: Police Torturers and Murderers Reconstruct Brazilian Atrocities, 2002; (with A.L. Weber and R.L. Johnson) Psychology: Core Concepts, 4th ed., 2003, 7th ed., 2012; (co-ed.) AP Psychology, 2005; Lucifer Effect: Understanding How Good People Turn Evil, 2007; (with J. Boyd) Time Paradox: The New Psychology of Time that will Change your Life, 2008; (foreword) Fixing Hell, 2008; (foreword) The Impact of 9, 2009. **Address:** Department of Psychology, Stanford University, Rm. 246, Jordan Hall, Bldg. 420, Stanford, CA 94305-2130, U.S.A. **Online address:** zim@standford.edu

ZIMBEROFF, Tom. American (born United States), b. 1951. **Genres:** Photography, Business/Trade/Industry, Transportation. **Career:** Vertex Software Inc., founder, 1993; Exactly Vertical Inc., founder, 1999; commercial photographer; photojournalist. Writer, 1971-; AOTC Corp., chief operating officer. **Publications:** Photography: Focus on Profit, 2002; Art of the Chopper, 2003; Art of the Chopper II, 2006; Art of the Chopper: Catalog for William J. Clinton Presidential Center, 2008. **Address:** AOTC Corp., 1364 45th Ave., Galtier Plz., Ste. 200, 380 Jackson St., San Francisco, CA 94122, U.S.A. **Online address:** tom@zimberoff.com

ZIMMER, Carl. American (born United States), b. 1966. **Genres:** Sciences, Documentaries/Reportage. **Career:** Discover magazine, senior editor, 1993-99; freelance writer, 1999-; Yale University, lecturer, fellow. **Publications:** At the Water's Edge: The Macroevolution of Life, 1998; Parasite Rex, 2000; Evolution: The Triumph of an Idea, 2001; Soul Made Flesh: The Discovery of the Brain and How it Changed the World, 2004; Smithsonian Intimate Guide to Human Origins, 2005; (co-ed.) Virus and the Whale: Exploring Evolution in Creatures Small and Large, 2006; (contrib.) The Descent of Man, 2007; Microcosm: E. Coli and the New Science of Life, 2008; The Tangled Bank: An Introduction to Evolution, 2010; Virus World, 2011; A Planet of Viruses, 2011; Contributor to periodicals. **Address:** c/o Eric Simonoff, Janklow & Nesbit Associates, 445 Park Ave., 13th Fl., New York, NY 10022-1614, U.S.A. **Online address:** mail@carlzimmer.com

ZIMMER, Paul J(erome). American (born United States), b. 1934. **Genres:**

Poetry, Essays. **Career:** Macy's Department Store, manager, 1961-63; San Francisco News Co., manager, 1963-65; University of California Bookstore, manager, 1963-67; University of Pittsburgh Press, assistant director, associate director, 1967-78; University of Georgia Press, director and editor, 1979-84; University of Iowa Press, director and editor, 1984-94, retired, 1994; Chico State College (now California State University), poet-in-residence; University of Montana, poet-in-residence, 1998. **Publications:** A Seed on the Wind: Poems, 1960; The Ribs of Death, 1967; The Republic of Many Voices, 1969; The Zimmer Poems, 1976; (contrib.) American Poets in 1976, 1976; With Wanda: Town and Country Poems, 1980; The Ancient Wars, 1981; Family Reunion: Selected and New Poems, 1983; Earthbound Zimmer, 1983; The American Zimmer, 1984; Live with Animals, 1987; The Great Bird of Love: Poems, 1989; Big Blue Train: Poems, 1993; Crossing to Sunlight: Selected Poems, 1996; After the Fire: A Writer Finds His Place, 2002; Trains in the Distance, 2004; Crossing To Sunlight Revisited: New And Selected Poems, 2007; Importance of Being Zimmer, 2010. **Address:** c/o Author Mail, Kent State University Press, 1118 Library, 1125 Risman Dr., PO Box 5190, Kent, OH 44242-0001, U.S.A.

ZIMMER, Tracie Vaughn. American (born United States), b. 1969. **Genres:** Poetry, Children's Fiction, Novels, Young Adult Non-fiction. **Career:** Lakota Local School District, teacher. Writer. **Publications:** Sketches from a Spy Tree, 2005; Reaching for Sun, 2007; The Floating Circus, 2008; 42 Miles, 2008; Steady Hands: Poems about Work, 2009; Cousins of Clouds: Elephant Poems, 2010. **Address:** Clarion Books, 215 Park Ave. S, New York, NY 10003, U.S.A. **Online address:** tvzimmer@mac.com

ZIMMERMAN, Cynthia (Diane). Canadian (born Canada), b. 1943. **Genres:** Theatre, Literary Criticism And History. **Career:** York University, Glendon College, lecturer, 1967-74, assistant professor, 1974-81, associate professor, 1981-99, professor of English, 1999-. Writer. **Publications:** (With R. Wallace) The Work: Conversations with English-Canadian Playwrights, 1982; Playwriting Women: Female Voices in English Canada, 1994. EDITOR: (with H. Zeifman) Contemporary British Drama, 1970-90: Essays from Modern Drama, 1993; (co-ed.) Taking the Stage: Selections from Plays by Canadian Women, 1994; (and intro.) Sharon Pallock: Collected Works, 2005, 3 vols., 2007; Betty Lambert Reader, 2007. **Address:** Department of English, Glendon College, York University, C224 York Hall, 2275 Bayview Ave., Toronto, ON M4N 3M6, Canada. **Online address:** czimmer@yorku.ca

ZIMMERMAN, Donald E(dward). American (born United States), b. 1944. **Genres:** Agriculture/Forestry, Communications/Media, Psychology, Sociology, Writing/Journalism. **Career:** Kansas State University, assistant director, 1964-68; Manhattan Mercury, reporter, editor and photographer, 1968; Pennsylvania Game Commission, wildlife education specialist, 1971-73; University of Wisconsin, teaching assistant, 1975-76; Colorado State University, assistant professor, 1976-82, associate professor, 1982-87, professor of technical journalism, 1987-, acting department head, 1993-94, Center for Research on Writing and Communication Technologies, co-director; University of New Mexico, technical communication professor, 2000; Brigham Young University, technical communication professor, 2000; University of Washington, technical communication professor, 2005; West Virginia Tech, technical communication professor, 2007. **Publications:** The Nature of Man: John Donne's Songs and Holy Sonnets, 1960; (ed. and contrib.) Farming Systems Research and Development: Guidelines for Developing Countries, 1982; (with D.G. Clark) The Random House Guide to Technical and Scientific Communication, with Instructor's Manual, 1987; (with D. Rodrigues) Research and Writing in the Disciplines, 1992; (with M.L. Muraski) The Element of Information Gathering: A Guide for Technical Communicators, Scientists and Engineers, 1995; (with M. Hassul) Electronic Devices and Circuits: Conventional Flow Version, 1997; (with M. Palmquist) Writing with a Computer, 1999. Works appear in anthologies. Contributor of articles and reviews to professional journals. **Address:** Dept. of Journalism & Tech. Communication, Colorado State University, C256B Clark Bldg., Fort Collins, CO 80523-1785, U.S.A. **Online address:** dzimmerman@vines.colostate.edu

ZIMMERMAN, Earl. American (born United States), b. 1950. **Genres:** Sociology, Theology/Religion, Humanities. **Career:** Shalom Mennonite Congregation, pastor; Eastern Mennonite University, faculty, 1998-, assistant professor of Bible and religion, associate professor, Justice, Peace and Conflict Studies Program, teacher, Conflict Resolution Center, director. Writer. **Publications:** (Ed. with R. Gingerich) Telling Our Stories: Personal Accounts of Engagements with Scripture, 2006; Practicing the Politics of Jesus: The Or-

igin and Significance of John Howard Yoder's Social Ethics, 2007. **Address:** Department of Bible and Religion, Eastern Mennonite University, 1200 Park Rd., Harrisonburg, VA 22802-2462, U.S.A.

ZIMMERMAN, Franklin (Bershir). American (born United States), b. 1923. **Genres:** Music, Biography, Autobiography/Memoirs. **Career:** State University of New York, assistant professor of music, 1958-59; University of Southern California, Department of History, Music and Literature, visiting associate professor, 1960, associate professor, chairman, 1961-64; Dartmouth College, professor of music, 1964-67; Dartmouth Collegium Musicum, director, 1964-67; University of Kentucky, professor of music, director of Pro Musica, Division of Music History and Musicology, director, Collegium Musicum, director, 1967-68, visiting professor, 1967-68; University of California, senior fellow, 1967, 1968; University of Pennsylvania, professor of music, 1968-, director of Pro Musica, Department of Music, chairman, 1968-, College of General Studies, lecturer, 1969-, now professor emeritus; Pennsylvania Pro Musica, founder and director, 1968-. Writer. **Publications:** Henry Purcell 1659-1695: An Analytical Catalogue of His Music, 1963; Henry Purcell, His Life and Times, 1967, 2nd ed., 1983; Sound and Sense in Purcell's Single Songs, 1968; The Anthems of Henry Purcell, 1971; Henry Purcell 1659-1695: Melodic and Intervallic Indexes to His Complete Works, 1975; Henry Purcell: A Guide to Research, 1989; Visible Music Sound Scapes Series, 1999; Henry Purcell's Opera, Dido and Aeneas, 2000; Handel's Vision: The Messiah; Beethoven's Ninth Symphony: As New View; J.S. Bach's Monumental Legacy: The Art of Fugue. EDITOR: Will Love Thee, O Lord, 1961; Introduction to the Skill of Music, 12th ed., 1972; John Playford's Introduction to the Skill of Music, 1973; A Facsimile Edition of the William Kennedy Gostling Manuscript, 1976; Serenata: There in Blissful Shades, 1982; There in Blissful Shade, 1983; The Symphonies of C.F. Abel's Opus I, 1983; Henry Purcell 1659-1695: An Analytical Catalog of His Complete Works, 1990. **Address:** Department of Music, University of Pennsylvania, Philadelphia, PA 19104, U.S.A. **Online address:** frank@pennsylvaniapromusica.com

ZIMMERMAN, Joseph Francis. American (born United States), b. 1928. **Genres:** Politics/Government, Public/Social Administration, Transportation, Women's Studies And Issues. **Career:** Clark University, lecturer, 1956-65; Worcester Polytechnic Institute, instructor, 1954-55, assistant professor, 1955-57, associate professor, 1957-62, professor of government, 1962-65; Visiting Nurse Association, corporator, 1960-65; Lincoln Neighborhood Center, director, 1960-65; State University of New York, Rockefeller College, professor of political science, 1965-, Local Government Studies Center, director, 1965-68, Department of Political Science, chairman, 1973-74, Graduate School of Public Affairs, chairman of the faculty; National Civic Review, contributing editor, 1968-95; Representation and Electoral Systems, editor; Citizens for Neighborhood Improvement, president; Citizens' Plan E Association, president. Consultant. **Publications:** State and Local Government, 1962, 3rd ed., 1978; Metropolitan Ecumenism: The Road to the Promised Land?, 1967; (with M.E. Snyder) The 1967 Survey of Metropolitan Planning: Emerging Trends, 1967; The Massachusetts Town Meeting, 1967; State Agencies for Local Affairs: The Institutionalization of State Assistance to Local Governments, 1968; The Federated City: Community Control in Large Cities, 1972; Pragmatic Federalism: The Reassignment of Functional Responsibility, 1976; (with F.W. Prescott) The Politics of the Veto of Legislation in New York, 2 vols., 1980; The Discretionary Authority of Local Governments, 1981; Measuring Local Discretionary Authority, 1981; The Government and Politics of New York State, 1981, 2nd ed., 2008; State-Local Relations: A Partnership Approach, 1983, 2nd ed., 1995; Participatory Democracy: Populism Revived, 1986; Federal Preemption: The Silent Revolution, 1991; Contemporary American Federalism: The Growth of National Power, 1992, 2nd ed., 2008; (with W. Rule) U.S. Electoral Systems: Their Impact on Women and Minorities, 1992; (with W. Rule) Electoral Systems in Comparative Perspective: Their Impact on Women and Minorities, 1994; Curbing Unethical Conduct in Government, 1994; Interstate Relations: The Neglected Dimension of Federalism, 1996; The Recall: Tribunal of the People, 1998; The New England Town Meeting: Democracy in Action, 1999; The Initiative: Citizen Law-Making, 1999; The Referendum: The People Decide Public Policy, 2001; Interstate Cooperation: Compacts and Administrative Agreements, 2002, 2nd ed., 2012; Interstate Economic Relations, 2004; (with A.J. Blasi) Transition from Vowed to Lay Ministry in American Catholicism, 2004; Congressional Preemption: Regulatory Federalism, 2005; Interstate Disputes: The Supreme Court's Original Jurisdiction, 2006; Silence of Congress: State Taxation of Interstate Commerce, 2007; Congress: Facilitator of State Action, 2010; Regulating the Business of Insurance in a Federal System, 2010; Horizontal

Federalism: Interstate Relations, 2011; Interstate Water Compacts: Intergovernmental Efforts to Manage America's Water Supply, 2012; State-local Governmental Interactions, 2012. EDITOR: Readings in State and Local Government, 1964; Metropolitan Charters, 1967; The Government of the Metropolis, 1968; Subnational Politics, 1970; The Crisis in Mass Transportation, 1971; (with D.A. Zimmerman) The Politics of Subnational Governance, 1983; (with W. Rule) United States Electoral Systems: Their Impact on Women and Minorities, 1992; (with W. Rule) The U.S. House of Representatives: Reform or Rebuild?, 2000. Contributor to books. **Address:** Rockefeller College, State University of New York, 135 Western Ave., Albany, NY 12222, U.S.A. **Online address:** zimmer@albany.edu

ZIMMERMAN, Muriel L. American (born United States), b. 1938. **Genres:** Communications/Media, Information Science/Computers. **Career:** Drexel Institute of Technology (now Drexel University), lecturer in writing, 1968-69; Energy Review, editor, 1973-83; University of California, lecturer in technical writing, 1980-83, senior lecturer in writing, 1986-2006; Massachusetts Institute of Technology, lecturer in writing, 1983-86, 2006-. **Publications:** (With J. Paradis) The MIT Guide to Science and Engineering Communication, 1997, 2nd ed., 2002. Contributor to books and journals. **Address:** University of California, 1822 Prospect Ave., Santa Barbara, CA 93103, U.S.A. **Online address:** mzimmer@writing.ucsb.edu

ZIMMERMAN, Robert. American (born United States), b. 1953. **Genres:** Air/Space Topics, Travel/Exploration, Astronomy. **Career:** Writer and historian. **Publications:** Genesis: The Story of Apollo 8, the First Manned Flight to Another World, 1998; The Chronological Encyclopedia of Discoveries in Space, 2000; Leaving Earth: Space Stations, Rival Superpowers, and the Quest for Interplanetary Travel, 2003; The Universe in a Mirror: The Saga of the Hubble Telescope and the Visionaries Who Built It, 2008. Contributor of articles to periodicals. **Address:** Princeton University Press, 6 Oxford St., Woodstock, Oxfordshire, OX20 1TW, England. **Online address:** zimmerman@nasw.org

ZIMMERMAN, Shirley Lee. American (born United States), b. 1925. **Genres:** Social Sciences, Politics/Government, Human Relations/Parenting, Public/Social Administration. **Career:** Minnesota Department of Public Welfare, consultant for the child welfare division to statewide organizations, 1967-69; Health and Welfare Planning Council, social planner, 1969; Interstudy, social welfare researcher, 1970-73; University of Minnesota, lecturer, 1970-72, assistant and lecturer, 1970-77, instructor, 1972-77, assistant director of continuing education in social work, 1977-84, assistant professor, 1982-83, associate professor, 1983-88, professor, 1988-2000, professor emeritus of family social science, 2000-. Writer. **Publications:** Understanding Family Policy: Theoretical Approaches, 1988; Family Policies and Family Well-Being: The Role of Political Culture, 1992; Understanding Family Policy: Theories & Applications, 1995; Family Policy: Constructed Solutions to Family Problems, 2001. Works appear in anthologies. Contributor of articles to journals and newspapers. **Address:** Department of Family Social Science, University of Minnesota, 299h McNeal Hall, 1985 Buford Ave., Saint Paul, MN 55108-6140, U.S.A. **Online address:** szimmerm@umn.edu

ZIMMERMANN, Arnold Walter. British (born England), b. 1913?. **Genres:** Novellas/Short Stories, Education, Geography, History, Theology/Religion, Literary Criticism And History, Young Adult Fiction. **Career:** Horsenden Junior School, head teacher, 1949-56; Newport Junior School, head teacher, 1957-72; California State University, professor. Writer. **Publications:** WITH F.M. MEADE: Spotlight Geography, 1966; (comp.) Illustrated Study Bible, 1973; (comp.) Illustrated Study Bible: With Today's English Version, 1977; Religions of the World, 1985; Time and Progress Histories-Books 1-6; School Study Bible Books 1-7; Panorama Readers; New English Study Bible. OTHER: Write Me a Story, 1962. **Address:** 8 Windmill Gardens, Enfield, GL EN2 7DU, England.

ZIMMERMANN, H(einz) Werner. Canadian/Austrian (born Austria), b. 1951. **Genres:** Children's Non-fiction, Illustrations, Children's Fiction, Picture/Board Books. **Career:** Sheridan College of Applied Arts and Technology, sessional and art instructor, 1986-; School of Craft and Design, art instructor, 1993-94. Writer. **Publications:** SELF-ILLUSTRATED FOR CHILDREN: Henny Penny, 1988; Alphonse Knows: A Circle Is Not a Valentine, 1990; Alphonse Knows: The Colour of Spring, 1990; Alphonse Knows: Zero is Not Enough, 1990; Alphonse Knows: Twelve Months Make a Year, 1990; (with J. Lawson) Whatever You Do, Don't Go Near that Canoe!, 1996; Snow Day,

1999; Porcupine in a Pine Tree; Pippin the Christmas Pig; Listen Said the Donkey; Brave Highland Heart; Farmer Joe; Farmer Joe Goes To The City; Farmer Joe Babysits; In My Backyard; Each One Special; Finster Frets. Illustrator of books by others. **Address:** 11 Glasgow St. S, Guelph, ON N1H 4T4, Canada. **Online address:** werner@wernerzimmermann.ca

ZIMMERMANN, Jens. German (born Germany), b. 1965?. **Genres:** Theology/Religion. **Career:** Trinity Western University, associate professor of English and modern languages; Canadian Council, research chair in interpretation, religion and culture, 2006-11. Academic and writer. **Publications:** Recovering Theological Hermeneutics: An Incarnational-Trinitarian Theory of Interpretation, 2004; (with N. Klassen) The Passionate Intellect: Incarnational Humanism and the Future of University Education, 2006. Contributor to journals. **Address:** Trinity Western University, 7600 Glover Rd., Langley, BC V2Y 1Y1, Canada. **Online address:** jensz@twu.ca

ZIMPEL, Lloyd. American (born United States), b. 1929. **Genres:** Novels, Business/Trade/Industry, Cultural/Ethnic Topics, Social Sciences, Young Adult Fiction, Literary Criticism And History. **Career:** West Coast Life Insurance Co., advertising director, 1959-63; State Department of Industrial Relations, Fair Employment Practice Commission, education director, 1964-81. Writer. **Publications:** (With D. Panger) Business and the Hardcore Unemployed: A Management Guide to Hiring, Training, and Motivating Minority Workers: Readings in Developing Minority Manpower, 1970; Meeting the Bear: Journal of the Black Wars, 1971; The Disadvantaged Worker, 1971; Man Against Work, 1974; Foundry Foreman, 1980; A Season of Fire & Ice: Excerpts from the Patriarch's Dakota Journal, with Addenda, 2006. Contributor to periodicals. **Address:** 61 Valley St., San Francisco, CA 94110, U.S.A.

ZINES, Leslie. Australian (born Australia), b. 1930. **Genres:** Law. **Career:** Department of the Attorney General, legal officer, 1952-62; Australian National University, senior lecturer, 1962-65, reader, 1965-67, professor of law, 1967-77, Robert Garran professor, 1977-92, dean, 1973-75 and 1984-86, professor emeritus, 1992-, Fleming Centre for the Advancement of Legal Research, visiting fellow; Cambridge University, Arthur Goodhart professor of legal science, 1992-93. Writer. **Publications:** Study of Law, 1968; (ed.) Commentaries on the Australian Constitution: A Tribute to Geoffrey Sawer, 1977; (with Z. Cowen) Federal Jurisdiction in Australia, 2nd ed., 1978, 3rd ed., 2002; The High Court and the Constitution, 1981, 5th ed., 2008; (with G. Lindell) Sawer's Australian Constitutional Cases, 4th ed., 1982; Constitutional Change in the Commonwealth, 1991; Cowen and Zines's Federal Jurisdiction in Australia, 2002. **Address:** Law Program, R.S.S.S., Australian National University, Rm. 282, Bldg. 5, Fellows Rd., Canberra, AC 0200, Australia. **Online address:** zinesl@law.anu.edu.au

ZINGG, Paul J(oseph). American (born United States), b. 1945. **Genres:** History, Sports/Fitness, Biography. **Career:** University of Georgia, Department of History, instructor, 1970-74; St. Bernard's College, Department of History and Political Science, chair and assistant professor, 1975-77; Southern Benedictine College, assistant professor of history, 1975-77; Williams University, executive dean for academic affairs, 1977-78; University of Pennsylvania, adjunct assistant professor, 1978-, adjunct associate professor of history, 1986, College of Arts and Sciences, vice-dean, 1979-83, assistant to the president, 1983-86; Saint Mary's College of California, professor of history and dean of liberal arts school, 1986-93; Hearst Art Gallery, board director, 1988-90; California Polytechnic State University, professor of history, 1993-2003, dean of liberal arts college, 1993-95, provost and vice president for academic affairs, 1995-2004; California State University, president, 2004-. Writer. **Publications:** SPORTS HISTORY: Pride of the Palestra, 1987; (ed. and contrib.) The Sporting Image: Readings in American Sport History, 1988; Harry Hooper, 1887-1974: An American Baseball Life, 1993; (with M.D. Medeiros) Runs, Hits, and an Era: The Pacific Coast League, 1903-1958, 1994; A Good Round: A Journey through the Landscapes and Memory of Golf, 1999; Emerald Odyssey: In Search of the Gods of Golf and Ireland, 2008. OTHER: (with J.J. Cooke and A.H. Miller) Through Foreign Eyes: Western Attitudes toward North Africa, 1982. EDITOR: In Search of the American National Character, 1984; (with T. Purdom) The Academic Penn, 1986. Contributor to periodicals. **Address:** California State University, 400 W 1st St., Chico, CA 95929-0020, U.S.A. **Online address:** pzingg@csuchico.edu

ZINIK, Zinovy. (Gluzberg-Zinik). British (born England), b. 1945. **Genres:** Novels, Novellas/Short Stories, Essays, Plays/Screenplays, Writing/Journalism. **Career:** Moscow University, teacher of creative writing, 1969-75;

Jerusalem University, Student Theatre Group, director, 1975-76; British Broadcasting Corp., editor and presenter of the Arts Programme, 1977-2011; University of Wesleyan, teacher of creative writing; Columbia University, teacher of creative writing. **Publications:** The Mushroom Picker (Russofobka i fungofil), 1987; The Lord and the Gamekeeper (Lord i eger), 1989; One-Way Ticket, 1995; Mind the Doors, 2001; History Thieves, 2011. Works appear in anthologies. Contributor of articles, essays, and stories to periodicals. **Address:** Anna Webber, United Agents, 12-26 Lexington St., London, GL W1F 0LE, England. **Online address:** zinovy.zinik@gmail.com

ZINK, Michelle. American (born United States), b. 1969?. **Genres:** Novels. **Career:** Writer. **Publications:** NOVELS: Prophecy of the Sisters, 2009; Guardian of the Gate, 2010. Contributor to books. **Address:** NY , U.S.A. **Online address:** prophecypress@aol.com

ZINNES, Harriet. American (born United States), b. 1919. **Genres:** Novels, Novellas/Short Stories, Poetry, Art/Art History, Literary Criticism And History, Translations, Psychiatry. **Career:** Raritan Arsenal, editor, 1942-43; Harper's Bazaar Magazine, associate editor, 1944-46; City University of New York, Hunter College, tutor, 1946-49, Queens College, professor of English, 1949-53, 1962-89, professor emeritus, 1989-; Rutgers University, lecturer, 1960-62; University of Geneva, visiting professor of American literature, 1968; Great Neck Library, poetry consultant, 1972-82; New York Arts Magazine, contributing writer and art critic. **Publications:** Waiting and Other Poems, 1964; An Eye for an I, 1966; I Wanted to See Something Flying, 1976; Entropisms, 1978; (ed. and intro.) Ezra Pound and the Visual Arts, 1980; Book of Ten, 1981; (trans.) Blood and Feathers: Selected Poems of Jacques Prevert, 1988-1993; Lover: Short Stories, 1988; Book of Twenty, 1992; My, Haven't the Flowers Been? (poems), 1995; The Radiant Absurdity of Desire (short stories), 1998; Plunge (poems), 2001; Drawing on the Wall (poems), 2002; Meaning, Extended (literary criticism), 2004; Whither Nonstopping (poems), 2006; Light Light, or, the Curvature of the Earth, 2009. Works appear in anthologies. Contributor to periodicals. **Address:** 25 W 54th St., Ste. 6A, New York, NY 10019-5404, U.S.A. **Online address:** hzinnes@rcn.com

ZINOVIEFF, Sofka. Greek/British (born England), b. 1961?. **Genres:** Anthropology/Ethnology, History. **Career:** The Independent Magazine, freelance journalist; The Telegraph Magazine, freelance journalist; The Times Literary Supplement, freelance journalist; The Financial Times, freelance journalist; The London Magazine, freelance journalist. Anthropologist. **Publications:** The History of Emigration from Greece, 1997; Eurydice Street: A Place in Athens, 2004; Red Princess: A Revolutionary Life, 2007. Contributor to periodicals. **Address:** c/o Caroline Dawnay, 130 Shaftesbury Ave., London, GL W1D 5EU, England.

ZINSSER, Caroline. American (born United States), b. 1930. **Genres:** Education, Women's Studies And Issues, Social Sciences. **Career:** Life, reporter, 1953-57; freelance editorial researcher, 1957-67; public school teacher, 1969-72; Yale University, lecturer, 1972-73, Center for the Study of Education, research associate, assistant director of primary teacher preparation program, 1972-73, Yale Child Study Center, research associate, 1973-80; Private Day School, director, 1973-78; Bank Street College of Education, Bank Street School for Children, director, 1978-81; Advocates for Children, director, 1979-80; Working Mother, contributing editor, 1982-85; University of Pennsylvania, lecturer, 1984, Baltimore Study of Adolescent Parenthood and the Transmission of Social Disadvantage, research assistant, 1985; Center for Public Advocacy Research, Child Care/Early Childhood Education Policy Study, project director, 1985-90; Rockefeller Brothers Fund, program officer, 1990-99, retired, 1999; Early Childhood Funders Collaborative, co-founder and chair; New York State Child Care Commission, consultant. **Publications:** A Study of New York Day Care Worker Salaries and Benefits, 1986; Day Care's Unfair Burden: How Low Wages Subsidize a Public Service, 1986; Over a Barrel: Working Mothers Talk About Child Care, 1987; (with B. Andrews) One Hundred Working Women, 1988; (with E. Marx) Raising Child Care Salaries and Benefits: An Evaluation of the New York State Salary Enhancement Legislation, 1990; Born and Raised in East Urban: A Community Study of Informal and Unregulated Child Care, 1990; Raised in East Urban: Child Care Changes in a Working Class Community, 1991; (ed. with S.D. Schachter and C.V.A. Schaffner) In the Company of Women: 100 Years at the Cosmopolitan Club, 2009. Contributor of articles to journals and magazines. **Address:** 45 E 62nd St., New York, NY 10065-8014, U.S.A.

ZINSSER, Judith P. American (born United States), b. 1943. **Genres:** Race

Relations, Women's Studies And Issues. **Career:** Brearley School, teacher, 1964-68; United Nations International School, Department of Humanities, teacher, 1969-93, Middle School, coordinator, 1970-76, acting head, 1973-74; Columbia University, Teacher's College, part-time instructor and advisor, 1989-90; United Nations conferences, assistant examiner, 1983-93; Rutgers University, Department of History, adjunct instructor and teaching assistant, 1990-93; Miami University, Department of history, assistant professor, professor, 1993-, now professor emeritus. Writer. **Publications:** (With P. Bergman) The Chronological History of the Negro in America, 1969; Understanding the Universal Declaration of Human Rights, 1978; Approaches to the Comparative History of the Americas, 1982; (with B.S. Anderson) A History of Their Own: Women in Europe from Prehistory to the Present, 1988, rev. ed., 2000; History and Feminism: A Glass Half Full, 1993; A New Partnership: Indigenous Peoples and the United Nations, 1994; (ed.) Men, Women and the Birthing of Modern Science, 2005; (ed. with J.C. Hayes) Emilie Du Châtelet: Rewriting Enlightenment Philosophy and Science, 2006; La dame d' esprit: A Biography of the Marquise Du Châtelet, 2006; (ed. and intro.) Emili, 2009; (ed. and intro.) Selected Philosophical and Scientific Writings, 2009. Contributor to journals. **Address:** Department of History, Miami University, 254 Upham Hall, Oxford, OH 45056, U.S.A. **Online address:** zinssejp@muohio.edu

ZIOLKOWSKI, Eric J(ozef). American/German (born Germany), b. 1958. **Genres:** Literary Criticism And History, Theology/Religion. **Career:** University of Chicago, instructor, 1984-87; University of Wisconsin, visiting assistant professor of comparative literature, 1987-88; Lafayette College, visiting assistant professor, 1988-89, assistant professor of religion and literature, 1989-94, Dana assistant professor, 1991-94, Thomas Roy and Lura Forrest Jones lecturer, 1992, associate professor, 1994-2000, professor, 2000-, Charles A. Dana professor of religious studies, department head, 2002-; De Gruyter's International Encyclopedia of the Bible, main editor of reception area, 2003-; Literature and Theology, North American editor, 2004-. **Publications:** The Sanctification of Don Quixote: From Hidalgo to Priest, 1991; (ed.) A Museum of Faiths: Histories and Legacies of the 1893 World's Parliament of Religions, 1993; Evil Children in Religion, Literature, and Art, 2001; (ed.) Literature, Religion, and East/West Comparison: Essays in Honor of Anthony C. Yu, 2005; (co-ed.) Encyclopedia of the Bible and Its Reception, 30 vols., 2008; Literary Kierkegaard, 2011. Works appear in anthologies. Contributor of articles to journals. **Address:** Department of Religious Studies, Lafayette College, Quad Dr., Easton, PA 18042-1770, U.S.A. **Online address:** ziolkowe@lafayette.edu

ZIOLKOWSKI, Jan M. American (born United States), b. 1956. **Genres:** History, Translations. **Career:** Harvard University, assistant professor, 1981-84, Loeb associate professor of the humanities, 1984-87, professor of Medieval Latin and comparative literature, 1987-2002, Arthur Kingsley Porter professor of Medieval Latin, 2002-, Department of Comparative Literature, acting chair, 1991-92, chair, 1993-2002, Department of the Classics, Walter Channing Cabot Fellow, 1996-97, acting chair, 2003-04, chair, 2006-07, Dumbarton Oaks Research Library and Collection, director, 2007-; Villa i Tatti, visiting professor, 1992-93, Lehman Foundation visiting professor, 1997-98; Netherlands Institute for Advanced Study (NIAS), fellow-in-residence, 2005-06. Writer. **Publications:** Alan of Lille's Grammar of Sex: The Meaning of Grammar to a Twelfth-Century Intellectual, 1985; (ed.) Nigel of Canterbury, Miracles of the Virgin Mary, in Verse=Miracula Sancte dei Genitricis Virginis Marie, Versifice, 1986; (ed.) Jezebel: A Norman Latin Poem of the Early Eleventh Century, 1989; (ed.) On Philology, 1990; Talking Animals: Medieval Latin Beast Poetry, 750-1150, 1993; (ed. and trans.) The Cambridge Songs (Carmina Cantabrigiensia), 1994; (ed. and trans.) Nigel of Canterbury, The Passion of St. Lawrence: Epigrams and Marginal Poems, 1994; (ed.) Obscenity: Social Control and Artistic Creation in the European Middle Ages, 1998; (ed. with M. Carruthers) The Medieval Craft of Memory: An Anthology of Texts and Pictures, 2002; (ed. and intro.) An Introduction to the Study of Medieval Latin Versification, 2004; Nota Bene: Reading Classics and Writing Melodies in the Early Middle Ages, 2007; Fairy Tales from before Fairy Tales: The Medieval Latin Past of Wonderful Lies, 2007; (ed. with B.K. Balint, J. Lake, L. Light and P. Piper) A Garland of Satire, Wisdom, and History: Latin Verse from Twelfth-Century France (Carmina Houghtoniensia), 2007; (trans.) Letters of Peter Abelard: Beyond the Personal, 2008; (ed. with M.C.J. Putnam) The Virgilian Tradition: The First Fifteen Hundred Years, 2008; Solomon and Marcolf, 2008. Contributor to books, journals and periodicals. **Ad-**

dress: Department of the Classics, Harvard University, 206 Boylston Hall, Cambridge, MA 02138, U.S.A. **Online address:** jmziolk@fas.harvard.edu

ZIOLKOWSKI, Theodore. American (born United States), b. 1932. **Genres:** Literary Criticism And History. **Career:** Yale University, instructor, 1956-60, assistant professor of German, 1960-62; Columbia University, associate professor, 1962-64; Princeton University, professor of German, 1964-69, Class of 1900 Professor of Modern Languages, 1969-, now Class of 1900 Professor Emeritus of Modern Language, professor of comparative literature, 1975, Department of German, chairperson, 1973-79, dean of graduate school, 1979-92, professor emeritus of Germanic languages and literatures and comparative literature, 1992-; University of Montevallo, Dancy memorial lecturer, 1973; University of Mississippi, Christopher Longest lecturer, 1979; Indiana University, Patten Foundation lecturer, 1980; University of Bristol, Benjamin Meaker visiting professor, 1987; University of Munich, visiting professor, 1992; Korean Ministry of Education, visiting lecturer, 1996; Leuphana University (Lueneburg), visiting professor. Writer. **Publications:** Hermann Broch, 1964; The Novels of Hermann Hesse: A Study in Theme and Structure, 1965; Hermann Hesse, 1966; (trans. with Y. Ziolkowski) H. Meyer, The Poetics of in the European Novel, 1968; Dimensions of the Modern Novel: German Texts and European Contexts, 1969; Fictional Transfigurations of Jesus, 1972; (trans. with Y. Ziolkowski) H. Hesse: A Pictorial Biography, 1975; Disenchanted Images: A Literary Iconology, 1977; Der Schriftsteller Hermann Hesse, 1979; The Classical German Elegy, 1795-1950, 1980; Varieties of Literary Thematics, 1983; German Romanticism and Its Institutions, 1990; Virgil and the Moderns, 1993; The Mirror of Justice: Literary Reflections of Legal Crises, 1997; Das Wunderjahr in Jena: Geist und Gesellschaft 1794/95, 1998; The View From the Tower: Origins of an Antimodernist Image, 1998; The Sin of Knowledge: Ancient Themes And Modern Variations, 2000; Berlin: Aufstieg eine Kulturmetropole um 1810, 2002; Clio the Romantic Muse: Historicizing the Faculties in Germany, 2004; Hesitant Heroes: Private Inhibition, Cultural Crisis, 2004; Ovid and the Moderns, 2005; Vorboten der Moderne: eine Kulturgeschichte der Fruhromantik, 2006; Modes of Faith: Secular Surrogates For Lost Religious Belief, 2007; Minos And The Moderns: Cretan Myth in Twentieth-Century Art and Literature, 2008; Mythologisierte Gegenwart: Deutsches Erleben Eit 1933 in Antikem Gewand, 2008; Scandal on Stage!: European Theater as Moral Trial, 2009; Heidelberger Romantik: Mythos und Symbol, 2009; Die Welt im Gedicht: Rilkes Sonette an Orpheus II.4, 2010; Dresdner Romantik: Politik und Harmonie, 2010; Gilgamesh Among Us: Modern Encounters with the Ancient Epic, 2012. EDITOR: Hermann Hesse, Spaete Prosa, 1966; Hermann Hesse: Stories of Five Decades, 1972; Hermann Hesse: Autobiographical Writings, 1972; Hesse: A Collection of Critical Essays, 1973; H. Hesse, My Belief: Essays of Art and Life, 1974, 2nd ed., 1976; H. Hesse, Tales of Student, 1975; (and intro.) H. Hesse, Pictor's Metamorphoses and Other Fantasies, 1982; (and intro.) Soul of the Age: Selected Letters from Hermann Hesse, 1891-1962, 1991; Friedrich Duerrenmatt: Selected Writings, 2006. Contributor of articles to journals. **Address:** Princeton University, C4J2 Firestone Library, 203 E Pyne Bldg., Princeton, NJ 08544, U.S.A. **Online address:** tjziol@aol.com

ZIRIN, Dave. American (born United States), b. 1975?. **Genres:** Sports/Fitness. **Career:** SLAM Magazine, columnist; The Score, sports commentator; Hard Core Sports Radio, commentator. Writer. **Publications:** What's My Name, Fool? Sports and Resistance in the United States, 2005; My Name is Erica Montoya de la Cruz, 2006; My Name is Erica Montoya de la Cruz, 2007; Welcome to the Terrordome: The Pain, Politics and Promise of Sports, 2007; A People's History of Sports in the United States: 250 Years of Politics, Protest, People, and Play, 2008; Bad Sports: How Owners are Ruining the Games We Love, 2010; (with J.W. Carlos) The John Carlos Story: The Sports Moment that Changed the World, 2011. Contributor to periodicals. **Address:** Washington, DC , U.S.A. **Online address:** editor@edgeofsports.com

ZISKIN, Harriet. American (born United States), b. 1933. **Genres:** Novels, Young Adult Non-fiction, History, Social Sciences. **Career:** Writer. **Publications:** The Blind Eagle: Stories From the Courtroom (nonfiction), 1982; The Adventures of Mona Pinsky (novel), 1995. **Address:** Calyx Books, 216 SW Madison, Ste. 7, PO Box B, Corvallis, OR 97333, U.S.A.

ZITTRAIN, Jonathan. American (born United States), b. 1969?. **Genres:** Information Science/Computers, Technology. **Career:** Harvard University, lecturer, 1997-99, assistant professor, 2000, Jack N. and Lillian R. Berkman assistant professor for entrepreneurial legal studies, 2001-07, Harvard Law School, professor of law, 2008-, Kennedy School of Government, professor

of law, 2008-, School of Engineering and Applied Sciences, professor of computer science, Berkman Center for Internet and Society, co-founder, 2000; Oxford University, professor of internet governance and regulation, 2005; Oxford Internet Institute, principal; New York University, School of Law, visiting professor; Stanford Law School, visiting professor. Writer. **Publications:** (With J.K. Harrison) The Torts Game: Defending Mean Joe Greene, 2004; Jurisdiction, 2005; Technological Complements to Copyright, 2005; The Future of the Internet and How to Stop It, 2008; (ed. with R. Deibert, J.G. Palfrey and R. Rohozinski) Access Denied: The Practice and Policy of Global Internet Filtering, 2008; The Richard S. Salant Lecture on Freedom of the Press with John Zittrain, 2009; (co-ed.) Access Controlled: The Shaping of Power, Rights, and Rule in Cyberspace, 2010. Contributor to journals. **Address:** U.S.A. **Online address:** zittrain@law.harvard.edu

ZIZEK, Slavoj. Slovenian (born Slovenia), b. 1949. **Genres:** Adult Nonfiction. **Career:** University of Ljubljana, Faculty for Social Sciences, Institute for Sociology and Philosophy, assistant researcher, 1971, researcher and professor, 1979-, senior researcher; Université Paris-VIII, Department of Psychoanalysis, visiting professor, 1982-83, 1985-86; Republic of Slovenia, ambassador of science, 1991; State University of New York, Centre for the Study of Psychoanalysis and Art, visiting professor, 1991-92; University of Minnesota, Department of Comparative Literature, visiting professor, 1992; Tulane University, visiting professor, 1993; European Graduate School, professor; University of London, Birkbeck Institute for the Humanities, director; Cardozo Law School, visiting professor, 1994; Columbia University, visiting professor, 1995; Princeton University, visiting professor, 1996; New York University, visiting professor; New School for Social Research, visiting professor, 1997; University of Michigan, visiting professor, 1998; Georgetown University, visiting professor, 1999. Writer. **Publications:** Bolec Oina razlike, 1972; Znak, Oznac Oitelj, Pismo: Prilog Materijalistic Okoj Teoriji Oznac Oiteljske Prakse, 1976; Zgodovina in Nezavedno, 1982; Jezik, Ideologija, Slovenci, 1987; (contrib.) Tout ce quevous avez toujours voulu savoir sur Lacan sans jamais oser le demander aHitchcock, 1988; Plus Sublime des Hystériques: Hegel Passe, 1988; Druga Smrt Josipa Broza-Tita, 1989; The Sublime Object of Ideology, 1989; Ils ne Savent pas ce Qu'ils Font: Le Sinthome Ideologique, 1990; Gestalten der Autoritat: Seminar der Laibacher Lacan-Schule, 1991; Erhabenste aller Hysteriker: Lacans Ruckkehr zu Hegel, 1991; For They Know Not What They Do: Enjoyment as a Political Factor, 1991; Looking Awry: An Introduction to Jacques Lacan through Popular Culture, 1991; Enjoy Your Symptom!: Jacques Lacan in Hollywood and Out, 1992; (co-author) Triumph des Blicks uber das Auge: Psychoanalyse bei Alfred-Hitchcock, 1992; Mehr-Geniessen: Lacan in der Popularkultur, 1993; Tarrying with the Negative: Kant, Hegel, and the Critique of Ideology, 1993; The Metastases of Enjoyment: Six Essays on Woman and Causality, 1994; Verweilen beim Negativen/ zweite, DurchgeseheneAuflage, 1994; The Indivisible Remainder: An Essay on Schelling and Related Matters, 1996; The Abyss of Freedom, 1997; Abyss of Freedom, 1997; (with P. Weibel) Inklusion, Exklusion: Probleme des Postkolonialismus und der globalen Migration, 1997; The Plague of Fantasies, 1998; The Ticklish Subject: An Essay in Political Ontology, 1999; The Zizek Reader, 1999; The Fragile Absolute, Or, Why is the Christian Legacy Worth Fighting For?, 2000; (with J. Butler and E.Laclau) Contingency, Hegemony, Universality: Contemporary Dialogues on the Left, 2000; The Art of the Ridiculous Sublime: On David Lynch's Lost Highway, 2000; Did Somebody Say Totalitarianism?, 2001; The Fright of Real Tears: Krzysztof Kie'slowski Between Theory and Post-Theory, 2001; On Belief, 2001; Welcome to the Desert of the Real!: Five Essays on 11 September and Related Dates, 2002; (with M. Dolar) Opera's Second Death, 2002; The Puppet and the Dwarf: The Perverse Core of Christianity, 2003; (with M.A. Rothenberg and D. Foster) Perversion and the Social Relation, 2003; (with G. Daly) Conversations with Zizek, 2003; Organs Without Bodies: Deleuze and Consequences, 2004; Iraq: The Borrowed Kettle, 2004; (with C. Davis and J. Milbank) Theology and the Political: The New Debate, 2005; Interrogating the Real: Selected Writings, 2005; Kako Biti Nihče, 2005; The Metastases of Enjoyment: Six Essays On Women and Causality, 2005; (with E.L. Santner and K. Reinhard) The Neighbor: Three Inquiries in Political Theology, 2005; The Parallax View, 2006; Škakljivi Subject, 2006; (intro.) On Practice and Contradiction, 2007; (intro.) Virtue and Terror/Maximilien Robespierre, 2007; Enjoy Your Symptom!: Jacques Lacan in Hollywood and Out, 2007; How to Read Lacan, 2007; The Indivisible Remainder: On Schelling and Related Matters, 2007; The Universal Exception, 2007; Ärger mit dem Realen, 2008; Violence: Six Sideways Reflections, 2008; Parallaxe, 2008; In Defense of Lost Causes, 2008; (with B. Gunjevic) Bog Na Mukama: Obrati Apokalipse, 2008; Ärger mit dem Realen=Troubles with the Real, 2008; First as

Tragedy, then as Farce, 2009; (with M. Gabriel) Mythology, Madness and Laughter: Subjectivity in German Idealism, 2009; (with A. Badiou) Philosophy in the Present, 2009; Monstrosity of Christ: Paradox or Dialectic?, 2009; Living in the end Times, 2010; A travers le réel, 2010; (with J. Milbank and C. Davis) Paul's New Moment: Continental Philosophy and the Future of Christian Theology, 2010; Najprej kot tragedija, nato kot farsa, 2010; Less than Nothing, 2012; (with B. Gunjević) God in Pain, 2012. EDITOR: Everything You Always Wanted to Know About Lacan: (But Were Afraid to Ask Hitchcock), 1992; Mapping Ideology, 1994; (with R. Salecl) Gaze and Voice as Love Objects, 1996; Cogito and the Unconscious, 1998; (intro. and afterword) Revolution at the Gates, 2002; (co-ed.) Lacan: The Silent Partners, 2006; Lenin Reloaded: Toward a Politics of Truth, 2007; (with J. Milbank) Monstrosity of Christ: Paradox or Dialectic?, 2009; (with C. Douzinas) Idea of Communism, 2010; Everything You Always Wanted to Know about Lacan: (but were afraid to ask Hitchcock), 2010; What Does a Jew want?: On Binationalism and Other Specters, 2011; (with C. Crockett and C. Davis) Hegel and the Infinite: Religion, Politics and Dialectic, 2011. **Address:** Department of Philosophy, University of Ljubljana, Kongresni trg 12, Ljubljana, 1000, Slovenia. **Online address:** slavoj.zizek@guest.arnes.si

ZMORA, Nurith. American/Israeli (born Israel), b. 1950. **Genres:** Children's Non-fiction, History, Social Work. **Career:** University of Delaware, assistant professor, 1990-93; Hamline University, assistant professor, 1993-97, associate professor, 1997-, professor. Writer. **Publications:** Orphanages Reconsidered: Child Care Institutions in Progressive Era Baltimore, 1994. **Address:** Hamline University, 1536 Hewitt Ave., Saint Paul, MN 55104-1284, U.S.A. **Online address:** nzmora@gw.hamline.edu

ZMUDA, Allison (G.). American (born United States), b. 1971. **Genres:** Education, How-to Books. **Career:** Newtown High School, teacher, 1994-2001; The Competent Classroom, president and education consultant, 1999-; Re: Learning by Design, staff consultant, 2001-; University of Bridgeport, adjunct professor, 2001-02; Association for Supervision and Curriculum Development, Understanding by Design Cadre, faculty, 2001-; Capitol Region Education Council, Institute of Teaching and Learning, senior education specialist, 2002-06; Education Connection, staff education specialist, 2006-09. Writer. **Publications:** (With M. Tomaino) The Competent Classroom: Aligning High School Curriculum, Standards, and Assessment-A Creative Teaching Guide, 2001; (with M. Tomaino and J. Miller) High Stakes High School: A Guide for the Perplexed Parent, 2001; (with R. Kuklis and E. Kline) Transforming Schools: Creating a Culture of Continuous Improvement, 2004; (co-author) Schooling by Design: An ASCD Action Tool, 2007; (with V.H. Harada) Librarians as Learning Specialists: Meeting the Learning Imperative for the 21st Century, 2008; Breaking Free from Myths about Teaching and Learning: Innovation as an Engine for Student Success, 2010. Contributor to books. **Address:** Association for Supervision and Curriculum, Development, 1703 N Beauregard St., Alexandria, VA 22311-1714, U.S.A. **Online address:** zmuda@competentclassroom.com

ZOLBERG, Vera L. American (born United States), b. 1932. **Genres:** Art/Art History, Sociology. **Career:** Edgewood College, instructor in sociology, 1962-63; St. Xavier College, assistant professor of sociology, 1964-67; Roosevelt University, lecturer, 1971; Purdue University-Calumet, associate professor of sociology, 1974-83; New School for Social Research, professor in sociology, 1983-; Ecole des Hautes Etudes en Sciences Sociales, visiting lecturer, 1979-80; Centre National de la Recherche Scientifique, research associate, 1986; Boekman Foundation Chair in Sociology of the Arts, 1992-94; University of Brasilia, Fulbright specialist, 1995; University of Amsterdam, Political and Social Sciences Institute, visiting professor. Writer. **Publications:** Constructing a Sociology of the Arts, 1990; (with J.M. Cherbo) Outsider Art: Contesting Boundaries in Contemporary Culture, 1997; (ed. with D.L. Schwartz) After Bourdieu: Influence, Critique, Elaboration, 2004. Works appear in anthologies. Contributor to books and journals. **Address:** Department of Sociology, New School for Social Reseaarch, 6 E 16th St., New York, NY 10003, U.S.A. **Online address:** zolbergv@newschool.edu

ZOLO, Danilo. Italian/Croatian (born Croatia), b. 1936. **Genres:** Politics/Government. **Career:** University of Florence, research assistant, 1965-71, associate professor, 1983-86, professor of philosophy of law, now retired; University of Sassari, associate professor, 1971-80; Boston University, associate researcher, 1981-82; University of Siena, professor of political philosophy, 1986-; University of Cambridge, visiting fellow, 1986-87; Princeton University, visiting fellow, 1993; Oxford University, Nuffield College, Centre for European Studies, Jemolo fellow, 1993. **Publications:** Il personalismo rosminiano. Studio sul pensiero politico di Antonio Rosmini, 1968; La teoria comunista della estinzione dello Stato, 1974; Stato socialista e liberta borghesi, 1976; Marxisti e lo Stato: dai classici ai contemporanei, 1977; Democrazia autoritaria e capitalismo maturo, 1978; Scienza e politica in Otto Neurath, 1986; Complessità e democrazia, 1987; La democrazia difficile, 1989; Il principato democratico, 1992; Cittadinanza: appartenenza, identità, diritti, 1994; Cosmopolis: la prospettiva del governo mondiale, 1995; Signori della pace: una critica del globalismo giuridico, 1998; Chi dice umanità: guerra, diritto e ordine globale, 2000; Stato di diritto: storia, teoria, critica, 2002; (contrib.) Guide: Cinque lezioni su Impero e dintorni, 2003; Globalizzazione: una mappa dei problemi, 2004; Señores de la paz: una crítica del globalismo jurídico, 2005; Mediterraneo: un dialogo fra le due sponde, 2005; Giustizia dei vincitori: da Norimberga a Baghdad, 2006; (ed. with F. Cassano) Alternativa mediterranea, 2007; (ed. with P. Costa) Rule of Law: History, Theory and Criticism, 2007; Da cittadini a sudditi: la cittadinanza politica vanificata, 2007; L'alito della libertà: su Bobbio, 2008; Terrorismo umanitario: dalla Guerra del Golfo alla strage di Gaza, 2009; Tramonto globale: La fame, il patibolo, la guerra, 2010; Un governo mondiale? Etica, diritto e potenza nelle relazioni internazionali, forthcoming; A Just World Government?, forthcoming. Contributor to journals. Works appears in anthologies. **Address:** Dipartimento di Filosofia e Scienze Sociali, Universita di Siena, Via Roma, 47, Siena, 53100, Italy. **Online address:** zolo@tsd.unifi.it

ZOLOTOW, Charlotte. Also writes as Charlotte Bookman, Sara Abbot. American (born United States), b. 1915. **Genres:** Children's Fiction, Poetry, Human Relations/Parenting, Humor/Satire, Literary Criticism And History, Young Adult Fiction. **Career:** Harper and Row Publishing, senior editor, 1938-44, 1962-76, Harper Junior Books Division, vice president, associate publisher, 1976-81, Charlotte Zolotow Books Division, consultant, editorial director, 1981-89, editorial advisor, publisher emeritus, 1991-. **Publications:** The Park Book, 1944; But Not Billy, 1947; The Storm Book, 1952; The Magic Word, 1952; (as Charlotte Bookman) The City Boy and the Country Horse, 1952; Indian, Indian, 1952; The Quiet Mother and the Noisy Little Boy, 1953; One Step, Two..., 1955, rev. ed., 1981; Over and Over, 1957; Not a Little Monkey, 1957, rev. ed., 1989; The Night When Mother Was Away, 1958 as The Summer Night, 1974, rev. ed., 1991; Do You Know What I'll Do?, 1958, rev. ed., 2000; The Sleepy Book, 1958, rev. ed., 2001; The Bunny Who Found Easter, 1959; The Little Black Puppy, 1960; Aren't You Glad?, 1960; In My Garden, 1960; Big Brother, 1960; The Man with the Purple Eyes, 1961; The Three Funny Friends, 1961; Mr. Rabbit and the Lovely Present, 1962; When the Wind Stops, 1962, rev. ed., 1995; The Sky Was Blue, 1963; The Quarreling Book, 1963; The White Marble, 1963; A Tiger Called Thomas, 1963, 2nd ed., 1988; I Have a Horse of My Own, 1964; The Poodle Who Barked at the Wind, 1964, 3rd ed., 2003; A Rose, a Bridge and a Wild Black Horse, 1964; Flocks of Birds, 1965; Someday, 1965; When I Have a Little Girl, 1965; If It Weren't for You, 1966, 2nd ed., 2006; Big Sister and Little Sister, 1966; I Want to Be Little, 1966, rev. ed. as I Like to Be Little, 1987; Summer Is ..., 1967; When I Have a Son: A Story, 1967; All That Sunlight, 1967; My Friend John, 1968, 2nd ed., 2000; The New Friend, 1968; Some Things Go Together, 1969, rev. ed., 1999; A Week in Yani's World: Greece, 1969; The Hating Book, 1969; (as Sara Abbot) Where I Begin, 1970, rev. ed. as This Quiet Lady, 1992; River Winding: Poems, 1970; A Week in Lateef's World: India, 1970; You and Me, 1971, as Here We Are, 1971; A Father Like That, 1971, rev. ed., 2000; Wake Up and Goodnight, 1971; William's Doll, 1972; Hold My Hand, 1972; (as Sarah Abbott) The Old Dog, 1972, 2nd ed., 1995; The Beautiful Christmas Tree, 1972; Janey, 1973; (ed.) An Overpraised Season: Ten Stories of Youth, 1973; My Grandson Lew, 1974; The Unfriendly Book, 1975; It's Not Fair, 1976; May I Visit?, 1976; Someone New, 1978; If You Listen, 1980; Say It!, 1980; The Song, 1982; I Know a Lady, 1984; Timothy Too!, 1986; (ed.) Early Sorrow: Ten Stories of Youth, 1986; Everything Glistens and Everything Sings: New and Selected Poems, 1987; I Like to Be Little, 1987; Something Is Going to Happen, 1988; The Seashore Book, 1992; Snippets, 1992; Snippets: A Gathering of Poems, Pictures and Possibilities, 1993; The Moon Was The Best, 1993; Peter and the Pigeons, 1993; Who Is Ben?, 1997; Seasons: A Book of Poems, 2002; The Poodle Who Barked at the Wind, 2002; Hold My Hand: Five Stories: Love and Family, 2003. Contributor to periodicals. **Address:** c/o Edite Kroll, Kroll Literary Agency, 20 Cross St., Saco, ME 04072, U.S.A. **Online address:** charlottesdaughter@charlottezolotow.com

ZONDERMAN, Jon. American (born United States), b. 1957. **Genres:** Medicine/Health, Adult Non-fiction, Children's Non-fiction, Business/Trade/Industry, Biography, Natural History, Sciences, Biology, Sports/Fitness,

Children's Fiction. **Career:** Writer, 1981-; Temple Emanuel, vice president, 1993-95, president, 1995-; Trinity Class of 1979, president, 1994-; Union of American Hebrew Congregations, Northeast Council director, 1996. **Publications:** Personal Computer Investment Handbook, 1984; (with L. Shader) Drugs and Disease, 1987; (with L. Shader) Mononucleosis and Other Infectious Diseases, 1989; (with L. Shader) Environmental Diseases, 1993; (with L. Shader) Nutritional Diseases, 1993; A Colonial Printer, 1994; A Whaling Captain, 1994; Helen Keller and Annie Sullivan: Working Miracles Together, 1994; (with R. Vender) Understanding Crohn Disease and Ulcerative Colitis, 2000; (with R. Alterowitz) Financing Your New or Growing Business: How to Find and Raise Capital for Your Venture, 2002; (with L. Shader) Legionnaires' Disease, 2006; (with L. Shader) Birth Control Pills, 2006; (co-author) Financing Your Business Made Easy, 2007. ADULT NON-FICTION: (with R. Alterowitz) New Corporate Ventures: How to Make Them Work, 1988; Beyond the Crime Lab: The New Science of Investigation, 1990, rev. ed., 1999. **Address:** 535 Howellton Rd., Orange, CT 06477, U.S.A.

ZOOK, Chris. American/Dutch (born Netherlands), b. 1951?. **Genres:** Economics, Business/Trade/Industry, Administration/Management. **Career:** Bain and Co., partner, director and head of the worldwide strategy practice, 1985-. Writer. **Publications:** (With J. Allen) Profit from the Core: Growth Strategy in an Era of Turbulence, 2001; Beyond the Core: Expand Your Market without Abandoning Your Roots, 2004; Unstoppable: Finding Hidden Assets to Renew the Core and Fuel Profitable Growth, 2007; (with J. Allen) Profit From the Core: A Return to Growth in Turbulent Times, 2010. **Address:** Bain & Company Inc., 131 Dartmouth St., Boston, MA 02116, U.S.A.

ZOOK, Kristal Brent. American (born United States) **Genres:** Social Sciences, Art/Art History, Literary Criticism And History. **Career:** University of California, reader in advanced composition, academic advisor, 1986, tutor in Spanish literature and composition, 1988-89, teacher's assistant, 1989, 1991, instructor, 1990, visiting assistant professor, 1995-96; Murdoch University, visiting lecturer, 1996; Columbia University, adjunct professor, 2002-07; Center for an Urban Future, editor-in-chief, 2002; Essence Magazine, contributing writer, 2002-; Connect Magazine, editor-in-chief, 2005-; Hofstra University, Department of Journalism, Public Relations, and Mass Media, associate professor of journalism, 2007-. Journalist. **Publications:** Color by Fox: The Fox Network and the Revolution in Black Television, 1999; Black Women's Lives: Stories of Power and Pain, 2006; I See Black People: The Rise and Fall of African American-Owned Television and Radio, 2008. **Address:** Department of Journalism, Public Relations, and, Mass Media, Hofstra University, 409 New Academic Bldg., 322C Dempster Hall, Hempstead, NY 11549-1000, U.S.A. **Online address:** kristal.zook@hofstra.edu

ZOOK, Matthew A. American (born United States) **Genres:** Geography, Information Science/Computers, Industrial Relations, Sciences, Sociology. **Career:** University of California, Department of City and Regional Planning, graduate student instructor, 1997-98, Public Policy Institute of California, visiting research fellow, 2001-02; University of Kentucky, Department of geography, assistant professor, 2002-07, associate professor, 2007-. Writer and geographer. **Publications:** The Geography of the Internet Industry: Venture Capital, Dot-Coms and Local Knowledge, 2005. Contributor to periodicals. **Address:** Department of Geography, University of Kentucky, 1457 Patterson Office Twr., Lexington, KY 40506-0027, U.S.A. **Online address:** zook@uky.edu

ZORACH, Rebecca. American (born United States), b. 1969. **Genres:** Art/Art History, Theology/Religion. **Career:** University of Chicago, preceptor, master of arts program in the humanities and lecturer in art history, 1999-2000, Harper-Schmidt Fellow and Collegiate assistant professor, 2001-03, director of undergraduate studies, 2005-06, assistant professor, 2003-07, associate professor of art history, 2007-; Yale University, Department of History of Art, visiting lecturer, 2002. Writer, art historian, curator and educator. **Publications:** (ed. with A. Bingaman and L. Sanders) Embodied Utopias: Gender, Social Change, and the Modern Metropolis, 2002; Blood, Milk, Ink, Gold: Abundance and Excess in the French Renaissance, 2005; (with E. Rodini) Paper Museums: The Reproductive Print in Europe, 1500-1800, 2005; (ed. with M.W. Cole) The Idol in the Age of Art: Objects, Devotions and the Early Modern World, 2009. Contributor to books, periodicals and journals. **Address:** Department of Art History, University of Chicago, Cochrane-Woods Art Ctr., 5540 S Greenwood Ave., Chicago, IL 60637-1506, U.S.A. **Online address:** rezorach@uchicago.edu

ZORNBERG, Avivah Gottlieb. British (born England), b. 1944. **Genres:** Novels, Theology/Religion. **Career:** Hebrew University, teacher of English literature, 1969-76; London School of Jewish Studies, visiting lecturer; Jerusalem College for Adults, teacher. Writer. **Publications:** Genesis: The Beginning of Desire, 1995; The Beginning of Desire: Reflections on Genesis, 1996; The Particulars of Rapture: Reflections on Exodus, 2001; Murmuring Deep: Reflections on the Biblical Unconscious, 2009. **Address:** c/o Author Mail, Doubleday, 1745 Broadway, New York, NY 10019, U.S.A.

ZOSS, Joel. (Alex Chadwick). American (born United States), b. 1944. **Genres:** Sports/Fitness, Novels, Adult Non-fiction, Music, Mythology/Folklore. **Career:** Video-Vision, audio producer, 1977-78; teacher of creative writing, 1985-87. Writer and musician. **Publications:** Chronicle (novel), 1980; (with J.S. Bowman) The National League, 1986; (with J.S. Bowman) The American League, 1986; (with J.S. Bowman) The Pictorial History of Baseball, 1986, rev. ed., 2002; Texas, 1986; Greatest Moments in Baseball, 1987; (as Alex Chadwick) The Illustrated History of Baseball, 1988; (with J.S. Bowman) Diamonds in the Rough: The Untold History of Baseball, 1989, 3rd ed., 2004; (with J.S. Bowman) The History of Major League Baseball, 1992. Contributor of articles to books and periodicals. **Address:** 138 S Part Rd., Conway, MA 01341, U.S.A. **Online address:** joelzoss@joelzoss.com

ZUBOK, Vladislav. American/Russian (born Russia), b. 1958?. **Genres:** Politics/Government, Social Commentary, Adult Non-fiction, History. **Career:** Carnegie Corp., Advanced Training Program for Russia, director, 2007-10; Temple University, Department of History, associate professor, professor, 2009-; George Washington University, National Security Archive, research fellow and summer projects organizer; Dmitry S. Likhachev Foundation, adviser and consultant. Writer. **Publications:** (With Y. Abramov) Political Parties and Executive Elites in the United States, 1990; (with V. Tsvetov and V. Levin) A Forest and the Trees: Outlines of Three National Ways of Life, 1991; (with C. Pleshakov) Inside the Kremlin's Cold War: From Stalin to Khruschev, 1996; (with E. Shiraev) Anti-Americanism: From Stalin to Putin, 2000; Gorbachev's Nuclear Learning, 2000; A Failed Empire: The Soviet Union in the Cold War from Stalin to Gorbachev, 2007; Zhivago's Children: The Last Russian Intelligentsia, 2009; (ed. with S. Savranskaya and T. Blanton) Masterpieces of History: The Peaceful End of the Cold War in Eastern Europe, 1989, 2010. Contributor to periodicals. **Address:** Department of History, Temple University, 922 Gladfelter Hall, 1115 W Berks St., Philadelphia, PA 19122-6089, U.S.A. **Online address:** zubok@temple.edu

ZUCCHI, John E. Canadian (born Canada), b. 1955. **Genres:** History, Music, Young Adult Non-fiction, Translations, Theology/Religion. **Career:** Cambridge University, Darwin College, junior research fellow, 1984-85; McGill University, assistant professor, 1985-88, associate professor of history, 1988-94, chair of the department of history, 1993-96, professor of history, 1994-; S.O.S. Boat People Canada, vice president, 1990-95; McGill-Queen's University Press, editor, 1996-; McGill-Queen's Studies in Ethnic History, general editor, 1996-. **Publications:** The Italian Immigrants of the St. John's Ward, 1875-1915: Patterns of Settlement and Neighbourhood Formation, 1988; Italians in Toronto: Development of A National Identity, 1875-1935, 1988; The Little Slaves of the Harp: Italian Child Street Musicians in Nineteenth-Century Paris, London And New York, 1992; (ed.) McGill-Queen's Studies in Ethnic History, 1996; (trans.) The Religious Sense, 1997; (trans., ed. and intro.) Pellegrino Stagni, The View from Rome: Archbishop Stagni's 1915 Reports on the Ontario Bilingual Schools Question, 2002; (trans.) Luigi Giussani, Cammino al vero è un'esperienza (title means: 'The Journey To Truth is an Experience'), 2006; A History Of Ethnic Enclaves In Canada, 2007; (ed.) Is it Possible to Live This Way? vol. II: Hope: An Unusual Approach to Christian Existence, 2008, vol. III: Charity: An Unusual Approach to Christian Existence, 2009. **Address:** Department of History, McGill University, Rm. 621, Leacock Bldg., 855 Sherbrooke W, Montreal, QC H3A 2T7, Canada. **Online address:** john.zucchi@mcgill.ca

ZUCCHINO, David. American (born United States), b. 1951. **Genres:** Novels, History, Military/Defense/Arms Control. **Career:** News & Observer, reporter, 1973-78; Detroit Free Press, reporter, 1978-80; Philadelphia Inquirer, foreign correspondent, 1980-; Los Angeles Times, foreign correspondent and national correspondent. **Publications:** Myth of the Welfare Queen: A Pulitzer Prize-winning Journalist's Portrait of Women on the Line, 1997; Thunder Run: The Armored Strike to Capture Baghdad, 2004. **Address:** c/o Author Mail, Grove/Atlantic Inc., 841 Broadway, 4th Fl., New York, NY 10003-4704, U.S.A.

ZUCKER, Naomi F(link). American (born United States), b. 1938. **Genres:** Civil Liberties/Human Rights, Politics/Government, Children's Fiction, Adult Non-fiction. **Career:** Houghton Mifflin Co., copy editor, 1961-64; Subscribe Editorial Service, director, 1964-82; University of Rhode Island, special instructor, 1978-85, lecturer in English, 1985-99, professor. Consultant. **Publications:** (With N.L. Zucker) The Guarded Gate: The Reality of American Refugee Policy, 1987; (with N.L. Zucker) Desperate Crossing: Seeking Refuge in America, 1996; Benno's Bear, 2001; Callie's Rules, 2009; Write On, Callie Jones, 2010. Contributor to periodicals. **Address:** c/o George Nicholson, Sterling Lord Literistic Inc., 65 Bleecker St., New York, NY 10012, U.S.A. **Online address:** nlzucker@uri.edu

ZUCKER, Norman Livingston. American (born United States), b. 1933. **Genres:** Politics/Government, History, Social Sciences, Biography. **Career:** Rutgers University, instructor, 1959-60; Northeastern University, instructor, 1960-61, assistant professor, 1961-62; Tufts University, assistant professor, 1962-66; University of Rhode Island, associate professor, 1966-69, professor, 1969-. Writer. **Publications:** George W. Norris: Gentle Knight of American Democracy, 1966; (comp.) The American Party Process: Readings and Comments, 1968; The Coming Crisis in Israel: Private Faith and Public Policy, 1973; The Voluntary Agencies and Refugee Resettlement in the United States, 1981; (with N.F. Zucker) The Guarded Gate: The Reality of American Refugee Policy, 1987; (with N.F. Zucker) Desperate Crossings: Seeking Refuge in America, 1996. **Address:** Department of Political Science, University of Rhode Island, Washburn Hall 80, Upper College Rd., Ste. 4, Kingston, RI 02881-0817, U.S.A. **Online address:** nlzucker@uri.edu

ZUCKERMAN, Harriet. American (born United States), b. 1937. **Genres:** Sciences, Biography, Sociology. **Career:** Barnard College, lecturer in sociology, 1964-65; Columbia University, assistant professor and project director of bureau of applied social research, 1965-72, associate professor, 1972-78, professor of sociology and chair of sociology department, 1978-92, College of Physicians and Surgeons, dean's distinguished lecturer, 1982, now professor emeritus; Annual Reviews Inc., board director, 1974-; Sigma Xi, national lecturer, 1975-76; Rockefeller University, adjunct faculty, 1979-; SIAM Institute for Mathematics and Society, board director, 1980-87; Harvard Medical School, Kass lecturer, 1984; ISI Press, board director, 1985-; University of Notre Dame, Exxon Series lecturer, 1986; Virginia Polytechnic Institute and State University, Nicholas C. Mullins lecturer, 1989; The Andrew W. Mellon Foundation, senior adviser, 1989-, vice-president, 1991-, senior vice president; American Savings Bank, board director; American Institute of Physics, consultant. Writer. **Publications:** Scientific Elite: Nobel Laureates in the United States, 1977, rev. ed., 1996; (co-ed.) Toward a Metric of Science: The Advent of Science Indicators, 1978; (ed. with R.B. Miller and contrib.) Science Indicators: Implications for Research and Policy, 1980; (ed. with J.R. Cole and J.T. Bruer) The Outer Circle: Women in the Scientific Community, 1991. Contributor of articles to periodicals. Works appear in anthologies. **Address:** The Andrew W. Mellon Foundation, 140 E 62nd St., New York, NY 10065, U.S.A.

ZUCKERMAN, Marvin. American (born United States), b. 1928. **Genres:** Psychology, Sports/Fitness. **Career:** Wayne County General Hospital, psychology intern, 1951-52; Norwich State Hospital, clinical psychologist, 1953-54; Larue D. Carter Memorial Hospital, clinical psychologist, 1954-56; Indiana University Medical Center, Institute of Psychiatric Research, assistant professor of psychology and research associate, 1956-60; City University of New York, Brooklyn College, assistant professor of psychology, 1960-62; Adelphi University, associate professor of psychology, 1962-63; Albert Einstein Medical Center, Northern Division, Department of Endocrinology and Human Reproduction, research associate in psychology, 1963-69; University of Delaware, associate professor, 1969-71, professor of psychology, 1971-2002, director of training program in clinical psychology, 1976-83, Institute for Advanced Study, Netherlands fellow, 1987-88, distinguished lecturer, 1993, professor emeritus, 2002-; Crittenton Drug Rehabilitation Center, consultant. Writer. **Publications:** (Co-author) Stress and Hallucinatory Effects of Perceptual Isolation and Confinement, 1962; (with B. Lubin) Test Manual for the Multiple Affect Adjective Check List, 1965; (ed. with C.D. Spielberger) Emotions and Anxiety: New Concepts, Methods and Applications, 1976; Sensation Seeking: Beyond the Optimal Level of Arousal, 1979; (ed.) The Biological Bases of Sensation Seeking, Impulsivity and Anxiety, 1983; (with B. Lubin) Manual for the MAACL-R: The Multiple Affect Adjective Check List, 1985; The Psychobiology of Personality, 1991, 2nd ed., 2005; Behavioral Manifestations and Biosocial Bases of Sensation Seeking, 1994; Behavioral

Expressions and Biosocial Bases of Sensation Seeking, 1994; Vulnerability to Psychopathology: A Biosocial Model, 1999; On the Psychobiology of Personality: Essays in Honor of Marvin Zuckerman, 2004; Sensation Seeking and Risky Behavior, 2007; Personality Science: Three Approaches and Their Applications to the Causes and Treatment of Depression, 2011. Contributor of articles to journals. **Address:** Department of Psychology, University of Delaware, 108 Wolf Hall, Newark, DE 19716, U.S.A. **Online address:** zuckerma@udel.edu

ZUCKERMAN, Mary Ellen. American (born United States), b. 1954. **Genres:** Marketing, History, Bibliography. **Career:** State University of New York College-Geneseo, School of Business, assistant professor, 1985-90, associate professor, 1990-99, professor of marketing, 1999-, dean, 1999-2008, distinguished service professor, 2009; Gannett Center for Media Studies, Freedom Forum Media Studies Center, research fellow, 1989-90; McGill University, Faculty of Management, visiting associate professor, 1990-91; Ithaca College, School of Business, dean, 2010-. Writer. **Publications:** (With J. Tebbel) The Magazine in America, 1741-1990, 1991; (comp.) Sources on the History of Women's Magazines, 1792-1960: An Annotated Bibliography, 1991; A History of Popular Women's Magazines in the United States, 1792-1995, 1998. Contributor to journals. **Address:** School of Business, Ithaca College, 308 Park Ctr., Ithaca, NY 14850, U.S.A. **Online address:** mzuckerman@ithaca.edu

ZUCKERMAN, Michael. American (born United States), b. 1939. **Genres:** History, Politics/Government. **Career:** Harvard University, teaching fellow in general education, 1963-64; University of Pennsylvania, instructor, 1965-67, assistant professor, 1967-70, associate professor, 1970-84, professor of history, 1984-; University of Oregon, visiting assistant professor of history, 1970; Johns Hopkins University, visiting associate professor of history, 1970; Hebrew University of Jerusalem, visiting professor of American studies, 1977-78; University of Richmond, visiting professor of history, 1981; University College, (Ireland), Mary Ball Washington Chair in American history, 2011. Writer. **Publications:** Peaceable Kingdoms: New England Towns in the Eighteenth Century, 1970; (ed.) Friends and Neighbors: Group Life in America's First Plural Society, 1982; Almost Chosen People: Oblique Biographies in the American Grain, 1993; (ed. with W. Koops) Beyond the Century of the Child: Cultural History and Developmental Psychology, 2003. **Address:** Department of History, University of Pennsylvania, Philadelphia, PA 19104, U.S.A. **Online address:** mzuckerm@history.upenn.edu

ZUCKERMANN, Wolfgang (Joachim). French/American/German (born Germany), b. 1922. **Genres:** Music, Environmental Sciences/Ecology, Children's Fiction, Young Adult Fiction. **Career:** Harpsichord Manufacturing Co., president, 1957-69; freelance writer, 1970-85; Shakespeare Bookstore, co-owner; Ecoplan, senior associate, writer and editor, 1987-97; Ducornet & Associates Intl., staff, now retired. **Publications:** The Modern Harpsichord: Twentieth Century Instruments and Their Makers, 1969; (with B. Rosen) The Mews of London: A Guide to the Hidden Byways of London's Past, 1982; End of the Road: The World Car Crisis and How We Can Solve It, 1991; Family Mouse behind the Wheel (juvenile), 1992; Alice in Underland, 2000. **Address:** 15-17 rue Cels, Paris, 75014, France.

ZUCKERT, Catherine H. American (born United States), b. 1942. **Genres:** Philosophy, Politics/Government. **Career:** Carleton College, instructor, 1971-, assistant professor, associate professor, department chair, 1985-88, professor of political science, through 1998; University of Notre Dame, professor of political science, 1998-, Nancy Reeves Dreux professor of political science, The Review of Politics, editor-in-chief, graduate placement director. Writer. **Publications:** (Ed.) Understanding the Political Spirit, 1988; Natural Right and the American Imagination: Political Philosophy in Novel Form, 1990; Postmodern Platos, 1996; (with M.P. Zuckert) The Truth about Leo Strauss: Political Philosophy and American Democracy, 2006; Plato's Philosophers, 2009; (ed.) Political Philosophy in the Twentieth Century: Authors and Arguments, 2011; Machiavellian Politics, forthcoming. **Address:** Department of Political Science, University of Notre Dame, 217 O'Shaughnessy Hall, Notre Dame, IN 46556, U.S.A. **Online address:** czuckert@nd.edu

ZUEHLKE, Mark. Canadian (born Canada), b. 1955. **Genres:** Mystery/Crime/Suspense, History, Military/Defense/Arms Control, Illustrations. **Career:** Journalist. Full-time writer, 1981-. **Publications:** SELF-ILLUSTRATED: Fun B.C. Facts for Kids, 1996. REGIONAL FACT BOOKS: The Vancouver Island South Explorer: The Outdoor Guide, 1994; The B.C. Fact

Book: Everything You Ever Wanted to Know about British Columbia, 1995; The Alberta Fact Book: Everything You Ever Wanted to Know about Alberta, 1997; The Yukon Fact Book: Everything You Ever Wanted to Know about the Yukon, 1998. ELIAS McCANN MYSTERY NOVELS: Hands Like Clouds, 2000; Carry Tiger to Mountain, 2002; Sweep Lotus, 2004. MILITARY HISTORY SERIES: Scoundrels, Dreamers & Second Sons: British Remittance Men in the Canadian West, 1994, 2nd ed., 2001; The Gallant Cause: Canadians in the Spanish Civil War, 1936-1939, 1996; Ortona: Canada's Epic World War II Battle, 1999; The Canadian Military Atlas: The Nation's Battlefields from the French and Indian Wars to Kosovo, 2001; The Liri Valley: Canada's World War II Breakthrough to Rome, 2001; The Gothic Line: Canada's Month of Hell in World War II Italy, 2003; Juno Beach: Canada's D-Day Victory, June 6, 1944, 2005; Holding Juno: Canada's Heroic Defence of the D-Day Beaches, June 7-12, 1944, 2005; For Honour's Sake: The War of 1812 and the Brokering of an Uneasy Peace, 2006; Terrible Victory: First Canadian Army and the Scheldt Estuary Campaign, 2007; Operation Husky: The Canadian Invasion of Sicily, July 10-August 7, 1943, 2007; Brave Battalion: The Remarkable Saga of the 16th Battalion (Canadian Scottish) in the First World War, 2008. OTHERS: (with L. Donnelly) Magazine Writing from the Boonies, 1992. **Address:** Carolyn Swayze Literary Agency, PO Box 39588, White Rock, BC V4A 9P3, Canada. **Online address:** mark@zuehlke.ca

ZUG, George R. American (born United States), b. 1938. **Genres:** Zoology, Natural History. **Career:** Smithsonian Institution, National Museum of Natural History, curator and curator-in-charge of vertebrate division, 1975-, now curator emeritus. Writer and herpetologist. **Publications:** The Penial Morphology and the Relationships of Cryptodiran Turtles, 1966; Geographic Variation in Rhineura floridana, 1968; Buoyancy, Locomotion, Morphology of the Pelvic Girdle and Hindlimb, and Systematics of Cryptodiran Turtles, 1971; The Distribution and Patterns of the Major Arteries of the Iguanids and Comments on the Intergeneric Relationships of Iguanids, 1971; (with C.J. Goin and O.B. Goin) Introduction to Herpetology, 3rd ed., 1978; Anuran Locomotion-Structure and Function, 1978; (with P.B. Zug) The Marine Toad, Bufo Marinus: A Natural History Resumé of Native Populations, 1979; (with S.B. Hedges and S. Sunkel) Variation in the Reproductive Parameters of Three Neotropical Snakes, Coniophanes fissidens, Dipsas catesbyi, and Imantodes cenchoa, 1979; (with A.H. Wynn and C. Ruckdeschel) Age Determination of Loggerhead Sea Turtles, Caretta Caretta, by Incremental Growth Marks in the Skeleton, 1986; Lizards of Fiji: Natural History and Systematics, 1991; Herpetology: An Introductory Biology of Amphibians and Reptiles, 1993, (with L.J. Vitt and J.P. Caldwell) 2nd ed., 2001; (with C.H. Ernst) Snakes in Question: The Smithsonian Answer Book, 1996; Sea Turtles of the Georgia Coast, 2000; Systematics of the Carlia Fusca Lizards, 2004; (with C.H. Ernst) Snakes: Smithsonian Answer Book, 2004; Speciation and Dispersal in a Low Diversity Taxon, 2010. Contributor to books. **Address:** National Museum of Natural History, Smithsonian Institution, MRC 162, 10th and Constitution Ave. NW, PO Box 37012, Washington, DC 20560-0162, U.S.A. **Online address:** zug.george@nmnh.si.edu

ZUIDERVAART, Lambert. American (born United States), b. 1950. **Genres:** Humanities, Philosophy, Young Adult Non-fiction, E-books. **Career:** KDCR-FM Radio, programmer and announcer, 1970-72; University of Toronto, director of music and liturgy for campus ministry, 1974-77, Graduate Faculty, associate faculty, 2003-, faculty associate, 2008-; King's University College, assistant professor of philosophy, 1981-85, Division of Humanities, chair, 1982-85; Roads Housing Cooperative Ltd., president of board of directors, 1982-85; Calvin College, associate professor, 1985-89, professor of philosophy, 1985-2002, chair, 1991-97, Calvin Center for Christian Scholarship, fellow, 1988-89, 1994-96, Faculty Senate, vice chairman, 1999-2002; Institute for Christian Studies, adjunct faculty, 1987-2002, visiting professor, 1991, chancellor and chair of senate, 1998-2001, professor of philosophy, 2002-, academic dean, 2003-04, Herman Dooyeweerd chair in social and political philosophy, 2006-, chair of faculty, 2007-09; Urban Institute for Contemporary Arts, board director, 1993-, president, 1994-98; German Academic Exchange Service, researcher, 1994, 2001; Toronto School of Theology, Advanced Degree Faculty, continuing faculty, 2003-. Writer. **Publications:** Kant's Critique of Beauty and Taste: Explorations into a Philosophical Aesthetics, 1977; Adorno's Aesthetic Theory: The Redemption of Illusion, 1991; (co-author) Dancing in the Dark: Youth, Popular Culture, and the Electronic Media, 1991; Artistic Truth: Aesthetics, Discourse, and Imaginative Disclosure, 2004; Social Philosophy after Adorno, 2007; (with C. Lafont and D.M. Rasmussen) Phenomenology and Critical Theory: The Twenty-fifth Annual Symposium of the Simon Silverman Phenomenology Center, 2008; Art in

Public: Politics, Economics, and A Democratic Culture, 2011. EDITOR/CO-EDITOR: (with H. Luttikhuizen) Pledges of Jubilee: Essays on the Arts and Culture, 1995; (with T. Huhn) The Semblance of Subjectivity, 1997; (with H. Luttikhuizen) The Arts, Community and Cultural Democracy, 2000. Works appear in anthologies. Contributor of articles and reviews to books and journals. **Address:** Institute for Christian Studies, 229 College St., Toronto, ON M5T 1R4, Canada. **Online address:** lambertz@icscanada.edu

ZUK, Marlene. American (born United States), b. 1956?. **Genres:** Sciences, Sex, Medicine/Health, Women's Studies And Issues, Zoology, Environmental Sciences/Ecology. **Career:** University of California, professor of biology, associate vice provost for faculty equity and diversity and principal investigator. Writer. **Publications:** (Ed. with J.E. Loye) Bird-Parasite Interactions: Ecology, Evolution, and Behaviour, 1991; Sexual Selections: What We Can and Can't Learn about Sex from Animals, 2002; Riddled with Life: Friendly Worms, Ladybug Sex, and the Parasites That Make Us Who We Are, 2007; Sex on Six Legs: Lessons on Life, Love, and Language from the Insect World, 2011. **Address:** Department of Biology, University of California, 3344 Spieth Hall, Riverside, CA 92521, U.S.A. **Online address:** marlene.zuk@ucr.edu

ZUKAV, Gary. American (born United States) **Genres:** Philosophy, Essays, Psychology, Human Relations/Parenting, Adult Non-fiction, Intellectual History, Physics, Self Help, Self Help. **Career:** Writer. **Publications:** The Dancing Wu Li Masters: An Overview of the New Physics, 1979; The Seat of the Soul, 1989; Thoughts from the Seat of the Soul: Meditations for Souls in Process, 1994; Soul Stories, 2000; (with L. Francis) The Heart of the Soul: Emotional Awareness, 2002; (with L. Francis) The Mind of the Soul: Responsible Choice, 2003; Soul to Soul: Communications from the Heart, 2007; Soul to Soul Meditations: Daily Reflections for Spiritual Growth, 2008; Spiritual Partnership: The Journey to Authentic Power, 2010. **Address:** The Seat of the Soul Institute, PO Box 3310, Ashland, OR 97520, U.S.A. **Online address:** info@seatofthesoul.com

ZUKIN, Sharon. American (born United States) **Genres:** Sociology, Urban Studies. **Career:** City University of New York, Department of Sociology, staff, Brooklyn College, Broeklundian professor of sociology, 1996-2008, professor of sociology. Writer. **Publications:** Beyond Marx and Tito: Theory and Practice in Yugoslav Socialism, 1975; Loft Living: Culture and Capital in Urban Change, 1982; (ed.) Industrial Policy: Business and Politics in the United States and France, 1985; (ed. with P. DiMaggio) Structures of Capital: The Social Organization of the Economy, 1990; Landscapes of Power: From Detroit to Disney World, 1991; The Cultures of Cities, 1995; (ed. with M. Sorkin) After the World Trade Center: Rethinking New York City, 2002; Point of Purchase: How Shopping Changed American Culture, 2004; Naked City: The Death and Life of Authentic Urban Places, 2010. Contributor to books and publications. **Address:** Department of Sociology, City University of New York, Brooklyn College, 3606 James Hall, 2900 Bedford Ave., Brooklyn, NY 11210-2813, U.S.A. **Online address:** zukin@brooklyn.cuny.edu

ZULAIKA, Joseba. American/Spanish (born Spain), b. 1948. **Genres:** Anthropology/Ethnology, Military/Defense/Arms Control. **Career:** University of Nevada, Center for Basque Studies, Basque Studies Program, adjunct professor of Basque studies, 1982-83, assistant professor, 1990-94, associate professor, 1994-2000, director, 2000-05, professor of Basque studies, 2001-; University of the Basque Country, associate professor, 1983-87. Writer. **Publications:** Adanen poema amaigabea (poems), 1975; Terranova: The Ethos and Luck of Deep-Sea Fishermen, 1981; Zu zara, 1982; Bertsolariaren Jokoa eta Jolasa, 1985; Tratado estético-ritual vasco, 1987; Basque Violence: Metaphor and Sacrament, 1988; Chivos y soldados: La mili como ritual de iniciacion, 1989; Ehiztariaren erotika, 1990; Caza, símbolo y eros, 1992; (with W.A. Douglass and S.M. Lyman) Migración, etnicidad y etnonacionalismo, 1995; (with W.A. Douglass) Terror and Taboo: The Follies, Fables, and Faces of Terrorism, 1996; Del Cromanon al Carnaval: Los vascos como museo antropologico, 1996; Crónica de una seducción: El Museo Guggenheim Bilbao, 1997; Enemigos, no hay enemigo, 1999; (ed.) Oteiza's Selected Writings, 2003; Guggenheim Bilbao Museoa: Museums, Architecture, and City Renewal, 2003; (ed. with A.M. Guasch) Learning from the Bilbao Guggenheim, 2005; (ed.) States of Terror: Begoña Aretxaga's Essays, 2005; (ed. with S.G. Armistead) Voicing the Moment: Improvised Oral Poetry and Basque Tradition, 2005; (with W. Douglass) Basque Culture: Anthropological Perspectives, 2007; Polvo de ETA, 2007; Terrorism: The Self-fulfilling Prophecy,

2009; Contraterrorismo USA, 2009. Works appear in anthologies. Contributor to journals. **Address:** Center for Basque Studies, University of Nevada, 1664 N Virginia St., Ste. 2322, Reno, NV 89557-0002, U.S.A. **Online address:** zulaika@unr.edu

ZULAWSKI, Ann. American (born United States), b. 1947. **Genres:** Politics/Government, History. **Career:** Smith College, Department of History, professor of history and Latin American studies, chair, 2010-11. Writer and historian. **Publications:** They Eat from Their Labor: Work and Social Change in Colonial Bolivia, 1995; Unequal Cures: Public Health and Political Change in Bolivia, 1900-1950, 2007. **Address:** Department of History, Smith College, 10 Prospect St., Ste. 201, Northampton, MA 01063, U.S.A. **Online address:** azulawsk@smith.edu

ZUMAS, Leni. American (born United States), b. 1972?. **Genres:** Novellas/Short Stories, Novels. **Career:** Portland State University, faculty; Juniper Summer Writing Institute, associate director; Columbia University, faculty; Hunter College, faculty; The New School, faculty; University of Massachusetts, faculty; Lower Manhattan Cultural Council, Workspace Program, artist-in-residence, 2008-09. Writer. **Publications:** Farewell Navigator: Stories, 2008; The Listeners, 2012. Contributor to journals. **Address:** Portland, OR , U.S.A. **Online address:** leni@lenizumas.com

ZUMOFF, Barnett. American (born United States), b. 1926. **Genres:** Translations. **Career:** Yeshiva University, Albert Einstein College of Medicine, professor of medicine, 1977-; Beth Israel Medical Center, attending physician and chief of endocrinology and metabolism, 1981-, emeritus chief; Mount Sinai School of Medicine, adjunct professor of medicine; NYU College of Medicine, adjunct professor of medicine; Folksbiene-Natilonal Yiddish Theatre, vice-president; Congress for Jewish Culture, president; The Forward Association, vice-president. Writer. **Publications:** TRANSLATOR: Sholem Aleichem, The Jackpot, 1989; I Keep Recalling: The Holocaust Poems of Jacob Glatstein, 1993; Laughter Beneath the Forest, 1995; God Hid His Face, 1996; Chaim Leiberman, In the Valley of Death, 1997; About Mother: Yiddish Poets Speak, 2003; Songs for Generations: More Pearls of Yiddish Song, 2003; Secular Jewishness for Our Time, 2003; Between Smile and Tear, 2004; Tsvi Eisenman, Pages From a Charred Notebook, 2004; Beneath the Trees, 2005; Memories: Autobiography of Abraham Zumoff, 2006; Songs to a Moonstruck Lady: Women in Yiddish Poetry, 2006; Tsvi Eisenman, At the Edge of Dreamland, 2008; Michael Lev, Sobibor: A Documentary Novel of the Sobibor Uprising, 2008; Motl Zelmanowicz, A Bundist Comments on History As It Was Being Made, 2008; Yiddish Literature in America, 1870-2000, vol. I, 2009; Pearls of Yiddish Poetry, 2010; Stones Don't Bear Witness: A Historical Novel of the Kishinev Pogrom, by Boris Sandler, 2011; The Waterfall: Rhymed Yiddish Couplets, 2011; The City in the Moonlight: Stories of the Old-Time Lithuanian Jews, 2011. Contributor of poems to magazines. **Address:** Division of Endocrinology and Metabolism, Beth Israel Medical Center, Rm. 8F03. Fierman Hall, 317 E 17th St., 7th Fl., New York, NY 10003, U.S.A. **Online address:** bzumoff@bethisraelny.org

ZUNSHINE, Lisa. American (born United States), b. 1968?. **Genres:** Literary Criticism And History, Cultural/Ethnic Topics. **Career:** University of Kentucky, Department of English, assistant professor, 2000-06, associate professor, 2006-08, Bush-Holbrook professor of English, 2008-. Writer. **Publications:** Bastards and Foundlings: Illegitimacy in Eighteenth-Century England, 2005; Why We Read Fiction: Theory of Mind and the Novel, 2006; Strange Concepts and the Stories They Make Possible: Cognition, Culture, Narrative, 2008; Getting Inside Your Head: What Cognitive Science can Tell Us about Popular Culture, 2012. EDITOR: Nabokov at the Limits: Redrawing Critical Boundaries, 1999; (co-ed.) Narratives of the Poor in Eighteenth-Century Britain, 2006; (with J. Harris) Approaches to Teaching the Novels of Samuel Richardson, 2006; (with T. Kishi) Acting Theory and the English Stage, 1700-1830, 5 vols., 2008; Introduction to Cognitive Cultural Studies, 2010. Contributor to books and journals. **Address:** Department of English, University of Kentucky, 1253 POT, 1215 Patterson Office Twr., Lexington, KY 40506-0027, U.S.A. **Online address:** lisa.zunshine@gmail.com

ZURBO, Matt. Australian (born Australia), b. 1967?. **Genres:** Young Adult Fiction, Children's Fiction, Science Fiction/Fantasy, Poetry, Novels, Picture/Board Books, Education. **Career:** Writer. **Publications:** Blow Kid, Blow! (picture book), 1996; Writing by Moonlight, 1996; Idiot Pride (young adult), 1997; I Got a Rocket, 1997 (picture book); Hot Nights Cool Dragons (young adult), 2004; Flyboy and The Invisible, 2002; Fred the Croc (picture book),

2008; Lulu's Wish (picture book), 2008; My Dad's A Wrestler (picture book), 2009. **Address:** Penguin Publicity, 80 Strand, London, GL WC2R 0RL, England. **Online address:** matt@mattzurbo.com

ZÜRCHER, Erik-Jan. Dutch (born Netherlands), b. 1953. **Genres:** History, Organized Labor, Politics/Government, Theology/Religion. **Career:** University of Nijmegen, lecturer, 1977-87, senior lecturer, 1987-97; International Institute of Social History, Turkish Department, head, 1989-99, senior research fellow, 1990-, director, 2008-; University of Amsterdam, professor of Ottoman and Turkish history, 1994-97, chair of Turkish history, 1993-97; University of Leiden, Faculty of Humanities, professor and chair of Turkish studies, 1997-. Writer. **Publications:** The Unionist Factor: The Rôle of the Committee of Union and Progress in the Turkish National Movement, 1905-1926, 1984; Milli Mücadelede Ittihatçilik, 1987; Political Opposition in the Early Turkish Republic: The Progressive Republican Party, 1924-1925, 1991; (ed. with M. Tunçay) Socialism and Nationalism in the Ottoman Empire, 1876-1923, 1994; Turkey: A Modern History, 1994, 3rd ed., 2004; (ed. with D. Quataert) Workers and the Working Class in the Ottoman Empire and the Turkish Republic, 1839-1950, 1995; (ed. with W. van Schendel) Identity Politics in Central Asia and the Muslim World: Nationalism, Ethnicity and Labour in the Twentieth Century, 2001; European Union, Turkey and Islam, 2004; (with T. Atabaki) Men of Order: Authoritarian Modernization under Ataturk and Reza Shah, 2004; (ed.) Knowledge in Ferment: Dilemmas in Science, Scholarship and Society, 2007; The Young Turk Legacy and Nation Building: From the Ottoman Empire to Atatürk's Turkey, 2010. Contributor to periodicals. **Address:** Institute for Area Studies, University of Leiden, Witte Singel-complex, Rm. 116B, Witte Singel 25/M. de Vrieshof 4, Leiden, 2311 BZ, Netherlands. **Online address:** e.j.zurcher@hum.leidenuniv.nl

ZUROFF, Efraim. Israeli/American (born United States), b. 1948. **Genres:** Adult Non-fiction. **Career:** Yad Vashem Studies, assistant editor, 1973-78; Yad Vashem (Israeli Holocaust Memorial), Department for Contacts with the Diaspora, director, 1978-80; Simon Wiesenthal Center, director, 1978-80, founding director of Israeli office, coordinator of Nazi war crimes research, 1986-; United States Department of Justice, Office of Special Investigations, researcher, 1980-86. **Publications:** (Ed. with Y. Gutman) Rescue Attempts During the Holocaust, 1977; Occupation: Nazi-Hunter, 1988, rev. ed., 1994; The Response of Orthodox Jewry in the United States to the Holocaust: The Activities of the Vaad ha-Hatzala Rescue Committee, 1939-1945, 2000; (with A. Duyck) Chasseur de Nazis, 2008; Operation Last Chance: One Man's Quest to Bring Nazi Criminals to Justice, 2009; Lovac na naciste, 2009; Lowac Nazistow, 2010; Operation Last Chance: Im Fadenkreuz des, Nazi-Jägers, 2011. Contributor of articles to journals and periodicals. **Address:** Simon Wiesenthal Center, 1 Mendele St., Jerusalem, 92147, Israel. **Online address:** swcjerus@netvision.net.il

ZUTSHI, Chitralekha. American/Indian (born India), b. 1972. **Genres:** Politics/Government, Language/Linguistics, History, Adult Non-fiction. **Career:** College of William and Mary, associate professor of history; National Endowment for the Humanities, fellow, 2005-06; Library of Congress, John W. Kluge Center, Kluge fellow, 2008. Writer, academic and historian. **Publications:** Languages of Belonging: Islam, Regional Identity and the Making of Kashmir, 2004. **Address:** Department of History, College of William & Mary, 306 Blair Hall, PO Box 8795, Williamsburg, VA 23185, U.S.A. **Online address:** cxzuts@wm.edu

ZWAHLEN, Diana. American (born United States), b. 1947. **Genres:** Children's Fiction, Education. **Career:** Shawnee Mission School District, elementary art teacher, 1973-; Baker University, graduate school teacher, through 1994. Writer. **Publications:** Pee-U I Think There is a Skunk in Our School, 1994. **Address:** 28118 W 88th Cir., De Soto, KS 66018, U.S.A.

ZWEIFEL, Thomas D. American/Swiss (born Switzerland), b. 1962. **Genres:** Business/Trade/Industry, International Relations/Current Affairs, Money/Finance, Politics/Government, Ethics, Administration/Management, Adult Non-fiction, Economics, inspirational/Motivational Literature. **Career:** Swiss Consulting Group, chief executive officer, 1997-; Columbia University, adjunct professor, 2000-; St. Gallen University, adjunct professor, 2004-. Writer. **Publications:** Democratic Deficit? Institutions and Regulation in the European Union, Switzerland and the United States, 2002; Culture Clash: Managing the Global High-Performance Team, 2003; Communicate or Die: Getting Results Through Speaking and Listening, 2003; International Organizations and Democracy: Accountability, Politics and Power, 2005;

The Rabbi and the CEO: The Ten Commandments for 21st Century Leaders, 2008; Leadership in 100 Days: A Systematic Self-Coaching Workbook, 2010. **Address:** Leugrueb 6, Zumikon-Zurich, 8126, Switzerland. **Online address:** thomasd.zweifel@gmail.com

ZWEIGENHAFT, Richard L. American (born United States), b. 1945. **Genres:** Psychology, Race Relations, Sociology. **Career:** Corning Community College, instructor in psychology and sociology, 1968-70; Guilford College, assistant professor to professor, 1974-93, Charles A. Dana professor of psychology, 1993-. Writer. **Publications:** WITH G.W. DOMHOFF: Jews in the Protestant Establishment, 1982; Blacks in the White Establishment?: A Study of Race and Class in America, 1991; Diversity in the Power Elite: Have Women and Minorities Reached the Top?, 1998; Blacks in the White Elite: Will the Progress Continue?, 2003; Diversity in the Power Elite: How It Happened, Why It Matters, 2006; The New CEOs: Women, African American, Latino and Asian American CEOs of Fortune 500 Companies, 2011. OTHER: Who Gets to the Top? Executive Suite Discrimination in the Eighties, 1984. Contributor to periodicals. **Address:** Department of Psychology, Guilford College, 228C King Hall, 5800 W Friendly Ave., Greensboro, NC 27410, U.S.A. **Online address:** rzweigen@guilford.edu

ZWINGE, Randall. *See* **RANDI, James.**

ZWINGER, Ann Haymond. American (born United States), b. 1925. **Genres:** Education, Environmental Sciences/Ecology, Natural History, Essays, Illustrations. **Career:** Smith College, instructor in art history, 1950-51; University of Kansas City, teacher of adult education courses, 1958-60; Benet Hill Academy, instructor in art, 1963-66; Colorado College, visiting lecturer, 1973-81, 1982-; Carleton College, naturalist-in-residence, 1985; University of Arizona, visiting lecturer, 1987; Southwest Studies Center, natural history consultant; American Electric Power Co., board director. Writer. **Publications:** SELF-ILLUSTRATED: Beyond the Aspen Grove, 1970; (with B.E. Willard) Land above the Trees: A Guide to American Alpine Tundra, 1972; Run, River, Run: A Naturalist's Journey Down One of the Great Rivers of the West, 1975; A Desert Country Near the Sea: A Natural History of the Cape Region of Baja California, 1983; Downcanyon: A Naturalist Explores the Colorado River Through the Grand Canyon, 1995; Mysterious Lands: A Naturalist Explores the Four Great Deserts of the Southwest, 1996; (contrib.) Portrait of Utah, 1999. OTHERS: Wind in the Rock: The Canyonlands of Southeastern Utah, 1978; (with E.W. Teale) A Conscious Stillness: Two Naturalists on Thoreau's Rivers, 1982; (ed.) John Xántus: The Fort Tejon Letters 1857-1859, 1986; The Letter of John Xantus to Spencer Fullerton Baird from San Francisco and Cabo San Lucas, 1986; Colorado II, 1987; The Mysterious Land: An Award-winning Naturalist Explores the Four Great Deserts of the Southwest, 1989; Aspen: Blazon of the High Country, 1991; (ed. and intro.) Writing the Western Landscape, 1994; (ed. with S. Zwinger) Women in Wilderness: Writings and Photographs, 1995; Yosemite: Valley of Thunder, 1996; (foreword) Reading the Forested Landscape, 1997; The Nearsighted Naturalist, 1998; Shaped by Wind and Water: Reflections of a Naturalist, 2000; (contrib.) Fall Colors across North America, 2001; Grand Canyon: Little Things in a Big Place, 2006. Works appear in anthologies. Contributor to periodicals. **Address:** 1825 Culebra Pl., Colorado Springs, CO 80907-7328, U.S.A.

ŻYGULSKI, Zdzislaw. Polish (born Poland), b. 1921. **Genres:** Art/Art History, History. **Career:** Museum of Princes Czartoryski, curator, 1950-; Museum of Adam Mickiewicz, organizer, 1955; University of Krakow, lecturer, 1973; Academy of Fine Arts, professor, 1989-91; Hagop Kevorkian Center for Near Eastern Art, New York University, lecturer, 1989; University of Connecticut, lecturer, 1994. Writer. **Publications:** (With M. Szyrocki) Silesiaca: Wybór z Dziel pisarszy sląsko-niemieckich XVII Wieku Wtekstach Originalnych i Polskich Przekladach, 1957; Poezje, 1960; Studia i Materialy Do Dziejów Dawnegouzbrojenia i Ubioru Wojskowego, 1963; Fryderyk Hölderlin, 1770-1843, 1964; Gerhard Hauptmann-Czlowiek i Twórca, 1968; Broń Jako Dzielosztuki, 1969; Fryderyk Hebbel: Obraz zycia i Twórczości, 1971; Kostiumologia, 1972; Jonasz Stern: katalog Wystawy, 1972; Mikolaj Koper-

nikw Krakowie: Przewodnik Po Wystawie, 1973; Broń w Dawnej Polsce: Na Tleuzbrojenia Europy i Bliskiego Wschodu, 1975; Muzeum Narodowe w Krakowie, Zbiory Czartoryskich: Historia i Wybór Zabytków, 1978; Starabroń w Polskich Zbiorach, 1982; Muzea Na świecie: Wstęp Domuzealnictwa, 1982; Stara Broń w Polskich Zbiorach, 1982; Dziejepolskiego Rzemiosla Artystycznego, 1987; Outline History of Polish Applied Art, 1987; Sztuka Turecka, 1988; Polski Mundur Wojskowy, 1988; Odsieczwiedeń; Ska 1683, 1988; Sztuka Islamu w Zbiorach Polskich, 1989; Ottoman Art in the Service of the Empire, 1992; światla Stambulu, 1999; Cracow: An Illustrated History, 2001; Princes Czartoryski Museum: A History of the Collections, 2001; Sztuka Perska, 2002; Polska, broń Wodzów i zolnierzy, 2003; (contrib.) Urbs celeberrima: ksiega pamiatkowa na 750-lecie lokacji Krakowa, 2008; Dzieje zbiorów pulawskich: światynia Sybilli i Dom Gotycki, 2009; Famous Battles in Art, forthcoming; Hussar's Book, forthcoming. **Address:** Museum of Princes Czartoryski, ul... Jana 19, Cracow, 31017, Poland.

ŻYLICZ, Tomasz. Polish (born Poland), b. 1951. **Genres:** Economics, Money/Finance, Adult Non-fiction, Natural History. **Career:** Warsaw University, Department of Economics, teaching assistant, 1974-78, lecturer, 1979-89, professor, 1989-, chair of microeconomics, 1996-2007, deputy dean, 1999-2005, dean, 2005-, Warsaw Ecological Economics Center, director, 1993-2008; University of Wisconsin, Department of Economics, honorary fellow, 1979; University of Colorado, Department of Economics, Fulbright visiting professor, 1988-89, Environment and Behavior Program, research associate, 1988-89; Ministry of Environment, director of economics, 1989-91, advisor, 1991-; Harvard University, Central and Eastern Europe Environmental Economics and Policy Project, project associate, 1995-98. Writer. **Publications:** Ekonomia Wobec Zagadnień Srodowiska Przyrodniczego: Elementy Teorii Oraz Implikacje Praktyczne, 1990; Costing Nature in a Transition Economy: Case Studies in Poland, 2000. Contributor to books. **Address:** Department of Economics, University of Warsaw, 44/50 Dluga St., Warsaw, 00-241, Poland. **Online address:** tzylicz@wne.uw.edu.pl

ZYSMAN, John. American (born United States), b. 1946?. **Genres:** Economics, Business/Trade/Industry, Industrial Relations. **Career:** Massachusetts Institute of Technology, Department of Political Science, lecturer, 1973-74; London School of Economics, visiting academic, 1976-77; University of California, assistant professor, 1974-82, associate professor of political science, 1982, professor of political science, 1995, Berkeley Roundtable on the International Economy, co-director. Writer. **Publications:** Political Strategies for Industrial Order: State, Market and Industry in France, 1977; (with M. Borrus and J. Millstein) U.S.-Japanese Competition in the Semi-Conductor Industry: A Study in International Trade and Technological Development, 1982; (with B. Michael) International Competition in Advanced Industrial Sectors: Trade and Development in the Semiconductor Industry: A Study, 1982; Governments, Markets and Growth: Finance and the Politics of Industrial Change, 1983; (with S.S. Cohen) Manufacturing Matters: The Myth of the Post-Industrial Economy, 1987; (with W. Sandholtz and Borrus) The Highest Stakes: The Economic Foundations of the Next Security System, 1992. EDITOR: (with L.D. Tyson) American Industry in International Competition: Government Policies and Corporate Strategies, 1983; (with Tyson and W.T. Dickens) The Dynamics of Trade and Employment, 1988; (with Tyson and C. Johnson) Politics and Productivity: The Real Story of Why Japan Works, 1989; (with A. Schwartz) Enlarging Europe: The Industrial Foundations of a New Political Reality, 1998; (with A. Schwartz and S.S. Cohen) The Tunnel at the End of the Light: Privatization, Business Networks and Economic Transformation in Russia, 1998; How Revolutionary was the Digital Revolution?: National Responses, Market Transitions and Global Technology, 2006. CONTRIBUTOR: European Industrial Policy, 1975; Twenty Years of Gaullism, 1980; France in the World Economy, 1982; Strategic Trade Policy and the New International Economics, 1986; The Politics of Industrial Policy, 1986. Contributor to periodicals. **Address:** Department of Political Science, University of Caliifornia-Berkeley, 716 Barrows, 2234 Piedmont Ave., Berkeley, CA 94720, U.S.A. **Online address:** zysman@berkeley.edu

OBITUARIES

ATWOOD, William G(oodson). American (born United States), b. 1932. **Genres:** Biography, History, Music. **Career:** University of Kansas Hospitals, intern, 1950-59; Columbia-Presbyterian Medical Center, resident, 1961-64; Columbia University, College of Physicians and Surgeons, associate professor, 1987-2011. Writer. **Publications:** The Lioness and the Little One: The Liaison of George Sand and Frédéric Chopin, 1980; Fryderyk Chopin, Pianist from Warsaw, 1987; The Parisian Worlds of Frédéric Chopin, 1999. Contributor to journals. *Died 2011.*

BACON, George Edward. British (born England), b. 1917. **Genres:** Chemistry, Physics. **Career:** Telecommunications Research Establishment of the Air Ministry, scientific officer, 1939-46; Atomic Energy Research Establishment, deputy chief scientific officer, 1946-63; University of Sheffield, professor of physics, 1963-81, dean of the faculty of pure science, 1969-71, professor emeritus of physics, 1981-2011. Writer. **Publications:** Neutron Diffraction 1955, 3rd ed. 1975; Applications of Neutron Diffraction in Chemistry, 1963; (ed.) X-ray and Neutron Diffraction, 1966; Neutron Physics, 1969; Neutron Scattering in Chemistry, 1977; The Architecture of Solids, 1981; (ed.) Fifty Years of Neutron Diffraction, 1986. *Died 2011.*

BAKEWELL, Kenneth (Graham Bartlett). British (born England), b. 1931. **Genres:** Administration/Management, Librarianship. **Career:** Dudley Public Libraries, assistant, 1947-52, branch librarian, 1953-55; Derbyshire County Library, senior assistant, 1952-53; Bexley Public Libraries, chief cataloguer, 1955-57; English Electric Co., chief cataloguer and publications editor, 1957-59; British Plaster Board (Holdings) Ltd., librarian, 1959-61; British Institute of Management, librarian, 1961-64; Liverpool City Libraries, technical documentation officer and librarian, 1964-66; Liverpool John Moores University, lecturer, 1966-68, senior lecturer, 1968-78, principal lecturer, 1978-87, reader, 1987-91, professor of information and library management, 1991-93, emeritus professor, 1993-2011; Society of Indexers, chairman, 1977-79, president, 1986-91. **Publications:** Productivity in British Industry, 1963; How to Find Out: Management and Productivity, A Guide to Sources of Information Arranged According to the Universal Decimal Classification, 1966, 2nd ed., 1970; (ed.) Classification for Information Retrieval: Papers Presented at an Intensive Course Held in September 1967 at the School of Librarianship, Liverpool College of Commerce, 1968; (ed.) Library and Information Services for Management: Papers Presented at a Short Course Held at the School of Librarianship and Information Work at Liverpool College of Commerce in December 1967, 1968; Industrial Libraries throughout the World, 1969; A Manual of Cataloguing Practice, 1972; (comp. with D.A. Cotton) The London Classification of Business Studies: An Introduction and Directory of Users, 1976, 2nd ed. as The London Classification of Business Studies: A Classification and Thesaurus for Business Libraries, 1979; (ed.) Management Principles and Practice: A Guide to Information Sources, 1977; Classification and Indexing Practice, 1978; (with J.M. Bibby, E.J. Hunter and V.P. Roper) A Study of Indexers' Reactions to the Precis Indexing System, 1978; (co-author) A Study of Indexers' Reactions to the PRECIS Indexing System (microfor): Final Report for the Period October 1976-December 1977, 1978; (with E.J. Hunter) Cataloguing, 1979, 3rd ed., 1991; (with G.A. Dare) The Manager's Guide to Getting the Answers, 1980, rev. ed., 1983; How to Organise Information: A Manager's Guide to Techniques and Sources, with a Checklist for Secretaries and Assistants, 1984; (with V.P. Roper) Business Information Services in Public Libraries: A Study of Services in London, the North-West of England and CLWYD Library Service: Final Report for the Period October 1982 to December 1983, 1984; Business Information and the Public Library, 1987; Information Sources and Reference Tools, 1988; Managing User-Centered Libraries and Information Services, 1990, 2nd ed., 1997; (with A.D. Rothwell) Information Needs for Combating Alcoholism: Report to the British Library Research and Development Department on Project SI/G/875, 1991; (with P.L. Williams) Indexing Children's Books, 2000. *Died 2011.*

BARRETT, Charles Kingsley. British (born England), b. 1917. **Genres:** Theology/Religion. **Career:** Minister-Darlington, 1943; University of Durham, lecturer in theology, 1945-58, professor of divinity, 1958-82, professor emeritus; Yale University, Shaffer Lecturer, 1965; Pittsburgh Theological Seminary, visiting professor, 1984; Emory University, Candler School of Theology, Woodruff Visiting Professor, 1986. Writer. **Publications:** The Holy Spirit and the Gospel Tradition, 1947; The Gospel According to St. John, 1955, 2nd ed., 1978; Biblical Preaching and Biblical Scholarship, 1957; A Commentary on the Epistle to the Romans, 1957; Westcott as Commentator, 1959; Luke the Historian in Recent Study, 1961; From First Adam to Last, 1962; The Pastoral Epistles in the New English Bible, 1963; Biblical Problems and Biblical Preaching, 1964; Christianity at Corinth, 1964; History and Faith: The Story of the Passion, 1967; Jesus and the Gospel Tradition, 1967; The First Epistle to the Corinthians, 1968; A Commentary on the First Epistle to the Corinthians, 1968; The Signs of an Apostle: The Cato Lecture, 1970; Das Johannesevangelium und das Judentum, 1970; New Testament Essays, 1972; A Commentary on the Second Epistle to the Corinthians, 1973; The Gospel of John and Judaism, 1975; Reading through Romans, 1977; Essays on Paul, 1982; Essays on John, 1982; Freedom and Obligation, 1985; Church, Ministry and Sacraments in the New Testament, 1985; (with M. Hengel) Conflicts and Challenges in Early Christianity, 1994; Paul: An Introduction to His Thought, 1994; Critical and Exegetical Commentary on the Acts of the Apostle, vol. I, 1994, vol. II, 1998; Jesus and the Word and Other Essays, 1995; Acts: A Shorter Commentary, 2002; On Paul: Aspects of his Life, Work and Influence in the Early Church, 2003. EDITOR: Wilbert Francis Howard, Fourth Gospel in Recent Criticism and Interpretation, 4th ed., 1955; (and intro.) The New Testament Background: Selected Documents, 1956, rev. ed., 1987; (with E. Bammel and W.D. Davis) Donum Gentilicium: New Testament Studies in Honour of David Daube, 1978; The Epistle to the Romans, 1991. *Died 2011.*

BERCOVITCH, Jacob. New Zealander (born New Zealand), b. 1946?. **Genres:** International Relations/Current Affairs. **Career:** University of Canterbury, professor of international relations, 1983-2011. Writer. **Publications:** Third Parties in Conflict, 1981; Resolving International Conflicts: The Theory & Practice of Mediation, 1996; (with R. Jackson) International Conflict: A Chronological Encyclopedia of Conflicts and their Management, 1945-1995, 1997. EDITOR: Social Conflicts and Third Parties: Strategies of Conflict Resolution, 1984; ANZUS in Crisis: Alliance Management in International Affairs, 1988; (with M. Efrat) Superpowers and Client States in the Middle East: The Imbalance of Influence, 1991; (with J.Z. Rubin) Mediation in International Relations: Multiple Approaches to Conflict Management, 1992; Resolving International Conflicts: The Theory and Practice of Mediation, 1996; (with J. Fretter) Studies in International Mediation: Essays in Honour of Jeffrey Z. Rubin, 2002; (with J. Fretter) Regional Guide to International Conflict Management from 1945 to 2003, 2004; (with K.B. Huang and C.C. Teng) Conflict Management, Security and Intervention in East Asia: Third-Party Mediation and Intervention Between China and Taiwan, 2008. OTHER: (contrib.) Preventing Violent Conflicts: Past Record and Future Challenges, 1998. *Died 2011.*

BOSCO, Monique. Canadian/Austrian (born Austria), b. 1927. **Genres:** Novels, Translations, Poetry. **Career:** Freelance journalist, 1949-59; National Film Board, writer; Radio Canada, writer; Université de Montréal, Department of French Studies, professor of literature, 1963-2007. **Publications:** Un Amour maladroit, 1961; Les Infusoires, 1965; La Femme de Loth, 1970; Jéricho; poèmes, 1971; New Medea, 1974; Lot's Wife, 1975; Charles Lévy, M.D., 1977; Schabbat 70-77, 1978; Portrait de Zeus peint par Minerve, 1982; Sara Sage, 1986; Boomerang, 1987; Clichés, 1988; Babel Opéra, 1989; Miserere, 1991; Remémoration, 1991; Ephémères, 1993; Ephémérides, 1993; Le jeu des sept familles, 1995; Lamento 90-97, 1997; Confiteor, 1998; Bis, 1999; Mea Culpa, 2001; L'attrape-rêves, 2002; Amen: Poèmes, 2002; Eh bien! la guerre, 2004; Ces gens-lá, 2006. Contributor to periodicals. *Died 2007.*

BRANSON, Gary D. American (born United States), b. 1933. **Genres:** Homes/Gardens, Architecture. **Career:** Family Handyman, senior editor; freelance writer. **Publications:** Home Maintenance & Repair: Walls, Ceilings, Floors, 1977; The Complete Guide to Remodeling Your Basement: How to Create New Living Space the Professional Way, 1990; The Complete Guide to Lumber Yards and Home Centers: A Consumer's Guide to Choosing and Using Building Materials and Tools, 1991; The Complete Guide to Recycling at Home: How to Take Responsibility, Save Money and Protect the Environment, 1991; (with H.W. Swinson) The Complete Guide to Barrier-free Housing: Convenient Living for the Elderly and Physically Handicapped, 1991; The Complete Guide to Manufactured Housing: The Affordable Alternative to Stick-built Construction, 1992; The Complete Guide to Floors, Walls and Ceilings: A Comprehensive Do-It-Yourself Handbook, 1992; (ed. with S. Willson) Popular Mechanics 101 Quick Home Improvement Tips, 1992; The Complete Guide to Log and Cedar Homes: All about Buying, Building, Decorating and Furnishing Log Cedar and Post Beam Homes, 1993; Popular Mechanics 125 Ways to Handle and Prevent Home Hazards and Emergencies, 1994; Gary Bransons Home Repairs and Improvements on a Budget, 1994; Home, Water & Moisture Problems: Prevention and Solutions, 2003; Solving Home Plumbing Problems, 2004. *Died 2011.*

BRITTAIN, William (E.). American (born United States), b. 1930. **Genres:** Children's Fiction, Children's Non-fiction, Horror. **Career:** English teacher, 1952-60; Lawrence Junior High School, remedial reading teacher, 1960-86; Ellery Queen's Mystery Magazine, staff, 1964-83. Writer. **Publications:** THE MAN WHO READ SERIES: The Man Who Read John Dickson Carr, 1965; The Man Who Read Ellery Queen, 1965; The Woman Who Read Rex Stout, 1966; The Boy Who Read Agatha Christie, 1966; The Man Who Read Sir Arthur Conan Doyle, 1969; The Man Who Read G.K. Chesterton, 1973; The Man Who Read Dashiell Hammett, 1974; The Man Who Read Georges Simenon, 1975; The Girl Who Read John Creasey, 1975; The Men Who Read Isaac Asimov, 1978. Mr. STRANG SERIES: Mr Strang Takes a Field Trip, 1968; Mr. Strang Checks a Record, 1972; Mr. Strang Examines a Legend, 1973; Mr. Strang Invents a Strange Device, 1973; Mr. Strang Discovers a Bug, 1973; Mr. Strang and the Cat Lady, 1975; Mr. Strang Performs an Experiment, 1975; Mr. Strang Accepts a Challenge, 1976; Mr. Strang Unlocks a Door, 1981; Mr. Strang Grasps at Straws, 1981; Mr. Strang Interprets a Picture, 1981; Mr. Strang and the Lost Ship, 1982; Mr. Strang Takes a Partner, 1982; Mr. Strang Studies Exhibit A, 1982; Mr. Strang and the Purloined Memo, 1983; Mr. Strang Takes a Tour, 1983; Mr. Strang Picks Up The Pieces, 1988. OTHERS: The Zaretski Chain, 1968; The Ferret Man, 1977; All The Money In The World, 1979; Devil's Donkey, 1981; Sherlock Holmes, Master Detective, 1982; The Wish Giver: Three Tales of Coven Tree, 1983; Who Knew There'd Be Ghosts?, 1985; Dr. Dredd's Wagon of Wonders, 1987; The Fantastic Freshman, 1988; My Buddy, The King, 1989; Professor Popkin's Prodigious Polish: A Tale of Coven Tree, 1990; Wings, 1991; The Ghost From Beneath The Sea, 1992; The Mystery Of The Several Sevens, 1994; Shape-Changer, 1994; The Wizards And The Monster, 1994; A Candle for the Bag Lady, 2006. *Died 2011.*

BRODY, Jean. American (born United States), b. 1930. **Genres:** Science Fiction/Fantasy, Novels. **Career:** Writer. **Publications:** (With G.B. Osborne) Twenty-Year Phenomenon: Men and Women Talk About the Breakup of Their Long-Term Marriages, 1980; Gideon's House, 1984; Braille Me, 1984; A Coven of Women, 1987; Elephants, 1993; Cleo, 1995; The Tropical Rainforest, 1995. *Died 2011.*

CHAMBERLAIN, Lorna M(arie). Canadian (born Canada), b. 1945. **Genres:** Animals/Pets, Medicine/Health. **Career:** Whitby Psychiatric Hospital, psychometrist, 1971; Addiction Research Foundation, community consultant, 1972-80; Sarnia General Hospital, associate director, 1980-92, director of addiction services, 1992-2011. Writer. **Publications:** (With R. Preece) Animal Welfare and Human Values, 1993. *Died 2011.*

CLEARY, Edward L. American (born United States), b. 1929. **Genres:** Area Studies, Theology/Religion, Politics/Government. **Career:** University of Pittsburgh, Center for Latin American Studies, assistant professor, assistant director, 1973-76, visiting professor; Aquinas Institute, academic dean, vice-president and professor, 1976-79; Pontifical College Josephinum, professor and director of Hispanic studies, 1985-93; Yale University, Graduate School, visiting professor, 1991-92; Providence College, professor of political science, 1993, professor emeritus, through 2011; Latin American Studies Program, director; University of California, Center for Latin American Studies, visiting professor, 2000-01; Bolivian Institute of Social Study and Action, president; New York University, visiting professor; Florida International University, visiting professor; Saint Xavier University, teacher and administrator; Catholic University, teacher and administrator. Writer. **Publications:** (Ed.) Shaping a New World: An Orientation to Latin America, 1971; Crisis and Change: The Church in Latin America Today, 1985; (ed.) Path from Puebla: Significant Documents of the Latin American Bishops since 1979, 1989; (ed.) Born of the Poor: The Latin American Church since Medellin, 1990; (ed.) Resonancias De Puebla: Documentos Significativos De Los Obispos Latino americanos Desde 1979, 1990; (ed. with H.W. Stewart-Gambino) Conflict and Competition: The Latin American Church in a Changing Environment, 1992; (ed. with H.W. Stewart-Gambino) Power, Politics and Pentecostals in Latin America, 1997; The Struggle for Human Rights in Latin America, 1997; (ed. with T.J. Steigenga) Resurgent Voices in Latin America: Indigenous Peoples, Political Mobilization and Religious Change, 2004; (ed. with A.D. Hertzke) Representing God at the Statehouse: Religion and Politics in the American States, 2006; Mobilizing for Human Rights in Latin America, 2007; (ed. with T.J. Steigenga) Conversion of a Continent: Contemporary Religious Change in Latin America, 2007; How Latin America Saved the Soul of the Catholic Church, 2009; Rise of Charismatic Catholicism in Latin America, 2011. *Died 2011.*

COFFIN, Tristram Potter. American (born United States), b. 1922. **Genres:** Mythology/Folklore, Sports/Fitness, Young Adult Fiction, Children's Fiction. **Career:** University of Pennsylvania, assistant instructor of English, 1946-49, associate professor of English, 1958-64, professor of English, 1964-84, Graduate School of Arts and Sciences, vice-dean, 1965-68, professor emeritus of English, 1984-2012; Denison University, varsity tennis coach, 1949-58, instructor of English, 1949-50, assistant professor of English, 1950-56, associate professor of English, 1956-58, varsity soccer coach, 1956-58; U.S. Military Academy, visiting professor of contemporary literature, 1962-63; Providence College, lecturer in folk studies, 1984-90. Writer. **Publications:** The British Traditional Ballad in North America, 1950, rev. ed., 1977; An Analytical Index to Journal Folklore, 1958; (with H.H. Flanders and B. Nettl) Ancient Ballads Traditionally Sung in New England, 4 vols., 1960; Uncertain Glory: Folklore and the American Revolution, 1971; The Old Ball Game: Baseball in Folklore and Fiction, 1971; The Book of Christmas Folklore, 1973; The Female Hero in Folklore and Legend, 1975; The Proper Book of Sexual Folklore, 1978; Great Game for a Girl, 1980; How to Play Tennis with What You Already Have, 1997; My Own Trumpet, 2001. EDITOR: (with M. Leach) The Critics and the Ballad, 1961; Indian Tales of North America, 1961; (with H. Cohen) Folklore in America: Tales, Songs, Superstitions, Proverbs, Riddles, Games, Folk Drama and Folk Festivals, 1966; Our Living Traditions, 1968; (with H. Cohen) Folklore from the Working Folk of America, 1972; (with H. Cohen) The Parade of Heroes: Legendary Figures in American Lore, 1978; (with H. Cohen) Folklore of the American Holidays, 1985, 3rd ed., 1999; (with H. Cohen) America Celebrates, 1991; Born Again, 2003. *Died 2012.*

COOKE, Jacob Ernest. American (born United States), b. 1924. **Genres:** History, Biography, Young Adult Non-fiction. **Career:** Columbia University, instructor, 1953-57, assistant professor of history, 1957-61, visiting professor, 1969; Carnegie Institute of Technology (now Carnegie-Mellon University), professor of history and chairperson of department, 1962-63; Lafayette College, John Henry MacCraken professor of history, 1962-90, chairperson of department, 1978-80, 1983-86, John Henry MacCraken professor emeritus of history, 1990-2011; Huntington Library, visiting fellow, 1987. Writer. **Publications:** Frederick Bancroft: Historian, 1957; A History of the U.S. 1946-1960, 1965; (co-author) The March of Democracy: A History of the United States, 1965; Tench Coxe and the Early Republic, 1978; Federalist: American State Papers, 1980; Alexander Hamilton, 1982. EDITOR: (with J.E. Cooke) The Papers of Alexander Hamilton, 1961; (and intro.) The Federalist, 1961; Reports of Alexander Hamilton, 1964; (with L.F. Shaefer and D.H. Fowler) Problems in Western Civilization: The Challenge of History, 1965; Alexander Hamilton: A Profile, 1967; A History of the American Colonies, 13 vols., 1973-86; (co-ed.) Encyclopedia of the North American Colonies, 1993; (with M.M. Klein) North America in Colonial Times: An Encyclopedia for Students, 1998. *Died 2011.*

COX, Patsi Bale. (G. F. Bale). American (born United States), b. 1945. **Genres:** Biography, Mystery/Crime/Suspense, Novels. **Career:** Plaza magazine, feature writer, 1967; Colorado Woman magazine, founder and editor, 1974-80; Rocky Mountain Country, editor, 1980; Tribute (film industry publication), editor, 1980-85. **Publications:** NONFICTION: (ed. with C. Pelletier and J. Glaser) A Country Music Christmas, 1996; (with J. Jones) Jenny Jones: My Story, 1997; (with T. Tucker) Nickel Dreams: My Life, 1997; (with R. Emery) The View from Nashville, 1998; (with R. Emery) Fifty Years Down a Country Road, 2000; (with L. Lynn) Loretta Lynn: Still Woman Enough, 2003; (with T. Orlando) Halfway to Paradise, 2003; (with W. Judd) Coming Home to Myself, 2005; (with W. Judd) Coming Home to Myself, 2006; Garth Factor: The Career Behind Country's Big Boom, 2009. NOVELS WITH G.B. WELLBROCK AS G.F. BALE: If Thoughts Could Kill, 1990; Cry, Baby, Cry, 1991. OTHERS: (with R. Emery) 50 Years Down a Country Road, 2000; (with P. Benatar) Between a Heart and a Rock Place: A Memoir, 2010; (with G. Jones) The Three of Us: Growing Up with Tammy and George, 2011. Contributor to periodicals. *Died 2011.*

CROWTHER, Harold Francis. American (born United States), b. 1920. **Genres:** Novels, Psychology, Music. **Career:** Salina County Juvenile Court, probation officer, 1956-59. Writer and lawyer. **Publications:** The Oblique Equalizer or Some for Me, 1965. *Died 2008.*

DALY, Leo (Arthur). Irish (born Ireland), b. 1920. **Genres:** Novels, Novellas/Short Stories, Plays/Screenplays, Area Studies, Literary Criticism And History, Travel/Exploration. **Career:** Mental Health Authority, psychiatric nurse, 1943-66; freelance photojournalist, 1966-69; Radio-Telefis-Eireann, broadcaster, 1969-75; writer and photographer, 1975-2010. **Publications:** (Trans.) Oileáin árann, 1975; James Joyce and the Mullingar Connection, 1975; Titles (essays), 1981; The Rock Garden (novel), 1984; The Stone-Cutter's Daughter (novel), 1991; James Joyce at the Cross Keys, 1991; Island Lovers (short stories), 1993; Austin Friars, 1994; The Jealous Wall (play), 1995. EDITOR: The Midlands, 1979; The Westmeath Examiner Centenary Edition, 1982; Life of Colman of Lynn, 1999. *Died 2010.*

DE HAMEL, Joan (Littledale). New Zealander/British (born England), b. 1924. **Genres:** Children's Fiction, Novels. **Career:** Francis Holland School, head of languages, 1945-48; Dunedin Teachers College, lecturer in French, 1967-79. Writer. **Publications:** SELF-ILLUSTRATED: X Marks the Spot, 1973. OTHERS: Take the Long Path, 1978; Hemi's Pet, 1985, 2nd ed., 1987; The Third Eye, 1987; Hideaway, 1992; Hemi and The Shortie Pyjamas, 1996. Contributor to periodicals and journals. *Died 2011.*

DEWALD, Paul A. American (born United States), b. 1920. **Genres:** Psychiatry. **Career:** Strong Memorial-Rochester Municipal Hospitals, chief resident in psychiatry, 1951-52, assistant psychiatrist, 1952-57, associate psychiatrist, 1957-61; University of Rochester, School of Medicine, instructor, 1952-57, assistant professor of psychiatry, 1957-61; Washington University, School of Medicine, assistant professor of clinical psychiatry, 1961-65; St. Louis University, School of Medicine, associate professor, 1965-69, professor of clinical psychiatry, 1969-2011; St. Louis Institute for Psychoanalysis, lecturer, 1961-2011, training and supervising analyst, 1965-2011, medical director, 1972-83, faculty, training analyst emeritus and supervising analyst; Psychoanalytic Foundation, director of low-cost treatment service. **Publications:** Psychotherapy: A Dynamic Approach, 1964, 2nd ed., 1971; The Psychoanalytic Process: A Case Illustration, 1972; Chŏngsin ChiryoU Iron Kwa Silche, 1978; Learning Process in Psychoanalytic Supervision: Complexities and Challenges: A Case Illustration, 1987; Supportive and Active Psychother-

apies: A Dynamic Approach, 1994; (ed. with R.W. Clark) Ethics Case Book of the American Psychoanalytic Association, 2002, 2nd ed., 2007. Contributor to journals. *Died 2011.*

DIX, Robin C. British (born England), b. 1956?. **Genres:** Poetry. **Career:** University of Durham, Department of English Studies, lecturer, 1991-2007. Writer. **Publications:** (Ed.) The Poetical Works of Mark Akenside, 1996; (ed.) Mark Akenside: A Reassessment, 2000; The Literary Career of Mark Akenside, Including an Edition of His Non-Medical Prose, 2006; (co-ed.) The Manuscripts of Adam Ferguson, 2006. Contributor of articles to periodicals. *Died 2007.*

DRUMMOND, June. South African (born South Africa), b. 1923. **Genres:** Mystery/Crime/Suspense, Romance/Historical, Young Adult Fiction. **Career:** Woman's Weekly and Natal Mercury, Journalist, 1946-48; Durban Civic Orchestra, secretary, 1950-53; Church Adoption Society, assistant secretary, 1954-60. Writer. **Publications:** The Black Unicorn, 1959; Thursday's Child, 1961; A Time to Speak, 1962; A Cage of Humming-Birds, 1964; Welcome, Proud Lady, 1968; Cable-Car, 1965; The Saboteurs, 1967; The Gantry Episode in US as Murder on a Bad Trip, 1968; The People in Glass House, 1970; Farewell Party, 1971; Bang! Bang! You're Dead, 1973; The Boon Companions, 1974; Drop Dead, 1976; Slowly the Poison, 1975; Funeral Urn: A Novel, 1977; The Patriots, 1979; I Saw Him Die, 1979; Such a Nice Family, 1980; The Trojan Mule, 1982; The Bluestocking: A Novel, 1985; Junta, 1989; The Unsuitable Miss Pelham, 1990; Burden of Guilt, 1991; Hidden Agenda, 1993; The Impostor: A Novel, 1993; Loose Cannon, 2003; The Meddlers, 2004; Old Bones Buried Under, 2006; Countdown Murder, 2006. Contributor to periodicals. *Died 2011.*

DUMMETT, Michael (Anthony Eardley). British (born England), b. 1925. **Genres:** Philosophy, Politics/Government, Race Relations, Recreation. **Career:** University of Birmingham, assistant lecturer, 1950-51; Oxford University, All Souls College, senior research fellow, 1974-79, sub-warden, 1974-76, New College, Wykehan professor of logic, 1979-92, reader in philosophy of mathematics, 1962-74, emeritus fellow, 1980-2011; University of Ghana, visiting lecturer, 1958; Stanford University, visiting professor, 1960-66; University of Minnesota, visiting professor, 1968; Princeton University, visiting professor; 1970; Rockefeller University, visiting professor, 1973; Harvard University, William James lecturer in philosophy, 1976. **Publications:** (Ed. with J.N. Crossley) Formal Systems and Recursive Functions: Proceedings, 1965; (contrib.) Justice First, 1969; Frege: Philosophy of Language, 1973, 2nd ed., 1981; The Justification of Deduction, 1974; Intuitionistic Mathematics and Logic, 1974; Elements of Intuitionism, 1977, 2nd ed., 2000; Truth and Other Enigmas, 1978; Immigration: Where the Debate Goes Wrong, 1978; Catholicism and the World Order: Some Reflections on the 1978 Reith Lectures, 1979; The Death of Blair Peach: The Supplementary Report of the Unofficial Committee of Enquiry, 1980; (with S. Mann) The Game of Tarot: From Ferrara to Salt Lake City, 1980; Twelve Tarot Games, 1980; The Interpretation of Frege's Philosophy, 1981; (contrib.) Ganjifa: The Playing Cards of India: A General Survey, with a Catalogue of the Victoria and Albert Museum Collection, 1982; Voting Procedures, 1984; The Visconti-Sforza Tarot Cards, 1986; Ursprunge Deranalytischen Philosophie, 1988; Frege and Other Philosophers, 1991; The Logical Basis of Metaphysics, 1991; Frege: Philosophy of Mathematics, 1991; Grammar and Style, 1993; The Seas of Language, 1993; Il Mondo El'Angelo: I Tarocchi e La Loro Storia, 1993; Origins of Analytical Philosophy, 1994; Tarocchi Siciliani, 1995, rev. ed., 2002; (with T. Depaulis and R. Decker) A Wicked Pack of Cards: The Origins of the Occult Tarot, 1996; Principles of Electoral Reform, 1997; La Natura e Il Futuro Di Filosofia, 2001; On Immigration and Refugees, 2001; (with R. Decker) A History of the Occult Tarot 1870-1970, 2002; Truth and the Past, 2004; (with J. McLeod) History of Games Played with the Tarot Pack: The Game of Triumphs, 2004; Thought and Reality, 2006; Nature and Future of Philosophy, 2010. Contributor to journals. *Died 2011.*

ENSLIN, Theodore (Vernon). American (born United States), b. 1925. **Genres:** Poetry, Novellas/Short Stories, Autobiography/Memoirs, Songs/Lyrics And Libretti, Music. **Career:** Writer. **Publications:** The Work Proposed, 1958; New Sharon's Prospect, 1962; The Place Where I Am Standing, 1964; This Do (and The Talents), 1966; New Sharon's Prospect and Journals, 1966; To Come to Have Become, 1966; The Dependencies, 1966; The Four Temperaments, 1966; Characters in Certain Places, 1967; The Diabelli Variations and Other Poems, 1967; Poems 1967, 1968; Agreement and Back: Sequences, 1969; The Poems, 1970; Forms, 4 vols., 1970-73; Views 1-7, 1970;

The Country of Our Consciousness, 1971; Etudes, 1972; Views, 1973; In the Keepers House, 1973; With Light Reflected, 1970-72, 1973; The Swamp Fox, 1973; The Mornings, 1974; Fever Poems, 1974; The Last Days of October, 1974; Sitio, 1974; The Median Flow: Poems 1943-73, 1975; Synthesis 1-24, 1975; Mahler, 1975; Some Pastorals: A New Year's Cycle for Jake, 1975; Ländler, 1975; Carmina, 1976; Papers, 1976; The July Book, 1976; Ascensions, 1977; Circles, 1977; Concentrations, 1977; The Further Regions, 1977; Tailings, 1978; Ranger, 2 vols., 1979-80; May Fault, 1979; Opus 31 No. 3, 1979; A Root in March, 1979; 16 Blossoms in February, 1979; Two Plus Twelve, 1979; The Flare of Beginning Is in November, 1980; Star Anise, 1980; The Fifth Direction, 1980; Two Geese, 1980; Axes 52, 1981; In Duo Concertante, 1981; Markings, 1981; Opus O, 1981; (co-author) Knee Deep in the Atlantic, 1981; Processionals, 1981; September's Bonfire, 1981; Fragments/ Epigrammata, 1982; F.P., 1982; A Man in Stir, 1983; To Come Here To, 1983; Meditations, 1983; Passacagila, 1983; Grey Days, 1984; Songs out Notes, 1984; Music for Several Occasions, 1985; (with K. Wilson) Meeting at Jal, 1985; For Mr. Walters, Master Mechanic, 1985; I Am You Are, 1985; Music for Several Occasions, 1985; The Path Between, 1986; The Waking of the Eye, 1986; The Weather Within, 1986; Case Book, 1987; From Near the Great Pine, 1989; Little Wandering Flake of Snow, 1990; Love and Science, 1990; Gamma UT, 1992; A Sonare, 1994; Communitas, 1995; Propositions for John Taggart, 1996; Thumbprint on Landscape, 1998; Then and Now: Selected Poems 1943-93, 1999; Re-Sounding: Selected Later Poems, 1999; Sequentiae, 1999; The Roads around Jenkins, 2000; Nine, 2000; Ring, 2001; Keep Sake, 2001; In Tandem, 2003; I, Benjamin: A Quasi-autobiographical Novella, 2010. *Died 2011.*

ESTES, William (Kaye). American (born United States), b. 1919. **Genres:** Psychology, Literary Criticism And History, Essays, Language/Linguistics. **Career:** Indiana University, faculty, 1946-62, professor of psychology, 1955-60, research professor, 1960-62, professor, 1999-2011; Journal of Experimental Psychology, associate editor, 1958-62; Journal of Comparative and Physiological Psychology, editor, 1962-68; Stanford University, professor of psychology, 1962-68, Institute of Mathematical Studies in Social Sciences, staff, 1962-68; Rockefeller University, professor of psychology, 1968-79; Psychological Review, editor, 1977-82; Harvard University, professor of psychology, 1979-94, professor emeritus of psychology, 1994-2011; Psychological Science, editor, 1990-94. **Publications:** An Experimental Study of Punishment, 1944; (co-author) Modern Learning Theory, 1954; (ed. with R.R. Bush) Studies in Mathematical Learning Theory, 1959; (with A. Binder) Transfer of Response in Visual Recognition Situations as a Function of Frequence Variables, 1966; Stimulus Sampling Theory, 1967; Learning Theory and Mental Development, 1970; Handbook of Learning and Cognitive Processes, 1975; (ed.) Attention and Memory, 1976; (ed.) Approaches to Human Learning and Motivation, 1976; (ed.) Human Information Processing, 1978; (ed.) Linguistic Functions in Cognitive Theory, 1978; Models of Learning, Memory and Choice, 1982; Statistical Models in Behavioral Research, 1991; (contrib.) Essays in Honor of William K. Estes, 1992; Classification and Cognition, 1994. *Died 2011.*

FENNER, Frank John. Australian (born Australia), b. 1914. **Genres:** Environmental Sciences/Ecology, Medicine/Health. **Career:** Walter and Eliza Hall Institute for Medical Research, Francis Haley Research Fellow, 1946-48; University of Melbourne, Francis Haley Research fellow, 1946-48; Australian National University, John Curtin School of Medical Research, professor of microbiology, 1949-67, university fellow, 1980-82, John Curtin School of Medical Research, director, 1967-73, visiting fellow, 1983-2010, emeritus professor; Australian Academy of Science, fellow, 1954; Royal Australasian College of Physicians, fellow, 1959; Royal College of Physicians, fellow, 1967; Centre for Resource and Environmental Studies, director, 1973-79, visiting fellow, 1980-2010. Writer. **Publications:** (With F.M. Burnet) The Production of Antibodies, 1949; (with F.N. Ratcliffe) Myxomatosis, 1965; Biology of Animal Viruses, 1968; Medical Virology, 1970, 4th ed., 1994; Your Pet's Complete Record Book, 1977; (co-author) Tofu-miso High Efficiency Diet, 1981; How to Be Your Cat's Best Friend, 1981; (with W.J. Kay) The Complete Book of Dog Health, 1985; (with W.J. Kay) The Complete Book of Cat Health, 1985; (with G. Hamilton) How to Help Your Puppy Grow Up to Be a Wonderful Dog, 1987; Sir Macfarlane Burnet, Scientist and Thinker, 1988; The Basic Bird Book, 1989; The Basic Book of Fish Keeping, 1991; (with B. Dibra) Dog Training by Bash: The Tried and True Techniques of the Dog Trainer to the Stars, 1991; Rabbits and Other Furry Pets, 1992; (with B. Dibra) Teach Your Dog to Behave: Simple Solutions to Over 300 Common Dog Behavior Problems from A to Z, 1993; (ed.) PDR Nurse's Dictionary,

1994; (ed.) A Community Response: Words Are the Bugles of Social Change, 1995; (ed.) First Forty Years, 1995; The Veterinarians' Guide to Your Cat's Symptoms, 1999; (with B. Fantini) Biological Control of Vertebrate Pests: The History of Myxomatosis: An Experiment in Evolution, 1999; The Veterinarians' Guide to Your Dog's Symptoms, 1999; (with B. Dibra) Cat Speak: How to Learn It, Speak It and Use It to Have a Happy, Healthy, Well-Mannered Cat, 2001; (co-author) Your Dream Dog: A Guide to Choosing the Right Breed for You, 2003; Nature, Nurture and Chance: The Lives of Frank And Charles Fenner, 2006. Contributor to magazines. *Died 2010.*

FERMOR, Patrick (Michael) Leigh. Greek/British (born England), b. 1915. **Genres:** Novels, Travel/Exploration, Translations, Autobiography/Memoirs, Literary Criticism And History, Reference. **Career:** British Institute, deputy director, 1947-48. Writer. **Publications:** Forever Ulysses, 1938; The Traveller's Tree: A Journey Through the Caribbean Islands, 1950; A Time to Keep Silence, 1953; The Violins of Saint-Jacques: A Tale of Antilles, 1954; Mani: Travels in the Southern Peloponnese, 1958; Ghika: Paintings, Drawings, Sculpture, 1964; Roumeli: Travels in Northern Greece, 1966; A Time of Gifts: On Foot to Constantinople: From the Hook of Holland to the Middle Danube, 1977; (foreword) Albanian Assignment, 1985; Between the Woods and the Water: On Foot to Constantinople from the Hook of Holland: The Middle Danube to the Iron Gates, 1986; Three Letters From the Andes, 1992; Vanishing Greece, 1995; (intro.) Greece 1940-41 Eyewitnessed, 1997; Words of Mercury, 2003; Giōrgos Sepheres, P.L. Fermor, and J. Rayner, 2007; In Tearing Haste: Letters Between Deborah Devonshire and Patrick Leigh Fermor, 2008. TRANSLATOR: Colette, Chance Acquaintances, 1952; G. Psychoundakis, The Cretan Runner, 1955; Colette, Gigi: Julie de Carneilhan: Chance Acquaintances, 2001. Contributor to periodicals. *Died 2011.*

FINN, R(alph) L(eslie). British (born England), b. 1912?. **Genres:** Novels, Sports/Fitness, Autobiography/Memoirs, Novellas/Short Stories. **Career:** Reynolds News, feature writer, 1937-40; People, feature writer, 1941-47; Birmingham Daily Mail, feature writer, 1953-55; creative director in advertising agencies, 1955-70; tutor in English. Freelance advertising and publicity consultant. **Publications:** Out of the Depths, 1943; Twenty Seven Stairs, 1949; Time Marches Sideways, 1950; Captive on the Flying Saucers: The Lunatic Lover and Poet, 1951; My Greatest Game, 1952; Spurs Supreme, 1961; No Tears in Aldgate, 1963; Spurs Go Marching On, 1963; Champions Again: Manchester United, 1965; England, World Champions, 1966, 1966; London's Cup Final 1967: How Chelsea and Spurs Reached Wembley, 1967; Spring in Aldgate, 1968; History of Chelsea Football Club, 1969; Arsenal: Chapman to Mee, 1969; World Cup, 1970, 1970; Spurs Again: The Story of the League Cup Season 1970-71, 1971; Tottenham Hotspur F.C.: The Official History, 1972; Time Remembered, Grief Forgotten, 1985; Down Oxford Street; He Said, What's Blue?; The Peephole; After the Sickness; And the Ants Came; Freaks v. Supermen; Waiting Room; And All Is Mist; Return to Earth; I Sent You Red Roses; Death of a Dream; Bleu; World Cup 1954. Contributor to magazines and newspapers. *Died 1999.*

FORD, Hilary. *See* **YOUD, Samuel.**

FREUND, Diane. American (born United States), b. 1944?. **Genres:** Novels, Young Adult Fiction. **Career:** University of Arizona South, Department of English, assistant professor, associate professor. Writer. **Publications:** Four Corners: A Novel, 2001; Special Mercy, 2009. *Died 2010.*

GLASS, Dee Dee. British/American (born United States), b. 1948. **Genres:** Human Relations/Parenting, Women's Studies And Issues. **Career:** Granada Television, researcher and script editor, 1976-78; Southern Television, producer and director, 1978-81; Reality Productions, producer and director, 1981-82; Glass Pictures, producer and director of documentary films, 1982-2004; Channel 4 News, producer, 1991. Writer. **Publications:** All My Fault: Why Women Don't Leave Abusive Men, 1995. Contributor to periodicals. *Died 2004.*

HALL, J(ohn) C(live). British (born England), b. 1920. **Genres:** Poetry, Literary Criticism And History, Biography. **Career:** John Lehmann Ltd., general manager, 1946-52; Michael Joseph Ltd., publicity manager, 1953-55; Encounter, business and advertising manager and reader, 1955-. Writer. **Publications:** (With K. Douglas and N. Nicholson) Selected Poems, 1943; The Summer Dance and Other Poems, 1951; (ed. with P. Dickinson and E. Marx) New Poems 1955, 1955; Edwin Muir, 1956; (ed. with W. Muir) Collected Poems of Edwin Muir, 1921-1958, 1960; The Burning Hare, 1966; (ed.

with G.S. Fraser and J. Waller) The Collected Poems of Keith Douglas, rev. ed., 1966; A House of Voices, 1973; Selected and New Poems 1939-84, 1985; Long Shadows: Poems 1938-2002, 2003. *Died 2001.*

HAMPSON, Norman. British (born England), b. 1922. **Genres:** History, Biography. **Career:** University of Manchester, lecturer, 1948-62, senior lecturer in French history, 1962-67; University of Newcastle upon Tyne, professor of modern history, 1967-74; University of York, professor of history, 1974-89, professor emeritus. Writer. **Publications:** La Marine de l'an II: Mobilisation de la flotte de l'Ocen, 1793-1794, 1959; A Social History of the French Revolution, 1963; A Cultural History of the Enlightenment, 1968 as Pelican History of European Thought, vol. IV: The Enlightenment, 1968; History As an Art: An Inaugural Lecture Delivered Before the University of Newcastle Upon Tyne on Monday 19 February 1968, 1968; The First European Revolution, 1776-1815, 1969; Siécle des Lumiéres, 1972; The Life and Opinions of Maxmillien Robespierre, 1974; French Revolution: A Concise History, 1975; The Enlightenment, 1976; Danton, 1978, rev. ed., 1988; The Terror in the French Revolution, 1981; Will & Circumstance: Montesquieu, Rousseau and the French Revolution, 1983; Prelude to Terror: The Constituent Assembly and the Failure of Consensus, 1789-1791, 1988; Saint-Just, 1991; The Perfidy of Albion: French Perceptions of England During the French Revolution, 1998; Not Really What You'd Call a War, 2001; (contrib.) Enlightenment and Revolution: Essays in Honour of Norman Hampson, 2004. Contributor to books, periodicals and journals. *Died 2011.*

HARRISON, Elizabeth Fancourt. British (born England), b. 1921. **Genres:** Romance/Historical. **Career:** Romantic Novelists' Association, chairman, 1977-79. Writer. **Publications:** Coffee at Dobree's, 1965; The Physicians, 1966; The Ravelston Affair, 1967; Corridors of Healing, 1968; Emergency Call, 1970; Accident Call, 1971; Ambulance Call, 1972; Surgeon's Call, 1973; On Call, 1974; Hospital Call, 1975; Dangerous Call, 1976; Love, Honour and Dismay, 1976; To Mend a Heart, 1977; Young Doctor Goddard, 1978; A Doctor Called Caroline, 1979; A Surgeon Called Amanda, 1982; A Surgeon's Life, 1983; Marrying a Doctor, 1984; Surgeon's Affair, 1985; A Surgeon at St. Marks, 1986; The Surgeon She Married, 1988; High Street Canada, 1990; The Faithful Type, 1993; The Senior Partner's Daughter, 1994; Made for Each Other, 1995. *Died 2008.*

HEADY, Harold F(ranklin). American (born United States), b. 1916. **Genres:** Environmental Sciences/Ecology, Natural History. **Career:** Montana State University, assistant professor, 1942-47; Texas University, associate professor, 1947-51; University of California, College of Natural Resources, associate dean, 1974-77, Agricultural Experiment Station, associate director, 1977-80, assistant vice-president and professor emeritus of range management and plant ecology; Widland Resources Center, staff, 1980-81; University of Idaho, Alumni Association, scientist. Writer. **Publications:** (With R.P. Gibbens) The Influence of Modern Man on the Vegetation of Yosemite Valley, 1964; Practices in Range Forage Production, 1967; (contrib.) Coat of the Earth: The Story of Grass, 1968; (ed. with W.M. Longhurst) Report of a Symposium on East African Range Problems, 1969; (with E.B. Heady) High Meadow: The Ecology of a Mountain Meadow, 1970; Rangeland Management, 1975; (with P.J. Zinke) Vegetational Changes in Yosemite Valley, 1979; (with E.B. Heady) Range and Wildlife Management in the Tropics, 1982; Rangeland Ecology and Management, 1994, rev. ed., 2001. *Died 2011.*

HEIDE, Florence Parry. Also writes as Jamie McDonald, Alex B. Allen. American (born United States), b. 1919. **Genres:** Children's Fiction, Novels, Animals/Pets. **Career:** Radio-Keith-Orpheum, staff; Pittsburgh Playhouse, public relations director. Writer. **Publications:** Benjamin Budge and Barnaby Ball, 1967; (with S.W. Van Clief) Maximilian, 1967; (with S.W. Van Clief) The Day It Snowed in Summer, 1968; (with S.W. Van Clief) How Big Am I?, 1968; (with S.W. Van Clief) It Never is Dark, 1968; (with S.W. Van Clief) Sebastian, 1968; (with S.W. Van Clief) That's What Friends Are For, 1968; (as Jamie McDonald with A. Thiess and W. Thiess) Hannibal, 1968; Maximilian Becomes Famous, 1969; (with S.W. Van Clief) The New Neighbor, 1970; Alphabet Zoop, 1970; Giants Are Very Brave People, 1970; The Little One, 1970; Sound of Sunshine, Sound of Rain, 1970; Look! Look! A Story Book, 1971; The Key, 1971; The Shrinking of Treehorn, 1971; Some Things Are Scary, 1971; Who Needs Me?, 1971; My Castle, 1972; (with S.W. Van Clief) The Mystery of the Missing Suitcase, 1972; (with S.W. Van Clief) The Mystery of the Silver Tag, 1972; (as Alex B. Allen with S.W. Van Clief) Basketball Toss Up, 1972; (as Alex B. Allen with S.W. Van Clief) No Place for Baseball, 1973; (with S.W. Van Clief) The Hidden Box Mystery, 1973; (with S.W. Van

Clief) Mystery at MacAdoo Zoo, 1973; (with R. Heide) Lost! (textbook), 1973; (with R. Heide) I See America Smiling (textbook), 1973; (with S.W. Van Clief) Mystery of the Whispering Voice, 1974; (with R. Heide) Mystery of the Melting Snowman, 1974; (with D.F. Parry) No Roads for the Wind (textbook), 1974; (with S.W. Van Clief) Who Can? (reader), 1974; (with S.W. Van Clief) Lost and Found (reader), 1974; (with S.W. Van Clief) Hats and Bears (reader), 1974; (with R. Heide) Tell about Someone You Love (textbook), 1974; (as Alex B. Allen with S.W. Van Clief) Danger on Broken Arrow Trail, 1974; (as Alex B. Allen with S.W. Van Clief) Fifth Down, 1974; (as Alex B. Allen with S.W. Van Clief and D. Heide) The Tennis Menace, 1975; God and Me (non-fiction), 1975; You and Me (non-fiction), 1975; (with R. Heide) Mystery of the Vanishing Visitor, 1975; (with R. Heide) Mystery of the Bewitched Bookmobile, 1975; When the Sad One Comes to Stay, 1975; Growing Anyway Up, 1976; (with R. Heide) Mystery of the Lonely Lantern, 1976; (with R. Heide) Mystery at Keyhole Carnival, 1977; (with R. Heide) Brillstone Break-In, 1977; (with R. Heide) Mystery of the Midnight Message, 1977; (with S.W. Van Clief) Fables You Shouldn't Pay Any Attention To, 1978; Banana Twist, 1978; Secret Dreamer, Secret Dreams, 1978; (with R. Heide) Fear at Brillstone, 1978; (with R. Heide) Mystery at Southport Cinema, 1978; (with R. Heide) I Love Every-People, 1978; Changes (non-fiction), 1978; Who Taught Me? Was It You, God? (non-fiction), 1978; By the Time You Count to Ten (non-fiction), 1979; (with R. Heide) Face at the Brillstone Window, 1979; (with R. Heide) Mystery of the Mummy's Mask, 1979; (with R. Heide) Body in the Brillstone Garage, 1980; (with R. Heide) Mystery of the Forgotten Island, 1980; (with R. Heide) A Monster Is Coming! A Monster Is Coming!, 1980; (with R. Heide) Black Magic at Brillstone, 1981; Treehorn's Treasure, 1981; Time's Up!, 1982; The Problem with Pulcifer, 1982; The Wendy Puzzle, 1982; (with R. Heide) Time Bomb at Brillstone, 1982; (with R. Heide) Mystery On Danger Road, 1983; Banana Blitz, 1983; Treehorn's Wish, 1984; Time Flies, 1984; Tales for the Perfect Child, 1985; (with J.H. Gilliland) The Day of Ahmed's Secret, 1990; (with J.H. Gilliland) Sami and the Time of the Troubles, 1992; Grim and Ghastly Goings-on (songs), 1992; Treehorn Times Three, 1992; The Bigness Contest, 1993; (with R. Heide Pierce) Timothy Twinge, 1993; (with R.H. Pierce) Oh, Grow Up: Poems to Help You Survive Parents, Chores, School and Other Afflictions, 1996; (with R.H. Pierce) Tio Armando, 1998; (with J.H. Gilliland) The House of Wisdom, 1999; (with J.H. Gilliland and R.H. Pierce) It's about Time: Poems, 1999; Some Things Are Scary, 2000; Treehorn Trilogy, 2006; A Promise is a Promise, 2007; Princess Hyacinth: (The Surprising Tale of a Girl Who Floated), 2009; One and Only Marigold, 2009; (with R.H. Pierce, D.F. Parry and J.M. Parry) Dillweed's Revenge, 2010; (with R. Heide) Always Listen to Your Mother, 2010. *Died 2011.*

HOBAN, Russell. British/American (born United States), b. 1925. **Genres:** Novels, Science Fiction/Fantasy, Children's Fiction, Songs/Lyrics And Libretti, Picture/Board Books, inspirational/Motivational Literature, Young Adult Fiction. **Career:** Fletcher Smith Film Studio, story board artist and character designer, 1951; Batten, Barton, Durstine & Osborn Inc., television art director, 1952-57; J. Walter Thompson Co., television art director, 1956; Time, freelance illustrator, 1957-65; Life, freelance illustrator, 1957-65; Fortune, freelance illustrator, 1957-65; Saturday Evening Post, freelance illustrator, 1957-65; True, freelance illustrator, 1957-65; Doyle, Dane, Bembach, copywriter, 1965-67; Famous Artists Schools, art instructor; School of Visual Arts, art instructor. Writer. **Publications:** What Does It Do and How Does It Work?, 1959; The Atomic Submarine, 1960; Bedtime for Frances, 1960; Herman the Loser, 1961; London Men and English Men, 1963; The Song in My Drum, 1963; Some Snow Said Hello, 1963; The Sorely Trying Day, 1964; A Baby Sister for Frances, 1964; Nothing to Do, 1964; Bread and Jam for Frances, 1964; Tom and the Two Handles, 1965; The Story of Hester Mouse, 1965; What Happened When Jack and Daisy Tried to Fool the Tooth Fairies, 1966; Goodnight, 1966; Henry and the Monstrous Din, 1966; The Little Brute Family, 1967; Save My Place, 1967; Charlie the Tramp, 1967; The Mouse and His Child, 1967; Birthday for Frances, 1968; The Pedaling Man and Other Poems, 1968; The Stone Doll of Sister Brute, 1968; Emmet Otters Jug Band Christmas, 1969; Harvey's Hideout, 1969; The Sea-thing Child, 1972, 2nd ed., 1999; Lion of Boaz-Jachin and Jachin-Boaz, 1973; Ten What?, 1974; How Tom Beat Captain Najork and His Hired Sportsmen, 1974; Kleinzeit (adult novel), 1974; Turtle Diary (adult novel), 1975; Dinner at Alberta's, 1975; A Near Thing for Captain Najork, 1975; (with S. Selig) Crocodile and Pierrot, 1975; The Dancing Tigers, 1978; Arthur's New Power, 1978; The Twenty-Elephant Restaurant, 1978; (with N. Bayley) La Corona and the Tin Frog, 1979; Riddley Walker (adult novel), 1980; Flat Cat, 1980; Ace Dragon Ltd., 1980; The Serpent Tower, 1981; (with L. Hoban) Arthur's Funny

Money, 1981; The Great Fruit Gum Robbery, 1981; They Came from Aargh!, 1981; The Battle of Zormla, 1982; The Flight of Bembel Rudzuk, 1982; Big John Turkle, 1983; Jim Frog, 1983; Pilgermann (adult novel), 1983; Ponders, 4 vols., 1983-84; Lavinia Bat, 1984; Charlie Meadows, 1984; The Rain Door, 1986; The Marzipan Pig, 1986; The Medusa Frequency (adult novel), 1987; Monsters, 1989; Jim Hedgehog's Supernatural Christmas, 1989; Jim Hedgehog and the Lonesome Tower, 1992; Emmet Otter's Jug Band Christmas, 1992; The Moment under the Moment (adult novel), 1992; A Bargain for Frances, 1992; I Thought I'd Take My Rat to School: Poems from September to June, 1993; M.O.L.E.: Much Overworked Little Earthmover, 1993; Egg Thoughts and Other Frances Songs, 1994; The Court of the Winged Serpent, 1994; Best Friends for Frances, 1994; Monster Film, 1995; Fremder, 1996; The Trokeville Way, 1996; The Last of the Wallendas: And Other Poems, 1997; Posterille Way, 1998; Mr Rinyo-Clacton's Offer, 1998; Trouble on Thunder Mountain, 1999; Angelica's Grotto (novel), 1999; Silly Sam, 2000; Jim's Lion, 2001; Amaryllis Night and Day, 2001; The Bat Tattoo, 2002; Her Name Was Lola, 2004; Come Dance with Me, 2005; Linger Awhile, 2006; My Tango with Barbara Strozzi, 2007; Angelica Lost and Found, 2010; Frances 50th Anniversary Collection, 2010. Contributor of articles to periodicals. *Died 2011.*

HOLBROOK, David (Kenneth). British (born England), b. 1923. **Genres:** Novels, Poetry, Songs/Lyrics And Libretti, Education, Literary Criticism And History, Philosophy, Art/Art History. **Career:** Our Time Magazine, assistant editor, 1947-48; Bureau of Current Affairs, assistant editor, 1948-51; Workers' Educational Association, tutor, 1951-54; Cambridgeshire Village College, tutor, 1954-61; Cambridge University, King's College, fellow, 1961-65, Senior Leverhulme Research Fellow, 1965, Leverhulme Emeritus Research Fellow, 1988-90, Jesus College, college lecturer in English, 1968-70, Downing College, fellow and director of English studies, 1981-88, emeritus fellow, 1989-2011; National Defense Education Act, English Programs in United States, consultant, 1966; University of Hull, Compton Poetry lecturer, 1969; Dartington Hall, Elmgrant Trust Grant, writer-in-residence, 1970-72; MacMaster University, Hooker distinguished visiting professor, 1984; Forum for the Advancement of Educational Therapy, president; Use of English Magazine, co-founder. **Publications:** The Borderline, 1959; English for Maturity, 1961, 2nd ed., 1967; Llareggub Revisited: Dylan Thomas and the State of Modern Poetry, 1962 as Dylan Thomas and Poetic Dissociation, 1964; Lights in the Sky Country, 1962; (co-author) Penguin Modern Poets, 4, 1963; The Secret Places, 1964; English in the C.S.E., 1964; English for the Rejected, 1964; The Quest for Love, 1964; The Quarry, An Opera For Young Players, 1966; The Flowers Shake Themselves Free, 1966; The Exploring Word: Creative Disciplines in the Education of Teachers of English, 1967; Children's Writing, 1967; Mr. Weston's Good Wine, 1967; (comp.) Plucking the Rushes, 1968; Human Hope and the Death Instinct: An Exploration of Psychoanalytical Theories of Human Nature and their Implications for Culture and Education, 1971; The Masks of Hate: The Problem of False Solutions in the Culture of an Acquisitive Society, 1972; Sex and Dehumanisation in Art, Thought and Life in Our Time, 1972; Dylan Thomas and the Code of Night, 1972; The Pseudo-Revolution: A Critical Study of Extremist Liberation in Sex, 1972; English in Australia Now, 1973; (co-author) Changing Attitudes to the Nature of Man, 1973; Gustav Mahler and the Courage to Be, 1975; Sylvia Plath: Poetry and Existence, 1976; (co-author) The Apple Tree, 1976; Lost Bearings in English Poetry, 1977; Education, Nihilism and Survival, 1977; English for Meaning, 1980; John Newton, Blasphemy, and Poetic Taste, 1984; Evolution and the Humanities, 1987; The Novel and Authenticity, 1987; Education and Philosophical Anthropology: Toward a New View of Man for the Humanities and English, 1987; Further Studies in Philosophical Anthropology, 1988; Images of Woman in Literature, 1989; Edith Wharton and the Unsatisfactory Man, 1991; The Skeleton in the Wardrobe: The Fantasies of C.S. Lewis, 1991; Where D.H. Lawrence Was Wrong about Woman, 1992; Charles Dickens and the Image of Woman, 1993; Creativity and Popular Culture, 1994; Tolstoy, Woman and Death: A Study of War and Peace and Anna Karenina, 1997; Wuthering Heights: A Drama of Being, 1997; Sex & Dehumanization, 1998; Bringing Everything Home (poems), 1999; George MacDonald and the Phantom Woman, 2000; A Study of George MacDonald and the Image of Woman, 2000; Nonsense Against Sorrow: Lewis Carroll's Alice Books, 2001; Education, Nihilism and Survival, 2002. NOVELS: Flesh Wounds, 1966; A Play of Passion, 1978; Nothing Larger Than Life, 1987; Worlds Apart, 1988; A Little Athens, 1990; Jennifer, 1991; The Gold in Father's Heart, 1992; Even If They Fail, 1993; Getting It Wrong with Uncle Tom, 1998; Going off the Rails, 2003. EDITOR: Children's Games, 1957; Iron Honey Gold, 1961; People and Diamonds, 1962; (comp.) Thieves and Angels: Dramatic Pieces for Use in

Schools, 1963; Visions of Life, 1964; Oliver Twist, 1965; Childhood, 1965; I've Got to Use Words, 1966; (with E. Poston) The Cambridge Hymnal, 1968; The Case Against Pornography, 1972; What Is It to Be Human?, 1990. POETRY: Imaginings, 1961; Get Your Hair Cut, 1962; Something to Sing About, 1962; Against the Cruel Frost, 1963; Object Relations, 1967; Old World, New World, 1969; Chance of a Lifetime, 1978; Moments in Italy: Poems and Sketches, 1978; Selected Poems, 1961-1978, 1980. CONTRIBUTOR: Discrimination and Popular Culture, 1965; Understanding Poetry, 1966; The World of the Child, 1966. Contributor to books, journals and newspapers. *Died 2011.*

INGHAM, Kenneth. British (born England), b. 1921. **Genres:** History. **Career:** Makerere University, lecturer, 1950-56, professor of history, 1956-62; Royal Military Academy, director of studies, 1962-67; University of Bristol, professor, 1967-86, emeritus professor of history, 1986-2010, Royal African Society, director. Writer. **Publications:** Europe and Africa: A School Certificate History, 1953; Reformers in India: 1793-1833: An Account of the Work of Christian Missionaries on Behalf of Social Reform, 1956; The Making of Modern Uganda, 1958; A History of East Africa, 1962, rev. ed., 1965; (ed.) Foreign Relations of African States: Proceedings of the Twenty-fifth Symposium of the Colston Research Society, 1974; The Kingdom of Toro in Uganda, 1975; Jan Christian Smuts: The Conscience of a South African, 1986; Politics in Modern Africa: The Uneven Tribal Dimension, 1990; Milton Obote, 1994; Obote: A Political Biography, 1994. Contributor to journals and periodicals. *Died 2010.*

JACKMAN, Sydney Wayne. Canadian/American (born United States), b. 1925. **Genres:** History, Politics/Government, Travel/Exploration, Biography. **Career:** Harvard University, tutor, 1949-52; Phillips Exeter Academy, instructor in history, 1952-56; Bates College, assistant professor, 1956-62, associate professor, 1962-64; University of Victoria, Department of history, associate professor, 1964-65, professor, 1965-91, acting head, 1971-72, director of liberal studies, 1975-78, Department of Creative Writing, acting chairman, 1976-77, Department of Slavonic Studies, acting chairman, professor emeritus, 1991-2011; University of Michigan, visiting professor, 1965; University of Tasmania, visiting professor, 1972; Australian National University, visiting fellow, 1975. Writer. **Publications:** Galloping Head, 1958; March to Saratoga, 1963; Man of Mercury: An Appreciation of the Mind of Henry St. John, Viscount Bolingbroke, 1965; Portraits of the Premiers: An Informal History of British Columbia, 1969; The Men at Cary Castle: A Series of Portrait Sketches of the Lieutenant-Governors of British Columbia from 1871 to 1971, 1972; Vancouver Island, 1972; Tasmania, 1974; Nicholas Cardinal Wiseman: A Victorian Prelate and His Writings, 1977; Slave to Duty: A Portrait Sketch of Sir George Arthur, Bart, PC, KCH, 1979; A People's Princess: A Portrait of H.R.H. Princess Mary, Duchess of Teck, 1984; (with H.S. Haase) Vreemdelinge in Den Haag, 1984; Romerov Relatie, 1987; Deviating Voices: Women and Orthodox Religious Tradition, 2003. EDITOR: (intro.) A Diary in America, with Remarks on Its Institutions, 1962; With Burgoyne from Quebec, 1963; The English Reform Tradition, 1790-1910, 1965; (intro.) The Idea of a Patriot King, 1965; (with R.R. Jeffels) Joseph Badenoch Clearihue, 1967; (with J.F. Freeman) American Voyageur: The Journal of David Bates Douglass, 1969; Romanov Relations: The Private Correspondence of Tsars Alexander I, Nicholas I and the Grand Dukes Constantine and Michael with Their Sister Queen Anna Pavlovna, 1817-1855, 1969; A Middle Passage, 1970; (intro.) The Journal of William Sturgis, 1978; Acton in America: The American Journal of Sir John Acton, 1853, 1979; (intro.) A Curious Cage, 1981; At Sea and By Land: The Reminiscences of William Balfour Macdonald, 1984; (with H. Haasse) Stranger in The Hague: The Letters of Queen Sophie of the Netherlands to Lady Malet, 1842-1877, 1989; (intro.) Chère Annette: Letters from St. Petersburg, 1820-1828: The Correspondence of the Empress Maria Feodorovna to Her Daughter the Grand Duchess Anna Pavlovna, the Princess of Orange, 1994; (intro.) Curious Cage: Life in a Japanese Internment Camp, 1943-1945, 2002. *Died 2011.*

KEYSERLINGK, Robert H. Canadian/German (born Germany), b. 1933. **Genres:** History, Young Adult Fiction. **Career:** Canadian Foreign Service, Germany and United Kingdom service officer, 1957-61; University of Ottawa, instructor, 1963-64, assistant professor, 1964-67, associate professor, 1968-87, professor of history, 1987, retired. Writer. **Publications:** Media Manipulation: The Press and Bismark in Imperial Germany, 1977; Austria in World War II: An Anglo-American Dilemma, 1988; (ed.) Breaking Ground: The 1956 Hungarian Refugee Movement to Canada, 1993. *Died 2009.*

KLEIN, Philip Alexander. American (born United States), b. 1927. **Genres:** Economics, Business/Trade/Industry, Money/Finance, Essays. **Career:** Carleton College, instructor, 1955; National Bureau of Economic Research, research staff, 1955-70, 1973-78; San Francisco State College (now University), visiting professor, 1962; Pennsylvania State University, instructor, 1955-58, assistant professor, 1958-61, associate professor, 1961-68, professor of economics, 1968-2000, professor emeritus of economics, 2000-11; University of London, London School of Economics, academic visitor, 1973-74; Columbia University, Center for International Business Cycle Research, research associate, 1978-96. Writer. **Publications:** Financial Adjustments to Unemployment, 1965; (with G.H. Moore) The Quality of Consumer Installment Credit, 1967; Pennsylvania Market Region, 1969; Statistics of the Pennsylvania Supply Region: 1963 Manufactures Census of Component Sources for Pennsylvania Industries, 1970; (with R.L. Gordon) The Steel Industry and U.S. Business Cycles, 1971; The Cyclical Timing of Consumer Credit, 1920-1967, 1971; (with R.L. Gordon) Impact of The Cyclical Activity in the Steel Industry, 1971; The Management of Market-Oriented Economics: A Comparative Perspective, 1973; Business Cycles in the Postwar World: Some Reflections on Recent Research, 1976; (with G.H. Moore) Monitoring Growth Cycles in Market-Oriented Countries: Developing and Using International Economic Indicators, 1985; (ed.) Analyzing Modern Business Cycles: Essays Honoring Geoffrey H. Moore, 1989, rev. ed., 2002; (with M.P. Niemira) Forecasting Financial and Economic Cycles, 1994; (ed.) The Role of Economic Theory, 1994; Beyond Dissent: Essays in Institutional Economics, 1994; Economics Confronts the Economy, 2005. *Died 2011.*

KLIMAN, Bernice W. American (born United States), b. 1933. **Genres:** Literary Criticism And History. **Career:** Long Island University, C.W. Post Campus, instructor, 1964, 1967-68; State University of New York, instructor, 1964-66, Nassau Community College, professor of English, 1976-99, professor emeritus, 1999-2011; City University of New York, Queens College, instructor, 1969-73, Bernard M. Baruch College, assistant professor, 1974-75; Yale University, Davenport College, visiting fellow, 1975, 1977, 1979; Massachusetts Institute of Technology, Shakespeare Interactive Research Group, consultant. Writer. **Publications:** Shakespeare on film newsletter, 1976; (contrib.) Shakespeare and the Arts: A Collection Essays from the Ohio Shakespeare Conference, 1981, 1982; Hamlet: Film, Television, and Audio Performance, 1988; (contrib.) Shakespeare on Television An Anthology of Essays and Reviews, 1988; (ed. with P. Bertram) The Three-Text Hamlet: Parallel Texts of the First and Second Quartos and First Folio, 1991, 2nd ed., 2003; Macbeth, 1992, 2nd ed., 2004; (contrib.) Screen Shakespeare, 1994; (contrib.) Reading Readings: Essays on Shakespeare Editing in the Eighteenth Century, 1998; (ed.) Approaches to Teaching Shakespeare's Hamlet, 2001; (ed.) Enfolded Hamlets, 2004; (ed. with R.J. Santos) Latin American Shakespeares, 2005; (ed. with J.H. Lake) Tragedy of Hamlet, Prince of Denmark, 2008; (ed. with L. Magnus and J.H. Lake) Tragedy of Romeo and Juliet, 2008; (ed. with L. Magnus and J.H. Lake) Measure for Measure, 2012. Contributor of articles to periodicals. Works appear in anthologies. *Died 2011.*

LANGMEAD, Donald. Australian (born Australia), b. 1939. **Genres:** Architecture. **Career:** University of Adelaide, South Australia Institute of Technology, lecturer, 1967-76, senior lecturer in architectural history, 1976-89, acting head of interior design, 1976-80; Group for Conservation and History of Australian Architecture, co-director, 1988-2011; Heritage Unit, registered consultant; Australian Architecture Archive and History Research Group, co-director; National Trust of South Australia, architectural history consultant; University of South Australia, principal lecturer, 1990-94, Louis Laybourne Smith School of Architecture, head, 1992-96, associate dean of research, 1998; associate professor, 1995-98, professor of architecture, 1998-2002, Louis Laybourne Smith School of Architecture and Design, professor of architectural history, 1999, adjunct professor of architectural history, 2002-11; public speaker on architecture and architectural history; architectural history consultant. Writer. **Publications:** (With J.R. Schenk) Guide to the Architecture of Adelaide, 1982; (with D.L. Johnson) The Adelaide City Plan: Fiction and Fact, 1986; English Language Sources on Dutch Modern Architecture, 1900-1940: Journal Articles Not by Dutch Authors, 1986; English Language Sources on Dutch Modern Architecture, 1900-1940: Monographs Not by Dutch Authors, 1986; Dutch Modern Architecture, 1900-1940: Perceptions of Dutch Architects, Writers and Editors, 1987; Accidental Architect, 1994; Willem Marinus Dudok: A Dutch Modernist: A Bio-Bibliography, 1996; Dutch Modernism: Architectural Resources in the English Language, 1996; (with Johnson) Makers of 20th Century Modern Architecture, 1997; J.J.P. Oud and the International Style: A Bio-Bibliography, 1999; (with D.L. Johnson) Ar-

chitectural Excursions: Frank Lloyd Wright, Holland, and Europe, 2000; The Artists of De Stijl: A Guide to the Literature, 2000; (with C. Garnaut) Encyclopedia of Architectural and Engineering Feats, 2001; Frank Lloyd Wright: A Bio-Bibliography, 2003; Icons of American Architecture: From the Alamo to the World Trade Center, 2009. Contributor to periodicals. *Died 2011.*

LLOBERA, Josep R. British/Cuban (born Cuba), b. 1939?. **Genres:** Anthropology/Ethnology, Novels. **Career:** University of London, Goldsmiths' College, visiting professor of anthropology, 1996-2010; Universitat Pompeu Fabra, visiting professor of anthropology, 1996-2010. Writer. **Publications:** Las sociedades primitives (title means: 'Primitive Societies'), 1974; (ed. with A.M. Bailey) The Asiatic Mode of Production: Science and Politics, 1981; (ed. with J.S. Kahn) The Anthropology of Pre-capitalist Societies, 1981; Caminos discordantes: Centralidad y marginalidad en la historia de las ciencias sociales, 1989; La identidad de la antropología, 1990; (ed., contrib., trans. and intro.) Family, Class and Nation in Catalonia, 1991; (ed. with V.A. Goddard and C. Shore) The Anthropology of Europe: Identity and Boundaries in Conflict, 1994; The God of Modernity: The Development of Nationalism in Western Europe, 1994; (co-author) Culturas, estados, ciudadanos: Una aproximación al multiculturalismo en Europa, 1995; Foundations of National Identity: From Catalonia to Europe, 2003; An Invitation to Anthropology: The Structure, Evolution and Cultural Identity of Human Societies, 2003; The Making of Totalitarian Thought, 2003; Reminiscences of a Distant Past (novel), 2006. Contributor of articles to books. *Died 2010.*

MACDONALD, Norman Malcolm. Scottish/Canadian (born Canada), b. 1927. **Genres:** Poetry, Novels, Adult Non-fiction, Plays/Screenplays. **Career:** New Zealand Air Force, affiliate, 1949-57; journalist, 1958-70; freelance writer, 1971-77; Gaelic Theatre, administrator, 1978-81; Gaelic College, writer-in-residence, 1982-83, 1986-87; Gaelic Arts Project, writer-in-residence, 1988-89. **Publications:** Calum Tod (novel), 1976; Iolaire Disaster (nonfiction), 1978; Call nah-Iolaire, 1978; Fad (poems), 1979; The Shutter Falls (play), 1983; The Brahan Seer (play), 1986; Clann-nighean an Sgadain, 1987; An Sgàineadh (novel), 1993; The Teuchter's Tale (play), 1994; Portrona (play), 1996; Beul nam Breug/Mouth of Lies (play), 1998. *Died 1998.*

MARSHALL, John. British (born England), b. 1922. **Genres:** Transportation, Biography, Law. **Career:** University of Manchester, Department Extra-Mural, lecturer in railway history, 1970-80. Writer. **Publications:** The Lancashire and Yorkshire Railway, 1969, rev. ed. as Railway History in Pictures: Lancashire and Yorkshire Railway, 1977; The Guinness Book of Railway Facts and Feats, 1971, 6th ed., (with R. Balkwill), 1993; Metre Gauge Railways in South and East Switzerland, 1974; Rail Facts and Feats, 1974; Biographical Dictionary of Railway Engineers, 1978, 2nd ed., 2003; Forgotten Railways: Northwest England, 1981, 2nd ed., 1992; The Cromford and High Peak Railway, 1982, 2nd ed., 1996; Rail: The Records, 1985; Guinness Fact Book: Rail, 1985; Guinness Rail: The Records, 1985; The Guinness Railway Book, 1989; The Severn Valley Railway, 1989; Guinness Railway Fact Book, 1994. *Died 2008.*

MASSINGHAM, Harold (William). British (born England), b. 1932. **Genres:** Poetry. **Career:** School teacher, 1955-70; freelance writer, 1970-2011; University of Manchester, Extra-Mural Department, part-time tutor, 1971-90; Wright Robinson High School, English teacher and head of department, 1974-75. Writer. **Publications:** Black Bull Guarding Apples, 1965; Creation, 1968; The Magician: A Poem Sequence, 1969; Storm: A Poem, 1970; Snow-Dream, 1971; The Pennine Way, 1971; Frost-Gods: Poems, 1971; Doomsday, 1972; The Magician's Chameleon, 1976; Mate in Two (on chess), 1976; Sonatas and Dreams, 1992. Works appear in anthologies. *Died 2011.*

MCCAFFREY, Anne (Inez). British/American (born United States), b. 1926. **Genres:** Novellas/Short Stories, Romance/Historical, Science Fiction/Fantasy, Food And Wine, Young Adult Non-fiction, Novels, Literary Criticism And History, Reference, Reference. **Career:** Liberty Music Shops, copywriter, layout designer, 1947-50; Helena Rubinstein, copywriter, secretary, 1950-52; Fin Film Productions, director, 1979-. **Publications:** NOVELS: Restoree, 1967; Dragonflight, 1969; Decision at Doona, 1969; The Ship Who Sang, 1969; (comp.) Alchemy And Academe: A Collection Of Original Stories Concerning Themselves With Transmutations, Mental And Elemental, Alchemical And Academic, 1970; The Mark of S, 1971; The Ring of Fear, 1971; Dragonquest: Being the Further Adventures of the Dragonriders of Pern, 1971; Demon Kind: Eleven New Stories Of Children With Strange And

Supernatural Powers, 1973; To Ride Pegasus, 1975; The Kilternan Legacy, 1975; Dragonsong, 1976; Dragonsinger, 1977; Dinosaur Planet, 1977; (with J.H. Holly and J.A. Carver) Futurelove: A Science Fiction Triad, 1977; The White Dragon, 1978; Dragondrums, 1979; The Harper Hall of Pern, 1979; Crystal Singer, 1982; The Coelura, 1983; Moreta: Dragonlady of Pern, 1983; Dinosaur Planet Survivors, 1984; The Ireta Adventure, 1984; Stitch in Snow, 1984; The Girl Who Heard Dragons, 1985; Killashandra, 1985; Nerilka's Story: A Pern Adventure, 1986; Habit Is An Old Horse, 1986; The Year of the Lucy, 1986; The Lady, 1987 in UK as The Carradyne Touch, 1988; Dragonfire, 1988; The Dragonriders of Pern, 1988; Dragonsdawn, 1988; The Renegades of Pern, 1989; (with J.L. Nye) The Death of Sleep, 1990; Pegasus in Flight, 1990; The Rowan, 1990; (with E. Moon) Sassinak, 1990; Three Gothic Novels, 1990; All the Weyrs of Pern, 1991; (with E. Moon) Generation Warriors, 1991; Wing of Pegasus, 1991; Damia, 1992; (with J.L. Nye) Crisis on Doona, 1992; Three Women, 1992; Crystal Line, 1992; PartnerShip, 1992; (with M. Ball) The Partnered Ship, 1992; (with M. Lackey) The Ship Who Searched, 1992; Damia's Children, 1993; (with S.M. Stirling) The City Who Fought, 1993; The Chronicles of Pern: First Fall, 1993; The Dolphins' Bell, 1993; (with E. Moon and J.L. Nye) The Planet Pirates, 1993; (with E.A. Scarborough) Powers That Be, 1993; The Dolphins of Pern, 1994; Lyon's Pride, 1994; (with E.A. Scarborough) Power Lines, 1994; (with J.L. Nye) The Ship Who Won, 1994; (with J.L. Nye) Treaty at Doona, 1994; An Exchange of Gifts, 1995; Freedom's Landing, 1995; (with E.A. Scarborough) Power Play, 1995; Black Horses for the King, 1996; No One Noticed the Cat, 1996; Red Star Rising, 1996; The Ship Avenged, 1997; Freedom's Choice, 1997; (with M. Ball) Acorna: The Unicorn Girl, 1997; Dragonseye, 1997; (with R. Woods) A Diversity of Dragons, 1997; Master Harper of Pern, 1998; Freedom's Challenge, 1998; (with M. Ball) Acorna's Quest, 1998; If Wishes Were Horses, 1998; The Tower and the Hive, 1999; (with M. Ball) Acorna's People, 1999; Nimisha's Ship, 1999; Pegasus in Space, 2000; (with E.A. Scarborough) Acorna's World, 2000; (with E.A. Scarborough) Acorna's Search, 2001; The Skies of Pern, 2001; Freedom's Ransom, 2002; Gift of Dragons, 2002; On Dragon Wings, 2003; (with E.A. Scarborough) Acorna's Rebels, 2003; (with T. McCaffrey) Dragon's Kin, 2003; (with J.L. Nye) The Ship Who Saved the Worlds, 2003; (with E.A. Scarborough) Acorna's Triumph, 2004; (with S.M. Stirling) The City and the Ship, 2004; (with J.L. Nye) Doona, 2004; (with E.A. Scarborough) First Warning: Acorna's Children, 2005; (with E.A. Scarborough) Changelings, 2006; (with E.A. Scarborough) Second Wave: Acorna's Children, 2006; (with E.A. Scarborough) Maelstrom, 2006; (with T. McCaffrey) Dragon Harper, 2007; (with E.A. Scarborough) Third Watch: Acorna's Children, 2007; (with E.A. Scarborough) Deluge, 2008; (with E.A. Scarborough) Catalyst: A Tale of the Barque Cats, 2010; (with T. McCaffrey) Dragon's Night, 2010; (with E.A. Scarborough) Catacombs, 2010; (with T. McCaffrey) Dragon's Time, 2011; (with T. McCaffrey) Sky Dragons, 2012. SHORT STORIES: A Time When: Being A Tale Of Young Lord Jaxom, His White Dragon, Ruth, And Various Fire-Lizards, 1975; Get off the Unicorn, 1977; The Worlds of Anne McCaffrey, 1981; Duty Calls, 1988; Rescue Run, 1991. OTHERS: (with R. Wood) The People of Pern, 1988; (with J.L. Nye) The Dragonlover's Guide to Pern, 1989; (with J.G. Betancourt) Serve It Forth: Cooking with Anne McCaffrey, 1996; Crystal Singer Trilogy, 1996. EDITOR: Cooking out of This World, 1973; (with E.A. Scarborough) Space Opera, 1996. Works appear in anthologies. Contributor to magazines. *Died 2011.*

MCDONALD, Jamie. *See* **HEIDE, Florence Parry.**

MCHUGH, John (Francis). British (born England), b. 1927. **Genres:** Theology/Religion, Translations. **Career:** Ordained Roman Catholic priest, 1953; Ushaw College, lecturer in biblical studies, 1957-76, director of studies, 1967-72; University of Durham, lecturer, 1976-78, senior lecturer in theology, 1978-88. Writer. **Publications:** (Trans.) Roland de Vaux, Ancient Israel: Its Life and Institutions, 1961; (trans. and ed.) Xavier Leon-Dufour, The Gospels and the Jesus of History, 1968; (ed.) The Bible and the Ancient Near East, 1971; (with V.E. Delnore) BOMEX: Period III Upper Ocean Soundings, 1972; The Mother of Jesus in the New Testament, 1975; Frases en inglés Para Defenderse, 1976; (contrib.) The Psalms: A New Translation for Worship, 1977; Critical and Exegetical Commentary on John 1-4, 2009. Contributor to books. *Died 2006.*

MILLER, J(ohn) D(onald) Bruce. Australian (born Australia), b. 1922. **Genres:** International Relations/Current Affairs, Politics/Government, Economics. **Career:** University of Sydney, staff tutor in adult education, 1946-52; University of London, London School of Economics and Political Science, assistant lecturer in government and international relations, 1953-55; University of Leicester, lecturer, 1955-57, professor of politics, 1957-62; Indian School of International Studies, visiting professor, 1959; Australian National University, professor of international relations, 1962-87, professor emeritus, 1987-2011; Columbia University, visiting professor, 1962, 1966, 1981; Yale University, visiting professor, 1977; Saint John's College, Cambridge University, Smuts visiting fellow, 1978; Princeton University, visiting professor, 1984; Academy of Social Sciences, executive director, 1989-91, professor emeritus, through 2011. Writer. **Publications:** Australian Government and Politics: An Introductory Survey, 1954, 4th ed., 1971; Richard Jebb and the Problem of Empire, 1956; The Commonwealth in the World, 1958, 3rd ed., 1965; Politicians: An Inaugural Lecture Delivered at the University, Leicester, 25 February, 1958, 1960; The Nature of Politics, 1963; Australia and Foreign Policy, 1963; Britain and the Old Dominions, 1966; Australia, 1966; The Politics of the Third World, 1966; Sir Winston Churchill and the Commonwealth of Nations, 1967; Survey of Commonwealth Affairs: Problems of Expansion and Attrition 1953-1969, 1974; The EEC and Australia, 1976; The World of States: Connected Essays, 1981; Ideology and Foreign Policy: Some Problems of the Reagan Administration, 1982; Norman Angell and the Futility of War: Peace and the Public Mind, 1986. EDITOR: Australian Trade Unionism: Addresses Delivered at Australia's First Trade Union School at Newport, 1952, 1952; (with T.H. Rigby) The Disintegrating Monolith: Pluralist Trends in the Communist World, 1965; India, Japan, Australia: Partners in Asia?: Papers from a Conference at the Australian National University, September 1967, 1968; Australia's Economic Relations, 1975; (with L.T. Evans) Policy and Practice: Essays in Honor of Sir John Crawford, 1987; Australians and British: Social and Political Connections, 1987; (with R.J. Vincent) Order and Violence: Hedley Bull and International Relations, 1990. *Died 2011.*

MILLS, Wilmer. American (born United States), b. 1969. **Genres:** Poetry. **Career:** University of North Carolina, teacher and Kenan visiting writer. **Publications:** Right as Rain, 1999; Light for the Orphans: Poems, 2002, 2nd ed., 2003. Contributor to periodicals. *Died 2011.*

MORNELL, Pierre. American (born United States), b. 1935. **Genres:** Novels, Business/Trade/Industry, Economics, Human Relations/Parenting. **Career:** Los Angeles County General Hospital, intern, 1963-64; Metro-Goldwyn-Mayer, ships doctor, location physician, 1965; University of California, Medical Center, Langley Porter Neuropsychiatric Institute, resident, 1965-68, chief resident, 1968-69, assistant professor, 1969-70, assistant clinical professor of medicine, 1970-2011; Veterans Administration Hospital, assistant chief, 1969-70; Trust for Public Land, director, 1973-85; Harvard Business School Advisory Board, 1997-2011; Young Presidents Organization International University, dean of faculty. Writer. **Publications:** The Lovebook, 1974; Passive Men and Wild Women, 1979; Thank God Its Monday! or, How to Prevent Success from Ruining Your Marriage, 1985; Hiring Smart, 1998; Forty-Five Effective Ways for Hiring Smart!: How to Predict Winners and Losers in The Incredibly Expensive People-Reading Game, 1998; Games Companies Play: The Job Hunters Guide to Playing Smart and Winning Big in the High-Stakes Hiring Game, 2000. *Died 2011.*

MUSGROVE, Frank. British (born England), b. 1922. **Genres:** Education, Sociology, History, Theology/Religion, Military/Defense/Arms Control. **Career:** Colonial Education Service, education officer, 1950-53; University of Leicester, lecturer, 1957-62; University of Leeds, senior lecturer, 1963-65; University of Bradford, professor of research in education, 1965-70; University of British Columbia, visiting professor, 1965; University of California, professor of sociology, 1969; University of Manchester, Sarah Fielden professor of education, 1970-82, Sarah Fielden professor emeritus of education, 1982-2011, Faculty of Education, dean, 1976-78. Writer. **Publications:** The Migratory Elite, 1963; Youth and the Social Order, 1965; The Family, Education and Society, 1966; Faith and Scepticism in English Education, 1966; (with P.H. Taylor) Society and the Teacher's Role, 1969; Patterns of Power and Authority in English Education, 1971; Ecstasy and Holiness: Counter Culture and the Open Society, 1974; Margins of the Mind, 1977; School and the Social Order, 1979; Education and Anthropology: Other Culture and Teacher, 1982; The North of England: A History from Roman Times to the Present, 1990; Dresden and the Heavy Bombers: An RAF Navigator's Perspective, 2005. *Died 2011.*

NAGEL, Paul C(hester). American (born United States), b. 1926. **Genres:** History, Biography, Human Relations/Parenting. **Career:** Augustana College, assistant professor of history, 1953-54; Eastern Kentucky University, associate professor of history, 1954-61; Amherst College, visiting professor, 1957-58; Vanderbilt University, visiting professor, 1959; University of Kentucky, associate professor of history, 1961-65, professor of history, 1964-69, College of Arts and Sciences, dean, 1965-69; University of Minnesota, visiting professor, 1964; Kentucky Arts Commission, research associate, 1966-69; University of Missouri, professor of history, 1969-78, vice president of academic affairs, 1970-74; Center for Research Libraries, vice chair and director, 1973-74; University of Georgia, professor of history and head of department, 1978-80; Virginia Historical Society, director, 1981-85; Carleton College, research associate, 1992-2011. Writer. **Publications:** One Nation Indivisible: The Union in American Thought, 1776-1861, 1964; This Sacred Trust: American Nationality, 1798-1898, 1971; Missouri: A Bicentennial History, 1977, rev. ed. as Missouri: A History, 1988; Descent from Glory: Four Generations of the John Adams Family, 1983; (co-author) Extraordinary Lives: The Art and Craft of American Biography, 1986; The Adams Women: Abigail and Louisa Adams, Their Sisters and Daughters, 1987, rev. ed., 1999; (co-author) George Caleb Bingham: Missouri's Famed Painter and Forgotten Politician, 1989; The Lees of Virginia: Seven Generations of an American Family, 1990; (co-author) Massachusetts and The New Nation, 1992; John Quincy Adams: A Public Life, A Private Life, 1997; The German Migration to Missouri, 2002; (contrib.) I Wish I'd Been There: Twenty Historians Bring to Life the Dramatic Events That Changed America, 2006. Contributor to periodicals. *Died 2011.*

NEMEC, James. American (born United States), b. 1953. **Genres:** Medicine/Health, Adult Non-fiction, inspirational/Motivational Literature, Psychology, Autobiography/Memoirs, Earth Sciences, Animals/Pets, Plays/Screenplays, Humor/Satire, Young Adult Non-fiction, Poetry, E-books, Theatre, Humanities. **Career:** Writer. **Publications:** Touch the Ocean: The Power of Our Collective Emotions, 2007; Journeys: Stories Our Bodies Can Tell, 2009; Awake and Asleep, 2010, The Hidden Meaning of License Plate, 2010. *Died 2011.*

NICHOLS, Peter. See **YOUD, Samuel.**

NITCHIE, George Wilson. American (born United States), b. 1921. **Genres:** Poetry, Education, Literary Criticism And History, Essays. **Career:** Simmons College, instructor, 1947-50, assistant professor, 1950-59, associate professor, 1959-66, professor, 1966-86, professor emeritus of English, 1986-2011. Writer. **Publications:** Seven Poems, 1959; Human Values in the Poetry of Robert Frost: A Study of a Poet's Convictions, 1960; (contrib.) Robert Frost: A Collection of Critical Essays, 1962; Marianne Moore: An Introduction to the Poetry, 1969. Contributor of articles to books and journals. *Died 2011.*

ODELL, George H. American (born United States), b. 1942. **Genres:** Archaeology/Antiquities, History. **Career:** International College, teacher of English, 1965-66; Institut Montana, social studies teacher, 1966-68; Winchester High School, social studies teacher, 1968-70; University of British Columbia, visiting assistant professor, 1977-78; Brown University, visiting assistant professor, 1978-79; Center for American Archaeology, director of lithics laboratory, 1979-84; Belize Archaic Archaeological Reconnaissance, director of lithics laboratory, 1983; University of Tulsa, assistant professor, 1984-90, associate professor, 1990-97, full professor of anthropology, 1997-2011. Writer. **Publications:** Stone Tools and Mobility in the Illinois Valley: From Hunter-Gatherer Camps to Agricultural Villages, 1996; La Harpe's Post: A Tale of French-Wichita Contact on the Eastern Plains, 2002; Lithic Analysis, 2004. EDITOR: (with D.O. Henry) Alternative Approaches to Lithic Analysis, 1989; Stone Tools: Theoretical Insights into Human Prehistory, 1996. Contributor to journals. *Died 2011.*

OPPENNEER, Betsy. American (born United States), b. 1943. **Genres:** Food And Wine. **Career:** The Breadworks Inc., principal. Writer. **Publications:** Betsy's Breads, 1987, rev. ed., 1991; The Bread Book, 1994; Breads from Betsy's Kitchen, 1998; The Oppenneer Family Cookbook, 1999; Celebration Breads: Recipes, Tales, and Traditions, 2003. *Died 2011.*

PARADIS, Adrian Alexis. American (born United States), b. 1912. **Genres:** Business/Trade/Industry, Children's Non-fiction, Young Adult Non-fiction, Economics, Money/Finance, Military/Defense/Arms Control. **Career:** American Airlines Inc., assistant secretary, 1942-68, executive secretary, 1969-73, chairman, 1974-75; New England Writing Associates, owner and director, 1968-72; Attaquechee Vermont Planning and Development Commission, director and chair, 1969-76; Phoenix Publishing Co., editor, 1972-2011; Sky Chefs Inc., secretary. **Publications:** 75 Ways for Boys to Earn Money, 1950;

Never Too Young to Earn, 1954; For Immediate Release: Careers in Public Relations, 1955; From High School to a Job, 1956; Americans at Work, 1958; Dollars for You: 150 Ways for Boys to Earn Money, 1958; Librarians Wanted: Careers in Library Service, 1959; The New Look in Banking, 1961; Business in Action, 1962; (with B. Burke) Life You Save, 1962; Labor in Action, 1963; The Problem Solvers, 1964; Gail Borden, 1964; You and the Next Decade, 1965; Government in Action, 1965; (with G. Paradis) Grow in Grace: The Reference Handbook, 1966; Toward a Better World, 1966; The Bulls and the Bears, 1967; Economics in Action Today, 1967; The Hungry Years, 1967; (with G. Paradis) Your Life: Make It Count, 1968; Harvey Firestone, 1968; Henry Ford, 1968; Jobs to Take You Places, Here and Abroad, 1968; Trade: The World's Lifeblood, 1969; Two Hundred Million Miles a Day, 1969; Job Opportunities for Young Negroes, 1969; Economics Reference Book, 1970; Gold: King of Metals, 1970; From Trails to Superhighways, 1971; How Money Works: The Federal Reserve System, 1972; Labor Reference Book, 1972; International Trade in Action, 1973; Inflation in Action, 1974; (with R.H. Wood) Social Security in Action, 1975; Opportunities in Banking, 1980; Opportunities in Aviation, 1980; Opportunities in Transportation, 1983; The Labor Almanac, 1983; Planning Your Military Career, 1984; Opportunities in Your Own Service Business, 1985; Ida Tarbell, 1985; Planning Your Career of Tomorrow, 1986; Opportunities in Part-Time and Summer Jobs, 1987; Small Business Information Source Book, 1987; Planning Your Vocational/Technical Career, 1987; Opportunities in Military Careers, 1989, rev. ed., 2006; Opportunities in Cleaning and Services Careers, 1992; Opportunities in Nonprofit Organizations Careers, 1993; Careers for Caregivers and Other Sensitive Types, 1995; (with J. Mills) Partnerships for Excellence, 1995; Careers For Caring People & Other Sensitive Types, 1996, 2nd ed., 2003; Opportunities in Airline Careers, 1997; Opportunities in Banking Careers, 2001; Opportunities in Transportation Careers, 2008. *Died 2011.*

PETERSON, Richard Austin. Indian (born India), b. 1932. **Genres:** Sociology, Music, History. **Career:** Washington University, research associate, 1959-60; University of Wisconsin, instructor, assistant professor of sociology, 1961-64; Vanderbilt University, associate professor, 1965-74, acting chair of department, 1968-69, professor of sociology, 1974-2010, chairman, 1982-85, professor emeritus; National Endowment for the Arts, consultant, 1975-2010; Leeds University, visiting senior lecturer, 1985-86; National Humanities Center, Mellon research fellow, 1989-90; College de France, Mellon research fellow, 1991-2010; American Journal of Sociology, associate editor; Journal of Popular Music, associate editor; Social Inquiry, associate editor; American Sociological Association, Sociology of Culture Section Newsletter, editor; University of Salford, senior research fellow, 2003. **Publications:** (With A.W. Gouldner) Notes on Technology and the Moral Order, 1962; (ed. with N.J. Demerath) System, Change and Conflict: A Reader on Contemporary Sociological Theory and the Debate Over Functionalism, 1967; (ed.) With the Indian Army in the Great War 1916-1919, 1970; (ed. with R.S. Denisoff) Sounds of Social Change: Studies in Popular Culture, 1972; (ed.) The Peterson Nursery: A Victorian Episode, 1972; The Industrial Order and Social Policy, 1972; The Dynamics of Industrial Society, 1973; (ed.) The Production of Culture, 1976; Nashville: Country Music City, 1977; Arts Audience Statistics and Culture Indicators, 1980; (ed. and contrib.) Patterns of Cultural Choice, 1984; (ed.) Contemporary Sociology, 1990; (ed. with M.A. McLaurin and contrib.) You Wrote My Life: Lyrical Themes in Country Music, 1992; (co-author) Age and Arts Participation with a Focus on the Baby Boom Cohort, 1996; Creating Country Music: Fabricating Authenticity, 1997; (with P.C. Hull and R.M. Kern) Age and Arts Participation: 1982-1997, 2000; (ed. with A. Bennett) Music Scenes: Local, Translocal and Virtual, 2004. Contributor to journals. *Died 2010.*

PETTY, W(illiam) H(enry). British (born England), b. 1921. **Genres:** Poetry, Administration/Management. **Career:** London County Council, Department of Education, senior assistant, 1946-47; Borough of Doncaster, administrative assistant, technical school English master and youth service worker, 1947-51; North Riding County Council, assistant education officer, 1951-57; West Riding County Council, assistant education officer, 1957-64; Kent County Council, deputy education officer, 1964-73, county education officer, 1973-84; International Training Services Ltd., director, 1974-97; Society of Education Officers, president, 1980-81; Canterbury Christ Church University, chair. Writer. **Publications:** No Bold Comfort, 1957; Conquest, and Other Poems, 1967; (co-author) Educational Administration, 1980; (ed.) Executive Summaries, 1985-90; Springfield: Pieces of the Past, 1994; (co-author) Genius Loci, 1995; The Louvre Imperial, 1997; Interpretations of History, 2000; No-one Listening, 2002; But Someone Liked Them, 2009. Contributor to periodicals. *Died 2011.*

PHILLIPS, Leroy. American (born United States), b. 1935. **Genres:** Law, History. **Career:** Phillips & Caputo, trial attorney. Writer. **Publications:** (With M. Curriden) Contempt of Court: The Turn-of-the-Century Lynching That Launched a Hundred Years of Federalism, 1999. *Died 2011.*

PIANKA, Eric R(odger). American (born United States), b. 1939. **Genres:** Animals/Pets, Environmental Sciences/Ecology, Zoology, Natural History, Biology, Autobiography/Memoirs. **Career:** University of Texas, School of Biological Sciences, assistant professor, 1968-72, associate professor, 1972-77, professor of zoology, 1977-86, Denton A. Cooley centennial professor of zoology, 1986-2011; The American Naturalist, managing editor, 1971-74. **Publications:** Evolutionary Ecology, 1973, 6th ed., 2000; (ed. with R.B. Huey and T.W. Schoener) Lizard Ecology: Studies of a Model Organism, 1983; Ecology and Natural History of Desert Lizards: Analyses of the Ecological Niche and Community Structure, 1986; (ed. with L.J. Vitt) Lizard Ecology: Historical and Experimental Perspectives, 1994; The Lizard Man Speaks, 1994; (with L.J. Vitt) Lizards: Windows to the Evolution of Diversity, 2003; (ed. with D.R. King and R.A. King) Varanoid Lizards of the World, 2004; (ed. with M. Hutchins and V. Geist) Grzimek's Animal Life Encyclopedia Evolution, 2011. *Died 2011.*

PRYBYLA, Jan S(tanislaw). American/Polish (born Poland), b. 1927. **Genres:** Economics, International Relations/Current Affairs, Business/Trade/Industry. **Career:** College of Free Europe, assistant, 1953-58; Pennsylvania State University, assistant professor, 1958-62, associate professor, 1962-65, professor of economics, 1965, now professor emeritus; U.S. Department of State, Foreign Service Institute, adjunct faculty. Writer. **Publications:** Basic Data, Economic, Governmental, Social, 1962; (with E. Atwater and K. Forster) World Tensions: Conflict and Accommodation, 1967, 2nd ed., 1972; (comp.) Comparative Economic Systems, 1969; The Societal Objectives of Wealth, Growth, Stability, and Equity in Taiwan, 1978; The Political Economy of Communist China, 1970; The Chinese Economy: Problems and Policies, 1978, 2nd ed., 1981; Issues in Socialist Economic Modernization, 1980; Market and Plan under Socialism: The Bird in the Cage, 1987; Reform in China and Other Socialist Economies, 1990; (co-author) China and the Crisis of Marxism-Leninism, 1990; (with C. Linden) Russia and China: On the Eve of a New Millennium, 1997; American Way of Peace: An Interpretation, 2005; When Angels Wept: The Rebirth and Dismemberment of Poland and Her People in the Early Decades of the Twentieth Century, 2009. EDITOR: Triangle of Power, Conflict, and Accommodation: The United States, the Soviet Union and Communist China: Papers, 1967; Communism at the Crossroads: Papers, 1968; (with H.G. Shaffer) From Underdevelopment to Affluence: Western, Soviet and Chinese Views, 1968; Communism and Nationalism; Papers, 1969. Contributor to books. *Died 2012.*

REJAI, Mostafa. American/Iranian (born Iran), b. 1931. **Genres:** Politics/Government, Cultural/Ethnic Topics, Military/Defense/Arms Control. **Career:** Miami University, assistant professor, 1964-67, associate professor, 1967-70, professor of political science, 1970-83, distinguished professor of political science, 1983, distinguished professor emeritus of political science. Writer. **Publications:** Democracy: The Contemporary Theories, 1967; (ed. and intro.) On Revolution and War, 1969; (co-author) Ideologies and Modern Politics, 1971, 3rd ed., 1981; (ed.) Decline of Ideology?, 1971; The Strategy of Political Revolution, 1973; The Comparative Study of Revolutionary Strategy, 1977; (with K. Phillips) Leaders of Revolution, 1979; (with K. Phillips) World Revolutionary Leaders, 1983; Comparative Political Ideologies, 1984; (with K. Phillips) Loyalists & Revolutionaries: Political Leaders Compared, 1988; Political Ideologies: A Comparative Approach, 1991, 2nd ed., 1995; (with K. Phillips and W.L. Mason) Demythologizing an Elite: American Presidents in Empirical, Comparative, and Historical Perspective, 1993; (with K. Phillips) World Military Leaders: A Collective and Comparative Analysis, 1996; (with K. Phillips) Leaders and Leadership: An Appraisal of Theory and Research, 1997; (with K. Phillips) The Young George Washington in Psychobiographical Perspective, 2000; (with K. Phillips) Concepts of Leadership in Western Political Thought, 2002; (ed.) Ideology: Comparative and Cultural Status, 2009. Contributor to journals. *Died 2011.*

RICHTER, Harvena. American (born United States), b. 1919. **Genres:** Novels, Novellas/Short Stories, Poetry, Literary Criticism And History. **Career:** Saks Fifth Avenue, copywriter, 1942-43; Macy's and Elizabeth Arden, copy writer, 1943-47; I. Miller, advertising director, 1947-48; New York Herald Tribune, North American Newspaper Alliance, Women's National News Service, reporter, 1948-49; freelance writer, 1949-52; New York University,

instructor in English, 1952-66; University of New Mexico, assistant professor of English, 1969-2011. Writer. **Publications:** The Human Shore (novel), 1959; Virginia Woolf: The Inward Voyage, 1970; (ed.) The Rawhide Knot and Other Stories, 1978; Writing to Survive: The Private Notebooks of Conrad Richter, 1988; The Yaddo Elegies and Other Poems, 1995; Green Girls, 1996; The Innocent Island, 1999; Frozen Light: The Crystal Poems, 2001; The Golden Fountains: Sources of Energy and Life Based on the Psycho-Energetics of Conrad Richter, 2002; Passage to Teheran, 2004. Contributor to periodicals. *Died 2011.*

RIFKIN, Shepard. (Jake Logan). American (born United States), b. 1918. **Genres:** Novels, Mystery/Crime/Suspense, Westerns/Adventure. **Career:** Writer. **Publications:** Texas: Blood Red, 1956; Desire Island, 1960; What Ship? Where Bound?, 1961; The Warring Breed, 1961; King Fisher's Road, 1963; (ed.) The Savage Years: Authorized First Hand Accounts of the Bloody Conflicts between the Whites and the Indians, 1967; Ladyfingers, 1969; The Murderer Vine, 1970; McQuaid, 1974; The Snow Rattlers, 1977; McQuaid in August, 1979. AS JAKE LOGAN: SLOCUM SERIES: Hanging Justice, 1975; Ride, Slocum, Ride, 1975; Slocum and the Widow Kate, 1975; Across the Rio Grande, 1975; The Comanche's Woman, 1975; Slocum's Gold, 1976; North to Dakota, 1976; Slocum's Woman, 1977; Ride for Revenge, 1980; White Hell, 1977; Montana Showdown, 1977; See Texas and Die, 1978; Iron Mustang, 1978; Slocum's Fire, 1979; Slocum's Revenge, 1979; Slocum's Hell, 1979; Slocum's Grave, 1979; Dead Man's Hand, 1979; Fighting Vengeance, 1981; Slocum's Slaughter, 1983; Roughrider, 1980; Slocum's Rage, 1980; Hellfire, 1981; Slocum's Code, 1981; Slocum's Flag, 1981; Slocum's Blood, 1981; Slocum's Raid, 1982; Slocum's Run, 1984; Outlaw Blood, 1981; Blazing Guns, 1981; Bloody Trail to Texas, 1987; Slocum's Gamble, 1982; Slocum and the Mad Major, 1982; The Necktie Party, 1982; The Canyon Bunch, 1982; Swamp Foxes, 1983; Law Comes to Cold Rain, 1983; Slocum's Drive, 1983; The Jackson Hole Trouble, 1983; Silver City Shootout, 1983; Slocum and the Law, 1983; Slocum's Justice, 1983; Nebraska Burnout, 1983; Slocum and the Cattle Queen, 1983; Slocum's Women, 1983; Slocum's Command, 1983; Slocum Gets Even, 1986; Slocum and the Lost Dutchman Mine, 1984; High Country Holdup, 1984; Guns of South Pass, 1984; Slocum and the Hatchet Men, 1984; Bandit Gold, 1984; South of the Border, 1984; The Dallas Madam, 1984; Texas Showdown, 1984; Slocum in Deadwood, 1984; Slocum's Winning Hand, 1984; Slocum and the Gun-Runners, 1984; Slocum's Pride, 1984; Slocum's Crime, 1985; The Nevada Swindle, 1985; Slocum's Good Deed, 1985; Slocum's Stampede, 1985; Gunplay At Hobb's Hole, 1985; The Journey of Death, 1985; Slocum Rides Alone, 1985; The Sunshine Basin War, 1985; Vigilante Justice, 1985; Jailbreak Moon, 1985; Mescalero Dawn, 1986; Denver Gold, 1986; Slocum and the Bozeman Trail, 1986; Slocum and the Horse Thieves, 1986; Slocum and the Noose of Hell, 1986; Cheyenne Bloodbath, 1986; The Blackmail Express, 1986; Slocum and the Silver Ranch Fight, 1986; Slocum and the Long Wagon Train, 1986; Slocum and the Deadly Feud, 1986; Rawhide Justice, 1986; Slocum and the Indian Ghost, 1986; Seven Graves to Laredo, 1987; Slocum's Deadly Game, 1987; Hell's Fury, 1987; High, Wide and Deadly, 1987; Slocum and the Wild Stallion Chase, 1987; Laredo Showdown, 1987; Slocum and the Claim Jumpers, 1987; Slocum and the Cherokee Manhunt, 1987; Sixguns At Silverado, 1987; Slocum and the El Paso Blood Feud, 1987; Slocum and the Blood Rage, 1988; Slocum and the Cracker Creek Killers, 1988; Slocum and the Red River Renegades, 1988; Slocum and the Gunfighters Greed, 1988; Sixgun Law, 1988; Slocum and the Arizona Kidnappers, 1988; Slocum and the Hanging Tree, 1988; Blood at the Crossing, 1988; Slocum and the Buffalo Hunters, 1988; Slocum and the Preacher's Daughter, 1988; Slocum and the Gunfighter's Return, 1988; The Rawhide Breed, 1988; Death Trap, 1989; Slocum and the Crooked Judge, 1989; Slocum and the Tong Warriors, 1989; Slocum and the Outlaw's Trail, 1989; Slow Death, 1989; Slocum and the Plains Massacre, 1989; Stalker's Moon, 1989; Mexican Silver, 1989; Slocum's Debt, 1989; Slocum and the Cattle War, 1989; Colorado Killers, 1990; Slocum Busts Out, 1990; Ride to Vengeance, 1990; Revenge of the Gunfighter, 1990; Texas Trail Drive, 1990; The Wyoming Cattle War, 1990; Vengeance Road, 1990; Slocum and the Town Tamer, 1990; A Noose for Slocum, 1990; Nevada Gunmen, 1990; The Horse Thief War, 1990; Slocum and the Plains Rampage, 1991; Slocum and the Death Dealer, 1991; Desolation Point, 1991; Slocum and the Apache Raiders, 1991; Slocum's Fortune, 1991; Slocum and the Deadwood Treasure, 1991; Slocum and the Trail of Death, 1991; Slocum and the Stagecoach Bandits, 1991; Slocum and the Hanging Party, 1991; The Grandville Bank Heist, 1991; Slocum and the Death Council, 1991; Slocum and the Timber King, 1992; Slocum and the Railroad Baron, 1992; Slocum and the River Chase, 1992; Tombstone Gold, 1992; Slocum and the Sharpshooter, 1992;

Silver Town Showdown, 1992; Slocum and the Bushwhackers, 1992; Slocum and the Wyoming Frame-Up, 1992; San Angelo Shoot-Out, 1992; Blood Fever, 1992; Helltown Trail, 1993; Sheriff Slocum, 1993; Virginia City Showdown, 1993; Slocum and the Forty Thieves, 1993; Powder River Massacre, 1993; Final Draw, 1993; Slocum and the Tin Star Swindle, 1993; Slocum and the Nightriders, 1993; Revenge At Devils Tower, 1993; Slocum At Outlaws' Haven, 1993; Ambush At Apache Rocks, 1993; Hell to Midnight, 1993; Slocum and the Phantom Gold, 1994; Ghost Town, 1994; Slocum and the Invaders, 1994; Slocum and the Mountain of Gold, 1994; Slocum and the Cow Town Kill, 1994; Pikes Peak Shoot-Out, 1994; Blood Trail, 1994; Slocum and the Gold Slaves, 1994; Slocum and Quantrill, 1994; Slocum and the Ghost Rustlers, 1994; Slocum and the Fort Worth Ambush, 1995; Slocum and the West Texas Plunder, 1995; Slocum and the Snake Gulch Swindlers, 1995; Slocum and the Shoshone Whiskey; 1995; Lady Niners, 1998; Boomtown Showdown, 1995; Slocum and the Pirates, 1995; The Silver Stallion, 1995; Slocum and the Spotted Horse, 1995; Slocum At Dog Leg Creek, 1996; Slocum's Silver, 1996; Renegade Trail, 1995; Slocum and the Dirty Game, 1995; Showdown At Drowning Creek, 1996; Slocum and the Bear Lake Monster, 1996; The Lady Gambler, 1996; Slocum in Paradise, 1996; Blood On the Rio Grande, 1996; Slocum and the Gold-Mine Gamble, 1996; Slocum and the Walapai War, 1996; Slocum's Folly, 1996; Slocum and the Frisco Killers, 1996; Slocum and the Great Southern Hunt, 1996; The Arizona Strip War, 1997; Slocum and the Apache Ransom, 1997; Slocum At Dead Dog, 1997; Slocum and the Town Boss, 1997; Slocum and the Lady in Blue, 1997; Slocum and the Powder River Gamble, 1997; Slocum and the Colorado Riverboat, 1997; Slocum's Inheritance, 1997; Slocum and Doc Holliday, 1997; The Aztec Priestess, 1997; Slocum and the Comanche Rescue, 1997; Louisiana Lovely, 1997; Prairie Fires, 1997; Slocum and the Real McCoy, 1998; Blood on the Brazos, 1998; Slocum and the Scalplock Trail, 1998; Slocum and the Comely Corpse, 1998; Blood in Kansas, 1998; Slocum and the Great Diamond Hoax, 1998; Slocum and the Lone Star Feud, 1998; The Last Gasp, 1998; Slocum and the Miners' Justice, 1998; Slocum At Hell's Acre, 1998; Slocum and the Wolf Hunt, 1998; Slocum and the Baroness, 1999; The Comanche Princess, 1999; Slocum and the Live Oak Boys, 1999; Slocum and the Big Three, 1999; Slocum At Scorpion Bend, 1999; Slocum and the Buffalo Hunter, 1999; Slocum and the Texas Rose, 1998; Slocum and the Yellow Rose of Texas, 1999; Slocum and the Lady from Abilene, 1999; Slocum and the Cattle King, 1999; Dead Man's Spurs, 1999; Showdown at Shiloh, 1999; Slocum and the Ketchem Gang, 1999; Slocum and the Jersey Lily, 1999; Slocum and the Gambler's Woman, 2000; Slocum and the Gunrunners (252), 2000; Slocum and the Nebraska Storm, 2000; Slocum's Close Call, 2000; Slocum and the Undertaker, 2000; Slocum and the Pomo Chief, 2000; Slocum and the Mountain Spirit, 2000; Slocum's Partner, 2000; Slocum and Wild Bill's Lady, 2000; Slocum and the Gila Rangers, 2000; Slocum and the Senorita, 2000; Slocum and the Ambush Trail, 2000; Showdown in Texas, 2001; Slocum and the Lakota Lady, 2001; Slocum and the Rich Man's Son, 2001; Slocum and the Blue-Eyed Hostage, 2001; Slocum's Sidekick, 2001; Slocum and the Hired Gun, 2001; The Hired Gun, 2002; Railroad to Hell, 2001; Slocum On Ghost Mesa, 2001; Slocum and the Friendly Foe, 2001; South of the Border (272), 2001; Two Coffins for Slocum, 2001; Valley of Skulls, 2001; Slocum and the Gravedigger Slocum, 2001; Slocum's Warpath, 2002; Slocum and the Deserter, 2002; Shoot-Out at Whiskey Springs, 2002; Hot on the Trail Slocum, 2002; Slocum and the Ranch War, 2002; Slocum and the Widow Maker, 2002; Slocum and the Lady in Black Slocum, 2002; Slocum and the Ghost Rustlers (283), 2002; Slocum, a Jury of One, 2002; Slocum's Disguise, 2002; Slocum and the Boomtown Bordello, 2002; Slocum and the Nebraska Swindle, 2003; Slocum Down Mexico Way, 2003; Slocum At Devil's Mouth, 2003; Slocum and the Treasure Chest, 2003; Slocum and the Bounty Jumpers, 2003; Slocum and the Bitterroot Belle, 2003; Slocum and the Circle Z Riders, 2003; Slocum and the Deadly Damsel, 2003; Dancer's Trail, 2003; Slocum and the Undertakers, 2003; Holding Down the Ranch, 2003; Slocum and the Tequila Rose, 2003; Slocum and the Bone Robbers, 2003; Slocum and the Storekeeper's Wife, 2004; Slocum and the Cayuse Squaw, 2004; Slocum and the Bad-News Brothers, 2004; Slocum and the Orphan Express, 2004; Slocum At Whiskey Lake, 2004; Slocum and the Rebel Yell, 2004; Slocum and the Sheriff of Guadalupe, 2004; Slocum and the Hangman's Lady, 2004; Slocum and the Crooked Sheriff, 2004; Slocum and the Teton Temptress, 2004; Slocum and the Slanderer, 2005; Slocum and the Bixby Battle, 2005; Slocum and the Runaway Bride, 2005; Slocum and the Deadwood Deal, 2005; Slocum's Gold Mountain, 2005; Slocum's Sweet Revenge, 2005; Slocum and the Sierra Madras Gold, 2005; Slocum and the Presidio Phantoms, 2005; Slocum and Lady Death, 2005; Slocum and the Sulfur Valley Widows, 2005; Slocum and the Vanished, 2005; Slocum and the Water Witch, 2005; Slocum and the Mojave Guns, 2005; Slocum and the Two Gold Bullets, 2006; Slocum and the Boss's Wife, 2006; Slocum and the Big Payback, 2006; Slocum and the Mescal Smugglers, 2006; Slocum and the Apache Border Incident, 2006; Slocum and the Horse Killers, 2006; Slocum and the Border War, 2006; Slocum and the Lost Command, 2006; Slocum and the Madhouse Madam, 2006; Slocum and the Land-Grabbers, 2006; Slocum At Hangdog, 2006; Slocum and the Tonto Basin War, 2006; Slocum and Hot Lead, 2007; Slocum and the Vengeful Widow, 2007; Slocum at Dead Dog 338, 2007; Slocum and the Apache Campaign, 2007; Slocum and the City Slickers, 2007; Slocum and the Highgraders, 2007; Slocum and the Gila River Hermit, 2007; Slocum and the Comanche Captive, 2007; Slocum in Shot Creek, 2007; Slocum and the Widow's Range Wars, 2007; Slocum's Revenge Trail, 2007; Slocum's Four Brides, 2007; Slocum and the Schoolmarm, 2007; Slocum and the Big Horn Trail, 2008; Slocum and the Killers, 2008; Slocum and the Tomboy, 2008; Slocum and the Frisby Flats, 2008; Slocum and the Rebel Cannon, 2008; Slocum and the Schuylkill Butchers, 2008; Slocum and Little Britches, 2008; Slocum and Pearl of the Rio Grande, 2008; Slocum and the Rancher's Daughter, 2008; Slocum and the Bandit Durango, 2008; Slocum's Bar-S Ranch, 2008; Slocum and El Loco, 2009; Slocum and the Lucky Lady, 2009; Slocum and the Witch of Westlake, 2009; Slocum and the British Bully, 2009; Slocum and the Dynamite Kid, 2009; Slocum and the Family Business, 2009; Slocum and the Rustler on the Run, 2009; Slocum and the Medicine Man, 2009; Slocum and Belle Starr, 2009; Slocum and the Living Dead Man, 2009; Slocum and the Four Peaks Range War, 2009; Slocum and the Backshooters, 2009; Slocum and the Sonoran Fugitive, 2010; Slocum and the Woman Sold to the Comanche, 2010; Slocum and the Gift Horse, 2010; Slocum's Snake Oil, 2010; Slocum and the Second Horse, 2010; Slocum and the Four Seasons, 2010; Slocum and the Teamster Lady, 2010; Slocum and the Yellowback Trail, 2010; Slocum and the Dirty Dozen, 2010; Slocum and the Forgetful Felon, 2010; Slocum and the James Gang, 2010; Slocum and the Trail to Tascosa, 2010; Slocum and the Terrors of White Pine County, 2011; Slocum and the Lady Detective, 2011; Slocum's Reward, 2011; Slocum and the Ghost of Adam Weyland, 2011; Slocum and the Bandit Cucaracha, 2011; Slocum and the Big Timber Belles, 2011; Slocum and the Cow Camp Killers, 2011. SLOCUM GIANT SERIES: Slocum's War, 1992; Slocum's Grubstake, 1996; Slocum and the Irish Lass, 1997; Slocum and the Three Wives, 1999; Sheriff Slocum (Giant), 2000; Slocum and the Helpless Harlots, 2001; Slocum and the Carnahan Boys, 2002; The Gunman and the Greenhorn, 2003; Slocum in the Secret Service, 2004; Slocum and the Larcenous Lady, 2005; Slocum and the Hanging Horse, 2006; Slocum and the Celestial Bones, 2007; Slocum and the Town Killers, 2008; Slocum's Great Race, 2009; Slocum Along Rotten Row, 2010. *Died 2011.*

ROONEY, Andy. American (born United States), b. 1919. **Genres:** Essays, Humor/Satire, Military/Defense/Arms Control, Biography, Reference, Young Adult Fiction. **Career:** Metro-Goldwyn-Mayer, staff; freelance magazine writer, 1947-49; Columbia Broadcasting System Inc., writer, 1949, producer, 1959-65, news writer, producer, 1962-70, 1972-2011, correspondent, commentator, 1978-2011; American Broadcasting Company Inc., staff, 1971-72; Tribune Co., Syndicate Newspaper, columnist, 1979-2011. **Publications:** (With B. Hutton) Air Gunner, 1944; (with B. Hutton) The Story of Stars and Stripes, 1946; (with B. Hutton) Conqueror's Peace: A Report to the American Stockholders, 1947; (co-author) Off the Record: The Best Stories of Foreign Correspondents, 1952; The Fortunes of War: Four Great Battles of World War II, 1962; A Few Minutes with Andy Rooney, 1981; And More by Andy Rooney, 1982; Pieces of My Mind, 1984; The Most of Andy Rooney, 1986; Word for Word, 1987; Not That You Asked, 1989; Sweet and Sour, 1992; My War, 1995; Sincerely, Andy Rooney, 1999; Common Nonsense, 2002; Years of Minutes, 2003; Out of My Mind, 2006; Andy Rooney: 60 Years of Wisdom and Wit, 2009. Contributor to periodicals. *Died 2011.*

ROSS, Stewart Halsey. American (born United States), b. 1928. **Genres:** Advertising/Public Relations, History, Transportation. **Career:** A.M.F., advertising manager, 1960-62; Fred Wittner Advertising, vice-president, 1962-65; James A. Ford Advertising, vice-president, 1965-70; Stewart H. Ross Advertising, president, 1970-92; Norwalk Community College, instructor; University of New Haven, adjunct instructor; Southern Connecticut State University, adjunct instructor. Writer. **Publications:** The Management of Business-to-Business Advertising: A Working Guide for Small to Mid-Size Companies, 1986; Propaganda for War: How the United States Was Conditioned to Fight the Great War of 1914-1918, 1996; Strategic Bombing by the United States in World War II: The Myths and the Facts, 2003; How Roosevelt Failed America in World War II, 2006; The Great Red Scare of 1919-1920. *Died 2010.*

RUSSELL, Norman H. American (born United States), b. 1921. **Genres:** Poetry, Botany. **Career:** Grinnell College, instructor, 1951-54, assistant professor, 1954-55, associate professor, 1955-56, professor of biology, 1957-59; Arizona State University, professor of botany and chairman of department, 1959-63; Rutgers University, visiting professor of botany, 1963-65; Central State University (now University of Central Oklahoma), associate professor, 1966-68, professor of biology, 1970-73, School of Math and Science, dean, 1973-76, vice-president for academic affairs, 1976-79, professor of biology and creative studies, 1979-88, professor emeritus, 1988-2011; Buena Vista College, visiting professor, 1968-70. Writer. **Publications:** SCIENTIFIC: An Introduction to the Plant Kingdom, 1958; (with P.C. Lemon) The Plant Kingdom: A Laboratory Manual, 1959, 3rd ed. as General Botany Manual: Exercises on the Life Histories, Structures, Physiology, and Ecology of the Plant Kingdom, 1970; Violets of Central and Eastern United States: An Introductory Survey, 1965; Introduction to Plant Science: A Humanistic and Ecological Approach, 1975. OTHERS: Night Dog and Other Poems, 1971; Open the Flower, 1974; The Ways of the World, 1974; Indian Thoughts: I Am Old, 1976; Indian Thoughts: The Children of God, 1976; Indian Thoughts: My Journey, 1980; The Longest March, 1980; From Star to Leaf, 1995. POETRY: At the Zoo, 1969; Indian Thoughts: The Small Songs of God, 1972; Russell, the Man, the Teacher, the Indian, 1975. Works appear in anthologies. Contributor of articles to journals. *Died 2011.*

RYE, Anthony. *See* YOUD, Samuel.

SAMUELS, Warren J(oseph). American (born United States), b. 1933. **Genres:** Economics, Law, Politics/Government, Essays. **Career:** University of Missouri, assistant professor of economics, 1957-58; Georgia State College, assistant professor of economics, 1958-59; University of Miami, assistant professor of economics, 1959-62, associate professor of economics, 1962-68; Michigan State University, Department of Economics, professor of economics, 1968-98, professor emeritus, 1998-2011, director of graduate programs and placement officer, 1969-73, adjunct professor, 1998-2001; Journal of Economic Issues, editor, 1971-81; Economics Society of Michigan, president, 1972-73; History of Economics Society, president, 1981-82; Association for Social Economics, president, 1988. Writer. **Publications:** The Classical Theory of Economic Policy, 1966; Pareto on Policy, 1974; (co-author) Institutionalismus heute: kritische Auseinandersetzung miteiner unorthodoxen wirtschaftswissenschaftlichen Bewegung; (with S.G. Medema) Gardiner C. Means, Institutionalist and Post Keynesian, 1990; (intro.) The Place of Science in Modern Civilization and Other Essays, 1990; Essays in the History of Heterodox Political Economy, 1992; Essays in the History of Mainstream Political Economy, 1992; Essays on the Economic Role of Government, 1992; Essays on the Methodology and Discourse of Economics, 1992; (with J. Biddle and T.W. Patchak-Schuster) Economic Thought and Discourse in the Twentieth Century, 1993; (with S.G. Medema and A.A. Schmid) The Economy as a Process of Valuation, 1997; (contrib.) Economics Broadly Considered: Essays in Honor of Warren J. Samuels, 2001; Economics, Governance, and Law: Essays on Theory and Policy, 2002; (co-author) Essays on the History of Economics, 2004; The Legal-economic Nexus: Fundamental Processes, 2007; Erasing the Invisible Hand: Essays on an Elusive and Misused Concept in Economics, 2011. EDITOR: (with H.M. Trebing) A Critique of Administrative Regulation of Public Utilities, 1972; The Chicago School of Political Economy, 1976; The Economy as a System of Power: Papers from the Journal of Economic Issues, 1979; (with L.L. Wade) Taxing and Spending Policy, 1980; The Methodology of Economic Thought: Critical Papers, 1980; (with A.A.A. Schimid) Law and Economics: An Institutional Perspective, 1981; Research in the History of Economic Thought and Methodology, vol. I, 1983; The Law of Power: Das Gesetz der Macht, 1983; (with H.W. Spiegel) Contemporary Economists in Perspective, 1984; (with A.S. Miller) Corporations and Society: Power and Responsibility, 1987; Institutional Economics, 1988; Economy as a System of Power, 1989; Fundamentals of the Economic Role of Government, 1989; (with M.R. Tool) State, Society, and Corporate Power, 2nd ed., 1989; Economics and Discourse: An Analysis of the Language of Economists, 1989; (with K. Hennings) Neoclassical Economic Theory, 1870 to 1930, 1990; New Horizons in Economic Thought: Appraisals of Leading Economists, 1992; (with F.S. Lee) The Heterodox Economics of Gardiner C. Means: A Collection, 1992; (with G.M. Hodgson and M.R. Tool) Elgar Companion to Institutional and Evolutionary Economics, 1994; (with F.S. Lee) A Monetary Theory of Employment, 1994; American Economists of the Late Twentieth Century, 1996; (with M. Rutherford) John R. Commons: Selected Essays, 1996; (with M. Rutherford) Classics in Institutional Economics: The Founders, 1890-1945, 1997; (with G.B. Davis) The Life and

Economics of David Ricardo, 1997; (with M. Rutherford) Classics in Institutional Economics II: Succeeding Generations, 1916-1978, 1998; (with S.G. Medema) A History of Economic Thought: The LSE Lectures, 1998; European Economists of the Early Twentieth Century: Studies of Neglected Thinkers of Belgium, France, The Netherlands and Scandinavia, 1998; (with N. Makasheva and V. Barnett) The Works of Nikolai D. Kondratiev, 1998; Law and Economics: The Early Journal Literature, 1998; Foundations of Research in Economics: How Do Economists Do Economics?, 1998; The Founding of Institutional Economics: The Leisure Class and Sovereignty, 1998; (with N. Mercuro) The Fundamental Interrelationships between Government and Property, 1999; Research in the History of Economic Thought and Methodology: American Economics, 2000; (with J.E. Biddle) Research in the History of Economic Thought and Methodology: A Research Annual, 2000; Research in the History of Economic Thought and Methodology: Twentieth-Century Economics, 2000; (with S.G. Medema) Historians of Economics and Economic Thought: The Construction of Disciplinary Memory, 2001; (with E.S. Miller) Institutionalist Approach to Public Utilities Regulation, 2002; (with M. Johnson and S.G. Medema) Foundations of the American Economy: The American Colonies from Inception to Independence, 2003; (with J.E. Biddle and J.B. Davis) Companion to the History of Economic Thought, 2003; (with S.G. Medema) History of Economic Thought: A Reader, 2003; (co-ed.) Emergence of a National Economy: The United States from Independence to the Civil War, 2004; (with M. Johnson) Documents from Glenn Johnson and F. Taylor Ostrander, 2009. Contributor of articles to books and journals. *Died 2011.*

SANJEK, David. British/American (born United States), b. 1952. **Genres:** Music, Business/Trade/Industry, Economics. **Career:** Washington University, instructor, through 1984; high school English teacher, 1985-87; New York University, adjunct professor, 1987-90; Iona College, adjunct professor, 1989-90; Manhattanville College, adjunct professor, 1988; Fordham University, assistant professor and adjunct professor, 1989-91; Broadcast Music Inc., BMI Archives, director, 1991-2007; New School for Social Research, visiting assistant professor, 1993; City University of New York, Hunter College, visiting assistant professor, 1994; Smithsonian Institution, Museum of American History, research associate, 1998; International Association for the Study of Popular Music, United States Branch, vice president, president and secretary; University of Salford, School of Media, Music and Performance, professor. Writer. **Publications:** (With R. Sanjek) The American Popular Music Business in the 20th Century, 1991; (with R. Sanjek) Pennies from Heaven: The American Popular Music Business in the Twentieth Century, 1996; Always on My Mind: Music, Memory and Money, 2003. Contributor of articles to journals. *Died 2011.*

SCALAPINO, Robert Anthony. American (born United States), b. 1919. **Genres:** International Relations/Current Affairs, Politics/Government, Education, Economics, History. **Career:** Santa Barbara College (now University of California, Santa Barbara), lecturer, 1940-41; Harvard University, instructor, 1948-49; University of California-Berkeley, Charles and Louise Travers Department of Political Science, assistant professor, 1949-51, associate professor, 1951-56, professor of political science, 1956-77, Robson research professor of government, 1978-90, Robson research professor emeritus of government, 1990-2011, chair, 1962-65, chair of group in Asian studies, 1959-61, Institute of East Asian Studies, founding director, 1978-90, Berkeley fellow, 1993; Institute for Korean-American Studies, distinguished fellow; American Academy of Arts and Sciences, fellow. Writer. **Publications:** Politics and Public Opinion in Japan, 1951; Democracy and the Party Movement in Prewar Japan, 1953; Reflections on American Relations with Japan: Prepared as a Background Paper for the Conference on Japanese-American Relations to be Held at Honolulu, January, 17-20, 1953, Under the Auspices of the Institute of Pacific Relations of Hawaii and the Japan Institute, 1953; (with G.T. Yu) Chinese Anarchist Movement, 1961; (with J. Masumi) Parties and Politics in Contemporary Japan, 1962; North Korea Today, 1963; Japan, Ally in the Far East, 1964; Japanese Communist Movement, 1920-1966, 1967; Communism in Korea, 1972; American-Japanese Relations in a Changing Era, 1972; Asia and the Major Powers: Implications for the International Order, 1972; Asia and the Road Ahead: Issues for the Major Powers, 1975; United States and Korea: Looking Ahead, 1979; (contrib.) Soviet Policy in Asia-Expansion or Accommodation?, 1980; Hanguk hyŏndaesa ŭi chae ChomyoAHCKng, 1982; Early Japanese Labor Movement: Labor and Politics in a Developing Society, 1983; Pukhan ŭionŭl Kwa Naeil, 1985; (with G.T. Yu) Modern China and Its Revolutionary Process: Recurrent Challenges to the Traditional Order, 1850-1920, 1985; Pukhan Kwa Onŭl ŭl Segye: 80-yŏndae ŭitaeoe chŏgŭng,

1986; Major Power Relations in Northeast Asia, 1987; Politics of Development: Perspectives on Twentieth-Century Asia, 1989; (co-author) Regional Dynamics: Security, Political, and Economic Issues in the Asia-Pacific Region, 1990; Last Leninists: The Uncertain Future of Asia's Communist States, 1992; (contrib.) Chinese: Mainland and Taiwan: A Study of Historical, Cultural, Economic and Political Relations with Documents, 1996; North Korea at a Crossroads, 1997; From Leavenworth to Lhasa: Living in a Revolutionary Era, 2008. EDITOR: Communist Revolution in Asia: Tactics, Goals, and Achievements, 1965, 2nd ed., 1969; Elites in the People's Republic of China, 1972; Foreign Policy of Modern Japan, 1977; (with J. Wanandi) Economic, Political, and Security Issues in Southeast Asia in the 1980s, 1982; (with J. Kim) North Korea Today: Strategic and Domestic Issues, 1983; (with S. Sato and J. Wanandi) Asian Economic Development-Present and Future, 1985; (with S. Sato and J. Wanandi) Asian Political Institutionalization, 1986; Economic Development in the Asia-Pacific Region: Appropriate Roles for Japan and the United States, 1986; (with S. Sato and J. Wanandi) Internal and External Security Issues in Asia, 1986; (with H. Lee) North Korea in a Regional and Global Context, 1986; (with H. Sung-joo) United States-Korea Relations, 1986; (co-ed.) Asia and the Major Powers: Domestic Politics and Foreign Policy, 1988; (with D. Kim) Asian Communism: Continuity and Transition, 1988; (with H. Lee) Korea-U.S. Relations: The Politics of Trade and Security, 1988; (co-ed.) Pacific-Asian Economic Policies and Regional Interdependence, 1988; (with M. Kosaka) Peace, Politics & Economics in Asia: The Challenge to Cooperate, 1988; (co-ed.) Asian Security Issues: Regional and Global, 1989; (with G.I. Chufrin) Asia in the 1990s: American and Soviet Perspectives, 1991; (co-ed.) Japan, Russia, and the United States: Prospects for Cooperative Relations in the New Era: A Conference Report, 1993. Contributor to journals. *Died 2011.*

SEARLE, Ronald (William Fordham). French/British (born England), b. 1920. **Genres:** Humor/Satire, Cartoons, Art/Art History, Education, Illustrations, Military/Defense/Arms Control, History, Business/Trade/Industry, Business/Trade/Industry. **Career:** Writer, graphic artist, cartoonist and pictorial satirist, 1935-2011. **Publications:** Forty Drawings, 1946; Le Nouveau Ballet Anglais, 1946; Hurrah for St. Trinian's and Other Lapses, 1948; The Female Approach, with Masculine Sidelights, 1949; Back to the Slaughterhouse and Other Ugly Moments, 1951; Souls in Torment, 1953; Medisances, 1953; The Female Approach: Cartoons, 1954; The Rake's Progress, 1955, new ed. as The Rake's Progress: Some Immoral Tales, 1968; Merry England, Etc., 1956; (ed. and intro.) The Biting Eye of Andre Francois, 1960; The Penguin Ronald Searle, 1960; (ed.) Toulouse-Lautrec: A Definitive Biography, 1960; (ed.) Cezanne: A Definitive Biography, 1961; Which Way Did He Go?, 1961; From Frozen North to Filthy Lucre: With Remarks by Groucho Marx and Commentaries by Jane Clapperton, 1964; Searle in the Sixties, 1964; Pardong, M'sieur: Paris et autres, 1965; Searle's Cats, 1967; The Square Egg, 1968; Take One Toad: A Book of Ancient Remedies, 1968; Hello-Where Did All the People Go?, 1969; Hommage a Toulouse-Lautrec, 1969 in UK as The Second Coming of Toulouse-Lautrec, 1970; Filles de Hambourg, 1969 in UK as Secret Sketchbook: The Back Streets of Hamburg, 1970; The Addict: A Terrible Tale, 1971; Weil noch das Laempchen glueht, 1972; Dick Deadeye, 1975; More Cats, 1975; Searle's Zoodiac, 1977 as Zoodiac, 1978; The King of Beasts and Other Creatures, 1980 as The Situation Is Hopeless, 1981; Ronald Searle's Big Fat Cat Book, 1982; The Illustrated Winespeak: Ronald Searle's Wicked World of Winetasting, 1983; Ronald Searle in Perspective, 1984; Ronald Searle's Golden Oldies, 1941-1961, 1985; Collins and the Imperial War Museum, 1986; To the Kwai and Back: War Drawings, 1939-1945, 1986; Something in the Cellar: Ronald Searle's Wonderful World of Wine, 1986; Ah Yes, I Remember It Well.: Paris 1961-1975, 1987; Ronald Searle's Non-Sexist Dictionary, 1988; Slightly Foxed-but Still Desirable: Ronald Searle's Wicked World of Book Collecting, 1989; Carnet de Croquis: Le Plaisir du trait, 1992; The Curse of St. Trinian's: The Best of the Drawings, 1993; Marquis de Sade Meets Goody Two-Shoes, 1994; Tales of Grandpa Cat, 1994; Hatless Man, 1995; Ronald Searle das Le Monde, 1998; The Face of War, 1999; Le Theatre a Paris (1954-1962), 2000; The Terror of St. Trinian's and Other Drawings, 2000; Ronald Searle in Le Monde, 2002; Beastly Feasts, 2007; Let's have a Bite!, 2010. CO-AUTHOR: (with K. Webb) Paris Sketchbook, 1950, rev. ed., 1957; (with T. Shy) The Terror of St. Trinian's; or, Angela's Prince Charming, 1952; (with K. Webb) Looking at London and People Worth Meeting, 1953; (with G. Willans) How to Be Topp: A Guide to Sukcess for Tiny Pupils, Including All Is to Kno About Space, 1954; (with G. Willans) Whizz for Atomms: A Guide to Survival in the Twentieth Century for Fellow Pupils, Their Doting Maters, Pompous Paters and Any Others Who Are Interested, 1956 as Molesworth's Guide to the Atomic Age, 1957; (with

G. Willans) The Dog's Ear Book: With Four Lugubrious Verses, 1958; (with A. Atkinson) The Big City; or, The New Mayhew, 1958; (with G. Willans) The Compleet Molesworth, 1958; (with G. Willans) Back in the Jug Agane, 1959 as Molesworth Back in the Jug Agane, 1960; (with A. Atkinson) USA for Beginners, 1959 as By Rocking Chair across America, 1959; (with A. Atkinson) Russia for Beginners: By Rocking Chair across Russia as By Rocking Chair across Russia, 1960; (with K. Webb) Refugees 1960, 1960; (with A. Atkinson) Escape from the Amazon!, 1964; (with H. Huber) Anatomie eines Adlers: Ein Deutschlandbuch as Haven't We Met before Somewhere?: Germany from the Inside and Out, 1966; (with K. Dobbs) The Great Fur Opera: Annals of the Hudson's Bay Company, 1670-1970, 1970; (with I. Shaw) Paris! Paris!, 1977. Contributor to periodicals. *Died 2011.*

ŠKVORECKÝ, Josef. Canadian/Czech (born Czech Republic), b. 1924. **Genres:** Novels, Film, Autobiography/Memoirs, Translations, inspirational/Motivational Literature. **Career:** Odeon Publishers, Anglo-American Department, editor, 1953-56; World Literature Magazine, assistant editor-in-chief, 1959-56; University of Toronto, Erindale College, special lecturer in English and Slavic drama, 1969-71, writer-in-residence, 1970-71, associate professor, 1971-75, professor of English, 1975-90, professor emeritus, 1990-2012; Sixty-Eight Publishers Corp., co-founder, 1971-2012; Northwestern University, writer-in-residence, 1984; University of British Columbia, writer-in-residence, 1984; Amherst College, writer-in-residence, 1985-86. Translator. **Publications:** Zbabělci, 1958, 4th ed., 1968; Legenda Emoke, 1963, 2nd ed., 1965; Sedmiramenný svícen, 1964, 2nd ed., 1965; Nápady čtenáře Detektivek, 1965; Ze života české společnosti, 1965; Babylónský přibeh, 1965; Smutek poručika Borůvky, 1966; Konec nylonového věku, 1967; O nich-o nas, 1968; Velká pov´idka o Americe, 1969; (with E. Schorm) Fararuv Konec, 1969; Lvíče, 1969; Hořkej svět: Povídky zlet, 1946-67, 1969; Tankový prapor, 1971; All the Bright Young Men and Women: A Personal History of the Czech Cinema, 1971; Mirákl, 1972; Hříchy pro pátera Knoxe, 1973; Prima Sezóna, 1974; Konec poručika Borůvky, 1975; Příběh Inženýra lidských duší: Entrtejnment na starátémata o životě, ženách, osudu, snění, dělnické třdě, fízlech, lásce a smrti, 1977; (with A. Brousek) Na brigádě, 1979; The Bass Saxophone; Bůh do domu: fraška o čt'yřech dějstvích, 1980; Návratporučika Borůvky: reakcionářská detektivka, 1980; Dvělegendy, 1982; Jiří Menzel and the History of the Closely Watched Trains, 1982; Scherzo capriccioso: veselý sen o Dvořákovi, 1983; Ze zivota ceskae spolecnosti, 1985; Franz Kafka, jazz a jiné marginálie, 1988; Talkin' Moscow Blues, 1988; Hlas z Ameriky, 1990; Nezoufejte, 1990; Divák v únorovénoci, 1991; Samožerbuch, 1991; Nevěsta z Texasu: Romantický přibeh ze skutečnosti, 1992; Povídky tenorsaxofonisty, 1993; Příběhy u Lize amladém Wertherovi a jiné povídky, 1994; The Bass Saxophone: Two Novellas, 1994; Pribech newspesneno saxofonisty, 1994; pribehy o Lizemladem Wertherovi a jine povidky, 1994; Headed for the Blues: A Memoir, 1996; Nove canterburske povidky a jine pribehy, 1996; The Tenor Saxophonist's Story, 1997; Nevysvetlitelny pribeh, aneb Vypraveni Questa Firma Sicula, 1999; When Eve Was Naked: Stories of a Life's Journey, 2000; (with Z. Salivarova) Kratke setkani, 2001; (with Z. Salivarova) Setkani po letech, 2001; Encounter After Many Years with Murder, 2001; Two Murders in My Double Life: A Crime Novel in Two Interlocking Movements, 2001; An Inexplicable Story, or, The Narrative of Questus Firmus Siculus, 2002; Pulchra: příběh o krásné planetě, 2003; Encounter in Prague, with Murder, 2004; Ordinary Lives, 2004. EDITOR: Selected Writings of Sinclair Lewis, 1964-69; (with P.L. Doruzka) Tvar Jazzu, 1966; Collected Writings of Ernest Hemingway, 1965-69; Three Times Hercule Poirot, 1965; (with P.L. Doruzka) Jazzovainspirace, 1966; Nachrichten aus der CSSR, 1968. Contributor to periodicals. *Died 2012.*

SPINK, Ian. British (born England), b. 1932. **Genres:** Music, History. **Career:** University of Sydney, Music Department, lecturer, senior lecturer, 1962-69; University of London, Royal Holloway, senior lecturer, 1969-72, head of department, 1969-92, reader, 1972-74, dean of faculty of arts, 1973-75, 1983-85, dean of faculty of music, 1974-78, professor of music, 1974-97, professor emeritus, 1997-. Writer. **Publications:** An Historical Approach to Musical Form, 1967; English Song: Dowland to Purcell, 1974; The Seventeenth Century, Blackwell History of Music in Britain, 1988; (intro.) Choice Ayres, Songs and Dialogues, 1989; Restoration Cathedral Music 1660-1714, 1995; Henry Lawes: Cavalier Songwriter, 2000. EDITOR: Ayres, Songs and Dialogues, 1961; Songs (1604) and Ayres (1618), 1962; Manuscript Songs, 1966; English Songs 1625-1660, 1971; The Judgment of Paris, 1978; The Athlone History of Music in Britain, 1981; The Works of Henry Purcell, vol. IV: A Song for the Duke of Gloucester's Birthday: 1695, 1990, vol. II, Timon of Athens, 1994; Dramatic Music, 1998; Catches, 2000. Contributor to journals. *Died 2011.*

STOLZ, Karen. American (born United States), b. 1957. **Genres:** Novels. **Career:** Austin Community College, adjunct instructor in English, 1994-2005; St. Edwards University, adjunct instructor, 2001-05; Pittsburgh State University, assistant professor, associate professor of English and creative writing, 2005-11. Writer. **Publications:** World of Pies, 2000; Fanny and Sue: A Novel, 2003; In One Word: Contemporary Writers on the Words They Love or Loathe, 2010. *Died 2011.*

STONE, Ruth. American (born United States), b. 1915. **Genres:** Poetry. **Career:** Radcliffe College, seminar teacher, 1963-65; Wellesley College, faculty, 1965; Brandies University, faculty of English department, 1965-66; University of Wisconsin, faculty, 1967-69; University of Illinois, faculty, 1971-73; Indiana University, visiting professor, 1973-74; Center College, creative writing, chair, 1975; Brandies University, Hurst visiting professor, 1976; University of Virginia, visiting professor, 1977-78; University of California, regent's lecturer, 1978, visiting lecturer, 1978, 1981; Old Dominion University, visiting professor, 1989-90; State University of New York, Binghamton University, department of English, professor of English and creative writing, 1990, now professor emeritus. Writer. **Publications:** In an Iridescent Time, 1959; Topography and Other Poems, 1971; Unknown Messages, 1973; Cheap: New Poems and Ballads, 1975; American Milk, 1986; Second-Hand Coat: Poems New and Selected, 1987; The Solution, 1989; Who is The Widow's Muse?, 1991; Nursery Rhymes From Mother Stone, 1992; Simplicity, 1995; House is Made of Poetry: The Art of Ruth Stone, 1996; Ordinary Words, 1999; In the Next Galaxy, 2002; In the Dark, 2004; What ILove Comes To: New and Selected Poems, 2008. Contributor to books and periodicals. *Died 2011.*

TAWA, Nicholas E. American (born United States), b. 1923. **Genres:** Music, History, Military/Defense/Arms Control. **Career:** Sonneck Society (now Society for American Music), co-founder, 1974, newsletter editor, 1975-80, vice president, 1975-80; University of Massachusetts, assistant professor, 1965-70, associate professor, 1970-77, professor of music, 1977-, professor emeritus. Writer. **Publications:** Sweet Songs for Gentle Americans: The Parlor Song in America, 1790-1860, 1980; A Sound of Strangers: Musical Culture, Acculturation, and the Post-Civil War Ethnic American, 1982; A Music for the Millions: Antebellum Democratic Attitudes and the Birth of American Popular Music, 1984; Serenading the Reluctant Eagle: American Musical Life, 1925-1945, 1984; A Most Wondrous Babble: American Art Composers, Their Music, and the American Scene, 1950-1985, 1987; Art Music in the American Society: The Condition of Art Music in the Late Twentieth Century, 1987; (ed.) American Solo Songs through 1865, 1989; (ed.) American Solo Songs 1866 through 1910, 1989; The Way to Tin Pan Alley: American Popular Song, 1866-1910, 1990; The Coming of Age of American Art Music: New England's Classical Romanticists, 1991; The Transitional American Composers of the Early Twentieth Century, 1992; Mainstream Music of Early Twentieth Century America: The Composers, Their Times, and Their Works, 1992; American Composers and Their Public: A Critical Look, 1995; Arthur Foote: A Musician in the Frame of Time and Place, 1997; High-Minded and Low-Down: Music in the Lives of Americans, 1800-1861, 2000; From Psalm to Symphony: A History of Music in New England, 2001; Supremely American: Popular Song in the 20th Century: Styles and Singers and What They Said About America, 2005; Great American Symphony: Music, the Depression, and War, 2009. Contributor to periodicals. *Died 2011.*

THOMAS, Edmund Barrington. Australian (born Australia), b. 1929?. **Genres:** Education, History. **Career:** Charlton High School, principal, 1966-67; Heywood High School, principal, 1968-70; University of Papua New Guinea, lecturer in education, 1971-72, sub-dean and dean of education, 1971-74, senior lecturer, 1973-76; Earle Page College, University of New England, master, 1976-79, senior lecturer in educational administration, 1976-84; Deakin University, senior lecturer in educational administration, 1984-86; The Professional Reading Guide for Educational Administrators, editor and publisher; Educational and Staff Development Services, director. Writer. **Publications:** Let's Talk of Many Things, 1966, 4th ed., 1986-87; Educational Research in Papua New Guinea: Priorities and Approaches: Papers Prepared for an Extraordinary Meeting of the Faculty of Education, UPNG, on October 25, 1974, 1977; (with W.S. Simpkins and A.R.Thomas) Principal and Task: An Australian Perspective, 1982. EDITOR: Papua New Guinea Education, 1976; Coping with Stress in Education, 1986; (with W.S. Simpkins and A.R. Thomas) Principal and Change: The Australian Experience, 1987; The School Principal's Handbook Series, 1992; The Principal's Treasury of Professional Reading: 101 Selected Summaries from the PRG 1990-2000, 2001. *Died 2009.*

VAN DYKE, Henry. American (born United States), b. 1928. **Genres:** Novels, Young Adult Fiction, History. **Career:** University Engineering Research Institute, associate editor, 1956-58; Crowell-Collier-Macmillan Inc., correspondent, 1959-67; writer, 1967-2011; Kent State University, writer-in-residence, 1969, emeritus; University of Michigan, associate editor. **Publications:** Ladies of the Rachmaninoff Eyes, 1965; Blood of Strawberries, 1969; Dead Piano, 1971; Lunacy and Caprice, 1987. Contributor to books and periodicals. *Died 2011.*

WARMINGTON, William Allan. British (born England), b. 1922. **Genres:** Administration/Management, History, Industrial Relations, Third World, Local History/Rural Topics, Natural History, Economics. **Career:** Building Research Station (DSIR), research assistant in economics, 1951-53; West Africa Institute of Social and Economic Research, freelance writer, lecturer and research fellow, 1953-56; Institute of Science and Technology, senior research fellow, 1956-69; London School of Economics, senior research officer, 1957-61; University of Manchester, Manchester School of Business, lecturer, 1969-83, senior research fellow. Writer. **Publications:** A West African Trade Union, 1960; (with Edwin and S. Ardener) Plantation and Village in the Cameroons, 1962; (with F.A. Wells) Studies in Industrialization: Nigeria and the Cameroons, 1962; (with T. Lupton and C. Gribbin) Organizational Behaviour and Performance: An Open System Approach to Change, 1977. Contributor to books. *Died 2007.*

WAYMAN, Vivienne. British (born England), b. 1926?. **Genres:** Mystery/Crime/Suspense, Children's Fiction. **Career:** Writer and educator. **Publications:** The Rose Boy at Penny Spring, 1968; Emma of Lark Water Hall, 1969; The Alabaster Princess, 1970; A Cage in the Apple Orchard, 1972; The Seventh Bull Maiden, 1974; Panchit's Secret, 1975; The Golden Duck (crime fiction), 1991. *Died 2003.*

WECKMANN, Luis. Mexican (born Mexico), b. 1923. **Genres:** History, Politics/Government, Biography. **Career:** National University of Mexico, lecturer, professor of history, 1944-64; University of the Americas, lecturer, associate professor, 1948-64, professor emeritus, 1991-95, dean of humanities; Mexican Foreign Service, foreign service officer, 1952-89, ambassador to Israel, 1967-69, ambassador to Austria, 1969-73, ambassador to West Germany, 1973-76, ambassador to Iran, 1976-79, ambassador to the United Nations, 1979-82, ambassador to Italy, 1982-86, ambassador to Belgium, 1986-88, consult general in Rio de Janeiro, 1988-89, eminent ambassador, 1989; El Colegiode Mexico, professor, 1960-79, director of graduate seminars in history, 1979-80. Writer. **Publications:** La Sociedad Feudal: Esencia y Supervivencias, 1944; Bulas Alejandrinas de 1493 y la teoría política del Papado medieval: Estudio de laSupremacía papal Sobre Islas, 1091-1493, 1949, 2nd ed. as Constantine the Great and Christopher Columbus, 1992; El Pensamiento Politico Medieval, 1950, 2nd ed., 1992; Las Relaciones Franco-Mexicanas, 1823-1885, 3 vols., 1972; Panorama de la Cultura Medieval, 1962; La herenciamedieval de Mexico, 1984; Mexico: Secretaria de Relaciones Exteriores, 1987; Carlotade Belgica: Correspondence, 1861-1868, 1989; Herencia medieval del Brasil, 1993; Glosario de terminusheraldicos, 1995; Diarios Politicos de un Embajador Mexicano, 1967-1988, 1997. *Died 1995.*

WESTCOTT, Jan (Vlachos). American (born United States), b. 1912. **Genres:** Novels, Mystery/Crime/Suspense, Romance/Historical, Young Adult Fiction. **Career:** Writer. **Publications:** The Border Lord, 1946, trans. as Det er maanelyst i nat, 1947; Jarl Og Elsker, 1947; Captain for Elizabeth, 1948; The Hepburn, 1950; Captain Barney, 1951; The Walsingham Woman, 1953; The Queen's Grace, 1959; Condottiere, 1962 in UK as The Mercenary, 1963; The White Rose, 1969 in UK as The Lion's Share, 1972; Set Her on a Throne, 1972; The Tower and the Dream, 1974; A Woman of Quality, 1978. *Died 2011.*

WICKER, Tom. (Paul Connolly). American (born United States), b. 1926. **Genres:** Novels, Politics/Government, Social Commentary, Biography, History. **Career:** Chamber of Commerce, Southern Pines Chamber, director, 1948-49; The Robesonian, managing editor, 1949-50; North Carolina Board of Public Welfare, public information director, 1950-51; Winston-Salem Journal, copy editor, 1951-52; U.S. Naval Reserves, sports editor, 1954-55, Sunday feature editor, 1955-56; Washington correspondent, 1957; Nieman fellow, 1957-58; editorial writer and city hall correspondent, 1958-59; Nashville Tennessean, associate editor, 1959-60; New York Times, staff of Washington bureau, 1960-64, chief of Washington bureau, 1964-68; political columnist and associate editor, 1968-91; Davidson College, James K. Batten visiting professor of public policy, 1998; Middle Tennessee State University, visiting professor of journalism, 1999; University of Southern California, visiting professor, 1999. Journalist. **Publications:** NOVELS AS PAUL CONNOLLY: Get Out of Town, 1951; Tears Are for Angels, 1952; So Fair, So Evil, 1955. NOVELS: The Kingpin, 1953; The Devil Must, 1957; The Judgement, 1961; On the World's Front Pages: The Behind-The-Scenes Story of The C.I.A., 1966; JFK and LBJ: The Influence of Personality Upon Politics, 1968; (with C.V. Woodward and S. Hook) Social Justice and the Problems of the Twentieth Century, 1968; Facing the Lions, 1973; A Time to Die, 1975; On Press, 1978; Politics and The Press, 1979; Unto This Hour: A Novel, 1984; Donovan's Wife, 1992; Time to Die: The Attica Prison Revolt, 1994; Easter Lilly: A Novel of the South Today, 1998. NON-FICTION: Kennedy without Tears, the Man beneath the Myth, 1964; JFK and LBJ: The Influence of Personality upon Politics, 1968; (intro.) U.S. Kerner Commission Report of the National Advisory Commission on Civil Disorders, 1968; (intro.) White House Enemies: Or How We Made the Dean's List, 1973; A Time to Die, 1975; On Press, 1978; One of Us: Richard Nixon and the American Dream, 1991; Time to Die: The Attica Prison Revolt, 1994; Tragic Failure: Racial Integration in America, 1996; (with W. Westfeldt) Indictment: The News Media and the Criminal Justice System, 1998; The Nixon Years, 1969-1974: White House to Watergate, 1999; Keeping the Record, 2001; Dwight D. Eisenhower, 2002; On the Record: An Insider's Guide to Journalism, 2002; (intro.) Four Days in November, 2003; George Herbert Walker Bush, 2004; Shooting Star: The Brief of Joseph McCarthy, 2006. Contributor of articles to magazines and books. *Died 2011.*

WILLIAMS, Michael. British (born England), b. 1935. **Genres:** Environmental Sciences/Ecology, Geography. **Career:** University of Adelaide, lecturer, 1960-65, senior lecturer, 1966-72, reader in geography, 1973-78; South Australian Institute of Technology, part-time lecturer, 1963-70; University College, lecturer, 1966-67, 1973; University of Wisconsin, visiting fellow, 1973-74; Oxford University, lecturer, 1978-90, reader in geography, 1990-96, professor of geography, 1996-2002, Environmental Change and Management Unit, director, 1993-98, Oriel College, fellow, 1993-2002, emeritus fellow, vice provost, 2000-02, emeritus professor of geography; St. Anne's College, lecturer in charge, 1978-96, Transactions of the Institute of British Geographers, editor, 1983-87; Flinders University, visiting fellow, 1984; University of Chicago, visiting fellow, 1989; University of California, visiting fellow; Global Environmental Change, joint editor, 1993-96; Progress in Human Geography, joint editor, 1999-2000; University of California, lecturer; Brandeis University, lecturer; University of Michigan, lecturer; Duke University, lecturer; North Carolina State University, lecturer. **Publications:** Adelaide, 1966; (ed.) South Australia from the Air, 1969; The Draining of the Somerset Levels, 1970; (with B.A. Badcock and D.H. Jaensch) Adelaide at the Census, 1971: The Making of the South Australian Landscape, 1974; (with J.M. Powell) Australian Space, Australian Time: Geographical Perspectives, 1788-1914, 1975; The Changing Rural Landscape of South Australia, 1977, rev. ed., 1992; A Social Atlas (monograph), 1977; The Americans and Their Forests: An Historical Geography, 1989; Wetlands: A Threatened Landscape, 1991; (ed.) Planet Management, 1993; (ed.) Understanding Geographical and Environmental Education: The Role of Research, 1996; The Landscapes of Lowland Britain, 1999; (ed.) The Relations of History and Geography: Studies in England, France and the United States, 2001; (ed. with R.H. Johnston) A Century of British Geography, 2003; Deforesting the Earth: Prehistoric to Present Crisis, 2003, rev. ed., 2006; (ed. with M. Robertson) Young People, Leisure and Place: Cross Cultural Perspectives, 2004; Galen Beknighted, 2004; (ed. with G. Humphrys) Presenting and Representing Environments, 2005; (ed. with J.C. Lee) School Improvement: International Perspectives, 2006; (ed. with J.C. Lee) Environmental and Geographical Education for Sustainability: Cultural Contexts, 2006; (with D.J. Meaker and R. Kimbrough) Extraordinary Old Testament People, 2006; (with G. Gooch) A Dictionary of Law Enforcement, 2007; Trajans Arch, 2010. Contributor to periodicals. *Died 2009.*

WINCHESTER, Stanley. *See* YOUD, Samuel.

WYNIA, Gary W. American (born United States), b. 1942. **Genres:** Economics, Politics/Government, History. **Career:** University of Minnesota, assistant professor, 1969-75, associate professor, 1975-78, professor of political science, 1978-84; Carleton College, Latin American Politics, professor and Kenan chairman, 1984-94, Department of Political Science, chairman, 1992-94. Writer. **Publications:** Politics and Planners: Economic Development Policy in Central America, 1972; Economic Policy-Making under Stress:

Conflict and Exchange in Argentina, 1974; The Politics of Latin American Development, 1978, 3rd ed., 1990; Argentina in the Postwar Era: Politics and Economic Policy Making in a Divided Society, 1978; Argentina: Illusions and Realities, 1986. *Died 2007.*

YATES, Nigel. Welsh/British (born England), b. 1944. **Genres:** Theology/Religion, Politics/Government, History, Essays. **Career:** University of Wales, professor of ecclesiastical history, University Research Center, keeper of archives and manuscripts. Writer and archivist. **Publications:** (Ed. with T. Barnes) Carmarthenshire Studies: Essays Presented to Major Francis Jones, 1974; Leeds and the Oxford Movement: A Study of High Church Activity in the Rural Deaneries of Allerton, Armley, Headingley and Whitkirk in the Diocese of Ripon, 1836-1934, 1975; (ed. with J. Webb and S. Quail) Hampshire Studies: Presented to Dorothy Dymond, C.B.E., M.A., D.Litt., on the Occasion of Her Ninetieth Birthday, 1981; Kent and the Oxford Movement: Selected Documents, 1983; (ed. with A. Detsicas) Studies in Modern Kentish History: Presented to Felix Hull and Elizabeth Melling on the Occasion of the Fiftieth Anniversary of the Kent Archives Office, 1983; The Later Kentish Seaside, 1840-1974: Selected Documents, 1985; Buildings, Faith, and Worship: The Liturgical Arrangement of Anglican Churches, 1600-1900, 1991, rev. ed., 2000; (ed. with W.M. Jacob and contrib.) Crown and Mitre: Religion and Society in Northern Europe since the Reformation, 1993; (with R. Hume and P. Hastings) Religion and Society in Kent, 1640-1914, 1994; (ed. with J.M. Gibson) Traffic and Politics: The Construction and Management of Rochester Bridge, AD 43-1993, 1994; (ed.) Faith and Fabric: A History of Rochester Cathedral, 604-1994, 1996; Anglican Ritualism in Victorian Britain, 1830-1910, 1999; (ed.) Kent in the Twentieth Century, 2001; The Religious Condition of Ireland, 1770-1850, 2006; (ed.) Bishop Burgess and His World: Culture, Religion, and Society in Britain, Europe, and North America in the Eighteenth and Nineteenth Centuries, 2007; Liturgical Space: Christian Worship and Church Buildings in Western Europe, 1500-2000, 2008; Eighteenth-Century Britain: Religion and Politics, 1714-1815, 2008. Contributor to books and periodicals. *Died 2009.*

YOUD, Samuel. Also writes as Hilary Ford, Anthony Rye, Stanley Winchester, Peter Nichols, John Christopher. British (born England), b. 1922. **Genres:** Novels, Novellas/Short Stories, Science Fiction/Fantasy, Young Adult Fiction, Bibliography. **Career:** Industrial Diamond Information Bureau of the Diamond Corp., staff, 1949-58; writer, 1958-2012. **Publications:** AS JOHN CHRISTOPHER: THE TRIPODS TRILOGY: The White Mountains, 1967, 2nd ed., 1988; The City of Gold and Lead, 1967, 2nd ed., 1988; The Pool of Fire, 1968, rev. ed., 1999. AS JOHN CHRISTOPHER: THE SWORD TRILOGY: The Prince in Waiting, 1970, 2nd ed., 1989; Beyond the Burning Lands, 1971, 2nd ed., 1989; The Sword of the Spirits, 1972, 2nd ed., 1989. AS JOHN CHRISTOPHER: THE FIREBALL TRILOGY: Fireball, 1981; New Found Land, 1983; Dragon Dance, 1986. ADULT NOVELS: The Winter Swan, 1949; Babel Itself, 1951; Brave Conquerors, 1952; Crown and Anchor, 1953; A Palace of Strangers, 1954; The Opportunist in UK as Holly Ash, 1955; (as Anthony Rye) Giant's Arrow, 1956; The Choice, 1961 in UK as The Burning Bird, 1964; Messages of Love, 1961; The Summers at Accorn, 1963. AS JOHN CHRISTOPHER FOR ADULTS: The Twenty-Second Century (stories), 1954; The Year of the Comet, 1955 in US as Planet in Peril, 1959; The Death of Grass, 1956 in US as No Blade of Grass, 1957; The Caves of Night, 1959; A Scent of White Poppies, 1959; The White Voyage in UK as The Long Voyage, 1960; The Long Winter in UK as The World in Winter, 1962; Sweeney's Island in UK as Cloud on Silver, 1964; The Possessors, 1965; A Wrinkle in the Skin, 1965 in US as The Ragged Edge, 1966; The Little People, 1967; Pendulum, 1968; Bad Dream, 2003. AS JOHN CHRISTOPHER FOR CHILDREN: The Lotus Caves, 1969, 2nd ed., 1992; The Guardians, 1970, 2nd ed., 1992; In the Beginning, 1972, rev. ed. as Dom and Va, 1973; Wild Jack, 1974, 2nd ed., 1991; Empty World, 1977; When the Tripods Came, 1988; A Dusk of Demons, 1993. AS HILARY FORD: Felix Walking, 1958; Felix Running, 1959; Bella on the Roof, 1965; A Figure in Grey, 1973; Sarnia, 1974; Castle Malindine, 1975; A Bride for Bedivere, 1976. AS WILLIAM GODFREY: Malleson at Melbourne, 1956; The Friendly Game, 1957. AS PETER GRAAF: Dust and the Curious Boy in US as Give the Devil His Due, 1957; Daughter Fair, 1958; The Sapphire Conference, 1959; The Gull's Kiss, 1962. AS PETER NICHOLS: Patchwork of Death, 1965; Piedmont and the English, 1967. AS STANLEY WINCHESTER: The Practice: A Novel, 1967; Man with a Knife, 1968; The Helpers, 1970; Ten Per Cent of Your Life, 1973. *Died 2012.*

YOUNG-BRUEHL, Elisabeth. American (born United States), b. 1946.

Genres: Novels, Philosophy, Biography, Essays, Psychology. **Career:** Wesleyan University, assistant professor, 1974-81, associate professor, 1981-86, professor, 1986-91; Yale University, Gardiner Seminar in Psychiatry and the Humanities, faculty, 1984-2011; Haverford College, professor of psychology, 1992-98; Columbia University, Center for Psychoanalytic Training and Research, faculty; Institute of Pennsylvania Hospital, psychotherapist. Writer. **Publications:** (With R. Hogan) Conor Cruise O'Brien: An Appraisal, 1974; Freedom and Karl Jaspers's Philosophy, 1981; Hannah Arendt: For Love of the World (biography), 1982, 2nd ed., 2004; Vigil: A Novel, 1983; Anna Freud: A Biography, 1988, 2nd ed., 2008; Mind and the Body Politic (essays), 1989; (ed. and intro.) Freud on Women: A Reader, 1990; Creative Characters (non-fiction), 1991; (ed. and intro.) Global Cultures: A Transnational Short Fiction Reader, 1994; The Anatomy of Prejudices, 1996; Subject to Biography: Psychoanalysis, Feminism, and Writing Women's Lives, 1998; (with F. Bethelard) Cherishment: A Psychology of the Heart, 2000; Where Do We Fall When We Fall in Love?, 2003; Why Arendt Matters, 2006. Contributor to journals. *Died 2011.*

WOLVERHAMPTON LIBRARIES

INDEX TO WRITING CATEGORIES

CONTENTS

Creative Writing

Novels
Novellas/Short stories
Mystery/Crime/Suspense
Horror
Romance/Historical
Science fiction/Fantasy
Westerns/Adventure
Children's fiction
Young adult fiction
Plays/Screenplays
Poetry
Songs/Lyrics and libretti

Non-fiction

Administration/Management
Adult non-fiction
Advertising/Public relations
Aerospace. *See* Air/Space topics
Aging. *See* Gerontology/Senior issues
Agriculture/Forestry
Air/Space topics
Animals/Pets
Anthropology/Ethnology
Antiques/Furnishings
Antiquities. *See* Archaeology/Antiquities
Archaeology/Antiquities
Architecture
Area studies
Arms control. *See* Military/Defense/Arms control
Art/Art history
Art history. *See* Art/Art history
Astronomy
Atmospheric sciences. *See* Meteorology/Atmospheric sciences
Ballet. *See* Dance/Ballet
Biology
Botany
Broadcasting. *See* Communications/Media
Business/Trade/Industry
Chemistry
Children's non-fiction
Cinema. *See* Film
City planning. *See* Regional/Urban planning
Civil liberties/Human rights
Classics
Communications/Media
Computers. *See* Information science/

Computers
Cookery. *See* Food and Wine
Costume. *See* Fashion/Costume
Country life. *See* Local history/Rural topics
Crafts
Criminology/True Crime
Cultural/Ethnic topics
Current affairs. *See* International relations/Current affairs
Dance/Ballet
Defense. *See* Military/Defense/Arms control
Demography
Design
Dictionaries. *See* Language/Linguistics
Earth sciences
Ecology. *See* Environmental sciences/Ecology
Economics
Education
Engineering
Environmental sciences/Ecology
Ethics
Ethnic topics. *See* Cultural/Ethnic topics
Ethnology. *See* Anthropology/Ethnology
Exploration. *See* Travel/Exploration
Facts. *See* Trivia/Facts
Fashion/Costume
Film
Finance. *See* Money/Finance
Fitness. *See* Sports/Fitness
Folklore. *See* Mythology/Folklore
Food and Wine
Forestry. *See* Agriculture/Forestry
Furnishings. *See* Antiques/Furnishings
Gardens. *See* Homes/Gardens
Gastronomy. *See* Food and Wine
Gay and lesbian issues
Genealogy/Heraldry
Geography
Gerontology/Senior issues
Government. *See* Politics/Government
Health. *See* Medicine/Health
Heraldry. *See* Genealogy/Heraldry
History
Hobbies. *See* Recreation
Homes/Gardens
Horticulture
How-to books
Human relations/Parenting
Human rights. *See* Civil liberties/Human rights

Humanities
Industrial relations
Industry. *See* Business/Trade/Industry
Information science/Computers
Inspirational/Motivational Literature
Institutions/Organizations
Intellectual history
International relations/Current affairs
Journalism. *See* Writing/Journalism
Justice. *See* Civil liberties/Human rights; Criminology/True Crime; Law
Language/Linguistics
Law
Leisure. *See* Recreation
Librarianship
Linguistics. *See* Language/Linguistics
Literary criticism and history
Local history/Rural topics
Management. *See* Administration/Management
Marine sciences/Oceanography
Marketing
Mathematics/Statistics
Media. *See* Communications/Media
Medicine/Health
Meteorology/Atmospheric sciences
Military/Defense/Arms control
Money/Finance
Motivational Literature. *See* Inspirational/Motivational Literature
Music
Mythology/Folklore
Natural history
Nonfiction. *See* Adult non-fiction; Children's non-fiction; Young adult nonfiction
Occult. *See* Paranormal
Oceanography. *See* Marine sciences/Oceanography
Organizations. *See* Institutions/Organizations
Organized labor
Paranormal
Parenting. *See* Human relations/Parenting
Parenting. *See* Human relations/Parenting; How-to books
Pets. *See* Animals/Pets
Philosophy
Photography
Physics
Politics/Government

Popular Culture
Psychiatry
Psychology
Public relations. *See* Advertising/Public relations
Public/Social administration
Race relations
Radio. *See* Communications/Media
Recreation
Regional/Urban planning
Religion. *See* Theology/Religion
Rhetoric. *See* Speech/Rhetoric
Rural topics. *See* Local history/Rural topics
Sciences
Self help
Senior issues. *See* Gerontology/Senior issues
Sex
Social administration. *See* Public/Social administration
Social commentary
Social sciences
Social work

Sociology
Space. *See* Air/Space topics
Speech/Rhetoric
Sports/Fitness
Statistics. *See* Mathematics/Statistics
Supernatural. *See* Paranormal
Technology
Television. *See* Communications/Media
Theatre
Theology/Religion
Third World
Town planning. *See* Regional/Urban planning
Trade. *See* Business/Trade/Industry
Transportation
Travel/Exploration
Trivia/Facts
True Crime. *See* Criminology/True Crime
Urban planning. *See* Regional/Urban planning
Urban studies
Wine. *See* Food and Wine
Women's studies and issues

Writing/Journalism
Young adult non-fiction
Zoology

Others

Autobiography/Memoirs
Bibliography
Biography
Board books. *See* Picture/board books
Cartoons
Documentaries/Reportage
e-Books
Essays
Ghost Writer
Graphic Novels
Humor/Satire
Illustrations
Picture/board books
Reference

Creative Writing

Novels

Aaron, Chester
Abajian, Kathryn J.
Abani, Chris
Abate, Carmine
Abbott, Hailey
Abbott, Karen
Abela, Deborah Anne
Abercrombie, Joe
Aberjhani
Abi-Ezzi, Nathalie
Abidi, Azhar
Abish, Walter
Ablow, Keith Russell
Abrahams, Peter
Abrams, Douglas Carlton
Abrams, Linsey
Abse, Dannie
Abu-Jaber, Diana
Accad, Evelyne
Achebe, Chinua
Ackroyd, Peter
Adair, Cherry
Adair, Vivyan Campbell
Adams, C. T.
Adams, Hazard
Adams, Jad
Adams, James (Macgregor David)
Adams, Jessica
Adams, Lorraine
Adams, Patch
Adams, Richard (George)
Adams, Sheila Kay
Adams, Will
Adamson, Gil
Adamson, M(ary) J(o)
Adderson, Caroline
Addonia, Sulaiman S. M. Y.
Addonizio, Kim (Theresa)
Adichie, Chimamanda Ngozi
Adickes, Sandra
Adlard, Mark
Adler, Elizabeth
Adnan, Etel
Agarwal, Shilpa
Agee, Jonis
Agell, Charlotte
Agha-Jaffar, Tamara
Agonito, Rosemary
Aidinoff, Elsie V.
Aira, César
Aird, Catherine
Akamatsu, Ken
Akins, Ellen
Akst, Daniel
Al-Ali, Nadje Sadig
al-Mohaimeed, Yousef
Al-Samman, Ghadah
Alameddine, Rabih
Alarcon, Daniel
Albahari, David
Albanese, Laurie Lico
Albarella, Joan K.
Albert, Bill
Albert, Susan Wittig
Alberts, Laurie

Novels-*cont.*

Alder, Ken(neth L.)
Aldridge, (Harold Edward) James
Alexander, Gary
Alexander, Meena
Alexander, Victoria N.
Alexie, Sherman (Joseph)
Alexis, Andre
Ali, Samina
Alkali, Zaynab
Allegretto, Michael
Allen, Edward (Hathaway)
Allen, John Jay
Allen, Preston L.
Allen, Roberta
Allen, Sarah Addison
Allende, Isabel
Allington, Maynard
Allison, Jennifer
Allison, Will
Allston, Aaron
Allyn, Doug
Almog, Ruth
Alonso, Eric Frattini
Alpert, Mark
Alphin, Elaine Marie
Alten, Steve
Altenburg, Matthias
Alter, Judy
Alther, Lisa
Alvarez, A(lfred)
Alvarez, Julia
Alvtegen, Karin
Amabile, George
Amadi, Elechi
Amato, Mary
Amery, Colin
Ames, Greg
Ames, Jonathan
Amick, Steve
Amirrezvani, Anita
Amis, Martin (Louis)
Amos, James H.
An, Na
Anam, Tahmima
Anania, Michael (Angelo)
Anastas, Benjamin
Anaya, Rudolfo A(lfonso)
Andersen, Kurt Byars
Anderson, Barth
Anderson, David Daniel
Anderson, Henry L(ee Norman)
Anderson, James G.
Anderson, Kevin J(ames)
Anderson, M. T(obin)
Anderson, Rachel
Anderson, Sheryl J.
Andoe, Joe
Andrews, J(ames) S(ydney)
Andrews, John (Malcolm)
Andrews, Sarah
Andrus, Jeff
Angelou, Maya
Ansa, Tina McElroy
Ansay, A. Manette
Anscombe, Roderick
Anshaw, Carol
Antal, Dan

Novels-*cont.*

Anthony, Crystal McCrary
Anthony, Evelyn
Anthony, Michael
Anthony, Patricia
Anthony, Piers
Anton, Maggie
Antoni, Brian
Antoni, Robert (William)
Antoon, Sinan
Antrim, Donald
Antrim, Taylor
Aoyama, Gosho
Appiah, (K.) Anthony
Apple, Max (Isaac)
Apple, Sam
Applegate, Katherine (Alice)
Appleman, Philip (Dean)
Appleyard, Bryan (Edward)
Araton, Harvey
Arbuthnott, Gill
Archer, Colleen Rutherford
Archer, Jeffrey (Howard)
Arden, John
Argers, Helen
Argiri, Laura
Aridjis, Chloe
Armah, Ayi Kwei
Armistead, John
Armstrong, Adam
Armstrong, Alan
Armstrong, David
Armstrong, Diane (Julie)
Armstrong, Jeannette C.
Armstrong, Jennifer
Armstrong, Judith (Mary)
Armstrong, Kelley L.
Armstrong, Luanne (A.)
Armstrong, Richard
Arnaud, Claude
Arnold, Elizabeth
Arnzen, Michael A.
Aronson, Sarah
Arthur, Keri
Arvin, Reed
Asante, Molefi K.
Aschan, Ulf
Ascher, Marcia
Ash, William Franklin
Ashbery, John (Lawrence)
Asher, Neal
Ashley, Bernard
Ashley, Leonard R. N.
Ashley, Trisha
Ashliman, D. L.
Asimov, Janet Jeppson
Aslam, Nadeem
Asner, Jules
Assefi, Nassim
Astley, Neil
Atabaki, Touraj
Athas, Daphne
Atkins, Charles
Atkinson, Kate
Attali, Jacques
Attema, Martha
Atwood, Margaret
Atxaga, Bernardo

Novels-*cont.*

Aubert, Jacques
Auel, Jean M(arie)
Auseon, Andrew
Auslander, Shalom
Austen, Catherine
Auster, Paul
Autry, Curt
Avi
Avishai, Bernard
Aw, Tash
Awoonor, Kofi
Axelrod, Mark (R.)
Ayres, Philip
Azriel, Yakov
Babbitt, Natalie
Baca, Ana
Bache, Ellyn
Bacho, Peter
Backer, Sara
Backscheider, Paula R(ice)
Bacon, Charlotte
Bacon, Margaret
Badami, Anita Rau
Badawi, Mohamed Mustafa
Baddock, James
Badeni, June
Badgley, John Herbert
Baecque, Antoine de
Baggott, Julianna
Bail, Murray
Bailey, Anne C.
Bailey, Anthony
Bailey, Charles Waldo
Bailey, F(rancis) Lee
Bailey, Hilary
Bailey, John
Bailey, Kathleen C.
Bailey, Linda
Bailey, Robin W(ayne)
Bailey-Williams, Nicole
Bailie, Grant
Baillie, Allan
Baird, Alison
Bajwa, Rupa
Baker, Calvin
Baker, Deirdre
Baker, Ellen
Baker, Kevin (Breen)
Baker, Larry
Baker, Lise S.
Baker, Lori
Baker, Sharlene
Baker, Susan P.
Bakker, Robert T.
Balaji, Murali
Baldeosingh, Kevin
Baldwin, Frank
Baldwin, John
Baldwin, Rosecrans
Bales, Richard F.
Ball, Karen
Ball, Terence
Ballantyne, Tony
Ballard, Michael B.
Balliett, Blue
Balmaseda, Liz
Balogh, Mary

Balutansky, Kathleen M(arie)
Bambola, Sylvia
Banbury, Jen(nifer Marie)
Bandele, Biyi
Bandyopadhyay, Bidisha
Banish, Roslyn
Banks, Kate
Banks, Leanne
Banks, Lynne Reid
Banks, Ray
Banks, Russell (Earl)
Banner, Catherine
Banville, John
Baraka, Imamu Amiri
Baratz-Logsted, Lauren
Barber, Benjamin R(eynolds)
Barber, Paul (Thomas)
Barber, Ronde
Barbieri, Elaine
Barden, Dan
Barer, Helen
Baricco, Alessandro
Barich, Bill
Barkan, Josh
Barker, Clive
Barker, Dennis (Malcolm)
Barker, Elspeth
Barker, M. P.
Barker, Pat(ricia)
Barker, Raffaella
Barlowe, Raleigh (Bruce)
Barmack, Erik S.
Barnacle, Hugo
Barnard, Judith
Barnard, Robert
Barnes, H. Lee
Barnes, Joyce Annette
Barnes, Lynard
Barnes, Mike
Barnes, Simon
Barnett, John Le Page
Barnwell, William (Curtis)
Barolini, Helen
Barr, Nevada
Barr, Patricia (Miriam)
Barre, Richard
Barrett, Andrea
Barrett, James R.
Barrett, Joyce Durham
Barron, Laird
Barron, T. A.
Barry, Dave
Barsamian, David
Barth, John (Simmons)
Barthelme, Frederick
Barthelme, Steve(n)
Bartlett, Anne
Bartlett, Eric George
Bartlett, Jennifer Losch
Barton, (Samuel) Wayne
Barton, Dan
Bartov, Omer
Barzak, Christopher
Basch, Rachel
Bascomb, Neal
Bass, Cynthia
Bass, Paul

Bass, Ronald
Bass, T. J.
Bassil, Andrea
Basta, Samir Sanad
Basu, Kunal
Bat-Ami, Miriam
Bataille, Christophe
Batchelor, David
Batchelor, John
Bate, Jonathan
Bateman, Tracey V.
Bates, Judy Fong
Bates, Karen Grigsby
Bates, Stephen
Batory, Joseph P.
Battle, Michael Jesse
Battles, Brett
Bauer, Belinda
Bauer, Marion Dane
Bauer, Tricia
Bauman, Beth Ann
Bauman, Bruce
Bauman, Christian
Baumbach, Jonathan
Bausch, Richard
Bawden, Nina (Mary)
Bax, Martin (Charles Owen)
Baxter, John
Baxter, Stephen
Baybars, Taner
Bayer, William
Bayley, John (Oliver)
Bazell, Josh
Beachy, Kyle
Beagle, Peter S(oyer)
Beagley, Brenda E.
Beahrs, Andrew
Beale, Elaine
Beale, Fleur
Beam, Matt
Bean, Gregory (K.)
Bear, Elizabeth
Bear, Greg(ory Dale)
Beard, Darleen Bailey
Beard, Jo Ann
Beard, Philip
Beard, Richard
Bearden, Milton
Beason, Doug
Beattie, Ann
Beaty, Andrea
Beaty, Betty (Smith)
Beauchard, Pierre François
Beauman, Nicola
Beauman, Sally
Beaumont, Maria
Beauseigneur, James
Bechard, Margaret
Beck, Ian
Becker, Robin
Beckhorn, Susan Williams
Beckman, John
Bedard, Michael
Bedford, Deborah
Bedford, Martyn
Bee, Ronald J.
Beer, Gillian Patricia Kempster

Begley, Dan
Begley, Louis
Behr, Ira Steven
Behrens, Ellen
Behrman, Greg
Beidler, Peter G.
Beinhart, Larry
Beland, Pierre
Belbin, David
Belkaoui, Ahmed R.
Belkin, Aaron
Bell, Betty Louise
Bell, Hilari
Bell, Ian Mackay
Bell, Madison Smartt
Bell, Mary Reeves
Bell, Nancy
Bell, William
Bellavia, David Gregory
Belletto, René
Belli, Gioconda
Bellows, Melina Gerosa
Bellows, Nathaniel
Belshaw, Patrick
Belton, Sandra (Yvonne)
Bemrose, John
Ben-Ner, Yitzhak
Benaïssa, Slimane
Benchley, Rob
Benedict, Elizabeth
Benedict, Helen
Benedict, Laura Philpot
Benedict, Pinckney
Benig, Irving
Benitez, Sandra (Ables)
Benjamin, Carol Lea
Benjamin, Saragail Katzman
Benmalek, Anouar
Bennassar, Bartolomé
Bennett, James B.
Bennett, R.G. Stephen
Bennett, Ronan
Bennett, Vanora
Benoit, Charles
Benson, Jackson J.
Benson, Peter
Benson, Richard
Bentley, Joyce
Benton, Jim
Benvenuto, Christine
Berberian, Viken
Berberick, Nancy Varian
Berg, Carol
Berg, Elizabeth
Berger, Fredericka
Berger, John (Peter)
Berger, Thomas (Louis)
Berger-Kiss, Andres
Berges, Emily Trafford
Bergland, Martha
Bergman, Andrew
Bergman, Eugene
Bergman, Tamar
Bergon, Frank
Bergonzi, Bernard
Bergstrom, Elaine
Berkoff, Steven

Berliner-Gluckman, Janet
Berlinger, Joe
Bernard, Kenneth
Bernardi, Adria
Bernardini, Joe
Bernhardt, William
Bernheim, Emmanuèle
Bernstein, Burton
Berry, Adrian M.
Berry, Brian Joe Lobley
Berry, Carole
Berry, Julie
Berry, Linda
Berry, Steve
Bertozzi, Nick
Bes-Shahar, Eluki
Bettis, Jerome Abram
Betts, Doris
Beverley, Jo
Bevis, William W.
Bhagat, Chetan
Bhattacharya, Nalinaksha
Bi, Feiyu
Biddle, Cordelia Frances
Biederman, Lynn
Bienes, Nicholas Peter
Biermann, Pieke
Biggs, Brian
Biggs, John Burville
Bigsby, C. W. E.
Bildner, Phil
Billetdoux, Raphaële
Billington, Rachel
Billone, Amy Christine
Billson, Anne
Binchy, Maeve
Binding, Paul
Binding, Tim
Bingham, Charlotte
Bingham, Sallie
Bingle, Donald J.
Birdsell, Sandra
Birmingham, John
Birstein, Ann
Bishop, Holley
Bishop, Michael
Bissell, Sallie
Bissette, Stephen
Bittner, Rosanne
Black, Ethan
Black, Michael A.
Black, Shane
Blackburn, Julia
Blackman, Malorie
Blackstock, Terri
Blades, John D.
Blaine, Michael
Blaise, Clark
Blake, Jon
Blake, Mark R.
Blake, Michael
Blake, Sarah
Blakely, Mary Kay
Blamires, Harry
Blanchard, Stephen (Thomas)
Blank, Jessica
Blatanis, Konstantinos

Burton, Wendy
Busbee, Shirlee (Elaine)
Busby, Mark
Buscall, Jon
Busch, Charles
Busfield, Andrea
Bush, Barney (Furman)
Bush, Catherine
Bush, Duncan
Bushell, Agnes
Busia, Akosua
Busiek, Kurt
Buslik, Gary
Butala, Sharon (Annette)
Butler, Dori Hillestad
Butler, Jack
Butler, Pierce A.
Butler, Robert Olen
Butlin, Ron
Buxbaum, Julie
Buxton, Jayne
Byatt, A(ntonia) S(usan)
Bye, Beryl (Joyce Rayment)
Byles, Jeff
Bynum, Laura
Bynum, Sarah Shun-lien
Byrd, Adrianne
Byrd, William Max
Byrne, Robert
Byrnes, Michael J.
Cabot, Meg(gin Patricia)
Cadnum, Michael
Cahalan, James Michael
Cail, Carol
Calasso, Roberto
Calder, Andrew
Calder, Marie D(onais)
Caldwell, Laura
Caletti, Deb
Callaghan, Barry
Calvert, Patricia
Cameron, Julia
Cameron, Stella
Cameron, Sue
Caminals-Heath, Roser
Camon, Ferdinando
Campbell, Alexandra
Campbell, Broos
Campbell, Christopher
Campbell, Drusilla
Campbell, Eric
Campbell, Gordon
Campbell, James
Campbell, Ramsey
Campbell, Rhonda
Campbell, Scott
Campbell, Stephen J.
Canham, Elizabeth
Canham, Marsha
Canin, Ethan
Cannell, Dorothy
Cannon, A. E.
Cannon, Eileen E(mily)
Cannon, Michael
Cano, Daniel
Canter, Mark
Cantu, Norma Elia

Cao, Lan
Capon, Robert Farrar
Cappellani, Ottavio
Cappello, Mary C.
Capriolo, Paola
Caputo, Philip
Carbin, Debbie
Carcaterra, Lorenzo
Card, Orson Scott
Cardieri, Anthony J.
Carens, Timothy L.
Carew, Jan (Rynveld)
Carey, Jacqueline
Carey, Jacqueline
Carey, Lisa
Carey, Peter
Cargill, Linda B.
Carin, Michael
Carkeet, David
Carlson, Laurie
Carlson, Lori Marie
Carlson, Ron
Carlton, Susan
Carlyon, David
Carman, Patrick
Carneci, Magda
Carr, Caleb
Carr, Duane
Carr, Lauren
Carr, Margaret
Carr, Marvin N.
Carranza, Andreu
Carrier, Roch
Carrillo, H. G.
Carrington, Roslyn
Carroll, Linda
Carroll, Michael
Carroll, Rodney (James)
Carroll, Susan
Carson, Anne
Carson, Donald W.
Carson, Paul
Carter, Alden R(ichardson)
Carter, Ally
Carter, Betty Smartt
Carter, Charlotte
Carter, David
Carter, Dean Vincent
Carter, Maureen
Carter, Mike
Carter, Raphael
Carton, Bernice
Cartwright, Anthony
Cartwright, Justin
Cary, Lorene
Casanova, Mary
Cascone, Annette
Case, George (Andrew Thomas)
Casey, Barbara
Casey, John (Dudley)
Casey, Maud
Cashdan, Linda
Cashill, Jack
Cashore, Kristin
Caskie, Kathryn
Casper, Claudia
Casper, Leonard (Ralph)

Caspers, Nona
Cassady, Marsh
Cassella, Carol Wiley
Cassidy, Anne
Cassidy, Cathy
Cassutt, Michael (Joseph)
Castel-Bloom, Orly
Castellucci, Cecil
Castillo, Mary
Castle, Linda
Castro, Brian (Albert)
Caswell, Brian
Cato, Heather
Caute, (John) David
Cavallaro, Michael J.
Cavanagh, Thomas B.
Cave, Emma
Cave, Kathryn
Cawthorne, Nigel
Cebulash, Mel
Center, Katherine Pannill
Cercas, Javier
Cerf, Muriel
Cervenka, Jarda
Chadbourn, Mark
Chadwick, Cydney
Chadwick, Whitney
Chai, Arlene J.
Chai, May-lee
Chalmers, Robert
Chamberlain, Marisha
Chamberlin, Ann
Chambers, Aidan
Chambers, Diane
Chambers, Veronica
Chamoiseau, Patrick
Champlin, Tim
Chance, Megan
Chandler, Glenn
Chandra, Vikram
Chang, Leonard
Chang, Leslie
Chang, Margaret
Chao, Patricia
Chapin, Sarah
Chapman, Herb
Chapman, Myriam
Chappell, Fred(erick Davis)
Charbonneau, Eileen
Charbonnet, Gabrielle
Chard, Judy (Gordon)
Charef, Mehdi
Chariandy, David
Charlesworth, Monique
Charlier, Roger Henri
Charlton-Trujillo, E. E.
Charlwood, D(onald) E(rnest Cameron)
Charnas, Suzy McKee
Charney, Noah
Charrette, Robert N.
Charters, Samuel
Charyn, Jerome
Chase, Joan
Chase, Kerry A.
Chattarji, Sampurna
Chatterjee, Upamanyu

Chaudhuri, Amit
Cheaney, J. B.
Cheever, Susan
Chehak, Susan Taylor
Chen, Patrizia
Chen, Ran
Chen, Ying
Cher, Ming
Chercover, Sean
Chernoff, Maxine
Cherry, Kelly
Cherry, Kittredge
Cherryh, C. J.
Cheshire, Simon
Chetwin, Grace
Cheuse, Alan
Chevalier, Tracy
Chiang, Lynette
Chieng, Chieh
Child, Lincoln B.
Child, Maureen
Childress, Mark
Chima, Cinda Williams
Chinodya, Shimmer
Chiocca, Olindo Romeo
Chippendale, Lisa A.
Chocolate, Debbi
Chodos, Robert
Cholodenko, Marc
Chopra, Deepak (K.)
Chouaki, Aziz
Choyce, Lesley
Christensen, Kate
Christensen, Lars Saabye
Christensen, Mark
Christian, Carol Cathay Tuttle
Christmas, Joyce
Christofferson, April
Chu, Tien-wen
Churchill, E. Richard
Chwin, Stefan
Ciment, Jill
Ciresi, Rita
Citro, Joseph A.
Citron, Stephen
Clabough, Casey Howard
Claire, Cherie
Clamp, Cathy
Clancy, Tom
Clark, Carol Higgins
Clark, Catherine
Clark, Eric
Clark, Martin Fillmore
Clark, Mary Higgins
Clark, Mary Jane Behrends
Clark, Roger Y.
Clark, Tom
Clark, Will
Clarke, (Victor) Lindsay
Clarke, Brock
Clarke, Judith
Clarke, Kenneth L.
Clarke, Margaret
Clausen, Andy
Clausen, Lowen
Clawson, Calvin C.
Claxton, Melvin

Novels-*cont.*

Clayton, Paul
Cleary, Beverly
Cleary, Christopher
Cleaver, Jerry
Clegg, Douglas
Clements, Andrew
Cleveland, Ceil
Clinch, Jon
Clipper Sethi, Robbie
Cloake, John (Cecil)
Close, Ajay
Cloudsley-Thompson, John (Leonard)
Côté, Richard N.
Coan, Richard W.
Cobb, Cathy
Cobb, James H(arvey)
Cobb, Thomas
Coben, Harlan
Coble, Colleen
Coburn, Andrew
Coburn, Ann
Cochran, Robert B(rady)
Cocquyt, Kathryn Marie
Codrescu, Andrei
Cody, Liza
Cody, Paul
Coe, Jonathan
Coelho, Ivo
Coetzee, J(ohn) M(ichael)
Cofer, Judith Ortiz
Cohen, Bernard
Cohen, Kerry
Cohen, Leah Hager
Cohen, Leonard
Cohen, Marcel
Cohen, Rachel
Cohen, Rich
Cohen, Richard
Cohen, Robert
Cohen, Stanley I.
Cohen, Stuart
Cohen, Tish
Cohn, David
Cohn, Rachel
Cokal, Susann
Colantuoni, Joe
Cole, Allan
Cole, Barry
Cole, Sheila R.
Colebank, Susan
Colegate, Isabel
Coleman, Carter
Coleman, Jane Candia
Coleman, Michael
Coleman, Terry
Coleridge, Nicholas (David)
Coles, Don
Colgan, Jenny
Colicchio, Joseph
Colin, Beatrice
Colin, Chris
Coll, Susan
Collee, John (Gerald)
Colletta, Lisa
Colley, Barbara
Collier, James Lincoln

Novels-*cont.*

Collier, Zena
Collignon, Jeff
Collignon, Rick
Collin, Marion (Cripps)
Collings, I. J.
Collings, Michael R(obert)
Collins, Ace
Collins, Floyd G.
Collins, Helen (Frances)
Collins, Jackie
Collins, Joan
Collins, Merle
Collins, Michael
Collins, Nancy A.
Collins, Paul
Collins, Richard (Wayne)
Collins, Stephen
Collins, Tess
Collinson, Alan S.
Collis, Louise (Edith)
Collison, Kerry B(oyd)
Colman, E. Adrian M.
Comfort, B(arbara)
Comfort, Ray
Compton, Patricia A.
Confiant, Raphaël
Conford, Ellen
Conlon, Evelyn
Conlon, Kathleen (Annie)
Conlon-McKenna, Marita
Conn, Andrew Lewis
Connell, Evan S(helby)
Connelly, Joe
Connelly, Michael
Connolly, Harry J.
Connolly, Joseph
Connolly, Ray
Connor, Joan
Connors, Bruton
Conquest, (George) Robert (Acworth)
Conquest, Ned
Conrad, Christine
Conrad, Peter
Conran, Shirley (Ida)
Conroy, (Donald) Pat(rick)
Constable, Kate
Constant, Paule
Constantine, David (John)
Constantine, Storm
Conway, Martha
Conway, Rosaleen D.
Cony, Carlos Heitor
Cook, Bob
Cook, Claire
Cook, David
Cook, Eileen
Cook, Glen (Charles)
Cook, Hugh
Cook, Jean Thor
Cook, Lorna J.
Cook, Marshall
Cook, Paul
Cook-Lynn, Elizabeth
Cooke, Carolyn
Cooke, John Peyton
Cooley, Martha S.

Novels-*cont.*

Coomer, Joe
Cooney, Doug
Cooney, Ellen
Coonts, Stephen (Paul)
Cooper, Dominic (Xavier)
Cooper, Ilene
Cooper, Jilly (Sallitt)
Cooper, Ron L.
Cooper, T.
Coover, Robert
Coplin, Keith
Copper, Basil
Corbett, Ben
Corcoran, Neil (Cornelius)
Cordelli, Franco
Corderoy, Conor
Cordesman, Anthony H.
Corey, Deborah Joy
Corin, Joshua
Corn, Alfred
Cornier, Nadia
Cornwell, Autumn
Corona, Laurel
Cory, Charlotte
Coscarelli, Don
Cosic, Dobrica
Cosper, Darcy
Costello, Matthew J.
Coster, Graham
Cotroneo, Roberto
Cotten, Cynthia
Cottle, Thomas J.
Cottonwood, Joe
Couch, Dick
Couloumbis, Audrey
Coulson, Juanita
Coupland, Douglas
Courtenay, Bryce
Courter, Gay (Eleanor)
Couvillon, Jacques
Covin, David L.
Covington, Dennis
Cowan, Shannon
Cowasjee, Saros
Cowell, Alan S.
Cowell, Stephanie
Cowley, (Cassia) Joy
Cox, Ana Marie
Cox, Anna-Lisa
Cox, Patsi Bale
Cox, Richard
Cox, Richard (Hubert Francis)
Cox, Vicki
Coy, John
Coyle, Beverly (Jones)
Crace, Jim
Craig, Amanda
Craig, Colleen
Craig, Daniel Edward
Craig, J. Marshall
Craig, Patricia
Cramer, W.
Crandall, Susan
Crandell, Doug
Craven, Michael
Craven, Sara
Crawford, Lynn

Novels-*cont.*

Crawley, Harriet
Creech, Sharon
Creel, Ann Howard
Cregan, David (Appleton Quartus)
Creighton, Joan Scott
Creighton, Kathleen
Crespi, Camilla T.
Crew, Gary
Crew, Linda
Crews, Harry (Eugene)
Crider, (Allen) Bill(y)
Croft, Barbara
Croker, Richard
Cron, Ian Morgan
Crosby, Harry W(illiams)
Cross, Gillian (Clare)
Cross, Helen
Cross, Ian (Robert)
Cross, Janine
Crowell, Jenn(ifer)
Crowley, Bridget
Crowley, Suzanne Carlisle
Crowther, Harold Francis
Crowther, Nick
Crozier, Brian
Crummey, Michael
Cruse, Howard
Cruse, Lonnie
Crusie, Jennifer
Crutcher, Chris(topher C.)
Cruz, Angie
Csányi, Vilmos
Csoori, Sandor
Culbert, Steven (Tye)
Cullen, Robert (B.)
Cullinane, Jan
Cumming, Charles
Cummins, Jeanine
Cumper, Patricia
Cunningham, Elizabeth
Cunningham, M. Allen
Cunningham, Valentine
Cuomo, George (Michael)
Curley, Marianne
Curnutt, Kirk
Currey, Richard
Currey-Wilson, Ellen
Currie, Edwina
Currie, Ron
Curry, Jane (Louise)
Curtis, Tony
Curtiss, A(rlene) B.
Cusk, Rachel
Cussler, Clive (Eric)
Cuthbert, Margaret
Cutler, Jane
Cutler, Stan
Cutting, Linda Katherine
Cyr, Myriam
D'Ath, Justin
d'Lacey, Chris
D'Souza, Tony
Dabydeen, Cyril
Dabydeen, David
Dahl, Victoria
Dahlberg, Maurine F.
Dailey, Janet

Daitch, Susan
Dalby, Liza Crihfield
Dale, Anna
Daley, Robert (Blake)
Dalton, Annie
Dalton, Sheila
Daly, Leo (Arthur)
Daly, Michael
Dalzell, Frederick
Dams, Jeanne M(artin)
Dangarembga, Tsitsi
Daniel, Tony
Daniels, Angie
Daniels, Jeff
Daniels, Sarah
Dann, Colin (Michael)
Dann, Jack
Dano, Linda
Danticat, Edwidge
Danziger, Daniel (Guggenheim)
Darby, Ann
Darling, Diana
Darlison, Bill
Darrieussecq, Marie
Darrow, Sharon
Dart, Iris Rainer
Dart-Thornton, Cecilia
Darton, Eric
Darty, Peggy
Darville, Helen (Fiona)
Dasgupta, Rana
Dasgupta, Subrata
Dash, Julie
Daugharty, Janice
Davenport, Roger (Hamilton)
David, Anna
David, Catherine
David, James F.
Davidar, David
Davidson, Dana
Davidson, Robyn
Davies, Hunter
Davies, Katharine
Davies, Linda
Davies, Nicola
Davies, Peter Ho
Davies, Stephanie
Davies-Mitchell, Margaret (Constance)
Davis, Albert Belisle
Davis, Bridgett M.
Davis, Christopher
Davis, Dee
Davis, Donald A.
Davis, Heather
Davis, Lexi
Davis, Lindsey
Davis, Margaret (Thomson)
Davis, Mildred (B.)
Davis, Philip Maurice
Davison, Liam
Dawes, Edna
Dawid, Annie
Dawson, Carol
Dawson, Geralyn
Day, Stacey B.
de Bernieres, Louis

de Blasi, Marlena
De Carvalho, Mário
de Grave, Kathleen
de Groen, Alma
de Hamel, Joan (Littledale)
De Haven, Tom
De La Cruz, Melissa
de los Santos, Marisa
De Marinis, Rick
de Rosnay, Tatiana
de Somogyi, Nick
de Souza, Eunice
de Vasconcelos, Erika
De Vries, Rachel (Guido)
Dean, Debra
Dean, Margaret Lazarus
Dean (Dyer-Bennett), Pamela (Collins)
DeAngelis, Camille
Deans, Bob
Dearie, John
Dearing, Sarah
Deaver, Jeffery Wilds
DeBuron, Nicole
DeCandido, Keith R. A.
Dee, Ed(ward J.)
Deford, Frank
DeGrazia, Emilio
Deighton, Len
DeJohn, Jacqueline
DeKeyser, Stacy
Del Paso, Fernando
del Toro, Guillermo
Delacroix, Claire
Delahaye, Michael (John)
Delahunt, Meaghan
Delaney, Edward J.
Delaney, Kathleen
Delano, Anthony
Delany, Samuel R(ay)
Delany, Vicki
Delbanco, Francesca
Delbanco, Nicholas F(ranklin)
Delerm, Philippe
DeLillo, Don
Delinsky, Barbara (Ruth Greenberg)
Dellasega, Cheryl
Delors, Catherine
Delson, Rudolph
Demarais, Ann
DeMarco, Kathy
DeMille, Nelson (Richard)
Deming, Sarah
Demott, Wes
Dendinger, Roger E.
Deng, Francis Mading
Deng Xiao hua
Denker, Henry
Denman, K. L.
Dennett, Nolan A.
Dent, Grace
DeParle, Jason
DePastino, Todd Allan
Derby, Pat
Desai, Anita
Desai, Boman

Desai, Kiran
Desarthe, Agnès
Desjarlais, John
Desmangles, Leslie G.
Desplechin, Marie
Despres, Loraine
DesRochers, Diane
Dessaix, Robert
Deuker, Carl
Devashish, Donald Acosta
Devereaux, Robert
DeVincent-Hayes, Nan
DeVita, James
Dewberry, Elizabeth
Dewey, Joseph (Owen)
Dewey, Scott Hamilton
Dewhurst, Eileen (Mary)
Dewitt, Helen
deWitt, Patrick
Dexter, Pete
Di Blasi, Debra
di Certo, J(oseph) J(ohn)
di Filippo, Paul
di Prima, Diane
Diamant, Anita
Diamond, Rickey Gard
Diaz, Tony
DiBartolomeo, Albert
Dibble, J(ames) Birney
Dickason, Christie
Dickey, Eric Jerome
Dickinson, Don(ald Percy)
Dickinson, John
Dickinson, Peter
Dickson, Athol
Didion, Joan
Dietrich, William A.
Dietz, Laura
Dietz, Steven
Dillard, Annie
Dillard, R(ichard) H(enry) W(ilde)
Dilmore, Kevin
DiMarco, Cris K. A.
Dimmick, Barbara
Dinh, Linh
Dintenfass, Mark L.
Diotalevi, Dave A.
DiRenzo, Anthony
DiSalvo, Jackie
Diski, Jenny
Ditchoff, Pamela J.
Divakaruni, Chitra Banerjee
Dix, Shane
Dixon, Larry
Dixon, Stephen
Djerassi, Carl
Djoleto, (Solomon Alexander) Amu
Doane, Janice (L.)
Dobbs, Michael
Dobson, Joanne
Doctorow, E(dgar) L(awrence)
Docx, Edward
Dodd, Christina
Dodd, Wayne
Doerr, Anthony

Doherty, Berlie
Doherty, Kieran
Doherty, P(aul) C.
Doig, Ivan
Dokey, Cameron
Dolan, David
Dolling-Mann, Patricia May
Dolnick, Ben
Donahue, Tina
Donald, Robyn Elaine
Donleavy, J(ames) P(atrick)
Donn, Linda
Donnelly, Jane
Donnelly, Joe
Donner, Rebecca
Donoghue, Emma
Donohue, Keith
Donovan, Anne
Donovan, Gerard
Dooling, Richard (Patrick)
Dorf, Fran
Dorner, Marjorie
Dorrestein, Renate
Dorros, Arthur (M.)
Dorset, Phyllis (Flanders)
Dorsey, Candas Jane
Dossey, Larry
Doudera, Vicki
Douglas, Kirk
Douglas, L. Warren
Dovalpage, Teresa
Dove, Rita (Frances)
Dowdy, Cecelia D.
Dower, Laura
Dowling, Terry
Downes, David A(nthony)
Downing, David A(lmon)
Downing, David C(laude)
Downing, Michael (Bernard)
Downs, Robert C. S.
Doyle, Debra
Doyle, Larry
Doyle, Roddy
Drabble, Margaret
Dracup, Angela
Dragomán, György
Drake, Albert (Dee)
Drake, David A.
Drakuli , Slavenka
Draper, Alfred Ernest
Draper, Robert
Dressler, Mylène
Drew, Alan
Drewe, Robert
Drexler, Rosalyn
Dreyer, Eileen
Driscoll, Jeremy
Driver, C(harles) J(onathan)
Drury, Tom
Du Brul, Jack B.
Dubens, Eugene (M.)
Duberstein, Helen (Laura)
Duberstein, Larry
Dubois, Muriel L.
Dubus, Andre
Ducharme, Diann
Duckworth, Marilyn

Duder, Tessa
Due, Tananarive
Duff, Alan
Duffy, Bruce
Duffy, James H(enry)
Duffy, Margaret
Duffy, Maureen (Patricia)
Dufresne, John
Dugoni, Robert
Duigan, John
Dully, Howard
Dumbleton, Mike
Dummett, (Agnes Margaret) Ann
Dunant, Sarah
Dunbar, Joyce
Duncan, Christine H.
Duncan, Dave
Duncan, Glen
Duncan, Hal
Duncan, Lois
Duncan, Patrick Sheane
Duncan, Sarah
Duncker, Patricia
Duncombe, Stephen
Dunham, Tracy
Dunlap, Susan D. (Sullivan)
Dunlap, Susanne Emily
Dunlop, Eileen (Rhona)
Dunn, Mark (Rodney)
Dunn, Suzannah
Duns, Jeremy
Durand, Alain-Philippe
Durban, Pam
Durcan, Liam
Durkee, Sarah
Durrant, Lynda
Durrow, Heidi W.
Durst, Sarah Beth
Dutton, J. T.
Dyer, Charles (Raymond)
Dyer, K. C.
Dyer, Wayne W(alter)
Eagleton, Terry
Eames, Anne
Earl, Maureen
Earley, Pete
Earley, Tony
Earls, Nick
Easterbrook, Gregg
Easton, Malcolm Coleman
Easton, Nina J(ane)
Eaves, Will
Ebbett, Eve
Eberle, Gary
Echenique, Alfredo Bryce
Echenoz, Jean
Eckler, Rebecca
Edelman, Amy Holman
Edgar, David
Edgecombe, David
Edgerton, Clyde
Edson, Russell
Edwards, (Kenneth) Martin
Edwards, Anne
Edwards, Brent Hayes
Edwards, Johanna
Edwards, Larry

Edwards, Louis
Edwards, Michael B.
Edwards, Sarah (Anne)
Egan, Ferol
Egan, Greg
Egan, Jennifer
Egbuna, Obi (Benedict)
Ehle, John
Ehrenberg, Pamela
Eichler, Selma
Eickhoff, Randy Lee
Eidinow, John
Eidson, Thomas
Eisen, Adrienne
Eisenberg, Nora
Eisler, Barry
Eisner, Michael Alexander
El-Moslimany, Ann P(axton)
el-Tahri, Jihan
Elboz, Stephen
Elder, Jo-Anne
Elegant, Robert (Sampson)
Elegant, Simon
Elkeles, Simone
Elkins, Charlotte
Ellenberg, Jordan S.
Ellerbeck, Rosemary
Elliott, Anna
Elliott, Charles
Ellis, Bret Easton
Ellis, David
Ellis, Ella Thorp
Ellis, Jamellah
Ellis, Kate
Ellis, Mark (Karl)
Ellis, Mary Relindes
Ellis, Peter Berresford
Ellis, Reuben J.
Ellis, Robert
Ellis, Royston
Ellis, Sarah
Ellis, Trey
Ellison, Harlan (Jay)
Ellroy, James
Elmer, Robert
Elmslie, Kenward
Else, Barbara
Ely, David
Emecheta, (Florence Onye) Buchi
Emerson, Earl W.
Emery, Clayton
Emmet, Alan
Emmett, Ayala
Emmons, Mary L.
Emshwiller, Carol (Fries)
Endlich, Lisa
Engdahl, Sylvia L(ouise)
Engel, Howard
Engel, Monroe
Engelberg, Alan (D.)
Engelhard, Jack
Enger, Leif
Engerman, David C.
Engle, Margarita
Engleman, Paul
English, Allan D.
English, Richard Ludlow

Engstrom, Elizabeth
Ennis, Garth
Eno, Will
Enquist, Per Olov
Epanomitis, Fotini
Ephron, Nora
Epping, Randy Charles
Eprile, Tony
Epstein, Jennifer Cody
Epstein, Leslie (Donald)
Epstein, Seymour
Erdrich, Louise
Erhard, Tom
Erickson, Carolly
Erickson, Steve
Ernaux, Annie
Erofeev, Viktor V.
Ershler, Phil
Erskine, Kathryn
Esch, Ben
Esckilsen, Erik E.
Eshun, Ekow
Eskridge, Ann E.
Eskridge, Kelley
Esler, Anthony James
Essex, Karen
Esterhazy, Peter
Estleman, Loren D.
Estrada, Rita Clay
Estrin, Allen
Euba, Femi
Eugenides, Jeffrey
Evanovich, Janet
Evans, Alan
Evans, Douglas
Evans, Jon
Evans, Justin
Evans, Liz
Evans, Mary Anna
Evans, Michael Robert
Evans, Mike
Evans, Sheila
Evans, Stephen
Evenson, Brian
Eversz, Robert (McLeod)
Ewan, Chris
Ewen, Pamela Binnings
Ewing, Lynne
Faas, K. Ekbert
Faber, Michel
Fagan, Louis J.
Fahnestock, Todd
Fahy, Thomas
Faigen, Anne G.
Fain, Michael
Fain, Sarah
Fairstein, Linda A.
Falco, Edward
Falcon, Mark
Falconer, Delia
Falconer, Helen
Fales-Hill, Susan
Falkner, Brian
Falla, Jonathan
Fallenberg, Evan
Fallon, Jennifer
Fallon, Peter

Fallowell, Duncan (Richard)
Fanchi, John R(ichard)
Fanning, Diane Lynn
Fante, Dan
Fanthorpe, R(obert) Lionel
Faqih, Ahmed
Faqir, Fadia A.M.
Farish, Terry
Farley, Terri
Farmer, Jerrilyn
Farmer, Penelope (Jane)
Farmiloe, Dorothy
Farooki, Roopa
Farr, Diane
Faschinger, Lilian
Fate, Robert
Faunce, John
Faust, Christa
Faust, Irvin
Favorite, Eileen
Fayer, Steve
Feeley, Gregory
Fehlbaum, Beth
Fehler, Gene
Feifer, George
Feiffer, Jules
Feinstein, Elaine
Feinstein, John
Feist, Raymond E(lias)
Felder, Deborah G.
Feldman, Ellen
Felinto (Barbosa De Lima),
   Marilene
Fell, Alison
Felske, Coerte V. W.
Felts, Susannah
Fennelly, Beth Ann
Fenske, Jennifer Manske
Fenton, Kate
Fenton, Margaret
Fenton, Peter
Fenton, Robert L.
Ferder, Fran
Ferguson, Alane
Ferguson, Andrew
Ferguson, Brad
Ferguson, Kitty
Ferguson, Robert (Thomas)
Ferguson, Ron
Ferguson, Sarah (Margaret)
Ferguson, Will
Ferlinghetti, Lawrence
Fermine, Maxence
Fermor, Patrick (Michael) Leigh
Ferner, Mike
Fernyhough, Charles
Ferrari, Mark J.
Ferraris, Zoë
Ferreiro, Carmen
Ferrell, Carolyn
Ferrigno, Robert
Ferris, Jean
Ferris, Joshua
Ferris, Paul
Fforde, Jasper
Fforde, Katie
Fiallos, Rosario

Ficera, Kim (M.)
Fickett, David C.
Field, Edward
Field, Thalia
Fielding, Helen
Fields, Jennie
Fields, Terri
Figes, Eva
Figiel, Sia
Filipacchi, Amanda
Filkins, Peter
Finch, Charles
Fine, Anne
Fink, Merton
Finlay, Peter (Warren)
Finley, Glenna
Finn, R(alph) L(eslie)
Finney, Ernest J.
Finnis, Jane
Fioretos, Aris
Firouz, Anahita (Homa)
Fischer, Debbie Reed
Fischer, Steven R.
Fischer, Tibor
Fischkin, Barbara
Fisher, Catherine
Fisher, David E.
Fisk, Pauline
Fister, Barbara
Fitch, Stona
Fitten, Marc
Fitzgerald, Astrid
Fitzgerald, Conor
Fitzpatrick, Becca
Fitzpatrick, Flo
Fitzpatrick, Tony
Flaherty, Liz
Flanagan, Erin
Flath, Carol (Apollonio)
Fleetwood, Hugh (Nigel)
Fleischer, Ari
Fleming, Anne
Fleming, Candace
Fleming, Thomas
Fletcher, Christine
Fletcher, Michael A.
Fletcher, Susan
Fletcher, Susan (Clemens)
Flinn, Alex
Flint, James
Flock, Elizabeth
Floegstad, Kjartan
Flores-Galbis, Enrique
Fluke, Joanne
Flynn, Joseph
Flynn, Laura M.
Foden, Giles
Foer, Jonathan Safran
Fogtdal, Peter H.
Foley, (Mary) Louise Munro
Foley, Gaelen
Foley, Mick
Foli, Karen J.
Follett, Ken(neth Martin)
Folsom, Allan (R.)
Fonda, Peter
Fone, Byrne R. S.

Fontes, Montserrat
Fontes, Ron
Foon, Dennis
Foos, Laurie
Force, Marie Sullivan
Ford, Darnella D.
Ford, G. M.
Ford, Jamie Mark
Ford, Marjorie Leet
Ford, Michael Curtis
Ford, Michael Thomas
Ford, Susan
Forde, Catherine
Foreman, Richard
Forman, Steven M.
Forrest, Christopher
Forrest, Katherine V(irginia)
Forrester, Helen
Forrester, Sandra
Forster, Margaret
Forsyth, Frederick
Forsyth, Kate
Foster, Alan Dean
Foster, Cecil (A.)
Foster, David Manning
Foster, Hal
Foster, Lori L.
Foster, Sesshu
Fowler, Christopher
Fowler, Connie May
Fowler, Earlene
Fox, Hugh (Bernard)
Fox, Les
Fox, Paula
Foy, George Michelsen
Foyt, Victoria
Fraiser, Jim
Frame, Ronald
Francis, Clare
Francis, Diana Pharaoh
Francis, Matthew (Charles)
Francis, Richard
Franey, Ros(alind)
Frank, Dana
Frank, Dorothea Benton
Frank, E(mily) R.
Frank, Joan
Frankel, Sandor
Frankel, Valerie
Franklin, Cheryl J.
Fraser, Anthea
Fraser, Antonia
Fraser, Margot
Fraser, Rebecca
Frayn, Michael
Frazer, Gail
Frazier, Charles (Robinson)
Frazier, Kit
Frazier, Sundee T.
Freda, Joseph
Freeborn, Richard (Harry)
Freed, Lynn
Freedman, Jeff
Freeman, Anne Hobson
Freeman, Castle (William)
Freeman, Gillian
Freeman, Martha

Freeman, Philip
Freemantle, Brian (Harry)
Freese, Mathias B(alogh)
Freireich, Valerie J.
French, Albert
French, Francis
French, Judith E.
French, Linda
French, Sean
French, Tana
French, Vivian
Freud, Esther
Freud, Sophie
Freund, Diane
Frewer, Glyn
Frey, James N.
Frey, Julia (Bloch)
Freydont, Shelley
Friedman, Aimee
Friedman, Bruce Jay
Friedman, C(elia) S.
Friedman, Kinky
Friedman, Paul (Alan)
Friedman, Philip (J.)
Friedman, Ron
Friedman, Rosemary
Friedmann, Patty
Friel, Brian
Friend, Theodore (Wood)
Friesen, Jonathan
Frisby, Terence
Fritchley, Alma
Fritz, Jean
Fromm, Pete
Frost, Mark C.
Frost, Scott
Fuchs, Michael Stephen
Fugard, Athol
Fugard, Lisa
Fukui, Isamu Carter
Fulghum, Robert (L.)
Fuller, Charles
Fuller, Jack (William)
Fuller, John (Leopold)
Fullerton, Alma
Fumento, Rocco
Fumizuki, Kou
Furey, Leo
Furutani, Dale
Fusilli, Jim
Fussell, E. Robert
Futcher, Jane P.
Futterman, Enid (Susan)
Gabbay, Tom
Gabriele, Lisa
Gadney, Reg
Gadol, Peter
Gaetz, Dayle Campbell
Gage, Eleni N.
Gagliani, William
Gagliano, Frank
Gagnon, Michelle
Gaillard, Frye
Gailly, Christian
Gaiman, Neil (Richard)
Gala (Y Velasco), Antonio
Galanes, Philip

Galant, Debra
Galbraith, Kathryn O(sebold)
Galdorisi, George V(ictor)
Galef, David
Gallagher, Liz
Gallagher, Stephen
Gallagher, Winifred
Gallaher, (William) Rhea
Gallaway, Morgana Bridget
Galleymore, Frances
Galli, Richard
Galloway, Janice
Galt, George
Gamble, Terry
Gander, Forrest
Gandt, Robert
Ganek, Danielle
Ganesan, Indira
Gangemi, Joseph G.
Gannon, Steve
Gansky, Alton
Gappah, Petina
Garbera, Katherine
Garbus, Cassandra
García, Cristina
Garcia, Diana
Garcia Y Robertson, R(odrigo)
Garcia-Aguilera, Carolina
García-Castañón, Santiago
Gardam, Jane
Garden, Nancy
Gardiner, Meg
Gardner, Craig Shaw
Gardner, Jerome
Gardner, Leonard
Gardner, Sandra
Gardner, Theodore Roosevelt
Gardon, Anne
Garland, Alex
Garland, Mark (A.)
Garland, Max
Garmaise, Freda
Garner, Alan
Garner, Helen
Garnett, Gale Zoë
Garwood, Julie
Gascoigne, Bamber
Gash, Jonathan
Gaskell, Jane
Gaskell, Whitney
Gaskill, Malcolm
Gass, William (Howard)
Gaston, Diane
Gateley, Edwina
Gates, David
Gathorne-Hardy, Jonathan
Gattey, Charles Neilson
Gau, Colleen
Gauch, Patricia Lee
Gaudé, Laurent
Gauldie, Enid Elizabeth
Gault, Peter
Gavronsky, Serge
Gayle, Stephanie
Gaylin, Alison
Geach, Christine
Gear, W. Michael

Geary, Joseph
Geary, Patricia (Carol)
Gedge, Pauline (Alice)
Gee, Maggie (Mary)
Gee, Maurice (Gough)
Gee, Sophie
Gehrig, Klaus
Gelb, Jeff
Genesse, Paul
Geniesse, Jane Fletcher
Gentle, Mary
Gentry, Christine
George, Elizabeth
George, Kathleen Elizabeth
George, Margaret
George, Robert P.
George, Rosemary
Geraghty, Paul
Gerard, Philip
Gerber, Merrill Joan
Gerdes, Eckhard
Gerhardt, Michael E.
Gershow, Miriam
Gershten, Donna M.
Gerson, Lloyd P.
Gersten-Vassilaros, Alexandra
Gerstler, Amy
Gervais, (George) Paul
Gerzina, Gretchen Holbrook
Geston, Mark S(ymington)
Getler, Warren
Getz, David
Ghahramani, Zarah
Ghose, Zulfikar
Ghosh, Amitav
Giardinelli, Mempo
Gibb, Camilla
Gibbons, Alan
Gibbons, Reginald
Gibson, Miles
Gibson, Tanya Egan
Giesbert, Franz-Olivier
Gifford, Barry (Colby)
Gilb, Dagoberto
Gilbert, Barbara Snow
Gilbert, Harriett
Gilbert, Sandra M(ortola)
Gilbert, W(illiam) Stephen
Gilchrist, Ellen
Gilden, Mel
Gildner, Gary
Gill, A. A.
Gill, Lakshmi
Giller, Marc D.
Gillespie, Diane Filby
Gillett, Margaret
Gillon, Adam
Gilman, Felix
Gilman, George G.
Gilman, Owen W(inslow)
Gilmore, Glenda Elizabeth
Gilmore, John
Gilmore, Rachna
Gilmore, Susan Gregg
Gilmour, David
Gilmour, David
Gilroy, Frank D(aniel)

Gilson, Christopher C.
Gilstrap, John
Gimferrer, Pere
Giorello, Sibella
Gipi
Gish, Robert F.
Gitlin, Todd
Gittlin, Adam
Glaister, Lesley (G.)
Glancy, Diane
Glancy, Ruth F(ergusson)
Glanville, Brian (Lester)
Glasco, Michael
Glass, Leslie
Glass, Rodge
Glatt, John
Glatt, Lisa
Gleiter, Jan
Glenn, Mel
Glenn, Sharlee Mullins
Glickman, James (A.)
Gliserman, Martin
Glisson, J(ake) T.
Gloag, Julian
Gloss, Molly
Glover, Douglas
Glover, Jane
Glucksmann, André
Glut, Don(ald) F.
Glynn, Alan
Gobbell, John J.
Godbout, Jacques
Goddard, Robert (William)
Goddard, Tariq
Godin, Seth Warren
Godshalk, C. S.
Godwin, Gail (Kathleen)
Godwin, Parke
Godwin, Rebecca T.
Goethe, Ann
Goff, Martyn
Going, Kelly L.
Goingback, Owl
Gold, Herbert
Gold, Jerome
Gold, Nora
Goldberg, Harold
Goldberg, Leonard S.
Golden, Arthur
Goldhagen, Shari
Golding, Theresa Martin
Goldman, Francisco
Goldman, William
Goldsmith, Andrea
Goldsmith, Barbara
Goldstein, Rebecca
Goldsworthy, Peter
Gomez, Jewelle
Gonzales, Laurence
Gonzalez, Genaro
Gooch, Brad
Goodfield, (Gwyneth) June
Goodison, Lorna (Gaye)
Goodkind, Terry
Goodman, Allegra
Goodman, Carol
Goodman, Eric

Goodman, Jo
Goodman, Joanna
Goodman, Matthew Aaron
Goodman, Susan E.
Goodstein, Judith R.
Goodstein, Phil
Goodwin, Doris (Helen) Kearns
Goonan, Kathleen Ann
Gordimer, Nadine
Gordon, Alan R.
Gordon, Deborah Hannes
Gordon, Graeme
Gordon, Jaimy
Gordon, Mary (Catherine)
Gordon, Robert
Gordon, Robert Ellis
Gordon, Sheila
Gore, Kristin (C.)
Gore, Patrick Wilson
Goto, Hiromi
Gottlieb, Annie
Gottlieb, Daphne
Gottlieb, Sherry Gershon
Gould, Bryan
Gould, Steven (Charles)
Gould, Terry
Gowan, Lee
Goyer, David S.
Grab, Daphne
Grabenstein, Chris
Grace, Alexander M.
Grace, Patricia (Frances)
Graff, Lisa
Grafton, Sue
Graham, Caroline
Graham, Laurie
Gralla, Cynthia
Gran, Sara
Granelli, Roger
Granger, (Patricia) Ann
Grant, Anne Underwood
Grant, Bruce (Alexander)
Grant, Graeme
Grant, Helen
Grant, James
Grant, Pete
Grant, Richard
Grant, Stephanie
Grant, Susan
Grant, Vanessa
Grass, Günter (Wilhelm)
Grassi, Maggi Lidchi
Gratus, Jack
Gratz, Alan
Grau, Shirley Ann
Graver, Elizabeth
Graves, Ralph (Augustus)
Gray, Alasdair (James)
Gray, Dulcie
Gray, Francine du Plessix
Gray, Robert (Curtis)
Grayson, Emily
Grazer, Gigi Levangie
Graziano, Michael S. A.
Greaney, Mark
Greeley, Andrew (Moran)
Green, (Charles Stuart) Jamison

Green, Angela
Green, Christine
Green, Cliff(ord)
Green, Connie Jordan
Green, Jane
Green, Jeffrey M.
Green, Jesse
Green, Joseph (Lee)
Green, Michael (Frederick)
Green, Norman
Green, Peter (Morris)
Green, Risa
Green, Simon R(ichard)
Green, Terence M(ichael)
Green, Timothy
Green, Toby
Greenberg, Alvin
Greenberg, Joanne
Greenberg, Mike
Greene, Amy
Greene, Bette
Greene, Constance C(larke)
Greene, Douglas G.
Greene, Sheldon L.
Greene, Thomas Christopher
Greenhall, Ken
Greenlaw, Lavinia (Elaine)
Greenleaf, Stephen (Howell)
Greeno, Gayle
Greenwood, Leigh
Greenwood, T.
Greer, Andrew Sean
Greer, Gaylon
Greer, Robert O.
Gregory, Dick
Gregory, Patrick
Gregory, Philippa
Gregory, Susanna
Gregson, Julia
Grescoe, Paul
Gresham, Stephen
Grey, Anthony
Griesemer, John
Griffin, Laura
Griffin, P(auline) M.
Griffin, Peni R(ae)
Griffith, Nicola
Griffiths, Niall
Griffiths, William G.
Griggs, Terry
Griggs, Vanessa Davis
Grihm, Amanda
Grimes, Martha
Grimes, Tom
Grimsley, Jim
Grindal, Richard
Grisham, John
Groff, Lauren
Groom, Winston (Francis)
Gross, Andrew
Gross, Jonathan David
Gross, Miss Anne Lasko
Grossinger, Tania
Grossman, Austin
Grossman, David
Grossman, Lev (Thomas)
Grossman, Richard

Grossmith, Robert (Anthony)
Grosz, Terry
Grotenstein, Jonathan
Groult, Benoite
Groundwater, Beth
Grover, Wayne
Grubb, Jeff
Grudin, Robert
Gruenenfelder, Kim
Grumbach, Doris
Grumman, Bob
Gruner, Wolf
Grusky, Scott T.
Guest, Christopher
Guest, Harry
Guest, Judith
Gugler, Laurel Dee
Guhrke, Laura Lee
Guilfoile, Kevin
Guill, Jane
Guillory, Dan
Guillou, Jan
Gumbrecht, Hans Ulrich
Gunn, James E(dwin)
Gunn, Kirsty
Gunn, Robin Jones
Gunning, Sally (Carlson)
Gunter, Pete (Addison Yancey)
Guo, Xiaolu
Guppy, Stephen (Anthony)
Gupta, Sunetra
Gurganus, Allan
Gurian, Naomi
Gurney, A(lbert) R(amsdell)
Gurr, David
Gurvis, Sandra J.
Gushee, David P.
Gussin, Patricia
Gustafson, Sid
Gustainis, Justin
Guterson, David
Guthrie, Allan
Gutteridge, Don(ald George)
Guy, Rosa (Cuthbert)
Haber, Julian Stuart
Haberman, Jacob
Habers, Walther A(drianus)
Habila, Helon
Hackett, Joyce
Hackl, Erich
Haddock, Lisa (Robyn)
Haenel, Wolfram
Hagan, Stephen
Hagedorn, Jessica Tarahata
Hagen, George
Hager, Betty
Hagy, Alyson
Hahn, Mary Downing
Hahn, Michael T.
Hailey, (Elizabeth) Kendall
Hailey, Elizabeth Forsythe
Haines, Kathryn Miller
Hairston, William
Haji, Nafisa
Haldeman, Joe (William)
Hale, John
Hale, Robert D(avid)

Hale, Shannon
Hales, Dianne R.
Hall, Brian
Hall, David C.
Hall, Douglas
Hall, Gimone
Hall, Karen L.
Hall, Lynn
Hall, Parnell
Hall, Rodney
Hall, Russ
Hall, Sarah
Hall, Steven
Hallahan, William H(enry)
Halligan, Marion (Mildred
    Crothall)
Hallinan, Timothy
Hallowell, Janis
Halperin, James L(ewis)
Halpern, Julie
Halpern, Sue
Halpin, Brendan
Halter, Marek
Hamamoto, Darrell Y.
Hamand, Maggie
Hambly, Barbara
Hamburger, Aaron
Hamid, Mohsin
Hamill, Pete
Hamilton, Carol (Jean Barber)
Hamilton, Hugo
Hamilton, Jane
Hamilton, Peter F.
Hamilton-Paterson, James
Hammel, Bob
Hammond, Andrew
Hammond, Gerald (Arthur
    Douglas)
Hammond, Warren
Hampton-Jones, Hollis
Han, Suzanne Crowder
Han Suyin
Hancock, Brian
Handeland, Lori
Handler, David
Hanes, Frank Borden
Hankin, Elizabeth Rosemary
Hanley, William
Hannah, Sophie
Hannan, Peter
Hannibal, Edward L.
Hannigan, Katherine
Hanscombe, Gillian E(ve)
Hänsel, Marion
Hansen, Brooks
Hansen, Jennifer
Hansen, Matthew Scott
Hansen-Hill, N. D.
Hanson, Neil
Hantover, Jeffrey Philip
Harada, Masako
Harbison, Beth
Hardcastle, Bob
Hardie, Sean
Harding, Paul
Harding, Robyn
Hardwick, Phil

Hardy, Barbara (Gladys)
Hardy, Edward
Hardy, Lyndon (Maurice)
Hareven, Gail
Harland, Richard
Harleman, Ann
Harley, Bill
Harmel, Kristin
Harmon, Sandra
Harnack, Curtis
Harner, Michael J(ames)
Harnum, Robert
Harper, Rachel M.
Harper, Tara K.
Harrell, Beatrice Orcutt
Harrington, Karen
Harrington, Kathleen
Harris, (Theodore) Wilson
Harris, Anne L.
Harris, C. Nelson
Harris, Deborah Turner
Harris, Denise Michelle
Harris, Elizabeth
Harris, Fred R(oy)
Harris, Jana
Harris, Leonard
Harris, Marion (Rose)
Harris, Paul
Harris, Philip Robert
Harris, Robert (Dennis)
Harris, Robert J.
Harris, Rosemary (Jeanne)
Harris, Ruth Elwin
Harris, Steve
Harris, Thomas Walter
Harrison, C. C.
Harrison, Colin
Harrison, Harry
Harrison, Jim
Harrison, Kathryn
Harrison, Kim
Harrison, Lisi
Harrison, Sarah
Harrison, Sue
Harrod-Eagles, Cynthia
Harrower, Elizabeth
Harsanyi, David
Harsch, Rich
Harsent, David
Hart, (Margaret Eleanor) Anne
Hart, Brian
Hart, Carolyn G(impel)
Hart, Christine
Hart, Ellen
Hart, JoeAnn
Hart, Lenore
Hart-Davis, Duff
Harte, Amanda
Harte, Lara
Harter, Karen
Hartland, Michael
Hartnett, Sonya
Haruf, Kent
Harvey, Clay
Harvey, John
Harvey, Kenneth J.
Harvor, Elisabeth

Harwood, John
Harwood, Ronald
Hasan, Anjum
Hasan, Ruqaiya
Hasburgh, Patrick
Haseley, Dennis
Haskell, Guy H.
Haskins, Michael
Haslam, Gerald William
Haslett, Adam
Hasluck, Nicholas
Hastings, Michael
Hatch, Michael F.
Hatcher, Robin Lee
Hathaway, Barbara
Hathorn, Libby
Hatoum, Milton
Hattersley, Roy (Sydney George)
Haughton, Rosemary Luling
Hauptman, William (Thornton)
Havazelet, Ehud
Havel, Harvey
Haverty, Anne
Haviaras, Stratis
Hawes, Louise
Hawke, Ethan
Hawke, Richard
Hawke, Rosanne Joy
Hawke, Simon
Hawkes, G(ary) W(arren)
Hawkes, Judith
Hawley, Ellen
Hawley, Noah
Hawley, Richard A.
Haworth-Attard, Barbara
Hay, Sheridan
Hayes, Bill
Hayes, Daniel
Hayes, Joe
Hayes, Rosemary
Haynes, David
Haynes, Duncan H(arold)
Haynes, Melinda
Hays, Tony
Haywood, Gar Anthony
Haywood, Steve
Hazard, Ann
Hazo, Samuel (John)
Hazuka, Tom
Hazzard, Shirley
Heacox, Kim
Head, Dominic
Head, John
Headley, Bernard D.
Headley, Jason
Headley, Victor
Heald, Tim(othy Villiers)
Healey, Judith Koll
Healy, Erin M.
Healy, Jeremiah
Healy, Sophia (Warner)
Hearn, Julie
Hearon, Shelby
Hearst, Dorothy
Heath, Jennifer
Heath, William
Heffron, Dorris

Hyde, Christopher
Hyde, Eleanor (M.)
Hynes, Charles J.
Hynes, Joel
Iagnemma, Karl
Iakovou, Takis
Iannuzzi, John Nicholas
Idov, Michael
Ignatieff, Michael
Ihimaera, Witi
Iida, Deborah
Ike, Vincent Chukwuemeka
Ilsley, George K.
Impola, Richard A(arre)
In-Ho, Choi
Indiana, Gary
Indridason, Arnaldur
Ing, Dean
Ingersoll, Earl G(eorge)
Ingham, R(ichard) A(rnison)
Inglis, Janet
Inness-Brown, Elizabeth (Ann)
Intrator, Sam M.
Ireland, David
Ireland, Kevin (Mark)
Irving, John (Winslow)
Irwin, Robert (Graham)
Isaacs, Anne
Isaacs, Susan
Isegawa, Moses
Isenberg, Nancy G.
Isenberg, Sheila
Ishiguro, Kazuo
Ittmann, John W.
Ivory, Judith
Iyer, Pico
Jabes, Sophie
Jackman, Stuart (Brooke)
Jackont, Amnon
Jackson, Angela
Jackson, Edwardo
Jackson, G. Mark
Jackson, Jane
Jackson, Lisa
Jackson, Monica
Jackson, Sheneska
Jackson, William J(oseph)
Jacobs, Anna
Jacobs, Barbara
Jacobs, David
Jacobs, Jonnie
Jacobs, Laura
Jacobs, Steve
Jacobson, Dan
Jacq, Christian
Jaffee, Annette Williams
Jakes, John
James, (William) Louis (Gabriel)
James, Brian
James, Caryn
James, Clive (Vivian Leopold)
James, Deana
James, Jamie
James, Julie
James, Kelvin Christopher
James, Marlon
James, P. D.

James, Peter
James, Russell
James, Stanlie
James, Syrie
Jameson, Marianna
Jance, J. A.
Janes, J(oseph) Robert
Janisch, Heinz
Janko, James
Janoda, Jeff
Janowitz, Tama
Jansen, Michael E(lin)
Jaramillo, Stephan
Jarman, Rosemary Hawley
Jarrar, Randa
Jason, Sonya
Jasper, Kenji (Nathaniel)
Jauncey, James
Jeal, (John Julian) Tim(othy)
Jeans, Peter D(ouglas)
Jecks, Michael
Jeffery, Anthea J.
Jeffreys, Diarmuid
Jeffries, Roderic
Jeffries, Sabrina
Jen, Gish
Jenkins, Amy
Jenkins, Beverly
Jenkins, Catherine
Jenkins, Sally
Jennings, Dana Andrew
Jennings, Kate
Jennings, Maureen
Jennings, Paul
Jennings, Phillip E.
Jensen, Emma
Jensen, Kathryn
Jensen, Muriel
Jensen, Ruby Jean
Jepson, Jill
Jernigan, Brenda K.
Jeschke, Wolfgang
Jhabvala, Ruth Prawer
Jin, Ha
Jinks, Catherine
Jirgens, Karl (E.)
Jo, Kyung-Ran
Jocelyn, Marthe
Joens, Michael R.
Johansen, Iris
John, Antony
Johns, Richard Alton
Johnson, Adam
Johnson, Alaya Dawn
Johnson, Allan G.
Johnson, Angela
Johnson, Annabel (Jones)
Johnson, Charles R(ichard)
Johnson, Cherry L(urae) F(lake)
Johnson, Chester L.
Johnson, Diane
Johnson, Fenton
Johnson, Freddie Lee
Johnson, Greg
Johnson, Jason
Johnson, Kenneth C.
Johnson, LouAnne

Johnson, Maureen
Johnson, Merri Lisa
Johnson, R(odney) M(arcus)
Johnson, R. Kikuo
Johnson, Rebecca L.
Johnson, Sandy
Johnson, Sherrie
Johnson, Susan (M.)
Johnson, Susan (Ruth)
Johnson, Todd
Johnston, Jennifer
Johnston, Joan
Johnston, Julie
Johnston, Ronald
Johnstone, Nick
Jolin, Paula
Jonell, Lynne
Jones, (Henry) John (Franklin)
Jones, (R.) Dennis
Jones, Allan Frewin
Jones, Bruce
Jones, Carrie
Jones, David
Jones, David Lee
Jones, Gayl
Jones, Gwyneth A(nn)
Jones, J. V.
Jones, Jenny
Jones, Jenny
Jones, Jill
Jones, Julia
Jones, Kaylie (Ann)
Jones, Keith
Jones, Larry
Jones, Linda Winstead
Jones, Louis B.
Jones, Madison
Jones, Matthew F.
Jones, Solomon
Jones, Tobias
Jong, Erica (Mann)
Jongman, Mariken
Jooste, Pamela
Jordan, Anne Devereaux
Jordan, Hillary
Jordan, Penny
Jordan, Richard Tyler
Jordan, Rosa
Joseph, Henry
Joseph, Lawrence
Josipovici, Gabriel (David)
Jovanovski, Meto
Joy, Camden
Joyce, Brenda
Joyce, Graham
Joyce, Michael
Juby, Susan
Judah, Aaron
Judd, Alan
Judd, Denis
Judson, D. Daniel
Judson, John
Jungman, Ann
Junkins, Donald (Arthur)
Just, Ward
Justiss, Julia
Kachtick, Keith

Kadare, Ismail
Kadrey, Richard
Kaduk, Kevin
Kafka, Kimberly
Kafka-Gibbons, Paul
Kagan, Elaine
Kahn, Michael A.
Kahn, Sharon
Kaimann, Diane S.
Kairys, David
Kaletski, Alexander
Kalin, Jim
Kallgren, Beverly Hayes
Kamakaris, Tina
Kamau, Kwadwo Agymah
Kamensky, Jane
Kan, Blossom
Kanar, Stephen (Patrick)
Kanazawa, Satoshi
Kandel, Michael
Kandel, Susan
Kane, Jessica Francis
Kane, John
Kang, K. Connie
Kanon, Joseph A.
Kanter, Lynn
Kantner, Seth
Kantor, Melissa
Kaplan, James
Kaplan, Mitchell James
Kaplan, Nelly
Kaplan-Maxfield, Thomas
Kaplow, Robert
Kapstein, Ethan B.
Kapur, Manju
Karasik, Paul
Karayianni, Lori
Karayianni, Tony
Karkala, John A.
Karlin, Wayne (Stephen)
Karodia, Farida
Karon, Jan
Karp, Larry
Karr, Kathleen
Kasischke, Laura
Kaslik, Ibolya Emma
Kassabova, Kapka
Katcher, Brian
Katz, Avner
Katz, Elia (Jacob)
Katz, Judith
Katz, Molly
Katz, Steve
Katz, Welwyn Wilton
Kauffman, Bill
Kauffman, Donna
Kauffman, Janet
Kauffmann, Stanley
Kaufman, Bel
Kaufman, Frederick L.
Kaufman, Lynne
Kaufmann, Dovid Yisroel Ber
Kavanagh, P(atrick) J(oseph)
Kavenna, Joanna
Kay, Alan N.
Kay, Guy Gavriel
Kay, Jackie

Laimo, Michael
Lain, Douglas
Laird, Nick
Laje, Zilia L.
Lake, M. D.
Lake, Paul
Lakhous, Amara
Lalicki, Tom
Lam, Vincent
Lamb, Karl A(llen)
Lamb, Nancy
Lamb, Wally
Lamba, Marie
Lambdin, Dewey (W.)
Lamberson, Gregory
Lambert, Page
Lambrecht, William
Lambrichs, Louise L.
Lambshead, John
Lamming, George (Eric)
Lamott, Anne
Lampitt, Dinah
Lanagan, Margo
Lancaster Brown, Peter
Lancelotta, Victoria
Land, Brad
Landers, Scott
Landesman, Peter
Landis, Catherine
Landis, Jill Marie
Landrum, Gene N.
Lane, Abbe
Lane, Dakota
Lane, Simon
Lane, Terry
Langa, Mandla
Langan, John P.
Langan, Mike
Langford, Gary R(aymond)
Langley, Andrew
Langton, Jane
Lanier, Drew Noble
Lankford, Terrill Lee
Lansdale, Joe R(ichard)
Lanthier, Jennifer
Lantigua, John
Lanyon, Anna
Lape, Noreen Groover
Lara, Adair
Larose, Lawrence
Larsen, Jeanne (Louise)
Larsgaard, Chris
Larson, Hope
Larson, Ingrid D(ana)
Lasenby, Jack
Lassiter, Rhiannon
Lathrop, John P.
Latuchie, Karen
Latynin, Leonid (Aleksandrovich)
Laubach, David C.
Laurant, Guillaume
Laurence, Janet
Laurie, Hugh
Laurimore, Jill Frances
Lauterstein, Ingeborg
Laux, Constance
Lavender, Will Ross

Law, Ingrid
Lawler, Jennifer
Lawrence, David
Lawrence, Kathleen Rockwell
Lawrence, Louise
Lawrence, Michael
Lawrence, Starling
Lawson, Dorie McCullough
Lawson, James
Lawson, JonArno Burhans
Lawton, John
Lazebnik, Claire Scovell
Lazenby, Edith P.
Lazuta, Gene
Le, Nam
le Carré, John
Le Guin, Ursula K(roeber)
Leaman, Celia A.
Leary, Ann (Lembeck)
Leavitt, Caroline
Leavitt, David
Lebor, Adam
Lebowitz, Albert
Lecesne, James
Leckie, Keith (Ross)
Leckie, Ross
LeClaire, Anne D(ickinson)
LeCompte, N(ancy) Jane
Ledbetter, Suzann
Leddy, Mary Jo
Ledwidge, Michael
Lee, A(rthur) Robert
Lee, Chang-rae
Lee, Don
Lee, Helen Elaine
Lee, J. Ardian
Lee, Jennifer
Lee, Marie G.
Lee, Mark
Lee, Mona
Lee, Rachel
Lee, Sky
Lee, Tonya Lewis
Lee, Wendy
Leegant, Joan
Leese, Jennifer L. B.
Leeson, Robert (Arthur)
Leeson, Ted
Lefcourt, Peter
Lefebure, Molly
Lehane, Cornelius
Lehane, Dennis
Lehman, Yvonne
Lehmann, Geoffrey (John)
Lehner, Lyndsay Farber
Lehrer, James (Charles)
Lehrer, Kate
Leib, Franklin A(llen)
Leigh, Ana
Leiner, Katherine
Leitch, Maurice
Leitch, Will
Leith, Linda Jane
Leithauser, Brad (Edward)
Lelchuk, Alan
Leleux, Robert
Lemov, Rebecca

Lennon, J. Robert
Lennon, Joan
Lent, John
Lentin, Ronit
Leo, Mabel R.
Leonard, Constance
Leonard, Elmore
Leoni, Giulio
Lerangis, Peter
Lerman, Rhoda
Lerner, Eric
Lerner, Eric J.
Lerner, Laurence (David)
Leroy, Margaret
Lescroart, John T.
Leslie, Roger (James)
Lesser, Wendy
Lessing, Doris (May)
Lester, Julius
Letessier, Dorothée
Lethem, Jonathan (Allen)
Leto, Julie Elizabeth
Letts, Billie
Leveritt, Thomas
Levesque, John
Leviant, Curt
Levin, Betty (Lowenthal)
Levin, Linda Lotridge
Levin, Mark
Levin, Michael (Graubart)
Levin, Miriam (Ramsfelder)
Levine, Gail Carson
Levine, Kristin
Levine, Paul
Levitin, Sonia (Wolff)
Levoy, Myron
Levy, Deborah
Levy, Elizabeth
Levy, JoAnn
Levy, Marc
Lewin, Leif
Lewin, Michael Z.
Lewis, J(ohn) P(aul) Lewis
Lewis, J(ohn) R(oyston)
Lewis, J. S.
Lewis, Linda (Joy)
Lewis, Norah L.
Lewis, Richard
Lewis, Simon
Lewis, Trudy
Li, Leslie
Libby, Alisa M.
Libera, Antoni
Licht, H. William (Bill)
Lichtenberg, Jacqueline
Lichtenstein, Alice
Lide, Mary
Lieberman, Herbert
Lieberman, Leanne
Lieberman, Richard K.
Liebreich, Karen
Lightman, Alan P.
Ligon, Samuel
Lilienfeld, Jane
Lim, Shirley Geok-lin
Limon, Jerzy
Limon, Martin

Limonov, E duard
Lin, Grace
Lin, Tan (Anthony)
Lindbergh, Judith
Linder, Marc
Lindquist, N(ancy) J(ane)
Lindsay, Frederic
Lindsay, James
Lindskold, Jane M.
Lindvall, Michael L(loyd)
Lingard, Joan (Amelia)
Links, Bo
Linzer, Anna
Lipkin, Randie
Lipman, Elinor
Lipman, Victoria M.
Lippi(-Green), Rosina
Lipsky, David
Lipsyte, Robert (Michael)
Lisle, Holly
Lisle, Rebecca
Liss, David
Lister, R(ichard) P(ercival)
Litman, Ellen
Littell, Robert
Little, (Flora) Jean
Little, Bentley
Littlefield, Bill
Littlefield, Holly
Littleton, Mark (R.)
Lively, Adam
Lively, Penelope
Llewellyn, Kate
Llewellyn, Sam
Lliteras, D. S.
Llobera, Josep R.
Lloyd, A(lan) R(ichard)
Lloyd, Saci
Llywelyn, Morgan
Lo, Malinda
Lo Scalzo, Jim
Lobanov-Rostovsky, Sergei
Lochte, Dick
Lock, Joan
Locke, Attica
Locklin, Gerald Ivan
Lockridge, Larry
Lodato, Victor
Lodge, David
Lodge, Jeff
Lofton, Ramona
Logan, Chuck
Logue, Mary
Loh, Sandra Tsing
Lohans, Alison
Löhr, Robert
Lombardo, Billy
London, Joan
London, Mark
Long, Jeff
Longyear, Barry B.
Lopez, Josefina
Lopez, Steve
Lordan, (Ellenora) Beth
Lordon, Randye
Lorey, Dean
Loriga, Ray

Lorrimer, Claire
Losse, Deborah N(ichols)
Lott, Bret
Louie, Andrea
Louie, David Wong
Louis, Cindi
Loundagin, Choeleen N.
Lourie, Richard
Lovegrove, James (Matthew Henry)
Lovelace, Earl
Lovelace, Merline (A.)
Lovell, Glenville
Lovell, Mary S(ybilla)
Lovely, Stephen
Lovric, Michelle
Low, Robert
Low, Shari
Lowden, Desmond Scott
Lowe, Helen
Lowe, Keith
Lowe, Sheila
Lowe, Tom
Lowell, Pamela
Lowenberg, Susan
Lowry, Lois (Hammersberg)
Lowy, Jonathan
Loy, Rosetta
Lubar, David
Lucas, Michele Claire
Lucashenko, Melissa
Luckett, Dave
Luddy, Karon
Ludwig, Jack
Luft, Lya Fett
Lund, Gerald N.
Lund, Michael
Lundin, Steve
Lupica, Mike
Lurie, Alison
Lurie, April
Lurie, Morris
Lusby, Jim
Lusk, John
Lustbader, Eric Van
Lusted, Marcia Amidon
Lustig, T(imothy) J(ohn)
Lutz, John (Thomas)
Lykins, Jenny
Lynch, Chris
Lynch, Daniel
Lynch, Janet Nichols
Lynds, Gayle (Hallenbeck)
Lynn, Jonathan
Lyon, Annabel
Lyon, Bentley
Lyon, Elizabeth
Lyon, George Ella
Lyons, Louis
Lytton, Deborah
Maas, Sharon
Maazel, Fiona
Mac, Carrie
Mac Donald, Laura M.
Macalister, Katie
MacCready, Robin Merrow
MacDonald, Ann-Marie

MacDonald, Anne Louise
Macdonald, James D.
Macdonald, Lyn
Macdonald, Marianne
Macdonald, Norman Malcolm
MacDonald, Patricia J.
Macdonald, Sharman
MacDougal, Bonnie
MacDowell, Heather
MacDowell, Rose
MacEnulty, Pat
MacEoin, Denis
Macgoye, Marjorie Oludhe
Machann, Clinton (John)
Machor, James L(awrence)
MacInnes, Mairi
MacInnes, Patricia
MacIntyre, Linden
MacIntyre, Wendy
Mack, Carol K.
Mack, David (A.)
MacKenna, John
MacKenzie, Sally
Mackin, Jeanne
Mackler, Carolyn
Macklin, Robert
MacLachlan, Patricia
MacLean, Glynne
MacLean, Judy Ellen
MacLean, Sarah
Maclear, Kyo
Macleod, Alison
Macleod, Ian R.
Macleod, Joan
MacLeod, Ken
MacNeill, Alastair
MacNish, Tracy
Macomber, Debbie
Macomber, James
Macomber, Robert N.
Macphail, Catherine
MacPherson, Andrea
MacRae, Molly
Madden, David
Madden, Deirdre
Madison, Bennett
Madsen, Svend Åge
Magee, Bryan
Magee, Doug
Maggio, Mike
Maginn, Simon
Magistrale, Tony
Magona, Sindiwe
Magorian, Michelle
Maguire, Gregory (Peter)
Magun, Carol
Mahajan, Karan
Maher, Eamon
Mahindra, Indira
Mailman, Erika
Maine, David
Mains, Randolph P.
Mairowitz, David Zane
Maisel, Eric
Maitland, Barry
Maitland, Karen
Majid, Anouar

Major, Andre
Major, Clarence
major, devorah
Majure, Janet
Makine, Andreï
Mallon, Thomas
Malmgren, Dallin
Malmont, Valerie S(kuse)
Malone, James Hiram
Malone, Susan (Mary)
Malouf, David
Malvasi, Mark G.
Mamet, David
Manaster, Benjamin
Mancusi, Mari
Mandanipour, Shahriar
Mandel, Emily St. John
Mandelman, Avner
Manea, Norman
Manhire, Bill
Manicka, Rani
Mann, (Anthony) Phillip
Mann, Catherine
Mann, Kenny
Mann, Paul (James)
Mann, William J.
Manning, Robert D.
Manotti, Dominique
Manrique (Ardila), Jaime
Mantel, Hilary (Mary)
Maracle, Lee
Maraniss, David
Marcantel, Pamela
Marchand, Philip (Edward)
Marchant, Ian
Marchessault, Jovette
Marciano, Francesca
Marcom, Micheline Aharonian
Marcus, Ben
Marcus, David L.
Marcus, James
Marder, Norma
Margam, Kate
Margolin, Phillip (Michael)
Margolis, Jonathan
Margolis, Leslie
Margolis, Seth J(acob)
Marias, Javier
Marin, Mindy
Marinick, Richard
Maristed, Kai
Markaris, Petros
Markham, Lynne
Markoe, Merrill
Markoosie
Markovits, Andrei S.
Marks, Graham
Marks, Stan(ley)
Marks-White, Judith
Markus, Julia
Marlis, Stefanie
Marlow, Joyce
Marolda, Edward J.
Maron, Margaret
Maron, Monika
Marouane, Leila
Marquis, Max

Marquit, Amanda
Marqusee, Mike
Marr, Maggie
Marr, Melissa
Marriott, Michel
Marriott, Zoë
Mars, Julie
Marsden, Carolyn
Marsden, John
Marsella, Anne (Francesca)
Marsh, Fabienne
Marshal, Nell
Marshall, Elizabeth Margaret
Marshall, Owen
Marshall, Peter
Marston, Cam
Martin, (Roy) Peter
Martin, Alex
Martin, Allana
Martin, Clancy M.
Martin, Courtney E.
Martin, Eric B.
Martin, George R.R.
Martin, Judith
Martin, Larry Jay
Martin, Man
Martin, Rhona
Martin, Russell
Martin, Stephen-Paul
Martin, Victoria Carolyn
Martin, William
Martinac, Paula
Martinez, Guillermo
Martínez, Manuel Luis
Martinez, Nancy C.
Martini, Steven (Paul)
Martini, Teri
Marton, Kati (Ilona)
Marusek, David
Marvin, Jay
Masello, Robert
Masini, Donna
Maso, Carole
Mason, Anita
Mason, Bobbie Ann
Mason, Daniel
Mason, David
Mason, Felicia
Mason, J. D.
Mason, Jeffrey D(aniel)
Mason, Sarah J.
Mason, Timothy
Mass, Wendy
Massey, Calvin R(andolph)
Massie, Elizabeth
Massie, Sonja
Masson, Sophie
Masters, Alexis
Masters, Susan Rowan
Mastras, George
Masud, Naiyer
Matalon, Ronit
Matas, Carol
Matera, Dary M.
Mather, Anne
Mathes, Charles (Elliott)
Matheson, Richard (Burton)

Index To Writing Categories

Mathews, Aidan (Carl)
Mathews, Ellie
Mathews, Lou
Mathis, Sharon Bell
Matlin, David
Matson, Suzanne
Matteson, John
Matthew, Christopher C. F.
Matthews, Alex
Matthews, Carole
Matthews, Greg
Matthews, Jack
Matthews, L. S.
Matthiessen, Peter
Maupin, Armistead
Maurensig, Paolo
Mauro, Nancy
Maxwell, Cathy
Maxwell, Patricia Anne
Maxwell, Robin
May, Derwent (James)
May, John
May, Julian
May, Wynne
Mayall, Beth
Maybury, Richard J.
Mayer, Bob
Mayer, Robert
Mayhar, Ardath (Hurst)
Mayhew, Margaret
Mayo, C(atherine) M(ansell)
Mayo, Wendell
Mayse, Susan
Mazer, Harry
Mazoyer, Deborah
Mazrui, Ali Al('Amin)
Mazza, Cris
Mazzuca Toops, Laura
Mbaye, Marietou (Bileoma)
McAdam, Colin
McAdams, Janet
McAfee, Carol
McAfee, John P.
McAlpine, Alistair
McAlpine, Rachel (Taylor)
McArthur, Nancy
McAulay, Alex
McAuley, Paul J.
McAuley, Roisin
McBride, Jule
McBride, Mary
McBride, Susan
McCafferty, Maureen
McCaffery, Steve
McCaffrey, Anne (Inez)
Mccaffrey, K. T.
McCain, Charles
McCall, Dan (Elliott)
McCann, Colum
Mccann, Maria
McCarry, Charles
McCarthy, Cormac
McCarthy, Gary
McCarthy, Nan
McCarthy, Thomas
McCarthy, Wil
McCartney, Alistair

McCaughrean, Geraldine (Jones)
McCauley, Sue
McClanahan, Jeffery
McCleary, Kathleen
McClendon, Lise (Webb)
McClure, Ken
McCollum, Michael (Allen)
McConkey, James (Rodney)
McConnochie, Mardi
McCorkle, Jill (Collins)
McCormack, Mike
McCormack, W(illiam) J(ohn)
McCouch, Hannah
McCoy, Max
McCoy, Sarah
McCracken, Elizabeth
McCray, W. Patrick
McCrumb, Sharyn
McCullough, Colleen
McCullough, David Willis
McCully, Emily Arnold
McCusker, Paul
McCutcheon, Sandy
McDaniel, Lurlene
McDermott, Alice
McDonald, Ian
McDonald, Ian (A.)
McDonald, Joyce
McDougal, Dennis
McEldowney, Eugene
McElmurray, Karen Salyer
McElroy, Colleen J.
McElroy, Joseph (Prince)
McEvilley, Thomas
McEwan, Ian
McEwen, Helena
McEwen, Todd
McFadden, David W.
McFarland, Dennis
McFarlane, Peter (William)
McFetridge, John
McGahan, Andrew
McGarrity, Michael
McGinniss, Joe
McGinniss, Joe
McGlothin, Victor
McGoogan, Ken
McGowan, Anthony
McGrath, Carmelita
McGrath, Kristina
McGrath, Patrick
McGraw, Erin
McGraw, Milena
Mcgregor, Jon
Mcgrory, Brian
McGuane, Thomas
McGuigan, Mary Ann
McGuire, Brian Patrick
McIlvoy, Kevin
McInerney, Jay
McIntosh, Fiona
McIntyre, Vonda N(eel)
McIvor, James
McKay, Claudia
McKay, Hilary
McKay, Ron
McKee, Annie

McKenna, Colleen
 O'Shaughnessy
McKenna, Lindsay Gvhdi
McKenzie, John D.
Mckenzie, Nancy Affleck
McKeon, Michael
McKinley, (Jennifer Carolyn)
 Robin
McKinney, Meagan
McKinney, Tina Brooks
McKissack, Patricia C(arwell)
McKittrick, David
McKown, Delos B.
McLain, Paula
McLaren, Clemence
McLaren, Philip
McLarey, Myra
McLarin, Kim
McLaughlin, Ann L.
Mclaughlin, Ritta
McLean, Duncan
McLeod, Grover S(tephen)
Mcmahan, Ian (D.)
McMahan, Janna
McMahon, Katharine
McMann, Lisa
McManus, Michael
McManus, Michael J.
McMaster, Juliet (Sylvia)
McMaster, Rhyll
McMillan, Rosalyn A.
McMillan, Terry
McMullan, Margaret
McMullen, Sean (Christopher)
McMurtry, Larry (Jeff)
McNab, Claire
McNamara, Eugene Joseph
McNamara, Mary
McNamee, Eoin
McNees, Kelly O'Connor
McNeish, James
McPhee, Martha (A.)
McPhee, Peter
McPherson, James A(lan)
McQueen, Rod
McReynolds, Glenna Jean
McShane, Mark
McTavish, Lianne
McWhirter, George
McWilliam, Candia
McWilliams, Karen
Mda, Zakes
Meade, Glenn
Meaker, Marijane (Agnes)
Meaney, John
Means, Howard
Mears, Gillian
Mebus, Scott
Mechling, Lauren
Meddeb, Abdelwahab
Medina, Nico
Mednick, Kevin
Medoff, Jillian
Medoff, Mark (Howard)
Medvedev, Grigori
Medwed, Mameve
Mee, Susie (B.)

Meeks, Christopher (Nelson)
Megged, Aharon
Mehta, Gita
Mehta, Ved (Parkash)
Meier, Diane
Meikle, William
Mekler, Eva
Melchior, Ib (Jorgen)
Melchiori, Barbara Arnett
Mellen, Joan
Melling, O.
Mellizo (Cuadrado), Carlos
Melman, Peter Charles
Melnyczuk, Askold
Melton, Brian C.
Melton, Buckner F.
Meltzer, Brad
Meltzer, David
Meluch, R(ebecca) M.
Melville, Pauline
Memmott, David R.
Mendelson, Cheryl
Mendes, Pedro Rosa
Menéndez, Ana (Maria)
Meno, Joe
Mercati, Cynthia
Mercer, Jeremy
Merriman, Catherine
Merullo, Roland
Merz, Jon F.
Messori, Vittorio
Messud, Claire
Metcalf, John (Wesley)
Mettam, Roger C.
Metz, Don
Metzger, Deena P.
Metzger, Robert A(lan)
Meyer, Carolyn
Meyer, Deon
Meyerowitz, Patricia
Meyers, Annette (Brafman)
Meyers, Kent
Meyers, Martin
Mezlekia, Nega
Michael, Livi
Michaels, Anne
Michaels, Lisa
Michaels, Rune
Michels, Sharry C.
Michelson, Richard
Mickelbury, Penny
Mickle, Shelley Fraser
Micklem, Sarah
Micou, Paul
Middleton, Haydn
Midwood, Bart(on A.)
Mihailovi, Dragoslav
Mikaelsen, Ben (John)
Miklowitz, Gloria D.
Miles, Keith
Miles, Rosalind
Milhorn, H. Thomas
Millen, Rochelle L.
Miller, Alyce
Miller, Christopher
Miller, David W.
Miller, Deborah

Nissenson, Hugh
Niven, Larry
Nixon, Cornelia
Nkala, Nathan
Nobbs, David
Nobisso, Josephine
Noel, Katharine
Nolan, William F(rancis)
Noll, Ingrid
Noon, Jeff
Norac, Carl
Nordan, Lewis
Norfleet, Celeste O.
Norfolk, Lawrence
Norman, Barry
Norman, Howard A.
Norman, Marsha
Norman, Rick (J.)
Norrell, Gregory T.
Norris, Frances
Norris, Pamela
Norris, Shana
Norris, William R.
North, Darian
Norton, Melissa
Norton, Sheila
Norwich, William
Novack, Sandra
Novak, Karen
Novak, Michael
Novaro, María
Novas, Himilce
Noyes, Deborah
Nunez, Sigrid
Nunnally, Tiina
Nutt, Paul C.
Nyamnjoh, Francis B.
Nye, Robert
Nye, Simon (Beresford)
Nylund, Eric S.
O Cuilleanain, Cormac
O'Brien, (Warren) Greg(ory)
O'Brien, Edna
O'Brien, Martin
O'Brien, Matthew
O'Brien, Maureen
O'Brien, Tim
O'Brien, Timothy L.
O'Callahan, Jay
O'Carroll, Brendan
O'Connell, Carol
O'Connell, Jack
O'Connell, Jennifer
O'Connell, Marvin R(ichard)
O'Connor, Rebecca K.
O'Connor, Robert
O'Dea, Brian
O'Dell, Tawni
O'Donnell, Sunshine
O'Donohoe, Nick
O'Faolain, Julia
O'Flynn, Catherine
O'Grady, John P.
O'Grady, Rohan
O'Hagan, Andrew
O'Hagan, Christine
O'Hanlon, Ardal

O'Hara, Marjorie (Doreen)
O'Keefe, Kevin
O'Keeffe, Frank
O'Leary, Patrick
O'Leary, Patsy Baker
O'Loughlin, Ed
O'Malley, Thomas
O'Neill, Jamie
O'Neill, Joseph
O'Neill, Tom
O'Neill, Tony
O'Reilly Herrera, (C.) Andrea
O'Rourke, Erin
O'Rourke, William
O'Shea, Donal B.
Oakes, Andy
Oakley, Ann
Oates, Joyce Carol
Obejas, Achy
Odaga, Asenath (Bole)
Odell, Jonathan
Odhiambo, David Nandi
o e, Kenzaburo
Ogunyemi, Yemi D(iploman)
Okimoto, Jean Davies
Okorafor-Mbachu, Nnedi
Okri, Ben
Oldfield, Jenny
Oldfield, Pamela
Oldham, June
Olds, Bruce
Oleksiw, Susan (Prince)
Oliveira, Robin Frazier
Oliver, Maria Antònia
Olmstead, Robert
Olsen, Lance (M.)
Olsen, Mark Andrew
Olshan, Matthew
Olson, Gretchen
Olson, Michael Keith
Olson, Toby
Oltion, Jerry
Omang, Joanne (Brenda)
Ondaatje, Michael
Oneal, Elizabeth
Oness, Elizabeth
Ong, Han
Onwueme, Tess Osonye
Onyeama, Dillibe
Oppegaard, David
Orban, Christine
Ordinans, Nicholas J.
Oren, Michael B(ornstein)
Orenstein, Catherine
Orlev, Uri
Orme, David John
Ormerod, Roger
Ormondroyd, Edward
Orr, Wendy
Ortego, Sheila
Orth, Lucia
Ortiz-Taylor, Sheila
Osborn, David (D.)
Osborn, Karen
Osborn, Susan (E.)
Osborne, Frances
Osborne-McKnight, Juilene

Ostow, Micol
Ostrom, Hans
Ott, Thomas
Otto, Lon
Otto, Whitney
Ouellette, Pierre
Oust, Gail
Overall, Sonia
Overmyer, Eric
Øvstedal, Barbara
Owen, Howard (Wayne)
Owens, Janis E(llen)
Ozick, Cynthia
Pace, Alison
Packer, Mez
Paczkowski, Andrzej
Padanilam, George J.
Paddock, Jennifer
Padfield, Peter
Padgett, Ron
Paetro, Maxine
Paffenroth, Kim
Page, Geoff(rey Donald)
Page, Katherine Hall
Pahor, Boris
Pairo, Preston (A.)
Paisner, Daniel
Palandri, Enrico
Palencia, Elaine Fowler
Palfrey, Evelyn
Palin, Michael (Edward)
Paling, Chris
Palliser, Charles
Palmer, Dexter
Palmer, Elizabeth
Palmer, Philip
Palmer, Stephen
Palmer, William J.
Palwick, Susan
Pancake, Ann
Pancol, Katherine
Papanikolas, Zeese
Pappano, Marilyn
Paquet, Laura Byrne
Paranjape, Makarand (Ramach-
  andra)
Parascandola, Louis J.
Paratore, Coleen Murtagh
Pardoe, Blaine
Paretsky, Sara
Pargin, Jason Keith
Pari, Susanne
Parini, Jay
Park, David
Park, Ed
Parker, Alan Michael
Parker, Barbara Keevil
Parker, Gary E.
Parker, Gordon
Parker, Jeff
Parker, Matthew
Parker, Peter (Robert Nevill)
Parker, Tom
Parker, Una-Mary
Parkhurst, Brooke
Parkin, Frank
Parkin, Gaile

Parkinson, Siobhan
Parks, Adele
Parks, Suzan Lori
Parotti, Phillip (Elliott)
Parrish, Richard
Partridge, Jenny (Lilian)
Partridge, Norman
Pascal, Francine
Pascoe, Bruce
Pashman, Susan
Pastan, Rachel
Pastor, Ben
Paterson, Alistair (Ian Hughes)
Paterson, Katherine (Womeldorf)
Patrick, Jennifer
Patrick, Robert
Patten, Brian
Patterson, (Horace) Orlando
Patterson, Glenn
Patterson, Jerry L.
Patterson, Kevin
Patterson, Richard North
Patterson, Sparrow L.
Patton, Robert H.
Pattou, Edith
Patzer, Gordon
Paul, Anthea
Paul, Caroline
Paulsen, Gary
Paulsson, Gunnar S.
Pausewang, Gudrun
Pavelich, Matt
Pavlou, Stel
Paxson, Diana L(ucile)
Payne, (William) David
Payne, Donald Gordon
Payne, Holly
Pazzi, Roberto
Peace, David
Peace, Richard (Arthur)
Peachment, Christopher
Peak, John A.
Pearce, Edward
Pearce, Margaret
Pearce, Mary E.
Pearl, Matthew
Pearlman, Daniel D.
Pears, Tim
Pearsall, Shelley
Pearson, Carol Lynn
Pearson, Diane (Margaret)
Pearson, John
Pearson, Kit
Pearson, Ridley
Pearson, T(homas) R(eid)
Peavler, Terry J.
Peck, Dale
Peck, Richard (Wayne)
Pedersen, Laura
Pedrazas, Allan
Peel, H(azel) M(ary)
Peery, Janet
Peet, Mal
Peeters, Frederik
Pekárková, Iva
Pekkanen, Sarah
Pelletier, Cathie

Reed, Paula
Reed, Ralph Eugene
Reeder, Carolyn
Reeman, Douglas (Edward)
Rees, Matt Beynon
Rees, Nigel (Thomas)
Reese, James
Reese, Laura
Reeve, F(ranklin) D(olier)
Reeves, Faye Couch
Reeves-Stevens, Garfield
Regan, Linda
Reginald, Robert
Rehder, Ben
Reich, Christopher
Reiche, Dietlof
Reid, Alastair
Reid, Elwood
Reid, Van
Reiken, Frederick
Reilly, Bernard F.
Reimann, Katya
Reiss, Kathryn
Reiter, Victoria (Kelrich)
Renaud, Jacques
Rendell, Ruth
Rennison, Louise
Renshaw, Corinne
Resnick, Mike
Resnick, Rachel
Resseguie, James L.
Reuland, Robert
Reusche, Taylor McCafferty
Reuss, Frederick
Reuter, Bjarne (B.)
Rey, Bret
Rey, Dennison
Reynald, Lance M.
Reynolds, (Richard) Clay
Reynolds, Arlene
Reynolds, Marjorie
Reynolds, Sheri
Reza, Yasmina
Rhodes, Richard (Lee)
Ribalow, M(eir) Z(vi)
Ricci, Nino
Rice, Anne
Rice, Bebe Faas
Rice, Earle
Rice, Linda Lightsey
Rice, Luanne
Rice, Zoe
Rich, Nathaniel
Rich, Simon
Richard, Adrienne
Richards, Dusty
Richards, Linda L.
Richardson, Nigel
Richardson, Robert
Richemont, Enid
Richie, Donald
Richler, Daniel
Richler, Nancy
Richman, Jana
Richmond, Michelle
Richtel, Matt
Richter, Harvena

Richter, Jutta
Richter, Roland Suso
Rickman, Philip
Riddle, Paxton
Riddles, Libby
Ridgway, Keith
Ridley, Elizabeth J(ayne)
Ridley, Philip
Riehecky, Janet Ellen
Rifbjerg, Klaus (Thorvald)
Rifkin, Shepard
Riggs, Cynthia
Riggs, Jack C.
Riley, Jess
Riley, Joan
Riley, Madeleine (Veronica)
Rinaldi, Ann
Rinder, Lenore
Rindo, Ron(ald J.)
Rinehart, Steven
Ringo, John
Rio, Michel
Riordan, James (William)
Riordan, Teresa
Rios, Julian
Ritchie, Harry
Rivard, Robert
Rivas, Manuel
Rivas, Mim Eichler
Rivenbark, Celia
Riverbend
Rivers, Francine (Sandra)
Rivers, Reggie
Rivière, William
Robb, B. R.
Robbins, Tom
Roberts, Alvin
Roberts, Denys (Tudor Emil)
Roberts, Diane
Roberts, Gregory David
Roberts, Katherine
Roberts, Kristina LaFerne
Roberts, Nora
Roberts, Paul William
Roberts, Tansy Rayner
Roberts, Yvonne
Robertson, C(harles) K(evin)
Robertson, Deborah
Robertson, Robin
Robins, Madeleine E.
Robins, Sari
Robinson, Cynthia
Robinson, Eden
Robinson, Jeremy
Robinson, Lee
Robinson, Roxana (Barry)
Robinson, Spider
Robotham, Michael
Robson, Lucia St. Clair
Rockland, Michael Aaron
Rodda, Emily
Rodgers, Alan (Paul)
Rodin, Robert L.
Rodrigues dos Santos, Jose
Roe, Caroline
Roe, Sue
Roe, Sue (Lynn)

Roessner, Michaela
Rogers, Franklin Robert
Rogers, Rebecca Elizabeth
Rogers, Rosemary
Rogow, Zack
Rohan, Michael Scott
Roiphe, Anne Richardson
Roiphe, Katie
Rolde, Neil
Roley, Brian Ascalon
Rollins, David A.
Romano, Tony
Romano-Lax, Andromeda
Rome, Margaret
Romero, George A.
Ronan, Frank
Rooke, Leon
Roorbach, Bill
Rorby, Ginny
Roripaugh, Robert (Alan)
Roschelle, Anne R.
Roscoe, Patrick
Rose, Elisabeth
Rose, Karen
Rosen, David J.
Rosen, James
Rosen, Louis H.
Rosen, Michael J(oel)
Rosen, Selina
Rosenberg, Joel C.
Rosenberg, Liz
Rosenberg, Robert Alan
Rosenthal, Lucy (Gabrielle)
Roshwald, Mordecai
Rosner, Elizabeth J.
Ross, JoAnn
Ross, Stuart
Ross-Macdonald, Malcolm (John)
Rossen, Jake
Rossi, Hozy (Joe)
Rossio, Terry
Rossiter, John
Rossman, Vadim
Rostkowski, Margaret I.
Rotenberg, Robert
Roth, Gerhard (Jurgen)
Roth, Philip
Rothenberg, David
Rothfuss, Pat J.
Rotter, Gabe
Rotter, Jeffrey
Rougeau, Remy
Rounds, David
Routley, (Bernarra) Jane
Rower, Ann
Rowland, Peter Kenneth
Rowling, J(oanne) K.
Rowse, Sharon
Rowson, Pauline
Roy, Archie E.
Roy, Arundhati
Roy, Jacqueline
Roy, Lucinda (H.)
Royal, Priscilla
Rozo, Marco Antonio Palacios
Rubin, Adam
Rubin, Larry (Jerome)

Rubright, Lynn
Rudolf, Anthony
Ruefle, Mary
Ruemmler, John D(avid)
Rule, Ann
Rumens, Carol
Rummel, Jack
Rumpf, Eva Augustin
Runcie, James
Rupp, Richard H.
Rusch, Kristine Kathryn
Rush, Christopher
Rushdie, Salman
Rushfield, Richard
Russell, Alan
Russell, Mary D(oria)
Russell, Paul
Russell, Roy
Russell Taylor, Elisabeth
Russo, Elena
Russo, John (A.)
Russo, Marisabina
Rutherfurd, Edward
Rutledge, Leigh W.
Rutsala, Vern A.
Ruyslinck, Ward
Ryan, Frank
Ryan, Pam Muñoz
Ryan, Patrick
Rydill, Jessica
S.D., Trav
Saban, Cheryl (Lynn)
Sabatini, Sandra
Sabin, Roger (John)
Sachs, Jeffrey D.
Sachs, Judith
Sachs, Marilyn (Stickle)
Sackett, Jeffrey
Saddler, Allen
Saenz, Benjamin Alire
Sæterøy, John Arne
Saferstein, Dan
Sagastizabal, Patricia
Sage, Angie
Sager, Mike
Sahgal, Nayantara (Pandit)
Sakamoto, Kerri
Saknussemm, Kris
Salak, Kira
Salaman, Nicholas
Salamon, Julie
Salazar, Dixie
Saldana, Rene
Saleem, Hiner
Saliers, Emily
Sallenave, Daniele
Salmansohn, Karen
Salutin, Rick
Salvatore, R(obert) A(nthony)
Salzman, Eva Frances
Sampson, Catherine
Sams, Ferrol
Sanchez, Patrick
Sandburg, Helga
Sanders, Ed(ward)
Sanders, Scott Loring
Sandford, John

Simons, Paullina
Simonson, Helen
Simpson, Dorothy
Simpson, Penny Claire
Sims, Elizabeth
Sims, Michael
Sinclair, Alison
Sinclair, Andrew (Annandale)
Sinclair, Iain
Sinclair, Olga (Ellen)
Singer, Alan
Singer, Judy Reene
Singleton, Janet Elyse
Singleton, Linda Joy
Sington, Philip
Sinha, Indra
Sinisalo, Johanna
Sinnett, Mark C.
Sipherd, Ray
Sirias, Silvio
Sisson, Rosemary Anne
Sittenfeld, Curtis
Skal, David J.
Skillingstead, Jack
Skinner, Margaret
Skinner, Michael
Skipp, John
Skloot, Floyd
Skrzynecki, Peter
Škvoreck , Josef
Skye, Christina
Skyler, Heather
Slade, Arthur G(regory)
Slader, John M.
Slattery, Brian Francis
Slattery, Dennis Patrick
Slaughter, Karin
Slavin, Helen
Slegman, Ann
Slepian, Jan(ice B.)
Sloan, Susan R.
Slosberg, Mike
Slote, Alfred
Slouka, Mark
Small, Hugh
Smarandache, Florentin
Smart, Ian Isidore
Smellie, Jim
Smigel, Robert
Smiley, Jane (Graves)
Smith, Ali
Smith, Bobbi
Smith, Charles R.
Smith, Craig
Smith, D. James
Smith, Dave
Smith, David Alexander
Smith, Deborah
Smith, Derek D.
Smith, Diane
Smith, Emily Wing
Smith, Emma
Smith, Faye McDonald
Smith, Frederick E(screet)
Smith, Greg Leitich
Smith, Gregory Blake
Smith, Jeanne Rosier

Smith, Joan Gerarda
Smith, Jonathan
Smith, Kirsten
Smith, Lora Roberts
Smith, Mark Haskell
Smith, Martin Cruz
Smith, Michael
Smith, Mitchell
Smith, Morris
Smith, Neil
Smith, Peter Charles Horstead
Smith, Peter Moore
Smith, Rupert
Smith, Sandra Lee
Smith, Scott
Smith, Sherri L.
Smith, Sherwood
Smith, Stephanie A.
Smith, Wilbur (Addison)
Smith, Zadie
Smither, Elizabeth
Smolens, John (Harrison)
Snadowsky, Daria
Snelling, Lauraine
Snicket, Lemony
Sniegoski, Thomas E.
Snow, Carol
Snyder, Cecil
Snyder, James D.
Snyder, Lucy A.
Snyder, Zilpha Keatley
Sobol, Donald J.
Sobol, Joshua
Sobott-Mogwe, Gaele
Soehnlein, Karl M.
Sofer, Barbara
Sohn, Amy
Sok-Kyong, Kang
Sokol, Julia
Solares, Ignacio
Solmssen, Arthur R(obert)
  G(eorge)
Solomita, Stephen
Solomon, Andrew
Solomon, Evan
Solomon, Nina
Somers, Jeff
Sonenberg, Maya
Sosnowski, David (J.)
Soto, Gary
Soueif, Ahdaf
Soule, Maris Anne
Souster, Raymond
Southey, Roz
Soyinka, Wole
Spacks, Barry
Spaeth, Anthony
Spalding, Andrea
Spangler, Catherine
Spanier, Sandra Whipple
Spanogle, Joshua
Sparkes, Ali
Sparks, Nicholas
Sparrow, Rebecca
Spatz, Gregory
Spaugh, Jean Christopher
Speck, Katie

Spence, William John Duncan
Spencer, Brent
Spencer, Colin
Spencer, Elizabeth
Spencer, Mark
Spencer, Scott
Spencer, William Browning
Spens, Christiana
Spiegelman, Ian
Spiegelman, Peter
Spielberg, Peter
Spinelli, Jerry
Spinner, Jackie
Spivack, Kathleen (Romola
  Drucker)
Spollen, Anne
Springer, Claudia
Sprinkle, Patricia Houck
Sproat, Robert
Sprott, Duncan
Spruill, Steven
Spufford, Francis
Spurling, John
St. John, Bob J.
Staats, Marilyn Dorn
Stableford, Brian M(ichael)
Stacey, Tom
Stachniak, Eva
Stackpole, Michael A(ustin)
Stamm, Peter
Stamp, Terence (Henry)
Stansberry, Domenic (Joseph)
Staples, Suzanne Fisher
Starer, Daniel
Stark, Marisa Kantor
Starmer, Aaron
Starr, Jason
Starr, Patti
Stashower, Daniel (Meyer)
Stathis, Pete
Statlander, Jane (B.)
Stead, C(hristian) K(arlson)
Stearns, Maureen
Steel, Danielle
Steele, Cynthia
Stefaniak, Mary Helen
Stein, Benjamin J.
Stein, Eugene
Stein, Leslie
Stein, Michael D.
Steinberg, Neil
Steiner, George
Steinhardt, Bernice
Steinke, Darcey
Steinman, David
Stengel, Joyce A.
Stenzel, Anabel
Stenzel Byrnes, Isabel
Stepakoff, Jeffrey
Stephen, Jaci
Stephens, Walter
Sterling, Bruce
Stern, Richard G(ustave)
Stern, Steve
Sterns, Kate
Stevens, Bryna
Stevens, David

Stevens, Diane
Stevens, Marcus
Stevens, Susan
Stevenson, James
Stevenson, Robin H.
Stevenson, Talitha
Stewart, Gary
Stewart, Kathleen
Stewart, Leah
Stewart, Lucretia
Stewart, Mary (Florence Elinor)
Stewart, Michael
Stiefvater, Maggie
Stillman, (John) Whit(ney)
Stimmler, Jane K.
Stimson, Tess
Stine, Scott A(aron)
Stinson, Jim
Stockbridge, Sara Jane
Stockenberg, Antoinette
Stoehr, Shelley
Stoker, Dacre
Stokoe, E(dward) G(eorge)
Stollman, Aryeh Lev
Stoltzfus, Ben
Stolz, Joëlle
Stolz, Karen
Stone, David Lee
Stone, Eric
Stone, Harry
Stone, Katherine
Stone, Laurie
Stone, Nick
Stone, Robert (Anthony)
Stone, Sarah
Stoner, Tom
Stonich, Sarah
Stoppard, Tom
Storey, David (Malcolm)
Storey, Gail Donohue
Stotter, Mike
Stourton, Ivo
Stout, Harry S.
Stout, Janis P.
Stover, Matthew Woodring
Strachan, Ian
Straight, Susan
Strange, Lily
Strasser, Todd
Strathern, Paul
Stratton, Allan
Straub, Peter (Francis)
Strelkoff, Tatiana
Strick, Wesley
Strieber, Anne
Stringer, Vickie M.
Stroby, Wallace
Strong, Albertine
Strong, Terence
Stroud, Carsten
Strube, Cordelia
Stuart, Alexander
Stuart, Anne
Stuart, Sally E(lizabeth)
Stuart, Sarah Payne
Stubbs, Jean
Stuckart, Diane A. S.

Index To Writing Categories

Van Scyoc, Sydney (Joyce)
Vanasse, Deb
Vance, Jack
Vance, Steve
Vandenburgh, Jane
Vanderbes, Jennifer (Chase)
Vankin, Jonathan
VanOosting, James
Vapnyar, Lara
Vardamis, Frances (Diem)
Vargas, Fred
Vargas Llosa, (Jorge) Mario
　(Pedro)
Varon, Sara
Vasquez, Ian
Vassanji, M(oyez) G.
Vasta, Edward
Vaughan, Brian K.
Vaughn, Ellen Santilli
Vaughn, Patrika
Vega, Ana Lydia
Veitch, Kate
Veitch, Rick
Velez, Ivan
Veltri, George (M.)
Verdelle, A. J.
Vermilye, Jerry
Verrier, Suzanne
Verrillo, Erica
Veryan, Patricia
Vickers, Adrian
Victor, Barbara
Vidal, Gore
Vijayaraghavan, Vineeta
Villa-Gilbert, Mariana
Villatoro, Marcos McPeek
Villegas, Halli
Vincent, Erin
Vincent, Rachel
Vincenzi, Penny
Vinge, Vernor (Steffen)
Viorst, Judith
Virgo, Seán
Vizenor, Gerald (Robert)
Voermans, Paul
Vogel, Steve
Voien, Steven
Voigt, Cynthia
Volk, Patricia (Gay)
Volsky, Paula
von Gunden, Kenneth
von Schlegell, Mark
von Unwerth, Matthew
von Ziegesar, Cecily
Vonnegut, Norb
Vornholt, John
Vowell, Sarah
Vreeland, Susan (Joyce)
Wachtel, Shirley Russak
Waddell, Dan
Waddell, Martin
Waddington-Feather, John Joseph
Wade, Susan
Wadia, Maneck S.
Wagner, Bruce
Wagner, Daniel
Wagner, Matt

Wagner, Sharon Blythe
Wagner-Martin, Linda C.
Wagoner, David (Russell)
Waisman, Sergio Gabriel
Waites, Martyn
Wakefield, Dan
Wakling, Christopher
Walden, Mark
Waldman, Ayelet
Waldo, Anna Lee
Walker, Kathryn
Walker, Martin
Walker, Sally M(acArt)
Walker, Wendy (Alison)
Wall, Kathryn R.
Wallace, Barbara Brooks
Wallace, Carey Jean
Wallace, Deborah
Wallace, Don
Wallace, Karen
Waller, Robert James
Wallingford, Lee
Wallis, Velma
Walsh, Ann
Walsh, Jill Paton
Walsh, P(atrick) G(erard)
Walter, Jess
Waltner-Toews, David
Walton, David
Waltzer, Jim
Wambaugh, Joseph
Wandor, Michelene
Wang, Anyi
Wang, Dong
Wang, Shuo
Ward, Amanda Eyre
Ward, David
Ward, Gregory
Ward, James M.
Ward, Jane (A.)
Ward, Jesmyn
Ward, Philip
Wardlaw, Lee
Wardman, Gordon
Warfield, Gallatin
Warlick, Ashley
Warneke, Sara
Warner, Jack
Warner, Marina
Warner, Sally
Warner, Sharon Oard
Warren, Rosanna
Warren, Sandra K.
Warren, Susan May
Warrington, Freda
Warsh, Lewis
Warsh, Sylvia E. Maultash
Washburn, Frances
Wasserman, Robin
Wästberg, Per
Waterfield, Robin Anthony
　Herschel
Waters, Sarah
Watkins, Graham
Watkins, Paul
Watman, Max
Watmough, David

Watson, C. G.
Watson, Ian
Watson, James
Watson, Jan Elizabeth
Watson, Jean
Watson, Kathy
Watson, Ken D.
Watson, Larry
Watson, Robert (Winthrop)
Watson, Sophia
Watson, Stephanie
Watt, Alan
Watt, Kelly
Wayman, Tom
Weales, Gerald
Wearne, Alan
Weatherly, Lee
Weaver, Will(iam Weller)
Weaver-Gelzer, Charlotte
Webb, Janeen (S.)
Webb, Michael (Jack)
Webb, Veronica
Weber, David
Weber, Doron
Weber, Katharine
Webster, Brenda
Webster, Ernest
Webster, Jason
Webster, Len
Wedde, Ian
Weeks, Sarah
Weems, David B(urnola)
Weinberg, Florence M(ay)
Weiner, Jennifer Agnes
Weiner, Marc A.
Weinstein, Philip M.
Weinstock, Nicholas
Weintraub, Sidney
Weir, Theresa
Weisberg, Joseph
Weisberger, Lauren
Weiss, Daniel Evan
Weissbach, Lee Shai
Welch, Robert
Welch-Tyson, Delorys
Weldon, Fay
Weldon, Phaedra M.
Weller, Vann K.
Wellman, John McDowell
Wells, Ken
Wells, Melanie
Wells, Rebecca
Wells, Rosemary
Wells, Shirley
Wells (Dimenstein), Catherine
Welsh, Irvine
Weltner, Peter (Nissen)
Wendt, Albert
Werber, Bernard
Wersba, Barbara
Wertenbaker, Timberlake
Wesker, Arnold
Wesley, Valerie Wilson
Wesselmann, Debbie Lee
West, Francis J.
Westburg, Barry (Richard)
Westcott, Jan (Vlachos)

Weston, Susan
Westrum, Dexter
Wetherell, W(alter) D(avid)
Wetmore, Kevin J. (Jr.)
Wexler, Robert Freeman
Weyland, Jack
Whalley, Peter
What, Leslie
Wheatcroft, John Stewart
Wheatle, Alex
Wheeler, Kate
Wheeler, Penny Estes
Wheeler, Richard S.
Wheeler, Susan
Wheeler, Thomas
Wheldon, David
Whisman, Dale
Whitaker, Katie
Whitaker, Phil
Whitcher, Susan (Godsil)
Whitcomb, Laura
White, Bailey
White, Caramine
White, Carolyn
White, Dave
White, Edmund
White, Franklin
White, Jenny
White, Jon Manchip
White, Jonathan (Bruce)
White, Karen
White, Kimberley
White, Michael C(harles)
White, Warren H.
White-Parks, Annette
Whitehead, Colson
Whitelaw, Stella
Whitlock, Dean
Whitmore, Benette
Whitson, Stephanie Grace (Irvin)
Whitten, Leslie Hunter
Whyman, Matt
Wicker, Christine
Wicker, Tom
Wicks, Susan
Wieck, Carl F.
Wieland, Liza
Wieler, Diana
Wiesel, Elie
Wiesenfarth, Joseph (John)
Wiesner, Karen Sue
Wiest, Andrew A.
Wiggin, Eric E(llsworth)
Wiggs, Susan
Wignall, Kevin
Wilcox, James
Wilcox, Laird (M.)
Wilcox, Stephen F.
Wild, Kate
Wilde, Kelley (Cotter)
Wildgen, Michelle
Wilding, Michael
Wildwind, Sharon Grant
Wile, Mary Lee
Wiles, Deborah
Wiley, Kim Wright
Wilhelm, Doug

Adelman, Deborah	Atxaga, Bernardo	Bell, Madison Smartt	Bradley, John Ed(mund)
Adnan, Etel	Auslander, Shalom	Beller, Tom	Brady, Catherine
Adoff, Arnold	Auster, Paul	Bellotti, Laura Golden	Brainard, Cecilia Manguerra
Afong, Milo S.	Avery, Gillian (Elise)	Belshaw, Patrick	Brandewyne, Rebecca
Agard, John	Avi	Benedict, Pinckney	Brandi, John
Agarwal, Shilpa	Awdry, Christopher Vere	Benjamin, Floella	Brandstetter, Alois
Agee, Jonis	Awoonor, Kofi	Bennett, Alan	Brantenberg, Gerd
Aguirre, Forrest	Ayres, Philip	Benson, Jackson J.	Braschi, Giannina
Aira, César	Bache, Ellyn	Benson, Peter	Brazaitis, Mark
Aitken, Rosemary	Bacho, Peter	Berberick, Nancy Varian	Brenna, Beverley
Akins, Ellen	Backer, Sara	Beresford-Kroeger, Diana	Brenner, Wendy
Alan, Theresa	Bacon, Charlotte	Berg, Leila	Brett, Brian
Albahari, David	Badawi, Mohamed Mustafa	Berger, John (Peter)	Brett, Edward T(racy)
Aldiss, Brian (Wilson)	Badt, Karin L(uisa)	Berger-Kiss, Andres	Brett, Simon (Anthony Lee)
Aldridge, (Harold Edward) James	Baehr, Kingsley M.	Berkman, Pamela Rafael	Brewster, Elizabeth (Winifred)
Alexander, Gary	Baez, Annecy	Berkoff, Steven	Brian, Cynthia
Alexie, Sherman (Joseph)	Baez, Fernando	Berliner-Gluckman, Janet	Briggs, John
Alexis, Andre	Bahal, Aniruddha	Bernard, Kenneth	Brin, David
Alford, Edna	Bahlmann, Shirley	Bernhardt, William	Briskin, Mae
Aliki	Bahr, Robert	Bernstein, Patricia	Brite, Poppy Z.
Alkali, Zaynab	Bail, Murray	Bertolino, James	Broderick, Damien
Allen, John Jay	Baker, Lori	Bes-Shahar, Eluki	Brodeur, Paul (Adrian)
Allen, Preston L.	Balderston, Daniel	Betts, Doris	Brooke, William J.
Allen, Roberta	Balogh, Mary	Beverley, Jo	Brooke-Rose, Christine
Allyn, Doug	Banks, Russell (Earl)	Bi, Feiyu	Brooker, Jewel Spears
Almog, Ruth	Banville, John	Biermann, Pieke	Brookner, Anita
Alofsin, Anthony	Barabtarlo, Gennady	Biggs, John Burville	Brooks, David (Gordon)
Altenburg, Matthias	Baratz-Logsted, Lauren	Binchy, Maeve	Brooks, Martha
Alther, Lisa	Barbarese, J. T.	Bingham, Sallie	Broughton, T. Alan
Alvarado, Lisa	Barbash, Tom	Birdsell, Sandra	Brown, Mary Ward
Alvarez, Rafael	Barber, Phyllis (Nelson)	Birstein, Ann	Brown, Murray
Amabile, George	Barbour, Douglas	Bishop, Michael	Brown, Richard E.
Amend, Allison	Barich, Bill	Bittner, Rosanne	Brown, Roberta Simpson
Amirrezvani, Anita	Barkan, Josh	Bjarkman, Peter C(hristian)	Brown, Rosellen
Amis, Martin (Louis)	Barker, Clive	Blackman, Malorie	Brown, Stewart
Amos, William (David)	Barnard, Robert	Blaise, Clark	Brownstein, Gabriel
Anaya, Rudolfo A(lfonso)	Barnes, H. Lee	Blake, Jon	Bruchac, Joseph
Anderson, Lauri (Arvid)	Barnes, Mike	Blauner, Peter	Brulotte, Gaetan
Andrews, Andy	Barr, Gonzalo	Blessington, Francis C(harles)	Bryan, Lynne
Andrews, William L(eake)	Barrett, Andrea	Block, Brett Ellen	Buccieri, Lisa Rojany
Ansay, A. Manette	Barron, Laird	Block, Francesca (Lia)	Buchanan, Edna
Antal, Dan	Bart, Michael	Block, Lawrence	Bucheister, Patt
Anthony, Michael	Barth, John (Simmons)	Bloor, Edward (William)	Buckhanon, Kalisha
Anthony, Patricia	Barthelme, Frederick	Blos, Joan W.	Budbill, David
Antieau, Kim	Barthelme, Steve(n)	Bluestein, Eleanor	Budnitz, Judy
Antoni, Robert (William)	Basta, Samir Sanad	Blythe, Ronald (George)	Buehler, Evelyn Judy
Appach, Anjana	Batchelor, David	Bobis, Merlinda Carullo	Buffett, Jimmy
Apple, Max (Isaac)	Bateman, Tracey V.	Bocardo, Claire	Bugeja, Michael J.
Archer, Jeffrey (Howard)	Bates, Judy Fong	Bolger, Dermot	Bujold, Lois McMaster
Arden, John	Bauer, Caroline Feller	Bond, Ruskin	Bukiet, Melvin Jules
Argers, Helen	Bauer, Tricia	Bordowitz, Hank	Bukoski, Anthony
Arksey, Neil	Baulenas, Lluís-Anton	Bosticco, (Isabel Lucy) Mary	Bull, Angela (Mary)
Armstrong, Adam	Bauman, Beth Ann	Boswell, Robert	Bullins, Ed
Armstrong, Kevin D.	Baumbach, Jonathan	Boullata, Issa J.	Burns, Jim
Arnold, Peter	Bausch, Richard	Bova, Ben(jamin William)	Busch, Charles
Arnzen, Michael A.	Baxter, Stephen	Bowen, Gail	Butala, Sharon (Annette)
Ash, Constance (Lee)	Bay, Jeanette Graham	Bowering, George	Butler, Dorothy
Asher, Jane	Beagle, Peter S(oyer)	Bowkett, Stephen	Butler, Geoff
Asher, Neal	Beale, Fleur	Bowman, David	Butler, Jack
Ashley, Bernard	Bear, Greg(ory Dale)	Bowyer, Mathew Justice	Butler, Robert Olen
Ashley, Leonard R. N.	Beattie, Ann	Boyd, Malcolm	Butlin, Ron
Ashton, Rosemary	Beck, Ian	Boyer, Jay	Byars, Betsy (Cromer)
Asim, Jabari	Becker, Jürgen	Boyers, Robert	Byatt, A(ntonia) S(usan)
Asimov, Janet Jeppson	Beeman, Robin	Boym, Svetlana	Cadnum, Michael
Atkinson, Kate	Beha, Christopher R.	Bradbury, Ray (Douglas)	Caldwell, Grant
Atlas, James (Robert)	Behrens, Ellen	Bradfield, Scott (Michael)	Callaghan, Barry
Atwood, Margaret	Bei Dao	Bradley, David (Henry)	Campbell, Ramsey

Index To Writing Categories

Fallon, Peter
Fanning, Diane Lynn
Fanthorpe, R(obert) Lionel
Farley, Terri
Farr, Diane
Faschinger, Lilian
Fatchen, Max
Faulkner, Colleen
Faust, Christa
Faust, Irvin
Fayer, Steve
Feiffer, Jules
Feinstein, Elaine
Felinto (Barbosa De Lima),
  Marilene
Felstein, Ivor
Ferguson, Brad
Fiallos, Rosario
Figes, Eva
Files, Meg
Finlayson, Iain (Thorburn)
Finn, R(alph) L(eslie)
Finney, Ernest J.
Fischer, Tibor
Fisk, Pauline
Fleetwood, Hugh (Nigel)
Fleischman, Paul
Flynn, Robert (Lopez)
Foege, Alec
Forbes, Camille F.
Foreman, Michael
Forrest, Katherine V(irginia)
Forsyth, Frederick
Foster, Alan Dean
Foster, David Manning
Foster, Ken
Foster, M(ichael) A(nthony)
Fourie, Corlia
Fowler, Christopher
Frame, Ronald
Francis, H(erbert) E(dward)
Frank, J. Suzanne
Frank, Joan
Frankel, Ellen
Fraser, Margot
Freeborn, Richard (Harry)
Freed, Lynn
Freedman, Adam
Freeman, Anne Hobson
Freeman, Castle (William)
Freireich, Valerie J.
Friedman, Bruce Jay
Friedman, Paul (Alan)
Friedmann, Patty
Friel, Brian
Friesen, Bernice (Sarah Anne)
Fromm, Pete
Fugard, Athol
Fuller, John (Leopold)
Gagliano, Eugene M.
Gailly, Christian
Galang, M. Evelina
Galef, David
Gallagher, Tess
Galleymore, Frances
Galloway, Janice
Galvin, Brendan

Garcia Y Robertson, R(odrigo)
Gardam, Jane
Gardaphé, Fred L(ouis)
Gardner, Craig Shaw
Gardner, Jerome
Garner, Helen
Garrison, Philip
Garwood, Julie
Gaskin, J. C. A.
Gass, William (Howard)
Gates, David
Gathorne-Hardy, Jonathan
Gauldie, Enid Elizabeth
Geddes, Gary
Gee, Maurice (Gough)
Gellis, Roberta (Leah Jacobs)
Geltmaker, Ty
George Bloomfield, Susanne K.
Geras, Adèle (Daphne Weston)
Gerber, Merrill Joan
Gerdes, Eckhard
Gessner, Lynne
Giardinelli, Mempo
Gibbons, Reginald
Gifford, Barry (Colby)
Gilbert, Elizabeth
Gilbert, Sandra M(ortola)
Gilchrist, Ellen
Gildner, Gary
Gillespie, Hollis
Gilmore, Rachna
Gioia, (Michael) Dana
Gish, Robert F.
Glancy, Diane
Glanville, Brian (Lester)
Glass, Charles
Glickman, James (A.)
Glover, Douglas
Godbout, Jacques
Godwin, Gail (Kathleen)
Godwin, Rebecca T.
Gold, Herbert
Gold, Jerome
Gold, Nora
Goldin, Barbara Diamond
Goldner, Beth
Goldstein, Naama
Goldstein, Rebecca
Goldsworthy, Peter
Golubhoff, Risa L.
Gomez, Jewelle
Gondry, Michel
Gonzales, Laurence
Gonzalez, Genaro
Gooch, Brad
Good, Timothy
Goodison, Lorna (Gaye)
Goodman, Allegra
Goodman, James
Goonetilleke, D. C. R. A.
Gordimer, Nadine
Gordon, Jaimy
Gordon, Mary (Catherine)
Gordon, Sheila
Goss, Theodora
Goto, Hiromi
Gould, John

Gowan, Lee
Grace, Patricia (Frances)
Graff, Laurie
Grafton, Sue
Graham, Frank
Granelli, Roger
Grant, Neil
Grant, Susan
Grassi, Maggi Lidchi
Gratus, Jack
Grau, Shirley Ann
Graver, Elizabeth
Gray, Alasdair (James)
Gray, Dulcie
Green, (Charles Stuart) Jamison
Green, Cliff(ord)
Green, Jesse
Green, Joseph (Lee)
Green, Peter (Morris)
Green, Risa
Green, Terence M(ichael)
Greenberg, Alvin
Greenberg, Joanne
Greene, Constance C(larke)
Greenside, Mark
Gregory, Philippa
Gresham, Stephen
Grey, Anthony
Grey, Beryl (Elizabeth)
Griesemer, John
Griffin, P(auline) M.
Griffiths, Niall
Griggs, Terry
Grimes, Martha
Griner, Paul
Grossinger, Harvey L.
Grossman, David
Grossmith, Robert (Anthony)
Grudin, Robert
Guest, Paul
Guista, Michael
Gunn, Eileen
Gunn, James E(dwin)
Guppy, Stephen (Anthony)
Gurganus, Allan
Gurney, A(lbert) R(amsdell)
Gustafson, Sid
Guterson, David
Guthrie, Allan
Habegger, Alfred (Carl)
Hagedorn, Jessica Tarahata
Hager, Alan
Hager, Betty
Hagger, Nicholas
Hagy, Alyson
Hairston, William
Haldeman, Joe (William)
Haley, Gail E(inhart)
Hall, Kirsten Marie
Hall, Lynn
Hall, Martha Lacy
Halligan, Marion (Mildred
  Crothall)
Halperin, James L(ewis)
Halpern, Daniel
Hamblin, Robert W(ayne)
Hamburger, Aaron

Hamill, Janet
Hamilton, Peter F.
Hamilton-Paterson, James
Hankin, C(herry) A(nne)
Hanley, William
Hannah, James
Hannibal, Edward L.
Hansen, Mark Victor
Harada, Masako
Hardy, John Philips
Hare-Duke, Michael (Geoffrey)
Hareven, Gail
Harleman, Ann
Harnack, Curtis
Harper, Susan (Rice)
Harris, Christine
Harris, Claire
Harris, Elizabeth
Harris, Rosemary (Jeanne)
Harrison, Harry
Harrison, Jim
Harrod-Eagles, Cynthia
Hart, (Margaret Eleanor) Anne
Hart, JoeAnn
Hart, Jonathan (Locke)
Hart, Lenore
Harvey, Kenneth J.
Harvor, Elisabeth
Harwood, Ronald
Hashmi, (Aurangzeb) Alamgir
Haslam, Gerald William
Haslett, Adam
Hasluck, Nicholas
Haswell, Richard H(enry)
Hatcher, Robin Lee
Hathorn, Libby
Hauptman, William (Thornton)
Havazelet, Ehud
Havel, Harvey
Haverty, Anne
Hawkes, G(ary) W(arren)
Hayden, Eric William
Hazuka, Tom
Hazzard, Shirley
Head, Dominic
Heald, Tim(othy Villiers)
Heaney, Seamus
Heffernan, Nancy Coffey
Heidel, R. Andrew
Hekkanen, Ernest
Heller, Michael
Helprin, Mark
Helwig, Maggie
Hely, Sara
Hemingway, Lorian
Henderson, Lauren
Hendricks, Vicki (Due)
Hendry, Diana
Henley, Patricia
Henry, DeWitt (Pawling)
Herman, Michelle
Hester, Katherine L.
Heyen, William
Hicks, Robert
Higgins, Aidan
Higgins, Joanna
High, Linda Oatman

Lott, Bret
Louie, David Wong
Louis, Laura Glen
Lourie, Richard
Lovegrove, James (Matthew Henry)
Lovelace, Earl
Lovesey, Peter (Harmer)
Lowe, Jack Phillips
Lucie-Smith, (John) Edward (McKenzie)
Luckett, Dave
Ludwig, Jack
Lundin, Steve
Lupoff, Richard A(llen)
Lurie, Alison
Lurie, Morris
Lustig, T(imothy) J(ohn)
Lutz, John (Thomas)
Lynch, Janet Nichols
Lynch, Thomas
Lynd, Staughton (Craig)
Lyon, Annabel
Macaulay, Teresa (E.)
MacDonald, Marylee
MacEnulty, Pat
MacEoin, Denis
Macgoye, Marjorie Oludhe
Machann, Clinton (John)
Mack, David (A.)
MacKenna, John
Mackler, Carolyn
MacLean, Glynne
Macleod, Ian R.
Madden, David
Madsen, Svend Åge
Maggio, Mike
Magorian, Michelle
Mahy, Margaret
Maio, Samuel (Joseph)
Mairowitz, David Zane
Major, Andre
Major, Clarence
major, devorah
Mallett, Daryl F(urumi)
Malouf, David
Malzahn, Manfred
Mandel, Charlotte
Mandel, Oscar
Mandelman, Avner
Manea, Norman
Manhire, Bill
Mann, (Anthony) Phillip
Mann, Jeff(rey A.)
Manrique (Ardila), Jaime
Maracle, Lee
Marcus, Ben
Mardon, Austin Albert
Mares, Theun
Margolis, Jonathan
Marias, Javier
Markus, Julia
Maron, Margaret
Maron, Monika
Marquart, Debra
Marr, Melissa
Marsden, Carolyn

Marsella, Anne (Francesca)
Marshall, Owen
Martin, Claire
Martin, George R.R.
Martin, Judith
Martin, Russell
Martin, Stephen-Paul
Martínez, Manuel Luis
Mason, Bobbie Ann
Mason, Haydn Trevor
Mass, Wendy
Matera, Lia
Mates, Susan Onthank
Matheson, Richard (Burton)
Mathews, Aidan (Carl)
Matthew, Christopher C. F.
Matthews, Carole
Matthews, Jack
Matthiessen, Peter
Mattingley, Christobel (Rosemary)
May, Julian
Mayne, Seymour
Mayo, C(atherine) M(ansell)
Mayo, Wendell
Mazetti, Katarina
Mazza, Cris
McAuley, Paul J.
McBratney, Sam
McCafferty, Jane
McCafferty, Maureen
McCaffrey, Anne (Inez)
McCann, Colum
McCann, Richard
McCaughrean, Geraldine (Jones)
McConkey, James (Rodney)
McCorkle, Jill (Collins)
McCormack, Derek
McCormack, Mike
McCracken, Elizabeth
McCrumb, Sharyn
McDonald, Collin
McDonald, Ian
McEwan, Ian
McFadden, David W.
McFarlane, Peter (William)
McGraw, Erin
McGuane, Thomas
McGuckian, Medbh (McCaughan)
McGuigan, Mary Ann
McHugh, Maureen F.
McInerney, Jay
McIntyre, Vonda N(eel)
McKee, David (John)
McKenzie, Barbara
McKinley, (Jennifer Carolyn) Robin
McKinney, Meagan
McLaughlin, Ann L.
McLean, Duncan
McLeod, Grover S(tephen)
McMahon, Maureen M.
McMullan, Margaret
McMullen, Sean (Christopher)
McMurtry, Larry (Jeff)
McNair, Wesley C.
McNamara, Eugene Joseph

McNamee, Eoin
McNett, Molly
McPherson, James A(lan)
McWhirter, George
Mears, Gillian
Medvedev, Grigori
Meehan, Paula
Mehta, Gita
Mehta, Ved (Parkash)
Meikle, William
Meinke, Peter
Melchior, Ib (Jorgen)
Mellizo (Cuadrado), Carlos
Melton, Brian C.
Meltzer, David
Melville, Pauline
Memmott, David R.
Meno, Joe
Mercati, Cynthia
Merriman, Catherine
Messud, Claire
Metcalf, John (Wesley)
Meyerowitz, Patricia
Meyers, Kent
Meyers, Martin
Mickelbury, Penny
Mickle, Shelley Fraser
Middleton, (John) Christopher
Midwood, Bart(on A.)
Mihailovi, Dragoslav
Miklowitz, Gloria D.
Miles, Keith
Miller, Alyce
Miller, Jane
Miller, Rebecca
Millhiser, Marlys
Millman, Joan (M.)
Millum, Trevor
Miltner, Robert
Mindt, Alex
Minot, Susan A.
Mishica, Clare
Misurella, Fred
Mitchard, Jacquelyn
Mittman, Stephanie
Mohin, Ann
Mohr, Nicholasa
Moira, Kate
Molina, Silvia
Momaday, N(avarre) Scott
Monesson, Harry S.
Montague, John (Patrick)
Montejo, Victor (D.)
Montpetit, Charles
Monzó, Quim
Moodie, Craig
Moody, Bill
Moon, Susan
Moorcock, Michael (John)
Moore, Alison
Moore, Dinty W.
Moore, James A.
Moore, Lorrie
Moore, Robin
Morales, Aaron Michael
Morden, Simon
Moreh, Shmuel

Morgan, Bernice
Morpurgo, Michael
Morris, Mark
Morris, Mary
Morson, Ian
Mortimer, Gavin
Moshiri, Farnoosh
Moskowitz, Faye (Stollman)
Mosley, Walter
Moss, Marissa
Moss, Stirling
Motley, Annette
Moulessehoul, Mohammed
Moye, Guan
Mueenuddin, Daniyal
Mueller, Daniel
Mukherjee, Bharati
Mulcahy, Greg
Muller, Herta
Muller, Marcia
Munevar, Gonzalo
Mungoshi, Charles L.
Munro, Alice
Murakami, Haruki
Murnane, Gerald
Murphy, Martha W(atson)
Murphy, Shirley R(ousseau)
Murphy, Sylvia
Murray, Victoria
Musgrave, Susan
Myers, Tamar
Na rang, Gopi Chand
Nádas, Péter
Nagem, Monique F.
Naha, Ed
Naidoo, Beverley
Najmabadi, Afsaneh
Nason, Tema
Natwar-Singh, K.
Nayman, Michele
Neenan, Colin
Nelson, Antonya
Nelson, Geoffrey Kenneth
Nesbitt, John D.
Nesbitt, Marc
Nesset, Kirk
Neugeboren, Jay
Neuhaus, Denise
Nevai, Lucia
Nevins, Francis M(ichael)
Newman, Andrea
Nicolson, Adam
Niederman, Derrick
Nigam, Sanjay (Kumar)
Niven, Larry
Nixon, Cornelia
Nkala, Nathan
Nolan, William F(rancis)
Noll, Ingrid
Nordan, Lewis
Norman, Howard A.
Norrell, Gregory T.
Northrup, Jim
Novakovich, Josip
Noyes, Deborah
Nye, Robert
Nylund, Eric S.

Sheard, Sarah
Sheehan, Aurelie
Shepard, Jim
Shepard, Sam
Sheppard, John L.
Sherman, Charlotte Watson
Sherman, Joe
Sherwood, Frances
Shields, Jody
Shigekuni, Julie
Shockley, Ann Allen
Shoesmith, Kathleen A.
Shomer, Enid
Shraer-Petrov, David
Sickels, Noelle
Sidney, Neilma
Silesky, Barry
Silman, Roberta
Silver, Marisa
Silverberg, Robert
Silverman, Jerry
Simic, Goran
Simmie, Lois (Ann)
Simon, Francesca
Simon, Rachel
Simonds, Merilyn
Simonelli, Jeanne M(arie)
Simpson, Penny Claire
Sinha, Indra
Sinisalo, Johanna
Sipherd, Ray
Skloot, Floyd
Skrzynecki, Peter
Skye, Christina
Slater, Judith (Carol)
Slote, Alfred
Slouka, Mark
Smarandache, Florentin
Smiley, Jane (Graves)
Smith, Ali
Smith, Charles R.
Smith, Dave
Smith, Deborah
Smith, Frederick E(screet)
Smith, Geof
Smith, Morris
Smith, Sherwood
Smith, Wanda VanHoy
Smolens, John (Harrison)
Snellgrove, Laurence Ernest
Snow, Philip (Albert)
Snyder, Lucy A.
Snyder, Zilpha Keatley
Sobol, Donald J.
Softly, Barbara (Charmian)
Solares, Ignacio
Sonenberg, Maya
Soto, Gary
Soueif, Ahdaf
Sparrow, Jeff
Spatz, Gregory
Speer, Laurel
Spence, William John Duncan
Spencer, Brent
Spencer, Elizabeth
Spencer, Mark

Spivack, Kathleen (Romola Drucker)
Sproat, Robert
Spruill, Steven
Spurling, Hilary
Staats, Marilyn Dorn
Stacey, Judith
Stacey, Tom
Stamm, Peter
Staples, Suzanne Fisher
Stead, C(hristian) K(arlson)
Steele, Cynthia
Steele, Mary
Stefaniak, Mary Helen
Steinberg, Susan
Steiner, Evgeny
Stern, Richard G(ustave)
Stern, Steve
Stevens, Karl
Stevenson, James
Stewart, Christopher S.
Stine, Catherine
Stine, Scott A(aron)
Stone, Eric
Stone, Robert (Anthony)
Stone, Sarah
Stoppard, Tom
Storey, David (Malcolm)
Stotter, Mike
Stout, Janis P.
Stover, Matthew Woodring
Straight, Susan
Straub, Peter (Francis)
Strickland, Craig (A.)
Strock, Ian Randal
Stuart, Dabney
Sullivan, Randall
Sultan, Stanley
Sussex, Lucy (Jane)
Sutherland, Margaret
Svoboda, Terese
Swartz, Jon David
Swetman, Glenn R(obert)
Swick, Marly
Swift, Graham
Swindells, Robert (Edward)
Taaffe, Sonya
Tapahonso, Luci
Tate, James (Vincent)
Tayleur, Karen
Taylor, Bruce
Taylor, Bruce
Taylor, Elizabeth Atwood
Taylor, Joe
Taylor, Liza Pennywitt
Taylor, Mildred D.
Taylor, Robert Larry
Taylor-Hall, Mary Ann
Te Awekotuku, Ngahuia
Teece, Philip
Tem, Melanie
Terry, Megan
Tervalon, Jervey
Tessaro, Kathleen
Tharoor, Shashi
Thomas, Abigail
Thomas, Audrey (Grace)

Thomas, D(onald) M(ichael)
Thomas, David St. John
Thomas, H(ubert) Nigel
Thomas, Sue
Thomasma, Kenneth R.
Thompson, E(rnest) V(ictor)
Thompson, Jean
Thomson, June
Thon, Melanie Rae
Thorsson, Örnólfur
Thurm, Marian
Tihanyi, Eva
Tillman, Lynne
Tindall, Gillian (Elizabeth)
Tipton, David
Title, Elise
Toews, Rita Y.
Tóibín, Colm
Toker, Leona
Tomalin, Ruth
Tong, Zhong Gui
Torres, Steven
Touré
Tourney, Leonard D(on)
Townsend Hall, Brenda P.
Tracey, Grant
Tracy, Lorna
Traxler, Patricia
Tremain, Rose
Tremblay, Paul G.
Trevor, William
Trillin, Calvin
Troop, Alan F.
Troy, Judy
Tsushima, Satoko
Tucker, Helen
Tucker, Judy H.
Turner, Megan Whalen
Turpin, Tom
Turtledove, Harry (Norman)
Tuttle, Lisa
Ty-Casper, Linda
Tyler, Anne
Ucko, Barbara
Ueda, Makoto
Ulitskaya, Ludmila
Underwood, Peter
Unwin, Peter
Ursell, Geoffrey
Ury, Allen B.
Vail, Rachel
Valentine, Mark
Valentino, Serena
Valeri, Laura
Vallbona, Rima de
Vallee, Lillian (Bozenna)
Vance, Jack
Vance, Steve
Vandenburgh, Jane
Vargas Llosa, (Jorge) Mario (Pedro)
Vassanji, M(oyez) G.
Vasta, Edward
Vidal, Gore
Virgo, Seán
Visson, Lynn
Vitiello, Justin

Vizenor, Gerald (Robert)
Voien, Steven
Volk, Patricia (Gay)
Vreeland, Susan (Joyce)
Vukcevich, Ray
Waddell, Martin
Walker, Wendy (Alison)
Wall, Cheryl A.
Wallace, Richard (Alan)
Waller, Robert James
Walton, David
Wandor, Michelene
Wang, Anyi
Wang, Shuo
Ward, Amanda Eyre
Ward, Chrissie
Ward, Philip
Warner, Marina
Warner, Sharon Oard
Warren, Dianne
Washington, Donna L.
Wasil, Kenneth
Watada, Terry
Watmough, David
Watson, Ian
Watson, James
Watson, Jean
Watson, Kathy
Watt, Kelly
Wayman, Tom
Wearne, Alan
Weaver, Will(iam Weller)
Webb, Janeen (S.)
Weber, Katharine
Webster, Brenda
Webster, Len
Wedde, Ian
Weenolsen, Patricia
Weiner, Marc A.
Welch, Robert
Weldon, Fay
Welsh, Irvine
Weltner, Peter (Nissen)
Wendt, Albert
Wesker, Arnold
Wesselmann, Debbie Lee
Westburg, Barry (Richard)
Weston, Susan
Westrum, Dexter
Wetherell, W(alter) D(avid)
Wexler, Merin
Wexler, Robert Freeman
Wheatcroft, John Stewart
Wheeler, Kate
White, Bailey
White, Michael C(harles)
White-Parks, Annette
Whitman, Sylvia (Choate)
Whittemore, (Edward) Reed
Whitty, Julia
Whyman, Matt
Wieland, Liza
Wilcox, Stephen F.
Wilding, Michael
Wilhelm, Kate
Wilks, Burrel Lee
Williams, Amanda Kyle

Carpenter, Lynette	Cook, Marshall	Doyle, Jeff	Fluke, Joanne
Carr, Lauren	Cooper, Brian (Newman)	Dreyer, Eileen	Flynn, Kevin
Carr, Margaret	Copeland, Rebecca L.	Drummond, June	Foley, (Mary) Louise Munro
Carr, Marvin N.	Copper, Basil	Du Brul, Jack B.	Follett, Ken(neth Martin)
Carter, Charlotte	Corn, David	Dubens, Eugene (M.)	Ford, G. M.
Carter, Maureen	Corrigan, John R.	Dubus, Andre	Ford, Susan
Carter, Steven R(ay)	Coulson, Juanita	Duffy, James H(enry)	Forrest, Christopher
Casey, Barbara	Coulter, Catherine	Duffy, Margaret	Forrest, Katherine V(irginia)
Casper, Claudia	Cowell, Alan S.	Dunant, Sarah	Forsyth, Frederick
Castle, Linda	Cox, Patsi Bale	Duncan, Christine H.	Fowler, Christopher
Cavanagh, Thomas B.	Cox, Richard	Duncan, Glen	Fowler, Connie May
Chalker, Dennis	Craig, Daniel Edward	Duncan, Lois	Fowler, Earlene
Chalmers, Robert	Crane, Caroline	Duncker, Patricia	Francis, Clare
Chambers, Christopher	Crawford, Gary W(illiam)	Dunham, Tracy	Francis, Dorothy Brenner
Chapman, Herb	Creed, William S.	Dunlap, Susan D. (Sullivan)	Frank, J. Suzanne
Charbonneau, Eileen	Creighton, Joan Scott	Dyer, Charles (Raymond)	Franklin, Yelena
Chard, Judy (Gordon)	Creighton, Kathleen	Easton, Malcolm Coleman	Fraser, Anthea
Charles, Kate	Crews, Harry (Eugene)	Edwards, (Kenneth) Martin	Fraser, Antonia
Charrette, Robert N.	Crider, (Allen) Bill(y)	Edwards, Larry	Fraser, Wynnette (McFaddin)
Chase, Elaine Raco	Crook, Marion	Edwards, Michael B.	Frazer, Gail
Chattam, Maxim	Crossman, David A.	Eichler, Selma	Freemantle, Brian (Harry)
Chercover, Sean	Cruse, Lonnie	Eisler, Barry	French, Judith E.
Chizmar, Richard T(homas)	Crusie, Jennifer	Elam, Jason	French, Linda
Choyce, Lesley	Cullen, Robert (B.)	Elkins, Charlotte	French, Vivian
Christianson, Sven-Åke	Cumbie, Pamela	Ellis, Kate	Frewer, Glyn
Christmas, Joyce	Cummings, Barbara	Ellis, Mark (Karl)	Freydont, Shelley
Christofferson, April	Cunningham, Keith	Ellis, Peter Berresford	Frezza, Robert (A.)
Clapp, Nicholas	Curry, Jane (Louise)	Ellory, R. J.	Friedman, Kinky
Clare, Alys	Cussler, Clive (Eric)	Ellroy, James	Frimansson, Inger
Clark, Andrew	Cuthbert, Margaret	Elrod, P(at) N.	Fritchley, Alma
Clark, Carol Higgins	Cutler, Stan	Ely, David	Fritz, Jean
Clark, Mary Higgins	Dams, Jeanne M(artin)	Emerson, Earl W.	Frum, David
Clark, Mary Jane Behrends	Dangarembga, Tsitsi	Emery, Clayton	Furutani, Dale
Clark, Will	Daniels, Angie	Ener, Güner	Fusilli, Jim
Clarke, Kenneth L.	David, James F.	Engel, Howard	Gabbay, Tom
Clausen, Lowen	Davidson, Diane Mott	Englade, Ken(neth Francis)	Gadney, Reg
Cleary, Melissa	Davies, Linda	Engleman, Paul	Gadol, Peter
Clemens, Brian (Horace)	Davis, Lindsey	Engstrom, Elizabeth	Gagliani, William
Cleveland, Ceil	Davis, Mildred (B.)	Essex-Cater, Antony John	Gagliano, Anthony
Cobb, James H(arvey)	Davis, Nageeba	Estleman, Loren D.	Gagnon, Michelle
Coben, Harlan	Dawson, Janet	Evanovich, Janet	Gailly, Christian
Coburn, Andrew	Day, Marele	Evans, Justin	Gallagher, Stephen
Cody, Liza	Dearing, Sarah	Evans, Liz	Galligan, John
Cohen, Mark	Deaver, Jeffery Wilds	Evans, Mary Anna	Gallo, Gina
Cohen, Stanley I.	Deaver, Julie Reece	Evans, Tammy	Gansky, Alton
Cohen, Stuart	Debin, David	Evenson, Brian	Garcia-Aguilera, Carolina
Cole, Allan	Dee, Ed(ward J.)	Eversz, Robert (McLeod)	Gardner, (Robert) Brian
Cole, Barry	Deighton, Len	Ewing, Lynne	Gardner, Theodore Roosevelt
Coleman, Reed Farrel	Delahaye, Michael (John)	Fahy, Thomas	Garfield, Brian (F. W.)
Collard, Sneed B.	Delaney, Kathleen	Faigen, Anne G.	Garwood, Julie
Colley, Barbara	Delany, Vicki	Fairstein, Linda A.	Gash, Jonathan
Collignon, Jeff	DeMille, Nelson (Richard)	Falconer, Helen	Gaskin, J. C. A.
Collings, Gillian	Deming, Sarah	Fanning, Diane Lynn	Gatiss, Mark
Collins, Barbara	Demott, Wes	Fante, Dan	Gaylin, Alison
Collins, Helen (Frances)	DePoy, Phillip	Fantoni, Barry (Ernest)	Geary, Joseph
Collins, Jackie	Dereske, Jo	Farmer, Jerrilyn	Gellis, Roberta (Leah Jacobs)
Collins, Max Allan	DeWeese, Gene	Faust, Christa	Gentry, Christine
Collins, Nancy A.	Dewhurst, Eileen (Mary)	Feinberg, Barbara	George, Elizabeth
Colt, George Howe	Dexter, (Norman) Colin	Feinstein, John	Gerritsen, Tess
Comfort, B(arbara)	Dibble, J(ames) Birney	Felstiner, Mary Lowenthal	Giancana, Sam
Compton, D(avid) G(uy)	Dickinson, Peter	Ferguson, Alane	Gill, Anton
Conn, Andrew Lewis	Dietz, Laura	Finch, Charles	Gillmeister, Heiner
Connolly, John	Dixon, Keith	Finstad, Suzanne	Gilman, George G.
Conway, Martha	Doherty, P(aul) C.	Fisher, Robin Gaby	Gilman, Keith
Conway, Simon	Donovan, Felicia	Flem-Ath, Rand	Gilstrap, John
Cook, Bob	Dorf, Fran	Fleming, Anne	Glaister, Lesley (G.)
Cook, Lorna J.	Dorner, Marjorie	Flores-Galbis, Enrique	Glass, Leslie

Ladd, Linda	Longmate, Norman Richard	Mccaffrey, K. T.	Murray, Yxta Maya
Lafavor, Carole S.	Longyear, Barry B.	McCaughren, Tom	Musk, Justine
Laguna, Sofie	Lopresti, Robert	McClure, Ken	Musto, Barry
Lake, M. D.	Lordon, Randye	McCullough, Colleen	Myers, Tamar
Lalicki, Tom	Lounsberry, Barbara	McCullough, David Willis	Myers, Tim
Lamb, Nancy	Lovelace, Merline (A.)	McCutcheon, Sandy	Mynton, Henry
Lamont-Brown, Raymond	Lovell, Glenville	McDonald, Collin	Nagy, Gloria
Lampitt, Dinah	Lovely, Stephen	McDougal, Dennis	Naha, Ed
Lamplugh, Lois	Lovesey, Peter (Harmer)	McGarrity, Michael	Needle, Jan
Lance, Peter	Lovett, Sarah	McGilloway, Brian	Neely, Barbara
Landesman, Peter	Lowden, Desmond Scott	McGrath, Patrick	Nesbitt, John D.
Lane, Dakota	Lowe, Sheila	McIntosh, Fiona	Nesbo, Jo
Langfield, Martin	Lowenthal, Gary T(obias)	McIntyre, Vonda N(eel)	Nevins, Francis M(ichael)
Langton, Jane	Lupica, Mike	McKay, Claudia	Newman, Sharan (Hill)
Lankford, Terrill Lee	Lupoff, Richard A(llen)	McKinney, Nadine	Nichols, Victoria (Sorensen)
Lansdale, Joe R(ichard)	Lustbader, Eric Van	McLean, Russel D.	Nicholson, Deborah L.
Lantigua, John	Lutz, John (Thomas)	McMahon, Maureen M.	Niebuhr, Gary Warren
Larios, Julie Hofstrand	Lutz, Lisa	McNab, Claire	Nighbert, David F(ranklin)
Larsgaard, Chris	Lynds, Gayle (Hallenbeck)	McNamara, Mary	Nir, Yossi
Lassiter, Rhiannon	Lynn, Jonathan	McRae, Cricket	Niven, Larry
Laurence, Janet	Lyon, Bentley	McShane, Mark	Nkala, Nathan
Laurie, Edward James	MacCready, Robin Merrow	Meikle, William	Noah, Robert
Lawrence, Caroline	Macdonald, James D.	Mekler, Eva	Nolan, William F(rancis)
Lawrence, David	MacDougal, Bonnie	Meltzer, Brad	Noll, Ingrid
Lawrence, Martha C.	MacEoin, Denis	Mender, Mona (Siegler)	North, Darian
Lawton, John	MacNeill, Alastair	Mercer, Jeremy	Nylund, Eric S.
Lazuta, Gene	MacRae, Molly	Mercer, Judy	O'Brien, Charles
le Carré, John	Madison, Bennett	Mertz, Barbara (Louise) G(ross)	O'Brien, Kevin
Leavy, Barbara Fass	Magee, Doug	Meyers, Annette (Brafman)	O'Brien, Martin
Lebsock, Suzanne (Dee)	Maier, Anne McDonald	Meyers, Martin	O'Brien, Maureen
Lecesne, James	Maier, Paul Luther	Michaels, Jamie	O'Connell, Carol
Ledbetter, Suzann	Maifair, Linda Lee	Micheels, Peter A.	O'Connell, Jack
Lee, Bernie	Mailman, Erika	Michels, Sharry C.	O'Donohoe, Nick
Lee, Sharon	Maitland, Barry	Mickelbury, Penny	O'Reilly, Victor
Leese, Jennifer L. B.	Majd, Kam	Mickolus, Edward (Francis)	O'Rourke, Erin
Lehane, Dennis	Mallett, Daryl F(urumi)	Micou, Paul	Oakes, Andy
Leib, Franklin A(llen)	Malmont, Valerie S(kuse)	Mikaelsen, Ben (John)	Odell, Robin Ian
Lellenberg, Jon L.	Manaster, Benjamin	Miles, Keith	Oleksiw, Susan (Prince)
Lennard, John (Chevening)	Mann, Jessica	Miller, Jeffrey	Olsen, Mark Andrew
Leo, Mabel R.	Marchand, Philip (Edward)	Millett, Kate	Ordinans, Nicholas J.
Leonard, Constance	Margolin, Leslie	Millhiser, Marlys	Ormerod, Roger
Leonard, Elmore	Margolis, Seth J(acob)	Mitchell, Chris	Osborn, David (D.)
Leppek, Christopher	Marinick, Richard	Mitchell, Nancy	Padgett, (Mary) Abigail
Lescroart, John T.	Maron, Margaret	Mitchell, Thomas R.	Padilla, Ignacio
Leslie, John	Marquis, Max	Mitcheltree, Tom	Page, Katherine Hall
Levine, Allan	Marriott, Michel	Moffat, Gwen	Pagel, Tempa
Levine, Laura (Sue)	Marshall, Peter	Moggach, Deborah	Pairo, Preston (A.)
Levine, Paul	Martin, (Roy) Peter	Moloney, Susie	Paling, Chris
Levy, Elizabeth	Martin, Allana	Monhollon, Michael L.	Paretsky, Sara
Lewin, Michael Z.	Martin, J(ulia) Wallis	Monroe, Steve	Parker, Gordon
Lewis, J(ohn) R(oyston)	Martin, Larry Jay	Monsour, Theresa	Parks, Brad
Lewis, Peter (Elvet)	Martin, Russell	Montes, Marisa	Patneaude, David
Lewis, Sherry	Martini, Steven (Paul)	Montpetit, Charles	Patterson, Richard North
Lewis, Simon	Martini, Teri	Moody, Bill	Paul, Barbara
Lewis, Stephen (C.)	Mason, David	Moore, Laurie	Paulsen, Gary
Lewis, Thomas P(arker)	Mason, Sarah J.	Morgan, Stacy T(owle)	Payne, Donald Gordon
Lide, Mary	Massie, Sonja	Moriarty, Michael	Peacock, Shane
Limon, Martin	Matera, Lia	Morson, Ian	Pearl, Matthew
Lindquist, N(ancy) J(ane)	Mathes, Charles (Elliott)	Moulessehoul, Mohammed	Pearson, Ridley
Lindsay, Frederic	Matheson, Richard (Burton)	Muggeson, Margaret Elizabeth	Pedrazas, Allan
Little, Bentley	Matteson, Stefanie (Newton)	Mullane, (R.) Mike	Pence, Joanne
Llewellyn, Sam	Matthews, Alex	Muller, Eddie	Pendleton, Thomas
Lochte, Dick	Matthews, Greg	Muller, Marcia	Penman, Sharon Kay
Lock, Joan	Maurensig, Paolo	Mundis, Hester (Jane)	Pennac, Daniel
Lodge, Jeff	Maxwell, Patricia Anne	Munson, Carol Barr Swayze	Pepper, Andrew
Logan, Chuck	May, Julian	Murdock, Linda	Perabo, Susan
Logue, Mary	McBride, Susan	Murphy, Shirley R(ousseau)	Perry, Anne

Perry, Steve
Petievich, Gerald
Pezzullo, Ralph
Philbrick, (W.) Rodman
Phillips, Clyde
Phillips, Scott
Piccirilli, Tom
Pickard, Nancy
Pine, Nicholas
Pineiro, R. J.
Poblocki, Dan
Poole, Josephine
Porter, Anna
Poskitt, Kjartan
Posner, Richard
Pottinger, Stanley
Poulson, Christine
Preston, Ivy (Alice)
Preston, Marcia K.
Price, Anthony
Price, Victor (Henry John)
Prickett, Stephen
Pritts, Kim Derek
Prowell, Sandra West
Prowse, Brad A.
Pugh, Dianne G.
Pullein-Thompson, Josephine
Pulsford, Petronella
Purser, Ann
Purser, Philip (John)
Pynchon, Thomas
Rabaté, Jean-Michel
Rabb, Jonathan
Rabb, Margo
Radin, Ruth Yaffe
Rae, Hugh C(rawford)
Raffel, Keith
Raine, Jerry
Raleigh, Michael
Ramsay, Caro
Ramsland, Katherine
Rankin, Ian (James)
Raphael, Lev
Reasoner, Livia Jane Washburn
Reed, Ishmael
Reed, Philip (Chandler)
Reeman, Douglas (Edward)
Rees, Matt Beynon
Reese, James
Reese, Laura
Regan, Linda
Reginald, Robert
Reid, Elwood
Reisman, Michael
Reiss, Kathryn
Reiter, Victoria (Kelrich)
Rendell, Ruth
Rennison, Louise
Reuland, Robert
Reusche, Taylor McCafferty
Reuter, Bjarne (B.)
Reynolds, Jan
Reynolds, Marjorie
Ricardo, Jack
Rice, Linda Lightsey
Richard, Adrienne
Richard, T. Dawn

Richards, Emilie
Richards, Linda L.
Richardson, Robert
Richmond, Michelle
Rickards, John
Rickman, Philip
Ridley, Elizabeth J(ayne)
Ridpath, Michael
Rifkin, Shepard
Riggs, Cynthia
Riordan, Rick
Riordon, Michael
Rips, Michael
Rivard, Robert
Rivers, Reggie
Robb, B. R.
Robb, Candace
Robenalt, James David
Roberts, Denys (Tudor Emil)
Robinson, David L.
Robinson, Frank M(alcolm)
Robinson, Leah Ruth
Robinson, Lynda S(uzanne)
Robinson, Roxana (Barry)
Rocha, Luis Miguel
Roe, Caroline
Rogow, Roberta
Romano, Ray
Rook, Tony
Rose, Karen
Roslund, Anders
Ross, Angus
Rossiter, John
Rothenberg, David
Rowling, J(oanne) K.
Rowse, Sharon
Royal, Priscilla
Rozan, S. J.
Rule, Ann
Russell, Alan
Russell, Martin (James)
Russell, Mary D(oria)
Sagastizabal, Patricia
Salaman, Nicholas
Sallis, James
Sammon, Paul M.
Sampson, Catherine
Sandford, John
Sandstrom, Eve K.
Santlofer, Jonathan
Saperstein, David
Sasser, Charles W(ayne)
Saulnier, Beth
Saum, Karen
Savage, Tom
Savarin, Julian Jay
Sawyer, Robert J(ames)
Saylor, Steven W(arren)
Scarpaci, Sherry
Schiffer, James (M.)
Schiller, Lawrence
Schmahmann, David
Schorsch, Laurence
Schrager, Sam(uel Alan)
Schuiten, François Louis Marie
Schwegel, Theresa
Scoppettone, Sandra

Scott, Amanda
Scott, Leonard B.
Scott, Manda
Scott, Trevor
Scott, Whitney S.
Seagrave, Sterling
Searls, Hank
Sears, Richard
Seay, Jody
Segriff, Larry
Sennett, Frank (Ronald)
Seymour, Gerald
Shaffer, Louise
Shaffer, Peter (Levin)
Shafquat, Sofia
Shahan, Sherry
Shannon, Doris
Shannon, Harry
Sharmat, Marjorie Weinman
Shefchik, Rick
Shelton, Connie
Sherbaniuk, Richard
Shoesmith, Kathleen A.
Shone, Anna
Shuman, George D.
Shuman, Malcolm K.
Sidor, Steven
Siegel, James
Siler, Jenny
Simon, Roger (Mitchell)
Simonetta, Marcello
Simpson, Dorothy
Sims, Michael
Sington, Philip
Sinnett, Mark C.
Sipherd, Ray
Siverling, Mike
Slade, Arthur G(regory)
Slan, Joanna Campbell
Slaughter, Karin
Slote, Alfred
Smith, Frederick E(screet)
Smith, Geof
Smith, Gordon
Smith, Gregory Blake
Smith, Joan Gerarda
Smith, Lora Roberts
Smith, Martin Cruz
Smith, Patricia
Smith, Sarah (W. R.)
Smith, Wilbur (Addison)
Sobol, Donald J.
Solomita, Stephen
Somerset, Anne
Soos, Troy
Soule, Maris Anne
South, Sheri Cobb
Spalding, Andrea
Spanogle, Joshua
Spicer, Michael
Sprinkle, Patricia Houck
Spruill, Steven
St. Antoine, Sara L.
St. George, Judith
Stabenow, Dana
Stacey, Cherylyn
Stanley, Autumn

Stanley, J. B.
Stanley, Kelli
Stansberry, Domenic (Joseph)
Starr, Jason
Stashower, Daniel (Meyer)
Staynes, Jill
Stein, Wendy
Stevens, Diane
Stewart, Elizabeth A.
Stewart, Mary (Florence Elinor)
Stewart, Michael
Stockley, Grif
Stodghill, Ron
Stone, Eric
Stone, Katherine
Stone, Nick
Stone, Rodney
Storey, Margaret
Stotter, Mike
Straight, Susan
Strickland, (William) Brad(ley)
Stroby, Wallace
Stroud, Carsten
Stubbs, Jean
Stukas, David
Sturman, Jennifer
Sullivan, M(ichael) J(ustin)
Sundstrand, David
Sussex, Lucy (Jane)
Swanson, Doug J.
Swanson, James L.
Swartz, Jon David
Swift, Graham
Takashima, Misako
Tallis, Frank
Tallman, Shirley
Taylor, Andrew (John Robert)
Taylor, Elizabeth Atwood
Taylor, Liza Pennywitt
Taylor, Sarah Stewart
Teller, Neville
Temple, Robert (Kyle Grenville)
Tepper, Sheri S.
Tesh, Jane
Thayer, Terri
Thomas, Will
Thomas-Graham, Pamela (Borders)
Thompson, Victoria
Thompson-Cannino, Jennifer
Thomson, June
Thor, Brad
Thurlo, Aimee
Title, Elise
Tomlinson, Theresa
Tonkin, Peter Francis
Tope, Rebecca
Torres, Steven
Tourney, Leonard D(on)
Tracy, Kristen
Travis, Lucille
Trembath, Don
Trenhaile, John Stevens
Tripp, David
Trollip, Stanley R.
Tucker, (Allan) James
Turnbull, Peter (John)

Turow, (L.) Scott
Tuttle, Lisa
Tyler, Anne
Tyre, Peg
Underwood, Blair
Uruburu, Paula
Vachss, Andrew H(enry)
van Allsburg, Chris
Van Dover, J(ames) K(enneth)
van Horn, Ray
Vance, Jack
Vance, Steve
Vanderbes, Jennifer (Chase)
Vankin, Jonathan
Vardamis, Frances (Diem)
Vaughan, Brian K.
Vidal, Gore
Viviano, Frank
Volkman, Ernest
Waddington-Feather, John Joseph
Wagner, Sharon Blythe
Wainwright, Jeffrey
Waites, Martyn
Waldman, Ayelet
Walker, Anne Collins
Walker, Kathryn
Walker, Sally M(acArt)
Wall, Kathryn R.
Wallace, Benjamin
Wallingford, Lee
Walsh, Jill Paton
Walsh, Lawrence
Walsh, Suella
Walter, Jess
Walton, Rick
Wambaugh, Joseph
Wang, Jen
Ward, Amanda Eyre
Ward, Gregory
Warfield, Gallatin
Warner, Penny
Warsh, Sylvia E. Maultash
Washburn, Livia J.
Washburn, Stan
Watada, Terry
Waters, John F(rederick)
Watkins, Ronald J(oseph)
Wayman, Vivienne
Webb, Betty
Webster, Ernest
Webster, Jason
Weenolsen, Patricia
Weinkauf, Mary S(tanley)
Weir, Charlene
Weldon, Phaedra M.
Welford, Sue
Wells, Melanie
Wells, Shirley
Wesley, Valerie Wilson
Westcott, Jan (Vlachos)
Whalley, Peter
Whitcher, Susan (Godsil)
White, Karen
White, Randy Wayne
Whitehead, David (Henry)
Whiteway, Doug(las) Alfred
Wiesner, Karen Sue

Wiggin, Eric E(llsworth)
Wignall, Kevin
Wilcox, Stephen F.
Wildwind, Sharon Grant
Wile, Mary Lee
Wiley, Michael
Wilhelm, Kate
Williams, Amanda Kyle
Williams, Jeanne
Williams, John Hartley
Williams, Len
Williams, Theresa
Williamson, Chet
Willis, Val
Wilson, Barbara (Ellen)
Wilson, David Niall
Wilson, Eric (P.)
Wilson, F(rancis) Paul
Wilson, Jacqueline (Aitken)
Wilson, John Morgan
Wimberley, (Amos) Darryl
Winckler, Martin
Winslow, Don
Winston, Daoma
Winston, Lois
Wolf, Sarah (Elizabeth)
Wolfe, Gene (Rodman)
Wolzien, Valerie
Womack, Steven (James)
Wood, Brian
Wood, Bridget
Wood, Edward John
Woodman, David C(harles)
Woodruff, Joan Leslie
Woods, Paula L.
Woodworth, Stephen
Worboys, Anne
Wright, Betty Ren
Wright, Eric
Wright, Keith
Wright, Nina
Wynne, John (Stewart)
Wynne, Marcus
Yaffe, James
Yarbro, Chelsea Quinn
Yorke, Margaret
Yurick, Sol
Zafón, Carlos Ruiz
Zelvin, Elizabeth
Zettler, Steve
Zigal, Thomas
Zuehlke, Mark

Horror

Adams, Abby
Adams, C. T.
Addison, Linda D.
Aguirre, Forrest
Albert, Neil
Allegretto, Michael
Allston, Aaron
Anderson, M. T(obin)
Arden, John
Armstead, Joseph

Arnold, Elizabeth
Arnzen, Michael A.
Ashley, Bernard
Bajoria, Paul
Bardsley, Michele
Barker, Clive
Barr, Nevada
Bedard, Anthony
Beere, Peter
Berliner-Gluckman, Janet
Bonansinga, Jay R.
Bowkett, Stephen
Boyer, Rick
Boyle, Josephine
Boyll, (James) Randall
Brandewyne, Rebecca
Brennan, J(ames) H(erbert)
Bridges, Laurie
Briggs, Patricia
Brite, Poppy Z.
Brittain, William (E.)
Brown, Alan
Brown, Roberta Simpson
Butler, Gwendoline (Williams)
Cacaci, Joe
Cadnum, Michael
Campbell, Ramsey
Cannon, Eileen E(mily)
Cantrell, Lisa W.
Carter, Dean Vincent
Chambers, Christopher
Chard, Judy (Gordon)
Charnas, Suzy McKee
Chercover, Sean
Chetwin, Grace
Churchill, E. Richard
Citro, Joseph A.
Clabough, Casey Howard
Clegg, Douglas
Clemens, Brian (Horace)
Collings, Michael R(obert)
Collins, Nancy A.
Corrigan, Eireann
Crawford, Gary W(illiam)
Cross, Gillian (Clare)
Crowley, Bridget
Dann, Jack
Davis, Nageeba
DeVincent-Hayes, Nan
DeWeese, Gene
Diver, Lucienne
Donnelly, Joe
Duffy, Margaret
Duncan, Hal
Edwards, (Kenneth) Martin
Egginton, Joyce
Elam, Jason
Ellis, Peter Berresford
Elrod, P(at) N.
Evans, Liz
Evenson, Brian
Fahy, Thomas
Fanning, Diane Lynn
Fanthorpe, R(obert) Lionel
Fate, Robert
Felske, Coerte V. W.
Fischer, Dennis

Forsyth, Frederick
Frank, Frederick S.
Frimansson, Inger
Furutani, Dale
Gagliani, William
Gallagher, Stephen
Garwood, Julie
Gelb, Jeff
Gibson, Marley
Gilden, Mel
Gilman, George G.
Glut, Don(ald) F.
Gold, Bernice
Gordon, John (William)
Gough, Laurence
Grant, Cynthia D.
Greenhall, Ken
Greer, Robert O.
Gresham, Eddie
Gresham, Stephen
Griffin, Peni R(ae)
Grimes, Martha
Grindal, Richard
Hahn, Mary Downing
Haldeman, Joe (William)
Hardcastle, Michael
Harris, Steve
Harrison, Kim
Hart, Carolyn G(impel)
Haught, James A(lbert)
Hawkes, Judith
Headley, Bernard D.
Healy, Erin M.
Hegarty, Frances
Herbert, James
Hill, Laban Carrick
Hill, William
Hilton, Matt
Hinton, S(usan) E(loise)
Hocking, Mary (Eunice)
Holder, Nancy L.
Holt, David
Holt, Ian
Hooper, Kay
Hoy, Linda
Hutchins, J. C.
Hutson, Shaun P.
James, Kelvin Christopher
James, Peter
Jancovich, Mark
Jensen, Ruby Jean
Johnston, Ronald
Jones, Gwyneth A(nn)
Jones, Stephen
Joyce, Graham
Kamau, Kwadwo Agymah
Kaye, Marvin
Kelleher, Victor Michael Kitch-
ener
Kelly, Ronald
Kenner, Julie
Kenyon, Nate
Kidd, Paul
Kiernan, Caitlín R(ebekah)
Killeen, Jarlath
Kilpatrick, Nancy
King, Gary C.

Coulter, Catherine
Crandall, Susan
Crane, Caroline
Craven, Sara
Crawley, Harriet
Cready, Gwyn
Creel, Ann Howard
Creighton, Kathleen
Cross, Helen
Crusie, Jennifer
Cummings, Barbara
D'Souza, Tony
Dahlberg, Maurine F.
Dailey, Janet
Daniels, Angie
Dann, Jack
Dano, Linda
Dart, Iris Rainer
Dart-Thornton, Cecilia
Darty, Peggy
Davidson, Dana
Davis, Anna
Davis, Dee
Davis, Lindsey
Dawes, Casey
Dawson, Geralyn
De Carvalho, Mário
Delacroix, Claire
DeVincent-Hayes, Nan
DeWeese, Gene
Dietrich, William A.
DiMarco, Cris K. A.
Dodd, Christina
Dolling-Mann, Patricia May
Dolnick, Barrie
Donahue, Tina
Donn, Linda
Donnelly, Jane
Dracup, Angela
Dreyer, Eileen
Drucker, Lisa
Drummond, June
Duncan, Carol Greene
Duncan, Sarah
Eames, Anne
Echenique, Alfredo Bryce
Edwards, Anne
Edwards, Louis
Edwards, P. D.
Elkins, Charlotte
Elliott, Elaine M.
Ellis, Royston
Elmer, Robert
Englund, Steven
Epstein, Seymour
Essex, Karen
Estrada, Rita Clay
Evanovich, Janet
Evans, Justin
Evanzz, Karl
Fain, Michael
Farr, Diane
Faulkner, Colleen
Fenton, Robert L.
Ferraro, Susan (Lyons)
Fforde, Katie
Field, Edward

Fields, Hillary
Fink, Merton
Finley, Glenna
Firouz, Anahita (Homa)
Flaherty, Liz
Flem, Lydia
Fleming, Candace
Flinn, Alex
Flokos, Nicholas
Fluke, Joanne
Foley, Gaelen
Fone, Byrne R. S.
Force, Marie Sullivan
Ford, Michael Curtis
Foster, Alan Dean
Foster, Lori L.
Francis, Dorothy Brenner
Frank, Dorothea Benton
Frank, Frederick S.
Frank, J. Suzanne
Fraser, Laura (Jane)
French, Judith E.
Freydont, Shelley
Friedman, Aimee
Gabhart, Ann Houchin
Galt, George
Garbera, Katherine
Garcia, Diana
Gardner, Theodore Roosevelt
Garfield, Brian (F. W.)
Garnett, Gale Zoë
Garwood, Julie
Gaston, Diane
Gattey, Charles Neilson
Geach, Christine
Gellis, Roberta (Leah Jacobs)
Gerritsen, Tess
Gersten-Vassilaros, Alexandra
Gilbert, Harriett
Gillespie, Gerald (Ernest Paul)
Gilson, Christopher C.
Gladstone, Arthur M.
Glaister, Lesley (G.)
Glendening, John
Glover, Judith
Godwin, Parke
Goldblatt, Stacey
Goldman, Mary Elizabeth
Golds, Cassandra
González, Aníbal
Goodman, Jo
Gordon, Deborah Hannes
Gould, Terry
Graham, Caroline
Grant, Susan
Grant, Vanessa
Gray, John
Grayson, Emily
Grazer, Gigi Levangie
Greene, Bette
Greene, Jennifer
Greenwood, Leigh
Grescoe, Paul
Grey, Anthony
Griesemer, John
Guhrke, Laura Lee
Gunn, Robin Jones

Gutman, Robert W.
Hackett, Helen
Hackett, Joyce
Haig, Kathryn
Hale, John
Hall, Gimone
Han Suyin
Harley, Willard F.
Harmel, Kristin
Harrington, Kathleen
Harris, Christine
Harris, Robert J.
Harris, Rosemary (Jeanne)
Harrison, C. C.
Harrison, Elizabeth Fancourt
Harrison, Sue
Harrod-Eagles, Cynthia
Hart, Catherine
Harte, Amanda
Harte, Lara
Hatcher, Robin Lee
Havens, Candace
Haynes, Sybille (Edith)
Heath, Lorraine
Hely, Sara
Henke, Shirl
Herman, Eleanor
Herring, Peg
Hess, Joan
Hiçyilmaz, Gaye
Hilderbrand, Elin
Hill, Pamela
Hill, Selima (Wood)
Hilton, Margery
Hines, Jeanne
Hoff, B. J.
Hoffman, Ronald
Hogan, Mary
Holder, Nancy L.
Holmes, Mary Z(astrow)
Hone, Joseph
Honnef, Klaus
Hood, Stuart (Clink)
Hooper, Kay
Howard, Audrey
Howe, Muriel
Hoyt, Elizabeth
Hughes, Dean
Humphreys, Helen (Caroline)
Hunt, Angela Elwell
Hutchinson, Bill
Ivory, Judith
Jackson, Jane
Jackson, Lisa
Jackson, Monica
Jacobs, Anna
Jakes, John
James, Deana
James, Reina
Janowitz, Brenda
Jansen, Marc C.
Jarman, Rosemary Hawley
Jenkins, Amy
Jenkins, Beverly
Jensen, Emma
Jensen, Kathryn
Jensen, Muriel

Jernigan, Brenda K.
Johansen, Iris
Johnson, Annabel (Jones)
Johnson, Maureen
Johnson, Susan (M.)
Johnson, Susan (Ruth)
Johnston, Joan
Jones, Jill
Jones, Linda Winstead
Jong, Erica (Mann)
Jordan, Penny
Joshi, S(unand) T(ryambak)
Joyce, Brenda
Justiss, Julia
Kaplow, Robert
Karayianni, Lori
Karayianni, Tony
Karr, Kathleen
Katz, Molly
Kauffman, Donna
Kauffman, Michael W.
Kaye, Barrington
Kemp, Kenny
Kerner, Elizabeth
Kessler, Julia Braun
Kiely, Robert (James)
Kiernan, Caitlín R(ebekah)
Kilworth, Garry
Kimmel, Daniel M.
King, Cassandra
King, Joy
Kingma, Daphne Rose
Kingston, Christina
Kirkland, Martha
Kitt, Sandra (E.)
Kleinsasser, Lois
Knight, Alanna (Cleet)
Knight, Angela
Kokoris, Jim
Kolpen, Jana (Fayne)
Krahn, Betina
Kricorian, Nancy
Krinard, Susan
Kuczkir, Mary
Kurtz, Katherine
Kyle, Susan S(paeth)
Ladd, Linda
Lafoy, Leslie
Lamba, Marie
Lambdin, Dewey (W.)
Lampitt, Dinah
Landis, Jill Marie
Lane, Abbe
Lateiner, Donald
Laux, Constance
Leckie, Ross
LeCompte, N(ancy) Jane
Lee, Rachel
Leigh, Ana
Lennard, John (Chevening)
Lennox-Smith, Judith (Elizabeth)
Leo, Mabel R.
Lerner, Laurence (David)
Leslie, John
Leto, Julie Elizabeth
Levy, Daniel S.
Lewis, Sherry

Romance/Historical-*cont.*

Waddington-Feather, John Joseph
Wagner, Sharon Blythe
Walker, Wendy (Alison)
Walters, Minette
Warneke, Sara
Warren, Susan May
Watford, Christopher M.
Wegmann, Peter
Wein, Elizabeth E(ve)
Weiner-Davis, Michele
Weir, Theresa
Wersba, Barbara
Westcott, Jan (Vlachos)
Westheimer, (Karola) Ruth
White, Karen
White, Kimberley
Whitehead, David (Henry)
Wiesepape, Betty Holland
Wiley, Michael
Williams, Bert (Nolan)
Williams, Dwight
Williams, Theresa
Wilson, Darryl B(abe)
Wilson, Frances Engle
Wilson, Sandra
Windsor, Linda
Winston, Daoma
Winston, Lois
Wisdom, Linda Randall
Wolfson, Susan J.
Wolper, Carol
Wolverton, Cheryl
Wood, Brian
Woodhouse, S(usan) T.
Woodhouse, Sarah
Woods, Stuart
Wootson, Alice (G.)
Worboys, Anne
Wright, (Mary) Patricia
Wright, Courtni C(rump)
Wright, Julie
Yarbro, Chelsea Quinn
Young, Bette Roth
Yurick, Sol

Science Fiction/Fantasy

Aamodt, Donald
Abbas, Jailan
Adams, C. T.
Addison, Linda D.
Adlard, Mark
Alai
Alama, Pauline J.
Aldiss, Brian (Wilson)
Alkiviades, Alkis
Allston, Aaron
Alschuler, William R.
Anderson, James G.
Anderson, Kevin J(ames)
Anderson, M. T(obin)
Anthony, Joseph Patrick
Anthony, Patricia
Anthony, Piers
Aponte, Harry J.

Science Fiction/Fantasy-*cont.*

Arbuthnott, Gill
Ash, Constance (Lee)
Asher, Neal
Auseon, Andrew
Bachorz, Pam
Bailey, Robin W(ayne)
Bains, William
Banner, Catherine
Barbour, Douglas
Barlowe, Wayne Douglas
Barnes, John (Allen)
Barnes, Lynard
Barnwell, William (Curtis)
Bass, T. J.
Bath, K. P.
Baxter, John
Baxter, Stephen
Bear, Greg(ory Dale)
Beauseigneur, James
Bechard, Margaret
Beck, Ian
Beere, Peter
Behr, Ira Steven
Bell, Betty Louise
Bell, Cathleen Davitt
Benford, Gregory (Albert)
Benz, Derek
Berberick, Nancy Varian
Berger-Kiss, Andres
Berlfein, Judy Reiss
Berliner-Gluckman, Janet
Berry, Adrian M.
Bingle, Donald J.
Bishop, Michael
Blamires, Harry
Block, Francesca (Lia)
Bohnhoff, Maya Kaathryn
Bova, Ben(jamin William)
Bowkett, Stephen
Boyll, (James) Randall
Bradbury, Ray (Douglas)
Brandewyne, Rebecca
Brennan, J(ames) H(erbert)
Brennan, Sarah Rees
Brenner, Mayer Alan
Bridges, Laurie
Brigg, Peter
Brin, David
Bristow, Robert O'Neil
Brittain, C. Dale
Broderick, Damien
Brody, Jean
Browne, Nicky Matthews
Bryant, Jennifer F(isher)
Buckell, Tobias S.
Buida, Yuri
Bujold, Lois McMaster
Bush, Anne Kelleher
Byars, Betsy (Cromer)
Callenbach, Ernest
Canavan, Trudi
Cantrell, Lisa W.
Capobianco, Michael
Card, Orson Scott
Carey, Jacqueline
Carter, Raphael
Casey, Barbara

Science Fiction/Fantasy-*cont.*

Cash, Steve
Casil, Amy Sterling
Cassady, Marsh
Cassutt, Michael (Joseph)
Castaneda, Christopher James
Caswell, Brian
Cavallaro, Michael J.
Cawthorne, Nigel
Charlesworth, Monique
Charnas, Suzy McKee
Charrette, Robert N.
Cherryh, C. J.
Chetwin, Grace
Chilson, Rob(ert) (Dean)
Choyce, Lesley
Chwedyk, Richard
Ciddor, Anna
Citro, Joseph A.
Clover, Peter
Colalillo-Kates, Isabella
Cole, Allan
Collier, James Lincoln
Collings, Michael R(obert)
Collins, Helen (Frances)
Collins, Robert
Compton, D(avid) G(uy)
Conquest, (George) Robert
  (Acworth)
Constantine, Storm
Cook, Glen (Charles)
Cook, Paul
Coombs, Patricia
Copper, Basil
Corderoy, Conor
Corran, Mary
Corrick, James A.
Coulson, Juanita
Creed, William S.
Croft, Barbara
Cross, Gillian (Clare)
Crouch, Katie
Culhane, John (William)
Czerneda, Julie E(lizabeth)
D'Ath, Justin
Daley, Michael J.
Dalton, Annie
Daniel, Tony
Daniels, Karen
Dann, Jack
Darnay, Arsen J.
Dart-Thornton, Cecilia
David, James F.
Davies, Linda
Davis, Sampson
Davis, Steven J(oseph)
Dean (Dyer-Bennett), Pamela
  (Collins)
DeCandido, Keith R. A.
Dedman, Stephen
Delany, Samuel R(ay)
Delgado, Ricardo
Dellamonica, A. M.
DesRochers, Diane
DeVincent-Hayes, Nan
DeVita, James
DeWeese, Gene
Dewey, Scott Hamilton

Science Fiction/Fantasy-*cont.*

di Filippo, Paul
Dickerson, Matthew T.
Dickinson, John
Dickinson, Peter
Dinello, Paul
Dix, Shane
Dixon, Dougal
Dixon, Larry
Donnelly, Deborah
Douglas, L. Warren
Douglas, Matthew M.
Dowling, Terry
Doyle, Debra
Doyle, Larry
Drake, David A.
Drucker, Mort
Duncan, Andy
Duncan, Dave
Duntemann, Jeff
Durgin, Doranna
Dwight, Jeffry
Dyson, Freeman (John)
Eason, Alethea
Easton, Malcolm Coleman
Ecklar, Julia (Marie)
Edgerton, Teresa (Ann)
Egan, Greg
Eisenstein, Phyllis (Kleinstein)
Elgin, Suzette Haden
Ellis, Ella Thorp
Ellison, Harlan (Jay)
Elrod, P(at) N.
Emery, Clayton
Emshwiller, Carol (Fries)
Engdahl, Sylvia L(ouise)
Engelberg, Alan (D.)
Epperson, Michael
Eriksson, Kjell
Eskridge, Kelley
Evans, Jon
Evans, Richard
Evenson, Brian
Eyer, Diane E(lizabeth)
Fahnestock, Todd
Fallon, Jennifer
Fan, Nancy Yi
Fancher, Jane S(uzanne)
Fantaskey, Beth
Fanthorpe, R(obert) Lionel
Faust, Jeff
Feeley, Gregory
Feist, Raymond E(lias)
Ferguson, Brad
Ferreiro, Carmen
Fickett, David C.
Fontes, Montserrat
Foreman, Lelia Rose
Forrest, Katherine V(irginia)
Forsyth, Kate
Foster, Alan Dean
Foster, M(ichael) A(nthony)
Fox, Helen
Fracis, Sohrab Homi
Franklin, Cheryl J.
Fraser, Mary Ann
Freireich, Valerie J.
Frezza, Robert (A.)

Okorafor-Mbachu, Nnedi
Oltion, Jerry
Otomo, Katsuhiro
Ouellette, Pierre
Palmer, John D.
Palumbo, Donald E.
Palwick, Susan
Pardoe, Blaine
Patneaude, David
Paul, Barbara
Pavlou, Stel
Paxson, Diana L(ucile)
Peabody, Richard (Myers)
Pearlman, Daniel D.
Pelan, John
Pélot, Pierre
Penrose, Roger
Perkins, Michael
Perkowitz, Sidney
Perrin, Don
Perry, Steve
Petrakis, Harry Mark
Philmus, Robert M(ichael)
Piercy, Marge
Pogue, Bill
Pohl, Frederik
Pon, Cindy
Posner, Richard
Powe, Bruce Allen
Pratchett, Terry
Price, Susan
Priest, Christopher (McKenzie)
Pringle, David (William)
Prowse, Brad A.
Ptacek, Kathryn
Radford, Irene
Raham, (R.) Gary
Ramsland, Katherine
Rankin, Robert
Rasmussen, Alis A.
Ratcliffe, Eric Hallam
Rawn, Melanie (Robin)
Reasoner, Livia Jane Washburn
Redick, Robert V.S.
Regan, Dian Curtis
Reginald, Robert
Reimann, Katya
Reisman, Michael
Resnick, Mike
Rettstatt, Chris
Rheingold, Howard (E.)
Riley, Martin
Ringo, John
Roberts, Katherine
Robinson, Frank M(alcolm)
Robinson, Spider
Rodgers, Alan (Paul)
Rodgers, Frank
Roessner, Michaela
Rogow, Roberta
Rohan, Michael Scott
Rohmer, Richard
Roshwald, Mordecai
Rossman, C. L.
Routley, (Bernarra) Jane
Rowling, J(oanne) K.
Rucker, Rudy

Ruddick, Nicholas
Rusch, Kristine Kathryn
Russell, Mary D(oria)
Russell, Sharon A.
Ryan, Frank
Saffer, Barbara
Sallis, James
Salvatore, R(obert) A(nthony)
Saperstein, David
Sargent, Pamela
Sarti, Ron
Sauter, Doris Elaine
Savage, Felicity
Sawyer, Cheryl
Sawyer, Robert J(ames)
Saxton, Josephine (Howard)
Schenck, Hilbert
Schmidt, Stanley (Albert)
Scott, Melissa
Searls, Hank
Sebanc, Mark
Seddon, Andrew M.
Seed, David
Segriff, Larry
Sendak, Maurice
Shelemay, Kay Kaufman
Shiina, Makoto
Shinn, Sharon
Shusterman, Neal (Douglas)
Silverberg, Robert
Sima, Carol Ann
Simmons, Jane
Sinclair, Alison
Sinisalo, Johanna
Sisk, David W.
Smigel, Robert
Smith, Marguerite
Smith, Mitchell
Smith, Sarah (W. R.)
Smith, Sherwood
Smith, Stephanie A.
Smith, Wesley J.
Snyder, Midori
Somers, Jeff
Spencer, William Browning
Stabenow, Dana
Stableford, Brian M(ichael)
Stackpole, Michael A(ustin)
Standiford, Natalie
Stathis, Pete
Sterling, Bruce
Stine, Scott A(aron)
Stover, Matthew Woodring
Strickland, (William) Brad(ley)
Strickland, Craig (A.)
Strock, Ian Randal
Stross, Charles
Sullivan, C(harles) W(illiam)
Sussex, Lucy (Jane)
Swartz, Jon David
Synge, Ursula
Taylor, Janelle (Diane Williams)
Taylor, Margaret
Tem, Steve Rasnic
Tepper, Sheri S.
Thurston, Robert (Donald)
Tilley, Patrick

Townsend, Wendy
Truman, Ruth
Turner, Megan Whalen
Turtledove, Harry (Norman)
Tuttle, Lisa
Tyler, C.
Tyson, Salinda
Valentine, Mark
Valentino, Serena
Van Scyoc, Sydney (Joyce)
Vance, Jack
Vance, Steve
Vasta, Edward
Verba, Joan Marie
Verniero, Joan C.
Vinge, Vernor (Steffen)
Voermans, Paul
Volsky, Paula
von Schlegell, Mark
Waitman, Katie
Walker, Wendy (Alison)
Warneke, Sara
Watkins, William John
Watson, Ian
Waugh, Sylvia
Webb, Janeen (S.)
Weber, David
Wein, Elizabeth E(ve)
Wells (Dimenstein), Catherine
Wharton, Thomas
What, Leslie
Wheeler, Deborah (Jean Ross)
Whitehead, David (Henry)
Whitelaw, Nancy
Whyte, Jack
Wiater, Stanley
Wilhelm, Kate
Willard, Dale C.
Williams, Liz
Williams, R. D.
Williams, Walter Jon
Williamson, Chet
Williamson, Philip G.
Willis, Connie
Wilson, David Niall
Wilson, F(rancis) Paul
Wisman, Ken
Wodhams, Jack
Wolfe, Gene (Rodman)
Wolverton, Dave
Womack, Jack
Wood, Brian
Wood, Bridget
Wood, N. Lee
Wrede, Patricia C(ollins)
Wullschläger, Jackie
Wurts, Janny
Yarbro, Chelsea Quinn
Yep, Laurence (Michael)
Yolen, Jane
Youd, Samuel
Youmans, Marly
Yourgrau, Palle
Zahn, Timothy
Zambreno, Mary Frances
Zebrowski, George
Zettel, Sarah

Zicree, Mark Scott
Zurbo, Matt

Westerns/Adventure

Anthony, Piers
Armstrong, Richard
Arrington, Stephen L(ee)
Barnes, John (Allen)
Barton, (Samuel) Wayne
Beauchamp, Cari
Bennett, R.G. Stephen
Berger, Thomas (Louis)
Blake, Michael
Bowers, Terrell L.
Brandewyne, Rebecca
Braun, Matt(hew)
Bride, Johnny Mack
Broomall, Robert W(alter)
Brown, J(oseph) P(aul)
    S(ummers)
Brundige, Sharron L(ea)
Burks, Brian
Canham, Marsha
Castle, Linda
Cervenka, Jarda
Champlin, Tim
Coulson, Juanita
Crider, (Allen) Bill(y)
Dailey, Janet
Dangarembga, Tsitsi
Day, Edward C.
Dickinson, Matt
Dix, Shane
Edson, J(ohn) T(homas)
Emshwiller, Carol (Fries)
Estleman, Loren D.
Estrada, Rita Clay
Eynon, Robert
Falcon, Mark
Fishman, Steve
Gardner, Jerome
Garfield, Brian (F. W.)
Gear, W. Michael
Gilman, George G.
Goss, Pete
Graham, Bob
Graves, Sarah
Gregory, Kristiana
Hansen, Eric K.
Harvey, John
Haydon, Elizabeth
Heminway, John
Hill, Janet Muirhead
Holmes, B(ryan) J(ohn)
Hunter, Gwen
Jakes, John
Johnston, Joan
Jong, Erica (Mann)
Keith, William H(enry)
Kittredge, William
Krieger, Michael J.
Lambdin, Dewey (W.)
Lansdale, Joe R(ichard)
Lawrence, Steven C.

Bond, Ruskin
Boniface, William
Boon, Debbie
Borchard, Therese Johnson
Borgenicht, David
Borntrager, Mary Christner
Bortnik, Aida (Beatriz)
Borton, Lady
Botting, Douglas
Bourgeois, Paulette
Bovaird, Anne E(lizabeth)
Bowen, John (Griffith)
Bowering, Marilyn (Ruthe)
Bowkett, Stephen
Bowler, Tim
Bowman, Crystal
Bowman, David
Boyd, Candy Dawson
Boyes, Vivien (Elizabeth)
Bradbury, Ray (Douglas)
Bradford, Karleen
Bradman, Tony
Brady, Kimberley S(mith)
Branch, Muriel Miller
Brand, Oscar
Brandenberg, Franz
Braun, Matt(hew)
Brayfield, Celia
Brazaitis, Mark
Bredsdorff, Bodil
Breen, Steve
Brennan, Herbie
Brennan, J(ames) H(erbert)
Brett, Jan (Churchill)
Bridgers, Sue Ellen (Hunsucker)
Bridwell, Norman (Ray)
Briggs, Raymond (Redvers)
Brill, Marlene Targ
Brisson, Pat
Brittain, William (E.)
Broach, Elise
Broderick, Tim
Brooke, William J.
Brooks, Erik
Brooks, Martha
Broome, Errol
Brouwer, Sigmund
Brown, Don
Brown, Jackie
Brown, Kevin
Brown, Ruth
Browne, Anthony (Edward Tudor)
Browne, Nicky Matthews
Brownjohn, Alan (Charles)
Brownridge, William R(oy)
Broyles, Anne
Bruchac, Joseph
Bruckner, Pascal
Brugman, Alyssa (F.)
Brusatte, Steve
Bryant, Jennifer F(isher)
Buccieri, Lisa Rojany
Buckey, Sarah Masters
Bucknall, Barbara Jane
Budbill, David
Buehner, Caralyn M.
Buffie, Margaret

Bujor, Flavia
Bull, Angela (Mary)
Bull, Schuyler M.
Bunting, (Anne) Eve(lyn Bolton)
Burgess, Colin
Burgess, Granville Wyche
Burnett, Gail Lemley
Burningham, John (Mackintosh)
Burns, Diane L.
Burns, Khephra
Burns, Marilyn
Burroway, Janet (Gay)
Burstein, Fred
Burton, Bonnie
Bushey, Jeanne
Bushnell, Jack
Busia, Akosua
Butcher, Kristin
Butler, Dori Hillestad
Butler, Dorothy
Butler, Geoff
Butterworth, Nick
Buzzeo, Toni
Byalick, Marcia
Byars, Betsy (Cromer)
Bye, Beryl (Joyce Rayment)
Cabot, Meg(gin Patricia)
Cabrera, Jane
Cadnum, Michael
Caduto, Michael J.
Cail, Carol
Calder, Marie D(onais)
Calhoun, B. B.
Calvert, Pam
Campbell, Rhonda
Campbell, Rod
Canham, Marsha
Cannon, A. E.
Cannon, Eileen E(mily)
Capacchione, Lucia
Capeci, Anne
Carbone, Elisa Lynn
Carew, Jan (Rynveld)
Carle, Eric
Carlton, Susan
Carr, Roger Vaughan
Carrick, Malcolm
Carrier, Roch
Carter, Betty Smartt
Carter, John T(homas)
Carusone, Al
Casanova, Mary
Cascone, Annette
Case, Chris
Cash, Steve
Cassidy, Cathy
Castaldo, Nancy Fusco
Castel-Bloom, Orly
Caswell, Brian
Catalanotto, Peter
Cato, Heather
Catrow, David J.
Cawthorne, Nigel
Cazet, Denys
Cebulash, Mel
Cerullo, Mary M.
Cervenka, Jarda

Chamberlin, Kate
Chan, Gillian
Chaney, Jill
Chao, Patricia
Chappell, Audrey
Charbonnet, Gabrielle
Charlip, Remy
Chase, Alyssa
Chataway, Carol
Chatterjee, Debjani
Cheney, Martha
Cheng, Andrea
Cheripko, Jan
Cheshire, Simon
Chetwin, Grace
Chiappe, Luis M.
Child, Maureen
Childress, Mark
Childs, Tera Lynn
Chin-Lee, Cynthia D.
Chinodya, Shimmer
Chitham, Edward (Harry Gordon)
Chocolate, Debbi
Chow, Claire S.
Choyce, Lesley
Christian, Carol Cathay Tuttle
Chwast, Seymour
Clark, Emma Chichester
Clarke, Gillian
Clarke, Gus
Clarke, Norma
Clarke-Rich, Elizabeth L.
Clayton, Elaine
Cleary, Beverly
Clem, Margaret H(ollingsworth)
Clements, Andrew
Clements, Bruce
Cleveland-Peck, Patricia
Clifford, Mary Louise
Climo, Shirley
Clover, Peter
Coburn, Ann
Cocks, Nancy L.
Cocquyt, Kathryn Marie
Coffin, Tristram Potter
Cohen, Bernard
Cohen, Jared
Cohen, Morton N(orton)
Cohen, Peter Zachary
Cohen, Sholom
Colalillo-Kates, Isabella
Cole, Betsy
Cole, Sheila R.
Coleman, Janet Wyman
Coleman, Michael
Collard, Sneed B.
Collicott, Sharleen
Collier, James Lincoln
Collings, Gillian
Collinson, Roger (Alfred)
Colquhoun, Glenn
Compestine, Ying Chang
Compton, Patricia A.
Conford, Ellen
Conlon-McKenna, Marita
Conn, Didi
Constable, Kate

Conway, Diana C(ohen)
Cook, Dawn
Cook, Jean Thor
Cooling, Wendy
Coombs, Patricia
Cooper, Helen
Cooper, Jilly (Sallitt)
Cornwell, Anita (R.)
Costello, Matthew J.
Cote, Nancy
Cotten, Cynthia
Cottonwood, Joe
Cottringer, Anne
Couloumbis, Audrey
Counsel, June
Cowell, Cressida
Cowie, Hamilton Russell
Cowley, (Cassia) Joy
Cowley, Marjorie
Cox, Judy
Coy, John
Crane, Richard (Arthur)
Creech, Sharon
Creeden, Sharon
Crenson, Victoria
Crew, Gary
Crew, Linda
Crews, Donald
Crews, Nina
Crider, (Allen) Bill(y)
Croall, Jonathan
Crook, Marion
Cross, Gillian (Clare)
Crossley-Holland, Kevin (John William)
Crowley, Bridget
Crunk, Tony
Crusie, Jennifer
Crutcher, Chris(topher C.)
Cuetara, Mittie
Cull, Mark E.
Cummings, Barbara
Cummings, Pat
Cunningham, Dru
Cuomo, Mario (Matthew)
Curlee, Lynn
Curley, Marianne
Currie, Stephen
Curry, Jane (Louise)
Curtis, Anthony
Curtis, Christopher (Paul)
Curtis, Jamie Lee
Curtiss, A(rlene) B.
Curzon, David
Cushman, Karen
Cutler, Jane
D'Ath, Justin
d'Lacey, Chris
Dahlberg, Maurine F.
Dailey, Janet
Daley, Michael J.
Dalton, Annie
Dalton, Sheila
Daly, Niki
Daniels, Karen
Dann, Colin (Michael)
Darke, Marjorie (Sheila)

Graff, Lisa
Graham, Bob
Graham, Frank
Grambs, David (Lawrence)
Granger, Michele
Grant, Cynthia D.
Graves, Sarah
Gray, Dianne E.
Greaves, Nick
Greeley, Andrew (Moran)
Green, Cliff(ord)
Greenberg, Joanne
Greene, Bette
Greene, Constance C(larke)
Greene, Jacqueline Dembar
Greene, Rhonda Gowler
Greenleaf, Stephen (Howell)
Greenlee, Sharon
Greenwood, Barbara
Gregor, Arthur
Gregory, Kristiana
Gregory, Valiska
Griffin, Adele
Griffin, Peni R(ae)
Griffin, Steven A(rthur)
Griffith, Helen V(irginia)
Grimes, Michael D.
Grisham, John
Griswold, Jerome
Grodin, Charles
Gross, Philip (John)
Grover, Wayne
Guest, Jacqueline
Guggenbühl, Allan
Gugler, Laurel Dee
Guile, Melanie
Gunn, Robin Jones
Guthrie, Donna W.
Gutman, Dan
Guy, Rosa (Cuthbert)
Haenel, Wolfram
Hahn, Mary Downing
Hajdusiewicz, Babs Bell
Hale, Shannon
Haley, Gail E(inhart)
Halfmann, Janet
Hall, Brian
Hall, Donald (Andrew)
Hall, Kirsten Marie
Hall, Lynn
Hall, Roger (Leighton)
Halligan, Marion (Mildred
    Crothall)
Hallowell, Edward McKey
Halpern, Julie
Halpin, Brendan
Halvorson, Marilyn
Hammerslough, Jane
Han, Suzanne Crowder
Hanbury-Tenison, Robin
Hannah, Sophie
Hannan, Peter
Hard, Charlotte (Ann)
Hardcastle, Michael
Hardy, Edward
Harley, Bill
Harlow, Michael

Harper, Jo
Harper, Piers
Harrill, Ronald
Harris, Christine
Harris, Robert J.
Harris, Robie H.
Harris, Rosemary (Jeanne)
Harrison, Colin
Harrison, Harry
Harrison, Michael
Harrison, Sarah
Hart, Alison
Hart, Carolyn G(impel)
Hart, Jan Siegel
Hart, Lenore
Haruf, Kent
Harvey, John
Harwood, (Henry) David
Haseley, Dennis
Haslam, Gerald William
Hasluck, Nicholas
Hatch, Lynda S.
Hathorn, Libby
Hatton, Caroline
Hauth, Katherine B.
Havel, Geoff
Hawes, Judy
Hawes, Louise
Hawke, Rosanne Joy
Hawkes, Kevin
Hawkins, Hunt
Haycock, Kate
Hayden, Eric William
Haydon, Elizabeth
Hayes, Joe
Hayes, Rosemary
Haywood, Gar Anthony
Heal, Gillian
Hearn, Julie
Hearth, Amy Hill
Heckert, Connie K(aye Delp)
Hedderwick, Mairi
Hegamin, Tonya C.
Heidbreder, Robert K.
Heide, Florence Parry
Heinz, Brian J(ames)
Helmer, Diana Star
Helmer, Marilyn
Henderson, J. A.
Hendry, Diana
Henney, Carolee Wells
Henning, Ann
Herndon, Ernest
Herrmanns, Ralph
Herron, Carolivia
Herschler, Mildred Barger
Hershenhorn, Esther
Hershey, Mary
Herzig, Alison Cragin
Herzog, Brad
Heslewood, Juliet
Hesse, Karen
Heuer, Karsten
Hewett, Joan
Heyer, Carol
Heyes, (Nancy) Eileen
Hezlep, William (Earl)

Hickey, Caroline
Hiçyilmaz, Gaye
Hieatt, Constance B(artlett)
Higdon, Hal
Higgins, Joanna
High, Linda Oatman
Hightower, Lynn S.
Highway, Tomson
Hill, Anthony (Robert)
Hill, David
Hill, Elizabeth Starr
Hill, Janet Muirhead
Hill, Susan (Elizabeth)
Hillman, Elizabeth
Hinds, Maurene J.
Hinds, P(atricia) Mignon
Hines, Jeanne
Hinton, S(usan) E(loise)
Ho, Minfong
Hoban, Russell
Hobbs, Valerie
Hoberman, Mary Ann
Hodgins, Jack
Hoehne, Marcia
Hoestlandt, Jo(celyne)
Hoff, Mary (King)
Hoffman, Alice
Hoffman, Mary (Margaret)
Holeman, Linda
Hollander, John
Hollander, Nicole
Hollindale, Peter
Hollingsworth, Mary
Holmes, Mary Z(astrow)
Holmes, Sara Lewis
Holt, Michael (Paul)
Holub, Joan
Honeycutt, Natalie
Hong, Lily Toy
Hook, Brendan
Hook, Geoffrey R(aynor)
Hooper, Maureen Brett
Hooper, Meredith Jean
Hoover, H(elen) M(ary)
Hope, Christopher (David Tully)
Hopkins, Antony
Hopkins, Lee Bennett
Hopkins, Mary R(ice)
Hopping Egan, Lorraine
Horniman, Joanne
Horowitz, Dave
Horvath, Betty
Hosozawa-Nagano, Elaine
Houghton, Eric
Houghton, Gordon
Houk, Randy
Houston, Gail Turley
Houston, Gloria
Houston, Velina Hasu
Hovey, Kate
Howard, Ellen
Howard, Maureen
Howarth, Lesley
Howe, Fanny
Howe, James
Hoy, Linda
Hoyle, Geoffrey

Hubbard, Woodleigh Marx
Hudak, Michal
Hughes, Dean
Hughes, Shirley
Hull, Nancy L.
Humphrey, Sandra McLeod
Hunkin, Tim(othy) Mark Tre-
    lawney
Hunt, Angela Elwell
Hunt, Janie Louise
Hunt, Peter (Leonard)
Hunter, Mollie
Hunter, Sara Hoagland
Hurwitz, Johanna (Frank)
Husain, Shahrukh
Huser, Glen
Hutchins, Hazel J.
Hutchins, Pat
Hwang, Jenny
Hynes, Pat
Iakovou, Takis
Ingves, Gunilla
Inkpen, Mick
Isaacs, Anne
Isadora, Rachel
Jablonski, Carla
Jackson, Kathy Merlock
Jackson, Lisa
Jacobs, Laura
Jacobs, Shannon K.
Jacobson, Jennifer Richard
James, Brian
Jance, J. A.
Janes, J(oseph) Robert
Janover, Caroline (Davis)
Jarman, Julia
Jarrow, Gail
Javernick, Ellen
Jeffries, Roderic
Jenkins, George
Jenkins, Jean
Jennings, Dana Andrew
Jennings, Patrick
Jennings, Paul
Jeram, Anita
Jerman, Jerry
Jinks, Catherine
Jobling, Curtis
Jocelyn, Marthe
Johnson, Angela
Johnson, Annabel (Jones)
Johnson, Dianne
Johnson, Dolores
Johnson, Kathleen Jeffrie
Johnson, Neil L.
Johnson, Sherrie
Jonas, Ann
Jonell, Lynne
Jones, Gerard
Jones, Gwyneth A(nn)
Jones, Jenny
Jones, Mary Voell
Jones, Naomi Brooks
Jones, Sally Roberts
Jones, Shane
Joosse, Barbara M(onnot)
Jordan, Anne Devereaux

Jordan, Sherryl
Jovanovski, Meto
Joyce, William
Judah, Aaron
Judd, Denis
Jungman, Ann
Jurmain, Suzanne
Juster, Norton
Kahl, Jonathan
Kahn, Sharon
Kalbacken, Joan
Kallen, Stuart A(rnold)
Kallevig, Christine Petrell
Kalman, Maira
Kandel, Michael
Kaplan, Andrew S.
Karon, Jan
Karr, Kathleen
Katin, Miriam
Katz, Avner
Katz, Bobbi
Katz, Susan
Katz, Welwyn Wilton
Kaufman, Scott S.
Kavanagh, P(atrick) J(oseph)
Kay, Alan N.
Kay, Betty Carlson
Kay, Elizabeth
Kaye, Geraldine
Keane, Nancy J.
Keaney, Brian
Keating, Frank
Keenan, Sheila
Keene, Ann T(odd)
Keens-Douglas, Richardo
Kefala, Antigone
Kelbaugh, Gretchen
Kelleher, Victor Michael Kitch-
ener
Keller, Debra
Keller, Holly
Kellogg, Steven
Kelly, Clint
Kelly, Joanne (W.)
Kelsay, Michael
Kemp, Gene
Kendall, Carol
Kendall, Jane (F.)
Keneally, Thomas (Michael)
Kennedy, William (Joseph)
Kennedy, X. J.
Kennemore, Tim
Kenward, Jean
Kerby, Mona
Kerr, (Anne) Judith
Kershen, (L.) Michael
Kertes, Joseph
Kerven, Rosalind
Kessler, Brad
Kevill-Davies, Sally
Khan, Rukhsana
Kherdian, David
Kilworth, Garry
Kimmel, Eric A.
Kimmel, Haven (Koontz)
King, Cynthia
King, Daniel (John)

King, Daren
King, Thomas
King, Wilma
Kingman, (Mary) Lee
Kingston, Christina
Kinney, Jeff
Kirby, Susan E.
Kisseloff, Jeff
Kitchen, Bert
Kittinger, Jo S(usenbach)
Kladstrup, Kristin
Klass, Sheila Solomon
Klaveness, Jan O'Donnell
Kleiman, Ed
Klein, Robin (McMaugh)
Klein, Zoe
Kleven, Elisa
Kline, Lisa Williams
Koch, Phyllis McCallum
Koff, Richard M.
Kogawa, Joy Nozomi
Koller, Jackie French
Kollin, Dani
Komaiko, Leah
Konigsburg, E(laine) L(obl)
Konzak, Burt
Koontz, Robin
Kopper, Lisa (Esther)
Korman, Bernice
Korman, Gordon (Richard)
Kornblatt, Marc
Koscielniak, Bruce
Koski, Mary B(ernadette)
Kotzwinkle, William
Koupal, Nancy Tystad
Kovach, Gay Haff
Kovacs, Deborah
Kovalski, Maryann
Kranendonk, Anke
Krantz, Hazel
Krasilovsky, Phyllis
Kraus, Joanna H.
Kress, Adrienne
Krishnaswami, Uma
Krohn, Katherine E(lizabeth)
Kroll, Virginia L(ouise)
Kroninger, Stephen
Kropp, Paul
Krupp, Robin Rector
Kuczkir, Mary
Kudlinski, Kathleen V.
Kuehnert, Stephanie
Kulling, Monica
Kumin, Maxine
Kunhardt, Edith
Kurlansky, Mark
Kurokawa, Mitsuhiro
Kushner, Ellen (Ruth)
Kusugak, Michael (Arvaarluk)
Kuyper, Sjoerd
Kvasnosky, Laura McGee
Lacey, Josh
Lachner, Dorothea
Ladd, Louise
LaFaye, A(lexandria R. T.)
LaFleur, Suzanne
Laguna, Sofie

Lake, M. D.
Lamb, Nancy
Lamplugh, Lois
Landon, Lucinda
Langa, Mandla
Langley, Charles P(itman)
Langley, Wanda
Langston, Laura
Langton, Jane
Lankford, Mary D.
Lanthier, Jennifer
Larson, Hope
Larson, Ingrid D(ana)
Larson, Kirby
Lasenby, Jack
Lassiter, Rhiannon
Lauture, Denizé
Lawrence, Michael
Lawson, JonArno Burhans
Layne, Steven L.
Le Guin, Ursula K(roeber)
Leacock, Elspeth
Lee, Dennis (Beynon)
Lee, Sally
Lee, Sky
Lee, Tonya Lewis
Leese, Jennifer L. B.
Leeson, Robert (Arthur)
Lehne, Judith Logan
Leiner, Katherine
Lemieux, A(nne) C(onnelly)
Lennard, John (Chevening)
Lennon, Joan
Leo, Mabel R.
Leonard, Constance
Leroux-Hugon, Hélène
Lester, Julius
Levin, Betty (Lowenthal)
Levin, Miriam (Ramsfelder)
Levine, Gail Carson
Levitin, Sonia (Wolff)
Levoy, Myron
Levy, Constance
Levy, Elizabeth
Lewis, Gregg (Allan)
Lewis, J. Patrick
Lewis, Linda (Joy)
Lewis, Paeony
Lewis, Thomas P(arker)
Li, Leslie
Liatsos, Sandra Olson
Liles, Maurine Walpole
Lindenbaum, Pija
Lindgren, Barbro
Lindsay, Frederic
Lindsay, William
Lingard, Joan (Amelia)
Lipsyte, Robert (Michael)
Lisandrelli, Elaine Slivinski
Lisle, Janet Taylor
Lisle, Rebecca
Lithgow, John (Arthur)
Little, (Flora) Jean
Littleton, Mark (R.)
Lively, Penelope
Llewellyn, Sam
Logue, Mary

Lohans, Alison
Lomonaco, Palmyra
Longfellow, Layne (A.)
Loomis, Christine
Lord, John Vernon
Lorenz, Lee (Sharp)
Lorrimer, Claire
Lourie, Richard
Love, D. Anne
Love, Douglas
Lovegrove, James (Matthew
Henry)
Lowry, Lois (Hammersberg)
Lucas, Celia
Luckett, Dave
Luddy, Karon
Lunge-Larsen, Lise
Lunn, Janet (Louise Swoboda)
Lurie, Morris
Ly, Many
Lycett Green, Candida
Lynch, Janet Nichols
Lyon, Annabel
Lyon, George Ella
MAC
Macaulay, Teresa (E.)
MacDonald, Amy
Macdonald, Marianne
Macgoye, Marjorie Oludhe
Macintosh, Brownie
Mackay, Claire (Bacchus)
MacLachlan, Patricia
MacLean, Glynne
Macleod, Alison
MacLeod, Elizabeth
Macphail, Catherine
Maddigan, Beth
Madenski, Melissa (Ann)
Madsen, Ross Martin
Maestro, Giulio
Magee, Doug
Maggio, Mike
Magnus, Erica
Maguire, Gregory (Peter)
Mahy, Margaret
Maifair, Linda Lee
Maitland, Barbara
Malone, James Hiram
Mamet, David
Mandel, Peter (Bevan)
Mango, Karin N.
Mania, Cathy
Marcus, Leonard S.
Marcuse, Aída E.
Markham, Lynne
Marko, Katherine McGlade
Markoosie
Marks, Alan
Marks, Graham
Marks, Stan(ley)
Marlow, Joyce
Marsden, Carolyn
Marsden, John
Marshall, Janet (Perry)
Martchenko, Michael
Martin, Alex
Martin, Claire

Martin, Francesca
Martin, George R.R.
Martin, Jacqueline Briggs
Martin, Nora
Martin, Phyllis R(odgers)
Martinez, Joseph G. R.
Martini, Teri
Marton, Jirina
Mason, Adrienne
Mass, Wendy
Massie, Elizabeth
Masson, Sophie
Masters, Susan Rowan
Matas, Carol
Matera, Dary M.
Mathis, Sharon Bell
Matott, Justin
Matthews, L. S.
Mattingley, Christobel (Rose-
   mary)
Mayer, Mercer
Mayfield, Sue
Mayhar, Ardath (Hurst)
Maynard, Christopher
Mayo, Gretchen Will
Mazer, Anne
Mazer, Harry
McAlpine, Rachel (Taylor)
McArthur, Nancy
McAulay, Alex
McBratney, Sam
McCafferty, Jim
McCafferty, Maureen
McCann, Michelle R.
McCarthy, Colin (John)
McCarthy, Wil
McCaughrean, Geraldine (Jones)
McCaughren, Tom
McClure, Gillian Mary
McConduit, Denise Walter
McConnochie, Mardi
McCord, Patricia
McCoy, Glenn
McCue, Lisa (Emiline)
McCullough, Sharon Pierce
McCully, Emily Arnold
McCutcheon, Elsie (Mary Jack-
   son)
McCutcheon, John
McCutcheon, Sandy
McDaniel, Lurlene
McDermott, Jeanne
McDonald, Brix
McDonald, Collin
McDonald, Forrest
McDonald, Joyce
Mcdonnell, Patrick
McFall, Gardner
McFarland, Henry O.
McGhee, Hallie M.
Mcgill, Alice
McGill, Angus
McGough, Roger
McGrath, Barbara B(arbieri)
McKaughan, Larry (Scott)
McKay, Hilary
McKay, Sharon E.

McKee, David (John)
McKenna, Colleen
   O'Shaughnessy
McKenzie, Evan
McKinley, (Jennifer Carolyn)
   Robin
McKissack, Fredrick L(emuel)
McKissack, Patricia C(arwell)
McLarey, Myra
McLean, Virginia Overton
McLerran, Alice
McMaster, Juliet (Sylvia)
McNab, Claire
McNicoll, Sylvia (Marilyn)
McWilliams, Karen
Meaker, Marijane (Agnes)
Meeker, Clare Hodgson
Meeks, Christopher (Nelson)
Meeks, Esther MacBain
Melnikoff, Pamela (Rita)
Melton, Marliss
Meltzer, David
Melzack, Ronald
Menéndez, Ana (Maria)
Merrill, Jean (Fairbanks)
Merriman, Catherine
Messner, Michael A.
Metzenthen, David
Meyer, Carolyn
Meyerhoff, Jenny
Midda, Sara
Mikaelsen, Ben (John)
Miklowitz, Gloria D.
Miles, Betty
Miles, Keith
Miles, Victoria
Miller, Laura
Miller, Robert H.
Millhiser, Marlys
Milligan, Bryce
Millman, Isaac
Minahan, John A.
Minar, Barbra (Goodyear)
Minarik, Else H(olmelund)
Minor, Wendell G.
Mishica, Clare
Mitchard, Jacquelyn
Mitchell, Margaree King
Mitton, Tony
Mo, Timothy
Mochizuki, Ken
Moeyaert, Bart
Mohr, Nicholasa
Mole, John
Molina, Silvia
Moloney, James
Monesson, Harry S.
Montenegro, Laura Nyman
Montes, Marisa
Montpetit, Charles
Moodie, Craig
Moon, Nicola
Moore, Ishbel (Lindsay)
Moore, Lorrie
Moore, Robin
Moore, Stephanie Perry
Moranville, Sharelle Byars

Mordecai, Pamela (Claire)
Morgan, Alison M.
Morgan, Robin
Morgan, Stacy T(owle)
Morgenstern, Susie Hoch
Morozumi, Atsuko
Morpurgo, Michael
Morris, Timothy
Morrison, (Philip) Blake
Morrison, Bill
Morrison, Martha A.
Morriss, Frank
Morse, Melvin (L.)
Mosher, Richard
Mosley, Shelley Elizabeth
Moss, Jenny
Moss, Marissa
Moss, Miriam
Mowat, Claire (Angel Wheeler)
Mowat, Farley (McGill)
Moxley, Sheila
Muchmore, Jo Ann
Muehl, Lois Baker
Muir, Helen
Mullen, Michael
Muller, (Lester) Robin
Muniz, Olga M.
Munsch, Robert
Murphy, Claire Rudolf
Murphy, Jill (Frances)
Murphy, Shirley R(ousseau)
Murphy, Sylvia
Musgrave, Susan
Musto, Barry
Myers, Bill
Myers, Walter Dean
Näaslund, Göorel Kristina
Naden, Corinne J.
Nagy, Gloria
Naidoo, Beverley
Namioka, Lensey
Naylor, Phyllis Reynolds
Needle, Jan
Nelson, D. A. Ann
Nelson, Peter N.
Nelson, Theresa
Nethery, Mary
Newcome, Robert
Newkirk, Ingrid E.
Newman, Jerry
Newth, Mette
Newton, Suzanne
Nicholls, Sally
Nichols, Grace
Nicieza, Fabian
Nickel, Barbara
Niditch, Susan
Nilsson, Eleanor
Nilsson, Jenny Lind
Nimmo, Jenny
Nishimura, Kae
Nissman, Blossom S.
Nobisso, Josephine
Nolan, Han
Norfolk, Lawrence
Norman, Lilith
Norment, Lisa

Northeast, Brenda V(ictoria)
Numeroff, Laura Joffe
Nutt, Paul C.
Nye, Naomi Shihab
Nye, Robert
O'Brien, Edna
O'Callahan, Jay
O'Hara, Marjorie (Doreen)
O'Hare, Jeff(rey A.)
O'Keeffe, Frank
O'Leary, Patsy Baker
Oakley, Graham
Odaga, Asenath (Bole)
Odhiambo, David Nandi
Ogunyemi, Yemi D(iploman)
Okimoto, Jean Davies
Okorafor-Mbachu, Nnedi
Okoro, Anezi
Olaleye, Isaac O.
Oldfield, Jenny
Oldfield, Pamela
Oldham, June
Oliver, Maria Antònia
Olmsted, Robert W(alsh)
Olson, Arielle North
Ondego, Ogova
Oneal, Elizabeth
Opie, Iona
Oppel, Kenneth
Orenstein, Ronald I.
Orgel, Doris
Orlev, Uri
Orme, David John
Ormondroyd, Edward
Orr, Wendy
Osborne, Will
Osterweil, Adam
Ostow, Micol
Ottaviani, Jim
Oughton, Jerrie
Overton, Jenny (Margaret Mary)
Oxenbury, Helen
Pace, Alison
Pale ek, Libuše
Palin, Michael (Edward)
Panik, Sharon
Parke, Marilyn
Parker, Nancy W(inslow)
Parkinson, Siobhan
Parsons, Alexandra
Partridge, Jenny (Lilian)
Paterson, Katherine (Womeldorf)
Patneaude, David
Paton, Priscilla
Patron, Susan
Patten, Brian
Pattou, Edith
Paul, Ann Whitford
Paulsen, Gary
Pearce, Margaret
Pearce, Mary E.
Pears, Tim
Pearson, Kit
Peck, Dale
Peck, Richard (Wayne)
Peck, Sylvia
Peel, H(azel) M(ary)

Sim, Dorrith M.
Simmie, Lois (Ann)
Simmons, Jane
Simon, Francesca
Simon, Seymour
Simonds, Merilyn
Simpson, Myrtle Lillias
Sinclair, Andrew (Annandale)
Sinclair, Carla
Sinclair, Olga (Ellen)
Singer, Marilyn
Sington, Philip
Sinykin, Sheril C.
Sipherd, Ray
Siracusa, Catherine (Jane)
Sirimarco, Elizabeth
Sisson, Rosemary Anne
Slater, Jim
Slepian, Jan(ice B.)
Sloat, Teri
Slote, Alfred
Smarandache, Florentin
Smiley, Bob
Smith, Andrew Anselmo
Smith, Cynthia Leitich
Smith, Emma
Smith, Greg Leitich
Smith, Joan Gerarda
Smith, Lane
Smith, Marya
Smith, Patricia
Smith, Sandra Lee
Smith, Tim(othy R.)
Smith, Wanda VanHoy
Smith, William Jay
Smith-Ankrom, M. E.
Smith-Ayala, Emilie
Smither, Elizabeth
Smyth, Iain
Snellgrove, Laurence Ernest
Snicket, Lemony
Snyder, Zilpha Keatley
Sobel, Ileene Smith
Sobol, Donald J.
Sobott-Mogwe, Gaele
Sofer, Barbara
Softly, Barbara (Charmian)
Solheim, James
Soos, Troy
Sorenson, Margo
Spalding, Andrea
Sparkes, Ali
Speck, Nancy
Spelman, Cornelia Maude
Spier, Peter (Edward)
Spinelli, Jerry
Spivak, Dawnine
Spollen, Anne
Springer, Margaret
St. Antoine, Sara L.
St. George, Judith
Staats, Marilyn Dorn
Stamm, Peter
Standiford, Natalie
Stanley, Autumn
Stanley, Diane
Stanley, Jerry

Staunton, Ted
Staynes, Jill
Steel, Danielle
Steele, Mary
Steele, Philip
Stengel, Joyce A.
Stern, Steve
Stevens, Diane
Stevenson, James
Stevenson, Sucie
Steward, H. Leighton
Stewart, Gail B.
Stewart, Mary (Florence Elinor)
Stewart, Sarah
Stinchecum, Amanda Mayer
Stine, Catherine
Stokoe, E(dward) G(eorge)
Stolz, Joëlle
Stone, Robert (Anthony)
Stops, Sue
Storey, Margaret
Strasser, Todd
Strauss, Gwen
Strauss, Susan (Elizabeth)
Strelkoff, Tatiana
Strickland, Craig (A.)
Striegel, Jana
Stroud, Bettye
Stroud, Jonathan
Stuart, Alexander
Sturtevant, Katherine
Stutson, Caroline
Stynes, Barbara White
Suen, Anastasia
Sumner, (Edith) Aurea
Sun, Chyng Feng
Susi, Geraldine Lee
Sussex, Lucy (Jane)
Sutherland, Margaret
Sutton, Jane
Svendsen, Linda
Swain, Gwenyth
Sweeney, Matthew
Swindells, Robert (Edward)
Swope, Sam
Sydor, Colleen
Synge, Ursula
Szekeres, Cyndy
Szymanski, Lois
Taback, Simms
Tafuri, Nancy
Tagg, Christine Elizabeth
Takahashi, Rumiko
Takayama, Sandi
Tamar, Erika
Tan, Amy
Tanen, Sloane A.
Tapahonso, Luci
Tashjian, Janet
Tate, Eleanora E(laine)
Taylor, Allegra
Taylor, Andrew (John Robert)
Taylor, Debbie A.
Taylor, Mildred D.
Taylor, Patrick
Taylor, Paul F.
Taylor, William

Teague, Mark (Christopher)
Temple, Charles
Terris, Susan
Theroux, Paul
Thomas, Abigail
Thomasma, Kenneth R.
Thomassie, Tynia
Thompson, Kate
Thompson, Richard
Thomson, Pat
Thurman, Mark (Gordon Ian)
Thwaite, Ann (Barbara)
Tingle, Tim
Tingum, Janice
Todd, Pamela A.
Toews, Rita Y.
Toksvig, Sandi
Tolbert, Steve
Tomalin, Ruth
Tomkins, Jasper
Tong, Gary S.
Topek, Susan Remick
Toriyama, Akira
Totten, Mark D.
Townsend, John Rowe
Tracy, Kristen
Tremain, Rose
Triggs, Tony D.
Tripp, Valerie
Trivizas, Eugene
Trott, Betty
Trottier, Maxine
Trout, Robert J(ay)
Trueit, Trudi Strain
Trueman, Terry
Tubb, Kristin O'Donnell
Tugendhat, Julia
Tulloch, Richard (George)
Tunnell, Michael O('Grady)
Turco, Lewis (Putnam)
Turner, Ann (Warren)
Turner, Megan Whalen
Turner, Robyn
Tuttle, Lisa
U'Ren, Andrea
Underdahl, S. T.
Ure, Jean
Ury, Allen B.
Vail, Rachel
Valentine, James
Valentino, Serena
Vallbona, Rima de
van Allsburg, Chris
Van Camp, Katie
Van Der Meer, Ron
van Heerden, Etienne
van Laan, Nancy
Van Rynbach, Iris
Vanak, Bonnie
Vanasse, Deb
Vanderwal, Andrew H.
Vapnyar, Lara
Vasta, Edward
Vatikiotis, Michael R. J.
Vaughan, Brian K.
Vaughan, Marcia (K.)
Vaughn, Patrika

Vejjajiva, Jane
Velásquez, Gloria (Louise)
Velez, Ivan
Verboven, Agnes
Verniero, Joan C.
Verrier, Suzanne
Vertreace-Doody, Martha Modena
Vincent, Erin
Vincenzi, Penny
Viorst, Judith
Voigt, Cynthia
Von Ahnen, Katherine
Vornholt, John
Waber, Bernard
Wachtel, Shirley Russak
Waddell, Martin
Waddington-Feather, John Joseph
Wadsworth, Ginger
Wagner, Sharon Blythe
Wahl, Jan
Waisman, Sergio Gabriel
Waite, Michael P(hillip)
Walden, Mark
Walker, Kate
Walkerdine, Valerie
Wall, Kathryn R.
Wallace, Barbara Brooks
Wallace, Ian
Wallace, John
Wallace, Karen
Wallace, Richard (Alan)
Waller, Jane (Ashton)
Walsh, Jill Paton
Walsh, Robb
Walsh, Suella
Walsh Shepherd, Donna
Walton, Rick
Ward, Ken
Wardlaw, Lee
Ware, Cheryl
Warner, Marina
Warner, Sally
Warren, Cathy
Warren, Sandra K.
Waterfield, Robin Anthony
  Herschel
Waterhouse, Carole A.
Waters, John F(rederick)
Waters, Tony
Watkins, William John
Watson, Clyde
Watson, Esther Pearl
Watson, Ken D.
Watson, Stephanie
Waugh, Sylvia
Wayman, Vivienne
Weales, Gerald
Weatherford, Carole Boston
Weaver-Gelzer, Charlotte
Weeks, Sarah
Welch, Sheila Kelly
Welcher, Rosalind
Weldon, Fay
Welford, Sue
Wellington, Monica
Wells, Rosemary
Welsbacher, Anne

Basch, Rachel
Base, Graeme (Rowland)
Bass, Ronald
Bat-Ami, Miriam
Bataille, Christophe
Bates, Judy Fong
Batnitzky, Leora
Baude, Jeannine
Bauer, Marion Dane
Bauer, Tricia
Bauman, Christian
Bawcutt, Priscilla (June)
Baxter, Mary Lynn
Baxter, Stephen
Bayda, Ezra
Beale, Fleur
Beaman, Joyce Proctor
Bear, Elizabeth
Beard, Darleen Bailey
Beard, Philip
Beauclerk, Charles
Bechard, Margaret
Beck, Ian
Beck, Mary L. (Giraudo)
Becker, Jürgen
Bedford, Deborah
Bedford, Martyn
Beere, Peter
Beha, Christopher R.
Behr, Ira Steven
Behrens, Ellen
Beifuss, John
Belasen, Amy
Belbin, David
Belgum, Erik
Belin, Esther G.
Bell, Hilary
Bell, Madison Smartt
Bell, William
Belli, Gioconda
Belting, Hans
Bemrose, John
Benaïssa, Slimane
Bender, Bert
Benedict, Helen
Benedict, Pinckney
Bennett, Cherie
Bennett, Holly
Bennett, Joe
Bennett, R.G. Stephen
Bensley, Connie
Bensman, David
Benson, Jackson J.
Benson, Judi
Benson, Peter
Benson, Richard
Benton, Jim
Benvenuto, Christine
Benz, Derek
Berger, John (Peter)
Berger-Kiss, Andres
Berges, Emily Trafford
Bergland, Martha
Bergman, Tamar
Bergon, Frank
Berkoff, Steven
Berman, Sanford

Bernard, Kenneth
Bernard, Patricia
Bernardini, Joe
Bernardo, Anilu
Bernhardt, William
Berry, Carole
Berry, Linda
Berry, Philippa
Bertagna, Julie
Bertematti, Richard
Bertrand, Diane Gonzales
Besner, Neil K.
Bettini, Maurizio
Beverley, Jo
Bhattacharya, Nalinaksha
Bianchi, Eugene Carl
Bieman, Elizabeth
Bienes, Nicholas Peter
Bierds, Linda
Biggs, Mary
Billington, James H(adley)
Billington, Rachel
Billson, Anne
Binchy, Maeve
Binnema, Theodore
Binns, Michael Ferrers Elliott
Birdsell, Sandra
Birmingham, Maisie
Bishop, Michael
Bissett, Bill
Bittner, Rosanne
Bjarkman, Peter C(hristian)
Blacklock, Dianne
Blackman, Malorie
Blaine, Michael
Blaise, Clark
Blake, Jon
Blake, Mark R.
Blamires, Harry
Blanchard, Stephen (Thomas)
Blank, Jessica
Blauner, Peter
Bledsoe, Alex
Bledsoe, Glen L(eonard)
Bledsoe, Karen E(lizabeth)
Blegen, Daniel M.
Blessington, Francis C(harles)
Blevins, Meredith
Blixt, David
Block, Francesca (Lia)
Block, Lawrence
Block, Thomas H(arris)
Block, Valerie
Bloodworth-Thomason, Linda
Bloom, Rebecca (S.)
Bloom, Steven
Bloor, Edward (William)
Blos, Joan W.
Blount, Roy (Alton)
Blume, Judy
Boast, Philip
Bocardo, Claire
Bock, Charles
Bodett, Tom
Bohlmeijer, Arno
Bohnhoff, Maya Kaathryn
Bojanowski, Marc

Bök, Christian
Bolden, Tonya
Boldt, Laurence G.
Boles, Philana Marie
Bonansinga, Jay R.
Bond, Nancy
Bonomelli, Charles J(ames)
Booth, Stanley
Borchard, Therese Johnson
Bordo, Susan (Rebecca)
Bortnik, Aida (Beatriz)
Bottke, Allison Gappa
Bottoms, David
Bourgeois, Paulette
Bovaird, Anne E(lizabeth)
Bowen, John (Griffith)
Bowering, George
Bowering, Marilyn (Ruthe)
Bowers, John
Bowers, Terrell L.
Bowker, Gordon
Bowler, Tim
Bowyer, Mathew Justice
Boyd, Blanche McCrary
Boyd, Candy Dawson
Boyd, Carl
Boyle, Josephine
Boym, Svetlana
Boyne, Walter J(ames)
Bradford, Barbara Taylor
Bradford, Karleen
Bradley, John Ed(mund)
Bradley, Shelley
Bradshaw, Anne
Braffet, Kelly
Brake, Mark L.
Brallier, Kate
Bramly, Serge
Brand, Dionne
Brandenberg, Franz
Brandewyne, Rebecca
Brandon, Ruth
Brandstetter, Alois
Brant, Jo-Ann A.
Brashear, Jean
Braswell, Elizabeth
Brault, Jacques
Braun, Matt(hew)
Braun, Richard Emil
Braund, Kathryn E. Holland
Braunmuller, A(lbert) R(ichard)
Braverman, Melanie
Brayfield, Celia
Brenna, Duff
Brennan, Frank
Brennan, J(ames) H(erbert)
Brenner, Mayer Alan
Brett, Peter V.
Brewer, Jeannie A.
Brice, Carleen
Brichoux, Karen
Bride, Johnny Mack
Bridgers, Sue Ellen (Hunsucker)
Bridges, Laurie
Briggs, Asa
Bright, Freda
Bright, Myron H.

Brimson, Dougie
Briskin, Jacqueline
Bristow, Robert O'Neil
Brittain, C. Dale
Britton, Celia (Margaret)
Brockway, Connie
Broderick, Damien
Brodeur, Paul (Adrian)
Broer, Lawrence R(ichard)
Brooke, William J.
Brooks, Andrée (Nicole) Aelion
Brooks, Betty
Brooks, Bruce (Delos)
Brooks, Fairleigh
Brooks, Kevin M.
Broomall, Robert W(alter)
Brophy, Grace
Brophy, Sarah
Broughton, T. Alan
Brouwer, Sigmund
Brown, Brooks
Brown, Dan
Brown, Gita
Brown, J(oseph) P(aul)
  S(ummers)
Brown, John
Brown, Mary Ward
Brown, Richard E.
Brown, Roberta Simpson
Brown, Sandra
Brown, Steve
Browne, Gerald A(ustin)
Browne, Hester
Browning, Pamela
Brownley, James
Bruchac, Joseph
Bruckner, Pascal
Brugman, Alyssa (F.)
Bryant, Sharon
Brzezinski, Matthew
Buccieri, Lisa Rojany
Buchanan, Roberta
Bucheister, Patt
Buckley, Gail Lumet
Bucknall, Barbara Jane
Bucuvalas, Tina
Buechner, (Carl) Frederick
Buffett, Jimmy
Buffie, Margaret
Bujold, Lois McMaster
Bujor, Flavia
Bukiet, Melvin Jules
Bulock, Lynn
Bunting, (Anne) Eve(lyn Bolton)
Burdett, John
Burgess, Colin
Burgh, Anita Lorna
Burke, Martyn
Burke, Shannon
Burks, Brian
Burman, Carina
Burney, Claudia Mair
Burningham, John (Mackintosh)
Burns, Anna
Burns, Jim
Burns, Marilyn
Burns, Ralph

Index To Writing Categories

Cummings, Pat
Cummins, Jeanine
Cunningham, Marion (Elizabeth)
Curnutt, Kirk
Curry, Jane (Louise)
Curtis, Christopher (Paul)
Cusk, Rachel
Cuthbert, Margaret
Cutler, Stan
Cytowic, Richard E(dmund)
D'Adamo, Francesco
D'Ambrosio, Charles
D'Ath, Justin
Dahlie, Hallvard
Dailey, Janet
Daitch, Susan
Dalsimer, Katherine
Dalton, Sheila
Daly, Brenda O.
Danakas, John
Dangarembga, Tsitsi
Daniels, Jeff
Dann, Jack
Danticat, Edwidge
Darke, Marjorie (Sheila)
Darling, Diana
Dart, Iris Rainer
Dart-Thornton, Cecilia
Darty, Peggy
Dasgupta, Amit
Davenport, Roger (Hamilton)
David, James F.
Davidar, David
Davidson, Craig
Davidson, Dana
Davidson, Pamela
Davidson, Sol M.
Davies, Linda
Davies, Peter Ho
Davies, Stephanie
Davies-Mitchell, Margaret (Con-
    stance)
Davis, (Elvis) Clark
Davis, Alan (R.)
Davis, Albert Belisle
Davis, Donald
Davis, Heather
Davis, Lindsey
Davis, Maggie S.
Davis, Nageeba
Dawe, Margaret
Dawson, Geralyn
Dawson, Greg
Day, Cathy
Day, Edward C.
de Blasi, Marlena
de Bono, Douglas
De La Cruz, Melissa
De Marinis, Rick
de Vasconcelos, Erika
De Vries, Rachel (Guido)
Dean (Dyer-Bennett), Pamela
    (Collins)
Deans, Sis Boulos
Dearie, John
Dearing, Sarah
Deaver, Jeffery Wilds

Deaver, Julie Reece
Dee, Barbara
Deem, James M(organ)
DeJohn, Jacqueline
Delahaye, Michael (John)
Delaney, Norman
Delano, Anthony
Delbanco, Francesca
DeMille, Nelson (Richard)
DePoy, Phillip
Dereske, Jo
Derksen, Jeff
Desai, Anita
Desai, Boman
Desena, Carmine
Deshpande, Chris
DeSpain, Pleasant
Desplechin, Marie
Desputeaux, Hélène
Deuker, Carl
DeVincent-Hayes, Nan
Devlin, Albert J.
DeWeese, Gene
Di Blasi, Debra
Diamant, Anita
Dibble, J(ames) Birney
Dickinson, Peter
Didion, Joan
Dieterich, Michele M.
Dietz, Peter (John)
Diller, Harriett
DiMarco, Cris K. A.
Dinello, Paul
Diski, Jenny
Diver, Lucienne
Dix, Shane
Dixon, Keith
Dixon, Stephen
Dobson, Jill
Doctorow, E(dgar) L(awrence)
Docx, Edward
Dodds, Bill
Doerr, Anthony
Doherty, Berlie
Dokey, Cameron
Dolan, Harry
Dolan, Sean J.
Dolling-Mann, Patricia May
Donaldson, Joan
Donleavy, J(ames) P(atrick)
Donn, Linda
Donnelly, Jane
Donnelly, Joe
Donovan, Katie
Dooley, David (Allen)
Dooling, Richard (Patrick)
Dorf, Fran
Dorflinger, Carolyn
Dorkin, Evan
Dorner, Marjorie
Dorrestein, Renate
Dorros, Arthur (M.)
dos Santos, Joyce Audy
Douglas, L. Warren
Dowell, Frances O'Roark
Downes, David A(nthony)
Downie, Mary Alice

Downing, David A(lmon)
Doyle, Brian
Drabble, Margaret
Dracup, Angela
Drake, Albert (Dee)
Drakuli , Slavenka
Draper, Polly
Draper, Sharon Mills
Draut, Tamara
Dressler, Mylène
Drexler, Rosalyn
Drucker, Lisa
Drucker, Mort
Drummond, June
Dubens, Eugene (M.)
Duberstein, Helen (Laura)
Dubosarsky, Ursula
Dubus, Andre
Duder, Tessa
Due, Tananarive
Dueck, Adele
Duey, Kathleen
Duff, Alan
Duffy, James H(enry)
Dufresne, John
Duncan, Christine H.
Duncan, Glen
Duncan, Lois
Duncan, Patrick Sheane
Duncan, Sarah
Dunlap, Susan D. (Sullivan)
Dunn, Peter Norman
Dunn, Suzannah
Durant, Michael J.
Durban, Pam
Durcan, Liam
Durrell, Julie
Durst, Sarah Beth
Dutton, J. T.
Dwight, Jeffry
Dyer, Sarah L.
Eames, Anne
Earl, Maureen
Earley, Pete
Earley, Tony
Earls, Nick
Easton, Malcolm Coleman
Ebbett, Eve
Ebisch, Glen Albert
Echenique, Alfredo Bryce
Eckler, Rebecca
Eddie, David
Ede, Piers Moore
Edgerton, Teresa (Ann)
Edson, J(ohn) T(homas)
Edson, Russell
Edwards, Anne
Edwards, Johanna
Edwards, Larry
Edwards, Michael B.
Edwards, P. D.
Egan, Greg
Egli, Ida Rae
Ehrlich, Amy
Eichler, Selma
Eidson, Thomas
Eisner, Michael Alexander

Elegant, Robert (Sampson)
Elegant, Simon
Elisha, Ron
Elium, Jeanne (Ann)
Ellenberg, Jordan S.
Ellerbeck, Rosemary
Ellingwood, Ken
Elliott, Elaine M.
Ellis, David
Ellis, Donald
Ellis, Jamellah
Ellis, Kate
Ellis, Keith
Ellis, Sarah
Elmer, Robert
Elmslie, Kenward
Else, Barbara
Eltringham, S(tewart) K(eith)
Emerson, Earl W.
Emery, Clayton
Emmet, Alan
Emmett, Ayala
Engdahl, Sylvia L(ouise)
Engel, Monroe
Engelberg, Alan (D.)
Enger, Leif
Engle, Margarita
Engleman, Paul
English, Allan D.
English, Sharon
Enquist, Per Olov
Ensor, Robert
Ephron, Nora
Eprile, Tony
Epstein, Joseph
Erdrich, Louise
Ereira, Alan
Erickson, Carolly
Erlbach, Arlene
Erskine, Kathryn
Eskridge, Kelley
Espaillat, Rhina P.
Essex, Karen
Esterhazy, Peter
Estrada, Rita Clay
Evans, Alan
Evans, Liz
Evans, Richard
Eyre, Peter
Fahnestock, Todd
Fahy, Thomas
Faig, Kenneth W(alter)
Fainlight, Ruth
Falcon, Mark
Falconer, Helen
Falk, Thomas H(einrich)
Falla, Jonathan
Fan, Nancy Yi
Fancher, Jane S(uzanne)
Farish, Terry
Farmer, Penelope (Jane)
Farnsworth, Clyde
Farr, Diane
Farthing-Knight, Catherine
Faust, Irvin
Fehler, Gene
Feiffer, Jules

Gosling, Paula
Goss, Theodora
Goto, Hiromi
Gottlieb, Daphne
Gough, Laurence
Gough, Sue
Gould, John
Gould, Steven (Charles)
Gowan, Lee
Grab, Daphne
Grace, Patricia (Frances)
Graff, Lisa
Graham, Jefferson
Gran, Sara
Granger, (Patricia) Ann
Granger, Michele
Grant, Andrew
Grant, Anne Underwood
Grant, Cynthia D.
Grant, Graeme
Grant, Pete
Grant, Richard
Grant, Vanessa
Grant-Adamson, Lesley (Hey-
cock)
Grau, Shirley Ann
Graves, Ralph (Augustus)
Graves, Sarah
Gray, Andrew
Gray, Dulcie
Gray, Richard J(ohn)
Gray, Robert (Curtis)
Grayson, Emily
Greacen, Lavinia
Greeley, Andrew (Moran)
Green, Angela
Green, Cliff(ord)
Green, Connie Jordan
Green, Duncan
Green, Joseph (Lee)
Green, Norman
Green, Terence M(ichael)
Green, Timothy
Greenberg, Alvin
Greene, Bette
Greene, Constance C(larke)
Greene, Harlan
Greene, Jacqueline Dembar
Greene, Rhonda Gowler
Greene, Sheldon L.
Greenhall, Ken
Greeno, Gayle
Greenwald, Sheila
Greenwood, Barbara
Greer, Andrew Sean
Gregg, Clark
Gregor, Arthur
Gregor, Neil
Gregory, Kristiana
Gregory, Susanna
Gresham, Stephen
Gresser, Seymour
Grey, Anthony
Griesemer, John
Griffin, Adele
Griffin, Peni R(ae)
Griffin, Steven A(rthur)

Griffith, Thomas Gwynfor
Griffiths, Niall
Griggs, Terry
Grimes, Martha
Grimes, Tom
Grindal, Richard
Gross, Philip (John)
Grossinger, Harvey L.
Grossman, Austin
Grossman, David
Grover, Wayne
Gruenenfelder, Kim
Grundy, Joan
Grusky, Scott T.
Guare, John
Guaspari, John
Guest, Jacqueline
Guest, Judith
Gugler, Laurel Dee
Gunn, Eileen
Gunn, Robin Jones
Gunter, Pete (Addison Yancey)
Guppy, Stephen (Anthony)
Gurganus, Allan
Gurr, Michael
Guterson, David
Gutteridge, Don(ald George)
Guy, Rosa (Cuthbert)
Guyatt, Nicholas
Gwyn, Richard
Gwynn, R(obert) S(amuel)
Haas, Dan
Haber, Karen
Habila, Helon
Hackl, Erich
Haddock, Lisa (Robyn)
Haffenden, John
Hagedorn, Jessica Tarahata
Hagy, Alyson
Hahn, Mary Downing
Hahn, Michael T.
Haines, Kathryn Miller
Hairston, William
Hakak, Lev
Hale, John
Hale, Robert D(avid)
Halkin, Ariela
Hall, Ann C.
Hall, Donald (Andrew)
Hall, Lincoln
Hall, Martha Lacy
Hall, Parnell
Hall, Rodney
Hallahan, William H(enry)
Halliday, Gemma
Hallinan, Timothy
Halperin, James L(ewis)
Halpern, Jake
Halvorson, Marilyn
Hamilton, Carol (Jean Barber)
Hamilton, Hugo
Hamilton, Jane
Hamilton, Marybeth
Hamilton, Peter F.
Hamm, Diane Johnston
Hankin, C(herry) A(nne)
Hannah, Sophie

Hannan, Peter
Hannigan, Katherine
Hansen, Brooks
Hansen-Hill, N. D.
Harada, Masako
Harding, Robyn
Harling, Robert
Harmel, Kristin
Harnack, Curtis
Harnum, Robert
Haroian-Guerin, Gil
Harper, Jo
Harper, Rachel M.
Harper, Susan (Rice)
Harrington, Kathleen
Harris, (Theodore) Wilson
Harris, Anne L.
Harris, Christine
Harris, Claire
Harris, Elizabeth
Harris, Rosemary (Jeanne)
Harrison, Harry
Harrison, Jim
Harrison, Kim
Harrison, Sue
Harrison, Suzan
Harrower, Elizabeth
Hart, Alison
Hart, Carolyn G(impel)
Hart, Lenore
Harte, Lara
Harter, Karen
Hartnett, Sonya
Harvey, Clay
Harvey, John
Harvey, Kenneth J.
Harvor, Elisabeth
Harwood, John
Haseley, Dennis
Haslam, Gerald William
Hastings, Michael
Hatch, Michael F.
Hatoum, Milton
Hattersley, Roy (Sydney George)
Hatton, Caroline
Haug, James
Haugen, Hayley Mitchell
Havazelet, Ehud
Haverty, Anne
Hawes, Louise
Hawke, Rosanne Joy
Hawke, Simon
Hawkins, Anne Hunsaker
Hawksley, Lucinda
Hay, Samuel A.
Hay, Sheridan
Hayashi, Nancy
Hayes, Daniel
Hayes, Rosemary
Hayman, Carol Bessent
Haynes, C. Rayfield
Haynes, David
Hays, Tony
Haywood, Gar Anthony
Hazuka, Tom
Head, Dominic
Headley, Jason

Headley, Victor
Healy, Jeremiah
Hearn, Julie
Hearon, Shelby
Heath, Lorraine
Heckert, Connie K(aye Delp)
Heffron, Dorris
Heidel, R. Andrew
Hein, Christoph
Heinrich, Will
Heisel, Sharon E(laine)
Heitzmann, Kristen
Helgeland, Brian
Heller, Zoë
Hellström, Börge
Hellyer, Jill
Helmer, Diana Star
Helprin, Mark
Hely, Sara
Hemingway, Lorian
Henderson, Meg
Hendricks, Patricia
Hendry, Diana
Heng, Liu
Henke, Shirl
Henley, Arthur
Henry, Maeve
Henry, Sue
Hentoff, Nat(han Irving)
Herbach, Geoff
Herbert, James
Herman, Richard
Hermann, Iselin C.
Hermes, Patricia
Herndon, Ernest
Herrin, Lamar
Herrmanns, Ralph
Herron, William G.
Herschler, Mildred Barger
Hershey, Kathleen M.
Hershey, Olive
Herzig, Alison Cragin
Hess, Joan
Hesse, Karen
Hessinger, Rodney
Hester, Katherine L.
Hettche, Thomas
Heuer, Karsten
Hewett, Joan
Heyes, (Nancy) Eileen
Hezlep, William (Earl)
Hiaasen, Carl
Hicken, Mandy
Hiçyilmaz, Gaye
Higgins, Simon (Richard)
Higginsen, Vy
Higgs, Liz Curtis
High, Linda Oatman
Highway, Tomson
Hilderbrand, Elin
Hildreth, Denise
Hill, Anthony (Robert)
Hill, David
Hill, Ingrid
Hill, Janet Muirhead
Hill, Justin
Hill, Laban Carrick

Hill, Marion Moore
Hill, Pamela
Hill, Reginald (Charles)
Hill, Russell
Hill, Thomas
Hill, Tracey
Hillman, Richard S.
Hilton, Margery
Hinde, Thomas
Hines, (Melvin) Barry
Hinton, Lynne
Hinton, S(usan) E(loise)
Hislop, Victoria
Ho, Minfong
Hoban, Russell
Hobbs, Valerie
Hockensmith, Steve
Hocking, Mary (Eunice)
Hodgins, Jack
Hoehne, Marcia
Hoestlandt, Jo(celyne)
Hoffman, Mat
Hogan, Mary
Hogan, Michael William
Holbrook, Teri
Holeman, Linda
Holland, David
Hollander, David
Hollingsworth, A. B.
Hollingsworth, Margaret
Holman, Sheri
Holmes, B(ryan) J(ohn)
Holmes, Sara Lewis
Holstad, Scott Cameron
Holt, David
Holt, Michael (Paul)
Holtz, Nairne
Holub, Joan
Homsher, Deborah
Hond, Paul
Hone, Joseph
Honeycutt, Natalie
Hooley, D(aniel) M.
Hooper, Maureen Brett
Hopkins, Cathy
Hopkins, Jackie (Mims)
Hopping Egan, Lorraine
Horan, Nancy
Hornby, Nick
Horniman, Joanne
Horovitz, Michael
Horowitz, Renee B(arbara)
Horspool, David
Horton, David (Edward)
Horvath, Betty
Hoskyns, Tam
Hosseini, Khaled
Houghton, Gordon
House, Tom
Houston, Gail Turley
Houston, Gloria
Howard, David M.
Howard, Maureen
Howard, Tracie
Howarth, Lesley
Howarth, William (Louis)
Howe, LeAnne

Howe, Marie
Howe, Melodie Johnson
Howe, Muriel
Howker, Janni
Howland, Ethan
Hoy, Linda
Hoyem, Andrew
Hubbard, Woodleigh Marx
Hucker, Hazel
Hudak, Michal
Hudgens, Dallas
Hughes, Dean
Hughes, Phillip William
Hughes, Richard (Edward)
Hughes, Shirley
Hugon, Anne
Huisinga, Roger
Humphreys, Emyr (Owen)
Humphreys, Helen (Caroline)
Hunt, Angela Elwell
Hunt, Samantha (J.)
Hunter, Jessie Prichard
Hurwitz, Johanna (Frank)
Husain, Shahrukh
Huss, Sandy
Hutchins, J. C.
Hutchins, Pat
Hutton, John (Harwood)
Huyler, Frank
Hynes, Joel
Hynes, Pat
Hyzy, Julie
Iakovou, Takis
Iannuzzi, John Nicholas
Ibbitson, John Perrie
Ifill, Sherrilyn A.
Iida, Deborah
Ike, Vincent Chukwuemeka
Ilie, Paul
Ingman, Nicholas
Inkpen, Mick
Intrator, Sam M.
Ireland, David
Irvine, Angela
Irving, John (Winslow)
Isaacs, Anne
Isaacs, Susan
Isegawa, Moses
Iyer, Pico
Jablonski, Carla
Jackman, Stuart (Brooke)
Jackson, Edwardo
Jackson, Lisa
Jackson, Sheneska
Jacobs, Barbara
Jacobs, Laura
Jaeck, Lois Marie
Jaffee, Annette Williams
Jakes, John
James, Brian
James, Caryn
James, Kelvin Christopher
James, Reina
Jandrey, G. Davies
Janeczko, Paul B(ryan)
Janes, J(oseph) Robert
Janko, James

Janover, Caroline (Davis)
Janowitz, Tama
Jaramillo, Stephan
Jauncey, James
Javernick, Ellen
Jen, Gish
Jenkins, Amy
Jenkins, George
Jenkins, T(erence) A(ndrew)
Jennings, Maureen
Jennings, Paul
Jennings, Phillip E.
Jensen, Emma
Jensen, Kathryn
Jensen, Muriel
Jensen, Ruby Jean
Jerman, Jerry
Jernigan, Brenda K.
Jhabvala, Ruth Prawer
Jin, Ha
Jinks, Catherine
Jobs, Daniel Steve
Jocelyn, Marthe
Johansen, Iris
Johnson, Annabel (Jones)
Johnson, Charles R(ichard)
Johnson, Cherry L(urae) F(lake)
Johnson, Chester L.
Johnson, Greg
Johnson, Je'Caryous
Johnson, Kathleen Jeffrie
Johnson, Maureen
Johnson, R(odney) M(arcus)
Johnson, Rob
Johnson, Sandy
Johnson, Susan (Ruth)
Johnston, Joan
Johnston, Julie
Johnstone, Nick
Jolin, Paula
Jonaitis, Aldona
Jonell, Lynne
Jones, Allan Frewin
Jones, Christopher S.
Jones, D(ouglas) G(ordon)
Jones, Daryl (Emrys)
Jones, David Lee
Jones, Evan (Lloyd)
Jones, Gayl
Jones, Gwyneth A(nn)
Jones, J(on) Sydney
Jones, Jill
Jones, Larry
Jones, Linda Winstead
Jones, Madison
Jones, Matthew F.
Jones, Naomi Brooks
Jones, R(obert) M(aynard)
Jones, Ted
Jongman, Mariken
Jooste, Pamela
Jordan, Sherryl
Jordan-Lake, Joy
Joseph, Henry
Joyce, Graham
Juarez, Tina
Judd, Alan

Judson, D. Daniel
Jurmain, Suzanne
Just, Ward
Ka, Olivier
Kabaservice, Geoffrey (M.)
Kachtick, Keith
Kafka, Kimberly
Kalin, Jim
Kalish, Irma
Kallen, Stuart A(rnold)
Kallgren, Beverly Hayes
Kamau, Kwadwo Agymah
Kandel, Susan
Kane, Penny
Kanter, Lynn
Kaplan, Jonathan
Kaplan, Nelly
Kaplan, Steven L.
Kaplan-Maxfield, Thomas
Kappes, Marcianne
Karem, Jeff
Karlin, Daniel
Karodia, Farida
Karon, Jan
Karr, Kathleen
Kashua, Sayed
Katin, Miriam
Katz, Steve
Katz, Welwyn Wilton
Kauffman, Janet
Kauffmann, Stanley
Kaufmann, Dovid Yisroel Ber
Kavanagh, P(atrick) J(oseph)
Kay, Betty Carlson
Kay, Elizabeth
Kaye, Geraldine
Kazantzis, Judith
Keaney, Brian
Keech, Thomas (Walton)
Keefauver, Larry
Keegan, John E.
Keens-Douglas, Richardo
Keith, Julie (Houghton)
Kelbaugh, Gretchen
Kelleher, Victor Michael Kitchener
Kelley, Douglas
Kellogg, Marne Davis
Kellogg, Steven
Kelly, Clint
Kelly, Ronald
Kelman, James
Kelman, Judith (Ann)
Kelsay, Michael
Kemp, (Bernard) Peter
Kemprecos, Paul
Kendall, Carol
Kendrick, Beth
Kennealy, Jerry
Kennedy, A(lison) L.
Kennedy, Pagan
Kennedy, Thomas E.
Kennemore, Tim
Kenton, Warren
Kershen, (L.) Michael
Kessler, Julia Braun
Keyes, Daniel

Keys, Mary M.
Keyserlingk, Robert H.
Khan, Adib
Khan, Rukhsana
Kherdian, David
Khoury-Ghata, Vénus
Kidd, Paul
Kiernan, Pauline
Kihn, Greg
Kilpatrick, Alan Edwin
Kilroy, Thomas
Kilworth, Garry
Kimbriel, Katharine Eliska
Kimmel, Daniel M.
Kimmel, Elizabeth Cody
Kindl, Patrice
King, A. S.
King, Cynthia
King, Daren
King, Joy
King, Mia Hsu
King, Wilma
Kingsbury, Donald (Macdonald)
Kingsolver, Barbara
Kingston, Christina
Kinnell, Galway
Kinney, Jeff
Kinsella, W(illiam) P(atrick)
Kirchner, Bharti
Kirk-Greene, Christopher
Kirkbright, Suzanne
Kirkland, Martha
Kissing, Steve
Kitchen, Bert
Kiteley, Brian
Kittredge, William
Klam, Matthew
Klass, Sheila Solomon
Klavan, Andrew
Klaveness, Jan O'Donnell
Kleiman, Ed
Klein, Adam
Klein, Marcus
Klein, Matthew
Klein, Rachel S.
Klein, Zachary
Klemm, Barry
Klempner, Joseph T(eller)
Kluger, Steve
Knecht, Robert Jean
Knight, Alanna (Cleet)
Knight, E. E.
Knight, Lynne
Knight, Roger
Knowles, Jo
Knox, Elizabeth (Fiona)
Koertge, Ron(ald)
Kogawa, Joy Nozomi
Koja, Kathe
Kolbaba, Ginger
Koller, Jackie French
Kollin, Eytan
Kolpen, Jana (Fayne)
Konig, Susan
Konigsberg, Bill
Koning, (Angela) Christina
Korelitz, Jean Hanff

Korman, Bernice
Kositsky, Lynne
Koski, Mary B(ernadette)
Koslow, Sally
Kossman, Nina
Kourilsky, Françoise
Krahn, Betina
Kramer, Lotte
Kramp, Michael
Kraus, Joanna H.
Krauss, Nicole
Kricorian, Nancy
Krinard, Susan
Krinsky, Natalie
Krisher, Trudy (B.)
Krizan, Kim
Kroll, Virginia L(ouise)
Kroninger, Stephen
Kropp, Paul
Krouse, Erika Dawn
Krovatin, Christopher
Krueger, Lesley
Krüger, Michael
Krusoe, Jim
Kuberski, Philip
Kuczkir, Mary
Kumin, Maxine
Kunzru, Hari
Kupfer, Allen C.
Kuppner, Frank
Kurz, Ron
Kushner, Lawrence
Kuvshinoff, Boris W.
La Fortune, Knolly Stephen
La Salle, Peter
Lacefield, Lori
Lachner, Dorothea
Lackey, Kris
Lackey, Mercedes R.
Ladd, Linda
Ladd, Louise
LaFaye, A(lexandria R. T.)
Lafoy, Leslie
Lain, Douglas
Laird, Holly A.
Laird, Nick
Lake, M. D.
Lalicki, Tom
Lamb, Nancy
Lamba, Marie
Lambrichs, Louise L.
Lambshead, John
Lamming, George (Eric)
Lampitt, Dinah
Lamppa, William R.
Lams, Victor
Lanagan, Margo
Lancashire, Anne Begor
Land, Brad
Landers, Scott
Landesman, Peter
Landsberg, Melvin
Lane, Dakota
Langa, Mandla
Langston, Laura
Langton, Jane
Lansdale, Joe R(ichard)

Lantigua, John
Lapcharoensap, Rattawut
Lape, Noreen Groover
Larsgaard, Chris
Larson, Ingrid D(ana)
Larson, Kirby
Laskin, Pamela L.
Lasky, Kathryn
Lassez, Sarah
Lathey, Gillian
Latreille, Stanley
Latuchie, Karen
Laux, Constance
Lawrence, Caroline
Lawrence, David
Lawrence, Kathleen Rockwell
Lawrence, Louise
Lawrence, Michael
Lawrence, Sara
Lawrence, Starling
Lawrence, Steven C.
Lawson, James
Le Guin, Ursula K(roeber)
Lear, Patricia
Leavitt, Caroline
Lebowitz, Albert
Lecesne, James
Ledbetter, Suzann
Lee, Dennis (Beynon)
Lee, J. Ardian
Lee, Leslie (E.)
Lee, Marie G.
Lee, Mark
Lee, Mona
Lee, Sky
Lee, Tommy W.
Leegant, Joan
Leese, Jennifer L. B.
Leeson, Ted
Lehane, Dennis
Lehman, Yvonne
Leidner, Alan C.
Leigh, Ana
Leith, Linda Jane
Lemieux, A(nne) C(onnelly)
Lemov, Rebecca
Lennard, John (Chevening)
Lennon, Joan
Lennox, John
Lepore, Jill
Lerangis, Peter
Lerman, Rhoda
Lerner, Eric
Leroy, Margaret
Lester, Julius
Letts, Billie
Levesque, John
Levi, Jan Heller
Leviant, Curt
Levin, Miriam (Ramsfelder)
Levine, Gail Carson
Levine, Philip
Levinson, Alan
Levoy, Myron
Levy, Elizabeth
Levy, Harry
Levy, Helen Fiddyment

Lewin, Michael Z.
Lewis, Linda (Joy)
Lewis, Robert W.
Lewis, Sherry
Lewis, Simon
Lewis, Trudy
Lewis, Ward B.
Lewis-Ferguson, Julinda
Lichtenberg, Jacqueline
Lide, Mary
Limon, Martin
Lindbergh, Judith
Lindquist, N(ancy) J(ane)
Lindsay, Frederic
Lindsey, Johanna
Lindskold, Jane M.
Lindvall, Michael L(loyd)
Lingard, Joan (Amelia)
Linzer, Anna
Lipman, Victoria M.
Lipsky, David
Lisle, Janet Taylor
Liss, David
Littell, Robert
Littleton, Mark (R.)
Livingston, Robert Henry
Lliteras, D. S.
Lloyd, A(lan) R(ichard)
Lloyd, Margaret Glynne
Lloyd, Saci
Lodge, Jeff
Loeb, Karen
Loeffelholz, Mary
Loewer, (Henry) Peter
Logan, Chuck
Logue, Christopher
Lohans, Alison
Löhr, Robert
Lomonaco, Palmyra
Loney, Glenn Meredith
López, Lorraine
Lopresti, Robert
Lorenz, Lee (Sharp)
Lorrimer, Claire
Lott, Bret
Loudon, Mary
Louie, Andrea
Louie, David Wong
Louis, Laura Glen
Lourie, Richard
Love, (Kathleen) Ann
Lovegrove, James (Matthew
  Henry)
Lovell, Glenville
Lovesey, Peter (Harmer)
Lowden, Desmond Scott
Lowe, Stephen
Lowe-Evans, Mary
Lowell, Pamela
Lowry, Lois (Hammersberg)
Lowy, Jonathan
Lubar, David
Lucas, Celia
Lucas, Eileen
Lucas, John
Lucas, Michele Claire
Lucie, Doug

Millett, John
Millhiser, Marlys
Milligan, Bryce
Millum, Trevor
Milne, Seumas
Milton, Giles
Mindt, Alex
Minogue, Valerie Pearson
Minot, Susan A.
Mirabelli, Eugene
Mishica, Clare
Mishkin, Tracy
Mishra, Sudesh (Raj)
Mitchard, Jacquelyn
Mitchell, Emily
Mitchell, Jay P.
Mitchell, Margaree King
Mitchell, Mark
Mitchell, Roger
Mitchell, Susanna (Ryland)
Mitchell, Thomas R.
Mitchell, Todd
Mitcheltree, Tom
Mo, Timothy
Moat, John
Mochizuki, Ken
Moeyaert, Bart
Moffat, Gwen
Moher, Frank
Mohin, Ann
Mohr, Nicholasa
Mok, Esther
Molina, Silvia
Moloney, James
Moloney, Susie
Monesson, Harry S.
Monk, Isabell
Monsour, Theresa
Montenegro, Laura Nyman
Montes, Marisa
Montpetit, Charles
Moodie, Craig
Moore, Alison
Moore, Carey Armstrong
Moore, Christopher
Moore, Ishbel (Lindsay)
Moore, Maureen (Audrey)
Moore, Rogan H.
Moore, Stephanie Perry
Moote, A. Lloyd
Moran, James P.
Moran, Michelle
Mordecai, Pamela (Claire)
Morehouse, Lyda
Morgan, Alison M.
Morgan, Diane
Morgan, Marlo
Morgan, Stacy T(owle)
Mori, Kyoko
Moriarty, Karen
Morley, Margaret
Morpurgo, Michael
Morris, Chris(topher Crosby)
Morris, Desmond
Morris, Keith Lee
Morris, Mark
Morris, Mary

Morris, Mary (Joan) McGarry
Morris, Michael
Morris, Rachel
Morrison, Bill
Morrow, Ann
Moses, Michael Valdez
Mosley, Nicholas
Mosley, Shelley Elizabeth
Moss, Thylias (Rebecca)
Motew, Becky Willis
Motion, Andrew (Peter)
Motley, Annette
Mould, Daphne D. C. Pochin
Mowat, Claire (Angel Wheeler)
Moye, Guan
Muggeson, Margaret Elizabeth
Muhanji, Cherry
Muir, Helen
Mullaney, James P.
Mullen, Michael
Muller, Marcia
Mundis, Hester (Jane)
Muñoz, Manuel
Munro, Alice
Munro, John M(urchison)
Munsch, Robert
Murakami, Haruki
Murnane, Gerald
Murphy, Claire Rudolf
Murphy, Patricia J.
Murphy, Shirley R(ousseau)
Murphy, Tom
Murray, Les(lie) (Allan)
Musgrave, Susan
Musto, Barry
Musto, Michael
Myers, Bill
Myers, Walter Dean
Myles, Eileen
Mynton, Henry
Nagai, Kaori
Naha, Ed
Naidoo, Beverley
Nails, Jennifer
Namioka, Lensey
Nancarrow, Mindy
Napoli, Donna Jo
Natusch, Sheila
Naughton, Jim
Navarro, Yvonne
Nayman, Michele
Neely, Barbara
Neenan, Colin
Neff, Lyle
Neighbour, Mary E.
Nelson, Dorothy
Nelson, Geoffrey Kenneth
Nelson, Peter N.
Nelson, Theresa
Neri, G.
Nesbitt, John D.
Nesbitt, Marc
Neuberger, Julia
Neuhaus, Denise
Nevai, Lucia
Newcomb, Robert
Newlyn, Lucy

Newman, Andrea
Newman, G(ordon) F.
Newton, Lionel
Newton, Nerida
Newton, Robert
Newton, Suzanne
Nichols, Grace
Niebuhr, Gary Warren
Niederhoffer, Galt
Niederman, Derrick
Nielson, James
Nigam, Sanjay (Kumar)
Nigro, August John
Nilsson, Jenny Lind
Nilsson, Per
Nimmo, Jenny
Niskala, Brenda
Nix, Garth
Nkala, Nathan
Noah, Robert
Nobbs, David
Nodelman, Perry
Nolan, Han
Noon, Jeff
Norman, Howard A.
Norman, Rick (J.)
Norment, Lisa
Norris, William R.
North, Darian
Novack, Sandra
Noyes, Deborah
Numeroff, Laura Joffe
Nunnally, Tiina
Nye, Naomi Shihab
Nye, Robert
Nyhart, Nina
O'Briant, Walter H(erbert)
O'Brien, George
O'Brien, Martin
O'Brien, Tim
O'Connell, Jennifer
O'Connell, Rebecca
O'Connor, Alan
O'Connor, Leo F.
O'Connor, Rebecca K.
O'Daly, William
O'Dell, Tawni
O'Faolain, Julia
O'Flynn, Catherine
O'Grady, John P.
O'Grady, Rohan
O'Hanlon, Ardal
O'Hara, Marjorie (Doreen)
O'Keefe, Deborah (Janney)
O'Keeffe, Frank
O'Neill, Jamie
O'Neill, Tom
Oakes, Andy
Oakley, Graham
Obika, Akili Addae
Obradovi , Nade da
Ochart (Torres), (Luz) Yvonne
Odell, Robin Ian
o e, Kenzaburo
Ogunyemi, Yemi D(iploman)
Okimoto, Jean Davies
Okker, Patricia

Okorafor-Mbachu, Nnedi
Oktenberg, Adrian
Olaleye, Isaac O.
Oldham, June
Olds, Bruce
Oliver, Bill
Olshan, Matthew
Olson, Toby
Oltion, Jerry
Omang, Joanne (Brenda)
Ondego, Ogova
Oneal, Elizabeth
Oness, Elizabeth
Oppel, Kenneth
Orgel, Doris
Orlev, Uri
Orlova, Alexandra (Anatol'evna)
Orr, Wendy
Orsenna, Érik
Osborn, David (D.)
Osborn, Karen
Osborne, Will
Osserman, Robert
Ostow, Micol
Otten, Charlotte F(ennema)
Otto, Lon
Otto, Whitney
Oughton, Jerrie
Overmyer, Eric
Owens, Rochelle
Oxendine, Bess Holland
Paddock, Jennifer
Padfield, Peter
Padgett, (Mary) Abigail
Page, Katherine Hall
Paine, Tom
Pairo, Preston (A.)
Palencia, Elaine Fowler
Paling, Chris
Palmer, Elizabeth
Palmer, Peter John
Palwick, Susan
Pari, Susanne
Parini, Jay
Park, Katharine
Parker, Gordon
Parker, Nancy W(inslow)
Parker, Peter (Robert Nevill)
Parker, Una-Mary
Parkinson, Siobhan
Parks, Adele
Parotti, Phillip (Elliott)
Parrish, Tim
Parsons, Alexandra
Partridge, Norman
Pascal, Francine
Pascoe, Bruce
Pashman, Susan
Paterson, Janet M.
Paterson, Ronald (William Keith)
Patneaude, David
Patron, Susan
Patten, Brian
Patterson, Jerry L.
Paul, Anthea
Pauley, Kimberly
Pausewang, Gudrun

Ross, Kent
Rossi, Hozy (Joe)
Rossio, Terry
Rossiter, John
Rostkowski, Margaret I.
Roth-Hano, Renée
Roughgarden, Tim
Routley, (Bernarra) Jane
Rowen, Michelle
Rower, Ann
Rowling, J(oanne) K.
Roy, Jacqueline
Roybal, Laura (Husby)
Rubin, Larry (Jerome)
Rubin, Susan Goldman
Rubin-Dorsky, Jeffrey
Rubinstein, Gillian (Margaret
   Hanson)
Rubio, Gwyn Hyman
Ruby, Lois
Ruefle, Mary
Rummel, Jack
Rumpf, Eva Augustin
Russell, Alan
Russell, Martin (James)
Russell Taylor, Elisabeth
Russo, Marisabina
Rust, Elissa Minor
Rutledge, Leigh W.
Ryder, Joanne (Rose)
Rylands, Jane Turner
Sabato, Haim
Sachs, Marilyn (Stickle)
Saddler, Allen
Sadiq, Nazneen
Sadler, Amy
Saenz, Benjamin Alire
Saenz, Gil
Saffer, Barbara
Sage, Angie
Sail, Lawrence (Richard)
Sakamoto, Kerri
Saknussemm, Kris
Salaman, Nicholas
Salwak, Dale (Francis)
Salzman, Eva Frances
Sampson, Catherine
Sanchez, Alex
Sanchez, Sonia
Sandburg, Helga
Sanders, David
Sanders, Scott Loring
Sandford, John
Sandy, Stephen
Sansom, C. J.
Sargent, Pamela
Saroyan, Aram
Sathre, Vivian
Saunders, Jean (Innes)
Savage, Felicity
Savage, Georgia
Savage, Tom
Savarin, Julian Jay
Savitzkaya, Eugne
Sawrey, Robert D.
Sawyer, (Frederick) Don(ald)
Sawyer, Cheryl

Sawyer, Kem Knapp
Sayer, Mandy Jane
Saylor, Steven W(arren)
Scarfe, Wendy (Elizabeth)
Schaffert, Timothy
Schaller, George B(eals)
Schellenberg, Betty A.
Schenker, Dona
Schenkkan, Robert (Frederic)
Schisgal, Murray
Schlesier, Karl H.
Schlessinger, Laura
Schlitz, Laura Amy
Schneider, Mindy
Schneider, Robert
Schneider, Robyn
Scholes, Ken
Schorsch, Laurence
Schrecker, Judie
Schroeder, Lucinda Delaney
Schulman, Audrey
Schwartz, Adam
Schwartz, Virginia Frances
Scoppettone, Sandra
Scott, Margaret (Allan Bennett)
Seals, David
Sears, Richard
Seay, Jody
See, Carolyn
Seed, Jenny
Seese, June Akers
Segal, Harriet
Segal, Lore
Segal, Susan
Segriff, Larry
Seguin, Marilyn W(eymouth)
Segun, Mabel D.
Seidel, Ross
Seigel, Catharine F.
Selig, Robert L.
Seligman, Craig
Seliy, Shauna
Sellers, Alexandra
Sellers-Garcia, Sylvia
Selman, Robyn
Seltzer, David
Seltzer, Mark
Selvadurai, Shyam
Semple, Andrea
Senior, W(illiam) A.
Servadio, Gaia (Cecilia Gem-
   malina)
Service, Pamela
Severance, John B(ridwell)
Sexton, Linda Gray
Shagan, Steve
Shahan, Sherry
Shakar, Alex
Shakespeare, Nicholas
Shalant, Phyllis
Shalit, Béatrice
Shannon, Doris
Shapiro, Harvey
Shapiro, Susan
Sharma, Poonam
Sharmat, Marjorie Weinman
Shatzky, Joel

Shaw, Carolyn V.
Shaw, Fiona
Shaw, Margret
Shaw, Patrick W.
Shay, Kathryn
Shea, Lisa
Sheehan, Aurelie
Shelby, Anne
Shelby, Graham
Shelden, Michael
Sheldon, Dyan
Sheldon, Mary
Shelton, Connie
Shepherd, Joel
Shepherd, John Scott
Sheppard, John L.
Sheppard, Mary C.
Sher, Ira G.
Sherlock, Patti
Sherman, Charlotte Watson
Sherman, Jason
Sherwood, Frances
Shiina, Makoto
Shimko, Bonnie
Shine, Frances L(ouise)
Shinn, Sharon
Shockley, Ann Allen
Shoesmith, Kathleen A.
Shomer, Enid
Shookman, Ellis
Shortt, Tim(othy Donald)
Shoup, Barbara
Showalter, Gena
Shraer-Petrov, David
Shreve, Susan R(ichards)
Shriver, Lionel
Shull, Steven A.
Shuman, Malcolm K.
Shusterman, Neal (Douglas)
Shuttle, Penelope (Diane)
Siddons, Anne Rivers
Sidney, Neilma
Siegel, James
Siler, Jenny
Silman, Roberta
Silva, Daniel (Joseph)
Silver, Marisa
Silver, Norman
Silverberg, Robert
Silverman, Robin L(andew)
Silverstein, Herma
Silverstein, Jake Phillip
Silvester, Peter (John)
Simmonds, Posy
Simmons, Jane
Simoen, Jan
Simon, Neil
Simonetta, Joseph R.
Simons, Paullina
Simpson, Dorothy
Sinclair, Iain
Sinclair, Olga (Ellen)
Singer, Alan
Singer, Marilyn
Singh, Amritjit
Singleton, Janet Elyse
Sington, Philip

Sipherd, Ray
Siverling, Mike
Sizemore, Christine Wick
Skinner, Gloria Dale
Skinner-Linnenberg, Virginia (M.)
Skloot, Floyd
Slade, Arthur G(regory)
Slater, Michael
Slattery, Brian Francis
Slavin, Helen
Sleigh, Tom
Slepian, Jan(ice B.)
Sloat, Teri
Sloman, Albert Edward
Slote, Alfred
Small, Bertrice
Smellie, Jim
Smiley, Jane (Graves)
Smith, Angela Thompson
Smith, Bobbi
Smith, D. James
Smith, Diane
Smith, Frederick E(screet)
Smith, Geof
Smith, Gordon Roland
Smith, Greg Leitich
Smith, Gregory Blake
Smith, Janna M(alamud)
Smith, Jeanne Rosier
Smith, Joan Gerarda
Smith, Lora Roberts
Smith, Martin Cruz
Smith, Mitchell
Smith, Morris
Smith, Rupert
Smith, Sarah (W. R.)
Smith, Sherwood
Smith, Tara Bray
Smith, Wanda VanHoy
Smith, Wilbur (Addison)
Smither, Elizabeth
Snelling, Dennis (Wayne)
Snelling, Lauraine
Snicket, Lemony
Snyder, Midori
Snyder, Zilpha Keatley
Sobott-Mogwe, Gaele
Soehnlein, Karl M.
Sofer, Barbara
Solares, Ignacio
Solmssen, Arthur R(obert)
   G(eorge)
Solomon, Nina
Somers, Jeff
Sommer, Jason
Sonenberg, Maya
Sonnevi, Göran
Soos, Troy
Sorenson, Margo
Soule, Maris Anne
Souster, Raymond
South, Sheri Cobb
Soyinka, Wole
Spalding, Andrea
Spangler, Catherine
Spaugh, Jean Christopher
Speer, Laurel

Wallace, Richard (Alan)
Wallach, Jeff
Waller, Jane (Ashton)
Wallingford, Lee
Walsh, Ann
Walsh, Jill Paton
Walsh, Lawrence
Walsh Shepherd, Donna
Walton, David
Walton, James
Wambaugh, Joseph
Ward, Gregory
Wardlaw, Alvia J.
Wardlaw, Lee
Ware, Sandra J.
Warfield, Gallatin
Warner, Sally
Warren, Dianne
Warren, Susan May
Warren, Victoria
Washburn, Stan
Wasserman, Robin
Watada, Terry
Waters, John F(rederick)
Waters, Tony
Watkins, Paul
Watkins, Steve
Watkins, William John
Watson, Clyde
Watson, Jean
Watson, Robert (Winthrop)
Watt, Kelly
Waugh, Sylvia
Weaver, Will(iam Weller)
Webb, Janeen (S.)
Webb, Michael (Jack)
Weber, Lori
Webster, Brenda
Wedde, Ian
Wein, Elizabeth E(ve)
Weinheimer, Beckie
Weinstein, Cindy
Weinstein, Philip M.
Weinstock, Nicholas
Weir, Charlene
Weir, Theresa
Weisberger, Lauren
Weiss, Daniel Evan
Welch, Robert
Welcher, Rosalind
Weldt-Basson, Helene Carol
Welford, Sue
Wells, Ken
Wells, Rebecca
Welsch, Roger L(ee)
Welsh, Frank (Reeson)
Welsh, Irvine
Weltner, Peter (Nissen)
Werber, Bernard
Werlock, Abby Holmes P(otter)
Wersba, Barbara
Wesker, Arnold
Wesley, Valerie Wilson
Westburg, Barry (Richard)
Westcott, Jan (Vlachos)
Westling, Louise (Hutchings)
Westrum, Dexter

Wetherington, Mark V.
Wexler, Merin
Weyermann, Debra
Weyland, Jack
Whalley, Peter
Wheeler, Elizabeth
Whelan, Gloria (Ann)
Whitcomb, Laura
White, Andrea
White, Bailey
White, Franklin
White, Jon Manchip
White, Karen
White, Michael J.
White, Randy Wayne
Whitlock, Dean
Whittington, Brad
Widdecombe, Ann (Noreen)
Wieler, Diana
Wiesenthal, Christine S.
Wiesepape, Betty Holland
Wilce, Ysabeau S.
Wilcox, Stephen F.
Wilde, Kelley (Cotter)
Wilde, Lyn Webster
Wilder, Gene
Wilding, Michael
Wildwind, Sharon Grant
Wile, Mary Lee
Willey, Margaret
Williams, (Henry) Nigel
Williams, Adam
Williams, Amanda Kyle
Williams, Arlene
Williams, Forman A.
Williams, Joy
Williams, Karen Lynn
Williams, Len
Williams, Mary E.
Williams, Niall
Williams, Sheila J.
Williams, Vera B.
Williamson, Denise
Willis, Barry
Willis, Connie
Wilson, A(ndrew) N.
Wilson, Barbara (Ellen)
Wilson, Budge
Wilson, D. Harlan
Wilson, David Henry
Wilson, Dolores J.
Wilson, Eric (P.)
Wilson, Frances Engle
Wilson, Gina
Wilson, Jacqueline (Aitken)
Wilson, Jonathan
Wilson, Martin
Wilson, N. D.
Wilson, Nancy Hope
Wilson, T. R.
Windley, Carol
Windsor, Linda
Winn, Tracy
Winnick, R. H.
Winston, Daoma
Winston, Lolly
Winter, John (Anthony)

Winter, Michael
Winterhalder, Edward
Witham, Larry
Withrow, Sarah
Witt, John Fabian
Witt, Martha
Wittlinger, Ellen
Wittmann, Rebecca
Wodhams, Jack
Wolf, Joan M.
Wolfe, Gene (Rodman)
Wolfe, Tom
Wolfer, Dianne
Wolff, Geoffrey
Wolfman, Judy
Wolfson, Jill
Wolitzer, Hilma
Wolper, Carol
Wolven, Scott
Wolverton, Cheryl
Womack, Jack
Wong, Janet S.
Wood, Brian
Wood, Marcia (Mae)
Woodford, Peggy
Woods, Paula L.
Woods, Stuart
Woodson, Jacqueline
Woodward, Margaret E.
Woodworth, Stephen
Woollen, Geoff
Woolley, Benjamin
Wootson, Alice (G.)
Worboys, Anne
Work, James C.
Wormser, Richard
Wo , Joanna H(elena)
Wray, John
Wright, (Mary) Patricia
Wright, Betty Ren
Wright, Franz
Wright, Kit
Wright, Nina
Wright, Vinita Hampton
Wronsky, Gail (F.)
Wu, Fan
Wuori, G. K.
Wurts, Janny
Wyatt, David M.
Wyeth, Sharon Dennis
Wyman, Max
Wymark, Olwen (Margaret)
Wyndham, Francis (Guy Percy)
Wynne, Marcus
Wynveen, Tim
Xingjian, Gao
Ya rid, Na zik Sa ba
Yablonsky, Linda
Yakhlif, Yahya
Yansky, Brian
Yarbro, Chelsea Quinn
Yarbrough, Steve
Yates, Dwight
Ye, Ting-Xing
Yep, Laurence (Michael)
Yglesias, Rafael
Yolen, Jane

York, Alissa
Yorke, Margaret
Yoshimoto, Banana
Youd, Samuel
Youmans, Marly
Young, David (Pollock)
Young, Dean (Wayne)
Young, Ian
Young, Ken
Young, Kevin
Young, Ruth
Yu, Miri
Yudkin, Leon Israel
Yurick, Sol
Zacharias, Karen Spears
Zafón, Carlos Ruiz
Zalben, Jane Breskin
Zambreno, Mary Frances
Zancanella, Don
Zangger, Eberhard
Zebrowski, George
Zechenter, Katarzyna Anna
Zeidner, Lisa
Zeier, Joan T(heresa)
Zeltserman, Dave
Zesch, Scott
Zettler, Steve
Zhu, Lin
Zicree, Mark Scott
Zietlow, E(dward) R(obert)
Zimmermann, Arnold Walter
Zimpel, Lloyd
Zolotow, Charlotte
Zuckermann, Wolfgang (Joachim)
Zurbo, Matt

Plays/Screenplays

Abbotson, Susan C.W.
Abresch, Peter E.
Abse, Dannie
Adams, James (Macgregor David)
Adderson, Caroline
Adnan, Etel
Aldridge, (Harold Edward) James
Alexander, Joseph H(ammond)
Alexis, Andre
Allen, Woody
Amabile, George
Amadi, Elechi
Anaya, Rudolfo A(lfonso)
Andersen, Kurt Byars
Anderson, Rachel
Andrews, Elmer
Angelou, Maya
Anthony, Patricia
Apple, Max (Isaac)
Archer, Jeffrey (Howard)
Arden, John
Argers, Helen
Arksey, Neil
Arnaud, Claude
Arnold, Peter
Arnott, Peter
Ashbery, John (Lawrence)
Asher, Sandy

Duncan, Patrick Sheane
Dunn, Mark (Rodney)
Durang, Christopher
Durschmied, Erik
Dyer, Charles (Raymond)
Eagleton, Terry
Earl, Maureen
Ebert, Roger (Joseph)
Echenoz, Jean
Edgar, David
Edgecombe, David
Edson, Russell
Edwards, Harvey
Egbuna, Obi (Benedict)
Ehle, John
Eisenberg, Deborah
Elder, Jo-Anne
Elisha, Ron
Ellis, Trey
Ellison, Harlan (Jay)
Elmslie, Kenward
Else, Barbara
Emery, Robert J.
Engel, Howard
Engelhard, Jack
England, Chris
Enquist, Per Olov
Ephron, Nora
Epstein, Leslie (Donald)
Erhard, Tom
Eskridge, Ann E.
Eskridge, Kelley
Euba, Femi
Falco, Edward
Fanthorpe, R(obert) Lionel
Fantoni, Barry (Ernest)
Faqih, Ahmed
Favreau, Jon
Fayer, Steve
Fedder, Norman Joseph
Feiffer, Jules
Ferguson, Robert (Thomas)
Ferlinghetti, Lawrence
Ferlita, Ernest
Ferris, Paul
Field, Dorothy
Fielding, Raymond
Fierstein, Harvey (Forbes)
Finch, Annie (Ridley Crane)
Finley, Karen
Fischerová, Daniela
Fisher, David E.
Fitch, Sheree
Fleetwood, Hugh (Nigel)
Fleming, Justin
Foley, (Mary) Louise Munro
Fonda, Peter
Foon, Dennis
Foreman, Richard
Forker, Charles R(ush)
Fornés, Maria Irene
Fowler, Christopher
Fox, Hugh (Bernard)
Frame, Ronald
Franzoni, David (H.)
Fraser, Robert (H.)
Fratti, Mario

Fraustino, Lisa Rowe
Frayn, Michael
Freeman, Gillian
Freemantle, Brian (Harry)
Freud, Esther
Frewer, Glyn
Friedman, Bruce Jay
Friedman, Philip (J.)
Friedman, Rosemary
Friel, Brian
Frisby, Terence
Frost, Mark C.
Fugard, Athol
Fuller, Charles
Fuller, John (Leopold)
Funkhouser, Erica
Futterman, Enid (Susan)
Gabbay, Tom
Gadney, Reg
Gagliano, Frank
Gaines, Jane (Marie)
Gala (Y Velasco), Antonio
Gallagher, Kathleen
Gallagher, Stephen
Galligan, John
Gangemi, Joseph G.
Gänzl, Kurt (Friedrich)
Gardaphé, Fred L(ouis)
Gardner, Leonard
Garfield, Brian (F. W.)
Garneau, Michel
Garner, Alan
Garner, Helen
Garnett, Gale Zoë
Garris, Mick
Gathorne-Hardy, Jonathan
Gattey, Charles Neilson
Gaunt, Kyra D.
Gay, Marie Louise
Gee, Shirley
Gerard, Philip
Gerritsen, Tess
Gersten-Vassilaros, Alexandra
Gibbs, Anthony Matthews
Gilbert, W(illiam) Stephen
Gill, Peter
Gilles, D. B.
Gillon, Adam
Gilmore, John
Gilroy, Frank D(aniel)
Gilstrap, John
Glancy, Diane
Glanville, Brian (Lester)
Glisson, J(ake) T.
Gloag, Julian
Goethe, Ann
Gold, Judy
Goldman, E(leanor) M(aureen)
Goldman, William
Goldsworthy, Peter
Gomez, Jewelle
Gooch, Steve
Goodman, Eric
Goodman, Lizbeth (L.)
Gordon, Charles F.
Gordon, Graeme
Gotanda, Philip Kan

Gottlieb, Annie
Gow, Michael
Gowan, Lee
Grafton, Sue
Graham, Caroline
Grange, William Marshall
Grass, Günter (Wilhelm)
Gratus, Jack
Gray, Alasdair (James)
Gray, Dulcie
Grazer, Gigi Levangie
Green, Cliff(ord)
Greenwood, David Luis Valdes
Gregg, Clark
Gregor, Arthur
Grey, Anthony
Griffiths, Linda
Griffiths, Trevor
Grimes, Tom
Grimsley, Jim
Grippo, Charles
Grodin, Charles
Grote, David (G.)
Grumman, Bob
Guare, John
Guest, Christopher
Guest, Harry
Guest, Judith
Guillen, Michael (Arthur)
Gurney, A(lbert) R(amsdell)
Gurr, David
Gurr, Michael
Guschov, Stephen D.
Guy, Ray
Guy, Rosa (Cuthbert)
Haenel, Wolfram
Hagedorn, Jessica Tarahata
Hagger, Nicholas
Hailey, (Elizabeth) Kendall
Hairston, William
Haldeman, Joe (William)
Hale, John
Hall, Roger (Leighton)
Hallett, Charles A(rthur)
Halligan, Marion (Mildred
    Crothall)
Hallwas, John E.
Hamill, Pete
Handler, David
Hanley, William
Hannan, Chris(topher John)
Hardie, Sean
Hare, David
Harling, Robert
Harris, Christine
Harris, Leonard
Harris, Thomas Walter
Harrison, Tony
Hart, Jonathan (Locke)
Hartley, Hal
Harwood, Ronald
Haskell, Molly
Hastings, Michael
Hathorn, Libby
Hauptman, William (Thornton)
Hawke, Ethan
Hawley, Noah

Hayman, Ronald
Hein, Christoph
Hekkanen, Ernest
Helgeland, Brian
Helmer, Diana Star
Heminway, John
Heng, Liu
Henley, Arthur
Henning, Ann
Henry, Chad
Herbert, Ivor
Herr, Michael
Herring, Peg
Herrmanns, Ralph
Hershey, Olive
Hewitt, Richard
Heyer, Carol
Hezlep, William (Earl)
Higginbotham, Jay
Higginsen, Vy
Highway, Tomson
Hill, Carol
Hill, David
Hill, Reginald (Charles)
Hill, Susan (Elizabeth)
Hillman, Barry (Leslie)
Hines, (Melvin) Barry
Hiro, Dilip
Hischak, Thomas S.
Hjortsberg, William
Hoffman, Alice
Hoffman, William M(oses)
Hoffmann, Roald
Hofmann, Michael
Hogan, Linda
Hoggard, James
Hollingsworth, Margaret
Hollingsworth, Mary
Homel, David
Hoodbhoy, Pervez
Horsfield, Debbie
Hotchner, A(aron) E(dward)
Houghton, Katharine
House, Silas D.
Houston, Velina Hasu
Howard, Elizabeth Jane
Howard, Roger
Hoy, Linda
Hoyle, Trevor
Huggett, Frank Edward
Hughart, Barry
Hughes, Declan
Humphreys, Emyr (Owen)
Hunter, Mollie
Hutchinson, Ron
Hutton, Paul Andrew
Hwang, David Henry
Hyde, Eleanor (M.)
Ibbitson, John Perrie
Indiana, Gary
Ingham, R(ichard) A(rnison)
Ione, Carole
Ireland, David
Isaacs, Susan
Ivory, James (Francis)
Jacker, Corinne
Jackman, Stuart (Brooke)

Plays/Screenplays-*cont.*

Jackson, Angela
Jackson, Edwardo
Jackson, Kevin
Jacobs, Shannon K.
James, Laurie
Jannuzzi, Luigi
Jason, Sonya
Jellicoe, Ann
Jensen, Erik
Jhabvala, Ruth Prawer
Jirgens, Karl (E.)
Johns, Richard Alton
Johnson, Charles R(ichard)
Johnston, Jennifer
Johnston, Julie
Jones, Gayl
Jones, Gerard
Jones, William B(ryan)
Jong, Erica (Mann)
Josipovici, Gabriel (David)
Judson, John
Kalb, Jonathan
Kane, Leslie
Kaplan, James
Kaplan, Nelly
Katz, Elia (Jacob)
Katz, Steve
Kauffmann, Stanley
Kaufman, Lynne
Kavanagh, P(atrick) J(oseph)
Kawin, Bruce F.
Kaye, Marvin
Keenan, Brian
Kein, Sybil
Kelbaugh, Gretchen
Kellerman, Jesse
Kellner, Bruce
Kellogg, Marjorie Bradley
Kelman, James
Kemp, Kenny
Kemp, Penn
Keneally, Thomas (Michael)
Kennedy, Adrienne
Kennedy, William (Joseph)
Kenworthy, Brian J(ohn)
Kesselman, Wendy
Kessler, Jascha (Frederick)
Ketron, Larry
Keys, Kerry Shawn
Kiarostami, Abbas
Kiernan, Pauline
Kilmer, Nicholas (John)
Kilroy, Thomas
King, Geoff
King, Roger (Frank Graham)
King, Stephen
Kirby, Michael Roger
Kitts, Thomas M(ichael)
Kluger, Steve
Knight, Alanna (Cleet)
Knight, Bernard
Knox, Elizabeth (Fiona)
Koch, Phyllis McCallum
Kopit, Arthur
Korder, Howard
Kornblatt, Marc
Kourilsky, Françoise

Plays/Screenplays-*cont.*

Kovel, Terry Horvitz
Kowalke, Kim H.
Kraus, Joanna H.
Krizan, Kim
Kruh, David
Kureishi, Hanif
Kurland, Michael (Joseph)
Kurz, Ron
Kushner, Ellen (Ruth)
Kushner, Tony
La Plante, Lynda
Labro, Philippe (Christian)
LaBute, Neil
Lahr, John (Henry)
Lan, David
Lane, John
Langford, Gary R(aymond)
Lapierre, Laurier L.
Laurie, Hugh
Laurimore, Jill Frances
Lavery, Bryony
Lavigne, Louis-Dominique
Law, Clara
Lawler, Patrick
Lawson, James
Laxdal, Vivienne
Leary, Ann (Lembeck)
Leckie, Keith (Ross)
Lee, Ang
Lee, Bernie
Lee, Leslie (E.)
Lefcourt, Peter
Leguizamo, John
Lehne, Judith Logan
Lehrer, James (Charles)
Leitch, Maurice
Leonard, Elmore
Lepage, Robert
Lerangis, Peter
Lessing, Doris (May)
Letessier, Dorothée
Levin, Irina
Levine, Paul
Lewin, Michael Z.
Libera, Antoni
Lieberman, Herbert
Liebman, Herbert
Lima, Robert (F.)
Lindenmuth, Kevin J.
Lindquist, N(ancy) J(ane)
Lindsay, Frederic
Lingard, Joan (Amelia)
Lively, Penelope
Livingston, Robert Henry
Lochte, Dick
Lock, Joan
Lockerbie, D(onald) Bruce
Locklin, Gerald Ivan
Lodge, David
Logue, Christopher
Loh, Sandra Tsing
Lopez, Josefina
Loriga, Ray
Love, Douglas
Lovelace, Earl
Lowden, Desmond Scott
Lowe, Stephen

Plays/Screenplays-*cont.*

Lucas, Craig
Lucie, Doug
Ludwig, Jack
Lurie, Morris
Lutz, John (Thomas)
Lycett Green, Candida
Lynn, Jonathan
Lyssiotis, Tes
MacDonald, Ann-Marie
Macdonald, Marianne
Macdonald, Norman Malcolm
Macdonald, Sharman
MacEnulty, Pat
MacEoin, Denis
Mack, Carol K.
Mack, David (A.)
Macleod, Alison
Macleod, Joan
Macleod, Wendy
Macphail, Catherine
Macsai, Gwen
Madden, David
Madsen, Svend Åge
Mairowitz, David Zane
Major, Andre
Makepeace, Anne
Maley, Willy
Malouf, David
Mamet, David
Mandel, Oscar
Mangold, James
Mann, (Anthony) Phillip
Mann, Emily
Marber, Patrick
Marchant, Ian
Marchessault, Jovette
Marcuse, Aída E.
Margulies, Donald
Marks, Stan(ley)
Maron, Monika
Marowitz, Charles
Marrs, Jim
Marsh, Derick Rupert Clement
Marshall, Owen
Martin, Alex
Martin, William
Mason, Jeffrey D(aniel)
Mason, Timothy
Matalon, Ronit
Matas, Carol
Mathison, Melissa
Matsen, Bradford (Conway)
Matthews, Jack
Maxwell, Robin
May, Daryl (Alden)
McAlpine, Rachel (Taylor)
McCarthy, Cormac
McCaughrean, Geraldine (Jones)
McCauley, Sue
McConnochie, Mardi
McCrea, Scott
McCusker, Paul
McCutcheon, Sandy
McDonagh, Martin
McDonald, Ian (A.)
McElroy, Colleen J.
McEwan, Ian

Plays/Screenplays-*cont.*

McGahan, Andrew
McGough, Roger
McGrath, Patrick
McGuane, Thomas
McKee, David (John)
McLean, Duncan
McLeod, Joseph (Bertram)
McMaster, Susan
McMullan, Margaret
McMurtry, Larry (Jeff)
McNally, Terrence
McNeish, James
Mda, Zakes
Medoff, Mark (Howard)
Meehan, Paula
Meeks, Christopher (Nelson)
Megged, Aharon
Mekler, Eva
Melchior, Ib (Jorgen)
Mercati, Cynthia
Merrill, Hugh (Davis)
Merwin, W(illiam) S(tanley)
Meserve, Walter Joseph
Metzger, Deena P.
Mickelbury, Penny
Mighton, John
Mihailovi , Dragoslav
Miles, Christopher (John)
Miles, Keith
Miller, Jonathan (Wolfe)
Miller, Lynn H.
Miller, Rebecca
Millner, Cork
Minot, Susan A.
Mishra, Sudesh (Raj)
Mitchard, Jacquelyn
Mitchell, (Charles) Julian
Mitchell, Margaree King
Mitchelson, Mitch
Moe, Christian H(ollis)
Moeyaert, Bart
Moggach, Deborah
Moher, Frank
Mohr, Nicholasa
Moira, Kate
Monk, Isabell
Montague, John (Patrick)
Monzó, Quim
Moore, Christine Palamidessi
Morency, Pierre
Morgan, Nicholas H.
Morgan, Robin
Moriarty, Michael
Morris, Stephen
Morrison, (Philip) Blake
Morrison, Bill
Morrison, Toni
Mosley, Philip
Moss, Thylias (Rebecca)
Mott, Robert L.
Moxley, Gina
Mu go, Mi cere Gi thae
Mulcahy, Lisa
Mungoshi, Charles L.
Murphy, Tom
Murrell, John
Myers, Robert Manson

Myles, Eileen
Naha, Ed
Naiden, James
Naidoo, Beverley
Navarra, Tova
Naylor, Gloria
Neale, Jonathan
Near, Holly
Nelson, Jill
Nelson, Peter N.
Nelson, Ray
Nemec, James
Neugeboren, Jay
Newman, Andrea
Newman, G(ordon) F.
Ngugi wa Thiong
Nichols, John
Nichols, Peter (Richard)
Nicosia, Gerald (Martin)
Nkala, Nathan
Nobbs, David
Nolan, William F(rancis)
Noon, Jeff
Norén, Lars
Norman, Lilith
Norman, Marsha
Novaro, María
Novas, Himilce
Nutt, Paul C.
Nye, Robert
Nye, Simon (Beresford)
O'Brien, Edna
O'Brien, Maureen
O'Connor, Patricia W.
O'Connor, Robert
O'Hare, Jeff(rey A.)
Oakes, Meredith
Oates, Joyce Carol
Ochart (Torres), (Luz) Yvonne
Odaga, Asenath (Bole)
Okimoto, Jean Davies
Oliver, Maria Antònia
Ondaatje, Michael
Ong, Han
Onwueme, Tess Osonye
Oppenheim, Michael
Osborn, David (D.)
Osborne, Will
Overmyer, Eric
Owens, Rochelle
Oxley, William
Ozick, Cynthia
Padgett, Ron
Palandri, Enrico
Pale ek, Libuše
Palin, Michael (Edward)
Palliser, Charles
Parker, Gordon
Parkes, Walter F.
Parks, Suzan Lori
Parlakian, Nishan
Paterek, Josephine
Paterson, Katherine (Womeldorf)
Patrick, Robert
Patten, Brian
Patterson, Jerry L.
Payne, Daniel G.

Peacock, Molly
Pearson, Sybille
Pelletier, Nancy
Pendergast, John S.
Penna, Dennis Roy
Perez, Rolando
Perry, Steve
Peters, Robert
Petievich, Gerald
Petrakis, Harry Mark
Pevsner, Stella
Pezzullo, Ralph
Phelan, Anna Hamilton
Philip, M(arlene) NourbeSe
Phillips, Caryl
Phillips, Mike
Pickard, Tom
Pickering, David (Hugh)
Pierce, Patricia Jobe
Piercy, Marge
Pike, R. William
Pinnock, Winsome
Pitcher, Harvey John
Platt, Randall
Pogue, Charles (Edward)
Pollock, (Mary) Sharon
Poole, Josephine
Poskitt, Kjartan
Pownall, David
Price, Richard
Price, Victor (Henry John)
Pritts, Kim Derek
Proulx, Monique
Prowse, Brad A.
Pugsley, Alex
Pullman, Philip
Purser, John W(hitley)
Purser, Philip (John)
Radzinsky, E dvard (Stanislav-
    ovich)
Rae, Hugh C(rawford)
Ragen, Naomi
Rakoff, Alvin
Ramsey, Jarold
Rangoussis, Steven
Raphael, Frederic (Michael)
Raucher, Herman
Rayson, Hannie
Read, Anthony
Read, Piers Paul
Read, Sylvia Joan
Rechy, John (Francisco)
Redhill, Michael H.
Redonnet, Marie
Reed, John
Reed, Philip (Chandler)
Reeves, Faye Couch
Reiter, Victoria (Kelrich)
Rendon, Marcie R.
Reuter, Bjarne (B.)
Reynolds, Kevin
Reza, Yasmina
Ribalow, M(eir) Z(vi)
Richards, Jeffrey H.
Richemont, Enid
Richter, Roland Suso
Ridley, Elizabeth J(ayne)

Ridley, Philip
Rifbjerg, Klaus (Thorvald)
Riley, Martin
Rio, Michel
Riordon, Michael
Robinette, Joseph A.
Roddam, Franc(is George)
Rodriguez, Judith (Green)
Romeril, John
Romero, George A.
Rooke, Leon
Roose-Evans, James
Rosen, Michael (Wayne)
Rosenthal, Lucy (Gabrielle)
Ross-Macdonald, Malcolm (John)
Rothman, William
Rubin, Bruce Joel
Rubinstein, Gillian (Margaret
    Hanson)
Rudkin, (James) David
Ruhl, Sarah
Rush, Christopher
Rushdie, Salman
Russell, Roy
Russell, Willy
Saban, Cheryl (Lynn)
Sacre, Antonio
Saddler, Allen
Sakamoto, Kerri
Salutin, Rick
Salzman, Eva Frances
Sanchez, Sonia
Sanford, Richard
Saperstein, David
Sardi, Jan
Saroyan, Aram
Sayer, Mandy Jane
Schaeffer, Mark
Schenkkan, Robert (Frederic)
Schiffer, James (M.)
Schisgal, Murray
Schlitz, Laura Amy
Schoenewolf, Gerald
Scholefield, Alan (A. T.)
Scholey, Arthur (Edward)
Schreiber, Joseph
Scoppettone, Sandra
Scott, (Robert James) Munroe
Seals, David
Searls, Hank
Sears, Joe
Sedaris, Amy
Sedaris, David
Selbourne, David
Sellars, Jane
Seltzer, David
Senior, Michael
Shafer, Yvonne
Shaffer, Peter (Levin)
Shagan, Steve
Shalit, Béatrice
Shandling, Garry
Shangé, Ntozake
Shank, Theodore
Shannon, Elizabeth (McNelly)
Shapcott, Thomas W(illiam)
Sheehy, Helen

Shem, Samuel
Shepard, Sam
Sherman, Jason
Shinn, Thelma J.
Shusterman, Neal (Douglas)
Shuttle, Penelope (Diane)
Sichrovsky, Peter
Sickels, Noelle
Sijie, Dai
Simic, Goran
Simon, Neil
Simpson, Michael Andrew
Sinclair, Andrew (Annandale)
Singer, Barry
Sisson, Rosemary Anne
Slade, Bernard
Slote, Alfred
Smarandache, Florentin
Smeliansky, Anatoly
Smith, Ali
Smith, Faye McDonald
Smith, Frederick E(screet)
Smith, Glenn Robert
Smith, Jonathan
Smith, Kevin
Smith, Marisa
Smith, Mark Haskell
Smith, Marya
Sobol, Joshua
Soto, Gary
Soyinka, Wole
Speer, Laurel
Spencer, Brent
Spencer, Elizabeth
Spencer, Stuart S.
Spurling, John
Stacey, Cherylyn
Stacey, Tom
Stansberry, Domenic (Joseph)
Stark, Marisa Kantor
Starkey, David
Starr, Jason
Staveacre, Tony
Steinman, Louise
Sternlicht, Sanford
Stillman, (John) Whit(ney)
Stirt, Joseph A.
Stone, Robert (Anthony)
Stonich, Sarah
Stoppard, Tom
Storey, David (Malcolm)
Strasser, Todd
Stratton, Allan
Street, Brian Jeffrey
Strelkoff, Tatiana
Stroud, Carsten
Stuart, Alexander
Stuart, Sarah Payne
Svendsen, Linda
Svenson, Bo
Sward, Robert S.
Sweeney, Terrance (Allen)
Syal, Meera
Szabó, Istvan
Szymczak, Leonard K.
Tagliavini, Gabriela
Tallman, Shirley

Index To Writing Categories

3351

Bei Dao
Beissel, Henry (Eric)
Belieu, Erin
Belin, Esther G.
Bell, Marvin (Hartley)
Bell, Robin
Belli, Gioconda
Bellm, Dan
Bellows, Nathaniel
Belshaw, Patrick
Bemrose, John
Bendall, Molly
Bender, Sheila
Benig, Irving
Bennett, John M(ichael)
Bensley, Connie
Benson, Gerard
Benson, Judi
Berdeshevsky, Margo Ann
Beresford, Anne
Berg, Stephen
Berger, Bruce
Berger-Kiss, Andres
Bergland, Martha
Bergonzi, Bernard
Berkson, Bill
Bernard, Kenneth
Bernard, Oliver
Bernstein, Charles
Berrigan, Daniel J.
Berry, John Stevens
Bertolino, James
Bertrand, Diane Gonzales
Besner, Neil K.
Bhatt, Sujata
Bidart, Frank
Bidney, Martin
Bielski, Alison (Joy Prosser)
Bieman, Elizabeth
Bierds, Linda
Biggs, Mary
Billson, Janet Mancini
Bina, Cyrus
Binding, Paul
Birenbaum, Barbara
Birney, Alice Lotvin
Birrell, Anne (Margaret)
Bishop, Michael
Bissett, Bill
Black, D(avid) M(acleod)
Blaisdell, Bob
Blake, Sarah
Blanco, Richard
Bland, Peter
Blank, G(regory) Kim
Blasing, Randy
Blei, Norbert
Blessington, Francis C(harles)
Block, Francesca (Lia)
Bloom, Harold
Blount, Roy (Alton)
Blunt, Giles
Bly, Robert (Elwood)
Bober, Natalie S.
Bobis, Merlinda Carullo
Bohnhoff, Maya Kaathryn
Bohntinsky, Dori

Boisseau, Michelle
Bolam, Robyn
Boland, Eavan (Aisling)
Bolger, Dermot
Bond, Edward
Bond, Ruskin
Bonomelli, Charles J(ames)
Boon, Debbie
Borenstein, Emily Schwartz
Borinsky, Alicia
Bornholdt, Jenny
Bornstein, George
Borntrager, Mary Christner
Boruch, Marianne
Bosco, Monique
Bosselaar, Laure Anne
Bottoms, David
Bouvard, Marguerite Guzman
Bowdring, Paul (Edward)
Bowering, George
Bowering, Marilyn (Ruthe)
Bowkett, Stephen
Brackenbury, Alison
Bradbury, Ray (Douglas)
Braham, (E.) Jeanne
Brand, Alice Glarden
Brand, Dionne
Brandi, John
Brandt, Di
Braschi, Giannina
Brault, Jacques
Braun, Richard Emil
Braverman, Melanie
Braxton, Joanne M(argaret)
Brazaitis, Mark
Breiner, Laurence A.
Brennan, Matthew C.
Brenton, Howard
Breskin, David
Brett, Brian
Brewer, Bob
Brewster, Elizabeth (Winifred)
Briggs, Raymond (Redvers)
Bringhurst, Robert
Britto, Paulo Henriques
Brochu, André
Brock, James
Brock-Broido, Lucie
Broer, Lawrence R(ichard)
Brooke-Rose, Christine
Brooker, Jewel Spears
Brooks, David (Gordon)
Broughton, T. Alan
Broumas, Olga
Brown, Lee Ann
Brown, Rita Mae
Brown, Rosellen
Brown, Stewart
Browne, Michael Dennis
Brownjohn, Alan (Charles)
Brox, Jane (Martha)
Bruce, Robert S.
Bruchac, Joseph
Bryant, Jennifer F(isher)
Buarque, Chico
Buccola, Regina M.
Buchanan, Oni

Buchanan, Roberta
Buckley, Christopher Howard
Bucknall, Barbara Jane
Budbill, David
Buehler, Evelyn Judy
Buell, Frederick (Henderson)
Bugan, Carmen
Bugeja, Michael J.
Buhner, Stephen Harrod
Burnett, Alfred David
Burns, Jim
Burns, Ralph
Burrow, J(ohn) A(nthony)
Burroway, Janet (Gay)
Burrs, Mick
Buscall, Jon
Bush, Barney (Furman)
Bush, Duncan
Butler, Geoff
Butler, Jack
Butlin, Ron
Butts, Anthony
Byer, Kathryn Stripling
Caddy, Caroline
Cadnum, Michael
Calbert, Cathleen
Calder, John (Mackenzie)
Caldwell, Grant
Callaghan, Barry
Cameron, Julia
Camlot, Jason
Camon, Ferdinando
Campbell, Mary B(aine)
Campbell, Siobhán
Camper, Carol
Campion, Dan(iel Ray)
Campo, Rafael
Cannon, A. E.
Cantu, Norma Elia
Carbo, Nick
Carew, Jan (Rynveld)
Carew, Rivers (Verain)
Carley, Lionel (Kenneth)
Carneci, Magda
Caron, Brane Mozetic
Carr, Duane
Carr, Julie
Carranza, Andreu
Carrier, Roch
Carson, Anne
Carson, Ciaran
Cartarescu, Mircea
Carter, Ally
Carter, Emily
Carter, Jared
Casey, John (Dudley)
Casil, Amy Sterling
Cassady, Marsh
Castro, Michael
Caulfield, Carlota
Chaleff, Ira
Chamberlain, Marisha
Chambers, Chris
Chappell, Fred(erick Davis)
Charlier, Roger Henri
Charlip, Remy
Charters, Samuel

Chase, Karen
Chattarji, Sampurna
Chatterjee, Debjani
Chen, Ken
Cheney, Patrick Gerard
Chernoff, Maxine
Cherry, Kelly
Chess, Richard
Chester, Tessa Rose
Chin, Justin
Chinodya, Shimmer
Chitwood, Michael
Chorlton, David
Christensen, Lars Saabye
Christensen, Paul
Christopher, Renny (Teresa)
Ciaravino, Helene
Citron, Stephen
Claire, Cherie
Clark, Emma Chichester
Clark, Tom
Clarke, Gillian
Clarke-Rich, Elizabeth L.
Clarvoe, Jennifer
Clary, Killarney
Clausen, Andy
Cleary, Brian P.
Clem, Margaret H(ollingsworth)
Cleveland, Leslie
Clewell, David
Clinton, James H(armon)
Clipper Sethi, Robbie
Cloutier, Cécile
Cluysenaar, Anne (Alice Andrée)
Coates, Robert Crawford
Cobb, Thomas
Cochran, Robert B(rady)
Codrescu, Andrei
Cofer, Judith Ortiz
Cohen, Leonard
Cohen, Susan
Colalillo-Kates, Isabella
Cole, Barry
Coleman, Jane Candia
Coles, Don
Coles, Robert
Colinas, Antonio
Collier, Michael
Collings, Michael R(obert)
Collins, Billy
Collins, Floyd G.
Collins, Martha
Collins, Merle
Collison, Kerry B(oyd)
Colman, E. Adrian M.
Colombo, John Robert
Colquhoun, Glenn
Comfort, Philip W(esley)
Confiant, Raphaël
Conn, Stewart
Connelly, Karen
Connor, Tony
Connors, Bruton
Conover, Roger L(loyd)
Conquest, (George) Robert
  (Acworth)
Conquest, Ned

Fry, William Finley
Fuller, John (Leopold)
Funkhouser, Erica
Gagliano, Eugene M.
Gala (Y Velasco), Antonio
Gale, Monica R(achel)
Galef, David
Galinsky, Karl
Gallagher, Tess
Gallas, John (Edward)
Galt, George
Galvin, Brendan
Gander, Forrest
García-Castañón, Santiago
Garland, Max
Garrison, David Lee
Garrison, Deborah (Gottlieb)
Garrison, Philip
Gaston, Patricia S.
Gatenby, Greg
Gavronsky, Serge
Geddes, Gary
George, Alice Rose
Geras, Adèle (Daphne Weston)
Gerstler, Amy
Gesner, Carol
Getty, Sarah Sovereign
Ghose, Zulfikar
Gibb, Robert
Gibbons, Reginald
Gibbs, Anthony Matthews
Gibson, Margaret
Gibson, Miles
Gifford, Barry (Colby)
Gifford, Peggy
Gilbert, Ruth
Gilbert, Sandra M(ortola)
Gilchrist, Ellen
Gildner, Gary
Giles, Gail
Gill, Lakshmi
Gillies, Valerie
Gillon, Adam
Gioia, (Michael) Dana
Giovanni, Nikki
Gizzi, Peter
Glancy, Diane
Glaser, Michael S.
Glatt, Lisa
Gleiter, Jan
Glenn, Mel
Glennon, Karen M.
Godbout, Jacques
Gold, Janet N(owakowski)
Gold, Jerome
Golden, Renny
Goldstein, Imre
Goldsworthy, Peter
Gomez, Jewelle
Gómez Rosa, Alexis
González, Ray
Gonzalez (Mandri), Flora
Gooch, Brad
Goodison, Lorna (Gaye)
Goodwin, Ken(neth Leslie)
Gordon, Jaimy
Goss, Theodora

Goto, Hiromi
Gottlieb, Daphne
Gould, Janice
Gourgouris, Stathis
Gragnolati, Manuele
Graham, Desmond
Graham, Henry
Graham, Jorie
Grandits, John
Grant, James Russell
Gray, Alasdair (James)
Gray, Andrew
Gray, Robert (Archibald Speir)
Green, Peter (Morris)
Greenberg, Alvin
Greenberg, Joanne
Greene, Jonathan (Edward)
Greening, John
Greenlaw, Lavinia (Elaine)
Greer, Germaine
Gregerson, Linda
Gregor, Arthur
Gregory, Valiska
Grenham, John
Grennan, Eamon
Gresser, Seymour
Griffiths, Jane
Griffiths, Steve
Grigg, Ray
Grimes, Martha
Gross, Philip (John)
Grossman, Richard
Grossman, Wendy
Grovier, Kelly
Grudin, Robert
Grumman, Bob
Grundy, Joan
Guest, Harry
Guevara, Maurice Kilwein
Guillory, Dan
Gundy, Jeff(rey Gene)
Guppy, Stephen (Anthony)
Gutteridge, Don(ald George)
Gwyn, Richard
Gwynn, R(obert) S(amuel)
Haar, James
Hacker, Marilyn
Hadas, Rachel
Hagedorn, Jessica Tarahata
Hagger, Nicholas
Hahn, Susan
Hainsworth, Peter (R. J.)
Hairston, William
Hajdusiewicz, Babs Bell
Hakak, Lev
Haldeman, Joe (William)
Hall, Donald (Andrew)
Hall, H(ugh) Gaston
Hall, J(ohn) C(live)
Hall, Kathleen (Mary)
Hall, Rodney
Halliday, Mark
Halpern, Daniel
Hamblin, Robert W(ayne)
Hamer, Forrest
Hamill, Janet
Hamill, Sam (Patrick)

Hamilton, Carol (Jean Barber)
Hamilton, Richard
Hamilton, Saskia
Hamilton-Paterson, James
Hampson, Robert (Gavin)
Hanes, Frank Borden
Hannah, Sophie
Hanscombe, Gillian E(ve)
Hardy, Barbara (Gladys)
Hardy, John Philips
Hare-Duke, Michael (Geoffrey)
Harleman, Ann
Harlow, Michael
Harnack, Curtis
Harper, Michael S(teven)
Harris, (Theodore) Wilson
Harris, Claire
Harris, Jana
Harrison, Antony H.
Harrison, Jim
Harrison, Michael
Harrison, Tony
Harsent, David
Hart, (Margaret Eleanor) Anne
Hart, Jonathan (Locke)
Hart, Kevin
Harteis, Richard
Harter, Penny
Hartman, Geoffrey H.
Harvey, John
Harvey, Kenneth J.
Harvey, Steven
Harvor, Elisabeth
Hasan, Anjum
Hashmi, (Aurangzeb) Alamgir
Hasluck, Nicholas
Hasselstrom, Linda (Michele)
Hassler, Donald M(ackey)
Hastings, Michael
Hatoum, Milton
Haug, James
Hauser, Susan Carol
Haverty, Anne
Haviaras, Stratis
Hawkins, Hunt
Hawley, Richard A.
Haxton, Brooks
Hayden, Eric William
Hayman, Carol Bessent
Hazo, Samuel (John)
Hazuka, Tom
Healey, Judith Koll
Heaney, Seamus
Heath, Malcolm (Frederick)
Heath, William
Hedin, Robert (Alexander)
Hefer, Hayim (Baruch)
Heidbreder, Robert K.
Heidel, R. Andrew
Heim, Scott
Heine, Steven
Hejinian, Lyn
Heller, Michael
Hellyer, Jill
Helwig, Maggie
Hendry, Diana
Hendry, Joy (McLaggan)

Henley, Patricia
Henney, Carolee Wells
Henning, Ann
Henry, Gordon D.
Henry, Paul
Herrick, Steven
Hershey, Olive
Hewitt, Geof
Heyen, William
Hibbs, John
Hicok, Bob
Hiestand, Emily (L.)
High, Linda Oatman
Hightower, Scott
Hilberry, Conrad Arthur
Hill, Barry
Hill, Carol
Hill, Geoffrey
Hill, Russell
Hill, Selima (Wood)
Hill, Tobias
Hilles, Rick
Hilles, Robert
Hillman, Barry (Leslie)
Hillman, Elizabeth
Hirata, Hosea
Hiro, Dilip
Hirsch, Edward
Hirschman, Jack
Hirshfield, Jane
Ho, Minfong
Hoberman, Mary Ann
Hodgson, Harriet
Høeck, Klaus
Hoeppner, Edward Haworth
Hoffman, Daniel
Hoffmann, Roald
Hofmann, Michael
Hogan, Linda
Hogg, Patrick Scott
Hoggard, James
Holahan, Susan
Holbrook, David (Kenneth)
Holbrook, Sara
Hollander, John
Hollenberg, Donna Krolik
Holley, Margaret
Hollingsworth, Mary
Hollo, Anselm (Paul Alexis)
Holloway, Sue (A.)
Holmes, Richard
Holst-Warhaft, Gail
Holstad, Scott Cameron
Hom, Sharon K.
Hooker, Jeremy
Hoover, Paul
Hope, Christopher (David Tully)
Hopkins, Lee Bennett
Hopler, Jay
Hord, Frederick (Lee)
Horovitz, Michael
Horváth, John
Houshmand, Zara
Houston, Velina Hasu
Hovey, Kate
Howard, Roger
Howe, Fanny

Howe, LeAnne
Howe, Marie
Howe, Susan
Howell, Anthony
Howell, Christopher
Hoyem, Andrew
Huddle, David
Hughes, Glenn
Hughey, Elizabeth
Huisinga, Roger
Hull, William E(dward)
Hulse, Michael (William)
Hummer, T(erry) R(andolph)
Humphreys, Emyr (Owen)
Humphreys, Helen (Caroline)
Hunter, R(ichard) L(awrence)
Hustvedt, Siri
Hutchins, Pat
Hwang, Tong-gyu
Hyde, (W.) Lewis
Igo, John (N.)
Inez, Colette
Ingham, R(ichard) A(rnison)
Ione, Carole
Ireland, Kevin (Mark)
Irion, Mary Jean
Isaacs, Anne
Isles, John A.
Izakson, Miron C.
Jackson, Angela
Jacobson, Dan
Jaffin, David
James, Clive (Vivian Leopold)
James, Kelvin Christopher
James, Sibyl
Jameson, W. C.
Jance, J. A.
Janeczko, Paul B(ryan)
Jarman, Mark (F.)
Jauss, David
Jeffers, Honorée Fanonne
Jenkins, Catherine
Jennings, Kate
Jin, Ha
Jinpa, Thupten
Jirgens, Karl (E.)
Johns, Linda
Johns, Richard Alton
Johnson, Angela
Johnson, Chester L.
Johnson, Greg
Johnson, Rob
Jones, D(ouglas) G(ordon)
Jones, Daryl (Emrys)
Jones, Evan (Lloyd)
Jones, Gayl
Jones, Naomi Brooks
Jones, Patricia Spears
Jones, R(obert) M(aynard)
Jones, Rodney
Jones, Sally Roberts
Jong, Erica (Mann)
Jordan, Anne Devereaux
Joseph, Lawrence
Joshi, S(unand) T(ryambak)
Joyce, Joyce Ann
Joyce, Michael

Judson, John
Junkins, Donald (Arthur)
Kadare, Ismail
Kalbacken, Joan
Kalin, Jim
Kallgren, Beverly Hayes
Kantaris, Sylvia (Mosley)
Kari, Daven M(ichael)
Karkala, John A.
Karr, Mary
Kasdorf, Julia
Kasischke, Laura
Kassabova, Kapka
Katz, Bobbi
Katz, Steve
Kauffman, Janet
Kavanagh, P(atrick) J(oseph)
Kawatski, Deanna
Kawin, Bruce F.
Kay, Guy Gavriel
Kay, Jackie
Kaye, Barrington
Kazantzis, Judith
Kearns, Josie
Kearns, Lionel (John)
Keats-Rohan, K. S. B.
Keene, John (R.)
Keery, James
Kefala, Antigone
Keil, Charles
Kein, Sybil
Kelbaugh, Gretchen
Kelley, (Kathleen) Alita
Kelley, Alec E(rvin)
Kelley, Ann
Kelley, Liam C.
Kelling, Hans Wilhelm
Kelly, Maeve
Kelly, Robert
Kemp, Penn
Kennedy, Sarah
Kennedy, X. J.
Kennelly, (Timothy) Brendan
Kenney, Richard (L.)
Kenny, Maurice (Francis)
Kent, Joseph (P.)
Kenward, Jean
Keplinger, David
Kessler, Jascha (Frederick)
Keys, Kerry Shawn
Khalvati, Mimi
Kherdian, David
Khoury-Ghata, Vénus
Khwaja, Waqas
Kidman, Fiona (Judith)
Kilmer, Nicholas (John)
Kim, Chi-Ha
Kim, Myung Mi
Kimball, Robert (Eric)
King, Brian
King, Dave
King, Jeanette (Margaret)
King, Martha
King-Hele, Desmond
Kingsolver, Barbara
Kingston, Maxine Hong
Kinnell, Galway

Kinsella, Thomas
Kinzie, Mary
Kirk, Pauline (M.)
Kissing, Steve
Kisubi, Alfred T(aligoola)
Kitchen, Judith
Kizer, Carolyn
Klappert, Peter
Kluger, Ruth
Knight, Lynne
Knighton, Ryan
Knoepfle, John
Ko, Tanya Hyonhye
Koch, Phyllis McCallum
Koertge, Ron(ald)
Koestenbaum, Wayne
Kogawa, Joy Nozomi
Kohler, Sandra
Koller, James
Kolosov, Jacqueline
Komunyakaa, Yusef
Koning, (Angela) Christina
Kooistra, Lorraine Janzen
Kooser, Ted
Korelitz, Jean Hanff
Korg, Jacob
Korman, Bernice
Kositsky, Lynne
Kossman, Nina
Kostelanetz, Richard (Cory)
Kramer, Lotte
Kronen, Steve
Kroninger, Stephen
Krouse, Erika Dawn
Krüger, Michael
Kuchar, Gary
Kulling, Monica
Kumin, Maxine
Kunin, Aaron
Kuppner, Frank
Kushner, Ellen (Ruth)
Kuusisto, Stephen
Kuvshinoff, Boris W.
Kuyper, Sjoerd
L'Heureux, John (Clarke)
La Fortune, Knolly Stephen
Lachs, John
LaFemina, Gerry
Laird, Holly A.
Laird, Nick
Lake, David (John)
Lamb, Nancy
Lamb, Patricia Clare
Lamb, Wally
Lammon, Martin
Lamplugh, Lois
Lamppa, William R.
Lane, John
Langa, Mandla
Lange, Arthur D.
Langford, Gary R(aymond)
Larios, Julie Hofstrand
Larkin, Joan
Larsen, Jeanne (Louise)
Laskin, Pamela L.
Latynin, Leonid (Aleksandrovich)
Lauterbach, Ann

Lauture, Denizé
Lawler, Patrick
Lawrence, Michael
Lawson, JonArno Burhans
Layne, Steven L.
Lazer, Hank
Le Guin, Ursula K(roeber)
Leader, Mary
Leader, Zachary
Lebow, Jeanne
Lederer, Katy
Lee, A(rthur) Robert
Lee, Dennis (Beynon)
Lee, Li Young
Leese, Jennifer L. B.
Leggo, Carl Derek
Lehmann, Geoffrey (John)
Leithauser, Brad (Edward)
LeMaster, J. R.
Lemay, Shawna
Lemon, Alex
Lennard, John (Chevening)
Leo, Teresa
Leong, Russell (C.)
Lerner, Laurence (David)
Lessing, Doris (May)
Lester, Julius
Levi, Jan Heller
Levine, Gail Carson
Levine, Philip
Levy, Andrew (Gordon)
Levy, Constance
Lewin, Michael Z.
Lewis, Carol F. Ra
Lewis, J. Patrick
Liatsos, Sandra Olson
Lieberman, Laurence (James)
Liebler, M. L.
Lifshin, Lyn
Lim, Shirley Geok-lin
Lima, Robert (F.)
Limonov, E duard
Lin, Tan (Anthony)
Lindgren, Barbro
Lindholdt, Paul J.
Lindsay, Frederic
Lindsay, Sarah
Linzer, Anna
Lister, R(ichard) P(ercival)
Little, (Flora) Jean
Little, Anne Colclough
Liu, Timothy
Llewellyn, Kate
Lliteras, D. S.
Lloyd, Margaret Glynne
Locklin, Gerald Ivan
Loeb, Karen
Lofton, Ramona
Logan, William
Logue, Christopher
Lohans, Alison
Lomas, Herbert
Lombardo, Mary A.
Loncraine, Rebecca
Longfellow, Layne (A.)
Longley, Michael
Lorrimer, Claire

Low, Anthony
Lowe, Jack Phillips
Lucas, John
Lucie-Smith, (John) Edward
  (McKenzie)
Luft, Lya Fett
Lunde, David (Eric)
Lynch, Thomas
Macainsh, Noel Leslie
Macaulay, Teresa (E.)
Macdonald, Norman Malcolm
MacGowan, Christopher (John)
Macgoye, Marjorie Oludhe
MacGuire, James
MacInnes, Mairi
Mack, Beverly (B.)
MacKenna, John
Mackler, Carolyn
MacLean, Glynne
MacLean, Jill
Macleod, Joan
MacPherson, Andrea
MacQueen, Winifred (Wallace)
Madden, David
Madgett, Naomi Long
Madhubuti, Haki R.
Madsen, Svend Åge
Magee, Bryan
Maggio, Mike
Magistrale, Tony
Magorian, Michelle
Mahy, Margaret
Mainone, Robert Franklin
Maio, Samuel (Joseph)
Mairs, Nancy (Pedrick)
Majaj, Lisa Suhair
Major, Clarence
major, devorah
Malone, Hank
Malone, James Hiram
Malouf, David
Malzahn, Manfred
Mamet, David
Mandel, Charlotte
Mandel, Oscar
Manhire, Bill
Mann, (Anthony) Phillip
Mann, Barbara E.
Mann, Charles F.
Mann, Jeff(rey A.)
Mann, Kenny
Manning, Joe
Manrique (Ardila), Jaime
Mansfield, Nick
Marchessault, Jovette
Marcuse, Aída E.
Marks, Corey
Marks, Graham
Marlis, Stefanie
Marotti, Arthur F(rancis)
Marquart, Debra
Marsden, Carolyn
Marsh, Jan
Martien, Jerry
Martin, Stephen-Paul
Martínez, Dionisio D.
Marting, Diane E.

Marty, Sid
Marvin, Cate
Marx, Steven
Masini, Donna
Mason, David
Massingham, Harold (William)
Matchett, William H(enry)
Mathes, Charles (Elliott)
Mathews, Aidan (Carl)
Mathis, Sharon Bell
Matlin, David
Matson, Suzanne
Mattawa, Khaled
Matthews, Jack
Matthews, Steven
Matthias, John (Edward)
Mattingley, Christobel (Rose-
  mary)
Maurer-Mathison, Diane V(ogel)
May, Steven W.
Mayer, Gerda (Kamilla)
Mayne, Seymour
Mazzaro, Jerome
McAdams, Janet
McAfee, John P.
McAlpine, Rachel (Taylor)
McAuley, James J.
McCaffery, Steve
McCain, Gillian
McCallum, Shara
McCann, Richard
McCarey, Peter
McCarthy, Sherri N.
McCarthy, Thomas
McClatchy, J(oseph) D(onald)
McColley, Diane Kelsey
McCormack, W(illiam) J(ohn)
McCoy, William C.
McCrorie, Edward (P.)
Mccrory, Donald P(eter)
McDonald, Ian (A.)
McElroy, Colleen J.
McEvilley, Thomas
McFadden, David W.
McFall, Gardner
McFarlane, Peter (William)
McGough, Roger
McGrath, Carmelita
McGregor, James H. S.
McGuckian, Medbh (McCaughan)
McHugh, Heather
McKay, Don
McKee, David (John)
Mckendrick, James (Stewart)
McKeon, Michael
McKeown, Tom
McKinlay, Brian John
McLane, Maureen N.
McLaughlin, Andrée Nicola
McLean, Sammy
McLeod, Joseph (Bertram)
McMaster, Rhyll
McMaster, Susan
McNair, Wesley C.
McNamara, Eugene Joseph
McNeill, Christine
McNeillie, Andrew

McPherson, Sandra
McWhirter, George
Mda, Zakes
Mead, Jane
Mead, Philip (Stirling)
Measham, Donald Charles
Meddeb, Abdelwahab
Medina, Tony
Medvedev, Grigori
Mee, Susie (B.)
Meehan, Paula
Mehrotra, Arvind Krishna
Meinke, Peter
Melançon, Robert
Melchiori, Barbara Arnett
Melnikoff, Pamela (Rita)
Meltzer, David
Memmott, David R.
Menes, Orlando Ricardo
Menninghaus, Winfried
Merrin, Jeredith
Merritt, Constance
Merwin, W(illiam) S(tanley)
Messer, Sarah
Metres, Philip
Metzger, Deena P.
Mezey, Robert
Michael, Colette V(erger)
Michaels, Anne
Middleton, (John) Christopher
Mikolyzk, Thomas A.
Miller, Anesa
Miller, Deborah
Miller, E. Ethelbert
Miller, Jane
Miller, Leslie Adrienne
Millett, John
Milligan, Bryce
Mills, Wilmer
Millum, Trevor
Miltner, Robert
Minar, Barbra (Goodyear)
Minarik, Else H(olmelund)
Minot, Susan A.
Mirikitani, Janice
Mishkin, Tracy
Mishra, Sudesh (Raj)
Mitcham, Judson
Mitchell, Roger
Moat, John
Moeyaert, Bart
Moffeit, Tony A.
Moffitt, Sharon McMahon
Mohin, Ann
Moldaw, Carol
Mole, John
Molesworth, Charles
Momaday, N(avarre) Scott
Monesson, Harry S.
Mong-Lan
Montague, John (Patrick)
Mordecai, Pamela (Claire)
Moreh, Shmuel
Morency, Pierre
Morgan, Elizabeth Seydel
Morgan, Nicholas H.
Morgan, Robert (R.)

Morgan, Robin
Mori, Kyoko
Morris, Bernard E.
Morris, Stephen
Morrison, (Philip) Blake
Morrison, Toni
Moshiri, Farnoosh
Mosley, Philip
Moss, Miriam
Moss, Stanley
Moss, Thylias (Rebecca)
Motion, Andrew (Peter)
Moxley, Jennifer
Moyer, Ann E.
Mu go, Mi cere Gi thae
Mudimbe, V. Y.
Muehl, Lois Baker
Mueller, Lisel
Muldoon, Paul
Munevar, Gonzalo
Muniz, Olga M.
Munro, John M(urchison)
Murdy, Louise Baughan
Murphy, Sylvia
Murray, Les(lie) (Allan)
Musgrave, Susan
Myers, Walter Dean
Myles, Eileen
Naiden, James
Napora, Joseph S.
Nash, Roger
Nasr, Seyyed Hossein
Nasrin, Taslima
Nayman, Michele
Neff, Lyle
Nelson, Geoffrey Kenneth
Nelson, Howard
Nemec, James
Nesbitt, John D.
Nesset, Kirk
Netifnet, Dadisi Mwende
New, William Herbert
Newcomer, James W.
Newlyn, Lucy
Newman, Jerry
Ní Chuilleanáin, Eiléan
Nichols, Grace
Nichols, John Gordon
Nichols, Peter (Richard)
Nickel, Barbara
Nicosia, Gerald (Martin)
Niskala, Brenda
Nitchie, George Wilson
Nolan, William F(rancis)
Norac, Carl
Norbrook, David
Nordhaus, Jean
Norén, Lars
Norrell, Gregory T.
Norris, Kathleen
Norris, Ken
Norris, Pamela
North, Charles
Northrup, Jim
Nurkse, D(ennis)
Nye, Naomi Shihab
Nye, Robert

Nyhart, Nina
O'Brien, Sean
O'Connor, Francis V(alentine)
O'Daly, William
O'Donoghue, Bernard
O'Driscoll, Dennis
O'Grady, Desmond (James Bernard)
O'Leary, Patrick
O'Neill, Tony
O'Riordan, Michelle
O'Rourke, P. J.
O'Siadhail, Micheal
Oates, Joyce Carol
Obika, Akili Addae
Ochart (Torres), (Luz) Yvonne
Odhiambo, David Nandi
Oguibe, Olu
Ogunyemi, Yemi D(iploman)
Ojaide, Tanure
Okri, Ben
Oktenberg, Adrian
Olaleye, Isaac O.
Olds, Sharon
Oliphant, Dave (Edward Davis)
Oliver, Mary
Olmsted, Robert W(alsh)
Olsen, Lance (M.)
Olson, Steven
Olson, Ted
Olson, Toby
Ondaatje, Michael
Ondego, Ogova
Oness, Elizabeth
Orlev, Uri
Ormondroyd, Edward
Ormsby, Frank
Orr, Gregory (Simpson)
Ortiz-Taylor, Sheila
Osborn, Karen
Osborne, Charles
Osers, Ewald
Osherow, Jacqueline
Osing, Gordon T.
Ostrom, Hans
Osundare, Niyi
Otten, Charlotte F(ennema)
Oughton, John P.
Overton, Ron
Owen, Maureen
Owens, Rochelle
Oxley, William
Pack, Robert
Padel, Ruth
Padgett, Ron
Padmore, Sandra
Page, Geoff(rey Donald)
Palencia, Elaine Fowler
Panofsky, Ruth
Paranjape, Makarand (Ramach-andra)
Parfitt, Will
Parini, Jay
Parry, Graham
Parson-Nesbitt, Julie
Parthasarathy, R(ajagopal)
Paschen, Elise (Maria)

Pastan, Linda
Paterson, Alistair (Ian Hughes)
Patten, Brian
Patterson, Jerry L.
Paul, Ann Whitford
Pawlak, Mark
Pazzi, Roberto
Peabody, Richard (Myers)
Peacock, Molly
Pearsall, Derek (Albert)
Pearson, Carol Lynn
Peeler, Tim
Peeradina, Saleem
Penelope, Julia
Perelman, Bob
Perez, Rolando
Pérez-Oramas, Luis
Perkins, Michael
Perloff, Marjorie (Gabrielle)
Peters, Lisa Westberg
Peters, Robert
Peterson, Richard S(cot)
Petrie, Paul (James)
Petty, W(illiam) H(enry)
Phelan, Joseph
Philip, M(arlene) NourbeSe
Phillippy, Patricia Berrahou
Phillips, Carl
Phillips, Patrick
Piccirilli, Tom
Pick, Alison
Pickard, Tom
Pickering, David (Hugh)
Pierce, Patricia Jobe
Piercy, Marge
Pierpoint, Katherine
Piirto, Jane
Pilling, Christopher (Robert)
Pinsker, Sanford S.
Pinsky, Robert
Pite, Ralph
Pitt-Kethley, (Helen) Fiona
Pizzichini, Lilian
Place, Milner
Platt, Donald
Plumly, Stanley (Ross)
Poch, John
Polito, Robert
Polkinhorn, Harry
Polukhina, Valentina
Pomerantz, Charlotte
Poole, Richard
Pope, Deborah
Poster, Jem
Potter, Carol
Powell, Craig
Powell, D. A.
Powell, Dannye Romine
Powell, Joseph
Powell, Kevin
Powell, Neil
Pownall, David
Powning, Beth
Prado, Holly
Pratt, John Clark
Pratt, Tim
Prelutsky, Jack

Presnell, Barbara
Price, Victor (Henry John)
Priestman, Martin
Prince, Alison
Protopopescu, Orel
Prynne, J. H.
Purdy, Dwight H(illiard)
Purpura, Lia
Purser, John W(hitley)
Putter, Ad
Pybus, Rodney
Quattlebaum, Mary
Queeney, Courtney
Quiatt, Duane
Quiñones, Magaly
Quinsey, Katherine M.
Rabassa, Gregory
Radzienda, Tom
Raine, Craig (Anthony)
Rajan, Tilottama
Ramazani, Jahan
Ramsay, Jay
Ramsey, Jarold
Rand, Harry
Randall, Margaret
Ransom, Jane (Reavill)
Rash, Ron
Ratcliff, Carter
Ratcliffe, Eric Hallam
Ravel, Edeet
Ray, David
Ray, Judy
Ray, Robert H.
Raz, Hilda
Read, David
Read, Sylvia Joan
Redhill, Michael H.
Redonnet, Marie
Reece, Erik
Reed, Ishmael
Reed, James
Reed, Thomas L.
Reeve, F(ranklin) D(olier)
Reibetanz, John
Reichertz, Ronald R.
Reid, Alastair
Reidel, James
Reinfeld, Linda M.
Reiss, Edward
Rekdal, Paisley
Renaux, Sigrid
Renker, Elizabeth
Revard, Carter (Curtis)
Rhodes, Martha
Riach, Alan
Ricapito, Joseph V.
Rich, Adrienne (Cecile)
Rich, Elaine Sommers
Rich, Susan
Richter, Gregory C.
Richter, Harvena
Riede, David G(eorge)
Rifbjerg, Klaus (Thorvald)
Rivard, David
Rivas, Manuel
Rivera, Eléna
Roberts, Francis X.

Robertson, Barbara Anne
Robertson, Robin
Robinson, Lee
Robson, Lloyd
Roddick, Alan
Rodriguez, Alejo
Rodríguez, Andrés
Rodriguez, Judith (Green)
Rodriguez, Luis J.
Roe, Sue
Roeske, Paulette
Rogovoy, Seth
Rogow, Zack
Ronk, Martha C(lare)
Rooksby, Rikky
Root, William Pitt
Root-Bernstein, Michèle
Roripaugh, Robert (Alan)
Rosemurgy, Catie
Rosen, Michael (Wayne)
Rosen, Michael J(oel)
Rosen, Stanley Howard
Rosenberg, John D(avid)
Rosenberg, Liz
Rosenblatt, Joseph
Rosner, Elizabeth J.
Ross, Stuart
Rothenberg, Jerome
Rouse, Anne (Barrett)
Roy, Lucinda (H.)
Rubin, Larry (Jerome)
Rucker, Rudy
Ruddell, Deborah
Rudolf, Anthony
Rudy, Jason R.
Ruefle, Mary
Rumens, Carol
Rupp, Joyce
Rush, Christopher
Russell, Norman H.
Rutledge, Leigh W.
Rutsala, Vern A.
Ryan, Gig (Elizabeth)
Ryan, Kay
Ryan, Margaret
Ryder, Joanne (Rose)
Rykwert, Joseph
Saenz, Benjamin Alire
Saenz, Gil
Sail, Lawrence (Richard)
Šalamun, Toma
Salazar, Dixie
Salinger, Michael
Sallis, James
Salter, Mary Jo
Salwak, Dale (Francis)
Salzman, Eva Frances
Sambrook, A(rthur) J(ames)
Sanchez, Sonia
Sandburg, Helga
Sanders, Ed(ward)
Sanders, Tony
Sandy, Stephen
Saner, Reg(inald Anthony)
Sansom, Peter
Santos, Sherod
Saroyan, Aram

Sato, Hiroaki
Savard, Jeannine
Savitzkaya, Eugne
Savren, Shelley
Sawyer-Laucanno, Christopher
Scarfe, Wendy (Elizabeth)
Schakel, Peter J.
Scheele, Roy
Schelling, Andrew
Scherf, Kathleen D.
Schiff, Robyn
Schmidt, Michael (Norton)
Schmitz, Dennis
Schor, Esther H.
Schott, Penelope Scambly
Schultz, Susan M.
Schwarcz, Vera
Schwartz, Lynne Sharon
Schwarz, Arturo (Samuele)
Schwarz, Daniel R(oger)
Scott, Whitney S.
Scully, James (Joseph)
Scupham, (John) Peter
Seals, David
Seaton, J(erome) P.
Seay, James
Sedgwick, Fred
Segun, Mabel D.
Seidel, Frederick (Lewis)
Seidman, Hugh
Seiferle, Rebecca
Sellers, Heather (Laurie)
Sellin, Eric
Selman, Robyn
Senior, Olive (Marjorie)
Serrano, Lucienne J.
Seshadri, Vijay
Seth, Vikram
Sewell, Lisa
Shafer, Audrey
Shammas, Anton
Shangé, Ntozake
Shankar, S.
Shapcott, Thomas W(illiam)
Shapiro, David (Joel)
Shapiro, Harvey
Shaughnessy, Brenda
Shaw, Carolyn V.
Shaw, Robert B.
Sheehan, Julie
Sheehan, Michael J.
Sheeler, Jackie
Shelby, Anne
Shelton, Richard
Shepard, Neil
Sherman, Arnold
Sherman, Jason
Shomer, Enid
Shookman, Ellis
Shreiber, Maeera Yaffa
Shumaker, Peggy
Shuttle, Penelope (Diane)
Sibum, Norm
Sikélianòs, Eleni
Silesky, Barry
Silver, Norman
Simic, Charles

Simic, Goran
Simmie, Lois (Ann)
Simonelli, Jeanne M(arie)
Simpson, Anne
Simpson, Michael Andrew
Sinclair, Iain
Singer, Marilyn
Sinister, Bucky
Sinnett, Mark C.
Sirowitz, Hal
Sirr, Peter
Skinner, Knute (Rumsey)
Skloot, Floyd
Skrzynecki, Peter
Slade, Leonard A.
Sleigh, Tom
Slesinger, Warren
Sloan, John
Sloat, Teri
Slosberg, Mike
Smarandache, Florentin
Smith, Annick
Smith, D. James
Smith, Dave
Smith, Gavin D.
Smith, Nigel
Smith, Patricia
Smith, Vivian (Brian)
Smith, William Jay
Smither, Elizabeth
Snyder, Gary (Sherman)
Snyder, Laurel
Snyder, Lucy A.
Snyder, Zilpha Keatley
Sommer, Jason
Sonnevi, Göran
Soto, Gary
Souster, Raymond
Soyinka, Wole
Spacks, Barry
Spahr, Juliana
Sparshott, Francis (Edward)
Speer, Laurel
Spencer, Brent
Spencer, John (Walter)
Spivack, Kathleen (Romola
    Drucker)
Spooner, Michael
Sprackland, Jean
St. John, David
Staley, Lynn
Stallworthy, Jon (Howie)
Stammers, John
Stanton, Joseph
Stark, Marisa Kantor
Starkey, David
Stead, C(hristian) K(arlson)
Steele, Cynthia
Steele, Timothy (Reid)
Stein, Kevin
Stepanchev, Stephen
Stephen, Martin
Stephens, Meic
Sterle, Francine
Stern, Gerald
Sternlicht, Sanford
Stevens, Bryna

Stevens, Peter (Stanley)
Stevenson, James
Stevenson (Lucas), Anne
Stewart, Jack (F.)
Stewart, Kathleen
Stewart, Mary (Florence Elinor)
Stewart, Susan
Stillinger, Jack
Stone, Ruth
Storey, Edward
Storey, Gail Donohue
Stowe, William W.
Straub, Peter (Francis)
Strauss, Gwen
Strauss, Jennifer (Wallace)
Strickland, Michael R.
Stryk, Lucien
Stuart, Dabney
Suen, Anastasia
Sundahl, Daniel James
Sunshine, Linda
Sutton, Dana F.
Sutton, David John
Svenvold, Mark
Svoboda, Terese
Sward, Robert S.
Sweeney, Matthew
Swetman, Glenn R(obert)
Sylvester, Janet
Sze, Arthur C.
Szirtes, George
Szybist, Mary
Szymborska, Wislawa
Taaffe, Sonya
Tabios, Eileen
Talbot, Emile J.
Tamblyn, Amber
Tapahonso, Luci
Tarn, Nathaniel
Tarnopolsky, Yuri
Tate, James (Vincent)
Taylor, Andrew (McDonald)
Taylor, Bruce
Taylor, Gary
Taylor, Henry
Taylor, Janelle (Diane Williams)
Taylor, Walter Kingsley
Teicher, Craig Morgan
Tellermann, Esther
Terpstra, John
Terris, Susan
Thalmann, William
Thesen, Sharon
Thibodeau, Serge Patrice
Thiel, Diane
Thomas, D(onald) M(ichael)
Thomas, H(ubert) Nigel
Thompson, Kate
Thompson, Robert Bruce
Thompson, William Irwin
Thomson, Derick S(mith)
Thwaite, Anthony (Simon)
Thynn, Alexander (George)
Tidwell, John Edgar
Tihanyi, Eva
Tillinghast, Richard
Tillman, Deborah Lindsay

Tipton, David
Tobias, Michael (Charles)
Tokarczyk, Michelle M.
Tomajczyk, S. F.
Tomalin, Ruth
Tomey, Ingrid
Tomlinson, (Alfred) Charles
Tong, Raymond
Townley, Wyatt
Townsend, Ann
Tranter, John (Ernest)
Trawick, Leonard M.
Traxler, Patricia
Trethewey, Natasha
Triggs, Tony D.
Trombley, Laura Skandera
Trueman, Terry
Truitt, Sam
Truman, Ruth
Tsaloumas, Dimitris
Tucker, Martin
Turco, Lewis (Putnam)
Turner, Ann (Warren)
Turner, Brian (Lindsay)
Turner, John Frayn
Turner, Martin
Ueda, Makoto
Ursell, Geoffrey
Valentine, Jean
Valle, Victor Manuel
Vallee, Lillian (Bozenna)
Vallejo, Armando
Van Clief-Stefanon, Lyrae N.
Van Domelen, John E(mory)
van Heerden, Etienne
vas Dias, Robert
Velásquez, Gloria (Louise)
Venclova, Tomas
Vendler, Helen (Hennessy)
Ventura, Michael
Vertreace-Doody, Martha Modena
Vicuna, Cecilia
Vigée, Claude (Andre Strauss)
Villatoro, Marcos McPeek
Viorst, Judith
Virgo, Seán
Viscusi, Robert
Vitiello, Justin
Vizenor, Gerald (Robert)
Voigt, Ellen Bryant
Von Ahnen, Katherine
Voss, Sarah (Henderson)
Waddington, Raymond B(ruce)
Waddington-Feather, John Joseph
Wade, Sidney
Wade, Stephen
Wagner-Martin, Linda C.
Wagoner, David (Russell)
Wahl, Jan
Wainwright, Jeffrey
Wakoski, Diane
Wald, Diane
Waldman, Anne
Waldoff, Leon
Wallace, Naomi (French)
Wallace-Crabbe, Christopher
    (Keith)

Near, Holly
Nelson, Ray
Nelson, Samuel H.
O'Callahan, Jay
O'Leary, Patrick
Osborne, Will
Padmore, Sandra
Palandri, Enrico
Palmer, Hap
Penner, Fred (Ralph Cornelius)
Pickard, Tom
Policoff, Stephen Phillip
Poole, Josephine
Poole, Richard

Raffi
Ramsey, Jarold
Riley, Martin
Roach, Archie
Rodriguez, Judith (Green)
Roscoe, Patrick
Ryan, Gig (Elizabeth)
Salzman, Eva Frances
Saperstein, David
Scheindlin, Raymond P.
Scholey, Arthur (Edward)
Seleshanko, Kristina
Shapcott, Thomas W(illiam)
Simic, Goran

Singer, Barry
Sparrowdancer, Mary
Sprinkle, Patricia Houck
Stevens, Bryna
Storey, Edward
Swain, Joseph P(eter)
Talalay, Kathryn M(arguerite)
Tapahonso, Luci
Taylor, Andrew (McDonald)
Terry, Megan
Thomas, Rob
Thomson, Derick S(mith)
Trawick, Leonard M.
Truman, Ruth

Turco, Lewis (Putnam)
Vachss, Andrew H(enry)
Walwicz, Ania
Wandor, Michelene
Watt, Ben
Weaver-Gelzer, Charlotte
Webber, Andrew Lloyd
Weber, Katharine
Wilbur, Richard (Purdy)
Wilson, (Brian) Geoffrey
Wilson, Sandy
Wolfe, George C.
Yolen, Jane
Young, Ruth

Non-fiction

Administration/Management

Adams, Roy J(oseph)
Agrawal, Arun
Albert, Michael
Alessandra, Tony
Anderson, Gary L.
Avolio, Bruce J.
Bacon, Lauren
Baer, Greg
Bailey, Martha (J.)
Bailyn, Lotte
Bakewell, Kenneth (Graham Bartlett)
Bashe, Philip (Scott)
Beatley, Timothy
Belkaoui, Ahmed R.
Benton, D(ebra) A.
Bhote, Keki R.
Birkland, Thomas A.
Bittlestone, Robert
Blair, Steven N.
Bolman, Lee G.
Bosticco, (Isabel Lucy) Mary
Boston, Jonathan
Boyett, Jimmie T.
Boyett, Joseph H.
Bragg, Steven M.
Brown, Robert G(oodell)
Bruns, William John
Brush, Kathleen (E.)
Burack, Elmer H(oward)
Burch, Geoff
Burns, James MacGregor
Camp, Robert C.
Caplan, Arthur L(eonard)
Caponigro, Jeffrey R.
Cespedes, Frank V.
Chaleff, Ira
Chorafas, Dimitris N.
Chowdhury, Subir
Clark, Will
Clawson, James G.
Cohen, Cary
Conway, Jill Ker
Cooper, Cary L.
Cooper, Terry L.
Copeman, George Henry
Corrington, Robert S.
Cox, Roger (Kenneth)
Crew, Rudy
Culp, Stephanie (Anne)
D'aveni, Richard
Davidson, Sol M.
de Bono, Edward (Francis Charles)
Desfor, Gene
Devlin, Albert J.
Devney, Darcy C(ampion)
DiRenzo, Anthony
Donnithorne, Larry R.
Doyle, Robert J.
Dreher, Henry
Dyer, Davis
Eaton, Jack
Eilon, Samuel
Elster, Kathi

Administration/Management-*cont.*

Fancutt, Walter
Feldman, Noah (R.)
Fiedler, Fred E(dward)
Flynn, Nancy L.
Fombrun, Charles J.
Frame, J. Davidson
Franklin, Daniel P.
Fremgen, James Morgan
Frigstad, David B.
Fruin, W. Mark
Fullan, Michael G.
Funakawa, Atsushi
Gabrieli, Christopher
Gannon, Martin John
Garten, Helen A.
Gecan, Michael
Ghosh, Arun Kumar
Giri, Ananta Kumar
Glantz, Kalman
Glen, Paul (Michael)
Gordon, Grant
Gottfredson, Mark Alan
Green, Charles H.
Green, Daryl D.
Greener, Michael John
Guaspari, John
Hackler, George
Hamel, Gary
Hamrin, Robert
Hannesson, Rögnvaldur
Harris, Philip Robert
Harris, Thomas (E.)
Harrison, J. Richard
Hatch, Michael F.
Heine, Arthur J.
Hiam, Alexander
Higham, Robin
Hoffman, Allan M.
Holmes, Leslie (Templeman)
Humphreys, George G(ary)
Hunt, Tristram
Ingram, Heather E(lizabeth)
Jarvis, William E.
Jay, Antony (Rupert)
Jensen, Clayne
Johns, Jeremy
Jones, Lawrence K.
Kambil, Ajit
Kanungo, R(abindra) N.
Kapferer, Jean-Noel
Kaplan, Robert S.
Katzenbach, Jon R.
Kemp, Roger L.
Kenjo, Takashi
Kerr, Steven
King, William Richard
Kotter, John P(aul)
Kraushar, Peter Maximilian
Kuczmarski, Thomas D(ale)
Kunda, Gideon
Kushnick, Louis
LeBoeuf, Michael
Leonard, Dorothy
Levinson, Harry
Lewis, (Norman) Douglas
Locke, Robert R.

Administration/Management-*cont.*

Lockerbie, D(onald) Bruce
Loen, Raymond O(rdell)
Loudon, David L.
Lowenstein, Michael W.
Lundman, Richard J.
Lynn, Adele B.
Maccoby, Michael
Maddison, Sarah
Maheshwari, Shriram
Malmgren, Dallin
Mann, Pamela
Mantel, Samuel J(oseph)
Manz, Charles C.
Manzoni, Jean-François
Marcuse, Gary
Margalit, Gilad
Markides, Constantinos C.
Marks, Mitchell Lee
Marriner Tomey, Ann
Martin, Roderick
Mason, Linda
Massie, Joseph Logan
Mayfield, Terry L.
Mazur, Laurie Ann
McColgan, John Joseph
McKenna, Patrick J.
McLean, J. W.
McNeal, Patricia
Mears, Emira
Melnyk, Steven A.
Merkhofer, Miley W(esson Lee)
Montgomery, David Bruce
Moonman, Eric
Moreau, David Merlin
Moskowitz, Robert A.
Mui, Chunka
Musgrave, Gerald L.
Neck, Christopher P.
Noer, David M.
Noltingk, Bernard Edward
Nutt, Paul C.
Ochart (Torres), (Luz) Yvonne
Oppenheim, Lois Hecht
Osterman, Paul
Palestini, Robert
Paludi, Michele A.
Park, Timothy K.
Parker, Glenn M.
Pascale, Richard Tanner
Pasewark, William Robert
Patten, Thomas H.
Patzer, Gordon
Peabody, Richard (Myers)
Peck, Merton Joseph
Pence, Joanne
Petty, W(illiam) H(enry)
Pollack, Kenneth M(ichael)
ReVelle, Jack B.
Roos, Johan
Rosaler, Robert C.
Rosner, Bob
Rossum, Ralph A.
Rothwell, William J.
Rowh, Mark
Rowland, Arthur Ray
Rowntree, Derek

Administration/Management-*cont.*

Roy, James (Henry Barstow)
Sanford, Kathleen (D.)
Schaefer, David Lewis
Schendel, Dan
Sebell, Mark Henry
Semler, Ricardo
Sessa, Valerie I.
Seybold, Patricia B.
Shim, Jae K.
Shivers, Jay Sanford
Shuman, Samuel I.
Simon, Harvey B(ruce)
Sims, Henry P.
Sjostrand, Sven-Erik
Smith, Douglas K.
Smith, H. Jeff
Smith, Steven
Snow, Philip (Albert)
Soden, Garrett
Spencer, Robert H.
St. Clair, William
Steel, D(avid) R(obert)
Steinberg, Erwin R.
Steiner, George A.
Steinmetz, Lawrence Leo
Sten, Christopher (W.)
Stening, Bruce W.
Stewart, Rosemary
Stewart, Thomas A(lan)
Stopford, John M(orton)
Susman, Gerald I.
Sutton, Robert I.
Thierauf, Robert James
Tripodi, Tony
Tropman, John E.
Troy, Tevi David
Truscott, Peter
Tulgan, Bruce L.
Tweed, Stephen C.
Vandermerwe, Sandra
Venardos, Thomas J(oseph)
Vroom, Victor H.
Wadia, Maneck S.
Walker, Kenneth Roland
Walton, Mary
Warmington, William Allan
Warner, Sharon Oard
Webber, Ross A.
Wellington, Sheila W(acks)
Wendover, Robert W(arren)
Wert, Jonathan (Maxwell)
Wettenhall, Roger L.
Whittle, Chris
Winnick, R. H.
Wolf, Sarah (Elizabeth)
Woll, Peter
Woodhull, Winifred
Wooldridge, Adrian
Zaremba, Alan Jay
Zook, Chris
Zweifel, Thomas D.

Eyetsemitan, Frank E.
Faber, Michel
Fabricant, Michael B.
Falk, Stanley Lawrence
Falsani, Cathleen
Farley, David
Farmer, Penelope (Jane)
Farmiloe, Dorothy
Faulkner, Mary
Fehler, Gene
Feinberg, Richard
Feinstein, Edward
Feinstein, Elaine
Feldman, Noah (R.)
Fell, Dafydd
Fenton, Alexander
Ferguson, Gary
Ferguson, Kitty
Ferguson, Will
Fernandez-Shaw, Carlos M(anuel)
Ferraro, Barbara
Ferreiro, Larrie D.
Ferrell, Jeff
Ferris, Jeri Chase
Fessler, Ann
Figes, Eva
Fink, Sheri
Finkel, Caroline
Finkelstein, Max W.
Finkle, Derek
Finnegan, Terrence J.
Finnegan, William (Patrick)
Finstad, Suzanne
Fischetti, Mark
Fitzpatrick, Mary Anne
Flaherty, Alice W.
Flamm, Michael W.
Flaste, Richard (Alfred)
Flayhart, William Henry
Fleming, Anne
Fleming, Justin
Flenley, John (Roger)
Flinders, Neil J.
Floegstad, Kjartan
Flood, (Nancy) Bo
Foley, Denise (M.)
Foran, John
Ford, Brian John
Ford, Michael Thomas
Forder, Anthony
Foreman, George
Forrester, Duncan B(aillie)
Forret, Jeff
Fortey, Richard
Foss, Sonja K.
Foster, Raymond E.
Fowler, Gene
Fowlkes, Diane L(owe)
Fox, Faulkner
Fox, John O.
Fox, Margalit
Fox, Mem
Foy, George Michelsen
Fraiser, Jim
Frame, J. Davidson
Francis, Dorothy Brenner
Francis, R(ichard) A.

Frank, Frederick S.
Frank, Robert
Frankel, Valerie
Frappier-Mazur, Lucienne
Fraser, Laura (Jane)
Frassetto, Michael
Freedman, Jonathan (Borwick)
Freedman, Russell (Bruce)
Freedman, Sarah Warshauer
Freeman, Marcia S.
Freese, Barbara
Frey, Julia (Bloch)
Fricchione, Gregory
Friedlander, Shems
Friedman, Bonnie
Friedman, George
Friedmann, Daniel
Friend, Craig Thompson
Fritz, Jean
Fritze, Ronald H.
Fromm, Pete
Frost, David (Paradine)
Frost, Helen
Frost, Linda
Frost, Shelley
Frueh, Joanna
Frye, Marilyn
Fulghum, Robert (L.)
Fussell, Paul
Futcher, Jane P.
Gaard, Greta
Gage, Eleni N.
Gagliano, Anthony
Galang, M. Evelina
Gall, Lothar
Gallagher, Tom
Galloway, Janice
Gamson, Joshua (Paul)
Gandt, Robert
Gansky, Alton
Gardam, Jane
Garner, Helen
Garrett, Leslie
Gaubatz, Kathlyn Taylor
Geist, Bill
Gelderman, Carol (Wettlaufer)
Gellis, Roberta (Leah Jacobs)
Gentleman, David
Gentry, Curt
Genya, Monica
Gerard, Philip
Gerrard, Michael B.
Gesch, Roy (George)
Getz, David
Gibson, Alan
Gibson, Chris
Gifford, Rob
Gilbert, Alma M.
Gilbert, John Raphael
Gillies, Valerie
Gimblett, Richard H.
Giovino, Andrea
Glancy, Diane
Glassman, Bruce
Goerner, Sally J.
Gold, Dore
Goldfarb, Jeffrey C.

Goldman, Ari L.
Goldstone, Patricia
Gommans, Jos J. L.
Goodall, Jane
Goodfield, (Gwyneth) June
Goodman, Richard
Goodstein, Phil
Goodwin, Neil
Gordimer, Nadine
Gordon, Mary (Catherine)
Gordon, Robert Ellis
Gorman, Martha
Gorup, Radmila J(ovanovi)
Gose, Peter
Grace, Alexander M.
Graham, Bob
Graham, Laurie
Graham, Ysenda (May) Maxtone
Gralla, Cynthia
Gran, Peter
Gray, Christopher
Gray, Clayton
Gray, Dulcie
Graydon, Shari
Grearson, Jessie Carroll
Green, Daryl D.
Green, Duncan
Green, J. Paul
Green, James
Green, Toby
Greene, Constance C(larke)
Greene, Melissa Fay
Greenhalgh, Susan
Greenwood, David Luis Valdes
Greif, Karen F.
Griffin, Jill
Grippo, Charles
Grisso, Thomas
Groom, Winston (Francis)
Gross, Michael L.
Gross, Philip (John)
Grossman, David
Grover, Jan(ice) Zita
Grover, Wayne
Grow, L(ynn) M(erle)
Gundy, Jeff(rey Gene)
Gurvis, Sandra J.
Guste, Roy F(rancis)
Haberman, Jacob
Hackett, Jeremy
Hackett, Joyce
Haidt, Jonathan
Haiken, Elizabeth
Haizlip, Shirlee Taylor
Hakala, Dee
Hall, Lesley A(nn)
Hallowell, Edward McKey
Hamilton, James
Hamilton, Sharon Jean
Han, Béatrice
Hankin, Elizabeth Rosemary
Hansen, Drew D.
Hansen, Maren Tonder
Hansen, Matthew Scott
Hardin, Russell
Harding, Les
Hardy, Gayle J.

Haring, Bruce
Harlan, Judith
Harmon, Daniel E(lton)
Harper, Judith E.
Harrington, Philip S(tuart)
Harris, C. Nelson
Harris, Marion (Rose)
Harris, Robie H.
Harrison, Jim
Harrison, Kathryn
Hart, Lenore
Harteis, Richard
Harter, Penny
Hartley, Hal
Hartmann, Thom
Harvey, David
Harvey, Steven
Harvey, Susan Ashbrook
Haskell, Molly
Hasselstrom, Linda (Michele)
Hatton, Caroline
Haugen, Hayley Mitchell
Hauser, Susan Carol
Hayden, C. J.
Hayduk, Ron
Haynes, C. Rayfield
Haynes, Gary (Anthony)
Head, John
Heckert, Connie K(aye Delp)
Hefer, Hayim (Baruch)
Heim, Michael Henry
Heising, Willetta L.
Hellenga, Robert
Heller, Michael
Helmreich, Anne
Henderson, Harold
Henneberger, Melinda
Henning, Ann
Herbert, James
Herding, Klaus
Herman, Barbara
Herman, Michelle
Hernandez, Jo Farb
Herndon, Terry (Eugene)
Herrick, James A.
Herrick, Steven
Herz, Rachel
Hess, Elizabeth
Hevia, James L.
Hicken, Mandy
Hickey, Caroline
Hickman, Bert G(eorge)
Higgs, Liz Curtis
High, Linda Oatman
Highfield, (John) Roger (Loxdale)
Hilberry, Conrad Arthur
Hildebrandt, Erik A(lan)
Hill, Anthony (Robert)
Hill, Marion Moore
Hilles, Robert
Hilmes, Michele
Hilsman, Gordon J.
Himelfarb, Richard
Himmel, Richard L.
Hinde, Thomas
Hinds, P(atricia) Mignon
Hinze, Bradford E.

Littlefield, Holly
Littleton, Mark (R.)
Livingston, Gordon (S.)
Locke, Robert R.
Lockwood, Jeffrey A(lan)
Logan, William
Lomas, Herbert
Long, Christopher
Looney, Dennis (Oscar)
Looser, Devoney
Lopez, Steve
Lord, Nancy J.
Lott, Bret
Loud, Patricia Cummings
Loudon, Mary
Loughery, John
Lounsberry, Barbara
Low, Brian J.
Lowe, Joy L.
Lowe, Mick
Lowe, Sheila
Lucado, Max (Lee)
Lucey, Michael
Luis, William
Lukken, Miriam
Lumer, Christoph
Lumry, Amanda (R.)
Lunde, Paul
Lunn, Janet (Louise Swoboda)
Luongo-Orlando, Katherine
Luper, Steven
Lusane, Clarence
Lustig, Nora Claudia
Lutz, Tom
Lux, Maureen K.
Lyon, Elizabeth
Lystra, Karen
Mac, Carrie
Mac Donald, Laura M.
MacDonald, Ann-Marie
Macdonald, Norman Malcolm
MacEoin, Denis
Macesich, George
MacGregor, Neil
Maclean, Rory
MacLeod, Ken
MacRae, Molly
Madden, David
Madenski, Melissa (Ann)
Madigan, Brian (Christoper)
Maharaj, Rabindranath
Maharidge, Dale (Dimitro)
Maher, Mary
Mahindra, Indira
Maier, Anne McDonald
Majaj, Lisa Suhair
Majors, Richard G.
Malvasi, Meg Greene
Mandler, Peter
Mann, Jessica
Mann, Judith (W.)
Mann, Pamela
Mann, Thomas E.
Manzoni, Jean-François
Maracle, Lee
Marcell, Jacqueline
Marcom, Micheline Aharonian

Marcum, David
Marcus, Ben
Margalit, Gilad
Margolis, Jonathan
Marin, Rosario
Marino, Anne (N.)
Markoosie
Marks, Kathy (L.)
Marks, Mitchell Lee
Marks, Paula Mitchell
Markus, Julia
Marrs, Jim
Mars, Julie
Mars, Perry
Marsa, Linda J.
Marshall, Bridget M(ary)
Marshall, Paul A.
Martin, Andy
Martin, Philip R.
Martin, Russell
Martin-Jones, David
Martinet, Jeanne
Martinez, Andrés
Martínez, Dionisio D.
Marty, Sid
Marvel, Thomas S.
Marzluff, John M.
Masco, Joseph P.
Mason, Adrienne
Mass, Wendy
Matott, Justin
Matsusaka, John G.
Maxford, Howard
May, Brian
May, Julian
Mayall, Beth
Mayer, Musa
Mazower, Mark
Mazzaro, Jerome
McAllen, Jack
McAlpine, Rachel (Taylor)
McCall, Jeffrey
Mccann, Maria
McCarthy, Mignon
McCartney, Scott
McCauley, Sue
McChesney, Robert Waterman
Mccoole, Sinéad
McCormick, Blaine
McCoy, Max
McCoy, William C.
McCullin, Don(ald)
Mccullough, Kate
McCutcheon, William Alan
Mcdaniel, Bruce A.
McDermott, Jeanne
McDonald, Brian
McElmurray, Karen Salyer
McElroy, Colleen J.
McGinniss, Joe
McGrath, Melanie
McGuane, Thomas
McIlwaine, John
McKenna, Patrick J.
McKie, Robin
McKittrick, David
Mclaren, Joseph

McLaughlin, Andrew
Mclaughlin, Martin L.
McLean, Stuart
McLerran, Alice
McManus, John C.
McManus, Michael
McMullan, Margaret
McNally, Patrick S.
McNutt, Randy
McPhee, Jenny
McPhee, John (Angus)
McPhee, Martha (A.)
McPhee, Norma H.
McWilliams, Karen
Meaker, Marijane (Agnes)
Means, D. Bruce
Megivern, James J(oseph)
Melady, Thomas (Patrick)
Melich, Tanya
Mellor, John W(illiams)
Melnyczuk, Askold
Melnyk, Andrew
Mendes, Irene Vilar
Mercer, Jeremy
Merser, Cheryl
Messer, Richard
Mester, Terri A.
Meyerson, Debra E.
Michaels, Walter Benn
Micheels, Peter A.
Michelson, Karin
Miele, Frank
Miklowitz, Gloria D.
Milis, Ludo(vicus) J. R.
Miller, Charles A.
Miller, David (Leslie)
Miller, Neil
Miller, Nina
Milligan, Bryce
Mills, Peter R.
Millum, Trevor
Milton, Giles
Misurella, Fred
Mitchell, Gillian
Mitchell, Helen Buss
Mitchell, Mark
Mitchell, Mark T.
Monahan, William G(regory)
Monmonier, Mark
Monoson, S. Sara
Montgomery, Sy
Montpetit, Charles
Moody, Fred
Mooney, Brian C.
Mooney, Robert
Moore, Lucy
Moreau, David Merlin
Morey, Melanie M.
Morgan, Dan
Morgan, Francesca
Morgan, Mary
Mori, Kyoko
Moro, Javier
Morrey, Douglas J.
Morris, Bob
Morris, Christopher W.
Morris, David

Morris, Jan
Morris, Jeffrey B(randon)
Morris, S(tephen) Brent
Morrisson, Mark S.
Morton, Bruce Rutherfurd
Morton, Patricia
Moschella, David C.
Moschis, George P.
Moses, Robert P(arris)
Mott, Robert L.
Muir, Helen
Mukherjee, Bharati
Mullett, John St. Hilary
Mullin, Robert Bruce
Munro, Donald J(acques)
Murakami, Haruki
Murarka, Shyam P.
Murphy, Austin
Murphy, Cullen
Murray, Bruce T.
Murray, Yxta Maya
Murren, Doug(las)
Mutz, Diana C.
Nadelmann, Ethan A.
Naden, Corinne J.
Nadler, John
Nason, Tema
Nasr, Kameel B.
Nasrin, Taslima
Naylor, Phyllis Reynolds
Neck, Christopher P.
Neder, Dennis W.
Negev, Eilat
Neiwert, David A.
Nelson, James L.
Nelson, Mariah Burton
Nemec, James
Nesbitt, John D.
Nesset, Kirk
Nevins, Joseph
Nevo, Joseph
Nguyên, Kiên
Nicholls, Henry
Nicholson, Lois P.
Nickel, Douglas R.
Nicosia, Gerald (Martin)
Niditch, Susan
Niemann, Greg
Nissman, Blossom S.
Nkala, Nathan
Nodelman, Perry
Nollen, Scott Allen
Norman, Barry
Nuechterlein, Jonathan E.
Nunez, Sigrid
Nussbaum, Jeff
Nyamnjoh, Francis B.
Nye, David E.
O'Brien, D(enis) P(atrick)
O'Connor, Stephen
O'Hagan, Andrew
O'Hearn, Denis
O'Keefe, Kevin
O'Leary, Patsy Baker
O'Reilly, Kenneth
O'Rourke, William
O'Toole, Patricia E.

Sherlock, Patti
Sherr, Lynn B(eth)
Sherrard-Johnson, Cherene
Shetterly, Aran
Shevelow, Kathryn
Shinagel, Michael
Shipman, John Marlin
Shlaes, Amity
Shone, Ronald
Short, Philip
Shrout, Richard Neil
Shuken, Julia
Shulman, Seth
Shumaker, Peggy
Shuman, George D.
Siegel, Daniel M.
Siemens, Alfred H.
Siggins, Lorna
Sikorski, Radek (Tomasz)
Silverblatt, Art
Simmons, Cynthia Francene
Simmons, Thomas
Simon, Francesca
Simon, Roger (Mitchell)
Simonds, Merilyn
Simonelli, Jeanne M(arie)
Simpson, John Warfield
Sinclair, Olga (Ellen)
Singer, Bayla
Singer, Marilyn
Sington, David
Sinyard, Neil
Siverson, Randolph M.
Skidmore, Max J(oseph)
Skinner, Stephen
Skloot, Floyd
Skreslet, Paula Youngman
Skyler, Heather
Sloane, Peter J(ames)
Slouka, Mark
Smiley, Jane (Graves)
Smith, Gordon Roland
Smith, Janna M(alamud)
Smith, M. J.
Smith, Mark Haskell
Smith, Scott
Smith, Stephanie A.
Smith, Wesley J.
Smith, William Jay
Smoley, Richard
Snelling, Lauraine
Snyder, James D.
Snyder, Jane McIntosh
Snyder, Laurel
Sobel, David T.
Soffer, Olga
Sokol, Julia
Solbrig, Dorothy J.
Solheim, James
Solomon, Evan
Solotaroff, Ivan
Somers, Jeff
Sorenson, Margo
Soto, Gary
South, Mary
Sowell, David (Lee)
Spalding, Andrea

Sparks, Randy J.
Speakes, Larry (Melvin)
Spedale, Darren R.
Speer, Laurel
Spencer, Elizabeth
Spiegelman, Annie
Spivack, Kathleen (Romola
   Drucker)
Spooner, Mary Helen
Spruyt, Hendrik
Spufford, Francis
Spurling, Hilary
St. George, Andrew
St. George, Judith
Stainback, Berry
Stallard, Michael L.
Stanton, Richard C.
Starita, Joe
Starr, Patti
Steavenson, Wendell
Steckel, Richard
Steele, Timothy (Reid)
Stein, Edward D.
Stein, Leslie
Steinberg, Neil
Steinberg, Warren
Steinman, David
Steinman, Louise
Stenger, Victor J.
Stern, Vivien
Sternberg, Robert J(effrey)
Stertz, Bradley A.
Stevens, Bryna
Stevens, Kathy
Stewart, Elizabeth A.
Stillman, David A.
Stine, Catherine
Stine, Scott A(aron)
Stingel, Janine
Story, Jonathan
Strathern, Paul
Strauss, Jennifer (Wallace)
Street, Brian Jeffrey
Streeten, Paul Patrick
Strelkoff, Tatiana
Stross, Randall E.
Stroud, Carsten
Stubbs, Jean
Stuever, Hank
Suen, Anastasia
Summers, Judith (Anne)
Summerscale, Kate
Surowiecki, James (Michael)
Sutcliffe, Jane
Sutton, Allan
Sutton, Roger
Svenvold, Mark
Swade, Doron
Swartz, Jon David
Swidey, Neil
Tabbi, Joseph
Taraborrelli, J. Randy
Tarnopolsky, Yuri
Tart, Charles T.
Taubes, Timothy
Taylor, Anne Marie
Taylor, Daniel (William)

Taylor, Margaret
Taylor, Nick
Taylor, William
Teiwes, Helga
Terasawa, Mizuho
Theroux, Paul
Thiel, Diane
Thomas, Leslie (John)
Thompson, Tracy
Thomson, Hugh
Thomson, Rodney M(alcolm)
Thon, Melanie Rae
Thornton, Naoko Fuwa
Thorsson, Örnólfur
Tikhomirov, Vladimir I.
Tillinghast, Richard
Tillman, Deborah Lindsay
Timms, Edward
Tisdale, Sallie
Tocher, Michelle
Tollefson, James W(illiam)
Tomajczyk, S. F.
Tomalin, Claire
Tompkins, Ptolemy (Christian)
Tone, John Lawrence
Topping, Keith A.
Totten, Mark D.
Townsend, Brad W.
Townsend, Elizabeth A.
Tranel, Virginia
Trebay, Guy
Treier, Daniel J.
Trimble, Stephen
Tripp, Charles R(ees) H(oward)
Tsomo, Karma Lekshe
Tudor, Andrew
Turner, Tom
Turney, Jon
Tyson, Salinda
Ulrich, Laurel Thatcher
Underhill, Lois Beachy
Usabiaga (Ibáñez), Carlos
Usborne, Cornelie
Vail, Rachel
Valenza, Joyce Kasman
Valerio, Anthony
Valle, Victor Manuel
van Den Brink, H(ans) M(aarten)
Vance, Jack
VanOosting, James
Vassanji, M(oyez) G.
Vaughn, Patrika
Velez-Mitchell, Jane
Venclova, Tomas
Verghese, Abraham
Vickers, Joanne F.
Victor, Barbara
Villasmil, Omar (Santiago)
Vincent, Norah
Vincenzi, Penny
Viscusi, Robert
Vitiello, Justin
Vittitow, Mary L(ou)
Viviano, Frank
Vlasich, James A(nthony)
Von Ward, Paul
Waber, Bernard

Waddell, Dan
Wadia, Maneck S.
Waiser, Bill
Wakefield, Dan
Walker, Anne Collins
Walker-Blondell, Becky
Wallace, Diana
Wallace, Mark I.
Wallace-Murphy, Tim
Walter, Jess
Walton, Mary
Waltzer, Jim
Wambaugh, Joseph
Warner, Brad
Warwick, Jacqueline
Wasil, Kenneth
Watson, Bruce
Watson, James
Watson, Sophia
Watson, William E.
Watt, Kelly
Waugh, Teresa (Lorraine)
Webb, T(erry) D(ouglas)
Webb, Veronica
Weber, Doron
Weber, Katharine
Weber, Sandra
Weber, William
Wecker, David
Wegman, William (George)
Weiner, Mark S(tuart)
Weiner, Stephen
Weinman, Lynda (Susan)
Weinreb, Michael
Weisblat, Tinky
Weiss, Raymond L.
Wekesser, Carol A.
Wellington, Sheila W(acks)
Wenderoth, Joe
Wendling, Ronald C(harles)
West, Diana
West, Francis J.
Weyr, Thomas
Wheatley, Nadia
Wheeler, Penny Estes
Whelan, Ruth
White, Edmund
White, Edward M.
Whiteley, Nigel
Whiting, Robert
Whitley, David S(cott)
Whynott, Douglas (Vernon)
Wick, Steve
Wicker, Christine
Wiener, Antje
Wiener, Nancy H.
Wilding, Michael
Wildman, Steven S.
Wildwind, Sharon Grant
Wiley, Peter (Booth)
Wilkins, Arnold
Wilkins, Sally (E. D.)
Wilkinson, Richard H(erbert)
Willett, Ralph
Williams, (Henry) Nigel
Williams, Geoff
Williams, Karen Lynn

Gruntman, Mike
Gunston, Bill
Hall, David Ian
Haynie, Barbara
Henbest, Nigel
Henriot, Christian
Heppenheimer, Thomas A.
Higham, Robin
Hitt, David
Hokanson, (Anthony) Drake
Hooper, Meredith Jean
Hopkins, George Emil
Horton, Madelyn (Stacey)
Ing, Dean
Jackson, Eve
Jaroff, Leon Morton
Jones, Thomas D.
Jones, Tobias
Jordan, Wendy A(dler)
Kanipe, Jeff
King, John
King-Hele, Desmond
Klerkx, Greg
Kozloski, Lillian D.
Kuntz, Jerry
Landis, Geoffrey A(lan)
Langley, Wanda
Launius, Roger D.
Lebow, Eileen F.
Levine, Joel S.
Lewis, John S.
Longyard, William H(enry)
Lorenz, Ralph
Lunan, Duncan
Mackowski, Maura Phillips
Mains, Randolph P.
Majd, Kam
Malusa, Jim
Mandeles, Mark D.
Mansfield, Howard
Marko, Katherine McGlade
Marrs, Jim
Marten, Michael
Maynard, Christopher
McCormick, Anita Louise
McPhee, John (Angus)
Miele, Angelo
Miller, Roger G.
Millspaugh, Ben P.
Miner, Ellis D(evere)
Mlodinow, Leonard
Moore, Philip N(icholas)
Morton, Oliver
Munevar, Gonzalo
Neufeld, Michael J.
Oster, Clinton Victor
Pape, Robert A.
Patterson, Dan
Peebles, Curtis
Peterson, Wallace C(arroll)
Pogue, Bill
Reeves-Stevens, Garfield
Robie, Bill
Rodgers, Eugene
Rusch, Elizabeth
Ryan, Craig
Salisbury, Frank B(oyer)

Sawyer, Kathy
Sherman, Arnold
Singer, Bayla
Sipiera, Paul P.
Spenser, Jay P.
Stambler, Irwin
Stamford Krause, Shari
Storer, James Donald
Strock, Ian Randal
Strong, John S.
Taubman, Philip
Taylor, Michael Ray
Thorne, Kip S.
Trimble, William F.
Turnill, Reginald
Tyson, Neil deGrasse
Vaughan, Brian K.
Verba, Joan Marie
Wang, Yun
Watts, Alan (James)
Watts, Anthony John
Wilford, John Noble
Wolverton, Mark
Yenne, Bill
Zimmerman, Robert

Animals/Pets

Abrahams, Peter
Ackerman, Lowell J.
Adams, Carol J.
Adlerman, Danny
Aleshire, Peter
Alexander, (Robert) McNeill
Allen, Fergus
Allen, Laura Jean
Allred, Alexandra Powe
Amato, Carol A.
Anderson, Joanne M.
Angela, Alberto
Arluke, Arnold
Armstrong, Alan
Arnold, Jennifer
Arruda, Suzanne M.
Ashby, Ruth
Axelrod, Amy
Bailey, Donna
Baker, Barbara
Bakker, Robert T.
Bang-Campbell, Monika
Banks, Geraldine
Barry, Robert Everett
Base, Graeme (Rowland)
Baur, Gene
Bearanger, Marie
Beard, Patricia
Beers, Diane L.
Beland, Pierre
Benjamin, Carol Lea
Benjamin, Saragail Katzman
Bennett, Joe
Bennett, Robin K.
Bensley, Connie
Berry, Andrew
Bethelard, Faith

Bishop, Nic
Blades, Ann
Blashford-Snell, John Nicholas
Bower, John Morton
Boysen, Sally T.
Brach, Tara
Brandenburg, Jim
Bridwell, Norman (Ray)
Brooks, Bill
Broome, Errol
Brown, Rita Mae
Brown, Ruth
Browne, Anthony (Edward Tudor)
Bruemmer, Fred
Brugman, Alyssa (F.)
Brundage, James A.
Budiansky, Stephen (Philip)
Burger, Joanna
Burnett, Alfred David
Burns, Diane L.
Burt, William
Burton, John Andrew
Bush, Barry (Michael)
Byers, John A.
Cadbury, Deborah
Callenbach, Ernest
Campbell, Eric
Campbell, Judith
Campbell, R(obert) Wayne
Capeci, Anne
Cato, Heather
Chaffey, Will
Chamberlain, Lorna M(arie)
Chase, Alyssa
Chataway, Carol
Cheney, Martha
Cheng, Christopher
Cheripko, Jan
Chiappe, Luis M.
Childs, Craig
Chinery, Michael
Clarke, Gus
Cleary, Melissa
Climo, Shirley
Cloudsley-Thompson, John
   (Leonard)
Clover, Peter
Cocker, Mark
Cocks, Nancy L.
Cohen, Peter Zachary
Cole, Betsy
Coleman, Loren (Elwood)
Collins, Miki (Dickey)
Cooper, Ann (Catharine)
Cooper, Paulette
Coren, Stanley
Craats, Rennay
Crenson, Victoria
Crosby, Alfred W.
Crump, Marty L.
Curlee, Lynn
Cutler, Jane
D'Aluisio, Faith
Danz, Harold P.
Darby, Ann
Dary, David Archie
Davies, Nicola

Davis, Patrick
Dee, Tim
DeGraaff, Robert M(ark)
DeMello, Margo
Derby, Pat
Desplechin, Marie
Dickey, Page
DiSilvestro, Roger L.
Dixon, Dougal
Dodman, Nicholas H.
Dombrowski, Daniel A.
Drew, Simon
Drisdelle, Rosemary
Dudzinski, Kathleen
Dugatkin, Lee Alan
Dunlap, Julie
Ellis, Barbara W.
Engel, Cindy
Eveleigh, Victoria
Fairley, James S(tewart)
Fairman, Joan A(lexandra)
Fan, Nancy Yi
Feiffer, Kate
Feld, Ellen F.
Fenton, M(elville) Brockett
Finley, Michael
Fishkin, Shelley Fisher
Fitzsimons, Cecilia (A. L.)
Fleisher, Paul
Fontanel, Béatrice
Ford, Barbara
Fox, Frank
Fox, M(ichael) W.
Fox, Paula
Freedman, Russell (Bruce)
Fried, Dennis F.
Frohoff, Toni
Frost, Shelley
Fudge, Erica
Fusilli, Jim
Gallardo, Evelyn
Gantschev, Ivan
Gattey, Charles Neilson
Geisert, Arthur (Frederick)
George, Jean Craighead
Gibbons, Anne R.
Gibbons, Gail (Gretchen)
Gilbert, Bil
Gillette, J(an) Lynett
Goodall, Jane
Goodavage, Maria
Goodman, Susan E.
Gould, James L.
Graham, Ada
Graham, Frank
Grambo, Rebecca L(ynn)
Grandin, Temple
Greaves, Nick
Greene, Jacqueline Dembar
Grice, Gordon
Grosz, Terry
Grover, Wayne
Grumbine, R. Edward
Gugler, Laurel Dee
Gurdon, Martin
Gustafson, Sid
Hajdusiewicz, Babs Bell

Animals/Pets-*cont.*

Tanen, Sloane A.
Tarantino, Quentin (Jerome)
Tarte, Bob
Terborgh, John W.
Thapar, Valmik
Thomas, David St. John
Thomas, William J.
Thomassie, Tynia
Thorington, Richard W.
Tobias, Michael (Charles)
Tomkins, Jasper
Trueit, Trudi Strain
Tudge, Colin
Turpin, Tom
van der Linde, Laurel
Vauclair, Jacques
Vaughan, Marcia (K.)
Von Ahnen, Katherine
Waber, Bernard
Wahl, Jan
Walker, Sally M(acArt)
Walkowicz, Chris
Wallace, Ian
Ward, Ken
Waters, Tony
Watson, Clyde
Wegman, William (George)
Wells, Susan (Mary)
Wersba, Barbara
West, Colin
Westrup, Hugh
Wheeler, Jill
Willey, Margaret
Williams, Arlene
Williams, Marcia (Dorothy)
Willingham, Bill
Wilson, Catherine
Wilson, David Henry
Wilson, Nancy Hope
Wolf, Gita
Wolfer, Dianne
Wormell, Mary
Woronov, Mary
Wright, Kit
Yoder, John C.
Yoerg, Sonja I.
Yorinks, Adrienne
Young, Carol

Anthropology/Ethnology

Adams, Kathleen M(arie)
Alexander, Jeffrey C(harles)
Alleyne, Mervyn C.
Anati, Emmanuel
Anderson, Duane
Anderson, William Louis
Appleman, Philip (Dean)
Apter, Andrew
Argyrou, Vassos
Arom, Simha
Averill, Gage
Awiakta, Marilou
Bada, Constantina
Baez, Fernando
Bailey, Frederick George

Anthropology/Ethnology-*cont.*

Bakalian, Anny
Baker, Hugh D(avid) R(oberts)
Banerjee, Mukulika
Barber, E(lizabeth) J. W(ayland)
Barclay, Robert
Barlett, Peggy F.
Barnhart, Terry A.
Barry, P(atricia) S(teepee)
Basso, Keith H(amilton)
Bastien, Joseph William
Bates, Craig D.
Bateson, Mary Catherine
Behar, Ruth
Bendall, Molly
Benson, Ophelia
Berger, Arthur A(sa)
Berman, Morris
Berry, J. W.
Bettini, Maurizio
Bieder, Robert E.
Binnema, Theodore
Birrell, Anne (Margaret)
Boaz, Noel T(homas)
Bock, Philip Karl
Boddy, Janice
Boellstorff, Tom
Bond, George C(lement)
Borneman, John W.
Bouquet, Mary (Rose)
Boyer, Rick
Brady, Patricia
Bragdon, Kathleen J.
Brener, Milton E(rnest)
Broch, Harald Beyer
Brook, Elaine (Isabel)
Brooks, George E.
Brotherston, Gordon
Brown, Jennifer S. H.
Brown, Michael F(obes)
Brownell, Susan
Bruchac, Marge M.
Bruemmer, Fred
Bruhns, Karen Olsen
Brundage, James A.
Buckser, Andrew (S.)
Burayidi, Michael A.
Burton, Thomas G(len)
Calhoun, Craig (Jackson)
Calvin, William H(oward)
Cannell, Fenella
Carneci, Magda
Carney, Judith A(nn)
Carrier, James G(olden)
Cartmill, Matt
Casey, James
Cassell, Joan
Castaneda, Christopher James
Ciochon, Russell L.
Clemmer, Richard O.
Clendinnen, Inga
Clifford, Mary Louise
Coe, Michael (Douglas)
Cole, Edmund Keith
Cole, Johnnetta B(etsch)
Coleman, Loren (Elwood)
Colson, Elizabeth
Comaroff, Jean

Anthropology/Ethnology-*cont.*

Connell, John
Copeland, Anne P.
Dalby, Liza Crihfield
Darnell, Regna (Diebold)
Dávila, Arlene M.
Davis, (Edmund) Wade
Davis, Nancy Yaw
Day, Michael Herbert
de Munck, Victor C.
Dent, Richard J.
Descola, Philippe
Díaz-Stevens, Ana María
Dibbell, Julian
Dillon, Wilton Sterling
Divale, William T(ulio)
Doak, Wade (Thomas)
Dunk, Thomas W.
Durrenberger, E. Paul
Ebert, James I(an)
Edmunds, R(ussell) David
Edwards, David B.
Ehret, Christopher
Eilberg-Schwartz, Howard
Eisenman, Stephen F.
El-Or, Tamar
Eldridge, John E. T.
Elisha, Ron
Emerson, Thomas E.
Emmett, Ayala
Ereira, Alan
Eriksen, Thomas Hylland
Evers, Larry
Fagan, Brian Murray
Faulkner, Charles Herman
Feinberg, Richard
Fenton, Alexander
Ferguson, R. Brian
Fienup-Riordan, Ann
Fikes, Jay C(ourtney)
Fink, Deborah
Fisher, Angela
Fluehr-Lobban, Carolyn
Ford, Brian John
Fowler, Don D.
Fox, Richard Allan
Fox, Robin
Franklin, David Byrd
Fraser, Evan D. G.
Fratkin, Elliot
Friedl, Erika (Loeffler)
Friedrich, Paul
Frisbie, Charlotte J(ohnson)
Fujimura, Joan H.
Gabriel (Loving), Kathryn (Ann)
Gamst, Frederick Charles
Gans, Eric L.
Gardner, Katy
Gates, Marilyn
Gay, John H.
Gewertz, Deborah B.
Gibbs, Tyson
Gibson, Thomas
Gillespie, Angus Kress
Gilmore, David D.
Glazier, Stephen D.
Gledhill, John
Gmelch, George

Anthropology/Ethnology-*cont.*

Gmelch, Sharon (Bohn)
Golomb, Jacob
Goodenough, Ward Hunt
Goody, John R(ankine)
Gordon, Lewis Ricardo
Gose, Peter
Gottlieb, Alma
Greenhill, Pauline
Greenhouse, Carol J(ane)
Gremillion, Helen
Griffin, P(auline) M.
Grobsmith, Elizabeth S.
Guillaumin, Colette
Guillemin, Jeanne (Harley)
Gustafson, Sid
Haines, David W.
Hall, Roger (Leighton)
Hallendy, Norman
Hamilton, J(ames) Scott
Handler, Richard
Hanlon, Gregory
Hare, David
Harner, Michael J(ames)
Harvey, Karen D.
Hastorf, Christine Ann
Haverty, Anne
Hayden, Brian (Douglas)
Haynes, Gary (Anthony)
Heald, Suzette
Heath, Dwight B.
Hecht, Jennifer Michael
Helms, Mary W.
Hemming, John Henry
Henare, Amiria J.M.
Hernandez, Jo Farb
Herzberg, Nancy K.
Herzfeld, Michael (F.)
Heyman, Josiah McC(onnell)
Hilbert, Richard A.
Hill, Jonathan D.
Hirabayashi, Lane Ryo
Hirschfeld, Lawrence A.
Hoddinott, R(alph) F(ield)
Hollos, Marida
Hook, Jonathan B(yron)
Hoopes, John W.
Huck, (Edwin) Arthur
Hudson, Charles
Hyman, Meryl
Jackson, Michael (Derek)
Jahoda, Gustav
Jarvis, William E.
Jett, Stephen Clinton
Jonaitis, Aldona
Joyce, Rosemary A.
Kan, Sergei
Karttunen, Frances
Kaye, Barrington
Keil, Charles
Kennedy, John C.
Kersenboom, Saskia
Keyser, James D.
Khalvati, Mimi
Khan, Aisha
Khare, R(avindra) S.
Khazanov, Anatoly M.
Kilpatrick, Alan Edwin

Antiques/Furnishings-*cont.*

Edwards, Clive D.
Ellis, Royston
Fabrizio, Timothy C(harles)
Franklin, Linda Campbell
Freund, Thatcher
Gabriel, Jüri (Evald)
Gao, Minglu
Godden, Geoffrey Arthur
Golden, Mark
Halperin, James L(ewis)
Haskins, Scott (M.)
Hernández, Lisa
Hill, Anthony (Robert)
Hirabayashi, Lane Ryo
Horne, R(alph) A(lbert)
Jonas, Susan
Kalyn, Wayne
Karp, Larry
Keller, Joe
Ketchum, William C.
Kevill-Davies, Sally
Kovel, Terry Horvitz
Loomes, Brian
Meijer, Fik
Mohr, Richard D(rake)
Nylander, Jane C.
Osborn, Susan (E.)
Paul, George F(ranklin)
Powell, Yolanda White
Poyer, Joe
Prown, Jonathan
Riley, Helene M.
Roberts, Derek Harry
Russo, Thomas A.
Schevill, Margot Blum
Schneider, Stuart L.
Scott, Amoret (Tanner)
Seleshanko, Kristina
Smith, Charles Robert Saumarez
Sturmer, Michael
Taylor, Elisabeth (D.)
Vaizey, Marina
van Lemmen, Hans
Wecker, David
Yarwood, Doreen
Young, Sheila

Archaeology/Antiquities

Abu El-Haj, Nadia
Adkins, Lesley
Adkins, Roy A(rthur)
Aldhouse-Green, Miranda Jane
Anati, Emmanuel
Anderson, Robert (David)
Assmann, Jan
Babich, Babette E.
Bahn, Paul (Gerard)
Bann, Stephen
Barber, E(lizabeth) J. W(ayland)
Berres, Thomas Edward
Bettini, Maurizio
Biddle, Martin
Blackburn, Fred M(onroe)
Blashford-Snell, John Nicholas

Archaeology/Antiquities-*cont.*

Boardman, John
Bracegirdle, Brian
Brilliant, Richard
Brooks, James F.
Brown, Michelle P(atricia)
Buchanan, Robert Angus
Carradice, Ian A.
Carter, John T(homas)
Carver, Martin
Castleden, Rodney
Chernykh, E(vgenij)
   N(ikolaevich)
Childs, Craig
Ciochon, Russell L.
Clancy, Flora Simmons
Clayton, Peter A(rthur)
Clendinnen, Inga
Cleveland, Ray L.
Coarelli, Filippo
Coe, Michael (Douglas)
Coles, John Morton
Coogan, Michael D(avid)
Crawford, Gregory A.
Cremo, Michael (A.)
Cunliffe, Barry
Davis, R(oland) P(arker) Stephen
Day, Alan
Day, Michael Herbert
de la Bédoyère, Guy
Deem, James M(organ)
Donohue, A. A.
Durrenberger, E. Paul
Dyer, James (Frederick)
Ebert, James I(an)
Ehret, Christopher
Elliott, Melinda
Elton, Hugh
Emerson, Thomas E.
Enslow, Sam
Evans, D(avid) Ellis
Fagan, Brian Murray
Faulkner, Charles Herman
Figueira, Thomas J.
Finkel, Caroline
Flem-Ath, Rand
Forte, Maurizio
Fox, Richard Allan
Frere, S(heppard) S(underland)
Gabriel (Loving), Kathryn (Ann)
Gallenkamp, Charles (Benton)
Geddes, Gary
Gilchrist, Roberta
Glazier, Stephen D.
Goodman, Susan E.
Grainger, John D(ownie)
Hagy, James William
Hallo, William W.
Hamilton, J(ames) Scott
Harris, Helen(a) (Barbara Mary)
Hastorf, Christine Ann
Hayden, Brian (Douglas)
Hayman, Richard
Haynes, Sybille (Edith)
Hays, Tony
Hays-Gilpin, Kelley
Heckman, Robert A.
Heminway, John

Archaeology/Antiquities-*cont.*

Hesse, Mary Brenda
Higham, Robin
Hoddinott, R(alph) F(ield)
Holtorf, Cornelius
Honerkamp, Nicholas
Hoopes, John W.
Horsley, Richard A.
Hughes, Meirion
Hume, John Robert
Hunter, Michael (Cyril William)
Hunter, R(ichard) L(awrence)
Jacq, Christian
Jenkins, Fred W(illiam)
Johnston, Alan (William)
Joyce, Rosemary A.
Kalfatovic, Martin R.
Keys, David
King, Philip J.
Kirch, Patrick V(inton)
Kleiner, Fred S.
Knecht, Heidi Katz
Koolhaas, Rem
Krentz, Edgar Martin
Kuntz, John Kenneth
Lancaster Brown, Peter
Leakey, Richard (Erskine Frere)
Lewis, Jack Pearl
Liebeschuetz, John Hugo W. G.
Ling, Roger (John)
Lippi, Ronald D.
Long, Cathryn J.
Lopez-Lujan, Leonardo
Ludwickson, John
Mallory, J(ames) P(atrick)
Malvasi, Meg Greene
Markoe, Glenn E.
Marrs, Jim
Marshall, Peter (H.)
Marx, Robert (Frank)
Mattusch, Carol C.
Mayor, Adrienne
McClendon, Charles B.
McCutcheon, William Alan
McGee, Marni
McGregor, James H. S.
Mckenzie, Judith (Sheila)
McLeod, Wallace
McMillan, Alan D.
Megarry, Tim
Meggers, Betty J.
Mertz, Barbara (Louise) G(ross)
Millard, Alan Ralph
Millett, Martin J(ohn)
Mitchell, Stephen (G.)
Mithen, Steven J.
Morwood, Mike
Muir, Richard
Nichols, Deborah L.
O'Connor, Mallory McCane
Odell, George H.
Oppelt, Norman T.
Ortner, Sherry B(eth)
Owens, E(dwin) J(ohn)
Pal, Pratapaditya
Panchyk, Richard
Pardue, Diana
Pastore, Christopher

Archaeology/Antiquities-*cont.*

Pauketat, Timothy R.
Phillipson, David W.
Pitblado, Bonnie L.
Platt, Colin
Porten, Bezalel
Porter, Barbara Nevling
Prag, John
Preston, Douglas
Randi, James
Randsborg, Klavs
Rapp, George (Robert)
Rathje, William (Laurens)
Renfrew, (Andrew) Colin
Rice, Michael
Ridley, Ronald T(homas)
Riesner, Rainer
Riley, Carroll L.
Riordan, Timothy B.
Robbins, Lawrence H.
Robinson, Andrew
Roehrig, Catharine H.
Romer, (Louis) John
Rook, Tony
Roth, Darlene R(ebecca)
Rowett, Helen (Graham Quiller)
Ruby, Jay
Russell, Ronald
Russell, Sharman Apt
Rutter, Jeremy B.
Ryan, Donald P.
Sale, Kirkpatrick
Salway, Peter
Saunders, Ann Loreille
Scarborough, Vernon L(ee)
Schlesier, Karl H.
Schofield, John A.
Schusky, Ernest L.
Shaw, Thurstan
Shipman, Pat
Shirley, Frances A.
Siliotti, Alberto
Simpson, Elizabeth
Smith, Christopher
Smith, Ryan K.
Snodgrass, Anthony McElrea
Snow, Philip (Albert)
Stafford-Deitsch, Jeremy
Stanley, Autumn
Stiebing, William H(enry)
Stone, Eric
Strouhal, Eugen
Tarlow, Sarah Alexandra
Taylor, Joan E(lizabeth)
Taylor, John H(ilton)
Thomas, (Antony) Charles
Thomas, David H(urst)
Thomas, Julian (Stewart)
Thompson, Thomas L.
Trollip, Stanley R.
Tsetskhladze, Gocha R(evazi)
Tubb, Jonathan N.
Turner, B. L.
Tyldesley, Joyce (Ann)
Ubelaker, Douglas H.
van De Mieroop, Marc
van Tilburg, Hans (Konrad)
Van Tilburg, Jo Anne

Architecture-*cont.*

Scott, John Beldon
Scruton, Roger
Scully, Vincent
Seale, William
Segre, Roberto
Sekler, Eduard F(ranz)
Shemie, Bonnie (Jean Brenner)
Shvidkovsky, Dimitri
Simpson, Marc
Smiles, Sam
Smith, Charles Robert Saumarez
Smith, Elizabeth A(ngele) T(aft)
Smith, James M.
Snadon, Patrick A.
Solomonson, Katherine M.
Spalding, Frances
Spreiregen, Paul (David)
Stein, Leslie
Steinhardt, Nancy Shatzman
Stern, Robert A. M.
Stevens, Garry
Stout, Nancy
Stretton, Hugh
Sudjic, Deyan
Swanson, Heather (Crichton)
Tavernor, Robert (William)
Taylor, Jennifer (Evelyn)
Temple, Wayne C(alhoun)
Testa, Judith (Anne)
Thurley, Simon
Tigerman, Stanley
Tinniswood, Adrian
Travis, Jack
van Lemmen, Hans
van Pelt, Robert-Jan
van Slyck, Abigail A(yres)
Vaughn, Patrika
Vilander, Barbara
Wach, Kenneth
Walton, James
Ward, (William) Peter
Ware, Jane (O.)
Warner, Malcolm
Watson, Amy Zakrzewski
Weisman, Leslie Kanes
White, Barbara Ehrlich
White, Christopher (John)
Williams, Carla
Winter, John (Anthony)
Wu Hung
Wurman, Richard Saul
Yarwood, Doreen
Yegül, Fikret K.
Young, Elizabeth
Zaborowska, Magdalena J.
Zaknic, Ivan
Zhuoyun Yu
Zietz, Karyl Lynn

Area Studies

Abouzeid, Leila
Abraham, A(ntoine) J.
Abrams, Ovid (S. McL.)
Abramson, Edward A.
Adams, Jerome R(obertson)

Area Studies-*cont.*

Addleton, Jonathan S.
Adepoju, Aderanti
Afkhami, Mahnaz
Akarli, Engin Deniz
Alagoa, Ebiegberi Joe
Allen, Philip M(ark)
Andrews, George Reid
Arai, Masami
Aronson, I(rwin) Michael
Aruri, Naseer H.
Ayittey, George B. N.
Bacik, Ivana
Baker, Paul R(aymond)
Ballendorf, Dirk Anthony
Bansemer, Roger
Baram, Amatzia
Barden, Thomas
Baron, Beth
Bassler, Gerhard P.
Baughan, Peter Edward
Beckerman, Paul
Bell, Ian Mackay
Berryman, Phillip E.
Betancourt, Ingrid
Bew, Paul Anthony
Bickford-Smith, Vivian
Biger, Gideon
Binnema, Theodore
Birrell, Anne (Margaret)
Blackbourn, David
Blumenfeld, Robert
Bonner, Arthur
Brading, D. A.
Braveboy-Wagner, Jacqueline
    Anne
Brezianu, Andrei
Bridgland, Fred
Brockington, J(ohn) L(eonard)
Brooks, Joanna
Bruce, (William) Harry
Butow, Robert J. C.
Campbell, James B.
Cannon, Michael
Castleden, Rodney
Chai, May-lee
Chamberlain, Mary (Christina)
Chaney, Edward (Paul de Gruyter)
Chang, Maria Hsia
Chapnick, Adam
Childs, David (Haslam)
Choudhury, Masudul Alam
Clark, Andrew F.
Cleary, Edward L.
Clements, Alan
Clifford, Mary Louise
Cohen, Lenard J.
Cohen, Youssef
Coney, Sandra
Connell, John
Coogan, Tim(othy) Pat(rick)
Cooper, Roger
Copeland, Anne P.
Coquery-Vidrovitch, Catherine
Corten, Irina H.
Cotman, John Walton
Covin, David L.
Craats, Rennay

Area Studies-*cont.*

Crabtree, John
Craig, Robert H.
Crecelius, Daniel
Cribb, Robert (Bridson)
Crossette, Barbara
Crossley, Pamela Kyle
Cuno, Kenneth M.
Daly, Leo (Arthur)
Daly, M(artin) W.
Darwish, Adel
Davies, Philip John
Davies, Robert William
de Gruchy, John W(esley)
de Varona, Frank J.
Deng, Francis Mading
Dillon, Wilton Sterling
Dolan, David
Doss, Erika
Dougherty, James E(dward)
Dower, John W(illiam)
Driedger, Leo
Duggan, Christopher
Dukes, Paul
Dunlop, Nic
Dussel Peters, Enrique
Dutton, Michael R.
Eaton, Richard M.
Eviota, Elizabeth Uy
Falola, Toyin
Finlay, Richard J(ason)
Fluehr-Lobban, Carolyn
Francis, Richard
Fraser, Ronald (Angus)
Frey, Marsha L.
Furniss, Graham (Lytton)
Gammer, Moshe
Gargan, Edward A.
Gay, John H.
Gelek, Ngawang
Gerlach, Larry R(euben)
Geyer, Georgie Anne
Gifford, Rob
Gilbert, Alan (Graham)
Glass, Charles
Glover, Judith
Gmelch, Sharon (Bohn)
Goodson, Larry P.
Goodstein, Phil
Gordon, Andrew D.
Greenfield, Jeanette
Greenhalgh, Paul
Grehan, Ida
Grenham, John
Grieb, Kenneth J.
Guillermoprieto, Alma
Gurtov, Melvin
Haddad, Gladys
Hall, Ivan P(arker)
Hallwas, John E.
Handelman, Stephen
Haring, Lee
Harris, Helen(a) (Barbara Mary)
Hart, John Mason
Haskell, Guy H.
Havet, Jose (L.)
Heffernan, Nancy Coffey
Hernandez, Jo Farb

Area Studies-*cont.*

Hoffmann, Stanley
Hokanson, (Anthony) Drake
Houston, Cecil J(ames)
Howard-Hassmann, Rhoda E.
Huang, Chun-chieh
Huber, Evelyne
Hupchick, Dennis P(aul)
Hutton, Drew
Ike, Vincent Chukwuemeka
Ioffe, Grigory
Jacobson, Joanne
Jalata, Asafa
Jameson, W. C.
Jarausch, Konrad H(ugo)
Kagarlitsky, Boris
Kalley, Jacqueline A(udrey)
Kaser, Michael Charles
Katagiri, Yasuhiro
Katouzian, Homa
Keegan, Marcia
Keene, Donald
Kelly, Brian
Khalid, Mansour
Kipp, Rita Smith
Kirk-Greene, Anthony
Klein, Anne Carolyn
Krauss, Clifford
Kremmer, Christopher
Laird, Thomas (Calvin)
Lakeland, Paul
Lee, A(rthur) Robert
Lee, Joann Faung Jean
Lee, Judith Yaross
Leiser, Gary
Lent, John A.
Lie, John
Lisk, Jill (Rosina Ann)
Lithman, Yngve Georg
Lobban, Richard A.
Lourie, Richard
Lowe, Ben(no P.)
Luciuk, Lubomyr Y(aroslav)
Lustig, T(imothy) J(ohn)
Mabbett, Ian William
MacEoin, Denis
Mack, Beverly (B.)
Mackerras, Colin Patrick
Magocsi, Paul Robert
Maier, Karl
Maingot, Anthony P.
Mallick, Ross
Mann, Kenny
Mars, Perry
Marting, Diane E.
Masalha, Nur
Maser, Chris
Matlock, Jack F.
Mauk, David C.
Mazower, Mark
Mbuende, Kaire (Munionganda)
McBeath, Gerald (Jerry) A.
McCann, James C.
McCarthy, Justin
McElroy, John Harmon
McLaughlin, Andrée Nicola
McNamara, Dennis L.
Mehta, Ved (Parkash)

Britain, Ian (Michael)
Britland, Karen
Brookner, Anita
Brower, Steven
Brown, Jonathan (Mayer)
Brown, Kevin
Brown, Michelle P(atricia)
Brown, Patricia Fortini
Brown, Stewart
Brownell, Charles E(dward)
Brownlee, Andrea Barnwell
Bruce, (William) Harry
Bryant, Mark
Bryson, Norman
Bucuvalas, Tina
Buddensieg, Tilmann
Budny, Mildred
Burkhardt, Joanna M.
Burks, Jean M.
Burningham, Bruce R.
Burns, Carol
Buskin, Richard
Butler, Geoff
Butler, Joseph T(homas)
Butler, Ruth (Ann)
Butlin, Martin (Richard Fletcher)
Byles, Jeff
Cahill, Nicholas D.
Calder, Andrew
Caldwell, David H(epburn)
Calkins, Robert G.
Cameron, Catherine M(ary)
Camnitzer, Luis
Canton, Katia
Capek, Michael
Capitan, William H(arry)
Carabelli, Giancarlo
Cardinal, Roger
Carnall, Geoffrey Douglas
Carney, Raymond
Carrera, Magali M.
Castile, Rand
Catterall, Lee
Caws, Mary Ann
Cawthorne, Nigel
Cevasco, G(eorge) A(nthony)
Chadwick, Whitney
Chalker, Sylvia
Chaney, Edward (Paul de Gruyter)
Chapin, Miles
Chartrand, Lili
Chave, Anna C.
Chayat, Sherry
Chen, Xiaoming
Cherry, Kittredge
Chester, Mark (S.)
Chester, Tessa Rose
Childs, Elizabeth C(atharine)
Choudhury, Ashok
Chu, Petra ten-Doesschate
Citron, Stephen
Clancy, Flora Simmons
Clark, David Lindsey
Clark, T(imothy) J(ames)
Clarke, John R.
Clarke, Mary
Clausen, Meredith L(eslie)

Clayson, (S.) Hollis
Clayton, Martin
Clemens, Brian (Horace)
Clubbe, John L(ouis) E(dwin)
Cohen, Hubert I.
Cohen, Jeffrey A.
Cohen, Lynne
Cohen, Milton A.
Cohen, Raymond
Cojocaru, Steven
Cole, Bruce
Coleman, A(llan) D(ouglass)
Collector, Stephen
Collings, Matthew
Collis, Louise (Edith)
Comini, Alessandra
Congdon, Kristin G.
Conklin, John E.
Conlin, Diane Atnally
Conn, Didi
Connelly, Frances S(usan)
Conner, Patrick (Roy Mountifort)
Connor, Carolyn L.
Cooper, Mark Garrett
Corbett, Patricia
Cordingly, David
Cork, Richard (Graham)
Corlett, Mary Lee
Corliss, Richard (Nelson)
Covington, Vicki
Cowart, Jack
Cox, Madison
Cranfield, Ingrid
Crawford, Alan
Crawford, Tad
Cray, Edward
Crean, Susan M.
Crook, J(oseph) Mordaunt
Cropper, Elizabeth
Crossan, G(regory) D(ixon)
Crouch, Tanja L.
Crow, Thomas E.
Crowley, David
Croyden, Margaret
Cumming, Elizabeth (Skeoch)
Cunningham, Keith
Cuno, James B.
Curl, James Stevens
Curran, Kathleen A.
Currid, Elizabeth
Curtis, J(ulie) A. E.
Curtis, Tony
Dabydeen, David
Daniel, Pete
Daniels, Sarah
Danziger, Daniel (Guggenheim)
Darby, William D(uane)
Daugherty, Greg(ory Ash)
Davenport-Hines, Richard (Peter
  Treadwell)
Davey, H. E.
David, Catherine
Davies, Kristian
Davis, Ann
Davis, Donald
Davis, Francis
Davis, Margaret Leslie

Davis, Peter G(raffam)
Davis, Robin W(orks)
Day, Holliday T.
Day-Lewis, Sean (Francis)
de Costa, Elena M.
De Long, David G.
de Marinis, Marco
De Zegher, M. Catherine
Demastes, William
Dembska, Anna
Demers, Patricia
Dempsey, Charles (Gates)
Deneuve, Catherine
des Vallires, Nathalie
Desser, David
Di Piero, W(illiam) S(imone)
Dial-Driver, Emily
Dickinson, Janice
Diehn, Gwen
Dimond, Peter
Divakaruni, Chitra Banerjee
Dixon, Steve
Dobrez, Patricia
Docherty, Jimmy
Doherty, Paul (Michael)
Donald, Diana
Donoghue, Mildred R(ansdorf)
Dorment, Richard
dos Santos, Joyce Audy
Doss, Erika
Downs, Dorothy
Drake, Alicia
Drew, Philip
Drew, Simon
Drexler, Rosalyn
Dromgoole, Dominic
Drucker, Johanna
Duckworth, William (Ervin)
Dufresne, Jim
Duggleby, John
Duncan, Carol Greene
Duncan, David Douglas
Dutoit, Ulysse
Dyrness, William A.
Easton, Elizabeth Wynne
Edwards, Clive D.
Edwards, Michael
Efimova, Alla
Eisenman, Stephen F.
Eisiminger, Sterling (Skip)
Eisler, Benita
Eliav, Yaron Z.
Ellis, Anita J.
Emmer, Michele
English, Darby
Ennulat, Egbert M.
Enslow, Sam
Eskilson, Stephen John
Etlin, Richard A.
Evangelisti, Silvia
Evans, Gary P.
Evans, Helen C.
Evans, Michael Robert
Fahey, David (Allen)
Failing, Patricia
Falk, Peter H(astings)
Farquhar, Mary Ann

Feaver, William (Andrew)
Ferlinghetti, Lawrence
Ferrer, Elizabeth
Field, Genevieve
Finch, Christopher
Fine, Jonathan
Finstad, Suzanne
Fisher, Allen
Fisher, Angela
Fisher, Paul
Fisher, Robert E.
Fishgall, Gary
Fitzgerald, Astrid
Fitzpatrick, Deanne
Flam, Jack D(onald)
Flanders, Judith
Flinn, Caryl
Floyd, Nancy
Foister, Susan Rosemary
Folgarait, Leonard
Folk, Thomas C.
Fontanel, Béatrice
Foot, Michael Richard Daniell
Foot, Mirjam M(ichaela)
Forsyth, Michael
Fort, Ilene Susan
Foster, Richard
Fraiser, Jim
Fraley, Tobin
Frankel, Ellen
Franklin, James L(ee)
Fraser, Harry
Fraser, Sarah E.
Freedman, Luba
Freeman, Garry
Frelinghuysen, Alice Cooney
Frey, Julia (Bloch)
Friedlander, Shems
Frueh, Joanna
Fry, Virginia Lynn
Fryd, Vivien Green
Gablik, Suzi
Gadney, Reg
Gaines, Jane (Marie)
Gaines, Thomas A.
Gallagher, Stephen
Gallas, John (Edward)
Gallo, Rubén
Gamson, William A(nthony)
Gao, Minglu
Garb, Tamar
Gardner, Theodore Roosevelt
Garelick, Rhonda K.
Garnham, Trevor
Gascoigne, Bamber
Gaskell, Ivan
Gattey, Charles Neilson
Gazetas, Aristides
Geary, Joseph
Gee, Maggie (Mary)
Gemunden, Gerd
Gentleman, David
George, Alice Rose
George, David (John)
Geronimus, Dennis
Getsy, David J.
Gibbon, Sean

Lipton, Eunice
Lisboa, Maria Manuel
Liscomb, Kathlyn Maurean
Lisle, Laurie
Litten, Julian
Loengard, John
Loney, Glenn Meredith
Lopes, Dominic (M. McIver)
Loshitzky, Yosefa
Loud, Patricia Cummings
Lovell, Margaretta M.
Lowenthal, Cynthia J.
Lubbock, Jules
Lucie-Smith, (John) Edward
  (McKenzie)
Lwin, Nanda Layos
Lynn, Jonathan
Macainsh, Noel Leslie
Macfarlane, Malcolm R.
Machotka, Pavel
Maclear, Kyo
Macmillan, (John) Duncan
Madigan, Brian (Christoper)
Madison, James H.
Mahony, Patrick J(oseph)
Maizels, John
Makepeace, Anne
Maltz, Diana
Malvern, Sue
Mamet, David
Man, Alfred Young
Mandel, Oscar
Mann, Judith (W.)
Marantz, Kenneth A.
Marantz, Sylvia S.
Marcus, Leonard S.
Marks, (Amelia) Lee
Marks, Richard
Marland, Hilary
Marling, Karal Ann
Marlor, Clark Strang
Marquardt, Virginia C. Hagelstein
Marr, David
Marshall, Nancy Rose
Martin, Ann Smart
Martin, Deana
Martin, F. David
Martin, Julie (Breyer)
Martin, Phyllis R(odgers)
Mason, Fran
Matera, Dary M.
Materson, Ray
Mathes, Charles (Elliott)
May, Gita
McAlpine, Alistair
McBride, Robert
McCannon, John
McCants, Clyde T.
McColley, Diane Kelsey
Mccully, Marilyn
McDonald, Craig
McDonough, Tom
McEvilley, Thomas
McEwen, Indra Kagis
Mcgee, Garry
McGurl, Mark J.
McIntyre, Ian (James)

McLeod, Scott Willard
McMaster, Gerald
McMaster, Juliet (Sylvia)
McRae, Barry (Donald)
Mead, Christopher Curtis
Meader, Jonathan
Melchior, Ib (Jorgen)
Melion, Walter S.
Menz, Deb
Mercer, Derrik
Merrill, Hugh (Davis)
Meserve, Walter Joseph
Messer, Thomas M.
Meyer, Richard E.
Meyerowitz, Patricia
Meyers, Jeffrey
Miller, Donna P.
Miller, John
Miller, Jonathan (Wolfe)
Miller, Kiri Mariah
Miller, Kit
Miller, R. Craig
Miller, Tice L.
Mills, Judith Christine
Mills, Robert
Mitchelson, Mitch
Miyares, Coco Emilia Fusco
Mizrahi, Isaac
Monaco, James
Moncrieff, Elspeth
Monda, Antonio
Mong-Lan
Montagu, Jennifer (Iris Rachel)
Montagu of Beaulieu
Montier, Jean-Pierre
Moran, Maya
Morgan, David
Morgan, Robert C.
Morris, Frances
Morrison, Keith
Morrison, Kristin Diane
Morrison, Taylor
Moskowitz, Anita F(iderer)
Mrazek, Robert J.
Mueller, Andrew
Mullins, Edwin B(randt)
Munhall, Edgar
Murray, Albert
Mustazza, Leonard
Myles, Eileen
Nahshon, Edna
Nancarrow, Mindy
Nasr, Seyyed Hossein
Neaverson, Bob
Nees, Lawrence
Nelson, Steven D.
Nelson, Tim Blake
Neufeld, James (E.)
Nickel, Douglas R.
Nilsen, Anders Brekhus
Nixon, Mignon
Noah, Robert
Nolan, David (Joseph)
Nolletti, Arthur (E.)
Noriega, Chon A.
Nornes, Abé Mark
Northeast, Brenda V(ictoria)

Norwich, John Julius (Cooper)
Novaro, María
Nunn, Pamela Gerrish
O'Connor, Francis V(alentine)
O'Driscoll, Dennis
O'Neal, Hank
O'Reilly Herrera, (C.) Andrea
O'Toole, Judith Hansen
Oakley, John H.
Ochart (Torres), (Luz) Yvonne
Ofrat, Gideon
Ogrin, Dušan
Oguibe, Olu
Olson, Lester C.
Oneal, Elizabeth
Oppenheimer, Gregg
Ortenberg, Veronica
Osborne, Roy Martin
Osmond, Jonathan
Ostrowski, Jan K.
Otis, Johnny
Ottenberg, Simon
Ovason, David
Paglia, Camille
Pal, Pratapaditya
Panchyk, Richard
Panzer, Mary (Caroline)
Pardue, Diana
Paris, Barry
Parry, Graham
Patin, Thomas A.
Patton, Phil
Patzer, Gordon
Paulson, Ronald (Howard)
Pauly, Rebecca M.
Pavey, Don
Peacock, Molly
Pear, David (Adrian)
Pearsall, Derek (Albert)
Pehnt, Wolfgang
Penrose, Antony
Pentcheva, Bissera V.
Perani, Judith
Perez, Rolando
Pérez-Oramas, Luis
Perkowitz, Sidney
Perl, Jed
Perloff, Marjorie (Gabrielle)
Peterson, Christian A.
Petro, Pamela J.
Petropoulos, Jonathan G.
Petsalis-Diomidis, Nicholas
Phillips, Derek L.
Phillips, Lisa
Phillipson, Michael
Pickering, David (Hugh)
Pickover, Clifford A.
Pierce, Patricia Jobe
Pierson, Melissa Holbrook
Pinsky, Mark I.
Piper, Adrian (Margaret Smith)
Pissarro, Joachim
Platt, Colin
Platt, Donald
Platzker, David
Plesch, Veronique Brigitte
Polisi, Joseph W.

Polizzotti, Mark
Ponsonby, Laura
Porter, Barbara Nevling
Poulson, Christine
Poupeye, Veerle
Powell, Neil
Powell, Robert
Powers, Alan
Powers, Martin J.
Poynor, Robin
Preston, Douglas
Priest, John Michael
Priestman, Martin
Principe, Lawrence M.
Probyn, Clive T.
Prown, Jonathan
Pultz, John Francis
Purvis, Alston W.
Quetchenbach, Bernard W.
Rabb, Theodore K.
Raeburn, Antonia
Raftery, Brian
Rajadhyaksha, Ashish
Rand, Harry
Ratcliff, Carter
Rathmell, George W(esley)
Raymond, C. Elizabeth
Reay, Barry
Reed, Christopher (G.)
Reeves, Eileen Adair
Renfrew, (Andrew) Colin
Reps, John W(illiam)
Reynolds, Graham
Reynolds, Jan
Rhodes, Colin
Richards, David P.
Richman, Irwin
Richmond, Robin
Riley, Charles A.
Rimler, Walter
Rinder, Lenore
Ring, Nancy G.
Rippley, LaVern J.
Robb, Peter
Robbin, Tony
Roberts, Jennifer L.
Robeson, Paul
Robinson, Andrew
Robinson, Frank M(alcolm)
Roche, Denis (Mary)
Roddam, Franc(is George)
Roehrig, Catharine H.
Rogan, Johnny
Rogers, Deborah D(ee)
Romanelli, Giandomenico
Root, Deborah
Root-Bernstein, Robert Scott
Rosand, David
Rosenak, Chuck
Rosenak, Jan(ice M.)
Rosenthal, Nan
Rosenthal, T(homas) G(abriel)
Ross, Lawrence C.
Rossol, Monona
Roston, Murray
Roth, Lorna
Rubin, Bruce Joel

Art/Art History-*cont.*

Wolf, Maryanne
Wolf, Reva
Wolfe, George C.
Wolff, Theodore F.
Wolfthal, Diane (Bette)
Wollen, Peter
Wolverton, Lisa
Wood, John A.
Woodbury, Heather
Woodger, Elin
Woods, Michael
Woronov, Mary
Worsham, Lynn
Wu, Chin-Tao
Wu Hung
Wynne, Frank
Yablonsky, Linda
Yamada, Nanako
Yanni, Carla
Yarwood, Doreen
Yenawine, Philip
Yorke, Malcolm
Young, John Sacret
Young, Sheila
Zaknic, Ivan
Zamora, Lois Parkinson
Zarucchi, Jeanne Morgan
Zevon, Crystal
Zicree, Mark Scott
Ziffrin, Marilyn J.
Zinnes, Harriet
Zolberg, Vera L.
Zook, Kristal Brent
Zorach, Rebecca
ygulski, Zdzislaw

Astronomy

Alschuler, William R.
Baillie, Allan
Banerjee, Asit
Banerji, S(riranjan)
Barrow, John D(avid)
Bash, Frank N(ess)
Begelman, Mitchell (Craig)
Bergland, Renee L.
Berry, Adrian M.
Bonnor, William Bowen
Boss, Alan Paul
Broughton, R(obert) Peter
Brownlee, Donald E(ugene)
Burgess, Colin
Calder, Nigel (David Ritchie)
Campion, Nicholas
Capobianco, Michael
Carter, William E.
Cawthorne, Nigel
Clotfelter, Beryl E(dward)
Coleman, James A.
Crowe, Michael J.
Darling, David J.
Dauber, Philip M.
De Pree, Christopher G.
Dickinson, Terence
Dunn, Robert J.
Eisenstaedt, Jean

Astronomy-*cont.*

Ellyard, David
Evans, Ben
Ferris, Timothy
Fleisher, Paul
Friedlander, Michael W.
Gaither, Carl C.
Gallant, Roy Arthur
Godwin, Robert
Goldschneider, Gary
Gorn, Michael H.
Goursac, Olivier de
Grabbe, Crockett L(ane)
Greenstein, George
Harrington, Philip S(tuart)
Harris, Alan
Henbest, Nigel
Henning, Ann
Hirshfeld, Alan
Hodge, Paul William
Hooper, Dan
Impey, Chris
Jackson, Eve
Jaroff, Leon Morton
Kanipe, Jeff
Krauss, Lawrence M.
Ladell, John L.
Lancaster Brown, Peter
Larcenet, Manu
Lattis, James M.
Lemonick, Michael D.
Levy, David H.
Lewis, John S.
Liller, William
Lingenfelter, Richard Emery
Lorenz, Ralph
Lovell, (Alfred Charles) Bernard
Lunan, Duncan
Maoz, Dan
Marshall, Peter (H.)
Marten, Michael
Masthay, Carl (David)
Miner, Ellis D(evere)
Munevar, Gonzalo
Nakayama, Shigeru
Napier, Bill
Odenwald, Sten F.
Panek, Richard
Parsons, Paul
Percy, John R(ees)
Perkowitz, Sidney
Rice, Prudence M.
Rotundo, Louis C.
Roy, Archie E.
Sakurai, Gail
Sawyer, Kathy
Sesti, Giuseppe Maria
Shipman, Henry Longfellow
Silk, Joseph (Ivor)
Sims, Michael
Sipiera, Paul P.
Smith, Roger T.
Sobel, Dava
Spolter, Pari (Dokht)
Sterken, Christiaan (L.)
Teece, Philip
Thorne, Kip S.
Tirion, Wil

Astronomy-*cont.*

Trefil, James
Tucker, Karen
Tyson, Neil deGrasse
Verschuur, Gerrit L(aurens)
Walsh Shepherd, Donna
Weinberg, Steven
Weintraub, David
Whitcomb, John C(lement)
Wickramasinghe, Nalin Chandra
Wilford, John Noble
Zeilik, Michael
Zimmerman, Robert

Biology

Agutter, Paul S.
Anderson, Trevor A(ndrew)
Appleman, Philip (Dean)
Ayala, Francisco J.
Bains, William
Barash, David P(hilip)
Beissinger, Steven R.
Belue, Ted Franklin
Bentley, Peter J.
Blackmore, Susan (Jane)
Blair, Steven N.
Blakemore, Colin (Brian)
Bledsoe, Karen E(lizabeth)
Bloom, Miriam
Bodmer, Walter (Fred)
Bonner, John Tyler
Bracegirdle, Brian
Brill, Marlene Targ
Brookes, Martin
Bruer, John T.
Brugger, E. Christian
Burger, Joanna
Burt, Austin
Burt, William
Burton, John Andrew
Campbell, G(aylon) S(anford)
Chinery, Michael
Chiras, Daniel D.
Clark, Jerome
Cloudsley-Thompson, John
  (Leonard)
Collinson, Alan S.
Coren, Stanley
Daniel, Wayne W.
Davis, (Edmund) Wade
Davis, Linda W.
De Lisle, Harold F.
Deichmann, Ute
Delves, Peter J(ohn)
Dewdney, A(lexander) K(eewatin)
Digregorio, Mario J.
Dolin, Eric Jay
Douglas, Matthew M.
Ehrlich, Paul (Ralph)
Engel, Michael S.
Ensminger, Peter A.
Entine, Jon
Farbman, Albert I.
Fausto-Sterling, Anne
Feder, Martin E(lliott)

Biology-*cont.*

Fenton, M(elville) Brockett
Ferguson, Mark W. J.
Ferreiro, Carmen
Fleisher, Paul
Ford, Brian John
Foster, Steven
Gaither, Carl C.
Galdikas, Birute
Gallant, Roy Arthur
Gallant, Stephen I.
Gaze, R(aymond) Michael
Geary, David C(yril)
Giampieri-Deutsch, Patrizia
Glick, Bernard R.
Goodall, Jane
Gorman, James
Gosden, Roger
Gould, James L.
Griffiths, Paul E(dmund)
Grimaldi, David
Grossmann, Atina
Gupta, Sunetra
Gupta, U. S.
Hanski, Ilkka
Harman, Oren Solomon
Hawkins, Bradford A(lan)
Hayflick, Leonard
Holdgate, Martin W.
Hölldobler, Bert(hold Karl)
James, Wilmot G.
Jaroff, Leon Morton
Johnsgard, Paul A.
Jones, Martin
Kamil, Alan C(urtis)
Kauffman, Stuart Alan
Kellert, Stephen R.
Kesseler, Rob
Kevles, Bettyann Holtzmann
Keynes, Randal
Kilham, Benjamin
Kimball, John (Ward)
King, Robert C(harles)
Kirkham, E. Bruce
Kirschner, Marc W.
Kitchen, Bert
Kohler, Robert E.
Kohn, Alan J(acobs)
Kormondy, Edward J(ohn)
Kratz, Martin P. J.
Kroll, Mark
Kruckeberg, Arthur R(ice)
Kushlan, James A.
Lamb, Marion J.
Landers, John
Larson, Edward J(ohn)
Laszlo, Pierre
Laurent, John (Angus)
Lebreton, J(ean) D(ominique)
Lee, Donald (Lewis)
Legato, Marianne J.
Legg, Gerald
LeVay, Simon
Lever, Christopher
Levin, Ted
Levitin, Daniel J.
Lippi, Ronald D.
Lloyd, Elisabeth A.

Benkler, Yochai
Benton, D(ebra) A.
Berger, Stefan
Bergquist, William Hastings
Bernstein, Jared
Bertrand, Marsha
Beynon, Huw
Bhala, Raj
Bhote, Keki R.
Bianco, Anthony
Bielefeld, Wolfgang
Billingsley, (Kenneth) Lloyd
Birnbaum, Jeffrey H.
Bishop, Jacqueline Kay
Black, Robert Perry
Blackford, Mansel G(riffiths)
Blank, Rebecca M.
Blinder, Alan S(tuart)
Blix, Jacqueline
Boldrin, Michele
Bonder, Nilton
Bonello, Frank J.
Bookstaber, Richard
Borjas, George J(esus)
Borkowski, Mark
Boschken, Herman L.
Bosticco, (Isabel Lucy) Mary
Boyett, Jimmie T.
Boyett, Joseph H.
Boyle, David (Courtney)
Bracewell-Milnes, (John) Barry
Brafman, Ori
Bragg, Steven M.
Branch, Alan E(dward)
Brandon, Ruth
Brandt, Allan M(orris)
Brenner, Philip (Joseph)
Brenner, Reuven
Brewer, Garry D(wight)
Brittan, Samuel
Broadman, Harry G.
Brobeck, Stephen
Brooks, Arthur C.
Brooks, George E.
Brown, Douglas Robert
Brown, Gregory N.
Brown, Jennifer S. H.
Brown, Rajeswary Ampalavanar
Brown, Robert G(oodell)
Bruck, Connie
Brunelle, Dorval
Bruns, William John
Brush, Kathleen (E.)
Bryce, Robert
Buchanan, Paul G.
Bucheli, Marcelo
Buchholz, Todd G.
Buddensieg, Tilmann
Buderi, Robert
Bulkowski, Thomas N.
Burch, Geoff
Burgess, Patricia
Burgess, Robert J(ohn)
Burkey, Stan
Burlingham, Bo
Burnett, Alan
Burrell, Brian

Burrough, Bryan
Burroughs, John
Burtless, Gary
Butman, John
Buxton, Jayne
Byrne, Frank J.
Caddy, (Michael) Douglas
Caferro, William
Calabro, Marian
Calomiris, Charles William
Cameron, Maxwell A(lan)
Camp, Robert C.
Campbell, Drusilla
Campbell, Mavis C.
Caplan, Suzanne H.
Caponigro, Jeffrey R.
Cappelli, Peter
Carless, Jennifer
Carothers, Thomas
Carroll, Rodney (James)
Casson, Mark (Christopher)
Castaneda, Christopher James
Cathcart, Jim
Caufield, Catherine
Cavallaro, Michael J.
Cell, Edward Charles
Center-Shabazz, Lois
Cerami, Charles A.
Ceruzzi, Paul Edward
Cespedes, Frank V.
Chaleff, Ira
Chanda, Nayan
Chang, Gordon G.
Chang, Ha-Joon
Chapman, Paul K.
Charan, Ram
Chethik, Neil
Childs, William R.
Chin-Lee, Cynthia D.
Choi, Frederick D. S.
Chorafas, Dimitris N.
Christensen, Mark
Christian, Jeffrey E.
Christie, Ian
Claire, Rodger W(illiam)
Clark, Eric
Clark, Gordon L.
Clarke, Sally H.
Clason, Marmy A.
Clawson, James G.
Clifford, Christine
Coates, Charles (K.)
Cobb, Clifford W(illiam)
Coburn, Pip
Cockburn, Patrick
Cohen, Allan R(ay)
Cohen, Cary
Cole, Diane
Collinge, Alan Michael
Collins, Hugh
Conger, Jay A.
Connor, Patrick E.
Cooley, Alexander
Cooper, Cary L.
Cooper, David A.
Cooperrider, Allen Y(ale)
Copeman, George Henry

Corley, Thomas Anthony Buchanan
Cowan, Brian William
Cox, Roger (Kenneth)
Craig, J. Marshall
Craig, Lee A(llen)
Crittenden, Ann
Crnobrnja (Tsernobernya), Mihailo
Cronin, Mary J.
Cross, Frank B.
Crowley, Katherine
Crowley, William R.
Cullinane, Jan
Culp, Stephanie (Anne)
Cummings, Sally (Nikoline)
Cunill, Onofre Martorell
Cunningham, Hugh
Currid, Elizabeth
Cycon, Dean
D'Anieri, Paul J. D.
D'aveni, Richard
Da Fonseca, Eduardo Giannetti
Dabney, Joseph Earl
Dallas, Roland
Daloz, Laurent A. Parks
Dalzell, Frederick
Danesh, Abol Hassan
Danley, John R(obert)
Darlington, Ralph
Davidson, Jeff
Davies, Robert William
Davis, Martyn P(aul)
Davis, Nancy Yaw
Davis, Steven J(oseph)
Dawes, Casey
Dawson, Carol
Dawson, George Glenn
Dawson, Roger
Day, Charles R.
Day, Laura (Globus)
de Bondt, Gabe J.
de Haas, Margaret
Dean, Cornelia
DeCredico, Mary A.
Delsen, Lei
Demski, Joel S.
Dent, Harry S.
Detz, Joan (Marie)
DeWilde, Dennis M.
Dibua, Jeremiah I.
Dicke, Thomas S(cott)
DiRenzo, Anthony
Dolnick, Barrie
Donaldson, Thomas
Donnachie, Ian
Donoghue, Frank J.
Dooley, Brian J.
Dore, Elizabeth W.
Doremus, Paul N.
Doriani, Beth Maclay
Doti, Lynne Pierson
Dover, Michael A.
Downey, Tom
Doyle, Paul I(gnatius)
Doyle, Robert J.
Dryfoos, Joy G.

Duncan, Cynthia M.
Duncan, William (Robert)
Dyer, Davis
Edelman, Ric
Edgerton, David
Edmunds, John C.
Edwards, Clive D.
Edwards, Sarah (Anne)
Eichengreen, Barry J.
Eilon, Samuel
Eisenson, Marc
Ellenberg, George B.
Ellis, Markman
Ellis, Royston
Elster, Kathi
Eltis, Walter (Alfred)
Emery, Robert Firestone
Endlich, Lisa
Engel, Margorie L(ouise)
English, Beth Anne
Entine, Jon
Epstein, Gene
Epstein, Rachel S.
Erickson, Edward J.
Erskine, Kathryn
Ertelt, Justin P.
Estevez-Abe, Margarita
Esty, Daniel C.
Fahlman, Clyde
Faith, Nicholas
Fallon, Ivan (Gregory)
Farber, Barry J.
Farkas, George
Farrell, Warren (Thomas)
Favreau, Jon
Felder, David W.
Feldman, Lynne B.
Fenn, Donna
Fetherston, Drew
Fiedler, Fred E(dward)
Fingleton, Eamonn
Fink, Leon
Finkel, Alvin
Finley, Michael
Fischel, William A.
Fischetti, Mark
Fishback, Price V(anmeter)
Fishman, Charles N.
Fishman, Steve
Fitzgerald, Cathy
Fix, Michael
Flint, Anthony
Florida, Richard (L.)
Flynn, Nancy L.
Flyvbjerg, Bent
Fogel, Robert William
Folster, David
Fombrun, Charles J.
Foot, Mirjam M(ichaela)
Foreman, George
Fox, Barry
Frader, Laura Levine
Frame, J. Davidson
Francis, Diane (Marie)
Fraser, George (C.)
Fratianni, Michele
Frazier, Shirley George

Loudon, David L.
Lowenberg, Anton D(avid)
Lowenstein, Michael W.
Lublin, Nancy
Lucsko, David
Lundvall, Bengt-Åke
Lustig, Nora Claudia
Lynch, Peter S.
Lynn, Adele B.
Lyons, Nick
MacDonald, Kyle
MacKay, Donald (Iain)
Mackay, Harvey (B.)
MacKenzie, Donald (Angus)
Magrath, Allan J.
Mahler, Jonathan
Mainiero, Lisa A.
Maitra, Priyatosh
Malloch, Theodore Roosevelt
Malseed, Mark
Mangan, Jane E.
Mann, John David
Mann, Judith (W.)
Manz, Charles C.
Marconi, Joe
Marcum, David
Margariti, Roxani Eleni
Marin, Dalia
Markaris, Petros
Markoff, John
Marks, Mitchell Lee
Marolda, Edward J.
Marsh, Robert Mortimer
Marshall, Adré
Marston, Cam
Martin, Roderick
Marx, Elisabeth
Maslon, Laurence
Massie, Joseph Logan
Masson, Paul R(obert)
Mathias, Peter
Matsen, Bradford (Conway)
Matson, Cathy
Matsumura, Takao
Matteo, Sherri
Matthee, Rudi
Maybury, Richard J.
Mayfield, Terry L.
Maynard, Geoffrey (Walter)
Mazzarella, William T. S.
Mazzeno, Laurence W.
McAllen, Jack
McCamant, Jim
McChesney, Robert Waterman
McClintick, David
McCormick, Ken
McCraw, Thomas K.
Mcdaniel, Bruce A.
McDonald, Forrest
McGinn, Daniel
McKenna, Patrick J.
McLean, J. W.
McNamara, Dennis L.
McQuown, Judith H.
Mears, Emira
Mele, Alfred R.
Mellan, Olivia

Mellor, John W(illiams)
Melnyk, Steven A.
Mendelsohn, Martin
Mertha, Andrew C.
Michaelowa, Axel
Michie, Jonathan
Miller, Geoffrey F.
Miller, Jeffrey G.
Miller, John G.
Miller, Seumas
Millman, Gregory J.
Millman, Joan (M.)
Mills, Vicki A.
Milne, Seumas
Minsky, Betty Jane
Modahl, Mary
Moise, Edwin E(variste)
Mollenkamp, Carrick
Mollick, Ethan Reuben
Montgomery, David Bruce
Montoya, Peter
Moon, Jeremy
Moonman, Eric
Moore, Thomas S(cott)
Morales, Rebecca (Hope)
Moreau, David Merlin
Morgan, Dan
Morison, Robert F.
Mornell, Pierre
Morris, Kenneth M.
Morton, Brian
Moschella, David C.
Moschis, George P.
Mosettig, Michael David
Moskowitz, Robert A.
Mrkvicka, Edward F(rancis)
Mui, Chunka
Murphy, James S.
Murphy, Joseph E.
Murphy, Mark A.
Murphy, Rae Allan
Murphy, Tom
Murray, James M.
Murray, Janet Horowitz
Myers, Walter Dean
Nagurney, Anna
Neal, Frank
Nehrt, Lee C(harles)
Nelson, Bobby Jack
Neubeck, Kenneth J.
Neufeld, Michael J.
Newell, Dianne
Nicholas, David M(ansfield)
Nichols, John
Nierenberg, Gerard I.
Nightingale, Pamela
Nissanoff, Daniel
Nissen, Bruce
Nixson, Frederick Ian
Nordlund, Willis J.
Norman, Rick (J.)
Novak, David
Nugent, Neill
Nutt, Paul C.
O'Brien, Timothy L.
O'donnell, Edward T.
O'Leary, Rosemary

O'Rourke, James S.
Ocampo, José Antonio
Odber (de Baubeta), Patricia (Anne)
Olasky, Marvin
Oliver, Richard W.
Olson, Michael Keith
Olwell, Russell B.
Ortner, Robert
Osborn, Susan (E.)
Oster, Clinton Victor
Osterman, Paul
Otto, Beatrice K.
Outland, Robert B.
Pacelle, Mitchell
Pack, Spencer J.
Packett, Charles Neville
Pae, Sung Moon
Paetro, Maxine
Page, Karen
Panford, Kwamina
Papadimitriou, Dimitri B.
Papes, Robert
Paradis, Adrian Alexis
Parker, Matthew
Parker, Tom
Parkin, Sara Lamb
Pascale, Richard Tanner
Pascarella, Perry
Pasewark, William Robert
Patel, Raj
Paturi, Felix R.
Patzer, Gordon
Pavlik, John V.
Paxton, John
Pedersen, Laura
Pencavel, John (H.)
Perdue, Peter C.
Perkins, John
Pierce, F(ranklin) David
Pierce, Patricia Jobe
Pitino, Rick
Pohl, Frederik
Polonsky, Michael Jay
Poorvu, William J.
Porter, Michael E(ugene)
Posner, Richard A.
Poundstone, William
Presser, Stephen B.
Pruett, Lynn
Prybyla, Jan S(tanislaw)
Pybrum, Steven (Mark)
Quandt, Richard (Emeric)
Quinlan, Mary Lou
Rachleff, Peter (J.)
Ramirez, Susan E(lizabeth)
Rao, Srikumar S.
Rapp, Steven A.
Rause, Vince
Rave, Tilmann
Raymond, C. Elizabeth
Razin, Assaf
Regehr, T(heodore) D.
Reichel, Aaron I(srael)
Reingold, Dan
Rennell, Tony
Renton, N(ick) E.

Reuber, Grant L.
Reynolds, Bill
Richards, Lawrence
Ries, Laura
Riley, Charles A.
Ring, Victoria A.
Rivkin, Steve
Rivlin, Paul Anthony
Roberts, Paul
Roberts, Russell D.
Robson, Brian Turnbull
Roodman, David Malin
Roos, Johan
Rosaler, Robert C.
Rosegrant, Susan
Rosen, Robert H.
Rosenberg, Nathan
Rosenfeld, Stephanie
Rosenstiel, Tom
Rosner, Bob
Ross, Angus
Rossman, Jeffrey J.
Rothkopf, David J.
Rothwell, William J.
Rowh, Mark
Rowland, Arthur Ray
Rubin, Gretchen (Craft)
Rubin, Rose M.
Rumer, Boris
Russell, Cheryl
Rust, H. Lee
Sable, Martin Howard
Sacknoff, Scott
Salter, David F.
Sanders, John H.
Sanjek, David
Sant, Thomas
Sawyer, Suzana
Sawyer-Laucanno, Christopher
Schell, Jim
Schendel, Dan
Schiavone, Giuseppe
Schier, Steven E.
Schioppa, Fiorella Kostoris Padoa
Schmieding, Holger
Schneider, Ben Ross
Schneiderman, David
Schoenfeldt, Beth
Schor, Juliet B.
Schumacher, Linda H.
Schumer, Fran
Schwartz, Evan I.
Schweber, Howard
Scott, David L(ogan)
Scott-Clark, Cathy
Scoville, James Griffin
Seabright, Paul
Searle, G(eoffrey) R(ussell)
Searle, Ronald (William Fordham)
Searls, David
Sebell, Mark Henry
Secretan, Lance H. K.
Sedaitis, Judith B.
Segal, Howard P.
Semler, Ricardo
Seybold, Patricia B.

Chemistry-*cont.*

Lide, David R.
March, N(orman) H(enry)
Masthay, Carl (David)
McIntyre, Lee C(ameron)
McNair, Harold M.
Miller, James M.
Mougios, Vassilis
Müller, Ingo
Myers, Drew(fus Young)
Ney, Ronald E.
Nicholls, Henry
Overend, William George
Principe, Lawrence M.
Reuben, Bryan G.
Roberts, Iolo Francis
Rybolt, Thomas R.
Scerri, Eric R.
Schramm, Laurier L.
Shneour, Elie Alexis
Sperling, L(es) H.
Sprackling, Michael Thomas
Streitwieser, Andrew
This, Herve
Trapp, Stefan (Alfred Josef)
Travis, Anthony S(tewart)
Trotman-Dickenson, Aubrey
  Fiennes
VanCleave, Janice
Vermerris, Wilfred
Verney, Douglas (Vernon)
von Zelewsky, Alexander
Wagner, Andreas
Walsh, Edward N.
Williams, R(obert) J(oseph)
  P(aton)
Wilson, Cynthia
Young, John K(arl)

Children's Non-fiction

Abbas, Jailan
Ackerman, Diane
Ackerman, Susan Yoder
Adler, David A.
Albahari, David
Aliki
Alkiviades, Alkis
Allen, John E(lliston)
Allen, Nancy Kelly
Allison, Amy
Alphin, Elaine Marie
Alter, Judy
Amato, Carol A.
Ancona, George
Andryszewski, Tricia
Ansary, Mir Tamim
Appelt, Kathi
Applegate, Katherine (Alice)
Armbruster, Ann
Armstrong, Jennifer
Artell, Mike
Ashabranner, Melissa
Ashby, Gwynneth Margaret
Ashby, Ruth
Asher, Sandy

Children's Non-fiction-*cont.*

Ashley, Bernard
Avery, Gillian (Elise)
Bailey, Donna
Balit, Christina
Barakat, Ibtisam
Barnes, Simon
Barrett, Tracy
Barrie, Alexander
Barron, Judy
Barth, Kelly L.
Bartoletti, Susan Campbell
Base, Graeme (Rowland)
Bassil, Andrea
Bauer, Caroline Feller
Bauer, Marion Dane
Bausum, Ann
Bawden, Nina (Mary)
Bedard, Anthony
Bell, David Owen
Bentley, Nancy
Berg, Leila
Berger, Samantha (Allison)
Bergman, Tamar
Bial, Raymond
Billington, Rachel
Birenbaum, Barbara
Blackman, Malorie
Blatchford, Claire H.
Bliss, Harry
Blocksma, Mary
Blos, Joan W.
Blumberg, Rhoda
Boelts, Maribeth
Bogart, Jo Ellen
Bond, Nancy
Bond, Ruskin
Bonsignore, Joan
Borgenicht, David
Borntrager, Mary Christner
Bortz, Fred
Bradford, Karleen
Branch, Muriel Miller
Brandenberg, Franz
Braun, Matt(hew)
Brennan, J(ames) H(erbert)
Brewster, Hugh
Brill, Marlene Targ
Brittain, William (E.)
Broome, Errol
Brouwer, Sigmund
Brown, Don
Brown, H. Jackson
Broyles, Anne
Bruchac, Joseph
Bruchac, Marge M.
Bruckner, Pascal
Bryant, Jennifer F(isher)
Buccieri, Lisa Rojany
Bull, Angela (Mary)
Bunkers, Suzanne L.
Burch, Joann J(ohansen)
Burns, Diane L.
Burns, Marilyn
Bushey, Jeanne
Busiek, Kurt
Butcher, Kristin
Butler, Dorothy

Children's Non-fiction-*cont.*

Butler, Lance St. John
Bye, Beryl (Joyce Rayment)
Cabrera, Jane
Capek, Michael
Caravantes, Peggy
Carle, Eric
Carlson, Laurie
Carson, Mary Kay
Carter, Alden R(ichardson)
Carter, John T(homas)
Carusone, Al
Casey, Barbara
Castaldo, Nancy Fusco
Catalanotto, Peter
Chappell, Audrey
Chappell, Ruth Paterson
Chase, Karen
Cheng, Andrea
Cheng, Christopher
Chiappe, Luis M.
Childs, Tera Lynn
Chin-Lee, Cynthia D.
Chippendale, Lisa A.
Chocolate, Debbi
Ciment, James D.
Clarke, Judith
Cleary, Brian P.
Clifford, Mary Louise
Climo, Shirley
Cloudsley-Thompson, John
  (Leonard)
Cobb, Nancy (Howard)
Cobb, Vicki
Cohen, Judith Love
Cohen, Sholom
Cole, Sheila R.
Coleman, Janet Wyman
Collard, Sneed B.
Collier, Christopher
Collier, James Lincoln
Collings, Gillian
Collins, Ace
Collinson, Roger (Alfred)
Cook, Jean Thor
Coombs, Patricia
Cooper, Ann (Catharine)
Cooper, Elisha
Cosby, Bill
Cowley, (Cassia) Joy
Cox, Vic
Cox, Vicki
Craats, Rennay
Craig, Joe Alexander
Cranfield, Ingrid
Crary, Elizabeth (Ann)
Crenson, Victoria
Crews, Donald
Crook, Marion
Crystal, David
Cummings, Pat
Cuomo, Mario (Matthew)
Currie, Stephen
Curtis, Jamie Lee
Darling, David J.
Davenport, Roger (Hamilton)
Davies, Nicola
Davis, Maggie S.

Children's Non-fiction-*cont.*

Davis, Sampson
de Medici, Lorenza
de Souza, Eunice
Deaver, Jeffery Wilds
Deem, James M(organ)
Deighton, Len
dePaola, Tomie
Deshpande, Chris
Diamond, Arthur
Dickinson, Terence
Dicks, Shirley
Diehn, Gwen
Diffily, Deborah
Ditchfield, Christin
Doak, Wade (Thomas)
Doherty, Craig A.
Doherty, Katherine M(ann)
Dolan, Sean J.
Dorros, Arthur (M.)
dos Santos, Joyce Audy
Dowell, Frances O'Roark
Dower, Laura
Downie, Mary Alice
Drake, Jane
Drake, Timothy A.
Driskill, J. Lawrence
Dubois, Muriel L.
Dubosarsky, Ursula
Duey, Kathleen
Duggleby, John
Duncan, Alice Faye
Duncan, Lois
Dunlap, Julie
Dunleavy, Deborah
DuPrau, Jeanne
Dyer, James (Frederick)
Dyson, John
Edwards, Anne
Edwards, Frank B.
Edwards, Harvey
Einhorn, Barbara
Elliott, David
Ellis, Gwen
Ellis, Sarah
Eoyang, Eugene Chen
Ephron, Delia
Epple, Anne Orth
Erickson, Betty J(ean)
Erlbach, Arlene
Fanthorpe, R(obert) Lionel
Felix, Antonia
Ferguson, Sarah (Margaret)
Ferris, Jeri Chase
Field, Dorothy
Field, Edward
Fine, Anne
Fisher, Leonard Everett
Fisher, Marshall Jon
Fishman, Cathy Goldberg
Fitzsimons, Cecilia (A. L.)
Fleischner, Jennifer
Fleisher, Paul
Fleming, Alice (Carew Mulcahey)
Floca, Brian
Flowers, Sarah
Foon, Dennis
Fourie, Corlia

Miklowitz, Gloria D.	Pinto, Jacqueline	Savage, Jeff	Suen, Anastasia
Miles, Betty	Piven, Hanoch	Sawyer, Kem Knapp	Sullivan, George E(dward)
Minarik, Else H(olmelund)	Points, Larry (Gene)	Schaefer, Lola M.	Sumner, (Edith) Aurea
Mishica, Clare	Polking, Kirk	Scheeres, Julia	Sutcliffe, Jane
Mitchard, Jacquelyn	Poploff, Michelle	Schmidt, Gary D.	Swain, Gwenyth
Mitchelson, Mitch	Porter, Sue	Schorsch, Laurence	Swanson, June
Mok, Esther	Potts, Richard	Schroeder, Alan	Swope, Sam
Montgomery, Sy	Powledge, Fred	Schulman, Arlene	Theroux, Paul
Morris, Deborah	Powling, Chris	Schuman, Michael A.	Thomson, Pat
Morris, Jeffrey B(randon)	Pratt, Pierre	Sharp, Anne Wallace	Thornley, Stew
Morrison, Bill	Preller, James	Sharratt, Nick	Tingum, Janice
Morrison, Taylor	Presnall, Judith (Ann) Janda	Shedd, Warner	Topek, Susan Remick
Morrison, Toni	Priest, Christopher (McKenzie)	Sheen, Barbara	Townsend, Brad W.
Morton, Alexandra (Hubbard)	Prime, Derek James	Shemie, Bonnie (Jean Brenner)	Townsend, John Rowe
Moss, Miriam	Prince, Alison	Shoesmith, Kathleen A.	Travis, Lucille
Mowat, Farley (McGill)	Pringle, Laurence P(atrick)	Siddons, Anne Rivers	Trottier, Maxine
Moxley, Sheila	Prior, Natalie Jane	Siegelson, Kim L.	Tugendhat, Julia
Mullane, (R.) Mike	Protopopescu, Orel	Sills, Leslie (Elka)	Tunnell, Michael O('Grady)
Munsch, Robert	Pullman, Philip	Silver, Norman	Turck, Mary C.
Murphy, Claire Rudolf	Putnam, Douglas	Silverberg, Robert	Turner, Ann (Warren)
Murphy, Patricia J.	Qualey, Marsha	Silverman, Robin L(andew)	Tweit, Susan J(oan)
Naden, Corinne J.	Quinlan, Susan E(lizabeth)	Silverstein, Herma	van der Linde, Laurel
Nathan, Amy	Quinsey, Mary Beth	Silvey, Diane F.	Van Der Meer, Ron
Naylor, Phyllis Reynolds	Rake, Jody	Simon, Francesca	VanMeter, Vandelia
Needham, Kate	Rand, Gloria	Simon, Seymour	Vaughan, Marcia (K.)
Nelson, Sharlene (P.)	Randell, Beverley	Sinclair, Olga (Ellen)	Vernerey, Denise
Nichols, Grace	Rappaport, Doreen	Singer, Marilyn	Verniero, Joan C.
Nielsen, Nancy J.	Rathmann, Peggy (Margaret	Sipiera, Paul P.	Vidrine, Beverly Barras
Nissman, Blossom S.	Crosby)	Sirimarco, Elizabeth	Viorst, Judith
Nobisso, Josephine	Razzell, Mary (Catherine)	Sita, Lisa	Vittitow, Mary L(ou)
Norgren, Jill	Read, Brian	Slavicek, Louise Chipley	Vogel, Carole Garbuny
Norman, Lilith	Reeder, Stephanie Owen	Smith, Gordon Roland	Waddell, Martin
O'Hare, Jeff(rey A.)	Rich, Francine Poppo	Smith, Vivian (Brian)	Wadsworth, Ginger
Oakley, Graham	Richards, Jean	Smith-Ankrom, M. E.	Waite, Michael P(hillip)
Olaleye, Isaac O.	Richardson, Midge Turk	Smith-Rex, Susan J.	Walker, Sally M(acArt)
Oldfield, Jenny	Ridgway, John M.	Snodgrass, Mary Ellen	Wallace, Karen
Olney, Ross R(obert)	Riehecky, Janet Ellen	Snow, Keith Ronald	Walsh Shepherd, Donna
Oneal, Elizabeth	Riordan, James (William)	Snyder, Midori	Walton, Richard J(ohn)
Orgel, Doris	Ripley, Catherine	Sobol, Donald J.	Wambaugh, Joseph
Osborne, Will	Robles, Harold E.	Sofer, Barbara	Ward, Chrissie
Oxendine, Bess Holland	Rockwell, Anne (Foote)	Softly, Barbara (Charmian)	Ward, Elizabeth Honor
Panchyk, Richard	Rodriguez, Alejo	Somervill, Barbara A(nn)	Wardlaw, Lee
Paradis, Adrian Alexis	Roehrig, Catharine H.	Sorenson, Margo	Warner, Penny
Parker, Barbara Keevil	Rogers, Bettye	Spelman, Cornelia Maude	Warren, Cathy
Parker, Nancy W(inslow)	Romano, Louis	Spencer, Colin	Watada, Terry
Parkinson, Siobhan	Roop, Connie	St. Antoine, Sara L.	Waters, John F(rederick)
Parks, Peggy J.	Roop, Peter	St. George, Judith	Waters, Sarah
Parsons, Alexandra	Ross, Michael Elsohn	Stambler, Irwin	Watson, Amy Zakrzewski
Paterson, Katherine (Womeldorf)	Ross, Stewart	Standiford, Natalie	Watson, Clyde
Patron, Susan	Rotner, Shelley	Stanley, Diane	Weatherford, Carole Boston
Patterson, Francine (G.)	Rowe, Lee Pelham	Steel, Danielle	Webber, Desiree Morrison
Paul, Ann Whitford	Rubin, Susan Goldman	Steele, Philip	Weber, Jennifer L.
Paulsen, Gary	Ruddell, Deborah	Stepakoff, Jeffrey	Weeks, Sarah
Pederson, William D(avid)	Russell, Helen Ross	Stern, Ellen Norman	Weidt, Maryann N.
Peppé, Rodney (Darrell)	Ruurs, Margriet	Stern, Judith M.	Weihs, Jean (Riddle)
Perdrizet, Marie-Pierre	Ryan, Pam Muñoz	Stevens, Bryna	Welch, Sheila Kelly
Perlman, Rhea	Rybolt, Thomas R.	Stewart, Gail B.	Weldon, Fay
Pernu, Dennis	Ryden, Hope	Stillerman, Marci	Wellford, Lin(da)
Perry, Bruce D.	Rylant, Cynthia	Stinchecum, Amanda Mayer	Wellington, Monica
Perry, Phyllis J.	Sabuda, Robert (James)	Stine, Catherine	Welton, Jude
Peters, Lisa Westberg	Sakurai, Gail	Stotter, Mike	Westrup, Hugh
Peterson, Cris	Salzberg, Allen	Strauss, Susan (Elizabeth)	Whalin, W. Terry
Pevsner, Stella	Samson, Suzanne M.	Strickland, Michael R.	Wheatley, Nadia
Pfeffer, Wendy	Sanderlin, George	Strother, Ruth	Wheeler, Jill
Pickering, Robert B.	Sanders, Bill	Stroud, Bettye	Wick, Walter
Pierce, Chonda	Sanna, Ellyn	Stutson, Caroline	Wiles, Deborah
Pike, Robert W(ilson)	Sauvain, Philip Arthur	Stynes, Barbara White	Wilkins, Sally (E. D.)

Children's Non-fiction-*cont.*

Williams, Terry Tempest
Wilson, Barbara Ker
Wing, Natasha
Winters, Kay
Wishinsky, Frieda
Wittmer, Pierre (Jean)
Wood, Douglas (Eric)
Woodson, Jacqueline
Woog, Adam
Wooldridge, Connie Nordhielm
Wormell, Mary
Wright, Alexandra
Wright, Cora M.
Wright, Leslie B(ailey)
Yagher, Kevin
Yancey, Diane
Ye, Ting-Xing
Ylvisaker, Anne
Yolen, Jane
Yoo, Paula
Yorke, Malcolm
Young, Dianne
Young, Donald R.
Young, Jeff C.
Yount, Lisa
Zeier, Joan T(heresa)
Zhang, Song Nan
Zimmermann, H(einz) Werner
Zmora, Nurith
Zonderman, Jon

Civil Liberties/Human Rights

Aberjhani
Abraham, Henry J.
Adams, Roy J(oseph)
Adler, David A.
Adshead, S(amuel) A(drian) M(iles)
Andrews, Kenneth T.
Archer of Sandwell
Bailey, Julius H.
Banash, Stan
Barber, Lucy G(race)
Bedau, Hugo Adam
Bennett, Georgette
Bennett, James Richard
Berg, Leila
Berger, Thomas R(odney)
Bernstein, David E(liot)
Bertrand, Jacques
Blundell, Sue
Bodenhamer, David J(ackson)
Bollinger, Lee C.
Boritt, Gabor
Bosmajian, Haig
Boyd, Malcolm
Bradley, Michael R.
Brennan, Frank
Bright, Myron H.
Brockett, Charles D.
Brook, Timothy (James)
Brown, David
Buchanan, Thomas C.
Burack, Elmer H(oward)
Campbell, Beatrix

Civil Liberties/Human Rights-*cont.*

Cashin, Joan E.
Chenut, Helen Harden
Clement, Priscilla Ferguson
Cohen, Jared
Connerly, Charles E.
Cook, Robert
Cottrell, Robert C.
Courter, Gay (Eleanor)
Craig, Robert H.
Cray, Edward
Crowder, George
Cunningham, James V.
D, John
Das, Suranjan
DeCrow, Karen
DelFattore, Joan
Dennis, Michael
Dershowitz, Alan M.
DesRochers, Diane
Devor, Aaron H.
Dobrin, Lyn
Donohue, William A.
Dorman, Michael L.
Dorsen, Norman
Dudziak, Mary L.
Dummett, (Agnes Margaret) Ann
Duncan, Alice Faye
Edelman, Marian Wright
Estes, Steve
Evans, Richard J(ohn)
Evans, Tammy
Faludi, Susan
Fayer, Steve
Finnegan, William (Patrick)
Flamm, Michael W.
Fones-Wolf, Elizabeth
Garrow, David J.
Gaubatz, Kurt Taylor
Gaylin, Willard
Giangreco, D. M.
Gillespie, J(ohn) David
Glass, Charles
Glasser, Ira
Gobodo-Madikizela, Pumla
Golden, Renny
Goldman, Arnold (Melvyn)
Goldstein, Robert Justin
Golubhoff, Risa L.
Graham, Patterson Toby
Grant, Gail Milissa
Green, (Charles Stuart) Jamison
Greer, Steven (Crawford)
Gregory, Dick
Grisso, Thomas
Guilhot, Nicolas
Hain, Peter
Hall, Simon
Hanbury-Tenison, Robin
Hannum, Hurst
Hardy, Gayle J.
Harer, John B.
Hayter, Teresa
Hentoff, Nat(han Irving)
Heuer, Jennifer Ngaire
Hope, Marjorie (Cecelia)
Horne, R(alph) A(lbert)

Civil Liberties/Human Rights-*cont.*

Howard-Hassmann, Rhoda E.
Humphrey-Keever, Mary Ann
Ignatieff, Michael
Jackson, David Cooper
Jacobs, Francis G(eoffrey)
Kairys, David
Kallen, Stuart A(rnold)
Kang, K. Connie
Kaplowitz, Craig A.
Katagiri, Yasuhiro
Kellough, J. Edward
Kersch, Ken I.
Klempner, Mark
Kuper, Jenny Riva
Kurasawa, Fuyuki
Le Breton, Binka
Lemus, Felicia Luna
Levitt, Matthew
Levy, Jill Meryl
Levy, Peter B.
Lewis, (Norman) Douglas
Lindsay-Poland, John
Ling, Peter J(ohn)
Lischer, Sarah Kenyon
Lyons, Thomas Tolman
Maltz, Earl M.
Mandel, Robert
Mandela, Nelson (Rolihlahla)
Manning, Robert D.
Markell, David L.
Marshall, Peter (H.)
Martin, Lisa L.
Marx, Gary T.
Matas, David
McDougall, Gay J.
McMullan, Margaret
McMullen, Jeremy
McPherson, Sandra
Melusky, Joseph A.
Meron, Theodor
Miller, Arthur R(aphael)
Miller, Douglas T.
Mohr, Richard D(rake)
Montpetit, Charles
Moore, John N(orton)
Morgan, Robin
Muravchik, Joshua
Murray, Paul T(hom)
Mutua, Makau wa
Neighbour, Mary E.
Nelson, Keith L(eBahn)
Nielsen, Nancy J.
Niman, Michael I.
Norgren, Jill
O'Brien, David M(ichael)
O'Rourke, William
Oliver, James (Anthony)
Patterson, E. Britt
Patzer, Gordon
Pauley, Garth E.
Peck, Robert S(tephen)
Pedahzur, Ami
Pelka, Fred
Pickus, Noah
Polsgrove, Carol
Potter, Harry (D.)

Civil Liberties/Human Rights-*cont.*

Powledge, Fred
Pritchard, R(obert) John
Ralph, James R.
Regan, Milton C.
Reger, James P.
Rendon, Armando B.
Roberts, J(ames) Deotis
Rosenfeld, Stephanie
Rothman, David J.
Rubin, Barry
Saunders, Gail
Sawyer, Roger
Scalmer, Sean
Schmeiser, Douglas A.
Schmidt, Winsor C.
Schulz, William F(rederick)
Semple, Andrea
Shepherd, George W.
Sikkink, Kathryn
Silverman, Jerry
Simmons, Beth A.
Simon, Roger (Mitchell)
Smith, Jean Edward
Smith, Robert Ellis
Soueif, Ahdaf
St. Aubyn, Giles (Rowan)
Statham, E. Robert
Stone, James S(tuart)
Strossen, Nadine
Sullivan, Patricia
Sundell, Joanne
Sussman, Peter Y.
Tate, Eleanora E(laine)
Taylor, Bron Raymond
Towers, Frank
Tribe, Laurence H(enry)
Trillin, Calvin
Trinkunas, Harold A.
Ungar, Sanford J.
Volpe, Vernon L(ewis)
Walker, Kenneth Roland
Weisbrot, Robert (S.)
Wellman, Carl Pierce
Wexler, Richard
Whitaker, Matthew C.
White, Pamela C.
Whitlock, Flint
Winter, Kari J.
Wood, Kieron
Wu, Harry
Yiannopoulos, A(thanassios) N.
Zaki, Hoda M.
Zucker, Naomi F(link)

Classics

Achenbach, Joel
Barr, Andrew
Barrett, Anthony A(rthur)
Barrow, Robin (St. Clair)
Baswell, Christopher
Bates, Craig D.
Beidler, Peter G.
Berger, Thomas (Louis)
Bettini, Maurizio

Birrell, Anne (Margaret)
Blamires, Alcuin (Godfrey)
Blessington, Francis C(harles)
Boardman, John
Boegehold, Alan L(indley)
Bokina, John
Brent, Allen
Briggs, Ward W(right)
Clabough, Casey Howard
Clayton, Peter A(rthur)
Cleveland, Ray L.
Coffey, Michael
Cox, Jim
Craik, Elizabeth M(ary)
Dawe, R(oger) D(avid)
Dickie, Matthew W(allace)
Dollimore, Jonathan
Dwyer, Richard A.
Dzielska, Maria
Evans, D(avid) Ellis
Evans, James Allan S.
Figueira, Thomas J.
Fogelmark, Staffan
Forsyth, Phyllis Young
Francis, James A.
Franklin, James L(ee)
Gale, Monica R(achel)
Galinsky, Karl
Gaskin, J. C. A.
Gerber, Douglas E.
Glenn, Cheryl
Goble, Paul
Golden, Mark
Goodkin, Richard E.
Grainger, John D(ownie)
Green, Peter (Morris)
Green, R. P. H.
Griffin, Jasper
Guest, Ivor (Forbes)
Gurval, Robert Alan
Habinek, Thomas N.
Hager, Alan
Handley, Eric Walter
Harrison, Kathryn
Hashmi, (Aurangzeb) Alamgir
Heath, Malcolm (Frederick)
Hinson, E. Glenn
Hinton, S(usan) E(loise)
Hooley, D(aniel) M.
Huby, Pamela Margaret
Hunter, R(ichard) L(awrence)
Hutchinson, G(regory) O(wen)
Huxley, George Leonard
Jenkins, Fred W(illiam)
Kagan, Donald
Kanigel, Robert
Kennell, Nigel M.
Kidd, I(an) G(ray)
Larson, Jennifer
Lateiner, Donald
Lazenby, J(ohn) F(rancis)
Lee, M. Owen
Lefkowitz, Mary (Rosenthal)
Ling, Roger (John)
Lisle, Janet Taylor
Long, A(nthony) A(rthur)
Lovric, Michelle

Lunge-Larsen, Lise
Lustig, T(imothy) J(ohn)
MacQueen, Winifred (Wallace)
Mayor, Adrienne
McCall, Marsh Howard
McClure, Laura (Kathleen)
McDowell, John (Henry)
McKechnie, Paul (Richard)
McLeod, Wallace
McNamee, Gregory
Mikalson, Jon D.
Millett, Martin J(ohn)
Millett, Paul
Mohr, Richard D(rake)
Moore, John Michael
Murphy, (Gavin) Martin (Hedd)
Netz, Reviel
Oakley, John H.
Panourgia, Neni K(onstantinou)
Parker, L. P. E.
Parkes, M(alcolm) B(eckwith)
Powell, Barry B.
Pucci, Pietro
Quinones, Sam
Ramaya, Shona
Rankin, Herbert David
Redford, Donald B(ruce)
Rinderle, Walter
Rosenmeyer, Patricia A.
Rowe, C(hristopher) J(ames)
Rucker, Patrick Michael
Rutter, Jeremy B.
Scholey, Arthur (Edward)
Smith, Nicholas D.
Snell, Daniel C.
Snyder, Jane McIntosh
Stray, Christopher
Sutton, Dana F.
Taplin, Oliver
Teller, Neville
Thomas, Rosalind
Thornton, Bruce S.
Tommasini, Anthony
Tsetskhladze, Gocha R(evazi)
Walsh, P(atrick) G(erard)
Welch, Kathleen E(thel)
Wellington, Jean Susorney
West, M(artin) L(itchfield)
White, Carolinne
Williamson, Margaret
Wiltshire, Susan Ford
Winterbottom, Michael
Wolverton, Robert E.
Wright, M(aureen) R(osemary)
Wright, Vinita Hampton

Communications/Media

Aaker, Everett
Allen, Craig M(itchell)
Altheide, David L.
Andrejevic, Mark
Andrews, Andy
Arnett, Ronald C.
Arthur, Chris

Auerbach, Loyd
Bagdikian, Ben H(aig)
Barer, Burl (Roger)
Barker, Dennis (Malcolm)
Barlow, William
Bechler, Curt
Bennett, James Richard
Bennett-England, Rodney
  (Charles)
Benoit, William L.
Berger, Arthur A(sa)
Berger, Charles R.
Berman, Sanford
Bernstein, Mark
Bicât, Tony
Bickerton, David M.
Birkby, Robert Corrie
Bordowitz, Hank
Brand, Oscar
Brewster, David (C.)
Brian, Cynthia
Brill, Marlene Targ
Burnett, Ron
Butsch, Richard (J.)
Calabro, Marian
Case, George (Andrew Thomas)
Cash, Anthony
Chernow, Barbara A.
Childs, William R.
Chinoy, Mike
Chorafas, Dimitris N.
Clark, Charles E.
Cleveland, Leslie
Coates, Charles (K.)
Coburn, Pip
Coleman, A(llan) D(ouglass)
Coleman, Loren (Elwood)
Collins, Kathleen
Copeland, Gary A.
Copeland, Peter
Coppa, Frank John
Cossolotto, Matthew
Costley, Bill
Cottrell, David
Cox, Stephen (LeRoy)
Crean, Susan M.
Culhane, John (William)
Cummings, Richard H.
Dary, David Archie
Dassanowsky, Robert
Davis, Andrew
Davis, Martyn P(aul)
Davis, Richard
Dawson, Melanie
Day, Stacey B.
Demers, David (Pearce)
Dessart, George Baldwin
DeVito, Joseph A.
di Certo, J(oseph) J(ohn)
Dibbell, Julian
Diehn, Gwen
Dintrone, Charles V.
Doig, Ivan
Dooley, Brian J.
Dotson, Bob
Douglas, Susan J(eanne)
Eastman, Susan Tyler

Edge, Marc
Ellis, Donald
Epstein, Gene
Erickson, Hal
Estrin, Allen
Euchner, Charles C.
Everett, Anna
Ezrahi, Yaron
Faigley, Lester
Farrar, Ronald T(ruman)
Farwell, Edith F.
Ferder, Fran
Ferre, John P.
Finnegan, Lisa
Fites, Philip
Fitzpatrick, Mary Anne
Flickenger, Rob
Foerstel, Herbert N.
Fournier, Marcel
Fox, Roy F.
Frankl, Razelle
Freedman, Eric
Freedman, Sarah Warshauer
Friedenberg, Robert V.
Frith, Katherine Toland
Fritzer, Penelope Joan
Gabriel, Jüri (Evald)
Garrison, Bruce
Gay, Kathlyn R.
Gilbert, Harriett
Gilbert, W(illiam) Stephen
Giles, Robert Hartmann
Gillman, Peter (Charles)
Gilman, Andrew D.
Gitlin, Todd
Glenn, Cheryl
Godfrey, Donald G.
Goldfarb, Ronald (Lawrence)
Golding, Peter
Goodman, Hirsh
Gordon, W. Terrence
Gottschall, Edward M(aurice)
Goulden, Joseph C.
Graham, Jefferson
Gratus, Jack
Green, John C.
Gross, Philip (John)
Gruner, Charles R.
Gurvis, Sandra J.
Guzzo, Lou(is Richard)
Hackbarth, Steven (L.)
Hacker, Kenneth L.
Hackett, Robert A(nthony)
Hamilton, John Maxwell
Hampton, Wilborn
Hannaford, Peter (Dor)
Harris, Leonard
Harris, Thomas (E.)
Harwit, Eric
Hayman, Carol Bessent
Hecht, Michael L.
Heidenry, John
Heinrich, Will
Hendry, Joy (McLaggan)
Hills, Philip James
Hilmes, Michele
Hinrichs, Ernest H(enry)

McCullough, Sharon Pierce
McQuay, Peri Phillips
Menz, Deb
Mohr, Richard D(rake)
Needham, Kate
Northrup, Jim
Oliver, Marilyn Tower
Peppé, Rodney (Darrell)
Peters, Rick
Platzker, David
Purvis, Alston W.
Robbins, Rogene A.
Rossol, Monona
Russo, Thomas A.
Schevill, Margot Blum
Schoeser, Mary
Seleshanko, Kristina
Simonds, Merilyn
Skye, Christina
Smiley, Jane (Graves)
Smith, Gordon Roland
Speel, Erika
Tayler, Jeffrey
Tong, Gary S.
Torres, Laura
Traig, Jennifer
Trottier, Maxine
Valentine, Fawn
van Lemmen, Hans
Verney, Michael Palmer
Vittitow, Mary L(ou)
Watson, Benjamin A.
Weiner, Kay Bain
Wellford, Lin(da)
Whalley, Joyce Irene
Wilkinson, Beth
Wilson, David M(ackenzie)
Winston, Lois
Young, Sheila

Criminology/True Crime

Abrahams, Peter
Abramson, Leslie W.
Adams, Mike S.
Adler, Jeffrey S(cott)
Adler, Patricia A.
Allason, Rupert (William Simon)
Altun, Selcuk
Anderson, Annelise Graebner
Armstrong, Bob
Armstrong, Kelley L.
Arnold, Peter
Bagdikian, Ben H(aig)
Bannon, David Race
Barer, Burl (Roger)
Beavan, Colin
Bedau, Hugo Adam
Benedict, Jeff
Bennett, Georgette
Bigelow, Brian J(ohn)
Bing, Leon
Bird, Brad
Black, Donald
Bledsoe, Jerry

Boessenecker, John
Bosco, Dominick
Botha, Ted
Botsman, Daniel V.
Brannigan, Augustine
Brant, Marley
Breslin, Jimmy
Brett, Edward T(racy)
Briskin, Mae
Broad, Kendal L.
Brode, Patrick
Brophy, Grace
Brown, Ethan
Brown, Tracy
Browne, Gerald A(ustin)
Bruce Lockhart, Robin
Buchanan, Edna
Burton, Thomas G(len)
Butler, Gwendoline (Williams)
Campbell, Beatrix
Candisky, Catherine A.
Cannell, Dorothy
Cannon, Eileen E(mily)
Carlson, Ron
Carr-Hill, Roy
Carstairs, Catherine
Casey, Barbara
Cathcart, Brian
Cawthorne, Nigel
Chapman, Samuel Greeley
Chase, Elaine Raco
Cohen, Henry
Cole, Simon A.
Conklin, John E.
Conley, Carolyn A.
Crews, Gordon A(rthur)
Crider, (Allen) Bill(y)
Crook, Marion
Crown, David Allan
Cullen, Robert (B.)
Cuomo, George (Michael)
Curry, G(len) David
Davies, Christie
Dawe, Margaret
Dee, Ed(ward J.)
Delano, Anthony
Deleon, Peter
Denham, James M.
Dershowitz, Alan M.
Dicks, Shirley
Dorman, Michael L.
Dressler, Joshua
Duffy, James H(enry)
Dummett, (Agnes Margaret) Ann
Duncan, Lois
Dutton, Donald G.
Egan, Timothy
Egginton, Joyce
Elam, Jason
Emsley, John
Engel, Howard
Englade, Ken(neth Francis)
English, T. J.
Fanning, Diane Lynn
Fanthorpe, R(obert) Lionel
Farmer, John J.
Faron, Fay

Farrington, David P.
Ferrell, Jeff
Ferrigno, Robert
Fido, Martin (Austin)
Fielding, Nigel G(oodwin)
Finkle, Derek
Flamm, Michael W.
Flint, Shamini Mahadevan
Fraenkel, Jack R.
Franceschini, Remo
Francis, Diane (Marie)
Frankel, Sandor
Friedland, Martin L(awrence)
Fritchley, Alma
Fuchs, Marek
Gabor, Thomas
Galeotti, Mark
Gallo, Gina
Gambetta, Diego
Gardner, Robert
Gaubatz, Kathlyn Taylor
Gaylin, Willard
Gentry, Curt
Gilligan, James F.
Gilman, George G.
Gilmore, John
Giovino, Andrea
Glatt, John
Glynn, Alan
Goff, M(adison) Lee
Gordon, Graeme
Graef, Roger (Arthur)
Gran, Sara
Guarnieri, Patrizia
Haas, Jeffrey
Hagedorn, John M.
Hallcox, Jarrett
Handler, Richard
Hanlon, Gregory
Hannah, Sophie
Harmon, Sandra
Hazelwood, Robert R.
Heide, Kathleen M.
Henry, Stuart (Dennis)
Hess, Joan
Hill, Barry
Hinojosa, Maria (de Lourdes)
Hobbs, Dick
Homsher, Deborah
Hood, Lynley (Jane)
Hopping Egan, Lorraine
Horton, David M.
Howard, Clark
Hoyle, Carolyn
Hubbard, Bill
Hunter, Mollie
Indridason, Arnaldur
Iserson, Kenneth Victor
Jackall, Robert
Jackson, G. Mark
Jackson, Marian J. A.
Jackson, Steve
Jaffee, Al(lan)
James, P. D.
Johansen, Iris
Jones, Ann (Maret)
Kahn, Michael A.

Kalin, Jim
Kelly, Jim
Kelly, Robert J.
Kidder, Tracy
King, Peter
Kleck, Gary
Kleinknecht, William
Kollmann, Dana D.
Kostelniuk, James
Krivich, Mikhail
Lacey, Nicola
Laird, Nick
Lake, M. D.
Langbein, John Harriss
Lange, James E(dward) T(homas)
Latzer, Barry
Laurence, Janet
Leake, John
Lee, Henry C.
Lefebure, Molly
Lennard, John (Chevening)
Leo, Richard A.
Levinson, Jay
Limon, Martin
Lock, Joan
Loo, Tina
Lui, Mary Ting Yi
Maeder, Thomas
Magee, Doug
Maier, Anne McDonald
Malin, Irving
Malkin, Michelle
Marchand, Philip (Edward)
Margolin, Phillip (Michael)
Margolis, Jeffrey A.
Marks, Kathy (L.)
Marx, Gary T.
Mason, Christopher
McCullough, Colleen
Meade, Glenn
Mercer, Jeremy
Meyer, Deon
Mihesuah, Devon Abbott
Mitchell, Chris
Moenssens, Andre A.
Moldea, Dan E.
Monzini, Paola
Moore, Christopher G.
Morey, Ann Janine
Morton, James (Severs)
Mowday, Bruce Edward
Murray, Raymond C.
Needle, Jan
Nesbo, Jo
O'Brien, Charles
O'Kane, James M.
Odell, Robin Ian
Opie, Anne
Ormerod, Roger
Ostrow, Ronald J.
Papke, David (Ray)
Paradise, Paul R.
Patterson, E. Britt
Peace, David
Petievich, Gerald
Phillips, Clyde
Posner, Gerald L.

Eliav, Yaron Z.
Elizondo, Virgil P.
Ellingson, Stephen
Ellison, Joan Audrey
Ely, Melvin Patrick
Encinias, Miguel
Epstein, Dan
Epstein, Mikhail N.
Erkkila, Betsy
Erlmann, Veit
Etlin, Richard A.
Evangelisti, Silvia
Evans, Martin
Evers, Larry
Ezrahi, Yaron
Fearnley-Whittingstall, Jane
Feldman, Lynne B.
Fenton, Alexander
Fernandez-Shaw, Carlos M(anuel)
Ferris, William (R.)
Feuerstein, Georg
Finlayson, Iain (Thorburn)
Fishman, Katharine Davis
Fitter, Chris
Fleurant, Gerdès
Flier, Michael S.
Foot, John
Forbes, Camille F.
Foster, John Wilson
Francaviglia, Richard V.
Francisco, Nia
Franklin, Robert M(ichael)
Fratkin, Elliot
Freccero, Carla
Freedman, Jonathan
Freudenthal, Gad
Frey, Julia (Bloch)
Fudge, Erica
Gaines, Thomas A.
Gallo, Patrick J.
Gamson, Joshua (Paul)
Ganas, Monica
Gardaphé, Fred L(ouis)
Gardell, Mattias
Gardner, Robert W(ayne)
Garrison, J. Ritchie
Gascoigne, John
Geller, Jaclyn
George Bloomfield, Susanne K.
Georgi-Findlay, Brigitte
Gerard, Charley
Gerhards, Jürgen
Gill, LaVerne McCain
Gill, Sam D.
Gillespie, Angus Kress
Gmelch, Sharon (Bohn)
Gold, Hazel
Gold, Michael
Goldman, Karla
Goodenough, Ward Hunt
Gootenberg, Paul
Gordon, Jacob U.
Gordon, Lewis Ricardo
Görlach, Manfred
Gottlieb, Annie
Gow, Andrew Colin
Grabill, Stephen J.

Gragnolati, Manuele
Graham, Gael
Grant, Barry Keith
Green, John C.
Greene, Victor
Greenfield, Jeanette
Greenhill, Pauline
Greenwald, Jeff
Grobman, Laurie
Groemer, Gerald
Gross, David
Gudorf, Christine E.
Gulbekian, Sevak E(dward)
Guttmann, Robert
Gwynelle (Dismukes), Gwynelle
Haeri, Shahla
Hall, Douglas
Hall, Thor
Hallissy, Margaret
Halpin, Marlene
Hammoudi, Abdellah
Hansen, G. Eric
Harner, Stephen M.
Harrell, Beatrice Orcutt
Harrison, J. Richard
Hartshorne, Thomas L.
Harvey, Karen D.
Harvey, Paul William
Hasty, Jennifer
Hauptman, Laurence Marc
Hayford, Charles W.
Hecht, Michael L.
Henry, Gordon D.
Hernandez, Jo Farb
Hershock, Martin J.
Hibbs, Thomas S.
Hine, Darlene Clark
Hinton, Michael
Hirabayashi, Lane Ryo
Hirschfelder, Arlene B.
Hoddinott, R(alph) F(ield)
Hoffman, Ronald
Hogan, Patrick Colm
Hoggart, Richard
Holli, Melvin George
Holmes, Diana
Holte, James Craig
Holter, Knut
Holtorf, Cornelius
Hooker, John
Hooks, Bell
Horne, Gerald
Houston, Cecil J(ames)
Houston, Velina Hasu
Howsam, Leslie
Huang, Nicole
Huck, (Edwin) Arthur
Hupchick, Dennis P(aul)
Hussey, Patricia (Ann)
Hutchinson, George B.
Hyde, (W.) Lewis
Illouz, Eva
Inge, M. Thomas
Ingle, Bob
Jacobson, Matthew Frye
Jafree, Mohammed Jawaid Iqbal
Jahoda, Gustav

Jalata, Asafa
Jalland, Pat(ricia)
Janowitz, Tama
Jarmakani, Amira
Jarvis, Brian
Jenkins, David L.
Jenkins, Virginia Scott
Jensen, Derrick
Jepson, Jill
Jett, Stephen Clinton
Johnson, Michael P(aul)
Jonas, Raymond
Jones, Bridget
Jones, Jacqueline
Joyce, Rosemary A.
Kamakahi, Jeffrey J(on)
Kanungo, R(abindra) N.
Kaplan, Janet A(nn)
Kaplan, Steven L.
Karras, Ruth Mazo
Katz, David
Katz, Steven T(heodore)
Kaufman, Suzanne K.
Kaufman, Will
Kawakami, Barbara Fusako
Kaye-Kantrowitz, Melanie
Keating, AnaLouise
Keeble, Neil H(oward)
Keegan, Marcia
Kefala, Antigone
Keil, Charles
Kelly, Robert J.
Kelsay, John
Kessner, Thomas
Kibler, M. Alison
Kimball, Roger
Kimura, Margaret
Klyza, Christopher McGrory
Knauft, Bruce M.
Kobel, Peter
Koegler, Hans Herbert
Koppel, Tom
Kornblatt, Judith Deutsch
Kramer, Hilton
Kurasawa, Fuyuki
Kushner, Barak
Kusugak, Michael (Arvaarluk)
Kwong, Peter
Lachman, Seymour P.
LaDuke, Betty
Lancaster, Roger N(elson)
Landry, Donna
Lanzmann, Claude
Larson, Wendy
Lavender, Abraham D(onald)
Ledgin, Stephanie P.
Lee, Joann Faung Jean
Lee, Judith Yaross
Lehrer, Stanley
Leistyna, Pepi
Lemons, James Stanley
Lerch, Patricia Barker
Letcher, Andy
Lewis, James R.
Li, Leslie
Libo, Kenneth (Harold)
Lindsay, James

Linn, Karen
Liscomb, Kathlyn Maurean
Little, J. I.
Liu, Lydia H.
Long, D. Stephen
Lovric, Michelle
Low, Setha M.
Lübbren, Nina
Lundin, Anne
Luria, Keith P.
Macfarlane, Robert
Mack, Beverly (B.)
Mackenney, Richard
Maffi, Mario
Majid, Anouar
Maley, Willy
Maly, Michael T.
Mancall, Peter C.
Manning, Roberta Thompson
Mansfield, Nick
Markham, Ian Stephen
Marks, Stan(ley)
Marland, Hilary
Marotti, Arthur F(rancis)
Marquardt, Virginia C. Hagelstein
Marshall, Peter (H.)
Martin, Ann Smart
Martin, Patricia Preciado
Martinez, D. P.
Matalin, Mary
Matovina, Timothy M.
Mayo, Wendell
McArthur, Judith N.
McBrien, Richard P(eter)
McCallum, Taffy Gould
McCarthy, Justin
McClellan, B(ernard) Edward
McClure, Laura (Kathleen)
McDonald, J. I(an) H.
McDougall, James
McFadden, Steven
McKay, Ian
McLaren, John
McMullan, Margaret
McNeill, William Hardy
McQuay, Peri Phillips
McWilliams, Margaret (Ann Edgar)
Mead, Rebecca
Meagher, Timothy J.
Meier, Diane
Melman, Billie
Meltzer, David
Mernissi, Fatima
Metge, (Alice) Joan
Meyer, Charles Robert
Meyer, Leisa D.
Meyer, Richard E.
Meyerson, Mark D.
Migliazzo, Arlin C.
Miles, William F. S.
Miller, Anesa
Miller, Robert H.
Miller-Lachmann, Lyn
Mills, Richard W.
Mills, Robert
Milne, Lorna

Cultural/Ethnic Topics-*cont.*

Winter, Kari J.
Witzel, Michael Karl
Wood, Gillen D'Arcy
Woody, Elizabeth
Wright, Helen L(ouise)
Wright, Robert Lee
Wu, David Y(en) H(o)
Wurst, Karin A.
Wyatt, Don J.
Wyman, Max
Yarbrough, Stephen R.
Yee, Shirley J.
Yeh, Catherine Vance
Youngman, Paul A.
Yuan, Gao
Zaborowska, Magdalena J.
Zabus, Chantal J.
Zack, Naomi
Zhang, Song Nan
Ziff, Larzer
Zimpel, Lloyd
Zunshine, Lisa

Dance/Ballet

Acosta, Carlos
Adair, Christy
Aloff, Mindy
Arens, Katherine (Marie)
Barber, E(lizabeth) J. W(ayland)
Barnhart, David K.
Bennahum, Judith Chazin
Berry, Chad
Bopp, Mary S.
Brissenden, Alan (Theo)
Clarke, Mary
Coussins, Craig
Dupuis, Robert
Emerson, Isabelle Putnam
Fishman, Katharine Davis
Flanders, Judith
Frank, Katherine
Gamble, Terry
Gänzl, Kurt (Friedrich)
Garfunkel, Trudy
Gill, Sam D.
Gray, Judith A(nne)
Greskovic, Robert
Grey, Beryl (Elizabeth)
Guest, Ivor (Forbes)
Hampton-Jones, Hollis
Holleran, Andrew
Johnson, Victoria
Kaye, Elizabeth
Kersenboom, Saskia
Kleh, Cindy (L.)
Kostelanetz, Richard (Cory)
Laird, Ross
Leiner, Katherine
Lewis-Ferguson, Julinda
Loney, Glenn Meredith
Millman, Cynthia R.
Nathan, Amy
Neufeld, James (E.)
Prevots, Naima
Quirk, Anne (E.)

Dance/Ballet-*cont.*

Rainer, Yvonne
Ravelhofer, Barbara
Riordan, James (William)
Sabatine, Jean A.
Schouvaloff, Alexander
Solomon, Andrew
Sparshott, Francis (Edward)
Spencer, Paul
Steinman, Louise
Striegel, Jana
Teachout, Terry
Wyman, Max

Demography

Adepoju, Aderanti
Appleman, Philip (Dean)
Becker, Charles M(axwell)
Brown, Lester R(ussell)
Cernada, George P.
Cohen, Henry
Crush, Jonathan
De Vos, Susan
Docherty, James C(airns)
Donaldson, Loraine
Falkingham, Jane (Cecelia)
Fassmann, Heinz
Feshbach, Murray
Fonseca, James W(illiam)
Francis, Diane (Marie)
Gardner, Robert W(ayne)
Goldstein, Sidney
Hanlon, Gregory
Harwood, (Henry) David
Heer, David M(acAlpine)
Ioffe, Grigory
Kane, Penny
Kritz, Mary M.
Kushner, James A(lan)
Lopreato, Joseph
Ness, Immanuel
Odell-Scott, David W.
Phillips, Roderick (Goler)
Pyle, Gerald F.
Richards, Eric
Richmond, Anthony Henry
Spencer, Paul
Struyk, Raymond J(ay)
Taeuber, Cynthia M.
Westoff, Charles F.

Design

Albarn, Keith
Aldersey-Williams, Hugh
Allen, John E(lliston)
Barnard, Nicholas
Baxter, Paula A.
Bayley, Stephen
Baynes, Ken
Bendix, Deanna Marohn
Black, Roger David
Brian, Cynthia

Design-*cont.*

Bringhurst, Robert
Brower, Steven
Burnett, Ron
Capshew, James H.
Cocks, Nancy L.
Cohen, Lizabeth (Ann)
Connolly, Joseph
Conran, Shirley (Ida)
Corio, David
Cowie, Colin
Crawford, Alan
Culhane, John (William)
Culp, Stephanie (Anne)
Curl, James Stevens
Danilowitz, Brenda
Dower, John W(illiam)
Drew, Philip
Eichorn, Rosemary D.
Flyvbjerg, Bent
Franklin, Linda Campbell
Frick, Carole Collier
Gentleman, David
Gikow, Jacqueline
Gonyea, Mark
Heller, Steven
Hill, Ann M.
Hockney, David
James, Warren A.
Kesseler, Rob
Kidd, Chip
Kidd, Paul
King, Carol Soucek
Lancaster, Michael (L.)
Latynin, Leonid (Aleksandrovich)
Lavin, Maud
Linton, Harold
MacCarthy, Fiona
Madden, Chris (Casson)
Mason, Christopher
McBride, Simon
McKean, J(ohn) M(aule)
Middlemas, (Robert) Keith
Miller, R. Craig
Monmonier, Mark
Patterson, Dan
Patton, Phil
Pavey, Don
Pence, Gregory E.
Petroski, Henry
Richards, Amelia M.
Riley, Charles A.
Rust, Graham (Redgrave)
Sabar, Ariel
Saville, Diana
Schmid, Wolfram George
Schoeser, Mary
Sparke, Penny
Tenner, Edward
Travis, Jack
van Lemmen, Hans
Velarde, Giles
Weiner, Kay Bain
Weltge, Sigrid W(ortmann)
Wilson, Eva

Earth Sciences

Allaby, (John) Michael
Backus, George Edward
Balling, Robert C.
Banks, Leslie
Barbash, Shepard
Behe, Michael J.
Bhatt, Jagdish J(eyshanker)
Blundell, Derek (John)
Botkin, Daniel B.
Bowen, Mark
Bowers, Janice Emily
Bradshaw, Michael
Bridgland, Fred
Brower, Kenneth
Brownlee, Donald E(ugene)
Brugioni, Dino A.
Bryant, Edward (Arnot)
Calder, Nigel (David Ritchie)
Calvin, William H(oward)
Carless, Jennifer
Carter, Martin R(oger)
Carter, William E.
Castaneda, Christopher James
Castleden, Rodney
Charlier, Roger Henri
Chiras, Daniel D.
Chociolko, Christina
Ciochon, Russell L.
Clayden, Andy
Cox, Christopher Barry
Crawford, Mark
Currie, Philip J(ohn)
Danson, Edwin
Davis, Richard A.
Dixon, Dougal
Douglas, L. Warren
Elias, Scott A.
Engel, Michael S.
Erwin, Douglas H.
Fanchi, John R(ichard)
Farlow, James O(rville)
Fawcett, Tina
Fitzsimons, Cecilia (A. L.)
Fleming, James Rodger
Flenley, John (Roger)
Fortey, Richard
Gallant, Roy Arthur
Gerrard, John
Gershuny, Grace
Gilbert, Bil
Glut, Don(ald) F.
Grayson, Donald K.
Grimaldi, David
Grubb, Michael (J.)
Hallé, Francis
Halliday, William R(oss)
Hambrey, Michael (John)
Hammond, Herb(ert L.)
Hartmann, Dennis L.
Heminway, John
Holdgate, Martin W.
Hopping Egan, Lorraine
Horton, J(ames) Wright
Jaccard, Mark
Janes, J(oseph) Robert
Johnson, Andrew
Kaiser, Ward L(ouis)

Christodoulou, Demetrios
Ciment, James D.
Clague, Christopher K.
Clapham, Christopher S.
Clark, Charles Michael Andres
Clark, Gordon L.
Clark, Gregory
Clarke, Peter Frederick
Cline, William R.
Clotfelter, Charles T.
Coatsworth, John H(enry)
Cobb, Clifford W(illiam)
Cohen, Alvin
Cohen, Cary
Cohen, Henry
Coker, Christopher
Coleman, William Oliver
Collini, Stefan
Collins, Hugh
Commoner, Barry
Conant, Michael
Conteh-Morgan, Earl
Cooper, Richard Newell
Copeman, George Henry
Corden, Warner Max
Corley, Thomas Anthony Buchanan
Cosgrove, Michael H.
Coulmas, Florian
Cowan, Brian William
Cowie, Hamilton Russell
Cox, Roger (Kenneth)
Cox, Stephen D.
Craig, J. Marshall
Craig, Lee A(llen)
Crittenden, Ann
Crnobrnja (Tsernobernya), Mihailo
Crowley, Katherine
Csaba, László
Csepeli, György
Culyer, A(nthony) J(ohn)
Cunill, Onofre Martorell
Cunningham, James V.
Currid, Elizabeth
Cutler, David M.
D'Anieri, Paul J. D.
D'aveni, Richard
Da Fonseca, Eduardo Giannetti
Dahl, Robert (Alan)
Danesh, Abol Hassan
Danley, John R(obert)
Darroch, James L.
Davenport, Paul
Davidson, Roger H(arry)
Davies, Robert William
Davis, Steven J(oseph)
Dawson, George Glenn
de Bondt, Gabe J.
de Vecchi, Nicolo
De Villiers, Marq
Delsen, Lei
Deng, Yong
Dennis, Michael
Detz, Joan (Marie)
Devaux, Claudia
Dibbell, Julian

Dibua, Jeremiah I.
Dicke, Thomas S(cott)
Dickman, Thomas
Dillon, Wilton Sterling
Dobbin, Murray
Donaldson, Loraine
Donnachie, Ian
Donnithorne, Audrey Gladys
Doti, Lynne Pierson
Downey, Tom
Doyle, Paul I(gnatius)
Dreher, Rod
Drèze, Jean
Driesen, David M.
Dryfoos, Joy G.
Dunaway, Wilma A.
Duncan, Cynthia M.
Dunkley, Graham (Royce)
Dussel Peters, Enrique
Dyer, Joel
Easterly, William
Edelman, Ric
Edwards, Sarah (Anne)
Egler, Claudio A. G.
Egnal, Marc
Eichengreen, Barry J.
Eilon, Samuel
Eisenson, Marc
Eisenstein, Hester
Eisner, Gisela
Eldridge, John E. T.
Ellis, Markman
Eltis, Walter (Alfred)
Emery, Robert Firestone
Emmerij, Louis (Johan)
Epping, Randy Charles
Epstein, Gene
Epstein, Rachel S.
Erickson, Edward J.
Erskine, Kathryn
Ertelt, Justin P.
Estevez-Abe, Margarita
Ezell, Margaret J. M.
Fahlman, Clyde
Fairbairn, Brett
Faith, Nicholas
Falk, Barbara J.
Falkingham, Jane (Cecelia)
Fallows, James Mackenzie
Farkas, George
Farmer, Roger E. A.
Farnsworth, Clyde
Faure, Michael G.
Federico, Giovanni
Feldman, Lynne B.
Fenn, Donna
Feuerwerker, Albert
Fialka, John J.
Fielding, Nigel G(oodwin)
Fingleton, Eamonn
Fink, Leon
Finkelstein, Stan N.
Finn, Margot C.
Fischel, William A.
Fischetti, Mark
Fishback, Price V(anmeter)
Fisher, Dana R.

Fisher, Franklin M.
Fishman, Charles N.
Fitzgerald, Cathy
Fitzpatrick, Tony
Fix, Michael
Florida, Richard (L.)
Floyd, John E(arl)
Fogel, Robert William
Folbre, Nancy
Foldvary, Fred E.
Fombrun, Charles J.
Fones-Wolf, Elizabeth
Foster, John Bellamy
Fotopoulos, Takis
Frame, J. Davidson
Francia, Peter L.
Francis, David J.
Francis, Diane (Marie)
Frank, Charles R(aphael)
Frank, Robert
Frank, Robert H.
Fraser, George (C.)
Fratianni, Michele
Fratkin, Elliot
Freeman, Harry M.
Fremgen, James Morgan
French, David
Freudenberger, Herman
Freyer, Tony (Allan)
Frieden, Jeffry
Friedman, Benjamin M.
Frigstad, David B.
Frost, Diane
Fukuda, Haruko
Furino, Antonio
Furubotn, Eirik G.
Gabor, Andrea (Anna Gisela)
Gaines, Thomas A.
Gallagher, Mary Elizabeth
Gallagher, Patricia C.
Gardner, Tom
Garnett, Richard (Duncan Carey)
Gerson, Kathleen
Ghilarducci, Teresa
Ghosh, Arun Kumar
Gibson, A(lex) J. S.
Gipson, Carolyn R.
Glahe, Fred R.
Glasmeier, Amy (K.)
Glickman, Norman J.
Godfrey, Neale S.
Goldman, Marshall I(rwin)
Goldstein-Jackson, Kevin
Goldwasser, Thomas
Goodman, Jordan E.
Goodwin, Michael
Gordon, Jennifer
Gorman, Michael E.
Gorringe, Timothy
Goto , Junichi
Gottfried, Robert R(ichard)
Gould, Bryan
Graham, Carol (Lee)
Graham, Daniel O.
Grampp, William D.
Grant, James
Grant, Jonathan A.

Gravelle, Jane G(ibson)
Greaves, Bettina Herbert Bien
Greener, Michael John
Greenwald, Bruce C.
Greenwald, G. Jonathan
Griffin, Keith B(roadwell)
Groenewegen, Peter
Grubb, Michael (J.)
Guinness, Jonathan (Bryan)
Gutteridge, Thomas G.
Guttmann, Robert
Gylfason, Thorvaldur
Gyohten, Toyoo
Haas, Lawrence J.
Hackler, George
Haenn, Nora
Hafner-Burton, Emilie M.
Hague, Douglas (Chalmers)
Hahn, Frank H(orace)
Hall, Carl W.
Hall, Stacey A.
Hamilton, John Maxwell
Hamrin, Robert
Hands, D. Wade
Handy, Rollo
Hanlon, Patrick
Hannesson, Rögnvaldur
Hansen, G. Eric
Hanson, David D.
Hanson, Philip
Harberger, Arnold C.
Harcourt, Geoffrey Colin
Harding, James
Hare, David
Harford, Tim
Harmon, Alexandra Sasha
Harner, Stephen M.
Harris, Walter A.
Harris, William V.
Hartley, Steven W.
Hastedt, Glenn Peter
Haveman, Robert Henry
Hawke, Gary Richard
Hayter, Teresa
Healey, Denis (Winston)
Heath, Chip
Heckscher, Charles
Heertje, Arnold
Held, Virginia
Helleiner, Gerald K(arl)
Hellyer, Paul T.
Helms, Robert B(rake)
Hepworth, Noel P.
Herzberg, Nancy K.
Heslam, Peter S.
Hey, Jeanne A. K.
Hibbs, John
Hickman, Bert G(eorge)
Hicks, Douglas A.
Hilton, (Andrew John) Boyd
Hilton, Boyd John Boyd
Hionidou, Violetta
Hirsch, Seev
Hitchcock, Tim
Hobbs, Dick
Hobson, John M.
Hodgson, Geoffrey M.

Nomani, Farhad
O'Brien, D(enis) P(atrick)
O'Brien, Patrick K.
O'Hearn, Denis
O'Leary, Rosemary
Ocampo, José Antonio
Odell, Peter R(andon)
Oelschlaeger, Max
Offer, Avner
Olsen, Edward A.
Olson, Michael Keith
Orr, David W.
Ortner, Robert
Outland, Robert B.
Owen, David
Pack, Spencer J.
Padgett, Stephen
Pae, Sung Moon
Palda, Filip
Palmer, Stanley H.
Panagariya, Arvind
Panford, Kwamina
Panitch, Leo (Victor)
Papadimitriou, Dimitri B.
Papes, Robert
Paradis, Adrian Alexis
Paradise, Paul R.
Parente, Stephen L.
Park, Jung-Dong
Parkin, Sara Lamb
Pascale, Richard Tanner
Patterson, Ian
Pauly, Louis W.
Pawel, Miriam
Peacock, Alan (Turner)
Pearson, Scott Roberts
Peck, Merton Joseph
Peetz, David
Pencak, William
Pencavel, John (H.)
Perez, Sofia A(na)
Perkins, Dwight Heald
Perkins, John
Peters, Michael (Adrian)
Peterson, Peter G.
Peterson, V. Spike
Peterson, Wallace C(arroll)
Phelps, Edmund S.
Philip, George
Philipsen, Dirk
Piderit, John J.
Pitts, Vincent J.
Pohl, Frederik
Pollitt, Michael G(erald)
Poorvu, William J.
Porter, Roger B.
Posner, Eric A.
Posner, Richard A.
Pospíšil, Leopold Jaroslav
Poundstone, William
Preda, Alex
Prestowitz, Clyde V.
Prindle, David F.
Prybyla, Jan S(tanislaw)
Putterman, Louis (G.)
Quandt, Richard (Emeric)
Quayle, (James) Dan(forth)

Ramos, Joseph R(afael)
Ranis, Gustav
Rao, J. N. K.
Rave, Tilmann
Ray, Daryll E.
Razin, Assaf
Redwood, John (Alan)
Regehr, T(heodore) D.
Reger, Gary
Reich, Robert B.
Reich, Simon (F.)
Renton, N(ick) E.
Reuben, Bryan G.
Reuber, Grant L.
Reynolds, Bill
Richards, Lawrence
Richardson, George Barclay
Ries, Laura
Righton, Caroline
Riley, Charles A.
Riley, James C.
Rinderle, Walter
Rivlin, Paul Anthony
Robb, Peter
Roberts, Alasdair Scott
Roberts, Paul
Roberts, Philip J.
Roberts, Russell D.
Robson, Brian Turnbull
Rodger, Richard
Root, Hilton L.
Rosenberg, Nathan
Roskamp, Karl Wilhelm
Rothkopf, David J.
Rothstein, Robert L.
Rothwell, William J.
Roubini, Nouriel
Rowley, Charles K(ershaw)
Rubin, Gretchen (Craft)
Rubin, Rose M.
Rumer, Boris
Russell, Cheryl
Sachs, Jeffrey D.
Sagalyn, Lynne B.
Samuels, Warren J(oseph)
Sanders, John H.
Sanford, Kathleen (D.)
Sanjek, David
Santoro, Michael A(nthony)
Scalapino, Robert Anthony
Schabas, Margaret
Scheiber, Harry N.
Schelling, Thomas C.
Schiavone, Giuseppe
Schier, Steven E.
Schioppa, Fiorella Kostoris Padoa
Schmieding, Holger
Schoenfeldt, Beth
Schor, Juliet B.
Schumacher, Linda H.
Scott, David L(ogan)
Scott, Tom
Scoville, James Griffin
Seabright, Paul
Searle, G(eoffrey) R(ussell)
Sebell, Mark Henry
Segal, Jerome M.

Selgin, George
Sellerberg, Ann Mari
Semler, Ricardo
Semyonov, Moshe
Seybold, Patricia B.
Shafer, D. Michael
Shafer, Neil
Shakoori, Ali
Shapiro, Eileen C.
Shapiro, Harold T(afler)
Sharkansky, Ira
Sharma, Nandita
Sharma, Poonam
Sharpe, Myron E(manuel)
Sharpe, William F(orsyth)
Shaw, Christine
Sheahan, John
Shear, Jeff
Sherman, Spencer D.
Shields, John M(ackie)
Shiller, Robert J.
Shim, Jae K.
Shmanske, Stephen
Shone, Ronald
Shoven, John B.
Shrestha, Nanda R.
Shughart, William F.
Shull, Steven A.
Shulman, Myra Ann
Shultz, George P(ratt)
Sichel, Werner
Sidak, J. Gregory
Siddiqa, Ayesha
Sikkink, Kathryn
Simmie, James (Martin)
Simon, Fritz B(ernhard)
Simon, Michele
Sims, Henry P.
Sinclair, Brett J(ason)
Singer, Max
Sinn, Hans Werner
Sirc, Ljubo
Sjostrand, Sven-Erik
Skidmore, David (G.)
Skipp, Victor (Henry Thomas)
Slemrod, Joel (B.)
Sloane, Peter J(ames)
Smart, S(tephen) Bruce
Smelser, Neil Joseph
Smiley, Gene
Smith, Christopher
Smith, Dale L.
Smith, George P(atrick)
Smith-Hunter, Andrea E.
Snell, Michael
Snow, Donald
Snyder, Francis Gregory
Sobel, Russell S(teven)
Solomon, Steven
Sonnenfeld, Jeffrey
Sowell, David (Lee)
Spar, Debora L.
Spash, Clive L(aurence)
Srivastava, Vinayak N.
Stark, Rodney
Stauber, John (Clyde)
Staubus, Martin

Stavrakis, Peter J(acob)
Steil, Benn
Stein, Benjamin J.
Steiner, George A.
Steinmetz, Lawrence Leo
Steuerle, C. Eugene
Stevenson, David
Stewart, David O.
Stewart, Matthew
Stewart, Michael (James)
Stewart, Rosemary
Stewart, Thomas A(lan)
Stoker, R. Bryan
Stoll, Steven
Stone, Dawna
Stone, Merlin (David)
Story, Jonathan
Strachman, Daniel A.
Streeten, Paul Patrick
Streever, Bill
Stretton, Hugh
Stroh, Linda K.
Stross, Randall E.
Struyk, Raymond J(ay)
Stubbs, Peter Charles
Stubbs, Richard W.
Stulberg, Adam N.
Sturmer, Michael
Suda, Zdenek Ludvik
Sullivan, Sherry E.
Sum, Ngai-Ling
Supple, Barry E(manuel)
Surowiecki, James (Michael)
Sutton, C(live) (Julian)
Sutton, Garrett
Sutton, Robert I.
Svallfors, Stefan
Swan, Claudia
Swanson, Gerald J.
Swedberg, Richard
Swift, Jamie
Szekely, Istvan P(al)
Szenberg, Michael
Szostak, Rick
Takenaka, Heizo
Targetti, Ferdinando
Tarr, Joel Arthur
Tatalovich, Raymond
Taverne, Dick
Taylor, Bob Pepperman
Taylor, Bron Raymond
Taylor, John A.
Taylor, Lester D.
Taylor, Ranald J.
Teece, David J(ohn)
Telser, Lester G(reenspan)
Temin, Peter
Tertzakian, Peter
Teske, Paul Eric
Thaler, Richard H.
Thierauf, Robert James
Thompson, Donald N.
Thompson, Kenneth W(infred)
Thornton, Mark
Thrift, Nigel
Thurow, Lester (Carl)
Tietenberg, T(homas) H(arry)

Burke, Sean
Burkhardt, Joanna M.
Burns, Marilyn
Burridge, Trevor David
Burtch, Brian
Burtchaell, James Tunstead
Bushey, Jeanne
Butler, Dorothy
Buzzeo, Toni
Byers, William
Byrt, Edwin Andrew
Caduto, Michael J.
Cahalan, James Michael
Callahan, Daniel (J.)
Camp, Robert C.
Campbell, Peter A.
Canada, Geoffrey
Canfield, Jack
Cantu, Norma Elia
Carbone, Elisa Lynn
Cardinal, Roger
Carr, Margaret
Carr-Hill, Roy
Carter, (Elizabeth) Susanne
Casagrande, June M.
Cave, Peter
Caws, Peter (James)
Cazden, Courtney B(orden)
Chafel, Judith A.
Chaitin, Gregory J.
Cheney, Martha
Cheripko, Jan
Chesters, Graham
Chilson, Peter
Chin, Justin
Chitham, Edward (Harry Gordon)
Chou, Tsu Wei
Christ, Henry I(rvine)
Chryssavgis, John
Church, Audrey P.
Churchill, E. Richard
Clark, Beverly Lyon
Clason, Marmy A.
Clawson, Calvin C.
Clotfelter, Charles T.
Clydesdale, Tim
Cobb, Clifford W(illiam)
Cobb, Vicki
Cockerill, A(rthur) W(illiam)
Colalillo-Kates, Isabella
Coles, Robert
Colfax, David (John)
Collier, Christopher
Collier, Graham
Collings, Gillian
Coloroso, Barbara
Comerford, Kathleen M.
Congdon, Kristin G.
Conley, Brenda Edgerton
Conroy, (Donald) Pat(rick)
Constantine-Simms, Delroy
Conway, Jill Ker
Cooling, Wendy
Cooper, Ilene
Copeland, Anne P.
Cordeiro, Patricia (A.)
Cormack, Robert J.

Cornell, Gary
Corten, Irina H.
Cottle, Thomas J.
Cottringer, Anne
Covington, James W.
Cowan, Gordon
Cowley, (Cassia) Joy
Cox, Vicki
Cramer, Stanley H.
Cranfield, Ingrid
Crawford, Alan
Crawley, Harriet
Creighton, Sarah Hammond
Crew, Rudy
Croissant, Jennifer L.
Cross, (Margaret) Claire
Cross, K. Patricia
Cullen, Dave
Cuomo, Mario (Matthew)
Currie, Stephen
Curthoys, Ann
Czerneda, Julie E(lizabeth)
D'Ambrosio, Jay S.
D'Anieri, Paul J. D.
Dahlen, Beverly
Daigle, Evelyne
Dale, Peter
Daloz, Laurent A. Parks
Daniels, Elizabeth Adams
Darby, Mary Ann
Date, C. J.
Davidson, Sol M.
Davies, Gareth
Davies, Jennifer (Eileen)
Davies, Martin L.
Davis, Andrew
Davis, Anita (Grey) P(rice)
Davis, Robin W(orks)
Davis, Rose Parkman
Dawson, George Glenn
Day, Alan
Day, Charles R.
Dayton, Charles (W.)
de Bono, Edward (Francis Charles)
de Costa, Elena M.
de Las Casas, Walter
DeCrow, Karen
Deem, James M(organ)
Del Re, Giuseppe
Delano, Anthony
deLara, Ellen
DelFattore, Joan
Delves, Peter J(ohn)
Demski, Joel S.
Dendinger, Roger E.
Devaux, Claudia
DeVincent-Hayes, Nan
Di, Zhu Xiao
Dial-Driver, Emily
Diffily, Deborah
Dillingham, William B.
Dines, Gail
Dintiman, George B.
Dolin, Sharon
Doman, Glenn
Donoghue, Mildred R(ansdorf)

Downie, R(obert) S(ilcock)
Dozier, Cheryl
Draper, Sharon Mills
Dressler, Joshua
Drum, Alice
Duchac, Joseph
Duckworth, Eleanor
Duggleby, John
Dulaney, W. Marvin
Dunbar, Joyce
Dunlop, Eileen (Rhona)
Dunmore, John
Dunn, John M.
DuPree, Sherry Sherrod
Duran, Jane
Dzielska, Maria
Echevarria, Jana
Edmunds, R(ussell) David
Edwards, Harvey
Egan, Kieran
Egler, Claudio A. G.
Eisen, Sydney
Elium, Jeanne (Ann)
Elkins, Dov Peretz
Ellenbecker, Todd S.
Ellis, Alec (Charles Owen)
Ellis, Mark (Karl)
Ellis, William E.
Emberley, Peter C.
Engell, James
English, Lyn D.
Ensor, Robert
Erard, Michael
Erickson, Betty J(ean)
Ettlinger, Steve
Evans, Brendan
Evans, Douglas
Evans, Earlene Green
Evans, Richard I(sadore)
Fabricant, Michael B.
Fairfield, Paul
Fairley, James S(tewart)
Farmaian, Sattareh Farman
Farrar, Ronald T(ruman)
Faruque, Cathleen Jo
Fay, Jim
Feder, Chris Welles
Feinberg, Rosa Castro
Feliciano, Hector
Fine, Doris Landau
Fink, Merton
Fishman, Katharine Davis
Flack, Jerry D(avid)
Fleisher, Paul
Flescher, Irwin
Fletcher, Ralph
Fleurant, Gerdès
Flinders, Neil J.
Flynn, Elizabeth A.
Fong, Bobby
Fonseca, James W(illiam)
Fontaine, Carole R.
Foust, J'aimé L.
Fowler, Alastair (David Shaw)
Fox, Margalit
Fox, Paula
Fraenkel, Jack R.

Fraser, Wynnette (McFaddin)
Freed, Anne O.
Freedman, Jonathan (Borwick)
Freedman, Sarah Warshauer
Freeman, Harry M.
French, Scot
Frey, Julia (Bloch)
Fried, Robert L.
Friedeberg-Seeley, Frank (J. B.)
Friedman, Lawrence M.
Fulghum, Robert (L.)
Fullan, Michael G.
Fuller, Jack (William)
Fuller, Mary Lou
Furino, Antonio
Gabbard, David A.
Gabrieli, Christopher
Gallagher, Kathleen
Gallagher, Liz
Gallagher, Patricia C.
Garber, Zev
Gascoigne, John
Gazetas, Aristides
Gelb, Michael J.
George, Judith W(ordsworth)
Gerdy, John R.
Getman, Julius (G.)
Gevisser, Mark
Geyer, Georgie Anne
Gibson, Ian
Gill, Walter
Gillett, Margaret
Gilman, Andrew D.
Gilpin, Geoff
Ginsburg, Mark B.
Giri, Ananta Kumar
Glancy, Ruth F(ergusson)
Glaser, William Arnold
Glenn, Cheryl
Gliserman, Martin
Gold, Penny Schine
Goldman, Arnold (Melvyn)
Goldschmidt, Arthur
Goldstein, Harvey
Goldstein, Larry Joel
Golubitsky, Martin
Goodlad, John I.
Goodman, Jesse
Goonetilleke, D. C. R. A.
Gordon, Deborah Hannes
Gordon, Haim
Gordon, Lewis Ricardo
Gordon, Mary (Catherine)
Gorman, Martha
Gorrell, Gena K.
Götz, Ignacio L.
Goulbourne, Harry
Graf, Mike
Grant, Cynthia D.
Grant, Daniel
Grant-Adamson, Lesley (Heycock)
Gray, Judith A(nne)
Grayson, Paul
Greeley, Andrew (Moran)
Green, Stephen J(ohn)
Greenberg, Elinor Miller

Marks, Paula Mitchell
Marshall, Christopher D(avid)
Marshall, Janet (Perry)
Marshall, Roy
Martin, Alex
Martin, David S.
Martin, Jack
Martínez, Dionisio D.
Martinez, Joseph G. R.
Martinez, Nancy C.
Marx, Eva
Mason, Anita
Masood, Maliha
Matalin, Mary
Matthews, Joseph R(onald)
Maxwell, Nicholas
McCall, Richard D.
McCants, William D.
McCarthy, Sherri N.
McCarty, Hanoch
McCaughrean, Geraldine (Jones)
McClellan, B(ernard) Edward
McConduit, Denise Walter
McCormick, Theresa Mickey (E.)
McCoy, William C.
McCullough, Donald W.
McDonald, J. I(an) H.
McDonnell, Kevin Lee
McFarlane, Peter (William)
McGrane, Bernard
McKeachie, Wilbert J.
McKinney, Sally (Brown)
McKinsey, Elizabeth
McLaren, John
Mcmanus, Antonia
McPhee, John (Angus)
McPhee, Norma H.
McQuain, Jeffrey Hunter
McQuay, Peri Phillips
McVey, Vicki
Meilman, Philip W(arren)
Mekler, Eva
Messel, Harry
Messner, Patricia A.
Meyer, Eugene L.
Michelson, Bruce (F.)
Michelson, William
Midwinter, Eric (Clare)
Mikolyzk, Thomas A.
Milgram, Gail Gleason
Miller, Kristie
Miller, Wilma Hildruth
Millman, Gregory J.
Millman, Joan (M.)
Mills, Richard W.
Minahan, John A.
Misa, Thomas J.
Mishica, Clare
Mitchell, Stephen (G.)
Mitroff, Ian I.
Moenssens, Andre A.
Mollenkott, Virginia Ramey
Mommsen, Hans
Monahan, William G(regory)
Montgomery, Diane
Montgomery, Scott L.
Moore, Cassandra Chrones

Moore-Hart, Margaret A.
Moran, Charles
Mordecai, Pamela (Claire)
Moreland, Richard C.
Morem, Susan
Moschonas, Andreas
Moses, Robert P(arris)
Moulakis, Athanasios
Muehl, Lois Baker
Muniz, Olga M.
Munro, John M(urchison)
Murphy, Austin
Murphy, Dervla Mary
Murphy, Sylvia
Murray, Elaine
Musgrove, Frank
Muuss, Rolf Eduard
Nadeau, Adel
Nahas, Gabriel G(eorges)
Needham, Kate
Neel, Jasper
Nehrt, Lee C(harles)
Nelson, Betty Palmer
Nelson, Jack Lee
Nersesian, Roy L.
Newton, Roger G(erhard)
Ney, Ronald E.
Nielsen, Nancy J.
Nissman, Blossom S.
Nitchie, George Wilson
Noah, Harold J.
Nobisso, Josephine
Northrup, Mary (Wirtz)
Norton, Robert L.
Nursten, Jean Patricia (Frobisher)
O'Donnell, Brennan (Patrick)
O'Shaughnessy, Ellen Cassels
Okoro, Anezi
Oliphant, Dave (Edward Davis)
Olitzky, Kerry M.
Oliver, Mary
Olson, David Richard
Olson, Gary A.
Olson, Linda
Oppelt, Norman T.
Oppenheimer, Todd
Orme, David John
Orme, Nicholas
Orton, Anthony
Ostrom, Hans
Ove, Robert S.
Overend, William George
Overton, Jenny (Margaret Mary)
Padilla, Raymond V.
Page, Penny B(ooth)
Page, Reba Neukom
Palestini, Robert
Paley, Vivian Gussin
Palmer, Frank Robert
Palmer, Hap
Paretsky, Sara
Paris, David C.
Park, Timothy K.
Parshall, Karen Hunger
Pascoe, C. J.
Pasework, William Robert
Pashkow, Fredric J.

Passeron, Jean Claude
Paterson, Ronald (William Keith)
Patey, Douglas Lane
Patzer, Gordon
Pauley, Garth E.
Pavey, Don
Peacock, Alan (Turner)
Peck, David R.
Peet, Mal
Penrod, Diane
Percy, John R(ees)
Perfetti, Charles A.
Perry, Phyllis J.
Peters, Michael (Adrian)
Peterson, Jean Sunde
Pfeiffer, Janet (B.)
Phillips, John Lawrence
Piderit, John J.
Piirto, Jane
Pike, R. William
Pine, Nicholas
Pirie, Bruce A.
Ploeger, Katherine (M.)
Pohlmann, Marcus D.
Pollard, Irina
Pong, David (B. P. T.)
Poortinga, Y(pe) H.
Pope, Deborah
Porter, Edgar A(dwell)
Posamentier, Alfred S.
Powers, Alan
Preston-Mafham, Rod(ney Arthur)
Price, Hugh B(ernard)
Price, Susan
Putnam, Constance E(lizabeth)
Quinn, Peter (John)
Ramsland, Katherine
Randi, James
Rathmell, George W(esley)
Ray, Robert H.
Ray, Ruth E.
Reed, John Shelton
Reed, Maureen G.
Reed-Danahay, Deborah
Rees, Brian
Reid, Loren
Rencher, Alvin C.
Renfield, Richard Lee
Renker, Elizabeth
Reyhner, Jon (Allan)
Reynolds, Aaron
Richardson, Peter
Ridd, Stephen (John)
Ridgway, John M.
Riedling, Ann Marlow
Rimmington, Gerald Thorneycroft
Rizzo, Margaret
Roberts, Alvin
Roberts, Iolo Francis
Roberts, Jon H.
Robins, Robert S.
Robinson, Ken
Robson, Derek Ian
Roche, Mark W.
Rockwell, Anne (Foote)
Rodden, John (Gallagher)
Roessner, Michaela

Romano, Louis
Roop, Peter
Roose, Kevin
Root-Bernstein, Robert Scott
Rose, Mike
Rosell, Steven A.
Rosenmeyer, Patricia A.
Ross, Lawrence C.
Rosser, Sue V(ilhauer)
Rossing, Barbara
Rowett, Helen (Graham Quiller)
Rowntree, Derek
Rozbicki, Michal J.
Russell, Helen Ross
Rutter, Michael (Llewellyn)
Ryan, Halford (Ross)
Ryder, Joanne (Rose)
Saffer, Barbara
Safransky, Sy
Saini, B(alwant) S(ingh)
Saloff, Jamie L.
Salsi, Lynn
Sampson, Michael
Sanchez-Eppler, Karen
Sanderlin, George
Sanders, Katrina M.
Sandman, Peter (Mark)
Sarkodie-Mensah, Kwasi
Sarno, Ronald Anthony
Saulnier, Karen Luczak
Sawyer, (Frederick) Don(ald)
Scalapino, Robert Anthony
Scales, Barbara
Schaafsma, David
Schaefer, William D.
Schaeffer, Mark
Schall, Lucy
Schank, Roger C(arl)
Scheindlin, Raymond P.
Schermbrucker, Bill
Scheuer, Jeffrey
Schiff, James A(ndrew)
Schimpff, Jill Wagner
Schmandt, Jurgen
Schmidt, Benno Charles
Schmidt, Peter
Schneider, Barbara
Schneider, Fred B.
Schneider, Robyn
Scholey, Arthur (Edward)
Schrag, Ariel
Schrock, Kathleen
Schwartz, Sheila R.
Schweickart, Patrocinio P.
Scott, Peter
Searle, Ronald (William Fordham)
Sears, James T(homas)
Sedgwick, Fred
Seguin, Marilyn W(eymouth)
Seligman, Martin E. P.
Sennett, Frank (Ronald)
Sewall, Gilbert T.
Shafer, Glenn (Ray)
Shallcross, John James
Shapiro, Bonnie L.
Shapiro, H. Svi

Buderi, Robert
Bugos, Glenn E.
Bungey, John Henry
Caldwell, David H(epburn)
Carter, C. Barry
Carter, Martin R(oger)
Charlier, Roger Henri
Chernykh, E(vgenij)
    N(ikolaevich)
Chorafas, Dimitris N.
Chou, Tsu Wei
Choudhury, Ashok
Chowdhury, Subir
Chu, Wai C.
Coburn, Pip
Cockerill, A(rthur) W(illiam)
Collinson, Alan S.
Commoner, Barry
Cook, James L(ister)
Craig, G(illian) M(ary)
de Neufville, Richard
des Rivières, Jim
Doran, David K.
Drew, Horace R.
Eberhart, Mark E.
Elliott, Clark A.
English, Lyn D.
Ezrahi, Yaron
Fanchi, John R(ichard)
Fenner, Roger T(heedham)
Ferrari, R(onald) L(eslie)
Ferreiro, Larrie D.
Ferrières, Madeleine
Fetherston, Drew
Fisher, Marshall Jon
Fisher, Robert E.
Fraser, Harry
Freeman, Harry M.
Galeotti, Mark
Grey, Jerry
Grove, Richard H(ugh)
Gruntman, Mike
Gunetti, Daniele
Hachigian, Nina L.
Haldar, Achintya
Hall, Carl W.
Halliday, Stephen
Hamid, Ahmad A.
Hammond, Herb(ert L.)
Harriott, Peter
Henderson, F(rancis) M(artin)
Heppenheimer, Thomas A.
Herring, Mark Youngblood
Heyman, Jacques
Hildt, Elisabeth
Horlock, John Harold
Hudson, John B.
Iagnemma, Karl
Ihde, Don
Ipsen, D. C.
Jain, Raj
Jin, Jian-Ming
Kasabov, Nikola K(irilov)
Kealey, Edward J.
Keller, Joe
Kemper, Steve
Kenjo, Takashi

Kent, James M.
Kentfield, J(ohn) A(lan) C.
King, John
Koff, Richard M.
Koya, Tatsuhito
Kratz, Martin P. J.
Kunda, Gideon
Kurzydłowski, Krzysztof Jan
Kuznetsov, Nickolaj
Ladell, John L.
Lauber, Volkmar
Lea, James F(ranklin)
Lebow, Eileen F.
Levin, Doron P.
Levy, Matthys
Linson, Art
Lorenz, Ralph
Lurquin, Paul F.
MacDonald, Marylee
Maggs, Colin Gordon
Malseed, Mark
Manzoni, Jean-François
Marangoni, Alejandro G.
March, N(orman) H(enry)
Markoff, John
Maughan, Jackie Johnson
McCutcheon, William Alan
McFarland, Stephen L.
McNerney, Gerald
Medvedev, Grigori
Michaelowa, Axel
Miele, Angelo
Milton, Pat
Misa, Thomas J.
Mitchell, John C.
Morales, Rebecca (Hope)
Moravec, Hans P(eter)
Motchenbacher, C(urt) D.
Müller, Ingo
Murarka, Shyam P.
Murphy, Gordon J.
Murray, G. T.
Myers, Drew(fus Young)
Nabhan, Gary Paul
Naidu, Prabhakar S.
Nayfeh, Ali Hasan
Negnevitsky, Michael
Nof, Shimon Y.
Norton, Robert L.
O'Connor, Colin
Panchyk, Richard
Parks, Deborah A.
Pecht, Michael G.
Perkowitz, Sidney
Perlin, John
Peterson, Chris(tine Louise)
Petroski, Henry
Pezeshki, Charles
Ponting, Clive
Prathap, G(angan)
Pritts, Kim Derek
Rabalais, J. Wayne
Rahman, Matiur
Raudkivi, A(rved) J(aan)
Roberts, Derek Harry
Rockwell, Theodore
Rosaler, Robert C.

Rossol, Monona
Rotundo, Louis C.
Ruddock, Ted
Sarfoh, Kwadwo A.
Schenck, Hilbert
Schnitter, Nicholas J.
Schott, John R.
Schramm, Laurier L.
Shah, Jami J.
Shlechter, Theodore M.
Sichel, Werner
Sindermann, Carl J(ames)
Slemon, Gordon Richard
Smarandache, Florentin
Smith, Julian C(leveland)
Smith, Peter Charles Horstead
Solomonson, Katherine M.
Stamford Krause, Shari
Storer, James Donald
Stroh, Linda K.
Sulston, John (Edward)
Summerhill, Thomas
Tang, Victor
Thompson, Francis George
Thompson, Marilyn W.
Thumann, Albert
Tidwell, Mike
Trapp, Stefan (Alfred Josef)
Tribus, Myron
Trzynadlowski, Andrzej M.
Turnill, Reginald
Uman, Myron F.
Valko, Peter
Vesper, Karl H(amptom)
Wajcman, Judy
Waldman, Harry
Watson, Bruce
Watts, Anthony John
Weems, David B(urnola)
Weinbaum, Marvin G.
Werbach, Adam
Williams, Forman A.
Wiseman, Alan
Zatsiorsky, Vladimir M.

Environmental Sciences/Ecology

Abdel-Magid, Isla m Mu ammad
Ableman, Michael
Adam, Paul
Adams, Carol J.
Allaby, (John) Michael
Allen, Patricia
Anderson, Duane
Antonetta, Susanne
Armbruster, Ann
Ashworth, (Lewis) William
Ayres, E. C.
Bach, David
Bacher, John
Bailey, Donna
Baker, Jeannie
Balling, Robert C.
Barbato, Joseph

Barnes, Burton V(erne)
Barnes, Peter
Barnes, Simon
Barnosky, Anthony D.
Barratt Brown, Michael
Barry, James P(otvin)
Bauckham, Richard J.
Beatley, Timothy
Begley, Ed James
Beissinger, Steven R.
Bell, David Owen
Benarde, Melvin Albert
Benson, Richard
Bentos, Carlos
Berger, Bruce
Bernstein, Ellen
Bevis, William W.
Bina, Cyrus
Birkland, Thomas A.
Black, Brian
Boag, Peter G.
Bolgiano, Chris(tina)
Bonta, Marcia Myers
Bortolotti, Dan
Botkin, Daniel B.
Bowden, Charles
Bowen, Mark
Boyd, Claude E.
Brandenburg, Jim
Brewer, Garry D(wight)
Brodeur, Paul (Adrian)
Brook, Elaine (Isabel)
Brower, Kenneth
Brown, Bryan T(urner)
Brown, Lester R(ussell)
Buck, Susan J.
Budiansky, Stephen (Philip)
Buell, Frederick (Henderson)
Buhner, Stephen Harrod
Burger, Joanna
Burt, Christopher Clinton
Burt, William
Burton, L(awrence) DeVere
Butala, Sharon (Annette)
Caduto, Michael J.
Calder, Nigel (David Ritchie)
Callenbach, Ernest
Callicott, J(ohn) Baird
Campbell, G(aylon) S(anford)
Campbell, R(obert) Wayne
Carless, Jennifer
Carroll, Matthew S.
Carter, Martin R(oger)
Castaneda, Christopher James
Caufield, Catherine
Cevasco, G(eorge) A(nthony)
Charlier, Roger Henri
Chertow, Marian R.
Childs, Christopher
Chiras, Daniel D.
Chu, Miyoko
Ciochon, Russell L.
Clark, Terry N(ichols)
Clayden, Andy
Cloudsley-Thompson, John
    (Leonard)

O'Leary, Rosemary
O'Malley, Penelope Grenoble
O'Neill, Kevin M.
Oates, Wallace Eugene
Obmascik, Mark
Odell, Robin Ian
Oelschlaeger, Max
Ogrin, Dušan
Oiwa, Keibo
Okoro, Anezi
Olson, Ted
Ophuls, William
Orenstein, Ronald I.
Orr, David W.
Parkin, Sara Lamb
Payne, Neil F.
Penney, Sue
Perkins, John H.
Perlin, John
Petuch, Edward J.
Pezeshki, Charles
Philp, Richard B(lain)
Pianka, Eric R(odger)
Pierson, Melissa Holbrook
Pimentel, David
Pimm, Stuart L(eonard)
Piper, Jon Kingsbury
Pitt, David Charles
Platt, Harold L.
Platt, Rutherford H.
Pollack, Henry N.
Popper, Frank James
Powledge, Fred
Prance, Ghillean Tolmie
Pregracke, Chad
Primack, Richard B.
Putnam, William L(owell)
Radcliffe Richards, Janet
Rahman, Matiur
Ramphal, Shridath (Surendranath)
Rathje, William (Laurens)
Raudkivi, A(rved) J(aan)
Reader, John
Redclift, Michael R.
Redford, Kent H(ubbard)
Reed, Maureen G.
Richardson, Bonham C.
Richardson, David (Horsfall Stuart)
Richerson, Peter J.
Riviere, Jim (E.)
Roach, Catherine M.
Roads, Michael J.
Robinson, Chuck
Rogers, Heather
Rohmer, Richard
Rose, Michael R.
Rotello, Gabriel
Royte, Elizabeth
Rubinoff, M. Lionel
Ruddiman, William F.
Russell, Helen Ross
Russell, Jeremy (Longmore)
Rybolt, Thomas R.
Sachs, Wolfgang
Safina, Carl

Sale, Kirkpatrick
Salisbury, Frank B(oyer)
Salzberg, Allen
Sandilands, Al P.
Sandman, Peter (Mark)
Sands, Philippe
Sanna, Ellyn
Sauvain, Philip Arthur
Scales, Barbara
Scheese, Donald
Schell, Orville (Hickok)
Schmandt, Jurgen
Schmid, Wolfram George
Sculle, Keith A.
Sellers, Christopher C.
Shabecoff, Philip
Shavelson, Lonny
Sheftel, Victor O.
Shelby, Anne
Sheldon, Joseph K(enneth)
Shellenberger, Michael
Shugart, Herman H(enry)
Sill, John
Simpson, John Warfield
Sindermann, Carl J(ames)
Singh, Chetan
Skolnikoff, Eugene B.
Smith, Annick
Smith, Anthony
Smith, Hobart Muir
Smith, Sheldon
Snow, Donald
Snowman, Daniel
Snyder, Gary (Sherman)
Solbrig, Otto Thomas
Soluri, John
Soper, Kate
Spash, Clive L(aurence)
Spellman, Frank R.
Spencer, Robert H.
Spretnak, Charlene
Stanford, Craig (Britton)
Stanish, Charles
Stapleton, Richard M.
Steinman, David
Sterling, Keir B(rooks)
Stern, Paul C(linton)
Stokes, Donald W.
Stonehouse, Bernard
Strauss, Susan (Elizabeth)
Stroud, Patricia Tyson
Szasz, Andrew
Taber, Stephen Welton
Tal, Alon
Tarr, Joel Arthur
Tatum, Beverly Daniel
Taylor, Bron Raymond
Taylor, Dave
Taylor, Michael Ray
Taylor, Sarah McFarland
Teece, David J(ohn)
Terborgh, John W.
Thiel, Diane
Thirsk, (Irene) Joan
Thompson, Claudia G(reig)
Thorson, John E.

Tisdell, Clement Allan
Tobias, Michael (Charles)
Tobin, Richard J.
Toffler, Heidi
Trapp, Stefan (Alfred Josef)
Travis, Anthony S(tewart)
Treat, James
Tribus, Myron
Tudge, Colin
Turco, Richard (Peter)
Turner, B. L.
Turner, Tom
Ulanski, Stan L.
Ulrich, Larry
Uman, Myron F.
van Duzer, Chet A.
Vaughn, Jacqueline
Vause, L(aurence) Mikel
Vayda, Andrew P.
Vileisis, Ann
Vogel, Carole Garbuny
Volk, Tyler
Walker, Lawrence R.
Wallace, Bruce
Wallace, Deborah
Waltner-Toews, David
Ward, Frank A.
Warren, Karen J.
Wedeen, Richard Peter
Weintraub, Linda
Wert, Jonathan (Maxwell)
Westmacott, Richard N.
Wheeler, Sara
White, Dan
White, Jonathan (Bruce)
Whitty, Julia
Williams, James C.
Williams, Martin Anthony Joseph
Williams, Michael
Williams, Wendy
Wilson, Cynthia
Wilson, Ken
Wolfson, Richard
Wood, Douglas (Eric)
Woodwell, George M.
Woody, Elizabeth
Woolfe, Jennifer A(nne)
Worcester, Robert
Wyman, Bruce C.
Yaroshinskaya, Alla
Young, John
Zencey, Eric
Zeveloff, Samuel I.
Zuckermann, Wolfgang (Joachim)
Zuk, Marlene
Zwinger, Ann Haymond

Ethics

Abbott, Karen
Adams, Roy J(oseph)
Agich, George J.
Albrecht, Gloria H.
Almond, Brenda

Amadi, Elechi
Anderson, Elizabeth (S.)
Andre, Judith
Arnett, Ronald C.
Arnold, Arnold F.
Attfield, Robin
Atwill, David G.
Baehr, Kingsley M.
Baggini, Julian
Bailey, Charles Waldo
Balswick, Judith K.
Battersby, Christine
Beckley, Harlan R.
Bedau, Hugo Adam
Berkowitz, Peter
Black, Donald
Bok, Sissela
Bonder, Nilton
Braine, David
Bronzino, Joseph D.
Brown, Montague
Brugger, E. Christian
Burnett, Alan
Busch, Lawrence (Michael)
Callahan, Daniel (J.)
Capitan, William H(arry)
Chociolko, Christina
Clough, David L.
Connell, George B(oyce)
Cook, Rebecca J.
Coyne, Michael
Craig, Robert H.
Culyer, A(nthony) J(ohn)
Dadlez, E(va) M(aria)
Davies, Christie
Dawid, Annie
DeGeorge, Richard T(homas)
DeWitt, Calvin B.
Donaldson, Thomas
Downie, R(obert) S(ilcock)
Drlica, Karl
Duffield, Gervase E.
Edgar, Stacey L.
Elfstrom, Gerard A.
Engelhardt, H(ugo) Tristram
Fasching, Darrell J.
Ferre, John P.
Fessler, Ann
Finnis, John M(itchell)
Fisk, Milton
Forrester, Duncan B(aillie)
Fritsch, Albert J(oseph)
Furnish, Victor Paul
Gaylin, Willard
Giampieri-Deutsch, Patrizia
Gill, LaVerne McCain
Gray, Chris Hables
Green, Ricky K(enneth)
Gross, Michael L.
Gustafson, Sid
Guy, Mary E.
Habgood, John Stapylton
Hampson, (Margaret) Daphne
Harpur, Tom
Harries, Karsten
Harris, James F.
Hartle, Anthony E.

Caws, Mary Ann
Chakravarty, Sumita S(inha)
Chambers, Veronica
Charles, John
Charney, Mark J.
Chatman, Seymour
Cherchi-Usai, Paolo
Chipman, Bruce Lewis
Clark, Paul John Abott
Cleveland, Leslie
Cloud, Darrah
Cohen, Gary P.
Cohen, Hubert I.
Cohen, Karl F.
Cohen, Paul (M.)
Coleman, Loren (Elwood)
Collison, Kerry B(oyd)
Cones, John W.
Conklin, John E.
Conley, Tom (Clark)
Conn, Didi
Cooper, Mark Garrett
Corliss, Richard (Nelson)
Cornis-Pope, Marcel (H.)
Cox, Paul(us)
Cox, Stephen (LeRoy)
Coyne, Michael
Crist, Judith
Crouch, Tanja L.
Culhane, John (William)
Cunningham, Frank R.
Dahl, Arlene
Daniels, Jeff
Darby, William D(uane)
Dassanowsky, Robert
Davis, Andrew
Dawid, Annie
De Stefano, George
Desser, David
Dick, Bernard F.
Dintrone, Charles V.
Drexler, Rosalyn
Dukore, Bernard F.
Ebert, Roger (Joseph)
Edwards, Anne
Edwards, Larry
Ellis, Gwen
Emery, Robert J.
Emmer, Michele
Engel, Joel
Erickson, Hal
Farquhar, Mary Ann
Fayer, Steve
Ferlita, Ernest
Field, Edward
Fielding, Raymond
Fienup-Riordan, Ann
Finch, Christopher
Fine, Marshall
Finstad, Suzanne
Fischer, Dennis
Flamini, Roland
Fleishman, Avrom
Flynn, Joseph
Folster, David
Fox, Barry
Fox, Jo

Foyt, Victoria
Franklin, Daniel P.
French, Philip (Neville)
French, Sean
Fromm, Pete
Fuegi, John
Fumento, Rocco
Gaines, Jane (Marie)
Gallagher, Tess
Gans, Eric L.
Garfield, Brian (F. W.)
Garner, Helen
Gazetas, Aristides
Gehring, Wes D(avid)
Gemunden, Gerd
Genini, Ronald
George, Terry
Gifford, James J.
Gillon, Adam
Gilman, Owen W(inslow)
Gilroy, Frank D(aniel)
Ginsburg, Faye D(iana)
Glancy, Diane
Glass, Charles
Glut, Don(ald) F.
Goble, Alan
Goldman, Steven
Gondry, Michel
Goodavage, Maria
Gorman, Lyn
Goyer, David S.
Grange, William Marshall
Grant, Barry Keith
Grazer, Gigi Levangie
Gregg, Clark
Griffiths, Linda
Guérif, François
Guzzetti, Alfred F.
Haddad, Gladys
Hajdu, David
Harburg, Ernie
Harmetz, Aljean
Haskell, Molly
Hatkoff, Amy
Hawke, Ethan
Haycock, Kate
Haynes, Jonathan
Helgeland, Brian
Hensley, Dennis
Hillier, Jim
Hirschhorn, Clive
Hischak, Thomas S.
Honri, Peter
Horak, Jan-Christopher
Howarth, William (Louis)
Hunt, Marjorie
Iaccino, James F(rancis)
Inge, M. Thomas
Isaacs, Susan
Ivory, James (Francis)
Jackson, Kathy Merlock
Jackson, Kevin
Jagose, Annamarie
Jancovich, Mark
Johnson-Smith, Jan
Jones, Stephen
Kaleta, Kenneth C.

Kaplan, James
Kaplan, Nelly
Kapsis, Robert E.
Kauffmann, Stanley
Kawin, Bruce F.
Kear, Lynn
Keeling, Kara
Kendrick, Stephen
Kenrick, Tony
Kimmel, Daniel M.
Kimura, Margaret
King, Geoff
Kingsland, Rosemary
Klempner, Mark
Kowalewski, Michael (John)
Krizan, Kim
LaBute, Neil
Landy, Marcia
Lanza, Joseph
Lanzmann, Claude
Lavery, David
Law, Clara
Lax, Eric
Lenney, Dinah
Lent, John A.
Leon, Sharon
Lev, Peter
Li, Leslie
Libo, Kenneth (Harold)
Libov, Charlotte Ann
Lindenmuth, Kevin J.
Linson, Art
Loshitzky, Yosefa
Low, Brian J.
Lukas, Christopher
Lynn, Jonathan
MacAdams, William
MacDougall, David
Maechler, Stefan
Magnus, Erica
Maher, Mary Z.
Makepeace, Anne
Mamet, David
Manchel, Frank
Mangold, James
Mann, William J.
Mapp, Edward
Marciano, Francesca
Marcus, Millicent
Martin-Jones, David
Martinez, D. P.
Mason, Fran
Mathison, Melissa
Maxford, Howard
McCann, Graham
McCarty, John
McClintick, David
McIlroy, Brian
McMahan, Alison
Mekler, Eva
Mellen, Joan
Menéndez, Ana (Maria)
Michael, Colette V(erger)
Mickolus, Edward (Francis)
Miller, Blair
Miyares, Coco Emilia Fusco
Monaco, James

Monaghan, David (Mark)
Morgan-Witts, Max
Morrey, Douglas J.
Morris, Nigel
Mosley, Philip
Muller, Eddie
Munby, Jonathan
Murdoch, David H.
Murkoff, Heidi Eisenberg
Murphy, Robert
Naha, Ed
Nathanson, Paul
Natoli, Joseph
Nelson, T. G. A.
Nericcio, William Anthony
Nevins, Francis M(ichael)
Nollen, Scott Allen
Nolletti, Arthur (E.)
Noriega, Chon A.
Norman, Barry
O'Leary, Patrick
Obst, Lynda (Rosen)
Ochart (Torres), (Luz) Yvonne
Oderman, Stuart (Douglas)
Olson, Ted
Ortenberg, Veronica
Paglia, Camille
Palmer, William J.
Paris, Michael
Parish, James Robert
Parkes, Walter F.
Patrick, Robert
Pauly, Rebecca M.
Pendreigh, Brian
Perez, Gilberto (Guillermo)
Petrie, Duncan
Phelan, Anna Hamilton
Pickett, Rex
Pike, David L.
Pitts, Michael R.
Poague, Leland
Polizzotti, Mark
Pollock, (Mary) Sharon
Pollock, Dale
Prawer, S(iegbert) S(alomon)
Priest, Christopher (McKenzie)
Prince, Stephen
Pye, Michael (Kenneth)
Quinlan, David
Rainer, Yvonne
Reynolds, Kevin
Rhodes, Gary Don
Rich, Nathaniel
Richie, Donald
Robb, David L.
Robinson, Andrew
Rockland, Michael Aaron
Roddam, Franc(is George)
Rothman, William
Ruddick, Nicholas
Russell, Catherine
Russell, Sharon A.
Russo, John (A.)
Saffle, Michael
Salamon, Julie
Salwolke, Scott
Sammon, Paul M.

Baron, Wendy
Barr, Alwyn
Barr, Andrew
Barr, Patricia (Miriam)
Barra, Allen
Barratt Brown, Michael
Barreto, Mascarenhas
Barrett, Anthony A(rthur)
Barrett, David M(arshall)
Barrett, John G(ilchrist)
Barrie, Alexander
Barrish, Phillip
Barrow, G. W. S.
Barrow, Robin (St. Clair)
Barry, James P(otvin)
Barry, Kathleen M.
Barry, Michael
Barry, P(atricia) S(teepee)
Barsamian, David
Barsky, Robert F(ranklin)
Barth, Robert Lawrence
Bartholomew-Feis, Dixee R.
Bartlett, Thomas
Barton, Carlin A.
Barton, Greg
Barton, Tamsyn (S.)
Bartoszewski, Wladyslaw T(eofil)
Bartov, Omer
Barzun, Jacques
Basil, John D.
Bass, Cynthia
Bass, Diana Butler
Bass, Gary J.
Bass, Jack
Bass, Thomas A.
Bassler, Gerhard P.
Baston, Lewis
Batchen, Geoffrey
Bateman, Robert L.
Bates, Stephen
Batnitzky, Leora
Battersby, Christine
Battestin, Martin Carey
Bauckham, Richard J.
Bauer, Yehuda
Bauerschmidt, Frederick Christian
Baughan, Peter Edward
Baughman, Michael
Baughman, T. H.
Bauman, Zygmunt
Bawcutt, Priscilla (June)
Baxter, John
Bayly, C. A.
Bayme, Steven
Beales, D(erek) E(dward) D(awson)
Bean, Jonathan J.
Beasley, Faith E(velyn)
Beattie, Judith Hudson
Beatty, Barbara (R.)
Beatty, Jack
Beaud, Michel
Beauman, Nicola
Beaumont, Matthew
Beauregard, Robert A.
Bebbington, D(avid) W(illiam)
Bechtol, Bruce E.

Beck, Mary L. (Giraudo)
Becker, Elizabeth
Becker, Jasper
Becker, Patti Clayton
Bederman, Gail
Bedford, Henry Frederick
Bedingfield, M. Bradford
Bee, Ronald J.
Beebe, Ralph K.
Beeby, James M.
Beecher, Maureen Ursenbach
Beer, Anna R.
Beers, Burton Floyd
Beers, Diane L.
Behdad, Sohrab
Behrens, John C.
Behringer, Wolfgang
Behuniak, James
Beisner, Robert L.
Beker, Avi
Belknap, Robert L.
Bell, Albert A.
Bell, Dean Phillip
Bell, Hazel K(athleen)
Bellamy, Alex J.
Bellamy, Christopher (David)
Bellamy, Richard (Paul)
Beller, Susan Provost
Bellesiles, Michael A.
Belloli, Andrea P. A.
Bellow, Adam
Bellows, Barbara L(awrence)
Beltman, Brian W.
Belue, Ted Franklin
Benavides, O. Hugo
Benbassa, Esther
Bender, Thomas
Benedict, Barbara M.
Benedict, Helen
Benedict, Philip (Joseph)
Benezra, Neal
Benn, Tony
Bennassar, Bartolomé
Bennett, Alan
Bennett, Edward M.
Bennett, G. H.
Bennett, James Richard
Bennett, Lerone
Bennett, Shelley M.
Bennett, W. Lance
Bennis, Phyllis
Bensel, Richard Franklin
Bensman, David
Benson, Ann
Benson, John
Bentley, Michael (John)
Bentsen, Cheryl
Berebitsky, Julie
Berenbaum, Michael
Berg, Manfred
Berg, Scott W.
Berger, Stefan
Bergerud, Eric M.
Berghahn, Volker R.
Bergin, Thomas J.
Bergman, Ronen
Bergonzi, Bernard

Bergquist, Charles
Bergreen, Laurence
Bergunder, Michael
Berinsky, Adam J.
Berkey, Jonathan P.
Berkovitz, Jay R.
Berkowitz, Edward D.
Berkowitz, Peter
Berman, David
Berman, David
Berman, Morris
Berman, Russell A.
Bernard, G. W.
Bernstein, David E(liot)
Bernstein, Frances Lee
Bernstein, Laurie
Bernstein, Mark
Bernstein, Richard
Bernstein, Richard B.
Berres, Thomas Edward
Berry, Andrew
Berry, Chad
Berry, J. Bill
Berry, Joanne
Berry, John Stevens
Berry, Stephen W.
Berryman, Jack W.
Bessel, Richard
Best, Antony
Best, Geoffrey (Francis Andrew)
Best, Wallace D.
Bettey, J(oseph) H(arold)
Betts, Clive
Bew, Paul Anthony
Biagini, Eugenio F.
Bialer, Uri
Bickerstaff, Steve
Bickerton, David M.
Bickford-Smith, Vivian
Bicks, Caroline
Biddiss, Michael Denis
Bieder, Robert E.
Biel, Steven
Biger, Gideon
Biggs, Chester M(axwell)
Biggs, John Burville
Bigham, Darrel E.
Bigsby, C. W. E.
Bilby, Joanne Stroud
Bilgrami, Akeel
Bilinkoff, Jodi
Billias, George Athan
Billinger, Robert D.
Billingsley, (Kenneth) Lloyd
Billingsley, Scott
Billington, David P(erkins)
Billington, James H(adley)
Binding, Paul
Binkley, Christina
Binnema, Theodore
Binski, Paul
Binstock, Robert H.
Binzen, Peter (Husted)
Bird, Christiane
Birdwell, Michael E.
Bireley, Robert
Birkland, Thomas A.

Birn, Raymond Francis
Birney, Alice Lotvin
Birrell, James Peter
Birzer, Bradley J.
Bitton-Jackson, Livia E(lvira)
Bizzarro, Tina Waldeier
Bjarkman, Peter C(hristian)
Bjorge, Gary J(ohn)
Bjork, Daniel W.
Black, Conrad
Black, Jeremy (Martin)
Black, Merle
Blackaby, Richard
Blackbourn, David
Blackburn, Fred M(onroe)
Blackford, Mansel G(riffiths)
Blackwell, Joyce
Blagojevic, Ljiljana
Blainey, Geoffrey Norman
Blair, E(lizabeth) Anne
Blake, Norman Francis
Blake, Quentin
Blake, Raymond B.
Blake, Stephen P.
Blanchard, James G.
Blanning, T. C. W.
Blaufarb, Rafe
Blauvelt, Martha Tomhave
Blee, Kathleen M.
Blegen, Daniel M.
Blenkinsopp, Joseph
Blethen, H(arold) Tyler
Blewett, Daniel K(eith)
Blickle, Peter
Blight, David W.
Blight, James G.
Blitzer, Wolf
Block, Sharon
Block, Thomas H(arris)
Blockson, Charles L(eRoy)
Blodgett, Peter J.
Blom, Philipp
Bloom, Clive
Bloom, Howard
Bloom, Jonathan M(ax)
Bloomfield, Lincoln P(almer)
Blosser, Susan Sokol
Blouet, Olwyn M(ary)
Bloxham, Donald
Blum, Edward J.
Blundell, Sue
Blythe, Martin
Blythe, Ronald (George)
Bo, Zhiyue
Boag, Peter G.
Boardman, John
Boast, Philip
Boatwright, Mary T.
Bober, Natalie S.
Bobrick, Benson
Bochin, Hal W(illiam)
Bock, Gisela
Bodansky, Yossef
Boddy, Janice
Bodek, Richard
Bodenhamer, David J(ackson)
Bodett, Tom

Bushnell, Rebecca W.
Buskin, Richard
Buss, David M.
Butler, Daniel Allen
Butler, David (Edgeworth)
Butler, Geoff
Butler, Gregory S.
Butler, Jon
Butler, Lance St. John
Butler, Leslie Ann
Butler, Linda
Butler, Pierce A.
Butler, Rex D.
Butow, Robert J. C.
Butts, Dennis
Byles, Jeff
Byman, Daniel L.
Bynum, Caroline Walker
Bynum, Victoria E.
Byrd, James P.
Cadbury, Deborah
Cadle, Farris W(illiam)
Caferro, William
Caffrey, Margaret M.
Cafruny, Alan W(eston)
Cahalan, James Michael
Cahill, Lisa Sowle
Cain, P. J.
Caine, Barbara
Calabro, Marian
Calder, Andrew
Calder, Marie D(onais)
Calder, Nigel (David Ritchie)
Calderwood, James Lee
Calhoun, Craig (Jackson)
Callahan, Bob
Callahan, Nelson J.
Callaway, Barbara J.
Calloway, Colin G(ordon)
Calvert, Patricia
Calvert, Peter (Anthony Richard)
Calvin, William H(oward)
Cambor, Kate
Cameron, Averil Millicent
Camlot, Jason
Camp, Helen C(ollier)
Camp, Stephanie M. H.
Campagna, Palmiro
Campbell, Christopher
Campbell, Colin
Campbell, Gwyn
Campbell, Ian Barclay
Campbell, James
Campbell, Jodi
Campbell, Malcolm
Campbell, Mavis C.
Campbell, Tracy (A.)
Campbell, Walter E.
Campbell-Kelly, Martin
Campos, Paul F.
Cannato, Vincent J.
Cannon, Dolores Eilene
Cannon, Garland
Cano, Daniel
Cao, Lan
Capek, Michael
Capitan, William H(arry)

Capp, Bernard (Stuart)
Capshew, James H.
Carabelli, Giancarlo
Carens, Timothy L.
Carew, Jan (Rynveld)
Carey, Patrick W.
Carey, Peter
Carley, James P.
Carlin, Martha
Carlisle, Elizabeth Pendergast
Carls, Stephen D(ouglas)
Carlsen, Spike
Carlson, Keith Thor
Carlson, Laurie
Carlson, Paul H.
Carlton, David
Carlyon, David
Carney, Judith A(nn)
Caro, Robert A.
Carone, Gabriela Roxana
Carpenter, Kenneth E(dward)
Carpenter, Mary Wilson
Carr, Caleb
Carr, J(ames) Revell
Carr, Jacqueline Barbara
Carradice, Ian A.
Carrier, Thomas J.
Carriker, S. David
Carroll, Francis M(artin)
Carroll, Stuart M.
Carstairs, Catherine
Carter, Alden R(ichardson)
Carter, Christine Jacobson
Carter, Jared
Carter, Miranda
Carter, W(illiam)
Carter, Walter
Carter, Warren
Carter, William E.
Cartledge, Mark J.
Carton, Bernice
Carver, Martin
Carver, Norman Francis
Carver, Terrell
Carwardine, Richard J(ohn)
Casey, Barbara
Casey, James
Casey, Shaun Allen
Cash, Anthony
Cashin, Joan E.
Cashore, Kristin
Casper, Scott E.
Cassel, Susie Lan
Cassels, Alan
Cassidy, David C(harles)
Cassidy, Robert M.
Castaneda, Christopher James
Casteel, Sarah Phillips
Castelli, Elizabeth A.
Castiglione, Caroline
Castile, George Pierre
Castle, Alfred L.
Castle, Gregory
Castle, Kathryn
Castleden, Rodney
Castor, Helen
Casway, Jerrold

Catherwood, Christopher
Catterall, Peter
Caughfield, Adrienne
Caughie, Pamela L.
Caute, (John) David
Cavazos-Gaither, Alma E(lisa)
Caveney, Graham
Cawthorne, Nigel
Cederlund, Johan
Ceruzzi, Paul Edward
Chadwick, Owen
Chafel, Judith A.
Chai, May-lee
Chalfont
Chalker, Dennis
Chamberlain, Mary (Christina)
Chambers, John Whiteclay
Champagne, Duane (Willard)
Champion, Craige B.
Champion, J(ustin) A. I.
Champion, Larry S.
Champlin, Peggy
Chan, Gerald
Chancy, Myriam J(osephe)
　　A(imee)
Chanda, Nayan
Chandler, Daniel Ross
Chaney, Edward (Paul de Gruyter)
Chang, Gordon G.
Chang, Ha-Joon
Chaniotis, Angelos
Chanoff, David
Chapin, Sarah
Chapman, Lynne F(erguson)
Chapman, Peter
Chapple, John Alfred Victor
Charbonnier, Rita
Charles, Douglas M.
Charles, John
Charlwood, D(onald) E(rnest
　　Cameron)
Charmley, John
Chatfield, E. Charles
Chatman, Seymour
Chatterji, Joya
Chauncey, George
Chaurette, Normand
Chávez-García, Miroslava
Cheathem, Mark R.
Cheers, D. Michael
Chen, Joseph T(ao)
Chénetier, Marc
Chenier, Elise
Chenut, Helen Harden
Cherny, Andrei
Cherny, Robert W(allace)
Chernykh, E(vgenij)
　　N(ikolaevich)
Cherry, Bridget (Katherine)
Chevalier, Tracy
Chiang, Lynette
Chibnall, Marjorie McCallum
Chidester, David
Childs, Craig
Childs, David (Haslam)
Childs, John Charles Roger
Childs, Matt D.

Childs, Michael J.
Childs, William R.
Chilson, Peter
Chinn, Carl
Chinoy, Mike
Chiocca, Olindo Romeo
Chipman, Donald
Chirot, Daniel
Chitham, Edward (Harry Gordon)
Chmielewski, Wendy E.
Choate, Jean (Marie)
Choi, Hyaeweol
Chomsky, Aviva
Chorbajian, Levon
Chow, Kai-wing
Christe, Ian
Christensen, Damascene
Christian, David Gilbert
Christian, Garna L.
Christiansen, Rupert
Christianson, Paul
Christoph, Peter R(ichard)
Churchill, E. Richard
Churchland, Paul M.
Ciepiela, Catherine
Ciment, James D.
Ciochon, Russell L.
Cirincione, Joseph
Claire, Cherie
Claire, Rodger W(illiam)
Clancy, Tom
Clapham, Christopher S.
Clapp, Nicholas
Clapp, Rodney
Clapper, Gregory S(cott)
Clark, (Carter) Blue
Clark, Andrew F.
Clark, Anna (K.)
Clark, Charles E.
Clark, Christopher M.
Clark, Dick
Clark, Emily
Clark, Gregory
Clark, J. C. D.
Clark, Jerome
Clark, Kathleen Ann
Clark, Paul John Abott
Clarke, (Victor) Lindsay
Clarke, Erskine
Clarke, Michael Tavel
Clarke, Patricia
Clarke, Peter Frederick
Clary, David A.
Clausen, Christopher (John)
Claxton, Melvin
Clayson, Alan
Clayton, Philip
Clear, Caitriona
Cleare, John S.
Cleary, Matthew R.
Clemens, Walter C.
Clément, Dominique
Clement, Priscilla Ferguson
Clements, Alan
Clements, Bruce
Clemmer, Richard O.
Clendinen, Dudley

Dalyell, Tam
Dalzell, Alexander
Danbom, David B.
Dance, Daryl Cumber
Danforth, John C(laggett)
Dangl, Benjamin
Dangler, Jean
Danson, Edwin
Danz, Harold P.
Darby, Andrew
Darby, John
Darlington, Ralph
Darlow, Steve
Darnton, Robert
Darton, Eric
Darwish, Adel
Dary, David Archie
Dascal, Marcelo
Daso, Dik A.
Davenport, John
Davidoff, Leonore
Davidson, Denise Z.
Davidson, Pamela
Davidson, Sol M.
Davies, Charlotte Aull
Davies, Gareth
Davies, J(ohn) D(avid)
Davies, Kristian
Davies, Martin L.
Davies, Owen
Davies, Philip John
Davies, Robert William
Davis, Allen F.
Davis, Anita (Grey) P(rice)
Davis, David Brion
Davis, Donald Edward
Davis, John W.
Davis, Julie Nelson
Davis, Kenneth C.
Davis, Margaret (Thomson)
Davis, Margaret Leslie
Davis, Nancy Yaw
Davis, Patrick
Davis, R(oland) P(arker) Stephen
Davis, Richard Whitlock
Davis, Robert C.
Davis, Rocio G.
Davis, Shelley L(orraine)
Davis, Steven L.
Davison, Eddy W.
Davison, Liam
Dawes, Gregory W.
Dawson, Melanie
Day, Alan
Day, Charles R.
Day, Richard J. F.
Day-Lewis, Sean (Francis)
de Bernieres, Louis
de Breadun, Deaglan
de Crespigny, (Richard) Rafe
  (Champion)
De Groot, Gerard J.
de Jonge, Alex
de la Bédoyère, Guy
de La Pedraja, René
de La Torre, Miguel A.
de Las Casas, Walter

De Syon, Guillaume
de Varona, Frank J.
De Villiers, Marq
De Vorsey, Louis
De Vries, Rachel (Guido)
De Zegher, M. Catherine
Deak, Istvan
Dean, Eric T.
Dean, Martin
Dean, Trevor
Deans, Bob
DeBonis, Steven
Debrix, François
DeBuron, Nicole
DeCaro, Louis A.
DeCredico, Mary A.
Deeb, Lara
Deem, James M(organ)
Deichmann, Ute
Deighton, Len
Del Negro, Giovanna P.
Delaney, Norman
Deletant, Dennis
Deligiorgi, Katerina
DeLillo, Don
Deloria, Philip J.
Demacopoulos, George E.
DeMarce, James L.
Demastes, William
Demers, David (Pearce)
Demos, John Putnam
Dempsey, Charles (Gates)
Deng, Francis Mading
Denham, James M.
Denson, Andrew
Dent, Harry S.
Denzey, Nicola
Derfler, (Arnold) Leslie
Derian, James (Arthur) Der
DeRogatis, Jim
Derr, Mark (Burgess)
Derrett, (John) Duncan (Martin)
Derry, John (Wesley)
Desai, Anita
Desan, Suzanne
Desch, Michael C.
Descola, Philippe
Deslandes, Paul R.
Desser, David
Deutsch, Sarah (Jane)
Deutscher, Irwin
Devji, Faisal Fatehali
Devor, Aaron H.
DeVries, Kelly
Dewart, Gilbert
Dewey, Donald O(dell)
Dewhirst, Ian
di Certo, J(oseph) J(ohn)
Diamond, Arthur
Diamond, Hanna Elizabeth
Dibua, Jeremiah I.
Dichtl, John R.
Dicke, Thomas S(cott)
Dickerson, Dennis C.
Dickie, Matthew W(allace)
Dickinson, Harry Thomas
Dickinson, John

Dickson, Paul (Andrew)
Dietrich, William A.
Dietz, Maribel
Dietz, Peter (John)
Dillon, Wilton Sterling
DiMarco, Damon
Dinan, Desmond
Dinan, Susan E.
Diner, Dan
Dinerman, Beatrice
Dinnerstein, Leonard
Dinsdale, Ann
Dintrone, Charles V.
DiPietro, Cary
Dippel, John V(an) H(outen)
Dipple, Geoffrey
DiSalvo, Jackie
DiSilvestro, Roger L.
Ditchoff, Pamela J.
Divine, Robert A(lexander)
Dixon, Simon M.
Dizikes, John
Doak, Wade (Thomas)
Dobbs, Ricky F.
Dobson, Alan P.
Dobson, R(ichard) Barrie
Docherty, James C(airns)
Docherty, Paddy
Docker, John
Dockery, Kevin
Dodd, Christopher J.
Dodge, Peter
Dodgshon, Robert A(ndrew)
Doherty, Craig A.
Doherty, Gillian M.
Doherty, Kieran
Doherty, P(aul) C.
Dolin, Eric Jay
Donald, Peter (Harry)
Donaldson, Gary A.
Donia, Robert J(ay)
Donnachie, Ian
Donoghue, Emma
Donoghue, Frank J.
Donovan, Brian
Doolen, Andy
Doran, Robert
Dorman, Michael L.
Dorril, Stephen
Dorset, Phyllis (Flanders)
Dotson, Bob
Dotson, Rand
Doughty, Robert A.
Douglas, Deborah G.
Douglas, John (Frederick James)
Douglas-Hamilton, James Alexander
Dower, John W(illiam)
Downer, Lesley
Downes, Alexander B.
Downes, David A(nthony)
Downey, Tom
Downing, Michael (Bernard)
Dowty, Alan K.
Doyle, Robert Charles
Doyle, William
Drakuli , Slavenka

Draper, Alfred Ernest
Drez, Ronald J(oseph)
Drogin, Bob
Dromgoole, Dominic
Drucker, Peter
Drummond, Michael
Drury, Sally
Duberman, Martin
Dubin, Michael J.
DuBois, Ellen Carol
Dubrow, Gail Lee
Ducey, Michael T.
Dudden, Alexis
Dudziak, Mary L.
Due, Tananarive
Duelfer, Charles A.
Duffield, Gervase E.
Duffield, John S.
Duffin, Jacalyn
Duffy, Eamon
Duffy, Maureen (Patricia)
Duffy, Michael
Duffy, Susan
Dugatkin, Lee Alan
Dugaw, Dianne
Duggan, Christopher
Duggleby, John
Duke, Martin
Duke, Michael S.
Dukes, Paul
Dulaney, W. Marvin
Dumbrell, John
Dunaway, Finis
Dunbar, Gary S(eamans)
Dunbar, Leslie W(allace)
Dunbar-Ortiz, Roxanne
Duncan, A. A. M.
Duncan, Colin A.M.
Dunlap, Susanne Emily
Dunlop, Eileen (Rhona)
Dunmore, John
Dunn, Douglas (Eaglesham)
Dunn, Durwood
Dunn, Joe P.
Dunn, John (Montfort)
Dunn, John M.
Dunn, Peter Norman
Dunnage, Jonathan (Michael)
DuPree, Sherry Sherrod
Durbach, Nadja
Durden, Robert F(ranklin)
Durham, Walter T.
Durrant, Lynda
Durschmied, Erik
Duthu, N. Bruce
Dutkina, Galina (Borisovna)
Dutton, Paul Edward
Dwyer, Richard A.
Dyal, Donald H(enriques)
Dyer, James (Frederick)
Dyson, John
Dyson, Michael Eric
Dzuback, Mary Ann
Eagles, Charles W.
Earl, Riggins R.
Earle, Jonathan
Earle, Rebecca

Flam, Jack D(onald)
Flamhaft, Ziva
Flamming, Douglas
Flanders, Judith
Flayhart, William Henry
Flem, Lydia
Fleming, James E.
Fleming, James Rodger
Fleming, Robert E.
Fleming, Thomas
Fletcher, Joel L.
Flinn, Kelly
Flint, John Edgar
Flores-Galbis, Enrique
Flory, David A.
Flowers, Sarah
Flynn, Thomas R.
Foden, Giles
Fogel, Robert William
Fogle, Jeanne
Foley, Robert T.
Folks, Jeffrey Jay
Folly, Martin H(arold)
Folster, David
Foner, Eric
Fontanel, Béatrice
Fontes, Ron
Foot, Michael Richard Daniell
Foote, David
Footitt, Hilary
Forbes, Bruce David
Ford, Barbara
Ford, Herbert (Paul)
Ford, Michael Curtis
Foreman, Amanda
Forment, Carlos A.
Forrest, Alan
Forrester, John
Forret, Jeff
Forsberg, Tuomas
Forstenzer, Thomas R.
Forster, Marc R.
Forster, Margaret
Forsyth, Kate
Forsyth, Michael
Forsyth, Phyllis Young
Fort, Ilene Susan
Foster, (William) Lawrence
Foster, Frances Smith
Foster, John Bellamy
Foster, John Wilson
Foster, Mark
Foulkes, Richard (George)
Fournier, Marcel
Fowler, Don D.
Fowler, Loretta
Fox, Barry
Fox, Frank
Fox, Jo
Fox, Paula
Fox, Richard Allan
Fox, Robert
Fox, William L.
Foxman, Abraham H.
Foxx, Daniel
Frader, Laura Levine
Fraiser, Jim

Frakes, George Edward
Francaviglia, Richard V.
Francis, H(erbert) E(dward)
Francis, Lesley Lee
Francis, Mark
Francis, R(ichard) A.
Francisco, Nia
Franco, Dean J.
Frankland, (Anthony) Noble
Franklin, Allan (David)
Franklin, David Byrd
Franklin, James L(ee)
Franklin, Jane (Morgan)
Fraser, Antonia
Fraser, Conon
Fraser, Rebecca
Fraser, Ronald (Angus)
Fraser, W. Hamish
Frassetto, Michael
Fravel, M. Taylor
Frazier, Alison Knowles
Frazier, Donald S(haw)
Frazier, Lessie Jo
Frederick, Jim
Freeborn, Richard (Harry)
Freed, Anne O.
Freedman, Eric
Freedman, Russell (Bruce)
Freehling, William W(ilhartz)
Freeman, Barbara M.
Freeman, Daniel E(van)
Freeman, Jo
Freeman, Joshua B.
Freeman, Michael
Freeman, Philip
Freese, Barbara
Freeze, Gregory L.
French, Albert
French, Howard W.
French, Patrick
French, Philip (Neville)
Frere, S(heppard) S(underland)
Freudenthal, Gad
Frey, Linda (Sue)
Frey, Marsha L.
Freyer, Tony (Allan)
Frick, Carole Collier
Fried, Dennis F.
Friedberg, Maurice
Frieden, Jeffry
Friedland, Martin L(awrence)
Friedland, William H(erbert)
Friedlander, Henry (Egon)
Friedman, Norman
Friedman, Rebecca
Friedman, Thomas L(oren)
Friedmann, Yohanan
Friend, Craig Thompson
Friend, Theodore (Wood)
Frisby, Terence
Frisch, Walter
Frith, David (Edward John)
Fritts, Mary Bahr
Fritz, Jean
Fritz, Stephen G.
Fritze, Ronald H.
Fritzsche, Peter

Frohnen, Bruce (P.)
Frommel, Christoph Lvitpold
Frommer, Benjamin
Frost, Diane
Frost, Ellen L.
Frost, Karolyn Smardz
Frost, Stanley Brice
Frost-Knappman, L. Elizabeth
Fry, William Finley
Fryer, Jonathan
Frykenberg, Robert E(ric)
Fuchs, Miriam
Fuchs, Rachel G(innis)
Fudge, Erica
Fuegi, John
Fukuyama, Francis
Fuller, Sophie
Fulton, Joe B.
Fumento, Rocco
Furdell, Elizabeth Lane
Furia, Philip (G.)
Furubotn, Eirik G.
Fussell, E. Robert
Gabbert, Wolfgang
Gabriel, Michael P.
Gabriel, Richard A(lan)
Gabriel, Theodore P. C.
Gabriel (Loving), Kathryn (Ann)
Gadney, Reg
Gaiduk, Ilya V(alerievich)
Gaillard, Frye
Gaines, Thomas A.
Galeotti, Mark
Galgano, Robert C.
Galison, Peter (Louis)
Gall, Lothar
Gall, Sandy
Gallagher, Gary W(illiam)
Gallagher, Tom
Gallenkamp, Charles (Benton)
Galli, Richard
Gallo, Patrick J.
Galston, William A.
Gamson, Joshua (Paul)
Ganji, Akbar
Ganz, Marshall
Gaposchkin, M. Cecilia
Garceau, Dee
García, Laura Gallego
Garcia, Luis M.
Gardella, Robert (P.)
Gardner, (Robert) Brian
Gardner, Mark L(ee)
Gardner, Michael R.
Gardner, Robert
Garfield, Brian (F. W.)
Garner, John S.
Garnett, Richard (Duncan Carey)
Garrard, Graeme
Garrett, Martin
Garrettson, Charles Lloyd
Garrison, J. Ritchie
Garthoff, Raymond L(eonard)
Gartner, Scott Sigmund
Garton Ash, Timothy
Garver, John W.
Garwood, Julie

Gaschnitz, Michael K.
Gascoigne, Bamber
Gascoigne, John
Gaskell, Ivan
Gat, Azar
Gateley, Edwina
Gates, Barbara T(imm)
Gathorne-Hardy, Jonathan
Gaudé, Laurent
Gaukroger, Stephen
Gauld, Alan (Ogilvie)
Gauldie, Enid Elizabeth
Gavronsky, Serge
Gawrych, George
Gay, John H.
Gay, Kathlyn R.
Gay, Peter
Gebhardt, James F(rederick)
Gedmin, Jeffrey (N.)
Gee, Sophie
Gelber, Yoav
Gelernter, David (Hillel)
Gellately, Robert
Geller, Jay Howard
Gelles, Edith B.
Gellman, Marc
Geltmaker, Ty
Gelvin, James L.
Gemunden, Gerd
Gentile, John S(amuel)
Gentry, Curt
George, Alice L.
George, David (John)
George Bloomfield, Susanne K.
Georgi-Findlay, Brigitte
Gerassi, John
Gerdy, John R.
Gerhards, Jürgen
Gerlach, Don R.
Gerlach, Larry R(euben)
Gernet, Jacques
Gerrish, Brian Albert
Gershoni, Israel
Gerstenberger, Erhard S.
Gessner, Lynne
Getis, Victoria
Getler, Warren
Getz, Christine S.
Getz, David
Getz, Marshall J(ay)
Getz, Trevor R.
Gewertz, Deborah B.
Geyer, Georgie Anne
Ghareeb, Edmund
Ghazvinian, John
Ghiglione, Loren
Ghose, Indira
Ghosh, Durba
Giampieri-Deutsch, Patrizia
Gibb, Lorna
Gibbons, Reginald
Gibbs, Anthony Matthews
Gibran, Daniel K.
Gibson, A(lex) J. S.
Gibson, Ian
Gibson, Robert
Gibson, Thomas

Giebel, Christoph
Gienow-Hecht, Jessica C. E.
Giglio, James N.
Gil, Moshe
Gilbert, Bil
Gilbert, Elizabeth
Gilbert, John Raphael
Gilbert, Martin
Gilbert, W(illiam) Stephen
Gilchrist, Roberta
Gildea, Robert
Giles, Paul
Gill, Anton
Gill, Gillian C(atherine)
Gillespie, Angus Kress
Gillespie, J(ohn) David
Gilley, Sheridan (Wayne)
Gillman, Peter (Charles)
Gillmeister, Heiner
Gillon, Steven M.
Gilmore, Glenda Elizabeth
Gilmore, Kate
Gilmore, Ruth Wilson
Gilstrap, John
Ginsborg, Paul (Anthony)
Ginzberg, Lori D.
Ginzburg, Carlo
Gipi
Girling, John (Lawrence Scott)
Gish, Robert F.
Gitter, Elisabeth
Giziowski, Richard (John)
Glantz, David M.
Glaser, James M.
Glassberg, David
Glasser, Ira
Glassie, Henry
Glassman, Jonathon P.
Glassman, Ronald M.
Glatthaar, Joseph T(homas)
Glazier, Stephen D.
Glees, Anthony
Glen, Frank Grenfell
Glener, Doug
Glenn, Jason Kahn
Glisson, J(ake) T.
Glock, Allison
Glover, Douglas
Glover, Judith
Glover, Lorri
Gobodo-Madikizela, Pumla
Godbold, E(dward) Stanly
Goddard, Hugh (P.)
Godson, Roy (S.)
Godwin, Parke
Goerler, Raimund E.
Goff, Barbara
Goff, Martyn
Golay, Michael
Gold, Bernice
Gold, Penny Schine
Goldberg, Bruce (Edward)
Goldberger, Avriel H.
Golden, Mark
Goldfarb, Michael
Goldman, Karla
Goldman, Lawrence

Goldman, Marshall I(rwin)
Goldschmidt, Arthur
Goldschneider, Gary
Goldsmith, Barbara
Goldstein, David B.
Goldstein, Nancy
Goldstein, Robert Justin
Goldstein, Sidney
Golinski, Jan
Gologorsky, Beverly
Gommans, Jos J. L.
Gonen, Jay Y.
Goñi, Uki
Gonzalez (Mandri), Flora
Gonzalez-Balado, Jose Luis
Goodhue, Thomas W.
Goodland, Katharine
Goodman, Amy
Goodman, James
Goodman, Jesse
Goodman, Martin (David)
Goodman, Susan
Goodrich, Amanda Jane
Goodson, Larry P.
Goodstein, Phil
Goodwin, Doris (Helen) Kearns
Goodwin, Joanne L.
Goodwin, Ken(neth Leslie)
Goody, John R(ankine)
Gooley, Dana
Goonetilleke, D. C. R. A.
Goossen, Rachel Waltner
Gootenberg, Paul
Gordin, Michael D.
Gordinier, Jeff
Gordis, Lisa M.
Gordon, Andrew D.
Gordon, Anne Wolrige
Gordon, Colin
Gordon, Deborah
Gordon, Haim
Gordon, Jacob U.
Gordon, Lois G.
Gordon, Philip H.
Gordon, Robert
Gordon, Wendy M.
Gordon, William A.
Goreham, Gary A.
Gorman, Lyn
Gorn, Elliott (J.)
Gorn, Michael H.
Gorriti, Gustavo
Goto , Junichi
Gott, Richard (Willoughby)
Gottlieb, Beatrice
Gottlieb, Sherry Gershon
Goudsouzian, Aram
Gough, Sue
Goulden, Joseph C.
Gow, Andrew Colin
Graber, Mark A.
Grace, Alexander M.
Graff, Henry Franklin
Grafton, Anthony T(homas)
Gragg, Rod
Graham, Frank
Graham, Patterson Toby

Graham, W(illiam) Fred
Grainger, John D(ownie)
Gran, Peter
Grange, William Marshall
Grann, David
Grant, Bruce (Alexander)
Grant, Gail Milissa
Grant, James Russell
Grant, Neil
Grant, Susan-Mary C.
Grassi, Maggi Lidchi
Grassian, Daniel
Gray, Chris Hables
Gray, Christopher
Gray, Clayton
Gray, Colin S.
Gray, Francine du Plessix
Gray, Robert (Archibald Speir)
Graybill, Andrew R.
Grayson, Donald K.
Grayson, Emily
Grebstein, Sheldon Norman
Greeley, Robin Adèle
Green, Adam
Green, Celia (Elizabeth)
Green, Elna C.
Green, Michael D.
Green, Peter (Morris)
Green, Scott E.
Green, Toby
Green Musselman, Elizabeth
Greenberg, Cheryl
Greenberg, Gerald S(tuart)
Greene, A. Wilson
Greene, Douglas G.
Greene, Jacqueline Dembar
Greene, Jody
Greene, Julie
Greene, Melissa Fay
Greene, Nathanael
Greene, Victor
Greenfeld, Liah
Greenwald, Jeff
Greenwood, Barbara
Greetham, David
Gregor, Neil
Gregorian, Raffi
Gregory, Frederick
Gregory, Kristiana
Grehan, Ida
Grenham, John
Grenier, John
Grescoe, Paul
Greshake, Gisbert
Grieb, Kenneth J.
Griffin, Jasper
Griffin, Patrick
Griffith, Nicola
Griffiths, Tom
Griffiths, Trevor
Grim, Ryan
Grinde, Donald A(ndrew)
Grob, Gerald N.
Grobsmith, Elizabeth S.
Groneman, Carol
Groom, Winston (Francis)
Grosbard, Ofer

Grose, Peter (Bolton)
Gross, Ariela J.
Gross, David
Gross, Ernie
Gross, Michael L.
Grosscup, Beau
Grossman, Dina
Grosz, Terry
Grovier, Kelly
Groys, Boris
Gruhn, George
Grundy, Pamela C.
Gruntman, Mike
Guardino, Peter
Guarnieri, Patrizia
Gubar, Susan (David)
Guest, Jacqueline
Guile, Melanie
Guill, Jane
Guillory, Dan
Guinier, Lani
Guinness, Desmond
Guinness, Jonathan (Bryan)
Gup, Ted (S.)
Gurney, Alan
Güse, Ernst Gerhard
Guste, Roy F(rancis)
Gutfreund, Owen D.
Guttenplan, D. D.
Guttmann, Allen
Gutzman, Kevin R.C.
Guyatt, Nicholas
Haar, James
Habito, Ruben L.F.
Hackelsberger, Christoph
Hacker, Barton C(lyde)
Hackett, Jeremy
Hackett, Robert A(nthony)
Hackler, George
Hackney, Rod(erick Peter)
Haddad, Gladys
Hadden, Sally E.
Hadley, Dawn M.
Haeger, John Denis
Hagerman, Edward
Hagerty, Devin T.
Hagger, Nicholas
Hagy, James William
Hahn, Steven C.
Haines, David W.
Hainsworth, D(avid) R(oger)
Hakak, Lev
Haldon, John F.
Hale, Douglas
Hale, Henry E.
Hale, John R.
Hale, Nathan G.
Halfmann, Janet
Hall, Bert S(tewart)
Hall, Douglas
Hall, Jonathan M.
Hall, Lee
Hall, Marie Beth
Hall, Simon
Hallahan, William H(enry)
Hallam, Elizabeth M.
Hallas, James H(enry)

Haller, Hermann (W)
Hallett, Michael A.
Halliburton, David (Garland)
Halliday, Stephen
Hallissy, Margaret
Hallo, William W.
Hallock, John W(esley) M(atthew)
Hallwas, John E.
Halpern, Cynthia Leone
Halsall, Guy
Halsey, A(lbert) H(enry)
Halstead, Ted
Halverson, Cathryn
Hamalainen, Pekka J.
Hamilton, Alastair
Hamilton, Bernard
Hamilton, J(ames) Scott
Hamm, Richard F.
Hampson, Norman
Hampton, Wilborn
Han, Béatrice
Hanc, John
Hancock, Ian (Robert)
Hand, Geoffrey Joseph Philip
Handler, Richard
Handley, Eric Walter
Hanhimäki, Jussi M.
Hankin, C(herry) A(nne)
Hanlon, Gregory
Hannaford, Peter (Dor)
Hannah, James
Hannant, Larry
Hansen, Ann Natalie
Hansen, Chadwick
Hansen, Debra Gold
Hansen, Drew D.
Hansen, James R.
Hanson, Neil
Hanson, Paul R.
Hanson, Susan F.
Hapke, Laura
Harberger, Arnold C.
Harclerode, Peter
Harden, Blaine
Harder, Robert O.
Hardin, John A.
Hardin, Russell
Harding, James
Harding, Les
Hardt, Michael
Hardy, B. Carmon
Hardy, Barbara (Gladys)
Hardy, Michael C.
Hargreaves, John D(esmond)
Harkins, Anthony
Harline, Craig E.
Harmetz, Aljean
Harmon, Alexandra Sasha
Harmon, Daniel E(lton)
Harnack, Curtis
Harpending, Henry
Harrell, Beatrice Orcutt
Harrigan, Patrick J.
Harrington, Anne
Harris, C. Nelson
Harris, Charles Wesley
Harris, Deborah Turner

Harris, Jonathan
Harris, Leslie M.
Harris, Neil
Harris, Paul
Harris, Robin
Harris, Roy
Harris, William V.
Harrison, Ann Tukey
Harrison, Brian (Howard)
Harrison, C. C.
Harrison, John F(letcher) C(lews)
Harrison, Lowell H.
Hart, Carolyn G(impel)
Hart, John Fraser
Hart, John Mason
Hart, Peter
Hart-Davis, Duff
Hartcup, Guy
Hartle, Anthony E.
Hartshorne, Thomas L.
Harvey, (Brian) Peter
Harvey, David
Harvey, Karen D.
Harvey, P(aul) D(ean) A(dshead)
Harvey, Susan Ashbrook
Harvie, Christopher (Thomas)
Hasenfeld, Yeheskel
Haskell, Molly
Haskett, Robert
Haskins, Scott (M.)
Haslam, Jonathan George
Hastings, Max M(acdonald)
Hasty, Will
Hatfield, Phyllis
Hattendorf, John B(rewster)
Hauptman, Judith
Hauptman, Laurence Marc
Haviaras, Stratis
Havil, Julian
Hawke, Gary Richard
Hawksley, Lucinda
Hay, William Anthony
Haycock, Kate
Hayes, Dawn Marie
Hayes, Derek
Hayford, Charles W.
Hayman, Richard
Haynes, John Earl
Haynes, Sybille (Edith)
Hays, Tony
Hayt, Elizabeth
Haythornthwaite, Philip John
Hazlehurst, Cameron
Head, David M.
Headley, John M.
Headrick, Daniel R.
Healey, Judith Koll
Healy, Maureen
Heard, Alex
Heard, Anthony Hazlitt
Hearden, Patrick J.
Hearn, Chester G.
Hearn, Julie
Heater, Derek Benjamin
Heath, Dwight B.
Heath, Malcolm (Frederick)
Heather, Peter

Hecht, Jennifer Michael
Hedderwick, Mairi
Hedeen, Stanley
Heefner, Wilson A.
Heerma van Voss, Lex
Heffer, Simon (James)
Heffernan, Nancy Coffey
Hegeman, Mary Theodore
Heidler, David S(tephen)
Heidler, Jeanne T(wiggs)
Heilbrunn, Jacob
Heim, S. Mark
Heimann, Judith M(oscow)
Heims, Steve J(oshua)
Heineman, Kenneth J.
Heising, Willetta L.
Heller, Agnes
Heller, Henry
Hellman, Hal
Hellman, Stephen
Helmer, Diana Star
Helms, Mary W.
Helvarg, David
Heminway, John
Hemming, John Henry
Hemming, Laurence Paul
Hen, Yitzhak
Henderson, Bonnie
Henderson, Kristin
Hendricks, Christopher E.
Hendrickson, Ryan C.
Hendrix, Scott H.
Hennessey, Thomas W.
Hennessy, John J(oseph)
Hennessy, Peter
Henriksen, Margot A.
Henriot, Christian
Hentoff, Nat(han Irving)
Heper, Metin
Heppenheimer, Thomas A.
Herbert, Sandra (Swanson)
Herbst, Jurgen
Herf, Jeffrey
Herman, Eleanor
Herman, Ellen
Herman, John E.
Hernandez-Ehrisman, Laura
Hero, Rodney E.
Herrin, Lamar
Herring, Adam
Hershock, Martin J.
Hertz, Deborah
Herzfeld, Michael (F.)
Herzig, Alison Cragin
Herzog, Dagmar
Herzog, Tobey C.
Hess, Alan
Hess, Bill
Hess, Gary R.
Hess, Richard S.
Hesse, Mary Brenda
Heuer, Jennifer Ngaire
Heuser, Beatrice
Hevia, James L.
Hewitt, W(arren) E(dward)
Heyes, (Nancy) Eileen
Heywood, Colin

Hickey, Donald R.
Hickey, Georgina
Hicks, Brian
Hietala, Thomas R.
Higgins, Michael W.
Higgins, Peter M.
Higham, Robin
Highfield, (John) Roger (Loxdale)
Hilburn, Robert
Hildebrand, Ann Meinzen
Hildebrand, Klaus
Hill, Anthony (Robert)
Hill, Barry
Hill, Brian W.
Hill, Charles E.
Hill, Geoff
Hill, Geoffrey
Hill, Gerald N.
Hill, Harvey
Hill, Kathleen Thompson
Hill, Sarah H.
Hillgarth, J(ocelyn) N(igel)
Hillman, Richard S.
Hiltermann, Joost R.
Hilton, (Andrew John) Boyd
Hilton, George Woodman
Hilton, Suzanne
Hilty, James W.
Himelstein, Shmuel
Himka, John-Paul
Himmel, Richard L.
Himmelfarb, Gertrude
Hinde, Thomas
Hindle, Steve
Hine, Darlene Clark
Hine, Robert V.
Hines, James R.
Hines, Thomas S(pight)
Hiney, Tom
Hinojosa, Gilberto Miguel
Hinrichs, Ernest H(enry)
Hinson, E. Glenn
Hinton, Michael
Hinze, Bradford E.
Hipperson, Carol Edgemon
Hirabayashi, Lane Ryo
Hirata, Hosea
Hiro, Dilip
Hirsch, James (S.)
Hirshfeld, Alan
Hise, Greg
Hislop, Victoria
Hitchcock, Tim
Hitchens, Peter Jonathan
Hitchins, Keith
Hitz, Frederick P(orter)
Hoare, Philip
Hobhouse, Hermione
Hobsbawm, Eric (John Ernest)
Hobson, Anthony Robert Alwyn
Hochman, Jiri
Hocking, Mary (Eunice)
Hoddinott, R(alph) F(ield)
Hodes, Martha
Hodge, Susie
Hodgkiss, Alan Geoffrey
Hoek, D. J.

Johnson, Clint
Johnson, Diane
Johnson, Freddie Lee
Johnson, Galen K.
Johnson, George Lloyd
Johnson, Joan Marie
Johnson, John L.
Johnson, Leland R(oss)
Johnson, Marilynn S.
Johnson, Michael P(aul)
Johnson, Neil L.
Johnson, Paul (Bede)
Johnson, Robert David
Johnson, Roger
Johnson, Sara Raup
Johnson, Stephen P.
Johnson, Whittington B.
Johnson, William Stacy
Johnston, Alan (William)
Johnston, Anna
Johnston, Barbara Rose
Johnston, Carolyn Ross
Johnston, Julie
Johnston, Lyle
Johnston, R(onald) J(ohn)
Johnston, William Murray
Johnstone, Bob
Joiner, Gary D.
Jolles, Michael Adam
Jonas, Manfred
Jones, Ann (Maret)
Jones, Charlotte Foltz
Jones, Constance
Jones, David Martin
Jones, J(on) Sydney
Jones, J. Gwynfor
Jones, Jacqueline
Jones, Jason B.
Jones, Jerry W.
Jones, John Henry
Jones, John Philip
Jones, Madison
Jones, Margaret C.
Jones, Matthew L.
Jones, Norman (Leslie)
Jones, Richard Allan
Jones, Ricky L.
Jones, Ted
Jones, Thai
Joppke, Christian
Jordan, Anne Devereaux
Jordan, Constance
Jordan, Daniel P(orter)
Jordan, David C.
Jordan, Mark D.
Jordan, Richard Tyler
Josipovici, Gabriel (David)
Joy, David (Anthony Welton)
Joyce, Davis D.
Joyce, Rosemary A.
Judd, Alan
Judd, Denis
Judge, Edward H.
Judge, Harry George
Judis, John B.
Juliani, Richard N.
Jung, Moon-Ho

Jung, Patrick J.
Junne, George H.
Jurmain, Suzanne
Kaartinen, Marjo
Kabaservice, Geoffrey (M.)
Kacowicz, Arie M.
Kadish, Alon
Kagan, Donald
Kagan, Frederick W.
Kahan, Alan S.
Kahn, David
Kaiser, David E.
Kale, Steven D(avid)
Kaler, Anne K(atherine)
Kalia, Ravi
Kallen, Stuart A(rnold)
Kallgren, Beverly Hayes
Kalmin, Richard
Kalpakli, Mehmet
Kamen, Henry
Kamensky, Jane
Kamil, Neil D.
Kamm, Henry
Kammen, Michael
Kamoie, Laura Croghan
Kampfner, John
Kamphoefner, Walter D.
Kamrava, Mehran
Kan, Sergei
Kanaaneh, Rhoda Ann
Kane, Larry
Kane, Penny
Kang, K. Connie
Kanigel, Robert
Kanipe, Jeff
Kantor, Jean-Michel
Kaplan, Alice Yaeger
Kaplan, Barbara Beigun
Kaplan, Edward S.
Kaplan, Elizabeth (A.)
Kaplan, Jonathan
Kaplan, Marion A.
Kaplan, Morton A.
Kaplan, Nelly
Kaplan, Steven L.
Kaplowitz, Craig A.
Karier, Thomas
Karlen, Neal (Stuart)
Karlin, Wayne (Stephen)
Karnow, Stanley
Karp, Larry
Karras, Ruth Mazo
Karttunen, Frances
Kaszynski, William
Katagiri, Yasuhiro
Katouzian, Homa
Katz, David
Katz, Esther
Katz, Lawrence S(anford)
Katz, Marshall P.
Kauffman, Michael W.
Kaufman, Joyce P.
Kaufman, Menahem
Kaufman, Suzanne K.
Kaufman, Victor S(cott)
Kaufman, Will
Kaufmann, Dovid Yisroel Ber

Kawakami, Barbara Fusako
Kay, Betty Carlson
Kay, George
Kay, Guy Gavriel
Kaye, Barrington
Kaye, Elizabeth
Kaye, Geraldine
Kaylin, Lucy
Keahey, John
Kealey, Edward J.
Keane, John
Kearns, Lionel (John)
Keates, Jonathan
Keay, John
Kee, Robert
Keeble, Neil H(oward)
Keegan, Marcia
Keeley, Edmund
Keeling, Kara
Keenan, Sheila
Keene, Donald
Keene, John (R.)
Keevak, Michael
Keillor, Steven J(ames)
Keith, Caroline H(elen)
Keller, Emily
Keller, William W(alton)
Kelley, Liam C.
Kelling, Hans Wilhelm
Kellogg, Frederick
Kelly, Catriona
Kelly, Christopher
Kelly, Liz
Kelly, Saul
Kelsay, John
Kendrick, Christopher
Keneally, Thomas (Michael)
Kennedy, David Michael
Kennedy, John C.
Kennedy, Kelly S.
Kennedy, Lawrence W.
Kennedy, Michael P. J.
Kennedy, Paul Michael
Kennedy, Robert Emmet
Kennedy, Scott
Kennedy, William (Joseph)
Kennefick, Daniel
Kennell, Nigel M.
Kenney, Michael
Kenney, Padraic (Jeremiah)
Kenney, William Howland
Kenslea, Timothy
Kent, Eliza F.
Kent, Homer Austin
Kent, Peter C.
Kent, Timothy J.
Keohane, Dan
Ker, Ian (Turnbull)
Kerbel, Matthew Robert
Kerber, Linda K(aufman)
Kerby, Mona
Kerkhoff, Blair
Kerner, Fred
Kerns, Thomas A.
Kerr, Andrea Moore
Kerr, K. Austin
Kerrison, Catherine M.

Kersaudy, François
Kershaw, Ian
Keshavarz, Fatemeh
Kessner, Thomas
Ketcham, Ralph Louis
Ketchum, Richard M.
Ketner, Kenneth Laine
Kettelkamp, Larry Dale
Kevill-Davies, Sally
Kevles, Daniel J.
Kevorkian, Martin
Keynes, Simon
Keys, David
Keyserlingk, Robert H.
Khan, Aisha
Khan, Mahmood H(asan)
Khan, Yasmin
Khlevniuk, Oleg V.
Khoroche, Peter (Andrew)
Kidd, Charles (William)
Kidd, Colin
Kidd, I(an) G(ray)
Kidd, Thomas S.
Kidder, Tracy
Kiddy, Elizabeth W.
Kidman, Fiona (Judith)
Kidwell, Clara Sue
Kiernan, Ben
Kierner, Cynthia A.
Killan, Gerald
Killen, Andreas
Kilpatrick, Andrew
Kim, Hakjoon
Kim, In S(oo)
Kim, Kyu Hyun
Kim, Young (Hum)
Kinealy, Christine
King, Brian
King, Gilbert
King, Iain
King, John
King, Sallie B.
King, Wilma
Kingseed, Cole C.
Kingsley, Sean A.
Kingston, Beverley
Kingston, Maxine Hong
Kingstone, Peter R.
Kingwell, Mark
Kinnear, Mary
Kinnell, Galway
Kinney, Arthur F.
Kiras, James D.
Kirby, David Peter
Kirch, Patrick V(inton)
Kirk, Donald
Kirk, Thomas Allison
Kirk-Greene, Anthony
Kirk-Greene, Christopher
Kirkland, Russell
Kirkley, Evelyn A(nne)
Kirkman, William Patrick
Kirsch, George B(enson)
Kirsch, Jonathan
Kirsner, Kim
Kiser, John W.
Kissel, Susan S.

Lesch, John E(mmett)
Lesjak, Carolyn
Lesourne, Jacques
Lester, Connie L.
Lester, Julius
Lesy, Michael
Letcher, Andy
Leupp, Gary P.
Levene, Mark
Leventhal, Judith
Lever, Christopher
Levere, Trevor H(arvey)
Levin, Michael (Graubart)
Levine, Alan J.
Levine, Allan
Levine, Bruce C.
Levitin, Sonia (Wolff)
Levy, Adrian
Levy, Allison
Levy, Daniel S.
Levy, JoAnn
Levy, Peter B.
Levy, Philip
Lewin, Rhoda G.
Lewis, Andrew B.
Lewis, Earl
Lewis, Herbert S.
Lewis, J(ohn) P(aul) Lewis
Lewis, J(ohn) Parry
Lewis, Johanna Miller
Lewis, Mark Edward
Lewis, Rupert
Lia, Brynjar
Liazos, Ariane
Libby, Alisa M.
Libo, Kenneth (Harold)
Lichtenstein, Alex
Lichtenstein, Nelson
Liddington, Jill
Liddle, Peter (Hammond)
Lide, Mary
Lie, John
Lieberman, Benjamin
Lieberman, Richard K.
Lieberthal, Kenneth G.
Liebeschuetz, John Hugo W. G.
Liebich, Andre
Lieven, Dominic
Lightfoot, Kent G.
Lightfoot Sizemore, Deborah
Lilley, Stephen R(ay)
Lim, Walter S. H.
Lincecum, Jerry Bryan
Lindemann, Mary
Lindenmeyer, Kriste
Linder, Marc
Linder, Robert D.
Lindgren, James M.
Ling, Peter J(ohn)
Lingard, Jeanette
Lingeman, Richard
Lingenfelter, Richard Emery
Link, William A.
Linklater, Magnus (Duncan)
Lipartito, Kenneth
Lippi, Ronald D.
Lipton, Eunice

Lisk, Jill (Rosina Ann)
Lister, R(ichard) P(ercival)
Litan, Robert E(li)
Litten, Julian
Little, Benerson
Little, J. I.
Litwack, Leon
Litwak, Robert S.
Liu, Xiaoyuan
Lively, Penelope
Llewellyn, Sam
Lliteras, D. S.
Lloyd, A(lan) R(ichard)
Lloyd, Geoffrey Ernest Richard
Lloyd, Peter Cutt
Lloyd, T(revor) O(wen)
Llywelyn, Morgan
Lo, Shiu-Hing
Loades, David Michael
Lobban, Richard A.
Lock, Joan
Locke, Hubert G.
Locke, Robert R.
Lockerbie, D(onald) Bruce
Lockhart, Paul Douglas
Loehr, Davidson
Loevy, Robert D(ickinson)
Loewe, Michael
Logan, George M(eredith)
London, Joan
Long, Alecia P.
Long, Carolyn Morrow
Long, Jeff
Long, Pamela O.
Longman, Jere
Longmate, Norman Richard
Longworth, Philip
Longyard, William H(enry)
Loo, Tina
Lookingbill, Brad D.
Looney, Dennis (Oscar)
Looser, Devoney
Lopez, Jonathan
Lopez-Lujan, Leonardo
LoPrete, Kimberly A.
Losse, Deborah N(ichols)
Lotchin, Roger W.
Lott, Eric
Lott, Jeremy
Loud, G(raham) A(nthony)
Loud, Patricia Cummings
Louër, Laurence
Loughery, John
Loughlin, James
Louis, William Roger
Love, Eric T. L.
Lovell, Julia
Lovell, Mary S(ybilla)
Low, Brian J.
Low, Kathleen
Lowe, Ben(no P.)
Lowe, Keith
Lowe, Rodney
Lowenthal, Cynthia J.
Lower, Michael T.
Lu, Suping
Lübbren, Nina

Lucado, Max (Lee)
Lucaites, John Louis
Lucero, Lisa Joyce
Lucey, Michael
Luchetti, Cathy
Luciak, Ilja Alexander
Luciuk, Lubomyr Y(aroslav)
Ludwickson, John
Luebke, Frederick Carl
Lui, Mary Ting Yi
Lukacs, John (Adalbert)
Lukacs, John D.
Lumsden, Linda J.
Lunde, Paul
Lundeberg, Philip (Karl)
Lundin, Roger
Lundstrom, John B(ernard)
Lunn, Janet (Louise Swoboda)
Luongo, F. Thomas
Luraghi, Raimondo
Luria, Keith P.
Lurie, Jonathan
Lurquin, Paul F.
Lusane, Clarence
Lusted, Marcia Amidon
Luttwak, Edward (Nicolae)
Lutz, John Sutton
Lutz, Tom
Lux, Maureen K.
Luxton, Donald
Lynch, Allen C.
Lynch, John
Lynch, Michael
Lynch, Michael P(atrick)
Lynch, Timothy J.
Lynd, Staughton (Craig)
Lynn, John A(lbert)
Lynn, Richard
Lyons, Martyn
Lyons, Thomas Tolman
Lystra, Karen
Lytle, Mark H.
Mabbett, Ian William
Mabee, Carleton
Mac Donald, Laura M.
MacClancy, Jeremy
Maccoby, Michael
MacCotter, Paul
Macdonald, Douglas J.
Macdonald, Lyn
Macdonald, Michael Patrick
MacDonald, Stuart
MacDonogh, Giles
MacEoin, Denis
MacFadden, Bruce J.
MacFadyen, David
Macfarlane, Alan (Donald James)
MacGuire, James
Mach, Thomas S.
Machedon, Luminita
Machoian, Ronald Glenn
Macintyre, Stuart (Forbes)
Mack, Beverly (B.)
Mack Smith, Denis
MacKenna, John
Mackenney, Richard
MacKenzie, Cameron A.

MacKenzie, Donald (Angus)
Mackenzie, G. Calvin
Mackerras, Colin Patrick
Mackesy, Piers Gerald
Mackey, Thomas
Mackin, Jeanne
Mackintosh-Smith, Tim
Mackowski, Maura Phillips
MacLachlan, Colin M.
MacLean, Glynne
Maclean, Rory
Maclear, Kyo
Macleod, John
MacMillan, Ken
Macniven, Ian S.
Macomber, Robert N.
MacPhee, Ross D(ouglas) E(arle)
MacQueen, John
MacQueen, Winifred (Wallace)
Macy, Sue
Madden, David
Madden, W. C.
Maddox, Robert James
Madigan, Charles M.
Madison, James H.
Madubuike, Ihechukwu (Chie-
   dozie)
Maestro, Giulio
Maffi, Mario
Magaloni, Beatriz
Magas, Branka
Mager, Hugo
Maggi, Armando
Maggio, Frank P.
Maghraoui, Abdeslam M.
Magida, Arthur J.
Magill, R. Jay
Magner, Lois N.
Magocsi, Paul Robert
Maharidge, Dale (Dimitro)
Mahler, Jonathan
Mahmood, Saba
Mahoney, Richard D.
Mahoney, Rosemary
Mahy, Margaret
Mai, Francois Martin
Maier, Karl
Maisel, Ivan
Majaj, Lisa Suhair
Majd, Hooman
Major, Andre
Major, John
Majumdar, Boria
Makari, George Jack
Makdisi, Saree
Makovsky, Michael
Malak, Amin
Malam, John
Malcolm, Elizabeth
Malcolm, Joyce Lee
Malcolm, Noel
Malefakis, Edward
Maley, Willy
Mallin, Jay
Mallon, Florencia E.
Malloy, Sean L.
Maloka, Eddy Tshidiso

Medway, Gareth J.	Migliazzo, Arlin C.	Moldea, Dan E.	Mortimer, Gavin
Meeks, Wayne A.	Mignolo, Walter D.	Molesworth, Carl	Mortimer, James Edward
Meer, Sarah	Mihm, Stephen	Molina, Silvia	Morton, Bruce Rutherfurd
Megarry, Tim	Miles, Dudley (Robert Alexander)	Mollenauer, Lynn Wood	Morton, Patricia
Megged, Aharon	Milis, Ludo(vicus) J. R.	Mommsen, Hans	Morton, Peter
Megivern, James J(oseph)	Millard, Candice	Monahan, William G(regory)	Morton, Ray
Mehaffey, Karen Rae	Miller, Donald L.	Monk, Robert C.	Moschonas, Andreas
Mehrotra, Sri Ram	Miller, Douglas T.	Monmonier, Mark	Mosier, John
Mehta, Ved (Parkash)	Miller, Edward A.	Montefiore, Janet	Mosley, Nicholas
Meijer, Fik	Miller, Glenn T(homas)	Montgomery, David	Moss, Carolyn (J.)
Meisel, Joseph S.	Miller, James Edward	Montgomery, M(aurice) R(ichard)	Motomura, Hiroshi
Melady, Thomas (Patrick)	Miller, Jim	Montgomery, Maureen E.	Moulakis, Athanasios
Melancon, Michael	Miller, Judith	Monzó, Quim	Mould, Daphne D. C. Pochin
Meldahl, Keith Heyer	Miller, Kerby A.	Mooney, Brian C.	Mountford, Kent
Mele, Christopher	Miller, Lynn H.	Moore, Andrew S.	Moure, Kenneth
Mellen, Joan	Miller, Paul D.	Moore, Brenda L(ee)	Moussalli, Ahmad S.
Mellows, Anthony (Roger)	Miller, Richard Lawrence	Moore, Harold G(regory)	Mowat, Claire (Angel Wheeler)
Melnick, Ralph	Miller, Robert H.	Moore, J. Stuart	Mowat, Farley (McGill)
Melnikoff, Pamela (Rita)	Miller, Roger G.	Moore, James T(almadge)	Moxham, Roy
Melonio, Francoise	Miller, Russell	Moore, John Michael	Moya, Jose C.
Melosh, Barbara	Miller, Shawn William	Moore, Lucy	Moye, J. Todd
Melton, Brian C.	Millet, Robert L.	Moore, Peter N.	Moyer, Ann E.
Melton, Buckner F.	Millett, John	Moore, Philip N(icholas)	Moynahan, Brian
Melville, Charles (Peter)	Millett, Paul	Moore, Robin	Mraz, John
Menache, Sophia	Millman, Brock	Moore, Rogan H.	Muehl, Lois Baker
Menand, Louis	Millman, Isaac	Moorhead, John (Anthony)	Mueller, Andrew
Mendenhall, George Emery	Mills, A(nthony) D(avid)	Moote, A. Lloyd	Muir, Richard
Mendilow, Jonathan	Mills, Greg	Morales, Waltraud Queiser	Mukherjee, Bharati
Mendyk, Stan A. E.	Mills, Peter R.	Moran, Bruce T.	Mulcahy, Matthew
Menon, Dilip M(adhav)	Mills, Robert	Moran, Charles	Mullan, David George
Menon, Rajan	Milne, Seumas	Morash, Christopher	Müller, Ingo
Mentz, Steve	Milsom, Stroud Francis Charles	Moreh, Shmuel	Muller, Jerry Z(ucker)
Mentzer, Raymond A.	Miltner, Robert	Morell, James B.	Mullett, John St. Hilary
Mercantini, Jonathan	Min, Anselm K.	Moreno, Paul D.	Mulligan, William
Mercati, Cynthia	Minc, Alain J. R.	Moreton, N. Edwina	Mullin, Robert Bruce
Mercer, Derrik	Minchin, Timothy J.	Morgan, Austen	Mullins, Edwin B(randt)
Mercer, Jeremy	Minear, Richard Hoffman	Morgan, Dan	Mulroy, Kevin
Meredith, Martin	Minetor, Randi (S.)	Morgan, Joseph G.	Munby, Jonathan
Merians, Linda E.	Miscamble, Wilson D.	Morgan, Lael	Munro, John M(urchison)
Merne, Oscar James	Mishkin, Tracy	Morgan, M. Gwyn	Muravchik, Joshua
Mernissi, Fatima	Mitchell, David (John)	Morgan, Michael L.	Murcott, Anne
Merridale, Catherine	Mitchell, Emily	Morgan, Neil	Murdoch, David H.
Merrill, Ellen C.	Mitchell, Helen Buss	Morgan, Philip	Murdoch, Lydia
Merrill, Jean (Fairbanks)	Mitchell, Jerome	Morgan, Philip D.	Murdoch, Norman H.
Merry, Robert William	Mitchell, John Hanson	Morgan, Robin	Murkoff, Bruce
Mertz, Barbara (Louise) G(ross)	Mitchell, Linda E.	Morgan-Witts, Max	Murphey, Rhoads
Meserve, Walter Joseph	Mitchell, Memory F.	Morillo, Stephen (Reeder)	Murphy, (Gavin) Martin (Hedd)
Metcalf, Allan (Albert)	Mitchell, Michele	Mörner, Magnus	Murphy, Claire Rudolf
Mettam, Roger C.	Mitchell, Nathan	Moro, Javier	Murphy, Cullen
Meyer, Charles Robert	Mitchell, Peter	Morrill, John S(tephen)	Murphy, Dervla Mary
Meyer, Eugene L.	Mitchell, Stephen	Morris, (Clifford) Eric	Murphy, Justin D.
Meyer, Leisa D.	Mitchell, Stephen (G.)	Morris, Charles R.	Murphy, Martha W(atson)
Meyer, Lysle E(dward)	Mitchell, William P.	Morris, Edmund	Murphy, Rae Allan
Meyer, Richard E.	Miura, Hiroshi	Morris, Jan	Murphy, Robert
Meyerowitz, Joanne	Mnookin, Robert H(arris)	Morris, Jeffrey B(randon)	Murray, James M.
Meyers, Annette (Brafman)	Moallem, Minoo	Morris, Larry E.	Murray, John E.
Meyerson, Mark D.	Mobley, Joe A.	Morris, Marilyn (A.)	Murray, Paul T(hom)
Mezlekia, Nega	Moch, Leslie Page	Morris, Rachel	Musgrove, Frank
Micale, Mark S.	Moe, Richard	Morris, Roger	Myers, Lois E.
Michael, Colette V(erger)	Moerman, D. Max	Morris, S(tephen) Brent	Myers, Robert Manson
Michaels, Walter Benn	Moffat, Wendy	Morrison, Jeffry H.	Myers, W. David
Middlebrook, Martin	Moffett, Samuel Hugh	Morrissey, Will	Myers, William
Middlemas, (Robert) Keith	Moggach, Deborah	Morritt, Hope	Myerson, Daniel
Middleton, Haydn	Moghaddam, Fathali M.	Morrow, Ann	Myint-U, Thant
Midwinter, Eric (Clare)	Mohun, Arwen Palmer	Morrow, John	Mylroie, Laurie
Miescher, Stephan F.	Moise, Edwin E(variste)	Morson, Ian	Myrick, David F.
Mighetto, Lisa	Mokyr, Joel	Mortimer, Edward	Nacos, Brigitte L.

Parrish, Tim
Parrish, William E.
Parry, Graham
Parshall, Jonathan B.
Parsons, (Quentin) Neil
Parsons, Alexandra
Parsons, George W.
Parsons, P. J.
Parsons, Paul
Parthasarathy, R(ajagopal)
Pascale, Richard Tanner
Pascoe, Bruce
Pastorello, Karen
Pate, J'Nell L(aVerne)
Patenaude, Bertrand M.
Paterek, Josephine
Paterson, Janet M.
Paterson, Katherine (Womeldorf)
Patey, Douglas Lane
Patten, Chris
Patterson, (Horace) Orlando
Patterson, Dan
Patterson, Michael
Patterson, Tiffany Ruby
Pattillo, Mary E.
Patton, Phil
Patton, Robert H.
Patton, Stacey
Pauketat, Timothy R.
Paul, George F(ranklin)
Paul, Tessa
Pauley, Garth E.
Paulsson, Martin W.
Pausewang, Gudrun
Pavey, Don
Pavlowitch, Stevan K.
Paxton, John
Payne, (William) David
Payne, Darwin
Payne, J. Gregory
Pearse, Meic
Pearson, John
Pearson, Roger A. G.
Pearson, Thomas S(pencer)
Pedersen, Vernon L.
Pederson, William D(avid)
Peebles, Curtis
Peel, Ellen S.
Peel, H(azel) M(ary)
Peerenboom, Randall
Pegram, Thomas R.
Pell, Ed(ward)
Peña, Charles V.
Pencak, William
Penn, Michael Philip
Penn, W(illiam) S.
Penslar, Derek J(onathan)
Pentcheva, Bissera V.
Penycate, John (Vincent George)
Perani, Judith
Peretti, Burton W(illiam)
Perez-Stable, Marifeli
Perin, Roberto
Perkins, Dwight Heald
Perkins, John H.
Perkins, Michael
Perkinson, Robert

Perrett, Bryan
Perrin, Dennis
Perry, Jeffrey B.
Persico, Joseph E.
Pessar, Patricia R.
Pestana, Carla Gardina
Peters, John Durham
Peters, Kate
Peters, Rudolph
Petersen, Tore T.
Peterson, Cris
Peterson, Fred W.
Peterson, Richard Austin
Petit, Susan
Petrie, Anne
Petroski, Henry
Petrucci, Armando
Petry, Yvonne
Petsalis-Diomidis, Nicholas
Pettifer, James
Pfaelzer, Jean
Pfaff, Steven
Pfaff, William (Wendel)
Phares, Walid
Pharies, David (Arnold)
Phayer, Michael
Phelan, Tom (Thomas Joseph)
Phelps, Barry
Philipsen, Dirk
Phillips, Derek L.
Phillips, Jason
Phillips, Jonathan P.
Phillips, Leroy
Phillips, Roderick (Goler)
Phillips, Sarah T.
Phillips, Sky
Phillips, Susan E.
Phillips, Timothy
Phillipson, Michael
Piascik, Andy
Pick, Hella
Pick, Lucy K.
Pickering, David (Hugh)
Pickus, Keith H.
Pierard, Richard V(ictor)
Pierce, David
Pierce, Nora Elena
Pierson, Christopher
Pietrusza, David
Piker, Joshua
Pilardi, Jo-Ann
Pilcher, Jeffrey M.
Pilling, Christopher (Robert)
Pinney, Lucy (Catherine)
Pinto, António Costa
Piotrowski, Thaddeus (Tadeusz)
Piott, Steven L.
Pipes, Daniel
Pipes, Richard
Pite, Ralph
Pitsula, James (Michael)
Pittock, Joan (Hornby)
Pitts, Jennifer G.
Pizer, John
Pizzichini, Lilian
Plach, Eva
Platt, Brian

Platt, Colin
Platt, Joshua Eli
Plaut, W. Gunther
Pletsch, Carl (Erich)
Plokhy, Serhii
Plotkin, Diane M.
Plowden, David
Plummer, Brenda Gayle
Pohl, Frederik
Pointer, Richard W(ayne)
Polakoff, Keith (Ian)
Polakow-Suransky, Sasha
Poling(-Kempes), Lesley
Polisi, Joseph W.
Pollack, Jill S.
Pollack, Kenneth M(ichael)
Polland, Madeleine A(ngela)
Pollard, A(nthony) J(ames)
Pollard, Helen Perlstein
Pollard, John (Richard Thornhill)
Pollard, Lisa
Pollen, Daniel A.
Pollock, John Charles
Polowetzky, Michael
Polsgrove, Carol
Polsky, Andrew J.
Pong, David (B. P. T.)
Poos, L. R.
Pope, Rebecca A.
Porter, Bernard (John)
Porter, Linda
Porter, Sheena
Post, Robert C(harles)
Postlewait, Heidi
Potkay, Adam
Potter, Franz J.
Potter, Harry (D.)
Potts, Stephen W(ayne)
Poulin, Stephane
Poulson, Stephen C.
Poultney, David
Poupeye, Veerle
Powell, Alan
Powell, Barry B.
Powell, Dannye Romine
Powell, H. Jefferson
Powell, Martyn J.
Power, Patrick C.
Power, Samantha
Powers, Lyall H(arris)
Powers, Richard Gid
Poynor, Robin
Prall, Stuart E.
Pratt, Anna
Pratt, David
Pratt, John Clark
Prazniak, Roxann
Premo, Bianca
Prendergast, Mark J(oseph Anthony)
Preston, Andrew
Preston, Diana
Prestwich, Michael (Charles)
Prevas, John
Prévaux, Aude Yung-De
Prevots, Naima
Price, Matthew A(rlen)

Price, Robert M.
Price, Roger (David)
Priest, John Michael
Prime, Jim H.
Prince, Hugh
Principe, Lawrence M.
Prior, Robin
Pritchard, R(obert) John
Pritchard, Ray
Prochaska, Frank
Proudfoot, Lindsay
Provence, Michael
Prowse, Brad A.
Prunier, Gerard
Pruter, Robert
Pryce-Jones, David
Prymak, Thomas M.
Pryor, Bonnie H.
Puar, Jasbir K.
Puff, Helmut
Pulzer, Peter George Julius
Pun, Ngai
Punke, Michael
Purcell, Anne G.
Purcell, Benjamin H.
Putnam, Constance E(lizabeth)
Putney, Clifford
Putterman, Louis (G.)
Puxley, Ray
Pybus, Cassandra
Pyenson, Lewis (Robert)
Pyle, Kenneth B.
Quale, G(ladys) Robina
Quick, William K(ellon)
Quigley, David
Quinn, D. Michael
Quirk, Joe
Quirk, Randolph
Quiroga, Alejandro
Quiroz, Anthony
Raab, David
Rabb, Theodore K.
Rabieh, Linda R.
Rabinbach, Anson (Gilbert)
Rabinowitz, Dorothy
Rabinyan, Dorit
Raboteau, Albert J(ordy)
Rabrenovic, Gordana
Rachleff, Peter (J.)
Racine, Philip N.
Rackham, Oliver
Radforth, Ian
Radin, Ruth Yaffe
Radovanovic, Ivan
Radulescu, Domnica
Radzinsky, E dvard (Stanislav-ovich)
Raeburn, Antonia
Rafuse, Ethan S.
Rahe, Paul A.
Raibmon, Paige Sylvia
Rainbolt, William
Rajtar, Steve
Rake, Alan
Ralph, James R.
Rambuss, Richard
Ramdin, Ron(ald Andrew)

Ramirez, Susan E(lizabeth)
Rampton, Sheldon M.
Ramsey, Rebecca S.
Ramsey, William L.
Randall, Adrian
Randall, Dale B(ertrand) J(onas)
Randall, Francis Ballard
Randall, Willard Sterne
Randell, Nigel
Randolph, Lewis A.
Randsborg, Klavs
Ranney, Joseph A.
Rappaport, Helen
Rapson, Richard L.
Rarick, Ethan
Rasanayagam, Angelo
Ratcliffe, Eric Hallam
Rath, Richard Cullen
Rathbone, Richard
Rausing, Sigrid
Ravetz, Alison
Ravitch, Norman
Rawlings, Helen
Ray, Krishnendu
Rayfield, Donald
Raymond, Barbara Bisantz
Raymond, C. Elizabeth
Razin, Assaf
Razzell, Mary (Catherine)
Read, Anthony
Read, Brian
Read, Christopher
Read, David
Read, Peter
Reader, John
Reagin, Nancy Ruth
Reardon-Anderson, James
Reasoner, Livia Jane Washburn
Reavis, Dick J.
Reay, Barry
Redford, Donald B(ruce)
Redinger, Matthew A.
Redshaw, Peggy A(nn)
Redwood, John (Alan)
Reed, Christopher (G.)
Reed, Christopher Robert
Reed, James
Reed, John
Reed, Linda
Reeder, Carolyn
Reeder, Stephanie Owen
Rees, Brian
Rees, Matt Beynon
Reese, Ellen
Reese, Roger R(oi)
Reeves, Thomas C.
Reeves-Stevens, Garfield
Regalbuto, Robert J.
Regehr, T(heodore) D.
Reger, James P.
Regis, Helen A.
Reich, Howard
Reich, Robert B.
Reichel, Aaron I(srael)
Reichert, Tom
Reid, John P(hillip)
Reid, Loren

Reid, Richard M.
Reid, T. R.
Reid, Van
Reilly, Bernard F.
Reilly, James
Reilly, Kevin
Rein, Raanan
Reinders, Eric
Reinhartz, Adele
Reinstedt, Randall A.
Reiss, Edward
Reiss, Tom
Renard, John
Renehan, Edward J(ohn)
Renfield, Richard Lee
Renfrew, (Andrew) Colin
Rennell, Tony
Rennie, Bradford James
Reps, John W(illiam)
Reséndez, Andrés
Resis, Albert
Restall, Matthew
Reuter, Christoph
Rév, István
Revels, Tracy J.
Revie, Linda Lee
Reynolds, Arlene
Reynolds, Bill
Reynolds, David
Reynolds, E. Bruce
Rhea, Gordon Campbell
Rhodes, Gary Don
Rhodes, Jane
Rhodes, Richard (Lee)
Rhyne, Nancy
Ribowsky, Mark
Ricci, Nino
Rice, Andrew
Rice, Earle
Rice, Michael
Rice, Stephen P.
Rich, Adrienne (Cecile)
Rich, Nathaniel
Richard, Carl J(ohn)
Richard-Allerdyce, Diane
Richards, Eric
Richards, Jeffrey H.
Richards, Judith M.
Richardson, Bonham C.
Richardson, Brian W.
Richardson, David (Horsfall Stuart)
Richardson, Heather Cox
Richardson, R. C.
Richardson, Robert Galloway
Richerson, Peter J.
Richetti, John J.
Richman, Irwin
Richter, Daniel K(arl)
Ridd, Stephen (John)
Riddell, Peter G.
Riddle, Paxton
Riddles, Libby
Ridley, Jane
Ridley, Ronald T(homas)
Ridlon, Florence
Rieder, Jonathan

Rieger, Bernhard
Rielage, Dale C.
Riesenberg, Peter N.
Riggsby, Andrew M.
Riley, Carroll L.
Riley, James A.
Riley, James C.
Rimstead, Roxanne L.
Rinderle, Walter
Rinpoche, Khandro
Riordan, Timothy B.
Riordon, Michael
Rippley, LaVern J.
Rips, Michael
Rischin, Moses
Rise, Eric W.
Risebero, Bill
Ritchie, Daniel E.
Ritchie, Pamela E.
Riter, Tim
Ritterhouse, Jennifer
Ritthaler, Shelly
Ritvo, Harriet
Riverbend
Rivers, Larry E.
Rivière, William
Rivlin, Paul Anthony
Robb, David L.
Robb, George
Robb, Peter
Robenalt, James David
Roberson, Houston Bryan
Robert, Dana L.
Roberts, (Ray) Clayton
Roberts, Adam
Roberts, Alvin
Roberts, Brian
Roberts, Callum
Roberts, Denys (Tudor Emil)
Roberts, Elizabeth
Roberts, Francis X.
Roberts, Geoffrey
Roberts, Jennifer L.
Roberts, Jon H.
Roberts, Madge Thornall
Roberts, Nancy N(orma)
Roberts, Philip J.
Roberts, Priscilla
Robertson, Barbara Anne
Robertson, Deborah
Robertson, Ian (Campbell)
Robertson, James I.
Robertson, Leslie A.
Robie, Bill
Robin, Corey
Robinson, Andrew
Robinson, Frank M(alcolm)
Robinson, H(enry) Basil
Robinson, Jennifer L.
Robinson, Lee
Robinson, Phyllis C(umins)
Robisheaux, Thomas
Robson, Derek Ian
Robson, Roy R(aymond)
Rocha, Luis Miguel
Rochberg, Francesca
Rock, Howard B.

Rockland, Michael Aaron
Rodger, N. A. M.
Rodger, Richard
Rodgers, Eamonn
Rodgers, Marion Elizabeth
Rodgers, Peter
Rodney, William
Rodriguez, Gregory
Rodriguez, Ileana
Rodriguez, Jarbel A.
Rodriguez, Julia
Rodriguez, Junius P.
Roe, JoAnn
Roediger, David R(andall)
Rogers, Colin D(arlington)
Rogers, Franklin Robert
Rogers, Rosemary
Rohrbough, Malcolm Justin
Rolde, Neil
Rolle, Andrew
Rollins, Alden M(ilton)
Roman, Peter
Romanelli, Giandomenico
Romano, Dennis
Romer, (Louis) John
Romeril, John
Roodenburg, Herman
Rook, Tony
Rooks, Judith P.
Rooks, Noliwe M.
Root, Hilton L.
Rose, David
Rose, Kenneth (Vivian)
Rose, Michael
Rose, Norman Anthony
Rose, Paul (Bernard)
Rosegrant, Susan
Rosen, Louis H.
Rosen, William S.
Rosenak, Jan(ice M.)
Rosenberg, Robert Alan
Rosenbloom, Joseph R.
Rosenfeld, Richard N.
Rosenkranz, Ze'ev
Roshwald, Aviel
Ross, Angus
Ross, Dorothy
Ross, Ellen
Ross, Ian Campbell
Ross, Lawrence C.
Ross, Rosetta E.
Ross, Stewart
Ross, Stewart Halsey
Rossman, Jeffrey J.
Rossman, Vadim
Rostker, Bernard D.
Roth, Darlene R(ebecca)
Roth, Norman
Roth, Randolph Anthony
Rothman, David J.
Rothman, William
Rothstein, Hy S.
Rothwell, Victor Howard
Rotter, Andrew J.
Rotundo, Louis C.
Roudinesco, Elisabeth
Rouse, Mary A(mes)

Rowan, Roy
Rowbotham, Sheila
Rowe, C(hristopher) J(ames)
Rowell, Douglas Geoffrey
Rowland, Arthur Ray
Rowland, Peter Kenneth
Roy, James Charles
Royal, Robert
Rozbicki, Michal J.
Rubens, Jim M.
Rubenstein, Richard Lowell
Rubin, Barry
Rubin, Hyman
Rubin, Joan Shelley
Ruby, Robert H.
Rucker, Walter C.
Ruckley, Brian
Ruddock, Ted
Rudgley, Richard
Rudwick, Martin J.S.
Ruedy, John
Ruemmler, John D(avid)
Rufus, Anneli S.
Rugeley, Terry
Rugg, Linda (Haverty)
Ruin, Hans
Rulon, Philip Reed
Rummel, Jack
Runco, Mark A.
Ruoff, A. LaVonne Brown
Ruotsila, Markku
Rush, Christopher
Rushing, Josh
Rusi, Alpo M.
Russell, Jeffrey Burton
Russell, Kenneth Victor
Russell, Richard L.
Russell, Sheldon
Russo, Elena
Russo, Thomas A.
Rustici, Craig M.
Rutgers, Leonard Victor
Ruthchild, Rochelle Goldberg
Rutherdale, Robert
Rutland, Suzanne D.
Rutledge, Ian
Rutledge, Leigh W.
Rutter, Jeremy B.
Ryan, Barbara
Ryan, Craig
Ryan, Donald P.
Ryan, Frank
Ryan, Halford (Ross)
Ryan, James G(ilbert)
Ryan, Peter Allen
Rychlak, Ronald (J.)
Ryczek, William J.
Rykwert, Joseph
Sabin, Roger (John)
Sable, Martin Howard
Sachs, Mendel
Sackman, Douglas Cazaux
Sacks, David Harris
Sadowsky, Jonathan Hal
Sadri, Ahmad
Sahgal, Nayantara (Pandit)
Sahlins, Peter

Saillant, John
Salam, Reihan
Sale, Kirkpatrick
Salerno, Beth A.
Salisbury, Joyce E(llen)
Salsi, Lynn
Salutin, Rick
Salway, Peter
Salyer, Lucy E.
Salzman, Michele Renee
Sambrook, A(rthur) J(ames)
Sampson, Curt
Samuels, Richard J.
Sanchez-Eppler, Karen
Sanderlin, George
Sanders, Andrew
Sanders, Charles W.
Sanders, Katrina M.
Sanders, Peter (Basil)
Sands, Philippe
Sandstrom, Alan R(ussell)
Sandweiss, Martha A(nn)
Sanneh, Lamin
Santos, Michael Wayne
Santosuosso, Antonio
Sapinsley, Barbara
Sargent, Lyman Tower
Sargent, Pamela
Sarna, Jonathan D(aniel)
Sarno, Ronald Anthony
Sarotte, Mary Elise
Sarris, Greg
Sarris, Jonathan Dean
Sarti, Ron
Sartre, Maurice
Sartwell, Crispin
Sass, Stephen L.
Sassoon, Donald
Sauder, Robert A(lden)
Sauers, Richard A(llen)
Saunders, Ann Loreille
Saunders, James Robert
Saunders, Nicholas J.
Saunt, Claudio
Sauro, Christy W.
Sauvain, Philip Arthur
Savage, Charlie
Savage, Kirk
Savage, Sean J.
Sawrey, Robert D.
Sawyer, Mary R.
Sawyer, Ralph D.
Sawyer, Roger
Sawyer, Suzana
Sax, Boria
Sayer, Ian (Keith Terence)
Sayre, Gordon M.
Scalapino, Robert Anthony
Scalmer, Sean
Scanlon, Jennifer
Scarborough, William Kauffman
Scarfe, Allan John
Scargill, David Ian
Scarr, Deryck (Antony)
Scates, Shelby
Schabas, Margaret
Schakel, Peter J.

Schaller, Lyle E(dwin)
Schama, Simon (Michael)
Scheck, Raffael
Schecter, Darrow
Scheese, Donald
Scheiber, Harry N.
Scheil, Katherine West
Scheindlin, Raymond P.
Schen, Claire S.
Schenken, Suzanne O'Dea
Schevill, Margot Blum
Schiff, James A(ndrew)
Schinto, Jeanne
Schlesier, Karl H.
Schlitz, Laura Amy
Schmidle, Nicholas
Schmidt, Benno Charles
Schmidt, Elizabeth
Schmidt, Leigh Eric
Schmidt, Peter
Schmidt, Samuel
Schmidt, Stanley (Albert)
Schmidt, Ulf
Schmidt, Vivien A.
Schmookler, Andrew Bard
Schneider, Deborah Lucas
Schneider, Gregory L.
Schneider, Robert
Schneider, Thomas E.
Schneiderman, David
Schoemer, Karen
Schoenfeld, Bruce
Schoenhals, Michael
Schofield, Brian
Schofield, Carey
Schofield, John A.
Scholefield, Alan (A. T.)
Schone, Robin
Schreiber, Roy E.
Schrijvers, Peter
Schroeder-Lein, Glenna R(uth)
Schryer, Frans J(ozsef)
Schubert, Frank N.
Schultz, Celia E.
Schumacher, John N(orbert)
Schusky, Ernest L.
Schutte, Anne Jacobson
Schwartz, Adam
Schwartz, E(arl) A(lbert)
Schwartz, Elliott S.
Schwartz, Joyce R.
Schwartz, Kessel
Schwartz, Marie Jenkins
Schwartz, Richard A(lan)
Schwartz, Stephen (Alfred)
Schwarz, Daniel R(oger)
Schwarz, Frederick A. O.
Schwarz, Henry G.
Schwarz, Philip J.
Schweikart, Larry (Earl)
Schweikart, Larry E.
Schweizer, Karl W.
Schweller, Randall
Scott, Alan (B.)
Scott, Amoret (Tanner)
Scott, Aurelia C.
Scott, Joan Wallach

Scott, Jonathan
Scott, P(aul) H(enderson)
Scott, Roy Vernon
Scott-Clark, Cathy
Sculle, Keith A.
Scully, Pamela (Frederika)
Seagrave, Sterling
Seale, William
Seaman, P. David
Searle, G(eoffrey) R(ussell)
Searle, John R(ogers)
Searle, Ronald (William Fordham)
Searles, P. D(avid)
Sears, James T(homas)
Sedaitis, Judith B.
Seddon, Andrew M.
Seed, David
Seed, Jenny
Segal, Howard P.
Seger, Linda
Seguin, Marilyn W(eymouth)
Sehene, Benjamin
Seib, Gerald
Seidman, Michael
Selbourne, David
Selcer, Richard F.
Seleshanko, Kristina
Self, Robert O.
Self, Will
Seligman, Craig
Semaan, Khalil I. H.
Semmes, Clovis E.
Senie, Harriet F.
Senior, Michael
Sennett, Richard
Senor, Dan
Seo, Audrey Yoshiko
Sepinwall, Alyssa Goldstein
Seraile, William
Serulnikov, Sergio
Settje, David E.
Severance, Ben H.
Seward, Desmond
Seward, Robert (Allen)
Seymour-Jones, Carole
Shabecoff, Philip
Shafer, Byron E.
Shafer, D. Michael
Shaffer, Donald R.
Shagan, Ethan H.
Shah, Sonia
Shahar, Yuval
Shain, Milton
Shakeri, Khosrow
Shakin, Ken
Shallcrass, John James
Shane, Scott
Shanker, Stuart G.
Shannon, Timothy J.
Shapin, Steven
Shapiro, Barbara J(une)
Shapiro, Barry M.
Shapiro, Edward S.
Shapiro, Harvey
Shapiro, Herbert
Shapiro, Ian

Stansky, Peter (David Lyman)
Stanton, Doug
Stanton, Shelby L(ee)
Stapleton, Timothy J.
Starnes, Richard D.
Statham, E. Robert
Stauber, John (Clyde)
Stave, Bruce M.
Stavrakis, Peter J(acob)
Stebenne, David
Stecker, Ann Page
Steedman, Carolyn (Kay)
Steege, Paul
Steel, David (Martin Scott)
Steel, Nigel
Steel, Ronald
Steele, Philip
Steidle, Brian
Steidle Wallace, Gretchen
Steiker, Valerie
Stein, Peter (Gonville)
Stein, Rebecca L.
Steinberg, Clarence B.
Steinberg, Erwin R.
Steinberg, Jonathan
Steinberg, Mark D(avid)
Steinbrook, Gordon L.
Steiner, George A.
Steiner, Michael C.
Steinlauf, Michael C.
Steinman, Ron
Steinmetz, Christian
Steins, Richard
Stepaniants, Marietta
Stephen, Martin
Stephens, Andy
Stephens, Randall J.
Stephens, Walter
Stephens, William Peter
Sterken, Christiaan (L.)
Sterling, Keir B(rooks)
Stern, Ellen Norman
Stern, Fritz
Stern, Kenneth S.
Stern, Robert A. M.
Stern, Sheldon M.
Stern, Steve J.
Sternlicht, Sanford
Sterritt, Laurence Lux
Stertz, Bradley A.
Stetson, Brad
Stevens, Bryna
Stevens, Garry
Stevenson, David
Stevenson, David
Stevenson, Garth
Stewart, Elizabeth A.
Stewart, Gary
Stewart, Harry E.
Stewart, Jeffrey C.
Stewart, Kenneth
Stewart, Mart A.
Stewart, Matthew
Stiebing, William H(enry)
Stiles, T. J.
Still, William N.
Stillman, Norman A(rthur)

Stiltner, Brian
Stinchecum, Amanda Mayer
Stine, Catherine
Stingel, Janine
Stinnett, Robert B.
Stjernø, Steinar
Stock, Gregory
Stockel, H. Henrietta
Stockley, Grif
Stokes, Gale
Stokes, Susan C.
Stoll, Steven
Stone, Cynthia L.
Stone, David R.
Stone, Gerald (Charles)
Stone, Harry
Stone, Judith F.
Stoner, K. Lynn
Stops, Sue
Storey, Margaret
Storey, Margaret M.
Storey, R(obin) L(indsay)
Stott, Annette
Stout, Harry S.
Stout, Joseph A.
Stovall, Tyler
Stow, Kenneth R.
Stowe, Steven M.
Stoyle, Mark
Stradling, R. A.
Strahinich, Helen C.
Strain, Christopher B.
Strane, Susan
Strausbaugh, John
Strauss, Jennifer (Wallace)
Stray, Christopher
Street, Brian Jeffrey
Strickland, Michael R.
Strieder, Leon F.
Stronach, Bruce
Strong, Albertine
Strong, Roy (Colin)
Stross, Randall E.
Stroud, Patricia Tyson
Strouhal, Eugen
Stubbs, Peter Charles
Sturtevant, Katherine
Subrahmanyam, Sanjay
Suda, Zdenek Ludvik
Sudjic, Deyan
Sullivan, (Donovan) Michael
Sullivan, David M.
Sullivan, Dolores P.
Sullivan, Garrett A.
Sullivan, M(ichael) J(ustin)
Sullivan, Michael Joseph
Sullivan, Patricia
Sultan, Stanley
Sumarsam
Summerhill, Thomas
Summers, Anthony (Bruce)
Summers, Judith (Anne)
Summers, Mark Wahlgren
Summerscale, Kate
Sumner, David E.
Sumner, George R.
Sumption, Jonathan

Sundiata, Ibrahim K.
Supple, Barry E(manuel)
Susi, Geraldine Lee
Sutherland, John
Sutphen, Mona
Sutter, Robert G.
Sutton, Matthew Avery
Sutton, Peter C.
Suzuki, Akihito
Swain, Gwenyth
Swanson, Heather (Crichton)
Swanson, James L.
Swanson, June
Sward, Robert S.
Swetman, Glenn R(obert)
Swett, Pamela E.
Swetz, Frank J.
Swick, Thomas
Swierenga, Robert P.
Swift, Donald C.
Swift, Will
Swindells, Robert (Edward)
Swinfen, Ann
Swinton, Elizabeth de Sabato
Switzer, Les
Sword, Wiley
Symonds, Deborah A(nn)
Symynkywicz, Jeffrey B(ruce)
Synan, (Harold) Vinson
Szalay, Miklós
Sze, Arthur C.
Szostak, Rick
Szyma ski, Leszek
T Hart, Marjolein C.
Ta V n Tài
Taeuber, Cynthia M.
Taguieff, Pierre André
Taheri, Amir
Taichert, Pari Noskin
Talese, Gay
Talley, Colin L.
Tamura, Linda
Tan, Sor-hoon
Tanaka, Stefan
Tanner, Karen Holliday (Olson)
Tanner, Marcus
Tanner, Norman P.
Tanner, Stephen L.
Tarling, (Peter) Nicholas
Tarnopolsky, Yuri
Tarnowski, Andrew
Tarr, Joel Arthur
Taruskin, Richard
Tate, Michael L.
Taubman, Philip
Tawa, Nicholas E.
Tawil, Ezra
Taylor, Andy
Taylor, Anne Marie
Taylor, Claire
Taylor, Diana
Taylor, Donathan
Taylor, Frederick
Taylor, Jean Gelman
Taylor, Joan E(lizabeth)
Taylor, John A.
Taylor, John H(ilton)

Taylor, Jon E.
Taylor, Justin
Taylor, Kathy
Taylor, Larissa J(uliet)
Taylor, Mark Lewis
Taylor, Michael J(oseph)
Taylor, Mildred D.
Taylor, Quintard
Taylor, Robert Allan
Taylor, Robert H(enry)
Taylor, Robert Larry
Taylor, Rogan
Taylor, Stephen
Taylor, Sue
Taylor, Welford Dunaway
Taylor, William R(obert)
Teague, Frances
Teahan, Sheila
Tehan, Arline Boucher
Teiser, Stephen F.
Teitelbaum, Matthew
Teja, Jesus F(rancisco) de la
Temperley, Nicholas
Temple, Brian
Temple, Robert (Kyle Grenville)
Temple, Wayne C(alhoun)
Tenner, Edward
Terpstra, John
Terrio, Susan J.
Teter, Magda
Thacker, Robert
Thackeray, Frank W.
Thaden, Barbara Z.
Thandeka
Tharu, Susie
Thayer, Bradley A.
Theiss, Janet M.
Theroux, Louis Sebastian
Thirsk, (Irene) Joan
Tholfsen, Trygve R(ainone)
Thom, James Alexander
Thomas, (Antony) Charles
Thomas, Adrian
Thomas, Clara McCandless
Thomas, David St. John
Thomas, Edmund Barrington
Thomas, G(regory) Scott
Thomas, H(ubert) Nigel
Thomas, Hugh
Thomas, Keith (Vivian)
Thomas, Rosalind
Thomas, Sue
Thomas, Velma Maia
Thomasma, Kenneth R.
Thompson, Alexander
Thompson, Christina
Thompson, Chuck
Thompson, Damian
Thompson, Francis George
Thompson, Janet A(nn)
Thompson, Jerry Don
Thompson, Nicholas
Thompson, Robert Farris
Thompson, Thomas L.
Thompson, William Irwin
Thomson, Alistair
Thomson, Andrew

Waller, John
Waller, P(hilip) J(ohn)
Walsh, Ann
Walsh, Jill Paton
Walsh, Stephen
Walshe, R(obert) D(aniel)
Waltenburg, Eric N.
Walter, John
Walton, James
Walton, Kendall L(ewis)
Walton, Richard J(ohn)
Waltz, Kenneth N.
Walvin, James
Wandel, Lee Palmer
Warburton, Nigel
Ward, (William) Peter
Ward, Alan J.
Ward, Brian
Ward, Chrissie
Ward, David
Ward, Geoffrey C(hampion)
Ward, Harry Merrill
Ward, Margaret
Ward, Matthew C.
Wardroper, John Edmund
Ware, Alan
Ware, Jane (O.)
Ware, Susan
Warmington, William Allan
Warne, Randi R(uth)
Warner, Francis
Warner, Judith
Warner, Marina
Warnicke, Retha M.
Warren, James Francis
Warren, Karen J.
Warren, Richard (Andrew)
Washburn, Stan
Wass, Douglas (William Gretton)
Wasserstein, Bernard (Mano
　Julius)
Wasserstrom, Jeffrey N.
Watada, Terry
Watenpaugh, Keith David
Waters, Claire M.
Waters, David Watkin
Watford, Christopher M.
Watman, Max
Watson, Don
Watson, J(ohn) R(ichard)
Watson, Kathy
Watson, Ritchie Devon
Watson, Steven
Watson, William E.
Watt, David Harrington
Watterson, John Sayle
Watts, Anthony John
Watts, Edward J.
Watts, Sheldon J.
Waugh, Alexander
Waugh, John C(linton)
Waugh, Teresa (Lorraine)
Wauzzinski, Robert A.
Wawro, Geoffrey
Waziyatawin
Weart, Spencer R(ichard)
Weaver, Karol K.

Webb, Clive
Webber, Mark (Alan)
Weber, Jennifer L.
Weber, Ralph E.
Weber, Sandra
Weber, Thomas
Weber, Thomas
Webster, Jason
Webster, Len
Weckmann, Luis
Weddle, Kevin J.
Weeks, Jeffrey
Wegman, William (George)
Wegmann, Peter
Weidensaul, Scott
Weinbaum, Marvin G.
Weinberg, Helene Barbara
Weinberger, Peter Ezra
Weiner, Hollace Ava
Weiner, Mark S(tuart)
Weiner, Stephanie Kuduk
Weiner, Stephen
Weinroth, Michelle
Weinstein, Allen
Weinstein, Miriam
Weintraub, Stanley
Weir, David A.
Weir, Gary E.
Weir, Ronald Blackwood
Weisbrot, Robert (S.)
Weisgall, Jonathan M.
Weiss, Andrea
Weissbach, Lee Shai
Weisskopf, Thomas E.
Weitz, Eric D.
Welch, David A.
Welch, Richard F.
Weldt-Basson, Helene Carol
Welland, Sasha Su-Ling
Wellington, Jean Susorney
Wells, Cheryl A.
Wells, Mary Ann
Wells, Peter S.
Wells, Roger
Wels, Susan
Welsh, Frank (Reeson)
Weltge, Sigrid W(ortmann)
Wen, Chihua
Wenham, David
Wert, Jonathan (Maxwell)
Wertheimer, Jack
West, Elliott
West, Sandra L.
Westad, Odd Arne
Westburg, Barry (Richard)
Westmeier, Karl-Wilhelm
Weston, Mark
Westwood, John Norton
Wetenhall, John
Wettig, Gerhard
Wexler, Alan
Wexler, Alice (Ruth)
Weyr, Thomas
Whalen, Richard James
Whalen, Thomas J.
Whalley, Joyce Irene
Wheeler, Lesley

Wheeler, Richard S.
Whelan, Irene
Whelan, Ruth
Whicker, Alan (Donald)
Whitaker, Matthew C.
Whitcomb, John C(lement)
White, Bill
White, C. Todd
White, Carolinne
White, Carolyn
White, Howard
White, Jon Manchip
White, Kevin
White, Mark J.
White, Peter (O. G.)
White, Phillip M.
White, Warren H.
White-Parks, Annette
Whitehead, Catherine Sarah
Whitehead, Colson
Whitehouse, David (Bryn)
Whiteley, Nigel
Whiteman, Robin
Whitlam, (Edward) Gough
Whitlock, Dean
Whitman, Sylvia (Choate)
Whitman, T(orrey) Stephen
Whynott, Douglas (Vernon)
Wick, Steve
Wicker, Tom
Wickham-Crowley, Timothy P.
Wiegand, Wayne A.
Wiener, Joel Howard
Wiesen, S. Jonathan
Wiesner-Hanks, Merry E.
Wild, Mark
Wilentz, Amy
Wilentz, Sean
Wiley, Peter (Booth)
Wilford, John Noble
Wilkins, Mira
Wilkins, Sally (E. D.)
Wilkinson, Marian
Wilkinson, Richard H(erbert)
Wilkinson, Sylvia J.
Wilkinson, Tracy
Will, George F.
Willbanks, James H.
Wille, Lois
Willett, Ralph
Williams, Adam
Williams, Alan Lee
Williams, Andrew
Williams, Austin
Williams, Barry
Williams, Bert (Nolan)
Williams, David
Williams, Duncan Ryûken
Williams, Geoff
Williams, Herbert (Lloyd)
Williams, Jacqueline (B.)
Williams, James C.
Williams, John A(lfred)
Williams, Kate
Williams, Lillian Serece
Williams, Marcia (Dorothy)
Williams, Marie S(heppard)

Williams, Martin Anthony Joseph
Williams, Paul K.
Williams, Robyn
Williams, Tony
Williams, Vernon J(ohnson)
Williams, Walter E(dward)
Williamson, Denise
Williamson, J(erry) W(ayne)
Williamson, Joel
Williamson, John (Gordon)
Williamson, Robert C(lifford)
Willimon, William H(enry)
Willis, Edgar E(rnest)
Willis, Resa
Willmott, Phyllis
Willrich, Mason
Wills, Alfred J(ohn)
Wills, Garry
Wilmot, Jeanne
Wilson, (Brian) Geoffrey
Wilson, Andrew
Wilson, Barbara Ker
Wilson, Barry K.
Wilson, Bronwen
Wilson, Budge
Wilson, Catharine Anne
Wilson, Catherine
Wilson, Colin (Henry)
Wilson, Darryl B(abe)
Wilson, David M(ackenzie)
Wilson, Des
Wilson, Eva
Wilson, Francille Rusan
Wilson, John K.
Wilson, Kathleen
Wilson, Lyle (Giles)
Wilson, Marc
Wilson, Peter H.
Wilson, Stephen G.
Wilson, Trevor Gordon
Wilson, Wesley M.
Wilson, William Scott
Wiltse, Jeff
Winckler, Edwin A.
Winder, Simon
Winkler, Henry Ralph
Winkler, Jonathan Reed
Winland, Daphne N.
Winnifrith, T(homas) J(ohn)
Winock, Michel
Winsey, Valentine Rossilli
Winship, Michael P.
Winter, Kari J.
Winterbottom, Michael
Winters, Kay
Wintz, Cary D.
Wirsing, Robert G.
Wise, Joe
Witham, Larry
Witherington, Ben
Wittner, Lawrence Stephen
Witzel, Michael Karl
Wixson, Douglas
Woell, Edward J.
Woirol, Gregory R.
Wokeck, Marianne Sophia
Wolensky, Kenneth C.

Homes/Gardens-*cont.*

Nice, Jill
Nold, Robert
Odenwald, Neil G.
Ogrin, Dušan
Orosz, Joel J.
Osborn, Susan (E.)
Pagán, Victoria Emma
Paul, George F(ranklin)
Paul, Tessa
Paulsen, Gary
Peacock, Molly
Peters, Rick
Peterson, Carol R.
Peterson, Fred W.
Pfanner, (Anne) Louise
Pleasant, Barbara
Powell, Dannye Romine
Prown, Jonathan
Ravetz, Alison
Read, Miss
Rice, Graham
Richards, Matt
Richman, Irwin
Robb, Daniel
Rose, Andrew (Wyness)
Russell Taylor, Elisabeth
Rybczynski, Witold
Sanecki, Kay Naylor
Saville, Diana
Saxton, Josephine (Howard)
Schmid, Wolfram George
Seleshanko, Kristina
Shemie, Bonnie (Jean Brenner)
Simonds, Merilyn
Spiegelman, Annie
Stamets, Paul
Stell, Elizabeth P(arker)
Stewart, Martha
Strong, Roy (Colin)
Sudjic, Deyan
Sullivan, John Jeremiah
Taylor, Walter Kingsley
Tinniswood, Adrian
Tomlinson, Harry
Tweit, Susan J(oan)
Valder, Peter
Van Kessel, Ineke
van Lemmen, Hans
Verney, Peter (Vivian Lloyd)
Walls, Ian G.
Wang, Sen
Ward, (William) Peter
Warren, Susan
Weems, David B(urnola)
Welton, Jude
Whiteman, Robin
Wiener, Nancy H.
Wilson, David S(cofield)
Wittmer, Pierre (Jean)
Yarwood, Doreen

Horticulture

Ackerman, James D.
Adams, Abby

Horticulture-*cont.*

Appell, Scott D.
Arvigo, Rosita
Barden, Dan
Benjamin, Joan
Biek, David E.
Bowers, Janice Emily
Bown, Deni
Brookes, John A.
Cabot, Francis H.
Campbell-Culver, Maggie
Clabough, Casey Howard
Cohen, Stephanie
Cootes, Jim E.
Corner, James
Cothran, James R(obert)
Coussins, Craig
Cox, Madison
Cranshaw, Whitney
Cullen, Mark
Davies, Jennifer (Eileen)
Davis, Linda W.
Dickey, Page
Digregorio, Mario J.
Drury, Sally
Ellis, Barbara W.
Emmet, Alan
Everitt, James H.
Fearnley-Whittingstall, Jane
Garber, Anne
Gershuny, Grace
Gervais, (George) Paul
Gilmore, Kate
Goodman, Richard
Grey-Wilson, Christopher
Grounds, Roger
Harris, Dudley Arthur
Holt, (Wilma) Geraldene
Jenkins, Virginia Scott
Johnston, Stanley H(oward)
Kennedy, Pagan
Kevles, Daniel J.
Khush, Gurdev S.
La Croix, I(sobyl) F.
Lacy, Allen
Laskin, David
Lawton, Barbara (Perry)
Lima, Patrick
Lin, Tan (Anthony)
Loewer, (Henry) Peter
Lord, Tony
Luebbermann, Mimi
Lycett Green, Candida
Matthews, Victoria (Ann)
McEwan, Barbara
Merser, Cheryl
Moran, James P.
Odenwald, Neil G.
Ogrin, Dušan
Ondra, Nancy J.
Pleasant, Barbara
Ponsonby, Laura
Reich, Lee
Rice, Graham
Salisbury, Frank B(oyer)
Samson, Suzanne M.
Sanecki, Kay Naylor
Saxton, Josephine (Howard)

Horticulture-*cont.*

Schmid, Wolfram George
Stell, Elizabeth P(arker)
Sweeney, Emma
Thirsk, (Irene) Joan
Tomlinson, Harry
Tweit, Susan J(oan)
Valder, Peter
Verrier, Suzanne
Walls, Ian G.
Watson, Benjamin A.
Westmacott, Richard N.
Whiteman, Robin
Wiggers, Raymond

How-to Books

Adamec, Christine
Adams, Carol J.
Adams, Marie
Allen, Roberta
Alphin, Elaine Marie
Arnold, Peter
Artell, Mike
Arterburn, Stephen
Ashabranner, Melissa
Barbato, Joseph
Baron, Wendy
Barrett, Andrea
Behrens, Ellen
Behrens, John C.
Bell, James Edward
Bentley, Nancy
Berg, Elizabeth
Berinstein, Paula
Bertrand, Marsha
Best, Don(ald M.)
Biesel, David B.
Blakey, Nancy
Blanchard, Robert
Bloch, Douglas
Bly, Robert (Elwood)
Bolden, Tonya
Bolles, Richard Nelson
Boorstein, Sylvia
Bouton, Gary David
Bowman, J. Wilson
Bradford, Barbara Taylor
Bradshaw, Anne
Breslin, Cathy
Brian, Cynthia
Brody, Jane E(llen)
Bromer, Anne C.
Brooke, Heather
Brookes, John A.
Buhner, Stephen Harrod
Canfield, Jack
Cannon, Michael F.
Carter, Steven
Casey, Barbara
Casey, Don
Cassady, Marsh
Chase, Elaine Raco
Chatfield, Cheryl A.
Chin-Lee, Cynthia D.
Chopra, Deepak (K.)

How-to Books-*cont.*

Clawson, Calvin C.
Cole, Diane
Collinge, William (B.)
Coloroso, Barbara
Comfort, Ray
Confer, Dennis W.
Cosman, Mark
Cossolotto, Matthew
Cottrell, David
Coussins, Craig
Cowan, Gordon
Cox, Richard (Hubert Francis)
Craig, Colleen
Cramer, Stanley H.
Cravey, Pamela J.
Crawford, Gregory A.
Davey, H. E.
Davidsen, Susanna L.
Davidson, Jeff
Davidson, Pamela
Dawson, Roger
Day, Laura (Globus)
De Becker, Gavin
De La Cruz, Melissa
Dervaes, Claudine
Desena, Carmine
Devney, Darcy C(ampion)
Diamant, Anita
Dodds, Bill
Doman, Glenn
Dresser, Norine
Dromgoole, Dominic
Duckworth, Eleanor
Duntemann, Jeff
Duvoisin, Roger C(lair)
Edwards, Frank B.
Ehrler, Brenda
Ellis, Barbara W.
Engel, Margorie L(ouise)
Ettlinger, Steve
Farrell, Warren (Thomas)
Fay, Jim
Fearnley-Whittingstall, Jane
Ferris, Jean
Fischer, Lynn
Fitzsimons, Cecilia (A. L.)
Fox, Barry
Fraser, Harry
Frazier, Shirley George
Gallagher, Patricia C.
Gallardo, Evelyn
Gallimore, Paul
Garber, Anne
Gelb, Michael J.
Gikow, Jacqueline
Godfrey, Neale S.
Goldman, Katherine (Wyse)
Goodman, Jordan E.
Gosline, Andrea Alban
Goulter, Barbara
Gow, Michael
Graham, Laurie
Gray, Judith A(nne)
Grenfell, Michael J.
Halpin, Marlene
Hamilton, Richard
Hanson, Susan F.

Human Relations/Parenting-
cont.

Human Relations/Parenting-
cont.

Human Relations/Parenting-
cont.

Human Relations/Parenting-
cont.

Burns, Ailsa (Milligan)
Bushong, Carolyn Nordin
Callenbach, Ernest
Campbell, Scott
Caplan, Mariana
Capon, Robert Farrar
Caponigro, Jeffrey R.
Carter, Steven
Casey, Maud
Cassidy, Michael
Cawthorne, Nigel
Chapman, J. Dudley
Charny, Israel Wolf
Cherlin, Andrew J.
Chin-Lee, Cynthia D.
Choi, Annie
Christian, Carol Cathay Tuttle
Christian, Jeffrey E.
Chryssavgis, John
Cline, Foster W.
Clinton, Hillary Rodham
Coates, Ta-Nehisi
Cochran, Heather
Cohen, Debra Nussbaum
Coles, Roberta L.
Coloroso, Barbara
Constantelos, Demetrios J.
Cook, Mark
Cooper, Jilly (Sallitt)
Cosby, Bill
Cosman, Mark
Counihan, Carole
Cowie, Colin
Crary, Elizabeth (Ann)
Crosland, Margaret
Cunningham, James V.
Curtis, Todd
Damon, William
Daniels, Karen
Davidson, Gordon
Davidson, Jeff
Davidson, Sol M.
Davies, Charlotte Aull
Davis, Dee
Davis, Rocio G.
de Vinck, José M. G. A.
Deats, Richard L.
Debin, David
deLara, Ellen
Derby, Pat
Dermond, Susan Usha
Diamant, Anita
Diamond, Jed
Dobson, James C.
Dockrey, Karen
Dodds, Bill
Dominian, Jack
Donnelly, Deborah
Douglas, Susan J(eanne)
Drewes, Athena A.
Durban, Pam
Eames, Anne
Easum, William M.
Edin, Kathryn
Ehrler, Brenda
Elbirt, Paula M.

Elium, Don
Elium, Jeanne (Ann)
Elizur, Joel
Ellington, Sara
Elliott, Elaine M.
Elster, Kathi
Emecheta, (Florence Onye) Buchi
Engel, Beverly
Engel, Joel
Engel, Margorie L(ouise)
Englund, Steven
Fain, Michael
Farber, Naomi
Farrell, Warren (Thomas)
Faulkner, Mary
Fay, Jim
Fearnley-Whittingstall, Jane
Feiffer, Kate
Feldman, Gayle
Fineman, Martha Albertson
Finley, Mitch
Firkatian, Mari A.
Fischer, Lucy Rose
Fitzpatrick, Mary Anne
Flescher, Irwin
Flinders, Neil J.
Foster, Brooke Lea
Foyster, Elizabeth A.
Frost, Jo
Fuess, Harald
Fullerton, Gail
Gabrieli, Christopher
Galligan, John
Gamble, Terry
Gammer, Moshe
Geer, Charlie
Gildner, Gary
Gilmour, David
Glass, Dee Dee
Glazer, Ellen Sarasohn
Gold, Michael
Goldberg, Jane G.
Goldhagen, Shari
Gordon, Grant
Gosline, Andrea Alban
Goulter, Barbara
Gray, John
Greeley, Andrew (Moran)
Green, Daryl D.
Green, Michael D.
Greenberg, Elinor Miller
Greene, Ross W.
Greenwood, David Luis Valdes
Greer, Jane
Greif, Geoffrey L.
Greiff, Barrie S(anford)
Greil, Arthur L(awrence)
Griffith, Gail
Griffith, Helen V(irginia)
Grigg, Ray
Grossinger, Tania
Grylls, Bear
Gurewitsch, Edna P.
Gwartney, Debra
Gwynelle (Dismukes), Gwynelle
Hacke, Daniela Alexandra

Haltzman, Scott
Hamrin, Robert
Hardy, Edward
Hardy, John Philips
Harley, Willard F.
Harrison, Kathryn
Hart, Charles (A.)
Hartwig, Michael J.
Hatkoff, Amy
Heckert, Connie K(aye Delp)
Hegeman, Mary Theodore
Helmer, Diana Star
Henggeler, Scott Walter
Heyman, Abigail
Hildebrand, Verna
Hill, Ann M.
Hillyer, Barbara
Hodgson, Harriet
Hoge, Hilary
Holloway, Sara
Holroyd, Michael
Honeycutt, Natalie
Honnold, RoseMary
Honoré, Carl
Hooper, Maureen Brett
Horvath, Betty
Houghton, Gordon
Howell, John Christian
Huffman, Jennifer Lee
Hunt, Angela Elwell
Huston, Nancy
Hutchinson, Earl Ofari
Isenberg, Sheila
Jacobsen, David
Jafree, Mohammed Jawaid Iqbal
Jamiolkowski, Raymond M.
Janko, (Kathleen) Susan
Jensen, Kathryn
Jepson, Bryan
Johnson, Cait
Johnson, Rebecca L.
Johnson, Susan (M.)
Jones, Charlotte Foltz
Jones, Thai
Joy, Donald Marvin
Kadushin, Alfred
Kapsis, Robert E.
Kaylin, Lucy
Keen, Sam
Kellerman, Jesse
Kenny, Lorraine Delia
Kent, Carol
Kertes, Joseph
Kilson, Marion D. de B.
Kim, Young (Hum)
Kingma, Daphne Rose
Kingston, Beverley
Kipnis, Aaron R.
Kirkwood, Annie
Kitzinger, Sheila
Kizer, Amber
Koenig, Harold G.
Koplewicz, Harold S.
Koski, Mary B(ernadette)
Kremenyuk, Victor (A.)
La Greca, Annette M(arie)

LaGrand, Louis E.
Lamb, Sharon
Lappé, Frances Moore
Larose, Lawrence
Larson, Ingrid D(ana)
Lasswell, Marcia
Lawrence-Lightfoot, Sara
Lazebnik, Claire Scovell
Lehmann-Haupt, Rachel
Lerner, Harriet
Levine, Barbara Hoberman
Levy, Barrie
Levy, Harry
Lewin, Roger A.
Lewis, Myron
Lichtenberg, Philip
Lieberman, Susan (Abel)
Lipper, Joanna
Little, Cynthia
Livingston, Gordon (S.)
Lofas, Jeannette
Lopreato, Joseph
Louv, Richard
Lukken, Miriam
Lynn, Adele B.
Mack, Dana
Mackey, Richard A.
Maital, Sharone L(evow)
Malone, Susan (Mary)
Marcell, Jacqueline
Marland, Hilary
Marquardt, Elizabeth
Martin, Judith
Maser, Shari
Mathabane, Mark
Mayer, Bob
Mayes, Linda C(arol)
McCall, Robert B.
McCarthy, Sherri N.
McCarty, Hanoch
Mccrory, Donald P(eter)
McCullough, Donald W.
McGraw, Phillip C.
McKee, Steve
McLain, Paula
McMillen, Sally G(regory)
McMullan, Margaret
Medved, Diane
Melville, Arabella
Merrell, Susan Scarf
Meyer, Donald J.
Millner, Denene
Minar, Barbra (Goodyear)
Minuchin, Salvador
Moore, Harold G(regory)
Moore, Kay
Moore, Louis
Moore-Colyer, Richard
Mornell, Pierre
Morris, Deborah
Morris, Desmond
Mountrose, Phillip
Muchmore, Jo Ann
Murkoff, Heidi Eisenberg
Muuss, Rolf Eduard
Nagel, Paul C(hester)

Castle, Kathryn
Cave, Eric M.
Caws, Peter (James)
Cerf, Muriel
Chaney, Edward (Paul de Gruyter)
Chapple, John Alfred Victor
Chase, Steven
Cherry, Mark J.
Chitham, Edward (Harry Gordon)
Chorbajian, Levon
Christensen, Kate
Cimino, Richard P.
Clabough, Casey Howard
Clark, David Lindsey
Clark, Kelly James
Clarke, Lee
Clubbe, John L(ouis) E(dwin)
Cochran, Gregory
Coffey, John Robert David
Cogliano, Francis D.
Cohen, Avner
Cohen, Henry
Colalillo-Kates, Isabella
Cole, Thomas R(ichard)
Coleman, James A.
Colin, Chris
Conley, Carolyn A.
Constantelos, Demetrios J.
Conway, Jill Ker
Cooper, Adam G.
Cornis-Pope, Marcel (H.)
Coyne, Michael
Creighton, Margaret S.
Crenshaw, James L.
Crow, Bill
Crowder, George
Cunliffe, Barry
Curl, James Stevens
Dacey, Austin
Daly, M(artin) W.
Danto, Elizabeth Ann
Dassanowsky, Robert
Davidoff, Leonore
Davies, Martin L.
Davis, (Elvis) Clark
de Gruchy, John W(esley)
DeGrazia, Emilio
Del Caro, Adrian
Dettmar, Kevin J(ohn)
   H(offmann)
DeVincent-Hayes, Nan
Di Gregorio, Mario A(urelio
   Umberto)
Dillingham, William B.
Dolan, Frederick Michael
Dolin, Sharon
Dolis, John
Dombrowski, Daniel A.
Donald, Diana
Donaldson, Gary A.
Donleavy, J(ames) P(atrick)
Dooley, Allan C(harles)
Downes, Jeremy M.
Downie, R(obert) S(ilcock)
Downs, Dorothy
Doyle, Dennis M(ichael)
Doyle, Robert Charles

Dreyer, Elizabeth A.
Dutton, Michael R.
Dutton, Paul Edward
Earle, Jonathan
Earnshaw, Steven
Ebadi, Shirin
Edmunds, R(ussell) David
Edwards, Clive D.
Ehrman, John
Eisen, Sydney
Eisiminger, Sterling (Skip)
Elie, Paul
Elliott, Melinda
Ellis, Keith
Elukin, Jonathan
Emanuel, James A(ndrew)
Emery, Tom
Engel, Joel
Engell, James
English, Barbara (Anne)
English, John A(lan)
Eno, Will
Esterhammer, Angela
Euba, Femi
Fandrich, Ina Johanna
Feis, William B.
Felstiner, Mary Lowenthal
Fetters, Thomas T.
Fieldhouse, David K(enneth)
Figes, Orlando (G.)
Fink, Sheri
Finlay, Peter (Warren)
Fischer, Klaus P.
Fischer, Steven R.
Fisdel, Steven A.
Fishkin, Shelley Fisher
Fishman, Lisa
Fletcher, John Walter James
Fleurant, Gerdès
Fontes, Manuel D(a Costa)
Fontes, Montserrat
Foster, Brooke Lea
Franklin, Jane (Morgan)
Fraser, Ronald (Angus)
Freccero, Carla
Freeman, Daniel E(van)
Freeman, Jo
Frey, Julia (Bloch)
Friedrich, Paul
Fritzell, Peter A(lgren)
Frueh, Joanna
Fuchs, Rachel G(innis)
Fudge, Erica
Furdell, Elizabeth Lane
Gaines, Thomas A.
Gallagher, Susan VanZanten
Gallo, Patrick J.
Gallo, Rubén
Gans, Eric L.
Gardella, Robert (P.)
Garrett, Martin
Gemunden, Gerd
Gerlach, Larry R(euben)
Gibbs, Anthony Matthews
Gibran, Daniel K.
Gibson, Alan
Gil, Moshe

Gill, Sam D.
Glatthaar, Joseph T(homas)
Glenn, Cheryl
Gliserman, Martin
Gold, Hazel
Goldberg, Jacob
Goldman, Arnold (Melvyn)
Golomb, Jacob
Gonzalez, Alexander G.
Goodman, Lizbeth (L.)
Goodman, Richard
Goody, John R(ankine)
Gordon, April A.
Gordon, Lewis Ricardo
Gordon, W. Terrence
Gorham, Deborah
Gorup, Radmila J(ovanovi)
Goshen-Gottstein, Esther
Gottlieb, Beatrice
Gottlieb, Freema (Peninah)
Gourgouris, Stathis
Grainger, John D(ownie)
Grant, Pete
Green, Arthur
Green, Peter (Morris)
Green, R. P. H.
Greenfeld, Liah
Greetham, David
Gregor, Neil
Grisso, Thomas
Gross, Ernie
Guardino, Peter
Hadas, Rachel
Haddad, Gladys
Hagerty, Barbara Bradley
Hagy, James William
Hallwas, John E.
Halperin, Joan Ungersma
Hamamoto, Darrell Y.
Hamlyn, D(avid) W(alter)
Hardy, John Philips
Hardy, Michael C.
Harlow, Michael
Harris, Fredrick C.
Harrison, Brian (Howard)
Hartman, Geoffrey H.
Hartman, Saidiya V.
Harwood, John
Hauptman, Laurence Marc
Hawkins, Anne Hunsaker
Hay, William Anthony
Hearn, Chester G.
Hennessey, Thomas W.
Henry, Gordon D.
Heppenheimer, Thomas A.
Herman, Barbara
Hick, John (Harwood)
Hill, Harvey
Hinchman, Lewis P(atrick)
Hodes, Martha
Hoff, Joan
Hogue, James K.
Holt, James Clarke
Hope, Marjorie (Cecelia)
Horlick, Allan S.
Hoy, David Couzens
Hoyle, Carolyn

Hunnicutt, Benjamin Kline
Hunt, Robert (William Gainer)
Hussey, Mark
Hutcheon, Linda
Hyam, Ronald
Inge, M. Thomas
Innis, Robert E(dward)
Iserson, Kenneth Victor
Isitt, Larry R.
Jackson, Mark
Jackson, William J(oseph)
Jacob, Merle (Lynn)
Jager, Eric
James, Alan
James, Caryn
Jarausch, Konrad H(ugo)
Jarvis, William E.
Jeffreys, Derek S.
Jirgens, Karl (E.)
Johnson, Donald Leslie
Johnson, Neil L.
Jones, Gayl
Jones, Madison
Jones, Norman (Leslie)
Jones, William B(ryan)
Judge, Harry George
Kamerick, Kathleen
Katagiri, Yasuhiro
Katz, Esther
Katz, Sanford N.
Kearns, Josie
Keating, AnaLouise
Keele, Alan (Frank)
Keil, Roger
Kelling, Hans Wilhelm
Kenney, Padraic (Jeremiah)
Ker, James
Ketner, Kenneth Laine
Kheirabadi, Masoud
King, Iain
Kinney, Arthur F.
Kitch, Sally L.
Klappert, Peter
Klein, Anne Carolyn
Klempner, Mark
Klingenstein, Susanne
Knox, George
Koehn, Peter H.
Koerner, Joseph Leo
Komporaly, Jozefina
Kostelanetz, Richard (Cory)
Kraft, Robert A(lan)
Kramp, Michael
Krystal, Arthur
Kuhn, Robert Lawrence
Kuper, Adam (Jonathan)
Lackey, Michael
LaDow, Beth
Lal, Brij V.
Lamb, Marion J.
Lamb, Wally
Lambert, Page
Lamphear, John
Langendoen, Donald Terence
Langley, Lester D(anny)
Laroche, Loretta
Lash, N. L. A.

Index To Writing Categories

Taylor, Joe
Taylor, John Russell
Taylor, Quintard
Thaden, Barbara Z.
Thiel, Diane
Thompson, Harry F.
Thomson, George Henry
Thornton, Bruce S.
Till, Nicholas
Torsney, Cheryl B.
Townley, Wyatt
Treat, James
Tsomo, Karma Lekshe
Tsutsui, William M.
Tuman, Myron C(hester)
Turner, Charles C.
Tuttle, William McCullough
Tyerman, Christopher
Tyrrell, Ian R(obert)
Tysdahl, Bjorn Johan
Tyson, Lois (M.)
Unger, Peter K(enneth)
Valente, Claire
Vallbona, Rima de
Van Ginneken, Jaap
van Ruler, J. A.
Vaughan, Megan
Velkley, Richard L.
Vendler, Helen (Hennessy)
Villamil, Victoria Etnier
Vincent, John (Russell)
Viola, Lynne
Vogt, Henri Hans Mikael
Waddington, Patrick (Haynes)
Wadell, Paul J(oseph)
Wainwright, Geoffrey
Waldman, Harry
Warner, Brad
Warren, Karen J.
Warren, Louis S.
Wasserstein, Bernard (Mano
    Julius)
Watson, Irene
Weiner, Marc A.
Weiner, Susan
Weinstein, Philip M.
Weir, Ronald Blackwood
Weiss, Raymond L.
Welch, Kathleen E(thel)
Wellington, Jean Susorney
Wernick, Andrew (Lee)
Weschler, Lawrence
Whelan, Ruth
White, Linda (Louise)
Whiting, Cécile
Williams, James C.
Williams, Stanley Tookie
Wilson, Barrie A.
Wininger, Kathleen J.
Wirzba, Norman
Wohlgelernter, Maurice
Wolf, Reva
Wolff, Cynthia Griffin
Wolverton, Robert E.
Wood, Anthony C.
Woolhouse, Roger
Wright, Alexis

Wright, C. D.
Wright, Donald R(ichard)
Wu, Chin-Tao
Wu, Harry
Wyatt-Brown, Anne M(arbury)
Wynyard, Robin (Norman)
Yancey, George
Yarbrough, Stephen R.
Young, James E.
Young, Margaret Labash
Yu, Anthony C.
Zaknic, Ivan
Zegura, Elizabeth Chesney
Zimmerman, Earl
Zuidervaart, Lambert

Industrial Relations

Abdel-Magid, Isla m Mu ammad
Adams, Roy J(oseph)
Alessandra, Tony
Arnold, Guy
Barnett, Correlli (Douglas)
Bealey, Frank (William)
Beynon, Huw
Bina, Cyrus
Boyett, Joseph H.
Casey, Don
Clark, Paul F.
Cohen, Cary
Cones, John W.
Darlington, Ralph
Eilon, Samuel
Foer, Franklin
Fraser, Harry
Fraser, W. Hamish
Friedland, William H(erbert)
Gabor, Andrea (Anna Gisela)
Gold, Michael Evan
Greco, Lidia
Grey, Jerry
Guttmann, Robert
Harris, Thomas (E.)
Hayter, Teresa
Hirsch, Seev
Honerkamp, Nicholas
Honri, Peter
Hopkins, George Emil
Hunt, Edward H.
Lateiner, Donald
LeBoeuf, Michael
Leider, Richard J.
Linder, Marc
Locke, Robert R.
Lowenstein, Michael W.
Lundman, Richard J.
Magrath, Allan J.
Maloka, Eddy Tshidiso
Marsa, Linda J.
Martin, Roderick
Matson, Cathy
Matsumura, Takao
McBride, Stephen
McMullen, Jeremy
Milne, Seumas
Mokyr, Joel

Mortimer, James Edward
Nelson, Daniel
O'Brien, D(enis) P(atrick)
O'Regan, Valerie R.
Pallis, Athanasios A.
Panitch, Leo (Victor)
Patten, Thomas H.
Peters, Rick
Presnell, Barbara
Pun, Ngai
Quigley, Declan
Schecter, Darrow
Schell, Jim
Schendel, Dan
Scoville, James Griffin
Sheridan, Thomas
Shultz, George P(ratt)
Sims, Henry P.
Sloane, Peter J(ames)
Slomp, Hans
Stening, Bruce W.
Susman, Gerald I.
Thompson, Gregory Lee
Turner, Lowell
Von Tunzelmann, G(eorge)
    N(icholas)
Walton, Mary
Warmington, William Allan
Welsh, Frank (Reeson)
Yudelman, David
Zook, Matthew A.
Zysman, John

Information Science/Computers

Aaland, Mikkel
Abramson, Bruce
Aguolu, Christian Chukwunedu
Alfino, Mark (R.)
Alkiviades, Alkis
Allen, Roberta
Alshawi, Hiyan
Ambler, Scott W.
Anderson, James G.
Apter, Michael John
Arnold, Kenneth L.
Baker, Christopher W.
Barfield, Woodrow
Baxter, Stephen
Benson, Frank Atkinson
Bentley, Peter J.
Bergin, Thomas J.
Berinstein, Paula
Bernstein, Mark
Bhagat, Chetan
Blatner, David
Blum, Bruce I(van)
Boczkowski, Pablo J.
Boden, Margaret A(nn)
Bookstaber, Richard
Borko, Harold
Bouton, Gary David
Bowman, David
Boyle, Thomas A.
Braga, Newton C.

Brooks, Rodney (A.)
Brown, Robert G(oodell)
Buderi, Robert
Bundesen, Lynne
Campbell-Kelly, Martin
Ceruzzi, Paul Edward
Chabris, Christopher F.
Chorafas, Dimitris N.
Clark, Andy
Clements, Alan
Cockerill, A(rthur) W(illiam)
Cohen, Daniel J.
Cohen, Norman J.
Cornell, Gary
Crevier, Daniel
Cronin, Mary J.
Crossman, William
Darnay, Arsen J.
Dasgupta, Subrata
Davidsen, Susanna L.
Davis, Robin W(orks)
Day, A(rthur) Colin
de Bono, Edward (Francis
    Charles)
de Kerckhove, Derrick
deBry, Roger K.
DeGeorge, Richard T(homas)
Dery, Mark
des Rivières, Jim
Dewdney, A(lexander) K(eewatin)
Dibbell, Julian
Dooley, Brian J.
Duntemann, Jeff
Duntemann, Jeff
Dyson, Esther
Edgar, Stacey L.
Fara, Patricia
Fenten, D. X.
Ferrell, John S.
Finley, Michael
Fites, Philip
Flickenger, Rob
Flood, Joe
Foust, Jeff
Frakes, William B.
Franklet, Duane
Freedman, David H.
Furino, Antonio
Gagné, Marcel
Garrison, Bruce
Gasser, Urs
Gelernter, David (Hillel)
Gemmell, Jim
Gerstein, Daniel M.
Goerner, Sally J.
Goldstein, Larry Joel
Gonzales, Laurence
Gottschall, Edward M(aurice)
Gray, Chris Hables
Greif, Karen F.
Grey, Jerry
Griffith, Jim
Gunetti, Daniele
Hafner, Katie
Haga, Enoch John
Hämäläinen, Pertti (Olavi)

inspirational/Motivational
Literature-*cont.*

inspirational/Motivational
Literature-*cont.*

inspirational/Motivational
Literature-*cont.*

inspirational/Motivational
Literature-*cont.*

Dickson, Athol
Diski, Jenny
Dockrey, Karen
Dwyer, Richard A.
Easum, William M.
Egan, Ken
Ehrler, Brenda
Ellis, Gwen
Emecheta, (Florence Onye) Buchi
Engstrom, Elizabeth
Epstein, Mikhail N.
Erickson, Steve
Erre, Mike
Estleman, Loren D.
Euba, Femi
Ezell, Lee
Fallon, Peter
Fanthorpe, R(obert) Lionel
Fisher, Roy
Fleischman, Paul
Fleischman, Paul R.
Foreman, George
Fornés, Maria Irene
Foust, J'aimé L.
Frame, J. Davidson
Frazee, Randy
Fritz, Robert
Frueh, Joanna
Fuller, Charles
Gabhart, Ann Houchin
Gallagher, Winifred
Gateley, Edwina
Gekoski, Rick
Gelek, Ngawang
Gellman, Marc
Gerber, Merrill Joan
Gilman, Andrew D.
Giovanni, Nikki
Glener, Doug
Gonzalez, Alexander G.
Grabbe, Crockett L(ane)
Graham, Billy
Gran, Peter
Greeley, Andrew (Moran)
Gregory, Valiska
Griggs, Vanessa Davis
Grow, L(ynn) M(erle)
Gulbekian, Sevak E(dward)
Hainsworth, Peter (R. J.)
Haley, Gail E(inhart)
Halpin, Marlene
Hansen, Mark Victor
Harris, Carla A.
Harrison, Sarah
Harvey, John
Harvor, Elisabeth
Hassler, Christine
Hayden, C. J.
Hayman, Carol Bessent
Hearn, Chester G.
Hichwa, John S.
Hightower, Lynn S.
Hilton, Joni
Hinds, P(atricia) Mignon
Hinson, E. Glenn
Hoban, Russell

Hockensmith, Sean M.
Hoff, B. J.
Hollingsworth, Mary
Holloway, Richard (Frederick)
Holmes, Megan
Hughes, Shirley
Hutchins, Pat
Intrator, Sam M.
Isaacs, Ronald (Howard)
Jacobs, Jonnie
Jhabvala, Ruth Prawer
Johnson, Cait
Johnson, Neil L.
Johnson, Sherrie
Johnson, Victoria
Johnston, Joan
Jones, Laurie Beth
Karon, Jan
Kazantzis, Judith
Keating, AnaLouise
Keefauver, Larry
Kegan, Robert G.
Keillor, Garrison (Edward)
Kelley, Tom
Kelly, Clint
Kelman, Judith (Ann)
Kemp, Gene
Kent, Carol
Kerner, Fred
Kidd, Sue Monk
Kimura, Margaret
Kincaid, Jamaica
King, Carol Soucek
Kinkade, Thomas
Kinsella, Thomas
Kirkwood, Annie
Kolpen, Jana (Fayne)
Komp, Diane M.
Kornfield, Jack
Kottler, Jeffrey (A.)
Kowalski, Gary A.
Lambert, Page
Landrum, Gene N.
Larkin, Joan
Le Guin, Ursula K(roeber)
LeCompte, N(ancy) Jane
Lee, Dennis (Beynon)
Leeman, Richard W.
Leidner, Gordon
Leonard, Elmore
Lewis, Sherry
Liebler, M. L.
Lief, Judith L.
Lombardo, Mary A.
Long, D. Stephen
Lotz, Anne Graham
Lucado, Max (Lee)
Lumpkin, Aaron
Machowicz, Richard J.
MacLaine, Shirley
Maclean, Rory
MacLeod, Ken
Mainone, Robert Franklin
Malam, John
Malvasi, Mark G.
Mann, John David

Mansfield, Nick
Margulies, Donald
Masson, Sophie
Maxwell, John C.
Mayfield, Terry L.
Mayo, C(atherine) M(ansell)
Mazzeno, Laurence W.
McBrien, Richard P(eter)
McCarty, Hanoch
McDonald, Ian
McEntyre, Marilyn Chandler
McIlvoy, Kevin
McKenna, Patrick J.
McNeill, Christine
McPhee, Martha (A.)
Measham, Donald Charles
Menache, Sophia
Minar, Barbra (Goodyear)
Minter, David Lee
Mitson, Eileen N(ora)
Monroe, Mary
Montague, John (Patrick)
Moore, Carey Armstrong
Moore, Louis
Moore, Stephanie Perry
Muniz, Olga M.
Murphey, Cecil B(laine)
Nappa, Mike
Navarra, Tova
Neck, Christopher P.
Nemec, James
Neuhouser, Frederick
Noble, Kathleen
Norris, Kathleen
O'Connor, Patricia W.
O'Faolain, Julia
O'Malley, Vincent (J.)
Opie, Iona
Orr, Gregory (Simpson)
Paquet, Laura Byrne
Parfitt, Will
Pastan, Linda
Patterson, Horace L.
Pearcey, Nancy
Peterson, Eugene H.
Pfeiffer, Janet (B.)
Pickard, Tom
Pierce, David
Pilling, Christopher (Robert)
Pritchard, Ray
Quilter, Deborah
Reed, Philip (Chandler)
Reinstedt, Randall A.
Rendell, Ruth
Renee, Janina
Robbins, Tom
Rosner, Bob
Rossant, Colette
Rubens, Jim M.
Rubinsky, Holley
Rule, Ann
Rupp, Joyce
Saloff, Jamie L.
Salzberg, Sharon
Sanna, Ellyn
Schaef, Anne Wilson

Schulze, Dallas
Seale, Alan
Secretan, Lance H. K.
Shaffer, Peter (Levin)
Shanley, Mary Kay
Shapiro, Eileen C.
Shapiro, Rami M.
Sheeler, Jim
Shepard, Sam
Sherrer, Quin(ton M.)
Shirley, Frances A.
Siggins, Lorna
Silverman, Robin L(andew)
Simonetta, Joseph R.
Škvoreck , Josef
Smith, J. Walker
Smith, Pamela (A.)
Smith, Steven
Stallard, Michael L.
Stewart, Mary (Florence Elinor)
Stratton, Allan
Stravinskas, Peter M. J.
Sutton, R. Anderson
Swope, Sam
Taylor, Henry
Tenbrook, Gretchen W.
Thomas, Audrey (Grace)
Thomas, Velma Maia
Topek, Susan Remick
Townsend, Sue
Trawick, Leonard M.
Treier, Daniel J.
Tropman, John E.
Truman, Ruth
Urch, Elizabeth
Vaughn, Ellen Santilli
Voss, Sarah (Henderson)
Wachsberger, Ken(neth)
Waite, Michael P(hillip)
Walton, Mary
Weldon, Fay
Wells (Dimenstein), Catherine
Whalin, W. Terry
Wheeler, Deborah (Jean Ross)
Wheldon, David
White, Franklin
Wile, Mary Lee
Wilkinson, Bruce H.
Wilkinson, Tracy
Wilson, Brandon
Winter, David Brian
Wise, Robert L.
Wolfman, Judy
Wong, Janet S.
Woodhouse, S(usan) T.
Wright, N. T(om)
Wright, Vinita Hampton
Wubbels, Lance
Zweifel, Thomas D.

Institutions/Organizations

Abt, Jeffrey
Allen, John E(lliston)
Bardwick, Judith M(arcia)

Intellectual History-*cont.*

Priest, Stephen
Pyenson, Lewis (Robert)
Rabb, Theodore K.
Rajan, Tilottama
Rapson, Richard L.
Ravitz, Abe (Carl)
Redfield, James
Reiss, Edward
Rickman, Hans Peter
Rigby, Nigel
Roark, Dallas M.
Roberts, Francis X.
Roger, Philippe
Root-Bernstein, Michèle
Rorty, Amélie Oksenberg
Roston, Murray
Roth, Norman
Rousseau, George S.
Roy, Donald H.
Rubin, Joan Shelley
Rudrum, Alan (William)
Ruotsila, Markku
Sandoz, (George) Ellis
Sax, Boria
Schofield, John A.
Schofield, Robert E(dwin)
Schreiber, Le Anne
Schrift, Alan D.
Schwarz, Daniel R(oger)
Sciabarra, Chris Matthew
Screech, M(ichael) A(ndrew)
Shakeri, Khosrow
Shanley, Mary L(yndon)
Shapiro, Judith
Shawver, Lois
Sheldon, Garrett Ward
Silver, Peter Rhoads
Skinner, Quentin (Robert Duthie)
Smith, Barbara Herrnstein
Smith, David Livingstone
Smoley, Richard
Smyth, William J.
Spretnak, Charlene
Stabile, Don
Stachel, John Jay
Stafford, Fiona (Jane)
Stephens, William Peter
Stevenson, Louise L.
Stout, Harry S.
Suleiman, Susan Rubin
Sullivan, Brad
Swett, Pamela E.
Talbot, Emile J.
Teja, Jesus F(rancisco) de la
Temple, Robert (Kyle Grenville)
Thaden, Barbara Z.
Thomas, Keith (Vivian)
Thompson, Thomas L.
Thompson, William Irwin
Tobias, Michael (Charles)
Toker, Leona
Turner, Marjorie Shepherd
Van Ginneken, Jaap
van Ruler, J. A.
Vitz, Robert C.
Von Ward, Paul
Walker, Paul E(rnest)

Intellectual History-*cont.*

Walker, R. B. J.
Warren, Louis S.
Waters, David Watkin
Weber, Katharine
Weiner, Marc A.
Weintraub, Stanley
Wendling, Ronald C(harles)
Wernick, Andrew (Lee)
White, Morton (Gabriel)
Whitelaw, Nancy
Wolf, Reva
Yarbrough, Stephen R.
Young, John
Zack, Naomi
Zegura, Elizabeth Chesney
Zukav, Gary

International Relations/Current Affairs

Abraham, Spencer
Abshire, David Manker
AbuKhalil, As'ad
Accinelli, Robert
Adamec, Ludwig W.
Adkin, Mark
Aggarwal, Ravina
Ahmed, Akbar S(alahudin)
Al-Azm, Sadik J.
Al-Marayati, Abid A(min)
Allason, Rupert (William Simon)
Anglin, Douglas G(eorge)
Applebaum, Anne
Appleton, Sheldon Lee
Arnold, Guy
Aruri, Naseer H.
Ascherson, (Charles) Neal
Avant, Deborah D.
Ayres, E. C.
Bacik, Ivana
Bahgat, Gawdat G.
Bailey, Norman (Alishan)
Bain, Kenneth (Ross)
Banisadr, Abol-Hassan
Bar-Joseph, Uri
Bareham, Lindsey
Barnaby, Charles Frank
Barnett, Michael N.
Barry, Tom
Baughman, John Russell
Baumann, Carol Edler
Bavly, Dan A(braham)
Baylis, John
Bayne, Nicholas (Peter)
Beck, Robert J.
Beckel, Bob
Becker, Jasper
Bee, Ronald J.
Beers, Burton Floyd
Bellush, Bernard
Benedict, Helen
Bennett, Edward M.
Bennett, Georgette
Bercovitch, Jacob
Bergeijk, Peter A.G. van

International Relations/Current Affairs-*cont.*

Berghahn, Volker R.
Berridge, G. R.
Bialer, Uri
Biddiss, Michael Denis
Biro, Andrew William
Blackmer, Donald L. M.
Blackwell, Joyce
Blackwill, Robert D.
Bledsoe, Timothy
Blight, James G.
Blitzer, Wolf
Bloomfield, Lincoln P(almer)
Blouet, Olwyn M(ary)
Blustein, Paul
Boraine, Alex(ander)
Borovik, Genrikh (Aviezerovich)
Bosdorff, Denise M.
Bosworth, R(ichard) J(ames) B(oon)
Boutros-Ghali, Boutros
Boyd, Carl
Bracey, Christopher Alan
Bradlee, Benjamin (Crowninshield)
Braunthal, Gerard
Braveboy-Wagner, Jacqueline Anne
Brecher, Michael
Brenner, Philip (Joseph)
Brett, Donna W(hitson)
Brightman, Carol
Bromke, Adam
Brooks, Stephen G.
Brown, Brian A.
Brysk, Alison
Brzezinski, Zbigniew (Kasimierz)
Buddensieg, Tilmann
Bugajski, Janusz
Burgess, Stephen F(ranklin)
Burk, Kathleen
Butow, Robert J. C.
Calvert, Peter (Anthony Richard)
Cao, Lan
Carlton, David
Cassels, Alan
Castaneda, Jorge G.
Champagne, Duane (Willard)
Chang, Maria Hsia
Chanoff, David
Charny, Israel Wolf
Chatfield, E. Charles
Childs, David (Haslam)
Chomsky, (Avram) Noam
Cirincione, Joseph
Clapham, Christopher S.
Clark, Andrew F.
Clark, Eric
Cleary, Matthew R.
Clemens, Walter C.
Cockburn, Patrick
Cohen, Lenard J.
Cohen, Michael A.
Cohen, Raymond
Cohrs, Patrick O.
Cole, Wayne S.
Collinson, Sarah

International Relations/Current Affairs-*cont.*

Collison, Kerry B(oyd)
Compton, James V(incent)
Conquest, (George) Robert (Acworth)
Conteh-Morgan, Earl
Cooper, Richard Newell
Cotman, John Walton
Cowie, Hamilton Russell
Cox, Richard (Hubert Francis)
Cranfield, Ingrid
Creswell, Michael
Cross, Frank B.
Crozier, Brian
Daalder, Ivo H.
Dale, Richard
Dallek, Robert
Dalyell, Tam
Darwish, Adel
Dassanowsky, Robert
Dauvergne, Peter
Davies, Charles E.
de Jouvenel, Hugues Alain
Deane-Drummond, Anthony (John)
Deats, Richard L.
Deng, Yong
Dibua, Jeremiah I.
Dikötter, Frank
Dimbleby, Jonathan
Dobson, Alan P.
Dougherty, James E(dward)
Dowty, Alan K.
Dukert, Joseph M(ichael)
Dunaway, Finis
Edelheit, Abraham J.
Edmisten, Patricia Taylor
El-Shazly, Nadia El-Sayed
Elegant, Robert (Sampson)
Emmerij, Louis (Johan)
Engel, Richard
Erkkila, Betsy
Falk, Stanley Lawrence
Farnsworth, Clyde
Faust, John R.
Feifer, George
Feigon, Lee
Finstad, Suzanne
Fisher, Roger (Dummer)
Flamhaft, Ziva
Foot, Michael Richard Daniell
Frank, Charles R(aphael)
Frankel, Glenn
Fravel, M. Taylor
Freeman, Charles Wellman
Frey, Julia (Bloch)
Friedberg, Maurice
Friedman, Thomas L(oren)
Galeotti, Mark
Gammer, Moshe
Garthoff, Raymond L(eonard)
Garton Ash, Timothy
Gaubatz, Kurt Taylor
Geldenhuys, Deon
Geyer, Georgie Anne
Girling, John (Lawrence Scott)
Glees, Anthony

International Relations/Current Affairs-*cont.*

Rothstein, Hy S.
Rubin, Barnett R(ichard)
Rubin, Barry
Rumer, Boris
Ruotsila, Markku
Russell, Jeremy (Longmore)
Russett, Bruce Martin
Sakamoto, Yoshikazu
Sanders, Alan J. K.
Sassen, Saskia
Sathasivam, Kanishkan
Savage, Sean J.
Savir, Uri
Scalapino, Robert Anthony
Scharf, Michael P(aul)
Schecter, Darrow
Schell, Orville (Hickok)
Schelling, Thomas C.
Schwartz, Stephen (Alfred)
Schweizer, Karl W.
Scipes, Kim
Scott, P(aul) H(enderson)
Seib, Gerald
Shafer, Byron E.
Shakeri, Khosrow
Shapiro, Robert Y.
Shapiro, Sidney
Shaw, Martin
Sheehan, Neil
Shemesh, Haim
Shepherd, George W.
Sher, Gilead
Shih, Chih-yu
Shipler, David K(arr)
Shlaim, Avi
Shogan, Colleen J.
Shorrock, Tim
Short, Kathy G(nagey)
Sibley, Katherine A. S.
Sick, Gary G(ordon)
Sicker, Martin
Silverburg, Sanford R.
Simons, Thomas W(inston)
Skeet, Ian
Skolnikoff, Eugene B.
Skoug, Kenneth N.
Smith, Arthur L.
Smith, Hedrick (Laurence)
Smyth, Denis
Solomon, Richard H(arvey)
Sørensen, Georg
Spanger, Hans-Joachim
Spar, Debora L.
St. John, Ronald Bruce
Staar, Richard F.
Steans, Jill A.
Stern, Paul C(linton)
Stopford, John M(orton)
Stout, Chris E.
Stronach, Bruce
Sturmer, Michael
Stützle, Walther
Sullivan, Michael Joseph
Sum, Ngai-Ling
Symynkywicz, Jeffrey B(ruce)
Taft, John (Thomas)

International Relations/Current Affairs-*cont.*

Taras, Raymond (C.)
Taylor, Robert
Thomas, A. M.
Thompson, Kenneth W(infred)
Tikhomirov, Vladimir I.
Tripp, Charles R(ees) H(oward)
Tulchin, Joseph S.
Turner, Frederick C.
Urban, Mark
Urquhart, Brian Edward
Urwin, Derek W(illiam)
Van Ginneken, Jaap
van Tuyll, Hubert P.
Vandenbroucke, Lucien S.
Verluise, Pierre
Vincent, John James
Viorst, Milton
Vital, David
Vogel, Ezra F.
Walker, Kenneth Roland
Walker, R. B. J.
Walt, Stephen M.
Walton, Richard J(ohn)
Waltz, Kenneth N.
Warner, Daniel
Wasserstein, Bernard (Mano Julius)
Weart, Spencer R(ichard)
Webber, Mark (Alan)
Weber, Ralph E.
Weber, Thomas
Weinstein, Allen
Weintraub, Sidney
Weiss, Thomas G.
Weschler, Lawrence
Westad, Odd Arne
Western, Jon W.
Wettig, Gerhard
Wicker, Brian John
Wildman, Steven S.
Willbanks, James H.
Willrich, Mason
Wilsford, David
Wilson, Andrew
Wilson, Wesley M.
Wolfers, Michael
Woods, Lawrence T(imothy)
Woolley, Peter J.
Wright, Clifford A.
Wright, Theodore Paul
Wu, Harry
Yang, Dali L.
Yarshater, Ehsan (Ollah)
Young, Elizabeth
Young, Margaret Labash
Young, Robert A.
Zawodny, J(anusz) K.
Zelikow, Philip
Zweifel, Thomas D.

Language/Linguistics

Adamson, Robin
Ainsworth, Patricia

Language/Linguistics-*cont.*

Alarcon, Francisco X.
Alber, Charles J.
Algeo, John
Allan, Keith
Alleyne, Mervyn C.
Alshawi, Hiyan
Ammer, Christine (Parker)
Anderson, Mark M.
Apple, Hope
Apter, Emily (S.)
Arens, Katherine (Marie)
Arnold, A(lbert) James
Asher, R. E.
Ashley, Leonard R. N.
Auger, C(harles) P(eter)
Baker, Hugh D(avid) R(oberts)
Balutansky, Kathleen M(arie)
Barber, E(lizabeth) J. W(ayland)
Barber, Karin
Barber, Katherine
Bardige, Betty S.
Barnette, Martha
Barnhart, David K.
Baron, Naomi S(usan)
Barreto, Amilcar Antonio
Barrett, Buckley Barry
Barzun, Jacques
Basso, Keith H(amilton)
Batchelor, R. E.
Bawcutt, Priscilla (June)
Beardsley, Theodore S.
Beeman, William O.
Bell, Susan
Bellos, David
Ben-Rafael, Eliezer
Berger, Charles R.
Berger, Thomas (Louis)
Berman, Jeffrey
Bertling, Tom
Betts, Clive
Bickerton, David M.
Bien, Peter
Bierhorst, John
Bizzell, Patricia (Lynn)
Blake, Norman Francis
Blamires, Harry
Blank, G(regory) Kim
Block, Cathy Collins
Bloom, Paul
Bolles, Edmund Blair
Bond, George C(lement)
Borko, Harold
Bosmajian, Haig
Boullata, Issa J.
Bovaird, Anne E(lizabeth)
Brandt, Deborah
Brayfield, Celia
Briggs, Ward W(right)
Britton, Celia (Margaret)
Brockington, J(ohn) L(eonard)
Brooks, Joanna
Brosnahan, L(eonard) F(rancis)
Buccini, Stefania
Buhner, Stephen Harrod
Burkhardt, Joanna M.
Burton, Betsy
Busby, Brian

Language/Linguistics-*cont.*

Byrne, Robert
Cachia, Pierre (Jacques Elie)
Cairns, Scott
Calder, Nigel (David Ritchie)
Cannon, Garland
Carter, Harold
Casagrande, June M.
Castle, Linda
Castor, Helen
Cazden, Courtney B(orden)
Cevasco, G(eorge) A(nthony)
Chafe, Wallace
Chalker, Sylvia
Charnon-Deutsch, Lou
Chomsky, (Avram) Noam
Christ, Henry I(rvine)
Ciaravino, Helene
Coffey, Michael
Cohen, Thomas V.
Colish, Marcia L(illian)
Comfort, Philip W(esley)
Confiant, Raphaël
Copeland, Gary A.
Cordeiro, Patricia (A.)
Cornis-Pope, Marcel (H.)
Corten, Irina H.
Coulmas, Florian
Cowser, Bob
Cranfield, Ingrid
Crystal, David
Dahlen, Beverly
Dandridge, Rita B(ernice)
Darnell, Regna (Diebold)
Dascal, Marcelo
Dassanowsky, Robert
Davis, Robin W(orks)
de Costa, Elena M.
DeCosta-Willis, Miriam
Deletant, Dennis
Demers, Patricia
Dervaes, Claudine
di Lella, Alexander Anthony
Divakaruni, Chitra Banerjee
Djwa, Sandra (Ann)
Doll, Mary A(swell)
Donker, Marjorie
Donleavy, J(ames) P(atrick)
Donoghue, Mildred R(ansdorf)
Doss, Erika
Dow, James
Dunn, Mark (Rodney)
Eaton, Trevor (Michael William)
Eble, Connie
Echeruo, Michael
Ehret, Christopher
Eisiminger, Sterling (Skip)
Elegant, Robert (Sampson)
Elgin, Suzette Haden
Ellis, Mark (Karl)
English, Sharon
Eoyang, Eugene Chen
Epstein, Mikhail N.
Erler, Mary C.
Estes, William (Kaye)
Evans, D(avid) Ellis
Everett, Daniel L.
Fausett, David

Shorto, Russell
Silva-Corvalán, Carmen
Silver, Carole G(reta)
Simmons, Cynthia Francene
Simpson, Jacqueline (Mary)
Sisk, David W.
Slade, Leonard A.
Slee, Debora A.
Slee, Vergil N(elson)
Smarandache, Florentin
Smith, Barbara Herrnstein
Smith, Neil(son) V(oyne)
Smith, Nigel
Smith, Paul Julian
Smith-Ankrom, M. E.
Snell, Daniel C.
Snellgrove, Laurence Ernest
Soto, Lourdes Díaz
Spack, Ruth
Spalding, Andrea
Speck, Bruce W.
Spencer, John (Walter)
Spurling, John
Stacks, Don W.
Stainton, Robert J. (H.)
Steinberg, Erwin R.
Steiner, Evgeny
Steiner, George
Steinmetz, Christian
Stephens, Meic
Stillman, Norman A(rthur)
Stivale, Charles J.
Stone, Gerald (Charles)
Strauss, Susan (Elizabeth)
Stromberg, Peter G.
Sutherland, John
Sutton, Dana F.
Svartvik, Jan
Swick, Marly
Tamburri, Anthony Julian
Tarnawsky, Maxim
Temianka, Dan(iel)
Thiel, Diane
Thier, Marlene
Thomas, (Antony) Charles
Thornton, Naoko Fuwa
Tidwell, John Edgar
Tollefson, James W(illiam)
Torsney, Cheryl B.
Trautmann, Thomas R(oger)
Trembath, Don
Tremblay, Florent A.
Tyler, Stephen Albert
Umstatter, Jack
Valesio, Paolo
Van Raden, Kristine
Venolia, Jan(et G.)
Vines, Lois Davis
Visson, Lynn
Waddington, Patrick (Haynes)
Waldman, Harry
Wallace, Vesna A.
Walshe, R(obert) D(aniel)
Walters, Joel
Wardhaugh, Ronald
Warren, Rosanna
Watson, Donald

Waziyatawin
Webster, Len
Weiner, Edmund
Whelan, Ruth
White, Linda (Louise)
Whitson, Kathy J.
Whitton, Kenneth S(tuart)
Wickham, Christopher J.
Williamson, Edwin
Wilson, Wesley M.
Winford, Donald C.
Wolf, Maryanne
Wolverton, Lisa
Wolverton, Robert E.
Wu, Yenna
Wurst, Karin A.
Wyatt-Brown, Anne M(arbury)
Yarbrough, Stephen R.
Yarshater, Ehsan (Ollah)
Young, John
Yudkin, Leon Israel
Zabus, Chantal J.
Ziefle, Helmut W(ilhelm)
Zutshi, Chitralekha

Law

Abraham, Henry J.
Abramson, Leslie W.
Acker, James R.
Adams, Charles
Adler, Stephen J.
Albert, Steve
Albrecht, Steve
Alderman, Ellen
Allen, Ronald J.
Amar, Akhil Reed
Anderson, Elizabeth (S.)
Anglim, Christopher Thomas
Archer of Sandwell
Arnold, A(lbert) James
Asim, Jabari
Asimow, Michael
Auger, C(harles) P(eter)
Avant, Deborah D.
Baderin, Mashood A.
Bailey, F(rancis) Lee
Baird, Vanessa A.
Baker, Mark
Baker, Tom
Barmash, Pamela
Barrett, Anthony A(rthur)
Bartholet, Elizabeth
Bascomb, Neal
Bauman, Richard W.
Beattie, L(inda) Elisabeth
Beck, Robert J.
Bedau, Hugo Adam
Belliotti, Raymond A(ngelo)
Bennett, Merit
Bennett, Robert S.
Bennett, Robert W.
Berg, Manfred
Berger, Thomas R(odney)
Bernstein, Richard B.

Berry, Jeffrey M.
Bessler, John D.
Best, Geoffrey (Francis Andrew)
Bhala, Raj
Biale, Rachel (Korati)
Bickerstaff, Steve
Birnbaum, Jeffrey H.
Biskupic, Joan
Black, Donald
Blakesley, Christopher L.
Blauw, Wim
Blecker, Robert A.
Blumberg, Phillip Irvin
Bogen, David S.
Boies, David
Bok, Derek Curtis
Bollinger, Lee C.
Boniface, William
Bordowitz, Hank
Bork, Robert H(eron)
Botsman, Daniel V.
Bowen, Michael
Boykin, Keith
Bozóki, András
Brannigan, Augustine
Brennan, Frank
Brenner, Reuven
Bright, Myron H.
Brooks, Arthur C.
Brooks, Karl Boyd
Brooks, Roy L(avon)
Brown, V(ictor) I(vy)
Brownlee, David B(ruce)
Buck, Susan J.
Buckley, John (F.)
Budge, Ian
Burroughs, John
Burtch, Brian
Burtchaell, James Tunstead
Byers, Michael
Cadle, Farris W(illiam)
Calavita, Kitty
Callahan, Daniel (J.)
Campbell, Ian Barclay
Campos, Paul F.
Cao, Lan
Caplan, Lincoln
Capon, Robert Farrar
Carlson, David J.
Carlson, Ron
Carnahan, Burrus M.
Carr, Patrick J.
Carrel, Annette Felder
Carrington, Paul D(ewitt)
Carter, Stephen L(isle)
Casto, William R.
Cessario, Romanus
Childs, William R.
Clark, (Carter) Blue
Clark, Andrew
Clark, Anna (K.)
Clark, Gordon L.
Clawson, Rosalee A.
Cleary, Matthew R.
Clement, Mary H.
Clinton, Hillary Rodham
Cohen, Cary

Cohn, Henry S.
Coleman, Mary DeLorse
Collins, Hugh
Collins, Ronald K. L.
Comiskey, Michael
Conant, Michael
Cones, John W.
Cook, Rebecca J.
Cooper, Roger
Cotterrell, Roger (B. M.)
Cowen, Zelman
Cox, Roger (Kenneth)
Crawford, Tad
Cray, Edward
Creeden, Sharon
Cromartie, Alan
Cross, Frank B.
Cullen, Robert (B.)
Cuno, Kenneth M.
D'Amato, Anthony
Daalder, Ivo H.
Damman, Gregory C.
Davies, Piers Anthony David
Davis, Margaret Leslie
Davis, Richard
de Haas, Margaret
DeCrow, Karen
DelFattore, Joan
Derrett, (John) Duncan (Martin)
Dershowitz, Alan M.
Desan, Suzanne
Diamond, Raymond T.
Dillow, Gordon
Dimock, Wai Chee
Dine, Janet
Dirck, Brian R.
Djwa, Sandra (Ann)
Dodd, Christopher J.
Dorman, Michael L.
Dorsen, Norman
Dow, David R.
Downie, Leonard
Drake, Charles D.
Dressler, Joshua
Driesen, David M.
Dubber, Markus Dirk
Duke, Steven B.
Duncan, William (Robert)
Duthu, N. Bruce
Dutton, Donald G.
Edwards, (Kenneth) Martin
Eisenberg, Jon B.
Eisgruber, Christopher L(udwig)
Eldridge, Colin Clifford
Ellis, Evelyn
Ellis, Ralph D.
Engel, Margorie L(ouise)
Epstein, Richard A(llen)
Eskridge, William N(ichol)
Eterno, John A.
Eula, Michael J(ames)
Evans, Gareth John
Evans, Richard J(ohn)
Faigman, David L.
Fairstein, Linda A.
Farrar, Ronald T(ruman)
Farrell, Warren (Thomas)

Mertus, Julie A.
Meyerson, Michael I.
Michelman, Kate
Miller, Abraham (H.)
Miller, Arthur R(aphael)
Miller, Jeffrey G.
Miller, William Ian
Millett, Paul
Mills, Linda G.
Milsom, Stroud Francis Charles
Mintz, Joel A(lan)
Mnookin, Robert H(arris)
Moenssens, Andre A.
Mohr, Richard D(rake)
Mollenkamp, Carrick
Monahan, John
Monahan, Patrick J.
Monet, Jean
Moore, John N(orton)
Moore, Roy L.
Morell, James B.
Moreno, Paul D.
Morgan, Austen
Morris, Jeffrey B(randon)
Morris, Rachel
Mortimer, James Edward
Morton, James (Severs)
Motomura, Hiroshi
Müller, Ingo
Murphy, Cullen
Murphy, James Bernard
Nadelmann, Ethan A.
Nahas, Gabriel G(eorges)
Nardulli, Peter F.
Nash, Patrick Gerard
Nathanson, Stephen (Lewis)
Neal, Bill
Neighbour, Mary E.
Nelson, Eric
Nevins, Francis M(ichael)
Newell, Coke
Newman, G(ordon) F.
Newman, Katherine S.
Newton, Merlin Owen
Norgren, Jill
Novick, Sheldon M.
O'Brien, David M(ichael)
O'Donnell, Pierce
O'Neil, Robert M.
Oaks, Dallin H.
Olson, Susan M.
Olson, Walter K.
Onuf, Nicholas
Opie, Anne
Oppenheim, Felix E.
Oppenheimer, Gregg
Orey, Michael
Orr, D. Alan
Oshinsky, David M.
Ostrow, Ronald J.
Ough, Richard N.
Owensby, Brian P(hilip)
Paddock, Lisa
Pallito, Robert M.
Palmer, Larry I.
Panford, Kwamina
Pannick, David

Paradise, Paul R.
Parloff, Roger (Harris)
Parrish, Richard
Pawlikowski, John Thaddeus
Pearl, David
Peck, Robert S(tephen)
Pederson, William D(avid)
Peerenboom, Randall
Peters, John Durham
Peters, Rudolph
Phillips, Leroy
Piatt, Bill
Pick, Hella
Pistor, Katharina
Platt, Rutherford H.
Pohlmann, Marcus D.
Polikoff, Nancy D.
Poos, L. R.
Posner, Eric A.
Posner, Richard A.
Pospíšil, Leopold Jaroslav
Potter, Harry (D.)
Power, Patrick C.
Premo, Bianca
Presser, Stephen B.
Pritchard, R(obert) John
Pritchett, Wendell
Quinn, Pat
Quirk, William J.
Quiroz, Anthony
Rabin, Robert L.
Rabinowitz, Dorothy
Rabkin, Jeremy A.
Ramos, Manuel
Ramphal, Shridath (Surendranath)
Ranney, Joseph A.
Ravitch, Frank S.
Redish, Martin H.
Regan, Milton C.
Regnery, Alfred S.
Reichel, Aaron I(srael)
Reid, John P(hillip)
Renauer, Albin (J.)
Rendon, Armando B.
Rice, Earle
Richards, David A. J.
Riggs, Robert E(dwon)
Rips, Michael
Rise, Eric W.
Robb, Peter
Roberts, Philip J.
Robertson Q.C., Geoffrey R.
Robinson, Paul H.
Rohrbough, Malcolm Justin
Rose, Paul (Bernard)
Rosell, Steven A.
Rosen, Jeffrey
Rosenkranz, E. Joshua
Rossum, Ralph A.
Rotenberg, Marc
Rozenberg, Joshua
Ruchelman, Leonard I.
Rudrum, Alan (William)
Russell, Kenneth Victor
Rychlak, Ronald (J.)
Sableman, Mark (Stephen)
Safir, Howard

Sakamoto, Yoshikazu
Salyer, Lucy E.
Samar, Vincent J(oseph)
Samuels, Warren J(oseph)
Sands, Philippe
Sarno, Ronald Anthony
Satter, Robert
Savage, Sean J.
Scalia, Antonin
Scharf, Michael P(aul)
Scheiber, Harry N.
Schiavone, Giuseppe
Schlink, Bernhard
Schmahmann, David
Schmeiser, Douglas A.
Schmidt, Benno Charles
Schmidt, Peter
Schmidt, Winsor C.
Schneiderman, David
Schoenbrod, David
Schrager, Sam(uel Alan)
Schroeder, Lucinda Delaney
Schudson, Charles B(enjamin)
Schwartz, Sunny
Schweizer, Karl W.
Scott, Elizabeth S.
Segal, Jeffrey A.
Seidman, Louis Michael
Shanley, Mary L(yndon)
Shapiro, Barry M.
Shapiro, Fred R(ichard)
Shapiro, Ian
Shapiro, Robert J.
Shapiro, Sidney
Shattuck, George C.
Shaw, James E.
Shaw, Mark
Sheridan, Lionel Astor
Sherry, Suzanna
Shimpock, Kathy E(lizabeth)
Shirk, David A.
Shoemaker, Robert B(rink)
Shorrock, Tim
Shropshire, Kenneth (L.)
Shulman, Mark R(ussell)
Shuman, Samuel I.
Sikes, Melvin P.
Silber, John (Robert)
Simon, James F.
Simon, Rita J(ames)
Simon, Roger (Mitchell)
Simpson, Michael Andrew
Sinclair, Brett J(ason)
Skover, David M.
Slaughter, Anne-Marie
Slee, Debora A.
Slee, Vergil N(elson)
Slemrod, Joel (B.)
Slovenko, Ralph
Smail, Daniel Lord
Smith, Bradley A.
Smith, Brenda
Smith, Clive Stafford
Smith, George P(atrick)
Smith, Robert Ellis
Smith, Wesley J.
Snyder, Francis Gregory

Solove, Daniel J.
Spriggs, James F.
Spring, Eileen
Stanley, Oliver
Stark, Evan
Statham, E. Robert
Stein, Edward D.
Stein, Leslie
Stein, Peter (Gonville)
Steinmetz, Devora
Stone, Alan A.
Stone, Judith F.
Streb, Matthew J(ustin)
Strossen, Nadine
Stubbs, Peter Charles
Stychin, Carl F.
Szasz, Thomas Stephen
Ta V n Tài
Tallis, Frank
Tan, Sor-hoon
Thompson, Augustine
Thornton, Margaret Rose
Thorson, John E.
Tierney, Kevin
Tollefsen, Christopher
Tomkins, Adam
Toobin, Jeffrey (Ross)
Torres, Gerald
Totani, Yuma
Towse, Ruth
Treitel, Guenter
Tribe, Laurence H(enry)
Tribe, Laurence H.
Trost, Jennifer Ann
Trotter, Michael H(amilton)
Trupp, Claudia
Turner, Amédée (Edward)
Turner, Tom
Turner, William Weyand
Turow, (L.) Scott
Ungar, Sanford J.
Vachss, Andrew H(enry)
Vallone, Ralph
van Alstyne, William W.
Ventura, Michael
Vermeule, Adrian
Wagner, Wenceslas J.
Waldman, Ayelet
Waldman, Steven
Walker, David (Maxwell)
Walker, Geoffrey de Q(uincey)
Waltenburg, Eric N.
Ware, Leland B.
Ware, Sandra J.
Warshauer, Matthew
Wasby, Stephen L(ewis)
Wass, Douglas (William Gretton)
Wax, Steven T.
Weber, Doron
Weddington, Sarah (Ragle)
Weimann, Gabriel
Weinberg, Louise
Weiner, Mark S(tuart)
Weiner, Susan
Weisstub, David N(orman)
Welch, D. Don
Wengert, Timothy J.

Law-*cont.*

West, Mark D.
Westervelt, Saundra D(avis)
Wettstein, Robert M.
Whittington, Keith E.
Wiber, Melanie G(ay)
Widner, Jennifer A(nne)
Wiener, Antje
Wiener, Jonathan B(aert)
Wiener, Joshua M(ark)
Wildenthal, Bryan H.
Williams, Gregory Howard
Williams, Patricia J(oyce)
Wilson, Duff
Wilson, Stephen G.
Wilson, Wesley M.
Winship, Michael P.
Witt, John Fabian
Wittes, Benjamin
Woll, Peter
Wolpert, Stanley Albert
Wood, Kieron
Wren, Jill Robinson
Yarnold, Barbara M(aria)
Yeager, Peter C(leary)
Yiannopoulos, A(thanassios) N.
Yoo, John C.
Zines, Leslie

Librarianship

Aguolu, Christian Chukwunedu
Ahearn, (Edward) Allen
Ahearn, Patricia
Alfino, Mark (R.)
Allan, Adrian R.
Anglim, Christopher Thomas
Armstrong, Diane (Julie)
Awe, Susan C.
Bahr, Alice Harrison
Bailey, Martha (J.)
Baird, Brian J.
Bakewell, Kenneth (Graham Bartlett)
Ballard, Terry
Barclay, Donald A.
Barker, Jonathan
Battles, Matthew
Becker, Patti Clayton
Berinstein, Paula
Berman, Sanford
Biggs, Mary
Blanchard, James G.
Blewett, Daniel K(eith)
Blockson, Charles L(eRoy)
Blodgett, Peter J.
Blouin, Lenora P.
Bobinski, George S.
Borko, Harold
Bracken, James K.
Breivik, Patricia Senn
Brown, Michelle P(atricia)
Burnett, Alfred David
Buzzeo, Toni
Carpenter, Kenneth E(dward)
Church, Audrey P.
Clausen, Tammy Hennigh

Librarianship-*cont.*

Cravey, Pamela J.
Crawford, Gregory A.
Credaro, Amanda
Davidsen, Susanna L.
Davis, Rose Parkman
DuPree, Sherry Sherrod
Edwards, Brendan Frederick R.
Elliott, Clark A.
Ellis, Alec (Charles Owen)
Fisher, Julieta Dias
Foust, J'aimé L.
Gasaway, Laura N.
Gatch, Milton McC
Graham, Patterson Toby
Greenberg, Gerald S(tuart)
Gregory, Vicki L.
Hall, Blaine H(ill)
Handy, Lowell K.
Hardesty, Larry (Lynn)
Harer, John B.
Harvey, John F(rederick)
Hauptman, Robert
Herring, Mark Youngblood
Hill, Ann M.
Hobson, Anthony Robert Alwyn
Hostrop, Richard W.
Hunter, Eric J.
Jacob, Merle (Lynn)
Jarvis, William E.
Johnson, Doug(las A.)
Jordan, Alma Theodora
Karetzky, Stephen
Kelly, Joanne (W.)
Kerby, Mona
Kitt, Sandra (E.)
Knapp, Sara D.
Kujoory, Parvin
Lamb, Connie
Lane, Nancy
Leerburger, Benedict A.
Lin, Tan (Anthony)
Lopresti, Robert
Low, Kathleen
Lumpkin, Betty S(tewart)
Mahmud, Shabana
Marantz, Sylvia S.
Matheson, Ann
Matthews, Elizabeth W(oodfin)
Matthews, Joseph R(onald)
McKitterick, David John
Mehaffey, Karen Rae
Meho, Lokman I.
Merrett, Christopher
Miller, Donna P.
Northrup, Mary (Wirtz)
Petrucci, Armando
Podell, Diane K(opperman)
Powell, David
Primack, Alice Lefler
Riedling, Ann Marlow
Rizzo, Margaret
Roberts, Francis X.
Rochman, Hazel
Rothstein, Samuel
Rowland, Arthur Ray
Sable, Martin Howard
Sarkodie-Mensah, Kwasi

Librarianship-*cont.*

Schaeffer, Mark
Schaffner, Bradley L(ewis)
Shapiro, Fred R(ichard)
Shavit, David
Shockley, Ann Allen
Shultz, Suzanne M.
Siebold, Jan
Sorrow, Barbara Head
Spratford, Becky Siegel
Stephens, Andy
Stewart, Sarah
Sutton, Roger
Thompson, Helen M.
Valenza, Joyce Kasman
Wagner, Ralph D.
Webb, T(erry) D(ouglas)
Webber, Desiree Morrison
Weihs, Jean (Riddle)
Weiner, Stephen
Wheeler, Helen Rippier
Wiegand, Shirley A.
Wiegand, Wayne A.
Wilson, Patricia Potter
Wood, Frances
Wren, Jill Robinson

Literary Criticism And History

Aaltonen, Sirkku
Abbotson, Susan C.W.
Abbott, Tony
Aberbach, David
Aberjhani
Abrams, M(eyer) H(oward)
Abramson, Edward A.
Abresch, Peter E.
Abu-Lughod, Lila
Accad, Evelyne
Achebe, Chinua
Achinstein, Sharon
Ackroyd, Peter
Adams, Carol J.
Adams, Hazard
Adams, James (Macgregor David)
Adams, Sheila Kay
Adams, Timothy Dow
Adamson, Donald
Addonizio, Kim (Theresa)
Adelman, Deborah
Adickes, Sandra
Agha-Jaffar, Tamara
Akins, Ellen
Alan, Theresa
Alaya, Flavia
Alazraki, Jaime
Albahari, David
Albanese, Laurie Lico
Alber, Charles J.
Albert, Susan Wittig
Alberts, Laurie
Alden, Patricia
Alexander, Floyce
Alexander, Harriet Semmes
Alexander, M(ichael) J(oseph)
Alexander, Meena

Literary Criticism And History-*cont.*

Alexander, Peter F.
Alexis, Andre
Alford, Edna
Ali, Samina
Alkali, Zaynab
Alkon, Paul K.
Allegretto, Michael
Allen, Ann Taylor
Allen, Dick
Allen, Fergus
Allen, John Jay
Allende, Isabel
Allgood, Myralyn F(rizzelle)
Aloff, Mindy
Alter, Robert B.
Alvarez, A(lfred)
Ambrosini, Richard
Ames, Christopher
Amoia, Alba della Fazia
Anam, Tahmima
Anania, Michael (Angelo)
Anastas, Benjamin
Anderson, David
Anderson, David Daniel
Anderson, Douglas A(llen)
Anderson, Jeffrey E.
Anderson, Mark M.
Anderson, Patricia J.
Anderson, Rachel
Anderson, Richard Lloyd
Anderson, Wilda (Christine)
Andrews, Elmer
Andrews, Nin
Andrews, William L(eake)
Anees, Munawar Ahmad
Anelli, Melissa
Antonette, Leslie
Applewhite, James
Apter, Emily (S.)
Apter, T(erri) E.
Arakawa, Yoichi
Arden, John
Arens, Katherine (Marie)
Arico, Santo L.
Armstrong, Judith (Mary)
Ash, Constance (Lee)
Asher, Jane
Asher, Neal
Asher, R. E.
Ashley, Leonard R. N.
Ashliman, D. L.
Ashrawi, Hanan (Mikhail)
Ashton, Dianne
Ashton, Rosemary
Asim, Jabari
Aslam, Nadeem
Aslan, Reza
Assael, Brenda
Assouline, Pierre
Astley, Neil
Atkinson, Michael (J.)
Atlas, James (Robert)
Atwood, Margaret
Aubert, Alvin
Aubert, Jacques
Auster, Paul

Austin, Linda Marilyn
Avery, Evelyn
Avery, Gillian (Elise)
Axelrod, Amy
Axelrod, Mark (R.)
Ayres, E. C.
Ayres, Pam
Ayres, Philip
Azriel, Yakov
Babb, Valerie (Melissa)
Bachman, W(illiam) Bryant
Backscheider, Paula R(ice)
Badami, Anita Rau
Badawi, Mohamed Mustafa
Baddock, James
Bagley, Mary (C.)
Bahr, Ehrhard
Bailey, Kathryn
Bailey, Peter J.
Bajwa, Rupa
Baker, Barbara
Baker, Richard E.
Baker, Rosalie F.
Baker, Russell (Wayne)
Baker, Sharlene
Baker, William
Bal, Mieke (Maria Gertrudis)
Balbo, Ned Clark
Balderston, Daniel
Ballentine, Lee (Kenney)
Balutansky, Kathleen M(arie)
Balzo, Sandra
Banash, Stan
Barabtarlo, Gennady
Bara czak, Stanisław
Barasch, Frances K.
Barbarese, J. T.
Barber, Phyllis (Nelson)
Barber, Richard (William)
Barbour, Douglas
Barbour, John D.
Barclay, Donald A.
Barden, Thomas
Bareham, Terence
Barer, Helen
Barish, Evelyn
Barker, Elspeth
Barker, Jonathan
Barley, Janet Crane
Barnard, Robert
Barnes, Christopher J(ohn)
Barnes, Linda (Joyce Appelblatt)
Barnes, Mike
Barnhill, David Landis
Barnie, John
Barolini, Helen
Barr, Patricia (Miriam)
Barranger, Milly S(later)
Barreto, Mascarenhas
Barrish, Phillip
Barry, P(atricia) S(teepee)
Barsky, Robert F(ranklin)
Bartolomeo, Joseph F(rancis)
Barton, Anne
Barton, Carlin A.
Barton, Dan

Baruch, Elaine Hoffman
Barzun, Jacques
Basinger, Jeanine (Deyling)
Basinski, Michael
Bass, Cynthia
Bass, Ronald
Bass, T. J.
Baswell, Christopher
Batchelor, John
Batchelor, R. E.
Bate, Jonathan
Battersby, Christine
Battestin, Martin Carey
Bauer, Caroline Feller
Bauer, Tricia
Bauerlein, Mark (Weightman)
Bauman, Bruce
Baumbach, Jonathan
Bawcutt, Priscilla (June)
Baybars, Taner
Bayley, John (Oliver)
Bayley, Peter (Charles)
Beal, Peter
Bean, Gregory (K.)
Beard, Jo Ann
Beardsell, Peter R.
Beardslee, Karen E.
Beardsley, Theodore S.
Beasley, Faith E(velyn)
Beattie, Ann
Beauman, Nicola
Beauman, Sally
Beavis, Mary Ann
Beckwith, Jonathan R(oger)
Bedingfield, M. Bradford
Beecher, Donald A(llen)
Beer, Gillian Patricia Kempster
Beiderwell, Bruce
Beidler, Peter G.
Beja, Morris
Belknap, Robert L.
Bell, Hilary
Bell, Ian Mackay
Bell, Marvin (Hartley)
Bellos, David
Bellows, Barbara L(awrence)
Belsey, Catherine
Bemrose, John
Benedict, Barbara M.
Bennassar, Bartolomé
Bennett, James Richard
Benson, Gerard
Benson, Jackson J.
Benstock, Shari
Bent, Timothy (David)
Bentley, Nancy Ann
Benton, Megan L.
Berberian, Viken
Berg, Leila
Berger, Arthur A(sa)
Berger, John (Peter)
Berger, Thomas (Louis)
Bergland, Martha
Bergon, Frank
Bergonzi, Bernard
Berkson, Bill

Berliner-Gluckman, Janet
Berman, Jeffrey
Bermann, Sandra L.
Bernard, Andre
Bernikow, Louise
Bernstein, Burton
Berry, Faith D.
Berry, J. Bill
Berry, Linda
Berry, Philippa
Bertolino, James
Besner, Neil K.
Betts, William Wilson
Bevis, William W.
Bhattacharya, Nalinaksha
Bicks, Caroline
Bidney, Martin
Bieman, Elizabeth
Bien, Peter
Bienes, Nicholas Peter
Biermann, Pieke
Biggs, Mary
Bigsby, C. W. E.
Bilby, Joanne Stroud
Binding, Paul
Bingham, Charlotte
Binns, Michael Ferrers Elliott
Birenbaum, Barbara
Birkerts, Sven
Birney, Alice Lotvin
Biro, Val
Birrell, Anne (Margaret)
Birrell, James Peter
Birringer, Johannes (H.)
Bitton-Jackson, Livia E(lvira)
Bjorge, Gary J(ohn)
Blackburn, Julia
Blades, John D.
Blake, Norman Francis
Blamires, Alcuin (Godfrey)
Blamires, Harry
Blanchard, Stephen (Thomas)
Blank, G(regory) Kim
Blank, Paula
Bledsoe, Glen L(eonard)
Bledsoe, Jerry
Blessington, Francis C(harles)
Blixt, David
Blockson, Charles L(eRoy)
Blodgett, (Anita) Jan
Bloom, Clive
Bloom, Harold
Bloom, James D.
Bloom, Lynn (Marie Zimmerman)
Blouin, Lenora P.
Blount, Roy (Alton)
Bluemel, Kristin
Blum, Edward J.
Blume, Judy
Blythe, Ronald (George)
Boast, Philip
Boehmer, Elleke
Bogacki, Tomek
Bogart, Jo Ellen
Boggs, Belle McQuade
Bohlmeijer, Arno

Bohm, Arnd
Boisseau, Michelle
Boitani, Piero
Bolam, Robyn
Boland, Eavan (Aisling)
Bolster, Richard (H.)
Bond, Nancy
Bonomelli, Charles J(ames)
Booker, Christopher
Booth, Brian
Booth, Stanley
Borden, Debra
Borinsky, Alicia
Bornstein, George
Bosselaar, Laure Anne
Bottoms, David
Boudreau, Kristin
Boullata, Issa J.
Boulton, James T(hompson)
Bourke, Angela
Bouson, J. Brooks
Bowden, Charles
Bowdring, Paul (Edward)
Bowen, Barbara C(herry)
Bowers, Jane Palatini
Bowie, Andrew (S.)
Bowker, Gordon
Bowlby, Rachel
Bowman, David
Bowness, Alan
Bowyer, Mathew Justice
Boyd, Blanche McCrary
Boyd, Brian (David)
Boyden, Amanda
Boyer, Jay
Boyers, Robert
Boyle, Josephine
Boyle, Kevin
Boyle, Nicholas
Bracken, Len
Bradbury, Jim
Bradford, Barbara Taylor
Bradley, Alan
Bradley, John Lewis
Brady, Rachel
Braham, (E.) Jeanne
Brake, Laurel
Brallier, Kate
Brand, Alice Glarden
Branden, Nathaniel
Brandt, Di
Brantenberg, Gerd
Brantley, Richard E.
Brantlinger, Patrick (Morgan)
Braudy, Leo
Brault, Jacques
Braun, Matt(hew)
Braunmuller, A(lbert) R(ichard)
Braxton, Joanne M(argaret)
Brebner, Philip
Breiner, Laurence A.
Breivik, Patricia Senn
Brennan, Matthew C.
Brennan, Michael G.
Brennan, Wendy
Brewer, David Allen

Literary Criticism And History-
cont.

Literary Criticism And History-
cont.

Literary Criticism And History-
cont.

Literary Criticism And History-
cont.

Cooke, Bernard
Cooke, Nathalie
Cooke, William
Cooley, Thomas (Winfield)
Coombs, Patricia
Coomer, Joe
Cooney, Ellen
Cooper, Barry (Anthony Raymond)
Cooper, Carolyn (Joy)
Cooper, David D.
Cooper, Helen
Cooper, Ron L.
Coquery-Vidrovitch, Catherine
Corbett, William
Corcoran, Neil (Cornelius)
Cordeiro, Patricia (A.)
Cordelli, Franco
Corn, Alfred
Corngold, Stanley
Cornis-Pope, Marcel (H.)
Cornyetz, Nina
Corran, Mary
Coscarelli, Don
Costello, Matthew John
Cotter, James Finn
Cottonwood, Joe
Cottringer, Anne
Coulson, Juanita
Cowasjee, Saros
Cowell, Stephanie
Cox, Ana Marie
Cox, Stephen D.
Cragg, (Albert) Kenneth
Craig, Daniel Edward
Craik, T(homas) W(allace)
Craven, Michael
Crawford, Lynn
Crawford, T. Hugh
Crew, Danny O(liver)
Crew, Louie
Crews, Donald
Crews, Frederick C(ampbell)
Crnobrnja (Tsernobernya),
    Mihailo
Croft, Barbara
Croft, Robert W(ayne)
Crosland, Margaret
Cross, Anthony Glenn
Cross, Helen
Cross, Richard K.
Crossan, G(regory) D(ixon)
Crow, Mary
Crow, Thomas E.
Crowder, Ashby Bland
Crowell, Jenn(ifer)
Crowl, Samuel
Croyden, Margaret
Crumbley, Paul
Crump, William D(rake)
Crusie, Jennifer
Culbert, Steven (Tye)
Cullen, Robert (B.)
Cumbie, Pamela
Cumming, Elizabeth (Skeoch)
Cunliffe, Barry

Cunningham, Frank R.
Cunningham, Valentine
Curry, Neil
Curtis, Anthony
Curtis, J(ulie) A. E.
Curtis, Rebecca
Curtis, Tony
Cusk, Rachel
Cuthbert, Margaret
Cutler, Jane
D'Ambrosio, Charles
Dabydeen, David
Dace, Tish
Dahlberg, Maurine F.
Dahlie, Hallvard
Dale, Peter
Daly, Brenda O.
Daly, Leo (Arthur)
Dalzell, Alexander
Dandridge, Rita B(ernice)
Dangler, Jean
Daniels, Karen
Danow, David K.
Darnton, Robert
Darty, Peggy
Dassanowsky, Robert
Dauer, Lesley
Davenport-Hines, Richard (Peter
    Treadwell)
David, Esther
Davidar, David
Davidson, Diane Mott
Davidson, Michael
Davidson, Pamela
Davies, J(ohn) D(avid)
Davies, Katharine
Davies, Martin L.
Davies, Stephanie
Davies-Mitchell, Margaret (Constance)
Davis, (Elvis) Clark
Davis, Albert Belisle
Davis, Anna
Davis, David Brion
Davis, Francis
Davis, Nancy Yaw
Davis, Steven J(oseph)
Davison, Carol Margaret
Davison, Peter (Hobley)
Dawe, R(oger) D(avid)
Dawick, John
Dawson, Geralyn
Day, Aidan
Dayan, Colin
de Costa, Elena M.
De Ferrari, Gabriella
de Grave, Kathleen
de Jonge, Alex
de Paor, Louis
de Souza, Eunice
de Waal, Ronald Burt
Dean, Debra
Dean, William Denard
Dearden, James Shackley
Deck, Allan Figueroa
DeCosta-Willis, Miriam

Deen, Hanifa
DeFazio, Albert J.
Deford, Frank
Del Caro, Adrian
Del Paso, Fernando
Delaney, Shelagh
Delbanco, Francesca
DeLillo, Don
Delson, Rudolph
DeMarr, Mary Jean
Demers, Patricia
DeMille, Nelson (Richard)
DeMott, Robert (James)
Demott, Wes
DePoy, Phillip
Derfler, (Arnold) Leslie
des Vallires, Nathalie
Desai, Kiran
Desautels, Denise
Desena, Carmine
Dessaix, Robert
Dettmar, Kevin J(ohn)
    H(offmann)
Devashish, Donald Acosta
Devlin, Albert J.
DeVries, Kelly
Deweese, Pamela J.
Dewey, Joseph (Owen)
Dewhurst, Eileen (Mary)
deWitt, Patrick
Dexter, Pete
di Prima, Diane
Diamant, Anita
Dick, Bernard F.
Dickerson, Vanessa D.
Dickinson, Don(ald Percy)
Dickinson, Peter
Dietz, Laura
Digby-Junger, Richard
Dillard, Annie
Dillard, R(ichard) H(enry)
    W(ilde)
Dillingham, William B.
Dimock, Wai Chee
Dintenfass, Mark L.
DioGuardi, Joseph J.
DiRenzo, Anthony
DiSalvo, Jackie
Divakaruni, Chitra Banerjee
Doane, Janice (L.)
Dobson, Joanne
Dodd, Wayne
Doebler, Bettie Anne
Doherty, Justin (Francis)
Dolan, Frederick Michael
Dolin, Sharon
Dolis, John
Doll, Mary A(swell)
Dolle, Raymond F.
Dollimore, Jonathan
Donaldson, Islay (Eila) Murray
Donaldson, Scott
Donker, Marjorie
Donleavy, J(ames) P(atrick)
Donoghue, Daniel
Donoghue, Emma

Donoghue, Frank J.
Donovan, Katie
Dooley, Allan C(harles)
Dooley, David (Allen)
Doriani, Beth Maclay
Dorré, Gina M.
Douglas, Ann
Dover, Michael A.
Dow, James
Downes, David A(nthony)
Downes, Jeremy M.
Downing, David C(laude)
Doyle, Brian
Doyle, Charles (Desmond)
Doyle, Debra
Dozier, Cheryl
Drabble, Margaret
Drew, Bettina
Drexler, Rosalyn
Dromgoole, Dominic
Duberman, Martin
Duberstein, Larry
Dubost, Thierry
Duchac, Joseph
Dufault, Peter Kane
Dufault, Roseanna Lewis
Duffy, Bruce
Dufresne, John
Duigan, John
Duke, Michael S.
Dukore, Bernard F.
Duncan, Carol Greene
Duncan, Christine H.
Duncker, Patricia
Dunn, Peter Norman
DuPlessis, Rachel Blau
Dupuis, Robert
Duyfhuizen, Bernard
Dwyer, Jim
Dyer, Joyce
Eady, Cornelius
Eagleton, Terry
Earnshaw, Steven
Eaton, Trevor (Michael William)
Ebisch, Glen Albert
Echeruo, Michael
Economou, George
Eddins, Dwight L.
Edelheit, Abraham J.
Edson, Russell
Edwards, Michael
Edwards, P. D.
Edwards, Philip (Walter)
Egan, Jennifer
Egan, Kieran
Egan, Linda
Egan, Ronald
Egli, Ida Rae
Ehrlich, Amy
Eigenbrod, Renate
Eisiminger, Sterling (Skip)
El-Enany, Rasheed
Elder, John
Eliav, Yaron Z.
Elliot, Alistair
Ellis, Bret Easton

Literary Criticism And History-
cont.

Literary Criticism And History-
cont.

Literary Criticism And History-
cont.

Literary Criticism And History-
cont.

Gilmour, Michael J.	Grant, Patrick	Hale, Robert D(avid)	Harsch, Rich
Gilson, Simon A.	Grass, Günter (Wilhelm)	Halkin, Ariela	Hart, Jan Siegel
Gioia, (Michael) Dana	Gray, Alasdair (James)	Hall, Ann C.	Hart, JoeAnn
Gish, Robert F.	Gray, Richard J(ohn)	Hall, Blaine H(ill)	Hart, Kevin
Glancy, Ruth F(ergusson)	Grayson, Emily	Hall, Donald (Andrew)	Harteis, Richard
Glanville, Brian (Lester)	Grebstein, Sheldon Norman	Hall, H(ugh) Gaston	Harter, Karen
Glatt, John	Greeley, Robin Adèle	Hall, J(ohn) C(live)	Hartman, Geoffrey H.
Gleiter, Jan	Green, Angela	Hall, Joan Wylie	Hartman, Saidiya V.
Glendening, John	Green, Joseph (Lee)	Hall, Kathleen (Mary)	Harvey, Clay
Glenn, Mel	Green, Norman	Hall, Martha Lacy	Hasan, Anjum
Gliserman, Martin	Green, R. P. H.	Hall, Rodney	Hashmi, (Aurangzeb) Alamgir
Gloag, Julian	Green, Scott E.	Hallett, Charles A(rthur)	Haskell, Molly
Glover, Douglas	Green, Sharony Andrews	Halliburton, David (Garland)	Haslam, Gerald William
Glut, Don(ald) F.	Greenberg, Martin	Halliday, Mark	Hassan, Ihab (Habib)
Glyer, Diana Pavlac	Greene, Gayle	Halligan, Marion (Mildred	Hassler, Donald M(ackey)
Godwin, Gail (Kathleen)	Greene, Jody	Crothall)	Hasty, Will
Godwin, Parke	Greenleaf, Stephen (Howell)	Hallissy, Margaret	Haswell, Janis Tedesco
Goering, Joseph	Greer, Germaine	Hallo, William W.	Hathaway, Barbara
Goethe, Ann	Gregerson, Linda	Hallock, John W(esley) M(atthew)	Haug, James
Gold, Hazel	Gregor, Arthur	Hallwas, John E.	Hauptman, Robert
Gold, Janet N(owakowski)	Gregory, Patrick	Halter, Marek	Havel, Harvey
Golding, Alan	Gregory, Tobias	Hamblin, Robert W(ayne)	Hawke, Simon
Goldman, Arnold (Melvyn)	Grennan, Eamon	Hamburger, Aaron	Hawkins, Anne Hunsaker
Goldman, William	Gretsch, Mechthild	Hamdani, Sumaiya A.	Hawley, John C(harles)
Goldner, Beth	Grieb, Kenneth J.	Hamid, Mohsin	Hay, Samuel A.
Goldstein, Naama	Griffin, Alice	Hamill, Sam (Patrick)	Hayman, David
Goldstein, Nancy	Griffin, Farah Jasmine	Hamilton, Jane	Hayman, Ronald
Gollin, Rita K.	Griffin, Susan M.	Hamilton, Peter F.	Haynes, Jonathan
Gonzalez, Alexander G.	Griffith, Thomas Gwynfor	Hammerschmidt-Hummel,	Haynes, Melinda
González, Aníbal	Griswold, Jerome	Hildegard	Haynie, Barbara
González, Ray	Groden, Michael (Lewis)	Hammond, Wayne G(ordon)	Hays, Peter L.
Gonzalez (Mandri), Flora	Gross, Jonathan David	Hampson, Robert (Gavin)	Hayward, Jennifer (Poole)
González-Echevarria, Roberto	Grosskurth, Phyllis	Han, Suzanne Crowder	Hazo, Samuel (John)
Goodheart, Eugene	Grote, David (G.)	Hanes, Frank Borden	Head, Dominic
Goodkin, Richard E.	Groth, Janet	Hankin, C(herry) A(nne)	Healy, Sophia (Warner)
Goodland, Katharine	Grow, L(ynn) M(erle)	Hannah, James	Heaney, Seamus
Goodman, Lizbeth (L.)	Grudin, Robert	Hanscombe, Gillian E(ve)	Heath, Jennifer
Goodman, Susan	Gruesser, John Cullen	Hansen, Ann Natalie	Heath, William
Goodwin, Ken(neth Leslie)	Grumbach, Doris	Hansen, Chadwick	Hegenberger, John
Goonetilleke, D. C. R. A.	Grumman, Bob	Hansen-Hill, N. D.	Heller, Michael
Gordimer, Nadine	Grundy, Joan	Hapke, Laura	Hellstrom, Ward
Gordis, Lisa M.	Guare, John	Hardy, Barbara (Gladys)	Helprin, Mark
Gordon, Anne Wolrige	Gubar, Susan (David)	Hardy, John Philips	Hely, Sara
Gordon, Eric A(rthur)	Guest, Harry	Hare, David	Hendra, Jessica
Gordon, Haim	Guevara, Maurice Kilwein	Haring, Lee	Hendry, Joy (McLaggan)
Gordon, Lois G.	Guignon, Charles B(urke)	Harleman, Ann	Henry, DeWitt (Pawling)
Gordon, Lyndall (Felicity)	Guilfoile, Kevin	Harmon, Maurice	Henry, Patrick
Gordon, Mary (Catherine)	Gunn, James E(dwin)	Haroian-Guerin, Gil	Herman, Richard
Gordon, Sheila	Gunning, Sally (Carlson)	Harper, Lila Marz	Hernández, Lisa
Gordon, W. Terrence	Gurr, A(ndrew) J(ohn)	Harrington, John P.	Herring, Phillip F.
Gore, Kristin (C.)	Gurr, Michael	Harris, (Theodore) Wilson	Herron, Carolivia
Gornick, Vivian	Gutteridge, Don(ald George)	Harris, Deborah Turner	Herzog, Tobey C.
Gorra, Michael (Edward)	Guttmann, Allen	Harris, Elizabeth	Hess, Bill
Gorrell, Robert (Mark)	Guy, Rosa (Cuthbert)	Harris, Rosemary	Hester, M(arvin) Thomas
Goss, Glenda Dawn	Gwynn, R(obert) S(amuel)	Harris, Rosemary (Jeanne)	Hewitt, Geof
Gottlieb, Annie	Haase, Donald	Harris, William V.	Heyen, William
Gottlieb, Lisa	Habegger, Alfred (Carl)	Harrison, Antony H.	Hicks, Barbara
Gougeon, Len (G.)	Habers, Walther A(drianus)	Harrison, Brady	Hieatt, Constance B(artlett)
Grace, Nancy McCampbell	Habinek, Thomas N.	Harrison, Gary	Higgins, Ian (Kevin)
Grafton, Anthony T(homas)	Hackett, Helen	Harrison, Jim	Higgins, Joanna
Gragnolati, Manuele	Hadas, Rachel	Harrison, Kathryn	Hildebrand, Ann Meinzen
Graham, Caroline	Haddad, Gladys	Harrison, Michael	Hildebrand, John
Graham, Desmond	Hagedorn, Jessica Tarahata	Harrison, Russell (T.)	Hill, Carol
Graham, Jefferson	Hager, Alan	Harrison, Suzan	Hill, Geoffrey
Grant, Anne Underwood	Haig, Kathryn	Harrison, Tony	Hill, Ingrid
Grant, James Russell	Hainsworth, Peter (R. J.)	Harrow, Kenneth W.	Hill, Lynda Marion

Literary Criticism And History-
cont.

Hill, Tracey
Hillgarth, J(ocelyn) N(igel)
Hilton, Margery
Himelstein, Morgan Y.
Hinchman, Sandra K(uracina)
Hines, Jeanne
Hinton, S(usan) E(loise)
Hirsch, E(ric) D(onald)
Hirsch, Pam
Hirshfield, Jane
Hischak, Thomas S.
Hitchcock, Tim
Hitz, Frederick P(orter)
Ho, Minfong
Hoare, Philip
Hobby, Elaine (Ann)
Hobson, Fred Colby
Hoeppner, Edward Haworth
Hoestlandt, Jo(celyne)
Hoffman, Alice
Hoffman, Andy
Hoffman, Daniel
Hoffman, Michael J.
Hofmann, Michael
Hogan, Patrick Colm
Hogg, Patrick Scott
Hoggart, Richard
Holahan, Susan
Holbrook, David (Kenneth)
Holden, Philip (Joseph)
Holdheim, W(illiam) Wolfgang
Holland, Norman N.
Hollander, John
Hollenberg, Donna Krolik
Holley, Margaret
Hollindale, Peter
Hollingsworth, Margaret
Hollis, Stephanie
Holloway, Karla F. C.
Holmes, Diana
Holmes, Katie
Holmes, Mary Tavener
Holmes, Richard
Holroyd, Michael
Holst-Warhaft, Gail
Holte, James Craig
Holthe, Tess Uriza
Homan, Sidney
Homberger, Eric
Honan, Park
Hond, Paul
Honeygosky, Stephen R(aymond)
Hook, Brendan
Hooker, Jeremy
Hoover, Paul
Hopkins, Antony
Hopkins, Lee Bennett
Hopkins, Lisa
Hopler, Jay
Horan, Elizabeth (Rosa)
Horan, Nancy
Hord, Frederick (Lee)
Hornby, Nick
Horne, Gerald
Horovitz, Michael
Horsfield, Debbie

Horsley, Lee
Horton, David (Edward)
Horváth, John
Hosozawa-Nagano, Elaine
House, Tom
Howard, Heather H.
Howard, Joan E.
Howard, Maureen
Howard, Roger
Howard, Todd
Howard, Walter T.
Howarth, William (Louis)
Howe, Fanny
Howe, Susan
Howes, Laura L(ouise)
Howker, Janni
Hoy, Linda
Hribal, C. J.
Hromic, Alma A.
Hubbard, Dolan
Hubbard, Thomas K.
Hucker, Hazel
Hudson, Wade
Hughes, Richard (Edward)
Huisinga, Roger
Hull, William E(dward)
Hulse, Michael (William)
Hume, Robert D.
Hummer, T(erry) R(andolph)
Humphreys, Emyr (Owen)
Hungerford, Rachael A.
Hunt, Marvin W.
Hunt, Peter (Leonard)
Hunt, Tony
Hunt, Walter H.
Hunter, J(ames) Paul
Hunter, Jessie Prichard
Hurley, Valerie
Hurwitz, Johanna (Frank)
Hussey, Mark
Hutcheon, Linda
Hutchings, Stephen
Hutchins, William
Hutchinson, G(regory) O(wen)
Hutchisson, James M.
Hutson, Lorna
Hutton, Frankie
Huxley, George Leonard
Hyde, (W.) Lewis
Hyde, Anthony
Hyman, Harold M(elvin)
Hynes, Joel
Hynes, Samuel
Ignatieff, Michael
Igo, John (N.)
Ilie, Paul
Impola, Richard A(arre)
In-Ho, Choi
Inge, M. Thomas
Ingersoll, Earl G(eorge)
Inglis, Janet
Inness-Brown, Elizabeth (Ann)
Intrator, Sam M.
Irmscher, Christoph
Irving, John (Winslow)
Irwin, Robert (Graham)

Isaacs, Anne
Isaacs, Susan
Isitt, Larry R.
Israel, Lee
Iyengar, Sujata
Jackson, Angela
Jackson, J. R. de J.
Jackson, John A.
Jackson, Marian J. A.
Jackson, Sheneska
Jacob, Merle (Lynn)
Jacobs, Alan
Jacobs, Kathryn
Jacobs, Steve
Jacobson, Dan
Jacobson, Joanne
Jacobus, Mary
Jaeck, Lois Marie
Jager, Eric
Jahme, Carole
Jakes, John
Jaksi , Iván
James, (William) Louis (Gabriel)
James, Clive (Vivian Leopold)
James, Laurie
James, Russell
James, Tania
Jancovich, Mark
Janko, James
Janoda, Jeff
Janowitz, Brenda
Jansen, Sharon L.
Janssen, Marian (L. M.)
Jaramillo, Stephan
Jarman, Mark (F.)
Jeffers, Thomas L.
Jenkins, Fred W(illiam)
Jennings, Maureen
Jennings, Phillip E.
Jensen, Ejner J.
Jensen, Kim
Jirgens, Karl (E.)
John, Juliet
Johnson, Alexandra
Johnson, Annabel (Jones)
Johnson, Charles R(ichard)
Johnson, Chester L.
Johnson, Diane
Johnson, Dianne
Johnson, Greg
Johnson, Rob
Johnson, Roger
Johnson, Todd
Jolly, Roslyn
Jonaitis, Aldona
Jones, (Henry) John (Franklin)
Jones, D(ouglas) G(ordon)
Jones, Daryl (Emrys)
Jones, Evan (Lloyd)
Jones, Gayl
Jones, Gwyneth A(nn)
Jones, Jason B.
Jones, Malcolm V(ince)
Jones, Margaret C.
Jones, Mary Voell
Jones, R(obert) M(aynard)

Jones, Sally Roberts
Jones, Ted
Jones, William B(ryan)
Jordan, Anne Devereaux
Jordan, Constance
Joseph, Diana
Joseph, Henry
Joseph, Lawrence
Joshi, S(unand) T(ryambak)
Josipovici, Gabriel (David)
Jouve, Nicole Ward
Jovanovski, Meto
Joven, Enrique
Joyce, Joyce Ann
Judah, Aaron
Judovitz, Dalia
Juraga, Dubravka
Jussawalla, Feroza
Jweid, Rosann
Kachtick, Keith
Kadare, Ismail
Kadir, Djelal
Kalaidjian, Walter B.
Kaler, Anne K(atherine)
Kalesniko, Mark G(aston)
Kallgren, Beverly Hayes
Kalson, Albert E(ugene)
Kane, Leslie
Kane, Penny
Kanigel, Robert
Kantaris, Sylvia (Mosley)
Kaplan, Alice Yaeger
Kaplan, Carter
Kaplan, Justin
Karem, Jeff
Kari, Daven M(ichael)
Karkala, John A.
Karlin, Daniel
Karlin, Wayne (Stephen)
Karnicky, Jeffrey
Kastely, James L.
Katrak, Ketu H.
Katritzky, M. A.
Katz, Michael Ray
Katz, Steve
Kauffman, Janet
Kauffmann, Stanley
Kaufman, Will
Kawin, Bruce F.
Kay, Betty Carlson
Kearns, Sheila M.
Keating, AnaLouise
Keeble, Neil H(oward)
Keegan, John E.
Keeley, Edmund
Keene, Donald
Keery, James
Kehler, Dorothea
Keilen, Sean
Keillor, Garrison (Edward)
Kelley, (Kathleen) Alita
Kelley, Liam C.
Kelling, Hans Wilhelm
Kellner, Bruce
Kelly, Catriona
Kelly, Linda

Kelly, Louis Gerard
Kelly, Maeve
Kelman, James
Kemp, (Bernard) Peter
Kenan, Randall (G.)
Kennedy, David Michael
Kennedy, Marlane
Kennedy, Pagan
Kennedy, Philip F.
Kennedy, X. J.
Kennelly, (Timothy) Brendan
Kennemore, Tim
Kenney, Catherine (McGehee)
Kenney, William Howland
Kenny, Maurice (Francis)
Kenrick, Tony
Kenward, Jean
Kenworthy, Brian J(ohn)
Ker, Ian (Turnbull)
Kesselman, Wendy
Kessler, Jascha (Frederick)
Khan, Adib
Khare, R(avindra) S.
Kherdian, David
Khilnani, Sunil
Khoo, Gaik Cheng
Khoury-Ghata, Vénus
Khwaja, Waqas
Kiberd, Declan
Kidwell, Carol (Evelyn Beryl)
Kiely, Robert (James)
Kiernan, Brian
Kiessling, Nicolas K.
Kihn, Greg
Killeen, Jarlath
Kim, Elaine H(aikyung)
Kimball, Roger
King, Bruce (Alvin)
King, Jeanette (Margaret)
King, Kathryn R.
King, Thomas
King-Hele, Desmond
Kingman, (Mary) Lee
Kingston, Maxine Hong
Kinnell, Galway
Kinney, Arthur F.
Kinsella, Thomas
Kinsella, W(illiam) P(atrick)
Kinzie, Mary
Kiraly, Sherwood
Kirk, Pauline (M.)
Kirkbright, Suzanne
Kirkham, E. Bruce
Kissel, Susan S.
Kitchen, Judith
Kittredge, William
Kitts, Thomas M(ichael)
Kizer, Carolyn
Klammer, Martin (P.)
Klappert, Peter
Kleiman, Ed
Klein, Kathleen Gregory
Klein, Marcus
Klein, Matthew
Klein, Robin (McMaugh)
Klempner, Joseph T(eller)

Kliman, Bernice W.
Klingenstein, Susanne
Kluger, Ruth
Koegler, Hans Herbert
Koelb, Clayton T.
Koestenbaum, Wayne
Koller, James
Kollin, Eytan
Konzak, Burt
Kopit, Arthur
Korder, Howard
Korg, Jacob
Kornblatt, Judith Deutsch
Korobkin, Laura Hanft
Kort, Wesley A.
Kositsky, Lynne
Koslow, Sally
Kostelanetz, Richard (Cory)
Kotker, Zane
Koupal, Nancy Tystad
Kowalewski, Michael (John)
Kramer, Dale
Kramp, Michael
Krashen, Stephen D.
Krich, Rochelle Majer
Krieg, Joann P(eck)
Kriegel, Leonard
Krinsky, Natalie
Krise, Thomas W(arren)
Kristal, Efrain
Kristeva, Julia
Kroker, Arthur (W.)
Kropp, Paul
Krovatin, Christopher
Krupp, Robin Rector
Krystal, Arthur
Kuberski, Philip
Kujoory, Parvin
Kumin, Maxine
Labanyi, Jo
Labrie, Ross
LaBute, Neil
Lackey, Kris
Lackey, Michael
Lahiri, Jhumpa
LaHood, Marvin J(ohn)
Lake, David (John)
Lake, Paul
Lambert, Page
Lammers, Wayne P.
Lampitt, Dinah
Lams, Victor
Land, Brad
Landers, Scott
Landry, Donna
Landsberg, Melvin
Landy, Marcia
Lane, Nancy
Langa, Mandla
Langbaum, Robert (Woodrow)
Lange, Arthur D.
Langford, David
Lanham, Richard Alan
Lankford, Mary D.
Lanzmann, Claude
Lapcharoensap, Rattawut

Lape, Noreen Groover
Larkin, Edward
Laroque, Francois G.
Larson, Gary
Larson, Sidner J.
Larson, Wendy
Laskin, Pamela L.
Lass, Roger
Lateiner, Donald
Lathey, Gillian
Latynin, Leonid (Aleksandrovich)
Laubach, David C.
Laurie, Edward James
Laurie, Hugh
Lauture, Denizé
Laux, Constance
Lavery, David
Lawlor, Clark
Lawson, James
Lazuta, Gene
le Carré, John
Le Guin, Ursula K(roeber)
Leach, William
Leader, Zachary
Leask, Nigel
Leatherbarrow, W(illiam) J(ohn)
Leavell, Linda
Leavitt, Caroline
Leavy, Barbara Fass
Lebor, Adam
Lebowitz, Albert
LeCompte, N(ancy) Jane
Lee, A(rthur) Robert
Lee, Anthony W.
Lee, Bernie
Lee, Dennis (Beynon)
Lee, Helen Elaine
Lee, Jeanne M.
Lee, Judith Yaross
Lee, Mona
Lee, Peter H.
Lee, Sky
Lee Six, Abigail (Etta)
Leeds, Barry H.
Leeson, Robert (Arthur)
Leggatt, Alexander
Leguizamo, John
Lehrer, Kate
Leib, Franklin A(llen)
Leidner, Alan C.
Leith, Linda Jane
Lelchuk, Alan
Lellenberg, Jon L.
LeMaster, J. R.
Lemon, Rebecca
Lennard, John (Chevening)
Lennox, John
Lennox-Smith, Judith (Elizabeth)
Leonard, James S.
Leonardi, Susan J.
Leong, Russell (C.)
Lerer, Seth
Lerner, Laurence (David)
Leseur, Geta
Lesjak, Carolyn
Lesser, Wendy

Lessing, Doris (May)
Lester, Julius
Letellier, Robert Ignatius
Lethbridge, Robert (David)
Levi, Jan Heller
Levin, Amy K.
Levin, Gerald
Levine, Stuart George
Levy, Andrew (Gordon)
Levy, Helen Fiddyment
Lewes, Darby
Lewin, Rhoda G.
Lewis, Peter (Elvet)
Lewis, Robert W.
Lewis, Trudy
Lewis, Ward B.
Lichtenstein, Alice
Lieberman, Herbert
Lieberman, Laurence (James)
Liebman, Herbert
Lilienfeld, Jane
Lim, Shirley Geok-lin
Lima, Robert (F.)
Limon, Jerzy
Lin, Tan (Anthony)
Lindemann, Mary
Lindholdt, Paul J.
Lindvall, Michael L(loyd)
Lingard, Jeanette
Lingeman, Richard
Linnell, David
Lisboa, Maria Manuel
Littell, Robert
Little, Anne Colclough
Little, Katherine C.
Little, Terra
Liu, Eric
Liu, Lydia H.
Liu, Timothy
Lively, Adam
Lloyd, Margaret Glynne
Lloyd, Rosemary
Lock, Charles (John Somerset)
Lockerbie, D(onald) Bruce
Locklin, Gerald Ivan
Lockridge, Larry
Lockyer, Judith (Ann)
Lodge, David
Loeb, Karen
Loeffelholz, Mary
Logan, George M(eredith)
Logan, Shirley Wilson
Loney, Glenn Meredith
Long, Jeff
Longley, Michael
Looby, Christopher
Looney, Dennis (Oscar)
Looser, Devoney
Losada (Goya), Jose Manuel
Losse, Deborah N(ichols)
Lounsberry, Barbara
Lovell, Glenville
Low, Anthony
Lowe-Evans, Mary
Lowenberg, Susan
Lowenthal, Cynthia J.

Miles, Barry
Miles, Leland
Miller, Anesa
Miller, David C.
Miller, E. Ethelbert
Miller, Paul D.
Miller-Lachmann, Lyn
Millet, Lydia
Millet, Richard
Millett, John
Millett, Paul
Millhiser, Marlys
Millman, Joan (M.)
Milne, Kevin Alan
Milne, Lorna
Milnor, Kristina
Minahan, John A.
Minock, Daniel
Minogue, Valerie Pearson
Minshall, Vera
Minter, David Lee
Mintz, Alan L.
Mishra, Sudesh (Raj)
Misurella, Fred
Mitchell, Jerome
Mitchell, Juliet
Mitchell, Margaree King
Mitchell, Roger
Mitchell, Thomas R.
Mo, Timothy
Moffat, Gwen
Moi, Toril
Mole, John
Molesworth, Charles
Mollenkott, Virginia Ramey
Molnar, Michael
Monaghan, David (Mark)
Monk, Isabell
Montefiore, Janet
Montgomery, Maureen E.
Montier, Jean-Pierre
Moore, J. Stuart
Moore-Gilbert, Bart
Moran, Charles
Moran, Mary (Molly) Hurley
Moran, Michelle
Morash, Christopher
Mordecai, Pamela (Claire)
Moreau, David Merlin
Moreh, Shmuel
Moreland, Richard C.
Morey, Ann Janine
Morgan, Nicholas H.
Morgan, Rosemarie (Anne Louise)
Moriarty, Michael
Morley, Margaret
Morris, Alan
Morris, Bill
Morris, Mary
Morris, S(tephen) Brent
Morris, Timothy
Morrison, (Philip) Blake
Morrison, Kristin Diane
Morrow, John
Morse, Donald E.

Morsi, Pamela
Morton, Brian
Morton, Richard Everett
Moses, Michael Valdez
Moskowitz, Faye (Stollman)
Mosley, Nicholas
Mosley, Philip
Moss, Carolyn (J.)
Moss, Thylias (Rebecca)
Motion, Andrew (Peter)
Mott, Wesley T.
Moulakis, Athanasios
Mowat, Farley (McGill)
Moy, James S.
Moynahan, Julian (Lane)
Mu go, Mi cere Gi thae
Mudimbe, V. Y.
Mullan, David George
Munro, John M(urchison)
Munsch, Robert
Murdoch, Brian (Oliver)
Murdy, Louise Baughan
Murphy, Claire Rudolf
Murphy, James H.
Murphy, Shirley R(ousseau)
Murray, David (J.)
Murray, Janet Horowitz
Murry, Katherine Middleton
Musacchio, George
Mustazza, Leonard
Myers, Eric
Myers, Robert Manson
Myers, William
Na rang, Gopi Chand
Naden, Corinne J.
Naiden, James
Nakhimovsky, Alice Stone
Nancarrow, Mindy
Nassar, Eugene Paul
Natarajan, Nalini
Naylor, Gloria
Neaverson, Bob
Needle, Jan
Neeld, Elizabeth Harper
Neely, Barbara
Nelson, Betty Palmer
Nelson, Claudia
Nelson, Howard
Nelson, Robert M(cDowell)
Nelson, T. G. A.
Nepaulsingh, Colbert I(vor)
Nericcio, William Anthony
Nesbitt, Marc
Netifnet, Dadisi Mwende
Neuberger, Julia
Nevins, Francis M(ichael)
New, Melvyn
New, William Herbert
Newcomb, Robert
Newcomer, James W.
Newlyn, Lucy
Ngugi wa Thiong
Nguyên, Kiên
Nichols, John Gordon
Nichols, Linda
Nichols, Peter (Richard)

Nicholson, Colin
Nicosia, Gerald (Martin)
Niebuhr, Gary Warren
Nielson, James
Nigam, Sanjay (Kumar)
Nigro, August John
Nitchie, George Wilson
Niven, Alastair (Neil Robertson)
Niven, Larry
Nixon, Cornelia
Nixon, Rob
Nobile, Philip
Nodelman, Perry
Noegel, Scott B.
Nolan, David (Joseph)
Norbrook, David
Nord, Deborah Epstein
Norman, Howard A.
Norris, Ken
Norris, Pamela
Norton, Rictor
Novak, Maximillian Erwin
Nunn, Frederick McKinley
Nye, Robert
Nye, Simon (Beresford)
O Cuilleanain, Cormac
O'Brien, George
O'Connell, Jack
O'Connor, Alan
O'Connor, Leo F.
O'Connor, Patricia W.
O'Daly, William
O'Donnell, Brennan (Patrick)
O'Donnell, Sunshine
O'Driscoll, Dennis
O'Grady, Rohan
O'Hara, David
O'Leary, Patrick
O'Neill, Joseph
O'Reilly Herrera, (C.) Andrea
O'Riordan, Michelle
O'Shaughnessy, Ellen Cassels
O'Toole, Judith Hansen
Oates, Joyce Carol
Oberndorf, Charles G.
Obika, Akili Addae
Obradovi , Nade da
Ochart (Torres), (Luz) Yvonne
Odaga, Asenath (Bole)
Odber (de Baubeta), Patricia (Anne)
Odhiambo, David Nandi
Ogbaa, Kalu
Ogede, Ode
Oguibe, Olu
Ogunyemi, Chikwenye Okonjo
Ojaide, Tanure
Okker, Patricia
Oktenberg, Adrian
Oldfield, Jenny
Oleksiw, Susan (Prince)
Oliphant, Dave (Edward Davis)
Oliver, Kelly
Oliver, Lawrence J.
Olsen, Lance (M.)
Olson, Arielle North

Olson, Kirby
Olson, Lester C.
Olson, Steven
Olson, Ted
Olson, Toby
Oltion, Jerry
Ondaatje, Michael
Ondego, Ogova
Oneal, Elizabeth
Opie, Iona
Orel, Harold
Ormsby, Frank
Orr, Gregory (Simpson)
Ortego, Sheila
Osborne, Charles
Ostow, Micol
Ostrom, Hans
Overton, Ron
Owens, Rochelle
Oxendine, Bess Holland
Oxley, William
Ozick, Cynthia
Ozsvath, Zsuzsanna
Pack, Robert
Packer, Joan Garrett
Paddock, Lisa
Padel, Ruth
Padgett, Ron
Padilla, Ignacio
Page, Clarence
Page, Geoff(rey Donald)
Page, Norman
Paietta, Ann C.
Palencia, Elaine Fowler
Palmer, William J.
Palumbo-Liu, David
Panofsky, Ruth
Paranjape, Makarand (Ramach-andra)
Parascandola, Louis J.
Paravisini-Gebert, Lizabeth
Pardue, Diana
Pari, Susanne
Parini, Jay
Paris, Barry
Paris, Bernard Jay
Parker, David
Parker, Gary E.
Parker, Nancy W(inslow)
Parker, Peter (Robert Nevill)
Parrish, Tim
Partridge, Jenny (Lilian)
Pascoe, Bruce
Passaro, Maria (C. Pastore)
Pastan, Linda
Paterson, Janet M.
Paterson, Katherine (Womeldorf)
Paterson, Ronald (William Keith)
Patey, Douglas Lane
Patten, Brian
Patterson, Michael
Paulson, Michael G.
Paulson, Ronald (Howard)
Pauly, Rebecca M.
Pawlak, Mark
Payne, Daniel G.

Literary Criticism And History- *cont.*

Payne, Donald Gordon
Payne, Ladell
Payne Fisk, Deborah C.
Payton, Rodney J.
Peabody, Richard (Myers)
Peace, Richard (Arthur)
Peachment, Christopher
Peacock, Molly
Peak, John A.
Pearl, Matthew
Pearlman, Daniel D.
Pearlman, Mickey
Pearsall, Derek (Albert)
Pearson, Kit
Peavler, Terry J.
Peck, Dale
Peck, David R.
Peck, Jeffrey M.
Peck, Richard (Wayne)
Peel, Ellen S.
Pelletier, Nancy
Pelli, Moshe
Pélot, Pierre
Pendergast, John S.
Perelman, Bob
Perez, Rolando
Perkins, George (Burton)
Perkins, Michael
Perloff, Marjorie (Gabrielle)
Perry, Curtis
Perry, Margaret
Perry, Paul
Perry, Phyllis Alesia
Peters, Margot (McCullough)
Peters, Robert
Peterson, Elmer
Peterson, Richard S(cot)
Petit, Susan
Petrie, Anne
Petro, Peter
Petry, Alice Hall
Petsalis-Diomidis, Nicholas
Pettit, Rhonda S(ue)
Pfaelzer, Jean
Pfanner, (Anne) Louise
Pflieger, Pat
Phillippy, Patricia Berrahou
Phillips, Clyde
Phillips, Delores
Phillips, Jayne Anne
Phillips, Kate
Phillips, Susan E.
Philmus, Robert M(ichael)
Pick, John Barclay
Pickering, Samuel F(rancis)
Pickett, Rex
Pierce, David
Pike, David L.
Pilipp, Frank
Pilling, John
Piñol, Albert Sánchez
Pinsker, Sanford S.
Pinsky, Robert
Pitcher, Harvey John
Pittock, Joan (Hornby)
Pizer, John

Plante, David (Robert)
Platt, Peter G(odfrey)
Plumly, Stanley (Ross)
Podhoretz, Norman
Pogue, Bill
Pogue, Charles (Edward)
Polhemus, Robert M(ackinlay)
Polito, Robert
Polizzotti, Mark
Pollack, Rachel
Pollak, Vivian R.
Polley, Judith Anne
Pollock, (Mary) Sharon
Polukhina, Valentina
Pool, Gail
Pope, Rebecca A.
Porte, Joan
Porter, Joe Ashby
Porter, Laurin
Porter, Sue
Portis, Charles (McColl)
Potter, Carol
Potts, Stephen W(ayne)
Poultney, David
Powell, D. A.
Powell, David
Powell, David A.
Powell, Eric
Powell, Neil
Power, Patrick C.
Powers, J. L.
Powers, Lyall H(arris)
Pratt, John Clark
Prawer, S(iegbert) S(alomon)
Prendergast, Mark J(oseph
   Anthony)
Price, Alan
Price, John (T.)
Prickett, Stephen
Priestman, Martin
Pritchard, William H.
Pritchett, Kay
Probyn, Clive T.
Promis, José
Prowse, Brad A.
Pruter, Robert
Pucci, Pietro
Pugh, Dianne G.
Pugsley, Alex
Pullein-Thompson, Diana
Pullein-Thompson, Josephine
Purdy, Dwight H(illiard)
Purkiss, Diane
Purser, John W(hitley)
Putter, Ad
Pynchon, Thomas
Qualey, Marsha
Quantic, Diane Dufva
Queeney, Courtney
Quetchenbach, Bernard W.
Quinn, Rob
Quiñones, Magaly
Quinones, Ricardo J(oseph)
Quintero, Ruben
Raban, Jonathan
Rabassa, Gregory

Rabaté, Jean-Michel
Rabb, Jonathan
Radano, Ronald M.
Raine, Craig (Anthony)
Rainey, Lawrence S.
Rajan, Tilottama
Rajic, Negovan
Ramazani, Jahan
Ramos, Luis Arturo
Ramsden, Herbert
Randall, Dale B(ertrand) J(onas)
Randall, Francis Ballard
Randall, Rona
Rankin, Herbert David
Raphael, Lev
Rapoport, Nessa
Rasmussen, Alis A.
Ratcliffe, Eric Hallam
Rathmell, George W(esley)
Ravitz, Abe (Carl)
Rawson, Claude Julien
Ray, Robert H.
Ray, Sheila G(raham)
Rayfield, Donald
Raymond, Jonathan
Read, David
Reay, Barry
Reddy, Maureen T.
Redhill, Michael H.
Redonnet, Marie
Reed, James
Reed, T(erence) J(ames)
Reed, Thomas L.
Reeder, Stephanie Owen
Reeve, F(ranklin) D(olier)
Regan, Stephen
Reginald, Robert
Reibetanz, John
Reichardt, Mary R.
Reichertz, Ronald R.
Reid, David
Reinfeld, Linda M.
Reizbaum, Marilyn
Rember, John
Remer, Gary
Renaux, Sigrid
Renker, Elizabeth
Resnick, Rachel
Reusche, Taylor McCafferty
Revard, Carter (Curtis)
Rey, Dennison
Reynolds, (Richard) Clay
Riach, Alan
Ribowsky, Mark
Ricapito, Joseph V.
Ricardo, Jack
Rice, Zoe
Rich, Adrienne (Cecile)
Rich, Francine Poppo
Rich, Nathaniel
Richard-Allerdyce, Diane
Richardson, Mark
Richardson, Peter
Richardson, Riché
Richetti, John J.
Richie, Donald

Richmond, Hugh Macrae
Richter, Daniel K(arl)
Richter, Gregory C.
Richter, Harvena
Rickards, John
Ricks, Christopher
Ricks, James
Ridgway, Keith
Riede, David G(eorge)
Riggs, Paula Detmer
Riley, Joan
Rimstead, Roxanne L.
Rippley, LaVern J.
Ritchie, Daniel E.
Ritchie, Harry
Ritthaler, Shelly
Rizzo, Margaret
Robb, Candace
Robbins, Bruce
Roberts, Daniel Sanjiv
Roberts, Diane
Roberts, Francis X.
Robinson, Andrew
Robinson, Spider
Rochman, Hazel
Rodden, John (Gallagher)
Roddick, Alan
Rodgers, Alan (Paul)
Rodgers, Audrey T(ropauer)
Rodgers, Eamonn
Rodgers, Marion Elizabeth
Rodriguez, Alfred
Rodríguez, Andrés
Rodriguez, Manuel
Roe, Nicholas
Roe, Sue
Roe, Sue (Lynn)
Roger, Philippe
Rogers, Deborah D(ee)
Rogers, Franklin Robert
Rogers, Katharine M.
Rogers, Pat
Rogers, Rosemary
Rollin, Roger B.
Romeril, John
Ronell, Avital
Rooke, Leon
Rooksby, Rikky
Rose, Mike
Rose, Phyllis
Rosen, David J.
Rosenak, Chuck
Rosenberg, John D(avid)
Rosenblatt, Jason P.
Rosenfeld, Nancy (G.)
Rosenthal, Debra J.
Rosenthal, Lucy (Gabrielle)
Roses, Lorraine Elena
Ross, Angus
Ross, Charles L(ouis)
Ross, Ian Campbell
Ross, Lawrence C.
Ross, Stephen M.
Rossi, Hozy (Joe)
Roston, Murray
Roth, Lorna

Literary Criticism And History-
cont.

Literary Criticism And History-
cont.

Literary Criticism And History-
cont.

Literary Criticism And History-
cont.

Roth, Norman
Rotter, Gabe
Rouse, Mary A(mes)
Rousseau, George S.
Rowland, Peter Kenneth
Rowlinson, Matthew
Royal, Robert
Royle, Nicholas
Rubin, Larry (Jerome)
Rubin-Dorsky, Jeffrey
Rucker, Mike
Ruddick, Nicholas
Rudolf, Anthony
Rudrum, Alan (William)
Rudy, Jason R.
Rudy, Susan Arlene
Rulon, Philip Reed
Rumens, Carol
Runyon, Randolph Paul
Ruoff, A. LaVonne Brown
Rupp, Richard H.
Rusch, Kristine Kathryn
Rushton, Julian (Gordon)
Russell, Martin (James)
Russell, Rinaldina
Russell, Sharon A.
Ryan, Barbara
Ryken, Leland
Sabin, Roger (John)
Sachs, Murray
Saddlemyer, (Eleanor) Ann
Sadler, Amy
Sadlier, Darlene J.
Sajdak, Bruce T.
Sallis, James
Salwak, Dale (Francis)
Salway, Peter
Salzman, Eva Frances
Sambrook, A(rthur) J(ames)
Sammon, Paul M.
Samuels, Shirley
Sanchez-Eppler, Karen
Sanders, Andrew
Sanders, Arlene
Sanders, David
Sanders, Eve Rachele
Sanders, Tony
Sandler, Irving (Harry)
Sandy, Stephen
Santos, Sherod
Sargent, Lyman Tower
Sargent, Pamela
Saslow, James M(axwell)
Sauer, Elizabeth M.
Saunders, George W.
Saunders, James Robert
Saunders, Max
Savage, Georgia
Savage, Tom
Saville, Diana
Sawyer-Laucanno, Christopher
Sayers, Valerie
Sayre, Gordon M.
Scaglione, Aldo
Scammell, Michael
Scarlett, Elizabeth

Schaefer, Claudia
Schapiro, Barbara
Scheele, Roy
Scheese, Donald
Scheil, Andrew P.
Scheindlin, Raymond P.
Schenkkan, Robert (Frederic)
Scherf, Kathleen D.
Schiff, James A(ndrew)
Schiffer, James (M.)
Schipper de Leeuw, W. J. J.
Schmid, Walter Thomas
Schmidt, Gary D.
Schmidt, Heidi
Schmidt, Michael (Norton)
Schmitz, Dennis
Schneider, Ben Ross
Schneider, Karen
Schneider, Robert
Schoffman, Nachum
Schone, Robin
Schulman, Ivan A(lbert)
Schultz, Susan M.
Schupack, Deborah
Schuster, Marilyn R.
Schwartz, Evan I.
Schwartz, Kessel
Schwartz, Richard A(lan)
Schwarz, Daniel R(oger)
Schweickart, Patrocinio P.
Scofield, Martin (Paul)
Scott, Grant F.
Scott, Margaret (Allan Bennett)
Scott, Nina M.
Scott, P(aul) H(enderson)
Scott, Whitney S.
Screech, M(ichael) A(ndrew)
Scrivener, Michael (Henry)
Scully, James (Joseph)
Seaman, Ann Rowe
Searle, Elizabeth
Sedia, Ekaterina
Seed, David
Seelye, John (Douglas)
Seese, June Akers
Segal, Susan
Seiferle, Rebecca
Seifrid, Thomas
Seigel, Catharine F.
Selig, Robert L.
Sellin, Christine Petra
Sellin, Eric
Seltzer, Leon F(rancis)
Selzer, Jack
Senior, W(illiam) A.
Senna, Danzy
Sensibar, Judith L(evin)
Serrano, Lucienne J.
Sessions, William
Sewell, Lisa
Sexton, Linda Gray
Shaaban, Bouthaina
Shafer, Neil
Shafer, Yvonne
Shaffer, Peter (Levin)
Shank, Theodore

Shapcott, Thomas W(illiam)
Shapiro, Harvey
Sharpe, Kevin
Sharpe, Tony
Sharpe, William Chapman
Shattuck, George C.
Shatzky, Joel
Shaul, David Leedom
Shaw, Carolyn V.
Shaw, Patrick W.
Shaw, Robert B.
Sheard, Sarah
Sheehan, Michael J.
Sheehy, Gail
Shelby, Anne
Sheldon, Mary
Shelton, Mark L(ogan)
Shem, Samuel
Shemie, Bonnie (Jean Brenner)
Shepard, Jim
Shepherd, John Scott
Sherry, Norman
Sherry, Patrick
Shevelow, Kathryn
Shields, Jody
Shillingsburg, Miriam (Carolyn)
   Jones
Shillingsburg, Peter L(eRoy)
Shinagel, Michael
Shinn, Thelma J.
Shirley, Frances A.
Shneidman, N(oah) N(orman)
Shone, Anna
Shookman, Ellis
Short, Robert Stuart
Shoup, Barbara
Showalter, Elaine
Showalter, Gena
Shrimsley, Bernard
Sicher, Efraim
Sicherman, Carol
Silberman, Marc (D.)
Silva, Daniel (Joseph)
Silver, Anna Krugovoy
Silver, Brenda R.
Silver, Carole G(reta)
Simmons, Cynthia Francene
Simmons, Diane E.
Simmons, James C(oleman)
Simmons, Thomas
Simon, Daniel (Martin)
Simon, Neil
Simpson, Dorothy
Sims, Michael
Singer, Alan
Singh, Amritjit
Sinyard, Neil
Sipherd, Ray
Siracusa, Catherine (Jane)
Sirowitz, Hal
Sisk, David W.
Sitter, John E(dward)
Sizemore, Christine Wick
Skerpan-Wheeler, Elizabeth
   (Penley)
Skinner, Michael

Skreslet, Paula Youngman
Slade, Bernard
Slade, Leonard A.
Slater, Michael
Slattery, Dennis Patrick
Slavin, Bill
Slavin, Helen
Sleigh, Tom
Slesinger, Warren
Slethaug, Gordon E.
Sloan, John
Sloman, Albert Edward
Slovic, Scott H.
Smart, Ian Isidore
Smigel, Robert
Smith, Ali
Smith, Barbara Herrnstein
Smith, Bruce R.
Smith, Christopher
Smith, Dave
Smith, Erin A(nn)
Smith, Faye McDonald
Smith, Janna M(alamud)
Smith, Jeanne Rosier
Smith, Martha Nell
Smith, Morris
Smith, Nicholas D.
Smith, Paul Julian
Smith, Robert Ellis
Smith, Sarah (W. R.)
Smith, Stephanie A.
Smith, Vivian (Brian)
Smith, William Jay
Smither, Elizabeth
Snodgrass, Mary Ellen
Snow, Donald
Sok-Kyong, Kang
Sokol, B. J.
Sokoloff, Naomi B.
Solmssen, Arthur R(obert)
   G(eorge)
Sonenberg, Maya
Sorkin, Adam J.
Soyinka, Wole
Spack, Ruth
Spacks, Barry
Spacks, Patricia Meyer
Spaeth, Anthony
Spahr, Juliana
Spanier, Sandra Whipple
Spear, Hilda D.
Speck, Nancy
Spelman, Cornelia Maude
Spencer, Elizabeth
Spencer, John (Walter)
Spencer, Scott
Spens, Christiana
Spiegelman, Willard
Spielberg, Peter
Spivack, Charlotte
Spivack, Kathleen (Romola
   Drucker)
Spurling, Hilary
Spurling, John
Spycket, Jerome
St. Clair, William

Literary Criticism And History-
cont.

Literary Criticism And History-
cont.

Literary Criticism And History-
cont.

Literary Criticism And History-
cont.

Stableford, Brian M(ichael)
Stacey, Tom
Stack, George
Stade, George
Stafford, Fiona (Jane)
Stainton, Leslie
Staley, Lynn
Stallworthy, Jon (Howie)
Stammers, John
Standen, John Derek
Stanley, Patricia H.
Stannard, Martin (J.)
Stansberry, Domenic (Joseph)
Stansky, Peter (David Lyman)
Stanton, Joseph
Stashower, Daniel (Meyer)
Stave, Shirley A.
Staynes, Jill
Stead, C(hristian) K(arlson)
Steel, Gayla R(uth)
Steele, Cynthia
Steele, Timothy (Reid)
Steggle, Matthew
Stein, Eugene
Stein, Kevin
Steinberg, Erwin R.
Steinberg, Mark D(avid)
Steiner, Evgeny
Steiner, George
Steinman, Louise
Sten, Christopher (W.)
Stepanchev, Stephen
Stephen, Martin
Stephens, Meic
Stern, David
Sterne, Richard Clark
Sternlicht, Sanford
Stevens, Dick
Stevens, Peter (Stanley)
Stevenson, Sucie
Stevenson, Talitha
Stevenson (Lucas), Anne
Stewart, Jack (F.)
Stewart, Susan
Stibbe, Mark W. G.
Stiles, T. J.
Stillinger, Jack
Stillman, (John) Whit(ney)
Stivale, Charles J.
Stokoe, E(dward) G(eorge)
Stokoe, James
Stollman, Arveh Lev
Stoltzfus, Ben
Stone, Cynthia L.
Stone, Harry
Stone, James S(tuart)
Stone, R. W.
Stone, Sarah
Stoneman, Richard (John)
Stoner, Tom
Storch, Margaret
Storey, David (Malcolm)
Storey, Dee
Storey, Edward
Storey, Gail Donohue
Storey, Mark

Stork, Francisco X.
Stourton, Ivo
Stout, Janis P.
Stowe, William W.
Strachan, Ian
Straub, Peter (Francis)
Strauss, Jennifer (Wallace)
Strieber, Anne
Stuart, Dabney
Stuhr(-Rommereim), Rebecca
  (Ann)
Sturges, Robert S(tuart)
Sturman, Jennifer
Suleiman, Susan Rubin
Sullivan, Brad
Sullivan, C(harles) W(illiam)
Sullivan, Garrett A.
Sullivan Harper, Donna Akiba
Sultan, Stanley
Sultana, Donald Edward
Summerhawk, Barbara
Sun, Yifeng
Sundahl, Daniel James
Sundelson, David
Sutcliffe, William
Swafford, Jan Johnson
Sward, Robert S.
Swartz, Jon David
Sweeney, Marvin A.
Swift, Graham
Swift, Sue
Swinfen, Ann
Swope, Sam
Sword, Wiley
Syal, Meera
Sze, Arthur C.
Szekeres, Cyndy
Taaffe, Sonya
Takayama, Sandi
Talbot, Emile J.
Talese, Gay
Tamblyn, Amber
Tamburri, Anthony Julian
Tanaka, Yukiko
Tanner, Jo A.
Tanner, John S.
Tanner, Stephen L.
Tanselle, G(eorge) Thomas
Taplin, Oliver
Targoff, Ramie
Tarlton, John S.
Tarn, Nathaniel
Tarnawsky, Maxim
Tate, Greg
Tawil, Ezra
Tayler, Irene
Taylor, Beverly (White)
Taylor, Diana
Taylor, Gary
Taylor, Helen
Taylor, Henry
Taylor, Jonathan
Taylor, Kathy
Taylor, Nick
Taylor, Welford Dunaway
Taylor, William

Te Awekotuku, Ngahuia
Teachout, Terry
Teahan, Sheila
Tellkamp, Uwe
Terasawa, Mizuho
Terpening, Ron
Thacker, Robert
Thaden, Barbara Z.
Tharu, Susie
Theisz, R. D.
Theroux, Paul
Thesen, Sharon
Thiemann, Ronald F.
Thomas, Audrey (Grace)
Thomas, Brook
Thomas, Chantal
Thomas, Clara McCandless
Thomas, D(onald) M(ichael)
Thomas, H(ubert) Nigel
Thomas, Keith (Vivian)
Thomas, Lyn
Thompson, Richard
Thomson, Derick S(mith)
Thomson, George Henry
Thomson, Pat
Thomson, Peter (William)
Thormählen, Marianne
Thorne-Smith, Courtney
Thorsson, Örnólfur
Thrailkill, Jane
Thwaite, Anthony (Simon)
Tindall, Gillian (Elizabeth)
Tingum, Janice
Tinkle, Theresa L.
Tjardes, Tamara J.
Todd, Olivier
Todd, Pamela A.
Toews, Miriam
Tokarczyk, Michelle M.
Toker, Leona
Tolson, Jay
Tomalin, Claire
Tomaselli, Sylvana
Tomlinson, (Alfred) Charles
Tope, Rebecca
Torrance, Lee
Torres, Steven
Torsney, Cheryl B.
Toulmin, Vanessa Elizabeth
Towne, Marian K(leinsasser)
Townsend, John Rowe
Tracy, Lorna
Trapp, Kenneth R.
Traub, Charles (Henry)
Travers, Paul J(oseph)
Travisano, Thomas (J.)
Trawick, Leonard M.
Tredell, Nicolas (Samuel)
Trela, D(ale) J(ohn)
Trevor, Douglas
Trevor, William
Trimpey, John P.
Trites, Roberta Seelinger
Troy, Judy
Trueman, Terry
Trzebinski, Errol

Tsushima, Satoko
Tucker, (Allan) James
Tucker, Judy H.
Tucker, Martin
Tunnell, Michael O('Grady)
Turco, Lewis (Putnam)
Turner, Brian (Lindsay)
Turner, Mark
Turner, Megan Whalen
Tydeman, William (Marcus)
Tye, Michael
Tyler, Anne
Tyler, Sandra
Tysdahl, Bjorn Johan
Tyson, Lois (M.)
Tyson, Salinda
Ueda, Makoto
Ulmer, Gregory L(eland)
Umland, Samuel J(oseph)
Unglaub, Jonathan
Unrue, Darlene Harbour
Uruburu, Paula
Vachss, Andrew H(enry)
Valdés, Mario J.
Valentine, Jean
Valentine, Mark
Vallone, Lynne
van Alphen, Ernst
Van Booy, Simon
Van Delden, Maarten
van der Zee, Karen
Van Domelen, John E(mory)
Van Dover, J(ames) K(enneth)
van Duzer, Chet A.
van Hensbergen, Gijs
van Itallie, Jean Claude
Vanderham, Paul
VanMeter, Vandelia
Vapnyar, Lara
vas Dias, Robert
Vasta, Edward
Vaughan, Alden T(rue)
Vause, L(aurence) Mikel
Vazsonyi, Nicholas
Velkley, Richard L.
Vella, Christina
Veltri, George (M.)
Venclova, Tomas
Vendler, Helen (Hennessy)
Venolia, Jan(et G.)
Vermilye, Jerry
Vertreace-Doody, Martha Modena
Vick, Helen Hughes
Vidal, Gore
Vigée, Claude (Andre Strauss)
Vines, Lois Davis
Vinge, Vernor (Steffen)
Virgo, Seán
Visotzky, Burton L.
Visram, Rozina
Viswanathan, S(ubrahmanyam)
Vitiello, Justin
Vizenor, Gerald (Robert)
Voigt, Ellen Bryant
Volk, Patricia (Gay)
Vollendorf, Lisa

Index To Writing Categories

von Gunden, Kenneth
Vondung, Klaus
Voss, Ralph F.
Vukcevich, Ray
Wachtel, Eleanor
Waddington, Patrick (Haynes)
Waddington, Raymond B(ruce)
Waddington-Feather, John Joseph
Waelti-Walters, Jennifer (Rose)
Wagner-Martin, Linda C.
Wagschal, Steven
Wainscott, Ronald H(arold)
Wakoski, Diane
Waldman, Harry
Waldoff, Leon
Walker, Greg
Walker, Marianne (Cascio)
Walker, Martin
Wall, Cheryl A.
Wallace, Diana
Wallace, Ian
Wallace-Crabbe, Christopher (Keith)
Walsh, P(atrick) G(erard)
Walton, Kendall L(ewis)
Walton, Priscilla L.
Wambaugh, Joseph
Wandor, Michelene
Wang, Jing
Ward, Elizabeth Honor
Wardman, Gordon
Wardroper, John Edmund
Warfield, Gallatin
Warlick, Ashley
Warner, Francis
Warner, Marina
Warren, Charles
Warren, Kenneth W.
Warren, Rosanna
Washburn, Stan
Wasiolek, Edward
Watada, Terry
Waters, Claire M.
Waters, Sarah
Watkins, John
Watkins, William John
Watson, Ben
Watson, Clyde
Watson, George (Grimes)
Watson, J(ohn) R(ichard)
Watson, Roderick
Watson, Stephanie
Watson, Stephen
Waugh, Teresa (Lorraine)
Wayman, Tom
Wayne, Valerie
Weaks, Mary Louise
Weales, Gerald
Weatherhead, A(ndrew) Kingsley
Weaver, Afaa Michael
Webb, Janeen (S.)
Webb, Phyllis
Weber, Katharine
Weimer, Joan
Weinberg, Florence M(ay)
Weiner, Stephen

Weiner, Susan
Weinkauf, Mary S(tanley)
Weinroth, Michelle
Weinstein, Cindy
Weinstein, Mark Allen
Weinstein, Philip M.
Weinstock, Nicholas
Weintraub, Stanley
Weiss, Timothy F.
Welch, Robert
Welcher, Rosalind
Weldt-Basson, Helene Carol
Welford, Sue
Welish, Marjorie
Wells, Rebecca
Wells, Stanley (William)
Wells (Dimenstein), Catherine
Welsh, Alexander
Welsh, Frank (Reeson)
Weltner, Peter (Nissen)
Wenderoth, Joe
Wendling, Ronald C(harles)
Werlock, Abby Holmes P(otter)
Werman, Golda
Werner, Marta L.
Werris, Wendy
Wershler-Henry, Darren Sean
Wessell, Eva
West, James L(emuel) W(ills)
West, Sandra L.
Westburg, Barry (Richard)
Westling, Louise (Hutchings)
Weston, Susan
Westrum, Dexter
Wetmore, Kevin J. (Jr.)
What, Leslie
Wheeler, Deborah (Jean Ross)
Wheeler, Thomas
Whelehan, Imelda
Whitaker, Katie
White, Andrea
White, Carolinne
White, Edward M.
White, Kenneth
White, Mary Wheeling
Whitehead, Catherine Sarah
Whiteman, (David) Bruce
Whitman, Sylvia (Choate)
Whitson, Kathy J.
Whittemore, (Edward) Reed
Whitton, Kenneth S(tuart)
Wick, Walter
Wicker, Brian John
Wickham, Christopher J.
Widdicombe, Toby
Wiedemann, Barbara
Wieland, Liza
Wiesenfarth, Joseph (John)
Wiesepape, Betty Holland
Wilbur, Richard (Purdy)
Wilde, Lyn Webster
Wilding, Michael
Wilkie, Pamela
Willett, Ralph
Williams, Gerhild Scholz
Williams, Hugh Steadman

Williams, John A(lfred)
Williams, John Hartley
Williams, Mark
Williams, R. D.
Williams, Vera B.
Williamson, Joel
Willis, Resa
Wills, Garry
Wilmer, Clive
Wilson, A(ndrew) N.
Wilson, Andrew
Wilson, Barbara Ker
Wilson, David Niall
Wilson, Frances Engle
Wilson, John Morgan
Wilson, Jonathan
Wilson, Robley
Wilson, Sharon Rose
Winchell, Donna Haisty
Winder, Simon
Winegarten, Renee
Wing, Betsy
Winnick, R. H.
Winnifrith, T(homas) J(ohn)
Winston, Daoma
Winter, Kari J.
Winter, Michael
Wisker, Gina
Witemeyer, Hugh Hazen
Wittenborn, Dirk
Wixson, Douglas
Wohlgelernter, Maurice
Wolf, Reva
Wolfe, Peter
Wolff, Cynthia Griffin
Wolff, Geoffrey
Wolff, Sally
Wolfson, Susan J.
Wollen, Peter
Wolven, Scott
Wolverton, Cheryl
Wolverton, Robert E.
Wolzien, Valerie
Wood, Bridget
Wood, Dennis (Michael)
Wood, Frances
Wood, Gerald C.
Wood, James
Wood, Marguerite N.
Wood, Michael
Wood, Patricia
Woodger, Elin
Woodhouse, S(usan) T.
Woodland, Malcolm
Woods, Brenda
Woody, Elizabeth
Woolfe, Sue
Woollen, Geoff
Worsham, Lynn
Wray, John
Wright, Alexis
Wright, Barbara
Wright, Cora M.
Wright, Franz
Wright, George Thaddeus
Wright, Helen L(ouise)

Wright, Julie
Wright, Michael J(ohn)
Wright, William Edward
Wu, Fan
Wu, Qingyun
Wu, Yenna
Wullschläger, Jackie
Wurst, Karin A.
Würzbach, Natascha
Wyatt, David M.
Wyatt-Brown, Anne M(arbury)
Wymark, Olwen (Margaret)
Wynne, Marcus
Xi, Xi
Ya rid, Na zik Sa ba
Yamashita, Karen Tei
Yarbrough, Stephen R.
Yazdanfar, Farzin
Yglesias, Rafael
York, R. A.
Yorke, Margaret
Yothers, Brian
Young, Bette Roth
Young, David (Pollock)
Young, James E.
Young, Robin
Young, Ruth
Yount, Steven
Yu, Anthony C.
Yudkin, Leon Israel
Yurick, Sol
Yuryenén, Sergey
Zaborowska, Magdalena J.
Zacharasiewicz, Waldemar
Zak, William F.
Zambreno, Mary Frances
Zamora, Bernice (B. Ortiz)
Zamora, Lois Parkinson
Zarucchi, Jeanne Morgan
Zegura, Elizabeth Chesney
Zelitch, Simone E.
Zettel, Sarah
Zettler, Steve
Zietlow, E(dward) R(obert)
Ziff, Larzer
Zilboorg, Caroline (Crawford)
Zimmerman, Cynthia (Diane)
Zimmermann, Arnold Walter
Zimpel, Lloyd
Zinnes, Harriet
Ziolkowski, Eric J(ozef)
Ziolkowski, Theodore
Zolotow, Charlotte
Zook, Kristal Brent
Zunshine, Lisa

Local History/Rural Topics

Aberjhani
Achenbach, Joel
Ackerman, Susan Yoder
Adepoju, Aderanti
Aird, Catherine
Allahar, Anton L.
Allen, John E(lliston)

Local History/Rural Topics-
cont.

Local History/Rural Topics-
cont.

Local History/Rural Topics-
cont.

Local History/Rural Topics-
cont.

Local History/Rural Topics-*cont.*

Scott, Nina M.
Sears, James T(homas)
Sehene, Benjamin
Selcer, Richard F.
Shandler, Jeffrey
Shirley, Shirley
Short, Brian (Michael)
Singh, Chetan
Slader, John M.
Smart, S(tephen) Bruce
Soffer, Olga
Spooner, Mary Helen
Stecker, Ann Page
Stepanchev, Stephen
Stout, Harry S.
Sward, Robert S.
Swierenga, Robert P.
Swift, Jamie
Teja, Jesus F(rancisco) de la
Tennyson, Brian
Thirsk, (Irene) Joan
Thom, James Alexander
Tillson, Albert H.
Tischauser, Leslie V.
Tisdell, Clement Allan
Towne, Marian K(leinsasser)
Tripp, Charles R(ees) H(oward)
van Onselen, Charles
Vaughan, Megan
Verluise, Pierre
Vitz, Robert C.
Walker, Kenneth Roland
Ware, Jane (O.)
Warmington, William Allan
Warren, Louis S.
Watson, Benjamin A.
Weaver, Frederick S(tirton)
Webster, Len
Wells, Mary Ann
Westmacott, Richard N.
Whelan, Ruth
Whynott, Douglas (Vernon)
Williams, Brooke
Williams, Jacqueline (B.)
Williams, James C.
Williamson, J(erry) W(ayne)
Willmott, Phyllis
Wilson, Barry K.
Winearls, Joan
Woog, Adam
Youst, Lionel
Zeier, Joan T(heresa)

Marine Sciences/Oceanography

Abrams, Douglas Carlton
Barry, James P(otvin)
Bell, David Owen
Bhatt, Jagdish J(eyshanker)
Bolster, W(illiam) Jeffrey
Burger, Joanna
Calder, Nigel (David Ritchie)
Charlier, Roger Henri
Clark, A(ilsa) M.

Marine Sciences/Oceanography-*cont.*

Corson, Trevor
Cox, Christopher Barry
Crockett, Rigel
Doak, Wade (Thomas)
Dunlap, Julie
Earle, Sylvia A.
Eltringham, S(tewart) K(eith)
Fitzsimons, Cecilia (A. L.)
Fleisher, Paul
Foster, Nora R(akestraw)
Gillespie, Angus Kress
Gleick, Peter H.
Halfmann, Janet
Hamilton-Paterson, James
Hattendorf, John B(rewster)
Hearn, Chester G.
Horne, R(alph) A(lbert)
Joyner, Tim(othy)
Kent, James M.
King, (William) Dennis
Kleh, Cindy (L.)
Kling, Christine
Launer, Donald
Llewellyn, Sam
Lord, Nancy J.
Merne, Oscar James
Meurn, Robert J.
Miller, Karl (Fergus Connor)
Moore, John N(orton)
Noble, Dennis L.
Patrick, Jim
Philbrick, Nathaniel
Pörtner, Hans O.
Raudkivi, A(rved) J(aan)
Reinstedt, Randall A.
Roberts, Callum
Robinson, Chuck
Robinson, Debbie
Sindermann, Carl J(ames)
Slader, John M.
Thompson, Mark L.
Thomson, James Miln
Vermeij, Geerat J.
Vogel, Carole Garbuny
Waters, David Watkin
Weisberg, Joseph
Williamson, Donald I.
Wu, Norbert

Marketing

Agins, Teri
Alessandra, Tony
Anderson, H(ugh) George
Ariff, Mohamed
Balter, Dave
Bertrand, Marsha
Bishop, Jacqueline Kay
Boutilier, Robert
Branch, Alan E(dward)
Brunelle, Dorval
Buscall, Jon
Cathcart, Jim
Cespedes, Frank V.

Marketing-*cont.*

Cohen, Debra Nussbaum
Cox, Roger (Kenneth)
Crawford, Mark
Davidson, Jeff
Day, Nancy
Dooley, Brian J.
Duggleby, John
Duncan, William (Robert)
Edwards, Sarah (Anne)
Frazier, Shirley George
Frigstad, David B.
Garber, Anne
Gilson, Christopher C.
Graham, Carol (Lee)
Graham, Jefferson
Green, Charles H.
Hanlon, Patrick
Hartley, Steven W.
Hauptman, Don
Hayden, C. J.
Heertje, Arnold
Hiam, Alexander
Hibbs, John
Huang, Gregory T.
Israel, Shel
Jiang, Fuming
Jones, John Philip
Kapferer, Jean-Noel
Kaynak, Erdener
Keller, Edward B.
Kimura, Margaret
King, William Richard
Kotler, Neil G.
Kotler, Philip
Kraushar, Peter Maximilian
Kruger, Arnd
Kuczmarski, Thomas D(ale)
Kuhre, W. Lee
Lauterborn, Robert F.
LeBoeuf, Michael
Leerburger, Benedict A.
Levinson, Jay Conrad
Levy, Robert A.
Locke, Christopher
Loudon, David L.
Lowenstein, Michael W.
Magrath, Allan J.
Malone, Susan (Mary)
Marconi, Joe
Marston, Cam
Mayfield, Terry L.
Mazur, Laurie Ann
McCarthy, Nan
McKenna, Patrick J.
Mellor, John W(illiams)
Mendelsohn, Martin
Montgomery, David Bruce
Montoya, Peter
Morison, Robert F.
Moschis, George P.
Nissanoff, Daniel
O'Leary, Patrick
Ocampo, José Antonio
Papes, Robert
Patel, Raj
Pavlik, John V.
Polonsky, Michael Jay

Marketing-*cont.*

Poundstone, William
Prince, Russ Alan
Reichert, Tom
Ries, Laura
Rivkin, Steve
Sant, Thomas
Sayre, Shay
Seabrook, John M.
Secretan, Lance H. K.
Sharpe, William F(orsyth)
Smart, Bradford D.
Smith, J. Walker
Steinmetz, Lawrence Leo
Stevens, Robert E(llis)
Stimmler, Jane K.
Stone, Merlin (David)
Tancer, Bill
Teller, Neville
Terpstra, Vern
Thompson, Donald N.
Towse, Ruth
Vandermerwe, Sandra
Vavra, Terry G.
Vinjamuri, David
Vitali, Julius
Ware, Leslie
Winkler, John
Worcester, Robert
Young, Antony
Zuckerman, Mary Ellen

Mathematics/Statistics

Aczel, Amir D.
Adams, Colin C.
Addison, Paul S.
Allen, Michael Patrick
Allen, Myron B.
Alligood, Kathleen T.
Arnold, Arnold F.
Arrow, Kenneth (Joseph)
Ascher, Marcia
Backus, George Edward
Baker, Alan
Balakrishnan, N.
Barbeau, Edward J(oseph)
Bartz, Albert
Berinstein, Paula
Blossfeld, Hans Peter
Blum, Lenore (Carol)
Boaler, Jo
Bonnor, William Bowen
Boot, John C. G.
Bressoud, David M(arius)
Burk, Frank
Burns, Marilyn
Byers, William
Byrt, Edwin Andrew
Carr-Hill, Roy
Carter, Martin R(oger)
Cassels, J(ohn) W(illiam) S(cott)
Chaitin, Gregory J.
Christodoulou, Demetrios
Clawson, Calvin C.
Cronon, William

Bodmer, Walter (Fred)
Boehmer, Ulrike
Bogdanich, Walt
Bonadio, William
Bondy, Andy
Bookchin, Debbie
Boone, Daniel R.
Borysenko, Joan
Bosco, Dominick
Bower, John Morton
Bowling, Lewis
Bown, Deni
Bowser, Benjamin P(aul)
Boxer, Arabella
Braham, (E.) Jeanne
Braine, David
Brandt, Allan M(orris)
Breeden, Joann Elizabeth
Brennan, Kate
Brewerton, Derrick (Arthur)
Brill, Marlene Targ
Brizendine, Louann
Brody, Jane E(llen)
Brody, Stuart
Bronzino, Joseph D.
Brookes, Tim
Brown, Douglas Robert
Brownlee, Shannon
Bruce, Robert S.
Brunelli, Jean
Bruno, Richard L(ouis)
Buhner, Stephen Harrod
Buller, David J.
Burak, Carl S.
Burnett, Gail Lemley
Burns, Richard Gordon
Burton, Wendy
Buser, Pierre
Bush, Barry (Michael)
Callahan, Daniel (J.)
Callaway, C. Wayne
Calvin, William H(oward)
Cameron, M(alcolm) L(aurence)
Cammermeyer, Margarethe
Campbell, Ian Barclay
Candland, Douglas Keith
Canin, Ethan
Cannon, Michael F.
Capacchione, Lucia
Caplan, Arthur L(eonard)
Capouya, John
Carlin, Vivian F.
Carling, Paul J.
Carlson, Laurie
Carr-Hill, Roy
Carson, Benjamin S(olomon)
Carson, Paul
Carter, Frances Monet
Carter, Rosalynn (Smith)
Cartmill, Matt
Cary, Margaret
Casey, Barbara
Casper, Monica J.
Cass, Dennis
Cassell, Eric J.
Cassell, Joan
Caster, Andrew I.

Cernada, George P.
Cerny, Frank J.
Chamberlain, Lorna M(arie)
Champion, J(ustin) A. I.
Chanoff, David
Charles, Sara C(onnor)
Cherry, Mark J.
Chesman, Andrea
Chia, Mantak
Chivian, Eric
Chopra, Deepak (K.)
Chris, Cynthia
Christakis, Nicholas A.
Clark, Andy
Clark, William R.
Claude-Pierre, Peggy
Clayton, David J.
Clayton, Lawrence (Otto)
Clegg, Holly Berkowitz
Clow, Barbara Hand
Cochrane, Peggy
Cohen, Richard M(artin)
Cohn, Jonathan
Cojocaru, Steven
Cole, Thomas R(ichard)
Coleman, C. Norman
Collin, Marion (Cripps)
Collinge, William (B.)
Collings, I. J.
Collins, Catherine Fisher
Collins, Joan
Colman, Carol
Connell, John
Connor, Daniel
Conrad, Peter
Cook, Rebecca J.
Cooper, Cary L.
Cooper, Kenneth H(ardy)
Coren, Stanley
Corrigan, Kelly
Corrington, Robert S.
Cournos, Francine
Cox, Ruth P.
Crabtree, Adam
Craig, Colleen
Crawford, Gregory A.
Croall, Jonathan
Cromwell, Rue L(eVelle)
Crosby, Donald G(ibson)
Crystal, David
Cullinane, Jan
Culyer, A(nthony) J(ohn)
Currey, Richard
Currie, Dwight
Curtis, Glade B.
D'Adamo, Peter J.
Dale, Rodney A. M.
Damasio, Antonio R.
Daniel, Wayne W.
Daniels, Anthony
Dantzer, Robert
Davenport, John (Chester)
Davey, H. E.
Davidson, Larry
Davies, Peter J.
Davies, Sharon L.
Davis, David Brion

Davis, Kathy E.
Davis, Mark H.
Day, Stacey B.
Dayton, Charles (W.)
de Angelis, Lissa G.
de Haas, Margaret
De Vos, Susan
Dean, Eric T.
Delaney, Gayle (M. V.)
Deller, John J.
Delves, Peter J(ohn)
Devor, Aaron H.
Diem, Max
Dierker, Larry
Dikötter, Frank
Dinerman, Beatrice
Dixon, Bernard
Dobrin, Lyn
Dobson, James C.
Dodge, Tom
Dodman, Nicholas H.
Doman, Glenn
Donaldson, Molla S(loane)
Donaldson, Ross I.
Dormandy, Thomas
Dossey, Larry
Downie, R(obert) S(ilcock)
Draper, Maureen McCarthy
Dreher, Henry
Drew, Horace R.
Drlica, Karl
Drummond, Edward H.
Duffin, Jacalyn
Duhl, Leonard J.
Duke, Martin
Duncan, Kirsty E.
Duvoisin, Roger C(lair)
Dyson, Esther
Eckard, Paula G.
Edlow, Jonathan A.
Edwards, Allen Jack
Edwards, Laurie Elizabeth
Edwards, Virginia
Eisenstein, Phyllis (Kleinstein)
Elbirt, Paula M.
Elias, Jason
Elizur, Joel
Ellenbecker, Todd S.
Ellis, Harold
Emmons, Henry
Emmons, Robert A.
Engel, Cindy
Engel, Jonathan
Engelhardt, H(ugo) Tristram
Engs, Ruth C(lifford)
Ensminger, Peter A.
Entine, Jon
Epstein, Helen
Epstein, Steven
Essex-Cater, Antony John
Evans, Richard J(ohn)
Eyer, Diane E(lizabeth)
Farber, Celia
Farber, Naomi
Farbman, Albert I.
Farley, Margaret A.
Faulkner, Mary

Feder, Bernard
Fedoroff, Nina (V.)
Feeney, Don J(oseph)
Feinstein, David
Feldman, Gayle
Felstein, Ivor
Felstiner, Mary Lowenthal
Fenner, Frank John
Ferber, Richard A.
Ferguson, Mark W. J.
Ferreiro, Carmen
Ferris, Paul
Feshbach, Murray
Field, Mark G(eorge)
Fine, Jonathan
Fink, Merton
Fink, Sheri
Finkel, Madelon Lubin
Finkelstein, Adrian
Finkelstein, Stan N.
Fischer, Lucy Rose
Fischer, Lynn
Fischetti, Mark
Fishman, Steve
Fitzsimons, Cecilia (A. L.)
Flaherty, Alice W.
Fleischman, Paul R.
Fleming, Alice (Carew Mulcahey)
Fleming, Anne
Flood, (Nancy) Bo
Foley, Denise (M.)
Forbes, Anna
Ford, Barbara
Foster, Steven
Fowers, Blaine J.
Fox, Barry
Fratkin, Elliot
Freed, Curt R(ichard)
Freedman, Michael R.
Fricchione, Gregory
Friedman, Paul (Alan)
Frist, William H.
Fritz, Robert
Fry, Virginia Lynn
Furdell, Elizabeth Lane
Furino, Antonio
Futcher, Jane P.
Galenorn, Yasmine
Gallagher, Patricia C.
Gallimore, Paul
Galvin, Matthew R(eppert)
Garrett, Laurie
Garrett, Susan
Garrison, Daniel H.
Gass, Thomas Edward
Gassenheimer, Linda
Gates, Ronda
Gaze, R(aymond) Michael
Gediman, Helen K.
Gerrig, Richard J.
Gesler, Wilbert M.
Getz, Marshall J(ay)
Geyman, John P.
Gifford, Rebecca
Gilbert, Harriett
Gillett, Grant (Randall)
Gilligan, James F.

Glantz, Kalman
Gochfeld, Michael
Goin, Suzanne
Golczewski, James A.
Gold, Michael
Goldberg, Bruce (Edward)
Goldberg, Jane G.
Goldberg, Leonard S.
Goldsmith, Jeff Charles
Gollaher, David L.
Goodwin, Frederick K(ing)
Gordon, April A.
Gordon, James S(amuel)
Gorman, James
Gosden, Roger
Gottlieb, Arthur
Goulbourne, Harry
Gould, K. Lance
Graeub, Ralph
Graham, John D.
Grant, James Russell
Grant, Pete
Graves, Joseph Lewis
Gravitz, Herbert L.
Green, (Charles Stuart) Jamison
Greene, Gayle
Greene, Melissa Fay
Greenhalgh, Susan
Greenwood-Waller, Judith
Greer, Jane
Greil, Arthur L(awrence)
Grierson, Bruce
Griffiths, Paul E(dmund)
Grob, Gerald N.
Growe, Sarah Jane
Guarnieri, Patrizia
Guggenbühl, Allan
Gullotta, Thomas P.
Gurvis, Sandra J.
Gustafson, Sid
Guthrie, Randolph H.
Habgood, John Stapylton
Hacker, Jacob S.
Haga, Enoch John
Haiken, Elizabeth
Hale, Nathan G.
Hales, Dianne R.
Halperin, Jonathan L.
Hamilton, Allan J.
Hanson, Peter G.
Hargarten, Stephen W.
Harpham, Wendy S(chlessel)
Harrington, Kathleen
Harrison, Ann Tukey
Harrison, Kathryn
Hart, Charles (A.)
Hartmann, Ernest L.
Harwood, (Henry) David
Haskell, Guy H.
Hassan, Aftab Syed
Hassen, Philip Charles
Hatton, Caroline
Häusler, Thomas
Havard, Cyril (William Holmes)
Hawkins, Anne Hunsaker
Hawthorne, Fran
Hayflick, Leonard

Haywood, Kathleen M.
Helms, Robert B(rake)
Henehan, Mary Pat
Henley, Arthur
Henry, Julie
Heppner, P(uncky) Paul
Herman, Ellen
Heyward, Vivian H.
Hiatt, Howard H(aym)
Hichwa, John S.
Hilden, Joanne (M.)
Hildt, Elisabeth
Hinnefeld, Joyce
Hobby, Elaine (Ann)
Hodgson, Harriet
Hoffman, Amy Beth
Holifield, E. Brooks
Holli, Betsy B.
Hollingsworth, A. B.
Holman, Susan R.
Houck, Judith A.
House, James S.
Howarth, Peter
Hoy, Claire
Huber, Jeffrey T(odd)
Humphreys, Margaret
Hundert, Edward M.
Hunt, Tony
Huston, James E(dward)
Hutcherson, Hilda
Huyghe, Patrick
Huyler, Frank
Hyman, Steven E(dward)
Iacoboni, Marco
Ireland, Patrick R(ichard)
Iserson, Kenneth Victor
Iversen, Leslie
Iyengar, Sujata
Jackson, Mark
Jackson, Marni
James, Oliver
Jamiolkowski, Raymond M.
Jamison, Kay R(edfield)
Janko, (Kathleen) Susan
Janowitz, Henry D.
Jaroff, Leon Morton
Jeffreys, Diarmuid
Jenike, Michael A.
Jensen, Arthur Robert
Jepson, Bryan
Johnson, Colin
Johnson, Sandy
Johnson, Victoria
Johnston, Joni E.
Jones, Richard Granville
Justman, Stewart
Kamil, Alan C(urtis)
Kandall, Stephen R.
Kane, Penny
Kannus, (Veli) Pekka
Kao, John J.
Kaplan, Jonathan
Kaplan, Kalman J.
Karkazis, Katrina
Karp, Larry
Kasabov, Nikola K(irilov)
Kaschak, Ellyn

Kassirer, Jerome P.
Katz, Jackson
Katzman, Melanie A.
Kaylin, Lucy
Keefe, Richard S.E.
Keen, Ernest
Kellerman, Jonathan
Kelman, Judith (Ann)
Kerner, Fred
Kessler, David A.
Kevill-Davies, Sally
Kevles, Bettyann Holtzmann
Khlentzos, Drew M.
Kilson, Marion D. de B.
Kimball, John (Ward)
Kincher, Jonni
King, Sorrel McElroy
Kipnis, Aaron R.
Kirkwood, Dianna
Kita, Joe
Kitzinger, Sheila
Klass, Perri (Elizabeth)
Klein, Allen
Klein, Donald F.
Klein, George
Klein, Sherwin
Klingenstein, Susanne
Klitzman, Robert (L.)
Knight, Bernard
Ko, Tanya Hyonhye
Kodis, Michelle R.
Koehn, Peter H.
Koenig, Harold G.
Koetzsch, Ronald E.
Kolata, Gina
Kolodny, Nancy J.
Komp, Diane M.
Kozol, Jonathan
Kraft, William F.
Kroll, Jerome
Kronenfeld, Jennie J(acobs)
Kuffel, Frances
Kulka, Richard A.
Kurland, Geoffrey
La Berge, Ann F.
La Greca, Annette M(arie)
LaDow, Beth
LaFevers, Stephen
Lance, James Waldo
Lang, Anthony E.
Lang, Susan S.
Laroche, Loretta
Larson, Edward J(ohn)
Lasswell, Marcia
Lax, Eric
Le Fanu, James
Leach, Penelope (Jane)
Leahy, Robert L.
Leaning, Jennifer
Leavitt, Caroline
Leavitt, Judith Walzer
LeClaire, Anne D(ickinson)
Leech, Kenneth
Legato, Marianne J.
Lehrer, Jonah
Leiblum, Sandra R.
Lemlin, Jeanne

Leonard, Annie
Lerner, Barron H.
Lerner, Henry M.
Lesch, John E(mmett)
Letcher, Andy
Leventhal, Bennett (L.)
Levi-Montalcini, Rita
Levine, Barbara Hoberman
Levinson, Harry
Levy, Thomas
Lewin, Roger A.
Lewis, Gregg (Allan)
Lewis, Myron
Lewis, Thomas H.
Libby, Ronald T(heodore)
Libov, Charlotte Ann
Lief, Judith L.
Lindell, Colleen
Lindemann, Mary
Lindner, Koenraad J(an)
Lingeman, Richard
Lipsyte, Robert (Michael)
Littman, Jonathan (Russell)
Livingston, Gordon (S.)
Livoti, Carol
Loewy, Erich H.
Longmate, Norman Richard
Loomis, Jennifer A.
Lorber, Judith
Love, Susan M.
Lovric, Michelle
Lubar, Joel F.
Lucas, Geralyn
Lucire, Yolande
Ludbrook, John
Luhrmann, T(anya) M(arie)
Lukas, Christopher
Lundberg, George D.
Lux, Maureen K.
Lyon, Elizabeth
Lyon, Jeff(rey R.)
Lysaught, Jerome P.
MacEoin, Denis
Machowicz, Richard J.
Mack, Arien
Mackey, Richard A.
Mackowski, Maura Phillips
MacMillan, Norma
MacPhee, Ross D(ouglas) E(arle)
Madrona, Lewis Mehl
Maeder, Thomas
Magner, Lois N.
Maher, Mary
Mahony, Patrick J(oseph)
Mahowald, Mary Briody
Mainiero, Lisa A.
Majure, Janet
Malone, Susan (Mary)
Mango, Karin N.
Manhein, Mary H(uffman)
Manning, Martha M.
Mantel, Samuel J(oseph)
Marangoni, Alejandro G.
Marble, Allan Everett
Marcell, Jacqueline
Marcus, Alan I.
Marion, Robert W.

Markel, Howard
Marks, David (Francis)
Marks, Gil(bert S.)
Marks, Lara Vivienne
Marland, Hilary
Marmot, Michael (Gideon)
Marriner Tomey, Ann
Marsa, Linda J.
Martell, Christopher R.
Martensen, Robert L.
Martin, Elizabeth A(nn)
Martinson, Ida M(arie)
Marx, Eva
Maskarinec, Gregory G.
Mason, Michael Paul
Massie, Elizabeth
Masters, Alexander
Mates, Susan Onthank
Matteo, Sherri
Maximovich, Stanley P.
Mayes, Linda C(arol)
Mayor, Federico
McCaffery, Margo
McCall, Robert B.
McCann, Richard
McClelland, Charles Edgar
McCormick, Sabrina
McCullough, Michael E.
McEntyre, Marilyn Chandler
McFadden, Steven
McKenna, Lindsay Gvhdi
McKenna, Maryn
McNeely, Ian F.
McQuown, Judith H.
McWilliams, Margaret (Ann Edgar)
Meckel, Richard A(lan)
Melville, Arabella
Mercati, Maria (B.)
Merz, Jon F.
Mesa-Lago, Carmelo
Mesibov, Gary B.
Metcalf, Donald
Metzl, Jonathan M.
Meyer, Dick
Midkiff, Mary D.
Mieth, Dietmar
Miles, Steven H.
Milhorn, H. Thomas
Miller, Jonathan (Wolfe)
Miller, Thomas W.
Minar, Barbra (Goodyear)
Mindell, Amy (Kaplan)
Minkler, Meredith
Mitchell, Ellinor R.
Mnookin, Seth
Mogil, Cindy R.
Montagnier, Luc
Montauredes, Rita
Moore, J. Stuart
Moore, Michele
Moreau, David Merlin
Morreim, E. Haavi
Morris, G. Scott
Morris, Lois B.
Mougios, Vassilis
Moyé, Lemuel A.

Mulgrew, Ian
Mundis, Hester (Jane)
Mundy, Liza
Munson, Ronald
Murcott, Anne
Murphy, Gregory L(eo)
Murphy, Martha W(atson)
Murphy, Patricia J.
Murphy, Shane M.
Musgrave, Gerald L.
Myss, Caroline
Nahas, Gabriel G(eorges)
Nash, Joyce D.
Nash, Michael R.
Navarra, Tova
Nemec, James
Nesse, Randolph M.
Nestler, Eric J.
Newcomer, Robert (J.)
Nice, Jill
Nicholls, Henry
Nichter, Mark (Andrew)
Nigam, Sanjay (Kumar)
Nobile, Philip
Noble, William Charles
Nuland, Sherwin
Nussbaum, Paul David
Nüsslein-Volhard, Christiane
O'Brien, Robyn
O'connell, David F.
O'Connor, Pat
O'Connor, Richard
O'Mara, Peggy (Noreen)
Oakley, Ann
Odets, Walt (Whitman)
Offit, Paul A.
Okoro, Anezi
Oldham, John (M.)
Oppenheim, Michael
Orent, Wendy
Ornish, Dean
Osborn, Ian
Oser, Marie
Owen, David (Anthony Llewellyn)
Palmer, Larry I.
Pampel, Fred C.
Park, Katharine
Park, Roberta J.
Parker, Steve
Parkinson, Stanley
Pashkow, Fredric J.
Patt, Richard B.
Patterson, Amy S.
Patterson, George N(eilson)
Patzer, Gordon
Pearl, David
Peddicord, Jo (Anne)
Pence, Gregory E.
Perloff, Richard M.
Perry, Paul
Peterson, Carol R.
Phillips, John Lawrence
Philp, Richard B(lain)
Picano, Felice
Pierce, F(ranklin) David
Pillemer, David B.

Pinch, Winifred J. Ellenchild
Pisani, Elizabeth
Plante, David (Robert)
Poëppel, Ernst
Polansky, Ronald M.
Pollack, Robert (Elliot)
Pollard, Irina
Pollen, Daniel A.
Pollock, Nancy J.
Postgate, John (Raymond)
Powers, William T.
Powter, Susan
Price-Smith, Andrew T.
Proulx, Suzanne
Prozan, Charlotte (Krause)
Pruett, Kyle D(ean)
Putnam, Constance E(lizabeth)
Pyle, Gerald F.
Pyle, Kevin C.
Quigley, Declan
Quilter, Deborah
Quinsey, Mary Beth
Rachman, Stanley Jack
Randall, John L(eslie)
Rapp, Rayna
Rapp, Steven A.
Raso, Jack
Ratey, John J(oseph)
Ray, Ruth E.
Raz, Aviad E.
Reaven, Gerald
Reid, Andrew H.
Reid, T. R.
Reinertsen, Sarah
Restak, Richard M(artin)
Reuben, Bryan G.
Ricciotti, Hope
Richard, Adrienne
Richardson, Robert Galloway
Richman, Kenneth A.
Ridley, Matt(hew White)
Riggs, Webster
Riley, James C.
Rinderle, Walter
Rinzler, Carol Ann
Rippe, James M.
Riviere, Jim (E.)
Robb, Christina
Robbers, James E.
Roberts, Derek Harry
Robertson, Joel C.
Robinson, Leah Ruth
Roche, Alex F.
Rodriguez, Julia
Rooks, Judith P.
Root-Bernstein, Robert Scott
Ropes, Linda Brubaker
Rose, Melody
Rosenau, Pauline Vaillancourt
Rosenthal, Ken S.
Rossol, Monona
Rotello, Gabriel
Rothman, David J.
Rous, Stephen N.
Roy, F. Hampton
Roy, James (Henry Barstow)
Rubin, Jordan

Rubin-Dorsky, Jeffrey
Rubinstein, Helge
Rubinstein, Hilary (Harold)
Russell, Ronald
Ruston, Sharon
Rutan, J. Scott
Rutter, Michael (Llewellyn)
Ryan, Frank
Ryle, Anthony
Sabbagh, Marwan Noel
Sachs, Judith
Sachs, Robert
Sacks, Oliver (Wolf)
Sadick, Neil (S.)
Saffer, Barbara
Saks, Mike
Saloff, Jamie L.
Sanders, Arthur
Sanders, Lisa
Sandford, John
Sandler, Merton
Sankar, Andrea (Patrice)
Sapinsley, Barbara
Sapolsky, Robert M.
Satter, Ellyn
Sauter, Doris Elaine
Scarry, Elaine (Margaret)
Schaef, Anne Wilson
Schaefer, Lola M.
Schafer, Elisabeth
Scheffer, Kathy J(ean)
Schiff, Isaac
Schlesinger, Benjamin
Schlosberg, Suzanne
Schmidt, Karl H.
Schmidt, Ulf
Schmidt, Winsor C.
Schmitz, Cecilia M.
Schreibman, Laura
Schulkin, Jay
Schulman, Michael D.
Schumacher, Jim
Schwartz, Gary E.
Schwartz, Samuel M.
Schwarzbein, Diana
Scott, David L.
Scott, Donald Fletcher
Sears, William P.
Secunda, Victoria (H.)
Seddon, Andrew M.
Segal, Julia (Clare)
Selak, Joy H.
Sellers, Christopher C.
Seltzer, Leon F(rancis)
Semchyshyn, Stefan
Severson, Kim
Shafquat, Sofia
Shainberg, Lawrence
Shapiro, Dan(iel)
Shapiro, Jerrold Lee
Shaw, Alison
Shay, Jonathan
Sheftel, Victor O.
Shelton, Mark L(ogan)
Shengold, Leonard
Shephard, Roy Jesse
Sherman, Janette D.

Bartov, Omer
Bass, Gary J.
Bateman, Robert L.
Baucom, Donald R.
Baylis, John
Bayly, C. A.
Beason, Doug
Beckel, Bob
Becker, Elizabeth
Becker, Patti Clayton
Bee, Ronald J.
Beeby, Dean
Bell, Robin
Bellamy, Alex J.
Bellamy, Christopher (David)
Benedict, Helen
Bennett, G. H.
Bennett, James Richard
Bergerud, Eric M.
Bergman, Ronen
Best, Antony
Best, Geoffrey (Francis Andrew)
Biank, Tanya
Biggs, Chester M(axwell)
Bird, Christiane
Bjorge, Gary J(ohn)
Black, Jeremy (Martin)
Blair, E(lizabeth) Anne
Blashford-Snell, John Nicholas
Blaufarb, Rafe
Bodansky, Yossef
Bogart, Eleanor A(nne)
Bohjalian, Chris
Bolotin, Norman (Phillip)
Bonadio, Felice A(nthony)
Bonekemper, Edward H.
Boritt, Gabor
Bostdorff, Denise M.
Botting, Douglas
Bowen, H. V.
Boyd, Carl
Boyne, Walter J(ames)
Braden, Nate
Bradley, Michael R.
Brandes, Stuart D.
Brands, Hal
Brenaman, Miriam
Broadwater, Robert P.
Brooks, Victor
Brown, Steve
Bruce, Colin John
Bruce Lockhart, Robin
Brugioni, Dino A.
Bryant, Mark
Bryden, John (Herbert)
Bucholz, Arden
Buckley, Cornelius M(ichael)
Buckley, Mary (Elizabeth Anne)
Budiansky, Stephen (Philip)
Burden, Matthew Currier
Burns, Ken(neth Lauren)
Burridge, Trevor David
Butler, Daniel Allen
Butler, Geoff
Butow, Robert J. C.
Byman, Daniel L.

Calder, Marie D(onais)
Calder, Nigel (David Ritchie)
Caldwell, David H(epburn)
Cameron, Christian
Cammermeyer, Margarethe
Campagna, Palmiro
Campbell, Duncan Andrew
Canney, Donald L.
Cannon, Carl M.
Carafano, James Jay
Carlton, David
Carr, Caleb
Carr, J(ames) Revell
Carter, Ashton B.
Carville, (Chester) James
Cassidy, Robert M.
Cavell, Richard
Cawthorne, Nigel
Chalfont
Chalker, Dennis
Chambers, John Whiteclay
Chanda, Nayan
Charlwood, D(onald) E(rnest Cameron)
Chilson, Rob(ert) (Dean)
Choate, Jean (Marie)
Christopher, Renny (Teresa)
Cimbala, Stephen J.
Clancy, Tom
Clark, Wesley K.
Clarke, (Victor) Lindsay
Clary, David A.
Clayton, Anthony
Clemens, Walter C.
Coers, Donald V.
Coffman, Edward M.
Cohen, Avner
Cohen, Jared
Cohen, Robin
Cohrs, Patrick O.
Coker, Christopher
Cole, Terrence (Michael)
Colley, David P.
Collier, Paul
Como, David R.
Connelly, Matthew
Conroy, John
Conway, Alan
Corona, Laurel
Cotham, Edward T.
Coulombe, Charles A.
Cozzens, Peter
Cramer, Clayton E.
Crane, Conrad C(harles)
Crawford, Mark
Crerar, Duff (Willis)
Cross, Coy F.
Crowley, Roger
Cumming, Carman
Curry, G(len) David
D'Este, Carlo
Dabney, Joseph Earl
Dallison, Robert L.
Danopoulos, Constantine P.
Darlow, Steve
Darwish, Adel

Davies, J(ohn) D(avid)
Davis, Anita (Grey) P(rice)
Davison, Eddy W.
de Bono, Douglas
De Groot, Gerard J.
de la Bédoyère, Guy
de La Pedraja, René
Dean, Martin
Deighton, Len
Delgado, Aidan
DeRogatis, Jim
Desch, Michael C.
DeVries, Kelly
Dickinson, W(illiam) Calvin
Dicks, Shirley
Dietz, Peter (John)
DiSilvestro, Roger L.
Dockery, Kevin
Donnithorne, Larry R.
Dorset, Phyllis (Flanders)
Dougherty, James E(dward)
Doughty, Robert A.
Douglas-Hamilton, James Alexander
Doyle, Robert Charles
Dudziak, Mary L.
Duffield, John S.
Duncan, Stephen M.
Durant, Michael J.
Dyer, Gwynne
Dysart, Joshua
Ebbett, Eve
Eck, Matthew
Edwards, Robert
Egan, Ferol
Egeland, Jan
Eggleston, Larry G.
Egli, Ida Rae
Eidinow, John
Eisenhower, John S(heldon) D(oud)
El-Shazly, Nadia El-Sayed
Eldridge, John E. T.
Ellwood, Sheelagh (Margaret)
Engel, Jeffrey A.
English, John A(lan)
Epstein, Robert M(orris)
Erickson, Edward J.
Esdaile, Charles J.
Evans, C. Wyatt
Evans, Stephen S(tewart)
Facey-Crowther, David R.
Falk, Stanley Lawrence
Fallows, James Mackenzie
Fehrenbach, T(heodore) R(eed)
Feith, Douglas J.
Ferling, John E.
Ferreiro, Larrie D.
Fialka, John J.
Fiennes, Ranulph
Filkins, Dexter
Finnegan, Terrence J.
Finnegan, William (Patrick)
Fisher, Ernest F.
Fleming, Thomas
Foden, Giles

Foot, Michael Richard Daniell
Forrest, Alan
Frank, Nathaniel
Frankland, (Anthony) Noble
Franklin, Jane (Morgan)
Frasca, Ralph
Frazier, Charles (Robinson)
Freedman, Lawrence (David)
Freedman, Russell (Bruce)
Freehling, William W(ilhartz)
Freeman, Philip
French, David
Frezza, Robert (A.)
Friedman, Brandon
Friedman, George
Fritz, Stephen G.
Gaiduk, Ilya V(alerievich)
Galli, Richard
Gandt, Robert
Gansler, Jacques Singleton
Garthoff, Raymond L(eonard)
Gartner, Scott Sigmund
Garver, John W.
Gat, Azar
Gaubatz, Kurt Taylor
Gawrych, George
Gay, Kathlyn R.
Gebhardt, James F(rederick)
Gerlach, Don R.
Gerstein, Daniel M.
Gibran, Daniel K.
Gibson, A(lex) J. S.
Gillespie, Angus Kress
Gimblett, Richard H.
Giziowski, Richard (John)
Glantz, David M.
Glatthaar, Joseph T(homas)
Glees, Anthony
Glen, Frank Grenfell
Goddard, Tariq
Goemans, Hein E.
Golay, Michael
Gold, Dore
Goldman, Roger L.
Goldstein, Lyle J.
Goñi, Uki
Goodson, Larry P.
Goulden, Joseph C.
Grace, Alexander M.
Gragg, Rod
Graham, Daniel O.
Grainger, John D(ownie)
Grant, Susan-Mary C.
Gray, Chris Hables
Gray, Colin S.
Green, Stephen J(ohn)
Greene, A. Wilson
Greene, Melissa Fay
Gregorian, Raffi
Grenier, John
Gunston, Bill
Guzzo, Lou(is Richard)
Hagerman, Edward
Halberstadt, Hans
Haldon, John F.
Hale, Douglas

Military/Defense/Arms Control-
cont.

Military/Defense/Arms Control-
cont.

Military/Defense/Arms Control-
cont.

Military/Defense/Arms Control-
cont.

Military/Defense/Arms Control-
cont.

Military/Defense/Arms Control-
cont.

Military/Defense/Arms Control-
cont.

Military/Defense/Arms Control-
cont.

Pagonis, William G.
Paldiel, Mordecai
Palmer, Alan Warwick
Pape, Robert A.
Paradis, Adrian Alexis
Pardoe, Blaine
Parillo, Mark P.
Parker, Peter (Robert Nevill)
Parrish, T(homas) Michael
Pate, J'Nell L(aVerne)
Patterson, Dan
Peden, W. Creighton
Peebles, Curtis
Peña, Charles V.
Pencak, William
Perrett, Bryan
Perrin, Dennis
Peterson, Wallace C(arroll)
Pezzullo, Ralph
Pfaff, William (Wendel)
Pollack, Kenneth M(ichael)
Posen, Barry R.
Powell, Alan
Poyer, Joe
Pozner, Vladimir
Pratt, Anna
Price, Anthony
Priest, John Michael
Priestley, Chris
Prior, Robin
Pritchard, R(obert) John
Rabb, Theodore K.
Racine, Philip N.
Ransom, Harry Howe
Ranstorp, Magnus
Raymond, Patrick (Ernest)
Read, Anthony
Reeder, Carolyn
Reese, Roger R(oi)
Reger, James P.
Reilly, Bernard F.
Reiss, Edward
Reiss, Mitchell
Rejai, Mostafa
Resis, Albert
Revels, Tracy J.
Reynolds, Arlene
Rhea, Gordon Campbell
Rice, Earle
Rieff, David Sontag
Rielage, Dale C.
Robbins, James S.
Roberts, Geoffrey
Roberts, Philip J.
Robertson, Ian (Campbell)
Robie, Bill
Rodger, N. A. M.
Rohmer, Richard
Rooney, Andy
Rosen, Leora N(adine)
Rosenthal, T(homas) G(abriel)
Rossman, C. L.
Rostker, Bernard D.
Rothstein, Hy S.
Rotter, Andrew J.
Rotundo, Louis C.

Russett, Bruce Martin
Rutherdale, Robert
Ryan, Peter Allen
Sakamoto, Yoshikazu
Sanders, Alan J. K.
Sanders, Charles W.
Sarris, Jonathan Dean
Sasser, Charles W(ayne)
Saunders, George W.
Sauro, Christy W.
Sawyer, Ralph D.
Sayer, Ian (Keith Terence)
Schaerf, Carlo
Schmookler, Andrew Bard
Schofield, Carey
Schreiber, Roy E.
Schroeder-Lein, Glenna R(uth)
Schubert, Frank N.
Schwarzbein, Diana
Schweikart, Larry (Earl)
Schweizer, Karl W.
Schweller, Randall
Scipes, Kim
Seagrave, Sterling
Searle, Ronald (William Ford-
ham)
Self, Robert O.
Severance, Ben H.
Seward, Desmond
Shachnow, Sid
Shaffer, Donald R.
Shaw, David W.
Shawver, Lois
Shehadeh, Lamia Rustrum
Sheriff, Carol
Sherman, Arnold
Sherman, Nancy
Shlaim, Avi
Shneour, Elie Alexis
Shrader, Charles R.
Shulman, Mark R(ussell)
Siddali, Silvana R.
Siddiqa, Ayesha
Silber, Nina
Silbey, David
Simpson, John (Cody Fidler)
Singer, P. W.
Sites, Kevin
Siverson, Randolph M.
Skelton, William B(arott)
Skiba, Katherine M.
Skinner, Michael
Slader, John M.
Slayton, Robert A(llen)
Slepyan, Kenneth D.
Small, Hugh
Smith, Dale L.
Smith, Hugh
Smith, Peter Charles Horstead
Smith, Steven Trent
Smith, Wilda M(axine)
Snellgrove, Laurence Ernest
Solomon, Richard H(arvey)
Spears, Sally
Spiers, Edward M(ichael)
Spikes, Daniel

Stafford, Edward Peary
Stanley, Peter W(illiam)
Stannard, Richard M.
Stansky, Peter (David Lyman)
Stanton, Shelby L(ee)
Stapleton, Timothy J.
Stauber, John (Clyde)
Steel, Nigel
Steinbrook, Gordon L.
Steins, Richard
Stentiford, Barry M.
Stephen, Martin
Stern, Kenneth S.
Sterritt, Laurence Lux
Stevens, Bryna
Stevenson, Jonathan
Stinnett, Robert B.
Stone, David R.
Stout, Jay A.
Street, Brian Jeffrey
Sturmer, Michael
Sullivan, David M.
Sumption, Jonathan
Sword, Wiley
Taubman, Philip
Tawa, Nicholas E.
Taylor, Robert Allan
Taylor, Robert Larry
Taylor, Stephen
Thomas, (Antony) Charles
Tiger, Lionel
Tirman, John
Tobias, Michael (Charles)
Toffler, Heidi
Tomajczyk, S. F.
Tombs, Robert P.
Tracy, (John) Nicholas
Trainor, Bernard E.
Traxel, David Stephens
Trenerry, Walter N.
Trevelyan, Raleigh
Tripp, Elise Forbes
Trout, Robert J(ay)
Trudeau, Noah Andre
Tucker, Spencer C.
Turnbull, Stephen (Richard)
Turner, John Frayn
Turner, William Weyand
Turse, Nick
Uldrich, Jack
Unterberger, Betty Miller
Valentine, Douglas
van Tuyll, Hubert P.
Vandenbroucke, Lucien S.
Vieira, Sergio
Vigh, Henrik
Vines, Lois Davis
Wade, Stephen
Wait, Eugene M(eredith)
Waldman, Sidney R.
Waldron, Arthur (Nelson)
Walker, Clarence Earl
Waller, Douglas C.
Waltz, Kenneth N.
Ward, Geoffrey C(hampion)
Ward, Harry Merrill

Warren, Susan May
Watts, Anthony John
Waugh, Joan
Wax, Steven T.
Weidenbaum, Murray
Wein, Elizabeth E(ve)
Weinbaum, Marvin G.
Weinberg, Louise
Weintraub, Stanley
Weir, Gary E.
Weisgall, Jonathan M.
Wells, Cheryl A.
West, Francis J.
Westwood, John Norton
Weyr, Thomas
White, Bill
White, Peter (O. G.)
Whitlock, Flint
Wicker, Brian John
Willbanks, James H.
Williams, Alan Lee
Williams, Cindy
Williams, John A(lfred)
Wills, Garry
Wilson, Andrew
Wilson, Marc
Wilson, Peter H.
Winder, Michael
Winkler, Jonathan Reed
Woell, Edward J.
Woodward, Bob
Worthing, Peter
Yeide, Harry
Yenne, Bill
Yoo, John C.
Young, Jeff C.
Zacharias, Karen Spears
Zagorski, Paul W.
Zaloga, Steven J(oseph)
Zangana, Haifa
Zechenter, Katarzyna Anna
Zedric, Lance Q.
Zeiler, Thomas W.
Zucchino, David
Zuehlke, Mark
Zulaika, Joseba

Money/Finance

Adams, Charles
Adler, David A.
Aliber, Robert Z(elwin)
Allen, Dean
Ariff, Mohamed
Armstrong, Alexandra
Baker, Tom
Baldassarri, Mario
Bale, Don
Barash, Samuel T.
Barr, Nicholas
Bartlett, Sarah
Bass, Thomas A.
Becker, Gary S.
Behrens, John C.
Belkaoui, Ahmed R.

Bond, C(hristopher Godfrey)
Booth, Stanley
Bordowitz, Hank
Bostock, Donald Ivan
Boulez, Pierre
Bourne, Joyce
Bowie, Andrew (S.)
Bowman, David
Boyd, Joe
Brand, Oscar
Brant, Marley
Brown, Christopher Boyd
Brown, Mick
Browne, David
Broyles, Michael
Budbill, David
Bulger, Peggy A.
Bullins, Ed
Burton, Humphrey (McGuire)
Burton, Thomas G(len)
Busch, Charles
Buskin, Richard
Campling, Christopher Russell
Carley, Lionel (Kenneth)
Carson, Ciaran
Carter, Walter
Case, George (Andrew Thomas)
Cash, Anthony
Cassady, Marsh
Castleden, Rodney
Catalano, Nick
Celenza, Anna Harwell
Chang, Kevin O'Brien
Chapin, Miles
Charters, Samuel
Chinen, Nate
Christe, Ian
Christian, Garna L.
Christiansen, Rupert
Churchill, Caryl
Clark, David Lindsey
Clark, Dick
Clausen, Andy
Clayson, Alan
Cleall, Charles
Cochran, Robert B(rady)
Cogan, Brian A.
Cohen, Leonard
Cole, Stephanie
Collier, Graham
Collis, Louise (Edith)
Collver, Michael
Conati, Marcello
Connell, John
Cooper, Barry (Anthony Raymond)
Coplan, David B.
Corgan, Billy Patrick
Cotterrell, Roger (B. M.)
Cowden, Robert H.
Cox, Gordon
Craggs, Stewart R.
Crew, Danny O(liver)
Crews, Nina
Crossan, G(regory) D(ixon)
Crouch, Tanja L.
Crow, Bill

Crowther, Harold Francis
Cusic, Don
Cutting, Linda Katherine
Cyr, Mary
Czekanowska, Anna
Dale, Rodney A. M.
Daniel, Wayne W.
Daniels, Sarah
Darden, Robert
Davies, Peter J.
Davis, Francis
Davis, Peter G(raffam)
Deathridge, John (William)
Deffaa, Chip
Dembska, Anna
Demers, Joanna Teresa
DeRogatis, Jim
Dettmar, Kevin J(ohn)
   H(offmann)
Dibbern, Mary
Dickerson, Matthew T.
Dimond, Peter
Dizikes, John
Donovan
Downie, R(obert) S(ilcock)
Draper, Maureen McCarthy
Draper, Robert
Duckworth, William (Ervin)
Dudley-Smith, Timothy
Dunleavy, Deborah
Dupuis, Robert
Earnshaw, Micky
Edgar, David
Edwards, Anne
Edwards, Larry
Ellison, Joan Audrey
Emerson, Isabelle Putnam
Emerson, Ken
England, Chris
Ennulat, Egbert M.
Enslin, Theodore (Vernon)
Erickson, Raymond (F.)
Erlmann, Veit
Evans, Gary P.
Fabrizio, Timothy C(harles)
Fair, David
Farr, Jory
Fernandez-Shaw, Carlos M(anuel)
Ferris, William (R.)
Fifield, Christopher G(eorge)
Finstad, Suzanne
Fleurant, Gerdès
Florita, Kira
Fox, Ted
Frank, Katherine
Freeman, Daniel E(van)
Freeman, Garry
French, Philip (Neville)
Friel, Brian
Frisch, Walter
Fuller, Sophie
Funderburg, Lise
Furia, Philip (G.)
Gaillard, Frye
Gänzl, Kurt (Friedrich)
Garden, Edward (James Clarke)
Gardner, Mark L(ee)

Gatti, Anne
Gaunt, Kyra D.
Gerard, Charley
Getz, Christine S.
Gilmour, Michael J.
Gish, Robert F.
Glixon, Jonathan Emmanuel
Goble, Alan
Godwin, Gail (Kathleen)
Goff, Martyn
Goldberg, Danny
Goldsmith, Lynn
Gooley, Dana
Gordon, Eric A(rthur)
Gorrell, Lorraine
Goss, Glenda Dawn
Gourgouris, Stathis
Green, J. Paul
Green, Sharony Andrews
Greene, Don
Greene, Victor
Greetham, David
Griffin, Farah Jasmine
Griffiths, Trevor
Gruhn, George
Guralnick, Peter
Gurney, A(lbert) R(amsdell)
Gutman, Robert W.
Guttmann, Hadassah
Haar, James
Hafner, Katie
Hager, Alan
Hajdusiewicz, Babs Bell
Hamill, Janet
Hansen, Chadwick
Hardy, Robert Earl
Haring, Bruce
Harlow, Michael
Harness, Kelley
Harper-Scott, J. P. E.
Harris, Stacy
Harvey, Steven
Haygood, Wil
Hayward, Philip
Hentoff, Nat(han Irving)
Herl, Joseph
Hilberry, Conrad Arthur
Himelstein, Morgan Y.
Hines, Robert S.
Hobsbawm, Eric (John Ernest)
Hoek, D. J.
Holland, James R.
Holmes, Jon Richard
Holmes, Rupert
Holst-Warhaft, Gail
Holt, David
Honri, Peter
Hooper, Maureen Brett
Hopkins, Antony
Horovitz, Michael
Howard, Patricia
Hsu, Madeleine (DeMory)
Hubbard, Woodleigh Marx
Hughes, Meirion
Hunter, Seb
Hurwitz, David
Hutcheon, Linda

Hutcheon, Michael
Ingman, Nicholas
Ishiguro, Kazuo
Isoardi, Steven L.
Jackson, Jeffrey H.
Jackson, John A.
Jakobson, Michael
Jefferson, Margo
Jones, David W(yn)
Jones, J. Barrie
Jones, Mary Voell
Jordan, James M.
Jordan, Richard Tyler
Jourdain, Robert
Jovanovic, Rob
Kallen, Stuart A(rnold)
Kane, Larry
Karlen, Neal (Stuart)
Karp, Larry
Kassler, Jamie C(roy)
Katz, Mark
Keates, Jonathan
Keil, Charles
Keiler, Allan Ronald
Kennedy, Michael
Kennedy, Rick
Kenney, William Howland
Kerman, Joseph
Kernfeld, Barry (Dean)
Kersenboom, Saskia
Kettelkamp, Larry Dale
Kimball, Robert (Eric)
Kimbrough, S. T.
King, Jonny
Kitts, Thomas M(ichael)
Knapp, Raymond
Knopper, Steve Aaron
Koestenbaum, Wayne
Kohler, Dean Ellis
Kostelanetz, Richard (Cory)
Kowalke, Kim H.
Kreitner, Kenneth
Kroll, Mark
Lachman, Barbara
Laird, Ross
Lamb, Andrew (Martin)
Lange, Arthur D.
Langfield, Valerie
Lanza, Joseph
Latham, Alison
Le Guin, Elisabeth
Ledgin, Stephanie P.
Lee, M. Owen
Leiby, Bruce R.
Lester, Julius
Letellier, Robert Ignatius
Letnanova, Elena
Levitin, Daniel J.
Lewis, Thomas P(arker)
Lie, John
Lieberman, Richard K.
Lightfoot, Gordon
Linn, Karen
Lipsyte, Robert (Michael)
Livingston, Robert Henry
LL Cool J
Logan, George M(eredith)

Music-*cont.*

Loney, Glenn Meredith
Lott, Eric
Loza, Steven (Joseph)
Lwin, Nanda Layos
Lynch, Janet Nichols
Mach, Elyse (Janet)
Mackerras, Colin Patrick
Macleod, Wendy
Magee, Bryan
Mai, Francois Martin
Maistros, Louis
Maltese, John Anthony
Maner, Martin
Marley, Rita
Marqusee, Mike
Marsalis, Wynton
Martin, George Whitney
Masekela, Hugh
Maslon, Laurence
Mason, David
Matera, Dary M.
McCants, Clyde T.
McClary, Susan
McColley, Diane Kelsey
McCutcheon, John
Mcgee, Garry
McKeen, William
McLean, Duncan
McMullen, Sean (Christopher)
McMullen, William Wallace
McNally, Terrence
McNamee, Gregory
McRae, Barry (Donald)
Meehan, Paula
Meintjes, Louise
Melnick, Jeffrey Paul
Meltzer, David
Mender, Mona (Siegler)
Merrill, Hugh (Davis)
Miles, Barry
Miller, Paul D.
Minahan, John A.
Mitchell, Gillian
Monk, Raymond
Monson, Ingrid (T.)
Montparker, Carol
Moody, Bill
Moore, Allan F.
Morgan, David
Morris, Edmund
Morrison, Toni
Moskowitz, David V.
Moynihan, Michael
Mullett, John St. Hilary
Myers, Helen
Myers, Robert Manson
Naha, Ed
Nathan, Amy
Nattiez, Jean Jacques
Neaverson, Bob
Nelson, Samuel H.
Nilsson, Jenny Lind
Norris, Geoffrey
O'Brien, Lucy
O'Neal, Hank
Oderman, Stuart (Douglas)
Ohl, Vicki

Oja, Carol J.
Oldfield, Michael
Oliphant, Dave (Edward Davis)
Olson, Ted
Orledge, Robert
Orlova, Alexandra (Anatol'evna)
Ortenberg, Veronica
Osborne, Charles
Otis, Johnny
Pack, Robert
Page, Christopher H.
Page, Tim
Palkovic, Mark
Parrott, Ian
Peacock, Alan (Turner)
Pear, David (Adrian)
Pearson, Roger A. G.
Pendle, Karin
Peretti, Burton W(illiam)
Perone, James E.
Perrone, Charles A.
Pesic, Peter
Peterson, Richard Austin
Petrusich, Amanda
Piazza, Tom
Pickering, David (Hugh)
Pinch, Trevor (John)
Plaut, Eric A.
Polisar, Barry Louis
Polizzotti, Mark
Pollack, Howard
Porter, Sue
Post, Jennifer C.
Poultney, David
Powell, Ardal
Powell, Craig
Previn, André (George)
Pruter, Robert
Purser, John W(hitley)
Pybus, Rodney
Quinn, Sunny
Raad, Virginia
Radano, Ronald M.
Raffi
Raftery, Brian
Ramsey, Doug(las K.)
Ratliff, Ben
Reich, Howard
Rezits, Joseph
Ribowsky, Mark
Richard, Cliff
Richmond, Peter
Richter, Gregory C.
Rimler, Walter
Rogan, Johnny
Rogovoy, Seth
Rooksby, Rikky
Rose, Elisabeth
Rosen, Louis H.
Rosenthal, Elizabeth J.
Ross, Alex
Rounds, David
Routh, Francis John
Rushton, Julian (Gordon)
Sacks, Howard L.
Saddler, Joseph Robert
Saffle, Michael

Saliers, Emily
Sallis, James
Sanders, Ed(ward)
Sanjek, David
Schoemer, Karen
Schoffman, Nachum
Schouvaloff, Alexander
Schulenberg, David
Schuller, Gunther
Schwartz, Elliott S.
Schweikart, Larry (Earl)
Scott, Frank
Seabrook, Mike
Seaman, Gerald Roberts
Seleshanko, Kristina
Selvin, Joel
Shafer, Neil
Shahan, Sherry
Shamas, Victor A.
Shaughnessy, Mary Alice
Shaw, Lisa
Shaw, William
Shelemay, Kay Kaufman
Sherman, Robert
Shiloah, Amnon
Shim, Eunmi
Shusterman, Richard (M.)
Silbiger, Alexander
Silverman, Jerry
Silvester, Peter (John)
Simmons, Earl
Simosko, Vladimir
Simpson, Adrienne
Singer, Barry
Smiraglia, Richard P(aul)
Smith, Carolyn Jeanne
Smith, Patricia
Smith, Ralph Lee
Smith, Rollin
Snowman, Daniel
Solum, John
Southey, Roz
Spencer, Jon Michael
Spink, Ian
Spycket, Jerome
Stambler, Irwin
Starr, Larry
Stell, Elizabeth P(arker)
Stetson, Brad
Stevens, Bryna
Stewart, Gary
Steyn, Mark
Stradling, R. A.
Such, David G.
Sutherland, Luke
Sutton, R. Anderson
Swafford, Jan Johnson
Swain, Joseph P(eter)
Tagg, Christine Elizabeth
Tanner, Michael (K.)
Taraborrelli, J. Randy
Taruskin, Richard
Tawa, Nicholas E.
Teachout, Terry
Temperley, David
Temperley, Nicholas
Thom, Paul

Thomas, Adrian
Thomas, D(onald) M(ichael)
Thompson, Jewel Taylor
Thomson, William
Till, Nicholas
Timbrell, Charles
Tommasini, Anthony
Treyz, Russell
Triggs, Tony D.
Tripp, Dawn Clifton
Trotter, William R.
Trudeau, Noah Andre
Tullos, Allen E.
Turbet, Richard
Van der Kiste, John (Patrick Guy)
Varesi, Anthony G.
Vaughan, Ronald G(eorge)
Vazsonyi, Nicholas
Villamil, Victoria Etnier
Visconti, Tony
Waddington, Patrick (Haynes)
Walsh, Stephen
Walton, Kendall L(ewis)
Wandor, Michelene
Ward, Geoffrey C(hampion)
Wareham, Dean Dean
Warner, Elizabeth (Ann)
Warrack, John (Hamilton)
Watson, Ben
Watt, Ben
Waugh, Alexander
Wearne, Alan
Webber, Andrew Lloyd
Weiner, Marc A.
Weintraub, Andrew N.
Weliver, Phyllis
Wesker, Arnold
West, Ewan (D.)
Whitton, Kenneth S(tuart)
Wilcken, Lois
Wilentz, Sean
Williams, Peter
Williams, Sheron
Williams, Vera B.
Williamson, John (Gordon)
Wilmot, Jeanne
Wilson, Christopher R.
Wilson, Frank R.
Wilson, Gretchen
Wingfield, Paul
Woodford, Peggy
Wright, Helen L(ouise)
Yanow, Scott
Yolen, Jane
York, Lynn
Zabor, Rafi
Zietz, Karyl Lynn
Ziffrin, Marilyn J.
Zimmerman, Franklin (Bershir)
Zoss, Joel
Zucchi, John E.
Zuckermann, Wolfgang (Joachim)

Mythology/Folklore

Abbas, Jailan

Aberjhani
Adams, Charles J.
Adkins, Roy A(rthur)
Aldhouse-Green, Miranda Jane
Anderson, Jeffrey E.
Armstrong, Jeannette C.
Ashe, Geoffrey Thomas
Auerbach, Loyd
Ayres, Thomas (R.)
Bachman, W(illiam) Bryant
Bailey, Greg
Bailey, Lee W.
Barber, E(lizabeth) J. W(ayland)
Barber, Paul (Thomas)
Barber, Richard (William)
Barden, Thomas
Barnet, Miguel
Bartlett, Sarah
Bastien, Joseph William
Batt, Tanya Robyn
Beardslee, Karen E.
Beck, Mary L. (Giraudo)
Berenzy, Alix
Berg, Leila
Bielski, Alison (Joy Prosser)
Bierhorst, John
Birrell, Anne (Margaret)
Bly, Robert (Elwood)
Booker, Christopher
Bowlby, Rachel
Brook, Elaine (Isabel)
Brown, Alan
Bruchac, Joseph
Bucuvalas, Tina
Bulger, Peggy A.
Burton, Thomas G(len)
Caduto, Michael J.
Castleden, Rodney
Chatterjee, Debjani
Citro, Joseph A.
Clabough, Casey Howard
Clarke, (Victor) Lindsay
Cleveland, Leslie
Climo, Shirley
Coffin, Tristram Potter
Coleman, Loren (Elwood)
Coren, Stanley
Cowley, Marjorie
Crawford, Tad
Cray, Edward
Creeden, Sharon
Crews, Nina
Crossley-Holland, Kevin (John
    William)
Curry, Jane (Louise)
Dabney, Joseph Earl
Dale, Rodney A. M.
Dance, Daryl Cumber
Dart-Thornton, Cecilia
Davidson, Sol M.
Deans, Sis Boulos
Del Negro, Giovanna P.
DeSpain, Pleasant
DiMarco, Cris K. A.
Doll, Mary A(swell)
Downie, Mary Alice
Dresser, Norine

Dunlop, Eileen (Rhona)
Egielski, Richard
Evers, Larry
Fanthorpe, R(obert) Lionel
Ferris, William (R.)
Fisher, Leonard Everett
Fleurant, Gerdès
Fontes, Manuel D(a Costa)
Fontes, Ron
Forsyth, Kate
Fourie, Corlia
Frankel, Ellen
Fritze, Ronald H.
Gabriel (Loving), Kathryn (Ann)
Gage, Eleni N.
Garner, Alan
Gaudet, Marcia
Gerber, Michael E.
Gillespie, Angus Kress
Glassie, Henry
Glazier, Stephen D.
Goble, Paul
Görlach, Manfred
Gottlieb, Freema (Peninah)
Grassi, Maggi Lidchi
Greaves, Nick
Greenhill, Pauline
Greer, John Michael
Hager, Alan
Hager, Betty
Hajdusiewicz, Babs Bell
Han, Suzanne Crowder
Handley, Eric Walter
Haring, Lee
Harrell, Beatrice Orcutt
Harris, Rosemary (Jeanne)
Harrison, Michael
Harrison, Sue
Haughton, Rosemary Luling
Heine, Steven
Hernandez, Jo Farb
Herrick, James A.
Heslewood, Juliet
Hoffman, Daniel
Holub, Joan
Hong, Lily Toy
Hooper, Meredith Jean
Igo, John (N.)
Jarvis, William E.
Jeans, Peter D(ouglas)
Jirgens, Karl (E.)
Jovanovski, Meto
Kaler, Anne K(atherine)
Karodia, Farida
Kerven, Rosalind
Kingston, Maxine Hong
Klempner, Mark
Kornblatt, Judith Deutsch
Krishnaswami, Uma
Kusugak, Michael (Arvaarluk)
Lambert, Page
Lamont-Brown, Raymond
Laubach, David C.
Leak, Andrew N.
Lee, Jeanne M.
Lester, Julius
Levine, Alan J.

Liles, Maurine Walpole
Lingenfelter, Richard Emery
Llewellyn, Sam
Longley, Kyle
Lunge-Larsen, Lise
Lurie, Alison
Mack, Carol K.
Maclean, Rory
Maranda, Pierre
Marcuse, Aída E.
Marks, Alan
Marshall, Peter (H.)
Martin, Francesca
Maskarinec, Gregory G.
Mayo, Wendell
Mayor, Adrienne
McCrumb, Sharyn
McFadden, Steven
McNamee, Gregory
Meeker, Clare Hodgson
Middleton, Haydn
Mills, Margaret A(nn)
Mitchell, John Hanson
Monesson, Harry S.
Montejo, Victor (D.)
Moynihan, Michael
Mullen, Patrick B.
Muller, (Lester) Robin
Murphy, Claire Rudolf
Noble, Kathleen
Norman, Howard A.
Odaga, Asenath (Bole)
Olson, Ted
Opie, Iona
Oughton, Jerrie
Panik, Sharon
Parkin, Frank
Pearson, Kit
Pickering, David (Hugh)
Powell, Barry B.
Price, Susan
Ramsey, Jarold
Rao, Sirish
Reed, James
Rhyne, Nancy
Rice, Michael
Rosenak, Chuck
Rosman, Steven M(ichael)
Rubright, Lynn
Sacre, Antonio
Salsi, Lynn
Sax, Boria
Scholey, Arthur (Edward)
Seed, Jenny
Sesti, Giuseppe Maria
Seth, Vikram
Shaw, Miranda Eberle
Shenkman, Richard (Bennett)
Silverman, Jerry
Simpson, Jacqueline (Mary)
Sims, Michael
Smith, Ali
Smith, Brian
Smoley, Richard
Spooner, Michael
Spretnak, Charlene
Stafford, Fiona (Jane)

Stave, Shirley A.
Strauss, Susan (Elizabeth)
Sullivan, C(harles) W(illiam)
Swartz, Jon David
Synge, Ursula
Temple, Robert (Kyle Grenville)
Thiel, Diane
Thomas, H(ubert) Nigel
Tjardes, Tamara J.
Tocher, Michelle
Tranter, John (Ernest)
Tyldesley, Joyce (Ann)
Urton, Gary
Vizenor, Gerald (Robert)
Von Ward, Paul
Warner, Marina
Washington, Donna L.
Wein, Elizabeth E(ve)
Welsch, Roger L(ee)
White, Carolyn
Whitten, Norman E.
Williams, Helen
Williams, R. D.
Wilmot, Jeanne
Wilson, Barbara Ker
Wilson, David S(cofield)
Wilson, Wesley M.
Wolf, Gita
Wolverton, Robert E.
Woodruff, Joan Leslie
Wright, Robert Lee
Yolen, Jane
Zambreno, Mary Frances
Zee, A.
Zhang, Song Nan
Zoss, Joel

Natural History

Ackerman, Jennifer G.
Anderson, Alun M.
Angel, Heather
Annerino, John
Appell, Scott D.
Armbruster, Ann
Armstrong, David Malet
Ashby, Ruth
Ashworth, (Lewis) William
Atherden, Margaret Ann
Avise, John C.
Backes, David James
Bailey, Donna
Bansemer, Roger
Barash, David P(hilip)
Barbash, Tom
Barlow, Maude
Barnes, Burton V(erne)
Barnes, Jay
Barnosky, Anthony D.
Barr, Stephen M.
Barreto, Mascarenhas
Barrett, Joyce Durham
Barron, T. A.
Baruchello, Gianfranco
Bates, Craig D.

Dobson, Andrew (Nicholas Howard)
Dolan, Frederick Michael
Dolis, John
Dombrowski, Daniel A.
Donaldson, Thomas
Dorrien, Gary J.
Douglas, Mark
Downie, R(obert) S(ilcock)
Draper, Robert
Drazin, Israel
Dukes, Paul
Dummett, Michael (Anthony Eardley)
Dunbar, Leslie W(allace)
Dunn, John (Montfort)
Dupré, Louis
Duquette, David A.
Duran, Jane
Durfee, Mary
Durschmied, Erik
Eck, Matthew
Ede, Piers Moore
Edgar, Stacey L.
Elliott, Clark A.
Ellis, Ralph D.
Engelhardt, H(ugo) Tristram
Engell, James
Epperson, Michael
Epstein, Mikhail N.
Erlmann, Veit
Evans, Calvin (Donald)
Evans, Stephen S(tewart)
Fairfield, Paul
Falck, Colin
Felder, David W.
Feldman, Lynne B.
Ferré, Frederick
Feuerstein, Georg
Finnis, John M(itchell)
Fisk, Milton
Fitch, David E.
Fitzgerald, Astrid
Flinders, Neil J.
Flynn, James Robert
Flynn, Thomas R.
Foldvary, Fred E.
Fonrobert, Charlotte Elisheva
Forsyth, Michael
Fotopoulos, Takis
Fox, M(ichael) W.
Franklin, Allan (David)
Franklin, Richard Langdon
Freadman, Richard
Freke, Timothy
Frohnen, Bruce (P.)
Frueh, Joanna
Frye, Marilyn
Fudge, Erica
Fuller, Steve William
Gabbard, David A.
Gabbert, Wolfgang
Galison, Peter (Louis)
Garaudy, Roger
Garrard, Graeme
Garver, Newton
Gascoigne, John

Gaskin, J. C. A.
Gaukroger, Stephen
Gauld, Alan (Ogilvie)
Gelek, Ngawang
Genasi, Chris
George, Rose
Gernet, Jacques
Giampieri-Deutsch, Patrizia
Gibson, Ann Eden
Gillett, Grant (Randall)
Gilmour, John C.
Ginsburg, Mark B.
Glossop, Ronald J.
Goldin, Owen
Goldin, Paul R.
Golomb, Jacob
Gooch, Paul W(illiam)
Goodrich, Amanda Jane
Gordon, Haim
Gordon, Lewis Ricardo
Gordon, Rivca
Gorman, Michael E.
Gorringe, Timothy
Gosling, J. C. B.
Gottlieb, Annie
Götz, Ignacio L.
Gourgouris, Stathis
Govier, Trudy
Gray, Chris Hables
Gray, John
Green, Kenneth Hart
Green, Ricky K(enneth)
Greer, Germaine
Greetham, David
Greil, Arthur L(awrence)
Grenfell, Michael J.
Grigg, Ray
Gross, David
Gross, Neil
Grunbaum, Adolf
Grundy, Joan
Guignon, Charles B(urke)
Gunter, Pete (Addison Yancey)
Gupta, Anil K.
Gwyn, William Brent
Gwynelle (Dismukes), Gwynelle
Hackbarth, Steven (L.)
Hagger, Nicholas
Hales, Steven D(ouglas)
Hamlyn, D(avid) W(alter)
Handy, Rollo
Hannay, Alastair
Hardt, Michael
Harkness, Deborah E.
Harries, Karsten
Harris, James F.
Harvey, (Brian) Peter
Hasler, Julie
Hatab, Lawrence J.
Haughton, Rosemary Luling
Haynes, Jim
Heather, Peter
Heine, Steven
Held, Virginia
Heller, Agnes
Hendry, Joy (McLaggan)
Herman, Barbara

Hershberger, Mary
Heslep, Robert Durham
Hesse, Mary Brenda
Hetherington, Stephen Cade
Heywood, Andrew
Hick, John (Harwood)
Higgins, Kathleen M(arie)
Hill, Thomas E(nglish)
Hinton, Michael
Hirshfeld, Alan
Hittinger, Russell (F.)
Hockensmith, Sean M.
Hofstadter, Douglas (Richard)
Holbrook, David (Kenneth)
Holdheim, W(illiam) Wolfgang
Holloway, Richard (Frederick)
Holmes, Arthur F(rank)
Honderich, Ted
Hooks, Bell
Hopkins, Jasper
Horowitz, Irving Louis
Hoy, David Couzens
Hoyningen-Huene, Paul
Huby, Pamela Margaret
Hughes, Gerard J.
Hughes, Glenn
Hurka, Thomas
Ihde, Don
Ihonvbere, Julius O.
Innis, Robert E(dward)
Isbister, John
Itzkoff, Seymour William
Jagose, Annamarie
Jaksi , Iván
Janis, Michael
Jarvis, William E.
Jay, Peter
Jeffreys, Derek S.
Joas, Hans
Johnson, Colin
Jones, Matthew L.
Jordan, James M.
Jordan, Mark D.
Joyce, Richard
Judovitz, Dalia
Kagan, Shelly
Kain, Philip J(oseph)
Kamakahi, Jeffrey J(on)
Kaplan, Morton A.
Karlen, Neal (Stuart)
Kastely, James L.
Katz, Steven T(heodore)
Kaye, Barrington
Kearney, Richard Marius
Keen, Sam
Keeton, Morris Teuton
Kegan, Robert G.
Kellenberger, J(ames)
Kellner, Menachem
Kenaan, Hagi
Kennedy, Robert Emmet
Kenny, Anthony (John Patrick)
Kessler, Brad
Ketner, Kenneth Laine
Khlentzos, Drew M.
Kidd, I(an) G(ray)
Kidwell, Carol (Evelyn Beryl)

Kirby, Michael Roger
Klein, Robin (McMaugh)
Kleinberg, Ethan
Knopp, Lisa
Koegler, Hans Herbert
Kornblatt, Judith Deutsch
Kornblith, Hilary
Kovel, Joel
Krausz, Ernest
Kraut, Richard
Kreml, William P.
Kricher, John C.
Lachs, John
Landy, Joshua
Langston, Douglas C.
Lara, Maria Pia
Lauder, Robert E(dward)
Lawler, Peter Augustine
Le Doeuff, Michèle
Leaman, Oliver
Leff, Gordon
Lemoncheck, Linda
Leplin, Jarrett
Lessnoff, Michael
Lethbridge, Robert (David)
Levinson, Jerrold
Lewis, James R.
Lindsay, James
Lingard, Jeanette
Linsky, Leonard
Livingston, Gordon (S.)
Lloyd, Elisabeth A.
Lloyd, Geoffrey Ernest Richard
Lockridge, Larry
Logan, George M(eredith)
Long, A(nthony) A(rthur)
Long, Eugene Thomas
Lopes, Dominic (M. McIver)
Louden, Robert B.
Lucas, John Randolph
Lukes, Steven M.
Lumer, Christoph
Luper, Steven
Lynch, Michael P(atrick)
Lyon, David
Lyons, David (Barry)
Lyons, William (Edward)
Macdonald, Copthorne
MacIntyre, Alasdair
Mackenzie, Craig
Madigan, Patrick
Magee, Bryan
Mahowald, Mary Briody
Malpas, J(effery) E(dward)
Mansfield, Nick
Marenbon, John (Alexander)
Marrone, Steven P(hillip)
Marshall, Donald G.
Marshall, Peter (H.)
Martin, Andy
Martin, Robert M.
Masalha, Nur
Masters, Roger D.
Matson, Wallace I.
Mautner, Thomas
Maxwell, Nicholas
May, Larry

Stangroom, Jeremy
Statham, E. Robert
Stein, Edward D.
Stepaniants, Marietta
Stevens, M. L. Tina (L.)
Stewart, Matthew
Stierlin, Helm
Stivale, Charles J.
Stock, Gregory
Strathern, Paul
Stryk, Lucien
Sturm, Douglas E.
Sturmer, Michael
Suleiman, Susan Rubin
Sullivan, Brad
Sullivan, M(ichael) J(ustin)
Sulmasy, Daniel P.
Sulston, John (Edward)
Susskind, Leonard
Swanson, Judith A(nn)
Sward, Robert S.
Swatuk, Larry A(nthony)
Sweet, William
Swidler, Ann
Swinburne, Richard (Granville)
Szasz, Thomas Stephen
Taguieff, Pierre André
Taliaferro, Charles
Tan, Kok-Chor
Tanner, Michael (K.)
Tarr, Joel Arthur
Tatalovich, Raymond
Taubes, Timothy
Taylor, Barbara Gold
Taylor, Bron Raymond
Taylor, Joan E(lizabeth)
Thagard, Paul
Thandeka
Thiele, Leslie Paul
Thiessen, Elmer John
This, Herve
Thiselton, Anthony C(harles)
Thom, Paul
Thomas, Bruce
Thomas, John Heywood
Thomas, Julian (Stewart)
Thompson, Kenneth W(infred)
Tierno, Michael
Tilghman, Benjamin R(oss)
Tomaselli, Sylvana
Tracy, Thomas F.
Trundle, Robert C(hristner)
Tsomo, Karma Lekshe
Tye, Michael
Tyson, Lois (M.)
Unger, Peter K(enneth)
Urbinati, Nadia
Valdés, Mario J.
van Fraassen, Bas C.
van Parijs, Philippe
van Ruler, J. A.
Varzi, Achille C.
Velkley, Richard L.
Versluis, Arthur
Vesey, Godfrey
Vicchio, Stephen (John)
Vincent, Andrew

Viney, Donald Wayne
Vogt, Henri Hans Mikael
Von Ward, Paul
Voss, Sarah (Henderson)
Wagner, Rudolf G.
Walker, Benjamin
Walker, Nigel (David)
Walker, R. B. J.
Walton, Kendall L(ewis)
Walzer, Michael
Warburton, Nigel
Ward, (John Stephen) Keith
Ware, Kallistos
Warner, Martin
Warnock, Mary
Warren, Karen J.
Watson, Ben
Wauzzinski, Robert A.
Weaver, Will(iam Weller)
Weber, Thomas
Weiss, Raymond L.
Wellman, Carl Pierce
Welsh, Alexander
West, Cornel (Ronald)
West, M(artin) L(itchfield)
Westervelt, Saundra D(avis)
Wetzel, James
Whitaker, Katie
White, Morton (Gabriel)
White, Stephen K.
Wicclair, Mark R.
Wicker, Brian John
Wiggins, David
Williams, Vernon J(ohnson)
Wilson, Catherine
Wimsatt, William C.
Winckler, Edwin A.
Wingerter, J. Richard
Wininger, Kathleen J.
Wirzba, Norman
Wolfe, Alan (Stephen)
Wolff, Robert P(aul)
Woolhouse, Roger
Wright, M(aureen) R(osemary)
Wyatt, Don J.
Wymelenberg, Suzanne
Yarbrough, Stephen R.
Young-Bruehl, Elisabeth
Youngblood, Ronald Fred
Yourgrau, Palle
Yusa, Michiko
Zack, Naomi
Zuckert, Catherine H.
Zuidervaart, Lambert
Zukav, Gary

Photography

Accattoli, Luigi
Adams, Charles
Ades, Dawn
Agins, Teri
Akinsha, Konstantin
Alinder, Mary Street
Alterman, Glenn
Amaki, Amalia K.

Anderson, Kent
Angel, Heather
Annerino, John
Armstrong, Richard B(yron)
Bair, Deirdre
Banish, Roslyn
Banker, James R.
Barbash, Shepard
Barnwell, Tim
Barry, James P(otvin)
Baruchello, Gianfranco
Batchelor, David
Batchen, Geoffrey
Battenfield, Jackie
Bayley, Stephen
Benezra, Neal
Bennett, Shelley M.
Berger, John (Peter)
Bial, Raymond
Bidner, Jenni
Billingsley, (Kenneth) Lloyd
Blank, Harrod
Bloom, Lisa E.
Blount, Roy (Alton)
Bochner, Mel
Bohn-Spector, Claudia
Booth, Stanley
Bourne, Joyce
Boyd, Steven R(ay)
Bracegirdle, Brian
Brandenburg, Jim
Braun, Marta (A.)
Brownlee, Andrea Barnwell
Bruemmer, Fred
Brugioni, Dino A.
Brumfield, William Craft
Brundage, James A.
Bucknall, Barbara Jane
Buehler, Evelyn Judy
Burnett, Ron
Burt, William
Butler, Linda
Butlin, Martin (Richard Fletcher)
Campling, Christopher Russell
Carlebach, Michael L(loyd)
Carter, Jared
Casey, Barbara
Chadwick, Whitney
Cheers, D. Michael
Chester, Mark (S.)
Childs, Elizabeth C(atharine)
Chinery, Michael
Christensen, Paul
Clarkson, Wensley
Clayton, Martin
Cleare, John S.
Cleveland, Leslie
Cohen, Leonard
Cole, Stephen A.
Coleman, A(llan) D(ouglass)
Collector, Stephen
Connelly, Frances S(usan)
Corio, David
Cothran, James R(obert)
Cottrell, David
Cox, Jim
Cox, Paul(us)

Cox, Steve
Crewdson, Gregory
Crist, Judith
Cumming, Elizabeth (Skeoch)
Curatola, Giovanni
Daniel, Pete
David, Catherine
David, Catherine
Davidson, Osha Gray
Davies, Kristian
Davis, Amelia
Davis, Harold
Dawid, Annie
Day, Holliday T.
Day-Lewis, Sean (Francis)
Devlin, Anne
Dickinson, Terence
Diehn, Gwen
Donovan
Dorment, Richard
Douglas, John (Frederick James)
Douglas, Susan J(eanne)
Dower, John W(illiam)
Drake, Alicia
Drury, John
Duncan, David Douglas
Dunlop, Nic
Eisler, Benita
Enyeart, James L.
Eppridge, Bill Alfredo Eduardo
Etheridge, Eric
Fabrizio, Timothy C(harles)
Fahey, David (Allen)
Fain, Michael
Feiler, Bruce
Fenton, Peter
Fermi, Rachel
Ferrer, Elizabeth
Fifield, Christopher G(eorge)
Fish, Charles (K.)
Fisher, Angela
Fleming, Kate
Floyd, Nancy
Foster, Steven
Fowler, Don D.
Fox, Ted
Fox, William L.
Fradin, Judith (Bernette) Bloom
Fraley, Tobin
Frega, Donnalee
Friedman, Debra
Frommel, Christoph Lvitpold
Fuegi, John
Gallardo, Evelyn
Gallas, John (Edward)
Gardiner, Jeremy
Gardon, Anne
Garner, Gretchen
Garrett, Susan
George, Alice Rose
Gilbert, Alma M.
Glassberg, David
Goin, Peter
Goldsmith, Lynn
Goodman, Lizbeth (L.)
Graham, Jorie
Grambo, Rebecca L(ynn)

Graves, Russell A.	Lavin, Maud	Pendreigh, Brian	Steele-Perkins, Christopher Horace
Gray, Christopher	Lee, Anthony W.	Penrose, Antony	Steinman, Louise
Griffin, Farah Jasmine	Lee, M. Owen	Peterson, Christian A.	Stevens, Bryna
Grosse, W. Jack	Lemann, Nicholas	Phillips, Lisa	Stevens, Dick
Gruen, Bob	Lerner, Martin	Pitts, Michael R.	Stout, Nancy
Gruhn, George	Lewis, Arnold	Plant, Sadie	Strong, Roy (Colin)
Gutman, Judith Mara	Lin, Tan (Anthony)	Platzker, David	Sullivan, Claudia
Hafertepe, Kenneth	Linnell, David	Plowden, David	Sullivan, George E(dward)
Hale, Robert D(avid)	Lipton, James	Powell, Robert	Sweeney, Emma
Hambourg, Maria Morris	Loengard, John	Powning, Beth	Symmons, Sarah
Hamill, Sam (Patrick)	Loney, Glenn Meredith	Poynor, Robin	Talese, Gay
Harker, Michael P.	Loomis, Jennifer A.	Prown, Jonathan	Tanner, Jo A.
Harris, Paul	Lopes, Dominic (M. McIver)	Pultz, John Francisco	Taylor, Jennifer (Evelyn)
Hart, John Fraser	Loud, Patricia Cummings	Quinn, Sunny	Taylor, Sue
Haseley, Dennis	Lucie-Smith, (John) Edward (McKenzie)	Randall, Margaret	Temperley, David
Heacox, Kim		Ratcliff, Carter	Terry, Megan
Hegenberger, John	Lwin, Nanda Layos	Ratliff, Ben	Thompson, Claudia G(reig)
Hentoff, Nat(han Irving)	Macgregor, James Murdoch	Richards, Eugene	Thurley, Simon
Hernandez, Jo Farb	Machedon, Luminita	Rippley, LaVern J.	Timmermans, Tricia
Hess, Alan	MacWeeney, Alen	Roberts, Jennifer L.	Toll, Robert Charles
Hillman, Barry (Leslie)	Maizels, John	Robertson, Janet (E.)	Toulmin, Vanessa Elizabeth
Hoagland, Edward	Marantz, Sylvia S.	Robinson, Frank M(alcolm)	Traub, Charles (Henry)
Hochman, Elaine S(chwartz)	Marcou, David J.	Romano, Ray	Trimble, Stephen
Hockney, David	Marcus, Jana	Roose-Evans, James	Tucker, Jennifer
Hokanson, (Anthony) Drake	Marks, (Amelia) Lee	Root, Deborah	Turan, Kenneth
Holmes, Jon Richard	Marlor, Clark Strang	Rosenak, Jan(ice M.)	Ulrich, Larry
Homberger, Eric	Marr, David	Roth, Lorna	Unglaub, Jonathan
Homer, William Innes	Marsh, Charles R.	Rubin, Bruce Joel	Vallee, Lillian (Bozenna)
Honnef, Klaus	Maso, Carole	Ruby, Jay	van Alphen, Ernst
Hopkinson, Amanda	Matthews, Victoria (Ann)	Rudkin, (James) David	van Hensbergen, Gijs
Howard, Kathleen L.	Maurer-Mathison, Diane V(ogel)	Rugg, Linda (Haverty)	Vatikiotis, Michael R. J.
Hume, John Robert	Mayer, Robert	Ryden, Hope	Vaughan, Ronald G(eorge)
Hunt, Robert (William Gainer)	McBride, Simon	Sabatine, Jean A.	Ventura, Michael
Hurwitz, David	McCullin, Don(ald)	Sandweiss, Martha A(nn)	Vermilye, Jerry
Imes, Birney	McEwan, Ian	Sarnoff, Irving	Vilander, Barbara
Isenberg, Barbara	McFall, Gardner	Sayre, Shay	Vornberger, Cal Calvin
Ivory, James (Francis)	McMullan, Margaret	Schiff, Nancy Rica	Walker, Robert
James, Russell	McNutt, Randy	Schinto, Jeanne	Waller, Robert James
Johns, Jeremy	Menzel, Peter	Schneider, Stuart L.	Watson, Steven
Johnson, Diane	Merne, Oscar James	Schoffman, Nachum	Weales, Gerald
Johnson, Neil L.	Midda, Sara	Schouvaloff, Alexander	Weber, Thomas
Jones, J. Barrie	Miller, Jonathan (Wolfe)	Seldon, Lynn	Wegman, William (George)
Jones, Thom	Miller, Tice L.	Sellars, Jane	Weideman, Ryan
Jourdain, Robert	Montier, Jean-Pierre	Selman, Robyn	Wek, Alek
Junker, Patricia	Morgan, Neil	Senn, Bryan	Wells, Spencer
Karnow, Stanley	Morton, Alexandra (Hubbard)	Shabazz, Jamel	West, Edward
Keegan, Marcia	Mott, Robert L.	Shavelson, Lonny	Whalley, Joyce Irene
Kelly, Franklin (Wood)	Mueller, Andrew	Sheppard, Rob	White, Christopher (John)
Kertess, Klaus	Muir, Richard	Shirley, Frances A.	Whitfield, Roderick
Keyser, James D.	Murphy, Sylvia	Sichel, Kim Deborah	Whitfield, Sarah
Khoroche, Peter (Andrew)	Nancarrow, Mindy	Silk, Gerald	Widdicombe, Toby
Kim, Elaine H(aikyung)	Navarra, Tova	Sills, Leslie (Elka)	Williams, Carla
Kimmelman, Michael Simon	Nericcio, William Anthony	Silverman, Stephen M.	Williamson, Kate T.
Kimura, Margaret	Nichols, John	Simmons, Sylvie	Willis, Deborah
King, David	Nickel, Douglas R.	Simon, Seymour	Willumson, Glenn
King, Gilbert	Nissenson, Marilyn	Sinden, Donald (Alfred)	Wilson, Christopher R.
Kleh, Cindy (L.)	Nixon, Mignon	Singer, Barry	Wolfe, Art
Knowles, Harry (Jay)	Nunn, Pamela Gerrish	Smith, Annick	Wood, John A.
Koenig, Karl P.	Nute, Kevin	Smith, David E(lvin)	Woodbury, Heather
Koontz, Robin	O'Kane, Bernard	Smith, Glenn D.	Woods, Michael
Kramer, Linda Konheim	O'Leary, Patrick	Smith, Glenn Robert	Wright, Michael J(ohn)
Kuklin, Susan	O'Neal, Hank	Smith, Zak	Wu, Norbert
Lahr, John (Henry)	O'Toole, Judith Hansen	Snyder, Gary (Sherman)	Wynne, Frank
Laird, Ross	Okwu, Julian C. R.	Sparke, Penny	Yamada, Nanako
Laird, Thomas (Calvin)	Olson, Ted	Spycket, Jerome	Yenawine, Philip
Lamplugh, Lois	Page, Geoff(rey Donald)	Staley, Allen (Percival Green)	Yolen, Jane
Lancaster, Michael (L.)	Patterson, Dan		

Photography-*cont.*

Zaccaria, Jerry A.
Zietz, Karyl Lynn
Ziffrin, Marilyn J.
Zimberoff, Tom

Physics

Aczel, Amir D.
Agrawal, Govind P.
Ahmed, Syed Naeem
Aitchison, Ian J(ohnston) R(hind)
Altmann, Simon L(eonardo)
Anderson, Katharine
Andrews, Edgar Harold
Armstrong, David Malet
Backus, George Edward
Bacon, George Edward
Balibar, Sebastien
Bandrauk, Andre D.
Banerjee, Asit
Banerji, S(riranjan)
Barabási, Albert-László
Barbour, Julian B.
Barr, Stephen M.
Bayley, Stephen
Begelman, Mitchell (Craig)
Bennett, Charles A.
Bertulani, Carlos A.
Bloembergen, Nicolaas
Bloomfield, Louis A(ub)
Boisvert, Raymond D.
Bonnor, William Bowen
Braginsky, Vladimir B.
Branover, Herman
Bube, Richard Howard
Buchanan, Mark
Burgess, Colin
Calder, Nigel (David Ritchie)
Cardona, Manuel
Cassidy, David C(harles)
Clotfelter, Beryl E(dward)
Cobb, Cathy
Coleman, James A.
Cook, Bob
Cooper, Leon N.
Cottrell, Alan (Howard)
Cramer, John G(leason)
Crowley-Milling, Michael C.
Darling, David J.
De Pree, Christopher G.
Dickinson, Terence
Drew, Horace R.
Dukert, Joseph M(ichael)
Dyson, Freeman (John)
Eisenstaedt, Jean
Epperson, Michael
Fanchi, John R(ichard)
Ferris, Timothy
Fontanella, John J.
Ford, Brian John
Freudenthal, Gad
Friedlander, Michael W.
Gaither, Carl C.
Gell-Mann, Murray
Ghirardi, G. C.

Physics-*cont.*

Goerner, Sally J.
Grabbe, Crockett L(ane)
Halpern, Paul
Hecht, Jeff(rey Charles)
Heims, Steve J(oshua)
Hellman, Hal
Heppenheimer, Thomas A.
Herman, Stephen L.
Hilborn, Robert C.
Hills, Philip James
Hodge, Paul William
Huizenga, John R(obert)
Hunt, Bruce J.
Jacker, Corinne
Jaroff, Leon Morton
Jones, D. S.
Kane, Gordon L.
Kevles, Daniel J.
Krauss, Lawrence M.
Krieger, Martin H.
Kumar, Alok
Lanouette, William (John)
Levi, Barbara Goss
Lide, David R.
Lovell, (Alfred Charles) Bernard
Lyons, Louis
Maoz, Dan
March, N(orman) H(enry)
Marion, Jean-Luc
Marten, Michael
Maxwell, Nicholas
McKay, Don
Melia, Fulvio
Messel, Harry
Mlodinow, Leonard
Modinos, Antonis
Morus, Iwan Rhys
Müller, Ingo
Newton, Roger G(erhard)
Nye, Mary Jo
Odenwald, Sten F.
Ohanian, Hans C.
Ouellette, Jennifer
Paesler, Michael
Penrose, Roger
Perkowitz, Sidney
Pesic, Peter
Polkinghorne, John Charlton
Quinn, Helen R.
Radin, Dean I.
Randall, Lisa
Raudkivi, A(rved) J(aan)
Reich, Eugenie Samuel
Rhodes, Richard (Lee)
Robinson, Andrew
Rosenkranz, Ze'ev
Rubinstein, Isaak
Rybolt, Thomas R.
Sachs, Mendel
Schaerf, Carlo
Schewe, Phillip F.
Segrè, Gino
Shasha, Dennis (E.)
Siegfried, Tom
Silverman, Mark P.
Smarandache, Florentin
Spall, James C.

Physics-*cont.*

Spolter, Pari (Dokht)
Sprackling, Michael Thomas
Stachel, John Jay
Sterken, Christiaan (L.)
Taylor, John (Gerald)
Thorne, Kip S.
Tipler, Frank J(ennings)
Tobias, Michael (Charles)
Trefil, James
Tribus, Myron
Tsipenyuk, Yuri M.
Uman, Myron F.
van Fraassen, Bas C.
VanCleave, Janice
Ward, Elizabeth Honor
Weart, Spencer R(ichard)
Weinberg, Steven
Weiss, Thomas Fischer
Welsbacher, Anne
Wickramasinghe, Nalin Chandra
Wilkinson, Denys (Haigh)
Will, Clifford M(artin)
Williams, Forman A.
Williams, W. S. C.
Wolfson, Richard
Zee, A.
Zukav, Gary

Politics/Government

Abegunrin, Olayiwola
Abraham, Henry J.
Abraham, Spencer
Abramsky, Sasha
Abramson, Bruce
Abshire, David Manker
AbuKhalil, As'ad
Accinelli, Robert
Achinstein, Sharon
Ackelsberg, Martha A.
Adams, James (Macgregor David)
Adams, Jerome R(obertson)
Adelman, Clifford
Adkin, Mark
Adler, Jeffrey S(cott)
Aggarwal, Ravina
Agha-Jaffar, Tamara
Agrawal, Arun
Agyeman, Opoku
Ajami, Fouad
Akarli, Engin Deniz
Akst, Daniel
Al-Marayati, Abid A(min)
Al-Rasheed, Madawi
Albert, Michael
Albert, Steve
Albritton, Robert
Alden, Chris
Alden, Edward H.
Alderman, Ellen
Alexseev, Mikhail A.
Ali, Ayaan Hirsi
Allison, Robert J.
Alterman, Eric (Ross)
Altman, Dennis

Politics/Government-*cont.*

Amar, Akhil Reed
Ambaras, David Richard
Amyx, Jennifer A.
Anders, Leslie
Anderson, Brian C.
Anderson, Elizabeth (S.)
Anderson, John B(ayard)
Anderson, Malcolm
Anderson, Wilda (Christine)
Andrew, Edward
Andrews, Molly
Anglin, Douglas G(eorge)
Antler, Joyce
Anunobi, Fredoline O.
Applebome, Peter
Appleton, Sheldon Lee
Archer, Keith (Allan)
Archer of Sandwell
Armitage, Ronda (Jacqueline)
Armstrong, Alan
Armstrong, Richard
Armstrong, Robert Laurence
Arnold, David
Arnold, Guy
Aron, Michael
Aronowitz, Stanley
Arsenault, Raymond
Arter, David
Aruri, Naseer H.
Ashford, Nigel (John Gladwell)
Aulich, James
Austin, Curtis J.
Avant, Deborah D.
Averill, Gage
Avery, Gillian (Elise)
Avishai, Bernard
Awoonor, Kofi
Ayittey, George B. N.
Ayres, E. C.
Babich, Babette E.
Bacon, Donald C(onrad)
Badger, Anthony J.
Badgley, John Herbert
Bagdikian, Ben H(aig)
Bageant, Joe
Bailey, Charles Waldo
Bailey, Frederick George
Bailey, Julius H.
Bailey, Kathleen C.
Bailey, Norman (Alishan)
Bain, Kenneth (Ross)
Baker, Raymond William
Baker, Richard A(llan)
Bakke, O. M.
Balen, Malcolm
Ball, Stuart
Ball, Terence
Ballard, Terry
Balz, Dan
Bandarage, Asoka
Banisadr, Abol-Hassan
Bannon, David Race
Baptist, Edward (E.)
Bar, Shmuel
Bar-Joseph, Uri
Bara czak, Stanisław
Barash, David P(hilip)

Carretta, Vincent (Albert)
Carrier, Thomas J.
Carroll, Francis M(artin)
Carswell, Sue
Carter, Jimmy
Carter, Warren
Carver, Terrell
Carville, (Chester) James
Cassell, Joan
Casstevens, Thomas William
Castaneda, Jorge G.
Castiglione, Caroline
Castle, Alfred L.
Castor, Helen
Caute, (John) David
Caws, Peter (James)
Cazden, Courtney B(orden)
Cerami, Charles A.
Chaleff, Ira
Chambers, Aidan
Chambers, John Whiteclay
Champagne, Duane (Willard)
Chan, Gerald
Chang, Gordon G.
Chang, Ha-Joon
Chang, Maria Hsia
Charmley, John
Chaves, Mark (Alan)
Checkel, Jeffrey T(aylor)
Chen, Calvin
Chester, Jeff
Chetkovich, Carol A.
Chidester, David
Chilcote, Ronald H.
Childs, David (Haslam)
Chinn, Carl
Chirot, Daniel
Chisholm, Michael
Chomsky, (Avram) Noam
Chomsky, Aviva
Chorbajian, Levon
Christian, William
Christie, Ian
Christie, Stuart
Christodoulou, Demetrios
Christoph, Peter R(ichard)
Cimbala, Stephen J.
Ciment, James D.
Cirincione, Joseph
Clague, Christopher K.
Clapham, Christopher S.
Clapp, Jennifer
Clark, Anna (K.)
Clark, Christopher M.
Clark, Paul F.
Clark, Terry N(ichols)
Clarke, Peter Frederick
Clausen, Christopher (John)
Clavel, Pierre
Clawson, Rosalee A.
Cleary, Edward L.
Cleary, Matthew R.
Clem, Alan L(eland)
Clément, Dominique
Clement, Mary H.
Clendinen, Dudley
Clinton, Hillary Rodham

Clinton, James W(illiam)
Clotfelter, Charles T.
Clouse, Robert Gordon
Coates, Charles (K.)
Coats, Wendell John
Coffey, John Robert David
Cogan, Brian A.
Cogliano, Francis D.
Cohen, David William
Cohen, Henry
Cohen, Jeffrey E.
Cohen, Lenard J.
Cohen, Michael A.
Cohen, Robin
Cohen, Stephen F(rand)
Cohen, Youssef
Cohrs, Patrick O.
Coker, Christopher
Coleman, Mary DeLorse
Coleman, Terry
Colfax, David (John)
Collette, Christine
Colley, Linda
Collier, Paul
Collini, Stefan
Collins, Gail
Collinson, Sarah
Colodny, Len
Comiskey, Michael
Commins, David Dean
Commoner, Barry
Connelly, Donald B.
Connolly, William E(ugene)
Conrad, Jessamyn
Conroy, John
Conteh-Morgan, Earl
Converse, Nathan
Converse, Philip E.
Coogan, Tim(othy) Pat(rick)
Cook, Chris(topher)
Cook, Philip J.
Cooley, Alexander
Coombes, Annie E.
Cooper, Roger
Copeland, Peter
Corbett, Richard (Graham)
Cormack, Patrick (Thomas)
Corn, David
Corrado, Anthony
Coryell, Janet L(ee)
Cossolotto, Matthew
Cotman, John Walton
Cottrell, Robert C.
Covin, David L.
Cowie, Hamilton Russell
Cox, Ana Marie
Cox, Gary W(alter)
Cox, Kevin Robert
Cox, Robert H(enry)
Coyne, James K(itchenman)
Crabtree, John
Craig, Robert H.
Craig, Stephen C.
Cramer, Richard Ben
Cranfield, Ingrid
Crawford, Craig
Creekmore, Marion V.

Crenson, Matthew A.
Creswell, Michael
Crew, Danny O(liver)
Cribb, Robert (Bridson)
Criddle, Byron
Critchley, Simon
Critchlow, Donald T.
Crnobrnja (Tsernobernya),
   Mihailo
Crockett, David A.
Cronin, Mike
Cronon, William
Crosby, Alfred W.
Crossley, James G.
Crowder, George
Crowley, Tony
Crozier, Michael (Paul)
Cruz, Consuelo
Csaba, László
Csepeli, György
Cunningham, James V.
Cuno, James B.
Cuomo, Mario (Matthew)
Curthoys, Ann
D'Amato, Anthony
D'Anieri, Paul J. D.
Dacey, Austin
Dahl, Robert (Alan)
Daily, David W.
Dale, Richard
Dalton, Russell J.
Dalyell, Tam
Danchev, Alex
Danforth, John C(laggett)
Dangler, Jean
Daniels, Mark R.
Danopoulos, Constantine P.
Darnell, Regna (Diebold)
Darwish, Adel
Das, Suranjan
Dauvergne, Peter
Davidson, Jamie S.
Davidson, Osha Gray
Davidson, Roger H(arry)
Davies, Charlotte Aull
Davies, Martin (Brett)
Davies, Philip John
Davies, Robert William
Davis, Alan (R.)
Davis, David (Howard)
Davis, Nancy Yaw
Davis, Richard
Davis, Richard Whitlock
Dawson, George Glenn
Day, Richard J. F.
De Becker, Gavin
de Breadun, Deaglan
de Vries, Hent
de-Shalit, Avner
Debrix, François
Defrank, Thomas M.
Delahaye, Michael (John)
Deleon, Peter
Deligiorgi, Katerina
Denham, Andrew
Derfler, (Arnold) Leslie
Derian, James (Arthur) Der

Desch, Michael C.
Desfor, Gene
Devalle, Susana B. C.
DeVincent-Hayes, Nan
Dew, Andrea J.
Dewey, Donald O(dell)
Dewey, Scott Hamilton
Diamond, Hanna Elizabeth
Diamond, Sara
Dibua, Jeremiah I.
Dickman, Thomas
Dietz, Peter (John)
Dillon, Sam(uel)
Dinan, Desmond
Dine, Janet
Dinerman, Beatrice
DioGuardi, Joseph J.
Dionne, E(ugene) J.
Dirck, Brian R.
Divine, Robert A(lexander)
Dixon, Steve
Djupe, Paul A.
Dobbin, Murray
Dobbs, Michael
Dobbs, Ricky F.
Dobson, Alan P.
Dobson, Andrew (Nicholas
   Howard)
Dobson, R(ichard) Barrie
Doherty, Brian
Doherty, Kieran
Dolan, Frederick Michael
Donohue, William A.
Donoughue, Bernard
Doolen, Andy
Doolittle, Amity A.
Dore, Elizabeth W.
Dorman, Michael L.
Dorrien, Gary J.
Dougherty, James E(dward)
Dowlah, Caf
Downes, Bryan T(revor)
Dowty, Alan K.
Doyle, Charles (Desmond)
Dreher, Rod
Dressler, Joshua
Dreyfuss, Robert
Drèze, Jean
Drezner, Daniel W.
Dryzek, John S.
Dubin, Michael J.
Dubose, Lou(is H.)
Dudziak, Mary L.
Duelfer, Charles A.
Duffield, John S.
Duffy, James H(enry)
Duffy, Susan
Duina, Francesco G.
Duke, Steven B.
Dulaney, W. Marvin
Dumbrell, John
Dummett, Michael (Anthony
   Eardley)
Dunaway, Finis
Dunbar, Leslie W(allace)
Duncan, Stephen M.
Dunkerley, James

Greene, Julie
Greene, Nathanael
Greenwald, Glenn
Greenwood-Waller, Judith
Greer, Steven (Crawford)
Greetham, David
Gregorian, Raffi
Grey, Anthony
Grieb, Kenneth J.
Griffith, Ivelaw L(loyd)
Griffith, Marlene
Griffiths, Steve
Grinde, Donald A(ndrew)
Grondahl, Paul
Grosbard, Ofer
Gross, David
Gross, Emanuel
Gruberg, Martin
Grundy, Pamela C.
Guardino, Peter
Guarnieri, Carlo
Guild, Elspeth
Guillou, Jan
Gurtov, Melvin
Gurval, Robert Alan
Gushee, David P.
Guttenplan, D. D.
Gutzman, Kevin R.C.
Guzzo, Lou(is Richard)
Gwyn, William Brent
Gylfason, Thorvaldur
Haas, Lawrence J.
Hacker, Jacob S.
Hacker, Kenneth L.
Hackett, Robert A(nthony)
Hagerty, Devin T.
Hague, William
Hahm, Sung Deuk
Hahn, Gordon M.
Hahn, Steven C.
Hain, Peter
Hale, Henry E.
Hall, Brian
Hall, David Locke
Halperin, Joan Ungersma
Halpern, Cynthia Leone
Halstead, Ted
Hamilton, Marci A.
Hamm, Theodore Alton
Hammond, John Craig
Hancock, Ian (Robert)
Handelman, Stephen
Handler, Richard
Hannaford, Peter (Dor)
Hannant, Larry
Hansford, Thomas G.
Hanson, Philip
Harding, James
Hardt, Michael
Hardy, Gayle J.
Hargrove, Erwin C.
Harmon, Louise
Harner, Stephen M.
Harriger, Katy J(ean)
Harris, Charles Wesley
Harris, Fred R(oy)
Harris, Fredrick C.

Harris, Jose
Harris, Robin
Harris, Walter A.
Harris-Lacewell, Melissa Victoria
Harrison, Kathy A.
Harrison, Neil E.
Harrison, Suzan
Harrison, Trevor (W.)
Harvey, David Allen
Harvey, Thomas
Harwood, John
Hasler, Julie
Hastedt, Glenn Peter
Hasty, Jennifer
Hattersley, Roy (Sydney George)
Hauptman, Laurence Marc
Hawthorne, Fran
Hay, William Anthony
Hayduk, Ron
Haynes, John Earl
Hays, Tony
Hayter, Teresa
Hazlehurst, Cameron
Heald, Suzette
Healey, Denis (Winston)
Healy, Gene
Heater, Derek Benjamin
Heath, Malcolm (Frederick)
Heather, Peter
Heertje, Arnold
Heidar, Knut (Martin)
Heidler, Jeanne T(wiggs)
Heilbrunn, Jacob
Heim, Michael Henry
Heineman, Kenneth J.
Held, Virginia
Hellman, Stephen
Hellyer, Paul T.
Helmke, Gretchen
Helms, Mary W.
Helms, Robert B(rake)
Heminway, John
Hendrickson, Ryan C.
Henig, Jeffrey R.
Henneberger, Melinda
Hennessy, Peter
Henry, Stuart (Dennis)
Heper, Metin
Hepworth, Noel P.
Herbst, Phil(ip H.)
Herf, Jeffrey
Herl, Joseph
Hero, Rodney E.
Heron, Ann
Herring, Eric
Hershberger, Mary
Herspring, Dale R.
Hertzke, Allen D.
Heryanto, Ariel
Herzog, Dagmar
Hewitt, W(arren) E(dward)
Hey, Jeanne A. K.
Heywood, Andrew
Hibbing, John R.
Hibbs, John
Hicks, L. Edward
Higgins, Rosalyn

Hill, Gerald N.
Hill, Harvey
Hill, Kathleen Thompson
Hillman, Richard S.
Hilsman, Roger
Hiltermann, Joost R.
Himelfarb, Richard
Himka, John-Paul
Hindess, Barry
Hing, Bill Ong
Hirsh, Michael
Hitchens, Peter Jonathan
Hitz, Frederick P(orter)
Hix, Simon
Hobsbawm, Eric (John Ernest)
Hochman, Jiri
Hoerr, John
Hoff, Joan
Hoffman, Bruce
Hoffman, Donna R.
Hoffman, Ronald
Hoffmann, Stanley
Hogan, J. Michael
Hoile, David
Hokanson, (Anthony) Drake
Holland, Max (Mendel)
Holland, Robert Gray
Hollifield, James F.
Hollings, Robert L.
Holloway, Harry (Albert)
Holloway, Richard (Frederick)
Holmes, Leslie (Templeman)
Holsti, Kalevi J.
Holsti, Ole Rudolf
Honderich, Ted
Hooft, Hendrik (G. A.)
Hooks, Bell
Hooks, Gregory M.
Hoover, H(elen) M(ary)
Hopcke, Robert H(enry)
Hope, Marjorie (Cecelia)
Hopkins, George Emil
Hormats, Robert D.
Horn, Gerd-Rainer
Horn, Michiel
Horne, Alistair (Allan)
Horner, David
Hornsby, Alton
Horowitz, Irving Louis
Horowitz, Shale A.
Horsey, David
Horsley, Lee
Houghton, David Patrick
Houston, Alan Craig
Howard, A(rthur) E(llsworth)
  Dick
Howard, Alison D.
Howard, J. Woodford
Howard, M(ichael) C.
Howard, Roger
Howard-Hassmann, Rhoda E.
Howe, (Richard Edward) Geoffrey
Howe, Neil
Howe, Stephen
Howell, Dorothy J(ulia)
Hoy, Claire
Hoyle, Russ

Hozic, Aida (A.)
Hsu, Albert Y.
Hsueh, Tien tung
Hubbard, Charles M.
Huber, Evelyne
Huck, (Edwin) Arthur
Huddleston, Mark W.
Hughes, Colin Anfield
Hughes, Steven C.
Huhne, Christopher
Hulsman, John C.
Hult, Karen
Humez, Nicholas (David)
Humphreys, George G(ary)
Hundley, Norris C.
Hung, Chang-tai
Hunt, Lynn (Avery)
Hunter, Shireen T.
Huntley, James Robert
Hurewitz, Daniel
Hurrell, Andrew
Hurtig, Mel
Huskey, Eugene
Hutchinson, Earl Ofari
Hutchinson, G(regory) O(wen)
Hutchinson, Peter
Hwang, Jenny
Hyde, Samuel C.
Hyde-Price, Adrian
Hyman, Harold M(elvin)
Ibata-Arens, Kathryn
Ibbitson, John Perrie
Igo, Sarah E.
Iheduru, Obioma M.
Ihonvbere, Julius O.
Ikenberry, G. John
Ilesanmi, Simeon O.
Imbroscio, David L.
Ingle, Bob
Ingram, Derek Thynne
Ireland, Patrick R(ichard)
Isaacs, Arnold R.
Jack, Andrew (John)
Jacker, Corinne
Jackman, Sydney Wayne
Jackson, Anthony
Jackson, Clare
Jackson, Robert J.
Jackson, William Keith
Jacob, Joseph M.
Jacobs, Dan(iel) N(orman)
Jacobs, David
Jacobs, Jack L.
Jaffrelot, Christophe
Jakobson, Michael
Jaksi , Iván
Jalata, Asafa
Jalland, Pat(ricia)
James, (William) Louis (Gabriel)
James, Alan
James, David Edward
James, Stanlie
James, W(illiam) Martin
Janken, Kenneth Robert
Jankowski, James P.
Jarvis, Sharon E.
Jasper, James M(acdonald)

Jay, Antony (Rupert)
Jay, Peter
Jefferies, Matthew (Martin)
Jeffery, Anthea J.
Jeffrey, Thomas E.
Jeffreys, Derek S.
Jelen, Ted G.
Jenkins, Brian Michael
Jenkins, T(erence) A(ndrew)
Jensen, Nathan M.
Jensen, Vickie (Dee)
Jervis, Robert
Jirgens, Karl (E.)
Johnson, A. Ross
Johnson, Cathy Marie
Johnson, Clint
Johnson, Freddie Lee
Johnson, George (Laclede)
Johnson, Robert David
Johnson-Cartee, Karen S.
Johnston, Barbara Rose
Johnston, R(onald) J(ohn)
Johnston, Richard
Jonas, Raymond
Jonasdottir, Anna G(uðrun)
Jones, Bryan D(avidson)
Jones, David (Erik) Hay
Jones, David Martin
Jones, J. Gwynfor
Jones, Ricky L.
Jordan, David C.
Jordan, Robert Smith
Joyce, Davis D.
Judd, Frank (Ashcroft)
Juffer, Jane
Kagan, Donald
Kagarlitsky, Boris
Kahan, Alan S.
Kahlenberg, Richard D.
Kain, Philip J(oseph)
Kaiser, David E.
Kaiser, Ward L(ouis)
Kalley, Jacqueline A(udrey)
Kalman, Laura
Kamieniecki, Sheldon
Kammen, Michael
Kampfner, John
Kamrava, Mehran
Kann, Mark E.
Kaplan, Edward S.
Kaplan, Morton A.
Kaplar, Richard T.
Kapstein, Ethan B.
Karch, Andrew
Kash, Don E.
Kasinitz, Philip
Katagiri, Yasuhiro
Katchanovski, Ivan
Katouzian, Homa
Katz, David
Katz, James Everett
Katz, Richard Stephen
Kauffman, Bill
Kaufman, Gerald (Bernard)
Kaufman, Menahem
Kaufman, Robert G.
Kaufman, Will

Kaufman-Osborn, Timothy
Kavanaugh, Andrea L(ee)
Keane, John
Kearney, Richard Marius
Keats-Rohan, K. S. B.
Keegan, William (James Gregory)
Keenan, Brian
Keeter, (Charles) Scott
Kehde, Ned
Keil, Roger
Kelleher, Victor Michael Kitchener
Keller, William W(alton)
Kelley, Liam C.
Kellough, J. Edward
Kemp, Roger L.
Kempe, Frederick
Kendrick, Paul Calvert
Kennedy, David Michael
Kennedy, Paul Michael
Kenney, Jeffrey T.
Kenney, Michael
Keohane, Dan
Kerbel, Matthew Robert
Kerr, K. Austin
Kersch, Ken I.
Kershaw, Alex
Kershaw, Ian
Kessler, Glenn
Kettell, Steven
Kevles, Daniel J.
Khalid, Mansour
Khilnani, Sunil
Khlevniuk, Oleg V.
Khwaja, Waqas
Kierner, Cynthia A.
Kiewe, Amos
Kim, Byoung-lo Philo
Kim, Thomas P.
Kimmel, Michael S(cott)
King, (William) Dennis
King, Anthony
Kingstone, Peter R.
Kirchner, Emil J(oseph)
Kirk, Thomas Allison
Kirk-Greene, Anthony
Kirshner, Jonathan
Kissinger, Henry (Alfred)
Kitfield, James C.
Kitts, Kenneth
Kitzinger, Uwe
Klare, Michael T(homas)
Klausen, Jytte
Klehr, Harvey
Klein, Norman M.
Kleinberg, S. J.
Klerkx, Greg
Kline, Michael
Klyza, Christopher McGrory
Kneeland, Timothy (W.)
Knowles, Helen
Koch, Edward I(rving)
Koehn, Peter H.
Kohn, Edward P.
Kolbert, Elizabeth
Kolinsky, Martin
Kolko, Joyce

Kornbluh, Peter
Korth, Philip A.
Kosar, Kevin R.
Kowalski, Kathiann M.
Krainz, Thomas A.
Kramer, Hilton
Kramer, Martin
Kramnick, Isaac
Kranish, Michael
Krasilovsky, Phyllis
Krauss, Clifford
Krebs, Ronald R.
Kremenyuk, Victor (A.)
Kreml, William P.
Kressel, Neil J.
Krislov, Samuel
Kroker, Arthur (W.)
Krooth, Richard
Kuhl, Stefan
Kukreja, Veena
Kumar, Martha Joynt
Kunich, John Charles
Kunze, Michael
Kupchan, Charles A.
Kupfer, Marcia A.
Kupferberg, Feiwel
Kurlantzick, Joshua
Kurtz, Donn M.
Kushner, James A(lan)
Kuttner, Robert (Louis)
Kydd, Andrew H.
Lachman, Seymour P.
LaFeber, Walter Frederick
Laffey, Steve
Laforest, Guy
Lai, David Chuenyan
Lal, Brij V.
Lamar, Howard Roberts
Lamb, Brian
Lamb, Karl A(llen)
Lambert, Josiah Bartlett
Lambrecht, William
Lamont, Michèle
Lampton, David M.
Lancaster, Carol J.
Lancaster, Roger N(elson)
Lander, Jack Robert
Landry, Donna
Lang, Gladys Engel
Lang, Kurt
Langley, Lester D(anny)
Lanouette, William (John)
Lape, Noreen Groover
Laponce, Jean
Lappé, Frances Moore
Lapping, Brian (Michael)
Laqueur, Walter
Larocca, Roger T.
Larsen, Timothy
Larson, Edward J(ohn)
Larson, Stephanie Greco
Lassiter, Matthew D.
Latell, Brian
Lathrop, Douglas A.
Lauber, Volkmar
Lauck, Jon K.
Laughland, John

Laurie, Peter
Laursen, John Christian
Lavender, Abraham D(onald)
Lawler, Peter Augustine
Lawless, Jennifer L.
Laybourn, Keith
Lazin, Fred A.
Le May, G(odfrey) H. L(ancelot)
Lea, James F(ranklin)
Leal, David L.
Leaning, Jennifer
Lee, Frances E.
Lee, Wei-chin
Leech, John
Legge, John David
Legro, Jeffrey W.
Lehrer, Stanley
Lehring, Gary L.
Leier, Mark
Leigh, David
Leiken, Robert S.
Leiner, Katherine
Lemay, Shawna
Lendon, J. E.
Lendvai, Paul
Leng, Russell J.
Lenz, Elinor
Leonard, Amy Elmore
Leonard, Mark
Leong, Russell (C.)
Lesch, David W.
Lesourne, Jacques
Lessnoff, Michael
Levene, Mark
Levin, Michael (Graubart)
Levin, Yuval
Levine, Alan J.
Levine, John R.
Levinson, David M.
Levitt, Matthew
Levy, Peter B.
Levy, Robert A.
Lewin, Leif
Lewis, (Norman) Douglas
Lewis, Herbert S.
Lewis, Michael
Lewis, Rupert
Li, Joyce H.S.
Libby, Ronald T(heodore)
Lichbach, Mark Irving
Lichtblau, Eric
Lieber, Robert J.
Lieberman, Benjamin
Lieberthal, Kenneth G.
Liebich, Andre
Liebovich, Louis W.
Lienesch, Michael
Lightfoot, Kent G.
Lilla, Mark
Lim, Elvin T.
Lim, Walter S. H.
Lind, Michael
Lindberg, Staffan I.
Lindenmeyer, Kriste
Linder, Marc
Linder, Robert D.
Lindsay, James

Lindsey, Brink
Link, William A.
Linklater, Magnus (Duncan)
Lintner, Bertil
Linzey, Andrew
Lipin, Lawrence M.
Lipman-Blumen, Jean
Lively, Adam
Livingston, Gordon (S.)
Livingston, James
Lloyd, T(revor) O(wen)
Lo, Shiu-Hing
Loades, David Michael
Lobel, Jules
Locke, Hubert G.
Loevy, Robert D(ickinson)
Lomnitz, Larissa Adler
London, Herbert I.
Long, Cathryn J.
Longley, Kyle
Lopach, James J.
Lord, Carnes
Lottman, Herbert
Louden, Robert B.
Louër, Laurence
Loughlin, James
Lounsberry, Barbara
Lowe, Rodney
Lowenberg, Anton D(avid)
Lowndes, Joseph E.
Lowry, William R.
Lu, Ning
Lu, Suping
Lubbock, Jules
Lucaites, John Louis
Luciak, Ilja Alexander
Ludwikowski, Rett R.
Lukes, Steven M.
Lundestad, Geir
Luongo, F. Thomas
Luraghi, Raimondo
Luria, Keith P.
Lurie, Jonathan
Lusane, Clarence
Lust-Okar, Ellen
Luttwak, Edward (Nicolae)
Lynch, Allen C.
Lynn, John A(lbert)
Lynn, Jonathan
Lyon, David
Lyons, Thomas Tolman
Lytle, Mark H.
Mabbett, Ian William
MacArthur, John R.
MacClancy, Jeremy
MacCotter, Paul
Macdonald, Douglas J.
Mace, Gordon
Macedo, Stephen
MacEoin, Denis
Macfarlane, Leslie John
Mach, Thomas S.
MacIntosh, Robert
Macintyre, Stuart (Forbes)
Mack, Dana
Mack Smith, Denis
MacKay, Donald (Iain)

Mackenzie, G. Calvin
Mackey, Thomas
MacKinnon, Catharine A.
MacKinnon, Mark
Macleod, Alison
Maddison, Sarah
Maddox, Bronwen
Maddox, Robert James
Madigan, Patrick
Magaloni, Beatriz
Magee, Bryan
Maghraoui, Abdeslam M.
Magnet, Myron
Maharidge, Dale (Dimitro)
Maheshwari, Shriram
Mahler, Jonathan
Mahmood, Saba
Mahoney, Richard D.
Mainwaring, Scott
Mairowitz, David Zane
Maitra, Priyatosh
Mallick, Ross
Mallios, Seth
Malloch, Theodore Roosevelt
Maloka, Eddy Tshidiso
Maltby, William S(aunders)
Maltese, John Anthony
Maltz, Earl M.
Mandel, Ruth Ellen
Mandle, Jay R.
Mandler, Peter
Manent, Pierre
Manheim, Jarol B(ruce)
Mann, Barbara E.
Mann, Brian
Mann, Thomas E.
Manna, Paul
Manning, Robert D.
Mansfield, Edward D.
Marcou, David J.
Marcus, Alan I.
Marcuse, Gary
Mardon, Austin Albert
Margalit, Gilad
Margolies, Daniel S.
Mark, David
Marks, Lara Vivienne
Marks, Thomas A.
Marling, Karal Ann
Marquardt, Virginia C. Hagelstein
Marqusee, Mike
Marr, Andrew
Marr, David G(eorge)
Marrs, Jim
Mars, Perry
Marsh, Peter T.
Marsh, Susan H.
Marshall, Paul A.
Marshall, Peter (H.)
Marszalek, John F.
Martin, Fenton S(trickland)
Martin, Lisa L.
Marx, Anthony W.
Masalha, Nur
Mason, Matthew
Mason, Robert
Masters, Roger D.

Mastny, Vojtech
Matalin, Mary
Matheny, Albert R(alston)
Matlin, David
Matray, James I(rving)
Matsusaka, John G.
Matteo, Sherri
Matthews, Chris John
Matthews, Mark
Mattson, Kevin
Mauceri, Philip
Mawdsley, Evan
Maxwell, Nicholas
May, Lary L.
May, Todd Gifford
Mayer, Jane
Mayers, David (Allan)
Mayhew, David Raymond
Mazrui, Ali Al('Amin)
Mazurana, Dyan E.
Mbuende, Kaire (Munionganda)
McAll, Christopher
McArthur, Judith N.
McBeath, Gerald (Jerry) A.
McBride, Stephen
McCall, Storrs
McCallum, Taffy Gould
McCargo, Duncan
McCarthy, John F.
McCartney, Scott
McCauley, Martin
McClay, Wilfred M(ark)
McClure, Ellen M.
McClure, Sandy
McColgan, John Joseph
McCraw, Thomas K.
McDonald, Forrest
McDonough, Peter
McDowell, Gary L.
McElroy, John Harmon
McEwen, Indra Kagis
McGinniss, Joe
McGrane, Bernard
McGrath, Carmelita
McGrew, W. C.
McIntyre, Ian (James)
McKean, Robert B.
McKenzie, Evan
McKeon, Michael
McKinlay, Brian John
McKinnon, Ronald I(an)
McKnight, David
McKnight, Stephen A.
McLaren, John
McLaughlin, Corinne
McLean, Iain (S.)
McLennan, Rebecca M.
McMillan, James
McMillen, Neil Raymond
McMullan, Gordon
McNeal, Patricia
McNutt, Patrick A.
McRae, Kenneth Douglas
Means, Howard
Medearis, John
Medhurst, Martin J.
Medved, Diane

Medvedev, Zhores (Alexandrov-
   ich)
Mehrotra, Sri Ram
Mele, Christopher
Melich, Tanya
Melman, Yossi
Melusky, Joseph A.
Menard, Orville D.
Mencimer, Stephanie
Mendilow, Jonathan
Menon, Dilip M(adhav)
Menon, Rajan
Merrett, Christopher
Merridale, Catherine
Metcalf, Allan (Albert)
Metz, Allan (Sheldon)
Meyerson, Mark D.
Meyerson, Michael I.
Michalak, Stanley J.
Michelman, Kate
Mickenberg, Julia L.
Mickolus, Edward (Francis)
Middlemas, (Robert) Keith
Miles, William F. S.
Miller, Aaron David
Miller, Abraham (H.)
Miller, Charles A.
Miller, David (Leslie)
Miller, J(ohn) D(onald) Bruce
Miller, James Edward
Miller, Lynn H.
Miller, Matthew
Miller, Richard Lawrence
Miller, Seumas
Miller, William L.
Millett, Paul
Millman, Brock
Millward, Robert
Milne, Lorna
Milofsky, Carl
Minc, Alain J. R.
Minear, Richard Hoffman
Minogue, Kenneth Robert
Minow, Newton N(orman)
Mirikitani, Janice
Miroff, Bruce
Miscamble, Wilson D.
Mitchell, Don
Mitchell, Memory F.
Mittelstadt, Jennifer
Moallem, Minoo
Moen, Matthew C.
Moldea, Dan E.
Monahan, Patrick J.
Monière, Denis
Monoson, S. Sara
Montgomery, Maureen E.
Moody, Peter R(ichard)
Moon, Jeremy
Mooney, Brian C.
Moonman, Eric
Moore, David W.
Moore, John N(orton)
Moore, Lisa Jean
Moore, Philip N(icholas)
Morales, Edmundo
Morales, Waltraud Queiser

Moravec, Ivo
Moreno, Jonathan D.
Moreton, N. Edwina
Morgan, Austen
Morgan, Glyn
Morgan, Janet
Morgan, Kimberly J.
Morgan, Robin
Morrill, John S(tephen)
Morris, Jeffrey B(randon)
Morris, Jiwe
Morris, Roger
Morrissey, Will
Morrow, John
Mortimer, Edward
Morton, Timothy
Moser, Edward P.
Mosettig, Michael David
Motomura, Hiroshi
Motyl, Alexander J(ohn)
Moure, Kenneth
Moussalli, Ahmad S.
Mowle, Thomas S.
Moyo, Dambisa
Moyser, George H.
Mukherjee, Bharati
Mukherjee, Rabin
Mullen, Bill V.
Muller, Jan-Werner
Mulroney, Brian
Muravchik, Joshua
Murchison, William
Murphy, Dervla Mary
Murphy, James Bernard
Murphy, Patricia J.
Murphy, Peter
Murphy, Rae Allan
Murray, William J(ames)
Mutz, Diana C.
Myerson, Daniel
Mylroie, Laurie
Nacos, Brigitte L.
Nadelmann, Ethan A.
Nader, Ralph
Nahas, Gabriel G(eorges)
Nahaylo, Bohdan
Naiden, James
Naím, Moisés
Nairn, Tom (Cunningham)
Nakash, Yitzhak
Nakhnikian, George
Nardulli, Peter F.
Nash, Gary B.
Nathanson, Stephen (Lewis)
Nation, Richard F.
Nau, Henry R(ichard)
Navasky, Victor
Navrozov, Andrei
Neilson, James Warren
Neiwert, David A.
Nelson, Eric
Nelson, Keith L(eBahn)
Ness, Immanuel
Nester, William R.
Netanyahu, Benjamin
Nevo, Joseph
Newell, Waller R.

Newman, Katherine S.
Newman, Rick
Newman, Stephen L.
Newton, Kenneth
Ngugi wa Thiong
Nice, David C.
Nicholas, David M(ansfield)
Nicholls, C(hristine) S(tephanie)
Nichols, Deborah L.
Noam, Eli Michael
Nogee, Joseph L(ippman)
Nojumi, Neamatollah
Noland, Marcus
Nomani, Farhad
Noonan, Peggy
Norrander, Barbara
Norton, Augustus Richard
Norton, Bryan G(eorge)
Norton, Philip
Nossiter, Adam
Nugent, Neill
Nunn, Frederick McKinley
Nye, Joseph S(amuel)
O'Brien, David M(ichael)
O'Donnell, Guillermo A.
O'Donovan, Oliver
O'Kane, Rosemary H.T.
O'Leary, Kevin
O'Malley, Padraig
O'Neil, Robert M.
O'Neill, Robert John
O'Regan, Valerie R.
O'Rourke, P. J.
O'Toole, Fintan
Ochart (Torres), (Luz) Yvonne
Ochoa, Enrique C(orrado)
Ocker, Christopher (Michael)
Offer, Avner
Ohaegbulam, Festus Ugboaja
Olasky, Marvin
Oldfield, J(ohn) R(ichard)
Oldmixon, Elizabeth Anne
Olick, Jeffrey K.
Oliver, James (Anthony)
Oliver, Lawrence J.
Olowu, (Claudius) Dele
Olson, Laura R.
Olson, Susan M.
Olson, Walter K.
Onuf, Nicholas
Oosterhuis, Harry
Ophuls, William
Oppelt, Norman T.
Oppenheim, Felix E.
Oppenheim, Lois Hecht
Orizio, Riccardo
Orkeny, Antal
Oros, Andrew L.
Orr, D. Alan
Ortner, Robert
Orttung, Robert W.
Osborne, Milton (Edgeworth)
Osgood, Kenneth
Ostrow, Joel M.
Ostrow, Ronald J.
Ostrower, Gary B.
Ottaway, David B.

Ottaway, Marina (Seassaro)
Overmyer, James E.
Owen, David (Anthony
 Llewellyn)
Owens, John E.
Oxhorn, Philip D.
Ozyurek, Esra
Padgett, Stephen
Pae, Sung Moon
Pagán, Victoria Emma
Paglen, Trevor
Palazzolo, Daniel J.
Palda, Filip
Palmer, Michael Denison
Panitch, Leo (Victor)
Pape, Robert A.
Paper, Lewis Jay
Paris, Roland
Parke, Marilyn
Parkinson, Alan F.
Parmelee, John H.
Pascale, Richard Tanner
Patten, Alan
Patten, Chris
Patterson, Amy S.
Patterson, Bradley H.
Patterson, E. Britt
Pattillo, Mary E.
Paxton, John
Payne, Donald Gordon
Payne, J. Gregory
Payne, Leigh A.
Pearlstine, Norman
Pearson, Thomas S(pencer)
Pedahzur, Ami
Peden, W. Creighton
Pedersen, Vernon L.
Pederson, William D(avid)
Peel, Ellen S.
Peetz, David
Pegram, Thomas R.
Peirce, Neal R.
Peleg, Ilan
Peña, Charles V.
Pencak, William
Penslar, Derek J(onathan)
Perez, Sofia A(na)
Perin, Roberto
Perloff, Richard M.
Peters, Michael (Adrian)
Petersen, Tore T.
Peterson, V. Spike
Peterson, Wallace C(arroll)
Petro, Nicolai N.
Petsalis-Diomidis, Nicholas
Pettifer, James
Pfaff, William (Wendel)
Phares, Walid
Phelan, Shane
Philip, George
Phillips, Christopher
Phillips, Derek L.
Pierard, Richard V(ictor)
Pierson, Christopher
Pierson, Paul
Pilger, John Richard
Pinto, António Costa

Piott, Steven L.
Pipes, Richard
Pitt, David Charles
Pitts, Vincent J.
Plach, Eva
Plant, Deborah G.
Plokhy, Serhii
Plutzer, Eric
Podhoretz, John
Pogge, Thomas
Pogrebin, Letty Cottin
Pohlmann, Marcus D.
Polakoff, Keith (Ian)
Polakow-Suransky, Sasha
Pollard, Lisa
Polsgrove, Carol
Polsky, Andrew J.
Poole, Elizabeth
Popkin, Samuel L(ewis)
Porter, Barbara Nevling
Porter, Bernard (John)
Porter, Roger B.
Posen, Barry R.
Posner, Daniel N.
Powell, Alan
Powell, H. Jefferson
Powell, Kevin
Powell, Martyn J.
Powers, Martin J.
Prag, John
Pratt, David
Prazniak, Roxann
Prechel, Harland
Prescott, J(ohn) R(obert) V(ictor)
Press, O(tto) Charles
Presser, Stephen B.
Pressman, Jeremy
Prestwich, Michael (Charles)
Prewitt, Kenneth
Price, Robert M.
Prindle, David F.
Pritchard, R(obert) John
Prochaska, Frank
Prothero, Stephen (Richard)
Prunier, Gerard
Puiggrós, Adriana (Victoria)
Pulzer, Peter George Julius
Pyle, Kenneth B.
Quandt, William Bauer
Quayle, (James) Dan(forth)
Queenan, Joe
Quigley, David
Quigley, Kevin F. F.
Quirk, William J.
Quiroga, Alejandro
Quiroz, Anthony
Qvortrup, Mads
Raab, David
Raadschelders, Jos C. N.
Rabinbach, Anson (Gilbert)
Rabkin, Jeremy A.
Raboy, Marc
Rainey, Gene Edward
Ramphal, Shridath (Surendranath)
Randall, Margaret
Randell, Nigel
Randolph, Lewis A.

Ransom, Harry Howe
Ranstorp, Magnus
Raphael, David Daiches
Rapp, George (Robert)
Rapp, Rayna
Rarick, Ethan
Rasanayagam, Angelo
Ratcliffe, Eric Hallam
Rathbone, Cristina
Rathbone, Richard
Rathbun, Brian C.
Rauch, Jonathan (Charles)
Rauch, William
Rayside, David
Read, Anthony
Reddaway, Peter (Brian)
Reddy, Maureen T.
Redfield, Marc
Redford, Kent H(ubbard)
Redwood, John (Alan)
Reed, Bruce
Reed, Ralph Eugene
Reeher, Grant
Rees-Mogg
Regan, Milton C.
Regenstreif, S(amuel) Peter
Reich, Robert B.
Reid, Harry M.
Reid, John P(hillip)
Reiss, Edward
Reiss, Tom
Rejai, Mostafa
Rejali, Darius M.
Relyea, Harold C.
Remer, Gary
Rennie, Bradford James
Renshon, Jonathan
Reséndez, Andrés
Resis, Albert
Reuber, Grant L.
Rév, István
Reynolds, Barrie (Gordon Robert)
Reynolds, David
Rhodes, R. A. W.
Rice, Prudence M.
Richards, David A. J.
Richardson, Richard Judson
Ridley, Matt(hew White)
Riesenberg, Peter N.
Riggs, Robert E(dwon)
Riley, Carroll L.
Rimstead, Roxanne L.
Ring, Jennifer
Ringquist, Evan J.
Ripley, Randall
Ritchie, Pamela E.
Rivlin, Gary
Robb, David L.
Robb, Peter
Roberts, (Edward) Adam
Roberts, Adam
Roberts, Alasdair Scott
Roberts, Elizabeth
Roberts, J(ames) Deotis
Robin, Corey
Robins, Robert S.
Robinson, Marguerite S(tern)

Robson, Brian Turnbull
Rodger, N. A. M.
Rodgers, Peter
Rodney, William
Rodriguez, Clara E.
Rohde, David S.
Rohrbough, Malcolm Justin
Rollin, Roger B.
Roman, Peter
Romano, Louis
Roop, Peter
Roosevelt, Selwa
Root, Hilton L.
Roschelle, Anne R.
Rose, Melody
Rose, Michael
Rose, Paul (Bernard)
Rose, Richard
Rosell, Steven A.
Rosenau, Pauline Vaillancourt
Rosenberg, Joel C.
Rosenblum, Nancy L.
Rosenkranz, E. Joshua
Rosenson, Beth A.
Rosenstiel, Tom
Rosenthal, Donald B.
Roshwald, Mordecai
Rossum, Ralph A.
Rothkopf, David J.
Rothstein, Robert L.
Rothwell, Victor Howard
Roubini, Nouriel
Rowbotham, Sheila
Roy, Arundhati
Roy, Donald H.
Royal, Robert
Rozell, Mark J.
Rozenberg, Joshua
Rubenstein, Richard Lowell
Rubin, Barry
Rubin, Hyman
Rubinoff, M. Lionel
Ruchelman, Leonard I.
Rudolph, Christopher
Rueschemeyer, Dietrich
Rusi, Alpo M.
Russell, Dick
Russett, Bruce Martin
Russo, Elena
Ryle, Michael
Sader, Emir
Safir, Howard
Salaita, Steven
Salam, Reihan
Salitan, Laurie P.
Salomon, Frank
Samples, John Curtis
Sampson, Geoffrey (Richard)
Samuels, Cynthia K(alish)
Samuels, David
Samuels, Richard J.
Samuels, Warren J(oseph)
Sanders, Alan J. K.
Sanders, Andrew
Sanders, Arthur
Sandoz, (George) Ellis
Sankar, Andrea (Patrice)

Sargent, Lyman Tower
Sartori, Anne E.
Sassoon, Donald
Sathasivam, Kanishkan
Saunt, Claudio
Savage, Charlie
Savage, Sean J.
Sawatsky, John
Sawyer, (Frederick) Don(ald)
Sawyer, Roger
Sawyer, Suzana
Scalapino, Robert Anthony
Scales-Trent, Judy
Scalmer, Sean
Scates, Shelby
Schabas, Margaret
Schaefer, David Lewis
Schaerf, Carlo
Schaffer, Frederic Charles
Schain, Martin A.
Scheck, Raffael
Schecter, Darrow
Scheiber, Harry N.
Schenken, Suzanne O'Dea
Schiavone, Giuseppe
Schier, Steven E.
Schilling, Mark R.
Schmeiser, Douglas A.
Schmidt, Samuel
Schmidt, Vivien A.
Schmidt, Winsor C.
Schneider, Ben Ross
Schneider, Thomas E.
Schneiderman, David
Schor, Mira
Schultz, (Reynolds) Bart(on)
Schulz, William F(rederick)
Schumaker, Paul
Schwartz, Joyce R.
Schwartz, Richard A(lan)
Schwartz, Stephen (Alfred)
Schwarz, Adam
Schwarz, Frederick A. O.
Schwarz, Henry G.
Schwarz, John E.
Schwedler, Jillian
Schweller, Randall
Scotchie, Joseph
Scott, Joan Wallach
Scott, Jonathan
Scott, P(aul) H(enderson)
Scruton, Roger
Searing, Donald D.
Searle, G(eoffrey) R(ussell)
Sears, David O('Keefe)
Segal, Howard P.
Segal, Jeffrey A.
Segal, Lynne
Sehene, Benjamin
Seib, Gerald
Seidman, Michael
Selbourne, David
Seward, Robert (Allen)
Shabecoff, Philip
Shafer, Byron E.
Shafer, D. Michael
Shain, Milton

Shain, Yossi
Shakeri, Khosrow
Shambaugh, David L.
Shane, Scott
Shanley, Mary L(yndon)
Shannon, Timothy J.
Shapiro, H. Svi
Shapiro, Ian
Shapiro, Judith
Shapiro, Robert Y.
Sharkansky, Ira
Sharlet, Jeff
Sharma, Nandita
Sharman, Russell Leigh
Shaw, Daron R.
Shawhan, Dorothy Sample
Sheard, Sarah
Sheerman, Barry
Shefter, Martin
Shelby, Tommie
Sheldon, Garrett Ward
Shell, Susan Meld
Shemesh, Haim
Shepard, Geoff Carroll
Shepherd, George W.
Shepherd, Robert
Sheridan, Thomas
Sherman, Arnold
Sherman, Joe
Shermer, Michael
Sherrill, Kenneth S.
Shesol, Jeff
Shiach, Morag
Shields, John M(ackie)
Shipp, Steve
Shipper, Apichai W.
Shirk, David A.
Shlaim, Avi
Shneidman, N(oah) N(orman)
Shneour, Elie Alexis
Shogan, Colleen J.
Shogan, Robert
Shohat, Ella Habiba
Shorrock, Tim
Short, Philip
Shoup, Donald
Shrader, Charles R.
Shughart, William F.
Shull, Steven A.
Shuman, Samuel I.
Sicker, Martin
Sidahmed, Abdel Salam
Siddiqa, Ayesha
Sidlow, Edward I.
Siegel, Jennifer
Siegel, Mona L.
Siegelbaum, Lewis H.
Silva, Noenoe
Silverburg, Sanford R.
Silverstein, Ken
Silverstone, Scott A.
Simien, Evelyn M.
Simon, Diane
Simon, Roger (Mitchell)
Simon, Scott
Simon, Sheldon Weiss
Simontacchi, Carol

Warber, Adam L.
Ward, (William) Peter
Ward, Alan J.
Ward, Lee
Ware, Alan
Warnicke, Retha M.
Warren, Richard (Andrew)
Warshauer, Matthew
Wasby, Stephen L(ewis)
Wass, Douglas (William Gretton)
Wasserstein, Bernard (Mano Julius)
Waterston, Alisse
Watson, Steven
Wattenberg, Martin P(aul)
Watts, Anthony John
Waziyatawin
Weaver, R(obert) Kent
Webber, Mark (Alan)
Weber, Ralph E.
Weber, Timothy P.
Weckmann, Luis
Weeks, Jeffrey
Weidenbaum, Murray
Weimann, Gabriel
Weinbaum, Marvin G.
Weinberger, Peter Ezra
Weiner, Mark S(tuart)
Weiner, Stephanie Kuduk
Weinrich, A. K. H.
Weinroth, Michelle
Weinstein, Allen
Weir, Gary E.
Weisberg, Herbert F.
Weisbrot, Robert (S.)
Weiss, Thomas G.
Weisskopf, Thomas E.
Werbner, Pnina
Werckmeister, O(tto) K(arl)
Weschler, Lawrence
West, Darrell M.
West, Harry G.
West, Michael Rudolph
Western, Jon W.
Wettenhall, Roger L.
Wettig, Gerhard
Wexler, Richard
Whalen, Richard James
Whalen, Thomas J.
Whelan, Yvonne
Whelpton, John Francis
Whigham, Thomas
White, John Kenneth
White, Stephen (Leonard)
White, Stephen K.
Whitehorn, Alan (James)
Whitlam, (Edward) Gough
Whitman, T(orrey) Stephen
Whittington, Keith E.
Wicker, Tom
Wickham, David
Widner, Jennifer A(nne)
Wiener, Antje
Wilcox, (William) Clyde
Wilcox, Laird (M.)
Wilkinson, Marian
Will, George F.

Williams, Alan Lee
Williams, Gregory Howard
Williams, Kristen P.
Williams, Walter E(dward)
Willrich, Mason
Wills, Alfred J(ohn)
Wilsford, David
Wilson, Andrew
Wilson, Barry K.
Wilson, Bronwen
Wilson, Jan Doolittle
Wilson, John K.
Wilson, Joseph (Charles)
Wilson, Trevor Gordon
Winckler, Edwin A.
Winegarten, Renee
Winock, Michel
Winter, Kari J.
Wintz, Cary D.
Wirsing, Robert G.
Wise, David
Wise, Tim J.
Wittes, Benjamin
Wittner, Lawrence Stephen
Wolfe, Alan (Stephen)
Wolff, Robert P(aul)
Wolfinger, Raymond E(dwin)
Woll, Peter
Wollen, Peter
Wolpert, Stanley Albert
Wood, Gordon S(tewart)
Woodard, J. David
Woods, Lawrence T(imothy)
Woodward, Bob
Wooldridge, Adrian
Woolf, Stuart Joseph
Woolley, Peter J.
Wootton, David
Worcester, Kent
Worcester, Robert
Worrell, (Rupert) DeLisle
Worsham, Lynn
Wrenn, Lynette Boney
Wreszin, Michael
Wright, Theodore Paul
Wright Austin, Sharon D.
Wunsch, James S(tevenson)
Wynia, Gary W.
Yaghmaian, Behzad
Yapp, Malcolm E(dward)
Yarnold, Barbara M(aria)
Yates, Nigel
Yellin, Emily
Yen, Ching-hwang
Yiftachel, Oren
Yoder, John C.
Yoo, John C.
York, Phyllis
Young, Donald R.
Young, Jeff C.
Young, John
Young, Ken
Young, Robert A.
Young, Robert J.C
Yudelman, David
Yurchak, Alexei
Zagorski, Paul W.

Zahariadis, Nikolaos
Zakaria, Fareed
Zakaria, Haji Ahmad
Zaki, Hoda M.
Zaretsky, Robert David
Zatlin, Jonathan R.
Zawodny, J(anusz) K.
Zeldin, Theodore
Zelizer, Julian E.
Zentner, Peter
Zhao, Yuezhi
Zimbalist, Andrew S.
Zimmerman, Joseph Francis
Zimmerman, Shirley Lee
Zolo, Danilo
Zubok, Vladislav
Zucker, Naomi F(link)
Zucker, Norman Livingston
Zuckerman, Michael
Zuckert, Catherine H.
Zulawski, Ann
Zürcher, Erik-Jan
Zutshi, Chitralekha
Zweifel, Thomas D.

Popular Culture

Aberjhani
Allen, Dick
Altheide, David L.
Asim, Jabari
Averill, Gage
Ayres, E. C.
Balbo, Ned Clark
Barreto, Mascarenhas
Barron, T. A.
Barton, Greg
Baxter, Paula A.
Bordowitz, Hank
Broussard, Meredith
Brugger, E. Christian
Burnett, Ron
Buskin, Richard
Butsch, Richard (J.)
Cohen, Daniel A.
Cohen, Debra Nussbaum
Conklin, John E.
Coombes, Annie E.
Cottrell, Robert C.
Cox, Alex
Crossley, James G.
Curatola, Giovanni
Dassanowsky, Robert
De Stefano, George
DeMello, Margo
Duggleby, John
Emerson, Ken
Entine, Jon
Epstein, Lawrence J(effrey)
Fahy, Thomas
Ferrell, Jeff
Ferris, Marcie Cohen
Fineman, Martha Albertson
Fishkin, Shelley Fisher
Fleurant, Gerdès
Fontes, Ron

Fraser, Sarah E.
Freidberg, Susanne
Frey, Julia (Bloch)
Gallagher, Kathleen
Gallo, Gina
Gamson, Joshua (Paul)
Gibson, Chris
Gibson, Thomas
Gillmeister, Heiner
Gillon, Steven M.
Gish, Robert F.
Gordon, W. Terrence
Grange, William Marshall
Greenberg, Gerald S(tuart)
Greetham, David
Gurvis, Sandra J.
Hamilton, Carl
Hernandez, Jo Farb
Herrick, James A.
Hollis, Tim
Hsiung, Ping-Chen
Hung, Chang-tai
Inge, M. Thomas
Jacobs, Andrew S.
James, Russell
Jancovich, Mark
Jarvis, William E.
Jones, Gerard
Jordan, Richard Tyler
Kaartinen, Marjo
Kaler, Anne K(atherine)
Karlen, Neal (Stuart)
Katz, Paul R.
Kellner, Bruce
Kimura, Margaret
Kitts, Thomas M(ichael)
Klerkx, Greg
Koestenbaum, Wayne
Kruger, Arnd
Kuntz, Jerry
Landy, Marcia
Libov, Charlotte Ann
Maclean, Rory
Maffi, Mario
Mann, Barbara E.
Marcus, Jana
Marqusee, Mike
Martin, Andy
Martinez, D. P.
Mayo, Wendell
Mayor, Adrienne
McCarthy, Nan
McDannell, Colleen
McMullan, Margaret
Meer, Sarah
Metz, Allan (Sheldon)
Mnookin, Seth
Mohr, Richard D(rake)
Monaghan, David (Mark)
Morey, Melanie M.
Moynihan, Michael
Munby, Jonathan
Natoli, Joseph
NightMare, M. Macha
Nissenson, Marilyn
Olson, Ted
Ortenberg, Veronica

Bennett-Goleman, Tara
Benson, Ophelia
Berger, Bruce
Bergquist, William Hastings
Berman, Claire
Berman, David
Berman, Morris
Berry, Carmen Renee
Berry, Carole
Berry, J. W.
Besner, Hilda F.
Bethelard, Faith
Biddle, Bruce Jesse
Bien, Thomas (H.)
Bigelow, Brian J(ohn)
Biggs, John Burville
Bilby, Joanne Stroud
Bjork, Daniel W.
Bjorklund, David F.
Blackmore, Susan (Jane)
Blakemore, Colin (Brian)
Blakeslee, Matthew
Blakeslee, Sandra
Blass, Thomas
Bloch, Douglas
Block, Joyce
Boden, Margaret A(nn)
Bok, Sissela
Bolles, Edmund Blair
Bonder, Nilton
Booker, Christopher
Borch-Jacobsen, Mikkel
Boteach, Shmuley
Bouvard, Marguerite Guzman
Boyd, Brian (David)
Boyll, (James) Randall
Brach, Tara
Braine, David
Brand, Alice Glarden
Branden, Nathaniel
Brannigan, Gary G(eorge)
Braverman, Terry
Breakwell, Glynis M(arie)
Brener, Milton E(rnest)
Breznitz, Shlomo
Broks, Paul
Bronson, Po
Brooks, Andrée (Nicole) Aelion
Brooks-Gunn, Jeanne
Brothers, Joyce (Diane)
Brown, Lyn Mikel
Brown, Richard E(arl)
Bruce, Robert S.
Brugger, E. Christian
Bruno, Richard L(ouis)
Brussat, Frederic
Brussat, Mary Ann
Buccieri, Lisa Rojany
Buckley, Francis Joseph
Bulkeley, Kelly
Buller, David J.
Burak, Carl S.
Burkitt, Ian
Burlew, A(nn) Kathleen
Burnham, Terence (Charles)
Burns, Ailsa (Milligan)
Burns, Richard Gordon

Burston, Daniel
Buser, Pierre
Bushong, Carolyn Nordin
Buss, David M.
Byalick, Marcia
Byrne, Donn
Cacioppo, John T.
Calder, Nigel (David Ritchie)
Calne, Donald B.
Calvin, William H(oward)
Campbell, Beatrix
Campion, Nicholas
Canada, Geoffrey
Candland, Douglas Keith
Capacchione, Lucia
Capshew, James H.
Carlin, Vivian F.
Carling, Paul J.
Carlson, Richard A.
Carroll, Michael P.
Carter, Rosalynn (Smith)
Carter, Steven
Cass, Dennis
Cathcart, Jim
Cavell, Marcia
Chamberlain, Lesley
Chapman, J. Dudley
Charny, Israel Wolf
Chia, Mantak
Chodorow, Nancy Julia
Chow, Claire S.
Christensen, Kathleen E(lizabeth)
Christianson, Sven-Åke
Clark, Andy
Claude-Pierre, Peggy
Clayton, Lawrence (Otto)
Coan, Richard W.
Cochrane, Peggy
Cohen, Henry
Colalillo-Kates, Isabella
Cole, Sheila R.
Coleman, Loren (Elwood)
Coles, Robert
Collier, Gary
Collinge, William (B.)
Coloroso, Barbara
Colt, George Howe
Condrell, Kenneth N.
Conigliaro, Vincenzo
Conley, Carolyn A.
Conrad, Peter
Cook, Mark
Cooper, Ilene
Copeland, Anne P.
Coren, Stanley
Cornyetz, Nina
Corrington, Robert S.
Cottle, Thomas J.
Cournos, Francine
Crabtree, Adam
Cramer, Stanley H.
Crawford, Mary
Crawford, Tad
Crews, Frederick C(ampbell)
Cromwell, Rue L(eVelle)
Crowther, Harold Francis
Dale, Peter

Damasio, Antonio R.
Damon, William
Daniels, Anthony
Danto, Elizabeth Ann
Dantzer, Robert
Dart, Iris Rainer
Dasgupta, Shamita Das
Dasgupta, Subrata
David, James F.
Davidson, Larry
Davies, Martin (Brett)
Davies, Peter J.
Davis, Hank
Davis, Mark H.
Day, Laura (Globus)
de Bono, Edward (Francis Charles)
de Marneffe, Daphne
Deans, Sis Boulos
DeBuron, Nicole
DeCrow, Karen
Delahunt, Meaghan
Delaney, Gayle (M. V.)
Demarais, Ann
Devor, Aaron H.
Diamond, Jed
DiFonzo, Nicholas
Dillon, Kathleen M. (Hynek)
DiSalvo, Jackie
Dobson, James C.
Doidge, Norman
Dolis, John
Dolnick, Barrie
Dominian, Jack
Donald, Merlin (Wilfred)
Dorf, Fran
Dorman, Daniel
Dossey, Larry
Douglas, Mark
Draper, Maureen McCarthy
Dreher, Henry
Drewes, Athena A.
Dryfoos, Joy G.
Dugan, Ellen
Duncan, Glen
Duncan, Karen A.
Dutton, Donald G.
Dyer, Wayne W(alter)
Eaton, Trevor (Michael William)
Edgette, Janet
Edwards, Allen Jack
El-Hai, Jack
Elium, Jeanne (Ann)
Elizur, Joel
Elkins, Dov Peretz
Ellis, Keith
Emmons, Robert A.
Engel, Beverly
Estes, Clarissa Pinkola
Estes, William (Kaye)
Evans, Richard I(sadore)
Eyer, Diane E(lizabeth)
Eysenck, Michael (William)
Fagan, Thomas K(evin)
Falk, Avner
Falzeder, Ernst
Faron, Fay

Farrell, Warren (Thomas)
Farrington, David P.
Faulkner, Howard J.
Feeney, Don J(oseph)
Feinstein, David
Feldman, Gayle
Felstein, Ivor
Ferder, Fran
Ferrara, Nadia
Ferriter, Diarmaid
Feuerstein, Georg
Fiedler, Fred E(dward)
Fields, Jennie
Finch, Caleb E(llicott)
Finkelstein, Adrian
Fischer, Lucy Rose
Fischer, Lynn
Fishman, Katharine Davis
Fitzpatrick, Mary Anne
Flem, Lydia
Flescher, Irwin
Flood, (Nancy) Bo
Flynn, James Robert
Fonagy, Peter
Forrester, John
Forrester, Michael A.
Fortes (De Leff), Jacqueline
Fowers, Blaine J.
Freed, Anne O.
Freedman, Michael R.
Freud, Sophie
Freyd, Jennifer J.(Joy)
Friedman, Norman
Friedman, Stewart D.
Fry, Virginia Lynn
Gabriel, Richard A(lan)
Gackenbach, Jayne
Gallagher, Shaun
Gallagher, Winifred
Galvin, Matthew R(eppert)
Garrison, Daniel H.
Gates, Barbara T(imm)
Gauld, Alan (Ogilvie)
Gault, Peter
Gaylin, Willard
Geary, David C(yril)
Gediman, Helen K.
Gelek, Ngawang
Geltmaker, Ty
Gerrig, Richard J.
Gerzon, Robert
Giampieri-Deutsch, Patrizia
Gillett, Grant (Randall)
Gilligan, Carol
Gilmore, David D.
Gindorf (Prof. Dr.), Rolf
Gladwell, Malcolm
Glaister, Lesley (G.)
Glantz, Kalman
Glazer, Ellen Sarasohn
Gliserman, Martin
Goldberg, Bruce (Edward)
Goldberg, Jane G.
Goldhagen, Shari
Goldstein, Niles Elliot
Golomb, Jacob
Gonen, Jay Y.

Murphy, Shane M.
Muuss, Rolf Eduard
Näaslund, Göorel Kristina
Nadelmann, Ethan A.
Nahas, Gabriel G(eorges)
Napier, Nancy J.
Nash, Michael R.
Nell, Victor
Nemec, James
Nerin, William F.
Nesse, Randolph M.
Neu, Jerome
Neugeboren, Jay
Newman, Susan
Nichter, Mark (Andrew)
Niemela, Pirkko
Noble, Kathleen
Nolen-Hoeksema, Susan
Noll, Richard
Norretranders, Tor
Norris, Kathleen
Nussbaum, Paul David
Nute, Kevin
O'connell, David F.
O'Connor, Francis V(alentine)
O'Connor, Richard
Oakley, Barbara A.
Oberlin, Loriann Hoff
Odets, Walt (Whitman)
Ohye, Bonnie
Okimoto, Jean Davies
Olkin, Rhoda
Olson, David Richard
Olson, Gretchen
Orenstein, Peggy
Ortner, Sherry B(eth)
Osborn, Ian
Padanilam, George J.
Paddison, Sara
Padel, Ruth
Paludi, Michele A.
Parfitt, Will
Paris, Bernard Jay
Parkinson, Stanley
Parrott, Les
Parrott, Leslie L.
Pascale, Richard Tanner
Patzer, Gordon
Pavey, Don
Pearson, Joanne (E.)
Pease, Allan
Penycate, John (Vincent George)
Perfetti, Charles A.
Peterson, Jean Sunde
Phillips, John Lawrence
Phongpaichit, Pasuk
Piirto, Jane
Pines, Ayala Malach
Pinker, Susan
Pipher, Mary (Bray)
Plaut, Eric A.
Poortinga, Y(pe) H.
Powers, William T.
Powles, William E(arnest)
Provine, Robert R(aymond)
Prozan, Charlotte (Krause)
Pruett, Kyle D(ean)

Quartz, Steven R.
Rachman, Stanley Jack
Radin, Dean I.
Rammohan, V.
Ramsland, Katherine
Randall, John L(eslie)
Randall, William Lowell
Raphael, Lev
Rapp, Steven A.
Raso, Jack
Ratey, John J(oseph)
Raz, Aviad E.
Real, Terrence
Regan, Pamela C.
Reuss, Frederick
Reynolds, Bill
Rhodes, Jean E.
Richard-Allerdyce, Diane
Rickels, Laurence A.
Riggs, Webster
Riley, Jess
Riter, Tim
Robb, Christina
Roberts, Yvonne
Robins, Robert S.
Robinson, Andrew
Robison, John Elder
Rodin, Robert L.
Rödl, Sebastian
Rogers, Annie G.
Rogers, Colin D(arlington)
Rogler, Lloyd Henry
Rohner, Ronald P.
Roiphe, Anne Richardson
Root-Bernstein, Michèle
Rosen, Leora N(adine)
Rosen, Robert H.
Rosenfield, Israel
Roudinesco, Elisabeth
Rubenstein, Richard Lowell
Rubin-Dorsky, Jeffrey
Rubinstein, Hilary (Harold)
Runco, Mark A.
Ruskan, John
Russell, Ronald
Rutan, J. Scott
Rutter, Michael (Llewellyn)
Rutter, Virginia Beane
Rychlak, Joseph F(rank)
Ryle, Anthony
Sachs, Judith
Sacks, Oliver (Wolf)
Salant, James
Salmon, Jacqueline L.
Sampson, Edward E.
Sapinsley, Barbara
Sarnoff, Irving
Sarvas, Mark
Satter, Ellyn
Sayers, Janet
Scarf, Maggie
Scarry, Elaine (Margaret)
Schacter, Daniel L.
Schaef, Anne Wilson
Schapiro, Barbara
Scharrer, Erica
Schlessinger, Laura

Schmidt, Karl H.
Schmidt, Winsor C.
Schoenewolf, Gerald
Schreibman, Laura
Schueler, G(eorge) F(rederick)
Schwartz, David B.
Schwartz, Gary E.
Scott, Donald Fletcher
Scott, Jill
Sears, David O('Keefe)
Secunda, Victoria (H.)
Seed, David
Segal, Julia (Clare)
Segal, Lynne
Seligman, Martin E. P.
Seltzer, Leon F(rancis)
Semans, Anne
Sensibar, Judith L(evin)
Serrano, Lucienne J.
Sexton, Linda Gray
Shamas, Victor A.
Shanahan, Daniel (A.)
Shapiro, Bonnie L.
Shapiro, Dan(iel)
Shapiro, Jerrold Lee
Shaver, Phillip (Robert)
Shawver, Lois
Shay, Jonathan
Sheehy, Gail
Shem, Samuel
Shengold, Leonard
Sher, Barbara
Sherman, Robert
Shermer, Michael
Shih, Chih-yu
Shlechter, Theodore M.
Shneour, Elie Alexis
Shontz, Franklin C(urtis)
Shore, Zachary
Shreve, Anita
Shrout, Richard Neil
Shute, Jenefer
Sidky, H.
Siegel, Bernard S(hepard)
Sills, Judith
Simmie, Lois (Ann)
Simmons, Jane
Simon, Fritz B(ernhard)
Simons, Daniel J.
Simpson, Michael Andrew
Singer, Jerome L(eonard)
Slattery, Dennis Patrick
Sloan, Tod (Stratton)
Slouka, Mark
Slovenko, Ralph
Smelser, Neil Joseph
Smith, Angela Thompson
Smith, David Livingstone
Smith, Douglas K.
Smith, Noel W.
Smith, Timothy B.
Soffer, Joshua
Sokol, B. J.
Sokol, Julia
Solomon, Andrew
Solter, Aletha
Spatz, Kenneth Christopher

Spear-Swerling, Louise
Spector, Jack Jerome
Spector, Sheila A.
Spencer, William Browning
Spiegel, David
Spindler, George Dearborn
Spungin, Charlotte I(sabelle)
Staddon, John (E. R.)
Steinberg, Blema S.
Steinberg, Laurence
Steinberg, Warren
Steinberg, Wendy
Stephens, Thomas M.
Stern, Daniel N.
Stern, Judith M.
Stern, Paul C(linton)
Sternberg, Robert J(effrey)
Stevens, Suzanne H.
Stevenson, Robert G.
Stoppard, Miriam
Stout, Martha
Straus, Murray A.
Strom, Robert
Stromberg, Peter G.
Sturgis, Ingrid
Subotnik, Rena F.
Suinn, Richard M.
Sullivan, Sherry E.
Sundelson, David
Suzuki, Akihito
Swartz, Jon David
Swidler, Ann
Sylvan, Dianne
Szalavitz, Maia
Szanton, Andrew (Emlen)
Szasz, Thomas Stephen
Taffel, Ron Walter
Tager-Flusberg, Helen
Tart, Charles T.
Taylor, Allegra
Taylor, John (Gerald)
Tefertiller, Casey (Orie)
Temple, Robert (Kyle Grenville)
Tenbrook, Gretchen W.
Terr, Lenore (C.)
Teyber, Edward C.
Thagard, Paul
Thaler, Richard H.
Theodore, Wayne
Theorell, (Per Gunnar) Toeres
Thomas, Barbara L(ee)
Thompson, Charles P.
Thompson, Janet A(nn)
Thompson, Tracy
Thondup, Tulku
Thone, Ruth Raymond
Timms, Edward
Ting, Windsor
Travers, Phil
Trehub, Arnold
Trice, Dawn Turner
Trimpey, John P.
Tripodi, Tony
Tuckman, Bruce Wayne
Turner, Ralph (Herbert)
Ugwuegbu, Denis Chima E.
Ullman, Ellen

Psychology-*cont.*

Ussher, Jane M.
Valenstein, Elliot S(piro)
Valentis, Mary (Arensberg)
Valle, Teresa Del
Van Beusekom, Janneke
Van Eenwyk, John R.
van Geert, Paul
Van Ginneken, Jaap
Vanderbilt, Tom
Vanzant, Iyanla
Vauclair, Jacques
Vaughan, Richard Patrick
Vaughan, Susan C.
Vazquez, Carmen Inoa
Victor, George
Vincent, Erin
Viney, Ethna
Viorst, Judith
Von Ward, Paul
Vos Savant, Marilyn
Vroom, Victor H.
Waehler, Charles A.
Wagman, Morton
Wagner, Daniel
Wakefield, Dan
Waldman, Mark Robert
Walker, Nigel (David)
Walker, Stephen
Walkerdine, Valerie
Walton, Henry John
Watkins, John Goodrich
Watson, Donald
Watson, Irene
Watson, Mary Ann
Watters, Ethan
Weber, Robert J(ohn)
Webster, Brenda
Weenolsen, Patricia
Wegela, Karen Kissel
Weingartner, Herbert J.
Weinrich, A. K. H.
Weiss, Brian L(eslie)
Weissbourd, Richard
Weitzman, Susan
Westen, Drew
Westheimer, (Karola) Ruth
Wettstein, Robert M.
White, Barbara Ehrlich
White, Kevin
White, Stephen E.
Wilcox, Sherman
Wilkins, Arnold
Wilkinson, Beth
Will, George F.
Williams, Donna
Williams, Lena (Marguerite)
Williams, Redford
Wilson, Colin (Henry)
Wilson, Melba (Jean)
Winder, Simon
Winsey, Valentine Rossilli
Winslade, John (Maxwell)
Wiseman, Richard
Wolin, Steven J.
Wolin, Sybil
Wood, Bridget
Woodman, Marion (Boa)

Psychology-*cont.*

Wooldridge, Adrian
Wright, Leslie B(ailey)
Wubbels, Lance
Wunderlich, Ray Charles
Wyer, Robert S.
Yalom, Irvin D(avid)
York, Phyllis
Young-Bruehl, Elisabeth
Young-Eisendrath, Polly
Youngs, Betty F.
Yuill, Nicola M.
Zaccaro, Stephen J.
Zarb, Janet M.
Zeidner, Moshe
Zimbardo, Philip G.
Zimmerman, Donald E(dward)
Zuckerman, Marvin
Zukav, Gary
Zweigenhaft, Richard L.

Public/Social Administration

Avant, Deborah D.
Bain, Kenneth (Ross)
Beasley, Vanessa B.
Behn, Robert Dietrich
Birkland, Thomas A.
Blau, Joel
Botsman, Daniel V.
Brzezinski, Zbigniew (Kasimierz)
Buck, Susan J.
Carling, Paul J.
Carr-Hill, Roy
Chang, Gordon G.
Chetkovich, Carol A.
Cockerill, A(rthur) W(illiam)
Coleman, Mary DeLorse
Colten, Craig E.
Cooper, Terry L.
Cormack, Robert J.
Culyer, A(nthony) J(ohn)
Cunningham, James V.
Cutler, David M.
Davidson, Roger H(arry)
Devney, Darcy C(ampion)
Downes, Bryan T(revor)
Elcock, Howard (James)
Feldman, Daniel L(ee)
Forder, Anthony
Gardner, James A.
Green, Daryl D.
Griffiths, Steve
Guarnieri, Carlo
Guy, Mary E.
Harrison, Trevor (W.)
Henry, Stuart (Dennis)
Huddleston, Mark W.
Hughes, Colin Anfield
Hult, Karen
Kaplowitz, Craig A.
Kash, Don E.
Kemp, Roger L.
Koehn, Peter H.
Lapping, Brian (Michael)
Lathrop, Douglas A.

Public/Social Administration-*cont.*

Lewis, (Norman) Douglas
Lowe, Rodney
Maheshwari, Shriram
Mesa-Lago, Carmelo
Moore, Cassandra Chrones
Murray, Charles (Alan)
Nice, David C.
O'Brien, David M(ichael)
O'Leary, Rosemary
Offer, Avner
Olowu, (Claudius) Dele
Peck, Merton Joseph
Peters, Michael (Adrian)
Press, O(tto) Charles
Raadschelders, Jos C. N.
Rappaport, Ann
Rhodes, R. A. W.
Ripley, Randall
Robbins, Hollis
Ruchelman, Leonard I.
Schmandt, Jurgen
Schmidt, Winsor C.
Schwartz, David B.
Secretan, Lance H. K.
Shivers, Jay Sanford
Shoup, Donald
Spruyt, Hendrik
Stanton, Richard C.
Stark, Evan
Steel, D(avid) R(obert)
Steiner, George A.
Stern, Vivien
Steuerle, C. Eugene
Streeten, Paul Patrick
Thomas, John Clayton
Tolchin, Susan J(ane)
Tosics, Ivan
Venardos, Thomas J(oseph)
Wang, XiaoHu
Wettenhall, Roger L.
Willrich, Mason
Wunsch, James S(tevenson)
Yarnold, Barbara M(aria)
Zimmerman, Joseph Francis
Zimmerman, Shirley Lee

Race Relations

Aberjhani
Adler, Jeffrey S(cott)
Aldridge, Delores P(atricia)
Alexander, Adele Logan
Anderson, Henry L(ee Norman)
Andrews, George Reid
Annerino, John
Aptheker, Bettina
Argers, Helen
Asim, Jabari
Audeh, Azmi S.
Bagdikian, Ben H(aig)
Bahal, Aniruddha
Baillie, Allan
Bain, Kenneth (Ross)
Banner-Haley, Charles T.

Race Relations-*cont.*

Baraka, Imamu Amiri
Barnes, Annie S.
Barr, Alwyn
Bean, Jonathan J.
Beary, Michael J.
Beidler, Peter G.
Benedict, Helen
Berry, Faith D.
Bethelard, Faith
Billingsley, Scott
Blauner, Bob
Blee, Kathleen M.
Blum, Edward J.
Bolton, Charles C.
Boskin, Joseph
Bowman, J. Wilson
Bowser, Benjamin P(aul)
Boyd, Malcolm
Boykin, Keith
Brand, Dionne
Brooks, Roy L(avon)
Brown, David
Browning, Christopher R(obert)
Bulbeck, Chilla
Burayidi, Michael A.
Carbo, Nick
Chetkovich, Carol A.
Cheyette, Bryan (Henry)
Cohen, Robin
Collins, Patricia Hill
Collum, Danny Duncan
Crais, Clifton C(harles)
Crean, Susan M.
Creighton, Margaret S.
Crouch, Stanley
Cunningham, James V.
Curthoys, Ann
Daniel, G. Reginald
Davies, Sharon L.
Davis, David Brion
De Villiers, Marq
DeCosta-Willis, Miriam
Diouf, Sylviane A.
Dorman, Michael L.
Dower, John W(illiam)
Dulaney, W. Marvin
Dummett, Michael (Anthony Eardley)
Dunbar, Leslie W(allace)
Eagles, Charles W.
Edwards, Brendan Frederick R.
Egbuna, Obi (Benedict)
Ehle, John
Ellis, Evelyn
Emerson, Michael O.
Eng, David L.
Eskew, Glenn T.
Essed, Philomena
Everett, Anna
Fayer, Steve
Feldman, Lynne B.
Finkenstaedt, Rose L. H.
Finnegan, William (Patrick)
Fishkin, Shelley Fisher
Fleurant, Gerdès
Foner, Eric
Forret, Jeff

Foster, Cecil (A.)
Frakes, George Edward
Frost, Diane
Fugard, Lisa
Fulton, Joe B.
Funderburg, Lise
Gallagher, Kathleen
Garrow, David J.
Gates, Henry Louis
Gerard, Charley
Gilens, Martin
Gilkes, Cheryl Townsend
Giovanni, Nikki
Glazer, Nathan
Goossen, Rachel Waltner
Gordon, Lewis Ricardo
Goulbourne, Harry
Gould, William B(enjamin)
Graves, Joseph Lewis
Green, Ricky K(enneth)
Greene, Melissa Fay
Gregory, Dick
Grinde, Donald A(ndrew)
Grundy, Pamela C.
Hall, Rodney
Hardy, B. Carmon
Hartigan, John
Hayter, Teresa
Hero, Rodney E.
Higginbotham, Elizabeth
Himka, John-Paul
Hiro, Dilip
Hodes, Martha
Hooks, Bell
Horne, R(alph) A(lbert)
Hornsby, Alton
Huang, Gregory T.
Huber, Richard Miller
Hutchinson, Earl Ofari
Hutchinson, George B.
Ignatiev, Noel
Ingham, John N.
Jackson, John P.
Jacobsen, David
Jacoby, Tamar
Jaffary, Nora E.
Jaffrelot, Christophe
Jahoda, Gustav
Jalata, Asafa
Johnson, Allan G.
Johnson, Whittington B.
Jones, Frank Lancaster
Jones, Jacqueline
Kahlenberg, Richard D.
Karp, Larry
Karttunen, Frances
Katagiri, Yasuhiro
Keating, AnaLouise
Kevane, Bridget
Khan, Aisha
Khan, Rukhsana
Kim, Thomas P.
Kitch, Sally L.
Koshiro, Yukiko
Krausz, Ernest
Krebs, Nina Boyd
Kujoory, Parvin

Kushnick, Louis
Lappé, Frances Moore
Lee, Josephine (D.)
Lentin, Ronit
Leonard, Richard James
Lewin, Rhoda G.
Lewis, Earl
Liazos, Ariane
Lin, Tan (Anthony)
Ling, Peter J(ohn)
Litwack, Leon
Lott, Eric
Loury, Glenn C(artman)
Lusane, Clarence
Lyons, Thomas Tolman
Mackerras, Colin Patrick
Madgett, Naomi Long
Madhubuti, Haki R.
Mandela, Nelson (Rolihlahla)
Mann, Paul (James)
Marks, Stan(ley)
Marqusee, Mike
Marszalek, John F.
Marx, Gary T.
Mason, Jim
Mathabane, Mark
Mattingley, Christobel (Rose-
    mary)
Mazrui, Ali Al('Amin)
McAll, Christopher
McDonald, J. I(an) H.
McFadden, Steven
Mcgreevy, John T.
McMullan, Margaret
McPherson, James Munro
Melady, Thomas (Patrick)
Melnick, Jeffrey Paul
Meyerson, Debra E.
Michaels, Walter Benn
Miele, Frank
Moore, Andrew S.
Moore, Brenda L(ee)
Moore, Carlos
Moreno, Paul D.
Mullen, Bill V.
Naidoo, Beverley
Neighbour, Mary E.
Nestel, Sheryl
Niman, Michael I.
Nolan, David (Joseph)
O'Reilly, Kenneth
O'Reilly Herrera, (C.) Andrea
Ochoa, Enrique C(orrado)
Olaleye, Isaac O.
Oliver, Kitty
Olson, Ted
Onyeama, Dillibe
Oren, Dan A.
Orme, Nicholas
Page, Clarence
Panayi, Panikos
Partow, Donna
Pattillo, Mary E.
Patton, Stacey
Pauley, Garth E.
Perry, Pamela
Phillips, Jonathan P.

Phillips, Mike
Pincus, Fred L.
Platt, Donald
Pohlmann, Marcus D.
Potter, Franz J.
Powledge, Fred
Radcliffe Richards, Janet
Rake, Alan
Reddy, Maureen T.
Rex, John Arderne
Richmond, Anthony Henry
Riddle, Paxton
Ring, Jennifer
Roberts, J(ames) Deotis
Rodriguez, Gregory
Roediger, David R(andall)
Rose, Peter I(saac)
Rose, Tricia
Roses, Lorraine Elena
Rubin, Hyman
Ruef, John Samuel
Sacre, Antonio
Salaita, Steven
Sanders, Peter (Basil)
Sankar, Andrea (Patrice)
Sawyer, Roger
Scales-Trent, Judy
Scarfe, Allan John
Scarfe, Wendy (Elizabeth)
Schipper de Leeuw, W. J. J.
Schreibman, Laura
Schusky, Ernest L.
Self, Robert O.
Shapiro, Herbert
Shaw, Alison
Shepherd, George W.
Sherman, Richard B.
Sherry, Patrick
Shipler, David K(arr)
Sikes, Melvin P.
Silverstein, Clara
Singh, Amritjit
Smedley, Audrey
Smith, David Livingstone
Smith, Judith E.
Smith, Patricia
Snay, Mitchell
Sorrenson, Maurice Peter Keith
Spencer, Jon Michael
Stanley, Susie Cunningham
Staples, Robert Eugene
Stark, Evan
Stern, Kenneth S.
Stewart, Kenneth
Strane, Susan
Talalay, Kathryn M(arguerite)
Tark, Ji-il
Tawil, Ezra
Taylor, Gary
Thobani, Sunera
Thomas, June Manning
Treat, James
Trigger, David S.
Tullos, Allen E.
Tuttle, William McCullough
Tutu, Desmond M(pilo)
Twine, France Winddance

Uekert, Brenda K.
Van Ausdale, Debra
Van Deburg, William L.
Vaughan, Alden T(rue)
Verniero, Joan C.
Vincent, John James
Viney, Donald Wayne
Vinikas, Vincent
Volpe, Vernon L(ewis)
Walker, Kenneth Roland
Walvin, James
Ward, Brian
Watkins, Steve
Watson, Ritchie Devon
Waziyatawin
Weinrich, A. K. H.
Weisbrot, Robert (S.)
Welsing, Frances Cress
West, Michael Rudolph
White, Peter (O. G.)
Whitten, Norman E.
Wilderson, Frank B.
Williams, Gregory Howard
Williams, Lena (Marguerite)
Williams, Lillian Serece
Williams, Patricia J(oyce)
Williams, Vernon J(ohnson)
Williams, Walter E(dward)
Williamson, Denise
Williamson, Joel
Winter, Kari J.
Wise, Tim J.
Wolf, Eva Sheppard
Wolfers, Michael
Woodard, Michael D.
Woodrum, Robert H.
Woods, Paula L.
Wright, (Mary) Patricia
Wright Austin, Sharon D.
Wylie, Diana
Wynes, Charles E.
Zinsser, Judith P.
Zweigenhaft, Richard L.

Recreation

Albrecht, Ernest (Jacob)
Allred, Alexandra Powe
Anderson, Lars
Arrington, Stephen L(ee)
Bale, Don
Block, Lawrence
Boyne, Daniel J.
Bradbury, J. C.
Brennan, Christine
Bruce Lockhart, Robin
Brundige, Donald G.
Brundige, Sharron L(ea)
Burk, Robert F(rederick)
Byrne, Robert
Churchill, E. Richard
Confer, Dennis W.
Cranfield, Ingrid
DeMott, Robert (James)
Dickson, Paul (Andrew)

Recreation-*cont.*

Dieterich, Michele M.
Divinsky, Nathan (Joseph)
Dombrowski, Daniel A.
Drake, Jane
Dudley, Ellen
Dummett, Michael (Anthony Eardley)
Dunlap, Julie
Dyson, John
Eckstein, Rick
Edwards, Harvey
Ellis, Reuben J.
Fisher, Marshall Jon
Florine, Hans E.
Ford, Jerry
Freedman, Eric
French, Sean
Fritsch, Albert J(oseph)
Gallagher, Patricia C.
Gehrig, Klaus
Gertridge, Allison
Goedecke, Christopher (John)
Goldstein-Jackson, Kevin
Gorman, Dave
Halliday, William R(oss)
Harrington, Philip S(tuart)
Harvey, Clay
Heminway, John
Henderson, Richard (Jud)
Holt, Michael (Paul)
Humphrey-Keever, Mary Ann
Hunnicutt, Benjamin Kline
Jensen, Clayne
Joy, Donald Marvin
Kay, George
Kaye, Marvin
Keene, Raymond D(ennis)
Kehde, Ned
Keller, Marian Jean
Kennedy, Michael P. J.
King, Daniel (John)
Knox-Johnston, Robin
Lecompte, Mary Lou
Lenskyj, Helen Jefferson
Maggio, Theresa (Marion)
Mccullough, Robert
McKinney, Sally (Brown)
Midkiff, Mary D.
Minetor, Randi (S.)
Moffat, Gwen
Montagu of Beaulieu
Morgan, Lael
Moss, Stirling
Nunn, John
Olney, Ross R(obert)
Ormondroyd, Edward
Perry, Roland
Pick, John Barclay
Piggott, Alan (Derek)
Pike, Robert W(ilson)
Pollak, Mark
Prime, Jim H.
Prosek, James
Resnick, Mike
Ridgway, John M.
Robertson, Janet (E.)
Rogers, Heather

Recreation-*cont.*

Rubinstein, Hilary (Harold)
Sampson, Curt
Scheft, Bill
Scott, Amoret (Tanner)
Seldon, Lynn
Setzer, (Cynthia) Lynn
Shivers, Jay Sanford
Spitz, Bob Stephen
Stambler, Irwin
Stebbins, Robert A.
Sultan, Stanley
Theobald, William F.
Thornley, Stew
Turner, Brian (Lindsay)
Turner, Marjorie Shepherd
Van der Plas, Rob(ert)
Verney, Michael Palmer
Wallach, Jeff
Waller, Jane (Ashton)
Waltham, Tony (A. C.)
Watts, Alan (James)
Williams, Wendy
Wilmer, Clive
Wilson, Jonathan
Wilson, Ken

Regional/Urban Planning

Adler, Richard
Askew, Thomas A(delbert)
Batali, Mario
Belkin, Lisa
Berry, Brian Joe Lobley
Betts, Clive
Birkland, Thomas A.
Blum, Kristen Raub
Bolton, Ruthie
Boskoff, Alvin
Boyle, David (Courtney)
Bradshaw, Michael
Burgess, Patricia
Chapin, F. Stuart
Clavel, Pierre
Cohen, Lizabeth (Ann)
Cunningham, James V.
Donnison, David Vernon
Drew, Philip
Duhl, Leonard J.
Ezell, Lee
Francis, David J.
Friend, Craig Thompson
Gilbert, Alan (Graham)
Glut, Don(ald) F.
Grant, Jill
Haar, Charles M(onroe)
Hall, Peter (Geoffrey)
Hasselstrom, Linda (Michele)
Hilty, James W.
Hooks, Gregory M.
Hough, Michael
Howey, John
Hu, Xu-wei
Huddleston, Mark W.
Jackson, John N.
Jackson, Kenneth T(erry)

Regional/Urban Planning-*cont.*

Johnson, Donald Leslie
Kanigel, Robert
Kavanaugh, Andrea L(ee)
Kemmis, Daniel (Orra)
Kemp, Roger L.
Kennedy, Lawrence W.
Kushner, James A(lan)
Langdon, Philip
Lewis, (Norman) Douglas
Lewis, J(ohn) Parry
Logan, Michael F.
Mango, Karin N.
Marcus, Alan I.
McGee, Terence Gary
Mohle, Robert L.
Nasar, Jack L.
Newcomer, Robert (J.)
Newton, Kenneth
O'Kane, Bernard
Olson, Ted
Palomino, Rafael
Phelan, Shane
Pindell, Terry
Pinner, Patty
Popper, Frank James
Portale, Alfred
Pushkarev, Boris S.
Ravetz, Alison
Regalbuto, Robert J.
Reps, John W(illiam)
Rinderle, Walter
Robinson, Phyllis C(umins)
Royte, Elizabeth
Sassen, Saskia
Simmie, James (Martin)
Smith, Peter J.
Steinlauf, Michael C.
Tarr, Joel Arthur
Thomas, June Manning
Timms, Edward
Tosics, Ivan
Tutu, Desmond M(pilo)
Warren, Kenneth
Weiss, Tamara
White, Randy Wayne
Whitzman, Carolyn
Wurman, Richard Saul

Sciences

Ackerman, Lowell J.
Ackerman, Michael J.
Aczel, Amir D.
Adams, Abby
Adams, Colin C.
Adams, Ernest Charles
Addison, Paul S.
Ahmed, Syed Naeem
Akera, Atsushi
Aldersey-Williams, Hugh
Alexander, (Robert) McNeill
Alexseev, Mikhail A.
Allen, John E(lliston)
Allen, Myron B.
Alligood, Kathleen T.

Sciences-*cont.*

Alpert, Mark
Altmann, Simon L(eonardo)
Anders, Charlie
Anderson, Alun M.
Andrews, Edgar Harold
Anees, Munawar Ahmad
Angela, Alberto
Annerino, John
Anton, Ted
Appleyard, Bryan (Edward)
Arellano, Juan Estevan
Arikha, Noga
Armbruster, Ann
Armstrong, David Malet
Ascher, Marcia
Ashall, Frank
Ashworth, (Lewis) William
Avise, John C.
Baatz, Simon
Backus, George Edward
Badeni, June
Baker, Nena
Bakker, Robert T.
Balaguru, P(erumalsamy) N(aidu)
Balakrishnan, N.
Balibar, Sebastien
Ban, Thomas Arthur
Bandrauk, Andre D.
Banerjee, Asit
Banks, Leslie
Baofu, Peter
Barabási, Albert-László
Barbour, Julian B.
Barnes, Burton V(erne)
Barnett, Cynthia
Baron-Cohen, Simon
Barr, Stephen M.
Barry, Susan R.
Bass, Thomas A.
Basta, Samir Sanad
Bauer, Henry H.
Bausell, R. Barker
Bechtel, Stefan D.
Beckwith, Jonathan R(oger)
Beerling, David
Begelman, Mitchell (Craig)
Behe, Michael J.
Behuniak, James
Bell, Mary Reeves
Bell, Suzanne
Benecke, Mark
Bengtson, Vern L.
Benjamin, Denis R(ichard)
Bennett, Charles A.
Bennett-Goleman, Tara
Benson, Frank Atkinson
Bentley, Peter J.
Bergland, Renee L.
Berkman, Michael B.
Berry, Adrian M.
Bertulani, Carlos A.
Berube, David M.
Best, Don(ald M.)
Biagioli, Mario
Bieder, Robert E.
Biek, David E.
Bierds, Linda

Binding, Paul
Bishop, Holley
Bjork, Daniel W.
Blackwell, Richard J.
Blair, Steven N.
Blakemore, Colin (Brian)
Blakeslee, Sandra
Bledsoe, Karen E(lizabeth)
Bloembergen, Nicolaas
Bloom, Howard
Bloom, Miriam
Bloomfield, Louis A(ub)
Blume, Harvey
Blundell, Derek (John)
Bök, Christian
Bonner, John Tyler
Bonnor, William Bowen
Bookchin, Debbie
Bortolotti, Dan
Bortz, Fred
Bostock, David
Bova, Ben(jamin William)
Bowen, Mark
Bown, Deni
Boyle, Thomas A.
Bracegirdle, Brian
Brady, Catherine
Braga, Newton C.
Braginsky, Vladimir B.
Branden, Nathaniel
Brandenburg, Jim
Braun, Stephen R.
Brenner, Mayer Alan
Bressoud, David M(arius)
Brewerton, Derrick (Arthur)
Bridges, Laurie
Brin, David
Brock, William Hodson
Broderick, Damien
Brodeur, Paul (Adrian)
Brookes, Martin
Brooks, David
Broom, Neil D.
Brothers, Joyce (Diane)
Brower, Kenneth
Brown, Richard E(arl)
Bruer, John T.
Bryant, Edward (Arnot)
Buchanan, Mark
Buchmann, Stephen L.
Buckelew, Albert R.
Buhs, Joshua Blu
Burgess, Patricia
Burk, Frank
Burke, James
Burnham, Terence (Charles)
Burns, Khephra
Burt, Austin
Burtless, Gary
Burton, John Andrew
Burton, L(awrence) DeVere
Buser, Pierre
Byers, John A.
Cacioppo, John T.
Cadbury, Deborah
Calder, Nigel (David Ritchie)
Calimani, Riccardo

Callaway, C. Wayne
Calle, Carlos I.
Calvin, William H(oward)
Cambie, R(ichard) C(onrad)
Campbell-Culver, Maggie
Cardona, Manuel
Carless, Jennifer
Carter, C. Barry
Carter, Martin R(oger)
Carter, Mike
Casey, Steven
Cass, Dennis
Cassels, J(ohn) W(illiam) S(cott)
Castaneda, Christopher James
Caster, Andrew I.
Cavazos-Gaither, Alma E(lisa)
Caws, Peter (James)
Cawthorne, Nigel
Chafel, Judith A.
Charles, Sara C(onnor)
Charlier, Roger Henri
Chiappe, Luis M.
Chiras, Daniel D.
Chociolko, Christina
Choudhury, Ashok
Chu, Wai C.
Clark, A(ilsa) M.
Clark, Andy
Clark, Jerome
Clark, William R.
Clayton, Lawrence (Otto)
Cleese, John (Marwood)
Cloudsley-Thompson, John
   (Leonard)
Côté, Richard N.
Cobb, Cathy
Cobb, Vicki
Cochran, Gregory
Cohen, Judith Love
Collard, Sneed B.
Collier, Gary
Collinson, Alan S.
Commoner, Barry
Coney, Sandra
Conley, Tom (Clark)
Conway, Erik M.
Cook, Hugh
Cooperrider, Allen Y(ale)
Coren, Stanley
Corfield, Richard
Corley, Thomas Anthony Bu-
   chanan
Corrick, James A.
Cottrell, Alan (Howard)
Coveney, Peter (Vivian)
Cox, Christopher Barry
Cox, Paul(us)
Coyne, Jerry A.
Craig, G(illian) M(ary)
Crane, Peter R(obert)
Crawford, Mark
Croissant, Jennifer L.
Crosby, Alfred W.
Crosland, Maurice P.
Crowe, Michael J.
Crowley-Milling, Michael C.
Crown, David Allan

Czerneda, Julie E(lizabeth)
D'Aluisio, Faith
Dabney, Joseph Earl
Dalyell, Tam
Daniel, Wayne W.
Daniell, Ellen
Darling, David J.
Date, C. J.
Dauber, Philip M.
Davenport, John (Chester)
David, Laurie
Davies, Nicola
Davis, David (Howard)
Day, Stacey B.
de Jouvenel, Hugues Alain
De Pree, Christopher G.
Dear, Peter
Dehaene, Stanislas
del Moral, Roger
Delaney, Michael
Delgado, Ricardo
Derr, Mark (Burgess)
Desalle, Rob
Devlin, Keith
Diamond, Jared (Mason)
Diamond, Jed
Dickinson, Terence
Diem, Max
Dixon, Bernard
Doerr, Anthony
Doherty, Paul (Michael)
Dombrowski, Daniel A.
Dormandy, Thomas
Dorset, Phyllis (Flanders)
Douglas, Matthew M.
Drake, Jane
Drawe, D. Lynn
Dressler, Alan (Michael)
Dreyfuss, Robert
Driesen, David M.
Drisdelle, Rosemary
Dugatkin, Lee Alan
Dunham, William
Dunn, Robert J.
Dunne, Pete
Dunster, Julian A.
Dupree, Stephen A.
Eastman, Susan Tyler
Eberhart, Mark E.
Edwards, Allen Jack
Eisenstaedt, Jean
El-Hai, Jack
Elbirt, Paula M.
Elias, Scott A.
Elliott, Clark A.
Ellis, Gwynn Pennant
Ellis, Harold
Ellyard, David
Eltringham, S(tewart) K(eith)
Emmer, Michele
Emsley, John
Engel, Cindy
Engell, James
English, Lyn D.
Ensminger, Peter A.
Entine, Jon
Epple, Anne Orth

Epstein, Steven
Evans, Ben
Everdell, William R(omeyn)
Ezrahi, Yaron
Faigman, David L.
Fairley, James S(tewart)
Fales-Hill, Susan
Falk, Dean
Fallows, James Mackenzie
Fanchi, John R(ichard)
Fanning, Philip Ashley
Fara, Patricia
Farber, Celia
Farbman, Albert I.
Farlow, James O(rville)
Farmelo, Graham
Fawcett, Tina
Feder, Bernard
Fedoroff, Nina (V.)
Felix, Antonia
Fenner, Roger T(heedham)
Fenton, M(elville) Brockett
Ferrari, R(onald) L(eslie)
Ferreiro, Carmen
Ferreiro, Larrie D.
Ferrières, Madeleine
Ferris, John (Stephen)
Ferris, Timothy
Fetherston, Drew
Finch, Caleb E(llicott)
Fink, Karl J.
Firsching, F. Henry
Fischetti, Mark
Fisher, Dana R.
Fisher, David E.
Fisher, Marshall Jon
Fishman, Charles N.
Fishman, Steve
Fitzsimons, Cecilia (A. L.)
Fleisher, Paul
Fleming, James Rodger
Flenley, John (Roger)
Florida, Richard (L.)
Fontanella, John J.
Ford, Brian John
Ford, Glyn
Forman, Richard T. T.
Forsdyke, Donald R.
Fortes (De Leff), Jacqueline
Fortey, Richard
Foster, Nora R(akestraw)
Fowler, James H.
Fox, Robert
Fox, Robin
Foy, George Michelsen
Franklin, Allan (David)
Fraser, Gordon
Fraser, Harry
Freed, Curt R(ichard)
Freeman, Harry M.
French, Francis
Freudenthal, Gad
Friedlander, Michael W.
Frist, William H.
Fry, William Finley
Fujimura, Joan H.
Fuller, Jack (William)

Lloyd, Elisabeth A.
Lloyd, Seth
Locke, Juliane Poirier
Loewer, (Henry) Peter
Lomnitz, Cinna
Lomnitz, Larissa Adler
Long, Benjamin
Long, Cathryn J.
Long, Pamela O.
Lord, Nancy J.
Louv, Richard
Lovell, (Alfred Charles) Bernard
Lubar, Joel F.
Lucire, Yolande
Ludbrook, John
Lunan, Duncan
Lundeberg, Philip (Karl)
Lurquin, Paul F.
Lynch, Michael
Lyon, Jeff(rey R.)
Lyons, Louis
Lysaught, Jerome P.
Mabey, Richard Thomas
MacFadden, Bruce J.
MacKenzie, Donald (Angus)
Madison, Gary (Brent)
Maeder, Thomas
Magner, Lois N.
Mahon, Basil
Mahony, Patrick J(oseph)
Majors, Richard G.
Mansfield, Howard
Maoz, Dan
Marangoni, Alejandro G.
Maranto, Gina (Lisa)
March, N(orman) H(enry)
Marcot, Bruce G.
Marcus, Alan I.
Markoff, John
Marks, Jonathan
Marmot, Michael (Gideon)
Marriner Tomey, Ann
Marriott, Edward
Marshall, Peter (H.)
Martell, Christopher R.
Marten, Michael
Martin, Claire
Martin, David S.
Massad, Joseph A.
Masthay, Carl (David)
Mathez, Edmond A.
Matsen, Bradford (Conway)
Maxwell, Nicholas
Maynard, Christopher
Mayor, Adrienne
McCall, Storrs
McCamant, Jim
McCormick, Anita Louise
McCormick, Sabrina
McCreery, Charles Anthony Selby
McDermott, Jeanne
McDonnell, Kevin Lee
McFadden, Johnjoe
McIntyre, Lee C(ameron)
McIntyre, Vonda N(eel)
McKie, Robin
McLeod, Carolyn

McMillan, Alan D.
McNair, Harold M.
McNamee, Gregory
McQuain, Jeffrey Hunter
Means, D. Bruce
Mearns, Barbara (Crawford)
Melko, Paul
Mellor, D. H.
Melville, Arabella
Merz, Jon F.
Messel, Harry
Metcalf, Donald
Metzinger, Thomas
Michod, Richard E.
Miele, Angelo
Miles, Steven H.
Milhorn, H. Thomas
Miller, Geoffrey F.
Millman, Joan (M.)
Mills, Stephanie
Mills, Stephen (Paul)
Millspaugh, Ben P.
Mirovitskaya, Natalia
Mirowski, Philip
Mitchell, Ellinor R.
Mithen, Steven J.
Mixon, Laura J.
Mlodinow, Leonard
Mnookin, Seth
Moenssens, Andre A.
Montaigne, Fen
Montandon, Mac
Montgomery, Scott L.
Moore, Randy Charles
Morrison, Taylor
Morton, Peter
Morton, Timothy
Morus, Iwan Rhys
Moss, Cynthia F.
Moss, Cynthia J(ane)
Motchenbacher, C(urt) D.
Mougios, Vassilis
Moyé, Lemuel A.
Muhanji, Cherry
Müller, Ingo
Munevar, Gonzalo
Murphy, Gregory L(eo)
Murphy, Patricia J.
Murray, Raymond C.
Myers, Drew(fus Young)
Myers, Greg
Myers, William
Nahas, Gabriel G(eorges)
Naidu, Prabhakar S.
Nakayama, Shigeru
Napier, Bill
Nash, Roger
Neale, Jonathan
Nelson, J. Bryan
Nelson, Sharlene (P.)
Nerlich, Graham C.
Neufeld, Michael J.
Newitz, Annalee
Newman, Arnold
Newman, William R.
Newsholme, Christopher (Man-
    sford)

Ney, Ronald E.
Nicholls, Henry
Niederhoffer, Galt
Nielsen, John
Niemela, Pirkko
Nighbert, David F(ranklin)
Nisbet, Jack
Nobile, Philip
Noble, William Charles
Nof, Shimon Y.
Norretranders, Tor
Norton, Bryan G(eorge)
Norton, M. Grant
Nüsslein-Volhard, Christiane
Nye, Mary Jo
O'Connell, Laurence J.
O'Dor, Ronald Keith
Oakley, Barbara A.
Odenwald, Sten F.
Offit, Paul A.
Ohanian, Hans C.
Olsen, Gary
Olsen, Klaus Malling
Olson, Steve E.
Ophuls, William
Oppelt, Norman T.
Oppenheim, Michael
Oren, Dan A.
Orenstein, Ronald I.
Orent, Wendy
Osserman, Robert
Ottaviani, Jim
Overend, William George
Pagán, Victoria Emma
Palmer, John D.
Palumbi, Stephen R.
Panek, Richard
Parberry, Ian
Park, Robert L.
Parsons, Alexandra
Parsons, Paul
Patt, Richard B.
Paul, George F(ranklin)
Payne, Daniel G.
Pecht, Michael G.
Peebles, Curtis
Penrose, Roger
Perkins, John H.
Perkins, Michael
Perlin, John
Petroski, Henry
Petuch, Edward J.
Peyton, A(nthony) J(oseph)
Phelan, Jay
Phillips, Kenneth J. H.
Pickover, Clifford A.
Pieribone, Vincent A.
Pike, R. William
Pimm, Stuart L(eonard)
Pinch, Richard G. E.
Pinch, Trevor (John)
Pisani, Elizabeth
Platt, Rutherford H.
Plotkin, Bill
Poëppel, Ernst
Pohl, Frederik
Poinar, Roberta

Polkinghorne, John Charlton
Pollack, Robert (Elliot)
Pollard, Irina
Pollen, Daniel A.
Pörtner, Hans O.
Postgate, John (Raymond)
Powell, Alan
Powell, Corey S.
Powledge, Fred
Preston-Mafham, Rod(ney Arthur)
Primack, Alice Lefler
Prince, Hugh
Prince-Hughes, Dawn
Principe, Lawrence M.
Prozan, Charlotte (Krause)
Pyenson, Lewis (Robert)
Quartz, Steven R.
Quinlan, Susan E(lizabeth)
Quinn, Helen R.
Quinn, Peter (John)
Rabalais, J. Wayne
Rabrenovic, Gordana
Rachman, Stanley Jack
Radcliffe Richards, Janet
Rader, Karen A.
Radick, Gregory M.
Rain, Patricia
Ramphal, Shridath (Surendranath)
Randi, James
Randles, Jenny
Rao, J. N. K.
Rapp, George (Robert)
Rapp, Rayna
Redford, Kent H(ubbard)
Redshaw, Peggy A(nn)
Reeves, Eileen Adair
Reeves-Stevens, Garfield
Regis, Edward
Reich, Eugenie Samuel
Reich, Lee
Reid, Julia
Reid, T. R.
Reinhardt, Carsten
Reiss, Mitchell
Restak, Richard M(artin)
Rhodes, Richard (Lee)
Rich, Thomas H(ewitt)
Richards, Matt
Richardson, Robert Galloway
Rigby, Susan
Riviere, Jim (E.)
Robbers, James E.
Roberts, Callum
Roberts, Charles E.
Roberts, Jon H.
Robinson, Chuck
Rodgers, Eugene
Rodriguez, Julia
Rooks, Judith P.
Root-Bernstein, Robert Scott
Rose, Michael R.
Rose, Steven
Roshwald, Mordecai
Ross-Macdonald, Malcolm (John)
Rowett, Helen (Graham Quiller)
Rowlands, Mark
Rowling, J(oanne) K.

Sciences-*cont.*

Roy, James (Henry Barstow)
Royte, Elizabeth
Rubin, Jordan
Rucker, Rudy
Ruddiman, William F.
Rudwick, Martin J.S.
Rue, Leonard Lee
Russell, Sharman Apt
Ryan, Frank
Ryan, Mark Dermot
Rybolt, Thomas R.
Ryder, Joanne (Rose)
Rylant, Cynthia
Sachs, Mendel
Sacknoff, Scott
Sakurai, Gail
Sale, Kirkpatrick
Salisbury, Frank B(oyer)
Sandler, Merton
Sanecki, Kay Naylor
Sankar, Andrea (Patrice)
Sarewitz, Daniel (R.)
Sass, Stephen L.
Sawyer, Kathy
Scarf, Maggie
Scarth, Alwyn
Schacter, Daniel L.
Scheffer, Kathy J(ean)
Schewe, Phillip F.
Schlesinger, Allen B(rian)
Schmid, Wolfram George
Schmidt, Stanley (Albert)
Schnitter, Jane T.
Schott, John R.
Schramm, Laurier L.
Schroeder, Gerald L.
Schwartz, Jeffrey H.
Scott, Donald Fletcher
Scott, Peter
Secretan, Lance H. K.
Seidl, Amy
Seife, Charles
Seligman, Martin E. P.
Sewell, Michael (John)
Shapiro, Bonnie L.
Shapiro, Jerrold Lee
Shedd, Warner
Sheftel, Victor O.
Shermer, Michael
Shipp, Steve
Shostak, Seth
Shulman, Seth
Sichel, Werner
Siegel, Daniel J.
Siegel, Daniel M.
Silk, Joseph (Ivor)
Silver, Lee M(errill)
Silverberg, Robert
Silverman, Joseph H.
Silverman, Mark P.
Simon, Seymour
Sims, Michael
Singer, Maxine
Singer, Peter
Singh, D(asharath)
Sirimarco, Elizabeth
Skolnikoff, Eugene B.

Sciences-*cont.*

Sleigh, Charlotte
Smartt, J(oseph)
Smith, Angela Thompson
Smith, Anthony
Smith, C(hristopher) U. M.
Smith, Lane
Smith, Rick
Smith, Roger T.
Smith, Rollin
Smoot, George Fitzgerald
Sobel, Dava
Sober, Elliott (Reuben)
Solbrig, Dorothy J.
Solbrig, Otto Thomas
Soluri, John
Sommers, Christina Hoff
Spall, James C.
Spear-Swerling, Louise
Sperling, L(es) H.
Spolter, Pari (Dokht)
Sprackling, Michael Thomas
Stachel, John Jay
Stahl, Saul
Stamets, Paul
Stangroom, Jeremy
Stapleton, Richard M.
Stell, Elizabeth P(arker)
Stenger, Victor J.
Stephens, William Peter
Sterken, Christiaan (L.)
Sterling, Keir B(rooks)
Stevens, Garry
Stock, Gregory
Stoddard, Robert H.
Stoff, David M.
Stokes, Donald W.
Stone, Linda
Stoskopf, Neal C.
Stout, Chris E.
Strathern, Paul
Strauss, Susan (Elizabeth)
Streitwieser, Andrew
Stringer, Christopher
Strock, Ian Randal
Strong, John S.
Stronge, James H.
Strother, Ruth
Stuckey, Peter J(ames)
Subotnik, Rena F.
Sullivan, Brad
Sullivan, George E(dward)
Sulston, John (Edward)
Sultan, Alan
Susskind, Leonard
Swetz, Frank J.
Sztompka, Piotr
Tagliaferro, Linda
Taubes, Gary
Taverne, Dick
Taylor, Dave
Taylor, Sarah McFarland
Temple, Robert (Kyle Grenville)
Thier, Marlene
This, Herve
Thompson, William J.
Thomson, James Miln
Thomson, Keith Stewart

Sciences-*cont.*

Thorne, Kip S.
Thumann, Albert
Thybony, Scott
Tierno, Philip M(ario)
Ting, Windsor
Tirion, Wil
Tobias, Michael (Charles)
Trefil, James
Trehub, Arnold
Tribus, Myron
Trimble, Michael R.
Triplehorn, Charles A(lbert)
Tucker, Karen
Tudge, Colin
Turchin, Peter
Turgeon, Pierre
Turner, John Christopher
Turner, Mark
Turney, Jon
Turok, Neil
Turpin, Tom
Tyson, Neil deGrasse
Uhlenbeck, Karen (Keskulla)
Ullmann-Margalit, Edna
Uman, Myron F.
Valenstein, Elliot S(piro)
Valko, Peter
Van der Plas, Rob(ert)
Van Eenwyk, John R.
van Fraassen, Bas C.
van Huyssteen, J. Wentzel
van Niel, Kimberly
VanCleave, Janice
Varmus, Harold E(lliot)
Vassberg, David E(rland)
Vauclair, Jacques
Velleman, Daniel J.
Vermerris, Wilfred
Vilander, Barbara
Vineyard, Jerry D.
Viorst, Judith
von Gunden, Kenneth
von Schlegell, Mark
Von Ward, Paul
von Zelewsky, Alexander
Vos Savant, Marilyn
Wachter, Kenneth W.
Wagman, Morton
Wagner, Andreas
Waldrop, M(orris) Mitchell
Walker, Benjamin
Walker, Sally M(acArt)
Walker, Stephen
Wallace, Bruce
Waller, John
Walsh Shepherd, Donna
Walton, John (Nicholas)
Ward, Frank A.
Warren, Susan
Watson, James D(ewey)
Watts, Alan (James)
Wayner, Peter
Weber, Robert J(ohn)
Weber, William
Weinberg, Steven
Weintraub, David
Weisgall, Jonathan M.

Sciences-*cont.*

Weiss, Thomas Fischer
Welland, Michael
Welton, Jude
Werber, Bernard
Wert, Jonathan (Maxwell)
Wess, Jane A.
Westrup, Hugh
Westwick, Peter J.
Wexler, Alan
Wexler, Bruce E.
Wheeler, Sara
White, Jonathan (Bruce)
White, Morton (Gabriel)
Wick, Steve
Widmaier, Eric P(aul)
Wiggers, Raymond
Wilford, John Noble
Wilkinson, Beth
Williams, Alan
Williams, Forman A.
Williams, Gerhild Scholz
Williams, Jacqueline (B.)
Williams, R(obert) J(oseph)
  P(aton)
Williams, Redford
Williams, Susan
Williams, Terry Tempest
Williams, Wendy
Williamson, Donald I.
Wilson, Catherine
Wilson, Frank R.
Wimsatt, William C.
Winckler, Edwin A.
Winston, Mark L.
Wolke, Robert L.
Woolfe, Jennifer A(nne)
Woolhouse, Roger
Wright, Michael J(ohn)
Wunderlich, Ray Charles
Wyllie, Peter J(ohn)
Wyman, Bruce C.
Wymelenberg, Suzanne
Wynn, Charles M.
Yeargers, Edward K.
Yellin, Emily
Yockey, Hubert P(almer)
Yolen, Jane
Young, John K(arl)
Young, Patrick
Younger, James
Yourdon, Jennifer
Zatsiorsky, Vladimir M.
Zihlman, Adrienne L.
Zimmer, Carl
Zonderman, Jon
Zook, Matthew A.
Zuckerman, Harriet
Zuk, Marlene

Self Help

Agonito, Rosemary
Alessandra, Tony
Ali, Shahrazad
Allen, Roberta

Alterman, Glenn
Anderson, Fil
Anderson, Maureen
Asper, Kathrin
Baer, Greg
Barker, Dennis (Malcolm)
Barratt, Iris K.
Barron, T. A.
Barron-Tieger, Barbara
Battle, Richard V.
Beaman, Joyce Proctor
Bennett, Hal Z(ina)
Bennett-Goleman, Tara
Berges, Emily Trafford
Berry, Carmen Renee
Biddle, Bruce Jesse
Birenbaum, Barbara
Blakey, Nancy
Blanco, Jodee
Blatchford, Claire H.
Bloch, Douglas
Boldt, Laurence G.
Boone, Daniel R.
Borchard, Therese Johnson
Branden, Nathaniel
Braverman, Terry
Breeden, Joann Elizabeth
Brehony, Kathleen A.
Brennan, J(ames) H(erbert)
Breslin, Cathy
Brian, Cynthia
Broks, Paul
Brooke, Jill
Browne-Miller, Angela
Buccieri, Lisa Rojany
Buck, Craig
Buhner, Stephen Harrod
Burns, Ailsa (Milligan)
Burns, Richard Gordon
Bushong, Carolyn Nordin
Byalick, Marcia
Byars, Betsy (Cromer)
Campbell, Colin
Campbell, Kellyna K.
Canfield, Jack
Capacchione, Lucia
Caplan, Mariana
Carling, Paul J.
Carlomagno, Mary
Carroll, Linda
Carter, Rosalynn (Smith)
Carter, Steven
Cathcart, Jim
Cell, Edward Charles
Cerami, Charles A.
Chethik, Neil
Chin-Lee, Cynthia D.
Chödrön, Pema
Chopra, Deepak (K.)
Ciaravino, Helene
Claude-Pierre, Peggy
Clayton, Lawrence (Otto)
Cleese, John (Marwood)
Clements, Alan
Clifford, Christine
Clow, Barbara Hand
Cobb, Nancy (Howard)

Cohen, Bernard
Cohen, Judith Love
Cossolotto, Matthew
Croall, Jonathan
Crouch, Tanja L.
Culp, Stephanie (Anne)
Currie, Dwight
Curtis, Jamie Lee
Dalai Lama
Damon, William
Davey, H. E.
Davidson, Gordon
Davidson, Jeff
Dayton, Charles (W.)
Deans, Sis Boulos
Delaney, Gayle (M. V.)
Demarais, Ann
DesRochers, Diane
Dolnick, Barrie
Draper, Maureen McCarthy
Driskill, J. Lawrence
Drummond, Edward H.
Dufresne, John
Edwards, Virginia
Ehrler, Brenda
Eisenson, Marc
Elgin, Suzette Haden
Emmons, Henry
Farrer-Halls, Gill
Feeney, Don J(oseph)
Ferder, Fran
Fisdel, Steven A.
Flem, Lydia
Flinders, Neil J.
France, Linda
Fritsch, Albert J(oseph)
Frueh, Joanna
Fry, Virginia Lynn
Gerzon, Robert
Gilbert, Harriett
Gladwell, Malcolm
Gleason, Katherine (A.)
Goldberg, Jane G.
Gordon, James S(amuel)
Gore, Ariel
Gottlieb, Annie
Grant, Cynthia D.
Gray, John
Green, James
Greenberg, Elinor Miller
Greene, Don
Greenlee, Sharon
Gremillion, Helen
Grierson, Bruce
Hakala, Dee
Hallowell, Edward McKey
Harley, Willard F.
Harpur, Tom
Harris, Carla A.
Hart, Charles (A.)
Hassler, Christine
Hausmann, Winifred Wilkinson
Hayden, C. J.
Hayman, Carol Bessent
Hazard, Ann
Hazlett-Stevens, Holly
Heine, Arthur J.

Heitmiller, David A.
Hinton, Michael
Hockensmith, Sean M.
Huber, Richard Miller
Illouz, Eva
Jacobs, Alan
Janko, (Kathleen) Susan
Jersild, Devon
Jinpa, Thupten
Johnson, Alexandra
Kanchier, Carole
Kaplan, Andrew S.
Katz, Jackson
Keen, Sam
Kent, Carol
Kerner, Fred
Kiefer, Louis
Kimball, Cheryl
Kimura, Margaret
Kingma, Daphne Rose
Kirkwood, Dianna
Klein, Allen
Kolodny, Nancy J.
Koman, Aleta
Kottler, Jeffrey (A.)
Kraft, William F.
Krasnow, Iris
Kuriansky, Judith (Anne Brodsky)
Landrum, Gene N.
Lang, Susan S.
LeBoeuf, Michael
Lee, Dorothy A.
Leerburger, Benedict A.
Lerner, Harriet
Lester, Margot Carmichael
Levin, Gerald
Levine, Barbara Hoberman
Lief, Judith L.
Little, Cynthia
LL Cool J
Longyear, Barry B.
Lotz, Anne Graham
Love, D. Anne
Lumpkin, Aaron
Lyon, Elizabeth
MacEachern, Diane
Marcell, Jacqueline
Mares, Theun
Marks, David (Francis)
Martinet, Jeanne
Maximovich, Stanley P.
Maxwell, John C.
McBratney, Sam
McClure, George W.
McCullough, Donald W.
McGraw, Phillip C.
McKenna, Patrick J.
McLean, J. W.
McNeil, Linda L.
Meckelson, Doug
Medved, Diane
Meier, Paul D.
Merriman, Catherine
Milhorn, H. Thomas
Millner, Cork
Mindell, Amy (Kaplan)
Mitchell, Ellinor R.

Molinary, Rosie
Moore, Lorrie
Morem, Susan
Morgan, Mary
Muchmore, Jo Ann
Murphey, Cecil B(laine)
Murphy, James S.
Murphy, Martha W(atson)
Muszynski, Stuart
Napier, Nancy J.
Neeld, Elizabeth Harper
Nerin, William F.
Ni Hua-Ching
Nicholson, Mavis
Nierenberg, Gerard I.
Norton, Augustus Richard
O'Connell, Rebecca
O'Connor, Richard
Olitzky, Kerry M.
Ornish, Dean
Paddison, Sara
Parfitt, Will
Pasick, Robert
Pavey, Don
Peddicord, Jo (Anne)
Pelosi, Nancy
Pelzer, Richard B.
Pfeiffer, Janet (B.)
Pitino, Rick
Plotkin, Bill
Pollack, Rachel
Powter, Susan
Pratt, Steven G.
Pruett, Kyle D(ean)
Quigley, Declan
Redding, David A(sbury)
Regnerus, Mark D.
Renee, Janina
Restak, Richard M(artin)
Reynolds, Bill
Richards, David P.
Riggs, Stephanie
Righton, Caroline
Rinzler, Carol Ann
Robertson, Joel C.
Robison, John Elder
Rogers, Colin D(arlington)
Rowan, Roy
Rubin, Gretchen (Craft)
Rubinstein, Helge
Ruskan, John
Rybolt, Thomas R.
Sachs, Judith
Sacks, Steven
Salmansohn, Karen
Saloff, Jamie L.
Sankar, Andrea (Patrice)
Schmitz, Cecilia M.
Schreiner, Samuel (Agnew)
Seale, Alan
Secretan, Lance H. K.
Secunda, Victoria (H.)
Seligman, Martin E. P.
Shafquat, Sofia
Shanahan, Michael Edward
Sheehy, Gail
Sheindlin, Judith

Ashley, Leonard R. N.
Ashman, Anastasia M.
Asimow, Michael
Aspinall, Edward
Austerlitz, Paul
Avery, Gillian (Elise)
Ayres, Thomas (R.)
Baca, Ana
Bacon, David
Bagley, Tennent H.
Bailey, Martha (J.)
Bailyn, Lotte
Baitz, Jon Robin
Baker, Paul R(aymond)
Baker, Raymond William
Baldassarri, Mario
Ballantyne, Tony
Ballard, John R.
Banerjee, Mukulika
Bar-Joseph, Uri
Barber, John (Douglass)
Barfield, Woodrow
Barker, Paul
Barlow, Maude
Barnard, Frederick Mechner
Barnes, Annie S.
Barnes, Samuel Henry
Barnet, Miguel
Barnett, Correlli (Douglas)
Barnhart, Terry A.
Barnwell, Tim
Barr, Andrew
Barr, Nicholas
Barreto, Mascarenhas
Barrow, Robin (St. Clair)
Barry, James P(otvin)
Barsamian, David
Bashe, Philip (Scott)
Bass, Jack
Bassler, Gerhard P.
Battle, Richard V.
Bauman, Christian
Bauman, Zygmunt
Baumgardner, Jennifer
Baumgartner, Frank R.
Bausell, R. Barker
Baxter, Paula A.
Bay, Jeanette Graham
Bayne, Nicholas (Peter)
Baynes, Kenneth R(ichard)
Beardslee, Karen E.
Bearman, Peter
Beattie, L(inda) Elisabeth
Beattie, Melody (Lynn)
Beck, Robert J.
Beckel, Bob
Beebe, Ralph K.
Beerling, David
Behar, Ruth
Belasen, Amy
Bell, David S.
Bell, James Edward
Bell, Madison Smartt
Belliotti, Raymond A(ngelo)
Bellotti, Laura Golden
Bellow, Adam
Bellows, Barbara L(awrence)

Beltman, Brian W.
Bendixson, Terence
Bennett, Colin J.
Bennett, Lerone
Bennett, Merit
Bentsen, Cheryl
Berendt, John
Berger, Arthur A(sa)
Berman, David
Bernstein, Jared
Bernstein, Richard
Berry, J. W.
Bertrand, Lynne
Best, Wallace D.
Bicchieri, Cristina
Biederman, Lynn
Bieler, Andreas
Bierhorst, John
Billington, James H(adley)
Billson, Janet Mancini
Binstock, Robert H.
Bird, Edward J.
Birkland, Thomas A.
Birnbaum, Jeffrey H.
Bizzell, Patricia (Lynn)
Black, D(avid) M(acleod)
Black, Robert Perry
Blackbourn, David
Blackburn, Fred M(onroe)
Blackmer, Donald L. M.
Blackwill, Robert D.
Blaisdell, Bob
Blakesley, Christopher L.
Blankley, Tony
Blasi, Anthony J(oseph)
Blass, Thomas
Blauw, Wim
Blodgett, Peter J.
Blondel, Jean (Fernand Pierre)
Bloxham, Donald
Blum, Deborah (Leigh)
Blumberg, Phillip Irvin
Bock, Gisela
Bodek, Richard
Boden, Margaret A(nn)
Bodenhamer, David J(ackson)
Boers, Arthur Paul
Boesche, Roger
Bohman, James F.
Bohntinsky, Dori
Bonner, Arthur
Bonner, Robert E.
Bonta, Marcia Myers
Boostrom, Robert E(dward)
Bornstein, David Neil
Boschken, Herman L.
Bosmajian, Haig
Boswell, Angela
Botha, Ted
Boucher, Philip P.
Bowen, John R.
Boyd, Candy Dawson
Boykin, Keith
Brace, Paul (R.)
Bracken, Len
Bradley, Patricia
Brady, Rose

Bramson, Leon
Brand, Alice Glarden
Branden, Nathaniel
Brannen, Julia (M.)
Brannigan, Augustine
Brantlinger, Patrick (Morgan)
Braschi, Giannina
Brauer, Ralph
Braun, Stephen R.
Braveboy-Wagner, Jacqueline
    Anne
Brawley, Robert L.
Brayfield, Celia
Breakwell, Glynis M(arie)
Brecher, Michael
Brener, Milton E(rnest)
Brenner, Philip (Joseph)
Brenner, Reuven
Breslin, Jimmy
Breton, Albert
Brewer, Carolyn
Brewer, John
Bridgers, Sue Ellen (Hunsucker)
Brizendine, Louann
Broad, Robin
Broch, Harald Beyer
Brockey, Liam Matthew
Brod, Harry
Brodeur, Paul (Adrian)
Brogan, Hugh
Bromann, Jennifer
Bromke, Adam
Brooks, Arthur C.
Brooks, George E.
Brooks, Karl Boyd
Brooks, Roy L(avon)
Brooks, Stephen G.
Brooks, Victor
Brown, Dale W.
Brown, Kathleen
Browne, Michael Dennis
Browne-Miller, Angela
Brownell, Susan
Brownlee, Andrea Barnwell
Bruns, William John
Bryant, Chris
Bryant, Jonathan M.
Bryden, John (Herbert)
Buchanan, Paul G.
Buchanan, Robert Angus
Buchholz, Todd G.
Buck, Craig
Buckley, Gail Lumet
Budge, Ian
Buettner, Dan
Bullins, Ed
Burack, Elmer H(oward)
Burchell, R(obert) A(rthur)
Burghardt, Linda
Burk, Robert F(rederick)
Burns, Jennifer L.
Burns, Kathryn (Jane)
Burr, David (Dwight)
Burtless, Gary
Burton, Anthony
Bush, M(ichael) L(accohee)
Bushong, Carolyn Nordin

Butler, Lance St. John
Buxton, Jayne
Byars, Betsy (Cromer)
Byrne, Donn
Cacioppo, John T.
Cafruny, Alan W(eston)
Calavita, Kitty
Calder, Nigel (David Ritchie)
Callahan, Bob
Cameron, Catherine M(ary)
Camp, Stephanie M. H.
Campbell, Beatrix
Campbell, Christopher
Campbell, David G.
Campbell, Ian Barclay
Canada, Geoffrey
Candilis, Wray O.
Canes-Wrone, Brandice
Carlin, Vivian F.
Carling, Alan H(ugh)
Carlson, Allen R.
Carney, Raymond
Carr, Jacqueline Barbara
Carr, Nicholas
Carr-Hill, Roy
Carroll, Michael P.
Carter, Timothy
Carter, W(illiam)
Cartmill, Matt
Cashill, Jack
Cassidy, Michael
Casstevens, Thomas William
Castaneda, Jorge G.
Castiglione, Caroline
Castile, Rand
Castle, Alfred L.
Castle, Kathryn
Castro, Daniel
Caughie, Pamela L.
Cernada, George P.
Chai, Arlene J.
Champion, J(ustin) A. I.
Chapin, F. Stuart
Chapman, Samuel Greeley
Chaves, Mark (Alan)
Chen, Joseph T(ao)
Chen, Victor Tan
Cherlin, Andrew J.
Cherry, Charles Conrad
Chethik, Neil
Childs, Matt D.
Chin, Rita
Chisholm, Michael
Chotzinoff, Robin
Chris, Cynthia
Christ, Carol P(atrice)
Christensen, Kit Richard
Christmas, Linda (Irene)
Cirincione, Joseph
Clague, Christopher K.
Claiborne, Shane
Clapham, Christopher S.
Clapp, Nicholas
Clapp, Rodney
Clark, Andrew
Clark, Charles E.
Clark, Kathleen Ann

Social Sciences-*cont.*

Clark, Paul F.
Clark, William R.
Clement, Priscilla Ferguson
Clemmer, Richard O.
Cleveland, Leslie
Cloutier, Cécile
Clunis, D. Merilee
Coates, Robert Crawford
Cobb, Kelton
Cochrane, Peggy
Coffey, John Robert David
Cohen, Andrew (Z.)
Cohen, Avner
Cohen, Bernard
Cohen, Daniel A.
Cohen, David William
Cohen, Elizabeth S.
Cohen, Jason
Cohen, Leah Hager
Cohen, Lisa R.
Cohen, Norman J.
Cohen, Stephen F(rand)
Cole, Simon A.
Cole, Susan Letzler
Coleman, Loren (Elwood)
Coleman, Mary DeLorse
Coles, Roberta L.
Colish, Marcia L(illian)
Colletta, Lisa
Collier, James Lincoln
Collins, Hugh
Collins, Irene
Collinson, Alan S.
Collinson, Sarah
Colquhoun, Kate
Colten, Craig E.
Compton, James V(incent)
Compton, Patricia A.
Condee, William Faricy
Condry, Ian Richard
Conklin, John E.
Connelly, Frances S(usan)
Conner, Patrick (Roy Mountifort)
Conrad, James H.
Conrad, Jessamyn
Conrad, Peter
Conway, Alan
Conway, Diana C(ohen)
Conway, Jill Ker
Coogan, Tim(othy) Pat(rick)
Cooley, Ronald W.
Coontz, Stephanie
Coren, Stanley
Corrado, Anthony
Cosman, Mark
Cottingham, John (Graham)
Cottrol, Robert J.
Coulmas, Florian
Cournos, Francine
Covey, Herbert C.
Cowan, Brian William
Cox, Anna-Lisa
Cox, Kevin Robert
Cozzens, Peter
Crabtree, John
Crary, Alice Marguerite
Crawford, Katherine

Social Sciences-*cont.*

Crawford, Lynn
Criddle, Byron
Critchlow, Donald T.
Croce, Paul Jerome
Croissant, Jennifer L.
Croker, Richard
Cronon, William
Cropper, Elizabeth
Crossley, James G.
Crowley, David
Crozier, Michael (Paul)
Crush, Jonathan
Csaba, László
Culyer, A(nthony) J(ohn)
Cummings, Sally (Nikoline)
Cunliffe, Barry
Cunningham, Patricia (A.)
Curtin, Deane
Czekanowska, Anna
D, John
D'Amato, Anthony
Daalder, Ivo H.
Dabashi, Hamid
Dabydeen, David
Dahl, Robert (Alan)
Dallaire, Romeo A.
Dallison, Robert L.
Danesh, Abol Hassan
Daniel, G. Reginald
Daniels, Anthony
Daniels, Mark R.
Danko, William D(avid)
Danquah, Meri Nana-Ama
Danto, Elizabeth Ann
Daoust, Jean-Paul
Darby, John
Darby, Mary Ann
Dary, David Archie
Davies, Philip John
Davis, Dick
Davis, Donald
Davis, Nancy Yaw
Davis, Robert C.
Davis, Robin W(orks)
Day, Nancy
Day, Richard J. F.
De Becker, Gavin
de Varona, Frank J.
de Vinck, José M. G. A.
De Vos, Susan
Debrix, François
DeCaro, Louis A.
Deck, Allan Figueroa
DeFrees, Madeline
del Moral, Roger
Del Paso, Fernando
Deloria, Philip J.
Delsohn, Gary
DeMello, Margo
Demos, John Putnam
Denham, Andrew
Denizet-Lewis, Benoit
Dent, David J.
dePaola, Tomie
Derfler, (Arnold) Leslie
Derickson, Alan
Dery, Mark

Social Sciences-*cont.*

Deshpande, Chris
Deutsch, Sarah (Jane)
Deutscher, Irwin
Devor, Aaron H.
Diallo, Kadiatou
Diamond, Arthur
Díaz-Stevens, Ana María
Dickman, Thomas
Diffily, Deborah
Diller, Harriett
Dillow, Gordon
DiMarco, Cris K. A.
Dine, Janet
Dinerman, Beatrice
Dinsdale, Ann
Dixon, John E.
Dixon, Steve
Dobie, Kathy
Dobson, Andrew (Nicholas Howard)
Dobson, R(ichard) Barrie
Docherty, Jimmy
Dolin, Eric Jay
Donaldson, Loraine
Donnison, David Vernon
Donohue, Laura K.
Donohue, William A.
Donovan, Brian
Dooley, Brendan Maurice
Doolittle, Amity A.
Dorrien, Gary J.
Dotson, Bob
Douglas, Susan J(eanne)
Doyle, Brian
Drake, Alicia
Draper, Sharon Mills
Dray, Philip
Dreher, Rod
Drew, Bettina
Drewes, Athena A.
Dreyfuss, Robert
Driedger, Leo
Driskill, J. Lawrence
Dryfoos, Joy G.
du Bois-Reymond, Manuela
Dubin, Michael J.
DuBois, Ellen Carol
Dudley, Ellen
Duff, Alan
Dumbrell, John
Duncan, A. A. M.
Duncan, Cynthia M.
Duncan, Karen A.
Duncan, William (Robert)
Dunk, Thomas W.
Dunlap, Julie
Dunlop, Eileen (Rhona)
Dunn, John (Montfort)
Dunn, John M.
Dunnage, Jonathan (Michael)
Dunne, Gillian A(nne)
DuPlessis, Rachel Blau
DuPree, Sherry Sherrod
Durrant, Lynda
Dutkina, Galina (Borisovna)
Dyer, James (Frederick)
Dyer, Joel

Social Sciences-*cont.*

Dzuback, Mary Ann
Earl, Riggins R.
Eason, Alethea
Easton, David
Eaton, Jack
Ebaugh, Helen Rose (Fuchs)
Ebbett, Eve
Ebel, Roland H.
Eberstadt, Nicholas (Nash)
Edin, Kathryn
Edwards, David B.
Eggleston, Larry G.
Eickhoff, Diane
Eisen, Sydney
Eldridge, John E. T.
Elizur, Joel
Elliott, Melinda
Ellis, Keith
Ellis, Ralph D.
Ellis, Richard (J.)
Ellwood, Sheelagh (Margaret)
Emanuel, James A(ndrew)
Eng, David L.
Ereira, Alan
Erickson, Hal
Erickson, Steve
Ericson, David F.
Erlbaum, Janice
Erofeev, Viktor V.
Erwin, Douglas H.
Estes, Steve
Esty, Daniel C.
Etheridge, Eric
Etlin, Richard A.
Eula, Michael J(ames)
Evans, James H.
Evans, Sara M(argaret)
Evans, Stephen S(tewart)
Eviota, Elizabeth Uy
Eyetsemitan, Frank E.
Ezell, Lee
Fairfield, Paul
Falkingham, Jane (Cecelia)
Farber, Celia
Farber, Naomi
Faron, Fay
Farris, William Wayne
Fassin, Didier
Feder, Bernard
Fell, Alison
Felstein, Ivor
Ferris, John (Stephen)
Ferris, Marcie Cohen
Feurer, Rosemary
Fielding, Nigel G(oodwin)
Fikes, Jay C(ourtney)
Fine, Doris Landau
Fingleton, Eamonn
Fink, Leon
Finkel, Alvin
Finkenstaedt, Rose L. H.
Finley, Randy
Finnegan, William (Patrick)
Finnis, John M(itchell)
Fischer, Steven R.
Fisher, Ernest F.
Fisher, Julieta Dias

Fisher, Marshall Jon
Fisher, Stephen L(ynn)
Fishman, Aryei
Fishman, Charles N.
Fishman, Katharine Davis
Fitzgerald, Mary Anne
Fitzgerald, Michael W(illiam)
Flanders, Laura
Flem-Ath, Rand
Flood, Pansie Hart
Florby, Gunilla
Florida, Richard (L.)
Fluehr-Lobban, Carolyn
Flynn, James Robert
Fong, Bobby
Fonseca, James W(illiam)
Foot, David
Foot, John
Foote, David
Foreman, Amanda
Forrester, Helen
Forstenzer, Thomas R.
Forte, Maurizio
Fortes (De Leff), Jacqueline
Fortna, Virginia Page
Foster, Brooke Lea
Foster, Richard
Fotopoulos, Takis
Fowers, Blaine J.
Fowler, Gene
Fox, Roy F.
Fox, William L.
Foxman, Abraham H.
Fradin, Judith (Bernette) Bloom
Fraenkel, Jack R.
Franceschini, Remo
Francia, Peter L.
Franey, Ros(alind)
Frank, Robert
Franklin, James L(ee)
Franklin, Robert M(ichael)
Fraser, Evan D. G.
Freehling, William W(ilhartz)
Freeman, Jo
Frey, Marsha L.
Frick, Carole Collier
Frisbie, Charlotte J(ohnson)
Frohnen, Bruce (P.)
Frost, Karolyn Smardz
Frye, Marilyn
Fuchs, Rachel G(innis)
Fullerton, Gail
Funk, Liz
Furino, Antonio
Gabor, Thomas
Gabriel, Theodore P. C.
Galasso, Vincenzo
Gall, Sandy
Gallagher, Susan VanZanten
Gambetta, Diego
Gammer, Moshe
Gamson, William A(nthony)
Gans, Chaim
Gans, Herbert J.
Gansler, Jacques Singleton
Garceau, Dee
Gardner, Michael R.

Gardner, Sandra
Garner, John S.
Garrett, Laurie
Garver, Newton
Gastil, John (Webster)
Gatenby, Greg
Gati, Charles
Gaubatz, Kurt Taylor
Gaunt, Kyra D.
Gay, John H.
Gazetas, Aristides
Gellately, Robert
Geller, Jaclyn
Geller, Jay Howard
Gemunden, Gerd
Gentry, Curt
Gerrard, John
Gerson, Michael J.
Gerstmann, Evan
Gerteis, Joseph
Getz, Trevor R.
Gewertz, Deborah B.
Ghareeb, Edmund
Gibbons, Reginald
Gibbs, Tyson
Gibson, Chris
Gifford, James J.
Giglio, James N.
Gil, David Georg
Gilbert, Alan (Graham)
Gilbert, Sandra M(ortola)
Gilens, Martin
Gilkes, Cheryl Townsend
Gillespie, Raymond
Gilligan, Carol
Gilmore, David D.
Ginsborg, Paul (Anthony)
Ginsburg, Mark B.
Ginzburg, Carlo
Girling, John (Lawrence Scott)
Glaser, William Arnold
Glassberg, David
Glazier, Stephen D.
Gleave, John T.
Gledhill, John
Glenn, Evelyn Nakano
Glennon, Robert Jerome
Glickman, Norman J.
Glossop, Ronald J.
Glucksmann, André
Godbold, E(dward) Stanly
Godwin, Gail (Kathleen)
Goerner, Sally J.
Goh, Evelyn
Golczewski, James A.
Gold, Michael Evan
Gold, Penny Schine
Golden, Renny
Golding, Peter
Goldman, Karla
Goldman, Marshall I(rwin)
Goldschmidt, Arthur
Goldstein, Robert Justin
Golubhoff, Risa L.
Gonen, Jay Y.
Goñi, Uki
González, Aníbal

Gonzalez (Mandri), Flora
Gonzalez-Balado, Jose Luis
Gooch, Paul W(illiam)
Good, Howard
Goodheart, Eugene
Goodwin, Doris (Helen) Kearns
Goody, John R(ankine)
Goossen, Rachel Waltner
Gootenberg, Paul
Gordinier, Jeff
Gordon, April A.
Gordon, Rivca
Gorham, Deborah
Gorman, Martha
Gott, Richard (Willoughby)
Gottlieb, Beatrice
Goulbourne, Harry
Gould, James L.
Govier, Trudy
Graham, Henry
Graham, Patterson Toby
Grant, James Russell
Grant, Patrick
Grassian, Daniel
Graves, Joseph Lewis
Gray, Francine du Plessix
Gray, John
Greeley, Andrew (Moran)
Green, (Charles Stuart) Jamison
Green, Celia (Elizabeth)
Green, Duncan
Green, G. Dorsey
Green, Ricky K(enneth)
Greenberg, Roger P(aul)
Greene, A. Wilson
Greene, Jody
Greene, Melissa Fay
Greenfeld, Liah
Greenwald, Marilyn S.
Greenwald, Ricky
Greenwood-Waller, Judith
Greetham, David
Greil, Arthur L(awrence)
Grewal, David Singh
Grimaldi, Janette Pienkny
Grimes, Michael D.
Grinde, Donald A(ndrew)
Grisso, Thomas
Grobsmith, Elizabeth S.
Gros, Jean-Germain
Grosbard, Ofer
Gross, Ernie
Gross, Michael L.
Guggenbühl, Allan
Guinier, Lani
Guo, Xiaolin
Gutman, Judith Mara
Guy, Mary E.
Gwynelle (Dismukes), Gwynelle
Hacker, Jacob S.
Hackett, Jeremy
Hackett, Robert A(nthony)
Haenn, Nora
Hagedorn, Jessica Tarahata
Hagerman, Edward
Hagerty, Devin T.
Hahn, Steven C.

Hajdusiewicz, Babs Bell
Hallendy, Norman
Haller, Hermann (W)
Halpern, Jake
Hamamoto, Darrell Y.
Hammoudi, Abdellah
Handelman, Stephen
Handler, Marisa
Handler, Richard
Hands, D. Wade
Hanlon, Gregory
Hannant, Larry
Hannay, Alastair
Hanscombe, Gillian E(ve)
Hansen, G. Eric
Hansen, Suzanne
Hanson, David D.
Hanson, Philip
Hapke, Laura
Harder, Leland
Hare-Duke, Michael (Geoffrey)
Hargrove, Erwin C.
Haring, Lee
Harlan, Judith
Harper, Hill
Harre, Rom
Harries, Patrick
Harriger, Katy J(ean)
Harris, Charles Wesley
Harris, Leslie M.
Harris, Margaret
Harris, Neil
Harris, Walter A.
Harrison, J. Richard
Harrison, John F(letcher) C(lews)
Harrison, Neil E.
Hart, Mitchell B.
Hartigan, John
Hartshorne, Thomas L.
Harvey, Karen D.
Harvey, P(aul) D(ean) A(dshead)
Hasenfeld, Yeheskel
Hashmi, (Aurangzeb) Alamgir
Haskell, Guy H.
Haskins, Scott (M.)
Haslam, Jonathan George
Hasler, Julie
Hatch, Lynda S.
Hattersley, Roy (Sydney George)
Hay, Samuel A.
Hayashi, Robert T.
Hayden, Brian (Douglas)
Hayes, Stephen F.
Haynes, John Earl
Hays-Gilpin, Kelley
Hayter, Teresa
Haythornthwaite, Philip John
Headley, John M.
Heald, Suzette
Heard, Alex
Heath, Dwight B.
Heath, Sebastian E.
Heckman, Robert A.
Hedin, Thomas F.
Heerma van Voss, Lex
Heffernan, Nancy Coffey
Hegeman, Mary Theodore

Lancaster, Carol J.
Lancaster Brown, Peter
Landau, Paul Stuart
Landers, John
Landrum, Gene N.
Lane, George
Langdon, E(sther) Jean Matteson
Lankford, Nelson D.
Lanyon, Anna
Lape, Noreen Groover
Lapping, Brian (Michael)
Lara, Maria Pia
Larocca, Roger T.
Laroche, Loretta
Lasserre, Philippe
Latourelle, René
Laughland, John
Laurence, Charles
Lause, Mark A.
Lawler, Peter Augustine
Lazerson, Joshua N(athaniel)
Lazin, Fred A.
Leader, Darian
Leahy, Robert L.
Leatherbarrow, W(illiam) J(ohn)
Leavitt, Judith Walzer
Leavy, Barbara Fass
Lee, Chae-Jin
Leeder, Elaine J.
Leen, Jeff
Lefkowitz, Mary (Rosenthal)
Legrain, Philippe
Lehmann, Wolfgang
Leiner, Katherine
Leira, Arnlaug
Lelchuk, Alan
Lemann, Nicholas
Lemons, James Stanley
Lende, Heather
Lenskyj, Helen Jefferson
Lentin, Ronit
Leonard, Gerald F.
Leonard, Karen Isaksen
Lerner, Michael A.
Lesourne, Jacques
Lessnoff, Michael
Lesy, Michael
Levene, Mark
Levin, Yuval
Levine, Alan J.
Levine, Bruce C.
Levy, Barrie
Levy, Peter B.
Lewis, Mark Edward
Lewis, Sarah Katherine
Lewis, Sydney
Li, Joyce H.S.
Lie, John
Lightfoot, Kent G.
Lilla, Mark
Lim, Shirley Geok-lin
Lind, Michael
Lindenbaum, Pija
Lindisfarne-Tapper, Nancy
Linebaugh, Peter
Linn, Karen
Linton, Simi

Lipman-Blumen, Jean
Lippi, Ronald D.
Litten, Julian
Little, Amanda
Little, Anne Colclough
Littlejohn, Duffy
Lloyd, Richard Douglas
Lockhart, Paul Douglas
Loevy, Robert D(ickinson)
Lofas, Jeannette
London, Herbert I.
London, Mark
Long, Carolyn Morrow
Lopreato, Joseph
Lorber, Judith
Louër, Laurence
Loury, Glenn C(artman)
Love, Eric T. L.
Lovelace, Earl
Low, Brian J.
Low, Setha M.
Lowenberg, Anton D(avid)
Lucero, Lisa Joyce
Luchetti, Cathy
Luciak, Ilja Alexander
Ludwickson, John
Lukes, Steven M.
Luria, Keith P.
Lynn, John A(lbert)
Lynn, Richard
Lyons, Thomas Tolman
Mabbett, Ian William
MacArthur, John R.
MacDonald, Hope
MacDonald, Jerry (Paul)
MacDonnell, Kathleen
Mace, Gordon
MacFadyen, David
Macfarlane, Robert
Mack, Arien
Mack, Dana
Mack, Raneta Lawson
Mackey, Richard A.
MacKinnon, Catharine A.
Maddox, Bronwen
Madhubuti, Haki R.
Magas, Branka
Magee, David
Maggi, Armando
Maghraoui, Abdeslam M.
Magistrale, Tony
Magnet, Myron
Magocsi, Paul Robert
Maharidge, Dale (Dimitro)
Maier, Karl
Mainiero, Lisa A.
Major, John
Mallick, Ross
Mallon, Florencia E.
Mallory, J(ames) P(atrick)
Malone, Hank
Malpezzi Price, Paola
Maltby, William S(aunders)
Maltese, John Anthony
Maly, Michael T.
Mandel, Oscar
Mandel, Robert

Manhein, Mary H(uffman)
Mann, Brian
Mann, Paul (James)
Mann, Reva
Mann, Thomas E.
Manna, Paul
Manning, Christel (J.)
Manning, Richard Dale
Mansfield, Edward D.
Manski, Charles F.
Marble, Allan Everett
March, Kathryn S.
Marcus, Paul
Margariti, Roxani Eleni
Margolick, David
Margolin, Leslie
Mark, David
Markoosie
Marks, Kathy (L.)
Marks, Lara Vivienne
Marks, Thomas A.
Marqusee, Mike
Mars, Perry
Marshall, Elizabeth Margaret
Martin, Francesca
Marx, Eva
Maser, Shari
Masini, Eleonora Barbieri
Maskarinec, Gregory G.
Mason, Matthew
Massey, Doreen Barbara
Matelski, Marilyn J.
Mathews, (Thomas) Jay
Mattingley, Christobel (Rose-
  mary)
Mauer, Marc
Mawdsley, Evan
Maxwell, Nicholas
May, Larry
Mazur, Laurie Ann
Mazurana, Dyan E.
Mazzarella, William T. S.
Mbuende, Kaire (Munionganda)
McAll, Christopher
McAllen, Jack
McCall, Storrs
McCallum, Taffy Gould
McCarthy, Sherri N.
McCarty, John
McColgan, John Joseph
McCormick, Theresa Mickey (E.)
McCutcheon, William Alan
McDonald, Patricia M.
McDonough, Peter
McDowell, Linda
McElroy, John Harmon
McEnery, John H.
McEwan, Barbara
McGrath, Melanie
McIntyre, W(illiam) David
McKay, Susan
McKean, Robert B.
McKechnie, Paul (Richard)
McKee, Steve
McKenzie, Evan
McKinlay, Brian John

McKinley, (Jennifer Carolyn)
  Robin
McKnight, David
McKown, Delos B.
McLeod, Grover S(tephen)
McLeod, Wallace
McMillen, Neil Raymond
McMillen, Sally G(regory)
McMullan, Margaret
McNally, Patrick S.
McNeil, William F.
McPhee, Jenny
McPherson, James Munro
McWhorter, John H.
Mead, Rebecca
Meer, Sarah
Megarry, Tim
Menard, Orville D.
Mender, Mona (Siegler)
Mendyk, Stan A. E.
Menzel, Peter
Merrell, Susan Scarf
Merrett, Christopher
Merridale, Catherine
Merrill, Ellen C.
Merrill, Hugh (Davis)
Mertus, Julie A.
Mesa-Lago, Carmelo
Messenger, Christian K(arl)
Messer, Donald E(dward)
Mettam, Roger C.
Meyer, Dick
Meyer, Leisa D.
Meyer, Lysle E(dward)
Meyer, Richard E.
Mezlekia, Nega
Michael, Colette V(erger)
Michaels, Walter Benn
Michalak, Stanley J.
Michelson, William
Miele, Frank
Milanovic, Branko
Milbank, (Alasdair) John
Miles, Tiya
Miller, Elmer S(chaffner)
Miller, Kristie
Miller, Lynn H.
Miller, Seumas
Millman, Brock
Mills, Richard W.
Minc, Alain J. R.
Minear, Richard Hoffman
Mingione, Enzo
Minogue, Kenneth Robert
Mitchel, Patrick
Mitchell, Don
Mitchell, Nancy
Mitchell, Nathan
Mitchell, Peter
Miyazaki, Hirokazu
Mnookin, Robert H(arris)
Moffett, Samuel Hugh
Moghaddam, Fathali M.
Mohun, Arwen Palmer
Molinary, Rosie
Mollenkott, Virginia Ramey
Monahan, John

Social Sciences-*cont.*

Montgomery, Maureen E.
Moore, Carey Armstrong
Moore, James T(almadge)
Moore, Peter N.
Moore, Thomas S(cott)
Moreno, Jonathan D.
Moreton, N. Edwina
Morey, Ann Janine
Morgan, Austen
Morgan, Jennifer L.
Morgan, Philip D.
Mormino, Gary R.
Morris, Jiwe
Morris, S(tephen) Brent
Morrison, Helen
Morrissey, Will
Morse, Melvin (L.)
Morton, Patricia
Moschis, George P.
Moskowitz, David V.
Moskowitz, Marina
Moy, James S.
Moya, Jose C.
Mrkvicka, Edward F(rancis)
Mulroney, Brian
Munro, John M(urchison)
Murdoch, David H.
Murdoch, Lydia
Murphey, Rhoads
Murphy, James Bernard
Murphy, Peter
Murray, Janet Horowitz
Murray, William J(ames)
Musselman, Jennifer
Muuss, Rolf Eduard
Myers, Eric
Myerson, Daniel
Nadelmann, Ethan A.
Naguib, Nefissa
Nahaylo, Bohdan
Naím, Moisés
Najmabadi, Afsaneh
Naraghi, Ehsan
Nash, (Cyril) Knowlton
Naureckas, Jim
Naves, Elaine Kalman
Naylor, Gloria
Neimanis, George J(uris)
Nelson, Jack Lee
Ness, Immanuel
Nestel, Sheryl
Newitz, Annalee
Newman, Felice
Newman, Isadore
Newman, Katherine S.
Newman, Susan
Newton, Diana
Ng, Franklin
Nichols, Deborah L.
Nichter, Mark (Andrew)
Niditch, Susan
Nightingale, Pamela
Nineham, Dennis Eric
Nissenson, Marilyn
Nobile, Philip
Noble, Kathleen
Norrander, Barbara

Social Sciences-*cont.*

Norton, Bryan G(eorge)
Nugent, Benjamin
Nuland, Sherwin
Nursten, Jean Patricia (Frobisher)
O'Callaghan, Sean
O'Doherty, Malachi
O'Kane, Rosemary H.T.
O'Rourke, William
Obaid, Nawaf E.
Ocampo, José Antonio
Odets, Walt (Whitman)
Oelschlaeger, Max
Ogletree, Thomas Warren
Oiwa, Keibo
Olaleye, Isaac O.
Olasky, Marvin
Olbermann, Keith
Oldenburg, Ray
Oldfield, J(ohn) R(ichard)
Oliver, Kitty
Oliver, Roland Anthony
Olkin, Rhoda
Olmstead, Earl P.
Olson, James S.
Olson, Jeannine E.
Olson, Karen
Olson, Robert W(illiam)
Ommundsen, Wenche
Oosterhuis, Harry
Opie, Anne
Oppelt, Norman T.
Oppenheim, Felix E.
Orenstein, Catherine
Orizio, Riccardo
Orr, David W.
Ortner, Sherry B(eth)
Osmond, John
Outhwaite, (Richard) William
Owens, John E.
Owings, Alison
Oxhorn, Philip D.
Packett, Charles Neville
Paczkowski, Andrzej
Padgett, (Mary) Abigail
Pae, Sung Moon
Page, Clarence
Palazzolo, Daniel J.
Palda, Filip
Palmer, Michael Denison
Palmié, Stephan
Panford, Kwamina
Panitch, Leo (Victor)
Pape, Robert A.
Paris, Roland
Parish, Steven M.
Parkin, Frank
Parkinson, Alan F.
Paschen, Elise (Maria)
Pascoe, C. J.
Passeron, Jean Claude
Patel, Eboo
Paterek, Josephine
Patin, Thomas A.
Patterson, E. Britt
Pavlik, John V.
Paxton, John
Payne, Ladell

Social Sciences-*cont.*

Payton, Rodney J.
Pearlstine, Norman
Peck, Robert S(tephen)
Pederson, William D(avid)
Pegram, Thomas R.
Pelka, Fred
Peña, Charles V.
Pensky, Max
Perry, Pamela
Person, James E(llis)
Pesantubbee, Michelene
Pessar, Patricia R.
Peters, Michael (Adrian)
Peters, Shawn Francis
Peterson, Peter G.
Pfeifer, Michael J.
Phayer, Michael
Phelan, Shane
Phillips, Christopher
Phillips, Stephen H.
Phillips, Susan E.
Pierson, Christopher
Pina-Cabral, João de
Pincus, Fred L.
Pinkwater, Daniel Manus
Pinto, António Costa
Piotrowski, Thaddeus (Tadeusz)
Pipes, Richard
Plank, Geoffrey
Plant, Sadie
Platt, Colin
Platt, Harold L.
Plaut, Joshua Eli
Plotkin, Diane M.
Pogge, Thomas
Pointer, Richard W(ayne)
Polakoff, Keith (Ian)
Polhemus, Robert M(ackinlay)
Pollack, Jill S.
Pollard, Helen Perlstein
Polletta, Francesca
Pollock, Nancy J.
Ponting, Clive
Poortinga, Y(pe) H.
Posner, Daniel N.
Posner, Gerald L.
Pospíšil, Leopold Jaroslav
Power, Patrick C.
Powers, William T.
Poynter, Jane
Prag, John
Prechel, Harland
Preda, Alex
Price, Hugh B(ernard)
Price, Robert M.
Priest, John Michael
Princess Anne
Prior, Kenneth Francis William
Prior, Natalie Jane
Pritchard, R(obert) John
Prozan, Charlotte (Krause)
Pruett, Kyle D(ean)
Prymak, Thomas M.
Pun, Ngai
Putnam, Constance E(lizabeth)
Putterman, Louis (G.)
Pybus, Cassandra

Social Sciences-*cont.*

Pyle, Kenneth B.
Qazwini, Hassan
Quale, G(ladys) Robina
Raadschelders, Jos C. N.
Rabie, Mohamed
Rabinbach, Anson (Gilbert)
Radano, Ronald M.
Radcliffe Richards, Janet
Radforth, Ian
Raeburn, Antonia
Raibmon, Paige Sylvia
Rake, Alan
Rampton, Sheldon M.
Randell, Beverley
Ranstorp, Magnus
Raphael, David Daiches
Rapp, Rayna
Rapson, Richard L.
Rarick, Ethan
Rasanayagam, Angelo
Rathbone, Cristina
Ravetz, Alison
Ravitz, Abe (Carl)
Ray, Sheila G(raham)
Read, Anthony
Real, Terrence
Reay, Barry
Reddaway, Peter (Brian)
Redish, Martin H.
Reeves, Marcus
Regan, Stephen
Regehr, T(heodore) D.
Regenstreif, S(amuel) Peter
Regnerus, Mark D.
Rehder, William J.
Reich, Robert B.
Reid, Elwood
Rejali, Darius M.
Rendon, Armando B.
Rendon, Marcie R.
Renshon, Jonathan
Reynolds, Barrie (Gordon Robert)
Rhodes, Jane
Rice, Prudence M.
Rice, Stephen P.
Richard, Adrienne
Richards, Amelia M.
Richardson, Miles
Richmond, Anthony Henry
Richter, Daniel K(arl)
Rickman, Hans Peter
Riddell, Roger C.
Rieger, Bernhard
Riley, Carroll L.
Riley, James C.
Rimmington, Gerald Thorneycroft
Rimstead, Roxanne L.
Ring, Jennifer
Ringquist, Evan J.
Riordon, Michael
Ripley, Randall
Ritter, Gretchen
Ritterhouse, Jennifer
Riverbend
Rivers, Larry E.
Roach, Catherine M.
Robb, James Harding

Roberts, Alvin
Roberts, Paul
Robertson, Barbara Anne
Robin, Corey
Robinson, Debbie
Robinson, H(enry) Basil
Robinson, Peter (Mark)
Robson, Brian Turnbull
Robson, Derek Ian
Rock, Howard B.
Rodger, Richard
Rodgers, Eamonn
Rodriguez, Clara E.
Rodriguez, Gregory
Rohner, Ronald P.
Rohrer, S. Scott
Romano, Louis
Rooks, Noliwe M.
Root, Deborah
Roscoe, Will
Rose, Paul (Bernard)
Rose, Tricia
Roselle, Mike
Rosenau, Pauline Vaillancourt
Rosenblum, Nancy L.
Rosenkranz, E. Joshua
Roslund, Anders
Ross, Lawrence C.
Ross, Oakland
Rosser, Sue V(ilhauer)
Rossman, Vadim
Rowlands, Mark
Roy, Donald H.
Royal, Robert
Rozbicki, Michal J.
Rubinoff, M. Lionel
Rubinstein, Ruth P.
Ruby, Robert H.
Rudgley, Richard
Rudolph, Christopher
Rulon, Philip Reed
Rushing, Josh
Rusi, Alpo M.
Rutan, J. Scott
Rutherdale, Robert
Ryan, Patrick
Rychlak, Joseph F(rank)
Rymph, Catherine E.
Sachs, Judith
Sachs, Wolfgang
Sakamoto, Yoshikazu
Salazar, Carles
Sale, Kirkpatrick
Salerno, Beth A.
Salisbury, Joyce E(llen)
Salitan, Laurie P.
Sampson, Edward E.
Samuels, David
Samuelson, Robert J(acob)
Sandel, Michael J.
Sander, Heather L.
Sanders, Clinton R.
Sandstrom, Alan R(ussell)
Sapinsley, Barbara
Sarnoff, Irving
Sarris, Greg
Sarris, Jonathan Dean

Sassoon, Donald
Sauers, Michael P(atrick)
Saums, Mary
Saunders, Gail
Saunt, Claudio
Savage, Sean J.
Sawatsky, John
Sawyer, Mary R.
Scalmer, Sean
Scarfe, Allan John
Scarr, Deryck (Antony)
Scarry, Elaine (Margaret)
Schaafsma, David
Schaefer, Claudia
Schain, Martin A.
Scheiber, Harry N.
Schellenberg, Betty A.
Schelling, Thomas C.
Schen, Claire S.
Scherer, Migael
Scheuer, Jeffrey
Schiller, Lawrence
Schlesier, Karl H.
Schlesinger, Benjamin
Schmidt, Arthur
Schmidt, Peter
Schmidt, Winsor C.
Schmitz, Cecilia M.
Schmookler, Andrew Bard
Schneider, Deborah Lucas
Schramm, Carl J.
Schroeder-Lein, Glenna R(uth)
Schryer, Frans J(ozsef)
Schubert, Frank N.
Schultz, (Reynolds) Bart(on)
Schumaker, Paul
Schusky, Ernest L.
Schwartz, Mel
Schwartz, Sunny
Schwartz-Nobel, Loretta
Sciabarra, Chris Matthew
Scott, Nina M.
Scott, P(aul) H(enderson)
Scott, Whitney S.
Scott-Clark, Cathy
Scully, Matthew
Seagrave, Sterling
Searle, G(eoffrey) R(ussell)
Sears, David O('Keefe)
Segal, Harriet
Segal, Lynne
Seidman, Louis Michael
Seltzer, Mark
Semyonov, Moshe
Sensibar, Judith L(evin)
Seymour, Tres
Shackelford, Renae Nadine
Shain, Milton
Shain, Yossi
Shalant, Phyllis
Shames, Germaine W.
Shankar, S.
Shanley, Mary L(yndon)
Shapiro, Sidney
Sharlet, Jeff
Shavelson, Lonny
Shaver, Phillip (Robert)

Shavit, David
Shaw, Alison
Shaw, Daron R.
Shaw, Deborah Anne
Shaw, Miranda Eberle
Shaw, William
Sheehan, Susan
Shelby, Tommie
Sheldon, Garrett Ward
Shell, Robert C.H.
Sheller, Mimi Beth
Shelton, Hal T(erry)
Shemesh, Haim
Shen, Fan (A.)
Shengold, Leonard
Shepherd, Robert
Sheppard, Alice
Sheridan, Thomas
Sherman, Joe
Sherman, John W.
Sherrill, Kenneth S.
Shrestha, Nanda R.
Shrimsley, Bernard
Shropshire, Kenneth (L.)
Siddali, Silvana R.
Sidky, H.
Siebold, Cathy
Siegel, Jennifer
Siegel, Mona L.
Sikes, Melvin P.
Silber, Nina
Silver, Carole G(reta)
Silverburg, Sanford R.
Silverman, Stephen M.
Silverstone, Scott A.
Simien, Evelyn M.
Simon, Sheldon Weiss
Singer, Benjamin D.
Singer, Mark
Singer, P. W.
Siniver, Asaf
Sirota, David
Sisson, Rosemary Anne
Sitkoff, Harvard
Sittser, Gerald L.
Siverson, Randolph M.
Skaria, Ajay
Skocpol, Theda (Ruth)
Skowronek, Stephen
Skrentny, John D.
Slatta, Richard W(ayne)
Slee, Debora A.
Smedley, Audrey
Smith, David A(lden)
Smith, Duane Allan
Smith, Erin A(nn)
Smith, Jeanne Rosier
Smith, Mark M.
Smith, Nigel
Smith, R. J.
Smith, Sheldon
Smith, Timothy B.
Smith, William Jay
Smith-Ayala, Emilie
Snider, J. H.
Snyder, Francis Gregory
Snyder, Jane McIntosh

Soffer, Olga
Sokol, Julia
Solinger, Rickie
Solomon, Evan
Solomon, Richard H(arvey)
Solotaroff, Ivan
Solove, Daniel J.
Soodalter, Ron
Soothill, Keith (Leonard)
Sorensen, Roy A.
Sorenson, John L.
Sorrow, Barbara Head
Soto, Lourdes Diáz
Soueif, Ahdaf
Spatz, Kenneth Christopher
Spellman, Frank R.
Spellman, W. M.
Spencer, Duncan
Spencer, Jon Michael
Spindler, George Dearborn
Spring, Eileen
Sprinkle, Annie (M.)
St. John, Warren
Stacey, Tom
Stafford, William
Stafford-Deitsch, Jeremy
Stanish, Charles
Stanley, Peter W(illiam)
Stanton, Richard C.
Staples, Robert Eugene
Stark, Evan
Stark, Rodney
Statham, E. Robert
Stavrakis, Peter J(acob)
Stebbins, Robert A.
Steel, D(avid) R(obert)
Steel, Gayla R(uth)
Steensland, Brian
Stein, Edward D.
Stein, Rebecca L.
Steinberg, Warren
Steinberg, Wendy
Steinhardt, Nancy Shatzman
Stepaniants, Marietta
Stephens, Thomas M.
Stern, Gerald
Stern, Paul C(linton)
Stern, Sol
Stetson, Brad
Stevens, Kathy
Stevenson, Garth
Stewart, Ron(nie)
Stockley, Grif
Stomfay-Stitz, Aline M.
Stone, James S(tuart)
Stone, Linda
Stoner, K. Lynn
Storch, Margaret
Stout, Chris E.
Stout, Martha
Stout, Maureen
Stovall, Tyler
Stoyle, Mark
Strange, Julie-Marie
Stromberg, Peter G.
Stronach, Bruce
Strong, Douglas M.

Social Work

Aponte, Harry J.
Blau, Joel
Boldt, Laurence G.
Brannigan, Augustine
Brown, Ethan
Coleman, Loren (Elwood)
Crittenden, Ann
Crocker, Ruth
Cunningham, James V.
Danto, Elizabeth Ann
Davies, Martin (Brett)
Dixon, John E.
Evans, Richard I(sadore)
Fabricant, Michael B.
Farmaian, Sattareh Farman
Faruque, Cathleen Jo
Fessler, Ann
Fitzgerald, Cathy
Foley, (Mary) Louise Munro
Forder, Anthony
Freed, Anne O.
Freudenheim, Ellen
Giddens, Anthony
Gil, David Georg
Glasberg, Davita Silfen
Glazer, Ellen Sarasohn
Gold, Nora
Gray, Deborah D.
Greif, Geoffrey L.
Hagedorn, John M.
Hatkoff, Amy
Hitchcock, Tim
Igo, Sarah E.
Jansson, Bruce S.
Jay, Ricky
Kadushin, Alfred
Kleiman, Mark A. R.
Klitzman, Robert (L.)
Kolodny, Nancy J.
Lappé, Frances Moore
Laskin, David
Leeder, Elaine J.
Lichtenberg, Philip
Lu, Ning
Lumpkin, Aaron
Lundvall, Bengt-Åke
Mac, Carrie
Marcell, Jacqueline
McKy, Katie
Meisel, Joseph S.
Montgomery, Maureen E.
Newcomer, Robert (J.)
Nursten, Jean Patricia (Frobisher)
Opie, Anne
Randall, John L(eslie)
Rappaport, Ann
Reitz, Miriam
Revie, Linda Lee
Saari, Carolyn
Schen, Claire S.
Schmidt, Winsor C.
Sherraden, Michael (Wayne)
Siebold, Cathy
Steckel, Richard
Stepaniants, Marietta
Tripodi, Tony
Van Beusekom, Janneke
von Hippel, Eric

Social Work-*cont.*

Wagner, David
Washburne, Carolyn Kott
Weissbach, Lee Shai
Welch, D. Don
Williams, Donna
Williams, Maurice
Willmott, Phyllis
Wolin, Steven J.
Yoshino, Kenji
Zmora, Nurith

Sociology

Abbott, Pamela
Adams, Gerald R.
Adams, James F(rederick)
Adams, Marie
Adler, Patricia A.
Adler, Peter
Aguirre, Forrest
Ahmed, Akbar S(alahudin)
Albert, Hans
Albrecht, Gary L(ouis)
Aldridge, Delores P(atricia)
Alexander, Jeffrey C(harles)
Allen, Craig M(itchell)
Allen, John L.
Allen, Kieran
Allen, Michael Patrick
Alt, Betty Sowers
Altheide, David L.
Ambert, Anne Marie
Ammerman, Nancy T(atom)
Anderson, Elijah
Anderson, James G.
Andryszewski, Tricia
Applebome, Peter
Archer, Margaret Scotford
Arluke, Arnold
Arnold, Eleanor
Averill, Gage
Avery, Gillian (Elise)
Ayres, E. C.
Badcock, Christopher Robert
Bagdikian, Ben H(aig)
Bailey, Greg
Bakalian, Anny
Baker, Maureen
Baldassarri, Mario
Ballantyne, Tony
Barker, Eileen (Vartan)
Barker, Paul
Barkey, Karen
Barnard, Frederick Mechner
Barnes, Annie S.
Barnhart, Terry A.
Barrow, Robin (St. Clair)
Basu, Alaka Malwade
Bauman, Zygmunt
Bayme, Steven
Bearman, Peter
Beck, Mary L. (Giraudo)
Beckert, Jens
Bedford, Henry Frederick
Beers, Diane L.

Sociology-*cont.*

Behar, Ruth
Bellotti, Laura Golden
Bellow, Adam
Ben-Rafael, Eliezer
Ben-Yehuda, Nachman
Bengtson, Vern L.
Benson, Richard
Berger, Arthur A(sa)
Berger, John (Peter)
Berkovitch, Nitza
Béteille, André
Beynon, Huw
Biddle, Bruce Jesse
Billson, Janet Mancini
Bird, Richard
Birkland, Thomas A.
Bishop, Bill
Black, Charlene Villasenor
Black, Donald
Blais, André
Blankenhorn, David (George)
Blasi, Anthony J(oseph)
Blauner, Bob
Blauw, Wim
Blee, Kathleen M.
Bloom, Clive
Blossfeld, Hans Peter
Boaz, Noel T(homas)
Bonner, Jeffrey P.
Bonner, Kieran (Martin)
Boskoff, Alvin
Bowe, John
Bowser, Benjamin P(aul)
Bramson, Leon
Brannen, Julia (M.)
Breakwell, Glynis M(arie)
Brewer, Garry D(wight)
Britnell, R(ichard) H.
Broad, Kendal L.
Brooks-Gunn, Jeanne
Brustein, William I.
Bryant, Christopher G. A.
Buckley, Francis Joseph
Burkey, Stan
Burkitt, Ian
Burwell, Jennifer
Busch, Lawrence (Michael)
Butsch, Richard (J.)
Byles, Jeff
Calder, Nigel (David Ritchie)
Calhoun, Craig (Jackson)
Cameron, Catherine M(ary)
Campbell, Beatrix
Champagne, Duane (Willard)
Chancer, Lynn S.
Chetkovich, Carol A.
Chirot, Daniel
Chodorow, Nancy Julia
Chorbajian, Levon
Christodoulou, Demetrios
Clark, Kathleen Ann
Clark, Terry N(ichols)
Clydesdale, Tim
Coarelli, Filippo
Cobb, Kelton
Cohen, Daniel A.
Cohen, Robin

Sociology-*cont.*

Cole, Sheila R.
Cole, Simon A.
Coles, Robert
Collin, Matthew
Comaroff, Jean
Comstock, Gary D(avid)
Conklin, John E.
Connerly, Charles E.
Conrad, Peter
Cottle, Thomas J.
Cowan, Brian William
Criddle, Byron
Croce, Paul Jerome
Crowley, David
Crozier, Michael (Paul)
Cunningham, James V.
Currid, Elizabeth
Danley, John R(obert)
Davidoff, Leonore
Davies, Christie
Davies, Martin (Brett)
Day, Richard J. F.
Day, Stacey B.
Deck, Allan Figueroa
Delage, Denys
Delgado, Hector L.
Deutscher, Irwin
Devor, Aaron H.
Dodge, Peter
Dreher, Rod
Driedger, Leo
du Bois-Reymond, Manuela
Duina, Francesco G.
Duncan, Cynthia M.
Dunk, Thomas W.
Durban, Pam
Ebaugh, Helen Rose (Fuchs)
Eckstein, Rick
Eisenstein, Hester
El-Or, Tamar
Eldridge, John E. T.
Emecheta, (Florence Onye) Buchi
Engel, Margorie L(ouise)
English, Camper
Erikson, Robert
Esterberg, Kristin G.
Etzioni, Amitai
Eviota, Elizabeth Uy
Eyer, Diane E(lizabeth)
Eyetsemitan, Frank E.
Farber, Naomi
Farrell, Warren (Thomas)
Fendrich, James Max
Ferree, Myra Marx
Ferrell, Jeff
Fessler, Ann
Field, Mark G(eorge)
Fielding, Nigel G(oodwin)
Fischer, Lucy Rose
Fischkin, Barbara
Fisher, Robin Gaby
Fishman, Aryei
Fisk, Milton
Flaherty, Michael G.
Fleurant, Gerdès
Foster, John Bellamy
Francis, Diane (Marie)

Sociology-*cont.*

Franklin, Samuel Harvey
Freeman, Gillian
Freeman, Jo
Frost, Diane
Fuess, Harald
Fulcher, James
Fuller, Steve William
Fullerton, Gail
Gabor, Andrea (Anna Gisela)
Gabor, Thomas
Gallagher, Tom
Gambetta, Diego
Gamson, Joshua (Paul)
Gamson, William A(nthony)
Gans, Herbert J.
Gates, Marilyn
Gaunt, Kyra D.
Gay, Kathlyn R.
Geismar, Ludwig Leo
Geller, Jaclyn
Gerson, Kathleen
Ghosh, Amitav
Giamo, Benedict
Gibbons, Reginald
Gilkes, Cheryl Townsend
Gilpin, Geoff
Gindorf (Prof. Dr.), Rolf
Gitlin, Todd
Glaister, Lesley (G.)
Glasberg, Davita Silfen
Glasser, Ira
Glassman, Ronald M.
Glazer, Nathan
Glenn, Richard A.
Goff, Martyn
Gold, Steven J(ames)
Golden, Renny
Golding, Peter
Goldman, Karla
Goldstein, Michael S.
Goldstein, Sidney
Gonzales, Phillip B.
Goodman, James
Goodman, Louis W.
Goody, John R(ankine)
Gordinier, Jeff
Gordon, April A.
Goulbourne, Harry
Graham, Patterson Toby
Gray, Ian
Greeley, Andrew (Moran)
Greenfeld, Liah
Greil, Arthur L(awrence)
Grimes, Michael D.
Guild, Elspeth
Guillaumin, Colette
Guillemin, Jeanne (Harley)
Gwynelle (Dismukes), Gwynelle
Halsey, A(lbert) H(enry)
Hansen, G. Eric
Hansen, Karen V.
Hardy, Richard Earl
Harris, Jose
Harrison, J. Richard
Harrison, Trevor (W.)
Hassen, Philip Charles
Havet, Jose (L.)

Sociology-*cont.*

Haynes, C. Rayfield
Heald, Suzette
Heath, Dwight B.
Heckman, Robert A.
Heller, Agnes
Henderson, William Darryl
Hendrix, Scott H.
Henley, Arthur
Henry, Stuart (Dennis)
Hewitt, W(arren) E(dward)
Hickey, Georgina
Hilbert, Richard A.
Hillyer, Barbara
Hooks, Gregory M.
Hope, Marjorie (Cecelia)
Horn, Stacy
Horowitz, Irving Louis
House, James S.
Hout, Michael
Hytrek, Gary J.
Igo, Sarah E.
Jackson, John P.
Jacobs, Jack L.
Jacoby, Tamar
Jalata, Asafa
James, David Edward
James, Wilmot G.
Jasper, James M(acdonald)
Joas, Hans
Johnson, Allan G.
Jonasdottir, Anna G(udrun)
Jones, Frank Lancaster
Jones, Naomi Brooks
Joppke, Christian
Juhasz, Anne McCreary
Kadushin, Alfred
Kamakahi, Jeffrey J(on)
Kavanaugh, Andrea L(ee)
Kaye, Barrington
Keil, Charles
Kelly, Deirdre M.
Kelly, Robert J.
Kendall, Diana
Kennedy, Kieran A.
Kenney, Jeffrey T.
Kent, James M.
Kimmel, Michael S(cott)
Kipnis, Aaron R.
Kirby, Michael Roger
Klein, Josephine (F. H.)
Knecht, Heidi Katz
Koehn, Peter H.
Kopinak, Kathryn
Korzenik, Diana
Krausz, Ernest
Kriesberg, Louis
Kritz, Mary M.
Kroeger, Brooke
Krooth, Richard
Kuhl, Stefan
Kumagai, Fumie
Kunda, Gideon
Kurien, Christopher (Thomas)
Ladell, John L.
Lakeland, Paul
Lamont, Michèle
Lang, Gladys Engel

Sociology-*cont.*

Lang, Kurt
Lara, Maria Pia
Lavender, Abraham D(onald)
Law, John
Lee, Jennifer
Leech, Kenneth
Leeder, Elaine J.
Lehmann, Wolfgang
Lehrer, Stanley
Lichbach, Mark Irving
Lie, John
Linder, Marc
Lippi, Ronald D.
Littleton, Darryl
Lloyd, Peter Cutt
Lockwood, David
Lomnitz, Larissa Adler
London, Charles
Lopreato, Joseph
Lorber, Judith
Loux, Ann Kimble
Lovelace, Earl
Lowry, Lois (Hammersberg)
Lowry, Ritchie Peter
Lukes, Steven M.
Lundman, Richard J.
Lyon, David
MacEachern, Diane
Macfarlane, Leslie John
Mack, Dana
MacKenzie, Donald (Angus)
Maghraoui, Abdeslam M.
Magnet, Myron
Mahindra, Indira
Mahoney, Rosemary
Maingot, Anthony P.
Majors, Richard G.
Malamud-Goti, Jaime
Manning, Christel (J.)
Manning, Robert D.
Marquardt, Elizabeth
Marsh, Robert Mortimer
Martin, David Alfred
Martin, Roderick
Martz, Linda
Marx, Gary T.
Mawhiney, Anne Marie
Mazzarella, William T. S.
McAll, Christopher
McEnery, John H.
McGrane, Bernard
McLaughlin, Corinne
McNamara, Dennis L.
McWhorter, John H.
Medved, Diane
Medvedev, Zhores (Alexandrovich)
Meeks, Wayne A.
Megarry, Tim
Melancon, Michael
Mele, Christopher
Mernissi, Fatima
Merry, Sally Engle
Messner, Michael A.
Mestrovic, Stjepan G.
Mettam, Roger C.
Michelson, William

Sociology-*cont.*

Miller, Abraham (H.)
Miller, Elmer S(chaffner)
Milofsky, Carl
Mingione, Enzo
Mishan, E. J.
Mitchell, Chris
Miyazaki, Hirokazu
Moberg, David O.
Mol, Johannis (Hans) J(acob)
Moore, Anne Elizabeth
Moore, Thomas S(cott)
Morales, Edmundo
Morales, Waltraud Queiser
Moravec, Hans P(eter)
Morton, Patricia
Moschis, George P.
Moschonas, Andreas
Mugny, Gabriel
Murcott, Anne
Murdoch, Lydia
Murray, Paul T(hom)
Murray, Stephen O.
Murren, Doug(las)
Musgrove, Frank
Naraghi, Ehsan
Nardi, Peter M.
Naylor, Phyllis Reynolds
Nelson, Geoffrey Kenneth
Nelson, Jack Lee
Nestel, Sheryl
Neubeck, Kenneth J.
Newell, William H.
Newton, Kenneth
Nolan, James L.
Nursten, Jean Patricia (Frobisher)
O'Connor, Pat
O'Kane, James M.
O'Malley, Padraig
Oakley, Ann
Olson, Linda
Orizio, Riccardo
Ottenberg, Simon
Outhwaite, (Richard) William
Page, Clarence
Pampel, Fred C.
Panitch, Leo (Victor)
Parkin, Frank
Parks, Gregory S.
Passeron, Jean Claude
Patten, Thomas H.
Patterson, (Horace) Orlando
Pena, Milagros
Pensky, Max
Perez-Stable, Marifeli
Perry, Pamela
Peterson, Richard Austin
Pfaff, Steven
Phillips, Derek L.
Phillips, Susan S.
Phillipson, Michael
Pinch, Trevor (John)
Pincus, Fred L.
Piotrowski, Thaddeus (Tadeusz)
Pitt, David Charles
Pogrebin, Letty Cottin
Poulson, Stephen C.
Powell, Ardal

Knox-Johnston, Robin
Kolata, Gina
Konigsberg, Bill
Konzak, Burt
Korman, Bernice
Kornheiser, Tony
Kriegel, Leonard
Kruger, Arnd
Krzyzewski, Mike
Kuntz, Jerry
Kurkjian, Tim Bell
Kyle, Donald G.
Lachner, Dorothea
LaFevers, Stephen
Lavender, Abraham D(onald)
Lazenby, Roland
Lecompte, Mary Lou
Lehrer, Jonah
Lenskyj, Helen Jefferson
Leo, Mabel R.
Levine, Barbara Hoberman
Liebreich, Karen
Linton, Simi
Lipsyte, Robert (Michael)
Liquori, Marty
Littlefield, Bill
Longman, Jere
Looney, Douglas S.
Loundagin, Choeleen N.
Lovesey, Peter (Harmer)
Lucas, John A.
Lucire, Yolande
Luckett, Dave
Ludwig, Jack
Lundin, Steve
Lupica, Mike
Lyon, Jeff(rey R.)
Lyons, Nick
Machowicz, Richard J.
MacIntosh, Robert
MacMillan, Norma
Macy, Sue
Madden, W. C.
Maggio, Frank P.
Maggio, Theresa (Marion)
Maisel, Ivan
Majumdar, Boria
Makowski, Silky
Mandel, Brett H.
Mandel, Peter (Bevan)
Marquis, Max
Marqusee, Mike
Marsden, Carolyn
Martin, Justin
Martin, Russell
Martino, Rick
Marx, Jeffrey
Maughan, Jackie Johnson
Maxwell, John C.
May, Jesse
Mayall, Beth
Mayne, Kenny
McConnochie, Mardi
McCrone, Kathleen E.
Mccullough, Robert
McDonell, Chris
McGurn, James (Edward)

McKinney, Sally (Brown)
McKy, Katie
McNeil, William F.
McPhee, John (Angus)
Mead, Chris
Mearns, Richard (James)
Melville, Arabella
Merrett, Christopher
Messner, Michael A.
Metcalf, Donald
Midwinter, Eric (Clare)
Miles, Steven H.
Mitchelson, Mitch
Mitman, Gregg
Mnookin, Seth
Molinary, Rosie
Moore, Kay
Moss, Stirling
Mowat, Farley (McGill)
Mulgrew, Ian
Murphy, Austin
Murphy, Shane M.
Murray, William J(ames)
Myerson, Daniel
Neale, Jonathan
Nelson, Mariah Burton
Nicholson, Lois P.
Norton, Melissa
O'Brien, Pat
O'Hare, Mick Richard
Oaksey
Oates, Joyce Carol
Oberle, Joseph
Olderr, Steven
Olney, Ross R(obert)
Oppenheim, Michael
Oser, Marie
Owens, Thomas S(heldon)
Pallone, Dave
Panik, Sharon
Paper, Lewis Jay
Park, Roberta J.
Parker, Tom
Pastore, Christopher
Pearlman, Jeff
Perry, Phyllis J.
Perry, Roland
Perry, Thomas Kennedy
Philbrick, (W.) Rodman
Pick, John Barclay
Pietrusza, David
Piggott, Alan (Derek)
Pike, R. William
Pitino, Rick
Platt, James R.
Plowden, Martha Ward
Pollak, Mark
Postman, Andrew
Powell, E. Sandy
Powell, Randy
Preller, James
Price, Christopher
Prime, Jim H.
Profumo, David
Prosek, James
Pruter, Robert
Purves, Libby

Putnam, Douglas
Quilter, Deborah
Rachman, Stanley Jack
Rann, Sheila
Rapp, Steven A.
Reback, Storms
Rees, C. Roger
Reid, Cindy
Reid, Elwood
Reid, Van
Resnick, Mike
Reynolds, Bill
Ribalow, M(eir) Z(vi)
Richard, Adrienne
Richmond, Peter
Riggs, Webster
Riley, James A.
Ring, Jennifer
Riordan, James (William)
Rippe, James M.
Robb, Daniel
Robbers, James E.
Rocks, Burton
Rosenfeld, Nancy (G.)
Rostkowski, Margaret I.
Roth, Eric
Rowett, Helen (Graham Quiller)
Roy, Alexander
Rusch, Elizabeth
Rutter, Michael (Llewellyn)
Ryczek, William J.
Sack, Allen L.
Sadick, Neil (S.)
Salter, David F.
Sampson, Curt
Satter, Ellyn
Savage, Jeff
Scanlon, Bill
Schenck, Hilbert
Schilling, Mark R.
Schilling, Peter
Schlosberg, Suzanne
Schnurnberger, Lynn
Schoenfeld, Bruce
Schulkin, Jay
Scovell, Brian (Souter)
Seabrook, Mike
Sears, William P.
Semchyshyn, Stefan
Shafquat, Sofia
Shahan, Sherry
Shanahan, Michael Edward
Sharpe, Graham
Sheeler, Jim
Shefchik, Rick
Shephard, Roy Jesse
Shermer, Michael
Shiner, David
Shipnuck, Alan
Shropshire, Kenneth (L.)
Shultz, Suzanne M.
Shusterman, Richard (M.)
Simon, Harvey B(ruce)
Simon, Scott
Simontacchi, Carol
Slee, Debora A.
Smart, S(tephen) Bruce

Smith, Brian
Smith, Sam
Smith, Tommie C.
Snelling, Dennis (Wayne)
Snow, Philip (Albert)
Snyder, Brad M.
Sobel, Dava
Soos, Troy
Sorenson, Margo
Souster, Raymond
Sowell, Mike
Spear-Swerling, Louise
Speck, Nancy
Spitz, Bob Stephen
St. Amant, Mark
St. James, Lyn
St. John, Bob J.
St. John, Warren
Stainback, Berry
Stambler, Irwin
Staten, Vince
Staurowsky, Ellen J.
Steele, Peter
Stephens, William Peter
Stevenson, Matthew
Stoddart, Brian
Stone, Eric
Stout, Nancy
Striegel, Jana
Stringer, C. Vivian
Strong, Carson
Suinn, Richard M.
Sullivan, George E(dward)
Sullivan, John Jeremiah
Sullivan, M(ichael) J(ustin)
Tamar, Erika
Taubman, Bruce
Taylor, Rogan
Terrill, Marshall
The Rock
Theismann, Joe
Thomas, Bruce
Thomas, Cornell
Thornley, Stew
Tofel, Richard J.
Torres, John A(lbert)
Townsend, Brad W.
Trecker, Jamie
Trengove, Alan Thomas
Tuaolo, Esera
Turner, Brian (Lindsay)
Ursano, Robert J.
Valiante, Gio
Van der Plas, Rob(ert)
van Derveer, Tara
van Hyning, Thomas E.
Vaz, Katherine
Vlasich, James A(nthony)
Vonderplanitz, Aajonus
Wade, (Sarah) Virginia
Waitzkin, Josh
Walker, Donald E(dwin)
Walker, Sam
Walker, Stephen
Wallace, Don
Wallace, Richard (Alan)
Wallach, Jeff

Sports/Fitness-*cont.*

Walvin, James
Waters, David Watkin
Watman, Max
Watterson, John Sayle
Webb, Lois Sinaiko
Weber, Robert J(ohn)
Weiner, William J(errold)
Weinreb, Michael
Welton, Jude
Westbrook, Peter (J.)
Westcott, Wayne L.
Wheeler, Lonnie
Wickham, David
Wiedman, John Charles
Wilkinson, Sylvia J.
Williams, Wendy
Wilson, Jonathan
Wilson, Ken
Wise, Joe
Wise, Mike
Wojnarowski, Adrian
Wolcott, Patty
Wolff, Craig (Thomas)
Wolverton, Robert E.
Woods, Tiger
Woog, Dan
Wubbels, Lance
Wunderlich, Ray Charles
Wymelenberg, Suzanne
Yaeger, Don
Yesalis, Charles E(dward)
Young, Jeff C.
Young, Ken
Young, Patrick
Zang, David W(illiam)
Zatsiorsky, Vladimir M.
Zimbalist, Andrew S.
Zingg, Paul J(oseph)
Zirin, Dave
Zonderman, Jon
Zoss, Joel
Zuckerman, Marvin

Technology

Aaland, Mikkel
Abbott, Elizabeth
Adams, Ernest Charles
Agrawal, Arun
Aldrich, Mark
Allen, John E(lliston)
Alshawi, Hiyan
Anderson, Alun M.
Anderson, H(ugh) George
Anderson, Trevor A(ndrew)
Arnold, Eleanor
Arnold, Kenneth L.
Auger, C(harles) P(eter)
Bahr, Alice Harrison
Bailey, Lee W.
Bain, Trevor
Bains, William
Baker, Christopher W.
Baker, Stephen
Balaguru, P(erumalsamy) N(aidu)
Bansemer, Roger

Technology-*cont.*

Baofu, Peter
Barfield, Woodrow
Barlow, Aaron
Barnett, Correlli (Douglas)
Baron, Naomi S(usan)
Bennahum, David S.
Benson, Frank Atkinson
Bentley, Peter J.
Bentsen, Cheryl
Berger, Fredericka
Bergerud, Eric M.
Berinstein, Paula
Berube, David M.
Bloembergen, Nicolaas
Bortz, Fred
Botting, Douglas
Bouton, Gary David
Bracken, James K.
Brin, David
Bronzino, Joseph D.
Browne, Cameron Bolitho
Brugioni, Dino A.
Brush, Kathleen (E.)
Budbill, David
Buderi, Robert
Burgess, Colin
Burke, James
Cadbury, Deborah
Calder, Nigel (David Ritchie)
Caldwell, David H(epburn)
Carless, Jennifer
Carlin, Martha
Carter, David
Ceruzzi, Paul Edward
Chiles, James R.
Chociolko, Christina
Chou, Tsu Wei
Clark, Andy
Clifford, Mary Louise
Cole, Stephen A.
Cossolotto, Matthew
Craig, G(illian) M(ary)
Cramer, Clayton E.
Croissant, Jennifer L.
Crosby, Alfred W.
Crossman, William
Crowley, William R.
Cummins, C. Lyle
Curtis, Todd
Czerneda, Julie E(lizabeth)
Dale, Rodney A. M.
Daley, Michael J.
Day-Lewis, Sean (Francis)
de Bono, Douglas
de Bono, Edward (Francis
  Charles)
de Jouvenel, Hugues Alain
de Neufville, Richard
DeVries, Kelly
Dewey, Scott Hamilton
Dibbell, Julian
Dooley, Brian J.
Doughty, Robert A.
Douglas, John (Frederick James)
Drew, Horace R.
Duguid, Paul
Dukert, Joseph M(ichael)

Technology-*cont.*

Duntemann, Jeff
Dyson, Esther
Eastman, Susan Tyler
Eberhart, Mark E.
Edgar, Stacey L.
Edwards, Clive D.
Egler, Claudio A. G.
Eilon, Samuel
Elliott, Clark A.
Ellyard, David
Evans, Ben
Ezrahi, Yaron
Faigley, Lester
Faust, Jeff
Fenner, Roger T(heedham)
Ferguson, Ron
Ferreiro, Larrie D.
Ferrières, Madeleine
Fetherston, Drew
Fetters, Thomas T.
Fialka, John J.
Fielding, Raymond
Finley, Michael
Fisher, Marshall Jon
Fisher, Robert E.
Fleming, James Rodger
Ford, Glyn
Foust, Jeff
Fox, Roy F.
Francis, Diane (Marie)
Franklin, Linda Campbell
Frantzich, Stephen E.
Fraser, Harry
Freedman, David H.
Freeman, Harry M.
French, Francis
Funk, Tom
Gagné, Marcel
Gaither, Carl C.
Galeotti, Mark
Gallimore, Paul
Gardner, Robert
Gasser, Urs
Gemmell, Jim
Gentry, Curt
Getz, David
Gleick, Peter H.
Glen, Paul (Michael)
Glick, Bernard R.
Goerner, Sally J.
Goldstein, Larry Joel
Gordon, Deborah
Gordon, W. Terrence
Gorman, Michael E.
Gorn, Michael H.
Gottschall, Edward M(aurice)
Grabbe, Crockett L(ane)
Graham, Jefferson
Green, Joseph (Lee)
Greetham, David
Grey, Jerry
Grossman, Wendy
Grove, Richard H(ugh)
Gunetti, Daniele
Gunston, Bill
Gupta, U. S.
Gurdon, Martin

Technology-*cont.*

Hachigian, Nina L.
Hacker, Kenneth L.
Hafner, Katie
Haga, Enoch John
Hagerman, Edward
Haldar, Achintya
Hall, Bert S(tewart)
Hall, Carl W.
Hanson, Philip
Hanzo, L(ajos)
Headrick, Daniel R.
Hecht, Jeff(rey Charles)
Heertje, Arnold
Hellman, Hal
Henderson, F(rancis) M(artin)
Heppenheimer, Thomas A.
Herrick, James A.
Hess, David J.
Hess, Mary E.
Hills, Philip James
Himrich, Brenda L.
Hofstadter, Douglas (Richard)
Holden, Greg
Hooper, Meredith Jean
Howell, David L.
Hrycej, Tomas
Hudson, John B.
Hunt, Bruce J.
Huston, James E(dward)
Iagnemma, Karl
Ihde, Don
Jacobs, David
Jain, Raj
Jaroff, Leon Morton
Jarvis, Jeff
Jenkins, Virginia Scott
Jensen, Geoffrey
Jensen, Vickie (Dee)
Jin, Jian-Ming
Johnson, Doug(las A.)
Johnstone, Bob
Jones, (R.) Dennis
Jones, Charlotte Foltz
Judkins, Phil(lip Edward)
Kahney, Leander
Karp, Larry
Kasabov, Nikola K(irilov)
Kash, Don E.
Kavanaugh, Andrea L(ee)
Kealey, Edward J.
Keith, William H(enry)
Kessler, Andy
Kevles, Daniel J.
Kevorkian, Martin
King, John
Koff, Richard M.
Koscielniak, Bruce
Koya, Tatsuhito
Kraeuter, David W.
Krupnick, Karen
Kuhre, W. Lee
Ladell, John L.
Lanouette, William (John)
Lebow, Eileen F.
Lecky-Thompson, Guy W.
Leerburger, Benedict A.
Lefebvre, Mario

3533

Levine, Joel S.
Levine, John R.
Li, Joyce H.S.
Lih, Andrew
Lindgren, David T(readwell)
Ling, Peter J(ohn)
Long, Cathryn J.
Long, Pamela O.
Lurquin, Paul F.
Lyon, David
Lysaught, Jerome P.
Macdonald, Copthorne
MacKenzie, Donald (Angus)
Maeder, Thomas
Maggs, Colin Gordon
Majd, Kam
Malmgren, Dallin
Malseed, Mark
Marangoni, Alejandro G.
Marcus, Alan I.
Markoff, John
Martel, William C.
Martinac, Paula
Maughan, Jackie Johnson
Maxwell, Nicholas
McCarthy, Nan
McCormick, Anita Louise
McCutcheon, William Alan
McKay, Claudia
Medvedev, Grigori
Michaelowa, Axel
Mills, Stephanie
Minetor, Randi (S.)
Misa, Thomas J.
Mitchell, John C.
Monmonier, Mark
Moody, Fred
Moravec, Hans P(eter)
Morgan, Dan
Moschella, David C.
Motchenbacher, C(urt) D.
Murarka, Shyam P.
Murphy, Gordon J.
Murray, G. T.
Murray, Janet Horowitz
Myers, Drew(fus Young)
Mylroie, Laurie
Naam, Ramez
Nabhan, Gary Paul
Nakayama, Shigeru
Nash, Roger
Nau, Henry R(ichard)
Nericcio, William Anthony
Nersesian, Roy L.
Newman, Dan
Nisbet, Jack
Noam, Eli Michael
Nof, Shimon Y.
Noltingk, Bernard Edward
Norton, Robert L.
Nunn, John
Nye, David E.
Nylund, Eric S.
Oliver, Richard W.
Olsen, Gary
Oneal, Elizabeth
Oppenheimer, Todd

Ottenberg, Simon
Parberry, Ian
Parsons, Paul
Pascarella, Perry
Pasework, William Robert
Patton, Phil
Paul, George F(ranklin)
Perlin, John
Peterson, Chris(tine Louise)
Petroski, Henry
Peyton, A(nthony) J(oseph)
Pickover, Clifford A.
Pinch, Trevor (John)
Pogue, Bill
Polkinghorne, John Charlton
Ponting, Clive
Post, Robert C(harles)
Pritts, Kim Derek
Rabalais, J. Wayne
Ragoné, Heléna
Regis, Edward
Reuben, Bryan G.
Rheingold, Howard (E.)
Richtel, Matt
Robbin, Tony
Rockwell, Theodore
Rosaler, Robert C.
Rotenberg, Marc
Rothwell, William J.
Rotundo, Louis C.
Rubin, Charles
Rubino, Anna
Ruchelman, Leonard I.
Rushkoff, Douglas
Ryan, Mark Dermot
Samuels, Richard J.
Sant, Thomas
Sarfoh, Kwadwo A.
Sargent, Ted H.
Sauers, Michael P(atrick)
Schnitter, Nicholas J.
Schramm, Laurier L.
Schwartau, Winn
Segal, Howard P.
Shallit, Jeffrey (Outlaw)
Shiller, Robert J.
Shim, Jae K.
Shlechter, Theodore M.
Shulman, Seth
Sichel, Werner
Sidak, J. Gregory
Singer, P. W.
Slemon, Gordon Richard
Smith, Martha Nell
Smith, Peter Charles Horstead
Snider, J. H.
Solove, Daniel J.
Stallman, Richard Matthew
Stamford Krause, Shari
Stanley, Autumn
Storer, James Donald
Stoskopf, Neal C.
Stout, Chris E.
Strong, John S.
Stubbs, Peter Charles
Summerhill, Thomas
Sundeen, Mark

Sutton, Roger
Swade, Doron
Szostak, Rick
Tang, Victor
Taylor, Lester D.
Teece, David J(ohn)
Temple, Brian
Tenner, Edward
Thompson, David C.
Thompson, Francis George
Thompson, Marilyn W.
Thompson, Richard A.
Tidwell, Mike
Tofts, Darren (John)
Travis, Anthony S(tewart)
Tribus, Myron
Trotter, William R.
Trzynadlowski, Andrzej M.
Tullos, Allen E.
Tunstall, C. Jeremy
Turney, Jon
Upton, Martin
Valenza, Joyce Kasman
Van der Plas, Rob(ert)
van Niel, Kimberly
Vavra, Terry G.
Vesper, Karl H(amptom)
Von Tunzelmann, G(eorge)
    N(icholas)
Waldman, Harry
Waldrop, M(orris) Mitchell
Ward, Ralph Gerard
Watkinson, John
Watson, Bruce
Weinbaum, Marvin G.
Weinman, Lynda (Susan)
Weiser, Philip J.
Wildman, Steven S.
Williams, Forman A.
Willrich, Mason
Winston, Wayne L.
Wolensky, Kenneth C.
Wu, C(hien-) F(u) Jeff
Wyman, Bruce C.
Young, E. L.
Youngman, Paul A.
Zangger, Eberhard
Zittrain, Jonathan

Theatre

Aaltonen, Sirkku
Abbotson, Susan C.W.
Amoia, Alba della Fazia
Argers, Helen
Arnott, Peter
Assael, Brenda
Atkey, Mel
Atkin, Flora B.
Ayckbourn, Alan
Aylen, Leo
Baker, Barbara
Barlow, William
Barnes, John (Allen)
Barranger, Milly S(later)

Bazzoni, Jana O'Keefe
Beacham, Richard C.
Beardsell, Peter R.
Beecher, Donald A(llen)
Berger, Sidney
Bergman, Eugene
Berry, Carmen Renee
Bert, Norman A(llen)
Beumers, Birgit
Bigsby, C. W. E.
Birringer, Johannes (H.)
Block, Geoffrey (Holden)
Bolam, Robyn
Bond, Edward
Bonds, Alexandra B.
Boyer, Jay
Branagh, Kenneth (Charles)
Brissenden, Alan (Theo)
Brodie, Leanna
Brown, Jared
Brustein, Robert
Burns, Edward
Canavaggio, Jean
Carter, Steven R(ay)
Cassady, Marsh
Castleden, Rodney
Chakravarty, Sumita S(inha)
Charney, Mark J.
Cohen, Gary P.
Cole, Susan Letzler
Condee, William Faricy
Craik, T(homas) W(allace)
Croyden, Margaret
Dace, Tish
Daniels, Rebecca
de Costa, Elena M.
de Marinis, Marco
Donoghue, Emma
Duffy, Susan
Dukore, Bernard F.
Eastman, Susan Tyler
Edwards, Anne
Eickhoff, Randy Lee
Elliot, Alistair
Emmer, Michele
Euba, Femi
Fahy, Thomas
Fedder, Norman Joseph
Ferlita, Ernest
Findlay, Alison
Finstad, Suzanne
Fishkin, Shelley Fisher
Forker, Charles R(ush)
Foulkes, Richard (George)
Freeman, Daniel E(van)
Frueh, Joanna
Gallagher, Kathleen
Gänzl, Kurt (Friedrich)
Garfunkel, Trudy
Gascoigne, Bamber
Gazetas, Aristides
Gelderman, Carol (Wettlaufer)
Gentile, John S(amuel)
George, Kathleen Elizabeth
Gifford, James J.
Glass, Charles
Goldman, William

Theatre-*cont.*

Goldstein, Imre
Goodland, Katharine
Gourgouris, Stathis
Grange, William Marshall
Greetham, David
Griffin, Alice
Griffiths, Linda
Grote, David (G.)
Gruber, William E.
Gurr, A(ndrew) J(ohn)
Hager, Alan
Hallett, Charles A(rthur)
Halpern, Cynthia Leone
Harburg, Ernie
Harrison, Tony
Hart, Jonathan (Locke)
Hashmi, (Aurangzeb) Alamgir
Hay, Samuel A.
Haycock, Kate
Hayman, Ronald
Haynes, Jim
Hendry, Joy (McLaggan)
Hilton, George Woodman
Himelstein, Morgan Y.
Hischak, Thomas S.
Homan, Sidney
Honri, Peter
Howard, Roger
Hume, Robert D.
Ionazzi, Daniel A.
Ione, Carole
Isenberg, Barbara
Jirgens, Karl (E.)
Jonas, Susan
Jordan, Richard Tyler
Kalb, Jonathan
Kalson, Albert E(ugene)
Kane, Leslie
Katritzky, M. A.
Keaney, Brian
Kear, Lynn
Keens-Douglas, Richardo
Kellogg, Marjorie Bradley
Kelly, Linda
Kenton, Warren
Kherdian, David
Kibler, M. Alison
Kiernan, Pauline
Kimball, Robert (Eric)
Knox, George
Koja, Kathe
Kourilsky, Françoise
Kowalke, Kim H.
Kritzer, Amelia Howe
Laguna, Sofie
Lahr, John (Henry)
Lamb, Andrew (Martin)
Lane, Terry
Lavigne, Louis-Dominique
Laxdal, Vivienne
Lee, Josephine (D.)
Leggatt, Alexander
Leidner, Alan C.
Lennard, John (Chevening)
Lepage, Robert
Levin, Igor
Levin, Irina

Theatre-*cont.*

Li, Leslie
Limon, Jerzy
Loney, Glenn Meredith
Loring, Kevin
Lott, Eric
Love, Douglas
Mackerras, Colin Patrick
Maher, Mary Z.
Mann, William J.
Marowitz, Charles
Marting, Diane E.
Mason, Jeffrey D(aniel)
Matas, Carol
McEwan, Ian
McIntyre, Ian (James)
McMullan, Gordon
McNally, Terrence
Mears, Gillian
Mekler, Eva
Meserve, Walter Joseph
Metzger, Deena P.
Miles, Keith
Miller, Jonathan (Wolfe)
Miller, Tice L.
Mitchelson, Mitch
Moe, Christian H(ollis)
Moher, Frank
Moreh, Shmuel
Morrison, Kristin Diane
Morton, Richard Everett
Mosley, Philip
Moy, James S.
Mulcahy, Lisa
Myers, Robert Manson
Nahshon, Edna
Naiden, James
Naidoo, Beverley
Nash, Elizabeth (Hamilton)
Nelson, T. G. A.
Nemec, James
Nericcio, William Anthony
Newey, Katherine
O'Connor, Patricia W.
O'Toole, Fintan
Olson, Kirby
Onwueme, Tess Osonye
Orledge, Robert
Ozick, Cynthia
Padel, Ruth
Palmer, William J.
Parish, James Robert
Paterek, Josephine
Patterson, Michael
Payne, J. Gregory
Payne Fisk, Deborah C.
Peters, Margot (McCullough)
Pickering, David (Hugh)
Pilling, Christopher (Robert)
Pollock, (Mary) Sharon
Porter, Sue
Prince, Stephen
Randall, Dale B(ertrand) J(onas)
Read, Anthony
Richmond, Hugh Macrae
Robinson, Ken
Roose-Evans, James
Rossol, Monona

Theatre-*cont.*

Roston, Murray
Sabatine, Jean A.
Sacre, Antonio
Saddlemyer, (Eleanor) Ann
Saddler, Allen
Santos, Sherod
Scales, Barbara
Schipper de Leeuw, W. J. J.
Schouvaloff, Alexander
Scully, James (Joseph)
Shafer, Yvonne
Shank, Theodore
Sheehy, Helen
Sherman, Jason
Shevelow, Kathryn
Shirley, Frances A.
Silberman, Marc (D.)
Sinden, Donald (Alfred)
Singer, Barry
Slide, Anthony (Clifford)
Smarandache, Florentin
Smeliansky, Anatoly
Smith, (John) Geddeth
Smith, Bruce R.
Smith, James L(eslie Clarke)
Smith, Marisa
Spencer, Charles
Spencer, Stuart S.
Spivack, Charlotte
Stainton, Leslie
Stamm, Peter
Steggle, Matthew
Steinman, Louise
Stewart, Harry E.
Stillson, Alan
Stone, Sarah
Sullivan, Claudia
Sullivan, Garrett A.
Sutton, Dana F.
Tanner, Jo A.
Taplin, Oliver
Taylor, John Russell
Teague, Frances
Terry, Megan
Thom, Paul
Thompson, Chuck
Thomson, Peter (William)
Till, Nicholas
Tillis, Steve
Toll, Robert Charles
Törnqvist, Egil
Towne, Marian K(leinsasser)
Tydeman, William (Marcus)
Vacche, Angela Dalle
Van Erven, Eugene
Versényi, Adam
Wagner, Nike
Wainscott, Ronald H(arold)
Wandor, Michelene
Wardle, (John) Irving
Weales, Gerald
Weintraub, Andrew N.
Wells, Stanley (William)
Wetmore, Kevin J. (Jr.)
Whitton, David
Whitton, Kenneth S(tuart)
Wood, Gerald C.

Theatre-*cont.*

Woods, Jeannie Marlin
Wortsman, Peter
Wright, Courtni C(rump)
Wymark, Olwen (Margaret)
Zaloga, Steven J(oseph)
Zimmerman, Cynthia (Diane)

Theology/Religion

Aaron, David
Aaronovitch, David
Abbas, Jailan
Aberbach, David
Abrams, Douglas Carl
Abrams, Jeanne E.
Abrams, Judith Z.
Abresch, Peter E.
Adam, David
Adams, Carol J.
Adams, Charles J.
Adams, Marilyn McCord
Adamz-Bogus, S. Diane
Addinall, Peter
Adshead, S(amuel) A(drian) M(iles)
Ahlgren, Gillian T. W.
Ahmed, Akbar S(alahudin)
Ajami, Fouad
Al-Rasheed, Madawi
Albert, Hans
Algeo, John
Allen, Diogenes
Allen, John L.
Allison, Dale C.
Allison, Robert J.
Alsdorf, Debbie
Altemeyer, Bob
Alter, Robert B.
Alvarez, Julia
Ammerman, Nancy T(atom)
Anders, Isabel
Anderson, Allan
Anderson, Fil
Anderson, H(ugh) George
Anderson, Richard Lloyd
Andrews, Edgar Harold
Andrus, Hyrum Leslie
Anees, Munawar Ahmad
Ansberry, Clare
Appleyard, Bryan (Edward)
Apter, Emily (S.)
Archer of Sandwell
Arinze, Francis
Arkin, Marcus
Armah, Ayi Kwei
Armstrong, Karen (Anderson)
Arruda, Suzanne M.
Arterburn, Stephen
Arthur, Chris
Arvigo, Rosita
Ashby, Godfrey W.
Ashton, Dianne
Aslan, Reza
Assmann, Jan
Astell, Ann W.

Atkinson, James
Atwood, Craig D.
Auerbach, Loyd
Avalos, Hector
Avella, Steven M.
Badcock, Gary D.
Baderin, Mashood A.
Badillo, David A.
Bailey, Gordon (Keith)
Bailey, Greg
Bailey, Lee W.
Bailey, Michael D.
Baker, Raymond William
Baker, Stuart Eddy
Bakke, O. M.
Bal, Mieke (Maria Gertrudis)
Balmer, Randall (Herbert)
Balswick, Judith K.
Bancroft, Anne
Banerjee, Mukulika
Bar, Shmuel
Bar-Yosef, Eitan
Barbour, John D.
Barker, Eileen (Vartan)
Barmann, Lawrence (Francis)
Barnes, Linda L.
Barnes, Michael (Anthony)
Barnet, Miguel
Barnett, Matthew
Barnett, Paul
Barnett, Victoria (Joan)
Barone, Joe
Barr, Andrew
Barrett, Charles Kingsley
Barrett, Mark
Barton, Carlin A.
Barton, Greg
Barton, John
Baskin, Judith R.
Bass, Diana Butler
Batchelor, Stephen
Bates, Stephen
Battle, Michael Jesse
Bauckham, Richard J.
Bauer, Yehuda
Bauerschmidt, Frederick Christian
Bauman, Richard
Baums, Roosevelt
Bayme, Steven
Beal, Timothy
Beary, Michael J.
Beaudoin, Tom
Beavis, Mary Ann
Bebbington, D(avid) W(illiam)
Beck, Edward L.
Becker, Palmer (Joseph)
Beckley, Harlan R.
Bedford, Deborah
Beebe, Ralph K.
Beecher, Maureen Ursenbach
Behdad, Sohrab
Behe, Michael J.
Bell, Albert A.
Bell, Dean Phillip
Bell, Richard H.
Benbassa, Esther
Bendroth, Margaret Lamberts

Bennett, Clinton
Bennett, James B.
Berenbaum, Michael
Berg, Leila
Berman, Morris
Bernstein, Ellen
Berrigan, Daniel J.
Berryman, Phillip E.
Best, Wallace D.
Bettey, J(oseph) H(arold)
Bevans, Stephen B(ennett)
Bewes, Richard
Bialer, Uri
Bianchi, Eugene Carl
Bieringer, R(eimund)
Billingsley, (Kenneth) Lloyd
Billington, Ray(mond John)
Binns, Michael Ferrers Elliott
Birrell, Anne (Margaret)
Bitton-Ashkelony, Brouria
Bivins, Jason C.
Black, Charlene Villasenor
Blackaby, Richard
Blair, Sheila
Blamires, Harry
Blasi, Anthony J(oseph)
Blatchford, Claire H.
Blenkinsopp, Joseph
Block, Daniel I.
Block, Thomas H(arris)
Bloom, Jonathan M(ax)
Blount, Brian K.
Blumhofer, Edith L.
Bobrick, Benson
Boers, Arthur Paul
Boersma, Hans
Boff, Leonardo (Genezio Darci)
Bonder, Nilton
Bookman, Terry Allen
Boorstein, Sylvia
Booth, Edward
Booth, Stanley
Borchard, Therese Johnson
Borelli, John
Borg, Marcus J(oel)
Boteach, Shmuley
Boullata, Issa J.
Bourdeaux, Michael Alan
Bourgeault, Cynthia
Bourgeois, Michael
Bovon, François
Bowley, Rex Lyon
Boyarin, Daniel
Boyd, Malcolm
Boynton, Susan
Brading, D. A.
Bradley, Michael R.
Bradshaw, Timothy
Brakke, David Bernhard
Bramsen, Paul D.
Branover, Herman
Brantley, Richard E.
Bratt, James D.
Brawley, Robert L.
Brenner, Michael
Brent, Allen
Breslin, Jimmy

Brett, Donna W(hitson)
Brett, Edward T(racy)
Breward, Ian
Brewer, Carolyn
Bridgers, Lynn
Britt, Brian (Michael)
Brockington, J(ohn) L(eonard)
Bronner, Leila Leah
Brooke, Rosalind B(eckford)
Brooks, Peter Newman
Broom, Neil D.
Brown, Christopher Boyd
Brown, Dale W.
Brown, H. Jackson
Brown, Jennifer S. H.
Brown, Michael F(obes)
Brown, Michelle P(atricia)
Brown, Robert G(oodell)
Brown, Steven Preston
Browne-Miller, Angela
Browning, Wilfrid (Robert
  Francis)
Broyles, Anne
Bruce, Steve
Bruce Lockhart, Robin
Brussat, Mary Ann
Bryant, Robert Harry
Bube, Richard Howard
Buchanan, Colin (Ogilvie)
Buck, Christopher
Buckley, Cornelius M(ichael)
Buckley, Francis Joseph
Budde, Michael L(eo)
Buechner, (Carl) Frederick
Buhner, Stephen Harrod
Bulkeley, Kelly
Bull, Malcolm
Bundesen, Lynne
Bunt, Gary R.
Burnett, Amy Nelson
Burns, Richard Gordon
Burr, David (Dwight)
Burtchaell, James Tunstead
Burton, Thomas G(len)
Bush, M(ichael) L(accohee)
Butler, Anthea D.
Butler, Jon
Butler, Judith P.
Butler, Rex D.
Bütz, Jeffrey J.
Bye, Beryl (Joyce Rayment)
Bynum, Caroline Walker
Byrd, James P.
Cahill, Lisa Sowle
Cairns, Scott
Calian, Carnegie Samuel
Callahan, Daniel (J.)
Callahan, Nelson J.
Campbell, Colleen Carroll
Campbell, James T.
Campling, Christopher Russell
Canham, Elizabeth
Cannell, Fenella
Cannon, Dolores Eilene
Capitan, William H(arry)
Caplan, Mariana
Capon, Robert Farrar

Carey, George (Leonard)
Carey, Patrick W.
Carling, Paul J.
Carlson, John V.
Carmichael, Liz
Carnley, Peter Frederick
Carpenter, Mary Wilson
Carr, David McLain
Carson, Anne (Regina)
Carson, Benjamin S(olomon)
Carson, D(onald) A(rthur)
Carter, J. Kameron
Carter, Warren
Cartledge, Mark J.
Carwardine, Richard J(ohn)
Cassidy, Michael
Castelli, Elizabeth A.
Castle, Alfred L.
Catherwood, (Henry) Frederick
  (Ross)
Catherwood, Christopher
Cauthen, (W.) Kenneth
Cell, Edward Charles
Cepero, Helen
Cessario, Romanus
Chadwick, Owen
Chandler, Daniel Ross
Chang, Maria Hsia
Charlesworth, James H(amilton)
Charmé, Stuart Zane
Charny, Israel Wolf
Chase, Steven
Chatellier, Louis
Chaves, Mark (Alan)
Chayat, Sherry
Chazan, Robert
Cheripko, Jan
Cherry, Charles Conrad
Cherry, Kittredge
Cherry, Mark J.
Chess, Richard
Cheyette, Bryan (Henry)
Chibnall, Marjorie McCallum
Chidester, David
Chiffolo, Anthony F.
Childs, Elizabeth C(atharine)
Chilton, Bruce
Chireau, Yvonne P.
Chodos, Robert
Chödrön, Pema
Choung, James
Christ, Carol P(atrice)
Christensen, Damascene
Christian, Carol Cathay Tuttle
Chryssavgis, John
Ciaravino, Helene
Cimino, Richard P.
Clapp, Rodney
Clapper, Gregory S(cott)
Clark, J. C. D.
Clark, Jerome
Clark, Kelly James
Clark, Mary Ann
Clark, Mary T.
Clarke, Erskine
Clayton, Mary
Clayton, Philip

Franco, Dean J.
Frankel, Ellen
Frankl, Razelle
Franklin, Robert M(ichael)
Frassetto, Michael
Frazee, Randy
Frazier, Sundee T.
Freitas, Donna
Freudenthal, Gad
Freundel, Barry
Friedmann, Yohanan
Frisbie, Charlotte J(ohnson)
Fritsch, Albert J(oseph)
Frost, Stanley Brice
Fryer, Jonathan
Fulton, Joe B.
Furnish, Victor Paul
Gabhart, Ann Houchin
Gabriel, Theodore P. C.
Gabriel (Loving), Kathryn (Ann)
Gaddis, Michael
Gal, Laszlo
Gallagher, Winifred
Garfunkel, Trudy
Gascoigne, John
Gaskin, J. C. A.
Gatch, Milton McC
Gateley, Edwina
Gauvreau, Michael
Gay, Peter
Geaves, Ronald Allan
Gelek, Ngawang
Gelernter, David (Hillel)
Geller, Jay Howard
Gellman, Marc
George, Robert P.
Gerassi, John
Gernet, Jacques
Gerrish, Brian Albert
Gerstenberger, Erhard S.
Gesch, Roy (George)
Gibson, Shimon
Gibson, Thomas
Gilbert, John Raphael
Gilbert, Martin
Gilchrist, Roberta
Gilkes, Cheryl Townsend
Gill, LaVerne McCain
Gill, Sam D.
Gilley, Sheridan (Wayne)
Gillis, Chester
Gillman, Abigail
Gilmour, Michael J.
Glancy, Jennifer A.
Glazier, Stephen D.
Gleason, Katherine (A.)
Glen, Frank Grenfell
Goddard, Hugh (P.)
Goff, Barbara
Gold, August
Gold, Judy
Gold, Michael
Goldin, Barbara Diamond
Goldman, Ari L.
Goldman, Karla
Goldman, Marshall I(rwin)
Goldstein, Sidney

Gombrich, Richard Francis
González, Justo L(uis)
Gonzalez-Balado, Jose Luis
Gooch, Paul W(illiam)
Good, Deirdre Joy
Goodhue, Thomas W.
Goody, John R(ankine)
Goossen, Rachel Waltner
Gordis, Lisa M.
Gordon, Lewis Ricardo
Gordon, Stewart
Gore, Ariel
Gorman, Lyn
Gorringe, Timothy
Gosline, Andrea Alban
Gosling, J. C. B.
Gottlieb, Annie
Götz, Ignacio L.
Gould, Kevin
Gow, Andrew Colin
Graff, Dale E(dward)
Graham, Billy
Graham, Gael
Graham, W(illiam) Fred
Graham, Ysenda (May) Maxtone
Grant, Patrick
Gratus, Jack
Gray, Francine du Plessix
Gray, John
Greeley, Andrew (Moran)
Green, Arthur
Green, John C.
Green, Kenneth Hart
Green, R. P. H.
Greenlee, J(acob) Harold
Greer, John Michael
Greet, Kenneth Gerald
Greetham, David
Gregory, Tobias
Grehan, Ida
Grenholm, Cristina
Greshake, Gisbert
Gresser, Seymour
Gretsch, Mechthild
Griffith, Arthur Leonard
Griffith, Jim
Griffiths, Paul J.
Grigg, Ray
Groseclose, Barbara
Gross, Ernie
Grossman, Dina
Gubar, Susan (David)
Gudorf, Christine E.
Guillen, Michael (Arthur)
Gulbekian, Sevak E(dward)
Habgood, John Stapylton
Habito, Ruben L.F.
Hagen, Steve
Hagerty, Barbara Bradley
Haight, Roger
Halbertal, Tova Hartman
Hall, Thor
Hall, Timothy L.
Halliday, Nigel Vaux
Hallo, William W.
Halpin, Marlene
Hamilton, Alastair

Hamilton, Bernard
Hammes, John A.
Hammoudi, Abdellah
Hampson, (Margaret) Daphne
Hand, Geoffrey Joseph Philip
Handy, Lowell K.
Hansen, Ann Natalie
Haqqani, Husain
Harakas, Stanley Samuel
Harder, Leland
Harding, Les
Hardy, B. Carmon
Hare-Duke, Michael (Geoffrey)
Harline, Craig E.
Harpur, Tom
Harris, Fredrick C.
Harris, James F.
Harris-Lacewell, Melissa Victoria
Harrison, Kathryn
Harrow, Judy
Harvey, (Brian) Peter
Harvey, Robert C.
Harvey, Thomas
Hastorf, Christine Ann
Haught, James A(lbert)
Haughton, Rosemary Luling
Hauptman, Judith
Hausmann, Winifred Wilkinson
Hawley, John C(harles)
Hayden, Eric William
Haynes, Stephen R.
Haywood, Gar Anthony
Headley, John M.
Hearn, Chester G.
Heim, S. Mark
Heller, Marvin J.
Helminski, Kabir
Hemming, Laurence Paul
Hemphill, Kenneth S.
Hendricks, Obery M(ack)
Hendricks, Patricia
Hendrix, Scott H.
Herrick, James A.
Hertz, Deborah
Heschel, Susannah
Heslam, Peter S.
Hess, Mary E.
Hess, Richard S.
Hewitt, W(arren) E(dward)
Hibbs, Thomas S.
Hick, John (Harwood)
Hicks, Douglas A.
Higgins, Michael W.
Hill, Charles E.
Hillis, Bryan V.
Hilsman, Gordon J.
Himelstein, Shmuel
Himka, John-Paul
Hines, Joanna
Hinn, Benny
Hinson, E. Glenn
Hinton, Michael
Hinze, Bradford E.
Hirota, Dennis
Hirschman, Jack
Hitchens, Peter Jonathan
Hittinger, Russell (F.)

Hodgson, Peter C.
Hoedemaker, Bert
Hoezee, Scott E.
Hoff, B. J.
Hoffman, Ronald
Hoffman, Valerie J.
Hogg, David S.
Holifield, E. Brooks
Holloway, Richard (Frederick)
Holmes, Arthur F(rank)
Holte, James Craig
Holter, Knut
Honeygosky, Stephen R(aymond)
Hooker, Morna Dorothy
Hopcke, Robert H(enry)
Hopkins, Dwight N(athaniel)
Hopkins, Jasper
Hopkins, Mary R(ice)
Horgan, John
Horsley, Lee
Horsley, Richard A.
Horton, Michael Scott
Hostetter, Joyce Moyer
Houghton, John T(heodore)
Houlbrooke, Ralph (A.)
Hovannisian, Richard G.
Howard, David M.
Howard, Thomas Albert
Howatch, Susan
Howe, Leo
Howell, John Christian
Howsam, Leslie
Hsu, Albert Y.
Hubbard, Steve (Albert)
Hudak, Michal
Hudnut, Robert K.
Hudnut-Beumler, James David
Huff, Toby E.
Hughes, Gerard J.
Hughes, Richard T(homas)
Hull, John M.
Hull, William E(dward)
Hunnicutt, Benjamin Kline
Hunt, Lynn (Avery)
Hur, Nam-lin
Hurtado, Larry W.
Hussey, Patricia (Ann)
Hutton, Ronald
Hvidt, Niels Christian
Ilesanmi, Simeon O.
Inch, Morris Alton
Ingram, Paul O.
Inkpen, Mick
Irion, Mary Jean
Isaacs, Ronald (Howard)
Isitt, Larry R.
Izzi Dien, Mawil
Jackman, Stuart (Brooke)
Jackson, Eve
Jackson, William J(oseph)
Jacobs, Alan
Jacobs, Andrew S.
Jacobs, Jack L.
Jacobs, Steven L(eonard)
Jacobsen, David
Jacobsen, Douglas G.
Jaffin, David

James, Jamie
Janzen, David
Jarvis, William E.
Jeeves, Malcolm
Jeffreys, Derek S.
Jeffries, Don
Jelen, Ted G.
Jenkins, David L.
Jenkins, Philip
Jensen, David H.
Jepson, Jill
Jiang, Tao
Jinpa, Thupten
Joas, Hans
Johns, Richard Alton
Johnson, Elizabeth A.
Johnson, Fenton
Johnson, Freddie Lee
Johnson, Galen K.
Johnson, John L.
Johnson, Sara Raup
Johnson, Sherrie
Johnson, William Stacy
Johnston, William Murray
Jones, Constance
Jones, Laurie Beth
Jones, Naomi Brooks
Jones, Norman (Leslie)
Jones, Richard Granville
Jones, Tony H.
Jordan, Mark D.
Joy, Donald Marvin
Kaartinen, Marjo
Kagan, Shelly
Kaiser, Ward L(ouis)
Kaltner, John
Kamil, Neil D.
Kappes, Marcianne
Karetzky, Patricia E(ichenbaum)
Kari, Daven M(ichael)
Katz, David
Katz, Steven T(heodore)
Kauffman, Stuart Alan
Kaufmann, Dovid Yisroel Ber
Kavanagh, Julie
Kearns, Lionel (John)
Keeble, Neil H(oward)
Keefauver, Larry
Keeler, Robert F.
Keen, Sam
Kelemen, Julie
Kellenberger, J(ames)
Keller, Timothy
Kelley, Alexia
Kellner, Menachem
Kemp, Penn
Kemsley, Deen
Kendrick, Stephen
Kenney, Charles
Kenney, Jeffrey T.
Kent, Carol
Kent, Eliza F.
Kent, Homer Austin
Kent, Peter C.
Kenton, Warren
Ker, Ian (Turnbull)
Kereszty, Roch A.

Keshavarz, Fatemeh
Kessler, Edward
Khan, Aisha
Khan, Hasan-Uddin
Khare, R(avindra) S.
Khoroche, Peter (Andrew)
Kiblinger, Kristin Beise
Kidd, Thomas S.
Kidwell, Clara Sue
Kim, In S(oo)
Kim, Rebecca Y.
Kimbrough, S. T.
King, Barbara J.
King, Karen L.
King, Nicholas
King, Philip J.
King, Sallie B.
Kinnaman, David
Kinnaman, Gary D.
Kirby, Michael Roger
Kirkland, Russell
Kirkley, Evelyn A(nne)
Kirkwood, Annie
Kiser, John W.
Kisly, Lorraine
Klauck, Hans-Josef
Klein, Anne Carolyn
Klein, Josephine (F. H.)
Klein, Zoe
Klempner, Mark
Kling, David W.
Knight, D(avid) M(arcus)
Knight, Mark J.
Knopp, Lisa
Knuth, Donald E.
Koch, Ebba
Kohn, Livia
Korb, Scott
Kornblatt, Judith Deutsch
Kornfield, Jack
Korngold, Jamie S.
Kort, Wesley A.
Korzen, Chris
Kovel, Joel
Kowalski, Gary A.
Kraft, Robert A(lan)
Kraft, William F.
Kramer, Martin
Krentz, Edgar Martin
Kressel, Neil J.
Krieg, Robert Anthony
Kripal, Jeffrey J.
Kritzler, Ed
Kroll, Jerome
Krondorfer, Björn
Kuchar, Gary
Kuefler, Mathew
Kugle, Scott
Kuhns, Elizabeth
Kuntz, John Kenneth
Kurian, George Thomas
Kurzman, Charles
Kushner, Harold S.
Kushner, Lawrence
Lachman, Seymour P.
Lamb, Ramdas
Lambert, Frank T.

Lamphear, John
Lams, Victor
Lang, Judith
Langdon, E(sther) Jean Matteson
Langer, Erick D.
Larsen, Timothy
Lash, N. L. A.
Latourelle, René
Lattin, Don
Lattis, James M.
Lauder, Robert E(dward)
Laursen, John Christian
Lawrence, Bruce B.
Lawrence, C(lifford) H(ugh)
Layton, Bentley
Lazar, Lance Gabriel
Lazenby, Edith P.
Leaman, Oliver
Lee, Dorothy A.
Lee, Jennifer
Lee, Tommy W.
Leech, Kenneth
Lefebure, Leo D.
Leff, Gordon
Leggett, Richard G.
Lehfeldt, Elizabeth A.
Lehrer, Stanley
Lemon, Rebecca
Lentz, John C(layton)
Leonard, Amy Elmore
Leonard, Bill J.
Lerner, Robert E(arl)
Leventhal, Judith
Levin, Gerald
Levin, Michael (Graubart)
Levin, Yuval
Levine, Amy-Jill
LeVine, Mark
Levinson, Jay
Lewis, Jack Pearl
Lewis, James R.
Licht, H. William (Bill)
Liebert, Elizabeth
Liebeschuetz, John Hugo W. G.
Lief, Judith L.
Lienesch, Michael
Lindsay, D. Michael
Lindvall, Michael L(loyd)
Lindvall, Terry R.
Linnea, Ann
Linzey, Andrew
Lippy, Charles H(oward)
Lister, R(ichard) P(ercival)
Locke, Hubert G.
Lockerbie, D(onald) Bruce
Loehr, Davidson
Lofton, Ramona
London, Charles
Long, Carolyn Morrow
Long, D. Stephen
Long, Edward Leroy
Long, Eugene Thomas
Long, Thomas G.
Losch, Richard R.
Lotz, Anne Graham
Loudon, Mary
Louër, Laurence

Lovett, Bobby L.
Lowe, Ben(no P.)
Loxley, James
Lucado, Max (Lee)
Ludwikowski, Rett R.
Lund, Gerald N.
Lunde, Paul
Lundin, Anne
Lundin, Roger
Luria, Keith P.
Luz, Ulrich
Lynch, Michael
Lyon, David
Lyons, Gabe
Mabbett, Ian William
MacDonald, Hope
MacEoin, Denis
MacGregor, Neil
MacKenzie, Cameron A.
Madigan, Patrick
Madsen, Susan A(rrington)
Magida, Arthur J.
Maher, Eamon
Mahmood, Saba
Maier, Paul Luther
Majid, Anouar
Malak, Amin
Malloch, Theodore Roosevelt
Malone, Mary T.
Mann, Charles F.
Manning, Christel (J.)
Mansbridge, Francis
Mansfield, Nick
March, Wallace Eugene
Margariti, Roxani Eleni
Margolf, Diane C.
Marion, Jean-Luc
Markham, Ian Stephen
Marks, Richard
Marlett, Jeffrey D.
Marotti, Arthur F(rancis)
Marrone, Steven P(hillip)
Marsh, Charles R.
Marshall, Christopher D(avid)
Marshall, Paul A.
Martin, Dale B.
Martin, David Alfred
Martin, Julie (Breyer)
Martin, Roger H(arry)
Martin, Troy
Martinez, D. P.
Marty, Martin E.
Masalha, Nur
Mason, Jim
Massa, Mark S(tephen)
Massey, James Earl
Mast, Gerald J.
Mathieson, Donald Lindsay
Matovina, Timothy M.
Matson, Wallace I.
Matur, Bejan
Maxwell, Jaclyn L.
May, Henry F(arnham)
Mayfield, Sue
Mazrui, Ali Al('Amin)
Mazzonis, Querciolo Odoardo
McBrien, Richard P(eter)

McCall, Richard D.
McClain, Lisa
McClelland, Vincent Alan
McCloud, Sean
McCullough, Donald W.
McCullough, Michael E.
McDaniel, Charles
McDannell, Colleen
McDonald, J. I(an) H.
McDonald, Patricia M.
McDonnell, Kevin Lee
McFeely, Eliza
McGee, Terence Gary
McGowan, Mark George
Mcgreevy, John T.
McHugh, John (Francis)
McIntire, C(arl) T(homas)
McKanan, Dan Patrick
McKibben, Bill
McKnight, Stephen A.
McKown, Delos B.
McLaughlin, Corinne
McNeal, Patricia
McPhee, Martha (A.)
McQuain, Jeffrey Hunter
Meacock, Heather
Meagher, Timothy J.
Medway, Gareth J.
Meeks, Wayne A.
Megivern, James J(oseph)
Mehta, Gita
Melnick, Ralph
Melosh, Barbara
Meltzer, David
Menache, Sophia
Mendenhall, George Emery
Menon, Ritu
Mentzer, Raymond A.
Mernissi, Fatima
Mesle, C. Robert
Messer, Donald E(dward)
Messer, Richard
Messori, Vittorio
Meyer, Charles Robert
Meynell, Hugo A(nthony)
Michael, George J.
Mieth, Dietmar
Mikalson, Jon D.
Milbank, (Alasdair) John
Miles, Jack
Miles, Leland
Milis, Ludo(vicus) J. R.
Millard, Alan Ralph
Millet, Robert L.
Min, Anselm K.
Minar, Barbra (Goodyear)
Mindell, Amy (Kaplan)
Mintz, Alan L.
Miscamble, Wilson D.
Mitchell, Chris
Mitchell, Nathan
Mitson, Eileen N(ora)
Moberg, David O.
Moen, Matthew C.
Moerman, D. Max
Moffett, Samuel Hugh
Mohr, Richard D(rake)

Mol, Johannis (Hans) J(acob)
Mollenkott, Virginia Ramey
Monda, Antonio
Monk, Robert C.
Montague, George T(homas)
Moore, Andrew S.
Moore, Carey Armstrong
Moore, Dinty W.
Moore, James T(almadge)
Moore, Peter N.
Moore, Philip N(icholas)
Moore, Stephanie Perry
Moore, T. M.
Moorhead, John (Anthony)
Morey, Ann Janine
Morgan, Kimberly J.
Morgan, Michael L.
Morimoto, Anri
Morinis, Alan
Morris, Lynn
Morrison, Martha A.
Morriss, Frank
Mosley, Nicholas
Mosley, Steven
Mould, Daphne D. C. Pochin
Moussalli, Ahmad S.
Moynahan, Brian
Moynihan, Michael
Moyser, George H.
Muddiman, John
Mueller, Joan
Mullan, David George
Mullett, John St. Hilary
Mullin, Robert Bruce
Murdoch, Brian (Oliver)
Murdoch, Norman H.
Murphy, (Gavin) Martin (Hedd)
Murray, Elaine
Murrell, Nathaniel S(amuel)
Murren, Doug(las)
Musacchio, George
Musgrove, Frank
Myers, Bill
Myss, Caroline
Nakash, Yitzhak
Nally, Susan W.
Napier, Nancy J.
Nasr, Seyyed Hossein
Nathanson, Paul
Nation, Mark
Nation, Richard F.
Nazir-Ali, Michael
Needleman, Jacob
Neeld, Elizabeth Harper
Nelson, Brent
Nelson, Geoffrey Kenneth
Nelson, Keith L(eBahn)
Nepstad, Sharon Erickson
Nersessian, V(rej) N.
Neuberger, Julia
Neufeld, Thomas R.
Neville, Robert C(ummings)
Ni Hua-Ching
Nichols, John Gordon
Nichols, Stephen J.
Nicholson, E(rnest) W(ilson)
Niditch, Susan

Niebuhr, Gustav
Nielsen, Niels Christian
NightMare, M. Macha
Nikkel, David H.
Nineham, Dennis Eric
Noble, Kathleen
Noltingk, Bernard Edward
Nomani, Asra Q.
Nomani, Farhad
Norman, Edward R(obert)
Norris, Pamela
Northrop, Douglas
Novak, Jana
Novak, Michael
Nugent, (Donald) Christopher
Nuland, Sherwin
O'Brien, David M(ichael)
O'Collins, Gerald Glynn
O'Connell, Laurence J.
O'Connell, Marvin R(ichard)
O'Doherty, Malachi
O'Donovan, Oliver
O'Hanlon, Michael E(dward)
O'Hara, David
O'Malley, Vincent (J.)
O'Murchu, Diarmuid
Ochs, Vanessa (L.)
Ocker, Christopher (Michael)
Ogletree, Thomas Warren
Olasky, Marvin
Oldenburg, Ray
Oldmixon, Elizabeth Anne
Olitzky, Kerry M.
Olivelle, Patrick
Olsen, Brad
Olsen, Mark Andrew
Olson, Jeannine E.
Olson, Laura R.
Olson, Steve E.
Olupona, Jacob K.
Oppenheim, Micha Falk
Orme, Nicholas
Ormerod, Neil
Ortenberg, Veronica
Osborn, David (D.)
Osen, James L.
Osmer, Richard Robert
Ostrander, Rick
Ottenberg, Simon
Ove, Robert S.
Oved, Yaacov
Overman, Dean L.
Packer, James Innell
Padel, Ruth
Paden, William E.
Padovano, Anthony T.
Pagels, Elaine
Painter, John
Pal, Pratapaditya
Paldiel, Mordecai
Palmer, Bryan D(ouglas)
Palmer, Catherine
Palmer, Martin (Giles)
Parfitt, Tudor (Vernon)
Parfitt, Will
Park, Timothy K.
Parker, D(avid) C.

Parker, Gary E.
Parker, Thomas (Henry Louis)
Parsons, Mikeal C.
Pascarella, Perry
Pasquarello, Michael
Paterson, Ronald (William Keith)
Patterson, George N(eilson)
Patterson, Horace L.
Paul, Tessa
Pawlikowski, John Thaddeus
Pearcey, Nancy
Pearson, Joanne (E.)
Peck, Jeffrey M.
Pecora, Vincent P.
Peden, W. Creighton
Pence, Gregory E.
Pendergast, John S.
Penn, Michael Philip
Penney, Sue
Penslar, Derek J(onathan)
Pentcheva, Bissera V.
Perry, Michael Charles
Perry, Paul
Pessar, Patricia R.
Pestana, Carla Gardina
Peters, Rudolph
Peterson, Eugene H.
Peterson, Michael L.
Pettifer, Julian
Phayer, Michael
Phillips, Jonathan P.
Phillips, Susan S.
Phillips, Timothy
Pick, Lucy K.
Pickering, David (Hugh)
Piderit, John J.
Pierard, Richard V(ictor)
Pierce, Chonda
Pinn, Anthony B(ernard)
Pinon, Nelida
Pinsky, Mark I.
Pinson, William M(eredith)
Pitluk, Adam
Plaut, Joshua Eli
Plaut, W. Gunther
Plokhy, Serhii
Plotkin, Bill
Podwal, Mark
Pogrebin, Letty Cottin
Polhemus, Robert M(ackinlay)
Polkinghorne, John Charlton
Pollack, Robert (Elliot)
Pollard, John (Richard Thornhill)
Pollock, John Charles
Poole, Elizabeth
Porten, Bezalel
Porter, Barbara Nevling
Potter, Harry (D.)
Powell, Barry B.
Powell, Yolanda White
Preston, Andrew
Price, Matthew A(rlen)
Priest, Stephen
Prime, Derek James
Prior, Charles W.A
Prior, Kenneth Francis William
Pritchard, Ray

Prokes, Mary T(imothy)
Prothero, Stephen (Richard)
Pulzer, Peter George Julius
Purcell, Anne G.
Purdy, Dwight H(illiard)
Purtill, Richard L.
Qazwini, Hassan
Quesada, Roberto
Quick, William K(ellon)
Quinn, D. Michael
Quinsey, Katherine M.
Raboteau, Albert J(ordy)
Radcliffe, Timothy
Rahe, Paul A.
Ramadan, Tariq
Ramirez, Susan E(lizabeth)
Ramsay, Frederick J.
Ramseyer, Valerie
Randall, John L(eslie)
Randall, William Lowell
Rapoport, Nessa
Rapoport, Sandra E.
Rasanayagam, Angelo
Raso, Jack
Ravitch, Frank S.
Ravitch, Norman
Rawlings, Helen
Raz, Simcha
Razzell, Mary (Catherine)
Read, Christopher
Redding, David A(sbury)
Redfield, James
Redinger, Matthew A.
Redwood, John (Alan)
Rees, Frank D.
Reeves, Faye Couch
Reeves, Thomas C.
Regehr, T(heodore) D.
Reger, Gary
Reichardt, Mary R.
Reichel, Aaron I(srael)
Reinders, Eric
Reinhart, Peter
Renard, John
Rennie, Bryan S.
Resseguie, James L.
Restall Orr, Emma
Rex, Richard
Reynolds, Thomas E.
Rhodes, Donna McKee
Rhodes, Tricia McCary
Rich, Elaine Sommers
Richard, Cliff
Richardson, James T.
Richardson, Mark
Riddell, Peter G.
Riesner, Rainer
Ringwald, Christopher D.
Rinpoche, Khandro
Rischin, Moses
Riter, Tim
Rivers, Larry E.
Roark, Dallas M.
Roberson, Houston Bryan
Robert, Dana L.
Roberts, J(ames) Deotis
Roberts, Yvonne

Robertson, C(harles) K(evin)
Robins, Glenn
Robinson, V. Gene
Robson, Roy R(aymond)
Rocha, Luis Miguel
Rodriguez, Jarbel A.
Rogers, Cindy
Rohrer, S. Scott
Rollins, Wayne Gilbert
Romano, Louis
Rooney, Lucy
Roose, Kevin
Rosenberg, Joel C.
Rosenbloom, Joseph R.
Rosenfeld, Dina
Roshwald, Mordecai
Rosman, Steven M(ichael)
Ross, Rosetta E.
Rossing, Barbara
Roth, Norman
Rottmann, Erik
Rougeau, Remy
Rounds, David
Rowell, Douglas Geoffrey
Roy, Olivier
Royal, Robert
Rozell, Mark J.
Rubenstein, Richard Lowell
Rubinoff, M. Lionel
Rudolph, Kurt
Rudy, Kathy
Ruef, John Samuel
Ruokanen, Miikka
Ruotsila, Markku
Russ, Daniel
Russell, Jeffrey Burton
Russell, Kenneth Victor
Russell, Mary D(oria)
Russell, Ronald
Rutland, Suzanne D.
Ryken, Leland
Saliba, George
Salisbury, Frank B(oyer)
Salisbury, Joyce E(llen)
Salzberg, Sharon
Sanders, Bill
Sandler, Lauren
Saner, Reg(inald Anthony)
Sanneh, Lamin
Sarna, Jonathan D(aniel)
Sarno, Ronald Anthony
Sasso, Sandy Eisenberg
Savage, Allan Maurice
Sawyer, Mary R.
Schaller, Lyle E(dwin)
Scheil, Andrew P.
Schifferdecker, Kathryn M.
Schmidt, Leigh Eric
Schmiechen, Peter
Schniedewind, William M.
Schnur, Steven
Schoen, Robert
Scholey, Arthur (Edward)
Schroeder, Gerald L.
Schroeder, Joy A.
Schryer, Frans J(ozsef)
Schubel, Vernon James

Schultz, Celia E.
Schumacher, Evelyn A(nn)
Schumacher, John N(orbert)
Schwab, George M.
Schwartz, Sanford
Schwartz, Shuly Rubin
Sciutto, Jim
Scott, Alan (B.)
Screech, M(ichael) A(ndrew)
Segal, Howard P.
Selbourne, David
Sellin, Christine Petra
Selmanovic, Samir
Selvidge, Marla J(ean)
Seymour-Jones, Carole
Shamas, Victor A.
Shapiro, Rami M.
Sharlet, Jeff
Sharma, Arvind
Shatzky, Joel
Shaw, Joseph M(inard)
Shaw, Miranda Eberle
Shaw, Russell B(urnham)
Shea, Mark P.
Shea, William M.
Sheldon, Garrett Ward
Sheldon, Joseph K(enneth)
Sherlock, Patti
Sherman, Steve (Barry)
Sherry, Patrick
Sherwin, Michael S.
Shire, Michael J.
Shraer-Petrov, David
Shreiber, Maeera Yaffa
Shuman, Joel James
Shuter, Jane Margaret
Silcott, Loma G. Davies
Simkins, Ronald A.
Simmer-Brown, Judith
Simmons, D(avid) R(oy)
Simon, Uriel
Simonetta, Joseph R.
Sinden, Donald (Alfred)
Singh, Nikhil Pal
Sinnott-Armstrong, Walter
Sita, Lisa
Sittser, Gerald L.
Skarsaune, Oskar
Skinner, Anthony David
Skinner, Stephen
Skipp, Victor (Henry Thomas)
Slawson, Douglas J.
Smalley, Stephen S(tewart)
Smith, Brian
Smith, Erin A(nn)
Smith, Gordon Roland
Smith, Gwen
Smith, James K. A.
Smith, Lori
Smith, Nicholas D.
Smith, Pamela (A.)
Smith, Ryan K.
Smith, Steven G(arry)
Smoak, Gregory E.
Smoley, Richard
Snay, Mitchell
Snell, Daniel C.

Snell, K. D. M.
Snell, Patricia
Snellgrove, David L(lewellyn)
Snyder, Graydon F.
Snyder, James D.
Sobel, Ileene Smith
Solvang, Elna K.
Sommerville, C(harles) John
Soussloff, Catherine M.
Spangler, David
Spangler, Jewel L.
Spellman, W. M.
Spencer, Jon Michael
Spretnak, Charlene
Sprinkle, Patricia Houck
Stanley, Susie Cunningham
Stark, Rodney
Steinlauf, Michael C.
Steinmann, Andrew E.
Stepaniants, Marietta
Stephens, William Peter
Sterk, Andrea
Stern, David
Stern, Gerald
Stern, Jessica Eve
Stern, Kenneth S.
Sterritt, Laurence Lux
Stevens, Susan
Stewart, Mary (Florence Elinor)
Stibbe, Mark W. G.
Stillman, Norman A(rthur)
Stingel, Janine
Stivender, Ed
Stoddard, Robert H.
Stone, Cynthia L.
Stoneman, Richard (John)
Stortz, Martha E.
Stout, Harry S.
Stow, Kenneth R.
Stravinskas, Peter M. J.
Strieder, Leon F.
Stromberg, Peter G.
Strong, Douglas M.
Stroup, George W.
Stryk, Lucien
Studdert-Kennedy, (William)
   Gerald
Sturm, Douglas E.
Stutzman, Linford L.
Sullivan, Winnifred Fallers
Sulmasy, Daniel P.
Sumner, George R.
Sumption, Jonathan
Sutton, Matthew Avery
Svartvik, Jesper
Swanson, Eric
Sward, Robert S.
Swearer, Donald K(eeney)
Sweeney, Marvin A.
Sweeney, Terrance (Allen)
Sweet, William
Swidler, Ann
Swierenga, Robert P.
Swinburne, Richard (Granville)
Switzer, Janet
Switzer, Les
Symynkywicz, Jeffrey B(ruce)

Synan, (Harold) Vinson
Szakolczai, árpád
Szekeres, Cyndy
Taheri, Amir
Taliaferro, Charles
Tanner, Kathryn
Tanner, Norman P.
Tark, Ji-il
Taylor, Allegra
Taylor, Bron Raymond
Taylor, Bruce
Taylor, Daniel (William)
Taylor, Joan E(lizabeth)
Taylor, Justin
Taylor, Larissa J(uliet)
Taylor, Mark Lewis
Taylor, Michael J(oseph)
Taylor, Sarah McFarland
Taylor, T(homas) F(ish)
Tehan, Arline Boucher
Teiser, Stephen F.
Temes, Peter S.
Temperley, Nicholas
Tenbrook, Gretchen W.
Terpstra, John
TeSelle, Eugene (Arthur)
Teter, Magda
Thatamanil, John J.
Thiemann, Ronald F.
Thiering, Barbara (Elizabeth)
Thiessen, Elmer John
Thiselton, Anthony C(harles)
Thomas, John Heywood
Thomas, Keith (Vivian)
Thomas, Lyn
Thompson, Damian
Thompson, Deanna A.
Thompson, Thomas L.
Thomson, George Henry
Thondup, Tulku
Tibbetts, Orlando L.
Tikhomirov, Vladimir I.
Till, Barry Dorn
Tirtha, Swami Sadashiva
Tisdale, Sallie
Tobias, Michael (Charles)
Tobin, Michael R.
Tolkin, Michael
Tollefsen, Christopher
Tomkins, Stephen
Topek, Susan Remick
Towne, Marian K(leinsasser)
Townsend, Craig D.
Tracy, Thomas F.
Travisano, Thomas (J.)
Treat, James
Trebilco, Paul R.
Treier, Daniel J.
Trevino, Roberto R.
Trible, Phyllis
Trifkovic, Serge
Trimiew, Darryl M.
Troy, Aidan
Truman, Ruth
Tsomo, Karma Lekshe
Tucker, Judy H.
Tucker, William Edward

Tully, (William) Mark
Turnbull, Stephen (Richard)
Turner, Richard Brent
Tutu, Desmond M(pilo)
Tyson, Joseph B.
Urch, Elizabeth
Utter, Glenn H.
Vahanian, Gabriel
van der Toorn, Karel
van Der Ven, Johannes A.
Van Eenwyk, John R.
van Huyssteen, J. Wentzel
Van Raden, Kristine
Vance, Laura L.
Vanderkam, James C(laire)
Vaughan, Richard Patrick
Vaughn, Ellen Santilli
Vermes, Géza
Versényi, Adam
Versluis, Arthur
Vicchio, Stephen (John)
Vidmar, John C.
Vigée, Claude (Andre Strauss)
Villafane, Eldin
Villasmil, Omar (Santiago)
Vincent, John James
Viney, Donald Wayne
Visotzky, Burton L.
Vital, David
Vittitow, Mary L(ou)
von Kellenbach, Katharina
Voss, Sarah (Henderson)
Wabuda, Susan
Wadell, Paul J(oseph)
Wahrman, Dror
Wainwright, Geoffrey
Waite, Michael P(hillip)
Wakefield, James L.
Waldman, Mark Robert
Walker, Benjamin
Walker, Joel Thomas
Walker, Kenneth Roland
Walker, Paul E(rnest)
Walker, Robert
Wall, James M(cKendree)
Wallace, B. Alan
Wallace, Catherine M(iles)
Wallace, Mark I.
Wallace, Vesna A.
Walsh, P(atrick) G(erard)
Walters, James W.
Wandel, Lee Palmer
Ward, (John Stephen) Keith
Ward, Elizabeth Honor
Ware, Kallistos
Warne, Randi R(uth)
Warner, Brad
Watson, Clyde
Watson, Donald
Wauzzinski, Robert A.
Weaver-Gelzer, Charlotte
Webb, Stephen H.
Weir, Ben(jamin M.)
Weir, David A.
Weiss, Avraham
Weiss, Raymond L.
Weissbach, Lee Shai

Wellington, Jean Susorney
Wells, Melanie
Wendling, Ronald C(harles)
Wenger, Beth S.
Wengert, Timothy J.
Wenham, David
Wernick, Andrew (Lee)
West, Cornel (Ronald)
Westmeier, Karl-Wilhelm
Wetzel, James
Wexler, Jay D.
Whalin, W. Terry
What, Leslie
Wheeler, Penny Estes
Whelan, Irene
Whitcomb, John C(lement)
White, Carolinne
White, David Gordon
White, Peter (O. G.)
White, Phillip M.
White, Stephen E.
Whitfield, Roderick
Whitlock, Luder (G.)
Wicker, Brian John
Wiebe, Katie Funk
Wiener, Nancy H.
Wiesel, Elie
Wiktorowicz, Quintan
Wile, Mary Lee
Wiley, Tatha
Wilhoit, James C.
Wilkinson, Bruce H.
Williams, Duncan Ryûken
Williamson, Denise
Williford, (G.) Craig
Willimon, William H(enry)
Willis, Alan Scot
Wills, Garry
Wilson, A(ndrew) N.
Wilson, Barrie A.
Wilson, Peter H.
Wilson, Stephen G.
Wingerter, J. Richard
Winner, Lauren F.
Winship, Michael P.
Winter, David Brian
Wise, Robert L.
Wiseman, James A.
Witham, Larry
Witherington, Ben
Wodhams, Jack
Wodzi ski, Marcin
Woell, Edward J.
Wogaman, J(ohn) Philip
Woiwode, Larry (Alfred)
Wold, Donald J.
Wolf, Kenneth Baxter
Wolfe, Tom
Wolverton, Cheryl
Wolverton, Robert E.
Wood, Ralph C.
Wouk, Herman
Wright, N. T(om)
Wright, Theodore Paul
Wright, Vinita Hampton
Wronsky, Gail (F.)
Wubbels, Lance

Yarbrough, Stephen R.
Yarnold, Barbara M(aria)
Yates, Nigel
Yong, Amos
Young, Bette Roth
Young, Glennys
Youngblood, Ronald Fred
Youngholm, Thomas
Yu, Anthony C.
Zacharias, Ravi K.
Zatti, Sergio
Ziefle, Helmut W(ilhelm)
Zimmerman, Earl
Zimmermann, Arnold Walter
Zimmermann, Jens
Ziolkowski, Eric J(ozef)
Zorach, Rebecca
Zornberg, Avivah Gottlieb
Zucchi, John E.
Zürcher, Erik-Jan

Third World

Accad, Evelyne
Agyeman, Opoku
Allen, Philip M(ark)
Allen, Roberta
Anees, Munawar Ahmad
Arnold, Guy
Bailey, Frederick George
Baillie, Allan
Bain, Kenneth (Ross)
Bickford-Smith, Vivian
Bina, Cyrus
Brainard, Cecilia Manguerra
Braveboy-Wagner, Jacqueline
  Anne
Brett, Edward T(racy)
Brook, Timothy (James)
Burkey, Stan
Carbo, Nick
Choudhury, Masudul Alam
Clark, Andrew F.
Clifford, Mary Louise
Cohen, Robin
Collison, Kerry B(oyd)
Cotman, John Walton
Crozier, Brian
Crush, Jonathan
Darwish, Adel
de Costa, Elena M.
Deats, Richard L.
Donaldson, Loraine
Drèze, Jean
Euba, Femi
Eviota, Elizabeth Uy
Fieldhouse, David K(enneth)
Finnegan, William (Patrick)
Fisher, Angela
Flint, John Edgar
Fryer, Jonathan
Fukuda, Haruko
Fukuyama, Francis
Girling, John (Lawrence Scott)
Goodman, Melvin A.
Gordon, Lewis Ricardo

Burch, Joann J(ohansen)
Burghardt, Linda
Burns, Khephra
Burton, Anthony
Burton, John Andrew
Butler, Geoff
Butler, Linda
Cahill, Tim
Calder, Martin
Calder, Nigel (David Ritchie)
Campbell, James
Campbell, James T.
Canfield, Jack
Canin, Ethan
Cannon, Eileen E(mily)
Capriolo, Paola
Carr, J(ames) Revell
Carrier, Thomas J.
Carter, W(illiam)
Carton, Bernice
Carver, Norman Francis
Chai, May-lee
Chalker, Sylvia
Chamberlain, Lesley
Chaney, Edward (Paul de Gruyter)
Chard, Judy (Gordon)
Charlier, Roger Henri
Charlwood, D(onald) E(rnest
  Cameron)
Chen, Patrizia
Choyce, Lesley
Christmas, Linda (Irene)
Chu, Miyoko
Churchill, E. Richard
Clabough, Casey Howard
Clark, Andrew F.
Cleare, John S.
Cleveland-Peck, Patricia
Cline, Lynn Hunter
Cody, Robin
Cohen, Morton N(orton)
Cole, Barry
Cole, Robert
Collins, Julie (Hubbard)
Confer, Dennis W.
Connelly, Karen
Conway, Diana C(ohen)
Cooke, John Peyton
Cooper, Derek (Macdonald)
Cooper, Paulette
Copeland, Anne P.
Corbett, Holly C.
Corona, Laurel
Coster, Graham
Cox, Richard (Hubert Francis)
Cox, Vic
Craats, Rennay
Cranfield, Ingrid
Crosby, Harry W(illiams)
Crossette, Barbara
Crossley-Holland, Kevin (John
  William)
Cudmore, Dana (D.)
Curiel, Jonathan
Cusick, Heidi Haughy
Dallas, Gregor
Dallas, Roland

Daly, Leo (Arthur)
Daniels, Anthony
David, Thomas
Davidson, Robyn
Davies, Hunter
Davis, Kenneth C.
Davis, Patrick
Davison, Liam
Dawidoff, Nicholas
Day, Edward C.
de Blasi, Marlena
de Blij, Harm J(an)
Deane-Drummond, Anthony
  (John)
DeAngelis, Camille
DeLyser, Dydia
Dendinger, Roger E.
Dervaes, Claudine
Dewart, Gilbert
Dibble, J(ames) Birney
Dickinson, Matt
Dietz, Maribel
Dilsaver, Lary M.
Dimbleby, Josceline (Rose)
DiSilvestro, Roger L.
Dobrin, Lyn
Docherty, Paddy
Doerr, Anthony
Doherty, Craig A.
Dolle, Raymond F.
Doudera, Vicki
Douglas, John (Frederick James)
Downer, Lesley
Dudley, Ellen
Dufresne, Jim
Duggleby, John
Dumas, Firoozeh
Duncan, William (Robert)
Dunlop, Eileen (Rhona)
Dwyer, Augusta (Maria)
Dyson, John
Eason, Alethea
Easton, Laird M.
Ede, Piers Moore
Edwards, Brendan Frederick R.
Edwards, Harvey
Edwards, Philip (Walter)
Egan, Ferol
Egan, Timothy
Ehret, Terry
Eisenberg, Robert
Eldon, Kathy
Elfers, James E.
Ellenblum, Ronnie
Ellis, Jerry
Ellis, Markman
Ellis, Royston
Elsy, (Winifred) Mary
Ely, David
Emmet, Alan
Emory, Jerry
England, Chris
Enslow, Sam
Ershler, Phil
Ershler, Susan
Etter, Dave
Fagan, Brian Murray

Fallowell, Duncan (Richard)
Farley, David
Fausett, David
Faust, Jeff
Feldman, Lynne B.
Felton, R. Todd
Ferguson, Gary
Ferguson, Will
Fermor, Patrick (Michael) Leigh
Fernández-Armesto, Felipe (Fer-
  min Ricardo)
Field, Edward
Fiennes, Ranulph
Filey, Mike
Finch, Peter
Finkelstein, Max W.
Firkatian, Mari A.
Fishback, Mary
Fishlock, Trevor
Fitch, Noel Riley
Fitzgerald, Astrid
FitzRoy, Charles (Patrick Hugh)
Fitzsimons, Cecilia (A. L.)
Flayhart, William Henry
Flinn, Kathleen
Flint, John Edgar
Foulkes, (Albert) Peter
Foy, George Michelsen
France, Miranda
Francis, Clare
Frank, Dorothea Benton
Fraser, Conon
Frayn, Michael
Frazier, Charles (Robinson)
Frazier, Donald S(haw)
Freed, Lynn
Freudenheim, Ellen
Fussell, Paul
Futcher, Jane P.
Gabriel, Jüri (Evald)
Gabriel (Loving), Kathryn (Ann)
Gage, Eleni N.
Gall, Sandy
Gallagher, Tess
Gallaher, (William) Rhea
Galt, George
Garber, Anne
Gardner, Katy
Gardner, Mark L(ee)
Geddes, Gary
Gehrig, Klaus
Geldard, Richard G.
Gentile, Olivia
Gentleman, David
Gesch, Roy (George)
Gibb, Lorna
Gifford, Rob
Gilbert, Harriett
Gilbert, John Raphael
Gill, A. A.
Gilman, George G.
Gilmour, David
Glazier, Stephen D.
Glen, Frank Grenfell
Glendening, John
Gold, Janet N(owakowski)
Goldstone, Patricia

Gooch, Brad
Goodavage, Maria
Goodman, Richard
Gordon, Sheila
Gordon, William A.
Gore, Ariel
Gough, Laurie
Grant, Neil
Grant-Adamson, Lesley (Hey-
  cock)
Graves, Ralph (Augustus)
Gray, Clayton
Gray, Dianne E.
Green, Jeffrey M.
Green, Timothy (S.)
Greenberg, Peter
Greenlaw, Lavinia (Elaine)
Greenside, Mark
Greenwald, Jeff
Grescoe, Paul
Grey, Beryl (Elizabeth)
Griffin, Peni R(ae)
Griffin, Steven A(rthur)
Grizzle, Ralph
Grossinger, Tania
Grossman, Dina
Grylls, Bear
Guest, Harry
Gunn, Robin Jones
Guralnick, Peter
Gurney, Alan
Gurvis, Sandra J.
Guste, Roy F(rancis)
Guy, Ray
Hager, Betty
Hagger, Nicholas
Hall, Brian
Hall, Susan Bard
Halliday, William R(oss)
Halpern, Jake
Hämäläinen, Pertti (Olavi)
Han, Suzanne Crowder
Han Suyin
Hanbury-Tenison, Robin
Hansen, Eric K.
Harnack, Curtis
Harrison, David Lakin
Harrison, Kathryn
Hart, John Fraser
Hatch, Lynda S.
Hathaway, Margaret
Hattendorf, John B(rewster)
Hauptman, Robert
Hauptman, William (Thornton)
Haynes, Duncan H(arold)
Haynes, Jim
Haynes, Sybille (Edith)
Haywood, Steve
Hazard, Ann
Heacox, Kim
Hedderwick, Mairi
Hekkanen, Ernest
Heminway, John
Henderson, Kristin
Henderson, Richard (Jud)
Henley, Arthur
Herbert, Ivor

Perkins, George (Burton)	Ryan, Craig	Stacey, Tom	Ure, John (Burns)
Pessar, Patricia R.	Ryan, Donald P.	Stambler, Irwin	Vanasse, Deb
Petro, Pamela J.	Saffer, Barbara	Stanley, Peter W(illiam)	Venables, Stephen
Pettifer, James	Sahgal, Nayantara (Pandit)	Steel, Nigel	Vincent, Norah
Peyer, Bernd C.	Salisbury, Mike	Steele, Peter	Vineyard, Jerry D.
Pfister, Patrick	Sanderlin, George	Stein, Rebecca L.	Wagener, Leon
Phillips, Caryl	Savage, (Maria) Ania	Stevenson, Matthew	Wagner, Michele R.
Philpott, Don	Sayre, Shay	Stevenson, Seth	Waldman, Stuart
Pickell, David	Scargill, David Ian	Stewart, Lucretia	Walker, Martin
Pindell, Terry	Scarlett, Elizabeth	Stewart, Sarah	Ward, Philip
Pinto, António Costa	Scherer, Migael	Stinchecum, Amanda Mayer	Ware, Jane (O.)
Pitt-Kethley, (Helen) Fiona	Schilling, Mark R.	Stone, Eric	Warren, Jeff
Pollard, John (Richard Thornhill)	Schine, Cathleen	Stonehouse, Bernard	Washburn, Stan
Pollock, John Charles	Schlosberg, Suzanne	Stoneman, Richard (John)	Wasil, Kenneth
Ponsonby, Laura	Schoenfeld, Bruce	Storey, Edward	Waterman, Jonathan
Poore, Carol	Schreiber, Joseph	Stout, Nancy	Waters, David Watkin
Pope, Hugh	Schroeder, Alan	Stowe, William W.	Waters, John F(rederick)
Potts, Rolf	Schuman, Michael A.	Strathern, Paul	Watson, Benjamin A.
Power, Patrick C.	Schwartz, Stephen (Alfred)	Streckert, Hal	Waugh, Louisa
Pownall, David	Scott, Amoret (Tanner)	Stuart, Alexander	Webster, Jason
Pressner, Amanda	Scott, David L(ogan)	Sturtevant, Katherine	Wecker, David
Preston, Diana	Scott, Kay W.	Sullivan, Michael Joseph	Weideman, Ryan
Prime, Derek James	Sealy, I(rwin) Allan	Sullivan, Randall	Weintraub, David
Pryce, Lois	Seddon, Andrew M.	Summerlin, Vernon	Wells, Ken
Pryce-Jones, David	Seed, David	Sutton, Allan	Wells, Mary Ann
Pye-Smith, Charlie	Seldon, Lynn	Swick, Thomas	Wells, Patricia
Quilter, Deborah	Seligson, Susan	Symons, Leslie John	Wels, Susan
Quindlen, Anna	Senior, Michael	Talese, Gay	West, Edward
Raban, Jonathan	Seret, Roberta	Tayler, Jeffrey	Westcott-Jones, Kenneth
Radforth, Ian	Servadio, Gaia (Cecilia Gem-malina)	Taylor, Allegra	Weston, Mark
Rajtar, Steve		Taylor, Daniel (William)	Wexler, Alan
Rake, Alan	Seth, Vikram	Taylor, Donathan	Wexler, Jay D.
Ramsey, Rebecca S.	Setzer, (Cynthia) Lynn	Taylor, Margaret	Wheeler, Kate
Rawson, Jacob	Seward, Robert (Allen)	Taylor, Michael Ray	Wheeler, Sara
Regalbuto, Robert J.	Shabazz, Jamel	Testa, Judith (Anne)	Whicker, Alan (Donald)
Reid, Robert Leonard	Shah, Sayed Tahir	Thayer, Helen	White, Dan
Rhyne, Nancy	Shalleck, David	Theobald, William F.	White, Howard
Richardson, Brian W.	Shavit, David	Theroux, Louis Sebastian	White, Kenneth
Richardson, Nigel	Sherman, Steve (Barry)	Theroux, Paul	Whiteman, Robin
Richardson, Paul	Sheward, Tamara	Theroux, Peter	Wiley, Peter (Booth)
Richie, Donald	Shirley, Shirley	Thomas, Leslie (John)	Williams, Brooke
Riddles, Libby	Sidney, Neilma	Thomas, Sue	Williams, David B.
Ridgway, John M.	Silcott, Loma G. Davies	Thomasma, Kenneth R.	Williams, Joy
Ritchie, Harry	Silverman, Robin L(andew)	Thompson, Chuck	Williams, Niall
Robb, Peter	Simeti, Mary Taylor	Thomson, Peter	Wilson, Barbara (Ellen)
Roberts, Paul William	Simmons, James C(oleman)	Thubron, Colin Gerald Dryden	Wilson, Brandon
Robertson, Ian (Campbell)	Simon, Lizzie	Thwaite, Anthony (Simon)	Wilson, Ken
Rodgers, Eugene	Simpson, Myrtle Lillias	Thybony, Scott	Wilson, Martin
Rodríguez, Andrés	Sims, Norman (Howard)	Tibbetts, Orlando L.	Wilson, Wesley M.
Roe, JoAnn	Singer, Mark	Tillinghast, Richard	Winchester, Simon
Rolde, Neil	Sirvaitis (Chernyaev), Karen (Ann)	Timmerman, Kelsey	Wise, Joe
Romano-Lax, Andromeda		Timmermans, Tricia	Wolfe, Art
Roop, Peter	Skeet, Ian	Tipton, David	Woodger, Elin
Rose, Peter I(saac)	Skidmore, Max J(oseph)	Tobias, Michael (Charles)	Woodman, David C(harles)
Rosenberg, Saralee	Skillman, Don	Tóibín, Colm	Woods, Stuart
Ross, Ellen	Skinner, Quentin (Robert Duthie)	Toksvig, Sandi	Wortsman, Peter
Ross, Kent	Skinner-Linnenberg, Virginia (M.)	Tong, Raymond	Wuori, G. K.
Roy, James Charles	Smith, Anthony	Townsend, Wendy	Wurman, Richard Saul
Royte, Elizabeth	Smith, Mark Haskell	Tracy, (John) Nicholas	Yenne, Bill
Rubinstein, Hilary (Harold)	Snow, Philip (Albert)	Travis, Anthony S(tewart)	Yockey, Hubert P(almer)
Rue, Leonard Lee	Sofer, Barbara	Travis, Frederick F.	Young, Donald R.
Rugeley, Terry	Souster, Raymond	Travis, Lucille	Young, Elizabeth
Rule, Ann	Spalding, Andrea	Trebay, Guy	Youngs, Tim
Rushdie, Salman	Spencer, Duncan	Tully, (William) Mark	Zaccaria, Jerry A.
Russell, Jeremy (Longmore)	Spender, Matthew	Turner, Brian (Lindsay)	Zimmerman, Robert
Russell, Ronald	St. George, Andrew	Turner, Jack Scott	
Russell Taylor, Elisabeth	St. James, Lyn	Turner, Marjorie Shepherd	

Trivia/Facts

Abusharaf, Rogaia Mustafa
Artell, Mike
Austin, Robyn M.
Ayres, Thomas (R.)
Bordowitz, Hank
Bryant, Mark
Caine, Michael
Dunbar-Ortiz, Roxanne
Epstein, Helen
Eshbaugh-Soha, Matthew
Fontes, Ron
French, Sean
Harding, Les
Harris, Paul
Horn, Michiel
Houck, Judith A.
Jay, Ricky
MacAdams, William
Maxford, Howard
Mogil, Cindy R.
Myint-U, Thant
Offley, Ed
Parish, James Robert
Pickering, David (Hugh)
Postman, Andrew
Poundstone, William
Raab, David
Rushing, Josh
Stillson, Alan
Underwood, Judy K.
Valentine, Fawn
Wojnarowski, Adrian

Urban Studies

Ackelsberg, Martha A.
Alaya, Flavia
Averill, Gage
Barden, Thomas
Barrie, Thomas (Matthew)
Becker, Charles M(axwell)
Bender, Thomas
Bendixson, Terence
Billson, Janet Mancini
Boskoff, Alvin
Bowser, Benjamin P(aul)
Brooks, Edwin
Brumfield, William Craft
Carter, Harold
Carver, Martin
Clubbe, John L(ouis) E(dwin)
Cohen, Thomas V.
Colfax, David (John)
Coppa, Frank John
Cox, Kevin Robert
Crowe, Norman
Cunningham, James V.
Cuomo, Mario (Matthew)
Curl, James Stevens
Darton, Eric
Davidson, Osha Gray
Dinerman, Beatrice
Downes, Bryan T(revor)
Downie, Leonard
Duhl, Leonard J.
Euchner, Charles C.

Urban Studies-*cont.*

Evans, Richard J(ohn)
Fairfield, John D.
Farmaian, Sattareh Farman
Ferrell, Jeff
Ferris, John (Stephen)
Fischel, William A.
Fix, Michael
Fraser, W. Hamish
Fuchs, Rachel G(innis)
Gallagher, Kathleen
Gilbert, Alan (Graham)
Gillespie, Angus Kress
Glazer, Nathan
Glickman, Norman J.
Goldstein, Sidney
Grant, Jill
Gutfreund, Owen D.
Hagedorn, John M.
Hamilton, Neil (W.)
Harris, Charles Wesley
Hayter, Teresa
Hewitt, W(arren) E(dward)
Hise, Greg
Homberger, Eric
Horowitz, Daniel
Horton, Frank E.
Ingham, John N.
Ireland, Patrick R(ichard)
Jackson, John N.
Jackson, Kenneth T(erry)
Jenkins, Simon
Kasinitz, Philip
Keil, Charles
Kemmis, Daniel (Orra)
Kemp, Roger L.
Kennedy, Lawrence W.
Kimura, Margaret
Kingsley, G. Thomas
Kirsch, George B(enson)
Kushner, James A(lan)
Ladd, Brian
Lappé, Frances Moore
Lloyd, Peter Cutt
Logan, Michael F.
Lotchin, Roger W.
Macedo, Stephen
Machor, James L(awrence)
Maffi, Mario
Maitland, Barry
Malone, Hank
Mandel, Brett H.
McGregor, James H. S.
McKean, Charles (Alexander)
McKenna, Marian Cecilia
McMullan, Margaret
Mead, Christopher Curtis
Meyer, Eugene L.
Michelson, William
Mingione, Enzo
Mukherjee, Rabin
Muth, Richard F(erris)
Ness, Immanuel
O'Malley, Penelope Grenoble
Oldenburg, Ray
Orlean, Susan
Owens, E(dwin) J(ohn)
Pike, David L.

Urban Studies-*cont.*

Popper, Frank James
Press, O(tto) Charles
Ravetz, Alison
Reay, Barry
Rieff, David Sontag
Risebero, Bill
Roberts, J(ames) Deotis
Robson, Brian Turnbull
Ruchelman, Leonard I.
Rybczynski, Witold
Sabar, Ariel
Safdie, Moshe
Sagalyn, Lynne B.
Saint, Andrew (John)
Schaller, Lyle E(dwin)
Schreck, Harley Carl
Segre, Roberto
Sekler, Eduard F(ranz)
Shackelford, Renae Nadine
Sharpe, William Chapman
Simmie, James (Martin)
Slayton, Robert A(llen)
Smerk, George M.
Smith, David Alexander
Spreiregen, Paul (David)
Stave, Bruce M.
Steinberg, Mark D(avid)
Steiner, Michael C.
Stretton, Hugh
Tavernor, Robert (William)
Thomas, G(regory) Scott
Thomas, John Clayton
Thomas, June Manning
Thrasher, Peter Adam
Tindall, Gillian (Elizabeth)
Valle, Teresa Del
van De Mieroop, Marc
Vincent, John James
Wästberg, Per
Watkins, William John
Weinrich, A. K. H.
Wille, Lois
Zukin, Sharon

Women's Studies And Issues

Abbott, Pamela
Abel, Emily K.
Abouzeid, Leila
Abrams, Judith Z.
Abu-Lughod, Lila
Abusharaf, Rogaia Mustafa
Accad, Evelyne
Ackelsberg, Martha A.
Ackerly, Brooke A.
Ackmann, Martha (A.)
Adair, Christy
Adair, Vivyan Campbell
Adams, Carol J.
Adamz-Bogus, S. Diane
Addonizio, Kim (Theresa)
Afkhami, Mahnaz
Agonito, Rosemary
Al-Ali, Nadje Sadig
Alaya, Flavia

Women's Studies And Issues-*cont.*

Alexander, Adele Logan
Alexander, Ruth M.
Alford, Edna
Ali, Ayaan Hirsi
Allen, Roberta
Als, Hilton
Amaki, Amalia K.
Andaya, Barbara Watson
Anderson, Elizabeth (S.)
Andes, Karen
Ansberry, Clare
Anthony, Crystal McCrary
Apple, Rima D.
Aptheker, Bettina
Armstrong, Karen (Anderson)
Arnold, Eleanor
Avakian, Arlene Voski
Awiakta, Marilou
Badami, Anita Rau
Baer, Richard K.
Baker, Christina Looper
Bal, Mieke (Maria Gertrudis)
Bancroft, Anne
Bardwick, Judith M(arcia)
Barlett, Peggy F.
Barlow, Tani E.
Baron, Beth
Barr, Patricia (Miriam)
Barreca, Regina
Bartky, Sandra Lee
Baruch, Elaine Hoffman
Baskin, Judith R.
Battersby, Christine
Bauermeister, Erica
Baumgardner, Jennifer
Beattie, L(inda) Elisabeth
Behar, Ruth
Belkin, Lisa
Bellows, Melina Gerosa
Bendroth, Margaret Lamberts
Benedict, Helen
Beneria, Lourdes
Berkovitch, Nitza
Bernikow, Louise
Biggs, Mary
Billson, Janet Mancini
Birrell, Anne (Margaret)
Blamires, Alcuin (Godfrey)
Blau, Francine D.
Blee, Kathleen M.
Blevins, Meredith
Block, Joyce
Bloom, Lisa E.
Bloom, Lynn (Marie Zimmerman)
Blundell, Sue
Bock, Gisela
Boddy, Janice
Bogin, Magda
Bolam, Robyn
Bonta, Marcia Myers
Boswell, Angela
Bourke, Dale Hanson
Bouvard, Marguerite Guzman
Bowers, Jane Palatini
Bowlby, Rachel
Brainard, Cecilia Manguerra

Women's Studies And Issues-
cont.

Women's Studies And Issues-
cont.

Women's Studies And Issues-
cont.

Women's Studies And Issues-
cont.

Price, Nancy
Prozan, Charlotte (Krause)
Purdy, Laura M.
Quinlan, Mary Lou
Quinsey, Katherine M.
Radcliffe Richards, Janet
Raeburn, Antonia
Ragoné, Heléna
Ramsay, Raylene
Rao, Aruna P.
Rapp, Rayna
Rappaport, Helen
Rech, Lindsay Faith
Reichardt, Mary R.
Restall Orr, Emma
Rich, Adrienne (Cecile)
Rich, Elaine Sommers
Richards, Amelia M.
Ridlon, Florence
Rimstead, Roxanne L.
Ring, Jennifer
Rodgers, Audrey T(ropauer)
Rogers, Deborah D(ee)
Roiphe, Katie
Rooks, Judith P.
Rooks, Noliwe M.
Rose, Phyllis
Rosenberg, Saralee
Rosenthal, Naomi B(raun)
Ross, Becki L.
Ross, Charles L(ouis)
Ross, Ellen
Rosser, Sue V(ilhauer)
Rowbotham, Sheila
Ruthchild, Rochelle Goldberg
Rutter, Virginia Beane
Rymph, Catherine E.
Saddlemyer, (Eleanor) Ann
Sadlier, Darlene J.
Samuels, Shirley
Sanchez, Sonia
Sargent, Pamela
Sawyer, Roger
Saxton, Josephine (Howard)
Sayers, Valerie
Scanlon, Jennifer
Schaef, Anne Wilson
Schein, Elyse
Schmidt, Elizabeth
Schone, Robin
Schultz, Celia E.
Schuster, Marilyn R.
Schweickart, Patrocinio P.
Scott, Margaret (Allan Bennett)
Scott, Robyn
Sears, James T(homas)
Segal, Lynne
Sellars, Jane
Selvidge, Marla J(ean)
Semyonov, Moshe
Sentilles, Sarah
Serrano, Lucienne J.
Sewell, Lisa
Sexton, Linda Gray
Shanley, Mary L(yndon)
Shannon, Elizabeth (McNelly)

Shaw, Miranda Eberle
Sheehan, Aurelie
Shehadeh, Lamia Rustrum
Sherwood, Dolly
Shevelow, Kathryn
Shogan, Colleen J.
Showalter, Elaine
Shreve, Anita
Shumaker, Peggy
Simkins, Ronald A.
Simon, Rita J(ames)
Sizemore, Christine Wick
Sklar, Kathryn Kish
Slayton, Robert A(llen)
Smith, Erin A(nn)
Smith, Marisa
Smith, Martha Nell
Smith, Patricia
Snellgrove, Laurence Ernest
Snyder, Jane McIntosh
Soffer, Olga
Sokol, Julia
Solinger, Rickie
Solvang, Elna K.
Sommers, Christina Hoff
Soper, Kate
Spar, Debora L.
Spretnak, Charlene
Sprinkle, Patricia Houck
Stacey, Judith
Stanley, Autumn
Stanley, Susie Cunningham
Staples, Robert Eugene
Stark, Evan
Steel, Gayla R(uth)
Steinberg, Blema S.
Stepp, Laura Sessions
Sterritt, Laurence Lux
Stevens, Bryna
Stevenson, Louise L.
Stockel, H. Henrietta
Stoltenberg, John (Vincent)
Stone, James S(tuart)
Stoner, K. Lynn
Strane, Susan
Sturgis, Ingrid
Sturtevant, Katherine
Suleiman, Susan Rubin
Sullivan, Sherry E.
Sullivan, Steve (Joseph)
Tallichet, Suzanne E.
Tanaka, Yukiko
Tattlin, Isadora
Tayler, Irene
Taylor, Allegra
Taylor, Helen
Taylor, Joan E(lizabeth)
Taylor, Liza Pennywitt
Teague, Frances
Tharu, Susie
Thirsk, (Irene) Joan
Thobani, Sunera
Thomas, Lyn
Thompson, Janet A(nn)
Thone, Ruth Raymond
Thorne, Barrie

Thornton, Margaret Rose
Thornton, Yvonne S.
Tokarczyk, Michelle M.
Towne, Marian K(leinsasser)
Trachtenberg, Peter
Tracy, Kristen
Tremain, Rose
Trible, Phyllis
Trimberger, E. Kay
Trinh, T. Min-Ha
Truman, Ruth
Tsomo, Karma Lekshe
Tsui, Bonnie
Tucker, Cynthia Grant
Turner, Marjorie Shepherd
Tusan, Michelle Elizabeth
Tuttle, Lisa
Twine, France Winddance
Tyrrell, Ian R(obert)
Usborne, Cornelie
Usry, Becky (S.)
Ussher, Jane M.
Valenti, Jessica
Valentis, Mary (Arensberg)
Valenze, Deborah M.
Valle, Teresa Del
Vallone, Lynne
Van Steenhouse, Andrea
Vance, Laura L.
Vanzant, Iyanla
Vargas, Margarita
Venarde, Bruce L.
Venet, Wendy Hamand
Verdon, Nicola
Vickers, Joanne F.
Vigil, James Diego
Visram, Rozina
Vitiello, Justin
Vogel, Lise
Vollendorf, Lisa
Wachtel, Eleanor
Waelti-Walters, Jennifer (Rose)
Wagner-Martin, Linda C.
Wajcman, Judy
Walker, Melissa A.
Wallace, Catherine M(iles)
Walton, Priscilla L.
Wandor, Michelene
Ward, Matthew C.
Ware, Susan
Warne, Randi R(uth)
Warner, Judith
Warner, Sharon Oard
Warnicke, Retha M.
Warren, Karen J.
Washburne, Carolyn Kott
Watson, Irene
Weber, Sandra
Weddington, Sarah (Ragle)
Weedman, Lauren
Weinrich, A. K. H.
Weisberger, Lauren
Weisman, Leslie Kanes
Weiss, Andrea
Weiss, Avraham
Weitekamp, Margaret A.

Weliver, Phyllis
Welland, Sasha Su-Ling
Wellington, Sheila W(acks)
Weltge, Sigrid W(ortmann)
Wexler, Alice (Ruth)
Wheeler, Helen Rippier
Wheeler, Penny Estes
Whelehan, Imelda
White, Evelyn C.
White, Merry (I.)
Wiener, Joshua M(ark)
Wiesner-Hanks, Merry E.
Wilde, Lyn Webster
Wilkins, Sally (E. D.)
Williams, Christine L.
Wilson, Jan Doolittle
Windle, Janice Woods
Winston-Allen, Anne
Winter, Kari J.
Wisker, Gina
Wolferman, Kristie C(arlson)
Wolff, Cynthia Griffin
Woodman, Marion (Boa)
Worsham, Lynn
Wronsky, Gail (F.)
Wu, Yenna
Yazdanfar, Farzin
Yee, Shirley J.
Yeh, Catherine Vance
Yount, Lisa
Yu, Michelle
Zaborowska, Magdalena J.
Zabus, Chantal J.
Zailckas, Koren
Zambrano, Myrna M.
Zamora, Bernice (B. Ortiz)
Zangana, Haifa
Zimmerman, Joseph Francis
Zinsser, Caroline
Zinsser, Judith P.
Zuk, Marlene

Writing/Journalism

Abbott, Tony
Aberjhani
Abresch, Peter E.
Addonizio, Kim (Theresa)
Aitchison, James
Albert, Michael
Albert, Susan Wittig
Allen, Roberta
Allington, Maynard
Allison, Amy
Allison, Will
Aloff, Mindy
Alther, Lisa
Argers, Helen
Aronie, Nancy S(lonim)
Ashe, Geoffrey Thomas
Asher, Sandy
Asim, Jabari
Asimov, Janet Jeppson
Ayittey, George B. N.

Badt, Karin L(uisa)
Bagdikian, Ben H(aig)
Bahr, Robert
Bain, David Haward
Bair, Deirdre
Baldasty, Gerald J.
Banks, Lynne Reid
Barbato, Joseph
Barker, Dennis (Malcolm)
Barnwell, William (Curtis)
Basta, Samir Sanad
Behrens, John C.
Bender, Sheila
Benedict, Elizabeth
Benedict, Helen
Bennett, Hal Z(ina)
Bennett, Holly
Bennett-England, Rodney
   (Charles)
Berck, Judith
Berg, Scott W.
Bergreen, Laurence
Berman, Jeffrey
Bernard, Andre
Bernikow, Louise
Berrigan, Daniel J.
Berry, Faith D.
Bertolino, James
Betts, Doris
Bieman, Elizabeth
Binzen, Peter (Husted)
Birstein, Ann
Bizzell, Patricia (Lynn)
Block, Lawrence
Bloom, Lynn (Marie Zimmerman)
Bogart, Eleanor A(nne)
Bok, Sissela
Bolam, Robyn
Bordowitz, Hank
Bower, Tom
Bowman, David
Boyer, Jay
Boyes, Vivien (Elizabeth)
Brampton, Sally Jane
Brand, Alice Glarden
Brett, Donna W(hitson)
Brett, Edward T(racy)
Briggs, John
Brody, Miriam
Brooks, Andrée (Nicole) Aelion
Brown, Roberta Simpson
Browne-Miller, Angela
Brugioni, Dino A.
Buchanan, Edna
Buhner, Stephen Harrod
Bundesen, Lynne
Burns, Eric
Byrne, Robert
Cairns, Scott
Calabro, Marian
Calloway, Colin G(ordon)
Casagrande, June M.
Caudill, (Charles) Edward
Cepero, Helen
Chappell, Fred(erick Davis)
Charlesworth, Monique
Checkoway, Julie

Chester, Mark (S.)
Chiarella, Tom
Chin, Justin
Christiansen, Rupert
Ciabattari, Jane
Clabough, Casey Howard
Claire, Rodger W(illiam)
Clarke, Patricia
Cleaver, Jerry
Cleveland-Peck, Patricia
Coates, Charles (K.)
Coburn, Andrew
Cockerill, A(rthur) W(illiam)
Cohen, Richard
Coleman, Deirdre
Connolly, Joseph
Cooke, William
Copeland, Peter
Costley, Bill
Craats, Rennay
Crawford, Tad
Crook, Marion
Cumming, Carman
Dace, Tish
Dandridge, Rita B(ernice)
Dawid, Annie
Day, Marele
De Villiers, Marq
Deem, James M(organ)
DeFrees, Madeline
Delano, Anthony
Delsohn, Gary
Demarco-Barrett, Barbara
Demers, David (Pearce)
Desena, Carmine
Desjarlais, John
DesRochers, Diane
Detz, Joan (Marie)
DeVincent-Hayes, Nan
Dial-Driver, Emily
Dibbell, Julian
Digby-Junger, Richard
Dils, Tracey E.
DiSalvo, Jackie
Dolle, Raymond F.
Dorman, Michael L.
Dorril, Stephen
Dorros, Arthur (M.)
Dovalpage, Teresa
Downie, Leonard
Drexler, Rosalyn
Duder, Tessa
Dufresne, John
Dyer, Joyce
Edge, Marc
Eisner, Peter (Norman)
Epstein, Gene
Etheridge, Eric
Euchner, Charles C.
Evans, James Allan S.
Faigley, Lester
Farish, Terry
Farmiloe, Dorothy
Faron, Fay
Ferris, Timothy
Figes, Eva
Fine, Richard

Finnegan, Lisa
Finnegan, William (Patrick)
Fiske, Robert H(artwell)
Flaherty, Alice W.
Fleisher, Paul
Fletcher, Ralph
Foerstel, Herbert N.
Foley, (Mary) Louise Munro
Fox, Sarah
Franco, Dean J.
Frank, Frederick S.
Freeman, Barbara M.
Freeman, Marcia S.
Frey, Julia (Bloch)
Friedman, Matthew
Friendly, Alfred
Fritts, Mary Bahr
Fritzell, Peter A(lgren)
Futterman, Enid (Susan)
Gaillard, Frye
Gale, Fredric G.
Gall, Sandy
Gardaphé, Fred L(ouis)
Gardner, Sandra
Garmaise, Freda
Garrison, Bruce
Gee, Maggie (Mary)
Geist, Bill
Gelderman, Carol (Wettlaufer)
Gerard, Philip
Giles, Frank (Thomas Robertson)
Giles, Robert Hartmann
Gill, Anton
Gillman, Peter (Charles)
Gitlin, Todd
Gjelten, Tom
Glenn, Cheryl
Godfrey, Donald G.
Gold, Jerome
Goldman, Marlene B.
Gooch, Steve
Goodman, Richard
Graham, Daniel O.
Gratus, Jack
Green, Jesse
Greenberg, Gerald S(tuart)
Greenwald, Jeff
Greenwald, Marilyn S.
Greetham, David
Griffith, Marlene
Grossinger, Tania
Grossman, Karl (H.)
Gurvis, Sandra J.
Gustafson, Sid
Guttenplan, D. D.
Guzzo, Lou(is Richard)
Haber, Karen
Hadas, Rachel
Haffenden, John
Hager, Alan
Halpern, Jake
Hamand, Maggie
Hamilton, John Maxwell
Harris, Brayton
Harrison, Sarah
Hart, JoeAnn
Hasty, Jennifer

Hatkoff, Amy
Havel, Harvey
Haynes, David
Haynes, Jane
Heffer, Simon (James)
Helmke, Gretchen
Hendry, Joy (McLaggan)
Herrington, Anne J.
Higginbotham, Jay
Hill-Miller, Katherine C(ecelia)
Hirsh, Michael
Hoar, Jere (Richmond)
Hodes, Martha
Hodgins, Jack
Hoffman, Mary (Margaret)
Hokanson, (Anthony) Drake
Horn, Tammy
Horning, Alice S.
Huddle, David
Humphrey, Carol Sue
Humphrys, Leslie George
Hutton, Frankie
Ike, Vincent Chukwuemeka
Ikenson, Ben
Isaacs, Susan
Israel, Betsy
Jackson, Marni
Janello, Amy (Elizabeth)
Jauss, David
Jenkins, Simon
Jepson, Jill
Johnson, Carla
Johnston, Anna
Jones, Alex S.
Kaler, Anne K(atherine)
Kanigel, Robert
Kantaris, Sylvia (Mosley)
Kaplan, James
Kaplan, Janet A(nn)
Kaplar, Richard T.
Karetzky, Stephen
Karlen, Neal (Stuart)
Kauffman, Michael W.
Keeler, Robert F.
Kemske, Floyd
Keneally, Thomas (Michael)
Kennedy, Rick
Kerner, Fred
King, (William) Dennis
Kleh, Cindy (L.)
Klempner, Mark
Klingenstein, Susanne
Knopp, Lisa
Koontz, Dean R(ay)
Koontz, Robin
Krashen, Stephen D.
Kraus, Joanna H.
Krimsky, George A.
Krisher, Trudy (B.)
Kroll, Virginia L(ouise)
Lambert, Page
Landrum, Gene N.
Lanham, Richard Alan
Lanouette, William (John)
Lappé, Frances Moore
Lathrop, Douglas A.
Lawlor, Clark

Lawson, Linda
Leab, Daniel Josef
Leader, Zachary
Lee, Chin-Chuan
Lee, Sharon
Leegant, Joan
Leff, David K.
Lent, John A.
Lesikar, Raymond Vincent
Levy, Jill Meryl
Lewin, Rhoda G.
Li, Guofang
Li, Leslie
Liberman, Rosette B.
Libov, Charlotte Ann
Liebovich, Louis W.
Lightfoot Sizemore, Deborah
Lindholdt, Paul J.
Lipton, Eunice
Lomazow, Steven
Longyear, Barry B.
Lord, Nancy J.
Lounsberry, Barbara
Lutz, John (Thomas)
Lyon, Elizabeth
MacDonald, Amy
Macgoye, Marjorie Oludhe
MacPherson, Andrea
Magida, Arthur J.
Magistrale, Tony
Manning, Richard Dale
Marcus, Jana
Martin, Rhona
Martinez, Joseph G. R.
Martinez, Nancy C.
Mason, Alane Salierno
Mason, Christopher
Matthiessen, Peter
Mayer, Bob
Mayer, Robert
McAlpine, Rachel (Taylor)
McCarthy, Nan
McChesney, Robert Waterman
McCoy, Max
McDonald, Ian (A.)
McElmeel, Sharron L.
McFarlane, Peter (William)
McKinney, Sally (Brown)
McPhee, John (Angus)
McQuay, Peri Phillips
McWilliam, Candia
Mehrabian, Albert
Melton, Judith
Merrill, Hugh (Davis)
Metcalf, Allan (Albert)
Metzger, Deena P.
Meyerowitz, Patricia
Michelson, Bruce (F.)
Milhorn, H. Thomas
Mnookin, Seth
Moher, Frank
Moreton, N. Edwina
Moriarty, Marilyn F(rances)
Mulcahy, Lisa
Murphy, Gregory L(eo)
Murphy, Sylvia
Musto, Michael

Natoli, Joseph
Navarra, Tova
Neel, Jasper
Neeld, Elizabeth Harper
Neighbour, Mary E.
Nelson, Carolyn W(illiamson)
Nelson, Peter N.
Nesbitt, John D.
Newman, Isadore
Nicholson, Colin
Niman, Michael I.
Nobisso, Josephine
Nuwer, Hank
O'Malley, Patrick R.
Obejas, Achy
Ochs, Vanessa (L.)
Offley, Ed
Ogden, Christopher
Olasky, Marvin
Oldfield, Michael
Olson, Gary A.
Olson, Ted
Ommundsen, Wenche
Ondego, Ogova
Orbach, Benjamin
Osborn, Susan (E.)
Overall, Christine
Owings, Alison
Packard, Robert
Pasti, Umberto
Pawlak, Mark
Payne, Daniel G.
Pearlstine, Norman
Penelope, Julia
Pesic, Peter
Peterson, Elmer
Pezzullo, Ralph
Phelps, Barry
Pickard, Nancy
Pincher, (Henry) Chapman
Pitt-Kethley, (Helen) Fiona
Ploeger, Katherine (M.)
Pogrebin, Letty Cottin
Policoff, Stephen Phillip
Polking, Kirk
Powell, Dannye Romine
Powers, Steve
Pozner, Vladimir
Pratt, John Clark
Price-Thompson, Tracy
Pullein-Thompson, Diana
Putnam, Constance E(lizabeth)
Rabinowitz, Dorothy
Radcliffe Richards, Janet
Ragen, Naomi
Raham, (R.) Gary
Ramsey, Doug(las K.)
Read, David
Reeder, Stephanie Owen
Reichel, Aaron I(srael)
Richards, Eric
Riess, Jana
Riley, Sam G.
Robinson, Spider
Rockland, Michael Aaron
Rocklin, Joanne
Rodgers, Peter

Rodríguez, Andrés
Ronell, Avital
Rosenfeld, Richard N.
Ross, Stephen M.
Rubino, Anna
Rusch, Kristine Kathryn
Ryan, Peter Allen
Salamon, Julie
Salzman, Eva Frances
Sanderlin, George
Sandman, Peter (Mark)
Saunders, Jean (Innes)
Sawatsky, John
Schmidt, Stanley (Albert)
Schreiber, Le Anne
Seguin, Marilyn W(eymouth)
Seleshanko, Kristina
Sellers, Heather (Laurie)
Sennett, Frank (Ronald)
Setterberg, Fred
Shaw, David W.
Sheehan, Michael J.
Sheehan, Susan
Shelton, Mark L(ogan)
Shine, Frances L(ouise)
Shipler, David K(arr)
Shipman, John Marlin
Shlaim, Avi
Shreve, Susan R(ichards)
Siebold, Jan
Silcott, Loma G. Davies
Simeti, Mary Taylor
Simmons, Charles A(lexander)
Simon, Daniel (Martin)
Simon, Roger (Mitchell)
Simpson, Myrtle Lillias
Sims, Norman (Howard)
Sims, Patsy
Singer, Barry
Skinner-Linnenberg, Virginia (M.)
Slovic, Scott H.
Smirnoff, Marc
Smith, Faye McDonald
Smith, Gavin D.
Soper, Tony
Spaeth, Anthony
Speck, Bruce W.
Spinner, Jackie
Stacey, Tom
Steinman, Louise
Sten, Christopher (W.)
Stone, Sarah
Stonich, Sarah
Strahinich, Helen C.
Strock, Ian Randal
Stuart, Sally E(lizabeth)
Summers, Judith (Anne)
Sussman, Peter Y.
Svoboda, Terese
Swanson, David
Sward, Robert S.
Swetz, Frank J.
Swope, Sam
Tate, Eleanora E(laine)
Taylor, Ronald B.
Tearle, John L.
Thomas, David St. John

Thomas, John Heywood
Thompson, Jerry Don
Tillinghast, Richard
Timmermans, Tricia
Tracy, Lorna
Tucker, Martin
Tuman, Myron C(hester)
Tusan, Michelle Elizabeth
Tweit, Susan J(oan)
Van Ginneken, Jaap
van Itallie, Jean Claude
van Praagh, David
Varsavsky, Paula
Vaughn, Patrika
Venolia, Jan(et G.)
Voss, Ralph F.
Wachsberger, Ken(neth)
Wachtel, Eleanor
Walshe, R(obert) D(aniel)
Wandor, Michelene
Warner, Penny
Watson, Irene
Weiner, Stephen
Weltge, Sigrid W(ortmann)
Weschler, Lawrence
What, Leslie
White, Edward M.
Whiteman, (David) Bruce
Wiater, Stanley
Wiesel, Elie
Wildgen, Michelle
Wiley, Peter (Booth)
Wilhelm, Kate
Wineapple, Brenda
Winer, Deborah Grace
Winkler, Anthony C.
Wisker, Gina
Wolton, Thierry
Wood, Monica
Wortsman, Peter
Wyatt, Clarence R.
Yansky, Brian
Youngs, Betty F.
Youngs, Tim
Yudelman, David
Zebrowski, George
Zhao, Yuezhi
Zimmerman, Donald E(dward)
Zinik, Zinovy

Young Adult Non-fiction

Abi-Ezzi, Nathalie
Abish, Walter
Accawi, Anwar F.
Ackroyd, Peter
Adair, Daryl John
Adams, Gerry
Adams, Jessica
Addinall, Peter
Addiscott, T. M.
Adkins, Lesley
Adler, David A.
Al-Rasheed, Madawi
Alan, Theresa

Cossolotto, Matthew
Couch, Dick
Covey, Herbert C.
Cowan, Shannon
Cowley, (Cassia) Joy
Cox, Vic
Cox, Vicki
Coy, John
Craats, Rennay
Craig, Colleen
Creighton, Joan Scott
Crenson, Victoria
Crews, Harry (Eugene)
Crook, Marion
Crummey, Michael
Cummings, Sally (Nikoline)
Cuomo, Mario (Matthew)
Curnutt, Kirk
Curry, Jane (Louise)
Dacey, Austin
Dailey, Janet
Daly, Michael
Dangl, Benjamin
Darling, David J.
Davies, Nicola
Davies, Stephanie
Davis, David R.
Davis, Francis
Davis, Maggie S.
Davison, Liam
Day, Nancy
de Breadun, Deaglan
de Vries, Hent
Dearing, Sarah
Deaver, Jeffery Wilds
Dellasega, Cheryl
Delman, Carmit
Deng, Yong
Denson, Andrew
Desai, Anita
Descola, Philippe
Devney, Darcy C(ampion)
Dexter, Pete
Dickason, Christie
Dickerson, Matthew T.
Dickie, John
Dickinson, Peter
Dickinson, Terence
Dickson, Paul (Andrew)
Dieckhoff, Alain
Dintiman, George B.
Dixon, Ann R.
Dixon, Larry
Djoleto, (Solomon Alexander) Amu
Djupe, Paul A.
Doak, Wade (Thomas)
Dobie, Kathy
Docker, John
Doherty, Brian
Doherty, P(aul) C.
Donn, Linda
Dornenburg, Andrew
Dorros, Arthur (M.)
dos Santos, Joyce Audy
Dott, Brian R.
Dower, Laura

Doyle, Roddy
Drabble, Margaret
Drake, Albert (Dee)
Draper, Alfred Ernest
Drosnin, Michael
Dudley, Ellen
Due, Tananarive
Duey, Kathleen
Dufault, Peter Kane
Duffy, Maureen (Patricia)
Duggan, Christopher
Dugoni, Robert
Dumbleton, Mike
Duncan, Cynthia M.
Duncan, David James
Duncan, Lois
Duncan, Stephen M.
Duncker, Patricia
Dunlap, Julie
Dunleavy, Deborah
Dunn, Mark (Rodney)
Dwight, Jeffry
Dyer, K. C.
Earl, Riggins R.
Earley, Pete
Easterbrook, Gregg
Eaton, Jack
Ebbett, Eve
Eck, Joe
Edgar, Stacey L.
Edmunds, John C.
Egan, Timothy
Ehrlich, Amy
Eickhoff, Diane
Eickhoff, Randy Lee
Eidse, Faith
Einhorn, Barbara
Eisenberg, Nora
Eisler, Benita
Elborough, Travis
Elliott, Charles
Ellis, Donald
Ellis, Peter Berresford
Ellison, Harlan (Jay)
Ellison, Joan Jarvis
Eltringham, S(tewart) K(eith)
Emecheta, (Florence Onye) Buchi
Emory, Jerry
Engdahl, Sylvia L(ouise)
Engel, Margorie L(ouise)
English, Darby
Erickson, Carolly
Erlbach, Arlene
Evey, Stuart
Fain, Sarah
Fairstein, Linda A.
Fales-Hill, Susan
Falk, Candace
Falkingham, Jane (Cecelia)
Faust, Jeff
Federico, Giovanni
Feinstein, John
Ferreiro, Carmen
Ferrer, Elizabeth
Ferris, Paul
Fessenden, Tracy
Fields, Terri

Figes, Eva
Fine, Anne
Fine, Doris Landau
Fisher, Leonard Everett
Fisher, Marshall Jon
Flamini, Roland
Fleetwood, Hugh (Nigel)
Fleischner, Jennifer
Fleisher, Paul
Fleishman, Avrom
Fleming, Keith
Fletcher, Ralph
Foley, Mick
Fontanel, Béatrice
Fornés, Maria Irene
Forster, Margaret
Forsyth, Frederick
Foster, Alan Dean
Fotopoulos, Takis
Fox, Les
Francis, Clare
Franco, Betsy
Frank, Jacquelyn
Frankel, Glenn
Frankel, Valerie
Frankfurter, David Thomas Munro
Franklin, Robert M(ichael)
Fraser, Antonia
Frazier, Sundee T.
Freeman, Jo
Freeman, Michael
Freitas, Donna
Freudenheim, Ellen
Frey, James N.
Fricker, Mary
Friedman, Philip (J.)
Fritts, Mary Bahr
Fritz, Jean
Frost, Scott
Frost-Knappman, L. Elizabeth
Fry, Virginia Lynn
Gadney, Reg
Gage, Leighton D.
Gallagher, Shaun
Galvin, Matthew R(eppert)
Ganz, Marshall
Garaudy, Roger
Gardam, Jane
Gardner, Robert
Gardner, Sandra
Garfunkel, Trudy
Garner, Alan
Garrison, Daniel H.
Garthoff, Raymond L(eonard)
Gaskill, Malcolm
Gass, William (Howard)
Gatenby, Greg
Gatti, Anne
Gay, Kathlyn R.
Gentry, Christine
Gertridge, Allison
Gibbons, Alan
Gilbert, Elizabeth
Gill, A. A.
Gilliland, Alexis A(rnaldus)
Gilmore, Dewitt
Gilstrap, John

Ginsburg, Mark B.
Gitter, Elisabeth
Gladwell, Malcolm
Goble, Paul
Godbout, Jacques
Godfrey, Neale S.
Godwin, Gail (Kathleen)
Going, Kelly L.
Goldberg, Jacob
Goldentyer, Debra
Goldman, Francisco
Goldman, William
Goldstein, Brandt
Goldstein, Rebecca
Golubhoff, Risa L.
Gondry, Michel
Gonzales, Laurence
Gooch, Brad
Good, Howard
Goodall, Jane
Gordievsky, Oleg
Gordon, April A.
Gordon, Deborah Hannes
Gorski, Philip S.
Goss, Kristin A.
Gottlieb, Lisa
Gottlieb, Sherry Gershon
Gough, Laurie
Gough, Sue
Grafton, Sue
Grant, Vanessa
Grau, Shirley Ann
Green, Ricky K(enneth)
Greenberg, Karen
Greene, Rhonda Gowler
Griggs, Vanessa Davis
Grindal, Richard
Grinde, Donald A(ndrew)
Grisham, John
Guest, Judith
Guillaumin, Colette
Guinn, Jeff Mason
Gup, Ted (S.)
Guy, Ray
Hackett, Robert A(nthony)
Hackl, Erich
Hague, Douglas (Chalmers)
Hajdu, David
Haley, Gail E(inhart)
Hall, Lynn
Hall, Martha Lacy
Hall, Rodney
Hallahan, William H(enry)
Halligan, Marion (Mildred Crothall)
Hamilton, Marybeth
Hamm, Diane Johnston
Hammerslough, Jane
Hampton, Wilborn
Han, Suzanne Crowder
Hannay, Alastair
Hansen, Matthew Scott
Haqqani, Husain
Harding, Les
Hareven, Gail
Harney, Elizabeth
Harper, Jo

Harris, (Theodore) Wilson
Harris, Robert (Dennis)
Harris, Robert J.
Harter, Penny
Hartle, Anthony E.
Hartman, Saidiya V.
Harvey, Kenneth J.
Harwood, Ronald
Haskell, Molly
Hatton, Caroline
Hayes, Stephen F.
Hazzard, Shirley
Heaney, Seamus
Hecht, Jeff(rey Charles)
Hein, Christoph
Heine, Arthur J.
Heller, Jane
Hemstock, Gillian
Henderson, Lauren
Henkin, Joshua
Henry, Charles P.
Hero, Rodney E.
Heron, Ann
Herr, Michael
Hewitt, W(arren) E(dward)
Hider, James
Higginsen, Vy
Higgs, Liz Curtis
Hildebrand, Verna
Hill-Miller, Katherine C(ecelia)
Hilton, Suzanne
Hing, Bill Ong
Hirschfelder, Arlene B.
Hodgins, Jack
Hodgson, Barbara L.
Hoehne, Marcia
Hoff, B. J.
Holbrook, Sara
Holland, JoJean
Holland, Max (Mendel)
Holroyd, Michael
Homes, A. M.
Hoose, Phillip M.
Hopkins, Jackie (Mims)
Hopkins, John
Hopping Egan, Lorraine
Hornby, Nick
Hornik, Heidi J.
Horspool, David
Horwitz, Tony
Horwood, William
Houston, Victoria
Howard, Clark
Howard, Elizabeth Jane
Howard, Maureen
Hubbard, Charles M.
Huby, Pamela Margaret
Hudak, Michal
Huff, Toby E.
Hughes, Gerard J.
Hughes, Kevin L.
Hughes, Shirley
Hughes, Susan
Hull, John M.
Hunter, Mollie
Huntley, James Robert
Husain, Shahrukh

Huston, Nancy
Hustvedt, Siri
Hutchings, Stephen
Hutchinson, Robert
Hutson, Shaun P.
Hwang, David Henry
Igoe, Jim Joseph
Ihimaera, Witi
Immell, Myra H.
Indiana, Gary
Inglis, Janet
Ipsen, D. C.
Isaacs, Arnold R.
Isaacs, Susan
Iyengar, Sheena
Jack, Andrew (John)
Jackson, Jesse
Jackson, Robert H.
Jacobs, Barry
Jacobson, Dan
Jacobson, Jennifer Richard
Jacq, Christian
Jaffe, Betsy
James, Clive (Vivian Leopold)
James, P. D.
Jamiolkowski, Raymond M.
Jancovich, Mark
Janes, J(oseph) Robert
Jankowski, James P.
Janover, Caroline (Davis)
Janowitz, Tama
Jarrow, Gail
Jarvis, Brian
Jason, Sonya
Jasper, Kenji (Nathaniel)
Jenkins, George
Jennaway, Megan
Jennings, Paul
Jeschke, Wolfgang
Jocelyn, Marthe
Johnson, Diane
Johnson, James W.
Johnson, Rebecca L.
Johnston, Julie
Johnston, Marilyn
Jones, Carrie
Jones, Charlotte Foltz
Jones, David
Jones, Madison
Jones, Tony H.
Jordan, Rosa
Jordan-Lake, Joy
Judd, Alan
Judge, Harry George
Kadrey, Richard
Kahn, Michael A.
Kallen, Stuart A(rnold)
Kalman, Maira
Kamenetz, Anya
Kane, Larry
Kantner, Seth
Kaplan, Andrew S.
Kassabova, Kapka
Kassell, Lauren
Katz, Judith
Kay, Alan N.
Kay, Betty Carlson

Kaye, Peggy
Kaylin, Lucy
Keaney, Brian
Keene, Ann T(odd)
Keevak, Michael
Keillor, Garrison (Edward)
Kellenberger, J(ames)
Kelly, Clint
Kemske, Floyd
Kendall, Carol
Keneally, Thomas (Michael)
Kennedy, Kieran A.
Kennedy, Pagan
Kennedy, Randall L.
Kennedy, Rick
Kennedy, Thomas E.
Kennedy, William (Joseph)
Keown, Tim
Kerner, Elizabeth
Kerr, Andrea Moore
Kerr, Audrey Elisa
Kessler, Liz
Killham, Edward L(eo)
Kimmel, Elizabeth Cody
King, Daren
King, Stephen
Kingsolver, Barbara
Kingston, Maxine Hong
Kirby, Susan E.
Kirkpatrick, Jane
Kirshner, Mia
Kitchen, Bert
Kleh, Cindy (L.)
Klein, Lisa M.
Klempner, Mark
Knight, Alanna (Cleet)
Knowles, Jo
Koestler-Grack, Rachel
Kolbaba, Ginger
Kolodny, Nancy J.
Kolosov, Jacqueline
Konigsburg, E(laine) L(obl)
Koppel, Tom
Kossman, Nina
Kowalski, Kathiann M.
Kranendonk, Anke
Kreml, William P.
Krieger, Michael J.
Krisher, Trudy (B.)
Krupp, Robin Rector
Kuh, Patric
Kuhl, Stefan
Kuklin, Susan
Kuppner, Frank
Kurlansky, Mark
Kurzweil, Allen
Lambert, Josiah Bartlett
Lamott, Anne
Lantier, Patricia
Lapham, Heather A.
Larios, Julie Hofstrand
Lasky, Kathryn
Lassiter, Rhiannon
Latko, David W.
Laubach, David C.
Laurens, Jeannine
Laurie, Hugh

Lawson, Dorie McCullough
Lazebnik, Claire Scovell
le Carré, John
Le Guin, Ursula K(roeber)
Leab, Daniel Josef
Leader, Darian
Leak, Andrew N.
Leaman, Celia A.
Lebor, Adam
LeClaire, Anne D(ickinson)
Lee, Helen Elaine
Lee, Sally
Leib, Franklin A(llen)
Lennard, John (Chevening)
Lenney, Dinah
Leonard, Elmore
Leonard, Frances
Leroy, Margaret
Lessing, Doris (May)
Lethem, Jonathan (Allen)
Letts, Billie
Leupp, Gary P.
Levin, Doron P.
Levin, Irina
Levitin, Daniel J.
Levy, Adrian
Levy, Elizabeth
Lewis, Simon
Lewis, Thomas H.
Lieber, Keir A.
Liebert, Elizabeth
Light, Alison Elizabeth
Lindquist, N(ancy) J(ane)
Linn, Karen
Lipsyte, Robert (Michael)
Lisandrelli, Elaine Slivinski
Lischer, Sarah Kenyon
Little, (Flora) Jean
Littleton, Mark (R.)
Lively, Adam
Lively, Penelope
Lobenstine, Margaret
Lock, Joan
Lodge, David
London, Herbert I.
London, Mark
Long, Cathryn J.
Longfellow, Layne (A.)
Lopresti, Robert
Love, (Kathleen) Ann
Low, Shari
Lowry, Lois (Hammersberg)
Lubet, Steven
Lukken, Miriam
Lupica, Mike
Lupoff, Richard A(llen)
Lurie, Alison
Lurie, April
Ly, Many
Lynd, Staughton (Craig)
Lyon, George Ella
Maass, Peter
Macdonald, James D.
MacDonald, Sam A.
Mackay, Claire (Bacchus)
Mackenzie, Craig
Mackin, Jeanne

Macomber, Debbie
Macy, Sue
Magee, David
Maharidge, Dale (Dimitro)
Mahoney, Rosemary
Mahy, Margaret
Mailman, Erika
Maley, Willy
Mallios, Seth
Mango, Karin N.
Marcus, Leonard S.
Margariti, Roxani Eleni
Marland, Hilary
Marquart, Debra
Marquis, Max
Marrone, Steven P(hillip)
Marsh, Fabienne
Marsh, Nigel
Martien, Jerry
Martin, Deborah L.
Martin, Jack
Martin, Julie (Breyer)
Martin, Rhona
Martin, Robert M.
Martin, Stephen-Paul
Martinez, Elizabeth Coonrod
Martínez, Manuel Luis
Masello, Robert
Masini, Donna
Mason, Bobbie Ann
Mason, Haydn Trevor
Mason, Prue
Massad, Joseph A.
Massey, Victoria
Massie, Sonja
Matera, Dary M.
Matheson, Richard (Burton)
Matlin, David
Matousek, Mark
Matovina, Timothy M.
Matthews, Chris John
Matthiessen, Peter
Mattingley, Christobel (Rose-
      mary)
Maurer-Mathison, Diane V(ogel)
Maxwell, Patricia Anne
May, Julian
Mayer, Barbara
Mayer, Robert
Mazer, Anne
McAfee, Carol
McAll, Christopher
McCaffrey, Anne (Inez)
McCallum, Taffy Gould
McCarthy, Thomas
McCaughrean, Geraldine (Jones)
McCleary, Kathleen
McClendon, Thomas V.
McCool, Daniel C.
McCormack, W(illiam) J(ohn)
McCormick, Anita Louise
McCrone, Kathleen E.
McCullough, David Willis
McEwan, Ian
McFadden, David W.
McGowan, Todd
McGrath, Patrick

McGuane, Thomas
Mckenzie, Nancy Affleck
McKinney, Nadine
McKnight, David
McMahan, Alison
McMillen, Christian W.
McMurtry, Larry (Jeff)
McNab, Claire
McNeely, Ian F.
McPhee, John (Angus)
McPhee, Norma H.
McReynolds, Glenna Jean
Mead, Rebecca
Meaker, Marijane (Agnes)
Megarry, Tim
Meltzer, Brad
Mercer, Judy
Metzger, Robert A(lan)
Metzinger, Thomas
Meyer, Carolyn
Meyer, Dick
Miles, Rosalind
Miller, Donalyn
Miller, Edward A.
Millner, Denene
Minshall, Vera
Mishica, Clare
Mitchelson, Mitch
Mithen, Steven J.
Mittelmark, Howard
Momaday, N(avarre) Scott
Monière, Denis
Montandon, Mac
Montpetit, Charles
Moorcock, Michael (John)
Moore, Perry
Mori, Kyoko
Morin, Paula
Morpurgo, Michael
Morreim, E. Haavi
Morris, Deborah
Morris, Jan
Morris, Jeffrey B(randon)
Morris, Mark
Morris, Mary (Joan) McGarry
Morrison, Toni
Morton, Peter
Moss, Marissa
Mourlevat, Jean-Claude
Moya, Jose C.
Mrazek, Robert J.
Mullen, Michael
Mullins, Hilary
Mulroney, Brian
Muñoz, Manuel
Murakami, Haruki
Murkoff, Bruce
Murphy, Patricia J.
Murphy, Shirley R(ousseau)
Murphy, Sylvia
Musgrave, Susan
Muuss, Rolf Eduard
Myers, Bill
Myers, Walter Dean
Mylroie, Laurie
Myrick, David F.
Napier, Bill

Naylor, Phyllis Reynolds
Naylor, Sean
Nayman, Michele
Neal, Bill
Neale, Jonathan
Neaverson, Bob
Neiwert, David A.
Nelson, Eric
Nelson, Peter N.
Nemec, James
Neri, G.
Nester, Daniel
Neubeck, Kenneth J.
Nevels, Cynthia Skove
Newey, Katherine
Newman, Andrea
Newton, Steven H.
Ng, Franklin
Nicholson, Lois P.
Nicolson, Adam
Nobbs, David
Norell, Mark A.
Norgren, Jill
Norrell, Robert J(efferson)
Nossiter, Adam
Noyes, Deborah
Nugent, Ted
O'Brien, Edna
O'Brien, Pat
O'Brien, Timothy L.
O'Connor, Rebecca K.
O'Hare, Jeff(rey A.)
O'Kane, James M.
O'Neal, Hank
Oakley, Graham
Oates, Joyce Carol
Oatis, Steven J.
Oberlin, Loriann Hoff
Oldham, June
Olney, Ross R(obert)
Olson, James S.
Olson, Laura R.
Oltion, Jerry
Oppenheimer, Todd
Orth, John V.
Orton, Anthony
Osborne, Will
Ozick, Cynthia
Pace, Robert F.
Paffenroth, Kim
Page, Katherine Hall
Palmer, Scott W.
Paradis, Adrian Alexis
Parfitt, Will
Parker, Barbara Keevil
Parker, Nancy W(inslow)
Parkes, Walter F.
Parkinson, Siobhan
Parloff, Roger (Harris)
Parmelee, John H.
Parr, Ann
Parsons, Alexandra
Pascal, Francine
Paterson, Katherine (Womeldorf)
Patterson, Glenn
Patterson, Kevin
Paulsen, Gary

Paxson, Diana L(ucile)
Pearl, Matthew
Pearson, Thomas S(pencer)
Peck, Dale
Peck, Jeffrey M.
Peck, Richard (Wayne)
Pederson, William D(avid)
Peet, Mal
Pegg, Mark Gregory
Pell, Ed(ward)
Perdrizet, Marie-Pierre
Peretti, Frank E.
Perez-Romero, Antonio
Perry, Dayn
Perry, Douglas
Perry, Roland
Persico, Joseph E.
Peterson, Cris
Peterson, Tracie
Petrie, Anne
Peyton, K. M.
Pickering, Samuel F(rancis)
Piercy, Marge
Pietrusza, David
Pilarz, Scott R.
Pilling, Ann
Pincher, (Henry) Chapman
Pinkard, Susan K.
Pinkwater, Daniel Manus
Pipkin, Turk
Pitcher, George
Ploeger, Katherine (M.)
Pohl, Frederik
Pollack, Rachel
Poortinga, Y(pe) H.
Powell, E. Sandy
Pratt, Geraldine
Preller, James
Presnall, Judith (Ann) Janda
Preston, Douglas
Preston-Mafham, Rod(ney Arthur)
Price, Anthony
Price, Christopher
Priestley, Chris
Prokes, Mary T(imothy)
Proulx, Suzanne
Purser, Ann
Quinlan, Patrick
Quinones, Sam
Quinsey, Mary Beth
Radosh, Daniel Lord
Radulescu, Domnica
Raffel, Keith
Raham, (R.) Gary
Rai, Bali
Rajah, Susi
Rake, Jody
Randell, Beverley
Rann, Sheila
Raphael, Lev
Rarick, Ethan
Rathbone, Cristina
Rathmell, George W(esley)
Ratto, Linda Lee
Raymond, Patrick (Ernest)
Read, Christopher
Reber, Deborah

Rechy, John (Francisco)
Redonnet, Marie
Redsand, Anna
Reed, Ishmael
Reeder, Carolyn
Reeves-Stevens, Garfield
Reger, James P.
Reiken, Frederick
Reilly, Kevin
Rejali, Darius M.
Relyea, Harold C.
Rendell, Ruth
Resnick, Mike
Rice, Earle
Richard, T. Dawn
Richards, Dusty
Richards, Jean
Ridd, Stephen (John)
Riehecky, Janet Ellen
Ritchie, Harry
Rivers, Reggie
Roberts, Adam
Roberts, Geoffrey
Roberts, Paul
Roberts, Yvonne
Robin, Corey
Robins, Sari
Robinson, Jennifer L.
Robisheaux, Thomas
Rodriguez, Clara E.
Roeske, Paulette
Rohan, Michael Scott
Roiphe, Anne Richardson
Roiphe, Katie
Romano, Louis
Romano-Lax, Andromeda
Roscoe, Patrick
Rosegrant, Susan
Rosen, Jeffrey
Rosen, Selina
Rosenberg, Howard
Rosenberg, Joel C.
Rosenkranz, E. Joshua
Roth, Philip
Rowh, Mark
Rubenstein, Richard Lowell
Ruby, Robert H.
Rudy, Jarrett
Rue, Loyal D.
Ruedy, John
Ruoff, A. LaVonne Brown
Rushdie, Salman
Russell, Richard L.
Russo, John (A.)
Ryan, Margaret
Rybolt, Thomas R.
Ryden, Hope
Sajdak, Bruce T.
Saldana, Rene
Salmon, Jacqueline L.
Salvatore, R(obert) A(nthony)
Salzberg, Sharon
Sammon, Paul M.
Samuels, Cynthia K(alish)
Sander, Heather L.
Sanders, Bill
Sanders, Katrina M.

Saner, Reg(inald Anthony)
Sanford, Richard
Sanna, Ellyn
Sawyer, Kem Knapp
Scarfe, Wendy (Elizabeth)
Scheck, Raffael
Scherf, Kathleen D.
Schnurnberger, Lynn
Schrefer, Eliot
Schroeder, Alan
Schubert, Frank N.
Schuman, Michael A.
Schupack, Deborah
Schwartz, Sheila R.
Scieszka, Jon
Scotch, Allison Winn
Scott, (Robert James) Munroe
See, Carolyn
Seidensticker, John
Sender Barayon, Ramon
Senior, Olive (Marjorie)
Senna, Danzy
Severance, John B(ridwell)
Shackelford, Renae Nadine
Shahan, Sherry
Shalant, Phyllis
Shamsie, Kamila
Shapiro, Karen Jo
Sharma, Poonam
Sharman, Cheryl Harris
Sharman, Russell Leigh
Sheen, Barbara
Shengold, Leonard
Shepard, Charles E.
Shepard, Sam
Shephard, Roy Jesse
Sherrett, James
Shields, Jody
Shockley, Ann Allen
Shorto, Russell
Shreve, Anita
Shreve, Susan R(ichards)
Shrum, Robert
Shulevitz, Judith Anne
Shuman, George D.
Shute, Jenefer
Shuter, Jane Margaret
Shuttle, Penelope (Diane)
Shvets, Yuri B.
Siddons, Anne Rivers
Silcott, Loma G. Davies
Silver, Brenda R.
Silver, Norman
Silverman, Robin L(andew)
Simmie, Lois (Ann)
Simmons, James C(oleman)
Simmons, Sylvie
Sims, Michael
Singer, Marcus George
Skal, David J.
Skiba, Katherine M.
Skipp, John
Skloot, Rebecca
Skorupski, John
Skye, Christina
Slegman, Ann
Sloan, Susan R.

Slote, Alfred
Smith, Andrew Anselmo
Smith, Bruce L. R.
Smith, Charles R.
Smith, Daniel Jordan
Smither, Elizabeth
Snodgrass, Mary Ellen
Sobol, Donald J.
Sohn, Amy
Somervill, Barbara A(nn)
Sorenson, John L.
Sorenson, Margo
Spanger, Hans-Joachim
Spencer, Colin
Spencer, Elizabeth
Spiegelman, Ian
Spindler, George Dearborn
Spinelli, Jerry
Spivak, Gayatri Chakravorty
Spollen, Anne
Stableford, Brian M(ichael)
Stack, George
Stampf, Günter
Stanley, Jerry
Stark, Evan
Statham, E. Robert
Steel, Danielle
Steele, Philip
Stein, Wendy
Stevens, Bryna
Stewart, Gail B.
Stimson, Tess
Stockley, Grif
Stoker, Gerry
Stomfay-Stitz, Aline M.
Stone, R. W.
Stone, Robert (Anthony)
Stout, Jay A.
Strahinich, Helen C.
Strasser, Todd
Straub, Peter (Francis)
Stringer, Vickie M.
Strong, Marilee
Strother, Ruth
Stubbs, Jean
Sturm, Circe
Sullivan, George E(dward)
Sullivan, Steve (Joseph)
Sumarsam
Summers, Anthony (Bruce)
Sundeen, Mark
Surridge, Lisa
Swan, Robert
Sweeney, Terrance (Allen)
Swindells, Robert (Edward)
Swinfen, Ann
Swope, Sam
Symynkywicz, Jeffrey B(ruce)
Szabó, Istvan
Tallichet, Suzanne E.
Tallis, Frank
Tan, Amy
Tappan, Mark B.
Tate, Eleanora E(laine)
Taylor, Allegra
Taylor, Andrew J.
Taylor, Carl S.

Taylor, Dave
Taylor, Frederick
Taylor, Ronald B.
Temes, Peter S.
Thapar, Valmik
The Rock
Theroux, Paul
Thomas, Barbara L(ee)
Thomas, Claudia E.
Thomas, Cornell
Thomas, D(onald) M(ichael)
Thomas, David St. John
Thomas, Rob
Thompson, Donald N.
Thompson, Mark L.
Thornton, Yvonne S.
Tighe, Carl
Toews, Miriam
Toffler, Alvin
Tomkins, Calvin
Tomlinson, Harry
Torres, John A(lbert)
Townsend, John Rowe
Townsend, Sue
Townsend, Wendy
Tracy, Kathleen
Tracy, Kristen
Treuer, David
Trevor, William
Tribe, Laurence H(enry)
Trillin, Calvin
Trinkunas, Harold A.
Tripodi, Tony
Tripp, Nathaniel
Tripp, Valerie
Tuaolo, Esera
Tuck, Lily
Tunnell, Michael O('Grady)
Turck, Mary C.
Turkel, William J.
Turner, Ann (Warren)
Turow, (L.) Scott
Turtledove, Harry (Norman)
Tutu, Desmond M(pilo)
Tweit, Susan J(oan)
Umstatter, Jack
Underwood, Deborah
Urbainczyk, Theresa
Ure, Jean
Vaill, Amanda
Valenza, Joyce Kasman
Valman, Nadia
Van Ausdale, Debra
van der Linde, Laurel
Van Der Meer, Ron
van der Toorn, Karel
Vanasse, Deb
Vance, Jack
VanMeter, Vandelia
Varounis, Athena
Vassanji, M(oyez) G.
Veitch, Kate
Vernerey, Denise
Verney, Michael Palmer
Vernon, Amelia Wallace
Victor, Barbara
Vincent, Isabel

Young Adult Non-fiction-*cont.*

Vincenzi, Penny
Vitebsky, Piers
Vogel, Carole Garbuny
Vornholt, John
Wachtel, Shirley Russak
Waddell, Dan
Walker, Kate
Walker, Sally M(acArt)
Wall, Cheryl A.
Wallace, Don
Walsh, Jill Paton
Walsh Shepherd, Donna
Wambaugh, Joseph
Wardlaw, Lee
Wasby, Stephen L(ewis)
Watkins, Graham
Watkins, Paul
Watson, Clyde
Watson, George (Grimes)
Watson, Ian
Weatherly, Lee
Weber, Sandra
Weddle, David
Weinbaum, Marvin G.
Weisgall, Jonathan M.
Weiss, Daniel Evan
Wekesser, Carol A.
Weldon, Fay
Welton, Jude
Wendt, Albert
Wernick, Andrew (Lee)
Werris, Wendy
Wersba, Barbara
Wesker, Arnold
Wesley, Valerie Wilson
Weston, Mark
Wexler, Richard
Whelehan, Imelda
Whitcomb, Laura
White, Edmund
White, Franklin
White, Jon Manchip
Whitelaw, Stella
Whiteway, Doug(las) Alfred
Whitson, Stephanie Grace (Irvin)
Whyman, Matt
Wijnberg, Ellen
Wilczek, Frank
Wilde, Lyn Webster
Wilding, Michael
Wilensky, Amy S.
Wiley, Kim Wright
Wilhelm, Doug
Wilhelm, Kate
Wilkins, Sally (E. D.)
Wilkinson, Carole
Williams, (Henry) Nigel
Williams, Bert (Nolan)
Williams, David
Williams, Ian
Williamson, Robert C(lifford)
Wilson, Andrew
Wilson, Antoine Leonide Thomas
Wilson, Colin (Henry)
Wilson, Diane
Wilson, Duff
Wilson, John Morgan

Young Adult Non-fiction-*cont.*

Wilson, N. D.
Wimsatt, William C.
Winder, Simon
Windle, Janice Woods
Winerip, Michael
Winterhalder, Edward
Wise, Robert L.
Wiseman, Rosalind
Wodzi ski, Marcin
Woginrich, Jenna
Wolf, Margery
Wolfe, Tom
Wolferman, Kristie C(arlson)
Wolff, Jonathan
Wolff, Robert P(aul)
Wolff, Theodore F.
Wolfman, Judy
Wolfson, Jill
Wong, Janet S.
Wood, Don
Wood, Monica
Woodruff, Joan Leslie
Woodson, Jacqueline
Woog, Adam
Wormser, Richard
Wouk, Herman
Wray, Matt
Wright, Cora M.
Wright, Kit
Wright, Theodore Paul
Wyman, Carolyn
Ya rid, Na zik Sa ba
Yagoda, Ben
Yancey, Diane
Ye, Ting-Xing
Yep, Laurence (Michael)
Yolen, Jane
Young, Jeff C.
Young, Robert A.
Yount, Lisa
Zellman, Shelley
Zimmer, Tracie Vaughn
Ziskin, Harriet
Zucchi, John E.
Zuidervaart, Lambert

Zoology

Alexander, (Robert) McNeill
Angela, Alberto
Avise, John C.
Bakker, Robert T.
Barash, David P(hilip)
Bearanger, Marie
Berra, Tim M.
Boysen, Sally T.
Brandenburg, Jim
Brown, Richard E(arl)
Buchmann, Stephen L.
Buckelew, Albert R.
Burger, Joanna
Burton, John Andrew
Byers, John A.
Campbell, R(obert) Wayne
Cerullo, Mary M.
Chinery, Michael

Zoology-*cont.*

Clark, A(ilsa) M.
Cloudsley-Thompson, John (Leonard)
Coleman, Loren (Elwood)
Coren, Stanley
Cox, Christopher Barry
Cranshaw, Whitney
Currie, Philip J(ohn)
Daigle, Evelyne
Danz, Harold P.
Derr, Mark (Burgess)
DeWitt, Calvin B.
Doak, Wade (Thomas)
Duggleby, John
Dunlap, Julie
Elias, Scott A.
Eltringham, S(tewart) K(eith)
Engel, Michael S.
Fairley, James S(tewart)
Ferguson, Mark W. J.
Finch, Caleb E(llicott)
Fitzsimons, Cecilia (A. L.)
Flannery, Tim(othy Fridtjof)
Gaither, Carl C.
Galdikas, Birute
Gallant, Roy Arthur
Gilbert, John Raphael
Goodall, Jane
Grambo, Rebecca L(ynn)
Grice, Gordon
Grosz, Terry
Gurdon, Martin
Heminway, John
Holden, Peter
Hölldobler, Bert(hold Karl)
Jarrow, Gail
Johnsgard, Paul A.
Kaufman, Kenn
Keller, Laurent
Kilham, Benjamin
King, (William) Dennis
King, Doreen
Kleh, Cindy (L.)
Kohn, Alan J(acobs)
Lamb, Marion J.
Landman, Jessica C.
Larsen, Torben B.
Lee, Donald (Lewis)
Legg, Gerald
Lever, Christopher
Levin, Ted
Lin, Tan (Anthony)
Loomis, Jennifer A.
Lovett, Sarah
MacFadden, Bruce J.
Macfadyen, Amyan
MacPhee, Ross D(ouglas) E(arle)
Marcot, Bruce G.
Maser, Chris
Mccarthy, Susan
McGowan, Christopher
Merne, Oscar James
Morris, Desmond
Morton, Alexandra (Hubbard)
Morton, Brian
Moss, Cynthia J(ane)
Murphy, John C.

Zoology-*cont.*

Naskrecki, Piotr
Nicholls, Henry
Norell, Mark A.
O'Dor, Ronald Keith
Olsen, Klaus Malling
Palumbi, Stephen R.
Pianka, Eric R(odger)
Pimm, Stuart L(eonard)
Pörtner, Hans O.
Preston-Mafham, Rod(ney Arthur)
Rich, Thomas H(ewitt)
Ride, W. D. L.
Roberts, Callum
Rossi, John V.
Rossi, Roxanne
Rowett, Helen (Graham Quiller)
Rue, Leonard Lee
Salzberg, Allen
Schaller, George B(eals)
Schwartz, Jeffrey H.
Shedd, Warner
Shine, Richard
Sims, Michael
Smith, Hobart Muir
Snow, Keith Ronald
Soulsby, E. J. L.
Stonehouse, Bernard
Strother, Ruth
Stroud, Patricia Tyson
Taylor, Dave
Taylor, Walter Kingsley
Thapar, Valmik
Thomson, James Miln
Triplehorn, Charles A(lbert)
Waldbauer, Gilbert (P.)
Welsbacher, Anne
Williamson, Donald I.
Yoerg, Sonja I.
Zeveloff, Samuel I.
Zug, George R.
Zuk, Marlene

Others

Autobiography/Memoirs

Aaker, Everett
Aaron, Chester
Abajian, Kathryn J.
Abbott, Tony
Aberjhani
Abildskov, Marilyn
Abinader, Elmaz
Abrahams, Peter
Abresch, Peter E.
Abse, Dannie
Abu-Jaber, Diana
Accad, Evelyne
Acheson, David C(ampion)
Ackerman, Susan Yoder
Adair, Aaron J.
Adams, Gerry
Adams, John
Adams, John Coolidge
Adams, Richard (George)
Adams, Timothy Dow
Adamson, Donald
Adamz-Bogus, S. Diane
Adell, Sandra
Adiele, Faith
Adoff, Arnold
Agassi, Andre Kirk
Agee, Jonis
Agran, Edward G.
Ahlquist, Dale
Akbar, Said Hyder
Alaya, Flavia
Albanese, Laurie Lico
Alberts, Laurie
Aldiss, Brian (Wilson)
Alexander, Ann Field
Alexander, Meena
Alexander, Peter F.
Alexander, Sally Hobart
Alfeyeva, Valeria
Ali, Ayaan Hirsi
Ali, Kazim
Alinder, Mary Street
Allen, Roberta
Allende, Isabel
Allgood, Myralyn F(rizzelle)
Alsamari, Lewis
Alson, Peter (H.)
Altman, Mara
Alvarez, A(lfred)
Amadi, Elechi
Amburn, Ellis
Ameisen, Olivier
Amiry, Suad
Anderson, Richard Lloyd
Anderson, Terry (A.)
Andoe, Joe
Andrews, Helena
Angelou, Maya
Angle, Kurt
Anglesey
Angus, Christopher (K.)
Antal, Dan
Anthony, Piers
Antonetta, Susanne
Antrim, Donald

Autobiography/Memoirs-*cont.*

Appelt, Kathi
Apple, Max (Isaac)
Aptheker, Bettina
Arico, Santo L.
Arkush, Michael
Armantrout, (Mary) Rae
Armstrong, Bob
Armstrong, Diane (Julie)
Armstrong, Heather B.
Armstrong, Karen (Anderson)
Armstrong, Luanne (A.)
Arnaud, Claude
Arnett, Peter (Gregg)
Arnold, David
Arnold, Eleanor
Arrington, Stephen L(ee)
Arterburn, Stephen
Asadi, Houshang
Aschan, Ulf
Ascher, Barbara Lazear
Ash, William Franklin
Ashrawi, Hanan (Mikhail)
Ashworth, (Lewis) William
Ashworth, Andrea
Asquith, Christina
Audeh, Azmi S.
Auster, Paul
Austin, Paul
Avakian, Arlene Voski
Avery, Tom
Avise, John C.
Awret, Irene
Bachrach, Nancy
Bagdikian, Ben H(aig)
Bageant, Joe
Baggett, Jennifer
Bagley, Tennent H.
Bahr, Iris
Bailey, Anthony
Bailey, Rosemary
Bain, Kenneth (Ross)
Bair, Deirdre
Baker, Christina Looper
Baker, Elna
Baker, Rosalie F.
Baker, Russell (Wayne)
Baker, William
Balbirer, Nancy
Ball, Stuart
Balmaseda, Liz
Banish, Roslyn
Barber, Charles
Barber, Phyllis (Nelson)
Bareham, Terence
Barham, Patte B.
Barich, Bill
Barley, Janet Crane
Barnes, Christopher J(ohn)
Barnhart, Terry A.
Barré, Jean-Luc
Barrett, John G(ilchrist)
Barry, Michael
Barthelme, Steve(n)
Bartlett, Anne
Baston, Lewis
Baszile, Jennifer Lynn
Bateman, Robert L.

Autobiography/Memoirs-*cont.*

Bateson, Mary Catherine
Baughman, T. H.
Bax, Martin (Charles Owen)
Baxter, John
Baybars, Taner
Beasley, Faith E(velyn)
Beattie, Ann
Beattie, Melody (Lynn)
Bechtel, Stefan D.
Beck, Mary L. (Giraudo)
Becker, Robin
Becker, Suzanne (Rose)
Beecher, Maureen Ursenbach
Beisner, Robert L.
Belkin, Lisa
Bell, Marvin (Hartley)
Bellos, Alex
Belshaw, Patrick
Bender, Sheila
Benson, Gerard
Bentley, Joanne
Bentley, Joyce
Beran, Michael Knox
Berg, A. Scott
Berg, Leila
Bergen, Candice
Berger, Barbara Helen
Berger, Thomas R(odney)
Berger-Kiss, Andres
Berkenstadt, Jim
Berkoff, Steven
Berlin, Leslie
Berman, Brooke
Bernard, Oliver
Bernstein, Burton
Bernstein, Paula
Berrigan, Daniel J.
Berry, Brian Joe Lobley
Berry, J. Bill
Bertolino, James
Bertschinger, Claire
Bessette, Roland L.
Best, Geoffrey (Francis Andrew)
Biank, Tanya
Bidini, Dave
Bieman, Elizabeth
Bierds, Linda
Biggs, Chester M(axwell)
Biggs, John Burville
Billetdoux, Raphaële
Binding, Paul
Bingham, Charlotte
Bingham, Howard L.
Bingham, Sallie
Bird, Christiane
Birrell, James Peter
Birstein, Ann
Birzer, Bradley J.
Bitton-Jackson, Livia E(lvira)
Bjork, Daniel W.
Bjornerud, Marcia
Black, William H.
Blackburn, Julia
Blackmore, Susan (Jane)
Blainey, Geoffrey Norman
Blair, E(lizabeth) Anne
Blakely, Mary Kay

Autobiography/Memoirs-*cont.*

Blanchard, Robert
Blashford-Snell, John Nicholas
Blass, Thomas
Blauner, Bob
Bloom, Lynn (Marie Zimmerman)
Blosser, Susan Sokol
Blum, Deborah (Leigh)
Blume, Harvey
Blundy, Anna
Bodansky, Yossef
Boers, Arthur Paul
Bogart, Stephen Humphrey
Bok, Sissela
Bolden, Abraham
Boller, Paul F.
Bolster, Richard (H.)
Bolton, Ruthie
Bonadio, William
Bond, Ruskin
Bonington, Chris(tian)
Booth, Stanley
Boraine, Alex(ander)
Borel, Kathryn
Borton, Lady
Bott, Caroline G.
Bowden, Keith
Bowering, Marilyn (Ruthe)
Bowers, John
Bowman, Christian
Boyd, Malcolm
Boyle, Brian
Boyt, Susie
Bradburd, Rus
Bradlee, Benjamin (Crownin-
    shield)
Bradley, Alan
Bradley, David (Henry)
Bradley, John Lewis
Braham, (E.) Jeanne
Branch, Taylor
Brands, H. W.
Branover, Herman
Braudis, Bob
Brennan, Christine
Brennan, Kate
Brett, Brian
Brett, Donna W(hitson)
Bretton, Barbara
Brewster, David (C.)
Brewster, Elizabeth (Winifred)
Brewster, Gurdon
Breznitz, Shlomo
Bridge, Andrew
Brkic, Courtney Angela
Brochu, André
Broderick, Colin
Brody, Richard
Brogan, Hugh
Brooke-Rose, Christine
Brooks, Peter Newman
Brower, Steven
Brown, David
Brown, Jared
Brown, Kevin
Brown, Mary Ward
Browne-Miller, Angela
Browner, Jesse

Brownlee, Andrea Barnwell
Bryant, John
Bryant, Mark
Brzezinski, Matthew
Bube, Richard Howard
Buchanan, Edna
Buchanan, Roberta
Buck, Rinker
Buckley, Gail Lumet
Buechner, (Carl) Frederick
Buffett, Jimmy
Bullitt, Dorothy
Bumsted, J(ohn) M(ichael)
Bundles, A'Lelia Perry
Bunkers, Suzanne L.
Burak, Carl S.
Burch, Joann J(ohansen)
Burchell, R(obert) A(rthur)
Burden, Wendy
Burns, Eric
Burns, James MacGregor
Burridge, Trevor David
Burrough, Bryan
Burroway, Janet (Gay)
Burston, Daniel
Burton, Betsy
Burton, Thomas G(len)
Busey-Hunt, Brook
Bushnell, Candace
Buskin, Richard
Butler, Dorothy
Butturini, Paula
Buzzell, Colby
Byer, Heather
Caine, Michael
Cairns, Scott
Calabro, Marian
Calasso, Roberto
Caldwell, Grant
Callow, Simon
Calvert, Patricia
Camp, Helen C(ollier)
Campbell, Colin
Campbell, Susan
Campion, Christopher John
Campling, Christopher Russell
Canfield, Oran
Canning, Peter
Cannon, Garland
Cantu, Norma Elia
Capotorto, Carl
Capouya, John
Cappello, Mary C.
Caputo, Philip
Carey, George (Leonard)
Carkeet, David
Carle, Eric
Carlson, David J.
Carney, Pat
Carnochan, W. B.
Carr, David
Carrier, Roch
Carson, Benjamin S(olomon)
Carswell, Sue
Carter, Abigail
Carter, Betty Smartt
Carter, Christine Jacobson

Carter, Jimmy
Carter, Joseph H(enry)
Carter, Rosalynn (Smith)
Carter, Tom
Carton, Bernice
Cary, Lorene
Casanova, Mary
Case, George (Andrew Thomas)
Cassutt, Michael (Joseph)
Castle, Alfred L.
Catanoso, Justin
Caws, Mary Ann
Cebulash, Mel
Chafee, Lincoln D.
Chamberlain, Lesley
Chambers, Aidan
Chamoiseau, Patrick
Chanoff, David
Chapin, Miles
Charlwood, D(onald) E(rnest Cameron)
Chasnoff, Joel
Châteaureynaud, Georges-Olivier
Cheathem, Mark R.
Checkoway, Julie
Cheers, D. Michael
Chen, Patrizia
Cheney, Terri
Chernow, Barbara A.
Cherry, Kelly
Cheuse, Alan
Chin, Staceyann
Chinen, Nate
Chinosole
Chiocca, Olindo Romeo
Chippendale, Lisa A.
Chitham, Edward (Harry Gordon)
Cho, Margaret
Cholodenko, Marc
Chotzinoff, Robin
Choyce, Lesley
Christensen, Damascene
Christman, Jill
Chyna
Ciment, Jill
Clark, Francesco
Clark, Gillian
Clarke, Margaret
Clear, Caitriona
Cleland, Max
Cleveland, Ceil
Cleveland-Peck, Patricia
Clinton, James W(illiam)
Close, Ajay
Cluysenaar, Anne (Alice Andrée)
Coates, Ta-Nehisi
Cockburn, Patrick
Cockrell, Alan
Codrescu, Andrei
Cofer, Judith Ortiz
Cohen, Aaron
Cohen, Kerry
Cohen, Morton N(orton)
Cohen, Rich
Cohen, Richard M(artin)
Cojocaru, Steven
Cole, Stephanie

Cole, Terrence (Michael)
Cole, Wayne S.
Coleman, Terry
Coleman, Verna (Scott)
Collins, Julie (Hubbard)
Collison, Kerry B(oyd)
Collum, Danny Duncan
Colodny, Len
Colson, Charles W(endell)
Colt, George Howe
Comfort, Ray
Comini, Alessandra
Coney, Sandra
Confer, Dennis W.
Conn, Stewart
Connelly, Karen
Conners, Peter
Connolly, Kevin Michael
Conroy, (Donald) Pat(rick)
Constant, Stephen
Conway, Jill Ker
Coogan, Tim(othy) Pat(rick)
Cook, Kevin Graeme
Cooper, Helene
Cooper, Polly Wylly
Copeland, Peter
Corbett, Holly C.
Corley, Thomas Anthony Buchanan
Corn, Alfred
Corp, Edward
Corrigan, Eireann
Corrigan, Kelly
Cosgrove, Brian
Cotton, Ronald
Cowen, Zelman
Cowley, (Cassia) Joy
Cox, Stephen (LeRoy)
Craggs, Stewart R.
Craig, Barry L.
Craig, J. Marshall
Creamer, Robert W.
Crean, Susan M.
Crenson, Victoria
Cress, Doug
Crews, Harry (Eugene)
Cron, Ian Morgan
Crosland, Margaret
Cross, Anthony Glenn
Crowder, Ashby Bland
Crozier, Lorna
Culkin, Jennifer
Cullen, Bill
Cummins, Jeanine
Currey-Wilson, Ellen
Curtis, Brian
Cutting, Linda Katherine
Cyr, Myriam
Cytowic, Richard E(dmund)
Dalai Lama
Dale, Rodney A. M.
Daly, Brenda O.
Damrosch, Phoebe
Dance, Daryl Cumber
Daniels, Anthony
Danquah, Meri Nana-Ama
Darwish, Adel

Dary, David Archie
Dasgupta, Subrata
Davenport, Randi
Davidson, Jeff
Davies, Hunter
Davis, Amelia
Davis, Donald
Davis, Margaret Leslie
Davis, Matthew J.
Davis, Patrick
Davis, Robert C.
Davis, Rocio G.
Davis, Sampson
Davison, Peter (Hobley)
Day, Stacey B.
Day-Lewis, Sean (Francis)
de Blasi, Marlena
de Herrera, Nancy Cooke
de la Billiere, Peter (Edgar de la Cour)
De Vries, Rachel (Guido)
de Waal, Ronald Burt
Deane-Drummond, Anthony (John)
Dearden, James Shackley
Debeljak, Erica Johnson
DeBuron, Nicole
Deffaa, Chip
Defrank, Thomas M.
DeFrees, Madeline
Delaney, Norman
Delany, Samuel R(ay)
Delbanco, Nicholas F(ranklin)
Delgado, Aidan
Delman, Carmit
Deneuve, Catherine
Dery, Dominika
Dessaix, Robert
Devereux, David
Di, Zhu Xiao
di Prima, Diane
Diallo, Kadiatou
Diamond, Arthur
Dibbell, Julian
Dickinson, Amy
Dickinson, Janice
Didion, Joan
Dietz, Peter (John)
Dillard, Annie
Dillard, R(ichard) H(enry) W(ilde)
Dillon, Kathleen M. (Hynek)
Dimbleby, Josceline (Rose)
Divale, William T(ulio)
Dixon, Simon M.
Djerassi, Carl
Djwa, Sandra (Ann)
Dobie, Kathy
Dobyns, Jay Jaybird
Doerr, Anthony
Doherty, Gillian M.
Doherty, Kieran
Doig, Ivan
Donaldson, Islay (Eila) Murray
Donn, Linda
Donofrio, Beverly
Donoughue, Bernard

Donovan
Dorman, Daniel
Dorset, Phyllis (Flanders)
Dotson, Bob
Doty, Mark
Dougan, Terrell Harris
Douglas, Kirk
Dow, David R.
Downer, Lesley
Downes, David A(nthony)
Doyle, Paul E.
Dracup, Angela
Drake, Alicia
Drake, Timothy A.
Draper, Alfred Ernest
Dreher, Henry
Dromgoole, Dominic
Drucker, Olga Levy
Drucker, Peter
Drummond, Michael
Dryden, Konrad
Duberstein, Helen (Laura)
Duberstein, Larry
Dubus, Andre
Duckworth, Marilyn
Dudley-Smith, Timothy
Due, Tananarive
Duff, Alan
Duffy, Maureen (Patricia)
Duke, Anna Marie
Dully, Howard
Dumas, Firoozeh
Dunbar-Ortiz, Roxanne
Duncan, Lois
Dunmore, John
Dunn, Stephen
Duntemann, Jeff
Durden, Robert F(ranklin)
Durschmied, Erik
Dutton, Paul Edward
Dyer, Joyce
Dyson, Freeman (John)
Eastburn, Kathryn
Easton, Nina J(ane)
Ebadi, Shirin
Ebbesmeyer, Curtis Charles
Edison, Mike
Edmisten, Patricia Taylor
Edwards, Anne
Edwards, Larry
Edwards, Philip (Walter)
Eggers, Kerry
Ehle, John
Ehrlich, Amy
Eidse, Faith
Eigenbrod, Renate
Eisenberg, John S.
Eisenberg, Nora
Eisenhower, John S(heldon)
   D(oud)
Elegant, Simon
Eley, Beverley
Ellis, Ella Thorp
Ellison, Joan Jarvis
Emanuel, James A(ndrew)
Emecheta, (Florence Onye) Buchi
Emerson, Ken

Emery, Tom
Emmons, Mary L.
Enslin, Theodore (Vernon)
Eprile, Tony
Epstein, Rachel S.
Erkkila, Betsy
Erlbaum, Janice
Ernaux, Annie
Esposito, Phil(ip Anthony)
Eteraz, Ali
Eugster, Sandra Lee
Evans, C. Wyatt
Evans, Danny
Evanzz, Karl
Fales-Hill, Susan
Fallon, Ivan (Gregory)
Fallowell, Duncan (Richard)
Faqir, Fadia A.M.
Farley, David
Farmaian, Sattareh Farman
Farrell, Mike Joseph
Farrell, Richard
Farthing-Knight, Catherine
Fassett, John D.
Faulkner, Howard J.
Febos, Melissa
Feder, Chris Welles
Federico, Meg
Feifer, George
Feiffer, Jules
Feinberg, Barbara
Feldman, Gayle
Feldman, Richard Jay
Ferguson, Ron
Ferguson, Will
Fermor, Patrick (Michael) Leigh
Field, Edward
Field, Ophelia
Fiennes, Ranulph
Figes, Eva
Fikes, Jay C(ourtney)
Fine, Jerramy Sage
Finley, Karen
Finley, Michael
Finn, R(alph) L(eslie)
Finstad, Suzanne
Fish, Charles (K.)
Fisher, Clive
Fisher, Robin Gaby
Fisher-Wirth, Ann W.
Fishgall, Gary
Fitzgerald, Cathy
Fitzpatrick, Sheila Mary
Fitzpatrick, Vincent (dePaul)
Flaste, Richard (Alfred)
Fleeson, Lucinda
Fleming, Kate
Fleming, Keith
Fleming, Thomas
Fletcher, Michael A.
Flinn, Kathleen
Flinn, Kelly
Flitter, Marc
Florita, Kira
Flowers, Pam
Flynn, Kevin
Flynn, Laura M.

Flynn, Robert (Lopez)
Foerstner, Abigail M.
Foley, Mick
Fonda, Peter
Foot, David
Forbes, Camille F.
Foreman, George
Forrester, Helen
Foster, Joanne Reckler
Foster, Ken
Fowler, Connie May
Fowler, Ruth
Fox, Barry
Fox, Faulkner
Fox, Hugh (Bernard)
Fox, Paula
Foxx, Daniel
Franceschini, Remo
Francis, Clare
Francis, R(ichard) A.
Frankel, Alona
Franklin, David Byrd
Fraser, Antonia
Fraser, Ronald (Angus)
Frassetto, Michael
Freadman, Richard
Freed, Anne O.
Freed, Lynn
Freedland, Michael
Freeman, Jo
French, Albert
French, Francis
Freud, Sophie
Frey, Julia (Bloch)
Friedland, Martin L(awrence)
Friedman, Andrew
Frisbie, Charlotte J(ohnson)
Frisby, Terence
Frist, William H.
Frith, David (Edward John)
Frueh, Joanna
Fugard, Athol
Fulda, Jennette
Fuller, Mary Lou
Funderburg, Lise
Gablik, Suzi
Gabor, Andrea (Anna Gisela)
Gage, Eleni N.
Gaillard, Frye
Gall, Pete
Gallenkamp, Charles (Benton)
Gallo, Gina
Galloway, Terry
Gänzl, Kurt (Friedrich)
Garbus, Martin
Garcia, J. Malcolm
Garnett, Richard (Duncan Carey)
Garrison, Bruce
Garthoff, Raymond L(eonard)
Garton Ash, Timothy
Gates, Henry Louis
Gathorne-Hardy, Jonathan
Gattey, Charles Neilson
Gaunt, Carole O'Malley
Gehring, Wes D(avid)
Gekoski, Rick
Gelpi, Albert

Gentile, Olivia
George, Margaret
Gerber, Merrill Joan
Gerlach, Don R.
German, Bill
Geronimus, Dennis
Gessel, Van C.
Getz, Marshall J(ay)
Geyer, Georgie Anne
Gherman, Beverly
Ghose, Zulfikar
Giancana, Sam
Gibbon, Sean
Giebel, Christoph
Gifford, Barry (Colby)
Gilbert, Ruth
Gilbert, Sandra M(ortola)
Gilbert, Suzie
Gildner, Gary
Giles, Frank (Thomas Robertson)
Gillett, Margaret
Gillies, Isabel Boyer
Gillman, Peter (Charles)
Gilmore, John
Gilmour, David
Gilpin, Geoff
Ginsberg, Blaze
Giovino, Andrea
Gish, Robert F.
Gitter, Elisabeth
Glatt, John
Glen, Frank Grenfell
Glendinning, Miles
Glock, Allison
Godbold, E(dward) Stanly
Gold, Herbert
Gold, Jerome
Goldberger, Avriel H.
Goodall, Jane
Goodhue, Thomas W.
Goodman, Hirsh
Goodman, Richard
Goodwin, Doris (Helen) Kearns
Gordievsky, Oleg
Gordon, Anne Wolrige
Gordon, Colin
Gordon, Eric A(rthur)
Gordon, John (William)
Gordon, Lyndall (Felicity)
Gordon, Mary (Catherine)
Gordon, Meryl
Gordon, Robert Ellis
Gordon, Sheila
Gore, Ariel
Gorham, Deborah
Gorlin, Eitan
Gornick, Vivian
Gorokhova, Elena
Gotfryd, Bernard
Gott, Richard (Willoughby)
Gottlieb, Alma
Goulden, Joseph C.
Grabbe, Crockett L(ane)
Graboys, Thomas B.
Grace, Nancy McCampbell
Graham, Billy
Graham, W(illiam) Fred

Grandin, Temple
Graves, Ralph (Augustus)
Gray, Dulcie
Gray, Francine du Plessix
Greacen, Lavinia
Green, (Charles Stuart) Jamison
Green, Michael (Frederick)
Green, Sharony Andrews
Greenberg, Elinor Miller
Greenberg, Mike
Greene, Bryan A.
Greene, Melissa Fay
Greenstein, George
Greer, Germaine
Greetham, David
Gregor, Arthur
Gregory, Dick
Gresser, Seymour
Grey, Anthony
Griffiths, William G.
Griggs, Vanessa Davis
Grimberg, Tina
Grodin, Charles
Groemer, Gerald
Grossinger, Tania
Grosz, Terry
Groult, Benoite
Grow, L(ynn) M(erle)
Gruber, William E.
Grumbach, Doris
Guidry, Cindy
Guinn, Jeff Mason
Gutman, Robert W.
Gwartney, Debra
Gyatso, Palden
Haddad, Gladys
Haffenden, John
Hafvenstein, Joel
Hagger, Nicholas
Hahn, Michael T.
Hajratwala, Minal
Hale, Robert D(avid)
Hall, Blaine H(ill)
Hall, Donald (Andrew)
Hall, Meredith
Hallock, John W(esley) M(atthew)
Hallwas, John E.
Hallwood, Jan
Halsey, A(lbert) H(enry)
Halter, Marek
Halverson, Cathryn
Hamilton, Hugo
Hamilton, Sharon Jean
Hammel, Bob
Hampton, Wilborn
Han Suyin
Handler, Marisa
Hänsel, Marion
Hansen, Chadwick
Hansen, Mark Victor
Hansen, Matthew Scott
Hansen, Suzanne
Hanson, Neil
Hardy, Barbara (Gladys)
Hardy, Gayle J.
Hardy, Robert Earl
Hargreaves, John D(esmond)

Haring, Bruce
Harline, Craig E.
Harman, Patricia
Harmon, Sandra
Harnack, Curtis
Harper, Jean
Harrill, Ronald
Harris, Brayton
Harris, Fred R(oy)
Harris, Stacy
Harrison, Kathryn
Harrison, Kathy A.
Harrison, Kyle
Hart, Bret
Hart, Melissa
Hartley, Aidan
Hartman, Saidiya V.
Harvey, Hazel (Mary)
Harvey, Steven
Harwood, John
Haskell, Guy H.
Haskell, Molly
Haslam, Gerald William
Haslam, Nicholas
Hassan, Ihab (Habib)
Hasselstrom, Linda (Michele)
Hatfield, Juliana
Hatfield, Phyllis
Hattersley, Roy (Sydney George)
Hauptman, Laurence Marc
Hauser, Susan Carol
Hawkins, Anne Hunsaker
Hawkins, Regina Trice
Hawksley, Lucinda
Hawley, Richard A.
Hay, Samuel A.
Hayes, Bill
Hayman, Carol Bessent
Hayman, Ronald
Haynes, C. Rayfield
Haynes, Jim
Hays, Peter L.
Hayslip, Le Ly
Haywood, Chelsea
Hazo, Samuel (John)
Heacox, Kim
Head, David M.
Hearon, Shelby
Heckler, Cheryl
Hein, Christoph
Hejinian, Lyn
Helfgott, Gillian
Heller, Michael
Helprin, Mark
Helvarg, David
Henderson, Kristin
Hendra, Jessica
Henley, Marian
Henriksson, John
Henry, DeWitt (Pawling)
Hensley, William L. Iggiagruk
Hentoff, Nat(han Irving)
Heppner, Cheryl M.
Herbert, Ivor
Herbst, Jurgen
Herr, Michael
Herrin, Lamar

Herrmanns, Ralph
Hershman, Marcie
Herzberg, Nancy K.
Heyman, Abigail
Hickman, Bert G(eorge)
Hietala, Thomas R.
Higginbotham, Jay
Higgins, Aidan
Hill, Brian W.
Hill, Lynn
Hill, Susan (Elizabeth)
Hilles, Robert
Him, Chanrithy
Hinde, Thomas
Hine, Robert V.
Hiney, Tom
Hinn, Benny
Hinojosa, Maria (de Lourdes)
Hinson, E. Glenn
Hoagland, Edward
Hobby, Elaine (Ann)
Hobson, J(ohn) Allan
Hochman, Jiri
Hodgkiss, Alan Geoffrey
Hoffman, Amy Beth
Hoffman, Eva
Hoffman, Mat
Hoffman, Ronald
Hogg, James (Dalby)
Holden, Anthony (Ivan)
Holdgate, Martin W.
Holland, James R.
Hollander, Samuel
Hollo, Anselm (Paul Alexis)
Holloway, Karla F. C.
Holroyd, Michael
Holt, Marilyn Irvin
Holyfield, Evander
Hom, Sharon K.
Hooker, Jeremy
Hopgood, Mei-Ling
Hopkins, Antony
Hopkins, George Emil
Horn, Mike
Horn, Stacy
Hornby, Nick
Horne, R(alph) A(lbert)
Horton, Madelyn (Stacey)
Horwood, William
Houghton, Katharine
Houshmand, Zara
Howard, Elizabeth Jane
Howard, Maureen
Hromic, Alma A.
Huber, Sonya
Huby, Pamela Margaret
Hughes, Shirley
Hughes-Hallett, Lucy
Hunt, Angela Elwell
Hunt, Rameck
Hunt, Richard (Patrick)
Huntley, Paula (Bowlin)
Hurtig, Mel
Hussey, Mark
Hutchinson, Bill
Hutchinson, Earl Ofari
Hutchinson, Samuel

Hutchinson, Timothy A.
Hutton, Ronald
Hynes, Samuel
Imbarrato, Susan Clair
Inez, Colette
Ireland, Kevin (Mark)
Irving, John (Winslow)
Isherwood, Charles
Israel, Lee
Ivanova, Tatyana G(rigoryevna)
Iyer, Pico
Jackson, Marni
Jacobs, Alan
Jacobson, Joanne
Jain, Anita
Jalland, Pat(ricia)
James, Catherine
James, Clive (Vivian Leopold)
James, Laura M.
James, P. D.
James, Sibyl
Janello, Amy (Elizabeth)
Janken, Kenneth Robert
Jares, Joe
Jasper, Kenji (Nathaniel)
Jellison, Katherine
Jenkins, George
Jenkins, Michael (Romilly Heald)
Jericho, Chris
Jiang, Ji li
Johnson, Fenton
Johnson, Joan Marie
Johnson, Rick L.
Johnston, Lyle
Johnston, Michael
Johnstone, Nick
Jokinen, Tom
Jolles, Michael Adam
Jones, Ben Lewis
Jones, Larry
Jones, Lisa
Jones, Malcolm
Jones, R(obert) M(aynard)
Joseph, Henry
Jourdan, Carolyn
Jouve, Nicole Ward
Jovanovic, Rob
Joy, Camden
Joya, Malalai
Joyce, Graham
Joyner, Hannah
Judson, John
Junger, Sebastian
Ka, Olivier
Kabaservice, Geoffrey (M.)
Kahlenberg, Richard D.
Kaiser, Ken
Kaleta, Kenneth C.
Kambalu, Samson
Kamoie, Laura Croghan
Kanafani, Deborah
Kang, K. Connie
Kaplan, Beth
Kaplan, James
Kaplan, Jonathan
Kaplan-Maxfield, Thomas
Karlin, Wayne (Stephen)

Karnow, Stanley
Karr, Mary
Kasparov, Garry (Kimovich)
Katouzian, Homa
Katz, Jesse
Kauffman, Michael W.
Kauffmann, Stanley
Kavanagh, P(atrick) J(oseph)
Kavenna, Joanna
Kawatski, Deanna
Kaysen, Susanna
Kearns, Lionel (John)
Kee, Robert
Keeble, Neil H(oward)
Keefe, Patrick Radden
Keillor, Steven J(ames)
Keith, Caroline H(elen)
Kelley, Alec E(rvin)
Kelly, Deirdre
Kelly, Ian
Kelly, Judith
Kenison, Katrina
Kennard, David
Kennedy, Adrienne
Kennedy, Dan
Kennedy, Michael
Kenslea, Timothy
Kent, Carol
Kerr, Ann Zwicker
Kessler, Glenn
Ketner, Kenneth Laine
Keyes, Daniel
Khosla, Dhillon
Kidd, Sue Monk
Kidder, Tracy
Kiddy, Elizabeth W.
Kilduff, Peter
Kimura, Margaret
Kindred, Dave
King, Sallie B.
King, Sorrel McElroy
King, William Davies
King-Hele, Desmond
Kingston, Maxine Hong
Kissinger, Henry (Alfred)
Kitaj, Karma
Kiteley, Brian
Klappert, Peter
Klass, Perri (Elizabeth)
Klass, Sheila Solomon
Klebanoff, Arthur
Kleh, Cindy (L.)
Kleinknecht, William
Klempner, Mark
Kluger, Ruth
Knighton, Ryan
Knowles, Harry (Jay)
Knox, Elizabeth (Fiona)
Koch, Edward I(rving)
Koch, Peter O.
Koerner, Lisbet
Kohler, Dean Ellis
Korda, Michael (Vincent)
Koren, Yehuda
Kossman, Nina
Kostelniuk, James
Kostman, Joel

Koterba, Jeffrey
Kraus, Caroline
Krej i, Jaroslav
Krieg, Joann P(eck)
Krieg, Robert Anthony
Kriegel, Leonard
Kuberski, Philip
Kull, Robert
Kuntz, Jerry
Kureishi, Hanif
Kurkjian, Tim Bell
Kurland, Geoffrey
L'Heureux, John (Clarke)
Laas, Virginia J(eans)
Lachman, Barbara
Ladd, Louise
Lahutsky, John
Lakos, Amos
Lamb, Karl A(llen)
Lambert, Page
Lambur, Joan
Lammon, Martin
Lamont-Brown, Raymond
Lampanelli, Lisa
Lamplugh, Lois
Lander, Ernest McPherson
Landsberg, Melvin
Lang, Lang
LaNier, Carlotta Walls
Lara, Adair
Lardner, Kate
Lassez, Sarah
Lassner, Phyllis
Lauren, Jillian
Lawday, David
Lawrence, C(lifford) H(ugh)
Laxer, James
Lay, Carol
Le Breton, Binka
Leak, Andrew N.
Leake, John
Leakey, Richard (Erskine Frere)
Leckie, Shirley A(nne)
Lederer, Katy
Lee, A(rthur) Robert
Lee, Barbara
Lee, Jid
Lee, M. Owen
Lehmann-Haupt, Rachel
Lehr, Jennifer
Lehrer, James (Charles)
Leiser, Gary
Lemay, Shawna
Lemon, Alex
Lende, Heather
Lenney, Dinah
Lennox, John
Lenskyj, Helen Jefferson
Leo, Mabel R.
Leonard, Stephen J.
Leonardi, Susan J.
Leslie, Kent A.
Lesser, Wendy
Lessing, Doris (May)
Lester, Julius
Letessier, Dorothée
Leve, Ariel

Levesque, John
Levin, Michael (Graubart)
Levy, Daniel S.
Lewis, Gregg (Allan)
Lewis, Rupert
Lewis-Ferguson, Julinda
Li, Leslie
Li, Moying
Lieberman, Robert C.
Liebman, Herbert
Lim, Shirley Geok-lin
Limonov, E duard
Lincecum, Jerry Bryan
Lindholdt, Paul J.
Lindstrom, Lamont (Carl)
Linnea, Ann
Linton, Simi
Lipsyte, Robert (Michael)
Lipton, Eunice
Lisle, Laurie
Littleton, Darryl
Littlewood, Clayton
Liu, Eric
Livingston, Gordon (S.)
LL Cool J
Llewellyn, Kate
Lloyd, T(revor) O(wen)
Lo Scalzo, Jim
Lock, Joan
Locke, Robert R.
Lockridge, Larry
Lofton, Rodney
Loh, Sandra Tsing
Long, Carolyn Morrow
Long, Michael G.
Longley, Michael
Longmate, Norman Richard
Lorrimer, Claire
Lourie, Richard
Loux, Ann Kimble
Lovell, (Alfred Charles) Bernard
Lovett, Bobby L.
Lucas, Geralyn
Lucas, John
Luft, Lya Fett
Lukas, Christopher
Luongo, F. Thomas
Lupica, Mike
Luyendijk, Joris
Lyden, Jacki
Lyon, Andrea D.
Lyon, Elizabeth
Lystra, Karen
Lytle, Mark H.
Mabee, Carleton
MacAdams, William
Macdonald, Michael Patrick
MacDonald, Sam A.
Macdonald, Sarah
MacEnulty, Pat
Macfarlane, Malcolm R.
Machoian, Ronald Glenn
MacInnes, Mairi
Macklin, Robert
MacLaine, Shirley
Madden, David
Madhubuti, Haki R.

Maes, Yvonne (M.)
Magee, Bryan
Mager, Hugo
Magliato, Kathy
Mahler, Jonathan
Mahon, Basil
Mahoney, Richard D.
Maier, Thomas
Mairs, Nancy (Pedrick)
Malcolm, Elizabeth
Malin, Irving
Mallin, Jay
Maltby, William S(aunders)
Mandela, Nelson (Rolihlahla)
Manetti, Larry
Manhein, Mary H(uffman)
Mann, Charles F.
Mann, Jeff(rey A.)
Mann, Reva
Manrique (Ardila), Jaime
Mansell, Darrel
Manzoor, Sarfraz
Maracle, Lee
Marcell, Jacqueline
Marcello, Patricia Cronin
Marcou, David J.
Marder, Norma
Mariano, Connie Concepcion
Marias, Javier
Marin, Rosario
Marker, Sherry
Marley, Rita
Marquart, Debra
Mars, Julie
Marsh, Jan
Marshall, John Douglas
Martin, Deana
Martin, Larry Jay
Martin, Lorna
Martinson, Deborah
Marty, Sid
Masekela, Hugh
Mason, Bobbie Ann
Mason, Robert C(averly)
Masood, Maliha
Massey, Victoria
Mathabane, Mark
Mayer, Musa
Mayer, Robert
McCaffrey, James M.
McCann, Graham
McCants, Clyde T.
McCargo, Duncan
McCarthy, Mignon
McCarthy, Nan
McCauley, Martin
McClintick, David
McClure, Tori Murden
McConica, James Kelsey
McConkey, James (Rodney)
Mccoole, Sinéad
McCorkindale, Susan
McCormick, Blaine
McCracken, Elizabeth
McCutcheon, Sandy
McDonald, Forrest
McElmeel, Sharron L.

Index To Writing Categories

McElroy, Colleen J.
McFarlane, Peter (William)
McGaughy, J. Kent
McGoogan, Ken
McGrath, Melanie
McGuane, Thomas
McKeen, William
McKenzie, John D.
McKinney, Sally (Brown)
McLendon, Jacquelyn Y.
McMaster, Susan
McMasters, Kelly
McMullan, Margaret
McNaron, Toni (A. H.)
McNeish, James
Mead, Chris
Mearns, Barbara (Crawford)
Measham, Donald Charles
Medicine-Eagle, Brooke
Meeink, Frank
Mehta, Gita
Mehta, Ved (Parkash)
Meier, Richard (Alan)
Melamed, Leo
Melchior, Ib (Jorgen)
Melion, Walter S.
Melosh, Barbara
Melton, Judith
Mercer, Jeremy
Meredith, Martin
Merrill, Wendy
Metcalf, John (Wesley)
Metz, Allan (Sheldon)
Metz, Julie
Metzger, Deena P.
Metzger, Michael M(oses)
Mezey, Robert
Mezlekia, Nega
Michaels, Lisa
Michelman, Kate
Middlemas, (Robert) Keith
Miklowitz, Gloria D.
Miller, Aaron David
Miller, Amie Klempnauer
Miller, Blair
Miller, Donald L.
Miller, E. Ethelbert
Miller, Edward A.
Miller, John
Miller, Laura
Miller, Richard Lawrence
Miller, Robert H.
Miller, Russell
Millett, Kate
Millman, Cynthia R.
Milne, David
Min, Anchee
Mintz, Alan L.
Mirvish, Dan
Missamou, Tchicaya
Mitchell, Thomas R.
Mitson, Eileen N(ora)
Moffat, Gwen
Momaday, N(avarre) Scott
Monk, Robert C.
Montagu of Beaulieu
Montague, John (Patrick)

Montgomery, David
Mooney, Brian C.
Moore, Carlos
Moore, Christine Palamidessi
Moore, Dinty W.
Moore, James T(almadge)
Moore, Laurie
Moore, Sam
Moran, Mary (Molly) Hurley
Moravec, Ivo
Morgan, Mary
Morgan, Robin
Mori, Kyoko
Moro, Javier
Morris, Bob
Morris, Edmund
Morris, Jan
Morris, Jeffrey B(randon)
Morris, Jiwe
Morris, Larry E.
Morris, Sylvia Jukes
Morrison, (Philip) Blake
Morritt, Hope
Morrow, Ann
Morton, James (Severs)
Moseley, Marcus
Mosley, Nicholas
Moss, Thylias (Rebecca)
Motion, Andrew (Peter)
Mould, Daphne D. C. Pochin
Mourlevat, Jean-Claude
Mowat, Claire (Angel Wheeler)
Mueller, Daniel
Muhlhahn, Cara
Mukherjee, Bharati
Mulgrew, Jason
Mullane, (R.) Mike
Mulroney, Brian
Murakami, Haruki
Murchie, Noël
Murphey, Cecil B(laine)
Murphy, Patrick J.
Murray, Albert
Murry, Katherine Middleton
Mustazza, Leonard
Muszynski, Stuart
Myers, Alyse
Myers, Kevin
Myers, Walter Dean
Naden, Corinne J.
Nahas, Gabriel G(eorges)
Naraghi, Ehsan
Narayan, Kirin
Nasdijj
Nash, Elizabeth (Hamilton)
Natusch, Sheila
Natwar-Singh, K.
Neale, Jonathan
Near, Holly
Neaverson, Bob
Necipoglu, Gulru
Neiman, Susan
Nelson, Geoffrey Kenneth
Nelson, Jill
Nemec, James
Nericcio, William Anthony
Neugeboren, Jay

Newell, William H.
Nguyên, Kiên
Nicholls, C(hristine) S(tephanie)
Nichols, John
Nichols, Peter (Richard)
Nicholson, Mavis
Niemann, Linda (Grant)
Nimoy, Adam
Nisbet, Jack
Nobbs, David
Noltingk, Bernard Edward
Nordan, Lewis
Norman, Michael Lewis
Norris, Kathleen
Novak, Jana
Nugent, Benjamin
Nunez, Sigrid
Nutt, Paul C.
Nutzle, Futzie
Nye, Robert
O'Brien, George
O'Callaghan, Sean
O'Connor, Rebecca K.
O'Dell, Carol D.
O'Doherty, Malachi
O'Donnell, Patrick K.
O'Driscoll, Dennis
O'Faolain, Julia
O'Hara, Kevin
O'Malley, Penelope Grenoble
O'Neal, Hank
O'Neill, Tony
O'Reilly Herrera, (C.) Andrea
O'Toole, Lawrence
Oakdale, Suzanne
Oakley, Ann
Oaksey
Oates, Stephen B(aery)
Obst, Lynda (Rosen)
Odber (de Baubeta), Patricia
  (Anne)
Oderman, Stuart (Douglas)
Ogden, Christopher
Ojaide, Tanure
Oleson, James A.
Oliver, Kitty
Oliver, Roland Anthony
Ollestad, Norman
Olmstead, Robert
Olson, Lynne
Olson, Ted
Ondego, Ogova
Onwueme, Tess Osonye
Onyeama, Dillibe
Orban, Christine
Orion, Doreen
Orizio, Riccardo
Orlova, Alexandra (Anatol'evna)
Orr, Gregory (Simpson)
Osborn, Ian
Osborne, Charles
Osen, James L.
Osgood, Kenneth
Overmyer, James E.
Owens, Thomas S(heldon)
Oxenhandler, Noelle
Oxley, William

Paddock, Lisa
Padfield, Peter
Paetro, Maxine
Pahor, Boris
Paisner, Daniel
Pakula, Hannah (Cohn)
Palazchenko, Pavel
Paldiel, Mordecai
Pallone, Dave
Palmer, Alan Warwick
Palmer, Beverly Wilson
Pantaeva, Irina
Pappas, Milt
Parillo, Mark P.
Paris, Barry
Parker, Tom
Parnell, Mary Davies
Parrish, T(homas) Michael
Patterson, George N(eilson)
Patterson, Horace L.
Patterson, Kevin
Paul, Caroline
Peabody, Richard (Myers)
Peacock, Molly
Pear, David (Adrian)
Pearson, Carol Lynn
Peck, Dale
Pederson, William D(avid)
Peeradina, Saleem
Pelosi, Nancy
Pennac, Daniel
Penrose, Antony
Perkins, Kelly
Perl, Ruth June
Perle, Liz
Perry, Roland
Peters, Robert
Petro, Pamela J.
Petsalis-Diomidis, Nicholas
Phayer, Michael
Pianka, Eric R(odger)
Pickering, David (Hugh)
Pickering, Samuel F(rancis)
Pierce, Chonda
Pierson, Melissa Holbrook
Piggott, Alan (Derek)
Pilling, John
Pindell, Terry
Pinney, Lucy (Catherine)
Pipher, Mary (Bray)
Pitcher, George
Plante, David (Robert)
Platt, James R.
Plaut, W. Gunther
Plitt, Jane R(uth)
Podhoretz, Norman
Pohl-Weary, Emily
Poirier-Bures, Simone
Polikoff, Barbara G(arland)
Polkinghorne, John Charlton
Pollard, A(nthony) J(ames)
Pollard, John (Richard Thornhill)
Pollock, John Charles
Ponce, Mary Helen
Poole, Eric
Potvin, Liza
Powell, D. A.

Stanley, Susie Cunningham
Stapleton, Timothy J.
Starzl, Thomas E(arl)
Stead, C(hristian) K(arlson)
Steavenson, Wendell
Steel, David (Martin Scott)
Steele, Mary
Steiker, Valerie
Steinbrook, Gordon L.
Steins, Richard
Stenzel, Anabel
Stephens, William Peter
Stern, Ellen Norman
Stevenson, James
Stewart, Kathleen
Stillerman, Marci
Stimpson, Jeff
Stockler, Bruce
Stodghill, Ron
Storey, Edward
Storlie, Erik Fraser
Stout, Jay A.
Stowe, Steven M.
Strane, Susan
Strathern, Paul
Streeter, Patrick
Stringer, C. Vivian
Strongin, Laurie
Stross, Randall E.
Stroud, Patricia Tyson
Stuart, Alexander
Stuart, Sarah Payne
Suleiman, Susan Rubin
Sullivan, David M.
Sullivan, George E(dward)
Sullivan, Randall
Summer, Lauralee
Sundeen, Mark
Sundquist, Josh
Sunee, Kim
Suskind, Ron(ald Steven)
Sussman, Peter Y.
Svoboda, Terese
Swafford, Jan Johnson
Sward, Robert S.
Sweeney, Eamonn
Swift, Graham
Swiller, Josh
Swope, Sam
Szanton, Andrew (Emlen)
Tabios, Eileen
Talese, Gay
Tarnopolsky, Yuri
Tarte, Bob
Tattlin, Isadora
Taylor, Andy
Taylor, Anne Marie
Taylor, Daniel (William)
Taylor, Jacqueline
Taylor, John Russell
Taylor, Jonathan
Taylor, Michael Ray
Taylor, Rogan
Taylor, Sarah Stewart
Taylor, Stephen
Teachout, Terry
Tearle, John L.

Tebbit, Norman
Teece, Philip
Tehan, Arline Boucher
Teller, Neville
Tenbrook, Gretchen W.
Tent, Pam
Terpstra, John
Thaden, Barbara Z.
Thatcher, Margaret (Hilda)
Thayer, Helen
Theodore, Wayne
Thomas, Abigail
Thomas, Adrian
Thomas, Bruce
Thomas, Clara McCandless
Thomas, D(onald) M(ichael)
Thomas, Leslie (John)
Thomas, Rosanne Daryl
Thompson, Christina
Thompson, Robert Farris
Thompson-Cannino, Jennifer
Thomson, Andrew
Thomson, George Henry
Thornton, Yvonne S.
Thrasher, Peter Adam
Thwe, Pascal Khoo
Thynn, Alexander (George)
Tindall, Gillian (Elizabeth)
Tippets, John M.
Toker, Leona
Tolson, Jay
Tomalin, Claire
Tomasulo, Daniel J.
Tombs, Robert P.
Tomkins, Calvin
Tompkins, Ptolemy (Christian)
Torsney, Cheryl B.
Toub, Micah
Towne, Marian K(leinsasser)
Transue, Emily R.
Tremlett, George (William)
Trevelyan, Raleigh
Tripp, Nathaniel
Trout, Robert J(ay)
Trudeau, Noah Andre
Truman, Ruth
Trump, Donald J.
Trzebinski, Errol
Tuaolo, Esera
Tucker, Cynthia Grant
Tucker, Judy H.
Tucker, Michael
Tucker, Neely
Turner, Ann (Warren)
Turner, Brian (Lindsay)
Turner, Marjorie Shepherd
Turvey, Roger
Tweed, Thomas A.
Tweit, Susan J(oan)
Tynan, Ronan
Tysdahl, Bjorn Johan
Ugel, Edward
Ullman, Ellen
Ullmann, Owen
Umland, Samuel J(oseph)
Underwood, Peter
Ung, Loung

Urch, Elizabeth
Ureneck, Lou
Urquhart, Brian Edward
Uruburu, Paula
Utley, Robert M(arshall)
Valk, Anne M.
Vallejo, Armando
Van der Kiste, John (Patrick Guy)
van der Kooi, Cornelis
Van Domelen, John E(mory)
van Praagh, David
van Vugt, William E.
Vandenburgh, Jane
Vasta, Edward
Vaughn, Patrika
Vazquez-Gomez, Juana
Velez-Mitchell, Jane
Vickers, Daniel
Vigée, Claude (Andre Strauss)
Vincent, Edgar
Vincent, Isabel
Visconti, Tony
Vizenor, Gerald (Robert)
Vollers, Maryanne
Wachsberger, Ken(neth)
Wachtel, Eleanor
Wade, (Sarah) Virginia
Wade, Stephen
Wagener, Leon
Wagner, Wenceslas J.
Wagner-Martin, Linda C.
Waisman, Sergio Gabriel
Wakefield, Dan
Waldman, Harry
Walker, Kenneth Roland
Walker, Nigel (David)
Wallace, James
Wallach, Jennifer Jensen
Wallin, Pamela
Walton, John (Nicholas)
Wapshott, Nicholas (Henry)
Ward, Gregory
Ward, Logan
Ware, Leland B.
Warnock, Mary
Warren, Louis S.
Warren, Sandra K.
Waters, Barbara
Watkins, Paul
Watson, Irene
Watt, Ben
Waugh, Alexander
Waugh, Joan
Waugh, Sylvia
Waxman, Henry Arnold
Weaver-Gelzer, Charlotte
Weber, Katharine
Webster, Brenda
Webster, Len
Weddington, Sarah (Ragle)
Weddle, David
Weddle, Kevin J.
Wedell, Eberhard George
Weimer, Joan
Weiner, Edmund
Weinstein, Philip M.
Weinstock, Nicholas

Weir, Ben(jamin M.)
Weir, Theresa
Wek, Alek
Weldon, Fay
Werbach, Adam
Werris, Wendy
Wesker, Arnold
Westbrook, Peter (J.)
Westheimer, (Karola) Ruth
Westling, Louise (Hutchings)
Westrum, Dexter
Wetenhall, John
Wexler, Alice (Ruth)
Wheeler, Lonnie
Whicker, Alan (Donald)
Whitaker, Katie
White, Edward M.
White, Emily
White, Evelyn C.
White, Kenneth
White, Neil
White-Parks, Annette
Whitelaw, Nancy
Whittemore, (Edward) Reed
Whitten, Leslie Hunter
Wickham, DeWayne
Wicks, Susan
Widner, Jennifer A(nne)
Wiebe, Katie Funk
Wieder, Alan
Wiesel, Elie
Wilder, Gene
Wilderson, Frank B.
Wildwind, Sharon Grant
Wilensky, Amy S.
Wilker, Josh
Williams, C(harles) K(enneth)
Williams, Donna
Williams, Dwight
Williams, Geoff
Williams, John A(lfred)
Williams, Kimmika L(yvette
  Hawes)
Williams, Niall
Williams, Robyn
Willis, Edgar E(rnest)
Willmott, Phyllis
Wilson, Brandon
Wilson, Darryl B(abe)
Wilson, Des
Wilson, G. Willow
Wilson, Gretchen
Wilson, Joseph (Charles)
Wilson, Ken
Wilson, Patricia Potter
Wilson, Sandy
Wiltshire, Susan Ford
Winans, Christopher
Winder, Michael
Wineapple, Brenda
Winik, Marion (Lisa)
Winner, Lauren F.
Winokur, Jon
Winship, Michael P.
Winter, Kari J.
Winter, Michael
Wise, Joe

Bibliography-*cont.*

Kramer, Dale
Kreitner, Kenneth
Kujoory, Parvin
Lachs, John
Lakos, Amos
Lamb, Connie
Lawler, Nancy Ellen
Leab, Daniel Josef
Lear, Linda J(ane)
Lengel, Edward G.
Lent, John A.
Leopold, Terry Ann Mood
Letellier, Robert Ignatius
Lewis, Ward B.
Lima, Robert (F.)
Lin, Tan (Anthony)
Lingenfelter, Richard Emery
Lippy, Charles H(oward)
Locklin, Gerald Ivan
Loewe, Michael
Lundeberg, Philip (Karl)
Mabbett, Ian William
Machoian, Ronald Glenn
Madden, David
Mahmud, Shabana
Makowski, Silky
Mallett, Daryl F(urumi)
Manchel, Frank
Marantz, Kenneth A.
Marantz, Sylvia S.
Marolda, Edward J.
Marr, David G(eorge)
Martin, Elizabeth A(nn)
Martin, Fenton S(trickland)
Marting, Diane E.
Matthews, Elizabeth W(oodfin)
May, Steven W.
McIlwaine, John
Mehaffey, Karen Rae
Meho, Lokman I.
Metz, Allan (Sheldon)
Meyers, Jeffrey
Michael, Colette V(erger)
Mickolus, Edward (Francis)
Mikolyzk, Thomas A.
Miles, Barry
Milgram, Gail Gleason
Moody, Fred
Moreh, Shmuel
Mörner, Magnus
Muniz, Olga M.
Navia, Luis E.
Nees, Lawrence
Nelson, Carolyn W(illiamson)
Nersessian, V(rej) N.
Noegel, Scott B.
Nolan, William F(rancis)
Norton, Augustus Richard
Nuechterlein, Jonathan E.
O'Day, Alan (Earl)
O'Neill, Robert John
O'Shea, Kathleen A.
Ogilvie, Marilyn Bailey
Olderr, Steven
Olson, James S.
Olson, Laura R.
Oppelt, Norman T.

Bibliography-*cont.*

Oppenheim, Micha Falk
Orenstein, Ronald I.
Ostler, Rosemarie
Packer, Joan Garrett
Paietta, Ann C.
Palkovic, Mark
Paravisini-Gebert, Lizabeth
Paris, Michael
Parkes, M(alcolm) B(eckwith)
Parrish, T(homas) Michael
Pearsall, Derek (Albert)
Perone, James E.
Perry, Margaret
Peters, Rudolph
Peterson, Christian A.
Pharies, David (Arnold)
Pierard, Richard V(ictor)
Poague, Leland
Podell, Diane K(opperman)
Powell, Ardal
Price, Glanville
Pringle, David (William)
Radelet, Michael L.
Rankin, Robert
Rapf, Joanna E.
Reasoner, Livia Jane Washburn
Reginald, Robert
Richmond, Hugh Macrae
Rimler, Walter
Ritchie, Pamela E.
Roberts, Francis X.
Robertson, James I.
Rodger, Richard
Rodríguez, Andrés
Rogers, Deborah D(ee)
Rohner, Ronald P.
Rollins, Alden M(ilton)
Roth, Klaus
Rowland, Arthur Ray
Ruoff, A. LaVonne Brown
Russell, Jeffrey Burton
Ruthchild, Rochelle Goldberg
Sable, Martin Howard
Sajdak, Bruce T.
Salwak, Dale (Francis)
Sanders, David
Sanecki, Kay Naylor
Sargent, Lyman Tower
Sarna, Jonathan D(aniel)
Scaglione, Aldo
Schaffner, Bradley L(ewis)
Schlesinger, Benjamin
Schmitz, Cecilia M.
Schumacher, John N(orbert)
Screech, M(ichael) A(ndrew)
Seaman, Gerald Roberts
Sensibar, Judith L(evin)
Server, Lee
Sessa, Valerie I.
Sheinin, David (M. K.)
Sheldon, Joseph K(enneth)
Shell, Robert C.H.
Shultz, Suzanne M.
Sicherman, Carol
Silver, Harold
Silverburg, Sanford R.
Simmie, James (Martin)

Bibliography-*cont.*

Simpson, Michael Andrew
Sinnette, Elinor Des Verney
Skemer, Don C.
Skreslet, Paula Youngman
Slater, Thomas J.
Sloan, Jane
Smith, Carolyn Jeanne
Smith, Hobart Muir
Smith, Hugh
Smith, Roger T.
Smith, Sarah (W. R.)
Smith, Vivian (Brian)
Snow, Philip (Albert)
Souster, Raymond
Speck, Bruce W.
Spector, Sheila A.
Stephens, Andy
Stevens, Peter (Stanley)
Stillinger, Jack
Stoner, K. Lynn
Storey, Dee
Storey, Mark
Stuhr(-Rommereim), Rebecca (Ann)
Tainter, Frank H(ugh)
Tanselle, G(eorge) Thomas
Thackeray, Frank W.
Tokarczyk, Michelle M.
Trattner, Walter I.
Trela, D(ale) J(ohn)
Tremblay, Florent A.
Tucker, Martin
Van der Kiste, John (Patrick Guy)
Van Willigen, John
Vanderwal, Andrew H.
VanMeter, Vandelia
Varzi, Achille C.
Vaughan, Alden T(rue)
Visotzky, Burton L.
Vizenor, Gerald (Robert)
Wakefield, James L.
Walker, Donald E(dwin)
Walters, James W.
Ward, Philip
Watson, George (Grimes)
Weihs, Jean (Riddle)
Weinrich, A. K. H.
Wells, Stanley (William)
Wert, Jonathan (Maxwell)
Wess, Jane A.
West, James L(emuel) W(ills)
Wheatley, Nadia
Wheeler, Helen Rippier
White, Phillip M.
Whiteman, (David) Bruce
Widdicombe, Toby
Wilcox, Laird (M.)
Williams, Gerhild Scholz
Willis, Deborah
Willoughby, Pamela R.
Wilson, Myoung Chung
Winearls, Joan
Woods, Jeannie Marlin
Youd, Samuel
Young, Ian
Zelinsky, Wilbur
Zuckerman, Mary Ellen

Bibliography-*cont.*

Biography

Aaker, Everett
Abajian, Kathryn J.
Abbotson, Susan C.W.
Abbott, Lynn
Abrahams, Peter
Ackroyd, Peter
Adair, Aaron J.
Adams, Jad
Adams, Jerome R(obertson)
Adams, Mark
Adams, Timothy Dow
Adamson, Donald
Adelson, Roger
Adler, David A.
Adler, Stephen J.
Adnan, Etel
Afong, Milo S.
Afzal, Omar
Agran, Edward G.
Ahlquist, Dale
Ahmad, Imran
Akbar, Said Hyder
Alaya, Flavia
Alber, Charles J.
Alberts, Laurie
Albom, Mitch
Albrecht, Ernest (Jacob)
Aldridge, (Harold Edward) James
Aleshire, Peter
Alexander, Ann Field
Alexander, John Thorndike
Alexander, Peter F.
Alexander, Sally Hobart
Ali, Ayaan Hirsi
Alinder, Mary Street
Allen, Jane
Allen, John L.
Allen, Nancy
Allfrey, Anthony
Allgood, Myralyn F(rizzelle)
Allison, Amy
Allmand, C. T.
Alofsin, Anthony
Als, Hilton
Alsamari, Lewis
Alson, Peter (H.)
Alter, Judy
Alter, Robert B.
Altman, Mara
Amabile, George
Amaki, Amalia K.
Ambrosini, Richard
Amburn, Ellis
Amoia, Alba della Fazia
Anders, Isabel
Anderson, David Daniel
Anderson, Donna K.
Anderson, M. T(obin)
Anderson, Maureen
Anderson, Richard Lloyd
Anderson, Terry (A.)
Andrews, William L(eake)

Bryant, Mark
Buccieri, Lisa Rojany
Buchanan, Roberta
Buck, Rinker
Buckley, Thomas
Budny, Mildred
Buechner, (Carl) Frederick
Buford, Bill
Buk-Swienty, Tom
Bull, Angela (Mary)
Bumiller, Elisabeth
Bumsted, J(ohn) M(ichael)
Bundles, A'Lelia Perry
Bundy, Carol
Bunkers, Suzanne L.
Burak, Carl S.
Burch, Joann J(ohansen)
Burgess, Charles
Burgess, Robert J(ohn)
Burk, Kathleen
Burk, Robert F(rederick)
Burke, Carolyn
Burlew, A(nn) Kathleen
Burlingame, Michael
Burman, Carina
Burns, James MacGregor
Burns, Khephra
Burns, Richard Gordon
Burridge, Trevor David
Burrough, Bryan
Burston, Daniel
Burton, Anthony
Burton, Betsy
Burton, Ivor (Flower)
Busey-Hunt, Brook
Buskin, Richard
Butcher, Kristin
Butler, Lance St. John
Butler, Rex D.
Butman, John
Byrne, Paula
Cahill, Tim
Caine, Barbara
Cairns, Scott
Calder, Marie D(onais)
Caldwell, Grant
Callanan, Frank
Callaway, Barbara J.
Callow, Simon
Calvert, Patricia
Cambor, Kate
Camp, Helen C(ollier)
Campbell, Colin
Campbell, Eddie
Campbell, James
Campbell, Judith
Campbell, Walter E.
Campbell-Culver, Maggie
Canfield, Oran
Canning, Peter
Cannon, Garland
Capouya, John
Capp, Bernard (Stuart)
Cappello, Mary C.
Caravantes, Peggy
Carcaterra, Lorenzo
Carey, Patrick W.

Carley, James P.
Carley, Lionel (Kenneth)
Carlisle, Elizabeth Pendergast
Carlson, Paul H.
Carlton, Jim
Carnall, Geoffrey Douglas
Carney, Judith A(nn)
Caro, Robert A.
Carr, Caleb
Carr, David
Carretta, Vincent (Albert)
Carrier, Roch
Carroll, Brendan G.
Carroll, Cathryn
Carson, Donald W.
Carter, Christine Jacobson
Carter, Joseph H(enry)
Carter, Miranda
Carter, Tom
Carter, William E.
Carver, Terrell
Cary, Lorene
Case, George (Andrew Thomas)
Cash, Jean W(ampler)
Cassady, Marsh
Cassutt, Michael (Joseph)
Casway, Jerrold
Catalano, Nick
Catanoso, Justin
Cathcart, Brian
Cavell, Marcia
Caveney, Graham
Caws, Mary Ann
Cevasco, G(eorge) A(nthony)
Chalfont
Champlin, Peggy
Chandler, Daniel Ross
Chanoff, David
Chapman, Lynne F(erguson)
Charles, Sara C(onnor)
Charmley, John
Charters, Ann
Chatfield, E. Charles
Chatman, Seymour
Cheathem, Mark R.
Cheever, Susan
Chehak, Susan Taylor
Chen, Patrizia
Chernow, Barbara A.
Cherny, Robert W(allace)
Chesler, Ellen
Cheuse, Alan
Chierichetti, David
Chin, Justin
Chiocca, Olindo Romeo
Chippendale, Lisa A.
Chitham, Edward (Harry Gordon)
Choi, Annie
Chowdhury, Bernie
Christ, Henry I(rvine)
Christensen, Damascene
Christian, Carol Cathay Tuttle
Christian, William
Christiansen, Rupert
Christoph, Peter R(ichard)
Ciepiela, Catherine
Clancy, Tom

Clark, Gillian
Clark, Mary T.
Clarke, Patricia
Clarkson, Wensley
Clary, David A.
Clayson, Alan
Clayton, Martin
Clayton, Michael
Cleland, Max
Clemmer, Richard O.
Cleveland-Peck, Patricia
Clifford, Christine
Cloake, John (Cecil)
Clubbe, John L(ouis) E(dwin)
Cluysenaar, Anne (Alice Andrée)
Côté, Richard N.
Coates, Carrol F(ranklin)
Coates, Ta-Nehisi
Cocker, Mark
Cockerill, A(rthur) W(illiam)
Cockrell, Thomas D(errell)
Coe, Jonathan
Coggeshall, Nancy
Cohen, Amy
Cohen, Henry
Cohen, Hubert I.
Cohen, Morton N(orton)
Cohen, Rich
Cohen, Richard M(artin)
Cohn, Henry S.
Cohn-Sherbok, Dan
Cole, Diane
Cole, Edmund Keith
Cole, Thomas R(ichard)
Cole, Wayne S.
Coleman, Jon
Coleman, Loren (Elwood)
Coleman, Terry
Coleman, Verna (Scott)
Coles, Don
Coles, Robert
Colley, Linda
Collier, James Lincoln
Collins, Bud
Collins, Joan
Collins, Julie (Hubbard)
Collins, Michael
Collins, Ronald K. L.
Collis, Louise (Edith)
Collis, Rose
Collum, Danny Duncan
Colman, Penny (Morgan)
Colvile, Georgiana M. M.
Comini, Alessandra
Conard, Rebecca
Coney, Sandra
Connell, Evan S(helby)
Connelly, Karen
Connolly, Ray
Conover, Roger L(loyd)
Conrad, Christine
Conroy, (Donald) Pat(rick)
Conroy, John
Constant, Stephen
Cony, Carlos Heitor
Cook, Kevin Graeme
Cook, William A.

Cooke, Jacob Ernest
Cooke, William
Cooper, David D.
Cooper, Floyd
Cooper, Ilene
Cooper, Kenneth H(ardy)
Copeland, Peter
Copeland, Rebecca L.
Coppa, Frank John
Corbett, Patricia
Corley, Thomas Anthony Buchanan
Corliss, Richard (Nelson)
Corn, David
Corp, Edward
Corrigan, Kelly
Corrington, Robert S.
Coryell, Janet L(ee)
Cotman, John Walton
Cotton, Ronald
Cottrell, Robert C.
Courtenay, Bryce
Cowan, Edward (James)
Cowden, Robert H.
Cox, Patsi Bale
Cox, Stephen (LeRoy)
Cox, Vicki
Craggs, Stewart R.
Craig, Barry L.
Cramer, Richard Ben
Crawford, Craig
Creamer, Robert W.
Crean, Susan M.
Crenson, Victoria
Crerar, Duff (Willis)
Crew, Danny O(liver)
Crewdson, Gregory
Crews, Harry (Eugene)
Croall, Jonathan
Crosland, Margaret
Crowder, Ashby Bland
Crowe, Michael J.
Crozier, Brian
Cullen, Bill
Cummins, C. Lyle
Cumper, Patricia
Cunningham, Frank R.
Curl, James Stevens
Curtis, Brian
Curtis, Susan
Cusic, Don
Cutting, Linda Katherine
D, John
D'Antonio, Michael
D'Orso, Michael
Dale, Peter
Dale, Rodney A. M.
Dallas, Roland
Dallek, Robert
Damrosch, Phoebe
Dance, Daryl Cumber
Daniels, Elizabeth Adams
Danko, William D(avid)
Darling, David J.
Darnell, Regna (Diebold)
Dary, David Archie

Davenport-Hines, Richard (Peter Treadwell)
David, Catherine
Davidson, Pamela
Davies, Hunter
Davies, Peter J.
Davis, Allen F.
Davis, Amelia
Davis, Anita (Grey) P(rice)
Davis, Margaret Leslie
Davis, Peter G(raffam)
Davis, Richard Whitlock
Davis, Sampson
Dawick, John
Dawidoff, Nicholas
Day-Lewis, Sean (Francis)
Dayan, Colin
de Blasi, Marlena
De Ferrari, Gabriella
de Gruchy, John W(esley)
de Jonge, Alex
De Vries, Rachel (Guido)
Deans, Sis Boulos
Dearden, James Shackley
Debs, Victor
Deck, Allan Figueroa
Defrank, Thomas M.
Del Paso, Fernando
Delaney, Norman
Delany, Samuel R(ay)
Delsohn, Gary
Demaray, Donald E(ugene)
Deneuve, Catherine
Denham, Andrew
Dennis, Felix
Derr, Mark (Burgess)
Derry, John (Wesley)
Dery, Dominika
Dessaix, Robert
Devaux, Claudia
Devor, Aaron H.
DeVries, Kelly
Dewey, Donald O(dell)
Diallo, Kadiatou
Diamond, Arthur
Dibble, J(ames) Birney
Dick, Bernard F.
Dickinson, Amy
Dickinson, Harry Thomas
Dickinson, Janice
Dicks, Shirley
Dierker, Larry
Dillon, Kathleen M. (Hynek)
Dimbleby, Jonathan
DiRenzo, Anthony
Divinsky, Nathan (Joseph)
Dixon, Simon M.
Djwa, Sandra (Ann)
Dobbin, Murray
Dobbs, Ricky F.
Dobrez, Patricia
Dodd, Christopher J.
Dodge, Peter
Doebler, Bettie Anne
Doerr, Anthony
Doherty, Kieran
Dolan, Sean J.

Donaldson, Islay (Eila) Murray
Donaldson, Scott
Donn, Linda
Donoughue, Bernard
Doriani, Beth Maclay
Dorman, Daniel
Dorril, Stephen
Douglas, Matthew M.
Douglas-Hamilton, James Alexander
Downer, Lesley
Downie, R(obert) S(ilcock)
Downing, David C(laude)
Doyle, Charles (Desmond)
Doyle, Debra
Drabble, Margaret
Dracup, Angela
Drake, Alicia
Draper, Alfred Ernest
Draper, Robert
Draper, Sharon Mills
Dromgoole, Dominic
Drosnin, Michael
Drucker, Joel
Drucker, Peter
Drummond, Michael
Dryden, Konrad
Duberstein, Larry
Dubose, Lou(is H.)
Duckworth, Marilyn
Duckworth, William (Ervin)
Dudley-Smith, Timothy
Duffy, Maureen (Patricia)
Duffy, Michael
Duggleby, John
Duke, Anna Marie
Dully, Howard
Dumas, Firoozeh
Duncan, A. A. M.
Dunham, William
Dunlap, Julie
Dunlop, Eileen (Rhona)
Dunlop, Ian (Geoffrey David)
Dunmore, John
Dunn, Durwood
DuPree, Sherry Sherrod
Dupuis, Robert
Durden, Robert F(ranklin)
Durham, Walter T.
Dutton, Paul Edward
Dwyer, Richard A.
Dyal, Donald H(enriques)
Dyer, Wayne W(alter)
Dyson, John
Early, Joseph E.
Easton, Nina J(ane)
Eaton, John Herbert
Eckler, Rebecca
Eddie, David
Edelstein, Robert
Edwards, Anne
Edwards, Larry
Edwards, Philip (Walter)
Edwards, Robert
Egan, Ferol
Eggers, Kerry
Ehle, John

Ehrlich, Amy
Eickhoff, Diane
Eidinow, John
Eisenman, Stephen F.
Eisler, Benita
Eisner, Peter (Norman)
El-Enany, Rasheed
Elegant, Robert (Sampson)
Eley, Beverley
Ellingham, Lewis
Elliott, Charles
Elliott, Clark A.
Ellis, Royston
Emanuel, James A(ndrew)
Emery, Tom
Endlich, Lisa
Epstein, Eric Joseph
Epstein, Jennifer Cody
Erickson, Carolly
Erkkila, Betsy
Erlbaum, Janice
Essex, Karen
Estow, Clara
Eugster, Sandra Lee
Evans, C. Wyatt
Evans, Eric J(ohn)
Evanzz, Karl
Falk, Avner
Falk, Candace
Fallon, Ivan (Gregory)
Fallows, James Mackenzie
Fanning, Philip Ashley
Faragher, John Mack
Farmaian, Sattareh Farman
Farrar, Ronald T(ruman)
Fassett, John D.
Faulkner, Howard J.
Fayer, Steve
Feifer, George
Feigon, Lee
Feinberg, Barbara
Feinstein, Elaine
Feis, William B.
Feldman, Lynne B.
Fenton, Peter
Ferguson, Robert (Thomas)
Ferguson, Ron
Ferling, John E.
Fernández-Armesto, Felipe (Fermin Ricardo)
Ferris, Jeri Chase
Ferris, Paul
Fiallos, Rosario
Fido, Martin (Austin)
Fifield, Christopher G(eorge)
Figley, Marty Rhodes
Fikes, Jay C(ourtney)
Finch, Christopher
Fine, Marshall
Fink, Carole (Kapiloff)
Fink, Karl J.
Fink, Mitchell
Fink, Sheri
Finlayson, Iain (Thorburn)
Finley, Michael
Finstad, Suzanne
Firkatian, Mari A.

Fisher, Clive
Fisher, Robin Gaby
Fishgall, Gary
Fitch, Noel Riley
Fitzgerald, Carol
Fitzgerald, Cathy
Fitzgerald-Hoyt, Mary
Fitzpatrick, Vincent (dePaul)
Flack, Jerry D(avid)
Flamini, Roland
Fleischner, Jennifer
Flem, Lydia
Fleming, Candace
Fleming, Kate
Fleming, Keith
Fleming, Thomas
Fletcher, Joel L.
Fletcher, Michael A.
Flinn, Kelly
Flint, John Edgar
Florita, Kira
Flynn, Kevin
Flynt, Mike
Foerstel, Karen
Foerstner, Abigail M.
Foley, Jack
Folly, Martin H(arold)
Fontes, Ron
Foot, David
Foot, Michael Richard Daniell
Forbes, Camille F.
Ford, Brian John
Ford, Herbert (Paul)
Foreman, Amanda
Forest, Jim
Forster, Margaret
Foster, Joanne Reckler
Foster, Richard
Fox, Barry
Fox, Faulkner
Foxx, Daniel
Fradin, Judith (Bernette) Bloom
Franceschini, Remo
Francis, R(ichard) A.
Frankland, (Anthony) Noble
Franklin, David Byrd
Franklin, Michael J(ohn)
Fraser, Antonia
Fraser, Laura (Jane)
Fraser, Rebecca
Freedland, Michael
Freedman, Russell (Bruce)
Freeman, Anne Hobson
Freeman, Philip
Frega, Donnalee
French, Albert
French, Francis
French, Patrick
Frey, James N.
Frey, Julia (Bloch)
Freyer, Tony (Allan)
Friedman, Lawrence S(amuel)
Frisbie, Charlotte J(ohnson)
Frist, William H.
Frith, David (Edward John)
Frost, Karolyn Smardz
Frueh, Joanna

Fryer, Jonathan
Fuegi, John
Fultz, James R.
Furia, Philip (G.)
Gablik, Suzi
Gabor, Andrea (Anna Gisela)
Gabriel, Michael P.
Gaddis-Rose, Marilyn
Gall, Pete
Gallant, Roy Arthur
Gallardo, Evelyn
Gallenkamp, Charles (Benton)
Gamson, Joshua (Paul)
Gänzl, Kurt (Friedrich)
Garceau, Dee
Garcia, J. Malcolm
Garcia, Luis M.
Gardner, (Robert) Brian
Gardner, Michael R.
Garfunkel, Trudy
Garnett, Richard (Duncan Carey)
Garrard, John (Gordon)
Garrett, Leslie
Gaschnitz, Michael K.
Gascoigne, John
Gathorne-Hardy, Jonathan
Gattey, Charles Neilson
Gaukroger, Stephen
Gay, Kathlyn R.
Geaves, Ronald Allan
Gehring, Wes D(avid)
Gekoski, Rick
Gelderman, Carol (Wettlaufer)
Gelpi, Albert
Geniesse, Jane Fletcher
Gentry, Curt
George Bloomfield, Susanne K.
Gerassi, John
Gerhart, Ann
Gerlach, Don R.
Geronimus, Dennis
Gerson, Lloyd P.
Gervais, (George) Paul
Gerzina, Gretchen Holbrook
Gessel, Van C.
Getz, Marshall J(ay)
Geyer, Georgie Anne
Gherman, Beverly
Ghiglione, Loren
Giancana, Sam
Gibb, Lorna
Gibbs, Anthony Matthews
Gibson, Ian
Gibson, Margaret
Gibson, Robert
Giesbert, Franz-Olivier
Gifford, Barry (Colby)
Gifford, Clive
Giglio, James N.
Gilbert, Elizabeth
Gilbert, John Raphael
Gilbert, Martin
Gilbert, Tom
Gilbert, W(illiam) Stephen
Gilchrist, Ellen
Gill, Anton
Gill, David Macinnis

Gill, Gillian C(atherine)
Gillespie, Angus Kress
Gillett, Margaret
Gilley, Sheridan (Wayne)
Gillman, Peter (Charles)
Gillmeister, Heiner
Gillon, Steven M.
Gilmour, David
Giovanni, Nikki
Giovino, Andrea
Gipson, Carolyn R.
Gitter, Elisabeth
Gjelten, Tom
Glassman, Bruce
Glatt, John
Gleiter, Jan
Glen, Frank Grenfell
Glock, Allison
Gmelch, Sharon (Bohn)
Godbold, E(dward) Stanly
Gold, Janet N(owakowski)
Goldberg, Jacob
Goldberger, Avriel H.
Golden, Arthur
Goldman, Elizabeth
Goldman, Mary Elizabeth
Goldschmidt, Arthur
Goldsmith, Barbara
Gollaher, David L.
Gollin, Rita K.
Gonzalez-Balado, Jose Luis
Gooch, Brad
Goodhue, Thomas W.
Goodwin, Doris (Helen) Kearns
Goodwin, Michael
Goodwin, Robert Theodore
   Chorley
Gordon, Anne Wolrige
Gordon, Colin
Gordon, Lois G.
Gordon, Lyndall (Felicity)
Gordon, W. Terrence
Gore, Ariel
Gorn, Elliott (J.)
Gorn, Michael H.
Goss, Pete
Gott, Richard (Willoughby)
Gottlieb, Freema (Peninah)
Goudsouzian, Aram
Gough, Sue
Goulden, Joseph C.
Grace, Nancy McCampbell
Graff, Henry Franklin
Grafton, Anthony T(homas)
Graham, Billy
Graham, Daniel O.
Graham, Desmond
Graham, Ysenda (May) Maxtone
Grainger, John D(ownie)
Gramer, Rod
Grant, Colin
Gray, Alasdair (James)
Gray, Francine du Plessix
Gray, Richard J(ohn)
Gray, Robert (Archibald Speir)
Greacen, Lavinia
Green, (Charles Stuart) Jamison

Green, Arthur
Green, Peter (Morris)
Green, Sharony Andrews
Greene, Bryan A.
Greene, Douglas G.
Greene, Gayle
Greenwald, G. Jonathan
Greenwald, Marilyn S.
Greenwood, Barbara
Greenwood, Norman Neill
Greer, Germaine
Gregory, Frederick
Gresser, Seymour
Grey, Rudolph
Griffin, Alice
Griffin, Susan M.
Griffith, Gail
Grodin, Charles
Grondahl, Paul
Gross, Neil
Grosskurth, Phyllis
Grosz, Terry
Groth, Janet
Groult, Benoite
Growe, Sarah Jane
Grumbach, Doris
Gruntman, Mike
Gubar, Susan (David)
Guérif, François
Guidry, Cindy
Guinness, Jonathan (Bryan)
Gunston, Bill
Guralnick, Peter
Gurewitsch, Edna P.
Gurney, A(lbert) R(amsdell)
Gutman, Judith Mara
Gutman, Robert W.
Habegger, Alfred (Carl)
Haberman, Jacob
Haddad, Gladys
Haeger, John Denis
Haffenden, John
Hafner, Katie
Hague, William
Hahn, Michael T.
Hailey, (Elizabeth) Kendall
Haizlip, Shirlee Taylor
Hajdu, David
Hajdusiewicz, Babs Bell
Hale, Douglas
Halfmann, Janet
Hall, Carl W.
Hall, Donald (Andrew)
Hall, J(ohn) C(live)
Hall, Lee
Hall, Meredith
Hall, Rodney
Hallock, John W(esley) M(atthew)
Hallwood, Jan
Hamblin, Robert W(ayne)
Hamilton, Carl
Hamilton, James
Hamilton, John Maxwell
Hammel, Bob
Hammond, Wayne G(ordon)
Hampson, Norman
Hanc, John

Hancock, Ian (Robert)
Handler, Marisa
Handley, Paul M.
Hankin, C(herry) A(nne)
Hannaford, Peter (Dor)
Hannam, June
Hansen, Chadwick
Hansen, Gregory
Hansen, James R.
Hansen, Jennifer
Hansen, Suzanne
Hanson, Neil
Hardwick, Phil
Hardy, Gayle J.
Hardy, Robert Earl
Hargreaves, John D(esmond)
Haring, Bruce
Harlan, Judith
Harline, Craig E.
Harmon, Daniel E(lton)
Harmon, Maurice
Harnack, Curtis
Harnois, Albert J.
Harper, Judith E.
Harrill, Ronald
Harris, Jose
Harris, Paul
Harris, Robert (Dennis)
Harris, Stacy
Harrison, Kathryn
Harrison, Kathy A.
Harrison, Kyle
Harrison, Lowell H.
Hart, (Margaret Eleanor) Anne
Hart, Bret
Hart-Davis, Duff
Hartje, Tod D(ale)
Harvey, Hazel (Mary)
Harvey, Robert C.
Harwood, John
Harwood, Ronald
Hastings, Max M(acdonald)
Hastings, Michael
Hasty, Will
Hatfield, Phyllis
Hattersley, Roy (Sydney George)
Hauptman, Laurence Marc
Haverty, Anne
Hawkins, Regina Trice
Hawksley, Lucinda
Hay, Elizabeth (Jean)
Hay, Samuel A.
Haygood, Wil
Hayman, Ronald
Haynes, C. Rayfield
Hays, Peter L.
Hazlehurst, Cameron
Heacox, Kim
Head, David M.
Headley, Maria Dahvana
Heald, Tim(othy Villiers)
Hearn, Chester G.
Hearon, Shelby
Hecht, Jennifer Michael
Heckler, Cheryl
Heefner, Wilson A.
Heffer, Simon (James)

Ketcham, Ralph Louis
Ketchum, Richard M.
Ketner, Kenneth Laine
Kettelkamp, Larry Dale
Keynes, Randal
Keyser, James D.
Kherdian, David
Khoroche, Peter (Andrew)
Kidd, Charles (William)
Kidd, Sue Monk
Kidder, Tracy
Kiddy, Elizabeth W.
Kidwell, Carol (Evelyn Beryl)
Kihn, Greg
Kilduff, Peter
Killan, Gerald
Kilpatrick, Andrew
King, Bruce (Alvin)
King, Don W.
King, William Davies
King-Hele, Desmond
Kingsley, Sean A.
Kingston, Maxine Hong
Kinnear, Mary
Kirkbright, Suzanne
Kirkpatrick, Rob
Kirsch, Jonathan
Kisseloff, Jeff
Kitaj, Karma
Kittinger, Jo S(usenbach)
Kline, David
Kline, Michael
Kline, Ronald R.
Klingenstein, Susanne
Kluger, Ruth
Knight, Alanna (Cleet)
Knight, D(avid) M(arcus)
Knight, Louise W.
Knightley, Phillip (George)
Knox, Elizabeth (Fiona)
Knox, Melissa
Koch, Edward I(rving)
Koch, Peter O.
Kohen, Arnold
Korda, Michael (Vincent)
Koren, Yehuda
Korg, Jacob
Kornheiser, Tony
Kossman, Nina
Kostman, Joel
Koupal, Nancy Tystad
Kramer, Dale
Kramer, Linda Konheim
Kranish, Michael
Krass, Peter
Kraus, Caroline
Kreitner, Kenneth
Krieg, Joann P(eck)
Krieg, Robert Anthony
Kroeger, Brooke
Krohn, Claus-Dieter
Krohn, Katherine E(lizabeth)
Kugler, Anne
Kurkjian, Tim Bell
Kurlansky, Mark
Kynaston, David
Laas, Virginia J(eans)

Lacey, Robert
Lachman, Charles
Ladd, Louise
Laffey, Steve
Lahr, John (Henry)
Lahutsky, John
Lai, Larissa
Lalicki, Tom
Lamb, Brian
Lamb, Karl A(llen)
Lambert, Katherine
Lambur, Joan
Lamont-Brown, Raymond
Lamplugh, Lois
Landsberg, Melvin
Lane, Abbe
Lane, Terry
Lang, Judith
Lang, Lang
Lang, Paul
Langley, Andrew
Langum, David J.
Lankford, Nelson D.
Lanouette, William (John)
Lantigua, John
Lanza, Joseph
Lanzmann, Claude
Larsen, Timothy
Larson, Edward J(ohn)
Larson, Kate Clifford
Laskas, Jeanne Marie
Laskin, David
Lassez, Sarah
Lasson, Kenneth (Lee)
Lattin, Don
Lawday, David
Lawrence, C(lifford) H(ugh)
Lawrence-Lightfoot, Sara
Lax, Eric
Lazerson, Joshua N(athaniel)
Le Guin, Elisabeth
Leach, William
Leake, John
Lear, Linda J(ane)
Leary, Ann (Lembeck)
Leatherbarrow, W(illiam) J(ohn)
Leavell, Linda
Lebow, Eileen F.
Leckie, Shirley A(nne)
Ledbetter, Suzann
Lee, A(rthur) Robert
Leeder, Elaine J.
Leen, Jeff
Lefebure, Molly
Lefkowitz, Mary (Rosenthal)
Legge, John David
Lehmberg, Stanford Eugene
Lehrer, Stanley
Leiby, Bruce R.
Leifer, Carol
Lellenberg, Jon L.
Lemann, Nicholas
LeMaster, Carolyn Gray
Lemonick, Michael D.
Lendvai, Paul
Lengel, Edward G.
Lennox, John

Lentz, Harris M(onroe)
Leo, Mabel R.
Leon, Sharon
Leonard, Stephen J.
Lesch, David W.
Leslie, Kent A.
Leslie, Roger (James)
Lesser, Wendy
Leve, Ariel
Levene, Mark
Levin, Doron P.
Levin, Gerald
Levin, Michael (Graubart)
Levine, Allan
Levy, Daniel S.
Levy, Evonne
Levy, JoAnn
Lewis, Gregg (Allan)
Lewis, Jeremy
Lewis, Margaret (B.)
Lewis, Norah L.
Lewis, Rupert
Lewis-Ferguson, Julinda
Libo, Kenneth (Harold)
Lichtenstein, Nelson
Liddington, Jill
Lieberman, Robert C.
Liebman, Herbert
Lightfoot Sizemore, Deborah
Lilley, Stephen R(ay)
Lima, Robert (F.)
Limonov, E duard
Lindskold, Jane M.
Lingeman, Richard
Linson, Art
Lipton, Eunice
Lisandrelli, Elaine Slivinski
Lisle, Laurie
Littlefield, Bill
Littleton, Darryl
Littlewood, Clayton
Lloyd, A(lan) R(ichard)
Llywelyn, Morgan
Lo Scalzo, Jim
Loades, David Michael
Locke, Juliane Poirier
Lockerbie, D(onald) Bruce
Lockridge, Larry
Loh, Sandra Tsing
Loncraine, Rebecca
Long, Carolyn Morrow
Long, Christopher
Long, Michael G.
Longmate, Norman Richard
Loomes, Brian
Looser, Devoney
Lorrimer, Claire
Lottman, Herbert
Loughery, John
Lounsberry, Barbara
Lourie, Richard
Loux, Ann Kimble
Lovell, Mary S(ybilla)
Lovett, Bobby L.
Lowenthal, Gary T(obias)
Lowery, Robert G.
Lucas, Celia

Lucas, Eileen
Lucas, Geralyn
Lucas, John
Luft, Lya Fett
Lundstrom, John B(ernard)
Luongo, F. Thomas
Lusk, John
Luyendijk, Joris
Lyden, Jacki
Lynch, Daniel
Lynch, Janet Nichols
Lyon, Andrea D.
Lystra, Karen
Lytle, Mark H.
Mabee, Carleton
MacAdams, William
MacCarthy, Fiona
Macdonald, Michael Patrick
Macdonald, Sarah
Macfarlane, Malcolm R.
Machotka, Pavel
Mack Smith, Denis
Macken, JoAnn Early
Macklin, Robert
MacLaine, Shirley
MacLeod, Elizabeth
Macniven, Ian S.
Macy, Sue
Maes, Yvonne (M.)
Magee, Bryan
Magee, David
Mager, Hugo
Maggio, Frank P.
Maharidge, Dale (Dimitro)
Mahon, Basil
Mahoney, Richard D.
Mai, Francois Martin
Maier, Paul Luther
Maier, Thomas
Mäkelä, Janne
Makepeace, Anne
Malcolm, Elizabeth
Malin, Irving
Mallin, Jay
Malone, Susan (Mary)
Malpezzi Price, Paola
Maltby, William S(aunders)
Malvasi, Meg Greene
Mandela, Nelson (Rolihlahla)
Manetti, Larry
Mango, Karin N.
Manhein, Mary H(uffman)
Mann, Charles F.
Mann, Reva
Manrique (Ardila), Jaime
Mansbridge, Francis
Mansfield, Bruce Edgar
Maraniss, David
Marble, Allan Everett
Marcello, Patricia Cronin
Marchessault, Jovette
Marcus, Leonard S.
Mardon, Austin Albert
Margolis, Jonathan
Marias, Javier
Marker, Sherry
Markus, Julia

Onyeama, Dillibe
Oppenheimer, Gregg
Orban, Christine
Orlova, Alexandra (Anatol'evna)
Osborne, Charles
Osborne, Frances
Osen, James L.
Ottaviani, Jim
Otten, Charlotte F(ennema)
Ove, Robert S.
Overend, William George
Overmyer, James E.
Owens, Kenneth N.
Oxendine, Bess Holland
Packer, Joan Garrett
Paddock, Lisa
Padfield, Peter
Padgett, Ron
Page, Geoff(rey Donald)
Page, Norman
Paisner, Daniel
Pakula, Hannah (Cohn)
Palazchenko, Pavel
Pallone, Dave
Palmer, Alan Warwick
Palmer, Beverly Wilson
Panchyk, Richard
Pannick, David
Paper, Lewis Jay
Paravisini-Gebert, Lizabeth
Pardes, Ilana
Parillo, Mark P.
Parini, Jay
Paris, Barry
Paris, Bernard Jay
Parish, James Robert
Parker, Peter (Robert Nevill)
Parks, Deborah A.
Parmet, Herbert S.
Parnell, Mary Davies
Parrish, T(homas) Michael
Parrish, William E.
Parsons, (Quentin) Neil
Pastorello, Karen
Pate, J'Nell L(aVerne)
Patel, Eboo
Paterson, Janet M.
Paterson, Ronald (William Keith)
Patey, Douglas Lane
Patterson, Horace L.
Payne, Darwin
Payne, Donald Gordon
Payne, J. Gregory
Payne, Ladell
Peabody, Richard (Myers)
Peachment, Christopher
Peacock, Molly
Peacock, Sandra J.
Peacock, Shane
Pear, David (Adrian)
Pearlman, Jeff
Pearsall, Derek (Albert)
Pearson, John
Peden, W. Creighton
Pell, Ed(ward)
Pelzer, Richard B.
Pendreigh, Brian

Penn, Michael Philip
Penna, Dennis Roy
Penrose, Antony
Perchard, Tom
Perle, Liz
Perone, James E.
Perrin, Dennis
Perry, Dayn
Perry, Jeffrey B.
Perry, Roland
Persico, Joseph E.
Person, James E(llis)
Peters, Margot (McCullough)
Peters, Robert
Petrakis, Harry Mark
Petrino, Elizabeth
Petro, Pamela J.
Petsalis-Diomidis, Nicholas
Pezeshki, Charles
Pfaff, Daniel W.
Phelps, Barry
Phelps, Christopher
Phillippy, Patricia Berrahou
Phillips, Hugh D.
Phillips, Kate
Phillips, Mike
Pick, Hella
Pick, John Barclay
Pickering, David (Hugh)
Pickus, Keith H.
Pierce, Patricia Jobe
Pietrusza, David
Pilbeam, Pamela M.
Pilling, John
Pinkwater, Daniel Manus
Piotrowski, Thaddeus (Tadeusz)
Pipkin, Turk
Pittock, Joan (Hornby)
Pizzichini, Lilian
Plant, Deborah G.
Plante, David (Robert)
Plaschke, Bill
Platt, James R.
Pletsch, Carl (Erich)
Plotkin, Diane M.
Plumly, Stanley (Ross)
Pogrebin, Letty Cottin
Pohl-Weary, Emily
Poirier-Bures, Simone
Polikoff, Barbara G(arland)
Polito, Robert
Polizzotti, Mark
Pollack, Jill S.
Pollak, Vivian R.
Pollard, A(nthony) J(ames)
Pollard, John (Richard Thornhill)
Pollock, Dale
Pollock, John Charles
Polukhina, Valentina
Ponce, Mary Helen
Poole, Scott
Porter, Linda
Posner, Gerald L.
Post, Robert C(harles)
Postgate, John (Raymond)
Potvin, Liza
Powell, Neil

Powers, Lyall H(arris)
Powling, Chris
Prager, Emily
Presnall, Judith (Ann) Janda
Press, O(tto) Charles
Prevas, John
Prévaux, Aude Yung-De
Prime, Jim H.
Prince, Alison
Princess Anne
Pritchard, William H.
Probyn, Clive T.
Profumo, David
Prosek, James
Prud'homme, Alex
Prymak, Thomas M.
Pullein-Thompson, Diana
Puls, Mark
Purcell, Anne G.
Purcell, Benjamin H.
Pushker, Gloria (Teles)
Putnam, Constance E(lizabeth)
Putnam, William L(owell)
Quantic, Diane Dufva
Quartz, Steven R.
Quaye, Kofi
Queller, Jessica
Quinlan, David
Quinn, D. Michael
Quinn, Rob
Raad, Virginia
Racine, Philip N.
Radcliffe Richards, Janet
Radovanovic, Ivan
Radzinsky, E dvard (Stanislav-
   ovich)
Raeder, Linda C.
Rake, Alan
Ramadan, Tariq
Ramdin, Ron(ald Andrew)
Rammohan, V.
Ramsey, Doug(las K.)
Ramsland, Katherine
Randall, Dale B(ertrand) J(onas)
Randall, Francis Ballard
Randall, Willard Sterne
Randell, Nigel
Raphael, Frederic (Michael)
Rapp, Anthony
Rappaport, Doreen
Rappaport, Helen
Ratcliff, Carter
Ratcliffe, Eric Hallam
Rathmell, George W(esley)
Ratto, Linda Lee
Rauch, William
Ravage, Barbara
Ravitz, Abe (Carl)
Rayfield, Donald
Raymond, Barbara Bisantz
Raz, Simcha
Read, Anthony
Read, Christopher
Read, Peter
Read, Piers Paul
Reasoner, Livia Jane Washburn
Reddaway, Peter (Brian)

Redsand, Anna
Reeder, Carolyn
Rees, Brian
Reeves, Thomas C.
Regehr, T(heodore) D.
Reger, James P.
Reich, Howard
Reid, John P(hillip)
Reid, Loren
Reidel, James
Reinertsen, Sarah
Reiss, Edward
Reiss, Tom
Rember, John
Renehan, Edward J(ohn)
Rennie, Bradford James
Resis, Albert
Reynolds, Bill
Rezits, Joseph
Rhodes, Richard (Lee)
Rhodes-Courter, Ashley Marie
Ribowsky, Mark
Rich, Elaine Sommers
Richard, Cliff
Richard-Allerdyce, Diane
Richards, Eric
Richards, Judith M.
Richardson, Brian W.
Richardson, Midge Turk
Richardson, Robert Galloway
Richmond, Robin
Ridgway, John M.
Ridley, Jane
Ridley, Ronald T(homas)
Ridlon, Florence
Rieder, Jonathan
Riley, James A.
Riley, Sam G.
Rimler, Walter
Ring, Nancy G.
Rischin, Moses
Roach, Catherine M.
Roark, Dallas M.
Robb, Peter
Robbins, Tom
Roberts, Brian
Roberts, Denys (Tudor Emil)
Roberts, Madge Thornall
Robertson, Barbara Anne
Robertson, Ian (Campbell)
Robertson, Janet (E.)
Robeson, Paul
Robins, Glenn
Robinson, Andrew
Robinson, Peter (Mark)
Robinson, Phyllis C(umins)
Robinson, Roxana (Barry)
Robison, John Elder
Robles, Harold E.
Rodger, N. A. M.
Rodgers, Marion Elizabeth
Rodney, William
Roe, Nicholas
Roe, Sue
Rogan, Johnny
Rogers, Deborah D(ee)
Rogers, Pat

Sprinkle, Annie (M.)
Spurling, Hilary
Spycket, Jerome
Squires, Richard D(onald)
Sragow, Michael
St. Amant, Mark
St. Aubyn, Giles (Rowan)
St. Clair, William
St. George, Andrew
St. John, Bob J.
St. John, Warren
Staar, Richard F.
Stainback, Berry
Stallworthy, Jon (Howie)
Stanley, Autumn
Stanley, Jerry
Stannard, Martin (J.)
Stansky, Peter (David Lyman)
Stanton, Joseph
Stapleton, Timothy J.
Stashower, Daniel (Meyer)
Staten, Vince
Stead, C(hristian) K(arlson)
Steavenson, Wendell
Stebenne, David
Steel, Danielle
Steel, Ronald
Steele, Mary
Steele, Peter
Steiker, Valerie
Steinberg, Blema S.
Steinberg, Jonathan
Steinbrook, Gordon L.
Steiner, Evgeny
Steinmann, Andrew E.
Steins, Richard
Stenzel, Anabel
Stephens, William Peter
Sterling, Keir B(rooks)
Stern, Ellen Norman
Sternlicht, Sanford
Stevens, Bryna
Stevenson, David
Stevenson (Lucas), Anne
Stewart, Kathleen
Stiles, T. J.
Stimpson, Jeff
Stivender, Ed
Stockel, H. Henrietta
Stockler, Bruce
Stockwin, J. A. A.
Stone, Eric
Stone, James S(tuart)
Stone, Judith F.
Stoppard, Tom
Storey, Edward
Storlie, Erik Fraser
Stout, Jay A.
Stowe, Steven M.
Strachman, Daniel A.
Strane, Susan
Strathern, Paul
Street, Brian Jeffrey
Streeter, Patrick
Strickland, Michael R.
Stringer, C. Vivian
Stross, Randall E.

Strother, Ruth
Stroud, Patricia Tyson
Stuart, Alexander
Stuart, Mark
Stuart, Sarah Payne
Stuhr(-Rommereim), Rebecca (Ann)
Stupples, Peter (Cecil)
Sullivan, (Donovan) Michael
Sullivan, David M.
Sullivan, Dolores P.
Sullivan, George E(dward)
Sullivan, Steve (Joseph)
Sultana, Donald Edward
Summers, Judith (Anne)
Summerscale, Kate
Sundquist, Josh
Sunee, Kim
Sussman, Peter Y.
Sutcliffe, Jane
Svenvold, Mark
Swafford, Jan Johnson
Swan, Annalyn
Sward, Robert S.
Swartz, Jon David
Sweeney, Fionnghuala
Swick, Thomas
Swidey, Neil
Swift, Graham
Swift, Will
Swiller, Josh
Swinton, Elizabeth de Sabato
Symynkywicz, Jeffrey B(ruce)
Sztompka, Piotr
Szyma ski, Leszek
Tabios, Eileen
Talalay, Kathryn M(arguerite)
Tanner, Karen Holliday (Olson)
Tanner, Marcus
Tanner, Stephen L.
Taraborrelli, J. Randy
Tarnopolsky, Yuri
Tarnowski, Andrew
Tarte, Bob
Tate, Eleanora E(laine)
Taylor, Andy
Taylor, Anne Marie
Taylor, John Russell
Taylor, Larissa J(uliet)
Taylor, Sarah Stewart
Taylor, Stephen
Taylor, T(homas) F(ish)
Taylor, Walter Kingsley
Taylor, Welford Dunaway
Teachout, Terry
Tearle, John L.
Tefertiller, Casey (Orie)
Tehan, Arline Boucher
Teller, Neville
Temple, Wayne C(alhoun)
Tennyson, Brian
Tent, Pam
Terrill, Marshall
Testa, Judith (Anne)
The Rock
Theisz, R. D.
Theodore, Wayne

Thesen, Sharon
Thomas, (Antony) Charles
Thomas, Abigail
Thomas, Adrian
Thomas, Bruce
Thomas, Clara McCandless
Thomas, Evan
Thomas, Hugh
Thompson, Charles P.
Thompson, Christina
Thompson, Jewel Taylor
Thompson, Marilyn W.
Thompson, Robert Farris
Thomson, Peter (William)
Thornley, Stew
Thrasher, Peter Adam
Thwaite, Ann (Barbara)
Thwe, Pascal Khoo
Tian, Hao Jiang
Tibbetts, Orlando L.
Tidwell, John Edgar
Tierney, Kevin
Tillyard, Stella
Timms, Edward
Tindall, Gillian (Elizabeth)
Tingle, Tim
Tingum, Janice
Tippets, John M.
Tipton, David
Tisdale, Sallie
Tobias, Michael (Charles)
Tocher, Michelle
Todd, Olivier
Tofel, Richard J.
Tolson, Jay
Tomalin, Claire
Tomalin, Ruth
Tombs, Robert P.
Tomkins, Calvin
Tomkins, Stephen
Tommasini, Anthony
Totten, Mark D.
Touré
Towne, Marian K(leinsasser)
Townend, Paul A.
Townsend, Brad W.
Townsend, John Rowe
Townsend, Sue
Tracy, Kathleen
Traig, Jennifer
Tranel, Virginia
Tremain, Rose
Tremlett, George (William)
Trenerry, Walter N.
Trengove, Alan Thomas
Trethewey, Rachel
Trevelyan, Raleigh
Triggs, Tony D.
Tripodi, Tony
Trout, Robert J(ay)
Trudeau, Noah Andre
Trzebinski, Errol
Tucker, Cynthia Grant
Tucker, Michael
Tucker, William Edward
Tully, (William) Mark
Turan, Kenneth

Turner, Brian (Lindsay)
Turner, John Frayn
Turner, Kathleen
Turner, Kathleen J.
Turner, Marjorie Shepherd
Turner, Robyn
Turow, (L.) Scott
Turvey, Roger
Tuttle, William McCullough
Ugel, Edward
Ullmann, Owen
Umland, Samuel J(oseph)
Underhill, Lois Beachy
Underwood, Peter
Unger, Harlow Giles
Unrue, Darlene Harbour
Ure, John (Burns)
Ureneck, Lou
Urquhart, Brian Edward
Uruburu, Paula
Usry, Becky (S.)
Vaill, Amanda
Vale-Allen, Charlotte
Valerio, Anthony
Valle-Ferrer, Norma
Van der Kiste, John (Patrick Guy)
van der Kooi, Cornelis
Van Domelen, John E(mory)
van Meter, Jonathan W.
Van Natta, Don
van Praagh, David
Van Rynbach, Iris
Van Tilburg, Jo Anne
van Vugt, William E.
Vassanji, M(oyez) G.
Vaughn, Patrika
Vazquez-Gomez, Juana
Velez-Mitchell, Jane
Vella, Christina
Venet, Wendy Hamand
Verney, Peter (Vivian Lloyd)
Verona, Stephen (Frederic)
Versényi, Adam
Villamil, Victoria Etnier
Vincent, Edgar
Vincent, Isabel
Vincent, John (Russell)
Vines, Lois Davis
Visconti, Tony
Vogel, Carole Garbuny
Vogel, Steve
Vollers, Maryanne
von Trier, Lars
von Tunzelmann, Alex
von Unwerth, Matthew
Vornholt, John
Wachtel, Eleanor
Waddington, Patrick (Haynes)
Wagener, Leon
Wagner, Nike
Wagner-Martin, Linda C.
Walcott, Charles E(liot)
Waldman, Harry
Walker, Kate
Walker, Nigel (David)
Wallace, James
Wallin, Pamela

Cartoons-*cont.*

Morrison, Grant
Nelson, Ray
Nitto, Tomio
Nutzle, Futzie
Otomo, Katsuhiro
Perez, George
Piraro, Dan
Rathje, William (Laurens)
Rayner, Mary (Yoma Grigson)
Rees, David
Schrag, Ariel
Searle, Ronald (William Fordham)
Simmonds, Posy
Siracusa, Catherine (Jane)
Smith, Wanda VanHoy
Sorel, Nancy Caldwell
Stathis, Pete
Stevenson, James
Swain, Gwenyth
Tinsley, Kevin (M.)
Van Citters, Darrell
Wagner, Matt
Wallmeyer, Dick
Welcher, Rosalind
Wershler-Henry, Darren Sean
Wheeler, Ron
Wheeler, Shannon L.
Woodring, Jim
Young, Dean (Wayne)

Documentaries/Reportage

Abrahams, Peter
Adiele, Faith
Albert, Steve
Alexander, Joseph H(ammond)
Angell, Roger
Anton, Ted
Arellano, Juan Estevan
Ash, Jennifer
Bacik, Ivana
Bagdikian, Ben H(aig)
Bailey, Anthony
Ball, Edward
Banazek, Jeanne M. (Carpenter)
Barker, Dennis (Malcolm)
Barry, John M.
Beifuss, John
Bellesiles, Michael A.
Benchley, Rob
Benedict, Helen
Bensman, David
Berlow, Alan
Bernstein, Burton
Bernstein, Richard
Betts, Clive
Bidini, Dave
Bienes, Nicholas Peter
Biermann, Pieke
Birnbaum, Jeffrey H.
Bledsoe, Jerry
Blitzer, Wolf
Blix, Jacqueline
Bonner, Arthur

Documentaries/Reportage-*cont.*

Booker, Christopher
Bowden, Mark
Bower, Tom
Brand, Oscar
Brener, Milton E(rnest)
Brenner, Joël Glenn
Breslin, Jimmy
Brett, Donna W(hitson)
Brightman, Carol
Brinkley, Douglas
Brown, Harriet N(ancy)
Bruce, Victoria
Bruck, Connie
Bumiller, Elisabeth
Burke, Martyn
Burns, Edward
Burns, Ken(neth Lauren)
Burrough, Bryan
Busch, Charles
Buskin, Richard
Calabro, Marian
Calder, Marie D(onais)
Calder, Nigel (David Ritchie)
Cantu, Norma Elia
Carlton, Jim
Chambers, John Whiteclay
Chitwood, Michael
Chowdhury, Bernie
Clapp, Nicholas
Clarkson, Wensley
Cohen, Andrew (Z.)
Cohen, Rich
Cohen, Richard M(artin)
Coleman, Jonathan (Mark)
Coleman, Terry
Coleridge, Nicholas (David)
Coll, Steve
Cooper, Elisha
Corbin, Jane
Corn, David
Costley, Bill
Coulmas, Florian
Courtenay, Bryce
Cox, Steve
Danner, Mark (David)
Darden, Robert
Dassanowsky, Robert
Dauber, Philip M.
Defrank, Thomas M.
Delano, Anthony
Dickinson, Matt
Dotson, Bob
Doyle, Robert Charles
Dray, Philip
Drosnin, Michael
Durschmied, Erik
Dyer, Joel
Earley, Pete
Eddie, David
Edwards, Anne
Edwards, David B.
Egginton, Joyce
Eisenberg, Robert
Elegant, Robert (Sampson)
Epstein, Rachel S.
Evans, Richard I(sadore)
Fadiman, Anne

Documentaries/Reportage-*cont.*

Faith, Nicholas
Fanthorpe, R(obert) Lionel
Fayer, Steve
Feiffer, Kate
Feiler, Bruce
Feliciano, Hector
Fetherston, Drew
Fialka, John J.
Field, Genevieve
Finkle, Derek
Finstad, Suzanne
Fisher, Marshall Jon
Fishlock, Trevor
Fitzgerald, Mary Anne
Fleming, Justin
Fogle, Jeanne
Franey, Ros(alind)
Freedman, Jonathan (Borwick)
Friendly, Alfred
Frisch, Walter
Fuegi, John
Gall, Sandy
Garner, Alan
Geltmaker, Ty
Gentleman, David
Gillman, Peter (Charles)
Glass, Charles
Good, Howard
Goodwin, Jan
Gordon, William A.
Gotfryd, Bernard
Gottlieb, Sherry Gershon
Graber Miller, Keith Allen
Graef, Roger (Arthur)
Grant, Barry Keith
Green, Scott E.
Grossman, Karl (H.)
Gup, Ted (S.)
Guttenplan, D. D.
Haddad, Gladys
Hafner, Katie
Hamblin, Robert W(ayne)
Hamill, Pete
Hargarten, Stephen W.
Harris, Paul
Hart, (Margaret Eleanor) Anne
Hastings, Max M(acdonald)
Haygood, Wil
Heitmiller, David A.
Heminway, John
Hermes, Jules
Hernandez, Jo Farb
Hess, Bill
Heyman, Abigail
Hillier, Jim
Hinojosa, Maria (de Lourdes)
Hirsch, James (S.)
Hockenberry, John
Hoffman, Carl
Honigsbaum, Mark
Horrie, Chris(topher)
Horton, Madelyn (Stacey)
Howes, Craig
Hubbard, Bill
James, W(illiam) Martin
Jennings, Charles
Johnson, LouAnne

Documentaries/Reportage-*cont.*

Jordan, Michele Anna
Kawakami, Barbara Fusako
Kelly, Brian
Kelly, Kevin (J.)
Kenney, Charles
Kessler, Judy
Kidder, Tracy
Kitfield, James C.
Kotlowitz, Alex
Kublicki, Nicolas M.
Kurlansky, Mark
Lamb, Brian
Lawson, James
Lax, Eric
Leigh, David
Leroi, Armand Marie
Lewis, Sydney
Li, Leslie
Lindvall, Michael L(loyd)
Lipper, Joanna
Lippman, Thomas W.
Logue, Christopher
Longman, Jere
Lounsberry, Barbara
Lucashenko, Melissa
Maffi, Mario
Maier, Anne McDonald
Majure, Janet
Makepeace, Anne
Mallin, Jay
Manning, Robert D.
Margolick, David
Margolis, Jeffrey A.
Markoff, John
Marshall, John Douglas
Martin, Russell
Marton, Kati (Ilona)
Mathews, (Thomas) Jay
Mays, John Bentley
McCaughren, Tom
McClintick, David
McClure, Sandy
McDougal, Dennis
McGoogan, Ken
McNutt, Randy
McPhee, John (Angus)
McQuay, Peri Phillips
Medvedev, Grigori
Meeks, Christopher (Nelson)
Miller, Kit
Molesworth, Carl
Mollenkamp, Carrick
Morgan-Witts, Max
Morton, Bruce Rutherfurd
Mosley, Philip
Moynihan, Michael
Mulgrew, Ian
Murchison, William
Nash, (Cyril) Knowlton
Naughton, Jim
Naureckas, Jim
Navarra, Tova
Neimanis, George J(uris)
Nobile, Philip
Nossiter, Adam
O'Dell, Tawni
O'Doherty, Malachi

Bara czak, Stanisław
Barasch, Frances K.
Barbash, Shepard
Barber, Phyllis (Nelson)
Baricco, Alessandro
Barich, Bill
Barth, John (Simmons)
Barton, John
Bashe, Philip (Scott)
Bate, Jonathan
Bayme, Steven
Beasley, Faith E(velyn)
Beattie, L(inda) Elisabeth
Beaud, Michel
Becker, Gary S.
Becker, Josh
Beissel, Henry (Eric)
Bell, Marvin (Hartley)
Bell, Susan
Belsey, Catherine
Benn, Tony
Benson, Jackson J.
Bentos, Carlos
Berger, Barbara Helen
Berger, John (Peter)
Bergonzi, Bernard
Berman, David
Bernard, G. W.
Bernstein, Charles
Berry, Faith D.
Bertrand, Diane Gonzales
Berube, Maurice R.
Betts, Doris
Biermann, Pieke
Billetdoux, Raphaële
Billias, George Athan
Bina, Cyrus
Bird, Christiane
Birstein, Ann
Bishop, Michael
Black, Arthur (Raymond)
Blades, John D.
Blake, Raymond B.
Blakely, Mary Kay
Blank, G(regory) Kim
Blanning, T. C. W.
Blei, Norbert
Blessington, Francis C(harles)
Bloom, Lynn (Marie Zimmerman)
Bly, Robert (Elwood)
Bodett, Tom
Bolgiano, Chris(tina)
Bolles, Edmund Blair
Bond, Ruskin
Boruch, Marianne
Boswell, Robert
Bovell, Andrew (John)
Bowering, George
Bowers, Janice Emily
Bowlby, Rachel
Bowyer, Mathew Justice
Boyd, Blanche McCrary
Boyers, Robert
Bradley, David (Henry)
Brainard, Cecilia Manguerra
Brand, Alice Glarden
Brantlinger, Patrick (Morgan)

Brett, Donna W(hitson)
Brewer, William D(ean)
Brewster, Elizabeth (Winifred)
Brochu, André
Bromann, Jennifer
Bromberg, Nicolette A.
Brombert, Victor (Henri)
Brooks, Bruce (Delos)
Brooks, David (Gordon)
Brooks, Peter Newman
Bross, Donald G.
Brown, Archibald Haworth
Brown, Canter
Brown, Harry Clifford
Brown, Michelle P(atricia)
Brown, Nickole
Brown, Rosellen
Brown, Stewart
Browning, Guy
Brox, Jane (Martha)
Bruckner, Pascal
Brulotte, Gaetan
Buchanan, Paul G.
Budny, Mildred
Buechner, (Carl) Frederick
Burnett, Alfred David
Burroughs, Franklin (Gorham)
Burrow, J(ohn) A(nthony)
Burroway, Janet (Gay)
Burtchaell, James Tunstead
Burton, Thomas G(len)
Burwell, Jennifer
Bushnell, Jack
Butala, Sharon (Annette)
Butler, David (Edgeworth)
Butler, Lance St. John
Butts, Dennis
Byalick, Marcia
Byrnes, Giselle
Cahill, Tim
Calderwood, James Lee
Campo, Rafael
Carbo, Nick
Carle, Eric
Carnall, Geoffrey Douglas
Carneci, Magda
Carpenter, Bogdana
Carroll, Noel
Carson, Anne
Carter, Harold
Cartledge, Mark J.
Case, George (Andrew Thomas)
Casey, John (Dudley)
Cassell, Eric J.
Castle, Alfred L.
Castro, Brian (Albert)
Caws, Mary Ann
Cazden, Courtney B(orden)
Cercas, Javier
Chambers, John Whiteclay
Charnas, Suzy McKee
Charny, Israel Wolf
Cherry, Kelly
Chevalier, Tracy
Chin, Justin
Chisholm, Michael
Chodorow, Nancy Julia

Chomsky, (Avram) Noam
Chorlton, David
Choyce, Lesley
Christensen, Paul
Chu, Tien-wen
Chupack, Cindy
Churchland, Paul M.
Chwin, Stefan
Ciochon, Russell L.
Clark, Beverly Lyon
Clark, Charles Michael Andres
Clausen, Christopher (John)
Clayton, Philip
Clendenen, Avis
Clendinnen, Inga
Clifford, Mary Louise
Clubbe, John L(ouis) E(dwin)
Codrescu, Andrei
Coelho, Ivo
Coers, Donald V.
Coetzee, J(ohn) M(ichael)
Coleman, Jane Candia
Colinas, Antonio
Collier, James Lincoln
Conn, Stewart
Connor, William S. P.
Conroy, (Donald) Pat(rick)
Cooper, Dominic (Xavier)
Corden, Warner Max
Cork, Richard (Graham)
Corn, Alfred
Cosic, Dobrica
Coupland, Douglas
Courtenay, Bryce
Covington, Vicki
Cowen, Zelman
Crenshaw, James L.
Crews, Harry (Eugene)
Crisp, Oliver D.
Crouch, Stanley
Crowder, Ashby Bland
Crowther, Hal
Cruz, Victor Hernandez
Culbert, Steven (Tye)
Cunningham, Frank R.
Curthoys, Ann
Cytowic, Richard E(dmund)
Czekanowska, Anna
D'Orso, Michael
Dale, Richard
Dance, Daryl Cumber
Daniel, Pete
Danow, David K.
Danto, Arthur C(oleman)
Davies, Brian
Davis, Amelia
Davis, Rose Parkman
De Vries, Rachel (Guido)
Dean, Margaret Lazarus
Dean, Trevor
Delany, Samuel R(ay)
Demers, David (Pearce)
Deming, Alison Hawthorne
Deming, Sarah
DeMott, Robert (James)
Demski, Joel S.
Derr, Mark (Burgess)

Derrett, (John) Duncan (Martin)
Dery, Mark
Desai, Boman
Desjarlais, John
Dexter, Pete
Di Piero, W(illiam) S(imone)
Diamant, Anita
Diamond, Rickey Gard
Dickinson, Matt
Didion, Joan
Dillard, Annie
Diner, Dan
Dipple, Geoffrey
DiRenzo, Anthony
Djerassi, Carl
Djwa, Sandra (Ann)
Dobson, R(ichard) Barrie
Docherty, Paddy
Doctorow, E(dgar) L(awrence)
Dodd, Elizabeth Caroline
Dolan, Frederick Michael
Dolin, Sharon
Donaldson, Thomas
Donovan, Katie
Dooley, Brian J.
Downie, Mary Alice
Downing, Michael (Bernard)
Drakuli , Slavenka
Dubber, Markus Dirk
Duberstein, Larry
Duckworth, Eleanor
Duffield, Gervase E.
Duke, Martin
Dunant, Sarah
Dunbar, Gary S(eamans)
Duncan, Lois
Dunkerley, James
Dunlap, Julie
Dunn, John (Montfort)
Dunn, Stephen
DuPlessis, Rachel Blau
Dutkina, Galina (Borisovna)
Dyer, Joyce
Dyson, Michael Eric
Eaton, Richard M.
Ede, Piers Moore
Edgerton, David
Edson, Russell
Edwards, Philip (Walter)
Egbuna, Obi (Benedict)
Egerton, Douglas R.
Eisiminger, Sterling (Skip)
Elder, John
Elie, Lolis Eric
Ellis, Jerry
Emanuel, James A(ndrew)
Emmer, Michele
Ensminger, Peter A.
Epstein, Joseph
Epstein, Leslie (Donald)
Epstein, Mikhail N.
Esfandiari, Haleh
Espada, Martín
Espaillat, Rhina P.
Estes, William (Kaye)
Evans, D(avid) Ellis
Evans, Helen C.

Essays-*cont.*

Faber, Michel
Fadiman, Anne
Faig, Kenneth W(alter)
Farley, Margaret A.
Farrar, Ronald T(ruman)
Feinstein, Sascha
Fenlon, Iain
Ferreiro, Alberto
Feuerstein, Georg
Field, Genevieve
Figiel, Sia
Finch, Christopher
Finch, Robert (Charles)
Fink, Leon
Fishkin, Shelley Fisher
Fishman, Katharine Davis
Fiss, Owen M(itchell)
Fitzmaurice, Gabriel
Fleischman, Paul R.
Fleisher, Paul
Fleishman, Lazar
Flenley, John (Roger)
Flynn, Elizabeth A.
Folster, David
Forrest, Alan
Foster, Edward Halsey
Foy, George Michelsen
Frank, Joan
Franklin, Caroline
Franklin, Linda Campbell
Fraser, Kathleen
Frayn, Michael
Freed, Lynn
Freedman, Jonathan (Borwick)
Freeman, Castle (William)
Frey, Julia (Bloch)
Fricker, Christophe E.
Fried, Dennis F.
Friedeberg-Seeley, Frank (J. B.)
Friedman, Bruce Jay
Fritzell, Peter A(lgren)
Frueh, Joanna
Frye, Marilyn
Fulghum, Robert (L.)
Fultz, James R.
Gala (Y Velasco), Antonio
Gallagher, Gary W(illiam)
Gallagher, Tess
Gallo, Gina
Gallo, Patrick J.
Gallo, Rubén
Galt, George
Garber, Zev
Garner, Alan
Garner, Helen
Garrison, Philip
Garton Ash, Timothy
Gass, William (Howard)
Gaudet, Marcia
Gaukroger, Stephen
Geddes, Gary
Geist, Bill
Geldard, Richard G.
Gelderman, Carol (Wettlaufer)
Geras, Norman (Myron)
Gerber, Merrill Joan
Gerrish, Brian Albert

Essays-*cont.*

Gianakaris, Constantine John
Giardinelli, Mempo
Gifford, Barry (Colby)
Gilbert, Glenn G(ordon)
Gilchrist, Ellen
Gill, A. A.
Gillespie, Diane Filby
Gilman, Owen W(inslow)
Giovanni, Nikki
Glancy, Diane
Glass, Charles
Godbout, Jacques
Godwin, Rebecca T.
Goethe, Ann
Gold, Herbert
Gold, Jerome
Goldberger, Avriel H.
Goldman, Katherine (Wyse)
Goldman, William
Goldsmith, Barbara
Goldstein, Rebecca
Gomez, Jewelle
Gomi, Taro
Gommans, Jos J. L.
Gonzales, Laurence
Gooch, Steve
Goodman, Ellen (Holtz)
Goodman, Richard
Gordimer, Nadine
Gordinier, Jeff
Gordon, Jaimy
Gordon, Lewis Ricardo
Gordon, Mary (Catherine)
Gordon, Sheila
Gorman, James
Gornick, Vivian
Gorup, Radmila J(ovanovi)
Gottlieb, Freema (Peninah)
Gourgouris, Stathis
Gow, Andrew Colin
Graff, Henry Franklin
Grant, Bruce (Alexander)
Grant, James Russell
Grass, Günter (Wilhelm)
Graver, Elizabeth
Grearson, Jessie Carroll
Grebstein, Sheldon Norman
Green, Peter (Morris)
Greenberg, Alvin
Greenberg, Elinor Miller
Greene, Jonathan (Edward)
Greenlee, J(acob) Harold
Greenwald, Jeff
Gridneff, Ilya
Grudin, Robert
Guest, Judith
Guidry, Cindy
Guillermoprieto, Alma
Guillory, Dan
Gundy, Jeff(rey Gene)
Guo, Xiaolu
Gurganus, Allan
Gurvis, Sandra J.
Gwyn, Richard
Haar, James
Haberman, David L.
Hackl, Erich

Essays-*cont.*

Hadas, Rachel
Haffenden, John
Haga, Enoch John
Hainsworth, Peter (R. J.)
Hajdu, David
Hakak, Lev
Hale, Robert D(avid)
Hall, H(ugh) Gaston
Halligan, Marion (Mildred
    Crothall)
Hamill, Pete
Hamill, Sam (Patrick)
Hamilton, John Maxwell
Hamrin, Robert
Hands, D. Wade
Hansen, Jennifer
Hardy, Barbara (Gladys)
Hardy, John Philips
Hargreaves, John D(esmond)
Harpur, Tom
Harris, (Theodore) Wilson
Harris, Claire
Harrison, John F(letcher) C(lews)
Harrison, Kathryn
Hart, Jonathan (Locke)
Hartman, Geoffrey H.
Hashmi, (Aurangzeb) Alamgir
Haslam, Gerald William
Hasluck, Nicholas
Hasselstrom, Linda (Michele)
Haswell, Richard H(enry)
Haught, James A(lbert)
Hauser, Susan Carol
Hawley, Richard A.
Haynes, Jim
Headley, John M.
Heffron, Dorris
Hein, Christoph
Heller, Michael
Helwig, Maggie
Hemming, Laurence Paul
Herman, Barbara
Herndon, Ernest
Hershman, Marcie
Heyen, William
Heyman, Jacques
Hiaasen, Carl
Hibbs, Thomas S.
Hill, Susan (Elizabeth)
Himka, John-Paul
Hinchman, Lewis P(atrick)
Hoagland, Edward
Hobsbawm, Eric (John Ernest)
Hobson, Fred Colby
Hoerder, Dirk
Hoffman, Elizabeth Cobbs
Hoffman, Michael J.
Hoffmann, Stanley
Hogan, Patrick Colm
Hoggard, James
Hoggart, Richard
Hokanson, (Anthony) Drake
Holli, Melvin George
Hollingshead, Greg
Hollo, Anselm (Paul Alexis)
Holloway, Sue (A.)
Holroyd, Michael

Essays-*cont.*

Holsti, Kalevi J.
Holtorf, Cornelius
Hom, Sharon K.
Homel, David
Honderich, Ted
Hooker, Jeremy
Hooks, Bell
Hord, Frederick (Lee)
Hornby, Nick
Horner, David
Horsley, Richard A.
Houston, Velina Hasu
Howard, A(rthur) E(llsworth)
    Dick
Howatch, Susan
Huddle, David
Hummer, T(erry) R(andolph)
Hundley, Norris C.
Hunt, Tom
Hurt, Harry
Hustvedt, Siri
Hynes, Samuel
Iggers, Georg G(erson)
Indiana, Gary
Intrator, Sam M.
Irion, Mary Jean
Iyer, Pico
Jacobs, Barbara
Jacobson, Dan
James, Russell
James, Sibyl
James, Warren A.
Jarman, Mark (F.)
Jason, Sonya
Jauss, David
Jennings, Kate
Jepson, Jill
Johnson, Michael P(aul)
Johnson, Paul (Bede)
Johnson, Susan (Ruth)
Jones, Gayl
Jones, Star(let Marie)
Jong, Erica (Mann)
Joosse, Barbara M(onnot)
Jordan, Michele Anna
Jordan, Robert Smith
Joseph, Diana
Joyce, Joyce Ann
Joyce, Michael
Kabira, Wanjiku Mukabi
Kadare, Ismail
Kaltner, John
Kanigel, Robert
Kantaris, Sylvia (Mosley)
Kaplan, James
Kasdorf, Julia
Katz, Steven T(heodore)
Kaufman, Bel
Kavanagh, P(atrick) J(oseph)
Kaza, Stephanie
Kearns, Lionel (John)
Keene, Donald
Keilen, Sean
Keillor, Steven J(ames)
Kelly, Louis Gerard
Kemp, Kenny
Kenaz, Yehoshua

Kendrick, Christopher
Kennedy, Randall L.
Kennedy, Rick
Ker, Ian (Turnbull)
Kerman, Joseph
Kertess, Klaus
Kessler, Edward
Ketner, Kenneth Laine
Kevles, Bettyann Holtzmann
Khare, R(avindra) S.
Kiberd, Declan
Kidd, I(an) G(ray)
Kidd, Sue Monk
Kiernan, Ben
Kiernan, Brian
Kincaid, Jamaica
Kingsolver, Barbara
Kingston, Maxine Hong
Kinsella, Thomas
Kitchen, Judith
Kittredge, William
Kitzinger, Uwe
Klass, Perri (Elizabeth)
Klein, Philip Alexander
Klempner, Mark
Klingenstein, Susanne
Knecht, Robert Jean
Knight, Roger
Knopp, Lisa
Knox, Elizabeth (Fiona)
Koerner, Joseph Leo
Kokoris, Jim
Koller, James
Kord, Susanne
Kowalke, Kim H.
Kraeuter, David W.
Kramer, Dale
Krasnow, Iris
Kreinin, Mordechai
Kriegel, Leonard
Krystal, Arthur
Kumin, Maxine
Kurtz, Howard
Kushner, Rachel
Lacey, Nicola
Ladd, Louise
LaHood, Marvin J(ohn)
Lahr, John (Henry)
Lamb, Nancy
Lamba, Marie
Lambert, Page
Landsberg, Melvin
Lane, John
Lane, Simon
Lang, William L.
Lange, Arthur D.
Lara, Adair
Lasson, Kenneth (Lee)
Lavin, Irving
Lawrence, Kathleen Rockwell
Le Doeuff, Michèle
Lea, James F(ranklin)
Leader, Zachary
Lebsock, Suzanne (Dee)
LeClaire, Anne D(ickinson)
Lee, A(rthur) Robert
Lee, Marie G.

Leithauser, Brad (Edward)
Lemann, Nicholas
Lemay, Shawna
Lende, Heather
Lennard, John (Chevening)
Lesser, Wendy
Lessing, Doris (May)
Levesque, John
Levine, Philip
Levinson, Jerrold
Levy, Evonne
Lewis, Jeremy
Lewis, Michael
Li, Leslie
Liberman, Rosette B.
Liebert, Elizabeth
Lindholdt, Paul J.
Lipton, Eunice
Lisle, Laurie
Livingston, Gordon (S.)
Llewellyn, Kate
Lodge, David
Logan, George M(eredith)
Loo, Tina
Lopez, Jack
Lord, Nancy J.
Lott, John R.
Louden, Robert B.
Loughery, John
Lounsberry, Barbara
Loury, Glenn C(artman)
Lowe-Evans, Mary
Lowery, Robert G.
Lucas, John A.
Lucas, John Randolph
Luft, Lya Fett
Lurie, Morris
Lutz, John Sutton
Lynch, Thomas
Lynd, Staughton (Craig)
MacIntyre, Alasdair
Macniven, Ian S.
Macphail, Catherine
Macsai, Gwen
Madden, David
Madden, Patrick
Madhubuti, Haki R.
Magistrale, Tony
Maguire, Laurie E.
Mahoney, Rosemary
Mairs, Nancy (Pedrick)
Major, Andre
major, devorah
Majure, Janet
Mallett, Daryl F(urumi)
Malone, James Hiram
Mamet, David
Mandel, Oscar
Mandelker, Amy
Mandler, Peter
Manea, Norman
Manetti, Larry
Mann, Jeff(rey A.)
Mansell, Darrel
Mansfield, Howard
Marshall, Paul A.
Marszalek, John F.

Martel, Gordon
Marting, Diane E.
Matthee, Rudi
Matthews, Jack
Mauer, Marc
Mauk, David C.
May, Gita
Mayor, Federico
McCann, Richard
McClelland, Vincent Alan
McDonald, Ian (A.)
McDowell, John (Henry)
McGowan, Mark George
McGrath, Carmelita
McIntire, C(arl) T(homas)
McKean, Robert B.
McKeen, William
McLaren, John
McLaughlin, Andrée Nicola
McMurry, Richard M.
McMurtry, Larry (Jeff)
McNair, Wesley C.
McPhee, John (Angus)
McPherson, James Munro
Mears, Gillian
Megged, Aharon
Meinke, Peter
Mele, Alfred R.
Mellizo (Cuadrado), Carlos
Mellor, D. H.
Mellor, John W(illiams)
Memmott, David R.
Merrill, Wendy
Merwin, W(illiam) S(tanley)
Messori, Vittorio
Metcalf, John (Wesley)
Metzger, Deena P.
Micale, Mark S.
Middleton, (John) Christopher
Mikalson, Jon D.
Mikolyzk, Thomas A.
Milis, Ludo(vicus) J. R.
Miller, Brenda
Miller, Charles A.
Miller, David (Leslie)
Miller, Jane
Millett, Kate
Millett, Paul
Milne, Seumas
Miltner, Robert
Minock, Daniel
Mishkin, Tracy
Mitchard, Jacquelyn
Mitchell, Mark
Mitchell, Nathan
Mitchell, Roger
Molesworth, Charles
Molina, Silvia
Monda, Antonio
Montague, John (Patrick)
Montefiore, Janet
Montpetit, Charles
Monzó, Quim
Moore, Philip N(icholas)
Morgan, Robert (R.)
Morgan, Robert C.
Morgan, Robin

Mori, Kyoko
Morriss, Frank
Morse, Donald E.
Moshiri, Farnoosh
Moskowitz, Faye (Stollman)
Motion, Andrew (Peter)
Muchmore, Jo Ann
Mudimbe, V. Y.
Mueller, Robert Emmett
Murphy, Cullen
Murphy, Martha W(atson)
Musgrave, Susan
Nádas, Péter
Nash, Gary B.
Nassar, Eugene Paul
Natwar-Singh, K.
Neeld, Elizabeth Harper
Neilan, Sarah
Nelson, Jill
Nersessian, V(rej) N.
Nesset, Kirk
Newcomer, James W.
Ngcobo, Lauretta
Nish, Ian Hill
Nitchie, George Wilson
Novakovich, Josip
O'Brien, D(enis) P(atrick)
O'Brien, Sean
O'Driscoll, Dennis
O'Grady, John P.
O'Mara, Peggy (Noreen)
Oates, Joyce Carol
Obejas, Achy
Obika, Akili Addae
o e, Kenzaburo
Oiwa, Keibo
Oktenberg, Adrian
Olson, David Richard
Onuf, Nicholas
Oppersdorff, Tony
Orel, Harold
Orr, Gregory (Simpson)
Osmer, Richard Robert
Ozick, Cynthia
Pack, Robert
Padmore, Sandra
Page, Clarence
Paglia, Camille
Pahor, Boris
Palencia, Elaine Fowler
Palmer, Stanley H.
Parrish, William E.
Pashman, Susan
Pastan, Linda
Patey, Douglas Lane
Peacock, Molly
Peavler, Terry J.
Penelope, Julia
Penn, W(illiam) S.
Pennac, Daniel
Perry, Michael Charles
Peters, Robert
Petry, Alice Hall
Pettigrew, Judy
Pettit, Rhonda S(ue)
Phelan, Tom (Thomas Joseph)
Philip, M(arlene) NourbeSe

Essays-*cont.*

Wallace-Crabbe, Christopher (Keith)
Waller, Robert James
Ward, Geoffrey C(hampion)
Warne, Randi R(uth)
Warner, Elizabeth (Ann)
Wasiolek, Edward
Wästberg, Per
Waters, John F(rederick)
Watson, George (Grimes)
Watson, J(ohn) R(ichard)
Watson, Stephen
Wayman, Tom
Webb, Phyllis
Webb, Veronica
Wedde, Ian
Weisskopf, Thomas E.
Wells, Ken
Wells, Rosemary
Wenderoth, Joe
Werckmeister, O(tto) K(arl)
Wesker, Arnold
West, Elliott
Westrum, Dexter
Wetherell, W(alter) D(avid)
What, Leslie
White, Dan
White, Edmund
White, Edward M.
White, Kenneth
Whittemore, (Edward) Reed
Wiesel, Elie
Wilentz, Sean
Wilkinson, Alec
Will, George F.
Willett, Ralph
Williams, C(harles) K(enneth)
Williams, Joy
Williams, Mark
Williams, Terry Tempest
Willimon, William H(enry)
Wilson, A(ndrew) N.
Wilson, David S(cofield)
Wilson, Stephen G.
Wiltshire, Susan Ford
Wineapple, Brenda
Winegarten, Renee
Winokur, Jon
Winston, Mark L.
Wohlgelernter, Maurice
Woiwode, Larry (Alfred)
Wolfe, Peter
Wolfinger, Raymond E(dwin)
Wood, Gerald C.
Wood, James
Woodruff, Lee McConaughy
Woods, Paula L.
Woody, Elizabeth
Woog, Dan
Woolf, D. R.
Woolley, Bryan
Worcester, Kent
Work, James C.
Wortsman, Peter
Wright, C. D.
Wu, Ningkun
Wunderlich, Ray Charles

Essays-*cont.*

Wuori, G. K.
Wynes, Charles E.
Wynyard, Robin (Norman)
Yarbro, Chelsea Quinn
Yates, Nigel
Yoder, Edwin Milton
Yoggy, Gary A.
Young, David (Pollock)
Young, Ian
Young-Bruehl, Elisabeth
Zaid, Gabriel
Zarnow, Teryl
Zenith, Richard
Ziegler, Philip (Sandeman)
Zigal, Thomas
Zilboorg, Caroline (Crawford)
Zimmer, Paul J(erome)
Zinik, Zinovy
Zukav, Gary
Zwinger, Ann Haymond

Ghost Writer

Adamec, Christine
Adams, Charles J.
Allie, Scott
Antol, Marie Nadine
Arnold, Peter
Becker, Jasper
Bellotti, Laura Golden
Bissell, Sallie
Bordowitz, Hank
Bosco, Dominick
Bryant, Mark
Buccieri, Lisa Rojany
Buffie, Margaret
Caputo, Philip
Cashdan, Linda
Cawthorne, Nigel
Clabough, Casey Howard
Cossolotto, Matthew
D'Antonio, Michael
Darden, Robert
Darrieussecq, Marie
Darwish, Adel
Davidson, Jeff
Deming, Sarah
Duggleby, John
Emerson, Ken
Evans, Justin
Foer, Jonathan Safran
Ford, G. M.
Fox, Barry
Gilman, George G.
Glut, Don(ald) F.
Goingback, Owl
Goldwasser, Thomas
Greene, Constance C(larke)
Gurvis, Sandra J.
Hahn, Mary Downing
Handler, David
Hart, Carolyn G(impel)
Harwood, John
Holder, Nancy L.
Hunter, Mollie
Jenkins, Garry

Ghost Writer-*cont.*

Jones, Gwyneth A(nn)
Jordan, Anne Devereaux
Kallen, Stuart A(rnold)
Keith, William H(enry)
Kessler, Julia Braun
King, Daren
Kleh, Cindy (L.)
Kurland, Michael (Joseph)
Ladd, Louise
Lassiter, Rhiannon
Lemire, Jeff
Lester, Julius
Lewis, J(ohn) R(oyston)
MacInnes, Mairi
Mack, David (A.)
McDonald, Collin
Moorcock, Michael (John)
Moore, James A.
Morris, Chris(topher Crosby)
Muller, (Lester) Robin
Murphey, Cecil B(laine)
Nolan, William F(rancis)
Pilling, Ann
Preller, James
Ragen, Naomi
Reed, Philip (Chandler)
Reiter, Victoria (Kelrich)
Ruelle, Karen Gray
Schnur, Steven
Schoenberg, Robert J.
Schweikart, Larry (Earl)
Shafquat, Sofia
Stackpole, Michael A(ustin)
Suen, Anastasia
Szanton, Andrew (Emlen)
Szymanski, Lois
Thorsson, Örnólfur
Vaughn, Patrika
Watkins, Graham
Watkins, Ronald J(oseph)
Watson, Kathy
Watson, William E.
Wein, Elizabeth E(ve)
Wilson, Des
Wood, Edward John
Wright, Betty Ren
Yenne, Bill

Graphic Novels

Akamatsu, Ken
Allan, Von
Allie, Scott
Bagge, Peter (Christian Paul)
Baker, Kevin (Breen)
Baker, Kyle
Baron, Mike
Beauchard, Pierre François
Bendis, Brian Michael
Bertozzi, Nick
Bouton, Gary David
Briggs, Patricia
Brill, Marlene Targ
Brown, Jeffrey
Butzer, C. M.

Graphic Novels-*cont.*

Campbell, Eddie
Card, Orson Scott
Carter, Steven R(ay)
Castellucci, Cecil
Colden, Kevin
Collins, Max Allan
Collins, Nancy A.
Cooper, Dave
Cruse, Howard
Culhane, John (William)
Davis, Eleanor
De Haven, Tom
Delgado, Ricardo
Donner, Rebecca
Dorkin, Evan
Doucet, Julie
Dowling, Terry
Drew, Simon
Dysart, Joshua
Elliott, David
Ellison, Harlan (Jay)
Ennis, Garth
Evans, Greg
Evans, Jon
Fancher, Jane S(uzanne)
Fontes, Ron
Foster, Alan Dean
Gay, Marie Louise
Gifford, Barry (Colby)
Gilliland, Alexis A(rnaldus)
Gipi
Groening, Matt
Hale, Shannon
Hamilton, Tim
Haspiel, Dean
Henley, Marian
Herbert, James
Hinds, Gareth
Hollander, Nicole
Holub, Joan
Hornschemeier, Paul
Horrocks, Dylan
Horsey, David
Inge, M. Thomas
Kadrey, Richard
Kalesniko, Mark G(aston)
Kaplan, Bruce Eric
Kneece, Mark
Kochalka, James
Koontz, Dean R(ay)
Krohn, Katherine E(lizabeth)
Kuitenbrouwer, Kathryn (Ann Frances)
Kuper, Peter
Lash, Batton
Lemire, Jeff
Liss, David
Lupoff, Richard A(llen)
Mackin, Jeanne
Mairowitz, David Zane
Margulies, Jimmy
Meltzer, Brad
Michelson, Richard
Montpetit, Charles
Moorcock, Michael (John)
Morrison, Grant
Moss, Marissa

Grant, Cynthia D.
Grant, Graeme
Grau, Shirley Ann
Green, Michael (Frederick)
Greenwald, Sheila
Griffith, Helen V(irginia)
Grodin, Charles
Groening, Matt
Grossman, Austin
Gruner, Charles R.
Guest, Christopher
Gurdon, Martin
Gurvis, Sandra J.
Guy, Ray
Hajdusiewicz, Babs Bell
Halliday, Ayun
Hanson, David D.
Harris, Christine
Harrison, Harry
Harrison, Michael
Hart, JoeAnn
Hartley, Hal
Hartman, Victoria
Harvey, Robert C.
Hasburgh, Patrick
Haslam, Gerald William
Hauptman, Don
Hawkes, Kevin
Hendra, Jessica
Henley, Arthur
Henley, Marian
Herbert, Brian
Hershenhorn, Esther
Hiaasen, Carl
Hill, Thomas
Hillier, Jim
Himelstein, Shmuel
Hoff, Al
Hofler, Robert
Hogg, James (Dalby)
Holden, Anthony (Ivan)
Hollander, Nicole
Holub, Joan
Horsey, David
Howard, Heather H.
Huggett, Frank Edward
Hunter, Seb
Hurwitz, David
Inge, M. Thomas
Isaacs, Anne
Israel, Lee
Jackson, Marni
Jacobs, David
Jaffee, Al(lan)
Jaffin, David
James, Clive (Vivian Leopold)
Jay, Ricky
Jennings, Charles
Johnson, Charles R(ichard)
Jones, Gerard
Jones, Merry Bloch
Jordan, Richard Tyler
Joy, David (Anthony Welton)
Judd, Alan
Juster, Norton
Kalson, Albert E(ugene)
Kaplan, Bruce Eric

Katz, Molly
Kaufman, Gerald (Bernard)
Keating, Frank
Keene, Raymond D(ennis)
Keillor, Garrison (Edward)
Keller, Holly
Kellogg, Marne Davis
Kellogg, Steven
Kelly, Maeve
Kendrick, Christopher
Kennedy, Dan
Kennedy, Sheila Suess
Kenney, William Howland
Kerner, Fred
Kidd, Paul
Kightlinger, Laura
Kimmel, Daniel M.
King, Daren
Kiraly, Sherwood
Kleh, Cindy (L.)
Klein, Allen
Kobel, Peter
Kochalka, James
Koller, Jackie French
Kuczkir, Mary
Kushner, Malcolm
Kvasnosky, Laura McGee
Lane, Terry
Langston, Cynthia
Lara, Adair
Larson, Gary
Leary, Ann (Lembeck)
Ledbetter, Suzann
Lederer, Richard
Leguizamo, John
Leifer, Carol
Leno, Jay
Lent, John A.
Lerner, Laurence (David)
Levesque, John
Lewis, Minty
Lipman, Elinor
Littleton, Darryl
Loh, Sandra Tsing
Longfellow, Layne (A.)
Longyear, Barry B.
Lopes, Dominic (M. McIver)
Lovric, Michelle
Lunn, Janet (Louise Swoboda)
Lynn, Jonathan
MacDonald, Kyle
Macfarlane, Malcolm R.
Mack, David (A.)
Macsai, Gwen
Madsen, Ross Martin
Maeder, Thomas
Malki, David
Malmgren, Dallin
Mamet, David
Mandel, Peter (Bevan)
Maner, Martin
Marcus, Leonard S.
Margulies, Jimmy
Markoe, Merrill
Marks, Stan(ley)
Marsh, Fabienne
Martchenko, Michael

Martin, Judith
Martinet, Jeanne
Mathews, Dan
Matthew, Christopher C. F.
Maxford, Howard
Mayne, Kenny
McCants, William D.
McCusker, Paul
McDermott, Alice
McGill, Angus
McGruder, Aaron
Mclaughlin, Ritta
McNamara, Mary
McShane, Mark
Meltzer, Brad
Mendoza, Lisa
Mercati, Cynthia
Merrill, Jean (Fairbanks)
Metz, Don
Meyerhoff, Jenny
Miller, Blair
Mizejewski, Linda
Mogelon, Ronna
Moggach, Deborah
Mone, Gregory
Monesson, Harry S.
Montandon, Mac
Montes, Marisa
Montpetit, Charles
Moon, Susan
Moore, Dinty W.
Morrey, Douglas J.
Morrow, Skip
Moser, Edward P.
Mowat, Farley (McGill)
Munsch, Robert
Murphy, Jill (Frances)
Myers, Robert Manson
Naureckas, Jim
Nelson, Arvid
Nelson, T. G. A.
Nemec, James
Nericcio, William Anthony
Nichols, Peter (Richard)
Nilsson, Eleanor
Nolan, William F(rancis)
Norris, Pamela
O'Hare, Jeff(rey A.)
O'Rourke, P. J.
Oberle, Joseph
Obst, Lynda (Rosen)
Oderman, Stuart (Douglas)
Olbermann, Keith
Oldenburg, Ray
Olson, Kirby
Oppenheimer, Gregg
Otomo, Katsuhiro
Ott, Thomas
Page, Tim
Palin, Michael (Edward)
Palmer, William J.
Payne, J. Julian
Peck, Richard (Wayne)
Perkins, George (Burton)
Perkins, Lynne Rae
Perlman, Rhea
Peters, Robert

Pick, John Barclay
Pickering, David (Hugh)
Pierce, Chonda
Pilcher, Robin
Pinkwater, Daniel Manus
Pipkin, Turk
Piraro, Dan
Platt, Randall
Powe, Bruce Allen
Pratt, John Clark
Preston, Caroline
Protopopescu, Orel
Provine, Robert R(aymond)
Puxley, Ray
Queenan, Joe
Rajah, Susi
Randolph, Elizabeth
Rayner, Hugh
Reback, Storms
Reed, Ishmael
Reed, John Shelton
Rees, David
Rees, Nigel (Thomas)
Rehder, William J.
Remkiewicz, Frank
Rennison, Louise
Rich, Simon
Richmond, Hugh Macrae
Richtel, Matt
Rickels, Laurence A.
Robb, David L.
Roberts, Denys (Tudor Emil)
Roberts, Diane
Robinson, Spider
Rodgers, Frank
Romano, Ray
Roodenburg, Herman
Rooney, Andy
Rosen, Michael (Wayne)
Rosen, Michael J(oel)
Rosenberg, Saralee
Rothman, William
Rouse, Wade
Russell, Alan
Russell, Roy
Rutledge, Leigh W.
Rylant, Cynthia
S.D., Trav
Sacre, Antonio
Saknussemm, Kris
Salmansohn, Karen
Sanchez, Patrick
Sarvas, Mark
Saums, Mary
Sawyer, (Frederick) Don(ald)
Scheil, Katherine West
Schiff, Nancy Rica
Schlosberg, Suzanne
Schnur, Steven
Schouvaloff, Alexander
Schuiten, François Louis Marie
Schwartz, Lynne Sharon
Searle, Ronald (William Fordham)
Sedaris, Amy
Sedaris, David
Sellers, Alexandra

Cote, Nancy
Cowley, (Cassia) Joy
Cox, Judy
Creech, Sharon
Crew, Gary
Crews, Nina
Cross, Gillian (Clare)
Crum, Shutta
Cruse, Howard
Cuetara, Mittie
Cummings, Pat
Curtiss, A(rlene) B.
Dann, Colin (Michael)
Day, Alexandra
dePaola, Tomie
Derby, Sally
DeSpain, Pleasant
Desputeaux, Hélène
Doherty, Berlie
Donaldson, Julia
Dorkin, Evan
Dorros, Arthur (M.)
Downie, Mary Alice
Drucker, Mort
Dubosarsky, Ursula
Duey, Kathleen
Dunbar, Joyce
Duncan, Lois
Dunlap, Julie
Dunlop, Eileen (Rhona)
Ehlert, Lois (Jane)
Elliott, David
Ellis, Gwen
Emmer, Michele
Englehart, Bob
Ephron, Delia
Erdrich, Louise
Farthing-Knight, Catherine
Feiffer, Kate
Ferguson, Sarah (Margaret)
Fields, Terri
Figes, Eva
Figley, Marty Rhodes
Fine, Anne
Fisher, Catherine
Fishman, Cathy Goldberg
Fitzsimons, Cecilia (A. L.)
Fleming, Candace
Foley, Mick
Ford, Carolyn (Mott)
Frankel, Alona
Fraustino, Lisa Rowe
Gagliano, Eugene M.
Galbraith, Kathryn O(sebold)
Gardella, Tricia
Garner, Alan
Gauch, Patricia Lee
Gay, Marie Louise
Geraghty, Paul
Gilbert, Alma M.
Gilmore, Rachna
Gleeson, Libby
Godkin, Celia (Marilyn)
Golding, Theresa Martin
Gomi, Taro
Gordon, Mike
Grace, Patricia (Frances)

Greene, Jacqueline Dembar
Greene, Rhonda Gowler
Griggs, Terry
Gugler, Laurel Dee
Guthrie, Donna W.
Hajdusiewicz, Babs Bell
Halfmann, Janet
Halpern, Julie
Harley, Bill
Harris, Christine
Harris, Robie H.
Hawes, Louise
Helmer, Marilyn
Herrick, Steven
Hesse, Karen
Higgs, Liz Curtis
High, Linda Oatman
Hill, Susan (Elizabeth)
Hinton, S(usan) E(loise)
Hoban, Russell
Hodgson, Barbara L.
Hoestlandt, Jo(celyne)
Hoffman, Alice
Holbrook, Sara
Hollingsworth, Mary
Holub, Joan
Hooper, Meredith Jean
Hopkins, Jackie (Mims)
Howe, James
Howker, Janni
Hughes, Shirley
Hunt, Angela Elwell
Hunter, Mollie
Hunter, Sara Hoagland
Hutchins, Hazel J.
Hutchins, Pat
Jarman, Julia
Jenkins, Jean
Jennings, Paul
Jocelyn, Marthe
Johnson, Angela
Jonell, Lynne
Jones, Allan Frewin
Joosse, Barbara M(onnot)
Jungman, Ann
Juster, Norton
Keillor, Garrison (Edward)
Keller, Holly
Kellogg, Steven
Khan, Rukhsana
Kittinger, Jo S(usenbach)
Komaiko, Leah
Konigsburg, E(laine) L(obl)
Koontz, Dean R(ay)
Koontz, Robin
Krasilovsky, Phyllis
Krishnaswami, Uma
Kroll, Virginia L(ouise)
Krupp, Robin Rector
Kudlinski, Kathleen V.
Kusugak, Michael (Arvaarluk)
Langston, Laura
Langton, Jane
Lasky, Kathryn
Lauture, Denizé
Lawrence, Michael
Le Guin, Ursula K(roeber)

Lee, Dennis (Beynon)
Lee, Sally
Levitin, Sonia (Wolff)
Lewis, Paeony
Lin, Grace
Lingard, Joan (Amelia)
Lisle, Rebecca
Little, (Flora) Jean
Littlefield, Holly
Lohans, Alison
Loomis, Christine
Lovelace, Earl
Lowry, Lois (Hammersberg)
Lunn, Janet (Louise Swoboda)
Lurie, Alison
Lyon, George Ella
MacDonald, Anne Louise
MacLachlan, Patricia
Macomber, Debbie
Mahy, Margaret
Mamet, David
Mandel, Peter (Bevan)
Marantz, Sylvia S.
Margulies, Jimmy
Marsden, John
Matott, Justin
Mattingley, Christobel (Rose-
   mary)
Mayer, Mercer
Mazer, Anne
McCaughrean, Geraldine (Jones)
McCullough, Sharon Pierce
McCully, Emily Arnold
Mcdonnell, Patrick
McEwan, Ian
McGrath, Barbara B(arbieri)
McGrath, Carmelita
McKay, Hilary
McKee, David (John)
McLerran, Alice
Messner, Patricia A.
Michelson, Richard
Monesson, Harry S.
Montenegro, Laura Nyman
Morpurgo, Michael
Morrison, Toni
Moss, Marissa
Munsch, Robert
Murphy, Jill (Frances)
Murphy, Shirley R(ousseau)
Murphy, Sylvia
Myers, Bill
Myers, Walter Dean
Namioka, Lensey
Napoli, Donna Jo
Nobisso, Josephine
Nodelman, Perry
Noyes, Deborah
Numeroff, Laura Joffe
O'Brien, Edna
O'Keefe, Susan Heyboer
Okimoto, Jean Davies
Okoro, Anezi
Oldfield, Jenny
Oldfield, Pamela
Oneal, Elizabeth
Oppel, Kenneth

Orgel, Doris
Orr, Wendy
Paratore, Coleen Murtagh
Paterson, Katherine (Womeldorf)
Patron, Susan
Pattou, Edith
Paul, Ann Whitford
Pearson, Kit
Peck, Richard (Wayne)
Peppé, Rodney (Darrell)
Peretti, Frank E.
Petersen, David
Petersen, P(eter) J(ames)
Peyton, K. M.
Pfanner, (Anne) Louise
Phelan, Anna Hamilton
Pinkwater, Daniel Manus
Pitcher, Caroline (Nell)
Poole, Josephine
Porte, Barbara Ann
Powell, Eric
Preller, James
Presnall, Judith (Ann) Janda
Protopopescu, Orel
Pulver, Robin
Quattlebaum, Mary
Rabe, Berniece (Louise)
Raham, (R.) Gary
Rand, Gloria
Randell, Beverley
Rappaport, Doreen
Razzell, Mary (Catherine)
Rees, David
Reynolds, Aaron
Richemont, Enid
Roach, Archie
Robinson, Frank M(alcolm)
Rodda, Emily
Roop, Connie
Rosen, Michael J(oel)
Rotner, Shelley
Ruddell, Deborah
Rugg, Linda (Haverty)
Rusch, Elizabeth
Russo, Marisabina
Rylant, Cynthia
Sabuda, Robert (James)
Samson, Suzanne M.
Scarry, Huck
Schaefer, Lola M.
Scheffler, Ursel
Schroeder, Alan
Scieszka, Jon
Segun, Mabel D.
Seidel, Ross
Sendak, Maurice
Serfozo, Mary
Sharmat, Marjorie Weinman
Short, Kathy G(nagey)
Shortt, Tim(othy Donald)
Simmonds, Posy
Simon, Francesca
Simon, Seymour
Smith, Charles R.
Smith, Greg Leitich
Snyder, Zilpha Keatley
Sorenson, Margo

Picture/Board Books-*cont.*

Soto, Gary
Spalding, Andrea
Spinelli, Jerry
St. John, Bob J.
Staunton, Ted
Steel, Danielle
Steele, Philip
Stengel, Joyce A.
Stevenson, Sucie
Stops, Sue
Strachan, Ian
Stroud, Bettye
Suen, Anastasia
Sutton, Jane
Swindells, Robert (Edward)
Swope, Sam
Tamar, Erika
Taylor, Debbie A.
Teague, Mark (Christopher)
Thomson, Pat
Tomkins, Jasper
Topek, Susan Remick
Toten, Teresa
Tracy, Kathleen
Trottier, Maxine
Tunnell, Michael O('Grady)
Turner, Ann (Warren)
U'Ren, Andrea
Underwood, Deborah
van Allsburg, Chris
Vanasse, Deb
Waddell, Martin
Walker, Kate
Wallace, Barbara Brooks
Walsh, Jill Paton
Walton, Rick
Wardlaw, Lee
Washington, Donna L.
Wasserman, Robin
Waters, John F(rederick)
Waters, Tony
Weeks, Sarah
Wellington, Monica
Weyland, Jack
Whitcher, Susan (Godsil)
Wick, Walter
Wieler, Diana
Wiles, Deborah
Willey, Margaret
Wing, Natasha
Wishinsky, Frieda
Withrow, Sarah
Woik, Julie
Wolfer, Dianne
Wynne-Jones, Tim(othy)
Yang, Belle
Ye, Ting-Xing
Yenne, Bill
Yep, Laurence (Michael)
Zalben, Jane Breskin
Zimmermann, H(einz) Werner
Zurbo, Matt

Reference

Reference-*cont.*

Aaker, Everett
Abbotson, Susan C.W.
Addington, Arthur Charles
Adkins, Roy A(rthur)
Aidells, Bruce
Alkon, Paul K.
Allason, Rupert (William Simon)
Allen, Jonathan B(urgess)
Ammer, Christine (Parker)
Apple, Hope
Arkin, Marcus
Asher, R. E.
Atkinson, Michael (J.)
Auger, C(harles) P(eter)
Awe, Susan C.
Ayres, Mary Jo
Bahr, Iris
Bailey, Martha (J.)
Baker, Christopher W.
Baker, Rosalie F.
Baker, William
Balswick, Judith K.
Barbato, Joseph
Barber, Richard (William)
Barbour, Julian B.
Barker, Jonathan
Barrett, Andrea
Barrett, Buckley Barry
Barsky, Robert F(ranklin)
Barthelme, Frederick
Barzun, Jacques
Basso, Keith H(amilton)
Bauer, Caroline Feller
Beaman, Joyce Proctor
Beard, Richard
Beck, Peggy
Becker, Gary S.
Belknap, Robert L.
Bell, Susan
Benedict, Pinckney
Bentley, Nancy
Bergquist, William Hastings
Berinstein, Paula
Berman, Jeffrey
Berube, Maurice R.
Bewes, Richard
Biesel, David B.
Blum, Kristen Raub
Blumberg, Phillip Irvin
Bogart, Eleanor A(nne)
Bolam, Robyn
Bolino, August C.
Bolles, Edmund Blair
Bolton, Charles C.
Bopp, Mary S.
Boschken, Herman L.
Brackman, Barbara
Branch, Alan E(dward)
Brandt, Di
Brannen, Julia (M.)
Brawley, Robert L.
Brennan, J(ames) H(erbert)
Breslow, Susan
Brooks, Betty
Browning, Wilfrid (Robert Francis)
Bruer, John T.

Reference-*cont.*

Bryant, Mark
Buckley, John (F.)
Bulson, Eric
Burghardt, Linda
Burns, Eric
Burns, Richard Gordon
Burr, David (Dwight)
Butman, John
Calderwood, James Lee
Campbell, Peter A.
Carlin, Martha
Cassutt, Michael (Joseph)
Castleden, Rodney
Cavazos-Gaither, Alma E(lisa)
Chalker, Sylvia
Chandler, Daniel Ross
Chanoff, David
Chapin, Miles
Charef, Mehdi
Chernow, Barbara A.
Chevalier, Tracy
Childs, David (Haslam)
Chow, Kai-wing
Christoph, Peter R(ichard)
Christopher, Renny (Teresa)
Clark, David Lindsey
Clason, Marmy A.
Cleveland, Ceil
Clotfelter, Charles T.
Coffey, Michael
Cohen, Norman J.
Coles, Robert
Collier, Christopher
Conati, Marcello
Constantine-Simms, Delroy
Cook, Chris(topher)
Cooling, Wendy
Cordeiro, Patricia (A.)
Cottringer, Anne
Cox, Vicki
Cramer, Clayton E.
Cranfield, Charles Ernest Burland
Crawford, Gary W(illiam)
Crenshaw, James L.
Crew, Danny O(liver)
Crossette, Barbara
Crossley, James G.
Crowley, Katherine
Crump, William D(rake)
Crusius, Timothy Wood
Crystal, David
Curl, James Stevens
Currie, Stephen
Curzon, David
Cutter, Charles
Cycon, Dean
Dale, Rodney A. M.
Danow, David K.
Darby, William D(uane)
Dassanowsky, Robert
Daugherty, Greg(ory Ash)
Davidson, Pamela
Davis, Lindsey
Davison, Liam
Dawson, George Glenn
Day, A(rthur) Colin
Day-Lewis, Sean (Francis)

Reference-*cont.*

Delano, Anthony
Demarco-Barrett, Barbara
Dervaes, Claudine
Dexter, Pete
Di, Zhu Xiao
Diamant, Anita
Dicke, Thomas S(cott)
Docherty, James C(airns)
Donker, Marjorie
Duckworth, William (Ervin)
Dudley-Smith, Timothy
Dufresne, Jim
DuPree, Sherry Sherrod
Dwyer, Augusta (Maria)
Dyal, Donald H(enriques)
Dyson, John
Eaton, John Herbert
Egan, Kieran
Eisen, Sydney
Elliott, Clark A.
Ellis, Gwynn Pennant
English, Lyn D.
Ennulat, Egbert M.
Epstein, Eric Joseph
Estes, Daniel J(ohn)
Estrada, Rita Clay
Estraikh, Gennady
Evans, Earlene Green
Fahnestock, Todd
Fanning, Philip Ashley
Farmaian, Sattareh Farman
Faron, Fay
Feiler, Bruce
Ferguson, Everett
Fermor, Patrick (Michael) Leigh
Fertig, Beth
Finello, Dominick
Finlayson, Iain (Thorburn)
Fischer, Dennis
Fisher, Julieta Dias
Fiske, Robert H(artwell)
Flint, John Edgar
Forrest, Alan
Fox, Roy F.
Fraenkel, Jack R.
France, Miranda
Franklin, Linda Campbell
Freeborn, Richard (Harry)
Freeman, Marcia S.
Freyer, Tony (Allan)
Fuchs, Miriam
Gabbard, David A.
Gall, Sandy
Gans, Chaim
Gänzl, Kurt (Friedrich)
Garnett, Richard (Duncan Carey)
Garrison, Bruce
Gates, Barbara T(imm)
Gay, Kathlyn R.
Gehrig, Klaus
Gelb, Michael J.
George, Alice L.
Ghiglione, Loren
Gibbs, Tyson
Gibson, Ian
Gill, LaVerne McCain
Gill, Walter

Translations-_cont._

Kendall, Carol
Kennedy, X. J.
Kenworthy, Brian J(ohn)
Keplinger, David
Kerr, Alex
Kersaudy, François
Kessler, Jascha (Frederick)
Keys, Kerry Shawn
Khoroche, Peter (Andrew)
Khwaja, Waqas
Kilmer, Nicholas (John)
Kim, Chi-Ha
Kinnell, Galway
Kinsella, Thomas
Klein, Anne Carolyn
Knoepfle, John
Kochan, Miriam (Louise)
Kossman, Nina
Kozameh, Alicia
Kugle, Scott
Kumar, Alok
Kuvshinoff, Boris W.
Laferrière, Dany
Lambrichs, Louise L.
Lammers, Wayne P.
Lan, David
Lane, Harlan
Larsen, Jeanne (Louise)
Latynin, Leonid (Aleksandrovich)
Le Doeuff, Michèle
Lee, Peter H.
Leith, Linda Jane
Leviant, Curt
Levieux, Eleanor
Libera, Antoni
Lima, Robert (F.)
Linder, Marc
Liu, Eric
Lloyd, Rosemary
Logue, Christopher
Lomas, Herbert
Looney, Dennis (Oscar)
Louden, Robert B.
Lourie, Richard
Lovric, Michelle
Lowe, Stephen
Lucie-Smith, (John) Edward (McKenzie)
Luker, Nicholas (John Lydgate)
Lunde, David (Eric)
Lunde, Paul
MacQueen, Winifred (Wallace)
Madigan, Patrick
Maffi, Mario
Maggi, Armando
Maher, Eamon
Maier, Paul Luther
Mairowitz, David Zane
Major, Andre
Mallon, Florencia E.
Mandel, Oscar
Mann, Charles F.
Marcus, K(aren) Melissa
Marcuse, Aída E.
Mardon, Austin Albert
Marias, Javier
Marineau, Michele

Marion, Robert W.
Markham, J. David
Martin, Clancy M.
Martin, Gerald Michael
Martinez, Elizabeth Coonrod
Marting, Diane E.
Masalha, Nur
Maskarinec, Gregory G.
Masthay, Carl (David)
Mattawa, Khaled
Mayne, Seymour
Mayo, C(atherine) M(ansell)
Mazzaro, Jerome
McCaughrean, Geraldine (Jones)
McCrorie, Edward (P.)
McHugh, Heather
McHugh, John (Francis)
McKechnie, Paul (Richard)
Mclaughlin, Martin L.
McLellan, David
McLoughlin, Leslie John
McNeill, Christine
McPhee, Jenny
McVaugh, Michael R(ogers)
McWhirter, George
Megged, Aharon
Mehrotra, Arvind Krishna
Melchior, Ib (Jorgen)
Mellizo (Cuadrado), Carlos
Melnyczuk, Askold
Menes, Orlando Ricardo
Mercer, Jeremy
Merwin, W(illiam) S(tanley)
Metres, Philip
Mezey, Robert
Micale, Mark S.
Michael, Colette V(erger)
Middleton, (John) Christopher
Minear, Richard Hoffman
Mitchell, Stephen
Molnar, Michael
Montague, John (Patrick)
Moore, Carey Armstrong
Moore, Greg
Moreh, Shmuel
Morency, Pierre
Morgenstern, Susie Hoch
Morse, Donald E.
Moser, Benjamin
Mosier, John
Mosley, Philip
Moxley, Jennifer
Mueller, Lisel
Muller, Herta
Mungoshi, Charles L.
Muniz, Olga M.
Murakami, Haruki
Murphy, (Gavin) Martin (Hedd)
Nagem, Monique F.
Nahas, Gabriel G(eorges)
Nakayama, Shigeru
Napora, Joseph S.
Navrozov, Andrei
Nersessian, V(rej) N.
Nesset, Kirk
Newth, Mette
Ni Hua-Ching

Nichols, John Gordon
Nielson, James
Nöel, Roger Arthur
Norman, Howard A.
Nunnally, Tiina
Nye, Robert
O Cuilleanain, Cormac
O'Briant, Walter H(erbert)
O'Connor, Patricia W.
O'Daly, William
O'Donoghue, Bernard
O'Faolain, Julia
O'Grady, Desmond (James Bernard)
Oakes, Meredith
Obejas, Achy
Obradovi , Nade da
Odber (de Baubeta), Patricia (Anne)
Oiwa, Keibo
Olivelle, Patrick
Olson, Kirby
Orgel, Doris
Orlev, Uri
Orme, Nicholas
Ortega, Julio
Osborne, Charles
Osers, Ewald
Osing, Gordon T.
Ostrovsky, Eugene
Ostrowski, Jan K.
Owens, Rochelle
Oxley, William
Ozsvath, Zsuzsanna
Padgett, Ron
Palandri, Enrico
Palkovic, Mark
Parsons, P. J.
Parthasarathy, R(ajagopal)
Passaro, Maria (C. Pastore)
Pasti, Umberto
Paterson, Janet M.
Paterson, Katherine (Womeldorf)
Patterson, Michael
Pausewang, Gudrun
Payton, Rodney J.
Pearson, Roger A. G.
Perdrizet, Marie-Pierre
Perloff, Marjorie (Gabrielle)
Perrone, Charles A.
Petro, Peter
Phillips, Carl
Pierce, David
Pilling, Christopher (Robert)
Pines, Ayala Malach
Pinsky, Robert
Pitcher, Harvey John
Plante, David (Robert)
Polastron, Lucien X.
Polizzotti, Mark
Ponce, Mary Helen
Porten, Bezalel
Poulin, Jacques
Prelutsky, Jack
Price, Victor (Henry John)
Pritchett, Kay
Purpura, Lia

Putnam, Constance E(lizabeth)
Pye, Michael (Kenneth)
Quandt, Richard (Emeric)
Rabassa, Gregory
Ramsay, Jay
Rand, Harry
Randall, Margaret
Raphael, Frederic (Michael)
Rayfield, Donald
Reed, T(erence) J(ames)
Reeve, F(ranklin) D(olier)
Reeves, Eileen Adair
Reid, Alastair
Reid, T. R.
Reidel, James
Reinfeld, Linda M.
Reiter, Victoria (Kelrich)
Renaud, Jacques
Renaux, Sigrid
Renfield, Richard Lee
Ricapito, Joseph V.
Rich, Adrienne (Cecile)
Rich, Nathaniel
Richter, Gregory C.
Ridley, Ronald T(homas)
Riordan, James (William)
Rios, Julian
Rippley, LaVern J.
Rivera, Eléna
Roberts, Nancy N(orma)
Robisheaux, Thomas
Rochberg, Francesca
Rockland, Michael Aaron
Rodriguez, Alfred
Rodriguez, Ileana
Rodriguez, Judith (Green)
Rogow, Zack
Root, William Pitt
Roses, Lorraine Elena
Rothenberg, Jerome
Rowe, C(hristopher) J(ames)
Rudkin, (James) David
Rudolf, Anthony
Rugeley, Terry
Russell, Rinaldina
Sachs, Murray
Šalamun, Toma
Sallenave, Daniele
Sallis, James
Sanderlin, George
Sanders, Peter (Basil)
Sandy, Stephen
Santos, Sherod
Sato, Hiroaki
Saviano, Roberto
Sawyer, Ralph D.
Sawyer-Laucanno, Christopher
Scammell, Michael
Schelling, Andrew
Schilling, Mark R.
Schmidt, Michael (Norton)
Schmidt, Samuel
Schneider, Deborah Lucas
Schrift, Alan D.
Schutte, Anne Jacobson
Schwartz, Lynne Sharon
Scott, John T.

Translations-*cont.*

Scott, Nina M.
Screech, M(ichael) A(ndrew)
Scully, James (Joseph)
Seaton, J(erome) P.
Sebanc, Mark
Sed-Rajna, Gabrielle
Segal, Lore
Seiferle, Rebecca
Selbourne, David
Shandler, Jeffrey
Shapiro, David (Joel)
Shapiro, Sidney
Shaw, Joseph M(inard)
Shen, Fan (A.)
Sherwin, Michael S.
Shukman, Harold
Silver, Harold
Silverman, Jerry
Simic, Charles
Simic, Goran
Simon, Daniel (Martin)
Simpson, Jacqueline (Mary)
Sinclair, Andrew (Annandale)
Sinha, Indra
Skinner, Anthony David
Škvoreck , Josef
Sluglett, Peter
Smarandache, Florentin
Smith, Sarah (W. R.)
Smith, William Jay
Sobel, Dava
Sorkin, Adam J.
Soueif, Ahdaf
Soyinka, Wole
Spivak, Gayatri Chakravorty
Stableford, Brian M(ichael)
Stallworthy, Jon (Howie)
Stanley, Patricia H.
Steele, Cynthia
Steger, Manfred B.
Steinberg, Jonathan
Steinhardt, Nancy Shatzman

Translations-*cont.*

Stephens, William Peter
Stewart, Ian (Nicholas)
Stewart, Susan
Stinchecum, Amanda Mayer
Stivale, Charles J.
Stockwin, J. A. A.
Stoltzfus, Ben
Stoppard, Tom
Strelkoff, Tatiana
Stryk, Lucien
Suleiman, Susan Rubin
Sun, Yifeng
Sutton, Dana F.
Suzuki, Ko ji
Svoboda, Terese
Swierenga, Robert P.
Swindells, Robert (Edward)
Szekely, Istvan P(al)
Szirtes, George
Tagliavini, Gabriela
Tanaka, Yukiko
Tanner, Norman P.
Taplin, Oliver
Tarn, Nathaniel
Tarnawsky, Maxim
Tavernor, Robert (William)
Taviani, Paolo
Taylor, Andrew (McDonald)
Taylor, Frederick
Taylor, Henry
Taylor, Patrick
Temple, Robert (Kyle Grenville)
Theroux, Peter
Thiel, Diane
Thomas, D(onald) M(ichael)
Thomson, Derick S(mith)
Thomson, Rodney M(alcolm)
Thondup, Tulku
Thormählen, Marianne
Thornton, Naoko Fuwa
Tipton, David
Tomaselli, Sylvana

Translations-*cont.*

Tong, Zhong Gui
Törnqvist, Egil
Trevelyan, Raleigh
Triggs, Tony D.
Tsaloumas, Dimitris
Tucker, Ernest S.
Turner, Martin
U'Ren, Andrea
Ueda, Makoto
Ure, Jean
Vahanian, Gabriel
Vallbona, Rima de
Vallee, Lillian (Bozenna)
van Itallie, Jean Claude
Vanderkam, James C(laire)
Vardamis, Frances (Diem)
Vargas, Margarita
Vasta, Edward
Venarde, Bruce L.
Venclova, Tomas
Versluis, Arthur
Visson, Lynn
Vitiello, Justin
Waelti-Walters, Jennifer (Rose)
Wainwright, Jeffrey
Waisman, Sergio Gabriel
Wallace, B. Alan
Walsh, P(atrick) G(erard)
Wang, Shuo
Ward, Philip
Ware, Kallistos
Warner, Val
Warren, Richard (Andrew)
Warsh, Lewis
Watson, Ellen Dore
Waugh, Teresa (Lorraine)
Weber, Samuel M.
Webster, Brenda
Wedde, Ian
Weissbort, Daniel
Werman, Golda
Wertenbaker, Timberlake

Translations-*cont.*

West, M(artin) L(itchfield)
Weyr, Thomas
White, Carolinne
White, Kenneth
White, Linda (Louise)
Whitfield, Roderick
Whitten, Leslie Hunter
Whitton, Kenneth S(tuart)
Wiesel, Elie
Wilbur, Richard (Purdy)
Williams, C(harles) K(enneth)
Wills, Garry
Wilmer, Clive
Wilson, Barbara (Ellen)
Wilson, Darryl B(abe)
Wilson, David Henry
Wilson, William Scott
Wing, Betsy
Winnifrith, T(homas) J(ohn)
Wolf, Kirsten
Wolfers, Michael
Wood, Frances
Woods, Jeannie Marlin
Woods, Macdara
Wootton, David
Wortsman, Peter
Wright, Charles (Penzel)
Wright, Franz
Wu, Ningkun
Wu, Qingyun
Wu, Yenna
Wynne, Frank
Xiaokang, Su
Yazdanfar, Farzin
Young, David (Pollock)
Young, Ian
Yu, Anthony C.
Zaknic, Ivan
Zenith, Richard
Zinnes, Harriet
Ziolkowski, Jan M.
Zucchi, John E.
Zumoff, Barnett

COUNTRY OF CITIZENSHIP INDEX

Afghanistan

Ayub, Awista
Joya, Malalai

Afghanistan-Canada

Perkel, Colin N.

Afghanistan-USA

Hafvenstein, Joel

Afghanistan-USA-Greece

Moulakis, Athanasios

American Samoa

Figiel, Sia

Argentina

Aira, César
Boczkowski, Pablo J.
Bortnik, Aida (Beatriz)
Giardinelli, Mempo
Martinez, Guillermo
Meyer, Gabriel Ray Henry
O'Donnell, Guillermo A.
Puiggrós, Adriana (Victoria)
Sagastizabal, Patricia
Sangalli, Arturo
Varsavsky, Paula

Argentina-Chile

Hagelin, Aiban

Argentina-China

Hopgood, Mei-Ling

Argentina-USA

Goñi, Uki
Kozameh, Alicia

Armenia-Canada

Neville, Helen F(rances Fowler)

Armenia-Israel

Semyonov, Moshe

Armenia-Netherlands

van der Zee, Karen

Armenia-South Africa-Canada

Winckler, Martin

Australia

Abela, Deborah Anne
Adair, Daryl John
Adamson, Robin
Ainsworth, Patricia
Allen, Jane
Altman, Dennis
Anderson, Kay
Anderson, Trevor A(ndrew)
Annear, Robyn
Arena, Felice
Ariff, Mohamed
Armstrong, David Malet
Armstrong, Judith (Mary)
Arthur, Keri
Aspinall, Edward
Ayres, Philip
Bail, Murray
Bailey, Greg
Bailey, John
Baillie, Allan
Balint, Ruth
Barnett, Paul
Bartlett, Anne

Barton, Greg
Bellamy, Alex J.
Bernard, Patricia
Biddulph, Steve
Biggs, John Burville
Birrell, James Peter
Blacklock, Dianne
Blainey, Geoffrey Norman
Blair, E(lizabeth) Anne
Bobis, Merlinda Carullo
Bosworth, R(ichard) J(ames) B(oon)
Brennan, Frank
Brennan, Wendy
Brewer, Carolyn
Brissenden, Alan (Theo)
Brooks, David (Gordon)
Broome, Errol
Brown, Deborah J.
Brugman, Alyssa (F.)
Bulbeck, Chilla
Burgess, Colin
Burke, Carolyn
Burns, Ailsa (Milligan)
Byrt, Edwin Andrew
Caddy, Caroline
Caldwell, Grant
Canavan, Trudi
Carnley, Peter Frederick
Carr, Roger Vaughan
Castro, Brian (Albert)
Charlwood, D(onald) E(rnest Cameron)
Cheng, Christopher
Chiang, Lynette
Ciddor, Anna
Clarke, Judith
Clarke, Patricia
Clendinnen, Inga
Cole, Edmund Keith
Coleman, David G.
Coleman, Deirdre
Coleman, Verna (Scott)
Coleman, William Oliver
Collison, Kerry B(oyd)
Connell, John
Constable, Kate
Cooper, Adam G.
Cooper, Michelle
Cootes, Jim E.
Cowen, Zelman

Credaro, Amanda
Crew, Gary
Cribb, Robert (Bridson)
Crozier, Michael (Paul)
Curthoys, Ann
Darby, Andrew
Darville, Helen (Fiona)
Davidson, Robyn
Davies, Peter J.
Davison, Liam
Dawe, (Donald) Bruce
Day, Marele
de Crespigny, (Richard) Rafe (Champion)
Dedman, Stephen
Deen, Hanifa
Denton, Terry
Dessaix, Robert
Dobrez, Patricia
Docherty, James C(airns)
Docker, John
Dowling, Terry
Doyle, Jeff
Drew, Philip
Drewe, Robert
Dubosarsky, Ursula
Dunkley, Graham (Royce)
Edwards, P. D
Egan, Greg
Eley, Beverley
Ellyard, David
Elson, R. E.
English, Lyn D.
Epanomitis, Fotini
Evans, Gareth John
Falconer, Delia
Fallon, Jennifer
Farthing-Knight, Catherine
Fatchen, Max
Fenner, Frank John
Fitzpatrick, Sheila Mary
Flannery, Tim(othy Fridtjof)
Fleming, Justin
Flynn, Pat
Forsyth, Kate
Foster, David Manning
Fox, Mem
Franklin, Richard Langdon
Freadman, Richard
Garner, Helen
Gaukroger, Stephen

Gibbs, Anthony Matthews
Gibson, Chris
Gill, Graeme J(oseph)
Gleeson, Libby
Golds, Cassandra
Goldsmith, Andrea
Goldsworthy, Peter
Goodwin, Ken(neth Leslie)
Gorman, Lyn
Gow, Michael
Graham, Bob
Grant, Bruce (Alexander)
Gray, Ian
Gray, Robert (Curtis)
Green, Cliff(ord)
Greenfield, Jeanette
Griffiths, Tom
Guile, Melanie
Gurr, Michael
Hagan, Stephen
Halford, Graeme S(ydney)
Hall, Lincoln
Halligan, Marion (Mildred Crothall)
Hancock, Ian (Robert)
Harcourt, Geoffrey Colin
Hardy, John Philips
Harland, Richard
Harris, Christine
Harrower, Elizabeth
Hartnett, Sonya
Harwood, John
Hasluck, Nicholas
Hathorn, Libby
Havel, Geoff
Hawke, Rosanne Joy
Helfgott, Gillian
Hellyer, Jill
Henderson, F(rancis) M(artin)
Herrick, Steven
Hetherington, Stephen Cade
Higgins, Ian (Kevin)
Higgins, Peter M.
Hill, Anthony (Robert)
Hill, Barry
Hill, Robert S.
Holmes, Katie
Holst-Warhaft, Gail
Holt, Stephen
Hook, Brendan
Hook, Geoffrey R(aynor)
Hooper, Chloe
Hooper, Meredith Jean
Hope, Janet
Horadam, Alwyn Francis
Horner, David
Horniman, Joanne
Huck, (Edwin) Arthur
Huggins, Jackie
Hughes, Phillip William
Hutton, Drew
Ireland, David
Irwin, Peter George
James, Clive (Vivian Leopold)
Jeans, Peter D(ouglas)
Jennaway, Megan
Jinks, Catherine
Johnson, Donald Leslie
Johnston, Anna
Jolly, Roslyn
Jones, Evan (Lloyd)

Jones, Frank Lancaster
Keane, John
Keneally, Thomas (Michael)
Kerr, Alexander McBride
Khlentzos, Drew M.
Khoo, Gaik Cheng
Kidd, Paul
Kiernan, Ben
Kiernan, Brian
King, Ross James
Kingston, Beverley
Kirsner, Kim
Klein, Robin (McMaugh)
Klemm, Barry
Kremmer, Christopher
Laguna, Sofie
Laird, Ross
Lake, Marilyn
Lanagan, Margo
Lance, James Waldo
Lane, Terry
Langmead, Donald
Lanyon, Anna
Laurent, John (Angus)
Lee, Dorothy A.
Legge, John David
Lehmann, Geoffrey (John)
Leonard, Richard James
Lingard, Jeanette
Little, Douglas
Llewellyn, Kate
London, Joan
Lovric, Michelle
Lucashenko, Melissa
Lucire, Yolande
Luckett, Dave
Lurie, Morris
Lyons, William (Edward)
Lyssiotis, Tes
Macdonald, Sarah
Macintyre, Stuart (Forbes)
Mackerras, Colin Patrick
Macklin, Robert
Maddison, Sarah
Malcolm, Elizabeth
Malouf, David
Mansfield, Bruce Edgar
Mansfield, Nick
Marr, David
Marriott, Kim
Marsden, John
Mason, Prue
Mattingley, Christobel (Rosemary)
McCalman, Iain
McCarthy, John F.
McConnochie, Mardi
McCullough, Colleen
McFarlane, Peter (William)
McGahan, Andrew
Mckenzie, Judith (Sheila)
McKinlay, Brian John
McKnight, David
McLagan, Jennifer
McLaren, Anne E.
McLaren, John
McLaren, Philip
McMaster, Rhyll
McMullen, Sean (Christopher)
Mead, Philip (Stirling)
Mears, Gillian

Metcalf, Donald
Metzenthen, David
Miller, Deborah
Miller, Glenn (W.)
Miller, J(ohn) D(onald) Bruce
Millett, John
Moloney, James
Moorhead, John (Anthony)
Morton, Kate
Morton, Peter
Murnane, Gerald
Murphy, Peter
Murphy, Shane M.
Murray, Les(lie) (Allan)
Murray, William J(ames)
Nash, Patrick Gerard
Negnevitsky, Michael
Nerlich, Graham C.
Newell, William H.
Newton, Nerida
Newton, Robert
Nix, Garth
Norman, Lilith
Nyiri, Pal
O'Connor, Colin
O'Shea, Mick
Ollier, Cliff(ord) David
Ormerod, Neil
Osborne, Milton (Edgeworth)
Page, Geoff(rey Donald)
Painter, John
Palmer, Peter John
Pascoe, Bruce
Pearce, Margaret
Pease, Allan
Peetz, David
Perry, Roland
Pfanner, (Anne) Louise
Pollard, Irina
Powell, Craig
Prescott, J(ohn) R(obert) V(ictor)
Prior, Natalie Jane
Prior, Robin
Purcell, Leah
Pybus, Cassandra
Quinn, Peter (John)
Rayson, Hannie
Read, Peter
Reeder, Stephanie Owen
Rees, Frank D.
Renton, N(ick) E.
Richards, Judith M.
Ricks, James
Ridley, Ronald T(homas)
Roach, Archie
Robb, Peter
Roberts, Gregory David
Roberts, Tansy Rayner
Robotham, Michael
Rodda, Emily
Rodgers, Peter
Rodriguez, Judith (Green)
Rollins, David A.
Romeril, John
Rose, Elisabeth
Rutland, Suzanne D.
Ryan, Gig (Elizabeth)
Ryan, Peter Allen
Sainsbury, Maurice Joseph
Sardi, Jan
Savage, Georgia

Sayer, Mandy Jane
Scalmer, Sean
Scarfe, Allan John
Scarfe, Wendy (Elizabeth)
Scott, Kim
Shapcott, Thomas W(illiam)
Shepherd, Joel
Shine, Richard
Smart, John Jamieson Carswell
Smith, Bernard (William)
Smith, Hugh
Smith, Vivian (Brian)
Sparrow, Jeff
Sparrow, Rebecca
Spens, Christiana
Stanton, Richard C.
Steele, Mary
Steger, Manfred B.
Stening, Bruce W.
Stephens, F(rank) Douglas
Stevens, Garry
Stewart, Kathleen
Strauss, Jennifer (Wallace)
Stretton, Hugh
Stuckey, Peter J(ames)
Tayleur, Karen
Taylor, Andrew (McDonald)
Taylor, Jean Gelman
Taylor, Jennifer (Evelyn)
Taylor, Ranald J.
Thiering, Barbara (Elizabeth)
Thom, Paul
Thomas, Edmund Barrington
Thomas, Hedley
Thomson, Alistair
Thomson, James Miln
Thomson, Rodney M(alcolm)
Thornton, Margaret Rose
Tisdell, Clement Allan
Tofts, Darren (John)
Toltz, Steve
Tranter, John (Ernest)
Trevor, Penelope
Trigger, David S.
Tulloch, Richard (George)
Tyrrell, Ian R(obert)
Valder, Peter
Valentine, James
van Niel, Kimberly
Vickers, Adrian
Vincent, Erin
Voermans, Paul
Wajcman, Judy
Walker, Geoffrey de Q(uincey)
Walker, Kate
Wallace-Crabbe, Christopher (Keith)
Walshe, R(obert) D(aniel)
Warneke, Sara
Watson, Don
Watson, Ken D.
Wearne, Alan
Webb, Janeen (S.)
Weber, Thomas
Wettenhall, Roger L.
Wheatley, Nadia
Whitlam, (Edward) Gough
Wilkinson, Marian
Williams, Donna
Wolfer, Dianne
Woodland, Alan D(onald)

Woolfe, Sue
Wright, Alexis
Young, E. L.
Zines, Leslie
Zurbo, Matt

Australia-Austria-Israel

Rosenkranz, Ze'ev

Australia-Bahamas

Hughes, Colin Anfield

Australia-Bangladesh

Khan, Adib

Australia-Canada

Kompridis, Nikolas
Lenskyj, Helen Jefferson
Mayse, Susan
Messel, Harry
Orr, Wendy

Australia-China

Farquhar, Mary Ann
Jiang, Fuming
Law, Clara
Lee, Lily Xiao Hong

Australia-Cuba

Garcia, Luis M.

Australia-England

Adam, Paul
Baker, Jeannie
Barnes, Rory
Base, Graeme (Rowland)
Bell, Hilary
Birmingham, John
Browne, Cameron Bolitho
Bruce, Robert S.
Chataway, Carol
Clark, Gordon L.
Crouch, Christopher
Dryzek, John S.
Dumbleton, Mike
Dutton, Michael R.
Fienberg, Anna
Gascoigne, John
Girling, John (Lawrence Scott)
Gough, Sue
Greenwood, Norman Neill
Hainsworth, D(avid) R(oger)
Hall, Rodney
Hayward, Philip
Hazlehurst, Cameron
Higgins, Simon (Richard)

Hindess, Barry
Holmes, Leslie (Templeman)
Jacobs, Anna
Jalland, Pat(ricia)
Jennings, Paul
Johnson, Rob
Kelleher, Victor Michael Kitchener
Lyons, Martyn
Mabbett, Ian William
Malpas, J(effery) E(dward)
Marks, Kathy (L.)
Marks, Stan(ley)
Marsh, Nigel
McIntosh, Fiona
McKechnie, Paul (Richard)
Minchin, Timothy J.
Nelson, T. G. A.
Northeast, Brenda V(ictoria)
Ordinans, Nicholas J.
Page, Tim
Pear, David (Adrian)
Probyn, Clive T.
Reynolds, Barrie (Gordon Robert)
Rhodes, Colin
Riddell, Peter G.
Ride, W. D. L.
Roads, Michael J.
Robson, Derek Ian
Rubinstein, Gillian (Margaret Hanson)
Scarr, Deryck (Antony)
Sheridan, Thomas
Trengove, Alan Thomas
Ussher, Jane M.
Wilkinson, Carole
Williams, Martin Anthony Joseph
Williams, Robyn
Wilson, Barbara Ker
Wodhams, Jack
Woods, Janet
Young, John

Australia-England-Ireland

Dart-Thornton, Cecilia

Australia-Fiji

Lal, Brij V.
Mishra, Sudesh (Raj)

Australia-France-Indonesia

Masson, Sophie

Australia-Germany

Corden, Warner Max
Skrzynecki, Peter
Wach, Kenneth

Australia-Greece

Tsaloumas, Dimitris

Australia-India

Britain, Ian (Michael)
Dasgupta, Amit
Hasan, Ruqaiya
Lake, David (John)
Majumdar, Boria
Saini, B(alwant) S(ingh)

Australia-Indonesia

Heryanto, Ariel

Australia-Ireland

Earls, Nick
O'Collins, Gerald Glynn

Australia-Israel

Elisha, Ron

Australia-Japan

Sugimoto, Yoshio

Australia-Kenya

Kane, Penny

Australia-Korea (South)

Kwon, O. Yul

Australia-Netherlands

Groenewegen, Peter
Mol, Johannis (Hans) J(acob)

Australia-New Zealand

Breward, Ian
Burnett, Alan
Campion, Jane
Cowie, Hamilton Russell
D'Ath, Justin
Langford, Gary R(aymond)
Lloyd, P(eter) J(ohn)
Ludbrook, John
McCutcheon, Sandy
Morton, Bruce Rutherfurd
Morwood, Mike
Powell, Alan
Sussex, Lucy (Jane)
Ward, Ralph Gerard

Australia-Norway

Ommundsen, Wenche

Australia-Pakistan

Abidi, Azhar

Australia-Poland

Armstrong, Diane (Julie)
Syktus, Jozef
Walwicz, Ania

Australia-Romania

Kefala, Antigone

Australia-Russia

Tikhomirov, Vladimir I.

Australia-Scotland

Campbell, Eddie
Colman, E. Adrian M.
Johnstone, Bob
Maitland, Barry
Miller, Seumas
Nilsson, Eleanor

Australia-South Africa

Alexander, Peter F.
Caine, Barbara
Coetzee, J(ohn) M(ichael)
Courtenay, Bryce
Marsh, Derick Rupert Clement

Australia-USA

Buchanan, Thomas C.
Cohen, Bernard
Dann, Jack
Dix, Shane
Drew, Horace R.
Johnston, William Murray
Kassler, Jamie C(roy)
MacDougall, David
Marr, David G(eorge)
McMahon, Maureen M.
Pegg, Mark Gregory
Polonsky, Michael Jay
Saknussemm, Kris
Sidney, Neilma
Stein, Leslie
Tolbert, Steve
Veitch, Kate
Warren, James Francis

Australia-USA-Canada

Bryant, Edward (Arnot)

Australia-Vietnam

Le, Nam

Australia-Wales

Brooks, Edwin
Caswell, Brian
Jones, David Martin
Knudsen, Margrethe June
Richards, Eric

Austria

Brandstetter, Alois
Falzeder, Ernst
Faschinger, Lilian
Janisch, Heinz
Koch, Ebba
Lachner, Dorothea
Lauber, Volkmar
Luciak, Ilja Alexander
Roth, Gerhard (Jurgen)
Sargent, Inge
Sichrovsky, Peter
Zacharasiewicz, Waldemar

Austria-England

Busfield, Andrea
Clarke, Alison (Jane)
Mortimer, Edward

Austria-France

Stolz, Joëlle

Austria-Germany

Fassmann, Heinz
Wagner, Nike

Austria-Hungary

David, Thomas
Lendvai, Paul

Austria-Italy

Giampieri-Deutsch, Patrizia

Austria-USA

Helnwein, Mercedes
Leake, John

Bahamas

Saunders, Gail

Barbados

Worrell, (Rupert) DeLisle

Barbados-England

Marshall, Roy

Belgium

Baert, Barbara
Clausen, Andy
Flem, Lydia
Laurens, Jeannine
Maes-Jelinek, Hena
Milis, Ludo(vicus) J. R.
Moeyaert, Bart
Overtveldt, Johan Van
Ruyslinck, Ward
Sante, Luc
Savitzkaya, Eugne
Schrijvers, Peter
Schuiten, François Louis Marie
Simoen, Jan
Sterken, Christiaan (L.)
van Geert, Paul
van Parijs, Philippe
Verboven, Agnes
Zabus, Chantal J.

Belgium-England

Grant, Helen

Belgium-France

Cumberlege, Marcus (Crossley)
Hänsel, Marion

Belgium-Italy

Schioppa, Fiorella Kostoris Padoa

Brazil

Boff, Leonardo (Genezio Darci)
Bonder, Nilton
Braga, Newton C.
Britto, Paulo Henriques
Buarque, Chico
Canton, Katia
Cony, Carlos Heitor
Da Fonseca, Eduardo Giannetti
Egler, Claudio A. G.
Felinto (Barbosa De Lima),
   Marilene
Hatoum, Milton
Luft, Lya Fett
Pinon, Nelida
Renaux, Sigrid
Sader, Emir
Trevisan, João Silvério

Brazil-Cuba

Moore, Carlos

Brazil-England

Le Breton, Binka

Brazil-Italy

Segre, Roberto

Brazil-USA

Langdon, E(sther) Jean Matteson

Canada

Abbott, Elizabeth
Adams, Marie
Adamson, Gil
Adderson, Caroline
Ahmed, Syed Naeem
Albahari, David
Alford, Edna
Allan, Von
Allen, Thomas M.
Allin, Lou
Ambert, Anne Marie
Ambler, Scott W.
Anderson, Christy
Anderson, James G.
Anderson, Katharine
Anderson, Patricia J.
Andrew, Edward
Anglin, Douglas G(eorge)
Archer, Colleen Rutherford
Archer, Keith (Allan)
Arends, Carolyn
Armstrong, Jeannette C.
Armstrong, Kelley L.
Armstrong, Kevin D.
Armstrong, Luanne (A.)
Ashenburg, Katherine
Atkey, Mel
Atwood, Margaret
Austen, Catherine
Azoulay, Dan
Babbitt, Susan E.
Bachelder, Thomas
Bacher, John
Backhouse, Constance B.
Bacon, Lauren
Badcock, Gary D.
Bailey, Linda
Baird, Alison
Baker, Deirdre
Ball, Nelson
Bannatyne-Cugnet, (Elizabeth)
   Jo(-Anne)
Barbeau, Edward J(oseph)
Barbour, Douglas
Barlow, Maude
Bassler, Gerhard P.
Bauman, Richard W.
Bazzana, Kevin
Beam, Matt
Beard, William

Beattie, Judith Hudson
Beavis, Mary Ann
Bedard, Michael
Bee, Samantha
Beeby, Dean
Beecher, Donald A(llen)
Beland, Pierre
Bell, William
Bemrose, John
Benidickson, Jamie
Bennett, Holly
Berger, Thomas R(odney)
Berry, J. W.
Bertrand, Jacques
Besner, Neil K.
Bidini, Dave
Bieman, Elizabeth
Bigelow, Brian J(ohn)
Binnema, Theodore
Bird, Richard
Birdsell, Sandra
Biro, Andrew William
Bissett, Bill
Black, Arthur (Raymond)
Black, Conrad
Blades, Ann
Blais, André
Blake, Raymond B.
Blanchard, James G.
Blanchet, Pascal
Blank, G(regory) Kim
Blunt, Giles
Boddy, Janice
Boers, Arthur Paul
Bohm, Arnd
Bök, Christian
Borel, Kathryn
Bortolotti, Dan
Bothwell, Robert (Selkirk)
Boudreau, R(obert) L(ouis)
Bourgeault, Cynthia
Bourgeois, Paulette
Boutilier, Robert
Bowdring, Paul (Edward)
Bowen, Gail
Bowering, George
Bowering, Marilyn (Ruthe)
Boyden, Joseph
Bradford, Karleen
Bradley, Alan
Brandt, Di
Brannigan, Augustine
Brault, Jacques
Braun, Marta (A.)
Brecher, Michael
Brenna, Beverley
Breton, Albert
Brett, Brian
Brewster, Elizabeth (Winifred)
Brigg, Peter
Brignall, Richard
Brochu, André
Brode, Patrick
Brodie, Leanna
Brook, Timothy (James)
Brooks, Martha
Brooks, Mary R.
Brophy, Sarah
Broughton, R(obert) Peter
Brousseau, Francine
Brown, Brian A.

Hart, Jonathan (Locke)
Harvey, Kenneth J.
Harvor, Elisabeth
Hasler, Julie
Haworth-Attard, Barbara
Hayes, Derek
Hellyer, Paul T.
Helmer, Marilyn
Hemstock, Gillian
Heuer, Karsten
Hewitt, W(arren) E(dward)
Higgins, Michael W.
Highway, Tomson
Hilles, Robert
Hillis, Bryan V.
Hodgins, Jack
Hodgson, Barbara L.
Holeman, Linda
Hollingshead, Greg
Holmes, Amanda
Holtz, Nairne
Howsam, Leslie
Hoy, Claire
Hughes, Susan
Hummel, Monte
Hunter, Douglas
Hur, Nam-lin
Hurka, Thomas
Hurtig, Mel
Huser, Glen
Hutcheon, Linda
Hutcheon, Michael
Hutchins, Hazel J.
Hyde, Anthony
Hyde, Christopher
Hynes, Joel
Iacovetta, Franca
Ibbitson, John Perrie
Ilsley, George K.
Inglis, Janet
Ingram, Heather E(lizabeth)
Jaccard, Mark
Jackson, Marni
Jackson, Robert J.
Jaeck, Lois Marie
Jaffary, Nora E.
Janes, J(oseph) Robert
Janoda, Jeff
Jenkins, Catherine
Jirgens, Karl (E.)
Jobs, Daniel Steve
Johns, Linda
Johnston, Julie
Johnston, Richard
Jokinen, Tom
Jones, (R.) Dennis
Jones, D(ouglas) G(ordon)
Jordan, Robert B.
Juby, Susan
Kanchier, Carole
Kaslik, Ibolya Emma
Katz, Welwyn Wilton
Kawatski, Deanna
Kay, Guy Gavriel
Kearns, Lionel (John)
Keil, Roger
Kelly, Deirdre
Kemp, Penn
Kennedy, Holly
Kennedy, Liv
Kennedy, Michael P. J.

Kent, Peter C.
Kerner, Fred
Kerr, Margaret (H.)
Kertes, Joseph
Khan, Rukhsana
Kingwell, Mark
Kinnear, Mary
Kinsella, W(illiam) P(atrick)
Kirby, John R.
Kirshner, Mia
Kleiman, Ed
Knighton, Ryan
Kogawa, Joy Nozomi
Kooistra, Lorraine Janzen
Kopinak, Kathryn
Koppel, Tom
Korman, Bernice
Kositsky, Lynne
Kostelniuk, James
Kramer, Reinhold
Kratz, Martin P. J.
Kress, Adrienne
Kroker, Arthur (W.)
Krueger, Lesley
Kuban, Ron
Kuchar, Gary
Kuitenbrouwer, Kathryn (Ann Frances)
Kulling, Monica
Kurasawa, Fuyuki
Kusugak, Michael (Arvaarluk)
Kynoch, Gary
Labrie, Ross
LaForest, Gerard V. (J.)
Laforest, Guy
Lake, Jo Anne
Lam, Vincent
Lambur, Joan
Lancashire, Anne Begor
Lang, Anthony E.
Langston, Laura
Lanthier, Jennifer
Lapierre, Laurier L.
Latourelle, René
Lavigne, Louis-Dominique
Lawson, JonArno Burhans
Laxdal, Vivienne
Leckie, Keith (Ross)
Leddy, Mary Jo
Lee, Dennis (Beynon)
Lee, Sky
Lefebvre, Mario
Leggatt, Alexander
Leggo, Carl Derek
Lehmann, Wolfgang
Leier, Mark
Lemay, Shawna
Lemire, Beverly
Lemire, Jeff
Lennox, John
Lent, John
Lepage, Robert
Lesjak, Carolyn
Levesque, John
Levine, Allan
Levy, David H.
Levy, Evonne
Lewis, Norah L.
Lieberman, Leanne
Lightfoot, Gordon
Lima, Patrick

Lindquist, N(ancy) J(ane)
Lippert, Randy K.
Little, J. I.
Lo, Shiu-Hing
Loo, Tina
Loring, Kevin
Love, (Kathleen) Ann
Low, Brian J.
Luciuk, Lubomyr Y(aroslav)
Lundin, Steve
Luongo-Orlando, Katherine
Lutz, John Sutton
Lux, Maureen K.
Luxton, Donald
Lwin, Nanda Layos
Lynch, Wayne
Lyon, Annabel
Mac, Carrie
MacDonald, Anne Louise
MacDonald, Stuart
Mace, Gordon
MacIntosh, Robert
MacIntyre, Linden
Mackay, Claire (Bacchus)
MacKinnon, J. B.
MacKinnon, Mark
MacLeod, Elizabeth
Macleod, Joan
MacMillan, Ken
MacPherson, Andrea
Maddigan, Beth
Madison, Gary (Brent)
Maes, Yvonne (M)
Magrath, Allan J.
Mai, Francois Martin
Major, Andre
Malak, Amin
Mallick, Ross
Maranda, Pierre
Marble, Allan Everett
Marchessault, Jovette
Marcotte, Gilles
Mardon, Austin Albert
Margolian, Howard T.
Marineau, Michele
Markoosie
Martel, Gordon
Martin, Jack
Martin, Robert M.
Maskalyk, James
Mason, Adrienne
Matas, Carol
Matas, David
Mawhiney, Anne Marie
Mayne, Seymour
McAdam, Ian
McCall, Storrs
McConica, James Kelsey
McCormack, Derek
McCrone, Kathleen E.
McDonell, Chris
McEwen, Indra Kagis
McFadden, David W.
McFetridge, John
McGoogan, Ken
McGowan, Mark George
McGrath, Carmelita
McKay, Don
McKay, Ian
McKay, Sharon E.
McKenna, Patrick J.

McKenzie, Andrea Katherine
McLean, Stuart
McLeod, Carolyn
McLeod, Joseph (Bertram)
McLeod, Wallace
McMaster, Gerald
McMaster, Lindsey
McMaster, Susan
McMillan, Alan D.
McNaughton, Janet
McNicoll, Sylvia (Marilyn)
McQuay, Peri Phillips
McQueen, Rod
McRae, Kenneth Douglas
McTavish, Lianne
Mears, Emira
Melançon, Robert
Mellin, Robert
Melzack, Ronald
Mendyk, Stan A. E.
Meyerson, Mark D.
Michaels, Anne
Michelson, Karin
Mighton, John
Miles, Victoria
Miller, Jeffrey
Millman, Brock
Mogelon, Ronna
Moher, Frank
Moloney, Susie
Monahan, Patrick J.
Monet, Jean
Monière, Denis
Montpetit, Charles
Moore, Christopher G.
Moore, Maureen (Audrey)
Morency, Pierre
Morgan, Bernice
Morinis, Alan
Morritt, Hope
Morton, Patricia
Mowat, Claire (Angel Wheeler)
Mowat, Farley (McGill)
Muller, (Lester) Robin
Mullin, Caryl Cude
Mulroney, Brian
Munro, Alice
Murphy, Rae Allan
Murray, Elaine
Nash, (Cyril) Knowlton
Nathanson, Paul
Naves, Elaine Kalman
Neff, Lyle
Nelson, Brent
Nestel, Sheryl
Neufeld, James (E.)
Neufeld, Thomas R.
New, William Herbert
Newell, Dianne
Newell, Waller R.
Newman, Jerry
Nicholson, Deborah L.
Nickel, Barbara
Niskala, Brenda
Nodelman, Perry
O'Dea, Brian
O'Grady, Rohan
O'Toole, Lawrence
Olson, David Richard
Oppel, Kenneth
Oughton, John P.

Woodland, Malcolm
Woodman, David C(harles)
Woodman, Marion (Boa)
Woods, Lawrence T(imothy)
Woodward, Caroline (Hendrika)
Worobec, Christine D.
Wright, Donald Andrew
Wynveen, Tim
Yekelchyk, Serhy
York, Alissa
Young, Dianne
Young, Robert A.
Young, T. Kue
Zellar, Gary
Zhao, Yuezhi
Zimmerman, Cynthia (Diane)
Zucchi, John E.
Zuehlke, Mark

Canada-Argentina

Smith-Ayala, Emilie

Canada-Australia

Gillett, Margaret
Timmermans, Tricia
Williams, Maurice

Canada-Austria

Bosco, Monique
Helleiner, Gerald K(arl)
Zimmermann, H(einz) Werner

Canada-Barbados

Foster, Cecil (A.)

Canada-Belgium

de Kerckhove, Derrick
Havet, Jose (L.)
Lakeland, Paul

Canada-British West Indies

Keens-Douglas, Richardo

Canada-China

Bates, Judy Fong
Carney, Pat
Chen, Ying
Lai, David Chuenyan
Wang, Sen
Ye, Ting-Xing
Zhang, Song Nan

Canada-Croatia

Novakovich, Josip

Toten, Teresa

Canada-Czech Republic

Barnard, Frederick Mechner
Moravec, Ivo
Škvorecký, Josef

Canada-Egypt

Raffi

Canada-England

Aberbach, David
Andrew, Sheila M.
Barber, Katherine
Barclay, Robert
Barker, Philip
Barnes, Christopher J(ohn)
Barrow, Robin (St. Clair)
Bennett, Colin J.
Beresford-Kroeger, Diana
Birch, Anthony Harold
Brandon, Laura
Brewster, Hugh
Bucknall, Barbara Jane
Burnett, Ron
Calne, Donald B.
Carter, Martin R(oger)
Carter, Timothy
Cassels, Alan
Chan, Gillian
Chatto, James
Cross, Janine
Crush, Jonathan
Dalton, Sheila
Doyle, Charles (Desmond)
Dunster, Julian A.
Elton, Hugh
Files, Gemma
Forrester, Helen
Frost, Stanley Brice
Gates, Marilyn
Gibb, Camilla
Godkin, Celia (Marilyn)
Godwin, Robert
Grant, Vanessa
Griffith, Arthur Leonard
Gurr, David
Hackett, Robert A(nthony)
Helwig, Maggie
Hewson, John
Hollingsworth, Margaret
Hughes, Matthew
Humphreys, Helen (Caroline)
Hutchinson, Allan C.
Jackson, Anthony
Jackson, John N.
Jennings, Maureen
Kennell, Nigel M.
Kentfield, J(ohn) A(lan) C.
Killan, Gerald
Kitchen, Martin
Lander, Jack Robert
Laughton, Bruce (Kyle Blake)
Leaman, Celia A.

Leggett, Richard G.
Levere, Trevor H(arvey)
Lloyd, T(revor) O(wen)
Lyon, David
MacLean, Jill
Maclean, Rory
Maclear, Kyo
Mansbridge, Francis
Marty, Sid
McAll, Christopher
McBride, Stephen
McGowan, Christopher
Metcalf, John (Wesley)
Meynell, Hugo A(nthony)
Monaghan, David (Mark)
Mullan, David George
Nash, Roger
Packer, James Innell
Richmond, Anthony Henry
Robinson, H(enry) Basil
Ruddick, Nicholas
Sinclair, Alison
Sinnett, Mark C.
Spalding, Andrea
Sparshott, Francis (Edward)
Springer, Margaret
Steele, Peter
Stevens, Peter (Stanley)
Stevenson, Robin H.
Temple, Norman J.
Unwin, Peter
Waelti-Walters, Jennifer (Rose)
Walker, R. B. J.
Watmough, David
Wernick, Andrew (Lee)
Williams, Helen
Winter, Michael
Wood, Edward John
Woolf, D. R.
Wright, Eric
Wyman, Max
Wynne-Jones, Tim(othy)
Young, Ian

Canada-England-Ireland

Taylor, Patrick

Canada-England-Kenya

McMaster, Juliet (Sylvia)

Canada-England-Scotland

Howard-Hassmann, Rhoda E.

Canada-Ethiopia

Mezlekia, Nega

Canada-France

Gardon, Anne
Hough, Michael
Laponce, Jean

Martchenko, Michael
Nattiez, Jean Jacques
Potvin, Liza
Walton, Priscilla L.

Canada-France-Czech Republic

Marton, Jirina

Canada-Germany

Bandrauk, Andre D.
Beissel, Henry (Eric)
Coupland, Douglas
Eigenbrod, Renate
Galdikas, Birute
Gehrig, Klaus
Hoffmann, Peter (Conrad Werner)
Keyserlingk, Robert H.
MacDonald, Ann-Marie
Plaut, W. Gunther
Schlesinger, Benjamin
Sibum, Norm
von Finckenstein, Maria
Warsh, Sylvia E. Maultash
Wishinsky, Frieda

Canada-Greece

Kamakaris, Tina

Canada-Guyana

Dabydeen, Cyril
Fenton, M(elville) Brockett

Canada-Haiti

Laferrière, Dany

Canada-Hong Kong

Kwong, Julia C.
McAdam, Colin

Canada-Hungary

Gabor, Thomas
Gal, Laszlo
Porter, Anna
Wiseman, Eva

Canada-India

Badami, Anita Rau
Balakrishnan, N.
Cooke, Nathalie
Gillies, David
Kanungo, R(abindra) N.
Mukherjee, Rabin
Rahman, Matiur
Rao, J. N. K.

Sharma, Arvind

Canada-Ireland

Bonner, Kieran (Martin)
Brady, John (Mary)
Clark, George
Dalzell, Alexander
Egan, Kieran
Grant, Patrick
Houston, Cecil J(ames)
Leith, Linda Jane
McIlroy, Brian
McWhirter, George
O'Connor, Alan
O'Keeffe, Frank
Orbinski, James Jude

Canada-Israel

Mandelman, Avner
Ravel, Edeet
Safdie, Moshe

Canada-Israel-France

Brenner, Reuven

Canada-Italy

Colalillo-Kates, Isabella
Ricci, Nino
Santosuosso, Antonio

Canada-Jamaica

Mordecai, Pamela (Claire)
Senior, Olive (Marjorie)

Canada-Japan

Powles, William E(arnest)

Canada-Kenya

Odhiambo, David Nandi
Vassanji, M(oyez) G.

Canada-Malta

Virgo, Seán

Canada-Netherlands

Alma, Ann
Attema, Martha
Boersma, Hans
Dallaire, Romeo A.
Hooft, Hendrik (G. A.)
Horn, Michiel
Ruurs, Margriet

Terpstra, John
van Pelt, Robert-Jan
Vanderwal, Andrew H.

Canada-New Zealand

Garnett, Gale Zoë
Gedge, Pauline (Alice)
McGee, Terence Gary
Phillips, Roderick (Goler)
Smith, Peter J.

Canada-Norway

Dahlie, Hallvard

Canada-Pakistan

Khan, Mahmood H(asan)
Sadiq, Nazneen

Canada-Philippines

Gill, Lakshmi

Canada-Poland

Bromke, Adam
Eisen, Sydney
Stachniak, Eva

Canada-Russia

Rothstein, Samuel

Canada-Scotland

Davison, Carol Margaret
Duncan, Dave
Gray, Andrew
Hamilton, Sharon Jean
Jackson, J. R. de J.
Lopes, Dominic (M. McIver)
MacIntyre, Wendy
Moore, Ishbel (Lindsay)
Mulgrew, Ian
Stewart, Jack (F.)
Watt, Alan
Whyte, Jack

Canada-Slovakia

Petro, Peter

Canada-Slovenia

Mohar, Bojan

Canada-South Africa

Buchanan, Roberta
De Villiers, Marq
Karodia, Farida
Laband, John (Paul Clow)
Rachman, Stanley Jack
Yudelman, David

Canada-Spain

Marangoni, Alejandro G.
Roscoe, Patrick

Canada-Sri Lanka

Ondaatje, Michael
Selvadurai, Shyam

Canada-Switzerland

Holsti, Kalevi J.
Paterson, Janet M.

Canada-Taiwan

Little, (Flora) Jean

Canada-Thailand

Ladell, John L.

Canada-Tibet

Jinpa, Thupten

Canada-Trinidad and Tobago

Alexis, Andre
Allahar, Anton L.
Brand, Dionne
Maharaj, Rabindranath
Philip, M(arlene) NourbeSe

Canada-Ukraine

Grimberg, Tina
Katchanovski, Ivan

Canada-USA

Ableman, Michael
Accinelli, Robert
Adams, Roy J(oseph)
Albritton, Robert
Alderson, Sue Ann
Alford, Jeffrey
Altemeyer, Bob
Amabile, George
Andre, Michael
Averill, Gage
Barnes, Mike
Barry, P(atricia) S(teepee)

Barsky, Robert F(ranklin)
Bourgeois, Michael
Braun, Richard Emil
Bringhurst, Robert
Brown, Jennifer S. H.
Bumsted, J(ohn) M(ichael)
Burrs, Mick
Bushey, Jeanne
Cameron, Christian
Charles, John
Checkel, Jeffrey T(aylor)
Choyce, Lesley
Christianson, Paul
Cohen, Thomas V.
Collier, Gary
Cook, Rebecca J.
Coren, Stanley
Crabtree, Adam
D'Elia, Anthony F.
Darnell, Regna (Diebold)
Delacroix, Claire
Desfor, Gene
Ditchoff, Pamela J.
Downes, Bryan T(revor)
Duke, Michael S.
Eddie, David
Egnal, Marc
Field, Dorothy
Finkle, Derek
Fites, Philip
Florida, Richard (L.)
Foon, Dennis
Forsyth, Phyllis Young
Francis, Diane (Marie)
Friedman, Matthew
Gackenbach, Jayne
Gage, S. R.
Gazetas, Aristides
Gerson, Lloyd P.
Goldman, E(leanor) M(aureen)
Gorham, Deborah
Gough, Laurie
Gould, Terry
Groden, Michael (Lewis)
Gross, Neil
Growe, Sarah Jane
Gugler, Laurel Dee
Hammond, Herb(ert L.)
Harrigan, Patrick J.
Hassen, Philip Charles
Hayden, Brian (Douglas)
Heidbreder, Robert K.
Hekkanen, Ernest
Heller, Henry
Hellman, Stephen
Himka, John-Paul
Holz, Cynthia
Homel, David
Hundert, E(dward) J.
Hunt, J. Timothy
Ingham, John N.
Isbister, John
Jackman, Sydney Wayne
Jensen, Vickie (Dee)
Jones, Amelia
Jones, David
Jones, Richard Allan
Jordan, Rosa
Kaplan, Beth
Keith, Julie (Houghton)
Kelbaugh, Gretchen

Kelly, Deirdre M.
Kilpatrick, Nancy
Kimball, Meredith M.
King, Thomas
Kingsbury, Donald (Macdonald)
Konzak, Burt
Kovalski, Maryann
Kropp, Paul
Kull, Robert
Ladd-Taylor, Molly
Lai, Larissa
Lassez, Sarah
Lee, M. Owen
Levitin, Daniel J.
Liscomb, Kathlyn Maurean
Logan, George M(eredith)
Lohans, Alison
Lowe, Mick
Lunn, Janet (Louise Swoboda)
Mac Donald, Laura M.
Macdonald, Copthorne
MacDonald, Kyle
MacDonnell, Kathleen
Magocsi, Paul Robert
Man, Alfred Young
Marchand, Philip (Edward)
Marcuse, Gary
Massumi, Brian
Mays, John Bentley
McIntire, C(arl) T(homas)
McLuhan, (Thomas) Eric (Marshall)
McNamara, Eugene Joseph
Michelson, William
Moriarty, Michael
Morton, Alexandra (Hubbard)
Moure, Kenneth
Munsch, Robert
Musgrave, Susan
Nielson, James
Norris, Ken
O'Dor, Ronald Keith
Parker, Jeff
Penslar, Derek J(onathan)
Philmus, Robert M(ichael)
Powning, Beth
Raboy, Marc
Rajan, Tilottama
Redhill, Michael H.
Reibetanz, John
Reichertz, Ronald R.
Reilly, James
Ridington, Robin
Robinson, Spider
Rooke, Leon
Root, Deborah
Rubinsky, Holley
Sawyer, (Frederick) Don(ald)
Sawyer, Robert J(ames)
Schabas, Margaret
Shallit, Jeffrey (Outlaw)
Shannon, Doris
Shapiro, Bonnie L.
Shemie, Bonnie (Jean Brenner)
Simosko, Vladimir
Simpson, Jeffrey (Carl)
Singer, Benjamin D.
Slethaug, Gordon E.
Stebbins, Robert A.
Sumner, George R.
Svendsen, Linda

Tarnawsky, Maxim
Thomas, Audrey (Grace)
Toub, Micah
Turner, Nancy J.
Valdés, Mario J.
Villegas, Halli
Walsh, Ann
Watson, Irene
White, Emily
Wildwind, Sharon Grant
Wilson, Bronwen
Zarb, Janet M.
Zietlow, E(dward) R(obert)

Canada-USA-Ireland

Mahony, Patrick J(oseph)

Canada-USA-Israel

Burston, Daniel

Canada-Wales

Balogh, Mary
Roberts, Paul William

Canada-Wales-Wales

Burridge, Trevor David

Canada-Yugoslavia

Rajic, Negovan

Chile

Jaksić, Iván

Chile-USA

Eason, Alethea

China

Alai
Bi, Feiyu
Compestine, Ying Chang
Deng Xiao hua
Heng, Liu
Hu, Xu-wei
Huang, Nicole
Lu, Ning
Moye, Guan
Ng, Man lun
Ni Hua-Ching
Shen, Dajun
Sun, Yifeng
Tong, Zhong Gui
Wang, Anyi
Wang, Shuo
Yen, Ching-hwang

Zhu, Lin
Zhuoyun Yu

China-England

Rudd, Anthony
Whelpton, John Francis

China-Netherlands

Lindner, Koenraad J(an)

China-Taiwan

Hsueh, Tien tung
Shih, Chih-yu

China-USA

Harner, Stephen M.
Lin-Liu, Jen
Liu, Xiaoyuan
Shapiro, Sidney
Wang, XiaoHu

Colombia

Betancourt, Ingrid

Colombia-England

Carradice, Ian A.

Colombia-USA

Ayarbe, Heidi

Croatia

Velickovic, Nenad

Cuba

Acosta, Carlos
Barnet, Miguel
de Varona, Frank J.
Perez-Stable, Marifeli

Cuba-USA

Moya, Jose C.

Cyprus

Argyrou, Vassos
Markides, Constantinos C.
Modinos, Antonis

Cyprus-Lebanon-England

Munro, John M(urchison)

Cyprus-USA

Christodoulou, Demetrios
Jansen, Michael E(lin)
Majaj, Lisa Suhair

Czech Republic

Dery, Dominika
Fischerová, Daniela
Hochman, Jiri
Kunze, Michael
Paleček, Libuše
Strouhal, Eugen

Czech Republic-USA

Frank, Charles R(aphael)
Gedmin, Jeffrey (N.)

Denmark

August, Bille
Bredsdorff, Bodil
Buk-Swienty, Tom
Bumiller, Elisabeth
Flyvbjerg, Bent
Hansen, Poul Einer
Hermann, Iselin C.
Høeck, Klaus
Høeg, Peter
Hvidt, Niels Christian
Lomborg, Bjørn
Madsen, Svend Åge
Nicolaisen, (Agnes) Ida (Benedicte)
Norretranders, Tor
Olsen, Klaus Malling
Randsborg, Klavs
Reuter, Bjarne (B.)
Rifbjerg, Klaus (Thorvald)
Schwarz, Jan
Sørensen, Georg
Vigh, Henrik
von Trier, Lars

Denmark-England

Larsen, Torben B.
Leese, Peter
Lock, Charles (John Somerset)

Denmark-Sweden

Lundvall, Bengt-Åke
Roos, Johan

Denmark-Sweden-Germany

Kupferberg, Feiwel

Denmark-USA

Kennedy, Thomas E.
Thompson, Thomas L.

Egypt

Abbas, Jailan
Boutros-Ghali, Boutros
El-Shazly, Nadia El-Sayed
Sabato, Haim

Egypt-Ireland

O'Kane, Bernard

Egypt-USA

Friedlander, Shems
Hamid, Ahmad A.

England

Aaronovitch, David
Abbott, John Patrick
Abercrombie, Joe
Ackroyd, Peter
Adair, Christy
Adam, David
Adams, Ernest Charles
Adams, Jad
Adams, Richard (George)
Adams, Will
Adamson, Donald
Addinall, Peter
Addington, Arthur Charles
Addiscott, T. M.
Addonia, Sulaiman S. M. Y.
Ades, Dawn
Adkin, Mark
Adkins, Lesley
Adkins, Roy A(rthur)
Adlard, Mark
Aird, Catherine
Aitchison, Ian J(ohnston) R(hind)
Aitken, Rosemary
Al-Ali, Nadje Sadig
Albarn, Keith
Alberti, Fay Bound
Alborough, Jez
Alden, Chris
Aldhouse-Green, Miranda Jane
Aldiss, Brian (Wilson)
Alexander, M(ichael) J(oseph)
Alford, Bernard William Ernest
Alkire, Sabina
Allan, Adrian R.
Allan, David
Allason, Rupert (William Simon)
Allen, Fergus
Allen, John E(lliston)
Allen, Jonathan B(urgess)
Allmand, C. T.

Almond, Brenda
Alsamari, Lewis
Alvarez, A(lfred)
Amery, Colin
Amis, Martin (Louis)
Amos, William (David)
Anderson, Allan
Anderson, Rachel
Anderson, Sarah
Andress, David
Andrews, Edgar Harold
Andrews, John (Malcolm)
Andrews, Molly
Angel, Heather
Angelov, Dimiter
Anthony, Evelyn
Appleby, Louis
Appleyard, Bryan (Edward)
Archer, Ian W.
Archer, Jeffrey (Howard)
Archer, Margaret Scotford
Archer of Sandwell
Arden, John
Arksey, Neil
Armstrong, Adam
Armstrong, Karen (Anderson)
Arnold, Arnold F.
Arnold, David
Arnold, Elizabeth
Arnold, Guy
Ashby, Gwynneth Margaret
Ashe, Geoffrey Thomas
Asher, Jane
Asher, Neal
Asher, R. E.
Ashley, Bernard
Ashley, Trisha
Ashton, Robert
Ashworth, Jenn
Astley, Neil
Atherden, Margaret Ann
Atkinson, Anthony Barnes
Atkinson, James
Attenborough, Richard (Samuel)
Auger, C(harles) P(eter)
Aulich, James
Austin, Gareth
Austin, Guy
Avery, Gillian (Elise)
Avery, Tom
Awdry, Christopher Vere
Ayckbourn, Alan
Ayres, Pam
Bacon, George Edward
Bacon, Margaret
Badcock, Christopher Robert
Baddock, James
Badeni, June
Baderin, Mashood A.
Badger, Anthony J.
Bahn, Paul (Gerard)
Bailey, Anthony
Bailey, Frederick George
Bailey, Gordon (Keith)
Bailey, Hilary
Bains, William
Bajoria, Paul
Baker, Alan
Baker, Barbara
Baker, Geoffrey
Baker, Hugh D(avid) R(oberts)

Baker, Margaret J(oyce)
Bakewell, Kenneth (Graham Bartlett)
Bale, John R.
Balen, Malcolm
Balit, Christina
Ball, Stuart
Ballantyne, Tony
Bancroft, Anne
Bandyopadhyay, Bidisha
Banerjee, Mukulika
Banfield, Stephen
Banks, Leslie
Banks, Lynne Reid
Bann, Stephen
Banner, Catherine
Bannister, Roger (Gilbert)
Bannock, Graham
Barber, John (Douglass)
Barber, Karin
Barber, Richard (William)
Barclay, Patrick
Bareham, Terence
Barker, David J. P.
Barker, Dennis (Malcolm)
Barker, Eileen (Vartan)
Barker, Jonathan
Barker, Pat(ricia)
Barker, Paul
Barker, Raffaella
Barlow, Paul
Barnaby, Charles Frank
Barnacle, Hugo
Barnard, Nicholas
Barnard, Robert
Barnard, Toby Christopher
Barnes, Douglas
Barnes, Hugh
Barnes, Jonathan
Barnes, Michael (Anthony)
Barnes, Simon
Barnett, Anthony
Barnett, Correlli (Douglas)
Baron, Denis Neville
Baron, Wendy
Baron-Cohen, Simon
Barr, Andrew
Barr, Nicholas
Barr, Patricia (Miriam)
Barratt Brown, Michael
Barrett, Charles Kingsley
Barrett, Mark
Barrett, Michèle
Barrow, John D(avid)
Barry, Kathleen M.
Barton, John
Barton, Tamsyn (S.)
Bartrum, Giulia
Bass, Howard
Bassil, Andrea
Baston, Lewis
Batchelor, David
Batchelor, John
Batchelor, R. E.
Bate, Jonathan
Bates, Stephen
Battersby, Christine
Battie, David
Baughan, Peter Edward
Bawcutt, Priscilla (June)
Bawden, Nina (Mary)

Bax, Martin (Charles Owen)
Baxter, Stephen
Baylis, John
Bayly, C. A.
Bayne, Nicholas (Peter)
Baynes, Ken
Beacham, Richard C.
Beal, Peter
Beales, D(erek) E(dward) D(awson)
Beard, Geoffrey
Beardsell, Peter R.
Beaty, Betty (Smith)
Beauclerk, Charles
Beaufoy, Simon
Beauman, Sally
Beaumont, Maria
Beaumont, Matthew
Beck, Ian
Becker, Jasper
Beckerman, Wilfred
Beckett, Francis
Bedford, Martyn
Beech, H. R(eginald)
Beer, Anna R.
Beer, Gillian Patricia Kempster
Beere, Peter
Beerling, David
Begbie, Jeremy
Belbin, David
Bell, David S.
Bell, Hazel K(athleen)
Bellamy, Christopher (David)
Bellamy, David James
Bellos, Alex
Bellos, David
Belshaw, Patrick
Bendixson, Terence
Benedetti, Jean (Norman)
Benn, Tony
Bennett, Alan
Bennett, G. H.
Bennett, Neville
Bennett, R.G. Stephen
Bennett, Vanora
Bennett-England, Rodney (Charles)
Bensley, Connie
Benson, Frank Atkinson
Benson, Gerard
Benson, John
Benson, Peter
Benson, Richard
Bentley, Joyce
Bentley, Peter J.
Beresford, Anne
Berg, Leila
Bergonzi, Bernard
Berkoff, Steven
Bernard, G. W
Bernard, Oliver
Berridge, G. R.
Berry, Adrian M.
Berry, Cicely
Berry, Philippa
Best, Antony
Best, Geoffrey (Francis Andrew)
Bettey, J(oseph) H(arold)
Bevan, James (Stuart)
Beverley, Jo
Beyfus, Drusilla

Biagini, Eugenio F.
Bicât, Tony
Biddiss, Michael Denis
Biddle, Martin
Bielski, Alison (Joy Prosser)
Bignell, Jonathan (Charles)
Bigsby, C. W. E.
Billington, Rachel
Billington, Ray(mond John)
Billson, Anne
Binding, Paul
Bingham, Charlotte
Binns, Michael Ferrers Elliott
Binski, Paul
Birrell, Anne (Margaret)
Bittlestone, Robert
Black, Jeremy (Martin)
Blackburn, Julia
Blackman, Malorie
Blackmore, Susan (Jane)
Blackstone
Blake, Mark R.
Blake, Quentin
Blakemore, Colin (Brian)
Blamires, Alcuin (Godfrey)
Blamires, Harry
Blanchard, Stephen (Thomas)
Bland, Peter
Blanning, T. C. W.
Blashford-Snell, John Nicholas
Bloom, Clive
Blundell, Sue
Blundy, Anna
Blythe, Ronald (George)
Boaler, Jo
Boardman, John
Boast, Philip
Boden, Margaret A(nn)
Boehmer, Elleke
Bogdanor, Vernon
Bolam, Robyn
Bolster, Richard (H.)
Bond, (Thomas) Michael
Bond, C(hristopher Godfrey)
Bond, Edward
Bond, Peter
Bonington, Chris(tian)
Bonnor, William Bowen
Booker, Christopher
Boon, Debbie
Borkowski, Mark
Bosticco, (Isabel Lucy) Mary
Bostock, David
Bostock, Donald Ivan
Botting, Douglas
Boulton, James T(hompson)
Bourdeaux, Michael Alan
Bourne, Joyce
Bowen, Barbara C(herry)
Bower, John Morton
Bower, Tom
Bowie, Andrew (S.)
Bowker, Gordon
Bowlby, Rachel
Bowler, Tim
Bowley, Rex Lyon
Bown, Deni
Bowness, Alan
Boxer, Arabella
Boyes, Vivien (Elizabeth)
Boyle, David (Courtney)

Boyle, Josephine
Boyle, Nicholas
Boyt, Susie
Bracegirdle, Brian
Bracewell-Milnes, (John) Barry
Brackenbury, Alison
Bradbury, Jim
Bradford, Chris
Bradford, Sarah (Mary Malet)
Brading, D. A.
Bradley, John Lewis
Bradley, Richard
Bradman, Tony
Bradshaw, Michael
Bradshaw, Timothy
Bragg, Melvyn
Brampton, Sally Jane
Branch, Alan E(dward)
Brandon, Ruth
Brannen, Julia (M.)
Brayfield, Celia
Breakwell, Glynis M(arie)
Brears, Peter C. D.
Brendon, Piers
Brennan, Michael G.
Brenton, Howard
Brett, Simon (Anthony Lee)
Breward, Christopher
Brewerton, Derrick (Arthur)
Bridgland, Fred
Briggs, Asa
Briggs, Raymond (Redvers)
Brimson, Dougie
Brindley, John
Britland, Karen
Britnell, R(ichard) H.
Brittan, Samuel
Brock, Michael (George)
Brock, William Hodson
Brogan, Hugh
Broks, Paul
Bromley, Simon
Brook, Elaine (Isabel)
Brook, Stephen
Brooke, Christopher N. L
Brooke, Heather
Brooke, Rosalind B(eckford)
Brookes, John A.
Brookes, Tim
Brookner, Anita
Brooks, Kevin M.
Brooks, Peter Newman
Brotherston, Gordon
Brown, David
Brown, Michelle P(atricia)
Brown, Mick
Brown, Ruth
Brown, Stewart
Browne, Anthony (Edward Tudor)
Browne, Hester
Browne, Nicky Matthews
Browning, Wilfrid (Robert
   Francis)
Brownjohn, Alan (Charles)
Brownlee, Nick
Brownley, James
Bruce Lockhart, Robin
Brunskill, Ronald William
Bryan, Lynne
Bryant, Christopher G. A.
Bryant, John

Bryant, Mark
Buchanan, Colin (Ogilvie)
Buchanan, Robert Angus
Buckley, Mary (Elizabeth Anne)
Budge, Ian
Bull, Angela (Mary)
Bull, Malcolm
Bungey, John Henry
Burch, Geoff
Burchardt, Jeremy
Burchell, R(obert) A(rthur)
Burchill, Julie
Burdett, John
Burgess, Melvin
Burgh, Anita Lorna
Burkitt, Ian
Burningham, John (Mackintosh)
Burns, Alan
Burns, Carol
Burns, Edward
Burns, Jim
Burrow, J(ohn) A(nthony)
Burt, Austin
Burton, Anthony
Burton, Humphrey (McGuire)
Burton, Ivor (Flower)
Burton, John Andrew
Buscall, Jon
Bush, Barry (Michael)
Bush, M(ichael) L(accohee)
Butler, David (Edgeworth)
Butler, Gwendoline (Williams)
Butler, Lance St. John
Butler, Marilyn (Speers)
Butlin, Martin (Richard Fletcher)
Butterworth, Jeremy
Butterworth, Nick
Butts, Dennis
Buxton, Jayne
Byatt, A(ntonia) S(usan)
Bye, Beryl (Joyce Rayment)
Byrne, Paula
Cabrera, Jane
Cachia, Pierre (Jacques Elie)
Cadbury, Deborah
Cain, P. J.
Caine, Michael
Calder, Andrew
Calder, John (Mackenzie)
Calder, Martin
Calder, Nigel (David Ritchie)
Callow, Simon
Calloway, Colin G(ordon)
Calvert, Peter (Anthony Richard)
Cameron, Averil Millicent
Campbell, Alexandra
Campbell, Eric
Campbell, Judith
Campbell, Ramsey
Campbell-Kelly, Martin
Campion, Nicholas
Cann, Kate
Cannell, Fenella
Canovan, Margaret Evelyn Leslie
Capp, Bernard (Stuart)
Carbin, Debbie
Cardinal, Roger
Carew, Rivers (Verain)
Carey, George (Leonard)
Carey, John
Carley, Lionel (Kenneth)

Carling, Alan H(ugh)
Carlton, David
Carmichael, Liz
Carnall, Geoffrey Douglas
Carr, Margaret
Carr-Hill, Roy
Carroll, Brendan G.
Carroll, Stuart M.
Carswell, Grace
Carter, Dean Vincent
Carter, Maureen
Carter, Mike
Carter, Miranda
Cartledge, Mark J.
Cartwright, Anthony
Cartwright, Justin
Carwardine, Richard J(ohn)
Casey, James
Cash, Anthony
Cassels, J(ohn) W(illiam) S(cott)
Cassidy, Anne
Cassidy, Cathy
Casson, Mark (Christopher)
Castleden, Rodney
Castor, Helen
Catherwood, Christopher
Catterall, Peter
Cave, Emma
Cave, Kathryn
Cave, Peter
Caveney, Graham
Cawthorne, Nigel
Chadbourn, Mark
Chadwick, Elizabeth E.
Chadwick, Owen
Chalker, Sylvia
Challis, Sarah
Chalmers, Alan D(ouglas)
Chalmers, Robert
Chamberlain, Lesley
Chamberlain, Mary (Christina)
Champion, J(ustin) A. I.
Chaney, Edward (Paul de
   Gruyter)
Chaney, Jill
Chapman, Peter
Chappell, Audrey
Chapple, John Alfred Victor
Chard, Judy (Gordon)
Charlesworth, Monique
Charmley, John
Cherry, Bridget (Katherine)
Cheshire, Simon
Chester, Tessa Rose
Chesters, Graham
Cheyette, Bryan (Henry)
Chibnall, Marjorie McCallum
Childs, David (Haslam)
Childs, John Charles Roger
Chinery, Michael
Chinn, Carl
Chisholm, Michael
Chitham, Edward (Harry Gordon)
Christiansen, Rupert
Christie, Ian
Christmas, Linda (Irene)
Churchett, Stephen
Churchill, Caryl
Clapham, Christopher S.
Clare, Alys
Clark, A(ilsa) M.

Clark, Andy
Clark, David Lindsey
Clark, Emma Chichester
Clark, Eric
Clark, J. C. D.
Clarke, (Victor) Lindsay
Clarke, Brenda
Clarke, Gus
Clarke, Mary
Clarke, Norma
Clarkson, Wensley
Clayden, Andy
Clayson, Alan
Clayton, Anthony
Clayton, Martin
Clayton, Michael
Clayton, Peter A(rthur)
Cleall, Charles
Cleare, John S.
Cleese, John (Marwood)
Clemens, Brian (Horace)
Clements, Alan
Cleveland-Peck, Patricia
Cloake, John (Cecil)
Clough, David L.
Clover, Peter
Coburn, Ann
Cockayne, Emily
Cocker, Mark
Cockerill, A(rthur) W(illiam)
Cody, Liza
Coe, Jonathan
Coffey, John Robert David
Coffey, Michael
Coker, Christopher
Cole, Barry
Cole, Stephanie
Colegate, Isabel
Coleman, Michael
Coleman, Terry
Coleridge, Nicholas (David)
Collee, John (Gerald)
Colley, Linda
Collier, Graham
Collier, Paul
Collin, Marion (Cripps)
Collingham, E. M.
Collings, Matthew
Collini, Stefan
Collins, Hugh
Collins, Irene
Collins, Jackie
Collins, Joan
Collinson, Alan S.
Collinson, Sarah
Collis, Rose
Cologne-Brookes, Gavin (John)
Colquhoun, Kate
Compton, D(avid) G(uy)
Conlon, Kathleen (Annie)
Conner, Patrick (Roy Mountifort)
Connolly, Joseph
Connolly, Peter
Connolly, Ray
Connor, Steven
Conradi, Peter J(ohn)
Conran, Shirley (Ida)
Constant, Stephen
Constantine, David (John)
Constantine, Storm
Cook, Bob

Cook, Chris(topher)
Cook, David
Cook, Robert
Cooke, William
Cooling, Wendy
Coombes, Annie E.
Cooney, Ray(mond George Alfred)
Cooper, Barry (Anthony Raymond)
Cooper, Brian (Newman)
Cooper, Derek (Macdonald)
Cooper, Helen
Cooper, Jilly (Sallitt)
Cooper, Kate
Cooper, Roger
Cope, Wendy
Copper, Basil
Copus, Julia
Corbett, Richard (Graham)
Corbin, Jane
Cordeiro, Patricia (A.)
Corderoy, Conor
Cordingly, David
Corfield, Richard
Cork, Richard (Graham)
Corley, Thomas Anthony Buchanan
Cormack, Patrick (Thomas)
Corran, Mary
Cory, Charlotte
Coster, Graham
Cotterrell, Roger (B. M.)
Cottingham, John (Graham)
Cottrell, Alan (Howard)
Coveney, Peter (Vivian)
Cowan, Gordon
Cowell, Cressida
Cox, Alex
Cox, Christopher Barry
Cox, Richard (Hubert Francis)
Cox, Roger (Kenneth)
Cox, Steve
Crabtree, John
Crace, Jim
Cragg, (Albert) Kenneth
Craggs, Stewart R.
Craig, Joe Alexander
Craik, T(homas) W(allace)
Crane, Richard (Arthur)
Cranfield, Charles Ernest Burland
Cranfield, Ingrid
Crang, Jeremy A.
Craven, Sara
Crawford, Alan
Crawley, Harriet
Cregan, David (Appleton Quartus)
Criddle, Byron
Crisp, Oliver D.
Cromartie, Alan
Crook, J(oseph) Mordaunt
Crosland, Margaret
Crosland, Maurice P.
Cross, (Margaret) Claire
Cross, Anthony Glenn
Cross, Gillian (Clare)
Cross, Helen
Crossley, James G.
Crossley-Holland, Kevin (John William)
Crowley, Bridget

Crowley, David
Crowley, Roger
Crowley, Tony
Crowther, Nick
Cruickshank, Dan
Culyer, A(nthony) J(ohn)
Cunliffe, Barry
Cunningham, Hugh
Cunningham, Valentine
Currie, Edwina
Curry, Neil
Curteis, Ian (Bayley)
Curtis, Anthony
Curtis, J(ulie) A. E.
D'Ancona, Matthew
Dabydeen, David
Dale, Anna
Dale, Peter
Dale, Rodney A. M
Dalton, Annie
Danchev, Alex
Daniels, Anthony
Daniels, Sarah
Dann, Colin (Michael)
Danson, Edwin
Darke, Marjorie (Sheila)
Darling, David J.
Darlington, Ralph
Darlow, Steve
Davenport, John (Chester)
Davenport, Roger (Hamilton)
Davenport-Hines, Richard (Peter Treadwell)
Davies, Christie
Davies, Gareth
Davies, Hunter
Davies, Jennifer (Eileen)
Davies, Katharine
Davies, Martin (Brett)
Davies, Martin L.
Davies, Nicola
Davies, Owen
Davies, Philip John
Davies, Robert William
Davies-Mitchell, Margaret (Constance)
Davis, Anna
Davis, Lindsey
Davis, Martyn P(aul)
Davis, Patrick
Davis, Philip Maurice
Davison, Peter (Hobley)
Dawe, R(oger) D(avid)
Dawes, Edna
Day, A(rthur) Colin
Day, Aidan
Day, Alan
Day, Michael Herbert
Day-Lewis, Sean (Francis)
de Bernieres, Louis
De Botton, Alain
de Haas, Margaret
de la Bédoyère, Guy
de Somogyi, Nick
Dean, Trevor
Deane-Drummond, Anthony (John)
Dearden, James Shackley
Deathridge, John (William)
Dee, Tim
Deighton, Len

Delahaye, Michael (John)
Delaney, Shelagh
Deletant, Dennis
Deligiorgi, Katerina
Delves, Peter J(ohn)
Denham, Andrew
Dennis, Felix
Dent, Grace
Derrett, (John) Duncan (Martin)
Derry, John (Wesley)
Deshpande, Chris
Devereux, David
Dewhirst, Ian
Dewhurst, Eileen (Mary)
Dexter, (Norman) Colin
Dhami, Narinder
Diamond, Hanna Elizabeth
Dickinson, Harry Thomas
Dickinson, John
Dickinson, Matt
Dietz, Peter (John)
Dillon, Anne
Dimbleby, Jonathan
Dimbleby, Josceline (Rose)
Dimond, Peter
Dine, Janet
Dinsdale, Ann
Diski, Jenny
Dix, Robin C.
Dixon, Bernard
Dixon, Simon M.
Dixon, Steve
Dobbs, Michael
Dobson, Andrew (Nicholas Howard)
Dobson, Jill
Dobson, R(ichard) Barrie
Docx, Edward
Doherty, Berlie
Doherty, Justin (Francis)
Doherty, P(aul) C.
Dollimore, Jonathan
Dolling-Mann, Patricia May
Donald, Diana
Donaldson, Julia
Donnelly, Jane
Donnithorne, Audrey Gladys
Donoughue, Bernard
Dooley, Maura
Doran, David K.
Dore, Elizabeth W.
Dormandy, Thomas
Douglas, John (Frederick James)
Downer, Lesley
Doyle, William
Drabble, Margaret
Dracup, Angela
Drake, Charles D.
Draper, Alfred Ernest
Drew, Simon
Dromgoole, Dominic
Drury, Sally
du Sautoy, Marcus Peter Francis
Dubens, Eugene (M.)
Dudley-Smith, Timothy
Duffield, Gervase E.
Duffy, Margaret
Duffy, Maureen (Patricia)
Duggan, Christopher
Dukes, Paul
Dumbrell, John

Dummett, (Agnes Margaret) Ann
Dummett, Michael (Anthony Eardley)
Dunant, Sarah
Dunbar, Joyce
Duncan, Glen
Duncan, Sarah
Duncan, William (Robert)
Dunkerley, James
Dunn, John (Montfort)
Dunn, Suzannah
Dunnage, Jonathan (Michael)
Dyer, Charles (Raymond)
Dyer, James (Frederick)
Dyer, Sarah L.
Eagleton, Terry
Earle, Rebecca
Earnshaw, Steven
Eaton, Jack
Eaton, John Herbert
Eaton, Trevor (Michael William)
Eatwell, Roger
Eaves, Will
Ede, Piers Moore
Edgar, David
Edson, J(ohn) T(homas)
Edwards, (Kenneth) Martin
Edwards, Clive D.
Edwards, Philip (Walter)
Edwards, Robert
Eidinow, John
Eilon, Samuel
Elborough, Travis
Elboz, Stephen
Elcock, Howard (James)
Elliot, Alistair
Elliott, John Huxtable
Elliott, Odette
Ellis, Alec (Charles Owen)
Ellis, Evelyn
Ellis, Harold
Ellis, Kate
Ellis, Keith
Ellis, Markman
Ellis, Peter Berresford
Ellis, Royston
Ellison, Joan Audrey
Ellory, R. J.
Ellwood, Sheelagh (Margaret)
Elsy, (Winifred) Mary
Emsley, Clive
Emsley, John
Engelke, Matthew Eric
England, Chris
Ereira, Alan
Esdaile, Charles J.
Eshun, Ekow
Essex-Cater, Antony John
Evans, Alan
Evans, Ben
Evans, Brendan
Evans, Eric J(ohn)
Evans, Liz
Evans, Martin
Evans, Richard
Evans, Richard J(ohn)
Eveleigh, Victoria
Ewan, Chris
Eysenck, Michael (William)
Faith, Nicholas
Falck, Colin

Falcon, Mark
Falkingham, Jane (Cecelia)
Fallowell, Duncan (Richard)
Fancutt, Walter
Fanthorpe, R(obert) Lionel
Fantoni, Barry (Ernest)
Faqih, Ahmed
Fara, Patricia
Farmer, Penelope (Jane)
Farrer-Halls, Gill
Farrington, David P.
Fawcett, Tina
Fearnley-Whittingstall, Jane
Feaver, William (Andrew)
Feinstein, Elaine
Fell, Dafydd
Fenby, Jonathan
Fenlon, Iain
Fenner, Roger T(heedham)
Fenton, Kate
Ferguson, Robert (Thomas)
Ferguson, Sarah (Margaret)
Fernández-Armesto, Felipe (Fermin Ricardo)
Fernyhough, Charles
Ferrari, R(onald) L(eslie)
Ferris, John (Stephen)
Fforde, Katie
Fielding, Helen
Fiennes, Ranulph
Fifield, Christopher G(eorge)
Figes, Kate
Figes, Orlando (G.)
Findlay, Alison
Fine, Anne
Fink, Merton
Finn, R(alph) L(eslie)
Finn, Richard
Finnis, Jane
Fischer, Tibor
Fishburn, Angela Mary
Fisher, Allen
Fisher, Roy
Fishlock, Trevor
Fisk, Pauline
Fitzgerald, William
FitzRoy, Charles (Patrick Hugh)
Fitzsimons, Cecilia (A. L.)
Fleetwood, Hugh (Nigel)
Fleming, Anne
Fleming, Jacky
Fleming, Kate
Fletcher, John Walter James
Fletcher, Susan
Flint, James
Foden, Giles
Foister, Susan Rosemary
Foley, Robert T.
Folly, Martin H(arold)
Foot, David
Foot, John
Foot, Michael Richard Daniell
Footitt, Hilary
Ford, Brian John
Ford, Glyn
Forder, Anthony
Foreman, Michael
Forrest, Alan
Forrester, John
Forster, Margaret
Forsyth, Frederick

Forsyth, Michael
Fortey, Richard
Foster, Richard
Foulkes, (Albert) Peter
Foulkes, Richard (George)
Fowler, Christopher
Fox, Jo
Fox, M(ichael) W.
Fox, Robert
Foyster, Elizabeth A.
France, Linda
France, Miranda
Francis, Clare
Francis, David J.
Francis, R(ichard) A.
Francis, Richard
Franey, Ros(alind)
Frankland, (Anthony) Noble
Fraser, Anthea
Fraser, Antonia
Fraser, Evan D. G.
Fraser, Harry
Fraser, Nicholas C(ampbell)
Fraser, Robert (H.)
Frayn, Michael
Freedland, Michael
Freedman, Lawrence (David)
Freeman, Gillian
Freeman, Michael
Freemantle, Brian (Harry)
Freke, Timothy
French, David
French, Fiona
French, Patrick
French, Philip (Neville)
French, Sean
Frere, S(heppard) S(underland)
Freud, Esther
Frewer, Glyn
Friedman, Rosemary
Frisby, Terence
Fritchley, Alma
Frith, David (Edward John)
Frost, David (Paradine)
Frost, Diane
Frost, Jo
Froud, Brian
Fryer, Jonathan
Fuchs, Michael Stephen
Fudge, Erica
Fulcher, James
Fuller, John (Leopold)
Fuller, Sophie
Furniss, Graham (Lytton)
Gadney, Reg
Gaiman, Neil (Richard)
Gallagher, Stephen
Galleymore, Frances
Gardam, Jane
Gardner, (Robert) Brian
Gardner, Katy
Gardner, Lyn
Garland, Alex
Garner, Alan
Garnett, Richard (Duncan Carey)
Garnham, Trevor
Garrett, Martin
Gascoigne, Bamber
Gash, Jonathan
Gaskell, Jane
Gaskill, Malcolm

Gateley, Edwina
Gatiss, Mark
Gattey, Charles Neilson
Gauld, Alan (Ogilvie)
Geach, Christine
Geaves, Ronald Allan
Gee, Maggie (Mary)
Gee, Shirley
Genasi, Chris
Gentle, Mary
Gentleman, David
George, Rose
George, Rosemary
Gerrard, John
Gervais, Ricky
Gibbons, Alan
Gibson, Miles
Gibson, Robert
Giddens, Anthony
Gifford, Clive
Gifford, Rob
Gilbert, Alan (Graham)
Gilbert, Harriett
Gilbert, John Raphael
Gilbert, Martin
Gilbert, W(illiam) Stephen
Gildea, Robert
Giles, Frank (Thomas Robertson)
Giles, Paul
Gill, Anton
Gillman, Peter (Charles)
Gilman, Felix
Gilman, George G.
Gilson, Simon A.
Girouard, Mark
Glaister, Lesley (G.)
Glanville, Brian (Lester)
Glatt, John
Gleave, John T.
Gledhill, John
Glees, Anthony
Glover, Jane
Glover, Judith
Goble, Alan
Goddard, Hugh (P.)
Goddard, Robert (William)
Goddard, Tariq
Godden, Geoffrey Arthur
Goff, Barbara
Goff, Martyn
Goh, Evelyn
Goldacre, Ben
Golding, Peter
Goldman, Lawrence
Goldrein, Iain S.
Goldstein, Harvey
Goldstein-Jackson, Kevin
Gombrich, Richard Francis
Gooch, Steve
Good, Timothy
Goodfield, (Gwyneth) June
Gooding, Mel
Goodman, Martin (David)
Goodrich, Amanda Jane
Goodwin, Robert Theodore Chorley
Goody, John R(ankine)
Gordievsky, Oleg
Gordon, Anne Wolrige
Gordon, Graeme
Gordon, Grant

Gordon, John (William)
Gorman, Dave
Gorringe, Timothy
Gosling, J. C. B.
Gott, Richard (Willoughby)
Gould, Kevin
Goulding, Edwin (John)
Graham, Caroline
Graham, Cosmo
Graham, Desmond
Graham, Henry
Graham, Ysenda (May) Maxtone
Grainger, John D(ownie)
Granger, (Patricia) Ann
Grant, Andrew
Grant, Neil
Grant-Adamson, Lesley (Hey-cock)
Gray, John
Gray, Richard J(ohn)
Gray, Robert (Archibald Speir)
Green, Celia (Elizabeth)
Green, Christine
Green, Duncan
Green, Jane
Green, Michael (Frederick)
Green, Peter (Morris)
Green, R. P. H.
Green, Simon R(ichard)
Green, Timothy (S.)
Green, Toby
Greenhalgh, Paul
Greenlaw, Lavinia (Elaine)
Greet, Kenneth Gerald
Gregor, Neil
Gregory, Derek John
Grenfell, Michael J.
Grey, Anthony
Grey, Beryl (Elizabeth)
Grey-Wilson, Christopher
Griffin, Jasper
Griffith, Nicola
Griffiths, Jane
Griffiths, Niall
Griffiths, Trevor
Gross, Philip (John)
Grounds, Roger
Grove, Richard H(ugh)
Grubb, Michael (J.)
Grundy, Joan
Grylls, Bear
Guest, Ivor (Forbes)
Guinness, Jonathan (Bryan)
Gulbekian, Sevak E(dward)
Gunn, Ali
Gunn, Kirsty
Gunston, Bill
Gurney, Alan
Guyatt, Nicholas
Habgood, John Stapylton
Hackett, Helen
Hackett, Jeremy
Hackney, Rod(erick Peter)
Hadley, Dawn M.
Haffenden, John
Hagger, Nicholas
Hague, Douglas (Chalmers)
Hague, William
Hailes, Julia
Hainsworth, Peter (R. J.)
Hale, John

Hall, David Ian
Hall, Edith
Hall, J(ohn) C(live)
Hall, Jonathan M.
Hall, Kathleen (Mary)
Hall, Lesley A(nn)
Hall, M. R.
Hall, Peter (Geoffrey)
Hall, Sarah
Hall, Simon
Hall, Steven
Hallam, Elizabeth M.
Halliday, Nigel Vaux
Halliday, Stephen
Hallwood, Jan
Halsall, Guy
Halsey, A(lbert) H(enry)
Hamand, Maggie
Hamblyn, Richard
Hamilton, Bernard
Hamilton, James
Hamilton, Marybeth
Hamilton, Peter F.
Hamlyn, D(avid) W(alter)
Hammond, Gerald (Arthur Douglas)
Hampson, (Margaret) Daphne
Hampson, Norman
Hampson, Robert (Gavin)
Hanbury-Tenison, Robin
Handley, Eric Walter
Hankin, Elizabeth Rosemary
Hannah, Sophie
Hannam, June
Hanson, Neil
Hanson, Philip
Harclerode, Peter
Hard, Charlotte (Ann)
Hardcastle, Michael
Harding, James
Hardy, Barbara (Gladys)
Hare, David
Harford, Tim
Harper, Piers
Harper-Scott, J. P. E.
Harris, Helen(a) (Barbara Mary)
Harris, Jonathan
Harris, Jose
Harris, Margaret
Harris, Robert (Dennis)
Harris, Rosemary (Jeanne)
Harris, Roy
Harris, Ruth Elwin
Harris, Steve
Harrison, Brian (Howard)
Harrison, David Lakin
Harrison, Elizabeth Fancourt
Harrison, John F(letcher) C(lews)
Harrison, Michael
Harrison, Roy M(ichael)
Harrison, Sarah
Harrison, Tony
Harrod-Eagles, Cynthia
Harsent, David
Hart, Peter
Hart-Davis, Duff
Hartcup, Guy
Hartland, Michael
Harvey, (Brian) Peter
Harvey, Hazel (Mary)
Harvey, John

Harvey, P(aul) D(ean) A(dshead)
Harwood, (Henry) David
Haslam, Jonathan George
Haslam, Nicholas
Hastings, Max M(acdonald)
Hastings, Michael
Hattersley, Roy (Sydney George)
Havard, Cyril (William Holmes)
Havil, Julian
Hawks, Tony
Hawksley, Lucinda
Haycock, Kate
Hayden, Eric William
Hayes, Rosemary
Hayman, Richard
Hayman, Ronald
Haynes, Jane
Hayter, Teresa
Haythornthwaite, Philip John
Haywood, Steve
Head, Dominic
Heal, Gillian
Heald, Tim(othy Villiers)
Healey, Denis (Winston)
Hearn, Julie
Heater, Derek Benjamin
Heath, Malcolm (Frederick)
Heath, Veronica
Heffer, Simon (James)
Hegarty, Frances
Hemming, Laurence Paul
Henare, Amiria J.M
Henbest, Nigel
Henderson, Lauren
Heneghan, Judith
Hennessy, Peter
Hepworth, Noel P.
Herbert, James
Herman, Michael
Herring, Eric
Heslewood, Juliet
Hesse, Mary Brenda
Heyman, Jacques
Heywood, Andrew
Heywood, Colin
Hibbs, John
Hick, John (Harwood)
Hicken, Mandy
Hiçyilmaz, Gaye
Higgins, Rosalyn
Highfield, (John) Roger (Lox-dale)
Hill, Brian W.
Hill, Reginald (Charles)
Hill, Selima (Wood)
Hill, Susan (Elizabeth)
Hill, Tobias
Hill, Tracey
Hillgarth, J(ocelyn) N(igel)
Hillier, Jim
Hillman, Barry (Leslie)
Hillman, Elizabeth
Hills, Philip James
Hilton, (Andrew John) Boyd
Hilton, Boyd John Boyd
Hilton, Margery
Hilton, Matt
Hinde, Thomas
Hindle, Steve
Hines, (Melvin) Barry
Hines, Joanna

Hinton, Michael
Hionidou, Violetta
Hirsch, Pam
Hislop, Victoria
Hitchens, Peter Jonathan
Hitchings, Henry
Hix, Simon
Hoare, Philip
Hobbs, Anne Stevenson
Hobbs, Dick
Hobby, Elaine (Ann)
Hobhouse, Hermione
Hobson, John M.
Hocking, Mary (Eunice)
Hoddinott, R(alph) F(ield)
Hodge, Susie
Hodges, Andrew
Hodgkiss, Alan Geoffrey
Hodgson, Geoffrey M.
Hoffman, Mary (Margaret)
Hofschröer, Peter
Hogg, James (Dalby)
Hoggart, Richard
Hoile, David
Holbrook, David (Kenneth)
Holden, Anthony (Ivan)
Holden, Peter
Holdgate, Martin W.
Hollindale, Peter
Hollis, Stephanie
Holloway, Sara
Holmes, B(ryan) J(ohn)
Holmes, Diana
Holmes, Jon Richard
Holmes, Richard
Holmes, Rupert
Holroyd, Michael
Holt, (Wilma) Geraldene
Holt, James Clarke
Holt, Michael (Paul)
Honigsbaum, Mark
Honoré, Tony
Honri, Peter
Hooker, Morna Dorothy
Hope, Ronald
Hopkins, Antony
Hopkins, Cathy
Hopkins, Lisa
Hopkinson, Amanda
Hopkinson, Christina
Horlock, John Harold
Horn, Gerd-Rainer
Hornby, Nick
Horne, Alistair (Allan)
Horne, Richard
Horrie, Chris(topher)
Horsfield, Debbie
Horspool, David
Horwood, William
Hoskyns, Tam
Hough, Peter A.
Houghton, Eric
Houghton, Gordon
Houlbrooke, Ralph (A.)
House, John
Howard, Elizabeth Jane
Howard, Michael (Eliot)
Howard, Patricia
Howard, Philip (Nicholas Charles)
Howard, Roger
Howarth, Lesley

Howarth, Peter
Howatch, Susan
Howe, Christine J.
Howe, Leo
Howell, Anthony
Hoy, Linda
Hoyle, Carolyn
Hoyle, Geoffrey
Hoyle, Trevor
Huby, Pamela Margaret
Hucker, Hazel
Huggett, Frank Edward
Hughes, James Raymond
Hughes, Shirley
Hughes-Hallett, Lucy
Huhne, Christopher
Hulse, Michael (William)
Humphrys, Leslie George
Hunkin, Tim(othy) Mark Tre-
lawney
Hunt, Edward H.
Hunt, Richard (Patrick)
Hunt, Robert (William Gainer)
Hunt, Tony
Hunt, Tristram
Hunter, Eric J.
Hunter, Michael (Cyril William)
Hunter, Seb
Hurrell, Andrew
Hutchings, Stephen
Hutchins, Pat
Hutchinson, G(regory) O(wen)
Hutchinson, Robert
Hutson, Shaun P.
Hutton, Barbara (Audrey)
Hyam, Ronald
Hyde-Price, Adrian
Hyman, Timothy
Iles, Jane
Ingham, Kenneth
Ingham, R(ichard) A(rnison)
Ingman, Nicholas
Ingram, Derek Thynne
Inkpen, Mick
Irwin, Robert (Graham)
Iversen, Leslie
Iyengar, Sujata
Jack, Malcolm Roy
Jackman, Stuart (Brooke)
Jackson, Ben
Jackson, David Cooper
Jackson, Jane
Jackson, Kevin
Jackson, Mark
Jacob, Joseph M.
Jacobs, Francis G(eoffrey)
Jacobus, Mary
Jacques, Martin
Jahme, Carole
James, (William) Louis (Gabriel)
James, Alan
James, David Edward
James, Laura M.
James, Oliver
James, P. D.
James, Peter
James, Reina
James, Russell
Jancovich, Mark
Jarman, Julia
Jarvis, Brian

Jay, Antony (Rupert)
Jay, Peter
Jeal, (John Julian) Tim(othy)
Jecks, Michael
Jefferies, Matthew (Martin)
Jeffreys, Diarmuid
Jeffs, Julian
Jeffs, Rae
Jellicoe, Ann
Jenkins, Amy
Jenkins, Garry
Jenkins, Michael (Romilly Heald)
Jenkins, Simon
Jenkins, T(erence) A(ndrew)
Jennings, Charles
Jeram, Anita
Jobling, Curtis
John, Juliet
Johns, Derek
Johns, Jeremy
Johnson, Andrew
Johnson, Colin
Johnson, Paul (Bede)
Johnston, Alan (William)
Johnston, R(onald) J(ohn)
Jolles, Michael Adam
Jolowicz, J(ohn) A(nthony)
Jones, (Henry) John (Franklin)
Jones, Allan Frewin
Jones, Andrew
Jones, Eileen
Jones, Gwyneth A(nn)
Jones, J. Barrie
Jones, Jenny
Jones, John Henry
Jones, Julia
Jones, Malcolm V(ince)
Jones, Margaret C.
Jones, Martin
Jones, Sally Roberts
Jones, Stephen
Jones, Tobias
Jordan, Penny
Jouve, Nicole Ward
Jovanovic, Rob
Joy, David (Anthony Welton)
Joyce, Graham
Judd, Alan
Judd, Denis
Judd, Frank (Ashcroft)
Judge, Harry George
Judkins, Phil(lip Edward)
Julius, Anthony (Robert)
Jungman, Ann
Kampfner, John
Kantaris, Sylvia (Mosley)
Karlin, Daniel
Karsh, Efraim
Kaser, Michael Charles
Kassell, Lauren
Katritzky, M. A.
Kaufman, Gerald (Bernard)
Kavanagh, P(atrick) J(oseph)
Kavenna, Joanna
Kay, Elizabeth
Kay, George
Kaye, Geraldine
Kazantzis, Judith
Keal, Jenny
Keegan, William (James Gregory)
Keene, Raymond D(ennis)

Kelley, Ann
Kelly, Catriona
Kelly, Chris
Kelly, Christopher
Kelly, Ian
Kelly, Jim
Kelly, Linda
Kemp, (Bernard) Peter
Kemp, Gene
Kennard, David
Kennedy, Michael
Kennedy, Philip F.
Kennemore, Tim
Kenny, Anthony (John Patrick)
Kent, Christobel
Kenton, Warren
Kenward, Jean
Kershaw, Ian
Kerven, Rosalind
Kesseler, Rob
Kessler, Edward
Kessler, Liz
Kettell, Steven
Kevill-Davies, Sally
Keynes, Simon
Keys, David
Khalid, Mansour
Khan, Yasmin
Khoroche, Peter (Andrew)
Kidd, Charles (William)
Kiernan, Pauline
Kilworth, Garry
King, Brian
King, Daniel (John)
King, Daren
King, Doreen
King, Geoff
King, Iain
King, Nicholas
King, Peter
King-Hele, Desmond
Kingsley, Sean A.
Kinsella, Sophie
Kirby, Michael Roger
Kirk, Pauline (M.)
Kirk-Greene, Anthony
Kirk-Greene, Christopher
Kirkbright, Suzanne
Kitchen, Bert
Kitzinger, Sheila
Klein, Adam
Kleinberg, S. J.
Knecht, Robert Jean
Knight, D(avid) M(arcus)
Knight, Mark J.
Knight, Roger
Knowles, Elizabeth
Knox, George
Knox-Johnston, Robin
Kochan, Miriam (Louise)
Komporaly, Jozefina
Koning, (Angela) Christina
Kraushar, Peter Maximilian
Kureishi, Hanif
Kushner, Barak
Kynaston, David
La Fortune, Knolly Stephen
La Plante, Lynda
Labanyi, Jo
Lacey, Andrew
Lacey, Josh

Lacey, Nicola
Lamb, Andrew (Martin)
Lamb, Marion J.
Lambert, Andrew D.
Lambshead, John
Lampitt, Dinah
Lamplugh, Lois
Lancaster, Michael (L.)
Lancaster Brown, Peter
Landers, John
Lane, Nick
Lane, Simon
Langfield, Valerie
Langford, David
Langley, Andrew
Lapping, Brian (Michael)
Lassiter, Rhiannon
Lathey, Gillian
Laurence, Janet
Laurence, Ray
Laurie, Hugh
Laurie, Peter
Lavery, Bryony
Law, John
Lawlor, Clark
Lawrence, C(lifford) H(ugh)
Lawrence, Caroline
Lawrence, David
Lawrence, Michael
Lawrence, Sara
Lawton, John
Laybourn, Keith
le Carré, John
Le Fanu, James
Leach, Neil
Leach, Penelope (Jane)
Leak, Andrew N.
Leatherbarrow, W(illiam) J(ohn)
Lee, A(rthur) Robert
Lee, Donald (Lewis)
Lee Six, Abigail (Etta)
Leech, Geoffrey Neil
Leech, Kenneth
Leeson, Robert (Arthur)
Lefebure, Molly
Leff, Gordon
Legg, Gerald
Leigh, David
Lennox-Smith, Judith (Elizabeth)
Leonard, Mark
Letcher, Andy
Letchford, Stanley
Levene, Mark
Lever, Christopher
Levinson, Alan
Levy, Adrian
Lewis, Jeremy
Lewis, Paeony
Lewis, Peter (Elvet)
Liddington, Jill
Liddle, Peter (Hammond)
Liebreich, Karen
Lieven, Dominic
Light, Alison Elizabeth
Lindsay, Geoff
Lindsay, William
Ling, Peter J(ohn)
Ling, Roger (John)
Linzey, Andrew
Lisk, Jill (Rosina Ann)
Lisle, Rebecca

Lister, R(ichard) P(ercival)
Litten, Julian
Littlewood, Clayton
Llewellyn, Sam
Lloyd, A(lan) R(ichard)
Lloyd, Geoffrey Ernest Richard
Lloyd, Peter Cutt
Lloyd, Saci
Loades, David Michael
Lock, Joan
Lockwood, David
Lodge, David
Loewe, Michael
Logue, Christopher
Lomas, Herbert
Loncraine, Rebecca
Longmate, Norman Richard
Longworth, Philip
Loomes, Brian
Lord, John Vernon
Lord, Tony
Lorrimer, Claire
Loud, G(raham) A(nthony)
Loudon, Mary
Lovegrove, James (Matthew
    Henry)
Lovell, (Alfred Charles) Bernard
Lovell, Julia
Lovell, Mary S(ybilla)
Lovesey, Peter (Harmer)
Lowden, Desmond Scott
Lowe, Keith
Lowe, Rodney
Lowe, Sheila
Lowe, Stephen
Lubbock, Jules
Lucas, John
Lucas, John Randolph
Lucie, Doug
Luker, Nicholas (John Lydgate)
Lustig, T(imothy) J(ohn)
Lynch, John
Lynch, Timothy J.
Lynn, Richard
Lyons, Louis
Mabey, Richard Thomas
MacCarthy, Fiona
MacClancy, Jeremy
Macdonald, Lyn
MacDonogh, Giles
Macfadyen, Amyan
Macfarlane, Leslie John
Macfarlane, Malcolm R.
Mack Smith, Denis
Mackintosh-Smith, Tim
Macleod, Alison
Macleod, Ian R.
Magee, Bryan
Mager, Hugo
Maggs, Colin Gordon
Maginn, Simon
Magorian, Michelle
Maguire, Laurie E.
Mahmud, Shabana
Maitland, Barbara
Maitland, Karen
Maizels, John
Major, John
Makinen, Merja
Malam, John
Malcolm, Noel

Malvern, Sue
Mandel, Ruth Ellen
Manlove, Colin (Nicholas)
Mann, Jessica
Mann, Pamela
Mantel, Hilary (Mary)
Marber, Patrick
March, N(orman) H(enry)
Marchant, Ian
Marcombe, David
Marenbon, John (Alexander)
Margam, Kate
Margolis, Jonathan
Markham, Ian Stephen
Markham, Lynne
Marks, Alan
Marks, David (Francis)
Marks, Graham
Marks, Lara Vivienne
Marks, Richard
Marland, Hilary
Marlow, Joyce
Marmot, Michael (Gideon)
Marquis, Max
Marriott, Edward
Marsh, Jan
Marshall, John
Marshall, Peter (H.)
Marten, Michael
Martin, (Roy) Peter
Martin, Andy
Martin, David Alfred
Martin, Elizabeth A(nn)
Martin, Francesca
Martin, J(ulia) Wallis
Martin, Joanna
Martin, Rhona
Martin, Victoria Carolyn
Martinez, D. P.
Mason, Anita
Mason, Christopher
Mason, Fran
Mason, Robert
Mason, Sarah J.
Massey, Doreen Barbara
Massey, Victoria
Massingham, Harold (William)
Mather, Anne
Mathias, Peter
Matthew, Christopher C. F
Matthews, Carole
Matthews, L. S.
Matthews, Peter (Hugoe)
Matthews, Steven
Maxford, Howard
Maxwell, Nicholas
May, Derwent (James)
Mayfield, Sue
Mayhew, Margaret
Maynard, Geoffrey (Walter)
McAlindon, Thomas
McAlpine, Alistair
McBride, Simon
McCann, Graham
Mccann, Maria
McCargo, Duncan
McCarthy, Colin (John)
McCaughrean, Geraldine (Jones)
McClelland, Vincent Alan
McClure, Gillian Mary
McCreery, Charles Anthony Selby

McCrone, John (Robert)
McCullin, Don(ald)
Mccully, Marilyn
McCutcheon, William Alan
McDonagh, Martin
McDonald, Patricia M.
McDougall, James
McDowell, Linda
McEwan, Ian
McGill, Angus
McGough, Roger
McGowan, Anthony
McGrath, Melanie
McGurn, James (Edward)
McHugh, John (Francis)
McIlwaine, John
McKay, Hilary
McKee, David (John)
Mckendrick, James (Stewart)
McKie, Robin
McKitterick, David John
McKitterick, Rosamond Deborah
Mclaughlin, Martin L.
McLellan, David
McLoughlin, Leslie John
McMahon, Katharine
McManus, Michael
McMullan, Gordon
McMullen, Jeremy
McRae, Barry (Donald)
Meacock, Heather
Meaney, John
Meer, Sarah
Megarry, Tim
Mellor, D. H.
Mellows, Anthony (Roger)
Melnikoff, Pamela (Rita)
Melville, Arabella
Melville, Charles (Peter)
Mendelsohn, Martin
Mercer, Derrik
Meredith, Richard A.
Merrett, Christopher
Merriman, Catherine
Messer, Richard
Mettam, Roger C.
Michael, Livi
Michie, Jonathan
Midda, Sara
Middlebrook, Martin
Middlemas, (Robert) Keith
Middleton, (John) Christopher
Middleton, Haydn
Midwinter, Eric (Clare)
Milbank, (Alasdair) John
Miles, Barry
Miles, Christopher (John)
Miles, Dudley (Robert Alexan-
    der)
Miles, Rosalind
Millard, Alan Ralph
Miller, Daniel
Miller, David (Leslie)
Miller, John
Miller, Jonathan (Wolfe)
Miller, Russell
Millett, Martin J(ohn)
Millett, Paul
Mills, Judith Christine
Mills, Richard W.
Mills, Robert

Mills, Stephen (Paul)
Millum, Trevor
Millward, Robert
Milne, David
Milne, Seumas
Milsom, Stroud Francis Charles
Milton, Giles
Minshall, Vera
Mishan, E. J.
Mitchell, (Charles) Julian
Mitchell, David (John)
Mitchell, Peter
Mitchell, Stephen (G.)
Mitchelson, Mitch
Mithen, Steven J.
Mitson, Eileen N(ora)
Mitton, Tony
Moffat, Gwen
Moggach, Deborah
Mole, John
Molnar, Michael
Monaghan, Nicola
Moncrieff, Elspeth
Monk, Raymond
Montagu, Jennifer (Iris Rachel)
Montagu of Beaulieu
Montefiore, Janet
Montgomery, David
Montgomery, Diane
Moody, David
Moon, Jeremy
Moon, Nicola
Moonman, Eric
Moore, Allan F.
Moore, John Michael
Moore, Tim
Morden, Simon
Moreton, N. Edwina
Morgan, Philip
Morpurgo, Michael
Morrill, John S(tephen)
Morris, Alan
Morris, Christopher Hugh
Morris, Desmond
Morris, Frances
Morris, Mark
Morris, Michael
Morris, Nigel
Morris, Rachel
Morrison, (Philip) Blake
Morson, Ian
Mortimer, James Edward
Morton, Andrew
Morton, James (Severs)
Morton, Oliver
Mosley, Nicholas
Moss, Miriam
Moss, Stirling
Motion, Andrew (Peter)
Motley, Annette
Moxham, Roy
Moxley, Sheila
Moynahan, Brian
Muddiman, John
Muggeson, Margaret Elizabeth
Muir, Helen
Muir, Richard
Mullett, John St. Hilary
Mullins, Edwin B(randt)
Munby, Jonathan
Murcott, Anne

Murdoch, Brian (Oliver)
Murdoch, David H.
Murphy, (Gavin) Martin (Hedd)
Murphy, Jill (Frances)
Murphy, Robert
Murray, Craig
Murray, David (J.)
Murry, Katherine Middleton
Musgrove, Frank
Musto, Barry
Myers, Greg
Nagai, Kaori
Neal, Frank
Needle, Jan
Neilan, Sarah
Neill, Fiona
Nelson, Geoffrey Kenneth
Nelson, Michael
Nelson, N. A.
Neuberger, Julia
Neuhaus, Denise
Newcome, Robert
Newman, Andrea
Newman, Andrew
Newman, G(ordon) F.
Newsholme, Christopher (Mansford)
Newton, Diana
Newton, Mark Charan
Nice, Jill
Nicholls, C(hristine) S(tephanie)
Nicholls, Henry
Nicholls, Sally
Nichols, John Gordon
Nichols, Peter (Richard)
Nicholson, Colin
Nicholson, E(rnest) W(ilson)
Nicolson, Adam
Nightingale, Pamela
Nineham, Dennis Eric
Nish, Ian Hill
Nixon, Mignon
Nixson, Frederick Ian
Nobbs, David
Noble, William Charles
Noltingk, Bernard Edward
Noon, Jeff
Norbrook, David
Norfolk, Lawrence
Norman, Barry
Norman, Edward R(obert)
Norris, Geoffrey
Norris, Pamela
Norton, Philip
Norton, Sheila
Norwich, John Julius (Cooper)
Nugent, Neill
Nunn, John
Nursten, Jean Patricia (Frobisher)
Nye, Simon (Beresford)
O'Brien, D(enis) P(atrick)
O'Brien, Lucy
O'Brien, Martin
O'Brien, Maureen
O'Brien, Patrick K.
O'Brien, Sean
O'Donovan, Oliver
O'Faolain, Julia
O'Flynn, Catherine
O'Hara, Marjorie (Doreen)
O'Hare, Mick Richard

O'Kane, Rosemary H.T
O'Malley, Thomas
Oakes, Andy
Oakley, Ann
Oakley, Graham
Oaksey
Odell, Robin Ian
Oldfield, Jenny
Oldfield, Michael
Oldfield, Pamela
Oldham, June
Oldridge, Darren
Oliver, James (Anthony)
Opie, Iona
Orledge, Robert
Orme, David John
Orme, Nicholas
Ormerod, Roger
Orton, Anthony
Osborne, Frances
Osborne, Roy Martin
Outhwaite, (Richard) William
Ovason, David
Overall, Sonia
Overend, William George
Overton, Jenny (Margaret Mary)
Øvstedal, Barbara
Owen, David (Anthony Llewellyn)
Owens, John E.
Oxenbury, Helen
Oxley, William
Packer, Mez
Packett, Charles Neville
Padel, Ruth
Page, Christopher H.
Page, Norman
Paget, Julian (Tolver)
Palin, Michael (Edward)
Paling, Chris
Palmer, Alan Warwick
Palmer, Elizabeth
Palmer, Frank Robert
Palmer, Martin (Giles)
Palmer, Philip
Panayi, Panikos
Pankhurst, Richard (Keir Pethick)
Pannick, David
Papineau, David
Parfitt, Tudor (Vernon)
Parfitt, Will
Paris, Michael
Parker, D(avid) C.
Parker, David
Parker, Gordon
Parker, L. P. E.
Parker, Peter (Robert Nevill)
Parker, Thomas (Henry Louis)
Parker, Una-Mary
Parkes, M(alcolm) B(eckwith)
Parkin, Frank
Parkinson, Alan F.
Parks, Adele
Parry, Graham
Parsons, (Quentin) Neil
Parsons, Alexandra
Parsons, P. J.
Parsons, Paul
Partridge, Jenny (Lilian)
Patten, Brian
Patten, Chris

Patterson, Ian
Patterson, Michael
Pattullo, Polly
Pavey, Don
Pavlou, Stel
Pavlowitch, Stevan K.
Paxton, John
Payne, Donald Gordon
Peace, Richard (Arthur)
Peacock, Alan (Turner)
Pearce, Edward
Pearce, Mary E.
Pearl, David
Pears, Tim
Pearsall, Derek (Albert)
Pearson, Diane (Margaret)
Pearson, John
Pearson, Roger A. G.
Peel, H(azel) M(ary)
Peet, Mal
Pemberton, Margaret
Penrose, Antony
Penycate, John (Vincent George)
Peppé, Rodney (Darrell)
Perchard, Tom
Perrett, Bryan
Perriam, Wendy
Perry, Michael Charles
Peters, Kate
Pettifer, James
Pettifer, Julian
Petty, W(illiam) H(enry)
Peyton, A(nthony) J(oseph)
Peyton, K. M.
Phelan, Joseph
Phelps, Barry
Philip, George
Phillips, Jonathan P.
Phillips, Kenneth J. H
Phillips, Marie
Phillipson, David W.
Phillipson, Michael
Pickard, Tom
Pickering, David (Hugh)
Pierce, David
Pierpoint, Katherine
Pierson, Christopher
Piggott, Alan (Derek)
Pilbeam, Pamela M.
Pilling, Ann
Pilling, Christopher (Robert)
Pilling, John
Pinch, Richard G. E.
Pinney, Lucy (Catherine)
Pinnock, Winsome
Pinto, Jacqueline
Pisani, Elizabeth
Pitcher, Caroline (Nell)
Pitcher, Harvey John
Pizzichini, Lilian
Place, Milner
Plank, Geoffrey
Plant, Sadie
Polkinghorne, John Charlton
Pollard, A(nthony) J(ames)
Pollitt, Michael G(erald)
Pollock, John Charles
Ponsonby, Laura
Poole, Elizabeth
Poole, Josephine
Poole, Richard

Porter, Bernard (John)
Porter, Linda
Porter, Sheena
Porter, Sue
Poskitt, Kjartan
Posner, Rebecca
Postgate, John (Raymond)
Potter, Simon J.
Potts, Richard
Poulson, Christine
Powell, David
Powell, Neil
Powers, Alan
Powling, Chris
Pownall, David
Prag, John
Prance, Ghillean Tolmie
Pratchett, Terry
Pratt, David
Preston, Andrew
Preston, Diana
Preston-Mafham, Rod(ney Arthur)
Prestwich, Michael (Charles)
Price, Anthony
Price, Susan
Priest, Christopher (McKenzie)
Priest, Stephen
Priestley, Chris
Priestman, Martin
Prime, Derek James
Prince, Hugh
Prince, Maggie
Princess Anne
Prior, Charles W.A
Prior, Kenneth Francis William
Profumo, David
Pryce, Lois
Prynne, J. H.
Pullein-Thompson, Diana
Pullein-Thompson, Josephine
Pullman, Philip
Pulsford, Petronella
Pulvertaft, (Isobel) Lalage
Purser, Ann
Purser, Philip (John)
Purves, Libby
Puxley, Ray
Pybus, Rodney
Pye-Smith, Charlie
Quigley, Declan
Quinlan, David
Rackham, Oliver
Radcliffe, Timothy
Radcliffe Richards, Janet
Raeburn, Antonia
Rai, Bali
Raine, Craig (Anthony)
Raine, Jerry
Rainey, Lawrence S.
Raisin, Ross
Rake, Alan
Ramsay, Jay
Ramsden, Herbert
Randall, Adrian
Randall, John L(eslie)
Randall, Rona
Randles, Jenny
Rankin, Robert
Raphael, David Daiches
Rappaport, Helen

Ratcliffe, Eric Hallam
Rathmell, Neil
Ravelhofer, Barbara
Ravetz, Alison
Ravilious, Robin
Rawle, Graham
Rawlings, Helen
Rayfield, Donald
Raymond, Patrick (Ernest)
Rayner, Hugh
Read, Anthony
Read, Brian
Read, Christopher
Read, Miss
Read, Piers Paul
Read, Sylvia Joan
Reader, John
Redclift, Michael R.
Redfern, Elizabeth
Redwood, John (Alan)
Reed, James
Reed, T(erence) J(ames)
Reeman, Douglas (Edward)
Rees, Nigel (Thomas)
Rees-Mogg
Regan, Linda
Regan, Stephen
Reid, Julia
Reiss, Edward
Rendell, Ruth
Renfrew, (Andrew) Colin
Rennell, Tony
Restall Orr, Emma
Reuben, Bryan G.
Rex, Richard
Rey, Bret
Reynolds, David
Reynolds, Dee
Reynolds, Graham
Reynolds, Jan
Rice, Graham
Rice, Michael
Richardson, David (Horsfall Stuart)
Richardson, George Barclay
Richardson, Mark
Richardson, Nigel
Richardson, R. C.
Richardson, Robert
Richardson, Robert Galloway
Richmond, Hugh Macrae
Rickman, Philip
Ridd, Stephen (John)
Riddell, Roger C.
Ridgway, John M.
Ridley, Jane
Ridley, Matt(hew White)
Ridley, Philip
Ridpath, Michael
Rieger, Bernhard
Rigby, Nigel
Righton, Caroline
Riley, Madeleine (Veronica)
Riley, Martin
Rimmington, Gerald Thorneycroft
Riordan, James (William)
Risebero, Bill
Roberts, (Edward) Adam
Roberts, Adam
Roberts, Brian
Roberts, Callum

Roberts, Denys (Tudor Emil)
Roberts, Derek Harry
Roberts, Elizabeth
Roberts, Iolo Francis
Roberts, Katherine
Roberts, Priscilla
Roberts, Yvonne
Robinson, Andrew
Robinson, Julian
Robson, Brian Turnbull
Roddam, Franc(is George)
Rodger, Richard
Roe, Sue
Rogan, Johnny
Rogers, Colin D(arlington)
Rome, Margaret
Rook, Tony
Rooksby, Rikky
Rooney, Jennie
Rooney, Lucy
Roose-Evans, James
Rose, Andrew (Wyness)
Rose, David
Rose, Kenneth (Vivian)
Rose, Michael
Rose, Nikolas S.
Rose, Paul
Rose, Paul (Bernard)
Rose, Steven
Rosen, Michael (Wayne)
Ross, Angus
Ross, Ian Campbell
Ross, Stewart
Ross, Tony
Rossiter, John
Routh, Francis John
Rowbotham, Sheila
Rowe, C(hristopher) J(ames)
Rowell, Douglas Geoffrey
Rowett, Helen (Graham Quiller)
Rowland, Peter Kenneth
Rowntree, Derek
Rowson, Pauline
Roy, Jacqueline
Roy, James (Henry Barstow)
Royle, Nicholas
Rozenberg, Joshua
Rubinstein, Hilary (Harold)
Rudgley, Richard
Rudolf, Anthony
Rumens, Carol
Rushton, Julian (Gordon)
Russell, Jeremy (Longmore)
Russell, Kenneth Victor
Russell, Martin (James)
Russell, Roy
Russell, Willy
Russell Taylor, Elisabeth
Rust, Graham (Redgrave)
Ruston, Sharon
Rutherfurd, Edward
Rutledge, Ian
Ryan, Mark Dermot
Rydill, Jessica
Ryle, Anthony
Ryle, Michael
Sabin, Roger (John)
Sacks, Oliver (Wolf)
Saddler, Allen
Sadler, Amy
Sail, Lawrence (Richard)

Saint, Andrew (John)
Saks, Mike
Salaman, Nicholas
Salisbury, Mike
Salway, Peter
Sambrook, A(rthur) J(ames)
Sampson, Catherine
Sampson, Geoffrey (Richard)
Sanders, Alan J. K.
Sanders, Andrew
Sanders, Peter (Basil)
Sandler, Merton
Sands, Philippe
Sandys, Celia
Sanecki, Kay Naylor
Sansom, Peter
Sant Cassia, Paul
Saunders, Ann Loreille
Saunders, Jean (Innes)
Saunders, Max
Saunders, Nicholas J.
Sauvain, Philip Arthur
Savage, Roz
Savarin, Julian Jay
Saville, Diana
Sawyer, Roger
Saxton, Josephine (Howard)
Sayer, Ian (Keith Terence)
Sayers, Janet
Scargill, David Ian
Scerri, Eric R.
Schecter, Darrow
Schmidt, Ulf
Schofield, Brian
Schofield, Carey
Schofield, John A.
Scholey, Arthur (Edward)
Schouvaloff, Alexander
Scofield, Martin (Paul)
Scott, David L.
Scott, Donald Fletcher
Scott, Peter
Scott, Robyn
Scott-Clark, Cathy
Scovell, Brian (Souter)
Screech, M(ichael) A(ndrew)
Scupham, (John) Peter
Seaford, Richard
Seaman, Gerald Roberts
Searle, G(eoffrey) R(ussell)
Seed, David
Segal, Julia (Clare)
Selbourne, David
Self, Will
Sellars, Jane
Semple, Andrea
Sewell, Michael (John)
Seymour, Gerald
Seymour-Jones, Carole
Shaffer, Peter (Levin)
Shah, Sayed Tahir
Shakespeare, Nicholas
Sharpe, Graham
Sharpe, Kevin
Sharratt, Nick
Shaw, Ali
Shaw, Alison
Shaw, Christine
Shaw, Deborah Anne
Shaw, Fiona
Shaw, James E.

Shaw, Lisa
Shaw, Margret
Shaw, Martin
Shaw, Thurstan
Shaw, Tony
Shaw, William
Sheehan, Sean
Sheerman, Barry
Shelby, Graham
Shepherd, Robert
Sherry, Norman
Sherry, Patrick
Sherry, Sylvia
Shiach, Morag
Shire, Michael J.
Shoesmith, Kathleen A.
Shone, Richard (N.)
Short, Brian (Michael)
Short, Robert Stuart
Shrimsley, Bernard
Shukman, Harold
Shuttle, Penelope (Diane)
Sidahmed, Abdel Salam
Silk, Joseph (Ivor)
Silver, Harold
Silvester, Peter (John)
Simmie, James (Martin)
Simmonds, Posy
Simmons, Jane
Simmons, Sylvie
Simpson, Jacqueline (Mary)
Simpson, John (Cody Fidler)
Simpson, Penny Claire
Sinclair, Andrew (Annandale)
Sinclair, Olga (Ellen)
Sinden, Donald (Alfred)
Singh, Simon
Sington, David
Sington, Philip
Siniver, Asaf
Sinyard, Neil
Sisson, Rosemary Anne
Skeet, Ian
Skinner, Quentin (Robert Duthie)
Skipp, Victor (Henry Thomas)
Slater, Jim
Slater, Michael
Slater, Nigel
Slavin, Helen
Sleigh, Charlotte
Sloman, Albert Edward
Smalley, Stephen S(tewart)
Smartt, J(oseph)
Smellie, Jim
Smiles, Sam
Smith, Adam I.P.
Smith, Anthony
Smith, C(hristopher) U. M.
Smith, Charles Robert Saumarez
Smith, Clive Stafford
Smith, David L(awrence)
Smith, Delia
Smith, Emma
Smith, Frederick E(screet)
Smith, Gordon Roland
Smith, James L(eslie Clarke)
Smith, Jonathan
Smith, Mark M.
Smith, Michael
Smith, Neil(son) V(oyne)
Smith, Paul

Smith, Peter Charles Horstead
Smith, Rupert
Smyth, Iain
Snell, K. D. M.
Snellgrove, David L(lewellyn)
Snellgrove, Laurence Ernest
Snodgrass, Anthony McElrea
Snow, Keith Ronald
Snow, Philip (Albert)
Snowman, Daniel
Softly, Barbara (Charmian)
Sokol, B. J.
Somerset, Anne
Soothill, Keith (Leonard)
Soper, Kate
Soper, Tony
Soueif, Ahdaf
Soulsby, E. J. L.
Souper, Patrick C(harles)
Soutar, Carolyn
Southey, Roz
Spalding, Frances
Sparke, Penny
Spash, Clive L(aurence)
Speel, Erika
Spence, William John Duncan
Spencer, Charles
Spencer, Colin
Spencer, John (Walter)
Spencer, Paul
Spicer, Michael
Spiers, Edward M(ichael)
Spink, Ian
Sprackland, Jean
Sprackling, Michael Thomas
Sprott, Duncan
Spufford, Francis
Spurling, Hilary
St. Aubyn, Giles (Rowan)
St. Clair, William
Stableford, Brian M(ichael)
Stacey, Tom
Stafford, Fiona (Jane)
Stallworthy, Jon (Howie)
Stammers, John
Stamp, Terence (Henry)
Standen, John Derek
Stangroom, Jeremy
Stanley, Oliver
Stannard, Martin (J.)
Stansfield, Gareth R.V.
Staynes, Jill
Steans, Jill A.
Steedman, Carolyn (Kay)
Steel, Nigel
Steggle, Matthew
Stein, Peter (Gonville)
Stephen, Jaci
Stephen, Martin
Stephens, Andy
Stephens, William Peter
Stern, Vivien
Stevenson, David
Stevenson, Talitha
Stewart, Ian (Nicholas)
Stewart, Mary (Florence Elinor)
Stewart, Michael (James)
Stewart, Rosemary
Stibbe, Mark W. G.
Stockbridge, Sara Jane
Stockwin, J. A. A.

Stoker, Gerry
Stokoe, E(dward) G(eorge)
Stone, Gerald (Charles)
Stone, Merlin (David)
Stone, Nick
Stone, Rodney
Stonehouse, Bernard
Stoneman, Richard (John)
Stopford, John M(orton)
Stoppard, Miriam
Stops, Sue
Storey, David (Malcolm)
Storey, Margaret
Storey, R(obin) L(indsay)
Stotter, Mike
Stourton, Ivo
Stoyle, Mark
Strachan, Ian
Strange, Julie-Marie
Strathern, Paul
Streeter, Patrick
Stringer, Christopher
Strong, Roy (Colin)
Strong, Terence
Stroud, Jonathan
Stuart, Mark
Stubbs, Jean
Stubbs, Peter Charles
Styles, John
Sulston, John (Edward)
Summers, Judith (Anne)
Summerscale, Kate
Sumner, (Edith) Aurea
Sumption, Jonathan
Supple, Barry E(manuel)
Sutherland, John
Sutherland, Luke
Sutton, C(live) (Julian)
Sutton, David John
Swain, Carol
Swan, Robert
Sweeney, Fionnghuala
Swift, Graham
Swinburne, Richard (Granville)
Swindells, Robert (Edward)
Sykes, Plum
Symmons, Sarah
Synge, Ursula
Tagg, Christine Elizabeth
Tanner, Marcus
Tanner, Michael (K.)
Taplin, Oliver
Tarlow, Sarah Alexandra
Tavernor, Robert (William)
Taylor, Andrew (John Robert)
Taylor, Barbara Gold
Taylor, Claire
Taylor, Frederick
Taylor, Helen
Taylor, John (Gerald)
Taylor, John H(ilton)
Taylor, John Russell
Taylor, Jonathan
Taylor, Robert
Taylor, Rogan
Tearle, John L.
Thatcher, Margaret (Hilda)
Thirsk, (Irene) Joan
Thiselton, Anthony C(harles)
Thomas, (Antony) Charles
Thomas, Bruce

Thomas, D(onald) M(ichael)
Thomas, David St. John
Thomas, Hugh
Thomas, Julian (Stewart)
Thomas, Lyn
Thomas, Rosalind
Thomas, Sue
Thompson, Damian
Thompson, E(rnest) V(ictor)
Thompson, Kate
Thomson, Hugh
Thomson, June
Thomson, Pat
Thomson, Peter (William)
Thrasher, Peter Adam
Thrift, Nigel
Thubron, Colin Gerald Dryden
Thurley, Simon
Thwaite, Anthony (Simon)
Thynn, Alexander (George)
Till, Barry Dorn
Till, Nicholas
Tilley, Patrick
Tillyard, Stella
Timms, Edward
Tindall, Gillian (Elizabeth)
Tinniswood, Adrian
Tipton, David
Tomalin, Claire
Tomkins, Stephen
Tomlinson, (Alfred) Charles
Tomlinson, Harry
Tomlinson, Theresa
Tong, Raymond
Tooze, J. Adam
Tope, Rebecca
Topping, Keith A.
Torrance, Lee
Toulmin, Vanessa Elizabeth
Townsend, John Rowe
Townsend, Lindsay
Townsend, Sue
Toynbee, Polly
Travis, Anthony S(tewart)
Tredell, Nicolas (Samuel)
Tremain, Rose
Tremlett, George (William)
Trenhaile, John Stevens
Triggs, Tony D.
Trimble, Michael R.
Tripp, Charles R(ees) H(oward)
Trollope, Joanna
Trotman-Dickenson, Aubrey
    Fiennes
Trotter, David
Truscott, Peter
Tsetskhladze, Gocha R(evazi)
Tubb, Jonathan N.
Tudge, Colin
Tugendhat, Christopher (Samuel)
Tugendhat, Julia
Tunstall, C. Jeremy
Turbet, Richard
Turnbull, Peter (John)
Turnbull, Stephen (Richard)
Turner, Amédée (Edward)
Turner, Barry
Turner, John Frayn
Turner, Martin
Turney, Jon
Turnill, Reginald

Turok, Neil
Tyerman, Christopher
Tyldesley, Joyce (Ann)
Underwood, Peter
Upton, Martin
Urban, Mark
Ure, Jean
Ure, John (Burns)
Valentine, Mark
Valman, Nadia
Van der Kiste, John (Patrick Guy)
Van der Vlies, Andrew
Van Der Zee, Barbara (Blanche)
Vaughan, Megan
Velarde, Giles
Venables, Stephen
Verdon, Nicola
Verney, Michael Palmer
Verney, Peter (Vivian Lloyd)
Vesey, Godfrey
Vieceli, Emma
Villa-Gilbert, Mariana
Vincent, John (Russell)
Vincent, John James
Vitebsky, Piers
von Tunzelmann, Alex
Waddell, Dan
Waddington-Feather, John Joseph
Wade, Stephen
Wagner, Gillian (Mary Millicent)
Wainwright, Geoffrey
Wainwright, Gordon Ray
Wainwright, Jeffrey
Waites, Martyn
Wakling, Christopher
Walden, Mark
Walker, Greg
Walker, Stephen
Wallace, John
Waller, Jane (Ashton)
Waller, P(hilip) J(ohn)
Walsh, Jill Paton
Walsh, Stephen
Walter, Andrew
Walter, John
Walters, Minette
Waltham, Tony (A. C.)
Walton, John (Nicholas)
Walvin, James
Wandor, Michelene
Wapshott, Nicholas (Henry)
Warburton, Nigel
Ward, (John Stephen) Keith
Ward, Elizabeth Honor
Ward, Gregory
Ward, Philip
Wardle, (John) Irving
Wardman, Gordon
Ware, Alan
Ware, Kallistos
Warmington, William Allan
Warner, Francis
Warner, Marina
Warner, Martin
Warner, Val
Warnock, Mary
Warrack, John (Hamilton)
Warren, Kenneth
Warrington, Freda
Wass, Douglas (William Gretton)
Waterfield, Robin Anthony

Herschel

Waterman, Andrew (John)
Waters, David Watkin
Watkins, Nicholas
Watkinson, John
Watson, Ben
Watson, Donald
Watson, Ian
Watson, J(ohn) R(ichard)
Watson, James
Watson, Kathy
Watson, Sophia
Watt, Ben
Watts, Alan (James)
Watts, Anthony John
Waugh, Alexander
Waugh, Sylvia
Waugh, Teresa (Lorraine)
Wayman, Vivienne
Webb, Clive
Webber, Andrew Lloyd
Webber, Mark (Alan)
Webster, Ernest
Webster, John
Webster, Len
Weiner, Edmund
Weir, Ronald Blackwood
Welch, Evelyn S.
Weldon, Fay
Welland, Michael
Wells, Roger
Wells, Shirley
Wells, Stanley (William)
Welsh, Frank (Reeson)
Welton, Jude
Wenham, David
Wesker, Arnold
Wess, Jane A.
West, Colin
West, Donald James
West, Ewan (D.)
West, Harry G.
West, M(artin) L(itchfield)
Westcott-Jones, Kenneth
Westwood, John Norton
Whalley, Joyce Irene
Whalley, Peter
Wheatle, Alex
Wheeler, Sara
Whelan, Yvonne
Wheldon, David
Whelehan, Imelda
Whitaker, Katie
Whitaker, Phil
White, Carolinne
White, Christopher (John)
White, Kevin
White, Mark J.
White, Peter (O. G.)
Whitehead, Catherine Sarah
Whitehead, David (Henry)
Whitelaw, Stella
Whiteley, Nigel
Whiteman, Robin
Whitfield, Roderick
Whitfield, Sarah
Whittington, Geoffrey
Whitton, David
Whyman, Matt
Wicker, Brian John
Wicks, Susan

Widdecombe, Ann (Noreen)
Wilby, Basil Leslie
Wilcox, Paula
Wild, Kate
Wilde, Lyn Webster
Wilford, Hugh
Wilkins, Arnold
Wilkinson, Denys (Haigh)
Wilks, Mike
Willett, Ralph
Williams, (Henry) Nigel
Williams, Alan
Williams, Alan Lee
Williams, Alex
Williams, Andrew
Williams, Austin
Williams, Barry
Williams, Charles
Williams, Charlie
Williams, Hugh Steadman
Williams, John Hartley
Williams, Kate
Williams, Liz
Williams, Marcia (Dorothy)
Williams, Michael
Williams, R(obert) J(oseph)
    P(aton)
Williams, W. S. C.
Williamson, Donald I.
Williamson, Edwin
Williamson, Philip G.
Willis, Val
Willmott, Phyllis
Wills, Alfred J(ohn)
Wilmer, Clive
Wilson, (Brian) Geoffrey
Wilson, A(ndrew) N.
Wilson, Andrew
Wilson, Andrew
Wilson, Christopher R.
Wilson, Colin (Henry)
Wilson, David Henry
Wilson, David M(ackenzie)
Wilson, Elizabeth
Wilson, Jacqueline (Aitken)
Wilson, Laura
Wilson, Peter H.
Wilson, Robin J.
Wilson, T. R.
Winder, Simon
Winegarten, Renee
Wingfield, Paul
Winkler, John
Winnifrith, T(homas) J(ohn)
Winter, David Brian
Winter, John (Anthony)
Winterbottom, Michael
Wiseman, Alan
Wiseman, Richard
Wisker, Gina
Wolfers, Michael
Wolff, Jonathan
Womack, Philip
Wood, Bridget
Wood, David
Wood, Dennis (Michael)
Wood, Frances
Wood, Gaby
Wood, Ian N(icholas)
Wood, James
Wood, Marguerite N.

Woodford, Peggy
Woodhouse, Sarah
Woods, Michael
Wooldridge, Adrian
Woolf, Stuart Joseph
Woolfe, Jennifer A(nne)
Woolhouse, Roger
Woollen, Geoff
Woolley, Benjamin
Wootton, David
Worboys, Anne
Worthen, John
Wright, (Mary) Patricia
Wright, Cliff
Wright, Daphne
Wright, Keith
Wright, Kit
Wright, M(aureen) R(osemary)
Wroughton, John Presbury
Wullschläger, Jackie
Wyke, Maria
Wyndham, Francis (Guy Percy)
Wynyard, Robin (Norman)
Yapp, Malcolm E(dward)
Yarwood, Doreen
Yorke, Malcolm
Yorke, Margaret
Youd, Samuel
Young, Elizabeth
Young, Sheila
Youngs, Tim
Yudkin, Leon Israel
Yuill, Nicola M.
Zephaniah, Benjamin (Obadiah
    Iqbal)
Ziegler, Philip (Sandeman)
Zimmermann, Arnold Walter
Zinik, Zinovy
Zornberg, Avivah Gottlieb

England-Argentina

Altmann, Simon L(eonardo)

England-Australia

Adams, Jessica
Aldridge, (Harold Edward) James
Allan, Keith
Brent, Allen
Campling, Christopher Russell
Carey, Peter
Clark, Christopher M.
Collings, I. J.
Conrad, Peter
Copeman, George Henry
Crozier, Brian
Dixon, John E.
Field, Ophelia
Finlay, Peter (Warren)
Fisher, Angela
Gilley, Sheridan (Wayne)
Greer, Germaine
Hanscombe, Gillian E(ve)
Howard, Audrey
Hull, John M.
Hunter, R(ichard) L(awrence)
Johnson, Susan (Ruth)

Joyce, Richard
Knightley, Phillip (George)
McShane, Mark
Mueller, Andrew
Nayman, Michele
Newey, Katherine
O'Neill, Robert John
Oakes, Meredith
Osborne, Charles
Palmer, Michael Denison
Pilger, John Richard
Purkiss, Diane
Rees, Brian
Rhodes, R. A. W.
Robertson Q.C., Geoffrey R.
Segal, Lynne
Taylor, Allegra
Vita-Finzi, Claudio
Walkerdine, Valerie
Watson, George (Grimes)
Wilding, Michael
Wyld, Evie

**England-Australia-New Zea-
land**

Minogue, Kenneth Robert

England-Austria

Chorlton, David
McNeill, Christine
Pick, Hella
Pryce-Jones, David
Pulzer, Peter George Julius

England-Bahamas

Hill, Justin

England-Bangladesh

Anam, Tahmima

England-Belgium

Daftary, Farhad
van Hensbergen, Gijs
Wignall, Kevin
Wilson, Andrew

England-Belgium-Germany

Wedell, Eberhard George

England-Belgium-USA

Bagley, Tennent H.

England-Bermuda

McGregor, Jon

England-Brazil

Blake, Norman Francis

England-Canada

Barrett, Anthony A(rthur)
Campbell, Beatrix
Clarke, Peter Frederick
Coles, John Morton
Cottringer, Anne
Cusk, Rachel
Eltringham, S(tewart) K(eith)
Gilchrist, Roberta
Glancy, Ruth F(ergusson)
Grant, Jill
Guild, Elspeth
Haywood, Chelsea
Heffron, Dorris
Hemming, John Henry
Herman, Didi
Honderich, Ted
Howard, M(ichael) C.
King, Anthony
Kolinsky, Martin
Lathrop, John P.
Macdonald, Marianne
Maynard, Christopher
Morgan, Janet
Morton, Richard Everett
Ough, Richard N.
Rakoff, Alvin
Richler, Daniel
Rudrum, Alan (William)
Scott, Amoret (Tanner)
Sellers, Alexandra
Stychin, Carl F.
Sullivan, (Donovan) Michael
Tomaselli, Sylvana
Wardroper, John Edmund
Williams, Stephanie

England-Canada-Scotland

Honoré, Carl

England-China

Guo, Xiaolu
Platt, Colin
Walker, Nigel (David)

England-Croatia

Magas, Branka

England-Cuba

Llobera, Josep R.

England-Cyprus

Alkiviades, Alkis
Arestis, Philip

Howker, Janni

England-Czech Republic

Eltis, Walter (Alfred)
Krejči, Jaroslav
Mayer, Gerda (Kamilla)
Osers, Ewald
Rickman, Hans Peter
Stoppard, Tom
Zentner, Peter

England-Denmark

Qvortrup, Mads
Toksvig, Sandi

England-Egypt

Badawi, Mohamed Mustafa
Caute, (John) David
Darwish, Adel
El-Enany, Rasheed
Hobsbawm, Eric (John Ernest)
Lang, Judith
Lively, Penelope
Moreau, David Merlin
Sassoon, Donald
Whicker, Alan (Donald)
Wickham, David

England-Estonia

Gabriel, Jüri (Evald)

England-France

Al-Rasheed, Madawi
Bickerton, David M.
Han, Béatrice
Josipovici, Gabriel (David)
Karmiloff-Smith, Annette Dionne
Keates, Jonathan
Krier, Léon
Seward, Desmond
Steiner, George
Tombs, Robert P.

England-France-Switzerland

Brooke-Rose, Christine

England-Germany

August, Oliver
Barrie, Alexander
Beumers, Birgit
Bieler, Andreas
Binding, Tim
Bodmer, Walter (Fred)
Eisner, Gisela
Figes, Eva
Garb, Tamar

Hahn, Frank H(orace)
Hayman, Walter Kurt
Haynes, Sybille (Edith)
Herrmann, Luke John
Kerr, (Anne) Judith
Klein, Josephine (F. H.)
Koenigsberger, Helmut Georg
Kord, Susanne
Kramer, Lotte
Leech, John
Liebeschuetz, John Hugo W. G.
Lübbren, Nina
Prawer, S(iegbert) S(alomon)
Quasthoff, Thomas
Quirk, Randolph
Rubinstein, Helge
Schmieding, Holger
Stuppy, Wolfgang
Treitel, Guenter
Usborne, Cornelie
Weinrich, A. K. H.

England-Greece

Chaniotis, Angelos
Dominian, Jack
Fotopoulos, Takis
Trivizas, Eugene
Tzouliadis, Tim

England-Guyana

Agard, John
Harris, (Theodore) Wilson
Melville, Pauline
Nichols, Grace
Ramphal, Shridath (Surendranath)

England-Hong Kong

Mo, Timothy
Sum, Ngai-Ling
Swanson, Heather (Crichton)

England-Hungary

Biro, Val
Fonagy, Peter
Szirtes, George
Vermes, Géza

England-India

Anderson, Robert (David)
Basu, Kunal
Birmingham, Maisie
Bowen, John (Griffith)
Chatterjee, Debjani
Chatterji, Joya
Chaudhuri, Amit
Ellis, Mark (Karl)
Fieldhouse, David K(enneth)
Gabriel, Theodore P. C.
Gupta, Sunetra
Hay, Elizabeth (Jean)

Hutton, Ronald
Judah, Aaron
Kee, Robert
Ker, Ian (Turnbull)
Kingsland, Rosemary
Kirkman, William Patrick
Lash, N. L. A.
Lazenby, J(ohn) F(rancis)
Macfarlane, Alan (Donald James)
Moat, John
Mohanti, Prafulla
Oliver, Roland Anthony
Padfield, Peter
Pincher, (Henry) Chapman
Richard, Cliff
Sinha, Indra
Studdert-Kennedy, (William)
    Gerald
Tatchell, Jo
Walker, Benjamin
Whitworth, John

England-Indonesia

Taverne, Dick

England-Iran

Katouzian, Homa
Khalvati, Mimi
Lessing, Doris (May)
Nersessian, V(rej) N.

England-Iraq

Zangana, Haifa

England-Ireland

Alexander, (Robert) McNeill
Andrews, J(ames) S(ydney)
Bennett, Ronan
Branagh, Kenneth (Charles)
Brennan, J(ames) H(erbert)
Burns, Anna
Cathcart, Brian
Catherwood, (Henry) Frederick
    (Ross)
Cockburn, Patrick
Cosgrove, Brian
Craig, Patricia
Devlin, Anne
Dunne, Gillian A(nne)
Elliott, Marianne
Fallon, Ivan (Gregory)
Ferguson, Mark W. J.
Gillespie, Raymond
Greer, Steven (Crawford)
Heather, Peter
Henry, Maeve
Hill, Geoff
Howe, Muriel
Johnson, Jason
Keaney, Brian
Keery, James
Keohane, Dan

Laird, Nick
Leitch, Maurice
Lewis, Margaret (B.)
Lycett Green, Candida
MacEoin, Denis
McAuley, Roisin
McCauley, Martin
Mccrory, Donald P(eter)
McDonald, Ian
McDonald, Ronan Daniel
McFadden, Johnjoe
McGilloway, Brian
McKittrick, David
Mitchell, Susanna (Ryland)
Morgan, Austen
Morrow, Ann
Myers, William
O'Brien, Edna
O'Donoghue, Bernard
O'Murchu, Diarmuid
Phillips, Timothy
Prendergast, Mark J(oseph
   Anthony)
Rankin, Herbert David
Ridgway, Keith
Ross-Macdonald, Malcolm (John)
Ryan, Frank
Sedgwick, Fred
Simms, Brendan
Staveacre, Tony
Stewart, Michael
Sweeney, Matthew
Tighe, Carl
Tomalin, Ruth
Tonkin, Peter Francis
Trevor, William
Vandermerwe, Sandra
Wallace-Murphy, Tim
Wright, Christopher J.H

England-Ireland-Scotland

Nairn, Tom (Cunningham)

England-Ireland-USA

Llywelyn, Morgan

England-Israel

Barbour, Julian B.
Geras, Adèle (Daphne Weston)
Offer, Avner
Pappé, Ilan
Roston, Murray
Teller, Neville
Zeldin, Theodore

England-Israel-Iraq

Shlaim, Avi

England-Italy

Antognazza, Maria Rosa

Coppolaro-Nowell, Annalisa
Evangelisti, Silvia
Gambetta, Diego
Gragnolati, Manuele
Hornby, Simonetta Agnello
Rivière, William
Rogers, Richard
Rylands, Philip
Servadio, Gaia (Cecilia Gem-
   malina)

England-Jamaica

Campbell, Colin
Cumper, Patricia
Duncker, Patricia
Goulbourne, Harry
Grant, Colin
Headley, Victor
Lucie-Smith, (John) Edward
   (McKenzie)
Riley, Joan

England-Japan

Fukuda, Haruko
Ishiguro, Kazuo
MacKay, Donald (Iain)
Morozumi, Atsuko

England-Kenya

Bewes, Richard
Gregory, Philippa
Hain, Peter
Hill, Pamela
Hunt, Janie Louise
Spurling, John

England-Korea (South)

Chang, Ha-Joon

England-Korea (South)-USA

Payne, Leigh A.

England-Lebanon

Abi-Ezzi, Nathalie
Khoury, Raymond
Rutter, Michael (Llewellyn)

England-Malawi

Allan, Robin
Kambalu, Samson

England-Malaysia

Bailey, Donna
Bott, Caroline G.

Brown, Rajeswary Ampalavanar
Gall, Sandy
Gray, Dulcie

England-Malta

d'Lacey, Chris
Mahon, Basil

England-Mexico

Schmidt, Michael (Norton)

England-Mozambique

Lisboa, Maria Manuel

England-Myanmar

Collis, Louise (Edith)
Rayner, Mary (Yoma Grigson)
Steele-Perkins, Christopher
   Horace
Thwe, Pascal Khoo

England-Netherlands

Davidson, Pamela
Heslam, Peter S.
Towse, Ruth
van Lemmen, Hans

England-New Zealand

Adcock, Fleur
Armitage, David
Armitage, Ronda (Jacqueline)
Dawick, John
Einhorn, Barbara
Kelly, Louis Gerard
Mitchell, Juliet
Robb, Peter
Rodger, N. A. M.
Thwaite, Ann (Barbara)
Urry, James
Whittle, Peter
Wilson, Des

England-New Zealand-Scotland

Petrie, Duncan

England-Nigeria

Emecheta, (Florence Onye) Buchi

England-Norway

Westad, Odd Arne

England-Pakistan

Ahmad, Imran
Alvi, Moniza
Aslam, Nadeem
Bayley, John (Oliver)
Cloudsley-Thompson, John
   (Leonard)
Farooki, Roopa
Hiro, Dilip
Husain, Shahrukh
Manzoor, Sarfraz
Shamsie, Kamila

England-Palestine

Masalha, Nur
Murphy, Sylvia

England-Poland

Bauman, Zygmunt

England-Romania

Antal, Dan
Bugan, Carmen
Ortenberg, Veronica

England-Russia

Golomstock, Igor (Naumovitch)
Medvedev, Zhores (Alexandrov-
   ich)
Polukhina, Valentina

England-Saudi Arabia-Swit-
zerland

Tarnowski, Andrew

England-Scotland

Addison, Paul S.
Anderson, Malcolm
Anderson, Olive Ruth
Arbuthnott, Gill
Ascherson, (Charles) Neal
Ashton, Rosemary
Banks, Ray
Barker, Elspeth
Bellamy, Richard (Paul)
Bowman, Christian
Britton, Celia (Margaret)
Brock, William Ranulf
Brown, Archibald Haworth
Brown, Gordon
Bruce, Colin John
Burnett, Alfred David
Carver, Martin
Chandler, Glenn
Christie, Stuart
Colgan, Jenny
Colin, Beatrice

Cumming, Charles
Dickie, John
Dixon, Dougal
Docherty, Paddy
English, Barbara (Anne)
Fell, Alison
Felstein, Ivor
Finkel, Caroline
Finlay, Richard J(ason)
Forrester, Michael A.
French, Vivian
Gallagher, Tom
Galloway, Janice
Garden, Edward (James Clarke)
Gathorne-Hardy, Jonathan
Gibb, Lorna
Gill, A. A
Grant, Susan-Mary C.
Grindal, Richard
Harlow, Rosie
Heald, Suzette
Hedderwick, Mairi
Henderson, J. A.
Hendry, Joy (McLaggan)
Impey, Chris
Kay, Jackie
Kay, John (A.)
Kelly, Mij
Leask, Nigel
Leveritt, Thomas
Lunan, Duncan
Macdonald, Sharman
MacGregor, Neil
MacIntyre, Alasdair
Mackesy, Piers Gerald
MacLeod, Ken
MacNeill, Alastair
Macphail, Catherine
Marshall, Peter
McClure, Ken
McCutcheon, Elsie (Mary Jackson)
McEnery, John H.
McEwen, Helena
McIntyre, Ian (James)
McKean, J(ohn) M(aule)
McLean, Iain (S.)
McWilliam, Candia
Mearns, Barbara (Crawford)
Miller, Karl (Fergus Connor)
Morrey, Douglas J.
Nelson, D. A. Ann
Newton, Kenneth
Niven, Alastair (Neil Robertson)
O'Hagan, Andrew
Odber (de Baubeta), Patricia (Anne)
Paterson, Ronald (William Keith)
Pelley, Kathleen T.
Potter, Harry (D.)
Pringle, David (William)
Ramsay, Caro
Rennie, Bryan S.
Robertson, Robin
Rohan, Michael Scott
Rothwell, Victor Howard
Ruckley, Brian
Sansom, C. J.
Sloan, John
Smith, Ali
Sproat, Robert

Steel, David (Martin Scott)
Taylor, Elisabeth (D.)
Taylor, T(homas) F(ish)
Thomson, D(aisy) H(icks)
Thomson, Richard
Tudor, Andrew
Whitton, Kenneth S(tuart)
Williamson, John (Gordon)

England-Scotland-Australia

Delahunt, Meaghan

England-Scotland-Slovenia

Sirc, Ljubo

England-Scotland-USA

McEwen, Todd

England-Singapore

Gibson, A(lex) J. S.
Skinner, Stephen
Stewart, Lucretia

England-South Africa

Aylen, Leo
Black, D(avid) M(acleod)
Counsel, June
Craig, Amanda
Driver, C(harles) J(onathan)
Ellerbeck, Rosemary
Geraghty, Paul
Gordon, Lyndall (Felicity)
Gratus, Jack
Harwood, Ronald
Herbert, Ivor
Hirschhorn, Clive
Jacobson, Dan
Kavanagh, Julie
King, David
Kuper, Adam (Jonathan)
Lan, David
Le May, G(odfrey) H. L(ancelot)
Lerner, Laurence (David)
Letellier, Robert Ignatius
Levy, Deborah
Naidoo, Beverley
Ngcobo, Lauretta
Parris, Matthew (Francis)
Pope, Hugh
Rex, John Arderne
Scholefield, Alan (A. T.)
Silver, Norman
Taylor, Stephen
Trapido, Barbara
Walton, Henry John
Werbner, Pnina

England-Spain

Pitt-Kethley, (Helen) Fiona
Quiroga, Alejandro
Sire, H. J. A.
Tremlett, Giles

England-Sweden

Jones, David (Erik) Hay
Rausing, Sigrid
Wilson, Eva

England-Switzerland

Bertschinger, Claire
Brandenberg, Franz

England-Taiwan

Aw, Tash

England-United Republic of Tanzania

Moore-Gilbert, Bart
Visram, Rozina

England-Thailand

Heuser, Beatrice

England-Trinidad and Tobago

Benjamin, Floella
Ramdin, Ron(ald Andrew)

England-Uganda

Newlyn, Lucy

England-Uruguay

Edgerton, David

England-USA

Abbotson, Susan C.W
Abramson, Edward A.
Achinstein, Sharon
Aliki
Anderson, Jon Lee
Apter, Michael John
Apter, T(erri) E.
Aridjis, Chloe
Ash, William Franklin
Ashworth, Andrea
Assael, Brenda
Bareham, Lindsey
Barton, Anne
Beard, Richard
Bessel, Richard
Brady, Joan

Brewer, John
Browning, Guy
Burk, Kathleen
Buxbaum, Julie
Carrier, James G(olden)
Castaldo, Nancy Fusco
Castle, Kathryn
Charles, Kate
Chernaik, Warren L(ewis)
Chevalier, Tracy
Colebank, Susan
Coleman, James A.
Collings, Gillian
Cooke, John Peyton
Davidoff, Leonore
Devlin, Keith
Dickason, Christie
Dorment, Richard
Elias, Scott A.
Engel, Cindy
Fainlight, Ruth
Fuller, Steve William
Gablik, Suzi
Gardner, Jerome
Ghose, Zulfikar
Glass, Dee Dee
Goldman, Arnold (Melvyn)
Goodman, Lizbeth (L.)
Gosling, Paula
Graef, Roger (Arthur)
Gray, Colin S.
Green, Angela
Green, Richard
Grossman, Wendy
Gurdon, Martin
Hall, H(ugh) Gaston
Hennessey, Thomas W.
Hill, Geoffrey
Hitchcock, Tim
Hoban, Russell
Homberger, Eric
Honan, Park
Horsley, Lee
Johnson-Smith, Jan
Kaufman, Will
Keats-Rohan, K. S. B.
Kelly, Saul
Kennedy, Leigh
Kinealy, Christine
Knevitt, Charles (Philip Paul)
Kopper, Lisa (Esther)
Krane, Jim
Kuper, Jenny Riva
Lahr, John (Henry)
Lambert, Katherine
Landry, Donna
Leader, Darian
Leader, Zachary
Legrain, Philippe
Lethbridge, Robert (David)
Lewin, Michael Z.
Lindisfarne-Tapper, Nancy
Lunde, Paul
Macfarlane, Robert
MacInnes, Mairi
MacMillan, Norma
Maddox, Bronwen
Majors, Richard G.
Mann, Kenny
Marqusee, Mike
Martin, Alex

Fermine, Maxence
Ferrières, Madeleine
Gailly, Christian
Garaudy, Roger
Gaudé, Laurent
Gernet, Jacques
Glucksmann, André
Gondry, Michel
Goursac, Olivier de
Grassi, Maggi Lidchi
Grimaldi, Janette Pienkny
Groult, Benoite
Guérif, François
Guillaumin, Colette
Hallé, Francis
Henriot, Christian
Hoestlandt, Jo(celyne)
Hugon, Anne
Hutchinson, Samuel
Jacob, Christian
Jaffrelot, Christophe
Ka, Olivier
Kadare, Ismail
Kantor, Jean-Michel
Kapferer, Jean-Noel
Kaplan, Rachel
Kersaudy, François
Kourilsky, Françoise
Kristeva, Julia
Labro, Philippe (Christian)
Lambrichs, Louise L.
Lanzmann, Claude
Larcenet, Manu
Laroque, Francois G.
Laszlo, Pierre
Laurant, Guillaume
Le Doeuff, Michèle
Lebreton, J(ean) D(ominique)
Leroux-Hugon, Hélène
Lesourne, Jacques
Letessier, Dorothée
Louër, Laurence
Manent, Pierre
Manotti, Dominique
Meddeb, Abdelwahab
Meinesz, Alexandre
Melonio, Francoise
Millet, Richard
Minc, Alain J. R.
Montier, Jean-Pierre
Moulessehoul, Mohammed
Mourlevat, Jean-Claude
Ndiaye, Marie
Orsenna, Érik
Passeron, Jean Claude
Pélot, Pierre
Perdrizet, Marie-Pierre
Polastron, Lucien X.
Prévaux, Aude Yung-De
Queffélec, Yann
Redonnet, Marie
Rio, Michel
Roger, Philippe
Roudinesco, Elisabeth
Rufin, Jean Christophe
Sallenave, Daniele
Sartre, Maurice
Sebbar, Leïla
Spycket, Jerome
Sterritt, Laurence Lux
Strauss, Gwen

Taguieff, Pierre André
Techiné, André
Tellermann, Esther
This, Herve
Thomas, Chantal
Todd, Emmanuel
Todd, Olivier
Tungate, Mark
Vahanian, Gabriel
Vargas, Fred
Verluise, Pierre
Vernerey, Denise
Werber, Bernard
Winock, Michel
Wittmer, Pierre (Jean)
Wolton, Thierry

France-Argentina

Kaplan, Nelly

France-Australia

Baxter, John

France-Austria

Durschmied, Erik
Gregor, Arthur

France-Belgium

Norac, Carl

France-Canada

Huston, Nancy
Kidwell, Carol (Evelyn Beryl)
Mercer, Jeremy
Sehene, Benjamin

France-China

Sijie, Dai
Xingjian, Gao

France-Cyprus

Baybars, Taner

France-Egypt

Basta, Samir Sanad

France-England

Bailey, Rosemary
Berger, John (Peter)
Campbell-Culver, Maggie
Collette, Christine
Corp, Edward

Dallas, Gregor
Edwards, Michael
Gloag, Julian
Laughland, John
Lawday, David
Morris, Stephen
Mortimer, Gavin
Needham, Kate
Petley, Dexter
Seabright, Paul
Seabrook, Mike
Searle, Ronald (William Fordham)
Shone, Anna
Short, Philip

France-England-Wales

Story, Jonathan

France-Finland-Romania

Sandu, Gabriel

France-Germany

Boulez, Pierre
Kamm, Henry
Karle, Hellmut (William Arthur)

France-Hungary

Sed-Rajna, Gabrielle

France-Iran

Abbas
Asadi, Houshang
Banisadr, Abol-Hassan
Naraghi, Ehsan
Nomani, Farhad
Shakeri, Khosrow

France-Iraq

Saleem, Hiner

France-Ireland

Madden, Deirdre

France-Israel

Vigée, Claude (Andre Strauss)

France-Israel-Germany

Arom, Simha

France-Italy

Jabes, Sophie

France-Japan

Robertson, Ian (Campbell)

France-Lebanon

el-Tahri, Jihan
Khoury-Ghata, Vénus

France-Morocco

Fontanel, Béatrice
Pancol, Katherine
Pennac, Daniel

France-Norway

Sæterøy, John Arne

France-Poland

Halter, Marek

France-Romania

Bujor, Flavia
Carneci, Magda

France-Russia

Limonov, Éduard
Makine, Andreï

France-Scotland

Batchelor, Stephen
Fraser, Gordon
White, Kenneth

France-South Africa

Chouaki, Aziz

France-Spain

Rios, Julian

France-Sweden

de Jouvenel, Hugues Alain

France-Switzerland

Vauclair, Jacques

France-Thailand

Phathanothai, Sirin

France-Tunisia

Bramly, Serge
DeBuron, Nicole
Marouane, Leila

France-Turkey

Benbassa, Esther

France-USA

Banks, Kate
Berdeshevsky, Margo Ann
Brawley, Ernest
Butturini, Paula
Daley, Robert (Blake)
Deàk, Erzsi
Drake, Alicia
Duncan, David Douglas
Emanuel, James A(ndrew)
Finkenstaedt, Rose L. H.
Forstenzer, Thomas R.
Giesbert, Franz-Olivier
Haynes, Jim
Holdefer, Charles
Kimmel, Allan J.
Levieux, Eleanor
Littell, Robert
Lottman, Herbert
Mairowitz, David Zane
Maristed, Kai
Micou, Paul
Morgenstern, Susie Hoch
Pfaff, William (Wendel)
Shalit, Béatrice
Spikes, Daniel
Steavenson, Wendell
Townsend Hall, Brenda P.
Viviano, Frank

France-USA-Germany

Zuckermann, Wolfgang (Joachim)

Germany

Albert, Hans
Allert, Tilman
Allred, Alexandra Powe
Altenburg, Matthias
Assmann, Jan
Becker, Jürgen
Beckert, Jens
Behringer, Wolfgang
Belting, Hans
Benecke, Mark
Berg, Manfred
Berger, Stefan
Bergunder, Michael
Biermann, Pieke

Birringer, Johannes (H.)
Blom, Philipp
Blossfeld, Hans Peter
Bock, Gisela
Brenner, Michael
Brinkbäumer, Klaus
Brunkhorst, Hauke
Buddensieg, Tilmann
Bürger, Peter
Chotjewitz, David
Deichmann, Ute
Diem, Max
Diner, Dan
Errington, R. Malcolm
Faas, K. Ekbert
Faroghi, Suraiya
Fischer, Klaus P.
Fraser, Ronald (Angus)
Fricker, Christophe E.
Gabbert, Wolfgang
Gabler, Hans Walter
Gall, Lothar
Gantschev, Ivan
Gardiner, Jeremy
Georgi-Findlay, Brigitte
Gerhards, Jürgen
Gerstenberger, Erhard S.
Gillmeister, Heiner
Gindorf (Prof. Dr.), Rolf
Görlach, Manfred
Greshake, Gisbert
Gretsch, Mechthild
Groys, Boris
Gruner, Wolf
Güse, Ernst Gerhard
Hackelsberger, Christoph
Haenel, Wolfram
Hammerschmidt-Hummel,
  Hildegard
Harries, Karsten
Hartwig, Manfred
Hein, Christoph
Herding, Klaus
Hettche, Thomas
Hildebrand, Klaus
Hildt, Elisabeth
Honnef, Klaus
Horovitz, Michael
Irmscher, Christoph
Joas, Hans
Kirchner, Emil J(oseph)
Kocka, Jürgen
Kramer, Fritz W.
Krohn, Claus-Dieter
Krug, Manfred
Kruger, Arnd
Krüger, Michael
Kuhl, Stefan
Laubenbacher, Reinhard C.
Löhr, Robert
Lumer, Christoph
Magill, R. Jay
Malzahn, Manfred
Maron, Monika
Mauch, Christof
Menninghaus, Winfried
Metzinger, Thomas
Mieth, Dietmar
Mommsen, Hans
Müller, Ingo
Nüsslein-Volhard, Christiane

Pausewang, Gudrun
Pehnt, Wolfgang
Pilipp, Frank
Poëppel, Ernst
Pörtner, Hans O.
Pressler, Mirjam
Rave, Tilmann
Reiche, Dietlof
Reinhardt, Carsten
Reuter, Christoph
Richter, Jutta
Riesner, Rainer
Roth, Klaus
Rudolph, Kurt
Ruepp, Krista
Sachs, Wolfgang
Scheck, Florian A.
Scheffler, Ursel
Schlink, Bernhard
Schulze, Ingo
Simon, Fritz B(ernhard)
Sinn, Hans Werner
Spanger, Hans-Joachim
Steinmetz, Christian
Sturmer, Michael
Stützle, Walther
Tellkamp, Uwe
Trapp, Stefan (Alfred Josef)
von Kellenbach, Katharina
Vondung, Klaus
Wagner, Rudolf G.
Wettig, Gerhard
Wiener, Antje
Würzbach, Natascha
Yuryenén, Sergey
Zimmermann, Jens

Germany-Austria

Marin, Dalia
Peyer, Bernd C.
Stampf, Günter

Germany-Bangladesh

Nasrin, Taslima

Germany-China

Noll, Ingrid

Germany-Czech Republic

Hrycej, Tomas
Jeschke, Wolfgang

Germany-England

Booth, Edward
Fuess, Harald

Germany-India

Bhatt, Sujata

Germany-Netherlands

de Bondt, Gabe J.

Germany-Poland

Grass, Günter (Wilhelm)
Paturi, Felix R.

Germany-Portugal

De Carvalho, Mário

Germany-Romania

Muller, Herta

Germany-Russia

Bronsky, Alina

Germany-Spain-USA

Cardona, Manuel

Germany-Switzerland

Hoyningen-Huene, Paul

Germany-USA

Cummings, Richard H.
Dewitt, Helen
Hulsman, John C.
Jaffin, David
Mathewson, Casey C. M.
Pagonis, William G.
Piper, Adrian (Margaret Smith)
Shakin, Ken
Winger, Anna
Zacharias, Karen Spears

Ghana

Agyeman, Opoku
Akyeampong, Emmanuel
  K(waku)
Armah, Ayi Kwei
Awoonor, Kofi
Djoleto, (Solomon Alexander)
  Amu

Greece

Bada, Constantina
Blatanis, Konstantinos
Broumas, Olga
Chorafas, Dimitris N.
Huffington, Arianna
Karamitroglou, Fotios
Moschonas, Andreas

Mougios, Vassilis
Pallis, Athanasios A.
Petsalis-Diomidis, Nicholas

Greece-England

Fermor, Patrick (Michael) Leigh
Zinovieff, Sofka

Greece-Israel-USA

Sherman, Arnold

Greece-Turkey

Markaris, Petros

Greece-USA

Macniven, Ian S.

Guyana

Confiant, Raphaël
Deena, Seodial F(rank) H(ubert)
Maas, Sharon
Mars, Perry
Phillips, Mike

Guyana-Trinidad and Tobago

McDonald, Ian (A.)

Hong Kong

Abraham, Thomas
Hung, Chang-tai
Parker, David

Hong Kong-China

Pun, Ngai

Hong Kong-England

Morton, Brian

Hong Kong-Taiwan

Hsiung, Ping-Chen

Hong Kong-USA

Weiss, Timothy F.

Hungary

Bozai, Ágota
Bozóki, András
Csaba, László
Csányi, Vilmos
Csepeli, György
Csoori, Sandor
Esterhazy, Peter
Hanzo, L(ajos)
Köves, András
Nádas, Péter
Orkeny, Antal
Rév, István
Szabó, Istvan
Szekely, Istvan P(al)
Takás, Tibor
Tosics, Ivan
Valko, Peter

Hungary-Canada

Nadler, John

Hungary-England

Lebor, Adam
Martin, Roderick

Hungary-Romania

Dragomán, György

Iceland

Gylfason, Thorvaldur
Indridason, Arnaldur
Michaels, Rune
Thorsson, Örnólfur

India

Amritanandamayi, Mataji
Appach, Anjana
Bahal, Aniruddha
Bajwa, Rupa
Banerjee, Asit
Banerji, S(riranjan)
Béteille, André
Bhagat, Chetan
Bhattacharya, Nalinaksha
Bond, Ruskin
Chatterjee, Upamanyu
Coelho, Ivo
Das, Suranjan
David, Esther
Davidar, David
de Souza, Eunice
Ghosh, Arun Kumar
Giri, Ananta Kumar
Guha-Thakurta, Tapati
Hasan, Anjum
Kapur, Manju
Khanna, Parag
Krishna, K. R.
Kukreja, Veena
Kurien, Christopher (Thomas)

Lalita, K
Maheshwari, Shriram
Masud, Naiyer
Mehrotra, Sri Ram
Menon, Dilip M(adhav)
Menon, Ritu
Mishra, Pankaj
Nārang, Gopī Chand
Naidu, Prabhakar S.
Natwar-Singh, K.
Paranjape, Makarand (Ramach-
andra)
Peterson, Richard Austin
Rajadhyaksha, Ashish
Rammohan, V.
Rana, Indira Higham
Rao, Sirish
Rinpoche, Khandro
Roy, Arundhati
Rushdie, Salman
Sahgal, Nayantara (Pandit)
Sealy, I(rwin) Allan
Seth, Vikram
Singh, Chetan
Singh, D(asharath)
Srivastava, Vinayak N.
Sukla, Ananta Charana
Syal, Meera
Thapar, Valmik
Tully, (William) Mark
Vijayaraghavan, Vineeta
Viswanathan, S(ubrahmanyam)
Wolf, Gita

India-Belgium

Drèze, Jean

India-England

Dasgupta, Rana
Tharoor, Shashi

India-Ethiopia

Chattarji, Sampurna

India-Pakistan

Mahindra, Indira
Mehrotra, Arvind Krishna

India-Singapore

Prathap, G(angan)

India-United Republic of Tanzania

Thomas, A. M.

India-Tibet

Dalai Lama

India-Uganda

Tharu, Susie

India-USA

Ashman, Anastasia M.
Halpern, Jake
Saraf, Sujit

Indonesia

Lewis, Richard

Indonesia-Canada-India

Choudhury, Masudul Alam

Indonesia-USA

Bacon, Charlotte
Darling, Diana
James, Jamie

Iran

Atabaki, Touraj
Ebadi, Shirin
Ganji, Akbar
Kiarostami, Abbas
Mandanipour, Shahriar
Najmabadi, Afsaneh
Perez, Sofia A(na)
Shakoori, Ali
Soroush, Abdolkarim
Taheri, Amir

Iran-Australia

Ghahramani, Zarah

Iran-England

de Bellaigue, Christopher

Iran-USA

Monshipouri, Mahmood

Iraq

Riverbend

Ireland

Adams, Gerry
Allen, Kieran

3626

Andrews, Elmer
Bacik, Ivana
Banville, John
Bew, Paul Anthony
Binchy, Maeve
Boland, Eavan (Aisling)
Bolger, Dermot
Bourke, Angela
Brennan, Herbie
Brennan, Sarah Rees
Breslin, Cathy
Burke, James
Butler, Pierce A.
Callanan, Frank
Campbell, Stephen J.
Carroll, Michael
Carson, Ciaran
Carson, Paul
Clear, Caitriona
Collins, Michael
Conlon, Evelyn
Conlon-McKenna, Marita
Connolly, John
Connolly, S(ean) J.
Coogan, Tim(othy) Pat(rick)
Corcoran, Neil (Cornelius)
Cullen, Bill
Curl, James Stevens
Daly, Leo (Arthur)
Darlison, Bill
de Breadun, Deaglan
de Paor, Louis
Devon, Paddie
Doherty, Gillian M.
Donovan, Katie
Doyle, Roddy
Dunlop, Nic
Egan, Desmond
English, Richard Ludlow
Farrell, David M.
Ferriter, Diarmaid
Fitzmaurice, Gabriel
Foster, John Wilson
Friel, Brian
Gatti, Anne
George, Terry
Glynn, Alan
Grehan, Ida
Grenham, John
Hamilton, Hugo
Harmon, Maurice
Harte, Lara
Haverty, Anne
Heaney, Seamus
Higgins, Aidan
Hughes, Declan
Hynes, Pat
Johnston, Jennifer
Keenan, Brian
Kelly, Maeve
Kennedy, Kieran A.
Kennelly, (Timothy) Brendan
Kiernan, Caitlín R(ebekah)
Killeen, Jarlath
Kilroy, Thomas
Kramer, Alan
Langdon, Gabrielle
Longley, Michael
LoPrete, Kimberly A.
Loughlin, James
MacKenna, John

MacWeeney, Alen
Magan, ManchAn
Maher, Mary
Malone, Mary T.
Mathews, Aidan (Carl)
McAuley, James J.
McBride, Robert
Mccaffrey, K. T.
McCarthy, Thomas
McCaughren, Tom
McCormack, Mike
McCormack, W(illiam) J(ohn)
McEldowney, Eugene
McGuckian, Medbh (McCaughan)
Mcmanus, Antonia
Mcmanus, Ruth
McNamee, Eoin
McNutt, Patrick A.
Meade, Glenn
Meehan, Paula
Melling, O.
Merne, Oscar James
Mitchel, Patrick
Morrison, Bill
Moxley, Gina
Mullen, Michael
Murphy, Tom
Nelson, Dorothy
Ní Chuilleanáin, Eiléan
O Cuilleanain, Cormac
O'Brien, George
O'Carroll, Brendan
O'Connor, Pat
O'Doherty, Malachi
O'Driscoll, Dennis
O'Grady, Desmond (James Bernard)
O'grady, Paul
O'Hanlon, Ardal
O'Leary, Don
O'Malley, Padraig
O'Neill, Jamie
O'Neill, Joseph
O'Riordan, Michelle
O'Siadhail, Micheal
O'Toole, Fintan
Ormsby, Frank
Parkinson, Siobhan
Pepper, Andrew
Power, Patrick C.
Price, Victor (Henry John)
Rodgers, Eamonn
Ronan, Frank
Scott, Michael
Sirr, Peter
Smith, Brian
Smyth, William J.
Sweeney, Eamonn
Tóibín, Colm
Troy, Aidan
Tynan, Ronan
Urbainczyk, Theresa
Viney, Ethna
Waddell, Martin
Welch, Robert
Whelan, Ruth
White, Stephen (Leonard)
Williams, Niall
Woods, Macdara
Wynne, Frank

Ireland-Australia

Fitzpatrick, David

Ireland-Canada

Donoghue, Emma
Morash, Christopher
O'Loughlin, Ed

Ireland-England

Adler, Elizabeth
Cronin, Mike
Ellis, Steven G.
Falconer, Helen
Gale, Monica R(achel)
Gaskin, J. C. A.
Graham, Laurie
Greacen, Lavinia
Guinness, Desmond
Hand, Geoffrey Joseph Philip
Hardie, Sean
Huxley, George Leonard
Lawrence, Louise
Lusby, Jim
MacCotter, Paul
Maher, Eamon
McBratney, Sam
Mould, Daphne D. C. Pochin
Myers, Kevin
Nye, Robert
Park, David
Patterson, Glenn
Proudfoot, Lindsay
Roberts, Geoffrey
Summers, Anthony (Bruce)
Tonkin, Elizabeth
Wood, Kieron
York, R. A.

Ireland-England-Germany

Ward, Margaret

Ireland-England-India

Roberts, Daniel Sanjiv

Ireland-England-Sweden

Henning, Ann

Ireland-Germany

Fallon, Peter

Ireland-Hungary

Szakolczai, árpád

Ireland-Scotland

Donovan
Siggins, Lorna
Welsh, Irvine

Ireland-South Africa

Guelke, Adrian

Ireland-USA

Agee, Chris
Clayton, Mary
Donleavy, J(ames) P(atrick)
French, Tana
Harrison, Harry
Kinsella, Thomas
Mallory, J(ames) P(atrick)
Mccoole, Sinéad
Montague, John (Patrick)
Phelan, Tom (Thomas Joseph)
Pinch, Trevor (John)
Stevenson, Jonathan

Ireland-USA-Zambia

Ohlmeyer, Jane H.

Ireland-Wales-Scotland

Napier, Bill

Israel

Aaron, David
Almog, Ruth
Avishai, Bernard
Bar, Shmuel
Bar-Joseph, Uri
Bar-Yosef, Eitan
Baram, Amatzia
Bavly, Dan A(braham)
Beker, Avi
Ben-Ner, Yitzhak
Ben-Yehuda, Nachman
Bergman, Ronen
Bergman, Tamar
Berkovitch, Nitza
Biale, Rachel (Korati)
Bialer, Uri
Biger, Gideon
Bitton-Ashkelony, Brouria
Castel-Bloom, Orly
Cohen, Raymond
Cohen-Shalev, Amir
de-Shalit, Avner
Ehrlich, Uri
El-Or, Tamar
Elad, Amikam
Elizur, Joel
Ellenblum, Ronnie
Ezrahi, Yaron
Falk, Avner
Freedman, Luba
Freudenthal, Gad
Friedmann, Daniel

Friedmann, Yohanan
Gans, Chaim
Gat, Azar
Gelber, Yoav
Gershoni, Israel
Gordon, Neve
Gordon, Rivca
Grosbard, Ofer
Gross, Michael L.
Grossman, David
Halkin, Ariela
Hareven, Gail
Harman, Oren Solomon
Hen, Yitzhak
Himelstein, Shmuel
Izakson, Miron C.
Jackont, Amnon
Ḳamir, Orit
Kashua, Sayed
Katz, Avner
Kenaan, Hagi
Kenaz, Yehoshua
Keret, Etgar
Lampert, Ada
Laskier, Michael M.
Loshitzky, Yosefa
Maoz, Dan
Margalit, Gilad
Matalon, Ronit
Meir, Avinoam
Melman, Billie
Netanyahu, Benjamin
Nevo, Joseph
Nir, Yossi
Ofrat, Gideon
Oved, Yaacov
Pardes, Ilana
Raab, David
Rabinowitz, Dan
Rabinyan, Dorit
Rein, Raanan
Sarna, Igal
Schroeder, Gerald L.
Shahar, Yuval
Shain, Yossi
Shenhav, Yehouda A.
Sher, Gilead
Shiloah, Amnon
Sicher, Efraim
Simon, Uriel
Sluhovsky, Moshe
Sobol, Joshua
Stevens, David
Ullmann-Margalit, Edna
Volkov, Shulamit
Weimann, Gabriel
Yiftachel, Oren

Israel-Argentina

Kacowicz, Arie M.
Menache, Sophia

Israel-Australia

Makler, Irris

Israel-Austria

Avni, Haim
Fahn, Abraham

Israel-Belgium

Ben-Rafael, Eliezer
Vanhuysse, Pieter

Israel-Brazil

Dascal, Marcelo

Israel-Canada

Golomb, Jacob
Halbertal, Tova Hartman

Israel-Canada-England

Hollander, Samuel

Israel-Czech Republic

Bauer, Yehuda

Israel-England

Cohen, Stuart
Gibson, Shimon
Hider, James
Mann, Reva
Rivlin, Paul Anthony
Rose, Norman Anthony
Sharot, Stephen
Vital, David

Israel-England-Germany

Goshen-Gottstein, Esther

Israel-Germany

Hirsch, Seev
Kaufman, Menahem
Zeidner, Moshe

Israel-Germany-USA

Werman, Golda

Israel-Iraq

Moreh, Shmuel

Israel-Ireland

Lentin, Ronit

Israel-Lithuania

Toker, Leona

Israel-Morocco

Illouz, Eva

Israel-Palestine

Gordon, Haim
Raz, Simcha

Israel-Poland

Fishman, Aryei
Frankel, Alona
Gil, Moshe
Hefer, Hayim (Baruch)
Megged, Aharon
Melman, Yossi
Orlev, Uri
Zamir, Israel

Israel-Puerto Rico

Mandel, Miriam B.

Israel-Romania

Gross, Emanuel
Krausz, Ernest

Israel-Russia

Gammer, Moshe
Pines, Ayala Malach
Rubinstein, Isaak
Sheftel, Victor O.
Shemesh, Haim

Israel-Slovakia

Breznitz, Shlomo

Israel-South Africa

Goodman, Hirsh
Herbert, Gilbert

Israel-Switzerland

Brunner, Jose

Israel-USA

Aronson, I(rwin) Michael
Bartov, Omer
Cohen, Jeremy
Cole, Peter

Fallenberg, Evan
Gold, Dore
Green, Jeffrey M.
Kadish, Alon
Katin, Miriam
Katz, David
Kellner, Menachem
Kramer, Martin
Lazin, Fred A.
Levinson, Jay
Negev, Eilat
Oren, Michael B(ornstein)
Porten, Bezalel
Ragen, Naomi
Rubin, Barry
Savir, Uri
Schmidt, Sarah
Schoffman, Nachum
Sharkansky, Ira
Singer, Max
Skinner, Anthony David
Statlander, Jane (B.)
Stow, Kenneth R.
Tal, Alon
Walters, Joel
Zuroff, Efraim

Israel-USA-Hungary

Goldstein, Imre

Italy

Abate, Carmine
Accattoli, Luigi
Ambrosini, Richard
Anati, Emmanuel
Baldassarri, Mario
Baricco, Alessandro
Baruchello, Gianfranco
Bettini, Maurizio
Boitani, Piero
Calasso, Roberto
Calimani, Riccardo
Camon, Ferdinando
Cappellani, Ottavio
Capriolo, Paola
Carabelli, Giancarlo
Casati, Roberto
Charbonnier, Rita
Coarelli, Filippo
Conati, Marcello
Conti, Gregory
Cordelli, Franco
Cotroneo, Roberto
Curatola, Giovanni
D'Adamo, Francesco
Dal Lago, Enrico
de Marinis, Marco
de Medici, Lorenza
de Vecchi, Nicolo
Del Re, Giuseppe
Emmer, Michele
Federico, Giovanni
Galasso, Vincenzo
Ghirardi, G. C.
Gipi
Greco, Lidia

Guarnieri, Carlo
Guarnieri, Patrizia
Gunetti, Daniele
Hey, Jeanne A. K.
Kanaaneh, Rhoda Ann
Kirk, Thomas Allison
Lakhous, Amara
Leoni, Giulio
Loy, Rosetta
Luraghi, Raimondo
Maffi, Mario
Marciano, Francesca
Maurensig, Paolo
Mazzonis, Querciolo Odoardo
Messori, Vittorio
Mingione, Enzo
Monzini, Paola
Orth, Lucia
Pahor, Boris
Palandri, Enrico
Pasti, Umberto
Pazzi, Roberto
Petrucci, Armando
Piersanti, Claudio
Romanelli, Giandomenico
Rylands, Jane Turner
Sarti, Raffaella
Saviano, Roberto
Schaerf, Carlo
Schiavone, Giuseppe
Sesti, Giuseppe Maria
Siliotti, Alberto
Targetti, Ferdinando
Taviani, Paolo
Tornabene, Wanda
Uvalić, Milica
Varzi, Achille C.
Villari, Rosario
Zatti, Sergio

Italy-Australia

Macainsh, Noel Leslie

Italy-Croatia

Zolo, Danilo

Italy-Egypt

Schwarz, Arturo (Samuele)

Italy-England

Burman, Edward
Di Gregorio, Mario A(urelio
   Umberto)
Fitzgerald, Conor
Ginsborg, Paul (Anthony)
Hamilton-Paterson, James
Melchiori, Barbara Arnett
Prantera, Amanda
Spender, Matthew
Tanner, Norman P.
Unsworth, Barry (Forster)

Italy-England-France

Blondel, Jean (Fernand Pierre)

Italy-England-USA

Elegant, Robert (Sampson)

Italy-France

Angela, Alberto
Roy, Olivier

Italy-Germany

Frommel, Christoph Lvitpold
Schneider, Helga

Italy-Guatemala

Masini, Eleonora Barbieri

Italy-India

Dhavamony, Mariasusai

Italy-Nigeria

Arinze, Francis

Italy-Russia

Navrozov, Andrei

Italy-USA

Allen, John L.
Amoia, Alba della Fazia
Anderson, Burton
Christensen, Allan Conrad
de Blasi, Marlena
Gervais, (George) Paul
Grant, Gail Milissa
Mitchell, Mark
Simeti, Mary Taylor
Strelkoff, Tatiana

Jamaica

Chang, Kevin O'Brien
Chin, Staceyann
Cooper, Carolyn (Joy)
Goodison, Lorna (Gaye)

Jamaica-Belgium

Poupeye, Veerle

Jamaica-Cuba

Marley, Rita

Jamaica-England

Constantine-Simms, Delroy
Lennard, John (Chevening)

**Jamaica-Puerto Rico-Trinidad
and Tobago**

Alleyne, Mervyn C.

Jamaica-South Africa

Abrahams, Peter

Jamaica-USA

Kritzler, Ed
Lewis, Rupert

Japan

Akamatsu, Ken
Aoyama, Gosho
Arai, Masami
Funakawa, Atsushi
Gomi, Tarō
Gotō, Junichi
Gyohten, Toyoo
Hirota, Dennis
Iwao, Sumiko
Kanazawa, Satoshi
Katagiri, Yasuhiro
Kumagai, Fumie
Kurokawa, Mitsuhiro
Matsumura, Takao
Miura, Hiroshi
Morimoto, Anri
Murakami, Haruki
Nakayama, Shigeru
Nitto, Tomio
ōe, Kenzaburō
Oiwa, Keibo
Otomo, Katsuhiro
Shiina, Makoto
Suzuki, Akihito
Suzuki, Kōji
Takahashi, Rumiko
Takenaka, Heizo
Terasawa, Mizuho
Thornton, Naoko Fuwa
Toriyama, Akira
Tsushima, Satoko
Urakami, Hiroko
Yabuki, Susumu
Yoshimoto, Banana
Yumoto, Kazumi

Japan-China

Harada, Masako

Japan-England

Iyer, Pico
Peace, David

Japan-Germany

Coulmas, Florian

Japan-Ireland

Fingleton, Eamonn

Japan-Jamaica-Argentina

Smith, Felipe

Japan-USA

Batten, Bruce L.
Groemer, Gerald
Halverson, Cathryn
Kennedy, Rick
Kerr, Alex
Koshiro, Yukiko
Richie, Donald
Sakamoto, Yoshikazu
Savage, Felicity
Schilling, Mark R.
Seward, Robert (Allen)
Whiting, Robert
Wilson, William Scott

Jordan-England

Faqir, Fadia A.M

Jordan-Iraq

Khedairi, Betool

Jordan-Pakistan

Addleton, Jonathan S.

Kenya

Genya, Monica
Hartley, Aidan
Kabira, Wanjiku Mukabi
Leakey, Richard (Erskine Frere)
Odaga, Asenath (Bole)
Ondego, Ogova

Kenya-England

Macgoye, Marjorie Oludhe
Trzebinski, Errol
Wells, Susan (Mary)

Kenya-Italy

Orizio, Riccardo

Kenya-South Africa

Thomson, Jennifer A.

Kenya-Sweden

Aschan, Ulf

Kenya-USA

Moss, Cynthia J(ane)

Korea (South)

Choi, Hyaeweol
Hahm, Sung Deuk
Hwang, Tong-gyu
In-Ho, Choi
Jo, Kyung-Ran
Kim, Byoung-lo Philo
Kim, Chi-Ha
Kim, Hakjoon
Kim, In S(oo)
Minnich, James M.
Park, Jung-Dong
Sok-Kyong, Kang
Tark, Ji-il
Yun, Ch'oe

Korea (South)-Japan

Yu, Miri

Korea (South)-USA

Cho, Margaret
Spaeth, Anthony

Lebanon

Al-Samman, Ghadah
Moussalli, Ahmad S.
Shehadeh, Lamia Rustrum

Lebanon-Lebanon

Khoury, Elias

Lebanon-Palestine

Yārid, Nāzik Sābā

Lebanon-USA

Makdisi, Saree
Meho, Lokman I.

Lithuania

Mango, Karin N.

Macedonia

Jovanovski, Meto

Malaysia

Mok, Esther

Malaysia-New Zealand

Stoddart, Brian

Malta-England

de Bono, Edward (Francis Charles)
Monsarrat, Ann Whitelaw

Mexico

Avalos, Hector
Del Paso, Fernando
del Toro, Guillermo
Fortes (De Leff), Jacqueline
Guillermoprieto, Alma
Jacobs, Barbara
Lara, Maria Pia
Lomnitz, Cinna
Lopez-Lujan, Leonardo
Molina, Silvia
Novaro, María
Solares, Ignacio
Weckmann, Luis
Zaid, Gabriel

Mexico-Argentina

Devalle, Susana B. C.

Mexico-Chile

Lomnitz, Larissa Adler

Mexico-Colombia

Rozo, Marco Antonio Palacios

Mexico-Germany-France

Dussel Peters, Enrique

Mexico-USA

Lopez, Josefina
Schmidt, Samuel

Morocco

Abouzeid, Leila
Mernissi, Fatima
Orban, Christine

Mozambique

Vieira, Sergio

Netherlands

Agutter, Paul S.
Bal, Mieke (Maria Gertrudis)
Bergeijk, Jeroen van
Bergeijk, Peter A.G. van
Blauw, Wim
Bohlmeijer, Arno
Bredero, Adriaan H(endrik)
Chu, Petra ten-Doesschate
Cox, Paul(us)
De Zegher, M. Catherine
Delsen, Lei
Dikötter, Frank
Dorrestein, Renate
Essed, Philomena
Goldschmidt, Tijs
Gommans, Jos J. L
Habers, Walther A(drianus)
Heerma van Voss, Lex
Heertje, Arnold
Hermans, Hubert J. M.
Hoedemaker, Bert
Hüttner, Harry J. M.
Jansen, Marc C.
Janssen, Marian (L. M.)
Jongman, Mariken
Kersenboom, Saskia
Koolhaas, Rem
Kranendonk, Anke
Kuyper, Sjoerd
Levelt, Willem J(ohannes) M(aria)
Luyendijk, Joris
Meijer, Fik
Oosterhuis, Harry
Oostindie, Gert
Peters, Rudolph
Pleij, Herman
Poortinga, Y(pe) H.
Prins, Harald E. L.
Riel, C. B. M. van
Roodenburg, Herman
Rutgers, Leonard Victor
Schipper de Leeuw, W. J. J.
Slomp, Hans
Spierenburg, Pieter (Cornelis)
Spruyt, Hendrik
T Hart, Marjolein C.
Tirion, Wil
van Alphen, Ernst
Van Delden, Maarten
van Den Brink, H(ans) M(aarten)
van der Kooi, Cornelis
Van Der Meer, Ron
van der Toorn, Karel
van Der Ven, Johannes A.
Van Erven, Eugene

Van Ginneken, Jaap
Van Kessel, Ineke
van Ruler, J. A.
Zürcher, Erik-Jan

Netherlands-Belgium

Faure, Michael G.

Netherlands-Canada-USA

Kolko, Joyce

Netherlands-England

Bouquet, Mary (Rose)
Hamilton, Alastair
Odell, Peter R(andon)

Netherlands-Germany

du Bois-Reymond, Manuela

Netherlands-New Zealand

Leroi, Armand Marie

Netherlands-Poland

Cwiertka, Katarzyna J.

Netherlands-Uganda

Isegawa, Moses

Netherlands-USA

Emmerij, Louis (Johan)
Forest, Jim
Goldschneider, Gary
Moser, Benjamin
Phillips, Derek L.
Robles, Harold E.
Schwartz, Gary (David)
Shorto, Russell
Siegal, Nina

New Zealand

Adshead, S(amuel) A(drian) M(iles)
Allen, Pamela (Kay)
Bain, Kenneth (Ross)
Ballantyne, Tony
Batt, Tanya Robyn
Beale, Fleur
Bercovitch, Jacob
Bornholdt, Jenny
Broom, Neil D.
Butler, Dorothy
Byrnes, Giselle

Cambie, R(ichard) C(onrad)
Campbell, Donald E.
Campbell, Ian Barclay
Campbell, Malcolm
Cato, Heather
Chan, Gerald
Cher, Ming
Clark, Paul John Abott
Colquhoun, Glenn
Coney, Sandra
Conway, Rosaleen D.
Cowley, (Cassia) Joy
Cross, Ian (Robert)
Crossan, G(regory) D(ixon)
Crowder, George
Curtis, Richard
Dawes, Gregory W.
de Groen, Alma
Doak, Wade (Thomas)
Dodd, Lynley Stuart (Weeks)
Donald, Robyn Elaine
Duckworth, Marilyn
Duder, Tessa
Duff, Alan
Dyson, John
Else, Barbara
Falkner, Brian
Fausett, David
Francis, Mark
Gallas, John (Edward)
Gänzl, Kurt (Friedrich)
Gee, Maurice (Gough)
Gilbert, Ruth
Gillett, Grant (Randall)
Glen, Frank Grenfell
Gould, Bryan
Grace, Patricia (Frances)
Hall, Roger (Leighton)
Hankin, C(herry) A(nne)
Hawke, Gary Richard
Hill, David
Hood, Lynley (Jane)
Horrocks, Dylan
Ihimaera, Witi
Ireland, Kevin (Mark)
Jackson, Michael (Derek)
Jackson, Richard D(ean) W(ells)
Jackson, William Keith
Jordan, Sherryl
Kasabov, Nikola K(irilov)
Kidman, Fiona (Judith)
King, Jeanette (Margaret)
King, John
Knox, Elizabeth (Fiona)
Knudson, Danny Alan
Lasenby, Jack
Lowe, Helen
Mackenzie, Anna
MacLean, Glynne
Mahy, Margaret
Mail, Audrey Maureen
Manhire, Bill
Marshall, Christopher D(avid)
Marshall, Owen
Mathieson, Donald Lindsay
McAlpine, Rachel (Taylor)
McCauley, Sue
McGregor, Andrew
McNeish, James
Metge, (Alice) Joan
Natusch, Sheila

Nunn, Pamela Gerrish
Opie, Anne
Page, Carl
Paterson, Alistair (Ian Hughes)
Perkins, Emily
Pitt, David Charles
Preston, Ivy (Alice)
Quinn, Pat
Ramsay, Raylene
Randell, Beverley
Robb, James Harding
Salmond, Mary Anne
Sawyer, Cheryl
Scott, Jonathan
Scott, Margaret (Allan Bennett)
Simmons, D(avid) R(oy)
Smither, Elizabeth
Sorrenson, Maurice Peter Keith
Stead, C(hristian) K(arlson)
Taylor, Justin
Taylor, William
Te Awekotuku, Ngahuia
Thompson, Robert Bruce
Trebilco, Paul R.
Turner, Brian (Lindsay)
Von Tunzelmann, G(eorge)
    N(icholas)
Ward, Chrissie
Watson, Jean
Wedde, Ian
Williams, Mark

New Zealand-Australia

Beder, Sharon
Cleveland, Leslie
Curley, Marianne
Davies, Piers Anthony David
Sutherland, Margaret

New Zealand-Canada

Baker, Maureen

New Zealand-China

Young, Antony

New Zealand-England

Bennett, Joe
Boston, Jonathan
Conway, Alan
de Hamel, Joan (Littledale)
Ebbett, Eve
Flenley, John (Roger)
Franklin, Samuel Harvey
Fraser, Conon
Gurr, A(ndrew) J(ohn)
Jagose, Annamarie
Mann, (Anthony) Phillip
McIntyre, W(illiam) David
Montgomery, Maureen E.
Morrow, John
Pollock, Nancy J.
Roddick, Alan

Stupples, Peter (Cecil)
Tarling, (Peter) Nicholas
Taylor, Joan E(lizabeth)
Turner, John Christopher
Waddington, Patrick (Haynes)
Welford, Sue
Wright, Michael J(ohn)

New Zealand-England-Australia

Reay, Barry

New Zealand-England-Ireland

Boyd, Brian (David)

New Zealand-Estonia

Raudkivi, A(rved) J(aan)

New Zealand-France

Dunmore, John

New Zealand-India

Maitra, Priyatosh

New Zealand-USA

Buchanan, Paul G.
Camp, Robert C.
Creegan, Nicola Hoggard
Fischer, Steven R.
Flynn, James Robert
Forster, Michelanne
Hansen-Hill, N. D.
Harlow, Michael
Thomson, Andrew
Wilson, Trevor Gordon

New Zealand-Western Samoa

Wendt, Albert

Nigeria

Adepoju, Aderanti
Adichie, Chimamanda Ngozi
Aguolu, Christian Chukwunedu
Alagoa, Ebiegberi Joe
Alkali, Zaynab
Amadi, Elechi
Ihonvbere, Julius O.
Ike, Vincent Chukwuemeka
Madubuike, Ihechukwu (Chie-
    dozie)
Nkala, Nathan
Ogunyemi, Chikwenye Okonjo
Okoro, Anezi
Okri, Ben

Olowu, (Claudius) Dele
Onwueme, Tess Osonye
Onyeama, Dillibe
Segun, Mabel D.

Nigeria-England

Habila, Helon

Nigeria-India

Gupta, U. S.

Nigeria-USA

Achebe, Chinua

Norway

Bakke, O. M.
Brantenberg, Gerd
Broch, Harald Beyer
Christensen, Lars Saabye
Egeland, Jan
Eriksen, Thomas Hylland
Floegstad, Kjartan
Heidar, Knut (Martin)
Holter, Knut
Leira, Arnlaug
Lia, Brynjar
Lundestad, Geir
Mark, Rebecca
Naguib, Nefissa
Newth, Mette
Petersen, Tore T.
Skarsaune, Oskar
Stjernø, Steinar
Tysdahl, Bjorn Johan
Wikan, Unni

Norway-England

Hannay, Alastair

Norway-Iceland

Hannesson, Rögnvaldur

Norway-Sweden

Hugdahl, Kenneth
Nesbo, Jo

Norway-USA

Cammermeyer, Margarethe
Mauk, David C.

Pakistan

Eteraz, Ali

Hashmi, (Aurangzeb) Alamgir
Hoodbhoy, Pervez
Mueenuddin, Daniyal
Siddiqa, Ayesha

Pakistan-England

Naqvi, H. M.

Pakistan-USA

Khan, Uzma Aslam

Palestine

Amiry, Suad
Ashrawi, Hanan (Mikhail)
Yakhlif, Yahya

Panama

Gorriti, Gustavo

Panama-USA

Sirias, Silvio

Papua New Guinea-Australia

Gridneff, Ilya

Philippines

Eviota, Elizabeth Uy
Schweickart, Patrocinio P.

Philippines-USA

Schumacher, John N(orbert)

Poland

Chwin, Stefan
Czekanowska, Anna
Dzielska, Maria
Kurzydłowski, Krzysztof Jan
Libera, Antoni
Limon, Jerzy
Ostrowski, Jan K.
Paczkowski, Andrzej
Sikorski, Radek (Tomasz)
Sztompka, Piotr
Szymański, Leszek
Szymborska, Wislawa
Wodziński, Marcin
Żygulski, Zdzislaw
Żylicz, Tomasz

Portugal

Barreto, Mascarenhas
Mendes, Pedro Rosa
Pina-Cabral, João de
Pinto, António Costa
Rocha, Luis Miguel

Portugal-England

Allfrey, Anthony
Brebner, Philip
Polley, Judith Anne
Pye, Michael (Kenneth)

Portugal-Mozambique

Rodrigues dos Santos, Jose

Portugal-USA

Zenith, Richard

Puerto Rico

Curet, L. Antonio
Echenique, Alfredo Bryce
Feliciano, Hector
Mendes, Irene Vilar
Montes, Marisa
Valle-Ferrer, Norma

Romania

Cartarescu, Mircea
Machedon, Luminita
Ursu, Liliana

Russia

Alfeyeva, Valeria
Biryukov, Nikolai (Ivanovich)
Borovik, Genrikh (Aviezerovich)
Boym, Svetlana
Braginsky, Vladimir B.
Buida, Yuri
Chernykh, E(vgenij)
  N(ikolaevich)
Dutkina, Galina (Borisovna)
Erofeev, Viktor V.
Kagarlitsky, Boris
Kasparov, Garry (Kimovich)
Kremenyuk, Victor (A.)
Krivich, Mikhail
Latynin, Leonid (Aleksandrovich)
Medvedev, Grigori
Medvedev, Roy (Alexandrovich)
Nefedova, Tatyana
Osokina, Elena A(leksandrovna)
Palazchenko, Pavel
Radzinsky, Ėdvard (Stanislav-
  ovich)
Shvidkovsky, Dimitri
Smeliansky, Anatoly
Stepaniants, Marietta
Ulitskaya, Ludmila

Russia-Australia

Lan'kov, Andreĭ N(ikolaevich)

Russia-Ukraine

Khlevniuk, Oleg V.
Tsipenyuk, Yuri M.
Yaroshinskaya, Alla
Zaslavskaia, Tatiana (Ivanovna)

Russia-USA

Tayler, Jeffrey

Saudi Arabia

Abdel-Magid, Islām Muḥammad
al-Mohaimeed, Yousef

Saudi Arabia-Egypt-Scotland

Hammond, Andrew

Saudi Arabia-England

Lacey, Robert

Scotland

Aitchison, James
Armstrong, John
Arnott, Peter
Bell, Ian Mackay
Bertagna, Julie
Bloxham, Donald
Butlin, Ron
Caldwell, David H(epburn)
Campbell, Rod
Collins, Roger
Conn, Stewart
Cook, James L(ister)
Cormack, Robert J.
Craik, Elizabeth M(ary)
Crawford, Robert
Crowther, Anne
Cumming, Elizabeth (Skeoch)
Dalyell, Tam
Davies, Linda
Davis, Margaret (Thomson)
Donald, Peter (Harry)
Donaldson, Islay (Eila) Murray
Donnachie, Ian
Donnelly, Joe
Donovan, Anne
Downie, R(obert) S(ilcock)
Duncan, A. A. M.
Duncan, Hal
Dunlop, Eileen (Rhona)
Dunn, Douglas (Eaglesham)
Esler, Philip F.
Ferguson, Ron
Forrester, Duncan B(aillie)
Fowler, Alastair (David Shaw)

Frame, Ronald
Fraser, W. Hamish
Grant, Graeme
Grant, James Russell
Gray, Alasdair (James)
Guthrie, Allan
Haig, Kathryn
Hannan, Chris(topher John)
Hansell, Mike
Harris, Robert J.
Harvie, Christopher (Thomas)
Henderson, Meg
Hogg, Patrick Scott
Holloway, Richard (Frederick)
Hood, Stuart (Clink)
Hughes, Gerard J.
Hume, John Robert
Hunter, Mollie
Jauncey, James
Johnston, Ronald
Kassabova, Kapka
Kemp, Martin (John)
Kennedy, A(lison) L.
Kuppner, Frank
La Croix, I(sobyl) F.
Leckie, Ross
Lessnoff, Michael
Lindsay, Frederic
Linklater, Magnus (Duncan)
Low, Shari
Loxley, James
Lynch, Michael
Macaulay, Ronald K. S.
Macgregor, James Murdoch
Macleod, John
Macmillan, (John) Duncan
MacQueen, John
MacQueen, Winifred (Wallace)
Maley, Willy
Marr, Andrew
Marshall, Elizabeth Margaret
Marshall, Rosalind Kay
Martin, Lorna
Martin-Jones, David
Matheson, Ann
Mawdsley, Evan
McDonald, J. I(an) H
McDowell, Lesley
McKay, Ron
McKean, Charles (Alexander)
McKean, Robert B.
McLean, Duncan
McLean, Russel D.
McPhee, Peter
Meikle, William
Miller, William L.
Milne, Lorna
Mitchell, Gillian
Morrison, Grant
Moskowitz, Marina
Parkin, Sara Lamb
Patterson, George N(eilson)
Preda, Alex
Purser, John W(hitley)
Rae, Hugh C(rawford)
Rankin, Ian (James)
Reid, David
Ritchie, Harry
Rodgers, Frank
Roy, Archie E.
Rush, Christopher

Scott, P(aul) H(enderson)
Scott, Tom
Skorupski, John
Smith, Neil
Stevenson, David
Thompson, Francis George
Thomson, Derick S(mith)
Walker, David (Maxwell)
Walls, Ian G.
Watson, Roderick

Scotland-Australia

Austin, M(ichel) M(ervyn)
Cannon, Michael

Scotland-Austria

Jahoda, Gustav

Scotland-Belgium

Willemen, Paul

Scotland-Canada

Gillies, Valerie
Lennon, Joan
Macdonald, Norman Malcolm

Scotland-England

Abbott, Pamela
Allaby, (John) Michael
Atkinson, Kate
Barrow, G. W. S.
Bauckham, Richard J.
Bayley, Peter (Charles)
Bealey, Frank (William)
Bebbington, D(avid) W(illiam)
Bentley, Michael (John)
Braine, David
Bride, Johnny Mack
Brockington, J(ohn) L(eonard)
Bruce, Steve
Close, Ajay
Cooper, Dominic (Xavier)
Coussins, Craig
Cowan, Edward (James)
Dobson, Alan P.
Docherty, Jimmy
Douglas-Hamilton, James Alexander
Eldridge, John E. T.
Fenton, Alexander
Forde, Catherine
Gauldie, Enid Elizabeth
Gaze, R(aymond) Michael
George, Judith W(ordsworth)
Gilmour, David
Glass, Rodge
Glendinning, Miles
Grossmith, Robert (Anthony)
Gunstone, Frank Denby
Hargreaves, John D(esmond)

Harris, Paul
Hely, Sara
Hendry, Diana
Hollis, Edward Christopher Rexworthy
Hutson, Lorna
Jeeves, Malcolm
Jones, D. S.
Keay, John
Keeble, Neil H(oward)
Kelman, James
Kennedy, Gavin
Kenworthy, Brian J(ohn)
Kidd, Colin
Knight, Alanna (Cleet)
Lamont-Brown, Raymond
Lingard, Joan (Amelia)
Low, Robert
Mackenney, Richard
MacKenzie, Donald (Angus)
McAuley, Paul J.
Mulligan, William
Nelson, J. Bryan
Padgett, Stephen
Perry, Anne
Pick, John Barclay
Pilcher, Robin
Pilcher, Rosamunde
Pittock, Joan (Hornby)
Prince, Alison
Rigby, Susan
Roe, Nicholas
Rowling, J(oanne) K.
Runcie, James
Russell, Ronald
Scott, Manda
Shone, Ronald
Simpson, Myrtle Lillias
Smith, Christopher
Smith, Gavin D.
Spear, Hilda D.
Steel, D(avid) R(obert)
Storer, James Donald
Stross, Charles
Sutcliffe, William
Tomkins, Adam
Urwin, Derek W(illiam)
Walsh, P(atrick) G(erard)
Ward, Matthew C.
Wilkie, Pamela
Wormell, Mary
Wright, N. T(om)

Scotland-England-Ireland

Bartlett, Thomas

Scotland-England-Pakistan

Nazir-Ali, Michael

Scotland-England-USA

Bell, Robin

Scotland-Germany

Sim, Dorrith M.
Waugh, Louisa
Weber, Thomas

Scotland-India

Dunlop, Ian (Geoffrey David)
Hare-Duke, Michael (Geoffrey)
Kidd, I(an) G(ray)

Scotland-Ireland

Arthur, Chris
Ruddock, Ted
Urch, Elizabeth

Scotland-Jamaica

Falla, Jonathan

Scotland-Malaysia

Mearns, Richard (James)

Scotland-Malta

Sultana, Donald Edward

Scotland-Myanmar

Donnison, David Vernon

Scotland-Netherlands

Faber, Michel

Scotland-New Zealand

Riach, Alan

Scotland-Sierra Leone

Prickett, Stephen

Scotland-USA

Arter, David
Cogliano, Francis D.
De Groot, Gerard J.
Harris, Deborah Turner
Lynch, Chris
Lynch, Peter S.
Swinfen, Ann

Senegal-Benin

Mbaye, Marietou (Bileoma)

Singapore

Lim, Walter S. H.
Ryan, Barbara
Tan, Sor-hoon
Zakaria, Haji Ahmad

Singapore-Canada-France

Manzoni, Jean-François

Singapore-China

Yeung, Henry Wai-Chung

Singapore-England

Holden, Philip (Joseph)
Powell, Robert

Singapore-France

Lasserre, Philippe

Singapore-Malaysia

Flint, Shamini Mahadevan

Singapore-USA

Davidson, Jamie S.
Harvey, Thomas
Schwarz, Adam

Singapore-USA-China

Bo, Zhiyue

Slovakia

Letnanova, Elena

Slovenia

Caron, Brane Mozetic
Ogrin, Dušan
Petkovšek, Marko
Prap, Lila
zizek, Slavoj

Slovenia-USA

Debeljak, Erica Johnson

Slovenia-Yugoslavia

Velikonja, Mitja

Somalia-Netherlands

Ali, Ayaan Hirsi

South Africa

Anthony, Lawrence
Arkin, Marcus
Brink, André (Philippus)
Cassidy, Michael
Cronin, Jeremy
Daly, Niki
de Gruchy, John W(esley)
Drummond, June
Fitzgerald, Mary Anne
Fourie, Corlia
Geldenhuys, Deon
Gevisser, Mark
Gobodo-Madikizela, Pumla
Gordimer, Nadine
Harris, Dudley Arthur
Heard, Anthony Hazlitt
Hiney, Tom
James, Wilmot G.
Jeffery, Anthea J.
Jooste, Pamela
Kalley, Jacqueline A(udrey)
Kaplan, Jonathan
Langa, Mandla
Mackenzie, Craig
Maloka, Eddy Tshidiso
Mandela, Nelson (Rolihlahla)
Marshall, Adré
Masekela, Hugh
McNulty, Bridget
Meyer, Deon
Mills, Greg
Nasson, Bill
Nyamnjoh, Francis B.
Seed, Jenny
Shain, Milton
Shell, Robert C.H
Simpson, Michael Andrew
Stein, Dan J(oseph)
Trollip, Stanley R.
Tutu, Desmond M(pilo)
van Heerden, Etienne
van Onselen, Charles
Walton, James
Watson, Stephen

South Africa-Australia

McDonnell, Kevin Lee
Sobott-Mogwe, Gaele

South Africa-England

Bickford-Smith, Vivian

South Africa-Ireland

Hope, Christopher (David Tully)

South Africa-Nigeria

Udjo, Eric O.

South Africa-Scotland

May, Wynne

South Africa-Scotland-USA

Lass, Roger

South Africa-Switzerland

Horn, Mike

South Africa-USA

Chidester, David
Coplan, David B.

South Africa-USA-Ireland

Nixon, Rob

South Africa-Zimbabwe

Mackenzie, Jassy
Mares, Theun
Nell, Victor

Spain

Alonso, Eric Frattini
Atxaga, Bernardo
Baulenas, Lluís-Anton
Carranza, Andreu
Cercas, Javier
Codina, Carles
Colinas, Antonio
Cooke, Lynne
Cunill, Onofre Martorell
Davis, Rocio G.
Fanés, Fèlix
Fernandez-Shaw, Carlos M(anuel)
Ferreiro, Carmen
Gala (Y Velasco), Antonio
García, Laura Gallego
García-Castañón, Santiago
Gimferrer, Pere
Gonzalez-Balado, Jose Luis
Joven, Enrique
Loriga, Ray
Marias, Javier
Mayor, Federico
Monzó, Quim
Moro, Javier
Oliver, Maria Antònia
Piñol, Albert Sánchez
Quesada, Roberto
Rivas, Manuel
Salazar, Carles
Soto, Hernando de
Usabiaga (Ibáñez), Carlos
Valle, Teresa Del

Vallvey, Ángela
Vargas Llosa, (Jorge) Mario
  (Pedro)

Spain-Austria

Gallhofer, Irmtraud N(ora)

Spain-England

Jeffries, Roderic
Losada (Goya), Jose Manuel
Taylor, Andy

Spain-France

Reza, Yasmina

Spain-Ireland

Gibson, Ian
Nash, Mary
Polland, Madeleine A(ngela)

Spain-Sweden

Sewell, Kitty

Spain-Uruguay

Piven, Hanoch

Spain-USA

Baez, Annecy
Beneria, Lourdes
Geer, Charlie
Hall, David C.
Pfister, Patrick
Richardson, Paul

Spain-USA-England

Kamen, Henry

Sri Lanka

Goonetilleke, D. C. R. A.

Sweden

Adler, Niclas
Adolphson, Mikael S.
Åkerman, Susanna (Kristina)
Alvtegen, Karin
Burman, Carina
Cederlund, Johan
Christianson, Sven-Åke
Enquist, Per Olov
Erikson, Robert

Eriksson, Kjell
Fioretos, Aris
Florby, Gunilla
Fogelmark, Staffan
Frimansson, Inger
Gardell, Mattias
Grenholm, Cristina
Guillou, Jan
Guo, Xiaolin
Hamilton, Carl
Hellström, Börge
Ingves, Gunilla
Jonsson, Lars O(ssian)
Klingberg, Torkel
Lewin, Leif
Lindbeck, (K.) Assar (E.)
Lindberg, Staffan I.
Lindenbaum, Pija
Lindgren, Barbro
Mautner, Thomas
Mazetti, Katarina
Mörner, Magnus
Näaslund, Göorel Kristina
Nilsson, Per
Norén, Lars
Ranstorp, Magnus
Roslund, Anders
Schoenhals, Michael
Schyffert, Bea
Sellerberg, Ann Mari
Sjostrand, Sven-Erik
Sonnevi, Göran
Svallfors, Stefan
Svartvik, Jan
Svartvik, Jesper
Theorell, (Per Gunnar) Toeres
Theorin, Johan
Thormählen, Marianne
Törnqvist, Egil
Wästberg, Per

Sweden-Croatia

Drakulić, Slavenka

Sweden-England

Duns, Jeremy

Sweden-Finland

Ruin, Hans

Sweden-Germany

Herrmanns, Ralph
Holtorf, Cornelius

Sweden-Ghana

Yamba, C(hristian) Bawa

Sweden-Hungary

Klein, George

Sweden-Iceland

Jonasdottir, Anna G(udrun)

Sweden-Norway

Lithman, Yngve Georg

Sweden-Slovakia

Hudak, Michal

Sweden-USA

Alsenas, Linas
Beach, Hugh

Switzerland

Bovon, François
Gasser, Urs
Graeub, Ralph
Guggenbühl, Allan
Hacke, Daniela Alexandra
Häusler, Thomas
Keller, Laurent
Luz, Ulrich
Maechler, Stefan
Mugny, Gabriel
Nihan, Christophe
Ott, Thomas
Otto, Beatrice K.
Peeters, Frederik
Plesch, Veronique Brigitte
Ramadan, Tariq
Sherwin, Michael S.
Stamm, Peter
Thevoz, Michel
von Zelewsky, Alexander
Wegmann, Peter

Switzerland-Austria

Hackl, Erich
Szpiro, George G.

Switzerland-Canada

Esterhammer, Angela

Switzerland-China

Han Suyin
Xiang, Lanxin

Switzerland-England

Liebich, Andre

Switzerland-France

Jacq, Christian

Switzerland-Germany

Ghose, Indira
Joppke, Christian
Michaelowa, Axel
Rödl, Sebastian
Zangger, Eberhard

Switzerland-Hungary

Szalay, Miklós

Switzerland-Italy

Schnitter, Nicholas J.

Switzerland-Poland

Zanussi, Krzysztof

Switzerland-Scotland

McCarey, Peter

Switzerland-South Africa

Harries, Patrick

Switzerland-USA

Benedict, Philip (Joseph)
Epping, Randy Charles
Hardt, Michael
Nelson, D-L. Lane
Rasanayagam, Angelo
Rosenbaum, Benjamin
Scarry, Huck
Smith, Craig
Stern, Daniel N.
Stevenson, Matthew
Wagner, Daniel
Warner, Daniel

Switzerland-Wales

Crowley-Milling, Michael C.

Switzerland-Zimbabwe

Gappah, Petina

Syrian Arab Republic

Al-Azm, Sadik J.
Shaaban, Bouthaina

Taiwan

Chang, Joan Chiung-huei
Chu, Tien-wen
Huang, Ch
Huang, Chun-chieh
Lee, Ang
Wu, Chin-Tao

Taiwan-USA

Katz, Paul R.
Keevak, Michael
Lee, Chin-Chuan

United Republic of Tanzania

Devji, Faisal Fatehali
Gardella, Robert (P.)

Thailand

Chia, Mantak
Phongpaichit, Pasuk
Radzienda, Tom
Vejjajiva, Jane

Thailand-Sweden

Lintner, Bertil

Tibet-USA

Gelek, Ngawang

Trinidad and Tobago

Anthony, Michael
Baldeosingh, Kevin
Carrington, Roslyn
Jordan, Alma Theodora
Lovelace, Earl
Nepaulsingh, Colbert I(vor)

Turkey

Aksin, Sina
Altun, Selcuk
Ener, Güner
Heper, Metin
Kalpakli, Mehmet
Kohn, Edward P.
Matur, Bejan
Sen, Zekai
Somel, Selcuk Akscin

Uganda

Kaguri, Twesigye Jackson

Uganda-USA

Burkey, Stan

Ukraine

Alexseev, Mikhail A.
Kuznetsov, Nickolaj

Ukraine-England-Poland

Bartoszewski, Wladyslaw T(eofil)

Ukraine-USA

Mycio, Mary

United States

Aaland, Mikkel
Aamodt, Donald
Aamodt, Michael G.
Aaron, Chester
Aaron, James E.
Abajian, Kathryn J.
Abbott, Hailey
Abbott, Karen
Abbott, Lynn
Abbott, Tony
Abel, Emily K.
Aberjhani
Abildskov, Marilyn
Abinader, Elmaz
Ablard, Jonathan D.
Ablow, Keith Russell
Abraham, A(ntoine) J.
Abraham, Spencer
Abrahams, Peter
Abramo, J(oe) L.
Abrams, Douglas Carl
Abrams, Douglas Carlton
Abrams, Judith Z.
Abrams, Linsey
Abrams, M(eyer) H(oward)
Abrams, Nita
Abramson, Bruce
Abramson, Leslie W.
Abresch, Peter E.
Abshire, David Manker
Abt, Jeffrey
Abu El-Haj, Nadia
Abu-Jaber, Diana
Abu-Lughod, Lila
AbuKhalil, As'ad
Abzug, Robert Henry
Accawi, Anwar F.
Achenbach, Joel
Acheson, David C(ampion)
Ackelsberg, Martha A.
Acker, James R.
Ackerly, Brooke A.
Ackerman, Diane
Ackerman, James D.
Ackerman, James S(loss)
Ackerman, Jennifer G.
Ackerman, Michael J.
Ackerman, Susan Yoder
Ackland, Len

Ackmann, Martha (A.)
Acuff, Jerry
Adair, Aaron J.
Adair, Vivyan Campbell
Adamchak, Raoul W.
Adamec, Christine
Adams, Abby
Adams, C. T.
Adams, Carol J.
Adams, Charles J.
Adams, Colin C.
Adams, Deborah
Adams, Gerald R.
Adams, Hazard
Adams, Jerome R(obertson)
Adams, John
Adams, John A.
Adams, John Coolidge
Adams, Kathleen M(arie)
Adams, Lorraine
Adams, Marilyn Jager
Adams, Marilyn McCord
Adams, Mark
Adams, Mike S.
Adams, Patch
Adams, Robert Merrihew
Adams, Scott
Adams, Sheila Kay
Adams, Timothy Dow
Adams, William James
Adamson, M(ary) J(o)
Adamz-Bogus, S. Diane
Addington, Larry Holbrook
Addison, Linda D.
Addonizio, Kim (Theresa)
Adell, Sandra
Adelman, Clifford
Adelman, Deborah
Adelson, Alan
Adelson, Roger
Adickes, Sandra
Adiele, Faith
Adler, David A.
Adler, Jeffrey S(cott)
Adler, Patricia A.
Adler, Peter
Adler, Richard
Adler, Stephen J.
Adlerman, Danny
Adlerman, Kimberly M.
Adoff, Arnold
Adoff, Jaime
Affron, Charles
Afong, Milo S.
Agassi, Andre Kirk
Agee, Jonis
Aggarwal, Ravina
Agich, George J.
Agins, Teri
Agnew, Eleanor
Agonito, Rosemary
Agran, Edward G.
Agrawal, Arun
Aguirre, Forrest
Ahearn, (Edward) Allen
Ahearn, Patricia
Ahlgren, Gillian T. W.
Ahlquist, Dale
Ahrons, Constance (Ruth)
Ahuja, Sunil
Aidells, Bruce

Aidinoff, Elsie V.
Aizley, Harlyn
Akarli, Engin Deniz
Akera, Atsushi
Akerlof, George A.
Akins, Ellen
Akst, Daniel
Alama, Pauline J.
Alan, Theresa
Alarcon, Daniel
Alarcon, Francisco X.
Alaya, Flavia
Albanese, Laurie Lico
Albarella, Joan K.
Alber, Charles J.
Albert, Michael
Albert, Michael
Albert, Neil
Albert, Steve
Albert, Susan Wittig
Alberts, Laurie
Albom, Mitch
Albrecht, Ernest (Jacob)
Albrecht, Gary L(ouis)
Albrecht, Gloria H.
Albrecht, Steve
Alchon, Suzanne Austin
Alcosser, Sandra (B.)
Alden, Edward H.
Alden, Patricia
Alder, Ken(neth L.)
Alderman, Ellen
Aldous, Richard
Aldrete, Gregory S.
Aldrich, Mark
Aldridge, Delores P(atricia)
Aleshire, Peter
Alessandra, Tony
Alexander, Adele Logan
Alexander, Ann Field
Alexander, Caroline
Alexander, Elizabeth
Alexander, Floyce
Alexander, Gary
Alexander, Greg
Alexander, Harriet Semmes
Alexander, Jeff
Alexander, Jeffrey C(harles)
Alexander, Jennifer Karns
Alexander, John Thorndike
Alexander, Joseph H(ammond)
Alexander, Ruth M.
Alexander, Sally Hobart
Alexander, Victoria N.
Alexie, Sherman (Joseph)
Alfino, Mark (R.)
Alford, Kenneth D.
Algeo, John
Ali, Saleem H.
Ali, Shahrazad
Aliber, Robert Z(elwin)
Alinder, Mary Street
Alkebulan, Paul
Alkon, Paul K.
Allcorn, Seth
Allegretto, Michael
Allen, Ann Taylor
Allen, Craig M(itchell)
Allen, Dean
Allen, Dick
Allen, Diogenes

Allen, Edward (Hathaway)
Allen, Jeffner
Allen, John Jay
Allen, Justin
Allen, Laura Jean
Allen, Michael Patrick
Allen, Myron B.
Allen, Nancy
Allen, Nancy Kelly
Allen, Patricia
Allen, Philip M(ark)
Allen, Preston L.
Allen, Richard William
Allen, Roberta
Allen, Ronald J.
Allen, Samuel W.
Allen, Sarah Addison
Allen, William Sheridan
Allen, Woody
Allgood, Myralyn F(rizzelle)
Allie, Scott
Alligood, Kathleen T.
Allington, Maynard
Allison, Amy
Allison, Dale C.
Allison, Henry E(dward)
Allison, Jennifer
Allison, Robert J.
Allison, Will
Allston, Aaron
Allyn, Doug
Allyn, Pam
Aloff, Mindy
Alofsin, Anthony
Alpert, Mark
Alphin, Elaine Marie
Als, Hilton
Alschuler, William R.
Alsdorf, Debbie
Alson, Peter (H.)
Alt, Betty Sowers
Alten, Steve
Alter, Judy
Alter, Robert B.
Alterman, Eric (Ross)
Alterman, Glenn
Altheide, David L.
Alther, Lisa
Altman, Mara
Altoff, Gerard T(homas)
Altschuler, Glenn C.
Alvarado, Lisa
Alvarez, Julia
Alvarez, Rafael
Alvarez, Walter
Alvis, Robert E.
Amaki, Amalia K.
Amann, Janet
Amar, Akhil Reed
Amato, Carol A.
Amato, Mary
Amato, Theresa Ann
Ambaras, David Richard
Ambrose, Bonnie Holt
Amburn, Ellis
Amend, Allison
Ames, Christopher
Ames, Greg
Ames, Jonathan
Ames, Kenneth L.
Amick, Steve

Ammerman, Nancy T(atom)
Amos, James H.
Amsden, David
Amster-Burton, Matthew
Amussen, Susan Dwyer
Amyx, Jennifer A.
Anania, Michael (Angelo)
Anastas, Benjamin
Anaya, Rudolfo A(lfonso)
Ancelet, Barry Jean
Ancona, George
Ande, Jan Lee
Anderegg, David
Anders, Charlie
Anders, Isabel
Anders, Leslie
Andersen, Kurt Byars
Andersen, Martin Edwin
Anderson, Amanda
Anderson, Annelise Graebner
Anderson, Barth
Anderson, Brian C.
Anderson, David
Anderson, David Daniel
Anderson, Donna K.
Anderson, Doug Douglas
Anderson, Douglas A(llen)
Anderson, Duane
Anderson, Elijah
Anderson, Elizabeth (S.)
Anderson, Fil
Anderson, Gary L.
Anderson, H(ugh) George
Anderson, Henry L(ee Norman)
Anderson, James G.
Anderson, Jeffrey E.
Anderson, Joanne M.
Anderson, John B(ayard)
Anderson, Judy
Anderson, Kent
Anderson, Kevin J(ames)
Anderson, Lars
Anderson, Lauri (Arvid)
Anderson, M. T(obin)
Anderson, Margaret Jean
Anderson, Marilyn D.
Anderson, Mark M.
Anderson, Maureen
Anderson, Molly D(elCarmen)
Anderson, Richard Lloyd
Anderson, Sheila E.
Anderson, Sheryl J.
Anderson, Terry (A.)
Anderson, Virginia DeJohn
Anderson, Wilda (Christine)
Anderson, William Louis
Andes, Karen
Andoe, Joe
Andre, Judith
Andreas, Peter
Andrejevic, Mark
Andrew, Joseph J(erald)
Andrews, Andy
Andrews, George Reid
Andrews, Helena
Andrews, Kenneth T.
Andrews, Nin
Andrews, Sam S.
Andrews, Sarah
Andrews, Thomas G.
Andrews, Walter G.

Andrews, William L(eake)
Andrus, Hyrum Leslie
Andrus, Jeff
Andryszewski, Tricia
Anelli, Melissa
Angel, Ann
Angell, Roger
Angelou, Maya
Angle, Kurt
Anglin, Patty
Angus, Christopher (K.)
Annerino, John
Annis, Barbara
Ansa, Tina McElroy
Ansay, A. Manette
Ansberry, Clare
Ansel, Talvikki
Anshaw, Carol
Anthes, Richard A.
Anthony, Crystal McCrary
Anthony, Joseph Patrick
Anthony, Patricia
Anthony, Ted
Antieau, Kim
Antler, Joyce
Antol, Marie Nadine
Anton, Maggie
Anton, Ted
Antonetta, Susanne
Antonette, Leslie
Antoni, Brian
Antrim, Donald
Antrim, Taylor
Anunobi, Fredoline O.
Apel, Dora
Aponte, Harry J.
Appell, Scott D.
Appelt, Kathi
Apple, Hope
Apple, Max (Isaac)
Apple, Rima D.
Apple, Sam
Applebome, Peter
Applegate, Katherine (Alice)
Appleman, Philip (Dean)
Appleton, Sheldon Lee
Applewhite, James
Appy, Christian G.
Apter, Andrew
Apter, Emily (S.)
Aptheker, Bettina
Araton, Harvey
Archer, Chalmers
Arellano, Gustavo
Arellano, Juan Estevan
Arens, Katherine (Marie)
Argers, Helen
Argiri, Laura
Arico, Santo L.
Ariely, Dan
Arkin, William M.
Arkush, Michael
Arluke, Arnold
Armantrout, (Mary) Rae
Armbruster, Ann
Armistead, John
Armstead, Joseph
Armstrong, Alan
Armstrong, Alan
Armstrong, Alexandra
Armstrong, Bob

Armstrong, Heather B.
Armstrong, Jennifer
Armstrong, Lori G.
Armstrong, Mary (Elizabeth)
    Willems
Armstrong, Richard
Armstrong, Richard B(yron)
Armstrong, Robert Laurence
Armstrong, Thomas Leigh
Arneson, Erik
Arnett, Ronald C.
Arnold, A(lbert) James
Arnold, Eleanor
Arnold, Elizabeth
Arnold, Jennifer
Arnold, Kenneth L.
Arnold, Oliver
Arnold, Peter
Arnold, Tedd
Arnzen, Michael A.
Aron, Michael
Aronie, Nancy S(lonim)
Aronoff, Craig E(llis)
Aronowitz, Stanley
Aronson, Sarah
Arrington, Stephen L(ee)
Arrow, Kenneth (Joseph)
Arruda, Suzanne M.
Arsenault, Raymond
Artell, Mike
Arterburn, Stephen
Arthur, W. Brian
Aruri, Naseer H.
Arvey, Michael
Arvigo, Rosita
Arvin, Reed
Asante, Molefi K.
Ascher, Barbara Lazear
Ascher, Marcia
Ascoli, Peter Max
Ash, Constance (Lee)
Ash, Jennifer
Ash, Stephen V.
Ashabranner, Melissa
Ashbery, John (Lawrence)
Ashby, Franklin C.
Ashby, Ruth
Asher, Catherine B.
Asher, Sandy
Ashley, Leonard R. N.
Ashliman, D. L.
Ashton, Dianne
Ashton, Dore
Ashworth, (Lewis) William
Ashworth, Heidi
Asim, Jabari
Asimov, Janet Jeppson
Asimow, Michael
Askew, Thomas A(delbert)
Asner, Jules
Asquith, Christina
Astell, Ann W.
Athas, Daphne
Atkin, Flora B.
Atkins, Charles
Atkins, E. Taylor
Atkins, Russell
Atkinson, Elizabeth Jane
Atkinson, Michael (J.)
Atlas, James (Robert)
Atlas, Nava

Atwill, David G.
Atwood, Craig D.
Atwood, William G(oodson)
Aubert, Alvin
Auch, Mary Jane
Auel, Jean M(arie)
Auerbach, Kimberlee
Auerbach, Loyd
Auerbach, Michael
Augenbraum, Harold
Augustine, Dolores L.
Auiler, Dan Rose
Aune, James Arnt
Auseon, Andrew
Auslander, Shalom
Auster, Paul
Austerlitz, Paul
Austin, Curtis J.
Austin, Dan
Austin, Jeannette Holland
Austin, Linda Marilyn
Austin, Paul
Austin, Robyn M.
Autry, Curt
Avakian, Arlene Voski
Avant, Deborah D.
Avella, Steven M.
Avery, Evelyn
Avery, Fiona Kai
Avery, Kevin J.
Avery, Martha
Avi
Avila, Eric
Avise, John C.
Avolio, Bruce J.
Avorn, Jerry
Avramides, Anita
Awe, Susan C.
Awiakta, Marilou
Awret, Irene
Axelrod, Amy
Axelrod, Mark (R.)
Ayala, Francisco J.
Ayers, William
Aylesworth, Jim
Ayres, E. C.
Ayres, Mary Jo
Ayres, Thomas (R.)
Azriel, Yakov
Baas, Jacquelynn
Baatz, Simon
Babb, Valerie (Melissa)
Babbitt, Natalie
Babich, Babette E.
Baca, Ana
Bach, David
Bache, Ellyn
Bachman, W(illiam) Bryant
Bacho, Peter
Bachorz, Pam
Bachrach, Nancy
Backer, Sara
Backes, David James
Backscheider, Paula R(ice)
Backus, George Edward
Bacon, David
Bacon, Donald C(onrad)
Badgley, John Herbert
Badillo, David A.
Baechle, Thomas R.
Baehr, Kingsley M.

Baer, Greg
Baer, Richard K.
Bageant, Joe
Bagert, Brod
Bagge, Peter (Christian Paul)
Baggett, Jennifer
Baggini, Julian
Baggott, Julianna
Bagley, Mary (C.)
Bahlmann, Shirley
Bahr, Alice Harrison
Bahr, Robert
Baicker-Mckee, Carol
Bailey, Blake
Bailey, Charles Waldo
Bailey, F(rancis) Lee
Bailey, Jerry
Bailey, Julius H.
Bailey, Kathleen C.
Bailey, Kathryn
Bailey, Lee W.
Bailey, Len
Bailey, Maria T.
Bailey, Martha (J.)
Bailey, Michael D.
Bailey, Nancy Fayrweather
Bailey, Norman (Alishan)
Bailey, Peter J.
Bailey, Robin W(ayne)
Bailey, Roz
Bailey-Williams, Nicole
Bailie, Grant
Bain, David Haward
Bain, Trevor
Bair, Deirdre
Baird, Brian J.
Baird, Vanessa A.
Baitz, Jon Robin
Baker, Barbara
Baker, Calvin
Baker, Christina Looper
Baker, Christopher W.
Baker, Deb
Baker, Ellen
Baker, Elna
Baker, John F.
Baker, Kevin (Breen)
Baker, Kyle
Baker, Larry
Baker, Lise S.
Baker, Lori
Baker, Mark
Baker, Nena
Baker, Paul R(aymond)
Baker, Raymond W.
Baker, Raymond William
Baker, Richard A(llan)
Baker, Richard E.
Baker, Rosalie F.
Baker, Russell (Wayne)
Baker, Sharlene
Baker, Stephen
Baker, Stuart Eddy
Baker, Susan P.
Baker, Tom
Baker, William
Baker-Cristales, Beth
Bakken, Kerry Neville
Bakker, Robert T.
Balaji, Murali
Balbirer, Nancy

Balbo, Ned Clark
Balch, James F.
Baldasty, Gerald J.
Balderston, Daniel
Baldwin, Frank
Baldwin, John
Baldwin, Rosecrans
Bale, Don
Bales, Richard F.
Balester, Valerie M.
Balian, Lorna
Ball, Angela
Ball, Donna Rochelle
Ball, Edward
Ball, Gordon
Ball, Karen
Ball, Terence
Ballard, John R.
Ballard, Michael B.
Ballard, Terry
Ballendorf, Dirk Anthony
Ballentine, Lee (Kenney)
Balliett, Blue
Balling, Robert C.
Balmer, Randall (Herbert)
Balswick, Judith K.
Balter, Dave
Balz, Dan
Balzo, Sandra
Bambach, Carmen C.
Banash, Stan
Banazek, Jeanne M. (Carpenter)
Banbury, Jen(nifer Marie)
Bandarage, Asoka
Bandelin, Oscar J.
Bando, Mark
Bang, Molly Garrett
Bang-Campbell, Monika
Bangs, Nina
Banish, Roslyn
Banker, James R.
Banker, Mark T(ollie)
Banks, Geraldine
Banks, Leanne
Banks, Russell (Earl)
Banner-Haley, Charles T.
Bannon, David Race
Bansemer, Roger
Banta, Trudy W.
Baofu, Peter
Baptist, Edward (E.)
Baracchi, Claudia
Baraka, Imamu Amiri
Barakat, Ibtisam
Barasch, Frances K.
Barash, David P(hilip)
Barash, Samuel T.
Baratta, Joseph Preston
Baratz-Logsted, Lauren
Barbarese, J. T.
Barbas, Samantha
Barbash, Shepard
Barbash, Tom
Barbato, Joseph
Barber, Benjamin R(eynolds)
Barber, Charles
Barber, David
Barber, E(lizabeth) J. W(ayland)
Barber, Lucy G(race)
Barber, Paul (Thomas)
Barber, Phyllis (Nelson)

Barber, Ronde
Barbieri, Elaine
Barbieri-Low, Anthony J.
Barbour, John D.
Barclay, Donald A.
Bard, Mitchell G.
Barden, Dan
Barden, Thomas
Bardige, Betty S.
Bardsley, Michele
Bardwick, Judith M(arcia)
Barer, Burl (Roger)
Barer, Helen
Barfield, Rhonda
Barfield, Woodrow
Barham, Patte B.
Barich, Bill
Barilleaux, Ryan J.
Barish, Evelyn
Barkan, Joanne
Barkan, Josh
Barker, M. P.
Barkow, Al
Barks, Coleman Bryan
Barlett, Peggy F.
Barley, Janet Crane
Barlow, Aaron
Barlow, Tani E.
Barlow, William
Barlowe, Raleigh (Bruce)
Barlowe, Wayne Douglas
Barmack, Erik S.
Barmann, Lawrence (Francis)
Barmash, Pamela
Barnard, Judith
Barnes, Annie S.
Barnes, Burton V(erne)
Barnes, Fred Wood
Barnes, H. Lee
Barnes, James J.
Barnes, Jay
Barnes, Jennifer Lynn
Barnes, John (Allen)
Barnes, Joyce Annette
Barnes, Linda (Joyce Appelblatt)
Barnes, Linda L.
Barnes, Lynard
Barnes, Peter
Barnes, Samuel Henry
Barnett, Cynthia
Barnett, Matthew
Barnett, Michael N.
Barnett, Sloan
Barnett, Victoria (Joan)
Barnette, Martha
Barnhart, David K.
Barnhart, Terry A.
Barnhill, David Landis
Barnosky, Anthony D.
Barnum, Barbara (J.) Stevens
Barnwell, Tim
Barnwell, William (Curtis)
Barolini, Helen
Baron, Beth
Baron, Kathi
Baron, Mike
Baron, Naomi S(usan)
Barone, Joe
Barot, Rick
Barr, Alwyn
Barr, Donald A.

Barr, Gonzalo
Barr, Nevada
Barr, Sheldon
Barr, Stephen M.
Barra, Allen
Barranger, Milly S(later)
Barratt, Iris K.
Barre, Richard
Barreca, Regina
Barrett, Andrea
Barrett, Buckley Barry
Barrett, David M(arshall)
Barrett, James R.
Barrett, John G(ilchrist)
Barrett, Joyce Durham
Barrett, Nancy Smith
Barrett, Tracy
Barrie, Thomas (Matthew)
Barrish, Phillip
Barron, Judy
Barron, Laird
Barron, Stephanie
Barron, T. A.
Barron-Tieger, Barbara
Barry, Dave
Barry, James P(otvin)
Barry, John M.
Barry, Michael
Barry, Robert Everett
Barry, Susan R.
Barry, Tom
Barsamian, David
Bart, Michael
Bartell, Karen Hulene
Bartels, Larry M.
Barth, John (Simmons)
Barth, Kelly L.
Barth, Robert Lawrence
Barthelme, Frederick
Barthelme, Steve(n)
Bartholet, Elizabeth
Bartholomew-Feis, Dixee R.
Bartky, Sandra Lee
Bartlett, Jennifer Losch
Bartlett, L. L.
Bartlett, Sarah
Bartoletti, Susan Campbell
Bartolomeo, Joseph F(rancis)
Barton, (Samuel) Wayne
Barton, Carlin A.
Barton, Dan
Bartz, Albert
Baruch, Elaine Hoffman
Baruth, Philip Edward
Barzak, Christopher
Basch, Rachel
Bascomb, Neal
Bash, Frank N(ess)
Bashe, Philip (Scott)
Basinger, Jeanine (Deyling)
Basinski, Michael
Bass, Cynthia
Bass, Diana Butler
Bass, Gary J.
Bass, Harold F.
Bass, Jack
Bass, Paul
Bass, Ronald
Bass, T. J.
Bass, Thomas A.
Bassett, Elizabeth

Basso, Keith H(amilton)
Bassoff, Evelyn S(ilten)
Basu, Alaka Malwade
Baswell, Christopher
Baszile, Jennifer Lynn
Bat-Ami, Miriam
Batali, Mario
Bateman, Robert L.
Bateman, Tracey V.
Bates, Craig D.
Bates, Karen Grigsby
Bateson, Mary Catherine
Bath, K. P.
Batnitzky, Leora
Batory, Joseph P.
Battenfield, Jackie
Battestin, Martin Carey
Battle, Michael Jesse
Battle, Richard V.
Battles, Brett
Battles, Matthew
Baucom, Donald R.
Bauer, Caroline Feller
Bauer, Douglas
Bauer, Marion Dane
Bauer, Susan Wise
Bauer, Tricia
Bauerlein, Mark (Weightman)
Bauermeister, Erica
Bauerschmidt, Frederick Christian
Baughman, John Russell
Baughman, Michael
Baughman, T. H.
Bauman, Beth Ann
Bauman, Bruce
Bauman, Christian
Bauman, Richard
Baumann, Carol Edler
Baumbach, Jonathan
Baumgardner, Jennifer
Baumgartner, Frank R.
Baumol, William J.
Baums, Roosevelt
Baumslag, Naomi
Baur, Gene
Bausch, Richard
Bausell, R. Barker
Bausum, Ann
Baxter, Mary Lynn
Baxter, Paula A.
Bay, Jeanette Graham
Bayda, Ezra
Bayer, William
Baylis, Janice H(inshaw)
Bayme, Steven
Baynes, Kenneth R(ichard)
Bazell, Josh
Bazzoni, Jana O'Keefe
Beachy, Kyle
Beagle, Peter S(oyer)
Beagley, Brenda E.
Beahrs, Andrew
Beal, Timothy
Beall, Anne E.
Beaman, Joyce Proctor
Bean, Gregory (K.)
Bean, Jonathan J.
Bear, Elizabeth
Bear, Greg(ory Dale)
Bear, Ray A. Young
Bearanger, Marie

Beard, Darleen Bailey
Beard, Jo Ann
Beard, Patricia
Beard, Philip
Bearden, Milton
Beardslee, Karen E.
Beardsley, Theodore S.
Bearman, Peter
Beary, Michael J.
Beaser, Richard S.
Beasley, Bruce
Beasley, Faith E(velyn)
Beasley, Sandra
Beasley, Vanessa B.
Beason, Doug
Beatie, Thomas
Beatley, Timothy
Beattie, Ann
Beattie, L(inda) Elisabeth
Beattie, Melody (Lynn)
Beatty, Barbara (R.)
Beatty, Jack
Beaty, Andrea
Beauchamp, Cari
Beauchamp, Kenneth
Beaudoin, Tom
Beauman, Nicola
Beauregard, Robert A.
Beauseigneur, James
Beavan, Colin
Beaver, Jim Norman
Bechler, Curt
Bechtel, Stefan D.
Bechtol, Bruce E.
Beck, Edward L.
Beck, John C.
Beck, Mary L. (Giraudo)
Beck, Peggy
Beck, Robert J.
Beckel, Bob
Becker, Charles M(axwell)
Becker, Elizabeth
Becker, Ethan
Becker, Gary S.
Becker, Josh
Becker, Palmer (Joseph)
Becker, Patti Clayton
Becker, Robin
Becker, Suzanne (Rose)
Beckerman, Paul
Beckhorn, Susan Williams
Beckley, Harlan R.
Beckman, John
Beckwith, Harry
Beckwith, Jonathan R(oger)
Bedard, Anthony
Bedau, Hugo Adam
Bederman, Gail
Bedford, Deborah
Bedford, Henry Frederick
Bedingfield, M. Bradford
Bee, Ronald J.
Beebe, Ralph K.
Beeby, James M.
Beeman, Robin
Beeman, William O.
Beers, Burton Floyd
Beers, Diane L.
Begelman, Mitchell (Craig)
Begley, Dan
Begley, Ed James

Beha, Christopher R.
Behe, Michael J.
Behn, Robert Dietrich
Behr, Ira Steven
Behrens, Ellen
Behrens, John C.
Behrman, Greg
Behuniak, James
Beiderwell, Bruce
Beidler, Peter G.
Beifuss, John
Beinhart, Larry
Beisner, Robert L.
Beissinger, Steven R.
Beja, Morris
Belasen, Amy
Belgum, Erik
Belieu, Erin
Belin, Esther G.
Belkin, Aaron
Belkin, Lisa
Belknap, Robert L.
Bell, Albert A.
Bell, Betty Louise
Bell, Cathleen Davitt
Bell, David Owen
Bell, Dean Phillip
Bell, Hilari
Bell, James Edward
Bell, Madison Smartt
Bell, Marvin (Hartley)
Bell, Mary Reeves
Bell, Nancy
Bell, Richard H.
Bell, Susan
Bell, Suzanne
Bellavia, David Gregory
Beller, Susan Provost
Beller, Tom
Bellesiles, Michael A.
Belli, Gioconda
Belliotti, Raymond A(ngelo)
Bellm, Dan
Belloli, Andrea P. A.
Bellotti, Laura Golden
Bellow, Adam
Bellows, Barbara L(awrence)
Bellows, Melina Gerosa
Bellows, Nathaniel
Bellush, Bernard
Belmonte, Kevin Charles
Belnap, Nuel
Beltman, Brian W.
Belton, Sandra (Yvonne)
Belue, Ted Franklin
Benarde, Melvin Albert
Benavides, O. Hugo
Benchley, Rob
Bendall, Molly
Bender, Bert
Bender, Sheila
Bender, Thomas
Bendis, Brian Michael
Bendix, Deanna Marohn
Bendroth, Margaret Lamberts
Benedict, Barbara M.
Benedict, Elizabeth
Benedict, Jeff
Benedict, Laura Philpot
Benedict, Pinckney
Benes, Rebecca C.

Benezra, Neal
Benford, Gregory (Albert)
Bengtson, Vern L.
Benig, Irving
Benitez, Sandra (Ables)
Benjamin, Carol Lea
Benjamin, Joan
Benjamin, Saragail Katzman
Bennahum, Judith Chazin
Bennett, Charles A.
Bennett, Cherie
Bennett, Edward M.
Bennett, Hal Z(ina)
Bennett, James B.
Bennett, James Richard
Bennett, John M(ichael)
Bennett, Lerone
Bennett, Merit
Bennett, Robert S.
Bennett, Robert W.
Bennett, Shelley M.
Bennett, W. Lance
Bennett-Goleman, Tara
Bennis, Phyllis
Benoit, Charles
Benoit, William L.
Bensel, Richard Franklin
Bensman, David
Benson, Ann
Benson, Jackson J.
Benson, Judi
Benson, Ophelia
Benstock, Shari
Bent, Timothy (David)
Bentley, Joanne
Bentley, Nancy
Bentley, Nancy Ann
Benton, D(ebra) A.
Benton, Jim
Benton, Megan L.
Bentsen, Cheryl
Benvenuto, Christine
Benz, Derek
Beran, Michael Knox
Berberian, Viken
Berberick, Nancy Varian
Berck, Judith
Berdanier, Carolyn D.
Berebitsky, Julie
Berenbaum, Michael
Berendt, John
Berenzy, Alix
Berg, A. Scott
Berg, Carol
Berg, Elizabeth
Berg, John C.
Berg, Scott W.
Berg, Stephen
Bergen, Candice
Berger, Arthur A(sa)
Berger, Barbara Helen
Berger, Bruce
Berger, Charles R.
Berger, Fredericka
Berger, Samantha (Allison)
Berger, Sidney
Berger, Thomas (Louis)
Bergerud, Eric M.
Berges, Emily Trafford
Bergin, Thomas J.
Bergland, Martha

Bergland, Renee L.
Bergman, Andrew
Bergner, Daniel
Bergon, Frank
Bergquist, Charles
Bergquist, William Hastings
Bergreen, Laurence
Bergstrom, Elaine
Berinsky, Adam J.
Berinstein, Paula
Berkenstadt, Jim
Berkey, Jonathan P.
Berkman, Michael B.
Berkman, Pamela Rafael
Berkovitz, Jay R.
Berkowitz, Edward D.
Berkowitz, Peter
Berkson, Bill
Berlfein, Judy Reiss
Berlin, Eric
Berlin, Leslie
Berlinger, Joe
Berlo, Janet Catherine
Berlow, Alan
Berman, Brooke
Berman, Claire
Berman, David
Berman, David
Berman, Jeffrey
Berman, Morris
Berman, Russell A.
Berman, Sanford
Bermann, Sandra L.
Bermeo, Nancy G(ina)
Bernard, Andre
Bernard, Kenneth
Bernardi, Daniel (Leonard)
Bernardini, Joe
Bernhardt, William
Bernikow, Louise
Bernstein, Burton
Bernstein, Charles
Bernstein, David E(liot)
Bernstein, Ellen
Bernstein, Frances Lee
Bernstein, Jake
Bernstein, Jared
Bernstein, Laurie
Bernstein, Mark
Bernstein, Patricia
Bernstein, Paula
Bernstein, Richard
Bernstein, Richard B.
Berra, Tim M.
Berres, Thomas Edward
Berrigan, Daniel J.
Berry, Carmen Renee
Berry, Carole
Berry, Chad
Berry, Faith D.
Berry, J. Bill
Berry, Jeffrey M.
Berry, John Stevens
Berry, Julie
Berry, Linda
Berry, Stephen W.
Berry, Steve
Berryman, Jack W.
Berryman, Phillip E.
Bert, Norman A(llen)
Bertematti, Richard

Bertling, Tom
Bertolino, James
Bertozzi, Nick
Bertrand, Diane Gonzales
Bertrand, Lynne
Bertrand, Marsha
Bertulani, Carlos A.
Berube, David M.
Berube, Maurice R.
Bes-Shahar, Eluki
Besner, Hilda F.
Bessette, Roland L.
Bessler, John D.
Best, Don(ald M.)
Best, Wallace D.
Bethelard, Faith
Bettis, Jerome Abram
Betts, Doris
Betts, William Wilson
Bevans, Stephen B(ennett)
Bevis, William W.
Bial, Raymond
Bianchi, Eugene Carl
Bianco, Anthony
Biank, Tanya
Bickerstaff, Steve
Bicks, Caroline
Bidart, Frank
Biddle, Bruce Jesse
Biddle, Cordelia Frances
Bidner, Jenni
Bidney, Martin
Bieder, Robert E.
Biederman, Lynn
Biek, David E.
Biel, Steven
Bielefeld, Wolfgang
Bien, Peter
Bien, Thomas (H.)
Bienvenu, Marcelle
Bierds, Linda
Bierhorst, John
Biesel, David B.
Biggs, Brian
Biggs, Chester M(axwell)
Biggs, Mary
Bigham, Darrel E.
Bilby, Joanne Stroud
Bildner, Phil
Bilinkoff, Jodi
Billias, George Athan
Billinger, Robert D.
Billingsley, Scott
Billington, David P(erkins)
Billington, James H(adley)
Billone, Amy Christine
Bing, Leon
Bingham, Howard L.
Bingham, Sallie
Bingle, Donald J.
Binkley, Christina
Binstock, Robert H.
Binzen, Peter (Husted)
Birchmore, Daniel A.
Bird, Brad
Bird, Christiane
Bird, Edward J.
Birdsall, Jeanne
Birdseye, Tom
Birdwell, Michael E.
Bireley, Robert

Birenbaum, Barbara
Birkby, Robert Corrie
Birkerts, Sven
Birkland, Thomas A.
Birn, Raymond Francis
Birnbaum, Jeffrey H.
Birney, Alice Lotvin
Birney, Betty G.
Birstein, Ann
Birzer, Bradley J.
Bishop, Bill
Bishop, Holley
Bishop, Jacqueline Kay
Bishop, Michael
Biskupic, Joan
Bissell, Sallie
Bissette, Stephen
Bittner, Rosanne
Bivins, Jason C.
Bizzarro, Tina Waldeier
Bizzell, Patricia (Lynn)
Bjarkman, Peter C(hristian)
Bjorge, Gary J(ohn)
Bjork, Daniel W.
Bjorklund, David F.
Bjornerud, Marcia
Black, Brian
Black, Charlene Villasenor
Black, Donald
Black, Ethan
Black, Keith Lanier
Black, Merle
Black, Michael A.
Black, Robert Perry
Black, Roger David
Black, Shane
Black, William H.
Blackburn, Fred M(onroe)
Blackford, Mansel G(riffiths)
Blackmer, Donald L. M.
Blackstock, Terri
Blackwell, Joyce
Blackwell, Richard J.
Blackwill, Robert D.
Blades, John D.
Blagojevic, Ljiljana
Blaine, Michael
Blair, Ann
Blair, Steven N.
Blaisdell, Bob
Blaise, Clark
Blake, Michael
Blake, Sarah
Blake, Stephen P.
Blakely, Mary Kay
Blakeslee, Matthew
Blakeslee, Sandra
Blakesley, Christopher L.
Blakey, Nancy
Blanchard, Melinda
Blanchard, Robert
Blanco, Jodee
Blank, Harrod
Blank, Jessica
Blank, Paula
Blank, Rebecca M.
Blasi, Anthony J(oseph)
Blasing, Randy
Blatchford, Claire H.
Blatner, David
Blau, Francine D.

Blau, Joel
Blaufarb, Rafe
Blauner, Bob
Blauner, Peter
Blauvelt, Martha Tomhave
Blech, Susan
Blechman, Elaine A(nn)
Blecker, Robert A.
Bledin, David
Bledsoe, Alex
Bledsoe, Glen L(eonard)
Bledsoe, Jerry
Bledsoe, Karen E(lizabeth)
Bledsoe, Timothy
Blee, Kathleen M.
Blegen, Daniel M.
Blei, Norbert
Blenk, Katie
Blessington, Francis C(harles)
Blethen, H(arold) Tyler
Blevins, Meredith
Blewett, Daniel K(eith)
Blight, David W.
Blight, James G.
Blinder, Alan S(tuart)
Blinn, William Frederick
Bliss, Harry
Bliss, Michael (J.)
Blix, Jacqueline
Blixt, David
Bloch, Douglas
Block, Brett Ellen
Block, Cathy Collins
Block, David
Block, Francesca (Lia)
Block, Geoffrey (Holden)
Block, Jennifer
Block, Joyce
Block, Lawrence
Block, Sharon
Block, Thomas H(arris)
Block, Valerie
Blocksma, Mary
Blockson, Charles L(eRoy)
Blodgett, (Anita) Jan
Blodgett, Peter J.
Bloodworth-Thomason, Linda
Bloom, Harold
Bloom, Howard
Bloom, James D.
Bloom, Jonathan M(ax)
Bloom, Lisa E.
Bloom, Lynn (Marie Zimmerman)
Bloom, Miriam
Bloom, Rebecca (S.)
Bloomfield, Lincoln P(almer)
Bloomfield, Louis A(ub)
Bloor, Edward (William)
Blos, Joan W.
Blosser, Susan Sokol
Blouin, Lenora P.
Blount, Brian K.
Blount, Roy (Alton)
Bluemel, Kristin
Bluestein, Eleanor
Blum, Bruce I(van)
Blum, Deborah (Leigh)
Blum, Edward J.
Blum, Howard
Blum, Kristen Raub
Blum, Lenore (Carol)

Blum, Louise A(gnes)
Blumberg, Phillip Irvin
Blumberg, Rhoda
Blume, Harvey
Blume, Judy
Blumenfeld, Robert
Blumenfeld-Kosinski, Renate
Blumhofer, Edith L.
Bly, Robert (Elwood)
Boag, Peter G.
Boatwright, Mary T.
Boaz, David
Boaz, Noel T(homas)
Bober, Natalie S.
Bobinski, George S.
Bobrick, Benson
Bocardo, Claire
Bochin, Hal W(illiam)
Bochner, Mel
Bock, Charles
Bock, Philip Karl
Bodek, Richard
Bodenhamer, David J(ackson)
Bodett, Tom
Boegehold, Alan L(indley)
Boehling, Rebecca L.
Boellstorff, Tom
Boelts, Maribeth
Boesche, Roger
Boessenecker, John
Bogart, Eleanor A(nne)
Bogart, Stephen Humphrey
Bogdanich, Walt
Bogen, David S.
Boggs, Belle McQuade
Bogin, Magda
Bogle, Donald
Bogosian, Eric
Bohjalian, Chris
Bohman, James F.
Bohn-Spector, Claudia
Bohnhoff, Maya Kaathryn
Bohntinsky, Dori
Bohrer, Frederick Nathaniel
Boice, James
Boies, David
Boisseau, Michelle
Boisvert, Raymond D.
Bojanowski, Marc
Bok, Derek Curtis
Bokina, John
Boland, Janice
Bolden, Abraham
Bolden, Tonya
Boldt, Laurence G.
Boles, Philana Marie
Bolgiano, Chris(tina)
Bolino, August C.
Boller, Paul F.
Bolles, Edmund Blair
Bolles, Richard Nelson
Bollier, David
Bollinger, Lee C.
Bolman, Lee G.
Bolotin, Norman (Phillip)
Bolster, W(illiam) Jeffrey
Bolton, Charles C.
Bolton, Ruthie
Bonadio, Felice A(nthony)
Bonadio, William
Bonansinga, Jay R.

Boncompagni, Tatiana
Bond, George C(lement)
Bond, Larry
Bond, Nancy
Bonds, Alexandra B.
Bondy, Andy
Bondy, Filip
Bonekemper, Edward H.
Bonello, Frank J.
Boniface, William
BonJour, Laurence Alan
Bonner, Arthur
Bonner, Jeffrey P.
Bonner, John Tyler
Bonner, Robert E.
Bonomelli, Charles J(ames)
Bonsignore, Joan
Bonta, Marcia Myers
Bookchin, Debbie
Bookman, Terry Allen
Bookstaber, Richard
Boone, Daniel R.
Boorstein, Sylvia
Boos, Ben
Boostrom, Robert E(dward)
Booth, Brian
Booth, Stanley
Bopp, Mary S.
Borchard, Therese Johnson
Borcz, Geri
Borden, Debra
Bordewich, Fergus M.
Bordo, Susan (Rebecca)
Bordowitz, Hank
Bordwell, David
Borelli, John
Borenstein, Emily Schwartz
Borg, Marcus J(oel)
Borgenicht, David
Boritt, Gabor
Bork, Lisa
Bork, Robert H(eron)
Borko, Harold
Borneman, John W.
Bornstein, George
Borntrager, Mary Christner
Borowitz, Andy
Borsch, Stuart J.
Borton, Lady
Bortz, Fred
Boruch, Marianne
Borysenko, Joan
Boschken, Herman L.
Bosco, Dominick
Bose, Purnima
Boskin, Joseph
Boskoff, Alvin
Bosmajian, Haig
Boss, Alan Paul
Boss, Pauline G.
Bostdorff, Denise M.
Boswell, Angela
Boswell, Robert
Boteach, Shmuley
Botha, Ted
Botkin, Daniel B.
Bottke, Allison Gappa
Bottoms, David
Boucher, Bruce (Ambler)
Boucher, Philip P.
Boudreau, Kristin

Boullata, Issa J.
Bourke, Dale Hanson
Bourne, Russell
Bouson, J. Brooks
Bouton, Gary David
Bouton, Marshall M.
Bouvard, Marguerite Guzman
Bova, Ben(jamin William)
Bovaird, Anne E(lizabeth)
Bowden, Charles
Bowden, Keith
Bowden, Mark
Bowe, John
Bowe, Julie
Bowen, John R.
Bowen, Mark
Bowen, Michael
Bowen, Roger W.
Bowen, William (Gordon)
Bowers, Jane Palatini
Bowers, Janice Emily
Bowers, John
Bowers, Terrell L.
Bowie, Phil
Bowles, Samuel
Bowling, Lewis
Bowman, Crystal
Bowman, J. Wilson
Bowman, James
Bowser, Benjamin P(aul)
Bowyer, Mathew Justice
Boyd, Blanche McCrary
Boyd, Candy Dawson
Boyd, Carl
Boyd, Claude E.
Boyd, Malcolm
Boyd, Nan Alamilla
Boyd, Steven R(ay)
Boyden, Amanda
Boyer, Jay
Boyer, Rick
Boyers, Robert
Boyett, Jimmie T.
Boyett, Joseph H.
Boykin, J. Robert
Boykin, Keith
Boyle, Brian
Boyle, Gerry
Boyle, Kevin
Boyle, Thomas A.
Boyll, (James) Randall
Boyne, Daniel J.
Boyne, Walter J(ames)
Boynton, Susan
Boysen, Sally T.
Brace, Paul (R.)
Bracey, Christopher Alan
Brach, Tara
Bracken, James K.
Bracken, Len
Brackman, Barbara
Bradburd, Rus
Bradbury, J. C.
Bradbury, Ray (Douglas)
Braden, Donna R.
Braden, Nate
Bradfield, Scott (Michael)
Bradlee, Benjamin (Crownin-
   shield)
Bradley, David (Henry)
Bradley, John Ed(mund)

Bradley, Michael R.
Bradley, Shelley
Brady, Catherine
Brady, Kimberley S(mith)
Brady, Patricia
Brady, Rachel
Brady, Rose
Bragdon, Kathleen J.
Bragg, Steven M.
Braham, (E.) Jeanne
Brake, Laurel
Brakke, David Bernhard
Brallier, Kate
Brame, Charles L.
Bramsen, Paul D.
Bramson, Leon
Branch, Muriel Miller
Branch, Taylor
Brand, Alice Glarden
Brandenburg, Jim
Brandes, Stanley H.
Brandes, Stuart D.
Brandewyne, Rebecca
Brandi, John
Brands, H. W.
Brands, Hal
Brandt, Allan M(orris)
Brandt, Clare
Brandt, Deborah
Brannigan, Gary G(eorge)
Branover, Herman
Branson, Gary D.
Brant, Jo-Ann A.
Brant, Marley
Brantley, Richard E.
Brantlinger, Patrick (Morgan)
Brashear, Jean
Brasseaux, Carl A(nthony)
Bratt, James D.
Braude, Stephen E.
Braudis, Bob
Braudy, Leo
Brauer, Jurgen
Brauer, Ralph
Braun, Matt(hew)
Braun, Stephen R.
Braund, Kathryn E. Holland
Braunmuller, A(lbert) R(ichard)
Braveboy-Wagner, Jacqueline
   Anne
Braverman, Melanie
Braverman, Terry
Brawley, Robert L.
Braxton, Joanne M(argaret)
Bray, Libba
Bray, Patricia
Bray, Robert C.
Brazaitis, Mark
Breckenridge-Haywood, Mae
Breeden, Joann Elizabeth
Breen, Steve
Breen, Susan
Brehony, Kathleen A.
Breiner, Laurence A.
Breivik, Patricia Senn
Bremer, L. Paul
Brenaman, Miriam
Brener, Milton E(rnest)
Brenna, Duff
Brennan, Christine
Brennan, Kate

Brennan, Mary C.
Brennan, Matthew C.
Brenner, Joël Glenn
Brenner, Mayer Alan
Brenner, Neil
Brenner, Philip (Joseph)
Brenner, Robert
Brenner, Wendy
Breskin, David
Breslin, Jimmy
Breslow, Susan
Bressoud, David M(arius)
Brett, Donna W(hitson)
Brett, Edward T(racy)
Brett, Jan (Churchill)
Brett, Peter V.
Bretton, Barbara
Brewer, Bob
Brewer, David Allen
Brewer, Garry D(wight)
Brewer, Heather
Brewer, Holly
Brewer, Jeannie A.
Brewer, Mark D.
Brewer, Sonny
Brewer, William D(ean)
Brewster, David (C.)
Brewster, Gurdon
Breyfogle, Nicholas B.
Breyman, Steve
Brian, Cynthia
Bribiescas, Richard G.
Brice, Carleen
Brichoux, Karen
Bridge, Andrew
Bridgers, Lynn
Bridgers, Sue Ellen (Hunsucker)
Bridges, Laurie
Bridwell, Norman (Ray)
Brierley, Barry
Briggs, John
Briggs, Patricia
Briggs, Ward W(right)
Brigham, Robert K.
Bright, Freda
Bright, Myron H.
Brightman, Carol
Brill, Marlene Targ
Brilliant, Richard
Brin, David
Brink, Jean R.
Brinkley, Alan
Brinkley, Douglas
Brinkman, Kiara
Briscoe, Connie
Briskin, Mae
Brisson, Pat
Bristow, Robert O'Neil
Brite, Poppy Z.
Britt, Brian (Michael)
Brittain, C. Dale
Brittain, William (E.)
Britton, Hannah E.
Brizendine, Louann
Brkic, Courtney Angela
Broach, Elise
Broad, Kendal L.
Broad, Robin
Broadhurst, Kent
Broadman, Harry G.
Broadwater, Robert P.

Brobeck, Stephen
Brock, James
Brock, Pope
Brock-Broido, Lucie
Brockett, Charles D.
Brockey, Liam Matthew
Brockway, Connie
Broderick, Tim
Brodeur, Adrienne
Brodeur, Paul (Adrian)
Brody, Jane E(llen)
Brody, Jean
Brody, Jessica
Brody, Miriam
Brody, Richard
Brody, Stuart
Broer, Lawrence R(ichard)
Brogan, Jan
Brom, Gerald
Bromann, Jennifer
Bromberg, Nicolette A.
Bromer, Anne C.
Bronleewe, Matt Ryan
Bronson, Po
Bronzino, Joseph D.
Brook, Vincent
Brooke, Jill
Brooke, William J.
Brooker, Jewel Spears
Brookes, Martin
Brookhiser, Richard
Brooks, Arthur C.
Brooks, Betty
Brooks, Bill
Brooks, Bruce (Delos)
Brooks, David
Brooks, Erik
Brooks, Fairleigh
Brooks, George E.
Brooks, James F.
Brooks, Joanna
Brooks, Karl Boyd
Brooks, Michael
Brooks, Roy L(avon)
Brooks, Stephen G.
Brooks, Victor
Brooks-Gunn, Jeanne
Broomall, Robert W(alter)
Brophy, Grace
Brophy, James M.
Bross, Donald G.
Brothers, Joyce (Diane)
Brotherton, Mike Sean
Broughton, T. Alan
Broussard, Meredith
Browder, Laura
Brower, Kenneth
Brower, Steven
Brown, Alan
Brown, Brooks
Brown, Bryan T(urner)
Brown, Canter
Brown, Christopher Boyd
Brown, Clair
Brown, Cynthia Stokes
Brown, Dale W.
Brown, Dan
Brown, Daniel James
Brown, David S.
Brown, Don
Brown, Dona

Brown, Douglas Robert
Brown, Ethan
Brown, Gita
Brown, Gregory N.
Brown, Gregory S.
Brown, H. Jackson
Brown, Harriet N(ancy)
Brown, Harry Clifford
Brown, Helen Gurley
Brown, Irene Quenzler
Brown, J(oseph) P(aul)
    S(ummers)
Brown, Jackie
Brown, Janelle
Brown, Jared
Brown, Jeffrey
Brown, John
Brown, John Gregory
Brown, Jonathan (Mayer)
Brown, Kathleen
Brown, Kevin
Brown, Lester R(ussell)
Brown, Lyn Mikel
Brown, Lynne P.
Brown, Margaret Lynn
Brown, Mary Ward
Brown, Michael F(obes)
Brown, Michael P.
Brown, Montague
Brown, Murray
Brown, Nancy Marie
Brown, Nicholas
Brown, Nickole
Brown, Parry Ann
Brown, Patricia Fortini
Brown, Peter A.
Brown, Richard E.
Brown, Rita Mae
Brown, Robert G(oodell)
Brown, Roberta Simpson
Brown, Rosellen
Brown, Ryan
Brown, Sandra
Brown, Steve
Brown, Steven Preston
Brown, Thomas J.
Brown, Tony
Brown, Tracy
Brown, V(ictor) I(vy)
Brown-Fleming, Suzanne
Browne, David
Browne, Gerald A(ustin)
Browne-Miller, Angela
Brownell, Charles E(dward)
Brownell, Susan
Browner, Jesse
Browning, Christopher R(obert)
Browning, Dixie Burrus
Browning, Pamela
Brownlee, Andrea Barnwell
Brownlee, David B(ruce)
Brownlee, Donald E(ugene)
Brownlee, Shannon
Brownmiller, Susan
Brownstein, Gabriel
Brox, Jane (Martha)
Broyles, Anne
Broyles, Michael
Broz, J. Lawrence
Bruce, Dickson Davies
Bruce, Victoria

Bruchac, Joseph
Bruck, Connie
Bruckheimer, Linda
Bruer, John T.
Brugger, E. Christian
Brugioni, Dino A.
Bruhns, Karen Olsen
Bruinius, Harry
Brumfield, William Craft
Brundage, James A.
Brundige, Donald G.
Brundige, Sharron L(ea)
Brunelli, Jean
Bruner, Jerome S(eymour)
Brunkhorst, Alex
Bruno, Richard L(ouis)
Bruns, Don
Bruns, Roger A.
Bruns, William John
Brusatte, Steve
Bruseth, James E.
Brush, Kathleen (E.)
Brush, Lisa D.
Brussat, Frederic
Brussat, Mary Ann
Brustein, Robert
Brustein, William I.
Bryant, Dorothy (Calvetti)
Bryant, Howard
Bryant, Jennifer F(isher)
Bryant, Jonathan M.
Bryant, Robert Harry
Bryant, Sharon
Bryce, Robert
Brysk, Alison
Bryson, Ellen
Bube, Richard Howard
Buccieri, Lisa Rojany
Buccola, Regina M.
Buchanan, Edna
Buchanan, Mark
Buchanan, Oni
Bucheister, Patt
Bucheli, Marcelo
Buchholz, Todd G.
Buchmann, Stephen L.
Bucholz, Arden
Buchwalter, Andrew
Buck, Craig
Buck, Rinker
Buck, Susan J.
Buckelew, Albert R.
Buckell, Tobias S.
Buckey, Sarah Masters
Buckhanon, Kalisha
Buckingham, Royce Scott
Buckley, Christopher Howard
Buckley, Cornelius M(ichael)
Buckley, Francis Joseph
Buckley, Gail Lumet
Buckley, Jay H.
Buckley, John (F.)
Buckley, Julia
Buckley, Thomas
Buckser, Andrew (S.)
Bucuvalas, Tina
Budbill, David
Budde, Michael L(eo)
Buderi, Robert
Budiansky, Stephen (Philip)
Budnitz, Judy

Budny, Mildred
Budz, Mark
Buechner, (Carl) Frederick
Buehler, Evelyn Judy
Buehner, Caralyn M.
Buell, Frederick (Henderson)
Buettner, Dan
Buffett, Jimmy
Buford, Bill
Bugeja, Michael J.
Bugos, Glenn E.
Buhner, Stephen Harrod
Buhs, Joshua Blu
Bujold, Lois McMaster
Bukey, Evan Burr
Bukiet, Melvin Jules
Bukoski, Anthony
Bulger, Peggy A.
Bulkeley, Kelly
Bulkowski, Thomas N.
Bull, Barry L.
Bull, Schuyler M.
Buller, David J.
Bullins, Ed
Bullitt, Dorothy
Bullough, Robert V.
Bulock, Lynn
Bulson, Eric
Bunck, Julie Marie
Bundles, A'Lelia Perry
Bundy, Carol
Bungert, D. Edward
Bunkers, Suzanne L.
Burack, Elmer H(oward)
Burak, Carl S.
Burch, Joann J(ohansen)
Burchard, Brendon
Burden, Barry C.
Burden, Matthew Currier
Burden, Wendy
Burg, Shana
Burg, Steven L.
Burger, Joanna
Burger, Michael
Burges, Dennis
Burgess, Charles
Burgess, Dean
Burgess, Granville Wyche
Burgess, Patricia
Burgess, Robert J(ohn)
Burgess, Stephen F(ranklin)
Burghardt, Linda
Burgos, Adrian
Burk, Frank
Burk, Josh D.
Burk, Robert F(rederick)
Burke, Richard E.
Burke, Shannon
Burke, Timothy M.
Burkhardt, Joanna M.
Burkman, Thomas W.
Burks, Brian
Burks, Jean M.
Burlew, A(nn) Kathleen
Burlingame, Michael
Burlingham, Bo
Burnett, Amy Nelson
Burnett, Gail Lemley
Burney, Claudia Mair
Burnham, Terence (Charles)
Burningham, Bruce R.

Carson, Barbara Harrell
Carson, Benjamin S(olomon)
Carson, Donald W.
Carson, Herbert L.
Carson, Mary Kay
Carswell, Sue
Carter, (Elizabeth) Susanne
Carter, Abigail
Carter, Alden R(ichardson)
Carter, Ally
Carter, Ashton B.
Carter, Betty
Carter, Betty Smartt
Carter, C. Barry
Carter, Charlotte
Carter, Christine Jacobson
Carter, David
Carter, Emily
Carter, Frances Monet
Carter, J. Kameron
Carter, Jared
Carter, Jimmy
Carter, John T(homas)
Carter, Joseph H(enry)
Carter, Julian B.
Carter, Raphael
Carter, Rosalynn (Smith)
Carter, Stephen L(isle)
Carter, Steven
Carter, Steven R(ay)
Carter, Tom
Carter, W(illiam)
Carter, Walter
Carter, William E.
Cartmill, Matt
Carton, Bernice
Carusone, Al
Carvell, Marlene
Carver, Norman Francis
Carver, Terrell
Carville, (Chester) James
Cary, Lorene
Cary, Margaret
Casagrande, June M.
Casanova, Mary
Cascone, Annette
Case, Chris
Casey, Barbara
Casey, Don
Casey, John (Dudley)
Casey, Maud
Casey, Shaun Allen
Casey, Steven
Cash, Jean W(ampler)
Cash, Steve
Cashdan, Linda
Cashill, Jack
Cashin, Joan E.
Cashore, Kristin
Casil, Amy Sterling
Caskie, Kathryn
Casper, Leonard (Ralph)
Casper, Monica J.
Casper, Scott E.
Caspers, Nona
Cass, Dennis
Cassady, Marsh
Cassell, Eric J.
Cassell, Joan
Cassella, Carol Wiley
Cassidy, David C(harles)

Cassidy, Robert M.
Casstevens, Thomas William
Cassutt, Michael (Joseph)
Castaneda, Christopher James
Castelli, Elizabeth A.
Castellucci, Cecil
Caster, Andrew I.
Castiglione, Caroline
Castile, George Pierre
Castillo, Mary
Castle, Alfred L.
Castle, Gregory
Castle, Linda
Casto, William R.
Castro, Daniel
Castro, Efren D.
Castro, Michael
Casway, Jerrold
Catalano, Nick
Catalanotto, Peter
Catanoso, Justin
Cathcart, Jim
Catrow, David J.
Catterall, Lee
Caudill, (Charles) Edward
Caufield, Catherine
Caughfield, Adrienne
Caughie, Pamela L.
Caulfield, Carlota
Cauthen, (W.) Kenneth
Cavallaro, Michael J.
Cavanagh, Thomas B.
Cavazos-Gaither, Alma E(lisa)
Cavell, Benjamin
Cavell, Marcia
Caves, Richard Earl
Caws, Mary Ann
Cayleff, Susan Evelyn
Cazden, Courtney B(orden)
Cazet, Denys
Cebulash, Mel
Celenza, Anna Harwell
Cell, Edward Charles
Center, Katherine Pannill
Center-Shabazz, Lois
Cepero, Helen
Cerami, Charles A.
Cernada, George P.
Cerny, Frank J.
Cerullo, Mary M.
Ceruzzi, Paul Edward
Cespedes, Frank V.
Cessario, Romanus
Cevasco, G(eorge) A(nthony)
Chabris, Christopher F.
Chadwick, Cydney
Chadwick, Whitney
Chafe, Wallace
Chafee, Lincoln D.
Chafel, Judith A.
Chaffey, Will
Chai, Arlene J.
Chai, May-lee
Chaitin, Gregory J.
Chaleff, Ira
Chalker, Dennis
Chamberlain, Lisa
Chamberlain, Marisha
Chamberlin, Ann
Chamberlin, Kate
Chambers, Aidan

Chambers, Christopher
Chambers, Diane
Chambers, John Whiteclay
Chambers, Veronica
Champagne, Duane (Willard)
Champion, Craige B.
Champion, Larry S.
Champlin, Peggy
Champlin, Tim
Chance, Megan
Chancer, Lynn S.
Chancy, Myriam J(osephe)
    A(imee)
Chandler, Daniel Ross
Chandler, James K.
Chandler, Marc
Chang, Gordon G.
Chang, Kang-i Sun
Chang, Leonard
Chang, Margaret
Chanoff, David
Chao, Patricia
Chapin, F. Stuart
Chapin, Miles
Chapin, Sarah
Chapman, Herb
Chapman, J. Dudley
Chapman, Myriam
Chapman, Paul K.
Chapman, Samuel Greeley
Chappell, Fred(erick Davis)
Chappell, Ruth Paterson
Charbonneau, Eileen
Charbonnet, Gabrielle
Charlebois, Lucile C.
Charles, Douglas M.
Charles, Sara C(onnor)
Charlesworth, James H(amilton)
Charlip, Remy
Charlot, Anita M.
Charlton-Trujillo, E. E.
Charmé, Stuart Zane
Charnas, Suzy McKee
Charney, Mark J.
Charney, Noah
Charnon-Deutsch, Lou
Charrette, Robert N.
Charters, Ann
Charters, Samuel
Chase, Alyssa
Chase, Joan
Chase, Karen
Chase, Karen Susan
Chase, Kerry A.
Chase, Loretta Lynda
Chase, Steven
Chasnoff, Joel
Chast, Roz
Chatfield, Cheryl A.
Chatfield, E. Charles
Chatman, Seymour
Chatzky, Jean
Chauncey, George
Chave, Anna C.
Chaves, Mark (Alan)
Chayat, Sherry
Chazan, Robert
Cheaney, J. B.
Cheathem, Mark R.
Checkoway, Julie
Cheers, D. Michael

Cheever, Susan
Chehak, Susan Taylor
Chen, Calvin
Chen, Ken
Chen, Victor Tan
Chen, Xiaoming
Cheney, Martha
Cheney, Patrick Gerard
Cheney, Terri
Cheng, Andrea
Chenut, Helen Harden
Cherchi-Usai, Paolo
Cheripko, Jan
Cherlin, Andrew J.
Chernoff, Maxine
Chernow, Barbara A.
Cherny, Andrei
Cherny, Robert W(allace)
Cherry, Charles Conrad
Cherry, Kelly
Cherry, Kittredge
Cherry, Mark J.
Cherryh, C. J.
Chertow, Marian R.
Chesler, Ellen
Chesman, Andrea
Chess, Richard
Chester, Jeff
Chester, Mark (S.)
Chethik, Neil
Chetkovich, Carol A.
Cheuse, Alan
Chiappe, Luis M.
Chiarello, Michael
Chierichetti, David
Chiffolo, Anthony F.
Chilcote, Ronald H.
Child, Lincoln B.
Child, Maureen
Childress, Mark
Childs, Christopher
Childs, Craig
Childs, Elizabeth C(atharine)
Childs, Matt D.
Childs, Tera Lynn
Childs, William R.
Chiles, James R.
Chilson, Peter
Chilson, Rob(ert) (Dean)
Chilton, Bruce
Chima, Cinda Williams
Chin, Rita
Chinen, Nate
Chinosole
Chinoy, Mike
Chipman, Bruce Lewis
Chipman, Donald
Chippendale, Lisa A.
Chira, Susan
Chiras, Daniel D.
Chireau, Yvonne P.
Chitwood, Michael
Chivian, Eric
Chizmar, Richard T(homas)
Choate, Jean (Marie)
Chocolate, Debbi
Chodorow, Nancy Julia
Chodos-Irvine, Margaret
Choi, Annie
Choi, Frederick D. S.
Choldenko, Gennifer

Chomsky, (Avram) Noam
Chomsky, Aviva
Chorbajian, Levon
Chotzinoff, Robin
Choung, James
Chow, Claire S.
Chris, Cynthia
Christ, Carol P(atrice)
Christ, Henry I(rvine)
Christ, Ronald
Christakis, Nicholas A.
Christensen, Damascene
Christensen, Kate
Christensen, Kathleen E(lizabeth)
Christensen, Kit Richard
Christensen, Mark
Christensen, Paul
Christenson, James A.
Christian, David Gilbert
Christian, Garna L.
Christian, Jeffrey E.
Christman, Jill
Christmas, Joyce
Christofferson, April
Christoph, Peter R(ichard)
Christopher, Renny (Teresa)
Chu, Miyoko
Chupack, Cindy
Church, Audrey P.
Churchill, E. Richard
Chwast, Seymour
Chwedyk, Richard
Chyna
Ciabattari, Jane
Ciaravino, Helene
Ciepiela, Catherine
Cimbala, Stephen J.
Cimino, Richard P.
Ciochon, Russell L.
Ciresi, Rita
Cirincione, Joseph
Citro, Joseph A.
Citron, Stephen
Clabough, Casey Howard
Clague, Christopher K.
Claiborne, Shane
Claire, Cherie
Claire, Rodger W(illiam)
Clamp, Cathy
Clancy, Flora Simmons
Clancy, Tom
Clapp, Nicholas
Clapp, Rodney
Clapper, Gregory S(cott)
Clark, (Carter) Blue
Clark, Andrew F.
Clark, Anna (K.)
Clark, Beverly Lyon
Clark, Carol Higgins
Clark, Catherine
Clark, Charles E.
Clark, Charles Michael Andres
Clark, Dick
Clark, Emily
Clark, Francesco
Clark, Geoffrey (D.)
Clark, Gillian
Clark, Jerome
Clark, Joshua
Clark, Kathleen Ann
Clark, Kelly James

Clark, Martin Fillmore
Clark, Mary Ann
Clark, Mary Higgins
Clark, Mary Jane Behrends
Clark, Mary T.
Clark, Paul F.
Clark, Suzanne
Clark, Terry N(ichols)
Clark, Tom
Clark, Wesley K.
Clark, Will
Clark, William R.
Clarke, Brock
Clarke, Erskine
Clarke, John R.
Clarke, Kenneth L.
Clarke, Lee
Clarke, Liz
Clarke, Sally H.
Clarke-Rich, Elizabeth L.
Clarvoe, Jennifer
Clary, David A.
Clary, Killarney
Clason, Marmy A.
Clausen, Christopher (John)
Clausen, Lowen
Clausen, Meredith L(eslie)
Clausen, Tammy Hennigh
Clavel, Pierre
Clawson, Calvin C.
Clawson, James G.
Clawson, Rosalee A.
Claxton, Melvin
Clayson, (S.) Hollis
Clayton, David J.
Clayton, Elaine
Clayton, Lawrence (Otto)
Clayton, Paul
Clayton, Philip
Cleary, Beverly
Cleary, Brian P.
Cleary, Christopher
Cleary, Edward L.
Cleary, Matthew R.
Cleary, Melissa
Cleaver, Jerry
Cleek, Richard K.
Clegg, Douglas
Clegg, Holly Berkowitz
Cleland, Max
Clem, Alan L(eland)
Clem, Margaret H(ollingsworth)
Clemens, Walter C.
Clement, Mary H.
Clement, Priscilla Ferguson
Clement-Moore, Rosemary
Clements, Alan
Clements, Andrew
Clements, Bruce
Clements, Jonathan
Clemmer, Richard O.
Clendenen, Avis
Clendenin, Daniel B.
Clendinen, Dudley
Cleveland, Ceil
Cleveland, Ray L.
Clewell, David
Clifford, Christine
Clifford, Mary Louise
Clifton, Chas S.
Climo, Shirley

Clinch, Jon
Cline, Foster W.
Cline, Wayne
Cline, William R.
Clinton, Catherine
Clinton, Hillary Rodham
Clinton, James H(armon)
Clinton, James W(illiam)
Clinton, Kate
Clipper Sethi, Robbie
Clippinger, Carol
Clippinger, John Henry
Clotfelter, Beryl E(dward)
Clotfelter, Charles T.
Cloud, Darrah
Clouse, Robert Gordon
Clouser, Roy A.
Clow, Barbara Hand
Clubbe, John L(ouis) E(dwin)
Clunis, D. Merilee
Clydesdale, Tim
Côté, Richard N.
Coan, Richard W.
Coates, Carrol F(ranklin)
Coates, Charles (K.)
Coates, Ta-Nehisi
Coats, Wendell John
Coatsworth, John H(enry)
Cobb, Cathy
Cobb, Clifford W(illiam)
Cobb, James H(arvey)
Cobb, Kelton
Cobb, Nancy (Howard)
Cobb, Thomas
Cobb, Vicki
Coben, Harlan
Coble, Colleen
Coburn, Andrew
Coburn, Pip
Cochran, Gregory
Cochran, Heather
Cochran, Robert B(rady)
Cochrane, Peggy
Cockrell, Alan
Cockrell, Thomas D(errell)
Cocquyt, Kathryn Marie
Cody, Jeffrey W.
Cody, Lisa Forman
Cody, Paul
Cody, Robin
Coe, Michael (Douglas)
Coers, Donald V.
Coffin, Tristram Potter
Coffman, Edward M.
Cogan, Brian A.
Cogan, Marc
Coggeshall, Nancy
Cohen, Allan R(ay)
Cohen, Alvin
Cohen, Amy
Cohen, Benyamin
Cohen, Cary
Cohen, Daniel A.
Cohen, Daniel J.
Cohen, David William
Cohen, Debra Nussbaum
Cohen, Elliot D.
Cohen, Gary P.
Cohen, Getzel M.
Cohen, Henry
Cohen, Hubert I.

Cohen, Jared
Cohen, Jason
Cohen, Jeffrey A.
Cohen, Jeffrey E.
Cohen, Judith Love
Cohen, Karl F.
Cohen, Kerry
Cohen, Leah Hager
Cohen, Lisa R.
Cohen, Lizabeth (Ann)
Cohen, Mark
Cohen, Michael A.
Cohen, Milton A.
Cohen, Norman J.
Cohen, Paul (M.)
Cohen, Peter Zachary
Cohen, Rachel
Cohen, Ralph
Cohen, Rich
Cohen, Richard
Cohen, Richard M(artin)
Cohen, Robert
Cohen, Shaye J. D.
Cohen, Sholom
Cohen, Stanley I.
Cohen, Stephanie
Cohen, Stephen F(rand)
Cohen, Stuart
Cohen, Susan
Cohn, David
Cohn, Henry S.
Cohn, Jonathan
Cohn, Rachel
Cohn-Sherbok, Dan
Cohrs, Patrick O.
Cokal, Susann
Coker, Joe L.
Colantuoni, Joe
Colasanti, Susane
Colden, Kevin
Cole, Allan
Cole, Betsy
Cole, Bruce
Cole, David
Cole, Diane
Cole, Johnnetta B(etsch)
Cole, Phyllis (Blum)
Cole, Robert
Cole, Simon A.
Cole, Stephen A.
Cole, Susan Letzler
Cole, Terrence (Michael)
Cole, Thomas R(ichard)
Cole, Wayne S.
Coleman, A(llan) D(ouglass)
Coleman, C. Norman
Coleman, Carter
Coleman, James W.
Coleman, Jane Candia
Coleman, Janet Wyman
Coleman, Jon
Coleman, Jonathan (Mark)
Coleman, Loren (Elwood)
Coleman, Mary DeLorse
Coleman, Reed Farrel
Coles, Robert
Coles, Roberta L.
Colfax, David (John)
Colicchio, Joseph
Colin, Chris
Colish, Marcia L(illian)

Coll, Steve
Coll, Susan
Collard, Sneed B.
Collector, Stephen
Colletta, Lisa
Colley, Barbara
Colley, David P.
Collicott, Sharleen
Collier, Christopher
Collier, James Lincoln
Collier, Michael
Collier-Thomas, Bettye
Collignon, Jeff
Collignon, Rick
Collinge, Alan Michael
Collinge, William (B.)
Collings, Michael R(obert)
Collins, Ace
Collins, Barbara
Collins, Billy
Collins, Bud
Collins, Catherine Fisher
Collins, Floyd G.
Collins, Gail
Collins, Helen (Frances)
Collins, Julie (Hubbard)
Collins, Kathleen
Collins, Max Allan
Collins, Merle
Collins, Miki (Dickey)
Collins, Nancy A.
Collins, Patricia Hill
Collins, Paul
Collins, Richard (Wayne)
Collins, Robert
Collins, Ronald K. L
Collins, Stephen
Collins, Tess
Collum, Danny Duncan
Collver, Michael
Colman, Carol
Colman, Penny (Morgan)
Colodny, Len
Coloroso, Barbara
Colson, Charles W(endell)
Colson, Elizabeth
Colt, George Howe
Colten, Craig E.
Comerford, Kathleen M.
Comfort, B(arbara)
Comfort, Philip W(esley)
Comini, Alessandra
Comiskey, Michael
Commins, David Dean
Commoner, Barry
Como, David R.
Compton, James V(incent)
Compton, Patricia A.
Comstock, Gary D(avid)
Conant, Michael
Conard, Rebecca
Condee, William Faricy
Condrell, Kenneth N.
Condry, Ian Richard
Cones, John W.
Confer, Dennis W.
Confino, Alon
Conford, Ellen
Conforti, Joseph A.
Congdon, Lee (Walter)
Conger, Jay A.

Conger, Syndy McMillen
Congress, Richard
Conklin, John E.
Conley, Brenda Edgerton
Conley, Carolyn A.
Conley, Tom (Clark)
Conlin, Diane Atnally
Conn, Andrew Lewis
Conn, Didi
Connell, Evan S(helby)
Connell, George B(oyce)
Connelly, Donald B.
Connelly, Frances S(usan)
Connelly, Joan Breton
Connelly, Joe
Connelly, Matthew
Connelly, Michael
Connerly, Charles E.
Conners, Peter
Connolly, Harry J.
Connolly, Kevin Michael
Connolly, William E(ugene)
Connor, Carolyn L.
Connor, Daniel
Connor, Joan
Connor, Patrick E.
Connor, William S. P
Conover, Roger L(loyd)
Conquest, Ned
Conrad, Christine
Conrad, James H.
Conrad, Jessamyn
Conrad, Peter
Conroy, (Donald) Pat(rick)
Conser, Walter H.
Conteh-Morgan, Earl
Converse, Nathan
Converse, Philip E.
Conway, Diana C(ohen)
Conway, Erik M.
Conway, Martha
Conway, Simon
Conybeare, Catherine
Coogan, Michael D(avid)
Cook, Claire
Cook, David Bryan
Cook, Dawn
Cook, Deanna F.
Cook, Ferris
Cook, Glen (Charles)
Cook, Jean Thor
Cook, Kevin Graeme
Cook, Lorna J.
Cook, Marshall
Cook, Noble David
Cook, Paul
Cook, Philip J.
Cook, Roger F.
Cook, Stephen L(loyd)
Cook, William A.
Cook-Lynn, Elizabeth
Cooke, Bernard
Cooke, Carolyn
Cooke, Jacob Ernest
Cool, Paul
Cooley, Alexander
Cooley, Martha S.
Cooley, Nicole (Ruth)
Cooley, Thomas (Winfield)
Coombs, Patricia
Coomer, Joe

Cooney, Doug
Cooney, Ellen
Coonts, Stephen (Paul)
Coontz, Stephanie
Cooper, Cary L.
Cooper, David A.
Cooper, David D.
Cooper, Elisha
Cooper, Floyd
Cooper, Helene
Cooper, Ilene
Cooper, Leon N.
Cooper, Mark Garrett
Cooper, Polly Wylly
Cooper, Richard Newell
Cooper, Ron L.
Cooper, T.
Cooper, Terry L.
Cooper, Wyn
Cooperrider, Allen Y(ale)
Coover, Robert
Cope, David
Copeland, Anne P.
Copeland, Gary A.
Copeland, Gloria
Copeland, Peter
Copeland, Rebecca L.
Copenhaver, John D.
Coplin, Keith
Coppa, Frank John
Corbett, Ben
Corbett, Holly C.
Corbett, Patricia
Corbett, William
Cordery, Stacy A.
Cordesman, Anthony H.
Cording, Robert
Corgan, Billy Patrick
Corin, Joshua
Corlett, Mary Lee
Corliss, Richard (Nelson)
Corn, Alfred
Corn, David
Cornell, Gary
Cornell, Jennifer C.
Corngold, Stanley
Cornier, Nadia
Cornwell, Anita (R.)
Cornwell, Autumn
Cornyetz, Nina
Corona, Laurel
Corrado, Anthony
Corrick, James A.
Corrigan, Eireann
Corrigan, John R.
Corrigan, Kelly
Corrington, Robert S.
Corsetti, Emilio
Corson, Trevor
Coryell, Janet L(ee)
Cosby, Bill
Cosgrove, Charles H.
Cosgrove, Michael H.
Cosic, Dobrica
Coskran, Kathleen
Cosman, Mark
Cosper, Darcy
Cossolotto, Matthew
Costa, Manuel J(oseph)
Costello, Matthew J.
Costello, Matthew John

Costley, Bill
Cotham, Edward T.
Cothran, James R(obert)
Cotman, John Walton
Cott, Nancy F(alik)
Cotten, Cynthia
Cotter, James Finn
Cottle, Thomas J.
Cotton, Ronald
Cottonwood, Joe
Cottrell, David
Cottrell, Robert C.
Cottrol, Robert J.
Couch, Dick
Coulombe, Charles A.
Couloumbis, Audrey
Coulson, Juanita
Coulter, Catherine
Counihan, Carole
Cournos, Francine
Courter, Gay (Eleanor)
Courtright, Nicola
Cousineau, Phil
Couto, Nancy Vieira
Couvillon, Jacques
Covell, Stephen G.
Covey, Herbert C.
Covin, David L.
Covington, Dennis
Covington, James W.
Covington, Vicki
Cowart, Jack
Cowden, Robert H.
Cowell, Stephanie
Cowen, Ron(ald)
Cowley, Marjorie
Cowser, Bob
Cox, Ana Marie
Cox, Anna-Lisa
Cox, Gary W(alter)
Cox, Jeffrey
Cox, Jim
Cox, Judy
Cox, Lynne
Cox, Madison
Cox, Mike
Cox, Patsi Bale
Cox, Richard
Cox, Robert H(enry)
Cox, Ruth P.
Cox, Stephen D.
Cox, Vic
Cox, Vicki
Coy, John
Coyle, Beverly (Jones)
Coyle, Bill
Coyne, James K(itchenman)
Coyne, Jerry A.
Cozzens, Peter
Craft, Michael
Craig, Lee A(llen)
Craig, Robert H.
Craig, Stephen C.
Crais, Clifton C(harles)
Cramer, Clayton E.
Cramer, John G(leason)
Cramer, Richard Ben
Cramer, Stanley H.
Cramer, W.
Cramsie, John
Crandall, Susan

Davidson, Michael
Davidson, Osha Gray
Davidson, Roger H(arry)
Davidson, Sol M.
Davies, Charles E.
Davies, Oliver
Davies, Sharon L.
Davis, (Elvis) Clark
Davis, Alan (R.)
Davis, Albert Belisle
Davis, Allen F.
Davis, Amelia
Davis, Andrew
Davis, Anita (Grey) P(rice)
Davis, Bridgett M.
Davis, Bryan
Davis, Christopher
Davis, David (Howard)
Davis, David Brion
Davis, David R.
Davis, Dee
Davis, Donald
Davis, Donald A.
Davis, Donald Edward
Davis, Eleanor
Davis, Ellen F.
Davis, Francis
Davis, Frank Joseph
Davis, Hank
Davis, Harold
Davis, Heather
Davis, James Calvin
Davis, Jennifer S.
Davis, John W.
Davis, Jon
Davis, Julie Nelson
Davis, Kathy E.
Davis, Kenneth C.
Davis, Lexi
Davis, Linda W.
Davis, Maggie S.
Davis, Margaret Leslie
Davis, Mark H.
Davis, Matthew J.
Davis, Mildred (B.)
Davis, Nageeba
Davis, Nancy Yaw
Davis, Peter G(raffam)
Davis, R(oland) P(arker) Stephen
Davis, Richard
Davis, Richard A.
Davis, Richard Whitlock
Davis, Robert C.
Davis, Robin W(orks)
Davis, Rose Parkman
Davis, Sampson
Davis, Shelley L(orraine)
Davis, Steven J(oseph)
Davis, Steven L.
Davison, Eddy W.
Dawe, Margaret
Dawes, Casey
Dawid, Annie
Dawidoff, Nicholas
Dawn, Marva J.
Dawson, Carol
Dawson, George Glenn
Dawson, Geralyn
Dawson, Greg
Dawson, Janet
Dawson, John David

Dawson, Melanie
Day, Alexandra
Day, Cathy
Day, Edward C.
Day, Holliday T.
Day, Laura (Globus)
Day, Nancy
Dayan, Colin
Dayton, Charles (W.)
de Angelis, Lissa G.
De Becker, Gavin
de Bono, Douglas
de Costa, Elena M.
De Ferrari, Gabriella
de Grave, Kathleen
De Haven, Tom
de Herrera, Nancy Cooke
de La Isla, José
De Lisle, Harold F.
De Long, David G.
de los Santos, Marisa
De Marinis, Rick
de Marneffe, Daphne
de Neufville, Richard
de Pillis, John E.
De Stefano, George
de Tagyos, Paul Rátz
De Vorsey, Louis
De Vries, Rachel (Guido)
de Waal, Ronald Burt
Dean, Cornelia
Dean, Debra
Dean, Eric T.
Dean, Margaret Lazarus
Dean, Martin
Dean, William Denard
Dean (Dyer-Bennett), Pamela
    (Collins)
DeAngelis, Camille
Deans, Bob
Deans, Sis Boulos
Dear, Peter
Dearie, John
Deats, Richard L.
Deaver, Jeffery Wilds
Deaver, Julie Reece
DeBerg, Betty A.
Debin, David
Debnam, Aaron
DeBonis, Steven
deBry, Roger K.
Debs, Victor
DeCandido, Keith R. A.
DeCaro, Louis A.
Deck, Allan Figueroa
DeCosta-Willis, Miriam
DeCredico, Mary A.
DeCrow, Karen
Dee, Barbara
Dee, Ed(ward J.)
Dee, Jonathan
Deeb, Lara
Deem, James M(organ)
DeFazio, Albert J.
Deffaa, Chip
Deford, Frank
Defrank, Thomas M.
DeFrees, Madeline
DeGeorge, Richard T(homas)
DeGraaff, Robert M(ark)
DeGrazia, Emilio

DeJohn, Jacqueline
Dejohnson, Shervene
DeKeyser, Stacy
Del Caro, Adrian
del Moral, Roger
Del Negro, Giovanna P.
Delaney, Edward J.
Delaney, Gayle (M. V.)
Delaney, Kathleen
Delaney, Michael
Delaney, Norman
Delany, Samuel R(ay)
deLara, Ellen
Delbanco, Francesca
Deleon, Peter
DelFattore, Joan
Delgado, Aidan
Delgado, Hector L.
Delgado, Ricardo
DeLillo, Don
Delinsky, Barbara (Ruth Green-
    berg)
Dellasega, Cheryl
Deller, John J.
DeLong-Bas, Natana J.
Deloria, Philip J.
Delors, Catherine
Delsohn, Gary
Delson, Rudolph
DeLyser, Dydia
Demacopoulos, George E.
Demarais, Ann
Demaray, Donald E(ugene)
DeMarce, James L.
DeMarco, Kathy
Demarco-Barrett, Barbara
DeMarr, Mary Jean
Demastes, William
Dembska, Anna
DeMello, Margo
Demers, David (Pearce)
Demers, Joanna Teresa
DeMille, Nelson (Richard)
Deming, Alison Hawthorne
Deming, Sarah
Demos, John Putnam
DeMott, Robert (James)
Demott, Wes
Dempsey, Charles (Gates)
Demski, Joel S.
Dendinger, Roger E.
Deng, Francis Mading
Denham, James M.
Denizet-Lewis, Benoit
Denker, Henry
Dennett, Nolan A.
Denson, Andrew
Dent, David J.
Dent, Harry S.
Dent, Richard J.
dePaola, Tomie
DeParle, Jason
DePastino, Todd Allan
DePoy, Phillip
Derby, Sally
Dereske, Jo
Derfler, (Arnold) Leslie
Derian, James (Arthur) Der
Derickson, Alan
Deriso, Christine Hurley
Dermond, Susan Usha

DeRogatis, Jim
Derr, Mark (Burgess)
Dershowitz, Alan M.
Dervaes, Claudine
Dery, Mark
Des Jardins, Julie
DeSaix, Deborah Durland
Desalle, Rob
Desan, Suzanne
Desch, Michael C.
Desena, Carmine
Deslandes, Paul R.
DeSpain, Pleasant
Despres, Loraine
DesRochers, Diane
Desser, David
DeStefano, Stephen
Dettmar, Kevin J(ohn)
    H(offmann)
Detz, Joan (Marie)
Deuker, Carl
Deutsch, Sarah (Jane)
Deutscher, Irwin
Devashish, Donald Acosta
Devaux, Claudia
Devereaux, Robert
DeVincent-Hayes, Nan
DeVita, James
Devlin, Albert J.
Devlin, Dean
Devney, Darcy C(ampion)
DeVries, Kelly
Dew, Andrea J.
Dewald, Paul A.
Dewalt, Gary W(eston)
Dewart, Gilbert
Dewberry, Elizabeth
DeWeese, Gene
Deweese, Pamela J.
Dewey, Donald O(dell)
Dewey, Joseph (Owen)
Dewey, Scott Hamilton
DeWilde, Dennis M.
DeWitt, Calvin B.
Dexter, Pete
Di Blasi, Debra
di Certo, J(oseph) J(ohn)
di Filippo, Paul
di Lella, Alexander Anthony
Di Piero, W(illiam) S(imone)
di Prima, Diane
Dial-Driver, Emily
Diamant, Anita
Diamond, Arthur
Diamond, Jared (Mason)
Diamond, Jed
Diamond, Raymond T.
Diamond, Rickey Gard
Diamond, Sara
Diaz, Tony
DiBartolomeo, Albert
Dibbell, Julian
Dibbern, Mary
Dichtl, John R.
Dick, Bernard F.
Dicke, Thomas S(cott)
Dickerson, Dennis C.
Dickerson, Matthew T.
Dickerson, Vanessa D.
Dickey, Eric Jerome
Dickey, Page

Dickinson, Amy
Dickinson, Janice
Dickinson, W(illiam) Calvin
Dickman, Thomas
Dicks, Shirley
Dickson, (W.) Michael
Dickson, Athol
Dickson, Paul (Andrew)
Didion, Joan
Diehn, Gwen
Dierker, Larry
Dieterich, Michele M.
Dietrich, William A.
Dietz, Laura
Dietz, Maribel
Dietz, Steven
Diffily, Deborah
DiFonzo, Nicholas
Digby-Junger, Richard
Digregorio, Mario J.
Dillard, Annie
Dillard, R(ichard) H(enry)
   W(ilde)
Diller, Harriett
Dillingham, William B.
Dillon, Kathleen M. (Hynek)
Dillon, Patrick
Dillon, Sam(uel)
Dillon, Wilton Sterling
Dillow, Gordon
Dilmore, Kevin
Dils, Tracey E.
Dilsaver, Lary M.
DiMarco, Cris K. A.
DiMarco, Damon
Dimmick, Barbara
Dinan, Susan E.
Dinello, Paul
Dinerman, Beatrice
Dinnerstein, Leonard
Dintenfass, Mark L.
Dintiman, George B.
Dintrone, Charles V.
DioGuardi, Joseph J.
Dionne, E(ugene) J.
Diotalevi, Dave A.
Dippel, John V(an) H(outen)
Dipple, Geoffrey
Dirck, Brian R.
DiSalvo, Jackie
DiSilvestro, Roger L.
DiSpirito, Rocco
Ditchfield, Christin
Dittmar, Trudy Addis
Divale, William T(ulio)
Diver, Lucienne
Divine, Robert A(lexander)
Dixon, Ann R.
Dixon, Keith
Dixon, Larry
Dixon, Stephen
Dizikes, John
Djupe, Paul A.
Doane, Janice (L.)
Dobbs, Ricky F.
Dobie, Kathy
Dobrin, Lyn
Dobson, James C.
Dobson, Joanne
Dobyns, Jay Jaybird
Dockery, Kevin

Dockrey, Karen
Doctorow, E(dgar) L(awrence)
Dodd, Christina
Dodd, Christopher J.
Dodd, Elizabeth Caroline
Dodd, Wayne
Dodds, Bill
Dodge, Peter
Dodge, Tom
Doebler, Bettie Anne
Doerr, Anthony
Doherty, Brian
Doherty, Craig A.
Doherty, Katherine M(ann)
Doherty, Kieran
Doherty, Paul (Michael)
Doig, Ivan
Dokey, Cameron
Dolan, David
Dolan, Frederick Michael
Dolan, Harry
Dolan, Sean J.
Dolin, Eric Jay
Dolin, Sharon
Dolis, John
Doll, Mary A(swell)
Dolle, Raymond F.
Dolnick, Barrie
Dolnick, Ben
Doman, Glenn
Dombrowski, Daniel A.
Donahue, Tina
Donaldson, Gary A.
Donaldson, Joan
Donaldson, Loraine
Donaldson, Molla S(loane)
Donaldson, Ross I.
Donaldson, Scott
Donaldson, Thomas
Donia, Robert J(ay)
Donker, Marjorie
Donn, Linda
Donnelly, Deborah
Donnithorne, Larry R.
Donofrio, Beverly
Donoghue, Daniel
Donoghue, Frank J.
Donoghue, Mildred R(ansdorf)
Donohue, A. A.
Donohue, Keith
Donohue, Laura K.
Donohue, William A.
Donovan, Brian
Donovan, Brian
Donovan, Felicia
Doolen, Andy
Dooley, Allan C(harles)
Dooley, Brian J.
Dooley, David (Allen)
Dooling, Richard (Patrick)
Doran, Colleen
Doran, Phil
Doremus, Paul N.
Dorf, Fran
Dorflinger, Carolyn
Doriani, Beth Maclay
Dorkin, Evan
Dorman, Daniel
Dorman, Michael L.
Dornenburg, Andrew
Dorner, Marjorie

Dorré, Gina M.
Dorrien, Gary J.
Dorril, Stephen
Dorros, Arthur (M.)
Dorsen, Norman
Dorset, Phyllis (Flanders)
dos Santos, Joyce Audy
Doss, Erika
Dossey, Larry
Doti, Lynne Pierson
Dotson, Bob
Dotson, Rand
Dott, Brian R.
Doty, Mark
Doudera, Vicki
Dougan, Terrell Harris
Dougherty, James E(dward)
Doughty, Robert A.
Douglas, Ann
Douglas, Deborah G.
Douglas, Kirk
Douglas, L. Warren
Douglas, Mark
Douglas, Susan J(eanne)
Doval, Alexis J.
Dove, Rita (Frances)
Dover, Michael A.
Dow, David R.
Dow, James
Dowdy, Cecelia D.
Dower, John W(illiam)
Dower, Laura
Downes, Alexander B.
Downes, David A(nthony)
Downes, Jeremy M.
Downey, Tom
Downie, Leonard
Downing, David A(lmon)
Downing, David C(laude)
Downing, Michael (Bernard)
Downs, Dorothy
Downs, Robert C. S
Dowty, Alan K.
Doyle, Debra
Doyle, Dennis M(ichael)
Doyle, Larry
Doyle, Paul E.
Doyle, Paul I(gnatius)
Doyle, Robert Charles
Doyle, Robert J.
Dozier, Cheryl
Drake, Albert (Dee)
Drake, David A.
Drake, Timothy A.
Draper, Maureen McCarthy
Draper, Polly
Draper, Robert
Draper, Sharon Mills
Draut, Tamara
Drawe, D. Lynn
Dray, Philip
Drazin, Israel
Dreher, Henry
Dreher, Rod
Drehle, David Von
Dresser, Norine
Dressler, Alan (Michael)
Dressler, Joshua
Drew, Alan
Drew, Bettina
Drewes, Athena A.

Drexler, Rosalyn
Dreyer, Eileen
Dreyer, Elizabeth A.
Dreyfuss, Robert
Drez, Ronald J(oseph)
Drezner, Daniel W.
Driesen, David M.
Driscoll, Jeremy
Driskill, J. Lawrence
Drlica, Karl
Drogin, Bob
Drosnin, Michael
Drucker, Johanna
Drucker, Lisa
Drucker, Mort
Drucker, Peter
Drum, Alice
Drummond, Edward H.
Drummond, Michael
Drury, Tom
Dryden, Konrad
Dryfoos, Joy G.
Du Brul, Jack B.
Dubber, Markus Dirk
Duberman, Martin
Duberstein, Helen (Laura)
Duberstein, Larry
Dubin, Michael J.
DuBois, Ellen Carol
Dubois, Muriel L.
Dubose, Lou(is H.)
Dubrow, Gail Lee
Dubrow, Heather
Dubus, Andre
Ducey, Michael T.
Duchac, Joseph
Ducharme, Diann
Duckworth, William (Ervin)
Dudden, Alexis
Dudley, Ellen
Dudziak, Mary L.
Dudzinski, Kathleen
Due, Tananarive
Duelfer, Charles A.
Duey, Kathleen
Dufault, Peter Kane
Dufault, Roseanna Lewis
Duffey, Betsy (Byars)
Duffield, John S.
Duffield, Wendell
Duffy, Bruce
Duffy, James H(enry)
Duffy, Michael
Duffy, Susan
Dufresne, Jim
Dufresne, John
Dugan, Ellen
Dugatkin, Lee Alan
Dugaw, Dianne
Duggleby, John
Dugoni, Robert
Duhl, Leonard J.
Duina, Francesco G.
Duke, Anna Marie
Duke, Steven B.
Dukert, Joseph M(ichael)
Dukore, Bernard F.
Dulaney, W. Marvin
Dully, Howard
Dunaway, Wilma A.
Dunbar, Gary S(eamans)

Dunbar, Leslie W(allace)
Dunbar-Ortiz, Roxanne
Duncan, Alice Faye
Duncan, Andy
Duncan, Carol Greene
Duncan, Christine H.
Duncan, Cynthia M.
Duncan, David James
Duncan, Karen A.
Duncan, Lois
Duncan, Patrick Sheane
Duncan, Stephen M.
Duncombe, Stephen
Dunham, Tracy
Dunham, William
Dunlap, Julie
Dunlap, Susan D. (Sullivan)
Dunlap, Susanne Emily
Dunn, Durwood
Dunn, Joe P.
Dunn, John M.
Dunn, Mark (Rodney)
Dunn, Robert J.
Dunn, Stephen
Dunne, John S(cribner)
Dunne, Pete
Duntemann, Jeff
Duntemann, Jeff
DuPlessis, Rachel Blau
DuPrau, Jeanne
Dupree, Nathalie
DuPree, Sherry Sherrod
Dupree, Stephen A.
Dupuis, Robert
Duquette, David A.
Duran, Jane
Durand, Alain-Philippe
Durang, Christopher
Durant, Michael J.
Durban, Pam
Durden, Robert F(ranklin)
Durfee, Mary
Durgin, Doranna
Durham, Walter T.
Durkee, Sarah
Durrant, Lynda
Durrell, Julie
Durrenberger, E. Paul
Durrow, Heidi W.
Durst, Sarah Beth
Dussling, Jennifer
Duthu, N. Bruce
Dutoit, Ulysse
Dutton, J. T.
Duvoisin, Roger C(lair)
Duyfhuizen, Bernard
Dwight, Jeffry
Dworkin, Shari L.
Dwyer, Jim
Dwyer, Richard A.
Dyal, Donald H(enriques)
Dychtwald, Maddy Kent
Dyer, Davis
Dyer, Joel
Dyer, Joyce
Dyer, Wayne W(alter)
Dyrness, William A.
Dysart, Joshua
Dyson, Michael Eric
Dzuback, Mary Ann
Eady, Cornelius

Eagles, Charles W.
Eakins, Patricia
Eames, Anne
Earl, Riggins R.
Earle, Jonathan
Earle, Sylvia A.
Earley, Pete
Earley, Tony
Early, Joseph E.
Earnshaw, Micky
Eastburn, Kathryn
Easter, Gerald M.
Easterbrook, Gregg
Easterly, William
Eastman, Susan Tyler
Easton, Elizabeth Wynne
Easton, Laird M.
Easton, Malcolm Coleman
Easton, Nina J(ane)
Easum, William M.
Eaton, Richard M.
Ebaugh, Helen Rose (Fuchs)
Ebbesmeyer, Curtis Charles
Ebel, Roland H.
Eberhart, Mark E.
Eberle, Gary
Eberstadt, Nicholas (Nash)
Ebert, James I(an)
Ebert, Roger (Joseph)
Ebisch, Glen Albert
Eble, Connie
Echevarria, Jana
Eck, Joe
Eck, Matthew
Eckard, Paula G.
Eckert, Kathryn Bishop
Ecklar, Julia (Marie)
Ecklund, Elaine Howard
Eckstein, Arthur M.
Eckstein, Rick
Economou, George
Eddins, Dwight L.
Edelheit, Abraham J.
Edelman, Amy Holman
Edelman, Marian Wright
Edelman, Ric
Edelstein, Robert
Edgar, Stacey L.
Edgecombe, David
Edgerton, Clyde
Edgerton, Teresa (Ann)
Edgette, Janet
Edin, Kathryn
Edinger, Ray
Edison, Mike
Edlow, Jonathan A.
Edmisten, Patricia Taylor
Edmunds, John C.
Edmunds, R(ussell) David
Edsel, Robert M.
Edson, Russell
Edwards, Allen Jack
Edwards, Anne
Edwards, Brent Hayes
Edwards, David B.
Edwards, Johanna
Edwards, Larry
Edwards, Laurie Elizabeth
Edwards, Louis
Edwards, Michael B.
Edwards, Mickey Henry

Edwards, Sarah (Anne)
Egan, Ferol
Egan, Jennifer
Egan, Ken
Egan, Linda
Egan, Ronald
Egan, Tim
Egan, Timothy
Egerton, Douglas R.
Eggers, Kerry
Egginton, William
Eggleston, Larry G.
Egielski, Richard
Egli, Ida Rae
Ehle, John
Ehlert, Lois (Jane)
Ehrenberg, John
Ehrenberg, Pamela
Ehret, Christopher
Ehret, Terry
Ehrler, Brenda
Ehrlich, Amy
Ehrlich, Paul (Ralph)
Ehrlich, Tracy L.
Ehrman, Bart D.
Ehrman, John
Eichengreen, Barry J.
Eichler, Selma
Eichorn, Rosemary D.
Eichstaedt, Peter H.
Eickhoff, Diane
Eickhoff, Randy Lee
Eidson, Thomas
Eilberg-Schwartz, Howard
Einolf, Christopher J.
Eisen, Adrienne
Eisenberg, Deborah
Eisenberg, Ellen M.
Eisenberg, John S.
Eisenberg, Jon B.
Eisenberg, Nora
Eisenberg, Robert
Eisenhower, John S(heldon)
  D(oud)
Eisenman, Stephen F.
Eisenson, Marc
Eisenstein, Hester
Eisenstein, Phyllis (Kleinstein)
Eisgruber, Christopher L(udwig)
Eisiminger, Sterling (Skip)
Eisler, Barry
Eisler, Benita
Eisner, Michael Alexander
Eisner, Peter (Norman)
El-Hai, Jack
El-Moslimany, Ann P(axton)
Elam, Jason
Elbirt, Paula M.
Elder, John
Eldon, Kathy
Elegant, Simon
Elfers, James E.
Elfstrom, Gerard A.
Elgin, Suzette Haden
Elias, Jason
Eliav, Yaron Z.
Elie, Lolis Eric
Elie, Paul
Elium, Don
Elium, Jeanne (Ann)
Elizondo, Virgil P.

Elkeles, Simone
Elkins, Charlotte
Elkins, Dov Peretz
Ellenbecker, Todd S.
Ellenberg, George B.
Ellenberg, Jordan S.
Ellenson, David Harry
Ellingham, Lewis
Ellingson, Stephen
Ellington, Sara
Elliott, Anna
Elliott, Charles
Elliott, Clark A.
Elliott, David
Elliott, Elaine M.
Elliott, Melinda
Ellis, Anita J.
Ellis, Barbara W.
Ellis, Bret Easton
Ellis, David
Ellis, Donald
Ellis, Ella Thorp
Ellis, Gwen
Ellis, Jamellah
Ellis, Jerry
Ellis, Mary Relindes
Ellis, Ralph D.
Ellis, Reuben J.
Ellis, Robert
Ellis, Trey
Ellis, William E.
Ellison, Elizabeth Stow
Ellison, Harlan (Jay)
Ellison, Joan Jarvis
Ellroy, James
Elmer, Robert
Elmslie, Kenward
Elrod, P(at) N.
Elster, Kathi
Elukin, Jonathan
Ely, Christopher
Ely, David
Ely, Melvin Patrick
Emerson, Claudia
Emerson, Earl W.
Emerson, Isabelle Putnam
Emerson, Ken
Emerson, Michael O.
Emerson, Thomas E.
Emery, Clayton
Emery, Robert Firestone
Emery, Robert J.
Emery, Tom
Emmet, Alan
Emmons, Henry
Emmons, Mary L.
Emmons, Robert A.
Emory, Jerry
Emshwiller, Carol (Fries)
Encinias, Miguel
Eng, David L.
Engdahl, Sylvia L(ouise)
Engel, Bernard F.
Engel, Beverly
Engel, Jeffrey A.
Engel, Joel
Engel, Jonathan
Engel, Margorie L(ouise)
Engel, Michael S.
Engel, Monroe
Engel, Richard

Fenton, Peter
Fenton, Robert L.
Ferber, Brenda Aaronson
Ferber, Richard A.
Ferder, Fran
Ferguson, Alane
Ferguson, Andrew
Ferguson, Brad
Ferguson, Everett
Ferguson, Gary
Ferguson, Kathy E.
Ferguson, Kitty
Ferguson, R. Brian
Ferling, John E.
Ferlinghetti, Lawrence
Ferlita, Ernest
Fermi, Rachel
Ferner, Mike
Ferrari, Mark J.
Ferraris, Zoë
Ferraro, Barbara
Ferraro, Susan (Lyons)
Ferre, John P.
Ferree, Myra Marx
Ferreiro, Larrie D.
Ferrell, Carolyn
Ferrell, Jeff
Ferrell, John S.
Ferrer, Elizabeth
Ferrigno, Robert
Ferris, Jean
Ferris, Jeri Chase
Ferris, Joshua
Ferris, Marcie Cohen
Ferris, William (R.)
Fertig, Beth
Feshbach, Murray
Fessenden, Tracy
Fessler, Ann
Fetherston, Drew
Fetters, Thomas T.
Feuerwerker, Albert
Feurer, Rosemary
Fialka, John J.
Fiallos, Rosario
Ficera, Kim (M.)
Fickett, David C.
Field, Edward
Field, Genevieve
Field, Mark G(eorge)
Field, Thalia
Fielding, Raymond
Fields, Hillary
Fields, Jennie
Fields, Terri
Fienup-Riordan, Ann
Fierstein, Harvey (Forbes)
Figley, Marty Rhodes
Figueira, Thomas J.
Filderman, Diane E(lizabeth)
Files, Meg
Filkins, Dexter
Filkins, Peter
Finch, Annie (Ridley Crane)
Finch, Charles
Finch, Robert (Charles)
Finchler, Judy
Fine, Jerramy Sage
Fine, Marshall
Fine, Richard
Finello, Dominick

Fineman, Martha Albertson
Fink, Carole (Kapiloff)
Fink, Deborah
Fink, Karl J.
Fink, Leon
Fink, Mitchell
Fink, Sheri
Finkel, David
Finkel, Madelon Lubin
Finkelstein, Adrian
Finkelstein, Stan N.
Finlan, Stephen
Finley, Glenna
Finley, Karen
Finley, Michael
Finley, Mitch
Finley, Randy
Finn, Margot C.
Finnegan, Lisa
Finnegan, Terrence J.
Finnegan, William (Patrick)
Finney, Ernest J.
Finstad, Suzanne
Firestone, Reuven
Firkatian, Mari A.
Firsching, F. Henry
Fischel, Jack R.
Fischel, William A.
Fischer, Debbie Reed
Fischer, Lucy Rose
Fischer, Lynn
Fischetti, Mark
Fischkin, Barbara
Fischler, Alan
Fisdel, Steven A.
Fish, Charles (K.)
Fish, Stanley E(ugene)
Fishback, Mary
Fishback, Price V(anmeter)
Fisher, Clive
Fisher, Dana R.
Fisher, David E.
Fisher, Donald M.
Fisher, Ernest F.
Fisher, Franklin M.
Fisher, Jessica
Fisher, Leonard Everett
Fisher, Louis
Fisher, Marshall Jon
Fisher, Marvin
Fisher, Paul
Fisher, Ralph Talcott
Fisher, Robert E.
Fisher, Robin Gaby
Fisher, Roger (Dummer)
Fisher, Stephen L(ynn)
Fisher-Wirth, Ann W.
Fishgall, Gary
Fishkin, Shelley Fisher
Fishman, Cathy Goldberg
Fishman, Charles N.
Fishman, David E.
Fishman, Katharine Davis
Fishman, Steve
Fishman, Sylvia Barack
Fisk, Milton
Fiske, Robert H(artwell)
Fiss, Owen M(itchell)
Fister, Barbara
Fitch, David E.
Fitch, Noel Riley

Fitch, Stona
Fitten, Marc
Fitzgerald, Carol
Fitzgerald, Cathy
Fitzgerald, Michael W(illiam)
Fitzgerald-Hoyt, Mary
Fitzpatrick, Becca
Fitzpatrick, Flo
Fitzpatrick, Frank
Fitzpatrick, Mary Anne
Fitzpatrick, Tony
Fitzpatrick, Vincent (dePaul)
Fix, Michael
Flack, Jerry D(avid)
Flaherty, Alice W.
Flaherty, Liz
Flaherty, Michael G.
Flam, Jack D(onald)
Flamini, Roland
Flamm, Michael W.
Flamming, Douglas
Flanagan, Erin
Flaste, Richard (Alfred)
Flayhart, William Henry
Fleeson, Lucinda
Fleischer, Ari
Fleischman, Paul
Fleischman, Paul R.
Fleischner, Jennifer
Fleisher, Paul
Fleishman, Avrom
Fleissner, Robert F.
Fleming, Alice (Carew Mulcahey)
Fleming, Candace
Fleming, James E.
Fleming, James Rodger
Fleming, Keith
Fleming, Robert E.
Fleming, Thomas
Fleming, Virginia (Edwards)
Flescher, Irwin
Fletcher, Christine
Fletcher, George P.
Fletcher, Joel L.
Fletcher, Michael A.
Fletcher, Ralph
Fletcher, Susan (Clemens)
Fleurant, Gerdès
Flieger, Verlyn
Flier, Michael S.
Flinders, Neil J.
Flinn, Alex
Flinn, Caryl
Flinn, Kathleen
Flinn, Kelly
Flint, Anthony
Flint, Richard
Flitter, Marc
Floca, Brian
Flock, Elizabeth
Flokos, Nicholas
Flood, (Nancy) Bo
Flood, Joe
Flood, Pansie Hart
Flora, Joseph M(artin)
Florine, Hans E.
Florita, Kira
Flory, David A.
Flowers, Pam
Flowers, Ronald B(ruce)
Flowers, Sarah

Floyd, Nancy
Fluehr-Lobban, Carolyn
Fluke, Joanne
Flynn, Elizabeth A.
Flynn, Joseph
Flynn, Kevin
Flynn, Laura M.
Flynn, Nancy L.
Flynn, Robert (Lopez)
Flynn, Thomas R.
Flynt, Mike
Foege, Alec
Foer, Franklin
Foer, Jonathan Safran
Foerstel, Herbert N.
Foerstel, Karen
Foerstner, Abigail M.
Fogel, Robert William
Fogle, Jeanne
Folbre, Nancy
Foldvary, Fred E.
Foley, Denise (M.)
Foley, Gaelen
Foley, Jack
Foley, Mick
Folgarait, Leonard
Foli, Karen J.
Folk, Thomas C.
Folks, Jeffrey Jay
Follett, CB
Folsom, Allan (R.)
Fonda, Peter
Fone, Byrne R. S.
Foner, Eric
Fones-Wolf, Elizabeth
Fong, Bobby
Fonseca, James W(illiam)
Fontaine, Carole R.
Fontanella, John J.
Fontes, Montserrat
Fontes, Ron
Foos, Laurie
Foote, David
Foran, John
Forbes, Anna
Forbes, Bruce David
Forbes, Camille F.
Force, Marie Sullivan
Forché, Carolyn (Louise)
Ford, Barbara
Ford, Carolyn (Mott)
Ford, Darnella D.
Ford, G. M.
Ford, Herbert (Paul)
Ford, Jamie Mark
Ford, Jennifer
Ford, Jerry
Ford, John C.
Ford, Katie
Ford, Marjorie Leet
Ford, Michael Curtis
Ford, Michael Thomas
Ford, Richard Thompson
Ford, Susan
Foreman, George
Foreman, Lelia Rose
Foreman, Richard
Forker, Charles R(ush)
Forman, Richard T. T.
Forman, Robert K. C.
Forman, Steven M.

Forment, Carlos A.
Forrest, Christopher
Forrester, Sandra
Forrester, Sibelan
Forret, Jeff
Forster, Marc R.
Fort, Ilene Susan
Fortna, Virginia Page
Foss, Sonja K.
Foster, (William) Lawrence
Foster, Alan Dean
Foster, Brooke Lea
Foster, David William
Foster, Edward Halsey
Foster, Frances Smith
Foster, Hal
Foster, Joanne Reckler
Foster, John Bellamy
Foster, Ken
Foster, Kennedy
Foster, Linda Nemec
Foster, Lori L.
Foster, M(ichael) A(nthony)
Foster, Mark
Foster, Nora R(akestraw)
Foster, Raymond E.
Foster, Sesshu
Foster, Steven
Foster, Thomas C.
Foust, J'aimé L.
Foust, Jeff
Fowers, Blaine J.
Fowler, Connie May
Fowler, Don D.
Fowler, Earlene
Fowler, Gene
Fowler, James H.
Fowler, Loretta
Fowler, Virginia C.
Fowlkes, Diane L(owe)
Fox, Andrew Jay
Fox, Barry
Fox, Faulkner
Fox, Hugh (Bernard)
Fox, John O.
Fox, Les
Fox, Margalit
Fox, Paula
Fox, Richard Allan
Fox, Richard L.
Fox, Roy F.
Fox, Sarah
Fox, Ted
Fox, William L.
Foxworthy, Jeff
Foxx, Daniel
Foyt, Victoria
Frader, Laura Levine
Fradin, Judith (Bernette) Bloom
Fraenkel, Jack R.
Fraiser, Jim
Frakes, George Edward
Frakes, William B.
Fraley, Tobin
Frame, J. Davidson
Francaviglia, Richard V.
Franceschini, Remo
Francia, Peter L.
Francis, Diana Pharaoh
Francis, Dorothy Brenner
Francis, James A.

Francis, Lesley Lee
Francisco, Nia
Franco, Betsy
Franco, Dean J.
Frank, Dana
Frank, Dorothea Benton
Frank, E(mily) R.
Frank, Frederick S.
Frank, J. Suzanne
Frank, Jacquelyn
Frank, Joan
Frank, Katherine
Frank, Nathaniel
Frank, Robert
Frank, Robert H.
Franke, William
Frankel, Ellen
Frankel, Glenn
Frankel, Sandor
Frankel, Valerie
Frankfurter, David Thomas Munro
Frankl, Razelle
Franklet, Duane
Franklin, Allan (David)
Franklin, Cheryl J.
Franklin, Daniel P.
Franklin, David Byrd
Franklin, James L(ee)
Franklin, Jane (Morgan)
Franklin, Linda Campbell
Franklin, Robert M(ichael)
Franklin, Yelena
Frantzen, Allen J.
Frantzich, Stephen E.
Franzoni, David (H.)
Frasca, Ralph
Fraser, George (C.)
Fraser, Kathleen
Fraser, Laura (Jane)
Fraser, Margot
Fraser, Mary Ann
Fraser, Rebecca
Fraser, Russell A(lfred)
Fraser, Sarah E.
Fraser, Wynnette (McFaddin)
Frassetto, Michael
Fratkin, Elliot
Fraustino, Lisa Rowe
Fravel, M. Taylor
Frazee, Randy
Frazer, Gail
Frazer, Megan
Frazer, Timothy C.
Frazier, Alison Knowles
Frazier, Charles (Robinson)
Frazier, Donald S(haw)
Frazier, Kit
Frazier, Lessie Jo
Frazier, Shirley George
Frazier, Sundee T.
Freccero, Carla
Freda, Joseph
Frederick, David C.
Frederick, Jim
Freed, Anne O.
Freed, Curt R(ichard)
Freedman, Adam
Freedman, Anne
Freedman, David H.
Freedman, Eric
Freedman, Jeff

Freedman, Jonathan
Freedman, Jonathan (Borwick)
Freedman, Michael R.
Freedman, Russell (Bruce)
Freedman, Sarah Warshauer
Freehling, William W(ilhartz)
Freeman, Anne Hobson
Freeman, Castle (William)
Freeman, Charles Wellman
Freeman, Daniel E(van)
Freeman, Harry M.
Freeman, Jo
Freeman, Joshua B.
Freeman, Marcia S.
Freeman, Martha
Freeman, Philip
Freese, Barbara
Freese, Mathias B(alogh)
Freeze, Gregory L.
Frega, Donnalee
Freidberg, Susanne
Freinkel, Susan Elizabeth
Freireich, Valerie J.
Freirich, Roy
Freitas, Donna
Frelinghuysen, Alice Cooney
Fremgen, James Morgan
French, Albert
French, Howard W.
French, Judith E.
French, Linda
French, Scot
Freudenheim, Ellen
Freund, Diane
Freund, Thatcher
Freundel, Barry
Frey, James N.
Frey, Julia (Bloch)
Frey, Linda (Sue)
Frey, Marsha L.
Frey, Stephen W.
Freyd, Jennifer J.(Joy)
Freydont, Shelley
Freyer, Tony (Allan)
Frezza, Robert (A.)
Fricchione, Gregory
Frick, Carole Collier
Fricker, Mary
Fried, Dennis F.
Fried, Robert L.
Frieden, Jeffry
Friedenberg, Robert V.
Friedland, William H(erbert)
Friedman, Aimee
Friedman, Alan Warren
Friedman, Andrew
Friedman, Barry E.
Friedman, Benjamin M.
Friedman, Bonnie
Friedman, Brandon
Friedman, Bruce Jay
Friedman, C(elia) S.
Friedman, Kinky
Friedman, Lawrence M.
Friedman, Lawrence S(amuel)
Friedman, Norman
Friedman, Paul (Alan)
Friedman, Philip (J.)
Friedman, Rebecca
Friedman, Ron
Friedman, Ronald S(amuel)

Friedman, Stewart D.
Friedman, Thomas L(oren)
Friedmann, Patty
Friedrich, Paul
Friend, Craig Thompson
Friend, Theodore (Wood)
Friendly, Alfred
Friesen, Jonathan
Frigstad, David B.
Frisbie, Charlotte J(ohnson)
Frisch, Walter
Frist, William H.
Frith, Katherine Toland
Fritsch, Albert J(oseph)
Fritts, Mary Bahr
Fritz, Robert
Fritz, Stephen G.
Fritze, Ronald H.
Fritzell, Peter A(lgren)
Fritzer, Penelope Joan
Fritzsche, Peter
Frohnen, Bruce (P.)
Frohoff, Toni
Frome, Michael
Fromm, Pete
Frommer, Benjamin
Frost, Ellen L.
Frost, Helen
Frost, Linda
Frost, Mark C.
Frost, Scott
Frost, Shelley
Frost-Knappman, L. Elizabeth
Frueh, Joanna
Fruin, W. Mark
Fry, Andrew C.
Fry, Joseph A.
Fry, Virginia Lynn
Fry, William Finley
Fryd, Vivien Green
Frye, Marilyn
Fuchs, Marek
Fuchs, Miriam
Fuchs, Rachel G(innis)
Fujimura, Joan H.
Fukui, Isamu Carter
Fukuyama, Francis
Fulani, Lenora (Branch)
Fulda, Jennette
Fulghum, Robert (L)
Fuller, Charles
Fuller, Jack (William)
Fuller, Mary Lou
Fullerton, Gail
Fulton, Joe B.
Fultz, James R.
Fumento, Rocco
Fumizuki, Kou
Funderburg, Lise
Funk, Liz
Funk, Tom
Funkhouser, Erica
Furdell, Elizabeth Lane
Furia, Philip (G.)
Furnish, Victor Paul
Furubotn, Eirik G.
Furutani, Dale
Fusilli, Jim
Fussell, E. Robert
Fussell, Paul
Futcher, Jane P.

Futterman, Enid (Susan)
Gaard, Greta
Gabbard, David A.
Gabbay, Tom
Gabhart, Ann Houchin
Gabor, Andrea (Anna Gisela)
Gabriel, Michael P.
Gabriel, Richard A(lan)
Gabriel (Loving), Kathryn (Ann)
Gabrieli, Christopher
Gaddis, Michael
Gaddis-Rose, Marilyn
Gadol, Peter
Gage, Leighton D.
Gagliani, William
Gagliano, Anthony
Gagliano, Eugene M.
Gagliano, Frank
Gagné, Marcel
Gagnon, Michelle
Gaillard, Frye
Gaines, Jane (Marie)
Gaines, Thomas A.
Gaither, Carl C.
Galanes, Philip
Galang, M. Evelina
Galant, Debra
Galbraith, Kathryn O(sebold)
Galdorisi, George V(ictor)
Gale, Fredric G.
Galef, David
Galenorn, Yasmine
Galgano, Robert C.
Galinsky, Karl
Galison, Peter (Louis)
Gall, Pete
Gallagher, Gary W(illiam)
Gallagher, Liz
Gallagher, Mary Elizabeth
Gallagher, Patricia C.
Gallagher, Shaun
Gallagher, Susan VanZanten
Gallagher, Tess
Gallagher, Winifred
Gallaher, (William) Rhea
Gallant, Roy Arthur
Gallant, Stephen I.
Gallardo, Evelyn
Gallas, Karen
Gallaway, Morgana Bridget
Gallenkamp, Charles (Benton)
Galli, Richard
Galligan, John
Gallimore, Paul
Gallo, Gina
Gallo, Patrick J.
Galston, William A.
Galvin, Brendan
Galvin, Matthew R(eppert)
Gamble, Ed
Gamble, Terry
Gamson, Joshua (Paul)
Gamson, William A(nthony)
Gamst, Frederick Charles
Ganas, Monica
Gander, Forrest
Gandt, Robert
Ganek, Danielle
Gangemi, Joseph G.
Gannett, Ruth Stiles
Gannon, Martin John

Gannon, Steve
Gans, Eric L.
Gansky, Alton
Gansler, Jacques Singleton
Ganson, Barbara
Ganz, Marshall
Gao, Minglu
Gaposchkin, M. Cecilia
Garber, Marjorie
Garber, Zev
Garbera, Katherine
Garbus, Cassandra
Garbus, Martin
Garceau, Dee
Garcia, Diana
Garcia, J. Malcolm
Garcia Y Robertson, R(odrigo)
Gardaphé, Fred L(ouis)
Gardella, Tricia
Garden, Nancy
Gardiner, Judith Kegan
Gardiner, Meg
Gardner, Craig Shaw
Gardner, James A.
Gardner, Leonard
Gardner, Mark L(ee)
Gardner, Michael R.
Gardner, Robert
Gardner, Robert W(ayne)
Gardner, Sandra
Gardner, Theodore Roosevelt
Gardner, Tom
Garelick, Rhonda K.
Garfield, Brian (F. W.)
Garfinkle, David
Garfunkel, Trudy
Gargan, Edward A.
Garland, Mark (A.)
Garland, Max
Garner, Gretchen
Garner, John S.
Garrard, John (Gordon)
Garrett, Laurie
Garrett, Susan
Garrettson, Charles Lloyd
Garris, Mick
Garrison, Bruce
Garrison, Daniel H.
Garrison, David Lee
Garrison, Deborah (Gottlieb)
Garrison, J. Ritchie
Garrison, Philip
Garrow, David J.
Garry, Patrick M.
Garten, Helen A.
Garten, Jeffrey E.
Gartner, Scott Sigmund
Garver, John W.
Garver, Newton
Garvey, John H.
Garwood, Julie
Gasaway, Laura N.
Gaskell, Whitney
Gaskins, Richard H.
Gass, Thomas Edward
Gass, William (Howard)
Gassenheimer, Linda
Gastil, John (Webster)
Gaston, Diane
Gaston, Patricia S.
Gatch, Milton McC

Gates, Barbara T(imm)
Gates, David
Gates, Henry Louis
Gates, Ronda
Gau, Colleen
Gaubatz, Kathlyn Taylor
Gaubatz, Kurt Taylor
Gauch, Patricia Lee
Gaudet, Marcia
Gaunt, Carole O'Malley
Gaunt, Kyra D.
Gawrych, George
Gay, John H.
Gay, Kathlyn R.
Gayle, Stephanie
Gaylin, Alison
Gaylin, Willard
Gear, W. Michael
Geary, David C(yril)
Geary, Patricia (Carol)
Gebhardt, James F(rederick)
Gecan, Michael
Gediman, Helen K.
Gehman, Mary W.
Gehring, Wes D(avid)
Geisert, Arthur (Frederick)
Geist, Bill
Gekoski, Rick
Gelb, Jeff
Gelb, Michael J.
Geldard, Richard G.
Gelderman, Carol (Wettlaufer)
Gelernter, David (Hillel)
Gell-Mann, Murray
Geller, Jaclyn
Geller, Jay Howard
Gelles, Edith B.
Gellis, Roberta (Leah Jacobs)
Gellman, Marc
Gelpi, Albert
Geltmaker, Ty
Gelvin, James L.
Gemmell, Jim
Genesse, Paul
Geniesse, Jane Fletcher
Genini, Ronald
Gentile, John S(amuel)
Gentile, Olivia
Gentry, Christine
Gentry, Curt
George, Alice L.
George, Alice Rose
George, Elizabeth
George, Jean Craighead
George, Kathleen Elizabeth
George, Margaret
George, Robert P.
George Bloomfield, Susanne K.
Gerard, Charley
Gerard, Philip
Gerber, Merrill Joan
Gerber, Michael E.
Gerdes, Eckhard
Gerdy, John R.
Gerhardt, Michael E.
Gerhart, Ann
Gerlach, Don R.
Gerlach, Douglas
Gerlach, Larry R(euben)
German, Bill
Geronimus, Dennis

Gerrard, Michael B.
Gerrig, Richard J.
Gerritsen, Tess
Gershow, Miriam
Gershten, Donna M.
Gershuny, Grace
Gerson, Kathleen
Gerson, Michael J.
Gerstein, Daniel M.
Gersten-Vassilaros, Alexandra
Gerstler, Amy
Gerstmann, Evan
Gerteis, Joseph
Gerzina, Gretchen Holbrook
Gerzon, Robert
Gesch, Roy (George)
Gessel, Van C.
Geston, Mark S(ymington)
Getis, Victoria
Getler, Warren
Getman, Julius (G.)
Getsy, David J.
Getty, Sarah Sovereign
Getz, Christine S.
Getz, David
Getz, Marshall J(ay)
Getz, Trevor R.
Gewertz, Deborah B.
Geyer, Georgie Anne
Geyman, John P.
Ghareeb, Edmund
Ghazvinian, John
Gherman, Beverly
Ghiglione, Loren
Ghilarducci, Teresa
Ghosh, Durba
Giamo, Benedict
Gianakaris, Constantine John
Giancana, Sam
Giangreco, D. M.
Gibb, Robert
Gibbon, Sean
Gibbons, Anne R.
Gibbons, Gail (Gretchen)
Gibbons, Reginald
Gibbs, David N.
Gibbs, Tyson
Gibson, Alan
Gibson, Ann Eden
Gibson, Margaret
Gibson, Marley
Gibson, Mary Ellis
Gibson, Tanya Egan
Gibson, Thomas
Gibson, Walter Samuel
Giebel, Christoph
Gier, Scott G.
Gifaldi, David
Gifford, Barry (Colby)
Gifford, James J.
Gifford, Peggy
Gifford, Rebecca
Giglio, James N.
Gikow, Jacqueline
Gilb, Dagoberto
Gilbert, Barbara Snow
Gilbert, Bil
Gilbert, Elizabeth
Gilbert, Glenn G(ordon)
Gilbert, Sandra M(ortola)
Gilbert, Sheri L.

Gilbert, Suzie
Gilbert, Tom
Gilchrist, Ellen
Gildea, William
Gilden, Mel
Gildner, Gary
Gilens, Martin
Giles, Gail
Giles, Robert Hartmann
Gilkes, Cheryl Townsend
Gill, David Macinnis
Gill, LaVerne McCain
Gill, Sam D.
Gill, Walter
Giller, Marc D.
Gilles, D. B.
Gillespie, Angus Kress
Gillespie, Carol Ann
Gillespie, Diane Filby
Gillespie, Gerald (Ernest Paul)
Gillespie, Hollis
Gillespie, J(ohn) David
Gillette, J(an) Lynett
Gillies, Isabel Boyer
Gilligan, Carol
Gilligan, James F.
Gilliland, Alexis A(rnaldus)
Gillis, Chester
Gillman, Abigail
Gillon, Adam
Gillon, Steven M.
Gilman, Andrew D.
Gilman, Keith
Gilman, Owen W(inslow)
Gilmore, David D.
Gilmore, Dewitt
Gilmore, Glenda Elizabeth
Gilmore, John
Gilmore, Kate
Gilmore, Ruth Wilson
Gilmore, Susan Gregg
Gilmour, John C.
Gilpin, Geoff
Gilreath, Shannon
Gilroy, Frank D(aniel)
Gilsdorf, Ethan
Gilson, Christopher C.
Gilstrap, John
Ginsberg, Blaze
Ginsburg, Faye D(iana)
Ginsburg, Mark B.
Ginzberg, Lori D.
Gioia, (Michael) Dana
Giorello, Sibella
Giovagnoli, Melissa (E.)
Giovanni, Nikki
Giovino, Andrea
Gipson, Carolyn R.
Gish, Robert F.
Gitlin, Todd
Gitter, Elisabeth
Gittlin, Adam
Giziowski, Richard (John)
Gizzi, Peter
Gjelten, Tom
Gladstone, Arthur M.
Glahe, Fred R.
Glancy, Diane
Glancy, Jennifer A.
Glantz, David M.
Glantz, Kalman

Glanville, Doug
Glasco, Michael
Glaser, James M.
Glaser, Michael S.
Glaser, William Arnold
Glasmeier, Amy (K.)
Glass, Leslie
Glassberg, David
Glasser, Ira
Glassie, Henry
Glassman, Bruce
Glassman, Jonathon P.
Glassman, Ronald M.
Glatt, Lisa
Glatthaar, Joseph T(homas)
Glazer, Ellen Sarasohn
Glazer, Nathan
Glazier, Stephen D.
Gleason, Katherine (A.)
Gleick, Peter H.
Gleiter, Jan
Glen, Paul (Michael)
Glendening, John
Glener, Doug
Glenn, Cheryl
Glenn, Evelyn Nakano
Glenn, Jason Kahn
Glenn, Patricia Brown
Glenn, Richard A.
Glenn, Sharlee Mullins
Glennon, Karen M.
Glennon, Robert Jerome
Glickman, James (A.)
Glickman, Norman J.
Gliserman, Martin
Glisson, J(ake) T.
Glixon, Jonathan Emmanuel
Glock, Allison
Gloss, Molly
Glossop, Ronald J.
Glover, Lorri
Glut, Don(ald) F.
Glyer, Diana Pavlac
Gmelch, George
Gobbell, John J.
Gochfeld, Michael
Godbold, E(dward) Stanly
Godfrey, Neale S.
Godfrey-June, Jean
Godin, Seth Warren
Godshalk, C. S.
Godson, Roy (S.)
Godwin, Gail (Kathleen)
Godwin, Parke
Godwin, Rebecca T.
Goedecke, Christopher (John)
Goehlert, Robert
Goerler, Raimund E.
Goerner, Sally J.
Goethe, Ann
Goff, M(adison) Lee
Goin, Peter
Goin, Suzanne
Going, Kelly L.
Goingback, Owl
Golant, Stephen M(yles)
Golay, Michael
Golczewski, James A.
Gold, August
Gold, Hazel
Gold, Herbert

Gold, Janet N(owakowski)
Gold, Jerome
Gold, Judy
Gold, Michael
Gold, Michael Evan
Gold, Penny Schine
Gold, Scott
Gold, Steven J(ames)
Goldberg, Bruce (Edward)
Goldberg, Danny
Goldberg, Harold
Goldberg, Jacob
Goldberg, Jane G.
Goldberg, Jonah Jacob
Goldberg, Leonard S.
Goldberger, Avriel H.
Goldblatt, Stacey
Golden, Arthur
Golden, Renny
Goldentyer, Debra
Goldfarb, Jeffrey C.
Goldfarb, Michael
Goldfarb, Ronald (Lawrence)
Goldhagen, Shari
Goldin, Barbara Diamond
Goldin, Owen
Goldin, Paul R.
Golding, Theresa Martin
Goldman, Ari L.
Goldman, Elizabeth
Goldman, Francisco
Goldman, Karla
Goldman, Katherine (Wyse)
Goldman, Marshall I(rwin)
Goldman, Mary Elizabeth
Goldman, Minton F.
Goldman, Roger L.
Goldman, Steven
Goldman, William
Goldner, Beth
Goldsborough, Robert (Gerald)
Goldschmidt, Arthur
Goldsmith, Barbara
Goldsmith, Jeff Charles
Goldsmith, Lynn
Goldstein, Brandt
Goldstein, Carl
Goldstein, David B.
Goldstein, Joshua S.
Goldstein, Larry Joel
Goldstein, Lyle J.
Goldstein, Michael S.
Goldstein, Naama
Goldstein, Nancy
Goldstein, Niles Elliot
Goldstein, Rebecca
Goldstein, Robert Justin
Goldstein, Sidney
Goldstone, Patricia
Goldwasser, Thomas
Gollaher, David L.
Gollin, Rita K.
Gologorsky, Beverly
Golubhoff, Risa L.
Golubitsky, Martin
Gomez, Jewelle
Gómez Rosa, Alexis
Gonyea, Mark
Gonzales, Laurence
Gonzales, Phillip B.
Gonzales-Day, Ken

Gonzalez, Alexander G.
Gonzalez, Genaro
González, Ray
Gooch, Brad
Good, Deirdre Joy
Good, Howard
Goodavage, Maria
Goodenough, Ward Hunt
Goodheart, Eugene
Goodhue, Thomas W.
Goodkin, Richard E.
Goodkind, Terry
Goodland, Katharine
Goodman, Allegra
Goodman, Amy
Goodman, Carol
Goodman, Ellen (Holtz)
Goodman, Eric
Goodman, James
Goodman, Jesse
Goodman, Jo
Goodman, Jordan E.
Goodman, Louis W.
Goodman, Matthew Aaron
Goodman, Melvin A.
Goodman, Richard
Goodman, Susan
Goodman, Susan E.
Goodson, Larry P.
Goodstein, Judith R.
Goodstein, Phil
Goodwill, Susan
Goodwin, Doris (Helen) Kearns
Goodwin, Frederick K(ing)
Goodwin, Joanne L.
Goodwin, Michael
Goodwin, Neil
Gooley, Dana
Goonan, Kathleen Ann
Goossen, Rachel Waltner
Gootenberg, Paul
Gordin, Michael D.
Gordinier, Jeff
Gordis, Lisa M.
Gordon, Alan R.
Gordon, Andrew D.
Gordon, April A.
Gordon, Charles F.
Gordon, Colin
Gordon, Deborah
Gordon, Deborah Hannes
Gordon, Eric A(rthur)
Gordon, Jaimy
Gordon, James S(amuel)
Gordon, Jennifer
Gordon, Lois G.
Gordon, Mary (Catherine)
Gordon, Meryl
Gordon, Philip H.
Gordon, Robert
Gordon, Robert Ellis
Gordon, Stewart
Gordon, Wendy M.
Gordon, William A.
Gore, Ariel
Gore, Kristin (C.)
Goreham, Gary A.
Gorini, Catherine A.
Gorlin, Eitan
Gorman, Carol
Gorman, James

Gorman, Martha
Gorman, Michael E.
Gorn, Elliott (J.)
Gorn, Michael H.
Gornick, Vivian
Gorra, Michael (Edward)
Gorrell, Lorraine
Gorrell, Robert (Mark)
Gorski, Philip S.
Gorup, Radmila J(ovanović)
Gosline, Andrea Alban
Goss, Kristin A.
Gotanda, Philip Kan
Gottfredson, Mark Alan
Gottfried, Paul Edward
Gottlieb, Alma
Gottlieb, Annie
Gottlieb, Arthur
Gottlieb, Beatrice
Gottlieb, Daphne
Gottlieb, Lisa
Gottlieb, Sherry Gershon
Gottlieb, Stephen E.
Gottschall, Edward M(aurice)
Götz, Ignacio L.
Goudsouzian, Aram
Gougeon, Len (G.)
Gough, Maria
Gough, Michael
Gould, James L.
Gould, Janice
Gould, K. Lance
Gould, Steven (Charles)
Gould, William B(enjamin)
Goulden, Joseph C.
Goulter, Barbara
Gowen, L. Kris
Goyer, David S.
Grab, Daphne
Grabbe, Crockett L(ane)
Grabenstein, Chris
Graber, Mark A.
Graber Miller, Keith Allen
Grabill, Stephen J.
Graboys, Thomas B.
Grace, Alexander M.
Grace, Nancy McCampbell
Grad, Laurie Burrows
Graf, Mike
Graf, William L.
Graff, Dale E(dward)
Graff, Garrett M.
Graff, Henry Franklin
Graff, Laurie
Graff, Lisa
Grafton, Anthony T(homas)
Grafton, Sue
Gragg, Rod
Graham, Ada
Graham, Barbara
Graham, Billy
Graham, Carol (Lee)
Graham, Daniel O.
Graham, Frank
Graham, Gael
Graham, Jefferson
Graham, John D.
Graham, Jorie
Graham, Patterson Toby
Graham, W(illiam) Fred
Gralla, Cynthia

Grambs, David (Lawrence)
Gramer, Rod
Grampp, William D.
Gran, Peter
Gran, Sara
Grandin, Temple
Grandits, John
Grange, William Marshall
Granger, Michele
Grann, David
Grant, Anne Underwood
Grant, Cynthia D.
Grant, Daniel
Grant, James
Grant, Jonathan A.
Grant, Michael Johnston
Grant, Pete
Grant, Richard
Grant, Stephanie
Grant, Susan
Grassian, Daniel
Gratz, Alan
Grau, Shirley Ann
Gravelle, Jane G(ibson)
Graver, Elizabeth
Graves, Joseph Lewis
Graves, Ralph (Augustus)
Graves, Russell A.
Graves, Sarah
Gravitz, Herbert L.
Gray, Chris Hables
Gray, Christopher
Gray, Deborah D.
Gray, Dianne E.
Gray, John
Gray, Richard A.
Graybill, Andrew R.
Grayson, Donald K.
Grayson, Emily
Grayson, Paul
Grazer, Gigi Levangie
Graziano, Michael S. A.
Greaney, Mark
Grearson, Jessie Carroll
Greaves, Bettina Herbert Bien
Grebstein, Sheldon Norman
Greeley, Andrew (Moran)
Greeley, Robin Adèle
Green, (Charles Stuart) Jamison
Green, Adam
Green, Arthur
Green, Bryan Clark
Green, Charles H.
Green, Connie Jordan
Green, Daryl D.
Green, December
Green, Elna C.
Green, G. Dorsey
Green, James
Green, Jesse
Green, John C.
Green, Joseph (Lee)
Green, Michael D.
Green, Norman
Green, Ricky K(enneth)
Green, Risa
Green, Scott E.
Green, Sharony Andrews
Green, Stephen J(ohn)
Green, Timothy
Green Musselman, Elizabeth

Greenberg, Alvin
Greenberg, Cheryl
Greenberg, Elinor Miller
Greenberg, Gerald S(tuart)
Greenberg, Joanne
Greenberg, Karen
Greenberg, Martin
Greenberg, Mike
Greenberg, Peter
Greenberg, Roger P(aul)
Greene, A. Wilson
Greene, Amy
Greene, Bette
Greene, Constance C(larke)
Greene, Don
Greene, Douglas G.
Greene, Gayle
Greene, Harlan
Greene, Jacqueline Dembar
Greene, Jennifer
Greene, Jody
Greene, Jonathan (Edward)
Greene, Julie
Greene, Melissa Fay
Greene, Nathanael
Greene, Rhonda Gowler
Greene, Ross W.
Greene, Sheldon L.
Greene, Thomas Christopher
Greene, Victor
Greenfeld, Liah
Greenhalgh, Susan
Greenhall, Ken
Greenhouse, Carol J(ane)
Greenleaf, Stephen (Howell)
Greenlee, J(acob) Harold
Greenlee, Sharon
Greeno, Gayle
Greenside, Mark
Greenstein, George
Greenwald, Bruce C.
Greenwald, G. Jonathan
Greenwald, Glenn
Greenwald, Jeff
Greenwald, Marilyn S.
Greenwald, Ricky
Greenwald, Sheila
Greenwood, David Luis Valdes
Greenwood, Leigh
Greenwood, T.
Greenwood-Waller, Judith
Greer, Andrew Sean
Greer, Gaylon
Greer, Jane
Greer, John Michael
Greer, Robert O.
Greetham, David
Gregerson, Linda
Gregg, Clark
Gregorian, Raffi
Gregory, Dick
Gregory, Frederick
Gregory, Kristiana
Gregory, Patrick
Gregory, Tobias
Gregory, Valiska
Gregory, Vicki L.
Greif, Geoffrey L.
Greif, Karen F.
Greiff, Barrie S(anford)
Greil, Arthur L(awrence)

Gremillion, Helen
Grenier, John
Gresham, Eddie
Gresham, Stephen
Greskovic, Robert
Gresser, Seymour
Grey, Jerry
Grey, Rudolph
Grice, Gordon
Grieb, Kenneth J.
Griesemer, John
Griest, Stephanie Elizondo
Griffin, Adele
Griffin, Alice
Griffin, Farah Jasmine
Griffin, H. Terrell
Griffin, Jill
Griffin, Laura
Griffin, P(auline) M.
Griffin, Patrick
Griffin, Peni R(ae)
Griffin, Steven A(rthur)
Griffin, Susan M.
Griffith, Gail
Griffith, Helen V(irginia)
Griffith, Jim
Griffiths, Fiona J.
Griffiths, William G.
Grigely, Joseph Constantine
Griggs, Vanessa Davis
Grihm, Amanda
Grim, Ryan
Grimaldi, David
Grimes, Martha
Grimes, Michael D.
Grimes, Tom
Grimsley, Jim
Grinde, Donald A(ndrew)
Griner, Paul
Grinspoon, David H.
Grippo, Charles
Grisham, John
Grisso, Thomas
Griswold, Jerome
Grizzle, Ralph
Grob, Gerald N.
Grobman, Laurie
Grobsmith, Elizabeth S.
Grodin, Charles
Groening, Matt
Groff, Lauren
Grondahl, Paul
Groneman, Carol
Groom, Gloria
Groom, Winston (Francis)
Gros, Jean-Germain
Grose, Peter (Bolton)
Groseclose, Barbara
Gross, Andrew
Gross, Ariela J.
Gross, David
Gross, Jonathan David
Gross, Kali N.
Gross, Miss Anne Lasko
Grosscup, Beau
Grosse, W. Jack
Grossinger, Harvey L.
Grossinger, Tania
Grossman, Austin
Grossman, Karl (H.)
Grossman, Lev (Thomas)

Grossman, Richard
Grossmann, Atina
Grosz, Terry
Grote, David (G.)
Grotenstein, Jonathan
Groth, Janet
Groundwater, Beth
Grover, Jan(ice) Zita
Grover, Wayne
Grow, L(ynn) M(erle)
Grubb, Jeff
Gruber, William E.
Gruberg, Martin
Grudin, Robert
Gruen, Bob
Gruenenfelder, Kim
Gruesser, John Cullen
Gruhn, George
Gruley, Bryan
Grumbach, Doris
Grumbine, R. Edward
Grumman, Bob
Grunbaum, Adolf
Grundy, Pamela C.
Gruner, Charles R.
Gruntman, Mike
Grusky, Scott T.
Guardino, Peter
Guare, John
Guaspari, John
Gubar, Susan (David)
Gudorf, Christine E.
Guernsey, Thomas F.
Guest, Christopher
Guest, Judith
Guest, Paul
Guhrke, Laura Lee
Guidry, Cindy
Guignon, Charles B(urke)
Guilfoile, Kevin
Guill, Jane
Guillemin, Jeanne (Harley)
Guillen, Michael (Arthur)
Guillory, Dan
Guinier, Lani
Guinn, Jeff Mason
Guista, Michael
Gullotta, Thomas P.
Gummer, Scott
Gundy, Jeff(rey Gene)
Gunn, Eileen
Gunn, James E(dwin)
Gunn, Moira A.
Gunn, Robin Jones
Gunning, Sally (Carlson)
Gunter, Pete (Addison Yancey)
Gunther, Robert E.
Gup, Ted (S.)
Gupta, Anil K.
Guralnick, Peter
Gurewitsch, Edna P.
Gurganus, Allan
Gurian, Naomi
Gurney, A(lbert) R(amsdell)
Gurtov, Melvin
Gurval, Robert Alan
Gurvis, Sandra J.
Guschov, Stephen D.
Gussin, Patricia
Gustafson, Chris
Gustafson, Sid

Gustainis, Justin
Guste, Roy F(rancis)
Guterson, David
Gutfreund, Owen D.
Guthman, Julie
Guthrie, Donna W.
Guthrie, Randolph H.
Gutman, Dan
Gutman, Judith Mara
Gutman, Robert W.
Gutmann, David L(eo)
Guttenplan, D. D
Gutteridge, Thomas G.
Guttmann, Allen
Guttmann, Hadassah
Guttmann, Robert
Gutzman, Kevin R.C.
Guy, Mary E.
Guzzetti, Alfred F.
Guzzo, Lou(is Richard)
Gwartney, Debra
Gwyn, William Brent
Gwynelle (Dismukes), Gwynelle
Gwynn, R(obert) S(amuel)
Haar, James
Haas, Dan
Haas, Jeffrey
Haas, Lawrence J.
Haase, Donald
Habegger, Alfred (Carl)
Haber, Julian Stuart
Haber, Karen
Haberman, David L.
Haberman, Richard
Habinek, Thomas N.
Habito, Ruben L.F
Hachigian, Nina L.
Hacker, Barton C(lyde)
Hacker, Jacob S.
Hacker, Kenneth L.
Hacker, Marilyn
Hackett, Joyce
Hackler, George
Hadas, Rachel
Haddad, Gladys
Hadden, Sally E.
Haddock, Lisa (Robyn)
Haeger, John Denis
Haenn, Nora
Hafertepe, Kenneth
Hafner, Katie
Hafner-Burton, Emilie M.
Haga, Enoch John
Hagedorn, John M.
Hagen, Steve
Hager, Alan
Hager, Betty
Hagerty, Barbara Bradley
Hagerty, Devin T.
Hagy, Alyson
Hagy, James William
Hahn, Mary Downing
Hahn, Michael T.
Hahn, Steven C.
Hahn, Susan
Haidt, Jonathan
Haight, Roger
Haiken, Elizabeth
Hailey, (Elizabeth) Kendall
Hailey, Elizabeth Forsythe
Haines, David W.

Haines, Kathryn Miller
Hairston, William
Haizlip, Shirlee Taylor
Hajdu, David
Hajdusiewicz, Babs Bell
Haji, Nafisa
Hajratwala, Minal
Hakak, Lev
Hakala, Dee
Halberstadt, Hans
Haldeman, Joe (William)
Hale, Douglas
Hale, Henry E.
Hale, Janice E(llen)
Hale, John R.
Hale, Nathan G.
Hale, Robert D(avid)
Hale, Shannon
Hales, Dianne R.
Hales, Steven D(ouglas)
Haley, Gail E(inhart)
Halfmann, Janet
Hall, Ann C.
Hall, Bert S(tewart)
Hall, Blaine H(ill)
Hall, Brian
Hall, Carl W.
Hall, David Locke
Hall, Donald (Andrew)
Hall, Douglas
Hall, Gimone
Hall, Ivan P(arker)
Hall, Joan Wylie
Hall, Karen L.
Hall, Kirsten Marie
Hall, Lee
Hall, Linley Erin
Hall, Lynn
Hall, Marie Beth
Hall, Martha Lacy
Hall, Matthew
Hall, Meredith
Hall, Parnell
Hall, Russ
Hall, Stacey A.
Hall, Susan Bard
Hall, Timothy L.
Hallahan, William H(enry)
Hallas, James H(enry)
Hallcox, Jarrett
Hallett, Charles A(rthur)
Hallett, Michael A.
Halliburton, David (Garland)
Halliday, Ayun
Halliday, Gemma
Halliday, Mark
Halliday, William R(oss)
Hallinan, Timothy
Hallissy, Margaret
Hallock, John W(esley)
  M(atthew)
Hallowell, Edward McKey
Hallowell, Janis
Hallwas, John E.
Halperin, James L(ewis)
Halperin, Joan Ungersma
Halperin, Jonathan L.
Halpern, Cynthia Leone
Halpern, Daniel
Halpern, Julie
Halpern, Paul

Halpern, Sue
Halpin, Brendan
Halpin, Marlene
Halstead, Ted
Haltzman, Scott
Hamalainen, Pekka J.
Hamamoto, Darrell Y.
Hamblin, Robert W(ayne)
Hambly, Barbara
Hambourg, Maria Morris
Hamburger, Aaron
Hamel, Gary
Hamer, Forrest
Hamill, Janet
Hamill, Pete
Hamill, Sam (Patrick)
Hamilton, Allan J.
Hamilton, Carol (Jean Barber)
Hamilton, Jane
Hamilton, John Maxwell
Hamilton, Marci A.
Hamilton, Neil (W.)
Hamilton, Richard
Hamilton, Saskia
Hamilton, Tim
Hamm, Diane Johnston
Hamm, Richard F.
Hamm, Theodore Alton
Hammel, Bob
Hammerslough, Jane
Hammes, John A.
Hammond, John Craig
Hammond, Warren
Hammond, Wayne G(ordon)
Hampton, Wilborn
Hampton-Jones, Hollis
Hamrin, Robert
Han, Suzanne Crowder
Hanc, John
Handeland, Lori
Handelman, Stephen
Handler, David
Handler, Richard
Handley, Paul M.
Hands, D. Wade
Handy, Lowell K.
Handy, Rollo
Hanes, Frank Borden
Hanley, William
Hanlon, Patrick
Hannaford, Peter (Dor)
Hannah, James
Hannan, Peter
Hannibal, Edward L.
Hannigan, Katherine
Hannum, Hurst
Hansen, Ann Larkin
Hansen, Ann Natalie
Hansen, Brooks
Hansen, Chadwick
Hansen, Debra Gold
Hansen, Drew D.
Hansen, Eric K.
Hansen, G. Eric
Hansen, Gregory
Hansen, James R.
Hansen, Jim Michael
Hansen, Karen V.
Hansen, Keith A.
Hansen, Maren Tonder
Hansen, Mark Victor

Hansen, Matthew Scott
Hansen, Suzanne
Hansford, Thomas G.
Hanson, David D.
Hanson, Paul R.
Hanson, Susan F.
Hantover, Jeffrey Philip
Hapke, Laura
Harakas, Stanley Samuel
Harberger, Arnold C.
Harbison, Beth
Harburg, Ernie
Hardcastle, Bob
Harden, Blaine
Harder, Leland
Harder, Robert O.
Hardesty, Larry (Lynn)
Hardin, John A.
Hardin, Russell
Harding, Paul
Hardwick, Phil
Hardy, B. Carmon
Hardy, Edward
Hardy, Gayle J.
Hardy, Lyndon (Maurice)
Hardy, Michael C.
Hardy, Richard Earl
Hardy, Robert Earl
Harer, John B.
Hargarten, Stephen W.
Hargrove, Erwin C.
Haring, Bruce
Haring, Lee
Harker, Michael P.
Harkins, Anthony
Harkness, Deborah E.
Harlan, Judith
Harleman, Ann
Harley, Bill
Harley, Willard F.
Harline, Craig E.
Harling, Robert
Harman, Patricia
Harmel, Kristin
Harmetz, Aljean
Harmon, Alexandra Sasha
Harmon, Daniel E(lton)
Harmon, Louise
Harmon, Sandra
Harnack, Curtis
Harner, Michael J(ames)
Harness, Kelley
Harnois, Albert J.
Harnum, Robert
Haroian-Guerin, Gil
Harold, Christine
Harpaz, Beth J.
Harpending, Henry
Harper, Hill
Harper, Jean
Harper, Jo
Harper, Judith E.
Harper, Lila Marz
Harper, Michael S(teven)
Harper, Rachel M.
Harper, Susan (Rice)
Harper, Tara K.
Harpham, Wendy S(chlessel)
Harrell, Beatrice Orcutt
Harriger, Katy J(ean)
Harrill, Ronald

Harrington, Anne
Harrington, John P.
Harrington, Karen
Harrington, Kathleen
Harrington, Philip S(tuart)
Harriott, Peter
Harris, Alan
Harris, Anne L.
Harris, Brayton
Harris, C. Nelson
Harris, Carla A.
Harris, Charles Wesley
Harris, Denise Michelle
Harris, Elizabeth
Harris, Fred R(oy)
Harris, Fredrick C.
Harris, George A.
Harris, James F.
Harris, Jana
Harris, Leonard
Harris, Leslie M.
Harris, Mary Emma
Harris, Neil
Harris, Paul
Harris, Philip Robert
Harris, Robie H.
Harris, Rosemary
Harris, Stacy
Harris, Thomas (E.)
Harris, Thomas Walter
Harris, Walter A.
Harris-Lacewell, Melissa Victoria
Harrison, Ann Tukey
Harrison, Antony H.
Harrison, Brady
Harrison, C. C.
Harrison, Colin
Harrison, Gary
Harrison, J. Richard
Harrison, Jim
Harrison, Kathryn
Harrison, Kathy A.
Harrison, Kim
Harrison, Kyle
Harrison, Lowell H.
Harrison, Russell (T.)
Harrison, Sue
Harrison, Suzan
Harrist, Robert E.
Harrod, Tanya
Harrow, Judy
Harrow, Kenneth W.
Harsanyi, David
Harsch, Rich
Hart, Alison
Hart, Brian
Hart, Carolyn G(impel)
Hart, Catherine
Hart, Charles (A.)
Hart, Christopher
Hart, Ellen
Hart, Jan Siegel
Hart, JoeAnn
Hart, John Fraser
Hart, John Mason
Hart, Lenore
Hart, Melissa
Hart, Mitchell B.
Harte, Amanda
Harteis, Richard
Harter, Karen

Harter, Penny
Hartig, John H.
Hartigan, John
Hartje, Tod D(ale)
Hartle, Anthony E.
Hartley, Hal
Hartley, Steven W.
Hartman, Donald K.
Hartman, Saidiya V.
Hartman, Victoria
Hartmann, Dennis L.
Hartmann, Thom
Hartoonian, Gevork
Hartshorne, Thomas L.
Hartwig, Michael J.
Haruf, Kent
Harvey, Clay
Harvey, David Allen
Harvey, John F(rederick)
Harvey, Karen D.
Harvey, Paul William
Harvey, Robert C.
Harvey, Steven
Harvey, Susan Ashbrook
Harwit, Eric
Harwood, John
Hasburgh, Patrick
Haseley, Dennis
Hasenfeld, Yeheskel
Haskell, Guy H.
Haskell, Molly
Haskett, Robert
Haskins, Michael
Haskins, Scott (M.)
Haslam, Gerald William
Haslett, Adam
Haspiel, Dean
Hasselstrom, Linda (Michele)
Hassler, Christine
Hassler, Donald M(ackey)
Hastedt, Glenn Peter
Hastorf, Christine Ann
Hasty, Jennifer
Hasty, Will
Haswell, Janis Tedesco
Haswell, Richard H(enry)
Hatab, Lawrence J.
Hatch, Lynda S.
Hatch, Michael F.
Hatcher, Robin Lee
Hatfield, Juliana
Hatfield, Phyllis
Hathaway, Barbara
Hathaway, Margaret
Hatkoff, Amy
Hattendorf, John B(rewster)
Haug, James
Haught, James A(lbert)
Hauptman, Don
Hauptman, Judith
Hauptman, Laurence Marc
Hauptman, Robert
Hauptman, William (Thornton)
Hauser, Marc D.
Hauser, Susan Carol
Hausmann, Winifred Wilkinson
Hauth, Katherine B.
Haveman, Robert Henry
Havens, Candace
Hawes, Judy
Hawes, Louise

Hawke, Ethan
Hawke, Richard
Hawke, Simon
Hawkes, G(ary) W(arren)
Hawkes, Judith
Hawkes, Kevin
Hawkins, Anne Hunsaker
Hawkins, Bradford A(lan)
Hawkins, Hunt
Hawkins, Regina Trice
Hawley, Ellen
Hawley, John C(harles)
Hawley, Noah
Hawley, Richard A.
Hawthorne, Fran
Haxton, Brooks
Hay, Samuel A.
Hay, William Anthony
Hayashi, Nancy
Hayashi, Robert T.
Hayden, C. J.
Haydon, Elizabeth
Hayduk, Ron
Hayes, Bill
Hayes, Christopher L.
Hayes, Daniel
Hayes, Dawn Marie
Hayes, Joe
Hayes, Stephen F.
Hayflick, Leonard
Hayford, Charles W.
Haygood, Wil
Hayman, Carol Bessent
Hayman, David
Haynes, C. Rayfield
Haynes, David
Haynes, Duncan H(arold)
Haynes, Gary (Anthony)
Haynes, John Earl
Haynes, Jonathan
Haynes, Melinda
Haynes, Stephen R.
Haynie, Barbara
Hays, Tommy
Hays, Tony
Hays-Gilpin, Kelley
Hayt, Elizabeth
Hayward, Jennifer (Poole)
Haywood, Gar Anthony
Haywood, Kathleen M.
Hazard, Ann
Hazelwood, Robert R.
Hazlett-Stevens, Holly
Hazo, Samuel (John)
Hazuka, Tom
Heacox, Kim
Head, David M.
Head, John
Headley, Bernard D.
Headley, Jason
Headley, John M.
Headley, Maria Dahvana
Headrick, Daniel R.
Heady, Harold F(ranklin)
Healey, Judith Koll
Healy, Erin M.
Healy, Gene
Healy, Jeremiah
Healy, Maureen
Healy, Sophia (Warner)
Heard, Alex

Hinds, P(atricia) Mignon
Hine, Darlene Clark
Hine, Robert V.
Hines, James R.
Hines, Jeanne
Hines, Robert S.
Hines, Thomas S(pight)
Hing, Bill Ong
Hingle, Metsy
Hinnefeld, Joyce
Hinojosa, Gilberto Miguel
Hinrichs, Ernest H(enry)
Hinson, E. Glenn
Hinton, Lynne
Hinton, S(usan) E(loise)
Hinze, Bradford E.
Hipperson, Carol Edgemon
Hirabayashi, Lane Ryo
Hirsch, E(ric) D(onald)
Hirsch, Edward
Hirsch, James (S.)
Hirschfeld, Lawrence A.
Hirschfelder, Arlene B.
Hirschman, Jack
Hirsh, Michael
Hirsh-Pasek, Kathy
Hirshfeld, Alan
Hirshfield, Jane
Hirshman, Linda R.
Hischak, Thomas S.
Hise, Greg
Hise, Phaedra
Hitchins, Keith
Hitt, David
Hittinger, Russell (F.)
Hitz, Frederick P(orter)
Hjortsberg, William
Hoag, Tami
Hoagland, Edward
Hoar, Jere (Richmond)
Hobbet, Anastasia
Hobbs, Valerie
Hoberman, Mary Ann
Hobson, Fred Colby
Hobson, J(ohn) Allan
Hochman, Elaine S(chwartz)
Hochman, Gloria
Hock, Randolph
Hockenberry, John
Hockensmith, Sean M.
Hockensmith, Steve
Hodel, Steve
Hodes, Martha
Hodge, Paul William
Hodgson, Harriet
Hodgson, Peter C.
Hoehne, Marcia
Hoek, D. J.
Hoeppner, Edward Haworth
Hoezee, Scott E.
Hoff, Al
Hoff, B. J.
Hoff, Joan
Hoff, Mary (King)
Hoffer, Peter T(homas)
Hoffman, Alice
Hoffman, Allan M.
Hoffman, Amy Beth
Hoffman, Andy
Hoffman, Bruce
Hoffman, Carl

Hoffman, Daniel
Hoffman, Donna R.
Hoffman, Elizabeth Cobbs
Hoffman, Jay
Hoffman, Mat
Hoffman, Michael J.
Hoffman, Paul E.
Hoffman, Ronald
Hoffman, Valerie J.
Hoffman, Wayne
Hoffman, William M(oses)
Hoffmann, Donald
Hoffschwelle, Mary S.
Hofler, Robert
Hofstadter, Douglas (Richard)
Hofstra, Warren R.
Hogan, David Gerard
Hogan, J. Michael
Hogan, Linda
Hogan, Mary
Hogan, Michael William
Hogan, Patrick Colm
Hogan, Ron
Hoge, Hilary
Hogeland, William
Hogendorn, Jan Stafford
Hogg, David S.
Hoggard, James
Hogue, James K.
Hokanson, (Anthony) Drake
Holahan, Susan
Holbrook, Sara
Holbrook, Teri
Holcomb, Brent H.
Holden, Craig
Holden, Greg
Holder, Nancy L.
Holifield, E. Brooks
Holland, Antonio F.
Holland, David
Holland, James R.
Holland, JoJean
Holland, Julie
Holland, Max (Mendel)
Holland, Norman N.
Holland, Noy
Holland, Robert Gray
Hollander, David
Hollander, Jack M.
Hollander, John
Hollander, Nicole
Hollandsworth, James G.
Hollar, David W(ason)
Holleran, Andrew
Holley, Margaret
Holli, Betsy B.
Holli, Melvin George
Holliday, Alesia
Hollifield, James F.
Hollings, Robert L.
Hollingsworth, A. B.
Hollingsworth, Mary
Hollins, Etta R(uth)
Hollis, Tim
Holloway, Harry (Albert)
Holloway, Karla F. C
Holloway, Sue (A.)
Holm, Tom
Holman, Sheri
Holman, Susan R.
Holmes, Hannah

Holmes, Mary Tavener
Holmes, Mary Z(astrow)
Holmes, Megan
Holmes, Sara Lewis
Holstad, Scott Cameron
Holt, David
Holt, Ian
Holt, Marilyn Irvin
Holte, James Craig
Holthe, Tess Uriza
Holton, Woody
Holtzman, Wayne Harold
Holub, Joan
Holyfield, Evander
Homan, Madeleine
Homan, Sidney
Homer, William Innes
Homes, A. M.
Homsher, Deborah
Hond, Paul
Honerkamp, Nicholas
Honeycutt, Natalie
Honeygosky, Stephen R(aymond)
Hong, Lily Toy
Honnold, RoseMary
Hood, Ann
Hood, Daniel
Hood, Mary
Hook, Jonathan B(yron)
Hooker, John
Hooks, Bell
Hooks, Gregory M.
Hooley, D(aniel) M.
Hooper, Dan
Hooper, Kay
Hooper, Maureen Brett
Hoopes, John W.
Hoose, Phillip M.
Hoover, Dwight Wesley
Hoover, H(elen) M(ary)
Hoover, Paul
Hopcke, Robert H(enry)
Hope, Marjorie (Cecelia)
Hopkins, Bruce R.
Hopkins, Dwight N(athaniel)
Hopkins, George Emil
Hopkins, Jackie (Mims)
Hopkins, Jasper
Hopkins, John
Hopkins, Lee Bennett
Hopkins, Mary R(ice)
Hopler, Jay
Hopper, Kim
Hopping Egan, Lorraine
Horack, Skip
Horan, Elizabeth (Rosa)
Horan, Ellen
Horan, Nancy
Hord, Frederick (Lee)
Horgan, John
Horlick, Allan S.
Hormats, Robert D.
Horn, James
Horn, Jeff
Horn, Miriam
Horn, Stacy
Horn, Tammy
Horne, Gerald
Horne, R(alph) A(lbert)
Horner, John R(obert)
Hornik, Heidi J.

Horning, Alice S.
Hornsby, Alton
Hornsby, Wendy
Hornschemeier, Paul
Hornstein, Gail A.
Horowitz, Daniel
Horowitz, Dave
Horowitz, Irving Louis
Horowitz, Mitch
Horowitz, Renee B(arbara)
Horowitz, Shale A.
Horsey, David
Horsley, Richard A.
Horton, David (Edward)
Horton, David M.
Horton, Frank E.
Horton, J(ames) Wright
Horton, Madelyn (Stacey)
Horton, Michael Scott
Horvath, Betty
Horváth, John
Horwitz, Gordon J.
Horwitz, Tony
Hosozawa-Nagano, Elaine
Hostetter, Joyce Moyer
Hostrop, Richard W.
Hotchner, A(aron) E(dward)
Houck, Davis W.
Houck, Judith A.
Houghton, David Patrick
Houghton, Katharine
Houk, Randy
House, James S.
House, Silas D.
House, Tom
Housewright, David
Houston, Alan Craig
Houston, Gail Turley
Houston, Gloria
Houston, Velina Hasu
Houston, Victoria
Houston, W. Robert
Hout, Michael
Hovannisian, Richard G.
Hovenkamp, Herbert
Hovey, Kate
Howard, A(rthur) E(llsworth)
  Dick
Howard, Alison D.
Howard, Clark
Howard, Clark
Howard, David A.
Howard, David M.
Howard, Ellen
Howard, Ginnah
Howard, Heather H.
Howard, J. Woodford
Howard, Jason
Howard, Joan E.
Howard, Maureen
Howard, Philip K.
Howard, Philip N.
Howard, Thomas Albert
Howard, Todd
Howard, Tracie
Howard, Walter T.
Howarth, William (Louis)
Howe, Fanny
Howe, James
Howe, Jeff P.
Howe, LeAnne

Howe, Marie
Howe, Melodie Johnson
Howe, Neil
Howe, Stephen
Howe, Susan
Howell, Christopher
Howell, David L.
Howell, Dorothy J(ulia)
Howell, John Christian
Howey, John
Howey, Noelle
Howland, Ethan
Hoy, David Couzens
Hoyem, Andrew
Hoyle, Russ
Hoyt, Elizabeth
Hribal, C. J.
Hromic, Alma A.
Hsieh, Tony
Hsu, Albert Y.
Hsu, Carolyn L.
Hsu, Madeleine (DeMory)
Huang, Gregory T.
Hubbard, Bill
Hubbard, Charles M.
Hubbard, Dolan
Hubbard, Steve (Albert)
Hubbard, Susan (S.)
Hubbard, Thomas K.
Hubbard, Woodleigh Marx
Huber, Jeffrey T(odd)
Huber, Richard Miller
Huber, Sonya
Huckabee, Mike Dale
Huddle, David
Huddleston, Mark W.
Hudgens, Dallas
Hudler, Ad
Hudnut, Robert K.
Hudnut-Beumler, James David
Hudson, Charles
Hudson, John B.
Hudson, Wade
Huff, Toby E.
Huffer, Lynne
Huffman, Jennifer Lee
Hughart, Barry
Hughes, Dean
Hughes, Glenn
Hughes, Judith M(arkham)
Hughes, Kevin L.
Hughes, Richard (Edward)
Hughes, Richard T(homas)
Hughes, Steven C.
Hughey, Elizabeth
Huisinga, Roger
Huizenga, John R(obert)
Hull, Isabel V.
Hull, Jonathan
Hull, Nancy L.
Hull, William E(dward)
Hulse, James Warren
Hult, Karen
Hume, Robert D.
Humez, Nicholas (David)
Hummel, Jeffrey Rogers
Hummer, T(erry) R(andolph)
Humphrey, Carol Sue
Humphrey, Sandra McLeod
Humphrey-Keever, Mary Ann
Humphreys, George G(ary)

Humphreys, Margaret
Hundert, Edward M.
Hundley, Jessica
Hundley, Norris C.
Hungerford, Rachael A.
Hunner, Jon
Hunnicutt, Benjamin Kline
Hunt, Angela Elwell
Hunt, Bruce J.
Hunt, Courtney
Hunt, Marjorie
Hunt, Marvin W.
Hunt, Rameck
Hunt, Samantha (J)
Hunt, Tom
Hunt, Walter H.
Hunter, Gwen
Hunter, J(ames) Paul
Hunter, Jessie Prichard
Hunter, Sara Hoagland
Huntley, James Robert
Huntley, Paula (Bowlin)
Hupchick, Dennis P(aul)
Hurewitz, Daniel
Hurley, Andrew
Hurley, Valerie
Hurt, Harry
Hurtado, Albert L.
Hurwitz, David
Hurwitz, Johanna (Frank)
Huskey, Eugene
Huss, Sandy
Hussain, Nasser
Hussey, Patricia (Ann)
Huston, James E(dward)
Huston, James W(ebb)
Hustvedt, Siri
Hutcherson, Hilda
Hutchins, J. C.
Hutchins, William
Hutchinson, Bill
Hutchinson, Earl Ofari
Hutchinson, George B.
Hutchinson, Peter
Hutchinson, Timothy A.
Hutchison, Kay Bailey
Hutchisson, James M.
Hutton, Frankie
Hutton, Paul Andrew
Huyghe, Patrick
Huyler, Frank
Hwang, David Henry
Hwang, Jenny
Hyde, (W.) Lewis
Hyde, Eleanor (M.)
Hyde, Samuel C.
Hyman, Harold M(elvin)
Hyman, Meryl
Hyman, Ronald T(erry)
Hyman, Steven E(dward)
Hynes, Charles J.
Hynes, Samuel
Hyson, Marion C.
Hytrek, Gary J.
Hyzy, Julie
Iaccino, James F(rancis)
Iagnemma, Karl
Iakovou, Judy
Iannuzzi, John Nicholas
Ibata-Arens, Kathryn
Ibbotson, Roger G.

Iber, Jorge
Ibrahim, Raymond
Idol, John L(ane)
Idov, Michael
Ifill, Sherrilyn A.
Ignatiev, Noel
Igo, John (N.)
Igo, Sarah E.
Igoe, Jim Joseph
Ihde, Don
Iida, Deborah
Ikenberry, G. John
Ikenson, Ben
Ilahiane, Hsain
Ilie, Paul
Imbarrato, Susan Clair
Imbroscio, David L.
Imes, Birney
Imhoff, Daniel
Immell, Myra H.
Impola, Richard A(arre)
Inch, Morris Alton
Indiana, Gary
Ing, Dean
Inge, M. Thomas
Ingersoll, Earl G(eorge)
Ingle, Bob
Ingram, Paul O.
Inness, Sherrie A.
Inness-Brown, Elizabeth (Ann)
Innis, Robert E(dward)
Intrator, Sam M.
Ionazzi, Daniel A.
Ione, Carole
Ipsen, D. C.
Ireland, Patrick R(ichard)
Ireland, R. Duane
Irion, Mary Jean
Irvine, Amy
Irvine, Angela
Irvine, William
Irving, John (Winslow)
Irving, Shae (Lyn)
Irving, Stephanie (Jean)
Isaacs, Anne
Isaacs, Arnold R.
Isaacs, Susan
Isadora, Rachel
Isenberg, Andrew C.
Isenberg, Barbara
Isenberg, Joan P.
Isenberg, Nancy G.
Isenberg, Sheila
Iserson, Kenneth Victor
Isherwood, Charles
Isitt, Larry R.
Isles, John A.
Isoardi, Steven L.
Israel, Betsy
Israel, Charles A.
Israel, Lee
Israel, Shel
Itano, Nicole
Ittmann, John W.
Itzkoff, Seymour William
Ivory, James (Francis)
Ivory, Judith
Jabine, Thomas B(oyd)
Jablonski, Carla
Jack, Dana Crowley
Jackall, Robert

Jacker, Corinne
Jackson, Angela
Jackson, Clare
Jackson, G. Mark
Jackson, Jeffrey H.
Jackson, Jesse
Jackson, John A.
Jackson, John P.
Jackson, Kathy Merlock
Jackson, Kenneth T(erry)
Jackson, Lisa
Jackson, Maggie
Jackson, Marian J. A.
Jackson, Monica
Jackson, Robert H.
Jackson, Sheneska
Jackson, Sherri L.
Jackson, Sid J.
Jackson, Steve
Jackson, Troy
Jackson, William J(oseph)
Jackson, William M.
Jacob, James R.
Jacob, Merle (Lynn)
Jacobs, Alan
Jacobs, Andrew S.
Jacobs, Barry
Jacobs, Bruce A.
Jacobs, Dan(iel) N(orman)
Jacobs, David
Jacobs, Jack L.
Jacobs, Joanne
Jacobs, Jonnie
Jacobs, Laura
Jacobs, Margaret (D.)
Jacobs, Shannon K.
Jacobs, Steven L(eonard)
Jacobsen, David
Jacobsen, Douglas G.
Jacobson, Jennifer Richard
Jacobson, Joanne
Jacobson, Judy
Jacobson, Matthew Frye
Jacoby, Karl
Jacoby, Tamar
Jaffe, Betsy
Jaffe, Mark
Jaffee, Al(lan)
Jaffee, Annette Williams
Jager, Eric
Jahn-Clough, Lisa
Jain, Raj
Jakes, John
Jalongo, Mary Renck
Jamail, Dahr
James, (Darryl) Dean
James, Brian
James, Caryn
James, Catherine
James, Deana
James, Julie
James, Laurie
James, Sibyl
James, Stanlie
James, Syrie
James, Tania
James, W(illiam) Martin
James, Warren A.
Jameson, Marianna
Jameson, W. C.
Jamieson, Kathleen Hall

Jamieson, Perry D.
Jamiolkowski, Raymond M.
Jamison, Bill
Jamison, Cheryl Alters
Jamison, Kay R(edfield)
Jance, J. A.
Jandrey, G. Davies
Janeczko, Paul B(ryan)
Janello, Amy (Elizabeth)
Janis, Michael
Janken, Kenneth Robert
Janko, (Kathleen) Susan
Janko, James
Jankowski, James P.
Janover, Caroline (Davis)
Janowitz, Brenda
Janowitz, Henry D.
Janowitz, Tama
Jansen, Sharon L.
Jansson, Bruce S.
Janzen, David
Jaramillo, Stephan
Jares, Joe
Jarmakani, Amira
Jarman, Mark (F.)
Jaroff, Leon Morton
Jarrar, Randa
Jarrow, Gail
Jarvik, Laurence
Jarvis, Christina S.
Jarvis, Jeff
Jarvis, Sharon E.
Jarvis, William E.
Jason, Sonya
Jasper, James M(acdonald)
Jasper, Kenji (Nathaniel)
Jasper, Margaret C.
Jaspin, Elliot
Jauss, David
Javernick, Ellen
Jay, Ricky
Jeffers, Honorée Fanonne
Jeffers, Thomas L.
Jefferson, Margo
Jeffrey, Francis
Jeffrey, Thomas E.
Jeffreys, Derek S.
Jeffries, Don
Jeffries, John C.
Jeffries, Judson L.
Jeffries, Sabrina
Jelen, Ted G.
Jellison, Katherine
Jen, Gish
Jencks, Charles (Alexander)
Jenkins, Beverly
Jenkins, Brian Michael
Jenkins, Carol
Jenkins, David L.
Jenkins, Fred W(illiam)
Jenkins, Gary W.
Jenkins, George
Jenkins, Jean
Jenkins, Mark
Jenkins, Sally
Jenkins, Steven
Jenkins, Virginia Scott
Jenkinson, Bill
Jennings, Dana Andrew
Jennings, Judith
Jennings, Patrick

Jennings, Phillip E.
Jensen, Arthur Robert
Jensen, Clayne
Jensen, David H.
Jensen, Derrick
Jensen, Ejner J.
Jensen, Emma
Jensen, Erik
Jensen, Geoffrey
Jensen, Kathryn
Jensen, Kim
Jensen, Muriel
Jensen, Nathan M.
Jensen, Ruby Jean
Jenson-Elliott, Cynthia L(ouise)
Jepson, Bryan
Jepson, Jill
Jericho, Chris
Jerman, Jerry
Jernigan, Brenda K.
Jernigan, Gisela (Evelyn)
Jersild, Devon
Jervey, Edward D(rewry)
Jervis, Robert
Jett, Stephen Clinton
Jiang, Tao
Jin, Jian-Ming
Joens, Michael R.
Joes, Anthony James
Johansen, Iris
Johansson, M. Jane
Johns, Richard Alton
Johnsgard, Paul A.
Johnson, A. Ross
Johnson, Adam
Johnson, Alaya Dawn
Johnson, Alexandra
Johnson, Allan G.
Johnson, Angela
Johnson, Annabel (Jones)
Johnson, Annette R.
Johnson, Barb
Johnson, Cait
Johnson, Carla
Johnson, Cathy Marie
Johnson, Charles R(ichard)
Johnson, Cherry L(urae) F(lake)
Johnson, Chester L.
Johnson, Clint
Johnson, David K.
Johnson, Diane
Johnson, Dianne
Johnson, Dick
Johnson, Dolores
Johnson, Doug(las A.)
Johnson, E. Patrick
Johnson, Elizabeth A.
Johnson, Fenton
Johnson, Freddie Lee
Johnson, Galen K.
Johnson, George (Laclede)
Johnson, George Lloyd
Johnson, Greg
Johnson, James W.
Johnson, Je'Caryous
Johnson, Joan Marie
Johnson, John L.
Johnson, John W.
Johnson, Jory (F.)
Johnson, Kathleen Jeffrie
Johnson, Kenneth C.

Johnson, Leland R(oss)
Johnson, LouAnne
Johnson, Marilynn S.
Johnson, Maureen
Johnson, Merri Lisa
Johnson, Michael P(aul)
Johnson, Neil L.
Johnson, R(odney) M(arcus)
Johnson, R. Kikuo
Johnson, Rebecca L.
Johnson, Rebecca L.
Johnson, Rick L.
Johnson, Robert David
Johnson, Roger
Johnson, Sandy
Johnson, Sara Raup
Johnson, Sherrie
Johnson, Stephen P.
Johnson, Steven F(orrest)
Johnson, Susan (M.)
Johnson, Todd
Johnson, Victoria
Johnson, Whittington B.
Johnson, William Stacy
Johnson-Cartee, Karen S.
Johnson-Freese, Joan
Johnston, Barbara Rose
Johnston, Carolyn Ross
Johnston, Joan
Johnston, Joni E.
Johnston, Lyle
Johnston, Marilyn
Johnston, Michael
Johnston, Stanley H(oward)
Johnstone, Nick
Joiner, Gary D.
Jolin, Paula
Jonaitis, Aldona
Jonas, Ann
Jonas, Raymond
Jonas, Susan
Jonell, Lynne
Jones, Alex S.
Jones, Ann (Maret)
Jones, Bart
Jones, Ben Lewis
Jones, Brian Jay
Jones, Bruce
Jones, Bryan D(avidson)
Jones, Caroly
Jones, Carrie
Jones, Charlotte Foltz
Jones, Constance
Jones, Daryl (Emrys)
Jones, David Lee
Jones, Denice
Jones, Gayl
Jones, Gerard
Jones, J(on) Sydney
Jones, Jacqueline
Jones, Jason B.
Jones, Jerry W.
Jones, Jill
Jones, K. F
Jones, Keith
Jones, Larry
Jones, Laurie Beth
Jones, Lawrence K.
Jones, Linda Winstead
Jones, Lisa
Jones, Louis B.

Jones, Madison
Jones, Malcolm
Jones, Mary Voell
Jones, Matthew F.
Jones, Matthew L.
Jones, Merry Bloch
Jones, Naomi Brooks
Jones, Norman (Leslie)
Jones, Pamela M.
Jones, Patricia Spears
Jones, Ricky L.
Jones, Rodney
Jones, Sabrina
Jones, Seth G.
Jones, Shane
Jones, Solomon
Jones, Star(let Marie)
Jones, Ted
Jones, Thai
Jones, Thom
Jones, Thomas D.
Jones, Tony H.
Jones, William B(ryan)
Jones, William P.
Jong, Erica (Mann)
Joosse, Barbara M(onnot)
Jordan, Anne Devereaux
Jordan, Constance
Jordan, Daniel P(orter)
Jordan, David C.
Jordan, Hillary
Jordan, James M.
Jordan, Ken
Jordan, Mark D.
Jordan, Michele Anna
Jordan, Pete
Jordan, Richard Tyler
Jordan, Robert Smith
Jordan, Wendy A(dler)
Jordan-Lake, Joy
Jorgensen-Earp, Cheryl R(uth)
Joseph, Diana
Joseph, Henry
Joseph, Lawrence
Josselson, Ruthellen (Lefkowitz)
Jourdain, Robert
Jourdan, Carolyn
Joy, Camden
Joy, Donald Marvin
Joyce, Brenda
Joyce, Davis D.
Joyce, Joyce Ann
Joyce, Michael
Joyce, Rosemary A.
Joyce, William
Joyner, Hannah
Joyner, Tim(othy)
Juarez, Tina
Judge, Edward H.
Judis, John B.
Judson, D. Daniel
Judson, John
Juffer, Jane
Jukofsky, Diane
Juliani, Richard N.
Jung, Moon-Ho
Jung, Patrick J.
Junger, Sebastian
Junker, Patricia
Junkins, Donald (Arthur)
Junne, George H.

Juris, Jeffrey S.
Jurmain, Suzanne
Just, Ward
Juster, Norton
Justiss, Julia
Justman, Stewart
Jweid, Rosann
Kabaservice, Geoffrey (M.)
Kacapyr, Elia
Kachtick, Keith
Kachur, Lewis
Kadel, Andrew
Kadrey, Richard
Kaduk, Kevin
Kadushin, Alfred
Kaempfer, William H.
Kafka, Kimberly
Kafka-Gibbons, Paul
Kagan, Elaine
Kagan, Frederick W.
Kagan, Jerome
Kagan, Shelly
Kagel, John H(enry)
Kahl, Jonathan
Kahlenberg, Richard D.
Kahn, David
Kahn, Michael A.
Kahn, Sharon
Kahne, Joseph
Kaimann, Diane S.
Kain, Philip J(oseph)
Kairys, David
Kaiser, David E.
Kaiser, Ken
Kalaidjian, Walter B.
Kalb, Jonathan
Kalbacken, Joan
Kale, Steven D(avid)
Kaler, Anne K(atherine)
Kaleta, Kenneth C.
Kalfatovic, Martin R.
Kalin, Jim
Kalish, Irma
Kallen, Stuart A(rnold)
Kallevig, Christine Petrell
Kallgren, Beverly Hayes
Kalman, Laura
Kalmin, Richard
Kalson, Albert E(ugene)
Kaltner, John
Kalyn, Wayne
Kamakahi, Jeffrey J(on)
Kambil, Ajit
Kamenetz, Anya
Kamensky, Jane
Kamerick, Kathleen
Kamieniecki, Sheldon
Kamil, Alan C(urtis)
Kamil, Neil D.
Kammen, Michael
Kamoie, Laura Croghan
Kamphoefner, Walter D.
Kan, Blossom
Kan, Sergei
Kanafani, Deborah
Kanar, Stephen (Patrick)
Kandall, Stephen R.
Kandel, Michael
Kandel, Susan
Kane, Gordon L.
Kane, Jessica Francis

Kane, John
Kane, Larry
Kane, Leslie
Kang, David C.
Kanigel, Robert
Kanipe, Jeff
Kann, Mark E.
Kanon, Joseph A.
Kanter, Lynn
Kantner, Seth
Kantor, Melissa
Kao, John J.
Kaplan, Alice Yaeger
Kaplan, Andrew S.
Kaplan, Barbara Beigun
Kaplan, Bruce Eric
Kaplan, Carter
Kaplan, Edward S.
Kaplan, Elizabeth (A.)
Kaplan, Ellen
Kaplan, James
Kaplan, Janet A(nn)
Kaplan, Jerry
Kaplan, Justin
Kaplan, Kalman J.
Kaplan, Louise J.
Kaplan, Marion A.
Kaplan, Mitchell James
Kaplan, Morton A.
Kaplan, Robert B.
Kaplan, Robert S.
Kaplan, Steven L.
Kaplan-Maxfield, Thomas
Kaplar, Richard T.
Kaplow, Louis
Kaplow, Robert
Kaplowitz, Craig A.
Kappes, Marcianne
Kapsis, Robert E.
Kapstein, Ethan B.
Karasik, Paul
Karayianni, Lori
Karch, Andrew
Karem, Jeff
Karetzky, Patricia E(ichenbaum)
Karetzky, Stephen
Kari, Daven M(ichael)
Karier, Thomas
Karkazis, Katrina
Karlen, Neal (Stuart)
Karlin, Wayne (Stephen)
Karnicky, Jeffrey
Karnow, Stanley
Karon, Jan
Karp, David A(llen)
Karp, Larry
Karpeles, Eric
Karr, Kathleen
Karr, Mary
Karras, Ruth Mazo
Karttunen, Frances
Kaschak, Ellyn
Kasdorf, Julia
Kash, Don E.
Kasinitz, Philip
Kasischke, Laura
Kassirer, Jerome P.
Kastely, James L.
Kaster, Robert A.
Kaszynski, William
Katcher, Brian

Katsh, M. Ethan
Katz, Bernard S.
Katz, Bobbi
Katz, Elia (Jacob)
Katz, Esther
Katz, Jackson
Katz, James Everett
Katz, Jesse
Katz, Judith
Katz, Lawrence S(anford)
Katz, Mark
Katz, Marshall P.
Katz, Michael Ray
Katz, Molly
Katz, Richard Stephen
Katz, Sanford N.
Katz, Steve
Katz, Steven T(heodore)
Katz, Susan
Katzen, Mollie
Katzenbach, Jon R.
Katzew, Ilona
Katzman, Melanie A.
Kauffman, Bill
Kauffman, Donna
Kauffman, Janet
Kauffman, Michael W.
Kauffman, Stuart Alan
Kauffmann, Stanley
Kaufman, Frederick L.
Kaufman, Joyce P.
Kaufman, Kenn
Kaufman, Lynne
Kaufman, Robert G.
Kaufman, Scott S.
Kaufman, Suzanne K.
Kaufman, Victor S(cott)
Kaufman-Osborn, Timothy
Kaufmann, Dovid Yisroel Ber
Kavanaugh, Andrea L(ee)
Kaveney, Roz J.
Kawin, Bruce F.
Kay, Alan N.
Kay, Betty Carlson
Kaye, Elizabeth
Kaye, Marvin
Kaye, Peggy
Kaye-Kantrowitz, Melanie
Kaylin, Lucy
Kays, Scott A.
Kaysen, Susanna
Kayyem, Juliette N.
Kaza, Stephanie
Keahey, John
Kealey, Edward J.
Keane, Nancy J.
Keane, Webb
Kear, Lynn
Kearns, Josie
Kearns, Sheila M.
Keating, AnaLouise
Keating, Frank
Keech, Thomas (Walton)
Keefauver, Larry
Keefe, Patrick Radden
Keefe, Richard S.E
Keegan, John E.
Keegan, Marcia
Keele, Alan (Frank)
Keeler, Robert F.
Keeling, Kara

Keen, Ernest
Keen, Sam
Keenan, Sheila
Keene, Ann T(odd)
Keene, John (R.)
Keeter, (Charles) Scott
Keeton, Morris Teuton
Keevers, Thomas J.
Kegan, Robert G.
Kehde, Ned
Kehler, Dorothea
Keil, Charles
Keilen, Sean
Keiler, Allan Ronald
Keillor, Garrison (Edward)
Keillor, Steven J(ames)
Kein, Sybil
Keith, Caroline H(elen)
Keith, William H(enry)
Kelemen, Julie
Kellenberger, J(ames)
Keller, Debra
Keller, Edward B.
Keller, Emily
Keller, Holly
Keller, Joe
Keller, Marian Jean
Keller, Richard C.
Keller, Timothy
Keller, William W(alton)
Kellerman, Jesse
Kellerman, Jonathan
Kellert, Stephen R.
Kelley, Alec E(rvin)
Kelley, Alexia
Kelley, Douglas
Kelley, Liam C.
Kelley, Tom
Kellner, Bruce
Kellogg, Frederick
Kellogg, Marjorie Bradley
Kellogg, Marne Davis
Kellogg, Steven
Kellough, J. Edward
Kelly, Brian
Kelly, Clint
Kelly, Franklin (Wood)
Kelly, James Patrick
Kelly, Joanne (W.)
Kelly, Kevin (J.)
Kelly, Liz
Kelly, Nataly E.
Kelly, Robert
Kelly, Robert J.
Kelly, Ronald
Kelman, Judith (Ann)
Kelner, Toni L. P
Kelsay, John
Kelsay, Michael
Kelty, Christopher M.
Kemmis, Daniel (Orra)
Kemp, Kenny
Kemp, Roger L.
Kempe, Frederick
Kemper, Steve
Kemprecos, Paul
Kemske, Floyd
Kemsley, Deen
Kenan, Randall (G.)
Kenda, Margaret
Kendall, Carol

Kendall, Diana
Kendall, Jane (F.)
Kendall, Joshua
Kendrick, Beth
Kendrick, Christopher
Kendrick, Paul Calvert
Kendrick, Stephen
Kenison, Katrina
Kennealy, Jerry
Kennedy, Adrienne
Kennedy, Dan
Kennedy, David Michael
Kennedy, Kelly S.
Kennedy, Lawrence W.
Kennedy, Marlane
Kennedy, Pagan
Kennedy, Randall L.
Kennedy, Robert Emmet
Kennedy, Sarah
Kennedy, Scott
Kennedy, Sheila Suess
Kennedy, William (Joseph)
Kennedy, X. J.
Kenner, Julie
Kenney, Catherine (McGehee)
Kenney, Charles
Kenney, Jeffrey T.
Kenney, Michael
Kenney, Padraic (Jeremiah)
Kenney, Richard (L.)
Kenney, William Howland
Kenny, Lorraine Delia
Kenny, Maurice (Francis)
Kenslea, Timothy
Kent, Carol
Kent, Eliza F.
Kent, Homer Austin
Kent, James M.
Kent, Joseph (P.)
Kent, Kathleen
Kent, Richard G.
Kenyon, Nate
Keown, Tim
Keplinger, David
Ker, James
Kerasote, Ted
Kerbel, Matthew Robert
Kerber, Linda K(aufman)
Kerby, Mona
Kerkhoff, Blair
Kerley, Jack
Kerner, Elizabeth
Kernfeld, Barry (Dean)
Kerns, Thomas A.
Kerr, Andrea Moore
Kerr, Ann Zwicker
Kerr, Audrey Elisa
Kerr, K. Austin
Kerr, Katharine
Kerr, Steven
Kerrison, Catherine M.
Kersch, Ken I.
Kershen, (L.) Michael
Kertess, Klaus
Kertscher, Kevin M.
Kessel, Brent
Kesselman, Wendy
Kessler, Andy
Kessler, Brad
Kessler, David A.
Kessler, Glenn

Kessler, Jackie H.
Kessler, Jascha (Frederick)
Kessler, Judy
Kessler, Julia Braun
Kessler, Suzanne J.
Ketcham, Ralph Louis
Ketchum, Richard M.
Ketchum, William C.
Ketner, Kenneth Laine
Ketron, Larry
Kettelkamp, Larry Dale
Kevles, Bettyann Holtzmann
Kevles, Daniel J.
Kevorkian, Martin
Keyes, Daniel
Keys, Kerry Shawn
Keys, Mary M.
Keyser, James D.
Khan, Aisha
Kherdian, David
Khwaja, Waqas
Kibler, M. Alison
Kiblinger, Kristin Beise
Kidd, Chip
Kidd, Sue Monk
Kidd, Thomas S.
Kidder, Tracy
Kiddy, Elizabeth W.
Kidwell, Clara Sue
Kiefer, Louis
Kiely, Robert (James)
Kierner, Cynthia A.
Kiessling, Nicolas K.
Kieves, Tama J.
Kiger, Patrick J.
Kightlinger, Laura
Kihn, Greg
Kijewski, Karen
Kilduff, Peter
Kiley, David
Kilgore, Evan
Kilham, Benjamin
Killen, Andreas
Killham, Edward L(eo)
Killough, (Karen) Lee
Kilmer, Nicholas (John)
Kilpatrick, Alan Edwin
Kilpatrick, Andrew
Kilson, Marion D. de B.
Kim, Elaine H(aikyung)
Kim, Thomas P.
Kimball, Cheryl
Kimball, John (Ward)
Kimball, Robert (Eric)
Kimball, Roger
Kimbriel, Katharine Eliska
Kimbrough, S. T.
Kimes, Martha
Kimmel, Daniel M.
Kimmel, Elizabeth Cody
Kimmel, Eric A.
Kimmel, Haven (Koontz)
Kimmel, Jordan L.
Kimmel, Michael S(cott)
Kimmelman, Michael Simon
Kincaid, Jamaica
Kincher, Jonni
Kinder, R. M.
Kindl, Patrice
Kindred, Dave
King, (William) Dennis

King, A. S.
King, Barbara J.
King, Bruce (Alvin)
King, Carol Soucek
King, Cassandra
King, Cynthia
King, Dave
King, Don W.
King, Francis P(aul)
King, Gary C.
King, Gilbert
King, Heather Donnellan
King, James
King, Jerry P.
King, Jonathon
King, Jonny
King, Joy
King, Karen L.
King, Kathryn R.
King, Laurie R.
King, Martha
King, Mia Hsu
King, Philip J.
King, R. Alan
King, Robert C(harles)
King, Sallie B.
King, Sarah Belk
King, Sorrel McElroy
King, Stephen
King, William Davies
King, William Richard
King, Wilma
Kingma, Daphne Rose
Kingman, (Mary) Lee
Kingseed, Cole C.
Kingsley, April
Kingsley, G. Thomas
Kingsolver, Barbara
Kingston, Christina
Kingston, Maxine Hong
Kingstone, Peter R.
Kinkade, Thomas
Kinnaman, David
Kinnaman, Gary D.
Kinnell, Galway
Kinney, Arthur F.
Kinney, Jeff
Kinzie, Mary
Kipnis, Aaron R.
Kipp, Rita Smith
Kiraly, Sherwood
Kiras, James D.
Kirby, Susan E.
Kirch, Patrick V(inton)
Kirk, Andrew G.
Kirk, Donald
Kirk, Paul
Kirkham, E. Bruce
Kirkland, Martha
Kirkland, Russell
Kirkley, Evelyn A(nne)
Kirkpatrick, Jane
Kirkpatrick, Rob
Kirkwood, Annie
Kirkwood, Catherine Mary
Kirkwood, Dianna
Kirsch, George B(enson)
Kirsch, Jonathan
Kirschner, Marc W.
Kirshner, Jonathan
Kiser, John W.

Kisly, Lorraine
Kissel, Susan S.
Kisseloff, Jeff
Kissing, Steve
Kita, Joe
Kitaj, Karma
Kitch, Sally L.
Kitchen, Judith
Kiteley, Brian
Kitfield, James C.
Kitt, Sandra (E.)
Kitterman, Barry
Kittinger, Jo S(usenbach)
Kittredge, William
Kitts, Kenneth
Kitts, Thomas M(ichael)
Kivelson, Valerie
Kizer, Amber
Kizer, Carolyn
Kladstrup, Kristin
Klahr, David
Klam, Julie
Klam, Matthew
Klammer, Martin (P.)
Klappert, Peter
Klare, Michael T(homas)
Klarman, Michael Joseph
Klass, David
Klass, Perri (Elizabeth)
Klass, Sheila Solomon
Klavan, Andrew
Klaveness, Jan O'Donnell
Klebanoff, Arthur
Kleck, Gary
Kleh, Cindy (L.)
Klehr, Harvey
Kleiman, Mark A. R.
Klein, Alan M.
Klein, Alec
Klein, Allen
Klein, Anne Carolyn
Klein, Cornelis
Klein, Donald F.
Klein, Kathleen Gregory
Klein, Lisa M.
Klein, Marcus
Klein, Matthew
Klein, Norman M.
Klein, Philip Alexander
Klein, Rachel S.
Klein, Richard
Klein, Sherwin
Klein, Zachary
Klein, Zoe
Kleinberg, Ethan
Kleiner, Diana E. E.
Kleiner, Fred S.
Kleinknecht, William
Kleinsasser, Lois
Klempner, Joseph T(eller)
Klempner, Mark
Klerkx, Greg
Kleven, Elisa
Kliem, Ralph L.
Kliman, Bernice W.
Kline, David
Kline, Lisa Williams
Kline, Michael
Kline, Ronald R.
Kling, Christine
Kling, David W.

Kvasnosky, Laura McGee
Kwong, Peter
Kydd, Andrew H.
Kyle, Donald G.
Kyle, Susan S(paeth)
L'Heureux, John (Clarke)
La Berge, Ann F.
La Greca, Annette M(arie)
La Salle, Peter
La Vere, David
Laas, Virginia J(eans)
LaBute, Neil
Lacefield, Lori
Lachman, Barbara
Lachman, Charles
Lachman, Seymour P.
Lachnit, Carroll
Lachs, John
Lackey, Kris
Lackey, Mercedes R.
Lackey, Michael
LaCour, Nina
Lacy, Allen
Ladd, Brian
Ladd, Linda
Ladd, Louise
LaDow, Beth
LaDuke, Betty
Laduke, Winona
Lafavor, Carole S.
LaFaye, A(lexandria R. T.)
LaFeber, Walter Frederick
LaFemina, Gerry
LaFevers, Stephen
Laffey, Steve
LaFleur, Suzanne
Lafoy, Leslie
Lagasse, Emeril
Lagatree, Kirsten M.
LaGrand, Louis E.
LaHood, Marvin J(ohn)
Laimo, Michael
Lain, Douglas
Laird, Holly A.
Laird, Thomas (Calvin)
Lake, M. D.
Lake, Paul
Lalicki, Tom
Lam, Truong Buu
Lamar, Howard Roberts
Lamay, Craig L.
Lamb, Brian
Lamb, Connie
Lamb, Karl A(llen)
Lamb, Nancy
Lamb, Patricia Clare
Lamb, Ramdas
Lamb, Sharon
Lamb, Wally
Lamba, Marie
Lambdin, Dewey (W.)
Lamberson, Gregory
Lambert, Frank T.
Lambert, Josiah Bartlett
Lambert, Page
Lambrecht, William
Lamm, Leonard Jonathan
Lammers, Wayne P.
Lammon, Martin
Lamott, Anne
Lampanelli, Lisa

Lamphear, John
Lamppa, William R.
Lampton, David M.
Lams, Victor
Lamster, Mark
Lancaster, Carol J.
Lancaster, Roger N(elson)
Lance, Peter
Lancelotta, Victoria
Lanctot, Neil J.
Land, Brad
Landau, Paul Stuart
Landau, Susan
Lander, Ernest McPherson
Landers, Scott
Landes, Richard
Landesman, Peter
Landis, Catherine
Landis, Dylan
Landis, Geoffrey A(lan)
Landis, Jill Marie
Landman, Jessica C.
Landon, Lucinda
Landrum, Gene N.
Landsberg, Brian K.
Landsberg, Melvin
Landsburg, Steven E(lliot)
Landy, Joshua
Landy, Marcia
Lane, Abbe
Lane, Dakota
Lane, George
Lane, Harlan
Lane, John
Lane, Nancy
Lang, Gladys Engel
Lang, Jenifer Harvey
Lang, Kurt
Lang, Paul
Lang, Susan S.
Lang, William L.
Langan, John P.
Langan, Mike
Langbaum, Robert (Woodrow)
Langbein, John Harriss
Langdon, Philip
Lange, Arthur D.
Lange, James E(dward) T(homas)
Langendoen, Donald Terence
Langer, Erick D.
Langer, Maria
Langley, Charles P(itman)
Langley, Lester D(anny)
Langley, Wanda
Langston, Cynthia
Langston, Douglas C.
Langton, Jane
Langum, David J.
Lanham, Richard Alan
LaNier, Carlotta Walls
Lanier, Drew Noble
Lanier, Jaron Zepel
Lankford, Mary D.
Lankford, Nelson D.
Lankford, Terrill Lee
Lanouette, William (John)
Lansdale, Joe R(ichard)
Lantier, Patricia
Lantigua, John
Lanza, Joseph
Lapcharoensap, Rattawut

Lape, Noreen Groover
Lapham, Heather A.
Lappé, Frances Moore
Lara, Adair
Lara, Jaime
Lardner, Kate
Lardy, Nicholas R.
Larios, Julie Hofstrand
Larkin, Edward
Larkin, Joan
Larocca, Roger T.
Laroche, Loretta
Larose, Lawrence
Larsen, Clark Spencer
Larsen, Jeanne (Louise)
Larsen, Timothy
Larsgaard, Chris
Larson, Edward J(ohn)
Larson, Gary
Larson, Hope
Larson, Ingrid D(ana)
Larson, Jennifer
Larson, Kate Clifford
Larson, Kirby
Larson, Sidner J.
Larson, Stephanie Greco
Larson, Wendy
LaRue, L. H.
Larzelere, Alex
Lasansky, D. Medina
Lash, Batton
Laskas, Jeanne Marie
Laskin, David
Laskin, Pamela L.
Lasky, Kathryn
Lassiter, Matthew D.
Lassner, Phyllis
Lasson, Kenneth (Lee)
Lasswell, Marcia
Last, Cynthia G.
Lateiner, Donald
Latell, Brian
Latham, Alison
Lather, Patti
Lathrop, Douglas A.
Latko, David W.
Latreille, Stanley
Lattin, Don
Lattis, James M.
Latuchie, Karen
Latzer, Barry
Lauck, Jon K.
Lauder, Robert E(dward)
Launer, Donald
Launius, Roger D.
Lauren, Jillian
Laurie, Clayton D.
Laurie, Edward James
Laurimore, Jill Frances
Laursen, John Christian
Lause, Mark A.
Lauterbach, Ann
Lauterborn, Robert F.
Lauture, Denizé
Laux, Constance
Lavender, Abraham D(onald)
Lavender, Will Ross
Lavery, David
Lavin, Irving
Lavin, Maud
Law, Ingrid

Lawler, Jennifer
Lawler, Patrick
Lawler, Peter Augustine
Lawless, Jennifer L.
Lawrence, Bruce B.
Lawrence, Kathleen Rockwell
Lawrence, Mark Atwood
Lawrence, Martha C.
Lawrence, Starling
Lawrence, Steven C.
Lawrence-Lightfoot, Sara
Lawson, Dorie McCullough
Lawson, James
Lawson, Laura J.
Lawson, Linda
Lawton, Barbara (Perry)
Laxer, James
Lay, Carol
Layne, Christopher
Layne, Steven L.
Layton, Bentley
Lazar, Lance Gabriel
Lazarus-Black, Mindie
Lazebnik, Claire Scovell
Lazenby, Edith P.
Lazenby, Roland
Lazer, Hank
Lazerson, Joshua N(athaniel)
Lazuta, Gene
Le Guin, Elisabeth
Le Guin, Ursula K(roeber)
Lea, James F(ranklin)
Leach, William
Leacock, Elspeth
Leader, Mary
Leahy, James E.
Leahy, Robert L.
Leal, David L.
Leaman, Oliver
Leaning, Jennifer
Lear, Linda J(ane)
Lear, Patricia
Leary, Ann (Lembeck)
Leavell, Linda
Leavitt, Caroline
Leavitt, David
Leavitt, Judith Walzer
Leavy, Barbara Fass
LeBoeuf, Michael
Lebow, Jeanne
Lebowitz, Albert
Lebsock, Suzanne (Dee)
Lecesne, James
Leckey, Andrew A.
Leckie, Shirley A(nne)
LeClaire, Anne D(ickinson)
Lecompte, Mary Lou
LeCompte, N(ancy) Jane
Ledbetter, Suzann
Lederer, Katy
Lederer, Richard
Ledgin, Stephanie P.
Ledoux, Joseph E.
Ledwidge, Michael
Lee, Anthony W.
Lee, Barbara
Lee, Bernie
Lee, Chae-Jin
Lee, Don
Lee, Frances E.
Lee, Helen Elaine

Lee, J(oseph) Edward
Lee, J. Ardian
Lee, Jennifer
Lee, Josephine (D.)
Lee, Judith Yaross
Lee, Leslie (E.)
Lee, Marie G.
Lee, Mark
Lee, Mona
Lee, Pamela M.
Lee, Peter H.
Lee, Rachel
Lee, Sally
Lee, Sharon
Lee, Tommy W.
Lee, Tonya Lewis
Lee, Wendy
Leeb, Donna
Leeb, Stephen
Leeder, Elaine J.
Leeds, Barry H.
Leegant, Joan
Leeman, Richard W.
Leen, Jeff
Leerburger, Benedict A.
Leese, Jennifer L. B
Leeson, Ted
Lefcourt, Peter
Lefebure, Leo D.
Lefens, Tim
Leff, David K.
Lefkowitz, Mary (Rosenthal)
Legato, Marianne J.
Leggiere, Michael V.
Legro, Jeffrey W.
Lehane, Cornelius
Lehane, Dennis
Lehfeldt, Elizabeth A.
Lehman, Yvonne
Lehmann-Haupt, Rachel
Lehmberg, Stanford Eugene
Lehne, Judith Logan
Lehner, Lyndsay Farber
Lehr, Jennifer
Lehrer, James (Charles)
Lehrer, Jonah
Lehrer, Kate
Lehrer, Stanley
Lehring, Gary L.
Leib, Franklin A(llen)
Leiblum, Sandra R.
Leiby, Bruce R.
Leider, Richard J.
Leidner, Alan C.
Leidner, Gordon
Leifer, Carol
Leigh, Ana
Leigh, Stephen
Leiken, Robert S.
Leiner, Katherine
Leiser, Gary
Leistyna, Pepi
Leitch, Will
Leithauser, Brad (Edward)
Lelchuk, Alan
Leleux, Robert
Lellenberg, Jon L.
Lemann, Nicholas
LeMaster, Carolyn Gray
LeMaster, J. R.
Lemieux, A(nne) C(onnelly)

Lemlin, Jeanne
Lemon, Alex
Lemon, Rebecca
Lemoncheck, Linda
Lemonick, Michael D.
Lemons, James Stanley
Lemov, Rebecca
Lemus, Felicia Luna
Lencioni, Patrick
Lende, Heather
Leng, Russell J.
Lengel, Edward G.
Lenney, Dinah
Lennon, Donald R.
Lennon, J. Robert
Leno, Jay
Lenski, Noel
Lent, John A.
Lentz, Harris M(onroe)
Lentz, John C(layton)
Lenz, Elinor
Leo, Mabel R.
Leo, Richard A.
Leo, Teresa
Leon, Sharon
Leonard, Amy Elmore
Leonard, Annie
Leonard, Bill J.
Leonard, Constance
Leonard, Dorothy
Leonard, Elmore
Leonard, Frances
Leonard, Gerald F.
Leonard, James S.
Leonard, Karen Isaksen
Leonard, Stephen J.
Leonardi, Susan J.
Leong, Russell (C.)
Leopold, Terry Ann Mood
Leplin, Jarrett
Lepore, Jill
Leppek, Christopher
Lerangis, Peter
Lerch, Patricia Barker
Lerer, Seth
Lerman, Rhoda
Lerner, Barron H.
Lerner, Edward M.
Lerner, Eric
Lerner, Eric J.
Lerner, Harriet
Lerner, Henry M.
Lerner, Martin
Lerner, Michael A.
Lerner, Robert E(arl)
Lerner, Steve
LeRoy, Greg
Leroy, Margaret
Lesch, David W.
Lesch, John E(mmett)
Lescroart, John T.
Lesikar, Raymond Vincent
Leslie, John
Leslie, Kent A.
Leslie, Roger (James)
Lesser, Wendy
Lester, Connie L.
Lester, Julius
Lester, June
Lester, Margot Carmichael
Lester, Richard K.

Lesy, Michael
Lethem, Jonathan (Allen)
Leto, Julie Elizabeth
Letts, Billie
Leupp, Gary P.
Lev, Peter
Leve, Ariel
Leventhal, Bennett (L.)
Leventhal, Judith
Levi, Barbara Goss
Levi, Jan Heller
Levin, Amy K.
Levin, Betty (Lowenthal)
Levin, Gerald
Levin, Linda Lotridge
Levin, Mark
Levin, Michael (Graubart)
Levin, Michael Eric
Levin, Miriam (Ramsfelder)
Levin, Ted
Levin, Yuval
Levine, Alan J.
Levine, Amy-Jill
Levine, Barbara Hoberman
Levine, Bruce C.
Levine, Gail Carson
Levine, Gustav
Levine, Jeffrey P.
Levine, Joel S.
Levine, John R.
Levine, Kristin
Levine, Laura (Sue)
LeVine, Mark
Levine, Paul
Levine, Philip
Levine, Stuart George
Levinson, David M.
Levinson, Harry
Levinson, Jay Conrad
Levinson, Jerrold
Levinson, Marc
Levitt, Matthew
Levitt, Steven D.
Levoy, Myron
Levy, Allison
Levy, Andrew (Gordon)
Levy, Barrie
Levy, Constance
Levy, Daniel S.
Levy, Elizabeth
Levy, Harry
Levy, Helen Fiddyment
Levy, Jill Meryl
Levy, JoAnn
Levy, Peter B.
Levy, Philip
Levy, Robert A.
Levy, Steven
Levy, Thomas
Lewes, Darby
Lewicki, Roy J.
Lewin, Rhoda G.
Lewin, Roger A.
Lewis, Adrian R.
Lewis, Andrew B.
Lewis, Arnold
Lewis, Carol F. Ra
Lewis, Earl
Lewis, Gregg (Allan)
Lewis, Herbert S.
Lewis, J(ohn) P(aul) Lewis

Lewis, J. Patrick
Lewis, J. S.
Lewis, Jack Pearl
Lewis, James R.
Lewis, Johanna Miller
Lewis, John S.
Lewis, Linda (Joy)
Lewis, Mark Edward
Lewis, Michael
Lewis, Minty
Lewis, Myron
Lewis, Robert W.
Lewis, Sarah Katherine
Lewis, Sherry
Lewis, Stephen (C.)
Lewis, Sydney
Lewis, Thomas H.
Lewis, Thomas P(arker)
Lewis, Trudy
Lewis, Ward B.
Lewis-Ferguson, Julinda
Li, Leslie
Liatsos, Sandra Olson
Liazos, Ariane
Libby, Alisa M.
Libby, Ronald T(heodore)
Libo, Kenneth (Harold)
Libov, Charlotte Ann
Lichbach, Mark Irving
Licht, H. William (Bill)
Lichtblau, Eric
Lichtenberg, Jacqueline
Lichtenberg, Peter A.
Lichtenberg, Philip
Lichtenstein, Alex
Lichtenstein, Alice
Lichtenstein, Nelson
Lichterman, Paul
Licklider, Roy
Lide, David R.
Lieber, Keir A.
Lieber, Robert J.
Lieberman, Benjamin
Lieberman, Herbert
Lieberman, Laurence (James)
Lieberman, Richard K.
Lieberman, Robert C.
Lieberman, Susan (Abel)
Liebert, Elizabeth
Lieberthal, Kenneth G.
Liebler, M. L.
Liebman, Herbert
Liebmann, George W.
Liebovich, Louis W.
Lief, Judith L.
Lienesch, Michael
Lifshin, Lyn
Lightfoot, Kent G.
Lightfoot Sizemore, Deborah
Lightman, Alan P.
Ligon, Samuel
Lih, Andrew
Lila, Kim
Liles, Maurine Walpole
Lilienfeld, Jane
Lilienfeld, Scott O.
Lilla, Mark
Liller, William
Lilley, Stephen R(ay)
Lim, Elvin T.
Limon, Martin

Lin, Grace
Lin, Jami
Lincecum, Jerry Bryan
Lincoln, Don
Lincoln, Edward J.
Lind, Michael
Lindbergh, Judith
Linde, Paul R.
Lindell, Colleen
Lindemann, Mary
Linden, David J.
Lindenmeyer, Kriste
Lindenmuth, Kevin J.
Linder, Marc
Linder, Robert D.
Lindgren, David T(readwell)
Lindgren, James M.
Lindholdt, Paul J.
Lindsay, D. Michael
Lindsay, James
Lindsay, Sarah
Lindsay-Poland, John
Lindsey, Brink
Lindskold, Jane M.
Lindstrom, Lamont (Carl)
Lindvall, Michael L(loyd)
Linebaugh, Peter
Lingeman, Richard
Lingenfelter, Richard Emery
Link, Kelly
Link, William A.
Links, Bo
Linn, Karen
Linnea, Ann
Linsky, Leonard
Linson, Art
Linton, Harold
Linton, Simi
Linzer, Anna
Lipartito, Kenneth
Lipin, Lawrence M.
Lipkin, Randie
Lipman, Elinor
Lipman, Victoria M.
Lipman-Blumen, Jean
Lipper, Joanna
Lippi, Ronald D.
Lippi(-Green), Rosina
Lippman, Thomas W.
Lippy, Charles H(oward)
Lipsky, David
Lipsyte, Robert (Michael)
Lipton, Eunice
Lipton, James
Liquori, Marty
Lisandrelli, Elaine Slivinski
Lischer, Sarah Kenyon
Lisle, Holly
Lisle, Janet Taylor
Lisle, Laurie
Liss, David
Litan, Robert E(li)
Lithgow, John (Arthur)
Little, Amanda
Little, Anne Colclough
Little, Benerson
Little, Bentley
Little, Cynthia
Little, Katherine C.
Little, Terra
Littlefield, Bill

Littlefield, Holly
Littlejohn, Duffy
Littleton, Darryl
Littleton, Mark (R.)
Littman, Jonathan (Russell)
Litwack, Leon
Litwak, Robert S.
Liu, Eric
Liu, Lydia H.
Liu, Timothy
Livingston, Gordon (S.)
Livingston, James
Livingston, Robert Henry
Livoti, Carol
LL Cool J
Lliteras, D. S.
Lloyd, Elisabeth A.
Lloyd, Richard Douglas
Lloyd, Seth
Lo Scalzo, Jim
Lobanov-Rostovsky, Sergei
Lobban, Richard A.
Lobel, Jules
Lobenstine, Margaret
Lochte, Dick
Locke, Attica
Locke, Christopher
Locke, Hubert G.
Locke, Juliane Poirier
Locke, Robert R.
Lockhart, Paul Douglas
Locklin, Gerald Ivan
Lockridge, Larry
Lockwood, Jeffrey A(lan)
Lockyer, Judith (Ann)
Lodato, Victor
Lodge, Jeff
Lodish, Leonard M.
Loeb, Jeph
Loeb, Karen
Loeffelholz, Mary
Loehr, Davidson
Loen, Raymond O(rdell)
Loengard, John
Loevy, Robert D(ickinson)
Loewer, (Henry) Peter
Lofas, Jeannette
Lofton, Ramona
Lofton, Rodney
Logan, Chuck
Logan, Michael F.
Logan, Shirley Wilson
Logan, William
Logston, Anne
Logue, Mary
Loh, Sandra Tsing
Lomazow, Steven
Lombardo, Billy
Lombardo, Mary A.
Lomonaco, Palmyra
London, Charles
London, Herbert I.
London, Mark
Loney, Glenn Meredith
Long, Alecia P.
Long, Benjamin
Long, Carolyn Morrow
Long, Cathryn J.
Long, Christopher
Long, D. Stephen
Long, Edward Leroy

Long, Eugene Thomas
Long, Jeff
Long, Michael G.
Long, Pamela O.
Long, Thomas G.
Longfellow, Layne (A.)
Longley, Kyle
Longman, Jere
Longyard, William H(enry)
Longyear, Barry B.
Looby, Christopher
Lookingbill, Brad D.
Loomis, Christine
Loomis, Jennifer A.
Loomis, Susan Herrmann
Looney, Dennis (Oscar)
Looney, Douglas S.
Looser, Devoney
Lopach, James J.
Lopez, Jack
Lopez, Jonathan
López, Lorraine
Lopez, Steve
Lopresti, Robert
Lorber, Judith
Lord, Carnes
Lord, Nancy J.
Lordan, (Ellenora) Beth
Lordon, Randye
Lorenz, Lee (Sharp)
Lorey, Dean
Losch, Richard R.
Losse, Deborah N(ichols)
Lotchin, Roger W.
Lott, Bret
Lott, Eric
Lott, Jeremy
Lott, John R.
Lotz, Anne Graham
Loud, Patricia Cummings
Louden, Robert B.
Loudon, David L.
Loughery, John
Louie, Andrea
Louie, David Wong
Louis, Cindi
Louis, William Roger
Loundagin, Choeleen N.
Lounsberry, Barbara
Lourie, Richard
Loury, Glenn C(artman)
Louv, Richard
Loux, Ann Kimble
Love, D. Anne
Love, Douglas
Love, Eric T. L.
Love, Susan M.
Lovelace, Merline (A.)
Lovell, Margaretta M.
Lovely, Stephen
Lovett, Bobby L.
Lovett, Sarah
Low, Anthony
Low, Kathleen
Low, Setha M.
Lowe, Ben(no P.)
Lowe, Jack Phillips
Lowe, Joy L.
Lowe, Tom
Lowe-Evans, Mary
Lowell, Pamela

Lowenberg, Susan
Lowenstein, Michael W.
Lowenthal, Cynthia J.
Lowenthal, Gary T(obias)
Lower, Michael T.
Lowery, Robert G.
Lowndes, Joseph E.
Lowry, Lois (Hammersberg)
Lowry, Ritchie Peter
Lowry, William R.
Lowy, Jonathan
Loza, Steven (Joseph)
Lu, Suping
Lubar, David
Lubar, Joel F.
Lubet, Steven
Lublin, Nancy
Lucado, Max (Lee)
Lucaites, John Louis
Lucas, Craig
Lucas, Eileen
Lucas, Geralyn
Lucas, John A.
Lucas, Michele Claire
Lucero, Lisa Joyce
Lucey, Michael
Luchetti, Cathy
Lucsko, David
Luddy, Karon
Ludwickson, John
Luebke, Frederick Carl
Luhrmann, T(anya) M(arie)
Lui, Mary Ting Yi
Luis, William
Lukacs, John D.
Lukas, Christopher
Lukken, Miriam
Lumpkin, Aaron
Lumpkin, Betty S(tewart)
Lumry, Amanda (R.)
Lumsden, Linda J.
Lund, Gerald N.
Lund, Michael
Lundberg, George D.
Lunde, David (Eric)
Lundeberg, Philip (Karl)
Lundin, Anne
Lundin, Roger
Lundman, Richard J.
Lundstrom, John B(ernard)
Luongo, F. Thomas
Luper, Steven
Lupica, Mike
Lupoff, Richard A(llen)
Luria, Keith P.
Lurie, Alison
Lurie, April
Lurie, Jonathan
Lurquin, Paul F.
Lusane, Clarence
Lusk, John
Lust-Okar, Ellen
Lustbader, Eric Van
Lusted, Marcia Amidon
Lutz, Catherine A.
Lutz, John (Thomas)
Lutz, Lisa
Lutz, Tom
Luxon, Thomas H.
Lyden, Jacki
Lyftogt, Kenneth L.

Lykins, Jenny
Lynch, Allen C.
Lynch, Daniel
Lynch, Jack
Lynch, Janet Nichols
Lynch, Michael
Lynch, Michael P(atrick)
Lynch, Thomas
Lynd, Staughton (Craig)
Lynds, Gayle (Hallenbeck)
Lynn, Adele B.
Lynn, David H.
Lynn, John A(lbert)
Lyon, Andrea D.
Lyon, Bentley
Lyon, Elizabeth
Lyon, George Ella
Lyon, Janet
Lyon, Jeff(rey R.)
Lyons, Dan
Lyons, David (Barry)
Lyons, Gabe
Lyons, Nick
Lyons, Thomas Tolman
Lysaught, Jerome P.
Lystra, Karen
Lytle, Elizabeth Stewart
Lytle, Mark H.
Lytton, Deborah
Maass, Peter
Maazel, Fiona
MAC
MacAdams, William
Macalister, Katie
MacArthur, John R.
Macaulay, Teresa (E.)
Maccoby, Michael
MacCready, Robin Merrow
MacDonald, Amy
Macdonald, Douglas J.
MacDonald, Hope
Macdonald, James D.
MacDonald, Jerry (Paul)
MacDonald, Marylee
MacDonald, Patricia J.
MacDonald, Sam A.
MacDougal, Bonnie
MacDowell, Heather
MacDowell, Rose
MacEachern, Diane
Macedo, Stephen
MacEnulty, Pat
Macesich, George
MacFadden, Bruce J.
MacFadyen, David
MacGillivray, Deborah
MacGuire, James
Mach, Elyse (Janet)
Mach, Thomas S.
Machann, Clinton (John)
Machoian, Ronald Glenn
Machor, James L(awrence)
Machowicz, Richard J.
Maciariello, Joseph A.
MacInnes, Patricia
Macintosh, Brownie
Mack, Arien
Mack, Beverly (B.)
Mack, Carol K.
Mack, Dana
Mack, David (A.)

Mack, Raneta Lawson
Mackay, Harvey (B.)
Macken, JoAnn Early
MacKenzie, Cameron A.
Mackenzie, G. Calvin
MacKenzie, Sally
Mackey, Richard A.
Mackey, Thomas
Mackin, Jeanne
MacKinnon, Catharine A.
Mackler, Carolyn
Mackowski, Maura Phillips
MacLachlan, Colin M.
MacLachlan, Patricia
MacLaine, Shirley
MacLean, Judy Ellen
MacLean, Sarah
Macleod, Wendy
MacNish, Tracy
Macomber, Debbie
Macomber, James
Macomber, Robert N.
Macquet, Dominique
MacRae, Molly
Macsai, Gwen
Macy, Sue
Madden, Chris (Casson)
Madden, David
Madden, Patrick
Madden, W. C.
Maddox, Robert James
Madenski, Melissa (Ann)
Madgett, Naomi Long
Madhubuti, Haki R.
Madigan, Brian (Christoper)
Madigan, Charles M.
Madigan, Mark J.
Madigan, Patrick
Madison, Bennett
Madison, James H.
Madrona, Lewis Mehl
Madsen, Ross Martin
Madsen, Susan A(rrington)
Maeder, Thomas
Maestro, Giulio
Magaloni, Beatriz
Magee, David
Magee, Doug
Maggio, Frank P.
Maggio, Mike
Maggio, Theresa (Marion)
Maghraoui, Abdeslam M.
Magida, Arthur J.
Magistrale, Tony
Magliato, Kathy
Magliocco, Sabina
Magnarelli, Sharon
Magner, Lois N.
Magnet, Myron
Magnus, Erica
Maguire, Gregory (Peter)
Magun, Carol
Mahajan, Karan
Maharidge, Dale (Dimitro)
Mahdavi, Pardis
Maher, Mary Z.
Mahler, Jonathan
Mahmood, Saba
Mahoney, Richard D.
Mahoney, Rosemary
Mahowald, Mary Briody

Maier, Anne McDonald
Maier, Karl
Maier, Paul Luther
Maier, Thomas
Maier-Katkin, Daniel
Maifair, Linda Lee
Mailman, Erika
Mainiero, Lisa A.
Mainone, Robert Franklin
Mains, Randolph P.
Mainwaring, Scott
Maio, Samuel (Joseph)
Mairs, Nancy (Pedrick)
Maisel, Eric
Maisel, Ivan
Maistros, Louis
Major, Clarence
major, devorah
Majure, Janet
Makari, George Jack
Makepeace, Anne
Makovsky, Michael
Makowski, Silky
Malamud, Randy
Malcolm, Joyce Lee
Malefakis, Edward
Malfi, Ronald Damien
Malin, Irving
Malki, David
Malkin, Michelle
Mallett, Daryl F(urumi)
Mallin, Jay
Mallios, Seth
Malloch, Theodore Roosevelt
Mallon, Thomas
Mallow, Judy M(ofield)
Malloy, Sean L.
Malmgren, Dallin
Malmont, Valerie S(kuse)
Malone, Hank
Malone, James Hiram
Malone, Susan (Mary)
Malseed, Mark
Maltby, William S(aunders)
Maltese, John Anthony
Maltz, Diana
Maltz, Earl M.
Malusa, Jim
Malvasi, Mark G.
Malvasi, Meg Greene
Maly, Michael T.
Mamet, David
Manaster, Benjamin
Mancall, Peter C.
Manchel, Frank
Mancusi, Mari
Mandel, Brett H.
Mandel, Charlotte
Mandel, Naomi
Mandel, Peter (Bevan)
Mandel, Robert
Mandelbaum, W.
Mandeles, Mark D.
Mandelker, Amy
Mandle, Jay R.
Mandler, Peter
Maner, Martin
Manetti, Larry
Mangan, Jane E.
Mangini (Gonzalez), Shirley
Mangold, James

Manheim, Jarol B(ruce)
Manhein, Mary H(uffman)
Mania, Cathy
Mania, Robert (C.)
Manjoo, Farhad
Mann, Barbara E.
Mann, Brian
Mann, Catherine
Mann, Charles F.
Mann, Emily
Mann, Jeff(rey A.)
Mann, John David
Mann, Judith (W.)
Mann, Thomas E.
Mann, William J.
Manna, Paul
Manne, Henry G.
Manning, Christel (J.)
Manning, Joe
Manning, Martha M.
Manning, Richard Dale
Manning, Robert D.
Manning, Roberta Thompson
Mansell, Darrel
Mansfield, Edward D.
Mansfield, Howard
Manski, Charles F.
Mansoor, Peter R.
Mantel, Samuel J(oseph)
Manz, Charles C.
Mapp, Edward
Maraniss, David
Maranto, Gina (Lisa)
Marantz, Kenneth A.
Marantz, Sylvia S.
Marcantel, Pamela
Marcell, Jacqueline
Marcello, Patricia Cronin
March, Kathryn S.
March, Wallace Eugene
Marconi, Joe
Marcot, Bruce G.
Marcou, David J.
Marcum, David
Marcus, Alan I.
Marcus, Ben
Marcus, David L.
Marcus, James
Marcus, Jana
Marcus, Leonard S.
Marcus, Millicent
Marcus, Paul
Marcus, Sharon
Marder, Norma
Mares, Michael A.
Margolf, Diane C.
Margolick, David
Margolies, Daniel S.
Margolin, Leslie
Margolin, Phillip (Michael)
Margolis, Jeffrey A.
Margolis, Leslie
Margolis, Seth J(acob)
Margulies, Donald
Margulies, Jimmy
Marin, Mindy
Marinick, Richard
Marino, Anne (N.)
Marion, Robert W.
Mark, David
Markel, Howard

Markell, David L.
Marken, William Riley
Marker, Sherry
Markham, J. David
Marko, Katherine McGlade
Markoe, Glenn E.
Markoe, Merrill
Markoff, John
Markowitz, Harry M.
Marks, (Amelia) Lee
Marks, Corey
Marks, Gil(bert S.)
Marks, Jonathan
Marks, Mitchell Lee
Marks, Paula Mitchell
Marks, Thomas A.
Marks-White, Judith
Markus, Julia
Marlett, Jeffrey D.
Marling, Karal Ann
Marlis, Stefanie
Marlor, Clark Strang
Marolda, Edward J.
Maron, Margaret
Marotti, Arthur F(rancis)
Marowitz, Charles
Marquardt, Elizabeth
Marquardt, Virginia C. Hagelstein
Marquart, Debra
Marquit, Amanda
Marr, Maggie
Marr, Melissa
Marr, Timothy
Marriner Tomey, Ann
Marriott, Michel
Marriott, Zoë
Marrone, Steven P(hillip)
Marrs, Jim
Mars, Julie
Marsa, Linda J.
Marsalis, Wynton
Marsella, Anne (Francesca)
Marsh, Charles R.
Marsh, Fabienne
Marsh, Joan F.
Marsh, Robert Mortimer
Marshal, Nell
Marshall, Alex
Marshall, Bridget M(ary)
Marshall, Donald G.
Marshall, Janet (Perry)
Marshall, John Douglas
Marshall, Nancy Rose
Marshall, W. Gerald
Marston, Cam
Marszalek, John F.
Martel, William C.
Martell, Christopher R.
Martens, Lorna
Martensen, Robert L.
Martien, Jerry
Martin, Adrian R.
Martin, Allana
Martin, Ann Smart
Martin, Carol A.
Martin, Claire
Martin, Courtney E.
Martin, Dale B.
Martin, David S.
Martin, Deana
Martin, Deborah L.

Martin, Eric B.
Martin, F. David
Martin, Fenton S(trickland)
Martin, George E.
Martin, George R.R
Martin, George Whitney
Martin, Gerald Michael
Martin, Jacqueline Briggs
Martin, Judith
Martin, Julie (Breyer)
Martin, Justin
Martin, Larry Jay
Martin, Lisa L.
Martin, Man
Martin, Nora
Martin, Patricia Preciado
Martin, Phyllis R(odgers)
Martin, Roger H(arry)
Martin, Russell
Martin, Stephen-Paul
Martin, Timothy (Peter)
Martin, Troy
Martin, William
Martin(-Berg), Laurey K(ramer)
Martinac, Paula
Martinet, Jeanne
Martinez, A. Lee
Martinez, Elizabeth Coonrod
Martinez, Joseph G. R.
Martínez, Manuel Luis
Martínez, Nancy C.
Marting, Diane E.
Martini, Steven (Paul)
Martini, Teri
Martino, Rick
Martinson, Deborah
Martinson, Ida M(arie)
Marty, Martin E.
Martz, Linda
Marusek, David
Marvel, Thomas S.
Marvin, Cate
Marvin, Jay
Marx, Anthony W.
Marx, Eva
Marx, Gary T.
Marx, Jeffrey
Marx, Robert (Frank)
Marx, Steven
Marzluff, John M.
Masco, Joseph P.
Masello, Robert
Maser, Chris
Maser, Shari
Masini, Donna
Maskarinec, Gregory G.
Maslon, Laurence
Maso, Carole
Mason, Alane Salierno
Mason, Bobbie Ann
Mason, Connie
Mason, Daniel
Mason, David
Mason, David
Mason, Felicia
Mason, J. D.
Mason, Jeffrey D(aniel)
Mason, Jim
Mason, Linda
Mason, Matthew
Mason, Michael Paul

Mason, Robert C(averly)
Mason, Timothy
Mass, Wendy
Massa, Mark S(tephen)
Massad, Joseph A.
Massey, Calvin R(andolph)
Massey, James Earl
Massie, Elizabeth
Massie, Joseph Logan
Massie, Sonja
Massie, Suzanne
Mast, Gerald J.
Masters, Alexis
Masters, Roger D.
Masters, Susan Rowan
Masterson, Daniel M.
Masthay, Carl (David)
Mastras, George
Matalin, Mary
Matarese, Susan M.
Matchett, William H(enry)
Matelski, Marilyn J.
Matera, Dary M.
Materson, Ray
Mates, Susan Onthank
Matheny, Albert R(alston)
Mathes, Charles (Elliott)
Matheson, Richard (Burton)
Mathews, (Thomas) Jay
Mathews, Dan
Mathews, Ellie
Mathews, Lou
Mathez, Edmond A.
Mathis, Sharon Bell
Mathison, Melissa
Matlin, David
Matlock, Jack F.
Matott, Justin
Matousek, Mark
Matovina, Timothy M.
Matray, James I(rving)
Matsen, Bradford (Conway)
Matson, Cathy
Matson, Suzanne
Matson, Wallace I.
Matsuda, Mari J.
Matsusaka, John G.
Mattawa, Khaled
Matteo, Sherri
Matteson, John
Matteson, Stefanie (Newton)
Matthews, Alex
Matthews, Chris John
Matthews, Elizabeth W(oodfin)
Matthews, Greg
Matthews, Jack
Matthews, Joseph R(onald)
Matthews, Lloyd J.
Matthews, Mark
Matthews, Victor H.
Matthias, John (Edward)
Matthiessen, Peter
Mattson, Kevin
Matusow, Allen J(oseph)
Mauceri, Philip
Mauer, Marc
Maughan, Jackie Johnson
Maupin, Armistead
Maurer, Warren R(ichard)
Maurer-Mathison, Diane V(ogel)
Mauro, Nancy

Maximovich, Stanley P.
Maxwell, Cathy
Maxwell, Jaclyn L.
Maxwell, Jessica
Maxwell, John C.
Maxwell, Patricia Anne
Maxwell, Robert A.
Maxwell, Robin
May, Brian
May, Daryl (Alden)
May, Gary
May, Henry F(arnham)
May, Jesse
May, John
May, Julian
May, Larry
May, Lary L.
May, Steven W.
May, Todd Gifford
Mayall, Beth
Maybury, Richard J.
Mayer, Barbara
Mayer, Bob
Mayer, Jane
Mayer, Mercer
Mayer, Musa
Mayer, Robert
Mayers, David (Allan)
Mayes, Linda C(arol)
Mayfield, Terry L.
Mayhar, Ardath (Hurst)
Mayhew, David Raymond
Mayhew, Robert
Mayne, Kenny
Mayo, C(atherine) M(ansell)
Mayo, Gretchen Will
Mayo, Wendell
Mayor, Adrienne
Mazer, Anne
Mazer, Harry
Mazoyer, Deborah
Mazur, Joseph
Mazur, Laurie Ann
Mazurana, Dyan E.
Mazza, Cris
Mazzarella, William T. S.
Mazzaro, Jerome
Mazzeno, Laurence W.
Mazzuca Toops, Laura
Mbuende, Kaire (Munionganda)
McAdams, Dan P.
McAdams, Janet
McAfee, Carol
McAfee, John P.
McAllen, Jack
McArthur, Judith N.
McArthur, Nancy
McBeath, Gerald (Jerry) A.
McBride, Genevieve G.
McBride, Jule
McBride, Susan
McBrien, Richard P(eter)
McCafferty, Jane
McCafferty, Jim
McCafferty, Maureen
McCaffery, Margo
McCaffrey, James M.
McCain, Charles
McCall, Dan (Elliott)
McCall, Jeffrey
McCall, Marsh Howard

Means, Howard
Mebus, Scott
Mechling, Lauren
Meckel, Richard A(lan)
Meckelson, Doug
Medearis, John
Medhurst, Martin J.
Medicine-Eagle, Brooke
Medina, Nico
Medina, Tony
Mednick, Kevin
Medoff, Jillian
Medoff, Mark (Howard)
Medved, Diane
Medway, Gareth J.
Medwed, Mameve
Mee, Susie (B.)
Meeink, Frank
Meeker, Clare Hodgson
Meeks, Christopher (Nelson)
Meeks, Esther MacBain
Meeks, Wayne A.
Meggers, Betty J.
Megivern, James J(oseph)
Mehrabian, Albert
Meier, Diane
Meier, Paul D.
Meier, Richard (Alan)
Meilman, Philip W(arren)
Meinke, Peter
Meisel, Joseph S.
Melady, Thomas (Patrick)
Melancon, Michael
Meldahl, Keith Heyer
Mele, Alfred R.
Mele, Christopher
Melich, Tanya
Melko, Paul
Mellan, Olivia
Mellen, Joan
Melman, Peter Charles
Melnick, Jeffrey Paul
Melnick, Ralph
Melnyczuk, Askold
Melnyk, Andrew
Melosh, Barbara
Melton, Brian C.
Melton, Buckner F.
Melton, Judith
Melton, Marliss
Meltzer, Brad
Meltzer, David
Meluch, R(ebecca) M.
Melusky, Joseph A.
Memmott, David R.
Menand, Louis
Menard, Orville D.
Mencimer, Stephanie
Mendelson, Cheryl
Mendenhall, George Emery
Mender, Mona (Siegler)
Mendoza, Lisa
Menéndez, Ana (Maria)
Menes, Orlando Ricardo
Meno, Joe
Menon, Rajan
Mentz, Steve
Mentzer, Raymond A.
Menz, Deb
Menzel, Peter
Mercantini, Jonathan

Mercati, Cynthia
Mercer, Joyce Ann
Mercer, Judy
Meredith, Martin
Meredith, Ted Jordan
Merians, Linda E.
Merkhofer, Miley W(esson Lee)
Meron, Theodor
Merrell, Susan Scarf
Merrill, Ellen C.
Merrill, Hugh (Davis)
Merrill, Jean (Fairbanks)
Merrill, Wendy
Merriman, John M.
Merrin, Jeredith
Merritt, Constance
Merry, Robert William
Merry, Sally Engle
Merser, Cheryl
Mertha, Andrew C.
Mertus, Julie A.
Mertz, Barbara (Louise) G(ross)
Merullo, Roland
Merwin, W(illiam) S(tanley)
Merz, Jon F.
Merz, Jon F.
Mesa-Lago, Carmelo
Meserve, Walter Joseph
Meshel, Jeffrey W.
Mesibov, Gary B.
Mesle, C. Robert
Messenger, Christian K(arl)
Messer, Donald E(dward)
Messer, Sarah
Messner, Michael A.
Messner, Patricia A.
Messud, Claire
Mester, Terri A.
Metcalf, Allan (Albert)
Metres, Philip
Metz, Allan (Sheldon)
Metz, Don
Metz, Julie
Metzger, Deena P.
Metzger, Robert A(lan)
Metzl, Jonathan M.
Meurn, Robert J.
Meyer, Carolyn
Meyer, Charles Robert
Meyer, Dick
Meyer, Donald J.
Meyer, Eugene L.
Meyer, Leisa D.
Meyer, Lysle E(dward)
Meyer, Michael
Meyer, Philipp
Meyer, Richard E.
Meyerhoff, Jenny
Meyering, Sheryl L.
Meyerowitz, Joanne
Meyers, Annette (Brafman)
Meyers, Jeffrey
Meyers, Kent
Meyers, Martin
Meyerson, Debra E.
Meyerson, Michael I.
Mezey, Robert
Micale, Mark S.
Michael, George J.
Michaels, Jamie
Michaels, Lisa

Michaels, Walter Benn
Michalak, Stanley J.
Micheels, Peter A.
Michelman, Kate
Michelson, Bruce (F.)
Michelson, Richard
Michod, Richard E.
Mickel, Emanuel J.
Mickelbury, Penny
Mickenberg, Julia L.
Mickle, Shelley Fraser
Micklem, Sarah
Mickolus, Edward (Francis)
Midkiff, Mary D.
Midwood, Bart(on A.)
Miele, Frank
Miescher, Stephan F.
Mighetto, Lisa
Migliazzo, Arlin C.
Mignolo, Walter D.
Mihesuah, Devon Abbott
Mihm, Stephen
Mijares, Sharon G.
Mikaelsen, Ben (John)
Mikalson, Jon D.
Miklowitz, Gloria D.
Mikolyzk, Thomas A.
Miles, Betty
Miles, Jack
Miles, Leland
Miles, Steven H.
Miles, Tiya
Miles, William F. S.
Milgram, Gail Gleason
Milhaupt, Curtis J.
Milhorn, H. Thomas
Millard, Candice
Millen, Rochelle L.
Miller, Aaron David
Miller, Abraham (H.)
Miller, Amie Klempnauer
Miller, Anesa
Miller, Arthur R(aphael)
Miller, Blair
Miller, Brenda
Miller, Charles A.
Miller, Christopher
Miller, David C.
Miller, David W.
Miller, Donald L.
Miller, Donalyn
Miller, Donna P.
Miller, Douglas T.
Miller, E. Ethelbert
Miller, Edward A.
Miller, Elmer S(chaffner)
Miller, Geoffrey F.
Miller, Glenn T(homas)
Miller, James Edward
Miller, James M.
Miller, Jane
Miller, Jeffrey G.
Miller, Jim
Miller, John G.
Miller, Judith
Miller, K(eith) Bruce
Miller, Kerby A.
Miller, Kiri Mariah
Miller, Kit
Miller, Kristie
Miller, Laura

Miller, Lee E.
Miller, Leslie Adrienne
Miller, Lynn H.
Miller, Matthew
Miller, Neil
Miller, Nina
Miller, Paul D.
Miller, R. Craig
Miller, Rebecca
Miller, Richard Lawrence
Miller, Robert H.
Miller, Roger G.
Miller, Shawn William
Miller, Thomas W.
Miller, Tice L.
Miller, William Ian
Miller, Wilma Hildruth
Miller-Lachmann, Lyn
Millet, Lydia
Millet, Robert L.
Millett, Kate
Millhiser, Marlys
Milligan, Bryce
Million, Joelle
Millman, Cynthia R.
Millman, Gregory J.
Millman, Joan (M.)
Millner, Cork
Millner, Denene
Mills, Linda G.
Mills, Margaret A(nn)
Mills, Patricia J(agentowicz)
Mills, Peter R.
Mills, Stephanie
Mills, Vicki A.
Mills, Wilmer
Millspaugh, Ben P.
Milne, Kevin Alan
Milnor, Kristina
Milofsky, Carl
Milofsky, David
Miltner, Robert
Milton, Pat
Min, Anselm K.
Minahan, John A.
Minar, Barbra (Goodyear)
Mindell, Amy (Kaplan)
Mindt, Alex
Minear, Richard Hoffman
Miner, Ellis D(evere)
Minetor, Randi (S.)
Minkler, Meredith
Minock, Daniel
Minor, Wendell G.
Minot, Susan A.
Minow, Newton N(orman)
Minsky, Betty Jane
Minter, David Lee
Mintz, Joel A(lan)
Mirabelli, Eugene
Mirikitani, Janice
Miroff, Bruce
Mirowski, Philip
Mirvish, Dan
Misa, Thomas J.
Mishica, Clare
Mishkin, Tracy
Misurella, Fred
Mitcham, Judson
Mitchard, Jacquelyn
Mitchell, Chris

Mitchell, Don
Mitchell, Helen Buss
Mitchell, Janet
Mitchell, Jay P.
Mitchell, Jerome
Mitchell, John C.
Mitchell, John Hanson
Mitchell, Linda E.
Mitchell, Margaree King
Mitchell, Mark T.
Mitchell, Mary E.
Mitchell, Memory F.
Mitchell, Michele
Mitchell, Nancy
Mitchell, Nathan
Mitchell, Roger
Mitchell, Sharon
Mitchell, Siri L.
Mitchell, Stephen
Mitchell, Thomas R.
Mitchell, Todd
Mitchell, William P.
Mitcheltree, Tom
Mitman, Gregg
Mitroff, Ian I.
Mittelmark, Howard
Mittelstadt, Jennifer
Mittman, Stephanie
Mix, Elizabeth K.
Mixon, Laura J.
Miyares, Coco Emilia Fusco
Miyazaki, Hirokazu
Mizejewski, Linda
Mizrahi, Isaac
Mlodinow, Leonard
Mnookin, Robert H(arris)
Mnookin, Seth
Moallem, Minoo
Moats, David
Moberg, David O.
Mobley, Joe A.
Moch, Leslie Page
Mochizuki, Ken
Modahl, Mary
Moe, Christian H(ollis)
Moe, Richard
Moen, Matthew C.
Moerman, D. Max
Moffat, Wendy
Moffeit, Tony A.
Moffitt, Sharon McMahon
Mogil, Cindy R.
Mohin, Ann
Mohle, Robert L.
Mohr, Jay
Mohr, Nicholasa
Mohr, Richard D(rake)
Mohun, Arwen Palmer
Moira, Kate
Moise, Edwin E(variste)
Mokyr, Joel
Moldaw, Carol
Molesworth, Carl
Molesworth, Charles
Molinary, Rosie
Mollenauer, Lynn Wood
Mollenkamp, Carrick
Mollenkott, Virginia Ramey
Mollick, Ethan Reuben
Momaday, N(avarre) Scott
Monaco, James

Monahan, John
Monahan, William G(regory)
Mone, Gregory
Monesson, Harry S.
Monfredo, Miriam Grace
Monhollon, Michael L.
Moning, Karen Marie
Monk, Isabell
Monk, Robert C.
Monmonier, Mark
Monoson, S. Sara
Monroe, Mary
Monroe, Steve
Monson, Ingrid (T.)
Monsour, Theresa
Montague, George T(homas)
Montaigne, Fen
Montandon, Mac
Montauredes, Rita
Montenegro, Laura Nyman
Montgomery, David Bruce
Montgomery, M(aurice) R(ichard)
Montgomery, Scott L.
Montgomery, Sy
Montoya, Peter
Montparker, Carol
Moodie, Craig
Moody, Bill
Moody, Fred
Moody, Martha
Moody, Peter R(ichard)
Moon, Susan
Moonen, Rick
Mooney, Brian C.
Mooney, Jonathan
Mooney, Robert
Moore, Alison
Moore, Andrew S.
Moore, Anne Elizabeth
Moore, Brenda L(ee)
Moore, Carey Armstrong
Moore, Cassandra Chrones
Moore, Christine Palamidessi
Moore, Christopher
Moore, David W.
Moore, Dinty W.
Moore, Greg
Moore, Hal G.
Moore, Harold G(regory)
Moore, J. Stuart
Moore, James A.
Moore, James T(almadge)
Moore, John N(orton)
Moore, Kay
Moore, Laurie
Moore, Lisa Jean
Moore, Lorrie
Moore, Louis
Moore, Michele
Moore, Perry
Moore, Peter N.
Moore, Philip N(icholas)
Moore, Phyllis
Moore, Randy Charles
Moore, Robin
Moore, Roy L.
Moore, Sam
Moore, Stephanie Perry
Moore, T. M.
Moore, Terry Terrell
Moore, Thomas S(cott)

Moore-Hart, Margaret A.
Morales, Aaron Michael
Morales, Edmundo
Morales, Rebecca (Hope)
Morales, Waltraud Queiser
Moran, Bruce T.
Moran, Charles
Moran, James P.
Moran, Johanna C.
Moran, Mary (Molly) Hurley
Moran, Michelle
Moranville, Sharelle Byars
Morehouse, Lyda
Moreland, Richard C.
Morell, James B.
Morem, Susan
Moreno, Jonathan D.
Moreno, Paul D.
Morey, Ann Janine
Morey, Melanie M.
Morgan, Dan
Morgan, David
Morgan, Diane
Morgan, Elizabeth Seydel
Morgan, Francesca
Morgan, Glyn
Morgan, Jennifer L.
Morgan, Joseph G.
Morgan, Kimberly J.
Morgan, Lael
Morgan, Marlo
Morgan, Mary
Morgan, Michael L.
Morgan, Neil
Morgan, Nicholas H.
Morgan, Philip D.
Morgan, Robert (R.)
Morgan, Robin
Morgan, Stacy T(owle)
Moriarty, Karen
Moriarty, Laura
Moriarty, Marilyn F(rances)
Morillo, Stephen (Reeder)
Morin, Paula
Morison, Robert F.
Mormino, Gary R.
Mornell, Pierre
Morreim, E. Haavi
Morris, Bernard E.
Morris, Bill
Morris, Bob
Morris, Bob
Morris, Charles R.
Morris, Chris(topher Crosby)
Morris, Christopher W.
Morris, David
Morris, Deborah
Morris, G. Scott
Morris, James McGrath
Morris, Janine A.
Morris, Jeffrey B(randon)
Morris, Jiwe
Morris, Keith Lee
Morris, Kenneth M.
Morris, Larry E.
Morris, Lois B.
Morris, Lynn
Morris, Marilyn (A.)
Morris, Mary
Morris, Mary (Joan) McGarry
Morris, Roger

Morris, S(tephen) Brent
Morris, Timothy
Morrison, Bill
Morrison, Helen
Morrison, Jeffry H.
Morrison, Kristin Diane
Morrison, Martha A.
Morrison, Taylor
Morrison, Toni
Morriss, Frank
Morrissey, Will
Morrisson, Mark S.
Morrow, Skip
Morse, Donald E.
Morse, Melvin (L.)
Morsi, Pamela
Morton, Brian
Morton, Ray
Morton, Timothy
Moschis, George P.
Moseley, Marcus
Moseley, Michael E(dward)
Moser, Edward P.
Moser, Laura
Moser, Paul K.
Moses, (Russell) Greg(ory)
Moses, Michael Valdez
Moses, Robert P(arris)
Mosettig, Michael David
Mosier, John
Moskin, Julia
Moskowitz, Anita F(iderer)
Moskowitz, David V.
Moskowitz, Faye (Stollman)
Moskowitz, Robert A.
Mosley, Philip
Mosley, Shelley Elizabeth
Mosley, Steven
Mosley, Walter
Moss, Carolyn (J.)
Moss, Cynthia F.
Moss, Eric Owen
Moss, Jenny
Moss, Marissa
Moss, Stanley
Moss, Thylias (Rebecca)
Most, Kenneth S.
Mostert, P(aul) S(tallings)
Motchenbacher, C(urt) D.
Motew, Becky Willis
Mott, Robert L.
Mott, Wesley T.
Mountford, Kent
Mountrose, Phillip
Mowday, Bruce Edward
Mowle, Thomas S.
Moxley, Jennifer
Moy, James S.
Moye, J. Todd
Moyé, Lemuel A.
Moyer, Ann E.
Moyer, Kermit
Moynahan, Julian (Lane)
Moynihan, Michael
Mrazek, Robert J.
Mrkvicka, Edward F(rancis)
Mucha, Zak
Muchmore, Jo Ann
Muckenhoupt, Margaret
Muehl, Lois Baker
Mueller, Daniel

Mueller, Joan
Mueller, Robert Emmett
Muhanji, Cherry
Muhlhahn, Cara
Muir, Star A.
Mulcahy, Greg
Mulcahy, Lisa
Mulcahy, Matthew
Mulgrew, Jason
Mullane, (R.) Mike
Mullaney, James P.
Mullen, Bill V.
Mullen, Patrick B.
Muller, Eddie
Muller, Jan-Werner
Muller, Marcia
Mullin, Robert Bruce
Mullins, Hilary
Mulroy, Kevin
Mundis, Hester (Jane)
Mundy, Liza
Munevar, Gonzalo
Munhall, Edgar
Muñoz, Manuel
Munro, Donald J(acques)
Munson, Carol Barr Swayze
Munson, Noel J.
Munson, Ronald
Munson, Sam
Muravchik, Joshua
Murchie, Noël
Murchison, William
Murdoch, Lydia
Murdoch, Norman H.
Murdock, Linda
Murdy, Louise Baughan
Murkoff, Bruce
Murkoff, Heidi Eisenberg
Murphey, Cecil B(laine)
Murphey, Rhoads
Murphy, Austin
Murphy, Claire Rudolf
Murphy, Cullen
Murphy, Gordon J.
Murphy, Gregory L(eo)
Murphy, James Bernard
Murphy, James H.
Murphy, James S.
Murphy, John C.
Murphy, Joseph E.
Murphy, Justin D.
Murphy, Mark A.
Murphy, Martha W(atson)
Murphy, Patricia J.
Murphy, Patrick J.
Murphy, Shirley R(ousseau)
Murray, Albert
Murray, Bruce T.
Murray, Charles (Alan)
Murray, G. T.
Murray, James M.
Murray, Janet Horowitz
Murray, John E.
Murray, Louise
Murray, Paul T(hom)
Murray, Raymond C.
Murray, Stephen O.
Murray, Victoria
Murray, Yxta Maya
Murrell, John
Murrell, Nathaniel S(amuel)

Murren, Doug(las)
Musgrave, Gerald L.
Mushet, Cindy
Musselman, Jennifer
Mustazza, Leonard
Musto, Michael
Muszynski, Stuart
Muth, Richard F(erris)
Mutz, Diana C.
Myers, Alyse
Myers, Bill
Myers, Drew(fus Young)
Myers, Eric
Myers, Helen
Myers, Lois E.
Myers, Robert Manson
Myers, Tim
Myers, W. David
Myers, Walter Dean
Myerson, Daniel
Myint-U, Thant
Myles, Eileen
Mylroie, Laurie
Mynton, Henry
Myrick, David F.
Myss, Caroline
Nabhan, Gary Paul
Nacos, Brigitte L.
Nadeau, Adel
Nadelmann, Ethan A.
Naden, Corinne J.
Nader, Ralph
Nadis, Fred
Nadkarni, Nalini
Nagata, Linda
Nagel, Paul C(hester)
Nagel, Susan
Nagorski, Tom
Nagy, Gloria
Naha, Ed
Nahaylo, Bohdan
Naiden, James
Nails, Jennifer
Nakash, Yitzhak
Nakhimovsky, Alice Stone
Nakhnikian, George
Nally, Susan W.
Nancarrow, Mindy
Napier, Nancy J.
Napora, Joseph S.
Nappa, Mike
Narayan, Kirin
Nardi, Peter M.
Nardulli, Peter F.
Nasar, Jack L.
Nasdijj
Nash, Elizabeth (Hamilton)
Nash, Gary B.
Nash, Joy
Nash, Joyce D.
Nash, Michael R.
Nash, Roderick Frazier
Naskrecki, Piotr
Nason, Tema
Nassar, Eugene Paul
Nathan, Amy
Nathan, John
Nathan, Linda F.
Nathanson, Stephen (Lewis)
Nation, Kaleb
Nation, Mark

Nation, Richard F.
Natoli, Joseph
Nau, Henry R(ichard)
Naughton, Jim
Naureckas, Jim
Navarra, Tova
Navarro, Yvonne
Navasky, Victor
Nayfeh, Ali Hasan
Naylor, Gloria
Naylor, Phyllis Reynolds
Neal, Bill
Nealon, Kevin
Near, Holly
Neaverson, Bob
Neck, Christopher P.
Neder, Dennis W.
Needleman, Jacob
Neel, Jasper
Neeld, Elizabeth Harper
Neely, Barbara
Neenan, Colin
Nees, Lawrence
Nehrt, Lee C(harles)
Neighbour, Mary E.
Neilson, James Warren
Neiman, Susan
Neiwert, David A.
Nelson, Antonya
Nelson, Arvid
Nelson, Betty Palmer
Nelson, Bobby Jack
Nelson, Carolyn W(illiamson)
Nelson, Claudia
Nelson, Daniel
Nelson, Eric
Nelson, Howard
Nelson, Jack Lee
Nelson, Jacquelyn S.
Nelson, James L.
Nelson, Jill
Nelson, Keith L(eBahn)
Nelson, Lynn A.
Nelson, Mariah Burton
Nelson, Megan Kate
Nelson, Peter N.
Nelson, Ray
Nelson, Robert M(cDowell)
Nelson, Samuel H.
Nelson, Sharlene (P.)
Nelson, Steven D.
Nelson, Theresa
Nelson, Tim Blake
Nemec, James
Nepstad, Sharon Erickson
Nerburn, Kent Michael
Neri, G.
Nericcio, William Anthony
Nerin, William F.
Nersesian, Roy L.
Nesbitt, John D.
Nesbitt, Marc
Ness, Immanuel
Nesse, Randolph M.
Nesset, Kirk
Nester, Daniel
Nester, William R.
Nestler, Eric J.
Nethery, Mary
Netifnet, Dadisi Mwende
Neu, Jerome

Neubeck, Kenneth J.
Neufeld, Josh
Neugeboren, Jay
Neuhouser, Frederick
Nevai, Lucia
Nevels, Cynthia Skove
Neville, Katherine
Neville, Leonora
Neville, Robert C(ummings)
Nevins, Francis M(ichael)
Nevins, Joseph
New, Melvyn
Newcomb, Robert
Newcomer, James W.
Newcomer, Robert (J.)
Newell, Clayton R.
Newell, Coke
Newitz, Annalee
Newman, Arnold
Newman, Dan
Newman, Felice
Newman, Isadore
Newman, James L.
Newman, Katherine S.
Newman, Rick
Newman, Sharan (Hill)
Newman, Stephen L.
Newman, Susan
Newman, William R.
Newmark, Leonard
Newton, Esther (Mary)
Newton, Lionel
Newton, Merlin Owen
Newton, Steven H.
Newton, Suzanne
Newton, Verne W.
Ney, Ronald E.
Ng, Fae Myenne
Ng, Franklin
Ng, Mei
Nicastro, Nicholas
Nice, David C.
Nicholas, David M(ansfield)
Nicholas, Sian (Helen)
Nichols, Deborah L.
Nichols, John
Nichols, Linda
Nichols, Stephen J.
Nichols, Victoria (Sorensen)
Nicholson, Lois P.
Nichter, Mark (Andrew)
Nickel, Douglas R.
Nicosia, Gerald (Martin)
Niditch, Susan
Niebuhr, Gary Warren
Niebuhr, Gustav
Niederhoffer, Galt
Niederman, Derrick
Nields, Nerissa
Nielsen, John
Nielsen, Kim E.
Nielsen, Nancy J.
Nielsen, Niels Christian
Niemann, Greg
Niemann, Linda (Grant)
Nierenberg, Gerard I.
Nighbert, David F(ranklin)
NightMare, M. Macha
Nigro, August John
Nikitas, Derek
Nikkel, David H.

Niklas, Karl J(oseph)
Niles, Steve
Nilsen, Anders Brekhus
Nilsson, Jenny Lind
Niman, Michael I.
Nimoy, Adam
Nisbet, Jack
Nishimura, Kae
Nissanoff, Daniel
Nissen, Bruce
Nissenson, Hugh
Nissenson, Marilyn
Nissman, Blossom S.
Nitchie, George Wilson
Niven, Larry
Nixon, Cornelia
Noah, Harold J.
Noah, Robert
Nobile, Philip
Noble, Dennis L.
Noble, Kathleen
Noe, Kenneth W.
Noegel, Scott B.
Noel, Katharine
Nöel, Roger Arthur
Noer, David M.
Nof, Shimon Y.
Nogee, Joseph L(ippman)
Nolan, David (Joseph)
Nolan, Han
Nolan, James L.
Nolan, William F(rancis)
Noland, Marcus
Nold, Robert
Nolen-Hoeksema, Susan
Noles, Jim
Noll, Richard
Nollen, Scott Allen
Nolletti, Arthur (E.)
Noonan, Peggy
Nord, Deborah Epstein
Nordan, Lewis
Nordhaus, Jean
Nordlund, Willis J.
Norell, Mark A.
Norfleet, Celeste O.
Norgren, Jill
Noriega, Chon A.
Norman, Howard A.
Norman, Marsha
Norman, Michael Lewis
Norman, Rick (J.)
Norment, Lisa
Nornes, Abé Mark
Norrander, Barbara
Norrell, Gregory T.
Norrell, Robert J(efferson)
Norris, Frances
Norris, Kathleen
Norris, Shana
Norris, William R.
North, Charles
North, Darian
Northcutt, Wayne
Northrop, Douglas
Northrup, Jim
Northrup, Mary (Wirtz)
Norton, Augustus Richard
Norton, Bryan G(eorge)
Norton, M. Grant
Norton, Melissa

Norton, Rictor
Norton, Robert L.
Norwich, William
Nossiter, Adam
Nostrand, Richard L(ee)
Notar, Beth E.
Novacek, Michael
Novack, Sandra
Novak, David
Novak, Jana
Novak, Karen
Novak, Maximillian Erwin
Novak, Michael
Novgorodoff, Danica
Novick, Sheldon M.
Noyes, Deborah
Nozaki, Yoshiko
Nuechterlein, Jonathan E.
Nugent, (Donald) Christopher
Nugent, Benjamin
Nugent, Ted
Nugent, Walter
Nuland, Sherwin
Numeroff, Laura Joffe
Nunberg, Geoffrey
Nunez, Sigrid
Nunn, Frederick McKinley
Nunnally, Tiina
Nurkse, D(ennis)
Nussbaum, Jeff
Nussbaum, Martha Craven
Nussbaum, Paul David
Nutt, Paul C.
Nutzle, Futzie
Nuwer, Hank
Nye, David E.
Nye, Joseph S(amuel)
Nye, Mary Jo
Nye, Naomi Shihab
Nyhart, Nina
Nylander, Jane C.
Nylund, Eric S.
O'Barr, Jean (Fox)
O'Beirne, Kate
O'Briant, Walter H(erbert)
O'Brien, (Warren) Greg(ory)
O'Brien, Charles
O'Brien, David M(ichael)
O'Brien, Kevin
O'Brien, Matthew
O'Brien, Pat
O'Brien, Robyn
O'Brien, Tim
O'Brien, Timothy L.
O'Callahan, Jay
O'Connell, Caitlin
O'Connell, Carol
O'connell, David F.
O'Connell, Jack
O'Connell, Jennifer
O'Connell, Laurence J.
O'Connell, Marvin R(ichard)
O'Connell, Rebecca
O'Connor, Carol A.
O'Connor, Erin
O'Connor, Francis V(alentine)
O'Connor, Laura
O'Connor, Leo F.
O'Connor, Mallory McCane
O'Connor, Patricia W.
O'Connor, Rebecca K.

O'Connor, Richard
O'Connor, Robert
O'Connor, Stephen
O'Connor, Timothy Edward
O'Daly, William
O'Dell, Carol D.
O'Dell, Holly
O'Dell, Tawni
O'Donnell, Brennan (Patrick)
O'donnell, Edward T.
O'Donnell, Patrick K.
O'Donnell, Pierce
O'Donnell, Sunshine
O'Donohoe, Nick
O'Donovan, Susan Eva
O'Grady, John P.
O'Hagan, Christine
O'Hanlon, Michael E(dward)
O'Hara, David
O'Hara, Kevin
O'Hare, Jeff(rey A.)
O'Hearn, Denis
O'Kane, James M.
O'Keefe, Deborah (Janney)
O'Keefe, Kevin
O'Keefe, Susan Heyboer
O'Leary, Kevin
O'Leary, Patrick
O'Leary, Patsy Baker
O'Leary, Rosemary
O'Malley, Patrick R.
O'Malley, Penelope Grenoble
O'Malley, Vincent (J.)
O'Mara, Peggy (Noreen)
O'Neal, Hank
O'Neil, Robert M.
O'Neill, Kevin M.
O'Neill, Tom
O'Neill, William L.
O'Regan, Valerie R.
O'Reilly, Kenneth
O'Reilly Herrera, (C.) Andrea
O'Rourke, Erin
O'Rourke, James S.
O'Rourke, P. J.
O'Rourke, William
O'Shaughnessy, Ellen Cassels
O'Shea, Kathleen A.
O'Toole, Judith Hansen
O'Toole, Patricia E.
Oakdale, Suzanne
Oakes, James
Oakes, Kaya
Oakley, Barbara A.
Oakley, John H.
Oaks, Dallin H.
Oates, Joyce Carol
Oates, Stephen B(aery)
Oates, Wallace Eugene
Oatis, Steven J.
Obadele-Starks, Ernest
Oberle, Joseph
Oberlin, Loriann Hoff
Oberly, James W.
Oberndorf, Charles G.
Obika, Akili Addae
Obmascik, Mark
Obradović, Nadežda
Obst, Lynda (Rosen)
Ochart (Torres), (Luz) Yvonne
Ochoa, Enrique C(orrado)

Ochs, Vanessa (L.)
Ocker, Christopher (Michael)
Odell, George H.
Odell, Jonathan
Odell-Scott, David W.
Odenwald, Neil G.
Odenwald, Sten F.
Oderman, Stuart (Douglas)
Odets, Walt (Whitman)
Oelschlaeger, Max
Offit, Paul A.
Offley, Ed
Ogawa, Dennis M.
Ogden, Christopher
Ogilvie, Brian W.
Ogilvie, Marilyn Bailey
Ogletree, Thomas Warren
Ohaegbulam, Festus Ugboaja
Ohl, Vicki
Ohye, Bonnie
Oja, Carol J.
Okimoto, Jean Davies
Okker, Patricia
Okorafor-Mbachu, Nnedi
Okrant, Robyn
Oktenberg, Adrian
Olasky, Marvin
Olbermann, Keith
Olcott, Jocelyn
Oldenburg, Ray
Olderr, Steven
Oldham, John (M.)
Oldman, Mark
Oldmixon, Elizabeth Anne
Olds, Bruce
Olds, Sharon
Oleksiw, Susan (Prince)
Oleson, James A.
Olick, Jeffrey K.
Oliphant, Dave (Edward Davis)
Olitzky, Kerry M.
Oliveira, Robin Frazier
Oliver, Bill
Oliver, Kelly
Oliver, Kitty
Oliver, Lawrence J.
Oliver, Marilyn Tower
Oliver, Mary
Olkin, Rhoda
Ollestad, Norman
Olmert, Michael
Olmstead, Earl P.
Olmstead, Robert
Olmsted, Robert W(alsh)
Olney, Ross R(obert)
Olsen, Edward A.
Olsen, Gary
Olsen, Lance (M.)
Olsen, Mark Andrew
Olshan, Matthew
Olson, Arielle North
Olson, Gary A.
Olson, Gretchen
Olson, James S.
Olson, Jeannine E.
Olson, Karen
Olson, Kirby
Olson, Laura R.
Olson, Lester C.
Olson, Linda
Olson, Lynne

Olson, Michael Keith
Olson, Robert W(illiam)
Olson, Steve E.
Olson, Steven
Olson, Susan M.
Olson, Ted
Olson, Toby
Olson, Walter K.
Oltion, Jerry
Olwell, Russell B.
Omang, Joanne (Brenda)
Ondra, Nancy J.
Oneal, Elizabeth
Oness, Elizabeth
Onstad, Chris
Onuf, Nicholas
Onuf, Peter S.
Ophuls, William
Oppegaard, David
Oppelt, Norman T.
Oppenheim, Lois Hecht
Oppenheim, Michael
Oppenheimer, Gregg
Oppenheimer, Todd
Oppenneer, Betsy
Orbach, Benjamin
Orel, Harold
Oren, Dan A.
Orenstein, Catherine
Orenstein, Peggy
Orenstein, Ronald I.
Orent, Wendy
Orey, Michael
Orion, Doreen
Orlean, Susan
Orleck, Annelise
Ormondroyd, Edward
Ornish, Dean
Oros, Andrew L.
Orosz, Joel J.
Orr, D. Alan
Orr, David W.
Orr, Gregory (Simpson)
Ortega, Julio
Ortego, Sheila
Orth, John V.
Ortiz, Paul
Ortiz-Taylor, Sheila
Ortner, Robert
Ortner, Sherry B(eth)
Orttung, Robert W.
Osborn, David (D.)
Osborn, Ian
Osborn, Karen
Osborn, Susan (E.)
Osborne, Thomas M.
Osborne, Will
Osborne-McKnight, Juilene
Osen, James L.
Oser, Marie
Osgood, Kenneth
Osherow, Jacqueline
Oshinsky, David M.
Osing, Gordon T.
Osmer, Richard Robert
Osserman, Robert
Oster, Clinton Victor
Osterman, Paul
Osterweil, Adam
Ostler, Rosemarie
Ostlund, Lori

Ostow, Micol
Ostrander, Rick
Ostrom, Hans
Ostrow, Joel M.
Ostrow, Ronald J.
Ostrower, Gary B.
Otis, Johnny
Ott, Victoria E.
Ottaviani, Jim
Ottaway, David B.
Otten, Charlotte F(ennema)
Ottenberg, Simon
Otto, Lon
Otto, Whitney
Ouellette, Jennifer
Ouellette, Pierre
Oughton, Jerrie
Oust, Gail
Outland, Robert B.
Ove, Robert S.
Overman, Dean L.
Overmyer, Eric
Overmyer, James E.
Overmyer-Velazquez, Mark
Overton, Ron
Owen, David
Owen, Howard (Wayne)
Owen, Maureen
Owens, David M.
Owens, Janis E(llen)
Owens, Kenneth N.
Owens, Rochelle
Owens, Thomas S(heldon)
Owensby, Brian P(hilip)
Owings, Alison
Oxendine, Bess Holland
Oxenhandler, Noelle
Oxhorn, Philip D.
Ozersky, Josh
Ozick, Cynthia
Ozsvath, Zsuzsanna
Ozyurek, Esra
Pace, Alison
Pace, Robert F.
Pacelle, Mitchell
Pack, Robert
Pack, Spencer J.
Packer, Joan Garrett
Pacult, F. Paul
Paddison, Sara
Paddock, Jennifer
Paddock, Lisa
Paden, William E.
Padgett, (Mary) Abigail
Padgett, Ron
Padilla, Mark Benjamin
Padilla, Tanalís
Padovano, Anthony T.
Paesler, Michael
Paetro, Maxine
Paffenroth, Kim
Pagán, Victoria Emma
Page, Clarence
Page, Karen
Page, Katherine Hall
Page, Penny B(ooth)
Page, Reba Neukom
Page, Tim
Page, Tyler
Pagel, Tempa
Pagels, Elaine

Paglen, Trevor
Paglia, Camille
Paietta, Ann C.
Paine, Tom
Pairo, Preston (A.)
Paisner, Daniel
Pakula, Hannah (Cohn)
Palazzolo, Daniel J.
Palencia, Elaine Fowler
Palestini, Robert
Paley, Vivian Gussin
Palfrey, Evelyn
Palkovic, Mark
Palliser, Charles
Pallito, Robert M.
Pallone, Dave
Palm, Carl
Palmer, Beverly Wilson
Palmer, Catherine
Palmer, Dexter
Palmer, Hap
Palmer, John D.
Palmer, Larry I.
Palmer, Scott W.
Palmer, Stanley H.
Palmer, William J.
Paludi, Michele A.
Palumbi, Stephen R.
Palumbo, Donald E.
Palumbo-Liu, David
Palwick, Susan
Pampel, Fred C.
Pancake, Ann
Panchyk, Richard
Panek, Richard
Panik, Sharon
Panzer, Mary (Caroline)
Papanikolas, Zeese
Pape, Robert A.
Paper, Lewis Jay
Papes, Robert
Papke, David (Ray)
Pappano, Marilyn
Pappas, Milt
Paradis, Adrian Alexis
Paradise, Paul R.
Parascandola, Louis J.
Paratore, Coleen Murtagh
Pardoe, Blaine
Pardue, Diana
Parente, Stephen L.
Paretsky, Sara
Pargin, Jason Keith
Pari, Susanne
Parillo, Mark P.
Parini, Jay
Paris, Barry
Paris, Bernard Jay
Paris, David C.
Paris, Jenell Williams
Parish, James Robert
Parish, Steven M.
Park, Ed
Park, Katharine
Park, Robert L.
Park, Roberta J.
Parke, Marilyn
Parker, Alan Michael
Parker, Barbara Keevil
Parker, Gary E.
Parker, Glenn M.

Parker, John W.
Parker, Julie Faith
Parker, Nancy W(inslow)
Parker, Steve
Parker, Tom
Parkes, Walter F.
Parkhurst, Brooke
Parkinson, Stanley
Parks, Brad
Parks, Deborah A.
Parks, Gregory S.
Parks, Peggy J.
Parks, Suzan Lori
Parlakian, Nishan
Parloff, Roger (Harris)
Parmelee, John H.
Parmet, Herbert S.
Parotti, Phillip (Elliott)
Parr, Ann
Parrish, Richard
Parrish, T(homas) Michael
Parrish, Tim
Parrish, William E.
Parrott, Les
Parrott, Leslie L.
Parshall, Jonathan B.
Parshall, Karen Hunger
Parson-Nesbitt, Julie
Parsons, George W.
Parsons, Mikeal C.
Partow, Donna
Partridge, Norman
Pascal, Francine
Pascarella, Perry
Paschen, Elise (Maria)
Pascoe, C. J.
Pasewark, William Robert
Pashkow, Fredric J.
Pashman, Susan
Pasick, Robert
Pasles, Paul C.
Pasquarello, Michael
Passet, Joanne E.
Pastan, Linda
Pastan, Rachel
Pastore, Christopher
Pastorello, Karen
Pate, J'Nell L(aVerne)
Patel, Eboo
Patenaude, Bertrand M.
Paterek, Josephine
Patey, Douglas Lane
Patin, Thomas A.
Patneaude, David
Paton, Priscilla
Patrick, Jennifer
Patrick, Jim
Patrick, Robert
Patron, Susan
Patt, Richard B.
Patten, Thomas H.
Patterson, Amy S.
Patterson, Bradley H.
Patterson, Dan
Patterson, E. Britt
Patterson, Francine (G.)
Patterson, Horace L.
Patterson, Jerry L.
Patterson, Martha H.
Patterson, Richard North
Patterson, Sparrow L.

Patterson, Tiffany Ruby
Pattillo, Mary E.
Patton, Phil
Patton, Robert H.
Patton, Stacey
Pattou, Edith
Patzer, Gordon
Pauketat, Timothy R.
Paul, Ann Whitford
Paul, Anthea
Paul, Barbara
Paul, Caroline
Paul, George F(ranklin)
Pauley, Garth E.
Pauley, Kimberly
Paulos, John A(llen)
Paulsen, Gary
Paulson, Michael G.
Paulson, Ronald (Howard)
Paulsson, Martin W.
Pauly, Rebecca M.
Pavelich, Matt
Pavlik, John V.
Pawel, Miriam
Pawlak, Mark
Pawlikowski, John Thaddeus
Paxson, Diana L(ucile)
Payne, (William) David
Payne, Daniel G.
Payne, Darwin
Payne, Holly
Payne, J. Gregory
Payne, Ladell
Payne, Neil F.
Payne Fisk, Deborah C.
Payton, Rodney J.
Peabody, Richard (Myers)
Peachment, Christopher
Peacock, Sandra J.
Peak, John A.
Pearcey, Nancy
Pearl, Matthew
Pearlman, Daniel D.
Pearlman, Jeff
Pearlman, Mickey
Pearlstine, Norman
Pearsall, Shelley
Pearson, Carol Lynn
Pearson, Ridley
Pearson, Scott Roberts
Pearson, T(homas) R(eid)
Pearson, Thomas S(pencer)
Peavler, Terry J.
Pecht, Michael G.
Peck, Dale
Peck, David R.
Peck, Jeffrey M.
Peck, Merton Joseph
Peck, Richard (Wayne)
Peck, Robert S(tephen)
Peck, Sylvia
Pecora, Vincent P.
Peddicord, Jo (Anne)
Pedelty, Mark
Peden, W. Creighton
Pedersen, Laura
Pedersen, Vernon L.
Pederson, Rena
Pedrazas, Allan
Peebles, Curtis
Peel, Ellen S.

Peeler, Tim
Peery, Janet
Pegram, Thomas R.
Peirce, Neal R.
Pekkanen, Sarah
Pelan, John
Pelka, Fred
Pell, Ed(ward)
Pelletier, Cathie
Pelletier, Nancy
Pelosi, Nancy
Pelzer, Richard B.
Peña, Charles V.
Pena, Milagros
Pencak, William
Pence, Caprial A.
Pence, Gregory E.
Pence, Joanne
Pendergast, John S.
Pendle, Karin
Pendleton, Thomas
Pendreigh, Brian
Penelope, Julia
Penman, Sharon Kay
Penn, Mark J.
Penn, Michael Philip
Penn, W(illiam) S.
Penna, Dennis Roy
Penner, Jonathan
Penrod, Diane
Pensky, Max
Pentcheva, Bissera V.
Perabo, Susan
Perani, Judith
Percy, Benjamin
Perdue, Peter C.
Perelman, Bob
Peretti, Burton W(illiam)
Perez, George
Perez, Marlene
Perfetti, Charles A.
Perkins, Dwight Heald
Perkins, George (Burton)
Perkins, John
Perkins, John H.
Perkins, Kelly
Perkins, Lynne Rae
Perkins, Michael
Perkins, Suzetta M.
Perkins, Tom James
Perkinson, Robert
Perkowitz, Sidney
Perl, Jed
Perl, Ruth June
Perle, Liz
Perlin, John
Perlman, Rhea
Perloff, Richard M.
Pernu, Dennis
Perone, James E.
Perrin, Dennis
Perrin, Kayla
Perrone, Charles A.
Perrotta, Tom
Perry, Bruce D.
Perry, Curtis
Perry, Dayn
Perry, Douglas
Perry, Jeffrey B.
Perry, Margaret
Perry, Pamela

Perry, Paul
Perry, Phyllis Alesia
Perry, Phyllis J.
Perry, Steve
Perry, Thomas Kennedy
Persico, Joseph E.
Person, James E(llis)
Pesantubbee, Michelene
Pesic, Peter
Pessar, Patricia R.
Pestana, Carla Gardina
Pete, Eric E.
Peters, Curtis H.
Peters, John Durham
Peters, Julie Anne
Peters, Lisa Westberg
Peters, Margot (McCullough)
Peters, Rick
Peters, Robert
Peters, Shawn Francis
Petersen, David
Petersen, P(eter) J(ames)
Petersilia, Joan
Peterson, Carol R.
Peterson, Chris(tine Louise)
Peterson, Christian A.
Peterson, Cris
Peterson, Elmer
Peterson, Eugene H.
Peterson, Fred W.
Peterson, Jean Sunde
Peterson, Michael L.
Peterson, Peter G.
Peterson, Tracie
Peterson, V. Spike
Peterson, Wallace C(arroll)
Petievich, Gerald
Petit, Susan
Petrakis, Harry Mark
Petrie, Paul (James)
Petrino, Elizabeth
Petro, Pamela J.
Petropoulos, Jonathan G.
Petroski, Henry
Petrusich, Amanda
Petry, Alice Hall
Pettigrew, Judy
Pettit, Rhonda S(ue)
Petuch, Edward J.
Pevsner, Stella
Pezeshki, Charles
Pezzullo, Ralph
Pfaelzer, Jean
Pfaff, Daniel W.
Pfaff, Steven
Pfeffer, Wendy
Pfeifer, Michael J.
Pfeiffer, Janet (B.)
Pflieger, Pat
Pharies, David (Arnold)
Phayer, Michael
Phelan, Anna Hamilton
Phelan, Jay
Phelan, Shane
Phelps, Christopher
Phelps, Edmund S.
Philbrick, (W.) Rodman
Philbrick, Nathaniel
Phillippy, Patricia Berrahou
Phillips, Carl
Phillips, Christopher

Phillips, Clyde
Phillips, Delores
Phillips, Hugh D.
Phillips, Jason
Phillips, Jayne Anne
Phillips, John Lawrence
Phillips, Kate
Phillips, Leroy
Phillips, Lisa
Phillips, Patrick
Phillips, Sarah T.
Phillips, Scott
Phillips, Sky
Phillips, Stephen H.
Phillips, Susan E.
Phillips, Susan S.
Phillips, Suzanne
Pianka, Eric R(odger)
Piascik, Andy
Piatt, Bill
Piazza, Tom
Picano, Felice
Piccirilli, Tom
Pickard, Nancy
Pickell, David
Pickering, Robert B.
Pickering, Samuel F(rancis)
Pickett, Rex
Pickover, Clifford A.
Pickus, Keith H.
Pickus, Noah
Piderit, John J.
Pielke, Roger A.
Pierard, Richard V(ictor)
Pierce, Chonda
Pierce, F(ranklin) David
Pierce, Nora Elena
Pierce, Patricia Jobe
Pierceson, Jason
Piercy, Marge
Pieribone, Vincent A.
Pierson, Melissa Holbrook
Pierson, Paul
Pietrusza, David
Piirto, Jane
Pike, David L.
Pike, R. William
Pike, Robert W(ilson)
Piker, Joshua
Pilardi, Jo-Ann
Pilarz, Scott R.
Pilcher, Jeffrey M.
Pillemer, David B.
Pimentel, David
Pinch, Winifred J. Ellenchild
Pincus, Fred L.
Pinczes, Elinor J(ane)
Pindell, Terry
Pine, Nicholas
Pinkard, Susan K.
Pinkwater, Daniel Manus
Pinn, Anthony B(ernard)
Pinner, Patty
Pinsker, Sanford S.
Pinsky, Mark I.
Pinsky, Robert
Pinson, William M(eredith)
Pinter, Jason
Piott, Steven L.
Piper, Jon Kingsbury
Pipes, Daniel

Pipher, Mary (Bray)
Pipkin, John
Pipkin, Turk
Piraro, Dan
Pitblado, Bonnie L.
Pitcher, George
Pitino, Rick
Pitluk, Adam
Pitts, Jennifer G.
Pitts, Michael R.
Pitts, Vincent J.
Pitzel, Steve
Pixley, Marcella
Pizer, John
Plant, Deborah G.
Plaschke, Bill
Platt, Brian
Platt, Donald
Platt, Harold L.
Platt, James R.
Platt, Peter G(odfrey)
Platt, Randall
Platt, Rutherford H.
Plattner, Andy
Plattner, Marc F.
Platzker, David
Plaut, Eric A.
Plaut, Joshua Eli
Plaut, Melissa
Pleasant, Barbara
Pless, Vera
Pletsch, Carl (Erich)
Plitt, Jane R(uth)
Ploeger, Katherine (M.)
Plotkin, Bill
Plotkin, Diane M.
Plowden, David
Plowden, Martha Ward
Plumley, Lisa
Plumly, Stanley (Ross)
Plummer, Brenda Gayle
Plummer, Louise
Plutzer, Eric
Poague, Leland
Poblocki, Dan
Poceski, Mario
Poch, John
Pochoda, Ivy
Podell, Diane K(opperman)
Podhoretz, John
Podhoretz, Norman
Podwal, Mark
Pogge, Thomas
Pogrebin, Letty Cottin
Pogue, Bill
Pogue, Charles (Edward)
Pohl, Frederik
Pohlmann, Marcus D.
Poinar, Roberta
Pointer, Richard W(ayne)
Points, Larry (Gene)
Poirier, Mark Jude
Polacco, Patricia
Polakoff, Keith (Ian)
Polakow-Suransky, Sasha
Polansky, Ronald M.
Polansky, Steven
Polaski, Sandra Hack
Polhemus, Robert M(ackinlay)
Policoff, Stephen Phillip
Polikoff, Barbara G(arland)

Polikoff, Nancy D.
Poling(-Kempes), Lesley
Polisar, Barry Louis
Polisi, Joseph W.
Polito, Robert
Polizzotti, Mark
Polking, Kirk
Polkinhorn, Harry
Pollack, Henry N.
Pollack, Howard
Pollack, Jill S.
Pollack, Kenneth M(ichael)
Pollack, Rachel
Pollack, Rachel (Grace)
Pollack, Robert (Elliot)
Pollak, Vivian R.
Pollard, Helen Perlstein
Pollard, Lisa
Pollen, Daniel A.
Polletta, Francesca
Pollock, Dale
Pollock, Donald Ray
Pollock, Leland W(ells)
Polsgrove, Carol
Polsky, Andrew J.
Pomerantz, Charlotte
Pong, David (B. P. T.)
Pool, Gail
Poole, Eric
Poole, Scott
Poor, Sara S.
Poore, Carol
Poorvu, William J.
Poos, L. R.
Pope, Deborah
Pope, Rebecca A.
Popkin, Samuel L(ewis)
Poploff, Michelle
Popper, Frank James
Porcellino, John
Portale, Alfred
Portales, Marco
Porte, Barbara Ann
Porte, Joan
Porter, Andrew
Porter, Barbara Nevling
Porter, Burton F.
Porter, Edgar A(dwell)
Porter, Joe Ashby
Porter, Laurin
Porter, Michael C.
Porter, Michael E(ugene)
Porter, Roger B.
Porter, Tracey
Portis, Charles (McColl)
Posamentier, Alfred S.
Posen, Barry R.
Posner, Daniel N.
Posner, Eric A.
Posner, Gerald L.
Posner, Richard
Posner, Richard A.
Post, Jennifer C.
Post, Robert C(harles)
Poster, Mark
Postlewait, Heidi
Postman, Andrew
Potkay, Adam
Potter, Carol
Potter, Franz J.
Pottinger, Stanley

Potts, Rolf
Potts, Stephen W(ayne)
Poulson, Stephen C.
Poultney, David
Poundstone, William
Poverman, C(harles) E.
Powell, Barry B.
Powell, Corey S.
Powell, D. A.
Powell, Dannye Romine
Powell, David A.
Powell, E. Sandy
Powell, Eric
Powell, H. Jefferson
Powell, Joseph
Powell, Kevin
Powell, Nate
Powell, Padgett
Powell, Randy
Powell, Yolanda White
Powers, J. L.
Powers, Janet M.
Powers, Lyall H(arris)
Powers, Martin J.
Powers, Richard (S.)
Powers, Richard Gid
Powers, Steve
Powers, William T.
Powledge, Fred
Powter, Susan
Poyer, Joe
Poynor, Robin
Prado, Holly
Prager, Emily
Prall, Stuart E.
Pratt, James Michael
Pratt, John Clark
Pratt, Steven G.
Pratt, Tim
Prazniak, Roxann
Prechel, Harland
Prechter, Robert R(ougelot)
Pregracke, Chad
Preller, James
Prelutsky, Jack
Premo, Bianca
Prendergast, John
Presnell, Barbara
Press, Frank
Press, O(tto) Charles
Presser, Stephen B.
Pressman, Jeremy
Pressner, Amanda
Preston, Caroline
Preston, Douglas
Preston, Marcia K.
Prestowitz, Clyde V.
Prevas, John
Prevots, Naima
Prewitt, Kenneth
Price, Alan
Price, Christopher
Price, Hugh B(ernard)
Price, John (T.)
Price, Matthew A(rlen)
Price, Nancy
Price, Richard
Price, Robert M.
Price-Thompson, Tracy
Priest, John Michael
Primack, Alice Lefler

Primack, Richard B.
Prince, Russ Alan
Prince, Stephen
Prince-Hughes, Dawn
Principe, Lawrence M.
Prindle, David F.
Pringle, Laurence P(atrick)
Pritchard, R(obert) John
Pritchard, Ray
Pritchard, William H.
Pritchett, Kay
Pritchett, Wendell
Pritts, Kim Derek
Probst, Mark
Prokes, Mary T(imothy)
Prosek, James
Prothero, Stephen (Richard)
Protopopescu, Orel
Proulx, E(dna) Annie
Proulx, Suzanne
Provence, Michael
Provine, Robert R(aymond)
Prowell, Sandra West
Prown, Jonathan
Prowse, Brad A.
Prozan, Charlotte (Krause)
Prud'homme, Alex
Pruett, Candace (J.)
Pruett, Kyle D(ean)
Pruett, Lynn
Pruter, Robert
Pryor, Bonnie H.
Ptacek, Kathryn
Puar, Jasbir K.
Puchner, Eric
Pugh, Dianne G.
Puls, Mark
Pultz, John Francisco
Pulver, Robin
Punke, Michael
Purcell, Anne G.
Purcell, Benjamin H.
Purdy, Dwight H(illiard)
Purdy, Laura M.
Purpura, Lia
Purtill, Richard L.
Purvis, Alston W.
Pushker, Gloria (Teles)
Putnam, Constance E(lizabeth)
Putnam, Douglas
Putnam, William L(owell)
Putney, Clifford
Putney, Mary Jo
Putterman, Louis (G.)
Pybrum, Steven (Mark)
Pyle, Gerald F.
Pyle, Kenneth B.
Pyle, Kevin C.
Pynchon, Thomas
Quale, G(ladys) Robina
Qualey, Marsha
Quandt, William Bauer
Quantic, Diane Dufva
Quartz, Steven R.
Quattlebaum, Mary
Quayle, (James) Dan(forth)
Queenan, Joe
Queeney, Courtney
Queller, Jessica
Quester, George (Herman)
Quetchenbach, Bernard W.

Quiatt, Duane
Quick, Matthew
Quick, William K(ellon)
Quigley, David
Quigley, Kevin F. F.
Quigley, Sarah
Quilter, Deborah
Quindlen, Anna
Quinlan, Mary Lou
Quinlan, Patrick
Quinlan, Susan E(lizabeth)
Quinn, D. Michael
Quinn, Rob
Quinn, Sunny
Quinn, Tara Taylor
Quinney, Richard
Quiñones, Magaly
Quinones, Ricardo J(oseph)
Quiñonez, Ernesto
Quinsey, Mary Beth
Quintero, Ruben
Quirk, Anne (E.)
Quirk, Joe
Quirk, William J.
Quiroz, Anthony
Raad, Virginia
Rabalais, J. Wayne
Rabasa, George
Rabassa, Gregory
Rabb, Jonathan
Rabb, Margo
Rabe, Berniece (Louise)
Rabe, Jean
Rabie, Mohamed
Rabieh, Linda R.
Rabin, Robert L.
Rabinbach, Anson (Gilbert)
Rabinowitz, Alan
Rabinowitz, Dorothy
Rabkin, Jeremy A.
Raboteau, Albert J(ordy)
Rabrenovic, Gordana
Rachleff, Peter (J.)
Racine, Philip N.
Radano, Ronald M.
Raday, Sophia
Radelet, Michael L.
Rader, Karen A.
Radford, Irene
Radick, Gregory M.
Radin, Dean I.
Radin, Ruth Yaffe
Radosh, Daniel Lord
Radulescu, Domnica
Raeder, Linda C.
Raffel, Keith
Raftery, Brian
Rafuse, Ethan S.
Ragoné, Heléna
Raham, (R.) Gary
Rahe, Paul A.
Rain, Patricia
Rainbolt, William
Rainer, Yvonne
Rainey, Gene Edward
Rajtar, Steve
Rake, Jody
Raleigh, Debbie
Raleigh, Michael
Rallison, Janette
Ralph, James R.

Ramazani, Jahan
Rambach, Peggy
Rambuss, Richard
Ramirez, Malin
Ramirez, Susan E(lizabeth)
Ramos, Manuel
Rampton, Sheldon M.
Ramsay, Frederick J.
Ramsey, Doug(las K.)
Ramsey, Jarold
Ramsey, Rebecca S.
Ramsey, William L.
Ramseyer, Valerie
Ramsland, Katherine
Rand, Gloria
Rand, Harry
Rand, Jacki Thompson
Randall, Dale B(ertrand) J(onas)
Randall, Francis Ballard
Randall, Lisa
Randall, Margaret
Randall, Willard Sterne
Randolph, Elizabeth
Randolph, Lewis A.
Rangoussis, Steven
Rann, Sheila
Ranney, Joseph A.
Ransom, Harry Howe
Ransom, Jane (Reavill)
Rao, Saira
Rao, Srikumar S.
Rapf, Joanna E.
Raphael, Lev
Rapoport, Sandra E.
Rapp, Anthony
Rapp, George (Robert)
Rapp, Rayna
Rapp, Steven A.
Rappaport, Ann
Rappaport, Doreen
Rappaport, Nancy
Rapson, Richard L.
Rarick, Ethan
Rash, Ron
Rasmussen, Alis A.
Raso, Jack
Ratcliff, Carter
Ratey, John J(oseph)
Rath, Richard Cullen
Rathbun, Brian C.
Rathje, William (Laurens)
Rathmann, Peggy (Margaret Crosby)
Rathmell, George W(esley)
Ratliff, Ben
Ratner, Austin
Ratto, Linda Lee
Rauch, Jonathan (Charles)
Rauch, William
Raucher, Herman
Rause, Vince
Ravage, Barbara
Ravitch, Frank S.
Ravitch, Norman
Ravitz, Abe (Carl)
Raviv, Dan
Rawn, Melanie (Robin)
Rawson, Claude Julien
Rawson, Jacob
Ray, Brian Christopher
Ray, Daryll E.

Ray, David
Ray, Jeanne
Ray, Robert H.
Ray, Ruth E.
Raymond, Barbara Bisantz
Raymond, C. Elizabeth
Raymond, Jonathan
Raz, Aviad E.
Raz, Hilda
Read, David
Reagin, Nancy Ruth
Real, Terrence
Reardon-Anderson, James
Reasoner, Livia Jane Washburn
Reaven, Gerald
Reavis, Dick J.
Reback, Storms
Reber, Deborah
Rech, Lindsay Faith
Rechy, John (Francisco)
Reck, Andrew Joseph
Redding, David A(sbury)
Reddy, Maureen T.
Redfield, James
Redfield, Marc
Redick, Robert V.S
Redinger, Matthew A.
Redish, Martin H.
Redsand, Anna
Redshaw, Peggy A(nn)
Reece, Erik
Reed, Amy
Reed, Bruce
Reed, Christopher (G.)
Reed, Christopher Robert
Reed, Ishmael
Reed, John
Reed, John Shelton
Reed, Linda
Reed, Paula
Reed, Philip (Chandler)
Reed, Ralph Eugene
Reed, Thomas L.
Reed-Danahay, Deborah
Reeder, Carolyn
Reeher, Grant
Rees, David
Reese, Ellen
Reese, James
Reese, Laura
Reese, Roger R(oi)
Reeve, F(ranklin) D(olier)
Reeves, Eileen Adair
Reeves, Faye Couch
Reeves, Marcus
Reeves, Thomas C.
Regalbuto, Robert J.
Regan, Dian Curtis
Regan, Milton C.
Regan, Pamela C.
Reger, Gary
Reger, James P.
Reginster, Bernard
Regis, Edward
Regis, Helen A.
Regnerus, Mark D.
Regnery, Alfred S.
Rehder, Ben
Rehder, William J.
Rehg, William (Richard)
Reich, Howard

Reich, Lee
Reich, Robert B.
Reichardt, Mary R.
Reichel, Aaron I(srael)
Reichenbach, Bruce
Reichert, Tom
Reid, Catherine
Reid, Cindy
Reid, Elwood
Reid, Harry M.
Reid, John P(hillip)
Reid, Loren
Reid, Robert Leonard
Reid, Theresa
Reid, Van
Reidel, James
Reiken, Frederick
Reilly, Bernard F.
Reilly, Kevin
Reimann, Katya
Reinders, Eric
Reinertsen, Sarah
Reinfeld, Linda M.
Reingold, Dan
Reinhart, Peter
Reinstedt, Randall A.
Reisman, Michael
Reiss, Ira Leonard
Reiss, Kathryn
Reiss, Mitchell
Reiss, Tom
Reiter, Victoria (Kelrich)
Reitman, Judith
Reizbaum, Marilyn
Rejali, Darius M.
Rekdal, Paisley
Relyea, Harold C.
Rember, John
Remer, Gary
Remkiewicz, Frank
Remnick, David (J.)
Renard, John
Renauer, Albin (J.)
Rencher, Alvin C.
Rendon, Armando B.
Renee, Janina
Renehan, Edward J(ohn)
Renfield, Richard Lee
Rengert, George F.
Renker, Elizabeth
Renshon, Jonathan
Reps, John W(illiam)
Resis, Albert
Resnick, Mike
Resnick, Rachel
Resseguie, James L.
Restak, Richard M(artin)
Rettstatt, Chris
Reuland, Robert
Reusche, Taylor McCafferty
Revard, Carter (Curtis)
ReVelle, Jack B.
Revels, Tracy J.
Rey, Dennison
Reyhner, Jon (Allan)
Reynald, Lance M.
Reynolds, (Richard) Clay
Reynolds, Aaron
Reynolds, Arlene
Reynolds, Bill
Reynolds, E. Bruce

Reynolds, Kevin
Reynolds, Marjorie
Reynolds, Sheri
Rezits, Joseph
Rhea, Gordon Campbell
Rheingold, Howard (E.)
Rhodes, Donna McKee
Rhodes, Gary Don
Rhodes, Jane
Rhodes, Jean E.
Rhodes, Martha
Rhodes, Richard (Lee)
Rhodes, Tricia McCary
Rhodes-Courter, Ashley Marie
Rhyne, Nancy
Ribalow, M(eir) Z(vi)
Ribowsky, Mark
Ricardo, Jack
Riccio, Dolores Stewart
Ricciotti, Hope
Rice, Andrew
Rice, Anne
Rice, Bebe Faas
Rice, Condoleezza
Rice, Earle
Rice, Linda Lightsey
Rice, Luanne
Rice, Prudence M.
Rice, Stephen P.
Rice, Zoe
Rich, Adrienne (Cecile)
Rich, Elaine Sommers
Rich, Francine Poppo
Rich, Nathaniel
Rich, Simon
Rich, Susan
Richard, Adrienne
Richard, Carl J(ohn)
Richard, T. Dawn
Richard-Allerdyce, Diane
Richards, Amelia M.
Richards, David A. J.
Richards, David P.
Richards, Dusty
Richards, Emilie
Richards, Eugene
Richards, Jean
Richards, Jeffrey H.
Richards, Lawrence
Richards, Matt
Richardson, Bonham C.
Richardson, Heather Cox
Richardson, James T.
Richardson, Justin
Richardson, Mark
Richardson, Midge Turk
Richardson, Miles
Richardson, Peter
Richardson, Richard Judson
Richardson, Riché
Richburg, Keith B(ernard)
Richerson, Peter J.
Richetti, John J.
Richman, Irwin
Richman, Jana
Richman, Kenneth A.
Richmond, Michelle
Richmond, Peter
Richtel, Matt
Richter, Daniel K(arl)
Richter, Gregory C.

Richter, Harvena
Rickels, Laurence A.
Riddle, Paxton
Riddles, Libby
Ridley, Elizabeth J(ayne)
Ridlon, Florence
Riede, David G(eorge)
Rieder, Jonathan
Riedling, Ann Marlow
Rieff, David Sontag
Riehecky, Janet Ellen
Rielage, Dale C.
Ries, Laura
Riesenberg, Peter N.
Riess, Jana
Rifkin, Shepard
Riggs, Cynthia
Riggs, Jack C.
Riggs, Paula Detmer
Riggs, Robert E(dwon)
Riggs, Stephanie
Riggs, Webster
Riggsby, Andrew M.
Rightmire, G. Philip
Riley, Carroll L.
Riley, Charles A.
Riley, James A.
Riley, James C.
Riley, Jess
Riley, Sam G.
Rimler, Walter
Rinaldi, Ann
Rinder, Lenore
Rinderle, Walter
Rindo, Ron(ald J.)
Rinehart, Steven
Ring, Jennifer
Ring, Nancy G.
Ring, Victoria A.
Ringgold, Faith
Ringo, John
Ringquist, Evan J.
Ringwald, Christopher D.
Rinzler, Carol Ann
Riordan, Rick
Riordan, Teresa
Riordan, Timothy B.
Ripley, Randall
Rippe, James M.
Rippley, LaVern J.
Rips, Michael
Rischin, Moses
Rise, Eric W.
Ritchie, Daniel E.
Ritchie, James A.
Riter, Tim
Ritter, Gretchen
Ritterhouse, Jennifer
Ritthaler, Shelly
Ritvo, Harriet
Rivard, David
Rivard, Robert
Rivas, Mim Eichler
Rivenbark, Celia
Rivers, Francine (Sandra)
Rivers, Larry E.
Rivers, Reggie
Riviere, Jim (E.)
Rivkin, Steve
Rivlin, Gary
Rizzo, Margaret

Roahen, Sara
Roark, Dallas M.
Robb, B. R.
Robb, Candace
Robb, Christina
Robb, Daniel
Robb, David L.
Robb, George
Robbers, James E.
Robbin, Tony
Robbins, Bruce
Robbins, Hollis
Robbins, James S.
Robbins, Lawrence H.
Robbins, Rogene A.
Robbins, Tom
Robenalt, James David
Roberson, Houston Bryan
Robert, Dana L.
Roberts, Alvin
Roberts, Charles E.
Roberts, Cokie
Roberts, Diane
Roberts, Francis X.
Roberts, J(ames) Deotis
Roberts, Jennifer L.
Roberts, Jon H.
Roberts, Kristina LaFerne
Roberts, Madge Thornall
Roberts, Nancy N(orma)
Roberts, Nora
Roberts, Paul
Roberts, Philip J.
Roberts, Russell D.
Robertson, C(harles) K(evin)
Robertson, James I.
Robertson, Janet (E.)
Robertson, Joel C.
Robeson, Paul
Robie, Bill
Robin, Corey
Robinette, Joseph A.
Robins, Glenn
Robins, Madeleine E.
Robins, Robert S.
Robins, Sari
Robinson, Chuck
Robinson, Cynthia
Robinson, David L.
Robinson, Debbie
Robinson, Frank M(alcolm)
Robinson, Holly
Robinson, Jennifer L.
Robinson, Jeremy
Robinson, Leah Ruth
Robinson, Lee
Robinson, Lynda S(uzanne)
Robinson, Marguerite S(tern)
Robinson, Michael F.
Robinson, Paul H.
Robinson, Peter (Mark)
Robinson, Phyllis C(umins)
Robinson, Roxana (Barry)
Robinson, V. Gene
Robinson, Wayne Alexander
Robisheaux, Thomas
Robison, John Elder
Robson, Lucia St. Clair
Robson, Roy R(aymond)
Rochberg, Francesca
Roche, Denis (Mary)

Roche, Mark W.
Rock, Howard B.
Rockland, Michael Aaron
Rocklin, Joanne
Rocks, Burton
Rockwell, Anne (Foote)
Rockwell, Theodore
Rodgers, Alan (Paul)
Rodgers, Audrey T(ropauer)
Rodgers, Eugene
Rodin, Robert L.
Rodrigue, George
Rodriguez, Alejo
Rodriguez, Alfred
Rodríguez, Andrés
Rodriguez, Clara E.
Rodriguez, Gregory
Rodriguez, Ileana
Rodriguez, Jarbel A.
Rodriguez, Julia
Rodriguez, Junius P.
Rodriguez, Luis J.
Rodriguez, Manuel
Roe, JoAnn
Roe, Sue (Lynn)
Roediger, David R(andall)
Roehrig, Catharine H.
Roesch, Mattox
Roeske, Paulette
Roessner, Michaela
Rogers, Annie G.
Rogers, Bettye
Rogers, Cindy
Rogers, Deborah D(ee)
Rogers, Franklin Robert
Rogers, Heather
Rogers, Katharine M.
Rogers, Rebecca Elizabeth
Rogers, Robert F.
Rogovoy, Seth
Rogow, Roberta
Rogow, Zack
Rohde, David S.
Rohner, Ronald P.
Rohrbough, Malcolm Justin
Rohrer, S. Scott
Roiphe, Anne Richardson
Roiphe, Katie
Rolde, Neil
Roley, Brian Ascalon
Rolle, Andrew
Rollin, Roger B.
Rollins, Alden M(ilton)
Rollins, Wayne Gilbert
Romack, Janice Reed
Roman, Peter
Romano, Christy Carlson
Romano, Dennis
Romano, Louis
Romano, Ray
Romano-Lax, Andromeda
Rombs, Ronnie J.
Romero, George A.
Romm, Robin
Ronk, Martha C(lare)
Roodman, David Malin
Rooks, Judith P.
Rooks, Noliwe M.
Rooney, Andy
Roop, Connie
Roop, Peter

Roorbach, Bill
Roose, Kevin
Roosevelt, Selwa
Root, Hilton L.
Root, Phyllis
Root, William Pitt
Root-Bernstein, Michèle
Root-Bernstein, Robert Scott
Ropes, Linda Brubaker
Rorby, Ginny
Roripaugh, Robert (Alan)
Rosaler, Robert C.
Rosand, David
Roschelle, Anne R.
Rosco, Jerry
Roscoe, Will
Rose, Alison (C.)
Rose, Karen
Rose, Melody
Rose, Mike
Rose, Peter I(saac)
Rose, Phyllis
Rose, Richard
Rose, Tricia
Rosegrant, Susan
Roselle, Mike
Rosemurgy, Catie
Rosen, David J.
Rosen, James
Rosen, Jeffrey
Rosen, Louis H.
Rosen, Michael J(oel)
Rosen, Robert H.
Rosen, Selina
Rosen, Stanley Howard
Rosen, William S.
Rosenak, Chuck
Rosenak, Jan(ice M.)
Rosenberg, Gerald N.
Rosenberg, Howard
Rosenberg, Joel C.
Rosenberg, John D(avid)
Rosenberg, Liz
Rosenberg, Nathan
Rosenberg, Robert Alan
Rosenberg, Saralee
Rosenblatt, Jason P.
Rosenbloom, Joseph R.
Rosenblum, Nancy L.
Rosenfeld, Dina
Rosenfeld, Nancy (G.)
Rosenfeld, Richard N.
Rosenfeld, Stephanie
Rosenfield, Israel
Rosengarten, David
Rosengren, John
Rosenkranz, E. Joshua
Rosenmeyer, Patricia A.
Rosenson, Beth A.
Rosenstiel, Tom
Rosenthal, Chuck P.
Rosenthal, Debra J.
Rosenthal, Donald B.
Rosenthal, Elizabeth J.
Rosenthal, Judy
Rosenthal, Ken S.
Rosenthal, Lucy (Gabrielle)
Rosenthal, Nan
Rosenthal, Naomi B(raun)
Rosenthal, T(homas) G(abriel)
Roses, Lorraine Elena

Roshwald, Aviel
Rosman, Katherine
Rosman, Steven M(ichael)
Rosner, Bob
Rosner, Elizabeth J.
Rosner, Lisa
Ross, Adam Thayer
Ross, Alex
Ross, Charles L(ouis)
Ross, Dennis
Ross, Dorothy
Ross, Ellen
Ross, James R(odman)
Ross, JoAnn
Ross, Kent
Ross, Lawrence C.
Ross, Michael Elsohn
Ross, Rosetta E.
Ross, Stephen M.
Ross, Stewart Halsey
Rossen, Jake
Rosser, Sue V(ilhauer)
Rossi, Hozy (Joe)
Rossi, John V.
Rossi, Roxanne
Rossing, Barbara
Rossio, Terry
Rossman, C. L.
Rossman, Jeffrey J.
Rossol, Monona
Rossum, Ralph A.
Rostker, Bernard D.
Rostkowski, Margaret I.
Rotello, Gabriel
Rotenberg, Marc
Roth, Darlene R(ebecca)
Roth, Eric
Roth, Norman
Roth, Philip
Roth, Randolph Anthony
Rothenberg, David
Rothenberg, Jerome
Rothfuss, Pat J.
Rothkopf, David J.
Rothman, David J.
Rothman, William
Rothstein, Hy S.
Rothstein, Robert L.
Rothwell, William J.
Rotner, Shelley
Rotter, Andrew J.
Rotter, Gabe
Rotter, Jeffrey
Rottmann, Erik
Rougeau, Remy
Rough, Bonnie J.
Roughgarden, Tim
Rounds, David
Rous, Stephen N.
Rouse, Mary A(mes)
Rouse, Wade
Rousseau, George S.
Rowan, Roy
Rowe, Lee Pelham
Rower, Ann
Rowh, Mark
Rowland, Arthur Ray
Roy, Alexander
Roy, Donald H.
Roy, F. Hampton
Roy, James Charles

Royal, Priscilla
Royal, Robert
Roybal, Laura (Husby)
Royte, Elizabeth
Rozan, S. J.
Rozell, Mark J.
Rubens, Jim M.
Rubenstein, Richard Lowell
Rubin, Adam
Rubin, Barnett R(ichard)
Rubin, Bruce Joel
Rubin, Charles
Rubin, Gretchen (Craft)
Rubin, Hyman
Rubin, Joan Shelley
Rubin, Jordan
Rubin, Larry (Jerome)
Rubin, Rose M.
Rubin, Susan Goldman
Rubin-Dorsky, Jeffrey
Rubinetti, Donald
Rubino, Anna
Rubio, Gwyn Hyman
Rubright, Lynn
Ruby, Jay
Ruby, Lois
Ruby, Robert H.
Ruchelman, Leonard I.
Rucker, Mike
Rucker, Patrick Michael
Rucker, Rudy
Rucker, Walter C.
Ruddell, Deborah
Ruddiman, William F.
Rudolph, Christopher
Rudy, Jason R.
Rudy, Kathy
Rue, Leonard Lee
Rue, Loyal D.
Ruedy, John
Ruef, John Samuel
Ruefle, Mary
Ruelle, Karen Gray
Ruemmler, John D(avid)
Rueschemeyer, Dietrich
Rufus, Anneli S.
Rugeley, Terry
Rugg, Linda (Haverty)
Ruhl, Sarah
Rule, Ann
Rulon, Philip Reed
Rumbaut, Hendle
Rummel, Jack
Rummel-Hudson, Robert
Rumpf, Eva Augustin
Runco, Mark A.
Runyon, Randolph Paul
Ruoff, A. LaVonne Brown
Rupp, Joyce
Rupp, Richard H.
Rusch, Elizabeth
Rusch, Kristine Kathryn
Rushfield, Richard
Rushing, Josh
Rushkoff, Douglas
Ruskan, John
Russ, Daniel
Russell, Alan
Russell, Dick
Russell, Helen Ross
Russell, Jan Jarboe

Russell, Jeffrey Burton
Russell, Mary D(oria)
Russell, Norman H.
Russell, Paul
Russell, Richard L.
Russell, Sharman Apt
Russell, Sharon A.
Russell, Sheldon
Russell-Brown, Katheryn
Russett, Bruce Martin
Russo, John (A.)
Russo, Marisabina
Russo, Thomas A.
Rust, Elissa Minor
Rust, H. Lee
Rustici, Craig M.
Rutan, J. Scott
Ruthchild, Rochelle Goldberg
Rutkoski, Marie
Rutledge, Leigh W.
Rutsala, Vern A.
Rutter, Jeremy B.
Rutter, Virginia Beane
Ryan, Craig
Ryan, Donald P.
Ryan, Halford (Ross)
Ryan, James G(ilbert)
Ryan, Kay
Ryan, Margaret
Ryan, Pam Muñoz
Ryan, Patrick
Ryan, Trish
Rybolt, Thomas R.
Rychlak, Joseph F(rank)
Rychlak, Ronald (J.)
Ryczek, William J.
Rydell, Katy
Ryden, Hope
Ryder, Joanne (Rose)
Ryken, Leland
Rylant, Cynthia
Rymph, Catherine E.
S.D., Trav
Saari, Carolyn
Saban, Cheryl (Lynn)
Sabar, Ariel
Sabatine, Jean A.
Sabbagh, Marwan Noel
Sable, Martin Howard
Sableman, Mark (Stephen)
Sabuda, Robert (James)
Sachs, Jeffrey D.
Sachs, Judith
Sachs, Marilyn (Stickle)
Sachs, Mendel
Sachs, Robert
Sack, Allen L.
Sackett, Jeffrey
Sackman, Douglas Cazaux
Sacknoff, Scott
Sacks, David Harris
Sacks, Howard L.
Sacks, Steven
Sacre, Antonio
Sadick, Neil (S.)
Sadlier, Darlene J.
Sadowsky, Jonathan Hal
Saenz, Benjamin Alire
Saenz, Gil
Saferstein, Dan
Saffle, Michael

Safina, Carl
Safir, Howard
Safransky, Sy
Sagalyn, Lynne B.
Sager, Mike
Sahlins, Peter
Saillant, John
Sajdak, Bruce T.
Sakurai, Gail
Salaita, Steven
Salak, Kira
Salam, Reihan
Salamon, Julie
Salamon, Sonya
Salant, James
Saldana, Rene
Sale, Kirkpatrick
Saler, Benson
Salerno, Beth A.
Saliba, George
Saliers, Emily
Salinger, Michael
Salisbury, Frank B(oyer)
Salisbury, Joyce E(llen)
Salitan, Laurie P.
Sallis, James
Sallis, John C(leveland)
Salmansohn, Karen
Salmon, Jacqueline L.
Saloff, Jamie L.
Salomon, Frank
Salsi, Lynn
Salter, David F.
Salter, Mary Jo
Salvatore, R(obert) A(nthony)
Salwak, Dale (Francis)
Salwen, Hannah
Salwen, Kevin
Salwolke, Scott
Salyer, Lucy E.
Salzberg, Allen
Salzberg, Sharon
Salzman, Michele Renee
Salzman, Neil
Samar, Vincent J(oseph)
Sammon, Paul M.
Samples, John Curtis
Sampsell, Kevin
Sampson, Curt
Sampson, Edward E.
Sampson, Michael
Sams, Ferrol
Samson, Suzanne M.
Samuels, Cynthia K(alish)
Samuels, David
Samuels, Richard J.
Samuels, Shirley
Samuels, Warren J(oseph)
Samuelson, Robert J(acob)
Sanchez, Ivan William
Sanchez, Patrick
Sanchez, Sonia
Sanchez-Eppler, Karen
Sánchez-Walsh, Arlene M.
Sanday, Peggy Reeves
Sandburg, Helga
Sandel, Michael J.
Sanderlin, George
Sanders, Arlene
Sanders, Arthur
Sanders, Bill

Sanders, Charles W.
Sanders, Clinton R.
Sanders, David
Sanders, Ed(ward)
Sanders, Eve Rachele
Sanders, James
Sanders, John H.
Sanders, Katrina M.
Sanders, Lisa
Sanders, Scott Loring
Sanders, Tony
Sandford, John
Sandler, Ellen
Sandler, Irving (Harry)
Sandler, Kevin S.
Sandler, Lauren
Sandman, Peter (Mark)
Sandor, Marjorie
Sandoz, (George) Ellis
Sandstrom, Alan R(ussell)
Sandstrom, Eve K.
Sandweiss, Martha A(nn)
Sandy, Stephen
Saner, Reg(inald Anthony)
Sanford, Kathleen (D.)
Sanford, Richard
Sankar, Andrea (Patrice)
Sanna, Ellyn
Sant, Thomas
Santlofer, Jonathan
Santos, Michael Wayne
Santos, Sherod
Saperstein, David
Sapinsley, Barbara
Sapolsky, Robert M.
Sarah, Edith
Sarewitz, Daniel (R.)
Sargent, Lyman Tower
Sargent, Pamela
Sarna, Jonathan D(aniel)
Sarno, Ronald Anthony
Sarnoff, Irving
Sarotte, Mary Elise
Saroyan, Aram
Sarris, Greg
Sarris, Jonathan Dean
Sarti, Ron
Sartori, Anne E.
Sartwell, Crispin
Sarvas, Mark
Saslow, James M(axwell)
Sass, Stephen L.
Sasser, Charles W(ayne)
Sasso, Sandy Eisenberg
Saterstrom, Selah
Sathre, Vivian
Satter, Ellyn
Satter, Robert
Sauder, Robert A(lden)
Sauers, Michael P(atrick)
Sauers, Richard A(llen)
Saulnier, Beth
Saulnier, Karen Luczak
Saums, Mary
Saunders, George W.
Saunders, James Robert
Saunt, Claudio
Sauro, Christy W.
Sauter, Doris Elaine
Savage, Charlie
Savage, Jeff

Savage, Kirk
Savage, Sean J.
Savage, Tom
Savard, Jeannine
Savren, Shelley
Sawrey, Robert D.
Sawyer, Kathy
Sawyer, Keith
Sawyer, Kem Knapp
Sawyer, Mary R.
Sawyer, Ralph D.
Sawyer, Suzana
Sawyer-Laucanno, Christopher
Sax, Boria
Sayers, Kari
Sayers, Valerie
Saylor, Steven W(arren)
Sayrafiezadeh, Said
Sayre, Shay
Scalapino, Robert Anthony
Scales, Barbara
Scales-Trent, Judy
Scaletta, Kurtis
Scalia, Antonin
Scanlon, Bill
Scanlon, Jennifer
Scannell, Christy
Scarborough, Vernon L(ee)
Scarborough, William Kauffman
Scarf, Maggie
Scarlett, Elizabeth
Scarpaci, Sherry
Scarry, Elaine (Margaret)
Scarth, Alwyn
Scates, Shelby
Schaafsma, David
Schacht, Richard
Schacter, Daniel L.
Schaef, Anne Wilson
Schaefer, Claudia
Schaefer, David Lewis
Schaefer, Eric
Schaefer, Lola M.
Schaefer, William D.
Schaeffer, Mark
Schafer, Elisabeth
Schaffer, Frederic Charles
Schaffert, Timothy
Schaffner, Bradley L(ewis)
Schain, Martin A.
Schakel, Peter J.
Schall, Lucy
Schaller, Lyle E(dwin)
Schank, Roger C(arl)
Schapiro, Barbara
Scharf, Michael P(aul)
Scharrer, Erica
Schatzkin, Paul
Schecter, Barnet
Scheele, Roy
Scheeres, Julia
Scheese, Donald
Scheffer, Kathy J(ean)
Scheft, Bill
Scheiber, Harry N.
Scheil, Andrew P.
Scheil, Katherine West
Schein, Elyse
Scheindlin, Raymond P.
Schell, Jim
Schell, Orville (Hickok)

Schelling, Andrew
Schelling, Thomas C.
Schen, Claire S.
Schenck, Hilbert
Schendel, Dan
Schenken, Suzanne O'Dea
Schenker, Dona
Schenkkan, Robert (Frederic)
Scherer, Marcia J.
Scherer, Migael
Scheuer, Jeffrey
Schevill, Margot Blum
Schewe, Phillip F.
Schiappa, (Anthony) Edward
Schickler, David
Schier, Steven E.
Schiff, James A(ndrew)
Schiff, Nancy Rica
Schiff, Robyn
Schiffer, James (M.)
Schifferdecker, Kathryn M.
Schiller, Lawrence
Schilling, Peter
Schimpff, Jill Wagner
Schine, Cathleen
Schinto, Jeanne
Schisgal, Murray
Schlesinger, Allen B(rian)
Schlessinger, Laura
Schlitz, Laura Amy
Schlosberg, Suzanne
Schmid, Walter Thomas
Schmidle, Nicholas
Schmidt, Arthur
Schmidt, Benno Charles
Schmidt, C. A.
Schmidt, Elizabeth
Schmidt, Gary D.
Schmidt, Heidi
Schmidt, Karl H.
Schmidt, Leigh Eric
Schmidt, Peter
Schmidt, Stanley (Albert)
Schmidt, Vivien A.
Schmidt, Winsor C.
Schmiechen, Peter
Schmitz, Cecilia M.
Schmitz, Dennis
Schmookler, Andrew Bard
Schnakenberg, Robert
Schneider, Barbara
Schneider, Ben Ross
Schneider, Deborah Lucas
Schneider, Fred B.
Schneider, Gregory L.
Schneider, Karen
Schneider, Mindy
Schneider, Richard J.
Schneider, Robert
Schneider, Robyn
Schneider, Stuart L.
Schneider, Thomas E.
Schniedewind, William M.
Schnitter, Jane T.
Schnur, Steven
Schnurnberger, Lynn
Schoemer, Karen
Schoen, Lawrence M.
Schoen, Robert
Schoenberg, Robert J.
Schoenbrod, David

Schoenewolf, Gerald
Schoenfeld, Bruce
Schoenfeldt, Beth
Schofield, Robert E(dwin)
Scholes, Ken
Schone, Robin
Schor, Esther H.
Schor, Juliet B.
Schor, Mira
Schorsch, Laurence
Schott, John R.
Schott, Penelope Scambly
Schrag, Ariel
Schrager, Sam(uel Alan)
Schramm, Carl J.
Schreck, Harley Carl
Schrecker, Judie
Schrefer, Eliot
Schreiber, Joseph
Schreiber, Le Anne
Schreiber, Roy E.
Schreiber, Terry
Schreibman, Laura
Schreiner, Samuel (Agnew)
Schrift, Alan D.
Schrock, Kathleen
Schroeder, Alan
Schroeder, Joy A.
Schroeder-Lein, Glenna R(uth)
Schubel, Vernon James
Schubert, Frank N.
Schubert, Leda
Schudson, Charles B(enjamin)
Schueler, G(eorge) F(rederick)
Schulenberg, David
Schuler, Douglas
Schulkin, Jay
Schuller, Gunther
Schulman, Arlene
Schulman, Ivan A(lbert)
Schulman, Michael D.
Schultz, (Reynolds) Bart(on)
Schultz, Celia E.
Schultz, Susan M.
Schultze, Quentin J(ames)
Schulz, William F(rederick)
Schulze, Dallas
Schulze, Franz
Schumacher, Evelyn A(nn)
Schumacher, Jim
Schumacher, Julie
Schumacher, Linda H.
Schumacher, Michael
Schumaker, Paul
Schumaker, Ward
Schuman, Michael A.
Schumer, Fran
Schupack, Deborah
Schusky, Ernest L.
Schuster, Marilyn R.
Schutt, Christine
Schutte, Anne Jacobson
Schwab, George M.
Schwantes, Carlos A(rnaldo)
Schwartau, Winn
Schwartz, Adam
Schwartz, David B.
Schwartz, E(arl) A(lbert)
Schwartz, Elliott S.
Schwartz, Evan I.
Schwartz, Gary E.

Schwartz, Jeffrey H.
Schwartz, Joan
Schwartz, John Burnham
Schwartz, Joyce R.
Schwartz, Kessel
Schwartz, Lynne Sharon
Schwartz, Marie Jenkins
Schwartz, Mel
Schwartz, Richard A(lan)
Schwartz, Sanford
Schwartz, Sheila R.
Schwartz, Shuly Rubin
Schwartz, Stephen (Alfred)
Schwartz, Sunny
Schwartz-Nobel, Loretta
Schwarz, Daniel R(oger)
Schwarz, Frederick A. O.
Schwarz, Henry G.
Schwarz, John E.
Schwarz, Philip J.
Schwarz, Robin
Schwarzbein, Diana
Schweber, Howard
Schwedler, Jillian
Schwegel, Theresa
Schweikart, Larry (Earl)
Schweikart, Larry E.
Schweller, Randall
Sciabarra, Chris Matthew
Scieszka, Jon
Scipes, Kim
Scofield, Sandra (Jean)
Scoppettone, Sandra
Scotch, Allison Winn
Scotchie, Joseph
Scott, Alan (B.)
Scott, Amanda
Scott, Aurelia C.
Scott, Darieck
Scott, David L(ogan)
Scott, Elizabeth
Scott, Elizabeth S.
Scott, Eugenie Carol
Scott, Grant F.
Scott, Joan Wallach
Scott, John Beldon
Scott, John T.
Scott, Kay W.
Scott, Melissa
Scott, Roy Vernon
Scott, Sophfronia
Scott, Trevor
Scott, Whitney S.
Scoville, James Griffin
Scrivener, Michael (Henry)
Sculle, Keith A.
Scully, Helen
Scully, James (Joseph)
Scully, Matthew
Scully, Vincent
Seabrook, John M.
Seagrave, Sterling
Seagraves, Donny Bailey
Seale, Alan
Seale, William
Seals, David
Seaman, Ann Rowe
Seaman, P. David
Searcy, David
Searing, Donald D.
Searle, Elizabeth

Searle, John R(ogers)
Searles, P. D(avid)
Searls, David
Searls, Hank
Sears, David O('Keefe)
Sears, Joe
Sears, Richard
Sears, William P.
Seaton, J(erome) P.
Seay, James
Seay, Jody
Sebell, Mark Henry
Secunda, Victoria (H.)
Sedaitis, Judith B.
Sedaris, Amy
Sedaris, David
See, Carolyn
Seelye, John (Douglas)
Seese, June Akers
Segal, Harriet
Segal, Howard P.
Segal, Jeffrey A.
Segal, Jerome M.
Segal, Susan
Seger, Linda
Segriff, Larry
Seguin, Marilyn W(eymouth)
Seib, Gerald
Seidel, Frederick (Lewis)
Seidel, George Joseph
Seidensticker, John
Seidl, Amy
Seidler, Ann
Seidman, Hugh
Seidman, Louis Michael
Seidman, Michael
Seife, Charles
Seiferle, Rebecca
Seifert, Lewis C.
Seifrid, Thomas
Seigel, Catharine F.
Seitz, Rebeca
Selak, Joy H.
Selcer, Richard F.
Seldon, Lynn
Seleshanko, Kristina
Self, Robert O.
Selfors, Suzanne
Selgin, Peter
Selig, Robert L.
Seligman, Craig
Seligman, Martin E. P.
Seligson, Susan
Seliy, Shauna
Sellers, Christopher C.
Sellers, Heather (Laurie)
Sellers, John
Sellers-Garcia, Sylvia
Sellin, Christine Petra
Sellin, Eric
Selman, Robyn
Selmanovic, Samir
Seltzer, David
Seltzer, Leon F(rancis)
Seltzer, Mark
Selvidge, Marla J(ean)
Selvin, Joel
Selzer, Adam
Selzer, Jack
Semans, Anne
Semchyshyn, Stefan

Semmes, Clovis E.
Semple, Maria
Semrud-Clikeman, Margaret
  (Elaine)
Senate, Melissa
Sendak, Maurice
Senie, Harriet F.
Senior, W(illiam) A.
Senn, Bryan
Senna, Danzy
Sennett, Frank (Ronald)
Sennett, Richard
Senor, Dan
Sensel, Joni
Sensibar, Judith L(evin)
Sentilles, Sarah
Seo, Audrey Yoshiko
Sepinwall, Alyssa Goldstein
Seraile, William
Seret, Roberta
Serfozo, Mary
Serling, Carol
Serrano, Richard A.
Serulnikov, Sergio
Server, Lee
Service, Pamela
Sessa, Valerie I.
Sessions, William
Setterberg, Fred
Settje, David E.
Setzer, (Cynthia) Lynn
Severance, Ben H.
Severance, John B(ridwell)
Severson, Kim
Severson, Richard
Sewall, Gilbert T.
Sewell, Lisa
Sexton, Linda Gray
Seybold, Patricia B.
Seymour, Tres
Shabazz, Jamel
Shabecoff, Philip
Shackelford, Renae Nadine
Shafer, Audrey
Shafer, Byron E.
Shafer, D. Michael
Shafer, Glenn (Ray)
Shafer, Neil
Shafer, Yvonne
Shaffer, Donald R.
Shaffer, Louise
Shagan, Ethan H.
Shagan, Steve
Shah, Sonia
Shahan, Sherry
Shaheen, Jack G.
Shainberg, Lawrence
Shakar, Alex
Shalant, Phyllis
Shalleck, David
Shambaugh, David L.
Shames, Germaine W.
Shanahan, Daniel (A.)
Shanahan, Michael Edward
Shandler, Jeffrey
Shandling, Garry
Shane, Scott
Shangé, Ntozake
Shank, Theodore
Shanley, Mary Kay
Shanley, Mary L(yndon)

Shannon, Elizabeth (McNelly)
Shannon, Harry
Shannon, Timothy J.
Shapin, Steven
Shapiro, Barbara J(une)
Shapiro, Barry M.
Shapiro, Dan(iel)
Shapiro, Dani (J.)
Shapiro, David (Joel)
Shapiro, Edward S.
Shapiro, Eileen C.
Shapiro, Fred R(ichard)
Shapiro, H. Svi
Shapiro, Harvey
Shapiro, Herbert
Shapiro, Jerrold Lee
Shapiro, Judith
Shapiro, Karen Jo
Shapiro, NancyKay
Shapiro, Rami M.
Shapiro, Robert J.
Shapiro, Robert Y.
Shapiro, Rochelle Jewel
Shapiro, Susan
Sharlet, Jeff
Sharma, Nandita
Sharma, Poonam
Sharman, Cheryl Harris
Sharman, Russell Leigh
Sharmat, Marjorie Weinman
Sharp, Anne Wallace
Sharp, Deborah
Sharpe, Myron E(manuel)
Sharpe, William Chapman
Sharpe, William F(orsyth)
Shasha, Dennis (E.)
Shattuck, George C.
Shatzky, Joel
Shaughnessy, Mary Alice
Shaul, David Leedom
Shavelson, Lonny
Shaver, Phillip (Robert)
Shavit, David
Shaw, Carolyn V.
Shaw, Daron R.
Shaw, Dash
Shaw, David W.
Shaw, Joseph M(inard)
Shaw, Mark
Shaw, Miranda Eberle
Shaw, Patrick W.
Shaw, Robert B.
Shaw, Russell B(urnham)
Shaw, Susan
Shawhan, Dorothy Sample
Shawl, Nisi
Shawver, Lois
Shay, Jonathan
Shay, Kathryn
Shea, Lisa
Shea, Mark P.
Shea, Pegi Deitz
Shea, Suzanne Strempek
Shea, William M.
Sheaffer, Mike
Sheahan, John
Shear, Jeff
Shedd, Warner
Sheehan, Jason
Sheehan, Julie
Sheehan, Michael J.

Sheehan, Neil
Sheehy, Gail
Sheehy, Helen
Sheeler, Jackie
Sheeler, Jim
Sheen, Barbara
Shefchik, Rick
Shefter, Martin
Sheindlin, Judith
Sheinmel, Courtney
Shelby, Anne
Shelby, Tommie
Shelden, Michael
Sheldon, Garrett Ward
Sheldon, Joseph K(enneth)
Sheldon, Mary
Shelemay, Kay Kaufman
Shell, Susan Meld
Shellenberger, Michael
Sheller, Mimi Beth
Shelton, Allen C.
Shelton, Beth Anne
Shelton, Connie
Shelton, Hal T(erry)
Shelton, Mark L(ogan)
Shelton, Richard
Shem, Samuel
Shengold, Leonard
Shenk, David
Shenkman, Richard (Bennett)
Shepard, Alicia C.
Shepard, Charles E.
Shepard, Geoff Carroll
Shepard, Jim
Shepard, Molly Dickinson
Shepard, Neil
Shepard, Sam
Shepherd, John Scott
Shepherd, Margaret
Shepherd, Sherri Evonne
Sheppard, Alice
Sheppard, John L.
Sheppard, Rob
Sher, Barbara
Sher, Ira G.
Sher, Richard B.
Sheriff, Carol
Sherlock, Patti
Sherman, Charlotte Watson
Sherman, Janette D.
Sherman, Joe
Sherman, John W.
Sherman, Nancy
Sherman, Richard B.
Sherman, Robert
Sherman, Spencer D.
Sherman, Steve (Barry)
Shermer, Michael
Sherr, Lynn B(eth)
Sherraden, Michael (Wayne)
Sherrard-Johnson, Cherene
Sherrer, Quin(ton M.)
Sherrill, Kenneth S.
Sherrill, Steven
Sherry, Suzanna
Sherwood, Ben
Sherwood, Dolly
Sherwood, Frances
Shesol, Jeff
Shetterly, Aran
Shevelow, Kathryn

Shevitz, Amy Hill
Sheward, Tamara
Shields, Jody
Shields, Jon A.
Shigekuni, Julie
Shiller, Robert J.
Shilling, Michael
Shillinglaw, Gordon
Shillingsburg, Miriam (Carolyn)
    Jones
Shimko, Bonnie
Shimpock, Kathy E(lizabeth)
Shine, Frances L(ouise)
Shinn, Sharon
Shinn, Thelma J.
Shipler, David K(arr)
Shipman, Henry Longfellow
Shipman, John Marlin
Shipman, Pat
Shipnuck, Alan
Shipp, Steve
Shipper, Apichai W.
Shirk, David A.
Shirky, Clay
Shirley, Dennis
Shirley, Frances A.
Shirley, Shirley
Shivers, Jay Sanford
Shlaes, Amity
Shlechter, Theodore M.
Shmanske, Stephen
Shockley, Ann Allen
Shoemaker, Robert B(rink)
Shogan, Colleen J.
Shogan, Robert
Shomer, Enid
Shontz, Franklin C(urtis)
Shookman, Ellis
Shore, Zachary
Shorrock, Tim
Shors, John
Short, Brendan
Short, Kathy G(nagey)
Shostak, Seth
Shoup, Barbara
Shoup, Donald
Shoven, John B.
Showalter, Elaine
Showalter, Gena
Shrader, Charles R.
Shreiber, Maeera Yaffa
Shreve, Anita
Shreve, Susan R(ichards)
Shriver, Jean Adair
Shropshire, Kenneth (L.)
Shrout, Richard Neil
Shrum, Robert
Shubin, Neil
Shubin, Seymour
Shugart, Herman H(enry)
Shughart, William F.
Shuken, Julia
Shulevitz, Judith Anne
Shull, Steven A.
Shulman, Mark R(ussell)
Shulman, Myra Ann
Shulman, Seth
Shultz, George P(ratt)
Shultz, Richard H.
Shultz, Suzanne M.
Shumaker, David M.

Shumaker, Peggy
Shuman, George D.
Shuman, Joel James
Shuman, Malcolm K.
Shuman, Samuel I.
Shusterman, Neal (Douglas)
Shusterman, Richard (M.)
Sibley, Katherine A. S.
Sichel, Kim Deborah
Sicherman, Carol
Sick, Gary G(ordon)
Sickels, Noelle
Sicker, Martin
Sidak, J. Gregory
Siddali, Silvana R.
Siddons, Anne Rivers
Sides, W(ade) Hampton
Sidky, H.
Sidlow, Edward I.
Sidor, Steven
Siebold, Cathy
Siebold, Jan
Siegel, Bernard S(hepard)
Siegel, Daniel J.
Siegel, Daniel M.
Siegel, James
Siegel, Jennifer
Siegel, Jonah
Siegel, Mona L.
Siegel, Robert Anthony
Siegelbaum, Lewis H.
Siegelson, Kim L.
Siegfried, Tom
Siegmund, Stefanie
Sikélianòs, Eleni
Sikes, Gini
Sikes, Melvin P.
Sikkink, Kathryn
Silber, John (Robert)
Silber, Lee T.
Silber, Nina
Silber, Sherman J(ay)
Silberman, Marc (D.)
Silbey, David
Silcott, Loma G. Davies
Siler, Jenny
Silesky, Barry
Siljander, Mark D.
Silk, Gerald
Sill, Isabel Shehadi
Sill, John
Silliman, Matthew R.
Sills, Judith
Sills, Leslie (Elka)
Silman, Roberta
Silva, Daniel (Joseph)
Silva, Noenoe
Silva-Corvalán, Carmen
Silver, Anna Krugovoy
Silver, Brenda R.
Silver, Carole G(reta)
Silver, Lee M(errill)
Silver, Marisa
Silver, Peter Rhoads
Silverberg, Robert
Silverblatt, Art
Silverburg, Sanford R.
Silverman, Jerry
Silverman, Joseph H.
Silverman, Mark P.
Silverman, Robin L(andew)

Silverman, Stephen M.
Silverman, Willa Z.
Silverstein, Amy
Silverstein, Clara
Silverstein, Herma
Silverstein, Jake Phillip
Silverstein, Ken
Silverstone, Scott A.
Silverton, Nancy
Sima, Carol Ann
Simic, Charles
Simien, Evelyn M.
Simkins, Ronald A.
Simmer-Brown, Judith
Simmons, Beth A.
Simmons, Cal
Simmons, Charles A(lexander)
Simmons, Curt
Simmons, Cynthia Francene
Simmons, Diane E.
Simmons, Earl
Simmons, James C(oleman)
Simmons, Marc (Steven)
Simmons, Thomas
Simon, Alvah
Simon, Diane
Simon, Harvey B(ruce)
Simon, James F.
Simon, Lizzie
Simon, Michele
Simon, Neil
Simon, Rachel
Simon, Rita J(ames)
Simon, Roger (Mitchell)
Simon, Scott
Simon, Seymour
Simon, Sheldon Weiss
Simonelli, Jeanne M(arie)
Simonetta, Joseph R.
Simons, Daniel J.
Simons, Thomas W(inston)
Simontacchi, Carol
Simpson, Brooks D.
Simpson, Dick
Simpson, Elizabeth
Simpson, John Warfield
Simpson, Marc
Sims, Anastatia
Sims, Elizabeth
Sims, Henry P.
Sims, Michael
Sims, Norman (Howard)
Sims, Patsy
Sinclair, Barbara Louise
Sinclair, Billy Wayne
Sinclair, Brett J(ason)
Sinclair, Carla
Sindermann, Carl J(ames)
Sine, Tom
Singer, Alan
Singer, Barry
Singer, Bayla
Singer, Jerome L(eonard)
Singer, Judy Reene
Singer, Marcus George
Singer, Marilyn
Singer, Mark
Singer, Maxine
Singer, P. W.
Singh, Nikhil Pal
Singleton, Janet Elyse

Singleton, Linda Joy
Sinister, Bucky
Sinnette, Elinor Des Verney
Sinnott-Armstrong, Walter
Sinykin, Sheril C.
Sipherd, Ray
Sipiera, Paul P.
Siple, Molly
Siracusa, Catherine (Jane)
Sirimarco, Elizabeth
Sirota, David
Sirowitz, Hal
Sirvaitis (Chernyaev), Karen
    (Ann)
Sisk, David W.
Sita, Lisa
Sites, Kevin
Sitkoff, Harvard
Sittenfeld, Curtis
Sitter, John E(dward)
Sittser, Gerald L.
Siverling, Mike
Siverson, Randolph M.
Sizemore, Christine Wick
Skal, David J.
Skelton, William B(arott)
Skemer, Don C.
Skerpan-Wheeler, Elizabeth
    (Penley)
Skiba, Katherine M.
Skidmore, David (G.)
Skidmore, Max J(oseph)
Skillingstead, Jack
Skillman, Don
Skinner, Gloria Dale
Skinner, Margaret
Skinner, Michael
Skinner-Linnenberg, Virginia (M.)
Skipp, John
Sklar, Kathryn Kish
Skloot, Floyd
Skloot, Rebecca
Skocpol, Theda (Ruth)
Skolnikoff, Eugene B.
Skoug, Kenneth N.
Skover, David M.
Skowronek, Stephen
Skrentny, John D.
Skreslet, Paula Youngman
Skultety, Nancy Laney
Skye, Christina
Skyler, Heather
Slade, Leonard A.
Slan, Joanna Campbell
Slater, Judith (Carol)
Slater, Thomas J.
Slatta, Richard W(ayne)
Slattery, Brian Francis
Slattery, Dennis Patrick
Slaughter, Anne-Marie
Slaughter, Karin
Slavicek, Louise Chipley
Slavin, Barbara
Slawson, Douglas J.
Slayton, Robert A(llen)
Slee, Debora A.
Slee, Vergil N(elson)
Slegman, Ann
Sleigh, Tom
Slemrod, Joel (B.)
Slepian, Jan(ice B.)

Slepyan, Kenneth D.
Slesinger, Warren
Slive, Seymour
Sloan, Cliff
Sloan, Don
Sloan, Jane
Sloan, Mark
Sloan, Susan R.
Sloan, Tod (Stratton)
Sloat, Teri
Slosberg, Mike
Slote, Alfred
Slotten, Ross A.
Slouka, Mark
Slovenko, Ralph
Slovic, Scott H.
Smail, Daniel Lord
Small, Bertrice
Small, Hugh
Smart, Bradford D.
Smart, Ian Isidore
Smart, S(tephen) Bruce
Smedley, Audrey
Smelser, Neil Joseph
Smerk, George M.
Smigel, Robert
Smiley, Bob
Smiley, Gene
Smiley, Jane (Graves)
Smiraglia, Richard P(aul)
Smirnoff, Marc
Smith, (John) Geddeth
Smith, Andrew Anselmo
Smith, Arthur L.
Smith, Barbara Herrnstein
Smith, Bobbi
Smith, Bradley A.
Smith, Bradley F.
Smith, Brenda
Smith, Bruce L. R.
Smith, Bruce R.
Smith, Carolyn Jeanne
Smith, Charles R.
Smith, Cynthia Leitich
Smith, D. James
Smith, Dale L.
Smith, Daniel Jordan
Smith, Dave
Smith, David A(lden)
Smith, David Alexander
Smith, David E(lvin)
Smith, David Livingstone
Smith, Deborah
Smith, Derek D.
Smith, Diane
Smith, Douglas K.
Smith, Duane Allan
Smith, Dustin Beall
Smith, Elizabeth A(ngele) T(aft)
Smith, Emily Wing
Smith, Erin A(nn)
Smith, F. Todd
Smith, Faye McDonald
Smith, Gary Scott
Smith, Geof
Smith, George P(atrick)
Smith, Glenn D.
Smith, Glenn Robert
Smith, Gordon
Smith, Greg Leitich
Smith, Gregory Blake

Smith, Gregory White
Smith, Gwen
Smith, H. Jeff
Smith, Hedrick (Laurence)
Smith, Hobart Muir
Smith, J. Walker
Smith, James M.
Smith, Janna M(alamud)
Smith, Jason Scott
Smith, Jean Edward
Smith, Jeanne Rosier
Smith, John M.
Smith, Judie R.
Smith, Judith E.
Smith, Julian C(leveland)
Smith, Kevin
Smith, Kirsten
Smith, Lane
Smith, Lee Harold
Smith, Lora Roberts
Smith, Lori
Smith, M. J
Smith, Marguerite
Smith, Marisa
Smith, Mark Haskell
Smith, Martha Nell
Smith, Martin Cruz
Smith, Marya
Smith, Mitchell
Smith, Morris
Smith, Nicholas D.
Smith, Nigel
Smith, Noel W.
Smith, Pamela (A.)
Smith, Patricia
Smith, R. J.
Smith, Ralph Lee
Smith, Richard L.
Smith, Robert Ellis
Smith, Roger T.
Smith, Rollin
Smith, Ryan K.
Smith, Sam
Smith, Sandra Lee
Smith, Sarah (W. R.)
Smith, Scott
Smith, Sherri L.
Smith, Sherry L.
Smith, Sherwood
Smith, Stephanie A.
Smith, Steven
Smith, Steven G(arry)
Smith, Steven Trent
Smith, Susan Arnout
Smith, Tara Bray
Smith, Tim(othy R.)
Smith, Timothy B.
Smith, Timothy B.
Smith, Tommie C.
Smith, Wanda VanHoy
Smith, Wesley J.
Smith, Wilda M(axine)
Smith, Zak
Smith-Ankrom, M. E.
Smith-Hunter, Andrea E.
Smith-Rex, Susan J.
Smoak, Gregory E.
Smock, Raymond W.
Smolens, John (Harrison)
Smoley, Richard
Smoot, George Fitzgerald

Snadon, Patrick A.
Snadowsky, Daria
Snay, Mitchell
Snell, Daniel C.
Snell, Michael
Snell, Patricia
Snelling, Dennis (Wayne)
Snelling, Lauraine
Snicket, Lemony
Snider, J. H.
Sniegoski, Thomas E.
Snodgrass, Mary Ellen
Snow, Carol
Snow, Donald
Snow, Kimberley
Snow, Robert L.
Snowdon, David A.
Snyder, Brad M.
Snyder, Cecil
Snyder, Gary (Sherman)
Snyder, Graydon F.
Snyder, Gregory J.
Snyder, James D.
Snyder, Jane McIntosh
Snyder, Laurel
Snyder, Lucy A.
Snyder, Midori
Snyder, Timothy
Snyder, Zilpha Keatley
Sobel, Dava
Sobel, David T.
Sobel, Ileene Smith
Sobel, Russell S(teven)
Sober, Elliott (Reuben)
Sobol, Donald J.
Soden, Dale E.(Edward)
Soden, Garrett
Soehnlein, Karl M.
Soerens, Matthew
Soffer, Joshua
Soffer, Olga
Sohn, Amy
Sokol, Julia
Sokoloff, Naomi B.
Solbrig, Dorothy J.
Soley, Lawrence C(harles)
Solheim, James
Solinger, Rickie
Solmssen, Arthur R(obert)
  G(eorge)
Solomita, Stephen
Solomon, Andrew
Solomon, Barry D.
Solomon, Marion F.
Solomon, Nina
Solomon, Richard H(arvey)
Solomon, Steven
Solomonson, Katherine M.
Solotaroff, Ivan
Solove, Daniel J.
Solter, Aletha
Soltis, Jonas F.
Solum, John
Soluri, John
Solvang, Elna K.
Somers, Jeff
Somervill, Barbara A(nn)
Sommer, Jason
Sommers, Christina Hoff
Sommers, Susan Mitchell
Sommerville, C(harles) John

Sonenberg, Maya
Sonn, Richard D.
Sonnenfeld, Jeffrey
Soodalter, Ron
Soos, Troy
Sorel, Nancy Caldwell
Sorensen, Roy A.
Sorenson, John L.
Sorenson, Margo
Sorkin, Adam J.
Sorrow, Barbara Head
Sosnowski, David (J.)
Soto, Gary
Soto, Lourdes Díaz
Soule, Maris Anne
Soussloff, Catherine M.
South, Mary
South, Sheri Cobb
Souther, J. Mark
Southwick, Leslie H.
Sowell, David (Lee)
Sowell, Mike
Spack, Ruth
Spacks, Barry
Spacks, Patricia Meyer
Spahr, Juliana
Spall, James C.
Spangler, Catherine
Spangler, David
Spanier, Sandra Whipple
Spanogle, Joshua
Spar, Debora L.
Sparks, John
Sparks, Kenton L.
Sparks, Nicholas
Sparks, Randy J.
Sparrowdancer, Mary
Spatz, Gregory
Spatz, Kenneth Christopher
Spaugh, Jean Christopher
Speakes, Larry (Melvin)
Spear-Swerling, Louise
Spears, Sally
Speck, Bruce W.
Speck, Katie
Speck, Nancy
Spector, Jack Jerome
Spector, Robert
Spector, Sheila A.
Spector, Stephen
Spedale, Darren R.
Speer, Laurel
Spehr, Paul C(hristopher)
Spellman, Frank R.
Spellman, W. M.
Spelman, Cornelia Maude
Spencer, Brent
Spencer, Duncan
Spencer, Elizabeth
Spencer, Irene
Spencer, Jon Michael
Spencer, Mark
Spencer, Robert H.
Spencer, Scott
Spencer, Stuart S.
Spencer, Wen
Spencer, William Browning
Spenser, Jay P.
Sperber, Jonathan
Sperling, Daniel
Sperling, L(es) H.

Spiegel, David
Spiegelman, Annie
Spiegelman, Ian
Spiegelman, Peter
Spiegelman, Willard
Spierling, Karen E.
Spindler, George Dearborn
Spinelli, Jerry
Spinner, Jackie
Spitz, Bob Stephen
Spivack, Charlotte
Spivack, Kathleen (Romola
  Drucker)
Spivak, Dawnine
Spollen, Anne
Spolter, Pari (Dokht)
Spooner, Mary Helen
Spooner, Michael
Spraggon, Julie
Spratford, Becky Siegel
Spreiregen, Paul (David)
Spretnak, Charlene
Spriggs, James F.
Springer, Claudia
Sprinkle, Annie (M.)
Sprinkle, Patricia Houck
Spruill, Steven
Spungin, Charlotte I(sabelle)
Squires, Richard D(onald)
Sragow, Michael
St. Amant, Mark
St. Antoine, Sara L.
St. George, Andrew
St. George, Judith
St. James, Lyn
St. John, Bob J.
St. John, David
St. John, Ronald Bruce
St. John, Warren
Staats, Marilyn Dorn
Stabenow, Dana
Stabile, Don
Stacey, Judith
Stachel, John Jay
Stack, George
Stack, Megan K.
Stackpole, Michael A(ustin)
Stacks, Don W.
Stade, George
Stafford, Edward Peary
Stainback, Berry
Stainton, Leslie
Staley, Allen (Percival Green)
Staley, Lynn
Stallard, Michael L.
Stallman, Richard Matthew
Stambler, Irwin
Stamets, Paul
Stamford Krause, Shari
Standiford, Natalie
Stanford, Craig (Britton)
Stanish, Charles
Stanley, Autumn
Stanley, Diane
Stanley, J. B.
Stanley, Jerry
Stanley, Kelli
Stanley, Patricia H.
Stanley, Peter W(illiam)
Stanley, Susie Cunningham
Stannard, Richard M.

Stansberry, Domenic (Joseph)
Stansky, Peter (David Lyman)
Stanton, Doug
Stanton, Joseph
Stanton, Shelby L(ee)
Staples, Robert Eugene
Staples, Suzanne Fisher
Stapleton, Richard M.
Starer, Daniel
Starita, Joe
Stark, Evan
Stark, Marisa Kantor
Stark, Rodney
Starkey, David
Starmer, Aaron
Starnes, Richard D.
Starr, Jason
Starr, Larry
Starzl, Thomas E(arl)
Stashower, Daniel (Meyer)
Staten, Vince
Statham, E. Robert
Stathis, Pete
Staub, Wendy Corsi
Stauber, John (Clyde)
Staubus, Martin
Staurowsky, Ellen J.
Stave, Bruce M.
Stave, Shirley A.
Stavitsky, Gail
Stavrakis, Peter J(acob)
Stearns, Maureen
Stebenne, David
Steckel, Richard
Stecker, Ann Page
Steege, Paul
Steel, Danielle
Steel, Gayla R(uth)
Steel, Ronald
Steele, Cynthia
Steele, Timothy (Reid)
Steensland, Brian
Stefaniak, Mary Helen
Steidle, Brian
Steidle Wallace, Gretchen
Steiker, Valerie
Steil, Benn
Stein, Benjamin J.
Stein, Edward D.
Stein, Eugene
Stein, Kevin
Stein, Mary Kay
Stein, Michael D.
Stein, Rebecca L.
Stein, Sherman K.
Stein, Wendy
Steinberg, Clarence B.
Steinberg, Erwin R.
Steinberg, Jonathan
Steinberg, Laurence
Steinberg, Mark D(avid)
Steinberg, Neil
Steinberg, Susan
Steinberg, Warren
Steinberg, Wendy
Steinbrook, Gordon L.
Steiner, George A.
Steiner, Michael C.
Steinhardt, Bernice
Steinhardt, Nancy Shatzman
Steinhoff, Judith B.

Steinke, Darcey
Steinlauf, Michael C.
Steinman, David
Steinman, Louise
Steinman, Michael
Steinman, Ron
Steinmann, Andrew E.
Steinmetz, Devora
Steinmetz, Lawrence Leo
Steins, Richard
Steketee, Gail
Sten, Christopher (W.)
Stengel, Joyce A.
Stenger, Victor J.
Stennett, Rob
Stentiford, Barry M.
Stenzel, Anabel
Stenzel Byrnes, Isabel
Stepakoff, Jeffrey
Stephens, John D(avid)
Stephens, Randall J.
Stephens, Thomas M.
Stephens, Walter
Stepp, Laura Sessions
Sterk, Andrea
Sterle, Francine
Sterling, Bruce
Sterling, Keir B(rooks)
Sterling, Susan Fisher
Stern, David
Stern, Fritz
Stern, Gerald
Stern, Jessica Eve
Stern, Judith M.
Stern, Kenneth S.
Stern, Paul C(linton)
Stern, Richard G(ustave)
Stern, Robert A. M.
Stern, Sheldon M.
Stern, Steve
Stern, Steve J.
Sternberg, Robert J(effrey)
Sterne, Richard Clark
Sterngold, James (S.)
Sternlicht, Sanford
Stertz, Bradley A.
Stetson, Brad
Steuerle, C. Eugene
Stevens, Bryna
Stevens, Diane
Stevens, Dick
Stevens, Karl
Stevens, Kathy
Stevens, Lawrence L.
Stevens, M. L. Tina (L.)
Stevens, Marcus
Stevens, Robert E(llis)
Stevens, Susan
Stevens, Suzanne H.
Stevenson, Doug
Stevenson, James
Stevenson, Louise L.
Stevenson, Robert G.
Stevenson, Seth
Stevenson, Sucie
Steward, H. Leighton
Stewart, Christopher S.
Stewart, David O.
Stewart, David W.
Stewart, Elizabeth A.
Stewart, Gail B.

Stewart, Gary
Stewart, Harry E.
Stewart, Jeffrey C.
Stewart, Kenneth
Stewart, Leah
Stewart, Martha
Stewart, Matthew
Stewart, Ron(nie)
Stewart, Susan
Stewart, Thomas A(lan)
Stidworthy, David Earl
Stiebing, William H(enry)
Stiefvater, Maggie
Stiles, T. J.
Still, William N.
Stillerman, Marci
Stillinger, Jack
Stillman, (John) Whit(ney)
Stillman, David A.
Stillman, Norman A(rthur)
Stillson, Alan
Stiltner, Brian
Stimmler, Jane K.
Stimpson, Jeff
Stinchecum, Amanda Mayer
Stine, Catherine
Stine, Scott A(aron)
Stinnett, Robert B.
Stinson, Jim
Stirt, Joseph A.
Stivale, Charles J.
Stivender, Ed
Stock, Gregory
Stockel, H. Henrietta
Stockenberg, Antoinette
Stockler, Bruce
Stockley, Grif
Stoddard, Robert H.
Stodghill, Ron
Stoehr, Shelley
Stoff, David M.
Stoker, R. Bryan
Stokes, Donald W.
Stokes, Gale
Stokes, Susan C.
Stoll, Steven
Stoller, Debbie
Stoltenberg, John (Vincent)
Stoltzfus, Ben
Stolz, Karen
Stomfay-Stitz, Aline M.
Stone, Alan A.
Stone, Cynthia L.
Stone, David R.
Stone, Dawna
Stone, Del
Stone, Eric
Stone, Glenn D(avis)
Stone, Harry
Stone, Judith F.
Stone, Katherine
Stone, Laurie
Stone, Linda
Stone, R. W.
Stone, Robert (Anthony)
Stone, Ruth
Stone, Sarah
Stonecash, Jeffrey M.
Stoner, K. Lynn
Stoner, Tom
Stonich, Sarah

Storey, Dee
Storey, Gail Donohue
Storey, Margaret M.
Stork, Francisco X.
Storlie, Erik Fraser
Stortz, Martha E.
Stott, Annette
Stout, Chris E.
Stout, Harry S.
Stout, Janis P.
Stout, Jay A.
Stout, Joseph A.
Stout, Martha
Stout, Nancy
Stovall, Tyler
Stover, Matthew Woodring
Stowe, Steven M.
Stowe, William W.
Strachman, Daniel A.
Strahinich, Helen C.
Straight, Susan
Strain, Christopher B.
Strane, Susan
Strange, Lily
Strasser, Todd
Straub, Peter (Francis)
Straus, Jillian
Straus, Murray A.
Strausbaugh, John
Strauss, David Levi
Strauss, Susan (Elizabeth)
Stravinskas, Peter M. J.
Straw, Deborah
Strawn, Martha A.
Streb, Matthew J(ustin)
Streckert, Hal
Streever, Bill
Streitwieser, Andrew
Strick, Wesley
Strickland, (William) Brad(ley)
Strickland, Craig (A.)
Strickland, Michael R.
Strieber, Anne
Strieder, Leon F.
Striegel, Jana
Strier, Karen B.
Stringer, C. Vivian
Stringer, Vickie M.
Stroby, Wallace
Strock, Ian Randal
Stroh, Linda K.
Strom, Robert
Strom, Yale
Stromberg, Peter G.
Stronach, Bruce
Strong, Albertine
Strong, Carson
Strong, Douglas M.
Strong, John S.
Strong, Marilee
Stronge, James H.
Strongin, Laurie
Stross, Randall E.
Strossen, Nadine
Strother, Ruth
Stroud, Bettye
Stroud, Patricia Tyson
Stroup, George W.
Struyk, Raymond J(ay)
Stuart, Anne
Stuart, Dabney

Stuart, Sally E(lizabeth)
Stuart, Sarah Payne
Stuckart, Diane A. S.
Stuever, Hank
Stuhr(-Rommereim), Rebecca
 (Ann)
Stukas, David
Stulberg, Adam N.
Sturges, Robert S(tuart)
Sturgis, Ingrid
Sturm, Circe
Sturm, Douglas E.
Sturma, Michael Thomas
Sturman, Jennifer
Sturtevant, Katherine
Stutson, Caroline
Stutzman, Linford L.
Stynes, Barbara White
Styron, Alexandra
Suarez, Daniel
Suarez, Ray
Subotnik, Rena F.
Such, David G.
Suen, Anastasia
Suinn, Richard M.
Sulkin, Tracy
Sullivan, Amy
Sullivan, Brad
Sullivan, C(harles) W(illiam)
Sullivan, Claudia
Sullivan, David M.
Sullivan, Dolores P.
Sullivan, Faith
Sullivan, Garrett A.
Sullivan, George E(dward)
Sullivan, John Jeremiah
Sullivan, M(ichael) J(ustin)
Sullivan, Michael Joseph
Sullivan, Patricia
Sullivan, Paul
Sullivan, Randall
Sullivan, Sherry E.
Sullivan, Steve (Joseph)
Sullivan, Winnifred Fallers
Sullivan Harper, Donna Akiba
Sullum, Jacob
Sulmasy, Daniel P.
Sultan, Alan
Sultan, Stanley
Summer, Lauralee
Summerhawk, Barbara
Summerhill, Thomas
Summerlin, Vernon
Summers, Mark Wahlgren
Sumner, David E.
Sumner, Mark (C.)
Sundahl, Daniel James
Sundeen, Mark
Sundell, Joanne
Sundelson, David
Sundiata, Ibrahim K.
Sundquist, James (Lloyd)
Sundquist, Josh
Sundstrand, David
Sunley, Christina
Sunshine, Linda
Surowiecki, James (Michael)
Susi, Geraldine Lee
Suskind, Ron(ald Steven)
Susman, Gerald I.
Susskind, Leonard

Sussman, Peter Y.
Sutcliffe, Jane
Sutcliffe, Katherine
Sutphen, Mona
Sutton, Allan
Sutton, Dana F.
Sutton, Garrett
Sutton, Jane
Sutton, Matthew Avery
Sutton, Peter C.
Sutton, R. Anderson
Sutton, Robert I.
Sutton, Roger
Svenvold, Mark
Svoboda, Terese
Swaab, Neil
Swafford, Jan Johnson
Swain, Gwenyth
Swain, Joseph P(eter)
Swan, Annalyn
Swan, Claudia
Swan, Sharon
Swanson, David
Swanson, Doug J.
Swanson, Eric
Swanson, Gerald J.
Swanson, James L.
Swanson, Judith A(nn)
Swanson, June
Sward, Robert S.
Swartz, Jon David
Swartz, Mark
Swasy, Alecia
Swearer, Donald K(eeney)
Sweeney, Aoibheann
Sweeney, Emma
Sweeney, Marvin A.
Sweeney, Terrance (Allen)
Sweet, O. Robin
Swenson, Kristin M.
Swetman, Glenn R(obert)
Swetz, Frank J.
Swick, Marly
Swick, Thomas
Swidey, Neil
Swidler, Ann
Swift, Donald C.
Swift, Sue
Swift, Will
Swiller, Josh
Swinton, Elizabeth de Sabato
Switzer, Janet
Switzer, Les
Swope, Sam
Sword, Wiley
Sykes, Charles J.
Sylvan, Dianne
Sylvester, Janet
Symonds, Deborah A(nn)
Symynkywicz, Jeffrey B(ruce)
Synan, (Harold) Vinson
Szalavitz, Maia
Szanton, Andrew (Emlen)
Szasz, Andrew
Sze, Arthur C.
Szekeres, Cyndy
Szybist, Mary
Szymanski, Lois
Szymczak, Leonard K.
Taaffe, Sonya
Taback, Simms

Tabbi, Joseph
Tabios, Eileen
Taeuber, Cynthia M.
Taffel, Ron Walter
Tafuri, Nancy
Tagliaferro, Linda
Taichert, Pari Noskin
Tainter, Frank H(ugh)
Takayama, Sandi
Talalay, Kathryn M(arguerite)
Talbot, Emile J.
Talese, Gay
Taliaferro, Charles
Talley, Colin L.
Tallichet, Suzanne E.
Tallis, Frank
Tallman, Shirley
Tamblyn, Amber
Tamburri, Anthony Julian
Tan, Amy
Tanaka, Stefan
Tancer, Bill
Tanen, Sloane A.
Tang, Victor
Tanner, Jo A.
Tanner, John S.
Tanner, Karen Holliday (Olson)
Tanner, Kathryn
Tanner, Stephen L.
Tanselle, G(eorge) Thomas
Tanzi, Rudolph E(mile)
Tanzman, Carol M.
Tapahonso, Luci
Tapia, Richard A(lfred)
Tappan, Mark B.
Taraborrelli, J. Randy
Tarantino, Quentin (Jerome)
Tarcov, Nathan
Targoff, Ramie
Tarlton, John S.
Tarr, Hope
Tarr, Joel Arthur
Tarrow, Sidney G.
Tart, Charles T.
Tarte, Bob
Taruskin, Richard
Tashjian, Janet
Tatalovich, Raymond
Tate, Eleanora E(laine)
Tate, Elodia
Tate, Greg
Tate, James (Vincent)
Tate, Michael L.
Tatham, David
Tattlin, Isadora
Tatum, Beverly Daniel
Taubes, Gary
Taubes, Timothy
Taubman, Bruce
Taubman, Philip
Tawa, Nicholas E.
Tawil, Ezra
Tayler, Irene
Taylor, Anne Marie
Taylor, Benjamin
Taylor, Beverly (White)
Taylor, Billy
Taylor, Bob Pepperman
Taylor, Bron Raymond
Taylor, Bruce
Taylor, Bruce

Taylor, Carl S.
Taylor, Daniel (William)
Taylor, Debbie A.
Taylor, Diana
Taylor, Donathan
Taylor, Elizabeth Atwood
Taylor, Gary
Taylor, Goldie
Taylor, Greg
Taylor, Henry
Taylor, Jacqueline
Taylor, Janelle (Diane Williams)
Taylor, Joe
Taylor, John A.
Taylor, Jon E.
Taylor, Karen E.
Taylor, Katherine
Taylor, Kathy
Taylor, Larissa J(uliet)
Taylor, Lester D.
Taylor, Mark Lewis
Taylor, Mary F.
Taylor, Michael J(oseph)
Taylor, Michael J.
Taylor, Michael Ray
Taylor, Mildred D.
Taylor, Nick
Taylor, Nick
Taylor, Paul F.
Taylor, Quintard
Taylor, Robert Allan
Taylor, Robert Larry
Taylor, Ronald B.
Taylor, Sarah McFarland
Taylor, Sarah Stewart
Taylor, Stuart
Taylor, Sue
Taylor, Terence
Taylor, Terry
Taylor, Walter Kingsley
Taylor, Welford Dunaway
Taylor, William R(obert)
Taylor-Hall, Mary Ann
Taze, James E.
Teachout, Terry
Teague, Mark (Christopher)
Teahan, Sheila
Tedrow, John C. F.
Tefertiller, Casey (Orie)
Tehan, Arline Boucher
Teicher, Craig Morgan
Teiser, Stephen F.
Telser, Lester G(reenspan)
Tem, Melanie
Tem, Steve Rasnic
Temes, Peter S.
Temianka, Dan(iel)
Temin, Peter
Temperley, David
Temple, Brian
Temple, Charles
Temple, Wayne C(alhoun)
Tenbrook, Gretchen W.
Tenenbaum, Shelly
Tennen, Howard
Tenner, Edward
Tenpas, Kathryn Dunn
Tent, Pam
Tepper, Sheri S.
Teran, Boston
Terborgh, John W.

Terpening, Ron
Terpstra, Vern
Terr, Lenore (C.)
Terrill, Marshall
Terrio, Susan J.
Terris, Susan
Terry, Ken J.
Terry, Megan
Tervalon, Jervey
TeSelle, Eugene (Arthur)
Tesh, Jane
Teske, Paul Eric
Testa, Judith (Anne)
Teter, Magda
Teyber, Edward C.
Thacker, Robert
Thackeray, Frank W.
Thaden, Barbara Z.
Thaler, Richard H.
Thalmann, William
Thandeka
Thatamanil, John J.
Thayer, Bradley A.
Thayer, Helen
Thayer, Terri
The Rock
Theismann, Joe
Theiss, Janet M.
Theobald, William F.
Theodore, Wayne
Theroux, Joseph (Peter)
Theroux, Paul
Theroux, Peter
Thiel, Diane
Thiemann, Ronald F.
Thier, Marian J.
Thier, Marlene
Thierauf, Robert James
Thoene, (William) Brock
Thoene, Bodie
Tholfsen, Trygve R(ainone)
Thom, James Alexander
Thomas, Abigail
Thomas, Adrian
Thomas, Barbara L(ee)
Thomas, Brook
Thomas, Claudia E.
Thomas, Cornell
Thomas, David H(urst)
Thomas, Evan
Thomas, G(regory) Scott
Thomas, John Clayton
Thomas, June Manning
Thomas, Laurence (Mordekhai)
Thomas, Michael A.
Thomas, Rob
Thomas, Rosanne Daryl
Thomas, Velma Maia
Thomas, Will
Thomas-Graham, Pamela (Borders)
Thomasma, Kenneth R.
Thomassie, Tynia
Thompson, Alexander
Thompson, Augustine
Thompson, Charles P.
Thompson, Christina
Thompson, Chuck
Thompson, Claudia G(reig)
Thompson, David C.
Thompson, Deanna A.

Tyson, Salinda
U'Ren, Andrea
Ubelaker, Douglas H.
Ucko, Barbara
Udall, Brady
Uekert, Brenda K.
Ugel, Edward
Uhlenbeck, Karen (Keskulla)
Uhlig, Richard
Ulanski, Stan L.
Uldrich, Jack
Ullman, Ellen
Ullmann, Owen
Ulmer, Gregory L(eland)
Ulrich, Larry
Ulrich, Laurel Thatcher
Uman, Myron F.
Umland, Samuel J(oseph)
Umstatter, Jack
Underdahl, S. T.
Underhill, Lois Beachy
Underwood, Blair
Underwood, Deborah
Underwood, Elizabeth Ann
Underwood, Judy K.
Ungar, Sanford J.
Unger, Harlow Giles
Unger, Peter K(enneth)
Ungerer, Miriam
Unglaub, Jonathan
Unrue, Darlene Harbour
Unruh, James A(rlen)
Upchurch, Charles
Upchurch, Michael
Urbinati, Nadia
Ureneck, Lou
Ursano, Robert J.
Urton, Gary
Uruburu, Paula
Ury, Allen B.
Usry, Becky (S.)
Utley, Robert M(arshall)
Utter, Glenn H.
Uviller, Daphne
Uzendoski, Michael
Uzzi, Brian
Vachss, Andrew H(enry)
Vadino, Diane
Vaidhyanathan, Siva
Vail, Rachel
Vaill, Amanda
Vaillant, Janet G.
Valelly, Richard M.
Valenstein, Elliot S(piro)
Valente, Claire
Valenti, Jessica
Valentine, Douglas
Valentine, Fawn
Valentine, Jean
Valentino, Serena
Valentis, Mary (Arensberg)
Valenza, Joyce Kasman
Valenze, Deborah M.
Valerio, Anthony
Valiante, Gio
Valk, Anne M.
Valle, Victor Manuel
Vallejo, Boris
Vallerand, April Hazard
Vallone, Lynne
Vallone, Ralph

van Allsburg, Chris
van Alstyne, William W.
Van Ausdale, Debra
Van Citters, Darrell
Van Clief-Stefanon, Lyrae N.
Van Cott, Donna Lee
Van Deburg, William L.
van der Linde, Laurel
van Derveer, Tara
Van Domelen, John E(mory)
Van Dover, J(ames) K(enneth)
van Duzer, Chet A.
van Dyke, Henry
Van Eenwyk, John R.
van Fraassen, Bas C.
van Horn, Ray
van Hyning, Thomas E.
van Laan, Nancy
van Meter, Jonathan W.
Van Natta, Don
Van Ness, Arthur Gordon
van Praagh, David
Van Raden, Kristine
Van Rynbach, Iris
Van Scyoc, Sydney (Joyce)
van Slyck, Abigail A(yres)
Van Steenhouse, Andrea
van Tilburg, Christopher
van Tilburg, Hans (Konrad)
Van Tilburg, Jo Anne
van Vugt, William E.
van Willigen, Anne
Van Willigen, John
Vanak, Bonnie
Vanasse, Deb
Vance, Jack
Vance, Laura L.
Vance, Steve
VanCleave, Janice
Vandenburgh, Jane
Vanderbes, Jennifer (Chase)
Vanderbilt, Tom
Vanderkam, James C(laire)
Vandevelder, Paul
Vandewalle, Dirk
Vankin, Jonathan
VanMeter, Vandelia
VanOosting, James
Vanzant, Iyanla
Vardamis, Frances (Diem)
Vareldzis, Georgia M.
Vargas, Margarita
Varmus, Harold E(lliot)
Varnum, Keith A.
Varon, Sara
Varounis, Athena
Vasquez, Ian
Vassberg, David E(rland)
Vasta, Edward
Vatikiotis, Michael R. J.
Vaughan, Alden T(rue)
Vaughan, Brian K.
Vaughan, Marcia (K.)
Vaughan, Richard Patrick
Vaughan, Susan C.
Vaughn, Carrie
Vaughn, Ellen Santilli
Vaughn, Jacqueline
Vaughn, Patrika
Vause, L(aurence) Mikel
Vavra, Terry G.

Vaz, Katherine
Vazquez, Carmen Inoa
Vazsonyi, Nicholas
Vega, Ana Lydia
Vega, Gina
Veitch, Rick
Velásquez, Gloria (Louise)
Velez, Ivan
Velez-Mitchell, Jane
Velkley, Richard L.
Vella, Christina
Velleman, Daniel J.
Veltri, George (M.)
Venarde, Bruce L.
Venardos, Thomas J(oseph)
Venditti, Robert
Vendler, Helen (Hennessy)
Venet, Wendy Hamand
Venolia, Jan(et G.)
Venter, J. Craig
Ventura, Michael
Verba, Joan Marie
Verdelle, A. J.
Verduin, John Richard
Vermaas, Lori
Vermerris, Wilfred
Vermeule, Adrian
Vermilye, Jerry
Verniero, Joan C.
Vernon, Amelia Wallace
Verona, Stephen (Frederic)
Verrier, Suzanne
Verrillo, Erica
Versényi, Adam
Versluis, Arthur
Vertreace-Doody, Martha Modena
Veseth, Michael
Vesper, Karl H(amptom)
Vest, Herb D.
Vicchio, Stephen (John)
Vick, Helen Hughes
Vickers, Joanne F.
Victor, George
Vidal, Gore
Vidmar, John C.
Vidrine, Beverly Barras
Vigil, James Diego
Vilander, Barbara
Vileisis, Ann
Villafane, Eldin
Villamil, Victoria Etnier
Villatoro, Marcos McPeek
Vincent, Edgar
Vincent, Norah
Vincent, Rachel
Vines, Lois Davis
Viney, Donald Wayne
Vineyard, Jerry D.
Vinge, Vernor (Steffen)
Vinikas, Vincent
Vinjamuri, David
Viola, Lynne
Viorst, Judith
Viorst, Milton
Visconti, Tony
Viscusi, Robert
Viscusi, W. Kip
Visotzky, Burton L.
Visson, Lynn
Visweswaran, Kamala
Vitali, Julius

Vitalis, Robert
Vitiello, Justin
Vittitow, Mary L(ou)
Vitz, Robert C.
Vizenor, Gerald (Robert)
Vlasich, James A(nthony)
Voeks, Robert A(llen)
Vogel, Carole Garbuny
Vogel, Ezra F.
Vogel, Lise
Vogel, Steve
Vogel, Steven Kent
Vogt, Peter
Voien, Steven
Voigt, Cynthia
Voigt, Ellen Bryant
Volanto, Keith J.
Volck, Brian
Volk, Patricia (Gay)
Volk, Tyler
Volkman, Ernest
Vollendorf, Lisa
Vollers, Maryanne
Vollstedt, Maryana
Volpe, Vernon L(ewis)
Volsky, Paula
Von Ahnen, Katherine
Von Bencke, Matthew Justin
von Gunden, Kenneth
von Hagen, Mark (L.)
von Hippel, Eric
von Schlegell, Mark
von Unwerth, Matthew
Von Ward, Paul
Von Wiesenberger, Arthur
von Ziegesar, Cecily
Vonderplanitz, Aajonus
Vonnegut, Norb
Voos, Paula B.
Vornberger, Cal Calvin
Vornholt, John
Vos Savant, Marilyn
Voss, Ralph F.
Voss, Sarah (Henderson)
Vosti, Stephen A.
Vowell, Sarah
Vreeland, Susan (Joyce)
Vuic, Jason
Vukcevich, Ray
Waber, Bernard
Wabuda, Susan
Wachsberger, Ken(neth)
Wachsmann, Shelley
Wachtel, Shirley Russak
Wachter, Kenneth W.
Waddington, Raymond B(ruce)
Wade, Sidney
Wade, Susan
Wadell, Paul J(oseph)
Wadia, Maneck S.
Wadsworth, Ginger
Waehler, Charles A.
Wagener, Leon
Wagman, Morton
Wagner, Bruce
Wagner, David
Wagner, Matt
Wagner, Michele R.
Wagner, Ralph D.
Wagner, Sharon Blythe
Wagner-Martin, Linda C.

Wagoner, David (Russell)
Wagschal, Steven
Wahl, Jan
Wahrman, Dror
Wainscott, Ronald H(arold)
Waisman, Sergio Gabriel
Wait, Eugene M(eredith)
Waite, Michael P(hillip)
Waitman, Katie
Waitzkin, Howard
Waitzkin, Josh
Wakefield, Dan
Wakefield, James L.
Wakoski, Diane
Walcott, Charles E(liot)
Wald, Diane
Waldbauer, Gilbert (P.)
Waldfogel, Joel
Waldinger, Roger (David)
Waldman, Anne
Waldman, Ayelet
Waldman, Mark Robert
Waldman, Sidney R.
Waldman, Steven
Waldman, Stuart
Waldo, Anna Lee
Waldoff, Leon
Waldrep, Christopher (Reef)
Waldron, Arthur (Nelson)
Waldrop, M(orris) Mitchell
Walker, Anne Collins
Walker, Charles F.
Walker, Clarence Earl
Walker, Donald E(dwin)
Walker, Henry M(acKay)
Walker, James R(obert)
Walker, Joel Thomas
Walker, Kathryn
Walker, Kenneth Roland
Walker, Lawrence R.
Walker, Marianne (Cascio)
Walker, Melissa A.
Walker, Paul E(rnest)
Walker, Randi Jones
Walker, Richard Averill
Walker, Sally M(acArt)
Walker, Sam
Walker, Susannah
Walker, Thomas W(oodley)
Walker, Wendy (Alison)
Walker-Blondell, Becky
Walkowicz, Chris
Wall, Cheryl A.
Wall, James M(cKendree)
Wall, James T.
Wall, Kathryn R.
Wallace, B. Alan
Wallace, Benjamin
Wallace, Bruce
Wallace, Carey Jean
Wallace, Catherine M(iles)
Wallace, Deborah
Wallace, Don
Wallace, James
Wallace, James D.(Donald)
Wallace, Mark I.
Wallace, Meredith
Wallace, Naomi (French)
Wallace, Richard (Alan)
Wallach, Alan
Wallach, Jeff

Wallach, Jennifer Jensen
Waller, Douglas C.
Waller, Robert James
Walley, Christine J.
Wallis, Velma
Wallmeyer, Dick
Walsh, Edward N.
Walsh, Kenneth T(homas)
Walsh, Lawrence
Walsh, Robb
Walsh, Suella
Walsh Shepherd, Donna
Walt, Stephen M.
Waltenburg, Eric N.
Walter, Jess
Walters, James W.
Walton, David
Walton, Kendall L(ewis)
Walton, Mary
Walton, Richard J(ohn)
Walton, Rick
Waltz, Kenneth N.
Waltzer, Jim
Walzer, Michael
Wambaugh, Joseph
Wandel, Lee Palmer
Wang, Dong
Wang, Jen
Wang, Lihua
Wang, Wallace E.
Wanko, Cheryl L.
Wapner, Leonard M.
Warber, Adam L.
Ward, Amanda Eyre
Ward, Frank A.
Ward, Geoffrey C(hampion)
Ward, Harry Merrill
Ward, James M.
Ward, Jane (A.)
Ward, Jesmyn
Ward, Logan
Wardell, Steven (William)
Wardlaw, Alvia J.
Wardlaw, Lee
Wardropper, Ian
Ware, Cheryl
Ware, Jane (O.)
Ware, Leland B.
Ware, Leslie
Ware, Sandra J.
Ware, Susan
Warfield, Gallatin
Waring, Belle
Warlick, Ashley
Warmuth, Donna Akers
Warner, Brad
Warner, Jack
Warner, Janine C.
Warner, Judith
Warner, Sally
Warner, Sharon Oard
Warnicke, Retha M.
Warren, Cathy
Warren, Charles
Warren, Karen J.
Warren, Kenneth W.
Warren, Louis S.
Warren, Richard (Andrew)
Warren, Rosanna
Warren, Sandra K.
Warren, Susan

Warren, Susan May
Warren, Victoria
Warsh, Lewis
Warshauer, Matthew
Wasby, Stephen L(ewis)
Washburn, Frances
Washburn, Livia J.
Washburn, Stan
Washburne, Carolyn Kott
Washington, Donna L.
Wasik, John F.
Wasil, Kenneth
Wasiolek, Edward
Wasserman, Robin
Wasserstrom, Jeffrey N.
Watenpaugh, Keith David
Waterhouse, Carole A.
Waterman, Jonathan
Waters, Barbara
Waters, Claire M.
Waters, John F(rederick)
Waters, Tony
Waterston, Alisse
Watford, Christopher M.
Watkins, Graham
Watkins, John
Watkins, John Goodrich
Watkins, Paul
Watkins, Ronald J(oseph)
Watkins, Steve
Watkins, William John
Watman, Max
Watrous, Livingston Vance
Watson, Amy Zakrzewski
Watson, Benjamin A.
Watson, Bruce
Watson, C. G.
Watson, Clyde
Watson, Ellen Dore
Watson, Esther Pearl
Watson, James D(ewey)
Watson, Jan Elizabeth
Watson, Larry
Watson, Mary Ann
Watson, Ritchie Devon
Watson, Robert (Winthrop)
Watson, Stephanie
Watson, Steven
Watson, William E.
Watt, David Harrington
Wattenberg, Martin P(aul)
Watters, Ethan
Watterson, John Sayle
Watts, Edward J.
Watts, Sheldon J.
Waugh, Joan
Waugh, John C(linton)
Wauzzinski, Robert A.
Wawro, Geoffrey
Wax, Amy L.
Wax, Steven T.
Waxman, Henry Arnold
Waycott, Edon
Wayne, Valerie
Wayner, Peter
Waziyatawin
Weaks, Mary Louise
Weales, Gerald
Weart, Spencer R(ichard)
Weatherford, Carole Boston
Weaver, Afaa Michael

Weaver, Frederick S(tirton)
Weaver, Karol K.
Weaver, R(obert) Kent
Weaver, Will(iam Weller)
Weaver-Gelzer, Charlotte
Webb, Betty
Webb, Lois Sinaiko
Webb, Michael (Jack)
Webb, Stephen H.
Webb, T(erry) D(ouglas)
Webb, Veronica
Webber, Alan M.
Webber, Desiree Morrison
Webber, Ross A.
Weber, David
Weber, Jennifer L.
Weber, Katharine
Weber, Ralph E.
Weber, Robert J(ohn)
Weber, Samuel M.
Weber, Sandra
Weber, Timothy P.
Weber, William
Webster, Brenda
Webster, Catherine
Wecker, David
Weddington, Sarah (Ragle)
Weddle, David
Weddle, Kevin J.
Wedeen, Richard Peter
Weedman, Lauren
Weeks, Sarah
Weems, David B(urnola)
Wegela, Karen Kissel
Wegman, William (George)
Weideman, Ryan
Weidenbaum, Murray
Weidensaul, Scott
Weidt, Maryann N.
Weil, Debbie
Weil, Elizabeth
Weimer, Joan
Wein, Elizabeth E(ve)
Weinbaum, Marvin G.
Weinberg, Florence M(ay)
Weinberg, Helene Barbara
Weinberg, Louise
Weinberg, Steve
Weinberg, Steven
Weinberger, Peter Ezra
Weiner, Hollace Ava
Weiner, Jennifer Agnes
Weiner, Kay Bain
Weiner, Marc A.
Weiner, Mark S(tuart)
Weiner, Stephanie Kuduk
Weiner, Stephen
Weiner, Susan
Weiner, William J(errold)
Weiner-Davis, Michele
Weinheimer, Beckie
Weinkauf, Mary S(tanley)
Weinman, Lynda (Susan)
Weinreb, Michael
Weinroth, Michelle
Weinstein, Allen
Weinstein, Cindy
Weinstein, Jay
Weinstein, Mark Allen
Weinstein, Miriam
Weinstein, Philip M.

Weinstock, Nicholas
Weintraub, Andrew N.
Weintraub, David
Weintraub, Linda
Weintraub, Sidney
Weintraub, Stanley
Weir, Ben(jamin M.)
Weir, Charlene
Weir, David A.
Weir, Gary E.
Weir, Theresa
Weis, Lois
Weisberg, Herbert F.
Weisberg, Joseph
Weisberger, Lauren
Weisblat, Tinky
Weisbrot, Robert (S.)
Weiser, Philip J.
Weisgall, Jonathan M.
Weisman, Brent Richards
Weisman, Leslie Kanes
Weiss, Avraham
Weiss, Brian L(eslie)
Weiss, Daniel Evan
Weiss, Raymond L.
Weiss, Tamara
Weiss, Thomas G.
Weissbourd, Richard
Weisskopf, Thomas E.
Weissman, Karen
Weitekamp, Margaret A.
Weitz, Eric D.
Weitzman, Susan
Wek, Alek
Wekesser, Carol A.
Welch, Amy
Welch, D. Don
Welch, Kathleen E(thel)
Welch, Richard F.
Welch, Sheila Kelly
Welch-Tyson, Delorys
Welcher, Rosalind
Weldon, Phaedra M.
Weldt-Basson, Helene Carol
Welish, Marjorie
Weliver, Phyllis
Welland, Sasha Su-Ling
Weller, Vann K.
Wellford, Lin(da)
Wellington, Jean Susorney
Wellington, Sheila W(acks)
Wellman, Carl Pierce
Wellman, John McDowell
Wells, Cheryl A.
Wells, Ken
Wells, Mary Ann
Wells, Melanie
Wells, Patricia
Wells, Peter S.
Wells, Rebecca
Wells, Rosemary
Wells, Simon
Wells, Spencer
Wells (Dimenstein), Catherine
Wels, Susan
Welsbacher, Anne
Welsch, Roger L(ee)
Welsh, Alexander
Welsing, Frances Cress
Weltner, Peter (Nissen)
Wen, Chihua

Wenderoth, Joe
Wendling, Ronald C(harles)
Wendover, Robert W(arren)
Wenger, Beth S.
Wengert, Timothy J.
Werbach, Adam
Werlock, Abby Holmes P(otter)
Werner, Marta L.
Werris, Wendy
Wersba, Barbara
Wert, Jonathan (Maxwell)
Werth, Barry
Wertheimer, Jack
Weschler, Lawrence
Wesley, Patricia Jabbeh
Wesley, Richard (Errol)
Wesley, Valerie Wilson
Wesselmann, Debbie Lee
West, Cornel (Ronald)
West, Darrell M.
West, Diana
West, Edward
West, Elliott
West, Francis J.
West, James L(emuel) W(ills)
West, Mark D.
West, Michael Rudolph
West, Sandra L.
Westbrook, Peter (J.)
Westburg, Barry (Richard)
Westcott, Jan (Vlachos)
Westcott, Wayne L.
Westen, Drew
Western, Jon W.
Westervelt, Saundra D(avis)
Westling, Louise (Hutchings)
Westoff, Charles F.
Weston, Mark
Weston, Susan
Westrum, Dexter
Westwick, Peter J.
Wetenhall, John
Wetherell, W(alter) D(avid)
Wetherington, Mark V.
Wetmore, Kevin J. (Jr.)
Wettstein, Robert M.
Wetzel, James
Wexler, Alan
Wexler, Alice (Ruth)
Wexler, Bruce E.
Wexler, Jay D.
Wexler, Merin
Wexler, Richard
Wexler, Robert Freeman
Weyermann, Debra
Weyland, Jack
Whalen, Richard James
Whalen, Thomas J.
Whalin, W. Terry
Wheatcroft, John Stewart
Wheeler, Deborah (Jean Ross)
Wheeler, Elizabeth
Wheeler, Helen Rippier
Wheeler, Jill
Wheeler, Kate
Wheeler, Lesley
Wheeler, Lonnie
Wheeler, Penny Estes
Wheeler, Richard S.
Wheeler, Ron
Wheeler, Shannon L.

Wheeler, Susan
Wheeler, Thomas
Whelan, Gloria (Ann)
Whelan, Irene
Whigham, Thomas
Whisman, Dale
Whitaker, Matthew C.
Whitcomb, John C(lement)
Whitcomb, Laura
White, Andrea
White, Bailey
White, Barbara Ehrlich
White, Bill
White, C. Todd
White, Caramine
White, Carolyn
White, Christopher
White, Courtney
White, Dan
White, Dave
White, David Gordon
White, Edmund
White, Edward M.
White, Evelyn C.
White, Franklin
White, John Kenneth
White, Jonathan (Bruce)
White, Joseph B.
White, Karen
White, Kimberley
White, Lawrence J.
White, Linda (Louise)
White, Mary Wheeling
White, Merry (I.)
White, Michael C(harles)
White, Michael J.
White, Mimi
White, Morton (Gabriel)
White, Neil
White, Pamela C.
White, Phillip M.
White, Randy Wayne
White, Stephen E.
White, Stephen K.
White, Warren H.
White-Parks, Annette
Whitehead, Barbara Dafoe
Whitehead, Colson
Whitelaw, Nancy
Whiting, Cécile
Whitley, David S(cott)
Whitley, Gershonah C.
Whitley, Peggy
Whitlock, Dean
Whitlock, Luder (G.)
Whitman, Nancy C(hong)
Whitman, Sylvia (Choate)
Whitman, T(orrey) Stephen
Whitmore, Benette
Whitson, Kathy J.
Whitson, Stephanie Grace (Irvin)
Whittemore, (Edward) Reed
Whitten, Leslie Hunter
Whitten, Norman E.
Whittington, Brad
Whittington, Keith E.
Whittle, Chris
Whitty, Julia
Whynott, Douglas (Vernon)
Whyte, Mary
Wiater, Stanley

Wicclair, Mark R.
Wick, Steve
Wick, Walter
Wicker, Christine
Wicker, Tom
Wickham, DeWayne
Wickham-Crowley, Timothy P.
Widdifield, Stacie G(raham)
Widmaier, Eric P(aul)
Widner, Jennifer A(nne)
Wiedemann, Barbara
Wieder, Alan
Wiedman, John Charles
Wiegand, Shirley A.
Wiegand, Wayne A.
Wieland, Liza
Wiener, Joel Howard
Wiener, Jonathan B(aert)
Wiener, Joshua M(ark)
Wiener, Nancy H.
Wiesen, S. Jonathan
Wiesenfarth, Joseph (John)
Wiesepape, Betty Holland
Wiesner, Karen Sue
Wiesner-Hanks, Merry E.
Wiest, Andrew A.
Wiggers, Raymond
Wiggin, Eric E(llsworth)
Wiggs, Susan
Wiktorowicz, Quintan
Wilbur, Richard (Purdy)
Wilce, Ysabeau S.
Wilcken, Lois
Wilcox, (William) Clyde
Wilcox, James
Wilcox, Laird (M.)
Wilcox, Sherman
Wilcox, Stephen F.
Wilczek, Frank
Wild, Mark
Wilde, Kelley (Cotter)
Wildenthal, Bryan H.
Wilder, Gene
Wilderson, Frank B.
Wildgen, Michelle
Wildman, Steven S.
Wile, Mary Lee
Wilensky, Amy S.
Wilentz, Amy
Wilentz, Sean
Wiles, Deborah
Wiley, Kim Wright
Wiley, Michael
Wiley, Peter (Booth)
Wiley, Tatha
Wilford, John Noble
Wilhelm, Doug
Wilhelm, Kate
Wilhoit, James C.
Wilker, Josh
Wilkie, Curtis
Wilkins, Mira
Wilkins, Sally (E. D.)
Wilkinson, Alec
Wilkinson, Beth
Wilkinson, Bruce H.
Wilkinson, Charles F.
Wilkinson, David Marion
Wilkinson, Richard H(erbert)
Wilkinson, Sylvia J.
Wilkinson, Tracy

Wilks, Burrel Lee
Will, Clifford M(artin)
Will, George F.
Willard, Dale C.
Willard, Pat
Willbanks, James H.
Wille, Lois
Willey, Margaret
Williams, Alan L(arson)
Williams, Amanda Kyle
Williams, Arlene
Williams, Brooke
Williams, C(harles) K(enneth)
Williams, Carla
Williams, Christine L.
Williams, Cindy
Williams, David
Williams, David B.
Williams, Diane
Williams, Dwight
Williams, Forman A.
Williams, Geoff
Williams, Gregory Howard
Williams, Jacqueline (B.)
Williams, James C.
Williams, Jeanne
Williams, John A(lfred)
Williams, Joy
Williams, Karen Lynn
Williams, Kathryn
Williams, Kimmika L(yvette Hawes)
Williams, Kristen P.
Williams, Lena (Marguerite)
Williams, Lillian Serece
Williams, Marie S(heppard)
Williams, Mark London
Williams, Mary E.
Williams, Nancy S.
Williams, Patricia J(oyce)
Williams, Paul K.
Williams, R. D.
Williams, Redford
Williams, Sheila J.
Williams, Sheron
Williams, Stanley Tookie
Williams, Susan
Williams, Terrie (Michelle)
Williams, Terry Tempest
Williams, Theresa
Williams, Vera B.
Williams, Vernon J(ohnson)
Williams, Walter E(dward)
Williams, Walter Jon
Williams, Wendy
Williamson, Chet
Williamson, Denise
Williamson, Greg
Williamson, J(erry) W(ayne)
Williamson, Joel
Williamson, Kate T.
Williamson, Miryam Ehrlich
Williamson, Robert C(lifford)
Williford, (G.) Craig
Williford, Lex
Willimon, William H(enry)
Willingham, Bill
Willis, Alan Scot
Willis, Barry
Willis, Connie
Willis, Deborah

Willis, Gerri
Willis, Jack D.
Willis, Julia
Willis, Paul J.
Willis, Resa
Willrich, Mason
Wills, Garry
Willumson, Glenn
Wilmot, Jeanne
Wilner, Isaiah
Wilsford, David
Wilson, Barbara (Ellen)
Wilson, Brandon
Wilson, Carter
Wilson, Catherine
Wilson, Cynthia
Wilson, D. Harlan
Wilson, Darryl B(abe)
Wilson, David Niall
Wilson, David S(cofield)
Wilson, Diane
Wilson, Dolores J.
Wilson, Duff
Wilson, Emma
Wilson, Eric (P.)
Wilson, F(rancis) Paul
Wilson, Frances Engle
Wilson, Francille Rusan
Wilson, Frank R.
Wilson, G. Willow
Wilson, Gretchen
Wilson, Jan Doolittle
Wilson, John K.
Wilson, John Morgan
Wilson, Joseph (Charles)
Wilson, Kathleen
Wilson, Ken
Wilson, Kevin
Wilson, Marc
Wilson, Martin
Wilson, Melba (Jean)
Wilson, N. D.
Wilson, Nancy Hope
Wilson, Patricia Potter
Wilson, Robley
Wilson, Sharon Rose
Wilson, Susan
Wilson, Wesley M.
Wilt, David (Edward)
Wiltse, Jeff
Wiltshire, Susan Ford
Wimberley, (Amos) Darryl
Wimsatt, William C.
Winans, Christopher
Winawer, Sidney Jerome
Winchell, Donna Haisty
Winckler, Edwin A.
Winder, Michael
Windle, Janice Woods
Windsor, Linda
Wineapple, Brenda
Winer, Andrew
Winer, Deborah Grace
Winerip, Michael
Winfield, Jess M.
Wing, Betsy
Wingate, Steven
Winik, Marion (Lisa)
Wininger, Kathleen J.
Winkler, Henry Ralph
Winkler, Jonathan Reed

Winn, Tracy
Winner, Lauren F.
Winnick, R. H.
Winokur, Jon
Winsey, Valentine Rossilli
Winship, Michael P.
Winslow, Barbara
Winslow, Don
Winston, Daoma
Winston, Lois
Winston, Lolly
Winston, Mark L.
Winston, Wayne L.
Winston-Allen, Anne
Winter, Kari J.
Winterhalder, Edward
Winters, Kay
Wintz, Cary D.
Wiprud, Brian M.
Wirsing, Robert G.
Wirzba, Norman
Wisdom, Linda Randall
Wise, David
Wise, Joe
Wise, Mike
Wise, Robert L.
Wise, Steven W.
Wise, Tim J.
Wise, Victoria (Jenanyan)
Wiseman, James A.
Wiseman, Rosalind
Wisman, Ken
Witek, Terri
Witemeyer, Hugh Hazen
Witham, Larry
Witherington, Ben
Witt, Christopher
Witt, John Fabian
Witt, Martha
Wittenborn, Dirk
Wittes, Benjamin
Wittlinger, Ellen
Wittner, Lawrence Stephen
Witzel, Michael Karl
Wixson, Douglas
Wizowaty, Suzi
Woell, Edward J.
Wogaman, J(ohn) Philip
Woginrich, Jenna
Woik, Julie
Woirol, Gregory R.
Woiwode, Larry (Alfred)
Wojahn, David (Charles)
Wojnarowski, Adrian
Wokeck, Marianne Sophia
Wolcott, Patty
Wold, Donald J.
Wolensky, Kenneth C.
Wolf, Allan
Wolf, Anthony E.
Wolf, Eva Sheppard
Wolf, Joan M.
Wolf, Kenneth Baxter
Wolf, Margery
Wolf, Maryanne
Wolf, Reva
Wolf, Sarah (Elizabeth)
Wolfe, Alan (Stephen)
Wolfe, Art
Wolfe, Barbara (Lea)
Wolfe, Gene (Rodman)

Wolfe, George C.
Wolfe, Linda
Wolfe, Peter
Wolfe, Tom
Wolferman, Kristie C(arlson)
Wolff, Craig (Thomas)
Wolff, Cynthia Griffin
Wolff, Edward N(athan)
Wolff, Geoffrey
Wolff, Justin
Wolff, Robert P(aul)
Wolff, Ruth
Wolff, Sally
Wolff, Theodore F.
Wolff, Tobias (Jonathan Ansell)
Wolfgang, Kurt
Wolfinger, Raymond E(dwin)
Wolfman, Judy
Wolfson, Jill
Wolfson, Richard
Wolfson, Susan J.
Wolfthal, Diane (Bette)
Wolin, Steven J.
Wolin, Sybil
Wolitzer, Hilma
Wolk, Josh
Wolke, Robert L.
Woll, Peter
Woloch, Cecilia G.
Woloch, Isser
Wolper, Carol
Wolpert, Stanley Albert
Wolters, Raymond
Wolven, Scott
Wolverton, Cheryl
Wolverton, Dave
Wolverton, Lisa
Wolverton, Mark
Wolverton, Robert E.
Wolverton, Terry
Wolzien, Valerie
Womack, Jack
Womack, Steven (James)
Wong, Janet S.
Wong, Shawn (Hsu)
Wood, (David) Ira
Wood, Ann
Wood, Anthony C.
Wood, Brian
Wood, C. E.
Wood, Curtis W(illiam)
Wood, Don
Wood, Douglas (Eric)
Wood, Frances M.
Wood, Gerald C.
Wood, Gordon S(tewart)
Wood, John A.
Wood, Marcia (Mae)
Wood, Margaret
Wood, Monica
Wood, N. Lee
Wood, Patricia
Wood, Ralph C.
Wood, Stephanie
Woodard, J. David
Woodard, Michael D.
Woodbury, Heather
Woodhouse, S(usan) T.
Woodhull, Winifred
Wooding, Sharon L(ouise)
Woodman, Allen

Woodman, Harold David
Woodring, Jim
Woodruff, Joan Leslie
Woodruff, Lee McConaughy
Woodruff, Nan Elizabeth
Woodruff, Nancy
Woodrum, Robert H.
Woods, Brenda
Woods, Jeannie Marlin
Woods, Paula L.
Woods, Stuart
Woods, Tiger
Woodson, Jacqueline
Woodward, Bob
Woodward, Kenneth L.
Woodward, Margaret E.
Woodward, Ralph Lee
Woodwell, George M.
Woodwell, William H.
Woodworth, Stephen
Woodworth, Steven E(dward)
Woody, Elizabeth
Woog, Adam
Woog, Dan
Wooldridge, Connie Nordhielm
Wooley, Marilyn J.
Wooley, Susan Frelick
Woolf, Greg
Woolf, Paula
Woolley, Bryan
Woolley, Peter J.
Woolverton, John F(rederick)
Wootson, Alice (G.)
Worcester, Kent
Worden, J. William
Work, James C.
Workman, Jeremiah W.
Wormser, Richard
Woronov, Mary
Worsham, Lynn
Worthen, Molly
Worthing, Peter
Worthington, Everett L.
Wortsman, Peter
Woś, Joanna H(elena)
Wouk, Herman
Wrangham, Richard W.
Wray, John
Wray, Matt
Wrede, Patricia C(ollins)
Wren, Jill Robinson
Wrenn, Lynette Boney
Wreszin, Michael
Wright, A(mos) J(asper)
Wright, Alex
Wright, Alexandra
Wright, Barbara
Wright, Betty Ren
Wright, C. D.
Wright, Charles (Penzel)
Wright, Clifford A.
Wright, Cora M.
Wright, Courtni C(rump)
Wright, Donald R(ichard)
Wright, Franz
Wright, George Thaddeus
Wright, Helen L(ouise)
Wright, James D(avid)
Wright, John S.
Wright, Julie
Wright, Kai

Wright, Leslie B(ailey)
Wright, Nina
Wright, Robert Lee
Wright, Theodore Paul
Wright, Vinita Hampton
Wright, William Edward
Wright Austin, Sharon D.
Wrigley, Robert
Wronsky, Gail (F.)
Wu, Norbert
Wubbels, Lance
Wuerch, William L.
Wulsin, Lawson R.
Wunderli, Richard (M.)
Wunderlich, Ray Charles
Wunsch, James S(tevenson)
Wuori, G. K.
Wurman, Richard Saul
Wurst, Karin A.
Wurts, Janny
Wurtzel, Elizabeth (Leigh)
Wyatt, Clarence R.
Wyatt, David M.
Wyatt, Don J.
Wyatt, Robert Lee
Wyatt-Brown, Anne M(arbury)
Wyer, Robert S.
Wyeth, Sharon Dennis
Wylie, Diana
Wyman, Andrea
Wyman, Bruce C.
Wyman, Carolyn
Wymark, Olwen (Margaret)
Wymelenberg, Suzanne
Wynes, Charles E.
Wynia, Gary W.
Wynn, Charles M.
Wynne, Ben
Wynne, John (Stewart)
Wynne, Marcus
Yablonsky, Linda
Yaeger, Don
Yaffe, James
Yagher, Kevin
Yagoda, Ben
Yalom, Irvin D(avid)
Yamashita, Karen Tei
Yan, Yunxiang
Yancey, Diane
Yancey, George
Yang, Belle
Yang, Dali L.
Yanni, Carla
Yanow, Scott
Yansky, Brian
Yarborough, Sharon C(lare)
Yarbro, Chelsea Quinn
Yarbrough, Stephen R.
Yarbrough, Steve
Yarnold, Barbara M(aria)
Yarrow, Andrew
Yates, Dwight
Yates, Jean
Yeager, Peter C(leary)
Yeargers, Edward K.
Yeats, Robert S(heppard)
Yee, Shirley J.
Yeh, Catherine Vance
Yeide, Harry
Yellin, Emily
Yenawine, Philip

Yenne, Bill
Yep, Laurence (Michael)
Yerxa, Donald A(llan)
Yesalis, Charles E(dward)
Yezzi, David Dalton
Yglesias, Rafael
Ylvisaker, Anne
Yockey, Hubert P(almer)
Yoder, Edwin Milton
Yoder, John C.
Yoerg, Sonja I.
Yoggy, Gary A.
Yolen, Jane
Yoo, Paula
Yorburg, Betty
Yorinks, Adrienne
York, Lynn
York, Phyllis
Yoshino, Kenji
Yost, J. T.
Yothers, Brian
Youmans, Marly
Young, Bette Roth
Young, C. Dale
Young, Carol
Young, David (Pollock)
Young, Dean
Young, Dean (Wayne)
Young, Donald R.
Young, Glennys
Young, James E.
Young, Jeff C.
Young, John K(arl)
Young, John Sacret
Young, Ken
Young, Kenneth Ray
Young, Kevin
Young, Margaret Labash
Young, Patrick
Young, Robert J.C
Young, Robin
Young, Roger (E.)
Young, Ruth
Young-Bruehl, Elisabeth
Young-Eisendrath, Polly
Youngblood, Denise J.
Youngblood, Ronald Fred
Youngblood, Shay
Youngholm, Thomas
Youngkin, Stephen D.
Youngman, Paul A.
Youngs, Betty F.
Younie, William J(ohn)
Yount, Lisa
Yount, Steven
Yourdon, Edward Nash
Yourdon, Jennifer
Youst, Lionel
Yow, Valerie Raleigh
Yu, Michelle
Yurick, Sol
Zabel, Diane
Zabor, Rafi
Zaccaria, Jerry A.
Zaccaro, Stephen J.
Zachary, G(regg) Pascal
Zachter, Mort
Zack, Naomi
Zacks, Shelemyahu
Zadoff, Allen
Zagorski, Paul W.

Zahariadis, Nikolaos
Zahn, Timothy
Zak, William F.
Zaki, Hoda M.
Zalben, Jane Breskin
Zald, Mayer Nathan
Zaloga, Steven J(oseph)
Zambrano, Myrna M.
Zambreno, Mary Frances
Zamora, Bernice (B. Ortiz)
Zamora, Lois Parkinson
Zamora, Narciso
Zancanella, Don
Zang, David W(illiam)
Zaremba, Alan Jay
Zaretsky, Natasha
Zaretsky, Robert David
Zarnow, Teryl
Zarr, Sara
Zarucchi, Jeanne Morgan
Zaslow, Jeffrey L.
Zatlin, Jonathan R.
Zavodnyik, Peter
Zazove, Philip
Zebrowski, George
Zechenter, Katarzyna Anna
Zedric, Lance Q.
Zegura, Elizabeth Chesney
Zeidner, Lisa
Zeier, Joan T(heresa)
Zeiler, Thomas W.
Zeilik, Michael
Zelikow, Philip
Zelinsky, Wilbur
Zelitch, Simone E.
Zelizer, Barbie
Zelizer, Julian E.
Zellman, Shelley
Zeltserman, Dave
Zelvin, Elizabeth
Zencey, Eric
Zentgraf, Kristine M.
Zepeda, Gwendolyn
Zesch, Scott
Zettel, Sarah
Zettler, Steve
Zeveloff, Samuel I.
Zevon, Crystal
Zheutlin, Peter
Zhu, Liping
Zicree, Mark Scott
Ziegler, Jennifer
Zielenziger, Michael
Zietz, Karyl Lynn
Ziff, Larzer
Ziffrin, Marilyn J.
Zigal, Thomas
Zigman, Laura
Zihlman, Adrienne L.
Zimbalist, Andrew S.
Zimbardo, Philip G.
Zimberoff, Tom
Zimmer, Carl
Zimmer, Paul J(erome)
Zimmer, Tracie Vaughn
Zimmerman, Donald E(dward)
Zimmerman, Earl
Zimmerman, Franklin (Bershir)
Zimmerman, Joseph Francis
Zimmerman, Muriel L.
Zimmerman, Robert

Gellately, Robert
Godfrey, Donald G.
Goodlad, John I.
Grant, Barry Keith
Harrison, Lisi
Henderson, William Darryl
Herz, Rachel
Hieatt, Constance B(artlett)
Hildebrand, Ann Meinzen
Hirata, Hosea
Hollenberg, Donna Krolik
Hossack, Joei Carlton
Howard, Kathleen L.
Howes, Craig
Hurtado, Larry W.
Hutchison, Linda Margaret
Ignatieff, Michael
Isaacs, Ronald (Howard)
Iyengar, Sheena
Jackson, Kate
Jocelyn, Marthe
Juhasz, Anne McCreary
Kaiser, Ward L(ouis)
Kalesniko, Mark G(aston)
Kelsey, Elin
Kennedy, John C.
Korman, Gordon (Richard)
Lamont, Michèle
Lax, Eric
Lockerbie, D(onald) Bruce
Ludwig, Jack
Mandel, Emily St. John
Maracle, Lee
Marcus, K(aren) Melissa
Marsh, Peter T.
Martin, Clancy M.
Masson, Paul R(obert)
Matera, Lia
McCain, Gillian
McKinnon, Ronald I(an)
McLennan, Rebecca M.
McNeill, William Hardy
Melnyk, Steven A.
Michels, Sharry C.
Moote, A. Lloyd
Muller, Jerry Z(ucker)
Musk, Justine
Nagurney, Anna
Naylor, Sean
Neufeld, Michael J.
O'Shea, Donal B.
Oliver, Richard W.
Packard, Robert
Patten, Alan
Pauly, Louis W.
Peacock, Molly
Peretti, Frank E.
Pick, Lucy K.
Poirier-Bures, Simone
Price-Smith, Andrew T.
Pyenson, Lewis (Robert)
Randi, James
Rapoport, Nessa
Redford, Donald B(ruce)
Regenstreif, S(amuel) Peter
Reitz, Miriam
Richardson, Brian W.
Roach, Catherine M.
Roberts, Alasdair Scott
Rosenau, Pauline Vaillancourt
Roth, Louise Marie

Sachs, Murray
Santoro, Michael A(nthony)
Schiff, Isaac
Schulman, Audrey
Schwartz, Samuel M.
Serels, M. Mitchell
Shaffer, Paul
Shapiro, Harold T(afler)
Slade, Bernard
Smith, James K. A.
Spring, Eileen
Staggenborg, Suzanne
Stewart, Mart A.
Steyn, Mark
Stoker, Dacre
Stollman, Arveh Lev
Taber, Stephen Welton
Taylor, Greg(ory Thomas)
Teague, Frances
Thiele, Leslie Paul
Tracey, Grant
Vaughan, Ronald G(eorge)
Victor, Barbara
Vroom, Victor H.
Wagman-Geller, Marlene
Wallace, Ian
Wallin, Pamela
Wallingford, Lee
Warren, Dianne
Williams, Len
Willis, Edgar E(rnest)
Wilson, Antoine Leonide Thomas
Wonnacott, Paul

United States-Canada-England

Durbach, Nadja
Verney, Douglas (Vernon)

United States-Canada-Ghana

Adjibolosoo, Senyo B. S. K.

United States-Canada-Hungary

Ban, Thomas Arthur

United States-Canada-Scotland

Rybczynski, Witold

United States-Chile

Allende, Isabel
Borzutzky, Silvia
Mallon, Florencia E.
Nutini, Hugo G(ino)
Perdue, Tito
Promis, José
Ramos, Joseph R(afael)
Rodgers, Marion Elizabeth
Vicuna, Cecilia

United States-China

Basil, John D.
Bei Dao
Chang, Leslie
Chen, Joseph T(ao)
Chen, Ran
Chieng, Chieh
Chin-Lee, Cynthia D.
Chou, Tsu Wei
Chu, Wai C.
Deng, Yong
Di, Zhu Xiao
Fan, Nancy Yi
Fritz, Jean
Hua, Gu
Jiang, Ji li
Jin, Ha
Lang, Lang
Lee, Henry C.
Li, Guofang
Li, Joyce H.S
Li, Moying
Lin, Tan (Anthony)
Lo, Malinda
Louis, Laura Glen
Ma, Liping
Mabee, Carleton
Marsh, Susan H.
Martin, Philip R.
Min, Anchee
Namioka, Lensey
Paterson, Katherine (Womeldorf)
Roberts, (Ray) Clayton
Shen, Aisling Juanjuan
Shen, Fan (A.)
Shepherd, George W.
Song, Yuwu
Tian, Hao Jiang
Ting, Windsor
Tribe, Laurence H(enry)
Tribe, Laurence H.
Wallace, Barbara Brooks
Wang, Yun
Wu, David Y(en) H(o)
Wu, Fan
Wu, Harry
Wu, Ningkun
Wu, Qingyun
Wu Hung
Xi, Xi
Xiaokang, Su
Yamada, Nanako
Yuan, Gao
Zee, A

United States-China-England

Lecky-Thompson, Guy W.

United States-Colombia

Guevara, Maurice Kilwein
Leguizamo, John
Manrique (Ardila), Jaime
Navia, Luis E.
Ocampo, José Antonio
Palomino, Rafael
Shillingsburg, Peter L(eRoy)

United States-Congo

Dongala, Emmanuel Boundzeki
Missamou, Tchicaya
Mudimbe, V. Y.

United States-Costa Rica

Vallbona, Rima de

United States-Croatia

Mestrovic, Stjepan G.
Wallace, Vesna A.
Zaknic, Ivan

United States-Cuba

Algaze, Guillermo
Balmaseda, Liz
Behar, Ruth
Bennett, Robin K.
Bernardo, Anilu
Borjas, George J(esus)
Carrillo, H. G.
de La Pedraja, René
de La Torre, Miguel A.
de Las Casas, Walter
Dovalpage, Teresa
Flores-Galbis, Enrique
Fornés, Maria Irene
García, Cristina
Garcia-Aguilera, Carolina
Gessner, Lynne
González, Justo L(uis)
Gonzalez (Mandri), Flora
González-Echevarria, Roberto
La Rosa, Pablo
Laje, Zilia L.
Lima, Robert (F.)
Martínez, Dionisio D.
Menocal, Narciso G(arcia)
Novas, Himilce
Obejas, Achy
Perez, Gilberto (Guillermo)
Perez, Rolando
Pineiro, R. J.
Prieto, Jose Manuel
Santiago, Fabiola
Shamas, Victor A.
Teja, Jesus F(rancisco) de la
Thurlo, Aimee

United States-Cyprus

Kadir, Djelal

United States-Czech Republic

Bronner, Leila Leah
Cervenka, Jarda
Lebovics, Herman
Mastny, Vojtech
McGraw, Milena
Messer, Thomas M.

Simonson, Helen
Simpson, Peter L. Phillips
Slide, Anthony (Clifford)
Sluglett, Peter
Smith, Angela Thompson
Smith, Paul
Sonnenberg, Susanna Sophia
Spence, Jonathan D(ermot)
Staddon, John (E. R.)
Stell, Elizabeth P(arker)
Stevenson (Lucas), Anne
Stone, David Lee
Storch, Margaret
Stuart, Alexander
Sudjic, Deyan
Taylor, Andrew J.
Taylor, Liza Pennywitt
Teller, Astro
Temperley, Nicholas
Thirlwell, Adam
Thomson, Keith Stewart
Thorpe, Helen
Tierney, Kevin
Todd, Pamela A.
Urquhart, Brian Edward
Van Booy, Simon
Vernon, James
Veryan, Patricia
Virden, Jenel
Wade, (Sarah) Virginia
Walker, Martin
Waller, John
Ward, Alan J.
Ward, Brian
Ward, David
Warner, Malcolm
Wasserstein, Bernard (Mano
    Julius)
Weatherhead, A(ndrew) Kingsley
Webster, Jason
Weiss, Andrea
Weissbort, Daniel
Wellington, Monica
Whitehouse, David (Bryn)
Wickham, Christopher J.
Widdicombe, Toby
Wiggins, David
Williams, Ian
Williams, Tony
Williamson, Margaret
Wilson, Jonathan
Wilson, Sandy
Winchester, Simon
Winner, Michael Robert
Wollen, Peter
Wood, Michael
Wrobel, David M.
Wyllie, Peter J(ohn)
Younger, James
Zilboorg, Caroline (Crawford)

United States-England-Australia

Delano, Anthony

United States-England-Barbados

Lamming, George (Eric)

United States-England-France

Guilhot, Nicolas

United States-England-Ireland

Hone, Joseph

United States-England-Italy

Luttwak, Edward (Nicolae)

United States-England-Netherlands

Foot, Mirjam M(ichaela)

United States-England-Nigeria

Euba, Femi

United States-England-Panama

Griffin, Keith B(roadwell)

United States-England-Scotland

Carter, Marie
Jenike, Michael A.

United States-England-South Africa

Swade, Doron

United States-Ethiopia

Jalata, Asafa
Reuss, Frederick
Verghese, Abraham

United States-Finland

Hollo, Anselm (Paul Alexis)

United States-France

Arikha, Noga
Barzun, Jacques
Bennahum, David S.
Borch-Jacobsen, Mikkel
Briefel, Aviva
Brombert, Victor (Henri)
Charyn, Jerome
Chirot, Daniel
Cohen, Jean-Louis
Dantzer, Robert

De Syon, Guillaume
Debrix, François
Diouf, Sylviane A.
Edwards, Harvey
Engelhard, Jack
Filipacchi, Amanda
Foy, George Michelsen
Frappier-Mazur, Lucienne
Gavronsky, Serge
Gerassi, John
Hatton, Caroline
Jones, Kaylie (Ann)
Kahan, Alan S.
Kuh, Patric
Levy, Marc
Marion, Jean-Luc
Mellor, John W(illiams)
Michael, Colette V(erger)
Milanovic, Branko
Millman, Isaac
Montagnier, Luc
Nagem, Monique F.
Nolan, Janne E.
Pissarro, Joachim
Pollak, Mark
Rabaté, Jean-Michel
Rossant, Colette
Roth-Hano, Renée
Sheehan, Aurelie
Shneour, Elie Alexis
Smith, Annick
Smith, William Jay
Tarn, Nathaniel
Trang, Corinne
Tuck, Lily
Vaite, Célestine Hitiura
Weenolsen, Patricia

United States-France-Greece

Kent, Timothy J.

United States-Gambia

Sanneh, Lamin

United States-Germany

Abraham, Henry J.
Amy, Lori E.
Atkinson, Rick
Bahr, Ehrhard
Berghahn, Volker R.
Bieringer, R(eimund)
Blankenhorn, David (George)
Blickle, Peter
Blitzer, Wolf
Bloom, Steven
Boehmer, Ulrike
Bradley, Ernestine
Braunthal, Gerard
Brod, Harry
Brückner, Martin
Desjarlais, John
Dessart, George Baldwin
Dooley, Brendan Maurice
Dowell, Frances O'Roark

Drucker, Olga Levy
Eckart, Gabriele
Erlmann, Veit
Etzioni, Amitai
Evans, Michael Robert
Falk, Thomas H(einrich)
Fandrich, Ina Johanna
Fasolt, Constantin
Ferré, Frederick
Feuerstein, Georg
Fine, Doris Landau
Fischer, Dennis
Fonrobert, Charlotte Elisheva
Freudenberger, Herman
Friedlander, Henry (Egon)
Galloway, Terry
Gans, Herbert J.
Gay, Peter
Geismar, Ludwig Leo
Gemunden, Gerd
Gienow-Hecht, Jessica C. E.
Glasberg, Davita Silfen
Gumbrecht, Hans Ulrich
Gushee, David P.
Hackbarth, Steven (L.)
Hahn, Gordon M.
Hallo, William W.
Hansen, Jennifer
Hartman, Geoffrey H.
Hays, Peter L.
Heims, Steve J(oshua)
Herbst, Jurgen
Hoerder, Dirk
Hofmann, Michael
Holdheim, W(illiam) Wolfgang
Hölldobler, Bert(hold Karl)
Horak, Jan-Christopher
Howes, Laura L(ouise)
Iggers, Georg G(erson)
Jacobs, Kathryn
Jarausch, Konrad H(ugo)
Jhabvala, Ruth Prawer
Jonas, Manfred
Kelling, Hans Wilhelm
Keogh, Pamela Clarke
Kessner, Thomas
Kissinger, Henry (Alfred)
Klauck, Hans-Josef
Klingenstein, Susanne
Kodis, Michelle R.
Koegler, Hans Herbert
Kohn, Livia
Krich, Rochelle Majer
Krohn, Katherine E(lizabeth)
Krondorfer, Björn
Kultermann, Udo
Laqueur, Walter
Laubach, David C.
Leab, Daniel Josef
Levitin, Sonia (Wolff)
Lindsey, Johanna
Mattusch, Carol C.
Medeiros, Teresa
Metzger, Michael M(oses)
Mueller, Lisel
Muuss, Rolf Eduard
Nasar, Sylvia
Newton, Roger G(erhard)
Ohanian, Hans C.
Oppenheim, Felix E.
Oppenheim, Micha Falk

Palmié, Stephan
Perrin, Don
Petro, Nicolai N.
Philipsen, Dirk
Pistor, Katharina
Previn, André (George)
Puff, Helmut
Quinones, Sam
Ranis, Gustav
Richter, Roland Suso
Rose, Michael R.
Roskamp, Karl Wilhelm
Russell, Cheryl
Saffer, Barbara
Schaller, George B(eals)
Scheck, Raffael
Schlesier, Karl H.
Schmid, Wolfram George
Schweizer, Karl W.
Scott, Leonard B.
Scott, Nina M.
Selz, Peter
Sichel, Werner
Smith, Helmut Walser
Stern, Ellen Norman
Stierlin, Helm
Teiwes, Helga
Vallee, Lillian (Bozenna)
Von Reden, Sitta
Weingartner, Herbert J.
Weltge, Sigrid W(ortmann)
Werckmeister, O(tto) K(arl)
Wessell, Eva
Westheimer, (Karola) Ruth
Westmeier, Karl-Wilhelm
What, Leslie
White, Jenny
Williams, Gerhild Scholz
Ziefle, Helmut W(ilhelm)
Ziolkowski, Eric J(ozef)

United States-Germany-England

Hoerr, John

United States-Ghana

Abrams, Ovid (S. McL.)
Ayittey, George B. N.
Burayidi, Michael A.
Busia, Akosua
Danquah, Meri Nana-Ama
Panford, Kwamina
Quaye, Kofi
Sarfoh, Kwadwo A.
Sarkodie-Mensah, Kwasi

United States-Greece

Bowman, David
Constantelos, Demetrios J.
Danopoulos, Constantine P.
Gage, Eleni N.
Gourgouris, Stathis
Haviaras, Stratis
Iakovou, Takis

Karayianni, Tony
Margariti, Roxani Eleni
Panourgia, Neni K(onstantinou)
Papadimitriou, Dimitri B.
Yiannopoulos, A(thanassios) N.

United States-Guatemala

Montejo, Victor (D.)

United States-Guyana

Carew, Jan (Rynveld)
Diallo, Kadiatou
Gibran, Daniel K.
Griffith, Ivelaw L(loyd)

United States-Haiti

Balutansky, Kathleen M(arie)
Desmangles, Leslie G.
Fombrun, Charles J.
Zéphir, Flore

United States-Hong Kong

Chang, Maria Hsia
Chow, Kai-wing
Chow, Rey
Davies, Kristian
De Pree, Christopher G.
Hom, Sharon K.
Lee, Joann Faung Jean
Mui, Chunka
Williams, Adam
Yu, Anthony C.

United States-Hungary

Bennett, Georgette
Berger-Kiss, Andres
Blass, Thomas
Darnay, Arsen J.
Deak, Istvan
Friedman, George
Gati, Charles
Goss, Theodora
Gross, Ernie
Hollos, Marida
Kereszty, Roch A.
Lukacs, John (Adalbert)
Marton, Kati (Ilona)
Plesko, Les
Quandt, Richard (Emeric)
Suleiman, Susan Rubin
Szasz, Thomas Stephen
Tong, Gary S.
Vayda, Andrew P.
von Habsburg(-Lothringen), Géza

United States-Hungary-Romania

Barabási, Albert-László

United States-India

Afzal, Omar
Agarwal, Shilpa
Agrawal, Govind P.
Ahmed, Akbar S(alahudin)
Alexander, Meena
Ali, Samina
Balaguru, P(erumalsamy) N(aidu)
Bardhan, Pranab Kumar
Bhabha, Homi K.
Bhatt, Jagdish J(eyshanker)
Bhote, Keki R.
Bilgrami, Akeel
Bruchac, Marge M.
Chakravarty, Sumita S(inha)
Chanda, Nayan
Chandra, Vikram
Charan, Ram
Chopra, Deepak (K.)
Choudhury, Ashok
Dasgupta, Shamita Das
Desai, Anita
Desai, Boman
Desai, Kiran
Dibble, J(ames) Birney
Divakaruni, Chitra Banerjee
Ferrell, Monica
Fracis, Sohrab Homi
Frykenberg, Robert E(ric)
Ganesan, Indira
Gesler, Wilbert M.
Ghosh, Amitav
Grewal, David Singh
Haldar, Achintya
Jain, Anita
Joshi, S(unand) T(ryambak)
Jussawalla, Feroza
Kalia, Ravi
Karkala, John A.
Katrak, Ketu H.
Khan, Hasan-Uddin
Khare, R(avindra) S.
Khilnani, Sunil
Khush, Gurdev S.
Kirchner, Bharti
Krishnaswami, Uma
Kumar, Alok
McEntyre, Marilyn Chandler
Mehta, Gita
Mehta, Suketu
Mehta, Ved (Parkash)
Mohan, Rakesh
Mosher, Richard
Mukherjee, Bharati
Murarka, Shyam P.
Natarajan, Nalini
Nigam, Sanjay (Kumar)
Nomani, Asra Q.
Padanilam, George J.
Panagariya, Arvind
Parthasarathy, R(ajagopal)
Peeradina, Saleem
Perkins, Mitali
Ramaya, Shona
Rao, Aruna P.
Ray, Krishnendu
Reddi, Rishi
Rendon, Marcie R.
Servid, Carolyn
Seshadri, Vijay

Shankar, S.
Singh, Amritjit
Skaria, Ajay
Spivak, Gayatri Chakravorty
Subrahmanyam, Sanjay
Trevelyan, Raleigh
Vaid, Urvashi
Wangmo, Tsering
Whitlock, Flint
Zacharias, Ravi K.
Zakaria, Fareed
Zutshi, Chitralekha

United States-India-France

Bastien, Joseph William

United States-Indonesia

Boot, John C. G
Lee, Li Young
Setiawan, Erick
Sumarsam

United States-Iran

Afary, Janet
Afkhami, Mahnaz
Amirrezvani, Anita
Askari, Hossein G.
Aslan, Reza
Assefi, Nassim
Azimi, Fakhreddin
Behdad, Sohrab
Bina, Cyrus
Dabashi, Hamid
Danesh, Abol Hassan
Dumas, Firoozeh
Esfandiari, Haleh
Farmaian, Sattareh Farman
Firouz, Anahita (Homa)
Haeri, Shahla
Houshmand, Zara
Hunter, Shireen T.
Kamrava, Mehran
Keshavarz, Fatemeh
Khadivi, Laleh
Khakpour, Porochista
Kheirabadi, Masoud
Kujoory, Parvin
Liberman, Rosette B.
Majd, Hooman
Majd, Kam
Moghaddam, Fathali M.
Moshiri, Farnoosh
Nasr, Seyyed Hossein
Rejai, Mostafa
Sadri, Ahmad
Seraji, Mahbod
Shahriari, Shahriar
Varzi, Roxanne
Yaghmaian, Behzad
Yarshater, Ehsan (Ollah)
Yazdanfar, Farzin

United States-Iraq

Agha-Jaffar, Tamara
Al-Marayati, Abid A(min)
Alshawi, Hiyan
Antoon, Sinan
Qazwini, Hassan

United States-Ireland

Anglim, Christopher Thomas
Bowden, Martha F.
Broderick, Colin
Bunting, (Anne) Eve(lyn Bolton)
Carr, Patrick J.
Congdon, Kristin G.
Dinan, Desmond
Donovan, Gerard
Duffy, Eamon
Ennis, Garth
Fairley, James S(tewart)
Ferris, Timothy
Grennan, Eamon
Hutchinson, Ron
Kearney, Richard Marius
Kennefick, Daniel
Kiberd, Declan
Macdonald, Michael Patrick
McCann, Colum
Muldoon, Paul
Murphy, Dervla Mary
O'Callaghan, Sean
O'Reilly, Victor
Pederson, William D(avid)
Power, Samantha
Rodden, John (Gallagher)
Shillue, Edith
Skinner, Knute (Rumsey)
Taft, John (Thomas)

United States-Israel

Aczel, Amir D.
Alon, Ilan
Bahr, Iris
Benkler, Yochai
Bitton-Jackson, Livia E(lvira)
Bodansky, Yossef
Boyarin, Daniel
Brafman, Ori
Charny, Israel Wolf
Cohen, Avner
Delman, Carmit
Ellingwood, Ken
Emmett, Ayala
Flamhaft, Ziva
Gonen, Jay Y.
Havazelet, Ehud
Hinn, Benny
Kalman, Maira
Kiewe, Amos
Koren, Yehuda
Kreinin, Mordechai
Kunda, Gideon
Levin, Doron P.
Maital, Sharone L(evow)
Myers, Tamar
Nahshon, Edna
Netz, Reviel
Noam, Eli Michael

Pedahzur, Ami
Peleg, Ilan
Pelli, Moshe
Razin, Assaf
Rotundo, Louis C.
Rubinstein, Ruth P.
Shammas, Anton
Sher, Gila
Shiner, David
Shohat, Ella Habiba
Sofer, Barbara
Stern, Sol
Weber, Doron
Weiner, Anita
Weissbach, Lee Shai
Zmora, Nurith

United States-Israel-Belgium

Paldiel, Mordecai

United States-Italy

Antonucci, Francesco
Astarita, Tommaso
Badt, Karin L(uisa)
Bastianich, Lidia Matticchio
Bernardi, Adria
Biagioli, Mario
Bicchieri, Cristina
Blevins, David
Boldrin, Michele
Bone, Eugenia
Buccini, Stefania
Chase, Elaine Raco
Chen, Patrizia
Chiarella, Tom
Conigliaro, Vincenzo
Conroy, John
de Palchi, Alfredo
DeVito, Joseph A.
DiRenzo, Anthony
Fales-Hill, Susan
Forni, P(ier) M(assimo)
Forte, Maurizio
Fratianni, Michele
Fratti, Mario
Furino, Antonio
Ginzburg, Carlo
Hohenegger, Beatrice
Iacoboni, Marco
Jannuzzi, Luigi
Kevane, Bridget
Levi-Montalcini, Rita
Lopreato, Joseph
Maestripieri, Dario
Maggi, Armando
Malpezzi Price, Paola
Melia, Fulvio
Miele, Angelo
Monda, Antonio
Musacchio, George
Napoli, Donna Jo
Nobisso, Josephine
Ottaway, Marina (Seassaro)
Passaro, Maria (C. Pastore)
Pastor, Ben
Pucci, Pietro

Ricapito, Joseph V.
Romano, Tony
Russell, Rinaldina
Russo, Elena
Scaglione, Aldo
Schaechter, Elio
Segrè, Gino
Selgin, George
Simonetta, Marcello
Sutter, Robert G.
Vacche, Angela Dalle
Valeri, Laura
Valesio, Paolo

United States-Italy-Czech Republic

Machotka, Pavel

United States-Italy-England

Romer, (Louis) John
Smith, Zadie

United States-Jamaica

Bailey, Anne C.
Campbell, Mavis C.
Gordon, Lewis Ricardo
James, Marlon
Leseur, Geta
McCallum, Shara
Morrison, Keith
Patterson, (Horace) Orlando
Winkler, Anthony C.

United States-Japan

Blustein, Paul
Brown, Lee Ann
Butow, Robert J. C
De Vos, Susan
Kawakami, Barbara Fusako
Keene, Donald
Kenjo, Takashi
Kibuishi, Kazu
Kimura, Margaret
Koya, Tatsuhito
Mori, Kyoko
Motomura, Hiroshi
Raichlen, Steven
Reginald, Robert
Reich, Christopher
Ryang, Sonia
Say, Allen
Shaughnessy, Brenda
Takashima, Misako
Tamura, Linda
Tanaka, Yukiko
Ueda, Makoto
Warner, Penny
Whitcher, Susan (Godsil)
Williams, Duncan Ryûken
Yagami, Kazuo
Yamaguchi, Yōji
Yusa, Michiko

United States-Kenya

Fisher, Julieta Dias
Mazrui, Ali Al('Amin)
Morris, Edmund
Mũgo, Mĩcere Gĩthae
Mutua, Makau wa
Ngugi wa Thiong

United States-Korea (South)

Adams, James F(rederick)
An, Na
Balgassi, Haemi
Kang, K. Connie
Kim, Kyu Hyun
Kim, Myung Mi
Kim, Rebecca Y.
Kim, Young (Hum)
Ko, Tanya Hyonhye
Lee, Chang-rae
Lee, Jennifer
Lee, Jid
Lie, John
Moffett, Samuel Hugh
Mun, Nami
Pae, Sung Moon
Park, Timothy K.
Shim, Eunmi
Shim, Jae K.
Sunee, Kim
Wilson, Myoung Chung
Woo, Sung J.
Yoo, John C.

United States-Latvia

Neimanis, George J(uris)

United States-Lebanon

Accad, Evelyne
Adnan, Etel
Ajami, Fouad
Alameddine, Rabih
Bakalian, Anny
Coscarelli, Don
Gerges, Fawaz A.
Lendon, J. E.
Malti-Douglas, Fedwa
Nasr, Kameel B.
Phares, Walid
Shehadi, Fadlou
Underwood, Marion K.

United States-Lithuania

Kagan, Donald
Shachnow, Sid
Venclova, Tomas

United States-Macao

Dimock, Wai Chee

United States-Malaysia

Chin, Justin
Lim, Shirley Geok-lin
Manicka, Rani
Woo, Wing Thye
Yong, Amos

United States-Mexico

Arakawa, Yoichi
Castaneda, Jorge G.
Chávez-García, Miroslava
Ferreiro, Alberto
Gallo, Rubén
Gilbert, Alma M.
Gottfried, Robert R(ichard)
Hinojosa, Maria (de Lourdes)
Marin, Rosario
Marsden, Carolyn
Martinez, Andrés
Mraz, John
Padilla, Ignacio
Padilla, Raymond V.
Ponce, Mary Helen
Ramos, Luis Arturo
Reséndez, Andrés
Rivera, Eléna
Sanchez, Alex
Stewart, Sarah
Vallejo, Armando
Vazquez-Gomez, Juana

United States-Morocco

Hammoudi, Abdellah
Majid, Anouar
Serrano, Lucienne J.

United States-Myanmar

Ho, Minfong

United States-Nepal

Shrestha, Nanda R.

United States-Netherlands

Baars, Bernard J(oseph)
Bloembergen, Nicolaas
Daalder, Ivo H.
de Blij, Harm J(an)
de Munck, Victor C.
de Vries, Hent
Dressler, Mylène
Erskine, Kathryn
Goemans, Hein E.
Hiltermann, Joost R.
Matthee, Rudi
Moran, Maya
Raadschelders, Jos C. N.
Sassen, Saskia
Silbiger, Alexander
Spier, Peter (Edward)

Swierenga, Robert P.
van Belle, Gerald
Van der Plas, Rob(ert)
van Tuyll, Hubert P.
Vermeij, Geerat J.
Zook, Chris

United States-Netherlands-Brazil

Van Beusekom, Janneke

United States-New Zealand

Arnett, Peter (Gregg)
Bishop, Nic
Blythe, Martin
Carter, Warren
Comfort, Ray
Gray, Judith A(nne)
Mintz, Alan L.
Peters, Michael (Adrian)
Shallcrass, John James
Simpson, Adrienne
Teece, David J(ohn)
Thompson, William J.
Vandenbroucke, Lucien S.
Wareham, Dean Dean
Winslade, John (Maxwell)

United States-Nigeria

Abani, Chris
Abegunrin, Olayiwola
Bandele, Biyi
Chude-Sokei, Louis Onuorah
Dibua, Jeremiah I.
Echeruo, Michael
Egbuna, Obi (Benedict)
Falola, Toyin
Gordon, Jacob U.
Iheduru, Obioma M.
Ilesanmi, Simeon O.
Nriagu, Jerome O.
Ogbaa, Kalu
Ogede, Ode
Oguibe, Olu
Ogunyemi, Yemi D(iploman)
Ojaide, Tanure
Olaleye, Isaac O.
Olupona, Jacob K.
Osundare, Niyi
Soyinka, Wole
Ugwuegbu, Denis Chima E

United States-Norway

Bundesen, Lynne
Hall, Thor
Lunge-Larsen, Lise
Moi, Toril

United States-Norway-Germany

Olsen, Brad

United States-Pakistan

Anees, Munawar Ahmad
Hamid, Mohsin
Haqqani, Husain
Hassan, Aftab Syed
Havel, Harvey
Jafree, Mohammed Jawaid Iqbal
Maine, David
Masood, Maliha
Shafquat, Sofia
Shah, Jami J.

United States-Palestine

Audeh, Azmi S.
Jones, Jenny

United States-Panama

Gmelch, Sharon (Bohn)
Hunt, Lynn (Avery)
Jackson, Edwardo
Johnson, Shoshana Nyree
Lebow, Eileen F.
Saum, Karen
Smith, Peter Moore
Thompson, Janet A(nn)

United States-Papua New Guinea

Botsman, Daniel V.

United States-Philippines

Brainard, Cecilia Manguerra
Carbo, Nick
De La Cruz, Melissa
Hagedorn, Jessica Tarahata
Mariano, Connie Concepcion
Melion, Walter S.
Ong, Han
Schroeder, Lucinda Delaney
Ty-Casper, Linda

United States-Poland

Barańczak, Stanisław
Begley, Louis
Bergman, Eugene
Bogacki, Tomek
Brandes, Joseph
Brzezinski, Zbigniew (Kasimierz)
Carpenter, Bogdana
Fox, Frank
Foxman, Abraham H.
Frajlich(-Zajac), Anna
Friedberg, Maurice
Gotfryd, Bernard
Gray, Francine du Plessix
Hoffman, Eva
Hoffmann, Roald
Ludwikowski, Rett R.
Mekler, Eva

Melamed, Leo
Piotrowski, Thaddeus (Tadeusz)
Pipes, Richard
Prybyla, Jan S(tanislaw)
Roshwald, Mordecai
Rozbicki, Michal J.
Rykwert, Joseph
Staar, Richard F.
Stryk, Lucien
Szenberg, Michael
Trzynadlowski, Andrzej M.
Wagner, Wenceslas J.
Waldman, Harry
Wohlgelernter, Maurice
Zaborowska, Magdalena J.
Zawodny, J(anusz) K.

United States-Poland-Slovakia

Presnall, Judith (Ann) Janda

United States-Portugal

Fontes, Manuel D(a Costa)

United States-Puerto Rico

Barreto, Amilcar Antonio
Braschi, Giannina
Cofer, Judith Ortiz
Dávila, Arlene M.
Díaz-Stevens, Ana María
González, Aníbal
Muniz, Olga M.
Paravisini-Gebert, Lizabeth
Rogler, Lloyd Henry

United States-Romania

Bambola, Sylvia
Bogdan, Radu J.
Brezianu, Andrei
Codrescu, Andrei
Cornis-Pope, Marcel (H.)
Flickenger, Rob
Judovitz, Dalia
Lakos, Amos
Manea, Norman
Markovits, Andrei S.
Moldea, Dan E.
Popescu, Petru
Schwarcz, Vera
Smarandache, Florentin
Tismaneanu, Vladimir
Wiesel, Elie

United States-Russia

Barabtarlo, Gennady
Berger, Joseph
Budman, Mark
Corten, Irina H.
Efimova, Alla
Epstein, Mikhail N.
Estraikh, Gennady

Gaiduk, Ilya V(alerievich)
Gorokhova, Elena
Grossman, Dina
Ioffe, Grigory
Ivanova, Tatyana G(rigoryevna)
Jakobson, Michael
Kaletski, Alexander
Khazanov, Anatoly M.
Kossman, Nina
Lahutsky, John
Levin, Igor
Levin, Irina
Litman, Ellen
Mirovitskaya, Natalia
Ostrovsky, Eugene
Pantaeva, Irina
Rossman, Vadim
Rumer, Boris
Sedia, Ekaterina
Shraer-Petrov, David
Shteyngart, Gary
Simons, Paullina
Turchin, Peter
Vapnyar, Lara
Yurchak, Alexei
Zatsiorsky, Vladimir M.
Zubok, Vladislav

United States-Russia-France

Pozner, Vladimir

United States-Russia-Germany

Kaufman, Bel

United States-Saudi Arabia

Marcom, Micheline Aharonian
Obaid, Nawaf E.
Zailckas, Koren

United States-Scotland

Barnett, John Le Page
Bryson, Norman
Campbell, John
Clark, Gregory
Comaroff, Jean
Cox, Caroline
Coyne, Michael
Dickie, Matthew W(allace)
Lorenz, Ralph
MacPhee, Ross D(ouglas) E(arle)
Mehaffey, Karen Rae
Peterson, Richard S(cot)
Unterberger, Betty Miller
Young, Jock

United States-Singapore

Tan, Kok-Chor
Theroux, Louis Sebastian
Westmacott, Richard N.

United States-Slovakia

Suda, Zdenek Ludvik

United States-Slovenia-Croatia

Šalamun, Tomaž

United States-Somalia

Mukhtar, Mohamed Haji

United States-South Africa

Adair, Cherry
Benjamin, Denis R(ichard)
Berliner-Gluckman, Janet
Boraine, Alex(ander)
Capon, Robert Farrar
Cassel, Susie Lan
Coates, Robert Crawford
Danilowitz, Brenda
Eprile, Tony
Freed, Lynn
Friedlander, Michael W.
Fugard, Athol
Fugard, Lisa
Gordon, Sheila
Greenberg, Allan
Hancock, Brian
Handler, Marisa
Hess, Alan
Jacobs, Steve
Lowenberg, Anton D(avid)
Magona, Sindiwe
Mathabane, Mark
McDowell, John (Henry)
Mda, Zakes
Meintjes, Louise
Philander, S. George H
Rochman, Hazel
Rosen, Leora N(adine)
Schmahmann, David
Scully, Pamela (Frederika)
Shapiro, Ian
Uys, Errol Lincoln
van Huyssteen, J. Wentzel
Verschuur, Gerrit L(aurens)
Walshe, Peter (Aubrey)
Yourgrau, Palle

United States-South Africa-England

Goodall, Jane

United States-Spain

Blanco, Richard
Francis, H(erbert) E(dward)
George, Lindsay Barrett
Gesner, Carol
Mellizo (Cuadrado), Carlos
Perez-Romero, Antonio
Salazar, Dixie

Sears, James T(homas)
Sender Barayon, Ramon
Zafón, Carlos Ruiz
Zulaika, Joseba

United States-Spain-Scotland

Reid, Alastair

United States-Sri Lanka

Olivelle, Patrick
Rogers, Rosemary
Sathasivam, Kanishkan

United States-Sweden

Abrams, Jeanne E.
Agell, Charlotte
Bok, Sissela
Cave, Eric M.
Cline, Lynn Hunter
Haller, Hermann (W)
Sayre, Gordon M.
Svenson, Bo
Swedberg, Richard

United States-Switzerland

Asper, Kathrin
Christe, Ian
Dyson, Esther
Fitzgerald, Astrid
Glenn, Mel
Haberman, Jacob
Holsti, Ole Rudolf
Huber, Evelyne
Levy, Matthys
Lindvall, Terry R.
Miller, Alyce
Mitchell, Ellinor R.
Wenger, Etienne
Zweifel, Thomas D.

United States-Syrian Arab Republic

Keeley, Edmund
Semaan, Khalil I. H.

United States-Taiwan

Lee, Wei-chin
Liou, K(uo-)N(an)
Pon, Cindy
Redford, Kent H(ubbard)
Sato, Hiroaki
Sun, Chyng Feng
Wang, Jing
Wu, C(hien-) F(u) Jeff
Wu, Yenna

United States-Thailand

Yang, Kao Kalia

United States-Tibet

Gyatso, Palden
Thondup, Tulku

United States-Trinidad and Tobago

Antoni, Robert (William)
Guy, Rosa (Cuthbert)
James, Kelvin Christopher
Maingot, Anthony P.
Rahaman, Vashanti
Smith, Sheldon
Winford, Donald C.

United States-Tunisia

Belkaoui, Ahmed R.

United States-Turkey

Bagdikian, Ben H(aig)
Barkey, Karen
Bicerano, Jozef
Demirguc-Kunt, Asli
Fikes, Jay C(ourtney)
Kaynak, Erdener
Laqueur, Thomas Walter
Necipoglu, Gulru
Roubini, Nouriel
Yegül, Fikret K.

United States-Uganda

Kisubi, Alfred T(aligoola)

United States-Ukraine

Akinsha, Konstantin
Fleishman, Lazar
Motyl, Alexander J(ohn)
Orlova, Alexandra (Anatol'evna)
Savage, (Maria) Ania
Shvets, Yuri B.
Tarnopolsky, Yuri
Wing, Natasha

United States-Uruguay

Bentos, Carlos
Crumbley, Paul
Marcuse, Aída E.

United States-USA

Douglas, Matthew M.
Entine, Jon